BASEBALL CARD PRICE GUIDE

EIGHTH EDITION – 1994

By the
Price Guide Editors
of Sports Collectors Digest
Edited by Bob Lemke

Library of Congress Catalog Number: 87-80033
ISBN: 0-87341-276-1

Krause Publications, Inc.
700 E. State St.
Iola, WI 54990

Printed in the United States of America

ACKNOWLEDGEMENTS

Dozens of individuals have made countless valuable contributions which have been incorporated into the *Sports Collectors Digest Baseball Card Price Guide.* While all cannot be acknowledged, special appreciation is extended to the following principal contributors who have exhibited a special dedication by creating, revising or verifying listings and technical data, reviewing market valuations or loaning cards for photography.

Johnny Adams, Jr.
Ken Agona
(Sports Cards Plus)
Gary Agostino
Lisa Albano
Dan Albaugh
Mark Anker
Steve Applebaum
Bill Ballew
John Beisiegel
Karen Bell
Cathy Black
Levi Bleam
Mike Bodner
Bill Bossert
(Mid-Atlantic Coin Exchange)
Brian Boston
Mike Boyd
Richard Bradley
Jon Brecka
John Brigandi
(Brigandi Coin Co.)
Lou Brown
Dan Bruner
(The Card King)
Greg Bussineau
(Superior Sports Cards)
Billy Caldwell
(Packman)
Len Caprisecca
Tony Carrafiell
(Delco Sports Cards)
Lee Champion
Dwight Chapin
Chriss Christiansen
Shane Cohen
(Grand Slam Sports Collectibles)
Rich Cole
Charles Conlon
Eric Cooper
(All Star Cards)
Bryan Couling
Marty Cramer
(Pacific Trading Cards)
Clyde Cripe
Jim Cumpton
Robert Curtiss
Tom Daniels
(T&J Sports Cards)
Tom Day
Dick DeCourcy
Ken Degnan
(Georgia Music & Sports)
Mike Del Gado
(All American Sportscards)
Frank DiRoberto
Larry Dluhy
(Texas Trading Cards)

John Dorsey
Curtis Earl
Mark Elliott
Brian Epstein
Joe Esposito
(B&E Collectibles)
Doak Ewing
David Festberg
(Baseball and Hobby Shop)
Jay Finglass
Nick Flaviano
Jeff Fritsch
Larry Fritsch
Richard Galasso
Tom Galic
Tony Galovich
(American Card Exchange)
Frank Giffune
Richard Gilkeson
Gerald J. Glasser
Dick Goddard
Jack Goodman
Bill Goodwin
(St. Louis Baseball Cards)
Audre Gold
(Au Sports Memorabilia)
Howard Gordon
Mike Gordon
Bob Gray
Paul Green
Wayne Grove
(First Base)
Gerry Guenther
Don Guilbert
Tom Guilfoile
Julie Haddon
David, Joel & Walter Hall
(Hall's Nostalgia)
Gary Hamilton
Tom Harbin
Don Harrison
Rick Hawksley
Herbert Hecht
Bill Henderson
Kathy Henry
Steve Hershkowitz
Gregg Hitesman
Jack Horkan
Jim Horne
Ron Hosmer
Marvin Huck
Robert Jacobsen
Donn Jennings
Scott Jensen
Jim Johnston
Stewart Jones
Larry Jordan
Judy Kay
(Kay's Baseball Cards)

Allan Kaye
Michael Keedy
Mark Kemmerle
Rick Kelinger
John King
John King
John Kitleson
(Sports Collectibles)
Bob Koehler
David Kohler
Jay Kurowski
John Kurowski
Steve Lacasse
Lee Lasseigne
Mark K. Larson
William Lawrence
Morley Leeking
Paul Lewicki
Howie Levy
(Blue Chip Sportscard)
Rob Lifson
Jeff Litteral
Paul Lohman
Mark MacRae
Ken Magee
Paul Marchant
Bill Mastro
Tony McLaughlin
Don McPherson
John Mehlin
Bill Mendel
Blake Meyer
(Lone Star Sportcard Co.)
Dick Millerd
Minnesota Sports Collectibles
Keith Mitchell
J.A. Monaco
Joe Morano
Brian Morris
Mike Mowery
Peter Mudavin
Mark Murphy
(The Baseball Card "Kid")
David Musser
(D.M.B.'s Baseball Cards)
Frank Nagy
Chuck Nobriga
Mark Nochta
Keith Olbermann
Joe Pasternack
(Card Collectors Co.)
Marty Perry
Marty Perry
Tom Pfirrman
(Baseball Card Corner)
Dan Piepenbrok
(Uneeda Hobbie)
Stan Pietruska
(Pro Sports Investments)

Paul Pollard
Ed Ransom
Fred Rapoport
(Yesterday's Heroes)
Tom Reid
Bob Richardson
Gavin Riley
Ron Ritzler
Mike Rodell
Mike Rogers
Chris Ronan
Rocky Rosato
Alan Rosen
John Rumierz
Bob Rund
Jon Sands
(Howard's Coin Shop)
Kevin Savage
(The Sports Gallery)
Stephen Schauer
Dave Schwartz
(Dave's Sportscards)
Robert Scott
Corey Shanus
Dan Shedrick
Barry Sloate
Joe Smith
Mark Soltan
John Spalding
Kevin Spears
Gene Speranza
David Spivack
Don Steinbach
Dan Stickney
Larry Stone
Todd Straughan
Doug Stultz
Joe Szeremet
Ted Taylor
(Fleer Corp.)
Erik Teller
K.J. Terplak
Dick Tinsley
Bud Tompkins
(Minnesota Connection)
Chuck Torrey
Rich Unruh
Jack Urban
Pete Waldman
Eric Waller
Gary Walter
Ken Weimer
Dale Weselowski
E.C. Wharton-Tigar
Chris Williams
Charles Williamson
Jay Yoder
Kit Young
Ted Zanidakis

Table of Contents

Acknowledgements 2
Catalalog Arrangement 10
Numbering 12
Grading 13
Valuations 14
Errors/Variations 16
Baseball Card History 18
Hobby Glossary 24
Steve Carlton Tribute 28

A

1988 Action Packed 30
1992 Action Packed All Star Gallery Series I 30
1992 Action Packed All Star Gallery Series II 31

B

1959 Bazooka 31
1960 Bazooka 32
1961 Bazooka 32
1962 Bazooka 33
1963 Bazooka 33
1963 Bazooka All-Time Greats 34
1964 Bazooka 34
1964 Bazooka Stamps 35
1965 Bazooka 35
1966 Bazooka 36
1967 Bazooka 36
1968 Bazooka 37
1969-70 Bazooka 37
1971 Bazooka Unnumbered Set 38
1971 Bazooka Numbered Set 38
1988 Bazooka 39
1989 Bazooka 39
1990 Bazooka 40
1991 Bazooka 40
1992 Bazooka 40
1948 Bowman 41
1949 Bowman 41
1950 Bowman 43
1951 Bowman 45
1952 Bowman 47
1953 Bowman Color 48
1953 Bowman Black & White 49
1954 Bowman 50
1955 Bowman 52
1989 Bowman 54
1989 Bowman Inserts 57
1990 Bowman 57
1990 Bowman Inserts 60
1991 Bowman 61
1992 Bowman 65
1993 Bowman 69
1978 Burger King Rangers 74
1978 Burger King Tigers 74
1978 Burger King Yankees 74
1979 Burger King Phillies 75
1979 Burger King Yankees 75
1980 Burger King Phillies 76
1980 Burger King Pitch, Hit & Run 76
1986 Burger King 76
1987 Burger King 77

C

1987 Classic Game 77
1987 Classic Travel Edition 78
1988 Classic - Blue 79
1988 Classic - Red 79
1989 Classic 80
1989 Classic Travel Update I 80
1989 Classic Travel Update II 81
1990 Classic 81
1990 Classic Series II 83
1990 Classic Series III 83
1991 Classic 84
1991 Classic Series II 85
1991 Classic Series III 85
1991 Classic Collector's Edition 86
1992 Classic Series I 88
1992 Classic Series II 88
1992 Classic Collector's Edition 89
1991 Conlon Collection 90
1992 Conlon Collection 92
1993 Conlon Collection 94
1993 Conlon Color 96
1994 Conlon Collection 97
1982 Cracker Jack 99
1991 Cracker Jack Topps I 99
1991 Cracker Jack Topps II 100
1992 Cracker Jack Donruss I 100
1992 Cracker Jack Donruss II 101
1993 Cracker Jack Anniversary 101

D

1992 Dairy Queen 101
1991 Denny's Grand Slam 102
1992 Denny's Grand Slam 102
1993 Denny's Grand Slam 102
1993 DiamondMarks 103
1993 DiamondMarks Inserts 104
1981 Donruss 104
1982 Donruss 108
1983 Donruss 112
1983 Donruss Action All-Stars 116
1983 Donruss Hall of Fame Heroes 117
1984 Donruss 117
1984 Donruss Action All-Stars 121
1984 Donruss Champions 122
1985 Donruss 122
1985 Donruss Action All-Stars 126
1985 Donruss Box Panels 127
1985 Donruss Diamond Kings Supers 127
1985 Donruss Highlights 128
1985 Donruss Sluggers 128
1986 Donruss 129
1986 Donruss All-Stars 133
1986 Donruss Box Panels 133
1986 Donruss Diamond Kings Supers 133
1986 Donruss Highlights 134
1986 Donruss Pop-Ups 135
1986 Donruss Rookies 135
1987 Donruss 136
1987 Donruss All-Stars 139
1987 Donruss Box Panels 140
1987 Donruss Diamond Kings Supers 140
1987 Donruss Highlights 141
1987 Donruss Opening Day 142
1987 Donruss Pop-Ups 143
1987 Donruss Rookies 144

1988 Donruss 144
1988 Donruss MVP 148
1988 Donruss All-Stars 149
1988 Donruss Baseball's Best 149
1988 Donruss Diamond Kings Supers 151
1988 Donruss Pop-Ups 152
1988 Donruss Rookies 152
1988 Donruss Red Sox Team Book 153
1988 Donruss Cubs Team Book 153
1988 Donruss Mets Team Book 153
1988 Donruss Yankees Team Book 154
1988 Donruss Oakland A's Team Book 154

1989 Donruss 154
1989 Donruss MVP 158
1989 Donruss All-Stars 159
1989 Donruss Grand Slammers 159
1989 Donruss Baseball's Best 160
1989 Donruss Pop-Ups 162
1989 Donruss Rookies 162
1989 Donruss Traded 163

1990 Donruss 163
1990 Donruss MVP 167
1990 Donruss Grand Slammers 168
1990 Donruss A.L. Best 168
1990 Donruss N.L. Best 169
1990 Donruss Diamond Kings Supers 170
1990 Donruss Learning Series 171
1990 Donruss Rookies 171

1991 Donruss 172
1991 Donruss Grand Slammers 176
1991 Donruss Highlights 176
1991 Donruss Elite 177
1991 Donruss Rookies 177

1992 Donruss 177
1992 Donruss Bonus Cards 182
1992 Donruss Diamond Kings 182
1992 Donruss Elite 183
1992 Donruss Rookies 183
1992 Donruss Rookie Phenoms 184
1992 Donruss Triple Play 184
1992 Donruss McDonald's 186
1992 Donruss Nolan Ryan 186

1993 Donruss 187
1993 Donruss Long Ball Leaders 191
1993 Donruss Diamond Kings 192
1993 Donruss MVP's 192
1993 Donruss Spirit of the Game 192
1993 Donruss Masters of the Game ... 193
1993 Donruss Elite 193
1993 Donruss Triple Play 193
1993 Triple Play Gallery 195
1993 Triple Play League Leaders 195
1993 Triple Play Nicknames 195
1993 Triple Play Action Baseball 196

1994 Donruss 196
1994 Donruss Decade Dominators 198
1994 Donruss Diamond Kings 198
1994 Donruss Elite ....
1994 Donruss MVPs ....
1994 Donruss Anniversary - 1984
1994 Donruss Special Edition - G
1994 Donruss Spirit of the Game

E

1939-46 Exhibit Supply Co. Salutation 200
1947-66 Exhibits 201
1962 Exhibits - Statistic Backs 203
1963 Exhibits - Statistic Backs 203
1948 Hall of Fame Exhibits 204
1953 Exhibits - Canadian 204
1961 Exhibits - Wrigley Field 205

F

1959 Fleer Ted Williams 205
1960 Fleer 206
1961-62 Fleer 207
1963 Fleer 208
1972 Fleer Famous Feats 208
1973 Fleer Wildest Days and Plays 209
1974 Fleer Baseball Firsts 209
1975 Fleer Pioneers of Baseball 210
1981 Fleer 210
1981 Fleer Star Stickers 214
1982 Fleer 215
1982 Fleer Stamps 219
1983 Fleer 221
1983 Fleer Stamps 225
1983 Fleer Stickers 226
1984 Fleer 227
1984 Fleer Update 231
1984 Fleer Stickers 232
1985 Fleer 233
1985 Fleer Stickers 238
1985 Fleer Update 237
1985 Fleer Limited Edition 239
1986 Fleer 240
1986 Fleer All Stars 244
1986 Fleer Box Panels 244
1986 Fleer Future Hall of Famers 244
1986 Fleer Update 244
1986 Fleer Baseball's Best 245
1986 Fleer League Leaders 246
1986 Fleer Limited Edition 246
1986 Fleer Mini 247
1986 Fleer Star Stickers 248
1986 Fleer Star Stickers Box Panels 249
1987 Fleer 249
1987 Fleer All Stars 253
1987 Fleer 1986 World Series 253
1987 Fleer Headliners 253
1987 Fleer Box Panels 254
1987 Fleer Update 254
1987 Fleer Baseball's Award Winners 255
1987 Fleer Baseballs All Stars 255
1987 Fleer Baseball's Best 256
1987 Fleer Baseball's Exciting Stars 256
1987 Fleer Baseball's Game Winners 257
1987 Fleer Baseball's Hottest Stars 257
1987 Fleer League Leaders 258
1987 Fleer Limited Edition 258
1987 Fleer Mini 259
1987 Fleer Star Stickers 260
1987 Fleer Baseball's Record Setters 260
1987 Fleer Star Sticker Box Panels 261
1988 Fleer 261
1988 Fleer All Stars 265
1988 Fleer Box Panels 266
1988 Fleer '87 World Series 266
1988 Fleer Headliners 266
1988 Fleer Update 267
1988 Fleer Award Winners 268
1988 Fleer MVP 269
1988 Fleer Baseball's Best 269
988 Fleer Baseball's Best Box Panel 270
Fleer Baseball's Exciting Stars 270
1988 Fleer Baseball's Hottest Stars 271
1988 Fleer League Leaders 271
1988 Fleer Mini 272
1988 Fleer Record Setters 272
1988 Fleer Star Stickers 273
1988 Fleer Star Stickers Box Panels 274
1988 Fleer Superstars 274
1989 Fleer 275
1989 Fleer All Stars 279
1989 Fleer For The Record 279
1989 Fleer '88 World Series 279
1989 Fleer Box Panels 280
1989 Fleer Update 280
1989 Fleer Baseball All Stars 281
1989 Fleer Baseball MVP 281
1989 Fleer Baseball's Exciting Stars 282
1989 Fleer Heroes of Baseball 282
1989 Fleer League Leaders 283
1989 Fleer Superstars 283
1990 Fleer 284
1990 Fleer All Stars 288
1990 Fleer '89 World Series 288
1990 Fleer League Standouts 288
1990 Fleer Box Panels 289
1990 Fleer Update 289
1991 Fleer 290
1991 Fleer All Stars 294
1991 Fleer Box Panels 295
1991 Fleer '90 World Series 295
1991 Fleer Pro Visions 295
1991 Fleer Update 295
1991 Fleer Ultra 296
1991 Fleer Ultra Gold 299
1991 Fleer Ultra Update 299
1992 Fleer 300
1992 Fleer All Stars 304
1992 Fller Roger Clemens 305
1992 Fleer Lumber Co. 305
1992 Fleer Rookie Sensations 305
1992 Fleer Smoke 'n Heat 305
1992 Fleer 7-Eleven 306
1992 Fleer Team Leaders 306
1992 Fleer Update 306
1992 Fleer Ultra 307
1992 Fleer Ultra Award Winners 311
1992 Fleer Ultra All-Rookies 311
1992 Fleer Ultra All-Stars 311
1992 Fleer Ultra Tony Gwynn 312
1993 Fleer 312
1993 Fleer Golden Moments I 316
1993 Fleer Golden Moments II 316
1993 Fleer Major League Prospects I 317
1993 Fleer Major League Prospects II 317
1993 Fleer All Stars 317
1993 Fleer ProVisions I 318
1993 Fleer ProVisions II 318
1993 Fleer Tom Glavine Highlights 318
1993 Fleer Rookie Sensations I 318
1993 Fleer Rookie Sensations II 319
1993 Fleer A.L. Team Leaders 319
1993 Fleer N.L. Team Leaders 319
1993 Fleer Ultra 319
1993 Fleer Ultra All-Rookies 323
1993 Fleer Ultra All-Stars 324
1993 Fleer Ultra Award Winners 324
1993 Fleer Ultra Dennis Eckersley 324
1993 Fleer Ultra Home Run Kings 325
1993 Fleer Ultra Performers 325
1993 Fleer Ultra Strikeout Kings 325
1993 Fleer Final Edition 325
1993 Fleer Flair 327
1993 Fleer Flair Wave of the Future 329
1994 Fleer 329
1994 Fleer Lumber Co. 334
1994 Fleer Rookie Sensations 334
1994 Fleer Smoke 'N Heat 334
1994 Fleer Team Leaders 335
1994 Fleer Award Winners 335
1994 Fleer League Leaders 335
1994 Fleer Major League Prospects 336
1994 Fleer All Stars 336
1994 Fleer Tim Salmon 336
1994 Fleer Golden Moments 337
1994 Fleer Golden Moments Super 337
1994 Fleer ProVisions 337
1994 Fleer Ultra 813
1994 Fleer Ultra Award Winners 814
1994 Fleer Ultra Home Run Kings 814
1994 Fleer Ultra RBI Kings 814
1994 Fleer Ultra League Leaders 814
1994 Fleer Ultra Phillies Finest 814
1994 Fleer Ultra 2nd Year Standouts 814

H

1975 Hostess 338
1975 Hostess Twinkies 339
1976 Hostess 340
1976 Hostess Twinkies 341
1977 Hostess 342
1977 Hostess Twinkies 343
1978 Hostess 344
1979 Hostess 345
1993 Hostess Twinkies 347

K

1970 Kellogg's 347
1971 Kellogg's 348
1972 Kellogg's 349
1972 Kellogg's Baseball Greats 349
1973 Kellogg's 350
1974 Kellogg's 350
1975 Kellogg's 351
1976 Kellogg's 351
1977 Kellogg's 352
1978 Kellogg's 352
1979 Kellogg's 353
1980 Kellogg's 354
1981 Kellogg's 354
1982 Kellogg's 355
1983 Kellogg's 355
1991 Kellogg's 3-D 356
1992 Kellogg's 3-D 356
1988 Kenner Starting Lineup 356
1989 Kenner Starting Lineup 357
1989 Starting Lineup Baseball Greats 359
1990 Kenner Starting Lineup 359
1991 Kenner Starting Lineup 360
1992 Kenner Starting Lineup 360
1993 Kenner Starting Lineup 361

L

1948 Leaf 361
1960 Leaf 361
1990 Leaf 363
1991 Leaf Previews 366
1991 Leaf 366
1992 Leaf Previews 370
1992 Leaf 370
1992 Leaf Gold Rookies 370
1992 Leaf Gold Edition 373
1993 Leaf 374
1993 Leaf Fasttrack 377
1993 Leaf Gold All-Stars 378

WHO AM I?

MY ACCOMPLISHMENTS

- Purchaser of over 60 million dollars in vintage cards and related memorabilia through 1993
- 14 years of full-time hobby experience
- Purchaser of the 1952 Topps find. What most people in the hobby consider the greatest find of baseball cards ever
- Appeared on "Good Morning America" on three different occasions
- Purchaser of Paris, Tennessee find, 250 unopened 1954-55 Topps and Bowman Football and Baseball Boxes and over 100 Mint condition sets
- Featured on hundreds of live T.V. and radio shows including, "Today," "Good Morning New York", "Live At Five," as well as ESPN, MSG, Sports Channel, etc.
- Appeared in over 300 different magazines and newspaper articles across the U.S.
- On the front pages of such prestigious newspapers as the Wall Street Journal, New York Times, New York Daily News
- Featured with major 8 page stories in popular magazines such as "Sports Illustrated" and "Sport"
- Participated in 12 national conventions in addition to over 400 regional baseball card conventions
- Have helped to form and develop some of the finest collections in the hobby including, Mr. James Copeland and Mr. Barry Halper
- The innovator of the "One Day Phone Auction," which runs 4 times a year and features only the finest in sports memorabilia

MY SERVICES

- We can buy your cards, for cold cash, check, money order, bank wire, whatever your needs may be.
- Appraise collections, or individual cards on a percentage basis.
- Counsel collectors at any time in person or by phone on any questions you may have about the hobby.
- Assist in any tax situation you might encounter in the dispersal of your collection.

NOBODY DOES IT BETTER THAN THE BUYING MACHINE!!

ALAN ROSEN 70 I Chestnut Ridge Road, Montvale, NJ 07645 • (201) 307-0700

1993 Leaf Gold Rookies 378
1993 Leaf Heading for the Hall 378
1993 Leaf Frank Thomas Super 379
1993 Leaf Update Gold All-Stars 379
1993 Leaf Update Gold Rookies 379

O

1991 O-Pee-Chee Premier 380
1992 O-Pee-Chee Premier 381
1993 O-Pee-Chee 382
1993 O-Pee-Chee Premier 385
1993 OPC Premier Star Performers 386
1993 OPC Premier Top Draft Picks 386
1993 O-Pee-Chee World Champs 384
1993 O-Pee-Chee World Series Heroes 385

P

1993 Pacific Spanish 386
1993 Pacific Spanish Gold Foil Stars .. 390
1993 Pacific Prism Inserts 390
1994 Pacific Crown 391
1994 Pacific Jewels of the Crown 395
1994 Pacific Homerun Leaders 395
1994 Pacific Latino All-Stars 395

S

1988 Score 396
1988 Score Box Panels 400
1988 Score Traded 400
1989 Score 401
1989 Score Traded 405
1990 Score 406
1990 Score Dream Team 410
1990 Score Traded 410
1991 Score 411
1991 Score Cooperstown 416
1991 Score Hot Rookies 416
1991 Score Mickey Mantle 417
1991 Score Traded 417
1992 Score 418
1992 Score Joe DiMaggio 423
1992 Score Factory Inserts 423
1992 Score Franchise 423
1992 Score Hot Rookies 424
1992 Score Impact Players 424
1992 Score Pinnacle 425
1992 Score Pinnacle Rookie Idols 430
1992 Score Pinnacle Slugfest 430
1992 Score Pinnacle Team Pinnacle .. 430
1992 Score Rookie/Traded 430
1993 Score 431
1993 Score Boys of Summer 435
1993 Score Franchise 436
1993 Score Gold Dream Team 436
1993 Score Select 436
1993 Score Select Aces 439
1993 Score Select Chase Rookies 439
1993 Score Select Chase Stars 439
1993 Score Select Stat Leaders 440
1993 Score Select Triple Crown 440
1993 Score Select Rookie/Traded 441
1993 Score Select All-Star Rookies 442
1993 Score Select Rookie/Traded Inserts ... 442
1993 Score Pinnacle 442
1993 Score Pinnacle Expansion Opening Day 446
1993 Score Pinnacle Rookie Team Pinnacle 446
1993 Score Pinnacle Slugfest 446
1993 Score Pinnacle Team Pinnacle .. 447
1993 Score Pinnacle Team 2001 447
1993 Score Pinnacle Tribute 447
1994 Score 449
1994 Score Boys of Summer 451
1994 Score Dream Team 451
1994 Score Gold Stars 451
1994 Score Gold Rush 452
1991 Studio Preview 452
1991 Studio 452
1992 Studio 454
1992 Studio Heritage 456
1993 Studio 456
1993 Studio Heritage 457
1993 Studio Frank Thomas 458
1993 Studio Silhouettes 458
1993 Studio Superstars on Canvas 458

T

1993 Ted Williams Card Co. 458
1951 Topps Red Backs 460
1951 Topps Blue Backs 461
1952 Topps 461
1953 Topps 464
1954 Topps 466
1955 Topps 467
1956 Topps 469
1956 Topps Pins 471
1957 Topps 471
1958 Topps 474
1959 Topps 478
1960 Topps 481
1960 Topps Baseball Tattoos 485
1961 Topps 486
1961 Topps Dice Game 489
1961 Topps Magic Rub-Offs 490
1961 Topps Stamps 490
1962 Topps 492
1962 Topps Baseball Bucks 495
1962 Topps Stamps 496
1963 Topps 498
1963 Topps Peel-Offs 501
1964 Topps 502
1964 Topps Coins 506
1964 Topps Giants 507
1964 Topps Photo Tattoos 508
1964 Topps Stand-Ups 508
1965 Topps 508
1965 Topps Embossed 512
1965 Topps Transfers 513
1966 Topps 514
1966 Topps Rub-Offs 518
1967 Topps 519
1967 Topps Pin-Ups 523
1967 Topps Stand-Ups 523
1967 Topps Stickers Pirates 524
1967 Topps Stickers Red Sox 524
1968 Topps 524
1968 Topps Action All-Star Stickers 528
1968 Topps Discs 529
1968 Topps Game 529
1968 Topps Plaks 530
1968 Topps Posters 530
1968 Topps Punchouts 530
1968 Topps 3-D 531
1969 Topps 531
1969 Topps Decals 536
1969 Topps Deckle Edge 537
1969 Topps 4-on-1 Stickers 537
1969 Topps Stamps 537
1969 Tops Super 538
1969 Topps Team Posters 539
1970 Topps 540
1970 Topps Candy Lids 544
1970 Topps Cloth Stickers 545
1970 Topps Posters 545
1970 Topps Scratch-Offs 545
1970 Topps Story Booklets 546
1970 Topps Super 546
1971 Topps 547
1971 Topps Coins 552
1971 Topps Greatest Moments 553
1971 Topps Super 553
1971 Topps Baseball Tattoos 554
1972 Topps 554
1972 Topps Cloth Stickers 559
1972 Topps Posters 560
1973 Topps 560
1973 Topps Candy Lids 565
1973 Topps Comics 565
1973 Topps 1953 Reprints 566
1973 Topps Pin-Ups 566
1973 Topps Team Checklists 566
1974 Topps 567
1974 Topps Deckle Edge 571
1974 Topps Puzzles 572
1974 Topps Stamps 572
1974 Topps Team Checklists 573
1974 Topps Traded 573
1975 Topps 574
1975 Topps Mini 578
1976 Topps 580
1976 Topps Traded 586
1977 Topps 587
1977 Topps Cloth Stickers 591
1978 Topps 591
1979 Topps 596
1979 Topps Comics 600
1980 Topps 601
1980 Topps Superstar 5x7 Photos 605
1981 Topps 606
1981 Topps Traded 610
1981 Topps Home Team 5x7 Photos . 611
1981 Topps National 5x7 Photos 612
1981 Topps Scratch-Offs 612
1981 Topps Stickers 613
1982 Topps 615
1982 Tops insert Stickers 621
1982 Topps Stickers 621
1982 Topps Traded 620
1983 Topps 623
1983 Topps Traded 628
1983 Topps All-Star Glossy set of 40 .. 628
1983 Topps Foldouts 629
1983 Topps Stickers 630
1983 Topps Stickers Boxes 632
1984 Topps 632
1984 Topps All-Star Glossy set of 22 .. 637
1984 Topps All-Star Glossy set of 40 .. 637
1984 Topps Traded 638
1984 Topps Gallery of Immortals 639
1984 Topps Rub Downs 639
1984 Topps Stickers 640
1984 Topps Stickers Boxes 642
1984 Topps Super 642
1985 Topps 643
1985 Topps All-Star Glossy set of 22 .. 648
1985 Topps All-Star Glossy set of 40 .. 648
1896 Topps Traded 648
1985 Topps All-Time Record Holders . 649
1985 Topps Gallery of Champions 650
1985 Topps Rub Downs 650
1985 Topps Stickers 651
1985 Topps Super 653
1985 Topps 3-D 654
1986 Topps 654
1986 Topps All-Star Glossy set of 22 .. 659
1986 Topps All-Star Glossy set of 60 .. 659
1986 Topps Traded 660
1986 Topps 3-D 660

1986 Topps Box Panels 661
1986 Topps Gallery of Champions 661
1986 Topps Mini League Leaders 661
1986 Topps Stickers 662
1986 Topps Super 664
1986 Topps Super Stars 665
1986 Topps Tattoos 665
1987 Topps 666
1987 Topps All-Star Glossy set of 22 .. 671
1987 Topps All-Star Glossy set of 60 .. 671
1987 Topps Traded 672
1987 Topps Baseball Highlights 673
1987 Topps Box Panels 673
1987 Topps Coins 674
1987 Topps Gallery of Champions 674
1987 Topps Glossy Rookies 674
1987 Topps Mini League Leaders 675
1987 Topps Stickers 676
1988 Topps 678
1988 Topps All-Star Glossy set of 22 .. 683
1988 Topps All-Star Glossy set of 60 .. 683
1988 Topps Traded 684
1988 Topps Box Panels 684
1988 Topps American Baseball 685
1988 Topps Big Baseball 686
1988 Topps Coins 687
1988 Topps Gallery of Champions 688
1988 Topps Glossy Rookies 689
1988 Topps Mini League Leaders 689
1988 Topps Sticker Cards 690
1988 Topps Stickers 690
1989 Topps 692
1989 Topps All-Star Glossy set of 22 .. 697
1989 Topps Glossy Rookie set of 22 .. 697
1989 Topps All-Star Glossy set of 60 .. 698
1989 Topps Traded 698
1989 Topps Box Panels 699
1989 Topps Batting Leaders 699
1989 Topps Big Baseball 700
1989 Topps Double Headers 702
1989 Topps Major League Debut 702
1989 Topps Mini League Leaders 703
1989 Topps American Baseball 704
1990 Topps 705
1990 Topps All-Star Glossy set of 22 .. 709
1990 Topps All-Star Glossy set of 60 .. 710
1990 Topps Traded 710
1990 Topps Big Baseball 711
1990 Topps Box Panels 711
1990 Topps Major League Debut 713
1990 Topps TV All-Stars 715
1990 Topps TV Cardinals 715
1990 Topps TV Cubs 716
1990 Topps TV Mets 716
1990 Topps TV Red Sox 717
1990 Topps TV Yankees 718
1990 Topps Heads Up! 718
1990 Topps Senior League 718
1991 Topps 719
1991 Topps Box Panels 724
1991 Topps Traded 724
1991 Topps Babe Ruth 725
1991 Topps Major League Debut 726
1991 Topps Stadium Club 727
1991 Topps 1953 Archives 730
1992 Topps 732
1992 Topps Gold 737
1992 Topps Traded 737
1992 Topps Kids 738
1992 Topps Triple Headers 739
1992 Topps Stadium Club Dome 740
1992 Topps Stadium Club 741
1996 Stadium Club First Day 746
1993 Topps 746
1993 Topps Gold 751
1993 Topps Black Gold 752
1993 Topps Stadium Club 753
1993 Topps Stadium Club Special 758
1993 Topps Stadium Club Team Sets . 759
1993 Topps Finest 762
1993 Topps Finest Refractors 763
1993 Topps Finest Jumbo All-Stars 763
1993 Topps Full Shot Super 764
1994 Topps Preview 764
1994 Topps 765
1987 Toys "R" Us 767
1988 Toys "R" Us Rookies 768
1989 Toys "R" Us Rookies 768
1990 Toys "R" Us Rookies 768
1991 Toys "R" Us Rookies 769
1993 Toys "R" Us Stadium Club 769

U

1989 Upper Deck Promos 770
1989 Upper Deck 771
1990 Upper Deck 775
1990 UD Reggie Jackson Heroes 780
1991 Upper Deck 780
1991 Upper Deck Final Edition 785
1991 Upper Deck Hank Aaron Heroes 786
1991 Upper Deck Nolan Ryan Heroes 786
1991 Upper Deck Hall of Fame Heroes 786
1991 Upper Deck Silver Sluggers 787
1992 Upper Deck 787
1992 UD College POY Holograms 792
1992 UD Bench/Morgan Heroes 792
1992 Upper Deck Fan Fest 793
1992 Upper Deck Hall of Fame Heroes 793
1992 Upper Deck Home Run Heroes . 793
1992 Upper Deck Scouting Report 793
1992 Upper Deck Ted Williams' Best . 794
1992 Upper Deck Ted Williams Heroes 794
1993 Upper Deck 794
1993 Upper Deck Clutch Performers .. 800
1993 Upper Deck 5th Anniversary 800
1993 Upper Deck Future Heroes 800
1993 Upper Deck Home Run Heroes . 800
1993 Upper Deck Iooss Collection 801
1993 Upper Deck On Deck 801
1993 UD Willie Mays Heroes 801
1993 Upper Deck 'Highlights' 802
1993 Upper Deck Then And Now 802
1993 Upper Deck Triple Crown 802
1993 Upper Deck All-Time Heroes 802
1993 Upper Deck All-Time Heroes T202 Reprints 804
1993 UD 5th Anniversary Super 804
1993 UD Iooss Collection Super 804
1993 UD Jackson Heroes Super 805
1993 Upper Deck Diamond Gallery 805
1993 Upper Deck SP 806
1993 Upper Deck SP Platinum Power 807
1993 Upper Deck Fun Packs 808
1993 Fun Packs All-Star Scratch-Offs . 809
1993 Fun Packs Mascot Madness 810
1994 Upper Deck Collector's Choice ... 810

Advertisers' Index

Larry Fritsch Cards .... IFC
Alan Rosen 5
Charles M. Conlon 7
Mark Jordan 9
Pro Sports Investments 11
Base Line Sports 15
Krause Publications 17
Krause Publications 19
Krause Publications 815
Card Collectors Co. 816
Power House Sports Cards .... IBC

Introduction

HOW TO USE THIS CATALOG

This catalog has been uniquely designed to serve the needs of all collectors, from beginning to advanced. It provides a comprehensive guide to nearly 50 years of baseball card issues, with a look back at the most significant cards prior to that time. The catalog is arranged so that even the most novice collector can consult it with confidence and ease.

The following explanations summarize the general practices used in preparing this catalog's listings. However, because of specialized requirements which may vary from card set to card set, these must not be considered ironclad. Where these standards have been set aside, appropriate notations are usually incorporated.

ARRANGEMENT

Because the most important feature in identifying, and pricing, a baseball card is its set of origin, the main body of this catalog, covering cards issued from 1948-date, has been alphabetically arranged according to the name by which the set is most popularly known to collectors.

Those sets which were issued for more than one year are then listed chronologically, from earliest to most recent.

Within each set, the cards are listed by their designated card number, or in the absence of card numbers, alphabetically according to the last name of the player pictured. Listing numbers found in parenthesis indicate the number does not appear on the card. Certain cards which fall outside the parameters of the normal card numbering for a specific set may be found at the beginnig or end of the listings for that set.

IDENTIFICATION

While most modern baseball cards are well identified on front, back or both, as to date and issue, such has not always been the case. In general, the back of the card is more useful in identifying the set of origin than the front. The issuer or sponsor's name will usually appear on the back since, after all, baseball cards were first produced as a promotional item to stimulate sales of other products. As often as not, that issuer's name is the name by which the set is known to collectors and under which it will be found listed in this catalog.

As a special feature, each set listed in this catalog has been cross-indexed by its date of issue. This will allow identification in some difficult cases because a baseball card's general age, if not specific year of issue, can usually be fixed by studying the biological or statistical information on the back of the card. The last year mentioned in either the biography or stats is usually the year which preceded the year of issue.

PHOTOGRAPHS

A photograph of the front and back of at least one representative card from virtually every set listed in this catalog has been incorporated into the listings to aid in identification.

Photographs have been printed in reduced size. The actual size of cards in each set is usually given in the introductory text preceding its listing. Cards which lack a specific mention of size should be presumed to be in the now-standard 2-1/2" x 3-1/2" format.

Stan Pietruska's

PRO SPORTS INVESTMENTS

Five times to think of Pro Sports Investments:

When Selling: When the time comes to sell, we'll be here to pay top dollar for your quality collectibles. Since 1980 Pro Sports Investments has consistently been one of the most aggressive buyers of both memorabilia and cards. We know what your items are worth.

Consignments: Our 10% consignment fee is the lowest in the hobby. Those dealers who charge 10% plus an additional 10% buyer's premium are actually taking 20% off the price realized. You pay double with those other guys!

Appraisals: Our 15 years in the hobby will give you the most accurate information as to the value of your quality memorabilia. We will travel anywhere in the world to view and appraisal large collections.

Consulting: Are you unsure what direction you wish to take with your memorabilia collection? Stan Pietruska can tell you where the market's been and where it's going. Put his 25 years of collecting in your corner.

When Buying: We get more quality material because we pay for it. If there's something you can't find anywhere, let us know. We'll locate it for you so you can add it to your collection. At a reasonable price.

Whether it's sets, singles, wax boxes, unopened packs, star cards, game used equipment, or any other sports memorabilia, we buy it all.

Stan Pietruska is a frequent guest on John L. Raybin's Sports Collectors Radio Show, and is currently a featured columnist in Wizard's Collectors Sportslook. His past writing credits include Baseball Card News, Baseball Cards Magazine and Sports Card Price Guide. A member of the SCD Price Guide Panel Since 1990. Stan received his Juris Doctor degree from Oklahoma City University in December of 1993. He is also a member of the American Bar Association and the American Trial Lawyers Association.

Stan Pietruska's

Pro Sports Investments

Box 3229, Bayonne, New Jersey 07002
(201) 433-1719

DATING

The dating of baseball cards by year of issue on the front or back of the card itself is a relatively new phenomenon. In most cases, to accurately determine a date of issue for an unidentified card, it must be studied for clues. As mentioned, the biography, career summary or statistics on the back of the card are the best way to pinpoint a year of issue. In most cases, the year of issue will be the year after the last season mentioned on the card.

Luckily for today's collector, earlier generations have done much of the research in determining year of issue for those cards which bear no clues. The painstaking task of matching players' listed and/or pictured team against their career records often allowed an issue date to be determined.

In some cases, particular card sets were issued over a period of more than one calendar year, but since they are collected together as a single set, their specific year of issue is not important. Such sets will be listed with their complete known range of issue years.

NUMBERING

While many baseball card issues as far back as the 1880s have contained card numbers assigned by the issuer, to facilitate the collecting of a complete set, the practice has by no means been universal. Even today, not every set bears card numbers.

Logically, those baseball cards which were numbered by their manufacturer are presented in that numerical order within the listings of this catalog. The many unnumbered issues, however, have been assigned Sports Collectors Digest Baseball Card Price Guide numbers to facilitate their universal identification within the hobby, especially when buying and selling by mail. In all cases, numbers which have been assigned, or which otherwise do not appear on the card through error or by design, are shown in this catalog within parentheses. In virtually all cases, unless a more natural system suggested itself by the unique matter of a particular set, the assignment of Sports Collectors Digest Baseball Card Price Guide numbers by the cataloging staff has been done by alphabetical arrangement of the players' last names or the card's principal title.

Significant collectible variations of any particular card are noted within the listings by the application of a suffix letter within parentheses. In instances of variations, the suffix "a" is assigned to the variation which was created first.

NAMES

The identification of a player by full name on the front of his baseball card has been a common practice only since the 1920s. Prior to that, the player's last name and team were the usual information found on the card front.

As a standard practice, the listings in the Sports Collectors Digest Baseball Card Price Guide present the player's name exactly as it appears on the front of the card. If the player's full name only appears on the back, rather than on the front of the card, the listing usually corresponds to that designation.

In cases where only the player's last name is given on the card, the cataloging staff has included the first name by which he was most often known for ease of identification.

Cards which contain misspelled first or last names, or even wrong initials, will usually have included in their listings the incorrect information, with a correction accompanying in parentheses. This extends, also, to cases where the name on the card does not correspond to the player actually pictured.

In some cases, to facilitate efficient presentations, to maintain ease of use for the reader, or to allow for proper computer sorting of data, a player's name or card title may be listed other than as it appears on the card.

GRADING

It is necessary that some sort of card grading standard be used so that buyer and seller (especially when dealing by mail) may reach an informed agreement on the value of a card.

Each card set's listings are generally priced in Krause Publications' price guides in three grades of preservation in which those cards are most commonly encountered in the daily buying and selling of the hobby marketplace.

Older cards (pre-1981) are listed in grades of Near Mint (NR MT), Excellent (EX) and Very Good (VG), reflecting the basic fact that few cards were able to survive for 25, 50 or even 100 years in close semblance to the condition of their issue.

The pricing of cards in these three conditions will allow readers to accurately price cards which fall in intermediate grades, such as EX-MT, or VG-EX.

More recent issues, which have been preserved in top condition in considerable number, are listed in the grades of Mint (MT), Near Mint and Excellent, reflective of the fact that there exists in the current market little or no demand for cards of the recent past in grades below Excellent.

In general, although grades below Very Good are not generally priced in price guides, close approximations of low-grade card values may be figured on the following formula: Good condition cards are valued at about 50 percent of VG price, with Fair cards about 50 percent of Good.

Cards in Poor condition have no market value except in the cases of the rarest and most expensive cards. In such cases, value has to be negotiated individually.

For the benefit of the reader, we present herewith the grading guide which was originally formulated by Baseball Cards (now Sports Cards) magazine and Sports Collectors Digest in 1981, and has been continually refined since that time.

These grading definitions have been used in the pricing of cards in this book, but they are by no means a universally-accepted grading standard.

The potential buyer of a baseball card should keep that in mind when encountering cards of nominally the same grade, but at a price which differs widely from that quoted in this book.

Ultimately, the collector himself must formulate his own personal grading standards in deciding whether cards available for purchase meet the needs of his own collection.

No collector is required to adhere to the grading standards presented herewith - or to any other published grading standards - but all are invited to do so. The editors of Krause Publications' sports books and price guides are eager to work toward the development of a standardized system of card grading that will be consistent with the realities of the hobby marketplace. Contact the editors.

Mint (MT): A perfect card. Well-centered, with parallel borders which appear equal to the naked eye. Four sharp, square corners. No creases, edge dents, surface scratches, paper flaws, loss of luster, yellowing or fading, regardless of age. No imperfectly printed card - out of register, badly cut or ink flawed - or card stained by contact with gum, wax or other substances can be considered truly Mint, even if new out of the pack. Generally, to be considered in Mint condition, a card's borders must exist in a ratio of 60/40 side to side and top to bottom.

Near Mint (NR MT): A nearly perfect card. At first glance, a Near Mint card appears perfect; upon closer examination, however, a minor flaw will be discovered. On well-centered cards, three of the four corners must be perfectly sharp; only one corner shows a minor imperfection upon close inspection. A slightly off-center card with one or more borders being noticeably unequal - but still present - would also fit this grade.

Excellent (EX): Corners are still fairly sharp with only moderate wear. Card borders may be off center. No creases. May have very minor gum, wax or product stains, front or back. Surfaces may show slight loss of luster from rubbing across other cards.

Very Good (VG): Show obvious handling. Corners rounded and/or perhaps showing minor creases. Other minor creases may be visible. Surfaces may exhibit loss of luster, but all printing is intact. May show major gum, wax or other packaging stains. No major creases, tape marks or extraneous markings or writing. Exhibits honest wear.

Good (G) (generally 50% of the VG price): A well-worn card, but exhibits no intentional damage or abuse. May have major or multiple creases. Corners rounded well beyond the border.

Fair (F) (generally 50% of the Good price): Shows excessive wear, along with damage or abuse. Will show all the wear characteristics of a Good card, along with such damage as thumb tack holes in or near margins, evidence of having been taped or pasted, perhaps small tears around the edges, or creases so heavy as to break the cardboard. Backs may show minor added pen or pencil writing, or be missing small bits of paper. Still, basically a complete card.

Poor (P): A card that has been tortured to death. Corners or other areas may be torn off. Card may have been trimmed, show holes from paper punch or have been used for BB gun practice. Front may have extraneous pen or pencil writing, or other defacement. Major portions of front or back design may be missing. Not a pretty sight.

In addition to these terms, collectors may encounter intermediate grades, such as VG-EX or EX-MT. These cards usually have characteristics of both the lower and higher grades, and are generally priced midway between those two values.

VALUATIONS

Values quoted in this book represent the current retail market at the time of compilation and are drawn from recommendations provided and verified through the editors' daily involvement in the publication of the hobby's leading advertising periodicals, as well as the input of specialized consultants, dealers and collectors.

It should be stressed, however, that this book is intended to serve only as an aid in evaluating cards; actual market conditions are constantly changing. This is especially true of the cards of current players, whose on-field performance during the course of a season can greatly affect the value of their cards - upwards or downwards.

Publication of this book is not intended as a solicitation to buy or sell the listed cards by the editors, publishers or contributors.

The values listed herein are retail prices - what a collector can expect to pay when buying a card from a dealer. The wholesale price, that which a collector can expect to receive from a dealer when selling cards, will be significantly lower.

Most dealers operate on a 100 percent mark-up, generally paying about 50 percent of a card's retail value. On some high-demand cards, dealers will pay up to 75 percent or even 100 percent or more of retail value, anticipating continued price increases. Conversely, for many low-demand cards, such as common players' cards of recent years, dealers may pay as little as 10 percent or even less of retail.

SETS

Collectors may note that the complete set prices for newer issues quoted in these listings are usually significantly lower than the total of the value of the individual cards which comprise the set.

This reflects two factors in the baseball card market. First, a seller is often willing to take a lower composite price for a complete set as a "volume discount" and to avoid inventorying a large number of common player or other lower-demand cards.

Second, to a degree, the value of common cards can be said to be inflated as a result of having a built-in overhead charge to justify the dealer's time in sorting cards, carrying them in stock and filling orders. This accounts for the fact that even brand new baseball cards, which cost the dealer around 1 cent each when bought in bulk, carry individual price tags of three to five cents or higher.

ERRORS/VARIATIONS

It is often hard for the beginning collector to understand that an error on a baseball card, in and of itself, does not usually add premium value to that card. It is usually only when the correcting of an error in the subsequent printing creates a variation that premium value attaches to an error.

Minor errors, such as wrong stats or personal data, misspellings, inconsistencies, etc. - usually affecting the back of the card - are very common, especially in recent years. Unless a corrected variation was also printed, these errors are not noted in the listings of this book because they are not generally perceived by collectors to have premium value.

On the other hand, major effort has been expended to include the most complete listings ever for collectible variation cards. Many scarce and valuable variations - dozens of them never before cataloged - are included in these listing because they are widely collected and often have significant premium value.

Beginning in the early 1990s, some card companies began production of their basic sets at more than one printing facility. This frequently resulted in numerous minor variations. Combined with a general decline in quality control from the mid-1980s through the early 1990s, which allowed unprecedented numbers of uncorrected error cards to be released, this caused a general softening of collector interest in errors and variations. No attempt has been made to catalog the dozens, perhaps even hundreds of minor variations in such sets as 1991 Topps and Fleer due to the fact that there exists no premium value for such cards.

COUNTERFEITS/REPRINTS

As the value of baseball cards has risen in the past 10-20 years, certain cards and sets have become too expensive for the average collector to obtain. This, along with changes in the technology of color printing, has given rise to increasing numbers of counterfeit and reprint cards.

While both terms describe essentially the same thing - a modern day copy which attempts to duplicate as closely as possible an original baseball card - there are differences which are important to the collector.

Generally, a counterfeit is made with the intention of deceiving somebody into believing it is genuine, and thus paying large amounts of money for it. The counterfeiter takes every pain to try to make his fakes look as authentic as possible. In recent years, the 1963 Pete Rose, 1984 Donruss Don Mattingly and more than 100 superstar cards of the late 1960s-early 1990s have been counterfeited - all were quickly detected because of the differences in quality of printing and the cardboard on which they were printed.

A reprint, on the other hand, while it may have been made to look as close as possible to an original card, is made with the intention of allowing collectors to buy them as substitutes for cards they may never be otherwise able to afford. The big difference is that a reprint is generally marked as such, usually on the back of the card. In other cases, like the Topps 1952 reprint set and 1953 Archives issue, the replicas are printed in a size markedly different from the originals.

Collectors should be aware, however, that unscrupulous persons will sometimes cut off or otherwise obliterate the distinguishing word - "Reprint," "Copy," - or modern copyright date on the back of a reprint card in an attempt to pass it as genuine.

A collector's best defense against reprints and counterfeits is to acquire a knowledge of the look and feel of genuine baseball cards of various eras and issues.

The publishers of this catalog also publish the Sportscard Counterfeit Detector book, listing more than 250 known counterfeit sportscards and providing details on identification of all known fakes. The book is available at card and hobby shops and many larger retail book outlets.

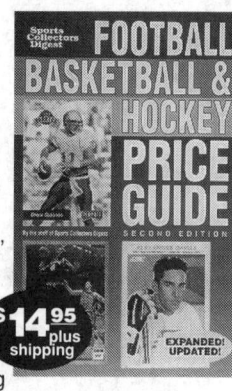

UNLISTED CARDS

Readers who have cards or sets which are not covered in this edition are invited to correspond with the editor for purposes of adding to the compilation work now in progress. Address: Sports Collectors Digest Baseball Card Price Guide, 700 E. State St., Iola, WI 54990.

Contributors will be acknowledged in future editions.

COLLECTORS ISSUES

There exists within the hobby a great body of cards which do not fall under the scope of this catalog by virtue of their nature of having been issued solely for the collector market. Known as "collector issues," these cards and sets are distinguished from "legitimate" issues in not having been created as a sales promotional item for another product or service - bubble gum, soda, snack cakes, dog food, cigarettes, gasoline, etc.

This distinction is no longer so easy to make since the early 1990s when many baseball card issues by even the major national companies began to be sold without an accompanying product.

Many collectors isuses are covered in the publisher's companion volume, Standard Catalog of Baseball Cards, available at card and hobby shops and in retail book outlets.

NEW ISSUES

Because new baseball cards are being issued all the time, the cataloging of them remains an on-going challenge. The editors will attempt to keep abreast of new issues so that they may be added to future editions of this book.

Readers are invited to submit news of new issues, especially limited-edition or regionally issued cards, to the editors. Address: Sports Collectors Digest Baseball Card Price Guide, 700 E. State St., Iola, WI 54990.

ROOKIE/FIRST CARD DESIGNATIONS

A player's name in *italic* type indicates a rookie card. An (FC) designation indicates a player's first card for that particular company. FCs will be found in major national regular-issue sets from 1981-94; generally Donruss, Fleer, Score, Topps and Upper Deck sets. They will also be located in the Donruss Rookies, Fleer Update, Topps Traded, Score Traded and Upper Deck Final Edition sets.

BASEBALL CARD HISTORY

In 1887 - more than 100 years ago - the first nationally-distributed baseball cards were issued by Goodwin & Co. of New York City. The 1 1/2" x 2 1/2" cards featured posed studio photographs glued to stiff cardboard. They were inserted into cigarette packages with such exotic brand names as Old Judge, Gypsy Queen and Dogs Head. Poses were formal, with artificial backgrounds and bare-handed players fielding balls suspended on strings to simulate action.

Then, as now, baseball cards were intended to stimulate product sales. What could be more American than using the diamond heroes of the national pastime to gain an edge on the competition? It is a tradition that has continued virtually unbroken for a century.

Following Goodwin's lead a year later, competitors began issuing baseball cards with their cigarettes, using full-color lithography to bring to life painted portraits of the era's top players.

After a few short years of intense competition, the cigarette industry's leading firms formed a monopoly and cornered the market. By the mid-1890s there was little competition, and no reason to issue baseball cards. The first great period of baseball card

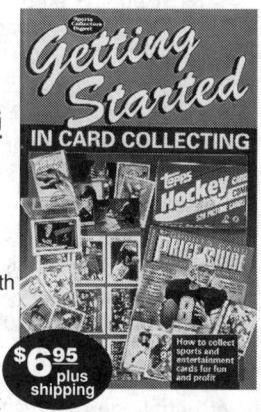

issues came to an end.

The importing of Turkish tobaccos in the years just prior to 1910 created a revolution in American smoking habits. With dozens of new firms entering the market, the idea of using baseball cards to boost sales was revived.

In the years from 1909-12, dozens of different sets of cards were produced to be given away in cigarette packages. There was a greater than ever variety in sizes, shapes and designs, from the extremely popular 1 1/2" x 2 5/8" color lithographed set of 500+ players which collectors call T206, to the large (5" x 8") Turkey Red premium cards given away to those sending in coupons found in cigarette packages.

There were double-folders, featuring two players on the same card, and triple-folders, which had two player portraits and an action scene. Gold ink and embossed designs were also tried to make competing companies' cards attractive and popular.

It was this era that saw the issue of the king of baseball cards, the T206 Honus Wagner card, worth as much as $400,000.

The zeal with which America's youngsters pursued their fathers, uncles and neighbors for cigarette cards in the years just prior to World War I convinced the nation's confectioners that baseball cards could also be used to boost candy sales.

While baseball cards had been produced by candy companies on a limited basis as far back as the 1880s, by the early 1920s the concept was being widely used in the industry. The highly competitive caramel business was a major force in this new marketing strategy, offering a baseball card in each nickel package of candy.

Not to be outdone, Cracker Jack began including baseball cards in each box. The 1914-15 Cracker Jack cards are important because they were the most popular of the candy cards to include players from a short-lived third major league, the Federal League.

Generally, candy cards of the era were not as colorful or well-printed as the earlier tobacco cards, due to the shortage of paper and ink-making ingredients caused by World War I.

The association of bubble gum and baseball cards is a phenomenon of only the past 60 years. In the early 1930s techniques were developed using rubber tree products to give chewing gum the elasticity necessary for blowing bubbles.

During this era the standard method of selling a slab of bubble gum and a baseball card in a colorfully wax-wrapped 1-cent package was developed. Bubble gum - and baseball card - production in this era was centered in Massachusetts, where National Chicle Co. (Cambridge) and Goudey Gum Co. (Boston) were headquartered.

Most bubble gum cards produced in the early 1930s featured a roughly square (about 2 1/2") format, with players depicted in colorful paintings. For the first time, considerable attention was paid to the backs of the cards, where biographical details, career highlights and past season statistics were presented.

In 1939, a new company entered the baseball card market - Gum Inc., of Philadelphia. Its "Play Ball" gum was the major supplier of baseball cards until 1941, when World War II caused a shortage of the materials necessary for both the production of bubble gum and the printing of baseball cards.

Three years after the end of World War II baseball cards returned on a national scale, with two companies competing for the bubble gum market. In Philadelphia, the former Gum Inc. reappeared on the market as Bowman Gum Inc.

Bowman's first baseball card set appeared in 1948, very similar in format to the cards which had existed prior to the war - black-and-white player photos on nearly square (2" x 2 1/2") cardboard. The 1948 Bowman effort was modest, with only 48 cards.

The following year, color was added to the photos. For 1950, Bowman replaced the retouched photos with original color paintings of players, many of which were repeated a year later in the 1951 issue. Also new for 1951 was a larger size card, 2" x 3 1/8".

Bowman had little national competition in this era. In 1948-49, Leaf Gum in Chicago produced a 98-card set that is the only bubble gum issue of the era to include a Joe DiMaggio card.

While Bowman dominated the post-war

era through 1951, in that year Topps began production of its first baseball cards, issuing three different small sets of cards and serving warning that it was going to become a major force in the baseball card field.

In 1952, Brooklyn-based Topps entered the baseball card market in a big way. Not only was its 407-card set the largest single-year issue ever produced, but its 2 5/8" x 3 3/4" format was the largest-sized baseball card ever offered for over-the-counter sale.

Other innovations in Topps' premiere issue for 1952 included the first-ever use of team logos in card design, and on the back of the card, the first use of line statistics to document the player's previous-year and career performance.

By contrast, Bowman's set for 1952 remained in the smaller format, had 72 fewer cards and showed little change in design from 1951.

Just as clearly as Topps won the 1952 baseball card battle, Bowman came back in 1953 with what is often considered the finest baseball card set ever produced. For the first time ever, actual color photographs were reproduced on baseball cards in Bowman's 160-card set.

To allow the full impact of the new technology, there were no other design elements on the front of the card and Bowman adopted a larger format, 2 1/2" x 3 3/4".

And so the competition went for five years, with each company trying to gain an edge by signing players to exclusive contracts and creating new and exciting card designs each year. Gradually, Topps became the dominant force in the card market. In late 1955, Bowman admitted defeat and the company was sold to Topps.

Baseball cards entered a new era in 1957. After years of intense competition, Topps enjoyed a virtual monopoly that was rarely seriously challenged in the next 25 years. One such challenge in the opening years of the 1960s came from Post cereal, which from 1961-63 issued 200-card sets on the backs of its cereal boxes.

In 1957, Topps' baseball cards were issued in a new size - 2 1/2" x 3 1/2" - that would become the industry-wide standard that prevails to this day. It was also the year that Topps first used full-color photographs for its cards, rather than paintings or retouched black-and-white photos.

Another innovation in the 1957 set was the introduction of complete major/and or minor league statistics on the card backs. This feature quickly became a favorite with youngsters and provided fuel for endless schoolyard debates about whether one player was better than the other.

In the ensuing five years, major league baseball underwent monumental changes. In 1958, the Giants and Dodgers left New York for California. In 1961-62 expansion came to the major leagues, with new teams springing up from coast to coast and border to border. The Topps baseball cards of the era preserve those days when modern baseball was in its formative stages.

In 1963, for the first time in seven years, it looked as if there might once again be two baseball card issues to choose from. After three years of issuing "old-timers" card sets, Fleer issued a 66-card set of current players.

Topps took Fleer to court, where the validity of Topps' exclusive contracts with baseball players to appear on bubble gum cards was upheld. It was the last major challenge to Topps for nearly 20 years.

The 1960s offered baseball card collecting at its traditional finest. Youngsters would wait and worry through the long winter, watching candy-store shelves for the first appearance of the brightly colored 5-cent card packs in the spring.

A cry of "They're in!" could empty a playground in seconds as youngsters rushed to the corner store to see what design innovations Topps had come up with for the new year.

Then, periodically during the summer, new series would be released, offering a new challenge to complete. As the seasons wore down, fewer and fewer stores carried the few final series, and it became a struggle to complete the "high numbers" from a given year's set. But it was all part of the fun of buying baseball cards in the 1960s.

The early 1970s brought some important changes to the baseball card scene. The decade's first two Topps issues were stunning in that the traditional white border was dropped in favor of gray in 1970, and black in 1971.

In 1972, Topps' card design was absolutely psychedelic, with brightly colored frames around the player photos, and comic book typography popping out all over. The design for the 1973 cards was more traditional, but the photos were not.

Instead of close-up portraits or posed "action" shots, many cards in the 1973 Topps set featured actual game action photos. Unfortunately, too many of those photos made it hard to tell which player was which, and the set was roundly panned by collectors.

But most significantly, 1973 marked the last year in which baseball cards were issued by series through the course of the summer. On the positive side, this eliminated the traditional scarce "high numbers" produced toward the end of the season.

On the negative side, it meant players who had been traded in the pre-season could no longer be shown in their correct uniforms, and outstanding new players had to wait a full year before their rookie cards would debut.

This marketing change made a significant impact on the hobby and helped spur a tremendous growth period in the late 1970s. By offering all of the cards at once, Topps made it easy for baseball card dealers to offer complete sets early in the year.

Previously, collectors had to either assemble their sets by buying packs of cards, or wait until all series had been issued to buy a set from a dealer. It was in this era that many of today's top baseball card dealers got their start or made the switch to baseball cards a full-time business.

During this era, the first national competition to Topps' baseball card monopoly in many years was introduced. Hostess, a bakery products company, began distributing baseball cards printed on the bottoms of packages of its snack cakes, while the Kellogg's company distributed simulated 3-D cards in boxes of its cereals.

The eagerness with which collectors gobbled up these issues showed that the hobby was ready for a period of unprecedented growth.

The baseball card hobby literally boomed in 1981. A federal court broke Topps' monopoly on the issue of baseball cards with bubble gum, and Fleer, from Philadelphia, and Donruss, of Memphis, entered the field as the first meaningful competition in nearly 20 years.

That same year also marked a beginning of the resurgence in the number of regional baseball card issues. Over the next few years, dozens of such sets came onto the market, helping to boost sales of everything from snack cakes to soda pop and police public relations.

By 1984, more than half of the teams in the major leagues were issuing some type of baseball cards on a regional basis. The hobby had not enjoyed such diversity of issues since the mid-1950s.

While yet another court decision cost Fleer and Donruss the right to sell their baseball cards with bubble gum, both companies remained in the market and gained strength.

Topps' major contribution in this era was the introduction of annual "Traded" sets which offered cards of the year's new rookies as well as cards of traded players in their correct uniforms.

The mid-1980s showed continued strong growth in the number of active baseball card collectors, as well as the number of new baseball card issues. Topps, still the industry's leader, expanded the number and variety of its baseball issues with many different test issues and on-going specialty sets, including oversize cards, 3-D plastic cards, metal "cards" and much more.

After three years of over-production of its baseball card sets, Donruss, in 1984, significantly limited the number of cards printed, creating a situation in which demand exceeded supply, causing the value of Donruss cards to rise above Topps for the first time.

In 1984, Fleer followed Topps' lead and produced a season's-end "Update" set. Because the quantity of sets printed was extremely limited, and because it contains some of today's hottest young players, the 1984 Fleer Update set has become the most valuable baseball card issue produced in recent times.

In 1986, a fourth company joined the baseball card wars. Called "Sportflics," the cards were produced by a subsidiary of the Wrigley Gum Co., and featured three different photos on each card in a simulated 3-D effect.

For 1988, a fourth national baseball card set, called Score, entered the scene. A fifth national baseball card set, Upper Deck, was created in 1989.

The early 1990s saw another explosion in baseball card supply. While the number of major national card-producing licensors remained static, each company attempted to carve a niche in the market by creating separate brands to appeal to base-level collectors, intermediate hobbyists, and - especially - those interested in high-tech premium quality cards for which money was no object. This trend peaked in late 1993 with the introduction of Topps Finest brand cards, which by virtue of an extremely limited press run were selling for more than $20 a pack soon after issue.

Another phenomenon of the early 1990s was the creation of extremely low-production specialty cards to be inserted in card packages on a random basis. Often showcasing the card companies' latest technology, the insert cards often achieved significant premium value as collectors pursued them for their relative rarity. This spawned the hobby term "chase card" to designate these wax-pack prizes. It also spawned a lottery mentality on the part of many card buyers who spurned the contents of any pack which did not contain the high-value inserts.

Glossary of hobby terms

Airbrushing: The touching up of a photo by an artist. Usually done on trading cards to show a player, who has changed teams, in his new uniform.

All-Star card: A special card identifying a player as a member of a National League, American League or Major League all-star team. Players shown on all-star cards may or may not be members of their league's official All-Star team. All-star cards can be part of a regular set or issued as an independent set.

Autographed card: A card that has actually been signed by the player pictured, as opposed to the facsimile signatures that are sometimes printed on cards as part of the design. The value of an autographed card is generally greater than that same card would be if it were unautographed.

Big cards: The trade name for Topps' oversized, glossy-finish card issues produced from 1988-1990. The cards are reminiscent of Topps cards from the 1950s.

Blank-back: Usually used to refer to a card that has no printing on the back because of a manufacturing mistake. Cards that were intentionally issued without printing on the back are also known as blank-backed.

Blister pack: A blister pack is a method of card packaging in which cards are packaged in hard plastic on a cardboard backing, Cards are usually visible through the plastic.

Book price: The retail selling price which appears in a price guide.

Borders: The portion of a card which surrounds the picture. Usually white but sometimes colored. The condition of a card's borders is one of the vital components in determining a card's grade.

Box-bottom cards: Cards printed on the bottom and/or sides of wax boxes. Box-bottom cards are not considered to be part of the regular set and generally are not valuable unless kept intact as a panel.

Boxed set: A set of cards, usually consisting of either 33 or 44 cards, issued as a complete set and sold in its own box at a large chain or discount store. Boxed sets are usually made by one of the major manufacturers and contain cards of only the biggest names or hottest rookies.

Brick: A wrapped lot of cards, usually all from one year. See "starter set."

Buy price: The price which a dealer is willing to pay for cards or memorabilia. A dealer's buy price is usually quite a bit lower than that item's catalog or retail price.

Caption: The title on a card which identifies or describes the subject pictured, but may also be a line of dialogue. It generally appears under the illustration and/or on the back.

Card stock: The paper or cardboard that baseball cards are printed on.

Case: A sealed case containing wax boxes or other product units which card companies sell at wholesale to dealers or retail stores. For instance, a 1990 Topps "wax case" is made up of 20 "wax boxes."

Cello box: A retail display box of cello packs, usually, but not always, containing 24 packs.

Cello case: A wholesale unit of cello boxes, usually, but not always, containing 16 boxes.

Cello pack: A cellophane-wrapped pack of cards. Usually contains more cards than a wax pack. Depending on packaging, the top and bottom card of a cello pack may be easily visible through the cellophane. Some collectors will pay a premium for a cello pack with a card of a star player or hot rookie showing on the top or bottom.

Centering: The positioning of a card picture between its borders. A well-centered card has even borders, an important factor in grading a card.

Checklist: A list of every card in a particular set, usually with a space allowing the collector to check whether he has the card. A checklist can appear on a card, in a book or elsewhere. Checklist cards are worth more if they're left unchecked.

Chipping: A card-grading term referring to a condition in which a portion of a card's dark-colored border is worn away. Chipping is a real problem, for instance, with 1953 and 1971 Topps cards, and more recent issues with colored borders.

Coin: A metal or plastic coin-sized disc which depicts a player. It can also refer to an actual coin or a coin-sized silver piece which commemorates an actual event.

Collation: The act of putting cards in order, usually numerical order.

Collectible: Something worth collecting. Baseball cards, programs, pennants, uniforms, and autographs are all examples of collectibles.

Collector issue: Cards produced primarily to be sold to collectors and not issued as a premium to be given away or sold with a commercial product. Collector issues fall into two categories: authorized (meaning the issue was made with the approval of professional sports and the players' association) or unauthorized (meaning the issue was made without approval).

Combination card: A single card which depicts two or more players, but is not a team card.

Common card: A card picturing a "common" or ordinary player — that is, not a star or superstar. "Commons" are the lowest-priced cards in a given series or set.

Condition: One of the major factors in determining the value of a card, this term applies to the wear and tear of a card.

Counterfeit card: A phony card made to look like a real card. Counterfeit cards have no collector value.

Crease: A bend mark in a card. usually due to mishandling. Creases substantially lower a card's grade and value.

CY: Cy Young Award.

Dealer: A person who buys, sells and trades baseball cards and other memorabilia for profit. A dealer may be full-time, part-time, own a shop, operate a mail-order business from his home, deal at baseball card shows on weekends or do any combination of the above.

Decollation: The act of putting cards in random order, usually for packaging.

Die-cut card: A baseball card in which the player's outline has been partially separated from the background, enabling the card to be folded into a "stand-up" figure. Die-cut cards that have never been folded are worth more to collectors.

Ding: Slight damage to the corner or edge of a card.

Disc set: A set of disc-shaped cards, usually showing head-and-shoulder shots of players.

Distributor: Persons or organizations which buy cards directly from the card companies or from other dealers and resells them on a large scale. Sometimes distributors receive exclusive products, and thus are the only source of distribution for the product.

Double-print: An individual card that, because of a particular printing configuration, appears twice on the same press sheet and is, therefore, twice as common as the other cards.

Doubles: A duplicate of a card in your collection. A card which, since you retain one for your set, can be traded or sold.

Error card: A card that contains a mistake, including wrong photos, misspelled words, incorrect statistics, and so forth. Usually error cards have no extra value unless they have been corrected, resulting in a "variation" card.

Exclusive: When a company makes an agreement that a distributor is the only one selling the company's cards at the offering price.

Exhibit cards: Postcard-size cards picturing baseball players and other celebrities and sold in penny-arcade machines. Exhibit cards were produced from the 1920s to the 1960s.

Extended set: A term used to describe a late-season series of cards added on to and numbered after a regular set. Also known as an extended series, update set or traded set.

Facsimile autograph: A reproduced autograph. Facsimile autographs are often found on sports cards as part of the card's design.

Factory set: A complete set of cards collated and packaged by the card company. A factory set may or may not be packaged in a special box. Usually factory sets are sealed or have sealed inner packs as an added security measure. Factory sets with intact seals or inner packs command a slight premium over hand-collated sets.

First card: The first card of a player in a national set. A first card may or may not be a player's rookie card; for instance, if a player appeared in a Fleer set one year and a Score set the next, the Fleer card would be that player's rookie card and his first Fleer card, while the Score card would be his first Score card but not his rookie card.

Foil: Foil-embossed stamp on a card.

Foil box: A retail display box of foil packs, usually, but not always, containing 36 packs.

Foil case: A wholesale unit of foil boxes, usually, but not always containing 24 boxes.

Foil pack: A pack of baseball cards packaged in a tamper-proof, shiny foil. Upper Deck packages its cards in foil packs.

Food set: A set either inserted in packages of food (hot dogs, cereal, popcorn, potato chips, candy, cookies, etc.) or offered as a send-in offer by a food company.

Full sheet: A full press sheet of cards that has never been cut; sometimes referred to as an "uncut" sheet. The number of cards on a sheet varies with the printing process, but most often contains 132 cards.

Gloss: The amount of surface shine on a card. All baseball cards are made with some surface gloss. Cards that keep more of their gloss keep more of their value.

Glossy card: A card with a special, extra-shiny finish.

Glossy set: A set of glossy cards. Glossy sets can be either small and common (Topps' sendaway all-star sets) or large and scarce. Fleer, Topps, Score and Bowman have made glossy versions of their regular baseball card sets.

Grade: The state of preservation of a card or piece of memorabilia. An item's value is based in large part on its grade (condition).

Grading service: A company that charges a fee to grade cards. Most grading services work like this: After a card is graded, it is placed in a tamper-proof plastic holder. A network of member-dealers then agrees to buy that card sight-unseen at that grade. Card grading services are a recent innovation, patterned after similar services in the coin collecting hobby.

Hall of Famer (HOFer): A member of the Baseball Hall of Fame in Cooperstown, N.Y., but also used to refer to a baseball card picturing a member of the Hall of Fame. Hall of Famer cards almost always command a premium over other cards.

Hand-collated set: A set assembled card-by-card by hand, usually by a collector or dealer putting the set together out of wax, cello or vending boxes.

High numbers: A term usually used to describe the final series in a particular set of cards. High numbers were generally produced in smaller quantities than other series and are, therefore, scarcer and more valuable.

Hologram: The silvery, laser-etched trademark printed as an anti-counterfeiting device on Upper Deck cards. Also, the disc with a team logo inserted into Upper Deck packs.

In-action card: A card showing a ballplayer in action, as opposed to posed.

Insert: A collectible included inside a regular pack of baseball cards to boost sales. Inserts have included posters, baseball player stamps, coins, stickers, comic books, special cards, and tattoos.

Key cards: The most important cards in a set.

Last card: The final card issued of a ballplayer (or the final card of any particular set).

Layering: A term used in card grading to describe the separation of the layers of paper that make up the cardboard stock. Layering is a sign of wear that is first noticeable at the corners of the card.

Legitimate issue: A licensed card set issued as a premium with a commercial product to increase sales; not a collector issue.

Limited edition: A term often used by makers of cards and memorabilia to indicate scarcity. A limited edition means just that — production of the item in question will be limited to a certain number. However, that number may be large or small.

Logo sticker: A peel-off, adhesive-backed reproduction of a team's symbol. Logo stickers are packed in Fleer wax packs.

Major set: A large, nationally-distributed set produced by a major card manufacturer, such as Tor

Fleer, Donruss, Score, or Upper Deck.

Mini: Small-size cards, sometimes miniature reproductions of regular cards (1975 Topps mini) and sometimes independent issues (1986-89 Topps Mini League Leaders).

Minor leaguer: A card depicting a player from the minor leagues. Minor league sets are a fast-growing segment of the hobby.

Miscut: A card that has been cut incorrectly from a press sheet during the manufacturing process and decreases in value as a result.

Multi-player card: A card picturing more than one player. Multi-player cards often show rookies or stars.

MVP: Most Valuable Player award winner.

Notching: A card-grading term used to describe indentations along the edge of a card, sometimes caused by a rubber band. Notching decreases a card's value.

Obverse: The front of the card displaying the picture.

Off-center: A term used in card grading to describe a card that has uneven borders.

Out of register: A term used to describe a printing error in which the various colors are not correctly superimposed upon one another, thereby decreasing the value of the card.

Panel: A strip of two or more uncut cards. Some card sets are issued in panels.

Police set: A regional card set made for a police department and given away to kids, usually one card at a time, to promote friendly relations. Police cards often carry a safety or anti-drug message on the back. Baseball, football, basketball and hockey police sets have been made of major league, minor league and college teams. Similar sets issued by fire departments are also generically called "police sets" or "safety sets."

Polyethylene: A type of plastic used to make card sheets and other collectors' supplies. Very flexible, but not as clear as other types of plastic. Safer than PVC for very long-term card storage.

Premium: An extra. In terms of cards, this can either refer to a card inserted in a package of some other product or something extra inserted in a package of cards. "Premium" can also refer to the extra money a high-series or star card commands.

Pre-rookie: Term sometimes used to refer to any card of a player issued before his rookie card – a minor league card, for example, or a high school, college or Olympic team card.

Press run: The total number of any one set of cards printed.

Price guide: A periodical or book which contains checklists of cards, sets and other memorabilia and their values in varying conditions.

Promo card: A card made for promotional purposes. Promo cards generally have very limited distribution and can be quite valuable.

Proof card: A card made not to be sold but to test the card presses, the card design, photography, colors, paper, statistical accuracy and so forth.

Puzzle piece, poster piece: The back of a card containing a partial design which, when pieced together with corresponding pieces, forms a large picture or poster.

Rack box: A retail display box of rack packs. There are usually 24 rack packs to a rack box.

Rack case: A wholesale case of rack boxes. There are usually three or six rack boxes in a rack case.

Rack pack: A cellophane-wrapped pack of cards, usually having three compartments, designed to be hung from a peg in a retail store. Rack packs vary in the number of cards in each pack; also, some rack packs consist of nothing but cello-wrapped wax packs.

Rare: Difficult to obtain and limited in number. See "Scarce."

Rated Rookie (RR): A Donruss subset featuring young players the company thinks are the top rookie players from a particular year (1984-present).

Record Breaker card: A special Topps card found in a regular issue set which commemorates a record-breaking performance by a player from the previous season.

Regional set: A card set limited in distribution to one geographical area. Regional sets often depict players from one team.

Reprint: A reproduction of a previously-issued sports card or set. Generally produced to satisfy collector demand, they usually – but not always – are labeled "reprint" and have little collector value.

Restored card: A card which has had "cosmetic surgery" – that is, a card which has had its imperfections fixed long after the card was issued. A card restorer can fix corners and restore gloss to card stock. Restored cards should be clearly labeled as such by whoever is selling them, and should be priced much less than unrestored cards in the same condition.

Reverse: The back of a card.

Reverse negative: A common error in which the picture negative is flip-flopped so the picture comes out backward, or reversed.

Rookie card: A player's first card issued by a major card producer in its regular annual set. It may or may not be issued during the player's actual rookie season. A rookie card is often a player's most valuable card.

ROY: Rookie of the Year.

Scuff: A rub or abrasion on a card which removes a portion of its gloss or printing. Scuffed cards are worth less than non-scuffed cards.

Second-year card: The second card of a player issued in the major sets. Usually, a second-year card is the most expensive card of a player, next to the rookie card.

Sell price: The price at which a dealer will sell cards. Generally much higher than his buy price.

Sepia: A dark reddish-brown coloration used in some card sets instead of traditional black-and-white.

Series: A group of cards that is part of a set and was issued at one time. The term is usually applied to Topps sets from 1952 through 1973, when sets were issued in various series.

Set: A complete run of cards, including one number of each card issued by a particular manufacturer in a particular year; for example, a 1985 Fleer set.

Short-print: A card that, for whatever reason, is not printed in as great a quantity as other cards in the set. The opposite of a double-print.

Skip-numbered: A set of cards not numbered in exact sequence, with some numbers missing. Some manufacturers have issued skip-numbered sets to trick collectors into buying more cards, looking for card numbers that didn't exist. Other sets became skip-numbered when one or more players were dropped from the set at the last minute and were not replaced.

Special card: A card in a set that depicts something other than a single player without mention of any special event that may involve that player; for example, a checklist card, All-Star card, team card or team leaders card.

Stamp: An adhesive-backed paper which depicts a player. When the stamp, which can be an individual or a sheet of many stamps, is moistened, it can be attached to another surface or corresponding stamp album.

Standard size card: A card which measures 2 1/2" by 3 1/2" tall. In 1957, Topps baseball cards were produced in the 2 1/2" by 3 1/2" size, which set the standard for modern baseball cards.

Star card: A designation used to describe a player of better-than-average skill and performance who isn't of "superstar" caliber. The term "minor star" may also be used to differentiate between various levels of skill and popularity. In terms of value, star cards fall between commons and superstars.

Starter kit: A prepackaged kit for new collectors. Often it contains a binder and plastic sheets, individual card protectors, plastic holders, a book or magazine on collecting or a price guide, and cards.

Starter set: A less-than-complete set of cards meant to give beginning collectors a start towards completing a certain set.

Sticker: An adhesive-backed card. Stickers can either be card-size or smaller. Topps, Fleer and Panini have issued major sports sticker sets in the last several years. Stickers are not tremendously popular with collectors.

Stock: The cardboard on which a card is printed.

Subset: A set of cards with the same theme within a larger set. Examples: Donruss Diamond Kings are a "subset" of the Donruss set; or Topps All-Star cards are a subset of the Topps set.

Super card: A designation referring to the physical size of a card. Generally, any card postcard size (3-1/2" x 5") or larger is referred to as a super.

Superstar card: A card picturing a player of Hall-of-Fame (current or future) caliber.

Tab: A portion of a card, usually perforated, which can be removed from the card without damaging the central part of the card.

Tattoos: Transfers showing ballplayers and/or team logos. Tattoos were a popular wax-pack premium in 1960s Topps wax packs; later Topps launched them as a stand-alone product, with little success.

Team card: A card picturing an entire team.

Team set: All the cards from a particular set showing members of a particular team. Team set collecting is becoming a very popular type of collecting.

Team-issued set: A set given away or sold by an individual team.

Test issue: A set of cards distributed on a limited basis to test its marketability. Topps has issued a variety of test products in the 1960s, 1970s and 1980s.

3-D card: Term used to refer to various types of cards and issues. A 3-D card may have a diffused background that lets the foreground image stand out (Kellogg's), multiple images (Sportflics) or a raised image (Topps 3-D).

Tiffany: Topps' name for its glossy version of its regular set. The first Tiffany set was issued in 1984.

Tin: Slang for a Fleer glossy set (1987-89), which are packaged in colorful, numbered tin boxes.

Traded set: An auxiliary set of cards issued toward the end of the season to reflect trades that were made after the printing of the regular set. Sometimes called "Update" sets, they also usually feature rookies not included in the regular set. The first stand-alone traded set was a baseball traded set issued by Topps in 1981.

Trimmed card: A card that has been cut down from its original size, greatly reducing its value.

Uncut sheet: A full press sheet of cards that has never been cut into individual cards.

Update set: See "Traded set."

Variation: A card that exists in two different forms within the same set. A "variation" frequently occurs when an error card has been corrected. Some variations are worth more than others, based on the quantity of each variation produced.

Vending case: A wholesale package containing nothing but cards, originally intended to be used to fill card-vending machines. Most often a vending case contains 24 boxes of 500 cards each.

Vending set: A set put together from cards in vending boxes. Such sets will not have cards that exhibit wax or gum stains.

Want list: A collector's or dealer's list of items he is wishing to buy. Often, a collector will send a dealer a "want list," and the dealer will try to locate the items on the list.

Wax box: A retail box of wax packs. There are usually 36 wax packs in a wax box.

Wax case: A wholesale case of wax boxes. There are usually 20 wax boxes in a wax case. Often the term is shortened to "wax."

Wax pack: The basic unit of retail baseball card packaging. A specific number of baseball cards, packaged with a premium (bubble gum, puzzle pieces, logo stickers and so forth) in a wax-coated wrapper.

Wax stain: A condition caused by wax from the pack wrapper melting onto a card. Wax stains lower the value of a card, but can be removed by rubbing with a pair of pantyhose or using a commercial wax-removal solution.

Wrapper: What wax packs are packaged in. A collectible item in itself.

Wrong backs: A card with the wrong back (the player on the front does not match the biography/statistics on the back). Most collectors think these cards are damaged and are worth less than a correctly-printed card, although some collectors will pay premiums on superstars or rookies.

Steve Norman Carlton

Dec. 22, 1944; 6-5, 210; throws and bats left; pitcher; retired; 24 seasons (St. Louis 1965-71, Philadelphia 1972-86, San Francisco 1986, Chicago White Sox 1986, Cleveland 1987, Minnesota 1987-88); Hall of Fame 1994.

Career statistics

W: 329 (9th); L: 244 (tied 13th); Pct.: .574; ERA: 3.22; G: 741 (29th); GS: 709; CG: 254; ShO: 55 (15th); IP: 5,216 1/3 (9th); H: 4,672; R: 2,130; ER: 1,864; BB: 1,833 (2nd); SO: 4,136 (2nd).

One of baseball's all-time best left-handed pitchers, Steve "Lefty" Carlton was the only player selected by the writers to enter Baseball's Hall of Fame in 1994.

The four-time Cy Young Award winner ranks only behind Warren Spahn (363) in victories by a left-hander, and trails only Nolan Ryan (5,714) in career strikeouts .

"Lefty" won his first Cy Young Award in 1972, posting a 27-10 record and league-leading 310 strikeouts and 1.98 ERA. His 27 wins tied the modern National League record for most games won by left-hander in a season and made him the only player to ever win a Cy Young Award for a last-place team.

Carlton captured his second award in 1977, with a 23-10 record and a 2.64 ERA. His 24-9 record, with a 2.34 ERA and league-leading 286 strikeouts, was enough for him to win his third award in 1980. After posting a 23-11 record and a league-leading 286 strikeouts, Carlton won his fourth award in 1982. His other 20-win seasons came in 1971 (20-9) and 1976 (20-7).

The 10-time all-star holds the National League lifetime record for games started (677), most years with 100 or more strikeouts (18), and most strikeouts by a left-hander (4,000). On Sept. 15, 1969, Carlton tied the N.L. record for most strikeouts in a game by a left-hander (19). He led the league in strikeouts and innings pitched five times.

Carlton posted a 4-2 record in five championship series playoffs, and participated in four World Series, playing on two winners - the 1967 St. Louis Cardinals and the 1980 Philadelphia Phillies, for which he posted a 2-0 record against the Kansas City Royals, including winning the clincher in Game Six.

Steve Carlton checklist

Set	#	NR MT	EX	VG
1965 Topps	477	600.00	300.00	175.00
1967 O-Pee-Chee	146	140.00	70.00	42.50
1967 Topps	146	125.00	62.50	37.50
1968 Topps	408	60.00	30.00	18.00
1969 Topps	255	60.00	30.00	18.00
1970 Major League Baseball stamps	137	2.00	1.00	.60
1970 O-Pee-Chee	67 (League Leader)	9.00	4.50	2.75
1970 O-Pee-Chee	220	50.00	25.00	15.00
1970 Topps	67 (League Leader)	3.00	1.50	.90
1970 Topps	220	40.00	20.00	12.00
1971 Major League Baseball stamps	271	2.00	1.00	.60
1971 O-Pee-Chee	55	38.00	19.00	11.50
1971 Topps	55	30.00	15.00	9.00
1971 Topps Coins	115	7.00	3.50	2.00
1972 Milton Bradley	unnumbered	20.00	10.00	6.00
1972 O-Pee-Chee	93 (League Leader)	6.00	3.00	1.75
1972 O-Pee-Chee	420	35.00	17.50	10.50
1972 Topps	93 (League Leader)	2.00	1.00	.60
1972 Topps	420	25.00	12.50	7.50
1972 Topps	751 (Traded)	60.00	30.00	18.00
1973 Kellogg's	7	4.00	2.00	1.25
1973 O-Pee-Chee	65 (League Leader)	5.00	2.50	1.50
1973 O-Pee-Chee	66 (League Leader)	5.00	2.50	1.50
1973 O-Pee-Chee	67 (League Leader)	22.00	11.00	6.50
1973 O-Pee-Chee	300	20.00	10.00	6.00
1973 Topps	65 (League Leader)	2.00	1.00	.60
1973 Topps	66 (League Leader)	2.00	1.00	.60
1973 Topps	67 (League Leader)	15.00	7.50	4.50
1973 Topps	300	15.00	7.50	4.50
1973 Topps Comics	4	125.00	62.50	37.50
1973 Topps Candy Lids	10	20.00	10.00	6.00
1973 Topps Pin-Ups	4	60.00	30.00	18.00
1974 Johnny Pro Phillies	32	20.00	10.00	6.00
1974 O-Pee-Chee	95	15.00	7.50	4.50
1974 Topps	95	10.00	5.00	3.00
1974 Topps Deckle Edge	5	80.00	40.00	25.00
1974 Topps Stickers	unnumbered	6.00	3.00	1.75
1975 Hostess	63	4.00	2.00	1.25
1975 O-Pee-Chee	185	12.00	6.00	3.50
1975 O-Pee-Chee	312 (League Leader)	20.00	10.00	6.00
1975 Topps	185	10.00	5.00	3.00
1975 Topps	312 (League Leader)	8.00	4.00	2.50
1975 Topps Mini	185	25.00	12.50	7.50
1975 Topps Mini	312 (League Leader)	2.50	1.25	.70
1975 SSPC	459	12.00	6.00	3.50
1976 Crane	10	1.25	.60	.40
1976 O-Pee-Chee	355	10.00	5.00	3.00
1976 Topps	355	7.00	3.50	2.00
1977 Hostess	117	5.00	2.50	1.50
1977 Kellogg's	57	5.00	2.50	1.50
1977 O-Pee-Chee	93	9.00	4.50	2.75
1977 Topps	110	8.00	4.00	2.50
1977 Topps cloth stickers	11	12.00	6.00	3.50
1978 Hostess	49	3.50	1.75	1.00
1978 Kellogg's	1	4.00	2.00	1.25
1978 O-Pee-Chee	5 (League Leader)	4.50	2.25	1.25
1978 O-Pee-Chee	170	7.00	3.50	2.00
1978 Topps	205 (League Leader)	1.50	.70	.40
1978 Topps	540	5.00	2.50	1.50
1979 Burger King Phillies	4	3.00	1.50	.90
1979 Hostess	71	3.50	1.75	1.00
1979 Kellogg's	18	2.50	1.25	.70
1979 O-Pee-Chee	9	5.00	2.50	1.50
1979 Topps	25	4.00	2.00	1.25

Note: 1980 prices and on are based on Mint, Near Mint and Excellent

Set	#	MT	NR MT	EX
1980 Burger King Phillies	15	4.00	2.00	1.25
1980 Burger King Pitch, Hit & Run	2	1.00	.50	.30
1980 Kellogg's	14	1.50	1.25	.60
1980 O-Pee-Chee	113	5.00	3.75	2.00
1980 Topps	210	4.00	3.00	1.50
1981 Coca-Cola	unnumbered	1.00	.70	.40
1981 Donruss	33	1.75	1.25	.60
1981 Donruss	481 (Cy Young)	.40	.30	.15
1981 Fleer	6	2.00	1.50	.80
1981 Fleer	660 (Milestone)	1.00	.70	.40
1981 Fleer stickers	85	5.00	3.75	2.00

Set	#	MT	NR MT	EX
1981 Kellogg's	50	.60	.45	.25
1981 O-Pee-Chee	203	3.00	2.25	1.25
1981 Perma-Graphics	CC-16	4.00	3.00	1.50
1981 Topps	5 (League Leader)	.20	.15	.08
1981 Topps	6 (League Leader)	.20	.15	.08
1981 Topps	202 (Highlight)	.40	.30	.15
1981 Topps	630	3.00	2.25	1.25
1981 Topps Home Team Supers	unnumbered	.70	.50	.30
1981 Topps scratch offs	104	.10	.08	.04
1981 Topps stickers	25	.20	.15	.08
1981 Topps stickers	28	.20	.15	.08
1981 Topps stickers	29	.20	.15	.08
1981 Topps stickers	261	.30	.25	.15
1982 Donruss	42	1.00	.70	.40
1982 Fleer	243	1.00	.70	.40
1982 Fleer	641	.50	.40	.20
1982 Fleer stickers	54	.20	.15	.08
1982 Fleer stickers	240	.12	.09	.05
1982 Fleer stickers	241	.12	.09	.05
1982 Kellogg's	45	.75	.60	.30
1982 O-Pee-Chee	68	1.50	1.25	.60
1982 O-Pee-Chee	122 (In Action)	.60	.45	.25
1982 Perma-Graphics	10	2.00	1.50	.80
1982 Topps	1 (Highlight)	.80	.60	.30
1982 Topps	480	1.00	.70	.40
1982 Topps	481 (In Action)	.40	.30	.15
1982 Topps	636 (Team leader)	.50	.40	.20
1982 Topps stickers	75	.20	.15	.08
1982 Topps stickers	129	.30	.25	.12
1983 Donruss	16 (Diamond Kings)	.40	.30	.15
1983 Donruss	219	1.00	.70	.40
1983 Donruss Action All-Stars	24	.30	.25	.12
1983 Fleer	155	.50	.40	.20
1983 Kellogg's	45	.50	.40	.20
1983 O-Pee-Chee	70	1.00	.70	.40
1983 O-Pee-Chee	71 (Super Veteran)	.50	.40	.20
1983 Perma-Graphics	2	3.00	2.25	1.25
1983 Topps	70	1.25	.90	.50
1983 Topps	71 (Super Veteran)	.30	.25	.12
1983 Topps	229 (Team Leader)	.20	.15	.08
1983 Topps	406 (All-Star)	.35	.25	.14
1983 Topps	705 (League Leaders)	.20	.15	.08
1983 Topps	706 (League Leaders)	.20	.15	.08
1983 Topps Glossy (40)	36	.50	.40	.20
1983 Topps stickers	203	.15	.11	.06
1983 Topps stickers	204	.12	.09	.05
1983 Topps stickers	267	.30	.25	.12
1984 Donruss	111	3.00	2.25	1.25
1984 Donruss Action All-Stars	24	.30	.25	.12
1984 Donruss Champions	38	.25	.20	.10
1984 Fleer	25	3.00	2.25	1.25
1984 Fleer	642 (In Action)	.20	.15	.08
1984 Fleer stickers	78	.20	.15	.08
1984 Fleer stickers	101	.20	.15	.08
1984 Fun Foods pins	30	1.00	.70	.40
1984 Milton Bradley	4	.40	.30	.15
1984 Nestle's	1 (Highlight)	1.75	1.25	.70
1984 Nestle's	4 (Highlight)	2.00	1.50	.80
1984 Nestle's	136 (League Leader)	1.00	.70	.40
1984 Nestle's	395 (All-Star)	2.00	1.50	.80
1984 Nestle's	706 (Career Leader)	1.75	1.25	.70
1984 Nestle's	707 Career Leader)	2.00	1.50	.80
1984 Nestle's	708 (Career Leader)	1.75	1.25	.70
1984 Nestle's	780	6.00	4.50	2.50
1984 Nestle's Dream Team	21	1.25	.90	.50
1984 O-Pee-Chee	214	.75	.60	.30
1984 O-Pee-Chee	395 (All-Star)	.75	.60	.30
1984 Tastykake Phillies	unnumbered (Hall of Fame)	1.50	1.25	.60
1984 Tastykake Phillies	unnumbered	2.00	1.50	.80
1984 Raltson	16	.30	.25	.12
1984 7-Eleven (Eastern)	3	2.50	2.00	1.00
1984 Topps	1 (Highlight)	.30	.25	.12
1984 Topps	4 (Highlight)	.30	.25	.12
1984 Topps	136 (League Leaders)	.25	.20	.10
1984 Topps	395 (All-Star)	.25	.20	.10
1984 Topps	706 (Career Leader)	.30	.25	.12
1984 Topps	707 (Career Leader)	.35	.25	.14
1984 Topps	708 (Career Leader)	.25	.20	.10
1984 Topps	780	1.00	.70	.40
1984 Topps Cereal	16	.60	.30	.20
1984 Topps Glossy (40)	27	.50	.40	.20
1984 Topps stickers	1	.15	.11	.06
1984 Topps stickers	2	.12	.09	.05
1984 Topps stickers	15	.12	.09	.05
1984 Topps stickers	119	.15	.11	.06
1984 Topps stickers	184	.25	.20	.10
1984 Topps Super	16	.50	.40	.20
1985 CIGNA Phillies	12	2.00	1.50	.80
1985 Donruss	305	.80	.60	.30
1985 Donruss Action All-Stars	55	.30	.25	.12
1985 Drake	35	.40	.30	.15
1985 Fleer	246	1.50	1.15	.60
1985 Fleer Limited Edition	6	.25	.20	.10
1985 Leaf	113	1.00	.70	.40
1985 O-Pee-Chee	360	.50	.40	.20
1985 Tastykake Phillies	9	.30	.25	.12
1985 Tastykake Phillies	14	2.00	1.50	.80
1985 7-Eleven Southeastern	2	3.00	2.25	1.25
1985 7-Eleven Eastern	3	2.00	1.50	.80
1985 Thom McAn discs	unnumbered	4.00	3.00	1.50
1985 Topps	360	.60	.45	.25
1985 Topps 3D	25	.60	.45	.25
1985 Topps stickers	112	.15	.11	.06
1985 Topps Supers	24	.50	.40	.20
1985 Topps Record Holders	6	.12	.09	.05
1986 Burger King	6	.50	.40	.20
1986 Donruss	183	.50	.40	.20
1986 Donruss Highlights	35	.25	.20	.12
1986 Fleer	435	.30	.25	.12
1986 Fleer Future Hall of Famers	2	1.75	1.25	.70
1986 Fleer Mini	91	.20	.15	.08
1986 FleerSluggers/ Pitchers box	M2	1.00	.70	.40
1986 Keller's Phillies	1	4.00	2.00	1.25
1986 Leaf	117	.30	.25	.12
1986 Meadow Milk	3	3.00	2.25	1.25
1986 O-Pee-Chee	120	.40	.30	.15
1986 Tastykake Phillies	32	1.50	1.25	.60
1986 Sportflics	27	.50	.40	.20
1986 Sportflics	70	.25	.20	.10
1986 Sportflics Decades Greats	54	.40	.30	.15
1986 Topps	120	.40	.30	.15
1986 Topps	246 (Team Leaders)	.15	.11	.06
1986 Topps stickers	116	.10	.08	.04
1987 Donruss	617	.25	.20	.10
1987 Fleer	490	.25	.20	.10
1987 Fleer	635 (Milestone)	.12	.09	.05
1987 Fleer Exciting Stars	8	.25	.20	.10
1987 Fleer Update	U17	.40	.30	.15
1987 K-Mart	15	.20	.15	.08
1987 O-Pee-Chee	271	.25	.20	.10
1987 O-Pee-Chee	Box	.30	.25	.12
1987 Sportflics	200	.75	.60	.30
1987 Topps	718	.15	.10	.05
1987 Topps	Box	.30	.25	.12
1987 Topps Highlight	1	.30	.25	.12
1987 Topps Traded	19T	.30	.25	.12
1988 Fleer	1	.30	.25	.12
1989 Swell	95	.30	.25	.12
1990 Baseball Wit	43	.15	.08	.05
1990 Pacific Legends	16	.25	.20	.10
1990 Swell Greats	110	.30	.25	.12
1990 Tastykake Phillies	30	1.00	.70	.40
1991 Kellogg's 3D	8	.75	.60	.30
1991 Kellogg's Stand Ups	5A small	2.00	1.50	.80
1991 Kellogg's Stand Ups	5B large	2.00	1.50	.80
1991 Line Drive	9	.50	.40	.20
1991 Swell Greats	17	.30	.25	.12

1988 Action Packed

Action Packed released this test set in an effort to receive a license from Major League Baseball. The cards are styled like the Action Packed football issues on the card fronts. The flip sides are styled like Score baseball cards. The Ozzie Smith card is considered scarcer than the other five cards in the test set. Action Packed did not receive a license to produce baseball cards.

		MT	NR MT	EX
Complete Set:		300.00	225.00	125.00
Common Player:		40.00	30.00	15.00
(1)	Wade Boggs	60.00	45.00	25.00
(2)	Andre Dawson	60.00	45.00	25.00
(3)	Dwight Gooden	50.00	37.00	20.00
(4)	Carney Lansford	40.00	30.00	15.00
(5)	Don Mattingly	60.00	45.00	25.00
(6)	Ozzie Smith	100.00	75.00	40.00

1992 Action Packed All-Star Gallery Series I

Action Packed, makers of a high quality, embossed style football card for several years, entered the baseball card field in 1992 with its 84-card All-Star Gallery, Series One. The cards feature former baseball greats, with 72 of the 84 cards in color and the remaining in sepia tone. Each foil pack of seven cards reportedly contained at least one Hall of Famer, and the company also made special 24K, gold leaf stamped cards of all of the HOFers that were randomly inserted in the packs.

		MT	NR MT	EX
Complete Set:		15.00	10.00	5.00
Common Player:		.15	.10	.05
1	Yogi Berra	.35	.20	.15
2	Lou Brock	.20	.12	.06
3	Bob Gibson	.25	.15	.05
4	Ferguson Jenkins	.15	.10	.05
5	Ralph Kiner	.20	.12	.05
6	Al Kaline	.20	.12	.05
7	Lou Boudreau	.15	.10	.05
8	Bobby Doerr	.15	.10	.05
9	Billy Herman	.15	.10	.05
10	Monte Irvin	.15	.10	.05
11	George Kell	.15	.10	.05
12	Robin Roberts	.20	.12	.05
13	Johnny Mize	.20	.12	.05
14	Willie Mays	.75	.50	.25
15	Enos Slaughter	.20	.12	.05
16	Warren Spahn	.30	.20	.10
17	Willie Stargell	.20	.12	.05
18	Billy Williams	.15	.10	.05
19	Vernon Law	.15	.10	.05
20	Virgil Trucks	.15	.10	.05
21	Mel Parnell	.15	.10	.05
22	Wally Moon	.15	.10	.05
23	Gene Woodling	.15	.10	.05
24	Richie Ashburn	.25	.15	.05
25	Mark Fidrych	.15	.10	.05
26	Elroy Face	.15	.10	.05
27	Larry Doby	.15	.10	.05
28	Dick Groat	.15	.10	.05
29	Cesar Cedeno	.15	.10	.05
30	Bob Horner	.15	.10	.05
31	Bobby Richardson	.15	.10	.05
32	Bobby Murcer	.15	.10	.05
33	Gil McDougald	.15	.10	.05
34	Roy White	.15	.10	.05
35	Bill Skowron	.15	.10	.05
36	Mickey Lolich	.15	.10	.05
37	Minnie Minoso	.15	.10	.05
38	Billy Pierce	.15	.10	.05
39	Ron Santo	.15	.10	.05
40	Sal Bando	.15	.10	.05
41	Ralph Branca	.15	.10	.05
42	Bert Campaneris	.15	.10	.05
43	Joe Garagiola	.25	.15	.05
44	Vida Blue	.20	.12	.05
45	Frank Crisetti	.15	.10	.05
46	Luis Tiant	.15	.10	.05
47	Maury Wills	.25	.15	.05
48	Sam McDowell	.25	.15	.05
49	Jimmy Piersall	.25	.15	.05
50	Jim Lonborg	.15	.10	.05
51	Don Newcombe	.15	.10	.05
52	Bobby Thomson	.20	.12	.05
53	Wilbur Wood	.20	.12	.05
54	Carl Erskine	.15	.10	.05
55	Chris Chambliss	.15	.10	.05
56	Dave Kingman	.15	.10	.05
57	Ken Holtzman	.15	.10	.05
58	Bud Harrelson	.15	.10	.05
59	Clem Labine	.15	.10	.05
60	Tony Oliva	.30	.20	.10
61	George Foster	.20	.12	.05
62	Bobby Bonds	.25	.15	.05
63	Harvey Haddix	.20	.12	.05
64	Steve Garvey	.20	.12	.05
65	Rocky Colavito	.20	.12	.05
66	Orlando Cepeda	.20	.12	.05
67	Ed Lopat	.15	.10	.05
68	Al Oliver	.15	.10	.05
69	Bill Mazeroski	.20	.10	.05
70	Al Rosen	.20	.10	.05
71	Bob Grich	.15	.10	.05
72	Curt Flood	.15	.10	.05
73	Willie Horton	.15	.10	.05
74	Rico Carty	.20	.12	.05
75	Davey Johnson	.15	.10	.05
76	Don Kessinger	.15	.10	.05
77	Frank Thomas	.15	.10	.05
78	Bobby Shantz	.15	.10	.05
79	Herb Score	.15	.10	.05
80	Boog Powell	.20	.12	.05
81	Rusty Staub	.20	.12	.05
82	Bill Madlock	.20	.12	.05
83	Manny Mota	.15	.10	.05
84	Bill White	.15	.10	.05

The values quoted are intended to reflect the market price.

1992 Action Packed All-Star Gallery Series II

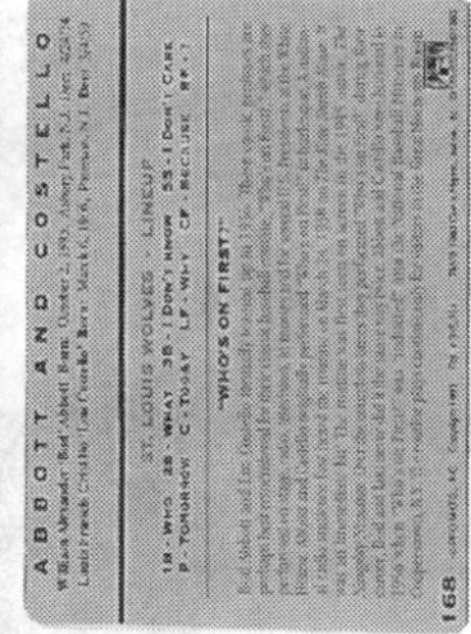

The Second Series of Action Packed All-Star Gallery was released in 1993, with cards numbered from 85 to 168. In a similar fashion to the First Series, Series Two features 52 cards in color, 31 in sepia tone and one as a colorized black and white. The series also includes two tongue-in-cheek cards - "Who's on First?" duo Bud Abbot and Lou Costello, and a card highlighting the TV and radio career of Bob Uecker.

		MT	NR MT	EX
Complete Set:		20.00	12.00	6.00
Common Player:		.15	.10	.05
85	Cy Young	.25	.15	.05
86	Honus Wagner	.25	.15	.05
87	Christy Mathewson	.15	.10	.05
88	Ty Cobb	.35	.20	.10
89	Eddie Collins	.15	.10	.05
90	Walter Johnson	.30	.20	.10
91	Tris Speaker	.30	.20	.10
92	Grover Alexander	.20	.12	.05
93	Edd Roush	.15	.10	.05
94	Babe Ruth	1.00	.60	.30
95	Rogers Hornsby	.40	.30	.15
96	Pie Traynor	.25	.15	.05
97	Lou Gehrig	.60	.40	.20
98	Mickey Cochrane	.20	.12	.05
99	Lefty Grove	.20	.12	.05
100	Jimmie Foxx	.25	.15	.05
101	Tony Lazzeri	.15	.10	.05
102	Mel ott	.15	.10	.05
103	Carl Hubbell	.15	.10	.05
104	Al Lopez	.15	.10	.05
105	Lefty Gomez	.20	.12	.05
106	Dizzy Dean	.20	.12	.05
107	Hank Greenberg	.20	.12	.05
108	Joe Medwick	.20	.12	.05
109	Arky Vaughan	.15	.10	.05
110	Bob Feller	.25	.15	.05
111	Hal Newhouser	.15	.10	.05
112	Early Wynn	.20	.12	.05
113	Bob Lemon	.20	.12	.05
114	Red Schoendienst	.20	.12	.05
115	Satchel Paige	.35	.20	.10
116	Whitey Ford	.25	.15	.05
117	Eddie Mathews	.25	.15	.05
118	Harmon Killebrew	.25	.15	.05
119	Roberto Clemente	.60	.40	.20
120	Brooks Robinson	.40	.30	.15
121	Don Drysdale	.25	.15	.05
122	Luis Aparicio	.15	.10	.05
123	Willie McCovey	.20	.12	.05
124	Juan Marichal	.20	.12	.05
125	Gaylord Perry	.20	.12	.05
126	Catfish Hunter	.15	.10	.05
127	Jim Palmer	.25	.15	.05
128	Rod Carew	.25	.15	.05
129	Tom Seaver	.30	.15	.05
130	Rollie Fingers	.20	.12	.05
131	Joe Jackson	.30	.20	.10
132	Pepper Martin	.15	.10	.05
133	Joe Gordon	.15	.10	.05
134	Marty Marion	.15	.10	.05
135	Allie Reynolds	.15	.10	.05
136	Johnny Sain	.25	.15	.05
137	Gil Hodges	.25	.15	.05
138	Ted Kluszewski	.20	.12	.05
139	Nellie Fox	.25	.12	.05
140	Billy Martin	.25	.12	.05
141	Smokey Burgess	.15	.10	.05
142	Lew Burdette	.15	.10	.05
143	Joe Black	.15	.10	.05
144	Don Larson	.20	.12	.05
145	Ken Boyer	.15	.10	.05
146	Johnny Callison	.15	.10	.05
147	Norm Cash	.15	.10	.05
148	Keith Hernandez	.15	.10	.05
149	Jim Kaat	.15	.10	.05
150	Bill Freehan	.15	.10	.05
151	Joe Torre	.15	.10	.05
152	Bob Uecker	.20	.12	.05
153	Dave McNally	.15	.10	.05
154	Denny McLain	.20	.12	.05
155	Dick Allen	.15	.10	.05
156	Jimmy Wynn	.15	.10	.05
157	Tommy John	.15	.10	.05
158	Paul Blair	.15	.10	.05
159	Reggie Smith	.15	.10	.05
160	Jerry Koosman	.15	.10	.05
161	Thurman Munson	.25	.15	.05
162	Graig Nettles	.15	.10	.05
163	Ron Cey	.15	.10	.05
164	Cecil Cooper	.15	.10	.05
165	Dave Parker	.20	.12	.05
166	Jim Rice	.15	.10	.05
167	Kent Tekulve	.15	.10	.05
168	Who's On First?	.25	.15	.05

1959 Bazooka

The 1959 Bazooka set, consisting of 23 full-color, unnumbered cards, was issued on boxes of Bazooka one-cent bubble gum. The individually wrapped pieces of Bazooka gum were produced by Topps Chewing Gum. The blank-backed cards measure 2-13/16" by 4-15/16" Nine cards were first issued, with 14 being added to the set later. The nine more plentiful cards are #'s 1, 5, 8, 9, 14, 15, 16, 17 and 22. Complete boxes would command 75 percent over the prices in the checklist that follows.

		NR MT	EX	VG
Complete Set:		8500.00	4250.00	2550.
Common Player:		125.00	62.00	37.00
(1a)	Hank Aaron (name in white)	650.00	325.00	195.00
(1b)	Hank Aaron (name in yellow)	650.00	325.00	195.00
(2)	Richie Ashburn	400.00	200.00	120.00
(3)	Ernie Banks	650.00	325.00	195.00
(4)	Ken Boyer	300.00	150.00	90.00
(5)	Orlando Cepeda	200.00	100.00	60.00
(6)	Bob Cerv	200.00	100.00	60.00
(7)	Rocco Colavito	500.00	250.00	150.00
(8)	Del Crandall	125.00	62.00	37.00

		NR MT	EX	VG
(9)	Jim Davenport	125.00	62.00	37.00
(10)	Don Drysdale	650.00	325.00	210.00
(11)	Nellie Fox	350.00	175.00	105.00
(12)	Jackie Jensen	250.00	125.00	75.00
(13)	Harvey Kuenn	250.00	125.00	75.00
(14)	Mickey Mantle	2000.00	1000.00	600.00
(15)	Willie Mays	500.00	250.00	150.00
(16)	Bill Mazeroski	150.00	75.00	45.00
(17)	Roy McMillan	125.00	62.00	37.00
(18)	Billy Pierce	200.00	100.00	60.00
(19)	Roy Sievers	200.00	100.00	60.00
(20)	Duke Snider	800.00	400.00	250.00
(21)	Gus Triandos	200.00	100.00	60.00
(22)	Bob Turley	125.00	62.00	37.00
(23)	Vic Wertz	200.00	100.00	60.00

1960 Bazooka

EARLY WYNN
CHICAGO WHITE SOX pitcher
NO. 28 OF 36 CARDS

Three-card panels were found on the bottoms of Bazooka bubble gum boxes in 1960. The blank- backed set is comprised of 36 cards with the card number located at the bottom of each full-color card. The individual cards measure 1-13/16" by 2-3/4"; the panels measure 2-3/4" by 5-1/2" in size. Prices, in the checklist that follows, are given for complete panels and individual cards.

		NR MT	EX	VG
	Complete panel set:	1800.00	900.00	540.00
	Complete singles set:	1200.00	600.00	360.00
	Common player:	5.00	2.50	1.50
	Panel 1	100.00	50.00	30.00
1	Ernie Banks	50.00	25.00	15.00
2	Bud Daley	5.00	2.50	1.50
3	Wally Moon	5.00	2.50	1.50
	Panel 2	150.00	75.00	45.00
4	Hank Aaron	80.00	40.00	25.00
5	Milt Pappas	5.00	2.50	1.50
6	Dick Stuart	8.00	4.00	2.25
	Panel 3	250.00	125.00	75.00
7	Bob Clemente	100.00	50.00	30.00
8	Yogi Berra	50.00	25.00	15.00
9	Ken Boyer	8.00	4.00	2.25
	Panel 4	55.00	22.50	13.50
10	Orlando Cepeda	15.00	7.50	4.50
11	Gus Triandos	5.00	2.50	1.50
12	Frank Malzone	5.00	2.50	1.50
	Panel 5	135.00	67.50	40.00
13	Willie Mays	80.00	40.00	24.00
14	Camilo Pascual	5.00	2.50	1.50
15	Bob Cerv	5.00	2.50	1.50
	Panel 6	100.00	50.00	30.00
16	Vic Power	5.00	2.50	1.50
17	Larry Sherry	5.00	2.50	1.50
18	Al Kaline	50.00	25.00	15.00
	Panel 7	130.00	65.00	39.00
19	Warren Spahn	40.00	20.00	12.50
20	Harmon Killebrew	30.00	15.00	9.00
21	Jackie Jensen	10.00	5.00	3.00
	Panel 8	135.00	65.00	39.00
22	Luis Aparicio	25.00	12.50	7.50
23	Gil Hodges	30.00	15.00	9.00
24	Richie Ashburn	30.00	15.00	9.00
	Panel 9	100.00	50.00	30.00
25	Nellie Fox	25.00	12.50	7.50
26	Robin Roberts	30.00	15.00	9.00
27	Joe Cunningham	5.00	2.50	1.50

		NR MT	EX	VG
	Panel 10	135.00	65.00	39.00
28	Early Wynn	25.00	12.50	7.50
29	Frank Robinson	50.00	25.00	15.00
30	Rocky Colavito	15.00	7.50	4.50
	Panel 11	475.00	235.00	140.00
31	Mickey Mantle	300.00	150.00	90.00
32	Glen Hobbie	5.00	2.50	1.50
33	Roy McMillan	5.00	2.50	1.50
	Panel 12	45.00	22.50	13.50
34	Harvey Kuenn	8.00	4.00	2.25
35	Johnny Antonelli	5.00	2.50	1.50
36	Del Crandall	8.00	4.00	2.25

1961 Bazooka

Similar in design to the 1960 Bazooka set, the 1961 edition consists of 36 cards issued in panels of three on the bottom of Bazooka bubble gum boxes. The full-color cards, which measure 1-13/16" by 2-3/4" individually and 2-3/4" by 5-1/2" as panels, are numbered 1 through 36. The backs are blank.

		NR MT	EX	VG
	Complete panel set:	1500.00	750.00	450.00
	Complete singles set:	750.00	375.00	225.00
	Common player:	5.00	2.50	1.50
	Panel 1	475.00	235.00	140.00
1	Art Mahaffey	5.00	2.50	1.50
2	Mickey Mantle	300.00	150.00	90.00
3	Ron Santo	12.00	6.00	3.50
	Panel 2	125.00	62.50	37.50
4	Bud Daley	5.00	2.50	1.50
5	Roger Maris	80.00	40.00	24.00
6	Eddie Yost	5.00	2.50	1.50
	Panel 3	50.00	25.00	15.00
7	Minnie Minoso	12.00	6.00	3.50
8	Dick Groat	8.00	4.00	2.25
9	Frank Malzone	5.00	2.50	1.50
	Panel 4	75.00	35.00	21.00
10	Dick Donovan	5.00	2.50	1.50
11	Ed Mathews	30.00	15.00	9.00
12	Jim Lemon	5.00	2.50	1.50
	Panel 5	50.00	25.00	15.00
13	Chuck Estrada	5.00	2.50	1.50
14	Ken Boyer	8.00	4.00	2.25
15	Harvey Kuenn	8.00	4.00	2.25
	Panel 6	60.00	30.00	18.00
16	Ernie Broglio	5.00	2.50	1.50
17	Rocky Colavito	15.00	7.50	4.50
18	Ted Kluszewski	15.00	7.50	4.50
	Panel 7	250.00	125.00	75.00
19	Ernie Banks	75.00	38.00	23.00
20	Al Kaline	50.00	25.00	15.00
21	Ed Bailey	5.00	2.50	1.50
	Panel 8	125.00	62.50	37.50
22	Jim Perry	5.00	2.50	1.50
23	Willie Mays	80.00	40.00	24.00
24	Bill Mazeroski	12.00	6.00	3.50
	Panel 9	75.00	37.50	22.50
25	Gus Triandos	5.00	2.50	1.50
26	Don Drysdale	25.00	12.50	7.50
27	Frank Herrera	5.00	2.50	1.50
	Panel 10	80.00	40.00	24.00
28	Earl Battey	5.00	2.50	1.50
29	Warren Spahn	35.00	17.50	10.50
30	Gene Woodling	8.00	4.00	2.25
	Panel 11	75.00	37.50	22.50

		NR MT	EX	VG
31	Frank Robinson	35.00	17.50	10.50
32	Pete Runnels	5.00	2.50	1.50
33	Woodie Held	5.00	2.50	1.50
	Panel 12	55.00	27.50	16.50
34	Norm Larker	5.00	2.50	1.50
35	Luis Aparicio	20.00	10.00	6.00
36	Bill Tuttle	5.00	2.50	1.50

1962 Bazooka

In 1962, Bazooka increased the size of its set to 45 full-color cards. The set is unnumbered and was issued in panels of three on the bottoms of bubble gum boxes. The individual cards measure 1-13/16" by 2-3/4" in size, whereas the panels are 2-3/4" by 5-1/2". In the checklist that follows the cards have been numbered alphabetically, using the name of the player who appears on the left end of the panel. Panel #s 1, 11 and 15 were issued in much shorter supply and command a higher price.

		NR MT	EX	VG
	Complete panel set:	5000.00	2500.00	1500.
	Complete singles set:	3150.00	1575.00	925.00
	Common player:	8.00	4.00	2.50
	Panel 1	1075.00	535.00	320.00
(1)	Bob Allison	150.00	75.00	45.00
(2)	Ed Mathews	350.00	175.00	105.00
(3)	Vada Pinson	150.00	75.00	45.00
	Panel 2	75.00	37.50	22.50
(4)	Earl Battey	8.00	4.00	2.50
(5)	Warren Spahn	30.00	15.00	9.00
(6)	Lee Thomas	8.00	4.00	2.50
	Panel 3	50.00	25.00	15.00
(7)	Orlando Cepeda	15.00	7.50	4.50
(8)	Woodie Held	8.00	4.00	2.50
(9)	Bob Aspromonte	8.00	4.00	2.50
	Panel 4	250.00	125.00	75.00
(10)	Dick Howser	10.00	5.00	3.00
(11)	Bob Clemente	100.00	50.00	30.00
(12)	Al Kaline	45.00	22.50	13.50
	Panel 5	165.00	82.50	50.00
(13)	Joey Jay	8.00	4.00	2.50
(14)	Roger Maris	75.00	37.50	22.50
(15)	Frank Howard	12.00	6.00	3.50
	Panel 6	150.00	75.00	45.00
(16)	Sandy Koufax	75.00	37.50	22.50
(17)	Jim Gentile	8.00	4.00	2.50
(18)	Johnny Callison	8.00	4.00	2.25
	Panel 7	45.00	22.50	13.50
(19)	Jim Landis	8.00	4.00	2.50
(20)	Ken Boyer	12.00	6.00	3.50
(21)	Chuck Schilling	8.00	4.00	2.50
	Panel 8	525.00	260.00	155.00
(22)	Art Mahaffey	8.00	4.00	2.25
(23)	Mickey Mantle	300.00	150.00	90.00
(24)	Dick Stuart	10.00	5.00	3.00
	Panel 9	110.00	55.00	33.00
(25)	Ken McBride	8.00	4.00	2.50
(26)	Frank Robinson	35.00	17.50	10.50
(27)	Gil Hodges	25.00	12.50	7.50
	Panel 10	200.00	100.00	60.00
(28)	Milt Pappas	8.00	4.00	2.25
(29)	Hank Aaron	100.00	50.00	30.00
(30)	Luis Aparicio	20.00	10.00	6.00
	Panel 11	1250.00	625.00	375.00
(31)	Johnny Romano	150.00	75.00	45.00
(32)	Ernie Banks	500.00	250.00	150.00
(33)	Norm Siebern	150.00	75.00	45.00
	Panel 12	50.00	25.00	15.00
(34)	Ron Santo	12.00	6.00	3.50
(35)	Norm Cash	10.00	5.00	3.00
(36)	Jim Piersall	10.00	5.00	3.00
	Panel 13	190.00	95.00	55.00
(37)	Don Schwall	8.00	4.00	2.50
(38)	Willie Mays	100.00	50.00	30.00
(39)	Norm Larker	8.00	4.00	2.50
	Panel 14	125.00	62.50	37.50
(40)	Bill White	10.00	5.00	3.00
(41)	Whitey Ford	50.00	25.00	15.00
(42)	Rocky Colavito	15.00	7.50	4.50
	Panel	1050.00	525.00	315.00
(43)	Don Zimmer	175.00	87.50	52.50
(44)	Harmon Killebrew	300.00	150.00	90.00
(45)	Gene Woodling	150.00	75.00	45.00

1963 Bazooka

FRANK ROBINSON
CINN. REDS OF
NO. 31 OF 36 CARDS

The 1963 Bazooka issue reverted back to a 12- panel, 36-card set, but saw a change in the size of the cards. Individual cards measure 1-9/16" by 2-1/2", while panels are 2-1/2" by 4-11/16" in size. The card design was altered also, with the player's name, team and position situated in a white oval space at the bottom of the card. The full-color, blank-backed set is numbered 1-36. Five Bazooka All-Time Greats cards were inserted in each box of bubble gum.

		NR MT	EX	VG
	Complete panel set:	1750.00	875.00	525.00
	Complete singles set:	1000.00	500.00	300.00
	Common player:	5.00	2.50	1.50
	Panel 1	575.00	275.00	170.00
1	Mickey Mantle (batting righty)	300.00	150.00	90.00
2	Bob Rodgers	5.00	2.50	1.50
3	Ernie Banks	50.00	25.00	15.00
	Panel 2	75.00	37.00	22.50
4	Norm Siebern	5.00	2.50	1.50
5	Warren Spahn (portrait)	30.00	15.00	9.00
6	Bill Mazeroski	10.00	5.00	3.00
	Panel 3	190.00	95.00	57.00
7	Harmon Killebrew (batting)	30.00	15.00	9.00
8	Dick Farrell (portrait)	5.00	2.50	1.50
9	Hank Aaron (glove in front)	80.00	40.00	24.00
	Panel 4	150.00	75.00	45.00
10	Dick Donovan	5.00	2.50	1.50
11	Jim Gentile (batting)	5.00	2.50	1.50
12	Willie Mays (bat in front)	80.00	40.00	24.00
	Panel 5	150.00	75.00	45.00
13	Camilo Pascual (hands at waist)	5.00	2.50	1.50
14	Roberto Clemente (portrait)	80.00	40.00	24.00
15	Johnny Callison (wearing pinstripe uniform)	5.00	2.50	1.50
	Panel 6	200.00	100.00	60.00
16	Carl Yastrzemski (kneeling)	75.00	37.50	22.50
17	Don Drysdale	45.00	22.50	13.50
18	Johnny Romano (portrait)	5.00	2.50	1.50
	Panel 7	30.00	15.00	9.00
19	Al Jackson	5.00	2.50	1.50
20	Ralph Terry	5.00	2.50	1.50
21	Bill Monbouquette	5.00	2.50	1.50
	Panel 8	115.00	57.50	35.00
22	Orlando Cepeda	15.00	7.50	4.50

		NR MT	EX	VG
23	Stan Musial	50.00	25.00	15.00
24	Floyd Robinson (no pinstripes on uniform)	5.00	2.50	1.50
	Panel 9	35.00	17.50	10.50
25	Chuck Hinton (batting)	5.00	2.50	1.50
26	Bob Purkey	5.00	2.50	1.50
27	Ken Hubbs	12.00	6.00	3.50
	Panel 10	80.00	40.00	24.00
28	Bill White	8.00	4.00	2.50
29	Ray Herbert	5.00	2.50	1.50
30	Brooks Robinson (glove in front)	35.00	17.50	10.50
	Panel 11	95.00	47.50	28.50
31	Frank Robinson (batting, uniform number doesn't show)	50.00	25.00	15.00
32	Lee Thomas	5.00	2.50	1.50
33	Rocky Colavito (Detroit)	12.00	6.00	3.50
	Panel 12	80.00	40.00	24.00
34	Al Kaline (kneeling)	35.00	17.50	10.50
35	Art Mahaffey	5.00	2.50	1.50
36	Tommy Davis (batting follow-through)	8.00	4.00	2.50

1963 Bazooka All-Time Greats

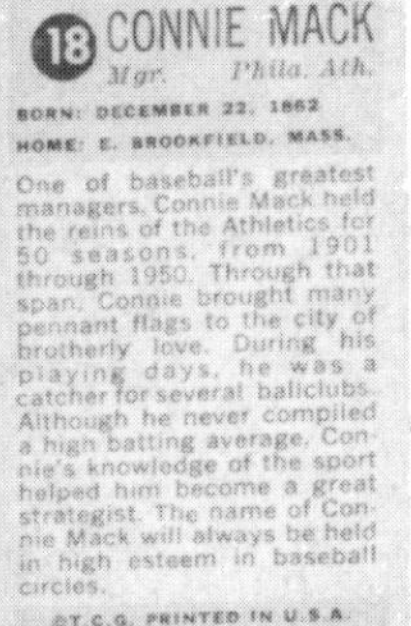

Consisting of 41 cards, the Bazooka All-Time Greats set was issued as inserts (5 per box) in boxes of Bazooka bubble gum. A black and white head-shot of the player is placed inside a gold plaque within a white border. The card backs have black print on white and white and yellow and contain a brief biography of the player. The numbered cards measure 1-9/16" by 2-1/2" in size. The cards can be found with silver fronts instead of gold. The silver are worth double the values listed in the following checklist.

		NR MT	EX	VG
	Complete set:	350.00	175.00	100.00
	Common player:	5.00	2.50	1.50
1	Joe Tinker	5.00	2.50	1.50
2	Harry Heilmann	5.00	2.50	1.50
3	Jack Chesbro	5.00	2.50	1.50
4	Christy Mathewson	8.00	4.00	2.25
5	Herb Pennock	5.00	2.50	1.50
6	Cy Young	6.00	3.00	1.75
7	Ed Walsh	5.00	2.50	1.50
8	Nap Lajoie	5.00	2.50	1.50
9	Eddie Plank	5.00	2.50	1.50
10	Honus Wagner	8.00	4.00	2.25
11	Chief Bender	5.00	2.50	1.50
12	Walter Johnson	8.00	4.00	2.25
13	Three-Fingered Brown	5.00	2.50	1.50
14	Rabbit Maranville	5.00	2.50	1.50
15	Lou Gehrig	40.00	20.00	12.00
16	Ban Johnson	5.00	2.50	1.50
17	Babe Ruth	55.00	27.00	16.50
18	Connie Mack	5.00	2.50	1.50
19	Hank Greenberg	5.00	2.50	1.50
20	John McGraw	5.00	2.50	1.50
21	Johnny Evers	5.00	2.50	1.50
22	Al Simmons	5.00	2.50	1.50
23	Jimmy Collins	5.00	2.50	1.50
24	Tris Speaker	5.00	2.50	1.50
25	Frank Chance	5.00	2.50	1.50
26	Fred Clarke	5.00	2.50	1.50
27	Wilbert Robinson	5.00	2.50	1.50
28	Dazzy Vance	5.00	2.50	1.50
29	Grover Alexander	5.00	2.50	1.50
30	Kenesaw Landis	5.00	2.50	1.50
31	Willie Keeler	5.00	2.50	1.50
32	Rogers Hornsby	5.00	2.50	1.50
33	Hugh Duffy	5.00	2.50	1.50
34	Mickey Cochrane	5.00	2.50	1.50
35	Ty Cobb	40.00	20.00	12.00
36	Mel Ott	5.00	2.50	1.50
37	Clark Griffith	5.00	2.50	1.50
38	Ted Lyons	5.00	2.50	1.50
39	Cap Anson	5.00	2.50	1.50
40	Bill Dickey	5.00	2.50	1.50
41	Eddie Collins	5.00	2.50	1.50

1964 Bazooka

The 1964 Bazooka set is identical in design and size to the previous year's effort. However, different photographs were used from year to year by Topps, issuer of Bazooka bubble gum. The 1964 set consists of 36 full-color, blank-backed cards numbered 1 through 36. Individual cards measure 1-9/16" by 2-1/2"; three-card panels measure 2-1/2" by 4-11/16". Sheets of ten full-color baseball stamps were inserted in each box of bubble gum.

		NR MT	EX	VG
	Complete panel set:	1450.00	725.00	435.00
	Complete singles set:	850.00	425.00	255.00
	Common player:	5.00	2.50	1.50
	Panel 1	350.00	175.00	100.00
1	Mickey Mantle (portrait)	200.00	100.00	60.00
2	Dick Groat	8.00	4.00	2.50
3	Steve Barber	5.00	2.50	1.50
	Panel 2	65.00	32.50	19.50
4	Ken McBride	5.00	2.50	1.50
5	Warren Spahn (head to waist shot)	30.00	15.00	9.00
6	Bob Friend	5.00	2.50	1.50
	Panel 3	175.00	87.50	52.50
7	Harmon Killebrew (portrait)	30.00	15.00	9.00
8	Dick Farrell (hands above head)	5.00	2.50	1.50
9	Hank Aaron (glove to left)	75.00	37.50	22.50
	Panel 4	125.00	62.50	37.50
10	Rich Rollins	5.00	2.50	1.50
11	Jim Gentile (portrait)	5.00	2.50	1.50
12	Willie Mays (looking to left)	75.00	37.50	22.50
	Panel 5	125.00	62.50	37.50
13	Camilo Pascual (pitching follow-through)	5.00	2.50	1.50
14	Roberto Clemente (throwing)	75.00	37.50	22.50
15	Johnny Callison (batting, screen showing)	5.00	2.50	1.50
	Panel 6	120.00	60.00	36.00
16	Carl Yastrzemski (batting)	45.00	22.50	13.50
17	Billy Williams (kneeling)	25.00	12.50	7.50
18	Johnny Romano (batting)	5.00	2.50	1.50
	Panel 7	70.00	35.00	21.00
19	Jim Maloney	5.00	2.50	1.50
20	Norm Cash	8.00	4.00	2.50
21	Willie McCovey	30.00	15.00	9.00
	Panel 8	30.00	15.00	9.00
22	Jim Fregosi (batting)	5.00	2.50	1.50
23	George Altman	5.00	2.50	1.50
24	Floyd Robinson (wearing pinstripe uniform)	5.00	2.50	1.50
	Panel 9	30.00	15.00	9.00
25	Chuck Hinton (portrait)	5.00	2.50	1.50

		NR MT	EX	VG
26	Ron Hunt (batting)	5.00	2.50	1.50
27	Gary Peters (pitching)	5.00	2.50	1.50
	Panel 10	75.00	37.50	22.50
28	Dick Ellsworth	5.00	2.50	1.50
29	Elston Howard (holding bat)	12.00	6.00	3.50
30	Brooks Robinson (kneeling with glove)	30.00	15.00	9.00
	Panel 11	180.00	90.00	54.00
31	Frank Robinson (uniforn number shows)	40.00	20.00	12.00
32	Sandy Koufax (glove in front)	60.00	30.00	18.00
33	Rocky Colavito (Kansas City)	12.00	6.00	3.50
	Panel 12	75.00	37.50	22.50
34	Al Kaline (holding two bats)	30.00	15.00	9.00
35	Ken Boyer (head to waist shot)	8.00	4.00	2.25
36	Tommy Davis (batting)	8.00	4.00	2.50

1964 Bazooka Stamps

Occasionally mislabeled "Topps Stamps," the 1964 Bazooka Stamps set was produced by Topps, but was found only in boxes of 1¢ Bazooka bubble gum. Issued in sheets of ten, 100 color stamps make up the set. Each stamp measures 1" by 1-1/2" in size. While the stamps are not individually numbered, the sheets are numbered one through ten. The stamps are commonly found as complete sheets of ten and are priced in that fashion in the checklist that follows.

		NR MT	EX	VG
	Complete sheet set:	500.00	250.00	150.00
	Common sheet:	25.00	12.50	7.50
1	Max Alvis, Ed Charles, Dick Ellsworth, Jimmie Hall, Frank Malzone, Milt Pappas, Vada Pinson, Tony Taylor, Pete Ward, Bill White	25.00	12.50	7.50
2	Bob Aspromonte, Larry Jackson, Willie Mays, Al McBean, Bill Monbouquette, Bobby Richardson, Floyd Robinson, Frank Robinson, Norm Siebern, Don Zimmer	40.00	20.00	12.00
3	Ernie Banks, Roberto Clemente, Curt Flood, Jesse Gonder, Woody Held, Don Lock, Dave Nicholson, Joe Pepitone, Brooks Robinson, Carl Yastrzemski	60.00	30.00	18.00
4	Hank Aguirre, Jim Grant, Harmon Killebrew, Jim Maloney, Juan Marichal, Bill Mazeroski, Juan Pizarro, Boog Powell, Ed Roebuck, Ron Santo	40.00	20.00	12.00
5	Jim Bouton, Norm Cash, Orlando Cepeda, Tommy Harper, Chuck Hinton, Albie Pearson, Ron Perranoski, Dick Radatz, Johnny Romano, Carl Willey	30.00	15.00	9.00
6	Steve Barber, Jim Fregosi, Tony Gonzalez, Mickey Mantle, Jim O'Toole, Gary Peters, Rich Rollins, Warren Spahn, Dick Stuart, Joe Torre	125.00	62.00	37.00
7	Felipe Alou, George Altman, Ken Boyer, Rocky Colavito, Jim Davenport, Tommy Davis, Bill Freehan, Bob Friend, Ken Johnson, Billy Moran	30.00	15.00	9.00
8	Earl Battey, Ernie Broglio, Johnny Callison, Donn Clendenon, Don Drysdale, Jim Gentile, Elston Howard, Claude Osteen, Billy Williams, Hal Woodeshick	35.00	17.50	10.50
9	Hank Aaron, Jack Baldschun, Wayne Causey, Moe Drabowsky, Dick Groat, Frank Howard, Al Jackson, Jerry Lumpe, Ken McBride, Rusty Staub	40.00	20.00	12.00
10	Ray Culp, Vic Davalillo, Dick Farrell, Ron Hunt, Al Kaline, Sandy Koufax, Eddie Mathews, Willie McCovey, Camilo Pascual, Lee Thomas	50.00	25.00	15.00

1965 Bazooka

The 1965 Bazooka set is identical to the 1963 and 1964 sets. Different players were added each year and different photographs were used for those players being included again. Individual cards cut from the boxes measure 1-9/16" by 2-1/2". Complete three-card panels measure 2-1/2" by 4-11/16". Thirty-six full-color, blank-backed, num- bered cards comprise the set. Prices are given for individual cards and complete panels in the checklist that follows.

		NR MT	EX	VG
	Complete panel set:	1200.00	600.00	360.00
	Complete singles set:	725.00	360.00	215.00
	Common player:	5.00	2.50	1.50
	Panel 1	300.00	150.00	90.00
1	Mickey Mantle (batting lefty)	200.00	100.00	60.00
2	Larry Jackson	5.00	2.50	1.50
3	Chuck Hinton	5.00	2.50	1.50
	Panel 2	30.00	15.00	9.00
4	Tony Oliva	10.00	5.00	3.00
5	Dean Chance	5.00	2.50	1.50
6	Jim O'Toole	5.00	2.50	1.50
	Panel 3	110.00	55.00	33.00
7	Harmon Killebrew (bat on shoulder)	25.00	12.50	7.50
8	Pete Ward	5.00	2.50	1.50
9	Hank Aaron (batting)	50.00	25.00	15.00
	Panel 4	100.00	50.00	30.00
10	Dick Radatz	5.00	2.50	1.50
11	Boog Powell	10.00	5.00	3.00
12	Willie Mays (looking down)	50.00	25.00	15.00
	Panel 5	100.00	50.00	30.00
13	Bob Veale	5.00	2.50	1.50
14	Roberto Clemente (batting)	50.00	25.00	15.00
15	Johnny Callison (batting, no screen in background)	5.00	2.50	1.50
	Panel 6	50.00	25.00	15.00
16	Joe Torre	5.00	2.50	1.50
17	Billy Williams (batting)	20.00	10.00	6.00
18	Bob Chance	5.00	2.50	1.50
	Panel 7	35.00	17.50	10.50
19	Bob Aspromonte	5.00	2.50	1.50
20	Joe Christopher	5.00	2.50	1.50
21	Jim Bunning	12.00	6.00	3.50
	Panel 8	80.00	40.00	24.00
22	Jim Fregosi (portrait)	5.00	2.50	1.50
23	Bob Gibson	25.00	12.50	7.50
24	Juan Marichal	20.00	10.00	6.00
	Panel 9	30.00	15.00	9.00
25	Dave Wickersham	5.00	2.50	1.50
26	Ron Hunt (throwing)	5.00	2.50	1.50
27	Gary Peters (portrait)	5.00	2.50	1.50
	Panel 10	85.00	42.50	25.00
28	Ron Santo	10.00	5.00	3.00
29	Elston Howard (with glove)	12.00	6.00	3.50
30	Brooks Robinson (portrait)	30.00	15.00	9.00
	Panel 11	130.00	65.00	39.00
31	Frank Robinson (portrait)	30.00	15.00	9.00
32	Sandy Koufax (hands over head)	45.00	22.50	13.50

		NR MT	EX	VG
33	Rocky Colavito (Cleveland)	10.00	5.00	3.00
	Panel 12	75.00	37.50	22.50
34	Al Kaline (portrait)	30.00	15.00	9.00
35	Ken Boyer (portrait)	8.00	4.00	2.25
36	Tommy Davis (fielding)	8.00	4.00	2.50

1966 Bazooka

The 1966 Bazooka set was increased to 48 cards. Issued in panels of three on the bottoms of boxes of bubble gum, the full-color cards are blank-backed and numbered. Individual cards measure 1-9/16" by 2-1/2", whereas panels measure 2-1/2" by 4-11/16".

		NR MT	EX	VG
	Complete panel set:	1200.00	600.00	360.00
	Complete singles set:	950.00	475.00	285.00
	Common player:	5.00	2.50	1.50
	Panel 1	80.00	40.00	24.00
1	Sandy Koufax	50.00	25.00	15.00
2	Willie Horton	5.00	2.50	1.50
3	Frank Howard	8.00	4.00	2.50
	Panel 2	40.00	20.00	12.00
4	Richie Allen	8.00	4.00	2.25
5	Mel Stottlemyre	5.00	2.50	1.50
6	Tony Conigliaro	15.00	7.50	4.50
	Panel 3	280.00	140.00	84.00
7	Mickey Mantle	200.00	100.00	60.00
8	Leon Wagner	5.00	2.50	1.50
9	Ed Kranepool	5.00	2.50	1.50
	Panel 4	70.00	35.00	21.00
10	Juan Marichal	20.00	10.00	6.00
11	Harmon Killebrew	25.00	12.50	7.50
12	Johnny Callison	5.00	2.50	1.50
	Panel 5	55.00	27.00	16.50
13	Roy McMillan	5.00	2.50	1.50
14	Willie McCovey	25.00	12.50	7.50
15	Rocky Colavito	10.00	5.00	3.00
	Panel 6	90.00	45.00	27.00
16	Willie Mays	50.00	25.00	15.00
17	Sam McDowell	8.00	4.00	2.50
18	Vern Law	5.00	2.50	1.50
	Panel 7	55.00	27.00	16.50
19	Jim Fregosi	5.00	2.50	1.50
20	Ron Fairly	5.00	2.50	1.50
21	Bob Gibson	25.00	12.50	7.50
	Panel 8	75.00	37.50	22.50
22	Carl Yastrzemski	40.00	20.00	12.00
23	Bill White	8.00	4.00	2.50
24	Bob Aspromonte	5.00	2.50	1.50
	Panel 9	85.00	42.50	25.00
25	Dean Chance (California)	5.00	2.50	1.50
26	Roberto Clemente	50.00	25.00	15.00
27	Tony Cloninger	5.00	2.50	1.50
	Panel 10	85.00	42.50	25.00
28	Curt Blefary	5.00	2.50	1.50
29	Milt Pappas	5.00	2.50	1.50
30	Hank Aaron	50.00	25.00	15.00
	Panel 11	70.00	35.00	21.00
31	Jim Bunning	12.00	6.00	3.50
32	Frank Robinson (portrait)	30.00	15.00	9.00
33	Bill Skowron	8.00	4.00	2.50
	Panel 12	60.00	30.00	18.00
34	Brooks Robinson	30.00	15.00	9.00
35	Jim Wynn	5.00	2.50	1.50
36	Joe Torre	5.00	2.50	1.50
	Panel 13	125.00	62.50	37.50
37	Jim Grant	5.00	2.50	1.50
38	Pete Rose	75.00	37.50	22.50
39	Ron Santo	10.00	5.00	3.00
	Panel 14	60.00	30.00	18.00
40	Tom Tresh	8.00	4.00	2.50
41	Tony Oliva	10.00	5.00	3.00
42	Don Drysdale	25.00	12.50	7.50
	Panel 15	25.00	12.50	7.50
43	Pete Richert	5.00	2.50	1.50
44	Bert Campaneris	8.00	4.00	2.50
45	Jim Maloney	5.00	2.50	1.50
	Panel 16	75.00	37.50	22.50
46	Al Kaline	30.00	15.00	9.00
47	Eddie Fisher	5.00	2.50	1.50
48	Billy Williams	20.00	10.00	6.00

1967 Bazooka

The 1967 Bazooka set is identical in design to the Bazooka sets of 1964-1966. Issued in panels of three on the bottoms of bubble gum boxes, the set is made up of 48 full-color, blank-backed, numbered cards. Individual cards measure 1-9/16" by 2-1/2"; complete panels measure 2-1/2" by 4-11/16" in size.

		NR MT	EX	VG
	Complete panel set:	1200.00	600.00	360.00
	Complete singles set:	850.00	425.00	255.00
	Common player:	5.00	2.50	1.50
	Panel 1	25.00	12.50	7.50
1	Rick Reichardt	5.00	2.50	1.50
2	Tommy Agee	5.00	2.50	1.50
3	Frank Howard	8.00	4.00	2.50
	Panel 2	40.00	20.00	12.00
4	Richie Allen	8.00	4.00	2.25
5	Mel Stottlemyre	5.00	2.50	1.50
6	Tony Conigliaro	15.00	7.50	4.50
	Panel 3	295.00	145.00	85.00
7	Mickey Mantle	200.00	100.00	60.00
8	Leon Wagner	5.00	2.50	1.50
9	Gary Peters	5.00	2.50	1.50
	Panel 4	70.00	35.00	21.00
10	Juan Marichal	20.00	10.00	6.00
11	Harmon Killebrew	25.00	12.50	7.50
12	Johnny Callison	5.00	2.50	1.50
	Panel 5	65.00	32.50	19.50
13	Denny McLain	12.00	6.00	3.50
14	Willie McCovey	25.00	12.50	7.50
15	Rocky Colavito	10.00	5.00	3.00
	Panel 6	80.00	40.00	24.00
16	Willie Mays	40.00	20.00	12.00
17	Sam McDowell	5.00	2.50	1.50
18	Jim Kaat	12.00	6.00	3.50
	Panel 7	50.00	25.00	15.00
19	Jim Fregosi	5.00	2.50	1.50
20	Ron Fairly	5.00	2.50	1.50
21	Bob Gibson	25.00	12.50	7.50
	Panel 8	70.00	35.00	21.00
22	Carl Yastrzemski	35.00	17.00	10.50
23	Bill White	8.00	4.00	2.25
24	Bob Aspromonte	5.00	2.50	1.50
	Panel 9	70.00	35.00	21.00
25	Dean Chance (Minnesota)	5.00	2.50	1.50
26	Roberto Clemente	40.00	20.00	12.00
27	Tony Cloninger	5.00	2.50	1.50

		NR MT	EX	VG
	Panel 10	70.00	35.00	21.00
28	Curt Blefary	5.00	2.50	1.50
29	Phil Regan	5.00	2.50	1.50
30	Hank Aaron	40.00	20.00	12.00
	Panel 11	60.00	30.00	18.00
31	Jim Bunning	12.00	6.00	3.50
32	Frank Robinson (batting)	25.00	12.50	7.50
33	Ken Boyer	8.00	4.00	2.25
	Panel 12	60.00	30.00	18.00
34	Brooks Robinson	30.00	15.00	9.00
35	Jim Wynn	5.00	2.50	1.50
36	Joe Torre	5.00	2.50	1.50
	Panel 13	105.00	52.50	31.50
37	Tommy Davis	5.00	2.50	1.50
38	Pete Rose	60.00	30.00	18.00
39	Ron Santo	10.00	5.00	3.00
	Panel 14	60.00	30.00	18.00
40	Tom Tresh	8.00	4.00	2.50
41	Tony Oliva	10.00	5.00	3.00
42	Don Drysdale	25.00	12.50	7.50
	Panel 15	25.00	12.50	7.50
43	Pete Richert	5.00	2.50	1.50
44	Bert Campaneris	5.00	2.50	1.50
45	Jim Maloney	5.00	2.50	1.50
	Panel 16	80.00	40.00	24.00
46	Al Kaline	30.00	15.00	9.00
47	Matty Alou	5.00	2.50	1.50
48	Billy Williams	20.00	10.00	6.00

1968 Bazooka

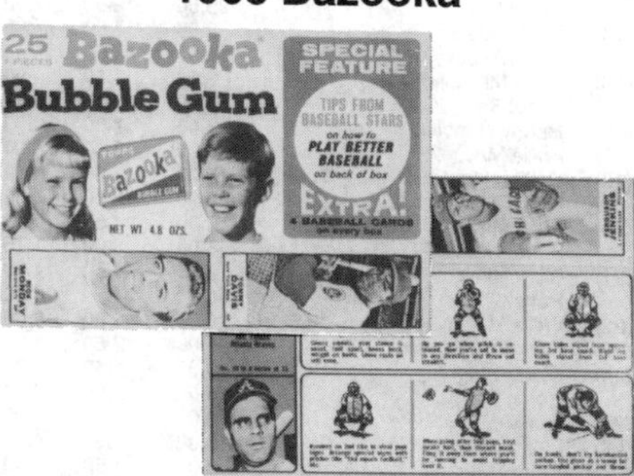

The design of the 1968 Bazooka set is radically different from previous years. The player cards are situated on the sides of the boxes with the box back containing "Tipps From The Topps." Four unnumbered player cards, measuring 1-1/4" by 3-1/8", are featured on each box. The box back includes a small player photo plus illustrated tips on various aspects of the game of baseball. The boxes are numbered 1-15 on the top panels. There are 56 different player cards in the set, with four of the cards (Agee, Drysdale, Rose, Santo) being used twice to round out the set of fifteen boxes.

		NR MT	EX	VG
	Complete box set:	2500.00	1250.00	750.00
	Complete singles set:	1500.00	750.00	450.00
	Common player:	5.00	2.50	1.50
	Box 1	200.00	100.00	60.00
1	Maury Wills (Bunting)	20.00	10.00	6.00
(1)	Clete Boyer	8.00	4.00	2.25
(2)	Paul Casanova	5.00	2.50	1.50
(3)	Al Kaline	30.00	15.00	9.00
(4)	Tom Seaver	70.00	35.00	21.00
	Box 2	115.00	57.50	35.00
2	Carl Yastrzemski (Batting)	40.00	20.00	12.00
(5)	Matty Alou	5.00	2.50	1.50
(6)	Bill Freehan	5.00	2.50	1.50
(7)	Catfish Hunter	20.00	10.00	6.00
(8)	Jim Lefebvre	5.00	2.50	1.50
	Box 3	95.00	47.50	28.50
3	Bert Campaneris (Stealing bases)	15.00	7.50	4.50
(9)	Bobby Knoop	5.00	2.50	1.50
(10)	Tim McCarver	12.00	6.00	3.50
(11)	Frank Robinson	25.00	12.50	7.50
(12)	Bob Veale	5.00	2.50	1.50
	Box 4	80.00	40.00	24.00
4	Maury Wills (Sliding)	20.00	10.00	6.00
(13)	Joe Azcue	5.00	2.50	1.50
(14)	Tony Conigliaro	15.00	7.50	4.50
(15)	Ken Holtzman	5.00	2.50	1.50
(16)	Bill White	8.00	4.00	2.25
	Box 5	135.00	67.50	40.00
5	Julian Javier (The Double Play)	15.00	7.50	4.50
(17)	Hank Aaron	40.00	20.00	12.00
(18)	Juan Marichal	20.00	10.00	6.00
(19)	Joe Pepitone	8.00	4.00	2.25
(20)	Rico Petrocelli	8.00	4.00	2.25
	Box 6	175.00	87.50	52.50
6	Orlando Cepeda (Playing 1st Base)	25.00	12.50	7.50
(21)	Tommie Agee	5.00	2.50	1.50
(22)	Don Drysdale	25.00	12.50	7.50
(23)	Pete Rose	50.00	25.00	15.00
(24)	Ron Santo	8.00	4.00	2.25
	Box 7	90.00	45.00	27.00
7	Bill Mazeroski (Playing 2nd Base)	20.00	10.00	6.00
(25)	Jim Bunning	12.00	6.00	3.50
(26)	Frank Howard	8.00	4.00	2.25
(27)	John Roseboro	9.00	4.50	2.75
(28)	George Scott	9.00	4.50	2.75
	Box 8	115.00	57.50	35.00
8	Brooks Robinson (Playing 3rd Base)	35.00	17.50	10.50
(29)	Tony Gonzalez	5.00	2.50	1.50
(30)	Willie Horton	5.00	2.50	1.50
(31)	Harmon Killebrew	25.00	12.50	7.50
(32)	Jim McGlothlin	5.00	2.50	1.50
	Box 9	90.00	45.00	27.00
9	Jim Fregosi (Playing Shortstop)	15.00	7.50	4.50
(33)	Max Alvis	5.00	2.50	1.50
(34)	Bob Gibson	20.00	10.00	6.00
(35)	Tony Oliva	10.00	6.00	3.50
(36)	Vada Pinson	10.00	6.00	3.50
	Box 10	75.00	37.50	22.50
10	Joe Torre (Catching)	15.00	7.50	4.50
(37)	Dean Chance	5.00	2.50	1.50
(38)	Tommy Davis	5.00	2.50	1.50
(39)	Ferguson Jenkins	20.00	10.00	6.00
(40)	Rick Monday	5.00	2.50	1.50
	Box 11	275.00	140.00	84.00
11	Jim Lonborg (Pitching)	15.00	7.50	4.50
(41)	Curt Flood	9.00	4.50	2.75
(42)	Joel Horlen	5.00	2.50	1.50
(43)	Mickey Mantle	150.00	75.00	45.00
(44)	Jim Wynn	5.00	2.50	1.50
	Box 12	120.00	60.00	36.00
12	Mike McCormick (Fielding the Pitcher's Position)	15.00	7.50	4.50
(45)	Roberto Clemente	40.00	20.00	12.00
(46)	Al Downing	5.00	2.50	1.50
(47)	Don Mincher	5.00	2.50	1.50
(48)	Tony Perez	15.00	7.50	4.50
	Box 13	120.00	60.00	36.00
13	Frank Crosetti (Coaching)	15.00	7.50	4.50
(49)	Rod Carew	30.00	15.00	9.00
(50)	Willie McCovey	25.00	12.50	7.50
(51)	Ron Swoboda	5.00	2.50	1.50
(52)	Earl Wilson	5.00	2.50	1.50
	Box 14	120.00	60.00	36.00
14	Willie Mays (Playing the Outfield)	35.00	17.50	10.50
(53)	Richie Allen	8.00	4.00	2.25
(54)	Gary Peters	5.00	2.50	1.50
(55)	Rusty Staub	10.00	5.00	3.00
(56)	Billy Williams	20.00	10.00	6.00
	Box 15	175.00	87.50	52.50
15	Lou Brock (Base Running)	25.00	12.50	7.50
(57)	Tommie Agee	5.00	2.50	1.50
(58)	Don Drysdale	25.00	12.50	7.50
(59)	Pete Rose	50.00	25.00	15.00
(60)	Ron Santo	8.00	4.00	2.25

1969 -70 Bazooka

Issued over a two-year span, the 1969-70 Bazooka set utilized the box bottom and sides. The box bottom, entitled "Baseball Extra," features an historic event in baseball. The bottom panels are numbered 1 through 12. Two "All-Time Great" cards were located on each side of the box. These cards are not numbered and have no

distinct borders. Individual cards measure 1-1/4" by 3-1/8"; the "Baseball Extra" panels measure 3" by 6-1/4". The prices in the checklist that follows are for complete boxes only. Cards/panels cut from the boxes have a greatly reduced value - 25 per cent of the complete box prices for all cut pieces.

		NR MT	EX	VG
	Complete box set:	250.00	125.00	75.00
	Common box:	15.00	7.50	4.50
1	No-Hit Duel By Toney And Vaughn (Mordecai Brown, Ty Cobb, Willie Keeler, Eddie Plank)	18.00	9.00	5.50
2	Alexander Conquers Yanks (Rogers Hornsby, Ban Johnson, Walter Johnson, Al Simmons)	15.00	7.50	4.50
3	Yanks Lazzeri Sets A.L. Hit Record (Hugh Duffy, Lou Gehrig, Tris Speaker, Joe Tinker)	18.00	9.00	5.50
4	Home Run Almost Hit Out Of Stadium (Grover Alexander, Chief Bender, Christy Mathewson, Cy Young)	15.00	7.50	4.50
5	Four Consecutive Homers By Gehrig (Frank Chance, Mickey Cochrane, John McGraw, Babe Ruth)	30.00	15.00	9.00
6	No-Hit Game By Walter Johnson (Johnny Evers, Walter Johnson, John McGraw, Cy Young)	15.00	7.50	4.50
7	Twelve RBI's By Bottomley (Ty Cobb, Eddie Collins, Johnny Evers, Lou Gehrig)	20.00	10.00	6.00
8	Ty Ties Record (Mickey Cochrane, Eddie Collins, Met Ott, Honus Wagner)	15.00	7.50	4.50
9	Babe Ruth Hits Three Homers In Game (Cap Anson, Jack Chesbro, Al Simmons, Tris Speaker)	25.00	12.50	7.50
10	Calls Shot In Series Game (Nap Lajoie, Connie Mack, Rabbit Maranville, Ed Walsh)	25.00	12.50	7.50
11	Ruth's 60th Homer Sets New Record (Frank Chance, Nap Lajoie, Mel Ott, Joe Tinker)	25.00	12.50	7.50
12	Double Shutout By Ed Reulbach (Rogers Hornsby, Rabbit Maranville, Christy Mathewson, Honus Wagner)	15.00	7.50	4.50

1971 Bazooka Unnumbered Set

This Bazooka set was issued in 1971, consisting of 36 full-color, blank-backed, unnumbered cards. Issued in panels of three on the bottoms of Bazooka bubble gum boxes, individual cards measure 2" by 2-5/8" whereas complete panels measure 2-5/8" by 5-5/16". In the checklist that follows, the cards have been numbered by panel using the name of the player who appears on the left portion of the panel.

		NR MT	EX	VG
	Complete panel set:	450.00	225.00	135.00
	Complete singles set:	400.00	200.00	120.00
	Common player:	3.00	1.50	.90
	Panel 1	55.00	27.50	16.50
(1)	Tommie Agee	3.00	1.50	.90
(2)	Harmon Killebrew	15.00	7.50	4.50
(3)	Reggie Jackson	30.00	15.00	9.00
	Panel 2	40.00	20.00	12.00
(4)	Bert Campaneris	3.00	1.50	.90
(5)	Pete Rose	25.00	12.50	7.50
(6)	Orlando Cepeda	9.00	4.50	2.75
	Panel 3	35.00	17.50	10.50
(7)	Rico Carty	3.00	1.50	.90
(8)	Johnny Bench	25.00	12.50	7.50
(9)	Tommy Harper	3.00	1.50	.90
	Panel 4	45.00	22.50	13.50
(10)	Bill Freehan	3.00	1.50	.90
(11)	Roberto Clemente	30.00	15.00	9.00
(12)	Claude Osteen	3.00	1.50	.90
	Panel 5	25.00	12.50	7.50
(13)	Jim Fregosi	3.00	1.50	.90
(14)	Billy Williams	15.00	7.50	4.50
(15)	Dave McNally	3.00	1.50	.90
	Panel 6	55.00	27.50	16.50
(16)	Randy Hundley	3.00	1.50	.90
(17)	Willie Mays	30.00	15.00	9.00
(18)	Catfish Hunter	15.00	7.50	4.50
	Panel 7	30.00	15.00	9.00
(19)	Juan Marichal	15.00	7.50	4.50
(20)	Frank Howard	6.00	3.00	1.75
(21)	Bill Melton	3.00	1.50	.90
	Panel 8	55.00	27.50	16.50
(22)	Willie McCovey	20.00	10.50	6.00
(23)	Carl Yastrzemski	25.00	12.50	7.50
(24)	Clyde Wright	3.00	1.50	.90
	Panel 9	25.00	12.50	7.50
(25)	Jim Merritt	3.00	1.50	.90
(26)	Luis Aparicio	15.00	7.50	4.50
(27)	Bobby Murcer	3.00	1.50	.90
	Panel 10	12.00	6.00	3.50
(28)	Rico Petrocelli	3.00	1.50	.90
(29)	Sam McDowell	3.00	1.50	.90
(30)	Cito Gaston	5.00	2.50	1.50
	Panel 11	65.00	32.50	19.50
(31)	Brooks Robinson	20.00	10.00	6.00
(32)	Hank Aaron	30.00	15.00	9.00
(33)	Larry Dierker	3.00	1.50	.90
	Panel 12	35.00	17.50	10.50
(34)	Rusty Staub	6.00	3.00	1.75
(35)	Bob Gibson	20.00	10.00	6.00
(36)	Amos Otis	5.00	2.50	1.50

1971 Bazooka Numbered Set

Photos not available at press time.

The 1971 Bazooka numbered set is a proof set produced by the company after the unnumbered set was released. The set is comprised of 48 cards as opposed to the 36 cards which make up the unnumbered set. Issued in panels of three, the nine cards not found in the unnumbered set are #'s 1-3, 13-15 and 43-45. All other cards are identical to those found in the unnumbered set. The cards, which measure 2" by 2-5/8", contain full-color photos and are blank-backed.

		NR MT	EX	VG
Complete panel set:		925.00	460.00	275.00
Complete singles set:		750.00	375.00	225.00
Common player:		5.00	2.50	1.50
	Panel 1	95.00	47.50	28.50
1	Tim McCarver	10.00	5.00	3.00
2	Frank Robinson	45.00	23.00	13.50
3	Bill Mazeroski	10.00	5.00	3.00
	Panel 2	75.00	37.50	22.50
4	Willie McCovey	25.00	12.50	7.50
5	Carl Yastrzemski	30.00	15.00	9.00
6	Clyde Wright	5.00	2.50	1.50
	Panel 3	35.00	17.50	10.50
7	Jim Merritt	5.00	2.50	1.50
8	Luis Aparicio	20.00	10.00	12.00
9	Bobby Murcer	5.00	2.50	1.50
	Panel 4	20.00	10.00	6.00
10	Rico Petrocelli	5.00	2.50	1.50
11	Sam McDowell	5.00	2.50	1.50
12	Cito Gaston	8.00	4.00	2.25
	Panel 5	60.00	30.00	18.00
13	Ferguson Jenkins	20.00	10.00	6.00
14	Al Kaline	25.00	12.50	7.50
15	Ken Harrelson	5.00	2.50	1.50
	Panel 6	65.00	32.50	19.50
16	Tommie Agee	5.00	2.50	1.50
17	Harmon Killebrew	20.00	10.00	6.00
18	Reggie Jackson	30.00	15.00	9.00
	Panel 7	40.00	20.00	12.00
19	Juan Marichal	20.00	10.00	6.00
20	Frank Howard	8.00	4.00	2.25
21	Bill Melton	5.00	2.50	1.50
	Panel 8	120.00	60.00	36.00
22	Brooks Robinson	45.00	22.50	13.50
23	Hank Aaron	50.00	25.00	15.00
24	Larry Dierker	5.00	2.50	1.50
	Panel 9	35.00	17.50	10.50
25	Jim Fregosi	5.00	2.50	1.50
26	Billy Williams	20.00	10.00	6.00
27	Dave McNally	5.00	2.50	1.50
	Panel 10	45.00	22.50	13.50
28	Rico Carty	5.00	2.50	1.50
29	Johnny Bench	25.00	12.50	7.50
30	Tommy Harper	5.00	2.50	1.50
	Panel 11	60.00	30.00	18.00
31	Bert Campaneris	5.00	2.50	1.50
32	Pete Rose	35.00	17.50	10.50
33	Orlando Cepeda	10.00	5.00	3.00
	Panel 12	60.00	30.00	18.00
34	Maury Wills	10.00	5.00	3.00
35	Tom Seaver	30.00	15.00	9.00
36	Tony Oliva	10.00	5.00	3.00
	Panel 13	75.00	37.50	22.50
37	Bill Freehan	5.00	2.50	1.50
38	Roberto Clemente	50.00	25.00	15.00
39	Claude Osteen	5.00	2.50	1.50
	Panel 14	45.00	22.50	13.50
40	Rusty Staub	8.00	4.00	2.25
41	Bob Gibson	20.00	10.00	6.00
42	Amos Otis	8.00	4.00	2.25
	Panel 15	30.00	15.00	9.00
43	Jim Wynn	5.00	2.50	1.50
44	Rich Allen	10.00	5.00	3.00
45	Tony Conigliaro	10.00	5.00	3.00
	Panel 16	90.00	45.00	27.00
46	Randy Hundley	5.00	2.50	1.50
47	Willie Mays	50.00	25.00	15.00
48	Catfish Hunter	20.00	10.00	6.00

1988 Bazooka

This 22-card set from Topps marks the first Bazooka issue since 1971. Full-color player photos are bordered in white, with the player name printed on a red, white and blue bubble gum box in the lower right corner. Flip sides are also red, white and blue, printed vertically. A large, but faint, Bazooka logo backs the Topps baseball logo team name, card number, player's name and position,

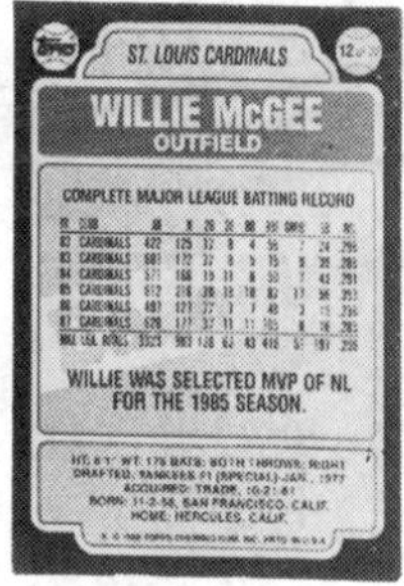

followed by batting records, personal information and brief career highlights. Cards were sold inside specially marked 59¢ and 79¢ Bazooka gum and candy boxes, one card per box.

		MT	NR MT	EX
Complete Set:		8.00	6.00	3.25
Common Player:		.20	.15	.08
1	George Bell	.25	.20	.10
2	Wade Boggs	.70	.50	.30
3	Jose Canseco	.75	.55	.25
4	Roger Clemens	.75	.55	.25
5	Vince Coleman	.20	.15	.08
6	Eric Davis	.25	.20	.10
7	Tony Fernandez	.20	.15	.08
8	Dwight Gooden	.40	.30	.15
9	Tony Gwynn	.30	.25	.12
10	Wally Joyner	.30	.25	.12
11	Don Mattingly	1.50	1.25	.60
12	Willie McGee	.20	.15	.08
13	Mark McGwire	.40	.30	.15
14	Kirby Puckett	.50	.40	.20
15	Tim Raines	.25	.20	.10
16	Dave Righetti	.20	.15	.08
17	Cal Ripken	.75	.55	.25
18	Juan Samuel	.20	.15	.08
19	Ryne Sandberg	.75	.55	.25
20	Benny Santiago	.20	.15	.08
21	Darryl Strawberry	.45	.35	.15
22	Todd Worrell	.20	.15	.08

1989 Bazooka

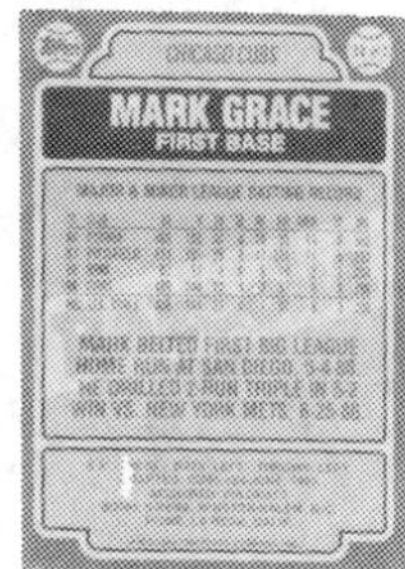

Topps produced this 22-card set in 1989 to be included (one card per box) in specially-marked boxes of its Bazooka brand bubblegum. The player photos have the words "Shining Star" along the top, while the player's name appears along the bottom of the card, along with the Topps Bazooka logo in the lower right corner. The cards are numbered alphabetically.

		MT	NR MT	EX
Complete Set:		5.00	3.75	2.00
Common Player:		.15	.11	.06
1	Tim Belcher	.15	.11	.06

		MT	NR MT	EX
2	Damon Berryhill	.15	.11	.06
3	Wade Boggs	.60	.45	.25
4	Jay Buhner	.15	.11	.06
5	Jose Canseco	.60	.45	.25
6	Vince Coleman	.15	.11	.06
7	Cecil Espy	.15	.11	.06
8	Dave Gallagher	.15	.11	.06
9	Ron Gant	.25	.20	.10
10	Kirk Gibson	.15	.11	.06
11	Paul Gibson	.15	.11	.06
12	Mark Grace	.35	.25	.12
13	Tony Gwynn	.25	.20	.10
14	Rickey Henderson	.30	.25	.12
15	Orel Hershiser	.25	.20	.10
16	Gregg Jefferies	.50	.40	.20
17	Ricky Jordan	.15	.11	.06
18	Chris Sabo	.15	.11	.06
19	Gary Sheffield	.35	.25	.12
20	Darryl Strawberry	.35	.25	.12
21	Frank Viola	.15	.11	.06
22	Walt Weiss	.15	.11	.06

1990 Bazooka

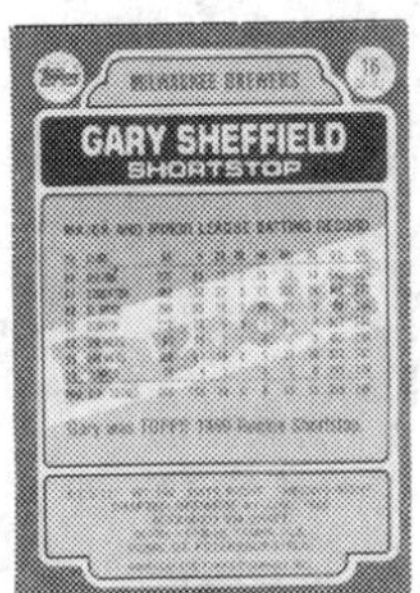

For the second consecutive year, Bazooka entitled its set "Shining Stars." Full color action and posed player shots are featured on the card fronts. The flip sides feature player statistics in a style much like the cards from the previous two Bazooka issues. Unlike the past two releases, the cards are not numbered alphabetically. The cards measure 2-1/2" by 3-1/2" in size and 22 cards complete the set.

		MT	NR MT	EX
Complete Set:		7.00	5.25	2.75
Common Player:		.15	.11	.06
1	Kevin Mitchell	.20	.15	.08
2	Robin Yount	.50	.40	.20
3	Mark Davis	.15	.11	.06
4	Bret Saberhagen	.15	.11	.06
5	Fred McGriff	.20	.15	.08
6	Tony Gwynn	.20	.15	.08
7	Kirby Puckett	.30	.25	.12
8	Vince Coleman	.15	.11	.06
9	Rickey Henderson	.30	.25	.12
10	Ben McDonald	.30	.25	.12
11	Gregg Olson	.15	.11	.06
12	Todd Zeile	.20	.15	.07
13	Carlos Martinez	.15	.11	.06
14	Gregg Jefferies	.25	.20	.10
15	Craig Worthington	.15	.11	.06
16	Gary Sheffield	.25	.20	.10
17	Greg Briley	.15	.11	.06
18	Ken Griffey,Jr.	2.00	1.50	.80
19	Jerome Walton	.15	.11	.06
20	Bob Geren	.15	.11	.06
21	Tom Gordon	.15	.11	.06
22	Jim Abbott	.25	.20	.10

Definitions for grading conditions are located in the Introduction of this price guide.

1991 Bazooka

For the third consecutive year Bazooka entitled its set "Shining Stars." The cards are styled like the 1990 issue, but include the Topps "40th Anniversary" logo. The 1991 issue is considered much scarcer than the previous releases. The cards measure 2-1/2" by 3-1/2" in size and 22 cards complete the set.

		MT	NR MT	EX
Complete Set:		15.00	11.00	6.00
Common Player:		.30	.25	.12
1	Barry Bonds	.80	.60	.30
2	Rickey Henderson	.50	.40	.20
3	Bob Welch	.30	.25	.12
4	Doug Drabek	.30	.25	.12
5	Alex Fernandez	.40	.30	.15
6	Jose Offerman	.30	.25	.12
7	Frank Thomas	3.00	2.25	1.25
8	Cecil Fielder	.60	.45	.25
9	Ryne Sandberg	.75	.55	.25
10	George Brett	.45	.35	.15
11	Willie McGee	.30	.25	.12
12	Vince Coleman	.30	.25	.12
13	Hal Morris	.30	.25	.12
14	Delino DeShields	.30	.25	.12
15	Robin Ventura	.30	.25	.12
16	Jeff Huson	.30	.25	.12
17	Felix Jose	.30	.25	.12
18	Dave Justice	.45	.35	.15
19	Larry Walker	.30	.25	.12
20	Sandy Alomar, Jr.	.30	.25	.12
21	Kevin Appier	.30	.25	.12
22	Scott Radinsky	.30	.25	.12

1992 Bazooka

This set of 22 cards features miniature versions of the 1953 Topps Archives issue. The mini-cards are set against a blue background on front and back. Besides reproductions of issued 1953 Topps cards, these "Quadracards" include minature versions of many of the special cards created for the Archives set. Cards feature the Bazooka logo on back, and were distributed in boxes of that bubble gum. They are readily available in complete set form.

		MT	NR MT	EX
Complete Set:		12.00	9.00	4.50
Common Player:		.50	.40	.20
1	Joe Adcock, Bob Lemon, Willie Mays, Vic Wertz	2.00	1.50	.75
2	Carl Furillo, Don Newcombe, Phil Rizzuto, Hank Sauer	.50	.40	.20
3	Ferris Fain, John Logan, Ed Mathews, Bobby Shantz	.50	.40	.20
4	Yogi Berra, Del Crandall, Howie Pollett, Gene Woodling	.50	.40	.20
5	Richie Ashburn, Leo Durocher, Allie Reynolds, Early Wynn	.50	.40	.20
6	Hank Aaron, Ray Boone, Luke Easter, Dick Williams	2.00	1.50	.75
7	Ralph Branca, Bob Feller, Rogers Hornsby, Bobby Thomson	.50	.40	.20
8	Jim Gilliam, Billy Martin, Orestes Minoso, Hal Newhouser	.50	.40	.20
9	Smoky Burgess, John Mize, Preacher Roe, Warren Spahn	.50	.40	.20
10	Monte Irvin, Bobo Newsom, Duke Snider, Wes Westrum	.50	.40	.20
11	Carl Erskine, Jackie Jensen, George Kell, Al Schoendienst	.50	.40	.20
12	Bill Bruton, Whitey Ford, Ed Lopat, Mickey Vernon	.50	.40	.20
13	Joe Black, Lew Burdette, Johnny Pesky, Enos Slaughter	.50	.40	.20
14	Gus Bell, Mike Garcia, Mel Parnell, Jackie Robinson	1.00	.75	.35
15	Alvin Dark, Dick Groat, Pee Wee Reese, John Sain	.50	.40	.20
16	Gil Hodges, Sal Maglie, Wilmer Mizell, Billy Pierce	.50	.40	.20
17	Nellie Fox, Ralph Kiner, Ted Kluszewski, Eddie Stanky	.50	.40	.20
18	Ewell Blackwell, Vern Law, Satchell Paige, Jim Wilson	.75	.55	.25
19	Lou Boudreau, Roy Face, Harvey Haddix, Bill Rigney	.50	.40	.20
20	Roy Campanella, Walt Dropo, Harvey Kuenn, Al Rosen	.50	.40	.20
21	Joe Garagiola, Robin Roberts, Casey Stengel, Hoyt Wilhelm	.50	.40	.20
22	John Antonelli, Bob Friend, Dixie Walker, Ted Williams	1.00	.75	.35

1948 Bowman

4 — JOHNNY MIZE
First Base—N. Y. Giants
Born: Demorest, Ga. Jan. 7, 1913
Bats: Left Throws: Right
Height: 6-02 Weight: 215
With a lifetime batting average of .326 he swings the heaviest bat in the National League. Tied with Ralph Kiner to lead all players with 51 home runs last year. He is the only National Leaguer who has 4 times hit 3 home runs in one game. He spent three years in the Navy. Married since 1937, he makes his home in Florida during the off season.
ASK FOR BLONY BUBBLE GUM
The Bubble Gum with the three different flavors
BOWMAN GUM, INC. Copyright 1948

Bowman Gum Co.'s premiere set was produced in 1948, making it one of the first major issues of the post-war period. Forty-eight black and white cards comprise the set, with each card measuring 2-1/16" by 2-1/2" in size. The card backs, printed in black ink on grey stock, include the card number and the player's name, team, position, and a short biography. Twelve cards (#'s 7, 8, 13, 16, 20, 22, 24, 26, 29, 30 and 34) were printed in short supply when they were removed from the 36-card printing sheet to make room for the set's high numbers (#'s 37-48). These 24 cards command a higher price than the remaining cards in the set.

		NR MT	EX	VG
Complete Set (48):		3500.00	1750.00	1000.
Common Player: 1-36		21.00	10.50	6.25
Common Player: 37-48		28.00	14.00	8.25
1	*Bob Elliott*	100.00	10.50	6.25
2	*Ewell Blackwell*	21.00	10.50	6.25
3	*Ralph Kiner*	180.00	90.00	54.00
4	Johnny Mize	110.00	55.00	33.00
5	Bob Feller	225.00	112.00	67.00
6	*Yogi Berra*	600.00	300.00	180.00
7	Pete Reiser	50.00	25.00	15.00
8	Phil Rizzuto	225.00	112.00	67.00
9	Walker Cooper	21.00	10.50	6.25
10	Buddy Rosar	21.00	10.50	6.25
11	Johnny Lindell	25.00	12.50	7.50
12	*Johnny Sain*	25.00	12.50	7.50
13	*Willard Marshall*	30.00	15.00	9.00
14	*Allie Reynolds*	40.00	20.00	12.00
15	Eddie Joost	21.00	10.50	6.25
16	Jack Lohrke	30.00	15.00	9.00
17	Enos Slaughter	100.00	50.00	30.00
18	*Warren Spahn*	350.00	175.00	105.00
19	Tommy Henrich	25.00	12.50	7.50
20	Buddy Kerr	30.00	15.00	9.00
21	*Ferris Fain*	21.00	10.50	6.25
22	Floyd (Bill) Bevens	40.00	20.00	12.00
23	Larry Jansen	21.00	10.50	6.25
24	Emil (Dutch) Leonard	30.00	15.00	9.00
25	Barney McCoskey (McCosky)	21.00	10.50	6.25
26	Frank Shea	40.00	20.00	12.00
27	Sid Gordon	21.00	10.50	6.25
28	Emil Verban	21.00	10.50	6.25
29	*Joe Page*	55.00	33.00	18.00
30	*"Whitey" Lockman*	30.00	15.00	9.00
31	Bill McCahan	21.00	10.50	6.25
32	*Bill Rigney*	21.00	10.50	6.25
33	Billy Johnson	25.00	12.50	7.50
34	Sheldon Jones	30.00	15.00	9.00
35	Snuffy Stirnweiss	25.00	12.50	7.50
36	*Stan Musial*	900.00	450.00	275.00
37	Clint Hartung	28.00	14.00	8.25
38	*Red Schoendienst*	175.00	87.50	52.50
39	Augie Galan	28.00	14.00	8.25
40	*Marty Marion*	55.00	27.50	16.50
41	Rex Barney	30.00	15.00	9.00
42	Ray Poat	28.00	14.00	8.25
43	Bruce Edwards	30.00	15.00	9.00
44	Johnny Wyrostek	28.00	14.00	8.25
45	Hank Sauer	28.00	14.00	8.25
46	Herman Wehmeier	28.00	14.00	8.25
47	*Bobby Thomson*	55.00	27.50	16.50
48	"Dave" Koslo	70.00	14.00	8.25

1949 Bowman

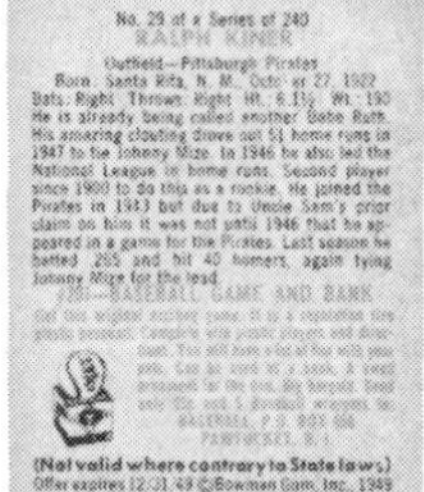

No. 29 of a Series of 240
RALPH KINER
Outfield—Pittsburgh Pirates
Born: Santa Rita, N. M., October 27, 1922
Bats: Right Throws: Right Ht.: 6-1½ Wt.: 190
He is already being called another Babe Ruth. His amazing clouting drove out 51 home runs in 1947 to tie Johnny Mize. In 1946 he also led the National League in home runs. Second player since 1900 to do this as a rookie. He joined the Pirates in 1943 but due to Uncle Sam's prior claim on him it was not until 1946 that he appeared in a game for the Pirates. Last season he batted .265 and hit 40 homers, again tying Johnny Mize for the lead.
(Not valid where contrary to State laws)
Offer expires 12/31/49 ©Bowman Gum, Inc., 1949

In 1949, Bowman increased the size of its issue to 240 numbered cards. The cards, which measure 2-1/16" by 2-1/2", are black and white photos overprinted with various pastel colors. Beginning with card #109 in the set, Bowman inserted the player's names on the card fronts. Twelve cards (#'s 4, 78, 83, 85, 88, 98, 109, 124, 127, 132 and 143), which were produced in the first four series of printings, were reprinted in the seventh series with either a card front or back modification. These variations are noted in the checklist that follows. Card #'s 1-3 and 5-73 can be found with either white or grey backs. The complete set of value in the following checklist does not include the higher priced variation cards.

	NR MT	EX	VG
Complete Set (240):	16500.00	8000.00	5250.
Common Player: 1-36	18.50	9.25	5.50
Common Player: 37-73	22.00	11.00	6.50
Common Player: 74-144	18.50	9.25	5.50
Common Player: 145-240	80.00	40.00	24.00

#	Player	NR MT	EX	VG
1	Vernon Bickford	100.00	9.25	5.50
2	"Whitey" Lockman	18.50	9.25	5.50
3	Bob Porterfield	22.00	11.00	6.50
4a	Jerry Priddy (no name on front)	18.50	9.25	5.50
4b	Jerry Priddy (name on front)	40.00	20.00	12.00
5	Hank Sauer	18.50	9.25	5.50
6	Phil Cavarretta	20.00	10.00	6.00
7	Joe Dobson	18.50	9.25	5.50
8	Murry Dickson	18.50	9.25	5.50
9	Ferris Fain	22.00	11.00	6.50
10	Ted Gray	18.50	9.25	5.50
11	Lou Boudreau(FC)	60.00	30.00	18.00
12	Cass Michaels	18.50	9.25	5.50
13	Bob Chesnes	18.50	9.25	5.50
14	*Curt Simmons*	30.00	15.00	9.00
15	*Ned Garver*	21.00	11.50	7.00
16	Al Kozar	18.50	9.25	5.50
17	Earl Torgeson	18.50	9.25	5.50
18	Bobby Thomson	30.00	15.00	9.00
19	*Bobby Brown*	60.00	30.00	18.00
20	Gene Hermanski	20.00	10.00	6.00
21	Frank Baumholtz	18.50	9.25	5.50
22	Harry "P-Nuts" Lowrey	18.50	9.25	5.50
23	Bobby Doerr(FC)	75.00	37.50	22.50
24	Stan Musial	600.00	300.00	180.00
25	Carl Scheib	18.50	9.25	5.50
26	George Kell(FC)	60.00	30.00	18.00
27	Bob Feller	150.00	75.00	45.00
28	Don Kolloway	18.50	9.25	5.50
29	Ralph Kiner	80.00	40.00	24.00
30	Andy Seminick	18.50	9.25	5.50
31	Dick Kokos	18.50	9.25	5.50
32	Eddie Yost	18.50	9.25	5.50
33	Warren Spahn	175.00	87.00	52.00
34	Dave Koslo	18.50	9.25	5.50
35	*Vic Raschi*	22.00	11.00	6.60
36	Pee Wee Reese(FC)	200.00	100.00	60.00
37	John Wyrostek	22.00	11.00	6.50
38	Emil Verban	22.00	11.00	6.50
39	Bill Goodman	22.00	11.00	6.50
40	"Red" Munger	22.00	11.00	6.50
41	Lou Brissie	22.00	11.00	6.50
42	"Hoot" Evers	22.00	11.00	6.50
43	Dale Mitchell	22.00	11.00	6.50
44	Dave Philley	22.00	11.00	6.50
45	Wally Westlake	22.00	11.00	6.50
46	*Robin Roberts*	275.00	137.00	82.00
47	Johnny Sain	24.00	12.00	7.20
48	Willard Marshall	22.00	11.00	6.50
49	Frank Shea	24.00	12.00	7.20
50	Jackie Robinson(FC)	900.00	450.00	275.00
51	Herman Wehmeier	22.00	11.00	6.50
52	Johnny Schmitz	22.00	11.00	6.50
53	Jack Kramer	22.00	11.00	6.50
54	Marty Marion	25.00	12.50	7.50
55	Eddie Joost	22.00	11.00	6.50
56	Pat Mullin	22.00	11.00	6.50
57	Gene Bearden	22.00	11.00	6.50
58	Bob Elliott	22.00	11.00	6.50
59	Jack Lohrke	22.00	11.00	6.50
60	Yogi Berra	350.00	175.00	105.00
61	Rex Barney	24.00	12.00	7.20
62	Grady Hatton	22.00	11.00	6.50
63	Andy Pafko	22.00	11.00	6.60
64	Dom DiMaggio(FC)	30.00	15.00	9.00
65	Enos Slaughter	60.00	30.00	18.00
66	Elmer Valo	22.00	11.00	6.50
67	Alvin Dark	24.00	12.00	7.20
68	Sheldon Jones	22.00	11.00	6.50
69	Tommy Henrich	25.00	12.50	7.50
70	*Carl Furillo*	75.00	37.50	22.50
71	Vern Stephens	22.00	11.00	6.50
72	Tommy Holmes	22.00	11.00	6.60
73	Billy Cox	24.00	12.00	7.20
74	Tom McBride	18.50	9.25	5.50
75	Eddie Mayo	18.50	9.25	5.50
76	Bill Nicholson	18.50	9.25	5.50
77	Ernie Bonham	18.50	9.25	5.50
78a	Sam Zoldak (no name on front)	18.50	9.25	5.50
78b	Sam Zoldak (name on front)	40.00	20.00	12.00
79	Ron Northey	18.50	9.25	5.50
80	Bill McCahan	18.50	9.25	5.50

#	Player	NR MT	EX	VG
81	Virgil "Red" Stallcup	18.50	9.25	5.50
82	Joe Page	24.00	12.00	7.20
83a	Bob Scheffing (no name on front)	18.50	9.25	5.50
83b	Bob Scheffing (name on front)	40.00	20.00	12.00
84	*Roy Campanella*	850.00	425.00	255.00
85a	Johnny Mize (no name on front)	65.00	32.50	19.50
85b	Johnny Mize (name on front)	125.00	62.00	37.00
86	Johnny Pesky	18.50	9.25	5.50
87	Randy Gumpert	18.50	9.25	5.50
88a	Bill Salkeld (no name on front)	18.50	9.25	5.50
88b	Bill Salkeld (name on front)	40.00	20.00	12.00
89	Mizell Platt	18.50	9.25	5.50
90	Gil Coan	18.50	9.25	5.50
91	Dick Wakefield	18.50	9.25	5.50
92	Willie Jones	18.50	9.25	5.50
93	Ed Stevens	18.50	9.25	5.50
94	*Mickey Vernon*	21.00	11.50	7.00
95	Howie Pollett	18.50	9.25	5.50
96	Taft Wright	18.50	9.25	5.50
97	Danny Litwhiler	18.50	9.25	5.50
98a	Phil Rizzuto (no name on front)	80.00	40.00	24.00
98b	Phil Rizzuto (name on front)	150.00	75.00	45.00
99	Frank Gustine	18.50	9.25	5.50
100	*Gil Hodges*	100.00	50.00	30.00
101	Sid Gordon	21.00	11.50	7.00
102	Stan Spence	18.50	9.25	5.50
103	Joe Tipton	18.50	9.25	5.50
104	Ed Stanky	21.00	11.50	7.00
105	Bill Kennedy	18.50	9.25	5.50
106	Jake Early	18.50	9.25	5.50
107	Eddie Lake	18.50	9.25	5.50
108	Ken Heintzelman	18.50	9.25	5.50
109a	Ed Fitz Gerald (script name on back)	18.50	9.25	5.50
109b	Ed Fitz Gerald (printed name on back)	40.00	20.00	12.00
110	*Early Wynn*	100.00	50.00	30.00
111	Red Schoendienst	65.00	32.50	19.50
112	Sam Chapman	18.50	9.25	5.50
113	Ray Lamanno	18.50	9.25	5.50
114	Allie Reynolds	25.00	12.50	7.50
115	Emil "Dutch" Leonard	18.50	9.25	5.50
116	Joe Hatten	22.00	11.00	6.50
117	Walker Cooper	18.50	9.25	5.50
118	Sam Mele	18.50	9.25	5.50
119	Floyd Baker	18.50	9.25	5.50
120	Cliff Fannin	18.50	9.25	5.50
121	Mark Christman	18.50	9.25	5.50
122	George Vico	18.50	9.25	5.50
123	Johnny Blatnick	18.50	9.25	5.50
124a	Danny Murtaugh (script name on back)	18.50	9.25	5.50
124b	Danny Murtaugh (printed name on back)	40.00	20.00	12.00
125	Ken Keltner	21.00	11.50	7.00
126a	Al Brazle (script name on back)	18.50	9.25	5.50
126b	Al Brazle (printed name on back)	40.00	20.00	12.00
127a	Henry Majeski (script name on back)	18.50	9.25	5.50
127b	Henry Majeski (printed name on back)	40.00	20.00	12.00
128	Johnny Vander Meer	21.00	11.50	7.00
129	Billy Johnson	24.00	12.00	7.20
130	Harry "The Hat" Walker	21.00	11.50	7.00
131	Paul Lehner	18.50	9.25	5.50
132a	Al Evans (script name on back)	18.50	9.25	5.50
132b	Al Evans (printed name on back)	40.00	20.00	12.00
133	Aaron Robinson	18.50	9.25	5.50
134	Hank Borowy	18.50	9.25	5.50
135	Stan Rojek	18.50	9.25	5.50
136	Hank Edwards	18.50	9.25	5.50
137	Ted Wilks	18.50	9.25	5.50
138	"Buddy" Rosar	18.50	9.25	5.50
139	Hank "Bow-Wow" Arft	18.50	9.25	5.50
140	Ray Scarborough	18.50	9.25	5.50
141	"Tony Lupien	18.50	9.25	5.50
142	Eddie Waitkus	18.50	9.25	5.50
143a	Bob Dillinger (script name on back)	18.50	9.25	5.50
143b	Bob Dillinger (printed name on back)	40.00	20.00	12.00
144	Mickey Haefner	18.50	9.25	5.50
145	"Blix" Donnelly	80.00	40.00	24.00
146	Mike McCormick	85.00	42.50	25.50
147	Elmer Singleton	80.00	40.00	24.00
148	Bob Swift	80.00	40.00	24.00
149	Roy Partee	90.00	45.00	27.00
150	Allie Clark	80.00	40.00	24.00
151	Mickey Harris	80.00	40.00	24.00

		NR MT	EX	VG
152	Clarence Maddern	80.00	40.00	24.00
153	Phil Masi	80.00	40.00	24.00
154	Clint Hartung	80.00	40.00	24.00
155	Mickey Guerra	80.00	40.00	24.00
156	Al Zarilla	80.00	40.00	24.00
157	Walt Masterson	80.00	40.00	24.00
158	Harry Brecheen	80.00	40.00	24.00
159	Glen Moulder	80.00	40.00	24.00
160	Jim Blackburn	80.00	40.00	24.00
161	"Jocko" Thompson	80.00	40.00	24.00
162	*Preacher Roe*	135.00	67.50	40.00
163	Clyde McCullough	80.00	40.00	24.00
164	*Vic Wertz*	80.00	40.00	24.00
165	"Snuffy" Stirnweiss	90.00	45.00	27.00
166	Mike Tresh	80.00	40.00	24.00
167	Boris "Babe" Martin	80.00	40.00	24.00
168	Doyle Lade	80.00	40.00	24.00
169	Jeff Heath	80.00	40.00	24.00
170	Bill Rigney	80.00	40.00	24.00
171	Dick Fowler	80.00	40.00	24.00
172	Eddie Pellagrini	80.00	40.00	24.00
173	Eddie Stewart	80.00	40.00	24.00
174	*Terry Moore*	90.00	45.00	27.00
175	Luke Appling(FC)	125.00	62.00	37.00
176	Ken Raffensberger	80.00	40.00	24.00
177	Stan Lopata	80.00	40.00	24.00
178	Tommy Brown	85.00	42.50	25.50
179	Hugh Casey	85.00	42.50	25.50
180	Connie Berry	80.00	40.00	24.00
181	Gus Niarhos	90.00	45.00	27.00
182	Hal Peck	80.00	40.00	24.00
183	Lou Stringer	80.00	40.00	24.00
184	Bob Chipman	80.00	40.00	24.00
185	Pete Reiser	85.00	42.50	25.00
186	"Buddy" Kerr	80.00	40.00	24.00
187	Phil Marchildon	80.00	40.00	24.00
188	Karl Drews	80.00	40.00	24.00
189	Earl Wooten	80.00	40.00	24.00
190	*Jim Hearn*	80.00	40.00	24.00
191	Joe Haynes	80.00	40.00	24.00
192	Harry Gumbert	80.00	40.00	24.00
193	Ken Trinkle	80.00	40.00	24.00
194	Ralph Branca	95.00	47.50	28.50
195	Eddie Bockman	80.00	40.00	24.00
196	Fred Hutchinson(FC)	80.00	40.00	24.00
197	Johnny Lindell	90.00	45.00	27.00
198	Steve Gromek	80.00	40.00	24.00
199	"Tex" Hughson	80.00	40.00	24.00
200	Jess Dobernic	80.00	40.00	24.00
201	Sibby Sisti	80.00	40.00	24.00
202	Larry Jansen	80.00	40.00	24.00
203	Barney McCosky	80.00	40.00	24.00
204	Bob Savage	80.00	40.00	24.00
205	Dick Sisler	80.00	40.00	24.00
206	Bruce Edwards	85.00	42.50	25.50
207	Johnny Hopp	80.00	40.00	24.00
208	"Dizzy" Trout	80.00	40.00	24.00
209	Charlie Keller	90.00	45.00	27.00
210	Joe Gordon	80.00	40.00	24.00
211	Dave "Boo" Ferris	80.00	40.00	24.00
212	Ralph Hamner	80.00	40.00	24.00
213	Charles "Red" Barrett	80.00	40.00	24.00
214	*Richie Ashburn*	550.00	275.00	165.00
215	Kirby Higbe	80.00	40.00	24.00
216	"Schoolboy" Rowe	85.00	42.50	25.00
217	Marino Pieretti	80.00	40.00	24.00
218	Dick Kryhoski	90.00	45.00	27.00
219	Virgil "Fire" Trucks(FC)	85.00	42.50	25.50
220	Johnny McCarthy	80.00	40.00	24.00
221	Bob Muncrief	80.00	40.00	24.00
222	Alex Kellner	80.00	40.00	24.00
223	Bob Hofman	80.00	40.00	24.00
224	*Satchel Paige*(FC)	1200.00	600.00	350.00
225	*Gerry Coleman*	100.00	50.00	30.00
226	Duke Snider	1000.00	500.00	300.00
227	Fritz Ostermueller	80.00	40.00	24.00
228	Jackie Mayo	80.00	40.00	24.00
229	Ed Lopat	100.00	50.00	30.00
230	Augie Galan	80.00	40.00	24.00
231	Earl Johnson	80.00	40.00	24.00
232	George McQuinn	90.00	45.00	27.00
233	Larry Doby(FC)	175.00	87.00	52.00
234	"Rip" Sewell	80.00	40.00	24.00
235	Jim Russell	80.00	40.00	24.00
236	Fred Sanford	90.00	45.00	27.00
237	Monte Kennedy	80.00	40.00	24.00
238	*Bob Lemon*	200.00	100.00	60.00
239	Frank McCormick	80.00	40.00	24.00
240	Norm "Babe" Young (Photo actually Bobby Young)	150.00	45.00	27.00

1950 Bowman

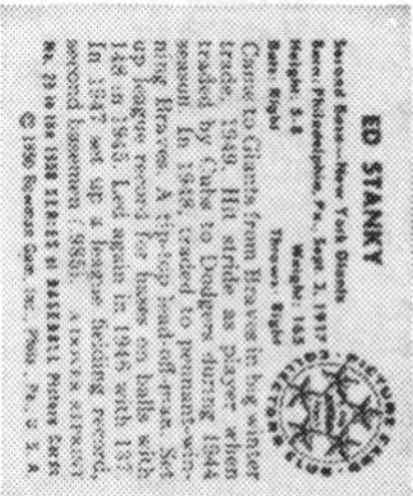

The quality of the 1950 Bowman issue showed a marked improvement over the company's previous efforts. The cards are beautiful color art reproductions of actual photographs and measure 2-1/16" by 2-1/2" in size. The card backs include the same type of information as found in the previous year's issue but are designed in a horizontal format. Cards found in the first two series of the set (#'s 1-72) are the scarcest in the issue. The backs of the final 72 cards in the set (#'s 181-252) can be found with or without the copyright line at the bottom of the card, the "without" version being the less common.

		NR MT	EX	VG
Complete Set (252):		10000.00	5000.00	3000.
Common Player: 1-72		55.00	27.00	16.50
Common Player: 73-252		18.00	9.00	5.50
1	Mel Parnell	200.00	27.50	5.50
2	Vern Stephens	55.00	27.00	16.50
3	Dom DiMaggio	75.00	37.50	22.50
4	Gus Zernial	55.00	27.00	16.50
5	Bob Kuzava	55.00	27.00	16.50
6	Bob Feller	225.00	112.00	67.00
7	Jim Hegan	55.00	27.00	16.50
8	George Kell	115.00	57.00	34.00
9	Vic Wertz	55.00	27.00	16.50
10	Tommy Henrich	60.00	30.00	18.00
11	Phil Rizzuto	165.00	82.00	49.00
12	Joe Page	60.00	30.00	18.00
13	Ferris Fain	55.00	27.00	16.50
14	Alex Kellner	55.00	27.00	16.50
15	Al Kozar	55.00	27.00	16.50
16	*Roy Sievers*	65.00	32.50	19.50
17	Sid Hudson	55.00	27.00	16.50
18	Eddie Robinson	55.00	27.00	16.50
19	Warren Spahn	225.00	112.50	67.50
20	Bob Elliott	55.00	27.00	16.50
21	Pee Wee Reese	225.00	112.50	67.50
22	Jackie Robinson	725.00	360.00	215.00
23	*Don Newcombe*	150.00	75.00	50.00
24	Johnny Schmitz	55.00	27.00	16.50
25	Hank Sauer	55.00	27.00	16.50
26	Grady Hatton	55.00	27.00	16.50
27	Herman Wehmeier	55.00	27.00	16.50
28	Bobby Thomson	75.00	37.50	22.50
29	Ed Stanky	55.00	27.00	16.50
30	Eddie Waitkus	55.00	27.00	16.50
31	*Del Ennis*	60.00	30.00	18.00
32	Robin Roberts	170.00	85.00	51.00
33	Ralph Kiner	150.00	75.00	45.00
34	Murry Dickson	55.00	27.00	16.50
35	Enos Slaughter	115.00	57.00	34.00
36	Eddie Kazak	55.00	27.00	16.50
37	Luke Appling	115.00	57.00	34.00
38	Bill Wight	55.00	27.00	16.50
39	Larry Doby	65.00	32.50	19.50
40	Bob Lemon	115.00	57.00	34.00
41	"Hoot" Evers	55.00	27.00	16.50
42	Art Houtteman	55.00	27.00	16.50
43	Bobby Doerr	115.00	57.00	34.00
44	Joe Dobson	55.00	27.00	16.50
45	Al Zarilla	55.00	27.00	16.50
46	Yogi Berra	425.00	212.00	125.00
47	Jerry Coleman	60.00	30.00	18.00
48	Lou Brissie	55.00	27.00	16.50
49	Elmer Valo	55.00	27.00	16.50

		NR MT	EX	VG
50	Dick Kokos	55.00	27.00	16.50
51	Ned Garver	55.00	27.00	16.50
52	Sam Mele	55.00	27.00	16.50
53	Clyde Vollmer	55.00	27.00	16.50
54	Gil Coan	55.00	27.00	16.50
55	"Buddy" Kerr	55.00	27.00	16.50
56	*Del Crandell* (Crandall)	70.00	35.00	21.00
57	Vernon Bickford	55.00	27.00	16.50
58	Carl Furillo	75.00	37.50	22.50
59	Ralph Branca	60.00	30.00	18.00
60	Andy Pafko	55.00	27.00	16.50
61	Bob Rush	55.00	27.00	16.50
62	Ted Kluszewski(FC)	70.00	35.00	21.00
63	Ewell Blackwell	55.00	27.00	16.50
64	Alvin Dark	55.00	27.00	16.50
65	Dave Koslo	55.00	27.00	16.50
66	Larry Jansen	55.00	27.00	16.50
67	Willie Jones	55.00	27.00	16.50
68	Curt Simmons	55.00	27.00	16.50
69	Wally Westlake	55.00	27.00	16.50
70	Bob Chesnes	55.00	27.00	16.50
71	Red Schoendienst	115.00	57.00	34.00
72	Howie Pollet	55.00	27.00	16.50
73	Willard Marshall	18.00	9.00	5.50
74	*Johnny Antonelli*	21.00	11.50	7.00
75	Roy Campanella	300.00	150.00	90.00
76	Rex Barney	20.00	10.00	6.00
77	Duke Snider	275.00	137.50	82.50
78	Mickey Owen	18.00	9.00	5.50
79	Johnny Vander Meer	18.00	9.00	5.50
80	Howard Fox	18.00	9.00	5.50
81	Ron Northey	18.00	9.00	5.50
82	"Whitey" Lockman	18.00	9.00	5.50
83	Sheldon Jones	18.00	9.00	5.50
84	Richie Ashburn	75.00	38.00	23.00
85	Ken Heintzelman	18.00	9.00	5.50
86	Stan Rojek	18.00	9.00	5.50
87	Bill Werle	18.00	9.00	5.50
88	Marty Marion	20.00	10.00	6.00
89	George Munger	18.00	9.00	5.50
90	Harry Brecheen	18.00	9.00	5.50
91	Cass Michaels	18.00	9.00	5.50
92	Hank Majeski	18.00	9.00	5.50
93	Gene Bearden	18.00	9.00	5.50
94	Lou Boudreau	55.00	27.00	16.50
95	Aaron Robinson	18.00	9.00	5.50
96	Virgil "Fire" Trucks	18.00	9.00	5.50
97	Maurice McDermott	18.00	9.00	5.50
98	Ted Williams(FC)	800.00	400.00	250.00
99	Billy Goodman	18.00	9.00	5.50
100	Vic Raschi	22.00	11.00	6.60
101	Bobby Brown	25.00	12.50	7.50
102	Billy Johnson	22.00	11.00	6.60
103	Eddie Joost	18.00	9.00	5.50
104	Sam Chapman	18.00	9.00	5.50
105	Bob Dillinger	18.00	9.00	5.50
106	Cliff Fannin	18.00	9.00	5.50
107	Sam Dente	18.00	9.00	5.50
108	Ray Scarborough	18.00	9.00	5.50
109	Sid Gordon	20.00	10.00	6.00
110	Tommy Holmes	18.00	9.00	5.50
111	Walker Cooper	18.00	9.00	5.50
112	Gil Hodges	80.00	40.00	24.00
113	Gene Hermanski	20.00	10.00	6.00
114	*Wayne Terwilliger*	21.00	11.50	7.00
115	Roy Smalley	18.00	9.00	5.50
116	Virgil "Red" Stallcup	18.00	9.00	5.50
117	Bill Rigney	18.00	9.00	5.50
118	Clint Hartung	18.00	9.00	5.50
119	Dick Sisler	18.00	9.00	5.50
120	Jocko Thompson	18.00	9.00	5.50
121	Andy Seminick	18.00	9.00	5.50
122	Johnny Hopp	18.00	9.00	5.50
123	Dino Restelli	18.00	9.00	5.50
124	Clyde McCullough	18.00	9.00	5.50
125	Del Rice	18.00	9.00	5.50
126	Al Brazle	18.00	9.00	5.50
127	Dave Philley	18.00	9.00	5.50
128	Phil Masi	18.00	9.00	5.50
129	Joe Gordon	21.00	11.50	7.00
130	Dale Mitchell	18.00	9.00	5.50
131	Steve Gromek	18.00	9.00	5.50
132	Mickey Vernon	18.00	9.00	5.50
133	Don Kolloway	18.00	9.00	5.50
134	"Dizzy" Trout	18.00	9.00	5.50
135	Pat Mullin	18.00	9.00	5.50
136	"Buddy" Rosar	18.00	9.00	5.50
137	Johnny Pesky	18.00	9.00	5.50
138	Allie Reynolds	40.00	20.00	12.00
139	Johnny Mize	60.00	30.00	18.00
140	Pete Suder	18.00	9.00	5.50

		NR MT	EX	VG
141	Joe Coleman	18.00	9.00	5.50
142	*Sherman Lollar*	22.00	11.00	6.60
143	Eddie Stewart	18.00	9.00	5.50
144	Al Evans	18.00	9.00	5.50
145	Jack Graham	18.00	9.00	5.50
146	Floyd Baker	18.00	9.00	5.50
147	*Mike Garcia*	25.00	12.50	7.50
148	Early Wynn	60.00	30.00	18.00
149	Bob Swift	18.00	9.00	5.50
150	George Vico	18.00	9.00	5.50
151	Fred Hutchinson	18.00	9.00	5.50
152	Ellis Kinder	18.00	9.00	5.50
153	Walt Masterson	18.00	9.00	5.50
154	Gus Niarhos	22.00	11.00	6.60
155	Frank "Spec" Shea	22.00	11.00	6.60
156	Fred Sanford	22.00	11.00	6.60
157	Mike Guerra	18.00	9.00	5.50
158	Paul Lehner	18.00	9.00	5.50
159	Joe Tipton	18.00	9.00	5.50
160	Mickey Harris	18.00	9.00	5.50
161	Sherry Robertson	18.00	9.00	5.50
162	Eddie Yost	18.00	9.00	5.50
163	Earl Torgeson	18.00	9.00	5.50
164	Sibby Sisti	18.00	9.00	5.50
165	Bruce Edwards	20.00	10.00	6.00
166	Joe Hatten	20.00	10.00	6.00
167	Preacher Roe	40.00	20.00	12.00
168	Bob Scheffing	18.00	9.00	5.50
169	Hank Edwards	18.00	9.00	5.50
170	Emil Leonard	18.00	9.00	5.50
171	Harry Gumbert	18.00	9.00	5.50
172	Harry Lowrey	18.00	9.00	5.50
173	Lloyd Merriman	18.00	9.00	5.50
174	*Henry Thompson*	18.00	9.00	5.50
175	Monte Kennedy	18.00	9.00	5.50
176	"Blix" Donnelly	18.00	9.00	5.50
177	Hank Borowy	18.00	9.00	5.50
178	Eddy Fitz Gerald	18.00	9.00	5.50
179	Charles Diering	18.00	9.00	5.50
180	Harry "The Hat" Walker	18.00	9.00	5.50
181	Marino Pieretti	18.00	9.00	5.50
182	Sam Zoldak	18.00	9.00	5.50
183	Mickey Haefner	18.00	9.00	5.50
184	Randy Gumpert	18.00	9.00	5.50
185	Howie Judson	18.00	9.00	5.50
186	Ken Keltner	20.00	10.00	6.00
187	Lou Stringer	18.00	9.00	5.50
188	Earl Johnson	18.00	9.00	5.50
189	Owen Friend	18.00	9.00	5.50
190	Ken Wood	18.00	9.00	5.50
191	Dick Starr	18.00	9.00	5.50
192	Bob Chipman	18.00	9.00	5.50
193	Pete Reiser	20.00	10.00	6.00
194	Billy Cox	20.00	10.00	6.00
195	Phil Cavarretta	18.00	9.00	5.50
196	Doyle Lade	18.00	9.00	5.50
197	Johnny Wyrostek	18.00	9.00	5.50
198	Danny Litwhiler	18.00	9.00	5.50
199	Jack Kramer	18.00	9.00	5.50
200	Kirby Higbe	18.00	9.00	5.50
201	Pete Castiglione	18.00	9.00	5.50
202	Cliff Chambers	18.00	9.00	5.50
203	Danny Murtaugh	18.00	9.00	5.50
204	Granny Hamner	18.00	9.00	5.50
205	Mike Goliat	18.00	9.00	5.50
206	Stan Lopata	18.00	9.00	5.50
207	Max Lanier	18.00	9.00	5.50
208	Jim Hearn	18.00	9.00	5.50
209	Johnny Lindell	18.00	9.00	5.50
210	Ted Gray	18.00	9.00	5.50
211	Charlie Keller	18.00	9.00	5.50
212	Gerry Priddy	18.00	9.00	5.50
213	Carl Scheib	18.00	9.00	5.50
214	Dick Fowler	18.00	9.00	5.50
215	Ed Lopat	22.00	11.00	6.60
216	Bob Porterfield	22.00	11.00	6.60
217	Casey Stengel(FC)	150.00	75.00	45.00
218	Cliff Mapes	22.00	11.00	6.60
219	*Hank Bauer*	70.00	35.00	20.00
220	Leo Durocher(FC)	50.00	25.00	15.00
221	Don Mueller	18.00	9.00	5.50
222	Bobby Morgan	20.00	10.00	6.00
223	Jimmy Russell	20.00	10.00	6.00
224	Jack Banta	20.00	10.00	6.00
225	Eddie Sawyer	18.00	9.00	5.50
226	*Jim Konstanty*	21.00	11.50	7.00
227	Bob Miller	18.00	9.00	5.50
228	Bill Nicholson	18.00	9.00	5.50
229	Frank Frisch	60.00	30.00	18.00
230	Bill Serena	18.00	9.00	5.50
231	Preston Ward	18.00	9.00	5.50

		NR MT	EX	VG
232	*Al Rosen*	50.00	25.00	15.00
233	Allie Clark	18.00	9.00	5.50
234	*Bobby Shantz*	25.00	12.50	7.50
235	Harold Gilbert	18.00	9.00	5.50
236	Bob Cain	18.00	9.00	5.50
237	Bill Salkeld	18.00	9.00	5.50
238	Nippy Jones	18.00	9.00	5.50
239	Bill Howerton	18.00	9.00	5.50
240	Eddie Lake	18.00	9.00	5.50
241	Neil Berry	18.00	9.00	5.50
242	Dick Kryhoski	18.00	9.00	5.50
243	Johnny Groth	18.00	9.00	5.50
244	Dale Coogan	18.00	9.00	5.50
245	Al Papai	18.00	9.00	5.50
246	*Walt Dropo*	25.00	12.50	7.50
247	*Irv Noren*	18.00	9.00	5.50
248	*Sam Jethroe*	21.00	11.50	7.00
249	"Snuffy" Stirnweiss	18.00	9.00	5.50
250	Ray Coleman	18.00	9.00	5.50
251	Les Moss	18.00	9.00	5.50
252	Billy DeMars	80.00	9.00	5.50

1951 Bowman

JAMES VERNON
First Base—Washington Senators
Born: Marcus Hook, Pa., April 22, 1918
Height: 6-2 Weight: 180
Bats: Left Throws: Left

James "Mickey" Vernon batted .281 in 118 games in 1950. Drove in 75 runs. Tied for top fielding percentage in the League with a .991 mark. Began the season with Cleveland, but after 28 games was switched back to Washington where all of major-league career has been spent except 1949 which was with Cleveland. First full season in the majors: 1941. Top AL batter, 1946. In service 2 years.

No. 65 in the 1951 SERIES
BASEBALL
PICTURE CARDS
©1951 Bowman Gum, Inc., Phila., Pa., U.S.A.

In 1951, Bowman increased the numbers of cards in its set for the third consecutive year when it issued 324 cards. The cards are, like 1950, color art reproductions of actual photographs but now measured 2-1/16" by 3-1/8" in size. The player's name is situated in a small, black box on the card front. Several of the card fronts are enlargements of the 1950 version. The high-numbered series of the set (#'s 253-324), which includes the rookie cards of Mantle and Mays, are the scarcest of the issue.

	NR MT	EX	VG
Complete Set (324):	22500.00	10000.00	6000.
Common Player: 1-36	22.00	11.00	6.50
Common Player: 37-252	15.00	7.50	4.50
Common Player: 253-324	60.00	30.00	18.00

		NR MT	EX	VG
1	*Whitey Ford*	1300.00	575.00	300.00
2	Yogi Berra	350.00	175.00	105.00
3	Robin Roberts	80.00	40.00	25.00
4	Del Ennis	22.00	11.00	6.50
5	Dale Mitchell	22.00	11.00	6.50
6	Don Newcombe	35.00	17.50	10.50
7	Gil Hodges	75.00	37.50	22.50
8	Paul Lehner	22.00	11.00	6.50
9	Sam Chapman	22.00	11.00	6.50
10	Red Schoendienst	80.00	40.00	25.00
11	"Red" Munger	22.00	11.00	6.50
12	Hank Majeski	22.00	11.00	6.50
13	Ed Stanky	24.00	12.00	7.25
14	Alvin Dark	24.00	12.00	7.25
15	Johnny Pesky	22.00	11.00	6.50
16	Maurice McDermott	22.00	11.00	6.50
17	Pete Castiglione	22.00	11.00	6.50
18	Gil Coan	22.00	11.00	6.50
19	Sid Gordon	24.00	12.00	7.25
20	Del Crandall	22.00	11.00	6.50
21	"Snuffy" Stirnweiss	22.00	11.00	6.50
22	Hank Sauer	22.00	11.00	6.50
23	"Hoot" Evers	22.00	11.00	6.50
24	Ewell Blackwell	22.00	11.00	6.50
25	Vic Raschi	30.00	15.00	9.00
26	Phil Rizzuto	100.00	50.00	30.00

		NR MT	EX	VG
27	Jim Konstanty	22.00	11.00	6.50
28	Eddie Waitkus	22.00	11.00	6.50
29	Allie Clark	22.00	11.00	6.50
30	Bob Feller	125.00	62.00	37.00
31	Roy Campanella	260.00	130.00	78.00
32	Duke Snider	250.00	125.00	75.00
33	Bob Hooper	22.00	11.00	6.50
34	Marty Marion	25.00	12.50	7.50
35	Al Zarilla	22.00	11.00	6.50
36	Joe Dobson	22.00	11.00	6.50
37	Whitey Lockman	15.00	7.50	4.50
38	Al Evans	15.00	7.50	4.50
39	Ray Scarborough	15.00	7.50	4.50
40	*Gus Bell*	20.00	10.00	6.00
41	Eddie Yost	15.00	7.00	4.50
42	Vern Bickford	15.00	7.50	4.50
43	Billy DeMars	15.00	7.50	4.50
44	Roy Smalley	15.00	7.50	4.50
45	Art Houtteman	15.00	7.50	4.50
46	George Kell	65.00	32.50	19.50
47	Grady Hatton	15.00	7.50	4.50
48	Ken Raffensberger	15.00	7.50	4.50
49	Jerry Coleman	20.00	10.00	6.00
50	Johnny Mize	60.00	30.00	18.00
51	Andy Seminick	15.00	7.50	4.50
52	Dick Sisler	15.00	7.50	4.50
53	Bob Lemon	60.00	30.00	18.00
54	*Ray Boone*	20.00	10.00	6.00
55	Gene Hermanski	18.00	9.00	5.50
56	Ralph Branca	30.00	15.00	9.00
57	Alex Kellner	15.00	7.50	4.50
58	Enos Slaughter	60.00	30.00	18.00
59	Randy Gumpert	15.00	7.50	4.50
60	"Chico" Carrasquel	15.00	7.50	4.50
61	Jim Hearn	15.00	7.50	4.50
62	Lou Boudreau	60.00	30.00	18.00
63	Bob Dillinger	15.00	7.50	4.50
64	Bill Werle	15.00	7.50	4.50
65	Mickey Vernon	18.00	9.00	5.50
66	Bob Elliott	15.00	7.50	4.50
67	Roy Sievers	18.00	9.00	5.50
68	Dick Kokos	15.00	7.50	4.50
69	Johnny Schmitz	15.00	7.50	4.50
70	Ron Northey	15.00	7.50	4.50
71	Jerry Priddy	15.00	7.50	4.50
72	Lloyd Merriman	15.00	7.50	4.50
73	Tommy Byrne	20.00	10.00	6.00
74	Billy Johnson	20.00	10.00	6.00
75	Russ Meyer	15.00	7.50	4.50
76	Stan Lopata	15.00	7.50	4.50
77	Mike Goliat	15.00	7.50	4.50
78	Early Wynn	60.00	30.00	18.00
79	Jim Hegan	15.00	7.50	4.50
80	Pee Wee Reese	150.00	75.00	50.00
81	Carl Furillo	30.00	15.00	9.00
82	Joe Tipton	15.00	7.50	4.50
83	Carl Scheib	15.00	7.50	4.50
84	Barney McCosky	15.00	7.50	4.50
85	Eddie Kazak	15.00	7.50	4.50
86	Harry Brecheen	15.00	7.50	4.50
87	Floyd Baker	15.00	7.50	4.50
88	Eddie Robinson	15.00	7.50	4.50
89	Henry Thompson	15.00	7.50	4.50
90	Dave Koslo	15.00	7.50	4.50
91	Clyde Vollmer	15.00	7.50	4.50
92	Vern Stephens	15.00	7.50	4.50
93	Danny O'Connell	15.00	7.50	4.50
94	Clyde McCullough	15.00	7.50	4.50
95	Sherry Robertson	15.00	7.50	4.50
96	Sandy Consuegra	15.00	7.50	4.50
97	Bob Kuzava	15.00	7.50	4.50
98	Willard Marshall	15.00	7.50	4.50
99	Earl Torgeson	15.00	7.50	4.50
100	Sherman Lollar	15.00	7.50	4.50
101	Owen Friend	15.00	7.50	4.50
102	Emil "Dutch" Leonard	15.00	7.50	4.50
103	Andy Pafko	15.00	7.50	4.50
104	Virgil "Fire" Trucks	15.00	7.50	4.50
105	Don Kolloway	15.00	7.50	4.50
106	Pat Mullin	15.00	7.50	4.50
107	Johnny Wyrostek	15.00	7.50	4.50
108	Virgil Stallcup	15.00	7.50	4.50
109	Allie Reynolds	25.00	12.50	7.50
110	Bobby Brown	30.00	15.00	9.00
111	Curt Simmons	15.00	7.50	4.50
112	Willie Jones	15.00	7.50	4.50
113	Bill "Swish" Nicholson	15.00	7.50	4.50
114	Sam Zoldak	15.00	7.50	4.50
115	Steve Gromek	15.00	7.50	4.50
116	Bruce Edwards	18.00	9.00	5.50
117	Eddie Miksis	18.00	9.00	5.50

		NR MT	EX	VG
118	Preacher Roe	25.00	12.50	7.50
119	Eddie Joost	15.00	7.50	4.50
120	Joe Coleman	15.00	7.50	4.50
121	Gerry Staley	15.00	7.50	4.50
122	*Joe Garagiola*	125.00	62.50	37.50
123	Howie Judson	15.00	7.50	4.50
124	Gus Niarhos	15.00	7.50	4.50
125	Bill Rigney	15.00	7.50	4.50
126	Bobby Thomson	30.00	15.00	9.00
127	*Sal Maglie*	45.00	22.50	13.50
128	Ellis Kinder	15.00	7.50	4.50
129	Matt Batts	15.00	7.50	4.50
130	Tom Saffell	15.00	7.50	4.50
131	Cliff Chambers	15.00	7.50	4.50
132	Cass Michaels	15.00	7.50	4.50
133	Sam Dente	15.00	7.50	4.50
134	Warren Spahn	125.00	62.50	37.50
135	Walker Cooper	15.00	7.50	4.50
136	Ray Coleman	15.00	7.50	4.50
137	Dick Starr	15.00	7.50	4.50
138	Phil Cavarretta	15.00	7.50	4.50
139	Doyle Lade	15.00	7.50	4.50
140	Eddie Lake	15.00	7.50	4.50
141	Fred Hutchinson	18.00	9.00	5.50
142	Aaron Robinson	15.00	7.50	4.50
143	Ted Kluszewski	30.00	15.00	9.00
144	Herman Wehmeier	15.00	7.50	4.50
145	Fred Sanford	20.00	10.00	6.00
146	Johnny Hopp	20.00	10.00	6.00
147	Ken Heintzelman	15.00	7.50	4.50
148	Granny Hamner	15.00	7.50	4.50
149	"Bubba" Church	15.00	7.50	4.50
150	Mike Garcia	18.00	9.00	5.50
151	Larry Doby	20.00	10.00	6.00
152	Cal Abrams	18.00	9.00	5.50
153	Rex Barney	18.00	9.00	5.50
154	Pete Suder	15.00	7.50	4.50
155	Lou Brissie	15.00	7.50	4.50
156	Del Rice	15.00	7.50	4.50
157	Al Brazle	15.00	7.50	4.50
158	Chuck Diering	15.00	7.50	4.50
159	Eddie Stewart	15.00	7.50	4.50
160	Phil Masi	15.00	7.50	4.50
161	Wes Westrum	15.00	7.50	4.50
162	Larry Jansen	15.00	7.50	4.50
163	Monte Kennedy	15.00	7.50	4.50
164	Bill Wight	15.00	7.50	4.50
165	Ted Williams	700.00	350.00	210.00
166	Stan Rojek	15.00	7.50	4.50
167	Murry Dickson	15.00	7.50	4.50
168	Sam Mele	15.00	7.50	4.50
169	Sid Hudson	15.00	7.50	4.50
170	Sibby Sisti	15.00	7.50	4.50
171	Buddy Kerr	15.00	7.50	4.50
172	Ned Garver	15.00	7.50	4.50
173	Hank Arft	15.00	7.50	4.50
174	Mickey Owen	15.00	7.50	4.50
175	Wayne Terwilliger	15.00	7.50	4.50
176	Vic Wertz	15.00	7.50	4.50
177	Charlie Keller	15.00	7.50	4.50
178	Ted Gray	15.00	7.50	4.50
179	Danny Litwhiler	15.00	7.50	4.50
180	Howie Fox	15.00	7.50	4.50
181	Casey Stengel	110.00	55.00	33.00
182	Tom Ferrick	18.00	9.00	5.50
183	Hank Bauer	30.00	15.00	9.00
184	Eddie Sawyer	15.00	7.50	4.50
185	Jimmy Bloodworth	15.00	7.50	4.50
186	Richie Ashburn	60.00	30.00	18.00
187	Al Rosen	20.00	10.00	6.00
188	*Roberto Avila*	20.00	10.00	6.00
189	Erv Palica	18.00	9.00	5.50
190	Joe Hatten	18.00	9.00	5.50
191	Billy Hitchcock	15.00	7.50	4.50
192	Hank Wyse	15.00	7.50	4.50
193	Ted Wilks	15.00	7.50	4.50
194	Harry "Peanuts" Lowrey	15.00	7.50	4.50
195	Paul Richards	25.00	12.50	7.50
196	*Bill Pierce*	20.00	10.00	6.00
197	Bob Cain	15.00	7.50	4.50
198	*Monte Irvin*	100.00	50.00	30.00
199	Sheldon Jones	15.00	7.50	4.50
200	Jack Kramer	15.00	7.50	4.50
201	Steve O'Neill	15.00	7.50	4.50
202	Mike Guerra	15.00	7.50	4.50
203	*Vernon Law*	22.00	11.00	6.50
204	Vic Lombardi	15.00	7.50	4.50
205	Mickey Grasso	15.00	7.50	4.50
206	Connie Marrero	15.00	7.50	4.50
207	Billy Southworth	15.00	7.50	4.50
208	"Blix" Donnelly	15.00	7.50	4.50

		NR MT	EX	VG
209	Ken Wood	15.00	7.50	4.50
210	Les Moss	15.00	7.50	4.50
211	Hal Jeffcoat	15.00	7.50	4.50
212	Bob Rush	15.00	7.50	4.50
213	Neil Berry	15.00	7.50	4.50
214	Bob Swift	15.00	7.50	4.50
215	Kent Peterson	15.00	7.50	4.50
216	Connie Ryan	15.00	7.50	4.50
217	Joe Page	20.00	10.00	6.00
218	Ed Lopat	20.00	10.00	6.00
219	*Gene Woodling*	40.00	20.00	12.00
220	Bob Miller	15.00	7.50	4.50
221	Dick Whitman	15.00	7.50	4.50
222	Thurman Tucker	15.00	7.50	4.50
223	Johnny Vander Meer	15.00	7.50	4.50
224	Billy Cox	18.00	9.00	5.50
225	*Dan Bankhead*	20.00	10.00	6.00
226	Jimmy Dykes	18.00	9.00	4.50
227	Bobby Shantz	18.00	9.00	4.50
228	*Cloyd Boyer*	15.00	7.50	4.50
229	Bill Howerton	15.00	7.50	4.50
230	Max Lanier	15.00	7.50	4.50
231	Luis Aloma	15.00	7.50	4.50
232	*Nellie Fox*	125.00	67.00	37.00
233	Leo Durocher	40.00	20.00	12.00
234	Clint Hartung	15.00	7.50	4.50
235	Jack Lohrke	15.00	7.50	4.50
236	"Buddy" Rosar	15.00	7.50	4.50
237	Billy Goodman	15.00	7.50	4.50
238	Pete Reiser	18.00	9.00	5.50
239	Bill MacDonald	15.00	7.50	4.50
240	Joe Haynes	15.00	7.50	4.50
241	Irv Noren	15.00	7.50	4.50
242	Sam Jethroe	15.00	7.50	5.50
243	Johnny Antonelli	15.00	7.50	4.50
244	Cliff Fannin	15.00	7.50	4.50
245	John Berardino	22.00	11.00	6.50
246	Bill Serena	15.00	7.50	4.50
247	Bob Ramazotti	15.00	7.50	4.50
248	*Johnny Klippstein*	15.00	7.50	4.50
249	Johnny Groth	15.00	7.50	4.50
250	Hank Borowy	15.00	7.50	4.50
251	Willard Ramsdell	15.00	7.50	4.50
252	"Dixie" Howell	15.00	7.50	4.50
253	*Mickey Mantle*	9000.00	4000.00	2400.
254	*Jackie Jensen*	100.00	50.00	30.00
255	Milo Candini	60.00	30.00	18.00
256	Ken Silvestri	60.00	30.00	18.00
257	Birdie Tebbetts	60.00	30.00	18.00
258	*Luke Easter*	60.00	30.00	18.00
259	Charlie Dressen	70.00	35.00	21.00
260	*Carl Erskine*	90.00	45.00	27.00
261	Wally Moses	60.00	30.00	18.00
262	Gus Zernial	60.00	30.00	18.00
263	Howie Pollet	60.00	30.00	18.00
264	Don Richmond	60.00	30.00	18.00
265	*Steve Bilko*	60.00	30.00	18.00
266	Harry Dorish	60.00	30.00	18.00
267	Ken Holcombe	60.00	30.00	18.00
268	Don Mueller	60.00	30.00	18.00
269	Ray Noble	60.00	30.00	18.00
270	Willard Nixon	60.00	30.00	18.00
271	Tommy Wright	60.00	30.00	18.00
272	Billy Meyer	60.00	30.00	18.00
273	Danny Murtaugh	60.00	30.00	18.00
274	George Metkovich	60.00	30.00	18.00
275	Bucky Harris	90.00	45.00	27.00
276	Frank Quinn	60.00	30.00	18.00
277	Roy Hartsfield	60.00	30.00	18.00
278	Norman Roy	60.00	30.00	18.00
279	Jim Delsing	60.00	30.00	18.00
280	Frank Overmire	60.00	30.00	18.00
281	Al Widmar	60.00	30.00	18.00
282	Frank Frisch	90.00	45.00	27.00
283	Walt Dubiel	60.00	30.00	18.00
284	Gene Bearden	60.00	30.00	18.00
285	Johnny Lipon	60.00	30.00	18.00
286	Bob Usher	60.00	30.00	18.00
287	Jim Blackburn	60.00	30.00	18.00
288	Bobby Adams	60.00	30.00	18.00
289	Cliff Mapes	70.00	35.00	21.00
290	Bill Dickey(FC)	175.00	70.00	44.00
291	Tommy Henrich	70.00	35.00	20.00
292	Eddie Pellagrini	60.00	30.00	18.00
293	Ken Johnson	60.00	30.00	18.00
294	Jocko Thompson	60.00	30.00	18.00
295	Al Lopez	90.00	45.00	25.00
296	Bob Kennedy	60.00	30.00	18.00
297	Dave Philley	60.00	30.00	18.00
298	Joe Astroth	60.00	30.00	18.00
299	Clyde King	65.00	32.50	19.50

		NR MT	EX	VG
300	Hal Rice	60.00	30.00	18.00
301	Tommy Glaviano	60.00	30.00	18.00
302	Jim Busby	60.00	30.00	18.00
303	Marv Rotblatt	60.00	30.00	18.00
304	Allen Gettel	60.00	30.00	18.00
305	*Willie Mays*	3500.00	1500.00	750.00
306	*Jim Piersall*	100.00	50.00	30.00
307	Walt Masterson	60.00	30.00	18.00
308	Ted Beard	60.00	30.00	18.00
309	Mel Queen	60.00	30.00	18.00
310	Erv Dusak	60.00	30.00	18.00
311	Mickey Harris	60.00	30.00	18.00
312	*Gene Mauch*	65.00	32.50	19.50
313	Ray Mueller	60.00	30.00	18.00
314	Johnny Sain	65.00	32.50	19.50
315	Zack Taylor	60.00	30.00	18.00
316	Duane Pillette	60.00	30.00	18.00
317	*Smoky Burgess*	70.00	35.00	20.00
318	Warren Hacker	60.00	30.00	18.00
319	Red Rolfe	60.00	30.00	18.00
320	Hal White	60.00	30.00	18.00
321	Earl Johnson	60.00	30.00	18.00
322	Luke Sewell	60.00	30.00	18.00
323	*Joe Adcock*	100.00	50.00	30.00
324	Johnny Pramesa	110.00	30.00	18.00

1952 Bowman

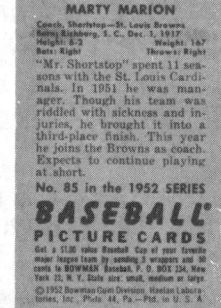

Bowman reverted back to a 252-card set in 1952, but retained the card size (2-1/16" by 3-1/8") employed the preceding year. The cards, which are color art reproductions of actual photographs, feature a facsimile autograph on the fronts.

	NR MT	EX	VG
Complete Set (252):	9500.00	4500.00	2700.
Common Player: 1-36	19.25	9.50	5.50
Common Player: 37-216	18.00	9.00	5.50
Common Player: 217-252	32.00	16.00	9.50

		NR MT	EX	VG
1	Yogi Berra	600.00	250.00	150.00
2	Bobby Thomson	27.00	13.50	8.00
3	Fred Hutchinson	19.25	9.50	5.50
4	Robin Roberts	60.00	30.00	18.00
5	*Minnie Minoso*	80.00	40.00	24.00
6	Virgil "Red" Stallcup	19.25	9.50	5.50
7	Mike Garcia	19.25	9.50	5.50
8	Pee Wee Reese	100.00	50.00	30.00
9	Vern Stephens	19.25	9.50	5.50
10	Bob Hooper	19.25	9.50	5.50
11	Ralph Kiner	60.00	30.00	18.00
12	Max Surkont	19.25	9.50	5.50
13	Cliff Mapes	19.25	9.50	5.50
14	Cliff Chambers	19.25	9.50	5.50
15	Sam Mele	19.25	9.50	5.50
16	Omar Lown	19.25	9.50	5.50
17	Ed Lopat	24.00	12.00	7.20
18	Don Mueller	19.25	9.50	5.50
19	Bob Cain	19.25	9.50	5.50
20	Willie Jones	19.25	9.50	5.50
21	Nellie Fox	30.00	15.00	9.00
22	Willard Ramsdell	19.25	9.50	5.50
23	Bob Lemon	45.00	22.50	13.50
24	Carl Furillo	30.00	15.00	9.00
25	Maurice McDermott	19.25	9.50	5.50
26	Eddie Joost	19.25	9.50	5.50
27	Joe Garagiola	70.00	35.00	23.00
28	Roy Hartsfield	19.25	9.50	5.50
29	Ned Garver	19.25	9.50	5.50
30	Red Schoendienst	60.00	30.00	18.00
31	Eddie Yost	19.25	9.50	5.50
32	Eddie Miksis	19.25	9.50	5.50
33	*Gil McDougald*	70.00	35.00	20.00
34	Al Dark	21.00	11.50	7.00
35	Granny Hamner	19.25	9.50	5.50
36	Cass Michaels	19.25	9.50	5.50
37	Vic Raschi	24.00	12.00	7.20
38	Whitey Lockman	18.00	9.00	5.50
39	Vic Wertz	18.00	9.00	5.50
40	"Bubba" Church	18.00	9.00	5.50
41	"Chico" Carrasquel	18.00	9.00	5.50
42	Johnny Wyrostek	18.00	9.00	5.50
43	Bob Feller	125.00	67.00	37.00
44	Roy Campanella	220.00	110.00	66.00
45	Johnny Pesky	18.00	9.00	5.50
46	Carl Scheib	18.00	9.00	5.50
47	Pete Castiglione	18.00	9.00	5.50
48	Vernon Bickford	18.00	9.00	5.50
49	Jim Hearn	18.00	9.00	5.50
50	Gerry Staley	18.00	9.00	5.50
51	Gil Coan	18.00	9.00	5.50
52	Phil Rizzuto	80.00	40.00	25.00
53	Richie Ashburn	50.00	25.00	15.00
54	Billy Pierce	20.00	10.00	6.00
55	Ken Raffensberger	18.00	9.00	5.50
56	Clyde King	22.00	11.00	6.50
57	Clyde Vollmer	18.00	9.00	5.50
58	Hank Majeski	18.00	9.00	5.50
59	Murry Dickson	18.00	9.00	5.50
60	Sid Gordon	20.00	10.00	6.00
61	Tommy Byrne	18.00	9.00	5.50
62	Joe Presko	18.00	9.00	5.50
63	Irv Noren	18.00	9.00	5.50
64	Roy Smalley	18.00	9.00	5.50
65	Hank Bauer	25.00	12.50	7.50
66	Sal Maglie	22.00	11.00	6.50
67	Johnny Groth	18.00	9.00	5.50
68	Jim Busby	18.00	9.00	5.50
69	Joe Adcock	20.00	10.00	6.00
70	Carl Erskine	24.00	12.00	7.20
71	Vernon Law	18.00	9.00	5.50
72	Earl Torgeson	18.00	9.00	5.50
73	Jerry Coleman	24.00	12.00	7.20
74	Wes Westrum	18.00	9.00	5.50
75	George Kell	50.00	25.00	15.00
76	Del Ennis	18.00	9.00	5.50
77	Eddie Robinson	18.00	9.00	5.50
78	Lloyd Merriman	18.00	9.00	5.50
79	Lou Brissie	18.00	9.00	5.50
80	Gil Hodges	80.00	40.00	25.00
81	Billy Goodman	18.00	9.00	5.50
82	Gus Zernial	18.00	9.00	5.50
83	Howie Pollet	18.00	9.00	5.50
84	Sam Jethroe	18.00	9.00	5.50
85	Marty Marion	20.00	10.00	6.00
86	Cal Abrams	22.00	11.00	6.50
87	Mickey Vernon	18.00	9.00	5.50
88	Bruce Edwards	18.00	9.00	5.50
89	Billy Hitchcock	18.00	9.00	5.50
90	Larry Jansen	18.00	9.00	5.50
91	Don Kolloway	18.00	9.00	5.50
92	Eddie Waitkus	18.00	9.00	5.50
93	Paul Richards	18.00	9.00	5.50
94	Luke Sewell	18.00	9.00	5.50
95	Luke Easter	18.00	9.00	5.50
96	Ralph Branca	24.00	12.00	7.20
97	Willard Marshall	18.00	9.00	5.50
98	Jimmy Dykes	18.00	9.00	5.50
99	Clyde McCullough	18.00	9.00	5.50
100	Sibby Sisti	18.00	9.00	5.50
101	Mickey Mantle	2750.00	1250.00	750.00
102	Peanuts Lowrey	18.00	9.00	5.50
103	Joe Haynes	18.00	9.00	5.50
104	Hal Jeffcoat	18.00	9.00	5.50
105	Bobby Brown	27.00	13.50	8.00
106	Randy Gumpert	18.00	9.00	5.50
107	Del Rice	18.00	9.00	5.50
108	George Metkovich	18.00	9.00	5.50
109	Tom Morgan	24.00	12.00	7.20
110	Max Lanier	18.00	9.00	5.50
111	"Hoot" Evers	18.00	9.00	5.50
112	"Smoky" Burgess	18.00	9.00	5.50
113	Al Zarilla	18.00	9.00	5.50
114	Frank Hiller	18.00	9.00	5.50
115	Larry Doby	25.00	12.50	7.50
116	Duke Snider	200.00	100.00	60.00
117	Bill Wight	18.00	9.00	5.50
118	Ray Murray	18.00	9.00	5.50
119	Bill Howerton	18.00	9.00	5.50

		NR MT	EX	VG
120	Chet Nichols	18.00	9.00	5.50
121	Al Corwin	18.00	9.00	5.50
122	Billy Johnson	18.00	9.00	5.50
123	Sid Hudson	18.00	9.00	5.50
124	Birdie Tebbetts	18.00	9.00	5.50
125	Howie Fox	18.00	9.00	5.50
126	Phil Cavarretta	18.00	9.00	5.50
127	Dick Sisler	18.00	9.00	5.50
128	Don Newcombe	25.00	12.50	7.50
129	Gus Niarhos	18.00	9.00	5.50
130	Allie Clark	18.00	9.00	5.50
131	Bob Swift	18.00	9.00	5.50
132	Dave Cole	18.00	9.00	5.50
133	Dick Kryhoski	18.00	9.00	5.50
134	Al Brazle	18.00	9.00	5.50
135	Mickey Harris	18.00	9.00	5.50
136	Gene Hermanski	18.00	9.00	5.50
137	Stan Rojek	18.00	9.00	5.50
138	Ted Wilks	18.00	9.00	5.50
139	Jerry Priddy	18.00	9.00	5.50
140	Ray Scarborough	18.00	9.00	5.50
141	Hank Edwards	18.00	9.00	5.50
142	Early Wynn	40.00	20.00	12.00
143	Sandy Consuegra	18.00	9.00	5.50
144	Joe Hatten	18.00	9.00	5.50
145	Johnny Mize	50.00	30.00	15.00
146	Leo Durocher	40.00	20.00	12.00
147	Marlin Stuart	18.00	9.00	5.50
148	Ken Heintzelman	18.00	9.00	5.50
149	Howie Judson	18.00	9.00	5.50
150	Herman Wehmeier	18.00	9.00	5.50
151	Al Rosen	20.00	10.00	6.00
152	Billy Cox	22.00	11.00	6.50
153	Fred Hatfield	18.00	9.00	5.50
154	Ferris Fain	18.00	9.00	5.50
155	Billy Meyer	18.00	9.00	5.50
156	Warren Spahn	125.00	62.50	37.50
157	Jim Delsing	18.00	9.00	5.50
158	Bucky Harris	45.00	22.50	13.50
159	Dutch Leonard	18.00	9.00	5.50
160	Eddie Stanky	20.00	10.00	6.00
161	Jackie Jensen	25.00	12.50	7.50
162	Monte Irvin	50.00	25.00	15.00
163	Johnny Lipon	18.00	9.00	5.50
164	Connie Ryan	18.00	9.00	5.50
165	Saul Rogovin	18.00	9.00	5.50
166	Bobby Adams	18.00	9.00	5.50
167	Bob Avila	20.00	10.00	6.00
168	Preacher Roe	25.00	12.50	7.50
169	Walt Dropo	18.00	9.00	5.50
170	Joe Astroth	18.00	9.00	5.50
171	Mel Queen	18.00	9.00	5.50
172	Ebba St. Claire	18.00	9.00	5.50
173	Gene Bearden	18.00	9.00	5.50
174	Mickey Grasso	18.00	9.00	5.50
175	Ransom Jackson	18.00	9.00	5.50
176	Harry Brecheen	18.00	9.00	5.50
177	Gene Woodling	20.00	10.00	6.00
178	Dave Williams	18.00	9.00	5.50
179	Pete Suder	18.00	9.00	5.50
180	Eddie Fitz Gerald	18.00	9.00	5.50
181	Joe Collins	24.00	12.00	7.20
182	Dave Koslo	18.00	9.00	5.50
183	Pat Mullin	18.00	9.00	5.50
184	Curt Simmons	18.00	9.00	5.50
185	Eddie Stewart	18.00	9.00	5.50
186	Frank Smith	18.00	9.00	5.50
187	Jim Hegan	18.00	9.00	5.50
188	Charlie Dressen	24.00	12.00	7.20
189	Jim Piersall	20.00	10.00	6.00
190	Dick Fowler	18.00	9.00	5.50
191	*Bob Friend*	20.00	10.00	6.00
192	John Cusick	18.00	9.00	5.50
193	Bobby Young	18.00	9.00	5.50
194	Bob Porterfield	18.00	9.00	5.50
195	Frank Baumholtz	18.00	9.00	5.50
196	Stan Musial	500.00	250.00	150.00
197	*Charlie Silvera*	24.00	12.00	7.20
198	Chuck Diering	18.00	9.00	5.50
199	Ted Gray	18.00	9.00	5.50
200	Ken Silvestri	18.00	9.00	5.50
201	Ray Coleman	18.00	9.00	5.50
202	Harry Perkowski	18.00	9.00	5.50
203	Steve Gromek	18.00	9.00	5.50
204	Andy Pafko	22.00	11.00	6.50
205	Walt Masterson	18.00	9.00	5.50
206	Elmer Valo	18.00	9.00	5.50
207	George Strickland	18.00	9.00	5.50
208	Walker Cooper	18.00	9.00	5.50
209	Dick Littlefield	18.00	9.00	5.50
210	Archie Wilson	18.00	9.00	5.50

		NR MT	EX	VG
211	Paul Minner	18.00	9.00	5.50
212	Solly Hemus	18.00	9.00	5.50
213	Monte Kennedy	18.00	9.00	5.50
214	Ray Boone	18.00	9.00	5.50
215	Sheldon Jones	18.00	9.00	5.50
216	Matt Batts	18.00	9.00	5.50
217	Casey Stengel	150.00	75.00	45.00
218	Willie Mays	1500.00	750.00	425.00
219	Neil Berry	32.00	16.00	9.50
220	Russ Meyer	32.00	16.00	9.50
221	Lou Kretlow	32.00	16.00	9.50
222	"Dixie" Howell	32.00	16.00	9.50
223	*Harry Simpson*	35.00	17.50	10.50
224	Johnny Schmitz	36.00	18.00	10.75
225	Del Wilber	32.00	16.00	9.50
226	Alex Kellner	32.00	16.00	9.50
227	Clyde Sukeforth	32.00	16.00	9.50
228	Bob Chipman	32.00	16.00	9.50
229	Hank Arft	32.00	16.00	9.50
230	Frank Shea	32.00	16.00	9.50
231	*Dee Fondy*	32.00	16.00	9.50
232	Enos Slaughter	90.00	45.00	25.00
233	Bob Kuzava	40.00	20.00	12.00
234	Fred Fitzsimmons	32.00	16.00	9.50
235	Steve Souchock	32.00	16.00	9.50
236	Tommy Brown	32.00	16.00	9.50
237	Sherman Lollar	32.00	16.00	9.50
238	*Roy McMillan*	32.00	16.00	9.50
239	Dale Mitchell	32.00	16.00	9.50
240	*Billy Loes*	36.00	18.00	10.75
241	Mel Parnell	32.00	16.00	9.50
242	Everett Kell	32.00	16.00	9.50
243	"Red" Munger	32.00	16.00	9.50
244	*Lew Burdette*	70.00	35.00	21.00
245	George Schmees	32.00	16.00	9.50
246	Jerry Snyder	32.00	16.00	9.50
247	John Pramesa	32.00	16.00	9.50
248	Bill Werle	32.00	16.00	9.50
249	Henry Thompson	32.00	16.00	9.50
250	Ike Delock	32.00	16.00	9.50
251	Jack Lohrke	32.00	12.50	7.50
252	Frank Crosetti	150.00	50.00	20.00

1953 Bowman Color

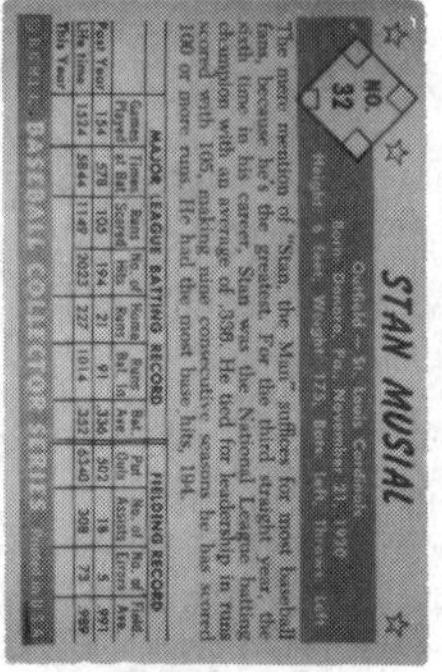

The first set of current major league players featuring actual color photographs, the 160-card 1953 Bowman Color set remains one of the most popular issues of the post-war era. The set is greatly appreciated for its uncluttered look; card fronts that contain no names, teams or facsimile autographs. Bowman increased the size of their cards to a 2-1/2" by 3-3/4" in order to better compete with Topps larger format. Bowman copied an idea from the 1952 Topps set and developed card backs that gave player career and previous-year statistics. The high-numbered cards (#s 113-160) are the scarcest of the set, with #s 113-128 being exceptionally difficult to find.

	NR MT	EX	VG
Complete Set (160):	12000.00	5500.00	3250.
Common Player: 1-112	30.00	15.00	9.00
Common Player: 113-128	50.00	25.00	15.00
Common Player: 129-160	40.00	20.00	12.00

		NR MT	EX	VG
1	Davey Williams	100.00	15.00	9.00

		NR MT	EX	VG
2	Vic Wertz	30.00	15.00	9.00
3	Sam Jethroe	30.00	15.00	9.00
4	Art Houtteman	30.00	15.00	9.00
5	Sid Gordon	32.00	16.00	9.50
6	Joe Ginsberg	30.00	15.00	9.00
7	Harry Chiti	30.00	15.00	9.00
8	Al Rosen	32.00	16.00	9.50
9	Phil Rizzuto	110.00	55.00	33.00
10	Richie Ashburn	85.00	42.00	26.00
11	Bobby Shantz	32.00	16.00	9.50
12	Carl Erskine	35.00	17.50	10.50
13	Gus Zernial	30.00	15.00	9.00
14	Billy Loes	35.00	17.50	10.50
15	Jim Busby	30.00	15.00	9.00
16	Bob Friend	30.00	15.00	9.00
17	Gerry Staley	30.00	15.00	9.00
18	Nellie Fox	75.00	38.00	23.00
19	Al Dark	32.00	16.00	9.50
20	Don Lenhardt	30.00	15.00	9.00
21	Joe Garagiola	80.00	40.00	25.00
22	Bob Porterfield	30.00	15.00	9.00
23	Herman Wehmeier	30.00	15.00	9.00
24	Jackie Jensen	40.00	20.00	12.00
25	"Hoot" Evers	30.00	15.00	9.00
26	Roy McMillan	30.00	15.00	9.00
27	Vic Raschi	40.00	20.00	12.00
28	"Smoky" Burgess	30.00	15.00	9.00
29	Roberto Avila	32.00	16.00	9.50
30	Phil Cavarretta	30.00	15.00	9.00
31	Jimmy Dykes	30.00	15.00	9.00
32	Stan Musial	550.00	275.00	165.00
33	Pee Wee Reese	500.00	250.00	150.00
34	Gil Coan	30.00	15.00	9.00
35	Maury McDermott	30.00	15.00	9.00
36	Minnie Minoso	40.00	20.00	12.00
37	Jim Wilson	30.00	15.00	9.00
38	Harry Byrd	30.00	15.00	9.00
39	Paul Richards	30.00	15.00	9.00
40	Larry Doby	40.00	20.00	12.00
41	Sammy White	30.00	15.00	9.00
42	Tommy Brown	30.00	15.00	9.00
43	Mike Garcia	30.00	15.00	9.00
44	Hank Bauer, Yogi Berra, Mickey Mantle	400.00	200.00	125.00
45	Walt Dropo	30.00	15.00	9.00
46	Roy Campanella	250.00	125.00	75.00
47	Ned Garver	30.00	15.00	9.00
48	Hank Sauer	30.00	15.00	9.00
49	Eddie Stanky	30.00	15.00	9.00
50	Lou Kretlow	30.00	15.00	9.00
51	Monte Irvin	60.00	30.00	18.00
52	Marty Marion	35.00	17.50	10.50
53	Del Rice	30.00	15.00	9.00
54	"Chico" Carrasquel	30.00	15.00	9.00
55	Leo Durocher	45.00	22.50	13.50
56	Bob Cain	30.00	15.00	9.00
57	Lou Boudreau	60.00	30.00	18.00
58	Willard Marshall	30.00	15.00	9.00
59	Mickey Mantle	2600.00	1300.00	750.00
60	Granny Hamner	30.00	15.00	9.00
61	George Kell	60.00	30.00	18.00
62	Ted Kluszewski	45.00	22.50	13.50
63	Gil McDougald	45.00	22.50	13.50
64	Curt Simmons	30.00	15.00	9.00
65	Robin Roberts	70.00	35.00	21.00
66	Mel Parnell	30.00	15.00	9.00
67	Mel Clark	30.00	15.00	9.00
68	Allie Reynolds	45.00	22.50	13.50
69	Charlie Grimm	30.00	15.00	9.00
70	Clint Courtney	30.00	15.00	9.00
71	Paul Minner	30.00	15.00	9.00
72	Ted Gray	30.00	15.00	9.00
73	Billy Pierce	32.00	16.00	9.50
74	Don Mueller	30.00	15.00	9.00
75	Saul Rogovin	30.00	15.00	9.00
76	Jim Hearn	30.00	15.00	9.00
77	Mickey Grasso	30.00	15.00	9.00
78	Carl Furillo	45.00	22.50	13.50
79	Ray Boone	30.00	15.00	9.00
80	Ralph Kiner	80.00	40.00	25.00
81	Enos Slaughter	70.00	35.00	21.00
82	Joe Astroth	30.00	15.00	9.00
83	Jack Daniels	30.00	15.00	9.00
84	Hank Bauer	45.00	22.50	13.50
85	Solly Hemus	30.00	15.00	9.00
86	Harry Simpson	30.00	15.00	9.00
87	Harry Perkowski	30.00	15.00	9.00
88	Joe Dobson	30.00	15.00	9.00
89	Sandalio Consuegra	30.00	15.00	9.00
90	Joe Nuxhall	30.00	15.00	9.00
91	Steve Souchock	30.00	15.00	9.00

		NR MT	EX	VG
92	Gil Hodges	110.00	55.00	33.00
93	Billy Martin, Phil Rizzuto	200.00	100.00	60.00
94	Bob Addis	30.00	15.00	9.00
95	Wally Moses	30.00	15.00	9.00
96	Sal Maglie	32.00	16.00	9.50
97	Eddie Mathews(FC)	200.00	100.00	60.00
98	Hector Rodriquez	30.00	15.00	9.00
99	Warren Spahn	200.00	100.00	60.00
100	Bill Wight	30.00	15.00	9.00
101	Red Schoendienst	80.00	40.00	25.00
102	Jim Hegan	30.00	15.00	9.00
103	Del Ennis	30.00	15.00	9.00
104	Luke Easter	30.00	15.00	9.00
105	Eddie Joost	30.00	15.00	9.00
106	Ken Raffensberger	30.00	15.00	9.00
107	Alex Kellner	30.00	15.00	9.00
108	Bobby Adams	30.00	15.00	9.00
109	Ken Wood	30.00	15.00	9.00
110	Bob Rush	30.00	15.00	9.00
111	Jim Dyck	30.00	15.00	9.00
112	Toby Atwell	30.00	15.00	9.00
113	Karl Drews	50.00	25.00	15.00
114	Bob Feller	300.00	150.00	90.00
115	Cloyd Boyer	50.00	25.00	15.00
116	Eddie Yost	50.00	25.00	15.00
117	Duke Snider	600.00	300.00	175.00
118	Billy Martin(FC)	300.00	150.00	90.00
119	Dale Mitchell	50.00	25.00	15.00
120	Marlin Stuart	50.00	25.00	15.00
121	Yogi Berra	500.00	250.00	150.00
122	Bill Serena	50.00	25.00	15.00
123	Johnny Lipon	50.00	25.00	15.00
124	Charlie Dressen	55.00	27.50	16.50
125	Fred Hatfield	50.00	25.00	15.00
126	Al Corwin	50.00	25.00	15.00
127	Dick Kryhoski	50.00	25.00	15.00
128	"Whitey" Lockman	50.00	25.00	15.00
129	Russ Meyer	45.00	22.50	13.50
130	Cass Michaels	40.00	20.00	12.00
131	Connie Ryan	40.00	20.00	12.00
132	Fred Hutchinson	40.00	20.00	12.00
133	Willie Jones	40.00	20.00	12.00
134	Johnny Pesky	40.00	20.00	12.00
135	Bobby Morgan	45.00	22.50	13.50
136	Jim Brideweser	50.00	25.00	15.00
137	Sam Dente	40.00	20.00	12.00
138	"Bubba" Church	40.00	20.00	12.00
139	Pete Runnels	40.00	20.00	12.00
140	Alpha Brazle	40.00	20.00	12.00
141	Frank "Spec" Shea	40.00	20.00	12.00
142	Larry Miggins	40.00	20.00	12.00
143	Al Lopez(FC)	60.00	30.00	18.00
144	Warren Hacker	40.00	20.00	12.00
145	George Shuba	45.00	22.50	13.50
146	Early Wynn	125.00	62.00	40.00
147	Clem Koshorek	40.00	20.00	12.00
148	Billy Goodman	40.00	20.00	12.00
149	Al Corwin	40.00	20.00	12.00
150	Carl Scheib	40.00	20.00	12.00
151	Joe Adcock	42.50	21.25	12.75
152	Clyde Vollmer	40.00	20.00	12.00
153	Whitey Ford	450.00	225.00	135.00
154	Omar "Turk" Lown	40.00	20.00	12.00
155	Allie Clark	40.00	20.00	12.00
156	Max Surkont	40.00	20.00	12.00
157	Sherman Lollar	40.00	20.00	12.00
158	Howard Fox	40.00	20.00	12.00
159	Mickey Vernon (Photo actually Floyd Baker)	40.00	17.50	10.50
160	Cal Abrams	90.00	20.00	12.00

1953 Bowman Black & White

The 1953 Bowman Black and White set is similar in all respects to the 1953 Bowman Color set, except that it lacks color. Purportedly, high costs in producing the color series forced Bowman to issue the set in black and white. Sixty-four cards, which measure 2-1/2" by 3-3/4", comprise the set.

	NR MT	EX	VG
Complete Set (64):	2500.00	1200.00	700.00
Common Player:	35.00	17.50	10.50

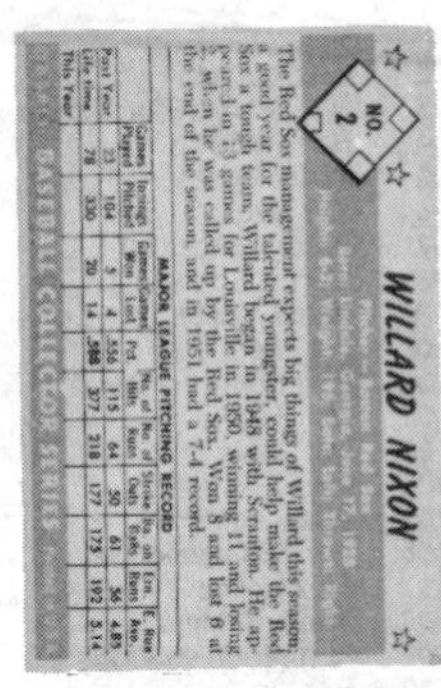

		NR MT	EX	VG
1	Gus Bell	125.00	17.50	10.50
2	Willard Nixon	35.00	17.50	10.50
3	Bill Rigney	35.00	17.50	10.50
4	Pat Mullin	35.00	17.50	10.50
5	Dee Fondy	35.00	17.50	10.50
6	Ray Murray	35.00	17.50	10.50
7	Andy Seminick	35.00	17.50	10.50
8	Pete Suder	35.00	17.50	10.50
9	Walt Masterson	35.00	17.50	10.50
10	Dick Sisler	35.00	17.50	10.50
11	Dick Gernert	35.00	17.50	10.50
12	Randy Jackson	35.00	17.50	10.50
13	Joe Tipton	35.00	17.50	10.50
14	Bill Nicholson	35.00	17.50	10.50
15	Johnny Mize	125.00	67.00	37.00
16	Stu Miller	35.00	17.50	10.50
17	Virgil Trucks	35.00	17.50	10.50
18	Billy Hoeft	35.00	17.50	10.50
19	Paul LaPalme	35.00	17.50	10.50
20	Eddie Robinson	35.00	17.50	10.50
21	Clarence "Bud" Podbielan	35.00	17.50	10.50
22	Matt Batts	35.00	17.50	10.50
23	Wilmer Mizell	37.50	18.75	11.25
24	Del Wilber	35.00	17.50	10.50
25	Johnny Sain	60.00	30.00	18.00
26	Preacher Roe	60.00	30.00	18.00
27	Bob Lemon	125.00	67.00	37.00
28	Hoyt Wilhelm(FC)	125.00	67.00	37.00
29	Sid Hudson	35.00	17.50	10.50
30	Walker Cooper	35.00	17.50	10.50
31	Gene Woodling	50.00	25.00	15.00
32	Rocky Bridges	35.00	17.50	10.50
33	Bob Kuzava	45.00	22.50	13.50
34	Ebba St. Clair (St. Claire)	35.00	17.50	10.50
35	Johnny Wyrostek	35.00	17.50	10.50
36	Jim Piersall	50.00	25.00	15.00
37	Hal Jeffcoat	35.00	17.50	10.50
38	Dave Cole	35.00	17.50	10.50
39	Casey Stengel	300.00	150.00	90.00
40	Larry Jansen	35.00	17.50	10.50
41	Bob Ramazotti	35.00	17.50	10.50
42	Howie Judson	35.00	17.50	10.50
43	Hal Bevan	35.00	17.50	10.50
44	Jim Delsing	35.00	17.50	10.50
45	Irv Noren	45.00	22.50	13.50
46	Bucky Harris	60.00	30.00	18.00
47	Jack Lohrke	35.00	17.50	10.50
48	Steve Ridzik	35.00	17.50	10.50
49	Floyd Baker	35.00	17.50	10.50
50	Emil "Dutch" Leonard	35.00	17.50	10.50
51	Lew Burdette	37.50	18.75	11.25
52	Ralph Branca	45.00	22.50	13.50
53	Morris Martin	35.00	17.50	10.50
54	Bill Miller	45.00	22.50	13.50
55	Don Johnson	35.00	17.50	10.50
56	Roy Smalley	35.00	17.50	10.50
57	Andy Pafko	35.00	17.50	10.50
58	Jim Konstanty	35.00	17.50	10.50
59	Duane Pillette	35.00	17.50	10.50
60	Billy Cox	40.00	20.00	12.00
61	Tom Gorman	45.00	22.50	13.50
62	Keith Thomas	35.00	17.50	10.50
63	Steve Gromek	35.00	17.50	10.50
64	Andy Hansen	50.00	17.50	10.50

Definitions for grading conditions are located in the Introduction of this price guide.

1954 Bowman

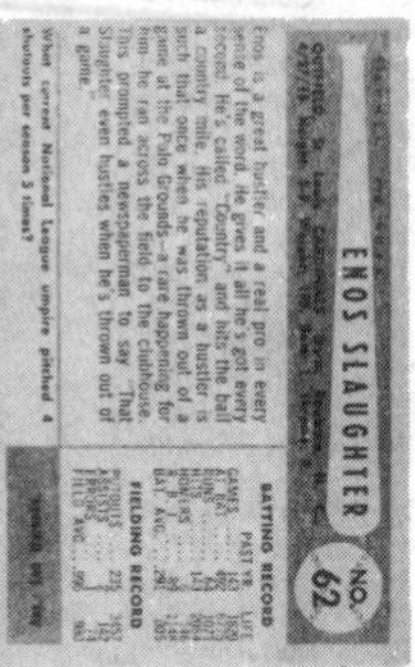

Bowman's 1954 set consists of 224 full-color cards that measure 2-1/2" by 3-3/4". It is believed that contractual problems caused the pulling of card #66 (Ted Williams) from the set, creating one of the most sought-after scarcities of the post-war era. The Williams card was replaced by Jim Piersall (who is also #210) in subsequent print runs. The set contains over 40 variations, most involving statistical errors on the card backs that were corrected. On most cards neither variation carries a premium value as both varieties appear to have been printed in equal amounts. The complete set price that follows does not include all variations or #66 Williams.

		NR MT	EX	VG
Complete Set (224):		4500.00	2250.00	1250.
Common Player: 1-112		9.00	4.50	2.75
Common Player:113-224		12.00	6.00	3.50
1	Phil Rizzuto	150.00	75.00	45.00
2	Jack Jensen	12.00	6.00	3.50
3	Marion Fricano	9.00	4.50	2.75
4	Bob Hooper	9.00	4.50	2.75
5	Billy Hunter	9.00	4.50	2.75
6	Nellie Fox	30.00	15.00	9.00
7	Walter Dropo	9.00	4.50	2.75
8	Jim Busby	9.00	4.50	2.75
9	Dave Williams	9.00	4.50	2.75
10	Carl Erskine	12.00	6.00	3.50
11	Sid Gordon	10.00	5.00	3.00
12a	Roy McMillan (551/1290 At Bat)	9.00	4.50	2.75
12b	Roy McMillan (557/1296 At Bat)	9.00	4.50	2.75
13	Paul Minner	9.00	4.50	2.75
14	Gerald Staley	9.00	4.50	2.75
15	Richie Ashburn	35.00	17.50	10.50
16	Jim Wilson	9.00	4.50	2.75
17	Tom Gorman	15.00	7.50	4.50
18	"Hoot" Evers	9.00	4.50	2.75
19	Bobby Shantz	10.00	5.00	3.00
20	Artie Houtteman	9.00	4.50	2.75
21	Vic Wertz	9.00	4.50	2.75
22a	Sam Mele (213/1661 Putouts)	9.00	4.50	2.75
22b	Sam Mele (217/1665 Putouts)	9.00	4.50	2.75
23	*Harvey Kuenn*	35.00	17.50	10.50
24	Bob Porterfield	9.00	4.50	2.75
25a	Wes Westrum (1.000/.987 Field Avg.)	9.00	4.50	2.75
25b	Wes Westrum (.982/.986 Field Avg.)	9.00	4.50	2.75
26a	Billy Cox (1.000/.960 Field Avg.)	12.00	6.00	3.50
26b	Billy Cox (.972/.960 Field Avg.)	12.00	6.00	3.50
27	Dick Cole	9.00	4.50	2.75
28a	Jim Greengrass (Birthplace Addison, N.J.)	9.00	4.50	2.75
28b	Jim Greengrass (Birthplace Addison, N.Y.)	9.00	4.50	2.75
29	Johnny Klippstein	9.00	4.50	2.75
30	Del Rice	9.00	4.50	2.75
31	"Smoky" Burgess	9.00	4.50	2.75
32	Del Crandall	9.00	4.50	2.75
33a	Vic Raschi (no trade line)	12.00	6.00	3.50
33b	Vic Raschi (traded line)	30.00	15.00	9.00
34	Sammy White	9.00	4.50	2.75
35a	Eddie Joost (quiz answer is 8)	9.00	4.50	2.75
35b	Eddie Joost (quiz answer is 33)	9.00	4.50	2.75
36	George Strickland	9.00	4.50	2.75

		NR MT	EX	VG
37	Dick Kokos	9.00	4.50	2.75
38a	Minnie Minoso (.895/.961 Field Avg.)	9.00	4.50	2.75
38b	Minnie Minoso (.963/.963 Field Avg.)	9.00	4.50	2.75
39	Ned Garver	9.00	4.50	2.75
40	Gil Coan	9.00	4.50	2.75
41a	Alvin Dark (.986/.960 Field Avg.)	10.00	5.00	3.00
41b	Alvin Dark (.968/.960 Field Avg.)	10.00	5.00	3.00
42	Billy Loes	12.00	6.00	3.50
43a	Bob Friend (20 shutouts in quiz question)	9.00	4.50	2.75
43b	Bob Friend (16 shutouts in quiz question)	9.00	4.50	2.75
44	Harry Perkowski	9.00	4.50	2.75
45	Ralph Kiner	40.00	20.00	12.00
46	"Rip" Repulski	9.00	4.50	2.75
47a	Granny Hamner (.970/.953 Field Avg.)	9.00	4.50	2.75
47b	Granny Hamner (.953/.951 Field Avg.)	9.00	4.50	2.75
48	Jack Dittmer	9.00	4.50	2.75
49	Harry Byrd	15.00	7.50	4.50
50	George Kell	30.00	15.00	9.00
51	Alex Kellner	9.00	4.50	2.75
52	Joe Ginsberg	9.00	4.50	2.75
53a	Don Lenhardt (.969/.984 Field Avg.)	9.00	4.50	2.75
53b	Don Lenhardt (.966/.983 Field Avg.)	9.00	4.50	2.75
54	"Chico" Carrasquel	9.00	4.50	2.75
55	Jim Delsing	9.00	4.50	2.75
56	Maurice McDermott	9.00	4.50	2.75
57	Hoyt Wilhelm	40.00	20.00	12.00
58	Pee Wee Reese	70.00	35.00	21.00
59	Bob Schultz	9.00	4.50	2.75
60	Fred Baczewski	9.00	4.50	2.75
61a	Eddie Miksis (.954/.962 Field Avg.)	9.00	4.50	2.75
61b	Eddie Miksis (.954/.961 Field Avg.)	9.00	4.50	2.75
62	Enos Slaughter	40.00	20.00	12.00
63	Earl Torgeson	9.00	4.50	2.75
64	Eddie Mathews	60.00	30.00	18.00
65	Mickey Mantle	900.00	450.00	275.00
66a	Ted Williams	4500.00	2000.00	1200.
66b	Jimmy Piersall	100.00	50.00	30.00
67a	Carl Scheib (.306 Pct. with two lines under bio)	9.00	4.50	2.75
67b	Carl Scheib (.306 Pct. with one line under bio)	9.00	4.50	2.75
67c	Carl Scheib (.300 Pct.)	9.00	4.50	2.75
68	Bob Avila	10.00	5.00	3.00
69	Clinton Courtney	9.00	4.50	2.75
70	Willard Marshall	9.00	4.50	2.75
71	Ted Gray	9.00	4.50	2.75
72	Ed Yost	9.00	4.50	2.75
73	Don Mueller	9.00	4.50	2.75
74	Jim Gilliam(FC)	18.00	9.00	6.50
75	Max Surkont	9.00	4.50	2.75
76	Joe Nuxhall	9.00	4.50	2.75
77	Bob Rush	9.00	4.50	2.75
78	Sal Yvars	9.00	4.50	2.75
79	Curt Simmons	9.00	4.50	2.75
80a	Johnny Logan (106 Runs)	9.00	4.50	2.75
80b	Johnny Logan (100 Runs)	9.00	4.50	2.75
81a	Jerry Coleman (1.000/.975 Field Avg.)	15.00	7.50	4.50
81b	Jerry Coleman (.952/.975 Field Avg.)	15.00	7.50	4.50
82a	Bill Goodman (.965/.986 Field Avg.)	9.00	4.50	2.75
82b	Bill Goodman (.972/.985 Field Avg.)	9.00	4.50	2.75
83	Ray Murray	9.00	4.50	2.75
84	Larry Doby	12.00	6.00	3.50
85a	Jim Dyck (.926/.956 Field Avg.)	9.00	4.50	2.75
85b	Jim Dyck (.947/.960 Field Avg.)	9.00	4.50	2.75
86	Harry Dorish	9.00	4.50	2.75
87	Don Lund	9.00	4.50	2.75
88	Tommy Umphlett	9.00	4.50	2.75
89	Willie Mays	400.00	200.00	125.00
90	Roy Campanella	175.00	87.50	52.00
91	Cal Abrams	9.00	4.50	2.75
92	Ken Raffensberger	9.00	4.50	2.75
93a	Bill Serena (.983/.966 Field Avg.)	9.00	4.50	2.75
93b	Bill Serena (.977/.966 Field Avg.)	9.00	4.50	2.75
94a	Solly Hemus (476/1343 Assists)	9.00	4.50	2.75
94b	Solly Hemus (477/1343 Assists)	9.00	4.50	2.75

		NR MT	EX	VG
95	Robin Roberts	40.00	20.00	12.00
96	Joe Adcock	10.00	5.00	3.00
97	Gil McDougald	15.00	7.50	4.50
98	Ellis Kinder	9.00	4.50	2.75
99a	Peter Suder (.985/.974 Field Avg.)	9.00	4.50	2.75
99b	Peter Suder (.978/.974 Field Avg.)	9.00	4.50	2.75
100	Mike Garcia	9.00	4.50	2.75
101	*Don Larsen*	40.00	20.00	12.00
102	Bill Pierce	10.00	5.00	3.00
103a	Stephen Souchock (144/1192 Putouts)	9.00	4.50	2.75
103b	Stephen Souchock (147/1195 Putouts)	9.00	4.50	2.75
104	Frank Spec Shea	9.00	4.50	2.75
105a	Sal Maglie (quiz answer is 8)	10.00	5.00	3.00
105b	Sal Maglie (quiz answer is 1904)	10.00	5.00	3.00
106	Clem Labine	12.00	6.00	3.50
107	Paul LaPalme	9.00	4.50	2.75
108	Bobby Adams	9.00	4.50	2.75
109	Roy Smalley	9.00	4.50	2.75
110	Red Schoendienst	40.00	20.00	12.00
111	Murry Dickson	9.00	4.50	2.75
112	Andy Pafko	9.00	4.50	2.75
113	Allie Reynolds	20.00	10.00	6.00
114	Willard Nixon	12.00	6.00	3.50
115	Don Bollweg	12.00	6.00	3.50
116	Luke Easter	12.00	6.00	3.50
117	Dick Kryhoski	12.00	6.00	3.50
118	Bob Boyd	12.00	6.00	3.50
119	Fred Hatfield	12.00	6.00	3.50
120	Mel Hoderlein	12.00	6.00	3.50
121	Ray Katt	12.00	6.00	3.50
122	Carl Furillo	20.00	10.00	6.00
123	Toby Atwell	12.00	6.00	3.50
124a	Gus Bell (15/27 Errors)	12.00	6.00	3.50
124b	Gus Bell (11/26 Errors)	12.00	6.00	3.50
125	Warren Hacker	12.00	6.00	3.50
126	Cliff Chambers	12.00	6.00	3.50
127	Del Ennis	12.00	6.00	3.50
128	Ebba St. Claire	12.00	6.00	3.50
129	Hank Bauer	20.00	10.00	6.00
130	Milt Bolling	12.00	6.00	3.50
131	Joe Astroth	12.00	6.00	3.50
132	Bob Feller	100.00	50.00	30.00
133	Duane Pillette	12.00	6.00	3.50
134	Luis Aloma	12.00	6.00	3.50
135	Johnny Pesky	12.00	6.00	3.50
136	Clyde Vollmer	12.00	6.00	3.50
137	Al Corwin	12.00	6.00	3.50
138a	Gil Hodges (.993/.991 Field Avg.)	70.00	50.00	25.00
138b	Gil Hodges (.992/.991 Field Avg.)	55.00	28.00	16.50
139a	Preston Ward (.961/.992 Field Avg.)	12.00	6.00	3.50
139b	Preston Ward (.990/.992 Field Avg.)	12.00	6.00	3.50
140a	Saul Rogovin (7-12 Won/Lost with 2 Strikeouts)	12.00	6.00	3.50
140b	Saul Rogovin (7-12 Won/Lost with 62 Strikeouts)	12.00	6.00	3.50
140c	Saul Rogovin (8-12 Won/Lost)	12.00	6.00	3.50
141	Joe Garagiola	40.00	20.00	12.00
142	Al Brazle	12.00	6.00	3.50
143	Willie Jones	12.00	6.00	3.50
144	Ernie Johnson	12.00	6.00	3.50
145a	Billy Martin (.985/.983 Field Avg.)	40.00	20.00	12.00
145b	Billy Martin (.983/.982 Field Avg.)	50.00	25.00	15.00
146	Dick Gernert	12.00	6.00	3.50
147	Joe DeMaestri	12.00	6.00	3.50
148	Dale Mitchell	12.00	6.00	3.50
149	Bob Young	12.00	6.00	3.50
150	Cass Michaels	12.00	6.00	3.50
151	Pat Mullin	12.00	6.00	3.50
152	Mickey Vernon	12.00	6.00	3.50
153a	"Whitey" Lockman (100/331 Assists)	12.00	6.00	3.50
153b	"Whitey" Lockman (102/333 Assists)	12.00	6.00	3.50
154	Don Newcombe	25.00	12.50	7.50
155	*Frank J. Thomas*	12.00	6.00	3.50
156a	Rocky Bridges (320/467 Assists)	12.00	6.00	3.50
156b	Rocky Bridges (328/475 Assists)	12.00	6.00	3.50
157	Omar Lown	12.00	6.00	3.50
158	Stu Miller	12.00	6.00	3.50

		NR MT	EX	VG
159	John Lindell	12.00	6.00	3.50
160	Danny O'Connell	12.00	6.00	3.50
161	Yogi Berra	175.00	87.00	52.00
162	Ted Lepcio	12.00	6.00	3.50
163a	Dave Philley (152 Games, no traded line)	12.00	6.00	3.50
163b	Dave Philley (152 Games, traded line)	25.00	12.50	7.50
163c	Dave Philley (157 Games, traded line)	12.00	6.00	3.50
164	Early Wynn	40.00	20.00	12.50
165	Johnny Groth	12.00	6.00	3.50
166	Sandy Consuegra	12.00	6.00	3.50
167	Bill Hoeft	12.00	6.00	3.50
168	Edward Fitz Gerald	12.00	6.00	3.50
169	Larry Jansen	12.00	6.00	3.50
170	Duke Snider	175.00	87.00	52.00
171	Carlos Bernier	12.00	6.00	3.50
172	Andy Seminick	12.00	6.00	3.50
173	Dee Fondy	12.00	6.00	3.50
174a	Pete Castiglione (.966/.959 Field Avg.)	12.00	6.00	3.50
174b	Pete Castiglione (.970/.959 Field Avg.)	12.00	6.00	3.50
175	Mel Clark	12.00	6.00	3.50
176	Vernon Bickford	12.00	6.00	3.50
177	Whitey Ford	110.00	55.00	33.00
178	Del Wilber	12.00	6.00	3.50
179a	Morris Martin (44 ERA)	12.00	6.00	3.50
179b	Morris Martin (4.44 ERA)	12.00	6.00	3.50
180	Joe Tipton	12.00	6.00	3.50
181	Les Moss	12.00	6.00	3.50
182	Sherman Lollar	12.00	6.00	3.50
183	Matt Batts	12.00	6.00	3.50
184	Mickey Grasso	12.00	6.00	3.50
185a	*Daryl Spencer* (.941/.944 Field Avg.)	12.00	6.00	3.50
185b	*Daryl Spencer* (.933/.936 Field Avg.)	12.00	6.00	3.50
186	Russ Meyer	15.00	7.50	4.50
187	Vern Law	12.00	6.00	3.50
188	Frank Smith	12.00	6.00	3.50
189	Ransom Jackson	12.00	6.00	3.50
190	Joe Presko	12.00	6.00	3.50
191	Karl Drews	12.00	6.00	3.50
192	Lew Burdette	14.00	7.00	4.25
193	Eddie Robinson	18.00	9.00	5.50
194	Sid Hudson	12.00	6.00	3.50
195	Bob Cain	12.00	6.00	3.50
196	Bob Lemon	40.00	20.00	12.00
197	Lou Kretlow	12.00	6.00	3.50
198	Virgil Trucks	12.00	6.00	3.50
199	Steve Gromek	12.00	6.00	3.50
200	Connie Marrero	12.00	6.00	3.50
201	Bob Thomson	15.00	7.50	4.50
202	George Shuba	15.00	7.50	4.50
203	Vic Janowicz	15.00	7.50	4.50
204	Jack Collum	12.00	6.00	3.50
205	Hal Jeffcoat	12.00	6.00	3.50
206	Steve Bilko	12.00	6.00	3.50
207	Stan Lopata	12.00	6.00	3.50
208	Johnny Antonelli	12.00	6.00	3.50
209	Gene Woodling (photo reversed)	18.00	9.00	5.50
210	Jimmy Piersall	15.00	7.50	4.50
211	Jim Robertson	12.00	6.00	3.50
212a	Owen Friend (.964/.957 Field Avg.)	12.00	6.00	3.50
212b	Owen Friend (.967/.958 Field Avg.)	12.00	6.00	3.50
213	Dick Littlefield	12.00	6.00	3.50
214	Ferris Fain	12.00	6.00	3.50
215	Johnny Bucha	12.00	6.00	3.50
216a	Jerry Snyder (.988/.988 Field Avg.)	12.00	6.00	3.50
216b	Jerry Snyder (.968/.968 Field Avg.)	12.00	6.00	3.50
217a	Henry Thompson (.956/.951 Field Avg.)	12.00	6.00	3.50
217b	Henry Thompson (.958/.952 Field Avg.)	12.00	6.00	3.50
218	Preacher Roe	15.00	7.50	4.50
219	Hal Rice	12.00	6.00	3.50
220	Hobie Landrith	12.00	6.00	3.50
221	Frank Baumholtz	12.00	6.00	3.50
222	Memo Luna	12.00	6.00	3.50
223	Steve Ridzik	12.00	6.00	3.50
224	Billy Bruton	30.00	6.00	3.50

A card number in parentheses () indicates the set is unnumbered.

1955 Bowman

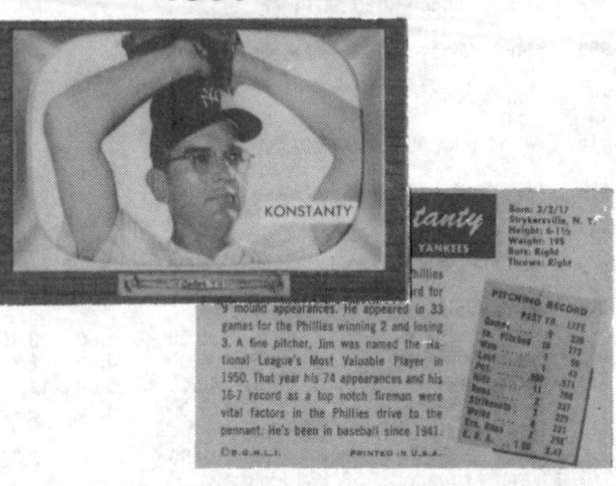

Bowman produced its final baseball card set in 1955, a popular issue which has player photographs placed inside a television set design. The set consists of 320 cards that measure 2-1/2" by 3-3/4" in size. High-numbered cards (#s 225-320) appear to have replaced certain low-numbered cards on the press sheets and are somewhat scarcer. The high series includes 31 umpire cards.

	NR MT	EX	VG
Complete Set (320):	5575.00	2750.00	1650.
Common Player: 1-224	9.00	4.50	2.75
Common Player: 225-320	20.00	10.00	6.00

		NR MT	EX	VG
1	Hoyt Wilhelm	100.00	20.00	12.00
2	Al Dark	10.00	5.00	3.00
3	Joe Coleman	9.00	4.50	2.75
4	Eddie Waitkus	9.00	4.50	2.75
5	Jim Robertson	9.00	4.50	2.75
6	Pete Suder	9.00	4.50	2.75
7	Gene Baker	9.00	4.50	2.75
8	Warren Hacker	9.00	4.50	2.75
9	Gil McDougald	15.00	7.50	4.50
10	Phil Rizzuto	30.00	15.00	9.00
11	Billy Bruton	9.00	4.50	2.75
12	Andy Pafko	9.00	4.50	2.75
13	Clyde Vollmer	9.00	4.50	2.75
14	Gus Keriazakos	9.00	4.50	2.75
15	*Frank Sullivan*	9.00	4.50	2.75
16	Jim Piersall	10.00	5.00	3.00
17	Del Ennis	9.00	4.50	2.75
18	Stan Lopata	9.00	4.50	2.75
19	Bobby Avila	10.00	5.00	3.00
20	Al Smith	9.00	4.50	2.75
21	Don Hoak(FC)	12.00	6.00	3.50
22	Roy Campanella	110.00	55.00	33.00
23	Al Kaline(FC)	125.00	62.50	37.50
24	Al Aber	9.00	4.50	2.75
25	Minnie Minoso	12.00	6.00	3.50
26	Virgil Trucks	9.00	4.50	2.75
27	Preston Ward	9.00	4.50	2.75
28	Dick Cole	9.00	4.50	2.75
29	Red Schoendienst	30.00	15.00	10.50
30	Bill Sarni	9.00	4.50	2.75
31	Johnny Temple	9.00	4.50	2.75
32	Wally Post	9.00	4.50	2.75
33	Nellie Fox	20.00	10.00	6.00
34	Clint Courtney	9.00	4.50	2.75
35	Bill Tuttle	9.00	4.50	2.75
36	Wayne Belardi	9.00	4.50	2.75
37	Pee Wee Reese	80.00	40.00	25.00
38	Early Wynn	30.00	15.00	9.00
39	Bob Darnell	12.00	6.00	3.50
40	Vic Wertz	9.00	4.50	2.75
41	Mel Clark	9.00	4.50	2.75
42	Bob Greenwood	9.00	4.50	2.75
43	Bob Buhl	9.00	4.50	2.75
44	Danny O'Connell	9.00	4.50	2.75
45	Tom Umphlett	9.00	4.50	2.75
46	Mickey Vernon	9.00	4.50	2.75
47	Sammy White	9.00	4.50	2.75
48a	Milt Bolling (Frank Bolling back)	10.00	5.00	3.00
48b	Milt Bolling (Milt Bolling back)	20.00	10.00	6.00
49	Jim Greengrass	9.00	4.50	2.75
50	Hobie Landrith	9.00	4.50	2.75
51	Elvin Tappe	9.00	4.50	2.75
52	Hal Rice	9.00	4.50	2.75
53	Alex Kellner	9.00	4.50	2.75

		NR MT	EX	VG
54	Don Bollweg	9.00	4.50	2.75
55	Cal Abrams	9.00	4.50	2.75
56	Billy Cox	10.00	5.00	3.00
57	Bob Friend	9.00	4.50	2.75
58	Frank J. Thomas	9.00	4.50	2.75
59	Whitey Ford	75.00	38.00	23.00
60	Enos Slaughter	30.00	15.00	9.00
61	Paul LaPalme	9.00	4.50	2.75
62	Royce Lint	9.00	4.50	2.75
63	Irv Noren	15.00	7.50	4.50
64	Curt Simmons	9.00	4.50	2.75
65	*Don Zimmer*	25.00	12.50	7.50
66	George Shuba	12.00	6.00	3.50
67	Don Larsen	18.00	9.00	5.50
68	*Elston Howard*	70.00	35.00	21.00
69	Bill Hunter	15.00	7.50	4.50
70	Lew Burdette	9.00	4.50	2.75
71	Dave Jolly	9.00	4.50	2.75
72	Chet Nichols	9.00	4.50	2.75
73	Eddie Yost	9.00	4.50	2.75
74	Jerry Snyder	9.00	4.50	2.75
75	Brooks Lawrence	9.00	4.50	2.75
76	Tom Poholsky	9.00	4.50	2.75
77	Jim McDonald	9.00	4.50	2.75
78	Gil Coan	9.00	4.50	2.75
79	Willie Miranda	9.00	4.50	2.75
80	Lou Limmer	9.00	4.50	2.75
81	Bob Morgan	9.00	4.50	2.75
82	Lee Walls	9.00	4.50	2.75
83	Max Surkont	9.00	4.50	2.75
84	George Freese	9.00	4.50	2.75
85	Cass Michaels	9.00	4.50	2.75
86	Ted Gray	9.00	4.50	2.75
87	Randy Jackson	9.00	4.50	2.75
88	Steve Bilko	9.00	4.50	2.75
89	Lou Boudreau	30.00	15.00	9.00
90	Art Ditmar	9.00	4.50	2.75
91	Dick Marlowe	9.00	4.50	2.75
92	George Zuverink	9.00	4.50	2.75
93	Andy Seminick	9.00	4.50	2.75
94	Hank Thompson	9.00	4.50	2.75
95	Sal Maglie	10.00	5.00	3.00
96	Ray Narleski	9.00	4.50	2.75
97	John Podres(FC)	15.00	7.50	4.50
98	Jim Gilliam	15.00	7.50	4.50
99	Jerry Coleman	15.00	7.50	4.50
100	Tom Morgan	15.00	7.50	4.50
101a	Don Johnson (Ernie Johnson (Braves) on front)	10.00	5.00	3.00
101b	Don Johnson (Don Johnson (Orioles) on front)	20.00	10.00	6.00
102	Bobby Thomson	10.00	5.00	3.00
103	Eddie Mathews	60.00	30.00	18.00
104	Bob Porterfield	9.00	4.50	2.75
105	Johnny Schmitz	9.00	4.50	2.75
106	Del Rice	9.00	4.50	2.75
107	Solly Hemus	9.00	4.50	2.75
108	Lou Kretlow	9.00	4.50	2.75
109	Vern Stephens	9.00	4.50	2.75
110	Bob Miller	9.00	4.50	2.75
111	Steve Ridzik	9.00	4.50	2.75
112	Granny Hamner	9.00	4.50	2.75
113	Bob Hall	9.00	4.50	2.75
114	Vic Janowicz	12.00	6.00	3.50
115	Roger Bowman	9.00	4.50	2.75
116	Sandy Consuegra	9.00	4.50	2.75
117	Johnny Groth	9.00	4.50	2.75
118	Bobby Adams	9.00	4.50	2.75
119	Joe Astroth	9.00	4.50	2.75
120	Ed Burtschy	9.00	4.50	2.75
121	Rufus Crawford	9.00	4.50	2.75
122	Al Corwin	9.00	4.50	2.75
123	Marv Grissom	9.00	4.50	2.75
124	Johnny Antonelli	9.00	4.50	2.75
125	Paul Giel	9.00	4.50	2.75
126	Billy Goodman	9.00	4.50	2.75
127	Hank Majeski	9.00	4.50	2.75
128	Mike Garcia	9.00	4.50	2.75
129	Hal Naragon	9.00	4.50	2.75
130	Richie Ashburn	20.00	10.00	6.00
131	Willard Marshall	9.00	4.50	2.75
132a	Harvey Kueen (misspelled last name)	10.00	5.00	3.00
132b	Harvey Kuenn (corrected)	30.00	15.00	9.00
133	Charles King	9.00	4.50	2.75
134	Bob Feller	60.00	30.00	18.00
135	Lloyd Merriman	9.00	4.50	2.75
136	Rocky Bridges	9.00	4.50	2.75
137	Bob Talbot	9.00	4.50	2.75
138	Davey Williams	9.00	4.50	2.75
139	Billy & Bobby Shantz	15.00	7.50	4.50
140	Bobby Shantz	10.00	5.00	3.00

		NR MT	EX	VG
141	Wes Westrum	9.00	4.50	2.75
142	Rudy Regalado	9.00	4.50	2.75
143	Don Newcombe	15.00	7.50	4.50
144	Art Houtteman	9.00	4.50	2.75
145	Bob Nieman	9.00	4.50	2.75
146	Don Liddle	9.00	4.50	2.75
147	Sam Mele	9.00	4.50	2.75
148	Bob Chakales	9.00	4.50	2.75
149	Cloyd Boyer	9.00	4.50	2.75
150	Bill Klaus	9.00	4.50	2.75
151	Jim Brideweser	9.00	4.50	2.75
152	Johnny Klippstein	9.00	4.50	2.75
153	Eddie Robinson	15.00	7.50	4.50
154	*Frank Lary*	9.00	4.50	2.75
155	Gerry Staley	9.00	4.50	2.75
156	Jim Hughes	9.00	4.50	2.75
157a	Ernie Johnson (Don Johnson (Orioles) picture on front)	10.00	5.00	3.00
157b	Ernie Johnson (Ernie Johnson (Braves) picture on front)	18.00	9.00	5.50
158	Gil Hodges	40.00	20.00	12.00
159	Harry Byrd	9.00	4.50	2.75
160	Bill Skowron(FC)	18.00	9.00	5.50
161	Matt Batts	9.00	4.50	2.75
162	Charlie Maxwell(FC)	9.00	4.50	2.75
163	Sid Gordon	10.00	5.00	3.00
164	Toby Atwell	9.00	4.50	2.75
165	Maurice McDermott	9.00	4.50	2.75
166	Jim Busby	9.00	4.50	2.75
167	Bob Grim	15.00	7.50	4.50
168	Yogi Berra	110.00	55.00	33.00
169	Carl Furillo	15.00	7.50	4.50
170	Carl Erskine	12.00	6.00	3.50
171	Robin Roberts	35.00	17.50	10.50
172	Willie Jones	9.00	4.50	2.75
173	"Chico" Carrasquel	9.00	4.50	2.75
174	Sherman Lollar	9.00	4.50	2.75
175	Wilmer Shantz	9.00	4.50	2.75
176	Joe DeMaestri	9.00	4.50	2.75
177	Willard Nixon	9.00	4.50	2.75
178	Tom Brewer	9.00	4.50	2.75
179	Hank Aaron	250.00	125.00	75.00
180	Johnny Logan	9.00	4.50	2.75
181	Eddie Miksis	9.00	4.50	2.75
182	Bob Rush	9.00	4.50	2.75
183	Ray Katt	9.00	4.50	2.75
184	Willie Mays	250.00	125.00	75.00
185	Vic Raschi	9.00	4.50	2.75
186	Alex Grammas	9.00	4.50	2.75
187	Fred Hatfield	9.00	4.50	2.75
188	Ned Garver	9.00	4.50	2.75
189	Jack Collum	9.00	4.50	2.75
190	Fred Baczewski	9.00	4.50	2.75
191	Bob Lemon	30.00	15.00	9.00
192	George Strickland	9.00	4.50	2.75
193	Howie Judson	9.00	4.50	2.75
194	Joe Nuxhall	9.00	4.50	2.75
195a	Erv Palica (no traded line)	9.00	4.50	2.75
195b	Erv Palica (traded line)	18.00	9.00	5.50
196	Russ Meyer	12.00	6.00	7.25
197	Ralph Kiner	35.00	17.50	10.50
198	Dave Pope	9.00	4.50	2.75
199	Vernon Law	9.00	4.50	2.75
200	Dick Littlefield	9.00	4.50	2.75
201	Allie Reynolds	15.00	7.50	4.50
202	Mickey Mantle	600.00	300.00	175.00
203	Steve Gromek	9.00	4.50	2.75
204a	Frank Bolling (Milt Bolling back)	10.00	5.00	3.00
204b	Frank Bolling (Frank Bolling back)	20.00	10.00	6.00
205	"Rip" Repulski	9.00	4.50	2.75
206	Ralph Beard	9.00	4.50	2.75
207	Frank Shea	9.00	4.50	2.75
208	Ed Fitz Gerald	9.00	4.50	2.75
209	"Smoky" Burgess	9.00	4.50	2.75
210	Earl Torgeson	9.00	4.50	2.75
211	John "Sonny" Dixon	9.00	4.50	2.75
212	Jack Dittmer	9.00	4.50	2.75
213	George Kell	30.00	15.00	9.00
214	Billy Pierce	10.00	5.00	3.00
215	Bob Kuzava	9.00	4.50	2.75
216	Preacher Roe	10.00	5.00	3.00
217	Del Crandall	9.00	4.50	2.75
218	Joe Adcock	10.00	5.00	3.00
219	"Whitey" Lockman	9.00	4.50	2.75
220	Jim Hearn	9.00	4.50	2.75
221	Hector "Skinny" Brown	9.00	4.50	2.75
222	Russ Kemmerer	9.00	4.50	2.75
223	Hal Jeffcoat	9.00	4.50	2.75
224	Dee Fondy	9.00	4.50	2.75
225	Paul Richards	20.00	10.00	6.00

		NR MT	EX	VG
226	W.F. McKinley (umpire)	24.00	12.00	7.25
227	Frank Baumholtz	20.00	10.00	6.00
228	John M. Phillips	20.00	10.00	6.00
229	Jim Brosnan	20.00	10.00	6.00
230	Al Brazle	20.00	10.00	6.00
231	Jim Konstanty	25.00	12.50	7.50
232	Birdie Tebbetts	20.00	10.00	6.00
233	Bill Serena	20.00	10.00	6.00
234	Dick Bartell	20.00	10.00	6.00
235	J.A. Paparella (umpire)	24.00	12.00	7.25
236	Murry Dickson	20.00	10.00	6.00
237	Johnny Wyrostek	20.00	10.00	6.00
238	Eddie Stanky	22.00	11.00	6.50
239	Edwin A. Rommel (umpire)	24.00	12.00	7.25
240	Billy Loes	22.00	11.00	6.50
241	John Pesky	20.00	10.00	6.00
242	Ernie Banks(FC)	400.00	200.00	125.00
243	Gus Bell	20.00	10.00	6.00
244	Duane Pillette	20.00	10.00	6.00
245	Bill Miller	20.00	10.00	6.00
246	Hank Bauer	30.00	15.00	9.00
247	Dutch Leonard	20.00	10.00	6.00
248	Harry Dorish	20.00	10.00	6.00
249	Billy Gardner	20.00	10.00	6.00
250	Larry Napp (umpire)	24.00	12.00	7.25
251	Stan Jok	20.00	10.00	6.00
252	Roy Smalley	20.00	10.00	6.00
253	Jim Wilson	20.00	10.00	6.00
254	Bennett Flowers	20.00	10.00	6.00
255	Pete Runnels	20.00	10.00	6.00
256	Owen Friend	20.00	10.00	6.00
257	Tom Alston	20.00	10.00	6.00
258	John W. Stevens (umpire)	24.00	12.00	7.25
259	*Don Mossi*	20.00	10.00	6.00
260	Edwin H. Hurley (umpire)	24.00	12.00	7.25
261	Walt Moryn	22.00	11.00	6.50
262	Jim Lemon	20.00	10.00	6.00
263	Eddie Joost	20.00	10.00	6.00
264	Bill Henry	20.00	10.00	6.00
265	Al Barlick (umpire)	60.00	30.00	18.00
266	Mike Fornieles	20.00	10.00	6.00
267	George Honochick (umpire)	50.00	25.00	15.00
268	Roy Lee Hawes	20.00	10.00	6.00
269	Joe Amalfitano	20.00	10.00	6.00
270	Chico Fernandez	22.00	11.00	6.50
271	Bob Hooper	20.00	10.00	6.00
272	John Flaherty (umpire)	24.00	12.00	7.25
273	"Bubba" Church	20.00	10.00	6.00
274	Jim Delsing	20.00	10.00	6.00
275	William T. Grieve (umpire)	24.00	12.00	7.25
276	Ike Delock	20.00	10.00	6.00
277	Ed Runge (umpire)	24.00	12.00	7.25
278	*Charles Neal*	22.00	11.00	6.50
279	Hank Soar (umpire)	24.00	12.00	7.25
280	Clyde McCullough	20.00	10.00	6.00
281	Charles Berry (umpire)	24.00	12.00	7.25
282	Phil Cavarretta	20.00	10.00	6.00
283	Nestor Chylak (umpire)	24.00	12.00	7.25
284	William A. Jackowski (umpire)	24.00	12.00	7.25
285	Walt Dropo	20.00	10.00	6.00
286	Frank Secory (umpire)	24.00	12.00	7.25
287	Ron Mrozinski	20.00	10.00	6.00
288	Dick Smith	20.00	10.00	6.00
289	Art Gore (umpire)	24.00	12.00	7.25
290	Hershell Freeman	20.00	10.00	6.00
291	Frank Dascoli (umpire)	24.00	12.00	7.25
292	Marv Blaylock	20.00	10.00	6.00
293	Thomas D. Gorman (umpire)	24.00	12.00	7.25
294	Wally Moses	20.00	10.00	6.00
295	Lee Ballanfant (umpire)	24.00	12.00	7.25
296	*Bill Virdon*	30.00	15.00	9.00
297	"Dusty" Boggess (umpire)	24.00	12.00	7.25
298	Charlie Grimm	20.00	10.00	6.00
299	Lonnie Warneke (umpire)	24.00	12.00	7.25
300	Tommy Byrne	25.00	12.50	7.50
301	William Engeln (umpire)	24.00	12.00	7.25
302	*Frank Malzone*	30.00	15.00	9.00
303	Jocko Conlan (umpire)	80.00	40.00	24.00
304	Harry Chiti	20.00	10.00	6.00
305	Frank Umont (umpire)	24.00	12.00	7.25
306	Bob Cerv	25.00	12.50	7.50
307	"Babe" Pinelli (umpire)	24.00	12.00	7.25
308	Al Lopez	40.00	20.00	12.00
309	Hal Dixon (umpire)	24.00	12.00	7.25
310	Ken Lehman	22.00	11.00	6.50
311	Larry Goetz (umpire)	24.00	12.00	7.25
312	Bill Wight	20.00	10.00	6.00
313	Augie Donatelli (umpire)	24.00	12.00	7.25
314	Dale Mitchell	20.00	10.00	6.00
315	Cal Hubbard (umpire)	80.00	40.00	24.00
316	Marion Fricano	20.00	10.00	6.00
317	Bill Summers (umpire)	24.00	12.00	7.25
318	Sid Hudson	20.00	10.00	6.00
319	Al Schroll	20.00	10.00	6.00
320	George Susce, Jr.	60.00	10.00	6.00

1989 Bowman

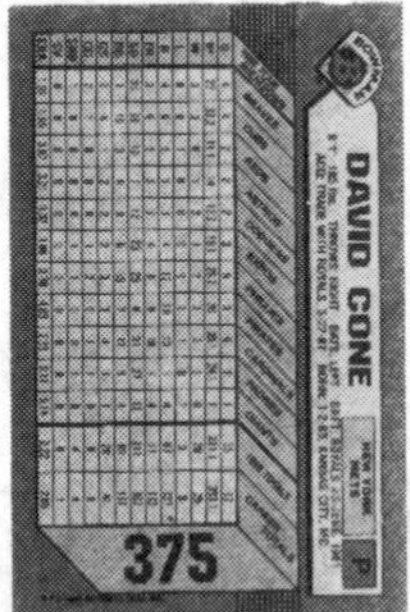

Topps, which purchased the Bowman Co. back in 1955, revived the Bowman name in 1989, issuing a 484-card set modeled after the 1953 Bowman cards. The cards are 2-1/2" by 3-3/4", slightly larger than a current standard-sized card. The fronts contain a full-color player photo, with facsimile autograph on the bottom and the Bowman logo in an upper corner. The unique card backs include a breakdown of the player's stats against each team in his league. A series of "Hot Rookie Stars" highlight the set. The cards were distributed in both wax packs and rack packs. Each pack included a special reproduction of a classic Bowman card with a sweepstakes on the back. The special cards said "reprint" on the front.

		MT	NR MT	EX
Complete Set (484):		10.00	7.50	4.00
Common Player:		.03	.02	.01
1	Oswald Peraza	.05	.04	.02
2	Brian Holton	.05	.04	.02
3	Jose Bautista	.05	.04	.02
4	*Pete Harnisch*	.20	.15	.08
5	Dave Schmidt	.03	.02	.01
6	Gregg Olson	.30	.25	.12
7	Jeff Ballard	.10	.08	.04
8	Bob Melvin	.03	.02	.01
9	Cal Ripken, Jr.	.40	.30	.15
10	Randy Milligan	.08	.06	.03
11	*Juan Bell*	.15	.11	.06
12	Billy Ripken	.05	.04	.02
13	Jim Trabor	.03	.02	.01
14	Pete Stanicek	.03	.02	.01
15	*Steve Finley*	.20	.15	.08
16	Larry Sheets	.03	.02	.01
17	Phil Bradley	.05	.04	.02
18	*Brady Anderson*	.30	.25	.12
19	Lee Smith	.03	.02	.01
20	Tom Fischer	.15	.11	.06
21	Mike Boddicker	.03	.02	.01
22	Rob Murphy	.03	.02	.01
23	Wes Gardner	.03	.02	.01
24	John Dopson	.10	.08	.04
25	Bob Stanley	.03	.02	.01
26	Roger Clemens	.35	.25	.14
27	Rich Gedman	.03	.02	.01
28	Marty Barrett	.03	.02	.01
29	Luis Rivera	.03	.02	.01
30	Jody Reed	.05	.04	.02
31	Nick Esasky	.05	.04	.02
32	Wade Boggs	.20	.15	.08
33	Jim Rice	.10	.08	.04
34	Mike Greenwell	.15	.11	.06
35	Dwight Evans	.15	.11	.06
36	Ellis Burks	.25	.20	.10
37	Chuck Finley	.05	.04	.02
38	Kirk McCaskill	.05	.04	.02
39	*Jim Abbott*	.60	.45	.25
40	*Bryan Harvey*	.35	.25	.14
41	Bert Blyleven	.08	.06	.03

		MT	NR MT	EX
42	Mike Witt	.03	.02	.01
43	Bob McClure	.03	.02	.01
44	Bill Schroeder	.03	.02	.01
45	Lance Parrish	.05	.04	.02
46	Dick Schofield	.03	.02	.01
47	Wally Joyner	.10	.08	.04
48	Jack Howell	.03	.02	.01
49	Johnny Ray	.03	.02	.01
50	Chili Davis	.05	.04	.02
51	Tony Armas	.03	.02	.01
52	Claudell Washington	.03	.02	.01
53	Brian Downing	.03	.02	.01
54	Devon White	.10	.08	.04
55	Bobby Thigpen	.08	.06	.03
56	Bill Long	.03	.02	.01
57	Jerry Reuss	.03	.02	.01
58	Shawn Hillegas	.03	.02	.01
59	Melido Perez	.10	.08	.04
60	Jeff Bittiger	.05	.04	.02
61	Jack McDowell	.25	.20	.10
62	Carlton Fisk	.10	.08	.04
63	Steve Lyons	.03	.02	.01
64	Ozzie Guillen	.05	.04	.02
65	*Robin Ventura*	1.25	.90	.50
66	Fred Manrique	.03	.02	.01
67	Dan Pasqua	.03	.02	.01
68	Ivan Calderon	.03	.02	.01
69	Ron Kittle	.03	.02	.01
70	Daryl Boston	.03	.02	.01
71	Dave Gallagher	.05	.04	.02
72	Harold Baines	.08	.06	.03
73	Charles Nagy	.20	.15	.08
74	John Farrell	.03	.02	.01
75	Kevin Wickander	.10	.08	.04
76	Greg Swindell	.15	.11	.06
77	Mike Walker	.15	.11	.06
78	Doug Jones	.05	.04	.02
79	Rich Yett	.03	.02	.01
80	Tom Candiotti	.03	.02	.01
81	Jesse Orosco	.03	.02	.01
82	Bud Black	.03	.02	.01
83	Andy Allanson	.03	.02	.01
84	Pete O'Brien	.05	.04	.02
85	Jerry Browne	.05	.04	.02
86	Brook Jacoby	.03	.02	.01
87	*Mark Lewis*	.25	.20	.10
88	Luis Aguayo	.03	.02	.01
89	Cory Snyder	.05	.04	.02
90	Oddibe McDowell	.05	.04	.02
91	Joe Carter	.25	.20	.10
92	Frank Tanana	.03	.02	.01
93	Jack Morris	.03	.02	.01
94	Doyle Alexander	.03	.02	.01
95	Steve Searcy	.08	.06	.03
96	Randy Bockus	.05	.04	.02
97	Jeff Robinson	.05	.04	.02
98	Mike Henneman	.05	.04	.02
99	Paul Gibson	.03	.02	.01
100	Frank Williams	.03	.02	.01
101	Matt Nokes	.05	.04	.02
102	Rico Brogna	.15	.11	.06
103	Lou Whitaker	.08	.06	.03
104	Al Pedrique	.03	.02	.01
105	Alan Trammell	.05	.04	.02
106	Chris Brown	.03	.02	.01
107	Pat Sheridan	.03	.02	.01
108	Gary Pettis	.03	.02	.01
109	Keith Moreland	.03	.02	.01
110	Mel Stottlemyre, Jr.	.15	.11	.06
111	Bret Saberhagen	.10	.08	.04
112	Floyd Bannister	.03	.02	.01
113	Jeff Montgomery	.05	.04	.02
114	Steve Farr	.05	.04	.02
115	Tom Gordon	.10	.08	.04
116	Charlie Leibrandt	.03	.02	.01
117	Mark Gubicza	.08	.06	.03
118	Mike MacFarlane	.03	.02	.01
119	Bob Boone	.05	.04	.02
120	Kurt Stillwell	.05	.04	.02
121	George Brett	.20	.15	.08
122	Frank White	.05	.04	.02
123	Kevin Seitzer	.08	.06	.03
124	Willie Wilson	.03	.02	.01
125	Pat Tabler	.03	.02	.01
126	Bo Jackson	.30	.25	.12
127	Hugh Walker	.20	.15	.08
128	Danny Tartabull	.05	.04	.02
129	Teddy Higuera	.08	.06	.03
130	Don August	.03	.02	.01
131	Juan Nieves	.03	.02	.01
132	Mike Birkbeck	.03	.02	.01

		MT	NR MT	EX
133	Dan Plesac	.05	.04	.02
134	Chris Bosio	.05	.04	.02
135	Bill Wegman	.03	.02	.01
136	Chuck Crim	.03	.02	.01
137	B.J. Surhoff	.05	.04	.02
138	Joey Meyer	.03	.02	.01
139	Dale Sveum	.03	.02	.01
140	Paul Molitor	.15	.11	.06
141	Jim Gantner	.03	.02	.01
142	Gary Sheffield	1.50	1.25	.60
143	Greg Brock	.03	.02	.01
144	Robin Yount	.25	.20	.10
145	Glenn Braggs	.03	.02	.01
146	Rob Deer	.03	.02	.01
147	Fred Toliver	.03	.02	.01
148	Jeff Reardon	.03	.02	.01
149	Allan Anderson	.05	.04	.02
150	Frank Viola	.15	.11	.06
151	Shane Rawley	.03	.02	.01
152	Juan Berenguer	.03	.02	.01
153	Johnny Ard	.20	.15	.08
154	Tim Laudner	.03	.02	.01
155	Brian Harper	.03	.02	.01
156	Al Newman	.03	.02	.01
157	Kent Hrbek	.08	.06	.03
158	Gary Gaetti	.08	.06	.03
159	Wally Backman	.03	.02	.01
160	Gene Larkin	.03	.02	.01
161	Greg Gagne	.03	.02	.01
162	Kirby Puckett	.35	.25	.14
163	Danny Gladden	.03	.02	.01
164	Randy Bush	.03	.02	.01
165	Dave LaPoint	.03	.02	.01
166	Andy Hawkins	.03	.02	.01
167	Dave Righetti	.05	.04	.02
168	Lance McCullers	.03	.02	.01
169	Jimmy Jones	.03	.02	.01
170	Al Leiter	.03	.02	.01
171	John Candelaria	.03	.02	.01
172	Don Slaught	.03	.02	.01
173	Jamie Quirk	.03	.02	.01
174	Rafael Santana	.03	.02	.01
175	Mike Pagliarulo	.03	.02	.01
176	Don Mattingly	.25	.20	.10
177	Ken Phelps	.03	.02	.01
178	Steve Sax	.08	.06	.03
179	Dave Winfield	.20	.15	.08
180	Stan Jefferson	.03	.02	.01
181	Rickey Henderson	.25	.20	.10
182	Bob Brower	.03	.02	.01
183	Roberto Kelly	.10	.08	.04
184	Curt Young	.03	.02	.01
185	Gene Nelson	.03	.02	.01
186	Bob Welch	.03	.02	.01
187	Rick Honeycutt	.03	.02	.01
188	Dave Stewart	.08	.06	.03
189	Mike Moore	.08	.06	.03
190	Dennis Eckersley	.08	.06	.03
191	Eric Plunk	.03	.02	.01
192	Storm Davis	.03	.02	.01
193	Terry Steinbach	.10	.08	.04
194	Ron Hassey	.03	.02	.01
195	Stan Royer	.15	.11	.06
196	Walt Weiss	.15	.11	.06
197	Mark McGwire	.30	.25	.12
198	Carney Lansford	.08	.06	.03
199	Glenn Hubbard	.03	.02	.01
200	Dave Henderson	.05	.04	.02
201	Jose Canseco	.40	.30	.15
202	Dave Parker	.05	.04	.02
203	Scott Bankhead	.05	.04	.02
204	Tom Niedenfuer	.03	.02	.01
205	Mark Langston	.15	.11	.06
206	*Erik Hanson*	.25	.20	.10
207	Mike Jackson	.03	.02	.01
208	Dave Valle	.03	.02	.01
209	Scott Bradley	.03	.02	.01
210	Harold Reynolds	.08	.06	.03
211	*Tino Martinez*	.30	.25	.12
212	Rich Renteria	.03	.02	.01
213	Rey Quinones	.03	.02	.01
214	Jim Presley	.03	.02	.01
215	Alvin Davis	.10	.08	.04
216	Edgar Martinez	.10	.08	.04
217	Darnell Coles	.03	.02	.01
218	Jeffrey Leonard	.08	.06	.03
219	Jay Buhner	.15	.11	.06
220	Ken Griffey, Jr.	3.00	2.25	1.25
221	Drew Hall	.03	.02	.01
222	Bobby Witt	.03	.02	.01
223	Jamie Moyer	.03	.02	.01

#	Player	MT	NR MT	EX
224	Charlie Hough	.03	.02	.01
225	Nolan Ryan	.70	.50	.30
226	Jeff Russell	.05	.04	.02
227	Jim Sundberg	.03	.02	.01
228	Julio Franco	.15	.11	.06
229	Buddy Bell	.03	.02	.01
230	Scott Fletcher	.03	.02	.01
231	Jeff Kunkel	.03	.02	.01
232	Steve Buechele	.03	.02	.01
233	Monty Fariss	.12	.09	.05
234	Rick Leach	.03	.02	.01
235	Ruben Sierra	.30	.25	.12
236	Cecil Espy	.05	.04	.02
237	Rafael Palmeiro	.20	.15	.08
238	Pete Incaviglia	.03	.02	.01
239	Dave Steib	.05	.04	.02
240	Jeff Musselman	.03	.02	.01
241	Mike Flanagan	.03	.02	.01
242	Todd Stottlemyre	.10	.08	.04
243	Jimmy Key	.05	.04	.02
244	Tony Castillo	.10	.08	.04
245	Alex Sanchez	.05	.04	.02
246	Tom Henke	.03	.02	.01
247	John Cerutti	.03	.02	.01
248	Ernie Whitt	.03	.02	.01
249	Bob Brenly	.03	.02	.01
250	Rance Mulliniks	.03	.02	.01
251	Kelly Gruber	.10	.08	.04
252	Ed Sprague	.40	.30	.15
253	Fred McGriff	.35	.25	.14
254	Tony Fernandez	.08	.06	.03
255	Tom Lawless	.03	.02	.01
256	George Bell	.10	.08	.04
257	Jesse Barfield	.05	.04	.02
258	Sandy Alomar	.20	.15	.08
259	Ken Griffey	1.00	.70	.40
260	Cal Ripken, Jr.	.15	.11	.06
261	Mel Stottlemyre	.15	.11	.06
262	Zane Smith	.03	.02	.01
263	Charlie Puleo	.03	.02	.01
264	Derek Lilliquist	.15	.11	.06
265	Paul Assenmacher	.03	.02	.01
266	John Smoltz	.60	.45	.25
267	Tom Glavine	.40	.30	.15
268	Steve Avery	1.00	.70	.40
269	*Pete Smith*	.15	.11	.06
270	Jody Davis	.03	.02	.01
271	Bruce Benedict	.03	.02	.01
272	Andres Thomas	.03	.02	.01
273	Gerald Perry	.05	.04	.02
274	Ron Gant	.35	.25	.14
275	Darrell Evans	.03	.02	.01
276	Dale Murphy	.10	.08	.04
277	Dion James	.03	.02	.01
278	Lonnie Smith	.08	.06	.03
279	Geronimo Berroa	.05	.04	.02
280	Steve Wilson	.20	.15	.08
281	Rick Suctcliffe	.05	.04	.02
282	Kevin Coffman	.03	.02	.01
283	Mitch Williams	.10	.08	.04
284	Greg Maddux	.20	.15	.08
285	Paul Kilgus	.03	.02	.01
286	Mike Harkey	.10	.08	.04
287	Lloyd McClendon	.05	.04	.02
288	Damon Berryhill	.05	.04	.02
289	Ty Griffin	.10	.08	.04
290	Ryne Sandberg	.35	.25	.14
291	Mark Grace	.30	.25	.12
292	Curt Wilkerson	.03	.02	.01
293	Vance Law	.03	.02	.01
294	Shawon Dunston	.08	.06	.03
295	Jerome Walton	.08	.06	.03
296	Mitch Webster	.03	.02	.01
297	Dwight Smith	.08	.06	.03
298	Andre Dawson	.15	.11	.06
299	Jeff Sellers	.03	.02	.01
300	Jose Rijo	.05	.04	.02
301	John Franco	.05	.04	.02
302	Rick Mahler	.03	.02	.01
303	Ron Robinson	.03	.02	.01
304	Danny Jackson	.03	.02	.01
305	Rob Dibble	.08	.06	.03
306	Tom Browning	.03	.02	.01
307	Bo Diaz	.03	.02	.01
308	Manny Trillo	.03	.02	.01
309	Chris Sabo	.15	.11	.06
310	Ron Oester	.03	.02	.01
311	Barry Larkin	.15	.11	.06
312	Todd Benzinger	.05	.04	.02
313	Paul O'Neil	.05	.04	.02
314	Kal Daniels	.05	.04	.02

#	Player	MT	NR MT	EX
315	Joel Youngblood	.03	.02	.01
316	Eric Davis	.12	.09	.05
317	Dave Smith	.05	.04	.02
318	Mark Portugal	.03	.02	.01
319	Brian Meyer	.03	.02	.01
320	Jim Deshaies	.05	.04	.02
321	Juan Agosto	.03	.02	.01
322	Mike Scott	.10	.08	.04
323	Rick Rhoden	.03	.02	.01
324	Jim Clancy	.03	.02	.01
325	Larry Andersen	.03	.02	.01
326	Alex Trevino	.03	.02	.01
327	Alan Ashby	.03	.02	.01
328	Craig Reynolds	.03	.02	.01
329	Bill Doran	.03	.02	.01
330	Rafael Ramirez	.03	.02	.01
331	Glenn Davis	.10	.08	.04
332	Willie Ansley	.25	.20	.10
333	Gerald Young	.03	.02	.01
334	Cameron Drew	.10	.08	.04
335	Jay Howell	.05	.04	.02
336	Tim Belcher	.05	.04	.02
337	Fernando Valenzuela	.05	.04	.02
338	Ricky Horton	.03	.02	.01
339	Tim Leary	.03	.02	.01
340	Bill Bene	.15	.11	.06
341	Orel Hershiser	.08	.06	.03
342	Mike Scioscia	.05	.04	.02
343	Rick Dempsey	.03	.02	.01
344	Willie Randolph	.03	.02	.01
345	Alfredo Griffin	.03	.02	.01
346	Eddie Murray	.15	.11	.06
347	Mickey Hatcher	.03	.02	.01
348	Mike Sharperson	.03	.02	.01
349	John Shelby	.03	.02	.01
350	Mike Marshall	.03	.02	.01
351	Kirk Gibson	.05	.04	.02
352	Mike Davis	.03	.02	.01
353	Bryn Smith	.03	.02	.01
354	Pascual Perez	.03	.02	.01
355	Kevin Gross	.03	.02	.01
356	Andy McGaffigan	.03	.02	.01
357	Brian Holman	.05	.04	.02
358	Dave Wainhouse	.20	.15	.08
359	Denny Martinez	.03	.02	.01
360	Tim Burke	.03	.02	.01
361	Nelson Santovenia	.08	.06	.03
362	Tim Wallach	.05	.04	.02
363	Spike Owen	.03	.02	.01
364	Rex Hudler	.03	.02	.01
365	Andres Galarraga	.15	.11	.06
366	Otis Nixon	.03	.02	.01
367	Hubie Brooks	.03	.02	.01
368	Mike Aldrete	.03	.02	.01
369	Rock Raines	.08	.06	.03
370	Dave Martinez	.03	.02	.01
371	Bob Ojeda	.03	.02	.01
372	Ron Darling	.05	.04	.02
373	Wally Whitehurst	.08	.06	.03
374	Randy Myers	.05	.04	.02
375	David Cone	.10	.08	.04
376	Doc Gooden	.12	.09	.05
377	Sid Fernandez	.05	.04	.02
378	Dave Proctor	.20	.15	.08
379	Gary Carter	.03	.02	.01
380	Keith Miller	.05	.04	.02
381	Gregg Jefferies	.40	.30	.15
382	Tim Teufel	.03	.02	.01
383	Kevin Elster	.03	.02	.01
384	Dave Magadan	.03	.02	.01
385	Keith Hernandez	.05	.04	.02
386	Mookie Wilson	.05	.04	.02
387	Darryl Strawberry	.15	.11	.06
388	Kevin McReynolds	.10	.08	.04
389	Mark Carreon	.05	.04	.02
390	Jeff Parrett	.05	.04	.02
391	Mike Maddux	.03	.02	.01
392	Don Carman	.03	.02	.01
393	Bruce Ruffin	.03	.02	.01
394	Ken Howell	.03	.02	.01
395	Steve Bedrosian	.05	.04	.02
396	Floyd Youmans	.03	.02	.01
397	Larry McWilliams	.03	.02	.01
398	Pat Combs	.10	.08	.04
399	Steve Lake	.03	.02	.01
400	Dickie Thon	.03	.02	.01
401	Ricky Jordan	.12	.09	.05
402	Mike Schmidt	.30	.25	.12
403	Tom Herr	.03	.02	.01
404	Chris James	.03	.02	.01
405	Juan Samuel	.08	.06	.03

		MT	NR MT	EX
406	Von Hayes	.08	.06	.03
407	Ron Jones	.15	.11	.06
408	Curt Ford	.03	.02	.01
409	Bob Walk	.03	.02	.01
410	Jeff Robinson	.03	.02	.01
411	Jim Gott	.03	.02	.01
412	Scott Medvin	.03	.02	.01
413	John Smiley	.03	.02	.01
414	Bob Kipper	.03	.02	.01
415	Brian Fisher	.03	.02	.01
416	Doug Drabek	.03	.02	.01
417	Mike Lavalliere	.03	.02	.01
418	Ken Oberkfell	.03	.02	.01
419	Sid Bream	.03	.02	.01
420	Austin Manahan	.20	.15	.08
421	Jose Lind	.03	.02	.01
422	Bobby Bonilla	.12	.09	.05
423	Glenn Wilson	.03	.02	.01
424	Andy Van Slyke	.12	.09	.05
425	Gary Redus	.03	.02	.01
426	Barry Bonds	.50	.40	.20
427	Don Heinkel	.03	.02	.01
428	Ken Dayley	.03	.02	.01
429	Todd Worrell	.05	.04	.02
430	Brad DuVall	.20	.15	.08
431	Jose DeLeon	.03	.02	.01
432	Joe Magrane	.10	.08	.04
433	John Ericks	.20	.15	.08
434	Frank DiPino	.03	.02	.01
435	Tony Pena	.05	.04	.02
436	Ozzie Smith	.12	.09	.05
437	Terry Pendleton	.03	.02	.01
438	Jose Oquendo	.03	.02	.01
439	Tim Jones	.05	.04	.02
440	Pedro Guerrero	.10	.08	.04
441	Milt Thompson	.03	.02	.01
442	Willie McGee	.05	.04	.02
443	Vince Coleman	.05	.04	.02
444	Tom Brunansky	.05	.04	.02
445	Walt Terrell	.03	.02	.01
446	Eric Show	.03	.02	.01
447	Mark Davis	.10	.08	.04
448	Andy Benes	.40	.30	.15
449	Eddie Whitson	.03	.02	.01
450	Dennis Rasmussen	.03	.02	.01
451	Bruce Hurst	.03	.02	.01
452	Pat Clements	.03	.02	.01
453	Benito Santiago	.10	.08	.04
454	Sandy Alomar, Jr.	.30	.25	.12
455	Garry Templeton	.03	.02	.01
456	Jack Clark	.05	.04	.02
457	Tim Flannery	.03	.02	.01
458	Roberto Alomar	.80	.60	.30
459	Camelo Martinez	.03	.02	.01
460	John Kruk	.03	.02	.01
461	Tony Gwynn	.25	.20	.10
462	Jerald Clark	.05	.04	.02
463	Don Robinson	.03	.02	.01
464	Craig Lefferts	.03	.02	.01
465	Kelly Downs	.03	.02	.01
466	Rick Rueschel	.05	.04	.02
467	Scott Garrelts	.03	.02	.01
468	Wil Tejada	.03	.02	.01
469	Kirt Manwaring	.10	.08	.04
470	Terry Kennedy	.03	.02	.01
471	Jose Uribe	.03	.02	.01
472	Royce Clayton	.75	.60	.30
473	Robby Thompson	.05	.04	.02
474	Kevin Mitchell	.12	.09	.05
475	Ernie Riles	.03	.02	.01
476	Will Clark	.25	.20	.10
477	Donnell Nixon	.03	.02	.01
478	Candy Maldonado	.03	.02	.01
479	Tracy Jones	.03	.02	.01
480	Brett Butler	.05	.04	.02
481	Checklist	.05	.04	.02
482	Checklist	.05	.04	.02
483	Checklist	.05	.04	.02
484	Checklist	.05	.04	.02

1989 Bowman Inserts

Bowman inserted sweepstakes cards in its 1989 packs. Each sweepstakes card features a reprint Bowman card on the front. The cards were by no means scarce.

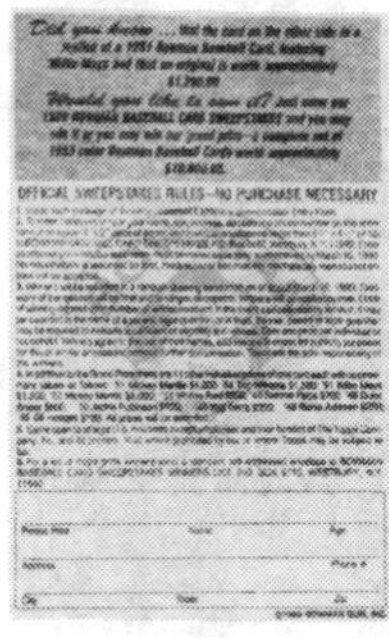

Complete Set:		1.50	1.25	.60
Common Player:		.10	.08	.04
(1)	Richie Ashburn	.10	.08	.04
(2)	Yogi Berra	.20	.15	.08
(3)	Whitey Ford	.10	.08	.04
(4)	Gil Hodges	.10	.08	.04
(5)	Mickey Mantle (1951)	.25	.20	.10
(6)	Mickey Mantle (1953)	.25	.20	.10
(7)	Willie Mays	.25	.20	.10
(8)	Satchel Paige	.15	.11	.06
(9)	Jackie Robinson	.20	.15	.08
(10)	Duke Snider	.15	.11	.06
(11)	Ted Williams	.25	.20	.10

1990 Bowman

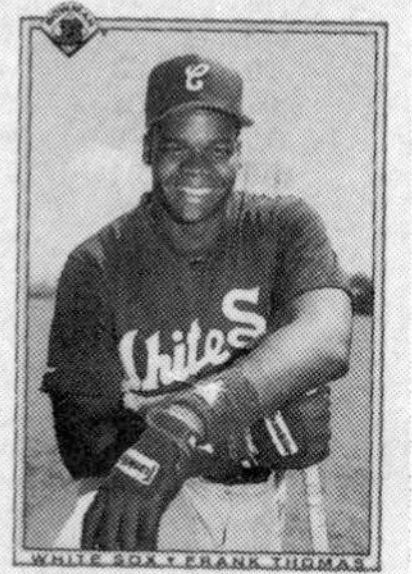

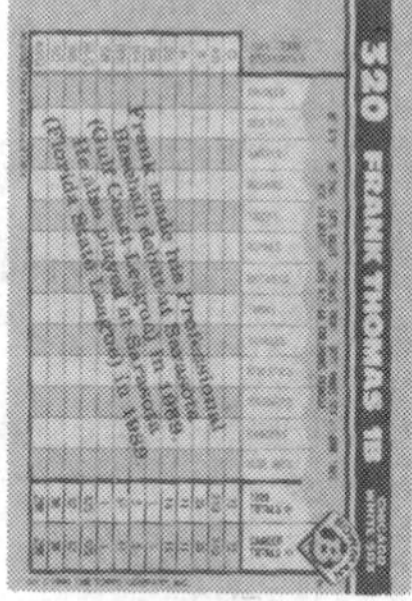

Bowman followed up its 1989 release with 528-card set in 1990. The 1990 cards follow the classic Bowman style featuring a full color photo bordered in white. The Bowman logo appears in the upper left corner. The player's team nickname and name appear on the bottom border of the card photo. Unlike the 1989 set, the 1990 cards measure 2-1/2" by 3-1/2" in size. The card backs are horizontal and display the player's statistics against the teams in his respective league. Included in the set are special insert cards that feature a reproduction of a painting of a modern-day superstar done in the style of the 1951 Bowman cards. The paintings were produced for Bowman by artist Craig Pursley. The card backs contain a sweepstakes offer with a chance to win a complete set of 11 lithographs made from these paintings.

		MT	NR MT	EX
Complete Set (528):		15.00	11.00	6.00
Common Player:		.05	.04	.02
1	Tommy Greene	.60	.45	.25
2	Tom Glavine	.25	.20	.10
3	Andy Nezelek	.08	.06	.03
4	Mike Stanton	.20	.15	.08
5	Rick Lueken	.08	.06	.03
6	Kent Mercker	.10	.08	.04
7	Derek Lilliquist	.06	.05	.02
8	Charlie Liebrandt	.05	.04	.02
9	Steve Avery	.60	.45	.25
10	John Smoltz	.25	.20	.10

		MT	NR MT	EX
11	Mark Lemke	.08	.06	.03
12	Lonnie Smith	.06	.05	.02
13	Oddibe McDowell	.05	.04	.02
14	Tyler Houston	.10	.08	.04
15	Jeff Blauser	.05	.04	.02
16	Ernie Whitt	.05	.04	.02
17	Alexis Infante	.10	.08	.04
18	Jim Presley	.06	.05	.02
19	Dale Murphy	.10	.08	.04
20	Nick Esasky	.06	.05	.02
21	Rick Sutcliffe	.06	.05	.02
22	Mike Bielecki	.06	.05	.02
23	Steve Wilson	.10	.08	.04
24	Kevin Blankenship	.10	.08	.04
25	Mitch Williams	.10	.08	.04
26	Dean Wilkins	.10	.08	.04
27	Greg Maddux	.20	.15	.08
28	Mike Harkey	.20	.15	.08
29	Mark Grace	.20	.15	.08
30	Ryne Sandberg	.40	.30	.15
31	Greg Smith	.20	.15	.08
32	Dwight Smith	.15	.11	.06
33	Damon Berryhill	.05	.04	.02
34	Earl Cunningham	.15	.11	.06
35	Jerome Walton	.08	.06	.03
36	Lloyd McClendon	.05	.04	.02
37	Ty Griffin	.20	.15	.08
38	Shawon Dunston	.10	.08	.04
39	Andre Dawson	.10	.08	.04
40	Luis Salazar	.05	.04	.02
41	Tim Layana	.20	.15	.08
42	Rob Dibble	.10	.08	.04
43	Tom Browning	.05	.04	.02
44	Danny Jackson	.05	.04	.02
45	Jose Rijo	.06	.05	.02
46	Scott Scudder	.20	.15	.08
47	Randy Myers	.06	.05	.02
48	Brian Lane	.15	.11	.06
49	Paul O'Neill	.05	.04	.02
50	Barry Larkin	.10	.08	.04
51	Reggie Jefferson	.40	.30	.15
52	Jeff Branson	.10	.08	.04
53	Chris Sabo	.08	.06	.03
54	Joe Oliver	.10	.08	.04
55	Todd Benzinger	.05	.04	.02
56	Rolando Roomes	.05	.04	.02
57	Hal Morris	.12	.09	.05
58	Eric Davis	.15	.11	.06
59	Scott Bryant	.20	.15	.08
60	Ken Griffey	.06	.05	.02
61	Darryl Kile	1.25	.90	.50
62	Dave Smith	.05	.04	.02
63	Mark Portugal	.05	.04	.02
64	Jeff Juden	.35	.25	.14
65	Bill Gullickson	.05	.04	.02
66	Danny Darwin	.05	.04	.02
67	Larry Andersen	.05	.04	.02
68	Jose Cano	.10	.08	.04
69	Dan Schatzeder	.05	.04	.02
70	Jim Deshaies	.05	.04	.02
71	Mike Scott	.06	.05	.02
72	Gerald Young	.05	.04	.02
73	Ken Caminiti	.05	.04	.02
74	Ken Oberkfell	.05	.04	.02
75	Dave Rhode	.20	.15	.08
76	Bill Doran	.06	.05	.02
77	Andujar Cedeno	.20	.15	.08
78	Craig Biggio	.08	.06	.03
79	Karl Rhodes	.15	.11	.06
80	Glenn Davis	.10	.08	.04
81	Eric Anthony	.30	.25	.12
82	John Wetteland	.20	.15	.08
83	Jay Howell	.06	.05	.02
84	Orel Hershiser	.10	.08	.04
85	Tim Belcher	.08	.06	.03
86	Kiki Jones	.25	.20	.10
87	Mike Hartley	.20	.15	.08
88	Ramon Martinez	.30	.25	.12
89	Mike Scioscia	.06	.05	.02
90	Willie Randolph	.06	.05	.02
91	Juan Samuel	.06	.05	.02
92	Jose Offerman	.30	.25	.12
93	Dave Hansen	.30	.25	.12
94	Jeff Hamilton	.05	.04	.02
95	Alfredo Griffin	.05	.04	.02
96	Tom Goodwin	.35	.25	.14
97	Kirk Gibson	.06	.05	.02
98	Jose Vizcaino	.20	.15	.08
99	Kal Daniels	.06	.05	.02
100	Hubie Brooks	.06	.05	.02
101	Eddie Murray	.08	.06	.03
102	Dennis Boyd	.05	.04	.02
103	Tim Burke	.06	.05	.02
104	Bill Sampen	.20	.15	.08
105	Brett Gideon	.06	.05	.02
106	Mark Gardner	.20	.15	.08
107	Howard Farmer	.15	.11	.06
108	Mel Rojas	.15	.11	.06
109	Kevin Gross	.05	.04	.02
110	Dave Schmidt	.05	.04	.02
111	Denny Martinez	.06	.05	.02
112	Jerry Goff	.10	.08	.04
113	Andres Galarraga	.08	.06	.03
114	Tim Welch	.12	.09	.05
115	Marquis Grissom	.50	.40	.20
116	Spike Owen	.05	.04	.02
117	Larry Walker	.60	.45	.25
118	Rock Raines	.08	.06	.03
119	Delino DeShields	.40	.30	.15
120	Tom Foley	.05	.04	.02
121	Dave Martinez	.05	.04	.02
122	Frank Viola	.10	.08	.04
123	Julio Valera	.15	.11	.06
124	Alejandro Pena	.05	.04	.02
125	David Cone	.08	.06	.03
126	Doc Gooden	.20	.15	.08
127	Kevin Brown	.20	.15	.08
128	John Franco	.08	.06	.03
129	Terry Bross	.25	.20	.10
130	Blaine Beatty	.20	.15	.08
131	Sid Fernandez	.08	.06	.03
132	Mike Marshall	.05	.04	.02
133	Howard Johnson	.10	.08	.04
134	Jaime Roseboro	.20	.15	.08
135	Alan Zinter	.20	.15	.08
136	Keith Miller	.06	.05	.02
137	Kevin Elster	.05	.04	.02
138	Kevin McReynolds	.06	.05	.02
139	Barry Lyons	.05	.04	.02
140	Gregg Jefferies	.25	.20	.10
141	Darryl Strawberry	.25	.20	.10
142	Todd Hundley	.25	.20	.10
143	Scott Service	.15	.11	.06
144	Chuck Malone	.15	.11	.06
145	Steve Ontiveros	.05	.04	.02
146	Roger McDowell	.06	.05	.02
147	Ken Howell	.05	.04	.02
148	Pat Combs	.15	.11	.06
149	Jeff Parrett	.05	.04	.02
150	Chuck McElroy	.15	.11	.06
151	Jason Grimsley	.15	.11	.06
152	Len Dykstra	.08	.06	.03
153	Mickey Morandini	.15	.11	.06
154	John Kruk	.05	.04	.02
155	Dickie Thon	.05	.04	.02
156	Ricky Jordan	.10	.08	.04
157	Jeff Jackson	.10	.08	.04
158	Darren Daulton	.05	.04	.02
159	Tom Herr	.05	.04	.02
160	Von Hayes	.06	.05	.02
161	Dave Hollins	.50	.40	.20
162	Carmelo Martinez	.05	.04	.02
163	Bob Walk	.05	.04	.02
164	Doug Drabek	.08	.06	.03
165	Walt Terrell	.05	.04	.02
166	Bill Landrum	.05	.04	.02
167	Scott Ruskin	.08	.06	.03
168	Bob Patterson	.05	.04	.02
169	Bobby Bonilla	.10	.08	.04
170	Jose Lind	.05	.04	.02
171	Andy Van Slyke	.08	.06	.03
172	Mike LaValliere	.05	.04	.02
173	Willie Greene	.20	.15	.08
174	Jay Bell	.06	.05	.02
175	Sid Bream	.05	.04	.02
176	Tom Prince	.05	.04	.02
177	Wally Backman	.05	.04	.02
178	Moises Alou	.40	.30	.15
179	Steve Carter	.08	.06	.03
180	Gary Redus	.05	.04	.02
181	Barry Bonds	.10	.08	.04
182	Don Slaught	.05	.04	.02
183	Joe Magrane	.06	.05	.02
184	Bryn Smith	.05	.04	.02
185	Todd Worrell	.06	.05	.02
186	Jose Deleon	.05	.04	.02
187	Frank DiPino	.05	.04	.02
188	John Tudor	.05	.04	.02
189	Howard Hilton	.10	.08	.04
190	John Ericks	.10	.08	.04
191	Ken Dayley	.05	.04	.02
192	Ray Lankford	.80	.60	.30

		MT	NR MT	EX
193	Todd Zeile	.80	.60	.30
194	Willie McGee	.06	.05	.02
195	Ozzie Smith	.10	.08	.04
196	Milt Thompson	.05	.04	.02
197	Terry Pendleton	.05	.04	.02
198	Vince Coleman	.06	.05	.02
199	Paul Coleman	.25	.20	.10
200	Jose Oquendo	.05	.04	.02
201	Pedro Guerrero	.06	.05	.02
202	Tom Brunansky	.06	.05	.02
203	Roger Smithberg	.10	.08	.04
204	Eddie Whitson	.05	.04	.02
205	Dennis Rasmussen	.05	.04	.02
206	Craig Lefferts	.05	.04	.02
207	Andy Benes	.15	.11	.06
208	Bruce Hurst	.06	.05	.02
209	Eric Show	.05	.04	.02
210	Rafael Valdez	.10	.08	.04
211	Joey Cora	.05	.04	.02
212	Thomas Howard	.20	.15	.08
213	Rob Nelson	.05	.04	.02
214	Jack Clark	.06	.05	.02
215	Garry Templeton	.05	.04	.02
216	Fred Lynn	.05	.04	.02
217	Tony Gwynn	.08	.06	.03
218	Benny Santiago	.08	.06	.03
219	Mike Pagliarulo	.05	.04	.02
220	Joe Carter	.08	.06	.03
221	Roberto Alomar	.08	.06	.03
222	Bip Roberts	.05	.04	.02
223	Rick Reuschel	.05	.04	.02
224	Russ Swan	.20	.15	.08
225	Eric Gunderson	.20	.15	.08
226	Steve Bedrosian	.05	.04	.02
227	Mike Remlinger	.40	.30	.15
228	Scott Garrelts	.05	.04	.02
229	Ernie Camacho	.05	.04	.02
230	Andres Santana	.25	.20	.10
231	Will Clark	.35	.25	.14
232	Kevin Mitchell	.25	.20	.10
233	Robby Thompson	.05	.04	.02
234	Bill Bathe	.06	.05	.02
235	Tony Perezchica	.08	.06	.03
236	Gary Carter	.05	.04	.02
237	Brett Butler	.05	.04	.02
238	Matt Williams	.15	.11	.06
239	Ernie Riles	.05	.04	.02
240	Kevin Bass	.05	.04	.02
241	Terry Kennedy	.05	.04	.02
242	Steve Hosey	.30	.25	.12
243	Ben McDonald	.40	.30	.15
244	Jeff Ballard	.05	.04	.02
245	Joe Price	.05	.04	.02
246	Curt Schilling	.05	.04	.02
247	Pete Harnisch	.06	.05	.02
248	Mark Williamson	.05	.04	.02
249	Gregg Olson	.15	.11	.06
250	Chris Myers	.15	.11	.06
251	David Segui	.40	.30	.15
252	Joe Orsulak	.05	.04	.02
253	Craig Worthington	.05	.04	.02
254	Mickey Tettleton	.06	.05	.02
255	Cal Ripken, Jr.	.20	.15	.08
256	Billy Ripken	.05	.04	.02
257	Randy Milligan	.06	.05	.02
258	Brady Anderson	.05	.04	.02
259	Chris Hoiles	.40	.30	.15
260	Mike Devereaux	.05	.04	.02
261	Phil Bradley	.05	.04	.02
262	Leo Gomez	.30	.25	.12
263	Lee Smith	.06	.05	.02
264	Mike Rochford	.06	.05	.02
265	Jeff Reardon	.06	.05	.02
266	Wes Gardner	.05	.04	.02
267	Mike Boddicker	.05	.04	.02
268	Roger Clemens	.25	.20	.10
269	Rob Murphy	.05	.04	.02
270	Mickey Pina	.25	.20	.10
271	Tony Pena	.06	.05	.02
272	Jody Reed	.06	.05	.02
273	Kevin Romine	.05	.04	.02
274	Mike Greenwell	.08	.06	.03
275	Maurice Vaughn	.80	.60	.30
276	Danny Heep	.05	.04	.02
277	Scott Cooper	.40	.30	.15
278	Greg Blosser	.25	.20	.10
279	Dwight Evans	.06	.05	.02
280	Ellis Burks	.08	.06	.03
281	Wade Boggs	.10	.08	.04
282	Marty Barrett	.05	.04	.02
283	Kirk McCaskill	.06	.05	.02

		MT	NR MT	EX
284	Mark Langston	.06	.05	.02
285	Bert Blyleven	.06	.05	.02
286	Mike Fetters	.08	.06	.03
287	Kyle Abbott	.20	.15	.08
288	Jim Abbott	.10	.08	.04
289	Chuck Finley	.06	.05	.02
290	Gary DiSarcina	.15	.11	.06
291	Dick Schofield	.05	.04	.02
292	Devon White	.06	.05	.02
293	Bobby Rose	.15	.11	.06
294	Brian Downing	.05	.04	.02
295	Lance Parrish	.06	.05	.02
296	Jack Howell	.05	.04	.02
297	Claudell Washington	.05	.04	.02
298	John Orton	.06	.05	.02
299	Wally Joyner	.08	.06	.03
300	Lee Stevens	.30	.25	.12
301	Chili Davis	.05	.04	.02
302	Johnny Ray	.05	.04	.02
303	Greg Hibbard	.15	.11	.06
304	Eric King	.06	.05	.02
305	Jack McDowell	.08	.06	.03
306	Bobby Thigpen	.08	.06	.03
307	Adam Peterson	.05	.04	.02
308	Scott Radinsky	.20	.15	.08
309	Wayne Edwards	.06	.05	.02
310	Melido Perez	.06	.05	.02
311	Robin Ventura	.50	.40	.20
312	Sammy Sosa	.30	.25	.12
313	Dan Pasqua	.05	.04	.02
314	Carlton Fisk	.08	.06	.03
315	Ozzie Guillen	.08	.06	.03
316	Ivan Calderon	.08	.06	.03
317	Daryl Boston	.05	.04	.02
318	Craig Grebeck	.15	.11	.06
319	Scott Fletcher	.05	.04	.02
320	Frank Thomas	3.00	2.25	1.25
321	Steve Lyons	.05	.04	.02
322	Carlos Martinez	.10	.08	.04
323	Joe Skalski	.08	.06	.03
324	Tom Candiotti	.05	.04	.02
325	Greg Swindell	.06	.05	.02
326	Steve Olin	.15	.11	.06
327	Kevin Wickander	.08	.06	.03
328	Doug Jones	.06	.05	.02
329	Jeff Shaw	.10	.08	.04
330	Kevin Bearse	.10	.08	.04
331	Dion James	.05	.04	.02
332	Jerry Browne	.06	.05	.02
333	Albert Belle	.60	.45	.25
334	Felix Fermin	.05	.04	.02
335	Candy Maldonado	.06	.05	.02
336	Cory Snyder	.06	.05	.02
337	Sandy Alomar	.30	.25	.12
338	Mark Lewis	.12	.09	.05
339	Carlos Baerga	.40	.30	.15
340	Chris James	.05	.04	.02
341	Brook Jacoby	.06	.05	.02
342	Keith Hernandez	.06	.05	.02
343	Frank Tanana	.05	.04	.02
344	Scott Aldred	.15	.11	.06
345	Mike Henneman	.06	.05	.02
346	Steve Wapnick	.15	.11	.06
347	Greg Gohr	.15	.11	.06
348	Eric Stone	.15	.11	.06
349	Brian DuBois	.10	.08	.04
350	Kevin Ritz	.10	.08	.04
351	Rico Brogna	.10	.08	.04
352	Mike Heath	.05	.04	.02
353	Alan Trammell	.08	.06	.03
354	Chet Lemon	.06	.05	.02
355	Dave Bergman	.05	.04	.02
356	Lou Whitaker	.08	.06	.03
357	Cecil Fielder	.40	.30	.15
358	Milt Cuyler	.20	.15	.08
359	Tony Phillips	.06	.05	.02
360	Travis Fryman	1.50	1.25	.60
361	Ed Romero	.05	.04	.02
362	Lloyd Moseby	.06	.05	.02
363	Mark Gubicza	.08	.06	.03
364	Bret Saberhagen	.10	.08	.04
365	Tom Gordon	.15	.11	.06
366	Steve Farr	.05	.04	.02
367	Kevin Appier	.30	.25	.12
368	Storm Davis	.05	.04	.02
369	Mark Davis	.05	.04	.02
370	Jeff Montgomery	.06	.05	.02
371	Frank White	.06	.05	.02
372	Brent Mayne	.20	.15	.08
373	Bob Boone	.06	.05	.02
374	Jim Eisenreich	.05	.04	.02

		MT	NR MT	EX
375	Danny Tartabull	.08	.06	.03
376	Kurt Stillwell	.05	.04	.02
377	Bill Pecota	.05	.04	.02
378	Bo Jackson	.40	.30	.15
379	Bob Hamelin	.20	.15	.08
380	Kevin Seitzer	.08	.06	.03
381	Rey Palacios	.05	.04	.02
382	George Brett	.12	.09	.05
383	Gerald Perry	.05	.04	.02
384	Teddy Higuera	.08	.06	.03
385	Tom Filer	.05	.04	.02
386	Dan Plesac	.06	.05	.02
387	Cal Eldred	1.00	.70	.40
388	Jaime Navarro	.06	.05	.02
389	Chris Bosio	.05	.04	.02
390	Randy Veres	.05	.04	.02
391	Gary Sheffield	.20	.15	.08
392	George Canale	.10	.08	.04
393	B.J. Surhoff	.06	.05	.02
394	Tim McIntosh	.15	.11	.06
395	Greg Brock	.05	.04	.02
396	Greg Vaughn	.50	.40	.20
397	Darryl Hamilton	.10	.08	.04
398	Dave Parker	.10	.08	.04
399	Paul Molitor	.08	.06	.03
400	Jim Gantner	.05	.04	.02
401	Rob Deer	.05	.04	.02
402	Billy Spiers	.15	.11	.06
403	Glenn Braggs	.06	.05	.02
404	Robin Yount	.15	.11	.06
405	Rick Aguilera	.05	.04	.02
406	Johnny Ard	.15	.11	.06
407	Kevin Tapani	.25	.20	.10
408	Park Pittman	.20	.15	.08
409	Allan Anderson	.05	.04	.02
410	Juan Berenguer	.05	.04	.02
411	Willie Banks	.40	.30	.15
412	Rich Yett	.05	.04	.02
413	Dave West	.08	.06	.03
414	Greg Gagne	.05	.04	.02
415	Chuck Knoblauch	.70	.50	.30
416	Randy Bush	.05	.04	.02
417	Gary Gaetti	.08	.06	.03
418	Kent Hrbek	.08	.06	.03
419	Al Newman	.05	.04	.02
420	Danny Gladden	.05	.04	.02
421	Paul Sorrento	.15	.11	.06
422	Derek Parks	.25	.20	.10
423	Scott Leius	.20	.15	.08
424	Kirby Puckett	.20	.15	.08
425	Willie Smith	.20	.15	.08
426	Dave Righetti	.08	.06	.03
427	Jeff Robinson	.05	.04	.02
428	Alan Mills	.20	.15	.08
429	Tim Leary	.05	.04	.02
430	Pascual Perez	.05	.04	.02
431	Alvaro Espinoza	.05	.04	.02
432	Dave Winfield	.12	.09	.05
433	Jesse Barfield	.06	.05	.02
434	Randy Velarde	.05	.04	.02
435	Rick Cerone	.05	.04	.02
436	Steve Balboni	.05	.04	.02
437	Mel Hall	.05	.04	.02
438	Bob Geren	.06	.05	.02
439	Bernie Williams	.40	.30	.15
440	Kevin Maas	.40	.30	.15
441	Mike Blowers	.15	.11	.06
442	Steve Sax	.08	.06	.03
443	Don Mattingly	.35	.25	.14
444	Roberto Kelly	.08	.06	.03
445	Mike Moore	.06	.05	.02
446	Reggie Harris	.15	.11	.06
447	Scott Sanderson	.05	.04	.02
448	Dave Otto	.05	.04	.02
449	Dave Stewart	.08	.06	.03
450	Rick Honeycutt	.05	.04	.02
451	Dennis Eckersley	.08	.06	.03
452	Carney Lansford	.06	.05	.02
453	Scott Hemond	.15	.11	.06
454	Mark McGwire	.20	.15	.08
455	Felix Jose	.15	.11	.06
456	Terry Steinbach	.06	.05	.02
457	Rickey Henderson	.25	.20	.10
458	Dave Henderson	.06	.05	.02
459	Mike Gallego	.05	.04	.02
460	Jose Canseco	.50	.40	.20
461	Walt Weiss	.06	.05	.02
462	Ken Phelps	.05	.04	.02
463	Darren Lewis	.40	.30	.15
464	Ron Hassey	.05	.04	.02
465	Roger Salkeld	.30	.25	.12

		MT	NR MT	EX
466	Scott Bankhead	.06	.05	.02
467	Keith Comstock	.05	.04	.02
468	Randy Johnson	.10	.08	.04
469	Erik Hanson	.10	.08	.04
470	Mike Schooler	.06	.05	.02
471	Gary Eave	.15	.11	.06
472	Jeffrey Leonard	.06	.05	.02
473	Dave Valle	.05	.04	.02
474	Omar Vizquel	.05	.04	.02
475	Pete O'Brien	.05	.04	.02
476	Henry Cotto	.05	.04	.02
477	Jay Buhner	.06	.05	.02
478	Harold Reynolds	.06	.05	.02
479	Alvin Davis	.08	.06	.03
480	Darnell Coles	.05	.04	.02
481	Ken Griffey, Jr.	1.50	1.25	.60
482	Greg Briley	.12	.09	.05
483	Scott Bradley	.05	.04	.02
484	Tino Martinez	.40	.30	.15
485	Jeff Russell	.06	.05	.02
486	Nolan Ryan	.40	.30	.15
487	Robb Nen	.20	.15	.08
488	Kevin Brown	.06	.05	.02
489	Brian Bohanon	.20	.15	.08
490	Ruben Sierra	.15	.11	.06
491	Pete Incaviglia	.06	.05	.02
492	Juan Gonzalez	2.00	1.50	.80
493	Steve Buechele	.05	.04	.02
494	Scott Coolbaugh	.15	.11	.06
495	Geno Petralli	.05	.04	.02
496	Rafael Palmeiro	.08	.06	.03
497	Julio Franco	.08	.06	.03
498	Gary Pettis	.05	.04	.02
499	Donald Harris	.20	.15	.08
500	Monty Fariss	.20	.15	.08
501	Harold Baines	.08	.06	.03
502	Cecil Espy	.05	.04	.02
503	Jack Daugherty	.08	.06	.03
504	Willie Blair	.15	.11	.06
505	Dave Steib	.06	.05	.02
506	Tom Henke	.06	.05	.02
507	John Cerutti	.05	.04	.02
508	Paul Kilgus	.05	.04	.02
509	Jimmy Key	.06	.05	.02
510	John Olerud	1.00	.70	.40
511	Ed Sprague	.25	.20	.10
512	Manny Lee	.05	.04	.02
513	Fred McGriff	.08	.06	.03
514	Glenallen Hill	.10	.08	.04
515	George Bell	.08	.06	.03
516	Mookie Wilson	.06	.05	.02
517	Luis Sojo	.15	.11	.06
518	Nelson Liriano	.05	.04	.02
519	Kelly Gruber	.08	.06	.03
520	Greg Myers	.06	.05	.02
521	Pat Borders	.06	.05	.02
522	Junior Felix	.25	.20	.10
523	Eddie Zosky	.25	.20	.10
524	Tony Fernandez	.06	.05	.02
525	Checklist	.05	.04	.02
526	Checklist	.05	.04	.02
527	Checklist	.05	.04	.02
528	Checklist	.05	.04	.02

1990 Bowman Inserts

Bowman inserted sweepstakes cards in its 1990 packs, much like in 1989. This 11-card set features current players displayed in drawings by Craig Pursley.

		MT	NR MT	EX
Complete Set:		1.00	.70	.40
Common Player:		.06	.05	.02
(1)	Will Clark	.10	.08	.04
(2)	Mark Davis	.06	.05	.02
(3)	Dwight Gooden	.08	.06	.03
(4)	Bo Jackson	.08	.06	.03
(5)	Don Mattingly	.08	.06	.03
(6)	Kevin Mitchell	.08	.06	.03
(7)	Gregg Olson	.08	.06	.03
(8)	Nolan Ryan	.15	.11	.06
(9)	Bret Saberhagen	.08	.06	.03
(10)	Jerome Walton	.06	.05	.02
(11)	Robin Yount	.10	.08	.04

1991 Bowman

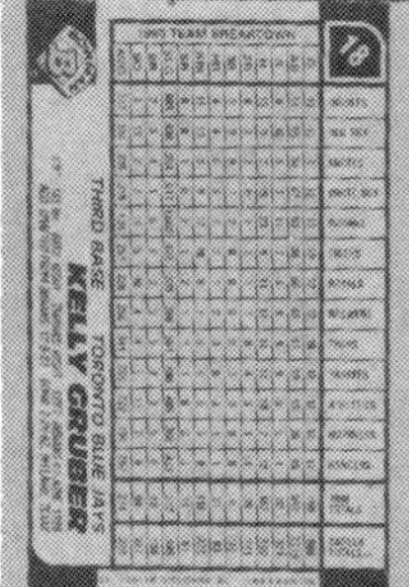

The 1991 Bowman set features 704 cards compared to 528 cards in the 1990 issue. The cards imitate the 1953 Bowman style. Special Rod Carew cards and gold foil-stamped cards are included. The set is numbered by teams. Like the 1989 and 1990 issues, the card backs feature a breakdown of performance against each other team in the league.

		MT	NR MT	EX
Complete Set (704):		15.00	11.00	6.00
Common Player:		.05	.04	.02
1	Rod Carew-I	.08	.06	.03
2	Rod Carew-II	.08	.06	.03
3	Rod Carew-III	.08	.06	.03
4	Rod Carew-IV	.08	.06	.03
5	Rod Carew-V	.08	.06	.03
6	Willie Fraser	.05	.04	.02
7	John Olerud	.30	.25	.12
8	William Suero	.10	.08	.04
9	Roberto Alomar	.20	.15	.08
10	Todd Stottlemyre	.06	.05	.02
11	Joe Carter	.12	.09	.05
12	Steve Karsay	.35	.25	.14
13	Mark Whiten	.20	.15	.08
14	Pat Borders	.05	.04	.02
15	Mike Timlin	.08	.06	.03
16	Tom Henke	.06	.05	.02
17	Eddie Zosky	.08	.06	.03
18	Kelly Gruber	.08	.06	.03
19	Jimmy Key	.06	.05	.02
20	Jerry Schunk	.12	.09	.05
21	Manny Lee	.05	.04	.02
22	Dave Steib	.08	.06	.03
23	Pat Hentgen	1.00	.70	.40
24	Glenallen Hill	.08	.06	.03
25	Rene Gonzales	.05	.04	.02
26	Ed Sprague	.15	.11	.06
27	Ken Dayley	.05	.04	.02
28	Pat Tabler	.05	.04	.02
29	*Denis Boucher*	.12	.09	.05
30	Devon White	.08	.06	.03
31	Dante Bichette	.05	.04	.02
32	Paul Molitor	.12	.09	.05
33	Greg Vaughn	.10	.08	.04
34	Dan Plesac	.05	.04	.02
35	Chris George	.10	.08	.04
36	Tim McIntosh	.08	.06	.03
37	Franklin Stubbs	.05	.04	.02
38	Bo Dodson	.15	.11	.06
39	Ron Robinson	.05	.04	.02
40	Ed Nunez	.05	.04	.02
41	Greg Brock	.05	.04	.02
42	Jaime Navarro	.06	.05	.02
43	Chris Bosio	.05	.04	.02
44	B.J. Surhoff	.06	.05	.02
45	Chris Johnson	.12	.09	.05
46	Willie Randolph	.06	.05	.02
47	Narciso Elvira	.10	.08	.04
48	Jim Gantner	.05	.04	.02
49	Kevin Brown	.05	.04	.02
50	Julio Machado	.05	.04	.02
51	Chuck Crim	.05	.04	.02
52	Gary Sheffield	.20	.15	.08
53	Angel Miranda	.25	.20	.10
54	Teddy Higuera	.06	.05	.02
55	Robin Yount	.10	.08	.04
56	Cal Eldred	.20	.15	.08
57	Sandy Alomar	.08	.06	.03
58	Greg Swindell	.06	.05	.02
59	Brook Jacoby	.06	.05	.02
60	Efrain Valdez	.08	.06	.03
61	Ever Magallanes	.10	.08	.04
62	Tom Candiotti	.05	.04	.02
63	Eric King	.05	.04	.02
64	Alex Cole	.05	.04	.02
65	Charles Nagy	.12	.09	.05
66	Mitch Webster	.05	.04	.02
67	Chris James	.05	.04	.02
68	Jim Thome	.40	.30	.15
69	Carlos Baerga	.20	.15	.08
70	Mark Lewis	.08	.06	.03
71	Jerry Browne	.05	.04	.02
72	Jesse Orosco	.05	.04	.02
73	Mike Huff	.06	.05	.02
74	Jose Escobar	.12	.09	.05
75	Jeff Manto	.06	.05	.02
76	*Turner Ward*	.10	.08	.04
77	Doug Jones	.05	.04	.02
78	*Bruce Egloff*	.12	.09	.05
79	Tim Costo	.20	.15	.08
80	Beau Allred	.06	.05	.02
81	Albert Belle	.30	.25	.12
82	John Farrell	.05	.04	.02
83	Glenn Davis	.08	.06	.03
84	Joe Orsulak	.05	.04	.02
85	Mark Williamson	.05	.04	.02
86	Ben McDonald	.12	.09	.05
87	Billy Ripken	.05	.04	.02
88	Leo Gomez	.08	.06	.03
89	Bob Melvin	.05	.04	.02
90	Jeff Robinson	.05	.04	.02
91	Jose Mesa	.05	.04	.02
92	Gregg Olson	.08	.06	.03
93	Mike Devereaux	.06	.05	.02
94	Luis Mercedes	.20	.15	.08
95	*Arthur Rhodes*	.20	.15	.08
96	Juan Bell	.05	.04	.02
97	Mike Mussina	1.25	.90	.50
98	Jeff Ballard	.05	.04	.02
99	Chris Hoiles	.12	.09	.05
100	Brady Anderson	.05	.04	.02
101	Bob Milacki	.05	.04	.02
102	David Segui	.06	.05	.02
103	Dwight Evans	.06	.05	.02
104	Cal Ripken, Jr.	.25	.20	.10
105	Mike Linskey	.12	.09	.05
106	*Jeff Tackett*	.12	.09	.05
107	Jeff Reardon	.08	.06	.03
108	Dana Kiecker	.05	.04	.02
109	Ellis Burks	.08	.06	.03
110	Dave Owen	.12	.09	.05
111	Danny Darwin	.05	.04	.02
112	Mo Vaughn	.50	.40	.20
113	Jeff McNeely	.25	.20	.10
114	Tom Bolton	.05	.04	.02
115	Greg Blosser	.12	.09	.05
116	Mike Greenwell	.10	.08	.04
117	Phil Plantier	.60	.45	.25
118	Roger Clemens	.15	.11	.06
119	John Marzano	.05	.04	.02
120	Jody Reed	.06	.05	.02
121	Scott Taylor	.12	.09	.05
122	Jack Clark	.06	.05	.02
123	Derek Livernois	.12	.09	.05
124	Tony Pena	.05	.04	.02
125	Tom Brunansky	.05	.04	.02
126	Carlos Quintana	.05	.04	.02
127	Tim Naehring	.10	.08	.04
128	Matt Young	.05	.04	.02

		MT	NR MT	EX
129	Wade Boggs	.12	.09	.05
130	Kevin Morton	.15	.11	.06
131	Pete Incaviglia	.05	.04	.02
132	Rob Deer	.05	.04	.02
133	Bill Gullickson	.05	.04	.02
134	Rico Brogna	.12	.09	.05
135	Lloyd Moseby	.05	.04	.02
136	Cecil Fielder	.15	.11	.06
137	Tony Phillips	.05	.04	.02
138	Mark Leiter	.05	.04	.02
139	John Cerutti	.05	.04	.02
140	Mickey Tettleton	.06	.05	.02
141	Milt Cuyler	.10	.08	.04
142	Greg Gohr	.10	.08	.04
143	Tony Bernazard	.05	.04	.02
144	Dan Gakeler	.12	.09	.05
145	Travis Fryman	.50	.40	.20
146	Dan Petry	.05	.04	.02
147	Scott Aldred	.08	.06	.03
148	John DeSilva	.12	.09	.05
149	Rusty Meacham	.12	.09	.05
150	Lou Whitaker	.06	.05	.02
151	Dave Haas	.06	.05	.02
152	Luis de los Santos	.05	.04	.02
153	Ivan Cruz	.12	.09	.05
154	Alan Trammell	.08	.06	.03
155	Pat Kelly	.15	.11	.06
156	Carl Everett	.35	.25	.14
157	Greg Cadaret	.05	.04	.02
158	Kevin Maas	.15	.11	.06
159	Jeff Johnson	.15	.11	.06
160	Willie Smith	.15	.11	.06
161	Gerald Williams	.20	.15	.08
162	Mike Humphreys	.15	.11	.06
163	Alvaro Espinoza	.05	.04	.02
164	Matt Nokes	.05	.04	.02
165	Wade Taylor	.12	.09	.05
166	Roberto Kelly	.08	.06	.03
167	John Habyan	.05	.04	.02
168	Steve Farr	.05	.04	.02
169	Jesse Barfield	.05	.04	.02
170	Steve Sax	.06	.05	.02
171	Jim Leyritz	.05	.04	.02
172	Robert Eenhoorn	.15	.11	.06
173	Bernie Williams	.15	.11	.06
174	Scott Lusader	.05	.04	.02
175	Torey Lovullo	.08	.06	.03
176	Chuck Cary	.05	.04	.02
177	Scott Sanderson	.05	.04	.02
178	Don Mattingly	.15	.11	.06
179	Mel Hall	.06	.05	.02
180	Juan Gonzalez	.70	.50	.30
181	Hensley Meulens	.08	.06	.03
182	Jose Offerman	.15	.11	.06
183	Jeff Bagwell	1.25	.90	.50
184	Jeff Conine	.30	.25	.12
185	Henry Rodriguez	.25	.20	.10
186	Jimmie Reese	.15	.11	.06
187	Kyle Abbott	.10	.08	.04
188	Lance Parrish	.06	.05	.02
189	Rafael Montalvo	.12	.09	.05
190	Floyd Bannister	.05	.04	.02
191	Dick Schofield	.05	.04	.02
192	Scott Lewis	.12	.09	.05
193	Jeff Robinson	.05	.04	.02
194	Kent Anderson	.05	.04	.02
195	Wally Joyner	.10	.08	.04
196	Chuck Finley	.08	.06	.03
197	Luis Sojo	.05	.04	.02
198	Jeff Richardson	.08	.06	.03
199	Dave Parker	.08	.06	.03
200	Jim Abbott	.12	.09	.05
201	Junior Felix	.06	.05	.02
202	Mark Langston	.08	.06	.03
203	Tim Salmon	2.00	1.50	.80
204	Cliff Young	.08	.06	.03
205	Scott Bailes	.05	.04	.02
206	Bobby Rose	.06	.05	.02
207	Gary Gaetti	.06	.05	.02
208	Ruben Amaro	.12	.09	.05
209	Luis Polonia	.06	.05	.02
210	Dave Winfield	.10	.08	.04
211	Bryan Harvey	.06	.05	.02
212	Mike Moore	.05	.04	.02
213	Rickey Henderson	.15	.11	.06
214	Steve Chitren	.15	.11	.06
215	Bob Welch	.06	.05	.02
216	Terry Steinbach	.06	.05	.02
217	Ernie Riles	.05	.04	.02
218	Todd Van Poppel	.60	.45	.25
219	Mike Gallego	.05	.04	.02
220	Curt Young	.05	.04	.02
221	Todd Burns	.05	.04	.02
222	Vance Law	.05	.04	.02
223	Eric Show	.05	.04	.02
224	*Don Peters*	.15	.11	.06
225	Dave Stewart	.10	.08	.04
226	Dave Henderson	.06	.05	.02
227	Jose Canseco	.15	.11	.06
228	Walt Weiss	.06	.05	.02
229	Dann Howitt	.06	.05	.02
230	Willie Wilson	.05	.04	.02
231	Harold Baines	.06	.05	.02
232	Scott Hemond	.06	.05	.02
233	Joe Slusarski	.12	.09	.05
234	Mark McGwire	.15	.11	.06
235	*Kirk Dressendorfer*	.12	.09	.05
236	*Craig Paquette*	.20	.15	.08
237	Dennis Eckersley	.10	.08	.04
238	Dana Allison	.12	.09	.05
239	Scott Bradley	.05	.04	.02
240	Brian Holman	.06	.05	.02
241	Mike Schooler	.06	.05	.02
242	Rich Delucia	.12	.09	.05
243	Edgar Martinez	.08	.06	.03
244	Henry Cotto	.05	.04	.02
245	Omar Vizquel	.05	.04	.02
246	Ken Griffey, Jr.	.70	.50	.30
247	Jay Buhner	.06	.05	.02
248	Bill Krueger	.05	.04	.02
249	Dave Fleming	.50	.40	.20
250	*Patrick Lennon*	.15	.11	.06
251	Dave Valle	.05	.04	.02
252	Harold Reynolds	.06	.05	.02
253	Randy Johnson	.08	.06	.03
254	Scott Bankhead	.06	.05	.02
255	Ken Griffey	.08	.06	.03
256	Greg Briley	.05	.04	.02
257	Tino Martinez	.12	.09	.05
258	Alvin Davis	.06	.05	.02
259	Pete O'Brien	.05	.04	.02
260	Erik Hanson	.08	.06	.03
261	*Bret Boone*	.50	.40	.20
262	Roger Salkeld	.15	.11	.06
263	Dave Burba	.08	.06	.03
264	*Kerry Woodson*	.15	.11	.06
265	Julio Franco	.08	.06	.03
266	Dan Peltier	.20	.15	.08
267	Jeff Russell	.05	.04	.02
268	Steve Buechele	.06	.05	.02
269	Donald Harris	.12	.09	.05
270	Robb Nen	.10	.08	.04
271	Rich Gossage	.06	.05	.02
272	Ivan Rodriguez	1.00	.70	.40
273	Jeff Huson	.06	.05	.02
274	Kevin Brown	.06	.05	.02
275	*Dan Smith*	.15	.11	.06
276	Gary Pettis	.05	.04	.02
277	Jack Daugherty	.05	.04	.02
278	Mike Jeffcoat	.05	.04	.02
279	Brad Arnsbarg	.06	.05	.02
280	Nolan Ryan	.50	.40	.20
281	Eric McCray	.12	.09	.05
282	Scott Chiamparino	.08	.06	.03
283	Ruben Sierra	.15	.11	.06
284	Geno Petralli	.05	.04	.02
285	Monty Fariss	.08	.06	.03
286	Rafael Palmeiro	.12	.09	.05
287	Bobb Witt	.06	.05	.02
288	Dean Palmer	.25	.20	.10
289	Tony Scruggs	.12	.09	.05
290	Kenny Rogers	.05	.04	.02
291	Bret Saberhagen	.08	.06	.03
292	Brian McRae	.25	.20	.10
293	Storm Davis	.05	.04	.02
294	Danny Tartabull	.08	.06	.03
295	David Howard	.12	.09	.05
296	Mike Boddicker	.06	.05	.02
297	Joel Johnston	.12	.09	.05
298	Tim Spehr	.15	.11	.06
299	Hector Wagner	.12	.09	.05
300	George Brett	.12	.09	.05
301	Mike Macfarlane	.06	.05	.02
302	Kirk Gibson	.06	.05	.02
303	Harvey Pulliam	.15	.11	.06
304	Jim Eisenreich	.05	.04	.02
305	Kevin Seitzer	.06	.05	.02
306	Mark Davis	.05	.04	.02
307	Kurt Stillwell	.05	.04	.02
308	Jeff Montgomery	.06	.05	.02
309	Kevin Appier	.06	.05	.02
310	Bob Hamelin	.10	.08	.04

		MT	NR MT	EX
311	Tom Gordon	.06	.05	.02
312	*Kerwin Moore*	.15	.11	.06
313	Hugh Walker	.12	.09	.05
314	Terry Shumpert	.05	.04	.02
315	Warren Cromartie	.05	.04	.02
316	Gary Thurman	.05	.04	.02
317	Steve Bedrosian	.05	.04	.02
318	Danny Gladden	.05	.04	.02
319	Jack Morris	.08	.06	.03
320	Kirby Puckett	.20	.15	.08
321	Kent Hrbek	.08	.06	.03
322	Kevin Tapani	.08	.06	.03
323	Denny Neagle	.12	.09	.05
324	Rich Garces	.12	.09	.05
325	Larry Casian	.10	.08	.04
326	Shane Mack	.08	.06	.03
327	Allan Anderson	.05	.04	.02
328	Junior Ortiz	.05	.04	.02
329	*Paul Abbott*	.10	.08	.04
330	Chuck Knoblauch	.20	.15	.08
331	Chili Davis	.08	.06	.03
332	*Todd Ritchie*	.15	.11	.06
333	Brian Harper	.06	.05	.02
334	Rick Aguilera	.06	.05	.02
335	Scott Erickson	.15	.11	.06
336	Pedro Munoz	.12	.09	.05
337	Scott Leuis	.10	.08	.04
338	Greg Gagne	.05	.04	.02
339	Mike Pagliarulo	.05	.04	.02
340	Terry Leach	.05	.04	.02
341	Willie Banks	.10	.08	.04
342	Bobby Thigpen	.06	.05	.02
343	Roberto Hernandez	.25	.20	.10
344	Melido Perez	.05	.04	.02
345	Carlton Fisk	.10	.08	.04
346	*Norberto Martin*	.12	.09	.05
347	*Johnny Ruffin*	.15	.11	.06
348	*Jeff Carter*	.12	.09	.05
349	Lance Johnson	.05	.04	.02
350	Sammy Sosa	.10	.08	.04
351	Alex Fernandez	.40	.30	.15
352	Jack McDowell	.10	.08	.04
353	Bob Wickman	.40	.30	.15
354	Wilson Alvarez	.15	.11	.06
355	Charlie Hough	.05	.04	.02
356	Ozzie Guillen	.06	.05	.02
357	Cory Snyder	.05	.04	.02
358	Robin Ventura	.15	.11	.06
359	Scott Fletcher	.05	.04	.02
360	Cesar Bernhardt	.12	.09	.05
361	Dan Pasqua	.05	.04	.02
362	Tim Raines	.08	.06	.03
363	Brian Drahman	.12	.09	.05
364	Wayne Edwards	.05	.04	.02
365	Scott Radinsky	.06	.05	.02
366	Frank Thomas	1.50	1.25	.60
367	Cecil Fielder	.10	.08	.04
368	Julio Franco	.10	.08	.04
369	Kelly Gruber	.08	.06	.03
370	Alan Trammell	.08	.06	.03
371	Rickey Henderson	.10	.08	.04
372	Jose Canseco	.10	.08	.04
373	Ellis Burks	.08	.06	.03
374	Lance Parrish	.06	.05	.02
375	Dave Parker	.08	.06	.03
376	Eddie Murray	.08	.06	.03
377	Ryne Sandberg	.12	.09	.05
378	Matt Williams	.10	.08	.04
379	Barry Larkin	.08	.06	.03
380	Barry Bonds	.15	.11	.06
381	Bobby Bonilla	.10	.08	.04
382	Darryl Strawberry	.10	.08	.04
383	Benny Santiago	.06	.05	.02
384	Don Robinson	.05	.04	.02
385	Paul Coleman	.10	.08	.04
386	Milt Thompson	.05	.04	.02
387	Lee Smith	.06	.05	.02
388	Ray Lankford	.15	.11	.06
389	Tom Pagnozzi	.06	.05	.02
390	Ken Hill	.06	.05	.02
391	Jamie Moyer	.05	.04	.02
392	*Greg Carmona*	.12	.09	.05
393	John Ericks	.10	.08	.04
394	Bob Tewksbury	.05	.04	.02
395	Jose Oquendo	.05	.04	.02
396	Rheal Cormier	.15	.11	.06
397	*Mike Milchin*	.12	.09	.05
398	Ozzie Smith	.10	.08	.04
399	Aaron Holbert	.15	.11	.06
400	Jose DeLeon	.05	.04	.02
401	Felix Jose	.08	.06	.03

		MT	NR MT	EX
402	Juan Agosto	.05	.04	.02
403	Pedro Guerrero	.08	.06	.03
404	Todd Zeile	.08	.06	.03
405	Gerald Perry	.05	.04	.02
406	Not issued			
407	Bryn Smith	.05	.04	.02
408	Bernard Gilkey	.20	.15	.08
409	Rex Hudler	.05	.04	.02
410a	Thomson/Branca	.10	.08	.04
410b	Donovan Osborne	.25	.20	.10
411	Lance Dickson	.15	.11	.06
412	Danny Jackson	.05	.04	.02
413	Jerome Walton	.06	.05	.02
414	Sean Cheetham	.12	.09	.05
415	Joe Girardi	.05	.04	.02
416	Ryne Sandberg	.20	.15	.08
417	Mike Harkey	.06	.05	.02
418	George Bell	.08	.06	.03
419	*Rick Wilkins*	.30	.25	.12
420	Earl Cunningham	.06	.05	.02
421	Heathcliff Slocumb	.12	.09	.05
422	Mike Bielecki	.05	.04	.02
423	*Jessie Hollins*	.12	.09	.05
424	Shawon Dunston	.06	.05	.02
425	Dave Smith	.05	.04	.02
426	Greg Maddux	.10	.08	.04
427	Jose Vizcaino	.05	.04	.02
428	Luis Salazar	.05	.04	.02
429	Andre Dawson	.10	.08	.04
430	Rick Sutcliffe	.05	.04	.02
431	Paul Assenmacher	.05	.04	.02
432	Erik Pappas	.12	.09	.05
433	Mark Grace	.10	.08	.04
434	Denny Martinez	.06	.05	.02
435	Marquis Grissom	.12	.09	.05
436	*Wil Cordero*	.35	.25	.14
437	Tim Wallach	.06	.05	.02
438	*Brian Barnes*	.15	.11	.06
439	Barry Jones	.05	.04	.02
440	Ivan Calderon	.08	.06	.03
441	*Stan Spencer*	.12	.09	.05
442	Larry Walker	.10	.08	.04
443	*Chris Haney*	.12	.09	.05
444	Hector Rivera	.12	.09	.05
445	Delino DeShields	.12	.09	.05
446	Andres Galarraga	.06	.05	.02
447	Gilberto Reyes	.06	.05	.02
448	Willie Greene	.10	.08	.04
449	Greg Colbrunn	.12	.09	.05
450	Rondell White	.75	.60	.30
451	Steve Frey	.06	.05	.02
452	*Shane Andrews*	.15	.11	.06
453	Mike Fitzgerald	.05	.04	.02
454	Spike Owen	.05	.04	.02
455	Dave Martinez	.05	.04	.02
456	Dennis Boyd	.05	.04	.02
457	Eric Bullock	.06	.05	.02
458	*Reid Cornelius*	.15	.11	.06
459	Chris Nabholz	.15	.11	.06
460	David Cone	.08	.06	.03
461	Hubie Brooks	.06	.05	.02
462	Sid Fernandez	.06	.05	.02
463	*Doug Simons*	.10	.08	.04
464	Howard Johnson	.10	.08	.04
465	Chris Donnels	.15	.11	.06
466	Anthony Young	.15	.11	.06
467	Todd Hundley	.12	.09	.05
468	Rick Cerone	.05	.04	.02
469	Kevin Elster	.05	.04	.02
470	Wally Whitehurst	.06	.05	.02
471	Vince Coleman	.08	.06	.03
472	Doc Gooden	.08	.06	.03
473	Charlie O'Brien	.05	.04	.02
474	Jeromy Burnitz	.60	.45	.25
475	John Franco	.08	.06	.03
476	Daryl Boston	.05	.04	.02
477	Frank Viola	.08	.06	.03
478	D.J. Dozier	.10	.08	.04
479	Kevin McReynolds	.06	.05	.02
480	Tom Herr	.05	.04	.02
481	Gregg Jefferies	.08	.06	.03
482	Pete Schourek	.12	.09	.05
483	Ron Darling	.06	.05	.02
484	Dave Magadan	.06	.05	.02
485	*Andy Ashby*	.10	.08	.04
486	Dale Murphy	.08	.06	.03
487	Von Hayes	.06	.05	.02
488	*Kim Batiste*	.12	.09	.05
489	*Tony Longmire*	.15	.11	.06
490	Wally Backman	.05	.04	.02
491	Jeff Jackson	.08	.06	.03

#	Player	MT	NR MT	EX
492	Mickey Morandini	.08	.06	.03
493	Darrel Akerfelds	.05	.04	.02
494	Ricky Jordan	.06	.05	.02
495	Randy Ready	.05	.04	.02
496	Darrin Fletcher	.06	.05	.02
497	Chuck Malone	.05	.04	.02
498	Pat Combs	.06	.05	.02
499	Dickie Thon	.05	.04	.02
500	Roger McDowell	.06	.05	.02
501	Len Dykstra	.06	.05	.02
502	Joe Boever	.05	.04	.02
503	John Kruk	.06	.05	.02
504	Terry Mulholland	.06	.05	.02
505	Wes Chamberlain	.20	.15	.08
506	*Mike Lieberthal*	.15	.11	.06
507	Darren Daulton	.15	.11	.06
508	Charlie Hayes	.06	.05	.02
509	John Smiley	.06	.05	.02
510	Gary Varsho	.05	.04	.02
511	Curt Wilkerson	.05	.04	.02
512	Orlando Merced	.25	.20	.10
513	Barry Bonds	.25	.20	.10
514	Mike Lavalliere	.05	.04	.02
515	Doug Drabek	.06	.05	.02
516	Gary Redus	.05	.04	.02
517	*William Pennyfeather*	.15	.11	.06
518	Randy Tomlin	.06	.05	.02
519	*Mike Zimmerman*	.12	.09	.05
520	Jeff King	.06	.05	.02
521	*Kurt Miller*	.20	.15	.08
522	Jay Bell	.06	.05	.02
523	Bill Landrum	.05	.04	.02
524	Zane Smith	.05	.04	.02
525	Bobby Bonilla	.10	.08	.04
526	Bob Walk	.05	.04	.02
527	Austin Manahan	.08	.06	.03
528	*Joe Ausanio*	.15	.11	.06
529	Andy Van Slyke	.08	.06	.03
530	Jose Lind	.05	.04	.02
531	*Carlos Garcia*	.50	.40	.20
532	Don Slaught	.05	.04	.02
533	Colin Powell	.25	.20	.10
534	*Frank Bolick*	.25	.20	.10
535	*Gary Scott*	.10	.08	.04
536	Nikco Riesgo	.10	.08	.04
537	Reggie Sanders	.60	.45	.25
538	*Tim Howard*	.10	.08	.04
539	*Ryan Bowen*	.15	.11	.06
540	Eric Anthony	.08	.06	.03
541	Jim Deshaies	.05	.04	.02
542	Tom Nevers	.12	.09	.05
543	Ken Caminiti	.05	.04	.02
544	Karl Rhodes	.12	.09	.05
545	Xavier Hernandez	.08	.06	.03
546	Mike Scott	.06	.05	.02
547	Jeff Juden	.15	.11	.06
548	Darryl Kile	.08	.06	.03
549	Willie Ansley	.10	.08	.04
550	*Luis Gonzalez*	.35	.25	.14
551	*Mike Simms*	.15	.11	.06
552	Mark Portugal	.05	.04	.02
553	Jimmy Jones	.05	.04	.02
554	Jim Clancy	.05	.04	.02
555	Pete Harnisch	.06	.05	.02
556	Craig Biggio	.08	.06	.03
557	Eric Yelding	.05	.04	.02
558	Dave Rohde	.06	.05	.02
559	Casey Candaele	.05	.04	.02
560	Curt Schilling	.05	.04	.02
561	Steve Finley	.06	.05	.02
562	Javier Ortiz	.08	.06	.03
563	Andujar Cedeno	.20	.15	.08
564	Rafael Ramirez	.05	.04	.02
565	*Kenny Lofton*	1.00	.70	.40
566	Steve Avery	.15	.11	.06
567	Lonnie Smith	.05	.04	.02
568	Kent Mercker	.06	.05	.02
569	*Chipper Jones*	1.00	.70	.40
570	Terry Pendleton	.06	.05	.02
571	Otis Nixon	.05	.04	.02
572	Juan Berenguer	.05	.04	.02
573	Charlie Leibrandt	.05	.04	.02
574	David Justice	.30	.25	.12
575	Keith Mitchell	.10	.08	.04
576	Tom Glavine	.15	.11	.06
577	Greg Olson	.05	.04	.02
578	Rafael Belliard	.05	.04	.02
579	Ben Rivera	.15	.11	.06
580	John Smoltz	.06	.05	.02
581	Tyler Houston	.05	.04	.02
582	*Mark Wohlers*	.15	.11	.06

#	Player	MT	NR MT	EX
583	Ron Gant	.12	.09	.05
584	Ramon Caraballo	.10	.08	.04
585	Sid Bream	.05	.04	.02
586	Jeff Treadway	.05	.04	.02
587	*Javier Lopez*	1.00	.70	.40
588	Deion Sanders	.20	.15	.08
589	Mike Heath	.05	.04	.02
590	*Ryan Klesko*	1.25	.90	.50
591	Bob Ojeda	.05	.04	.02
592	Alfredo Griffin	.05	.04	.02
593	*Raul Mondesi*	.40	.30	.15
594	Greg Smith	.05	.04	.02
595	Orel Hershiser	.08	.06	.03
596	Juan Samuel	.06	.05	.02
597	Brett Butler	.06	.05	.02
598	Gary Carter	.06	.05	.02
599	Stan Javier	.05	.04	.02
600	Kal Daniels	.08	.06	.03
601	*Jamie McAndrew*	.15	.11	.06
602	Mike Sharperson	.05	.04	.02
603	Jay Howell	.05	.04	.02
604	*Eric Karros*	.80	.60	.30
605	Tim Belcher	.06	.05	.02
606	Dan Opperman	.12	.09	.05
607	Lenny Harris	.05	.04	.02
608	Tom Goodwin	.10	.08	.04
609	Darryl Strawberry	.10	.08	.04
610	Ramon Martinez	.12	.09	.05
611	Kevin Gross	.05	.04	.02
612	Zakary Shinall	.12	.09	.05
613	Mike Scioscia	.05	.04	.02
614	Eddie Murray	.08	.06	.03
615	Ronnie Walden	.15	.11	.06
616	Will Clark	.20	.15	.08
617	Adam Hyzdu	.15	.11	.06
618	Matt Williams	.08	.06	.03
619	Don Robinson	.05	.04	.02
620	Jeff Brantley	.05	.04	.02
621	Greg Litton	.05	.04	.02
622	Steve Decker	.10	.08	.04
623	Robby Thompson	.06	.05	.02
624	*Mark Leonard*	.12	.09	.05
625	Kevin Bass	.05	.04	.02
626	Scott Garrelts	.05	.04	.02
627	Jose Uribe	.05	.04	.02
628	Eric Gunderson	.08	.06	.03
629	Steve Hosey	.15	.11	.06
630	Trevor Wilson	.06	.05	.02
631	Terry Kennedy	.05	.04	.02
632	Dave Righetti	.06	.05	.02
633	Kelly Downs	.05	.04	.02
634	Johnny Ard	.08	.06	.03
635	*Eric Christopherson*	.12	.09	.05
636	Kevin Mitchell	.10	.08	.04
637	John Burkett	.05	.04	.02
638	*Kevin Rogers*	.15	.11	.06
639	Bud Black	.05	.04	.02
640	Willie McGee	.06	.05	.02
641	Royce Clayton	.15	.11	.06
642	Tony Fernandez	.06	.05	.02
643	Ricky Bones	.12	.09	.05
644	Thomas Howard	.06	.05	.02
645	Dave Staton	.15	.11	.06
646	Jim Presley	.05	.04	.02
647	Tony Gwynn	.12	.09	.05
648	Marty Barrett	.05	.04	.02
649	Scott Coolbaugh	.06	.05	.02
650	Craig Lefferts	.05	.04	.02
651	Eddie Whitson	.05	.04	.02
652	Oscar Azocar	.05	.04	.02
653	Wes Gardner	.05	.04	.02
654	Bip Roberts	.06	.05	.02
655	*Robbie Beckett*	.15	.11	.06
656	Benny Santiago	.06	.05	.02
657	Greg W. Harris	.05	.04	.02
658	Jerald Clark	.06	.05	.02
659	Fred McGriff	.20	.15	.08
660	Larry Andersen	.05	.04	.02
661	Bruce Hurst	.06	.05	.02
662	Steve Martin	.12	.09	.05
663	Rafael Valdez	.06	.05	.02
664	*Paul Faries*	.10	.08	.04
665	Andy Benes	.08	.06	.03
666	Randy Myers	.06	.05	.02
667	Rob Dibble	.08	.06	.03
668	Glenn Sutko	.12	.09	.05
669	Glenn Braggs	.05	.04	.02
670	Billy Hatcher	.05	.04	.02
671	Joe Oliver	.05	.04	.02
672	Freddie Benavides	.12	.09	.05
673	Barry Larkin	.10	.08	.04

		MT	NR MT	EX
674	Chris Sabo	.08	.06	.03
675	Mariano Duncan	.05	.04	.02
676	*Chris Jones*	.15	.11	.06
677	*Gino Minutelli*	.12	.09	.05
678	Reggie Jefferson	.12	.09	.05
679	Jack Armstrong	.06	.05	.02
680	Chris Hammond	.15	.11	.06
681	Jose Rijo	.08	.06	.03
682	Bill Doran	.05	.04	.02
683	Terry Lee	.06	.05	.02
684	Tom Browning	.06	.05	.02
685	Paul O'Neill	.08	.06	.03
686	Eric Davis	.10	.08	.04
687	*Dan Wilson*	.15	.11	.06
688	Ted Power	.05	.04	.02
689	Tim Layana	.05	.04	.02
690	Norm Charlton	.06	.05	.02
691	Hal Morris	.10	.08	.04
692	Rickey Henderson	.10	.08	.04
693	*Sam Militello*	.30	.25	.12
694	*Matt Mieske*	.40	.30	.15
695	*Paul Russo*	.25	.20	.10
696	*Domingo Mota*	.12	.09	.05
697	*Todd Guggiana*	.12	.09	.05
698	Marc Newfield	.25	.20	.10
699	Checklist	.05	.04	.02
700	Checklist	.05	.04	.02
701	Checklist	.05	.04	.02
702	Checklist	.05	.04	.02
703	Checklist	.05	.04	.02
704	Checklist	.05	.04	.02

1992 Bowman

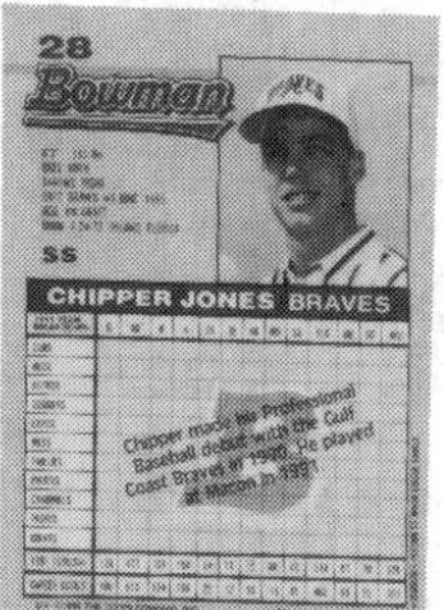

Topps introduced several changes with the release of its 1992 Bowman set. The 705-card set features 45 special insert cards stamped with gold foil. The cards are printed with a premium UV coated glossy card stock. Several players without major league experience are featured in the set. Included in this group are 1991 MVP's of the minor leagues and first round draft choices.

		MT	NR MT	EX
Complete Set (704):		400.00	300.00	150.00
Common Player:		.25	.20	.10
1	Ivan Rodriguez	4.00	3.00	1.50
2	Kirk McCaskill	.25	.20	.10
3	Scott Livingstone	.40	.30	.15
4	Salomon Torres	4.00	3.00	1.50
5	Carlos Hernandez	.25	.20	.10
6	Dave Hollins	3.00	2.25	1.25
7	Scott Fletcher	.25	.20	.10
8	Jorge Fabregas	.40	.30	.15
9	Andujar Cedeno	.50	.40	.20
10	Howard Johnson	.25	.20	.10
11	Trevor Hoffman	.60	.45	.25
12	Roberto Kelly	.25	.20	.10
13	Gregg Jefferies	.75	.60	.30
14	Marquis Grissom	1.00	.70	.40
15	Mike Ignasiak	.40	.30	.15
16	Jack Morris	.40	.30	.15
17	William Pennyfeather	.40	.30	.15
18	Todd Stottlemyre	.25	.20	.10
19	Chito Martinez	.25	.20	.10
20	Roberto Alomar	2.50	2.00	1.00
21	Sam Militello	1.00	.70	.40
22	Hector Fajardo	.30	.25	.12
23	Paul Quantrill	.80	.60	.30
24	Chuck Knoblauch	1.00	.70	.40
25	Reggie Jefferson	1.00	.70	.40
26	Jeremy McGarity	.40	.30	.15
27	Jerome Walton	.25	.20	.10
28	Chipper Jones	7.50	5.75	3.00
29	Brian Barber	2.00	1.50	.80
30	Ron Darling	.25	.20	.10
31	Robert Petagine	1.00	.70	.40
32	Chuck Finley	.25	.20	.10
33	Edgar Martinez	.40	.30	.15
34	Napolean Robinson	.40	.30	.15
35	Andy Van Slyke	.25	.20	.10
36	Bobby Thigpen	.25	.20	.10
37	Travis Fryman	4.00	3.00	1.50
38	Eric Christopherson	.40	.30	.15
39	Terry Mulholland	.25	.20	.10
40	Darryl Strawberry	.40	.30	.15
41	Manny Alexander	.60	.45	.25
42	Tracey Sanders	.60	.45	.25
43	Pete Incaviglia	.25	.20	.10
44	Kim Batiste	.40	.30	.15
45	Frank Rodriguez	1.25	.90	.50
46	Greg Swindell	.25	.20	.10
47	Delino DeShields	.75	.60	.30
48	John Ericks	.25	.20	.10
49	Franklin Stubbs	.25	.20	.10
50	Tony Gwynn	.75	.60	.30
51	Clifton Garrett	.50	.40	.20
52	Mike Gardella	.30	.25	.12
53	Scott Erickson	.40	.30	.15
54	Gary Caballo	.40	.30	.15
55	Jose Oliva	.80	.60	.30
56	Brook Fordyce	.40	.30	.15
57	Mark Whiten	.75	.60	.30
58	Joe Slusarski	.25	.20	.10
59	J.R. Phillips	2.50	2.00	1.00
60	Barry Bonds	4.00	3.00	1.50
61	Bob Milacki	.25	.20	.10
62	Keith Mitchell	.40	.30	.15
63	Angel Miranda	.40	.30	.15
64	Raul Mondesi	2.00	1.50	.80
65	Brian Koelling	.40	.30	.15
66	Brian McRae	.60	.45	.25
67	John Patterson	.30	.25	.12
68	John Wetteland	.25	.20	.10
69	Wilson Alvarez	.75	.60	.30
70	Wade Boggs	.75	.60	.30
71	Darryl Ratliff	.30	.25	.12
72	Jeff Jackson	.40	.30	.15
73	Jeremy Hernandez	.40	.30	.15
74	Darryl Hamilton	.25	.20	.10
75	Rafael Belliard	.25	.20	.10
76	Ricky Trlicek	.30	.25	.12
77	Felipe Crespo	.80	.60	.30
78	Carney Lansford	.25	.20	.10
79	Ryan Long	.60	.45	.25
80	Kirby Puckett	3.00	2.25	1.25
81	Earl Cunningham	.25	.20	.10
82	Pedro Martinez	1.00	.70	.40
83	Scott Hatteberg	.50	.40	.20
84	Juan Gonzalez	10.00	7.50	4.00
85	Robert Nutting	.40	.30	.15
86	Calvin Reese	.50	.40	.20
87	Dave Silvestri	.40	.30	.15
88	Scott Ruffcorn	3.00	2.25	1.25
89	Rick Aguilera	.25	.20	.10
90	Cecil Fielder	1.25	.90	.50
91	Kirk Dressendorfer	.25	.20	.10
92	Jerry DiPoto	.40	.30	.15
93	Mike Felder	.25	.20	.10
94	Craig Paquette	.80	.60	.30
95	Elvin Paulino	.40	.30	.15
96	Donovan Osborne	2.00	1.50	.80
97	Hubie Brooks	.25	.20	.10
98	Derek Lowe	.40	.30	.15
99	David Zancanaro	.40	.30	.15
100	Ken Griffey, Jr.	10.00	7.50	4.00
101	Todd Hundley	.25	.20	.10
102	Mike Trombley	.60	.45	.25
103	Ricky Gutierrez	.80	.60	.30
104	Braulio Castillo	.40	.30	.15
105	Craig Lefferts	.25	.20	.10
106	Rick Sutcliffe	.25	.20	.10
107	Dean Palmer	2.25	1.75	.90
108	Henry Rodriguez	.40	.30	.15
109	Mark Clark	.40	.30	.15
110	Kenny Lofton	3.50	2.75	1.50
111	Mark Carreon	.25	.20	.10
112	J.T. Bruett	.40	.30	.15
113	Gerald Williams	.40	.30	.15

		MT	NR MT	EX
114	Frank Thomas	18.00	13.50	7.25
115	Kevin Reimer	.25	.20	.10
116	Sammy Sosa	2.00	1.50	.80
117	Mickey Tettleton	.25	.20	.10
118	Reggie Sanders	2.00	1.50	.80
119	Trevor Wilson	.25	.20	.10
120	Cliff Brantley	.30	.25	.12
121	Spike Owen	.25	.20	.10
122	Jeff Montgomery	.25	.20	.10
123	Alex Sutherland	.30	.25	.12
124	Brien Taylor	7.00	5.25	2.75
125	Brian Williams	.60	.45	.25
126	Kevin Seitzer	.25	.20	.10
127	Carlos Delgado	12.00	9.00	4.75
128	Gary Scott	.25	.20	.10
129	Scott Cooper	1.50	1.25	.60
130	Domingo Jean	2.00	1.50	.80
131	Pat Mahomes	.80	.60	.30
132	Mike Boddicker	.25	.20	.10
133	Roberto Hernandez	.80	.60	.30
134	Dave Valle	.25	.20	.10
135	Kurt Stillwell	.25	.20	.10
136	Brad Pennington	.80	.60	.30
137	Jermaine Swifton	.40	.30	.15
138	Ryan Hawblitzel	.80	.60	.30
139	Tito Navarro	.40	.30	.15
140	Sandy Alomar	.25	.20	.10
141	Todd Benzinger	.25	.20	.10
142	Danny Jackson	.25	.20	.10
143	Melvin Nieves	4.00	3.00	1.50
144	Jim Campanis	.30	.25	.12
145	Luis Gonzalez	.40	.30	.15
146	Dave Doorneweerd	.40	.30	.15
147	Charlie Hayes	.40	.30	.15
148	Greg Maddux	1.00	.70	.40
149	Brian Harper	.25	.20	.10
150	Brent Miller	.40	.30	.15
151	Shawn Estes	.40	.30	.15
152	Mike Williams	.60	.45	.25
153	Charlie Hough	.25	.20	.10
154	Randy Myers	.25	.20	.10
155	Kevin Young	2.50	2.00	1.00
156	Rick Wilkins	1.50	1.25	.60
157	Terry Schumpert	.25	.20	.10
158	Steve Karsay	2.00	1.50	.80
159	Gary DiSarcina	.25	.20	.10
160	Deion Sanders	1.00	.70	.40
161	Tom Browning	.25	.20	.10
162	Dickie Thon	.25	.20	.10
163	Luis Mercedes	.40	.30	.15
164	Ricardo Ingram	.40	.30	.15
165	Tavo Alavarez	1.00	.70	.40
166	Rickey Henderson	1.00	.70	.40
167	Jaime Navarro	.25	.20	.10
168	Billy Ashley	4.00	3.00	1.50
169	Phil Dauphin	.60	.45	.25
170	Ivan Cruz	.40	.30	.15
171	Harold Baines	.25	.20	.10
172	Bryan Harvey	.25	.20	.10
173	Alex Cole	.25	.20	.10
174	Curtis Shaw	.30	.25	.12
175	Matt Williams	1.00	.70	.40
176	Felix Jose	.30	.25	.12
177	Sam Horn	.25	.20	.10
178	Randy Johnson	.25	.20	.10
179	Ivan Calderon	.25	.20	.10
180	Steve Avery	2.00	1.50	.80
181	William Suero	.25	.20	.10
182	Bill Swift	.25	.20	.10
183	Howard Battle	.80	.60	.30
184	Ruben Amaro	.25	.20	.10
185	Jim Abbott	1.00	.70	.40
186	Mike Fitzgerald	.25	.20	.10
187	Bruce Hurst	.25	.20	.10
188	Jeff Juden	.60	.45	.25
189	Jeromy Burnitz	1.50	1.25	.60
190	Dave Burba	.25	.20	.10
191	Kevin Brown	.25	.20	.10
192	Patrick Lennon	.30	.25	.12
193	Jeffrey McNeely	.40	.30	.15
194	Wil Cordero	2.00	1.50	.80
195	Chili Davis	.25	.20	.10
196	Milt Cuyler	.25	.20	.10
197	Von Hayes	.25	.20	.10
198	Todd Revening	.40	.30	.15
199	Joel Johnson	.25	.20	.10
200	Jeff Bagwell	3.00	2.25	1.25
201	Alex Fernandez	2.00	1.50	.80
202	Todd Jones	.40	.30	.15
203	Charles Nagy	.40	.30	.15
204	Tim Raines	.25	.20	.10
205	Kevin Maas	.25	.20	.10
206	Julio Franco	.25	.20	.10
207	Randy Velarde	.25	.20	.10
208	Lance Johnson	.25	.20	.10
209	Scott Leius	.25	.20	.10
210	Derek Lee	.40	.30	.15
211	Joe Sondrini	.30	.25	.12
212	Royce Clayton	1.50	1.25	.60
213	Chris George	.25	.20	.10
214	Gary Sheffield	2.50	2.00	1.00
215	Mark Gubicza	.25	.20	.10
216	Mike Moore	.25	.20	.10
217	Rick Huisman	.60	.45	.25
218	Jeff Russell	.25	.20	.10
219	D.J. Dozier	.25	.20	.10
220	Dave Martinez	.25	.20	.10
221	Al Newman	.25	.20	.10
222	Nolan Ryan	6.00	4.50	2.50
223	Teddy Higuera	.25	.20	.10
224	Damon Buford	.80	.60	.30
225	Ruben Sierra	.80	.60	.30
226	Tom Nevers	.30	.25	.12
227	Tommy Greene	1.50	1.25	.60
228	Nigel Wilson	7.50	5.75	3.00
229	John DeSilva	.40	.30	.15
230	Bobby Witt	.25	.20	.10
231	Greg Cadaret	.25	.20	.10
232	John VanderWal	.50	.40	.20
233	Jack Clark	.25	.20	.10
234	Bill Doran	.25	.20	.10
235	Bobby Bonilla	.50	.40	.20
236	Steve Olin	.25	.20	.10
237	Derek Bell	2.00	1.50	.80
238	David Cone	.40	.30	.15
239	Victor Cole	.30	.25	.12
240	Rod Bolton	.60	.45	.25
241	Tom Pagnozzi	.25	.20	.10
242	Rob Dibble	.25	.20	.10
243	Michael Carter	.40	.30	.15
244	Don Peters	.30	.25	.12
245	Mike LaValliere	.25	.20	.10
246	Joe Perona	.30	.25	.12
247	Mitch Williams	.25	.20	.10
248	Jay Buhner	.50	.40	.20
249	Andy Benes	.40	.30	.15
250	Alex Ochoa	.80	.60	.30
251	Greg Blosser	1.50	1.25	.60
252	Jack Armstrong	.25	.20	.10
253	Juan Samuel	.25	.20	.10
254	Terry Pendleton	.40	.30	.15
255	Ramon Martinez	.40	.30	.15
256	Rico Brogna	.30	.25	.12
257	John Smiley	.25	.20	.10
258	Carl Everett	.60	.45	.25
259	Tim Salmon	20.00	15.00	8.00
260	Will Clark	2.00	1.50	.80
261	Ugueth Urbina	1.50	1.25	.60
262	Jason Wood	.30	.25	.12
263	Dave Magadan	.25	.20	.10
264	Dante Bichette	.50	.40	.20
265	Jose DeLeon	.25	.20	.10
266	Mike Neill	1.50	1.25	.60
267	Paul O'Neill	.25	.20	.10
268	Anthony Young	.25	.20	.10
269	Greg Harris	.25	.20	.10
270	Todd Van Poppel	.90	.70	.35
271	Pete Castellano	.60	.45	.25
272	Tony Phillips	.25	.20	.10
273	Mike Gallego	.25	.20	.10
274	Steve Cooke	1.00	.70	.40
275	Robin Ventura	1.50	1.25	.60
276	Kevin Mitchell	.40	.30	.15
277	Doug Linton	.30	.25	.12
278	Robert Eenhorn	.30	.25	.12
279	Gabe White	1.50	1.25	.60
280	Dave Stewart	.25	.20	.10
281	Mo Sanford	.30	.25	.12
282	Greg Perschke	.30	.25	.12
283	Kevin Flora	.40	.30	.15
284	Jeff Williams	.30	.25	.12
285	Keith Miller	.25	.20	.10
286	Andy Ashby	.30	.25	.12
287	Doug Dascenzo	.25	.20	.10
288	Eric Karros	2.50	2.00	1.00
289	Glenn Murray	2.50	2.00	1.00
290	Troy Percival	.40	.30	.15
291	Orlando Merced	1.00	.70	.40
292	Peter Hoy	.80	.60	.30
293	Tony Fernandez	.08	.06	.03
294	Juan Guzman	2.50	2.00	1.00
295	Jesse Barfield	.25	.20	.10

		MT	NR MT	EX
296	Sid Fernandez	.08	.06	.03
297	Scott Cepicky	.80	.60	.30
298	Garret Anderson	.80	.60	.30
299	Cal Eldred	1.75	1.25	.70
300	Ryne Sandberg	2.50	2.00	1.00
301	Jim Gantner	.25	.20	.10
302	Mariano Rivera	.80	.60	.30
303	Ron Lockett	.80	.60	.30
304	David Nied, Jose Offerman	.08	.06	.03
305	Denny Martinez	.08	.06	.03
306	Luis Ortiz	.80	.60	.30
307	David Howard	.08	.06	.03
308	Russ Springer	.40	.30	.15
309	Chris Howard	.60	.45	.25
310	Kyle Abbott	.50	.40	.20
311	Aaron Sele	12.00	9.00	4.75
312	David Justice	2.50	2.00	1.00
313	Pete O'Brien	.25	.20	.10
314	Greg Hansell	.80	.60	.30
315	Dave Winfield	1.50	1.25	.60
316	Lance Dickson	.50	.40	.20
317	Eric King	.25	.20	.10
318	Vaughn Eshelman	.80	.60	.30
319	Tim Belcher	.08	.06	.03
320	Andres Galarraga	.08	.06	.03
321	Scott Bullett	.80	.60	.30
322	Doug Strange	.08	.06	.03
323	Jerald Clark	.08	.06	.03
324	Dave Righetti	.08	.06	.03
325	Greg Hibbard	.08	.06	.03
326	Eric Dillman	.80	.60	.30
327	Shane Reynolds	.80	.60	.30
328	Chris Hammond	.08	.06	.03
329	Albert Belle	4.00	3.00	1.50
330	Rich Becker	1.00	.70	.40
331	Eddie Williams	.08	.06	.03
332	Donald Harris	.08	.06	.03
333	Dave Smith	.08	.06	.03
334	Steve Fireovoid	.80	.60	.30
335	Steve Buechele	.25	.20	.10
336	Mike Schooler	.25	.20	.10
337	Kevin McReynolds	.08	.06	.03
338	Hensley Meulens	.08	.06	.03
339	Benji Gil	3.00	2.25	1.25
340	Don Mattingly	.75	.60	.30
341	Alvin Davis	.25	.20	.10
342	Alan Mills	.25	.20	.10
343	Kelly Downs	.25	.20	.10
344	Leo Gomez	.40	.30	.15
345	Tarrik Brock	.80	.60	.30
346	Ryan Turner	1.75	1.25	.70
347	John Smoltz	.40	.30	.15
348	Bill Sampen	.25	.20	.10
349	Paul Byrd	.80	.60	.30
350	Mike Bordick	.40	.30	.15
351	Jose Lind	.08	.06	.03
352	David Wells	.25	.20	.10
353	Barry Larkin	.60	.45	.25
354	Bruce Ruffin	.25	.20	.10
355	Luis Rivera	.25	.20	.10
356	Sid Bream	.25	.20	.10
357	Julian Vasquez	.80	.60	.30
358	Jason Bere	8.50	6.50	3.50
359	Ben McDonald	.40	.30	.15
360	Scott Stahoviak	.80	.60	.30
361	Kirt Manwaring	.08	.06	.03
362	Jeff Johnson	.40	.30	.15
363	Rob Deer	.25	.20	.10
364	Tony Pena	.25	.20	.10
365	Melido Perez	.25	.20	.10
366	Clay Parker	.25	.20	.10
367	Dale Sveum	.25	.20	.10
368	Mike Scioscia	.25	.20	.10
369	Roger Salkeld	.50	.40	.20
370	Mike Stanley	.25	.20	.10
371	Jack McDowell	1.00	.70	.40
372	Tim Wallach	.25	.20	.10
373	Billy Ripken	.25	.20	.10
374	Mike Christopher	.80	.60	.30
375	Paul Molitor	.40	.30	.15
376	Dave Stieb	.08	.06	.03
377	Pedro Guerrero	.40	.30	.15
378	Russ Swan	.25	.20	.10
379	Bob Ojeda	.25	.20	.10
380	Donn Pall	.25	.20	.10
381	Eddie Zosky	.40	.30	.15
382	Darnell Coles	.25	.20	.10
383	Tom Smith	.60	.45	.25
384	Mark McGwire	.60	.45	.25
385	Gary Carter	.40	.30	.15
386	Rich Amarel	.40	.30	.15

		MT	NR MT	EX
387	Alan Embree	.60	.45	.25
388	Jonathan Hurst	.60	.45	.25
389	Bobby Jones	2.50	2.00	1.00
390	Rico Rossy	.60	.45	.25
391	Dan Smith	.60	.45	.25
392	Terry Steinbach	.08	.06	.03
393	Jon Farrell	.25	.20	.10
394	Dave Anderson	.25	.20	.10
395	Benito Santiago	.40	.30	.15
396	Mark Wohlers	.40	.30	.15
397	Mo Vaughn	2.50	2.00	1.00
398	Randy Kramer	.40	.30	.15
399	John Jaha	1.50	1.25	.60
400	Cal Ripken, Jr.	3.00	2.25	1.25
401	Ryan Bowen	.60	.45	.25
402	Tim McIntosh	.25	.20	.10
403	Bernard Gilkey	.08	.06	.03
404	Junior Felix	.08	.06	.03
405	Cris Colon	.80	.60	.30
406	Marc Newfield	3.50	2.75	1.50
407	Bernie Williams	.40	.30	.15
408	Jay Howell	.25	.20	.10
409	Zane Smith	.25	.20	.10
410	Jeff Shaw	.25	.20	.10
411	Kerry Woodson	.08	.06	.03
412	Wes Chamberlain	.40	.30	.15
413	Dave Mulicki	.80	.60	.30
414	Benny Distefano	.08	.06	.03
415	Kevin Rogers	.80	.60	.30
416	Tim Naehring	.40	.30	.15
417	Clemente Nunez	.80	.60	.30
418	Luis Sojo	.25	.20	.10
419	Kevin Ritz	.25	.20	.10
420	Omar Oliveras	.25	.20	.10
421	Manuel Lee	.25	.20	.10
422	Julio Valera	.40	.30	.15
423	Omar Vizquel	.25	.20	.10
424	Darren Burton	.60	.45	.25
425	Mel Hall	.08	.06	.03
426	Dennis Powell	.25	.20	.10
427	Lee Stevens	.08	.06	.03
428	Glenn Davis	.08	.06	.03
429	Willie Greene	1.50	1.25	.60
430	Kevin Wickander	.08	.06	.03
431	Dennis Eckersley	.40	.30	.15
432	Joe Orsulak	.25	.20	.10
433	Eddie Murray	.08	.06	.03
434	Matt Stairs	.40	.30	.15
435	Wally Joyner	.40	.30	.15
436	Rondell White	7.50	5.75	3.00
437	Rob Mauer	.40	.30	.15
438	Joe Redfield	.60	.45	.25
439	Mark Lewis	.08	.06	.03
440	Darren Daulton	.40	.30	.15
441	Mike Henneman	.08	.06	.03
442	John Cangelosi	.25	.20	.10
443	Vince Moore	1.50	1.25	.60
444	John Wehner	.08	.06	.03
445	Kent Hrbek	.08	.06	.03
446	Mark McLemore	.25	.20	.10
447	Bill Wegman	.25	.20	.10
448	Robby Thompson	.25	.20	.10
449	Mark Anthony	.60	.45	.25
450	Archi Cianfrocco	.80	.60	.30
451	Johnny Ruffin	.50	.40	.20
452	Javier Lopez	4.00	3.00	1.50
453	Greg Gohr	.60	.45	.25
454	Tim Scott	.60	.45	.25
455	Stan Belinda	.08	.06	.03
456	Darrin Jackson	.08	.06	.03
457	Chris Gardner	.50	.40	.20
458	Esteban Beltre	.40	.30	.15
459	Phil Plantier	.60	.45	.25
460	Jim Thome	3.00	2.25	1.25
461	Mike Piazza	40.00	30.00	16.00
462	Matt Sinatro	.25	.20	.10
463	Scott Servais	.40	.30	.15
464	Brian Jordan	1.75	1.25	.70
465	Doug Drabek	.40	.30	.15
466	Carl Willis	.25	.20	.10
467	Bret Barbarie	.08	.06	.03
468	Hal Morris	.08	.06	.03
469	Steve Sax	.08	.06	.03
470	Jerry Willard	.25	.20	.10
471	Dan Wilson	.80	.60	.30
472	Chris Hoiles	.60	.45	.25
473	Rheal Cormier	.08	.06	.03
474	John Morris	.25	.20	.10
475	Jeff Reardon	.08	.06	.03
476	Mark Leiter	.25	.20	.10
477	Tom Gordon	.25	.20	.10

		MT	NR MT	EX
478	Kent Bottenfield	.60	.45	.25
479	Gene Larkin	.25	.20	.10
480	Dwight Gooden	.60	.45	.25
481	B.J. Surhoff	.40	.30	.15
482	Andy Stankiewicz	.40	.30	.15
483	Tino Martinez	.40	.30	.15
484	Craig Biggio	.40	.30	.15
485	Denny Neagle	.40	.30	.15
486	Rusty Meacham	.40	.30	.15
487	Kal Daniels	.08	.06	.03
488	Dave Henderson	.08	.06	.03
489	Tim Costo	.40	.30	.15
490	Doug Davis	.60	.45	.25
491	Frank Viola	.40	.30	.15
492	Cory Snyder	.08	.06	.03
493	Chris Martin	.60	.45	.25
494	Dion James	.25	.20	.10
495	Randy Tomlin	.08	.06	.03
496	Greg Vaughn	.40	.30	.15
497	Dennis Cook	.25	.20	.10
498	Rosario Rodriguez	.25	.20	.10
499	Dave Staton	.25	.20	.10
500	George Brett	1.50	1.25	.60
501	Brian Barnes	.08	.06	.03
502	Butch Henry	.08	.06	.03
503	Harold Reynolds	.08	.06	.03
504	David Nied	5.00	3.75	2.00
505	Lee Smith	.08	.06	.03
506	Steve Chitren	.25	.20	.10
507	Ken Hill	.40	.30	.15
508	Robbie Beckett	.60	.45	.25
509	Troy Afenir	.25	.20	.10
510	Kelly Gruber	.08	.06	.03
511	Bret Boone	1.75	1.25	.70
512	Jeff Branson	.80	.60	.30
513	Mike Jackson	.25	.20	.10
514	Pete Harnisch	.08	.06	.03
515	Chad Kreuter	.25	.20	.10
516	Joe Vitko	.60	.45	.25
517	Orel Hershiser	.40	.30	.15
518	John Doherty	1.50	1.25	.60
519	Jay Bell	.40	.30	.15
520	Mark Langston	.40	.30	.15
521	Dann Howitt	.25	.20	.10
522	Bobby Reed	.40	.30	.15
523	Roberto Munoz	.60	.45	.25
524	Todd Ritchie	.25	.20	.10
525	Bip Roberts	.08	.06	.03
526	Pat Listach	1.00	.70	.40
527	Scott Brosius	.08	.06	.03
528	John Roper	.60	.45	.25
529	Phil Hiatt	4.00	3.00	1.50
530	Denny Walling	.25	.20	.10
531	Carlos Baerga	4.00	3.00	1.50
532	Manny Ramirez	8.00	6.00	3.25
533	Pat Clements	.25	.20	.10
534	Ron Gant	.75	.60	.30
535	Pat Kelly	.25	.20	.10
536	Billy Spiers	.25	.20	.10
537	Darren Reed	.40	.30	.15
538	Ken Caminiti	.08	.06	.03
539	Butch Husky	2.50	2.00	1.00
540	Matt Nokes	.25	.20	.10
541	John Kruk	.08	.06	.03
542	John Jaha (Foil)	3.00	2.25	1.25
543	Justin Thompson	.80	.60	.30
544	Steve Hosey	1.50	1.25	.60
545	Joe Kmak	.40	.30	.15
546	John Franco	.08	.06	.03
547	Devon White	.08	.06	.03
548	Elston Hansen (Foil)	1.50	1.25	.60
549	Ryan Klesko	5.00	3.75	2.00
550	Danny Tartabull	.08	.06	.03
551	Frank Thomas (Foil)	50.00	37.00	20.00
552	Kevin Tapani	.08	.06	.03
553	Willie Banks	.08	.06	.03
554	B.J. Wallace (Foil)	5.00	3.75	2.00
555	Orlando Miller	.80	.60	.30
556	Mark Smith	1.00	.70	.40
557	Tim Wallach (Foil)	.80	.60	.30
558	Bill Gullickson	.08	.06	.03
559	Derek Bell (Foil)	3.00	2.25	1.25
560	Joe Randa (Foil)	1.00	.70	.40
561	Frank Seminara	.40	.30	.15
562	Mark Gardner	.08	.06	.03
563	Rick Greene (Foil)	1.00	.70	.40
564	Gary Gaetti	.08	.06	.03
565	Ozzie Guillen	.08	.06	.03
566	Charles Nagy (Foil)	.75	.60	.30
567	Mike Milchin	.60	.45	.25
568	Ben Shelton (Foil)	.80	.60	.30

		MT	NR MT	EX
569	Chris Roberts (Foil)	2.00	1.50	.80
570	Ellis Burks	.08	.06	.03
571	Scott Scudder	.25	.20	.10
572	Jim Abbott (Foil)	1.50	1.25	.60
573	Joe Carter	1.00	.70	.40
574	Steve Finley	.40	.30	.15
575	Jim Olander (Foil)	.60	.45	.25
576	Carlos Garcia	1.00	.70	.40
577	Greg Olson	.08	.06	.03
578	Greg Swindell (Foil)	.80	.60	.30
579	Matt Williams (Foil)	1.50	1.25	.60
580	Mark Grace	1.00	.70	.40
581	Howard House (Foil)	.90	.70	.35
582	Luis Polonia	.25	.20	.10
583	Erik Hanson	.08	.06	.03
584	Salomon Torres (Foil)	3.00	2.25	1.25
585	Carlton Fisk	.40	.30	.15
586	Bret Saberhagen	.40	.30	.15
587	Chad McDonnell (Foil)	2.00	1.50	.80
588	Jimmy Key	.08	.06	.03
589	Mike MacFarlane	.08	.06	.03
590	Barry Bonds (Foil)	6.00	4.50	2.50
591	Jamie McAndrew	.80	.60	.30
592	Shane Mack	.40	.30	.15
593	Kerwin Moore	.60	.45	.25
594	Joe Oliver	.25	.20	.10
595	Chris Sabo	.08	.06	.03
596	Alex Gonzalez	5.00	3.75	2.00
597	Brett Butler	.08	.06	.03
598	Mark Hutton	.60	.45	.25
599	Andy Benes (Foil)	.80	.60	.30
600	Jose Canseco	1.00	.70	.40
601	Darryl Kile	1.50	1.25	.60
602	Matt Stairs (Foil)	1.50	1.25	.60
603	Robert Butler (Foil)	1.00	.70	.40
604	Willie McGee	.08	.06	.03
605	Jack McDowell	1.50	1.25	.60
606	Tom Candiotti	.08	.06	.03
607	Ed Martel	.60	.45	.25
608	Matt Mieske (Foil)	.80	.60	.30
609	Darrin Fletcher	.08	.06	.03
610	Rafael Palmeiro	.08	.06	.03
611	Bill Swift (Foil)	.80	.60	.30
612	Mike Mussina	7.00	5.25	2.75
613	Vince Coleman	.08	.06	.03
614	Scott Cepicky (Foil)	.80	.60	.30
615	Mike Greenwell	.08	.06	.03
616	Kevin McGehee	.60	.45	.25
617	Jeffrey Hammonds (Foil)	11.00	8.25	4.50
618	Scott Taylor	.60	.45	.25
619	Dave Otto	.25	.20	.10
620	Mark McGwire (Foil)	2.00	1.50	.80
621	Kevin Tatar	.80	.60	.30
622	Steve Farr	.25	.20	.10
623	Ryan Klesko (Foil)	5.00	3.75	2.00
625	Andre Dawson	.75	.60	.30
626	Tino Martinez (Foil)	1.50	1.25	.60
627	Chad Curtis	4.00	3.00	1.50
628	Mickey Morandini	.40	.30	.15
629	Gregg Olson (Foil)	.80	.60	.30
630	Lou Whitaker	.08	.06	.03
631	Arthur Rhodes	.60	.45	.25
632	Brandon Wilson	.80	.60	.30
633	Lance Jennings	.80	.60	.30
634	Allen Watson	4.00	3.00	1.50
635	Len Dykstra	.50	.40	.20
636	Joe Girardi	.25	.20	.10
637	Kiki Hernandez (Foil)	1.50	1.25	.60
638	Mike Hampton	.40	.30	.15
639	Al Osuna	.25	.20	.10
640	Kevin Appier	.40	.30	.15
641	Rick Helling (Foil)	2.00	1.50	.80
642	Jody Reed	.25	.20	.10
643	Ray Lankford	1.00	.70	.40
644	John Olerud	5.00	3.75	2.00
645	Paul Molitor (Foil)	2.50	2.00	1.00
646	Pat Borders	.25	.20	.10
647	Mike Morgan	.25	.20	.10
648	Larry Walker	1.50	1.25	.60
649	Pete Castellano	2.00	1.50	.80
650	Fred McGriff	1.50	1.25	.60
651	Walt Weiss	.25	.20	.10
652	Calvin Murray	4.00	3.00	1.50
653	Dave Nilsson	.60	.45	.25
654	Greg Pirkl	.80	.60	.30
655	Robin Ventura	3.00	2.25	1.25
656	Mark Portugal	.25	.20	.10
657	Roger McDowell	.25	.20	.10
658	Rick Hirtensteiner (Foil)	1.50	1.25	.60
659	Glenallen Hill	.25	.20	.10
660	Greg Gagne	.25	.20	.10

		MT	NR MT	EX
661	Charles Johnson (Foil)	6.00	4.50	2.50
662	Brian Hunter	.40	.30	.15
663	Mark Lemke	.25	.20	.10
664	Tim Belcher (Foil)	1.25	.90	.50
665	Rich DeLucia	.25	.20	.10
666	Bob Walk	.25	.20	.10
667	Joe Carter (Foil)	2.50	2.00	1.00
668	Jose Guzman	.25	.20	.10
669	Otis Nixon	.25	.20	.10
670	Phil Nevin (Foil)	8.00	6.00	3.25
671	Eric Davis	.25	.20	.10
672	Damion Easley	3.00	2.25	1.25
673	Will Clark (Foil)	3.00	2.25	1.25
674	Mark Kiefer	.30	.25	.12
675	Ozzie Smith	1.00	.70	.40
676	Manny Ramirez (Foil)	10.00	7.50	4.00
677	Gregg Olson	.25	.20	.10
678	Cliff Floyd	25.00	18.50	10.00
679	Duane Singleton	.50	.40	.20
680	Jose Rijo	.25	.20	.10
681	Willie Randolph	.25	.20	.10
682	Michael Tucker (Foil)	6.00	4.50	2.50
683	Darren Lewis	.25	.20	.10
684	Dale Murphy	.25	.20	.10
685	Mike Pagliarulo	.25	.20	.10
686	Paul Miller	.30	.25	.12
687	Mike Robertson	.40	.30	.15
688	Mike Devereaux	.25	.20	.10
689	Pedro Astacio	1.50	1.25	.60
690	Alan Trammell	.25	.20	.10
691	Roger Clemens	2.50	2.00	1.00
692	Bud Black	.25	.20	.10
693	Turk Wendell	.50	.40	.20
694	Barry Larkin (Foil)	4.00	3.00	1.50
695	Todd Zeile	.25	.20	.10
696	Pat Hentgen	4.00	3.00	1.50
697	Eddie Taubensee	.40	.30	.15
698	Guillermo Vasquez	.50	.40	.20
699	Tom Glavine	1.00	.70	.40
700	Robin Yount	1.50	1.25	.60
701	Checklist	.25	.20	.10
702	Checklist	.25	.20	.10
703	Checklist	.25	.20	.10
704	Checklist	.25	.20	.10
705	Checklist	.25	.20	.10

1993 Bowman

Bowman's 708-card 1993 set once again features a premium UV-coated glossy stock. There are also 48 special insert cards, with gold foil stamping, randomly inserted one per pack or two per jumbo pack. The foil cards, numbered 339-374 and 693-704, feature top prospects and rookie-of-the-year candidates, as do several regular cards in the set. Cards are standard size.

	MT	NR MT	EX
Complete Set (708):	130.00	97.00	52.00
Common Player:	.15	.11	.06

		MT	NR MT	EX
1	Glenn Davis	.15	.11	.06
2	*Hector Roa*	.25	.20	.10
3	*Ken Ryan*	.30	.25	.12
4	*Derek Wallace*	.50	.40	.20
5	Jorge Fabregas	.15	.11	.06
6	Joe Oliver	.15	.11	.06
7	Brandon Wilson	.25	.20	.10
8	*Mark Thompson*	.60	.45	.25
9	Tracy Sanders	.15	.11	.06
10	Rich Renteria	.15	.11	.06
11	Lou Whitaker	.15	.11	.06
12	*Brian Hunter*	.75	.60	.30
13	Joe Vitiello	.50	.40	.20
14	Eric Karros	.50	.40	.20
15	Joe Kmak	.15	.11	.06
16	Tavo Alvarez	.15	.11	.06
17	*Steve Dunn*	.60	.45	.25
18	Tony Fernandez	.15	.11	.06
19	Melido Perez	.15	.11	.06
20	Mike Lieberthal	.15	.11	.06
21	Terry Steinbach	.15	.11	.06
22	Stan Belinda	.15	.11	.06
23	Jay Bohner	.15	.11	.06
24	Allen Watson	1.50	1.25	.60
25	*Daryl Henderson*	.25	.20	.10
26	*Ray McDavid*	1.00	.70	.40
27	Shawn Green	.75	.60	.30
28	Bud Black	.15	.11	.06
29	*Sherman Obando*	.50	.40	.20
30	*Mike Hostetler*	.15	.11	.06
31	*Nate Hinchey*	.75	.60	.30
32	Randy Myers	.15	.11	.06
33	*Brian Grebeck*	.40	.30	.15
34	John Roper	.15	.11	.06
35	Larry Thomas	.40	.30	.15
36	Alex Cole	.15	.11	.06
37	*Tom Kramer*	.50	.40	.20
38	*Matt Whisenant*	.25	.20	.10
39	*Chris Gomez*	.30	.25	.12
40	Luis Gonzalez	.15	.11	.06
41	Kevin Appier	.15	.11	.06
42	*Omar Daal*	.25	.20	.10
43	Duane Singleton	.15	.11	.06
44	Bill Risley	.15	.11	.06
45	*Pat Meares*	.30	.25	.12
46	Butch Huskey	.75	.60	.30
47	Bobby Munoz	.15	.11	.06
48	Juan Bell	.15	.11	.06
49	*Scott Lydy*	.40	.30	.15
50	Dennis Moeller	.15	.11	.06
51	Marc Newfield	1.25	.90	.50
52	*Tripp Croner*	.20	.15	.08
53	Kurt Miller	.15	.11	.06
54	Jim Pena	.15	.11	.06
55	Juan Guzman	.75	.60	.30
56	Matt Williams	.20	.15	.08
57	Harold Reynolds	.15	.11	.06
58	*Donnie Elliott*	.40	.30	.15
59	*Jon Shave*	.30	.25	.12
60	*Kevin Roberson*	1.00	.70	.40
61	*Hilly Hathaway*	.75	.60	.30
63	*Kerry Taylor*	.30	.25	.12
64	Ryan Hawblitzel	.15	.11	.06
65	Glenallen Hill	.15	.11	.06
66	Ramon Martinez	.15	.11	.06
67	Travis Fryman	1.00	.70	.40
68	Tom Nevers	.15	.11	.06
69	Phil Hiatt	.75	.60	.30
70	Tim Wallach	.15	.11	.06
71	B.J. Surhoff	.15	.11	.06
72	Rondell White	2.00	1.50	.80
73	*Denny Hocking*	.25	.20	.10
74	*Mike Oquist*	.25	.20	.10
75	Paul O'Neill	.15	.11	.06
76	Willie Banks	.15	.11	.06
77	Bob Welch	.15	.11	.06
78	*Jose Sandoval*	.25	.20	.10
79	Bill Haselman	.15	.11	.06
80	Rheal Cormier	.15	.11	.06
81	Dean Palmer	.50	.40	.20
82	*Pat Gomez*	.30	.25	.12
83	Steve Karsay	1.00	.70	.40
84	*Carl Hanselman*	.30	.25	.12
85	*T.R. Lewis*	.75	.60	.30
86	Chipper Jones	2.00	1.50	.80
87	Scott Hatteberg	.20	.15	.08
88	Greg Hibbard	.15	.11	.06
89	*Lance Painter*	.30	.25	.12
90	*Chad Mottola*	3.50	2.75	1.50
91	Jason Bere	2.00	1.50	.80
92	Dante Bichette	.15	.11	.06
93	Sandy Alomar	.15	.11	.06
94	Carl Everett	.30	.25	.12
95	*Danny Bautista*	.50	.40	.20
96	Steve Finley	.15	.11	.06
97	David Cone	.15	.11	.06
98	Todd Hollandsworth	.75	.60	.30
99	Matt Mieske	.15	.11	.06
100	Larry Walker	.50	.40	.20
101	Shane Mack	.15	.11	.06
102	*Aaron Ledesma*	.40	.30	.15

		MT	NR MT	EX
103	*Andy Pettitte*	.60	.45	.25
104	Kevin Stocker	2.50	2.00	1.00
105	Mike Mobler	.30	.25	.12
106	Tony Menedez	.15	.11	.06
107	Derek Lowe	.15	.11	.06
108	Basil Shabazz	.30	.25	.12
109	Dan Smith	.15	.11	.06
110	*Scott Sanders*	.20	.15	.08
111	Todd Stottlemyre	.15	.11	.06
112	*Benji Sikonton*	.60	.45	.25
113	Rick Sutcliffe	.15	.11	.06
114	*Lee Heath*	.40	.30	.15
115	Jeff Russell	.15	.11	.06
116	*Dave Stevens*	.25	.20	.10
117	*Mark Holzemer*	.25	.20	.10
118	Tim Belcher	.15	.11	.06
119	Bobby Thigpen	.15	.11	.06
120	*Roger Bailey*	.25	.20	.10
121	*Tony Mitchell*	.25	.20	.10
122	Junior Felix	.15	.11	.06
123	*Rich Robertson*	.25	.20	.10
124	*Andy Cook*	.25	.20	.10
125	*Brian Bevil*	.25	.20	.10
126	Darryl Strawberry	.15	.11	.06
127	Cal Eldred	.30	.25	.12
128	Cliff Floyd	7.50	5.75	3.00
129	Alan Newman	.15	.11	.06
130	Howard Johnson	.15	.11	.06
131	Jim Abbott	.30	.25	.12
132	Chad McConnell	.75	.60	.30
133	*Miguel Jimenez*	1.00	.70	.40
134	*Brett Backlund*	1.00	.70	.40
135	*John Cummings*	.30	.25	.12
136	Brian Barber	.60	.45	.25
137	Rafael Palmeiro	.20	.15	.08
138	*Tim Worrell*	.30	.25	.12
139	*Jose Pett*	1.75	1.25	.70
140	Barry Bonds	1.50	1.25	.60
141	Damon Buford	.15	.11	.06
142	Jeff Blauser	.15	.11	.06
143	Frankie Rodriguez	.50	.40	.20
144	Mike Morgan	.15	.11	.06
145	Gary DeSarcina	.15	.11	.06
146	Calvin Reese	.15	.11	.06
147	Johnny Ruffin	.15	.11	.06
148	David Nied	1.50	1.25	.60
149	Charles Nagy	.15	.11	.06
150	*Mike Myers*	.30	.25	.12
151	*Kenny Carlyle*	.25	.20	.10
152	Eric Anthony	.15	.11	.06
153	Jose Lind	.15	.11	.06
154	Pedro Martinez	.20	.15	.08
155	Mark Kiefer	.15	.11	.06
156	*Tim Laker*	.30	.25	.12
157	Pat Mahomes	.15	.11	.06
158	Bobby Bonilla	.15	.11	.06
159	Domingo Jean	1.00	.70	.40
160	Darren Daulton	.15	.11	.06
161	Mark McGwire	.30	.25	.12
162	*Jason Kendall*	1.25	.90	.50
163	Desi Relaford	.25	.20	.10
164	Ozzie Canseco	.15	.11	.06
165	Rick Helling	.75	.60	.30
166	*Steve Pegues*	.30	.25	.12
167	Paul Molitor	.40	.30	.15
168	*Larry Carter*	.25	.20	.10
169	Arthur Rhodes	.15	.11	.06
170	*Damon Hollins*	.30	.25	.12
171	Frank Viola	.15	.11	.06
172	*Steve Tracheel*	.30	.25	.12
173	*J.T. Snow*	3.50	2.75	1.50
174	*Keith Gordon*	.25	.20	.10
175	Carlton Fisk	.15	.11	.06
176	*Jason Bates*	.25	.20	.10
177	*Mike Crosby*	.25	.20	.10
178	Benny Santiago	.15	.11	.06
179	Mike Moore	.15	.11	.06
180	Jeff Juden	.15	.11	.06
181	Darren Burton	.15	.11	.06
182	*Todd Williams*	.25	.20	.10
183	John Jaha	.25	.20	.10
184	*Mike Lansing*	.90	.70	.35
185	*Pedro Grifol*	.25	.20	.10
186	Vince Coleman	.15	.11	.06
187	Pat Kelly	.15	.11	.06
188	*Clemente Alvarez*	.25	.20	.10
189	Ron Darling	.15	.11	.06
190	Orlando Merced	.15	.11	.06
191	Chris Bosio	.15	.11	.06
192	*Steve Dixon*	.25	.20	.10
193	Doug Dascenzo	.15	.11	.06

		MT	NR MT	EX
194	*Ray Holbert*	.50	.40	.20
195	Howard Battle	.25	.20	.10
196	Willie McGee	.15	.11	.06
197	*John O'Donoghue*	.25	.20	.10
198	Steve Avery	.75	.60	.30
199	Greg Blosser	.30	.25	.12
200	Ryne Sandberg	1.25	.90	.50
201	Joe Grahe	.15	.11	.06
202	Dan Wilson	.15	.11	.06
203	*Domingo Martinez*	.25	.20	.10
204	Andres Galarraga	.20	.15	.08
205	*Jamie Taylor*	.25	.20	.10
206	*Darrell Whitmore*	1.50	1.25	.60
207	*Ben Blomdahl*	.25	.20	.10
208	Doug Drabek	.15	.11	.06
209	Keith Miller	.15	.11	.06
210	Billy Ashley	1.75	1.25	.70
211	*Mike Farrell*	.25	.20	.10
212	John Wetteland	.15	.11	.06
213	Randy Tomlin	.15	.11	.06
214	Sid Fernandez	.15	.11	.06
215	*Quilvio Veras*	1.00	.70	.40
216	Dave Hollins	.30	.25	.12
217	Mike Neill	.25	.20	.10
218	Andy Van Slyke	.15	.11	.06
219	Bret Boone	.50	.40	.20
220	Tom Pagnozzi	.15	.11	.06
221	*Mike Welch*	.30	.25	.12
222	Frank Seminara	.15	.11	.06
223	Ron Villone	.50	.40	.20
224	*D.J. Thielen*	.50	.40	.20
225	Cal Ripken, Jr.	1.25	.90	.50
226	*Pedro Borbon*	.30	.25	.12
227	Carlos Quintana	.15	.11	.06
228	*Tommy Shields*	.25	.20	.10
229	Tim Salmon	6.00	4.50	2.50
230	John Smiley	.15	.11	.06
231	Ellis Burks	.15	.11	.06
232	Pedro Castellano	.15	.11	.06
233	Paul Byrd	.15	.11	.06
234	Bryan Harvey	.15	.11	.06
235	Scott Livingstone	.15	.11	.06
236	*James Mouton*	1.00	.70	.40
237	Joe Randa	.25	.20	.10
238	Pedro Astacio	.60	.45	.25
239	Darryl Hamilton	.15	.11	.06
240	*Joey Eischen*	.75	.60	.30
241	*Edgar Herrera*	.30	.25	.12
242	Doc Gooden	.15	.11	.06
243	Sam Militello	.15	.11	.06
244	*Ron Blazier*	.25	.20	.10
245	Ruben Sierra	.15	.11	.06
246	Al Martin	.15	.11	.06
247	Mike Felder	.15	.11	.06
248	Bob Tewksbury	.15	.11	.06
249	Craig Lefferts	.15	.11	.06
250	Luis Lopez	.15	.11	.06
251	Devon White	.15	.11	.06
252	Will Clark	.75	.60	.30
253	Mark Smith	.50	.40	.20
254	Terry Pendleton	.15	.11	.06
255	Aaron Sele	3.50	2.75	1.50
256	*Jose Viera*	.25	.20	.10
257	Damion Easley	.20	.15	.08
258	*Rod Lofton*	.25	.20	.10
259	*Chris Snopek*	.70	.50	.30
260	*Quinton McCracken*	.30	.25	.12
261	*Mike Matthews*	.30	.25	.12
262	*Hector Carrasco*	.40	.30	.15
263	Rick Greene	.25	.20	.10
264	*Chris Bolt*	.25	.20	.10
265	George Brett	.60	.45	.25
266	*Rick Gorecki*	.75	.60	.30
267	*Francisco Gamez*	.25	.20	.10
268	Marquis Grissom	.40	.30	.15
269	Kevin Tapani	.15	.11	.06
270	Ryan Thompson	.25	.20	.10
271	Gerald Williams	.15	.11	.06
272	*Paul Fletcher*	.30	.25	.12
273	Lance Blankenship	.15	.11	.06
274	*Marty Neff*	.30	.25	.12
275	Shawn Estes	.15	.11	.06
276	*Rene Arocha*	1.50	1.25	.60
277	*Scott Eyre*	.60	.45	.25
278	Phil Plantier	.15	.11	.06
279	*Paul Spoljaric*	1.00	.70	.40
280	Chris Gahbs	.25	.20	.10
281	Harold Baines	.15	.11	.06
282	*Jose Oliva*	.30	.25	.12
283	Matt Whiteside	.40	.30	.15
284	*Brant Brown*	.75	.60	.30

		MT	NR MT	EX
285	Russ Springer	.15	.11	.06
286	Chris Sabo	.15	.11	.06
287	Ozzie Guillen	.15	.11	.06
288	*Marcus Moore*	.40	.30	.15
289	Chad Ogea	.75	.60	.30
290	Walt Weiss	.15	.11	.06
291	Brian Edmondson	.15	.11	.06
292	Jimmy Gonzalez	.15	.11	.06
293	*Danny Hiceli*	.30	.25	.12
294	Jose Offerman	.15	.11	.06
295	Greg Vaughn	.15	.11	.06
296	Frank Bolick	.15	.11	.06
297	*Mike Maksudian*	.25	.20	.10
298	John Franco	.15	.11	.06
299	Danny Tartabull	.15	.11	.06
300	Len Dykstra	.25	.20	.10
301	Bobby Witt	.15	.11	.06
302	*Trey Beamon*	1.25	.90	.50
303	Tino Martinez	.15	.11	.06
304	Aaron Holbert	.15	.11	.06
305	Juan Gonzalez	5.00	3.75	2.00
306	*Billy Hall*	.25	.20	.10
307	Duane Ward	.15	.11	.06
308	Rod Beck	.20	.15	.08
309	*Jose Mercedes*	.40	.30	.15
310	Otis Nixon	.15	.11	.06
311	*Gettys Glaze*	.25	.20	.10
312	Candy Maldonado	.15	.11	.06
313	Chad Curtis	.60	.45	.25
314	Tim Costo	.15	.11	.06
315	Mike Robertson	.15	.11	.06
316	Nigel Wilson	2.00	1.50	.80
317	*Greg McMichael*	1.00	.70	.40
318	*Scott Pose*	.30	.25	.12
319	Ivan Cruz	.15	.11	.06
320	Greg Swindell	.15	.11	.06
321	Kevin McReynolds	.15	.11	.06
322	Tom Candiotti	.15	.11	.06
323	*Bob Wishnevski*	.25	.20	.10
324	Ken Hill	.15	.11	.06
325	Kirby Puckett	1.25	.90	.50
326	*Tim Bogar*	.30	.25	.12
327	Mariano Rivera	.15	.11	.06
328	Mitch Williams	.15	.11	.06
329	Craig Paquette	.25	.20	.10
330	Jay Bell	.15	.11	.06
331	*Jose Martinez*	.75	.60	.30
332	Rob Deer	.15	.11	.06
333	Brook Fordyce	.15	.11	.06
334	Matt Nokes	.15	.11	.06
335	Derek Lee	.15	.11	.06
336	*Paul Ellis*	.25	.20	.10
337	*Desi Wilson*	.40	.30	.15
338	Roberto Alomar	1.50	1.25	.60
339	Jim Tatum (Foil)	.50	.40	.20
340	J.T. Snow (Foil)	4.00	3.00	1.50
341	Tim Salmon (Foil)	9.00	6.75	3.50
342	*Russ Davis* (Foil)	1.00	.70	.40
343	Javy Lopez (Foil)	3.00	2.25	1.25
344	*Troy O'Leary* (Foil)	1.00	.70	.40
345	*Marty Cordova* (Foil)	.75	.60	.30
346	*Bubba Smith* (Foil)	.60	.45	.25
347	Chipper Jones (Foil)	4.00	3.00	1.50
348	Jessie Hollins (Foil)	.20	.15	.08
349	Willie Greene (Foil)	.40	.30	.15
350	Mark Thompson (Foil)	.75	.60	.30
351	Nigel Wilson (Foil)	2.50	2.00	1.00
352	Todd Jones (Foil)	.25	.20	.10
353	Raul Mondesi (Foil)	1.00	.70	.40
354	Cliff Floyd (Foil)	9.00	6.75	3.50
355	Bobby Jones (Foil)	1.50	1.25	.60
356	Kevin Stocker (Foil)	4.00	3.00	1.50
357	Midre Cummings (Foil)	1.50	1.25	.60
358	Allen Watson (Foil)	2.50	2.00	1.00
359	Ray McDavid (Foil)	1.00	.70	.40
360	Steve Hosey (Foil)	.75	.60	.30
361	Brad Pennington (Foil)	.25	.20	.10
362	Frankie Rodriguez (Foil)	.60	.45	.25
363	Troy Percival (Foil)	.25	.20	.10
364	Jason Bere (Foil)	3.00	2.25	1.25
365	Manny Ramirez (Foil)	4.00	3.00	1.50
366	Justin Thompson (Foil)	.25	.20	.10
367	Joe Vitello (Foil)	1.25	.90	.50
368	Tyrone Hill (Foil)	.75	.60	.30
369	David McCarty (Foil)	2.00	1.50	.80
370	Brien Taylor (Foil)	3.00	2.25	1.25
371	Todd Van Poppel (Foil)	1.00	.70	.40
372	Marc Newfield (Foil)	1.50	1.25	.60
373	*Terrell Lowery* (Foil)	.60	.45	.25
374	Alex Gonzalez (Foil)	2.00	1.50	.80
375	Ken Griffey Jr.	5.00	3.75	2.00

		MT	NR MT	EX
376	Donovan Osborne	.30	.25	.12
377	*Ritchie Moody*	.40	.30	.15
378	Shane Andrews	.40	.30	.15
379	Carlos Delgado	4.00	3.00	1.50
380	Bill Swift	.15	.11	.06
381	Leo Gomez	.15	.11	.06
382	Ron Gant	.25	.20	.10
383	Scott Fletcher	.15	.11	.06
384	*Matt Walbreck*	.30	.25	.12
385	Chuck Finley	.15	.11	.06
386	Kevin Mitchell	.15	.11	.06
387	Wilson Alvarez	.25	.20	.10
388	*John Burke*	.60	.45	.25
389	Alan Embree	.15	.11	.06
390	Trevor Hoffman	.15	.11	.06
391	Alan Trammell	.15	.11	.06
392	Todd Jones	.15	.11	.06
393	Felix Jose	.15	.11	.06
394	Orel Hershiser	.15	.11	.06
395	Pat Listach	.25	.20	.10
396	Gabe White	.50	.40	.20
397	*Dan Berafini*	.60	.45	.25
398	Todd Hundley	.15	.11	.06
399	Wade Boggs	.30	.25	.12
400	Tyler Green	.15	.11	.06
401	Mike Bordick	.15	.11	.06
402	Scott Bullett	.15	.11	.06
403	*Lagrande Russell*	.25	.20	.10
404	Ray Lankford	.15	.11	.06
405	Nolan Ryan	4.00	3.00	1.50
406	Robbie Beckett	.15	.11	.06
407	*Brent Bowers*	.25	.20	.10
408	*Adell Davenport*	.50	.40	.20
409	Brady Anderson	.15	.11	.06
410	Tom Glavine	.75	.60	.30
411	*Doug Hecker*	.40	.30	.15
412	Jose Guzman	.15	.11	.06
413	Luis Polonia	.15	.11	.06
414	Brian Williams	.15	.11	.06
415	Bo Jackson	.25	.20	.10
416	Eric Young	.40	.30	.15
417	Kenny Lofton	.75	.60	.30
418	Orestes Destrade	.15	.11	.06
419	Tony Phillips	.15	.11	.06
420	Jeff Bagwell	.75	.60	.30
421	Hark Gardner	.15	.11	.06
422	Brett Butler	.15	.11	.06
423	*Graeme Lloyd*	.50	.40	.20
424	Delino DeShields	.25	.20	.10
425	Scott Erickson	.15	.11	.06
426	Jeff Kent	.15	.11	.06
427	Jimmy Key	.15	.11	.06
428	Mickey Horandini	.15	.11	.06
429	*Marcos Arkas*	.75	.60	.30
430	Don Slaught	.15	.11	.06
431	Randy Johnson	.20	.15	.08
432	Omar Olivares	.15	.11	.06
433	Charlie Leibrandt	.15	.11	.06
434	Kurt Stillwell	.15	.11	.06
435	*Scott Brow*	.25	.20	.10
436	Robby Thompson	.15	.11	.06
437	Ben McDonald	.15	.11	.06
438	Deion Sanders	.30	.25	.12
439	Tony Pena	.15	.11	.06
440	Mark Grace	.30	.25	.12
441	Eduardo Perez	3.00	2.25	1.25
442	*Tim Pugh*	.75	.60	.30
443	Scott Ruffcorn	1.25	.90	.50
444	*Jay Gainer*	.60	.45	.25
445	Albert Belle	1.25	.90	.50
446	Bret Barberie	.15	.11	.06
447	Justin Mashore	.15	.11	.06
448	Pete Harnisch	.15	.11	.06
449	Greg Gagne	.15	.11	.06
450	Eric Davis	.15	.11	.06
451	Dave Mlicki	.15	.11	.06
452	Moises Alou	.20	.15	.08
453	Rick Aguilera	.15	.11	.06
454	Eddie Murray	.15	.11	.06
455	Bob Wickhan	.40	.30	.15
456	Wes Chamberlain	.15	.11	.06
457	Brent Gates	1.50	1.25	.60
458	Paul Weber	.15	.11	.06
459	Mike Hampton	.15	.11	.06
460	Ozzie Smith	.30	.25	.12
461	Tom Henke	.15	.11	.06
462	Ricky Gutuerrez	.25	.20	.10
463	Jack Morris	.15	.11	.06
464	*Joel Chimelis*	.25	.20	.10
465	Gregg Olson	.15	.11	.06
466	Javy Lopez	2.00	1.50	.80

		MT	NR MT	EX
467	Scott Cooper	.15	.11	.06
468	Willie Wilson	.15	.11	.06
469	Mark Langston	.15	.11	.06
470	Barry Larkin	.15	.11	.06
471	Rod Bolton	.15	.11	.06
472	Freddie Benavides	.15	.11	.06
473	*Ken Ramos*	.25	.20	.10
474	Chuck Carr	.15	.11	.06
475	Cecil Fielder	.50	.40	.20
476	Eddie Taubensee	.15	.11	.06
477	*Chris Eddy*	.25	.20	.10
478	Greg Hansell	.15	.11	.06
479	Kevin Reimer	.15	.11	.06
480	Denny Martinez	.15	.11	.06
481	Chuck Knoblauch	.25	.20	.10
482	Mike Draper	.15	.11	.06
483	Spike Owen	.15	.11	.06
484	Terry Mulholland	.15	.11	.06
485	Dennis Eckersley	.15	.11	.06
486	Blas Minor	.15	.11	.06
487	Dave Fleming	.25	.20	.10
488	Dan Cholonsky	.30	.25	.12
489	Ivan Rodriguez	.60	.45	.25
490	Gary Sheffield	.50	.40	.20
491	Ed Sprague	.15	.11	.06
492	Steve Hosey	.75	.60	.30
493	*Jimmy Haynes*	.50	.40	.20
494	John Smoltz	.15	.11	.06
495	Andre Dawson	.30	.25	.12
496	Rey Sanchez	.15	.11	.06
497	*Ty Van Durkleo*	.25	.20	.10
498	*Bobby Ayala*	.40	.30	.15
499	Tim Raines	.15	.11	.06
500	Charlie Hayes	.15	.11	.06
501	Paul Sorrento	.15	.11	.06
502	*Richie Lewis*	.30	.25	.12
503	*Jason Pfaff*	.40	.30	.15
504	Ken Caminiti	.15	.11	.06
505	Mike Macfarlane	.15	.11	.06
506	Jody Reed	.15	.11	.06
507	*Bobby Hughes*	.50	.40	.20
508	Wil Cordero	.15	.11	.06
509	*George Tsanis*	.25	.20	.10
510	Bret Saberhagen	.15	.11	.06
511	*Derek Jeter*	3.00	2.25	1.25
512	Gene Schall	.60	.45	.25
513	Curtis Shan	.15	.11	.06
514	Steve Cooke	.30	.25	.12
515	Edgar Martinez	.15	.11	.06
516	Nike Milchin	.15	.11	.06
517	Billy Ripken	.15	.11	.06
518	Andy Benes	.15	.11	.06
519	*Juan de la Rosa*	.30	.25	.12
520	John Burkett	.15	.11	.06
521	Alex Ochoa	.40	.30	.15
522	*Tony Tarasco*	1.75	1.25	.70
523	Luis Ortiz	.25	.20	.10
524	Rick Williams	.15	.11	.06
525	*Chris Turner*	.50	.40	.20
526	Rob Dibble	.15	.11	.06
527	Jack McDowell	.50	.40	.20
528	Daryl Boston	.15	.11	.06
529	*Bill Wertz*	.30	.25	.12
530	Charlie Hough	.15	.11	.06
531	Sean Bergman	.25	.20	.10
532	Doug Jones	.15	.11	.06
533	Jeff Montgomery	.15	.11	.06
534	*Roger Cedeno*	1.00	.70	.40
535	Robin Yount	.50	.40	.20
536	Mo Vaughn	.50	.40	.20
537	Brian Harper	.15	.11	.06
538	Juan Castillo	.15	.11	.06
539	Steve Farr	.15	.11	.06
540	John Kruk	.20	.15	.08
541	Troy Neel	.75	.60	.30
542	*Danny Clyburn*	.60	.45	.25
543	*Jim Converse*	.30	.25	.12
544	Gregg Jefferies	.15	.11	.06
545	Jose Canseco	.25	.20	.10
546	*Julio Bruno*	.30	.25	.12
547	Rob Butler	.20	.15	.08
548	Royce Clayton	.25	.20	.10
549	Chris Hoiles	.15	.11	.06
550	Greg Maddux	.40	.30	.15
551	*Joe Ciccarella*	.25	.20	.10
552	Ozzie Timmons	.40	.30	.15
553	Chili Davis	.15	.11	.06
554	Brian Koelling	.30	.25	.12
555	Frank Thomas	6.50	5.00	2.50
556	Vinny Castilla	.15	.11	.06
557	Reggie Jefferson	.15	.11	.06

		MT	NR MT	EX
558	Rob Natal	.15	.11	.06
559	Mike Henneman	.15	.11	.06
560	Craig Biggio	.15	.11	.06
561	*Billy Brewer*	.20	.15	.08
562	Dan Melendez	.20	.15	.08
563	*Kenny Felder*	1.00	.70	.40
564	*Miguel Batista*	.50	.40	.20
565	Dave Winfield	.40	.30	.15
566	Al Shirley	.25	.20	.10
567	Robert Eenhoorn	.15	.11	.06
568	Mike Williams	.15	.11	.06
569	*Tanyon Sturtze*	.40	.30	.15
570	Tim Wakefield	.15	.11	.06
571	Greg Pirkl	.20	.15	.08
572	*Sean Lowe*	.60	.45	.25
573	*Terry Burows*	.50	.40	.20
574	*Kevin Higgins*	.30	.25	.12
575	Joe Carter	.30	.25	.12
576	Kevin Rogers	.15	.11	.06
577	Manny Alexander	.15	.11	.06
578	David Justice	1.00	.70	.40
579	*Brian Conroy*	.30	.25	.12
580	*Jessie Hollins*	.25	.20	.10
581	*Ron Watson*	.25	.20	.10
582	Bip Roberts	.15	.11	.06
583	*Tom Urbani*	.25	.20	.10
584	*Jason Hutchins*	.30	.25	.12
585	Carlos Baerga	1.50	1.25	.60
586	Jeff Mutis	.25	.20	.10
587	Justin Thompson	.25	.20	.10
588	Orlando Miller	.20	.15	.08
589	Brian McRae	.15	.11	.06
590	Ramon Martinez	.15	.11	.06
591	Dave Nilsson	.15	.11	.06
592	*Jose Vidro*	.50	.40	.20
593	Rich Becker	.15	.11	.06
594	*Preston Wilson*	1.75	1.25	.70
595	Don Mattingly	.50	.40	.20
596	Tony Langmire	.15	.11	.06
597	Kevin Seitzer	.15	.11	.06
598	*Midre Cummings*	.90	.70	.35
599	Omar Vizquel	.15	.11	.06
600	Lee Smith	.15	.11	.06
601	*David Hulse*	.75	.60	.30
602	*Darrell Sherman*	.50	.40	.20
603	Alex Gonzalez	1.00	.70	.40
604	Geronimo Pena	.15	.11	.06
605	Mike Devereaux	.15	.11	.06
606	*Sterling Hitchcock*	.90	.70	.35
607	Mike Greenwell	.15	.11	.06
608	Steve Buechele	.15	.11	.06
609	Troy Percival	.15	.11	.06
610	Bobby Kelly	.15	.11	.06
611	*James Baldwin*	1.25	.90	.50
612	Jerald Clark	.15	.11	.06
613	*Albie Lopez*	.75	.60	.30
614	Dave Magadan	.15	.11	.06
615	Mickey Tettleton	.15	.11	.06
616	*Sean Runyan*	.25	.20	.10
617	Bob Hamelin	.15	.11	.06
618	Raul Mondesi	.75	.60	.30
619	Tyrone Hill	.25	.20	.10
620	Darrin Fletcher	.15	.11	.06
621	Mike Trombley	.15	.11	.06
622	Jeromy Burnitz	.50	.40	.20
623	Bernie Williams	.15	.11	.06
624	*Mike Farmer*	.30	.25	.12
625	Rickey Henderson	.40	.30	.15
626	Carlos Garcia	.20	.15	.08
627	*Jeff Darwin*	.40	.30	.15
628	Todd Zeile	.15	.11	.06
629	Benji Gil	.90	.70	.35
630	Tony Gwynn	.40	.30	.15
631	*Aaron Small*	.25	.20	.10
632	*Joe Rosselli*	.30	.25	.12
633	Mike Mussina	1.00	.70	.40
634	Ryan Klesko	1.50	1.25	.60
635	Roger Clemens	.90	.70	.35
636	Sammy Sosa	.20	.15	.08
637	*Orlando Palmeiro*	.30	.25	.12
638	Willie Greene	.15	.11	.06
639	George Bell	.15	.11	.06
640	*Garvin Alston*	.30	.25	.12
641	*Pete Janicki*	.40	.30	.15
642	*Chris Sheff*	.25	.20	.10
643	*Felipe Lira*	.40	.30	.15
644	Roberto Petagine	.50	.40	.20
645	Wally Joyner	.15	.11	.06
646	Mike Piazza	11.00	8.25	4.50
647	Jaime Navarro	.15	.11	.06
648	*Jeff Hartsock*	.25	.20	.10

		MT	NR MT	EX
649	David McCarty	1.25	.90	.50
650	Bobby Jones	1.00	.70	.40
651	Mark Hutton	.15	.11	.06
652	Kyle Abbott	.15	.11	.06
653	*Steve Cox*	.50	.40	.20
654	Jeff King	.15	.11	.06
655	Norm Charlton	.15	.11	.06
656	*Mike Gulan*	.30	.25	.12
657	Julio Franco	.15	.11	.06
658	*Cameron Cairncross*	.30	.25	.12
659	John Olerud	1.75	1.25	.70
660	Salomon Torres	1.00	.70	.40
661	Brad Pennington	.15	.11	.06
662	Melvin Nieves	1.50	1.25	.60
663	Ivan Calderon	.15	.11	.06
664	Turk Wendell	.15	.11	.06
665	Chris Pritchett	.30	.25	.12
666	Reggie Sanders	.30	.25	.12
667	Robin Ventura	.30	.25	.12
668	Joe Girardi	.15	.11	.06
669	Manny Rodriguez	3.50	2.75	1.50
670	Jeff Conine	.15	.11	.06
671	Greg Gohr	.15	.11	.06
672	Andujar Cedeno	.15	.11	.06
673	*Les Norman*	.40	.30	.15
674	*Mike James*	.25	.20	.10
675	*Marshall Boze*	.75	.60	.30
676	B.J. Wallace	.90	.70	.35
677	Kent Hrbek	.15	.11	.06
678	Jack Voight	.15	.11	.06
679	Brien Taylor	2.00	1.50	.80
680	Curt Schilling	.15	.11	.06
681	Todd Van Poppel	.50	.40	.20
682	Kevin Young	.80	.60	.30
683	Tommy Adams	.15	.11	.06
684	Bernard Gilkey	.15	.11	.06
685	Kevin Brown	.15	.11	.06
686	Fred McGriff	.60	.45	.25
687	Pat Borders	.15	.11	.06
688	Kirt Manwaring	.15	.11	.06
689	Sid Bream	.15	.11	.06
690	John Valentin	.15	.11	.06
691	*Steve Olsen*	.40	.30	.15
692	*Roberto Mejia*	1.50	1.25	.60
693	Carlos Delgado (Foil)	5.00	3.75	2.00
694	*Steve Gibralter* (Foil)	.50	.40	.20
695	Gary Mota (Foil)	.25	.20	.10
696	*Jose Malave* (Foil)	.90	.70	.35
697	*Larry Sutton* (Foil)	.50	.40	.20
698	*Dan Frye* (Foil)	.50	.40	.20
699	*Tim Clark* (Foil)	.90	.70	.35
700	*Brian Rupp* (Foil)	.60	.45	.25
701	Alou's (Foil)	.25	.20	.10
702	Bond's (Foil)	1.00	.70	.40
703	Griffey's (Foil)	2.00	1.50	.80
704	McRae's (Foil)	.25	.20	.10
705	Checklist 1	.15	.11	.06
706	Checklist 2	.15	.11	.06
707	Checklist 3	.15	.11	.06
718	Checklist 4	.15	.10	.05

1977 Burger King Yankees

The first Topps-produced set for Burger King restaurants was issued in the New York area in 1977 and featured the A.L. champion New York Yankees. Twenty-two players plus an unnumbered checklist were issued at the beginning of the promotion with card #23 (Lou Piniella) being added to the set at a later date. The Piniella card was issued in limited quantities. The cards, numbered 1 through 23, are 2-1/2" by 3-1/2" in size and have fronts identical to the regular 1977 Topps set except for the following numbers: 2, 6, 7, 13, 14, 15, 17, 20 and 21. These cards feature different poses or major picture-cropping variations. It should be noted that very minor cropping variations between the regular Topps sets and the Burger King issues exist throughout the years the sets were produced.

		NR MT	EX	VG
Complete Set:		45.00	22.00	13.50
Common Player:		.30	.15	.09
1	Yankees Team (Billy Martin)	1.00	.50	.30
2	Thurman Munson	7.00	3.50	2.00
3	Fran Healy	.30	.15	.09
4	Jim Hunter	2.00	1.00	.60
5	Ed Figueroa	.30	.15	.09
6	Don Gullett	.30	.15	.09
7	Mike Torrez	.30	.15	.09
8	Ken Holtzman	.30	.15	.09
9	Dick Tidrow	.30	.15	.09
10	Sparky Lyle	.50	.25	.15
11	Ron Guidry	.75	.35	.20
12	Chris Chambliss	.30	.15	.09
13	Willie Randolph	.75	.35	.20
14	Bucky Dent	.75	.35	.20
15	Graig Nettles	.75	.35	.20
16	Fred Stanley	.30	.15	.09
17	Reggie Jackson	8.00	4.00	2.50
18	Mickey Rivers	.30	.15	.09
19	Roy White	.50	.25	.15
20	Jim Wynn	.50	.25	.15
21	Paul Blair	.30	.15	.09
22	Carlos May	.30	.15	.09
23	Lou Piniella	20.00	10.00	6.00
——	Checklist	.10	.05	.03

1978 Burger King Astros

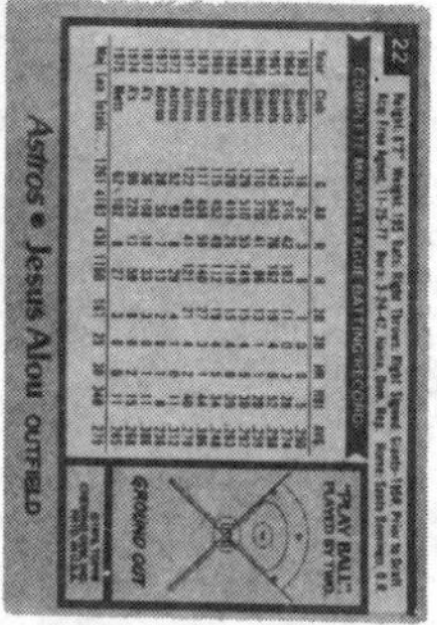

Burger King restaurants in the Houston area distributed a Topps-produced 23-card set showcasing the Astros in 1978. The cards are standard size (2-1/2" by 3-1/2") and are numbered 1 through 22. The checklist card is unnumbered. The card fronts are identical to the regular 1978 Topps set with the exception of card numbers 21 and 22, which have different poses. Although not noted in the following checklist, it should be remembered that very minor picture-cropping variations between the regular Topps issues and the 1977-1980 Burger King sets do exist.

		NR MT	EX	VG
Complete Set:		12.00	6.00	3.50
Common Player:		.35	.20	.11
1	Bill Virdon	.50	.25	.15
2	Joe Ferguson	.35	.20	.11
3	Ed Herrmann	.35	.20	.11
4	J.R. Richard	.60	.30	.20
5	Joe Niekro	.60	.30	.20
6	Floyd Bannister	.35	.20	.11

		NR MT	EX	VG
7	Joaquin Andujar	.35	.20	.11
8	Ken Forsch	.35	.20	.11
9	Mark Lemongello	.35	.20	.11
10	Joe Sambito	.35	.20	.11
11	Gene Pentz	.35	.20	.11
12	Bob Watson	.40	.20	.12
13	Julio Gonzalez	.35	.20	.11
14	Enos Cabell	.35	.20	.11
15	Roger Metzger	.35	.20	.11
16	Art Howe	.40	.20	.11
17	Jose Cruz	.75	.35	.20
18	Cesar Cedeno	.75	.35	.20
19	Terry Puhl	.35	.20	.11
20	Wilbur Howard	.35	.20	.11
21	Dave Bergman	.35	.20	.11
22	Jesus Alou	.50	.25	.15
----	Checklist	.04	.02	.01

1978 Burger King Rangers

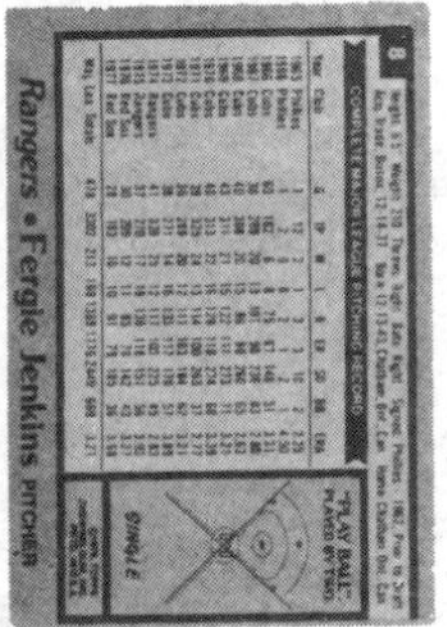

Issued by Burger King restaurants in the Dallas-Fort Worth area, this 23-card Topps-produced set features the Texas Rangers. The cards are standard size (2-1/2" by 3-1/2") and are identical in style to the regular 1978 Topps set with the following exceptions: #'s 5, 8, 10, 12, 17, 21 and 22. An unnumbered checklist card was included with the set.

		NR MT	EX	VG
	Complete Set:	12.00	6.00	3.50
	Common Player:	.35	.20	.11
1	Billy Hunter	.35	.20	.11
2	Jim Sundberg	.35	.20	.11
3	John Ellis	.35	.20	.11
4	Doyle Alexander	.35	.20	.11
5	Jon Matlack	.35	.20	.11
6	Dock Ellis	.35	.20	.11
7	George Medich	.35	.20	.11
8	Fergie Jenkins	2.50	1.25	.75
9	Len Barker	.35	.20	.11
10	Reggie Cleveland	.35	.20	.11
11	Mike Hargrove	.50	.25	.15
12	Bump Wills	.60	.30	.20
13	Toby Harrah	.50	.25	.15
14	Bert Campaneris	.50	.25	.15
15	Sandy Alomar	.50	.25	.15
16	Kurt Bevacqua	.35	.20	.11
17	Al Oliver	1.00	.50	.30
18	Juan Beniquez	.35	.20	.11
19	Claudell Washington	.35	.20	.11
20	Richie Zisk	.35	.20	.11
21	John Lowenstein	.35	.20	.11
22	Bobby Thompson	.35	.20	.11
----	Checklist	.04	.02	.01

A player's name in italic indicates a rookie card. An (FC) indicates a player's first card for that particular card company.

1978 Burger King Tigers

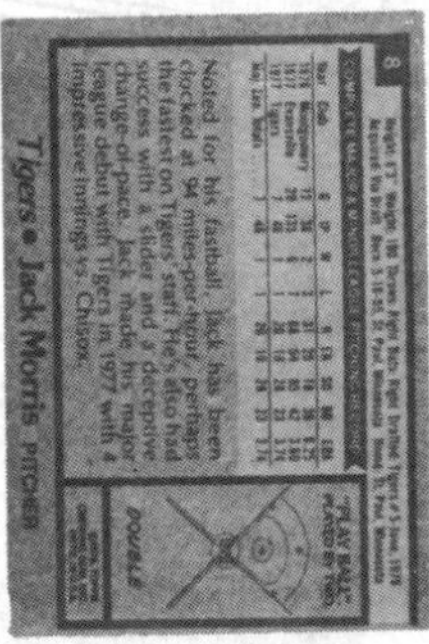

Rookie cards of Morris, Trammell and Whitaker make the Topps-produced 1978 Burger King Detroit Tigers issue the most popular of the BK sets. Twenty-two player cards and an unnumbered checklist make up the set which was issued in the Detroit area. The cards measure 2-1/2" by 3-1/2", and are identical to the regular 1978 Topps issue with the following exceptions - card #'s 6, 7, 8, 13, 15 and 16. Collectors are reminded that numerous minor picture-cropping variations between the regular Topps issues and the Burger King sets appear from the 1977 through 1980. These minor variations are not noted in the following checklist.

		NR MT	EX	VG
	Complete Set:	60.00	30.00	18.00
	Common Player:	.40	.20	.12
1	Ralph Houk	.50	.25	.15
2	Milt May	.40	.20	.12
3	John Wockenfuss	.40	.20	.12
4	Mark Fidrych	1.00	.50	.30
5	Dave Rozema	.40	.20	.12
6	Jack Billingham	.40	.20	.12
7	Jim Slaton	.40	.20	.12
8	Jack Morris	15.00	7.50	4.50
9	John Hiller	.40	.20	.12
10	Steve Foucault	.40	.20	.12
11	Milt Wilcox	.40	.20	.12
12	Jason Thompson	.40	.20	.12
13	Lou Whitaker	15.00	7.50	4.50
14	Aurelio Rodriguez	.40	.20	.12
15	Alan Trammell	20.00	10.00	6.00
16	Steve Dillard	.40	.20	.12
17	Phil Mankowski	.40	.20	.12
18	Steve Kemp	.40	.20	.12
19	Ron LeFlore	.50	.25	.15
20	Tim Corcoran	.40	.20	.12
21	Mickey Stanley	.40	.20	.12
22	Rusty Staub	1.00	.50	.30
---)	Checklist	.10	.05	.03

1978 Burger King Yankees

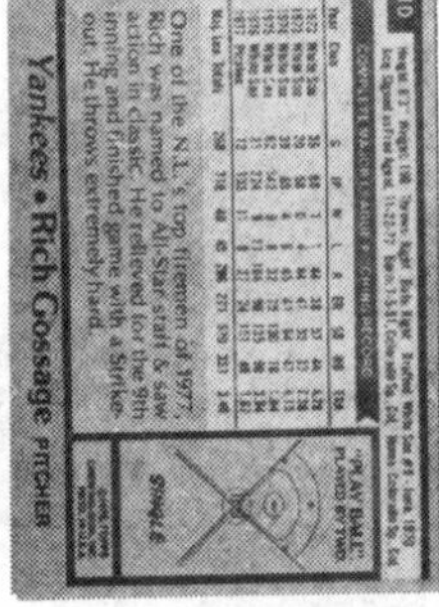

Produced by Topps for Burger King outlets in the New York area for the second year in a row, the 1978 Yankees set contains 22 cards plus an unnumbered checklist. The cards are numbered 1 through 22 and are the standard size of 2-1/2" by 3-1/2". The cards feature the same pictures found in the regular 1978 Topps set except for numbers 10, 11 and 16. Only those variations containing different poses or major picture-cropping differences are noted. Numerous minor picture-cropping variations, that are very insignificant in nature, exist between the regular Topps sets and the Burger King issues of 1977-1980.

		NR MT	EX	VG
Complete Set:		10.00	5.00	3.00
Common Player:		.30	.15	.09
1	Billy Martin	.80	.40	.25
2	Thurman Munson	3.00	1.50	.90
3	Cliff Johnson	.30	.15	.09
4	Ron Guidry	.50	.25	.15
5	Ed Figueroa	.30	.15	.09
6	Dick Tidrow	.30	.15	.09
7	Jim Hunter	1.00	.50	.30
8	Don Gullett	.30	.15	.09
9	Sparky Lyle	.50	.25	.15
10	Rich Gossage	.75	.35	.20
11	Rawly Eastwick	.30	.15	.09
12	Chris Chambliss	.30	.15	.09
13	Willie Randolph	.50	.25	.15
14	Graig Nettles	.50	.25	.15
15	Bucky Dent	.50	.25	.15
16	Jim Spencer	.30	.15	.09
17	Fred Stanley	.30	.15	.09
18	Lou Piniella	.60	.30	.18
19	Roy White	.50	.25	.15
20	Mickey Rivers	.30	.15	.09
21	Reggie Jackson	4.00	2.00	1.25
22	Paul Blair	.30	.15	.09
---	Checklist	.04	.02	.01

1979 Burger King Phillies

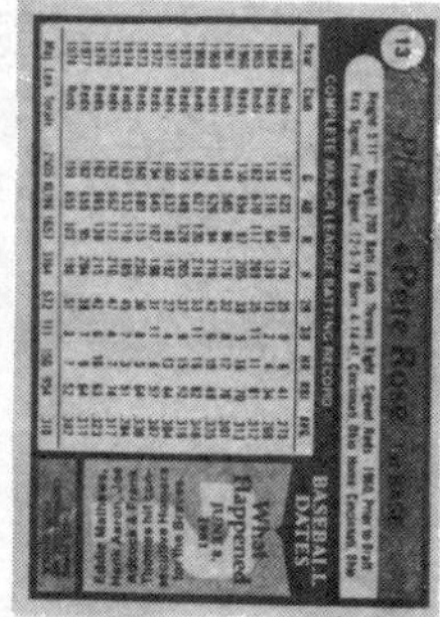

Twenty-two Philadelphia Phillies players are featured in the 1979 Burger King issue given out in the Philadelphia area. The Topps-produced set, whose cards measure 2-1/2" by 3-1/2", also includes an unnumbered checklist. The cards are identical to the regular 1979 Topps set except in seven instances. Card numbers 1, 11, 12, 13, 14, 17 and 22 have different poses. Very minor picture-cropping variations between the regular Topps issues and the Burger King sets can be found throughout the four years the cards were produced, but only those variations featuring major changes are noted in the following checklist.

		NR MT	EX	VG
Complete Set:		10.00	5.00	3.00
Common Player:		.20	.10	.06
1	Danny Ozark	.20	.10	.06
2	Bob Boone	.45	.25	.15
3	Tim McCarver	.40	.20	.10
4	Steve Carlton	3.00	1.50	.90
5	Larry Christenson	.20	.10	.06
6	Dick Ruthven	.20	.10	.06
7	Ron Reed	.20	.10	.06
8	Randy Lerch	.20	.10	.06
9	Warren Brusstar	.20	.10	.06
10	Tug McGraw	.30	.15	.09
11	Nino Espinosa	.20	.10	.06
12	Doug Bird	.20	.10	.06
13	Pete Rose	4.00	2.00	1.25
14	Manny Trillo	.40	.20	.12
15	Larry Bowa	.50	.25	.15
16	Mike Schmidt	4.00	2.00	1.25
17	Pete Mackanin	.20	.10	.06
18	Jose Cardenal	.20	.10	.06
19	Greg Luzinski	.40	.20	.12
20	Garry Maddox	.20	.10	.06
21	Bake McBride	.20	.10	.06
22	Greg Gross	.20	.10	.06
---	Checklist	.04	.02	.01

1979 Burger King Yankees

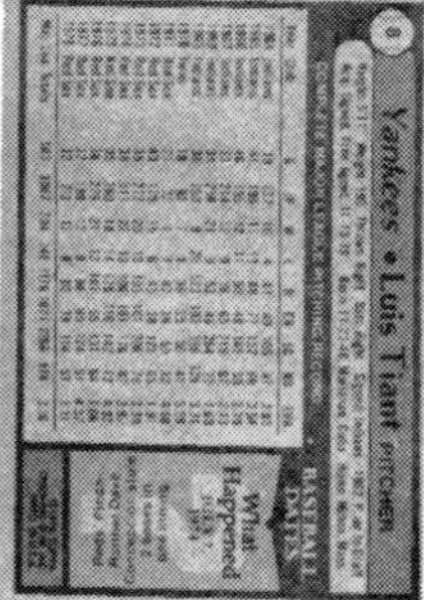

The New York Yankees were featured in a Topps-produced Burger King set for the third consecutive year in 1979. Once again, 22 numbered player cards and an unnumbered checklist made up the set. The cards, which measure 2-1/2" by 3-1/2", are identical to the 1979 Topps regular set except for card numbers 4, 8, 9 and 22 which included new poses. Only different poses or major picture-cropping variations between the regular Topps set and the Burger King issue are recognized in the checklist that follows. Numerous minor picture cropping variations between the regular Topps issue and the Burger King sets of 1977-1980 exist.

		NR MT	EX	VG
Complete Set:		10.00	5.00	3.00
Common Player:		.30	.15	.09
1	Yankees Team (Bob Lemon)	.50	.25	.15
2	Thurman Munson	2.00	1.00	.60
3	Cliff Johnson	.30	.15	.09
4	Ron Guidry	.75	.35	.20
5	Jay Johnstone	.40	.20	.12
6	Jim Hunter	1.00	.50	.30
7	Jim Beattie	.30	.15	.09
8	Luis Tiant	.50	.25	.15
9	Tommy John	.75	.35	.20
10	Rich Gossage	.75	.35	.20
11	Ed Figueroa	.30	.15	.09
12	Chris Chambliss	.30	.15	.09
13	Willie Randolph	.50	.25	.15
14	Bucky Dent	.50	.25	.15
15	Graig Nettles	.50	.25	.15
16	Fred Stanley	.30	.15	.09
17	Jim Spencer	.30	.15	.09
18	Lou Piniella	.60	.30	.18
19	Roy White	.50	.25	.15
20	Mickey Rivers	.30	.15	.09
21	Reggie Jackson	3.00	1.50	.90
22	Juan Beniquez	.30	.15	.09
---	Checklist	.04	.02	.01

A card number in parentheses () indicates the set is unnumbered.

1980 Burger King Phillies

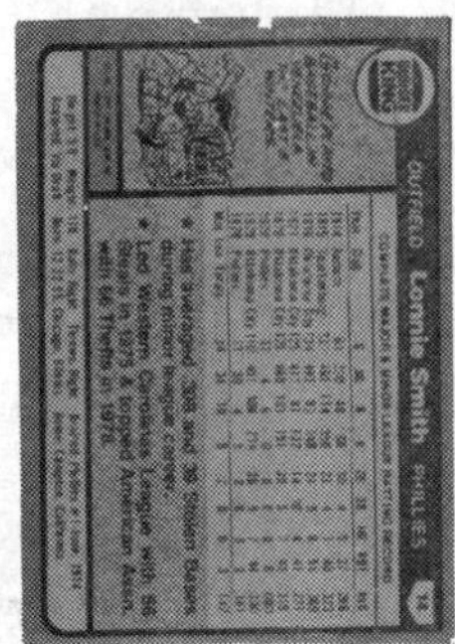

Philadelphia-area Burger King outlets issued a 23-card set featuring the Phillies for the second in a row in 1980. The Topps-produced set, whose cards measure 2-1/2" by 3-1/2", contains 22 player cards and an unnumbered checklist. The card fronts are identical in design to the regular 1980 Topps sets with the following exceptions - card numbers 1, 3, 8, 14 and 22 feature new poses. Collectors should note that very minor picture-cropping variations between the regular Topps issues and the Burger King sets exist in all years. Those minor differences are not noted in the checklist that follows. The 1980 Burger King sets were the first to include the Burger King logo on the card backs.

		NR MT	EX	VG
Complete Set:		8.00	4.00	2.50
Common Player:		.15	.08	.05
1	Dallas Green	.50	.25	.15
2	Bob Boone	.50	.25	.15
3	Keith Moreland	.30	.15	.09
4	Pete Rose	3.00	1.50	.90
5	Manny Trillo	.20	.10	.06
6	Mike Schmidt	3.00	1.50	.90
7	Larry Bowa	.25	.12	.07
8	John Vukovich	.15	.08	.05
9	Bake McBride	.15	.08	.05
10	Garry Maddox	.15	.08	.05
11	Greg Luzinski	.30	.15	.09
12	Greg Gross	.15	.08	.05
13	Del Unser	.15	.08	.05
14	Lonnie Smith	.50	.25	.15
15	Steve Carlton	1.75	.90	.50
16	Larry Christenson	.15	.08	.05
17	Nino Espinosa	.15	.08	.05
18	Randy Lerch	.15	.08	.05
19	Dick Ruthven	.15	.08	.05
20	Tug McGraw	.20	.10	.06
21	Ron Reed	.15	.08	.05
22	Kevin Saucier	.15	.08	.05
----	Checklist	.04	.02	.01

1980 Burger King Pitch, Hit & Run

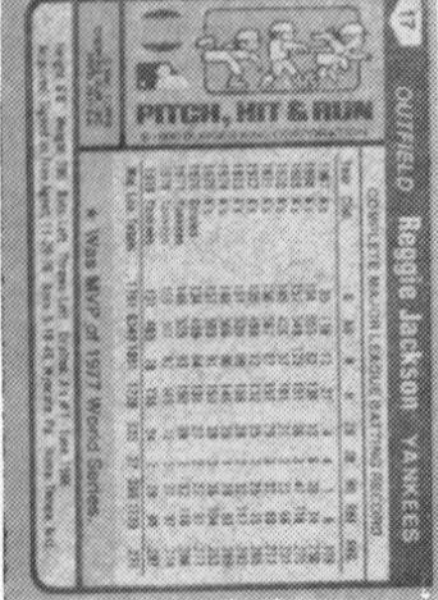

In 1980, Burger King issued, in conjunction with its "Pitch, Hit & Run" promotion, a Topps-produced 34-card set featuring pitchers (card #'s 1-11), hitters (#'s 12-22), and base stealers (#'s 23-33). The card fronts, which carry the Burger King logo, are identical in nature to the regular 1980 Topps set except for numbers 1, 4, 5, 7, 9, 10, 16, 17, 18, 22, 23, 27, 28, 29 and 30, which feature different poses. The cards, which are numbered 1 through 33, measure 2-1/2" by 3-1/2" in size. An unnumbered checklist was included with the set.

		NR MT	EX	VG
Complete Set:		25.00	12.50	7.50
Common Player:		.20	.10	.06
1	Vida Blue	.30	.15	.09
2	Steve Carlton	1.50	.75	.45
3	Rollie Fingers	1.50	.75	.45
4	Ron Guidry	.30	.15	.09
5	Jerry Koosman	.30	.15	.09
6	Phil Niekro	.75	.35	.20
7	Jim Palmer	2.00	1.00	.60
8	J.R. Richard	.20	.10	.06
9	Nolan Ryan	8.00	4.00	2.50
10	Tom Seaver	1.50	.75	.45
11	Bruce Sutter	.20	.10	.06
12	Don Baylor	.25	.13	.08
13	George Brett	1.50	.70	.45
14	Rod Carew	1.50	.75	.45
15	George Foster	.20	.10	.06
16	Keith Hernandez	.30	.15	.09
17	Reggie Jackson	2.25	1.25	.70
18	Fred Lynn	.50	.25	.15
19	Dave Parker	.50	.25	.15
20	Jim Rice	.80	.40	.25
21	Pete Rose	2.50	1.25	.70
22	Dave Winfield	1.50	.75	.45
23	Bobby Bonds	.50	.25	.15
24	Enos Cabell	.20	.10	.06
25	Cesar Cedeno	.20	.10	.06
26	Julio Cruz	.20	.10	.06
27	Ron LeFlore	.30	.15	.09
28	Dave Lopes	.30	.15	.09
29	Omar Moreno	.20	.10	.06
30	Joe Morgan	1.00	.50	.30
31	Bill North	.20	.10	.06
32	Frank Taveras	.20	.10	.06
33	Willie Wilson	.25	.13	.08
----	Checklist	.04	.02	.01

1986 Burger King

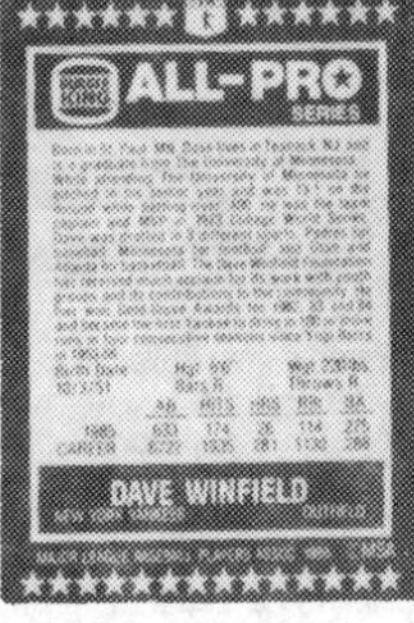

Burger King restaurants in the Pennsylvania and New Jersey areas issued a 20-card set entitled "All-Pro Series". The cards were issued with the purchase of a Whopper sandwich and came in folded panels of two cards each, along with a coupon card. The card fronts feature a color photo and contain the player's name, team and position plus the Burger King logo. Due to a licensing problem, the team insignias on the players' caps were airbrushed away. The card backs feature black print on white stock and contain brief biographical and statistical information.

		MT	NR MT	EX
Complete Panel Set		9.00	6.75	3.50
Complete Singles Set		6.00	4.50	2.50
Common Panel		.75	.60	.30
Common Single Player		.10	.08	.04
	Panel	.70	.50	.30
1	Tony Pena	.10	.08	.04
2	Dave Winfield	.20	.15	.08
	Panel	2.00	1.50	.80
3	Fernando Valenzuela	.10	.08	.04
4	Pete Rose	.50	.40	.20
	Panel	1.50	1.25	.60
5	Mike Schmidt	1.00	.70	.40
6	Steve Carlton	.50	.40	.20
	Panel	.75	.60	.30
7	Glenn Wilson	.10	.08	.04
8	Jim Rice	.20	.15	.08
	Panel	2.00	1.50	.75
9	Wade Boggs	.75	.55	.25
10	Juan Samuel	.10	.08	.04
	Panel	1.50	1.25	.60
11	Dale Murphy	.40	.30	.15
12	Reggie Jackson	.50	.35	.20
	Panel	1.25	.90	.50
13	Kirk Gibson	.20	.15	.08
14	Eddie Murray	.30	.25	.12
	Panel	1.50	1.25	.60
15	Cal Ripken, Jr.	.50	.40	.20
16	Willie McGee	.10	.08	.04
	Panel	1.50	1.25	.60
17	Dwight Gooden	.25	.20	.10
18	Steve Garvey	.20	.15	.08
	Panel	2.50	2.00	1.00
19	Don Mattingly	1.00	.70	.40
20	George Brett	.50	.40	.20

1987 Burger King

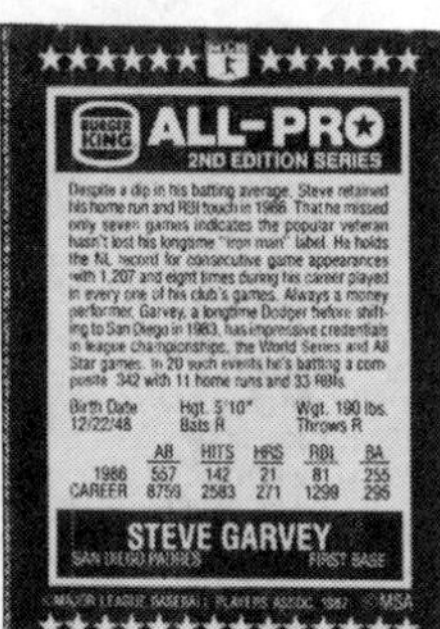

The 1987 Burger King "All-Pro 2nd Edition Series" set was part of a giveaway promotion at participating Burger King restaurants. The set is comprised of 20 players on ten different panels. The cards measure 2-1/2" by 3-1/2" each with a three-card panel (includes a coupon card) measuring 7-5/8" by 3-1/2". The card fronts feature a full-color photo and the Burger King logo surrounded by a blue stars-and-stripes border. The babcks contain black print on white stock and carry a brief player biography and 1986 career statistics. The set was produced by Mike Schecter Associates and, as with many MSA issues, all team insignias were airbrushed away.

		MT	NR MT	EX
Complete Panel Set:		8.00	6.00	3.25
Complete Singles Set:		4.00	3.00	1.50
Common Panel:		.25	.20	.10
Common Single Player:		.05	.04	.02
	Panel	1.25	.90	.50
1	Wade Boggs	.40	.30	.15
2	Gary Carter	.10	.07	.03
	Panel	1.00	.70	.40
3	Will Clark	.50	.40	.20
4	Roger Clemens	.20	.15	.08
	Panel	.50	.40	.20
5	Steve Garvey	.10	.07	.03
6	Ron Darling	.05	.04	.02
	Panel	.25	.20	.10
7	Pedro Guerrero	.06	.04	.02
8	Von Hayes	.05	.04	.02
	Panel	.60	.45	.25
9	Rickey Henderson	.25	.20	.10
10	Keith Hernandez	.06	.04	.02
	Panel	.60	.45	.25
11	Wally Joyner	.20	.15	.08
12	Mike Krukow	.05	.04	.02
	Panel	1.75	1.25	.70
13	Don Mattingly	.75	.55	.25
14	Ozzie Smith	.15	.11	.06
	Panel	.50	.40	.20
15	Tony Pena	.05	.04	.02
16	Jim Rice	.15	.11	.06
	Panel	1.50	1.15	.55
17	Ryne Sandberg	.50	.40	.20
18	Mike Schmidt	.40	.30	.15
	Panel	.80	.60	.30
19	Darryl Strawberry	.15	.11	.06
20	Fernando Valenzuela	.05	.04	.02

1987 Classic Major League Baseball Game

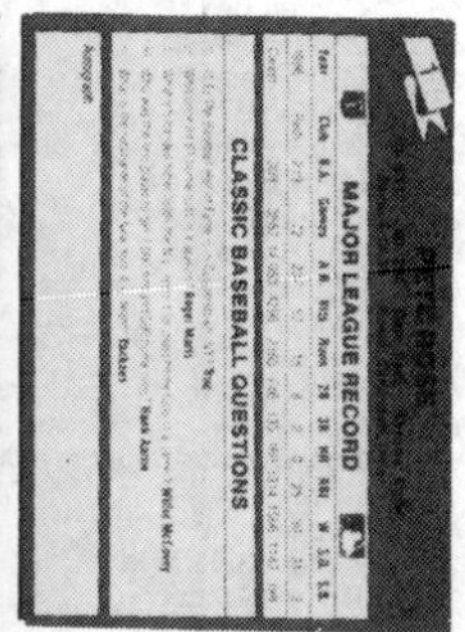

The "Classic Major League Baseball Board Game" set consists of 100 full-color cards which were used to play the game. Game participants were required to answer trivia questions found on the backs of the cards. The attractive cards measure 2 1/2" by 3-1/2" and are printed on glossy card stock. The card backs carry the player's career statistics besides the Classic Baseball Questions. The game was produced by Game Time, Ltd. of Marietta, Ga., and sold for $19.95 in most retail outlets.

		MT	NR MT	EX
Complete Set (100):		225.00	175.00	90.00
Common Player:		.10	.08	.04
1	Pete Rose	3.00	2.25	1.25
2	Len Dykstra	2.00	1.50	.80
3	Darryl Strawberry	4.00	3.00	1.50
4	Keith Hernandez	.20	.15	.08
5	Gary Carter	.30	.25	.12
6	Wally Joyner	1.00	.70	.40
7	Andres Thomas	.10	.08	.04
8	Pat Dodson	.10	.08	.04
9	Kirk Gibson	.30	.25	.12
10	Don Mattingly	4.00	3.00	1.50
11	Dave Winfield	1.00	.70	.40
12	Rickey Henderson	6.00	4.50	2.25
13	Dan Pasqua	.10	.08	.04
14	Don Baylor	.15	.11	.06
15	Bo Jackson	80.00	60.00	30.00
16	Pete Incaviglia	.20	.15	.08
17	Kevin Bass	.10	.08	.04
18	Barry Larkin	1.00	.70	.40
19	Dave Magadan	.80	.60	.30
20	Steve Sax	.20	.15	.08

		MT	NR MT	EX
21	Eric Davis	1.00	.70	.40
22	Mike Pagliarulo	.10	.08	.04
23	Fred Lynn	.20	.15	.08
24	Reggie Jackson	1.00	.70	.40
25	Larry Parrish	.10	.08	.04
26	Tony Gwynn	.80	.60	.30
27	Steve Garvey	.30	.20	.10
28	Glenn Davis	.10	.08	.04
29	Tim Raines	.25	.20	.10
30	Vince Coleman	.20	.15	.08
31	Willie McGee	.10	.08	.04
32	Ozzie Smith	.80	.60	.30
33	Dave Parker	.60	.45	.25
34	Tony Pena	.10	.08	.04
35	Ryne Sandberg	10.00	7.50	4.00
36	Brett Butler	.10	.08	.04
37	Dale Murphy	.50	.40	.20
38	Bob Horner	.10	.08	.04
39	Pedro Guerrero	.15	.11	.06
40	Brook Jacoby	.10	.08	.04
41	Carlton Fisk	.30	.25	.12
42	Harold Baines	.15	.11	.06
43	Rob Deer	.10	.08	.04
44	Robin Yount	6.00	4.50	2.25
45	Paul Molitor	2.00	1.50	.80
46	Jose Canseco	30.00	22.50	11.25
47	George Brett	6.00	4.50	2.25
48	Jim Presley	.10	.08	.04
49	Rich Gedman	.10	.08	.04
50	Lance Parrish	.10	.08	.04
51	Eddie Murray	.50	.40	.20
52	Cal Ripken, Jr.	8.00	5.50	2.75
53	Kent Hrbek	.25	.20	.10
54	Gary Gaetti	.10	.08	.04
55	Kirby Puckett	6.00	4.50	2.25
56	George Bell	.20	.15	.08
57	Tony Fernandez	.20	.15	.08
58	Jesse Barfield	.10	.08	.04
59	Jim Rice	.40	.30	.15
60	Wade Boggs	2.00	1.50	.80
61	Marty Barrett	.10	.08	.04
62	Mike Schmidt	8.00	5.50	2.75
63	Von Hayes	.10	.08	.04
64	Jeff Leonard	.10	.08	.04
65	Chris Brown	.10	.08	.04
66	Dave Smith	.10	.08	.04
67	Mike Krukow	.10	.08	.04
68	Ron Guidry	.15	.11	.06
69	Rob Woodward (photo actually Pat Dodson)	.10	.08	.04
70	Rob Murphy	.10	.08	.04
71	Andres Galarraga	.25	.20	.10
72	Dwight Gooden	1.00	.70	.40
73	Bob Ojeda	.10	.08	.04
74	Sid Fernandez	.10	.08	.04
75	Jesse Orosco	.10	.08	.04
76	Roger McDowell	.10	.08	.04
77	John Tutor (Tudor)	.10	.08	.04
78	Tom Browning	.10	.08	.04
79	Rick Aguilera	.10	.08	.04
80	Lance McCullers	.10	.08	.04
81	Mike Scott	.10	.08	.04
82	Nolan Ryan	12.00	9.00	4.75
83	Bruce Hurst	.15	.11	.06
84	Roger Clemens	5.00	3.75	2.00
85	Oil Can Boyd	.10	.08	.04
86	Dave Righetti	.20	.15	.08
87	Dennis Rasmussen	.10	.08	.04
88	Bret Saberhagan (Saberhagen)	.20	.15	.08
89	Mark Langston	.20	.15	.08
90	Jack Morris	.15	.11	.06
91	Fernando Valenzuela	.15	.11	.06
92	Orel Hershiser	.30	.25	.12
93	Rick Honeycutt	.10	.08	.04
94	Jeff Reardon	.15	.11	.06
95	John Habyan	.10	.08	.04
96	Goose Gossage	.15	.11	.06
97	Todd Worrell	.20	.15	.08
98	Floyd Youmans	.10	.08	.04
99	Don Aase	.10	.08	.04
100	John Franco	.15	.11	.06

A player's name in italic indicates a rookie card. An (FC) indicates a player's first card for that particular card company.

1987 Classic Travel Edition

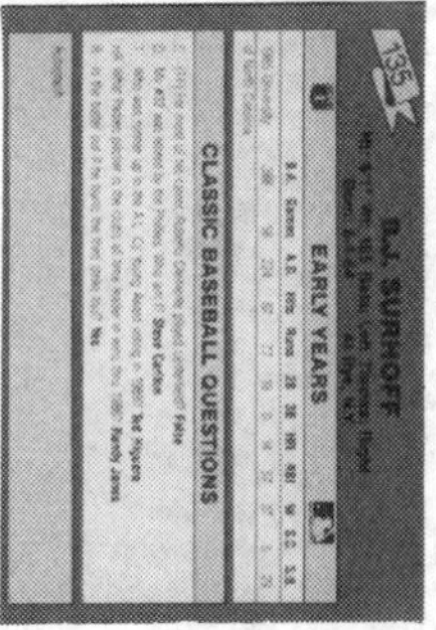

Game Time, Ltd. of Marietta, Ga., issued as an update to their Classic Baseball Board Game a 50- card set entitled "Travel Edition." The cards measure 2-1/2" by 3-1/2" and feature the same outstanding quality characteristic of the first release. Numbered from 101 to 150, the "Travel Edition" is an extension of the original set. Besides updating player trades and showcasing rookies, the set offers several highlights from the 1987 season, including Andre Dawson's beaning. All new trivia questions are contained on the card backs.

		MT	NR MT	EX
Complete Set (50):		30.00	22.00	12.00
Common Player:		.08	.06	.03
101	Mike Schmidt	2.00	1.50	.80
102	Eric Davis	1.00	.70	.40
103	Pete Rose	2.00	1.50	.80
104	Don Mattingly	2.00	1.50	.80
105	Wade Boggs	1.50	1.25	.60
106	Dale Murphy	.40	.30	.15
107	Glenn Davis	.08	.06	.03
108	Wally Joyner	2.00	1.50	.80
109	Bo Jackson	6.00	4.50	2.25
110	Cory Snyder	.08	.06	.03
111	Jim Lindeman	.08	.06	.03
112	Kirby Puckett	2.00	1.50	.80
113	Barry Bonds	8.00	5.50	2.25
114	Roger Clemens	2.00	1.50	.80
115	Oddibe McDowell	.08	.06	.03
116	Bret Saberhagen	.20	.15	.08
117	Joe Magrane	.08	.06	.03
118	Scott Fletcher	.08	.06	.03
119	Mark McLemore	.08	.06	.03
120	Who Me? (Joe Niekro)	.25	.20	.10
121	Mark McGwire	2.00	1.50	.80
122	Darryl Strawberry	1.50	1.25	.60
123	Mike Scott	.08	.06	.03
124	Andre Dawson	.40	.30	.15
125	Jose Canseco	4.00	3.00	1.50
126	Kevin McReynolds	.15	.11	.06
127	Joe Carter	.50	.40	.20
128	Casey Candaele	.08	.06	.03
129	Matt Nokes	.15	.11	.06
130	Kal Daniels	.15	.11	.06
131	Pete Incaviglia	.25	.20	.10
132	Benito Santiago	1.00	.70	.40
133	Barry Larkin	1.00	.70	.40
134	Gary Pettis	.08	.06	.03
135	B.J. Surhoff	.15	.11	.06
136	Juan Nieves	.08	.06	.03
137	Jim Deshaies	.08	.06	.03
138	Pete O'Brien	.08	.06	.03
139	Kevin Seitzer	.08	.06	.03
140	Devon White	.25	.20	.10
141	Rob Deer	.08	.06	.03
142	Kurt Stillwell	.08	.06	.03
143	Edwin Correa	.08	.06	.03
144	Dion James	.08	.06	.03
145	Danny Tartabull	.40	.30	.15
146	Jerry Browne	.08	.06	.03
147	Ted Higuera	.15	.11	.06
148	Jack Clark	.15	.11	.06
149	Ruben Sierra	2.00	1.50	.80

		MT	NR MT	EX
150	McGwire/Davis, (Mark McGwire, Eric Davis)	1.50	1.25	.60
189	John Marzano	.08	.06	.03
190	Kevin Elster	.08	.06	.03
191	Vincente Palacios	.08	.06	.03
192	Kent Hrbek	.25	.20	.10
193	Eric Bell	.08	.06	.03
194	Kelly Downs	.08	.06	.03
195	Jose Lind	.10	.08	.04
196	Dave Stewart	.20	.15	.08
197	Jose Canseco, Mark McGwire	1.50	1.25	.60
198	Phil Niekro	.25	.20	.10
199	Phil Niekro	.25	.20	.10
200	Phil Niekro	.25	.20	.10

1988 Classic - Red

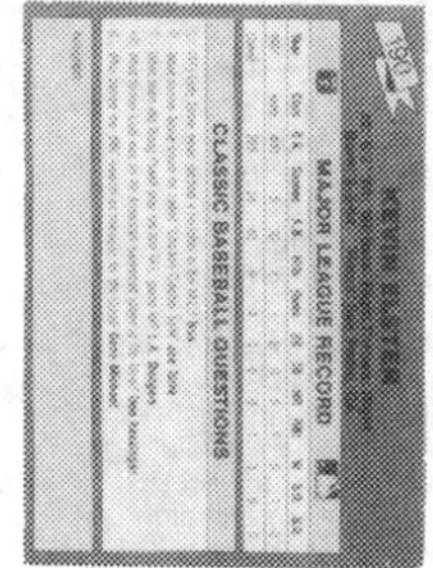

This 50-card set, numbered 151-200, was produced for use with the travel edition of Game Time's Classic Baseball Board Game. Special cards in the set include a McGwire/Mattingly, an instruction card with McGwire/Canseco and three different cards featuring Phil Niekro (in different uniforms). A follow-up to the first edition in 1987, the 1988 Red Series was designed for use with the 1988 Blue Series (#'s 201-250). Red Series card fronts have red borders, a yellow Classic logo in the upper left corner and a black and beige player banner beneath the photo. The card backs are printed in red and pink on white and include the player name, personal info, major league records, a baseball question and space for the player autograph. Classic card series sold via hobby dealers and retail toy stores nationwide. Game Time Ltd., the set's producer, was purchased by Scoreboard of Cherry Hill, N.J. in 1988.

		MT	NR MT	EX
Complete Set (50):		16.00	12.00	6.50
Common Player:		.08	.06	.03
151	Don Mattingly, Mark McGwire,	1.00	.70	.40
152	Don Mattingly	.75	.55	.25
153	Mark McGwire	.50	.40	.20
154	Eric Davis	.50	.40	.20
155	Wade Boggs	1.00	.70	.40
156	Dale Murphy	.50	.40	.20
157	Andre Dawson	.40	.30	.15
158	Roger Clemens	1.50	1.25	.60
159	Kevin Seitzer	.08	.06	.03
160	Benito Santiago	.08	.06	.03
161	Kal Daniels	.08	.06	.03
162	John Kruk	.20	.15	.08
163	Bill Ripken	.08	.06	.03
164	Kirby Puckett	.50	.40	.20
165	Jose Canseco	3.00	2.25	1.25
166	Matt Nokes	.15	.11	.06
167	Mike Schmidt	2.00	1.50	.80
168	Tim Raines	.25	.20	.10
169	Ryne Sandberg	2.00	1.50	.80
170	Dave Winfield	.50	.40	.20
171	Dwight Gooden	.50	.40	.20
172	Bret Saberhagen	.15	.11	.06
173	Willie McGee	.08	.06	.03
174	Jack Morris	.08	.06	.03
175	Jeff Leonard	.08	.06	.03
176	Cal Ripken, Jr.	3.00	2.25	1.25
177	Pete Incaviglia	.08	.06	.03
178	Devon White	.10	.08	.04
179	Nolan Ryan	5.00	3.75	2.00
180	Ruben Sierra	1.50	1.25	.60
181	Todd Worrell	.08	.06	.03
182	Glenn Davis	.08	.06	.03
183	Frank Viola	.15	.11	.06
184	Cory Snyder	.08	.06	.03
185	Tracy Jones	.08	.06	.03
186	Terry Steinbach	.15	.11	.06
187	Julio Franco	.15	.11	.06
188	Larry Sheets	.08	.06	.03

1988 Classic - Blue

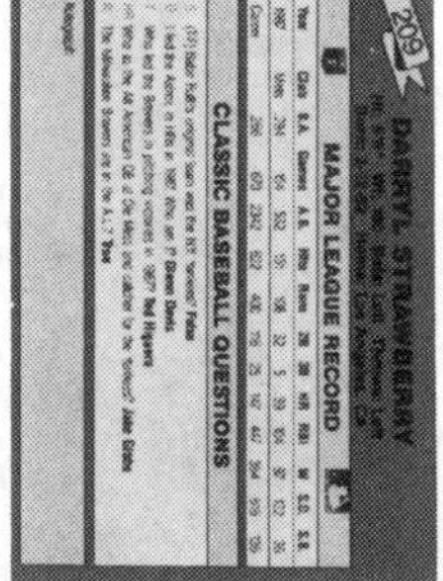

This 50-card set, numbered 201-250, was produced for use with the travel edition of Game Time's Classic Baseball Board Game. Two cards in the set feature two players: Davis/Murphy and McGwire/Mattingly. A follow-up to the first edition in 1987, the 1988 Blue was designed for use with the 1988 Red Series (151-200). Blue Series card fronts have blue borders, a yellow classic logo in the upper left corner and a black and beige player name banner beneath the photo. The card backs are printed in blue on white and include the player name, personal info, major league records, a baseball question and space for the player autograph. Classic card series are sold via hobby dealers and retail toy stores nationwide. Game Time Ltd., the set's producer, was purchased by Scoreboard of Cherry Hill, N.J. in 1988.

		MT	NR MT	EX
Complete Set (50):		20.00	15.00	8.00
Common Player:		.15	.11	.06
201	Davis/Murphy (Eric Davis, Dale Murphy)	.40	.30	.15
202	B.J. Surhoff	.15	.11	.06
203	John Kruk	.20	.15	.08
204	Sam Horn	.15	.11	.06
205	Jack Clark	.15	.11	.06
206	Wally Joyner	.40	.30	.15
207	Matt Nokes	.25	.20	.10
208	Bo Jackson	4.00	3.00	1.50
209	Darryl Strawberry	1.00	.70	.40
210	Ozzie Smith	.25	.20	.10
211	Don Mattingly	1.00	.70	.40
212	Mark McGwire	1.00	.70	.40
213	Eric Davis	.70	.50	.30
214	Wade Boggs	1.50	1.25	.60
215	Dale Murphy	.30	.25	.12
216	Andre Dawson	.30	.25	.12
217	Roger Clemens	1.00	.70	.40
218	Kevin Seitzer	.15	.11	.06
219	Benito Santiago	.25	.20	.10
220	Tony Gwynn	1.00	.70	.40
221	Mike Scott	.15	.11	.06
222	Steve Bedrosian	.15	.11	.06
223	Vince Coleman	.25	.20	.10
224	Rick Sutcliffe	.15	.11	.06
225	Will Clark	7.00	5.25	2.75
226	Pete Rose	1.50	1.25	.60
227	Mike Greenwell	.30	.25	.15
228	Ken Caminiti	.15	.11	.06

		MT	NR MT	EX
229	Ellis Burks	.50	.40	.20
230	Dave Magadan	.15	.11	.06
231	Alan Trammell	.30	.25	.12
232	Paul Molitor	.40	.30	.15
233	Gary Gaetti	.15	.11	.06
234	Rickey Henderson	1.25	.90	.50
235	Danny Tartabull	.60	.45	.25
236	Bobby Bonilla	1.00	.70	.40
237	Mike Dunne	.15	.11	.06
238	Al Leiter	.15	.11	.06
239	John Farrell	.15	.11	.06
240	Joe Magrane	.15	.11	.06
241	Mike Henneman	.15	.11	.06
242	George Bell	.25	.20	.10
243	Gregg Jefferies	.60	.45	.25
244	Jay Buhner	.40	.30	.15
245	Todd Benzinger	.15	.11	.06
246	Matt Williams	.80	.60	.30
247	Don Mattingly, Mark McGwire (no card number on back)	1.00	.70	.40
248	George Brett	1.00	.70	.40
249	Jimmy Key	.15	.11	.06
250	Mark Langston	.20	.15	.08

1989 Classic

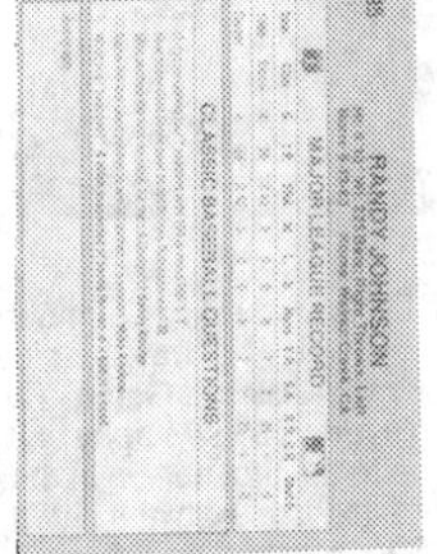

This 100-card set was released by The Score Board to accompany trivia board games. Fronts have a wide border which is pink at the top and blue at the bottom. Card backs are printed in blue. The player's name appears beneath the color photo. The flip side includes the card number in the upper left, personal information, and the player's major league record in a boxed area. Another boxed area below the record presents five trivia questions. The lower border of the flip side provides an autograph space. The Classic card series was sold by retail stores and hobby dealers nationwide.

		MT	NR MT	EX
Complete set (100):		20.00	15.00	8.00
Common player:		.08	.06	.03
1	Orel Hershiser	.30	.25	.12
2	Wade Boggs	.60	.45	.25
3	Jose Canseco	1.50	1.25	.60
4	Mark McGwire	.40	.30	.15
5	Don Mattingly	.60	.45	.25
6	Gregg Jefferies	.50	.40	.20
7	Dwight Gooden	.60	.45	.25
8	Darryl Strawberry	.40	.30	.15
9	Eric Davis	.40	.30	.15
10	Joey Meyer	.08	.06	.03
11	Joe Carter	.20	.15	.08
12	Paul Molitor	.40	.30	.15
13	Mark Grace	.30	.25	.12
14	Kurt Stillwell	.08	.06	.03
15	Kirby Puckett	.60	.45	.25
16	Keith Miller	.08	.06	.03
17	Glenn Davis	.08	.06	.03
18	Will Clark	.75	.55	.25
19	Cory Snyder	.08	.06	.03
20	Jose Lind	.08	.06	.03
21	Andres Thomas	.08	.06	.03
22	Dave Smith	.08	.06	.03
23	Mike Scott	.08	.06	.03
24	Kevin McReynolds	.08	.06	.03
25	B.J. Surhoff	.08	.06	.03
26	Mackey Sasser	.08	.06	.03
27	Chad Kreuter	.20	.15	.08
28	Hal Morris	.60	.45	.25
29	Wally Joyner	.20	.15	.08
30	Tony Gwynn	.40	.30	.15
31	Kevin Mitchell	.20	.15	.08
32	Dave Winfield	.40	.30	.15
33	Billy Bean	.08	.06	.03
34	Steve Bedrosian	.08	.06	.03
35	Ron Gant	.20	.15	.08
36	Len Dykstra	.20	.15	.08
37	Andre Dawson	.30	.25	.12
38	Brett Butler	.08	.06	.03
39	Rob Deer	.08	.06	.03
40	Tommy John	.20	.15	.08
41	Gary Gaetti	.15	.11	.06
42	Tim Raines	.20	.15	.08
43	George Bell	.20	.15	.08
44	Dwight Evans	.15	.11	.06
45	Denny Martinez	.15	.11	.06
46	Andres Galarraga	.20	.15	.08
47	George Brett	.50	.40	.20
48	Mike Schmidt	1.25	.90	.50
49	Dave Steib	.08	.06	.03
50	Rickey Henderson	.50	.40	.20
51	Craig Biggio	.40	.30	.15
52	Mark Lemke	.08	.06	.03
53	Chris Sabo	.40	.30	.15
54	Jeff Treadway	.08	.06	.03
55	Kent Hrbek	.15	.11	.06
56	Cal Ripken, Jr.	1.00	.70	.40
57	Tim Belcher	.08	.06	.03
58	Ozzie Smith	.40	.30	.15
59	Keith Hernandez	.08	.06	.03
60	Pedro Guerrero	.08	.06	.03
61	Greg Swindell	.08	.06	.03
62	Bret Saberhagen	.20	.15	.08
63	John Tudor	.08	.06	.03
64	Gary Carter	.15	.11	.06
65	Kevin Seitzer	.08	.06	.03
66	Jesse Barfield	.08	.06	.03
67	Luis Medina	.08	.06	.03
68	Walt Weiss	.20	.15	.08
69	Terry Steinbach	.08	.06	.03
70	Barry Larkin	.20	.15	.08
71	Pete Rose	.80	.60	.30
72	Luis Salazar	.08	.06	.03
73	Benito Santiago	.20	.15	.08
74	Kal Daniels	.08	.06	.03
75	Kevin Elster	.08	.06	.03
76	Rob Dibble	.25	.20	.10
77	Bobby Witt	.15	.11	.06
78	Steve Searcy	.08	.06	.03
79	Sandy Alomar	.15	.11	.06
80	Chili Davis	.20	.15	.08
81	Alvin Davis	.08	.06	.03
82	Charlie Leibrandt	.08	.06	.03
83	Robin Yount	.80	.60	.30
84	Mark Carreon	.08	.06	.03
85	Pascual Perez	.08	.06	.03
86	Dennis Rasmussen	.08	.06	.03
87	Ernie Riles	.08	.06	.03
88	Melido Perez	.08	.06	.03
89	Doug Jones	.08	.06	.03
90	Dennis Eckersley	.15	.11	.06
91	Bob Welch	.08	.06	.03
92	Bob Milacki	.08	.06	.03
93	Jeff Robinson	.08	.06	.03
94	Mike Henneman	.08	.06	.03
95	Randy Johnson	.40	.30	.15
96	Ron Jones	.08	.06	.03
97	Jack Armstrong	.08	.06	.03
98	Willie McGee	.08	.06	.03
99	Ryne Sandberg	.80	.60	.30
100	David Cone/ Danny Jackson	.70	.50	.25

1989 Classic Travel Update I

Sold only as a 50-card complete set under the official name of "Travel Update I," these cards are identical in format to the 1989 Classic 100-card set with the exception that the borders are orange at the top and maroon at the bottom. Backs are maroon. Like the Update I orange series, cards are numbered contiguously from 101-150.

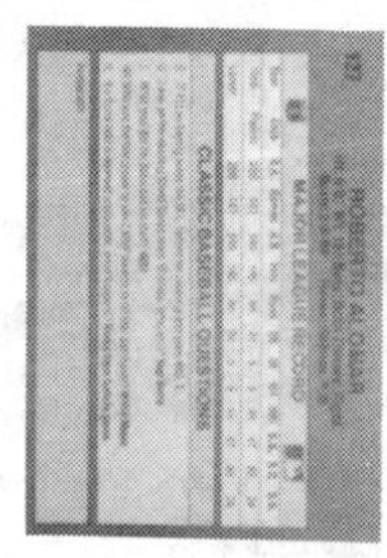

		MT	NR MT	EX
Complete Set (50):		10.00	7.00	3.50
Common Player:		.08	.06	.03
101	Gary Sheffield	1.25	.90	.50
102	Wade Boggs	.80	.60	.30
103	Jose Canseco	.60	.40	.20
104	Mark McGwire	.60	.40	.20
105	Orel Hershiser	.20	.15	.08
106	Don Mattingly	1.25	.90	.50
107	Dwight Gooden	.50	.40	.20
108	Darryl Strawberry	.40	.30	.15
109	Eric Davis	.40	.30	.15
110	Bam Bam Meulens	.08	.06	.03
111	Andy Van Slyke	.15	.11	.06
112	Al Leiter	.08	.06	.03
113	Matt Nokes	.15	.11	.06
114	Mike Krukow	.08	.06	.03
115	Tony Fernandez	.15	.11	.06
116	Fred McGriff	.25	.20	.10
117	Barry Bonds	.80	.60	.20
118	Gerald Perry	.08	.06	.03
119	Roger Clemens	.30	.25	.12
120	Kirk Gibson	.12	.09	.05
121	Greg Maddux	.20	.15	.08
122	Bo Jackson	1.25	.90	.50
123	Danny Jackson	.08	.06	.03
124	Dale Murphy	.20	.15	.08
125	David Cone	.15	.11	.06
126	Tom Browning	.08	.06	.03
127	Roberto Alomar	1.00	.70	.40
128	Alan Trammell	.15	.11	.06
129	Rickey Jordan	.08	.06	.03
130	Ramon Martinez	.50	.40	.20
131	Ken Griffey, Jr.	5.00	3.75	2.00
132	Gregg Olson	.50	.40	.20
133	Carlos Quintana	.08	.06	.03
134	Dave West	.15	.11	.06
135	Cameron Drew	.08	.06	.03
136	Ted Higuera	.08	.06	.03
137	Sil Campusano	.08	.06	.03
138	Mark Gubicza	.15	.11	.06
139	Mike Boddicker	.08	.06	.03
140	Paul Gibson	.08	.06	.03
141	Jose Rijo	.20	.15	.08
142	John Costello	.08	.06	.03
143	Cecil Espy	.08	.06	.03
144	Frank Viola	.15	.11	.08
145	Erik Hanson	.30	.25	.12
146	Juan Samuel	.08	.06	.03
147	Harold Reynolds	.15	.11	.06
148	Joe Magrane	.08	.06	.03
149	Mike Greenwell	.15	.11	.06
150	Darryl Strawberry/ Will Clark	1.00	.70	.40

1989 Classic Travel Update II

Numbered from 151-200, this 50-card set features rookies and traded players with their new teams. The cards are purple and gray and were sold as part of a board game with baseball trivia questions.

		MT	NR MT	EX
Complete Set (50):		10.00	7.50	4.00
Common Player:		.05	.04	.02
151	Jim Abbott	.50	.40	.20
152	Ellis Burks	.10	.08	.04

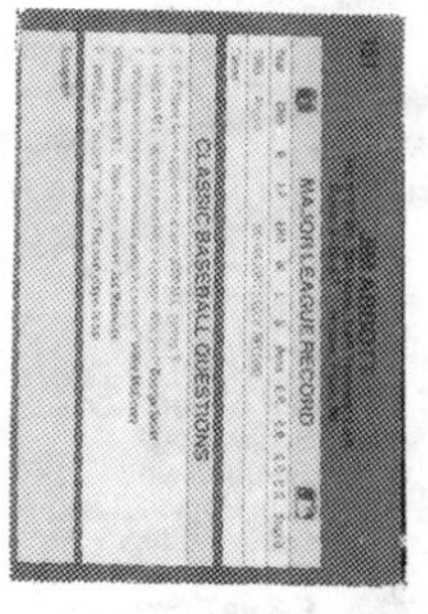

		MT	NR MT	EX
153	Mike Schmidt	1.00	.70	.30
154	Gregg Jefferies	.20	.15	.08
155	Mark Grace	.20	.15	.08
156	Jerome Walton	.05	.04	.02
157	Bo Jackson	1.00	.70	.40
158	Jack Clark	.05	.04	.02
159	Tom Glavine	.10	.08	.04
160	Eddie Murray	.15	.11	.06
161	John Dopson	.05	.04	.02
162	Ruben Sierra	.20	.15	.08
163	Rafael Palmeiro	.25	.20	.10
164	Nolan Ryan	1.50	1.25	.60
165	Barry Larkin	.20	.15	.08
166	Tommy Herr	.05	.04	.02
167	Roberto Kelly	.20	.15	.08
168	Glenn Davis	.05	.04	.02
169	Glenn Braggs	.05	.04	.02
170	Juan Bell	.05	.04	.02
171	Todd Burns	.05	.04	.02
172	Derek Lilliquist	.05	.04	.02
173	Orel Hershiser	.20	.15	.08
174	John Smoltz	.25	.20	.10
175	Ozzie Guillen/ Ellis Burks	.30	.25	.12
176	Kirby Puckett	.50	.40	.20
177	Robin Ventura	.75	.55	.25
178	Allan Anderson	.05	.04	.02
179	Steve Sax	.05	.04	.02
180	Will Clark	.75	.55	.25
181	Mike Devereaux	.05	.04	.02
182	Tom Gordon	.05	.04	.02
183	Rob Murphy	.05	.04	.02
184	Pete O'Brien	.05	.04	.02
185	Cris Carpenter	.05	.04	.02
186	Tom Brunansky	.05	.04	.02
187	Bob Boone	.15	.11	.06
188	Lou Whitaker	.10	.08	.04
189	Dwight Gooden	.20	.15	.08
190	Mark McGwire	.40	.30	.15
191	John Smiley	.05	.04	.02
192	Tommy Gregg	.05	.04	.02
193	Ken Griffey, Jr.	4.00	3.00	1.50
194	Bruce Hurst	.05	.04	.02
195	Greg Swindell	.10	.08	.04
196	Nelson Liriano	.05	.04	.02
197	Randy Myers	.05	.04	.02
198	Kevin Mitchell	.20	.15	.08
199	Dante Bichette	.10	.08	.04
200	Deion Sanders	.70	.50	.30

1990 Classic Baseball

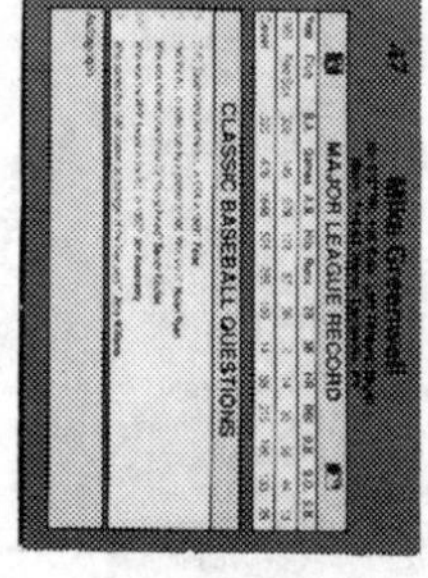

Classic Baseball returned in 1990 with another 150-card set. The cards were again sold as part of a baseball trivia game, and each game included a box designed to store all the cards in the set.

		MT	NR MT	EX
Complete set (154):		15.00	11.00	6.00
Common player:		.05	.04	.02
1	Nolan Ryan	2.00	1.50	.80
2	Bo Jackson	.50	.40	.20
3	Gregg Olson	.10	.08	.04
4	Tom Gordon	.05	.04	.02
5	Robin Ventura	.20	.15	.08
6	Will Clark	.50	.40	.20
7	Ruben Sierra	.20	.15	.08
8	Mark Grace	.25	.20	.10
9	Luis de los Santos	.05	.04	.02
10	Bernie Williams	.25	.20	.10
11	Eric Davis	.20	.15	.08
12	Carney Lansford	.05	.04	.02
13	John Smoltz	.10	.08	.04
14	Gary Sheffield	.25	.20	.10
15	Kent Merker	.25	.20	.10
16	Don Mattingly	.75	.55	.25
17	Tony Gwynn	.15	.11	.06
18	Ozzie Smith	.25	.20	.10
19	Fred McGriff	.25	.20	.10
20	Ken Griffey, Jr.	2.00	1.50	.80
21a	Deion Sanders ("Prime Time")	4.00	3.00	1.50
21b	Deion Sanders (Deion "Prime Time" Sanders)	.70	.50	.30
22	Jose Canseco	.40	.30	.15
23	Mitch Williams	.15	.11	.06
24	Cal Ripken, Jr.	.75	.55	.25
25	Bob Geren	.10	.08	.04
26	Wade Boggs	.50	.40	.20
27	Ryne Sandberg	.60	.45	.25
28	Kirby Puckett	.50	.40	.20
29	Mike Scott	.05	.04	.02
30	Dwight Smith	.05	.04	.02
31	Craig Worthington	.05	.04	.02
32	Ricky Jordan	.05	.04	.02
33	Darryl Strawberry	.25	.20	.10
34	Jerome Walton	.05	.04	.02
35	John Olerud	.70	.50	.30
36	Tom Glavine	.10	.08	.04
37	Rickey Henderson	.40	.30	.15
38	Rolando Roomes	.05	.04	.02
39	Mickey Tettleton	.10	.08	.04
40	Jim Abbott	.50	.40	.20
41	Dave Righetti	.05	.04	.02
42	Mike LaValliere	.05	.04	.02
43	Rob Dibble	.15	.11	.06
44	Pete Harnisch	.05	.04	.02
45	Jose Offerman	.20	.15	.08
46	Walt Weiss	.05	.04	.02
47	Mike Greenwell	.15	.11	.06
48	Barry Larkin	.15	.11	.06
49	Dave Gallagher	.05	.04	.02
50	Junior Felix	.05	.04	.02
51	Roger Clemens	.20	.15	.08
52	Lonnie Smith	.05	.04	.02
53	Jerry Browne	.05	.04	.02
54	Greg Briley	.05	.04	.02
55	Delino DeShields	.75	.55	.25
56	Carmelo Martinez	.05	.04	.02
57	Craig Biggio	.10	.08	.04
58	Dwight Gooden	.20	.15	.08
59a	Bo Jackson, Ruben Sierra, Mark McGwire (Bo, Ruben, Mark)	2.00	1.50	.80
59b	Bo Jackson, Ruben Sierra, Mark McGwire (A.L. Fence Busters)	.60	.45	.25
60	Greg Vaughn	.25	.20	.10
61	Roberto Alomar	.25	.20	.10
62	Steve Bedrosian	.05	.04	.02
63	Devon White	.10	.08	.04
64	Kevin Mitchell	.20	.15	.08
65	Marquis Grissom	.40	.30	.15
66	Brian Holman	.05	.04	.02
67	Julio Franco	.05	.04	.02
68	Dave West	.10	.08	.04
69	Harold Baines	.10	.08	.04
70	Eric Anthony	.30	.25	.12
71	Glenn Davis	.05	.04	.02
72	Mark Langston	.15	.11	.06
73	Matt Williams	.25	.20	.10
74	Rafael Palmeiro	.20	.15	.08
75	Pete Rose, Jr.	.20	.15	.08
76	Ramon Martinez	.15	.11	.06
77	Dwight Evans	.10	.08	.04
78	Mackey Sasser	.05	.04	.02
79	Mike Schooler	.05	.04	.02
80	Dennis Cook	.05	.04	.02
81	Orel Hershiser	.20	.15	.08
82	Barry Bonds	.50	.40	.20
83	Geronimo Berroa	.05	.04	.02
84	George Bell	.10	.08	.04
85	Andre Dawson	.20	.15	.08
86	John Franco	.05	.04	.02
87a	Will Clark, Tony Gwynn (Clark/Gwynn)	3.00	2.25	1.25
87b	Will Clark, Tony Gwynn (N.L. Hit Kings)	.40	.30	.15
88	Glenallen Hill	.05	.04	.02
89	Jeff Ballard	.05	.04	.02
90	Todd Zeile	.30	.25	.12
91	Frank Viola	.15	.11	.06
92	Ozzie Guillen	.10	.08	.04
93	Jeff Leonard	.05	.04	.02
94	Dave Smith	.05	.04	.02
95	Dave Parker	.20	.15	.08
96	Jose Gonzalez	.05	.04	.02
97	Dave Steib	.05	.04	.02
98	Charlie Hayes	.15	.11	.06
99	Jesse Barfield	.05	.04	.02
100	Joey Belle	1.00	.70	.40
101	Jeff Reardon	.05	.04	.02
102	Bruce Hurst	.05	.04	.02
103	Luis Medina	.05	.04	.02
104	Mike Moore	.05	.04	.02
105	Vince Coleman	.10	.08	.04
106	Alan Trammell	.15	.11	.06
107	Randy Myers	.05	.04	.02
108	Frank Tanana	.05	.04	.02
109	Craig Lefferts	.05	.04	.02
110	John Wetteland	.20	.15	.08
111	Chris Gwynn	.05	.04	.02
112	Mark Carreon	.05	.04	.02
113	Von Hayes	.05	.04	.02
114	Doug Jones	.05	.04	.02
115	Andres Galarraga	.10	.08	.04
116	Carlton Fisk	.20	.15	.08
117	Paul O'Neill	.05	.04	.02
118	Tim Raines	.10	.08	.04
119	Tom Brunansky	.05	.04	.02
120	Andy Benes	.35	.25	.14
121	Mark Portugal	.05	.04	.02
122	Willie Randolph	.05	.04	.02
123	Jeff Blauser	.05	.04	.02
124	Don August	.05	.04	.02
125	Chuck Cary	.05	.04	.02
126	John Smiley	.05	.04	.02
127	Terry Mullholland	.05	.04	.02
128	Harold Reynolds	.05	.04	.02
129	Hubie Brooks	.05	.04	.02
130	Ben McDonald	.30	.25	.12
131	Kevin Ritz	.05	.04	.02
132	Luis Quinones	.05	.04	.02
133	Bam Bam Muelens ((Muelens - error))	4.00	3.00	1.50
133	Bam Bam Meulens ((Meulens - correct))	.20	.15	.08
134	Bill Spiers	.05	.04	.02
135	Andy Hawkins	.05	.04	.02
136	Alvin Davis	.05	.04	.02
137	Lee Smith	.15	.11	.06
138	Joe Carter	.15	.11	.06
139	Bret Saberhagen	.10	.08	.04
140	Sammy Sosa	.30	.25	.12
141	Matt Nokes	.10	.08	.04
142	Bert Blyleven	.10	.08	.04
143	Bobby Bonilla	.25	.20	.10
144	Howard Johnson	.10	.08	.04
145	Joe Magrane	.05	.04	.02
146	Pedro Guerrero	.05	.04	.02
147	Robin Yount	.45	.35	.15
148	Dan Gladden	.05	.04	.02
149	Steve Sax	.05	.04	.02
150a	Will Clark, Kevin Mitchell (Clark/Mitchell)	1.00	.70	.40
150b	Will Clark, Kevin Mitchell (Bay Bombers)	.50	.40	.20

Definitions for grading conditions are located in the Introduction of this price guide.

1990 Classic Series II

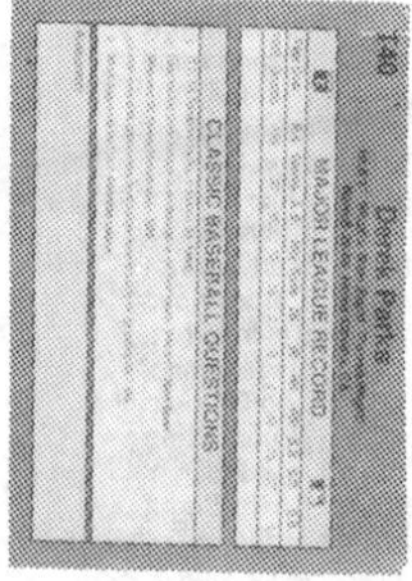

Like in previous years, Classic released a 50-card second series set for use with its baseball trivia game. Unlike the 1989 update set, the 1990 Classic Series II set is numbered 1-50 with a "T" designation accompanying the card number. The cards measure 2-1/2" by 3-1/2" and are designed after the original 1990 Classic cards. Series II cards have pink borders with a blue design, while the cards from the regular issue feature the opposite color combination. The cards are issued in a complete Series II set form.

		MT	NR MT	EX
Complete Set (50):		8.00	6.00	3.25
Common Player:		.05	.04	.02
1	Gregg Jefferies	.15	.11	.06
2	Steve Adkins	.05	.04	.02
3	Sandy Alomar, Jr.	.10	.08	.04
4	Steve Avery	.50	.40	.20
5	Mike Blowers	.20	.15	.08
6	George Brett	.50	.40	.20
7	Tom Browning	.05	.04	.02
8	Ellis Burks	.10	.08	.04
9	Joe Carter	.15	.11	.06
10	Jerald Clark	.05	.04	.02
11	"Hot Corners" (Matt Williams, Will Clark)	.40	.30	.15
12	Pat Combs	.05	.04	.02
13	Scott Cooper	.15	.11	.06
14	Mark Davis	.05	.04	.02
15	Storm Davis	.05	.04	.02
16	Larry Walker	.15	.11	.06
17	Brian DuBois	.05	.04	.02
18	Len Dykstra	.15	.11	.06
19	John Franco	.10	.08	.04
20	Kirk Gibson	.10	.08	.04
21	Juan Gonzalez	2.00	1.50	.80
22	Tommy Greene	.05	.04	.02
23	Kent Hrbek	.15	.11	.06
24	Mike Huff	.05	.04	.02
25	Bo Jackson	.70	.50	.30
26	Nolan Knows Bo (Bo Jackson, Nolan Ryan)	2.00	1.50	.80
27	Roberto Kelly	.10	.08	.04
28	Mark Langston	.10	.08	.04
29	Ray Lankford	.60	.45	.25
30	Kevin Maas	.20	.15	.08
31	Julio Machado	.05	.04	.02
32	Greg Maddux	.10	.08	.04
33	Mark McGwire	.20	.15	.08
34	Paul Molitor	.20	.15	.08
35	Hal Morris	.10	.08	.04
36	Dale Murphy	.25	.20	.10
37	Eddie Murray	.25	.20	.10
38	Jaime Navarro	.05	.04	.02
39	Dean Palmer	.40	.30	.15
40	Derek Parks	.05	.04	.02
41	Bobby Rose	.05	.04	.02
42	Wally Joyner	.15	.11	.06
43	Chris Sabo	.10	.08	.04
44	Benito Santiago	.10	.08	.04
45	Mike Stanton	.05	.04	.02
46	Terry Steinbach	.05	.04	.02
47	Dave Stewart	.10	.08	.04
48	Greg Swindell	.05	.04	.02
49	Jose Vizcaino	.05	.04	.02
---	"Royal Flush" (Bret Saberhagen)	.25	.20	.10
---	"Royal Flush" (Mark Davis)	.25	.20	.10

1990 Classic Series III

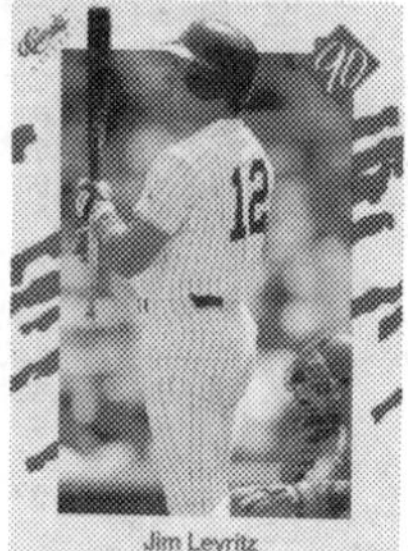

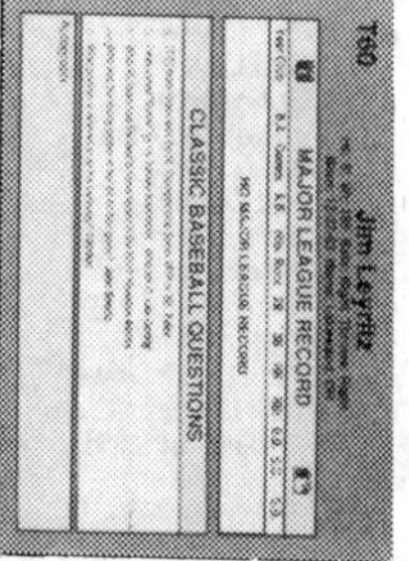

Classic's third series of 1990, features the same style as the previous two releases. The only major difference is the border color. Series III features yellow borders with blue accent. One hundred trivia playing cards are included in Series III. the cards are numbered 1T-100T. No card 51T or 57T exists. Two cards in the set are unnumbered. Like all other Classic issues, the cards are designed for use with the trivia board game.

		MT	NR MT	EX
Complete Set (100):		10.00	7.50	4.00
Common Player:		.05	.04	.02
1	Ken Griffey Jr.	1.50	1.25	.60
2	John Tudor	.05	.04	.02
3	John Kruk	.10	.08	.04
4	Mark Gardner	.05	.04	.02
5	Scott Radinsky	.20	.15	.08
6	John Burkett	.20	.15	.08
7	Will Clark	.40	.30	.15
8	Gary Carter	.10	.08	.04
9	Ted Higuera	.05	.04	.02
10	Dave Parker	.20	.15	.08
11	Dante Bichette	.05	.04	.02
12	Don Mattingly	.50	.40	.20
13	Greg Harris	.05	.04	.02
14	David Hollins	.10	.08	.04
15	Matt Nokes	.10	.08	.04
16	Kevin Tapani	.05	.04	.02
17	Shane Mack	.05	.04	.02
18	Randy Myers	.05	.04	.02
19	Greg Olson	.05	.04	.02
20	Shawn Abner	.05	.04	.02
21	Jim Presley	.05	.04	.02
22	Randy Johnson	.10	.08	.04
23	Edgar Martinez	.05	.04	.02
24	Scott Coolbaugh	.05	.04	.02
25	Jeff Treadway	.05	.04	.02
26	Joe Klink	.05	.04	.02
27	Rickey Henderson	.30	.25	.12
28	Sam Horn	.05	.04	.02
29	Kurt Stillwell	.05	.04	.02
30	Andy Van Slyke	.10	.08	.04
31	Willie Banks	.20	.15	.08
32	Jose Canseco	.30	.25	.12
33	Felix Jose	.05	.04	.02
34	Candy Maldonado	.05	.04	.02
35	Carlos Baerga	.30	.25	.12
36	Keith Hernandez	.05	.04	.02
37	Frank Viola	.10	.08	.04
38	Pete O'Brien	.05	.04	.02
39	Pat Borders	.05	.04	.02
40	Mike Heath	.05	.04	.02
41	Kevin Brown	.05	.04	.02
42	Chris Bosio	.05	.04	.02
43	Shawn Boskie	.05	.04	.02
44	Carlos Quintana	.05	.04	.02
45	Juan Samuel	.05	.04	.02
46	Tim Layana	.05	.04	.02
47	Mike Harkey	.05	.04	.02
48	Gerald Perry	.05	.04	.02
49	Mike Witt	.05	.04	.02
50	Joe Orsulak	.05	.04	.02

		MT	NR MT	EX
51	(Not issued)			
52	Willie Blair	.10	.08	.04
53	Gene Larkin	.05	.04	.02
54	Jody Reed	.05	.04	.02
55	Jeff Reardon	.05	.04	.02
56	Kevin McReynolds	.05	.04	.02
57	(Not issued)			
58	Eric Yelding	.05	.04	.02
59	Fred Lynn	.05	.04	.02
60	Jim Leyritz	.05	.04	.02
61	John Orton	.05	.04	.02
62	Mike Lieberthal	.20	.15	.08
63	Mike Hartley	.05	.04	.02
64	Kal Daniels	.05	.04	.02
65	Terry Shumpert	.05	.04	.02
66	Sil Campusano	.05	.04	.02
67	Tony Pena	.05	.04	.02
68	Barry Bonds	.35	.25	.14
69	Oddibe McDowell	.05	.04	.02
70	Kelly Gruber	.05	.04	.02
71	Willie Randolph	.05	.04	.02
72	Rick Parker	.05	.04	.02
73	Bobby Bonilla	.20	.15	.08
74	Jack Armstrong	.05	.04	.02
75	Hubie Brooks	.05	.04	.02
76	Sandy Alomar, Jr.	.10	.08	.04
77	Ruben Sierra	.20	.15	.08
78	Erik Hanson	.08	.06	.03
79	Tony Phillips	.05	.04	.02
80	Rondell White	.25	.20	.10
81	Bobby Thigpen	.05	.04	.02
82	Ron Walden	.05	.04	.02
83	Don Peters	.20	.15	.08
84	#6 (Nolan Ryan)	1.00	.70	.40
85	Lance Dickson	.05	.04	.02
86	Ryne Sandberg	.40	.30	.15
87	Eric Christopherson	.05	.04	.02
88	Shane Andrews	.05	.04	.02
89	Marc Newfield	.60	.45	.25
90	Adam Hyzdu	.25	.20	.10
91	"Texas Heat" (Nolan Ryan, Reid Ryan)	2.00	1.50	.80
92	Chipper Jones	.50	.40	.20
93	Frank Thomas	3.00	2.25	1.25
94	Cecil Fielder	.25	.20	.10
95	Delino DeShields	.20	.15	.08
96	John Olerud	.20	.15	.08
97	Dave Justice	1.00	.70	.40
98	Joe Oliver	.10	.08	.04
99	Alex Fernandez	.40	.30	.15
100	Todd Hundley	.20	.15	.08
—	Mike Marshall (Game Instructions On Back)	.05	.04	.02
—	4 in 1 (Frank Viola)	.30	.25	.12
—	4 in 1 (Nolan/Reid Ryan)	.30	.25	.12
—	4 in 1 (Chipper Jones)	.30	.25	.12
—	4 in 1 (Don Mattingly)	.30	.25	.12

1991 Classic

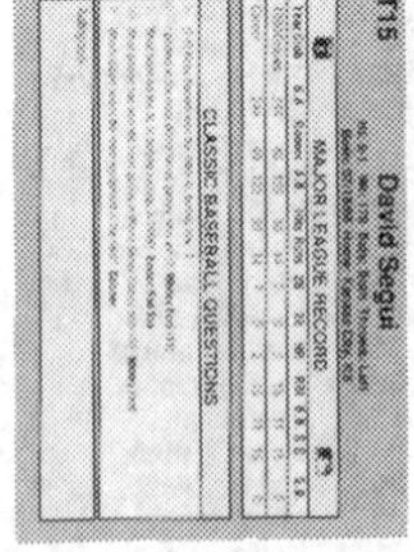

Top rookies and draft picks highlight this 99-card set from Classic. The cards come along with a board game and accessories designed for trivia game use. The card fronts feature fading blue borders with a touch of red. A "4-in-1" micro-player piece is included with each game set.

		MT	NR MT	EX
	Complete set (99):	8.00	6.00	3.25
	Common player:	.08	.06	.03
1	John Olerud	.20	.15	.08
2	Tino Martinez	.20	.15	.08
3	Ken Griffey,Jr.	1.00	.70	.40
4	Jeromy Burnitz	.25	.20	.10
5	Ron Gant	.15	.11	.06
6	Mike Benjamin	.08	.06	.03
7	Steve Decker	.10	.08	.04
8	Matt Williams	.10	.08	.04
9	Rafael Novoa	.08	.06	.03
10	Kevin Mitchell	.10	.08	.04
11	Dave Justice	.20	.15	.08
12	Leo Gomez	.20	.15	.08
13	Chris Hoiles	.20	.15	.08
14	Ben McDonald	.10	.08	.04
15	David Segui	.08	.06	.03
16	Anthony Telford	.25	.20	.10
17	Mike Mussina	.60	.45	.25
18	Roger Clemens	.20	.15	.08
19	Wade Boggs	.30	.25	.12
20	Tim Naehring	.10	.08	.04
21	Joe Carter	.10	.08	.04
22	Phil Plantier	.50	.40	.20
23	Rob Dibble	.08	.06	.03
24	Mo Vaughn	.50	.40	.20
25	Lee Stevens	.08	.06	.03
26	Chris Sabo	.10	.08	.04
27	Mark Grace	.15	.11	.06
28	Derrick May	.30	.25	.12
29	Ryne Sandberg	.30	.25	.12
30	Matt Stark	.08	.06	.03
31	Bobby Thigpen	.08	.06	.03
32	Frank Thomas	1.50	1.25	.60
33	Don Mattingly	.04	.11	.06
34	Eric Davis	.15	.11	.06
35	Reggie Jefferson	.20	.15	.08
36	Alex Cole	.08	.06	.03
37	Mark Lewis	.08	.06	.03
38	Tim Costo	.08	.06	.03
39	Sandy Alomar,Jr.	.10	.08	.04
40	Travis Fryman	.50	.40	.20
41	Cecil Fielder	.15	.11	.06
42	Milt Cuyler	.08	.06	.03
43	Andujar Cedeno	.20	.15	.08
44	Danny Darwin	.08	.06	.03
45	Randy Henis	.10	.08	.04
46	George Brett	.04	.08	.04
47	Jeff Conine	.20	.15	.08
48	Bo Jackson	.40	.30	.15
49	Brian McRae	.40	.30	.15
50	Brent Mayne	.20	.15	.08
51	Eddie Murray	.10	.08	.04
52	Ramon Martinez	.10	.08	.04
53	Jim Neidlinger	.10	.08	.04
54	Jim Poole	.10	.08	.04
55	Tim McIntosh	.08	.06	.03
56	Randy Veres	.08	.06	.03
57	Kirby Puckett	.30	.25	.12
58	Todd Ritchie	.08	.06	.03
59	Rich Garces	.08	.06	.03
60	Moises Alou	.12	.09	.05
61	Delino DeShields	.15	.11	.06
62	Oscar Azocar	.08	.06	.03
63	Kevin Maas	.10	.08	.04
64	Alan Mills	.08	.06	.03
65	John Franco	.08	.06	.03
66	Chris Jelic	.20	.15	.08
67	Dave Magadan	.08	.06	.03
68	Darryl Strawberry	.12	.09	.05
69	Hensley Meulens	.08	.06	.03
70	Juan Gonzalez	1.25	.90	.50
71	Reggie Harris	.08	.06	.03
72	Rickey Henderson	.20	.15	.08
73	Mark McGwire	.20	.15	.08
74	Willie McGee	.08	.06	.03
75	Todd Van Poppel	.75	.55	.25
76	Bob Welch	.08	.06	.03
77	"Future Aces" (Todd Van Poppel, Don Peters, David Zancanaro, Kirk Dressendorfer)	1.00	.70	.40
78	Lenny Dykstra	.15	.11	.06
79	Mickey Morandini	.20	.15	.08
80	Wes Chamberlain	.20	.15	.08
81	Barry Bonds	.30	.25	.12
82	Doug Drabek	.08	.06	.03
83	Randy Tomlin	.08	.06	.03
84	Scott Chiamparino	.08	.06	.03
85	Rafael Palmeiro	.15	.11	.06
86	Nolan Ryan	.50	.40	.20

		MT	NR MT	EX
87	Bobby Witt	.08	.06	.03
88	Fred McGriff	.15	.11	.06
89	Dave Steib	.08	.06	.03
90	Ed Sprague	.15	.11	.06
91	Vince Coleman	.08	.06	.03
92	Rod Brewer	.08	.06	.03
93	Bernard Gilkey	.35	.25	.14
94	Roberto Alomar	.20	.15	.08
95	Chuck Finley	.08	.06	.03
96	Dale Murphy	.20	.15	.08
97	Jose Rijo	.10	.08	.04
98	Hal Morris	.08	.06	.03
99	"Friendly Foes" (Dwight Gooden, Darryl Strawberry)	.15	.11	.06

1991 Classic Series II

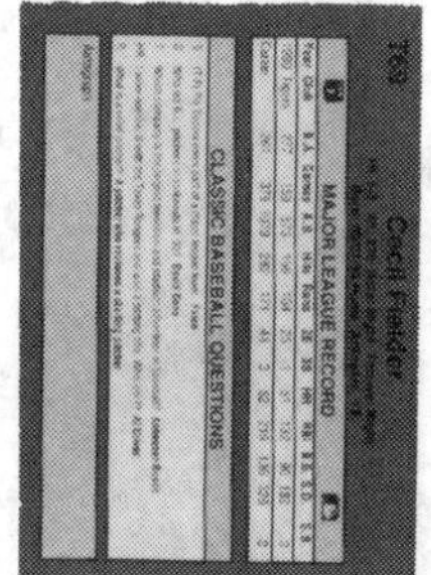

Classic released a 100-card second series in 1991 compared to a 50-card second series in 1990. The cards feature the same style as the first Classic series of 1991 with the exception of the border color. The first series featured blue borders, while Series II features maroon borders. The cards are designed for trivia game use. Series II includes several players with new teams and top rookies. Special Four-In-One, 300 Game Winner and Strikout Kings cards are included with each set.

		MT	NR MT	EX
Complete set (100):		8.00	6.00	3.25
Common player:		.08	.06	.03
1	Ken Griffey, Jr.	.80	.60	.30
2	Wilfredo Cordero	.25	.20	.10
3	Cal Ripken, Jr.	.40	.30	.15
4	D.J. Dozier	.15	.11	.06
5	Darrin Fletcher	.08	.06	.03
6	Glenn Davis	.08	.06	.03
7	Alex Fernandez	.10	.08	.04
8	Cory Snyder	.08	.06	.03
9	Tim Raines	.10	.08	.04
10	Greg Swindell	.08	.06	.03
11	Mark Lewis	.08	.06	.03
12	Rico Brogna	.20	.15	.08
13	Gary Sheffield	.15	.11	.06
14	Paul Molitor	.15	.11	.06
15	Kent Hrbek	.15	.11	.08
16	Scott Erickson	.20	.15	.08
17	Steve Sax	.08	.06	.03
18	Dennis Eckersley	.10	.08	.04
19	Jose Canseco	.25	.20	.10
20	Kirk Dressendorfer	.20	.15	.08
21	Ken Griffey,Sr.	.08	.06	.03
22	Erik Hanson	.10	.08	.04
23	Dan Peltier	.08	.06	.03
24	John Olerud	.10	.08	.04
25	Eddie Zosky	.15	.11	.06
26	Steve Avery	.20	.15	.08
27	John Smoltz	.10	.08	.04
28	Frank Thomas	1.00	.70	.40
29	Jerome Walton	.08	.06	.03
30	George Bell	.08	.06	.03
31	Jose Rijo	.08	.06	.03
32	Randy Myers	.08	.06	.03
33	Barry Larkin	.10	.08	.04
34	Eric Anthony	.08	.06	.03
35	Dave Hansen	.08	.06	.03
36	Eric Karros	.50	.40	.20
37	Jose Offerman	.08	.06	.03
38	Marquis Grissom	.10	.08	.04
39	Dwight Gooden	.15	.11	.06
40	Gregg Jefferies	.10	.08	.04
41	Pat Combs	.08	.06	.03
42	Todd Zeile	.10	.08	.04
43	Benito Santiago	.10	.08	.04
44	Dave Staton	.08	.06	.03
45	Tony Fernandez	.08	.06	.03
46	Fred McGriff	.10	.08	.04
47	Jeff Brantley	.08	.06	.03
48	Junior Felix	.08	.06	.03
49	Jack Morris	.10	.08	.04
50	Chris George	.10	.08	.04
51	Henry Rodriguez	.25	.20	.10
52	Paul Marak	.10	.08	.04
53	Ryan Klesko	.50	.40	.20
54	Darren Lewis	.15	.11	.06
55	Lance Dickson	.08	.06	.03
56	Anthony Young	.08	.06	.03
57	Willie Banks	.10	.08	.04
58	Mike Bordick	.08	.06	.03
59	Roger Salkeld	.20	.15	.08
60	Steve Karsay	.20	.15	.08
61	Bernie Williams	.08	.06	.03
62	Mickey Tettleton	.10	.08	.04
63	Dave Justice	.15	.11	.06
64	Steve Decker	.08	.06	.03
65	Roger Clemens	.15	.11	.06
66	Phil Plantier	.10	.08	.04
67	Ryne Sandberg	.50	.40	.20
68	Sandy Alomar,Jr.	.10	.08	.04
69	Cecil Fielder	.15	.11	.06
70	George Brett	.50	.40	.20
71	Delino DeShields	.10	.08	.04
72	Dave Magadan	.08	.06	.03
73	Darryl Strawberry	.15	.11	.06
74	Juan Gonzalez	.30	.25	.12
75	Rickey Henderson	.20	.15	.08
76	Willie McGee	.08	.06	.03
77	Todd Van Poppel	.50	.40	.20
78	Barry Bonds	.30	.25	.12
79	Doug Drabek	.08	.06	.03
80	Nolan Ryan (300 games)	.40	.30	.15
81	Roberto Alomar	.15	.11	.06
82	Ivan Rodriguez	1.00	.70	.40
83	Dan Opperman	.08	.06	.03
84	Jeff Bagwell	.50	.40	.20
85	Braulio Castillo	.08	.06	.03
86	Doug Simons	.08	.06	.03
87	Wade Taylor	.15	.11	.06
88	Gary Scott	.08	.06	.03
89	Dave Stewart	.10	.08	.04
90	Mike Simms	.08	.06	.03
91	Luis Gonzalez	.25	.20	.10
92	Bobby Bonilla	.15	.11	.06
93	Tony Gwynn	.15	.11	.06
94	Will Clark	.25	.20	.10
95	Rich Rowland	.08	.06	.03
96	Alan Trammell	.15	.11	.06
97	"Strikeout Kings" (Nolan Ryan, Roger Clemens)	.40	.30	.15
98	Joe Carter	.15	.11	.06
99	Jack Clark	.08	.06	.03
100	Four-In-One	.25	.20	.10

1991 Classic Series III

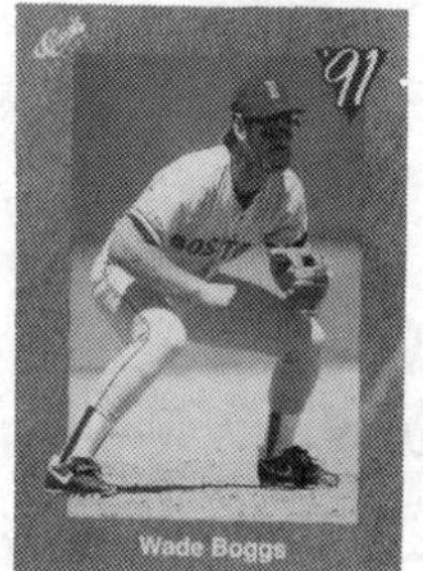

Green borders highlight Classic's third series of cards

for 1991. The set includes a gameboard and player cards featuring trivia questions on the back. Statistics, biographical information and card numbers are also found on the card backs.

		MT	NR MT	EX
Complete Set (100):		8.00	6.00	3.25
Common Player:		.06	.05	.02
1	Jim Abbott	.12	.09	.05
2	Craig Biggio	.06	.05	.02
3	Wade Boggs	.30	.25	.12
4	Bobby Bonilla	.15	.11	.06
5	Ivan Calderon	.06	.05	.02
6	Jose Canseco	.20	.15	.08
7	Andy Benes	.12	.09	.05
8	Wes Chamberlain	.12	.09	.05
9	Will Clark	.20	.15	.08
10	Royce Clayton	.20	.15	.08
11	Gerald Alexander	.06	.05	.02
12	Chili Davis	.08	.06	.03
13	Eric Davis	.12	.09	.05
14	Andre Dawson	.15	.11	.06
15	Rob Dibble	.06	.05	.02
16	Chris Donnels	.20	.15	.08
17	Scott Erickson	.12	.09	.05
18	Monty Fariss	.06	.05	.02
19	Ruben Amaro, Jr.	.25	.20	.10
20	Chuck Finley	.08	.06	.03
21	Carlton Fisk	.12	.09	.05
22	Carlos Baerga	.10	.08	.04
23	Ron Gant	.12	.09	.05
24	Dave Justice/ Ron Gant	.30	.25	.12
25	Mike Gardiner	.06	.05	.02
26	Tom Glavine	.10	.08	.04
27	Joe Grahe	.15	.11	.06
28	Derek Bell	.20	.15	.08
29	Mike Greenwell	.08	.06	.03
30	Ken Griffey, Jr.	.50	.40	.20
31	Leo Gomez	.06	.05	.02
32	Tom Goodwin	.15	.11	.06
33	Tony Gwynn	.12	.09	.05
34	Mel Hall	.06	.05	.02
35	Brian Harper	.08	.06	.03
36	Dave Henderson	.06	.05	.02
37	Albert Belle	.20	.15	.08
38	Orel Hershiser	.08	.06	.03
39	Brian Hunter	.12	.09	.05
40	Howard Johnson	.08	.06	.03
41	Felix Jose	.06	.05	.02
42	Wally Joyner	.10	.08	.04
43	Jeff Juden	.15	.11	.06
44	Pat Kelly	.12	.09	.05
45	Jimmy Key	.06	.05	.02
46	Chuck Knoblauch	.15	.11	.06
47	John Kruk	.12	.09	.05
48	Ray Lankford	.20	.15	.08
49	Ced Landrum	.06	.05	.02
50	Scott Livingstone	.12	.09	.05
51	Kevin Maas	.06	.05	.02
52	Greg Maddux	.08	.06	.03
53	Dennis Martinez	.06	.05	.02
54	Edgar Martinez	.06	.05	.02
55	Pedro Martinez	.08	.06	.03
56	Don Mattingly	.30	.25	.12
57	Orlando Merced	.30	.25	.12
58	Keith Mitchell	.10	.08	.04
59	Kevin Mitchell	.10	.08	.04
60	Paul Molitor	.12	.09	.05
61	Jack Morris	.08	.06	.03
62	Hal Morris	.06	.05	.02
63	Kevin Morton	.12	.09	.05
64	Pedro Munoz	.20	.15	.08
65	Eddie Murray	.15	.11	.06
66	Jack McDowell	.10	.08	.04
67	Jeff McNeely	.25	.20	.10
68	Brian McRae	.20	.15	.08
69	Kevin McReynolds	.06	.05	.02
70	Gregg Olson	.06	.05	.02
71	Rafael Palmeiro	.12	.09	.05
72	Dean Palmer	.12	.09	.05
73	Tony Phillips	.06	.05	.02
74	Kirby Puckett	.20	.15	.08
75	Carlos Quintana	.06	.05	.02
76	Pat Rice	.06	.05	.02
77	Cal Ripken, Jr.	.30	.25	.12
78	Ivan Rodriguez	1.00	.70	.40
79	Nolan Ryan	.50	.40	.20
80	Bret Saberhagen	.08	.06	.03
81	Tim Salmon	.75	.55	.25
82	Juan Samuel	.06	.05	.02
83	Ruben Sierra	.12	.09	.05
84	Heathcliff Slocumb	.06	.05	.02
85	Joe Slusarski	.12	.09	.05
86	John Smiley	.06	.05	.02
87	Dave Smith	.06	.05	.02
88	Ed Sprague	.08	.06	.03
89	Todd Stottlemyre	.06	.05	.02
90	Mike Timlin	.12	.09	.05
91	Greg Vaughn	.08	.06	.03
92	Frank Viola	.08	.06	.03
93	John Wehner	.08	.06	.03
94	Devon White	.08	.06	.03
95	Matt Williams	.15	.11	.06
96	Rick Wilkins	.15	.11	.06
97	Bernie Williams	.12	.09	.05
98	Starter & Stopper (Nolan Ryan, Goose Gossage)	.20	.15	.08
99	Gerald Williams	.30	.25	.12
----	4-In-1 (Bobby Bonilla, Will Clark, Cal Ripken Jr., Scott Erickson)	.20	.15	.08

1991 Classic Collector's Edition

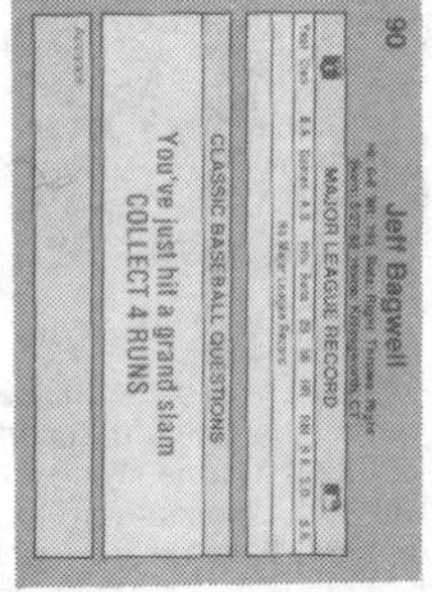

The Classic Collector's edition made its debut in 1991. This package includes a board game, trivia baseball cards, a baseball tips booklet and a certificate of authenticity. It is all packaged in an attractive collector's edition box. Each box is individually and sequentially numbered on the outside. This issue was limited with only 100,000 available. The card set features 200 trivia baseball cards. Mickey Morandini's card features a photo of Darren Daulton.

		MT	NR MT	EX
Complete Set (200):		25.00	18.00	13.00
Common Player:		.08	.06	.03
1	Frank Viola	.10	.08	.04
2	Tim Wallach	.08	.06	.03
3	Lou Whitaker	.10	.08	.04
4	Brett Butler	.08	.06	.03
5	Jim Abbott	.10	.08	.04
6	Jack Armstrong	.08	.06	.03
7	Craig Biggio	.08	.06	.03
8	Brian Barnes	.08	.06	.03
9	Dennis "Oil Can" Boyd	.08	.06	.03
10	Tom Browning	.08	.06	.03
11	Tom Brunansky	.08	.06	.03
12	Ellis Burks	.08	.06	.03
13	Harold Baines	.10	.08	.04
14	Kal Daniels	.08	.06	.03
15	Mark Davis	.08	.06	.03
16	Storm Davis	.08	.06	.03
17	Tom Glavine	.12	.09	.05
18	Mike Greenwell	.10	.08	.04
19	Kelly Gruber	.08	.06	.03
20	Mark Gubicza	.08	.06	.03
21	Pedro Guerrero	.08	.06	.03
22	Mike Harkey	.08	.06	.03
23	Orel Hershiser	.10	.08	.04
24	Ted Higuera	.08	.06	.03
25	Von Hayes	.08	.06	.03
26	Andre Dawson	.15	.11	.06
27	Shawon Dunston	.08	.06	.03
28	Roberto Kelly	.10	.08	.04

		MT	NR MT	EX
29	Joe Magrane	.08	.06	.03
30	Dennis Martinez	.10	.08	.04
31	Kevin McReynolds	.08	.06	.03
32	Matt Nokes	.10	.08	.04
33	Dan Plesac	.08	.06	.03
34	Dave Parker	.15	.11	.06
35	Randy Johnson	.10	.08	.04
36	Bret Saberhagen	.10	.08	.04
37	Mackey Sasser	.08	.06	.03
38	Mike Scott	.08	.06	.03
39	Ozzie Smith	.15	.11	.06
40	Kevin Seitzer	.08	.06	.03
41	Ruben Sierra	.12	.09	.05
42	Kevin Tapani	.08	.06	.03
43	Danny Tartabull	.12	.09	.05
44	Robby Thompson	.08	.06	.03
45	Andy Van Slyke	.12	.09	.05
46	Greg Vaughn	.12	.09	.05
47	Harold Reynolds	.10	.08	.04
48	Will Clark	.40	.30	.15
49	Gary Gaetti	.10	.08	.04
50	Joe Grahe	.08	.06	.03
51	Carlton Fisk	.20	.15	.08
52	Robin Ventura	.12	.09	.05
53	Ozzie Guillen	.10	.08	.04
54	Tom Candiotti	.08	.06	.03
55	Doug Jones	.08	.06	.03
56	Eric King	.08	.06	.03
57	Kirk Gibson	.12	.09	.05
58	Tim Costo	.08	.06	.03
59	Robin Yount	.25	.20	.10
60	Sammy Sosa	.20	.15	.08
61	Jesse Barfield	.08	.06	.03
62	Marc Newfield	.50	.40	.20
63	Jimmy Key	.08	.06	.03
64	Felix Jose	.08	.06	.03
65	Mark Whiten	.50	.40	.20
66	Tommy Greene	.08	.06	.03
67	Kent Mercker	.08	.06	.03
68	Greg Maddux	.10	.08	.04
69	Danny Jackson	.08	.06	.03
70	Reggie Sanders	.25	.20	.10
71	Eric Yelding	.08	.06	.03
72	Karl Rhodes	.20	.15	.08
73	Fernando Valenzuela	.10	.08	.04
74	Chris Nabholz	.10	.08	.04
75	Andres Galarraga	.10	.08	.04
76	Howard Johnson	.12	.09	.05
77	Hubie Brooks	.08	.06	.03
78	Terry Mulholland	.08	.06	.03
79	Paul Molitor	.15	.11	.06
80	Roger McDowell	.08	.06	.03
81	Darren Daulton	.10	.08	.04
82	Zane Smith	.08	.06	.03
83	Ray Lankford	.12	.09	.05
84	Bruce Hurst	.08	.06	.03
85	Andy Benes	.12	.09	.05
86	John Burkett	.10	.08	.04
87	Dave Righetti	.08	.06	.03
88	Steve Karsay	.40	.30	.15
89	D.J. Dozier	.40	.30	.15
90	Jeff Bagwell	.50	.40	.20
91	Joe Carter	.20	.15	.08
92	Wes Chamberlain	.12	.09	.05
93	Vince Coleman	.10	.08	.04
94	Pat Combs	.08	.06	.03
95	Jerome Walton	.08	.06	.03
96	Jeff Conine	.40	.30	.15
97	Alan Trammell	.15	.11	.06
98	Don Mattingly	.40	.30	.15
99	Ramon Martinez	.10	.08	.04
100	Dave Magadan	.08	.06	.03
101	Greg Swindell	.08	.06	.03
102	Dave Stewart	.10	.08	.04
103	Gary Sheffield	.15	.11	.06
104	George Bell	.10	.08	.04
105	Mark Grace	.15	.11	.06
106	Steve Sax	.08	.06	.03
107	Ryne Sandberg	.50	.40	.20
108	Chris Sabo	.10	.08	.04
109	Jose Rijo	.10	.08	.04
110	Cal Ripken, Jr.	.80	.60	.30
111	Kirby Puckett	.40	.30	.15
112	Eddie Murray	.20	.15	.08
113	Roberto Alomar	.30	.25	.12
114	Randy Myers	.08	.06	.03
115	Rafael Palmeiro	.15	.11	.06
116	John Olerud	.15	.11	.06
117	Gregg Jefferies	.12	.09	.05
118	Kent Hrbek	.12	.09	.05
119	Marquis Grissom	.12	.09	.05

		MT	NR MT	EX
120	Ken Griffey, Jr.	1.50	1.25	.60
121	Dwight Gooden	.20	.15	.08
122	Juan Gonzalez	.30	.25	.12
123	Ron Gant	.12	.09	.05
124	Travis Fryman	.12	.09	.05
125	John Franco	.08	.06	.03
126	Dennis Eckersley	.12	.09	.05
127	Cecil Fielder	.15	.11	.06
128	Phil Plantier	.50	.40	.20
129	Kevin Mitchell	.12	.09	.05
130	Kevin Maas	.08	.06	.03
131	Mark McGwire	.20	.15	.08
132	Ben McDonald	.10	.08	.04
133	Lenny Dykstra	.12	.09	.05
134	Delino DeShields	.12	.09	.05
135	Jose Canseco	.40	.30	.15
136	Eric Davis	.20	.15	.08
137	George Brett	.40	.30	.15
138	Steve Avery	.12	.09	.05
139	Eric Anthony	.10	.08	.04
140	Bobby Thigpen	.08	.06	.03
141	Ken Griffey, Sr.	.08	.06	.03
142	Barry Larkin	.12	.09	.05
143	Jeff Brantley	.08	.06	.03
144	Bobby Bonilla	.15	.11	.06
145	Jose Offerman	.08	.06	.03
146	Mike Mussina	.30	.25	.12
147	Erik Hanson	.10	.08	.04
148	Dale Murphy	.25	.20	.10
149	Roger Clemens	.30	.25	.12
150	Tino Martinez	.25	.20	.10
151	Todd Van Poppel	.75	.55	.25
152	Mo Vaughn	1.00	.70	.40
153	Derrick May	.20	.15	.08
154	Jack Clark	.08	.06	.03
155	Dave Hansen	.08	.06	.03
156	Tony Gwynn	.15	.11	.06
157	Brian McRae	.30	.25	.12
158	Matt Williams	.15	.11	.06
159	Kirk Dressendorfer	.30	.25	.12
160	Scott Erickson	.20	.15	.08
161	Tony Fernandez	.10	.08	.04
162	Willie McGee	.08	.06	.03
163	Fred McGriff	.12	.09	.05
164	Leo Gomez	.08	.06	.03
165	Bernard Gilkey	.30	.25	.12
166	Bobby Witt	.08	.06	.03
167	Doug Drabek	.08	.06	.03
168	Rob Dibble	.08	.06	.03
169	Glenn Davis	.08	.06	.03
170	Danny Darwin	.08	.06	.03
171	Eric Karros	.50	.40	.20
172	Eddie Zosky	.20	.15	.08
173	Todd Zeile	.12	.09	.05
174	Tim Raines	.12	.09	.05
175	Benito Santiago	.12	.09	.05
176	Dan Peltier	.20	.15	.08
177	Darryl Strawberry	.30	.25	.12
178	Hal Morris	.08	.06	.03
179	Hensley Meulens	.08	.06	.03
180	John Smoltz	.10	.08	.04
181	Frank Thomas	2.50	2.00	1.00
182	Dave Staton	.15	.11	.06
183	Scott Chiamparino	.08	.06	.03
184	Alex Fernandez	.30	.25	.12
185	Mark Lewis	.08	.06	.03
186	Bo Jackson	1.25	.90	.50
187	Mickey Morandini (photo actually Darren Daulton)	.30	.25	.12
188	Cory Snyder	.08	.06	.03
189	Rickey Henderson	.25	.20	.10
190	Junior Felix	.08	.06	.03
191	Milt Cuyler	.08	.06	.03
192	Wade Boggs	.30	.25	.12
193	"Justice Prevails" (David Justice)	.30	.25	.12
194	Sandy Alomar, Jr.	.12	.09	.05
195	Barry Bonds	.40	.30	.15
196	Nolan Ryan	1.00	.70	.40
197	Rico Brogna	.15	.11	.06
198	Steve Decker	.08	.06	.03
199	Bob Welch	.10	.08	.04
200	Andujar Cedeno	.12	.09	.05

The values quoted are intended to reflect the market price.

1992 Classic Series I

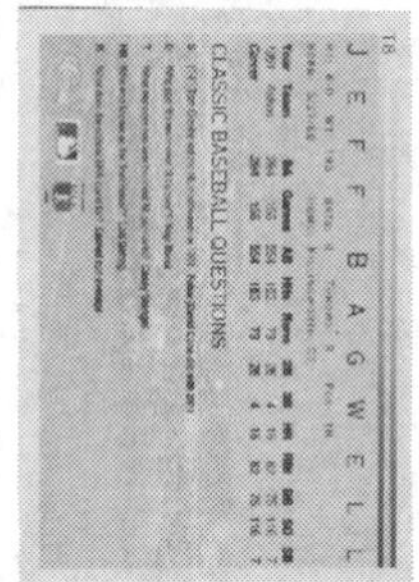

Classic introduced a new innovative design with the release of its 1992 set. The card fronts feature full-color photos bordered in white, while the flip sides feature statistics, biographical information and trivia questions accented by a fading stadium shot. The cards were released with a gameboard and are numbered on the back with a "T" prefix.

		MT	NR MT	EX
Complete set (100):		8.00	6.00	3.25
Common player:		.06	.05	.02
1	Jim Abbott	.12	.09	.05
2	Kyle Abbott	.10	.08	.04
3	Scott Aldred	.06	.05	.02
4	Roberto Alomar	.20	.15	.08
5	Wilson Alvarez	.08	.06	.03
6	Andy Ashby	.06	.05	.02
7	Steve Avery	.12	.09	.05
8	Jeff Bagwell	.12	.09	.05
9	Bret Barberie	.12	.09	.05
10	Kim Batiste	.10	.08	.04
11	Derek Bell	.10	.08	.04
12	Jay Bell	.10	.08	.04
13	Albert Belle	.15	.11	.06
14	Andy Benes	.10	.08	.04
15	Sean Berry	.08	.06	.03
16	Barry Bonds	.25	.20	.10
17	Ryan Bowen	.10	.08	.04
18	Trifecta (Alejandro Pena, Mark Wohlers, Kent Mercker)	.06	.05	.02
19	Scott Brosius	.06	.05	.02
20	Jay Buhner	.10	.08	.04
21	David Burba	.06	.05	.02
22	Jose Canseco	.25	.20	.10
23	Andujar Cedeno	.08	.06	.03
24	Will Clark	.25	.20	.10
25	Royce Clayton	.06	.05	.02
26	Roger Clemens	.20	.15	.08
27	David Cone	.08	.06	.03
28	Scott Cooper	.08	.06	.03
29	Chris Cron	.06	.05	.02
30	Len Dykstra	.10	.08	.04
31	Cal Eldred	.08	.06	.03
32	Hector Fajardo	.10	.08	.04
33	Cecil Fielder	.10	.08	.04
34	Dave Fleming	.10	.08	.04
35	Steve Foster	.06	.05	.02
36	Julio Franco	.06	.05	.02
37	Carlos Garcia	.06	.05	.02
38	Tom Glavine	.10	.08	.04
39	Tom Goodwin	.06	.05	.02
40	Ken Griffey, Jr.	.60	.45	.25
41	Chris Haney	.06	.05	.02
42	Bryan Harvey	.08	.06	.03
43	Rickey Henderson	.25	.20	.10
44	Carlos Hernandez	.06	.05	.02
45	Roberto Hernandez	.06	.05	.02
46	Brook Jacoby	.06	.05	.02
47	Howard Johnson	.10	.08	.04
48	Pat Kelly	.06	.05	.02
49	Darryl Kile	.08	.06	.03
50	Chuck Knoblauch	.12	.09	.05
51	Ray Lankford	.12	.09	.05
52	Mark Leiter	.06	.05	.02
53	Darren Lewis	.08	.06	.03
54	Scott Livingstone	.08	.06	.03
55	Shane Mack	.10	.08	.04
56	Chito Martinez	.20	.15	.08
57	Dennis Martinez	.06	.05	.02
58	Don Mattingly	.25	.20	.10
59	Paul McClellan	.06	.05	.02
60	Chuck McElroy	.06	.05	.02
61	Fred McGriff	.12	.09	.05
62	Orlando Merced	.10	.08	.04
63	Luis Mercedes	.08	.06	.03
64	Kevin Mitchell	.08	.06	.03
65	Hal Morris	.08	.06	.03
66	Jack Morris	.08	.06	.03
67	Mike Mussina	.12	.09	.05
68	Denny Neagle	.20	.15	.08
69	Tom Pagnozzi	.06	.05	.02
70	Terry Pendleton	.08	.06	.03
71	Phil Plantier	.10	.08	.04
72	Kirby Puckett	.15	.11	.06
73	Carlos Quintana	.06	.05	.02
74	Willie Randolph	.06	.05	.02
75	Arthur Rhodes	.08	.06	.03
76	Cal Ripken	.25	.20	.10
77	Ivan Rodriguez	.15	.11	.06
78	Nolan Ryan	.35	.25	.12
79	Ryne Sandberg	.25	.20	.10
80	Deion Sanders	.20	.15	.08
81	Reggie Sanders	.20	.15	.08
82	Mo Sanford	.15	.11	.06
83	Terry Shumpert	.06	.05	.02
84	Tim Spehr	.06	.05	.02
85	Lee Stevens	.06	.05	.02
86	Darryl Strawberry	.15	.11	.06
87	Kevin Tapani	.06	.05	.02
88	Danny Tartabull	.08	.06	.03
89	Frank Thomas	.80	.60	.30
90	Jim Thome	.20	.15	.08
91	Todd Van Poppel	.20	.15	.08
92	Andy Van Slyke	.08	.06	.03
93	John Wehner	.06	.05	.02
94	John Wetteland	.06	.05	.02
95	Devon White	.08	.06	.03
96	Brian Williams	.10	.08	.04
97	Mark Wohlers	.10	.08	.04
98	Robin Yount	.25	.20	.10
99	Eddie Zosky	.08	.06	.03
---	4-in-1 (Barry Bonds, Roger Clemens, Steve Avery, Nolan Ryan)	.12	.09	.05

1992 Classic Series II

The 100-cards in Classic's 1992 Series II came packaged with a gameboard and spinner. In a completely different format from Classic's other '92 issues, Series II features player photos bordered at left and right with red or blue color bars which fade toward top and bottom. The player's name is presented in a blue bar beneath the photo. Card backs have biographical data, previous-year and career statistics and five trivia questions, along with a color representation of the team's uniform. Cards, except the 4-In-1, are numbered with a "T" prefix.

		MT	NR MT	EX
Complete set (100):		8.00	6.00	3.00
Common player:		.06	.05	.02
1	Jim Abbott	.15	.11	.06
2	Jeff Bagwell	.12	.09	.05
3	Jose Canseco	.35	.25	.14
4	Julio Valera	.06	.05	.02

		MT	NR MT	EX
5	Scott Brosius	.06	.05	.02
6	Mark Langston	.10	.08	.04
7	Andy Stankiewicz	.06	.05	.02
8	Gary DiSarcina	.06	.05	.02
9	Pete Harnisch	.08	.06	.03
10	Mark McGwire	.20	.15	.08
11	Ricky Bones	.10	.08	.04
12	Steve Avery	.15	.11	.06
13	Deion Sanders	.25	.20	.10
14	Mike Mussina	.12	.09	.05
15	Dave Justice	.15	.11	.06
16	Pat Hentgen	.06	.05	.02
17	Tom Glavine	.12	.09	.05
18	Juan Guzman	.08	.06	.03
19	Ron Gant	.10	.08	.04
20	Kelly Gruber	.06	.05	.02
21	Eric Karros	.12	.09	.05
22	Derrick May	.08	.06	.03
23	Dave Hansen	.06	.05	.02
24	Andre Dawson	.12	.09	.05
25	Eric Davis	.15	.11	.06
26	Ozzie Smith	.15	.11	.06
27	Sammy Sosa	.10	.08	.04
28	Lee Smith	.10	.08	.04
29	Ryne Sandberg	.25	.20	.10
30	Robin Yount	.20	.15	.08
31	Matt Williams	.12	.09	.05
32	John Vander Wal	.06	.05	.02
33	Bill Swift	.06	.05	.02
34	Delino DeShields	.10	.08	.04
35	Royce Clayton	.06	.05	.02
36	Moises Alou	.08	.06	.03
37	Will Clark	.20	.15	.08
38	Darryl Strawberry	.20	.15	.08
39	Larry Walker	.10	.08	.04
40	Ramon Martinez	.06	.05	.02
41	Howard Johnson	.10	.08	.04
42	Tino Martinez	.06	.05	.02
43	Dwight Gooden	.15	.11	.06
44	Ken Griffey, Jr.	.45	.35	.20
45	David Cone	.08	.06	.03
46	Kenny Lofton	.06	.05	.02
47	Bobby Bonilla	.12	.09	.05
48	Carlos Baerga	.10	.08	.04
49	Don Mattingly	.25	.20	.10
50	Sandy Alomar, Jr.	.08	.06	.03
51	Lenny Dykstra	.12	.09	.05
52	Tony Gwynn	.15	.11	.06
53	Felix Jose	.06	.05	.02
54	Rick Sutcliffe	.06	.05	.02
55	Wes Chamberlain	.06	.05	.02
56	Cal Ripken, Jr.	.25	.20	.10
57	Kyle Abbott	.06	.05	.02
58	Leo Gomez	.06	.05	.02
59	Gary Sheffield	.12	.09	.05
60—	Anthony Young	.06	.05	.02
61—	Roger Clemens	.15	.11	.06
62—	Rafael Palmeiro	.15	.11	.06
63—	Wade Boggs	.20	.15	.08
64—	Andy Van Slyke	.12	.09	.05
65—	Ruben Sierra	.12	.09	.05
66—	Denny Neagle	.06	.05	.02
67—	Nolan Ryan	.45	.35	.20
68—	Doug Drabek	.08	.06	.03
69—	Ivan Rodriguez	.10	.08	.04
70—	Barry Bonds	.20	.15	.08
71—	Chuck Knoblauch	.10	.08	.04
72—	Reggie Sanders	.08	.06	.03
73—	Cecil Fielder	.15	.11	.06
74—	Barry Larkin	.12	.09	.05
75—	Scott Aldred	.06	.05	.02
76—	Rob Dibble	.06	.05	.02
77—	Brian McRae	.10	.08	.04
78—	Tim Belcher	.06	.05	.02
79—	George Brett	.25	.20	.10
80—	Frank Viola	.08	.06	.03
81—	Roberto Kelly	.08	.06	.03
82—	Jack McDowell	.10	.08	.04
83—	Mel Hall	.06	.05	.02
84—	Esteban Beltre	.15	.11	.06
85—	Robin Ventura	.12	.09	.05
86—	George Bell	.10	.08	.04
87—	Frank Thomas	.45	.35	.20
88—	John Smiley	.06	.05	.02
89—	Bobby Thigpen	.06	.05	.02
90—	Kirby Puckett	.20	.15	.08
91—	Kevin Mitchell	.08	.06	.03
92—	Peter Hoy	.15	.11	.06
93—	Russ Springer	.15	.11	.06
94—	Donovan Osborne	.06	.05	.02
95—	Dave Silvestri	.15	.11	.06
96—	Chad Curtis	.15	.11	.06
97—	Pat Mahomes	.06	.05	.02
98—	Danny Tartabull	.10	.08	.04
99—	John Doherty	.15	.11	.06
-----	4-In-1 (Ryne Sandberg, Mike Mussina, Reggie Sanders, Jose Canseco)	.20	.15	.08

1992 Classic Collector's Edition

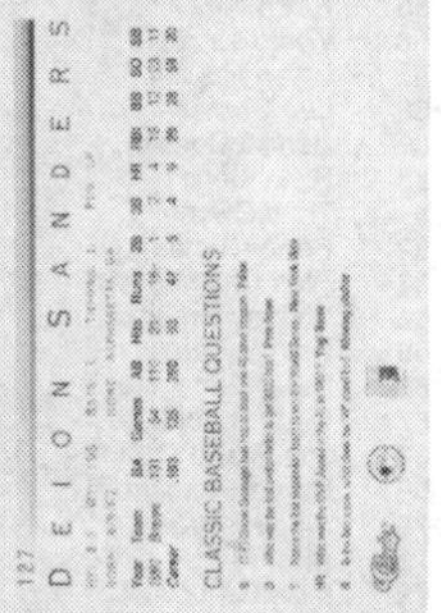

The second annual 200-card "Collector's Edition" set was packaged with a gameboard, spinner, generic player pieces a mechanical scoreboard and a book of tips from star players. The UV-coated card fronts feature color player photos against a deep purple border. The Classic logo, year of issue and player's name aare reversed out of the top and bottom borders. Card backs have a few biographical details, stats from the previous season and career totals, plus five trivia questions in case anyone actually decided to play the game.

		MT	NR MT	EX
Complete Set (200):		20.00	15.00	8.00
Common Player:		.06	.05	.02
1	Chuck Finley	.06	.05	.02
2	Craig Biggio	.08	.06	.03
3	Luis Gonzalez	.06	.05	.02
4	Pete Harnisch	.08	.06	.03
5	Jeff Juden	.06	.05	.02
6	Harold Baines	.08	.06	.03
7	Kirk Dressendorfer	.06	.05	.02
8	Dennis Eckersley	.10	.08	.04
9	Dave Henderson	.06	.05	.02
10	Dave Stewart	.10	.08	.04
11	Joe Carter	.15	.11	.06
12	Juan Guzman	.08	.06	.03
13	Dave Stieb	.06	.05	.02
14	Todd Stottlemyre	.06	.05	.02
15	Ron Gant	.12	.05	.02
16	Brian Hunter	.06	.05	.02
17	Dave Justice	.15	.11	.06
18	John Smoltz	.10	.08	.04
19	Mike Stanton	.06	.05	.02
20	Chris George	.06	.05	.02
21	Paul Molitor	.15	.11	.06
22	Omar Olivares	.06	.05	.02
23	Lee Smith	.08	.06	.03
24	Ozzie Smith	.15	.11	.06
25	Todd Zeile	.08	.06	.03
26	George Bell	.08	.06	.03
27	Andre Dawson	.15	.11	.06
28	Shawon Dunston	.06	.05	.02
29	Mark Grace	.12	.05	.02
30	Greg Maddux	.12	.05	.02
31	Dave Smith	.06	.05	.02
32	Brett Butler	.06	.05	.02
33	Orel Hershiser	.12	.05	.02
34	Eric Karros	.10	.08	.04
35	Ramon Martinez	.06	.05	.02
36	Jose Offerman	.06	.05	.02
37	Juan Samuel	.06	.05	.02
38	Delino DeShields	.12	.05	.02
39	Marquis Grissom	.08	.06	.03
40	Tim Wallach	.06	.05	.02
41	Eric Gunderson	.06	.05	.02

		MT	NR MT	EX
42	Willie McGee	.08	.06	.03
43	Dave Righetti	.06	.05	.02
44	Robby Thompson	.08	.06	.03
45	Matt Williams	.10	.08	.04
46	Sandy Alomar Jr.	.08	.06	.03
47	Reggie Jefferson	.06	.05	.02
48	Mark Lewis	.06	.05	.02
49	Robin Ventura	.12	.05	.02
50	Tino Martinez	.06	.05	.02
51	Roberto Kelly	.08	.06	.03
52	Vince Coleman	.08	.06	.03
53	Dwight Gooden	.15	.11	.06
54	Todd Hundley	.06	.05	.02
55	Kevin Maas	.06	.05	.02
56	Wade Taylor	.06	.05	.02
57	Bryan Harvey	.08	.06	.03
58	Leo Gomez	.06	.05	.02
59	Ben McDonald	.08	.06	.03
60	Ricky Bones	.06	.05	.02
61	Tony Gwynn	.12	.05	.02
62	Benito Santiago	.10	.08	.04
63	Wes Chamberlain	.06	.05	.02
64	Tommy Greene	.06	.05	.02
65	Dale Murphy	.15	.11	.06
66	Steve Buechele	.06	.05	.02
67	Doug Drabek	.06	.05	.02
68	Joe Grahe	.06	.05	.02
69	Rafael Palmeiro	.15	.11	.06
70	Wade Boggs	.20	.15	.08
71	Ellis Burks	.08	.06	.03
72	Mike Greenwell	.08	.06	.03
73	Mo Vaughn	.12	.05	.02
74	Derek Bell	.06	.05	.02
75	Rob Dibble	.06	.05	.02
76	Barry Larkin	.12	.05	.02
77	Jose Rijo	.10	.08	.04
78	Doug Henry	.06	.05	.02
79	Chris Sabo	.08	.06	.03
80	Pedro Guerrero	.06	.05	.02
81	George Brett	.20	.15	.08
82	Tom Gordon	.06	.05	.02
83	Mark Gubicza	.06	.05	.02
84	Mark Whiten	.06	.05	.02
85	Brian McRae	.08	.06	.03
86	Danny Jackson	.06	.05	.02
87	Milt Cuyler	.06	.05	.02
88	Travis Fryman	.10	.08	.04
89	Mickey Tettleton	.10	.08	.04
90	Alan Trammell	.15	.11	.06
91	Lou Whitaker	.12	.05	.02
92	Chili Davis	.10	.08	.04
93	Scott Erickson	.06	.05	.02
94	Kent Hrbek	.12	.05	.02
95	Alex Fernandez	.08	.06	.03
96	Carlton Fisk	.12	.05	.02
97	Ramon Garcia	.06	.05	.02
98	Ozzie Guillen	.08	.06	.03
99	Tim Raines	.12	.05	.02
100	Bobby Thigpen	.06	.05	.02
101	Kirby Puckett	.15	.11	.06
102	Bernie Williams	.06	.05	.02
103	Dave Hansen	.06	.05	.02
104	Kevin Tapani	.06	.05	.02
105	Don Mattingly	.20	.15	.08
106	Frank Thomas	.50	.40	.20
107	Monty Fariss	.06	.05	.02
108	Bo Jackson	.45	.35	.20
109	Jim Abbott	.15	.11	.06
110	Jose Canseco	.25	.20	.10
111	Phil Plantier	.10	.08	.04
112	Brian Williams	.06	.05	.02
113	Mark Langston	.06	.05	.02
114	Wilson Alvarez	.06	.05	.02
115	Roberto Hernandez	.06	.05	.02
116	Darryl Kile	.08	.06	.03
117	Ryan Bowen	.15	.11	.06
118	Rickey Henderson	.15	.11	.06
119	Mark McGwire	.15	.11	.06
120	Devon White	.10	.08	.04
121	Roberto Alomar	.15	.11	.06
122	Kelly Gruber	.06	.05	.02
123	Eddie Zosky	.06	.05	.02
124	Tom Glavine	.08	.06	.03
125	Kal Daniels	.06	.05	.02
126	Cal Eldred	.06	.05	.02
127	Deion Sanders	.25	.20	.10
128	Robin Yount	.20	.15	.08
129	Cecil Fielder	.15	.11	.06
130	Ray Lankford	.08	.06	.03
131	Ryne Sandberg	.25	.20	.10
132	Darryl Strawberry	.20	.15	.08

		MT	NR MT	EX
133	Chris Haney	.06	.05	.02
134	Dennis Martinez	.06	.05	.02
135	Bryan Hickerson	.06	.05	.02
136	Will Clark	.15	.11	.06
137	Hal Morris	.06	.05	.02
138	Charles Nagy	.06	.05	.02
139	Jim Thome	.06	.05	.02
140	Albert Belle	.15	.11	.06
141	Reggie Sanders	.12	.05	.02
142	Scott Cooper	.10	.08	.04
143	David Cone	.06	.05	.02
144	Anthony Young	.06	.05	.02
145	Howard Johnson	.12	.05	.02
146	Arthur Rhodes	.08	.06	.03
147	Scott Aldred	.06	.05	.02
148	Mike Mussina	.10	.08	.04
149	Fred McGriff	.15	.11	.06
150	Andy Benes	.10	.08	.04
151	Ruben Sierra	.15	.11	.06
152	Len Dykstra	.15	.11	.06
153	Andy Van Slyke	.10	.08	.04
154	Orlando Merced	.06	.05	.02
155	Barry Bonds	.20	.15	.08
156	John Smiley	.06	.05	.02
157	Julio Franco	.06	.05	.02
158	Juan Gonzalez	.25	.20	.10
159	Ivan Rodriguez	.15	.11	.06
160	Willie Banks	.06	.05	.02
161	Eric Davis	.15	.11	.06
162	Eddie Murray	.15	.11	.06
163	Dave Fleming	.06	.05	.02
164	Wally Joyner	.15	.11	.06
165	Kevin Mitchell	.08	.06	.03
166	Ed Taubensee	.06	.05	.02
167	Danny Tartabull	.10	.08	.04
168	Ken Hill	.06	.05	.02
169	Willie Randolph	.06	.05	.02
170	Kevin McReynolds	.08	.06	.03
171	Gregg Jefferies	.12	.05	.02
172	Patrick Lennon	.06	.05	.02
173	Luis Mercedes	.06	.05	.02
174	Glenn Davis	.06	.05	.02
175	Bret Saberhagen	.08	.06	.03
176	Bobby Bonilla	.12	.05	.02
177	Kenny Lofton	.08	.06	.03
178	Jose Lind	.08	.06	.03
179	Royce Clayton	.06	.05	.02
180	Scott Scudder	.06	.05	.02
181	Chuck Knoblauch	.08	.06	.03
182	Terry Pendleton	.08	.06	.03
183	Nolan Ryan	.50	.40	.20
184	Rob Maurer	.06	.05	.02
185	Brian Bohanon	.06	.05	.02
186	Ken Griffey Jr.	.50	.40	.20
187	Jeff Bagwell	.10	.08	.04
188	Steve Avery	.12	.05	.02
189	Roger Clemens	.15	.11	.06
190	Cal Ripken	.25	.20	.10
191	Kim Batiste	.06	.05	.02
192	Bip Roberts	.06	.05	.02
193	Greg Swindell	.06	.05	.02
194	Dave Winfield	.15	.11	.06
195	Steve Sax	.06	.05	.02
196	Frank Viola	.08	.06	.03
197	Mo Sanford	.06	.05	.02
198	Kyle Abbott	.06	.05	.02
199	Jack Morris	.08	.06	.03
200	Andy Ashby	.06	.05	.02

1991 Conlon Collection

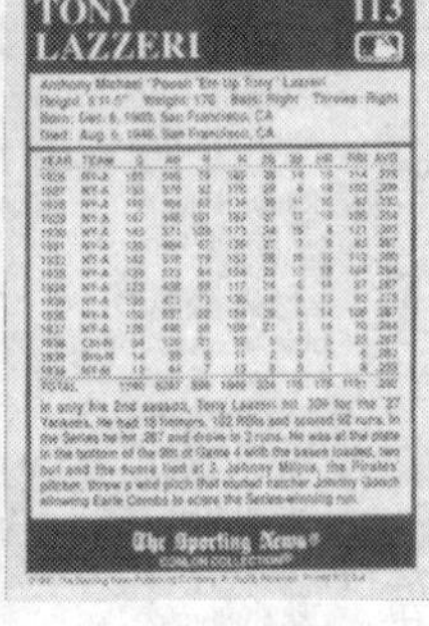

This 330-card set features the photography of Charles Martin Conlon, who was active from the before 1910

through the early 1940s. Black-and-white photos are set against black borders on the UV-coated card fronts. Megacards worked with The Sporting News, (owners of the Conlon photos) to release the set. Several subsets are featured such as Hall of Famers, 1927 New York Yankees, MVP's and more. The backs feature statistics and career highlights.

		MT	NR MT	EX
Complete set (330):		30.00	22.50	11.00
Common player:		.10	.08	.04
1	Rogers Hornsby	.10	.08	.04
2	James E. Foxx	.10	.08	.04
3	Jay H. Dean	.10	.08	.04
4	Walter J.V. Maranville	.10	.08	.04
5	Paul G. Waner	.10	.08	.04
6	Lloyd J. Waner	.10	.08	.04
7	Melvin T. Ott	.10	.08	.04
8	John P. Wagner	.10	.08	.04
9	Walter P. Johnson	.10	.08	.04
10	Carol O. Hubbell	.10	.08	.04
11	Frank F. Frisch	.10	.08	.04
12	Hazen S. Cuyler	.10	.08	.04
13	Charles H. Ruffing	.10	.08	.04
14	Henry B. Greenberg	.10	.08	.04
15	John J. Evers	.10	.08	.04
16	Hugh A. Jennings	.10	.08	.04
17	David J. Bancroft	.10	.08	.04
18	Joseph M. Medwick	.10	.08	.04
19	Theodore A. Lyons	.10	.08	.04
20	Charles A. Bender	.10	.08	.04
21	Edward T. Collins	.10	.08	.04
22	James L. Bottomley	.10	.08	.04
23	Robert M. Grove	.10	.08	.04
24	Max Carey	.10	.08	.04
25	Burleigh A. Grimes	.10	.08	.04
26	Ross M. Youngs	.10	.08	.04
27	Ernest N. Lombardi	.10	.08	.04
28	Joseph V. McCarthy	.10	.08	.04
29	Lewis R. Wilson	.10	.08	.04
30	Charles H. Klein	.10	.08	.04
31	Howard E. Averill Sr.	.10	.08	.04
32	Grover C. Alexander	.10	.08	.04
33	Charles J. Hafey	.10	.08	.04
34	William B. Mckechnie	.10	.08	.04
35	Robert W.A. Feller	.10	.08	.04
36	Harold J. Traynor	.10	.08	.04
37	Charles D. Stengel	.10	.08	.04
38	Joseph F. Vaughan	.10	.08	.04
39	Eppa Rixey	.10	.08	.04
40	Joseph W. Sewell	.10	.08	.04
41	Urban C. Faber	.10	.08	.04
42	Travis C. Jackson	.10	.08	.04
43	Jesse J. Haines	.10	.08	.04
44	Tristram E. Speaker	.10	.08	.04
45	Cornelius Mack	.10	.08	.04
46	Cornelius Mack	.10	.08	.04
47	Cornelius Mack	.10	.08	.04
48	Raymond W. Schalk	.10	.08	.04
49	Aloysius H. Simmons	.10	.08	.04
50	Joseph E. Cronin	.10	.08	.04
51	Gordon S. Cochrane	.10	.08	.04
52	Harry E. Heilmann	.10	.08	.04
53	John R. Mize	.10	.08	.04
54	Edgar C. Rice	.10	.08	.04
55	Edd J. Roush	.10	.08	.04
56	Enos B. Slaughter	.10	.08	.04
57	Christopher Mathewson	.10	.08	.04
58	Fred C. Lindstrom	.10	.08	.04
59	Charles L. Hartnett	.10	.08	.04
60	George L. Kelly	.10	.08	.04
61	Stanley R. Harris	.10	.08	.04
62	Leon A. Goslin	.10	.08	.04
63	Henry E. Manush	.10	.08	.04
64	William H. Terry	.10	.08	.04
65	John J. McGraw	.10	.08	.04
66	George H. Sisler	.10	.08	.04
67	Vernon L. Gomez	.10	.08	.04
68	Joseph I. Judge	.10	.08	.04
69	Thomas J. Thevenow	.10	.08	.04
70	Charles M. Gelbert	.10	.08	.04
71	Minter C. Hayes	.10	.08	.04
72	Robert R. Fothergill	.10	.08	.04
73	Adam A. Comorosky	.10	.08	.04
74	Earl S. Smith	.10	.08	.04
75	Samuel D. Gray	.10	.08	.04
76	Peter W. Appleton	.10	.08	.04
77	Eugene Moore Jr.	.10	.08	.04
78	Arndt L. Jorgens	.10	.08	.04
79	William H. Knickerbocker	.10	.08	.04

		MT	NR MT	EX
80	Carl N. Reynolds	.10	.08	.04
81	Oscar D. Melillo	.10	.08	.04
82	John H. Burnett	.10	.08	.04
83	Alvin J. Powell	.10	.08	.04
84	John J. Murphy	.10	.08	.04
85	Leroy E. Parmelee	.10	.08	.04
86	James A. Ripple	.10	.08	.04
87	Gerald H. Walker	.10	.08	.04
88	George L. Earnshaw	.10	.08	.04
89	William H. Southworth	.10	.08	.04
90	Wallace Moses	.10	.08	.04
91	George E. Walberg	.10	.08	.04
92	James J. Dykes	.10	.08	.04
93	Charles H. Root	.10	.08	.04
94	John W. Cooney	.10	.08	.04
95	Charles J. Grimm	.10	.08	.04
96	Robert L. Johnson	.10	.08	.04
97	John W. Scott	.10	.08	.04
98	Raymond A. Radcliff	.10	.08	.04
99	Frederick R. Ostermueller	.10	.08	.04
100	Julian V. Wera	.10	.08	.04
101	Miller J. Huggins	.10	.08	.04
102	Raymond A. Morehart	.10	.08	.04
103	Bernard O. Bengough	.10	.08	.04
104	Walter H. Ruether	.10	.08	.04
105	Earle B. Combs	.10	.08	.04
106	Myles L. Thomas	.10	.08	.04
107	Benjamin E. Paschal	.10	.08	.04
108	Cedric M. Durst	.10	.08	.04
109	William W. Moore	.10	.08	.04
110	George H. Ruth	.50	.40	.20
111	Louis H. Gehrig	.50	.40	.20
112	Joseph A. Dugan	.10	.08	.04
113	Anthony M. Lazzeri	.10	.08	.04
114	Urban J. Shocker	.10	.08	.04
115	Waite C. Hoyt	.10	.08	.04
116	Charles T. O'Leary	.10	.08	.04
117	Arthur Fletcher	.10	.08	.04
118	Tharon L. Collins	.10	.08	.04
119	Joseph O. Giard	.10	.08	.04
120	Herbert J. Pennock	.10	.08	.04
121	Michael Gazella	.10	.08	.04
122	Robert W. Meusel	.10	.08	.04
123	George W. Pipgras	.10	.08	.04
124	John P. Grabowski	.10	.08	.04
125	Mark A. Koenig	.10	.08	.04
126	Stanley C. Hack	.10	.08	.04
127	Earl O. Whitehill	.10	.08	.04
128	William C. Lee	.10	.08	.04
129	Frank O. Mancuso	.10	.08	.04
130	Francis R. Blades	.10	.08	.04
131	John I. Burns	.10	.08	.04
132	Clinton H. Brown	.10	.08	.04
133	William J. Dietrich	.10	.08	.04
134	Darrell E. Blanton	.10	.08	.04
135	Harry B. Hooper	.10	.08	.04
136	Charles H. Shorten	.10	.08	.04
137	Clarence W. Walker	.10	.08	.04
138	George Foster	.10	.08	.04
139	John J. Barry	.10	.08	.04
140	Samuel P. Jones	.10	.08	.04
141	Ernest G. Shore	.10	.08	.04
142	Hubert B. Leonard	.10	.08	.04
143	Herbert J. Pennock	.10	.08	.04
144	Harold C. Janvrin	.10	.08	.04
145	George H. Ruth	.40	.30	.15
146	George E. Lewis	.10	.08	.04
147	William L. Gardner	.10	.08	.04
148	Richard C. Hoblitzel	.10	.08	.04
149	Lewis E. Scott	.10	.08	.04
150	Carl W. Mays	.10	.08	.04
151	John A. Niehoff	.10	.08	.04
152	Burton E. Shotton	.10	.08	.04
153	Leon K. Ames	.10	.08	.04
154	Fred Williams	.10	.08	.04
155	William W. Hinchman	.10	.08	.04
156	James R. Shawkey	.10	.08	.04
157	Walter C. Pipp	.10	.08	.04
158	George J. Burns	.10	.08	.04
159	Robert H. Veach	.10	.08	.04
160	Harold H. Chase	.10	.08	.04
161	Thomas L. Hughes	.10	.08	.04
162	Derrill B. Pratt	.10	.08	.04
163	Henry K. Groh	.10	.08	.04
164	Zachariah D. Wheat	.10	.08	.04
165	Francis J. O'Doul	.10	.08	.04
166	William E. Kamm	.10	.08	.04
167	Paul G. Waner	.10	.08	.04
168	Fred C. Snodgrass	.10	.08	.04
169	Floyd C. Herman	.10	.08	.04
170	Albert H. Bridwell	.10	.08	.04

		MT	NR MT	EX
171	John T. Meyers	.10	.08	.04
172	John B. Lobert	.10	.08	.04
173	Raymond B. Bressler	.10	.08	.04
174	Samuel P. Jones	.10	.08	.04
175	Robert A. O'Farrell	.10	.08	.04
176	George Toporcer	.10	.08	.04
177	George E. McNeely	.10	.08	.04
178	John H. Knott	.10	.08	.04
179	Clarence F. Mueller	.10	.08	.04
180	Thomas J.D. Bridges	.10	.08	.04
181	Lloyd A. Brown	.10	.08	.04
182	Lawrence J. Benton	.10	.08	.04
183	Max F. Bishop	.10	.08	.04
184	Morris Berg	.10	.08	.04
185	Ralph F. Perkins	.10	.08	.04
186	Stephen F. O'Neill	.10	.08	.04
187	Glenn C. Myatt	.10	.08	.04
188	Joseph A. Kuhel	.10	.08	.04
189	Martin J. McManus	.10	.08	.04
190	Charles F. Lucas	.10	.08	.04
191	John P. McInnis	.10	.08	.04
192	Edmund J. Miller	.10	.08	.04
193	James L. Sewell	.10	.08	.04
194	William H. Sherdel	.10	.08	.04
195	Harold J. Rhyne	.10	.08	.04
196	Guy T. Bush	.10	.08	.04
197	Ervin Fox	.10	.08	.04
198	Wesley C. Ferrell	.10	.08	.04
199	Roy C. Johnson	.10	.08	.04
200	William Wambsganss	.10	.08	.04
201	George H. Burns	.10	.08	.04
202	Clarence E. Mitchell	.10	.08	.04
203	Cornelius Ball	.10	.08	.04
204	John H. Neun	.10	.08	.04
205	Homer W. Summa	.10	.08	.04
206	Ernest K. Padgett	.10	.08	.04
207	Walter H. Holke	.10	.08	.04
208	Forrest G. Wright	.10	.08	.04
209	Henry M. Gowdy	.10	.08	.04
210	James W. Taylor	.10	.08	.04
211	Benjamin C. Cantwell	.10	.08	.04
212	Joseph F. Demaree	.10	.08	.04
213	Samuel P. Derringer	.10	.08	.04
214	William A. Hallahan	.10	.08	.04
215	Daniel K. MacFayden	.10	.08	.04
216	Harry F. Rice	.10	.08	.04
217	Robert Eldridge Smith	.10	.08	.04
218	Jackson R. Stephenson	.10	.08	.04
219	Perce L. Malone	.10	.08	.04
220	Henry B. Tate	.10	.08	.04
221	Joseph F. Vosmik	.10	.08	.04
222	George A. Watkins	.10	.08	.04
223	James Wilson	.10	.08	.04
224	George E. Uhle	.10	.08	.04
225	Melvin T. Ott	.10	.08	.04
226	Nicholas Altrock	.10	.08	.04
227	Charles H. Ruffing	.10	.08	.04
228	Joseph V.L. Krakauskas	.10	.08	.04
229	Walter A. Berger	.10	.08	.04
230	Norman L. Newsom	.10	.08	.04
231	Lonnie Warneke	.10	.08	.04
232	Frank E. Snyder	.10	.08	.04
233	Myril O. Hoag	.10	.08	.04
234	Baldomero M. Almada	.10	.08	.04
235	Ivy B. Wingo	.10	.08	.04
236	James P. Austin	.10	.08	.04
237	Henry J. Bonura	.10	.08	.04
238	Russell G. Wrightstone	.10	.08	.04
239	Alfred C. Todd	.10	.08	.04
240	Harold B. Warstler	.10	.08	.04
241	Samuel F. West	.10	.08	.04
242	Arthur C. Reinhart	.10	.08	.04
243	Walter C. Stewart	.10	.08	.04
244	John B. Gooch	.10	.08	.04
245	Eugene F. Hargrave	.10	.08	.04
246	George W. Harper	.10	.08	.04
247	George W. Connally	.10	.08	.04
248	Edgar G. Braxton	.10	.08	.04
249	Walter H. Schang	.10	.08	.04
250	Tyrus R. Cobb	.50	.40	.20
251	Rogers Hornsby	.10	.08	.04
252	Richard W. Marquard	.10	.08	.04
253	Carl O. Hubbell	.10	.08	.04
254	Joe Wood	.10	.08	.04
255	Robert M. Grove	.10	.08	.04
256	Lynwood T. Rowe	.10	.08	.04
257	Alvin F. Crowder	.10	.08	.04
258	Walter P. Johnson	.10	.08	.04
259	Charles J. Hafey	.10	.08	.04
260	Frederick L. Fitzsimmons	.10	.08	.04
261	William E. Webb	.10	.08	.04
262	Earle B. Combs	.10	.08	.04
263	Edward J. Konetchy	.10	.08	.04
264	Taylor L. Douthit	.10	.08	.04
265	Lloyd J. Waner	.10	.08	.04
266	Gordon S. Cochrane	.10	.08	.04
267	John O. Wilson	.10	.08	.04
268	Harold J. Traynor	.10	.08	.04
269	Virgil L. Davis	.10	.08	.04
270	Henry E. Manush	.10	.08	.04
271	Michael F. Higgins	.10	.08	.04
272	Adrian Joss	.10	.08	.04
273	Edward Augustine Walsh	.10	.08	.04
274	Johnny L.R. Martin	.10	.08	.04
275	Joseph W. Sewell	.10	.08	.04
276	Hubert B. Leonard	.10	.08	.04
277	Clifford C. Cravath	.10	.08	.04
278	Oral C. Hildebrand	.10	.08	.04
279	Remy P. Kremer	.10	.08	.04
280	Frank A. Pytlak	.10	.08	.04
281	Samuel D. Byrd	.10	.08	.04
282	Curtis B. Davis	.10	.08	.04
283	Lewis A. Fonseca	.10	.08	.04
284	Herold D. Ruel	.10	.08	.04
285	Julius J. Solters	.10	.08	.04
286	Fred W. Schulte	.10	.08	.04
287	John P. Quinn	.10	.08	.04
288	Arthur C. Whitney	.10	.08	.04
289	Jonathon T. Stone	.10	.08	.04
290	Hugh M. Critz	.10	.08	.04
291	Ira J. Flagstead	.10	.08	.04
292	George F. Grantham	.10	.08	.04
293	Samuel D. Hale	.10	.08	.04
294	James F. Hogan	.10	.08	.04
295	Oswald L. Bluege	.10	.08	.04
296	Debs Garms	.10	.08	.04
297	Augistaf B. Friberg	.10	.08	.04
298	Edward A. Brandt	.10	.08	.04
299	Ralston B. Hemsley	.10	.08	.04
300	Charles H. Klein	.10	.08	.04
301	Morton C. Cooper	.10	.08	.04
302	James L. Bottomley	.10	.08	.04
303	James E. Foxx	.10	.08	.04
304	Frank Schulte	.10	.08	.04
305	Frank F. Frisch	.10	.08	.04
306	Frank A. McCormick	.10	.08	.04
307	Jacob E. Daubert	.10	.08	.04
308	Roger T. Peckinpaugh	.10	.08	.04
309	George H. Burns	.10	.08	.04
310	Louis H. Gehrig	.40	.30	.15
311	Aloysius H. Simmons	.10	.08	.04
312	Edward T. Collins	.10	.08	.04
313	Charles L. Hartnett	.10	.08	.04
314	Joseph E. Cronin	.10	.08	.04
315	Paul G. Waner	.10	.08	.04
316	Robert A. O'Farrell	.10	.08	.04
317	Lawrence J. Doyle	.10	.08	.04
318	Lynford H. Lary	.10	.08	.04
319	Frank S. May	.10	.08	.04
320	Roy H. Spencer	.10	.08	.04
321	Samuel R. Coffman	.10	.08	.04
322	Peter J. Donohue	.10	.08	.04
323	George W. Haas	.10	.08	.04
324	Edward S. Farrell	.10	.08	.04
325	Charles F. Rhem	.10	.08	.04
326	Frederick Marberry	.10	.08	.04
327	Charles Martin Conlon	.10	.08	.04
328	Checklist 1-110	.10	.08	.04
329	Checklist 111-220	.10	.08	.04
330	Checklist 221-330	.10	.08	.04

1992 Conlon Collection

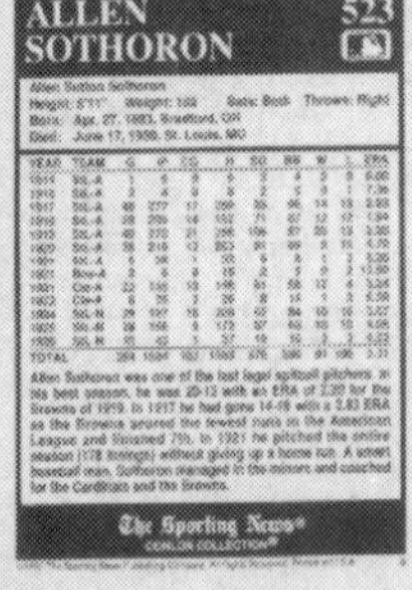

In their second season, the 330 cards of the Conlon Collection were numbered consecutively where the 1991 premiere issue ended. Cards 331-660 also maintained the high-gloss black-and-white format of the previous year. Many subsets within the issue carry special designations on the card fronts. Subsets included no-hitters, Triple Crown winners, "Great Stories," nicknames and more.

		MT	NR MT	EX
Complete set (330):		24.00	18.00	9.00
Common player:		.10	.08	.04
331	Christopher Mathewson	.10	.08	.04
332	George L. Wiltse	.10	.08	.04
333	George N. Rucker	.10	.08	.04
334	Leon K. Ames	.10	.08	.04
335	Charles A. Bender	.10	.08	.04
336	Joe Wood	.10	.08	.04
337	Edward Augstine Walsh	.10	.08	.04
338	George J. Mullin	.10	.08	.04
339	Earl A. Hamilton	.10	.08	.04
340	Charles M Tesreau	.10	.08	.04
341	James Scott	.10	.08	.04
342	Richard W. Marquard	.10	.08	.04
343	Claude R. Hendrix	.10	.08	.04
344	James S. Lavender	.10	.08	.04
345	Leslie A. Bush	.10	.08	.04
346	Hubert B. Leonard	.10	.08	.04
347	Fred A. Toney	.10	.08	.04
348	James L. Vaughn	.10	.08	.04
349	Ernest G. Koob	.10	.08	.04
350	Robert Groom	.10	.08	.04
351	Ernest G. Shore	.10	.08	.04
352	Horace O. Eller	.10	.08	.04
353	Walter P. Johnson	.10	.08	.04
354	Charles C. Robertson	.10	.08	.04
355	Jesse L. Barnes	.10	.08	.04
356	Samuel P. Jones	.10	.08	.04
357	Howard J. Ehmke	.10	.08	.04
358	Jesse J. Haines	.10	.08	.04
359	Theodore A. Lyons	.10	.08	.04
360	Carl O. Hubbell	.10	.08	.04
361	Wesley C. Ferrell	.10	.08	.04
362	Robert J. Burke	.10	.08	.04
363	Paul D. Dean	.10	.08	.04
364	Norman L. Newsom	.10	.08	.04
365	Lloyd V. Kennedy	.10	.08	.04
366	William J. Dietrich	.10	.08	.04
367	John S. Vander Meer	.10	.08	.04
368	John S. Vander Meer	.10	.08	.04
369	Montgomery M. Pearson	.10	.08	.04
370	Robert W.A. Feller	.10	.08	.04
371	Lonnie Warneke	.10	.08	.04
372	James A. Tobin	.10	.08	.04
373	Earl A. Moore	.10	.08	.04
374	William H. Dineen	.10	.08	.04
375	Malcolm W. Eason	.10	.08	.04
376	George A. Mogridge	.10	.08	.04
377	Clarence A. Vance	.10	.08	.04
378	James O. Carleton	.10	.08	.04
379	Clyde M. Shoun	.10	.08	.04
380	Franklin W. Hayes	.10	.08	.04
381	Benjamin R. Frey	.10	.08	.04
382	Henry W. Johnson	.10	.08	.04
383	Ralph Kress	.10	.08	.04
384	John T. Allen	.10	.08	.04
385	Harold A. Trosky Sr.	.10	.08	.04
386	Eugene E. Robertson	.10	.08	.04
387	Lemuel F. Young	.10	.08	.04
388	George A. Selkirk	.10	.08	.04
389	Edwin L. Wells	.10	.08	.04
390	James D. Weaver	.10	.08	.04
391	George H. McQuinn	.10	.08	.04
392	John B. Lobert	.10	.08	.04
393	Ernest E. Swanson	.10	.08	.04
394	Ernest A. Nevers	.10	.08	.04
395	James J. Levey	.10	.08	.04
396	Hugo F. Bezdek	.10	.08	.04
397	Walter E. French	.10	.08	.04
398	Charles F. Berry	.10	.08	.04
399	Franklin T. Grube	.10	.08	.04
400	Charles W. Dressen	.10	.08	.04
401	Alfred E. Neale	.10	.08	.04
402	Henry A. Vick	.10	.08	.04
403	James F. Thorpe	.50	.40	.20
404	Walter J. Gilbert	.10	.08	.04
405	John L. Urban	.10	.08	.04
406	Everett V. Purdy	.10	.08	.04
407	Albert O. Wright	.10	.08	.04
408	William M. Urbanski	.10	.08	.04

		MT	NR MT	EX
409	Charles W. Fischer	.10	.08	.04
410	John R. Warner	.10	.08	.04
411	Chalmer W. Cissell	.10	.08	.04
412	Mervin D.J. Shea	.10	.08	.04
413	Adolfo Luque	.10	.08	.04
414	John L. Bassler	.10	.08	.04
415	Arvel O. Hale	.10	.08	.04
416	Lawrence R. French	.10	.08	.04
417	William C. Walker	.10	.08	.04
418	Allen L. Cooke	.10	.08	.04
419	Philip J. Todt	.10	.08	.04
420	Ivy P. Andrews	.10	.08	.04
421	William J. Herman	.10	.08	.04
422	Tristram E. Speaker	.10	.08	.04
423	Aloysius H. Simmons	.10	.08	.04
424	Lewis R. Wilson	.10	.08	.04
425	Tyrus R. Cobb	.40	.30	.15
426	George H. Ruth	.50	.40	.20
427	Ernest N. Lombardi	.10	.08	.04
428	Jay H. Dean	.10	.08	.04
429	Lloyd J. Waner	.10	.08	.04
430	Henry B. Greenberg	.10	.08	.04
431	Robert M. Grove	.10	.08	.04
432	Gordon S. Cochrane	.10	.08	.04
433	Burleigh A. Grimes	.10	.08	.04
434	Harold J. Traynor	.10	.08	.04
435	John R. Mize	.10	.08	.04
436	Edgar C. Rice	.10	.08	.04
437	Leon A. Goslin	.10	.08	.04
438	Charles H. Klein	.10	.08	.04
439	Cornelius Mack	.10	.08	.04
440	James L. Bottomley	.10	.08	.04
441	Jackson R. Stephenson	.10	.08	.04
442	Kenneth R. Williams	.10	.08	.04
443	Charles B. Adams	.10	.08	.04
444	Joseph J. Jackson	.50	.40	.20
445	Harold Newhouser	.10	.08	.04
446	Wesley C. Ferrell	.10	.08	.04
447	Francis J. O'Doul	.10	.08	.04
448	Walter H. Schang	.10	.08	.04
449	Sherwood R. Magee	.10	.08	.04
450	Michael J. Donlin	.10	.08	.04
451	Roger M. Cramer	.10	.08	.04
452	Richard W. Bartell	.10	.08	.04
453	Earle T. Mack	.10	.08	.04
454	Walter G. Brown	.10	.08	.04
455	John A. Heving	.10	.08	.04
456	Percy L. Jones	.10	.08	.04
457	Theodore Blankenship	.10	.08	.04
458	Absalom H. Wingo	.10	.08	.04
459	Roger P. Bresnahan	.10	.08	.04
460	William J. Klem	.10	.08	.04
461	Charles L. Gehringer	.10	.08	.04
462	Stanley A. Coveleski	.10	.08	.04
463	Edward S. Plank	.10	.08	.04
464	Clark C.F. Griffith	.10	.08	.04
465	Herbert J. Pennock	.10	.08	.04
466	Earle B. Combs	.10	.08	.04
467	Robert P. Doerr	.10	.08	.04
468	Waite C. Hoyt	.10	.08	.04
469	Thomas H. Connolly	.10	.08	.04
470	Harry B. Hooper	.10	.08	.04
471	Richard B. Ferrell	.10	.08	.04
472	William G. Evans	.10	.08	.04
473	William J. Herman	.10	.08	.04
474	William M. Dickey	.10	.08	.04
475	Lucius B. Appling	.10	.08	.04
476	Ralph A. Pinelli	.10	.08	.04
477	Donald E. McNair	.10	.08	.04
478	John F. Blake	.10	.08	.04
479	Valentine J. Picinich	.10	.08	.04
480	Fred A. Heimach	.10	.08	.04
481	John G. Graney	.10	.08	.04
482	Ewell A. Russell	.10	.08	.04
483	Urban C. Faber	.10	.08	.04
484	Benjamin M. Kauff	.10	.08	.04
485	Clarence L. Rowland	.10	.08	.04
486	Robert H. Veach	.10	.08	.04
487	James C. Bagby	.10	.08	.04
488	William D. Perritt	.10	.08	.04
489	Charles L. Herzog	.10	.08	.04
490	Arthur Fletcher	.10	.08	.04
491	Walter H. Holke	.10	.08	.04
492	Arthur N. Nehr	.10	.08	.04
493	Lafayette F. Thompson	.10	.08	.04
494	James D. Welsh	.10	.08	.04
495	Oscar J. Vitt	.10	.08	.04
496	Owen T. Carroll	.10	.08	.04
497	James K. O'Dea	.10	.08	.04
498	Fredrick M. Frankhouse	.10	.08	.04
499	Jewel W. Ens	.10	.08	.04

		MT	NR MT	EX
500	Morris Arnovich	.10	.08	.04
501	Walter Gerber	.10	.08	.04
502	George W. Davis	.10	.08	.04
503	Charles S. Myer	.10	.08	.04
504	Samuel A. Leslie	.10	.08	.04
505	William C. Bolton	.10	.08	.04
506	Fred Walker	.10	.08	.04
507	John W. Smith	.10	.08	.04
508	Irving D. Hadley	.10	.08	.04
509	Clyde E. Crouse	.10	.08	.04
510	Joseph C. Glenn	.10	.08	.04
511	Clyde E. Kimsey	.10	.08	.04
512	Louis K. Finney	.10	.08	.04
513	Alfred V. Lawson	.10	.08	.04
514	Charles P. Fullis	.10	.08	.04
515	Earl H. Sheely	.10	.08	.04
516	George Gibson	.10	.08	.04
517	John J. Broaca	.10	.08	.04
518	Bibb A. Falk	.10	.08	.04
519	Frank O. Hurst	.10	.08	.04
520	Grover A. Hartley	.10	.08	.04
521	Donald H. Heffner	.10	.08	.04
522	Harvey L. Hendrick	.10	.08	.04
523	Allen S. Sothoron	.10	.08	.04
524	Anthony F. Piet	.10	.08	.04
525	Tyrus R. Cobb	.40	.30	.15
526	James E. Foxx	.10	.08	.04
527	Rogers Hornsby	.10	.08	.04
528	Napoleon LaJoie	.10	.08	.04
529	Louis H. Gehrig	.40	.30	.15
530	Henry Zimmerman	.10	.08	.04
531	Charles H. Klein	.10	.08	.04
532	Hugh Duffy	.10	.08	.04
533	Robert M. Grove	.10	.08	.04
534	Grover C. Alexander	.10	.08	.04
535	Amos W. Rusie	.10	.08	.04
536	Vernon L. Gomez	.10	.08	.04
537	William H. Walters	.10	.08	.04
538	Urban J. Hodapp	.10	.08	.04
539	Bruce D. Campbell	.10	.08	.04
540	Horace M. Lisenbee	.10	.08	.04
541	John F. Fournier	.10	.08	.04
542	James R. Tabor	.10	.08	.04
543	John H. Burnett	.10	.08	.04
544	Roy A. Hartzell	.10	.08	.04
545	Walter P. Gautreau	.10	.08	.04
546	Emil O. Yde	.10	.08	.04
547	Robert L. Johnson	.10	.08	.04
548	Joseph J. Hauser	.10	.08	.04
549	Edward M. Reulbach	.10	.08	.04
550	Baldomero M. Almada	.10	.08	.04
551	Gordon S. Cochrane	.10	.08	.04
552	Carl O. Hubbell	.10	.08	.04
553	Charles L. Gehringer	.10	.08	.04
554	Aloysius H. Simmons	.10	.08	.04
555	Mordecai P.C. Brown	.10	.08	.04
556	Hugh A. Jennings	.10	.08	.04
557	Norman A. Elberfeld	.10	.08	.04
558	Charles D. Stengel	.10	.08	.04
559	Alexander Schacht	.10	.08	.04
560	James E. Foxx	.10	.08	.04
561	George L. Kelly	.10	.08	.04
562	Lloyd J. Waner	.10	.08	.04
563	Paul G. Waner	.10	.08	.04
564	Walter P. Johnson	.10	.08	.04
565	John Franklin Baker	.10	.08	.04
566	Roy J. Hughes	.10	.08	.04
567	Lewis S. Riggs	.10	.08	.04
568	John H. Whitehead	.10	.08	.04
569	Elam R. Vangilder	.10	.08	.04
570	William A. Zitzmann	.10	.08	.04
571	Walter J. Schmidt	.10	.08	.04
572	John A. Tavener	.10	.08	.04
573	Joseph E. Genewich	.10	.08	.04
574	John A. Marcum	.10	.08	.04
575	Fred Hofmann	.10	.08	.04
576	Robert A. Rolfe	.10	.08	.04
577	Victor G. Sorrell	.10	.08	.04
578	Floyd J. Scott	.10	.08	.04
579	Alphonse Thomas	.10	.08	.04
580	Alfred J. Smith	.10	.08	.04
581	Walter J. Henline	.10	.08	.04
582	Edward T. Collins	.10	.08	.04
583	Earle B. Combs	.10	.08	.04
584	John J. McGraw	.10	.08	.04
585	Lewis R. Wilson	.10	.08	.04
586	Charles L. Hartnett	.10	.08	.04
587	Hazen S. Cuyler	.10	.08	.04
588	William H. Terry	.10	.08	.04
589	Joseph V. McCarthy	.10	.08	.04
590	Henry B. Greenberg	.10	.08	.04
591	Tristram E. Speaker	.10	.08	.04
592	William B. McKechnie	.10	.08	.04
593	Stanley R. Harris	.10	.08	.04
594	Herbert J. Pennock	.10	.08	.04
595	George H. Sisler	.10	.08	.04
596	Fred C. Lindstrom	.10	.08	.04
597	Howard E. Averill Sr.	.10	.08	.04
598	David J. Bancroft	.10	.08	.04
599	Cornelius Mack	.10	.08	.04
600	Joseph E. Cronin	.10	.08	.04
601	Kenneth L. Ash	.10	.08	.04
602	Alfred R. Spohrer	.10	.08	.04
603	Lee R. Mahaffey	.10	.08	.04
604	James F. O'Rourke	.10	.08	.04
605	Ulysses S.G. Stoner	.10	.08	.04
606	Frank H. Gabler	.10	.08	.04
607	Thomas F. Padden	.10	.08	.04
608	Charles A. Shires	.10	.08	.04
609	Sherrod M. Smith	.10	.08	.04
610	Philip Weintraub	.10	.08	.04
611	Russell Van Atta	.10	.08	.04
612	Joyner C. White	.10	.08	.04
613	Clifford G. Melton	.10	.08	.04
614	James J. Ring	.10	.08	.04
615	John H. Sand	.10	.08	.04
616	David D. Alexander	.10	.08	.04
617	Kent Greenfield	.10	.08	.04
618	Edwin H. Dyer	.10	.08	.04
619	William H. Sherdel	.10	.08	.04
620	Hubert M. Lanier	.10	.08	.04
621	Robert A. O'Farrell	.10	.08	.04
622	Rogers Hornsby	.10	.08	.04
623	William A. Beckman	.10	.08	.04
624	Morton C. Cooper	.10	.08	.04
625	William P. Delancey	.10	.08	.04
626	Martin W. Marion	.10	.08	.04
627	William H. Southworth	.10	.08	.04
628	John R. Mize	.10	.08	.04
629	Joseph M. Medwick	.10	.08	.04
630	Grover C. Alexander	.10	.08	.04
631	Paul D. Dean	.10	.08	.04
632	Herman S. Bell	.10	.08	.04
633	William W. Cooper	.10	.08	.04
634	Frank F. Frisch	.10	.08	.04
635	Jay H. Dean	.10	.08	.04
636	Donald J. Gutteridge	.10	.08	.04
637	Johnny L.R. Martin	.10	.08	.04
638	Edward J. Konetchy	.10	.08	.04
639	William A. Hallahan	.10	.08	.04
640	Lonnie Warneke	.10	.08	.04
641	Terry B. Moore	.10	.08	.04
642	Enos B. Slaughter	.10	.08	.04
643	Clarence F. Mueller	.10	.08	.04
644	George Toporcer	.10	.08	.04
645	James L. Bottomely	.10	.08	.04
646	Francis R. Blades	.10	.08	.04
647	Jesse J. Haines	.10	.08	.04
648	Andrew A. High	.10	.08	.04
649	Miller J. Huggins	.10	.08	.04
650	Ernesto R. Orsatti	.10	.08	.04
651	Lester R. Bell	.10	.08	.04
652	Charles E. Street	.10	.08	.04
653	Walter H. Roettger	.10	.08	.04
654	Sylvester W. Johnson	.10	.08	.04
655	Miguel A. Gonzalez	.10	.08	.04
656	James A. Collins	.10	.08	.04
657	Charles J. Hafey	.10	.08	.04
658	Checklist 331-440	.10	.08	.04
659	Checklist 441-550	.10	.08	.04
660	Checklist 551-660	.10	.08	.04

1993 Conlon Collection

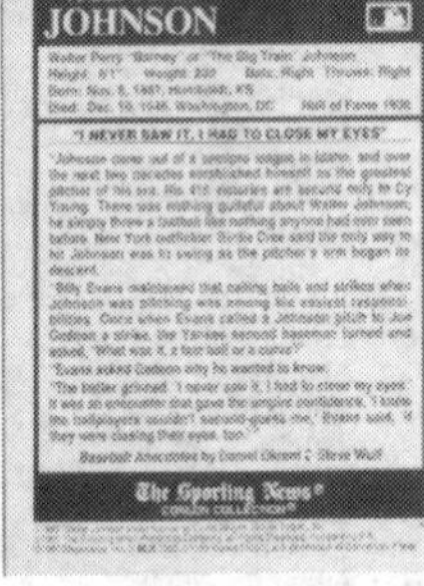

The third annual Conlon Collection issue of 330 cards is

numbered 661-990, a continuation of the series produced in 1991-92. The format of black-and-white photos produced 50-90 years ago by Charles Martin Conlon and surrounded by a wide black border and UV coating was continued. As with earlier issues, card backs contain brief biographical data, a few stats and well-written career highlights. The 1993 set also featured many subsets arranged by topic, such as spitballers, native Americans, players who overcame handicaps, etc. One subset compared Nolan Ryan with star pitchers in baseball history and included a fantasy photo of Ryan shaking hands in the dugout with Walter Johnson (card #934).

		MT	NR MT	EX
Complete set (330):		20.00	15.00	7.50
Common player:		.10	.08	.04
661	William H. Terry	.10	.08	.04
662	Vernon L. Gomez	.10	.08	.04
663	George H. Ruth	.50	.40	.20
664	Frank F. Frisch	.10	.08	.04
665	Carl O. Hubbell	.10	.08	.04
666	Aloysius H. Simmons	.10	.08	.04
667	Charles L. Gehringer	.10	.11	.06
668	Howard E. Averill Sr.	.10	.08	.04
669	Robert M. Grove	.10	.08	.04
670	Harold J. Traynor	.10	.08	.04
671	Charles H. Klein	.10	.08	.04
672	Paul G. Waner	.10	.08	.04
673	Louis H. Gehrig	.40	.30	.15
674	Richard B. Ferrell	.10	.08	.04
675	Charles L. Hartnett	.10	.08	.04
676	Joseph E. Cronin	.10	.08	.04
677	Charles J. Hafey	.10	.08	.04
678	James J. Dykes	.10	.08	.04
679	Samuel F. West	.10	.08	.04
680	Johnny L.R. Martin	.10	.08	.04
681	Francis J. O'Doul	.10	.08	.04
682	Alvin F. Crowder	.10	.08	.04
683	James Wilson	.10	.08	.04
684	Richard W. Bartell	.10	.08	.04
685	William A. Hallahan	.10	.08	.04
686	Walter A. Berger	.10	.08	.04
687	Lonnie Warneke	.10	.08	.04
688	William B. Chapman	.10	.08	.04
689	Elwood G. English	.10	.08	.04
690	James H. Reese	.10	.08	.04
691	Roscoe A. Holm	.10	.08	.04
692	Charles D. Jamieson	.10	.08	.04
693	Jonathan T.W. Zachary	.10	.08	.04
694	John C. Ryan	.10	.08	.04
695	Earl J. Adams	.10	.08	.04
696	William E. Hunnefield	.10	.08	.04
697	Henry L. Meadows	.10	.08	.04
698	Thomas F. Carey	.10	.08	.04
699	John W. Rawlings	.10	.08	.04
700	Kenneth E. Holloway	.10	.08	.04
701	Lance C. Richbourg	.10	.08	.04
702	Raymond L. Fisher	.10	.08	.04
703	Edward Augustine Walsh	.10	.08	.04
704	Richard Rudolph	.10	.08	.04
705	Raymond B. Caldwell	.10	.08	.04
706	Burleigh A. Grimes	.10	.08	.04
707	Stanley A. Coveleski	.10	.08	.04
708	George A. Hildebrand	.10	.08	.04
709	John P. Quinn	.10	.08	.04
710	Urban C. Faber	.10	.08	.04
711	Urban J. Shocker	.10	.08	.04
712	Hubert B. Leonard	.10	.08	.04
713	Louis L. Koupal	.10	.08	.04
714	James C. Wasdell	.10	.08	.04
715	John H. Lindell	.10	.08	.04
716	Don W. Padgett	.10	.08	.04
717	Nelson T. Potter	.10	.08	.04
718	Lynwood T. Rowe	.10	.08	.04
719	David C. Danforth	.10	.08	.04
720	Claude W. Passeau	.10	.08	.04
721	Harry L. Kelley	.10	.08	.04
722	John T. Allen	.10	.08	.04
723	Thomas J.D. Bridges	.10	.08	.04
724	William C. Lee	.10	.08	.04
725	Fredrick M. Frankhouse	.10	.08	.04
726	John J. McCarthy	.10	.08	.04
727	Glen D. Russell	.10	.08	.04
728	Emory E. Rigney	.10	.08	.04
729	Howard S. Shanks	.10	.08	.04
730	Lucius B. Appling	.10	.08	.04
731	William J. Byron	.10	.08	.04
732	Earle B. Combs	.10	.08	.04

		MT	NR MT	EX
733	Henry B. Greenberg	.10	.11	.06
734	Walter W. Beck	.10	.08	.04
735	Hollis J. Thurston	.10	.08	.04
736	Lewis R. Wilson	.10	.08	.04
737	William A. McGowan	.10	.08	.04
738	Henry J. Bonura	.10	.08	.04
739	Thomas C. Baker	.10	.08	.04
740	William C. Jacobson	.10	.08	.04
741	Hazen S. Cuyler	.10	.08	.04
742	George F. Blaeholder	.10	.08	.04
743	Wilson D. Miles	.10	.08	.04
744	Lee E. Handley	.10	.08	.04
745	John F. Collins	.10	.08	.04
746	Wilfred P. Ryan	.10	.08	.04
747	Aaron L. Ward	.10	.08	.04
748	Montgomery M. Pearson	.10	.08	.04
749	Jacob W. Early	.10	.08	.04
750	William F. Atwood	.10	.08	.04
751	Mark A. Koenig	.10	.08	.04
752	John A. Hassett	.10	.08	.04
753	David J. Jones	.10	.08	.04
754	John P. Wagner	.10	.08	.04
755	William M. Dickey	.10	.08	.04
756	Albert M. Butcher	.10	.08	.04
757	Waite C. Hoyt	.10	.08	.04
758	Walter P. Johnson	.10	.15	.08
759	Howard J. Ehmke	.10	.08	.04
760	Norman L. Newsom	.10	.08	.04
761	Anthony M. Lazzeri	.10	.08	.04
762	Anthony M. Lazzeri	.10	.08	.04
763	Spurgeon F. Chandler	.10	.08	.04
764	Walter K. Higbe	.10	.08	.04
765	Paul R. Richards	.10	.08	.04
766	Rogers Hornsby	.10	.08	.04
767	Joseph F. Vosmik	.10	.08	.04
768	Jesse J. Haines	.10	.08	.04
769	William H. Walters	.10	.08	.04
770	Thomas D. Henrich	.10	.08	.04
771	James F. Thorpe	.40	.30	.15
772	Euel W. Moore	.10	.40	.20
773	Rudolph P. York	.10	.40	.20
774	Charles A. Bender	.10	.40	.20
775	John T. Meyers	.10	.40	.20
776	Robert L. Johnson	.10	.40	.20
777	Roy C. Johnson	.10	.40	.20
778	Richard T. Porter	.10	.40	.20
779	Ethan N. Allen	.10	.40	.20
780	Harry F. Sallee	.10	.40	.20
781	Roy C. Bell	.10	.40	.20
782	Arnold J. Statz	.10	.40	.20
783	Frank J. Henry	.10	.40	.20
784	Charles L. Woodall	.10	.40	.20
785	Philip E. Collins	.10	.40	.20
786	Joseph W. Sewell	.10	.40	.20
787	William J. Herman	.10	.40	.20
788	Rueben H. Oldring	.10	.40	.20
789	William H. Walker	.10	.40	.20
790	Joseph C. Schultz	.10	.40	.20
791	Fred E. Maguire	.10	.40	.20
792	Claude W. Willoughby	.10	.40	.20
793	James A. Ferguson	.10	.40	.20
794	John D. Morrison	.10	.40	.20
795	Tristram E. Speaker	.10	.11	.06
796	Tyrus R. Cobb	.40	.30	.15
797	Max Carey	.10	.08	.04
798	George H. Sisler	.10	.08	.04
799	Charles J. Hollocher	.10	.08	.04
800	James L. Vaughn	.10	.08	.04
801	Samuel P. Jones	.10	.08	.04
802	Harry B. Hooper	.10	.08	.04
803	Clifford C. Cravath	.10	.08	.04
804	Walter P. Johnson	.10	.11	.06
805	Jacob E. Daubert	.10	.08	.04
806	Jesse C. Milan	.10	.08	.04
807	Hugh A. McQuillan	.10	.08	.04
808	George F. Brickell	.10	.08	.04
809	Joseph V. Stripp	.10	.08	.04
810	Urban J. Hodapp	.10	.08	.04
811	John L. Vergez	.10	.08	.04
812	Linus R. Frey	.10	.08	.04
813	William W. Regan	.10	.08	.04
814	Norman R. Young	.10	.08	.04
815	Charles C. Robertson	.10	.08	.04
816	Walter F. Judnich	.10	.08	.04
817	Joseph B. Tinker	.10	.08	.04
818	John Evers	.10	.08	.04
819	Frank L. Chance	.10	.08	.04
820	John J. McGraw	.10	.08	.04
821	Charles J. Grimm	.10	.08	.04
822	Ted Lyons	.10	.08	.04
823	Joe McCarthy	.10	.08	.04

		MT	NR MT	EX
824	Connie Mack	.10	.08	.04
825	George Gibson	.10	.08	.04
826	Steve O'Neill	.10	.08	.04
827	Tristram E. Speaker	.10	.11	.06
828	William F. Carrigan	.10	.08	.04
829	Charles D. Stengel	.10	.08	.04
830	Miller J. Huggins	.10	.08	.04
831	William B. McKechnie	.10	.08	.04
832	Charles W. Dressen	.10	.08	.04
833	Charles E. Street	.10	.08	.04
834	Melvin T. Ott	.10	.08	.04
835	Frank F. Frisch	.10	.08	.04
836	George H. Sisler	.10	.08	.04
837	Napoleon LaJoie	.10	.08	.04
838	Tyrus R. Cobb	.40	.30	.15
839	William H. Southworth	.10	.08	.04
840	Clark C.F. Griffith	.10	.08	.04
841	William H. Terry	.10	.08	.04
842	Rogers Hornsby	.10	.08	.04
843	Joseph E. Cronin	.10	.08	.04
844	Alfonso R. Lopez	.10	.08	.04
845	Stanley R. Harris	.10	.08	.04
846	Wilbert Robinson	.10	.08	.04
847	Hugh A. Jennings	.10	.08	.04
848	James J. Dykes	.10	.08	.04
849	Roy J. Cullenbine	.10	.08	.04
850	Graham E. Moore	.10	.08	.04
851	John H. Rothrock	.10	.08	.04
852	William H. Lamar	.10	.08	.04
853	Monte Weaver	.10	.08	.04
854	Ival R. Goodman	.10	.08	.04
855	Henry L. Severeid	.10	.08	.04
856	Fred G. Haney	.10	.08	.04
857	Joseph B. Shaute	.10	.08	.04
858	Smead P. Jolley	.10	.08	.04
859	Edwin D. Williams	.10	.08	.04
860	Bernard O. Bengough	.10	.08	.04
861	Richard B. Ferrell	.10	.08	.04
862	Robert A. O'Farrell	.10	.08	.04
863	Virgil L. Davis	.10	.08	.04
864	Franklin W. Hayes	.10	.08	.04
865	Herold D. Ruel	.10	.08	.04
866	Gordon S. Cochrane	.10	.08	.04
867	John Kling	.10	.08	.04
868	Ivy B. Wingo	.10	.08	.04
869	William M. Dickey	.10	.08	.04
870	Frank E. Snyder	.10	.08	.04
871	Roger P. Bresnahan	.10	.08	.04
872	Walter H. Schang	.10	.08	.04
873	Alfonso R. Lopez	.10	.08	.04
874	James Wilson	.10	.08	.04
875	Valentine J. Picinich	.10	.08	.04
876	Stephen F. O'Neill	.10	.08	.04
877	Ernest N. Lombardi	.10	.08	.04
878	John L. Bassler	.10	.08	.04
879	Raymond W. Schalk	.10	.08	.04
880	Charles L. Hartnett	.10	.08	.04
881	Bruce D. Campbell	.10	.08	.04
882	Charles H. Ruffing	.10	.08	.04
883	Mordecai P.C. Brown	.10	.08	.04
884	Peter J. Archer	.10	.08	.04
885	David E. Keefe	.10	.08	.04
886	Nathan H. Andrews	.10	.08	.04
887	Edgar C. Rice	.10	.08	.04
888	George H. Ruth	.50	.40	.20
889	Charles J. Hafey	.10	.08	.04
890	Oscar D. Melillo	.10	.08	.04
891	Joe Wood	.10	.08	.04
892	John J. Evers	.10	.08	.04
893	George Toporcer	.10	.08	.04
894	Myril O. Hoag	.10	.08	.04
895	Robert G. Weiland	.10	.08	.04
896	Joseph A. Marty	.10	.08	.04
897	Sherwood R. Magee	.10	.08	.04
898	Daniel T. Taylor	.10	.08	.04
899	William E. Kamm	.10	.08	.04
900	Samuel J.T. Sheckard	.10	.08	.04
901	Sylvester W. Johnson	.10	.08	.04
902	Stephen R. Sundra	.10	.08	.04
903	Roger M. Cramer	.10	.08	.04
904	Hubert S. Pruett	.10	.08	.04
905	Russell A. Blackburne	.10	.08	.04
906	Eppa Rixey	.10	.08	.04
907	Leon A. Goslin	.10	.08	.04
908	George L. Kelly	.10	.08	.04
909	James L. Bottomley	.10	.08	.04
910	Christopher Mathewson	.10	.11	.06
911	Anthony M. Lazzeri	.10	.08	.04
912	John A. Mostil	.10	.08	.04
913	Robert P. Doerr	.10	.08	.04
914	Walter J.V. Maranville	.10	.08	.04

		MT	NR MT	EX
915	Harry E. Heilmann	.10	.08	.04
916	Rodrick J. Wallace	.10	.08	.04
917	James E. Foxx	.10	.08	.04
918	John R. Mize	.10	.08	.04
919	John N. Bentley	.10	.08	.04
920	Alexander Schacht	.10	.08	.04
921	Parke E. Coleman	.10	.08	.04
922	George H. Paskert	.10	.08	.04
923	Horace H. Ford	.10	.08	.04
924	Randolph E. Moore	.10	.08	.04
925	Milburn J. Shoffner	.10	.08	.04
926	Richard W. Siebert	.10	.08	.04
927	Anthony C. Kaufmann	.10	.08	.04
928	Jay H. Dean/ Nolan Ryan	.25	.20	.10
929	Clarence A. Vance/ Nolan Ryan	.25	.20	.10
930	Robert M. Grove/ Nolan Ryan	.25	.20	.10
931	George E. Waddell/ Nolan Ryan	.25	.20	.10
932	Grover C. Alexander/ Nolan Ryan	.25	.20	.10
933	Robert W.A. Feller/ Nolan Ryan	.25	.20	.10
934	Walter P. Johnson/ Nolan Ryan	.50	.40	.20
935	Theodore A. Lyons/ Nolan Ryan	.25	.20	.10
936	James C. Bagby	.10	.08	.04
937	Joseph Sugden	.10	.08	.04
938	Robert E. Grace	.10	.08	.04
939	John G. Heath	.10	.08	.04
940	Kenneth R. Williams	.10	.08	.04
941	Marvin J. Owen	.10	.08	.04
942	Cyril R. Weatherly	.10	.08	.04
943	Edward C. Morgan	.10	.08	.04
944	John C. Rizzo	.10	.08	.04
945	Archie R. McKain	.10	.08	.04
946	Robert M. Garbark	.10	.08	.04
947	John B. Osborn	.10	.08	.04
948	John S. Podgajny	.10	.08	.04
949	Joseph P. Evans	.10	.08	.04
950	George A. Rensa	.10	.08	.04
951	John H. Humphries	.10	.08	.04
952	Merritt P. Cain	.10	.08	.04
953	Roy E. Hansen	.10	.08	.04
954	John A. Niggeling	.10	.08	.04
955	Harold J. Wiltse	.10	.08	.04
956	Alejandro A.A.E. Carrasquel	.10	.08	.04
957	George A. Grant	.10	.08	.04
958	Philip W. Weinert	.10	.08	.04
959	Ervin B. Brame	.10	.08	.04
960	Raymond J. Harrell	.10	.08	.04
961	Edward K. Linke	.10	.08	.04
962	Samuel B. Gibson	.10	.08	.04
963	John C. Watwood	.10	.08	.04
964	James T. Prothro	.10	.08	.04
965	Julio G. Bonetti	.10	.08	.04
966	Howard R. Mills	.10	.08	.04
967	Clarence E. Galloway	.10	.08	.04
968	Harold J. Kelleher	.10	.08	.04
969	Elon C. Hogsett	.10	.08	.04
970	Edward B. Heusser	.10	.08	.04
971	Edward J. Baecht	.10	.08	.04
972	Otto H. Saltzgaver	.10	.08	.04
973	Leroy G. Herrmann	.10	.08	.04
974	Beveric B. Bean	.10	.08	.04
975	Harry Seibold	.10	.08	.04
976	Howard V. Keen	.10	.08	.04
977	William J. Barrett	.10	.08	.04
978	Patrick H. McNulty	.10	.08	.04
979	George E. Turbeville	.10	.08	.04
980	Edward D. Phillips	.10	.08	.04
981	Garland M. Buckeye	.10	.08	.04
982	Victor P. Frasier	.10	.08	.04
983	John G. Rhodes	.10	.08	.04
984	Emile D. Barnes	.10	.08	.04
985	James C. Edwards	.10	.08	.04
986	Herschel E. Bennett	.10	.08	.04
987	Carmen P. Hill	.10	.08	.04
988	Checklist 661-770	.10	.08	.04
989	Checklist 771-880	.10	.08	.04
990	Checklist 881-990	.10	.08	.04

1993 Conlon Color

The cards in this 23-card set were previously released in black and white in either the 1991 or 1992 regular Conlon sets. The distribution of the color cards is unique. Cards 1-12 were issued as bonus cards in Megacards accessory items. 250,000 of cards 1-12 were produced. Cards 13-20 were randomly inserted in 1993 Conlon counter and blister packs. Only 100,000 of cards 13-20 were produced. Cards 21 and 22 were only available through a send-away offer and card 23 was available exclusively in the Seventh Edition SCD Baseball Card Price Guide. Only 60,000 of card number 23 were available.

through a send-away offer and card 23 was available exclusively in the Seventh Edition SCD Baseball Card Price Guide. Only 60,000 of card number 23 were available.

		MT	NR MT	EX
Complete Set:		50.00	37.00	20.00
Common Player:		1.50	1.25	.60
1	Sunny Jim Bottomley	1.50	1.25	.60
2	Lefty Grove	2.00	1.50	.80
3	Lou Gehrig	3.00	2.25	1.25
4	Babe Ruth	5.00	3.75	2.00
5	Casey Stengel	2.00	1.50	.80
6	Rube Marquard	1.50	1.25	.60
7	Walter Johnson	2.00	1.50	.80
8	Lou Gehrig	3.00	2.25	1.25
9	Christy Mathewson	2.00	1.50	.80
10	Ty Cobb	3.00	2.25	1.25
11	Mel Ott	2.00	1.50	.80
12	Carl Hubbell	2.00	1.50	.80
13	Al Simmons	2.00	1.50	.80
14	Connie Mack	2.00	1.50	.80
15	Grover C. Alexander	2.00	1.50	.80
16	Jimmie Foxx	2.00	1.50	.80
17	Lloyd Waner	2.00	1.50	.80
18	Tris Speaker	3.00	2.25	1.25
19	Dizzy Dean	2.00	1.50	.80
20	Rogers Hornsby	2.00	1.50	.80
21	Shoeless Joe Jackson	4.00	3.00	1.50
22	Jim Thorpe	4.00	3.00	1.50
23	Bob Feller	5.00	3.75	2.00

1994 Conlon Collection

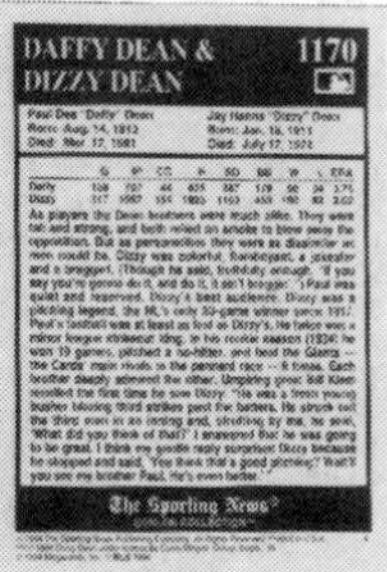

The production of "old-timers" cards based on the baseball photography of Charles M. Conlon from the 1910s through the 1930s continued into a fourth year in 1994 with another 330-card series, numbered 991-1320. Once again the format of previous years was continued. Subsets included the 1919 Chicago White Sox, major league brothers and action photos.

		MT	NR MT	EX
Complete set (330):		20.00	15.00	8.00
Common player:		.10	.08	.04
991	Johnny L.R. Martin	.10	.08	.04
992	Joseph W. Sewell	.10	.08	.04
993	Edd J. Roush	.10	.08	.04
994	Richard B. Ferrell	.10	.08	.04
995	John J. Broaca	.10	.08	.04
996	James L. Swewll	.10	.08	.04
997	Burleigh A. Grimes	.10	.08	.04
998	Lewis R. Wilson	.10	.08	.04
999	Robert M. Grove	.10	.08	.04
1000	Tyrus R. Cobb			
1001	John J. McGraw	.10	.08	.04
1002	Edward S. Plank	.10	.08	.04
1003	Samuel P. Jones	.10	.08	.04
1004	James L. Bottomley	.10	.08	.04
1005	Henry B. Greenberg	.10	.08	.04
1006	Lloyd J. Waner	.10	.08	.04
1007	William W. Moore	.10	.08	.04
1008	Lucius B. Appling	.10	.08	.04
1009	Harold Newhouser	.10	.08	.04
1010	Alfonso R. Lopez	.10	.08	.04
1011	Tyrus R. Cobb	.40	.30	.15
1012	Charles A. Nichols	.10	.08	.04
1013	Edward Augustine Walsh	.10	.08	.04
1014	Hugh Duffy	.10	.08	.04
1015	Richard W. Marquard	.10	.08	.04
1016	Adrian Joss	.10	.08	.04
1017	Rodrick J. Wallace	.10	.08	.04
1018	William H. Keeler	.10	.08	.04
1019	Jacob E. Daubert	.10	.08	.04
1020	Harry F. Sallee	.10	.08	.04
1021	Adolfo Luque	.10	.08	.04
1022	Ivy B. Wingo	.10	.08	.04
1023	Edd J. Roush	.10	.08	.04
1024	William A. Rariden	.10	.08	.04
1025	Sherwood R. Magee	.10	.08	.04
1026	Louis B. Duncan	.10	.08	.04
1027	Horace O. Eller	.10	.08	.04
1028	Alfred E. Neale	.10	.08	.04
1029	George D. Weaver	.10	.08	.04
1030	Joseph J. Jackson	.50	.40	.20
1031	Arnold Gandil	.10	.08	.04
1032	Charles A. Risberg	.10	.08	.04
1033	Raymond W. Schalk	.10	.08	.04
1034	Edward V. Cicotte	.10	.08	.04
1035	William H. James	.10	.08	.04
1036	Harry L. Leibold	.10	.08	.04
1037	Richard H. Kerr	.10	.08	.04
1038	William J. Gleason	.10	.08	.04
1039	Frederick W. McMullin	.10	.08	.04
1040	Edward T. Collins	.10	.08	.04
1041	Sox Pitchers (Lefty Williams, Bill James, Ed Cicotte, Dicky Kerr)	.10	.08	.04
1042	Sox Outfielders (Nemo Leibold, Happy Felsch, Shano Collins)	.10	.08	.04
1043	Kenneth F. Keltner	.10	.08	.04
1044	Charles F. Berry	.10	.08	.04
1045	Walter J. Lutzke	.10	.08	.04
1046	John C. Schulte	.10	.08	.04
1047	John V. Welch	.10	.08	.04
1048	Jack E. Russell	.10	.08	.04
1049	John J. Murray	.10	.08	.04
1050	Harold J. Traynor	.10	.08	.04
1051	Michael J. Donlin	.10	.08	.04
1052	Charles L. Hartnett	.10	.08	.04
1053	Anthony M. Lazzeri	.10	.08	.04
1054	Lawrence H. Miller	.10	.08	.04
1055	Clarence A. Vance	.10	.08	.04
1056	Williams F. Carrigan	.10	.08	.04
1057	John J. Murphy	.10	.08	.04
1058	Clifton E Heathcote	.10	.08	.04
1059	Joseph A. Dugan	.10	.08	.04
1060	Walter J.V. Maranville	.10	.08	.04
1061	Thomas D. Henrich	.10	.08	.04
1062	Leroy E. Parmelee	.10	.08	.04
1063	Vernon L. Gomez	.10	.08	.04
1064	Ernest N. Lombardi	.10	.08	.04
1065	David J. Bancroft	.10	.08	.04
1066	William B. McKechnie	.10	.08	.04
1067	John A. Hassett	.10	.08	.04
1068	Spurgeon F. Chandler	.10	.08	.04
1069	Roy J. Hughes	.10	.08	.04
1070	George A. Dauss	.10	.08	.04
1071	Joseph J. Hauser	.10	.08	.04
1072	Virgil L. Davis	.10	.08	.04
1073	Albert M. Butcher	.10	.08	.04
1074	Louis P. Chiozza	.10	.08	.04
1075	Center Field Bleachers	.10	.08	.04
1076	Charles L. Gehringer	.10	.08	.04
1077	Henry E. Manush	.10	.08	.04
1078	Charles H. Ruffing	.10	.08	.04
1079	Melvin L. Harder	.10	.08	.04
1080	George H. Ruth	.50	.40	.20

		MT	NR MT	EX
1081	William B. Chapman	.10	.08	.04
1082	Louis H. Gehrig	.40	.30	.15
1083	James E. Foxx	.10	.08	.04
1084	Aloysius H. Simmons	.10	.08	.04
1085	Joseph E. Cronin	.10	.08	.04
1086	William M. Dickey	.10	.08	.04
1087	Gordon S. Cochrane	.10	.08	.04
1088	Vernon L. Gomez	.10	.08	.04
1089	Howard E. Averill Sr.	.10	.08	.04
1090	Samuel F. West	.10	.08	.04
1091	Frank F. Frisch	.10	.08	.04
1092	William J. Herman	.10	.08	.04
1093	Harold J. Traynor	.10	.08	.04
1094	Joseph M. Medwick	.10	.08	.04
1095	Charles H. Klein	.10	.08	.04
1096	Hazen S. Cuyler	.10	.08	.04
1097	Melvin T. Ott	.10	.08	.04
1098	Walter T. Ott	.10	.08	.04
1099	Paul G. Waner	.10	.08	.04
1100	William H. Terry	.10	.08	.04
1101	Travis C. Jackson	.10	.08	.04
1102	Joseph F. Vaughan	.10	.08	.04
1103	Charles L. Hartnett	.10	.08	.04
1104	Alfonso R. Lopez	.10	.08	.04
1105	Carl O. Hubbell	.10	.08	.04
1106	Lonnie Warneke	.10	.08	.04
1107	Van L. Mungo	.10	.08	.04
1108	Johnny J.R. Martin	.10	.08	.04
1109	Jay H. Dean	.10	.08	.04
1110	Fredrick M. Frankhouse	.10	.08	.04
1111	Giullaedeau Spink Heydler	.10	.08	.04
1112	JG Taylor Spink/ Mrs. Spink	.10	.08	.04
1113	Hirchman and Keller	.10	.08	.04
1114	Victor E. Aldridge	.10	.08	.04
1115	Michael F. Higgins	.10	.08	.04
1116	Harold G. Carlson	.10	.08	.04
1117	Frederick L. Fitzsimmons	.10	.08	.04
1118	William H. Walters	.10	.08	.04
1119	Nicholas Altrock	.10	.08	.04
1120	Charles W. Dressen	.10	.08	.04
1121	Mark A. Koenig	.10	.08	.04
1122	Charles L. Gehringer	.10	.08	.04
1123	Lloyd V. Kennedy	.10	.08	.04
1124	Harlond B. Clift	.10	.08	.04
1125	Ernest G. Phelps	.10	.08	.04
1126	John R. Mize	.10	.08	.04
1127	Harold H. Schumacher	.10	.08	.04
1128	Ethan N. Allen	.10	.08	.04
1129	William A. Wambsganss	.10	.08	.04
1130	Frederick Leach	.10	.08	.04
1131	John W. Clancy	.10	.08	.04
1132	John F. Stewart	.10	.08	.04
1133	Wilbur L. Brubaker	.10	.08	.04
1134	Leslie Mann	.10	.08	.04
1135	Howard J. Ehmke	.10	.08	.04
1136	Aloysius H. Simmons	.10	.08	.04
1137	George W. Haas	.10	.08	.04
1138	George W. Haas	.10	.08	.04
1139	Edmund J. Miller	.10	.08	.04
1140	Robert M. Grove	.10	.08	.04
1141	John P. Boley	.10	.08	.04
1142	Edward T. Collins Sr.	.10	.08	.04
1143	Walter E. French	.10	.08	.04
1144	Donald E. McNair	.10	.08	.04
1145	William D. Shores	.10	.08	.04
1146	Gordon S. Cochrane	.10	.08	.04
1147	Homer W. Summa	.10	.08	.04
1148	John P. Quinn	.10	.08	.04
1149	Max F. Bishop	.10	.08	.04
1150	James J. Dykes	.10	.08	.04
1151	George E. Walberg	.10	.08	.04
1152	James E. Foxx	.10	.08	.04
1153	George H. Burns	.10	.08	.04
1154	Roger M. Cramer	.10	.08	.04
1155	Samuel D. Hale	.10	.08	.04
1156	Edwin A. Rommel	.10	.08	.04
1157	Ralph F. Perkins	.10	.08	.04
1158	James J. Cronin	.10	.08	.04
1159	Cornelios Mack	.10	.08	.04
1160	Raymond C. Kolp	.10	.08	.04
1161	Clyde J. Manion	.10	.08	.04
1162	Franklin T. Grube	.10	.08	.04
1163	Stephen A. Swetonic	.10	.08	.04
1164	Joseph B. Tinker	.10	.08	.04
1165	John J. Evers	.10	.08	.04
1166	Frank L. Chance	.10	.08	.04
1167	Emerson Dickman	.10	.08	.04
1168	John T. Tobin	.10	.08	.04
1169	Wesley C. Ferrell	.10	.08	.04
1170	Jay H. Dean	.10	.08	.04
1171	Tony & Al Cuccinello	.10	.08	.04

		MT	NR MT	EX
1172	Harry & Stan Coveleski	.10	.08	.04
1173	Bob & Roy Johnson	.10	.08	.04
1174	Andy & Hugh High	.10	.08	.04
1175	Joe & Luke Sewell	.10	.08	.04
1176	John & Joe Heving	.10	.08	.04
1177	Ab & Ivy Wingo	.10	.08	.04
1178	Wade & Bill Killefer	.10	.08	.04
1179	Bubbles & Pinky Hargrave	.10	.08	.04
1180	Paul G. & Lloyd Waner	.10	.08	.04
1181	John S. Vander Meer	.10	.08	.04
1182	Joe G. Moore	.10	.08	.04
1183	Robert J. Burke	.10	.08	.04
1184	John F. Moore	.10	.08	.04
1185	John J. Egan	.10	.08	.04
1186	Thomas H. Connolly	.10	.08	.04
1187	Frank H. O'Loughlin	.10	.08	.04
1188	John E. Reardon	.10	.08	.04
1189	Charles B. Moran	.10	.08	.04
1190	William J. Klem	.10	.08	.04
1191	Albert D. Stark	.10	.08	.04
1192	Albert L. Orth	.10	.08	.04
1193	William E. Bransfield	.10	.08	.04
1194	Roy Van Graflan	.10	.08	.04
1195	Eugene F. Hart	.10	.08	.04
1196	John B. Conlan	.10	.08	.04
1197	Ralph A. Pinelli	.10	.08	.04
1198	John F. Sheridan	.10	.08	.04
1199	Richard F. Nallin	.10	.08	.04
1200	William H. Dineen	.10	.08	.04
1201	Henry F. O'Day	.10	.08	.04
1202	Charles Rigler	.10	.08	.04
1203	Robert D. Emslie	.10	.08	.04
1204	Charles H. Pfirman	.10	.08	.04
1205	Harry C. Geisel	.10	.08	.04
1206	Ernest C. Quigley	.10	.08	.04
1207	Emmett T. Ormsby	.10	.08	.04
1208	George A. Hildebrand	.10	.08	.04
1209	George J. Moriarty	.10	.08	.04
1210	William G. Evans	.10	.08	.04
1211	Clarence B. Owens	.10	.08	.04
1212	William A. McGowan	.10	.08	.04
1213	Walter K. Higbe	.10	.08	.04
1214	Taylor L. Douthit	.10	.08	.04
1215	Delmar D. Baker	.10	.08	.04
1216	Albert W. Demaree	.10	.08	.04
1217	Cornelius Mack	.10	.08	.04
1218	Napoleon Lajoie	.10	.08	.04
1219	John P. Wagner	.10	.08	.04
1220	Christopher Mathewson	.10	.08	.04
1221	Samuel E. Crawford	.10	.08	.04
1222	Tristram E. Speaker	.10	.08	.04
1223	Grover C. Alexander	.10	.08	.04
1224	Joseph E. Bowman	.10	.08	.04
1225	John D. Rigney	.10	.08	.04
1226	William E. Webb	.10	.08	.04
1227	Lloyd A. Moore	.10	.08	.04
1228	Bruce D. Campbell	.10	.08	.04
1229	Luzerne A. Blue	.10	.08	.04
1230	Mark A. Koenig	.10	.08	.04
1231	Walter H. Schang	.10	.08	.04
1232	Max Carey	.10	.08	.04
1233	Frank F. Frisch	.10	.08	.04
1234	Owen J. Bush	.10	.08	.04
1235	Goerge S. Davis	.10	.08	.04
1236	William G. Rogell	.10	.08	.04
1237	James A. Collins	.10	.08	.04
1238	Mauricel L. Burrus	.10	.08	.04
1239	Ernest E. Swanson	.10	.08	.04
1240	Elwood G. English	.10	.08	.04
1241	Joseph Harris	.10	.08	.04
1242	Harry H. McCurdy	.10	.08	.04
1243	Richard W. Bartell	.10	.08	.04
1244	Rupert L. Thompson	.10	.08	.04
1245	Charles B. Adams	.10	.08	.04
1246	Arthur N. Nehf	.10	.08	.04
1247	John G. Graney	.10	.08	.04
1248	Theodore A. Lyons	.10	.08	.04
1249	Louis H. Gehrig	.40	.30	.15
1250	Michael F. Welch	.10	.08	.04
1251	Urban C. Faber	.10	.08	.04
1252	Joseph J. McGinnity	.10	.08	.04
1253	Rogers Hornsby	.10	.08	.04
1254	Melvin T. Ott	.10	.08	.04
1255	Walter P. Johnson	.10	.08	.04
1256	Edgar C. Rice	.10	.08	.04
1257	James A. Tobin	.10	.08	.04
1258	Roger T. Peckinpaugh	.10	.08	.04
1259	George T. Stovall	.10	.08	.04
1260	Fredrick C. Merkle	.10	.08	.04
1261	Harry W. Collins	.10	.08	.04
1262	Henry C. Lind	.10	.08	.04

		MT	NR MT	EX
1263	George N. Rucker	.10	.08	.04
1264	Hollis J. Thurston	.10	.08	.04
1265	Alexander Metzler	.10	.08	.04
1266	Charles Martin Conlon	.10	.08	.04
1267	McCarty gets Magee	.10	.08	.04
1268	Sliding Home	.10	.08	.04
1269	Kauff safe at 3rd	.10	.08	.04
1270	Groh out at 3rd	.10	.08	.04
1271	Mollwitz out at the plate	.10	.08	.04
1272	Burns safe at home	.10	.08	.04
1273	Lee Magee out stealing 3rd	.10	.08	.04
1274	Killefer out at plate	.10	.08	.04
1275	John M. Warhop	.10	.08	.04
1276	Emil J. Leonard	.10	.08	.04
1277	Alvin F. Crowder	.10	.08	.04
1278	Chester P. Laabs	.10	.08	.04
1279	Leslie A. Bush	.10	.08	.04
1280	Raymond B. Bressler	.10	.08	.04
1281	Robret M. Brown	.10	.08	.04
1282	Bernard Deviveiros	.10	.08	.04
1283	Leslie W. Tietje	.10	.08	.04
1284	Charles Devens	.10	.08	.04
1285	Elliott A. Bigelow	.10	.08	.04
1286	John O. Dickshot	.10	.08	.04
1287	Charles L. Chatham	.10	.08	.04
1288	Walter E. Beall	.10	.08	.04
1289	Richard D. Attreau	.10	.08	.04
1290	Anthony V. Brief	.10	.08	.04
1291	James J. Gleason	.10	.08	.04
1292	Walter D. Shaner	.10	.08	.04
1293	Clifford R. Crawford	.10	.08	.04
1294	Manuel Salvo	.10	.08	.04
1295	Calvin L. Dorsett	.10	.08	.04
1296	Russell D. Peters	.10	.08	.04
1297	John D. Couch	.10	.08	.04
1298	Frank W. Ulrich	.10	.08	.04
1299	James M. Bivin	.10	.08	.04
1300	Paul E. Strand	.10	.08	.04
1301	John Y. Lanning	.10	.08	.04
1302	William R. Brenzel	.10	.08	.04
1303	Don Songer	.10	.08	.04
1304	Emil H. Levsen	.10	.08	.04
1305	Otto A. Bluege	.10	.08	.04
1306	Fabian S. Gaffke	.10	.08	.04
1307	Maurice J. Archdeacon	.10	.08	.04
1308	James B. Chaplin	.10	.08	.04
1309	Lawrence J. Rosenthal	.10	.08	.04
1310	William M. Bagwell	.10	.08	.04
1311	Ralph F. Dawson	.10	.08	.04
1312	John P.J. Sturm	.10	.08	.04
1313	Haskell C. Billings	.10	.08	.04
1314	Vernon S. Wilshere	.10	.08	.04
1315	Robert A. Asbjornson	.10	.08	.04
1316	Henry J. Steinbacher	.10	.08	.04
1317	Stanwood F. Baumgartner	.10	.08	.04
1318	Checklist 991-1100	.10	.08	.04
1319	Checklist 1101-1210	.10	.08	.04
1320	Checklist 1211-1320	.10	.08	.04

1982 Cracker Jack

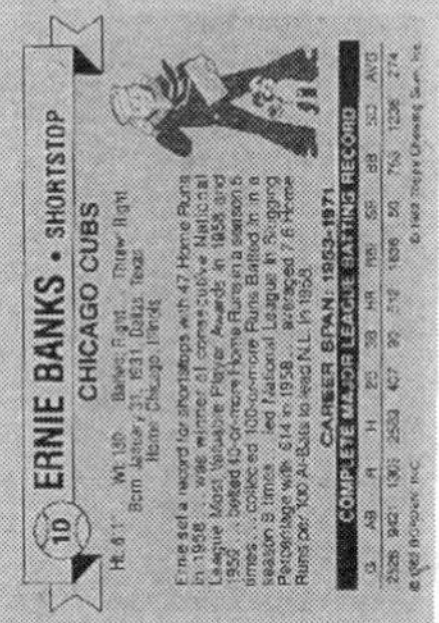

The Topps-produced 1982 Cracker Jack set was issued to promote the first "Old Timers Baseball Classic, held in Washington, D.C. Sixteen cards comprise the set which was issued in two sheets of eight cards, plus an advertising card located in the center. The individual cards are 2-1/2" by 3-1/2" in size with the complete sheets measuring 7-1/2" by 10-1/2". Card #'s 1-8 feature American League players with #'s 9-16 being former National League stars. The card fronts feature a full-color photo inside a Cracker Jack border. The backs contain the Cracker Jack logo plus a short player biography and his lifetime pitching or batting record. Complete sheets were available through a write-in offer.

		MT	NR MT	EX
Complete Panel Set:		10.00	7.50	4.00
Complete Singles Set:		4.00	3.00	1.50
Common Single Player:		.05	.04	.02
	Panel	5.00	3.75	2.00
1	Larry Doby	.05	.04	.02
2	Bob Feller	.10	.08	.04
3	Whitey Ford	.10	.08	.04
4	Al Kaline	.10	.08	.04
5	Harmon Killebrew	.10	.08	.04
6	Mickey Mantle	2.50	2.00	1.00
7	Tony Oliva	.05	.04	.02
8	Brooks Robinson	.10	.08	.04
	Panel	4.00	3.00	1.50
9	Hank Aaron	1.25	.90	.50
10	Ernie Banks	.10	.08	.04
11	Ralph Kiner	.10	.08	.04
12	Eddie Mathews	.10	.08	.04
13	Willie Mays	1.00	.70	.40
14	Robin Roberts	.10	.08	.04
15	Duke Snider	.10	.08	.04
16	Warren Spahn	.10	.08	.04
----	Advertising Card	.02	.02	.01

1991 Cracker Jack Topps I

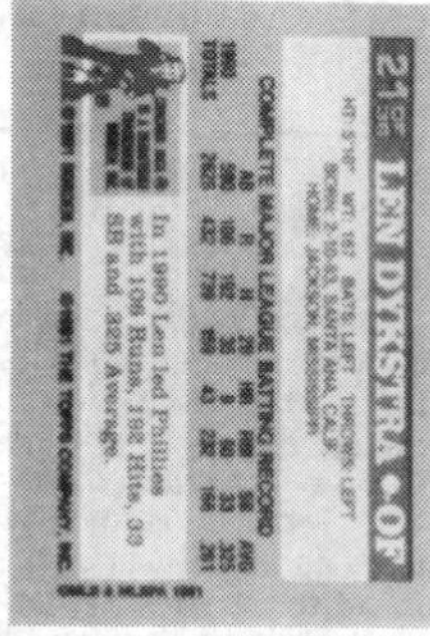

In their first issue in almost 10 years, Cracker Jack inserted miniature cards (1-1/4" x 1-3/4") as the toy surprise in packages of the famous snack. In 1991 the company produced two 36-card series, portraying many of the top stars in the game. The card fronts are identical to the corresponding regular issue Topps card, but the backs are significantly different because of the small amount of space available for statistics. The Cracker Jack sailor logo appears on the bright red backs, along with copyright information listing Borden, Cracker Jack's parent company.

		MT	NR MT	EX
Complete Set:		12.00	9.00	4.50
Common Player:		.25	.20	.10
1	Nolan Ryan	2.00	1.50	.80
2	Paul Molitor	.35	.25	.12
3	Tim Raines	.25	.20	.10
4	Frank Viola	.25	.20	.10
5	Sandy Alomar Jr.	.25	.20	.10
6	Ryne Sandberg	1.00	.75	.40
7	Don Mattingly	.75	.55	.25
8	Pedro Guerrero	.25	.20	.10
9	Jose Rijo	.25	.20	.10
10	Jose Canseco	.50	.40	.20
11	Dave Parker	.35	.25	.12
12	Doug Drabek	.25	.20	.10
13	Cal Ripken	1.00	.75	.40
14	Dave Justice	.30	.25	.12
15	George Brett	.60	.45	.25
16	Eric Davis	.25	.20	.10

		MT	NR MT	EX
17	Mark Langston	.25	.20	.10
18	Rickey Henderson	.50	.40	.20
19	Barry Bonds	.50	.40	.20
20	Kevin Maas	.25	.20	.10
21	Len Dykstra	.30	.25	.12
22	Roger Clemens	.35	.25	.12
23	Robin Yount	.35	.25	.12
24	Mark Grace	.30	.25	.12
25	Bo Jackson	.45	.35	.15
26	Tony Gwynn	.35	.25	.12
27	Mark McGwire	.35	.25	.12
28	Dwight Gooden	.30	.25	.12
29	Wade Boggs	.45	.35	.15
30	Kevin Mitchell	.25	.20	.10
31	Cecil Fielder	.35	.25	.12
32	Bobby Thigpen	.25	.20	.10
33	Benito Santiago	.25	.20	.10
34	Kirby Puckett	.45	.35	.15
35	Will Clark	.35	.25	.12
36	Ken Griffey Jr.	1.00	.75	.40

1991 Cracker Jack Topps II

Photos not available at press time

A second series of 36 micro cards was found in Cracker Jack boxes later in the 1991 season. Again numbered from 1-18, the 1-1/4" x 1-3/4" cards carry a "2nd Series" designation on the back above the card number. Like the first series, these cards replicate the front of the 1991 Topps issue and have modified back design which includes the "Sailor Jack" logo of the candy company. Because the Cracker Jack micro cards were not made available in any fashion other than one-per-box, they are difficult to find. Low collector demand has kept prices down.

		MT	NR MT	EX
Complete Set (36):		9.00	6.75	3.25
Common Player:		.25	.20	.10
1	Eddie Murray	.35	.25	.14
2	Carlton Fisk	.35	.25	.14
3	Eric Anthony	.25	.20	.10
4	Kelly Gruber	.25	.20	.10
5	Von Hayes	.25	.20	.10
6	Ben McDonald	.25	.20	.10
7	Andre Dawson	.35	.25	.14
8	Ellis Burks	.25	.20	.10
9	Matt Williams	.30	.25	.12
10	Dave Stewart	.25	.20	.10
11	Barry Larkin	.30	.25	.12
12	Chuck Finley	.25	.20	.10
13	Shane Andrews	.25	.20	.10
14	Bret Saberhagen	.25	.20	.10
15	Bobby Bonilla	.30	.25	.12
16	Roberto Kelly	.25	.20	.10
17	Orel Hershiser	.30	.25	.12
18	Ruben Sierra	.30	.25	.12
19	Ron Gant	.30	.25	.12
20	Frank Thomas	2.00	1.50	.80
21	Tim Wallach	.25	.20	.10
22	Gregg Olson	.25	.20	.10
23	Shawon Dunston	.25	.20	.10
24	Kent Hrbek	.30	.25	.12
25	Ramon Martinez	.25	.20	.10
26	Alan Trammell	.30	.25	.12

		MT	NR MT	EX
27	Ozzie Smith	.35	.25	.14
28	Bob Welch	.25	.20	.10
29	Chris Sabo	.25	.20	.10
30	Steve Sax	.25	.20	.10
31	Bip Roberts	.25	.20	.10
32	Dave Steib	.25	.20	.10
33	Howard Johnson	.30	.25	.12
34	Mike Greenwell	.25	.20	.10
35	Delino DeShields	.30	.25	.12
36	Alex Fernandez	.25	.20	.10

1992 Cracker Jack Donruss I

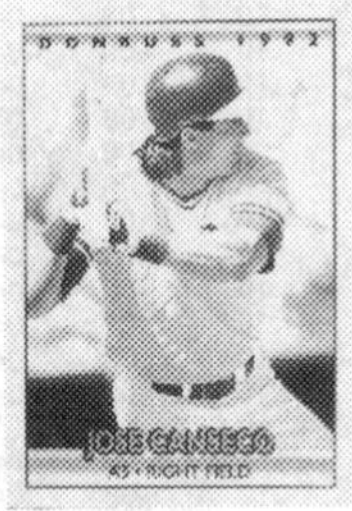

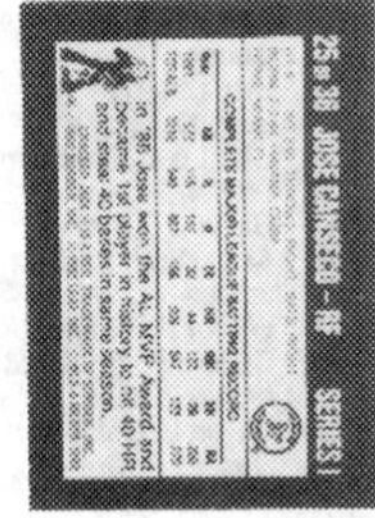

In 1992, Cracker Jack turned to Donruss to produce the cards for the surprise in their packages. The first series of micro cards (1-1/4" x 1-3/4") was numbered 1-36 and featured many of the top players. The fronts of the cards are identical to the regular issue 1992 Donruss, but the backs have a different format and much less information because of the tiny space available. The backs have a blue border, with some spot red printing and the Cracker Jack sailor logo in the lower left corner.

		MT	NR MT	EX
Complete Set:		12.00	9.00	4.50
Common Player:		.25	.20	.10
1	Jeff Bagwell	.25	.20	.10
2	Terry Pendleton	.25	.20	.10
3	Ozzie Smith	.35	.25	.14
4	Steve Avery	.25	.20	.10
5	Todd Zeile	.25	.20	.10
6	Lance Dickson	.25	.20	.10
7	Ryne Sandberg	1.00	.75	.40
8	Brett Butler	.25	.20	.10
9	Ramon Martinez	.25	.20	.10
10	Marquis Grissom	.25	.20	.10
11	Travis Fryman	.30	.25	.12
12	Will Clark	.45	.35	.15
13	Tony Gwynn	.35	.25	.14
14	Wes Chamberlain	.25	.20	.10
15	Doug Drabek	.25	.20	.10
16	Barry Larkin	.30	.25	.12
17	Hal Morris	.25	.20	.10
18	Dwight Gooden	.35	.25	.14
19	Dennis Eckersley	.30	.25	.12
20	Jose Canseco	.60	.45	.25
21	Jim Abbott	.35	.25	.14
22	Kelly Gruber	.25	.20	.10
23	Robin Yount	.50		
24	Sandy Alomar Jr.	.25	.20	.10
25	Ken Griffey Jr.	1.00	.75	.40
26	Cal Ripken	1.00	.75	.40
27	Nolan Ryan	2.00	1.50	.80
28	Ivan Rodriguez	.35	.25	.14
29	Roger Clemens	.35	.25	.14
30	Brian McRae	.25	.20	.10
31	Kent Hrbek	.30	.25	.12
32	Cecil Fielder	.40	.30	.15
33	Chuck Knoblauch	.30	.25	.12
34	Frank Thomas	2.00	1.50	.80
35	Don Mattingly	.75	.55	.30
36	Robin Ventura	.30	.25	.12

1992 Cracker Jack Donruss II

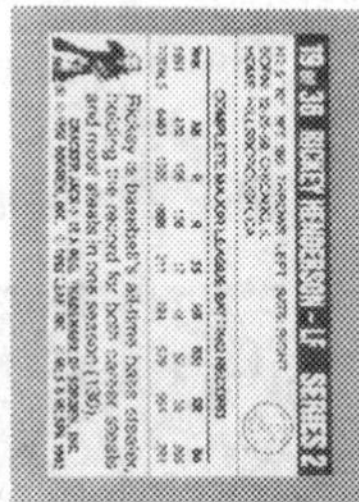

The Second Series of the 1992 Crack Jack Donruss set is almost identical to the first series, with the only change being different players and red border on the back instead of blue. The micro cards are numbered 1-36, just as in the first series.

		MT	NR MT	EX
Complete Set:		8.00	6.00	3.00
Common Player:		.25	.20	.10
1	Craig Biggio	.30	.25	.12
2	Tom Glavine	.25	.20	.10
3	David Justice	.30	.25	.12
4	Lee Smith	.25	.20	.10
5	Mark Grace	.35	.25	.14
6	George Bell	.25	.20	.10
7	Darryl Strawberry	.45	.35	.15
8	Eric Davis	.25	.20	.10
9	Ivan Calderon	.25	.20	.10
10	Royce Clayton	.25	.20	.10
11	Matt Williams	.30	.25	.12
12	Fred McGriff	.30	.25	.12
13	Len Dykstra	.30	.25	.12
14	Barry Bonds	.45	.35	.15
15	Reggie Sanders	.30	.25	.12
16	Chris Sabo	.25	.20	.10
17	Howard Johnson	.30	.25	.12
18	Bobby Bonilla	.30	.25	.12
19	Rickey Henderson	.45	.35	.15
20	Mark Langston	.25	.20	.10
21	Joe Carter	.30	.25	.12
22	Paul Molitor	.35	.25	.14
23	Glenallen Hill	.25	.20	.10
24	Edgar Martinez	.30	.25	.12
25	Gregg Olson	.25	.20	.10
26	Ruben Sierra	.30	.25	.12
27	Julio Franco	.25	.20	.10
28	Phil Plantier	.30	.25	.12
29	Wade Boggs	.40	.30	.15
30	George Brett	.50	.40	.20
31	Alan Trammell	.30	.25	.12
32	Kirby Puckett	.45	.35	.15
33	Scott Erickson	.25	.20	.10
34	Matt Nokes	.25	.20	.10
35	Danny Tartabull	.30	.25	.12
36	Jack McDowell	.30	.25	.12

1993 Cracker Jack Anniversary

In 1993, as part of the company's 100th anniversary celebration, Cracker Jack issued a 24-card set of mini replicas of its famous 1915 cards. The cards, measuring 1-1/4" x 1-3/4", were included in specially-marked packages of the famous snack. The set, taken from the original 176-card Cracker Jack set, features Hall of Famers such as Cobb, Mathewson, Walter Johnson and others, plus the Joe Jackson card.

3 of 24 WAGNER
PITTSBURGH-NATIONALS
1915 SET #68

John P. (Hans) Wagner, shortstop of the Pittsburgh National League team, was born in Carnegie, Pa., February 24, 1874. At the age of eighteen he began to play professional ball with his home team. He became a member of the Louisville team in 1897, and remained there until 1900, when he signed with Pittsburgh. Has batted over 300 for ten years.

© 1993 Borden Inc.
© 1993 MLB
© 1993 Wagner by Curtis Mngmt., Indpls., IN

		MT	NR MT	EX
Complete Set:		10.00	7.50	4.00
Common Player:		.50	.40	.20
(1)	Ty Cobb	2.00	1.50	.80
(2)	Nap Lajoie	.50	.40	.20
(3)	Connie Mack	.50	.40	.20
(4)	Leslie Bush	.50	.40	.20
(5)	Tris Speaker	.50	.40	.20
(6)	Harry Hooper	.50	.40	.20
(7)	Eddie Collins	.50	.40	.20
(8)	Ed Walsh	.50	.40	.20
(9)	Joe Jackson	2.00	1.50	.80
(10)	Branch Rickey	.50	.40	.20
(11)	Walter Johnson	.75	.55	.30
(12)	Honus Wagner	.75	.55	.30
(13)	Fred Clarke	.50	.40	.20
(14)	Christy Mathewson	.60	.45	.25
(15)	John McGraw	.50	.40	.20
(16)	Johnny Evers	.50	.40	.20
(17)	Walter Maranville	.50	.40	.20
(18)	Zack Wheat	.50	.40	.20
(19)	Miller Huggins	.50	.40	.20
(20)	Grover Alexander	.50	.40	.20
(21)	Joe Tinker	.50	.40	.20
(22)	Mordecai Brown	.50	.40	.20
(23)	Eddie Plank	.50	.40	.20
(24)	Rube Marquard	.50	.40	.20

1992 Dairy Queen Team USA

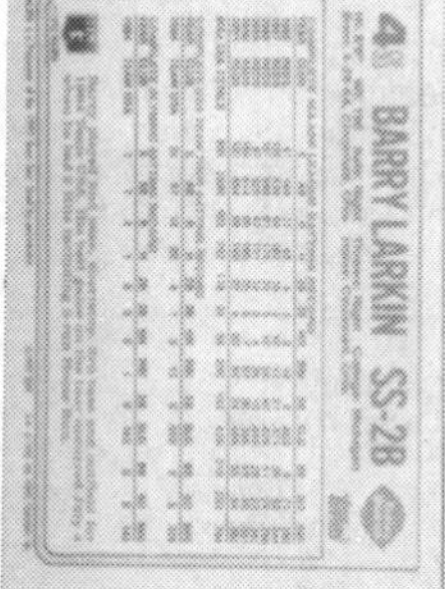

In 1992, in conjunction with the Dairy Queen Team USA Sundae-in-a-Helmet promotion, customers received a four-card pack of Team USA cards, part of a 33-card set manufactured by Topps for the company. Included in the set are 16 Team USA players from the 1984 and 1988 Olympics who have gone on to major league stardom. The set also has 15 Team USA Prospects, a 1988 Gold Medal team celebration card and a card of 1992 coach Ron Fraser. The front of the card features each player in their Team USA uniform and the backs include statistics from amateur, Team USA and professional competition.

		MT	NR MT	EX
Complete Set:		20.00	15.00	7.50
Common Player:		.25	.20	.10
1	Mark McGwire (1984)	2.00	1.50	.80
2	Will Clark (1984)	3.00	2.25	1.20
3	John Marzano (1984)	.25	.20	.10
4	Barry Larkin (1984)	1.00	.75	.40
5	Bobby Witt (1984)	.50	.40	.20
6	Scott Bankhead (1984)	.25	.20	.10
7	B.J. Surhoff (1984)	.50	.40	.20
8	Shane Mack (1984)	.75	.60	.30
9	Jim Abbott (1988)	1.50	1.25	.60
10	Ben McDonald (1988)	.50	.40	.20
11	Robin Ventura (1988)	.50	.40	.20
12	Charles Nagy (1988)	.35	.25	.14
13	Andy Benes (1988)	.50	.40	.20
14	Joe Slusarski (1988)	.35	.25	.14
15	Ed Sprague (1988)	.35	.25	.14
16	Bret Barberie (1988)	.35	.25	.14
17	Gold Medal (1988)	.25	.20	.10
18	Jeff Granger (1992)	.25	.20	.10
19	John Dettmer (1992)	.25	.20	.10
20	Todd Greene (1992)	.25	.20	.10
21	Jeffrey Hammonds (1992)	.75	.60	.30
22	Dan Melendez (1992)	.50	.40	.20
23	Kennie Steenstra (1992)	.25	.20	.10
24	Todd Johnson (1992)	.25	.20	.10
25	Chris Roberts (1992)	.35	.25	.14
26	Steve Rodriguez (1992)	.25	.20	.10
27	Charles Johnson (1992)	.35	.25	.14
28	Chris Wimmer (1992)	.25	.20	.10
29	Tony Phillips (1992)	.35	.25	.14
30	Craig Wilson (1992)	.35	.25	.14
31	Jason Giambi (1992)	.25	.20	.10
32	Paul Shuey (1992)	.25	.20	.10
33	Ron Fraser (1992 coach)	.25	.20	.10

1991 Denny's Grand Slam

Photos not available at press time

This 26-card set was produced by Upper Deck and features one player from each Major League team. One hologram card was distributed with the purchase of a Grand Slam meal. The cards are numbered on the front and are 3-D. The card backs describe grand slams hit by the featured player.

		MT	NR MT	EX
Complete Set:		50.00	37.00	20.00
Common Player:		1.50	1.25	.60
1	Ellis Burks	1.50	1.25	.60
2	Cecil Fielder	3.00	2.25	1.25
3	Will Clark	4.00	3.00	1.50
4	Eric Davis	2.00	1.50	.80
5	Dave Parker	2.00	1.50	.80
6	Kelly Gruber	1.50	1.25	.60
7	Kent Hrbek	2.00	1.50	.80
8	Don Mattingly	4.00	3.00	1.50
9	Brook Jacoby	1.50	1.25	.60
10	Mark McGwire	3.00	2.25	1.25
11	Howard Johnson	2.00	1.50	.80
12	Tim Wallach	1.50	1.25	.60
13	Ricky Jordan	1.50	1.25	.60
14	Andre Dawson	2.50	2.00	1.00
15	Eddie Murray	2.50	2.00	1.00
16	Danny Tartabull	2.00	1.50	.80
17	Bobby Bonilla	2.50	2.00	1.00
18	Benito Santiago	2.00	1.50	.80
19	Alvin Davis	1.50	1.25	.60
20	Cal Ripken	5.00	3.00	1.50
21	Ruben Sierra	2.00	1.50	.80
22	Pedro Guererro	1.50	1.25	.60
23	Wally Joyner	2.00	1.50	.80
24	Craig Biggio	2.00	1.50	.80
25	Dave Justice	2.50	2.00	1.00
26	Tim Raines	1.50	1.25	.60

1992 Denny's Grand Slam

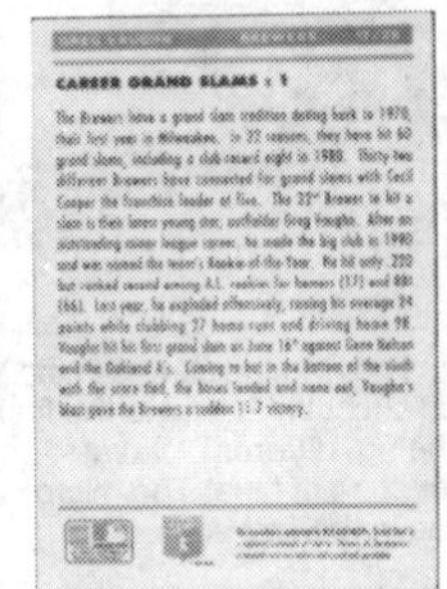

The second year of the Denny's Gland Slam promotion featured one power hitter from each major league team in 1992, portrayed on a hologram in front of a scene from his team's city. As in the first year, the cards were produced by Upper Deck and given away, one at a time, with a Denny's purchase during the middle of the summer. The set totals 26 cards.

		MT	NR MT	EX
Complete Set:		50.00	37.50	20.00
Common Player:		1.50	1.25	.60
1	Marquis Grissom	1.50	1.25	.60
2	Kem Caminiti	1.50	1.25	.60
3	Fred McGriff	2.50	2.00	1.00
4	Felix Jose	1.50	1.25	.60
5	Jack Clark	1.50	1.25	.60
6	Albert Belle	2.50	2.00	1.00
7	Sid Bream	1.50	1.25	.60
8	Robin Ventura	2.00	1.50	.80
9	Cal Ripken Jr.	5.00	3.75	2.00
10	Ryne Sandberg	5.00	3.75	2.00
11	Paul O'Neill	1.50	1.25	.60
12	Luis Polonia	1.50	1.25	.60
13	Cecil Fielder	3.00	2.25	1.25
14	Kal Daniels	1.50	1.25	.60
15	Brian McRae	2.00	1.50	.80
16	Howard Johnson	2.00	1.50	.80
17	Greg Vaughn	1.50	1.25	.60
18	Dale Murphy	2.50	2.00	1.00
19	Kent Hrbek	2.00	1.50	.80
20	Barry Bonds	3.00	2.25	1.25
21	Matt Nokes	1.50	1.25	.60
22	Jose Canseco	3.00	2.25	1.25
23	Jay Buhner	2.00	1.50	.80
24	Will Clark	3.00	2.25	1.25
25	Ruben Sierra	2.00	1.50	.80
26	Joe Carter	2.00	1.50	.80

1993 Denny's Grand Slam Holograms

The 1993 Denny's Gland Slam set expanded to 28 cards with the addition of the Florida and Colorado expansion teams. The featured color photos of one grand slam slugger for each team superimposed over a hologram background. The reverse of each card gives anecdotes about the player's grand slams along with his career total. The cards were distributed at participating Denny's restaurants during mid-summer.

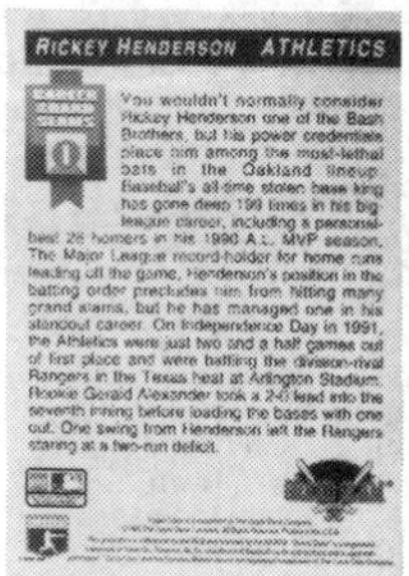

		MT	NR MT	EX
Complete Set:		50.00	37.50	20.00
Common Player:		1.50	1.25	.60
1	Chili Davis	1.50	1.25	.60
2	Eric Anthony	1.50	1.25	.60
3	Rickey Henderson	3.00	2.25	1.25
4	Joe Carter	2.00	1.50	.80
5	Terry Pendleton	1.50	1.25	.60
6	Robin Yount	4.00	3.00	1.50
7	Ray Lankford	2.00	1.50	.80
8	Ryne Sandberg	5.00	3.75	2.00
9	Darryl Strawberry	2.50	2.00	1.00
10	Marquis Grissom	1.50	1.25	.60
11	Will Clark	3.00	2.25	1.25
12	Albert Belle	2.00	1.50	.80
13	Edgar Martinez	1.50	1.25	.60
14	Benito Santiago	2.00	1.50	.80
15	Eddie Murray	2.50	2.00	1.00
16	Cal Ripken Jr.	5.00	3.75	2.00
17	Gary Sheffield	2.50	2.00	1.00
18	Dave Hollins	2.00	1.50	.80
19	Andy Van Slyke	2.00	1.50	.80
20	Juan Gonzalez	3.00	2.25	1.25
21	John Valentin	1.50	1.25	.60
22	Joe Oliver	1.50	1.25	.60
23	Dante Bichette	2.00	1.50	.80
24	Wally Joyner	2.00	1.50	.80
25	Cecil Fielder	2.50	2.00	1.00
26	Kirby Puckett	4.00	3.00	1.50
27	Robin Ventura	2.00	1.50	.80
28	Danny Tartabull	2.00	1.50	.80

1993 DiamondMarks

While they look like baseball cards and were sold in foil packs like baseball cards, DaimondMarks were licensed as book marks. Issued by Barry Colla Productions, the 2-1/2" x 5" cards feature Barry Colla's trademark high-quality player photos on front and back. The UV-coated fronts feature black borders with the player's name in white above the photo and a color team logo beneath. Backs, also bordered in black, feature two color player photos in an open book design. There is a portrait photo on the left and a head-and-shoulders reproduction of the front photo at right. A bookmark with team lofo is incorporated in the design. The 120-card set is unnumbered and is arranged in the checklist below alphabetically within league and team.

		MT	NR MT	EX
Complete Set:		30.00	22.50	11.25
Common Player:		.15	.11	.06
	ATLANTA BRAVES			
(1)	Steve Avery	.25	.20	.10
(2)	Ron Gant	.25	.20	.10
(3)	Tom Glavine	.25	.20	.10
(4)	David Justice	.35	.25	.12
(5)	Terry Pendleton	.15	.11	.06
(6)	Deion Sanders	.30	.25	.12
(7)	John Smoltz	.25	.20	.10
	CHICAGO CUBS			
(8)	Mark Grace	.25	.20	.10
(9)	Randy Myers	.15	.11	.06
(10)	Ryne Sandberg	.75	.55	.25
(11)	Jose Vizcaino	.15	.11	.06
	CINCINNATI REDS			
(12)	Bobby Kelly	.15	.11	.06
(13)	Barry Larkin	.25	.20	.10
(14)	Kevin Mitchell	.15	.11	.06
(15)	Jose Rijo	.25	.20	.10
(16)	Reggie Sanders	.15	.11	.06
	COLORADO ROCKIES			
(17)	Dante Bichette	.15	.11	.06
(18)	Daryl Boston	.15	.11	.06
(19)	Andres Galarraga	.30	.25	.12
(20)	Charlie Hayes	.15	.11	.06
	FLORIDA MARLINS			
(21)	Orestes Destrade	.15	.11	.06
(22)	Dave Magadan	.15	.11	.06
(23)	Benito Santiago	.15	.11	.06
(24)	Walt Weiss	.15	.11	.06
	HOUSTON ASTROS			
(25)	Jeff Bagwell	.25	.20	.10
(26)	Craig Biggio	.15	.11	.06
(27)	Ken Caminiti	.15	.11	.06
(28)	Luis Gonzalez	.15	.11	.06
	LOS ANGELES DODGERS			
(29)	Brett Butler	.15	.11	.06
(30)	Eric Davis	.15	.11	.06
(31)	Orel Hershiser	.25	.20	.10
(32)	Eric Karros	.15	.11	.06
(33)	Ramon Martinez	.15	.11	.06
(34)	Mike Piazza	1.00	.75	.35
(35)	Darryl Strawberry	.45	.35	.15
	MONTREAL EXPOS			
(36)	Moises Alou	.15	.11	.06
(37)	Delino DeShields	.25	.20	.10
(38)	Marquis Grissom	.25	.20	.10
(39)	Dennis Martinez	.15	.11	.06
(40)	Larry Walker	.15	.11	.06
	NEW YORK METS			
(41)	Bobby Bonilla	.25	.20	.10
(42)	Dwight Gooden	.25	.20	.10
(43)	Howard Johnson	.25	.20	.10
(44)	Eddie Murray	.30	.25	.12
	PHILADELPHIA PHILLIES			
(45)	Darren Daulton	.25	.20	.10
(46)	Lenny Dykstra	.35	.25	.12
(47)	Dale Hollins	.15	.11	.06
(48)	John Kruk	.35	.25	.12
	PITTSBURGH PIRATES			
(49)	Jay Bell	.15	.11	.06
(50)	Al Martin	.15	.11	.06
(51)	Orlando Merced	.15	.11	.06
(52)	Andy Van Slyke	.25	.20	.10
	ST. LOUIS CARDINALS			
(53)	Gregg Jefferies	.25	.20	.10
(54)	Tom Pagnozzi	.15	.11	.06
(55)	Ozzie Smith	.30	.25	.12
(56)	Todd Zeile	.15	.11	.06
	SAN DIEGO PADRES			
(57)	Derek Bell	.15	.11	.06
(58)	Tony Gwynn	.25	.20	.10
(59)	Fred McGriff	.30	.25	.12
(60)	Gary Sheffield	.30	.25	.12
	SAN FRANCISCO GIANTS			
(61)	Barry Bonds	.60	.45	.25
(62)	John Burkett	.20	.20	.10
(63)	Will Clark	.45	.35	.15
(64)	Matt Williams	.25	.20	.10
	BALTIMORE ORIOLES			
(65)	Brady Anderson	.15	.11	.06
(66)	Mike Mussina	.15	.11	.06
(67)	Cal Ripken Jr.	.75	.55	.25
	BOSTON RED SOX			
(68)	Roger Clemens	.40	.30	.15
(69)	Andre Dawson	.25	.20	.10
(70)	Mike Greenwell	.15	.11	.06
(71)	Mo Vaughn	.25	.20	.10
	DETROIT TIGERS			
(72)	Cecil Fielder	.35	.25	.12

		MT	NR MT	EX
(73)	Tony Phillips	.15	.11	.06
(74)	Mickey Tettleton	.25	.20	.10
(75)	Alan Trammell	.30	.25	.12
	CLEVELAND INDIANS			
(76)	Sandy Alomar Jr.	.15	.11	.06
(77)	Carlos Baerga	.15	.11	.06
(78)	Albert Belle	.25	.20	.10
(79)	Kenny Lofton	.15	.11	.06
	CHICAGO WHITE SOX			
(80)	Bo Jackson	.45	.35	.15
(81)	Frank Thomas	.60	.45	.25
(82)	Robin Ventura	.25	.20	.10
	CALIFORNIA ANGELS			
(83)	Chad Curtis	.15	.11	.06
(84)	Gary DiSarcina	.15	.11	.06
(85)	Tim Salmon	.50	.40	.20
(86)	J.T. Snow	.15	.11	.06
	KANSAS CITY ROYALS			
(87)	George Brett	.60	.45	.25
(88)	Wally Joyner	.25	.20	.10
(89)	Mike MacFarlane	.15	.11	.06
(90)	Brian McRae	.25	.20	.10
	MILWAUKEE BREWERS			
(91)	Darryl Hamilton	.15	.11	.06
(92)	Pat Listach	.15	.11	.06
(93)	B.J. Surhoff	.15	.11	.06
(94)	Robin Yount	.60	.45	.25
	MINNESOTA TWINS			
(95)	Kent Hrbek	.25	.20	.10
(96)	Chuck Knoblauch	.15	.11	.06
(97)	Kirby Puckett	.50	.40	.20
(98)	Dave Winfield	.40	.30	.15
	NEW YORK YANKEES			
(99)	Wade Boggs	.50	.40	.20
(100)	Don Mattingly	.60	.45	.25
(101)	Danny Tartabull	.25	.20	.10
	OAKLAND ATHLETICS			
(102)	Dennis Eckersley	.25	.20	.10
(103)	Rickey Henderson	.35	.25	.12
(104)	Mark McGwire	.40	.30	.15
(105)	Ruben Sierra	.25	.20	.10
(106)	Terry Steinbach	.15	.11	.06
	SEATTLE MARINERS			
(107)	Ken Griffey Jr.	.60	.45	.25
(108)	Edgar Martinez	.15	.11	.06
(109)	Pete O'Brien	.15	.11	.06
(110)	David Valle	.15	.11	.06
	TEXAS RANGERS			
(111)	Jose Canseco	.45	.35	.15
(112)	Juan Gonzalez	.50	.40	.20
(113)	Ivan Rodriguez	.25	.20	.10
(114)	Nolan Ryan	.75	.55	.25
	TORONTO BLUE JAYS			
(115)	Roberto Alomar	.50	.40	.20
(116)	Pat Borders	.15	.11	.06
(117)	Joe Carter	.30	.25	.12
(118)	Juan Guzman	.25	.20	.10
(119)	Paul Molitor	.45	.35	.15
(120)	Dave Stewart	.25	.20	.10

1993 DiamondMarks Inserts

Randomly inserted into packs of DiamondMarks cards was a series of seven cards featuring the baseball artwork of Terry Smith. The inserts are the same 2-1/2" x 5" size as the regular issue and carry on with the basic black bordered design, though the inserts are UV-coated both front and back. Beneath the fantasy-design player art on the front is the player's name. On back the open book design is seen again, with a short player profile on the left and a Barry Colla photo portrait on the right, along with the appropriate team logo.

		MT	NR MT	EX
Complete set:		65.00	45.00	22.50
Common player:		10.00	7.50	3.75
(1)	Barry Bonds	12.00	9.00	4.50
(2)	Ken Griffey, Jr.	12.00	9.00	4.50
(3)	David Justice	10.00	7.50	3.75
(4)	John Olerud	10.00	7.50	3.75
(5)	Nolan Ryan	15.00	11.25	5.50
(6)	Frank Thomas	12.00	9.00	4.50
(7)	Robin Yount	12.00	9.00	4.50

1981 Donruss

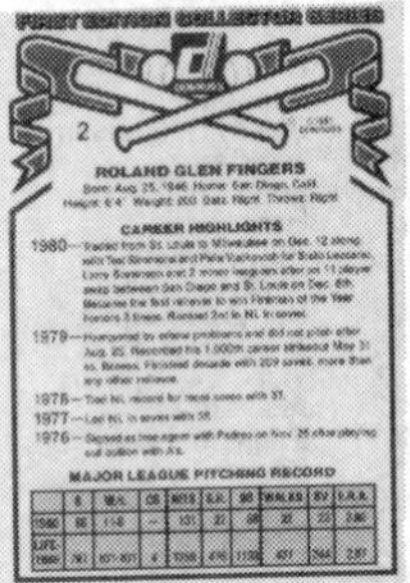

The Donruss Co. of Memphis, Tenn., produced its premiere baseball card issue in 1981 with a set that consisted of 600 numbered cards and five unnumbered checklists. The cards, which measure 2-1/2" by 3-1/2", are printed on thin stock. The card fronts contain the Donruss logo plus the year of issue. The card backs are designed on a vertical format and have black print on red and white. The set, entitled "First Edition Collector Series," contains nearly 40 variations, those being first-printing errors that were corrected in a subsequent print run. The cards were issued in gum wax packs, with hobby dealer sales being coordinated by TCMA of Amawalk, N.Y. The complete set price does not include the higher priced variations.

		MT	NR MT	EX
Complete Set (605):		60.00	45.00	25.00
Common Player:		.06	.05	.02
1	Ozzie Smith	3.00	2.25	1.25
2	Rollie Fingers	1.00	.70	.40
3	Rick Wise	.08	.06	.03
4	Gene Richards	.06	.05	.02
5	Alan Trammell	.80	.60	.30
6	Tom Brookens	.08	.06	.03
7a	Duffy Dyer (1980 Avg. .185)	1.00	.70	.40
7b	Duffy Dyer (1980 Avg. 185)	.10	.08	.04
8	Mark Fidrych	.08	.06	.03
9	Dave Rozema	.06	.05	.02
10	Ricky Peters	.06	.05	.02
11	Mike Schmidt	2.50	2.00	1.00
12	Willie Stargell	.80	.60	.30
13	Tim Foli	.06	.05	.02
14	Manny Sanguillen	.06	.05	.02
15	Grant Jackson	.06	.05	.02
16	Eddie Solomon	.06	.05	.02
17	Omar Moreno	.06	.05	.02
18	Joe Morgan	.60	.45	.25
19	Rafael Landestoy	.06	.05	.02
20	Bruce Bochy	.06	.05	.02
21	Joe Sambito	.06	.05	.02
22	Manny Trillo	.08	.06	.03
23a	*Dave Smith* (incomplete box around stats)	1.00	.70	.40
23b	*Dave Smith* (complete box around stats)	.30	.25	.12
24	Terry Puhl	.06	.05	.02

No.	Player	MT	NR MT	EX
25	Bump Wills	.06	.05	.02
26a	John Ellis (Danny Walton photo - with bat)	1.25	.90	.50
26b	John Ellis (John Ellis photo - with glove)	.10	.08	.04
27	Jim Kern	.06	.05	.02
28	Richie Zisk	.08	.06	.03
29	John Mayberry	.08	.06	.03
30	Bob Davis	.06	.05	.02
31	Jackson Todd	.06	.05	.02
32	Al Woods	.06	.05	.02
33	Steve Carlton	1.75	1.25	.60
34	Lee Mazzilli	.08	.06	.03
35	John Stearns	.06	.05	.02
36	Roy Jackson	.06	.05	.02
37	Mike Scott	.70	.50	.30
38	Lamar Johnson	.06	.05	.02
39	Kevin Bell	.06	.05	.02
40	Ed Farmer	.06	.05	.02
41	Ross Baumgarten	.06	.05	.02
42	Leo Sutherland	.06	.05	.02
43	Dan Meyer	.06	.05	.02
44	Ron Reed	.06	.05	.02
45	Mario Mendoza	.06	.05	.02
46	Rick Honeycutt	.06	.05	.02
47	Glenn Abbott	.06	.05	.02
48	Leon Roberts	.06	.05	.02
49	Rod Carew	1.50	1.25	.60
50	Bert Campaneris	.10	.08	.04
51a	Tom Donahue (incorrect spelling)	1.00	.70	.40
51b	Tom Donohue (Donohue on front)	.10	.08	.04
52	Dave Frost	.06	.05	.02
53	Ed Halicki	.06	.05	.02
54	Dan Ford	.06	.05	.02
55	Garry Maddox	.10	.08	.04
56a	Steve Garvey (Surpassed 25 HR..)	1.75	1.25	.70
56b	Steve Garvey (Surpassed 21 HR..)	.60	.45	.25
57	Bill Russell	.08	.06	.03
58	Don Sutton	.30	.25	.12
59	Reggie Smith	.10	.08	.04
60	Rick Monday	.10	.08	.04
61	Ray Knight	.10	.08	.04
62	Johnny Bench	1.25	.90	.50
63	Mario Soto	.08	.06	.03
64	Doug Bair	.06	.05	.02
65	George Foster	.20	.15	.08
66	Jeff Burroughs	.08	.06	.03
67	Keith Hernandez	.40	.30	.15
68	Tom Herr	.10	.08	.04
69	Bob Forsch	.08	.06	.03
70	John Fulgham	.06	.05	.02
71a	Bobby Bonds (lifetime HR 986)	.30	.20	.10
71b	Bobby Bonds (lifetime HR 326)	.15	.11	.06
72a	Rennie Stennett ("...breaking broke leg..." on back)	1.00	.70	.40
72b	Rennie Stennett ("...breaking leg..." on back)	.10	.08	.04
73	Joe Strain	.06	.05	.02
74	Ed Whitson	.06	.05	.02
75	Tom Griffin	.06	.05	.02
76	Bill North	.06	.05	.02
77	Gene Garber	.06	.05	.02
78	Mike Hargrove	.06	.05	.02
79	Dave Rosello	.06	.05	.02
80	Ron Hassey	.06	.05	.02
81	Sid Monge	.06	.05	.02
82a	*Joe Charboneau* ("For some reason, Phillies..." on back)	1.00	.70	.40
82b	*Joe Charboneau* ("Phillies..." on back)	.12	.09	.05
83	Cecil Cooper	.15	.11	.06
84	Sal Bando	.10	.08	.04
85	Moose Haas	.06	.05	.02
86	Mike Caldwell	.06	.05	.02
87a	Larry Hisle ("...Twins with 28 RBI." on back)	1.00	.70	.40
87b	Larry Hisle ("...Twins with 28 HR" on back)	.10	.08	.04
88	Luis Gomez	.06	.05	.02
89	Larry Parrish	.10	.08	.04
90	Gary Carter	.50	.40	.20
91	*Bill Gullickson*	.15	.11	.06
92	Fred Norman	.06	.05	.02
93	Tommy Hutton	.06	.05	.02
94	Carl Yastrzemski	1.00	.70	.40
95	Glenn Hoffman	.06	.05	.02
96	Dennis Eckersley	2.00	1.50	.80
97a	Tom Burgmeier (Throws: Right)	1.00	.70	.40
97b	Tom Burgmeier (Throws: Left)	.10	.08	.04
98	Win Remmerswaal	.06	.05	.02

No.	Player	MT	NR MT	EX
99	Bob Horner	.12	.09	.05
100	George Brett	4.00	3.00	1.50
101	Dave Chalk	.06	.05	.02
102	Dennis Leonard	.08	.06	.03
103	Renie Martin	.06	.05	.02
104	Amos Otis	.08	.06	.03
105	Graig Nettles	.15	.11	.06
106	Eric Soderholm	.06	.05	.02
107	Tommy John	.20	.15	.08
108	Tom Underwood	.06	.05	.02
109	Lou Piniella	.12	.09	.05
110	Mickey Klutts	.06	.05	.02
111	Bobby Murcer	.10	.08	.04
112	Eddie Murray	3.00	2.25	1.25
113	Rick Dempsey	.08	.06	.03
114	Scott McGregor	.08	.06	.03
115	Ken Singleton	.10	.08	.04
116	Gary Roenicke	.06	.05	.02
117	Dave Revering	.06	.05	.02
118	Mike Norris	.06	.05	.02
119	Rickey Henderson	10.00	7.50	4.00
120	Mike Heath	.06	.05	.02
121	Dave Cash	.06	.05	.02
122	Randy Jones	.08	.06	.03
123	Eric Rasmussen	.06	.05	.02
124	Jerry Mumphrey	.06	.05	.02
125	Richie Hebner	.06	.05	.02
126	Mark Wagner	.06	.05	.02
127	Jack Morris	2.00	1.50	.80
128	Dan Petry	.08	.06	.03
129	Bruce Robbins	.06	.05	.02
130	Champ Summers	.06	.05	.02
131a	Pete Rose (ERR see card 251 on back)	2.25	1.75	.90
131b	Pete Rose (COR card 371)	1.25	.90	.50
132	Willie Stargell	.40	.30	.15
133	Ed Ott	.06	.05	.02
134	Jim Bibby	.06	.05	.02
135	Bert Blyleven	.12	.09	.05
136	Dave Parker	.30	.25	.12
137	Bill Robinson	.06	.05	.02
138	Enos Cabell	.06	.05	.02
139	Dave Bergman	.06	.05	.02
140	J R Richard	.10	.08	.04
141	Ken Forsch	.06	.05	.02
142	Larry Bowa	.15	.11	.06
143	Frank LaCorte (photo actually Randy Niemann)	.06	.05	.02
144	Dennis Walling	.06	.05	.02
145	Buddy Bell	.12	.09	.05
146	Fergie Jenkins	.50	.40	.30
147	Danny Darwin	.06	.05	.02
148	John Grubb	.06	.05	.02
149	Alfredo Griffin	.08	.06	.03
150	Jerry Garvin	.06	.05	.02
151	*Paul Mirabella*(FC)	.10	.08	.04
152	Rick Bosetti	.06	.05	.02
153	Dick Ruthven	.06	.05	.02
154	Frank Taveras	.06	.05	.02
155	Craig Swan	.06	.05	.02
156	*Jeff Reardon*	5.00	3.75	2.00
157	Steve Henderson	.06	.05	.02
158	Jim Morrison	.06	.05	.02
159	Glenn Borgmann	.06	.05	.02
160	*Lamarr Hoyt (LaMarr)*	.10	.08	.04
161	Rich Wortham	.06	.05	.02
162	Thad Bosley	.06	.05	.02
163	Julio Cruz	.06	.05	.02
164a	Del Unser (no 3B in stat heads)	1.00	.70	.40
164b	Del Unser (3B in stat heads)	.10	.08	.04
165	Jim Anderson	.06	.05	.02
166	Jim Beattie	.06	.05	.02
167	Shane Rawley	.10	.08	.04
168	Joe Simpson	.06	.05	.02
169	Rod Carew	1.50	1.25	.60
170	Fred Patek	.06	.05	.02
171	Frank Tanana	.10	.08	.04
172	Alfredo Martinez	.06	.05	.02
173	Chris Knapp	.06	.05	.02
174	Joe Rudi	.10	.08	.04
175	Greg Luzinski	.15	.11	.06
176	Steve Garvey	.50	.40	.20
177	Joe Ferguson	.06	.05	.02
178	Bob Welch	.60	.45	.25
179	Dusty Baker	.10	.08	.04
180	Rudy Law	.06	.05	.02
181	Dave Concepcion	.15	.11	.06
182	Johnny Bench	1.00	.70	.40
183	Mike LaCoss	.06	.05	.02
184	Ken Griffey	.12	.09	.05
185	Dave Collins	.08	.06	.03

		MT	NR MT	EX
186	Brian Asselstine	.06	.05	.02
187	Garry Templeton	.10	.08	.04
188	Mike Phillips	.06	.05	.02
189	Pete Vukovich	.08	.06	.03
190	John Urrea	.06	.05	.02
191	Tony Scott	.06	.05	.02
192	Darrell Evans	.12	.09	.05
193	Milt May	.06	.05	.02
194	Bob Knepper	.08	.06	.03
195	Randy Moffitt	.06	.05	.02
196	Larry Herndon	.08	.06	.03
197	Rick Camp	.06	.05	.02
198	Andre Thornton	.10	.08	.04
199	Tom Veryzer	.06	.05	.02
200	Gary Alexander	.06	.05	.02
201	Rick Waits	.06	.05	.02
202	Rick Manning	.06	.05	.02
203	Paul Molitor	3.00	2.25	1.25
204	Jim Gantner	.08	.06	.03
205	Paul Mitchell	.06	.05	.02
206	Reggie Cleveland	.06	.05	.02
207	Sixto Lezcano	.06	.05	.02
208	Bruce Benedict	.06	.05	.02
209	Rodney Scott	.06	.05	.02
210	John Tamargo	.06	.05	.02
211	Bill Lee	.08	.06	.03
212	Andre Dawson	1.75	1.25	.70
213	Rowland Office	.06	.05	.02
214	Carl Yastrzemski	1.25	.90	.50
215	Jerry Remy	.06	.05	.02
216	Mike Torrez	.08	.06	.03
217	Skip Lockwood	.06	.05	.02
218	Fred Lynn	.20	.15	.08
219	Chris Chambliss	.08	.06	.03
220	Willie Aikens	.06	.05	.02
221	John Wathan	.08	.06	.03
222	Dan Quisenberry	.15	.11	.06
223	Willie Wilson	.15	.11	.06
224	Clint Hurdle	.06	.05	.02
225	Bob Watson	.08	.06	.03
226	Jim Spencer	.06	.05	.02
227	Ron Guidry	.25	.20	.10
228	Reggie Jackson	4.00	3.00	1.50
229	Oscar Gamble	.08	.06	.03
230	Jeff Cox	.06	.05	.02
231	Luis Tiant	.12	.09	.05
232	Rich Dauer	.06	.05	.02
233	Dan Graham	.06	.05	.02
234	Mike Flanagan	.10	.08	.04
235	John Lowenstein	.06	.05	.02
236	Benny Ayala	.06	.05	.02
237	Wayne Gross	.06	.05	.02
238	Rick Langford	.06	.05	.02
239	Tony Armas	.10	.08	.04
240a	Bob Lacy (incorrect spelling)	1.00	.70	.40
240b	Bob Lacey (correct spelling)	.10	.08	.04
241	Gene Tenace	.08	.06	.03
242	Bob Shirley	.06	.05	.02
243	Gary Lucas	.08	.06	.03
244	Jerry Turner	.06	.05	.02
245	John Wockenfuss	.06	.05	.02
246	Stan Papi	.06	.05	.02
247	Milt Wilcox	.06	.05	.02
248	Dan Schatzeder	.06	.05	.02
249	Steve Kemp	.08	.06	.03
250	Jim Lentine	.06	.05	.02
251	Pete Rose	1.00	.70	.40
252	Bill Madlock	.12	.09	.05
253	Dale Berra	.06	.05	.02
254	Kent Tekulve	.08	.06	.03
255	Enrique Romo	.06	.05	.02
256	Mike Easler	.08	.06	.03
257	Chuck Tanner	.06	.05	.02
258	Art Howe	.06	.05	.02
259	Alan Ashby	.06	.05	.02
260	Nolan Ryan	8.00	6.00	3.25
261a	Vern Ruhle (Ken Forsch photo - head shot)	1.25	.90	.50
261b	Vern Ruhle (Vern Ruhle photo - waist to head shot)	.10	.08	.04
262	Bob Boone	.10	.08	.04
263	Cesar Cedeno	.12	.09	.05
264	Jeff Leonard	.12	.09	.05
265	Pat Putnam	.06	.05	.02
266	Jon Matlack	.08	.06	.03
267	Dave Rajsich	.06	.05	.02
268	Billy Sample	.06	.05	.02
269	*Damaso Garcia*	.10	.08	.04
270	Tom Buskey	.06	.05	.02
271	Joey McLaughlin	.06	.05	.02
272	Barry Bonnell	.06	.05	.02

		MT	NR MT	EX
273	Tug McGraw	.10	.08	.04
274	Mike Jorgensen	.06	.05	.02
275	Pat Zachry	.06	.05	.02
276	Neil Allen	.08	.06	.03
277	Joel Youngblood	.06	.05	.02
278	Greg Pryor	.06	.05	.02
279	*Britt Burns*	.10	.08	.04
280	*Rich Dotson*	.25	.20	.10
281	Chet Lemon	.08	.06	.03
282	Rusty Kuntz	.06	.05	.02
283	Ted Cox	.06	.05	.02
284	Sparky Lyle	.10	.08	.04
285	Larry Cox	.06	.05	.02
286	Floyd Bannister	.10	.08	.04
287	Byron McLaughlin	.06	.05	.02
288	Rodney Craig	.06	.05	.02
289	Bobby Grich	.10	.08	.04
290	Dickie Thon	.08	.06	.03
291	Mark Clear	.06	.05	.02
292	Dave Lemanczyk	.06	.05	.02
293	Jason Thompson	.06	.05	.02
294	Rick Miller	.06	.05	.02
295	Lonnie Smith	.08	.06	.03
296	Ron Cey	.12	.09	.05
297	Steve Yeager	.06	.05	.02
298	Bobby Castillo	.06	.05	.02
299	Manny Mota	.08	.06	.03
300	Jay Johnstone	.08	.06	.03
301	Dan Driessen	.08	.06	.03
302	Joe Nolan	.06	.05	.02
303	Paul Householder	.06	.05	.02
304	Harry Spilman	.06	.05	.02
305	Cesar Geronimo	.06	.05	.02
306a	Gary Mathews (Mathews on front)	1.25	.90	.50
306b	Gary Matthews (Matthews on front)	.10	.08	.04
307	Ken Reitz	.06	.05	.02
308	Ted Simmons	.12	.09	.05
309	John Littlefield	.06	.05	.02
310	George Frazier	.06	.05	.02
311	Dane Iorg	.06	.05	.02
312	Mike Ivie	.06	.05	.02
313	Dennis Littlejohn	.06	.05	.02
314	Gary LaVelle (Lavelle)	.06	.05	.02
315	Jack Clark	.25	.20	.10
316	Jim Wohlford	.06	.05	.02
317	Rick Matula	.06	.05	.02
318	Toby Harrah	.08	.06	.03
319a	Dwane Kuiper (Dwane on front)	1.00	.70	.40
319b	Duane Kuiper (Duane on front)	.10	.08	.04
320	Len Barker	.08	.06	.03
321	Victor Cruz	.06	.05	.02
322	Dell Alston	.06	.05	.02
323	Robin Yount	4.00	3.00	1.50
324	Charlie Moore	.06	.05	.02
325	Lary Sorensen	.06	.05	.02
326a	Gorman Thomas ("...30-HR mark 4th..." on back)	1.25	.90	.50
326b	Gorman Thomas ("...30-HR mark 3rd..." on back)	.10	.08	.04
327	Bob Rodgers	.08	.06	.03
328	Phil Niekro	.30	.25	.12
329	Chris Speier	.06	.05	.02
330a	Steve Rodgers (Rodgers on front)	1.00	.70	.40
330b	Steve Rogers (Rogers on front)	.10	.08	.04
331	Woodie Fryman	.08	.06	.03
332	Warren Cromartie	.06	.05	.02
333	Jerry White	.06	.05	.02
334	Tony Perez	.20	.15	.08
335	Carlton Fisk	1.75	1.25	.70
336	Dick Drago	.06	.05	.02
337	Steve Renko	.06	.05	.02
338	Jim Rice	.50	.40	.20
339	Jerry Royster	.06	.05	.02
340	Frank White	.10	.08	.04
341	Jamie Quirk	.06	.05	.02
342a	Paul Spittorff (Spittorff on front)	1.00	.70	.40
342b	Paul Splittorff (Splittorff on front)	.08	.06	.03
343	Marty Pattin	.06	.05	.02
344	Pete LaCock	.06	.05	.02
345	Willie Randolph	.10	.08	.04
346	Rick Cerone	.06	.05	.02
347	Rich Gossage	.20	.15	.08
348	Reggie Jackson	2.50	2.00	1.00
349	Ruppert Jones	.06	.05	.02
350	Dave McKay	.06	.05	.02
351	Yogi Berra	.15	.11	.06
352	Doug Decinces (DeCinces)	.10	.08	.04
353	Jim Palmer	1.00	.70	.40
354	Tippy Martinez	.06	.05	.02

		MT	NR MT	EX
355	Al Bumbry	.08	.06	.03
356	Earl Weaver	.10	.08	.04
357a	Bob Picciolo (Bob on front)	1.00	.70	.40
357b	Rob Picciolo (Rob on front)	.10	.08	.04
358	Matt Keough	.06	.05	.02
359	Dwayne Murphy	.08	.06	.03
360	Brian Kingman	.06	.05	.02
361	Bill Fahey	.06	.05	.02
362	Steve Mura	.06	.05	.02
363	Dennis Kinney	.06	.05	.02
364	Dave Winfield	3.00	2.25	1.25
365	Lou Whitaker	.40	.30	.15
366	Lance Parrish	.35	.25	.14
367	Tim Corcoran	.06	.05	.02
368	Pat Underwood	.06	.05	.02
369	Al Cowens	.06	.05	.02
370	Sparky Anderson	.10	.08	.04
371	Pete Rose	1.50	1.25	.65
372	Phil Garner	.08	.06	.03
373	Steve Nicosia	.06	.05	.02
374	John Candelaria	.10	.08	.04
375	Don Robinson	.08	.06	.03
376	Lee Lacy	.06	.05	.02
377	John Milner	.06	.05	.02
378	Craig Reynolds	.06	.05	.02
379a	Luis Pujols (Pujois on front)	1.00	.70	.40
379b	Luis Pujols (Pujols on front)	.10	.08	.04
380	Joe Niekro	.12	.09	.05
381	Joaquin Andujar	.10	.08	.04
382	*Keith Moreland*	.35	.25	.14
383	Jose Cruz	.12	.09	.05
384	Bill Virdon	.06	.05	.02
385	Jim Sundberg	.08	.06	.03
386	Doc Medich	.06	.05	.02
387	Al Oliver	.15	.11	.06
388	Jim Norris	.06	.05	.02
389	Bob Bailor	.06	.05	.02
390	Ernie Whitt	.08	.06	.03
391	Otto Velez	.06	.05	.02
392	Roy Howell	.06	.05	.02
393	*Bob Walk*	.35	.25	.14
394	Doug Flynn	.06	.05	.02
395	Pete Falcone	.06	.05	.02
396	Tom Hausman	.06	.05	.02
397	Elliott Maddox	.06	.05	.02
398	Mike Squires	.06	.05	.02
399	Marvis Foley	.06	.05	.02
400	Steve Trout	.06	.05	.02
401	Wayne Nordhagen	.06	.05	.02
402	Tony Larussa (LaRussa)	.08	.06	.03
403	Bruce Bochte	.06	.05	.02
404	Bake McBride	.06	.05	.02
405	Jerry Narron	.06	.05	.02
406	Rob Dressler	.06	.05	.02
407	Dave Heaverlo	.06	.05	.02
408	Tom Paciorek	.06	.05	.02
409	Carney Lansford	.10	.08	.04
410	Brian Downing	.10	.08	.04
411	Don Aase	.06	.05	.02
412	Jim Barr	.06	.05	.02
413	Don Baylor	.12	.09	.05
414	Jim Fregosi	.08	.06	.03
415	Dallas Green	.08	.06	.03
416	Dave Lopes	.10	.08	.04
417	Jerry Reuss	.10	.08	.04
418	Rick Sutcliffe	.20	.15	.08
419	Derrel Thomas	.06	.05	.02
420	Tommy LaSorda (Lasorda)	.10	.08	.04
421	*Charlie Leibrandt*	.40	.30	.15
422	Tom Seaver	2.00	1.50	.80
423	Ron Oester	.06	.05	.02
424	Junior Kennedy	.06	.05	.02
425	Tom Seaver	2.00	1.50	.80
426	Bobby Cox	.06	.05	.02
427	*Leon Durham*	.20	.15	.08
428	Terry Kennedy	.08	.06	.03
429	Silvio Martinez	.06	.05	.02
430	George Hendrick	.08	.06	.03
431	Red Schoendienst	.08	.06	.03
432	John LeMaster	.06	.05	.02
433	Vida Blue	.12	.09	.05
434	John Montefusco	.08	.06	.03
435	Terry Whitfield	.06	.05	.02
436	Dave Bristol	.06	.05	.02
437	Dale Murphy	.90	.70	.35
438	Jerry Dybzinski	.06	.05	.02
439	Jorge Orta	.06	.05	.02
440	Wayne Garland	.06	.05	.02
441	Miguel Dilone	.06	.05	.02
442	Dave Garcia	.06	.05	.02
443	Don Money	.06	.05	.02

		MT	NR MT	EX
444a	Buck Martinez (photo reversed)	1.00	.70	.40
444b	Buck Martinez (photo correct)	.10	.08	.04
445	Jerry Augustine	.06	.05	.02
446	Ben Oglivie	.08	.06	.03
447	Jim Slaton	.06	.05	.02
448	Doyle Alexander	.10	.08	.04
449	Tony Bernazard	.06	.05	.02
450	Scott Sanderson	.06	.05	.02
451	Dave Palmer	.06	.05	.02
452	Stan Bahnsen	.06	.05	.02
453	Dick Williams	.06	.05	.02
454	Rick Burleson	.08	.06	.03
455	Gary Allenson	.06	.05	.02
456	Bob Stanley	.06	.05	.02
457a	*John Tudor* (lifetime W/L 9.7)	1.50	1.25	.60
457b	*John Tudor* (lifetime W/L 9-7)	1.00	.70	.40
458	Dwight Evans	.15	.11	.06
459	Glenn Hubbard	.08	.06	.03
460	U L Washington	.06	.05	.02
461	Larry Gura	.06	.05	.02
462	Rich Gale	.06	.05	.02
463	Hal McRae	.10	.08	.04
464	Jim Frey	.06	.05	.02
465	Bucky Dent	.10	.08	.04
466	Dennis Werth	.06	.05	.02
467	Ron Davis	.08	.06	.03
468	Reggie Jackson	3.50	2.75	1.50
469	Bobby Brown	.06	.05	.02
470	*Mike Davis*	.20	.15	.08
471	Gaylord Perry	.50	.40	.20
472	Mark Belanger	.08	.06	.03
473	Jim Palmer	.80	.60	.30
474	Sammy Stewart	.06	.05	.02
475	Tim Stoddard	.06	.05	.02
476	Steve Stone	.08	.06	.03
477	Jeff Newman	.06	.05	.02
478	Steve McCatty	.06	.05	.02
479	Billy Martin	.12	.09	.05
480	Mitchell Page	.06	.05	.02
481	Steve Carlton (CY)	.40	.30	.15
482	Bill Buckner	.12	.09	.05
483a	Ivan DeJesus (lifetime hits 702)	1.00	.70	.40
483b	Ivan DeJesus (lifetime hits 642)	.10	.08	.04
484	Cliff Johnson	.06	.05	.02
485	Lenny Randle	.06	.05	.02
486	Larry Milbourne	.06	.05	.02
487	Roy Smalley	.06	.05	.02
488	John Castino	.06	.05	.02
489	Ron Jackson	.06	.05	.02
490a	Dave Roberts (1980 highlights begins "Showed pop...")	1.00	.70	.40
490b	Dave Roberts (1980 highlights begins "Declared himself...")	.10	.08	.04
491	George Brett (MVP)	2.50	2.00	1.00
492	Mike Cubbage	.06	.05	.02
493	Rob Wilfong	.06	.05	.02
494	Danny Goodwin	.06	.05	.02
495	Jose Morales	.06	.05	.02
496	Mickey Rivers	.08	.06	.03
497	Mike Edwards	.06	.05	.02
498	Mike Sadek	.06	.05	.02
499	Lenn Sakata	.06	.05	.02
500	Gene Michael	.06	.05	.02
501	Dave Roberts	.06	.05	.02
502	Steve Dillard	.06	.05	.02
503	Jim Essian	.06	.05	.02
504	Rance Mulliniks	.06	.05	.02
505	Darrell Porter	.08	.06	.03
506	Joe Torre	.08	.06	.03
507	Terry Crowley	.06	.05	.02
508	Bill Travers	.06	.05	.02
509	Nelson Norman	.06	.05	.02
510	Bob McClure	.06	.05	.02
511	*Steve Howe*	.10	.08	.04
512	Dave Rader	.06	.05	.02
513	Mick Kelleher	.06	.05	.02
514	Kiko Garcia	.06	.05	.02
515	Larry Biittner	.06	.05	.02
516a	Willie Norwood (1980 highlights begins "Spent most...")	1.00	.70	.40
516b	Willie Norwood (1980 highlights begins "Traded to...")	.10	.08	.04
517	Bo Diaz	.08	.06	.03
518	Juan Beniquez	.06	.05	.02
519	Scot Thompson	.06	.05	.02
520	Jim Tracy	.06	.05	.02
521	Carlos Lezcano	.06	.05	.02
522	Joe Amalfitano	.06	.05	.02
523	Preston Hanna	.06	.05	.02
524a	Ray Burris (1980 highlights begins "Went on...")	1.00	.70	.40

		MT	NR MT	EX
524b	Ray Burris (1980 highlights begins "Drafted by...")	.10	.08	.04
525	Broderick Perkins	.06	.05	.02
526	Mickey Hatcher	.08	.06	.03
527	John Goryl	.06	.05	.02
528	Dick Davis	.06	.05	.02
529	Butch Wynegar	.06	.05	.02
530	Sal Butera	.06	.05	.02
531	Jerry Koosman	.10	.08	.04
532a	Jeff Zahn (Geoff) (1980 highlights begins "Was 2nd in...")	1.00	.70	.40
532b	Jeff Zahn (Geoff) (1980 highlights begins "Signed a 3 year...")	.10	.08	.04
533	Dennis Martinez	.08	.06	.03
534	Gary Thomasson	.06	.05	.02
535	Steve Macko	.06	.05	.02
536	Jim Kaat	.15	.11	.06
537	Best Hitters (George Brett, Rod Carew)	2.00	1.50	.80
538	*Tim Raines*	7.00	5.00	2.50
539	Keith Smith	.06	.05	.02
540	Ken Macha	.06	.05	.02
541	Burt Hooton	.08	.06	.03
542	Butch Hobson	.06	.05	.02
543	Bill Stein	.06	.05	.02
544	Dave Stapleton	.06	.05	.02
545	Bob Pate	.06	.05	.02
546	Doug Corbett	.06	.05	.02
547	Darrell Jackson	.06	.05	.02
548	Pete Redfern	.06	.05	.02
549	Roger Erickson	.06	.05	.02
550	Al Hrabosky	.08	.06	.03
551	Dick Tidrow	.06	.05	.02
552	Dave Ford	.06	.05	.02
553	Dave Kingman	.15	.11	.06
554a	Mike Vail (1980 highlights begins "After...")	1.00	.70	.40
554b	Mike Vail (1980 highlights begins "Traded...")	.10	.08	.04
555a	Jerry Martin (1980 highlights begins "Overcame...")	1.00	.70	.40
555b	Jerry Martin (1980 highlights begins "Traded...")	.10	.08	.04
556a	Jesus Figueroa (1980 highlights begins "Had...")	1.00	.70	.40
556b	Jesus Figueroa (1980 highlights begins "Traded...")	.10	.08	.04
557	Don Stanhouse	.06	.05	.02
558	Barry Foote	.06	.05	.02
559	Tim Blackwell	.06	.05	.02
560	Bruce Sutter	.15	.11	.06
561	Rick Reuschel	.10	.08	.04
562	Lynn McGlothen	.06	.05	.02
563a	Bob Owchinko (1980 highlights begins "Traded...")	1.00	.70	.40
563b	Bob Owchinko (1980 highlights begins "Involved...")	.10	.08	.04
564	John Verhoeven	.06	.05	.02
565	Ken Landreaux	.06	.05	.02
566a	Glen Adams (Glen on front)	1.00	.70	.40
566b	Glenn Adams (Glenn on front)	.10	.08	.04
567	Hosken Powell	.06	.05	.02
568	Dick Noles	.06	.05	.02
569	*Danny Ainge*	2.50	2.00	1.00
570	Bobby Mattick	.06	.05	.02
571	Joe LeFebvre (Lefebvre)	.06	.05	.02
572	Bobby Clark	.06	.05	.02
573	Dennis Lamp	.06	.05	.02
574	Randy Lerch	.06	.05	.02
575	*Mookie Wilson*	.60	.45	.25
576	Ron LeFlore	.08	.06	.03
577	Jim Dwyer	.06	.05	.02
578	Bill Castro	.06	.05	.02
579	Greg Minton	.06	.05	.02
580	Mark Littell	.06	.05	.02
581	Andy Hassler	.06	.05	.02
582	Dave Stieb	.60	.45	.25
583	Ken Oberkfell	.06	.05	.02
584	Larry Bradford	.06	.05	.02
585	Fred Stanley	.06	.05	.02
586	Bill Caudill	.06	.05	.02
587	Doug Capilla	.06	.05	.02
588	George Riley	.06	.05	.02
589	Willie Hernandez	.10	.08	.04
590	Mike Schmidt (MVP)	1.00	.70	.40
591	Cy Young 1980 (Steve Stone)	.08	.06	.03
592	Rick Sofield	.06	.05	.02
593	Bombo Rivera	.06	.05	.02
594	Gary Ward	.08	.06	.03
595a	Dave Edwards (1980 highlights begins "Sidelined...")	1.00	.70	.40
595b	Dave Edwards (1980 highlights begins "Traded...")	.10	.08	.04
596	Mike Proly	.06	.05	.02
597	Tommy Boggs	.06	.05	.02
598	Greg Gross	.06	.05	.02
599	Elias Sosa	.06	.05	.02
600	Pat Kelly	.06	.05	.02
---a	Checklist 1-120 (51 Tom Donohue)	2.00	1.50	.80
---b	Checklist 1-120 (51 Tom Donahue)	.10	.08	.04
——	Checklist 121-240	.06	.05	.02
---a	Checklist 241-360 (306 Gary Mathews)	.70	.50	.30
---b	Checklist 241-360 (306 Gary Matthews)	.10	.08	.04
---a	Checklist 361-480 (379 Luis Pujois)	.70	.50	.30
---b	Checklist 361-480 (379 Luis Pujols)	.10	.08	.04
---a	Checklist 481-600 (566 Glen Adams)	.70	.50	.30
---b	Checklist 481-600 (566 Glenn Adams)	.10	.08	.04

1982 Donruss

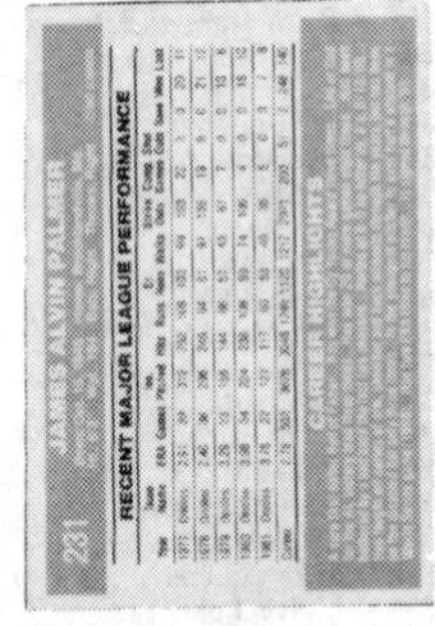

Using card stock thicker than the previous year, Donruss issued a 660-card set which includes 653 numbered cards and seven unnumbered checklists. The cards, which measure 2-1/2" by 3-1/2", were sold with puzzle pieces rather than gum as a result of a lawsuit by Topps. The puzzle pieces (three pieces on one card per pack) feature Babe Ruth. The first 26 cards of the set, entitled Diamond Kings, showcase the artwork of Dick Perez of Perez-Steele Galleries. The card fronts display the Donruss logo and the year of issue. The card backs have black and blue ink on white stock and include the player's career highlights. The complete set price does not include the higher priced variations.

		MT	NR MT	EX
	Complete Set (660):	100.00	75.00	40.00
	Common Player:	.06	.05	.02
1	Pete Rose (DK)	2.00	1.50	.80
2	Gary Carter (DK)	.50	.40	.20
3	Steve Garvey (DK)	.50	.40	.20
4	Vida Blue (DK)	.12	.09	.05
5a	Alan Trammel (DK name incorrect)	1.50	1.25	.60
5b	Alan Trammell (DK COR)	.40	.30	.15
6	Len Barker (DK)	.08	.06	.03
7	Dwight Evans (DK)	.15	.11	.06
8	Rod Carew (DK)	.60	.45	.25
9	George Hendrick (DK)	.08	.06	.03
10	Phil Niekro (DK)	.30	.25	.12
11	Richie Zisk (DK)	.08	.06	.03
12	Dave Parker (DK)	.30	.25	.12
13	Nolan Ryan (DK)	4.00	3.00	1.50
14	Ivan DeJesus (DK)	.08	.06	.03
15	George Brett (DK)	1.50	1.25	.60
16	Tom Seaver (DK)	.80	.60	.30
17	Dave Kingman (DK)	.15	.11	.06
18	Dave Winfield (DK)	1.50	1.25	.60
19	Mike Norris (DK)	.08	.06	.03
20	Carlton Fisk (DK)	.80	.60	.30

		MT	NR MT	EX
21	Ozzie Smith (DK)	.20	.15	.08
22	Roy Smalley (DK)	.08	.06	.03
23	Buddy Bell (DK)	.12	.09	.05
24	Ken Singleton (DK)	.10	.08	.04
25	John Mayberry (DK)	.08	.06	.03
26	Gorman Thomas (DK)	.10	.08	.04
27	Earl Weaver	.10	.08	.04
28	Rollie Fingers	.80	.60	.30
29	Sparky Anderson	.10	.08	.04
30	Dennis Eckersley	1.25	.90	.50
31	Dave Winfield	2.50	2.00	1.00
32	Burt Hooton	.08	.06	.03
33	Rick Waits	.06	.05	.02
34	George Brett	3.00	2.25	1.25
35	Steve McCatty	.06	.05	.02
36	Steve Rogers	.08	.06	.03
37	Bill Stein	.06	.05	.02
38	Steve Renko	.06	.05	.02
39	Mike Squires	.06	.05	.02
40	George Hendrick	.08	.06	.03
41	Bob Knepper	.08	.06	.03
42	Steve Carlton	1.00	.70	.40
43	Larry Biittner	.06	.05	.02
44	Chris Welsh	.06	.05	.02
45	Steve Nicosia	.06	.05	.02
46	Jack Clark	.25	.20	.10
47	Chris Chambliss	.08	.06	.03
48	Ivan DeJesus	.06	.05	.02
49	Lee Mazzilli	.08	.06	.03
50	Julio Cruz	.06	.05	.02
51	Pete Redfern	.06	.05	.02
52	Dave Stieb	.12	.09	.05
53	Doug Corbett	.06	.05	.02
54	*George Bell*(FC)	4.00	3.00	1.50
55	Joe Simpson	.06	.05	.02
56	Rusty Staub	.10	.08	.04
57	Hector Cruz	.06	.05	.02
58	Claudell Washington(FC)	.10	.08	.04
59	Enrique Romo	.06	.05	.02
60	Gary Lavelle	.06	.05	.02
61	Tim Flannery	.06	.05	.02
62	Joe Nolan	.06	.05	.02
63	Larry Bowa	.15	.11	.06
64	Sixto Lezcano	.06	.05	.02
65	Joe Sambito	.06	.05	.02
66	Bruce Kison	.06	.05	.02
67	Wayne Nordhagen	.06	.05	.02
68	Woodie Fryman	.08	.06	.03
69	Billy Sample	.06	.05	.02
70	Amos Otis	.08	.06	.03
71	Matt Keough	.06	.05	.02
72	Toby Harrah	.08	.06	.03
73	*Dave Righetti*(FC)	.60	.45	.25
74	Carl Yastrzemski	1.00	.70	.40
75	Bob Welch	.12	.09	.05
76a	Alan Trammel (ERR)	2.00	1.50	.80
76b	Alan Trammell (COR)	.60	.45	.25
77	Rick Dempsey	.08	.06	.03
78	Paul Molitor	3.00	2.25	1.25
79	Dennis Martinez	.08	.06	.03
80	Jim Slaton	.06	.05	.02
81	Champ Summers	.06	.05	.02
82	Carney Lansford	.08	.06	.03
83	Barry Foote	.06	.05	.02
84	Steve Garvey	.50	.40	.20
85	Rick Manning	.06	.05	.02
86	John Wathan	.08	.06	.03
87	Brian Kingman	.06	.05	.02
88	Andre Dawson	1.25	.90	.50
89	Jim Kern	.06	.05	.02
90	Bobby Grich	.10	.08	.04
91	Bob Forsch	.08	.06	.03
92	Art Howe	.06	.05	.02
93	Marty Bystrom	.06	.05	.02
94	Ozzie Smith	2.00	1.50	.80
95	Dave Parker	.30	.25	.12
96	Doyle Alexander	.10	.08	.04
97	Al Hrabosky	.08	.06	.03
98	Frank Taveras	.06	.05	.02
99	Tim Blackwell	.06	.05	.02
100	Floyd Bannister	.10	.08	.04
101	Alfredo Griffin	.08	.06	.03
102	Dave Engle	.06	.05	.02
103	Mario Soto	.08	.06	.03
104	Ross Baumgarten	.06	.05	.02
105	Ken Singleton	.10	.08	.04
106	Ted Simmons	.12	.09	.05
107	Jack Morris	.50	.35	.20
108	Bob Watson	.08	.06	.03
109	Dwight Evans	.15	.11	.06
110	Tom Lasorda	.10	.08	.04

		MT	NR MT	EX
111	Bert Blyleven	.12	.09	.05
112	Dan Quisenberry	.15	.11	.06
113	Rickey Henderson	4.00	3.00	1.50
114	Gary Carter	.70	.50	.30
115	Brian Downing	.10	.08	.04
116	Al Oliver	.15	.11	.06
117	LaMarr Hoyt	.06	.05	.02
118	Cesar Cedeno	.12	.09	.05
119	Keith Moreland	.10	.08	.04
120	Bob Shirley	.06	.05	.02
121	Terry Kennedy	.08	.06	.03
122	Frank Pastore	.06	.05	.02
123	Gene Garber	.06	.05	.02
124	Tony Pena(FC)	.25	.20	.10
125	Allen Ripley	.06	.05	.02
126	Randy Martz	.06	.05	.02
127	Richie Zisk	.08	.06	.03
128	Mike Scott	.15	.11	.06
129	Lloyd Moseby(FC)	.20	.15	.08
130	Rob Wilfong	.06	.05	.02
131	Tim Stoddard	.06	.05	.02
132	Gorman Thomas	.10	.08	.04
133	Dan Petry	.08	.06	.03
134	Bob Stanley	.06	.05	.02
135	Lou Piniella	.12	.09	.05
136	Pedro Guerrero(FC)	.70	.50	.30
137	Len Barker	.08	.06	.03
138	Richard Gale	.06	.05	.02
139	Wayne Gross	.06	.05	.02
140	*Tim Wallach*(FC)	2.00	1.50	.80
141	Gene Mauch	.08	.06	.03
142	Doc Medich	.06	.05	.02
143	Tony Bernazard	.06	.05	.02
144	Bill Virdon	.06	.05	.02
145	John Littlefield	.06	.05	.02
146	Dave Bergman	.06	.05	.02
147	Dick Davis	.06	.05	.02
148	Tom Seaver	1.50	1.25	.60
149	Matt Sinatro	.06	.05	.02
150	Chuck Tanner	.06	.05	.02
151	Leon Durham	.08	.06	.03
152	Gene Tenace	.08	.06	.03
153	Al Bumbry	.08	.06	.03
154	Mark Brouhard	.06	.05	.02
155	Rick Peters	.06	.05	.02
156	Jerry Remy	.06	.05	.02
157	Rick Reuschel	.10	.08	.04
158	Steve Howe	.08	.06	.03
159	Alan Bannister	.06	.05	.02
160	U L Washington	.06	.05	.02
161	Rick Langford	.06	.05	.02
162	Bill Gullickson	.08	.06	.03
163	Mark Wagner	.06	.05	.02
164	Geoff Zahn	.06	.05	.02
165	Ron LeFlore	.08	.06	.03
166	Dane Iorg	.06	.05	.02
167	Joe Niekro	.12	.09	.05
168	Pete Rose	1.50	1.25	.60
169	Dave Collins	.08	.06	.03
170	Rick Wise	.08	.06	.03
171	Jim Bibby	.06	.05	.02
172	Larry Herndon	.08	.06	.03
173	Bob Horner	.12	.09	.05
174	Steve Dillard	.06	.05	.02
175	Mookie Wilson	.12	.09	.05
176	Dan Meyer	.06	.05	.02
177	Fernando Arroyo	.06	.05	.02
178	Jackson Todd	.06	.05	.02
179	Darrell Jackson	.06	.05	.02
180	Al Woods	.06	.05	.02
181	Jim Anderson	.06	.05	.02
182	Dave Kingman	.15	.11	.06
183	Steve Henderson	.06	.05	.02
184	Brian Asselstine	.06	.05	.02
185	Rod Scurry	.06	.05	.02
186	Fred Breining	.06	.05	.02
187	Danny Boone	.06	.05	.02
188	Junior Kennedy	.06	.05	.02
189	Sparky Lyle	.10	.08	.04
190	Whitey Herzog	.08	.06	.03
191	Dave Smith	.10	.08	.04
192	Ed Ott	.06	.05	.02
193	Greg Luzinski	.15	.11	.06
194	Bill Lee	.08	.06	.03
195	Don Zimmer	.06	.05	.02
196	Hal McRae	.12	.09	.05
197	Mike Norris	.06	.05	.02
198	Duane Kuiper	.06	.05	.02
199	Rick Cerone	.06	.05	.02
200	Jim Rice	.40	.30	.15
201	Steve Yeager	.06	.05	.02

		MT	NR MT	EX
202	Tom Brookens	.06	.05	.02
203	Jose Morales	.06	.05	.02
204	Roy Howell	.06	.05	.02
205	Tippy Martinez	.06	.05	.02
206	Moose Haas	.06	.05	.02
207	Al Cowens	.06	.05	.02
208	Dave Stapleton	.06	.05	.02
209	Bucky Dent	.10	.08	.04
210	Ron Cey	.12	.09	.05
211	Jorge Orta	.06	.05	.02
212	Jamie Quirk	.06	.05	.02
213	Jeff Jones	.06	.05	.02
214	Tim Raines	1.50	1.25	.60
215	Jon Matlack	.08	.06	.03
216	Rod Carew	1.00	.70	.40
217	Jim Kaat	.15	.11	.06
218	Joe Pittman	.06	.05	.02
219	Larry Christenson	.06	.05	.02
220	Juan Bonilla	.06	.05	.02
221	Mike Easler	.08	.06	.03
222	Vida Blue	.12	.09	.05
223	Rick Camp	.06	.05	.02
224	Mike Jorgensen	.06	.05	.02
225	*Jody Davis*(FC)	.30	.25	.12
226	Mike Parrott	.06	.05	.02
227	Jim Clancy	.08	.06	.03
228	Hosken Powell	.06	.05	.02
229	Tom Hume	.06	.05	.02
230	Britt Burns	.06	.05	.02
231	Jim Palmer	.70	.50	.30
232	Bob Rodgers	.08	.06	.03
233	Milt Wilcox	.06	.05	.02
234	Dave Revering	.06	.05	.02
235	Mike Torrez	.08	.06	.03
236	Robert Castillo	.06	.05	.02
237	*Von Hayes*(FC)	.40	.30	.15
238	Renie Martin	.06	.05	.02
239	Dwayne Murphy	.08	.06	.03
240	Rodney Scott	.06	.05	.02
241	Fred Patek	.06	.05	.02
242	Mickey Rivers	.08	.06	.03
243	Steve Trout	.06	.05	.02
244	Jose Cruz	.12	.09	.05
245	Manny Trillo	.08	.06	.03
246	Lary Sorensen	.06	.05	.02
247	Dave Edwards	.06	.05	.02
248	Dan Driessen	.08	.06	.03
249	Tommy Boggs	.06	.05	.02
250	Dale Berra	.06	.05	.02
251	Ed Whitson	.06	.05	.02
252	*Lee Smith*(FC)	12.00	9.00	4.75
253	Tom Paciorek	.06	.05	.02
254	Pat Zachry	.06	.05	.02
255	Luis Leal	.06	.05	.02
256	John Castino	.06	.05	.02
257	Rich Dauer	.06	.05	.02
258	Cecil Cooper	.15	.11	.06
259	Dave Rozema	.06	.05	.02
260	John Tudor	.15	.11	.06
261	Jerry Mumphrey	.06	.05	.02
262	Jay Johnstone	.08	.06	.03
263	Bo Diaz	.08	.06	.03
264	Dennis Leonard	.08	.06	.03
265	Jim Spencer	.06	.05	.02
266	John Milner	.06	.05	.02
267	Don Aase	.06	.05	.02
268	Jim Sundberg	.08	.06	.03
269	Lamar Johnson	.06	.05	.02
270	Frank LaCorte	.06	.05	.02
271	Barry Evans	.06	.05	.02
272	Enos Cabell	.06	.05	.02
273	Del Unser	.06	.05	.02
274	George Foster	.20	.15	.08
275	*Brett Butler*(FC)	2.50	2.00	1.00
276	Lee Lacy	.06	.05	.02
277	Ken Reitz	.06	.05	.02
278	Keith Hernandez	.40	.30	.15
279	Doug DeCinces	.10	.08	.04
280	Charlie Moore	.06	.05	.02
281	Lance Parrish	.35	.25	.14
282	Ralph Houk	.08	.06	.03
283	Rich Gossage	.20	.15	.08
284	Jerry Reuss	.10	.08	.04
285	Mike Stanton	.06	.05	.02
286	Frank White	.10	.08	.04
287	Bob Owchinko	.06	.05	.02
288	Scott Sanderson	.06	.05	.02
289	Bump Wills	.06	.05	.02
290	Dave Frost	.06	.05	.02
291	Chet Lemon	.08	.06	.03
292	Tito Landrum	.06	.05	.02

		MT	NR MT	EX
293	Vern Ruhle	.06	.05	.02
294	Mike Schmidt	2.50	2.00	1.00
295	Sam Mejias	.06	.05	.02
296	Gary Lucas	.06	.05	.02
297	John Candelaria	.10	.08	.04
298	Jerry Martin	.06	.05	.02
299	Dale Murphy	.90	.70	.35
300	Mike Lum	.06	.05	.02
301	Tom Hausman	.06	.05	.02
302	Glenn Abbott	.06	.05	.02
303	Roger Erickson	.06	.05	.02
304	Otto Velez	.06	.05	.02
305	Danny Goodwin	.06	.05	.02
306	John Mayberry	.08	.06	.03
307	Lenny Randle	.06	.05	.02
308	Bob Bailor	.06	.05	.02
309	Jerry Morales	.06	.05	.02
310	Rufino Linares	.06	.05	.02
311	Kent Tekulve	.08	.06	.03
312	Joe Morgan	.50	.40	.20
313	John Urrea	.06	.05	.02
314	Paul Householder	.06	.05	.02
315	Garry Maddox	.10	.08	.04
316	Mike Ramsey	.06	.05	.02
317	Alan Ashby	.06	.05	.02
318	Bob Clark	.06	.05	.02
319	Tony LaRussa	.08	.06	.03
320	Charlie Lea	.08	.06	.03
321	Danny Darwin	.06	.05	.02
322	Cesar Geronimo	.06	.05	.02
323	Tom Underwood	.06	.05	.02
324	Andre Thornton	.10	.08	.04
325	Rudy May	.06	.05	.02
326	Frank Tanana	.10	.08	.04
327	Davey Lopes	.10	.08	.04
328	Richie Hebner	.06	.05	.02
329	Mike Flanagan	.10	.08	.04
330	Mike Caldwell	.06	.05	.02
331	Scott McGregor	.08	.06	.03
332	Jerry Augustine	.06	.05	.02
333	Stan Papi	.06	.05	.02
334	Rick Miller	.06	.05	.02
335	Graig Nettles	.15	.11	.06
336	Dusty Baker	.10	.08	.04
337	Dave Garcia	.06	.05	.02
338	Larry Gura	.06	.05	.02
339	Cliff Johnson	.06	.05	.02
340	Warren Cromartie	.06	.05	.02
341	Steve Comer	.06	.05	.02
342	Rick Burleson	.08	.06	.03
343	John Martin	.06	.05	.02
344	Craig Reynolds	.06	.05	.02
345	Mike Proly	.06	.05	.02
346	Ruppert Jones	.06	.05	.02
347	Omar Moreno	.06	.05	.02
348	Greg Minton	.06	.05	.02
349	*Rick Mahler*(FC)	.25	.20	.10
350	Alex Trevino	.06	.05	.02
351	Mike Krukow	.08	.06	.03
352a	Shane Rawley (Jim Anderson photo — shaking hands)	1.25	.90	.50
352b	Shane Rawley (correct photo - kneeling)	.15	.11	.06
353	Garth Iorg	.06	.05	.02
354	Pete Mackanin	.06	.05	.02
355	Paul Moskau	.06	.05	.02
356	Richard Dotson	.10	.08	.04
357	Steve Stone	.08	.06	.03
358	Larry Hisle	.08	.06	.03
359	Aurelio Lopez	.06	.05	.02
360	Oscar Gamble	.08	.06	.03
361	Tom Burgmeier	.06	.05	.02
362	Terry Forster	.08	.06	.03
363	Joe Charboneau	.08	.06	.03
364	Ken Brett	.08	.06	.03
365	Tony Armas	.10	.08	.04
366	Chris Speier	.06	.05	.02
367	Fred Lynn	.20	.15	.08
368	Buddy Bell	.12	.09	.05
369	Jim Essian	.06	.05	.02
370	Terry Puhl	.06	.05	.02
371	Greg Gross	.06	.05	.02
372	Bruce Sutter	.15	.11	.06
373	Joe Lefebvre	.06	.05	.02
374	Ray Knight	.10	.08	.04
375	Bruce Benedict	.06	.05	.02
376	Tim Foli	.06	.05	.02
377	Al Holland	.06	.05	.02
378	Ken Kravec	.06	.05	.02
379	Jeff Burroughs	.08	.06	.03
380	Pete Falcone	.06	.05	.02

		MT	NR MT	EX
381	Ernie Whitt	.08	.06	.03
382	Brad Havens	.06	.05	.02
383	Terry Crowley	.06	.05	.02
384	Don Money	.06	.05	.02
385	Dan Schatzeder	.06	.05	.02
386	Gary Allenson	.06	.05	.02
387	Yogi Berra	.15	.11	.06
388	Ken Landreaux	.06	.05	.02
389	Mike Hargrove	.06	.05	.02
390	Darryl Motley	.06	.05	.02
391	Dave McKay	.06	.05	.02
392	Stan Bahnsen	.06	.05	.02
393	Ken Forsch	.06	.05	.02
394	Mario Mendoza	.06	.05	.02
395	Jim Morrison	.06	.05	.02
396	Mike Ivie	.06	.05	.02
397	Broderick Perkins	.06	.05	.02
398	Darrell Evans	.15	.11	.06
399	Ron Reed	.06	.05	.02
400	Johnny Bench	.60	.45	.25
401	*Steve Bedrosian*(FC)	.50	.40	.20
402	Bill Robinson	.06	.05	.02
403	Bill Buckner	.12	.09	.05
404	Ken Oberkfell	.06	.05	.02
405	*Cal Ripken, Jr.*(FC)	50.00	37.00	20.00
406	Jim Gantner	.08	.06	.03
407	Kirk Gibson(FC)	.90	.70	.35
408	Tony Perez	.20	.15	.08
409	Tommy John	.20	.15	.08
410	*Dave Stewart*(FC)	3.50	2.50	1.25
411	Dan Spillner	.06	.05	.02
412	Willie Aikens	.06	.05	.02
413	Mike Heath	.06	.05	.02
414	Ray Burris	.06	.05	.02
415	Leon Roberts	.06	.05	.02
416	*Mike Witt*(FC)	.35	.25	.14
417	Bobby Molinaro	.06	.05	.02
418	Steve Braun	.06	.05	.02
419	Nolan Ryan	9.00	6.75	3.50
420	Tug McGraw	.12	.09	.05
421	Dave Concepcion	.12	.09	.05
422a	Juan Eichelberger (Gary Lucas photo — white player)	1.25	.90	.50
422b	Juan Eichelberger (correct photo - black player)	.08	.06	.03
423	Rick Rhoden	.10	.08	.04
424	Frank Robinson	.12	.09	.05
425	Eddie Miller	.06	.05	.02
426	Bill Caudill	.06	.05	.02
427	Doug Flynn	.06	.05	.02
428	Larry Anderson (Andersen)	.06	.05	.02
429	Al Williams	.06	.05	.02
430	Jerry Garvin	.06	.05	.02
431	Glenn Adams	.06	.05	.02
432	Barry Bonnell	.06	.05	.02
433	Jerry Narron	.06	.05	.02
434	John Stearns	.06	.05	.02
435	Mike Tyson	.06	.05	.02
436	Glenn Hubbard	.08	.06	.03
437	Eddie Solomon	.06	.05	.02
438	Jeff Leonard	.10	.08	.04
439	Randy Bass	.06	.05	.02
440	Mike LaCoss	.06	.05	.02
441	Gary Matthews	.10	.08	.04
442	Mark Littell	.06	.05	.02
443	Don Sutton	.30	.25	.12
444	John Harris	.06	.05	.02
445	Vada Pinson	.08	.06	.03
446	Elias Sosa	.06	.05	.02
447	Charlie Hough	.10	.08	.04
448	Willie Wilson	.15	.11	.06
449	Fred Stanley	.06	.05	.02
450	Tom Veryzer	.06	.05	.02
451	Ron Davis	.06	.05	.02
452	Mark Clear	.06	.05	.02
453	Bill Russell	.08	.06	.03
454	Lou Whitaker	.40	.30	.15
455	Dan Graham	.06	.05	.02
456	Reggie Cleveland	.06	.05	.02
457	Sammy Stewart	.06	.05	.02
458	Pete Vuckovich	.08	.06	.03
459	John Wockenfuss	.06	.05	.02
460	Glenn Hoffman	.06	.05	.02
461	Willie Randolph	.10	.08	.04
462	Fernando Valenzuela(FC)	.80	.60	.30
463	Ron Hassey	.06	.05	.02
464	Paul Splittorff	.06	.05	.02
465	Rob Picciolo	.06	.05	.02
466	Larry Parrish	.10	.08	.04
467	Johnny Grubb	.06	.05	.02
468	Dan Ford	.06	.05	.02

		MT	NR MT	EX
469	Silvio Martinez	.06	.05	.02
470	Kiko Garcia	.06	.05	.02
471	Bob Boone	.10	.08	.04
472	Luis Salazar	.08	.06	.03
473	Randy Niemann	.06	.05	.02
474	Tom Griffin	.06	.05	.02
475	Phil Niekro	.30	.25	.12
476	Hubie Brooks(FC)	.25	.20	.10
477	Dick Tidrow	.06	.05	.02
478	Jim Beattie	.06	.05	.02
479	Damaso Garcia	.06	.05	.02
480	Mickey Hatcher	.08	.06	.03
481	Joe Price	.06	.05	.02
482	Ed Farmer	.06	.05	.02
483	Eddie Murray	2.00	1.50	.80
484	Ben Oglivie	.08	.06	.03
485	Kevin Saucier	.06	.05	.02
486	Bobby Murcer	.10	.08	.04
487	Bill Campbell	.06	.05	.02
488	Reggie Smith	.10	.08	.04
489	Wayne Garland	.06	.05	.02
490	Jim Wright	.06	.05	.02
491	Billy Martin	.12	.09	.05
492	Jim Fanning	.06	.05	.02
493	Don Baylor	.12	.09	.05
494	Rick Honeycutt	.06	.05	.02
495	Carlton Fisk	1.50	1.25	.60
496	Denny Walling	.06	.05	.02
497	Bake McBride	.06	.05	.02
498	Darrell Porter	.08	.06	.03
499	Gene Richards	.06	.05	.02
500	Ron Oester	.06	.05	.02
501	*Ken Dayley*(FC)	.20	.15	.08
502	Jason Thompson	.06	.05	.02
503	Milt May	.06	.05	.02
504	Doug Bird	.06	.05	.02
505	Bruce Bochte	.06	.05	.02
506	Neil Allen	.06	.05	.02
507	Joey McLaughlin	.06	.05	.02
508	Butch Wynegar	.06	.05	.02
509	Gary Roenicke	.06	.05	.02
510	Robin Yount	3.00	2.25	1.25
511	Dave Tobik	.06	.05	.02
512	*Rich Gedman*(FC)	.25	.20	.10
513	*Gene Nelson*(FC)	.06	.05	.02
514	Rick Monday	.10	.08	.04
515	Miguel Dilone	.06	.05	.02
516	Clint Hurdle	.06	.05	.02
517	Jeff Newman	.06	.05	.02
518	Grant Jackson	.06	.05	.02
519	Andy Hassler	.06	.05	.02
520	Pat Putnam	.06	.05	.02
521	Greg Pryor	.06	.05	.02
522	Tony Scott	.06	.05	.02
523	Steve Mura	.06	.05	.02
524	Johnnie LeMaster	.06	.05	.02
525	Dick Ruthven	.06	.05	.02
526	John McNamara	.06	.05	.02
527	Larry McWilliams	.06	.05	.02
528	*Johnny Ray*(FC)	.10	.08	.04
529	*Pat Tabler*(FC)	.10	.08	.04
530	Tom Herr	.10	.08	.04
531a	San Diego Chicken (w/trademark symbol)(FC)	1.25	.90	.50
531b	San Diego Chicken (no trademark symbol)(FC)	.80	.60	.30
532	Sal Butera	.06	.05	.02
533	Mike Griffin	.06	.05	.02
534	Kelvin Moore	.06	.05	.02
535	Reggie Jackson	2.00	1.50	.80
536	Ed Romero	.06	.05	.02
537	Derrel Thomas	.06	.05	.02
538	Mike O'Berry	.06	.05	.02
539	Jack O'Connor	.06	.05	.02
540	*Bob Ojeda*	.50	.40	.20
541	Roy Lee Jackson	.06	.05	.02
542	Lynn Jones	.06	.05	.02
543	Gaylord Perry	.40	.30	.15
544a	Phil Garner (photo reversed)	1.25	.90	.50
544b	Phil Garner (photo correct)	.10	.08	.04
545	Garry Templeton	.10	.08	.04
546	Rafael Ramirez(FC)	.10	.08	.04
547	Jeff Reardon	1.25	.90	.50
548	Ron Guidry	.25	.20	.10
549	*Tim Laudner*(FC)	.25	.20	.10
550	John Henry Johnson	.06	.05	.02
551	Chris Bando	.06	.05	.02
552	Bobby Brown	.06	.05	.02
553	Larry Bradford	.06	.05	.02
554	*Scott Fletcher*(FC)	.40	.30	.15
555	Jerry Royster	.06	.05	.02

		MT	NR MT	EX
556	Shooty Babbitt	.06	.05	.02
557	*Kent Hrbek*(FC)	2.50	2.00	1.00
558	Yankee Winners (Ron Guidry, Tommy John)	.15	.11	.06
559	Mark Bomback	.06	.05	.02
560	Julio Valdez	.06	.05	.02
561	Buck Martinez	.06	.05	.02
562	*Mike Marshall*(FC)	.25	.20	.10
563	Rennie Stennett	.06	.05	.02
564	Steve Crawford	.06	.05	.02
565	Bob Babcock	.06	.05	.02
566	Johnny Podres	.08	.06	.03
567	Paul Serna	.06	.05	.02
568	Harold Baines(FC)	1.25	.90	.50
569	Dave LaRoche	.06	.05	.02
570	Lee May	.08	.06	.03
571	Gary Ward(FC)	.10	.08	.04
572	John Denny	.06	.05	.02
573	Roy Smalley	.06	.05	.02
574	*Bob Brenly*(FC)	.20	.15	.08
575	Bronx Bombers (Reggie Jackson, Dave Winfield)	2.00	1.50	.80
576	Luis Pujols	.06	.05	.02
577	Butch Hobson	.06	.05	.02
578	Harvey Kuenn	.08	.06	.03
579	Cal Ripken, Sr.	.08	.06	.03
580	Juan Berenguer	.08	.06	.03
581	Benny Ayala	.06	.05	.02
582	Vance Law(FC)	.15	.11	.06
583	*Rick Leach*(FC)	.12	.09	.05
584	George Frazier	.06	.05	.02
585	Phillies Finest (Pete Rose, Mike Schmidt)	.70	.50	.30
586	Joe Rudi	.10	.08	.04
587	Juan Beniquez	.06	.05	.02
588	*Luis DeLeon*(FC)	.08	.06	.03
589	Craig Swan	.06	.05	.02
590	Dave Chalk	.06	.05	.02
591	Billy Gardner	.06	.05	.02
592	Sal Bando	.08	.06	.03
593	Bert Campaneris	.10	.08	.04
594	Steve Kemp	.08	.06	.03
595a	Randy Lerch (Braves)	1.25	.90	.50
595b	Randy Lerch (Brewers)	.08	.06	.03
596	Bryan Clark	.06	.05	.02
597	Dave Ford	.06	.05	.02
598	Mike Scioscia(FC)	.20	.15	.08
599	John Lowenstein	.06	.05	.02
600	Rene Lachmann (Lachemann)	.06	.05	.02
601	Mick Kelleher	.06	.05	.02
602	Ron Jackson	.06	.05	.02
603	Jerry Koosman	.10	.08	.04
604	Dave Goltz	.08	.06	.03
605	Ellis Valentine	.06	.05	.02
606	Lonnie Smith	.08	.06	.03
607	Joaquin Andujar	.08	.06	.03
608	Garry Hancock	.06	.05	.02
609	Jerry Turner	.06	.05	.02
610	Bob Bonner	.06	.05	.02
611	Jim Dwyer	.06	.05	.02
612	Terry Bulling	.06	.05	.02
613	Joel Youngblood	.06	.05	.02
614	Larry Milbourne	.06	.05	.02
615	Phil Roof (Gene)	.06	.05	.02
616	Keith Drumright	.06	.05	.02
617	Dave Rosello	.06	.05	.02
618	Rickey Keeton	.06	.05	.02
619	Dennis Lamp	.06	.05	.02
620	Sid Monge	.06	.05	.02
621	Jerry White	.06	.05	.02
622	*Luis Aguayo*(FC)	.10	.08	.04
623	Jamie Easterly	.06	.05	.02
624	*Steve Sax*(FC)	2.00	1.50	.80
625	Dave Roberts	.06	.05	.02
626	Rick Bosetti	.06	.05	.02
627	*Terry Francona*(FC)	.10	.08	.04
628	Pride of the Reds (Johnny Bench, Tom Seaver)	.80	.60	.30
629	Paul Mirabella	.06	.05	.02
630	Rance Mulliniks	.06	.05	.02
631	Kevin Hickey	.06	.05	.02
632	Reid Nichols	.06	.05	.02
633	Dave Geisel	.06	.05	.02
634	Ken Griffey	.12	.09	.05
635	Bob Lemon	.10	.08	.04
636	Orlando Sanchez	.06	.05	.02
637	Bill Almon	.06	.05	.02
638	Danny Ainge	1.25	.90	.50
639	Willie Stargell	.40	.30	.15
640	Bob Sykes	.06	.05	.02
641	Ed Lynch	.06	.05	.02
642	John Ellis	.06	.05	.02
643	Fergie Jenkins	.15	.11	.06
644	Lenn Sakata	.06	.05	.02
645	Julio Gonzales	.06	.05	.02
646	Jesse Orosco(FC)	.15	.11	.06
647	Jerry Dybzinski	.06	.05	.02
648	Tommy Davis	.08	.06	.03
649	Ron Gardenhire	.06	.05	.02
650	Felipe Alou	.08	.06	.03
651	Harvey Haddix	.08	.06	.03
652	Willie Upshaw(FC)	.15	.11	.06
653	Bill Madlock	.12	.09	.05
---a	Checklist 1-26 DK (5 Trammel)	.70	.50	.30
---b	Checklist 1-26 DK (5 Trammell)	.08	.06	.03
---	Checklist 27-130	.06	.05	.02
---	Checklist 131-234	.06	.05	.02
---	Checklist 235-338	.06	.05	.02
---	Checklist 339-442	.06	.05	.02
---	Checklist 443-544	.06	.05	.02
---	Checklist 545-653	.06	.05	.02

1983 Donruss

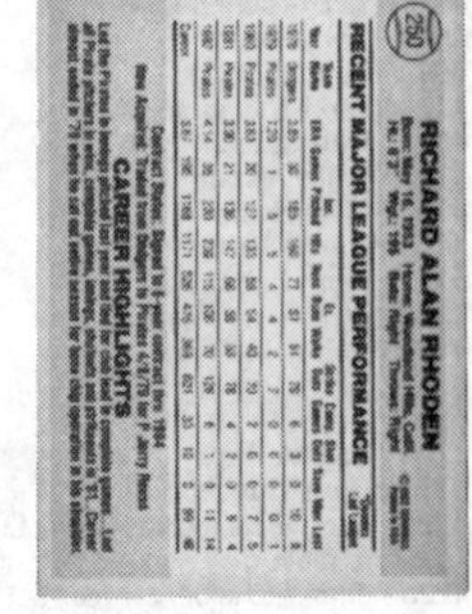

The 1983 Donruss set consists of 653 numbered cards plus seven unnumbered checklists. The cards, which measure 2-1/2" by 3-1/2", were issued with puzzle pieces (three pieces on one card per pack) that feature Ty Cobb. The first 26 cards in the set were once again the Diamond Kings series. The card fronts display the Donruss logo and the year of issue. The card backs have black print on yellow and white and include statistics, career highlights, and the player's contract status. (DK) in the checklist that follows indicates cards which belong to the Diamond Kings series.

		MT	NR MT	EX
Complete Set (660):		125.00	94.00	50.00
Common Player:		.06	.05	.02
1	Fernando Valenzuela (DK)	.40	.30	.15
2	Rollie Fingers (DK)	.20	.15	.08
3	Reggie Jackson (DK)	.60	.45	.25
4	Jim Palmer (DK)	.40	.30	.15
5	Jack Morris (DK)	.30	.25	.12
6	George Foster (DK)	.20	.15	.08
7	Jim Sundberg (DK)	.08	.06	.03
8	Willie Stargell (DK)	.40	.30	.15
9	Dave Stieb (DK)	.12	.09	.05
10	Joe Niekro (DK)	.12	.09	.05
11	Rickey Henderson (DK)	2.00	1.50	.80
12	Dale Murphy (DK)	.50	.40	.20
13	Toby Harrah (DK)	.08	.06	.03
14	Bill Buckner (DK)	.12	.09	.05
15	Willie Wilson (DK)	.15	.11	.06
16	Steve Carlton (DK)	.40	.30	.15
17	Ron Guidry (DK)	.25	.20	.10
18	Steve Rogers (DK)	.08	.06	.03
19	Kent Hrbek (DK)	.40	.30	.15
20	Keith Hernandez (DK)	.40	.30	.15
21	Floyd Bannister (DK)	.10	.08	.04
22	Johnny Bench (DK)	.40	.30	.15
23	Britt Burns (DK)	.08	.06	.03
24	Joe Morgan (DK)	.30	.25	.12
25	Carl Yastrzemski (DK)	.80	.60	.30
26	Terry Kennedy (DK)	.08	.06	.03
27	Gary Roenicke	.06	.05	.02

		MT	NR MT	EX
28	Dwight Bernard	.06	.05	.02
29	Pat Underwood	.06	.05	.02
30	Gary Allenson	.06	.05	.02
31	Ron Guidry	.25	.20	.10
32	Burt Hooton	.08	.06	.03
33	Chris Bando	.06	.05	.02
34	Vida Blue	.12	.09	.05
35	Rickey Henderson	3.00	2.25	1.25
36	Ray Burris	.06	.05	.02
37	John Butcher	.06	.05	.02
38	Don Aase	.06	.05	.02
39	Jerry Koosman	.10	.08	.04
40	Bruce Sutter	.15	.11	.06
41	Jose Cruz	.12	.09	.05
42	Pete Rose	1.50	1.25	.60
43	Cesar Cedeno	.12	.09	.05
44	Floyd Chiffer	.06	.05	.02
45	Larry McWilliams	.06	.05	.02
46	Alan Fowlkes	.06	.05	.02
47	Dale Murphy	.70	.50	.30
48	Doug Bird	.06	.05	.02
49	Hubie Brooks	.12	.09	.05
50	Floyd Bannister	.10	.08	.04
51	Jack O'Connor	.06	.05	.02
52	Steve Senteney	.06	.05	.02
53	*Gary Gaetti*(FC)	.80	.60	.30
54	Damaso Garcia	.06	.05	.02
55	Gene Nelson	.06	.05	.02
56	Mookie Wilson	.10	.08	.04
57	Allen Ripley	.06	.05	.02
58	Bob Horner	.12	.09	.05
59	Tony Pena	.10	.08	.04
60	Gary Lavelle	.06	.05	.02
61	Tim Lollar	.06	.05	.02
62	Frank Pastore	.06	.05	.02
63	Garry Maddox	.10	.08	.04
64	Bob Forsch	.08	.06	.03
65	Harry Spilman	.06	.05	.02
66	Geoff Zahn	.06	.05	.02
67	Salome Barojas	.06	.05	.02
68	David Palmer	.06	.05	.02
69	Charlie Hough	.10	.08	.04
70	Dan Quisenberry	.15	.11	.06
71	Tony Armas	.10	.08	.04
72	Rick Sutcliffe	.12	.09	.05
73	Steve Balboni(FC)	.15	.11	.06
74	Jerry Remy	.06	.05	.02
75	Mike Scioscia	.08	.06	.03
76	John Wockenfuss	.06	.05	.02
77	Jim Palmer	.80	.60	.30
78	Rollie Fingers	.60	.45	.25
79	Joe Nolan	.06	.05	.02
80	Pete Vuckovich	.08	.06	.03
81	Rick Leach	.06	.05	.02
82	Rick Miller	.06	.05	.02
83	Graig Nettles	.15	.11	.06
84	Ron Cey	.12	.09	.05
85	Miguel Dilone	.06	.05	.02
86	John Wathan	.08	.06	.03
87	Kelvin Moore	.06	.05	.02
88a	Byrn Smith (first name incorrect)	.70	.50	.30
88b	Bryn Smith (first name correct)	.08	.06	.03
89	Dave Hostetler	.06	.05	.02
90	Rod Carew	1.00	.70	.40
91	Lonnie Smith	.08	.06	.03
92	Bob Knepper	.08	.06	.03
93	Marty Bystrom	.06	.05	.02
94	Chris Welsh	.06	.05	.02
95	Jason Thompson	.06	.05	.02
96	Tom O'Malley	.06	.05	.02
97	Phil Niekro	.30	.25	.12
98	Neil Allen	.06	.05	.02
99	Bill Buckner	.12	.09	.05
100	*Ed Vande Berg*(FC)	.10	.08	.04
101	Jim Clancy	.08	.06	.03
102	Robert Castillo	.06	.05	.02
103	Bruce Berenyi	.06	.05	.02
104	Carlton Fisk	1.25	.90	.50
105	Mike Flanagan	.10	.08	.04
106	Cecil Cooper	.15	.11	.06
107	Jack Morris	.80	.60	.30
108	Mike Morgan(FC)	.12	.09	.05
109	Luis Aponte	.06	.05	.02
110	Pedro Guerrero	.25	.20	.10
111	Len Barker	.08	.06	.03
112	Willie Wilson	.15	.11	.06
113	Dave Beard	.06	.05	.02
114	Mike Gates	.06	.05	.02
115	Reggie Jackson	1.50	1.25	.60
116	George Wright	.06	.05	.02
117	Vance Law	.08	.06	.03
118	Nolan Ryan	8.50	6.50	3.50
119	Mike Krukow	.08	.06	.03
120	Ozzie Smith	1.50	1.25	.60
121	Broderick Perkins	.06	.05	.02
122	Tom Seaver	1.50	1.25	.60
123	Chris Chambliss	.08	.06	.03
124	Chuck Tanner	.06	.05	.02
125	Johnnie LeMaster	.06	.05	.02
126	*Mel Hall*(FC)	1.00	.70	.40
127	Bruce Bochte	.06	.05	.02
128	*Charlie Puleo*(FC)	.12	.09	.05
129	Luis Leal	.06	.05	.02
130	John Pacella	.06	.05	.02
131	Glenn Gulliver	.06	.05	.02
132	Don Money	.06	.05	.02
133	Dave Rozema	.06	.05	.02
134	Bruce Hurst(FC)	.25	.20	.10
135	Rudy May	.06	.05	.02
136	Tom LaSorda (Lasorda)	.10	.08	.04
137	Dan Spillner (photo actually Ed Whitson)	.06	.05	.02
138	Jerry Martin	.06	.05	.02
139	Mike Norris	.06	.05	.02
140	Al Oliver	.15	.11	.06
141	Daryl Sconiers	.06	.05	.02
142	Lamar Johnson	.06	.05	.02
143	Harold Baines	.15	.11	.06
144	Alan Ashby	.06	.05	.02
145	Garry Templeton	.10	.08	.04
146	Al Holland	.06	.05	.02
147	Bo Diaz	.08	.06	.03
148	Dave Concepcion	.12	.09	.05
149	Rick Camp	.06	.05	.02
150	Jim Morrison	.06	.05	.02
151	Randy Martz	.06	.05	.02
152	Keith Hernandez	.40	.30	.15
153	John Lowenstein	.06	.05	.02
154	Mike Caldwell	.06	.05	.02
155	Milt Wilcox	.06	.05	.02
156	Rich Gedman	.08	.06	.03
157	Rich Gossage	.20	.15	.08
158	Jerry Reuss	.10	.08	.04
159	Ron Hassey	.06	.05	.02
160	Larry Gura	.06	.05	.02
161	Dwayne Murphy	.08	.06	.03
162	Woodie Fryman	.08	.06	.03
163	Steve Comer	.06	.05	.02
164	Ken Forsch	.06	.05	.02
165	Dennis Lamp	.06	.05	.02
166	David Green	.06	.05	.02
167	Terry Puhl	.06	.05	.02
168	Mike Schmidt	2.00	1.50	.80
169	*Eddie Milner*(FC)	.10	.08	.04
170	John Curtis	.06	.05	.02
171	Don Robinson	.08	.06	.03
172	Richard Gale	.06	.05	.02
173	Steve Bedrosian	.12	.09	.05
174	Willie Hernandez	.08	.06	.03
175	Ron Gardenhire	.06	.05	.02
176	Jim Beattie	.06	.05	.02
177	Tim Laudner	.08	.06	.03
178	Buck Martinez	.06	.05	.02
179	Kent Hrbek	.80	.60	.30
180	Alfredo Griffin	.08	.06	.03
181	Larry Andersen	.06	.05	.02
182	Pete Falcone	.06	.05	.02
183	Jody Davis	.10	.08	.04
184	Glenn Hubbard	.08	.06	.03
185	Dale Berra	.06	.05	.02
186	Greg Minton	.06	.05	.02
187	Gary Lucas	.06	.05	.02
188	Dave Van Gorder	.06	.05	.02
189	Bob Dernier(FC)	.10	.08	.04
190	*Willie McGee*(FC)	3.00	2.25	1.25
191	Dickie Thon	.08	.06	.03
192	Bob Boone	.10	.08	.04
193	Britt Burns	.06	.05	.02
194	Jeff Reardon	.80	.60	.30
195	Jon Matlack	.08	.06	.03
196	*Don Slaught*(FC)	.20	.15	.08
197	Fred Stanley	.06	.05	.02
198	Rick Manning	.06	.05	.02
199	Dave Righetti	.25	.20	.10
200	Dave Stapleton	.06	.05	.02
201	Steve Yeager	.06	.05	.02
202	Enos Cabell	.06	.05	.02
203	Sammy Stewart	.06	.05	.02
204	Moose Haas	.06	.05	.02
205	Lenn Sakata	.06	.05	.02
206	Charlie Moore	.06	.05	.02
207	Alan Trammell	.40	.30	.15

		MT	NR MT	EX
208	Jim Rice	.40	.30	.15
209	Roy Smalley	.06	.05	.02
210	Bill Russell	.08	.06	.03
211	Andre Thornton	.10	.08	.04
212	Willie Aikens	.06	.05	.02
213	Dave McKay	.06	.05	.02
214	Tim Blackwell	.06	.05	.02
215	Buddy Bell	.12	.09	.05
216	Doug DeCinces	.10	.08	.04
217	Tom Herr	.10	.08	.04
218	Frank LaCorte	.06	.05	.02
219	Steve Carlton	1.00	.70	.40
220	Terry Kennedy	.08	.06	.03
221	Mike Easler	.08	.06	.03
222	Jack Clark	.25	.20	.10
223	Gene Garber	.06	.05	.02
224	Scott Holman	.06	.05	.02
225	Mike Proly	.06	.05	.02
226	Terry Bulling	.06	.05	.02
227	Jerry Garvin	.06	.05	.02
228	Ron Davis	.06	.05	.02
229	Tom Hume	.06	.05	.02
230	Marc Hill	.06	.05	.02
231	Dennis Martinez	.08	.06	.03
232	Jim Gantner	.08	.06	.03
233	Larry Pashnick	.06	.05	.02
234	Dave Collins	.08	.06	.03
235	Tom Burgmeier	.06	.05	.02
236	Ken Landreaux	.06	.05	.02
237	John Denny	.06	.05	.02
238	Hal McRae	.12	.09	.05
239	Matt Keough	.06	.05	.02
240	Doug Flynn	.06	.05	.02
241	Fred Lynn	.20	.15	.08
242	Billy Sample	.06	.05	.02
243	Tom Paciorek	.06	.05	.02
244	Joe Sambito	.06	.05	.02
245	Sid Monge	.06	.05	.02
246	Ken Oberkfell	.06	.05	.02
247	Joe Pittman (photo actually Juan Eichelberger)	.06	.05	.02
248	Mario Soto	.08	.06	.03
249	Claudell Washington	.08	.06	.03
250	Rick Rhoden	.10	.08	.04
251	Darrell Evans	.15	.11	.06
252	Steve Henderson	.06	.05	.02
253	Manny Castillo	.06	.05	.02
254	Craig Swan	.06	.05	.02
255	Joey McLaughlin	.06	.05	.02
256	Pete Redfern	.06	.05	.02
257	Ken Singleton	.10	.08	.04
258	Robin Yount	3.00	2.25	1.25
259	Elias Sosa	.06	.05	.02
260	Bob Ojeda	.12	.09	.05
261	Bobby Murcer	.10	.08	.04
262	*Candy Maldonado*(FC)	.80	.60	.30
263	Rick Waits	.06	.05	.02
264	Greg Pryor	.06	.05	.02
265	Bob Owchinko	.06	.05	.02
266	Chris Speier	.06	.05	.02
267	Bruce Kison	.06	.05	.02
268	Mark Wagner	.06	.05	.02
269	Steve Kemp	.10	.08	.04
270	Phil Garner	.08	.06	.03
271	Gene Richards	.06	.05	.02
272	Renie Martin	.06	.05	.02
273	Dave Roberts	.06	.05	.02
274	Dan Driessen	.08	.06	.03
275	Rufino Linares	.06	.05	.02
276	Lee Lacy	.06	.05	.02
277	*Ryne Sandberg*(FC)	40.00	30.00	16.00
278	Darrell Porter	.08	.06	.03
279	Cal Ripken, Jr.	15.00	11.00	6.00
280	Jamie Easterly	.06	.05	.02
281	Bill Fahey	.06	.05	.02
282	Glenn Hoffman	.06	.05	.02
283	Willie Randolph	.10	.08	.04
284	Fernando Valenzuela	.30	.25	.12
285	Alan Bannister	.06	.05	.02
286	Paul Splittorff	.06	.05	.02
287	Joe Rudi	.10	.08	.04
288	Bill Gullickson	.06	.05	.02
289	Danny Darwin	.06	.05	.02
290	Andy Hassler	.06	.05	.02
291	Ernesto Escarrega	.06	.05	.02
292	Steve Mura	.06	.05	.02
293	Tony Scott	.06	.05	.02
294	Manny Trillo	.08	.06	.03
295	Greg Harris(FC)	.08	.06	.03
296	Luis DeLeon	.06	.05	.02
297	Kent Tekulve	.08	.06	.03

		MT	NR MT	EX
298	Atlee Hammaker(FC)	.12	.09	.05
299	Bruce Benedict	.06	.05	.02
300	Fergie Jenkins	.15	.11	.06
301	Dave Kingman	.15	.11	.06
302	Bill Caudill	.06	.05	.02
303	John Castino	.06	.05	.02
304	Ernie Whitt	.08	.06	.03
305	Randy S. Johnson	.06	.05	.02
306	Garth Iorg	.06	.05	.02
307	Gaylord Perry	.40	.30	.15
308	Ed Lynch	.06	.05	.02
309	Keith Moreland	.08	.06	.03
310	Rafael Ramirez	.06	.05	.02
311	Bill Madlock	.12	.09	.05
312	Milt May	.06	.05	.02
313	John Montefusco	.06	.05	.02
314	Wayne Krenchicki	.06	.05	.02
315	George Vukovich	.06	.05	.02
316	Joaquin Andujar	.08	.06	.03
317	Craig Reynolds	.06	.05	.02
318	Rick Burleson	.08	.06	.03
319	Richard Dotson	.10	.08	.04
320	Steve Rogers	.08	.06	.03
321	Dave Schmidt(FC)	.10	.08	.04
322	*Bud Black*(FC)	.20	.15	.08
323	Jeff Burroughs	.08	.06	.03
324	Von Hayes	.15	.11	.06
325	Butch Wynegar	.06	.05	.02
326	Carl Yastrzemski	.80	.60	.30
327	Ron Roenicke	.06	.05	.02
328	*Howard Johnson*(FC)	2.50	2.00	1.00
329	Rick Dempsey	.08	.06	.03
330a	Jim Slaton (one yellow box on back)	.70	.50	.30
330b	Jim Slaton (two yellow boxes on back)	.08	.06	.03
331	Benny Ayala	.06	.05	.02
332	Ted Simmons	.12	.09	.05
333	Lou Whitaker	.40	.30	.15
334	Chuck Rainey	.06	.05	.02
335	Lou Piniella	.12	.09	.05
336	Steve Sax	.30	.25	.12
337	Toby Harrah	.08	.06	.03
338	George Brett	3.00	2.25	1.25
339	Davey Lopes	.10	.08	.04
340	Gary Carter	.40	.30	.15
341	John Grubb	.06	.05	.02
342	Tim Foli	.06	.05	.02
343	Jim Kaat	.15	.11	.06
344	Mike LaCoss	.06	.05	.02
345	Larry Christenson	.06	.05	.02
346	Juan Bonilla	.06	.05	.02
347	Omar Moreno	.06	.05	.02
348	Charles Davis(FC)	.20	.15	.08
349	Tommy Boggs	.06	.05	.02
350	Rusty Staub	.10	.08	.04
351	Bump Wills	.06	.05	.02
352	Rick Sweet	.06	.05	.02
353	*Jim Gott*(FC)	.20	.15	.08
354	Terry Felton	.06	.05	.02
355	Jim Kern	.06	.05	.02
356	Bill Almon	.06	.05	.02
357	Tippy Martinez	.06	.05	.02
358	Roy Howell	.06	.05	.02
359	Dan Petry	.08	.06	.03
360	Jerry Mumphrey	.06	.05	.02
361	Mark Clear	.06	.05	.02
362	Mike Marshall	.20	.15	.08
363	Lary Sorensen	.06	.05	.02
364	Amos Otis	.08	.06	.03
365	Rick Langford	.06	.05	.02
366	Brad Mills	.06	.05	.02
367	Brian Downing	.10	.08	.04
368	Mike Richardt	.06	.05	.02
369	Aurelio Rodriguez	.08	.06	.03
370	Dave Smith	.08	.06	.03
371	Tug McGraw	.12	.09	.05
372	Doug Bair	.06	.05	.02
373	Ruppert Jones	.06	.05	.02
374	Alex Trevino	.06	.05	.02
375	Ken Dayley	.06	.05	.02
376	Rod Scurry	.06	.05	.02
377	Bob Brenly(FC)	.08	.06	.03
378	Scot Thompson	.06	.05	.02
379	Julio Cruz	.06	.05	.02
380	John Stearns	.06	.05	.02
381	Dale Murray	.06	.05	.02
382	*Frank Viola*(FC)	2.25	1.75	.90
383	Al Bumbry	.08	.06	.03
384	Ben Oglivie	.08	.06	.03
385	Dave Tobik	.06	.05	.02

		MT	NR MT	EX
386	Bob Stanley	.06	.05	.02
387	Andre Robertson	.06	.05	.02
388	Jorge Orta	.06	.05	.02
389	Ed Whitson	.06	.05	.02
390	Don Hood	.06	.05	.02
391	Tom Underwood	.06	.05	.02
392	Tim Wallach	.20	.15	.08
393	Steve Renko	.06	.05	.02
394	Mickey Rivers	.08	.06	.03
395	Greg Luzinski	.12	.09	.05
396	Art Howe	.06	.05	.02
397	Alan Wiggins	.06	.05	.02
398	Jim Barr	.06	.05	.02
399	Ivan DeJesus	.06	.05	.02
400	*Tom Lawless*(FC)	.08	.06	.03
401	Bob Walk	.08	.06	.03
402	Jimmy Smith	.06	.05	.02
403	Lee Smith	2.00	1.50	.80
404	George Hendrick	.08	.06	.03
405	Eddie Murray	.80	.60	.30
406	Marshall Edwards	.06	.05	.02
407	Lance Parrish	.35	.25	.14
408	Carney Lansford	.08	.06	.03
409	Dave Winfield	3.00	2.25	1.25
410	Bob Welch	.12	.09	.05
411	Larry Milbourne	.06	.05	.02
412	Dennis Leonard	.08	.06	.03
413	Dan Meyer	.06	.05	.02
414	Charlie Lea	.06	.05	.02
415	Rick Honeycutt	.06	.05	.02
416	Mike Witt	.15	.11	.06
417	Steve Trout	.06	.05	.02
418	Glenn Brummer	.06	.05	.02
419	Denny Walling	.06	.05	.02
420	Gary Matthews	.10	.08	.04
421	Charlie Liebrandt (Leibrandt)	.08	.06	.03
422	Juan Eichelberger	.06	.05	.02
423	*Matt Guante (Cecilio)*(FC)	.15	.11	.06
424	Bill Laskey	.06	.05	.02
425	Jerry Royster	.06	.05	.02
426	Dickie Noles	.06	.05	.02
427	George Foster	.15	.11	.06
428	*Mike Moore*(FC)	1.00	.70	.40
429	Gary Ward	.08	.06	.03
430	Barry Bonnell	.06	.05	.02
431	Ron Washington	.06	.05	.02
432	Rance Mulliniks	.06	.05	.02
433	Mike Stanton	.06	.05	.02
434	Jesse Orosco	.10	.08	.04
435	Larry Bowa	.12	.09	.05
436	Biff Pocoroba	.06	.05	.02
437	Johnny Ray	.12	.09	.05
438	Joe Morgan	.40	.30	.15
439	*Eric Show*(FC)	.30	.25	.12
440	Larry Biittner	.06	.05	.02
441	Greg Gross	.06	.05	.02
442	Gene Tenace	.08	.06	.03
443	Danny Heep	.06	.05	.02
444	Bobby Clark	.06	.05	.02
445	Kevin Hickey	.06	.05	.02
446	Scott Sanderson	.06	.05	.02
447	Frank Tanana	.10	.08	.04
448	Cesar Geronimo	.06	.05	.02
449	Jimmy Sexton	.06	.05	.02
450	Mike Hargrove	.06	.05	.02
451	Doyle Alexander	.10	.08	.04
452	Dwight Evans	.15	.11	.06
453	Terry Forster	.08	.06	.03
454	Tom Brookens	.06	.05	.02
455	Rich Dauer	.06	.05	.02
456	Rob Picciolo	.06	.05	.02
457	Terry Crowley	.06	.05	.02
458	Ned Yost	.06	.05	.02
459	Kirk Gibson	.40	.30	.15
460	Reid Nichols	.06	.05	.02
461	Oscar Gamble	.08	.06	.03
462	Dusty Baker	.10	.08	.04
463	Jack Perconte	.06	.05	.02
464	Frank White	.10	.08	.04
465	Mickey Klutts	.06	.05	.02
466	Warren Cromartie	.06	.05	.02
467	Larry Parrish	.10	.08	.04
468	Bobby Grich	.10	.08	.04
469	Dane Iorg	.06	.05	.02
470	Joe Niekro	.12	.09	.05
471	Ed Farmer	.06	.05	.02
472	Tim Flannery	.06	.05	.02
473	Dave Parker	.30	.25	.12
474	Jeff Leonard	.10	.08	.04
475	Al Hrabosky	.08	.06	.03
476	Ron Hodges	.06	.05	.02
477	Leon Durham	.08	.06	.03
478	Jim Essian	.06	.05	.02
479	Roy Lee Jackson	.06	.05	.02
480	Brad Havens	.06	.05	.02
481	Joe Price	.06	.05	.02
482	Tony Bernazard	.06	.05	.02
483	Scott McGregor	.08	.06	.03
484	Paul Molitor	1.50	1.25	.60
485	Mike Ivie	.06	.05	.02
486	Ken Griffey	.12	.09	.05
487	Dennis Eckersley	1.00	.70	.40
488	Steve Garvey	.40	.30	.15
489	Mike Fischlin	.06	.05	.02
490	U.L. Washington	.06	.05	.02
491	Steve McCatty	.06	.05	.02
492	Roy Johnson	.06	.05	.02
493	Don Baylor	.12	.09	.05
494	Bobby Johnson	.06	.05	.02
495	Mike Squires	.06	.05	.02
496	Bert Roberge	.06	.05	.02
497	Dick Ruthven	.06	.05	.02
498	Tito Landrum	.06	.05	.02
499	Sixto Lezcano	.06	.05	.02
500	Johnny Bench	1.00	.70	.40
501	Larry Whisenton	.06	.05	.02
502	Manny Sarmiento	.06	.05	.02
503	Fred Breining	.06	.05	.02
504	Bill Campbell	.06	.05	.02
505	Todd Cruz	.06	.05	.02
506	Bob Bailor	.06	.05	.02
507	Dave Stieb	.12	.09	.05
508	Al Williams	.06	.05	.02
509	Dan Ford	.06	.05	.02
510	Gorman Thomas	.10	.08	.04
511	Chet Lemon	.08	.06	.03
512	Mike Torrez	.08	.06	.03
513	Shane Rawley	.10	.08	.04
514	Mark Belanger	.08	.06	.03
515	Rodney Craig	.06	.05	.02
516	Onix Concepcion	.06	.05	.02
517	Mike Heath	.06	.05	.02
518	Andre Dawson	1.25	.90	.50
519	Luis Sanchez	.06	.05	.02
520	Terry Bogener	.06	.05	.02
521	Rudy Law	.06	.05	.02
522	Ray Knight	.10	.08	.04
523	Joe Lefebvre	.06	.05	.02
524	Jim Wohlford	.06	.05	.02
525	*Julio Franco*(FC)	5.00	3.75	2.00
526	Ron Oester	.06	.05	.02
527	Rick Mahler	.08	.06	.03
528	Steve Nicosia	.06	.05	.02
529	Junior Kennedy	.06	.05	.02
530a	Whitey Herzog (one yellow box on back)	.70	.50	.30
530b	Whitey Herzog (two yellow boxes on back)	.10	.08	.04
531a	Don Sutton (blue frame)	1.00	.70	.40
531b	Don Sutton (green frame)	.30	.25	.12
532	Mark Brouhard	.06	.05	.02
533a	Sparky Anderson (one yellow box on back)	.70	.50	.30
533b	Sparky Anderson (two yellow boxes on back)	.10	.08	.04
534	Roger LaFrancois	.06	.05	.02
535	George Frazier	.06	.05	.02
536	Tom Niedenfuer	.08	.06	.03
537	Ed Glynn	.06	.05	.02
538	Lee May	.08	.06	.03
539	Bob Kearney	.06	.05	.02
540	Tim Raines	.35	.25	.14
541	Paul Mirabella	.06	.05	.02
542	Luis Tiant	.12	.09	.05
543	Ron LeFlore	.08	.06	.03
544	*Dave LaPoint*(FC)	.30	.25	.12
545	Randy Moffitt	.06	.05	.02
546	Luis Aguayo	.06	.05	.02
547	Brad Lesley	.06	.05	.02
548	Luis Salazar	.06	.05	.02
549	John Candelaria	.10	.08	.04
550	Dave Bergman	.06	.05	.02
551	Bob Watson	.08	.06	.03
552	Pat Tabler	.06	.05	.02
553	Brent Gaff	.06	.05	.02
554	Al Cowens	.06	.05	.02
555	Tom Brunansky(FC)	.10	.08	.04
556	Lloyd Moseby	.06	.05	.02
557a	Pascual Perez (Twins)	.90	.70	.35
557b	Pascual Perez (Braves)	.15	.11	.06
558	Willie Upshaw	.08	.06	.03
559	Richie Zisk	.08	.06	.03

		MT	NR MT	EX
560	Pat Zachry	.06	.05	.02
561	Jay Johnstone	.08	.06	.03
562	Carlos Diaz	.06	.05	.02
563	John Tudor	.10	.08	.04
564	Frank Robinson	.12	.09	.05
565	Dave Edwards	.06	.05	.02
566	Paul Householder	.06	.05	.02
567	Ron Reed	.06	.05	.02
568	Mike Ramsey	.06	.05	.02
569	Kiko Garcia	.06	.05	.02
570	Tommy John	.20	.15	.08
571	Tony LaRussa	.08	.06	.03
572	Joel Youngblood	.06	.05	.02
573	*Wayne Tolleson*(FC)	.12	.09	.05
574	Keith Creel	.06	.05	.02
575	Billy Martin	.12	.09	.05
576	Jerry Dybzinski	.06	.05	.02
577	Rick Cerone	.06	.05	.02
578	Tony Perez	.20	.15	.08
579	*Greg Brock*(FC)	.35	.25	.14
580	*Glen Wilson* (Glenn)	.35	.25	.14
581	Tim Stoddard	.06	.05	.02
582	Bob McClure	.06	.05	.02
583	Jim Dwyer	.06	.05	.02
584	Ed Romero	.06	.05	.02
585	Larry Herndon	.08	.06	.03
586	*Wade Boggs*(FC)	25.00	18.50	10.00
587	Jay Howell(FC)	.15	.11	.06
588	Dave Stewart	.80	.60	.30
589	Bert Blyleven	.12	.09	.05
590	Dick Howser	.06	.05	.02
591	Wayne Gross	.06	.05	.02
592	Terry Francona	.06	.05	.02
593	Don Werner	.06	.05	.02
594	Bill Stein	.06	.05	.02
595	Jesse Barfield(FC)	.70	.50	.30
596	Bobby Molinaro	.06	.05	.02
597	Mike Vail	.06	.05	.02
598	*Tony Gwynn*(FC)	25.00	18.50	10.00
599	Gary Rajsich	.06	.05	.02
600	Jerry Ujdur	.06	.05	.02
601	Cliff Johnson	.06	.05	.02
602	Jerry White	.06	.05	.02
603	Bryan Clark	.06	.05	.02
604	Joe Ferguson	.06	.05	.02
605	Guy Sularz	.06	.05	.02
606a	Ozzie Virgil (green frame around photo)(FC)	.90	.70	.35
606b	Ozzie Virgil (orange frame around photo)(FC)	.08	.06	.03
607	Terry Harper(FC)	.06	.05	.02
608	Harvey Kuenn	.08	.06	.03
609	Jim Sundberg	.08	.06	.03
610	Willie Stargell	.40	.30	.15
611	Reggie Smith	.10	.08	.04
612	Rob Wilfong	.06	.05	.02
613	Niekro Brothers (Joe Niekro, Phil Niekro)	.15	.11	.06
614	Lee Elia	.06	.05	.02
615	Mickey Hatcher	.08	.06	.03
616	Jerry Hairston	.06	.05	.02
617	John Martin	.06	.05	.02
618	Wally Backman(FC)	.15	.11	.06
619	*Storm Davis*(FC)	.30	.25	.12
620	Alan Knicely	.06	.05	.02
621	John Stuper	.06	.05	.02
622	Matt Sinatro	.06	.05	.02
623	*Gene Petralli*(FC)	.15	.11	.06
624	Duane Walker	.06	.05	.02
625	Dick Williams	.06	.05	.02
626	Pat Corrales	.06	.05	.02
627	Vern Ruhle	.06	.05	.02
628	Joe Torre	.08	.06	.03
629	Anthony Johnson	.06	.05	.02
630	Steve Howe	.08	.06	.03
631	Gary Woods	.06	.05	.02
632	Lamarr Hoyt (LaMarr)	.06	.05	.02
633	Steve Swisher	.06	.05	.02
634	Terry Leach(FC)	.12	.09	.05
635	Jeff Newman	.06	.05	.02
636	Brett Butler	.10	.08	.04
637	Gary Gray	.06	.05	.02
638	Lee Mazzilli	.08	.06	.03
639a	Ron Jackson (A's)	6.00	4.50	2.50
639b	Ron Jackson (Angels - green frame around photo)	.90	.70	.35
639c	Ron Jackson (Angels - red frame around photo)	.20	.15	.08
640	Juan Beniquez	.06	.05	.02
641	Dave Rucker	.06	.05	.02
642	Luis Pujols	.06	.05	.02
643	Rick Monday	.10	.08	.04
644	Hosken Powell	.06	.05	.02
645	San Diego Chicken	.20	.15	.08
646	Dave Engle	.06	.05	.02
647	Dick Davis	.06	.05	.02
648	MVP's (Vida Blue, Joe Morgan, Frank Robinson)	.15	.11	.06
649	Al Chambers	.06	.05	.02
650	Jesus Vega	.06	.05	.02
651	Jeff Jones	.06	.05	.02
652	Marvis Foley	.06	.05	.02
653	Ty Cobb Puzzle	.06	.05	.02
---a	Dick Perez/DK Checklist (no word "Checklist" on back)	.70	.50	.30
---b	Dick Perez/DK Checklist (word "Checklist" on back)	.08	.06	.03
----	Checklist 27-130	.06	.05	.02
----	Checklist 131-234	.06	.05	.02
----	Checklist 235-338	.06	.05	.02
----	Checklist 339-442	.06	.05	.02
----	Checklist 443-546	.06	.05	.02
----	Checklist 547-653	.06	.05	.02

1983 Donruss Action All-Stars

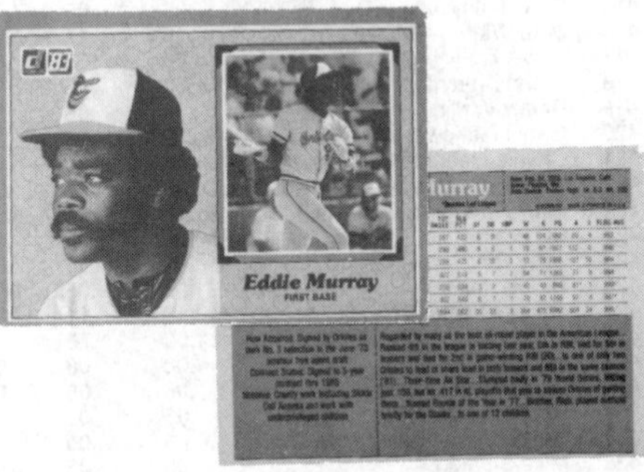

The cards in this 60-card set are designed on a horizontal format and contain a large close-up photo of the player on the left and a smaller action photo on the right. The cards, which measure 3-1/2" by 5", have deep red borders and contain the Donruss logo and the year of issue. The card backs have black print on red and white and contain various statistical and biographical information. The cards were sold with puzzle pieces (three pieces on one card per pack) that feature Mickey Mantle.

		MT	NR MT	EX
	Complete Set:	9.00	6.75	3.50
	Common Player:	.10	.08	.04
1	Eddie Murray	.30	.25	.12
2	Dwight Evans	.15	.11	.06
3a	Reggie Jackson (red covers part of statistics on back)	.60	.45	.25
3b	Reggie Jackson (red does not cover any statistics on back)	.60	.45	.25
4	Greg Luzinski	.12	.09	.05
5	Larry Herndon	.10	.08	.04
6	Al Oliver	.12	.09	.05
7	Bill Buckner	.10	.08	.04
8	Jason Thompson	.10	.08	.04
9	Andre Dawson	.20	.15	.08
10	Greg Minton	.10	.08	.04
11	Terry Kennedy	.10	.08	.04
12	Phil Niekro	.20	.15	.08
13	Willie Wilson	.12	.09	.05
14	Johnny Bench	.60	.45	.25
15	Ron Guidry	.15	.11	.06
16	Hal McRae	.10	.08	.04
17	Damaso Garcia	.10	.08	.04
18	Gary Ward	.10	.08	.04
19	Cecil Cooper	.12	.09	.05
20	Keith Hernandez	.25	.20	.10
21	Ron Cey	.12	.09	.05
22	Rickey Henderson	1.00	.70	.40

		MT	NR MT	EX
23	Nolan Ryan	2.50	2.00	1.00
24	Steve Carlton	.30	.25	.12
25	John Stearns	.10	.08	.04
26	Jim Sundberg	.10	.08	.04
27	Joaquin Andujar	.10	.08	.04
28	Gaylord Perry	.15	.11	.06
29	Jack Clark	.15	.11	.06
30	Bill Madlock	.12	.09	.05
31	Pete Rose	.60	.45	.25
32	Mookie Wilson	.10	.08	.04
33	Rollie Fingers	.15	.11	.06
34	Lonnie Smith	.10	.08	.04
35	Tony Pena	.10	.08	.04
36	Dave Winfield	.30	.25	.12
37	Tim Lollar	.10	.08	.04
38	Rod Carew	.60	.45	.25
39	Toby Harrah	.10	.08	.04
40	Buddy Bell	.10	.08	.04
41	Bruce Sutter	.12	.09	.05
42	George Brett	.70	.50	.30
43	Carlton Fisk	.60	.45	.25
44	Carl Yastrzemski	.70	.50	.30
45	Dale Murphy	.25	.20	.10
46	Bob Horner	.12	.09	.05
47	Dave Concepcion	.12	.09	.05
48	Dave Stieb	.12	.09	.05
49	Kent Hrbek	.20	.15	.08
50	Lance Parrish	.15	.11	.06
51	Joe Niekro	.12	.09	.05
52	Cal Ripken Jr.	.80	.60	.30
53	Fernando Valenzuela	.12	.09	.05
54	Rickie Zisk	.10	.08	.04
55	Leon Durham	.10	.08	.04
56	Robin Yount	.70	.50	.30
57	Mike Schmidt	1.25	.90	.50
58	Gary Carter	.15	.11	.06
59	Fred Lynn	.15	.11	.06
60	Checklist	.10	.08	.04

1983 Donruss Hall Of Fame Heroes

The artwork of Dick Perez is featured in the 44- card Donruss Hall of Fame Heroes set issued in 1983. The standard-size cards (2-1/2" by 3-1/2") were available in wax packs that contained eight cards plus a Mickey Mantle puzzle piece card (three pieces on one card per pack). The backs, which display red and blue print on white stock, contain a short player biograpical sketch derived from the Hall of Fame yearbook. The numbered set consists of 44 player cards, a Mantle puzzle card, and a checklist.

		MT	NR MT	EX
Complete Set:		8.00	6.00	3.25
Common Player:		.05	.04	.02
1	Ty Cobb	.70	.50	.30
2	Walter Johnson	.15	.11	.06
3	Christy Mathewson	.15	.11	.06
4	Josh Gibson	.10	.08	.04
5	Honus Wagner	.15	.11	.06
6	Jackie Robinson	.50	.40	.20
7	Mickey Mantle	1.00	.70	.40
8	Luke Appling	.05	.04	.02
9	Ted Williams	.70	.50	.30
10	Johnny Mize	.15	.11	.06
11	Satchel Paige	.15	.11	.06
12	Lou Boudreau	.15	.11	.06
13	Jimmie Foxx	.15	.11	.06
14	Duke Snider	.70	.50	.30
15	Monte Irvin	.15	.11	.06
16	Hank Greenberg	.15	.11	.06
17	Roberto Clemente	.50	.40	.20
18	Al Kaline	.50	.40	.20
19	Frank Robinson	.50	.40	.20
20	Joe Cronin	.09	.07	.04
21	Burleigh Grimes	.05	.04	.02
22	The Waner Brothers (Lloyd Waner, Paul Waner)	.09	.07	.04
23	Grover Alexander	.09	.07	.04
24	Yogi Berra	.50	.40	.20
25	James Bell	.05	.04	.02
26	Bill Dickey	.09	.07	.04
27	Cy Young	.15	.11	.06
28	Charlie Gehringer	.09	.07	.04
29	Dizzy Dean	.15	.11	.06
30	Bob Lemon	.15	.11	.06
31	Red Ruffing	.05	.04	.02
32	Stan Musial	.70	.50	.30
33	Carl Hubbell	.15	.11	.06
34	Hank Aaron	.70	.50	.30
35	John McGraw	.09	.07	.04
36	Bob Feller	.50	.40	.20
37	Casey Stengel	.15	.11	.06
38	Ralph Kiner	.15	.11	.06
39	Roy Campanella	.15	.11	.06
40	Mel Ott	.09	.07	.04
41	Robin Roberts	.15	.11	.06
42	Early Wynn	.15	.11	.06
43	Mickey Mantle Puzzle Card	.09	.07	.04
—	Checklist	.09	.07	.04

1984 Donruss

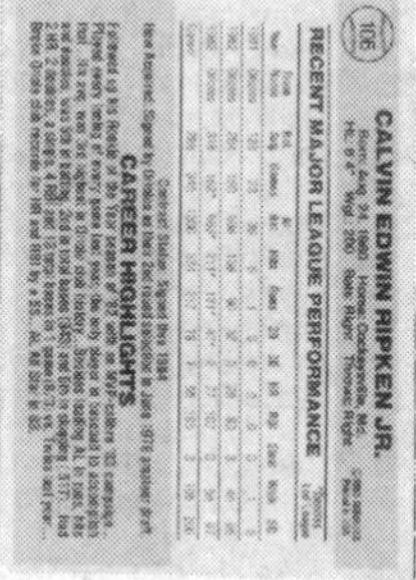

The 1984 Donruss set consists of 651 numbered cards, seven unnumbered checklists and two "Living Legends" cards (designated A and B). The A and B cards were issued only in wax packs and were not available to hobby dealers purchasing factory sets. The card fronts differ in style from the previous years, however the Donruss logo and year of issue are still included. The card backs have black print on green and white and are identical in format to the preceding year. The standard-size cards (2-1/2" by 3-1/2") were issued with a 63-piece puzzle of Duke Snider. A limited print run of the issue by Donruss has caused the set to escalate in price in recent years. The complete set price in the checklist that follows does not include the higher priced variations. Cards marked with (DK) or (RR) in the checklist refer to the Diamond Kings and Rated Rookies subsets. Each of the Diamond Kings cards and the DK checklist can be found in two varieties. The more common has Frank Steele's name misspelled "Steel" in the credit line at the bottom-right corner on the back. The error was later corrected.

		MT	NR MT	EX
Complete Set (660):		400.00	300.00	160.00
Common Player:		.12	.09	.05
A	Living Legends (Rollie Fingers, Gaylord Perry)	5.00	3.75	2.00

		MT	NR MT	EX
B	Living Legends (Johnny Bench, Carl Yastrzemski)	7.00	5.25	2.75
1a	Robin Yount ((DK) Steel)	3.00	2.25	1.25
1b	Robin Yount ((DK) Steele)	4.00	3.00	1.50
2a	Dave Concepcion ((DK) Steel)	.30	.25	.12
2b	Dave Concepcion ((DK) Steele)	.60	.45	.25
3a	Dwayne Murphy ((DK) Steel)	.25	.20	.10
3b	Dwayne Murphy ((DK) Steele)	.60	.45	.25
4a	John Castino ((DK) Steel)	.20	.15	.08
4b	John Castino ((DK) Steele)	.60	.45	.25
5a	Leon Durham ((DK) Steel)	.25	.20	.10
5b	Leon Durham ((DK) Steele)	.60	.45	.25
6a	Rusty Staub ((DK) Steel)	.30	.25	.12
6b	Rusty Staub ((DK) Steele)	.60	.45	.25
7a	Jack Clark ((DK) Steel)	.25	.20	.10
7b	Jack Clark ((DK) Steele)	.60	.45	.25
8a	Dave Dravecky ((DK) Steel)	.25	.20	.10
8b	Dave Dravecky ((DK) Steele)	.60	.45	.25
9a	Al Oliver ((DK) Steel)	.35	.25	.14
9b	Al Oliver ((DK) Steele)	.70	.50	.30
10a	Dave Righetti ((DK) Steel)	.25	.20	.10
10b	Dave Righetti ((DK) Steele)	.60	.45	.25
11a	Hal McRae ((DK) Steel)	.30	.25	.12
11b	Hal McRae ((DK) Steele)	.60	.45	.25
12a	Ray Knight ((DK) Steel)	.25	.20	.10
12b	Ray Knight ((DK) Steele)	.60	.45	.25
13a	Bruce Sutter ((DK) Steel)	.35	.25	.14
13b	Bruce Sutter ((DK) Steele)	.70	.50	.30
14a	Bob Horner ((DK) Steel)	.25	.20	.10
14b	Bob Horner ((DK) Steele)	.60	.45	.25
15a	Lance Parrish ((DK) Steel)	.25	.20	.10
15b	Lance Parrish ((DK) Steele)	.60	.45	.25
16a	Matt Young ((DK) Steel)	.25	.20	.10
16b	Matt Young ((DK) Steele)	.60	.45	.25
17a	Fred Lynn ((DK) Steel)	.35	.25	.14
17b	Fred Lynn ((DK) Steele)	.70	.50	.30
18a	Ron Kittle ((DK) Steel)(FC)	.35	.25	.14
18b	Ron Kittle ((DK) Steele)(FC)	.70	.50	.30
19a	Jim Clancy ((DK) Steel)	.25	.20	.10
19b	Jim Clancy ((DK) Steele)	.60	.45	.25
20a	Bill Madlock ((DK) Steel)	.30	.25	.12
20b	Bill Madlock ((DK) Steele)	.60	.45	.25
21a	Larry Parrish ((DK) Steel)	.25	.20	.10
21b	Larry Parrish ((DK) Steele)	.60	.45	.25
22a	Eddie Murray ((DK) Steel)	1.25	.90	.50
22b	Eddie Murray ((DK) Steele)	2.50	2.00	1.00
23a	Mike Schmidt ((DK) Steel)	6.00	4.50	2.50
23b	Mike Schmidt ((DK) Steele)	4.00	3.00	1.50
24a	Pedro Guerrero ((DK) Steel)	.25	.20	.10
24b	Pedro Guerrero ((DK) Steele)	.60	.45	.25
25a	Andre Thomton ((DK) Steel)	.25	.20	.10
25b	Andre Thomton ((DK) Steele)	.60	.45	.25
26a	Wade Boggs ((DK) Steel)	3.00	2.25	1.25
26b	Wade Boggs ((DK) Steele)	4.00	3.00	1.50
27	*Joel Skinner* (RR)(FC)	.12	.09	.05
28	Tom Dunbar (RR)	.12	.09	.05
29a	Mike Stenhouse ((RR) no number on back)	.15	.11	.06
29b	Mike Stenhouse ((RR) 29 on back)	4.00	3.00	1.50
30a	*Ron Darling* ((RR) no number on back)	5.00	3.75	2.00
30b	*Ron Darling* ((RR) 30 on back)	10.00	7.50	4.00
31	*Dion James* (RR)(FC)	.15	.11	.06
32	*Tony Fernandez* (RR)	6.00	4.50	2.50
33	Angel Salazar (RR)	.12	.09	.05
34	*Kevin McReynolds* (RR)	1.50	1.25	.60
35	*Dick Schofield* (RR)	.40	.30	.15
36	*Brad Komminsk* (RR)(FC)	.12	.09	.05
37	*Tim Teufel* (RR)(FC)	.30	.25	.12
38	Doug Frobel (RR)	.12	.09	.05
39	*Greg Gagne* (RR)	.60	.45	.25
40	Mike Fuentes (RR)	.12	.09	.05
41	*Joe Carter* (RR)(FC)	58.00	43.00	23.00
42	Mike Brown (RR)	.12	.09	.05
43	Mike Jeffcoat (RR)	.12	.09	.05
44	*Sid Fernandez* (RR)(FC)	4.00	3.00	1.50
45	Brian Dayett (RR)	.12	.09	.05
46	Chris Smith (RR)	.12	.09	.05
47	Eddie Murray	5.00	3.75	2.00
48	Robin Yount	10.00	7.50	4.00
49	Lance Parrish	.50	.40	.20
50	Jim Rice	.90	.70	.35
51	Dave Winfield	11.00	8.25	4.50
52	Fernando Valenzuela	.50	.40	.20
53	George Brett	10.00	7.50	4.00
54	Rickey Henderson	12.00	9.00	4.75
55	Gary Carter	1.00	.70	.40
56	Buddy Bell	.20	.15	.08
57	Reggie Jackson	6.00	4.50	2.50
58	Harold Baines	.25	.20	.10
59	Ozzie Smith	5.00	3.75	2.00
60	Nolan Ryan	30.00	22.00	12.00
61	Pete Rose	3.00	2.25	1.25
62	Ron Oester	.12	.09	.05
63	Steve Garvey	.90	.70	.35
64	Jason Thompson	.12	.09	.05
65	Jack Clark	.35	.25	.14
66	Dale Murphy	2.00	1.50	.80
67	Leon Durham	.12	.09	.05
68	*Darryl Strawberry*(FC)	25.00	18.50	10.00
69	Richie Zisk	.12	.09	.05
70	Kent Hrbek	.60	.45	.25
71	Dave Stieb	.25	.20	.10
72	Ken Schrom	.12	.09	.05
73	George Bell	2.00	1.50	.80
74	John Moses	.15	.11	.06
75	Ed Lynch	.12	.09	.05
76	Chuck Rainey	.12	.09	.05
77	Biff Pocoroba	.12	.09	.05
78	Cecilio Guante	.12	.09	.05
79	Jim Barr	.12	.09	.05
80	Kurt Bevacqua	.12	.09	.05
81	Tom Foley	.12	.09	.05
82	Joe Lefebvre	.12	.09	.05
83	*Andy Van Slyke*(FC)	10.00	7.50	4.00
84	Bob Lillis	.12	.09	.05
85	Rick Adams	.12	.09	.05
86	Jerry Hairston	.12	.09	.05
87	Bob James	.12	.09	.05
88	Joe Altobelli	.12	.09	.05
89	Ed Romero	.12	.09	.05
90	John Grubb	.12	.09	.05
91	John Henry Johnson	.12	.09	.05
92	Juan Espino	.12	.09	.05
93	Candy Maldonado	.20	.15	.08
94	Andre Thomton	.20	.15	.08
95	Onix Concepcion	.12	.09	.05
96	*Don Hill*(FC)	.20	.15	.08
97	Andre Dawson	5.00	3.75	2.00
98	Frank Tanana	.15	.11	.06
99	*Curt Wilkerson*(FC)	.15	.11	.06
100	Larry Gura	.12	.09	.05
101	Dwayne Murphy	.12	.09	.05
102	Tom Brennan	.12	.09	.05
103	Dave Righetti	.40	.30	.15
104	Steve Sax	.30	.25	.12
105	Dan Petry	.12	.09	.05
106	Cal Ripken, Jr.	25.00	18.50	10.00
107	Paul Molitor	6.00	4.50	2.50
108	Fred Lynn	.35	.25	.14
109	Neil Allen	.12	.09	.05
110	Joe Niekro	.20	.15	.08
111	Steve Carlton	3.00	2.25	1.25
112	Terry Kennedy	.15	.11	.06
113	Bill Madlock	.20	.15	.08
114	Chili Davis	.15	.11	.06
115	Jim Gantner	.12	.09	.05
116	Tom Seaver	6.00	4.50	2.50
117	Bill Buckner	.20	.15	.08
118	Bill Caudill	.12	.09	.05
119	Jim Clancy	.15	.11	.06
120	John Castino	.12	.09	.05
121	Dave Concepcion	.20	.15	.08
122	Greg Luzinski	.20	.15	.08
123	Mike Boddicker(FC)	.20	.15	.08
124	Pete Ladd	.12	.09	.05
125	Juan Berenguer	.12	.09	.05
126	John Montefusco	.12	.09	.05
127	Ed Jurak	.12	.09	.05
128	Tom Niedenfuer	.12	.09	.05
129	Bert Blyleven	.30	.25	.12
130	Bud Black	.12	.09	.05
131	Gorman Heimueller	.12	.09	.05
132	Dan Schatzeder	.12	.09	.05
133	Ron Jackson	.12	.09	.05
134	*Tom Henke*(FC)	3.00	2.25	1.25
135	Kevin Hickey	.12	.09	.05
136	Mike Scott	.30	.25	.12
137	Bo Diaz	.12	.09	.05
138	Glenn Brummer	.12	.09	.05
139	Sid Monge	.12	.09	.05
140	Rich Gale	.12	.09	.05
141	Brett Butler	.15	.11	.06
142	Brian Harper	2.00	1.50	.80
143	John Rabb	.12	.09	.05
144	Gary Woods	.12	.09	.05
145	Pat Putnam	.12	.09	.05
146	*Jim Acker*(FC)	.15	.11	.06
147	Mickey Hatcher	.12	.09	.05
148	Todd Cruz	.12	.09	.05
149	Tom Tellmann	.12	.09	.05
150	John Wockenfuss	.12	.09	.05

		MT	NR MT	EX
151	Wade Boggs	18.00	13.50	7.25
152	Don Baylor	.20	.15	.08
153	Bob Welch	.20	.15	.08
154	Alan Bannister	.12	.09	.05
155	Willie Aikens	.12	.09	.05
156	Jeff Burroughs	.12	.09	.05
157	Bryan Little	.12	.09	.05
158	Bob Boone	.15	.11	.06
159	Dave Hostetler	.12	.09	.05
160	Jerry Dybzinski	.12	.09	.05
161	Mike Madden	.12	.09	.05
162	Luis DeLeon	.12	.09	.05
163	Willie Hernandez	.15	.11	.06
164	Frank Pastore	.12	.09	.05
165	Rick Camp	.12	.09	.05
166	Lee Mazzilli	.12	.09	.05
167	Scot Thompson	.12	.09	.05
168	Bob Forsch	.12	.09	.05
169	Mike Flanagan	.15	.11	.06
170	Rick Manning	.12	.09	.05
171	Chet Lemon	.12	.09	.05
172	Jerry Remy	.12	.09	.05
173	Ron Guidry	.35	.25	.14
174	Pedro Guerrero	.50	.40	.20
175	Willie Wilson	.25	.20	.10
176	Carney Lansford	.20	.15	.08
177	Al Oliver	.30	.25	.12
178	Jim Sundberg	.12	.09	.05
179	Bobby Grich	.20	.15	.08
180	Richard Dotson	.20	.15	.08
181	Joaquin Andujar	.12	.09	.05
182	Jose Cruz	.20	.15	.08
183	Mike Schmidt	15.00	11.00	6.00
184	*Gary Redus*(FC)	.30	.25	.12
185	Garry Templeton	.15	.11	.06
186	Tony Pena	.20	.15	.08
187	Greg Minton	.12	.09	.05
188	Phil Niekro	.50	.40	.20
189	Fergie Jenkins	.30	.25	.12
190	Mookie Wilson	.15	.11	.06
191	Jim Beattie	.12	.09	.05
192	Gary Ward	.12	.09	.05
193	Jesse Barfield	.40	.30	.15
194	Pete Filson	.12	.09	.05
195	Roy Lee Jackson	.12	.09	.05
196	Rick Sweet	.12	.09	.05
197	Jesse Orosco	.15	.11	.06
198	*Steve Lake*(FC)	.12	.09	.05
199	Ken Dayley	.12	.09	.05
200	Manny Sarmiento	.12	.09	.05
201	Mark Davis(FC)	.25	.20	.10
202	Tim Flannery	.12	.09	.05
203	Bill Scherrer	.12	.09	.05
204	Al Holland	.12	.09	.05
205	David Von Ohlen	.12	.09	.05
206	Mike LaCoss	.12	.09	.05
207	Juan Beniquez	.12	.09	.05
208	*Juan Agosto*(FC)	.20	.15	.08
209	Bobby Ramos	.12	.09	.05
210	Al Bumbry	.12	.09	.05
211	Mark Brouhard	.12	.09	.05
212	Howard Bailey	.12	.09	.05
213	Bruce Hurst	.20	.15	.08
214	Bob Shirley	.12	.09	.05
215	Pat Zachry	.12	.09	.05
216	Julio Franco	4.50	3.50	1.75
217	Mike Armstrong	.12	.09	.05
218	Dave Beard	.12	.09	.05
219	Steve Rogers	.12	.09	.05
220	John Butcher	.12	.09	.05
221	*Mike Smithson*(FC)	.20	.15	.08
222	Frank White	.20	.15	.08
223	Mike Heath	.12	.09	.05
224	Chris Bando	.12	.09	.05
225	Roy Smalley	.12	.09	.05
226	Dusty Baker	.20	.15	.08
227	Lou Whitaker	.60	.45	.25
228	John Lowenstein	.12	.09	.05
229	Ben Oglivie	.12	.09	.05
230	Doug DeCinces	.15	.11	.06
231	Lonnie Smith	.12	.09	.05
232	Ray Knight	.15	.11	.06
233	Gary Matthews	.20	.15	.08
234	Juan Bonilla	.12	.09	.05
235	Rod Scurry	.12	.09	.05
236	Atlee Hammaker	.12	.09	.05
237	Mike Caldwell	.12	.09	.05
238	Keith Hernandez	.80	.60	.30
239	Larry Bowa	.25	.20	.10
240	Tony Bernazard	.12	.09	.05
241	Damaso Garcia	.12	.09	.05

		MT	NR MT	EX
242	Tom Brunansky	.35	.25	.14
243	Dan Driessen	.12	.09	.05
244	Ron Kittle(FC)	.30	.25	.12
245	Tim Stoddard	.12	.09	.05
246	Bob L. Gibson	.12	.09	.05
247	Marty Castillo	.12	.09	.05
248	*Don Mattingly*(FC)	50.00	37.00	20.00
249	Jeff Newman	.12	.09	.05
250	*Alejandro Pena*(FC)	.70	.50	.30
251	Toby Harrah	.12	.09	.05
252	Cesar Geronimo	.12	.09	.05
253	Tom Underwood	.12	.09	.05
254	Doug Flynn	.12	.09	.05
255	Andy Hassler	.12	.09	.05
256	Odell Jones	.12	.09	.05
257	Rudy Law	.12	.09	.05
258	Harry Spilman	.12	.09	.05
259	Marty Bystrom	.12	.09	.05
260	Dave Rucker	.12	.09	.05
261	Ruppert Jones	.12	.09	.05
262	Jeff Jones	.12	.09	.05
263	*Gerald Perry*(FC)	.50	.40	.20
264	Gene Tenace	.12	.09	.05
265	Brad Wellman	.12	.09	.05
266	Dickie Noles	.12	.09	.05
267	Jamie Allen	.12	.09	.05
268	Jim Gott	.15	.11	.06
269	Ron Davis	.12	.09	.05
270	Benny Ayala	.12	.09	.05
271	Ned Yost	.12	.09	.05
272	Dave Rozema	.12	.09	.05
273	Dave Stapleton	.12	.09	.05
274	Lou Piniella	.20	.15	.08
275	Jose Morales	.12	.09	.05
276	Brod Perkins	.12	.09	.05
277	Butch Davis	.12	.09	.05
278	*Tony Phillips*(FC)	3.00	2.25	1.25
279	Jeff Reardon	.25	.20	.10
280	Ken Forsch	.12	.09	.05
281	*Pete O'Brien*(FC)	1.00	.70	.40
282	Tom Paciorek	.12	.09	.05
283	Frank LaCorte	.12	.09	.05
284	Tim Lollar	.12	.09	.05
285	Greg Gross	.12	.09	.05
286	Alex Trevino	.12	.09	.05
287	Gene Garber	.12	.09	.05
288	Dave Parker	.50	.40	.20
289	Lee Smith	3.00	2.25	1.25
290	Dave LaPoint	.15	.11	.06
291	*John Shelby*(FC)	.25	.20	.10
292	Charlie Moore	.12	.09	.05
293	Alan Trammell	.60	.45	.25
294	Tony Armas	.20	.15	.08
295	Shane Rawley	.20	.15	.08
296	Greg Brock	.15	.11	.06
297	Hal McRae	.20	.15	.08
298	Mike Davis	.12	.09	.05
299	Tim Raines	.80	.60	.30
300	Bucky Dent	.15	.11	.06
301	Tommy John	.35	.25	.14
302	Carlton Fisk	4.00	3.00	1.50
303	Darrell Porter	.12	.09	.05
304	Dickie Thon	.12	.09	.05
305	Garry Maddox	.12	.09	.05
306	Cesar Cedeno	.20	.15	.08
307	Gary Lucas	.12	.09	.05
308	Johnny Ray	.20	.15	.08
309	Andy McGaffigan	.12	.09	.05
310	Claudell Washington	.12	.09	.05
311	Ryne Sandberg	25.00	18.50	10.00
312	George Foster	.30	.25	.12
313	*Spike Owen*(FC)	.70	.50	.30
314	Gary Gaetti	.40	.30	.15
315	Willie Upshaw	.12	.09	.05
316	Al Williams	.12	.09	.05
317	Jorge Orta	.12	.09	.05
318	Orlando Mercado	.12	.09	.05
319	*Junior Ortiz*(FC)	.12	.09	.05
320	Mike Proly	.12	.09	.05
321	Randy S. Johnson	.12	.09	.05
322	Jim Morrison	.12	.09	.05
323	Max Venable	.12	.09	.05
324	Tony Gwynn	18.00	13.50	7.25
325	Duane Walker	.12	.09	.05
326	Ozzie Virgil	.12	.09	.05
327	Jeff Lahti	.12	.09	.05
328	*Bill Dawley*(FC)	.12	.09	.05
329	Rob Wilfong	.12	.09	.05
330	Marc Hill	.12	.09	.05
331	Ray Burris	.12	.09	.05
332	Allan Ramirez	.12	.09	.05

		MT	NR MT	EX
333	Chuck Porter	.12	.09	.05
334	Wayne Krenchicki	.12	.09	.05
335	Gary Allenson	.12	.09	.05
336	*Bob Meacham*(FC)	.20	.15	.08
337	Joe Beckwith	.12	.09	.05
338	Rick Sutcliffe	.25	.20	.10
339	*Mark Huismann*(FC)	.15	.11	.06
340	*Tim Conroy*(FC)	.15	.11	.06
341	Scott Sanderson	.12	.09	.05
342	Larry Biittner	.12	.09	.05
343	Dave Stewart	2.00	1.50	.80
344	Darryl Motley	.12	.09	.05
345	*Chris Codiroli*(FC)	.12	.09	.05
346	Rick Behenna	.12	.09	.05
347	Andre Robertson	.12	.09	.05
348	Mike Marshall	.25	.20	.10
349	Larry Herndon	.12	.09	.05
350	Rich Dauer	.12	.09	.05
351	Cecil Cooper	.25	.20	.10
352	Rod Carew	4.00	3.00	1.50
353	Willie McGee	.40	.30	.15
354	Phil Garner	.12	.09	.05
355	Joe Morgan	.60	.45	.25
356	Luis Salazar	.12	.09	.05
357	John Candelaria	.20	.15	.08
358	Bill Laskey	.12	.09	.05
359	Bob McClure	.12	.09	.05
360	Dave Kingman	.30	.25	.12
361	Ron Cey	.20	.15	.08
362	*Matt Young*(FC)	.20	.15	.08
363	Lloyd Moseby	.20	.15	.08
364	Frank Viola	2.00	1.50	.80
365	Eddie Milner	.12	.09	.05
366	Floyd Bannister	.20	.15	.08
367	Dan Ford	.12	.09	.05
368	Moose Haas	.12	.09	.05
369	Doug Bair	.12	.09	.05
370	*Ray Fontenot*(FC)	.12	.09	.05
371	Luis Aponte	.12	.09	.05
372	Jack Fimple	.12	.09	.05
373	*Neal Heaton*(FC)	.20	.15	.08
374	Greg Pryor	.12	.09	.05
375	Wayne Gross	.12	.09	.05
376	Charlie Lea	.12	.09	.05
377	Steve Lubratich	.12	.09	.05
378	Jon Matlack	.12	.09	.05
379	Julio Cruz	.12	.09	.05
380	John Mizerock	.12	.09	.05
381	*Kevin Gross*(FC)	.50	.40	.20
382	Mike Ramsey	.12	.09	.05
383	Doug Gwosdz	.12	.09	.05
384	Kelly Paris	.12	.09	.05
385	Pete Falcone	.12	.09	.05
386	Milt May	.12	.09	.05
387	Fred Breining	.12	.09	.05
388	*Craig Lefferts*(FC)	.25	.20	.10
389	Steve Henderson	.12	.09	.05
390	Randy Moffitt	.12	.09	.05
391	Ron Washington	.12	.09	.05
392	Gary Roenicke	.12	.09	.05
393	*Tom Candiotti*(FC)	1.00	.70	.40
394	Larry Pashnick	.12	.09	.05
395	Dwight Evans	.30	.25	.12
396	Goose Gossage	.40	.30	.15
397	Derrel Thomas	.12	.09	.05
398	Juan Eichelberger	.12	.09	.05
399	Leon Roberts	.12	.09	.05
400	Davey Lopes	.15	.11	.06
401	Bill Gullickson	.12	.09	.05
402	Geoff Zahn	.12	.09	.05
403	Billy Sample	.12	.09	.05
404	Mike Squires	.12	.09	.05
405	Craig Reynolds	.12	.09	.05
406	Eric Show	.15	.11	.06
407	John Denny	.12	.09	.05
408	Dann Bilardello	.12	.09	.05
409	Bruce Benedict	.12	.09	.05
410	Kent Tekulve	.12	.09	.05
411	Mel Hall	.20	.15	.08
412	John Stuper	.12	.09	.05
413	Rick Dempsey	.12	.09	.05
414	Don Sutton	1.00	.70	.40
415	Jack Morris	3.00	2.25	1.25
416	John Tudor	.20	.15	.08
417	Willie Randolph	.20	.15	.08
418	Jerry Reuss	.15	.11	.06
419	Don Slaught	.12	.09	.05
420	Steve McCatty	.12	.09	.05
421	Tim Wallach	.25	.20	.10
422	Larry Parrish	.20	.15	.08
423	Brian Downing	.20	.15	.08

		MT	NR MT	EX
424	Britt Burns	.12	.09	.05
425	David Green	.12	.09	.05
426	Jerry Mumphrey	.12	.09	.05
427	Ivan DeJesus	.12	.09	.05
428	Mario Soto	.12	.09	.05
429	Gene Richards	.12	.09	.05
430	Dale Berra	.12	.09	.05
431	Darrell Evans	.25	.20	.10
432	Glenn Hubbard	.12	.09	.05
433	Jody Davis	.15	.11	.06
434	Danny Heep	.12	.09	.05
435	*Ed Nunez*(FC)	.20	.15	.08
436	Bobby Castillo	.12	.09	.05
437	Ernie Whitt	.12	.09	.05
438	Scott Ullger	.12	.09	.05
439	Doyle Alexander	.15	.11	.06
440	Domingo Ramos	.12	.09	.05
441	Craig Swan	.12	.09	.05
442	Warren Brusstar	.12	.09	.05
443	Len Barker	.12	.09	.05
444	Mike Easler	.12	.09	.05
445	Renie Martin	.12	.09	.05
446	*Dennis Rasmussen*(FC)	.70	.50	.30
447	Ted Power(FC)	.15	.11	.06
448	*Charlie Hudson*(FC)	.25	.20	.10
449	*Danny Cox*(FC)	.70	.50	.30
450	Kevin Bass(FC)	.30	.25	.12
451	Daryl Sconiers	.12	.09	.05
452	Scott Fletcher	.12	.09	.05
453	Bryn Smith	.12	.09	.05
454	Jim Dwyer	.12	.09	.05
455	Rob Picciolo	.12	.09	.05
456	Enos Cabell	.12	.09	.05
457	*Dennis Boyd*(FC)	.70	.50	.30
458	Butch Wynegar	.12	.09	.05
459	Burt Hooton	.12	.09	.05
460	Ron Hassey	.12	.09	.05
461	*Danny Jackson*(FC)	1.00	.70	.40
462	Bob Kearney	.12	.09	.05
463	Terry Francona	.12	.09	.05
464	Wayne Tolleson	.12	.09	.05
465	Mickey Rivers	.12	.09	.05
466	John Wathan	.12	.09	.05
467	Bill Almon	.12	.09	.05
468	George Vukovich	.12	.09	.05
469	Steve Kemp	.15	.11	.06
470	Ken Landreaux	.12	.09	.05
471	Milt Wilcox	.12	.09	.05
472	Tippy Martinez	.12	.09	.05
473	Ted Simmons	.20	.15	.08
474	Tim Foli	.12	.09	.05
475	George Hendrick	.12	.09	.05
476	Terry Puhl	.12	.09	.05
477	Von Hayes	.25	.20	.10
478	Bobby Brown	.12	.09	.05
479	Lee Lacy	.12	.09	.05
480	Joel Youngblood	.12	.09	.05
481	Jim Slaton	.12	.09	.05
482	*Mike Fitzgerald*(FC)	.20	.15	.08
483	Keith Moreland	.12	.09	.05
484	Ron Roenicke	.12	.09	.05
485	Luis Leal	.12	.09	.05
486	Bryan Oelkers	.12	.09	.05
487	Bruce Berenyi	.12	.09	.05
488	LaMarr Hoyt	.12	.09	.05
489	Joe Nolan	.12	.09	.05
490	Marshall Edwards	.12	.09	.05
491	*Mike Laga*(FC)	.12	.09	.05
492	Rick Cerone	.12	.09	.05
493	Mike Miller (Rick)	.12	.09	.05
494	Rick Honeycutt	.12	.09	.05
495	Mike Hargrove	.12	.09	.05
496	Joe Simpson	.12	.09	.05
497	*Keith Atherton*(FC)	.25	.20	.10
498	Chris Welsh	.12	.09	.05
499	Bruce Kison	.12	.09	.05
500	Bob Johnson	.12	.09	.05
501	Jerry Koosman	.15	.11	.06
502	Frank DiPino	.12	.09	.05
503	Tony Perez	.40	.30	.15
504	Ken Oberkfell	.12	.09	.05
505	*Mark Thurmond*(FC)	.12	.09	.05
506	Joe Price	.12	.09	.05
507	Pascual Perez	.15	.11	.06
508	*Marvell Wynne*(FC)	.25	.20	.10
509	Mike Krukow	.12	.09	.05
510	Dick Ruthven	.12	.09	.05
511	Al Cowens	.12	.09	.05
512	Cliff Johnson	.12	.09	.05
513	*Randy Bush*(FC)	.20	.15	.08
514	Sammy Stewart	.12	.09	.05

		MT	NR MT	EX
515	*Bill Schroeder*(FC)	.25	.20	.10
516	Aurelio Lopez	.12	.09	.05
517	Mike Brown	.12	.09	.05
518	Graig Nettles	.35	.25	.14
519	Dave Sax	.12	.09	.05
520	Gerry Willard	.12	.09	.05
521	Paul Splittorff	.12	.09	.05
522	Tom Burgmeier	.12	.09	.05
523	Chris Speier	.12	.09	.05
524	Bobby Clark	.12	.09	.05
525	George Wright	.12	.09	.05
526	Dennis Lamp	.12	.09	.05
527	Tony Scott	.12	.09	.05
528	Ed Whitson	.12	.09	.05
529	Ron Reed	.12	.09	.05
530	Charlie Puleo	.12	.09	.05
531	Jerry Royster	.12	.09	.05
532	Don Robinson	.12	.09	.05
533	Steve Trout	.12	.09	.05
534	Bruce Sutter	.30	.25	.12
535	Bob Horner	.20	.15	.08
536	Pat Tabler	.15	.11	.06
537	Chris Chambliss	.12	.09	.05
538	Bob Ojeda	.15	.11	.06
539	Alan Ashby	.12	.09	.05
540	Jay Johnstone	.12	.09	.05
541	Bob Dernier	.12	.09	.05
542	*Brook Jacoby*(FC)	1.50	1.25	.60
543	U.L. Washington	.12	.09	.05
544	Danny Darwin	.12	.09	.05
545	Kiko Garcia	.12	.09	.05
546	Vance Law	.12	.09	.05
547	Tug McGraw	.20	.15	.08
548	Dave Smith	.12	.09	.05
549	Len Matuszek	.12	.09	.05
550	Tom Hume	.12	.09	.05
551	Dave Dravecky	.15	.11	.06
552	Rick Rhoden	.15	.11	.06
553	Duane Kuiper	.12	.09	.05
554	Rusty Staub	.20	.15	.08
555	Bill Campbell	.12	.09	.05
556	Mike Torrez	.12	.09	.05
557	Dave Henderson(FC)	.25	.20	.10
558	Len Whitehouse	.12	.09	.05
559	Barry Bonnell	.12	.09	.05
560	Rick Lysander	.12	.09	.05
561	Garth Iorg	.12	.09	.05
562	Bryan Clark	.12	.09	.05
563	Brian Giles	.12	.09	.05
564	Vern Ruhle	.12	.09	.05
565	Steve Bedrosian	.20	.15	.08
566	Larry McWilliams	.12	.09	.05
567	Jeff Leonard	.15	.11	.06
568	Alan Wiggins	.12	.09	.05
569	*Jeff Russell*(FC)	.25	.20	.10
570	Salome Barojas	.12	.09	.05
571	Dane Iorg	.12	.09	.05
572	Bob Knepper	.15	.11	.06
573	Gary Lavelle	.12	.09	.05
574	Gorman Thomas	.15	.11	.06
575	Manny Trillo	.12	.09	.05
576	Jim Palmer	4.00	3.00	1.50
577	Dale Murray	.12	.09	.05
578	Tom Brookens	.12	.09	.05
579	Rich Gedman	.15	.11	.06
580	*Bill Doran*(FC)	1.00	.70	.40
581	Steve Yeager	.12	.09	.05
582	Dan Spillner	.12	.09	.05
583	Dan Quisenberry	.15	.11	.06
584	Rance Mulliniks	.12	.09	.05
585	Storm Davis	.15	.11	.06
586	Dave Schmidt	.12	.09	.05
587	Bill Russell	.12	.09	.05
588	*Pat Sheridan*(FC)	.20	.15	.08
589	Rafael Ramirez	.12	.09	.05
590	Bud Anderson	.12	.09	.05
591	George Frazier	.12	.09	.05
592	*Lee Tunnell*(FC)	.12	.09	.05
593	Kirk Gibson	1.00	.70	.40
594	Scott McGregor	.12	.09	.05
595	Bob Bailor	.12	.09	.05
596	Tom Herr	.20	.15	.08
597	Luis Sanchez	.12	.09	.05
598	Dave Engle	.12	.09	.05
599	*Craig McMurtry*(FC)	.15	.11	.06
600	Carlos Diaz	.12	.09	.05
601	Tom O'Malley	.12	.09	.05
602	*Nick Esasky*(FC)	.70	.50	.30
603	Ron Hodges	.12	.09	.05
604	Ed Vande Berg	.12	.09	.05
605	Alfredo Griffin	.12	.09	.05
606	Glenn Hoffman	.12	.09	.05
607	Hubie Brooks	.20	.15	.08
608	Richard Barnes (photo actually Neal Heaton)	.12	.09	.05
609	*Greg Walker*(FC)	.40	.30	.15
610	Ken Singleton	.20	.15	.08
611	Mark Clear	.12	.09	.05
612	Buck Martinez	.12	.09	.05
613	Ken Griffey	.15	.11	.06
614	Reid Nichols	.12	.09	.05
615	*Doug Sisk*(FC)	.12	.09	.05
616	Bob Brenly	.12	.09	.05
617	Joey McLaughlin	.12	.09	.05
618	Glenn Wilson	.12	.09	.05
619	Bob Stoddard	.12	.09	.05
620	Len Sakata (Lenn)	.12	.09	.05
621	*Mike Young*(FC)	.25	.20	.10
622	John Stefero	.12	.09	.05
623	*Carmelo Martinez*(FC)	.30	.25	.12
624	Dave Bergman	.12	.09	.05
625	Runnin' Reds (David Green, Willie McGee, Lonnie Smith, Ozzie Smith)	.30	.25	.12
626	Rudy May	.12	.09	.05
627	Matt Keough	.12	.09	.05
628	*Jose DeLeon*(FC)	.50	.40	.20
629	Jim Essian	.12	.09	.05
630	*Darnell Coles*(FC)	.15	.11	.06
631	Mike Warren	.12	.09	.05
632	Del Crandall	.12	.09	.05
633	Dennis Martinez	.12	.09	.05
634	Mike Moore	.12	.09	.05
635	Lary Sorensen	.12	.09	.05
636	Ricky Nelson	.12	.09	.05
637	Omar Moreno	.12	.09	.05
638	Charlie Hough	.15	.11	.06
639	Dennis Eckersley	5.00	3.75	2.00
640	*Walt Terrell*(FC)	.20	.15	.08
641	Denny Walling	.12	.09	.05
642	*Dave Anderson*(FC)	.20	.15	.08
643	*Jose Oquendo*(FC)	.25	.20	.10
644	Bob Stanley	.12	.09	.05
645	Dave Geisel	.12	.09	.05
646	*Scott Garrelts*(FC)	.40	.30	.15
647	*Gary Pettis*(FC)	.40	.30	.15
648	Duke Snider Puzzle Card	.12	.09	.05
649	Johnnie LeMaster	.12	.09	.05
650	Dave Collins	.12	.09	.05
651	San Diego Chicken	.25	.20	.10
---a	Checklist 1-26 DK (Perez-Steel on back)	.12	.09	.05
---b	Checklist 1-26 DK (Perez-Steele on back)	.40	.30	.15
----	Checklist 27-130	.12	.09	.05
----	Checklist 131-234	.12	.09	.05
----	Checklist 235-338	.12	.09	.05
----	Checklist 339-442	.12	.09	.05
----	Checklist 443-546	.12	.09	.05
----	Checklist 547-651	.12	.09	.05

1984 Donruss Action All-Stars

Full-color photos on the card fronts and backs make the 1984 Donruss Action All-Stars set somewhat unusual. The fronts contain a large action photo plus the Donruss logo and year of issue inside a deep red border. The top half of the card backs feature a close-up photo with the bottom portion containing biographical and statistical information. The cards, which measure 3-1/2" by 5", were sold with Ted Williams puzzle pieces.

		MT	NR MT	EX
Complete Set:		9.00	6.75	3.50
Common Player:		.09	.07	.04
1	Gary Lavelle	.09	.07	.04
2	Willie McGee	.15	.11	.06
3	Tony Pena	.09	.07	.04
4	Lou Whitaker	.15	.11	.06
5	Robin Yount	.35	.25	.14
6	Doug DeCinces	.09	.07	.04
7	John Castino	.09	.07	.04
8	Terry Kennedy	.09	.07	.04
9	Rickey Henderson	.50	.40	.20
10	Bob Horner	.12	.09	.05
11	Harold Baines	.15	.11	.06
12	Buddy Bell	.09	.07	.04
13	Fernando Valenzuela	.12	.09	.05
14	Nolan Ryan	2.00	1.50	.80
15	Andre Thornton	.09	.07	.04
16	Gary Redus	.09	.07	.04
17	Pedro Guerrero	.15	.11	.06
18	Andre Dawson	.20	.15	.08
19	Dave Stieb	.12	.09	.05
20	Cal Ripken	.60	.45	.25
21	Ken Griffey	.12	.09	.05
22	Wade Boggs	.70	.50	.30
23	Keith Hernandez	.25	.20	.10
24	Steve Carlton	.30	.25	.12
25	Hal McRae	.12	.09	.05
26	John Lowenstein	.09	.07	.04
27	Fred Lynn	.15	.11	.06
28	Bill Buckner	.09	.07	.04
29	Chris Chambliss	.09	.07	.04
30	Richie Zisk	.09	.07	.04
31	Jack Clark	.15	.11	.06
32	George Hendrick	.09	.07	.04
33	Bill Madlock	.12	.09	.05
34	Lance Parrish	.15	.11	.06
35	Paul Molitor	.15	.11	.06
36	Reggie Jackson	.35	.25	.14
37	Kent Hrbek	.20	.15	.08
38	Steve Garvey	.20	.15	.08
39	Carney Lansford	.09	.07	.04
40	Dale Murphy	.30	.25	.12
41	Greg Luzinski	.12	.09	.05
42	Larry Parrish	.09	.07	.04
43	Ryne Sandberg	.60	.45	.25
44	Dickie Thon	.09	.07	.04
45	Bert Blyleven	.12	.09	.05
46	Ron Oester	.09	.07	.04
47	Dusty Baker	.09	.07	.04
48	Steve Rogers	.09	.07	.04
49	Jim Clancy	.09	.07	.04
50	Eddie Murray	.15	.11	.06
51	Ron Guidry	.15	.11	.06
52	Jim Rice	.15	.11	.06
53	Tom Seaver	.30	.25	.12
54	Pete Rose	.30	.25	.12
55	George Brett	.40	.30	.15
56	Dan Quisenberry	.09	.07	.04
57	Mike Schmidt	.60	.45	.25
58	Ted Simmons	.12	.09	.05
59	Dave Righetti	.15	.11	.06
60	Checklist	.09	.07	.04

1984 Donruss Champions

The 60-card Donruss Champions set includes ten Hall of Famers, forty-nine current players and one numbered checklist. The ten Hall of Famers' cards (called Grand Champions) feature the artwork of Dick Perez, while cards of the current players (called Champions) are color photos. The cards measure 3-1/2" by 5". The Grand Champions represent hallmarks of excellence in various statistical categories, while the Champions are the leaders among active players in each category. The ten Grand Champion cards are #'s 1, 8, 14, 20, 26, 31, 37, 43, 50 and 55. The cards were issued with Duke Snider puzzle pieces.

		MT	NR MT	EX
Complete Set:		7.00	5.25	275.00
Common Player:		.07	.05	.03
1	Babe Ruth	1.00	.70	.40
2	George Foster	.10	.08	.04
3	Dave Kingman	.10	.08	.04
4	Jim Rice	.10	.08	.04
5	Gorman Thomas	.10	.08	.04
6	Ben Oglivie	.07	.05	.03
7	Jeff Burroughs	.07	.05	.03
8	Hank Aaron	.35	.25	.14
9	Reggie Jackson	.30	.25	.12
10	Carl Yastrzemski	.50	.40	.20
11	Mike Schmidt	.50	.40	.20
12	Graig Nettles	.14	.11	.06
13	Greg Luzinski	.10	.08	.04
14	Ted Williams	1.00	.70	.40
15	George Brett	.35	.25	.14
16	Wade Boggs	.50	.40	.20
17	Hal McRae	.10	.08	.04
18	Bill Buckner	.10	.08	.04
19	Eddie Murray	.10	.08	.04
20	Rogers Hornsby	.14	.11	.06
21	Rod Carew	.20	.15	.08
22	Bill Madlock	.10	.08	.04
23	Lonnie Smith	.07	.05	.03
24	Cecil Cooper	.10	.08	.04
25	Ken Griffey	.10	.08	.04
26	Ty Cobb	.40	.30	.15
27	Pete Rose	.40	.30	.15
28	Rusty Staub	.10	.08	.04
29	Tony Perez	.10	.08	.04
30	Al Oliver	.10	.08	.04
31	Cy Young	.14	.11	.06
32	Gaylord Perry	.14	.11	.06
33	Ferguson Jenkins	.10	.08	.04
34	Phil Niekro	.14	.11	.06
35	Jim Palmer	.30	.25	.12
36	Tommy John	.10	.08	.04
37	Walter Johnson	.20	.15	.08
38	Steve Carlton	.25	.20	.10
39	Nolan Ryan	.50	.40	.20
40	Tom Seaver	.25	.20	.10
41	Don Sutton	.14	.11	.06
42	Bert Blyleven	.10	.08	.04
43	Frank Robinson	.35	.25	.14
44	Joe Morgan	.25	.20	.10
45	Rollie Fingers	.14	.11	.06
46	Keith Hernandez	.10	.08	.04
47	Robin Yount	.50	.40	.20
48	Cal Ripken	.25	.20	.10
49	Dale Murphy	.35	.25	.14
50	Mickey Mantle	1.00	.70	.40
51	Johnny Bench	.50	.40	.20
52	Carlton Fisk	.30	.25	.12
53	Tug McGraw	.10	.08	.04
54	Paul Molitor	.10	.08	.04
55	Carl Hubbell	.14	.11	.06
56	Steve Garvey	.15	.11	.06
57	Dave Parker	.14	.11	.06
58	Gary Carter	.15	.11	.06
59	Fred Lynn	.14	.11	.06
60	Checklist	.10	.08	.04

1985 Donruss

The black-bordered 1985 Donruss set includes 653 numbered cards and seven unnumbered checklists. Displaying the artwork of Dick Perez for the fourth consecutive year, card #'s 1-26 feature the Diamond Kings series. Donruss, realizing the hobby craze over rookie cards, included a Rated Rookies subset (card

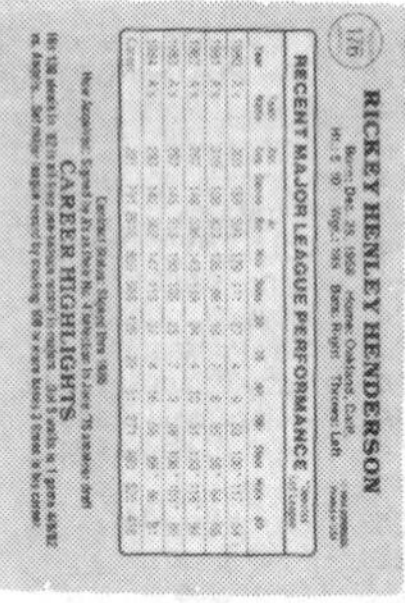

#'s 27-46). The cards, which are the standard size of 2-1/2" by 3-1/2", were issued with a Lou Gehrig puzzle. The backs of the cards have black print on yellow and white. The complete set price does not include the higher priced variations. (DK) and (RR) refer to the Diamond Kings and Rated Rookies subsets.

		MT	NR MT	EX
Complete Set (660):		200.00	150.00	80.00
Common Player:		.08	.06	.03
1	Ryne Sandberg (DK)	4.00	3.00	1.50
2	Doug DeCinces (DK)	.10	.08	.04
3	Rich Dotson (DK)	.12	.09	.05
4	Bert Blyleven (DK)	.15	.11	.06
5	Lou Whitaker (DK)	.30	.25	.12
6	Dan Quisenberry (DK)	.15	.11	.06
7	Don Mattingly (DK)	3.50	2.75	1.50
8	Carney Lansford (DK)	.10	.08	.04
9	Frank Tanana (DK)	.12	.09	.05
10	Willie Upshaw (DK)	.10	.08	.04
11	Claudell Washington (DK)	.10	.08	.04
12	Mike Marshall (DK)	.20	.15	.08
13	Joaquin Andujar (DK)	.10	.08	.04
14	Cal Ripken, Jr. (DK)	4.00	3.00	1.50
15	Jim Rice (DK)	.50	.40	.20
16	Don Sutton (DK)	.30	.25	.12
17	Frank Viola (DK)	.15	.11	.06
18	Alvin Davis (DK)(FC)	.10	.08	.04
19	Mario Soto (DK)	.10	.08	.04
20	Jose Cruz (DK)	.12	.09	.05
21	Charlie Lea (DK)	.10	.08	.04
22	Jesse Orosco (DK)	.10	.08	.04
23	Juan Samuel (DK)(FC)	.25	.20	.10
24	Tony Pena (DK)	.12	.09	.05
25	Tony Gwynn (DK)	1.75	1.25	.70
26	Bob Brenly (DK)	.10	.08	.04
27	*Danny Tartabull* (RR)	10.00	7.50	4.00
28	*Mike Bielecki* (RR)(FC)	.15	.11	.06
29	*Steve Lyons* (RR)(FC)	.20	.15	.08
30	*Jeff Reed* (RR)(FC)	.15	.11	.06
31	Tony Brewer (RR)	.08	.06	.03
32	*John Morris* (RR)(FC)	.08	.06	.03
33	*Daryl Boston* (RR)(FC)	.25	.20	.10
34	Alfonso Pulido (RR)	.08	.06	.03
35	*Steve Kiefer* (RR)(FC)	.08	.06	.03
36	*Larry Sheets* (RR)(FC)	.08	.06	.03
37	*Scott Bradley* (RR)(FC)	.08	.06	.03
38	*Calvin Schiraldi* (RR)(FC)	.08	.06	.03
39	*Shawon Dunston* (RR)	1.00	.70	.40
40	Charlie Mitchell (RR)	.08	.06	.03
41	*Billy Hatcher* (RR)	.60	.45	.25
42	Russ Stephans (RR)	.08	.06	.03
43	Alejandro Sanchez (RR)	.08	.06	.03
44	*Steve Jeltz* (RR)(FC)	.08	.06	.03
45	*Jim Traber* (RR)(FC)	.08	.06	.03
46	Doug Loman (RR)	.08	.06	.03
47	Eddie Murray	1.50	1.25	.60
48	Robin Yount	4.00	3.00	1.50
49	Lance Parrish	.30	.25	.12
50	Jim Rice	.50	.40	.20
51	Dave Winfield	4.00	3.00	1.50
52	Fernando Valenzuela	.35	.25	.14
53	George Brett	4.00	3.00	1.50
54	Dave Kingman	.15	.11	.06
55	Gary Carter	.40	.30	.15
56	Buddy Bell	.12	.09	.05
57	Reggie Jackson	.60	.45	.25
58	Harold Baines	.20	.15	.08
59	Ozzie Smith	1.50	1.25	.60
60	Nolan Ryan	10.00	7.50	4.00
61	Mike Schmidt	4.00	3.00	1.50
62	Dave Parker	.35	.25	.14
63	Tony Gwynn	5.00	3.75	2.00
64	Tony Pena	.12	.09	.05
65	Jack Clark	.25	.20	.10
66	Dale Murphy	.80	.60	.30
67	Ryne Sandberg	10.00	7.50	4.00
68	Keith Hernandez	.40	.30	.15
69	*Alvin Davis*(FC)	.50	.40	.20
70	Kent Hrbek	.30	.25	.12
71	Willie Upshaw	.10	.08	.04
72	Dave Engle	.08	.06	.03
73	Alfredo Griffin	.10	.08	.04
74a	Jack Perconte (last line of highlights begins "Batted .346...")	.10	.08	.04
74b	Jack Perconte (last line of highlights begins "Led the...")	1.25	.90	.50
75	Jesse Orosco	.10	.08	.04
76	Jody Davis	.12	.09	.05
77	Bob Horner	.12	.09	.05
78	Larry McWilliams	.08	.06	.03
79	Joel Youngblood	.08	.06	.03
80	Alan Wiggins	.08	.06	.03
81	Ron Oester	.08	.06	.03
82	Ozzie Virgil	.08	.06	.03
83	*Ricky Horton*(FC)	.10	.08	.04
84	Bill Doran	.12	.09	.05
85	Rod Carew	1.00	.70	.40
86	LaMarr Hoyt	.08	.06	.03
87	Tim Wallach	.15	.11	.06
88	Mike Flanagan	.12	.09	.05
89	Jim Sundberg	.10	.08	.04
90	Chet Lemon	.10	.08	.04
91	Bob Stanley	.08	.06	.03
92	Willie Randolph	.12	.09	.05
93	Bill Russell	.10	.08	.04
94	Julio Franco	1.50	1.25	.60
95	Dan Quisenberry	.12	.09	.05
96	Bill Caudill	.08	.06	.03
97	Bill Gullickson	.08	.06	.03
98	Danny Darwin	.08	.06	.03
99	Curtis Wilkerson	.08	.06	.03
100	Bud Black	.08	.06	.03
101	Tony Phillips	.40	.30	.15
102	Tony Bernazard	.08	.06	.03
103	Jay Howell	.10	.08	.04
104	Burt Hooton	.10	.08	.04
105	Milt Wilcox	.08	.06	.03
106	Rich Dauer	.08	.06	.03
107	Don Sutton	.35	.25	.14
108	Mike Witt	.15	.11	.06
109	Bruce Sutter	.15	.11	.06
110	Enos Cabell	.08	.06	.03
111	John Denny	.08	.06	.03
112	Dave Dravecky	.10	.08	.04
113	Marvell Wynne	.08	.06	.03
114	Johnnie LeMaster	.08	.06	.03
115	Chuck Porter	.08	.06	.03
116	John Gibbons	.08	.06	.03
117	Keith Moreland	.10	.08	.04
118	Darnell Coles	.12	.09	.05
119	Dennis Lamp	.08	.06	.03
120	Ron Davis	.08	.06	.03
121	Nick Esasky	.10	.08	.04
122	Vance Law	.10	.08	.04
123	Gary Roenicke	.08	.06	.03
124	Bill Schroeder	.08	.06	.03
125	Dave Rozema	.08	.06	.03
126	Bobby Meacham	.08	.06	.03
127	Marty Barrett(FC)	.25	.20	.10
128	*R.J. Reynolds*(FC)	.30	.25	.12
129	Ernie Camacho	.08	.06	.03
130	Jorge Orta	.08	.06	.03
131	Lary Sorensen	.08	.06	.03
132	Terry Francona	.08	.06	.03
133	Fred Lynn	.25	.20	.10
134	Bobby Jones	.08	.06	.03
135	Jerry Hairston	.08	.06	.03
136	Kevin Bass	.12	.09	.05
137	Garry Maddox	.08	.06	.03
138	Dave LaPoint	.10	.08	.04
139	Kevin McReynolds	.25	.20	.10
140	Wayne Krenchicki	.08	.06	.03
141	Rafael Ramirez	.08	.06	.03
142	Rod Scurry	.08	.06	.03
143	Greg Minton	.08	.06	.03
144	Tim Stoddard	.08	.06	.03
145	Steve Henderson	.08	.06	.03
146	George Bell	.70	.50	.30
147	Dave Meier	.08	.06	.03

		MT	NR MT	EX
148	Sammy Stewart	.08	.06	.03
149	Mark Brouhard	.08	.06	.03
150	Larry Herndon	.10	.08	.04
151	Oil Can Boyd	.10	.08	.04
152	Brian Dayett	.08	.06	.03
153	Tom Niedenfuer	.10	.08	.04
154	Brook Jacoby	.15	.11	.06
155	Onix Concepcion	.08	.06	.03
156	Tim Conroy	.08	.06	.03
157	*Joe Hesketh*(FC)	.15	.11	.06
158	Brian Downing	.12	.09	.05
159	Tommy Dunbar	.08	.06	.03
160	Marc Hill	.08	.06	.03
161	Phil Garner	.10	.08	.04
162	Jerry Davis	.08	.06	.03
163	Bill Campbell	.08	.06	.03
164	*John Franco*(FC)	1.00	.70	.40
165	Len Barker	.10	.08	.04
166	*Benny Distefano*(FC)	.10	.08	.04
167	George Frazier	.08	.06	.03
168	Tito Landrum	.08	.06	.03
169	Cal Ripken, Jr.	10.00	7.50	4.00
170	Cecil Cooper	.15	.11	.06
171	Alan Trammell	.40	.30	.15
172	Wade Boggs	5.00	3.75	2.00
173	Don Baylor	.15	.11	.06
174	Pedro Guerrero	.30	.25	.12
175	Frank White	.12	.09	.05
176	Rickey Henderson	4.00	3.00	1.50
177	Charlie Lea	.08	.06	.03
178	Pete O'Brien	.20	.15	.08
179	Doug DeCinces	.12	.09	.05
180	Ron Kittle	.12	.09	.05
181	George Hendrick	.10	.08	.04
182	Joe Niekro	.12	.09	.05
183	Juan Samuel(FC)	.60	.45	.25
184	Mario Soto	.10	.08	.04
185	Goose Gossage	.25	.20	.10
186	Johnny Ray	.15	.11	.06
187	Bob Brenly	.08	.06	.03
188	Craig McMurtry	.08	.06	.03
189	Leon Durham	.10	.08	.04
190	*Dwight Gooden*(FC)	8.00	6.00	3.25
191	Barry Bonnell	.08	.06	.03
192	Tim Teufel	.12	.09	.05
193	Dave Stieb	.15	.11	.06
194	Mickey Hatcher	.08	.06	.03
195	Jesse Barfield	.25	.20	.10
196	Al Cowens	.08	.06	.03
197	Hubie Brooks	.12	.09	.05
198	Steve Trout	.08	.06	.03
199	Glenn Hubbard	.08	.06	.03
200	Bill Madlock	.15	.11	.06
201	*Jeff Robinson*(FC)	.10	.08	.04
202	Eric Show	.10	.08	.04
203	Dave Concepcion	.15	.11	.06
204	Ivan DeJesus	.08	.06	.03
205	Neil Allen	.08	.06	.03
206	Jerry Mumphrey	.08	.06	.03
207	Mike Brown	.08	.06	.03
208	Carlton Fisk	.40	.30	.15
209	Bryn Smith	.08	.06	.03
210	Tippy Martinez	.08	.06	.03
211	Dion James	.10	.08	.04
212	Willie Hernandez	.10	.08	.04
213	Mike Easler	.10	.08	.04
214	Ron Guidry	.10	.08	.04
215	Rick Honeycutt	.08	.06	.03
216	Brett Butler	.12	.09	.05
217	Larry Gura	.08	.06	.03
218	Ray Burris	.08	.06	.03
219	Steve Rogers	.10	.08	.04
220	Frank Tanana	.12	.09	.05
221	Ned Yost	.08	.06	.03
222	*Bret Saberhagen*	3.00	2.25	1.25
223	Mike Davis	.10	.08	.04
224	Bert Blyleven	.15	.11	.06
225	Steve Kemp	.10	.08	.04
226	Jerry Reuss	.10	.08	.04
227	Darrell Evans	.15	.11	.06
228	Wayne Gross	.08	.06	.03
229	Jim Gantner	.10	.08	.04
230	Bob Boone	.10	.08	.04
231	Lonnie Smith	.10	.08	.04
232	Frank DiPino	.08	.06	.03
233	Jerry Koosman	.12	.09	.05
234	Graig Nettles	.20	.15	.08
235	John Tudor	.12	.09	.05
236	John Rabb	.08	.06	.03
237	Rick Manning	.08	.06	.03
238	Mike Fitzgerald	.08	.06	.03

		MT	NR MT	EX
239	Gary Matthews	.12	.09	.05
240	*Jim Presley*(FC)	.20	.15	.08
241	Dave Collins	.10	.08	.04
242	Gary Gaetti	.30	.25	.12
243	Dann Bilardello	.08	.06	.03
244	Rudy Law	.08	.06	.03
245	John Lowenstein	.08	.06	.03
246	Tom Tellmann	.08	.06	.03
247	Howard Johnson	.50	.40	.20
248	Ray Fontenot	.08	.06	.03
249	Tony Armas	.12	.09	.05
250	Candy Maldonado	.12	.09	.05
251	*Mike Jeffcoat*(FC)	.10	.08	.04
252	Dane Iorg	.08	.06	.03
253	Bruce Bochte	.08	.06	.03
254	Pete Rose	1.75	1.25	.70
255	Don Aase	.08	.06	.03
256	George Wright	.08	.06	.03
257	Britt Burns	.08	.06	.03
258	Mike Scott	.20	.15	.08
259	Len Matuszek	.08	.06	.03
260	Dave Rucker	.08	.06	.03
261	Craig Lefferts	.10	.08	.04
262	*Jay Tibbs*(FC)	.20	.15	.08
263	Bruce Benedict	.08	.06	.03
264	Don Robinson	.10	.08	.04
265	Gary Lavelle	.08	.06	.03
266	Scott Sanderson	.08	.06	.03
267	Matt Young	.08	.06	.03
268	Ernie Whitt	.10	.08	.04
269	Houston Jimenez	.08	.06	.03
270	*Ken Dixon*(FC)	.12	.09	.05
271	Peter Ladd	.08	.06	.03
272	Juan Berenguer	.08	.06	.03
273	*Roger Clemens*(FC)	50.00	37.00	20.00
274	Rick Cerone	.08	.06	.03
275	Dave Anderson	.08	.06	.03
276	George Vukovich	.08	.06	.03
277	Greg Pryor	.08	.06	.03
278	Mike Warren	.08	.06	.03
279	Bob James	.08	.06	.03
280	Bobby Grich	.12	.09	.05
281	*Mike Mason*(FC)	.12	.09	.05
282	Ron Reed	.08	.06	.03
283	Alan Ashby	.08	.06	.03
284	Mark Thurmond	.08	.06	.03
285	Joe Lefebvre	.08	.06	.03
286	Ted Power	.08	.06	.03
287	Chris Chambliss	.10	.08	.04
288	Lee Tunnell	.08	.06	.03
289	Rich Bordi	.08	.06	.03
290	Glenn Brummer	.08	.06	.03
291	Mike Boddicker	.12	.09	.05
292	Rollie Fingers	.25	.20	.10
293	Lou Whitaker	.40	.30	.15
294	Dwight Evans	.15	.11	.06
295	Don Mattingly	6.00	4.50	2.50
296	Mike Marshall	.15	.11	.06
297	Willie Wilson	.15	.11	.06
298	Mike Heath	.08	.06	.03
299	Tim Raines	.50	.40	.20
300	Larry Parrish	.12	.09	.05
301	Geoff Zahn	.08	.06	.03
302	Rich Dotson	.12	.09	.05
303	David Green	.08	.06	.03
304	Jose Cruz	.12	.09	.05
305	Steve Carlton	.80	.60	.30
306	Gary Redus	.10	.08	.04
307	Steve Garvey	.50	.40	.20
308	Jose DeLeon	.10	.08	.04
309	Randy Lerch	.08	.06	.03
310	Claudell Washington	.10	.08	.04
311	Lee Smith	1.00	.70	.40
312	Darryl Strawberry	2.50	2.00	1.00
313	Jim Beattie	.08	.06	.03
314	John Butcher	.08	.06	.03
315	Damaso Garcia	.10	.08	.04
316	Mike Smithson	.08	.06	.03
317	Luis Leal	.08	.06	.03
318	Ken Phelps(FC)	.25	.20	.10
319	Wally Backman	.10	.08	.04
320	Ron Cey	.12	.09	.05
321	Brad Komminsk	.08	.06	.03
322	Jason Thompson	.08	.06	.03
323	*Frank Williams*(FC)	.20	.15	.08
324	Tim Lollar	.08	.06	.03
325	*Eric Davis*(FC)	7.00	5.25	2.75
326	Von Hayes	.12	.09	.05
327	Andy Van Slyke	1.00	.70	.40
328	Craig Reynolds	.08	.06	.03
329	Dick Schofield	.10	.08	.04

		MT	NR MT	EX
330	Scott Fletcher	.10	.08	.04
331	Jeff Reardon	.15	.11	.06
332	Rick Dempsey	.10	.08	.04
333	Ben Oglivie	.10	.08	.04
334	Dan Petry	.10	.08	.04
335	Jackie Gutierrez	.08	.06	.03
336	Dave Righetti	.10	.08	.04
337	Alejandro Pena	.10	.08	.04
338	Mel Hall	.10	.08	.04
339	Pat Sheridan	.08	.06	.03
340	Keith Atherton	.08	.06	.03
341	David Palmer	.08	.06	.03
342	Gary Ward	.10	.08	.04
343	Dave Stewart	.15	.11	.06
344	*Mark Gubicza*(FC)	.50	.40	.20
345	Carney Lansford	.12	.09	.05
346	Jerry Willard	.08	.06	.03
347	Ken Griffey	.12	.09	.05
348	*Franklin Stubbs*(FC)	.20	.15	.08
349	Aurelio Lopez	.08	.06	.03
350	Al Bumbry	.10	.08	.04
351	Charlie Moore	.08	.06	.03
352	Luis Sanchez	.08	.06	.03
353	Darrell Porter	.10	.08	.04
354	Bill Dawley	.08	.06	.03
355	Charlie Hudson	.10	.08	.04
356	Garry Templeton	.10	.08	.04
357	Cecilio Guante	.08	.06	.03
358	Jeff Leonard	.12	.09	.05
359	Paul Molitor	3.00	2.25	1.25
360	Ron Gardenhire	.08	.06	.03
361	Larry Bowa	.12	.09	.05
362	Bob Kearney	.08	.06	.03
363	Garth Iorg	.08	.06	.03
364	Tom Brunansky	.15	.11	.06
365	Brad Gulden	.08	.06	.03
366	Greg Walker	.12	.09	.05
367	Mike Young	.10	.08	.04
368	Rick Waits	.08	.06	.03
369	Doug Bair	.08	.06	.03
370	Bob Shirley	.08	.06	.03
371	Bob Ojeda	.12	.09	.05
372	Bob Welch	.15	.11	.06
373	Neal Heaton	.08	.06	.03
374	Danny Jackson (photo actually Steve Farr)	.80	.60	.30
375	Donnie Hill	.08	.06	.03
376	Mike Stenhouse	.08	.06	.03
377	Bruce Kison	.08	.06	.03
378	Wayne Tolleson	.08	.06	.03
379	Floyd Bannister	.12	.09	.05
380	Vern Ruhle	.08	.06	.03
381	Tim Corcoran	.08	.06	.03
382	Kurt Kepshire	.08	.06	.03
383	Bobby Brown	.08	.06	.03
384	Dave Van Gorder	.08	.06	.03
385	Rick Mahler	.08	.06	.03
386	Lee Mazzilli	.10	.08	.04
387	Bill Laskey	.08	.06	.03
388	Thad Bosley	.08	.06	.03
389	Al Chambers	.08	.06	.03
390	Tony Fernandez	.70	.50	.30
391	Ron Washington	.08	.06	.03
392	Bill Swaggerty	.08	.06	.03
393	Bob L. Gibson	.08	.06	.03
394	Marty Castillo	.08	.06	.03
395	Steve Crawford	.08	.06	.03
396	Clay Christiansen	.08	.06	.03
397	Bob Bailor	.08	.06	.03
398	Mike Hargrove	.08	.06	.03
399	Charlie Leibrandt	.10	.08	.04
400	Tom Burgmeier	.08	.06	.03
401	Razor Shines	.08	.06	.03
402	Rob Wilfong	.08	.06	.03
403	Tom Henke	.12	.09	.05
404	Al Jones	.08	.06	.03
405	Mike LaCoss	.08	.06	.03
406	Luis DeLeon	.08	.06	.03
407	Greg Gross	.08	.06	.03
408	Tom Hume	.08	.06	.03
409	Rick Camp	.08	.06	.03
410	Milt May	.08	.06	.03
411	*Henry Cotto*(FC)	.20	.15	.08
412	Dave Von Ohlen	.08	.06	.03
413	Scott McGregor	.10	.08	.04
414	Ted Simmons	.15	.11	.06
415	Jack Morris	.30	.25	.12
416	Bill Buckner	.15	.11	.06
417	Butch Wynegar	.08	.06	.03
418	Steve Sax	.25	.20	.10
419	Steve Balboni	.10	.08	.04

		MT	NR MT	EX
420	Dwayne Murphy	.10	.08	.04
421	Andre Dawson	1.75	1.25	.70
422	Charlie Hough	.10	.08	.04
423	Tommy John	.25	.20	.10
424a	Tom Seaver (Floyd Bannister photo ERR)	3.00	2.25	1.25
424b	Tom Seaver (COR)	30.00	22.00	12.00
425	Tom Herr	.12	.09	.05
426	Terry Puhl	.08	.06	.03
427	Al Holland	.08	.06	.03
428	Eddie Milner	.08	.06	.03
429	Terry Kennedy	.10	.08	.04
430	John Candelaria	.12	.09	.05
431	Manny Trillo	.10	.08	.04
432	Ken Oberkfell	.08	.06	.03
433	Rick Sutcliffe	.15	.11	.06
434	Ron Darling	.40	.30	.15
435	Spike Owen	.10	.08	.04
436	Frank Viola	.25	.20	.10
437	Lloyd Moseby	.12	.09	.05
438	*Kirby Puckett*(FC)	55.00	41.00	22.00
439	Jim Clancy	.10	.08	.04
440	Mike Moore	.08	.06	.03
441	Doug Sisk	.08	.06	.03
442	Dennis Eckersley	1.50	1.25	.60
443	Gerald Perry	.25	.20	.10
444	Dale Berra	.08	.06	.03
445	Dusty Baker	.10	.08	.04
446	Ed Whitson	.08	.06	.03
447	Cesar Cedeno	.12	.09	.05
448	*Rick Schu*(FC)	.20	.15	.08
449	Joaquin Andujar	.10	.08	.04
450	*Mark Bailey*(FC)	.12	.09	.05
451	*Ron Romanick*(FC)	.12	.09	.05
452	Julio Cruz	.08	.06	.03
453	Miguel Dilone	.08	.06	.03
454	Storm Davis	.12	.09	.05
455	Jaime Cocanower	.08	.06	.03
456	Barbaro Garbey	.12	.09	.05
457	Rich Gedman	.12	.09	.05
458	Phil Niekro	.30	.25	.12
459	Mike Scioscia	.10	.08	.04
460	Pat Tabler	.10	.08	.04
461	Darryl Motley	.08	.06	.03
462	Chris Codoroli (Codiroli)	.08	.06	.03
463	Doug Flynn	.08	.06	.03
464	Billy Sample	.08	.06	.03
465	Mickey Rivers	.10	.08	.04
466	John Wathan	.10	.08	.04
467	Bill Krueger	.08	.06	.03
468	Andre Thornton	.12	.09	.05
469	Rex Hudler	.12	.09	.05
470	*Sid Bream*(FC)	.80	.60	.30
471	Kirk Gibson	.40	.30	.15
472	John Shelby	.10	.08	.04
473	Moose Haas	.08	.06	.03
474	Doug Corbett	.08	.06	.03
475	Willie McGee	.35	.25	.14
476	Bob Knepper	.10	.08	.04
477	Kevin Gross	.12	.09	.05
478	Carmelo Martinez	.10	.08	.04
479	Kent Tekulve	.10	.08	.04
480	Chili Davis	.12	.09	.05
481	Bobby Clark	.08	.06	.03
482	Mookie Wilson	.12	.09	.05
483	Dave Owen	.08	.06	.03
484	Ed Nunez	.08	.06	.03
485	Rance Mulliniks	.08	.06	.03
486	Ken Schrom	.08	.06	.03
487	Jeff Russell	.08	.06	.03
488	Tom Paciorek	.08	.06	.03
489	Dan Ford	.08	.06	.03
490	Mike Caldwell	.08	.06	.03
491	Scottie Earl	.08	.06	.03
492	*Jose Rijo*(FC)	2.00	1.50	.80
493	Bruce Hurst	.15	.11	.06
494	Ken Landreaux	.08	.06	.03
495	Mike Fischlin	.08	.06	.03
496	Don Slaught	.08	.06	.03
497	Steve McCatty	.08	.06	.03
498	Gary Lucas	.08	.06	.03
499	Gary Pettis	.10	.08	.04
500	Marvis Foley	.08	.06	.03
501	Mike Squires	.08	.06	.03
502	*Jim Pankovitz*(FC)	.15	.11	.06
503	Luis Aguayo	.08	.06	.03
504	Ralph Citarella	.08	.06	.03
505	Bruce Bochy	.08	.06	.03
506	Bob Owchinko	.08	.06	.03
507	Pascual Perez	.10	.08	.04
508	Lee Lacy	.08	.06	.03

		MT	NR MT	EX
509	Atlee Hammaker	.08	.06	.03
510	Bob Dernier	.08	.06	.03
511	Ed Vande Berg	.08	.06	.03
512	Cliff Johnson	.08	.06	.03
513	Len Whitehouse	.08	.06	.03
514	Dennis Martinez	.10	.08	.04
515	Ed Romero	.08	.06	.03
516	Rusty Kuntz	.08	.06	.03
517	Rick Miller	.08	.06	.03
518	Dennis Rasmussen	.15	.11	.06
519	Steve Yeager	.08	.06	.03
520	Chris Bando	.08	.06	.03
521	U.L. Washington	.08	.06	.03
522	*Curt Young*(FC)	.15	.11	.06
523	Angel Salazar	.08	.06	.03
524	Curt Kaufman	.08	.06	.03
525	Odell Jones	.08	.06	.03
526	Juan Agosto	.08	.06	.03
527	Denny Walling	.08	.06	.03
528	Andy Hawkins(FC)	.20	.15	.08
529	Sixto Lezcano	.08	.06	.03
530	Skeeter Barnes	.08	.06	.03
531	Randy Johnson S.	.08	.06	.03
532	Jim Morrison	.08	.06	.03
533	Warren Brusstar	.08	.06	.03
534a	*Jeff Pendleton* (ERR)	8.00	6.00	3.25
534b	*Terry Pendleton* (COR)	20.00	15.00	8.00
535	Vic Rodriguez	.08	.06	.03
536	Bob McClure	.08	.06	.03
537	Dave Bergman	.08	.06	.03
538	Mark Clear	.08	.06	.03
539	*Mike Pagliarulo*(FC)	1.00	.70	.40
540	Terry Whitfield	.08	.06	.03
541	Joe Beckwith	.08	.06	.03
542	Jeff Burroughs	.10	.08	.04
543	Dan Schatzeder	.08	.06	.03
544	Donnie Scott	.08	.06	.03
545	Jim Slaton	.08	.06	.03
546	Greg Luzinski	.12	.09	.05
547	*Mark Salas*(FC)	.15	.11	.06
548	Dave Smith	.10	.08	.04
549	John Wockenfuss	.08	.06	.03
550	Frank Pastore	.08	.06	.03
551	Tim Flannery	.08	.06	.03
552	Rick Rhoden	.12	.09	.05
553	Mark Davis	.08	.06	.03
554	*Jeff Dedmon*(FC)	.15	.11	.06
555	Gary Woods	.08	.06	.03
556	Danny Heep	.08	.06	.03
557	*Mark Langston*(FC)	5.00	3.75	2.00
558	Darrell Brown	.08	.06	.03
559	*Jimmy Key*(FC)	4.00	3.00	1.50
560	Rick Lysander	.08	.06	.03
561	Doyle Alexander	.12	.09	.05
562	Mike Stanton	.08	.06	.03
563	Sid Fernandez	.50	.40	.20
564	Richie Hebner	.08	.06	.03
565	Alex Trevino	.08	.06	.03
566	Brian Harper	.08	.06	.03
567	*Dan Gladden*(FC)	.60	.45	.25
568	Luis Salazar	.08	.06	.03
569	Tom Foley	.08	.06	.03
570	Larry Andersen	.08	.06	.03
571	Danny Cox	.12	.09	.05
572	Joe Sambito	.08	.06	.03
573	Juan Beniquez	.08	.06	.03
574	Joel Skinner	.08	.06	.03
575	*Randy St. Claire*(FC)	.15	.11	.06
576	Floyd Rayford	.08	.06	.03
577	Roy Howell	.08	.06	.03
578	John Grubb	.08	.06	.03
579	Ed Jurak	.08	.06	.03
580	John Montefusco	.08	.06	.03
581	*Orel Hershiser*(FC)	3.00	2.25	1.25
582	*Tom Waddell*(FC)	.08	.06	.03
583	Mark Huismann	.08	.06	.03
584	Joe Morgan	.30	.25	.12
585	Jim Wohlford	.08	.06	.03
586	Dave Schmidt	.08	.06	.03
587	*Jeff Kunkel*(FC)	.12	.09	.05
588	Hal McRae	.12	.09	.05
589	Bill Almon	.08	.06	.03
590	Carmen Castillo(FC)	.10	.08	.04
591	Omar Moreno	.08	.06	.03
592	*Ken Howell*(FC)	.20	.15	.08
593	Tom Brookens	.08	.06	.03
594	Joe Nolan	.08	.06	.03
595	Willie Lozado	.08	.06	.03
596	*Tom Nieto*(FC)	.12	.09	.05
597	Walt Terrell	.10	.08	.04
598	Al Oliver	.15	.11	.06

		MT	NR MT	EX
599	Shane Rawley	.12	.09	.05
600	*Denny Gonzalez*(FC)	.10	.08	.04
601	*Mark Grant*(FC)	.15	.11	.06
602	Mike Armstrong	.08	.06	.03
603	George Foster	.15	.11	.06
604	Davey Lopes	.10	.08	.04
605	Salome Barojas	.08	.06	.03
606	Roy Lee Jackson	.08	.06	.03
607	Pete Filson	.08	.06	.03
608	Duane Walker	.08	.06	.03
609	Glenn Wilson	.10	.08	.04
610	*Rafael Santana*(FC)	.20	.15	.08
611	Roy Smith	.08	.06	.03
612	Ruppert Jones	.08	.06	.03
613	Joe Cowley(FC)	.08	.06	.03
614	*Al Nipper* (photo actually Mike Brown)(FC)	.20	.15	.08
615	Gene Nelson	.08	.06	.03
616	Joe Carter	13.00	9.75	5.25
617	Ray Knight	.12	.09	.05
618	Chuck Rainey	.08	.06	.03
619	Dan Driessen	.10	.08	.04
620	Daryl Sconiers	.08	.06	.03
621	Bill Stein	.08	.06	.03
622	Roy Smalley	.08	.06	.03
623	Ed Lynch	.08	.06	.03
624	*Jeff Stone*(FC)	.15	.11	.06
625	Bruce Berenyi	.08	.06	.03
626	Kelvin Chapman	.08	.06	.03
627	Joe Price	.08	.06	.03
628	Steve Bedrosian	.12	.09	.05
629	Vic Mata	.08	.06	.03
630	Mike Krukow	.10	.08	.04
631	*Phil Bradley*(FC)	.20	.15	.08
632	Jim Gott	.08	.06	.03
633	Randy Bush	.08	.06	.03
634	*Tom Browning*(FC)	.60	.45	.25
635	Lou Gehrig Puzzle Card	.08	.06	.03
636	Reid Nichols	.08	.06	.03
637	*Dan Pasqua*(FC)	.60	.45	.25
638	German Rivera	.08	.06	.03
639	*Don Schulze*(FC)	.10	.08	.04
640a	Mike Jones (last line of highlights begins "Was 11-7...")	.10	.08	.04
640b	Mike Jones (last line of highlights begins "Spent some ...")	1.25	.90	.50
641	Pete Rose	2.00	1.50	.80
642	*Wade Rowdon*(FC)	.10	.08	.04
643	Jerry Narron	.08	.06	.03
644	*Darrell Miller*(FC)	.15	.11	.06
645	*Tim Hulett*(FC)	.15	.11	.06
646	Andy McGaffigan	.08	.06	.03
647	Kurt Bevacqua	.08	.06	.03
648	*John Russell*(FC)	.20	.15	.08
649	*Ron Robinson*(FC)	.25	.20	.10
650	Donnie Moore(FC)	.08	.06	.03
651a	Two for the Title (Don Mattingly, Dave Winfield) (Mattingly Yellow Letters)	3.00	2.25	1.25
651b	Two for the Title (Don Mattingly, Dave Winfield) (Mattingly White Letters)	6.00	4.50	2.50
652	Tim Laudner	.08	.06	.03
653	*Steve Farr*(FC)	.40	.30	.15
—	Checklist 1-26 DK	.08	.06	.03
—	Checklist 27-130	.08	.06	.03
—	Checklist 131-234	.08	.06	.03
—	Checklist 235-338	.08	.06	.03
—	Checklist 339-442	.08	.06	.03
—	Checklist 443-546	.08	.06	.03
—	Checklist 547-653	.08	.06	.03

1985 Donruss Action All-Stars

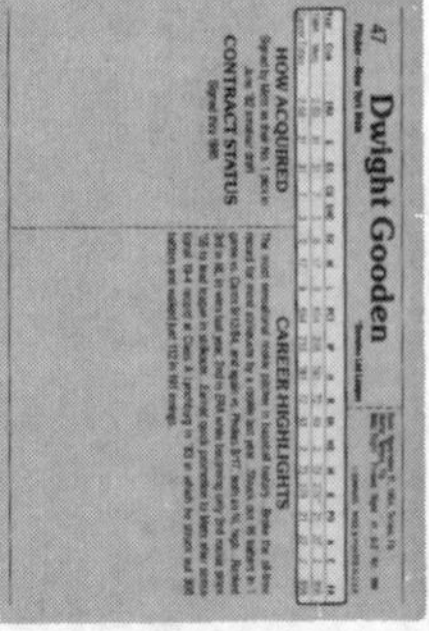

In 1985, Donruss issued an Action All-Stars set for the third consecutive year. The card fronts feature an action photo with an inset head-shot of the player inside a black border with grey boxes through it. The card backs have black print on blue and white and include statistical and biographical information. The cards were issued with a Lou Gehrig puzzle.

		MT	NR MT	EX
Complete Set:		8.00	6.00	3.25
Common Player:		.09	.07	.04
1	Tim Raines	.25	.20	.10
2	Jim Gantner	.09	.07	.04
3	Mario Soto	.09	.07	.04
4	Spike Owen	.09	.07	.04
5	Lloyd Moseby	.09	.07	.04
6	Damaso Garcia	.09	.07	.04
7	Cal Ripken	.60	.45	.25
8	Dan Quisenberry	.09	.07	.04
9	Eddie Murray	.12	.09	.05
10	Tony Pena	.09	.07	.04
11	Buddy Bell	.09	.07	.04
12	Dave Winfield	.30	.25	.12
13	Ron Kittle	.12	.09	.05
14	Rich Gossage	.12	.09	.05
15	Dwight Evans	.15	.11	.06
16	Al Davis	.15	.11	.06
17	Mike Schmidt	.40	.30	.15
18	Pascual Perez	.09	.07	.04
19	Tony Gwynn	.30	.25	.12
20	Nolan Ryan	1.25	.90	.50
21	Robin Yount	.50	.40	.20
22	Mike Marshall	.12	.09	.05
23	Brett Butler	.09	.07	.04
24	Ryne Sandberg	.50	.40	.20
25	Dale Murphy	.40	.30	.15
26	George Brett	.40	.30	.15
27	Jim Rice	.15	.11	.06
28	Ozzie Smith	.15	.11	.06
29	Larry Parrish	.09	.07	.04
30	Jack Clark	.15	.11	.06
31	Manny Trillo	.09	.07	.04
32	Dave Kingman	.12	.09	.05
33	Geoff Zahn	.09	.07	.04
34	Pedro Guerrero	.15	.11	.06
35	Dave Parker	.20	.15	.08
36	Rollie Fingers	.15	.11	.06
37	Fernando Valenzuela	.12	.09	.05
38	Wade Boggs	.60	.45	.25
39	Reggie Jackson	.30	.25	.12
40	Kent Hrbek	.20	.15	.08
41	Keith Hernandez	.25	.20	.10
42	Lou Whitaker	.15	.11	.06
43	Tom Herr	.09	.07	.04
44	Alan Trammell	.20	.15	.08
45	Butch Wynegar	.09	.07	.04
46	Leon Durham	.09	.07	.04
47	Dwight Gooden	.80	.60	.30
48	Don Mattingly	1.00	.70	.40
49	Phil Niekro	.20	.15	.08
50	Johnny Ray	.09	.07	.04
51	Doug DeCinces	.09	.07	.04
52	Willie Upshaw	.09	.07	.04
53	Lance Parrish	.15	.11	.06
54	Jody Davis	.09	.07	.04
55	Steve Carlton	.30	.25	.12
56	Juan Samuel	.09	.07	.04
57	Gary Carter	.12	.09	.05
58	Harold Baines	.15	.11	.06
59	Eric Show	.09	.07	.04
60	Checklist	.09	.07	.04

1985 Donruss Box Panels

In 1985, Donruss placed on the bottoms of their wax pack boxes a four-card panel which included three player cards and a Lou Gehrig puzzle card. The player cards, numbered PC 1 through PC 3, have backs identical to the regular 1985 Donruss issue. The card fronts are identical in design to the regular issue, but carry different picture poses.

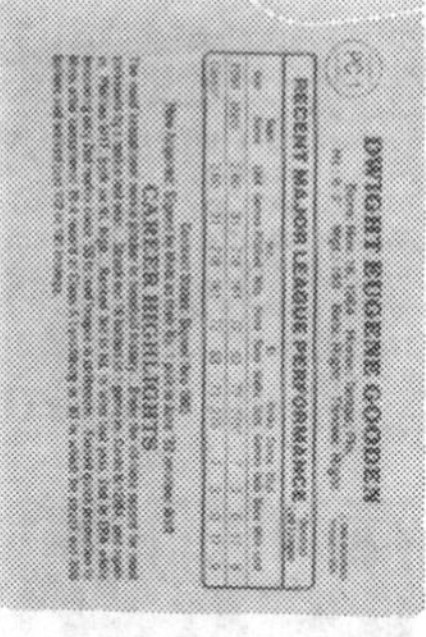

		MT	NR MT	EX
Complete Panel Set:		7.00	5.25	2.75
Complete Singles Set:		5.00	3.75	2.00
Common Single Player:		.10	.08	.04
	Panel	7.00	5.25	2.75
1	Dwight Gooden	3.00	2.25	1.25
2	Ryne Sanberg	2.00	1.50	.80
3	Ron Kittle	.10	.08	.04
----	Lou Gehrig Puzzle Card	.05	.04	.02

1985 Donruss Diamond Kings Supers

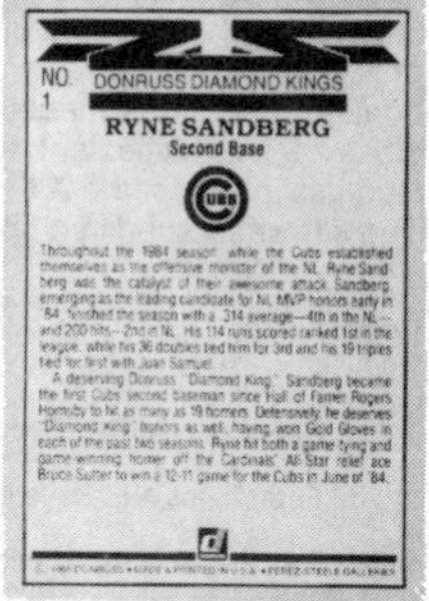

The 1985 Donruss Diamond Kings Supers are enlarged versions of the Diamond Kings card (#'s 1-26) in the regular 1985 Donruss set. The cards measure 4-15/16" by 6-3/4". The Diamond Kings series features the artwork of Dick Perez. Twenty-eight cards make up the set - 26 DK cards, an unnumbered checklist, and an unnumbered Dick Perez card. The back of the Perez card contains a brief history of Dick Perez and the Perez-Steele Galleries. The set could be obtained through a write-in offer found on the wrappers of the regular issue wax packs.

		MT	NR MT	EX
Complete Set:		15.00	11.00	6.00
Common Player:		.20	.15	.08
1	Ryne Sandberg	2.00	1.50	.80
2	Doug DeCinces	.20	.15	.08
3	Richard Dotson	.20	.15	.08
4	Bert Blyleven	.25	.20	.10
5	Lou Whitaker	.30	.25	.12
6	Dan Quisenberry	.20	.15	.08
7	Don Mattingly	3.00	2.25	1.25
8	Carney Lansford	.20	.15	.08
9	Frank Tanana	.20	.15	.08
10	Willie Upshaw	.20	.15	.08
11	Claudell Washington	.20	.15	.08
12	Mike Marshall	.25	.20	.10
13	Joaquin Andujar	.20	.15	.08
14	Cal Ripken, Jr.	2.00	1.50	.80
15	Jim Rice	.35	.25	.14
16	Don Sutton	.30	.25	.12
17	Frank Viola	.35	.25	.14
18	Alvin Davis	.30	.25	.12
19	Mario Soto	.20	.15	.08

		MT	NR MT	EX
20	Jose Cruz	.20	.15	.08
21	Charlie Lea	.20	.15	.08
22	Jesse Orosco	.20	.15	.08
23	Juan Samuel	.20	.15	.08
24	Tony Pena	.20	.15	.08
25	Tony Gwynn	.40	.30	.15
26	Bob Brenly	.20	.15	.08
——	Checklist	.12	.09	.05
——	Dick Perez (DK artist)	.12	.09	.05

1985 Donruss Highlights

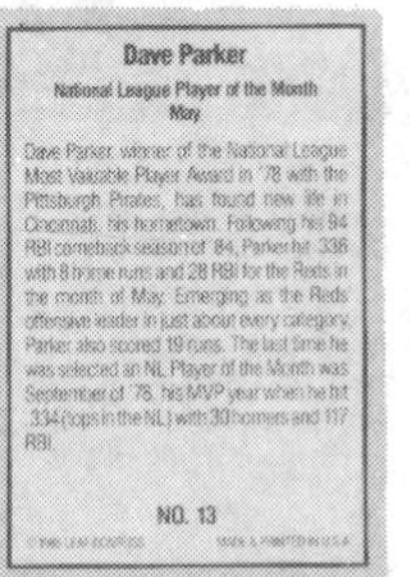

Designed in the style of the regular 1985 Donruss set, this issue features the Player of the Month in the major leagues plus highlight cards of special baseball events and milestones that occurred during the 1985 season. Fifty-six cards, including an unnumbered checklist, comprise the set which was available only through hobby dealers. The cards measure 2-1/2" by 3-1/2" and have glossy fronts. The last two cards in the set feature Donruss' picks for the A.L. and N.L. Rookies of the Year. The set was issued in a specially designed box.

	MT	NR MT	EX
Complete Set:	30.00	22.00	12.00
Common Player:	.12	.09	.05

		MT	NR MT	EX
1	Sets Opening Day Record (Tom Seaver)	.40	.30	.15
2	Establishes A.L. Save Mark (Rollie Fingers)	.15	.11	.06
3	A.L. Player of the Month - April (Mike Davis)	.12	.09	.05
4	A.L. Pitcher of the Month - April (Charlie Leibrandt)	.12	.09	.05
5	N.L. Player of the Month - April (Dale Murphy)	.40	.30	.15
6	N.L. Pitcher of the Month - April (Fernando Valenzuela)	.12	.09	.05
7	N.L. Shortstop Record (Larry Bowa)	.12	.09	.05
8	Joins Reds 2000 Hit Club (Dave Concepcion)	.12	.09	.05
9	Eldest Grand Slammer (Tony Perez)	.15	.11	.06
10	N.L. Career Run Leader (Pete Rose)	1.25	.90	.50
11	A.L. Player of the Month - May (George Brett)	.90	.70	.35
12	A.L. Pitcher of the Month - May (Dave Stieb)	.12	.09	.05
13	N.L. Player of the Month - May (Dave Parker)	.20	.15	.08
14	N.L. Pitcher of the Month - May (Andy Hawkins)	.12	.09	.05
15	Records 11th Straight Win (Andy Hawkins)	.12	.09	.05
16	Two Homers In First Inning (Von Hayes)	.15	.11	.06
17	A.L. Player of the Month - June (Rickey Henderson)	1.00	.70	.40
18	A.L. Pitcher of the Month - June (Jay Howell)	.12	.09	.05
19	N.L. Player of the Month - June (Pedro Guerrero)	.20	.15	.08
20	N.L. Pitcher of the Month - June (John Tudor)	.12	.09	.05
21	Marathon Game Iron Men (Gary Carter, Keith Hernandez)	.35	.25	.14
22	Records 4000th K (Nolan Ryan)	1.25	.90	.50
23	All-Star Game MVP (LaMarr Hoyt)	.12	.09	.05
24	1st Ranger To Hit For Cycle (Oddibe McDowell)	.40	.30	.15
25	A.L. Player of the Month - July (George Brett)	.90	.70	.35
26	A.L. Pitcher of the Month - July (Bret Saberhagen)	1.50	1.25	.60
27	N.L. Player of the Month - July (Keith Hernandez)	.35	.25	.14
28	N.L. Pitcher of the Month - July (Fernando Valenzuela)	.12	.09	.05
29	Record Setting Base Stealers (Vince Coleman, Willie McGee)	.80	.60	.30
30	Notches 300th Career Win (Tom Seaver)	.35	.25	.14
31	Strokes 3000th Hit (Rod Carew)	.40	.30	.15
32	Establishes Met Record (Dwight Gooden)	2.25	1.75	.90
33	Achieves Strikeout Milestone (Dwight Gooden)	2.25	1.75	.90
34	Explodes For 9 RBI (Eddie Murray)	.70	.50	.30
35	A.L. Career Hbp Leader (Don Baylor)	.15	.11	.06
36	A.L. Player of the Month - August (Don Mattingly)	3.25	2.50	1.25
37	A.L. Pitcher of the Month - August (Dave Righetti)	.20	.15	.08
38	N.L. Player of the Month (Willie McGee)	.20	.15	.08
39	N.L. Pitcher of the Month - August (Shane Rawley)	.12	.09	.05
40	Ty-Breaking Hit (Pete Rose)	.90	.70	.35
41	Hits 3 Hrs Drives In 8 Runs (Andre Dawson)	.20	.15	.08
42	Sets Yankee Theft Mark (Rickey Henderson)	1.00	.70	.40
43	20 Wins In Rookie Season (Tom Browning)	.35	.25	.14
44	Yankee Milestone For Hits (Don Mattingly)	3.25	2.50	1.25
45	A.L. Player of the Month - September (Don Mattingly)	3.25	2.50	1.25
46	A.L. Pitcher of the Month - September (Charlie Leibrandt)	.12	.09	.05
47	N.L. Player of the Month - September (Gary Carter)	.12	.09	.05
48	N.L. Pitcher of the Month - September (Dwight Gooden)	2.25	1.75	.90
49	Major League Record Setter (Wade Boggs)	2.00	1.50	.80
50	Hurls Shutout For 300th Win (Phil Niekro)	.30	.25	.12
51	Venerable HR King (Darrell Evans)	.15	.11	.06
52	N.L. Switch-hitting Record (Willie McGee)	.20	.15	.08
53	Equals DiMaggio Feat (Dave Winfield)	.30	.25	.12
54	Donruss N.L. Rookie of the Year (Vince Coleman)	2.25	1.75	.90
55	Donruss A.L. Rookie of the Year (Ozzie Guillen)	.50	.40	.20
——	Checklist	.20	.15	.08

1985 Donruss Sluggers Of The Hall of Fame

In much the same manner as the first Bazooka

cards were issued in 1959, this eight-player set from Donruss consists of cards which formed the bottom panel of a box of bubble gum. When cut off the box, cards measure 3-1/2" by 6-1/2", with blank backs. Players are pictured on the cards in paintings done by Dick Perez.

		MT	NR MT	EX
Complete Set:		12.00	9.00	4.75
Common Player:		.60	.45	.25
1	Babe Ruth	2.00	1.50	.80
2	Ted Williams	1.00	.70	.40
3	Lou Gehrig	1.75	1.25	.70
4	Johnny Mize	.60	.45	.25
5	Stan Musial	1.00	.70	.40
6	Mickey Mantle	3.00	2.25	1.25
7	Hank Aaron	2.00	1.50	.80
8	Frank Robinson	.90	.70	.35

1986 Donruss

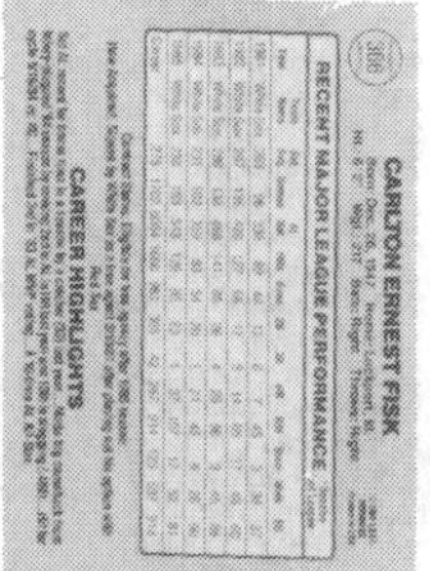

In 1986, Donruss issued a 660-card set which included 653 numbered cards and seven unnum- bered checklists. The cards, which measure 2-1/2" by 3-1/2", have fronts that feature blue borders and backs that have black print on blue and white. For the fifth year in a row, the first 26 cards in the set are Diamond Kings. The Rated Rookies subset (card #'s 27-46) appears once a-gain. The cards were distributed with a Hank Aaron puzzle. The complete set price does not include the higher priced variations. In the checklist that follows, (DK) and (RR) refer to the Diamond Kings and Rated Rookies series.

		MT	NR MT	EX
Complete Set (660):		175.00	131.00	70.00
Common Player:		.06	.05	.02
1	Kirk Gibson (DK)	.30	.25	.12
2	Goose Gossage (DK)	.20	.15	.08
3	Willie McGee (DK)	.15	.11	.06
4	George Bell (DK)	.30	.25	.12
5	Tony Armas (DK)	.10	.08	.04
6	Chili Davis (DK)	.10	.08	.04
7	Cecil Cooper (DK)	.12	.09	.05
8	Mike Boddicker (DK)	.10	.08	.04
9	Davey Lopes (DK)	.10	.08	.04
10	Bill Doran (DK)	.12	.09	.05
11	Bret Saberhagen (DK)	.25	.20	.10
12	Brett Butler (DK)	.10	.08	.04
13	Harold Baines (DK)	.15	.11	.06
14	Mike Davis (DK)	.10	.08	.04
15	Tony Perez (DK)	.15	.11	.06
16	Willie Randolph (DK)	.12	.09	.05
17	Bob Boone (DK)	.10	.08	.04
18	Orel Hershiser (DK)	.20	.15	.08
19	Johnny Ray (DK)	.12	.09	.05
20	Gary Ward (DK)	.10	.08	.04
21	Rick Mahler (DK)	.08	.06	.03
22	Phil Bradley (DK)	.20	.15	.08
23	Jerry Koosman (DK)	.12	.09	.05
24	Tom Brunansky (DK)	.15	.11	.06
25	Andre Dawson (DK)	.30	.25	.12
26	Dwight Gooden (DK)	.40	.30	.15
27	*Kal Daniels* (RR)	.15	.11	.06
28	*Fred McGriff* (RR)	35.00	26.00	14.00
29	*Cory Snyder* (RR)	.40	.30	.15
30	*Jose Guzman* (RR)	.75	.60	.30
31	*Ty Gainey* (RR)(FC)	.10	.08	.04
32	*Johnny Abrego* (RR)(FC)	.06	.05	.02
33a	*Andres Galarraga* ((RR) accent mark over e of Andres on back)	6.00	4.50	2.50
33b	*Andres Galarraga* ((RR) no accent mark)	7.00	5.25	2.75
34	*Dave Shipanoff* (RR)(FC)	.06	.05	.02
35	*Mark McLemore* (RR)	.30	.25	.12
36	*Marty Clary* (RR)(FC)	.08	.06	.03
37	*Paul O'Neill* (RR)	2.50	2.00	1.00
38	Danny Tartabull (RR)	2.00	1.50	.80
39	*Jose Canseco* (RR)	28.00	21.00	11.00
40	*Juan Nieves* (RR)(FC)	.10	.08	.04
41	*Lance McCullers* (RR)(FC)	.35	.25	.14
42	*Rick Surhoff* (RR)(FC)	.08	.06	.03
43	*Todd Worrell* (RR)	.40	.30	.15
44	Bob Kipper (RR)(FC)	.20	.15	.08
45	*John Habyan* (RR)(FC)	.15	.11	.06
46	*Mike Woodard* (RR)(FC)	.06	.05	.02
47	Mike Boddicker	.10	.08	.04
48	Robin Yount	2.00	1.50	.80
49	Lou Whitaker	.30	.25	.12
50	Dennis Boyd	.08	.06	.03
51	Rickey Henderson	2.00	1.50	.80
52	Mike Marshall	.15	.11	.06
53	George Brett	2.00	1.50	.80
54	Dave Kingman	.15	.11	.06
55	Hubie Brooks	.10	.08	.04
56	*Oddibe McDowell*(FC)	.20	.15	.08
57	Doug DeCinces	.10	.08	.04
58	Britt Burns	.06	.05	.02
59	Ozzie Smith	1.00	.70	.40
60	Jose Cruz	.10	.08	.04
61	Mike Schmidt	2.00	1.50	.80
62	Pete Rose	1.00	.70	.40
63	Steve Garvey	.40	.30	.15
64	Tony Pena	.10	.08	.04
65	Chili Davis	.10	.08	.04
66	Dale Murphy	.60	.45	.25
67	Ryne Sandberg	4.00	3.00	1.50
68	Gary Carter	.35	.25	.14
69	Alvin Davis	.30	.25	.12
70	Kent Hrbek	.25	.20	.10
71	George Bell	.30	.25	.12
72	Kirby Puckett	10.00	7.50	4.00
73	Lloyd Moseby	.10	.08	.04
74	Bob Kearney	.06	.05	.02
75	Dwight Gooden	1.00	.70	.40
76	Gary Matthews	.10	.08	.04
77	Rick Mahler	.06	.05	.02
78	Benny Distefano	.06	.05	.02
79	Jeff Leonard	.08	.06	.03
80	Kevin McReynolds	.30	.25	.12
81	Ron Oester	.06	.05	.02
82	John Russell	.06	.05	.02
83	Tommy Herr	.10	.08	.04
84	Jerry Mumphrey	.06	.05	.02
85	Ron Romanick	.06	.05	.02
86	Daryl Boston	.08	.06	.03
87	Andre Dawson	1.00	.70	.40
88	Eddie Murray	1.00	.70	.40
89	Dion James	.08	.06	.03
90	Chet Lemon	.08	.06	.03
91	Bob Stanley	.06	.05	.02
92	Willie Randolph	.10	.08	.04
93	Mike Scioscia	.08	.06	.03
94	Tom Waddell	.06	.05	.02
95	Danny Jackson	.30	.25	.12
96	Mike Davis	.08	.06	.03
97	Mike Fitzgerald	.06	.05	.02
98	Gary Ward	.08	.06	.03
99	Pete O'Brien	.10	.08	.04
100	Bret Saberhagen	.60	.45	.25
101	Alfredo Griffin	.08	.06	.03
102	Brett Butler	.08	.06	.03
103	Ron Guidry	.20	.15	.08
104	Jerry Reuss	.08	.06	.03
105	Jack Morris	.30	.25	.12
106	Rick Dempsey	.08	.06	.03
107	Ray Burris	.06	.05	.02
108	Brian Downing	.10	.08	.04
109	Willie McGee	.15	.11	.06
110	Bill Doran	.10	.08	.04
111	Kent Tekulve	.08	.06	.03
112	Tony Gwynn	2.00	1.50	.80
113	Marvell Wynne	.06	.05	.02
114	David Green	.06	.05	.02
115	Jim Gantner	.08	.06	.03

#	Player	MT	NR MT	EX
116	George Foster	.15	.11	.06
117	Steve Trout	.06	.05	.02
118	Mark Langston	.30	.25	.12
119	Tony Fernandez	.20	.15	.08
120	John Butcher	.06	.05	.02
121	Ron Robinson	.08	.06	.03
122	Dan Spillner	.06	.05	.02
123	Mike Young	.06	.05	.02
124	Paul Molitor	1.75	1.25	.70
125	Kirk Gibson	.35	.25	.14
126	Ken Griffey	.12	.09	.05
127	Tony Armas	.08	.06	.03
128	*Mariano Duncan*(FC)	.15	.11	.06
129	Mr. Clutch (Pat Tabler)	.08	.06	.03
130	Frank White	.10	.08	.04
131	Carney Lansford	.10	.08	.04
132	Vance Law	.08	.06	.03
133	Dick Schofield	.06	.05	.02
134	Wayne Tolleson	.06	.05	.02
135	Greg Walker	.10	.08	.04
136	Denny Walling	.06	.05	.02
137	Ozzie Virgil	.06	.05	.02
138	Ricky Horton	.08	.06	.03
139	LaMarr Hoyt	.06	.05	.02
140	Wayne Krenchicki	.06	.05	.02
141	Glenn Hubbard	.06	.05	.02
142	Cecilio Guante	.06	.05	.02
143	Mike Krukow	.08	.06	.03
144	Lee Smith	.10	.08	.04
145	Edwin Nunez	.06	.05	.02
146	Dave Stieb	.12	.09	.05
147	Mike Smithson	.06	.05	.02
148	Ken Dixon	.06	.05	.02
149	Danny Darwin	.06	.05	.02
150	Chris Pittaro	.06	.05	.02
151	Bill Buckner	.12	.09	.05
152	Mike Pagliarulo	.20	.15	.08
153	Bill Russell	.08	.06	.03
154	Brook Jacoby	.10	.08	.04
155	Pat Sheridan	.06	.05	.02
156	*Mike Gallego*(FC)	.15	.11	.06
157	Jim Wohlford	.06	.05	.02
158	Gary Pettis	.06	.05	.02
159	Toby Harrah	.08	.06	.03
160	Richard Dotson	.10	.08	.04
161	Bob Knepper	.08	.06	.03
162	Dave Dravecky	.08	.06	.03
163	Greg Gross	.06	.05	.02
164	Eric Davis	1.50	1.25	.60
165	Gerald Perry	.15	.11	.06
166	Rick Rhoden	.10	.08	.04
167	Keith Moreland	.08	.06	.03
168	Jack Clark	.20	.15	.08
169	Storm Davis	.10	.08	.04
170	Cecil Cooper	.12	.09	.05
171	Alan Trammell	.35	.25	.14
172	Roger Clemens	9.00	6.75	3.50
173	Don Mattingly	3.00	2.25	1.25
174	Pedro Guerrero	.20	.15	.08
175	Willie Wilson	.12	.09	.05
176	Dwayne Murphy	.08	.06	.03
177	Tim Raines	.40	.30	.15
178	Larry Parrish	.10	.08	.04
179	Mike Witt	.10	.08	.04
180	Harold Baines	.15	.11	.06
181	*Vince Coleman*(FC)	.75	.60	.30
182	*Jeff Heathcock*(FC)	.10	.08	.04
183	Steve Carlton	.50	.40	.20
184	Mario Soto	.08	.06	.03
185	Goose Gossage	.20	.15	.08
186	Johnny Ray	.12	.09	.05
187	Dan Gladden	.08	.06	.03
188	Bob Horner	.12	.09	.05
189	Rick Sutcliffe	.12	.09	.05
190	Keith Hernandez	.25	.20	.10
191	Phil Bradley	.20	.15	.08
192	Tom Brunansky	.12	.09	.05
193	Jesse Barfield	.20	.15	.08
194	Frank Viola	.20	.15	.08
195	Willie Upshaw	.08	.06	.03
196	Jim Beattie	.06	.05	.02
197	Darryl Strawberry	1.50	1.25	.60
198	Ron Cey	.10	.08	.04
199	Steve Bedrosian	.12	.09	.05
200	Steve Kemp	.08	.06	.03
201	Manny Trillo	.08	.06	.03
202	Garry Templeton	.08	.06	.03
203	Dave Parker	.25	.20	.10
204	John Denny	.06	.05	.02
205	Terry Pendleton	.15	.11	.06
206	Terry Puhl	.06	.05	.02

#	Player	MT	NR MT	EX
207	Bobby Grich	.10	.08	.04
208	*Ozzie Guillen*(FC)	.90	.70	.35
209	Jeff Reardon	.12	.09	.05
210	Cal Ripken, Jr.	5.00	3.75	2.00
211	Bill Schroeder	.06	.05	.02
212	Dan Petry	.08	.06	.03
213	Jim Rice	.40	.30	.15
214	Dave Righetti	.20	.15	.08
215	Fernando Valenzuela	.35	.25	.14
216	Julio Franco	.50	.40	.20
217	Darryl Motley	.06	.05	.02
218	Dave Collins	.08	.06	.03
219	Tim Wallach	.12	.09	.05
220	George Wright	.06	.05	.02
221	Tommy Dunbar	.06	.05	.02
222	Steve Balboni	.08	.06	.03
223	Jay Howell	.08	.06	.03
224	Joe Carter	3.00	2.25	1.25
225	Ed Whitson	.06	.05	.02
226	Orel Hershiser	.30	.25	.12
227	Willie Hernandez	.08	.06	.03
228	Lee Lacy	.06	.05	.02
229	Rollie Fingers	.20	.15	.08
230	Bob Boone	.08	.06	.03
231	Joaquin Andujar	.08	.06	.03
232	Craig Reynolds	.06	.05	.02
233	Shane Rawley	.10	.08	.04
234	Eric Show	.08	.06	.03
235	Jose DeLeon	.08	.06	.03
236	*Jose Uribe*(FC)	.25	.20	.10
237	Moose Haas	.06	.05	.02
238	Wally Backman	.08	.06	.03
239	Dennis Eckersley	.12	.09	.05
240	Mike Moore	.06	.05	.02
241	Damaso Garcia	.06	.05	.02
242	Tim Teufel	.06	.05	.02
243	Dave Concepcion	.12	.09	.05
244	Floyd Bannister	.10	.08	.04
245	Fred Lynn	.20	.15	.08
246	Charlie Moore	.06	.05	.02
247	Walt Terrell	.08	.06	.03
248	Dave Winfield	1.75	1.25	.70
249	Dwight Evans	.12	.09	.05
250	*Dennis Powell*(FC)	.10	.08	.04
251	Andre Thornton	.10	.08	.04
252	Onix Concepcion	.06	.05	.02
253	Mike Heath	.06	.05	.02
254a	David Palmer (2B on front)	.06	.05	.02
254b	David Palmer (P on front)	1.00	.70	.40
255	Donnie Moore	.06	.05	.02
256	Curtis Wilkerson	.06	.05	.02
257	Julio Cruz	.06	.05	.02
258	Nolan Ryan	6.00	4.50	2.50
259	Jeff Stone	.06	.05	.02
260a	John Tudor (1981 Games is .18)	.10	.08	.04
260b	John Tudor (1981 Games is 18)	1.00	.70	.40
261	Mark Thurmond	.06	.05	.02
262	Jay Tibbs	.06	.05	.02
263	Rafael Ramirez	.06	.05	.02
264	Larry McWilliams	.06	.05	.02
265	Mark Davis	.06	.05	.02
266	Bob Dernier	.06	.05	.02
267	Matt Young	.06	.05	.02
268	Jim Clancy	.08	.06	.03
269	Mickey Hatcher	.06	.05	.02
270	Sammy Stewart	.06	.05	.02
271	Bob L. Gibson	.06	.05	.02
272	Nelson Simmons	.06	.05	.02
273	Rich Gedman	.10	.08	.04
274	Butch Wynegar	.06	.05	.02
275	Ken Howell	.06	.05	.02
276	Mel Hall	.08	.06	.03
277	Jim Sundberg	.08	.06	.03
278	Chris Codiroli	.06	.05	.02
279	*Herman Winningham*(FC)	.15	.11	.06
280	Rod Carew	.70	.50	.30
281	Don Slaught	.06	.05	.02
282	Scott Fletcher	.08	.06	.03
283	Bill Dawley	.06	.05	.02
284	Andy Hawkins	.06	.05	.02
285	Glenn Wilson	.08	.06	.03
286	Nick Esasky	.08	.06	.03
287	Claudell Washington	.08	.06	.03
288	Lee Mazzilli	.08	.06	.03
289	Jody Davis	.10	.08	.04
290	Darrell Porter	.08	.06	.03
291	Scott McGregor	.08	.06	.03
292	Ted Simmons	.12	.09	.05
293	Aurelio Lopez	.06	.05	.02
294	Marty Barrett	.10	.08	.04
295	Dale Berra	.06	.05	.02

		MT	NR MT	EX
296	Greg Brock	.08	.06	.03
297	Charlie Leibrandt	.08	.06	.03
298	Bill Krueger	.06	.05	.02
299	Bryn Smith	.06	.05	.02
300	Burt Hooton	.08	.06	.03
301	*Stu Cliburn*(FC)	.12	.09	.05
302	Luis Salazar	.06	.05	.02
303	Ken Dayley	.06	.05	.02
304	Frank DiPino	.06	.05	.02
305	Von Hayes	.10	.08	.04
306a	Gary Redus (1983 2B is .20)	.08	.06	.03
306b	Gary Redus (1983 2B is 20)	1.00	.70	.40
307	Craig Lefferts	.06	.05	.02
308	Sam Khalifa	.06	.05	.02
309	Scott Garrelts	.06	.05	.02
310	Rick Cerone	.06	.05	.02
311	Shawon Dunston	.20	.15	.08
312	Howard Johnson	.12	.09	.05
313	Jim Presley	.15	.11	.06
314	Gary Gaetti	.25	.20	.10
315	Luis Leal	.06	.05	.02
316	Mark Salas	.06	.05	.02
317	Bill Caudill	.06	.05	.02
318	Dave Henderson	.10	.08	.04
319	Rafael Santana	.06	.05	.02
320	Leon Durham	.08	.06	.03
321	Bruce Sutter	.15	.11	.06
322	Jason Thompson	.06	.05	.02
323	Bob Brenly	.06	.05	.02
324	Carmelo Martinez	.08	.06	.03
325	Eddie Milner	.06	.05	.02
326	Juan Samuel	.15	.11	.06
327	Tom Nieto	.06	.05	.02
328	Dave Smith	.08	.06	.03
329	*Urbano Lugo*(FC)	.08	.06	.03
330	Joel Skinner	.06	.05	.02
331	Bill Gullickson	.06	.05	.02
332	Floyd Rayford	.06	.05	.02
333	Ben Oglivie	.08	.06	.03
334	Lance Parrish	.30	.25	.12
335	Jackie Gutierrez	.06	.05	.02
336	Dennis Rasmussen	.12	.09	.05
337	Terry Whitfield	.06	.05	.02
338	Neal Heaton	.06	.05	.02
339	Jorge Orta	.06	.05	.02
340	Donnie Hill	.06	.05	.02
341	Joe Hesketh	.06	.05	.02
342	Charlie Hough	.10	.08	.04
343	Dave Rozema	.06	.05	.02
344	Greg Pryor	.06	.05	.02
345	*Mickey Tettleton*	3.00	2.25	1.25
346	George Vukovich	.06	.05	.02
347	Don Baylor	.12	.09	.05
348	Carlos Diaz	.06	.05	.02
349	Barbaro Garbey	.06	.05	.02
350	Larry Sheets	.12	.09	.05
351	*Ted Higuera*(FC)	.15	.11	.06
352	Juan Beniquez	.06	.05	.02
353	Bob Forsch	.08	.06	.03
354	Mark Bailey	.06	.05	.02
355	Larry Andersen	.06	.05	.02
356	Terry Kennedy	.08	.06	.03
357	Don Robinson	.08	.06	.03
358	Jim Gott	.06	.05	.02
359	*Earnest Riles*(FC)	.30	.25	.12
360	*John Christensen*(FC)	.10	.08	.04
361	Ray Fontenot	.06	.05	.02
362	Spike Owen	.06	.05	.02
363	Jim Acker	.06	.05	.02
364a	Ron Davis (last line in highlights ends with "...in May.")	.08	.06	.03
364b	Ron Davis (last line in highlights ends with "...relievers (9).")	1.00	.70	.40
365	Tom Hume	.06	.05	.02
366	Carlton Fisk	.60	.45	.25
367	Nate Snell	.06	.05	.02
368	Rick Manning	.06	.05	.02
369	Darrell Evans	.15	.11	.06
370	Ron Hassey	.06	.05	.02
371	Wade Boggs	3.00	2.25	1.25
372	Rick Honeycutt	.06	.05	.02
373	Chris Bando	.06	.05	.02
374	Bud Black	.06	.05	.02
375	Steve Henderson	.06	.05	.02
376	Charlie Lea	.06	.05	.02
377	Reggie Jackson	1.00	.70	.40
378	Dave Schmidt	.06	.05	.02
379	Bob James	.06	.05	.02
380	Glenn Davis(FC)	.40	.30	.15
381	Tim Corcoran	.06	.05	.02
382	Danny Cox	.10	.08	.04

		MT	NR MT	EX
383	Tim Flannery	.06	.05	.02
384	Tom Browning	.20	.15	.08
385	Rick Camp	.06	.05	.02
386	Jim Morrison	.06	.05	.02
387	Dave LaPoint	.08	.06	.03
388	Davey Lopes	.08	.06	.03
389	Al Cowens	.06	.05	.02
390	Doyle Alexander	.10	.08	.04
391	Tim Laudner	.06	.05	.02
392	Don Aase	.06	.05	.02
393	Jaime Cocanower	.06	.05	.02
394	Randy O'Neal(FC)	.08	.06	.03
395	Mike Easler	.08	.06	.03
396	Scott Bradley	.06	.05	.02
397	Tom Niedenfuer	.08	.06	.03
398	Jerry Willard	.06	.05	.02
399	Lonnie Smith	.08	.06	.03
400	Bruce Bochte	.06	.05	.02
401	Terry Francona	.06	.05	.02
402	Jim Slaton	.06	.05	.02
403	Bill Stein	.06	.05	.02
404	Tim Hulett	.06	.05	.02
405	Alan Ashby	.06	.05	.02
406	Tim Stoddard	.06	.05	.02
407	Garry Maddox	.08	.06	.03
408	Ted Power	.06	.05	.02
409	Len Barker	.08	.06	.03
410	Denny Gonzalez	.06	.05	.02
411	George Frazier	.06	.05	.02
412	Andy Van Slyke	.15	.11	.06
413	Jim Dwyer	.06	.05	.02
414	Paul Householder	.06	.05	.02
415	Alejandro Sanchez	.06	.05	.02
416	Steve Crawford	.06	.05	.02
417	Dan Pasqua	.15	.11	.06
418	Enos Cabell	.06	.05	.02
419	Mike Jones	.06	.05	.02
420	Steve Kiefer	.06	.05	.02
421	*Tim Burke*(FC)	.30	.25	.12
422	Mike Mason	.06	.05	.02
423	Ruppert Jones	.06	.05	.02
424	Jerry Hairston	.06	.05	.02
425	Tito Landrum	.06	.05	.02
426	Jeff Calhoun	.06	.05	.02
427	*Don Carman*(FC)	.20	.15	.08
428	Tony Perez	.15	.11	.06
429	Jerry Davis	.06	.05	.02
430	Bob Walk	.06	.05	.02
431	Brad Wellman	.06	.05	.02
432	Terry Forster	.08	.06	.03
433	Billy Hatcher	.10	.08	.04
434	Clint Hurdle	.06	.05	.02
435	*Ivan Calderon*(FC)	1.00	.70	.40
436	Pete Filson	.06	.05	.02
437	Tom Henke	.08	.06	.03
438	Dave Engle	.06	.05	.02
439	Tom Filer	.06	.05	.02
440	Gorman Thomas	.10	.08	.04
441	*Rick Aguilera*(FC)	1.25	.90	.50
442	Scott Sanderson	.06	.05	.02
443	Jeff Dedmon	.06	.05	.02
444	*Joe Orsulak*(FC)	.15	.11	.06
445	Atlee Hammaker	.06	.05	.02
446	Jerry Royster	.06	.05	.02
447	Buddy Bell	.10	.08	.04
448	Dave Rucker	.06	.05	.02
449	Ivan DeJesus	.06	.05	.02
450	Jim Pankovits	.06	.05	.02
451	Jerry Narron	.06	.05	.02
452	Bryan Little	.06	.05	.02
453	Gary Lucas	.06	.05	.02
454	Dennis Martinez	.08	.06	.03
455	Ed Romero	.06	.05	.02
456	*Bob Melvin*(FC)	.12	.09	.05
457	Glenn Hoffman	.06	.05	.02
458	Bob Shirley	.06	.05	.02
459	Bob Welch	.12	.09	.05
460	Carmen Castillo	.06	.05	.02
461	Dave Leeper	.06	.05	.02
462	*Tim Birtsas*(FC)	.12	.09	.05
463	Randy St. Claire	.06	.05	.02
464	Chris Welsh	.06	.05	.02
465	Greg Harris	.06	.05	.02
466	Lynn Jones	.06	.05	.02
467	Dusty Baker	.08	.06	.03
468	Roy Smith	.06	.05	.02
469	Andre Robertson	.06	.05	.02
470	Ken Landreaux	.06	.05	.02
471	Dave Bergman	.06	.05	.02
472	Gary Roenicke	.06	.05	.02
473	Pete Vuckovich	.08	.06	.03

		MT	NR MT	EX
474	*Kirk McCaskill*(FC)	.40	.30	.15
475	Jeff Lahti	.06	.05	.02
476	Mike Scott	.20	.15	.08
477	*Darren Daulton*(FC)	5.00	3.75	2.00
478	Graig Nettles	.15	.11	.06
479	Bill Almon	.06	.05	.02
480	Greg Minton	.06	.05	.02
481	Randy Ready(FC)	.10	.08	.04
482	*Len Dykstra*	7.00	5.25	2.75
483	Thad Bosley	.06	.05	.02
484	*Harold Reynolds*	1.00	.70	.40
485	Al Oliver	.12	.09	.05
486	Roy Smalley	.06	.05	.02
487	John Franco	.15	.11	.06
488	Juan Agosto	.06	.05	.02
489	Al Pardo	.06	.05	.02
490	*Bill Wegman*(FC)	.25	.20	.10
491	Frank Tanana	.10	.08	.04
492	*Brian Fisher*(FC)	.08	.06	.03
493	Mark Clear	.06	.05	.02
494	Len Matuszek	.06	.05	.02
495	Ramon Romero	.06	.05	.02
496	John Wathan	.08	.06	.03
497	Rob Picciolo	.06	.05	.02
498	U.L. Washington	.06	.05	.02
499	John Candelaria	.10	.08	.04
500	Duane Walker	.06	.05	.02
501	Gene Nelson	.06	.05	.02
502	John Mizerock	.06	.05	.02
503	Luis Aguayo	.06	.05	.02
504	Kurt Kepshire	.06	.05	.02
505	Ed Wojna	.06	.05	.02
506	Joe Price	.06	.05	.02
507	*Milt Thompson*(FC)	.30	.25	.12
508	Junior Ortiz	.06	.05	.02
509	Vida Blue	.10	.08	.04
510	Steve Engel	.06	.05	.02
511	Karl Best	.06	.05	.02
512	*Cecil Fielder*(FC)	28.00	21.00	11.00
513	Frank Eufemia	.06	.05	.02
514	Tippy Martinez	.06	.05	.02
515	*Billy Robidoux*(FC)	.10	.08	.04
516	Bill Scherrer	.06	.05	.02
517	Bruce Hurst	.12	.09	.05
518	Rich Bordi	.06	.05	.02
519	Steve Yeager	.06	.05	.02
520	Tony Bernazard	.06	.05	.02
521	Hal McRae	.10	.08	.04
522	Jose Rijo	.10	.08	.04
523	*Mitch Webster*(FC)	.08	.06	.03
524	*Jack Howell*(FC)	.08	.06	.03
525	Alan Bannister	.06	.05	.02
526	Ron Kittle	.10	.08	.04
527	Phil Garner	.08	.06	.03
528	Kurt Bevacqua	.06	.05	.02
529	Kevin Gross	.08	.06	.03
530	Bo Diaz	.08	.06	.03
531	Ken Oberkfell	.06	.05	.02
532	Rick Reuschel	.10	.08	.04
533	Ron Meridith	.06	.05	.02
534	Steve Braun	.06	.05	.02
535	Wayne Gross	.06	.05	.02
536	Ray Searage	.06	.05	.02
537	Tom Brookens	.06	.05	.02
538	Al Nipper	.06	.05	.02
539	Billy Sample	.06	.05	.02
540	Steve Sax	.20	.15	.08
541	Dan Quisenberry	.10	.08	.04
542	Tony Phillips	.06	.05	.02
543	*Floyd Youmans*(FC)	.20	.15	.08
544	*Steve Buechele*(FC)	.70	.50	.30
545	Craig Gerber	.06	.05	.02
546	Joe DeSa	.06	.05	.02
547	Brian Harper	.06	.05	.02
548	Kevin Bass	.10	.08	.04
549	Tom Foley	.06	.05	.02
550	Dave Van Gorder	.06	.05	.02
551	Bruce Bochy	.06	.05	.02
552	R.J. Reynolds	.08	.06	.03
553	*Chris Brown*(FC)	.20	.15	.08
554	Bruce Benedict	.06	.05	.02
555	Warren Brusstar	.06	.05	.02
556	Danny Heep	.06	.05	.02
557	Darnell Coles	.08	.06	.03
558	Greg Gagne	.08	.06	.03
559	Ernie Whitt	.08	.06	.03
560	Ron Washington	.06	.05	.02
561	Jimmy Key	.15	.11	.06
562	Billy Swift(FC)	.15	.11	.06
563	Ron Darling	.15	.11	.06
564	Dick Ruthven	.06	.05	.02

		MT	NR MT	EX
565	Zane Smith(FC)	.15	.11	.06
566	Sid Bream	.10	.08	.04
567a	Joel Youngblood (P on front)	.08	.06	.03
567b	Joel Youngblood (IF on front)	1.00	.70	.40
568	Mario Ramirez	.06	.05	.02
569	Tom Runnells	.06	.05	.02
570	Rick Schu	.06	.05	.02
571	Bill Campbell	.06	.05	.02
572	Dickie Thon	.08	.06	.03
573	Al Holland	.06	.05	.02
574	Reid Nichols	.06	.05	.02
575	Bert Roberge	.06	.05	.02
576	Mike Flanagan	.10	.08	.04
577	Tim Leary(FC)	.35	.25	.14
578	Mike Laga	.06	.05	.02
579	Steve Lyons	.06	.05	.02
580	Phil Niekro	.30	.25	.12
581	Gilberto Reyes	.06	.05	.02
582	Jamie Easterly	.06	.05	.02
583	Mark Gubicza	.12	.09	.05
584	*Stan Javier*(FC)	.15	.11	.06
585	Bill Laskey	.06	.05	.02
586	Jeff Russell	.06	.05	.02
587	Dickie Noles	.06	.05	.02
588	Steve Farr	.08	.06	.03
589	*Steve Ontiveros*(FC)	.15	.11	.06
590	Mike Hargrove	.06	.05	.02
591	Marty Bystrom	.06	.05	.02
592	Franklin Stubbs	.08	.06	.03
593	Larry Herndon	.08	.06	.03
594	Bill Swaggerty	.06	.05	.02
595	Carlos Ponce	.06	.05	.02
596	*Pat Perry*(FC)	.12	.09	.05
597	Ray Knight	.08	.06	.03
598	*Steve Lombardozzi*(FC)	.15	.11	.06
599	Brad Havens	.06	.05	.02
600	*Pat Clements*(FC)	.12	.09	.05
601	Joe Niekro	.12	.09	.05
602	Hank Aaron Puzzle Card	.06	.05	.02
603	*Dwayne Henry*(FC)	.10	.08	.04
604	Mookie Wilson	.10	.08	.04
605	Buddy Biancalana	.06	.05	.02
606	Rance Mulliniks	.06	.05	.02
607	Alan Wiggins	.06	.05	.02
608	Joe Cowley	.06	.05	.02
609a	Tom Seaver (green stripes around name COR)	1.00	.70	.40
609b	Tom Seaver (yellow stripes around name ERR)	3.00	2.25	1.25
610	Neil Allen	.06	.05	.02
611	Don Sutton	.30	.25	.12
612	*Fred Toliver*(FC)	.15	.11	.06
613	Jay Baller	.06	.05	.02
614	Marc Sullivan	.06	.05	.02
615	John Grubb	.06	.05	.02
616	Bruce Kison	.06	.05	.02
617	Bill Madlock	.12	.09	.05
618	Chris Chambliss	.08	.06	.03
619	Dave Stewart	.12	.09	.05
620	Tim Lollar	.06	.05	.02
621	Gary Lavelle	.06	.05	.02
622	Charles Hudson	.06	.05	.02
623	*Joel Davis*(FC)	.08	.06	.03
624	*Joe Johnson*(FC)	.08	.06	.03
625	Sid Fernandez	.12	.09	.05
626	Dennis Lamp	.06	.05	.02
627	Terry Harper	.06	.05	.02
628	Jack Lazorko	.06	.05	.02
629	*Roger McDowell*(FC)	.30	.25	.12
630	Mark Funderburk	.06	.05	.02
631	Ed Lynch	.06	.05	.02
632	Rudy Law	.06	.05	.02
633	*Roger Mason*(FC)	.08	.06	.03
634	*Mike Felder*(FC)	.15	.11	.06
635	Ken Schrom	.06	.05	.02
636	Bob Ojeda	.08	.06	.03
637	Ed Vande Berg	.06	.05	.02
638	Bobby Meacham	.06	.05	.02
639	Cliff Johnson	.06	.05	.02
640	Garth Iorg	.06	.05	.02
641	Dan Driessen	.08	.06	.03
642	Mike Brown	.06	.05	.02
643	John Shelby	.06	.05	.02
644	Pete Rose (RB)	.50	.40	.20
645	Knuckle Brothers (Joe Niekro, Phil Niekro)	.15	.11	.06
646	Jesse Orosco	.08	.06	.03
647	*Billy Beane*(FC)	.06	.05	.02
648	Cesar Cedeno	.10	.08	.04
649	Bert Blyleven	.15	.11	.06
650	Max Venable	.06	.05	.02

		MT	NR MT	EX
651	Fleet Feet (Vince Coleman, Willie McGee)	.35	.25	.14
652	Calvin Schiraldi	.08	.06	.03
653	King of Kings (Pete Rose)	1.00	.70	.40
——	Checklist 1-26 DK	.06	.05	.02
---a	Checklist 27-130 (45 is Beane)	.08	.06	.03
---b	Checklist 27-130 (45 is Habyan)	.60	.45	.25
——	Checklist 131-234	.06	.05	.02
——	Checklist 235-338	.06	.05	.02
——	Checklist 339-442	.06	.05	.02
——	Checklist 443-546	.06	.05	.02
——	Checklist 547-653	.06	.05	.02

1986 Donruss All-Stars

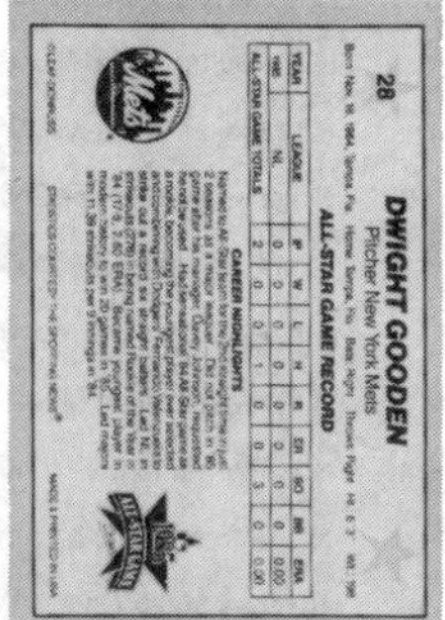

Issued in conjunction with the 1986 Donruss Pop-Ups set, the Donruss All-Stars set consists of 60 cards that measure 3-1/2" by 5". Fifty-nine players involved in the 1985 All-Star game plus an unnumbered checklist comprise the set. The card fronts have the same blue border found on the regular 1986 Donruss issue. Retail packs included one Pop-up card, three All-Star cards and one Hank Aaron puzzle card.

		MT	NR MT	EX
	Complete Set:	8.00	6.00	3.25
	Common Player:	.09	.07	.04
1	Tony Gwynn	.30	.25	.12
2	Tommy Herr	.09	.07	.04
3	Steve Garvey	.30	.25	.12
4	Dale Murphy	.40	.30	.15
5	Darryl Strawberry	.60	.45	.25
6	Graig Nettles	.12	.09	.05
7	Terry Kennedy	.09	.07	.04
8	Ozzie Smith	.15	.11	.06
9	LaMarr Hoyt	.09	.07	.04
10	Rickey Henderson	1.25	.90	.50
11	Lou Whitaker	.15	.11	.06
12	George Brett	.40	.30	.15
13	Eddie Murray	.12	.09	.05
14	Cal Ripken, Jr.	.35	.25	.14
15	Dave Winfield	.25	.20	.10
16	Jim Rice	.12	.09	.05
17	Carlton Fisk	.15	.11	.06
18	Jack Morris	.15	.11	.06
19	Jose Cruz	.09	.07	.04
20	Tim Raines	.25	.20	.10
21	Nolan Ryan	1.25	.90	.50
22	Tony Pena	.09	.07	.04
23	Jack Clark	.15	.11	.06
24	Dave Parker	.15	.11	.06
25	Tim Wallach	.12	.09	.05
26	Ozzie Virgil	.09	.07	.04
27	Fernando Valenzuela	.12	.09	.05
28	Dwight Gooden	.40	.30	.15
29	Glenn Wilson	.09	.07	.04
30	Garry Templeton	.09	.07	.04
31	Goose Gossage	.12	.09	.05
32	Ryne Sandberg	.25	.20	.10
33	Jeff Reardon	.12	.09	.05
34	Pete Rose	.35	.25	.14
35	Scott Garrelts	.09	.07	.04
36	Willie McGee	.12	.09	.05
37	Ron Darling	.12	.09	.05
38	Dick Williams	.09	.07	.04
39	Paul Molitor	.15	.11	.06
40	Damaso Garcia	.09	.07	.04
41	Phil Bradley	.12	.09	.05
42	Dan Petry	.09	.07	.04
43	Willie Hernandez	.09	.07	.04
44	Tom Brunansky	.12	.09	.05
45	Alan Trammell	.20	.15	.08
46	Donnie Moore	.09	.07	.04
47	Wade Boggs	.60	.45	.25
48	Ernie Whitt	.09	.07	.04
49	Harold Baines	.15	.11	.06
50	Don Mattingly	1.50	1.25	.60
51	Gary Ward	.09	.07	.04
52	Bert Blyleven	.12	.09	.05
53	Jimmy Key	.12	.09	.05
54	Cecil Cooper	.12	.09	.05
55	Dave Stieb	.12	.09	.05
56	Rich Gedman	.09	.07	.04
57	Jay Howell	.09	.07	.04
58	Sparky Anderson	.09	.07	.04
59	Minneapolis Metrodome	.09	.07	.04
——	Checklist	.09	.07	.04

1986 Donruss Box Panels

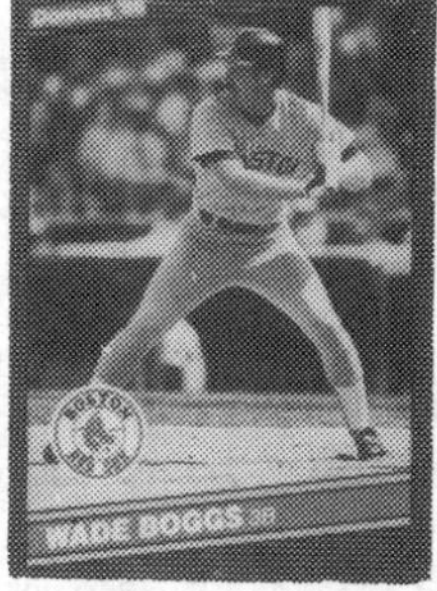
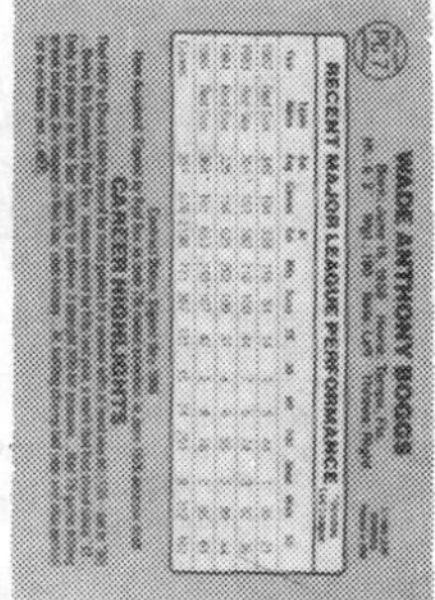

For the second year in a row, Donruss placed baseball cards on the bottom of their wax and cello pack boxes. The cards, which come four to a panel, are the standard 2-1/2" by 3-1/2" in size. With numbering that begins where Donruss left off in 1985, cards PC 4 through PC 6 were found on boxes of regular Donruss issue wax packs. Cards PC 7 through PC 9 were found on boxes of the 1986 All- Star/Pop-up packs. An unnumbered Hank Aaron puzzle card was included on each box.

		MT	NR MT	EX
	Complete Panel Set:	5.00	3.75	2.00
	Complete Singles Set:	3.00	2.25	1.25
	Common Single Player:	.15	.11	.06
	Panel	1.00	.70	.40
4	Kirk Gibson	.35	.25	.14
5	Willie Hernandez	.15	.11	.06
6	Doug DeCinces	.15	.11	.06
——	Aaron Puzzle Card	.04	.03	.02
	Panel	3.00	2.25	1.25
7	Wade Boggs	1.00	.70	.40
8	Lee Smith	.15	.11	.06
9	Cecil Cooper	.20	.15	.08
——	Aaron Puzzle Card	.04	.03	.02

1986 Donruss Diamond Kings Supers

Donruss produced a set of giant-size Diamond Kings in 1986 for the second year in a row. The cards, which measure 4-11/6" by 6-3/4", are enlarged versions of the 26 Diamond Kings cards found in the regular 1986 Donruss set. Featuring the artwork of Dick Perez, the set consists of 28 cards - 26 DKs, an unnumbered checklist and an unnumbered Pete Rose "King of Kings" card.

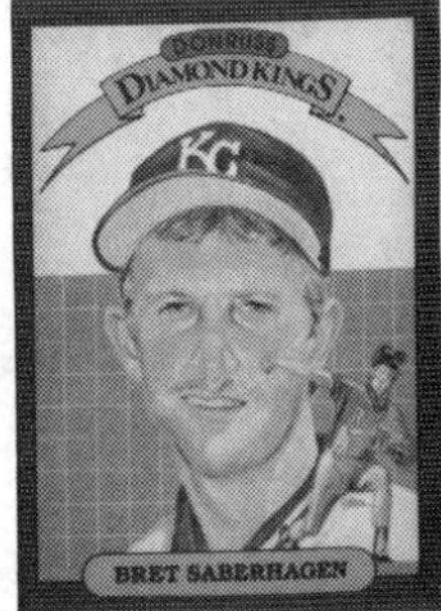

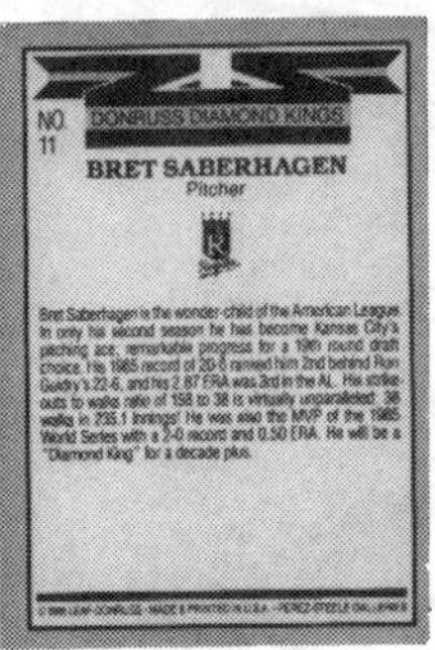

	MT	NR MT	EX
Complete Set:	10.00	7.50	4.00
Common Player:	.20	.15	.08

		MT	NR MT	EX
1	Kirk Gibson	.50	.40	.20
2	Goose Gossage	.30	.25	.12
3	Willie McGee	.30	.25	.12
4	George Bell	.30	.25	.12
5	Tony Armas	.20	.15	.08
6	Chili Davis	.20	.15	.08
7	Cecil Cooper	.25	.20	.10
8	Mike Boddicker	.20	.15	.08
9	Davey Lopes	.20	.15	.08
10	Bill Doran	.25	.20	.10
11	Bret Saberhagen	.70	.50	.30
12	Brett Butler	.20	.15	.08
13	Harold Baines	.30	.25	.12
14	Mike Davis	.20	.15	.08
15	Tony Perez	.25	.20	.10
16	Willie Randolph	.25	.20	.10
18	Orel Hershiser	.70	.50	.30
19	Johnny Ray	.25	.20	.10
20	Gary Ward	.20	.15	.08
21	Rick Mahler	.20	.15	.08
22	Phil Bradley	.30	.25	.12
23	Jerry Koosman	.20	.15	.08
24	Tom Brunansky	.25	.20	.10
25	Andre Dawson	.35	.25	.14
26	Dwight Gooden	1.00	.70	.40
——	Checklist	.15	.11	.06
——	King of Kings (Pete Rose)	1.50	1.25	.60

1986 Donruss Highlights

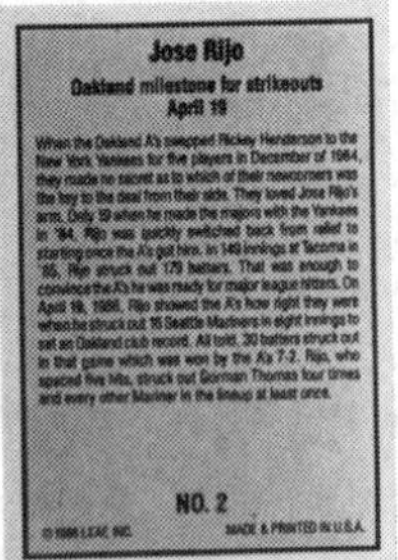

Donruss, for the second year in a row, issued a 56-card highlights set which featured cards of the A.L. and N.L. Player of the Month plus significant events that took place during the 1986 season. The cards, which measure 2-1/2" by 3-1/2" in size, are similar in design to the regular 1986 Donruss set but have a gold border instead of blue. A "Highlights" logo appears in the lower left corner of each card front. The card backs are designed on a vertical format and feature black print on a yellow background. As in 1985, the set includes Donruss' picks for the Rookies of the Year awards. A new feature was three cards honoring the 1986 Hall of Fame inductees. The set, available only through hobby dealers, was issued in a specially designed box.

	MT	NR MT	EX
Complete Set:	12.00	9.00	4.75
Common Player:	.10	.08	.04

		MT	NR MT	EX
1	Homers In First At-Bat (Will Clark)	2.00	1.50	.80
2	Oakland Milestone For Strikeouts (Jose Rijo)	.10	.08	.04
3	Royals' All-Time Hit Man (George Brett)	.20	.15	.08
4	Phillies RBI Leader (Mike Schmidt)	.30	.25	.12
5	KKKKKKKKKKKKKKKKKKK (Roger Clemens)	.75	.55	.20
6	A.L. Pitcher of the Month-April (Roger Clemens)	.50	.40	.20
7	A.L. Player of the Month-April (Kirby Puckett)	.50	.40	.20
8	N.L. Pitcher of the Month-April (Dwight Gooden)	.50	.40	.20
9	N.L. Player of the Month-April (Johnny Ray)	.10	.08	.04
10	Eclipses Mantle HR Record (Reggie Jackson)	.25	.20	.10
11	First Five Hit Game of Career (Wade Boggs)	.50	.40	.20
12	A.L. Pitcher of the Month-May (Don Aase)	.10	.08	.04
13	A.L. Player of the Month-May (Wade Boggs)	.50	.40	.20
14	N.L. Pitcher of the Month-May (Jeff Reardon)	.15	.11	.06
15	N.L. Player of the Month-May (Hubie Brooks)	.10	.08	.04
16	Notches 300th Career Win (Don Sutton)	.10	.08	.04
17	Starts Season 14-0 (Roger Clemens)	.50	.40	.20
18	A.L. Pitcher of the Month-June (Roger Clemens)	.50	.40	.20
19	A.L. Player of the Month-June (Kent Hrbek)	.10	.08	.04
20	N.L. Pitcher of the Month-June (Rick Rhoden)	.10	.08	.04
21	N.L. Player of the Month-June (Kevin Bass)	.10	.08	.04
22	Blasts 4 HRS in 1 Game (Bob Horner)	.10	.08	.04
23	Starting All Star Rookie (Wally Joyner)	.50	.40	.20
24	Starts 3rd Straight All Star Game (Darryl Strawberry)	.25	.20	.10
25	Ties All Star Game Record (Fernando Valenzuela)	.10	.08	.04
26	All Star Game MVP (Roger Clemens)	.50	.40	.20
27	A.L. Pitcher of the Month-July (Jack Morris)	.10	.08	.04
28	A.L. Player of the Month-July (Scott Fletcher)	.10	.08	.04
29	N.L. Pitcher of the Month-July (Todd Worrell)	.25	.20	.10
30	N.L. PLayer of the Month-July (Eric Davis)	.40	.30	.15
31	Records 3000th Strikeout (Bert Blyleven)	.15	.11	.06
32	1986 Hall of Fame Inductee (Bobby Doerr)	.15	.11	.06
33	1986 Hall of Fame Inductee (Ernie Lombardi)	.15	.11	.06
34	1986 Hall of Fame Inductee (Willie McCovey)	.20	.15	.08
35	Notches 4000th K (Steve Carlton)	.25	.20	.10
36	Surpasses DiMaggio Record (Mike Schmidt)	.40	.30	.15
37	Records 3rd "Quadruple Double" (Juan Samuel)	.10	.08	.04
38	A.L. Pitcher of the Month-August (Mike Witt)	.10	.08	.04
39	A.L. Player of the Month-August (Doug DeCinces)	.10	.08	.04
40	N.L. Pitcher of the Month-August (Bill Gullickson)	.10	.08	.04
41	N.L. Player of the Month-August (Dale Murphy)	.20	.15	.08
42	Sets Tribe Offensive Record (Joe Carter)	.25	.20	.10
43	Longest HR In Royals Stadium (Bo Jackson)	2.00	1.50	.80
44	Majors 1st No-Hitter In 2 Years (Joe Cowley)	.10	.08	.04

		MT	NR MT	EX
45	Sets M.L. Strikeout Record (Jim Deshaies)	.15	.11	.06
46	No Hitter Clinches Division (Mike Scott)	.10	.08	.04
47	A.L. Pitcher of the Month-September (Bruce Hurst)	.10	.08	.04
48	A.L. Player of the Month-September (Don Mattingly)	1.00	.70	.40
49	N.L. Pitcher of the Month-September (Mike Krukow)	.10	.08	.04
50	N.L. Player of the Month-September (Steve Sax)	.10	.08	.04
51	A.L. Record For Steals By A Rookie (John Cangelosi)	.10	.08	.04
52	Shatters M.L. Save Mark (Dave Righetti)	.10	.08	.04
53	Yankee Record For Hits & Doubles (Don Mattingly)	1.00	.70	.40
54	Donruss N.L. Rookie of the Year (Todd Worrell)	.25	.20	.10
55	Donruss A.L. Rookie of the Year (Jose Canseco)	3.00	2.25	1.25
56	Highlight Checklist	.10	.08	.04

1986 Donruss Pop-Ups

Issued in conjunction with the 1986 Donruss All-Stars set, the Donruss Pop-Ups (18 unnumbered cards) feature the 1985 All-Star Game starting lineups. The cards, which measure 2-1/2" by 5", are die-cut and fold out to form a three-dimensional stand-up card. The background for the cards is the Minneapolis Metrodome, site of the 1985 All-Star Game. Retail packs included one Pop-Up card, three All-Star cards and one Hank Aaron puzzle card.

		MT	NR MT	EX
Complete Set:		5.00	3.75	2.00
Common Player:		.20	.15	.08
(1)	George Brett	.60	.45	.25
(2)	Carlton Fisk	.30	.25	.12
(3)	Steve Garvey	.20	.15	.08
(4)	Tony Gwynn	.50	.40	.20
(5)	Rickey Henderson	.70	.50	.30
(6)	Tommy Herr	.20	.15	.08
(7)	LaMarr Hoyt	.20	.15	.08
(8)	Terry Kennedy	.20	.15	.08
(9)	Jack Morris	.20	.15	.08
(10)	Dale Murphy	.30	.25	.12
(11)	Eddie Murray	.30	.25	.12
(12)	Graig Nettles	.20	.15	.08
(13)	Jim Rice	.20	.15	.08
(14)	Cal Ripken Jr.	.50	.40	.20
(15)	Ozzie Smith	.30	.25	.12
(16)	Darryl Strawberry	.70	.50	.30
(17)	Lou Whitaker	.30	.25	.12
(18)	Dave Winfield	.30	.25	.12

1986 Donruss Rookies

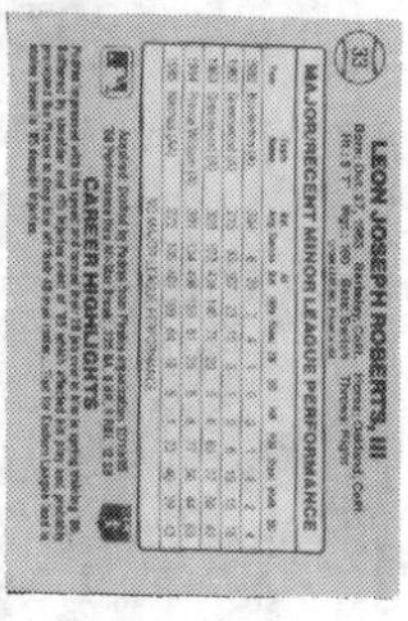

Entitled "The Rookies," this 56-card set includes the top 55 rookies of 1986 plus an unnumbered checklist. The cards, which measure 2-1/2" by 3-1/2", are similar to the format used for the 1986 Donruss regular issue, except that the borders are green rather than blue. Several of the rookies who had cards in the regular 1986 Donruss set appear again in "The Rookies" set. The sets, which were only available through hobby dealers, came in a specially designed box.

		MT	NR MT	EX
Complete Set (56):		50.00	37.00	20.00
Common Player:		.15	.11	.06
1	Wally Joyner(FC)	2.00	1.50	.80
2	Tracy Jones(FC)	.15	.11	.06
3	Allan Anderson(FC)	.20	.15	.08
4	Ed Correa(FC)	.15	.11	.06
5	Reggie Williams	.15	.11	.06
6	Charlie Kerfeld(FC)	.15	.11	.06
7	Andres Galarraga	3.00	2.25	1.25
8	Bob Tewksbury(FC)	.80	.60	.30
9	Al Newman	.15	.11	.06
10	Andres Thomas(FC)	.15	.11	.06
11	Barry Bonds(FC)	16.00	12.00	6.50
12	Juan Nieves	.15	.11	.06
13	Mark Eichhorn(FC)	.25	.20	.10
14	Dan Plesac(FC)	.25	.20	.10
15	Cory Snyder	.40	.30	.15
16	Kelly Gruber	.25	.20	.10
17	Kevin Mitchell(FC)	2.50	2.00	1.00
18	Steve Lombardozzi	.15	.11	.06
19	Mitch Williams	.50	.40	.20
20	John Cerutti(FC)	.25	.20	.10
21	Todd Worrell	.15	.11	.06
22	Jose Canseco	5.00	3.75	2.00
23	Pete Incaviglia(FC)	1.00	.70	.40
24	Jose Guzman	.25	.20	.10
25	Scott Bailes(FC)	.15	.11	.06
26	Greg Mathews(FC)	.15	.11	.06
27	Eric King(FC)	.20	.15	.08
28	Paul Assenmacher	.20	.15	.08
29	Jeff Sellers	.15	.11	.06
30	Bobby Bonilla(FC)	4.00	3.00	1.50
31	Doug Drabek(FC)	1.50	1.25	.60
32	Will Clark(FC)	9.00	6.75	3.50
33	Bip Roberts	.90	.70	.35
34	Jim Deshaies(FC)	.25	.20	.10
35	Mike LaValliere(FC)	.40	.30	.15
36	Scott Bankhead(FC)	.20	.15	.08
37	Dale Sveum(FC)	.15	.11	.06
38	Bo Jackson(FC)	6.00	4.50	2.50
39	Rob Thompson(FC)	1.75	1.25	.70
40	Eric Plunk(FC)	.20	.15	.08
41	Bill Bathe	.15	.11	.06
42	John Kruk(FC)	5.00	3.75	2.00
43	Andy Allanson(FC)	.20	.15	.08
44	Mark Portugal	.15	.11	.06
45	Danny Tartabull	2.00	1.50	.80
46	Bob Kipper	.15	.11	.06
47	Gene Walter	.15	.11	.06
48	Rey Quinonez	.15	.11	.06
49	Bobby Witt(FC)	.30	.25	.12
50	Bill Mooneyham	.15	.11	.06
51	John Cangelosi(FC)	.15	.11	.06
52	Ruben Sierra(FC)	7.00	5.25	2.75
53	Rob Woodward	.15	.11	.06
54	Ed Hearn	.15	.11	.06
55	Joel McKeon	.15	.11	.06
56	Checklist 1-56	.05	.04	.02

1987 Donruss

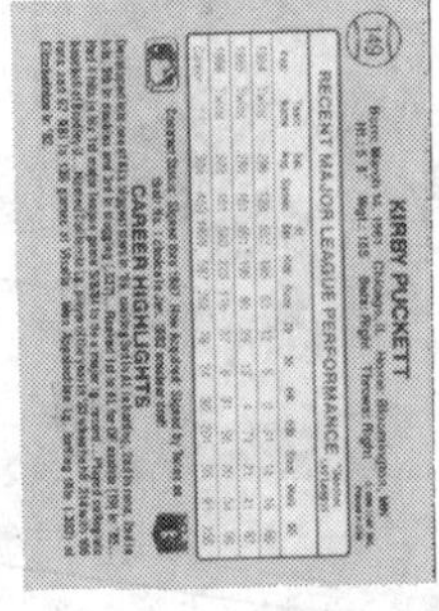

The 1987 Donruss set consists of 660 numbered cards, each measuring 2-1/2" by 3-1/2" in size. Full color photos are surrounded by a bold black border separated by two narrow bands of yellow which enclose a brown area filled with baseballs. The player's name, team and team logo appear on the card fronts along with the words "Donruss '87". The card backs are designed on a horizontal format and contain black print on a yellow and white background. The backs are very similar to those in previous years' sets. Backs of cards issued in wax and rack packs face to the left when turned over, while those issued in factory sets face to the right.

		MT	NR MT	EX
Complete Set (660):		60.00	45.00	24.00
Common Player:		.05	.04	.02
1	Wally Joyner (DK)	.25	.20	.10
2	Roger Clemens (DK)	.70	.50	.30
3	Dale Murphy (DK)	.12	.09	.05
4	Darryl Strawberry (DK)	.12	.09	.05
5	Ozzie Smith (DK)	.20	.15	.08
6	Jose Canseco (DK)	.40	.30	.15
7	Charlie Hough (DK)	.07	.05	.03
8	Brook Jacoby (DK)	.10	.08	.04
9	Fred Lynn (DK)	.12	.09	.05
10	Rick Rhoden (DK)	.10	.08	.04
11	Chris Brown (DK)	.10	.08	.04
12	Von Hayes (DK)	.10	.08	.04
13	Jack Morris (DK)	.10	.08	.04
14a	Kevin McReynolds ((DK) no yellow stripe on back)	1.25	.90	.50
14b	Kevin McReynolds ((DK) yellow stripe on back)	.20	.15	.08
15	George Brett (DK)	.40	.30	.15
16	Ted Higuera (DK)	.05	.04	.02
17	Hubie Brooks (DK)	.10	.08	.04
18	Mike Scott (DK)	.12	.09	.05
19	Kirby Puckett (DK)	.60	.45	.25
20	Dave Winfield (DK)	.25	.20	.10
21	Lloyd Moseby (DK)	.10	.08	.04
22a	Eric Davis ((DK) no yellow stripe on back)	1.00	.70	.40
22b	Eric Davis ((DK) yellow stripe on back)	.15	.11	.06
23	Jim Presley (DK)	.12	.09	.05
24	Keith Moreland (DK)	.07	.05	.03
25a	Greg Walker ((DK) no yellow stripe on back)	.50	.40	.20
25b	Greg Walker ((DK) yellow stripe on back)	.10	.08	.04
26	Steve Sax (DK)	.12	.09	.05
27	Checklist 1-27	.05	.04	.02
28	*B.J. Surhoff*(FC)	.30	.25	.12
29	*Randy Myers*(FC)	.30	.25	.12
30	*Ken Gerhart*(FC)	.15	.11	.06
31	Benito Santiago(FC)	.60	.45	.25
32	*Greg Swindell*	.60	.45	.25
33	*Mike Birkbeck*(FC)	.20	.15	.08
34	*Terry Steinbach*	.40	.30	.15
35	*Bo Jackson*	3.00	2.25	1.25
36	*Greg Maddux*	7.00	5.25	2.75
37	*Jim Lindeman*(FC)	.15	.11	.06
38	*Devon White*	1.00	.70	.40
39	*Eric Bell*(FC)	.12	.09	.05
40	*Will Fraser*(FC)	.20	.15	.08
41	*Jerry Browne*	.25	.20	.10

		MT	NR MT	EX
42	*Chris James*	.20	.15	.08
43	*Rafael Palmeiro*	6.00	4.50	2.50
44	*Pat Dodson*(FC)	.12	.09	.05
45	*Duane Ward*	.80	.60	.30
46	*Mark McGwire*	4.50	3.50	1.75
47	*Bruce Fields* (Photo actually Darnell Coles)(FC)	.10	.08	.04
48	Eddie Murray	.50	.40	.20
49	Ted Higuera	.06	.05	.02
50	Kirk Gibson	.15	.11	.06
51	Oil Can Boyd	.07	.05	.03
52	Don Mattingly	1.00	.70	.40
53	Pedro Guerrero	.15	.11	.06
54	George Brett	.60	.45	.25
55	Jose Rijo	.07	.05	.03
56	Tim Raines	.30	.25	.12
57	*Ed Correa*	.15	.11	.06
58	Mike Witt	.10	.08	.04
59	Greg Walker	.10	.08	.04
60	Ozzie Smith	.40	.30	.15
61	Glenn Davis	.06	.05	.02
62	Glenn Wilson	.07	.05	.03
63	Tom Browning	.10	.08	.04
64	Tony Gwynn	1.00	.70	.40
65	R.J. Reynolds	.07	.05	.03
66	*Will Clark*	7.00	5.25	2.75
67	Ozzie Virgil	.05	.04	.02
68	Rick Sutcliffe	.12	.09	.05
69	Gary Carter	.15	.11	.06
70	Mike Moore	.05	.04	.02
71	Bert Blyleven	.12	.09	.05
72	Tony Fernandez	.12	.09	.05
73	Kent Hrbek	.15	.11	.06
74	Lloyd Moseby	.10	.08	.04
75	Alvin Davis	.12	.09	.05
76	Keith Hernandez	.25	.20	.10
77	Ryne Sandberg	1.25	.90	.50
78	Dale Murphy	.15	.11	.06
79	Sid Bream	.07	.05	.03
80	Chris Brown	.07	.05	.03
81	Steve Garvey	.25	.20	.10
82	Mario Soto	.07	.05	.03
83	Shane Rawley	.07	.05	.03
84	Willie McGee	.12	.09	.05
85	Jose Cruz	.10	.08	.04
86	Brian Downing	.07	.05	.03
87	Ozzie Guillen	.10	.08	.04
88	Hubie Brooks	.10	.08	.04
89	Cal Ripken, Jr.	1.25	.90	.50
90	Juan Nieves	.07	.05	.03
91	Lance Parrish	.06	.05	.02
92	Jim Rice	.15	.11	.06
93	Ron Guidry	.15	.11	.06
94	Fernando Valenzuela	.08	.06	.03
95	*Andy Allanson*	.15	.11	.06
96	Willie Wilson	.12	.09	.05
97	Jose Canseco	3.50	2.75	1.50
98	Jeff Reardon	.10	.08	.04
99	*Bobby Witt*	.20	.15	.08
100	Checklist 28-133	.05	.04	.02
101	Jose Guzman	.10	.08	.04
102	Steve Balboni	.07	.05	.03
103	Tony Phillips	.05	.04	.02
104	Brook Jacoby	.10	.08	.04
105	Dave Winfield	.60	.45	.25
106	Orel Hershiser	.15	.11	.06
107	Lou Whitaker	.25	.20	.10
108	Fred Lynn	.15	.11	.06
109	Bill Wegman	.07	.05	.03
110	Donnie Moore	.05	.04	.02
111	Jack Clark	.15	.11	.06
112	Bob Knepper	.07	.05	.03
113	Von Hayes	.10	.08	.04
114	*Bip Roberts*	.40	.30	.15
115	Tony Pena	.08	.06	.03
116	Scott Garrelts	.05	.04	.02
117	Paul Molitor	.50	.40	.20
118	Darryl Strawberry	.30	.25	.12
119	Shawon Dunston	.10	.08	.04
120	Jim Presley	.10	.08	.04
121	Jesse Barfield	.06	.05	.02
122	Gary Gaetti	.15	.11	.06
123	*Kurt Stillwell*	.15	.11	.06
124	Joel Davis	.05	.04	.02
125	Mike Boddicker	.07	.05	.03
126	Robin Yount	.60	.45	.25
127	Alan Trammell	.25	.20	.10
128	Dave Righetti	.15	.11	.06
129	Dwight Evans	.12	.09	.05
130	Mike Scioscia	.07	.05	.03
131	Julio Franco	.10	.08	.04

		MT	NR MT	EX
132	Bret Saberhagen	.15	.11	.06
133	Mike Davis	.07	.05	.03
134	Joe Hesketh	.05	.04	.02
135	*Wally Joyner*	1.00	.70	.40
136	Don Slaught	.05	.04	.02
137	Daryl Boston	.05	.04	.02
138	Nolan Ryan	2.00	1.50	.80
139	Mike Schmidt	1.00	.70	.40
140	Tommy Herr	.10	.08	.04
141	Garry Templeton	.07	.05	.03
142	Kal Daniels	.20	.15	.08
143	Billy Sample	.05	.04	.02
144	Johnny Ray	.10	.08	.04
145	*Rob Thompson*	.75	.60	.30
146	Bob Dernier	.05	.04	.02
147	Danny Tartabull	.25	.20	.10
148	Ernie Whitt	.07	.05	.03
149	Kirby Puckett	2.00	1.50	.80
150	Mike Young	.05	.04	.02
151	Ernest Riles	.05	.04	.02
152	Frank Tanana	.07	.05	.03
153	Rich Gedman	.10	.08	.04
154	Willie Randolph	.10	.08	.04
155a	Bill Madlock (name in brown band)	.12	.09	.05
155b	Bill Madlock (name in red band)	.70	.50	.30
156a	Joe Carter (name in brown band)	.15	.11	.06
156b	Joe Carter (ERR)	1.00	.70	.40
157	Danny Jackson	.15	.11	.06
158	Carney Lansford	.10	.08	.04
159	Bryn Smith	.05	.04	.02
160	Gary Pettis	.05	.04	.02
161	Oddibe McDowell	.10	.08	.04
162	*John Cangelosi*	.12	.09	.05
163	Mike Scott	.15	.11	.06
164	Eric Show	.07	.05	.03
165	Juan Samuel	.12	.09	.05
166	Nick Esasky	.07	.05	.03
167	Zane Smith	.07	.05	.03
168	Mike Brown	.05	.04	.02
169	Keith Moreland	.07	.05	.03
170	John Tudor	.10	.08	.04
171	Ken Dixon	.05	.04	.02
172	Jim Gantner	.07	.05	.03
173	Jack Morris	.20	.15	.08
174	Bruce Hurst	.10	.08	.04
175	Dennis Rasmussen	.10	.08	.04
176	Mike Marshall	.12	.09	.05
177	Dan Quisenberry	.07	.05	.03
178	Eric Plunk(FC)	.10	.08	.04
179	Tim Wallach	.12	.09	.05
180	Steve Buechele	.07	.05	.03
181	Don Sutton	.20	.15	.08
182	Dave Schmidt	.05	.04	.02
183	Terry Pendleton	.35	.25	.14
184	*Jim Deshaies*	.15	.11	.06
185	Steve Bedrosian	.12	.09	.05
186	Pete Rose	.60	.45	.25
187	Dave Dravecky	.07	.05	.03
188	Rick Reuschel	.10	.08	.04
189	Dan Gladden	.05	.04	.02
190	Rick Mahler	.05	.04	.02
191	Thad Bosley	.05	.04	.02
192	Ron Darling	.15	.11	.06
193	Matt Young	.05	.04	.02
194	Tom Brunansky	.10	.08	.04
195	Dave Stieb	.12	.09	.05
196	Frank Viola	.15	.11	.06
197	Tom Henke	.07	.05	.03
198	Karl Best	.05	.04	.02
199	Dwight Gooden	.25	.20	.10
200	Checklist 134-239	.05	.04	.02
201	Steve Trout	.05	.04	.02
202	Rafael Ramirez	.05	.04	.02
203	Bob Walk	.05	.04	.02
204	Roger Mason	.05	.04	.02
205	Terry Kennedy	.07	.05	.03
206	Ron Oester	.05	.04	.02
207	John Russell	.05	.04	.02
208	*Greg Mathews*	.20	.15	.08
209	Charlie Kerfeld	.10	.08	.04
210	Reggie Jackson	.35	.25	.14
211	Floyd Bannister	.10	.08	.04
212	Vance Law	.07	.05	.03
213	Rich Bordi	.05	.04	.02
214	*Dan Plesac*	.10	.08	.04
215	Dave Collins	.07	.05	.03
216	Bob Stanley	.05	.04	.02
217	Joe Niekro	.10	.08	.04
218	Tom Niedenfuer	.07	.05	.03
219	Brett Butler	.07	.05	.03
220	Charlie Leibrandt	.07	.05	.03
221	Steve Ontiveros	.05	.04	.02
222	Tim Burke	.05	.04	.02
223	Curtis Wilkerson	.05	.04	.02
224	*Pete Incaviglia*	.50	.40	.20
225	Lonnie Smith	.07	.05	.03
226	Chris Codiroli	.05	.04	.02
227	*Scott Bailes*	.08	.06	.03
228	Rickey Henderson	.60	.45	.25
229	Ken Howell	.05	.04	.02
230	Darnell Coles	.07	.05	.03
231	Don Aase	.05	.04	.02
232	Tim Leary	.07	.05	.03
233	Bob Boone	.07	.05	.03
234	Ricky Horton	.07	.05	.03
235	Mark Bailey	.05	.04	.02
236	Kevin Gross	.07	.05	.03
237	Lance McCullers	.07	.05	.03
238	Cecilio Guante	.05	.04	.02
239	Bob Melvin	.05	.04	.02
240	Billy Jo Robidoux	.05	.04	.02
241	Roger McDowell	.12	.09	.05
242	Leon Durham	.07	.05	.03
243	Ed Nunez	.05	.04	.02
244	Jimmy Key	.12	.09	.05
245	Mike Smithson	.05	.04	.02
246	Bo Diaz	.07	.05	.03
247	Carlton Fisk	.20	.15	.08
248	Larry Sheets	.08	.06	.03
249	*Juan Castillo*(FC)	.10	.08	.04
250	*Eric King*	.08	.06	.03
251	*Doug Drabek*	.90	.70	.35
252	Wade Boggs	.80	.60	.30
253	Mariano Duncan	.05	.04	.02
254	Pat Tabler	.07	.05	.03
255	Frank White	.10	.08	.04
256	Alfredo Griffin	.07	.05	.03
257	Floyd Youmans	.07	.05	.03
258	Rob Wilfong	.05	.04	.02
259	Pete O'Brien	.10	.08	.04
260	Tim Hulett	.05	.04	.02
261	Dickie Thon	.07	.05	.03
262	Darren Daulton	1.00	.70	.40
263	Vince Coleman	.12	.09	.05
264	Andy Hawkins	.05	.04	.02
265	Eric Davis	.30	.25	.12
266	*Andres Thomas*	.15	.11	.06
267	*Mike Diaz*(FC)	.15	.11	.06
268	Chili Davis	.07	.05	.03
269	Jody Davis	.07	.05	.03
270	Phil Bradley	.12	.09	.05
271	George Bell	.25	.20	.10
272	Keith Atherton	.05	.04	.02
273	Storm Davis	.10	.08	.04
274	Rob Deer(FC)	.20	.15	.08
275	Walt Terrell	.07	.05	.03
276	Roger Clemens	2.00	1.50	.80
277	Mike Easler	.07	.05	.03
278	Steve Sax	.15	.11	.06
279	Andre Thornton	.07	.05	.03
280	Jim Sundberg	.07	.05	.03
281	Bill Bathe	.05	.04	.02
282	Jay Tibbs	.05	.04	.02
283	Dick Schofield	.05	.04	.02
284	Mike Mason	.05	.04	.02
285	Jerry Hairston	.05	.04	.02
286	Bill Doran	.10	.08	.04
287	Tim Flannery	.05	.04	.02
288	Gary Redus	.05	.04	.02
289	John Franco	.10	.08	.04
290	*Paul Assenmacher*	.15	.11	.06
291	Joe Orsulak	.05	.04	.02
292	Lee Smith	.15	.11	.06
293	Mike Laga	.05	.04	.02
294	Rick Dempsey	.07	.05	.03
295	Mike Felder	.05	.04	.02
296	Tom Brookens	.05	.04	.02
297	Al Nipper	.05	.04	.02
298	Mike Pagliarulo	.10	.08	.04
299	Franklin Stubbs	.07	.05	.03
300	Checklist 240-345	.05	.04	.02
301	Steve Farr	.05	.04	.02
302	*Bill Mooneyham*	.10	.08	.04
303	Andres Galarraga	.60	.45	.25
304	Scott Fletcher	.07	.05	.03
305	Jack Howell	.07	.05	.03
306	*Russ Morman*(FC)	.10	.08	.04
307	Todd Worrell	.20	.15	.08
308	Dave Smith	.07	.05	.03
309	Jeff Stone	.05	.04	.02
310	Ron Robinson	.05	.04	.02
311	Bruce Bochy	.05	.04	.02

		MT	NR MT	EX
312	Jim Winn	.05	.04	.02
313	Mark Davis	.05	.04	.02
314	Jeff Dedmon	.05	.04	.02
315	*Jamie Moyer*(FC)	.20	.15	.08
316	Wally Backman	.07	.05	.03
317	Ken Phelps	.07	.05	.03
318	Steve Lombardozzi	.05	.04	.02
319	Rance Mulliniks	.05	.04	.02
320	Tim Laudner	.05	.04	.02
321	*Mark Eichhorn*	.15	.11	.06
322	*Lee Guetterman*	.15	.11	.06
323	Sid Fernandez	.12	.09	.05
324	Jerry Mumphrey	.05	.04	.02
325	David Palmer	.05	.04	.02
326	Bill Almon	.05	.04	.02
327	Candy Maldonado	.07	.05	.03
328	*John Kruk*	2.00	1.50	.80
329	John Denny	.05	.04	.02
330	Milt Thompson	.07	.05	.03
331	*Mike LaValliere*	.25	.20	.10
332	Alan Ashby	.05	.04	.02
333	Doug Corbett	.05	.04	.02
334	*Ron Karkovice*(FC)	.10	.08	.04
335	Mitch Webster	.07	.05	.03
336	Lee Lacy	.05	.04	.02
337	*Glenn Braggs*(FC)	.15	.11	.06
338	Dwight Lowry	.05	.04	.02
339	Don Baylor	.12	.09	.05
340	Brian Fisher	.07	.05	.03
341	*Reggie Williams*	.10	.08	.04
342	Tom Candiotti	.05	.04	.02
343	Rudy Law	.05	.04	.02
344	Curt Young	.07	.05	.03
345	Mike Fitzgerald	.05	.04	.02
346	*Ruben Sierra*	4.00	3.00	1.50
347	*Mitch Williams*	.40	.30	.15
348	Jorge Orta	.05	.04	.02
349	Mickey Tettleton	.10	.08	.04
350	Ernie Camacho	.05	.04	.02
351	Ron Kittle	.10	.08	.04
352	Ken Landreaux	.05	.04	.02
353	Chet Lemon	.07	.05	.03
354	John Shelby	.05	.04	.02
355	Mark Clear	.05	.04	.02
356	Doug DeCinces	.07	.05	.03
357	Ken Dayley	.05	.04	.02
358	Phil Garner	.05	.04	.02
359	Steve Jeltz	.05	.04	.02
360	Ed Whitson	.05	.04	.02
361	*Barry Bonds*	11.00	8.25	4.50
362	Vida Blue	.10	.08	.04
363	Cecil Cooper	.12	.09	.05
364	Bob Ojeda	.07	.05	.03
365	Dennis Eckersley	.15	.11	.06
366	Mike Morgan	.05	.04	.02
367	Willie Upshaw	.07	.05	.03
368	*Allan Anderson*(FC)	.10	.08	.04
369	Bill Gullickson	.07	.05	.03
370	*Bobby Thigpen*(FC)	.08	.06	.03
371	Juan Beniquez	.05	.04	.02
372	Charlie Moore	.05	.04	.02
373	Dan Petry	.07	.05	.03
374	Rod Scurry	.05	.04	.02
375	Tom Seaver	.40	.30	.15
376	Ed Vande Berg	.05	.04	.02
377	Tony Bernazard	.05	.04	.02
378	Greg Pryor	.05	.04	.02
379	Dwayne Murphy	.07	.05	.03
380	Andy McGaffigan	.05	.04	.02
381	Kirk McCaskill	.07	.05	.03
382	Greg Harris	.05	.04	.02
383	Rich Dotson	.07	.05	.03
384	Craig Reynolds	.05	.04	.02
385	Greg Gross	.05	.04	.02
386	Tito Landrum	.05	.04	.02
387	Craig Lefferts	.05	.04	.02
388	Dave Parker	.20	.15	.08
389	Bob Horner	.10	.08	.04
390	Pat Clements	.05	.04	.02
391	Jeff Leonard	.07	.05	.03
392	Chris Speier	.05	.04	.02
393	John Moses	.05	.04	.02
394	Garth Iorg	.05	.04	.02
395	Greg Gagne	.05	.04	.02
396	Nate Snell	.05	.04	.02
397	*Bryan Clutterbuck*(FC)	.10	.08	.04
398	Darrell Evans	.12	.09	.05
399	Steve Crawford	.05	.04	.02
400	Checklist 346-451	.05	.04	.02
401	*Phil Lombardi*(FC)	.10	.08	.04
402	Rick Honeycutt	.05	.04	.02

		MT	NR MT	EX
403	Ken Schrom	.05	.04	.02
404	Bud Black	.05	.04	.02
405	Donnie Hill	.05	.04	.02
406	Wayne Krenchicki	.05	.04	.02
407	*Chuck Finley*(FC)	.35	.25	.14
408	Toby Harrah	.07	.05	.03
409	Steve Lyons	.05	.04	.02
410	Kevin Bass	.10	.08	.04
411	Marvell Wynne	.05	.04	.02
412	Ron Roenicke	.05	.04	.02
413	*Tracy Jones*	.25	.20	.10
414	Gene Garber	.05	.04	.02
415	Mike Bielecki	.05	.04	.02
416	Frank DiPino	.05	.04	.02
417	Andy Van Slyke	.25	.20	.10
418	Jim Dwyer	.05	.04	.02
419	Ben Oglivie	.07	.05	.03
420	Dave Bergman	.05	.04	.02
421	Joe Sambito	.05	.04	.02
422	*Bob Tewksbury*	.20	.15	.08
423	Len Matuszek	.05	.04	.02
424	*Mike Kingery*(FC)	.15	.11	.06
425	Dave Kingman	.12	.09	.05
426	*Al Newman*	.07	.05	.03
427	Gary Ward	.07	.05	.03
428	Ruppert Jones	.05	.04	.02
429	Harold Baines	.15	.11	.06
430	Pat Perry	.05	.04	.02
431	Terry Puhl	.05	.04	.02
432	Don Carman	.07	.05	.03
433	Eddie Milner	.05	.04	.02
434	LaMarr Hoyt	.05	.04	.02
435	Rick Rhoden	.10	.08	.04
436	Jose Uribe	.07	.05	.03
437	Ken Oberkfell	.05	.04	.02
438	Ron Davis	.05	.04	.02
439	Jesse Orosco	.07	.05	.03
440	Scott Bradley	.05	.04	.02
441	Randy Bush	.05	.04	.02
442	*John Cerutti*	.20	.15	.08
443	Roy Smalley	.05	.04	.02
444	Kelly Gruber	.25	.20	.10
445	Bob Kearney	.05	.04	.02
446	*Ed Hearn*	.10	.08	.04
447	Scott Sanderson	.05	.04	.02
448	Bruce Benedict	.05	.04	.02
449	Junior Ortiz	.05	.04	.02
450	*Mike Aldrete*	.15	.11	.06
451	Kevin McReynolds	.15	.11	.06
452	*Rob Murphy*(FC)	.20	.15	.08
453	Kent Tekulve	.07	.05	.03
454	Curt Ford(FC)	.07	.05	.03
455	Davey Lopes	.07	.05	.03
456	Bobby Grich	.10	.08	.04
457	Jose DeLeon	.07	.05	.03
458	Andre Dawson	.30	.25	.12
459	Mike Flanagan	.07	.05	.03
460	*Joey Meyer*(FC)	.06	.05	.02
461	*Chuck Cary*(FC)	.10	.08	.04
462	Bill Buckner	.10	.08	.04
463	Bob Shirley	.05	.04	.02
464	*Jeff Hamilton*(FC)	.06	.05	.02
465	Phil Niekro	.15	.11	.06
466	Mark Gubicza	.12	.09	.05
467	Jerry Willard	.05	.04	.02
468	*Bob Sebra*(FC)	.10	.08	.04
469	Larry Parrish	.10	.08	.04
470	Charlie Hough	.07	.05	.03
471	Hal McRae	.10	.08	.04
472	*Dave Leiper*(FC)	.10	.08	.04
473	Mel Hall	.07	.05	.03
474	Dan Pasqua	.10	.08	.04
475	Bob Welch	.10	.08	.04
476	Johnny Grubb	.05	.04	.02
477	Jim Traber	.07	.05	.03
478	*Chris Bosio*(FC)	.40	.30	.15
479	Mark McLemore	.07	.05	.03
480	John Morris	.05	.04	.02
481	Billy Hatcher	.07	.05	.03
482	Dan Schatzeder	.05	.04	.02
483	Rich Gossage	.15	.11	.06
484	Jim Morrison	.05	.04	.02
485	Bob Brenly	.05	.04	.02
486	Bill Schroeder	.05	.04	.02
487	Mookie Wilson	.10	.08	.04
488	*Dave Martinez*(FC)	.25	.20	.10
489	Harold Reynolds	.10	.08	.04
490	Jeff Hearron	.05	.04	.02
491	Mickey Hatcher	.05	.04	.02
492	*Barry Larkin*(FC)	3.00	2.25	1.25
493	Bob James	.05	.04	.02

		MT	NR MT	EX
494	John Habyan	.05	.04	.02
495	*Jim Adduci*(FC)	.07	.05	.03
496	Mike Heath	.05	.04	.02
497	Tim Stoddard	.05	.04	.02
498	Tony Armas	.07	.05	.03
499	Dennis Powell	.05	.04	.02
500	Checklist 452-557	.05	.04	.02
501	Chris Bando	.05	.04	.02
502	*David Cone*(FC)	2.50	2.00	1.00
503	Jay Howell	.07	.05	.03
504	Tom Foley	.05	.04	.02
505	*Ray Chadwick*(FC)	.10	.08	.04
506	*Mike Loynd*(FC)	.15	.11	.06
507	Neil Allen	.05	.04	.02
508	Danny Darwin	.05	.04	.02
509	Rick Schu	.05	.04	.02
510	Jose Oquendo	.05	.04	.02
511	Gene Walter	.07	.05	.03
512	*Terry McGriff*(FC)	.12	.09	.05
513	Ken Griffey	.10	.08	.04
514	Benny Distefano	.05	.04	.02
515	*Terry Mulholland*(FC)	.80	.60	.30
516	Ed Lynch	.05	.04	.02
517	Bill Swift	.25	.20	.10
518	Manny Lee(FC)	.07	.05	.03
519	Andre David	.05	.04	.02
520	Scott McGregor	.07	.05	.03
521	Rick Manning	.05	.04	.02
522	Willie Hernandez	.07	.05	.03
523	Marty Barrett	.10	.08	.04
524	Wayne Tolleson	.05	.04	.02
525	*Jose Gonzalez*(FC)	.15	.11	.06
526	Cory Snyder	.12	.09	.05
527	Buddy Biancalana	.05	.04	.02
528	Moose Haas	.05	.04	.02
529	*Wilfredo Tejada*(FC)	.10	.08	.04
530	Stu Cliburn	.05	.04	.02
531	*Dale Mohorcic*(FC)	.20	.15	.08
532	Ron Hassey	.05	.04	.02
533	Ty Gainey	.05	.04	.02
534	Jerry Royster	.05	.04	.02
535	*Mike Maddux*(FC)	.20	.15	.08
536	Ted Power	.05	.04	.02
537	Ted Simmons	.12	.09	.05
538	*Rafael Belliard*(FC)	.12	.09	.05
539	Chico Walker	.05	.04	.02
540	Bob Forsch	.07	.05	.03
541	John Stefero	.05	.04	.02
542	*Dale Sveum*	.08	.06	.03
543	Mark Thurmond	.05	.04	.02
544	*Jeff Sellers*	.20	.15	.08
545	Joel Skinner	.05	.04	.02
546	Alex Trevino	.05	.04	.02
547	*Randy Kutcher*(FC)	.10	.08	.04
548	Joaquin Andujar	.07	.05	.03
549	*Casey Candaele*(FC)	.15	.11	.06
550	Jeff Russell	.05	.04	.02
551	John Candelaria	.10	.08	.04
552	Joe Cowley	.05	.04	.02
553	Danny Cox	.07	.05	.03
554	Denny Walling	.05	.04	.02
555	*Bruce Ruffin*(FC)	.20	.15	.08
556	Buddy Bell	.10	.08	.04
557	*Jimmy Jones*(FC)	.20	.15	.08
558	*Bobby Bonilla*	2.00	1.50	.80
559	Jeff Robinson	.07	.05	.03
560	Ed Olwine	.05	.04	.02
561	*Glenallen Hill*(FC)	.30	.25	.12
562	Lee Mazzilli	.07	.05	.03
563	Mike Brown	.05	.04	.02
564	George Frazier	.05	.04	.02
565	*Mike Sharperson*(FC)	.10	.08	.04
566	*Mark Portugal*	.10	.08	.04
567	Rick Leach	.05	.04	.02
568	Mark Langston	.12	.09	.05
569	Rafael Santana	.05	.04	.02
570	Manny Trillo	.07	.05	.03
571	Cliff Speck	.05	.04	.02
572	Bob Kipper	.05	.04	.02
573	*Kelly Downs*(FC)	.10	.08	.04
574	*Randy Asadoor*(FC)	.10	.08	.04
575	*Dave Magadan*(FC)	.40	.30	.15
576	*Marvin Freeman*(FC)	.12	.09	.05
577	Jeff Lahti	.05	.04	.02
578	Jeff Calhoun	.05	.04	.02
579	Gus Polidor(FC)	.07	.05	.03
580	Gene Nelson	.05	.04	.02
581	Tim Teufel	.05	.04	.02
582	Odell Jones	.05	.04	.02
583	Mark Ryal	.05	.04	.02
584	Randy O'Neal	.05	.04	.02

		MT	NR MT	EX
585	*Mike Greenwell*(FC)	1.25	.90	.50
586	Ray Knight	.07	.05	.03
587	*Ralph Bryant*(FC)	.12	.09	.05
588	Carmen Castillo	.05	.04	.02
589	Ed Wojna	.05	.04	.02
590	Stan Javier	.05	.04	.02
591	*Jeff Musselman*(FC)	.20	.15	.08
592	*Mike Stanley*(FC)	.75	.60	.30
593	Darrell Porter	.07	.05	.03
594	*Drew Hall*(FC)	.20	.15	.08
595	*Rob Nelson*(FC)	.10	.08	.04
596	Bryan Oelkers	.05	.04	.02
597	*Scott Nielsen*(FC)	.10	.08	.04
598	*Brian Holton*(FC)	.20	.15	.08
599	*Kevin Mitchell*	1.50	1.25	.60
600	Checklist 558-660	.05	.04	.02
601	Jackie Gutierrez	.05	.04	.02
602	*Barry Jones*(FC)	.12	.09	.05
603	Jerry Narron	.05	.04	.02
604	Steve Lake	.05	.04	.02
605	Jim Pankovits	.05	.04	.02
606	Ed Romero	.05	.04	.02
607	Dave LaPoint	.07	.05	.03
608	Don Robinson	.07	.05	.03
609	Mike Krukow	.07	.05	.03
610	*Dave Valle*(FC)	.12	.09	.05
611	Len Dykstra	.80	.60	.30
612	Roberto Clemente Puzzle Card	.05	.04	.02
613	Mike Trujillo(FC)	.05	.04	.02
614	Damaso Garcia	.05	.04	.02
615	Neal Heaton	.05	.04	.02
616	Juan Berenguer	.05	.04	.02
617	Steve Carlton	.25	.20	.10
618	Gary Lucas	.05	.04	.02
619	Geno Petralli	.05	.04	.02
620	Rick Aguilera	.20	.15	.08
621	Fred McGriff	4.00	3.00	1.50
622	Dave Henderson	.10	.08	.04
623	*Dave Clark*(FC)	.08	.06	.03
624	Angel Salazar	.05	.04	.02
625	Randy Hunt	.05	.04	.02
626	John Gibbons	.05	.04	.02
627	*Kevin Brown*(FC)	1.50	1.25	.60
628	Bill Dawley	.05	.04	.02
629	Aurelio Lopez	.05	.04	.02
630	Charlie Hudson	.05	.04	.02
631	Ray Soff	.05	.04	.02
632	*Ray Hayward*(FC)	.12	.09	.05
633	Spike Owen	.05	.04	.02
634	Glenn Hubbard	.05	.04	.02
635	*Kevin Elster*(FC)	.08	.06	.03
636	Mike LaCoss	.05	.04	.02
637	Dwayne Henry	.05	.04	.02
638	*Rey Quinones*	.15	.11	.06
639	Jim Clancy	.07	.05	.03
640	Larry Andersen	.05	.04	.02
641	Calvin Schiraldi	.05	.04	.02
642	*Stan Jefferson*(FC)	.15	.11	.06
643	Marc Sullivan	.05	.04	.02
644	Mark Grant	.05	.04	.02
645	Cliff Johnson	.05	.04	.02
646	Howard Johnson	.25	.20	.10
647	Dave Sax	.05	.04	.02
648	Dave Stewart	.10	.08	.04
649	Danny Heep	.05	.04	.02
650	Joe Johnson	.05	.04	.02
651	*Bob Brower*(FC)	.15	.11	.06
652	Rob Woodward	.07	.05	.03
653	John Mizerock	.05	.04	.02
654	*Tim Pyznarski*(FC)	.10	.08	.04
655	*Luis Aquino*(FC)	.10	.08	.04
656	Mickey Brantley(FC)	.10	.08	.04
657	Doyle Alexander	.07	.05	.03
658	Sammy Stewart	.05	.04	.02
659	Jim Acker	.05	.04	.02
660	Pete Ladd	.05	.04	.02

1987 Donruss All-Stars

Issued in conjunction with the Donruss Pop-Ups set for the second consecutive year, the 1987 Donruss All-Stars set consists of 59 players (plus a checklist) who were selected to the 1986 All-Star Game. Measuring 3-1/2" by 5" in size, the card fronts feature black borders and American or National League logos. Included on the backs are the player's career highlights and All-Star Game statistics. Retail packs included one pop-Up card,

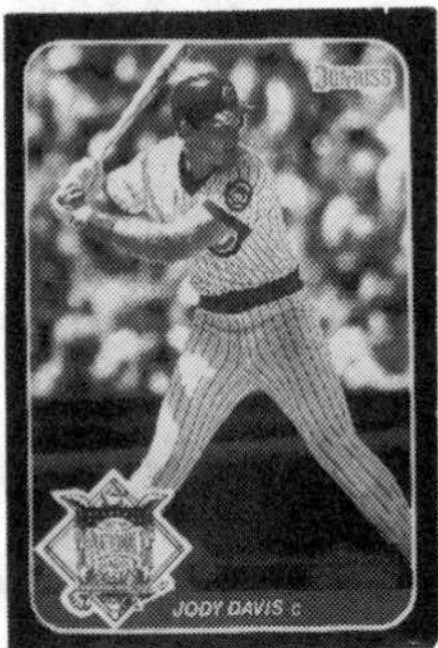

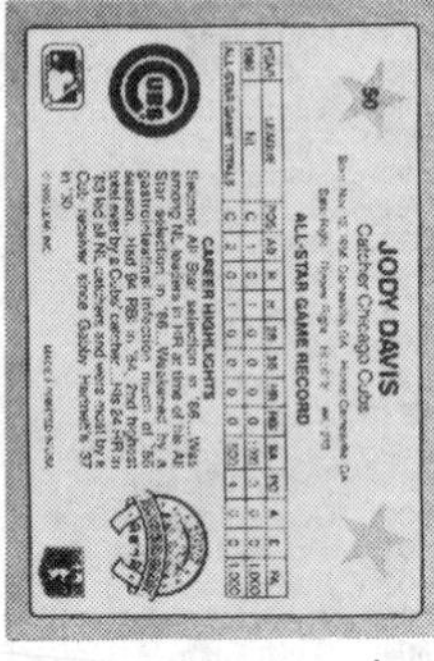

three All-Star cards and one Roberto Clemente puzzle.

		MT	NR MT	EX
Complete Set:		7.00	5.25	2.75
Common Player:		.09	.07	.04
1	Wally Joyner	.80	.60	.30
2	Dave Winfield	.25	.20	.10
3	Lou Whitaker	.15	.11	.06
4	Kirby Puckett	.50	.40	.20
5	Cal Ripken, Jr.	.60	.45	.25
6	Rickey Henderson	.50	.40	.20
7	Wade Boggs	.60	.45	.25
8	Roger Clemens	.50	.40	.20
9	Lance Parrish	.09	.07	.04
10	Dick Howser	.09	.07	.04
11	Keith Hernandez	.10	.08	.04
12	Darryl Strawberry	.50	.40	.20
13	Ryne Sandberg	.60	.45	.25
14	Dale Murphy	.40	.30	.15
15	Ozzie Smith	.15	.11	.06
16	Tony Gwynn	.30	.25	.12
17	Mike Schmidt	.40	.30	.15
18	Dwight Gooden	.60	.45	.25
19	Gary Carter	.15	.11	.06
20	Whitey Herzog	.09	.07	.04
21	Jose Canseco	1.50	1.25	.60
22	John Franco	.09	.07	.04
23	Jesse Barfield	.12	.09	.05
24	Rick Rhoden	.09	.07	.04
25	Harold Baines	.15	.11	.06
26	Sid Fernandez	.12	.09	.05
27	George Brett	.40	.30	.15
28	Steve Sax	.15	.11	.06
29	Jim Presley	.12	.09	.05
30	Dave Smith	.09	.07	.04
31	Eddie Murray	.10	.08	.04
32	Mike Scott	.12	.09	.05
33	Don Mattingly	1.00	.70	.40
34	Dave Parker	.15	.11	.06
35	Tony Fernandez	.15	.11	.06
36	Tim Raines	.25	.20	.10
37	Brook Jacoby	.12	.09	.05
38	Chili Davis	.09	.07	.04
39	Rich Gedman	.09	.07	.04
40	Kevin Bass	.09	.07	.04
41	Frank White	.09	.07	.04
42	Glenn Davis	.15	.11	.06
43	Willie Hernandez	.09	.07	.04
44	Chris Brown	.09	.07	.04
45	Jim Rice	.10	.08	.04
46	Tony Pena	.09	.07	.04
47	Don Aase	.09	.07	.04
48	Hubie Brooks	.09	.07	.04
49	Charlie Hough	.09	.07	.04
50	Jody Davis	.09	.07	.04
51	Mike Witt	.09	.07	.04
52	Jeff Reardon	.12	.09	.05
53	Ken Schrom	.09	.07	.04
54	Fernando Valenzuela	.10	.08	.04
55	Dave Righetti	.15	.11	.06
56	Shane Rawley	.09	.07	.04
57	Ted Higuera	.12	.09	.05
58	Mike Krukow	.09	.07	.04
59	Lloyd Moseby	.09	.07	.04
60	Checklist	.09	.07	.04

1987 Donruss Box Panels

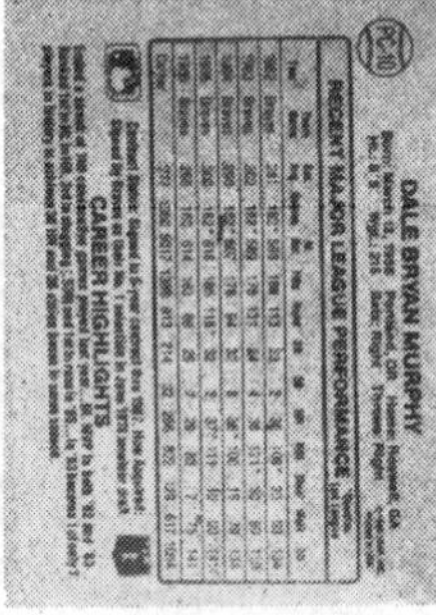

Continuing with an idea they initiated in 1985, Donruss once again placed baseball cards on the bottoms of their retail boxes. The cards, which are 2-1/2" by 3-1/2" in size, come four to a panel with each panel containing an unnumbered Roberto Clemente puzzle card. With numbering that begins where Donruss left off in 1986, cards PC 10 through PC 12 were found on boxes of Donruss regular issue wax packs. Cards PC 13 through PC 15 were located on boxes of the 1987 All-Star/Pop-Up packs.

		MT	NR MT	EX
Complete Panel Set:		5.00	3.75	2.00
Complete Singles Set:		3.00	2.25	1.25
Common Single Player:		.15	.11	.06
	Panel	4.00	3.00	1.50
10	Dale Murphy	.35	.25	.14
11	Jeff Reardon	.20	.15	.08
12	Jose Canseco	2.00	1.50	.80
---	Roberto Clemente Puzzle Card	.04	.03	.02
	Panel	2.25	1.75	.90
13	Mike Scott	.20	.15	.08
14	Roger Clemens	1.00	.70	.40
15	Mike Krukow	.15	.11	.06
---	Roberto Clemente Puzzle Card	.04	.03	.02

1987 Donruss Diamond Kings Supers

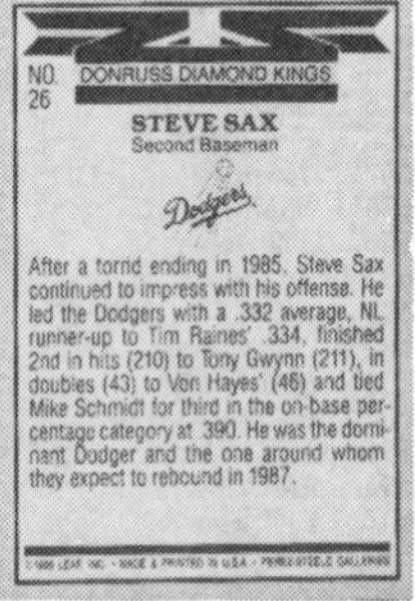

For a third straight baseball card season, Donruss produced a set of enlarged size Diamond Kings. The cards, which measure 4-11/16" by 6-3/4", are giant versions of the Diamond Kings subset found in the regular 1987 Donruss set. The 28-card set, which features the artwork of Dick Perez, contains 26 player cards, a checklist and a Roberto Clemente puzzle card. The set was available through a mail-in offer for $9.50 plus three wrappers.

	MT	NR MT	EX
Complete Set:	12.00	9.00	4.75

		MT	NR MT	EX
Common Player:		.20	.15	.08
1	Wally Joyner	.90	.70	.35
2	Roger Clemens	1.00	.70	.40
3	Dale Murphy	.40	.30	.15
4	Darryl Strawberry	.90	.70	.35
5	Ozzie Smith	.30	.25	.12
6	Jose Canseco	2.00	1.50	.80
7	Charlie Hough	.20	.15	.08
8	Brook Jacoby	.20	.15	.08
9	Fred Lynn	.20	.15	.08
10	Rick Rhoden	.20	.15	.08
11	Chris Brown	.25	.20	.10
12	Von Hayes	.25	.20	.10
13	Jack Morris	.20	.15	.08
14	Kevin McReynolds	.35	.25	.14
15	George Brett	.70	.50	.30
16	Ted Higuera	.20	.15	.08
17	Hubie Brooks	.20	.15	.08
18	Mike Scott	.20	.15	.08
19	Kirby Puckett	.90	.70	.35
20	Dave Winfield	.30	.25	.12
21	Lloyd Moseby	.20	.15	.08
22	Eric Davis	.90	.70	.35
23	Jim Presley	.25	.20	.10
24	Keith Moreland	.20	.15	.08
25	Greg Walker	.20	.15	.08
26	Steve Sax	.30	.25	.12
27	Checklist	.15	.11	.06
—	Roberto Clemente Puzzle Card	.15	.11	.06

1987 Donruss Highlights

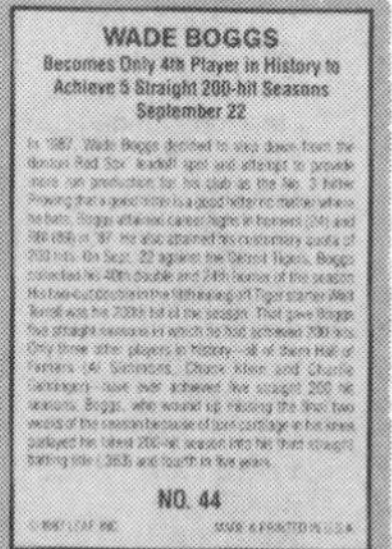

For a third consecutive year, Donruss produced a 56-card set which highlighted the special events of the 1987 baseball season. The cards, which measure 2-1/2" by 3-1/2", have a front design similar to the regular 1987 Donruss set. A blue border and the "Highlights" logo are the significant differences. The card backs feature black print on a white background and include the date the event took place plus the particulars about it. As in the past, the set includes Donruss' picks for the A.L. and N.L. Rookies of the Year. The set was issued in a specially designed box and was available only through hobby dealers.

		MT	NR MT	EX
Complete Set:		8.00	6.00	3.25
Common Player:		.10	.08	.04
1	First No-Hitter For Brewers (Juan Nieves)	.15	.11	.06
2	Hits 500th Homer (Mike Schmidt)	.40	.30	.15
3	N.L. Player of the Month - April (Eric Davis)	.50	.40	.20
4	N.L. Pitcher of the Month - April (Sid Fernandez)	.10	.08	.04
5	A.L. Player of the Month - April (Brian Downing)	.10	.08	.04
6	A.L. Pitcher of the Month - April (Bret Saberhagen)	.30	.25	.12
7	Free Agent Holdout Returns (Tim Raines)	.25	.20	.10
8	N.L. Player of the Month - May (Eric Davis)	.50	.40	.20
9	N.L. Pitcher of the Month - May (Steve Bedrosian)	.15	.11	.06
10	A.L. Player of the Month - May (Larry Parrish)	.10	.08	.04
11	A.L. Pitcher of the Month - May (Jim Clancy)	.10	.08	.04
12	N.L. Player of the Month - June (Tony Gwynn)	.30	.25	.12
13	N.L. Pitcher of the Month - June (Orel Hershiser)	.25	.20	.10
14	A.L. Player of the Month - June (Wade Boggs)	.80	.60	.30
15	A.L. Pitcher of the Month - June (Steve Ontiveros)	.10	.08	.04
16	All Star Game Hero (Tim Raines)	.25	.20	.10
17	Consecutive Game Homer Streak (Don Mattingly)	1.00	.70	.40
18	1987 Hall of Fame Inductee (Jim "Catfish" Hunter)	.20	.15	.08
19	1987 Hall of Fame Inductee (Ray Dandridge)	.10	.08	.04
20	1987 Hall of Fame Inductee (Billy Williams)	.20	.15	.08
21	N.L. Player of the Month - July (Bo Diaz)	.10	.08	.04
22	N.L. Pitcher of the Month - July (Floyd Youmans)	.10	.08	.04
23	A.L. Player of the Month - July (Don Mattingly)	1.00	.70	.40
24	A.L. Pitcher of the Month - July (Frank Viola)	.20	.15	.08
25	Strikes Out 4 Batters In 1 Inning (Bobby Witt)	.15	.11	.06
26	Ties A.L. 9-Inning Game Hit Mark (Kevin Seitzer)	.50	.40	.20
27	Sets Rookie Home Run Record (Mark McGwire)	1.25	.90	.50
28	Sets Cubs' 1st Year Homer Mark (Andre Dawson)	.20	.15	.08
29	Hits In 39 Straight Games (Paul Molitor)	.15	.11	.06
30	Record Weekend (Kirby Puckett)	.50	.40	.20
31	N.L. Player of the Month - August (Andre Dawson)	.20	.15	.08
32	N.L. Pitcher of the Month - August (Doug Drabek)	.10	.08	.04
33	A.L. Player of the Month - August (Dwight Evans)	.15	.11	.06
34	A.L. Pitcher of the Month - August (Mark Langston)	.25	.20	.10
35	100 RBI In 1st 2 Major League Seasons (Wally Joyner)	.40	.30	.15
36	100 SB In 1st 3 Major League Seasons (Vince Coleman)	.20	.15	.08
37	Orioles' All Time Homer King (Eddie Murray)	.10	.08	.04
38	Ends Consecutive Innings Streak (Cal Ripken)	.30	.25	.12
39	Blue Jays Hit Record 10 Homers In 1 Game (Rob Ducey, Fred McGriff, Ernie Whitt)	.50	.40	.20
40	Equal A's RBI Marks (Jose Canseco, Mark McGwire)	2.50	2.00	1.00
41	Sets All-Time Catching Record (Bob Boone)	.10	.08	.04
42	Sets Mets' One-Season HR Mark (Darryl Strawberry)	.50	.40	.20
43	N.L.'s All-Time Switch Hit HR King (Howard Johnson)	.15	.11	.06
44	Five Straight 200-Hit Seasons (Wade Boggs)	.80	.60	.30
45	Eclipses Rookie Game Hitting Streak (Benito Santiago)	.40	.30	.15
46	Eclipses Jackson's A's HR Record (Mark McGwire)	1.25	.90	.50
47	13th Rookie To Collect 200 Hits (Kevin Seitzer)	.50	.40	.20
48	Sets Slam Record (Don Mattingly)	1.00	.70	.40
49	N.L. Player of the Month - September (Darryl Strawberry)	.50	.40	.20
50	N.L. Pitcher of the Month - September (Pascual Perez)	.10	.08	.04
51	A.L. Player of the Month - September (Alan Trammell)	.20	.15	.08
52	A.L. Pitcher of the Month - September (Doyle Alexander)	.10	.08	.04
53	Strikeout King - Again (Nolan Ryan)	1.00	.70	.40
54	Donruss A.L. Rookie of the Year (Mark McGwire)	1.25	.90	.50
55	Donruss N.L. Rookie of the Year (Benito Santiago)	.40	.30	.15

		MT	NR MT	EX
56	Highlight Checklist	.10	.08	.04

1987 Donruss Opening Day

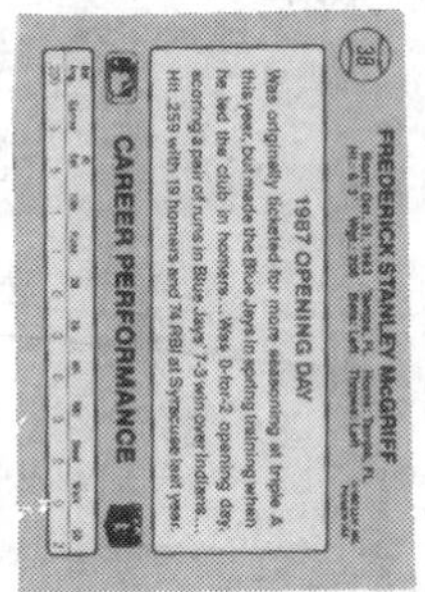

The Donruss Opening Day set includes all players in major league baseball's starting lineups on the opening day of the 1987 baseball season. Cards in the 272-piece set measure 2-1/2" by 3-1/2" and have a glossy coating. The card fronts are identical in design to the regular Donruss set, but new photos were utilized and the fronts contain maroon borders as opposed to black. The backs carry black printing on white and yellow and carry a brief player biography plus the player's career statistics. The set was packaged in a sturdy 15" by 5" by 2" box with a clear acetate lid.

		MT	NR MT	EX
Complete Set:		25.00	18.50	10.00
Common Player:		.05	.04	.02
1	Doug DeCinces	.07	.05	.03
2	Mike Witt	.12	.09	.05
3	George Hendrick	.07	.05	.03
4	Dick Schofield	.05	.04	.02
5	Devon White	.50	.40	.20
6	Butch Wynegar	.05	.04	.02
7	Wally Joyner	.75	.55	.30
8	Mark McLemore	.05	.04	.02
9	Brian Downing	.07	.05	.03
10	Gary Pettis	.05	.04	.02
11	Bill Doran	.07	.05	.03
12	Phil Garner	.05	.04	.02
13	Jose Cruz	.07	.05	.03
14	Kevin Bass	.07	.05	.03
15	Mike Scott	.12	.09	.05
16	Glenn Davis	.15	.11	.06
17	Alan Ashby	.05	.04	.02
18	Billy Hatcher	.07	.05	.03
19	Craig Reynolds	.05	.04	.02
20	Carney Lansford	.07	.05	.03
21	Mike Davis	.05	.04	.02
22	Reggie Jackson	.30	.25	.12
23	Mickey Tettleton	.07	.05	.03
24	Jose Canseco	2.50	2.00	1.00
25	Rob Nelson	.05	.04	.02
26	Tony Phillips	.05	.04	.02
27	Dwayne Murphy	.05	.04	.02
28	Alfredo Griffin	.07	.05	.03
29	Curt Young	.05	.04	.02
30	Willie Upshaw	.05	.04	.02
31	Mike Sharperson	.05	.04	.02
32	Rance Mulliniks	.05	.04	.02
33	Ernie Whitt	.05	.04	.02
34	Jesse Barfield	.12	.09	.05
35	Tony Fernandez	.12	.09	.05
36	Lloyd Moseby	.07	.05	.03
37	Jimmy Key	.10	.08	.04
38	Fred McGriff	1.50	1.25	.60
39	George Bell	.25	.20	.10
40	Dale Murphy	.40	.30	.15
41	Rick Mahler	.05	.04	.02
42	Ken Griffey	.07	.05	.03
43	Andres Thomas	.10	.08	.04
44	Dion James	.05	.04	.02
45	Ozzie Virgil	.05	.04	.02
46	Ken Oberkfell	.05	.04	.02
47	Gary Roenicke	.05	.04	.02
48	Glenn Hubbard	.05	.04	.02
49	Bill Schroeder	.05	.04	.02
50	Greg Brock	.07	.05	.03
51	Billy Jo Robidoux	.05	.04	.02
52	Glenn Braggs	.12	.09	.05
53	Jim Gantner	.05	.04	.02
54	Paul Molitor	.15	.11	.06
55	Dale Sveum	.15	.11	.06
56	Ted Higuera	.12	.09	.05
57	Rob Deer	.07	.05	.03
58	Robin Yount	.35	.25	.14
59	Jim Lindeman	.10	.08	.04
60	Vince Coleman	.15	.11	.06
61	Tommy Herr	.07	.05	.03
62	Terry Pendleton	.07	.05	.03
63	John Tudor	.10	.08	.04
64	Tony Pena	.07	.05	.03
65	Ozzie Smith	.15	.11	.06
66	Tito Landrum	.05	.04	.02
67	Jack Clark	.15	.11	.06
68	Bob Dernier	.05	.04	.02
69	Rick Sutcliffe	.10	.08	.04
70	Andre Dawson	.20	.15	.08
71	Keith Moreland	.07	.05	.03
72	Jody Davis	.07	.05	.03
73	Brian Dayett	.05	.04	.02
74	Leon Durham	.07	.05	.03
75	Ryne Sandberg	.25	.20	.10
76	Shawon Dunston	.20	.15	.08
77	Mike Marshall	.10	.08	.04
78	Bill Madlock	.07	.05	.03
79	Orel Hershiser	.30	.25	.12
80	Mike Ramsey	.05	.04	.02
81	Ken Landreaux	.05	.04	.02
82	Mike Scioscia	.05	.04	.02
83	Franklin Stubbs	.07	.05	.03
84	Mariano Duncan	.05	.04	.02
85	Steve Sax	.15	.11	.06
86	Mitch Webster	.07	.05	.03
87	Reid Nichols	.05	.04	.02
88	Tim Wallach	.10	.08	.04
89	Floyd Youmans	.07	.05	.03
90	Andres Galarraga	.25	.20	.10
91	Hubie Brooks	.07	.05	.03
92	Jeff Reed	.05	.04	.02
93	Alonzo Powell	.05	.04	.02
94	Vance Law	.05	.04	.02
95	Bob Brenly	.05	.04	.02
96	Will Clark	2.50	2.00	1.00
97	Chili Davis	.07	.05	.03
98	Mike Krukow	.05	.04	.02
99	Jose Uribe	.05	.04	.02
100	Chris Brown	.07	.05	.03
101	Rob Thompson	.10	.08	.04
102	Candy Maldonado	.07	.05	.03
103	Jeff Leonard	.07	.05	.03
104	Tom Candiotti	.05	.04	.02
105	Chris Bando	.05	.04	.02
106	Cory Snyder	.30	.25	.12
107	Pat Tabler	.07	.05	.03
108	Andre Thornton	.07	.05	.03
109	Joe Carter	.25	.20	.10
110	Tony Bernazard	.05	.04	.02
111	Julio Franco	.10	.08	.04
112	Brook Jacoby	.10	.08	.04
113	Brett Butler	.07	.05	.03
114	Donnell Nixon	.05	.04	.02
115	Alvin Davis	.12	.09	.05
116	Mark Langston	.25	.20	.10
117	Harold Reynolds	.07	.05	.03
118	Ken Phelps	.05	.04	.02
119	Mike Kingery	.10	.08	.04
120	Dave Valle	.07	.05	.03
121	Rey Quinones	.07	.05	.03
122	Phil Bradley	.12	.09	.05
123	Jim Presley	.12	.09	.05
124	Keith Hernandez	.12	.09	.05
125	Kevin McReynolds	.12	.09	.05
126	Rafael Santana	.05	.04	.02
127	Bob Ojeda	.07	.05	.03
128	Darryl Strawberry	.60	.45	.25
129	Mookie Wilson	.07	.05	.03
130	Gary Carter	.15	.11	.06
131	Tim Teufel	.05	.04	.02
132	Howard Johnson	.20	.15	.08
133	Cal Ripken	.30	.25	.12
134	Rick Burleson	.05	.04	.02
135	Fred Lynn	.12	.09	.05

		MT	NR MT	EX
136	Eddie Murray	.15	.11	.06
137	Ray Knight	.07	.05	.03
138	Alan Wiggins	.05	.04	.02
139	John Shelby	.05	.04	.02
140	Mike Boddicker	.07	.05	.03
141	Ken Gerhart	.07	.05	.03
142	Terry Kennedy	.07	.05	.03
143	Steve Garvey	.30	.25	.12
144	Marvell Wynne	.05	.04	.02
145	Kevin Mitchell	1.50	1.25	.60
146	Tony Gwynn	.35	.25	.14
147	Joey Cora	.10	.08	.04
148	Benito Santiago	.60	.45	.25
149	Eric Show	.07	.05	.03
150	Garry Templeton	.07	.05	.03
151	Carmelo Martinez	.05	.04	.02
152	Von Hayes	.10	.08	.04
153	Lance Parrish	.10	.08	.04
154	Milt Thompson	.07	.05	.03
155	Mike Easler	.05	.04	.02
156	Juan Samuel	.10	.08	.04
157	Steve Jeltz	.05	.04	.02
158	Glenn Wilson	.05	.04	.02
159	Shane Rawley	.07	.05	.03
160	Mike Schmidt	.40	.30	.15
161	Andy Van Slyke	.10	.08	.04
162	Johnny Ray	.07	.05	.03
163a	Barry Bonds (dark jersey, photo actually Johnny Ray)	125.00	94.00	50.00
163b	Barry Bonds (white jersey, correct photo)	.50	.40	.20
164	Junior Ortiz	.05	.04	.02
165	Rafael Belliard	.05	.04	.02
166	Bob Patterson	.05	.04	.02
167	Bobby Bonilla	.50	.40	.20
168	Sid Bream	.07	.05	.03
169	Jim Morrison	.05	.04	.02
170	Jerry Browne	.10	.08	.04
171	Scott Fletcher	.05	.04	.02
172	Ruben Sierra	1.50	1.25	.60
173	Larry Parrish	.07	.05	.03
174	Pete O'Brien	.07	.05	.03
175	Pete Incaviglia	.35	.25	.14
176	Don Slaught	.05	.04	.02
177	Oddibe McDowell	.10	.08	.04
178	Charlie Hough	.07	.05	.03
179	Steve Buechele	.05	.04	.02
180	Bob Stanley	.05	.04	.02
181	Wade Boggs	1.00	.70	.40
182	Jim Rice	.10	.08	.04
183	Bill Buckner	.07	.05	.03
184	Dwight Evans	.10	.08	.04
185	Spike Owen	.05	.04	.02
186	Don Baylor	.10	.08	.04
187	Marc Sullivan	.05	.04	.02
188	Marty Barrett	.07	.05	.03
189	Dave Henderson	.07	.05	.03
190	Bo Diaz	.05	.04	.02
191	Barry Larkin	.90	.70	.35
192	Kal Daniels	.25	.20	.10
193	Terry Francona	.05	.04	.02
194	Tom Browning	.07	.05	.03
195	Ron Oester	.05	.04	.02
196	Buddy Bell	.07	.05	.03
197	Eric Davis	.60	.45	.25
198	Dave Parker	.15	.11	.06
199	Steve Balboni	.05	.04	.02
200	Danny Tartabull	.30	.25	.12
201	Ed Hearn	.05	.04	.02
202	Buddy Biancalana	.05	.04	.02
203	Danny Jackson	.05	.04	.02
204	Frank White	.08	.06	.03
205	Bo Jackson	2.50	2.00	1.00
206	George Brett	.40	.30	.15
207	Kevin Seitzer	.90	.70	.35
208	Willie Wilson	.10	.08	.04
209	Orlando Mercado	.05	.04	.02
210	Darrell Evans	.07	.05	.03
211	Larry Herndon	.05	.04	.02
212	Jack Morris	.15	.11	.06
213	Chet Lemon	.07	.05	.03
214	Mike Heath	.05	.04	.02
215	Darnell Coles	.07	.05	.03
216	Alan Trammell	.20	.15	.08
217	Terry Harper	.05	.04	.02
218	Lou Whitaker	.15	.11	.06
219	Gary Gaetti	.15	.11	.06
220	Tom Nieto	.05	.04	.02
221	Kirby Puckett	.80	.60	.30
222	Tom Brunansky	.10	.08	.04
223	Greg Gagne	.05	.04	.02

		MT	NR MT	EX
224	Dan Gladden	.07	.05	.03
225	Mark Davidson	.07	.05	.03
226	Bert Blyleven	.10	.08	.04
227	Steve Lombardozzi	.05	.04	.02
228	Kent Hrbek	.15	.11	.06
229	Gary Redus	.05	.04	.02
230	Ivan Calderon	.10	.08	.04
231	Tim Hulett	.05	.04	.02
232	Carlton Fisk	.15	.11	.06
233	Greg Walker	.07	.05	.03
234	Ron Karkovice	.05	.04	.02
235	Ozzie Guillen	.07	.05	.03
236	Harold Baines	.12	.09	.05
237	Donnie Hill	.05	.04	.02
238	Rich Dotson	.07	.05	.03
239	Mike Pagliarulo	.10	.08	.04
240	Joel Skinner	.05	.04	.02
241	Don Mattingly	1.50	1.25	.60
242	Gary Ward	.05	.04	.02
243	Dave Winfield	.20	.15	.08
244	Dan Pasqua	.10	.08	.04
245	Wayne Tolleson	.05	.04	.02
246	Willie Randolph	.07	.05	.03
247	Dennis Rasmussen	.07	.05	.03
248	Rickey Henderson	.50	.40	.20
249	Angels Checklist	.05	.04	.02
250	Astros Checklist	.05	.04	.02
251	Athletics Checklist	.05	.04	.02
252	Blue Jays Checklist	.05	.04	.02
253	Braves Checklist	.05	.04	.02
254	Brewers Checklist	.05	.04	.02
255	Cardinals Checklist	.05	.04	.02
256	Dodgers Checklist	.05	.04	.02
257	Expos Checklist	.05	.04	.02
258	Giants Checklist	.05	.04	.02
259	Indians Checklist	.05	.04	.02
260	Mariners Checklist	.05	.04	.02
261	Orioles Checklist	.05	.04	.02
262	Padres Checklist	.05	.04	.02
263	Phillies Checklist	.05	.04	.02
264	Pirates Checklist	.05	.04	.02
265	Rangers Checklist	.05	.04	.02
266	Red Sox Checklist	.05	.04	.02
267	Reds Checklist	.05	.04	.02
268	Royals Checklist	.05	.04	.02
269	Tigers Checklist	.05	.04	.02
270	Twins Checklist	.05	.04	.02
271	White Sox/Cubs Checklist	.05	.04	.02
272	Yankees/Mets Checklist	.05	.04	.02

1987 Donruss Pop-Ups

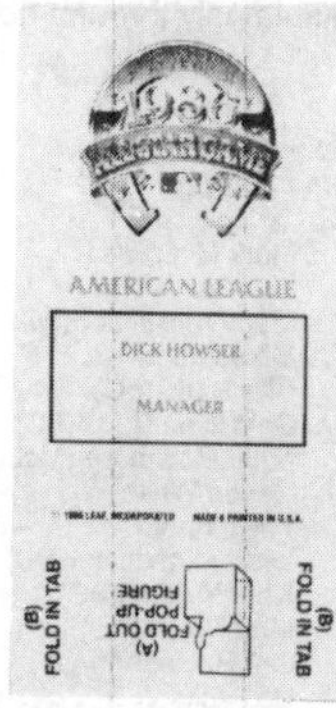

For the second straight year, Donruss released in conjunction with its All-Stars issue a set of cards designed to fold out to form a three-dimensional stand-up card. Consisting of 20 cards, as opposed to the previous year's 18, the 1987 Donruss Pop-Ups set contains players selected to the 1986 All-Star Game. Background for the 2-1/2" by 5" cards is the Houston Astrodome, site of the 1986 mid-summer classic. Retail packs included one Pop-Up card, three All-Star cards and one Roberto Clemente puzzle card.

	MT	NR MT	EX
Complete Set:	4.00	3.00	1.50
Common Player:	.20	.15	.08

		MT	NR MT	EX
(1)	Wade Boggs	.70	.50	.30
(2)	Gary Carter	.25	.20	.10
(3)	Roger Clemens	.80	.60	.30
(4)	Dwight Gooden	.80	.60	.30
(5)	Tony Gwynn	.50	.40	.20
(6)	Rickey Henderson	.75	.55	.30
(7)	Keith Hernandez	.25	.20	.10
(8)	Whitey Herzog	.20	.15	.08
(9)	Dick Howser	.20	.15	.08
(10)	Wally Joyner	.40	.30	.15
(11)	Dale Murphy	.40	.30	.15
(12)	Lance Parrish	.20	.15	.08
(13)	Kirby Puckett	.75	.55	.30
(14)	Cal Ripken	.50	.40	.20
(15)	Ryne Sandberg	.80	.60	.30
(16)	Mike Schmidt	.60	.45	.25
(17)	Ozzie Smith	.30	.25	.12
(18)	Darryl Strawberry	.50	.40	.20
(19)	Lou Whitaker	.20	.15	.08
(20)	Dave Winfield	.30	.25	.12

1987 Donruss Rookies

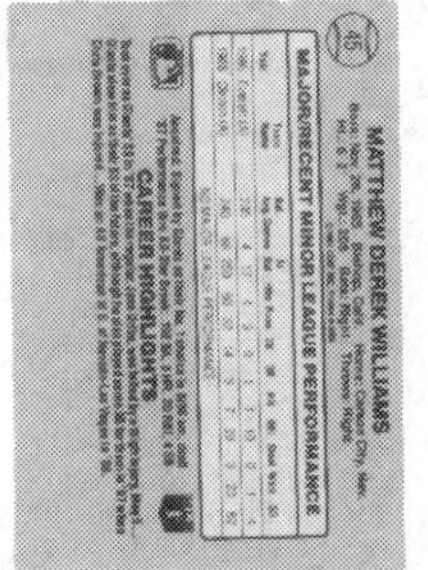

As they did in 1986, Donruss issued a 56-card set highlighting the major league's most promising rookies. The cards are the standard 2-1/2" by 3-1/2" size and are identical in design to the regular Donruss issue. The card fronts have green borders as opposed to the black found in the regular issue and carry the words "The Rookies" in the lower left portion of the card. The set came housed in a specially designed box and was available only through hobby dealers.

		MT	NR MT	EX
Complete Set (56):		20.00	15.00	8.00
Common Player:		.10	.08	.04
1	Mark McGwire	3.25	2.00	1.00
2	Eric Bell	.10	.08	.04
3	Mark Williamson(FC)	.10	.08	.04
4	Mike Greenwell	1.00	.70	.40
5	Ellis Burks(FC)	1.00	.70	.40
6	DeWayne Buice(FC)	.10	.08	.04
7	Mark Mclemore (McLemore)	.10	.08	.04
8	Devon White	.50	.40	.20
9	Willie Fraser	.15	.11	.06
10	Lester Lancaster(FC)	.15	.11	.06
11	Ken Williams(FC)	.10	.08	.04
12	Matt Nokes(FC)	.50	.40	.20
13	Jeff Robinson(FC)	.15	.11	.06
14	Bo Jackson	2.50	2.00	1.00
15	Kevin Seitzer(FC)	.15	.11	.06
16	Billy Ripken(FC)	.15	.11	.06
17	B.J. Surhoff	.15	.11	.06
18	Chuck Crim(FC)	.10	.08	.04
19	Mike Birbeck	.10	.08	.04
20	Chris Bosio	.15	.11	.06
21	Les Straker(FC)	.10	.08	.04
22	Mark Davidson(FC)	.10	.08	.04
23	Gene Larkin(FC)	.35	.25	.14
24	Ken Gerhart	.10	.08	.04
25	Luis Polonia(FC)	.50	.40	.20
26	Terry Steinbach	.25	.20	.10
27	Mickey Brantley	.10	.08	.04
28	Mike Stanley	.60	.40	.20
29	Jerry Browne	.10	.08	.04
30	Todd Benzinger(FC)	.15	.11	.06
31	Fred McGriff	4.00	3.00	1.50
32	Mike Henneman(FC)	.35	.25	.14
33	Casey Candaele	.10	.08	.04
34	Dave Magadan	.25	.15	.05
35	David Cone	1.50	1.00	.50
36	Mike Jackson(FC)	.20	.15	.08
37	John Mitchell(FC)	.10	.08	.04
38	Mike Dunne(FC)	.10	.08	.04
39	John Smiley(FC)	1.00	.70	.40
40	Joe Magrane(FC)	.20	.12	.06
41	Jim Lindeman	.10	.08	.04
42	Shane Mack(FC)	.80	.50	.25
43	Stan Jefferson	.10	.08	.04
44	Benito Santiago	.25	.15	.05
45	Matt Williams(FC)	5.00	3.75	2.00
46	Dave Meads(FC)	.10	.08	.04
47	Rafael Palmeiro	3.50	2.25	1.25
48	Bill Long(FC)	.10	.08	.04
49	Bob Brower	.10	.08	.04
50	James Steels(FC)	.10	.08	.04
51	Paul Noce(FC)	.10	.08	.04
52	Greg Maddux	5.00	3.75	2.00
53	Jeff Musselman	.15	.11	.06
54	Brian Holton	.10	.08	.04
55	Chuck Jackson(FC)	.10	.08	.04
56	Checklist 1-56	.10	.08	.04

1988 Donruss

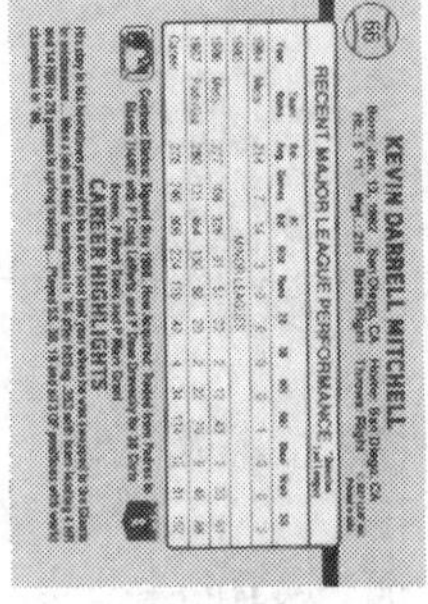

The 1988 Donruss set consists of 660 cards, each measuring 2-1/2" by 3-1/2" in size. The card fronts feature a full-color photo surrounded by a colorful border - alternating stripes of black, red, black, blue, black, blue, black, red and black (in that order) - separated by soft-focus edges and airbrushed fades. The player's name and position appear in a red band at the bottom of the card. The Donruss logo is situated in the upper left corner of the card, while the team logo is located in the lower right corner. For the seventh consecutive season, Donruss included a subset of "Diamond Kings" cards (#'s 1-27) in the issue. And for the fifth straight year, Donruss incorporated their highly popular "Rated Rookies" (card #'s 28-47) with the set.

		MT	NR MT	EX
Complete Set (660):		20.00	15.00	8.00
Common Player		.05	.04	.02
1	Mark McGwire (DK)	.25	.20	.10
2	Tim Raines (DK)	.08	.06	.03
3	Benito Santiago (DK)	.08	.06	.03
4	Alan Trammell (DK)	.08	.06	.03
5	Danny Tartabull (DK)	.10	.08	.04
6	Ron Darling (DK)	.12	.09	.05
7	Paul Molitor (DK)	.12	.09	.05
8	Devon White (DK)	.10	.08	.04
9	Andre Dawson (DK)	.10	.08	.04
10	Julio Franco (DK)	.10	.08	.04
11	Scott Fletcher (DK)	.07	.05	.03
12	Tony Fernandez (DK)	.12	.09	.05
13	Shane Rawley (DK)	.07	.05	.03
14	Kal Daniels (DK)	.06	.05	.02
15	Jack Clark (DK)	.06	.05	.02
16	Dwight Evans (DK)	.08	.06	.03
17	Tommy John (DK)	.08	.06	.03
18	Andy Van Slyke (DK)	.10	.08	.04
19	Gary Gaetti (DK)	.06	.05	.02

		MT	NR MT	EX
20	Mark Langston (DK)	.06	.05	.02
21	Will Clark (DK)	.25	.20	.10
22	Glenn Hubbard (DK)	.07	.05	.03
23	Billy Hatcher (DK)	.07	.05	.03
24	Bob Welch (DK)	.10	.08	.04
25	Ivan Calderon (DK)	.10	.08	.04
26	Cal Ripken, Jr. (DK)	.35	.25	.14
27	Checklist 1-27	.05	.04	.02
28	*Mackey Sasser* (RR)	.10	.08	.04
29	*Jeff Treadway* (RR)	.10	.08	.04
30	*Mike Campbell* (RR)(FC)	.12	.09	.05
31	*Lance Johnson* (RR)	.50	.40	.20
32	*Nelson Liriano* (RR)(FC)	.08	.06	.03
33	Shawn Abner (RR)(FC)	.08	.06	.03
34	*Roberto Alomar* (RR)	4.00	3.00	1.50
35	*Shawn Hillegas* (RR)(FC)	.08	.06	.03
36	Joey Meyer (RR)	.06	.05	.02
37	Kevin Elster (RR)	.08	.06	.03
38	*Jose Lind* (RR)	.12	.09	.05
39	*Kirt Manwaring* (RR)	.15	.11	.06
40	*Mark Grace* (RR)	1.25	.90	.50
41	*Jody Reed* (RR)	.20	.15	.08
42	*John Farrell* (RR)(FC)	.08	.06	.03
43	*Al Leiter* (RR)(FC)	.12	.09	.05
44	*Gary Thurman* (RR)(FC)	.08	.06	.03
45	*Vicente Palacios* (RR)	.10	.08	.04
46	*Eddie Williams* (RR)(FC)	.06	.05	.02
47	*Jack McDowell* (RR)	1.25	.90	.50
48	Ken Dixon	.05	.04	.02
49	Mike Birkbeck	.07	.05	.03
50	Eric King	.07	.05	.03
51	Roger Clemens	.60	.45	.25
52	Pat Clements	.05	.04	.02
53	Fernando Valenzuela	.06	.05	.02
54	Mark Gubicza	.12	.09	.05
55	Jay Howell	.07	.05	.03
56	Floyd Youmans	.05	.04	.02
57	Ed Correa	.05	.04	.02
58	*DeWayne Buice*	.15	.11	.06
59	Jose DeLeon	.07	.05	.03
60	Danny Cox	.07	.05	.03
61	Nolan Ryan	.50	.40	.20
62	Steve Bedrosian	.12	.09	.05
63	Tom Browning	.10	.08	.04
64	Mark Davis	.05	.04	.02
65	R.J. Reynolds	.05	.04	.02
66	Kevin Mitchell	.15	.11	.06
67	Ken Oberkfell	.05	.04	.02
68	Rick Sutcliffe	.10	.08	.04
69	Dwight Gooden	.12	.09	.05
70	Scott Bankhead	.07	.05	.03
71	Bert Blyleven	.12	.09	.05
72	Jimmy Key	.10	.08	.04
73	*Les Straker*	.15	.11	.06
74	Jim Clancy	.07	.05	.03
75	Mike Moore	.05	.04	.02
76	Ron Darling	.12	.09	.05
77	Ed Lynch	.05	.04	.02
78	Dale Murphy	.10	.08	.04
79	Doug Drabek	.07	.05	.03
80	Scott Garrelts	.05	.04	.02
81	Ed Whitson	.05	.04	.02
82	Rob Murphy	.07	.05	.03
83	Shane Rawley	.07	.05	.03
84	Greg Mathews	.07	.05	.03
85	Jim Deshaies	.07	.05	.03
86	Mike Witt	.07	.05	.03
87	Donnie Hill	.05	.04	.02
88	Jeff Reed	.05	.04	.02
89	Mike Boddicker	.07	.05	.03
90	Ted Higuera	.10	.08	.04
91	Walt Terrell	.07	.05	.03
92	Bob Stanley	.05	.04	.02
93	Dave Righetti	.15	.11	.06
94	Orel Hershiser	.08	.06	.03
95	Chris Bando	.05	.04	.02
96	Bret Saberhagen	.10	.08	.04
97	Curt Young	.07	.05	.03
98	Tim Burke	.05	.04	.02
99	Charlie Hough	.07	.05	.03
100a	Checklist 28-137	.05	.04	.02
100b	Checklist 28-133	.10	.08	.04
101	Bobby Witt	.10	.08	.04
102	George Brett	.40	.30	.15
103	Mickey Tettleton	.15	.11	.06
104	Scott Bailes	.07	.05	.03
105	Mike Pagliarulo	.10	.08	.04
106	Mike Scioscia	.07	.05	.03
107	Tom Brookens	.05	.04	.02
108	Ray Knight	.07	.05	.03
109	Dan Plesac	.10	.08	.04
110	Wally Joyner	.12	.09	.05

		MT	NR MT	EX
111	Bob Forsch	.07	.05	.03
112	Mike Scott	.12	.09	.05
113	Kevin Gross	.07	.05	.03
114	Benito Santiago	.10	.08	.04
115	Bob Kipper	.05	.04	.02
116	Mike Krukow	.07	.05	.03
117	Chris Bosio	.07	.05	.03
118	Sid Fernandez	.10	.08	.04
119	Jody Davis	.07	.05	.03
120	Mike Morgan	.05	.04	.02
121	Mark Eichhorn	.07	.05	.03
122	Jeff Reardon	.10	.08	.04
123	John Franco	.10	.08	.04
124	Richard Dotson	.07	.05	.03
125	Eric Bell	.05	.04	.02
126	Juan Nieves	.07	.05	.03
127	Jack Morris	.12	.09	.05
128	Rick Rhoden	.07	.05	.03
129	Rich Gedman	.07	.05	.03
130	Ken Howell	.05	.04	.02
131	Brook Jacoby	.10	.08	.04
132	Danny Jackson	.12	.09	.05
133	Gene Nelson	.05	.04	.02
134	Neal Heaton	.05	.04	.02
135	Willie Fraser	.05	.04	.02
136	Jose Guzman	.07	.05	.03
137	Ozzie Guillen	.07	.05	.03
138	Bob Knepper	.07	.05	.03
139	*Mike Jackson*	.20	.15	.08
140	*Joe Magrane*	.08	.06	.03
141	Jimmy Jones	.07	.05	.03
142	Ted Power	.05	.04	.02
143	Ozzie Virgil	.05	.04	.02
144	*Felix Fermin*(FC)	.15	.11	.06
145	Kelly Downs	.10	.08	.04
146	Shawon Dunston	.10	.08	.04
147	Scott Bradley	.05	.04	.02
148	Dave Stieb	.10	.08	.04
149	Frank Viola	.15	.11	.06
150	Terry Kennedy	.07	.05	.03
151	Bill Wegman	.05	.04	.02
152	*Matt Nokes*	.25	.20	.10
153	Wade Boggs	.25	.20	.10
154	Wayne Tolleson	.05	.04	.02
155	Mariano Duncan	.05	.04	.02
156	Julio Franco	.10	.08	.04
157	Charlie Leibrandt	.07	.05	.03
158	Terry Steinbach	.10	.08	.04
159	Mike Fitzgerald	.05	.04	.02
160	Jack Lazorko	.05	.04	.02
161	Mitch Williams	.07	.05	.03
162	Greg Walker	.07	.05	.03
163	Alan Ashby	.05	.04	.02
164	Tony Gwynn	.35	.25	.14
165	Bruce Ruffin	.07	.05	.03
166	Ron Robinson	.05	.04	.02
167	Zane Smith	.07	.05	.03
168	Junior Ortiz	.05	.04	.02
169	Jamie Moyer	.07	.05	.03
170	Tony Pena	.07	.05	.03
171	Cal Ripken	.50	.40	.20
172	B.J. Surhoff	.12	.09	.05
173	Lou Whitaker	.08	.06	.03
174	*Ellis Burks*	.35	.25	.14
175	Ron Guidry	.15	.11	.06
176	Steve Sax	.15	.11	.06
177	Danny Tartabull	.20	.15	.08
178	Carney Lansford	.10	.08	.04
179	Casey Candaele	.05	.04	.02
180	Scott Fletcher	.07	.05	.03
181	Mark McLemore	.05	.04	.02
182	Ivan Calderon	.10	.08	.04
183	Jack Clark	.15	.11	.06
184	Glenn Davis	.08	.06	.03
185	Luis Aguayo	.05	.04	.02
186	Bo Diaz	.07	.05	.03
187	Stan Jefferson	.07	.05	.03
188	Sid Bream	.07	.05	.03
189	Bob Brenly	.05	.04	.02
190	Dion James	.07	.05	.03
191	Leon Durham	.07	.05	.03
192	Jesse Orosco	.07	.05	.03
193	Alvin Davis	.12	.09	.05
194	Gary Gaetti	.12	.09	.05
195	Fred McGriff	.40	.30	.15
196	Steve Lombardozzi	.05	.04	.02
197	Rance Mulliniks	.05	.04	.02
198	Rey Quinones	.05	.04	.02
199	Gary Carter	.10	.08	.04
200a	Checklist 138-247	.05	.04	.02
200b	Checklist 134-239	.10	.08	.04

		MT	NR MT	EX
201	Keith Moreland	.07	.05	.03
202	Ken Griffey	.07	.05	.03
203	*Tommy Gregg*(FC)	.08	.06	.03
204	Will Clark	.30	.25	.12
205	John Kruk	.12	.09	.05
206	Buddy Bell	.07	.05	.03
207	Von Hayes	.07	.05	.03
208	Tommy Herr	.07	.05	.03
209	Craig Reynolds	.05	.04	.02
210	Gary Pettis	.05	.04	.02
211	Harold Baines	.12	.09	.05
212	Vance Law	.07	.05	.03
213	Ken Gerhart	.07	.05	.03
214	Jim Gantner	.05	.04	.02
215	Chet Lemon	.07	.05	.03
216	Dwight Evans	.12	.09	.05
217	Don Mattingly	.30	.25	.12
218	Franklin Stubbs	.07	.05	.03
219	Pat Tabler	.07	.05	.03
220	Bo Jackson	.30	.25	.12
221	Tony Phillips	.05	.04	.02
222	Tim Wallach	.10	.08	.04
223	Ruben Sierra	.30	.25	.12
224	Steve Buechele	.05	.04	.02
225	Frank White	.07	.05	.03
226	Alfredo Griffin	.07	.05	.03
227	Greg Swindell	.12	.09	.05
228	Willie Randolph	.07	.05	.03
229	Mike Marshall	.12	.09	.05
230	Alan Trammell	.08	.06	.03
231	Eddie Murray	.20	.15	.08
232	Dale Sveum	.07	.05	.03
233	Dick Schofield	.05	.04	.02
234	Jose Oquendo	.05	.04	.02
235	Bill Doran	.07	.05	.03
236	Milt Thompson	.05	.04	.02
237	Marvell Wynne	.05	.04	.02
238	Bobby Bonilla	.20	.15	.08
239	Chris Speier	.05	.04	.02
240	Glenn Braggs	.10	.08	.04
241	Wally Backman	.07	.05	.03
242	Ryne Sandberg	.40	.30	.15
243	Phil Bradley	.10	.08	.04
244	Kelly Gruber	.05	.04	.02
245	Tom Brunansky	.10	.08	.04
246	Ron Oester	.05	.04	.02
247	Bobby Thigpen	.10	.08	.04
248	Fred Lynn	.15	.11	.06
249	Paul Molitor	.15	.11	.06
250	Darrell Evans	.10	.08	.04
251	Gary Ward	.07	.05	.03
252	Bruce Hurst	.10	.08	.04
253	Bob Welch	.10	.08	.04
254	Joe Carter	.15	.11	.06
255	Willie Wilson	.10	.08	.04
256	Mark McGwire	.30	.25	.12
257	Mitch Webster	.07	.05	.03
258	Brian Downing	.07	.05	.03
259	Mike Stanley	.10	.08	.04
260	Carlton Fisk	.20	.15	.08
261	Billy Hatcher	.07	.05	.03
262	Glenn Wilson	.07	.05	.03
263	Ozzie Smith	.15	.11	.06
264	Randy Ready	.05	.04	.02
265	Kurt Stillwell	.10	.08	.04
266	David Palmer	.05	.04	.02
267	Mike Diaz	.07	.05	.03
268	Rob Thompson	.07	.05	.03
269	Andre Dawson	.20	.15	.08
270	Lee Guetterman	.05	.04	.02
271	Willie Upshaw	.07	.05	.03
272	Randy Bush	.05	.04	.02
273	Larry Sheets	.07	.05	.03
274	Rob Deer	.07	.05	.03
275	Kirk Gibson	.08	.06	.03
276	Marty Barrett	.07	.05	.03
277	Rickey Henderson	.20	.15	.08
278	Pedro Guerrero	.15	.11	.06
279	Brett Butler	.07	.05	.03
280	Kevin Seitzer	.08	.06	.03
281	Mike Davis	.07	.05	.03
282	Andres Galarraga	.15	.11	.06
283	Devon White	.12	.09	.05
284	Pete O'Brien	.07	.05	.03
285	Jerry Hairston	.05	.04	.02
286	Kevin Bass	.07	.05	.03
287	Carmelo Martinez	.07	.05	.03
288	Juan Samuel	.12	.09	.05
289	Kal Daniels	.06	.05	.02
290	Albert Hall	.05	.04	.02
291	Andy Van Slyke	.12	.09	.05

		MT	NR MT	EX
292	Lee Smith	.10	.08	.04
293	Vince Coleman	.08	.06	.03
294	Tom Niedenfuer	.07	.05	.03
295	Robin Yount	.30	.25	.12
296	*Jeff Robinson*	.08	.06	.03
297	*Todd Benzinger*	.10	.08	.04
298	Dave Winfield	.35	.25	.14
299	Mickey Hatcher	.05	.04	.02
300a	Checklist 248-357	.05	.04	.02
300b	Checklist 240-345	.10	.08	.04
301	Bud Black	.05	.04	.02
302	Jose Canseco	.30	.25	.12
303	Tom Foley	.05	.04	.02
304	Pete Incaviglia	.15	.11	.06
305	Bob Boone	.07	.05	.03
306	*Bill Long*	.08	.06	.03
307	Willie McGee	.12	.09	.05
308	*Ken Caminiti*(FC)	.40	.30	.15
309	Darren Daulton	.05	.04	.02
310	Tracy Jones	.12	.09	.05
311	Greg Booker	.07	.05	.03
312	Mike LaValliere	.07	.05	.03
313	Chili Davis	.07	.05	.03
314	Glenn Hubbard	.05	.04	.02
315	*Paul Noce*	.10	.08	.04
316	Keith Hernandez	.08	.06	.03
317	Mark Langston	.12	.09	.05
318	Keith Atherton	.05	.04	.02
319	Tony Fernandez	.12	.09	.05
320	Kent Hrbek	.15	.11	.06
321	John Cerutti	.07	.05	.03
322	Mike Kingery	.05	.04	.02
323	Dave Magadan	.12	.09	.05
324	Rafael Palmeiro	.40	.30	.15
325	Jeff Dedmon	.05	.04	.02
326	Barry Bonds	.50	.40	.20
327	Jeffrey Leonard	.07	.05	.03
328	Tim Flannery	.05	.04	.02
329	Dave Concepcion	.07	.05	.03
330	Mike Schmidt	.30	.25	.12
331	Bill Dawley	.05	.04	.02
332	Larry Andersen	.05	.04	.02
333	Jack Howell	.07	.05	.03
334	*Ken Williams*	.06	.05	.02
335	Bryn Smith	.05	.04	.02
336	*Billy Ripken*	.10	.08	.04
337	Greg Brock	.07	.05	.03
338	Mike Heath	.05	.04	.02
339	Mike Greenwell	.12	.09	.05
340	Claudell Washington	.07	.05	.03
341	Jose Gonzalez	.05	.04	.02
342	Mel Hall	.07	.05	.03
343	Jim Eisenreich	.07	.05	.03
344	Tony Bernazard	.05	.04	.02
345	Tim Raines	.08	.06	.03
346	Bob Brower	.07	.05	.03
347	Larry Parrish	.07	.05	.03
348	Thad Bosley	.05	.04	.02
349	Dennis Eckersley	.12	.09	.05
350	Cory Snyder	.06	.05	.02
351	Rick Cerone	.05	.04	.02
352	John Shelby	.05	.04	.02
353	Larry Herndon	.05	.04	.02
354	John Habyan	.05	.04	.02
355	*Chuck Crim*	.12	.09	.05
356	Gus Polidor	.05	.04	.02
357	Ken Dayley	.05	.04	.02
358	Danny Darwin	.05	.04	.02
359	Lance Parrish	.15	.11	.06
360	*James Steels*	.12	.09	.05
361	*Al Pedrique*(FC)	.15	.11	.06
362	Mike Aldrete	.07	.05	.03
363	Juan Castillo	.05	.04	.02
364	Len Dykstra	.15	.11	.06
365	Luis Quinones	.05	.04	.02
366	Jim Presley	.10	.08	.04
367	Lloyd Moseby	.07	.05	.03
368	Kirby Puckett	.50	.40	.20
369	Eric Davis	.12	.09	.05
370	Gary Redus	.05	.04	.02
371	Dave Schmidt	.05	.04	.02
372	Mark Clear	.05	.04	.02
373	Dave Bergman	.05	.04	.02
374	Charles Hudson	.05	.04	.02
375	Calvin Schiraldi	.05	.04	.02
376	Alex Trevino	.05	.04	.02
377	Tom Candiotti	.05	.04	.02
378	Steve Farr	.05	.04	.02
379	Mike Gallego	.05	.04	.02
380	Andy McGaffigan	.05	.04	.02
381	Kirk McCaskill	.07	.05	.03

		MT	NR MT	EX
382	Oddibe McDowell	.07	.05	.03
383	Floyd Bannister	.07	.05	.03
384	Denny Walling	.05	.04	.02
385	Don Carman	.07	.05	.03
386	Todd Worrell	.10	.08	.04
387	Eric Show	.07	.05	.03
388	Dave Parker	.08	.06	.03
389	Rick Mahler	.05	.04	.02
390	*Mike Dunne*	.08	.06	.03
391	Candy Maldonado	.07	.05	.03
392	Bob Dernier	.05	.04	.02
393	Dave Valle	.05	.04	.02
394	Ernie Whitt	.07	.05	.03
395	Juan Berenguer	.05	.04	.02
396	Mike Young	.05	.04	.02
397	Mike Felder	.05	.04	.02
398	Willie Hernandez	.07	.05	.03
399	Jim Rice	.08	.06	.03
400a	Checklist 358-467	.05	.04	.02
400b	Checklist 346-451	.10	.08	.04
401	Tommy John	.15	.11	.06
402	Brian Holton	.07	.05	.03
403	Carmen Castillo	.05	.04	.02
404	Jamie Quirk	.05	.04	.02
405	Dwayne Murphy	.07	.05	.03
406	*Jeff Parrett*(FC)	.08	.06	.03
407	Don Sutton	.20	.15	.08
408	Jerry Browne	.07	.05	.03
409	Jim Winn	.05	.04	.02
410	Dave Smith	.07	.05	.03
411	*Shane Mack*	.15	.11	.06
412	Greg Gross	.05	.04	.02
413	Nick Esasky	.07	.05	.03
414	Damaso Garcia	.05	.04	.02
415	Brian Fisher	.07	.05	.03
416	Brian Dayett	.05	.04	.02
417	Curt Ford	.05	.04	.02
418	*Mark Williamson*	.12	.09	.05
419	Bill Schroeder	.05	.04	.02
420	*Mike Henneman*	.25	.20	.10
421	*John Marzano*(FC)	.08	.06	.03
422	Ron Kittle	.07	.05	.03
423	Matt Young	.05	.04	.02
424	Steve Balboni	.07	.05	.03
425	*Luis Polonia*	.30	.25	.12
426	Randy St. Claire	.05	.04	.02
427	Greg Harris	.05	.04	.02
428	Johnny Ray	.07	.05	.03
429	Ray Searage	.05	.04	.02
430	Ricky Horton	.07	.05	.03
431	*Gerald Young*(FC)	.08	.06	.03
432	Rick Schu	.05	.04	.02
433	Paul O'Neill	.07	.05	.03
434	Rich Gossage	.15	.11	.06
435	John Cangelosi	.05	.04	.02
436	Mike LaCoss	.05	.04	.02
437	Gerald Perry	.10	.08	.04
438	Dave Martinez	.07	.05	.03
439	Darryl Strawberry	.20	.15	.08
440	John Moses	.05	.04	.02
441	Greg Gagne	.05	.04	.02
442	Jesse Barfield	.12	.09	.05
443	George Frazier	.05	.04	.02
444	Garth Iorg	.05	.04	.02
445	Ed Nunez	.05	.04	.02
446	Rick Aguilera	.05	.04	.02
447	Jerry Mumphrey	.05	.04	.02
448	Rafael Ramirez	.05	.04	.02
449	*John Smiley*	.30	.25	.12
450	Atlee Hammaker	.05	.04	.02
451	Lance McCullers	.07	.05	.03
452	Guy Hoffman(FC)	.07	.05	.03
453	Chris James	.12	.09	.05
454	Terry Pendleton	.10	.08	.04
455	*Dave Meads*	.15	.11	.06
456	Bill Buckner	.10	.08	.04
457	*John Pawlowski*(FC)	.10	.08	.04
458	Bob Sebra	.05	.04	.02
459	Jim Dwyer	.05	.04	.02
460	*Jay Aldrich*(FC)	.12	.09	.05
461	Frank Tanana	.07	.05	.03
462	Oil Can Boyd	.07	.05	.03
463	Dan Pasqua	.10	.08	.04
464	*Tim Crews*(FC)	.15	.11	.06
465	Andy Allanson	.07	.05	.03
466	*Bill Pecota*(FC)	.15	.11	.06
467	Steve Ontiveros	.05	.04	.02
468	Hubie Brooks	.10	.08	.04
469	*Paul Kilgus*(FC)	.15	.11	.06
470	Dale Mohorcic	.05	.04	.02
471	Dan Quisenberry	.07	.05	.03
472	Dave Stewart	.10	.08	.04
473	Dave Clark	.07	.05	.03
474	Joel Skinner	.05	.04	.02
475	Dave Anderson	.05	.04	.02
476	Dan Petry	.07	.05	.03
477	*Carl Nichols*(FC)	.12	.09	.05
478	Ernest Riles	.05	.04	.02
479	George Hendrick	.07	.05	.03
480	John Morris	.05	.04	.02
481	*Manny Hernandez*(FC)	.10	.08	.04
482	Jeff Stone	.05	.04	.02
483	Chris Brown	.07	.05	.03
484	Mike Bielecki	.05	.04	.02
485	Dave Dravecky	.07	.05	.03
486	Rick Manning	.05	.04	.02
487	Bill Almon	.05	.04	.02
488	Jim Sundberg	.07	.05	.03
489	Ken Phelps	.07	.05	.03
490	Tom Henke	.07	.05	.03
491	Dan Gladden	.05	.04	.02
492	Barry Larkin	.25	.20	.10
493	*Fred Manrique*(FC)	.06	.05	.02
494	Mike Griffin	.05	.04	.02
495	*Mark Knudson*(FC)	.10	.08	.04
496	Bill Madlock	.10	.08	.04
497	Tim Stoddard	.05	.04	.02
498	*Sam Horn*(FC)	.10	.08	.04
499	*Tracy Woodson*(FC)	.06	.05	.02
500a	Checklist 468-577	.05	.04	.02
500b	Checklist 452-557	.10	.08	.04
501	Ken Schrom	.05	.04	.02
502	Angel Salazar	.05	.04	.02
503	Eric Plunk	.05	.04	.02
504	Joe Hesketh	.05	.04	.02
505	Greg Minton	.05	.04	.02
506	Geno Petralli	.05	.04	.02
507	Bob James	.05	.04	.02
508	*Robbie Wine*(FC)	.12	.09	.05
509	Jeff Calhoun	.05	.04	.02
510	Steve Lake	.05	.04	.02
511	Mark Grant	.05	.04	.02
512	Frank Williams	.05	.04	.02
513	*Jeff Blauser*(FC)	.40	.30	.15
514	Bob Walk	.05	.04	.02
515	Craig Lefferts	.05	.04	.02
516	Manny Trillo	.07	.05	.03
517	Jerry Reed	.05	.04	.02
518	Rick Leach	.05	.04	.02
519	*Mark Davidson*	.12	.09	.05
520	*Jeff Ballard*(FC)	.08	.06	.03
521	*Dave Stapleton*(FC)	.10	.08	.04
522	Pat Sheridan	.05	.04	.02
523	Al Nipper	.05	.04	.02
524	Steve Trout	.05	.04	.02
525	Jeff Hamilton	.07	.05	.03
526	*Tommy Hinzo*(FC)	.15	.11	.06
527	Lonnie Smith	.07	.05	.03
528	*Greg Cadaret*(FC)	.08	.06	.03
529	Rob McClure (Bob)	.05	.04	.02
530	Chuck Finley	.10	.08	.04
531	Jeff Russell	.05	.04	.02
532	Steve Lyons	.05	.04	.02
533	Terry Puhl	.05	.04	.02
534	*Eric Nolte*(FC)	.15	.11	.06
535	Kent Tekulve	.07	.05	.03
536	*Pat Pacillo*(FC)	.15	.11	.06
537	Charlie Puleo	.05	.04	.02
538	*Tom Prince*(FC)	.15	.11	.06
539	Greg Maddux	.15	.11	.06
540	Jim Lindeman	.07	.05	.03
541	*Pete Stanicek*(FC)	.15	.11	.06
542	Steve Kiefer	.05	.04	.02
543	Jim Morrison	.05	.04	.02
544	Spike Owen	.05	.04	.02
545	*Jay Buhner*(FC)	.70	.50	.30
546	*Mike Devereaux*(FC)	.50	.40	.20
547	Jerry Don Gleaton	.05	.04	.02
548	Jose Rijo	.07	.05	.03
549	Dennis Martinez	.05	.04	.02
550	Mike Loynd	.05	.04	.02
551	Darrell Miller	.05	.04	.02
552	Dave LaPoint	.07	.05	.03
553	John Tudor	.10	.08	.04
554	*Rocky Childress*(FC)	.12	.09	.05
555	*Wally Ritchie*(FC)	.15	.11	.06
556	Terry McGriff	.05	.04	.02
557	Dave Leiper	.05	.04	.02
558	Jeff Robinson	.07	.05	.03
559	Jose Uribe	.05	.04	.02
560	Ted Simmons	.10	.08	.04
561	*Lester Lancaster*	.15	.11	.06

		MT	NR MT	EX
562	*Keith Miller*(FC)	.10	.08	.04
563	Harold Reynolds	.07	.05	.03
564	*Gene Larkin*	.10	.08	.04
565	Cecil Fielder	.30	.25	.12
566	Roy Smalley	.05	.04	.02
567	Duane Ward	.07	.05	.03
568	*Bill Wilkinson*(FC)	.15	.11	.06
569	Howard Johnson	.10	.08	.04
570	Frank DiPino	.05	.04	.02
571	*Pete Smith*(FC)	.20	.15	.08
572	Darnell Coles	.07	.05	.03
573	Don Robinson	.07	.05	.03
574	Rob Nelson	.05	.04	.02
575	Dennis Rasmussen	.10	.08	.04
576	Steve Jeltz (photo actually Juan Samuel)	.05	.04	.02
577	*Tom Pagnozzi*(FC)	.15	.11	.06
578	Ty Gainey	.05	.04	.02
579	Gary Lucas	.05	.04	.02
580	Ron Hassey	.05	.04	.02
581	Herm Winningham	.05	.04	.02
582	*Rene Gonzales*(FC)	.15	.11	.06
583	Brad Komminsk	.05	.04	.02
584	Doyle Alexander	.07	.05	.03
585	Jeff Sellers	.07	.05	.03
586	Bill Gullickson	.05	.04	.02
587	Tim Belcher(FC)	.10	.08	.04
588	*Doug Jones*(FC)	.25	.20	.10
589	*Melido Perez*(FC)	.30	.25	.12
590	Rick Honeycutt	.05	.04	.02
591	Pascual Perez	.07	.05	.03
592	Curt Wilkerson	.05	.04	.02
593	Steve Howe	.07	.05	.03
594	*John Davis*(FC)	.08	.06	.03
595	Storm Davis	.10	.08	.04
596	Sammy Stewart	.05	.04	.02
597	Neil Allen	.05	.04	.02
598	Alejandro Pena	.07	.05	.03
599	Mark Thurmond	.05	.04	.02
600a	Checklist 578-BC26	.05	.04	.02
600b	Checklist 558-660	.10	.08	.04
601	*Jose Mesa*(FC)	.10	.08	.04
602	*Don August*(FC)	.15	.11	.06
603	Terry Leach	.10	.08	.04
604	*Tom Newell*(FC)	.08	.06	.03
605	*Randall Byers*(FC)	.08	.06	.03
606	Jim Gott	.05	.04	.02
607	Harry Spilman	.05	.04	.02
608	John Candelaria	.07	.05	.03
609	*Mike Brumley*(FC)	.06	.05	.02
610	Mickey Brantley	.07	.05	.03
611	*Jose Nunez*(FC)	.08	.06	.03
612	Tom Nieto	.05	.04	.02
613	Rick Reuschel	.10	.08	.04
614	Lee Mazzilli	.12	.09	.05
615	*Scott Lusader*(FC)	.08	.06	.03
616	Bobby Meacham	.05	.04	.02
617	Kevin McReynolds	.15	.11	.06
618	Gene Garber	.05	.04	.02
619	*Barry Lyons*(FC)	.15	.11	.06
620	Randy Myers	.10	.08	.04
621	Donnie Moore	.05	.04	.02
622	Domingo Ramos	.05	.04	.02
623	Ed Romero	.05	.04	.02
624	*Greg Myers*(FC)	.10	.08	.04
625	Ripken Baseball Family, (Cal Ripken, Jr., Cal Ripken, Sr.)	.15	.11	.06
626	Pat Perry	.05	.04	.02
627	Andres Thomas	.10	.08	.04
628	*Matt Williams*	2.00	1.50	.80
629	*Dave Hengel*(FC)	.08	.06	.03
630	Jeff Musselman	.07	.05	.03
631	Tim Laudner	.05	.04	.02
632	Bob Ojeda	.07	.05	.03
633	Rafael Santana	.05	.04	.02
634	*Wes Gardner*(FC)	.08	.06	.03
635	*Roberto Kelly*(FC)	1.25	.90	.50
636	Mike Flanagan	.12	.09	.05
637	*Jay Bell*(FC)	.50	.40	.20
638	Bob Melvin	.05	.04	.02
639	*Damon Berryhill*(FC)	.15	.11	.06
640	*David Wells*(FC)	.25	.20	.10
641	Stan Musial Puzzle Card	.05	.04	.02
642	Doug Sisk	.05	.04	.02
643	*Keith Hughes*(FC)	.08	.06	.03
644	*Tom Glavine*(FC)	2.50	2.00	1.00
645	Al Newman	.05	.04	.02
646	Scott Sanderson	.05	.04	.02
647	Scott Terry	.10	.08	.04
648	Tim Teufel	.12	.09	.05
649	Garry Templeton	.12	.09	.05
650	Manny Lee	.05	.04	.02
651	Roger McDowell	.10	.08	.04
652	Mookie Wilson	.15	.11	.06
653	David Cone	.60	.45	.25
654	*Ron Gant*	2.50	2.00	1.00
655	Joe Price	.12	.09	.05
656	George Bell	.12	.09	.05
657	*Gregg Jefferies*	2.00	1.50	.80
658	*Todd Stottlemyre*	.50	.40	.20
659	*Geronimo Berroa*	.10	.08	.04
660	Jerry Royster	.12	.09	.05

1988 Donruss MVP

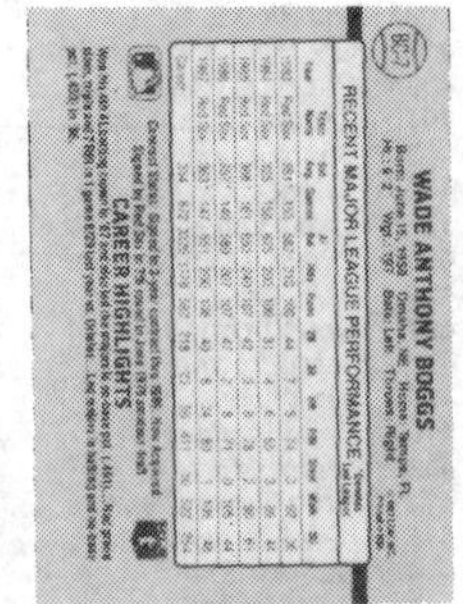

This 26-card set of standard-size player cards replaced the Donruss box-bottom cards in 1988. Instead of box-bottoms, the bonus cards (numbered BC-1 through BC-26) were randomly inserted in Donruss wax or rack packs. Cards feature the company's choice of Most Valuable Player for each major league team and are titled "Donruss MVP." The MVP cards were not included in the factory-collated sets. Card fronts carry the same basic red-blue-black flowing border design as the 1988 Donruss basic 660-card issue (with the exception of the Donruss MVP logo). Card backs are the same as the regular issue, except for the numbering system.

		MT	NR MT	EX
Complete Set (26):		7.00	5.25	2.75
Common Player:		.15	.11	.06
1	Cal Ripken	.30	.25	.12
2	Eric Davis	.50	.40	.20
3	Paul Molitor	.20	.15	.08
4	Mike Schmidt	.35	.25	.14
5	Ivan Calderon	.15	.11	.06
6	Tony Gwynn	.30	.25	.12
7	Wade Boggs	.75	.55	.30
8	Andy Van Slyke	.15	.11	.06
9	Joe Carter	.25	.20	.10
10	Andre Dawson	.25	.20	.10
11	Alan Trammell	.25	.20	.10
12	Mike Scott	.15	.11	.06
13	Wally Joyner	.25	.20	.10
14	Dale Murphy	.35	.25	.14
15	Kirby Puckett	.50	.40	.30
16	Pedro Guerrero	.20	.15	.08
17	Kevin Seitzer	.50	.40	.30
18	Tim Raines	.25	.20	.10
19	George Bell	.25	.20	.10
20	Darryl Strawberry	.50	.40	.30
21	Don Mattingly	1.00	.70	.40
22	Ozzie Smith	.20	.15	.08
23	Mark McGwire	.70	.50	.30
24	Will Clark	.90	.70	.35
25	Alvin Davis	.15	.11	.06
26	Ruben Sierra	.35	.25	.14

A player's name in italic indicates a rookie card. An (FC) indicates a player's first card for that particular card company.

1988 Donruss All-Stars

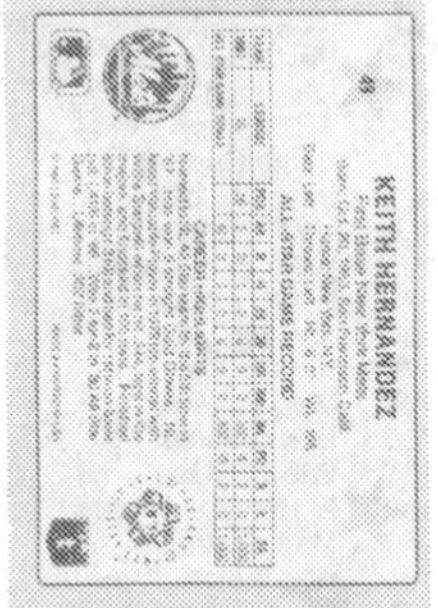

For the third consecutive year, this set of 64 cards featuring major league All-Stars was marketed in conjunction with Donruss Pop-Ups. The 1988 issue included a major change - the cards were reduced in size from 3-1/2" x 5" to a standard 2-1/2" x 3-1/2". The set features players from the 1987 All-Star Game starting lineup. Card fronts feature full-color photos, framed in blue, black and white, with a Donruss logo upper left. Player name and position appear in a red banner below the photo, along with the appropriate National or American League logo. All-Stars card backs include player stats and All-Star Game record. In 1988, All-Stars cards were distributed in individual packages containing three All-Stars, one Pop-Up and three Donruss puzzle pieces.

		MT	NR MT	EX
Complete Set:		7.00	5.25	2.75
Common Player:		.09	.07	.04
1	Don Mattingly	1.25	.90	.50
2	Dave Winfield	.25	.20	.10
3	Willie Randolph	.09	.07	.04
4	Rickey Henderson	.50	.40	.20
5	Cal Ripken, Jr.	.30	.25	.12
6	George Bell	.20	.15	.08
7	Wade Boggs	.80	.60	.30
8	Bret Saberhagen	.15	.11	.06
9	Terry Kennedy	.09	.07	.04
10	John McNamara	.09	.07	.04
11	Jay Howell	.09	.07	.04
12	Harold Baines	.12	.09	.05
13	Harold Reynolds	.09	.07	.04
14	Bruce Hurst	.09	.07	.04
15	Kirby Puckett	.50	.40	.20
16	Matt Nokes	.20	.15	.08
17	Pat Tabler	.09	.07	.04
18	Dan Plesac	.12	.09	.05
19	Mark McGwire	.60	.45	.25
20	Mike Witt	.09	.07	.04
21	Larry Parrish	.09	.07	.04
22	Alan Trammell	.20	.15	.08
23	Dwight Evans	.12	.09	.05
24	Jack Morris	.12	.09	.05
25	Tony Fernandez	.12	.09	.05
26	Mark Langston	.20	.15	.08
27	Kevin Seitzer	.40	.30	.15
28	Tom Henke	.09	.07	.04
29	Dave Righetti	.12	.09	.05
30	Oakland Coliseum	.09	.07	.04
31	Top Vote Getter (Wade Boggs)	.60	.45	.25
32	Checklist 1-32	.09	.07	.04
33	Jack Clark	.15	.11	.06
34	Darryl Strawberry	.40	.30	.15
35	Ryne Sandberg	.20	.15	.08
36	Andre Dawson	.20	.15	.08
37	Ozzie Smith	.15	.11	.06
38	Eric Davis	.50	.40	.20
39	Mike Schmidt	.80	.60	.30
40	Mike Scott	.12	.09	.05
41	Gary Carter	.12	.09	.05
42	Davey Johnson	.09	.07	.04
43	Rick Sutcliffe	.12	.09	.05
44	Willie McGee	.12	.09	.05
45	Hubie Brooks	.09	.07	.04
46	Dale Murphy	.40	.30	.15
47	Bo Diaz	.09	.07	.04
48	Pedro Guerrero	.15	.11	.06
49	Keith Hernandez	.15	.11	.06
50	Ozzie Virgil	.09	.07	.04
51	Tony Gwynn	.25	.20	.10
52	Rick Reuschel	.12	.09	.05
53	John Franco	.12	.09	.05
54	Jeffrey Leonard	.09	.07	.04
55	Juan Samuel	.15	.11	.06
56	Orel Hershiser	.20	.15	.08
57	Tim Raines	.20	.15	.08
58	Sid Fernandez	.12	.09	.05
59	Tim Wallach	.12	.09	.05
60	Lee Smith	.09	.07	.04
61	Steve Bedrosian	.12	.09	.05
62	MVP (Tim Raines)	.20	.15	.08
63	Top Vote Getter (Ozzie Smith)	.15	.11	.06
64	Checklist 33-64	.09	.07	.04

1988 Donruss Baseball's Best

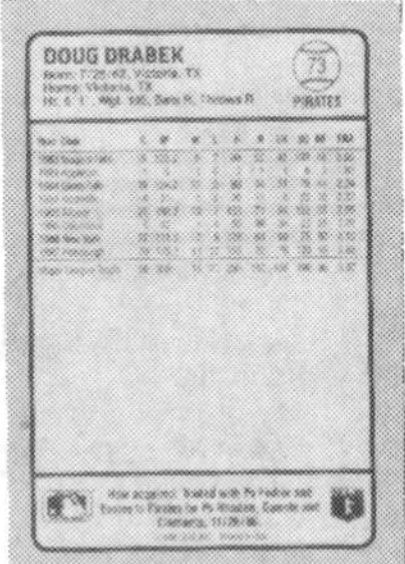

The design of this 336-card set (2-1/2" by 3-1/2") is similar to the regular 1988 Donruss issue with the exception of the borders which are orange, instead of blue. Full-color player photos are framed by the Donruss logo upper left, team logo lower right and a bright red and white player name that spans the bottom margin. The backs are black and white, framed by a yellow border, and include personal information, year-by-year stats and major league totals. This set was packaged in a bright red cardboard box (10" x 11" x 12") that contained six individually shrink-wrapped packs of 56 cards. Donruss marketed the set via retail chain outlets including Walgreens, Venture, Wall-Mart, Ben Frank- lin, Shopko, Super X, Target, McCrory's, Osco, Woolworth and J.C. Murphy.

		MT	NR MT	EX
Complete Set:		8.00	13.50	7.25
Common Player:		.05	.04	.02
1	Don Mattingly	.50	.40	.20
2	Ron Gant	.25	.20	.10
3	Bob Boone	.05	.04	.02
4	Mark Grace	.35	.25	.14
5	Andy Allanson	.05	.04	.02
6	Kal Daniels	.05	.04	.02
7	Floyd Bannister	.05	.04	.02
8	Alan Ashby	.05	.04	.02
9	Marty Barrett	.05	.04	.02
10	Tim Belcher	.05	.04	.02
11	Harold Baines	.07	.05	.03
12	Hubie Brooks	.05	.04	.02
13	Doyle Alexander	.05	.04	.02
14	Gary Carter	.09	.07	.04
15	Glenn Braggs	.05	.04	.02
16	Steve Bedrosian	.05	.04	.02
17	Barry Bonds	.50	.40	.20
18	Bert Blyleven	.07	.05	.03
19	Tom Brunansky	.05	.04	.02
20	John Candelaria	.05	.04	.02
21	Shawn Abner	.05	.04	.02
22	Jose Canseco	.45	.35	.20
23	Brett Butler	.05	.04	.02

		MT	NR MT	EX
24	Scott Bradley	.05	.04	.02
25	Ivan Calderon	.07	.05	.03
26	Rich Gossage	.07	.05	.03
27	Brian Downing	.05	.04	.02
28	Jim Rice	.10	.08	.04
29	Dion James	.05	.04	.02
30	Terry Kennedy	.05	.04	.02
31	George Bell	.07	.05	.03
32	Scott Fletcher	.05	.04	.02
33	Bobby Bonilla	.20	.15	.08
34	Tim Burke	.05	.04	.02
35	Darrell Evans	.07	.05	.03
36	Mike Davis	.05	.04	.02
37	Shawon Dunston	.07	.05	.03
38	Kevin Bass	.05	.04	.02
39	George Brett	.40	.30	.15
40	David Cone	.09	.07	.04
41	Ron Darling	.05	.04	.02
42	Roberto Alomar	.20	.15	.08
43	Dennis Eckersley	.10	.08	.04
44	Vince Coleman	.09	.07	.04
45	Sid Bream	.05	.04	.02
46	Gary Gaetti	.07	.05	.03
47	Phil Bradley	.05	.04	.02
48	Jim Clancy	.05	.04	.02
49	Jack Clark	.07	.05	.03
50	Mike Krukow	.05	.04	.02
51	Henry Cotto	.05	.04	.02
52	Rich Dotson	.05	.04	.02
53	Jim Gantner	.05	.04	.02
54	John Franco	.05	.04	.02
55	Pete Incaviglia	.07	.05	.03
56	Joe Carter	.10	.08	.04
57	Roger Clemens	.25	.20	.10
58	Gerald Perry	.05	.04	.02
59	Jack Howell	.05	.04	.02
60	Vance Law	.05	.04	.02
61	Jay Bell	.07	.05	.03
62	Eric Davis	.12	.09	.05
63	Gene Garber	.05	.04	.02
64	Glenn Davis	.05	.04	.02
65	Wade Boggs	.40	.30	.15
66	Kirk Gibson	.10	.08	.04
67	Carlton Fisk	.10	.08	.04
68	Casey Candaele	.05	.04	.02
69	Mike Heath	.05	.04	.02
70	Kevin Elster	.05	.04	.02
71	Greg Brock	.05	.04	.02
72	Don Carman	.05	.04	.02
73	Doug Drabek	.09	.07	.04
74	Greg Gagne	.07	.05	.03
75	Danny Cox	.05	.04	.02
76	Rickey Henderson	.30	.25	.12
77	Chris Brown	.05	.04	.02
78	Terry Steinbach	.05	.04	.02
79	Will Clark	.40	.30	.15
80	Mickey Brantley	.05	.04	.02
81	Ozzie Guillen	.07	.05	.03
82	Greg Maddux	.12	.09	.05
83	Kirk McCaskill	.05	.04	.02
84	Dwight Evans	.09	.07	.04
85	Ozzie Virgil	.05	.04	.02
86	Mike Morgan	.05	.04	.02
87	Tony Fernandez	.07	.05	.03
88	Jose Guzman	.05	.04	.02
89	Mike Dunne	.05	.04	.02
90	Andres Galarraga	.07	.05	.03
91	Mike Henneman	.05	.04	.02
92	Alfredo Griffin	.05	.04	.02
93	Rafael Palmeiro	.12	.09	.05
94	Jim Deshaies	.05	.04	.02
95	Mark Gubicza	.05	.04	.02
96	Dwight Gooden	.20	.15	.08
97	Howard Johnson	.10	.08	.04
98	Mark Davis	.05	.04	.02
99	Dave Stewart	.09	.07	.04
100	Joe Magrane	.05	.04	.02
101	Brian Fisher	.05	.04	.02
102	Kent Hrbek	.10	.08	.04
103	Kevin Gross	.05	.04	.02
104	Tom Henke	.05	.04	.02
105	Mike Pagliarulo	.05	.04	.02
106	Kelly Downs	.05	.04	.02
107	Alvin Davis	.05	.04	.02
108	Willie Randolph	.07	.05	.03
109	Rob Deer	.05	.04	.02
110	Bo Diaz	.05	.04	.02
111	Paul Kilgus	.05	.04	.02
112	Tom Candiotti	.05	.04	.02
113	Dale Murphy	.20	.15	.08
114	Rick Mahler	.05	.04	.02

		MT	NR MT	EX
115	Wally Joyner	.20	.15	.08
116	Ryne Sandberg	.25	.20	.10
117	John Farrell	.05	.04	.02
118	Nick Esasky	.05	.04	.02
119	Bo Jackson	.40	.30	.15
120	Bill Doran	.05	.04	.02
121	Ellis Burks	.15	.11	.06
122	Pedro Guerrero	.05	.04	.02
123	Dave LaPoint	.05	.04	.02
124	Neal Heaton	.05	.04	.02
125	Willie Hernandez	.05	.04	.02
126	Roger McDowell	.07	.05	.03
127	Ted Higuera	.05	.04	.02
128	Von Hayes	.07	.05	.03
129	Mike LaValliere	.05	.04	.02
130	Dan Gladden	.07	.05	.03
131	Willie McGee	.09	.07	.04
132	Al Lieter	.05	.04	.02
133	Mark Grant	.05	.04	.02
134	Bob Welch	.07	.05	.03
135	Dave Dravecky	.05	.04	.02
136	Mark Langston	.07	.05	.03
137	Dan Pasqua	.07	.05	.03
138	Rick Sutcliffe	.07	.05	.03
139	Dan Petry	.05	.04	.02
140	Rich Gedman	.05	.04	.02
141	Ken Griffey	.05	.04	.02
142	Eddie Murray	.10	.08	.04
143	Jimmy Key	.07	.05	.03
144	Dale Mohoric	.05	.04	.02
145	Jose Lind	.10	.08	.04
146	Dennis Martinez	.07	.05	.03
147	Chet Lemon	.05	.04	.02
148	Orel Hershiser	.10	.08	.04
149	Dave Martinez	.05	.04	.02
150	Billy Hatcher	.07	.05	.03
151	Charlie Leibrandt	.05	.04	.02
152	Keith Hernandez	.07	.05	.03
153	Kevin McReynolds	.07	.05	.03
154	Tony Gwynn	.15	.11	.06
155	Stan Javier	.05	.04	.02
156	Tony Pena	.05	.04	.02
157	Andy Van Slyke	.10	.08	.04
158	Gene Larkin	.07	.05	.03
159	Chris James	.05	.04	.02
160	Fred McGriff	.25	.20	.10
161	Rick Rhoden	.05	.04	.02
162	Scott Garrelts	.05	.04	.02
163	Mike Campbell	.05	.04	.02
164	Dave Righetti	.07	.05	.03
165	Paul Molitor	.15	.11	.06
166	Danny Jackson	.07	.05	.03
167	Pete O'Brien	.05	.04	.02
168	Julio Franco	.05	.04	.02
169	Mark McGwire	.35	.25	.14
170	Zane Smith	.05	.04	.02
171	Johnny Ray	.05	.04	.02
172	Lester Lancaster	.05	.04	.02
173	Mel Hall	.05	.04	.02
174	Tracy Jones	.05	.04	.02
175	Kevin Seitzer	.05	.04	.02
176	Bob Knepper	.05	.04	.02
177	Mike Greenwell	.15	.11	.06
178	Mike Marshall	.07	.05	.03
179	Melido Perez	.05	.04	.02
180	Tim Raines	.15	.11	.06
181	Jack Morris	.07	.05	.03
182	Darryl Strawberry	.25	.20	.10
183	Robin Yount	.35	.25	.14
184	Lance Parrish	.09	.07	.04
185	Darnell Coles	.05	.04	.02
186	Kirby Puckett	.30	.25	.12
187	Terry Pendleton	.07	.05	.03
188	Don Slaught	.05	.04	.02
189	Jimmy Jones	.05	.04	.02
190	Dave Parker	.15	.11	.06
191	Mike Aldrete	.05	.04	.02
192	Mike Moore	.05	.04	.02
193	Greg Walker	.05	.04	.02
194	Calvin Schiraldi	.05	.04	.02
195	Dick Schofield	.05	.04	.02
196	Jody Reed	.07	.05	.03
197	Pete Smith	.05	.04	.02
198	Cal Ripken, Jr.	.50	.40	.20
199	Lloyd Moseby	.05	.04	.02
200	Ruben Sierra	.15	.11	.06
201	R.J. Reynolds	.05	.04	.02
202	Bryn Smith	.05	.04	.02
203	Gary Pettis	.05	.04	.02
204	Steve Sax	.05	.04	.02
205	Frank DiPino	.05	.04	.02

		MT	NR MT	EX
206	Mike Scott	.05	.04	.02
207	Kurt Stillwell	.05	.04	.02
208	Mookie Wilson	.05	.04	.02
209	Lee Mazzilli	.05	.04	.02
210	Lance McCullers	.05	.04	.02
211	Rick Honeycutt	.05	.04	.02
212	John Tudor	.07	.05	.03
213	Jim Gott	.07	.05	.03
214	Frank Viola	.09	.07	.04
215	Juan Samuel	.07	.05	.03
216	Jesse Barfield	.05	.04	.02
217	Claudell Washington	.05	.04	.02
218	Rick Reuschel	.05	.04	.02
219	Jim Presley	.05	.04	.02
220	Tommy John	.12	.09	.05
221	Dan Plesac	.05	.04	.02
222	Barry Larkin	.10	.08	.04
223	Mike Stanley	.05	.04	.02
224	Cory Snyder	.07	.05	.03
225	Andre Dawson	.20	.15	.08
226	Ken Oberkfell	.05	.04	.02
227	Devon White	.09	.07	.04
228	Jamie Moyer	.05	.04	.02
229	Brook Jacoby	.07	.05	.03
230	Rob Murphy	.05	.04	.02
231	Bret Saberhagen	.10	.08	.04
232	Nolan Ryan	.50	.40	.20
233	Bruce Hurst	.07	.05	.03
234	Jesse Orosco	.05	.04	.02
235	Bobby Thigpen	.05	.04	.02
236	Pascual Perez	.05	.04	.02
237	Matt Nokes	.09	.07	.04
238	Bob Ojeda	.07	.05	.03
239	Joey Meyer	.05	.04	.02
240	Shane Rawley	.05	.04	.02
241	Jeff Robinson	.05	.04	.02
242	Jeff Reardon	.09	.07	.04
243	Ozzie Smith	.15	.11	.06
244	Dave Winfield	.35	.25	.14
245	John Kruk	.07	.05	.03
246	Carney Lansford	.05	.04	.02
247	Candy Maldonado	.05	.04	.02
248	Ken Phelps	.05	.04	.02
249	Ken Williams	.05	.04	.02
250	Al Nipper	.05	.04	.02
251	Mark McLemore	.05	.04	.02
252	Lee Smith	.07	.05	.03
253	Albert Hall	.05	.04	.02
254	Billy Ripken	.05	.04	.02
255	Kelly Gruber	.05	.04	.02
256	Charlie Hough	.07	.05	.03
257	John Smiley	.07	.05	.03
258	Tim Wallach	.10	.08	.04
259	Frank Tanana	.07	.05	.03
260	Mike Scioscia	.05	.04	.02
261	Damon Berryhill	.05	.04	.02
262	Dave Smith	.05	.04	.02
263	Willie Wilson	.07	.05	.03
264	Len Dykstra	.09	.07	.04
265	Randy Myers	.07	.05	.03
266	Keith Moreland	.05	.04	.02
267	Eric Plunk	.05	.04	.02
268	Todd Worrell	.05	.04	.02
269	Bob Walk	.05	.04	.02
270	Keith Atherton	.05	.04	.02
271	Mike Schmidt	.40	.30	.15
272	Mike Flanagan	.05	.04	.02
273	Rafael Santana	.05	.04	.02
274	Rob Thompson	.07	.05	.03
275	Rey Quinones	.05	.04	.02
276	Cecilio Guante	.05	.04	.02
277	B.J. Surhoff	.05	.04	.02
278	Chris Sabo	.10	.08	.04
279	Mitch Williams	.07	.05	.03
280	Greg Swindell	.07	.05	.03
281	Alan Trammell	.12	.09	.05
282	Storm Davis	.05	.04	.02
283	Chuck Finley	.07	.05	.03
284	Dave Stieb	.07	.05	.03
285	Scott Bailes	.05	.04	.02
286	Larry Sheets	.05	.04	.02
287	Danny Tartabull	.10	.08	.04
288	Checklist	.05	.04	.02
289	Todd Benzinger	.07	.05	.03
290	John Shelby	.05	.04	.02
291	Steve Lyons	.05	.04	.02
292	Mitch Webster	.05	.04	.02
293	Walt Terrell	.05	.04	.02
294	Pete Stanicek	.05	.04	.02
295	Chris Bosio	.07	.05	.03
296	Milt Thompson	.07	.05	.03
297	Fred Lynn	.12	.09	.05
298	Juan Berenguer	.05	.04	.02
299	Ken Dayley	.05	.04	.02
300	Joel Skinner	.05	.04	.02
301	Benito Santiago	.15	.11	.06
302	Ron Hassey	.05	.04	.02
303	Jose Uribe	.05	.04	.02
304	Harold Reynolds	.07	.05	.03
305	Dale Sveum	.05	.04	.02
306	Glenn Wilson	.05	.04	.02
307	Mike Witt	.05	.04	.02
308	Ron Robinson	.05	.04	.02
309	Denny Walling	.05	.04	.02
310	Joe Orsulak	.05	.04	.02
311	David Wells	.07	.05	.03
312	Steve Buechele	.05	.04	.02
313	Jose Oquendo	.05	.04	.02
314	Floyd Youmans	.05	.04	.02
315	Lou Whitaker	.10	.08	.04
316	Fernando Valenzuela	.07	.05	.03
317	Mike Boddicker	.05	.04	.02
318	Gerald Young	.05	.04	.02
319	Frank White	.07	.05	.03
320	Bill Wegman	.05	.04	.02
321	Tom Niedenfuer	.05	.04	.02
322	Ed Whitson	.05	.04	.02
323	Curt Young	.05	.04	.02
324	Greg Mathews	.05	.04	.02
325	Doug Jones	.07	.05	.03
326	Tommy Herr	.05	.04	.02
327	Kent Tekulve	.05	.04	.02
328	Rance Mulliniks	.05	.04	.02
329	Checklist	.05	.04	.02
330	Craig Lefferts	.05	.04	.02
331	Franklin Stubbs	.05	.04	.02
332	Rick Cerone	.05	.04	.02
333	Dave Schmidt	.05	.04	.02
334	Larry Parrish	.05	.04	.02
335	Tom Browning	.07	.05	.03
336	Checklist	.05	.04	.02

1988 Donruss Diamond Kings Supers

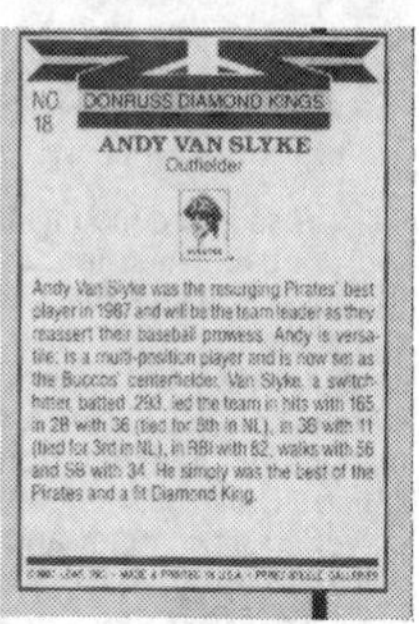

This 28-card set (including the checklist) marks the fourth edition of Donruss' super-size (5"x7") set. These cards, exact duplicates of the 1988 Diamond Kings that feature player portraits by Dick Perez, have a red, blue and black striped border. A gold Diamond Kings banner curves above the player portrait and a matching oval name banner is printed below. Each card features a large player closeup and a smaller full-figure inset on a split background that is white at the top and striped with multi-colors on the lower portion. Card backs are black and white with a blue border and contain the card number, DK logo, player name, team logo and a paragraph style career summary. A 12-piece Stan Musial puzzle was also included with the purchase of the super-size set which was marketed via a mail-in offer printed on Donruss wrappers.

	MT	NR MT	EX
Complete Set:	10.00	7.50	4.00
Common Player:	.20	.15	.08

		MT	NR MT	EX
1	Mark McGwire	.70	.50	.30
2	Tim Raines	.30	.25	.12
3	Benito Santiago	.30	.25	.12
4	Alan Trammell	.30	.25	.12
5	Danny Tartabull	.35	.25	.14
6	Ron Darling	.30	.25	.12
7	Paul Molitor	.30	.25	.12
8	Devon White	.35	.25	.14
9	Andre Dawson	.30	.25	.12
10	Julio Franco	.25	.20	.10
11	Scott Fletcher	.20	.15	.08
12	Tony Fernandez	.30	.25	.12
13	Shane Rawley	.20	.15	.08
14	Kal Daniels	.30	.25	.12
15	Jack Clark	.30	.25	.12
16	Dwight Evans	.25	.20	.10
17	Tommy John	.25	.20	.10
18	Andy Van Slyke	.25	.20	.10
19	Gary Gaetti	.30	.25	.12
20	Mark Langston	.35	.25	.14
21	Will Clark	1.75	1.25	.70
22	Glenn Hubbard	.20	.15	.08
23	Billy Hatcher	.20	.15	.08
24	Bob Welch	.20	.15	.08
25	Ivan Calderon	.20	.15	.08
26	Cal Ripken, Jr.	.60	.45	.25
27	Checklist	.20	.15	.08
641	Stan Musial Puzzle Card	.20	.15	.08

1988 Donruss Pop-Ups

Donruss introduced its Pop-Up cards in 1986. The first two annual issues featured 2-1/2" x 5" cards. In 1988, Donruss reduced the size of the Pop-Ups cards to a standard 2-1/2"x 3-1/2". The 1988 set includes 20 cards that fold out so that the upper portion of the player stands upright, giving a three-dimensional effect. Pop-ups feature players from the All-Star Game starting lineup. Card fronts feature full-color photos, with the player's name, team and position printed in black on a yellow banner near the bottom of the card front. As in previous issues, the card backs contain only the player's name, league and position. Pop-Ups were distributed in individual packages containing one Pop-Up, three puzzle pieces and three All-Star cards.

		MT	NR MT	EX
Complete Set:		4.00	3.00	1.50
Common Player:		.15	.11	.06
(1)	George Bell	.20	.15	.08
(2)	Wade Boggs	.50	.40	.20
(3)	Gary Carter	.20	.15	.08
(4)	Jack Clark	.20	.15	.08
(5)	Eric Davis	.30	.25	.12
(6)	Andre Dawson	.20	.15	.08
(7)	Rickey Henderson	.50	.40	.20
(8)	Davey Johnson	.15	.11	.06
(9)	Don Mattingly	.50	.40	.20
(10)	Terry Kennedy	.15	.11	.06
(11)	John McNamara	.15	.11	.06
(12)	Willie Randolph	.15	.11	.06
(13)	Cal Ripken, Jr.	.60	.45	.25
(14)	Bret Saberhagen	.35	.25	.14
(15)	Ryne Sandberg	.60	.45	.25
(16)	Mike Schmidt	.60	.45	.25
(17)	Mike Scott	.15	.11	.06
(18)	Ozzie Smith	.30	.25	.12
(19)	Darryl Strawberry	.50	.40	.20
(20)	Dave Winfield	.25	.20	.10

1988 Donruss Rookies

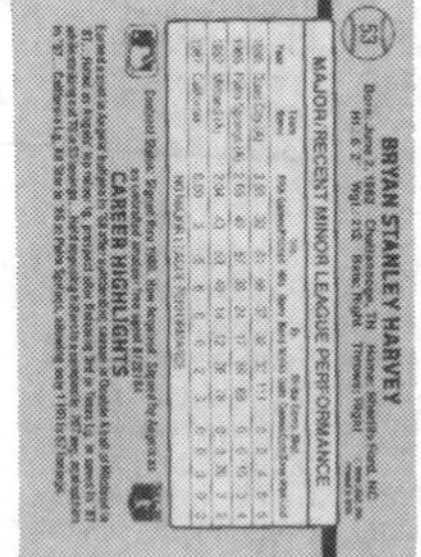

For the third consecutive year, Donruss issued this 56-card boxed set highlighting current rookies. The complete set includes a checklist and a 15-piece Stan Musial Diamond Kings puzzle. As in previous years, the set is similar to the company's basic issue, with the exception of the logo and border color. Card fronts feature red, green and black-striped borders, with a red-and-white player name printed in the lower left corner beneath the full-color photo. "The Rookies" logo is printed in red, white and black in the lower right corner. The card backs are printed in black on bright aqua and include personal data, recent performance stats and major league totals, as well as 1984-88 year-by-year minor league stats. The cards are the standard 2-1/2" by 3-1/2" size.

		MT	NR MT	EX
Complete Set (56):		20.00	15.00	8.00
Common Player:		.10	.08	.04
1	Mark Grace	2.50	2.00	1.00
2	Mike Campbell	.10	.08	.04
3	Todd Frowirth(FC)	.20	.15	.08
4	Dave Stapleton	.10	.08	.04
5	Shawn Abner	.10	.08	.04
6	Jose Cecena(FC)	.10	.08	.04
7	Dave Gallagher(FC)	.10	.08	.04
8	Mark Parent(FC)	.10	.08	.04
9	Cecil Espy(FC)	.15	.11	.06
10	Pete Smith	.10	.08	.04
11	Jay Buhner	1.25	.75	.40
12	Pat Borders(FC)	.40	.30	.15
13	Doug Jennings(FC)	.10	.08	.04
14	Brady Anderson(FC)	.90	.60	.30
15	Pete Stanicek	.15	.11	.06
16	Roberto Kelly	1.00	.70	.40
17	Jeff Treadway	.10	.08	.04
18	Walt Weiss(FC)	.30	.25	.12
19	Paul Gibson(FC)	.15	.11	.06
20	Tim Crews	.10	.08	.04
21	Melido Perez	.15	.11	.06
22	Steve Peters(FC)	.10	.08	.04
23	Craig Worthington(FC)	.10	.08	.04
24	John Trautwein(FC)	.10	.08	.04
25	DeWayne Vaughn(FC)	.10	.08	.04
26	David Wells	.15	.11	.06
27	Al Leiter	.10	.08	.04
28	Tim Belcher	.20	.15	.08
29	Johnny Paredes(FC)	.10	.08	.04
30	Chris Sabo(FC)	.80	.50	.25
31	Damon Berryhill	.15	.11	.06
32	Randy Milligan(FC)	.50	.40	.20
33	Gary Thurman	.10	.08	.04
34	Kevin Elster	.10	.08	.04
35	Roberto Alomar	12.00	9.00	4.75
36	Edgar Martinez(FC)	1.25	.75	.40
37	Todd Stottlemyre	.40	.20	.10
38	Joey Meyer	.10	.08	.04
39	Carl Nichols	.10	.08	.04
40	Jack McDowell	2.00	1.50	.80

		MT	NR MT	EX
41	Jose Bautista(FC)	.20	.15	.08
42	Sil Campusano(FC)	.15	.11	.06
43	John Dopson(FC)	.20	.15	.08
44	Jody Reed	.35	.25	.14
45	Darrin Jackson(FC)	.20	.15	.08
46	Mike Capel(FC)	.10	.08	.04
47	Ron Gant	2.50	1.50	.80
48	John Davis	.10	.08	.04
49	Kevin Coffman(FC)	.10	.08	.04
50	Cris Carpenter(FC)	.20	.15	.08
51	Mackey Sasser	.10	.08	.04
52	Luis Alicea(FC)	.25	.20	.10
53	Bryan Harvey(FC)	1.50	.90	.50
54	Steve Ellsworth(FC)	.10	.08	.04
55	Mike Macfarlane(FC)	.35	.20	.10
56	Checklist 1-56	.10	.08	.04

1988 Donruss Boston Red Sox Team Book

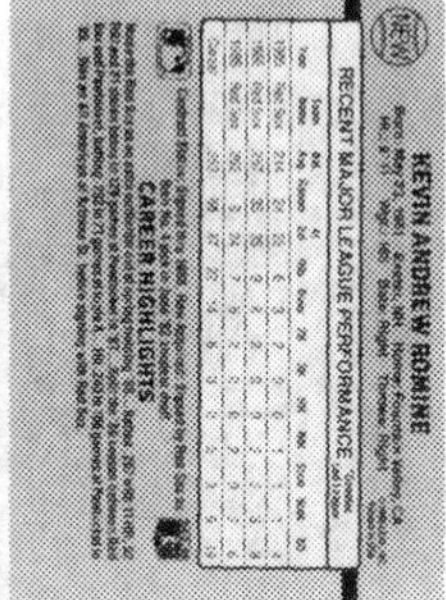

Three pages of nine cards each and a Stan Musial puzzle highlight this special team collection book. The cards feature the same design as the regular 1988 Donruss cards, but contain a 1988 copyright date instead of 1987 like the regular set. The cards are numbered like the regular issue with the exception of eight new cards which were produced especially for the Red Sox collection book. The book is commonly found complete with the cards and puzzle. The puzzle pieces are perforated for removal, but the card sheets are not.

		MT	NR MT	EX
Complete Set:		4.00	3.00	1.50
Common Player:		.08	.06	.03
-N1	Brady Anderson	.20	.15	.08
-N2	Rick Cerone	.08	.06	.03
-N3	Steve Ellsworth	.08	.06	.03
-N4	Dennis Lamp	.08	.06	.03
-N5	Kevin Romine	.15	.11	.06
-N6	Lee Smith	.20	.15	.08
-N7	Mike Smithson	.08	.06	.03
-N8	John Trautwein	.08	.06	.03
41	Jody Reed	.35	.25	.14
51	Roger Clemens	.80	.60	.30
92	Bob Stanley	.08	.06	.03
129	Rich Gedman	.08	.06	.03
153	Wade Boggs	.80	.60	.30
174	Ellis Burks	1.00	.70	.40
216	Dwight Evans	.25	.20	.10
252	Bruce Hurst	.25	.20	.10
276	Marty Barrett	.12	.09	.05
297	Todd Benzinger	.15	.11	.06
339	Mike Greenwell	.90	.70	.35
399	Jim Rice	.20	.15	.08
421	John Marzano	.12	.09	.05
462	Oil Can Boyd	.12	.09	.05
498	Sam Horn	.20	.15	.08
544	Spike Owen	.12	.09	.05
585	Jeff Sellers	.08	.06	.03
623	Ed Romero	.08	.06	.03
634	Wes Gardner	.12	.09	.05

The values quoted are intended to reflect the market price.

1988 Donruss Chicago Cubs Team Book

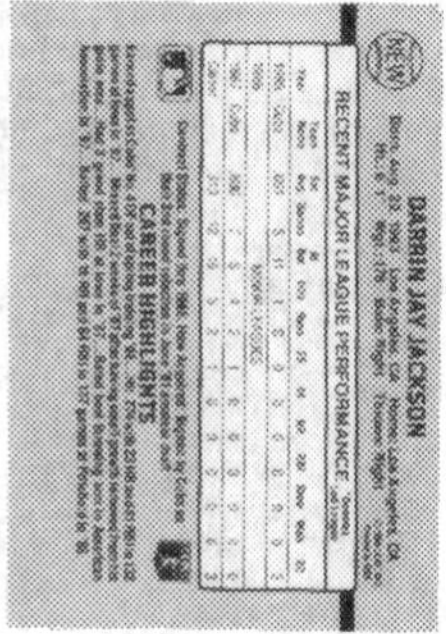

Primarily sold intact, the 1988 Donruss Chicago Cubs team book features three pages of cards and a fourth page featuring a Stan Musial puzzle. The inside cover provides space for autographs and the back inside cover provides team and ballpark history. The card fronts feature the design of the regular Donruss set. Eight "New" players are included in the team book. The cards have a 1988 copyright on the back in contrast with the 1987 copyright on the regular Donruss cards.

		MT	NR MT	EX
Complete Set:		5.00	3.75	2.00
Common Player:		.08	.06	.03
-N1	Mike Bielecki	.20	.15	.08
-N2	Rich Gossage	.10	.08	.04
-N3	Drew Hall	.10	.08	.04
-N4	Darrin Jackson	.10	.08	.04
-N5	Vance Law	.08	.06	.03
-N6	Al Nipper	.08	.06	.03
-N7	Angel Salazar	.08	.06	.03
-N8	Calvin Schiraldi	.08	.06	.03
40	Mark Grace	1.75	1.25	.70
68	Rick Sutcliffe	.15	.11	.06
119	Jody Davis	.08	.06	.03
146	Shawon Dunston	.35	.25	.14
169	Jamie Moyer	.08	.06	.03
191	Leon Durham	.08	.06	.03
242	Ryne Sandberg	.70	.50	.30
269	Andre Dawson	.40	.30	.15
315	Paul Noce	.08	.06	.03
324	Rafael Palmeiro	.70	.50	.30
438	Dave Martinez	.15	.11	.06
447	Jerry Mumphrey	.08	.06	.03
488	Jim Sundberg	.08	.06	.03
516	Manny Trillo	.10	.08	.04
539	Greg Maddux	.50	.40	.20
561	Les Lancaster	.08	.06	.03
570	Frank DiPino	.08	.06	.03
639	Damon Berryhill	.30	.25	.12
646	Scott Sanderson	.08	.06	.03

1988 Donruss New York Mets Team Book

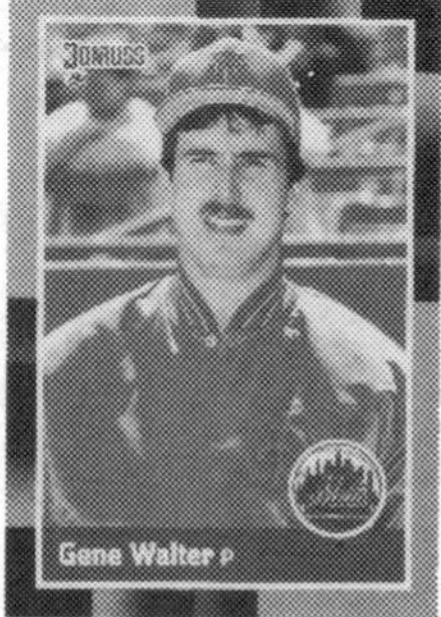

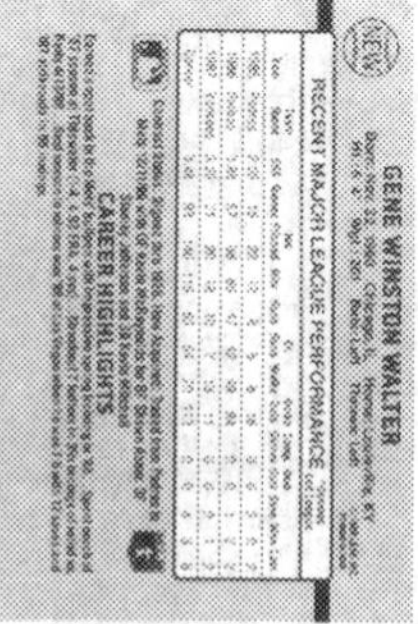

Distributed in book form, the 1988 Donruss New York

Mets team book is still usually found intact. The team book features three pages of player cards, a full page featuring a perforated Stan Musial puzzle, space for autographs on the inside cover and team history information on the back inside cover. The outside covers of the Donruss team books are bright red. The player cards are the same as the regular Donruss issue with the exception of the copyright date. Three "New" Mets are featured in the team book.

		MT	NR MT	EX
Complete Set:		4.00	3.00	1.50
Common Player:		.08	.06	.03
-N1	Jeff Innis	.15	.11	.06
-N2	Mackey Sasser	.30	.25	.12
-N3	Gene Walter	.08	.06	.03
37	Kevin Elster	.10	.08	.04
69	Dwight Gooden	.60	.45	.25
76	Ron Darling	.10	.08	.04
118	Sid Fernandez	.15	.11	.06
199	Gary Carter	.20	.15	.08
241	Wally Backman	.08	.06	.03
316	Keith Hernandez	.20	.15	.08
323	Dave Magadan	.30	.25	.12
364	Len Dykstra	.15	.11	.06
439	Darryl Strawberry	.70	.50	.30
446	Rick Aguilera	.10	.08	.04
562	Keith Miller	.10	.08	.04
569	Howard Johnson	.25	.20	.10
603	Terry Leach	.08	.06	.03
614	Lee Mazzilli	.08	.06	.03
617	Kevin McReynolds	.20	.15	.08
619	Barry Lyons	.08	.06	.03
620	Randy Myers	.20	.15	.08
632	Bob Ojeda	.08	.06	.03
648	Tim Teufel	.08	.06	.03
651	Roger McDowell	.15	.11	.06
652	Mookie Wilson	.10	.08	.04
653	David Cone	.30	.25	.12
657	Gregg Jefferies	2.00	1.50	.80

1988 Donruss New York Yankees Team Book

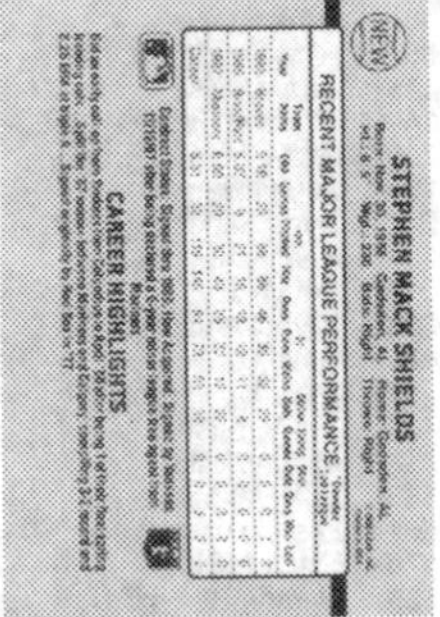

The 1988 Donruss New York Yankees team book includes the same features as the other team collection books. Three pages of cards, a Stan Musial puzzle, autograph space and team history information are provided. The team book is updated for 1988 trades. Nine "New" Yankees are included. The player cards are the same as the regular Donruss cards with the exception of the copyright dates. The team collection books are most often sold intact.

		MT	NR MT	EX
Complete Set:		5.00	3.75	2.00
Common Player:		.08	.06	.03
-N1	John Candelaria	.10	.08	.04
-N2	Jack Clark	.25	.20	.10
-N3	Jose Cruz	.08	.06	.03
-N4	Richard Dotson	.08	.06	.03
-N5	Cecilio Guante	.08	.06	.03
-N6	Lee Guetterman	.08	.06	.03
-N7	Rafael Santana	.08	.06	.03
-N8	Steve Shields	.08	.06	.03
-N9	Don Slaught	.10	.08	.04
43	Al Leiter	.08	.06	.03
93	Dave Righetti	.15	.11	.06
105	Mike Pagliarulo	.10	.08	.04
128	Rick Rhoden	.08	.06	.03
175	Ron Guidry	.15	.11	.06
217	Don Mattingly	1.25	.90	.50
228	Willie Randolph	.15	.11	.06
251	Gary Ward	.08	.06	.03
277	Rickey Henderson	.70	.50	.30
278	Dave Winfield	.25	.20	.10
340	Claudell Washington	.08	.06	.03
374	Charles Hudson	.08	.06	.03
401	Tommy John	.15	.11	.06
474	Joel Skinner	.08	.06	.03
497	Tim Stoddard	.08	.06	.03
545	Jay Buhner	.30	.25	.12
616	Bobby Meacham	.08	.06	.03
635	Roberto Kelly	.90	.70	.35

1988 Donruss Oakland A's Team Book

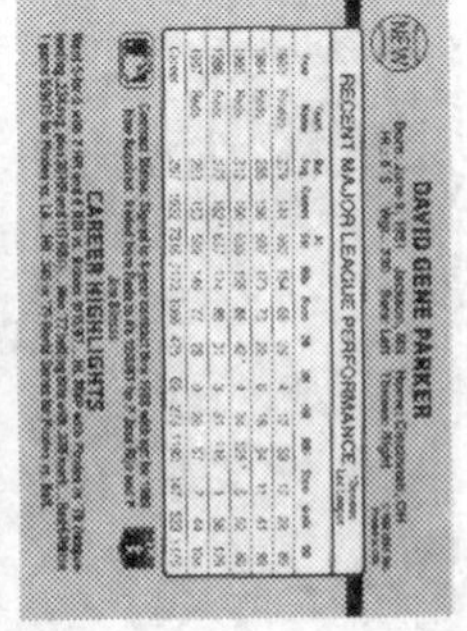

Eleven "New" players are among the featured cards in this unique collectible. The team book includes three pages of player cards, a Stan Musial puzzle, autograph space and team history information. The team books are most often sold intact. The player cards feature the same design as the regular Donruss cards.

		MT	NR MT	EX
Complete Set:		6.00	4.50	2.50
Common Player:		.08	.06	.03
-N1	Don Baylor	.20	.15	.08
-N1	Bob Welch	.30	.25	.12
-N1	Matt Young	.08	.06	.03
-N2	Ron Hassey	.12	.09	.05
-N3	Dave Henderson	.20	.15	.08
-N4	Glenn Hubbard	.08	.06	.03
-N5	Stan Javier	.10	.08	.04
-N6	Doug Jennings	.20	.15	.08
-N7	Edward Jurak	.08	.06	.03
-N8	Dave Parker	.35	.25	.14
-N9	Walt Weiss	.80	.60	.30
97	Curt Young	.08	.06	.03
133	Gene Nelson	.08	.06	.03
158	Terry Steinbach	.20	.15	.08
178	Carney Lansford	.20	.15	.08
221	Tony Phillips	.08	.06	.03
256	Mark McGwire	.80	.60	.30
302	Jose Canseco	1.75	1.25	.70
349	Dennis Eckersley	.40	.30	.15
379	Mike Gallego	.08	.06	.03
425	Luis Polonia	.08	.06	.03
467	Steve Ontiveros	.08	.06	.03
472	Dave Stewart	.40	.30	.15
503	Eric Plunk	.08	.06	.03
528	Greg Cadaret	.08	.06	.03
590	Rick Honeycutt	.08	.06	.03
595	Storm Davis	.08	.06	.03

1989 Donruss

This basic annual issue consists of 660 standard-size (2-1/2" by 3-1/2") cards, including 26 Diamond Kings portrait cards and 20 Rated Rookies cards. Top and bottom borders of the cards are printed in a variety of colors that fade from dark to light (i.e. dark blue to light purple, bright red to pale yellow). A white-lettered player name is printed across the top margin. The team logo appears upper right and the Donruss logo lower left. A black

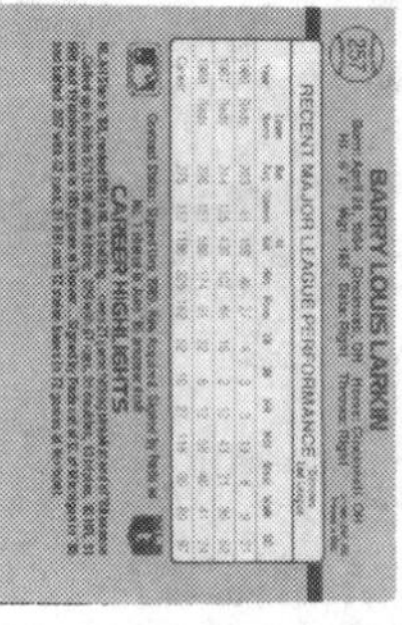

stripe and thin white line make up the vertical side borders. The black outer stripe varnish that gives faintly visible filmstrip texture to the border. The backs (horizontal format) are printed in orange and black, similar to the 1988 design, with personal info, recent stats and major league totals. Team logo sticker cards (22 total) and Warren Spahn puzzle cards (63 total) are included in individual wax packs of cards.

		MT	NR MT	EX
Complete Set (660):		15.00	11.00	6.00
Common Player:		.04	.03	.02
1	Mike Greenwell (DK)	.08	.06	.03
2	Bobby Bonilla (DK)	.12	.09	.05
3	Pete Incaviglia (DK)	.12	.09	.05
4	Chris Sabo (DK)	.08	.06	.03
5	Robin Yount (DK)	.10	.08	.04
6	Tony Gwynn (DK)	.12	.09	.05
7	Carlton Fisk (DK)	.12	.09	.05
8	Cory Snyder (DK)	.15	.11	.06
9	David Cone (DK)	.08	.06	.03
10	Kevin Seitzer (DK)	.08	.06	.03
11	Rick Reuschel (DK)	.10	.08	.04
12	Johnny Ray (DK)	.10	.08	.04
13	Dave Schmidt (DK)	.08	.06	.03
14	Andres Galarraga (DK)	.15	.11	.06
15	Kirk Gibson (DK)	.08	.06	.03
16	Fred McGriff (DK)	.15	.11	.06
17	Mark Grace (DK)	.12	.09	.05
18	Jeff Robinson (DK)	.12	.09	.05
19	Vince Coleman (DK)	.06	.05	.02
20	Dave Henderson (DK)	.10	.08	.04
21	Harold Reynolds (DK)	.08	.06	.03
22	Gerald Perry (DK)	.10	.08	.04
23	Frank Viola (DK)	.08	.06	.03
24	Steve Bedrosian (DK)	.10	.08	.04
25	Glenn Davis (DK)	.08	.06	.03
26	Don Mattingly (DK)	.15	.11	.06
27	Checklist 1-27	.04	.03	.02
28	*Sandy Alomar, Jr.* (RR)	.30	.25	.12
29	*Steve Searcy* (RR)(FC)	.15	.11	.06
30	*Cameron Drew* (RR)(FC)	.15	.11	.06
31	*Gary Sheffield* (RR)	1.75	1.25	.70
32	*Erik Hanson* (RR)	.40	.30	.15
33	*Ken Griffey, Jr.* (RR)	4.00	3.00	1.50
34	*Greg Harris* (RR)	.15	.11	.06
35	Gregg Jefferies (RR)	.40	.30	.15
36	*Luis Medina* (RR)(FC)	.08	.06	.03
37	*Carlos Quintana* (RR)	.12	.09	.05
38	*Felix Jose* (RR)	.25	.20	.10
39	*Cris Carpenter* (RR)	.10	.08	.04
40	*Ron Jones* (RR)(FC)	.10	.08	.04
41	*Dave West* (RR)	.12	.09	.05
42	*Randy Johnson* (RR)	.75	.60	.30
43	*Mike Harkey* (RR)	.15	.11	.06
44	*Pete Harnisch* (RR)	.25	.20	.10
45	*Tom Gordon* (RR)	.10	.08	.04
46	*Gregg Olson* (RR)	.25	.20	.10
47	*Alex Sanchez* (RR)(FC)	.15	.11	.06
48	Ruben Sierra	.35	.25	.14
49	Rafael Palmeiro	.25	.20	.10
50	Ron Gant	.35	.25	.14
51	Cal Ripken, Jr.	.50	.40	.20
52	Wally Joyner	.10	.08	.04
53	Gary Carter	.10	.08	.04
54	Andy Van Slyke	.12	.09	.05
55	Robin Yount	.25	.20	.10
56	Pete Incaviglia	.10	.08	.04
57	Greg Brock	.06	.05	.02
58	Melido Perez	.08	.06	.03
59	Craig Lefferts	.04	.03	.02
60	Gary Pettis	.04	.03	.02
61	Danny Tartabull	.15	.11	.06
62	Guillermo Hernandez	.06	.05	.02
63	Ozzie Smith	.12	.09	.05
64	Gary Gaetti	.12	.09	.05
65	Mark Davis	.04	.03	.02
66	Lee Smith	.08	.06	.03
67	Dennis Eckersley	.10	.08	.04
68	Wade Boggs	.25	.20	.10
69	Mike Scott	.10	.08	.04
70	Fred McGriff	.40	.30	.15
71	Tom Browning	.08	.06	.03
72	Claudell Washington	.06	.05	.02
73	Mel Hall	.06	.05	.02
74	Don Mattingly	.25	.20	.10
75	Steve Bedrosian	.08	.06	.03
76	Juan Samuel	.10	.08	.04
77	Mike Scioscia	.06	.05	.02
78	Dave Righetti	.12	.09	.05
79	Alfredo Griffin	.06	.05	.02
80	Eric Davis	.12	.09	.05
81	Juan Berenguer	.04	.03	.02
82	Todd Worrell	.08	.06	.03
83	Joe Carter	.15	.11	.06
84	Steve Sax	.12	.09	.05
85	Frank White	.06	.05	.02
86	John Kruk	.06	.05	.02
87	Rance Mulliniks	.04	.03	.02
88	Alan Ashby	.04	.03	.02
89	Charlie Leibrandt	.06	.05	.02
90	Frank Tanana	.06	.05	.02
91	Jose Canseco	.30	.25	.12
92	Barry Bonds	.50	.40	.20
93	Harold Reynolds	.06	.05	.02
94	Mark McLemore	.04	.03	.02
95	Mark McGwire	.30	.25	.12
96	Eddie Murray	.20	.15	.08
97	Tim Raines	.08	.06	.03
98	Rob Thompson	.06	.05	.02
99	Kevin McReynolds	.12	.09	.05
100	Checklist 28-137	.04	.03	.02
101	Carlton Fisk	.12	.09	.05
102	Dave Martinez	.06	.05	.02
103	Glenn Braggs	.06	.05	.02
104	Dale Murphy	.10	.08	.04
105	Ryne Sandberg	.40	.30	.15
106	Dennis Martinez	.06	.05	.02
107	Pete O'Brien	.06	.05	.02
108	Dick Schofield	.04	.03	.02
109	Henry Cotto	.04	.03	.02
110	Mike Marshall	.12	.09	.05
111	Keith Moreland	.06	.05	.02
112	Tom Brunansky	.10	.08	.04
113	Kelly Gruber	.04	.03	.02
114	Brook Jacoby	.08	.06	.03
115	*Keith Brown*(FC)	.15	.11	.06
116	Matt Nokes	.15	.11	.06
117	Keith Hernandez	.08	.06	.03
118	Bob Forsch	.06	.05	.02
119	Bert Blyleven	.10	.08	.04
120	Willie Wilson	.08	.06	.03
121	Tommy Gregg	.08	.06	.03
122	Jim Rice	.08	.06	.03
123	Bob Knepper	.06	.05	.02
124	Danny Jackson	.12	.09	.05
125	Eric Plunk	.04	.03	.02
126	Brian Fisher	.06	.05	.02
127	Mike Pagliarulo	.08	.06	.03
128	Tony Gwynn	.30	.25	.12
129	Lance McCullers	.06	.05	.02
130	Andres Galarraga	.15	.11	.06
131	Jose Uribe	.04	.03	.02
132	Kirk Gibson	.08	.06	.03
133	David Palmer	.04	.03	.02
134	R.J. Reynolds	.04	.03	.02
135	Greg Walker	.06	.05	.02
136	Kirk McCaskill	.06	.05	.02
137	Shawon Dunston	.08	.06	.03
138	Andy Allanson	.04	.03	.02
139	Rob Murphy	.04	.03	.02
140	Mike Aldrete	.06	.05	.02
141	Terry Kennedy	.06	.05	.02
142	Scott Fletcher	.06	.05	.02
143	Steve Balboni	.06	.05	.02
144	Bret Saberhagen	.12	.09	.05
145	Ozzie Virgil	.04	.03	.02
146	Dale Sveum	.06	.05	.02
147	Darryl Strawberry	.15	.11	.06
148	Harold Baines	.10	.08	.04

		MT	NR MT	EX
149	George Bell	.10	.08	.04
150	Dave Parker	.12	.09	.05
151	Bobby Bonilla	.12	.09	.05
152	Mookie Wilson	.06	.05	.02
153	Ted Power	.04	.03	.02
154	Nolan Ryan	.60	.45	.25
155	Jeff Reardon	.08	.06	.03
156	Tim Wallach	.08	.06	.03
157	Jamie Moyer	.04	.03	.02
158	Rich Gossage	.10	.08	.04
159	Dave Winfield	.25	.20	.10
160	Von Hayes	.08	.06	.03
161	Willie McGee	.10	.08	.04
162	Rich Gedman	.06	.05	.02
163	Tony Pena	.06	.05	.02
164	Mike Morgan	.04	.03	.02
165	Charlie Hough	.06	.05	.02
166	Mike Stanley	.10	.08	.04
167	Andre Dawson	.20	.15	.08
168	Joe Boever(FC)	.04	.03	.02
169	Pete Stanicek	.08	.06	.03
170	Bob Boone	.06	.05	.02
171	Ron Darling	.10	.08	.04
172	Bob Walk	.04	.03	.02
173	Rob Deer	.06	.05	.02
174	Steve Buechele	.04	.03	.02
175	Ted Higuera	.08	.06	.03
176	Ozzie Guillen	.06	.05	.02
177	Candy Maldonado	.06	.05	.02
178	Doyle Alexander	.06	.05	.02
179	Mark Gubicza	.10	.08	.04
180	Alan Trammell	.08	.06	.03
181	Vince Coleman	.15	.11	.06
182	Kirby Puckett	.30	.25	.12
183	Chris Brown	.06	.05	.02
184	Marty Barrett	.06	.05	.02
185	Stan Javier	.04	.03	.02
186	Mike Greenwell	.08	.06	.03
187	Billy Hatcher	.06	.05	.02
188	Jimmy Key	.08	.06	.03
189	Nick Esasky	.06	.05	.02
190	Don Slaught	.04	.03	.02
191	Cory Snyder	.15	.11	.06
192	John Candelaria	.06	.05	.02
193	Mike Schmidt	.40	.30	.15
194	Kevin Gross	.06	.05	.02
195	John Tudor	.08	.06	.03
196	Neil Allen	.04	.03	.02
197	Orel Hershiser	.08	.06	.03
198	Kal Daniels	.15	.11	.06
199	Kent Hrbek	.15	.11	.06
200	Checklist 138-247	.04	.03	.02
201	Joe Magrane	.08	.06	.03
202	Scott Bailes	.04	.03	.02
203	Tim Belcher	.10	.08	.04
204	George Brett	.30	.25	.12
205	Benito Santiago	.12	.09	.05
206	Tony Fernandez	.10	.08	.04
207	Gerald Young	.10	.08	.04
208	Bo Jackson	.30	.25	.12
209	Chet Lemon	.06	.05	.02
210	Storm Davis	.08	.06	.03
211	Doug Drabek	.06	.05	.02
212	Mickey Brantley (photo actually Nelson Simmons)	.04	.03	.02
213	Devon White	.10	.08	.04
214	Dave Stewart	.08	.06	.03
215	Dave Schmidt	.04	.03	.02
216	Bryn Smith	.04	.03	.02
217	Brett Butler	.06	.05	.02
218	Bob Ojeda	.06	.05	.02
219	*Steve Rosenberg*(FC)	.08	.06	.03
220	Hubie Brooks	.08	.06	.03
221	B.J. Surhoff	.08	.06	.03
222	Rick Mahler	.04	.03	.02
223	Rick Sutcliffe	.08	.06	.03
224	Neal Heaton	.04	.03	.02
225	Mitch Williams	.06	.05	.02
226	Chuck Finley	.08	.06	.03
227	Mark Langston	.10	.08	.04
228	Jesse Orosco	.06	.05	.02
229	Ed Whitson	.04	.03	.02
230	Terry Pendleton	.10	.08	.04
231	Lloyd Moseby	.06	.05	.02
232	Greg Swindell	.10	.08	.04
233	John Franco	.08	.06	.03
234	Jack Morris	.15	.11	.06
235	Howard Johnson	.08	.06	.03
236	Glenn Davis	.12	.09	.05
237	Frank Viola	.12	.09	.05
238	Kevin Seitzer	.06	.05	.02
239	Gerald Perry	.08	.06	.03
240	Dwight Evans	.10	.08	.04
241	Jim Deshaies	.04	.03	.02
242	Bo Diaz	.06	.05	.02
243	Carney Lansford	.06	.05	.02
244	Mike LaValliere	.06	.05	.02
245	Rickey Henderson	.20	.15	.08
246	Roberto Alomar	.80	.60	.30
247	Jimmy Jones	.04	.03	.02
248	Pascual Perez	.06	.05	.02
249	Will Clark	.35	.25	.14
250	Fernando Valenzuela	.08	.06	.03
251	Shane Rawley	.06	.05	.02
252	Sid Bream	.06	.05	.02
253	Steve Lyons	.04	.03	.02
254	Brian Downing	.06	.05	.02
255	Mark Grace	.40	.30	.15
256	Tom Candiotti	.04	.03	.02
257	Barry Larkin	.12	.09	.05
258	Mike Krukow	.06	.05	.02
259	Billy Ripken	.06	.05	.02
260	Cecilio Guante	.04	.03	.02
261	Scott Bradley	.04	.03	.02
262	Floyd Bannister	.06	.05	.02
263	Pete Smith	.08	.06	.03
264	Jim Gantner	.04	.03	.02
265	Roger McDowell	.08	.06	.03
266	Bobby Thigpen	.08	.06	.03
267	Jim Clancy	.06	.05	.02
268	Terry Steinbach	.08	.06	.03
269	Mike Dunne	.08	.06	.03
270	Dwight Gooden	.10	.08	.04
271	Mike Heath	.04	.03	.02
272	Dave Smith	.06	.05	.02
273	Keith Atherton	.04	.03	.02
274	Tim Burke	.04	.03	.02
275	Damon Berryhill	.12	.09	.05
276	Vance Law	.06	.05	.02
277	Rich Dotson	.06	.05	.02
278	Lance Parrish	.15	.11	.06
279	Denny Walling	.04	.03	.02
280	Roger Clemens	.30	.25	.12
281	Greg Mathews	.06	.05	.02
282	Tom Niedenfuer	.06	.05	.02
283	Paul Kilgus	.10	.08	.04
284	Jose Guzman	.08	.06	.03
285	Calvin Schiraldi	.04	.03	.02
286	Charlie Puleo	.04	.03	.02
287	Joe Orsulak	.04	.03	.02
288	Jack Howell	.06	.05	.02
289	Kevin Elster	.08	.06	.03
290	Jose Lind	.10	.08	.04
291	Paul Molitor	.20	.15	.08
292	Cecil Espy	.08	.06	.03
293	Bill Wegman	.04	.03	.02
294	Dan Pasqua	.08	.06	.03
295	Scott Garrelts	.04	.03	.02
296	Walt Terrell	.06	.05	.02
297	Ed Hearn	.04	.03	.02
298	Lou Whitaker	.08	.06	.03
299	Ken Dayley	.04	.03	.02
300	Checklist 248-357	.04	.03	.02
301	Tommy Herr	.06	.05	.02
302	Mike Brumley	.06	.05	.02
303	Ellis Burks	.10	.08	.04
304	Curt Young	.06	.05	.02
305	Jody Reed	.10	.08	.04
306	Bill Doran	.06	.05	.02
307	David Wells	.06	.05	.02
308	Ron Robinson	.04	.03	.02
309	Rafael Santana	.04	.03	.02
310	Julio Franco	.10	.08	.04
311	Jack Clark	.15	.11	.06
312	Chris James	.08	.06	.03
313	Milt Thompson	.04	.03	.02
314	John Shelby	.04	.03	.02
315	Al Leiter	.15	.11	.06
316	Mike Davis	.06	.05	.02
317	*Chris Sabo*	.30	.25	.12
318	Greg Gagne	.04	.03	.02
319	Jose Oquendo	.04	.03	.02
320	John Farrell	.10	.08	.04
321	Franklin Stubbs	.04	.03	.02
322	Kurt Stillwell	.06	.05	.02
323	Shawn Abner	.10	.08	.04
324	Mike Flanagan	.06	.05	.02
325	Kevin Bass	.06	.05	.02
326	Pat Tabler	.06	.05	.02
327	Mike Henneman	.08	.06	.03
328	Rick Honeycutt	.04	.03	.02
329	John Smiley	.10	.08	.04

		MT	NR MT	EX
330	Rey Quinones	.04	.03	.02
331	Johnny Ray	.06	.05	.02
332	Bob Welch	.08	.06	.03
333	Larry Sheets	.06	.05	.02
334	Jeff Parrett	.08	.06	.03
335	Rick Reuschel	.08	.06	.03
336	Randy Myers	.10	.08	.04
337	Ken Williams	.06	.05	.02
338	Andy McGaffigan	.04	.03	.02
339	Joey Meyer	.08	.06	.03
340	Dion James	.04	.03	.02
341	Les Lancaster	.06	.05	.02
342	Tom Foley	.04	.03	.02
343	Geno Petralli	.04	.03	.02
344	Dan Petry	.06	.05	.02
345	Alvin Davis	.12	.09	.05
346	Mickey Hatcher	.04	.03	.02
347	Marvell Wynne	.04	.03	.02
348	Danny Cox	.06	.05	.02
349	Dave Stieb	.08	.06	.03
350	Jay Bell	.06	.05	.02
351	Jeff Treadway	.10	.08	.04
352	Luis Salazar	.04	.03	.02
353	Lenny Dykstra	.15	.11	.06
354	Juan Agosto	.04	.03	.02
355	Gene Larkin	.10	.08	.04
356	Steve Farr	.04	.03	.02
357	Paul Assenmacher	.04	.03	.02
358	Todd Benzinger	.12	.09	.05
359	Larry Andersen	.04	.03	.02
360	Paul O'Neill	.04	.03	.02
361	Ron Hassey	.04	.03	.02
362	Jim Gott	.04	.03	.02
363	Ken Phelps	.06	.05	.02
364	Tim Flannery	.04	.03	.02
365	Randy Ready	.04	.03	.02
366	*Nelson Santovenia*(FC)	.08	.06	.03
367	Kelly Downs	.08	.06	.03
368	Danny Heep	.04	.03	.02
369	Phil Bradley	.08	.06	.03
370	Jeff Robinson	.06	.05	.02
371	Ivan Calderon	.06	.05	.02
372	Mike Witt	.06	.05	.02
373	Greg Maddux	.25	.20	.10
374	Carmen Castillo	.04	.03	.02
375	Jose Rijo	.06	.05	.02
376	Joe Price	.04	.03	.02
377	R.C. Gonzalez	.04	.03	.02
378	Oddibe McDowell	.06	.05	.02
379	Jim Presley	.06	.05	.02
380	Brad Wellman	.04	.03	.02
381	Tom Glavine	.30	.25	.12
382	Dan Plesac	.08	.06	.03
383	Wally Backman	.06	.05	.02
384	*Dave Gallagher*	.08	.06	.03
385	Tom Henke	.06	.05	.02
386	Luis Polonia	.06	.05	.02
387	Junior Ortiz	.04	.03	.02
388	David Cone	.12	.09	.05
389	Dave Bergman	.04	.03	.02
390	Danny Darwin	.04	.03	.02
391	Dan Gladden	.04	.03	.02
392	*John Dopson*	.08	.06	.03
393	Frank DiPino	.04	.03	.02
394	Al Nipper	.04	.03	.02
395	Willie Randolph	.06	.05	.02
396	Don Carman	.06	.05	.02
397	Scott Terry	.06	.05	.02
398	Rick Cerone	.04	.03	.02
399	Tom Pagnozzi	.06	.05	.02
400	Checklist 358-467	.04	.03	.02
401	Mickey Tettleton	.10	.08	.04
402	Curtis Wilkerson	.04	.03	.02
403	Jeff Russell	.04	.03	.02
404	Pat Perry	.04	.03	.02
405	*Jose Alvarez*(FC)	.06	.05	.02
406	Rick Schu	.04	.03	.02
407	*Sherman Corbett*(FC)	.08	.06	.03
408	Dave Magadan	.10	.08	.04
409	Bob Kipper	.04	.03	.02
410	Don August	.08	.06	.03
411	Bob Brower	.04	.03	.02
412	Chris Bosio	.04	.03	.02
413	Jerry Reuss	.06	.05	.02
414	Atlee Hammaker	.04	.03	.02
415	Jim Walewander(FC)	.06	.05	.02
416	*Mike Macfarlane*	.25	.20	.10
417	Pat Sheridan	.04	.03	.02
418	Pedro Guerrero	.15	.11	.06
419	Allan Anderson	.06	.05	.02
420	*Mark Parent*	.08	.06	.03

		MT	NR MT	EX
421	Bob Stanley	.04	.03	.02
422	Mike Gallego	.04	.03	.02
423	Bruce Hurst	.08	.06	.03
424	Dave Meads	.04	.03	.02
425	Jesse Barfield	.10	.08	.04
426	*Rob Dibble*(FC)	.20	.15	.08
427	Joel Skinner	.04	.03	.02
428	Ron Kittle	.06	.05	.02
429	Rick Rhoden	.08	.06	.03
430	Bob Dernier	.04	.03	.02
431	Steve Jeltz	.04	.03	.02
432	Rick Dempsey	.06	.05	.02
433	Roberto Kelly	.10	.08	.04
434	Dave Anderson	.04	.03	.02
435	Herm Winningham	.04	.03	.02
436	Al Newman	.04	.03	.02
437	Jose DeLeon	.06	.05	.02
438	Doug Jones	.10	.08	.04
439	Brian Holton	.06	.05	.02
440	Jeff Montgomery(FC)	.15	.11	.06
441	Dickie Thon	.04	.03	.02
442	Cecil Fielder	.25	.20	.10
443	*John Fishel*(FC)	.08	.06	.03
444	Jerry Don Gleaton	.04	.03	.02
445	*Paul Gibson*	.15	.11	.06
446	Walt Weiss	.10	.08	.04
447	Glenn Wilson	.06	.05	.02
448	Mike Moore	.04	.03	.02
449	Chili Davis	.06	.05	.02
450	Dave Henderson	.08	.06	.03
451	*Jose Bautista*	.06	.05	.02
452	Rex Hudler	.04	.03	.02
453	Bob Brenly	.04	.03	.02
454	Mackey Sasser	.06	.05	.02
455	Daryl Boston	.04	.03	.02
456	Mike Fitzgerald	.04	.03	.02
457	Jeffery Leonard	.06	.05	.02
458	Bruce Sutter	.08	.06	.03
459	Mitch Webster	.06	.05	.02
460	Joe Hesketh	.04	.03	.02
461	Bobby Witt	.08	.06	.03
462	Stew Cliburn	.04	.03	.02
463	Scott Bankhead	.04	.03	.02
464	*Ramon Martinez*(FC)	.40	.30	.15
465	Dave Leiper	.04	.03	.02
466	*Luis Alicea*	.20	.15	.08
467	John Cerutti	.06	.05	.02
468	Ron Washington	.04	.03	.02
469	Jeff Reed	.04	.03	.02
470	Jeff Robinson	.12	.09	.05
471	Sid Fernandez	.08	.06	.03
472	Terry Puhl	.04	.03	.02
473	Charlie Lea	.04	.03	.02
474	*Israel Sanchez*(FC)	.15	.11	.06
475	Bruce Benedict	.04	.03	.02
476	Oil Can Boyd	.06	.05	.02
477	Craig Reynolds	.04	.03	.02
478	Frank Williams	.04	.03	.02
479	Greg Cadaret	.10	.08	.04
480	*Randy Kramer*(FC)	.15	.11	.06
481	*Dave Eiland*(FC)	.12	.09	.05
482	Eric Show	.06	.05	.02
483	Garry Templeton	.06	.05	.02
484	Wallace Johnson(FC)	.04	.03	.02
485	Kevin Mitchell	.15	.11	.06
486	Tim Crews	.06	.05	.02
487	Mike Maddux	.04	.03	.02
488	Dave LaPoint	.06	.05	.02
489	Fred Manrique	.06	.05	.02
490	Greg Minton	.04	.03	.02
491	*Doug Dascenzo*(FC)	.08	.06	.03
492	Willie Upshaw	.06	.05	.02
493	*Jack Armstrong*(FC)	.10	.08	.04
494	Kirt Manwaring	.10	.08	.04
495	Jeff Ballard	.06	.05	.02
496	Jeff Kunkel	.04	.03	.02
497	Mike Campbell	.08	.06	.03
498	Gary Thurman	.10	.08	.04
499	Zane Smith	.06	.05	.02
500	Checklist 468-577	.04	.03	.02
501	Mike Birkbeck	.04	.03	.02
502	Terry Leach	.04	.03	.02
503	Shawn Hillegas	.06	.05	.02
504	Manny Lee	.04	.03	.02
505	*Doug Jennings*	.08	.06	.03
506	Ken Oberkfell	.04	.03	.02
507	Tim Teufel	.04	.03	.02
508	Tom Brookens	.04	.03	.02
509	Rafael Ramirez	.04	.03	.02
510	Fred Toliver	.04	.03	.02
511	*Brian Holman*(FC)	.12	.09	.05

		MT	NR MT	EX
512	Mike Bielecki	.04	.03	.02
513	*Jeff Pico*(FC)	.06	.05	.02
514	Charles Hudson	.04	.03	.02
515	Bruce Ruffin	.04	.03	.02
516	Larry McWilliams	.04	.03	.02
517	Jeff Sellers	.04	.03	.02
518	*John Costello*(FC)	.15	.11	.06
519	*Brady Anderson*	.40	.30	.15
520	Craig McMurtry	.04	.03	.02
521	Ray Hayward	.08	.06	.03
522	Drew Hall	.08	.06	.03
523	*Mark Lemke*(FC)	.15	.11	.06
524	*Oswald Peraza*(FC)	.08	.06	.03
525	*Bryan Harvey*	.40	.30	.15
526	Rick Aguilera	.04	.03	.02
527	Tom Prince	.06	.05	.02
528	Mark Clear	.04	.03	.02
529	Jerry Browne	.04	.03	.02
530	Juan Castillo	.04	.03	.02
531	Jack McDowell	.15	.11	.06
532	Chris Speier	.04	.03	.02
533	Darrell Evans	.08	.06	.03
534	Luis Aquino	.04	.03	.02
535	Eric King	.04	.03	.02
536	*Ken Hill*(FC)	.40	.30	.15
537	Randy Bush	.04	.03	.02
538	Shane Mack	.06	.05	.02
539	Tom Bolton(FC)	.06	.05	.02
540	Gene Nelson	.04	.03	.02
541	Wes Gardner	.06	.05	.02
542	Ken Caminiti	.06	.05	.02
543	Duane Ward	.04	.03	.02
544	*Norm Charlton*(FC)	.15	.11	.06
545	*Hal Morris*(FC)	.25	.20	.10
546	Rich Yett(FC)	.04	.03	.02
547	*Hensley Meulens*(FC)	.20	.15	.08
548	Greg Harris	.04	.03	.02
549	Darren Daulton	.04	.03	.02
550	Jeff Hamilton	.06	.05	.02
551	Luis Aguayo	.04	.03	.02
552	Tim Leary	.06	.05	.02
553	Ron Oester	.04	.03	.02
554	Steve Lombardozzi	.04	.03	.02
555	*Tim Jones*(FC)	.15	.11	.06
556	Bud Black	.04	.03	.02
557	Alejandro Pena	.04	.03	.02
558	*Jose DeJesus*(FC)	.15	.11	.06
559	Dennis Rasmussen	.08	.06	.03
560	*Pat Borders*	.20	.15	.08
561	*Craig Biggio*(FC)	.35	.25	.14
562	*Luis de los Santos*(FC)	.10	.08	.04
563	Fred Lynn	.10	.08	.04
564	*Todd Burns*(FC)	.20	.15	.08
565	Felix Fermin	.06	.05	.02
566	Darnell Coles	.06	.05	.02
567	Willie Fraser	.04	.03	.02
568	Glenn Hubbard	.04	.03	.02
569	*Craig Worthington*	.08	.06	.03
570	*Johnny Paredes*	.15	.11	.06
571	Don Robinson	.04	.03	.02
572	Barry Lyons	.04	.03	.02
573	Bill Long	.06	.05	.02
574	Tracy Jones	.10	.08	.04
575	Juan Nieves	.06	.05	.02
576	Andres Thomas	.06	.05	.02
577	*Rolando Roomes*(FC)	.15	.11	.06
578	Luis Rivera(FC)	.04	.03	.02
579	*Chad Kreuter*(FC)	.15	.11	.06
580	Tony Armas	.06	.05	.02
581	Jay Buhner	.12	.09	.05
582	Ricky Horton	.06	.05	.02
583	Andy Hawkins	.04	.03	.02
584	*Sil Campusano*	.15	.11	.06
585	Dave Clark	.06	.05	.02
586	*Van Snider*(FC)	.15	.11	.06
587	Todd Frohwirth(FC)	.06	.05	.02
588	Warren Spahn Puzzle Card	.04	.03	.02
589	*William Brennan*(FC)	.15	.11	.06
590	*German Gonzalez*(FC)	.15	.11	.06
591	Ernie Whitt	.06	.05	.02
592	Jeff Blauser	.08	.06	.03
593	Spike Owen	.04	.03	.02
594	Matt Williams	.40	.30	.15
595	Lloyd McClendon(FC)	.04	.03	.02
596	Steve Ontiveros	.04	.03	.02
597	*Scott Medvin*(FC)	.15	.11	.06
598	*Hipolito Pena*(FC)	.15	.11	.06
599	*Jerald Clark*(FC)	.15	.11	.06
600a	Checklist 578-BC26 (#635 is Kurt Schilling)	.15	.11	.06
600b	Checklist 578-BC26 (#635 is Curt Schilling)	.06	.05	.02
601	Carmelo Martinez	.04	.03	.02
602	Mike LaCoss	.04	.03	.02
603	Mike Devereaux	.15	.11	.06
604	*Alex Madrid*(FC)	.15	.11	.06
605	Gary Redus	.04	.03	.02
606	Lance Johnson	.06	.05	.02
607	*Terry Clark*(FC)	.15	.11	.06
608	Manny Trillo	.04	.03	.02
609	*Scott Jordan*(FC)	.15	.11	.06
610	Jay Howell	.06	.05	.02
611	*Francisco Melendez*(FC)	.15	.11	.06
612	Mike Boddicker	.06	.05	.02
613	Kevin Brown	.20	.15	.08
614	Dave Valle	.04	.03	.02
615	Tim Laudner	.04	.03	.02
616	*Andy Nezelek*(FC)	.15	.11	.06
617	Chuck Crim	.04	.03	.02
618	Jack Savage(FC)	.10	.08	.04
619	Adam Peterson(FC)	.10	.08	.04
620	Todd Stottlemyre	.15	.11	.06
621	*Lance Blankenship*	.10	.08	.04
622	*Miguel Garcia*(FC)	.15	.11	.06
623	Keith Miller	.06	.05	.02
624	*Ricky Jordan*	.10	.08	.04
625	Ernest Riles	.04	.03	.02
626	John Moses	.04	.03	.02
627	Nelson Liriano	.06	.05	.02
628	Mike Smithson	.04	.03	.02
629	Scott Sanderson	.04	.03	.02
630	Dale Mohorcic	.04	.03	.02
631	Marvin Freeman	.04	.03	.02
632	Mike Young	.04	.03	.02
633	Dennis Lamp	.04	.03	.02
634	*Dante Bichette*	.40	.30	.15
635	*Curt Schilling*	.15	.11	.06
636	*Scott May*(FC)	.15	.11	.06
637	*Mike Schooler*	.15	.11	.06
638	Rick Leach	.04	.03	.02
639	*Tom Lampkin*(FC)	.08	.06	.03
640	*Brian Meyer*(FC)	.15	.11	.06
641	Brian Harper	.04	.03	.02
642	*John Smoltz*	.80	.60	.30
643	Jose Canseco (40/40)	.15	.11	.06
644	Bill Schroeder	.04	.03	.02
645	*Edgar Martinez*	.25	.20	.10
646	*Dennis Cook*	.10	.08	.04
647	Barry Jones	.04	.03	.02
648	59 and Counting (Orel Hershiser)	.15	.11	.06
649	*Rod Nichols*(FC)	.15	.11	.06
650	Jody Davis	.06	.05	.02
651	*Bob Milacki*	.12	.09	.05
652	Mike Jackson	.06	.05	.02
653	*Derek Lilliquist*	.15	.11	.06
654	Paul Mirabella	.04	.03	.02
655	Mike Diaz	.06	.05	.02
656	Jeff Musselman	.06	.05	.02
657	Jerry Reed	.04	.03	.02
658	*Kevin Blankenship*(FC)	.08	.06	.03
659	Wayne Tolleson	.04	.03	.02
660	*Eric Hetzel*(FC)	.15	.11	.06

1989 Donruss MVP

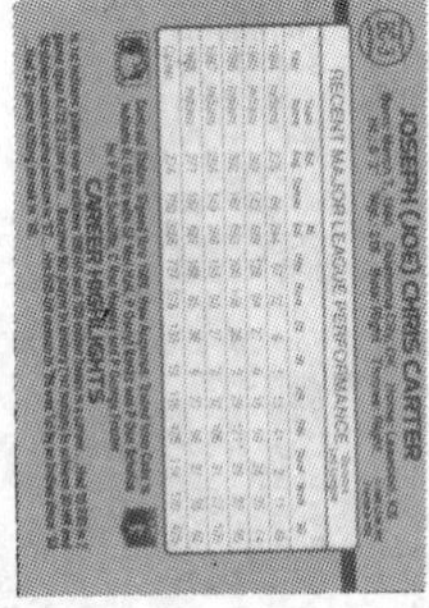

This 26-card set, numbered BC-1 through BC-26, was randomly packed in Donruss wax packs, but were not included in factory sets or other card packs. Players highlighted in this set are selected by Donruss, one player per team. MVP cards feature a variation of the design in the basic Donruss issue, with multi-color upper and lower borders and black side borders. The player name and Donruss '89 logos appear in the upper margin with the team logo appearing lower right. The "MVP" designation in large, bright letters serves as a backdrop for the full-color player photo. The cards measure 2-1/2" by 3-1/2" in size.

		MT	NR MT	EX
Complete Set (26):		1.00	.60	.30
Common Player:		.04	.03	.02
1	Kirby Puckett	.30	.20	.10
2	Mike Scott	.15	.11	.06
3	Joe Carter	.30	.25	.12
4	Orel Hershiser	.25	.20	.10
5	Jose Canseco	.75	.55	.30
6	Darryl Strawberry	.60	.45	.25
7	George Brett	.15	.10	.05
8	Andre Dawson	.25	.20	.10
9	Paul Molitor	.20	.15	.08
10	Andy Van Slyke	.15	.11	.06
11	Dave Winfield	.20	.15	.08
12	Kevin Gross	.15	.11	.06
13	Mike Greenwell	.30	.25	.12
14	Ozzie Smith	.10	.06	.03
15	Cal Ripken	.30	.20	.10
16	Andres Galarraga	.15	.11	.06
17	Alan Trammell	.25	.20	.10
18	Kal Daniels	.20	.15	.08
19	Fred McGriff	.25	.15	.10
20	Tony Gwynn	.10	.06	.03
21	Wally Joyner	.30	.25	.12
22	Will Clark	.15	.10	.05
23	Ozzie Guillen	.15	.11	.06
24	Gerald Perry	.15	.11	.06
25	Alvin Davis	.15	.11	.06
26	Ruben Sierra	.25	.20	.10

1989 Donruss Grand Slammers

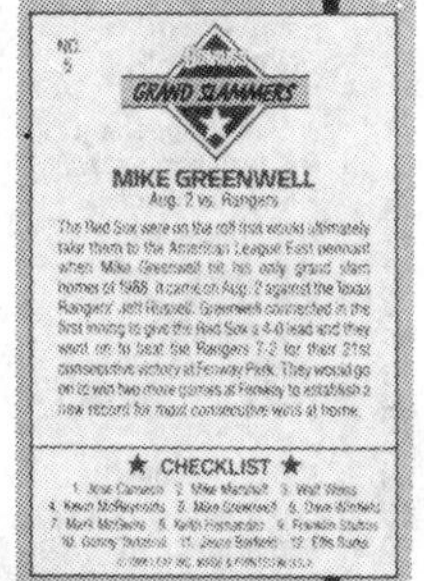

One card from this 12-card set was included in each Donruss cello pack. The complete insert set was included in factory sets. The featured players all hit grand slams in 1988. The 2-1/2" by 3-1/2" cards feature full color action photos. The card backs feature the story of the player's grand slam. Border variations on the front of the card have been discovered, but the prices are consistent with all forms of the cards.

		MT	NR MT	EX
Complete Set (12):		2.50	1.50	.75
Common Player:		.12	.09	.05
1	Jose Canseco	.20	.12	.06
2	Mike Marshall	.12	.09	.05
3	Walt Weiss	.12	.09	.05
4	Kevin McReynolds	.15	.11	.06
5	Mike Greenwell	.25	.20	.10
6	Dave Winfield	.25	.15	.10
7	Mark McGwire	.25	.15	.10
8	Keith Hernandez	.15	.11	.06
9	Franklin Stubbs	.12	.09	.05
10	Danny Tartabull	.25	.15	.10
11	Jesse Barfield	.15	.11	.06
12	Ellis Burks	.30	.25	.12

1989 Donruss All-Stars

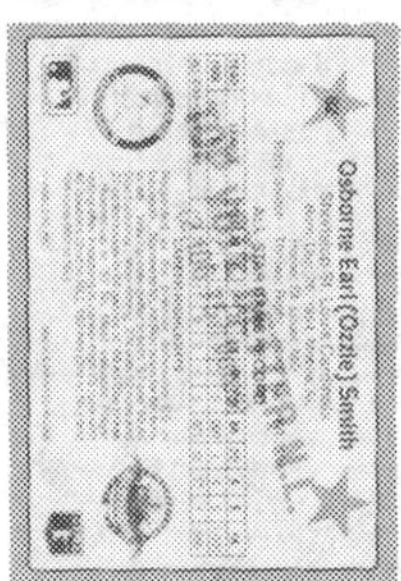

For the fourth consecutive year in conjunction with the Pop-Ups, Donruss featured a 64-card set with players from the 1988 All-Star Game. The card fronts include a red- to-gold fade or gold-to-red fade border and blue vertical side borders. The top border features the player's name and position along with the "Donruss 89" logo. Each full-color player photo is highlighted by a thin white line and includes a league logo in the lower right corner. Card backs reveal an orange-gold border and black and white printing. The player's ID and personal information is displayed with a gold star on both sides. The star in the left corner includes the card number. 1988 All-Star game statistics and run totals follow along with a career highlights feature surrounded by the team, All-Star Game MLB, MLBPA, and Leaf Inc. logos. The All-Stars were distributed in wax packages containing five All-Stars, one Pop-Up, and one three-piece Warren Spahn puzzle card.

		MT	NR MT	EX
Complete Set:		9.00	6.75	3.50
Common Player:		.09	.07	.04
1	Mark McGwire	.50	.40	.20
2	Jose Canseco	1.00	.70	.40
3	Paul Molitor	.12	.09	.05
4	Rickey Henderson	.30	.25	.12
5	Cal Ripken, Jr.	.30	.25	.12
6	Dave Winfield	.20	.15	.08
7	Wade Boggs	.50	.40	.20
8	Frank Viola	.15	.11	.06
9	Terry Steinbach	.09	.07	.04
10	Tom Kelly	.09	.07	.04
11	George Brett	.12	.09	.05
12	Doyle Alexander	.09	.07	.04
13	Gary Gaetti	.12	.09	.05
14	Roger Clemens	.40	.30	.15
15	Mike Greenwell	.25	.20	.10
16	Dennis Eckersley	.12	.09	.05
17	Carney Lansford	.09	.07	.04
18	Mark Gubicza	.09	.07	.04
19	Tim Laudner	.09	.07	.04
20	Doug Jones	.09	.07	.04
21	Don Mattingly	1.00	.70	.40
22	Dan Plesac	.12	.09	.05
23	Kirby Puckett	.30	.25	.12
24	Jeff Reardon	.09	.07	.04
25	Johnny Ray	.09	.07	.04
26	Jeff Russell	.09	.07	.04
27	Harold Reynolds	.09	.07	.04
28	Dave Stieb	.09	.07	.04
29	Kurt Stillwell	.09	.07	.04
30	Jose Canseco	1.00	.70	.40
31	Terry Steinbach	.09	.07	.04
32	AL Checklist	.09	.07	.05
33	Will Clark	1.00	.70	.40
34	Darryl Strawberry	.60	.45	.25
35	Ryne Sandberg	.40	.30	.15
36	Andre Dawson	.20	.15	.08
37	Ozzie Smith	.20	.15	.08
38	Vince Coleman	.15	.11	.06
39	Bobby Bonilla	.15	.11	.06
40	Dwight Gooden	.40	.30	.15
41	Gary Carter	.10	.08	.04
42	Whitey Herzog	.09	.07	.05

		MT	NR MT	EX
43	Shawon Dunston	.09	.07	.05
44	David Cone	.12	.09	.05
45	Andres Galarraga	.09	.07	.04
46	Mark Davis	.09	.07	.04
47	Barry Larkin	.12	.09	.05
48	Kevin Gross	.09	.07	.04
49	Vance Law	.09	.07	.04
50	Orel Hershiser	.20	.15	.08
51	Willie McGee	.09	.07	.04
52	Danny Jackson	.09	.07	.04
53	Rafael Palmeiro	.20	.15	.08
54	Bob Knepper	.09	.07	.04
55	Lance Parrish	.09	.07	.04
56	Greg Maddux	.15	.11	.06
57	Gerald Perry	.09	.07	.04
58	Bob Walk	.09	.07	.04
59	Chris Sabo	.12	.09	.04
60	Todd Worrell	.09	.07	.04
61	Andy Van Slyke	.12	.09	.04
62	Ozzie Smith	.20	.15	.08
63	Riverfront Stadium	.09	.07	.04
64	NL Checklist	.09	.07	.04

1989 Donruss Baseball's Best

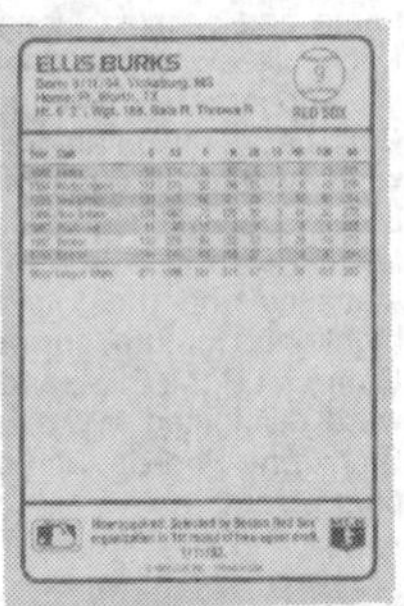

For the second consecutive year, Donruss issued a "Baseball's Best" set in 1989 to highlight the game's top players. The special 336-card set was packaged in a special box and was sold at various retail chains nationwide following the conclusion of the 1989 baseball season. The cards are styled after the regular 1989 Donruss set with green borders and a glossy finish. The set included a Warren Spahn puzzle.

		MT	NR MT	EX
Complete Set:		20.00	15.00	8.00
Common Player:		.05	.04	.02
1	Don Mattingly	1.00	.70	.40
2	Tom Glavine	.15	.11	.06
3	Bert Blyleven	.08	.06	.03
4	Andre Dawson	.10	.08	.04
5	Pete O'Brien	.05	.04	.02
6	Eric Davis	.40	.30	.15
7	George Brett	.10	.08	.04
8	Glenn Davis	.10	.08	.04
9	Ellis Burks	.30	.25	.12
10	Kirk Gibson	.08	.06	.03
11	Carlton Fisk	.08	.06	.03
12	Andres Galarraga	.08	.06	.03
13	Alan Trammell	.06	.05	.02
14	Dwight Gooden	.30	.25	.12
15	Paul Molitor	.10	.08	.04
16	Roger McDowell	.05	.04	.02
17	Doug Drabek	.05	.04	.02
18	Kent Hrbek	.08	.06	.03
19	Vince Coleman	.08	.06	.03
20	Steve Sax	.08	.06	.03
21	Roberto Alomar	.30	.25	.12
22	Carney Lansford	.06	.05	.02
23	Will Clark	1.50	1.25	.60
24	Alvin Davis	.08	.06	.03
25	Bobby Thigpen	.08	.06	.03
26	Ryne Sandberg	.60	.45	.25
27	Devon White	.08	.06	.03
28	Mike Greenwell	.40	.30	.15
29	Dale Murphy	.10	.08	.04
30	Jeff Ballard	.10	.08	.04
31	Kelly Gruber	.08	.06	.03
32	Julio Franco	.15	.11	.06
33	Bobby Bonilla	.15	.11	.06
34	Tim Wallach	.05	.04	.02
35	Lou Whitaker	.07	.05	.03
36	Jay Howell	.07	.05	.03
37	Greg Maddux	.30	.25	.12
38	Bill Doran	.07	.05	.03
39	Danny Tartabull	.12	.09	.05
40	Darryl Strawberry	.50	.40	.20
41	Ron Darling	.10	.08	.06
42	Tony Gwynn	.30	.25	.12
43	Mark McGwire	.40	.30	.15
44	Ozzie Smith	.15	.11	.06
45	Andy Van Slyke	.12	.09	.05
46	Juan Berenguer	.05	.04	.02
47	Von Hayes	.08	.06	.03
48	Tony Fernandez	.12	.09	.05
49	Eric Plunk	.05	.04	.02
50	Ernest Riles	.05	.04	.02
51	Harold Reynolds	.07	.05	.03
52	Andy Hawkins	.06	.05	.02
53	Robin Yount	.35	.25	.14
54	Danny Jackson	.06	.05	.02
55	Nolan Ryan	1.25	.90	.50
56	Joe Carter	.12	.09	.05
57	Jose Canseco	1.00	.70	.40
58	Jody Davis	.05	.04	.02
59	Lance Parrish	.06	.05	.02
60	Mitch Williams	.15	.11	.06
61	Brook Jacoby	.06	.05	.02
62	Tom Browning	.10	.08	.06
63	Kurt Stillwell	.06	.05	.02
64	Rafael Ramirez	.05	.04	.02
65	Roger Clemens	.50	.40	.20
66	Mike Scioscia	.07	.05	.02
67	Dave Gallagher	.07	.05	.02
68	Mark Langston	.15	.11	.06
69	Chet Lemon	.06	.05	.02
70	Kevin McReynolds	.25	.20	.10
71	Rob Deer	.06	.05	.02
72	Tommy Herr	.07	.05	.03
73	Barry Bonds	.12	.09	.05
74	Frank Viola	.15	.11	.06
75	Pedro Guerrero	.15	.11	.06
76	Dave Righetti	.07	.05	.03
77	Bruce Hurst	.08	.06	.03
78	Rickey Henderson	.40	.30	.15
79	Robby Thompson	.08	.06	.03
80	Randy Johnson	.25	.20	.10
81	Harold Baines	.12	.09	.05
82	Calvin Schiraldi	.05	.04	.02
83	Kirk McCaskill	.05	.04	.02
84	Lee Smith	.07	.05	.03
85	John Smoltz	.25	.20	.10
86	Mickey Tettleton	.20	.15	.08
87	Jimmy Key	.08	.06	.03
88	Rafael Palmeiro	.10	.08	.04
89	Sid Bream	.05	.04	.02
90	Dennis Martinez	.05	.04	.02
91	Frank Tanana	.05	.04	.02
92	Eddie Murray	.15	.11	.06
93	Shawon Dunston	.15	.11	.06
94	Mike Scott	.10	.08	.04
95	Bret Saberhagen	.25	.20	.10
96	David Cone	.20	.15	.08
97	Kevin Elster	.05	.04	.02
98	Jack Clark	.20	.15	.08
99	Dave Stewart	.20	.15	.08
100	Jose Oquendo	.06	.05	.02
101	Jose Lind	.05	.04	.02
102	Gary Gaetti	.12	.09	.05
103	Ricky Jordan	.25	.20	.10
104	Fred McGriff	.50	.40	.20
105	Don Slaught	.05	.04	.02
106	Jose Uribe	.05	.04	.02
107	Jeffrey Leonard	.07	.05	.02
108	Lee Guetterman	.05	.04	.02
109	Chris Bosio	.08	.06	.03
110	Barry Larkin	.15	.11	.06
111	Ruben Sierra	.30	.25	.12
112	Greg Swindell	.12	.09	.05
113	Gary Sheffield	.40	.30	.15
114	Lonnie Smith	.10	.08	.04
115	Chili Davis	.08	.06	.03
116	Damon Berryhill	.08	.06	.03
117	Tom Candiotti	.05	.04	.02
118	Kal Daniels	.10	.08	.04
119	Mark Gubicza	.10	.08	.04

		MT	NR MT	EX
120	Jim Deshaies	.08	.06	.03
121	Dwight Evans	.10	.08	.04
122	Mike Morgan	.05	.04	.02
123	Dan Pasqua	.05	.04	.02
124	Bryn Smith	.07	.05	.03
125	Doyle Alexander	.07	.05	.03
126	Howard Johnson	.25	.20	.10
127	Chuck Crim	.07	.05	.03
128	Darren Daulton	.05	.04	.02
129	Jeff Robinson	.08	.06	.03
130	Kirby Puckett	.50	.40	.20
131	Joe Magrane	.10	.08	.04
132	Jesse Barfield	.07	.05	.03
133	Mark Davis (Photo actually Dave Leiper)	.25	.20	.10
134	Dennis Eckersley	.10	.08	.04
135	Mike Krukow	.05	.04	.02
136	Jay Buhner	.10	.08	.04
137	Ozzie Guillen	.08	.06	.03
138	Rick Sutcliffe	.12	.09	.05
139	Wally Joyner	.25	.20	.10
140	Wade Boggs	.60	.45	.25
141	Jeff Treadway	.08	.06	.05
142	Cal Ripken	.30	.25	.12
143	Dave Steib	.10	.08	.04
144	Pete Incaviglia	.07	.05	.03
145	Bob Walk	.05	.04	.02
146	Nelson Santovenia	.10	.08	.04
147	Mike Heath	.05	.04	.02
148	Willie Randolph	.08	.06	.03
149	Paul Kilgus	.05	.04	.02
150	Billy Hatcher	.07	.05	.03
151	Steve Farr	.05	.04	.02
152	Gregg Jefferies	.40	.30	.15
153	Randy Myers	.06	.05	.02
154	Garry Templeton	.06	.05	.02
155	Walt Weiss	.10	.08	.04
156	Terry Pendleton	.10	.08	.04
157	John Smiley	.08	.06	.03
158	Greg Gagne	.05	.04	.02
159	Lenny Dykstra	.08	.06	.03
160	Nelson Liriano	.05	.04	.02
161	Alvaro Espinoza	.10	.08	.04
162	Rick Reuschel	.08	.06	.03
163	Omar Vizquel	.15	.11	.06
164	Clay Parker	.15	.11	.06
165	Dan Plesac	.06	.05	.02
166	John Franco	.06	.05	.02
167	Scott Fletcher	.06	.05	.02
168	Cory Snyder	.12	.09	.05
169	Bo Jackson	1.00	.70	.40
170	Tommy Gregg	.08	.06	.03
171	Jim Abbott	.50	.40	.20
172	Jerome Walton	.50	.40	.20
173	Doug Jones	.06	.05	.02
174	Todd Benzinger	.08	.06	.03
175	Frank White	.08	.06	.03
176	Craig Biggio	.20	.15	.08
177	John Dopson	.10	.08	.06
178	Alfredo Griffin	.06	.05	.02
179	Melido Perez	.06	.05	.02
180	Tim Burke	.06	.05	.02
181	Matt Nokes	.10	.08	.04
182	Gary Carter	.10	.08	.04
183	Ted Higuera	.08	.06	.03
184	Ken Howell	.05	.04	.02
185	Rey Quinones	.05	.04	.02
186	Wally Backman	.07	.05	.03
187	Tom Brunansky	.07	.05	.03
188	Steve Balboni	.05	.04	.02
189	Marvell Wynne	.05	.04	.02
190	Dave Henderson	.08	.06	.03
191	Don Robinson	.05	.04	.02
192	Ken Griffey, Jr.	4.00	3.00	1.50
193	Ivan Calderon	.05	.04	.02
194	Mike Bielecki	.07	.05	.03
195	Johnny Ray	.07	.05	.03
196	Rob Murphy	.05	.04	.02
197	Andres Thomas	.05	.04	.02
198	Phil Bradley	.06	.05	.02
199	Junior Felix	.30	.25	.12
200	Jeff Russell	.08	.06	.03
201	Mike LaValliere	.05	.04	.02
202	Kevin Gross	.06	.05	.02
203	Keith Moreland	.06	.05	.02
204	Mike Marshall	.06	.05	.02
205	Dwight Smith	.30	.25	.12
206	Jim Clancy	.05	.04	.02
207	Kevin Seitzer	.10	.08	.04
208	Keith Hernandez	.10	.08	.04
209	Bob Ojeda	.06	.05	.02

		MT	NR MT	EX
210	Ed Whitson	.06	.05	.02
211	Tony Phillips	.06	.05	.02
212	Milt Thompson	.05	.04	.02
213	Randy Kramer	.05	.04	.02
214	Randy Bush	.05	.04	.02
215	Randy Ready	.05	.04	.02
216	Duane Ward	.05	.04	.02
217	Jimmy Jones	.05	.04	.02
218	Scott Garrelts	.08	.06	.03
219	Scott Bankhead	.10	.08	.04
220	Lance McCullers	.06	.05	.02
221	B.J. Surhoff	.06	.05	.02
222	Chris Sabo	.06	.05	.02
223	Steve Buechele	.06	.05	.02
224	Joel Skinner	.05	.04	.02
225	Orel Hershiser	.15	.11	.06
226	Derek Lilliquist	.10	.08	.06
227	Claudell Washington	.08	.06	.05
228	Lloyd McClendon	.10	.08	.04
229	Felix Fermin	.05	.04	.02
230	Paul O'Neill	.08	.06	.03
231	Charlie Leibrandt	.05	.04	.02
232	Dave Smith	.06	.05	.02
233	Bob Stanley	.05	.04	.02
234	Tim Belcher	.15	.11	.06
235	Eric King	.05	.04	.02
236	Spike Owen	.05	.04	.02
237	Mike Henneman	.05	.04	.02
238	Juan Samuel	.06	.05	.02
239	Greg Brock	.06	.05	.02
240	John Kruk	.06	.05	.02
241	Glenn Wilson	.06	.05	.02
242	Jeff Reardon	.06	.05	.02
243	Todd Worrell	.08	.06	.03
244	Dave LaPoint	.05	.04	.02
245	Walt Terrell	.05	.04	.02
246	Mike Moore	.08	.06	.03
247	Kelly Downs	.05	.04	.02
248	Dave Valle	.05	.04	.02
249	Ron Kittle	.06	.05	.04
250	Steve Wilson	.10	.08	.04
251	Dick Schofield	.05	.04	.02
252	Marty Barrett	.06	.05	.02
253	Dion James	.06	.05	.02
254	Bob Milacki	.10	.08	.04
255	Ernie Whitt	.06	.05	.02
256	Kevin Brown	.08	.06	.03
257	R.J. Reynolds	.05	.04	.02
258	Tim Raines	.10	.08	.04
259	Frank Williams	.05	.04	.02
260	Jose Gonzalez	.05	.04	.02
261	Mitch Webster	.05	.04	.02
262	Ken Caminiti	.07	.05	.03
263	Bob Boone	.07	.05	.03
264	Dave Magadan	.07	.05	.03
265	Rick Aguilera	.05	.04	.02
266	Chris James	.05	.04	.02
267	Bob Welch	.07	.05	.03
268	Ken Dayley	.05	.04	.02
269	Junior Ortiz	.05	.04	.02
270	Allan Anderson	.08	.06	.03
271	Steve Jeltz	.05	.04	.02
272	George Bell	.10	.08	.04
273	Roberto Kelly	.10	.08	.04
274	Brett Butler	.07	.05	.03
275	Mike Schooler	.07	.05	.02
276	Ken Phelps	.05	.04	.02
277	Glenn Braggs	.06	.05	.02
278	Jose Rijo	.06	.05	.02
279	Bobby Witt	.06	.05	.02
280	Jerry Browne	.06	.05	.02
281	Kevin Mitchell	.40	.30	.15
282	Craig Worthington	.15	.11	.06
283	Greg Minton	.05	.04	.02
284	Nick Esasky	.07	.05	.03
285	John Farrell	.05	.04	.02
286	Rick Mahler	.05	.04	.02
287	Tom Gordon	.40	.30	.15
288	Gerald Young	.05	.04	.02
289	Jody Reed	.08	.06	.03
290	Jeff Hamilton	.05	.04	.02
291	Gerald Perry	.05	.04	.02
292	Hubie Brooks	.05	.04	.02
293	Bo Diaz	.05	.04	.02
294	Terry Puhl	.05	.04	.02
295	Jim Gantner	.05	.04	.02
296	Jeff Parrett	.05	.04	.02
297	Mike Boddicker	.05	.04	.02
298	Dan Gladden	.05	.04	.02
299	Tony Pena	.07	.05	.03
300	Checklist	.05	.04	.02

		MT	NR MT	EX
301	Tom Henke	.05	.04	.02
302	Pascual Perez	.05	.04	.02
303	Steve Bedrosian	.05	.04	.02
304	Ken Hill	.10	.08	.04
305	Jerry Reuss	.07	.05	.03
306	Jim Eisenreich	.05	.04	.02
307	Jack Howell	.05	.04	.02
308	Rick Cerone	.05	.04	.02
309	Tim Leary	.05	.04	.02
310	Joe Orsulak	.05	.04	.02
311	Jim Dwyer	.05	.04	.02
312	Geno Petralli	.05	.04	.02
313	Rick Honeycutt	.05	.04	.02
314	Tom Foley	.05	.04	.02
315	Kenny Rogers	.10	.08	.04
316	Mike Flanagan	.06	.05	.02
317	Bryan Harvey	.06	.05	.02
318	Billy Ripken	.05	.04	.02
319	Jeff Montgomery	.05	.04	.02
320	Erik Hanson	.12	.09	.05
321	Brian Downing	.06	.05	.02
322	Gregg Olson	.40	.30	.15
323	Terry Steinbach	.12	.09	.05
324	Sammy Sosa	.40	.30	.15
325	Gene Harris	.05	.04	.02
326	Mike Devereaux	.10	.08	.04
327	Dennis Cook	.12	.09	.05
328	David Wells	.08	.06	.03
329	Checklist	.05	.04	.02
330	Kirt Manwaring	.10	.08	.04
331	Jim Presley	.05	.04	.02
332	Checklist	.05	.04	.02
333	Chuck Finley	.05	.04	.02
334	Rob Dibble	.08	.06	.03
335	Cecil Espy	.06	.05	.02
336	Dave Parker	.08	.06	.02

1989 Donruss Pop-Ups

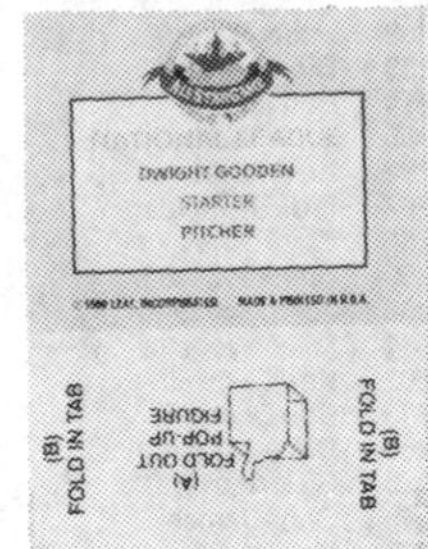

This set features the eighteen starters from the 1988 Major League All-Star game. The cards are designed with a perforated outline so each player can be popped out and made to stand upright. On the front side, each player's name, team, and position is featured in an orange-and-yellow rectangle below the borderless full-color photo. Each Pop-Up includes a unique double card, folded over and glued together on the back. The flip side features a red, white, and blue "Cincinnati Reds All-Star Game" logo at the top, a blue-lettered league designation, and the player's name and position in red. The lower portion of the flip side displays illustrated instructions for creating the base of the Pop-Up. The Pop-Ups were marketed in conjunction with All-Star and Warren Spahn Puzzle Cards.

		MT	NR MT	EX
Complete Set:		5.00	3.75	2.00
Common Player:		.20	.15	.08
(1)	Mark McGwire	.40	.30	.15
(2)	Jose Canseco	.80	.60	.30
(3)	Paul Molitor	.30	.25	.12
(4)	Rickey Henderson	.50	.40	.20
(5)	Cal Ripken, Jr.	.50	.40	.20
(6)	Dave Winfield	.40	.30	.15
(7)	Wade Boggs	.50	.40	.20
(8)	Frank Viola	.25	.20	.10
(9)	Terry Steinbach	.20	.15	.08
(10)	Tom Kelly	.20	.15	.08
(11)	Will Clark	1.00	.70	.40
(12)	Darryl Strawberry	.50	.40	.20
(13)	Ryne Sandberg	.50	.40	.20
(14)	Andre Dawson	.35	.25	.14
(15)	Ozzie Smith	.30	.25	.12
(16)	Vince Coleman	.20	.15	.08
(17)	Bobby Bonilla	.30	.25	.12
(18)	Dwight Gooden	.50	.40	.20
(19)	Gary Carter	.20	.15	.08
(20)	Whitey Herzog	.20	.15	.08

1989 Donruss Rookies

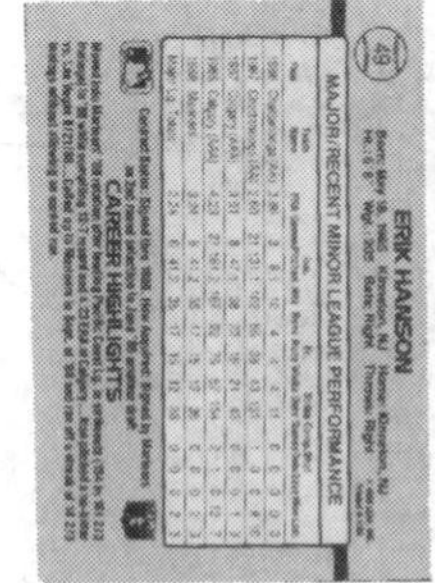

For the fourth straight year, Donruss issued a 56-card "Rookies" set in 1989. As in previous years, the set is similar in design to the regular Donruss set, except for a new "The Rookies" logo and a green and black border.

		MT	NR MT	EX
Complete Set (56):		15.00	11.00	6.00
Common Player:		.10	.08	.04
1	Gary Sheffield	3.00	2.25	1.25
2	Gregg Jefferies	.60	.45	.25
3	Ken Griffey, Jr.	8.00	6.00	3.25
4	Tom Gordon	.12	.09	.05
5	Billy Spiers(FC)	.10	.08	.04
6	Deion Sanders(FC)	2.00	1.50	.80
7	Donn Pall(FC)	.20	.15	.08
8	Steve Carter(FC)	.20	.15	.08
9	Francisco Oliveras(FC)	.15	.11	.06
10	Steve Wilson(FC)	.20	.15	.08
11	Bob Geren(FC)	.20	.15	.08
12	Tony Castillo(FC)	.15	.11	.06
13	Kenny Rogers(FC)	.20	.15	.08
14	Carlos Martinez(FC)	.30	.25	.12
15	Edgar Martinez	.25	.20	.10
16	Jim Abbott(FC)	1.50	1.25	.60
17	Torey Lovullo(FC)	.20	.15	.08
18	Mark Carreon(FC)	.15	.11	.06
19	Geronimo Berroa	.10	.08	.04
20	Luis Medina	.10	.08	.04
21	Sandy Alomar, Jr.	.30	.25	.12
22	Bob Milacki	.10	.08	.04
23	Joe Girardi(FC)	.30	.25	.12
24	German Gonzalez	.10	.08	.04
25	Craig Worthington	.15	.11	.06
26	Jerome Walton(FC)	.12	.09	.05
27	Gary Wayne(FC)	.20	.15	.08
28	Tim Jones	.10	.08	.04
29	Dante Bichette	.50	.40	.20
30	Alexis Infante(FC)	.15	.11	.06
31	Ken Hill	.50	.40	.20
32	Dwight Smith(FC)	.12	.09	.05
33	Luis de los Santos	.10	.08	.04
34	Eric Yelding(FC)	.08	.06	.03
35	Gregg Olson	.40	.30	.15
36	Phil Stephenson(FC)	.15	.11	.06
37	Ken Patterson(FC)	.15	.11	.06
38	Rick Wrona(FC)	.15	.11	.06
39	Mike Brumley	.10	.08	.04
40	Cris Carpenter	.10	.08	.04
41	Jeff Brantley(FC)	.20	.15	.08
42	Ron Jones	.10	.08	.04
43	Randy Johnson	.75	.60	.30
44	Kevin Brown	.10	.08	.04

		MT	NR MT	EX
45	Ramon Martinez	.50	.40	.20
46	Greg Harris	.10	.08	.04
47	Steve Finley(FC)	.40	.30	.15
48	Randy Kramer	.10	.08	.04
49	Erik Hanson	.30	.25	.12
50	Matt Merullo(FC)	.15	.11	.06
51	Mike Devereaux	.15	.11	.06
52	Clay Parker(FC)	.15	.11	.06
53	Omar Vizquel(FC)	.20	.15	.08
54	Derek Lilliquist	.12	.09	.05
55	Junior Felix(FC)	.15	.11	.06
56	Checklist	.10	.08	.04

1989 Donruss Traded

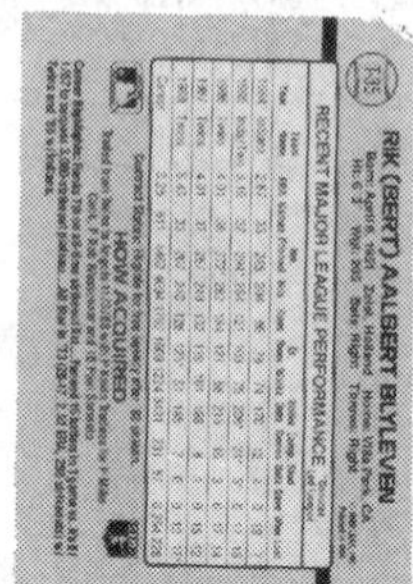

Donruss issued its first "Traded" set in 1989, releasing a 56-card boxed set designed in the same style as the regular 1989 Donruss set. The set included a Stan Musial puzzle card and a checklist.

		MT	NR MT	EX
Complete Set:		4.00	3.00	1.50
Common Player:		.06	.05	.02
1	Jeffrey Leonard	.08	.06	.03
2	Jack Clark	.15	.11	.06
3	Kevin Gross	.06	.05	.02
4	Tommy Herr	.08	.06	.03
5	Bob Boone	.10	.08	.04
6	Rafael Palmeiro	.30	.25	.12
7	John Dopson	.15	.11	.06
8	Willie Randolph	.08	.06	.03
9	Chris Brown	.06	.05	.02
10	Wally Backman	.06	.05	.02
11	Steve Ontiveros	.06	.05	.02
12	Eddie Murray	.30	.25	.12
13	Lance McCullers	.08	.06	.03
14	Spike Owen	.06	.05	.02
15	Rob Murphy	.06	.05	.02
16	Pete O'Brien	.08	.06	.03
17	Ken Williams	.06	.05	.02
18	Nick Esasky	.06	.05	.02
19	Nolan Ryan	1.50	1.25	.60
20	Brian Holton	.06	.05	.02
21	Mike Moore	.08	.06	.03
22	Joel Skinner	.06	.05	.02
23	Steve Sax	.15	.11	.06
24	Rick Mahler	.06	.05	.02
25	Mike Aldrete	.06	.05	.02
26	Jesse Orosco	.08	.06	.03
27	Dave LaPoint	.06	.05	.02
28	Walt Terrell	.08	.06	.03
29	Eddie Williams	.08	.06	.03
30	Mike Devereaux	.10	.08	.04
31	Julio Franco	.15	.11	.06
32	Jim Clancy	.06	.05	.02
33	Felix Fermin	.06	.05	.02
34	Curtis Wilkerson	.06	.05	.02
35	Bert Blyleven	.12	.09	.05
36	Mel Hall	.08	.06	.03
37	Eric King	.06	.05	.02
38	Mitch Williams	.12	.09	.05
39	Jamie Moyer	.06	.05	.02
40	Rick Rhoden	.08	.06	.03
41	Phil Bradley	.08	.06	.03
42	Paul Kilgus	.08	.06	.03
43	Milt Thompson	.06	.05	.02
44	Jerry Browne	.08	.06	.03

		MT	NR MT	EX
45	Bruce Hurst	.08	.06	.03
46	Claudell Washington	.08	.06	.03
47	Todd Benzinger	.12	.09	.05
48	Steve Balboni	.06	.05	.02
49	Oddibe McDowell	.08	.06	.03
50	Charles Hudson	.06	.05	.02
51	Ron Kittle	.08	.06	.03
52	Andy Hawkins	.06	.05	.02
53	Tom Brookens	.06	.05	.02
54	Tom Niedenfuer	.06	.05	.02
55	Jeff Parrett	.08	.06	.03
56	Checklist	.06	.05	.02

1990 Donruss

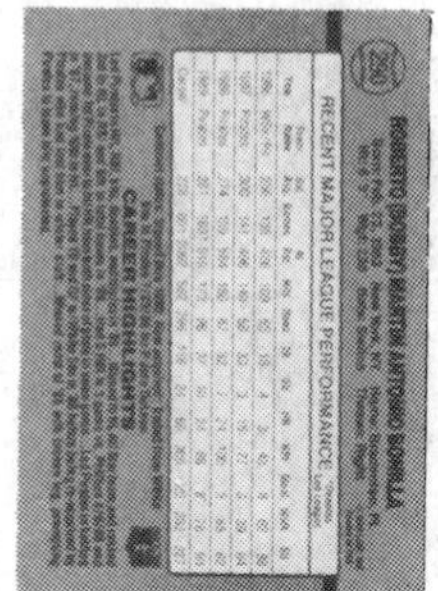

Donruss marked its 10th anniversary in the baseball card hobby with a 715-card set in 1990, up from previous 660-card sets. The standard-size cards feature bright red borders with the player's name in script at the top. The set includes 26 "Diamond Kings", 20 "Rated Rookies" and a Carl Yastrzemski puzzle. Each All-Star card back has two variations. The more common has the stats box headed "All-Star Performance". Slightly scarcer versions say "Recent Major League Performance", and are worth about twice the value of the correct version.

		MT	NR MT	EX
Complete Set (716):		18.00	13.50	7.25
Common Player:		.04	.03	.02
1	Bo Jackson (DK)	.20	.15	.08
2	Steve Sax (DK)	.12	.09	.05
3a	Ruben Sierra ((DK) no vertical black line at top-right on back)	1.00	.70	.40
3b	Ruben Sierra ((DK) vertical line at top right on back)	.30	.25	.12
4	Ken Griffey, Jr. (DK)	.40	.30	.15
5	Mickey Tettleton (DK)	.12	.09	.05
6	Dave Stewart (DK)	.12	.09	.05
7	Jim Deshaies (DK)	.07	.05	.03
8	John Smoltz (DK)	.15	.11	.06
9	Mike Bielecki (DK)	.07	.05	.03
10a	Brian Downing ((DK) reversed negative)	1.00	.70	.40
10b	Brian Downing ((DK) corrected)	.25	.20	.10
11	Kevin Mitchell (DK)	.06	.05	.02
12	Kelly Gruber (DK)	.08	.06	.03
13	Joe Magrane (DK)	.08	.06	.03
14	John Franco (DK)	.08	.06	.03
15	Ozzie Guillen (DK)	.08	.06	.03
16	Lou Whitaker (DK)	.08	.06	.03
17	John Smiley (DK)	.08	.06	.03
18	Howard Johnson (DK)	.06	.05	.02
19	Willie Randolph (DK)	.08	.06	.03
20	Chris Bosio (DK)	.07	.05	.03
21	Tommy Herr (DK)	.07	.05	.03
22	Dan Gladden (DK)	.07	.05	.03
23	Ellis Burks (DK)	.08	.06	.03
24	Pete O'Brien (DK)	.08	.06	.03
25	Bryn Smith (DK)	.07	.05	.03
26	Ed Whitson (DK)	.07	.05	.03
27	Checklist 1-27	.04	.03	.02
28	*Robin Ventura* (RR)	.80	.60	.30
29	*Todd Zeile* (RR)	.20	.15	.08
30	Sandy Alomar, Jr. (RR)	.20	.15	.08
31	*Kent Mercker* (RR)	.10	.08	.04
32	*Ben McDonald* (RR)	.50	.40	.20
33a	*Juan Gonzalez* ((RR) reversed negative)	4.00	3.00	1.50

		MT	NR MT	EX
33b	*Juan Gonzalez* ((RR) corrected)	2.00	1.50	.80
34	*Eric Anthony* (RR)	.50	.40	.20
35	*Mike Fetters* (RR)	.20	.15	.08
36	*Marquis Grissom* (RR)	.60	.45	.25
37	*Greg Vaughn* (RR)	.30	.25	.12
38	*Brian Dubois* (RR)(FC)	.15	.11	.06
39	*Steve Avery* (RR)	.60	.45	.25
40	*Mark Gardner* (RR)	.20	.15	.08
41	*Andy Benes* (RR)	.40	.30	.15
42	*Delino DeShields* (RR)	.80	.60	.30
43	*Scott Coolbaugh* (RR)	.08	.06	.03
44	*Pat Combs* (RR)	.12	.09	.05
45	*Alex Sanchez* (RR)	.15	.11	.06
46	*Kelly Mann* (RR)(FC)	.10	.08	.04
47	*Julio Machado* (RR)(FC)	.08	.06	.03
48	Pete Incaviglia	.05	.04	.02
49	Shawon Dunston	.07	.05	.03
50	Jeff Treadway	.05	.04	.02
51	Jeff Ballard	.10	.08	.04
52	Claudell Washington	.08	.06	.03
53	Juan Samuel	.10	.08	.04
54	John Smiley	.08	.06	.03
55	Rob Deer	.06	.05	.02
56	Geno Petralli	.04	.03	.02
57	Chris Bosio	.10	.08	.04
58	Carlton Fisk	.12	.09	.05
59	Kirt Manwaring	.10	.08	.04
60	Chet Lemon	.06	.05	.02
61	Bo Jackson	.30	.25	.12
62	Doyle Alexander	.05	.04	.02
63	Pedro Guerrero	.12	.09	.05
64	Allan Anderson	.07	.05	.03
65	Greg Harris	.07	.05	.03
66	Mike Greenwell	.10	.08	.04
67	Walt Weiss	.08	.06	.03
68	Wade Boggs	.30	.25	.12
69	Jim Clancy	.04	.03	.02
70	*Junior Felix*	.08	.06	.03
71	Barry Larkin	.12	.09	.05
72	Dave LaPoint	.05	.04	.02
73	Joel Skinner	.04	.03	.02
74	Jesse Barfield	.08	.06	.03
75	Tommy Herr	.08	.06	.03
76	Ricky Jordan	.10	.08	.04
77	Eddie Murray	.15	.11	.06
78	Steve Sax	.10	.08	.04
79	Tim Belcher	.10	.08	.04
80	Danny Jackson	.06	.05	.02
81	Kent Hrbek	.10	.08	.04
82	Milt Thompson	.05	.04	.02
83	Brook Jacoby	.07	.05	.03
84	Mike Marshall	.08	.06	.03
85	Kevin Seitzer	.12	.09	.05
86	Tony Gwynn	.15	.11	.06
87	Dave Steib	.08	.06	.03
88	Dave Smith	.06	.05	.02
89	Bret Saberhagen	.08	.06	.03
90	Alan Trammell	.10	.08	.04
91	Tony Phillips	.05	.04	.02
92	Doug Drabek	.05	.04	.02
93	Jeffrey Leonard	.09	.07	.04
94	Wally Joyner	.15	.11	.06
95	Carney Lansford	.09	.07	.04
96	Cal Ripken, Jr.	.25	.20	.10
97	Andres Galarraga	.15	.11	.06
98	Kevin Mitchell	.10	.08	.04
99	Howard Johnson	.15	.11	.06
100a	Checklist 28-129	.04	.03	.02
100b	Checklist 28-125	.04	.03	.02
101	Melido Perez	.07	.05	.03
102	Spike Owen	.05	.04	.02
103	Paul Molitor	.20	.15	.08
104	Geronimo Berroa	.06	.05	.02
105	Ryne Sandberg	.25	.20	.10
106	Bryn Smith	.06	.05	.02
107	Steve Buechele	.04	.03	.02
108	Jim Abbott	.30	.25	.12
109	Alvin Davis	.10	.08	.04
110	Lee Smith	.05	.04	.02
111	Roberto Alomar	.50	.40	.20
112	Rick Reuschel	.09	.07	.04
113a	Kelly Gruber (Born 2/22)	.08	.06	.03
113b	Kelly Gruber (Born 2/26)	.25	.20	.10
114	Joe Carter	.09	.07	.04
115	Jose Rijo	.06	.05	.02
116	Greg Minton	.04	.03	.02
117	Bob Ojeda	.04	.03	.02
118	Glenn Davis	.08	.06	.03
119	Jeff Reardon	.05	.04	.02
120	Kurt Stillwell	.05	.04	.02
121	John Smoltz	.15	.11	.06
122	Dwight Evans	.08	.06	.03

		MT	NR MT	EX
123	Eric Yelding	.08	.06	.03
124	John Franco	.05	.04	.02
125	Jose Canseco	.25	.20	.10
126	Barry Bonds	.25	.20	.10
127	Lee Guetterman	.04	.03	.02
128	Jack Clark	.10	.08	.04
129	Dave Valle	.04	.03	.02
130	Hubie Brooks	.05	.04	.02
131	Ernest Riles	.04	.03	.02
132	Mike Morgan	.04	.03	.02
133	Steve Jeltz	.04	.03	.02
134	Jeff Robinson	.05	.04	.02
135	Ozzie Guillen	.05	.04	.02
136	Chili Davis	.06	.05	.02
137	Mitch Webster	.04	.03	.02
138	Jerry Browne	.06	.05	.02
139	Bo Diaz	.04	.03	.02
140	Robby Thompson	.07	.05	.03
141	Craig Worthington	.09	.07	.04
142	Julio Franco	.09	.07	.04
143	Brian Holman	.05	.04	.02
144	George Brett	.15	.11	.06
145	Tom Glavine	.15	.11	.06
146	Robin Yount	.20	.15	.08
147	Gary Carter	.06	.05	.02
148	Ron Kittle	.06	.05	.02
149	Tony Fernandez	.07	.05	.03
150	Dave Stewart	.07	.05	.03
151	Gary Gaetti	.07	.05	.03
152	Kevin Elster	.04	.03	.02
153	Gerald Perry	.05	.04	.02
154	Jesse Orosco	.05	.04	.02
155	Wally Backman	.05	.04	.02
156	Dennis Martinez	.05	.04	.02
157	Rick Sutcliffe	.08	.06	.03
158	Greg Maddux	.12	.09	.05
159	Andy Hawkins	.05	.04	.02
160	John Kruk	.05	.04	.02
161	Jose Oquendo	.05	.04	.02
162	John Dopson	.08	.06	.03
163	Joe Magrane	.08	.06	.03
164	Billy Ripken	.04	.03	.02
165	Fred Manrique	.04	.03	.02
166	Nolan Ryan	.40	.30	.15
167	Damon Berryhill	.06	.05	.02
168	Dale Murphy	.09	.07	.04
169	Mickey Tettleton	.08	.06	.03
170a	Kirk McCaskill (Born 4/19)	.06	.05	.02
170b	Kirk McCaskill	.25	.20	.10
171	Dwight Gooden	.15	.11	.06
172	Jose Lind	.04	.03	.02
173	B.J. Surhoff	.07	.05	.03
174	Ruben Sierra	.15	.11	.06
175	Dan Plesac	.08	.06	.03
176	Dan Pasqua	.05	.04	.02
177	Kelly Downs	.05	.04	.02
178	Matt Nokes	.08	.06	.03
179	Luis Aquino	.04	.03	.02
180	Frank Tanana	.04	.03	.02
181	Tony Pena	.07	.05	.03
182	Dan Gladden	.05	.04	.02
183	Bruce Hurst	.05	.04	.02
184	Roger Clemens	.20	.15	.08
185	Mark McGwire	.25	.20	.10
186	Rob Murphy	.04	.03	.02
187	Jim Deshaies	.06	.05	.02
188	Fred McGriff	.20	.15	.08
189	Rob Dibble	.06	.05	.02
190	Don Mattingly	.25	.20	.10
191	Felix Fermin	.04	.03	.02
192	Roberto Kelly	.08	.06	.03
193	Dennis Cook	.08	.06	.03
194	Darren Daulton	.04	.03	.02
195	Alfredo Griffin	.05	.04	.02
196	Eric Plunk	.05	.04	.02
197	Orel Hershiser	.20	.15	.08
198	Paul O'Neil	.07	.05	.03
199	Randy Bush	.04	.03	.02
200a	Checklist 130-231	.04	.03	.02
200b	Checklist 126-223	.04	.03	.02
201	Ozzie Smith	.10	.08	.04
202	Pete O'Brien	.06	.05	.02
203	Jay Howell	.06	.05	.02
204	Mark Gibicza	.08	.06	.03
205	Ed Whitson	.04	.03	.02
206	George Bell	.09	.07	.04
207	Mike Scott	.09	.07	.04
208	Charlie Leibrandt	.04	.03	.02
209	Mike Heath	.04	.03	.02
210	Dennis Eckersley	.09	.07	.04
211	Mike LaValliere	.04	.03	.02

		MT	NR MT	EX
212	Darnell Coles	.04	.03	.02
213	Lance Parrish	.07	.05	.03
214	Mike Moore	.07	.05	.03
215	*Steve Finley*	.20	.15	.08
216	Tim Raines	.09	.07	.04
217a	Scott Garrelts (Born 10/20)	.06	.05	.02
217b	Scott Garrelts (Born 10/30)	.25	.20	.10
218	Kevin McReynolds	.09	.07	.04
219	Dave Gallagher	.08	.06	.03
220	Tim Wallach	.08	.06	.03
221	Chuck Crim	.04	.03	.02
222	Lonnie Smith	.08	.06	.03
223	Andre Dawson	.12	.09	.05
224	Nelson Santovenia	.07	.05	.03
225	Rafael Palmeiro	.12	.09	.05
226	Devon White	.07	.05	.03
227	Harold Reynolds	.07	.05	.03
228	Ellis Burks	.15	.11	.06
229	Mark Parent	.04	.03	.02
230	Will Clark	.40	.30	.15
231	Jimmy Key	.08	.06	.03
232	John Farrell	.04	.03	.02
233	Eric Davis	.10	.08	.04
234	Johnny Ray	.05	.04	.02
235	Darryl Strawberry	.20	.15	.08
236	Bill Doran	.05	.04	.02
237	Greg Gagne	.05	.04	.02
238	Jim Eisenreich	.04	.03	.02
239	Tommy Gregg	.06	.05	.02
240	Marty Barrett	.05	.04	.02
241	Rafael Ramirez	.05	.04	.02
242	Chris Sabo	.10	.08	.04
243	Dave Henderson	.07	.05	.03
244	Andy Van Slyke	.07	.05	.03
245	Alvaro Espinoza	.10	.08	.04
246	Garry Templeton	.06	.05	.02
247	Gene Harris	.04	.03	.02
248	Kevin Gross	.05	.04	.02
249	Brett Butler	.09	.07	.04
250	Willie Randolph	.07	.05	.03
251	Roger McDowell	.05	.04	.02
252	Rafael Belliard	.04	.03	.02
253	Steve Rosenberg	.04	.03	.02
254	Jack Howell	.04	.03	.02
255	Marvell Wynne	.04	.03	.02
256	Tom Candiotti	.05	.04	.02
257	Todd Benzinger	.05	.04	.02
258	Don Robinson	.04	.03	.02
259	Phil Bradley	.08	.06	.03
260	Cecil Espy	.05	.04	.02
261	Scott Bankhead	.05	.04	.02
262	Frank White	.07	.05	.03
263	Andres Thomas	.05	.04	.02
264	Glenn Braggs	.05	.04	.02
265	David Cone	.10	.08	.04
266	Bobby Thigpen	.07	.05	.03
267	Nelson Liriano	.04	.03	.02
268	Terry Steinbach	.09	.07	.04
269	Kirby Puckett	.30	.25	.12
270	Gregg Jefferies	.25	.20	.10
271	Jeff Blauser	.05	.04	.02
272	Cory Snyder	.07	.05	.03
273	Roy Smith	.05	.04	.02
274	Tom Foley	.04	.03	.02
275	Mitch Williams	.09	.07	.04
276	Paul Kilgus	.04	.03	.02
277	Don Slaught	.04	.03	.02
278	Von Hayes	.08	.06	.03
279	Vince Coleman	.10	.08	.04
280	Mike Boddicker	.05	.04	.02
281	Ken Dayley	.04	.03	.02
282	Mike Devereaux	.07	.05	.03
283	*Kenny Rogers*	.09	.07	.04
284	Jeff Russell	.07	.05	.03
285	*Jerome Walton*	.15	.11	.06
286	Derek Lilliquist	.08	.06	.03
287	Joe Orsulak	.04	.03	.02
288	Dick Schofield	.04	.03	.02
289	Ron Darling	.09	.07	.04
290	Bobby Bonilla	.10	.08	.04
291	Jim Gantner	.05	.04	.02
292	Bobby Witt	.05	.04	.02
293	Greg Brock	.05	.04	.02
294	Ivan Calderon	.05	.04	.02
295	Steve Bedrosian	.06	.05	.02
296	Mike Henneman	.06	.05	.02
297	Tom Gordon	.08	.06	.03
298	Lou Whitaker	.08	.06	.03
299	Terry Pendleton	.07	.05	.03
300	Checklist 232-333	.04	.03	.02
300	Checklist 224-321	.04	.03	.02

		MT	NR MT	EX
301	Juan Berenguer	.04	.03	.02
302	Mark Davis	.09	.07	.04
303	Nick Esasky	.09	.07	.04
304	Rickey Henderson	.15	.11	.06
305	Rick Cerone	.04	.03	.02
306	Craig Biggio	.15	.11	.06
307	Duane Ward	.04	.03	.02
308	Tom Browning	.07	.05	.03
309	Walt Terrell	.05	.04	.02
310	Greg Swindell	.10	.08	.04
311	Dave Righetti	.07	.05	.03
312	Mike Maddux	.04	.03	.02
313	Lenny Dykstra	.12	.09	.05
314	Jose Gonzalez	.08	.06	.03
315	Steve Balboni	.04	.03	.02
316	Mike Scioscia	.07	.05	.03
317	Ron Oester	.04	.03	.02
318	*Gary Wayne*	.09	.07	.04
319	Todd Worrell	.06	.05	.02
320	Doug Jones	.05	.04	.02
321	Jeff Hamilton	.05	.04	.02
322	Danny Tartabull	.09	.07	.04
323	Chris James	.05	.04	.02
324	Mike Flanagan	.05	.04	.02
325	Gerald Young	.05	.04	.02
326	Bob Boone	.09	.07	.04
327	Frank Williams	.04	.03	.02
328	Dave Parker	.09	.07	.04
329	Sid Bream	.04	.03	.02
330	Mike Schooler	.06	.05	.02
331	Bert Blyleven	.08	.06	.03
332	Bob Welch	.07	.05	.03
333	Bob Milacki	.06	.05	.02
334	Tim Burke	.05	.04	.02
335	Jose Uribe	.05	.04	.02
336	Randy Myers	.05	.04	.02
337	Eric King	.04	.03	.02
338	Mark Langston	.12	.09	.05
339	Ted Higuera	.08	.06	.03
340	Oddibe McDowell	.06	.05	.02
341	Lloyd McClendon	.07	.05	.03
342	Pascual Perez	.05	.04	.02
343	Kevin Brown	.08	.06	.03
344	Chuck Finley	.05	.04	.02
345	Erik Hanson	.09	.07	.04
346	Rich Gedman	.05	.04	.02
347	Bip Roberts	.10	.08	.04
348	Matt Williams	.20	.15	.08
349	Tom Henke	.05	.04	.02
350	Brad Komminsk	.05	.04	.02
351	Jeff Reed	.04	.03	.02
352	Brian Downing	.05	.04	.02
353	Frank Viola	.09	.07	.04
354	Terry Puhl	.05	.04	.02
355	Brian Harper	.05	.04	.02
356	Steve Farr	.05	.04	.02
357	Joe Boever	.05	.04	.02
358	Danny Heep	.04	.03	.02
359	Larry Andersen	.04	.03	.02
360	Rolando Roomes	.10	.08	.04
361	Mike Gallego	.05	.04	.02
362	Bob Kipper	.04	.03	.02
363	Clay Parker	.07	.05	.03
364	Mike Pagliarulo	.05	.04	.02
365	Ken Griffey, Jr.	1.25	.90	.50
366	Rex Hudler	.04	.03	.02
367	Pat Sheridan	.04	.03	.02
368	Kirk Gibson	.09	.07	.04
369	Jeff Parrett	.05	.04	.02
370	Bob Walk	.05	.04	.02
371	Ken Patterson	.04	.03	.02
372	Bryan Harvey	.05	.04	.02
373	Mike Bielecki	.07	.05	.03
374	*Tom Magrann*(FC)	.12	.09	.05
375	Rick Mahler	.05	.04	.02
376	Craig Lefferts	.05	.04	.02
377	Gregg Olson	.20	.15	.08
378	Jamie Moyer	.04	.03	.02
379	Randy Johnson	.12	.09	.05
380	Jeff Montgomery	.06	.05	.02
381	Marty Clary	.06	.05	.02
382	*Bill Spiers*	.15	.11	.06
383	Dave Magadan	.06	.05	.02
384	*Greg Hibbard*(FC)	.10	.08	.04
385	Ernie Whitt	.05	.04	.02
386	Rick Honeycutt	.04	.03	.02
387	Dave West	.08	.06	.03
388	Keith Hernandez	.07	.05	.03
389	Jose Alvarez	.04	.03	.02
390	*Albert Belle*(FC)	1.00	.70	.40
391	Rick Aguilera	.05	.04	.02

		MT	NR MT	EX
392	Mike Fitzgerald	.04	.03	.02
393	*Dwight Smith*	.08	.06	.03
394	*Steve Wilson*	.09	.07	.04
395	*Bob Geren*	.08	.06	.03
396	Randy Ready	.04	.03	.02
397	Ken Hill	.07	.05	.03
398	Jody Reed	.05	.04	.02
399	Tom Brunansky	.07	.05	.03
400	Checklist 334-435	.04	.03	.02
400	Checklist 322-419	.04	.03	.02
401	Rene Gonzales	.04	.03	.02
402	Harold Baines	.09	.07	.04
403	Cecilio Guante	.04	.03	.02
404	Joe Girardi	.15	.11	.06
405a	*Sergio Valdez* (black line crosses S in Sergio)(FC)	.25	.20	.10
405b	Sergio Valdez (corrected)	.08	.06	.03
406	Mark Williamson	.04	.03	.02
407	Glenn Hoffman	.04	.03	.02
408	*Jeff Innis*(FC)	.10	.08	.04
409	Randy Kramer	.04	.03	.02
410	Charlie O'Brien(FC)	.04	.03	.02
411	Charlie Hough	.06	.05	.02
412	Gus Polidor	.04	.03	.02
413	Ron Karkovice	.04	.03	.02
414	Trevor Wilson(FC)	.07	.05	.03
415	*Kevin Ritz*(FC)	.10	.08	.04
416	Gary Thurman	.04	.03	.02
417	Jeff Robinson	.04	.03	.02
418	Scott Terry	.05	.04	.02
419	Tim Laudner	.04	.03	.02
420	Dennis Rasmussen	.04	.03	.02
421	Luis Rivera	.04	.03	.02
422	Jim Corsi(FC)	.07	.05	.03
423	Dennis Lamp	.04	.03	.02
424	Ken Caminiti	.06	.05	.02
425	David Wells	.06	.05	.02
426	Norm Charlton	.09	.07	.04
427	*Deion Sanders*	.40	.30	.15
428	Dion James	.05	.04	.02
429	Chuck Cary	.05	.04	.02
430	Ken Howell	.04	.03	.02
431	Steve Lake	.04	.03	.02
432	Kal Daniels	.09	.07	.04
433	Lance McCullers	.05	.04	.02
434	Lenny Harris(FC)	.10	.08	.04
435	*Scott Scudder*(FC)	.10	.08	.04
436	Gene Larkin	.04	.03	.02
437	Dan Quisenberry	.05	.04	.02
438	*Steve Olin*(FC)	.15	.11	.06
439	Mickey Hatcher	.05	.04	.02
440	Willie Wilson	.05	.04	.02
441	Mark Grant	.05	.04	.02
442	Mookie Wilson	.07	.05	.03
443	Alex Trevino	.04	.03	.02
444	Pat Tabler	.05	.04	.02
445	Dave Bergman	.04	.03	.02
446	Todd Burns	.05	.04	.02
447	R.J. Reynolds	.04	.03	.02
448	Jay Buhner	.08	.06	.03
449	*Lee Stevens*(FC)	.10	.08	.04
450	Ron Hassey	.04	.03	.02
451	Bob Melvin	.04	.03	.02
452	Dave Martinez	.05	.04	.02
453	*Greg Litton*(FC)	.08	.06	.03
454	Mark Carreon	.10	.08	.04
455	Scott Fletcher	.05	.04	.02
456	Otis Nixon	.04	.03	.02
457	*Tony Fossas*(FC)	.10	.08	.04
458	John Russell	.04	.03	.02
459	Paul Assenmacher	.04	.03	.02
460	Zane Smith	.04	.03	.02
461	*Jack Daugherty*	.08	.06	.03
462	*Rich Monteleone*(FC)	.08	.06	.03
463	Greg Briley(FC)	.08	.06	.03
464	Mike Smithson	.04	.03	.02
465	Benito Santiago	.09	.07	.04
466	*Jeff Brantley*	.10	.08	.04
467	Jose Nunez	.07	.05	.03
468	Scott Bailes	.04	.03	.02
469	Ken Griffey	.06	.05	.02
470	Bob McClure	.04	.03	.02
471	Mackey Sasser	.04	.03	.02
472	Glenn Wilson	.04	.03	.02
473	*Kevin Tapani*(FC)	.20	.15	.08
474	Bill Buckner	.05	.04	.02
475	Ron Gant	.12	.09	.05
476	Kevin Romine(FC)	.05	.04	.02
477	Juan Agosto	.04	.03	.02
478	Herm Winningham	.04	.03	.02
479	Storm Davis	.05	.04	.02

		MT	NR MT	EX
480	Jeff King(FC)	.09	.07	.04
481	*Kevin Mmahat*(FC)	.08	.06	.03
482	Carmelo Martinez	.05	.04	.02
483	*Omar Vizquel*	.10	.08	.04
484	Jim Dwyer	.04	.03	.02
485	Bob Knepper	.04	.03	.02
486	Dave Anderson	.04	.03	.02
487	Ron Jones	.09	.07	.04
488	Jay Bell	.05	.04	.02
489	*Sammy Sosa*(FC)	.60	.45	.25
490	*Kent Anderson*(FC)	.08	.06	.03
491	Domingo Ramos	.04	.03	.02
492	Dave Clark	.05	.04	.02
493	Tim Birtsas	.04	.03	.02
494	Ken Oberkfell	.04	.03	.02
495	Larry Sheets	.04	.03	.02
496	Jeff Kunkel	.04	.03	.02
497	Jim Presley	.04	.03	.02
498	Mike Macfarlane	.04	.03	.02
499	Pete Smith	.05	.04	.02
500	Checklist 436-537	.04	.03	.02
500	Checklist 420-517	.04	.03	.02
501	Gary Sheffield	.35	.25	.14
502	*Terry Bross*(FC)	.08	.06	.03
503	*Jerry Kutzler*(FC)	.06	.05	.02
504	Lloyd Moseby	.05	.04	.02
505	Curt Young	.04	.03	.02
506	Al Newman	.04	.03	.02
507	Keith Miller	.04	.03	.02
508	*Mike Stanton*(FC)	.20	.15	.08
509	Rich Yett	.04	.03	.02
510	*Tim Drummond*(FC)	.08	.06	.03
511	Joe Hesketh	.04	.03	.02
512	*Rick Wrona*	.10	.08	.04
513	Luis Salazar	.04	.03	.02
514	Hal Morris	.06	.05	.02
515	Terry Mullholland	.07	.05	.03
516	John Morris	.05	.04	.02
517	Carlos Quintana	.08	.06	.03
518	Frank DiPino	.04	.03	.02
519	Randy Milligan	.06	.05	.02
520	Chad Kreuter	.07	.05	.03
521	Mike Jeffcoat	.04	.03	.02
522	Mike Harkey	.10	.08	.04
523	Andy Nezelek (Born 1985)	.06	.05	.02
523	Andy Nezelek (Born 1965)	.25	.20	.10
524	Dave Schmidt	.04	.03	.02
525	Tony Armas	.04	.03	.02
526	Barry Lyons	.04	.03	.02
527	*Rick Reed*(FC)	.08	.06	.03
528	Jerry Reuss	.06	.05	.02
529	*Dean Palmer*(FC)	.75	.60	.30
530	*Jeff Peterek*(FC)	.06	.05	.02
531	*Carlos Martinez*	.08	.06	.03
532	Atlee Hammaker	.05	.04	.02
533	Mike Brumley	.04	.03	.02
534	Terry Leach	.04	.03	.02
535	*Doug Strange*(FC)	.08	.06	.03
536	Jose DeLeon	.05	.04	.02
537	Shane Rawley	.05	.04	.02
538	Joey Cora(FC)	.10	.08	.04
539	Eric Hetzel	.08	.06	.03
540	Gene Nelson	.04	.03	.02
541	Wes Gardner	.04	.03	.02
542	Mark Portugal	.04	.03	.02
543	Al Leiter	.05	.04	.02
544	Jack Armstrong	.04	.03	.02
545	Greg Cadaret	.04	.03	.02
546	Rod Nichols	.04	.03	.02
547	Luis Polonia	.05	.04	.02
548	Charlie Hayes(FC)	.20	.15	.08
549	Dickie Thon	.04	.03	.02
550	Tim Crews	.04	.03	.02
551	Dave Winfield	.20	.15	.08
552	Mike Davis	.04	.03	.02
553	Ron Robinson	.04	.03	.02
554	Carmen Castillo	.04	.03	.02
555	John Costello	.04	.03	.02
556	Bud Black	.04	.03	.02
557	Rick Dempsey	.04	.03	.02
558	Jim Acker	.04	.03	.02
559	Eric Show	.06	.05	.02
560	Pat Borders	.06	.05	.02
561	Danny Darwin	.04	.03	.02
562	*Rick Luecken*(FC)	.06	.05	.02
563	Edwin Nunez	.05	.04	.02
564	Felix Jose	.09	.07	.04
565	John Cangelosi	.04	.03	.02
566	Billy Swift	.04	.03	.02
567	Bill Schroeder	.04	.03	.02
568	Stan Javier	.04	.03	.02

		MT	NR MT	EX
569	Jim Traber	.04	.03	.02
570	Wallace Johnson	.04	.03	.02
571	Donell Nixon	.04	.03	.02
572	Sid Fernandez	.08	.06	.03
573	Lance Johnson	.09	.07	.04
574	Andy McGaffigan	.04	.03	.02
575	Mark Knudson	.04	.03	.02
576	*Tommy Greene*(FC)	.50	.40	.20
577	Mark Grace	.25	.20	.10
578	*Larry Walker*(FC)	.75	.60	.30
579	Mike Stanley	.04	.03	.02
580	Mike Witt	.05	.04	.02
581	Scott Bradley	.04	.03	.02
582	Greg Harris	.07	.05	.03
583	Kevin Hickey	.04	.03	.02
584	Lee Mazzilli	.04	.03	.02
585	Jeff Pico	.04	.03	.02
586	*Joe Oliver*(FC)	.12	.09	.05
587	Willie Fraser	.04	.03	.02
588	Puzzle Card	.04	.03	.02
589	Kevin Bass	.06	.05	.02
590	John Moses	.04	.03	.02
591	Tom Pagnozzi	.04	.03	.02
592	*Tony Castillo*	.10	.08	.04
593	Jerald Clark	.06	.05	.02
594	Dan Schatzeder	.04	.03	.02
595	Luis Quinones	.04	.03	.02
596	Pete Harnisch	.08	.06	.03
597	Gary Redus	.04	.03	.02
598	Mel Hall	.05	.04	.02
599	Rick Schu	.04	.03	.02
600a	Checklist 538-639	.04	.03	.02
600b	Checklist 518-617	.04	.03	.02
601	Mike Kingery	.04	.03	.02
602	Terry Kennedy	.04	.03	.02
603	Mike Sharperson	.06	.05	.02
604	Don Carman	.04	.03	.02
605	Jim Gott	.05	.04	.02
606	Donn Pall	.05	.04	.02
607	Rance Mulliniks	.04	.03	.02
608	Curt Wilkerson	.04	.03	.02
609	Mike Felder	.04	.03	.02
610	Guillermo Hernandez	.04	.03	.02
611	Candy Maldonado	.05	.04	.02
612	Mark Thurmond	.04	.03	.02
613	Rick Leach	.04	.03	.02
614	Jerry Reed	.04	.03	.02
615	Franklin Stubbs	.05	.04	.02
616	Billy Hatcher	.05	.04	.02
617	Don August	.05	.04	.02
618	Tim Teufel	.04	.03	.02
619	Shawn Hillegas	.04	.03	.02
620	Manny Lee	.04	.03	.02
621	Gary Ward	.05	.04	.02
622	*Mark Guthrie*(FC)	.08	.06	.03
623	Jeff Musselman	.05	.04	.02
624	Mark Lemke	.07	.05	.03
625	Fernando Valenzuela	.07	.05	.03
626	*Paul Sorrento*(FC)	.20	.15	.08
627	Glenallen Hill	.20	.15	.08
628	Les Lancaster	.05	.04	.02
629	Vance Law	.04	.03	.02
630	Randy Velarde(FC)	.10	.08	.04
631	Todd Frohwirth	.04	.03	.02
632	Willie McGee	.06	.05	.02
633	Oil Can Boyd	.06	.05	.02
634	Cris Carpenter	.09	.07	.04
635	Brian Holton	.04	.03	.02
636	Tracy Jones	.05	.04	.02
637	Terry Steinbach ((AS))	.08	.06	.03
638	Brady Anderson	.09	.07	.04
639a	Jack Morris (black line crosses J of Jack)	.25	.20	.10
639b	Jack Morris (corrected)	.08	.06	.03
640	*Jaime Navarro*(FC)	.12	.09	.05
641	Darrin Jackson	.05	.04	.02
642	*Mike Dyer*(FC)	.10	.08	.04
643	Mike Schmidt	.30	.25	.12
644	Henry Cotto	.04	.03	.02
645	John Cerutti	.05	.04	.02
646	*Francisco Cabrera*(FC)	.12	.09	.05
647	Scott Sanderson	.05	.04	.02
648	Brian Meyer	.05	.04	.02
649	Ray Searage	.05	.04	.02
650	Bo Jackson ((AS))	.15	.11	.06
651	Steve Lyons	.04	.03	.02
652	Mike LaCoss	.04	.03	.02
653	Ted Power	.04	.03	.02
654	Howard Johnson ((AS))	.08	.06	.03
655	*Mauro Gozzo*(FC)	.08	.06	.03
656	*Mike Blowers*(FC)	.15	.11	.06

		MT	NR MT	EX
657	Paul Gibson	.05	.04	.02
658	Neal Heaton	.05	.04	.02
659a	Nolan Ryan 5,000 K's (King of Kings (#665) back)	2.50	2.00	1.00
659b	Nolan Ryan 5,000 K's (correct back)	.50	.40	.20
660a	Harold Baines ((AS) black line through star on front, Recent Major League Performance on back)	2.00	1.50	.80
660b	Harold Baines ((AS) black line through star on front, All-Star Game Performance on back)	3.00	2.25	1.25
660c	Harold Baines ((AS) black line behind star on front, Recent Major League Performance on back)	1.50	1.25	.60
660d	Harold Baines ((AS) black line behind star on front, All-Star Game Performance on back)	.10	.08	.04
661	Gary Pettis	.05	.04	.02
662	*Clint Zavaras*(FC)	.08	.06	.03
663	Rick Reuschel ((AS))	.08	.06	.03
664	Alejandro Pena	.05	.04	.02
665a	Nolan Ryan ((King of Kings) 5,000 K's (#659) back)	2.50	2.00	1.00
665b	Nolan Ryan ((King of Kings) correct back)	.50	.40	.20
665c	Nolan Ryan ((King of Kings) no number on back)	1.00	.70	.40
666	Ricky Horton	.04	.03	.02
667	Curt Schilling	.06	.05	.02
668	Bill Landrum(FC)	.05	.04	.02
669	Todd Stottlemyre	.05	.04	.02
670	Tim Leary	.05	.04	.02
671	*John Wetteland*	.30	.25	.12
672	Calvin Schiraldi	.04	.03	.02
673	Ruben Sierra (AS)	.09	.07	.04
674	Pedro Guerrero (AS)	.09	.07	.04
675	Ken Phelps	.04	.03	.02
676	Cal Ripken (AS)	.30	.25	.12
677	Denny Walling	.04	.03	.02
678	Goose Gossage	.04	.03	.02
679	*Gary Mielke*(FC)	.20	.15	.08
680	Bill Bathe	.04	.03	.02
681	Tom Lawless	.04	.03	.02
682	*Xavier Hernandez*	.20	.15	.08
683	Kirby Puckett (AS)	.20	.15	.08
684	Mariano Duncan	.05	.04	.02
685	Ramon Martinez	.10	.08	.04
686	Tim Jones	.05	.04	.02
687	Tom Filer	.04	.03	.02
688	Steve Lombardozzi	.04	.03	.02
689	*Bernie Williams*(FC)	.25	.20	.10
690	*Chip Hale*(FC)	.08	.06	.03
691	*Beau Allred*(FC)	.10	.08	.04
692	Ryne Sandberg (AS)	.25	.20	.10
693	*Jeff Huson*(FC)	.10	.08	.04
694	Curt Ford	.04	.03	.02
695	Eric Davis (AS)	.09	.07	.04
696	Scott Lusader	.05	.04	.02
697	Mark McGwire (AS)	.09	.07	.04
698	*Steve Cummings*(FC)	.15	.11	.06
699	*George Canale*(FC)	.15	.11	.06
700	Checklist 640-715/BC1-BC26	.04	.03	.02
700	Checklist 640-716/BC1-BC-26	.04	.03	.02
700	Checklist 618-716	.04	.03	.02
701	Julio Franco (AS)	.09	.07	.04
702	*Dave Johnson*(FC)	.10	.08	.04
703	Dave Stewart (AS)	.08	.06	.03
704	*Dave Justice*(FC)	1.25	.90	.50
705	Tony Gwynn (AS)	.15	.11	.06
706	Greg Myers	.06	.05	.02
707	Will Clark (AS)	.15	.11	.06
708	Benito Santiago (AS)	.08	.06	.03
709	Larry McWilliams	.04	.03	.02
710	Ozzie Smith (AS)	.08	.06	.03
711	*John Olerud*(FC)	1.50	1.25	.60
712	Wade Boggs (AS)	.09	.07	.04
713	*Gary Eave*(FC)	.15	.11	.06
714	Bob Tewksbury	.05	.04	.02
715	Kevin Mitchell (AS)	.09	.07	.04
716	A. Bartlett Giamatti	.35	.25	.14

1990 Donruss MVP

This special 26-card set includes one player from each Major League team. Numbered BC-1 (the "BC" stands for "Bonus Card") through BC-26, the cards from this set were randomly packed in 1990 Donruss wax packs

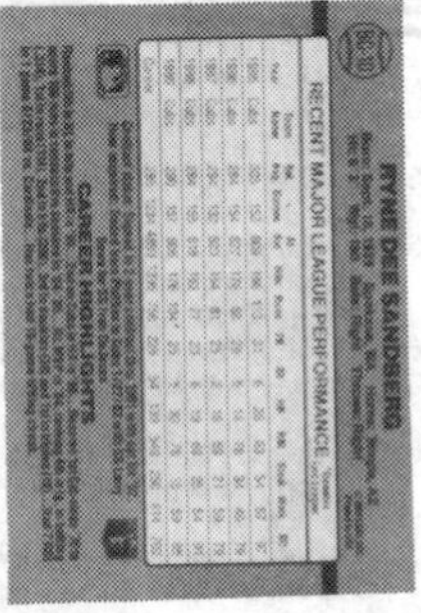

and were not available in factory sets or other types of packaging. The red-bordered cards are similar in design to the regular 1990 Donruss set, except the player photos are set against a special background made up of the "MVP" logo.

		MT	NR MT	EX
Complete Set (26):		1.25	.75	.40
Common MVP:		.04	.03	.02
1	Bo Jackson	.30	.25	.12
2	Howard Johnson	.10	.08	.04
3	Dave Stewart	.08	.06	.03
4	Tony Gwynn	.15	.11	.06
5	Orel Hershiser	.10	.08	.04
6	Pedro Guerrero	.10	.08	.04
7	Tim Raines	.10	.08	.04
8	Kirby Puckett	.30	.25	.12
9	Alvin Davis	.08	.06	.03
10	Ryne Sandberg	.30	.25	.12
11	Kevin Mitchell	.20	.15	.08
12a	John Smoltz (photo of Tom Glavine)	2.00	1.50	.80
12b	John Smoltz (corrected)	.40	.30	.15
13	George Bell	.10	.08	.04
14	Julio Franco	.15	.11	.06
15	Paul Molitor	.20	.12	.06
16	Bobby Bonilla	.15	.11	.06
17	Mike Greenwell	.15	.11	.06
18	Cal Ripken	.30	.25	.12
19	Carlton Fisk	.12	.09	.05
20	Chili Davis	.08	.06	.03
21	Glenn Davis	.10	.08	.04
22	Steve Sax	.10	.08	.04
23	Eric Davis	.20	.15	.08
24	Greg Swindell	.08	.06	.03
25	Von Hayes	.08	.06	.03
26	Alan Trammell	.10	.08	.04

1990 Donruss Grand Slammers

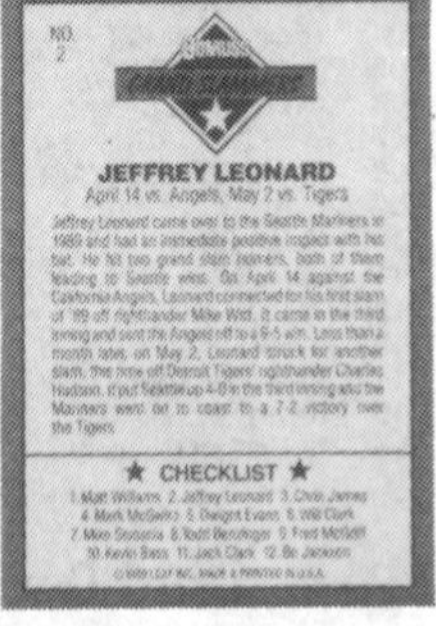

For the second consecutive year Donruss produced a set in honor of players who hit grand slams in the previous season. The cards are styled after the 1990 Donruss regular issue. The cards were inserted into 1990 Donruss factory sets, and one card per cello pack.

		MT	NR MT	EX
Complete Set (12):		2.00	1.50	.80
Common Player:		.10	.06	.03
1	Matt Williams	.25	.20	.10
2	Jeffrey Leonard	.12	.09	.05
3	Chris James	.12	.09	.05
4	Mark McGwire	.30	.25	.12
5	Dwight Evans	.15	.11	.06
6	Will Clark	.25	.15	.10
7	Mike Scioscia	.12	.09	.05
8	Todd Benzinger	.12	.09	.05
9	Fred McGriff	.40	.30	.15
10	Kevin Bass	.12	.09	.05
11	Jack Clark	.12	.09	.05
12	Bo Jackson	.25	.15	.10

1990 Donruss A.L. Best

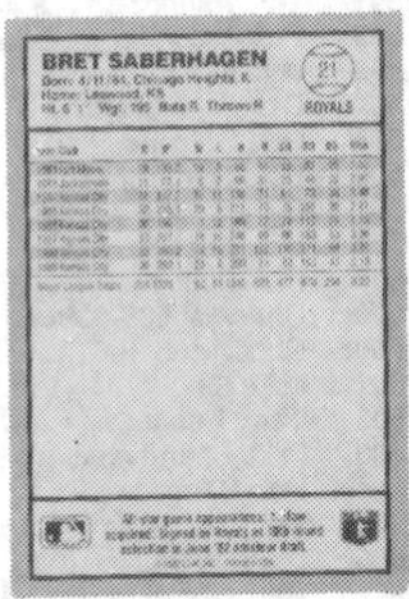

This 144-card set features the top players of the American League. The cards measure 2-1/2" by 3-1/2" and feature the same card front design as the regular Donruss set with the exception of having blue borders instead of red. The card backs feature a yellow frame with complete statistics and biogra- phical information provided. 1990 marks the first year that Donruss divided its baseball best issue into two sets designated by league.

		MT	NR MT	EX
Complete Set:		12.00	9.00	4.75
Common Player:		.04	.03	.02
1	Ken Griffey,Jr.	1.50	1.25	.90
2	Bob Milacki	.04	.03	.02
3	Mike Boddicker	.06	.05	.02
4	Bert Blyleven	.08	.06	.03
5	Carlton Fisk	.10	.08	.04
6	Greg Swindell	.06	.05	.02
7	Alan Trammell	.10	.08	.04
8	Mark Davis	.05	.04	.02
9	Chris Bosio	.04	.03	.02
10	Gary Gaetti	.10	.08	.04
11	Matt Nokes	.06	.05	.02
12	Dennis Eckersley	.10	.08	.04
13	Kevin Brown	.08	.06	.03
14	Tom Henke	.06	.05	.02
15	Mickey Tettleton	.08	.06	.03
16	Jody Reed	.08	.06	.03
17	Mark Langston	.08	.06	.03
18	Melido Perez	.06	.05	.02
19	John Farrell	.04	.03	.02
20	Tony Phillips	.04	.03	.02
21	Bret Saberhagen	.10	.08	.04
22	Robin Yount	.10	.08	.04
23	Kirby Puckett	.15	.11	.06
24	Steve Sax	.10	.08	.04
25	Dave Stewart	.10	.08	.04
26	Alvin Davis	.08	.06	.03
27	Geno Petralli	.04	.03	.02
28	Mookie Wilson	.05	.04	.02
29	Jeff Ballard	.04	.03	.02
30	Ellis Burks	.10	.08	.04
31	Wally Joyner	.08	.06	.03
32	Bobby Thigpen	.10	.08	.04
33	Keith Hernandez	.06	.05	.02
34	Jack Morris	.06	.05	.02

		MT	NR MT	EX
35	George Brett	.10	.08	.04
36	Dan Plesac	.08	.06	.03
37	Brian Harper	.05	.04	.02
38	Don Mattingly	.25	.20	.10
39	Dave Henderson	.08	.06	.03
40	Scott Bankhead	.06	.05	.02
41	Rafael Palmeiro	.10	.08	.04
42	Jimmy Key	.06	.05	.02
43	Gregg Olson	.10	.08	.04
44	Tony Pena	.06	.05	.02
45	Jack Howell	.04	.03	.02
46	Eric King	.04	.03	.02
47	Cory Snyder	.06	.05	.02
48	Frank Tanana	.04	.03	.02
49	Nolan Ryan	.60	.45	.25
50	Bob Boone	.06	.05	.02
51	Dave Parker	.10	.08	.04
52	Allan Anderson	.04	.03	.02
53	Tim Leary	.05	.04	.02
54	Mark McGwire	.25	.20	.10
55	Dave Valle	.04	.03	.02
56	Fred McGriff	.25	.20	.10
57	Cal Ripken	.15	.11	.06
58	Roger Clemens	.30	.25	.12
59	Lance Parrish	.08	.06	.03
60	Robin Ventura	.30	.25	.12
61	Doug Jones	.08	.06	.03
62	Lloyd Moseby	.06	.05	.02
63	Bo Jackson	.80	.60	.30
64	Paul Molitor	.08	.06	.03
65	Kent Hrbek	.08	.06	.03
66	Mel Hall	.04	.03	.02
67	Bob Welch	.10	.08	.04
68	Erik Hanson	.10	.08	.04
69	Harold Baines	.08	.06	.03
70	Junior Felix	.10	.08	.04
71	Craig Worthington	.06	.05	.02
72	Jeff Reardon	.08	.06	.03
73	Johnny Ray	.05	.04	.02
74	Ozzie Guillen	.10	.08	.04
75	Brook Jacoby	.08	.06	.03
76	Chet Lemon	.05	.04	.02
77	Mark Gubicza	.08	.06	.03
78	B.J. Surhoff	.08	.06	.03
79	Rick Aguilera	.05	.04	.02
80	Pascual Perez	.04	.03	.02
81	Jose Canseco	.70	.50	.30
82	Mike Schooler	.08	.06	.03
83	Jeff Huson	.12	.09	.05
84	Kelly Gruber	.15	.11	.06
85	Randy Milligan	.08	.06	.03
86	Wade Boggs	.35	.25	.14
87	Dave Winfield	.20	.15	.08
88	Scott Fletcher	.04	.03	.02
89	Tom Candiotti	.04	.03	.02
90	Mike Heath	.04	.03	.02
91	Kevin Seitzer	.08	.06	.03
92	Ted Higuera	.08	.06	.03
93	Kevin Tapani	.15	.11	.06
94	Roberto Kelly	.08	.06	.03
95	Walt Weiss	.06	.05	.02
96	Checklist	.04	.03	.02
97	Sandy Alomar	.30	.25	.12
98	Pete O'Brien	.05	.04	.02
99	Jeff Russell	.06	.05	.02
100	John Olerud	.50	.40	.20
101	Pete Harnisch	.05	.04	.02
102	Dwight Evans	.08	.06	.03
103	Chuck Finley	.08	.06	.03
104	Sammy Sosa	.25	.20	.10
105	Mike Henneman	.06	.05	.02
106	Kurt Stillwell	.06	.05	.02
107	Greg Vaughn	.30	.25	.12
108	Dan Gladden	.05	.04	.02
109	Jesse Barfield	.06	.05	.02
110	Willie Randolph	.06	.05	.02
111	Randy Johnson	.08	.06	.03
112	Julio Franco	.08	.06	.03
113	Tony Fernandez	.08	.06	.03
114	Ben McDonald	.50	.40	.20
115	Mike Greenwell	.20	.15	.08
116	Luis Polonia	.04	.03	.02
117	Carney Lansford	.06	.05	.02
118	Bud Black	.05	.04	.02
119	Lou Whitaker	.08	.06	.03
120	Jim Eisenreich	.04	.03	.02
121	Gary Sheffield	.25	.20	.10
122	Shane Mack	.08	.06	.03
123	Alvaro Espinoza	.04	.03	.02
124	Rickey Henderson	.40	.30	.15
125	Jeffrey Leonard	.05	.04	.02
126	Gary Pettis	.04	.03	.02
127	Dave Steib	.08	.06	.03
128	Danny Tartabull	.08	.06	.03
129	Joe Orsulak	.04	.03	.02
130	Tom Brunansky	.06	.05	.02
131	Dick Schofield	.04	.03	.02
132	Candy Maldonado	.06	.05	.02
133	Cecil Fielder	.30	.25	.12
134	Terry Shumpert	.20	.15	.08
135	Greg Gagne	.05	.04	.02
136	Dave Righetti	.08	.06	.03
137	Terry Steinbach	.06	.05	.02
138	Harold Reynolds	.08	.06	.03
139	George Bell	.08	.06	.03
140	Carlos Quintana	.06	.05	.02
141	Ivan Calderon	.08	.06	.03
142	Greg Brock	.04	.03	.02
143	Ruben Sierra	.15	.11	.06
144	Checklist	.04	.03	.02

1990 Donruss N.L. Best

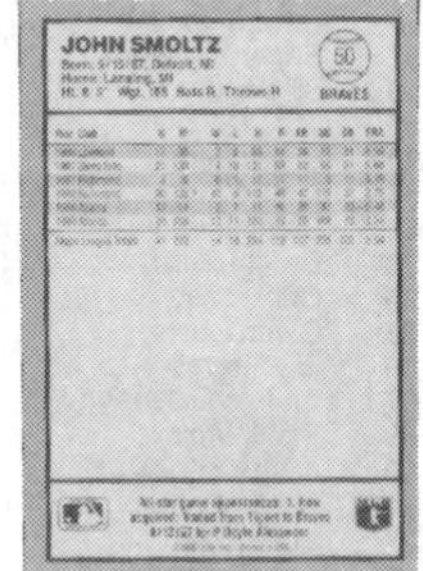

This 144-card set features the top players in the National League for 1990. The cards measure 2-1/2" by 3-1/2" and feature the same design as the regular Donruss cards. The only difference on the card fronts is the border color. The N.L. Best cards contain blue borders, while the regular cards featured red borders. Traded players are featured with their new teams. This set along with the A.L. Best set was available at select retail stores and within the hobby.

	MT	NR MT	EX
Complete Set:	12.00	9.00	4.75
Common Player:	.04	.03	.02

		MT	NR MT	EX
1	Eric Davis	.20	.15	.08
2	Tom Glavine	.10	.08	.04
3	Mike Bielecki	.05	.04	.02
4	Jim Deshaies	.05	.04	.02
5	Mike Scioscia	.05	.04	.02
6	Spike Owen	.05	.04	.02
7	Dwight Gooden	.20	.15	.08
8	Ricky Jordan	.08	.06	.03
9	Doug Drabek	.10	.08	.04
10	Bryn Smith	.04	.03	.02
11	Tony Gwynn	.10	.08	.04
12	John Burkett	.10	.08	.04
13	Nick Esasky	.06	.05	.02
14	Greg Maddux	.08	.06	.03
15	Joe Oliver	.08	.06	.03
16	Mike Scott	.08	.06	.03
17	Tim Belcher	.08	.06	.03
18	Kevin Gross	.06	.05	.02
19	Howard Johnson	.10	.08	.04
20	Darren Daulton	.06	.05	.02
21	John Smiley	.06	.05	.02
22	Ken Dayley	.05	.04	.02
23	Craig Lefferts	.05	.04	.02
24	Will Clark	.60	.45	.25
25	Greg Olson	.12	.09	.05
26	Ryne Sandberg	.50	.40	.20
27	Tom Browning	.06	.05	.02
28	Eric Anthony	.20	.15	.08
29	Juan Samuel	.06	.05	.02
30	Dennis Martinez	.06	.05	.02

		MT	NR MT	EX
31	Kevin Elster	.05	.04	.02
32	Tom Herr	.06	.05	.02
33	Sid Bream	.06	.05	.02
34	Terry Pendleton	.06	.05	.02
35	Roberto Alomar	.20	.15	.08
36	Kevin Bass	.06	.05	.02
37	Jim Presley	.06	.05	.02
38	Les Lancaster	.04	.03	.02
39	Paul O'Neill	.08	.06	.03
40	Dave Smith	.06	.05	.02
41	Kirk Gibson	.10	.08	.04
42	Tim Burke	.06	.05	.02
43	David Cone	.10	.08	.04
44	Ken Howell	.06	.05	.02
45	Barry Bonds	.20	.15	.08
46	Joe Magrane	.08	.06	.03
47	Andy Benes	.08	.06	.03
48	Gary Carter	.10	.08	.04
49	Pat Combs	.08	.06	.03
50	John Smoltz	.10	.08	.04
51	Mark Grace	.10	.08	.04
52	Barry Larkin	.10	.08	.04
53	Danny Darwin	.08	.06	.03
54	Orel Hershiser	.10	.08	.04
55	Tim Wallach	.08	.06	.03
56	Dave Magadan	.10	.08	.04
57	Roger McDowell	.08	.06	.03
58	Bill Landrum	.06	.05	.02
59	Jose DeLeon	.06	.05	.02
60	Bip Roberts	.06	.05	.02
61	Matt Williams	.10	.08	.04
62	Dale Murphy	.08	.06	.03
63	Dwight Smith	.08	.06	.03
64	Chris Sabo	.10	.08	.04
65	Glenn Davis	.10	.08	.04
66	Jay Howell	.06	.05	.02
67	Andres Galarraga	.08	.06	.03
68	Frank Viola	.10	.08	.04
69	John Kruk	.06	.05	.02
70	Bobby Bonilla	.15	.11	.06
71	Todd Zeile	.60	.45	.25
72	Joe Carter	.10	.08	.04
73	Robby Thompson	.06	.05	.02
74	Jeff Blauser	.04	.03	.02
75	Mitch Williams	.08	.06	.03
76	Rob Dibble	.10	.08	.04
77	Rafael Ramirez	.04	.03	.02
78	Eddie Murray	.10	.08	.04
79	Dave Martinez	.05	.04	.02
80	Darryl Strawberry	.50	.40	.20
81	Dickie Thon	.04	.03	.02
82	Jose Lind	.05	.04	.02
83	Ozzie Smith	.10	.08	.04
84	Bruce Hurst	.06	.05	.02
85	Kevin Mitchell	.20	.15	.08
86	Lonnie Smith	.05	.04	.02
87	Joe Girardi	.08	.06	.03
88	Randy Myers	.10	.08	.04
89	Craig Biggio	.08	.06	.03
90	Fernando Valenzuela	.06	.05	.02
91	Larry Walker	.20	.15	.08
92	John Franco	.10	.08	.04
93	Dennis Cook	.06	.05	.02
94	Bob Walk	.05	.04	.02
95	Pedro Guerrero	.08	.06	.03
96	Checklist	.04	.03	.02
97	Andre Dawson	.10	.08	.04
98	Ed Whitson	.06	.05	.02
99	Steve Bedrosian	.06	.05	.02
100	Oddibe McDowell	.06	.05	.02
101	Todd Benzinger	.06	.05	.02
102	Bill Doran	.08	.06	.03
103	Alfredo Griffin	.04	.03	.02
104	Tim Raines	.10	.08	.04
105	Sid Fernandez	.08	.06	.03
106	Charlie Hayes	.08	.06	.03
107	Mike LaValliere	.05	.04	.02
108	Jose Oquendo	.04	.03	.02
109	Jack Clark	.08	.06	.03
110	Scott Garrelts	.06	.05	.02
111	Ron Gant	.10	.08	.04
112	Shawon Dunston	.10	.08	.04
113	Mariano Duncan	.06	.05	.02
114	Eric Yelding	.10	.08	.04
115	Hubie Brooks	.08	.06	.03
116	Delino DeShields	.25	.20	.10
117	Gregg Jefferies	.20	.15	.08
118	Len Dykstra	.10	.08	.04
119	Andy Van Slyke	.10	.08	.04
120	Lee Smith	.08	.06	.03
121	Benito Santiago	.10	.08	.04
122	Jose Uribe	.04	.03	.02
123	Jeff Treadway	.05	.04	.02
124	Jerome Walton	.10	.08	.04
125	Billy Hatcher	.06	.05	.02
126	Ken Caminiti	.04	.03	.02
127	Kal Daniels	.08	.06	.03
128	Marquis Grissom	.30	.25	.12
129	Kevin McReynolds	.08	.06	.03
130	Wally Backman	.04	.03	.02
131	Willie McGee	.10	.08	.04
132	Terry Kennedy	.04	.03	.02
133	Garry Templeton	.04	.03	.02
134	Lloyd McClendon	.04	.03	.02
135	Daryl Boston	.04	.03	.02
136	Jay Bell	.08	.06	.03
137	Mike Pagliarulo	.06	.05	.02
138	Vince Coleman	.08	.06	.03
139	Brett Butler	.06	.05	.02
140	Von Hayes	.08	.06	.03
141	Ramon Martinez	.20	.15	.08
142	Jack Armstrong	.10	.08	.04
143	Franklin Stubbs	.05	.04	.02
144	Checklist	.04	.03	.02

1990 Donruss Diamond Kings Supers

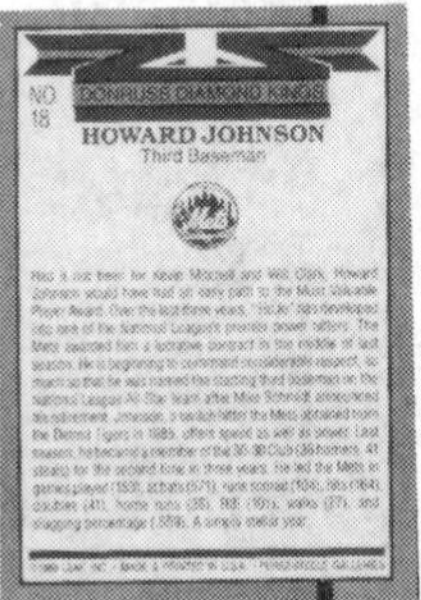

Donruss made this set available through a mail-in offer. Three wrappers, $10 and $2 for postage were necessary to obtain this set. The cards are exactly the same design as the regular Donruss Diamond Kings except they measure approximately 5" by 6-3/4" in size. The artwork of Dick Perez is featured.

		MT	NR MT	EX
Complete Set:		10.00	7.50	4.00
Common Player:		.10	.08	.04
1	Bo Jackson	1.25	.90	.50
2	Steve Sax	.15	.11	.06
3	Ruben Sierra	.35	.25	.12
4	Ken Griffey,Jr.	2.00	1.50	.80
5	Mickey Tettleton	.10	.08	.04
6	Dave Stewart	.20	.15	.08
7	Jim Deshaies	.10	.08	.04
8	John Smoltz	.20	.15	.08
9	Mike Bielecki	.10	.08	.04
10	Brian Downing	.10	.08	.04
11	Kevin Mitchell	.20	.15	.08
12	Kelly Gruber	.25	.20	.10
13	Joe Magrane	.15	.11	.06
14	John Franco	.15	.11	.06
15	Ozzie Guillen	.20	.15	.08
16	Lou Whitaker	.15	.11	.06
17	John Smiley	.10	.08	.04
18	Howard Johnson	.25	.20	.10
19	Willie Randolph	.10	.08	.04
20	Chris Bosio	.10	.08	.04
21	Tommy Herr	.10	.08	.04
22	Dan Gladden	.10	.08	.04
23	Ellis Burks	.20	.15	.08
24	Pete O'Brien	.10	.08	.04
25	Bryn Smith	.10	.08	.04
26	Ed Whitson	.10	.08	.04

1990 Donruss Learning Series

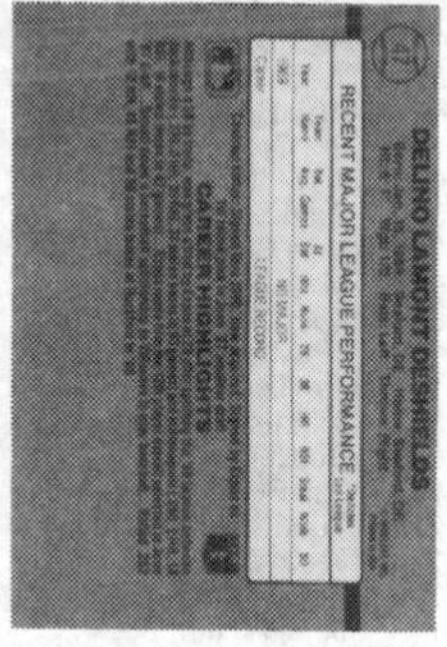

Cards from this 55-card set were released as a part of an educational package available to schools. The cards are styled like the regular-issue 1990 Donruss cards, but feature a special "learning series" logo on the front. The backs feature career highlights, statistics and card numbers. The cards were not released directly to the hobby.

		MT	NR MT	EX
Complete Set:		55.00	40.00	20.00
Common Player:		.40	.30	.15
1	George Brett (DK)	2.50	2.00	1.00
2	Kevin Mitchell	.60	.45	.25
3	Andy Van Slyke	.80	.60	.30
4	Benito Santiago	.60	.45	.25
5	Gary Carter	.80	.60	.30
6	Jose Canseco	5.00	3.75	2.00
7	Rickey Henderson	5.00	3.75	2.00
8	Ken Griffey,Jr.	10.00	7.50	4.00
9	Ozzie Smith	4.00	3.00	1.50
10	Dwight Gooden	3.00	2.25	1.25
11	Ryne Sandberg (DK)	8.00	6.00	3.25
12	Don Mattingly	6.00	4.50	2.50
13	Ozzie Guillen	.50	.40	.20
14	Dave Righetti	.40	.30	.15
15	Rick Dempsey	.40	.30	.15
16	Tom Herr	.40	.30	.15
17	Julio Franco	.40	.30	.15
18	Von Hayes	.40	.30	.15
19	Cal Ripken	8.00	6.00	3.25
20	Alan Trammell	.80	.60	.30
21	Wade Boggs	5.00	3.75	2.00
22	Glenn Davis	.40	.30	.15
23	Will Clark	6.00	4.50	2.50
24	Nolan Ryan	12.00	9.00	4.75
25	George Bell	.60	.45	.25
26	Cecil Fielder	2.00	1.50	.80
27	Gregg Olson	.40	.30	.15
28	Tim Wallach	.40	.30	.15
29	Ron Darling	.40	.30	.15
30	Kelly Gruber	.40	.30	.15
31	Shawn Boskie	.40	.30	.15
32	Mike Greenwell	.60	.45	.25
33	Dave Parker	.60	.45	.25
34	Joe Magrane	.40	.30	.15
35	Dave Stewart	.60	.45	.25
36	Kent Hrbek	.50	.40	.20
37	Robin Yount	3.00	2.25	1.25
38	Bo Jackson	1.50	1.25	.60
39	Fernando Valenzuela	.40	.30	.15
40	Sandy Alomar, Jr.	.50	.40	.20
41	Lance Parrish	.40	.30	.15
42	Candy Maldonado	.40	.30	.15
43	Mike LaValliere	.40	.30	.15
44	Jim Abbott	1.50	1.25	.60
45	Edgar Martinez	.60	.45	.25
46	Kirby Puckett	5.00	3.75	2.00
47	Delino DeShields	.80	.60	.30
48	Tony Gwynn	2.00	1.50	.80
49	Carlton Fisk	2.00	1.50	.80
50	Mike Scott	.40	.30	.15
51	Barry Larkin	1.50	1.25	.60
52	Andre Dawson	2.00	1.50	.80
53	Tom Glavine	.80	.60	.30
54	Tom Browning	.40	.30	.15
55	Checklist	.40	.30	.15

1990 Donruss Rookies

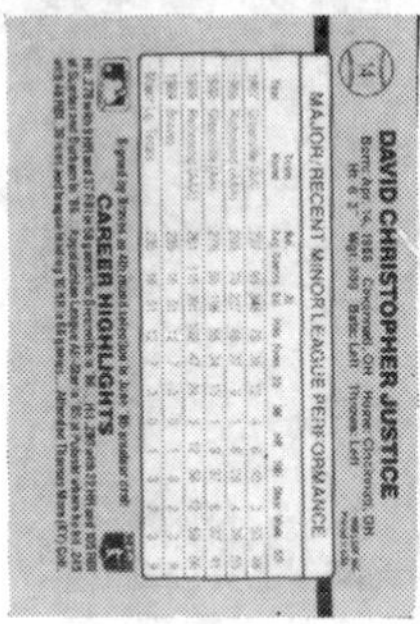

For the fifth straight year, Donruss issued a 56-card "Rookies" set in 1990. As in previous years, the set is similar in design to the regular Donruss set, except for a new "The Rookies" logo and green borders instead of red. The set is packaged in a special box and includes a special Carl Yastrzemski puzzle card.

		MT	NR MT	EX
Complete Set (56):		8.00	6.00	3.25
Common Player:		.10	.08	.04
1	Sandy Alomar	.15	.11	.06
2	John Olerud	1.50	1.25	.60
3	Pat Combs	.20	.15	.08
4	Brian Dubois	.10	.08	.04
5	Felix Jose	.12	.09	.05
6	Delino DeShields	.50	.40	.20
7	Mike Stanton	.10	.08	.04
8	Mike Munoz(FC)	.10	.08	.04
9	Craig Grebeck(FC)	.15	.11	.06
10	Joe Kraemer(FC)	.10	.08	.04
11	Jeff Huson	.10	.08	.04
12	Bill Sampen(FC)	.30	.25	.12
13	Brian Bohanon(FC)	.12	.09	.05
14	Dave Justice	1.25	.90	.50
15	Robin Ventura	.80	.60	.30
16	Greg Vaughn	.60	.45	.25
17	Wayne Edwards(FC)	.15	.11	.06
18	Shawn Boskie	.25	.20	.10
19	Carlos Baerga(FC)	1.50	1.25	.60
20	Mark Gardner	.20	.15	.08
21	Kevin Appier(FC)	.30	.25	.12
22	Mike Harkey	.20	.15	.08
23	Tim Layana(FC)	.20	.15	.08
24	Glenallen Hill	.20	.15	.08
25	Jerry Kutzler	.10	.08	.04
26	Mike Blowers	.15	.11	.06
27	Scott Ruskin(FC)	.25	.20	.10
28	Dana Kiecker(FC)	.15	.11	.06
29	Willie Blair(FC)	.10	.08	.04
30	Ben McDonald	.60	.45	.25
31	Todd Zeile	.40	.30	.15
32	Scott Coolbaugh	.12	.09	.05
33	Xavier Hernandez	.10	.08	.04
34	Mike Hartley(FC)	.15	.11	.06
35	Kevin Tapani	.30	.25	.12
36	Kevin Wickander(FC)	.10	.08	.04
37	Carlos Hernandez(FC)	.15	.11	.06
38	Brian Traxler(FC)	.20	.15	.08
39	Marty Brown(FC)	.10	.08	.04
40	Scott Radinsky(FC)	.25	.20	.10
41	Julio Machado	.15	.11	.06
42	Steve Avery	.80	.60	.30
43	Mark Lemke	.12	.09	.05
44	Alan Mills(FC)	.25	.20	.10
45	Marquis Grissom	.50	.40	.20
46	Greg Olson(FC)	.15	.11	.06
47	Dave Hollins(FC)	.80	.60	.30
48	Jerald Clark	.10	.08	.04
49	Eric Anthony	.20	.15	.08
50	Tim Drummond	.10	.08	.04
51	John Burkett(FC)	.20	.15	.08
52	Brent Knackert(FC)	.12	.09	.05
53	Jeff Shaw(FC)	.12	.09	.05
54	John Orton(FC)	.10	.08	.04
55	Terry Shumpert(FC)	.15	.11	.06
56	Checklist	.10	.08	.04

1991 Donruss

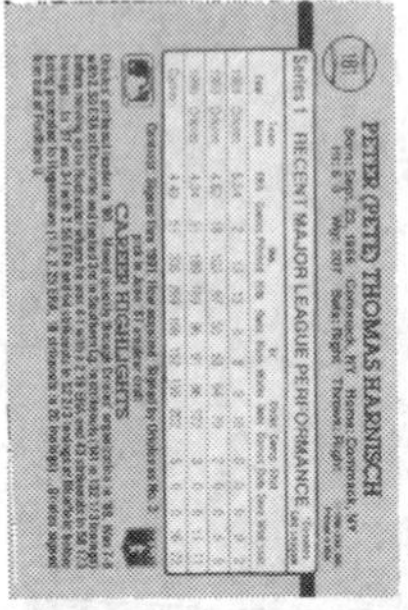

Donruss decided to use a two series format in 1991. The first series was released in December and the second in February. The 1991 design is somewhat reminiscent of the 1986 set. Blue borders are used. Limited edition cards including an autographed Ryne Sandberg card (5,000) were randomly inserted in wax packs. Other features of the set include 40 Rated Rookies, a "Legends Series," Elite Series, and another Diamond King subset. Collectors could also take part in Donruss' Instant Win promotion.

		MT	NR MT	EX
Complete Set (792):		18.00	13.50	7.25
Common Player:		.04	.03	.02
1	Dave Steib (DK)	.04	.03	.02
2	Craig Biggio (DK)	.05	.04	.02
3	Cecil Fielder (DK)	.15	.11	.06
4	Barry Bonds (DK)	.10	.08	.04
5	Barry Larkin (DK)	.06	.05	.02
6	Dave Parker (DK)	.05	.04	.02
7	Len Dykstra (DK)	.06	.05	.02
8	Bobby Thigpen (DK)	.05	.04	.02
9	Roger Clemens (DK)	.10	.08	.04
10	Ron Gant (DK)	.08	.06	.03
11	Delino DeShields (DK)	.08	.06	.03
12	Roberto Alomar (DK)	.10	.08	.04
13	Sandy Alomar (DK)	.12	.09	.05
14	Ryne Sandberg (DK)	.15	.11	.06
15	Ramon Martinez (DK)	.06	.05	.02
16	Edgar Martinez (DK)	.08	.06	.03
17	Dave Magadan (DK)	.04	.03	.02
18	Matt Williams (DK)	.12	.09	.05
19	Rafael Palmeiro (DK)	.05	.04	.02
20	Bob Welch (DK)	.06	.05	.02
21	Dave Righetti (DK)	.04	.03	.02
22	Brian Harper (DK)	.04	.03	.02
23	Gregg Olson (DK)	.05	.04	.02
24	Kurt Stillwell (DK)	.04	.03	.02
25	Pedro Guerrero (DK)	.05	.04	.02
26	Chuck Finley (DK)	.05	.04	.02
27	DK Checklist	.04	.03	.02
28	Tino Martinez (RR)	.10	.08	.04
29	Mark Lewis (RR)	.10	.08	.04
30	*Bernard Gilkey* (RR)	.20	.15	.08
31	Hensley Meulens (RR)	.08	.06	.03
32	*Derek Bell* (RR)	.40	.30	.15
33	Jose Offerman (RR)	.10	.08	.04
34	Terry Bross (RR)	.10	.08	.04
35	*Leo Gomez* (RR)	.12	.09	.05
36	Derrick May (RR)	.35	.25	.14
37	*Kevin Morton* (RR)	.10	.08	.04
38	Moises Alou (RR)	.25	.20	.10
39	*Julio Valera* (RR)(FC)	.06	.05	.02
40	Milt Cuyler (RR)(FC)	.10	.08	.04
41	*Phil Plantier* (RR)	.50	.40	.20
42	*Scott Chiamparino* (RR)(FC)	.08	.06	.03
43	*Ray Lankford* (RR)	.20	.15	.08
44	*Mickey Morandini* (RR)(FC)	.08	.06	.03
45	Dave Hansen (RR)(FC)	.10	.08	.04
46	*Kevin Belcher* (RR)	.15	.11	.06
47	Darrin Fletcher (RR)(FC)	.10	.08	.04
48	Steve Sax (AS)	.05	.04	.02
49	Ken Griffey,Jr. (AS)	.40	.30	.15
50	Jose Canseco (AS)	.12	.09	.05
51	Sandy Alomar (AS)	.10	.08	.04
52	Cal Ripken, Jr. (AS)	.15	.11	.06
53	Rickey Henderson (AS)	.15	.11	.06
54	Bob Welch (AS)	.05	.04	.02
55	Wade Boggs (AS)	.10	.08	.04
56	Mark McGwire (AS)	.10	.08	.04
57	Jack McDowell	.06	.05	.02
58	Jose Lind	.05	.04	.02
59	*Alex Fernandez*(FC)	.50	.40	.20
60	Pat Combs	.08	.06	.03
61	*Mike Walker*(FC)	.06	.05	.02
62	Juan Samuel	.05	.04	.02
63	Mike Blowers	.05	.04	.02
64	Mark Guthrie	.05	.04	.02
65	Mark Salas	.04	.03	.02
66	Tim Jones	.04	.03	.02
67	Tim Leary	.05	.04	.02
68	Andres Galarraga	.08	.06	.03
69	Bob Milacki	.05	.04	.02
70	Tim Belcher	.08	.06	.03
71	Todd Zeile	.06	.05	.02
72	Jerome Walton	.08	.06	.03
73	Kevin Seitzer	.06	.05	.02
74	Jerald Clark	.06	.05	.02
75	John Smoltz	.10	.08	.04
76	Mike Henneman	.05	.04	.02
77	Ken Griffey,Jr.	.70	.50	.30
78	Jim Abbott	.06	.05	.02
79	Gregg Jefferies	.15	.11	.06
80	Kevin Reimer(FC)	.08	.06	.03
81	Roger Clemens	.20	.15	.08
82	Mike Fitzgerald	.04	.03	.02
83	Bruce Hurst	.06	.05	.02
84	Eric Davis	.15	.11	.06
85	Paul Molitor	.12	.09	.05
86	Will Clark	.25	.20	.10
87	Mike Bielecki	.04	.03	.02
88	Bret Saberhagen	.10	.08	.04
89	Nolan Ryan	.35	.25	.14
90	Bobby Thigpen	.08	.06	.03
91	Dickie Thon	.04	.03	.02
92	Duane Ward	.04	.03	.02
93	Luis Polonia	.04	.03	.02
94	Terry Kennedy	.04	.03	.02
95	Kent Hrbek	.08	.06	.03
96	Danny Jackson	.06	.05	.02
97	Sid Fernandez	.08	.06	.03
98	Jimmy Key	.06	.05	.02
99	Franklin Stubbs	.05	.04	.02
100	Checklist	.04	.03	.02
101	R.J. Reynolds	.04	.03	.02
102	Dave Stewart	.08	.06	.03
103	Dan Pasqua	.05	.04	.02
104	Dan Plesac	.06	.05	.02
105	Mark McGwire	.15	.11	.06
106	John Farrell	.04	.03	.02
107	Don Mattingly	.20	.15	.08
108	Carlton Fisk	.10	.08	.04
109	Ken Oberkfell	.04	.03	.02
110	Darrel Akerfelds	.04	.03	.02
111	Gregg Olson	.08	.06	.03
112	Mike Scioscia	.06	.05	.02
113	Bryn Smith	.04	.03	.02
114	Bob Geren	.05	.04	.02
115	Tom Candiotti	.04	.03	.02
116	Kevin Tapani	.08	.06	.03
117	Jeff Treadway	.05	.04	.02
118	Alan Trammell	.08	.06	.03
119	Pete O'Brien	.04	.03	.02
120	Joel Skinner	.04	.03	.02
121	Mike LaValliere	.05	.04	.02
122	Dwight Evans	.08	.06	.03
123	Jody Reed	.08	.06	.03
124	Lee Guetterman	.04	.03	.02
125	Tim Burke	.05	.04	.02
126	Dave Johnson	.04	.03	.02
127	Fernando Valenzuela	.08	.06	.03
128	Jose DeLeon	.06	.05	.02
129	Andre Dawson	.10	.08	.04
130	Gerald Perry	.05	.04	.02
131	Greg Harris	.04	.03	.02
132	Tom Glavine	.15	.11	.06
133	Lance McCullers	.04	.03	.02
134	Randy Johnson	.08	.06	.03
135	Lance Parrish	.08	.06	.03
136	Mackey Sasser	.08	.06	.03
137	Geno Petralli	.04	.03	.02
138	Dennis Lamp	.04	.03	.02
139	Dennis Martinez	.06	.05	.02
140	Mike Pagliarulo	.05	.04	.02
141	Hal Morris	.10	.08	.04
142	Dave Parker	.10	.08	.04
143	Brett Butler	.06	.05	.02

		MT	NR MT	EX
144	Paul Assenmacher	.04	.03	.02
145	Mark Gubicza	.06	.05	.02
146	Charlie Hough	.05	.04	.02
147	Sammy Sosa	.15	.11	.06
148	Randy Ready	.04	.03	.02
149	Kelly Gruber	.08	.06	.03
150	Devon White	.06	.05	.02
151	Gary Carter	.08	.06	.03
152	Gene Larkin	.05	.04	.02
153	Chris Sabo	.08	.06	.03
154	David Cone	.08	.06	.03
155	Todd Stottlemyre	.06	.05	.02
156	Glenn Wilson	.05	.04	.02
157	Bob Walk	.05	.04	.02
158	Mike Gallego	.04	.03	.02
159	Greg Hibbard	.06	.05	.02
160	Chris Bosio	.05	.04	.02
161	Mike Moore	.06	.05	.02
162	Jerry Browne	.06	.05	.02
163	Steve Sax	.08	.06	.03
164	Melido Perez	.06	.05	.02
165	Danny Darwin	.05	.04	.02
166	Roger McDowell	.06	.05	.02
167	Bill Ripken	.04	.03	.02
168	Mike Sharperson	.05	.04	.02
169	Lee Smith	.08	.06	.03
170	Matt Nokes	.06	.05	.02
171	Jesse Orosco	.05	.04	.02
172	Rick Aguilera	.06	.05	.02
173	Jim Presley	.06	.05	.02
174	Lou Whitaker	.08	.06	.03
175	Harold Reynolds	.08	.06	.03
176	Brook Jacoby	.06	.05	.02
177	Wally Backman	.05	.04	.02
178	Wade Boggs	.10	.08	.04
179	Chuck Cary	.04	.03	.02
180	Tom Foley	.04	.03	.02
181	Pete Harnisch	.05	.04	.02
182	Mike Morgan	.05	.04	.02
183	Bob Tewksbury	.05	.04	.02
184	Joe Girardi	.06	.05	.02
185	Storm Davis	.05	.04	.02
186	Ed Whitson	.06	.05	.02
187	Steve Avery	.25	.20	.10
188	Lloyd Moseby	.06	.05	.02
189	Scott Bankhead	.06	.05	.02
190	Mark Langston	.08	.06	.03
191	Kevin McReynolds	.06	.05	.02
192	Julio Franco	.08	.06	.03
193	John Dopson	.05	.04	.02
194	Oil Can Boyd	.05	.04	.02
195	Bip Roberts	.06	.05	.02
196	Billy Hatcher	.06	.05	.02
197	Edgar Diaz(FC)	.08	.06	.03
198	Greg Litton	.05	.04	.02
199	Mark Grace	.10	.08	.04
200	Checklist	.04	.03	.02
201	George Brett	.10	.08	.04
202	Jeff Russell	.06	.05	.02
203	Ivan Calderon	.08	.06	.03
204	Ken Howell	.04	.03	.02
205	Tom Henke	.08	.06	.03
206	Bryan Harvey	.06	.05	.02
207	Steve Bedrosian	.08	.06	.03
208	Al Newman	.04	.03	.02
209	Randy Myers	.08	.06	.03
210	Daryl Boston	.04	.03	.02
211	Manny Lee	.06	.05	.02
212	Dave Smith	.06	.05	.02
213	Don Slaught	.04	.03	.02
214	Walt Weiss	.06	.05	.02
215	Donn Pall	.04	.03	.02
216	Jamie Navarro	.06	.05	.02
217	Willie Randolph	.06	.05	.02
218	Rudy Seanez(FC)	.08	.06	.03
219	*Jim Leyritz*(FC)	.08	.06	.03
220	Ron Karkovice	.05	.04	.02
221	Ken Caminiti	.05	.04	.02
222	Von Hayes	.08	.06	.03
223	Cal Ripken, Jr.	.25	.20	.10
224	Lenny Harris	.06	.05	.02
225	Milt Thompson	.05	.04	.02
226	Alvaro Espinoza	.05	.04	.02
227	Chris James	.06	.05	.02
228	Dan Gladden	.06	.05	.02
229	Jeff Blauser	.05	.04	.02
230	Mike Heath	.04	.03	.02
231	Omar Vizquel	.05	.04	.02
232	Doug Jones	.08	.06	.03
233	Jeff King	.06	.05	.02
234	Luis Rivera	.04	.03	.02

		MT	NR MT	EX
235	Ellis Burks	.10	.08	.04
236	Greg Cadaret	.04	.03	.02
237	Dave Martinez	.05	.04	.02
238	Mark Williamson	.04	.03	.02
239	Stan Javier	.05	.04	.02
240	Ozzie Smith	.10	.08	.04
241	*Shawn Boskie*	.15	.11	.06
242	Tom Gordon	.10	.08	.04
243	Tony Gwynn	.10	.08	.04
244	Tommy Gregg	.04	.03	.02
245	Jeff Robinson	.05	.04	.02
246	Keith Comstock	.04	.03	.02
247	Jack Howell	.05	.04	.02
248	Keith Miller	.05	.04	.02
249	Bobby Witt	.08	.06	.03
250	Rob Murphy	.04	.03	.02
251	Spike Owen	.06	.05	.02
252	Garry Templeton	.06	.05	.02
253	Glenn Braggs	.06	.05	.02
254	Ron Robinson	.06	.05	.02
255	Kevin Mitchell	.08	.06	.03
256	Les Lancaster	.04	.03	.02
257	*Mel Stottlemyre*(FC)	.10	.08	.04
258	Kenny Rogers	.06	.05	.02
259	Lance Johnson	.06	.05	.02
260	John Kruk	.06	.05	.02
261	Fred McGriff	.20	.15	.08
262	Dick Schofield	.04	.03	.02
263	Trevor Wilson	.05	.04	.02
264	Scott Scudder, David West	.05	.04	.02
266	Dwight Gooden	.08	.06	.03
267	*Willie Blair*(FC)	.08	.06	.03
268	Mark Portugal	.04	.03	.02
269	Doug Drabek	.10	.08	.04
270	Dennis Eckersley	.10	.08	.04
271	Eric King	.05	.04	.02
272	Robin Yount	.10	.08	.04
273	Carney Lansford	.08	.06	.03
274	*Carlos Baerga*	.30	.25	.12
275	Dave Righetti	.08	.06	.03
276	Scott Fletcher	.04	.03	.02
277	Eric Yelding	.08	.06	.03
278	Charlie Hayes	.08	.06	.03
279	Jeff Ballard	.05	.04	.02
280	Orel Hershiser	.10	.08	.04
281	Jose Oquendo	.04	.03	.02
282	Mike Witt	.05	.04	.02
283	Mitch Webster	.04	.03	.02
284	Greg Gagne	.05	.04	.02
285	*Greg Olson*	.10	.08	.04
286	Tony Phillips	.05	.04	.02
287	Scott Bradley	.04	.03	.02
288	Cory Snyder	.08	.06	.03
289	Jay Bell	.06	.05	.02
290	Kevin Romine	.04	.03	.02
291	Jeff Robinson	.05	.04	.02
292	Steve Frey(FC)	.06	.05	.02
293	Craig Worthington	.05	.04	.02
294	Tim Crews	.04	.03	.02
295	Joe Magrane	.08	.06	.03
296	*Hector Villanueva*(FC)	.08	.06	.03
297	*Terry Shumpert*	.10	.08	.04
298	Joe Carter	.10	.08	.04
299	Kent Mercker	.10	.08	.04
300	Checklist	.04	.03	.02
301	Chet Lemon	.05	.04	.02
302	Mike Schooler	.08	.06	.03
303	Dante Bichette	.06	.05	.02
304	Kevin Elster	.05	.04	.02
305	Jeff Huson	.06	.05	.02
306	Greg Harris	.05	.04	.02
307	Marquis Grissom	.12	.09	.05
308	Calvin Schiraldi	.04	.03	.02
309	Mariano Duncan	.06	.05	.02
310	Bill Spiers	.06	.05	.02
311	Scott Garrelts	.06	.05	.02
312	Mitch Williams	.08	.06	.03
313	Mike Macfarlane	.05	.04	.02
314	Kevin Brown	.06	.05	.02
315	Robin Ventura	.15	.11	.06
316	Darren Daulton	.10	.08	.04
317	PUuat Borders	.06	.05	.02
318	Mark Eichhorn	.04	.03	.02
319	Jeff Brantley	.08	.06	.03
320	Shane Mack	.05	.04	.02
321	Rob Dibble	.10	.08	.04
322	John Franco	.10	.08	.04
323	Junior Felix	.08	.06	.03
324	Casey Candaele	.04	.03	.02
325	Bobby Bonilla	.10	.08	.04
326	Dave Henderson	.06	.05	.02

		MT	NR MT	EX
327	Wayne Edwards	.06	.05	.02
328	Mark Knudson	.04	.03	.02
329	Terry Steinbach	.06	.05	.02
330	*Colby Ward*(FC)	.06	.05	.02
331	*Oscar Azocar*(FC)	.08	.06	.03
332	*Scott Radinsky*	.15	.11	.06
333	Eric Anthony	.10	.08	.04
334	Steve Lake	.04	.03	.02
335	Bob Melvin	.04	.03	.02
336	Kal Daniels	.08	.06	.03
337	Tom Pagnozzi	.05	.04	.02
338	*Alan Mills*	.06	.05	.02
339	Steve Olin	.06	.05	.02
340	Juan Berenguer	.04	.03	.02
341	Francisco Cabrera	.06	.05	.02
342	Dave Bergman	.04	.03	.02
343	Henry Cotto	.04	.03	.02
344	Sergio Valdez	.08	.06	.03
345	Bob Patterson	.04	.03	.02
346	John Marzano	.05	.04	.02
347	*Dana Kiecker*	.08	.06	.03
348	Dion James	.04	.03	.02
349	Hubie Brooks	.08	.06	.03
350	Bill Landrum	.05	.04	.02
351	*Bill Sampen*	.08	.06	.03
352	Greg Briley	.05	.04	.02
353	Paul Gibson	.04	.03	.02
354	Dave Eiland	.04	.03	.02
355	Steve Finley	.06	.05	.02
356	Bob Boone	.06	.05	.02
357	Steve Buechele	.06	.05	.02
358	*Chris Hoiles*(FC)	.20	.15	.08
359	Larry Walker	.15	.11	.06
360	Frank DiPino	.04	.03	.02
361	Mark Grant	.04	.03	.02
362	Dave Magadan	.08	.06	.03
363	Robby Thompson	.06	.05	.02
364	Lonnie Smith	.05	.04	.02
365	Steve Farr	.05	.04	.02
366	Dave Valle	.05	.04	.02
367	*Tim Naehring*(FC)	.08	.06	.03
368	Jim Acker	.04	.03	.02
369	Jeff Reardon	.08	.06	.03
370	Tim Teufel	.04	.03	.02
371	Juan Gonzalez	.70	.50	.30
372	Luis Salazar	.04	.03	.02
373	Rick Honeycutt	.04	.03	.02
374	Greg Maddux	.10	.08	.04
375	Jose Uribe	.05	.04	.02
376	Donnie Hill	.04	.03	.02
377	Don Carman	.04	.03	.02
378	*Craig Grebeck*	.06	.05	.02
379	Willie Fraser	.05	.04	.02
380	Glenallen Hill	.08	.06	.03
381	Joe Oliver	.06	.05	.02
382	Randy Bush	.04	.03	.02
383	Alex Cole(FC)	.08	.06	.03
384	Norm Charlton	.08	.06	.03
385	Gene Nelson	.04	.03	.02
386	Checklist	.04	.03	.02
387	Rickey Henderson (MVP)	.15	.11	.06
388	Lance Parrish (MVP)	.05	.04	.02
389	Fred McGriff (MVP)	.15	.11	.06
390	Dave Parker (MVP)	.10	.08	.04
391	Candy Maldonado	.05	.04	.02
392	Ken Griffey,Jr. (MVP)	.40	.30	.15
393	Gregg Olson (MVP)	.10	.08	.04
394	Rafael Palmeiro (MVP)	.10	.08	.04
395	Roger Clemens (MVP)	.15	.11	.06
396	George Brett (MVP)	.10	.08	.04
397	Cecil Fielder (MVP)	.15	.11	.06
398	Brian Harper (MVP)	.05	.04	.02
399	Bobby Thigpen (MVP)	.06	.05	.02
400	Roberto Kelly (MVP)	.08	.06	.03
401	Danny Darwin (MVP)	.05	.04	.02
402	Dave Justice (MVP)	.25	.20	.10
403	Lee Smith (MVP)	.05	.04	.02
404	Ryne Sandberg (MVP)	.15	.11	.06
405	Eddie Murray (MVP)	.10	.08	.04
406	Tim Wallach (MVP)	.06	.05	.02
407	Kevin Mitchell (MVP)	.10	.08	.04
408	Darryl Strawberry (MVP)	.10	.08	.04
409	Joe Carter (MVP)	.06	.05	.02
410	Len Dykstra (MVP)	.06	.05	.02
411	Doug Drabek (MVP)	.06	.05	.02
412	Chris Sabo (MVP)	.08	.06	.03
413	*Paul Marak* (RR)(FC)	.06	.05	.02
414	Tim McIntosh (RR)(FC)	.10	.08	.04
415	*Brian Barnes* (RR)	.10	.08	.04
416	*Eric Gunderson* (RR)(FC)	.08	.06	.03
417	*Mike Gardiner* (RR)	.10	.08	.04
418	Steve Carter (RR)	.08	.06	.03
419	*Gerald Alexander* (RR)	.15	.11	.06
420	*Rich Garces* (RR)	.10	.08	.04
421	*Chuck Knoblauch* (RR)	.25	.20	.10
422	*Scott Aldred* (RR)	.15	.11	.06
423	*Wes Chamberlain* (RR)	.20	.15	.08
424	*Lance Dickson* (RR)	.10	.08	.04
425	*Greg Colbrunn* (RR)	.15	.11	.06
426	*Rich Delucia* (RR)(FC)	.08	.06	.03
427	*Jeff Conine* (RR)	.35	.25	.14
428	*Steve Decker* (RR)	.10	.08	.04
429	*Turner Ward* (RR)	.10	.08	.04
430	*Mo Vaughn* (RR)	.50	.40	.20
431	*Steve Chitren* (RR)	.10	.08	.04
432	Mike Benjamin (RR)(FC)	.10	.08	.04
433	Ryne Sandberg (AS)	.10	.08	.04
434	Len Dykstra (AS)	.06	.05	.02
435	Andre Dawson (AS)	.10	.08	.04
436	Mike Scioscia (AS)	.06	.05	.02
437	Ozzie Smith (AS)	.10	.08	.04
438	Kevin Mitchell (AS)	.10	.08	.04
439	Jack Armstrong (AS)	.06	.05	.02
440	Chris Sabo (AS)	.08	.06	.03
441	Will Clark (AS)	.10	.08	.04
442	Mel Hall	.05	.04	.02
443	Mark Gardner	.06	.05	.02
444	Mike Devereaux	.06	.05	.02
445	Kirk Gibson	.06	.05	.02
446	Terry Pendleton	.08	.06	.03
447	Mike Harkey	.08	.06	.03
448	Jim Eisenreich	.04	.03	.02
449	Benito Santiago	.08	.06	.03
450	Oddibe McDowell	.04	.03	.02
451	Cecil Fielder	.20	.15	.08
452	Ken Griffey,Sr.	.08	.06	.03
453	Bert Blyleven	.06	.05	.02
454	Howard Johnson	.10	.08	.04
455	Monty Farris(FC)	.08	.06	.03
456	Tony Pena	.05	.04	.02
457	Tim Raines	.08	.06	.03
458	Dennis Rasmussen	.04	.03	.02
459	Luis Quinones	.04	.03	.02
460	B.J. Surhoff	.06	.05	.02
461	Ernest Riles	.04	.03	.02
462	Rick Sutcliffe	.06	.05	.02
463	Danny Tartabull	.10	.08	.04
464	Pete Incaviglia	.06	.05	.02
465	Carlos Martinez	.05	.04	.02
466	Ricky Jordan	.06	.05	.02
467	John Cerutti	.04	.03	.02
468	Dave Winfield	.12	.09	.05
469	Francisco Oliveras	.04	.03	.02
470	Roy Smith	.04	.03	.02
471	Barry Larkin	.12	.09	.05
472	Ron Darling	.06	.05	.02
473	David Wells	.06	.05	.02
474	Glenn Davis	.10	.08	.04
475	Neal Heaton	.04	.03	.02
476	Ron Hassey	.04	.03	.02
477	Frank Thomas(FC)	1.25	.90	.50
478	Greg Vaughn	.15	.11	.06
479	Todd Burns	.04	.03	.02
480	Candy Maldonado	.05	.04	.02
481	Dave LaPoint	.04	.03	.02
482	Alvin Davis	.08	.06	.03
483	Mike Scott	.06	.05	.02
484	Dale Murphy	.12	.09	.05
485	Ben McDonald	.10	.08	.04
486	Jay Howell	.06	.05	.02
487	Vince Coleman	.08	.06	.03
488	Alfredo Griffin	.05	.04	.02
489	Sandy Alomar	.08	.06	.03
490	Kirby Puckett	.15	.11	.06
491	Andres Thomas	.04	.03	.02
492	Jack Morris	.08	.06	.03
493	Matt Young	.04	.03	.02
494	Greg Myers	.04	.03	.02
495	Barry Bonds	.25	.20	.10
496	Scott Cooper(FC)	.20	.15	.08
497	Dan Schatzeder	.04	.03	.02
498	Jesse Barfield	.06	.05	.02
499	Jerry Goff(FC)	.05	.04	.02
500	Checklist	.04	.03	.02
501	*Anthony Telford*(FC)	.15	.11	.06
502	Eddie Murray	.12	.09	.05
503	*Omar Olivares*(FC)	.12	.09	.05
504	Ryne Sandberg	.20	.15	.08
505	Jeff Montgomery	.06	.05	.02
506	Mark Parent	.04	.03	.02
507	Ron Gant	.15	.11	.06
508	Frank Tanana	.05	.04	.02

		MT	NR MT	EX
509	Jay Buhner	.06	.05	.02
510	Max Venable	.04	.03	.02
511	Wally Whitehurst	.06	.05	.02
512	Gary Pettis	.04	.03	.02
513	Tom Brunansky	.06	.05	.02
514	Tim Wallach	.08	.06	.03
515	Craig Lefferts	.05	.04	.02
516	*Tim Layana*	.10	.08	.04
517	Darryl Hamilton	.08	.06	.03
518	Rick Reuschel	.05	.04	.02
519	Steve Wilson	.06	.05	.02
520	Kurt Stillwell	.05	.04	.02
521	Rafael Palmeiro	.12	.09	.05
522	Ken Patterson	.04	.03	.02
523	Len Dykstra	.12	.09	.05
524	Tony Fernandez	.06	.05	.02
525	Kent Anderson	.04	.03	.02
526	*Mark Leonard*(FC)	.10	.08	.04
527	Allan Anderson	.04	.03	.02
528	Tom Browning	.06	.05	.02
529	Frank Viola	.12	.09	.05
530	John Olerud	.35	.25	.14
531	Juan Agosto	.04	.03	.02
532	Zane Smith	.06	.05	.02
533	Scott Sanderson	.06	.05	.02
534	Barry Jones	.05	.04	.02
535	Mike Felder	.04	.03	.02
536	Jose Canseco	.15	.11	.06
537	Felix Fermin	.04	.03	.02
538	Roberto Kelly	.08	.06	.03
539	Brian Holman	.05	.04	.02
540	Mark Davidson	.04	.03	.02
541	Terry Mulholland	.06	.05	.02
542	Randy Milligan	.06	.05	.02
543	Jose Gonzalez	.04	.03	.02
544	*Craig Wilson*(FC)	.10	.08	.04
545	Mike Hartley	.04	.03	.02
546	Greg Swindell	.06	.05	.02
547	Gary Gaetti	.08	.06	.03
548	Dave Justice	.50	.40	.20
549	Steve Searcy	.04	.03	.02
550	Erik Hanson	.12	.09	.05
551	Dave Stieb	.08	.06	.03
552	Andy Van Slyke	.08	.06	.03
553	Mike Greenwell	.12	.09	.05
554	Kevin Maas	.10	.08	.04
555	Delino Deshields	.20	.15	.08
556	Curt Schilling	.05	.04	.02
557	Ramon Martinez	.08	.06	.03
558	Pedro Guerrero	.08	.06	.03
559	Dwight Smith	.05	.04	.02
560	Mark Davis	.04	.03	.02
561	Shawn Abner	.05	.04	.02
562	Charlie Leibrandt	.05	.04	.02
563	John Shelby	.04	.03	.02
564	Bill Swift	.05	.04	.02
565	Mike Fetters	.06	.05	.02
566	Alejandro Pena	.05	.04	.02
567	Ruben Sierra	.15	.11	.06
568	Calos Quintana	.08	.06	.03
569	Kevin Gross	.05	.04	.02
570	Derek Lilliquist	.04	.03	.02
571	Jack Armstrong	.06	.05	.02
572	Greg Brock	.04	.03	.02
573	Mike Kingery	.04	.03	.02
574	Greg Smith(FC)	.06	.05	.02
575	*Brian McRae*(FC)	.25	.20	.10
576	Jack Daugherty	.05	.04	.02
577	Ozzie Guillen	.06	.05	.02
578	Joe Boever	.04	.03	.02
579	Luis Sojo	.06	.05	.02
580	Chili Davis	.06	.05	.02
581	Don Robinson	.04	.03	.02
582	Brian Harper	.06	.05	.02
583	Paul O'Neill	.06	.05	.02
584	Bob Ojeda	.05	.04	.02
585	Mookie Wilson	.05	.04	.02
586	Rafael Ramirez	.04	.03	.02
587	Gary Redus	.04	.03	.02
588	Jamie Quirk	.04	.03	.02
589	Shawn Hilligas	.04	.03	.02
590	*Tom Edens*(FC)	.08	.06	.03
591	Joe Klink(FC)	.05	.04	.02
592	Charles Nagy(FC)	.12	.09	.05
593	Eric Plunk	.04	.03	.02
594	Tracy Jones	.04	.03	.02
595	Craig Biggio	.08	.06	.03
596	Jose DeJesus	.06	.05	.02
597	Mickey Tettleton	.08	.06	.03
598	Chris Gwynn	.05	.04	.02
599	Rex Hudler	.06	.05	.02

		MT	NR MT	EX
600	Checklist	.04	.03	.02
601	Jim Gott	.04	.03	.02
602	Jeff Manto(FC)	.12	.09	.05
603	Nelson Liriano	.04	.03	.02
604	Mark Lemke	.06	.05	.02
605	Clay Parker	.04	.03	.02
606	Edgar Martinez	.08	.06	.03
607	*Mark Whiten*(FC)	.35	.25	.14
608	Ted Power	.04	.03	.02
609	Tom Bolton	.05	.04	.02
610	Tom Herr	.05	.04	.02
611	Andy Hawkins	.04	.03	.02
612	Scott Ruskin	.04	.03	.02
613	Ron Kittle	.05	.04	.02
614	John Wetteland	.06	.05	.02
615	*Mike Perez*(FC)	.12	.09	.05
616	Dave Clark	.04	.03	.02
617	Brent Mayne(FC)	.12	.09	.05
618	Jack Clark	.08	.06	.03
619	Marvin Freeman	.04	.03	.02
620	Edwin Nunez	.04	.03	.02
621	Russ Swan(FC)	.08	.06	.03
622	Johnny Ray	.04	.03	.02
623	Charlie O'Brien	.04	.03	.02
624	*Joe Bitker*(FC)	.12	.09	.05
625	Mike Marshall	.04	.03	.02
626	Otis Nixon	.05	.04	.02
627	Andy Benes	.15	.11	.06
628	Ron Oester	.04	.03	.02
629	Ted Higuera	.06	.05	.02
630	Kevin Bass	.05	.04	.02
631	Damon Berryhill	.05	.04	.02
632	Bo Jackson	.20	.15	.08
633	Brad Arnsberg	.05	.04	.02
634	Jerry Willard	.04	.03	.02
635	Tommy Greene	.06	.05	.02
636	*Bob MacDonald*(FC)	.10	.08	.04
637	Kirk McCaskill	.05	.04	.02
638	John Burkett	.05	.04	.02
639	*Paul Abbott*(FC)	.06	.05	.02
640	Todd Benzinger	.05	.04	.02
641	Todd Hundley(FC)	.10	.08	.04
642	George Bell	.10	.08	.04
643	*Javier Ortiz*(FC)	.12	.09	.05
644	Sid Bream	.05	.04	.02
645	Bob Welch	.06	.05	.02
646	Phil Bradley	.05	.04	.02
647	Bill Krueger	.04	.03	.02
648	Rickey Henderson	.12	.09	.05
649	Kevin Wickander	.05	.04	.02
650	Steve Balboni	.04	.03	.02
651	Gene Harris	.05	.04	.02
652	Jim Deshaies	.04	.03	.02
653	Jason Grimsley(FC)	.12	.09	.05
654	Joe Orsulak	.05	.04	.02
655	*Jimmy Poole*(FC)	.12	.09	.05
656	Felix Jose	.10	.08	.04
657	Dennis Cook	.05	.04	.02
658	Tom Brookens	.04	.03	.02
659	Junior Ortiz	.04	.03	.02
660	Jeff Parrett	.04	.03	.02
661	Jerry Don Gleaton	.04	.03	.02
662	Brent Knackert	.04	.03	.02
663	Rance Mulliniks	.04	.03	.02
664	John Smiley	.06	.05	.02
665	Larry Andersen	.04	.03	.02
666	Willie McGee	.08	.06	.03
667	*Chris Nabholz*(FC)	.10	.08	.04
668	Brady Anderson	.04	.03	.02
669	*Darren Holmes*(FC)	.12	.09	.05
670	Ken Hill	.06	.05	.02
671	Gary Varsho	.04	.03	.02
672	Bill Pecota	.05	.04	.02
673	Fred Lynn	.05	.04	.02
674	Kevin D. Brown(FC)	.10	.08	.04
675	Dan Petry	.04	.03	.02
676	Mike Jackson	.05	.04	.02
677	Wally Joyner	.06	.05	.02
678	Danny Jackson	.05	.04	.02
679	*Bill Haselman*(FC)	.12	.09	.05
680	Mike Boddicker	.06	.05	.02
681	*Mel Rojas*(FC)	.12	.09	.05
682	Roberto Alomar	.20	.15	.08
683	Dave Justice (R.O.Y.)	.25	.20	.10
684	Chuck Crim	.04	.03	.02
685	Matt Williams	.12	.09	.05
686	Shawon Dunston	.06	.05	.02
687	*Jeff Schulz*(FC)	.08	.06	.03
688	*John Barfield*(FC)	.08	.06	.03
689	Gerald Young	.04	.03	.02
690	*Luis Gonzalez*(FC)	.40	.30	.15

		MT	NR MT	EX
691	Frank Wills	.05	.04	.02
692	Chuck Finley	.08	.06	.03
693	Sandy Alomar (R.O.Y.)	.06	.05	.02
694	Tim Drummond	.05	.04	.02
695	Herm Winningham	.04	.03	.02
696	Darryl Strawberry	.10	.08	.04
697	Al Leiter	.04	.03	.02
698	*Karl Rhodes*(FC)	.08	.06	.03
699	Stan Belinda(FC)	.08	.06	.03
700	Checklist	.04	.03	.02
701	Lance Blankenship	.04	.03	.02
702	Willie Stargell (Puzzle Card)	.10	.08	.04
703	Jim Gantner	.05	.04	.02
704	*Reggie Harris*(FC)	.06	.05	.02
705	Rob Ducey	.04	.03	.02
706	Tim Hulett	.04	.03	.02
707	Atlee Hammaker	.04	.03	.02
708	Xavier Hernandez	.04	.03	.02
709	Chuck McElroy(FC)	.08	.06	.03
710	John Mitchell	.04	.03	.02
711	Carlos Hernandez	.05	.04	.02
712	Geronimo Pena(FC)	.10	.08	.04
713	*Jim Neidlinger*(FC)	.06	.05	.02
714	John Orton	.04	.03	.02
715	Terry Leach	.04	.03	.02
716	Mike Stanton	.06	.05	.02
717	Walt Terrell	.04	.03	.02
718	Luis Aquino	.05	.04	.02
719	Bud Black	.05	.04	.02
720	Bob Kipper	.04	.03	.02
721	*Jeff Gray*(FC)	.08	.06	.03
722	Jose Rijo	.08	.06	.03
723	Curt Young	.04	.03	.02
724	Jose Vizcaino(FC)	.08	.06	.03
725	*Randy Tomlin*(FC)	.15	.11	.06
726	Junior Noboa	.05	.04	.02
727	Bob Welch (Award Winner)	.08	.06	.03
728	Gary Ward	.04	.03	.02
729	Rob Deer	.05	.04	.02
730	*David Segui*(FC)	.08	.06	.03
731	Mark Carreon	.04	.03	.02
732	Vicente Palacios	.04	.03	.02
733	Sam Horn	.05	.04	.02
734	*Howard Farmer*(FC)	.08	.06	.03
735	Ken Dayley	.04	.03	.02
736	Kelly Mann	.08	.06	.03
737	*Joe Grahe*(FC)	.12	.09	.05
738	Kelly Downs	.04	.03	.02
739	*Jimmy Kremers*(FC)	.06	.05	.02
740	Kevin Appier	.12	.09	.05
741	Jeff Reed	.04	.03	.02
742	Jose Rijo (World Series)	.08	.06	.03
743	*Dave Rohde*(FC)	.06	.05	.02
744	Dr. Dirt/ Mr. Clean (Len Dykstra, Dale Murphy)	.08	.06	.03
745	Paul Sorrento	.06	.05	.02
746	Thomas Howard(FC)	.10	.08	.04
747	*Matt Stark*(FC)	.10	.08	.04
748	Harold Baines	.08	.06	.03
749	Doug Dascenzo	.05	.04	.02
750	Doug Drabek (Award Winner)	.08	.06	.03
751	Gary Sheffield	.20	.15	.08
752	*Terry Lee*(FC)	.06	.05	.02
753	*Jim Vatcher*(FC)	.08	.06	.03
754	Lee Stevens	.12	.09	.05
755	Randy Veres(FC)	.08	.06	.03
756	Bill Doran	.06	.05	.02
757	Gary Wayne	.04	.03	.02
758	*Pedro Munoz*(FC)	.10	.08	.04
759	Chris Hammond(FC)	.12	.09	.05
760	Checklist	.04	.03	.02
761	Rickey Henderson (MVP)	.12	.09	.05
762	Barry Bonds (MVP)	.20	.15	.08
763	Billy Hatcher (World Series)	.05	.04	.02
764	Julio Machado	.05	.04	.02
765	Jose Mesa	.05	.04	.02
766	Willie Randolph (World Series)	.05	.04	.02
767	*Scott Erickson*(FC)	.12	.09	.05
768	*Travis Fryman*(FC)	.60	.45	.25
769	*Rich Rodriguez*(FC)	.12	.09	.05
770	Checklist	.04	.03	.02

1991 Donruss Highlights

This 22-card subset features highlights from the 1990 season. The cards feature a "BC" designation along with the number and are styled after the 1991 regular issue Donruss Cards. Cards 1-10 feature blue borders due to their release with Series I cards. Cards 11-22 feature green borders and were released with Series II cards. A highlight logo appears on the front of the card. Each highlight is explained in depth on the card back.

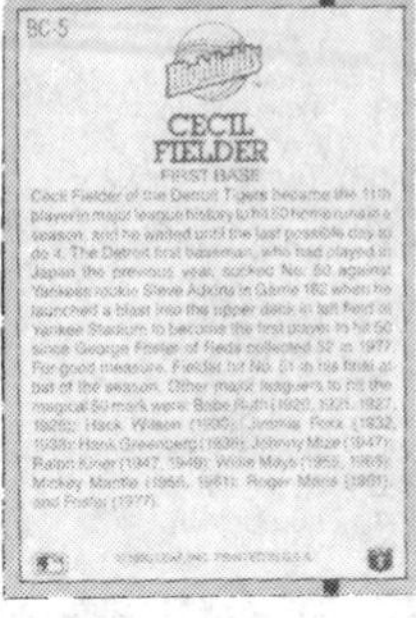

		MT	NR MT	EX
	Complete Set:	3.00	2.25	1.25
	Common Player:	.10	.08	.04
1	Mark Langston/ Mike Witt (No-Hit Mariners)	.15	.11	.06
2	Randy Johnson (No-Hits Tigers)	.15	.11	.06
3	Nolan Ryan (No-Hits A's)	.40	.30	.15
4	Dave Stewart (No-Hits Blue Jays)	.15	.11	.06
5	Cecil Fielder (50 Homer Club)	.25	.20	.10
6	Carlton Fisk (Record Home Run)	.20	.15	.08
7	Ryne Sandberg (Sets Fielding Records)	.20	.15	.08
8	Gary Carter (Breaks Catching Mark)	.15	.11	.06
9	Mark McGwire (Home Run Milestone)	.15	.11	.06
10	Bo Jackson (4 Consecutive HRs)	.25	.20	.10
11	Fernando Valenzuela (No-Hits Cardinals)	.15	.11	.06
12	Andy Hawkins (No-Hits White Sox)	.10	.08	.04
13	Melido Perez (No-Hits Yankees)	.10	.08	.04
14	Terry Mulholland (No-Hits Giants)	.10	.08	.04
15	Nolan Ryan (300th Win)	.40	.30	.15
16	Delino DeShields (4 Hits In Debut)	.15	.11	.06
17	Cal Ripken (Errorless Games)	.20	.15	.08
18	Eddie Murray (Switch Hit Homers)	.15	.11	.06
19	George Brett (3 Decade Champ)	.20	.15	.08
20	Bobby Thigpen (Shatters Save Mark)	.15	.11	.06
21	Dave Stieb (No-Hits Indians)	.10	.08	.06
22	Willie McGee (NL Batting Champ)	.10	.08	.04

1991 Donruss Grand Slammers

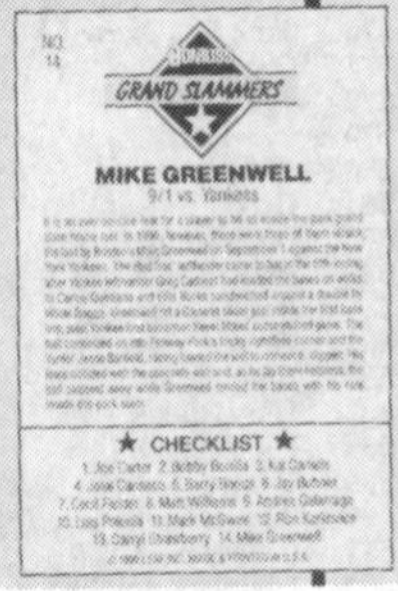

This 14-card set features players who hit grand slams in 1990. The cards are styled after the 1991 Donruss regular issue cards. The featured player is showcased with a star in the background. The set was included in factory sets and randomly in jumbo packs.

		MT	NR MT	EX
Complete Set (14):		2.50	2.00	1.00
Common Player:		.10	.08	.04
1	Joe Carter	.20	.15	.08
2	Bobby Bonilla	.20	.15	.08
3	Kal Daniels	.15	.11	.06
4	Jose Canseco	.30	.25	.12
5	Barry Bonds	.25	.20	.10
6	Jay Buhner	.15	.11	.06
7	Cecil Fielder	.30	.25	.12
8	Matt Williams	.20	.15	.08
9	Andres Galarraga	.10	.08	.04
10	Luis Polonia	.10	.08	.04
11	Mark McGwire	.20	.15	.08
12	Ron Karkovice	.10	.08	.04
13	Darryl Strawberry	.25	.20	.10
14	Mike Greenwell	.20	.15	.06

1991 Donruss Elite

Photos not available at press time

Donruss released a series of special inserts in 1991. Ten thousand of each Elite card was released, while 7,500 Legend cards and 5,000 Signature cards were issued. Cards were inserted in wax packs and feature marble borders. The Legend card features a Dick Perez drawing. Each card is designated with a serial number on the back.

		MT	NR MT	EX
Complete Set (10):		1400.00	1000.00	600.00
Common Player:		50.00	30.00	15.00
1	Barry Bonds	150.00	100.00	50.00
2	George Brett	100.00	75.00	40.00
3	Jose Canseco	75.00	50.00	25.00
4	Andre Dawson	80.00	60.00	40.00
5	Doug Drabek	75.00	55.00	30.00
6	Cecil Fielder	90.00	60.00	30.00
7	Rickey Henderson	80.00	60.00	30.00
8	Matt Williams	70.00	55.00	30.00
—	Nolan Ryan (Legend)	375.00	300.00	140.00
—	Ryne Sandberg (Signature)	400.00	260.00	140.00

1991 Donruss Rookies

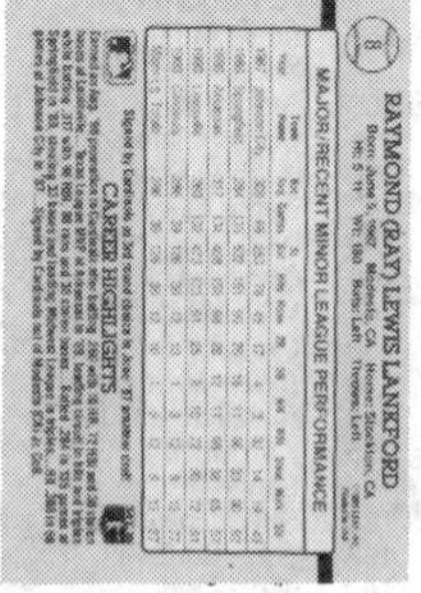

Red borders highlight the 1991 Donruss Rookies cards. This set marks the sixth year that Donruss has produced such an issue. Like in past years, "The Rookies" logo appears on the card fronts. The set is packaged in a special box and includes a Willie Stargell puzzle card.

		MT	NR MT	EX
Complete Set (56):		6.00	4.50	2.50
Common Player:		.10	.08	.04
1	Pat Kelly(FC)	.15	.10	.07
2	Rich DeLucia	.10	.08	.04
3	Wes Chamberlain	.20	.15	.07
4	Scott Leius(FC)	.10	.08	.04
5	Darryl Kile(FC)	.15	.11	.06
6	Milt Cuyler	.15	.11	.06
7	Todd Van Poppel(FC)	.50	.35	.20
8	Ray Lankford	.30	.25	.12
9	Brian Hunter(FC)	.40	.30	.15
10	Tony Perezchica	.10	.08	.04
11	Ced Landrum(FC)	.10	.08	.04
12	Dave Burba(FC)	.10	.08	.04
13	Ramon Garcia(FC)	.20	.15	.08
14	Ed Sprague(FC)	.15	.11	.06
15	Warren Newson(FC)	.15	.11	.06
16	Paul Faries(FC)	.10	.08	.04
17	Luis Gonzalez	.35	.25	.14
18	Charles Nagy	.15	.11	.06
19	Chris Hammond	.10	.08	.04
20	Frank Castillo(FC)	.25	.20	.10
21	Pedro Munoz	.20	.15	.08
22	Orlando Merced(FC)	.30	.20	.12
23	Jose Melendez(FC)	.10	.08	.04
24	Kirk Dressendorfer(FC)	.30	.25	.12
25	Heathcliff Slocumb(FC)	.10	.08	.04
26	Doug Simons(FC)	.10	.08	.04
27	Mike Timlin(FC)	.20	.15	.08
28	Jeff Fassero(FC)	.15	.10	.07
29	Mark Leiter(FC)	.10	.08	.04
30	Jeff Bagwell(FC)	1.00	.70	.40
31	Brian McRae	.35	.25	.14
32	Mark Whiten	.20	.15	.08
33	Ivan Rodriguez(FC)	1.00	.70	.40
34	Wade Taylor(FC)	.10	.08	.04
35	Darren Lewis(FC)	.35	.25	.12
36	Mo Vaughn	.40	.30	.15
37	Mike Remlinger(FC)	.10	.08	.04
38	Rick Wilkins(FC)	.20	.15	.08
39	Chuck Knoblauch	.40	.30	.15
40	Kevin Morton	.15	.11	.06
41	Carlos Rodriguez(FC)	.10	.08	.04
42	Mark Lewis	.20	.15	.08
43	Brent Mayne	.10	.08	.04
44	Chris Haney(FC)	.15	.11	.06
45	Denis Boucher(FC)	.15	.11	.06
46	Mike Gardiner	.10	.08	.04
47	Jeff Johnson(FC)	.15	.11	.06
48	Dean Palmer	.30	.25	.12
49	Chuck McElroy	.10	.08	.04
50	Chris Jones(FC)	.10	.08	.04
51	Scott Kamieniecki(FC)	.10	.08	.04
52	Al Osuna(FC)	.10	.08	.04
53	Rusty Meacham(FC)	.15	.11	.06
54	Chito Martinez(FC)	.25	.20	.10
55	Reggie Jefferson(FC)	.25	.20	.10
56	Checklist	.05	.04	.02

1992 Donruss

For the second consecutive year, Donruss chose

to release its card set in two series. The 1992 cards feature improved stock, an anti-couterfeit feature and include both front and back photos. Once again Rated Rookies and All-Stars are included in the set. Special highlight cards also can be found in the 1992 Donruss set. Production was reduced in 1992 compared to 1988-1991.

		MT	NR MT	EX
Complete Set (784):		30.00	22.00	12.00
Common Player:		.05	.04	.02
1	*Mark Wohlers* (RR)	.15	.11	.06
2	Will Cordero (RR)	.30	.25	.12
3	Kyle Abbott (RR)	.08	.06	.03
4	*Dave Nilsson* (RR)	.12	.09	.05
5	*Kenny Lofton* (RR)	.60	.45	.25
6	*Luis Mercedes* (RR)	.20	.15	.08
7	*Roger Salkeld* (RR)	.15	.11	.06
8	Eddie Zosky (RR)(FC)	.25	.20	.10
9	*Todd Van Poppel* (RR)	.30	.25	.12
10	*Frank Seminara* (RR)	.10	.08	.04
11	*Andy Ashby* (RR)(FC)	.20	.15	.08
12	Reggie Jefferson (RR)(FC)	.35	.25	.14
13	*Ryan Klesko* (RR)	.50	.40	.20
14	*Carlos Garcia* (RR)	.15	.11	.06
15	*John Ramos* (RR)(FC)	.10	.08	.04
16	*Eric Karros* (RR)	.35	.25	.14
17	*Pat Lennon* (RR)(FC)	.10	.08	.04
18	*Eddie Taubensee* (RR)	.10	.08	.04
19	*Roberto Hernandez* (RR)	.10	.08	.04
20	D.J. Dozier (RR)(FC)	.20	.15	.08
21	Dave Henderson (AS)	.10	.08	.04
22	Cal Ripken, Jr. (AS)	.20	.15	.08
23	Wade Boggs (AS)	.20	.15	.08
24	Ken Griffey,Jr. (AS)	.60	.45	.25
25	Jack Morris (AS)	.10	.08	.04
26	Danny Tartabull (AS)	.10	.08	.04
27	Cecil Fielder (AS)	.20	.15	.08
28	Roberto Alomar (AS)	.20	.15	.08
29	Sandy Alomar (AS)	.10	.08	.04
30	Rickey Henderson (AS)	.20	.15	.08
31	Ken Hill	.06	.05	.02
32	John Habyan	.05	.04	.02
33	Otis Nixon (Highlight)	.10	.08	.04
34	Tim Wallach	.08	.06	.03
35	Cal Ripken, Jr.	.30	.25	.12
36	Gary Carter	.08	.06	.03
37	Juan Agosto	.05	.04	.02
38	Doug Dascenzo	.05	.04	.02
39	Kirk Gibson	.08	.06	.03
40	Benito Santiago	.08	.06	.03
41	Otis Nixon	.06	.05	.02
42	Andy Allanson	.05	.04	.02
43	Brian Holman	.06	.05	.02
44	Dick Schofield	.05	.04	.02
45	Dave Magadan	.08	.06	.03
46	Rafael Palmeiro	.10	.08	.04
47	Jody Reed	.06	.05	.02
48	Ivan Calderon	.08	.06	.03
49	Greg Harris	.05	.04	.02
50	Chris Sabo	.08	.06	.03
51	Paul Molitor	.15	.11	.06
52	Robby Thompson	.06	.05	.02
53	Dave Smith	.05	.04	.02
54	Mark Davis	.05	.04	.02
55	Kevin Brown	.06	.05	.02
56	Donn Pall	.05	.04	.02
57	Lenny Dykstra	.08	.06	.03
58	Roberto Alomar	.25	.20	.10
59	Jeff Robinson	.05	.04	.02
60	Willie McGee	.08	.06	.03
61	Jay Buhner	.08	.06	.03
62	Mike Pagliarulo	.05	.04	.02
63	Paul O'Neill	.08	.06	.03
64	Hubie Brooks	.06	.05	.02
65	Kelly Gruber	.08	.06	.03
66	Ken Caminiti	.06	.05	.02
67	Gary Redus	.05	.04	.02
68	Harold Baines	.08	.06	.03
69	Charlie Hough	.06	.05	.02
70	B.J. Surhoff	.06	.05	.02
71	Walt Weiss	.06	.05	.02
72	Shawn Hillegas	.05	.04	.02
73	Roberto Kelly	.08	.06	.03
74	Jeff Ballard	.05	.04	.02
75	Craig Biggio	.08	.06	.03
76	Pat Combs	.06	.05	.02
77	Jeff Robinson	.05	.04	.02
78	Tim Belcher	.06	.05	.02
79	Cris Carpenter	.06	.05	.02
80	Checklist	.05	.04	.02

		MT	NR MT	EX
81	Steve Avery	.30	.25	.12
82	Chris James	.05	.04	.02
83	Brian Harper	.06	.05	.02
84	Charlie Leibrandt	.06	.05	.02
85	Mickey Tettleton	.08	.06	.03
86	Pete O'Brien	.06	.05	.02
87	Danny Darwin	.05	.04	.02
88	Bob Walk	.05	.04	.02
89	Jeff Reardon	.08	.06	.03
90	Bobby Rose	.08	.06	.03
91	Danny Jackson	.06	.05	.02
92	John Morris	.05	.04	.02
93	Bud Black	.06	.05	.02
94	Tommy Greene (Highlight)	.10	.08	.04
95	Rick Aguilera	.08	.06	.03
96	Gary Gaetti	.08	.06	.03
97	David Cone	.08	.06	.03
98	John Olerud	.25	.20	.10
99	Joel Skinner	.05	.04	.02
100	Jay Bell	.08	.06	.03
101	Bob Milacki	.05	.04	.02
102	Norm Charlton	.06	.05	.02
103	Chuck Crim	.05	.04	.02
104	Terry Steinbach	.06	.05	.02
105	Juan Samuel	.08	.06	.03
106	Steve Howe	.06	.05	.02
107	Rafael Belliard	.05	.04	.02
108	Joey Cora	.05	.04	.02
109	Tommy Greene	.08	.06	.03
110	Gregg Olson	.08	.06	.03
111	Frank Tanana	.06	.05	.02
112	Lee Smith	.08	.06	.03
113	Greg Harris	.05	.04	.02
114	Dwayne Henry	.05	.04	.02
115	Chili Davis	.08	.06	.03
116	Kent Mercker	.08	.06	.03
117	Brian Barnes	.08	.06	.03
118	Rich DeLucia	.06	.05	.02
119	Andre Dawson	.15	.11	.06
120	Carlos Baerga	.25	.20	.10
121	Mike LaValliere	.06	.05	.02
122	Jeff Gray	.06	.05	.02
123	Bruce Hurst	.08	.06	.03
124	Alvin Davis	.08	.06	.03
125	John Candelaria	.06	.05	.02
126	Matt Nokes	.08	.06	.03
127	George Bell	.10	.08	.04
128	Bret Saberhagen	.10	.08	.04
129	Jeff Russell	.08	.06	.03
130	Jim Abbott	.10	.08	.04
131	Bill Gullickson	.06	.05	.02
132	Todd Zeile	.15	.11	.06
133	Dave Winfield	.10	.08	.04
134	Wally Whitehurst	.06	.05	.02
135	Matt Williams	.15	.11	.06
136	Tom Browning	.08	.06	.03
137	Marquis Grissom	.15	.11	.06
138	Erik Hanson	.10	.08	.04
139	Rob Dibble	.08	.06	.03
140	Don August	.05	.04	.02
141	Tom Henke	.08	.06	.03
142	Dan Pasqua	.06	.05	.02
143	George Brett	.15	.11	.06
144	Jerald Clark	.06	.05	.02
145	Robin Ventura	.25	.20	.10
146	Dale Murphy	.10	.08	.04
147	Dennis Eckersley	.10	.08	.04
148	Eric Yelding	.05	.04	.02
149	Mario Diaz	.05	.04	.02
150	Casey Candaele	.05	.04	.02
151	Steve Olin	.06	.05	.02
152	Luis Salazar	.05	.04	.02
153	Kevin Maas	.15	.11	.06
154	Nolan Ryan (HL)	.40	.30	.15
155	Barry Jones	.05	.04	.02
156	Chris Hoiles	.15	.11	.06
157	Bobby Ojeda	.06	.05	.02
158	Pedro Guerrero	.08	.06	.03
159	Paul Assenmacher	.05	.04	.02
160	Checklist	.05	.04	.02
161	Mike Macfarlane	.06	.05	.02
162	Craig Lefferts	.06	.05	.02
163	*Brian Hunter*	.20	.15	.08
164	Alan Trammell	.10	.08	.04
165	Ken Griffey,Jr.	.75	.60	.30
166	Lance Parrish	.08	.06	.03
167	Brian Downing	.05	.04	.02
168	John Barfield	.06	.05	.02
169	Jack Clark	.08	.06	.03
170	Chris Nabholz	.06	.05	.02
171	Tim Teufel	.05	.04	.02

		MT	NR MT	EX
172	Chris Hammond	.08	.06	.03
173	Robin Yount	.20	.15	.08
174	Dave Righetti	.08	.06	.03
175	Joe Girardi	.06	.05	.02
176	Mike Boddicker	.06	.05	.02
177	Dean Palmer	.25	.20	.10
178	Greg Hibbard	.06	.05	.02
179	Randy Ready	.05	.04	.02
180	Devon White	.08	.06	.03
181	Mark Eichhorn	.05	.04	.02
182	Mike Felder	.05	.04	.02
183	Joe Klink	.05	.04	.02
184	Steve Bedrosian	.06	.05	.02
185	Barry Larkin	.15	.11	.06
186	John Franco	.08	.06	.03
187	*Ed Sprague*	.15	.11	.06
188	Mark Portugal	.05	.04	.02
189	Jose Lind	.05	.04	.02
190	Bob Welch	.08	.06	.03
191	Alex Fernandez	.25	.20	.10
192	Gary Sheffield	.25	.20	.10
193	Rickey Henderson	.20	.15	.08
194	Rod Nichols	.05	.04	.02
195	*Scott Kamieniecki*	.15	.11	.06
196	Mike Flanagan	.05	.04	.02
197	Steve Finley	.08	.06	.03
198	Darren Daulton	.06	.05	.02
199	Leo Gomez	.15	.11	.06
200	Mike Morgan	.06	.05	.02
201	Bob Tewksbury	.05	.04	.02
202	Sid Bream	.08	.06	.03
203	Sandy Alomar	.15	.11	.06
204	Greg Gagne	.05	.04	.02
205	Juan Berenguer	.05	.04	.02
206	Cecil Fielder	.25	.20	.10
207	Randy Johnson	.08	.06	.03
208	Tony Pena	.06	.05	.02
209	Doug Drabek	.10	.08	.04
210	Wade Boggs	.20	.15	.08
211	Bryan Harvey	.08	.06	.03
212	Jose Vizcaino	.06	.05	.02
213	*Alonzo Powell*(FC)	.15	.11	.06
214	Will Clark	.30	.25	.12
215	Rickey Henderson (HL)	.20	.15	.08
216	Jack Morris	.08	.06	.03
217	Junior Felix	.06	.05	.02
218	Vince Coleman	.08	.06	.03
219	Jimmy Key	.08	.06	.03
220	Alex Cole	.08	.06	.03
221	Bill Landrum	.06	.05	.02
222	Randy Milligan	.08	.06	.03
223	Jose Rijo	.08	.06	.03
224	Greg Vaughn	.10	.08	.04
225	Dave Stewart	.08	.06	.03
226	Lenny Harris	.06	.05	.02
227	Scott Sanderson	.06	.05	.02
228	Jeff Blauser	.06	.05	.02
229	Ozzie Guillen	.08	.06	.03
230	John Kruk	.08	.06	.03
231	Bob Melvin	.05	.04	.02
232	Milt Cuyler	.15	.11	.06
233	Felix Jose	.15	.11	.06
234	Ellis Burks	.10	.08	.04
235	Pete Harnisch	.06	.05	.02
236	Kevin Tapani	.08	.06	.03
237	Terry Pendleton	.08	.06	.03
238	Mark Gardner	.08	.06	.03
239	Harold Reynolds	.06	.05	.02
240	Checklist	.05	.04	.02
241	Mike Harkey	.06	.05	.02
242	Felix Fermin	.05	.04	.02
243	Barry Bonds	.30	.25	.12
244	Roger Clemens	.25	.20	.10
245	Dennis Rasmussen	.05	.04	.02
246	Jose DeLeon	.06	.05	.02
247	Orel Hershiser	.10	.08	.04
248	Mel Hall	.06	.05	.02
249	*Rick Wilkins*	.25	.20	.10
250	Tom Gordon	.08	.06	.03
251	Kevin Reimer	.06	.05	.02
252	Luis Polonia	.06	.05	.02
253	Mike Henneman	.06	.05	.02
254	Tom Pagnozzi	.06	.05	.02
255	Chuck Finley	.10	.08	.04
256	Mackey Sasser	.05	.04	.02
257	John Burkett	.06	.05	.02
258	Hal Morris	.15	.11	.06
259	Larry Walker	.10	.08	.04
260	Billy Swift	.06	.05	.02
261	Joe Oliver	.06	.05	.02
262	Julio Machado	.05	.04	.02
263	Todd Stottlemyre	.08	.06	.03
264	Matt Merullo	.05	.04	.02
265	Brent Mayne	.08	.06	.03
266	Thomas Howard	.06	.05	.02
267	Lance Johnson	.06	.05	.02
268	Terry Mulholland	.08	.06	.03
269	Rick Honeycutt	.05	.04	.02
270	Luis Gonzalez	.25	.20	.10
271	Jose Guzman	.06	.05	.02
272	Jimmy Jones	.05	.04	.02
273	Mark Lewis	.20	.15	.08
274	Rene Gonzales	.05	.04	.02
275	*Jeff Johnson*	.25	.20	.10
276	Dennis Martinez (Highlight)	.10	.08	.04
277	Delino DeShields	.08	.06	.03
278	Sam Horn	.05	.04	.02
279	Kevin Gross	.06	.05	.02
280	Jose Oquendo	.05	.04	.02
281	Mark Grace	.15	.11	.06
282	Mark Gubicza	.08	.06	.03
283	Fred McGriff	.15	.11	.06
284	Ron Gant	.15	.11	.06
285	Lou Whitaker	.08	.06	.03
286	Edgar Martinez	.08	.06	.03
287	Ron Tingley	.05	.04	.02
288	Kevin McReynolds	.08	.06	.03
289	*Ivan Rodriguez*	.30	.25	.12
290	Mike Gardiner	.08	.06	.03
291	*Chris Haney*	.20	.15	.08
292	Darrin Jackson	.06	.05	.02
293	Bill Doran	.08	.06	.03
294	Ted Higuera	.08	.06	.03
295	Jeff Brantley	.08	.06	.03
296	Les Lancaster	.05	.04	.02
297	Jim Eisenreich	.05	.04	.02
298	Ruben Sierra	.10	.08	.04
299	Scott Radinsky	.08	.06	.03
300	Jose DeJesus	.08	.06	.03
301	*Mike Timlin*	.20	.15	.08
302	Luis Sojo	.08	.06	.03
303	Kelly Downs	.05	.04	.02
304	Scott Bankhead	.06	.05	.02
305	Pedro Munoz	.20	.15	.08
306	Scott Scudder	.06	.05	.02
307	Kevin Elster	.06	.05	.02
308	Duane Ward	.06	.05	.02
309	*Darryl Kile*	.15	.11	.06
310	Orlando Merced	.12	.09	.05
311	Dave Henderson	.10	.08	.04
312	Tim Raines	.10	.08	.04
313	Mark Lee(FC)	.06	.05	.02
314	Mike Gallego	.06	.05	.02
315	Charles Nagy	.10	.08	.04
316	Jesse Barfield	.08	.06	.03
317	Todd Frohwirth	.05	.04	.02
318	Al Osuna	.06	.05	.02
319	Darrin Fletcher	.06	.05	.02
320	Checklist	.05	.04	.02
321	David Segui	.10	.08	.04
322	Stan Javier	.05	.04	.02
323	Bryn Smith	.05	.04	.02
324	Jeff Treadway	.06	.05	.02
325	Mark Whiten	.15	.11	.06
326	Kent Hrbek	.08	.06	.03
327	David Justice	.35	.25	.14
328	Tony Phillips	.06	.05	.02
329	Rob Murphy	.05	.04	.02
330	Kevin Morton	.10	.08	.04
331	John Smiley	.08	.06	.03
332	Luis Rivera	.05	.04	.02
333	Wally Joyner	.15	.11	.06
334	*Heathcliff Slocumb*	.15	.11	.06
335	Rick Cerone	.05	.04	.02
336	*Mike Remlinger*(FC)	.15	.11	.06
337	Mike Moore	.06	.05	.02
338	Lloyd McClendon	.05	.04	.02
339	Al Newman	.05	.04	.02
340	Kirk McCaskill	.08	.06	.03
341	Howard Johnson	.15	.11	.06
342	Greg Myers	.05	.04	.02
343	Kal Daniels	.08	.06	.03
344	Bernie Williams	.10	.08	.04
345	Shane Mack	.10	.08	.04
346	Gary Thurman	.05	.04	.02
347	Dante Bichette	.06	.05	.02
348	Mark McGwire	.12	.09	.05
349	Travis Fryman	.25	.20	.10
350	Ray Lankford	.15	.11	.06
351	Mike Jeffcoat	.05	.04	.02
352	Jack McDowell	.10	.08	.04
353	Mitch Williams	.08	.06	.03

		MT	NR MT	EX
354	Mike Devereaux	.06	.05	.02
355	Andre Galarraga	.06	.05	.02
356	Henry Cotto	.05	.04	.02
357	Scott Bailes	.05	.04	.02
358	*Jeff Bagwell*	.30	.25	.12
359	Scott Leius	.08	.06	.03
360	Zane Smith	.06	.05	.02
361	Bill Pecota	.06	.05	.02
362	Tony Fernandez	.08	.06	.03
363	Glenn Braggs	.06	.05	.02
364	Bill Spiers	.06	.05	.02
365	Vicente Palacios	.05	.04	.02
366	Tim Burke	.06	.05	.02
367	Randy Tomlin	.06	.05	.02
368	Kenny Rogers	.06	.05	.02
369	Brett Butler	.08	.06	.03
370	Pat Kelly	.20	.15	.08
371	Bip Roberts	.06	.05	.02
372	Gregg Jefferies	.15	.11	.06
373	Kevin Bass	.06	.05	.02
374	Ron Karkovice	.05	.04	.02
375	Paul Gibson	.05	.04	.02
376	Bernard Gilkey	.10	.08	.04
377	Dave Gallagher	.06	.05	.02
378	Bill Wegman	.06	.05	.02
379	Pat Borders	.06	.05	.02
380	Ed Whitson	.06	.05	.02
381	Gilberto Reyes	.08	.06	.03
382	Russ Swan	.08	.06	.03
383	Andy Van Slyke	.10	.08	.04
384	Wes Chamberlain	.20	.15	.08
385	Steve Chitren	.08	.06	.03
386	Greg Olson	.06	.05	.02
387	Brian McRae	.10	.08	.04
388	Rich Rodriguez	.06	.05	.02
389	Steve Decker	.15	.11	.06
390	Chuck Knoblauch	.12	.09	.05
391	Bobby Witt	.06	.05	.02
392	Eddie Murray	.10	.08	.04
393	Juan Gonzalez	.75	.60	.30
394	Scott Ruskin	.05	.04	.02
395	Jay Howell	.06	.05	.02
396	Checklist	.05	.04	.02
397	Royce Clayton	.20	.15	.08
398	*John Jaha*(FC)	.15	.11	.06
399	Dan Wilson (RR)(FC)	.15	.11	.06
400	*Archie Corbin*	.10	.08	.04
401	*Barry Manuel*	.20	.15	.08
402	Kim Batiste (RR)(FC)	.10	.08	.04
403	*Pat Mahomes*	.15	.11	.06
404	Dave Fleming	.25	.20	.10
405	Jeff Juden	.15	.11	.06
406	*Jim Thome*	.15	.11	.06
407	Sam Militello (RR)(FC)	.10	.08	.04
408	Jeff Nelson (RR)(FC)	.10	.08	.04
409	Anthony Young (RR)	.15	.11	.06
410	Tino Martinez (RR)	.15	.11	.06
411	*Jeff Mutis* (RR)(FC)	.15	.11	.06
412	*Rey Sanchez* (RR)(FC)	.15	.11	.06
413	*Chris Gardner*	.25	.20	.10
414	*John Vander Wal*	.12	.09	.05
415	Reggie Sanders	.15	.11	.06
416	*Brian Williams*	.20	.15	.08
417	Mo Sanford (RR)(FC)	.15	.11	.06
418	*David Weathers*	.15	.11	.06
419	*Hector Fajardo*	.10	.08	.04
420	*Steve Foster*	.10	.08	.04
421	Lance Dickson (RR)	.10	.08	.04
422	Andre Dawson (AS)	.10	.08	.04
423	Ozzie Smith (AS)	.10	.08	.04
424	Chris Sabo (AS)	.08	.06	.03
425	Tony Gwynn (AS)	.10	.08	.04
426	Tom Glavine (AS)	.10	.08	.04
427	Bobby Bonilla (AS)	.10	.08	.04
428	Will Clark (AS)	.15	.11	.06
429	Ryne Sandberg (AS)	.15	.11	.06
430	Benito Santiago (AS)	.08	.06	.03
431	Ivan Calderon (AS)	.08	.06	.03
432	Ozzie Smith	.08	.06	.03
433	Tim Leary	.05	.04	.02
434	Bret Saberhagen (HL)	.08	.06	.03
435	Mel Rojas	.06	.05	.02
436	Ben McDonald	.10	.08	.04
437	Tim Crews	.05	.04	.02
438	Rex Hudler	.05	.04	.02
439	Chico Walker	.05	.04	.02
440	Kurt Stillwell	.05	.04	.02
441	Tony Gwynn	.15	.11	.06
442	John Smoltz	.08	.06	.03
443	Lloyd Moseby	.05	.04	.02
444	Mike Schooler	.06	.05	.02

		MT	NR MT	EX
445	Joe Grahe	.06	.05	.02
446	Dwight Gooden	.10	.08	.04
447	Oil Can Boyd	.05	.04	.02
448	John Marzano	.05	.04	.02
449	Bret Barberie	.10	.08	.04
450	Mike Maddux	.05	.04	.02
451	Jeff Reed	.05	.04	.02
452	Dale Sveum	.05	.04	.02
453	Jose Uribe	.05	.04	.02
454	Bob Scanlan	.05	.04	.02
455	Kevin Appier	.08	.06	.03
456	Jeff Huson	.05	.04	.02
457	Ken Patterson	.05	.04	.02
458	Ricky Jordan	.08	.06	.03
459	Tom Candiotti	.06	.05	.02
460	Lee Stevens	.08	.06	.03
461	*Rod Beck*(FC)	.15	.11	.06
462	Dave Valle	.05	.04	.02
463	Scott Erickson	.25	.20	.10
464	Chris Jones	.06	.05	.02
465	Mark Carreon	.05	.04	.02
466	Rob Ducey	.05	.04	.02
467	Jim Corsi	.05	.04	.02
468	Jeff King	.05	.04	.02
469	Curt Young	.05	.04	.02
470	Bo Jackson	.15	.11	.06
471	Chris Bosio	.06	.05	.02
472	Jamie Quirk	.05	.04	.02
473	Jesse Orosco	.05	.04	.02
474	Alvaro Espinoza	.05	.04	.02
475	Joe Orsulak	.05	.04	.02
476	Checklist	.05	.04	.02
477	Gerald Young	.05	.04	.02
478	Wally Backman	.05	.04	.02
479	Juan Bell	.05	.04	.02
480	Mike Scioscia	.06	.05	.02
481	Omar Olivares	.06	.05	.02
482	Francisco Cabrera	.05	.04	.02
483	Greg Swindell	.08	.06	.03
484	Terry Leach	.05	.04	.02
485	Tommy Gregg	.05	.04	.02
486	Scott Aldred	.05	.04	.02
487	Greg Briley	.05	.04	.02
488	Phil Plantier	.20	.15	.08
489	Curtis Wilkerson	.05	.04	.02
490	Tom Brunansky	.06	.05	.02
491	Mike Fetters	.05	.04	.02
492	Frank Castillo	.08	.06	.03
493	Joe Boever	.05	.04	.02
494	Kirt Manwaring	.05	.04	.02
495	Wilson Alvarez (HL)	.06	.05	.02
496	Gene Larkin	.05	.04	.02
497	Gary DiSarcina	.06	.05	.02
498	Frank Viola	.08	.06	.03
499	Manuel Lee	.05	.04	.02
500	Albert Belle	.25	.20	.10
501	Stan Belinda	.05	.04	.02
502	Dwight Evans	.06	.05	.02
503	Eric Davis	.10	.08	.04
504	Darren Holmes	.05	.04	.02
505	Mike Bordick	.12	.09	.05
506	Dave Hansen	.06	.05	.02
507	Lee Guetterman	.05	.04	.02
508	*Keith Mitchell*(FC)	.15	.11	.06
509	Melido Perez	.05	.04	.02
510	Dickie Thon	.05	.04	.02
511	Mark Williamson	.05	.04	.02
512	Mark Salas	.05	.04	.02
513	Milt Thompson	.05	.04	.02
514	Mo Vaughn	.20	.15	.08
515	Jim Deshaies	.05	.04	.02
516	Rich Garces	.05	.04	.02
517	Lonnie Smith	.05	.04	.02
518	Spike Owen	.06	.05	.02
519	Tracy Jones	.05	.04	.02
520	Greg Maddux	.08	.06	.03
521	Carlos Martinez	.05	.04	.02
522	Neal Heaton	.05	.04	.02
523	Mike Greenwell	.08	.06	.03
524	Andy Benes	.08	.06	.03
525	Jeff Schaefer	.05	.04	.02
526	Mike Sharperson	.06	.05	.02
527	Wade Taylor	.06	.05	.02
528	Jerome Walton	.06	.05	.02
529	Storm Davis	.05	.04	.02
530	*Jose Hernandez*	.10	.08	.04
531	Mark Langston	.08	.06	.03
532	Rob Deer	.06	.05	.02
533	Geronimo Pena	.06	.05	.02
534	*Juan Guzman*	.25	.20	.10
535	Pete Schourek	.08	.06	.03

		MT	NR MT	EX
536	Todd Benzinger	.05	.04	.02
537	Billy Hatcher	.05	.04	.02
538	Tom Foley	.05	.04	.02
539	Dave Cochrane	.05	.04	.02
540	Mariano Duncan	.05	.04	.02
541	Edwin Nunez	.05	.04	.02
542	Rance Mulliniks	.05	.04	.02
543	Carlton Fisk	.10	.08	.04
544	Luis Aquino	.05	.04	.02
545	Ricky Bones	.08	.06	.03
546	Craig Grebeck	.05	.04	.02
547	Charlie Hayes	.06	.05	.02
548	Jose Canseco	.15	.11	.06
549	Andujar Cedeno	.10	.08	.04
550	Geno Petralli	.05	.04	.02
551	Javier Ortiz	.05	.04	.02
552	Rudy Seanez	.06	.05	.02
553	Rich Gedman	.05	.04	.02
554	Eric Plunk	.05	.04	.02
555	Nolan Ryan, Rich Gossage (HL)	.20	.15	.08
556	Checklist	.05	.04	.02
557	Greg Colbrunn	.06	.05	.02
558	*Chito Martinez*(FC)	.20	.15	.08
559	Darryl Strawberry	.20	.15	.08
560	Luis Alicea	.05	.04	.02
561	Dwight Smith	.06	.05	.02
562	Terry Shumpert	.05	.04	.02
563	Jim Vatcher	.05	.04	.02
564	Deion Sanders	.08	.06	.03
565	Walt Terrell	.05	.04	.02
566	Dave Burba	.05	.04	.02
567	Dave Howard	.05	.04	.02
568	Todd Hundley	.08	.06	.03
569	Jack Daugherty	.05	.04	.02
570	Scott Cooper	.10	.08	.04
571	Bill Sampen	.05	.04	.02
572	Jose Melendez	.10	.08	.04
573	Freddie Benavides	.05	.04	.02
574	Jim Gantner	.05	.04	.02
575	Trevor Wilson	.05	.04	.02
576	Ryne Sandberg	.20	.15	.08
577	Kevin Seitzer	.05	.04	.02
578	Gerald Alexander	.05	.04	.02
579	Mike Huff	.05	.04	.02
580	Von Hayes	.06	.05	.02
581	Derek Bell	.30	.25	.12
582	Mike Stanley	.05	.04	.02
583	Kevin Mitchell	.08	.06	.03
584	Mike Jackson	.05	.04	.02
585	Dan Gladden	.05	.04	.02
586	Ted Power	.05	.04	.02
587	Jeff Innis	.05	.04	.02
588	Bob MacDonald	.08	.06	.03
589	*Jose Tolentino*(FC)	.08	.06	.03
590	Bob Patterson	.05	.04	.02
591	*Scott Brosius*(FC)	.10	.08	.04
592	Frank Thomas	1.00	.70	.40
593	Darryl Hamilton	.08	.06	.03
594	Kirk Dressendorfer	.08	.06	.03
595	Jeff Shaw	.08	.06	.03
596	Don Mattingly	.12	.09	.05
597	Glenn Davis	.06	.05	.02
598	Andy Mota	.10	.08	.04
599	Jason Grimsley	.05	.04	.02
600	Jimmy Poole	.06	.05	.02
601	Jim Gott	.05	.04	.02
602	Stan Royer	.08	.06	.03
603	Marvin Freeman	.05	.04	.02
604	Denis Boucher	.08	.06	.03
605	Denny Neagle	.10	.08	.04
606	Mark Lemke	.06	.05	.02
607	Jerry Don Gleaton	.05	.04	.02
608	Brent Knackert	.05	.04	.02
609	Carlos Quintana	.05	.04	.02
610	Bobby Bonilla	.12	.09	.05
611	Joe Hesketh	.05	.04	.02
612	Daryl Boston	.05	.04	.02
613	Shawon Dunston	.08	.06	.03
614	Danny Cox	.05	.04	.02
615	Darren Lewis	.12	.09	.05
616	Alejandro Pena, Kent Mercker, Mark Wohlers (HL)	.10	.08	.04
617	Kirby Puckett	.15	.11	.06
618	Franklin Stubbs	.05	.04	.02
619	Chris Donnels	.10	.08	.04
620	David Wells	.05	.04	.02
621	Mike Aldrete	.05	.04	.02
622	Bob Kipper	.05	.04	.02
623	Anthony Telford	.05	.04	.02
624	Randy Myers	.05	.04	.02
625	Willie Randolph	.05	.04	.02

		MT	NR MT	EX
626	Joe Slusarski	.08	.06	.03
627	John Wetteland	.06	.05	.02
628	Greg Cadaret	.05	.04	.02
629	Tom Glavine	.10	.08	.04
630	Wilson Alvarez	.10	.08	.04
631	Wally Ritchie	.05	.04	.02
632	Mike Mussina	.35	.25	.14
633	Mark Leiter	.05	.04	.02
634	Gerald Perry	.05	.04	.02
635	Matt Young	.05	.04	.02
636	Checklist	.05	.04	.02
637	Scott Hemond	.05	.04	.02
638	David West	.05	.04	.02
639	Jim Clancy	.05	.04	.02
640	Doug Piatt(FC)	.10	.08	.04
641	Omar Vizquel	.05	.04	.02
642	Rick Sutcliffe	.08	.06	.03
643	Glenallen Hill	.08	.06	.03
644	Gary Varsho	.05	.04	.02
645	Tony Fossas	.05	.04	.02
646	Jack Howell	.05	.04	.02
647	*Jim Campanis*(FC)	.15	.11	.06
648	Chris Gwynn	.05	.04	.02
649	Jim Leyritz	.05	.04	.02
650	Chuck McElroy	.05	.04	.02
651	Sean Berry(FC)	.08	.06	.03
652	Donald Harris(FC)	.10	.08	.04
653	Don Slaught	.05	.04	.02
654	*Rusty Meacham*	.10	.08	.04
655	Scott Terry	.05	.04	.02
656	Ramon Martinez	.12	.09	.05
657	Keith Miller	.05	.04	.02
658	Ramon Garcia(FC)	.08	.06	.03
659	*Milt Hill*(FC)	.10	.08	.04
660	Steve Frey	.05	.04	.02
661	Bob McClure	.05	.04	.02
662	*Ced Landrum*	.08	.06	.03
663	*Doug Henry*	.15	.11	.06
664	Candy Maldonado	.05	.04	.02
665	Carl Willis	.05	.04	.02
666	Jeff Montgomery	.08	.06	.03
667	*Craig Shipley*(FC)	.10	.08	.04
668	*Warren Newson*	.08	.06	.03
669	Mickey Morandini	.08	.06	.03
670	Brook Jacoby	.05	.04	.02
671	*Ryan Bowen*	.10	.08	.04
672	Bill Krueger	.05	.04	.02
673	Rob Mallicoat	.05	.04	.02
674	Doug Jones	.05	.04	.02
675	Scott Livingstone	.10	.08	.04
676	Danny Tartabull	.10	.08	.04
677	Joe Carter (HL)	.08	.06	.03
678	Cecil Espy	.05	.04	.02
679	Randy Velarde	.05	.04	.02
680	Bruce Ruffin	.05	.04	.02
681	*Ted Wood*	.10	.08	.04
682	Dan Plesac	.05	.04	.02
683	Eric Bullock	.05	.04	.02
684	Junior Ortiz	.05	.04	.02
685	Dave Hollins	.06	.05	.02
686	Dennis Martinez	.08	.06	.03
687	Larry Andersen	.05	.04	.02
688	Doug Simons	.05	.04	.02
689	*Tim Spehr*	.08	.06	.03
690	*Calvin Jones*(FC)	.12	.09	.05
691	Mark Guthrie	.05	.04	.02
692	Alfredo Griffin	.05	.04	.02
693	Joe Carter	.12	.09	.05
694	*Terry Mathews*(FC)	.08	.06	.03
695	Pascual Perez	.05	.04	.02
696	Gene Nelson	.05	.04	.02
697	Gerald Williams	.15	.11	.06
698	*Chris Cron*(FC)	.15	.11	.06
699	Steve Buechele	.06	.05	.02
700	Paul McClellan(FC)	.08	.06	.03
701	Jim Lindeman	.05	.04	.02
702	Francisco Oliveras	.05	.04	.02
703	*Rob Maurer*	.25	.20	.10
704	*Pat Hentgen*	.35	.25	.14
705	Jaime Navarro	.06	.05	.02
706	*Mike Magnante*(FC)	.10	.08	.04
707	Nolan Ryan	.30	.25	.12
708	Bobby Thigpen	.08	.06	.03
709	John Cerutti	.05	.04	.02
710	Steve Wilson	.05	.04	.02
711	Hensley Meulens	.08	.06	.03
712	*Rheal Cormier*(FC)	.20	.15	.08
713	Scott Bradley	.05	.04	.02
714	Mitch Webster	.05	.04	.02
715	Roger Mason	.05	.04	.02
716	Checklist	.05	.04	.02

		MT	NR MT	EX
717	*Jeff Fassero*	.08	.06	.03
718	Cal Eldred	.20	.15	.08
719	Sid Fernandez	.08	.06	.03
720	*Bob Zupcic*	.15	.11	.06
721	Jose Offerman	.08	.06	.03
722	*Cliff Brantley*	.20	.15	.08
723	Ron Darling	.06	.05	.02
724	Dave Stieb	.06	.05	.02
725	Hector Villanueva	.06	.05	.02
726	Mike Hartley	.05	.04	.02
727	*Arthur Rhodes*	.15	.11	.06
728	Randy Bush	.05	.04	.02
729	Steve Sax	.08	.06	.03
730	Dave Otto	.05	.04	.02
731	*John Wehner*	.10	.08	.04
732	Dave Martinez	.05	.04	.02
733	*Ruben Amaro*	.10	.08	.04
734	Billy Ripken	.05	.04	.02
735	Steve Farr	.05	.04	.02
736	Shawn Abner	.05	.04	.02
737	*Gil Heredia*(FC)	.10	.08	.04
738	Ron Jones	.05	.04	.02
739	Tony Castillo	.05	.04	.02
740	Sammy Sosa	.08	.06	.03
741	Julio Franco	.08	.06	.03
742	Tim Naehring	.08	.06	.03
743	*Steve Wapnick*(FC)	.10	.08	.04
744	Craig Wilson	.08	.06	.03
745	*Darrin Chapin*(FC)	.15	.11	.06
746	*Chris George*(FC)	.08	.06	.03
747	Mike Simms	.08	.06	.03
748	Rosario Rodriguez	.08	.06	.03
749	Skeeter Barnes	.05	.04	.02
750	Roger McDowell	.05	.04	.02
751	Dann Howitt	.05	.04	.02
752	Paul Sorrento	.05	.04	.02
753	*Braulio Castillo*(FC)	.15	.11	.06
754	*Yorkis Perez*(FC)	.15	.11	.06
755	Willie Fraser	.05	.04	.02
756	*Jeremy Hernandez*(FC)	.10	.08	.04
757	Curt Schilling	.05	.04	.02
758	Steve Lyons	.05	.04	.02
759	Dave Anderson	.05	.04	.02
760	Willie Banks	.12	.09	.05
761	Mark Leonard	.05	.04	.02
762	Jack Armstrong	.06	.05	.02
763	Scott Servais	.08	.06	.03
764	Ray Stephens	.08	.06	.03
765	Junior Noboa	.05	.04	.02
766	*Jim Olander*(FC)	.10	.08	.04
767	Joe Magrane	.06	.05	.02
768	Lance Blankenship	.05	.04	.02
769	*Mike Humphreys*(FC)	.10	.08	.04
770	*Jarvis Brown*(FC)	.12	.09	.05
771	Damon Berryhill	.05	.04	.02
772	Alejandro Pena	.06	.05	.02
773	Jose Mesa	.05	.04	.02
774	*Gary Cooper*(FC)	.10	.08	.04
775	Carney Lansford	.06	.05	.02
776	Mike Bielecki	.05	.04	.02
777	Charlie O'Brien	.05	.04	.02
778	Carlos Hernandez	.05	.04	.02
779	Howard Farmer	.05	.04	.02
780	Mike Stanton	.05	.04	.02
781	Reggie Harris	.05	.04	.02
782	Xavier Hernandez	.05	.04	.02
783	*Bryan Hickerson*(FC)	.10	.08	.04
784	Checklist	.05	.04	.02

True Mint condition cards issued prior to 1980 will sell at a significant premium over the listed Near Mint price. Mint specimens may be worth 20% to 100% more than the Near Mint price shown.

1992 Donruss Bonus Cards

These eight bonus cards were randomly inserted in 1992 foil packs and are numbered with a BC prefix. Both leagues' Cy Young and Rookie of the Year award winners are featured, as are cards for the new expansion teams, the Colorado Rockies and the Florida Marlins. A Cal Ripken MVP card is also included. Cards are standard size.

		MT	NR MT	EX
Complete Set (8):		1.50	1.00	.60
Common Player		.15	.10	.05
1	Cal Ripken, Jr. (MVP)	.20	.15	.08
2	Terry Pendleton (MVP)	.15	.10	.05
3	Roger Clemens (CY)	.30	.20	.10
4	Tom Glavine (CY)	.30	.20	.10
5	Chuck Knoblauch (ROY)	.20	.15	.08
6	Jeff Bagwell (ROY)	.50	.40	.20
7	Colorado Rockies	.50	.40	.20
8	Florida Marlins	.50	.40	.20

1992 Donruss Diamond Kings

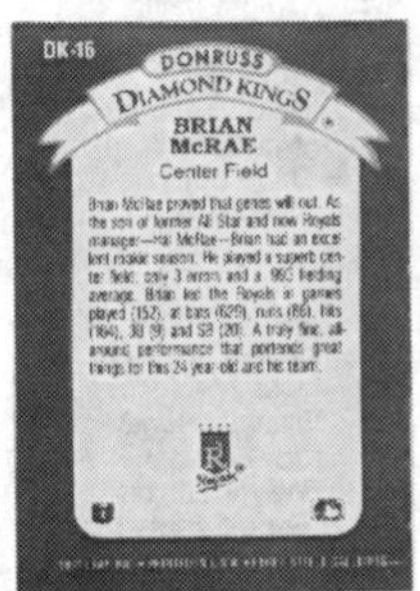

Donruss changed its Diamond Kings style and distribution in 1992. The cards still featured the art of Dick Perez, but quality was improved from past years. The cards were randomly inserted in foil packs. One player from each team is featured. Card numbers have a DK prefix.

		MT	NR MT	EX
Complete Set (27):		30.00	20.00	10.00
Complete Series 1 (14):		20.00	12.00	6.00
Complete Series 2 (13):		10.00	6.00	3.00
Common Player:		.75	.50	.25
1	Paul Molitor	2.50	2.00	1.00
2	Will Clark	2.50	1.50	.75
3	Joe Carter	2.50	2.00	1.00
4	Julio Franco	.75	.50	.25
5	Cal Ripken, Jr.	3.50	2.00	1.00
6	Dave Justice	3.00	2.00	1.00
7	George Bell	.75	.50	.25
8	Frank Thomas	9.00	6.00	3.00
9	Wade Boggs	1.25	.75	.40
10	Scott Sanderson	.75	.50	.25
11	Jeff Bagwell	3.00	2.00	1.00
12	John Kruk	1.25	.75	.40
13	Felix Jose	.75	.50	.25
14	Harold Baines	.75	.50	.25
15	Dwight Gooden	.75	.50	.25
16	Brian McRae	.90	.60	.30
17	Jay Bell	.75	.50	.25
18	Brett Butler	.75	.50	.25
19	Hal Morris	.75	.50	.25
20	Mark Langston	.75	.50	.25
21	Scott Erickson	.75	.50	.25
22	Randy Johnson	1.00	.60	.30
23	Greg Swindell	.75	.50	.25
24	Dennis Martinez	.75	.50	.25
25	Tony Phillips	.75	.50	.25
26	Fred McGriff	2.50	2.00	1.00
27	Checklist	.50	.30	.15

A card number in parentheses () indicates the set is unnumbered.

1992 Donruss Elite

Donruss continued its Elite series in 1992 by inserting cards in foil packs. Each card was released in the same quantity as the 1991 cards - 10,000 Elite, 7,500 Legend and 5,000 Signature. The Elite cards, now featuring a prismatic border, are numbered as a continuation of the 1991 issue Rickey Henderson and Cal Ripken are the subjects of the Legend card and Signature card, respectively.

		MT	NR MT	EX
Complete Set (12):		1400.00	1000.00	400.00
Common Player:		30.00	22.00	12.00
9	Wade Boggs	60.00	45.00	24.00
10	Joe Carter	70.00	52.00	28.00
11	Will Clark	100.00	75.00	40.00
12	Dwight Gooden	40.00	30.00	16.00
13	Ken Griffey, Jr.	200.00	150.00	80.00
14	Tony Gwynn	60.00	45.00	24.00
15	Howard Johnson	30.00	22.00	12.00
16	Terry Pendleton	40.00	30.00	16.00
17	Kirby Puckett	120.00	90.00	48.00
18	Frank Thomas	250.00	187.00	100.00
----	Rickey Henderson (Legend)	125.00	90.00	45.00
----	Cal Ripken (Signature)	400.00	300.00	120.00

1992 Donruss Rookies

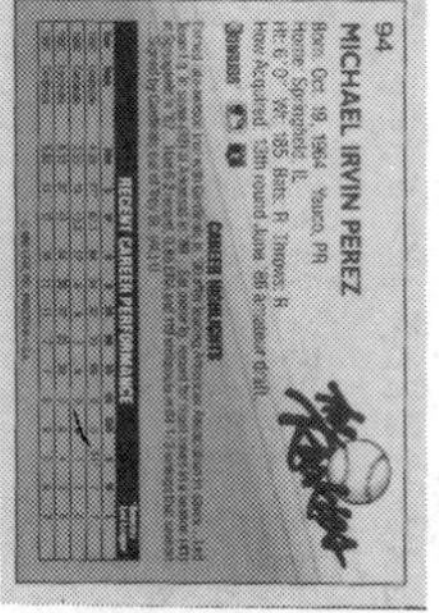

Donruss increased the size of its Rookies set in 1992 to include 132 cards. In the past the cards were released only in boxed set form, but the 1992 cards were available in packs. Special phenoms insert cards were randomly inserted into Rookies packs. The phenoms cards feature black borders, while the Rookies cards are styled after the regular 1992 Donruss issue. The cards are numbered alphabetically.

		MT	NR MT	EX
Complete Set (132):		15.00	11.00	6.00
Common Player:		.08	.06	.03
1	Kyle Abbott	.08	.06	.03
2	Troy Afenir	.08	.06	.03
3	Rich Amaral(FC)	.12	.09	.05
4	Ruben Amaro(FC)	.12	.09	.05
5	Billy Ashley(FC)	.50	.40	.20
6	Pedro Astacio(FC)	.25	.20	.10
7	Jim Austin(FC)	.08	.06	.03
8	Robert Ayrault(FC)	.10	.08	.04
9	Kevin Baez(FC)	.10	.08	.04
10	Estaban Beltre	.08	.06	.03
11	Brian Bohanon(FC)	.08	.06	.03
12	Kent Bottenfield(FC)	.12	.09	.05
13	Jeff Branson(FC)	.20	.15	.08
14	Brad Brink	.08	.06	.03
15	John Briscoe(FC)	.10	.08	.04
16	Doug Brocail(FC)	.10	.08	.04
17	Rico Brogna(FC)	.15	.11	.06
18	J.T. Bruett(FC)	.15	.11	.06
19	Jacob Brumfield	.12	.09	.05
20	Jim Bullinger(FC)	.12	.09	.05
21	Kevin Campbell(FC)	.08	.06	.03
22	Pedro Castellano(FC)	.20	.15	.08
23	Mike Christopher(FC)	.08	.06	.03
24	Archi Cianfrocco(FC)	.40	.30	.15
25	Mark Clark(FC)	.12	.09	.05
26	Craig Colbert(FC)	.08	.06	.03
27	Victor Cole(FC)	.12	.09	.05
28	Steve Cooke(FC)	.12	.09	.05
29	Tim Costo(FC)	.15	.11	.06
30	Chad Curtis(FC)	.60	.45	.25
31	Doug Davis(FC)	.10	.08	.04
32	Gary DiSarcina	.08	.06	.03
33	John Doherty(FC)	.10	.08	.04
34	Mike Draper(FC)	.20	.15	.08
35	Monty Fariss	.08	.06	.03
36	Bien Figueroa(FC)	.10	.08	.04
37	John Flaherty(FC)	.08	.06	.03
38	Tim Fortugno(FC)	.10	.08	.04
39	Eric Fox(FC)	.10	.08	.04
40	Jeff Frye(FC)	.10	.08	.04
41	Ramon Garcia(FC)	.12	.09	.05
42	Brent Gates(FC)	.50	.25	.14
43	Tom Goodwin(FC)	.10	.08	.04
44	Buddy Groom(FC)	.12	.09	.05
45	Jeff Grotewold(FC)	.20	.15	.08
46	Juan Guerrero(FC)	.20	.15	.08
47	Johnny Guzman(FC)	.10	.08	.04
48	Shawn Hare(FC)	.12	.09	.05
49	Ryan Hawblitzel(FC)	.20	.15	.08
50	Bert Heffernan(FC)	.08	.06	.03
51	Butch Henry(FC)	.10	.08	.04
52	Cesar Hernandez(FC)	.10	.08	.04
53	Vince Horsman(FC)	.10	.08	.04
54	Steve Hosey(FC)	.10	.08	.04
55	Pat Howell(FC)	.10	.08	.04
56	Peter Hoy(FC)	.10	.08	.04
57	Jon Hurst(FC)	.10	.08	.04
58	Mark Hutton(FC)	.30	.25	.12
59	Shawn Jeter(FC)	.12	.09	.05
60	Joel Johnston(FC)	.08	.06	.03
61	Jeff Kent(FC)	.30	.25	.12
62	Kurt Knudsen(FC)	.08	.06	.03
63	Kevin Koslofski(FC)	.20	.15	.08
64	Danny Leon(FC)	.10	.08	.04
65	Jesse Levis(FC)	.20	.15	.08
66	Tom Marsh(FC)	.10	.08	.04
67	Ed Martel(FC)	.10	.08	.04
68	Al Martin(FC)	.50	.40	.20
69	Pedro Martinez(FC)	.25	.20	.10
70	Derrick May	.10	.08	.04
71	Matt Maysey	.12	.09	.05
72	Russ McGinnis	.08	.06	.03
73	Tim McIntosh	.08	.06	.03
74	Jim McNamara(FC)	.08	.06	.03
75	Jeff McNeely(FC)	.30	.25	.12
76	Rusty Meacham	.08	.06	.03
77	Tony Melendez(FC)	.10	.08	.04
78	Henry Mercedes(FC)	.10	.08	.04
79	Paul Miller(FC)	.10	.08	.04
80	Joe Millette(FC)	.10	.08	.04
81	Blas Minor(FC)	.10	.08	.04
82	Dennis Moeller(FC)	.10	.08	.04
83	Raul Mondesi(FC)	.35	.25	.14
84	Rob Natal(FC)	.20	.15	.08
85	Troy Neel(FC)	.25	.20	.10
86	David Nied(FC)	1.00	.60	.30
87	Jerry Nielsen(FC)	.20	.15	.08
88	Donovan Osborne(FC)	.25	.20	.10
89	John Patterson(FC)	.12	.09	.05
90	Roger Pavlik(FC)	.10	.08	.04
91	Dan Peltier(FC)	.20	.15	.08
92	Jim Pena(FC)	.10	.08	.04
93	William Pennyfeather(FC)	.30	.25	.12
94	Mike Perez	.08	.06	.03
95	Hipolito Pichardo(FC)	.20	.15	.08

		MT	NR MT	EX
96	Greg Pirkl(FC)	.08	.06	.03
97	Harvey Pulliam(FC)	.08	.06	.03
98	Manny Ramirez(FC)	.50	.40	.20
99	Pat Rapp(FC)	.12	.09	.05
100	Jeff Reboulet(FC)	.10	.08	.04
101	Darren Reed(FC)	.10	.08	.04
102	Shane Reynolds(FC)	.10	.08	.04
103	Bill Risley(FC)	.10	.08	.04
104	Ben Rivera(FC)	.10	.08	.04
105	Henry Rodriguez(FC)	.10	.08	.04
106	Rico Rossy(FC)	.10	.08	.04
107	Johnny Ruffin(FC)	.10	.08	.04
108	Steve Scarsone(FC)	.20	.15	.08
109	Tim Scott(FC)	.08	.06	.03
110	Steve Shifflett(FC)	.10	.08	.04
111	Dave Silvestri(FC)	.20	.15	.08
112	Matt Stairs(FC)	.08	.06	.03
113	William Suero(FC)	.08	.06	.03
114	Jeff Tackett(FC)	.10	.08	.04
115	Eddie Taubensee(FC)	.12	.09	.05
116	Rick Trlicek(FC)	.10	.08	.04
117	Scooter Tucker(FC)	.10	.08	.04
118	Shane Turner(FC)	.10	.08	.04
119	Julio Valera(FC)	.10	.08	.04
120	Paul Wagner(FC)	.10	.08	.04
121	Tim Wakefield(FC)	.25	.15	.10
122	Mike Walker(FC)	.08	.06	.03
123	Bruce Walton(FC)	.08	.06	.03
124	Lenny Webster	.08	.06	.03
125	Bob Wickman(FC)	.50	.40	.20
126	Mike Williams(FC)	.10	.08	.04
127	Kerry Woodson(FC)	.10	.08	.04
128	Eric Young(FC)	.12	.09	.05
129	Kevin Young(FC)	.50	.40	.20
130	Pete Young(FC)	.10	.08	.04
131	Checklist	.08	.06	.03
132	Checklist	.08	.06	.03

1992 Donruss Rookie Phenoms

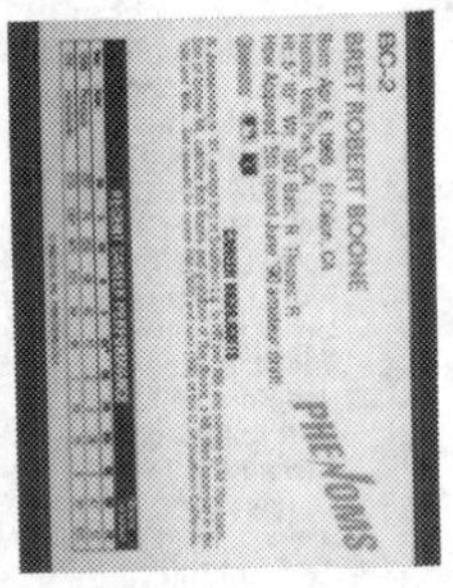

The first 12 cards in this insert set were available in Donruss Rookies foil packs. Cards 13-20 were found randomly packed in jumbo packs. Predominantly black on both front and back, the borders are highlighted with gold. A gold-foil "Phenoms" appears at top front.

		MT	NR MT	EX
	Complete Set (20):	50.00	37.00	20.00
	Common Player:	.50	.40	.20
1	Moises Alou	2.00	1.50	.80
2	Bret Boone	1.50	1.25	.60
3	Jeff Conine	2.50	2.00	1.00
4	Dave Fleming	2.00	1.50	.80
5	Tyler Green	1.00	.70	.40
6	Eric Karros	3.00	2.25	1.25
7	Pat Listach	1.50	1.25	.60
8	Kenny Lofton	4.00	3.00	1.50
9	Mike Piazza	18.00	13.50	7.25
10	Tim Salmon	10.00	7.50	4.00
11	Andy Stankiewicz	.50	.40	.20
12	Dan Walters	.50	.40	.20
13	Ramon Caraballo	1.00	.70	.40
14	Brian Jordan	2.00	1.50	.80
15	Ryan Klesko	4.00	3.00	1.50
16	Sam Militello	1.00	.70	.40
17	Frank Seminara	1.00	.70	.40
18	Salomon Torres	3.00	2.25	1.25
19	John Valentin	2.00	1.50	.80
20	Wil Cordero	1.50	1.25	.60

1992 Donruss Triple Play

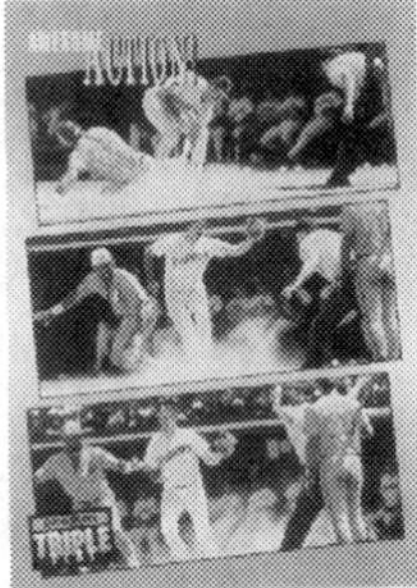

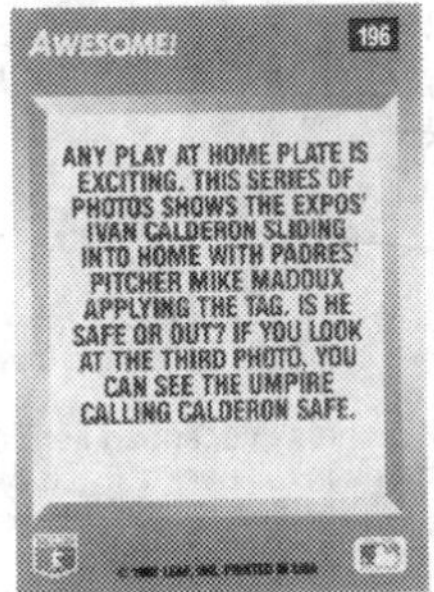

This 264-card set was released in wax pack form only by Donruss. The cards feature red borders and mark the first release of its kind by Donruss. Boyhood photos, mascots and ballparks are among the featured cards. This set was designed to give collectors an alternative product to the high end card sets. The cards are standard sized.

		MT	NR MT	EX
	Complete Set (264):	12.00	9.00	4.75
	Common Player:	.05	.04	.02
1	SkyDome	.05	.04	.02
2	Tom Foley	.05	.04	.02
3	Scott Erickson	.20	.15	.08
4	Matt Williams	.15	.11	.06
5	Dave Valle	.05	.04	.02
6	Andy Van Slyke (Little Hotshot)	.08	.06	.03
7	Tom Glavine	.15	.11	.06
8	Kevin Appier	.08	.06	.03
9	Pedro Guerrero	.08	.06	.03
10	Terry Steinbach	.06	.05	.02
11	Terry Mulholland	.06	.05	.02
12	Mike Boddicker	.05	.04	.02
13	Gregg Olson	.12	.09	.05
14	Tim Burke	.05	.04	.02
15	Candy Maldonado	.05	.04	.02
16	Orlando Merced	.15	.11	.06
17	Robin Ventura	.15	.10	.05
18	Eric Anthony	.10	.08	.04
19	Greg Maddux	.12	.09	.05
20	Erik Hanson	.06	.05	.02
21	Bob Ojeda	.05	.04	.02
22	Nolan Ryan	.40	.30	.15
23	Dave Righetti	.06	.05	.02
24	Reggie Jefferson	.20	.15	.08
25	Jody Reed	.06	.05	.02
26	Awesome Action 1 (Steve Finley/ Gary Carter)	.05	.04	.02
27	Chili Davis	.05	.04	.02
28	Hector Villanueva	.05	.04	.02
29	Cecil Fielder	.20	.15	.10
30	Hal Morris	.12	.09	.05
31	Barry Larkin	.15	.11	.06
32	Bobby Thigpen	.12	.09	.05
33	Andy Benes	.12	.09	.05
34	Harold Baines	.08	.06	.03
35	David Cone	.12	.09	.05
36	Mark Langston	.08	.06	.03
37	Bryan Harvey	.08	.06	.03
38	John Kruk	.12	.09	.05
39	Scott Sanderson	.05	.04	.02
40	Lonnie Smith	.06	.05	.02
41	Awesome Action 2 (Rex Hudler)	.05	.04	.02
42	George Bell	.08	.06	.03
43	Steve Finley	.06	.05	.02
44	Mickey Tettleton	.08	.06	.03
45	Robby Thompson	.05	.04	.02
46	Pat Kelly	.10	.08	.04
47	Marquis Grissom	.12	.09	.05
48	Tony Pena	.05	.04	.02

		MT	NR MT	EX
49	Alex Cole	.05	.04	.02
50	Steve Buechele	.05	.04	.02
51	Ivan Rodriguez	.25	.15	.08
52	John Smiley	.05	.04	.02
53	Gary Sheffield	.20	.15	.08
54	Greg Olson	.08	.06	.03
55	Ramon Martinez	.08	.06	.03
56	B.J. Surhoff	.08	.06	.03
57	Bruce Hurst	.06	.05	.02
58	Todd Stottlemyre	.05	.04	.02
59	Brett Butler	.06	.05	.02
60	Glenn Davis	.10	.08	.04
61	Awesome Action 3 (Glenn Braggs/ Kirt Manwaring)	.05	.04	.02
62	Lee Smith	.08	.06	.03
63	Rickey Henderson	.15	.10	.05
64	Fun at the Ballpark	.05	.04	.02
65	Rick Aguilera	.05	.04	.02
66	Kevin Elster	.05	.04	.02
67	Dwight Evans	.08	.06	.03
68	Andujar Cedeno	.15	.11	.06
69	Brian McRae	.15	.11	.06
70	Benito Santiago	.12	.09	.05
71	Randy Johnson	.06	.05	.02
72	Roberto Kelly	.12	.09	.05
73	Awesome Action 4 (Juan Samuel)			
74	Alex Fernandez	.15	.11	.06
75	Felix Jose	.15	.11	.06
76	Brian Harper	.06	.05	.02
77	Scott Sanderson (Little Hotshot)	.05	.04	.02
78	Ken Caminiti	.06	.05	.02
79	Mo Vaughn	.15	.11	.06
80	Roger McDowell	.05	.04	.02
81	Robin Yount	.12	.09	.05
82	Dave Magadan	.06	.05	.02
83	Julio Franco	.12	.09	.05
84	Roberto Alomar	.25	.15	.06
85	Steve Avery	.20	.15	.08
86	Travis Fryman	.30	.25	.12
87	Fred McGriff	.15	.11	.06
88	Dave Stewart	.06	.05	.02
89	Larry Walker	.15	.11	.06
90	Chris Sabo	.15	.11	.06
91	Chuck Finley	.06	.05	.02
92	Dennis Martinez	.06	.05	.02
93	Jeff Johnson	.06	.05	.02
94	Len Dykstra	.15	.11	.06
95	Mark Whiten	.08	.06	.03
96	Wade Taylor	.08	.06	.03
97	Lance Dickson	.08	.06	.03
98	Kevin Tapani	.06	.05	.02
99	Awesome Action 5 (Luis Polonia/ Tony Phillips)	.05	.04	.02
100	Milt Cuyler	.05	.04	.02
101	Willie McGee	.05	.04	.02
102	Awesome Action 6 (Tony Fernandez)	.05	.04	.02
103	Albert Belle	.25	.20	.10
104	Todd Hundley	.08	.06	.03
105	Ben McDonald	.15	.11	.06
106	Doug Drabek	.12	.09	.05
107	Tim Raines	.06	.05	.02
108	Joe Carter	.12	.09	.05
109	Reggie Sanders	.20	.15	.08
110	John Olerud	.25	.15	.06
111	Darren Lewis	.15	.11	.06
112	Juan Gonzalez	.75	.40	.20
113	Awesome Action 7 (Andre Dawson)	.05	.04	.02
114	Mark Grace	.12	.09	.05
115	George Brett	.12	.09	.05
116	Barry Bonds	.30	.20	.10
117	Lou Whitaker	.06	.05	.02
118	Jose Oquendo	.05	.04	.02
119	Lee Stevens	.06	.05	.02
120	Phil Plantier	.15	.10	.05
121	Awesome Action 8 (Matt Merullo)	.05	.04	.02
122	Greg Vaughn	.12	.09	.05
123	Royce Clayton	.25	.20	.10
124	Bob Welch	.06	.05	.02
125	Juan Samuel	.05	.04	.02
126	Ron Gant	.20	.15	.08
127	Edgar Martinez	.08	.06	.03
128	Andy Ashby	.08	.06	.03
129	Jack McDowell	.08	.06	.03
130	Awesome Action 9 (Dave Henderson/ Jerry Browne)	.05	.04	.02
131	Leo Gomez	.12	.09	.05
132	Checklist	.05	.04	.02
133	Phillie Mascot	.05	.04	.02
134	Bret Barbarie	.08	.06	.03
135	Kent Hrbek	.06	.05	.02

		MT	NR MT	EX
136	Hall Of Fame	.05	.04	.02
137	Omar Vizquel	.05	.04	.02
138	The Chicken	.05	.04	.02
139	Terry Pendleton	.08	.06	.03
140	Jim Eisenreich	.05	.04	.02
141	Todd Zeile	.06	.05	.02
142	Todd Van Poppel	.20	.15	.08
143	Darren Daulton	.08	.06	.03
144	Mike Macfarlane	.05	.04	.02
145	Luis Mercedes	.20	.15	.08
146	Trevor Wilson	.05	.04	.02
147	Dave Steib	.05	.04	.02
148	Andy Van Slyke	.08	.06	.03
149	Carlton Fisk	.15	.11	.06
150	Craig Biggio	.08	.06	.03
151	Joe Girardi	.05	.04	.02
152	Ken Griffey, Jr.	.75	.50	.25
153	Jose Offerman	.08	.06	.03
154	Bobby Witt	.06	.05	.02
155	Will Clark	.20	.15	.08
156	Steve Olin	.08	.06	.03
157	Greg Harris	.05	.04	.02
158	Dale Murphy (Little Hotshot)	.08	.06	.03
159	Don Mattingly	.20	.15	.08
160	Shawon Dunston	.08	.06	.03
161	Bill Gullickson	.06	.05	.02
162	Paul O'Neill	.06	.05	.02
163	Norm Charlton	.06	.05	.02
164	Bo Jackson	.30	.25	.12
165	Tony Fernandez	.06	.05	.02
166	Dave Henderson	.06	.05	.02
167	Dwight Gooden	.15	.11	.06
168	Junior Felix	.06	.05	.02
169	Lance Parrish	.06	.05	.02
170	Pat Combs	.06	.05	.02
171	Chuck Knoblauch	.12	.09	.05
172	John Smoltz	.10	.08	.04
173	Wrigley Field	.05	.04	.02
174	Andre Dawson	.12	.09	.05
175	Pete Harnisch	.05	.04	.02
176	Alan Trammell	.08	.06	.03
177	Kirk Dressendorfer	.08	.06	.03
178	Matt Nokes	.06	.05	.02
179	Wil Cordero	.25	.20	.10
180	Scott Cooper	.08	.06	.03
181	Glenallen Hill	.06	.05	.02
182	John Franco	.06	.05	.02
183	Rafael Palmeiro	.12	.09	.05
184	Jay Bell	.06	.05	.02
185	Bill Wegman	.06	.05	.02
186	Deion Sanders	.15	.11	.06
187	Darryl Strawberry	.10	.08	.04
188	Jaime Navarro	.06	.05	.02
189	Darren Jackson	.06	.05	.02
190	Eddie Zosky	.06	.05	.02
191	Mike Scioscia	.05	.04	.02
192	Chito Martinez	.15	.11	.06
193	Awesome Action 10 (Pat Kelly/ Ron Tingley)	.05	.04	.02
194	Ray Lankford	.12	.09	.05
195	Dennis Eckersley	.10	.08	.04
196	Awesome Action 11 (Ivan Calderon/ Mike Maddux)	.05	.04	.02
197	Shane Mack	.06	.05	.02
198	Checklist	.05	.04	.02
199	Cal Ripken, Jr.	.25	.15	.08
200	Jeff Bagwell	.25	.15	.08
201	David Howard	.05	.04	.02
202	Kirby Puckett	.25	.15	.08
203	Harold Reynolds	.06	.05	.02
204	Jim Abbott	.12	.09	.05
205	Mark Lewis	.08	.06	.03
206	Frank Thomas	1.25	.90	.50
207	Rex Hudler	.05	.04	.02
208	Vince Coleman	.06	.05	.02
209	Delino DeShields	.10	.08	.04
210	Luis Gonzalez	.15	.11	.06
211	Wade Boggs	.12	.09	.05
212	Orel Hershiser	.08	.06	.03
213	Cal Eldred	.25	.20	.10
214	Jose Canseco	.10	.05	.02
215	Jose Guzman	.06	.05	.02
216	Roger Clemens	.20	.15	.08
217	Dave Justice	.30	.25	.14
218	Tony Phillips	.06	.05	.02
219	Tony Gwynn	.15	.10	.05
220	Mitch Williams	.06	.05	.02
221	Bill Sampen	.05	.04	.02
222	Billy Hatcher	.05	.04	.02
223	Gary Gaetti	.06	.05	.02
224	Tim Wallach	.06	.05	.02

		MT	NR MT	EX
225	Kevin Maas	.06	.05	.02
226	Kevin Brown	.06	.05	.02
227	Sandy Alomar	.15	.11	.06
228	John Habyan	.05	.04	.02
229	Ryne Sandberg	.20	.15	.08
230	Greg Gagne	.05	.04	.02
231	Autographs (Mark McGwire)	.05	.04	.02
232	Mike LaValliere	.05	.04	.02
233	Mark Gubicza	.05	.04	.02
234	Lance Parrish (Little Hotshot)	.06	.05	.02
235	Carlos Baerga	.25	.15	.08
236	Howard Johnson	.12	.09	.05
237	Mike Mussina	.30	.20	.10
238	Ruben Sierra	.10	.08	.04
239	Lance Johnson	.06	.05	.02
240	Devon White	.06	.05	.02
241	Dan Wilson	.25	.20	.10
242	Kelly Gruber	.12	.09	.05
243	Brett Butler (Little Hotshot)	.06	.05	.02
244	Ozzie Smith	.15	.11	.06
245	Chuck McElroy	.05	.04	.02
246	Shawn Boskie	.06	.05	.02
247	Mark Davis	.05	.04	.02
248	Bill Landrum	.05	.04	.02
249	Frank Tanana	.05	.04	.02
250	Darryl Hamilton	.08	.06	.03
251	Gary DiSarcina	.05	.04	.02
252	Mike Greenwell	.12	.09	.05
253	Cal Ripken, Jr. (Little Hotshot)	.25	.15	.06
254	Paul Molitor	.12	.09	.05
255	Tim Teufel	.05	.04	.02
256	Chris Hoiles	.35	.25	.14
257	Rob Dibble	.12	.09	.05
258	Sid Bream	.05	.04	.02
259	Chito Martinez	.08	.06	.03
260	Dale Murphy	.08	.06	.03
261	Greg Hibbard	.06	.05	.02
262	Mark McGwire	.15	.10	.05
263	Oriole Park	.05	.04	.02
264	Checklist	.05	.04	.02

1992 Donruss McDonald's

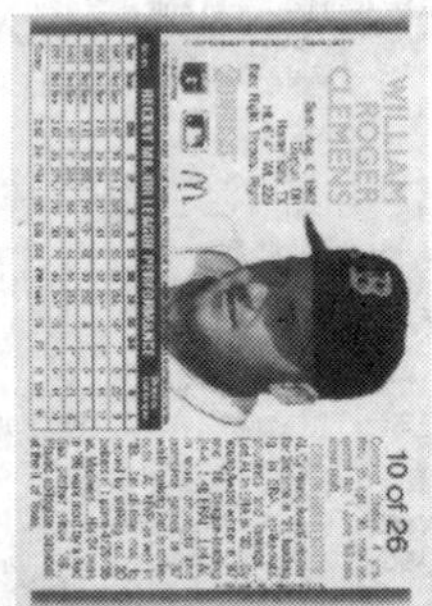

McDonald's restaurants in Ontario released a 26-card All-Star baseball card set in 1992 featuring many of the top players in the game. The cards were sold at Canadian McDonald's in packs of four with the purchase of a meal. Additionally, the company offered a six-card Toronto Blue Jays subset.

		MT	NR MT	EX
	Complete Set:	20.00	15.00	8.00
	Common Player:	.25	.20	.10
1	Cal Ripken Jr.	.75	.60	.30
2	Frank Thomas	1.00	.75	.40
3	George Brett	.60	.45	.25
4	Roberto Kelly	.25	.20	.10
5	Nolan Ryan	1.00	.75	.40
6	Ryne Sandberg	.75	.60	.30
7	Darryl Strawberry	.35	.25	.14
8	Len Dykstra	.35	.25	.14
9	Fred McGriff	.35	.25	.14
10	Roger Clemens	.35	.25	.14
11	Sandy Alomar Jr.	.25	.20	.10
12	Robin Yount	.60	.45	.25
13	Jose Canseco	.60	.45	.25
14	Jimmy Key	.25	.20	.10
15	Barry Larkin	.35	.25	.14
16	Don Mattingly	.60	.45	.25
17	Andy Van Slyke	.35	.25	.14
18	Will Clark	.50	.40	.20
19	Mark Langston	.25	.20	.10
20	Cecil Fielder	.50	.40	.20
21	Kirby Puckett	.50	.40	.20
22	Ken Griffey	.75	.60	.30
23	Dave Justice	.35	.25	.14
24	Jeff Bagwell	.35	.25	.14
25	Howard Johnson	.25	.20	.10
26	Ozzie Smith	.35	.25	.14
	Gold Blue Jays			
1	Roberto Alomar	.75	.60	.30
2	Joe Carter	.60	.45	.25
3	Kelly Gruber	.50	.40	.20
4	Jack Morris	.50	.40	.20
5	Tom Henke	.50	.40	.20
6	Devon White	.60	.45	.25

1992 Donruss Nolan Ryan Career Series

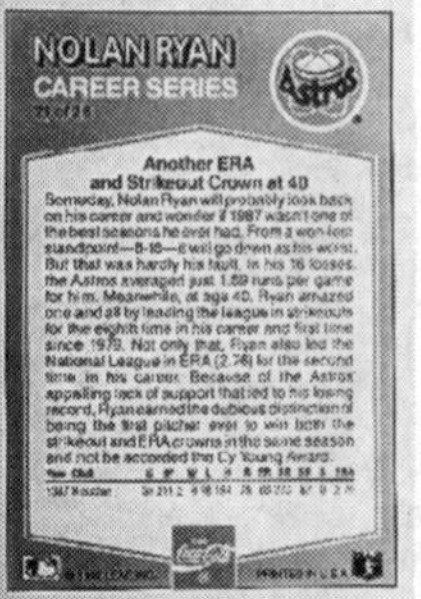

This 26-card set was issued iu conjunction with Coca-Cola to honor Nolan Ryan's 26 major league seasons. One Nolan Ryan card was packaged with three regular 1992 Donruss cards in special 12-packs of Coke. Complete Sets, in a black, red and gold box, were available through a mail-in offer. The 2-1/2" x 3-1/2" cards have a full-color photo on front, framed by a gold border. Ryan's name is printed in gold toward the bottom, above a blue bar which presents a team and year. The Coke logo is at upper right. One back there are details of Ryan's performance in the indicated year, the card number, and team and Coke logos.

		MT	NR MT	EX
	Complete Set (26):	25.00	19.00	10.00
	Common Card:	1.00	.70	.40
	NEW YORK METS			
1	1966 Breaking In (Nolan Ryan)	1.00	.70	.40
2	1968 Record-Setting Rookie (Nolan Ryan)	1.00	.70	.40
3	1969 World Champions (Nolan Ryan)	1.00	.70	.40
4	1970 Growing Pains (Nolan Ryan)	1.00	.70	.40
5	1971 Traded' (Nolan Ryan)	1.00	.70	.40
	CALIFORNIA ANGELS			
6	1972 Fitted For a Halo (Nolan Ryan)	1.00	.70	.40
7	1973 The First Two No-Nos and a Record (Nolan Ryan)	1.00	.70	.40
8	1974 No-Hitter No. 3/Another K Record (Nolan Ryan)	1.00	.70	.40
9	1975 Tying Koufax (Nolan Ryan)	1.00	.70	.40
10	1976 Back on Track (Nolan Ryan)	1.00	.70	.40
11	1977 Carrying the Load (Nolan Ryan)	1.00	.70	.40
12	1978 A Year of Injuries (Nolan Ryan)	1.00	.70	.40
13	1979 California Farewell (Nolan Ryan)	1.00	.70	.40
	HOUSTON ASTROS			
14	1980 Coming Home (Nolan Ryan)	1.00	.70	.40
15	1981 A Gusher in Houston (Nolan Ryan)	1.00	.70	.40

		MT	NR MT	EX
16	1982 Mounting 'Em Up (Nolan Ryan)	1.00	.70	.40
17	1983 Passing the Big Train (Nolan Ryan)	1.00	.70	.40
18	1984 Misleading Signs of Age (Nolan Ryan)	1.00	.70	.40
19	1985 Another Milestone/a New Contract (Nolan Ryan)	1.00	.70	.40
20	1986 The Elbow Flares Up Again (Nolan Ryan)	1.00	.70	.40
21	1987 Another ERA/Strikeout Crown at 40 (Nolan Ryan)	1.00	.70	.40
22	1988 Leaving Home Again (Nolan Ryan)	1.00	.70	.40
	TEXAS RANGERS			
23	1989 5,000 Strikeouts at Texas (Nolan Ryan)	1.00	.70	.40
24	1990 Win No. 300, No-hitter No. 6 (Nolan Ryan)	1.00	.70	.40
25	1991 No-hitter No. 7 (Nolan Ryan)	1.00	.70	.40
26	1992 Man of Records (Nolan Ryan)	1.00	.70	.40

1993 Donruss

Rated Rookies and a randomly inserted Diamond Kings subset once again are featured in the 1993 Donruss set. Series I of the set was released first and includes 396 cards. The card fronts feature white borders surrounding a full-color player photo. The player's name and position appear at the bottom of the photo along with a diamond featuring the team logo. The flip sides feature an additional photo, biographical information and career statistics. The cards are numbered on the back and the series the card appears in is given with the number. The cards are UV coated.

		MT	NR MT	EX
Complete Set (792):		30.00	22.00	12.00
Common Player:		.05	.04	.02
1	Craig Lefferts	.05	.04	.02
2	Kent Mercker	.06	.05	.02
3	Phil Plantier	.10	.08	.04
4	*Alex Arias*(FC)	.15	.11	.06
5	Julio Valera	.08	.06	.03
6	Dan Wilson(FC)	.12	.09	.05
7	Frank Thomas	.75	.60	.30
8	Eric Anthony	.08	.06	.03
9	Derek Lilliquist	.05	.04	.02
10	*Rafael Bournigal*	.15	.11	.06
11	*Manny Alexander*(FC)	.15	.11	.06
12	Bret Barberie	.08	.06	.03
13	Mickey Tettleton	.08	.06	.03
14	Anthony Young	.08	.06	.03
15	Tim Spehr	.08	.06	.03
16	*Bob Ayrault*	.10	.08	.04
17	Bill Wegman	.06	.05	.02
18	Jay Bell	.08	.06	.03
19	Rick Aguilera	.08	.06	.03
20	Todd Zeile	.08	.06	.03
21	Steve Farr	.06	.05	.02
22	Andy Benes	.08	.06	.03
23	Lance Blankenship	.05	.04	.02
24	Ted Wood	.08	.06	.03
25	Omar Vizquel	.05	.04	.02
26	Steve Avery	.08	.06	.03
27	Brian Bohanon	.08	.06	.03
28	Rick Wilkins	.08	.06	.03
29	Devon White	.08	.06	.03
30	*Bobby Ayala*(FC)	.12	.09	.05
31	Leo Gomez	.08	.06	.03
32	Mike Simms	.08	.06	.03
33	Ellis Burks	.08	.06	.03
34	Steve Wilson	.05	.04	.02
35	Jim Abbott	.08	.06	.03
36	Tim Wallach	.06	.05	.02
37	Wilson Alvarez	.06	.05	.02
38	Daryl Boston	.05	.04	.02
39	Sandy Alomar Jr.	.10	.08	.04
40	Mitch Williams	.08	.06	.03
41	Rico Brogna	.10	.08	.04
42	Gary Varsho	.05	.04	.02
43	Kevin Appier	.08	.06	.03
44	Eric Wedge	.12	.09	.05
45	Dante Bichette	.05	.04	.02
46	Jose Oquendo	.05	.04	.02
47	*Mike Trombley*(FC)	.12	.09	.05
48	Dan Walters	.08	.06	.03
49	Gerald Williams	.08	.06	.03
50	Bud Black	.05	.04	.02
51	Bobby Witt	.06	.05	.02
52	Mark Davis	.05	.04	.02
53	*Shawn Barton*(FC)	.15	.11	.06
54	Paul Assenmacher	.05	.04	.02
55	Kevin Reimer	.06	.05	.02
56	*Billy Ashley*(FC)	.30	.25	.12
57	Eddie Zosky	.08	.06	.03
58	Chris Sabo	.08	.06	.03
59	Billy Ripken	.05	.04	.02
60	*Scooter Tucker*	.12	.09	.05
61	*Tim Wakefield*	.10	.08	.04
62	Mitch Webster	.05	.04	.02
63	Jack Clark	.06	.05	.02
64	Mark Gardner	.06	.05	.02
65	Lee Stevens	.06	.05	.02
66	Todd Hundley	.08	.06	.03
67	Bobby Thigpen	.08	.06	.03
68	Dave Hollins	.10	.08	.04
69	Jack Armstrong	.06	.05	.02
70	Alex Cole	.06	.05	.02
71	Mark Carreon	.05	.04	.02
72	Todd Worrell	.06	.05	.02
73	*Steve Shifflett*	.12	.09	.05
74	Jerald Clark	.06	.05	.02
75	Paul Molitor	.08	.06	.03
76	*Larry Carter*(FC)	.15	.11	.06
77	Rich Rowland(FC)	.10	.08	.04
78	Damon Berryhill	.06	.05	.02
79	Willie Banks	.08	.06	.03
80	Hector Villanueva	.06	.05	.02
81	Mike Gallego	.06	.05	.02
82	Tim Belcher	.06	.05	.02
83	Mike Bordick	.08	.06	.03
84	Criag Biggio	.08	.06	.03
85	Lance Parrish	.06	.05	.02
86	Brett Butler	.06	.05	.02
87	Mike Timlin	.06	.05	.02
88	Brian Barnes	.06	.05	.02
89	Brady Anderson	.08	.06	.03
90	D.J. Dozier	.08	.06	.03
91	Frank Viola	.08	.06	.03
92	Darren Daulton	.08	.06	.03
93	Chad Curtis	.15	.11	.06
94	Zane Smith	.05	.04	.02
95	George Bell	.08	.06	.03
96	Rex Hudler	.05	.04	.02
97	Mark Whiten	.08	.06	.03
98	Tim Teufel	.05	.04	.02
99	Kevin Ritz	.05	.04	.02
100	Jeff Brantley	.05	.04	.02
101	Jeff Conine	.08	.06	.03
102	*Vinny Castilla*(FC)	.15	.11	.06
103	Greg Vaughn	.08	.06	.03
104	Steve Buechele	.06	.05	.02
106	Darren Reed, Bip Roberts	.08	.06	.03
107	John Habyan	.05	.04	.02
108	Scott Servais	.05	.04	.02
109	Walt Weiss	.05	.04	.02
110	*J.T. Snow*(FC)	.75	.60	.30
111	Jay Buhner	.08	.06	.03
112	Darryl Strawberry	.08	.06	.03
113	*Roger Pavlik*	.12	.09	.05
114	Chris Nabholz	.06	.05	.02
115	Pat Borders	.06	.05	.02
116	*Pat Howell*	.12	.09	.05
117	Gregg Olson	.08	.06	.03
118	Curt Schilling	.08	.06	.03

		MT	NR MT	EX
119	Roger Clemens	.15	.11	.06
120	*Victor Cole*	.12	.09	.05
121	Gary DiSarcina	.05	.04	.02
122	Checklist	.05	.04	.02
123	Steve Sax	.08	.06	.03
124	Chuck Carr(FC)	.08	.06	.03
125	Mark Lewis	.08	.06	.03
126	Tony Gwynn	.08	.06	.03
127	Travis Fryman	.12	.09	.05
129	Dave Burba	.06	.05	.02
130	John Smoltz	.08	.06	.03
131	Cal Eldred	.15	.11	.06
132	Checklist	.05	.04	.02
133	Arthur Rhodes	.10	.08	.04
134	Jeff Blauser	.06	.05	.02
135	Scott Cooper	.06	.05	.02
136	Doug Strange	.06	.05	.02
137	Luis Sojo	.06	.05	.02
138	*Jeff Branson*	.15	.11	.06
139	Alex Fernandez	.08	.06	.03
140	Ken Caminiti	.06	.05	.02
141	Charles Nagy	.08	.06	.03
142	Tom Candiotti	.06	.05	.02
143	Willie Green	.10	.08	.04
144	*Kurt Knudsen*	.10	.08	.04
146	John Franco	.06	.05	.02
147	*Eddie Pierce*(FC)	.15	.11	.06
148	Kim Batiste	.08	.06	.03
149	Darren Holmes	.05	.04	.02
150	*Steve Cooke*	.15	.11	.06
151	Terry Jorgensen	.08	.06	.03
152	*Mark Clark*	.12	.09	.05
153	Randy Velarde	.05	.04	.02
154	Greg Harris	.05	.04	.02
155	*Kevin Campbell*	.10	.08	.04
156	John Burkett	.06	.05	.02
157	Kevin Mitchell	.08	.06	.03
158	Deion Sanders	.10	.08	.04
159	Jose Canseco	.10	.08	.04
160	*Jeff Hartsock*(FC)	.15	.11	.06
161	*Tom Quinlan*(FC)	.15	.11	.06
162	*Tim Pugh*(FC)	.25	.20	.10
163	Glenn Davis	.08	.06	.03
164	*Shane Reynolds*	.12	.09	.05
165	Jody Reed	.06	.05	.02
166	Mike Sharperson	.06	.05	.02
167	Scott Lewis	.06	.05	.02
168	Dennis Martinez	.06	.05	.02
169	Scott Radinsky	.06	.05	.02
170	Dave Gallagher	.05	.04	.02
171	Jim Thome	.08	.06	.03
172	Terry Mulholland	.06	.05	.02
173	Milt Cuyler	.06	.05	.02
174	Bob Patterson	.05	.04	.02
175	Jeff Montgomery	.06	.05	.02
176	*Tim Salmon*	1.50	1.25	.60
177	Franklin Stubbs	.05	.04	.02
178	Donovan Osborne	.10	.08	.04
179	*Jeff Reboulet*	.10	.08	.04
180	*Jeremy Hernandez*(FC)	.15	.11	.06
181	Charlie Hayes	.06	.05	.02
182	Matt Williams	.08	.06	.03
183	Mike Raczka	.15	.11	.06
184	Francisco Cabrera	.05	.04	.02
185	Rich DeLucia	.05	.04	.02
186	Sammy Sosa	.06	.05	.02
187	Ivan Rodriguez	.20	.15	.08
188	*Bret Boone*(FC)	.20	.15	.08
189	Juan Guzman	.20	.15	.08
190	Randy Milligan	.06	.05	.02
191	Ivan Calderon	.08	.06	.03
197	Junior Felix	.06	.05	.02
198	Pete Schourek	.06	.05	.02
199	Craig Grebeck	.06	.05	.02
200	Juan Bell	.06	.05	.02
201	Glenallen Hill	.06	.05	.02
202	Danny Jackson	.06	.05	.02
203	John Kiely	.12	.09	.05
204	Bob Tewksbury	.08	.06	.03
205	*Kevin Koslofski*(FC)	.15	.11	.06
206	Craig Shipley	.08	.06	.03
207	John Jaha(FC)	.20	.15	.08
208	Royce Clayton	.10	.08	.04
209	*Mike Piazza*(FC)	2.50	2.00	1.00
210	Ron Gant	.08	.06	.03
211	Scott Erickson	.08	.06	.03
212	Doug Dascenzo	.05	.04	.02
213	Andy Stankiewicz(FC)	.12	.09	.05
214	Geronimo Berroa	.05	.04	.02
215	Dennis Eckersley	.08	.06	.03
216	Al Osuna	.05	.04	.02

		MT	NR MT	EX
217	Tino Martinez	.08	.06	.03
218	*Henry Rodriguez*	.12	.09	.05
219	Ed Sprague	.08	.06	.03
220	Ken Hill	.08	.06	.03
221	Chito Martinez	.08	.06	.03
222	Bret Saberhagen	.08	.06	.03
223	Mike Greenwell	.08	.06	.03
224	Mickey Morandini	.08	.06	.03
225	Chuck Finley	.08	.06	.03
226	Denny Neagle	.08	.06	.03
227	Kirk McCaskill	.06	.05	.02
228	Rheal Cormier	.08	.06	.03
229	Paul Sorrento	.08	.06	.03
230	Darrin Jackson	.06	.05	.02
231	Rob Deer	.06	.05	.02
232	Bill Swift	.06	.05	.02
233	Kevin McReynolds	.08	.06	.03
234	Terry Pendleton	.08	.06	.03
235	Dave Nilsson	.12	.09	.05
236	Chuck McElroy	.05	.04	.02
237	Derek Parks	.06	.05	.02
238	Norm Charlton	.08	.06	.03
239	Matt Nokes	.06	.05	.02
240	*Juan Guerrero*	.15	.11	.06
241	Jeff Parrett	.05	.04	.02
242	*Ryan Thompson*(FC)	.20	.15	.08
243	Dave Fleming	.10	.08	.04
244	Dave Hansen	.05	.04	.02
245	Monty Fariss	.05	.04	.02
246	*Archi Cianfrocco*	.15	.11	.06
247	*Pat Hentgen*(FC)	.15	.11	.06
248	Bill Pecota	.05	.04	.02
249	Ben McDonald	.08	.06	.03
250	Cliff Brantley	.08	.06	.03
251	*John Valentin*(FC)	.15	.11	.06
252	Jeff King	.06	.05	.02
253	*Reggie Williams*(FC)	.15	.11	.06
254	Checklist	.05	.04	.02
255	Ozzie Guillen	.08	.06	.03
256	Mike Perez	.06	.05	.02
257	Thomas Howard	.06	.05	.02
258	Kurt Stillwell	.06	.05	.02
259	Mike Henneman	.06	.05	.02
260	Steve Decker	.06	.05	.02
261	Brent Mayne	.06	.05	.02
262	Otis Nixon	.08	.06	.03
263	*Mark Keifer*(FC)	.15	.11	.06
264	Checklist	.05	.04	.02
265	*Richie Lewis*(FC)	.15	.11	.06
266	*Pat Gomez*(FC)	.15	.11	.06
267	*Scott Taylor*(FC)	.15	.11	.06
268	Shawon Dunston	.06	.05	.02
269	Greg Myers	.05	.04	.02
270	Tim Costo	.10	.08	.04
271	Greg Hibbard	.06	.05	.02
272	Pete Harnisch	.06	.05	.02
273	*Dave Mlicki*(FC)	.12	.09	.05
274	Orel Hershiser	.08	.06	.03
275	Sean Berry	.08	.06	.03
276	Doug Simons	.08	.06	.03
277	*John Doherty*	.10	.08	.04
278	Eddie Murray	.08	.06	.03
279	Chris Haney	.08	.06	.03
280	Stan Javier	.05	.04	.02
281	Jaime Navarro	.08	.06	.03
282	Orlando Merced	.08	.06	.03
283	Kent Hrbek	.08	.06	.03
284	Bernard Gilkey	.08	.06	.03
285	Russ Springer	.06	.05	.02
286	Mike Maddux	.05	.04	.02
287	*Eric Fox*	.12	.09	.05
288	Mark Leonard	.05	.04	.02
289	Tim Leary	.05	.04	.02
290	Brian Hunter	.08	.06	.03
291	Donald Harris	.08	.06	.03
292	Bob Scanlan	.05	.04	.02
293	Turner Ward	.08	.06	.03
294	Hal Morris	.08	.06	.03
295	Jimmy Poole	.08	.06	.03
296	Doug Jones	.06	.05	.02
297	Tony Pena	.06	.05	.02
298	Ramon Martinez	.08	.06	.03
299	*Tim Fortugno*	.12	.09	.05
300	Marquis Grissom	.10	.08	.04
301	Lance Johnson	.06	.05	.02
302	*Jeff Kent*	.15	.11	.06
303	Reggie Jefferson	.08	.06	.03
304	Wes Chamberlain	.08	.06	.03
305	*Shawn Hare*	.12	.09	.05
306	Mike LaValliere	.05	.04	.02
307	Gregg Jefferies	.08	.06	.03

		MT	NR MT	EX
308	*Troy Neel*	.20	.15	.08
309	*Pat Listach*(FC)	.10	.08	.04
310	Geronimo Pena	.06	.05	.02
311	Pedro Munoz	.08	.06	.03
312	*Guillermo Pena*(FC)	.15	.11	.06
313	Roberto Kelly	.08	.06	.03
314	Mike Jackson	.05	.04	.02
315	Rickey Henderson	.12	.09	.05
316	Mark Lemke	.06	.05	.02
317	Erik Hanson	.08	.06	.03
318	Derrick May	.08	.06	.03
319	Geno Petralli	.05	.04	.02
320	*Melvin Nieves*(FC)	.20	.15	.08
321	*Doug Linton*(FC)	.15	.11	.06
322	Rob Dibble	.08	.06	.03
323	Chris Hoiles	.10	.08	.04
324	Jimmy Jones	.05	.04	.02
325	Dave Staton	.06	.05	.02
326	Pedro Martinez	.10	.08	.04
327	*Paul Quantrill*(FC)	.15	.11	.06
328	Greg Colbrunn	.05	.04	.02
329	*Hilly Hathaway*(FC)	.25	.20	.10
330	Jeff Innis	.06	.05	.02
331	Ron Karkovice	.06	.05	.02
332	*Keith Shepherd*(FC)	.15	.11	.06
333	*Alan Embree*(FC)	.15	.11	.06
334	*Paul Wagner*	.15	.11	.06
335	*Dave Haas*(FC)	.15	.11	.06
336	Ozzie Canseco	.10	.08	.04
337	Bill Sampen	.05	.04	.02
338	Rich Rodriguez	.05	.04	.02
339	Dean Palmer	.08	.06	.03
340	Greg Litton	.05	.04	.02
341	*Jim Tatum*(FC)	.20	.15	.08
342	*Todd Haney*(FC)	.10	.08	.04
343	Larry Casian	.06	.05	.02
344	Ryne Sandberg	.12	.09	.05
345	*Sterling Hitchcock*(FC)	.30	.25	.12
346	Chris Hammond	.06	.05	.02
347	*Vince Horseman*	.12	.09	.05
348	*Butch Henry*	.12	.09	.05
349	Dann Howitt	.05	.04	.02
350	Roger McDowell	.05	.04	.02
351	Jack Morris	.08	.06	.03
352	Bill Krueger	.05	.04	.02
353	*Cris Colon*(FC)	.15	.11	.06
354	*Joe Vitko*(FC)	.15	.11	.06
355	Willie McGee	.08	.06	.03
356	Jay Baller	.06	.05	.02
357	Pat Mahomes	.10	.08	.04
358	Roger Mason	.05	.04	.02
359	*Jerry Nielsen*	.15	.11	.06
360	Tom Pagnozzi	.06	.05	.02
361	*Kevin Baez*	.15	.11	.06
362	*Tim Scott*	.15	.11	.06
363	*Domingo Martinez*(FC)	.20	.15	.08
364	Kirt Manwaring	.05	.04	.02
365	Rafael Palmeiro	.08	.06	.03
366	Ray Lankford	.12	.09	.05
367	Tim McIntosh	.08	.06	.03
368	*Jessie Hollins*(FC)	.15	.11	.06
369	Scott Leius	.06	.05	.02
370	Bill Doran	.05	.04	.02
371	*Sam Militello*(FC)	.10	.08	.04
372	Ryan Bowen	.08	.06	.03
373	Dave Henderson	.08	.06	.03
374	Dan Smith(FC)	.12	.09	.05
375	*Steve Reed*(FC)	.12	.09	.05
376	Jose Offerman	.08	.06	.03
377	Kevin Brown	.08	.06	.03
378	Darrin Fletcher	.05	.04	.02
379	Duane Ward	.06	.05	.02
380	Wayne Kirby(FC)	.12	.09	.05
381	*Steve Scarsone*	.15	.11	.06
382	Mariano Duncan	.06	.05	.02
383	*Ken Ryan*(FC)	.15	.11	.06
384	Lloyd McClendon	.05	.04	.02
385	Brian Holman	.05	.04	.02
386	Braulio Castillo	.08	.06	.03
387	*Danny Leon*	.12	.09	.05
388	Omar Olivares	.05	.04	.02
389	Kevin Wickander	.05	.04	.02
390	Fred McGriff	.10	.08	.04
391	Phil Clark(FC)	.12	.09	.05
392	Darren Lewis	.06	.05	.02
393	*Phil Hiatt*(FC)	.40	.30	.15
394	Mike Morgan	.06	.05	.02
395	Shane Mack	.08	.06	.03
396	Checklist	.05	.04	.02
397	David Segui	.05	.04	.02
398	Rafael Belliard	.05	.04	.02

		MT	NR MT	EX
399	Tim Naehring	.05	.04	.02
400	Frank Castillo	.05	.04	.02
401	Joe Grahe	.05	.04	.02
402	Reggie Sanders	.10	.08	.04
403	Roberto Hernandez	.05	.04	.02
404	Luis Gonzalez	.05	.04	.02
405	Carlos Baerga	.20	.15	.08
406	Carlos Hernandez	.05	.04	.02
407	*Pedro Astacio*	.10	.08	.04
408	Mel Rojas	.05	.04	.02
409	Scott Livingstone	.05	.04	.02
410	Chico Walker	.05	.04	.02
411	Brian McRae	.05	.04	.02
412	Ben Rivera	.05	.04	.02
413	Ricky Bones	.05	.04	.02
414	Andy Van Slyke	.05	.04	.02
415	Chuck Knoblauch	.12	.09	.05
416	Luis Alicea	.05	.04	.02
417	Bob Wickman	.12	.09	.05
418	Doug Brocail	.05	.04	.02
419	Scott Brosius	.05	.04	.02
420	Rod Beck	.05	.04	.02
421	Edgar Martinez	.05	.04	.02
422	Ryan Klesko	.25	.20	.10
423	Nolan Ryan	.30	.25	.12
424	Rey Sanchez	.05	.04	.02
425	Roberto Alomar	.20	.15	.08
426	Barry Larkin	.10	.08	.04
427	Mike Mussina	.05	.04	.02
428	Jeff Bagwell	.15	.11	.06
429	Mo Vaughn	.10	.08	.04
430	Eric Karros	.15	.11	.06
431	John Orton	.05	.04	.02
432	Wil Cordero	.15	.11	.06
433	Jack McDowell	.08	.06	.03
434	Howard Johnson	.05	.04	.02
435	Albert Belle	.10	.08	.04
436	John Kruk	.05	.04	.02
437	Skeeter Barnes	.05	.04	.02
438	Don Slaught	.05	.04	.02
439	Rusty Meacham	.05	.04	.02
440	*Tim Laker*(FC)	.15	.11	.06
441	Robin Yount	.10	.08	.04
442	Brian Jordan	.15	.11	.06
443	Kevin Tapani	.05	.04	.02
444	Gary Sheffield	.15	.11	.06
445	Rich Monteleone	.05	.04	.02
446	Will Clark	.15	.11	.06
447	Jerry Browne	.05	.04	.02
448	Jeff Treadway	.05	.04	.02
449	Mike Schooler	.05	.04	.02
450	Mike Harkey	.05	.04	.02
451	Julio Franco	.05	.04	.02
452	*Kevin Young*	.25	.20	.10
453	Kelly Gruber	.05	.04	.02
454	Jose Rijo	.05	.04	.02
455	Mike Devereaux	.05	.04	.02
456	Andujar Cedeno	.05	.04	.02
457	*Damion Easley*	.25	.20	.10
458	Kevin Gross	.05	.04	.02
459	Matt Young	.05	.04	.02
460	Matt Stairs	.05	.04	.02
461	Luis Polonia	.05	.04	.02
462	Dwight Gooden	.05	.04	.02
463	Warren Newson	.05	.04	.02
464	Jose DeLeon	.05	.04	.02
465	Jose Mesa	.05	.04	.02
466	Danny Cox	.05	.04	.02
467	Dan Gladden	.05	.04	.02
468	Gerald Perry	.05	.04	.02
469	Mike Boddicker	.05	.04	.02
470	Jeff Gardner	.05	.04	.02
471	Doug Henry	.05	.04	.02
472	Mike Benajmin	.05	.04	.02
473	Dan Peltier	.05	.04	.02
474	Mike Stanton	.05	.04	.02
475	John Smiley	.05	.04	.02
476	Dwight Sith	.05	.04	.02
477	Jim Leyritz	.05	.04	.02
478	Dwayne Henry	.05	.04	.02
479	Mark McGwire	.10	.08	.04
480	Pete Incaviglia	.05	.04	.02
481	Dave Cochrane	.05	.04	.02
482	Eric Davis	.05	.04	.02
483	John Olerud	.25	.20	.10
484	Ken Bottenfield	.12	.09	.05
485	Mark McLemore	.05	.04	.02
486	Dave Magadan	.05	.04	.02
487	John Marzano	.05	.04	.02
488	Ruben Amaro	.05	.04	.02
489	Rob Ducey	.05	.04	.02

		MT	NR MT	EX
490	Stan Belinda	.05	.04	.02
491	Dan Pasqua	.05	.04	.02
492	Joe Magrane	.05	.04	.02
493	Brook Jacoby	.05	.04	.02
494	Gene Harris	.05	.04	.02
495	Mark Leiter	.05	.04	.02
496	Bryan Hickerson	.05	.04	.02
497	Tom Gordon	.05	.04	.02
498	Pete Smith	.05	.04	.02
499	Chris Bosio	.05	.04	.02
500	Shawn Boskie	.05	.04	.02
501	Dave West	.05	.04	.02
502	Milt Hill	.05	.04	.02
503	Pat Kelly	.05	.04	.02
504	Joe Boever	.05	.04	.02
505	Terry Steinbach	.05	.04	.02
506	*Butch Huskey*(FC)	.20	.15	.08
507	David Valle	.05	.04	.02
508	Mike Scioscia	.05	.04	.02
509	Kenny Rogers	.05	.04	.02
510	Moises Alou	.05	.04	.02
511	David Wells	.05	.04	.02
512	Mackey Sasser	.05	.04	.02
513	Todd Frohwirth	.05	.04	.02
514	Ricky Jordan	.05	.04	.02
515	Mike Gardiner	.05	.04	.02
516	Gary Redus	.05	.04	.02
517	Gary Gaetti	.05	.04	.02
518	Checklist	.05	.04	.02
519	Carlton Fisk	.08	.06	.03
520	Ozzie Smith	.08	.06	.03
521	Rod Nichols	.05	.04	.02
522	Benito Santiago	.05	.04	.02
523	Bill Gullickson	.05	.04	.02
524	Robby Thompson	.05	.04	.02
525	Mike Macfarlane	.05	.04	.02
526	Sid Bream	.05	.04	.02
527	Darryl Hamilton	.05	.04	.02
528	Checklist	.05	.04	.02
529	Jeff Tackett	.05	.04	.02
530	Greg Olson	.05	.04	.02
531	Bob Zupcic	.08	.06	.03
532	Mark Grace	.08	.06	.03
533	Steve Frey	.05	.04	.02
534	Dave Martinez	.05	.04	.02
535	Robin Ventura	.12	.09	.05
536	Casey Candaele	.05	.04	.02
537	Kenny Lofton	.20	.15	.08
538	Jay Howell	.05	.04	.02
539	*Fernando Ramsey*(FC)	.15	.11	.06
540	Larry Walker	.12	.09	.05
541	Cecil Fielder	.12	.09	.05
542	Lee Guetterman	.05	.04	.02
543	Keith Miller	.05	.04	.02
544	Lenny Dykstra	.05	.04	.02
545	B.J. Surhoff	.05	.04	.02
546	Bob Walk	.05	.04	.02
547	Brian Harper	.05	.04	.02
548	Lee Smith	.05	.04	.02
549	Danny Tartabull	.05	.04	.02
550	Frank Seminara	.05	.04	.02
551	Henry Mercedes	.05	.04	.02
552	Dave Righetti	.05	.04	.02
553	Ken Griffey, Jr.	.50	.40	.20
554	Tom Glavine	.12	.09	.05
555	Juan Gonzalez	.50	.40	.20
556	Jim Bullinger	.05	.04	.02
557	Derek Bell	.05	.04	.02
558	Cesar Hernandez	.05	.04	.02
559	Cal Ripken, Jr.	.20	.15	.08
560	Eddie Taubensee	.05	.04	.02
561	John Flaherty	.05	.04	.02
562	Todd Benzinger	.05	.04	.02
563	Hubie Brooks	.05	.04	.02
564	Delino DeShields	.05	.04	.02
565	Tim Raines	.05	.04	.02
567	Steve Olin	.05	.04	.02
568	Tommy Greene	.05	.04	.02
569	Buddy Groom	.05	.04	.02
570	Randy Tomlin	.05	.04	.02
571	Hipolito Pichardo	.05	.04	.02
572	*Rene Arocha*(FC)	.25	.20	.10
573	Mike Fetters	.05	.04	.02
574	Felix Jose	.05	.04	.02
575	Gene Larkin	.05	.04	.02
576	Bruce Hurst	.05	.04	.02
577	Bernie Williams	.05	.04	.02
578	Trevor Wilson	.05	.04	.02
579	Bon Welch	.05	.04	.02
580	Dave Justice	.25	.20	.10
581	Randy Johnson	.05	.04	.02
582	Jose Vizcaino	.05	.04	.02
583	Jeff Huson	.05	.04	.02
584	Rob Maurer	.05	.04	.02
585	Todd Stottlemyre	.05	.04	.02
586	Joe Oliver	.05	.04	.02
587	Bob Milacki	.05	.04	.02
588	Rob Murphy	.05	.04	.02
589	*Greg Pirkl*	.12	.09	.05
590	Lenny Harris	.05	.04	.02
591	Luis Rivera	.05	.04	.02
592	John Wetteland	.05	.04	.02
593	Mark Langston	.05	.04	.02
594	Bobby Bonilla	.05	.04	.02
595	Este Beltre	.05	.04	.02
596	Mike Hartley	.05	.04	.02
597	Felix Fermin	.05	.04	.02
598	Carlos Garcia	.05	.04	.02
599	Frank Tanana	.05	.04	.02
600	Pedro Guerrero	.05	.04	.02
601	Terry Shumpert	.05	.04	.02
602	Wally Whitehurst	.05	.04	.02
603	Kevin Seitzer	.05	.04	.02
604	Chris James	.05	.04	.02
605	Greg Gohr	.05	.04	.02
606	Mark Wohlers	.05	.04	.02
607	Kirby Puckett	.15	.11	.06
608	Greg Maddux	.10	.08	.04
609	Don Mattingly	.12	.09	.05
610	Greg Cadaret	.05	.04	.02
611	Dave Stewart	.05	.04	.02
612	Mark Portugal	.05	.04	.02
613	Pete O'Brien	.05	.04	.02
614	Bobby Ojeda	.05	.04	.02
615	Joe Carter	.10	.08	.04
616	Pete Young	.05	.04	.02
617	Sam Horn	.05	.04	.02
618	Vince Coleman	.05	.04	.02
619	Checklist (Wade Boggs)	.05	.04	.02
620	*Todd Pratt*(FC)	.15	.11	.06
621	Ron Tingley	.05	.04	.02
622	Doug Drabek	.05	.04	.02
623	Scott Hemond	.05	.04	.02
624	Tim Jones	.05	.04	.02
625	Dennis Cook	.05	.04	.02
626	Jose Melendez	.05	.04	.02
627	Mike Munoz	.05	.04	.02
628	Jim Pena	.05	.04	.02
629	Gary Thurman	.05	.04	.02
630	Charlie Leibrandt	.05	.04	.02
631	Scott Fletcher	.05	.04	.02
632	Andre Dawson	.10	.08	.04
633	Greg Gagne	.05	.04	.02
634	Greg Swindell	.05	.04	.02
635	Kevin Maas	.05	.04	.02
636	Xavier Hernandez	.05	.04	.02
637	Ruben Sierra	.12	.09	.05
638	Dimitri Young(FC)	.15	.11	.06
639	Harold Reynolds	.05	.04	.02
640	Tom Goodwin	.05	.04	.02
641	Todd Burns	.05	.04	.02
642	Jeff Fassero	.05	.04	.02
643	Dave Winfield	.10	.08	.04
644	Willie Randolph	.05	.04	.02
645	Luis Mercedes	.05	.04	.02
646	Dale Murphy	.05	.04	.02
647	Danny Darwin	.05	.04	.02
648	Dennis Moeller	.05	.04	.02
649	Chuck Crim	.05	.04	.02
650	Checklist	.05	.04	.02
651	Shawn Abner	.05	.04	.02
652	Tracy Woodson	.05	.04	.02
653	Scott Scudder	.05	.04	.02
654	Tom Lampkin	.05	.04	.02
655	Alan Trammell	.05	.04	.02
656	Cory Snyder	.05	.04	.02
657	Chris Gwynn	.05	.04	.02
658	Lonnie Smith	.05	.04	.02
659	Jim Austin	.05	.04	.02
660	Checklist	.05	.04	.02
661	Checklist (Tim Hulett)	.05	.04	.02
662	Marvin Freeman	.05	.04	.02
663	Greg Harris	.05	.04	.02
664	Heathcliff Slocumb	.05	.04	.02
665	Mike Butcher	.05	.04	.02
666	Steve Foster	.05	.04	.02
667	Donn Pall	.05	.04	.02
668	Darryl Kile	.05	.04	.02
669	Jesse Levis	.10	.08	.04
670	Jim Gott	.05	.04	.02
671	*Mark Hutton*	.15	.11	.06
672	Brian Drahman	.05	.04	.02

		MT	NR MT	EX
673	Chad Kreuter	.05	.04	.02
674	Tony Fernandez	.05	.04	.02
675	Jose Lind	.05	.04	.02
676	Kyle Abbott	.05	.04	.02
677	Dan Plesac	.05	.04	.02
678	Barry Bonds	.30	.25	.12
679	Chili Davis	.05	.04	.02
680	Stan Royer	.05	.04	.02
681	Scott Kamieniecki	.05	.04	.02
682	Carlos Martinez	.05	.04	.02
683	Mike Moore	.05	.04	.02
684	Candy Maldanado	.05	.04	.02
685	Jeff Nelson	.05	.04	.02
686	Lou Whitaker	.05	.04	.02
687	Jose Guzman	.05	.04	.02
688	Manuel Lee	.05	.04	.02
689	Bob MacDonald	.05	.04	.02
690	Scott Bankhead	.05	.04	.02
691	Alan Mills	.05	.04	.02
692	Brian Williams	.05	.04	.02
693	Tom Brunansky	.05	.04	.02
694	Lenny Webster	.05	.04	.02
695	Greg Briley	.05	.04	.02
696	Paul O'Neill	.05	.04	.02
697	Joey Cora	.05	.04	.02
698	Charlie O'Brien	.05	.04	.02
699	Junior Ortiz	.05	.04	.02
700	Ron Darling	.05	.04	.02
701	Tony Phillips	.05	.04	.02
702	William Pennyfeather	.05	.04	.02
703	Mark Gubicza	.05	.04	.02
704	Steve Hosey(FC)	.15	.11	.06
705	Henry Cotto	.05	.04	.02
706	*David Hulse*(FC)	.20	.15	.08
707	Mike Pagliarulo	.05	.04	.02
708	Dave Stieb	.05	.04	.02
709	Melido Perez	.05	.04	.02
710	Jimmy Key	.05	.04	.02
711	Jeff Russell	.05	.04	.02
712	David Cone	.05	.04	.02
713	Russ Swan	.05	.04	.02
714	Mark Guthrie	.05	.04	.02
715	Checklist	.05	.04	.02
716	*Al Martin*(FC)	.30	.25	.12
717	Randy Knorr	.05	.04	.02
718	Mike Stanley	.05	.04	.02
719	Rick Sutcliffe	.05	.04	.02
720	Terry Leach	.05	.04	.02
721	Chipper Jones	.40	.30	.15
722	Jim Eisenreich	.05	.04	.02
723	Tom Henke	.05	.04	.02
724	Jeff Frye	.05	.04	.02
725	Harold Baines	.05	.04	.02
726	Scott Sanderson	.05	.04	.02
727	Tom Foley	.05	.04	.02
728	Bryan Harvey	.05	.04	.02
729	Tom Edens	.05	.04	.02
730	*Eric Young*	.20	.15	.08
731	Dave Weathers	.05	.04	.02
732	Spike Owen	.05	.04	.02
733	Scott Aldred	.05	.04	.02
734	Cris Carpenter	.05	.04	.02
735	Dion James	.05	.04	.02
736	Joe Girardi	.05	.04	.02
737	Nigel Wilson	.60	.45	.25
738	Scott Chiamparino	.05	.04	.02
739	Jeff Reardon	.05	.04	.02
740	Willie Blair	.05	.04	.02
741	Jim Corsi	.05	.04	.02
742	Ken Patterson	.05	.04	.02
743	Andy Ashby	.05	.04	.02
744	Rob Natal	.05	.04	.02
745	Kevin Bass	.05	.04	.02
746	Freddie Benavides	.05	.04	.02
747	Chris Donnels	.05	.04	.02
748	*Kerry Woodson*	.15	.11	.06
749	Calvin Jones	.05	.04	.02
750	Gary Scott	.05	.04	.02
751	Joe Orsulak	.05	.04	.02
752	Armando Reynoso	.05	.04	.02
753	Monty Farriss	.05	.04	.02
754	Billy Hatcher	.05	.04	.02
755	Denis Boucher	.05	.04	.02
756	Walt Weiss	.05	.04	.02
757	Mike Fitzgerald	.05	.04	.02
758	Rudy Seanez	.05	.04	.02
759	Bret Barberie	.05	.04	.02
760	Mo Sanford	.05	.04	.02
761	*Pete Castellano*(FC)	.15	.11	.06
762	Chuck Carr	.05	.04	.02
763	Steve Howe	.05	.04	.02
764	Andres Galarraga	.05	.04	.02
765	Jeff Conine	.05	.04	.02
766	Ted Power	.05	.04	.02
767	Butch Henry	.05	.04	.02
768	Steve Decker	.05	.04	.02
769	Storm Davis	.05	.04	.02
770	Vinny Castilla	.05	.04	.02
771	Junior Felix	.05	.04	.02
772	Walt Terrell	.05	.04	.02
773	*Brad Ausmus*	.15	.11	.06
774	Jamie McAndrew	.05	.04	.02
775	Milt Thompson	.05	.04	.02
776	Charlie Hayes	.05	.04	.02
777	Jack Armstrong	.05	.04	.02
778	Dennis Rasmussen	.05	.04	.02
779	Darren Holmes	.05	.04	.02
780	*Alex Arias*	.15	.11	.06
781	Randy Bush	.05	.04	.02
782	*Javy Lopez*	.50	.40	.20
783	Dante Bichette	.05	.04	.02
784	*John Johnstone*(FC)	.25	.20	.10
785	Rene Gonzales	.05	.04	.02
786	Alex Cole	.05	.04	.02
787	Jeromy Burnitz	.15	.11	.06
788	Michael Huff	.05	.04	.02
789	Anthony Telford	.05	.04	.02
790	Jerald Clark	.05	.04	.02
791	Joel Johnston	.05	.04	.02
792	*David Nied*	.80	.60	.30

1993 Donruss Long Ball Leaders

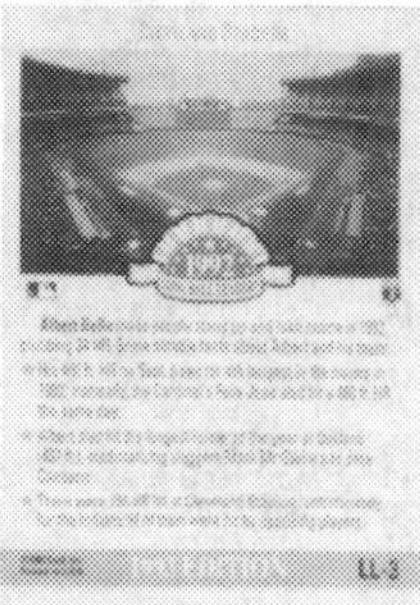

Carrying a prefix of "LL" before the card number, these inserts were released in Series I (LL1-9) and Series II (LL10-18) jumbo packs.

		MT	NR MT	EX
Complete Set (18):		75.00	56.00	30.00
Common Player:		2.00	1.50	.80
1	Rob Deer	2.00	1.50	.80
2	Fred McGriff	6.00	4.50	2.50
3	Albert Belle	5.00	3.75	2.00
4	Mark McGwire	2.50	2.00	1.00
5	David Justice	5.00	3.75	2.00
6	Jose Canseco	2.50	2.00	1.00
7	Kent Hrbek	2.00	1.50	.80
8	Roberto Alomar	8.00	6.00	3.25
9	Ken Griffey Jr.	14.00	10.50	5.50
10	Frank Thomas	20.00	15.00	8.00
11	Darryl Strawberry	2.00	1.50	.80
12	Felix Jose	2.00	1.50	.80
13	Cecil Fielder	3.50	2.75	1.50
14	Juan Gonzalez	14.00	10.50	5.50
15	Ryne Sandberg	4.00	3.00	1.50
16	Gary Sheffield	3.00	2.25	1.25
17	Jeff Bagwell	4.50	3.50	1.75
18	Larry Walker	3.00	2.25	1.25

Definitions for grading conditions are located in the Introduction of this price guide.

1993 Donruss MVP's

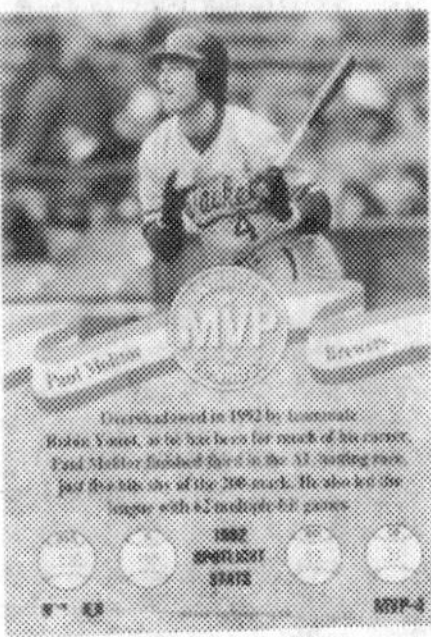

This 26-card set was inserted in jumbo packs of both Series I and Series II. Cards carry a MVP prefix to the card number.

		MT	NR MT	EX
Complete Set (26):		50.00	37.00	20.00
Complete Series 1 (13):		18.00	13.50	7.25
Complete Series 2 (13):		32.00	24.00	13.00
Common Player:		.75	.60	.30
1	Luis Polonia	.75	.60	.30
2	Frank Thomas	7.50	5.75	3.00
3	George Brett	2.50	2.00	1.00
4	Paul Molitor	2.50	2.00	1.00
5	Don Mattingly	2.00	1.50	.80
6	Roberto Alomar	3.00	2.25	1.25
7	Terry Pendleton	1.00	.70	.40
8	Eric Karros	1.25	.90	.50
9	Larry Walker	1.00	.70	.40
10	Eddie Murray	1.00	.70	.40
11	Darren Daulton	1.50	1.25	.60
12	Ray Lankford	1.00	.70	.40
13	Will Clark	2.00	1.50	.80
14	Cal Ripken, Jr.	3.00	2.25	1.25
15	Roger Clemens	2.50	2.00	1.00
16	Carlos Baerga	3.00	2.25	1.25
17	Cecil Fielder	2.00	1.50	.80
18	Kirby Puckett	3.50	2.75	1.50
19	Mark McGwire	1.00	.70	.40
20	Ken Griffey Jr.	7.00	5.25	2.75
21	Juan Gonzalez	7.00	5.25	2.75
22	Ryne Sandberg	3.00	2.25	1.25
23	Bip Roberts	.75	.60	.30
24	Jeff Bagwell	2.00	1.50	.80
25	Barry Bonds	4.00	3.00	1.50
26	Gary Sheffield	1.50	1.25	.60

1993 Donruss Spirit of the Game

Series I and Series II foil and jumbo packs could be found with these cards randomly inserted. Several multi-player cards are included in the set. Card numbers bear an SG prefix.

		MT	NR MT	EX
Complete Set (20):		45.00	34.00	18.00
Common Player:		1.00	.70	.40
1	Turning Two (Dave Winfield, Mike Bordick)	1.50	1.25	.60
2	Play at the Plate (David Justice)	3.00	2.25	1.25
3	In There (Roberto Alomar)	4.00	3.00	1.50
4	Pumped (Dennis Eckersley)	2.00	1.50	.80
5	Dynamic Duo (Juan Gonzalez, Jose Canseco)	7.00	5.25	2.75
6	Gone (Frank Thomas, George Bell)	5.00	3.75	2.00
7	Safe or Out? (Wade Boggs)	2.00	1.50	.80
8	The Thrill (Will Clark)	4.00	3.00	1.50
9	Safe at Home (Damon Berryhill, Bip Roberts, Glenn Braggs)	2.00	1.50	.80
10	Thirty X 31 (Cecil Fielder, Mickey Tettleton, Rob Deer)	2.00	1.50	.80
11	Bag Bandit (Kenny Lofton)	3.00	2.25	1.25
12	Back to Back (Fred McGriff, Gary Sheffield)	3.00	2.25	1.25
13	Range Rovers (Greg Gagne, Barry Larkin)	2.00	1.50	.80
14	The Ball Stops Here (Ryne Sandberg)	5.00	3.75	2.00
15	Over the Top (Carlos Baerga, Gary Gaetti)	3.00	2.25	1.25
16	At the Wall (Danny Tartabull)	1.00	.70	.40
17	Head First (Brady Anderson)	1.00	.70	.40
18	Big Hurt (Frank Thomas)	12.00	9.00	4.75
19	No-Hitter (Kevin Gross)	1.00	.70	.40
20	3,000 (Robin Yount)	3.50	2.75	1.50

1993 Donruss Diamond Kings

The traditional Donruss Diamond Kings cards were again used as an insert in Series I and Series II foil packs in 1993. The first 15 cards were found in Series I packs, while cards 16-31 were available in the second series packs.

		MT	NR MT	EX
Complete Set (31):		60.00	45.00	25.00
Common Player:		1.00	.70	.40
1	Ken Griffey, Jr.	8.00	6.00	3.25
2	Ryne Sandberg	5.00	3.75	2.00
3	Roger Clemens	5.00	3.75	2.00
4	Kirby Puckett	4.00	3.00	1.50
5	Bill Swift	1.25	.90	.50
6	Larry Walker	3.00	2.25	1.25
7	Juan Gonzalez	5.00	3.75	2.00
8	Wally Joyner	2.00	1.50	.80
9	Andy Van Slyke	2.00	1.50	.80
10	Robin Ventura	2.50	2.00	1.00
11	Bip Roberts	2.00	1.50	.80
12	Roberto Kelly	2.00	1.50	.80
13	Carlos Baerga	4.00	3.00	1.50
14	Orel Hershiser	2.00	1.50	.80
15	Cecil Fielder	3.00	2.25	1.25
16	Robin Yount	2.50	2.00	1.00
17	Darren Daulton	2.00	1.50	.80
18	Mark McGwire	4.00	3.00	1.50
19	Tom Glavine	2.50	2.00	1.00
20	Roberto Alomar	4.00	3.00	1.50
21	Gary Sheffield	4.00	3.00	1.50
22	Bob Tewksbury	2.00	1.50	.80
23	Brady Anderson	2.00	1.50	.80
24	Craig Biggio	2.00	1.50	.80

		MT	NR MT	EX
25	Eddie Murray	3.00	2.25	1.25
26	Luis Polonia	2.00	1.50	.80
27	Nigel Wilson	3.00	2.25	1.25
28	David Nied	3.00	2.25	1.25
29	Pat Listach	1.00	.70	.40
30	Eric Karros	2.25	1.75	.90
31	Checklist	1.00	.70	.40

1993 Donruss Masters of the Game

Donruss issued a series of 16 "Masters of the Game" art cards that were available only at WalMart stores. The oversized cards (3-1/2" by 5") feature the artwork of noted artist Dick Perez, creator of the Diamond Kings cards for the same company. The cards came issued one to a pack, along with a foil pack of 1993 Donruss cards for a retail price of about $2.96.

		MT	NR MT	EX
Complete Set:		50.00	37.00	20.00
Common Player:		2.00	1.50	.80
1	Frank Thomas	6.00	4.50	2.50
2	Nolan Ryan	6.00	4.50	2.50
3	Gary Sheffield	2.00	1.50	.80
4	Fred McGriff	3.00	2.25	1.25
5	Ryne Sandberg	5.00	3.75	2.00
6	Cal Ripken, Jr.	5.00	3.75	2.00
7	Jose Canseco	3.00	2.25	1.25
8	Ken Griffey, Jr.	6.00	4.50	2.50
9	Will Clark	4.00	3.00	1.50
10	Roberto Alomar	3.00	2.25	1.25
11	Juan Gonzalez	4.00	3.00	1.50
12	David Justice	2.50	2.00	1.00
13	Kirby Puckett	3.00	2.25	1.25
14	Barry Bonds	4.00	3.00	1.50
15	Robin Yount	4.00	3.00	1.50
16	Deion Sanders	3.00	2.25	1.25

1993 Donruss Elite

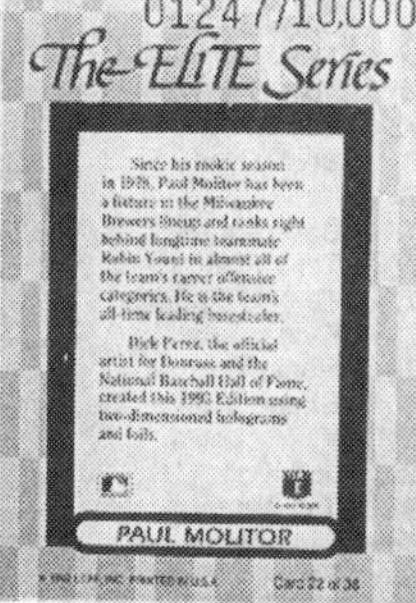

Continuing the card numbering from the 1992 Elite set, the Elite '93 inserts utilized a silver-foil front border look with blue back printing, as opposed to the gold/green scheme of the previous year. Each card is serial numbered as one of 10,000; this identified production number helping to make the Elites among the most valuable of insert cards.

		MT	NR MT	EX
Complete Set (20):		1500.00	1100.00	600.00
Common Player:		40.00	30.00	15.00
19	Fred McGriff	85.00	64.00	34.00
20	Ryne Sandberg	140.00	105.00	56.00
21	Eddie Murray	60.00	45.00	24.00
22	Paul Molitor	90.00	67.00	36.00
23	Barry Larkin	60.00	45.00	24.00
24	Don Mattingly	100.00	75.00	40.00
25	Dennis Eckersley	50.00	37.00	20.00
26	Roberto Alomar	120.00	90.00	48.00
27	Edgar Martinez	40.00	30.00	16.00
28	Gary Sheffield	65.00	49.00	26.00
29	Darren Daulton	60.00	45.00	24.00
30	Larry Walker	40.00	30.00	16.00
31	Barry Bonds	150.00	112.00	60.00
32	Andy Van Slyke	40.00	30.00	16.00
33	Mark McGwire	65.00	49.00	26.00
34	Cecil Fielder	60.00	45.00	24.00
35	Dave Winfield	75.00	56.00	30.00
36	Juan Gonzalez	175.00	131.00	70.00
—	Robin Yount (Legend)	150.00	115.00	45.00
—	Will Clark (Signature)	300.00	225.00	90.00

1993 Donruss Triple Play

For the second year, Leaf-Donruss used the "Triple Play" brand name for its base-level card set aimed at the younger collector. The 264-card set was available in several types of retail packaging and included a number of special subsets, such as childhood photos (labeled LH - Little Hotshots in the checklist) and insert sets. Checklist card #264 incorrectly show card #129, Joe Robbie Stadium, as #259. There is a second card, "Equipment," which also bears #129. An "Action Baseball" scratch-off game card was included in each foil pack.

		MT	NR MT	EX
Complete Set (264):		15.00	11.00	6.00
Common Player:		.05	.04	.02
1	Ken Griffey Jr.	.50	.40	.20
2	Roberto Alomar	.25	.20	.10
3	Cal Ripken, Jr.	.50	.40	.20
4	Eric Karros	.15	.11	.06
5	Cecil Fielder	.20	.15	.08
6	Gary Sheffield	.15	.11	.06
7	Darren Daulton	.10	.08	.04
8	Andy Van Slyke	.10	.08	.04
9	Dennis Eckersley	.07	.05	.03
10	Ryne Sandberg	.50	.40	.20
11	Mark Grace (LH)	.35	.25	.14
12	Awesome Action #1 (Luis Polonia/ Diego Segui)	.05	.04	.02
13	Mike Mussina	.07	.05	.03
14	Vince Coleman	.07	.05	.03
15	Rafael Belliard	.05	.04	.02
16	Ivan Rodriguez	.15	.11	.06
17	Eddie Taubensee	.05	.04	.02
18	Cal Eldred	.05	.04	.02

		MT	NR MT	EX
19	Rick Wilkins	.05	.04	.02
20	Edgar Martinez	.07	.05	.03
21	Brian McRae	.07	.05	.03
22	Darren Holmes	.05	.04	.02
23	Mark Whiten	.05	.04	.02
24	Todd Zeile	.07	.05	.03
25	Scott Cooper	.05	.04	.02
26	Frank Thomas	.75	.55	.30
27	Wil Cordero	.15	.11	.06
28	Juan Guzman	.05	.04	.02
29	Pedro Astacio	.05	.04	.02
30	Steve Avery	.10	.08	.04
31	Barry Larkin	.12	.09	.05
32	President Clinton	.25	.20	.10
33	Scott Erickson	.05	.04	.02
34	Mike Devereaux	.07	.05	.03
35	Tino Martinez	.05	.04	.02
36	Brent Mayne	.07	.05	.03
37	Tim Salmon	.35	.25	.14
38	Dave Hollins	.07	.05	.03
39	Royce Clayton	.05	.04	.02
40	Shawon Dunston	.05	.04	.02
41	Eddie Murray	.10	.08	.04
42	Larry Walker	.07	.05	.03
43	Jeff Bagwell	.10	.08	.04
44	Milt Cuyler	.05	.04	.02
45	Mike Bordick	.05	.04	.02
46	Mike Greenwell	.07	.05	.03
47	Steve Sax	.05	.04	.02
48	Chuck Knoblauch	.10	.08	.04
49	Charles Nagy	.05	.04	.02
50	Tim Wakefield	.05	.04	.02
51	Tony Gwynn	.10	.08	.04
52	Rob Dibble	.05	.04	.02
53	Mickey Morandini	.05	.04	.02
54	Steve Hosey	.07	.05	.03
55	Mike Piazza	.40	.30	.15
56	Bill Wegman	.05	.04	.02
57	Kevin Maas	.05	.04	.02
58	Gary DiSarcina	.07	.05	.03
59	Travis Fryman	.10	.08	.04
60	Ruben Sierra	.15	.11	.06
61	Awesome Action #2 (Ken Caminiti)	.05	.04	.02
62	Brian Jordan	.10	.08	.04
63	Scott Chiamparino	.05	.04	.02
64	Awesome Action #3 (Mike Bordick/ George Brett)	.10	.08	.04
65	Carlos Garcia	.07	.05	.03
66	Checklist 1-66	.05	.04	.02
67	John Smoltz	.07	.05	.03
68	Awesome Action #4 (Mark McGwire/ Brian Harper)	.10	.08	.04
69	Kurt Stillwell	.05	.04	.02
70	Chad Curtis	.10	.08	.04
71	Rafael Palmeiro	.20	.15	.08
72	Kevin Young	.05	.04	.02
73	Glenn Davis	.05	.04	.02
74	Dennis Martinez	.07	.05	.03
75	Sam Militello	.05	.04	.02
76	Mike Morgan	.05	.04	.02
77	Frank Thomas (LH)	.50	.40	.20
78	Staying Fit (Bip Roberts/ Mike Devereaux)	.05	.04	.02
79	Steve Buechele	.05	.04	.02
80	Carlos Baerga	.10	.08	.04
81	Robby Thompson	.07	.05	.03
82	Kirk McCaskill	.05	.04	.02
83	Lee Smith	.07	.05	.03
84	Gary Scott	.05	.04	.02
85	Tony Pena	.05	.04	.02
86	Howard Johnson	.07	.05	.03
87	Mark McGwire	.15	.11	.06
88	Bip Roberts	.07	.05	.03
89	Devon White	.10	.08	.04
90	John Franco	.05	.04	.02
91	Tom Browning	.05	.04	.02
92	Mickey Tettleton	.10	.08	.04
93	Jeff Conine	.07	.05	.03
94	Albert Belle	.15	.11	.06
95	Fred McGriff	.12	.09	.05
96	Nolan Ryan	.60	.45	.25
97	Paul Molitor (LH)	.25	.20	.10
98	Juan Bell	.05	.04	.02
99	Dave Fleming	.05	.04	.02
100	Craig Biggio	.07	.05	.03
101	Andy Stankiewicz (white name on front)	.05	.04	.02
101b	Andy Stankiewicz (red name on front)	.25	.20	.10
102	Delino DeShields	.10	.08	.04
103	Damion Easley	.07	.05	.03
104	Kevin McReynolds	.07	.05	.03
105	David Nied	.12	.09	.05
106	Rick Sutcliffe	.05	.04	.02
107	Will Clark	.20	.15	.08
108	Tim Raines	.12	.09	.05
109	Eric Anthony	.05	.04	.02
110	Mike LaValliere	.05	.04	.02
111	Dean Palmer	.07	.05	.03
112	Eric Davis	.12	.09	.05
113	Damon Berryhill	.05	.04	.02
114	Felix Jose	.05	.04	.02
115	Ozzie Guillen	.07	.05	.03
116	Pat Listach	.07	.05	.03
117	Tom Glavine	.07	.05	.03
118	Roger Clemens	.15	.11	.06
119	Dave Henderson	.05	.04	.02
120	Don Mattingly	.45	.35	.15
121	Orel Hershiser	.15	.11	.06
122	Ozzie Smith	.15	.11	.06
123	Joe Carter	.15	.11	.06
124	Bret Saberhagen	.07	.05	.03
125	Mitch Williams	.07	.05	.03
126	Jerald Clark	.05	.04	.02
127	Mile High Stadium	.05	.04	.02
128	Kent Hrbek	.10	.08	.04
129	Equipment (Curt Schilling/ Mark Whiten)	.05	.04	.02
129	Joe Robbie Stadium	.05	.04	.02
130	Gregg Jefferies	.10	.08	.04
131	John Orton	.05	.04	.02
132	Checklist 67-132	.05	.04	.02
133	Bret Boone	.07	.05	.03
134	Pat Borders	.05	.04	.02
135	Gregg Olson	.05	.04	.02
136	Brett Butler	.07	.05	.03
137	Rob Deer	.05	.04	.02
138	Darrin Jackson	.07	.05	.03
139	John Kruk	.10	.08	.04
140	Jay Bell	.07	.05	.03
141	Bobby Witt	.05	.04	.02
142	New Cubs (Dan Plesac/ Randy Myers/ Jose Guzman)	.15	.11	.06
143	Wade Boggs (LH)	.25	.20	.10
144	Awesome Action #5 (Kenny Lofton)	.05	.04	.02
145	Ben McDonald	.07	.05	.03
146	Dwight Gooden	.15	.11	.06
147	Terry Pendleton	.07	.05	.03
148	Julio Franco	.05	.04	.02
149	Ken Caminiti	.07	.05	.03
150	Greg Vaughn	.07	.05	.03
151	Sammy Sosa	.07	.05	.03
152	David Valle	.05	.04	.02
153	Wally Joyner	.12	.09	.05
154	Dante Bichette	.07	.05	.03
155	Mark Lewis	.05	.04	.02
156	Bob Tewksbury	.07	.05	.03
157	Billy Hatcher	.07	.05	.03
158	Jack McDowell	.10	.08	.04
159	Marquis Grissom	.07	.05	.03
160	Jack Morris	.07	.05	.03
161	Ramon Martinez	.05	.04	.02
162	Deion Sanders	.15	.11	.06
163	Tim Belcher	.05	.04	.02
164	Mascots	.10	.08	.04
165	Scott Leius	.05	.04	.02
166	Brady Anderson	.07	.05	.03
167	Randy Johnson	.07	.05	.03
168	Mark Gubicza	.05	.04	.02
169	Chuck Finley	.05	.04	.02
170	Terry Mulholland	.05	.04	.02
171	Matt Williams	.12	.09	.05
172	Dwight Smith	.05	.04	.02
173	Bobby Bonilla	.12	.09	.05
174	Ken Hill	.05	.04	.02
175	Doug Jones	.05	.04	.02
176	Tony Phillips	.05	.04	.02
177	Terry Steinbach	.07	.05	.03
178	Frank Viola	.07	.05	.03
179	Robin Ventura	.12	.09	.05
180	Shane Mack	.10	.08	.04
181	Kenny Lofton	.07	.05	.03
182	Jeff King	.05	.04	.02
183	Tim Teufel	.05	.04	.02
184	Chris Sabo	.07	.05	.03
185	Lenny Dykstra	.15	.11	.06
186	Trevor Wilson	.05	.04	.02
187	Darryl Strawberry	.15	.11	.06
188	Robin Yount	.35	.25	.14
189	Bob Wickman	.07	.05	.03
190	Luis Polonia	.07	.05	.03

		MT	NR MT	EX
191	Alan Trammell	.20	.15	.08
192	Bob Welch	.07	.05	.03
193	Awesome Action #6	.05	.04	.02
194	Tom Pagnozzi	.05	.04	.02
195	Bret Barberie	.05	.04	.02
196	Awesome Action #7 (Mike Scioscia)	.05	.04	.02
197	Randy Tomlin	.05	.04	.02
198	Checklist 133-198	.05	.04	.02
199	Ron Gant	.10	.08	.04
200	Awesome Action #8 (Roberto Alomar)	.10	.08	.04
201	Andy Benes	.07	.05	.03
202	Pepper	.05	.04	.02
203	Steve Finley	.07	.05	.03
204	Steve Olin	.05	.04	.02
205	Chris Hoiles	.07	.05	.03
206	John Wetteland	.05	.04	.02
207	Danny Tartabull	.07	.05	.03
208	Bernard Gilkey	.10	.08	.04
209	Tom Glavine (LH)	.10	.08	.04
210	Benito Santiago	.10	.08	.04
211	Mark Grace	.12	.09	.05
212	Glenallen Hill	.05	.04	.02
213	Jeff Brantley	.05	.04	.02
214	George Brett	.50	.40	.20
215	Mark Lemke	.05	.04	.02
216	Ron Karkovice	.07	.05	.03
217	Tom Brunansky	.05	.04	.02
218	Todd Hundley	.05	.04	.02
219	Rickey Henderson	.25	.20	.10
220	Joe Oliver	.05	.04	.02
221	Juan Gonzalez	.35	.25	.14
222	John Olerud	.15	.11	.06
223	Hal Morris	.07	.05	.03
224	Lou Whitaker	.10	.08	.04
225	Bryan Harvey	.07	.05	.03
226	Mike Gallego	.05	.04	.02
227	Willie McGee	.07	.05	.03
228	Jose Oquendo	.05	.04	.02
229	Darren Daulton (LH)	.10	.08	.04
230	Curt Schilling	.05	.04	.02
231	Jay Buhner	.10	.08	.04
232	New Astros (Doug Drabek/ Greg Swindell)	.05	.04	.02
233	Jaime Navarro	.05	.04	.02
234	Kevin Appier	.05	.04	.02
235	Mark Langston	.07	.05	.03
236	Jeff Montgomery	.05	.04	.02
237	Joe Girardi	.05	.04	.02
238	Ed Sprague	.05	.04	.02
239	Dan Walters	.05	.04	.02
240	Kevin Tapani	.05	.04	.02
241	Pete Harnisch	.07	.05	.03
242	Al Martin	.05	.04	.02
243	Jose Canseco	.25	.20	.10
244	Moises Alou	.10	.08	.04
245	Mark McGwire (LH)	.15	.11	.06
246	Luis Rivera	.07	.05	.03
247	George Bell	.07	.05	.03
248	B.J. Surhoff	.05	.04	.02
249	David Justice	.12	.09	.05
250	Brian Harper	.07	.05	.03
251	Sandy Alomar Jr.	.07	.05	.03
252	Kevin Brown	.05	.04	.02
253	New Dodgers (Tim Wallach/ Jody Reed/ Todd Worrell)	.05	.04	.02
254	Ray Lankford	.15	.11	.06
255	Derek Bell	.05	.04	.02
256	Joe Grahe	.05	.04	.02
257	Charlie Hayes	.07	.05	.03
258	New Yankees (Wade Boggs/ Jim Abbott)	.25	.20	.10
259	Not issued	.05	.04	.02
260	Kirby Puckett	.35	.25	.14
261	Fun at the Ballpark (Jay Bell/ Vince Coleman)	.05	.04	.02
262	Bill Swift	.07	.05	.03
263	Fun at the Ballpark (Roger McDowell)	.05	.04	.02
264	Checklist 199-264	.05	.04	.02

1993 Triple Play Gallery

The Gallery of Stars cards were found as random inserts in Triple Play jumbo packs. There are 10 cards in the set, featuring painted representations of the players.

Photos not available at press time

		MT	NR MT	EX
Complete Set (10):		25.00	15.00	10.00
Common Player:		1.00	.60	.30
1	Barry Bonds	7.00	5.00	3.00
2	Andre Dawson	1.25	.75	.40
3	Wade Boggs	1.75	1.00	.50
4	Greg Maddux	2.00	1.50	.75
5	Dave Winfield	2.50	1.50	.75
6	Paul Molitor	2.50	1.50	.75
7	Jim Abbott	1.75	1.00	.50
8	J.T. Snow	3.00	2.00	1.00
9	Benito Santiago	1.00	.60	.30
10	David Nied	3.50	2.50	1.25

1993 Triple Play League Leaders

These "double-headed" cards feature one player on each side. The six cards were random inserts in Triple Play retail packs and are currently the most popular of that brand's inserts.

		MT	NR MT	EX
Complete Set (6):		28.00	16.00	10.00
Common Player:		2.50	1.50	.75
1	Barry Bonds/ Dennis Eckersley	7.50	5.00	2.50
2	Greg Maddux/ Dennis Eckersley	3.00	2.00	1.00
3	Eric Karros/ Pat Listach	2.50	1.50	.75
4	Fred McGriff/ Juan Gonzalez	11.00	6.00	4.00
5	Darren Daulton/ Cecil Fielder	3.00	2.00	1.00
6	Gary Sheffield/ Edgar Martinez	3.00	2.00	1.00

1993 Triple Play Nicknames

Donruss marked its 10th anniversary in the baseball Popular nicknames of 10 of the game's top stars are featured in silver foil on this insert set found in Triple Play foil packs.

	MT	NR MT	EX
Complete Set (10):	30.00	20.00	10.00

		MT	NR MT	EX
Common Player:		1.00	.60	.30
1	Frank Thomas (Big Hurt)	8.00	6.00	3.00
2	Roger Clemens (Rocket)	3.00	2.00	1.00
3	Ryne Sandberg (Ryno)	3.50	2.50	1.25
4	Will Clark (Thrill)	2.50	1.50	.75
5	Ken Griffey Jr. (Junior)	7.00	4.00	2.50
6	Dwight Gooden (Doc)	1.00	.60	.30
7	Nolan Ryan (Express)	7.50	5.00	3.00
8	Deion Sanders (Prime Time)	1.50	1.00	.50
9	Ozzie Smith (Wizard)	2.00	1.50	.75
10	Fred McGriff (Crime Dog)	3.00	2.00	1.00

1994 Donruss

Donruss released its 1994 set in two series; the first includes 330 cards, 50 Special Edition gold cards and several insert sets. The regular cards have full-bleed photos and are UV coated and foil stamped. The Special Edition cards are gold-foil stamped on both sides and are included in each pack. Insert sets are titled Spirit of the Game, MVPs, and Decade Dominators, which were also issued in a larger (3 1/2" by 5") format. Diamond Kings, in both regular and super size, and an Elite series of cards, continuing from previous years with #s 37-42, were also issued as inserts. A 1984 Donruss Anniversary insert set features 10 popular 1984 Donruss cards.

		MT	NR MT	EX
Complete Set (330):		20.00	15.00	8.00
Common Player:		.05	.04	.02
1	Nolan Ryan (Career Salute 27 Years)	1.00	.70	.40
2	Mike Piazza	3.00	2.25	1.25
3	Moises Alou	.15	.11	.06
4	Ken Griffey, Jr.	1.50	1.25	.60
5	Gary Sheffield	.25	.20	.10
6	Roberto Alomar	.40	.30	.15
7	John Kruk	.10	.08	.04
8	Gregg Olson	.05	.04	.02
9	Gregg Jefferies	.05	.04	.02
10	Tony Gwynn	.25	.20	.10
11	Chad Curtis	.15	.11	.06
12	Craig Biggio	.05	.04	.02
13	John Burkett	.05	.04	.02
14	Carlos Baerga	.25	.20	.10
15	Robin Yount	.25	.20	.10
16	Dennis Eckersley	.05	.04	.02
17	Dwight Gooden	.05	.04	.02
18	Ryne Sandberg	.40	.30	.15
19	Rickey Henderson	.20	.15	.08
20	Jack McDowell	.10	.08	.04
21	Jay Bell	.05	.04	.02
22	Kevin Brown	.05	.04	.02
23	Robin Ventura	.10	.08	.04
24	Paul Molitor	.25	.20	.10
25	David Justice	.30	.25	.12
26	Rafael Palmeiro	.15	.11	.06
27	Cecil Fielder	.15	.11	.06
28	Chuck Knoblauch	.05	.04	.02
29	Dave Hollins	.10	.08	.04
30	Jimmy Key	.05	.04	.02
31	Mark Langston	.05	.04	.02
32	Darryl Kile	.05	.04	.02
33	Ruben Sierra	.10	.08	.04
34	Ron Gant	.10	.08	.04
35	Ozzie Smith	.15	.11	.06
36	Wade Boggs	.15	.11	.06
37	Marquis Grissom	.10	.08	.04
38	Will Clark	.15	.11	.06
39	Kenny Lofton	.20	.15	.08
40	Cal Ripken, Jr.	.35	.25	.14
41	Steve Avery	.15	.11	.06
42	Mo Vaughn	.15	.11	.06
43	Brian McRae	.05	.04	.02
44	Mickey Tettleton	.05	.04	.02
45	Barry Larkin	.05	.04	.02
46	Charlie Hayes	.05	.04	.02
47	Kevin Appier	.05	.04	.02
48	Robby Thompson	.05	.04	.02
49	Juan Gonzalez	1.50	1.25	.60
50	Paul O'Neill	.05	.04	.02
51	Marcos Armas	.05	.04	.02
52	Mike Butcher	.05	.04	.02
53	Ken Caminiti	.05	.04	.02
54	Pat Borders	.05	.04	.02
55	Pedro Munoz	.05	.04	.02
56	Tim Belcher	.05	.04	.02
57	Paul Assenmacher	.05	.04	.02
58	Damon Berryhill	.05	.04	.02
59	Ricky Bones	.05	.04	.02
60	Rene Arocha	.25	.20	.10
61	Shawn Boskie	.05	.04	.02
62	Pedro Astacio	.05	.04	.02
63	Frank Bolick	.05	.04	.02
64	Bud Black	.05	.04	.02
65	Sandy Alomar, Jr.	.05	.04	.02
66	Rich Amaral	.05	.04	.02
67	Luis Aquino	.05	.04	.02
68	Kevin Baez	.05	.04	.02
69	Mike Devereaux	.05	.04	.02
70	Andy Ashby	.05	.04	.02
71	Larry Andersen	.05	.04	.02
72	Steve Cooke	.05	.04	.02
73	Mario Daiz	.05	.04	.02
74	Rob Deer	.05	.04	.02
75	Bobby Ayala	.05	.04	.02
76	Freddie Benavides	.05	.04	.02
77	Stan Belinda	.05	.04	.02
78	John Doherty	.05	.04	.02
79	Willie Banks	.05	.04	.02
80	Spike Owen	.05	.04	.02
81	Mike Bordick	.05	.04	.02
82	Chili Davis	.05	.04	.02
83	Luis Gonzalez	.05	.04	.02
84	Ed Sprague	.05	.04	.02
85	Jeff Reboulet	.05	.04	.02
86	Jason Bere	1.00	.70	.40
87	Mark Hutton	.05	.04	.02
88	Jeff Blauser	.05	.04	.02
89	Cal Eldred	.20	.15	.08
90	Bernard Gilkey	.05	.04	.02
91	Frank Castillo	.05	.04	.02
92	Jim Gott	.05	.04	.02
93	Greg Colbrunn	.05	.04	.02
94	Jeff Brantley	.05	.04	.02
95	Jeremy Hernandez	.05	.04	.02
96	Norm Charlton	.05	.04	.02
97	Alex Arias	.05	.04	.02
98	John Franco	.05	.04	.02
99	Chris Hoiles	.05	.04	.02
100	Brad Ausmus	.05	.04	.02
101	Wes Chamberlain	.05	.04	.02
102	Mark Dewey	.05	.04	.02
103	Benji Gil (Rated Rookie)	.60	.45	.25
104	John Dopson	.05	.04	.02
105	John Smiley	.05	.04	.02
106	David Nied	.40	.30	.15
107	George Brett (Career Salute 21 Years)	.25	.20	.10

#	Player	MT	NR MT	EX
108	Kirk Gibson	.05	.04	.02
109	Larry Casian	.05	.04	.02
110	Checklist (Ryne Sandberg 2,000 Hits)	.05	.04	.02
111	Brent Gates	.15	.11	.06
112	Damion Easley	.10	.08	.04
113	Pete Harnisch	.05	.04	.02
114	Danny Cox	.05	.04	.02
115	Kevin Tapani	.05	.04	.02
116	Roberto Hernandez	.05	.04	.02
117	Domingo Jean	.05	.04	.02
118	Sid Bream	.05	.04	.02
119	Doug Henry	.05	.04	.02
120	Omar Olivares	.05	.04	.02
121	Mike Harkey	.05	.04	.02
122	Carlos Hernandez	.05	.04	.02
123	Jeff Fassero	.20	.15	.08
124	Dave Burba	.05	.04	.02
125	Wayne Kirby	.05	.04	.02
126	John Cummings	.05	.04	.02
127	Bret Barberie	.05	.04	.02
128	Todd Hundley	.05	.04	.02
129	Tim Hulett	.05	.04	.02
130	Phil Clark	.05	.04	.02
131	Danny Jackson	.05	.04	.02
132	Tom Foley	.05	.04	.02
133	Donald Harris	.15	.11	.06
134	Scott Fletcher	.05	.04	.02
135	Johnny Ruffin (Rated Rookie)	.05	.04	.02
136	Jerald Clark	.05	.04	.02
137	Billy Brewer	.05	.04	.02
138	Dan Gladden	.05	.04	.02
139	Eddie Guardado	.05	.04	.02
140	Checklist (Cal Ripken, Jr. 2,000 Hits)	.05	.04	.02
141	Scott Hemond	.05	.04	.02
142	Steve Frey	.05	.04	.02
143	Xavier Hernandez	.05	.04	.02
144	Mark Eichhorn	.05	.04	.02
145	Ellis Burks	.05	.04	.02
146	Jim Leyritz	.05	.04	.02
147	Mark Lemke	.05	.04	.02
148	Pat Listach	.15	.11	.06
149	Donovan Osborne	.05	.04	.02
150	Glenallen Hill	.05	.04	.02
151	Orel Hershiser	.05	.04	.02
152	Darrin Fletcher	.05	.04	.02
153	Royce Clayton	.15	.11	.06
154	Derek Lilliquist	.05	.04	.02
155	Mike Felder	.05	.04	.02
156	Jeff Conine	.05	.04	.02
157	Ryan Thompson	.05	.04	.02
158	Ben McDonald	.10	.08	.04
159	Ricky Gutierrez	.05	.04	.02
160	Terry Mulholland	.05	.04	.02
161	Carlos Garcia	.20	.15	.08
162	Tom Henke	.05	.04	.02
163	Mike Greenwell	.05	.04	.02
164	Thomas Howard	.05	.04	.02
165	Joe Girardi	.05	.04	.02
166	Hubie Brooks	.05	.04	.02
167	Greg Gohr	.05	.04	.02
168	Chip Hale	.05	.04	.02
169	Rick Honeycutt	.05	.04	.02
170	Hilly Hathaway	.05	.04	.02
171	Todd Jones	.05	.04	.02
172	Tony Fernandez	.05	.04	.02
173	Bo Jackson	.20	.15	.08
174	Bobby Munoz	.05	.04	.02
175	Greg McMichael	.25	.20	.10
176	Graeme Lloyd	.10	.08	.04
177	Tom Pagnozzi	.05	.04	.02
178	Derrick May	.05	.04	.02
179	Pedro Martinez	.20	.15	.08
180	Ken Hill	.05	.04	.02
181	Bryan Hickerson	.05	.04	.02
182	Jose Mesa	.05	.04	.02
183	Dave Fleming	.05	.04	.02
184	Henry Cotto	.05	.04	.02
185	Jeff Kent	.05	.04	.02
186	Mark McLemore	.05	.04	.02
187	Trevor Hoffman	.15	.11	.06
188	Todd Pratt	.15	.11	.06
189	Blas Minor	.05	.04	.02
190	Charlie Leibrandt	.05	.04	.02
191	Tony Pena	.05	.04	.02
192	Larry Luebbers	.05	.04	.02
193	Greg Harris	.05	.04	.02
194	David Cone	.05	.04	.02
195	Bill Gullickson	.05	.04	.02
196	Brian Harper	.05	.04	.02
197	Steve Karsay (Rated Rookie)	.05	.04	.02
198	Greg Myers	.05	.04	.02
199	Mark Portugal	.05	.04	.02
200	Pat Hentgen	.40	.30	.15
201	Mike La Valliere	.05	.04	.02
202	Mike Stanley	.10	.08	.04
203	Kent Mercker	.05	.04	.02
204	Dave Nilsson	.05	.04	.02
205	Erik Pappas	.05	.04	.02
206	Mike Morgan	.05	.04	.02
207	Roger McDowell	.05	.04	.02
208	Mike Lansing	.20	.15	.08
209	Kirt Manwaring	.05	.04	.02
210	Randy Milligan	.05	.04	.02
211	Erik Hanson	.05	.04	.02
212	Orestes Destrade	.05	.04	.02
213	Mike Maddux	.05	.04	.02
214	Alan Mills	.05	.04	.02
215	Tim Mauser	.05	.04	.02
216	Ben Rivera	.05	.04	.02
217	Don Slaught	.05	.04	.02
218	Bob Patterson	.05	.04	.02
219	Carlos Quintana	.05	.04	.02
220	Checklist (Tim Raines 2,000 Hits)	.05	.04	.02
221	Hal Morris	.05	.04	.02
222	Darren Holmes	.05	.04	.02
223	Chris Gwynn	.05	.04	.02
224	Chad Kreuter	.05	.04	.02
225	Mike Hartley	.05	.04	.02
226	Scott Lydy	.05	.04	.02
227	Eduardo Perez	.05	.04	.02
228	Greg Swindell	.05	.04	.02
229	Al Leiter	.05	.04	.02
230	Scott Radinsky	.05	.04	.02
231	Bob Wickman	.05	.04	.02
232	Otis Nixon	.05	.04	.02
233	Kevin Reimer	.05	.04	.02
234	Geronimo Pena	.05	.04	.02
235	Kevin Roberson (Rated Rookie)	.20	.15	.08
236	Jody Reed	.05	.04	.02
237	Kirk Rueter (Rated Rookie)	.05	.04	.02
238	Willie McGee	.05	.04	.02
239	Charles Nagy	.05	.04	.02
240	Tim Leary	.05	.04	.02
241	Carl Everett	.05	.04	.02
242	Charlie O'Brien	.05	.04	.02
243	Mike Pagliarulo	.05	.04	.02
244	Kerry Taylor	.05	.04	.02
245	Kevin Stocker	.20	.15	.08
246	Joel Johnston	.05	.04	.02
247	Geno Petralli	.05	.04	.02
248	Jeff Russell	.05	.04	.02
249	Joe Oliver	.05	.04	.02
250	Robert Mejia	.40	.30	.15
251	Chris Haney	.05	.04	.02
252	Bill Krueger	.05	.04	.02
253	Shane Mack	.05	.04	.02
254	Terry Steinbach	.05	.04	.02
255	Luis Polonia	.05	.04	.02
256	Eddie Taubensee	.05	.04	.02
257	Dave Stewart	.05	.04	.02
258	Tim Raines	.05	.04	.02
259	Bernie Williams	.05	.04	.02
260	John Smoltz	.10	.08	.04
261	Kevin Seitzer	.05	.04	.02
262	Bob Tewksbury	.05	.04	.02
263	Bob Scanlan	.05	.04	.02
264	Henry Rodriguez	.05	.04	.02
265	Tim Scott	.05	.04	.02
266	Scott Sanderson	.05	.04	.02
267	Eric Plunk	.05	.04	.02
268	Edgar Martinez	.05	.04	.02
269	Charlie Hough	.05	.04	.02
270	Joe Orsulak	.05	.04	.02
271	Harold Reynolds	.05	.04	.02
272	Tim Teufel	.05	.04	.02
273	Bobby Thigpen	.05	.04	.02
274	Randy Tomlin	.05	.04	.02
275	Gary Redus	.05	.04	.02
276	Ken Ryan	.05	.04	.02
277	Tim Pugh	.05	.04	.02
278	Jayhawk Owens	.05	.04	.02
279	Phil Hiatt (Rated Rookie)	.20	.15	.08
280	Alan Trammell	.05	.04	.02
281	Dave McCarty (Rated Rookie)	.20	.15	.08
282	Bob Welch	.05	.04	.02
283	J.T. Snow	.60	.45	.25
284	Brian Williams	.05	.04	.02
285	Devon White	.05	.04	.02
286	Steve Sax	.05	.04	.02
287	Tony Tarasco	.30	.25	.12

		MT	NR MT	EX
288	Bill Spiers	.05	.04	.02
289	Allen Watson	.40	.30	.15
290	Checklist (Rickey Henderson 2,000 Hits)	.05	.04	.02
291	Joe Vizcaino	.05	.04	.02
292	Darryl Strawberry	.05	.04	.02
293	John Wetteland	.05	.04	.02
294	Bill Swift	.05	.04	.02
295	Jeff Treadway	.05	.04	.02
296	Tino Martinez	.05	.04	.02
297	Richie Lewis	.05	.04	.02
298	Bret Saberhagen	.05	.04	.02
299	Arthur Rhodes	.05	.04	.02
300	Guillermo Velasquez	.05	.04	.02
301	Milt Thompson	.05	.04	.02
302	Doug Strange	.05	.04	.02
303	Aaron Sele	.60	.45	.25
304	Bip Roberts	.05	.04	.02
305	Bruce Ruffin	.05	.04	.02
306	Jose Lind	.05	.04	.02
307	David Wells	.05	.04	.02
308	Bobby Witt	.05	.04	.02
309	Mark Wohlers	.05	.04	.02
310	B.J. Surhoff	.05	.04	.02
311	Mark Whiten	.10	.08	.04
312	Turk Wendell	.05	.04	.02
313	Raul Mondesi	.15	.11	.06
314	Brian Turang	.05	.04	.02
315	Chris Hammond	.05	.04	.02
316	Tim Bogar	.05	.04	.02
317	Brad Pennington	.05	.04	.02
318	Tim Worrell	.05	.04	.02
319	Mitch Williams	.05	.04	.02
320	Rondell White (Rated Rookie)	.50	.40	.20
321	Frank Viola	.05	.04	.02
322	Manny Ramirez (Rated Rookie)	1.00	.70	.40
323	Gary Wayne	.05	.04	.02
324	Mike Macfarlane	.05	.04	.02
325	Russ Springer	.05	.04	.02
326	Tim Wallach	.05	.04	.02
327	Salomon Torres (Rated Rookie)	.25	.20	.10
328	Omar Vizquel	.05	.04	.02
329	Andy Tomberlin	.05	.04	.02
330	Chris Sabo	.05	.04	.02

1994 Donruss Decade Dominators

Donruss has selected 10 top home run hitters from the 1990s for this insert set. Cards were issued in all types of 94 Series I packs. The Dominators were also issued in a large format (3 1/2 by 5), with every box of hobby foil packs containing one of the serially-numbered (10,000 each) cards.

		MT	NR MT	EX
	Complete Set (10):	25.00	15.00	8.00
	Common Player:	1.50	1.25	.60
1	Cecil Fielder	2.00	1.50	.75
2	Barry Bonds	5.00	3.50	2.00
3	Fred McGriff	2.50	1.75	.90
4	Matt Williams	1.50	1.25	.60
5	Joe Carter	2.50	1.75	.90
6	Juan Gonzalez	6.00	4.50	2.25
7	Jose Canseco	2.00	1.60	.75
8	Ron Gant	2.00	1.60	.75
9	Ken Griffey, Jr.	8.00	6.00	3.00
10	Mark McGwire	2.00	1.60	.75

Values listed are a national average. Cards of players, especially minor stars, which might be priced as commons throughout most of the country will often sell for a premium in the player's hometown and in cities where he played.

1994 Donruss Elite

Donruss continues its popular Elite Series with six more players in 1994. The cards, numbered #37-42, were inserted in foil packs only. The cards feature the player in a diamond on the front; the back offers an opinion of why the player is considered an elite and is serially numbered from 1-10,000.

		MT	NR MT	EX
	Complete Set (6):	450.00	300.00	145.00
	Common Player:	40.00	30.00	15.00
37	Frank Thomas	150.00	125.00	60.00
38	Tony Gwynn	55.00	40.00	20.00
39	Tim Salmon	125.00	100.00	45.00
40	Albert Belle	50.00	35.00	18.00
41	John Kruk	40.00	30.00	15.00
42	Juan Gonzalez	100.00	75.00	40.00

1994 Donruss Diamond Kings

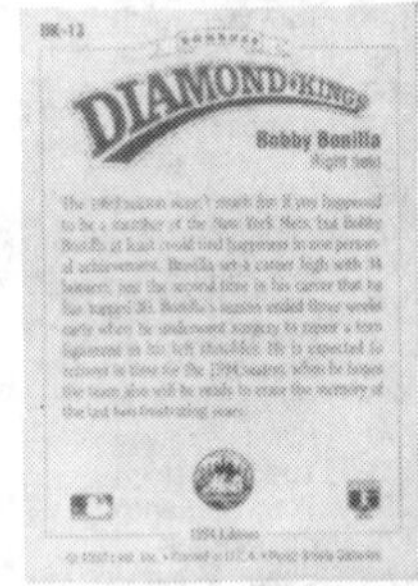

The artwork of Dick Perez is again featured on this insert set included in foil packs. Player art is set against garnish color backgrounds with a red-and-silver "Diamond Kings" foil logo above, and the player's name in script at bottom. Backs are printed in red on pale yellow and feature a 1993 season summary. Cards have a DK preface to the number. Card #1-14 were included in Series I packaging, cards 15-28 were found in Series II. A 29th card, honoring Dave Winfield, was also produced.

		MT	NR MT	EX
	Complete Set (14):	30.00	22.50	11.00
	Common Player:	1.50	1.25	.60
1	Barry Bonds	4.00	3.00	1.60
2	Mo Vaughn	2.50	1.75	1.00
3	Steve Avery	2.50	1.75	1.00
4	Tim Salmon	7.50	5.75	3.50
5	Rick Wilkins	1.50	1.25	.60

		MT	NR MT	EX
6	Brian Harper	1.50	1.25	.60
7	Andres Galarraga	1.50	1.25	.60
8	Albert Belle	3.00	2.25	1.25
9	John Kruk	1.75	1.35	.80
10	Ivan Rodriguez	2.50	1.75	.90
11	Tony Gwynn	2.50	1.75	.90
12	Brian McRae	1.50	1.25	.60
13	Bobby Bonilla	1.50	1.25	.60
14	Ken Griffey, Jr.	8.00	6.00	3.00

1994 Donruss MVPs

These 1994 Donruss insert cards were included in 1994 jumbo packs only. The fronts have a large metallic blue MVP logo, beneath which is a red stripe with the player's name and position in white. At the upper-left border are six vertical white stars. A gold-foil Donruss logo is at upper-right. Backs have a portrait photo bordered at left by a metallic blue strip with a row of seven vertical white stars. Stats for 1993 are in a red-and-white banner at bottom, and there is a short summary of why the player was selected as team MVP.

		MT	NR MT	EX
Complete Set (14):		25.00	15.00	8.00
Common Player:		1.00	.70	.40
1	David Justice	2.00	1.50	.80
2	Mark Grace	1.25	1.00	.50
3	Jose Rijo	1.00	.70	.40
4	Andres Galarraga	1.00	.70	.40
5	Bryan Harvey	1.00	.70	.40
6	Jeff Bagwell	2.00	1.50	.80
7	Mike Piazza	10.00	7.00	4.00
8	Moises Alou	1.50	1.25	.60
9	Bobby Bonilla	1.25	1.00	.45
10	Lenny Dykstra	2.00	1.50	.80
11	Jeff King	1.00	.70	.40
12	Gregg Jefferies	1.50	1.25	.60
13	Tony Gwynn	2.50	2.00	1.00
14	Barry Bonds	4.00	3.00	1.50

1994 Donruss Anniversary-1984

Photos not available at press time

This set commemorates and features 10 of the most popular cards from Donruss' 1984 set. The cards, inserted in hobby foil packs only, are "holographically enhanced" with foil stamping and UV coating.

		MT	NR MT	EX
1	Complete Set (10):, Don Mattingly			
		6.00	4.50	2.50
2	Joe Carter	6.00	4.50	2.50
3	Cal Ripken, Jr.	5.00	3.50	2.00
4	Ryne Sandberg	5.00	3.50	2.00
5	Robin Yount	4.00	3.00	1.75
6	Nolan Ryan	6.00	4.50	2.50
7	Tony Gwynn	3.00	2.25	1.25
8	Wade Boggs	2.50	1.75	1.00
9	Rickey Henderson	3.00	2.25	1.25
10	George Brett	6.00	4.50	2.50

1994 Donruss Spirit of the Game

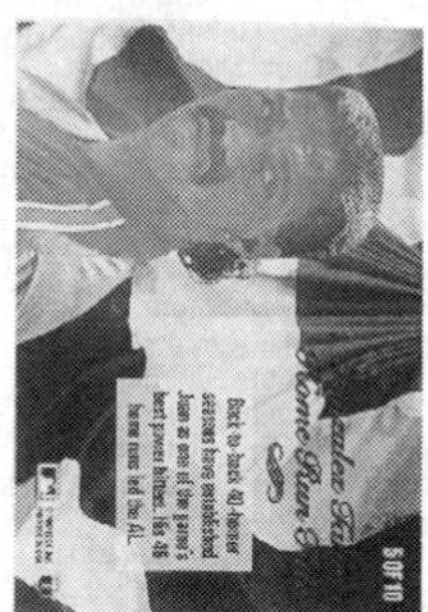

Ten players are featured in this 1994 Donruss insert set, packaged exclusively in retail boxes. Horizontal in format, fronts feature a color player action photo set against a gold-tone background which has the appearance of a multiple-exposure photo. The Donruss logo at upper-right and the bottom strip carrying the "Spirit of the Game" title are holographic foil. On back a player portrait photo is set against a backdrop of red, white and blue bunting. There is a short previous-season write-up at right. Cards #1-5 were included with Series I, cards 6-10 were in Series II packs.

		MT	NR MT	EX
Complete Set (10):		150.00	110.00	60.00
Common player:		12.00	9.00	4.75
1	John Olerud	12.00	9.00	4.75
2	Barry Bonds	18.00	13.50	7.25
3	Ken Griffey, Jr.	25.00	18.50	10.00
4	Mike Piazza	18.00	13.50	7.25
5	Juan Gonzalez	18.00	13.50	7.25
6	Frank Thomas	25.00	18.50	10.00
7	Tim Salmon	18.00	13.50	7.25
8	David Justice	12.00	9.00	4.75
9	Don Mattingly	15.00	11.00	6.00
10	Lenny Dykstra	12.00	9.00	4.75

1994 Donruss Special Edition-Gold

In 1994 Donruss added a Special Edition subset of 100 of the game's top players. The first 50 cards were included one or two per pack in all types of Donruss' Series I 1994 packaging. THe cards have special gold-foil stamping on front in the area of the team logo and player name, and on back in a "Special Edition" number box in the upper-left corner.

		MT	NR MT	EX
Complete Set (50):		40.00	30.00	15.00
Common Player:		.25	.20	.10
1	Nolan Ryan	4.00	3.00	1.75
2	Mike Piazza	10.00	7.00	4.00
3	Moises Alou	.60	.45	.25
4	Ken Griffey, Jr.	4.00	3.00	1.75
5	Gary Sheffield	.50	.35	.20
6	Roberto Alomar	1.00	.70	.40
7	John Kruk	.50	.35	.20
8	Gregg Olson	.25	.20	.10
9	Gregg Jefferies	.40	.30	.15
10	Tony Gwynn	.60	.45	.25
11	Chad Curtis	1.00	.70	.40
12	Craig Biggio	.25	.20	.10
13	John Burkett	.25	.20	.10
14	Carlos Baerga	1.00	.70	.40
15	Robin Yount	1.00	.70	.40
16	Dennis Eckersley	.25	.20	.10
17	Dwight Gooden	.25	.20	.10
18	Ryne Sandberg	1.00	.70	.40
19	Rickey Henderson	1.00	.70	.40
20	Jack McDowell	.40	.30	.15
21	Jay Bell	.25	.20	.10
22	Kevin Brown	.25	.20	.10
23	Robin Ventura	.60	.45	.25
24	Paul Molitor	1.00	.70	.40
25	David Justice	.80	.60	.35
26	Rafael Palmeiro	.40	.30	.15
27	Cecil Fielder	.40	.30	.15
28	Chuck Knoblauch	.25	.20	.10
29	Dave Hollins	.40	.30	.15
30	Jimmy Key	.25	.20	.10
31	Mark Langston	.25	.20	.10
32	Darryl Kile	.25	.20	.10
33	Ruben Sierra	.35	.20	.10
34	Ron Gant	.50	.35	.20
35	Ozzie Smith	.50	.35	.20
36	Wade Boggs	.50	.35	.20
37	Marquis Grissom	.40	.30	.15
38	Will Clark	.75	.60	.30
39	Kenny Lofton	.50	.35	.20
40	Cal Ripken, Jr.	1.00	.70	.40
41	Steve Avery	.40	.30	.15
42	Mo Vaughn	.25	.20	.10
43	Brian McRae	.25	.20	.10
44	Mickey Tettleton	.25	.20	.10
45	Barry Larkin	.25	.20	.10
46	Charlie Hayes	.25	.20	.10
47	Kevin Appier	.25	.20	.10
48	Robby Thompson	.25	.20	.10
49	Juan Gonzalez	4.00	3.00	1.75
50	Paul O'Neill	.25	.20	.10

Values for recent cards and sets are listed in Mint (MT), Near Mint (NM) and Excellent (EX), reflecting the fact that many cards from recent years have been preserved in top condition. Recent cards and sets in less than Excellent condition have little collector interest.

1939 -46 Exhibit Supply Co. Salutation

Referred to as "Exhibits" because they were issued by the Exhibit Supply Co. of Chicago, Ill., this group was produced over an 8-year span. They are frequently called "Salutations" because of the personalized greeting found on the card. The black and white cards, which measure 3-3/8" by 5-3/8", are unnumbered and blank-backed. Most exhibits were sold through vending machines for a penny. The complete set price includes all variations.

		NR MT	EX	VG
Complete Set:		4750.00	2375.00	1425.
Common Player:		5.00	2.50	1.50
(1a)	Luke Appling ("Made In U.S.A." in left corner)	12.00	6.00	3.50
(1b)	Luke Appling ("Made In U.S.A." in right corner)	7.00	3.50	2.00
(2)	Earl Averill	375.00	175.00	100.00
(3)	Charles "Red" Barrett	5.00	2.50	1.50
(4)	Henry "Hank" Borowy	5.00	2.50	1.50
(5)	Lou Boudreau	8.00	4.00	2.50
(6)	Adolf Camilli	25.00	12.50	7.50
(7)	Phil Cavarretta	6.00	3.00	1.75
(8)	Harland Clift (Harlond)	12.00	6.00	3.50
(9)	Tony Cuccinello	25.00	12.50	7.50
(10)	Dizzy Dean	80.00	40.00	24.00
(11)	Paul Derringer	5.00	2.50	1.50
(12a)	Bill Dickey ("Made In U.S.A." in left corner)	25.00	12.50	7.50
(12b)	Bill Dickey ("Made In U.S.A." in right corner)	25.00	12.50	7.50
(13)	Joe DiMaggio	125.00	60.00	40.00
(14)	Bob Elliott	5.00	2.50	1.50
(15)	Bob Feller (portrait)	100.00	50.00	30.00
(16)	Bob Feller (pitching)	30.00	15.00	9.00
(17)	Dave Ferriss	5.00	2.50	1.50
(18)	Jimmy Foxx	100.00	50.00	30.00
(19)	Lou Gehrig	1000.00	500.00	300.00
(20)	Charlie Gehringer	125.00	56.00	35.00
(21)	Vernon Gomez	180.00	90.00	55.00
(22a)	Joe Gordon (Cleveland)	25.00	12.50	7.50
(22b)	Joe Gordon (New York)	6.00	3.00	1.75
(23)	Hank Greenberg (Truly yours)	20.00	10.00	6.00
(24)	Hank Greenberg (Very truly yours)	80.00	40.00	24.00
(25)	Robert Grove	50.00	25.00	15.00
(26)	Gabby Hartnett	275.00	150.00	80.00
(27)	Buddy Hassett	15.00	7.50	4.50
(28a)	Jeff Heath (large projection)	25.00	12.50	7.50
(28b)	Jeff Heath (small projection)	5.00	2.50	1.50
(29)	Kirby Higbe	15.00	7.50	4.50
(30a)	Tommy Holmes (Yours truly)	5.00	2.50	1.50
(30b)	Tommy Holmes (Sincerely yours)	125.00	60.00	40.00
(31)	Carl Hubbell	25.00	12.50	7.50
(32)	Bob Johnson	15.00	7.50	4.50
(33)	Charles Keller	5.00	2.50	1.50
(34)	Ken Keltner	25.00	12.50	7.50
(35)	Chuck Klein	175.00	90.00	50.00
(36)	Mike Kreevich	80.00	40.00	24.00
(37)	Joe Kuhel	20.00	10.00	6.00
(38)	Bill Lee	20.00	10.00	6.00
(39)	Ernie Lombardi (Cordially)	200.00	100.00	60.00
(40)	Ernie Lombardi (Cordially yours)	8.00	4.00	2.50

		NR MT	EX	VG
(41a)	Martin Marion ("Made in U.S.A." in left corner)	6.00	3.00	1.75
(41b)	Martin Marion ("Made In U.S.A." in right corner)	6.00	3.00	1.75
(42)	Merrill May	20.00	10.00	6.00
(43a)	Frank McCormick ("Made In U.S.A." in left corner)	20.00	10.00	6.00
(43b)	Frank McCormick ("Made In U.S.A." in right corner)	6.00	3.00	1.75
(44a)	George McQuinn ("Made In U.S.A." in left corner)	20.00	10.00	6.00
(44b)	George McQuinn ("Made In U.S.A." in right corner)	6.00	3.00	1.75
(45)	Joe Medwick	30.00	15.00	9.00
(46a)	Johnny Mize ("Made In U.S.A." in left corner)	25.00	12.50	7.50
(46b)	Johnny Mize ("Made In U.S.A." in right corner)	15.00	7.50	4.50
(47)	Hugh Mulcahy	80.00	40.00	24.00
(48)	Hal Newhouser	7.50	3.75	2.25
(49)	Buck Newson (Newsom)	175.00	90.00	50.00
(50)	Louis (Buck) Newsom	5.00	2.50	1.50
(51a)	Mel Ott ("Made In U.S.A." in left corner)	50.00	25.00	15.00
(51b)	Mel Ott ("Made In U.S.A." in right corner)	25.00	12.50	7.50
(52a)	Andy Pafko ("C" on cap)	5.00	2.50	1.50
(52b)	Andy Pafko (plain cap)	5.00	2.50	1.50
(53)	Claude Passeau	6.00	3.00	1.75
(54a)	Howard Pollet ("Made In U.S.A." in left corner)	11.00	5.50	3.25
(54b)	Howard Pollet ("Made In U.S.A." in right corner)	5.00	2.50	1.50
(55a)	Pete Reiser ("Made In U.S.A." in left corner)	80.00	40.00	24.00
(55b)	Pete Reiser ("Made In U.S.A." in right corner)	5.00	2.50	1.50
(56)	Johnny Rizzo	90.00	45.00	27.00
(57)	Glenn Russell	90.00	45.00	27.00
(58)	George Stirnweiss	5.00	2.50	1.50
(59)	Cecil Travis	15.00	7.50	4.50
(60)	Paul Trout	5.00	2.50	1.50
(61)	Johnny Vander Meer	40.00	20.00	12.00
(62)	Arky Vaughn (Vaughan)	20.00	10.00	6.00
(63a)	Fred "Dixie" Walker ("D" on cap)	5.00	2.50	1.50
(63b)	Fred "Dixie" Walker ("D" blanked out)	50.00	25.00	15.00
(64)	"Bucky" Walters	5.00	2.50	1.50
(65)	Lon Warneke	6.50	3.25	2.00
(66)	Ted Williams (#9 shows)	350.00	175.00	105.00
(67)	Ted Williams (#9 not showing)	60.00	30.00	18.00
(68)	Rudy York	5.00	2.50	1.50

1947 -66 Exhibits

Called "Exhibits" as they were produced by the Exhibit Supply Co. of Chicago, Ill., this group covers a span of twenty years. Each unnumbered, black and white card, printed on heavy stock, measures 3-3/8" by 5-3/8" and is blank-backed. The Exhibit Supply Co. issued new sets each year, with many players being repeated year after year. Other players appeared in only one or two years, thereby creating levels of scarcity. Many variations of the same basic pose are found in the group. Those cards are listed in the checklist that follows with an "a", "b", etc. following the assigned card number. The complete set includes all variations.

		NR MT	EX	VG
Complete Set:		5000.00	2500.00	1500.
Common Player:		4.25	2.25	1.25
(1)	Hank Aaron	30.00	15.00	9.00
(2a)	Joe Adcock (script signature)	4.25	2.25	1.25
(2b)	Joe Adcock (plain signature)	5.00	2.50	1.50
(3)	Max Alvis	25.00	12.50	7.50
(4)	Johnny Antonelli (Braves)	4.25	2.25	1.25
(5)	Johnny Antonelli (Giants)	5.00	2.50	1.50
(6)	Luis Aparicio (portrait)	7.00	3.50	2.00
(7)	Luis Aparicio (batting)	25.00	12.50	7.50
(8)	Luke Appling	7.00	3.50	2.00
(9a)	Ritchie Ashburn (Phillies, first name incorrect)	7.00	3.50	2.00
(9b)	Richie Ashburn (Phillies, first name correct)	10.00	5.00	3.00
(10)	Richie Ashburn (Cubs)	13.00	6.50	4.00
(11)	Bob Aspromonte	4.25	2.25	1.25
(12)	Toby Atwell	4.25	2.25	1.25
(13)	Ed Bailey (with cap)	5.00	2.50	1.50
(14)	Ed Bailey (no cap)	4.25	2.25	1.25
(15)	Gene Baker	4.25	2.25	1.25
(16a)	Ernie Banks (bat on shoulder, script signature)	25.00	12.50	7.50
(16b)	Ernie Banks (bat on shoulder, plain signature)	15.00	7.50	4.50
(17)	Ernie Banks (portrait)	25.00	12.50	7.50
(18)	Steve Barber	4.25	2.25	1.25
(19)	Earl Battey	5.00	2.50	1.50
(20)	Matt Batts	4.25	2.25	1.25
(21a)	Hank Bauer (N.Y. cap)	5.00	2.50	1.50
(21b)	Hank Bauer (plain cap)	7.00	3.50	2.00
(22)	Frank Baumholtz	4.25	2.25	1.25
(23)	Gene Bearden	4.25	2.25	1.25
(24)	Joe Beggs	12.00	6.00	3.50
(25)	Larry "Yogi" Berra	30.00	15.00	9.00
(26)	Yogi Berra	20.00	10.00	6.00
(27)	Steve Bilko	5.00	2.50	1.50
(28)	Ewell Blackwell (pitching)	7.00	3.50	2.00
(29)	Ewell Blackwell (portrait)	4.25	2.25	1.25
(30a)	Don Blasingame (St. Louis cap)	4.25	2.25	1.25
(30b)	Don Blasingame (plain cap)	6.00	3.00	1.75
(31)	Ken Boyer	7.00	3.50	2.00
(32)	Ralph Branca	7.00	3.50	2.00
(33)	Jackie Brandt	50.00	25.00	15.00
(34)	Harry Brecheen	4.25	2.25	1.25
(35)	Tom Brewer	12.00	6.00	3.50
(36)	Lou Brissie	5.00	2.50	1.50
(37)	Bill Bruton	4.25	2.25	1.25
(38)	Lew Burdette (pitching, side view)	4.25	2.25	1.25
(39)	Lew Burdette (pitching, front view)	6.00	3.00	1.75
(40)	Johnny Callison	7.00	3.50	2.00
(41)	Roy Campanella	20.00	10.00	6.00
(42)	Chico Carrasquel (portrait)	13.00	6.50	4.00
(43)	Chico Carrasquel (leaping)	4.25	2.25	1.25
(44)	George Case	12.00	6.00	3.50
(45)	Hugh Casey	5.00	2.50	1.50
(46)	Norm Cash	7.00	3.50	2.00
(47)	Orlando Cepeda (portrait)	10.00	5.00	3.00
(48)	Orlando Cepeda (batting)	10.00	5.00	3.00
(49a)	Bob Cerv (A's cap)	7.00	3.50	2.00
(49b)	Bob Cerv (plain cap)	16.00	8.00	4.75
(50)	Dean Chance	4.25	2.25	1.25
(51)	Spud Chandler	12.00	6.00	3.50
(52)	Tom Cheney	4.25	2.25	1.25
(53)	Bubba Church	5.00	2.50	1.50
(54)	Roberto Clemente	30.00	15.00	9.00
(55)	Rocky Colavito (portrait)	30.00	15.00	9.00
(56)	Rocky Colavito (batting)	7.00	3.50	2.00
(57)	Choo Choo Coleman	13.00	6.50	4.00
(58)	Gordy Coleman	25.00	12.50	7.50
(59)	Jerry Coleman	5.00	2.50	1.50
(60)	Mort Cooper	12.00	6.00	3.50
(61)	Walker Cooper	4.25	2.25	1.25
(62)	Roger Craig	12.00	6.00	3.50
(63)	Delmar Crandall	4.25	2.25	1.25
(64)	Joe Cunningham (batting)	30.00	15.00	9.00
(65)	Joe Cunningham (portrait)	7.00	3.50	2.00
(66)	Guy Curtwright (Curtright)	5.00	2.50	1.50
(67)	Bud Daley	35.00	17.50	10.50
(68a)	Alvin Dark (Braves)	7.00	3.50	2.00
(68b)	Alvin Dark (Giants)	5.00	2.50	1.50
(69)	Alvin Dark (Cubs)	7.00	3.50	2.00
(70)	Murray Dickson (Murry)	5.00	2.50	1.50
(71)	Bob Dillinger	7.00	3.50	2.00
(72)	Dom DiMaggio	18.00	9.00	5.50
(73)	Joe Dobson	7.00	3.50	2.00

		NR MT	EX	VG
(74)	Larry Doby	4.25	2.25	1.25
(75)	Bobby Doerr	12.00	6.00	3.50
(76)	Dick Donovan (plain cap)	7.00	3.50	2.00
(77)	Dick Donovan (Sox cap)	4.25	2.25	1.25
(78)	Walter Dropo	4.25	2.25	1.25
(79)	Don Drysdale (glove at waist)	30.00	15.00	9.00
(80)	Don Drysdale (portrait)	30.00	15.00	9.00
(81)	Luke Easter	5.00	2.50	1.50
(82)	Bruce Edwards	5.00	2.50	1.50
(83)	Del Ennis	4.25	2.25	1.25
(84)	Al Evans	4.50	2.25	1.25
(85)	Walter Evers	4.25	2.25	1.25
(86)	Ferris Fain (fielding)	7.00	3.50	2.00
(87)	Ferris Fain (portrait)	4.25	2.25	1.25
(88)	Dick Farrell	4.25	2.25	1.25
(89)	Ed "Whitey" Ford	25.00	12.50	7.50
(90)	Whitey Ford (pitching)	15.00	7.50	4.50
(91)	Whitey Ford (portrait)	60.00	30.00	17.50
(92)	Dick Fowler	7.00	3.50	2.00
(93)	Nelson Fox	5.00	2.50	1.50
(94)	Tito Francona	4.25	2.25	1.25
(95)	Bob Friend	4.25	2.25	1.25
(96)	Carl Furillo	10.00	5.00	3.00
(97)	Augie Galan	7.00	3.50	2.00
(98)	Jim Gentile	4.25	2.25	1.25
(99)	Tony Gonzalez	4.25	2.25	1.25
(100)	Billy Goodman (leaping)	4.25	2.25	1.25
(101)	Billy Goodman (batting)	7.00	3.50	2.00
(102)	Ted Greengrass (Jim)	4.25	2.25	1.25
(103)	Dick Groat	7.00	3.50	2.00
(104)	Steve Gromek	4.25	2.25	1.25
(105)	Johnny Groth	4.25	2.25	1.25
(106)	Orval Grove	13.00	6.50	4.00
(107a)	Frank Gustine (Pirates uniform)	5.00	2.50	1.50
(107b)	Frank Gustine (plain uniform)	5.00	2.50	1.50
(108)	Berthold Haas	13.00	6.50	4.00
(109)	Grady Hatton	5.00	2.50	1.50
(110)	Jim Hegan	4.25	2.25	1.25
(111)	Tom Henrich	7.00	3.50	2.00
(112)	Ray Herbert	25.00	12.50	7.50
(113)	Gene Hermanski	4.50	2.25	1.25
(114)	Whitey Herzog	7.00	3.50	2.00
(115)	Kirby Higbe	13.00	6.50	4.00
(116)	Chuck Hinton	4.25	2.25	1.25
(117)	Don Hoak	13.00	6.50	4.00
(118a)	Gil Hodges ("B" on cap)	12.00	6.00	3.50
(118b)	Gil Hodges ("LA" on cap)	10.00	5.00	3.00
(119)	Johnny Hopp	12.00	6.00	3.50
(120)	Elston Howard	7.00	3.50	2.00
(122)	Ken Hubbs	35.00	17.50	10.50
(123)	Tex Hughson	12.00	6.00	3.50
(124)	Fred Hutchinson	4.50	2.25	1.25
(125)	Monty Irvin (Monte)	7.00	3.50	2.00
(126)	Joey Jay	4.25	2.25	1.25
(127)	Jackie Jensen	30.00	15.00	9.00
(128)	Sam Jethroe	5.00	2.50	1.50
(129)	Bill Johnson	5.00	2.50	1.50
(130)	Walter Judnich	12.00	6.00	3.50
(131)	Al Kaline (kneeling)	30.00	15.00	9.00
(132)	Al Kaline (portrait)	30.00	15.00	9.00
(133)	George Kell	7.00	3.50	2.00
(134)	Charley Keller	4.50	2.25	1.25
(135)	Alex Kellner	4.25	2.25	1.25
(136)	Kenn Keltner (Ken)	5.00	2.50	1.50
(137)	Harmon Killebrew (batting)	30.00	15.00	9.00
(138)	Harmon Killebrew (throwing)	30.00	15.00	9.00
(139)	Harmon Killibrew (Killebrew) (portrait)	30.00	15.00	9.00
(140)	Ellis Kinder	4.25	2.25	1.25
(141)	Ralph Kiner	7.00	3.50	2.00
(142)	Billy Klaus	25.00	12.50	7.50
(143)	Ted Kluzewski (Kluszewski) (batting)	7.00	3.50	2.00
(144a)	Ted Kluzewski (Kluszewski) (Pirates uniform)	7.00	3.50	2.00
(144b)	Ted Kluzewski (Kluszewski) (plain uniform)	13.00	6.50	4.00
(145)	Don Kolloway	7.00	3.50	2.00
(146)	Jim Konstanty	5.00	2.50	1.50
(147)	Sandy Koufax	25.00	12.50	7.50
(148)	Ed Kranepool	50.00	25.00	15.00
(149a)	Tony Kubek (light background)	7.00	3.50	2.00
(149b)	Tony Kubek (dark background)	5.00	2.50	1.50
(150a)	Harvey Kuenn ("D" on cap)	12.00	6.00	3.50
(150b)	Harvey Kuenn (plain cap)	13.00	6.50	4.00
(151)	Harvey Kuenn ("SF" on cap)	7.00	3.50	2.00
(152)	Kurowski (Whitey)	4.50	2.25	1.25
(153)	Eddie Lake	5.00	2.50	1.50
(154)	Jim Landis	4.25	2.25	1.25
(155)	Don Larsen	7.00	3.50	2.00
(156)	Bob Lemon (glove not visible)	7.00	3.50	2.00
(157)	Bob Lemon (glove partially visible)	30.00	15.00	9.00
(158)	Buddy Lewis	12.00	6.00	3.50
(159)	Johnny Lindell	25.00	12.50	7.50
(160)	Phil Linz	25.00	12.50	7.50
(161)	Don Lock	25.00	12.50	7.50
(162)	Whitey Lockman	4.25	2.25	1.25
(163)	Johnny Logan	4.25	2.25	1.25
(164)	Dale Long ("P" on cap)	4.25	2.25	1.25
(165)	Dale Long ("C" on cap)	7.00	3.50	2.00
(166)	Ed Lopat	5.00	2.50	1.50
(167a)	Harry Lowery (name misspelled)	5.00	2.50	1.50
(167b)	Harry Lowrey (name correct)	5.00	2.50	1.50
(168)	Sal Maglie	4.25	2.25	1.25
(169)	Art Mahaffey	5.00	2.50	1.50
(170)	Hank Majeski	4.25	2.25	1.25
(171)	Frank Malzone	4.25	2.25	1.25
(172)	Mickey Mantle (batting, pinstriped uniform)	100.00	50.00	30.00
(173a)	Mickey Mantle (batting, no pinstripes, first name outlined in white)	75.00	38.00	23.00
173b	Mickey Mantle (batting, no pinstripes, first name not outlined in white)	75.00	38.00	23.00
(174)	Mickey Mantle (portrait)	400.00	200.00	120.00
(175)	Martin Marion	7.00	3.50	2.00
(176)	Roger Maris	25.00	12.50	7.50
(177)	Willard Marshall	5.00	2.50	1.50
(178a)	Eddie Matthews (name incorrect)	12.00	6.00	3.50
(178b)	Eddie Mathews (name correct)	13.00	6.50	4.00
(179)	Ed Mayo	5.00	2.50	1.50
(180)	Willie Mays (batting)	30.00	15.00	9.00
(181)	Willie Mays (portrait)	35.00	17.50	10.50
(182)	Bill Mazeroski (portrait)	10.00	5.00	3.00
(183)	Bill Mazeroski (batting)	10.00	5.00	3.00
(184)	Ken McBride	4.25	2.25	1.25
(185a)	Barney McCaskey (McCosky)	13.00	6.50	4.00
(185b)	Barney McCoskey (McCosky)	90.00	45.00	27.00
(186)	Lindy McDaniel	4.25	2.25	1.25
(187)	Gil McDougald	7.00	3.50	2.00
(188)	Albert Mele	13.00	6.50	4.00
(189)	Sam Mele	5.00	2.50	1.50
(190)	Orestes Minoso ("C" on cap)	7.00	3.50	2.00
(191)	Orestes Minoso (Sox on cap)	4.25	2.25	1.25
(192)	Dale Mitchell	4.25	2.25	1.25
(193)	Wally Moon	7.00	3.50	2.00
(194)	Don Mueller	5.00	2.50	1.50
(195)	Stan Musial (kneeling)	25.00	12.50	7.50
(196)	Stan Musial (batting)	35.00	17.50	10.50
(197)	Charley Neal	18.00	9.00	5.50
(198)	Don Newcombe (shaking hands)	7.00	3.50	2.00
(199a)	Don Newcombe (Dodgers on jacket)	5.00	2.50	1.50
(199b)	Don Newcombe (plain jacket)	5.00	2.50	1.50
(200)	Hal Newhouser	7.00	3.50	2.00
(201)	Ron Northey	12.00	6.00	3.50
(202)	Bill O'Dell	4.25	2.25	1.25
(203)	Joe Page	12.00	6.00	3.50
(204)	Satchel Paige	40.00	20.00	12.00
(205)	Milt Pappas	4.25	2.25	1.25
(206)	Camilo Pascual	4.25	2.25	1.25
(207)	Albie Pearson	25.00	12.50	7.50
(208)	Johnny Pesky	4.25	2.25	1.25
(209)	Gary Peters	25.00	12.50	7.50
(210)	Dave Philley	4.25	2.25	1.25
(211)	Billy Pierce	4.25	2.25	1.25
(212)	Jimmy Piersall	16.00	8.00	4.75
(213)	Vada Pinson	7.00	3.50	2.00
(214)	Bob Porterfield	4.25	2.25	1.25
(215)	John "Boog" Powell	35.00	17.50	10.50
(216)	Vic Raschi	4.50	2.25	1.25
(217a)	Harold "Peewee" Reese (fielding, ball partially visible)	15.00	7.50	4.50
(217b)	Harold "Peewee" Reese (fielding, ball not visible)	15.00	7.50	4.50
(218)	Del Rice	4.25	2.25	1.25
(219)	Bobby Richardson	55.00	28.00	16.50
(220)	Phil Rizzuto	15.00	7.50	4.50
(221a)	Robin Roberts (script signature)	12.00	6.00	3.50
(221b)	Robin Roberts (plain signature)	7.00	3.50	2.00
(222)	Brooks Robinson	30.00	15.00	9.00
(223)	Eddie Robinson	4.25	2.25	1.25
(224)	Floyd Robinson	25.00	12.50	7.50
(225)	Frankie Robinson	20.00	10.00	6.00
(226)	Jackie Robinson	30.00	15.00	9.00
(227)	Preacher Roe	7.00	3.50	2.00
(228)	Bob Rogers (Rodgers)	25.00	12.50	7.50
(229)	Richard Rollins	25.00	12.50	7.50
(230)	Pete Runnels	12.00	6.00	3.50
(231)	John Sain	5.00	2.50	1.50
(232)	Ron Santo	7.00	3.50	2.00

	NR MT	EX	VG
(233) Henry Sauer	5.00	2.50	1.50
(234a) Carl Sawatski ("M" on cap)	4.25	2.25	1.25
(234b) Carl Sawatski ("P" on cap)	4.25	2.25	1.25
(234c) Carl Sawatski (plain cap)	13.00	6.50	4.00
(235) Johnny Schmitz	5.00	2.50	1.50
(236a) Red Schoendeinst (Schoendienst) (fielding, name in white)	7.00	3.50	2.00
(236b) Red Schoendeinst (Schoendienst) (fielding, name in red-brown)	10.00	5.00	3.00
(237) Red Schoendinst (Schoendienst) (batting)	7.00	3.50	2.00
(238a) Herb Score ("C" on cap)	5.00	2.50	1.50
(238b) Herb Score (plain cap)	12.00	6.00	3.50
(239) Andy Seminick	4.25	2.25	1.25
(240) Rip Sewell	7.00	3.50	2.00
(241) Norm Siebern	4.25	2.25	1.25
(242) Roy Sievers (batting)	5.00	2.50	1.50
(243a) Roy Sievers (portrait, "W" on cap, light background)	7.00	3.50	2.00
(243b) Roy Sievers (portrait, "W" on cap, dark background)	5.00	2.50	1.50
(243c) Roy Sievers (portrait, plain cap)	4.50	2.25	1.25
(244) Curt Simmons	5.00	2.50	1.50
(245) Dick Sisler	5.00	2.50	1.50
(246) Bill Skowron	7.00	3.50	2.00
(247) Bill "Moose" Skowron	55.00	28.00	16.50
(248) Enos Slaughter	7.00	3.50	2.00
(249a) Duke Snider ("B" on cap)	15.00	7.50	4.50
(249b) Duke Snider ("LA" on cap)	18.00	9.00	5.50
(250a) Warren Spahn ("B" on cap)	10.00	5.00	3.00
(250b) Warren Spahn ("M" on cap)	12.00	6.00	3.50
(251) Stanley Spence	13.00	6.50	4.00
(252) Ed Stanky (plain uniform)	5.00	2.50	1.50
(253) Ed Stanky (Giants uniform)	5.00	2.50	1.50
(254) Vern Stephens (batting)	5.00	2.50	1.50
(255) Vern Stephens (portrait)	5.00	2.50	1.50
(256) Ed Stewart	5.00	2.50	1.50
(257) Snuffy Stirnweiss	13.00	6.50	4.00
(258) George "Birdie" Tebbetts	12.00	6.00	3.50
(259) Frankie Thomas (photo actually Bob Skinner)	30.00	15.00	9.00
(260) Frank Thomas (portrait)	13.00	6.50	4.00
(261) Lee Thomas	4.25	2.25	1.25
(262) Bobby Thomson	7.00	3.50	2.00
(263a) Earl Torgeson (Braves uniform)	4.25	2.25	1.25
(263b) Earl Torgeson (plain uniform)	5.00	2.50	1.50
(264) Gus Triandos	7.00	3.50	2.00
(265) Virgil Trucks	4.25	2.25	1.25
(266) Johnny Vandermeer (VanderMeer)	13.00	6.50	4.00
(267) Emil Verban	7.00	3.50	2.00
(268) Mickey Vernon (throwing)	4.25	2.25	1.25
(269) Mickey Vernon (batting)	4.25	2.25	1.25
(270) Bill Voiselle	7.00	3.50	2.00
(271) Leon Wagner	4.25	2.25	1.25
(272a) Eddie Waitkus (throwing, Chicago uniform)	7.00	3.50	2.00
(272b) Eddie Waitkus (throwing, plain uniform)	5.00	2.50	1.50
(273) Eddie Waitkus (portrait)	13.00	6.50	4.00
(274) Dick Wakefield	5.00	2.50	1.50
(275) Harry Walker	7.00	3.50	2.00
(276) Bucky Walters	4.50	2.25	1.25
(277) Pete Ward	30.00	15.00	9.00
(278) Herman Wehmeier	5.00	2.50	1.50
(279) Vic Wertz (batting)	4.25	2.25	1.25
(280) Vic Wertz (portrait)	4.25	2.25	1.25
(281) Wally Westlake	5.00	2.50	1.50
(282) Wes Westrum	13.00	6.50	4.00
(283) Billy Williams	13.00	6.50	4.00
(284) Maurice Wills	12.00	6.00	3.50
(285a) Gene Woodling (script signature)	4.25	2.25	1.25
(285b) Gene Woodling (plain signature)	7.00	3.50	2.00
(286) Taffy Wright	5.00	2.50	1.50
(287) Carl Yastrazemski (Yastrzemski)	175.00	90.00	50.00
(288) Al Zarilla	5.00	2.50	1.50
(289a) Gus Zernial (script signature)	4.25	2.25	1.25
(289b) Gus Zernial (plain signature)	7.00	3.50	2.00
(290) Braves Team - 1948	18.00	9.00	5.50
(291) Dodgers Team - 1949	25.00	12.50	7.50
(292) Dodgers Team - 1952	25.00	12.50	7.50
(293) Dodgers Team - 1955	25.00	12.50	7.50
(294) Dodgers Team - 1956	25.00	12.50	7.50
(295) Giants Team - 1951	18.00	9.00	5.50
(296) Giants Team - 1954	18.00	9.00	5.50
(297) Indians Team - 1948	18.00	9.00	5.50
(298) Indians Team - 1954	18.00	9.00	5.50
(299) Phillies Team - 1950	18.00	9.00	5.50
(300) Yankees Team - 1949	30.00	15.00	9.00
(301) Yankees Team - 1950	30.00	15.00	9.00
(302) Yankees Team - 1951	30.00	15.00	9.00
(303) Yankees Team - 1952	30.00	15.00	9.00
(304) Yankees Team - 1955	30.00	15.00	9.00
(305) Yankees Team - 1956	30.00	15.00	9.00

1962 Exhibit Supply Co. Statistic Backs

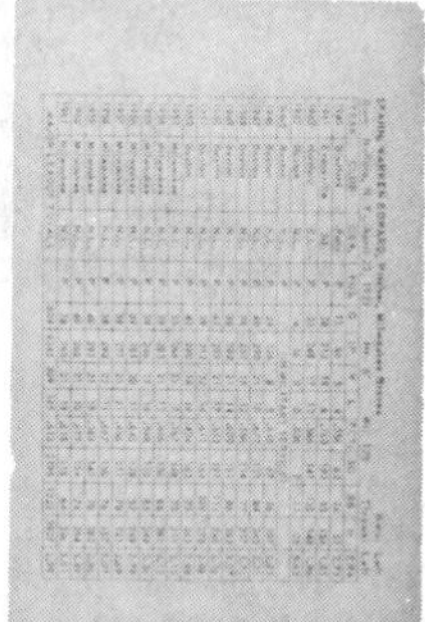

In 1962, the Exhibit Supply Co. added career statistics to the yearly set they produced. The black and white, unnumbered cards measure 3-3/8" by 5-3/8". The statistics found on the back are printed in black or red. The red backs are three times greater in value. The set is comprised of 32 cards.

	NR MT	EX	VG
Complete Set:	425.00	212.00	127.00
Common Player:	3.00	1.50	.90
(1) Hank Aaron	35.00	17.50	10.50
(2) Luis Aparicio	7.00	3.50	2.00
(3) Ernie Banks	20.00	10.00	6.00
(4) Larry "Yogi" Berra	15.00	7.50	4.50
(5) Ken Boyer	4.00	2.00	1.25
(6) Lew Burdette	3.50	1.75	1.00
(7) Norm Cash	3.50	1.75	1.00
(8) Orlando Cepeda	6.00	3.00	1.75
(9) Roberto Clemente	35.00	17.50	10.50
(10) Rocky Colavito	6.00	3.00	1.75
(11) Ed "Whitey" Ford	10.00	5.00	3.00
(12) Nelson Fox	6.00	3.00	1.75
(13) Tito Francona	3.00	1.50	.90
(14) Jim Gentile	3.00	1.50	.90
(15) Dick Groat	3.50	1.75	1.00
(16) Don Hoak	3.50	1.75	1.00
(17) Al Kaline	10.00	5.00	3.00
(18) Harmon Killebrew	10.00	5.00	3.00
(19) Sandy Koufax	25.00	12.50	7.50
(20) Jim Landis	3.00	1.50	.90
(21) Art Mahaffey	3.00	1.50	.90
(22) Frank Malzone	3.00	1.50	.90
(23) Mickey Mantle	90.00	45.00	27.00
(24) Roger Maris	10.00	5.00	3.00
(25) Eddie Mathews	10.00	5.00	3.00
(26) Willie Mays	35.00	17.50	10.50
(27) Wally Moon	3.50	1.75	1.00
(28) Stan Musial	35.00	17.50	10.50
(29) Milt Pappas	3.50	1.75	1.00
(30) Vada Pinson	4.00	2.00	1.25
(31) Norm Siebern	3.00	1.50	.90
(32) Warren Spahn	10.00	5.00	3.00

1963 Exhibit Supply Co. Statistic Backs

The Exhibit Supply Co. issued a 64-card set with career statistics on the backs of the cards in 1963. The unnumbered, black and white cards are printed on thick cardboard and measure 3-3/8" by 5-3/8" in size. The statistics on the back are printed in black.

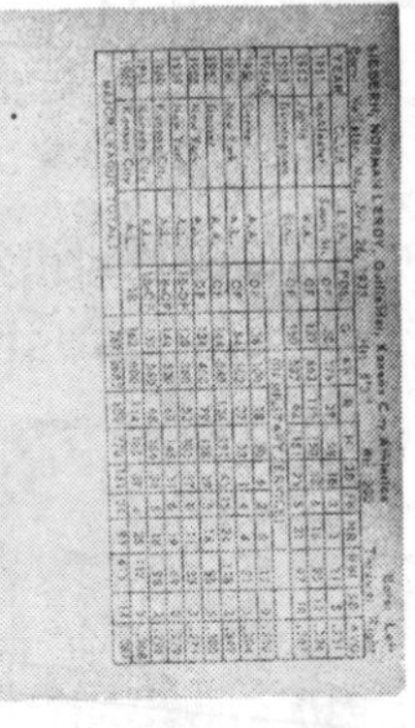

		NR MT	EX	VG
Complete Set:		500.00	250.00	150.00
Common Player:		3.00	1.50	.90
(1)	Hank Aaron	35.00	17.50	10.50
(2)	Luis Aparicio	7.00	3.50	2.00
(3)	Bob Aspromonte	3.00	1.50	.90
(4)	Ernie Banks	20.00	10.00	6.00
(5)	Steve Barber	3.00	1.50	.90
(6)	Earl Battey	3.00	1.50	.90
(7)	Larry "Yogi" Berra	15.00	7.50	4.50
(8)	Ken Boyer	4.00	2.00	1.25
(9)	Lew Burdette	3.50	1.75	1.00
(10)	Johnny Callison	3.50	1.75	1.00
(11)	Norm Cash	3.50	1.75	1.00
(12)	Orlando Cepeda	6.00	3.00	1.75
(13)	Dean Chance	3.00	1.50	.90
(14)	Tom Cheney	3.00	1.50	.90
(15)	Roberto Clemente	35.00	17.50	10.50
(16)	Rocky Colavito	6.00	3.00	1.75
(17)	Choo Choo Coleman	3.00	1.50	.90
(18)	Roger Craig	3.50	1.75	1.00
(19)	Joe Cunningham	3.00	1.50	.90
(20)	Don Drysdale	10.00	5.00	3.00
(21)	Dick Farrell	3.00	1.50	.90
(22)	Ed "Whitey" Ford	10.00	5.00	3.00
(23)	Nelson Fox	6.00	3.00	1.75
(24)	Tito Francona	3.00	1.50	.90
(25)	Jim Gentile	3.00	1.50	.90
(26)	Tony Gonzalez	3.00	1.50	.90
(27)	Dick Groat	3.50	1.75	1.00
(28)	Ray Herbert	3.00	1.50	.90
(29)	Chuck Hinton	3.00	1.50	.90
(30)	Don Hoak	3.50	1.75	1.00
(31)	Frank Howard	4.00	2.00	1.25
(32)	Ken Hubbs	3.50	1.75	1.00
(33)	Joey Jay	3.00	1.50	.90
(34)	Al Kaline	10.00	5.00	3.00
(35)	Harmon Killebrew	10.00	5.00	3.00
(36)	Sandy Koufax	25.00	12.50	7.50
(37)	Harvey Kuenn	4.00	2.00	1.25
(38)	Jim Landis	3.00	1.50	.90
(39)	Art Mahaffey	3.00	1.50	.90
(40)	Frank Malzone	3.00	1.50	.90
(41)	Mickey Mantle	100.00	50.00	30.00
(42)	Roger Maris	10.00	5.00	3.00
(43)	Eddie Mathews	10.00	5.00	3.00
(44)	Willie Mays	35.00	17.50	10.50
(45)	Bill Mazeroski	4.00	2.00	1.25
(46)	Ken McBride	3.00	1.50	.90
(47)	Wally Moon	3.50	1.75	1.00
(48)	Stan Musial	35.00	17.50	10.50
(49)	Charlie Neal	3.00	1.50	.90
(50)	Bill O'Dell	3.00	1.50	.90
(51)	Milt Pappas	3.50	1.75	1.00
(52)	Camilo Pascual	3.50	1.75	1.00
(53)	Jimmy Piersall	4.00	2.00	1.25
(54)	Vada Pinson	4.00	2.00	1.25
(55)	Brooks Robinson	15.00	7.50	4.50
(56)	Frankie Robinson	15.00	7.50	4.50
(57)	Pete Runnels	3.50	1.75	1.00
(58)	Ron Santo	4.00	2.00	1.25
(59)	Norm Siebern	3.00	1.50	.90
(60)	Warren Spahn	12.00	6.00	3.50
(61)	Lee Thomas	3.00	1.50	.90
(62)	Leon Wagner	3.00	1.50	.90
(63)	Billy Williams	7.00	3.50	2.00
(64)	Maurice Wills	3.00	1.50	.90

1948 Exhibits Baseball's Great Hall Of Fame

Titled "Baseball's Great Hall of Fame," this 32-player set features black and white player photos against a gray background. The photos are accented by Greek columns on either side with brief player information printed at the bottom. The blank-backed cards are unnumbered and are listed here alphabetically. The cards measure 3-3/8" by 5-3/8". Collectors should be aware that 24 of the cards in this set were reprinted on white stock in the mid-1970s.

		NR MT	EX	VG
Complete Set:		550.00	275.00	165.00
Common Player:		4.00	2.00	1.25
(1)	Grover Cleveland Alexander	7.00	3.50	2.00
(2)	Roger Bresnahan	4.00	2.00	1.25
(3)	Frank Chance	5.00	2.50	1.50
(4)	Jack Chesbro	4.00	2.00	1.25
(5)	Fred Clarke	4.00	2.00	1.25
(6)	Ty Cobb	50.00	25.00	15.00
(7)	Mickey Cochrane	5.00	2.50	1.50
(8)	Eddie Collins	4.00	2.00	1.25
(9)	Hugh Duffy	4.00	2.00	1.25
(10)	Johnny Evers	4.00	2.00	1.25
(11)	Frankie Frisch	4.00	2.00	1.25
(12)	Lou Gehrig	50.00	25.00	15.00
(13)	Clark Griffith	4.00	2.00	1.25
(14)	Robert "Lefty" Grove	6.00	3.00	1.75
(15)	Rogers Hornsby	10.00	5.00	3.00
(16)	Carl Hubbell	5.00	2.50	1.50
(17)	Hughie Jennings	4.00	2.00	1.25
(18)	Walter Johnson	15.00	7.50	4.50
(19)	Willie Keeler	4.00	2.00	1.25
(20)	Napolean Lajoie	7.00	3.50	2.00
(21)	Connie Mack	7.00	3.50	2.00
(22)	Christy Matthewson (Mathewson)	15.00	7.50	4.50
(23)	John J. McGraw	5.00	2.50	1.50
(24)	Eddie Plank	4.00	2.00	1.25
(25)	Babe Ruth (batting)	75.00	37.00	22.00
(26)	Babe Ruth (standing with bats)	200.00	100.00	60.00
(27)	George Sisler	5.00	2.50	1.50
(28)	Tris Speaker	7.00	3.50	2.00
(29)	Joe Tinker	4.00	2.00	1.25
(30)	Rube Waddell	4.00	2.00	1.25
(31)	Honus Wagner	15.00	7.50	4.50
(32)	Ed Walsh	4.00	2.00	1.25
(33)	Cy Young	9.00	4.50	2.75

1953 Exhibits - Canadian

This Canadian-issued set consists of 64 cards and includes both major leaguers and player from the Montreal Royals of the International League. The cards are slightly smaller than the U.S. exhibit cards, measuring 3-1/4" by 5-1/4", and are numbered. The blank-backed cards were printed on gray stock. Card numbers 1-32 have a green or red tint, while card numbers 33-64 have a blue or reddish-brown tint.

		NR MT	EX	VG
Complete Set:		1300.00	650.00	390.00
Common Player: 1-32		6.00	3.00	1.75
Common Player: 33-64		4.00	2.00	1.25
1	Preacher Roe	9.00	4.50	2.75
2	Luke Easter	6.00	3.00	1.75
3	Gene Bearden	6.00	3.00	1.75
4	Chico Carrasquel	6.00	3.00	1.75
5	Vic Raschi	9.00	4.50	2.75
6	Monty Irvin	18.00	9.00	5.50
7	Henry Sauer	6.00	3.00	1.75
8	Ralph Branca	9.00	4.50	2.75
9	Ed Stanky	7.00	3.50	2.00
10	Sam Jethroe	6.00	3.00	1.75
11	Larry Doby	7.00	3.50	2.00
12	Hal Newhouser	6.00	3.00	1.75
13	Gil Hodges	25.00	12.50	7.50
14	Harry Brecheen	6.00	3.00	1.75
15	Ed Lopat	9.00	4.50	2.75
16	Don Newcombe	9.00	4.50	2.75
17	Bob Feller	35.00	17.50	10.50
18	Tommy Holmes	6.00	3.00	1.75
19	Jackie Robinson	110.00	55.00	33.00
20	Roy Campanella	110.00	55.00	33.00
21	Harold "Peewee" Reese	30.00	15.00	9.00
22	Ralph Kiner	25.00	12.50	7.50
23	Dom DiMaggio	8.00	4.00	2.50
24	Bobby Doerr	18.00	9.00	5.50
25	Phil Rizzuto	25.00	12.50	7.50
26	Bob Elliott	6.00	3.00	1.75
27	Tom Henrich	9.00	4.50	2.75
28	Joe DiMaggio	350.00	175.00	105.00
29	Harry Lowery (Lowrey)	6.00	3.00	1.75
30	Ted Williams	150.00	75.00	45.00
31	Bob Lemon	20.00	10.00	6.00
32	Warren Spahn	30.00	15.00	9.00
33	Don Hoak	5.00	2.50	1.50
34	Bob Alexander	4.00	2.00	1.25
35	Simmons	4.00	2.00	1.25
36	Steve Lembo	4.00	2.00	1.25
37	Norman Larker	4.50	2.25	1.25
38	Bob Ludwick	4.00	2.00	1.25
39	Walter Moryn	4.00	2.00	1.25
40	Charlie Thompson	4.00	2.00	1.25
41	Ed Roebuck	4.50	2.25	1.25
42	Rose	4.00	2.00	1.25
43	Edmundo Amoros	4.50	2.25	1.25
44	Bob Milliken	4.00	2.00	1.25
45	Art Fabbro	4.00	2.00	1.25
46	Jacobs	4.00	2.00	1.25
47	Mauro	4.00	2.00	1.25
48	Walter Fiala	4.00	2.00	1.25
49	Rocky Nelson	4.00	2.00	1.25
50	Tom La Sorda (Lasorda)	40.00	20.00	12.00
51	Ronnie Lee	4.00	2.00	1.25
52	Hampton Coleman	4.00	2.00	1.25
53	Frank Marchio	4.00	2.00	1.25
54	Sampson	4.00	2.00	1.25
55	Gil Mills	4.00	2.00	1.25
56	Al Ronning	4.00	2.00	1.25
57	Stan Musial	70.00	35.00	21.00
58	Walker Cooper	4.50	2.25	1.25
59	Mickey Vernon	5.00	2.50	1.50
60	Del Ennis	5.00	2.50	1.50
61	Walter Alston	20.00	10.00	6.00
62	Dick Sisler	4.50	2.25	1.25
63	Billy Goodman	4.50	2.25	1.25
64	Alex Kellner	4.00	2.00	1.25

1961 Exhibits - Wrigley Field

Distributed at Chicago's Wrigley Field circa 1961, this 24-card set features members of the Baseball Hall of Fame. The cards measure 3-3/8" by 5-3/8" and include the player's full name along the bottom. They were printed on gray stock and have a postcard back. The set is unnumbered.

		NR MT	EX	VG
Complete Set:		325.00	162.00	97.00
Common Player:		4.00	2.00	1.25
(1)	Grover Cleveland Alexander	6.00	3.00	1.75
(2)	Adrian Constantine Anson	6.00	3.00	1.75
(3)	John Franklin Baker	4.00	2.00	1.25
(4)	Roger Phillip Bresnahan	4.00	2.00	1.25
(5)	Mordecai Peter Brown	4.00	2.00	1.25
(6)	Frank Leroy Chance	5.00	2.50	1.50
(7)	Tyrus Raymond Cobb	50.00	25.00	15.00
(8)	Edward Trowbridge Collins	4.00	2.00	1.25
(9)	James J. Collins	4.00	2.00	1.25
(10)	John Joseph Evers	4.00	2.00	1.25
(11)	Henry Louis Gehrig	50.00	25.00	15.00
(12)	Clark C. Griffith	4.00	2.00	1.25
(13)	Walter Perry Johnson	10.00	5.00	3.00
(14)	Anthony Michael Lazzeri	4.00	2.00	1.25
(15)	James Walter Vincent Maranville	4.00	2.00	1.25
(16)	Christopher Mathewson	10.00	5.00	3.00
(17)	John Joseph McGraw	5.00	2.50	1.50
(18)	Melvin Thomass Ott	5.00	2.50	1.50
(19)	Herbert Jeffries Pennock	4.00	2.00	1.25
(20)	George Herman Ruth	70.00	35.00	21.00
(21)	Aloysius Harry Simmons	4.00	2.00	1.25
(22)	Tristram Speaker	12.00	6.00	3.50
(23)	Joseph B. Tinker	4.00	2.00	1.25
(24)	John Peter Wagner	10.00	5.00	3.00

1959 Fleer Ted Williams

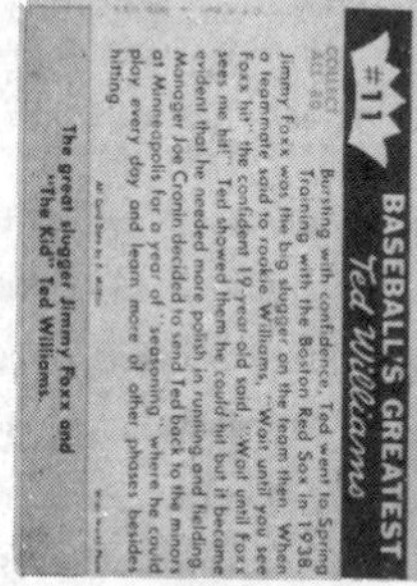

This 80-card 1959 Fleer set tells of the life of baseball great Ted Williams, from his childhood years up to 1958.

The full-color cards measure 2-1/2" by 3-1/2" in size and make use of both horizontal and vertical formats. The card backs, all designed horizontally, contain a continuing biography of Williams. Card #68 was withdrawn from the set early in production and is scarce. Counterfeit cards of #68 have been produced and can be distinguished by a cross-hatch pattern which appears over the photo on the card fronts.

		NR MT	EX	VG
Complete Set:		1050.00	525.00	315.00
Common Player:		6.50	3.25	2.00
1	The Early Years	30.00	12.50	7.50
2	Ted's Idol - Babe Ruth	40.00	20.00	12.00
3	Practice Makes Perfect	6.50	3.25	2.00
4	1934 - Ted Learns The Fine Points	6.50	3.25	2.00
5	Ted's Fame Spreads - 1935-36	6.50	3.25	2.00
6	Ted Turns Professional	6.50	3.25	2.00
7	1936 - From Mound To Plate	6.50	3.25	2.00
8	1937 - First Full Season	6.50	3.25	2.00
9	1937 - First Step To The Majors	6.50	3.25	2.00
10	1938 - Gunning As A Pastime	6.50	3.25	2.00
11	1938 - First Spring Training	6.50	3.25	2.00
12	1939 - Burning Up The Minors	6.50	3.25	2.00
13	1939 - Ted Shows He Will Stay	6.50	3.25	2.00
14	Outstanding Rookie of 1939	6.50	3.25	2.00
15	1940 - Williams Licks Sophomore Jinx	6.50	3.25	2.00
16	1941 - Williams' Greatest Year	6.50	3.25	2.00
17	1941 - How Ted Hit .400	6.50	3.25	2.00
18	1941 - All-Star Hero	6.50	3.25	2.00
19	1942 - Ted Wins Triple Crown	6.50	3.25	2.00
20	1942 - On To Naval Training	6.50	3.25	2.00
21	1943 - Honors For Williams	6.50	3.25	2.00
22	1944 - Ted Solos	6.50	3.25	2.00
23	1944 - Williams Wins His Wings	6.50	3.25	2.00
24	1945 - Sharpshooter	6.50	3.25	2.00
25	1945 - Ted Is Discharged	6.50	3.25	2.00
26	1946 - Off To A Flying Start	6.50	3.25	2.00
27	July 9, 1946 - One Man Show	6.50	3.25	2.00
28	July 14, 1946 - The Williams Shift	6.50	3.25	2.00
29	July 21, 1946, Ted Hits For The Cycle	6.50	3.25	2.00
30	1946 - Beating The Williams Shift	6.50	3.25	2.00
31	Oct. 1946 - Sox Lose The Series	6.50	3.25	2.00
32	1946 - Most Valuable Player	6.50	3.25	2.00
33	1947 - Another Triple Crown For Ted	6.50	3.25	2.00
34	1947 - Ted Sets Runs-Scored Record	6.50	3.25	2.00
35	1948 - The Sox Miss The Pennant	6.50	3.25	2.00
36	1948 - Banner Year For Ted	6.50	3.25	2.00
37	1949 - Sox Miss Out Again	6.50	3.25	2.00
38	1949 - Power Rampage	6.50	3.25	2.00
39	1950 - Great Start	6.50	3.25	2.00
40	July 11, 1950 - Ted Crashes Into Wall	6.50	3.25	2.00
41	1950 - Ted Recovers	6.50	3.25	2.00
42	1951 - Williams Slowed By Injury	6.50	3.25	2.00
43	1951 - Leads Outfielders In Double Plays	6.50	3.25	2.00
44	1952 - Back To The Marines	6.50	3.25	2.00
45	1952 - Farewell To Baseball?	6.50	3.25	2.00
46	1952 - Ready For Combat	6.50	3.25	2.00
47	1953 - Ted Crash Lands Jet	6.50	3.25	2.00
48	July 14, 1953 - Ted Returns	6.50	3.25	2.00
49	1953 - Smash Return	6.50	3.25	2.00
50	March 1954 - Spring Injury	6.50	3.25	2.00
51	May 16, 1954 - Ted Is Patched Up	6.50	3.25	2.00
52	1954 - Ted's Comeback	6.50	3.25	2.00
53	1954 - Ted's Comeback Is A Sucess	6.50	3.25	2.00
54	Dec. 1954, Fisherman Ted Hooks a Big One	6.50	3.25	2.00
55	1955 - Ted Decides Retirement Is "No Go"	6.50	3.25	2.00
56	1956 - Ted Reaches 400th Homer,	6.50	3.25	2.00
58	1957 - Williams Hits .388	6.50	3.25	2.00
59	1957 - Hot September For Ted	6.50	3.25	2.00
60	1957 - More Records For Ted	6.50	3.25	2.00
61	1957 - Outfielder Ted	6.50	3.25	2.00
62	1958 - 6th Batting Title For Ted	6.50	3.25	2.00
63	Ted's All-Star Record	6.50	3.25	2.00
64	1958 - Daughter And Famous Daddy	6.50	3.25	2.00
65	August 30, 1958	6.50	3.25	2.00
66	1958 - Powerhouse	6.50	3.25	2.00
67	Two Famous Fisherman (with Sam Snead)	15.00	7.50	4.50
68	Jan. 23, 1959 - Ted Signs For 1959	600.00	300.00	180.00
69	A Future Ted Williams?	6.50	3.25	2.00
70	Ted Williams & Jim Thorpe	25.00	12.50	7.50
71	Ted's Hitting Fundamentals #1	6.50	3.25	2.00
72	Ted's Hitting Fundamentals #2	6.50	3.25	2.00
73	Ted's Hitting Fundamentals #3	6.50	3.25	2.00
74	Here's How!	6.50	3.25	2.00
75	Williams' Value To Red Sox (with Babe Ruth, Eddie Collins)	20.00	10.00	6.00
76	Ted's Remarkable "On Base" Record	6.50	3.25	2.00
77	Ted Relaxes	6.50	3.25	2.00
78	Honors For Williams	6.50	3.25	2.00
79	Where Ted Stands	6.50	3.25	2.00
80	Ted's Goals For 1959	15.00	4.00	2.50

1960 Fleer

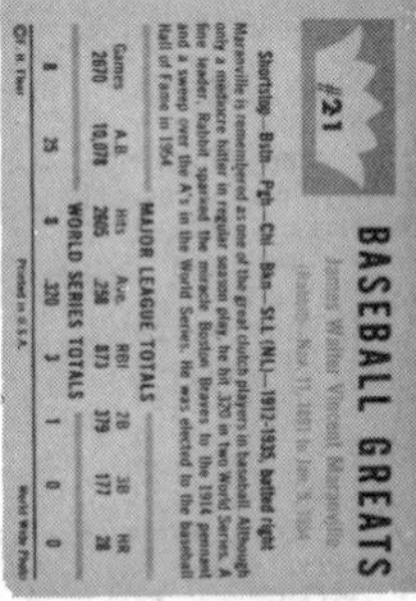

The 1960 Fleer Baseball Greats set consists of 79 cards of the game's top players from the past. (The set does include a card of Ted Williams, who was in his final major league season). The cards are standard size (2-1/2" by 3-1/2") and feature color photos inside blue, green, red or yellow borders. The card backs carry a short player biography plus career hitting or pitching statistics. Cards with a Pepper Martin back (#80), but with another player pictured on the front are in existence.

		NR MT	EX	VG
Complete Set (132):		425.00	200.00	120.00
Common Player:		3.00	1.50	.90
1	Nap Lajoie	10.00	5.00	3.00
2	Christy Mathewson	10.00	5.00	3.00
3	Babe Ruth	85.00	40.00	24.00
4	Carl Hubbell	3.00	1.50	.90
5	Grover Cleveland Alexander	5.00	2.50	1.50
6	Walter Johnson	10.00	5.00	3.00
7	Chief Bender	3.00	1.50	.90
8	Roger Bresnahan	3.00	1.50	.90
9	Mordecai Brown	3.00	1.50	.90
10	Tris Speaker	3.00	1.50	.90
11	Arky Vaughan	3.00	1.50	.90
12	Zack Wheat	3.00	1.50	.90
13	George Sisler	3.00	1.50	.90
14	Connie Mack	4.00	2.00	1.25
15	Clark Griffith	3.00	1.50	.90
16	Lou Boudreau	3.00	1.50	.90
17	Ernie Lombardi	3.00	1.50	.90
18	Heinie Manush	3.00	1.50	.90
19	Marty Marion	3.00	1.50	.90
20	Eddie Collins	3.00	1.50	.90
21	Rabbit Maranville	3.00	1.50	.90
22	Joe Medwick	3.00	1.50	.90
23	Ed Barrow	3.00	1.50	.90
24	Mickey Cochrane	3.00	1.50	.90
25	Jimmy Collins	3.00	1.50	.90
26	Bob Feller	7.00	3.50	2.00
27	Luke Appling	3.00	1.50	.90
28	Lou Gehrig	45.00	22.50	13.50
29	Gabby Hartnett	3.00	1.50	.90
30	Chuck Klein	3.00	1.50	.90
31	Tony Lazzeri	3.00	1.50	.90

#	Player	NR MT	EX	VG
32	Al Simmons	3.00	1.50	.90
33	Wilbert Robinson	3.00	1.50	.90
34	Sam Rice	3.00	1.50	.90
35	Herb Pennock	3.00	1.50	.90
36	Mel Ott	3.00	1.50	.90
37	Lefty O'Doul	3.00	1.50	.90
38	Johnny Mize	3.00	1.50	.90
39	Bing Miller	3.00	1.50	.90
40	Joe Tinker	3.00	1.50	.90
41	Frank Baker	3.00	1.50	.90
42	Ty Cobb	35.00	17.50	10.50
43	Paul Derringer	3.00	1.50	.90
44	Cap Anson	3.00	1.50	.90
45	Jim Bottomley	3.00	1.50	.90
46	Eddie Plank	3.00	1.50	.90
47	Cy Young	5.00	2.50	1.50
48	Hack Wilson	3.00	1.50	.90
49	Ed Walsh	3.00	1.50	.90
50	Frank Chance	3.00	1.50	.90
51	Dazzy Vance	3.00	1.50	.90
52	Bill Terry	3.00	1.50	.90
53	Jimmy Foxx	4.00	2.00	1.25
54	Lefty Gomez	3.00	1.50	.90
55	Branch Rickey	3.00	1.50	.90
56	Ray Schalk	3.00	1.50	.90
57	Johnny Evers	3.00	1.50	.90
58	Charlie Gehringer	3.00	1.50	.90
59	Burleigh Grimes	3.00	1.50	.90
60	Lefty Grove	3.00	1.50	.90
61	Rube Waddell	3.00	1.50	.90
62	Honus Wagner	10.00	5.00	3.00
63	Red Ruffing	3.00	1.50	.90
64	Judge Landis	3.00	1.50	.90
65	Harry Heilmann	3.00	1.50	.90
66	John McGraw	3.00	1.50	.90
67	Hughie Jennings	3.00	1.50	.90
68	Hal Newhouser	3.00	1.50	.90
69	Waite Hoyt	3.00	1.50	.90
70	Bobo Newsom	3.00	1.50	.90
71	Earl Averill	3.00	1.50	.90
72	Ted Williams	55.00	27.00	16.50
73	Warren Giles	3.00	1.50	.90
74	Ford Frick	3.00	1.50	.90
75	Ki Ki Cuyler	3.00	1.50	.90
76	Paul Waner	3.00	1.50	.90
77	Pie Traynor	3.00	1.50	.90
78	Lloyd Waner	3.00	1.50	.90
79	Ralph Kiner	3.00	1.50	.90

1961 -62 Fleer

Over a two-year period, Fleer issued another set utilizing the Baseball Greats theme. The 154-card set was issued in two series and features a color player portrait against a color background. The player's name is located in a pennant set at the bottom of the card. The card backs feature orange and black on white stock and contain player biographical and statistical information. The cards measure 2-1/2" by 3-1/2" in size. The second series cards (#'s 89-154) were issued in 1962.

	NR MT	EX	VG
Complete Set (154):	1100.00	500.00	300.00
Common Player: 1-88	4.00	2.00	1.25
Common Player: 89-154	10.00	5.00	3.00

#	Player	NR MT	EX	VG
1	Checklist (Frank Baker/Ty Cobb/Zach Wheat)	55.00	20.00	10.50
2	G.C. Alexander	6.00	3.00	1.75
3	Nick Altrock	4.00	2.00	1.25
4	Cap Anson	4.00	2.00	1.25
5	Earl Averill	4.00	2.00	1.25
6	Home Run Baker	4.00	2.00	1.25
7	Dave Bancroft	4.00	2.00	1.25
8	Chief Bender	4.00	2.00	1.25
9	Jim Bottomley	4.00	2.00	1.25
10	Roger Bresnahan	4.00	2.00	1.25
11	Mordecai Brown	4.00	2.00	1.25
12	Max Carey	4.00	2.00	1.25
13	Jack Chesbro	4.00	2.00	1.25
14	Ty Cobb	45.00	20.00	12.00
15	Mickey Cochrane	4.00	2.00	1.25
16	Eddie Collins	4.00	2.00	1.25
17	Earle Combs	4.00	2.00	1.25
18	Charles Comiskey	4.00	2.00	1.25
19	Ki Ki Cuyler	4.00	2.00	1.25
20	Paul Derringer	4.00	2.00	1.25
21	Howard Ehmke	4.00	2.00	1.25
22	Billy Evans	4.00	2.00	1.25
23	Johnny Evers	4.00	2.00	1.25
24	Red Faber	4.00	2.00	1.25
25	Bob Feller	6.00	3.00	1.75
26	Wes Ferrell	4.00	2.00	1.25
27	Lew Fonseca	4.00	2.00	1.25
28	Jimmy Foxx	6.00	3.00	1.75
29	Ford Frick	4.00	2.00	1.25
30	Frankie Frisch	4.00	2.00	1.25
31	Lou Gehrig	50.00	25.00	15.00
32	Charlie Gehringer	4.00	2.00	1.25
33	Warren Giles	4.00	2.00	1.25
34	Lefty Gomez	4.00	2.00	1.25
35	Goose Goslin	4.00	2.00	1.25
36	Clark Griffith	4.00	2.00	1.25
37	Burleigh Grimes	4.00	2.00	1.25
38	Lefty Grove	4.00	2.00	1.25
39	Chick Hafey	4.00	2.00	1.25
40	Jesse Haines	4.00	2.00	1.25
41	Gabby Hartnett	4.00	2.00	1.25
42	Harry Heilmann	4.00	2.00	1.25
43	Rogers Hornsby	4.00	2.00	1.25
44	Waite Hoyt	4.00	2.00	1.25
45	Carl Hubbell	4.00	2.00	1.25
46	Miller Huggins	4.00	2.00	1.25
47	Hughie Jennings	4.00	2.00	1.25
48	Ban Johnson	4.00	2.00	1.25
49	Walter Johnson	10.00	5.00	3.00
50	Ralph Kiner	4.00	2.00	1.25
51	Chuck Klein	4.00	2.00	1.25
52	Johnny Kling	4.00	2.00	1.25
53	Judge Landis	4.00	2.00	1.25
54	Tony Lazzeri	4.00	2.00	1.25
55	Ernie Lombardi	4.00	2.00	1.25
56	Dolf Luque	4.00	2.00	1.25
57	Heinie Manush	4.00	2.00	1.25
58	Marty Marion	4.00	2.00	1.25
59	Christy Mathewson	10.00	5.00	3.00
60	John McGraw	4.00	2.00	1.25
61	Joe Medwick	4.00	2.00	1.25
62	Bing Miller	4.00	2.00	1.25
63	Johnny Mize	4.00	2.00	1.25
64	Johnny Mostil	4.00	2.00	1.25
65	Art Nehf	4.00	2.00	1.25
66	Hal Newhouser	4.00	2.00	1.25
67	Bobo Newsom	4.00	2.00	1.25
68	Mel Ott	4.00	2.00	1.25
69	Allie Reynolds	4.00	2.00	1.25
70	Sam Rice	4.00	2.00	1.25
71	Eppa Rixey	4.00	2.00	1.25
72	Edd Roush	4.00	2.00	1.25
73	Schoolboy Rowe	4.00	2.00	1.25
74	Red Ruffing	4.00	2.00	1.25
75	Babe Ruth	85.00	40.00	24.00
76	Joe Sewell	4.00	2.00	1.25
77	Al Simmons	4.00	2.00	1.25
78	George Sisler	4.00	2.00	1.25
79	Tris Speaker	4.00	2.00	1.25
80	Fred Toney	4.00	2.00	1.25
81	Dazzy Vance	4.00	2.00	1.25
82	Jim Vaughn	4.00	2.00	1.25
83	Big Ed Walsh	4.00	2.00	1.25
84	Lloyd Waner	4.00	2.00	1.25
85	Paul Waner	4.00	2.00	1.25
86	Zach Wheat	4.00	2.00	1.25
87	Hack Wilson	4.00	2.00	1.25
88	Jimmy Wilson	4.00	2.00	1.25
89	Checklist (George Sisler/Pie Traynor)	35.00	17.50	10.50
90	Babe Adams	10.00	5.00	3.00
91	Dale Alexander	10.00	5.00	3.00
92	Jim Bagby	10.00	5.00	3.00

		NR MT	EX	VG
93	Ossie Bluege	10.00	5.00	3.00
94	Lou Boudreau	10.00	5.00	3.00
95	Tommy Bridges	10.00	5.00	3.00
96	Donnie Bush (Donie)	10.00	5.00	3.00
97	Dolph Camilli	10.00	5.00	3.00
98	Frank Chance	10.00	5.00	3.00
99	Jimmy Collins	10.00	5.00	3.00
100	Stanley Coveleskie (Coveleski)	10.00	5.00	3.00
101	Hughie Critz	10.00	5.00	3.00
102	General Crowder	10.00	5.00	3.00
103	Joe Dugan	10.00	5.00	3.00
104	Bibb Falk	10.00	5.00	3.00
105	Rick Ferrell	10.00	5.00	3.00
106	Art Fletcher	10.00	5.00	3.00
107	Dennis Galehouse	10.00	5.00	3.00
108	Chick Galloway	10.00	5.00	3.00
109	Mule Haas	10.00	5.00	3.00
110	Stan Hack	10.00	5.00	3.00
111	Bump Hadley	10.00	5.00	3.00
112	Billy Hamilton	10.00	5.00	3.00
113	Joe Hauser	10.00	5.00	3.00
114	Babe Herman	10.00	5.00	3.00
115	Travis Jackson	10.00	5.00	3.00
116	Eddie Joost	10.00	5.00	3.00
117	Addie Joss	10.00	5.00	3.00
118	Joe Judge	10.00	5.00	3.00
119	Joe Kuhel	10.00	5.00	3.00
120	Nap Lajoie	12.00	6.00	3.50
121	Dutch Leonard	10.00	5.00	3.00
122	Ted Lyons	10.00	5.00	3.00
123	Connie Mack	10.00	5.00	3.00
124	Rabbit Maranville	10.00	5.00	3.00
125	Fred Marberry	10.00	5.00	3.00
126	Iron Man McGinnity	10.00	5.00	3.00
127	Oscar Melillo	10.00	5.00	3.00
128	Ray Mueller	10.00	5.00	3.00
129	Kid Nichols	10.00	5.00	3.00
130	Lefty O'Doul	10.00	5.00	3.00
131	Bob O'Farrell	10.00	5.00	3.00
132	Roger Peckinpaugh	10.00	5.00	3.00
133	Herb Pennock	10.00	5.00	3.00
134	George Pipgras	10.00	5.00	3.00
135	Eddie Plank	10.00	5.00	3.00
136	Ray Schalk	10.00	5.00	3.00
137	Hal Schumacher	10.00	5.00	3.00
138	Luke Sewell	10.00	5.00	3.00
139	Bob Shawkey	10.00	5.00	3.00
140	Riggs Stephenson	10.00	5.00	3.00
141	Billy Sullivan	10.00	5.00	3.00
142	Bill Terry	10.00	5.00	3.00
143	Joe Tinker	10.00	5.00	3.00
144	Pie Traynor	10.00	5.00	3.00
145	George Uhle	10.00	5.00	3.00
146	Hal Troskey (Trosky)	10.00	5.00	3.00
147	Arky Vaughan	10.00	5.00	3.00
148	Johnny Vander Meer	10.00	5.00	3.00
149	Rube Waddell	10.00	5.00	3.00
150	Honus Wagner	35.00	17.50	10.50
151	Dixie Walker	10.00	5.00	3.00
152	Ted Williams	65.00	32.00	19.50
153	Cy Young	12.00	6.00	3.50
154	Ross Young (Youngs)	12.00	4.00	2.50

1963 Fleer

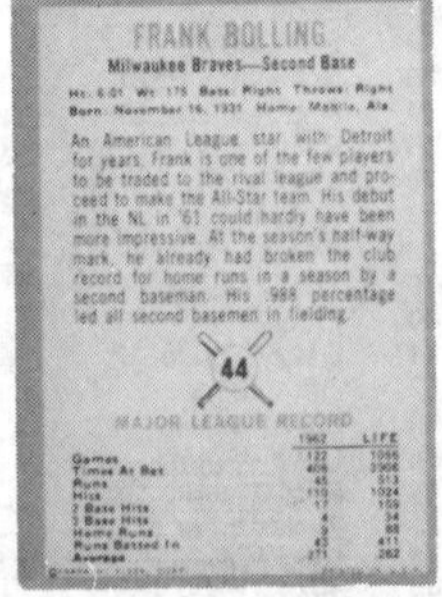

A lawsuit by Topps stopped Fleer's 1963 set at one series of 66 cards. Issued with a cookie rather than gum, the set features color photos of current players. The card backs include statistical information for 1962 and career plus a brief player biography. The cards, which measure 2-1/2" by 3-1/2", are numbered 1-66. An unnumbered checklist was issued with the set and is included in the complete set price in the checklist that follows. The checklist and #46 Adcock are scarce.

		NR MT	EX	VG
Complete Set (67):		1500.00	750.00	425.00
Common Player:		10.00	5.00	3.00
1	Steve Barber	20.00	10.00	6.00
2	Ron Hansen	10.00	5.00	3.00
3	Milt Pappas	10.00	5.00	3.00
4	Brooks Robinson	50.00	25.00	15.00
5	Willie Mays	150.00	75.00	52.00
6	Lou Clinton	10.00	5.00	3.00
7	Bill Monbouquette	10.00	5.00	3.00
8	Carl Yastrzemski	95.00	47.50	28.50
9	Ray Herbert	10.00	5.00	3.00
10	Jim Landis	10.00	5.00	3.00
11	Dick Donovan	10.00	5.00	3.00
12	Tito Francona	10.00	5.00	3.00
13	Jerry Kindall	10.00	5.00	3.00
14	Frank Lary	10.00	5.00	3.00
15	Dick Howser	15.00	7.50	4.50
16	Jerry Lumpe	10.00	5.00	3.00
17	Norm Siebern	10.00	5.00	3.00
18	Don Lee	10.00	5.00	3.00
19	Albie Pearson	10.00	5.00	3.00
20	Bob Rodgers	10.00	5.00	3.00
21	Leon Wagner	10.00	5.00	3.00
22	Jim Kaat	15.00	7.50	4.50
23	Vic Power	10.00	5.00	3.00
24	Rich Rollins	10.00	5.00	3.00
25	Bobby Richardson	15.00	7.50	4.50
26	Ralph Terry	15.00	7.50	4.50
27	Tom Cheney	12.50	6.25	3.75
28	Chuck Cottier	10.00	5.00	3.00
29	Jimmy Piersall	10.00	5.00	3.00
30	Dave Stenhouse	10.00	5.00	3.00
31	Glen Hobbie	10.00	5.00	3.00
32	Ron Santo	20.00	10.00	6.00
33	Gene Freese	10.00	5.00	3.00
34	Vada Pinson	15.00	7.50	4.50
35	Bob Purkey	10.00	5.00	3.00
36	Joe Amalfitano	10.00	5.00	3.00
37	Bob Aspromonte	10.00	5.00	3.00
38	Dick Farrell	10.00	5.00	3.00
39	Al Spangler	10.00	5.00	3.00
40	Tommy Davis	10.00	5.00	3.00
41	Don Drysdale	40.00	20.00	12.00
42	Sandy Koufax	150.00	75.00	45.00
43	Maury Wills	50.00	25.00	15.00
44	Frank Bolling	10.00	5.00	3.00
45	Warren Spahn	50.00	20.00	12.00
46	Joe Adcock	150.00	75.00	45.00
47	Roger Craig	10.00	5.00	3.00
48	Al Jackson	10.00	5.00	3.00
49	Rod Kanehl	10.00	5.00	3.00
50	Ruben Amaro	10.00	5.00	3.00
51	John Callison	10.00	5.00	3.00
52	Clay Dalrymple	10.00	5.00	3.00
53	Don Demeter	10.00	5.00	3.00
54	Art Mahaffey	10.00	5.00	3.00
55	"Smoky" Burgess	10.00	5.00	3.00
56	Roberto Clemente	175.00	87.50	52.50
57	Elroy Face	10.00	5.00	3.00
58	Vernon Law	10.00	5.00	3.00
59	Bill Mazeroski	20.00	10.00	6.00
60	Ken Boyer	20.00	10.00	6.00
61	Bob Gibson	40.00	20.00	12.00
62	Gene Oliver	10.00	5.00	3.00
63	Bill White	15.00	7.50	4.50
64	Orlando Cepeda	20.00	10.00	6.00
65	Jimmy Davenport	10.00	5.00	3.00
66	Billy O'Dell	10.00	5.00	3.00
—-	Checklist	400.00	200.00	120.00

1972 Fleer Famous Feats

This 40-card set by sports artist R.G. Laughlin is oversized, 2-1/2" x 4". It features the pen and ink work of the artist, with several colors added to the front. The backs are printed in blue on white card stock. The Major League Baseball logo appears on the front of the card, one of the few Laughlin issues to do so.

		NR MT	EX	VG
COMPLETE SET (40)		25.00	11.50	3.10
COMMON PLAYER (1-40)		.50	.23	.06
1	Joe McGinnity	.60	.25	.08
2	Rogers Hornsby	1.25	.55	.16
3	Christy Mathewson	1.25	.55	.16
4	Dazzy Vance	.60	.25	.08
5	Lou Gehrig	2.00	.90	.25
6	Jim Bottomley	.60	.25	.08
7	Johnny Evers	.60	.25	.08
8	Walter Johnson	1.25	.55	.16
9	Hack Wilson	.75	.35	.09
10	Wilbert Robinson	.60	.25	.08
11	Cy Young	1.00	.45	.13
12	Rudy York	.50	.23	.06
13	Grover C. Alexander	.75	.35	.09
14	Fred Toney, Hippo Vaughn	.50	.23	.06
15	Ty Cobb	2.00	.90	.25
16	Jimmie Foxx	1.25	.55	.16
17	Hub Leonard	.50	.23	.06
18	Eddie Collins	.60	.25	.08
19	Joe Oeschger, Leon Cadore	.50	.23	.06
20	Babe Ruth	3.00	1.35	.40
21	Honus Wagner	1.25	.55	.16
22	Red Rolfe	.50	.23	.06
23	Ed Walsh	.60	.25	.08
24	Paul Waner	.60	.25	.08
25	Mel Ott	1.00	.45	.13
26	Eddie Plank	.75	.35	.09
27	Sam Crawford	.60	.25	.08
28	Napoleon Lajoie	1.00	.45	.13
29	Ed Reulbach	.50	.23	.06
30	Pinky Higgins	.50	.23	.06
31	Bill Klem	.60	.25	.08
32	Tris Speaker	1.00	.45	.13
33	Hank Gowdy	.50	.23	.06
34	Lefty O'Doul	.50	.23	.06
35	Lloyd Waner	.60	.25	.08
36	Chuck Klein	.60	.25	.08
37	Deacon Phillippe	.50	.23	.06
38	Ed Delahanty	.60	.25	.08
39	Jack Chesbro	.60	.25	.08
40	Willie Keeler	.75	.35	.09

1973 Fleer Wildest Days and Plays

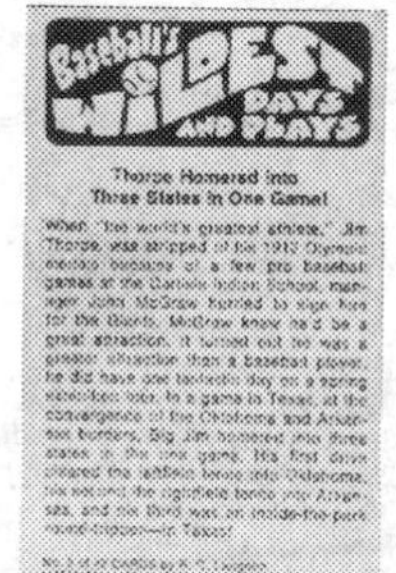

Baseball's
WILDEST
DAYS AND PLAYS
Thorpe Homered into Three States in One Game!

This 42-card set highlights unusual plays and happenings in baseball history, with the fronts featuring artwork by R.G. Laughlin. The cards are 2-1/2" x 4" and printed with color on the front and in red on the back.

		NR MT	EX	VG
COMPLETE SET (42)		20.00	9.00	2.50
COMMON PLAYER (1-42)		.50	.23	.06
1	Cubs and Phillies Score 49 Runs in Game	.75	.35	.09
2	Frank Chance Five HBP's in One Day	2.00	.90	.25
3	Jim Thorpe Homered into 3 States	1.00	.45	.13
4	Eddie Gaedel Midget in Majors	1.00	.45	.13
5	Most Tied Game Ever	.50	.23	.06
6	Seven Errors in One Inning	.50	.23	.06
7	Four 20-Game Winners But No Pennant	.50	.23	.06
8	Dummy Hoy Umpires Signal Strikes	1.00	.45	.13
9	Fourteen Hits in One Inning	.50	.23	.06
10	Yankees Not Shut Out For Two Years	.50	.23	.06
11	Buck Weaver 17 Straight Fouls	1.00	.45	.13
12	George Sisler Greatest Thrill Was as a Pitcher	.60	.25	.08
13	Wrong-Way Baserunner	.50	.23	.06
14	Kiki Cuyler Sits Out Series	.60	.25	.08
15	Grounder Climbed Wall	.50	.23	.06
16	Gabby Street Washington Monument	.60	.25	.08
17	Mel Ott Ejected Twice	1.00	.45	.13
18	Shortest Pitching Career	.50	.23	.06
19	Three Homers in One Inning	.50	.23	.06
20	Bill Byron Singing Umpire	.50	.23	.06
21	Fred Clarke Walking Steal of Home	.60	.25	.08
22	Christy Mathewson 373rd Win Discovered	1.00	.45	.13
23	Hitting Through the Unglaub Arc	.50	.23	.06
24	Jim O'Rourke Catching at 52	.50	.23	.06
25	Fired for Striking Out in Series	.50	.23	.06
26	Eleven Run Inning on One Hit	.50	.23	.06
27	58 Innings in 3 Days	.50	.23	.06
28	Homer on Warm-Up Pitch	.50	.23	.06
29	Giants Win 26 Straight But Finish Fourth	.50	.23	.06
30	Player Who Stole First Base	.50	.23	.06
31	Ernie Shore Perfect Game in Relief	.60	.25	.08
32	Greatest Comeback	.50	.23	.06
33	All-Time Flash-In-The-Pan	.50	.23	.06
34	Pruett Fanned Ruth 19 out of 31	1.00	.45	.13
35	Fixed Batting Race Cobb/Lajoie	1.00	.45	.13
36	Wild-Pitch Rebound Play	.50	.23	.06
37	17 Straight Scoring Innings	.50	.23	.06
38	Wildest Opening Day	.50	.23	.06
39	Baseball's Strike One	.50	.23	.06
40	Opening Day No Hitter That Didn't Count	.50	.23	.06
41	Jimmie Foxx Six Straight Walks in One Game	1.00	.45	.13
42	Entire Team Hit and Scored in Inning	.75	.35	.09

1974 Fleer Baseball Firsts

Photos not available at press time

This 42-card set from Fleer is titled "Baseball Firsts" and features several historical moments in baseball, as captured through the artwork of sports artist R.G.

Laughlin. The cards are 2 1/2" by 4" and are numbered on the back, which is gray card stock with black printing. The set is not licensed by Major League Baseball.

		NR MT	EX	VG
COMPLETE SET (42)		10.00	4.50	1.25
COMMON PLAYER (1-42)		.25	.11	.03
1	Slide	.50	.23	.06
2	Spring Training	.25	.11	.03
3	Bunt	.25	.11	.03
4	Catcher's Mask	.25	.11	.03
5	Four Straight Homers (Lou Gehrig)	1.50	.65	.19
6	Radio Broadcast	.25	.11	.03
7	Numbered Uniforms	.25	.11	.03
8	Shin Guards	.25	.11	.03
9	Players Association	.25	.11	.03
10	Knuckleball	.25	.11	.03
11	Player With Glasses	.25	.11	.03
12	Baseball Cards	2.00	.90	.25
13	Standardized Rules	.25	.11	.03

1975 Fleer Pioneers of Baseball

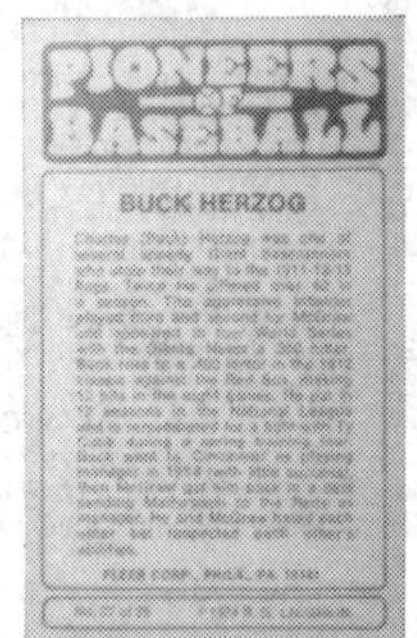

This 28-card set did not draw a great deal of interest in the hobby. The cards are slightly oversized and feature sepia-toned photographs of old baseball players. The backs feature information about the player and the card number. A "Pioneers of Baseball" banner appears at the top of the card back.

		NR MT	EX	VG
Complete Set:		15.00	7.50	4.50
Common Player:		.50	.25	.15
1	Cap Anson	.50	.25	.15
2	Harry Wright	.50	.25	.15
3	Buck Ewing	.50	.25	.15
4	A.G. Spalding	.50	.25	.15
5	Old Hoss Radbourn	.50	.25	.15
6	Dan Brouthers	.50	.25	.15
7	Roger Bresnahan	.50	.25	.15
8	Mike Kelly	.50	.25	.15
9	Ned Hanton	.50	.25	.15
10	Ed Delahanty	.50	.25	.15
11	Pud Galvin	.50	.25	.15
12	Amos Rusie	.50	.25	.15
13	Tommy McCarthy	.50	.25	.15
14	Ty Cobb	1.00	.50	.30
15	John McGraw	.50	.25	.15
16	Home Run Baker	.50	.25	.15
17	Johnny Evers	.50	.25	.15
18	Nap Lajoie	.50	.25	.15
19	Cy Young	.50	.25	.15
20	Eddie Collins	.50	.25	.15
21	John Glasscock	.50	.25	.15
22	Hal Chase	.50	.25	.15
23	Mordecai Brown	.50	.25	.15
24	Jake Daubert	.50	.25	.15
25	Mike Donlin	.50	.25	.15
26	John Clarkson	.50	.25	.15
27	Buck Herzog	.50	.25	.15
28	Art Nehf	.50	.25	.15

1981 Fleer

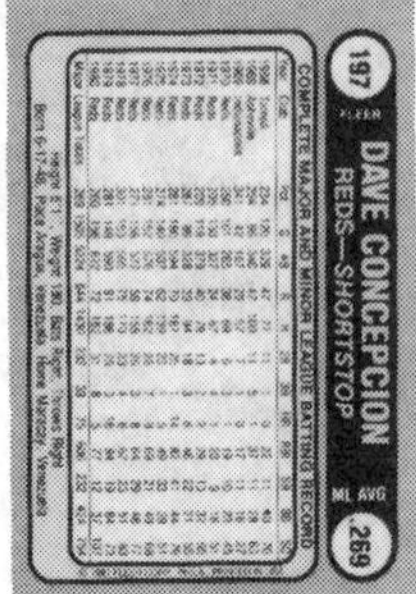

For the first time in 18 years, Fleer issued a baseball card set featuring current players. Fleer's 660-card effort included numerous errors in the first printing run which were subsequently corrected in additional runs. The cards, which measure 2-1/2" by 3-1/2", are numbered alphabetically by team. The card fronts feature a full-color photo inside a border which is color-coded by team. The card backs have black, grey and yellow ink on white stock and carry player statistical information. The player's batting average or earned run average is located in a circle in the upper right corner of the card. The complete set price in the checklist that follows does not include the higher priced variations.

		MT	NR MT	EX
Complete Set (660):		60.00	45.00	25.00
Common Player:		.06	.05	.02
1	Pete Rose	1.75	1.25	.70
2	Larry Bowa	.15	.11	.06
3	Manny Trillo	.08	.06	.03
4	Bob Boone	.10	.08	.04
5a	Mike Schmidt (portrait)	2.00	1.50	.80
5b	Mike Schmidt (batting)	2.00	1.50	.80
6a	Steve Carlton ("Lefty" on front)	1.00	.70	.40
6b	Steve Carlton (Pitcher of the Year on front, date 1066 on back)	2.00	1.50	.80
6c	Steve Carlton (Pitcher of the Year on front, date 1966 on back)	3.00	2.25	1.25
7a	Tug McGraw (Game Saver on front)	.50	.40	.20
7b	Tug McGraw (Pitcher on front)	.12	.09	.05
8	Larry Christenson	.06	.05	.02
9	Bake McBride	.06	.05	.02
10	Greg Luzinski	.15	.11	.06
11	Ron Reed	.06	.05	.02
12	Dickie Noles	.06	.05	.02
13	*Keith Moreland*	.08	.06	.03
14	*Bob Walk*	.10	.08	.04
15	Lonnie Smith	.08	.06	.03
16	Dick Ruthven	.06	.05	.02
17	Sparky Lyle	.10	.08	.04
18	Greg Gross	.06	.05	.02
19	Garry Maddox	.10	.08	.04
20	Nino Espinosa	.06	.05	.02
21	George Vukovich	.06	.05	.02
22	John Vukovich	.06	.05	.02
23	Ramon Aviles	.06	.05	.02
24a	Kevin Saucier (Ken Saucier on back)	.15	.11	.06
24b	Kevin Saucier (Kevin Saucier on back)	.70	.50	.30
25	Randy Lerch	.06	.05	.02
26	Del Unser	.06	.05	.02
27	Tim McCarver	.15	.11	.06
28a	George Brett (batting)	4.00	3.00	1.50
28b	George Brett (portrait)	1.00	.70	.40
29a	Willie Wilson (portrait)	.60	.45	.25
29b	Willie Wilson (batting)	.15	.11	.06
30	Paul Splittorff	.06	.05	.02
31	Dan Quisenberry	.15	.11	.06
32a	Amos Otis (batting)	.50	.40	.20
32b	Amos Otis (portrait)	.10	.08	.04
33	Steve Busby	.08	.06	.03
34	U.L. Washington	.06	.05	.02
35	Dave Chalk	.06	.05	.02

		MT	NR MT	EX
36	Darrell Porter	.08	.06	.03
37	Marty Pattin	.06	.05	.02
38	Larry Gura	.06	.05	.02
39	Renie Martin	.06	.05	.02
40	Rich Gale	.06	.05	.02
41a	Hal McRae (dark blue "Royals" on front)	.40	.30	.15
41b	Hal McRae (light blue "Royals" on front)	.10	.08	.04
42	Dennis Leonard	.08	.06	.03
43	Willie Aikens	.06	.05	.02
44	Frank White	.10	.08	.04
45	Clint Hurdle	.06	.05	.02
46	John Wathan	.08	.06	.03
47	Pete LaCock	.06	.05	.02
48	Rance Mulliniks	.06	.05	.02
49	Jeff Twitty	.06	.05	.02
50	Jamie Quirk	.06	.05	.02
51	Art Howe	.06	.05	.02
52	Ken Forsch	.06	.05	.02
53	Vern Ruhle	.06	.05	.02
54	Joe Niekro	.12	.09	.05
55	Frank LaCorte	.06	.05	.02
56	J.R. Richard	.10	.08	.04
57	Nolan Ryan	8.00	6.00	3.25
58	Enos Cabell	.06	.05	.02
59	Cesar Cedeno	.12	.09	.05
60	Jose Cruz	.12	.09	.05
61	Bill Virdon	.06	.05	.02
62	Terry Puhl	.06	.05	.02
63	Joaquin Andujar	.10	.08	.04
64	Alan Ashby	.06	.05	.02
65	Joe Sambito	.06	.05	.02
66	Denny Walling	.06	.05	.02
67	Jeff Leonard	.12	.09	.05
68	Luis Pujols	.06	.05	.02
69	Bruce Bochy	.06	.05	.02
70	Rafael Landestoy	.06	.05	.02
71	*Dave Smith*	.10	.08	.04
72	*Danny Heep*	.10	.08	.04
73	Julio Gonzalez	.06	.05	.02
74	Craig Reynolds	.06	.05	.02
75	Gary Woods	.06	.05	.02
76	Dave Bergman	.06	.05	.02
77	Randy Niemann	.06	.05	.02
78	Joe Morgan	.70	.50	.30
79a	Reggie Jackson (portrait)	4.00	3.00	1.50
79b	Reggie Jackson (batting)	2.00	1.50	.80
80	Bucky Dent	.10	.08	.04
81	Tommy John	.20	.15	.08
82	Luis Tiant	.12	.09	.05
83	Rick Cerone	.06	.05	.02
84	Dick Howser	.06	.05	.02
85	Lou Piniella	.12	.09	.05
86	Ron Davis	.08	.06	.03
87a	Graig Nettles (Craig on back)	10.00	7.50	4.00
87b	Graig Nettles (Graig on back)	.30	.25	.12
88	Ron Guidry	.25	.20	.10
89	Rich Gossage	.20	.15	.08
90	Rudy May	.06	.05	.02
91	Gaylord Perry	.60	.45	.25
92	Eric Soderholm	.06	.05	.02
93	Bob Watson	.08	.06	.03
94	Bobby Murcer	.10	.08	.04
95	Bobby Brown	.06	.05	.02
96	Jim Spencer	.06	.05	.02
97	Tom Underwood	.06	.05	.02
98	Oscar Gamble	.08	.06	.03
99	Johnny Oates	.06	.05	.02
100	Fred Stanley	.06	.05	.02
101	Ruppert Jones	.06	.05	.02
102	Dennis Werth	.06	.05	.02
103	Joe Lefebvre	.06	.05	.02
104	Brian Doyle	.06	.05	.02
105	Aurelio Rodriguez	.08	.06	.03
106	Doug Bird	.06	.05	.02
107	Mike Griffin	.06	.05	.02
108	Tim Lollar	.06	.05	.02
109	Willie Randolph	.10	.08	.04
110	Steve Garvey	.70	.50	.30
111	Reggie Smith	.10	.08	.04
112	Don Sutton	.30	.25	.12
113	Burt Hooton	.08	.06	.03
114a	Davy Lopes (Davey) (no finger on back)	.10	.08	.04
114b	Davy Lopes (Davey) (small finger on back)	1.00	.70	.40
115	Dusty Baker	.10	.08	.04
116	Tom Lasorda	.10	.08	.04
117	Bill Russell	.08	.06	.03
118	Jerry Reuss	.10	.08	.04

		MT	NR MT	EX
119	Terry Forster	.08	.06	.03
120a	Bob Welch (Bob on back)	.60	.45	.25
120b	Bob Welch (Robert)	1.00	.70	.40
121	Don Stanhouse	.06	.05	.02
122	Rick Monday	.10	.08	.04
123	Derrel Thomas	.06	.05	.02
124	Joe Ferguson	.06	.05	.02
125	Rick Sutcliffe	.20	.15	.08
126a	Ron Cey (no finger on back)	.12	.09	.05
126b	Ron Cey (small finger on back)	1.00	.70	.40
127	Dave Goltz	.08	.06	.03
128	Jay Johnstone	.08	.06	.03
129	Steve Yeager	.06	.05	.02
130	Gary Weiss	.06	.05	.02
131	*Mike Scioscia*	.25	.20	.10
132	Vic Davalillo	.08	.06	.03
133	Doug Rau	.06	.05	.02
134	Pepe Frias	.06	.05	.02
135	Mickey Hatcher	.08	.06	.03
136	*Steve Howe*	.10	.08	.04
137	Robert Castillo	.06	.05	.02
138	Gary Thomasson	.06	.05	.02
139	Rudy Law	.06	.05	.02
140	*Fernand Valenzuela* (Fernando)	2.50	2.00	1.00
141	Manny Mota	.08	.06	.03
142	Gary Carter	.70	.50	.30
143	Steve Rogers	.08	.06	.03
144	Warren Cromartie	.06	.05	.02
145	Andre Dawson	2.00	1.50	.80
146	Larry Parrish	.10	.08	.04
147	Rowland Office	.06	.05	.02
148	Ellis Valentine	.06	.05	.02
149	Dick Williams	.06	.05	.02
150	*Bill Gullickson*	.15	.11	.06
151	Elias Sosa	.06	.05	.02
152	John Tamargo	.06	.05	.02
153	Chris Speier	.06	.05	.02
154	Ron LeFlore	.08	.06	.03
155	Rodney Scott	.06	.05	.02
156	Stan Bahnsen	.06	.05	.02
157	Bill Lee	.08	.06	.03
158	Fred Norman	.06	.05	.02
159	Woodie Fryman	.08	.06	.03
160	Dave Palmer	.06	.05	.02
161	Jerry White	.06	.05	.02
162	Roberto Ramos	.06	.05	.02
163	John D'Acquisto	.06	.05	.02
164	Tommy Hutton	.06	.05	.02
165	*Charlie Lea*	.12	.09	.05
166	Scott Sanderson	.06	.05	.02
167	Ken Macha	.06	.05	.02
168	Tony Bernazard	.06	.05	.02
169	Jim Palmer	1.00	.70	.40
170	Steve Stone	.08	.06	.03
171	Mike Flanagan	.10	.08	.04
172	Al Bumbry	.08	.06	.03
173	Doug DeCinces	.10	.08	.04
174	Scott McGregor	.08	.06	.03
175	Mark Belanger	.08	.06	.03
176	Tim Stoddard	.06	.05	.02
177a	Rick Dempsey (no finger on front)	.10	.08	.04
177b	Rick Dempsey (small finger on front)	1.00	.70	.40
178	Earl Weaver	.10	.08	.04
179	Tippy Martinez	.06	.05	.02
180	Dennis Martinez	.08	.06	.03
181	Sammy Stewart	.06	.05	.02
182	Rich Dauer	.06	.05	.02
183	Lee May	.08	.06	.03
184	Eddie Murray	3.00	2.25	1.25
185	Benny Ayala	.06	.05	.02
186	John Lowenstein	.06	.05	.02
187	Gary Roenicke	.06	.05	.02
188	Ken Singleton	.10	.08	.04
189	Dan Graham	.06	.05	.02
190	Terry Crowley	.06	.05	.02
191	Kiko Garcia	.06	.05	.02
192	Dave Ford	.06	.05	.02
193	Mark Corey	.06	.05	.02
194	Lenn Sakata	.06	.05	.02
195	Doug DeCinces	.10	.08	.04
196	Johnny Bench	1.00	.70	.40
197	Dave Concepcion	.15	.11	.06
198	Ray Knight	.10	.08	.04
199	Ken Griffey	.12	.09	.05
200	Tom Seaver	2.00	1.50	.80
201	Dave Collins	.08	.06	.03
202	George Foster	.20	.15	.08
203	Junior Kennedy	.06	.05	.02
204	Frank Pastore	.06	.05	.02
205	Dan Driessen	.08	.06	.03

		MT	NR MT	EX
206	Hector Cruz	.06	.05	.02
207	Paul Moskau	.06	.05	.02
208	*Charlie Leibrandt*	.25	.20	.10
209	Harry Spilman	.06	.05	.02
210	*Joe Price*	.08	.06	.03
211	Tom Hume	.06	.05	.02
212	Joe Nolan	.06	.05	.02
213	Doug Bair	.06	.05	.02
214	Mario Soto	.08	.06	.03
215a	Bill Bonham (no finger on back)	.08	.06	.03
215b	Bill Bonham (small finger on back)	1.00	.70	.40
216a	George Foster (Slugger on front)	.25	.20	.10
216b	George Foster (Outfield on front)	.20	.15	.08
217	Paul Householder	.06	.05	.02
218	Ron Oester	.06	.05	.02
219	Sam Mejias	.06	.05	.02
220	Sheldon Burnside	.06	.05	.02
221	Carl Yastrzemski	1.25	.90	.50
222	Jim Rice	.50	.40	.20
223	Fred Lynn	.20	.15	.08
224	Carlton Fisk	2.00	1.50	.80
225	Rick Burleson	.08	.06	.03
226	Dennis Eckersley	1.50	1.25	.60
227	Butch Hobson	.06	.05	.02
228	Tom Burgmeier	.06	.05	.02
229	Garry Hancock	.06	.05	.02
230	Don Zimmer	.06	.05	.02
231	Steve Renko	.06	.05	.02
232	Dwight Evans	.15	.11	.06
233	Mike Torrez	.08	.06	.03
234	Bob Stanley	.06	.05	.02
235	Jim Dwyer	.06	.05	.02
236	Dave Stapleton	.06	.05	.02
237	Glenn Hoffman	.06	.05	.02
238	Jerry Remy	.06	.05	.02
239	Dick Drago	.06	.05	.02
240	Bill Campbell	.06	.05	.02
241	Tony Perez	.20	.15	.08
242	Phil Niekro	.30	.25	.12
243	Dale Murphy	.90	.70	.35
244	Bob Horner	.12	.09	.05
245	Jeff Burroughs	.08	.06	.03
246	Rick Camp	.06	.05	.02
247	Bob Cox	.06	.05	.02
248	Bruce Benedict	.06	.05	.02
249	Gene Garber	.06	.05	.02
250	Jerry Royster	.06	.05	.02
251a	Gary Matthews (no finger on back)	.12	.09	.05
251b	Gary Matthews (small finger on back)	1.00	.70	.40
252	Chris Chambliss	.08	.06	.03
253	Luis Gomez	.06	.05	.02
254	Bill Nahorodny	.06	.05	.02
255	Doyle Alexander	.10	.08	.04
256	Brian Asselstine	.06	.05	.02
257	Biff Pocoroba	.06	.05	.02
258	Mike Lum	.06	.05	.02
259	Charlie Spikes	.06	.05	.02
260	Glenn Hubbard	.08	.06	.03
261	Tommy Boggs	.06	.05	.02
262	Al Hrabosky	.08	.06	.03
263	Rick Matula	.06	.05	.02
264	Preston Hanna	.06	.05	.02
265	Larry Bradford	.06	.05	.02
266	*Rafael Ramirez*	.08	.06	.03
267	Larry McWilliams	.06	.05	.02
268	Rod Carew	1.50	1.25	.60
269	Bobby Grich	.10	.08	.04
270	Carney Lansford	.10	.08	.04
271	Don Baylor	.12	.09	.05
272	Joe Rudi	.10	.08	.04
273	Dan Ford	.06	.05	.02
274	Jim Fregosi	.08	.06	.03
275	Dave Frost	.06	.05	.02
276	Frank Tanana	.10	.08	.04
277	Dickie Thon	.08	.06	.03
278	Jason Thompson	.06	.05	.02
279	Rick Miller	.06	.05	.02
280	Bert Campaneris	.10	.08	.04
281	Tom Donohue	.06	.05	.02
282	Brian Downing	.10	.08	.04
283	Fred Patek	.06	.05	.02
284	Bruce Kison	.06	.05	.02
285	Dave LaRoche	.06	.05	.02
286	Don Aase	.06	.05	.02
287	Jim Barr	.06	.05	.02
288	Alfredo Martinez	.06	.05	.02
289	Larry Harlow	.06	.05	.02
290	Andy Hassler	.06	.05	.02
291	Dave Kingman	.15	.11	.06

		MT	NR MT	EX
292	Bill Buckner	.12	.09	.05
293	Rick Reuschel	.10	.08	.04
294	Bruce Sutter	.15	.11	.06
295	Jerry Martin	.06	.05	.02
296	Scot Thompson	.06	.05	.02
297	Ivan DeJesus	.06	.05	.02
298	Steve Dillard	.06	.05	.02
299	Dick Tidrow	.06	.05	.02
300	Randy Martz	.06	.05	.02
301	Lenny Randle	.06	.05	.02
302	Lynn McGlothen	.06	.05	.02
303	Cliff Johnson	.06	.05	.02
304	Tim Blackwell	.06	.05	.02
305	Dennis Lamp	.06	.05	.02
306	Bill Caudill	.06	.05	.02
307	Carlos Lezcano	.06	.05	.02
308	Jim Tracy	.06	.05	.02
309	Doug Capilla	.06	.05	.02
310	Willie Hernandez	.10	.08	.04
311	Mike Vail	.06	.05	.02
312	Mike Krukow	.08	.06	.03
313	Barry Foote	.06	.05	.02
314	Larry Biittner	.06	.05	.02
315	Mike Tyson	.06	.05	.02
316	Lee Mazzilli	.08	.06	.03
317	John Stearns	.06	.05	.02
318	Alex Trevino	.06	.05	.02
319	Craig Swan	.06	.05	.02
320	Frank Taveras	.06	.05	.02
321	Steve Henderson	.06	.05	.02
322	Neil Allen	.08	.06	.03
323	Mark Bomback	.06	.05	.02
324	Mike Jorgensen	.06	.05	.02
325	Joe Torre	.08	.06	.03
326	Elliott Maddox	.06	.05	.02
327	Pete Falcone	.06	.05	.02
328	Ray Burris	.06	.05	.02
329	Claudell Washington	.08	.06	.03
330	Doug Flynn	.06	.05	.02
331	Joel Youngblood	.06	.05	.02
332	Bill Almon	.06	.05	.02
333	Tom Hausman	.06	.05	.02
334	Pat Zachry	.06	.05	.02
335	*Jeff Reardon*	5.00	3.75	2.00
336	*Wally Backman*	.35	.25	.14
337	Dan Norman	.06	.05	.02
338	Jerry Morales	.06	.05	.02
339	Ed Farmer	.06	.05	.02
340	Bob Molinaro	.06	.05	.02
341	Todd Cruz	.06	.05	.02
342a	*Britt Burns* (no finger on front)	.20	.15	.08
342b	*Britt Burns* (small finger on front)	1.00	.70	.40
343	Kevin Bell	.06	.05	.02
344	Tony LaRussa	.08	.06	.03
345	Steve Trout	.06	.05	.02
346	*Harold Baines*	4.00	3.00	1.50
347	Richard Wortham	.06	.05	.02
348	Wayne Nordhagen	.06	.05	.02
349	Mike Squires	.06	.05	.02
350	Lamar Johnson	.06	.05	.02
351	Rickey Henderson	7.00	5.25	2.75
352	Francisco Barrios	.06	.05	.02
353	Thad Bosley	.06	.05	.02
354	Chet Lemon	.08	.06	.03
355	Bruce Kimm	.06	.05	.02
356	*Richard Dotson*	.08	.06	.03
357	Jim Morrison	.06	.05	.02
358	Mike Proly	.06	.05	.02
359	Greg Pryor	.06	.05	.02
360	Dave Parker	.30	.25	.12
361	Omar Moreno	.06	.05	.02
362a	Kent Tekulve (1071 Waterbury on back)	.15	.11	.06
362b	Kent Tekulve (1971 Waterbury on back)	.70	.50	.30
363	Willie Stargell	.40	.30	.15
364	Phil Garner	.08	.06	.03
365	Ed Ott	.06	.05	.02
366	Don Robinson	.08	.06	.03
367	Chuck Tanner	.06	.05	.02
368	Jim Rooker	.06	.05	.02
369	Dale Berra	.06	.05	.02
370	Jim Bibby	.06	.05	.02
371	Steve Nicosia	.06	.05	.02
372	Mike Easler	.08	.06	.03
373	Bill Robinson	.06	.05	.02
374	Lee Lacy	.06	.05	.02
375	John Candelaria	.10	.08	.04
376	Manny Sanguillen	.06	.05	.02
377	Rick Rhoden	.10	.08	.04
378	Grant Jackson	.06	.05	.02

		MT	NR MT	EX
379	Tim Foli	.06	.05	.02
380	*Rod Scurry*	.08	.06	.03
381	Bill Madlock	.12	.09	.05
382a	Kurt Bevacqua (photo reversed, backwards "P" on cap)	.15	.11	.06
382b	Kurt Bevacqua (correct photo)	.70	.50	.30
383	Bert Blyleven	.12	.09	.05
384	Eddie Solomon	.06	.05	.02
385	Enrique Romo	.06	.05	.02
386	John Milner	.06	.05	.02
387	Mike Hargrove	.06	.05	.02
388	Jorge Orta	.06	.05	.02
389	Toby Harrah	.08	.06	.03
390	Tom Veryzer	.06	.05	.02
391	Miguel Dilone	.06	.05	.02
392	Dan Spillner	.06	.05	.02
393	Jack Brohamer	.06	.05	.02
394	Wayne Garland	.06	.05	.02
395	Sid Monge	.06	.05	.02
396	Rick Waits	.06	.05	.02
397	*Joe Charboneau*	.10	.08	.04
398	Gary Alexander	.06	.05	.02
399	Jerry Dybzinski	.06	.05	.02
400	Mike Stanton	.06	.05	.02
401	Mike Paxton	.06	.05	.02
402	Gary Gray	.06	.05	.02
403	Rick Manning	.06	.05	.02
404	Bo Diaz	.08	.06	.03
405	Ron Hassey	.06	.05	.02
406	Ross Grimsley	.06	.05	.02
407	Victor Cruz	.06	.05	.02
408	Len Barker	.08	.06	.03
409	Bob Bailor	.06	.05	.02
410	Otto Velez	.06	.05	.02
411	Ernie Whitt	.08	.06	.03
412	Jim Clancy	.08	.06	.03
413	Barry Bonnell	.06	.05	.02
414	Dave Stieb	.60	.45	.25
415	*Damaso Garcia*	.10	.08	.04
416	John Mayberry	.08	.06	.03
417	Roy Howell	.06	.05	.02
418	*Dan Ainge*	4.00	2.00	1.25
419a	Jesse Jefferson (Pirates on back)	.10	.08	.04
419b	Jesse Jefferson (Blue Jays on back)	.50	.40	.20
420	Joey McLaughlin	.06	.05	.02
421	*Lloyd Moseby*	.10	.08	.04
422	Al Woods	.06	.05	.02
423	Garth Iorg	.06	.05	.02
424	Doug Ault	.06	.05	.02
425	*Ken Schrom*	.06	.05	.02
426	Mike Willis	.06	.05	.02
427	Steve Braun	.06	.05	.02
428	Bob Davis	.06	.05	.02
429	Jerry Garvin	.06	.05	.02
430	Alfredo Griffin	.08	.06	.03
431	Bob Mattick	.06	.05	.02
432	Vida Blue	.12	.09	.05
433	Jack Clark	.25	.20	.10
434	Willie McCovey	.40	.30	.15
435	Mike Ivie	.06	.05	.02
436a	Darrel Evans (Darrel on front)	.15	.11	.06
436b	Darrell Evans (Darrell on front)	.70	.50	.30
437	Terry Whitfield	.06	.05	.02
438	Rennie Stennett	.06	.05	.02
439	John Montefusco	.08	.06	.03
440	Jim Wohlford	.06	.05	.02
441	Bill North	.06	.05	.02
442	Milt May	.06	.05	.02
443	Max Venable	.06	.05	.02
444	Ed Whitson	.06	.05	.02
445	*Al Holland*	.08	.06	.03
446	Randy Moffitt	.06	.05	.02
447	Bob Knepper	.08	.06	.03
448	Gary Lavelle	.06	.05	.02
449	Greg Minton	.06	.05	.02
450	Johnnie LeMaster	.06	.05	.02
451	Larry Herndon	.08	.06	.03
452	Rich Murray	.06	.05	.02
453	Joe Pettini	.06	.05	.02
454	Allen Ripley	.06	.05	.02
455	Dennis Littlejohn	.06	.05	.02
456	Tom Griffin	.06	.05	.02
457	Alan Hargesheimer	.06	.05	.02
458	Joe Strain	.06	.05	.02
459	Steve Kemp	.08	.06	.03
460	Sparky Anderson	.10	.08	.04
461	Alan Trammell	1.00	.70	.40
462	Mark Fidrych	.08	.06	.03
463	Lou Whitaker	.40	.30	.15
464	Dave Rozema	.06	.05	.02

		MT	NR MT	EX
465	Milt Wilcox	.06	.05	.02
466	Champ Summers	.06	.05	.02
467	Lance Parrish	.35	.25	.14
468	Dan Petry	.08	.06	.03
469	Pat Underwood	.06	.05	.02
470	Rick Peters	.06	.05	.02
471	Al Cowens	.06	.05	.02
472	John Wockenfuss	.06	.05	.02
473	Tom Brookens	.08	.06	.03
474	Richie Hebner	.06	.05	.02
475	Jack Morris	1.75	1.25	.70
476	Jim Lentine	.06	.05	.02
477	Bruce Robbins	.06	.05	.02
478	Mark Wagner	.06	.05	.02
479	Tim Corcoran	.06	.05	.02
480a	Stan Papi (Pitcher on front)	.15	.11	.06
480b	Stan Papi (Shortstop on front)	.70	.50	.30
481	*Kirk Gibson*	3.00	2.25	1.25
482	Dan Schatzeder	.06	.05	.02
483	Amos Otis	.70	.50	.30
484	Dave Winfield	3.00	2.25	1.25
485	Rollie Fingers	1.00	.70	.40
486	Gene Richards	.06	.05	.02
487	Randy Jones	.08	.06	.03
488	Ozzie Smith	2.00	1.50	.80
489	Gene Tenace	.08	.06	.03
490	Bill Fahey	.06	.05	.02
491	John Curtis	.06	.05	.02
492	Dave Cash	.06	.05	.02
493a	Tim Flannery (photo reversed, batting righty)	.15	.11	.06
493b	Tim Flannery (photo correct, batting lefty)	.70	.50	.30
494	Jerry Mumphrey	.06	.05	.02
495	Bob Shirley	.06	.05	.02
496	Steve Mura	.06	.05	.02
497	Eric Rasmussen	.06	.05	.02
498	Broderick Perkins	.06	.05	.02
499	Barry Evans	.06	.05	.02
500	Chuck Baker	.06	.05	.02
501	*Luis Salazar*	.15	.11	.06
502	Gary Lucas	.08	.06	.03
503	Mike Armstrong	.06	.05	.02
504	Jerry Turner	.06	.05	.02
505	Dennis Kinney	.06	.05	.02
506	Willy Montanez (Willie)	.06	.05	.02
507	Gorman Thomas	.10	.08	.04
508	Ben Oglivie	.08	.06	.03
509	Larry Hisle	.08	.06	.03
510	Sal Bando	.10	.08	.04
511	Robin Yount	4.00	3.00	1.50
512	Mike Caldwell	.06	.05	.02
513	Sixto Lezcano	.06	.05	.02
514a	Jerry Augustine (Billy Travers photo)	.15	.11	.06
514b	Billy Travers (correct name with photo)	.70	.50	.30
515	Paul Molitor	3.00	2.25	1.25
516	Moose Haas	.06	.05	.02
517	Bill Castro	.06	.05	.02
518	Jim Slaton	.06	.05	.02
519	Lary Sorensen	.06	.05	.02
520	Bob McClure	.06	.05	.02
521	Charlie Moore	.06	.05	.02
522	Jim Gantner	.08	.06	.03
523	Reggie Cleveland	.06	.05	.02
524	Don Money	.06	.05	.02
525	Billy Travers	.06	.05	.02
526	Buck Martinez	.06	.05	.02
527	Dick Davis	.06	.05	.02
528	Ted Simmons	.12	.09	.05
529	Garry Templeton	.10	.08	.04
530	Ken Reitz	.06	.05	.02
531	Tony Scott	.06	.05	.02
532	Ken Oberkfell	.06	.05	.02
533	Bob Sykes	.06	.05	.02
534	Keith Smith	.06	.05	.02
535	John Littlefield	.06	.05	.02
536	Jim Kaat	.15	.11	.06
537	Bob Forsch	.08	.06	.03
538	Mike Phillips	.06	.05	.02
539	*Terry Landrum*	.06	.05	.02
540	*Leon Durham*	.10	.08	.04
541	Terry Kennedy	.08	.06	.03
542	George Hendrick	.08	.06	.03
543	Dane Iorg	.06	.05	.02
544	Mark Littell (photo actually Jeff Little)	.06	.05	.02
545	Keith Hernandez	.40	.30	.15
546	Silvio Martinez	.06	.05	.02
547a	Pete Vuckovich (photo actually Don Hood)	.15	.11	.06

		MT	NR MT	EX
547b	Don Hood (correct name with photo)	.70	.50	.30
548	Bobby Bonds	.10	.08	.04
549	Mike Ramsey	.06	.05	.02
550	Tom Herr	.10	.08	.04
551	Roy Smalley	.06	.05	.02
552	Jerry Koosman	.10	.08	.04
553	Ken Landreaux	.06	.05	.02
554	John Castino	.06	.05	.02
555	Doug Corbett	.06	.05	.02
556	Bombo Rivera	.06	.05	.02
557	Ron Jackson	.06	.05	.02
558	Butch Wynegar	.06	.05	.02
559	Hosken Powell	.06	.05	.02
560	Pete Redfern	.06	.05	.02
561	Roger Erickson	.06	.05	.02
562	Glenn Adams	.06	.05	.02
563	Rick Sofield	.06	.05	.02
564	Geoff Zahn	.06	.05	.02
565	Pete Mackanin	.06	.05	.02
566	Mike Cubbage	.06	.05	.02
567	Darrell Jackson	.06	.05	.02
568	Dave Edwards	.06	.05	.02
569	Rob Wilfong	.06	.05	.02
570	Sal Butera	.06	.05	.02
571	Jose Morales	.06	.05	.02
572	Rick Langford	.06	.05	.02
573	Mike Norris	.06	.05	.02
574	Rickey Henderson	10.00	7.50	4.00
575	Tony Armas	.10	.08	.04
576	Dave Revering	.06	.05	.02
577	Jeff Newman	.06	.05	.02
578	Bob Lacey	.06	.05	.02
579	Brian Kingman (photo actually Alan Wirth)	.06	.05	.02
580	Mitchell Page	.06	.05	.02
581	Billy Martin	.12	.09	.05
582	Rob Picciolo	.06	.05	.02
583	Mike Heath	.06	.05	.02
584	Mickey Klutts	.06	.05	.02
585	Orlando Gonzalez	.06	.05	.02
586	*Mike Davis*	.25	.20	.10
587	Wayne Gross	.06	.05	.02
588	Matt Keough	.06	.05	.02
589	Steve McCatty	.06	.05	.02
590	Dwayne Murphy	.08	.06	.03
591	Mario Guerrero	.06	.05	.02
592	Dave McKay	.06	.05	.02
593	Jim Essian	.06	.05	.02
594	Dave Heaverlo	.06	.05	.02
595	Maury Wills	.10	.08	.04
596	Juan Beniquez	.06	.05	.02
597	Rodney Craig	.06	.05	.02
598	Jim Anderson	.06	.05	.02
599	Floyd Bannister	.10	.08	.04
600	Bruce Bochte	.06	.05	.02
601	Julio Cruz	.06	.05	.02
602	Ted Cox	.06	.05	.02
603	Dan Meyer	.06	.05	.02
604	Larry Cox	.06	.05	.02
605	Bill Stein	.06	.05	.02
606	Steve Garvey	.50	.40	.20
607	Dave Roberts	.06	.05	.02
608	Leon Roberts	.06	.05	.02
609	Reggie Walton	.06	.05	.02
610	Dave Edler	.06	.05	.02
611	Larry Milbourne	.06	.05	.02
612	Kim Allen	.06	.05	.02
613	Mario Mendoza	.06	.05	.02
614	Tom Paciorek	.06	.05	.02
615	Glenn Abbott	.06	.05	.02
616	Joe Simpson	.06	.05	.02
617	Mickey Rivers	.08	.06	.03
618	Jim Kern	.06	.05	.02
619	Jim Sundberg	.08	.06	.03
620	Richie Zisk	.08	.06	.03
621	Jon Matlack	.08	.06	.03
622	Fergie Jenkins	.50	.40	.20
623	Pat Corrales	.06	.05	.02
624	Ed Figueroa	.06	.05	.02
625	Buddy Bell	.12	.09	.05
626	Al Oliver	.15	.11	.06
627	Doc Medich	.06	.05	.02
628	Bump Wills	.06	.05	.02
629	Rusty Staub	.10	.08	.04
630	Pat Putnam	.06	.05	.02
631	John Grubb	.06	.05	.02
632	Danny Darwin	.06	.05	.02
633	Ken Clay	.06	.05	.02
634	Jim Norris	.06	.05	.02
635	John Butcher	.06	.05	.02
636	Dave Roberts	.06	.05	.02
637	Billy Sample	.06	.05	.02
638	Carl Yastrzemski	1.00	.70	.40
639	Cecil Cooper	.15	.11	.06
640	Mike Schmidt	2.00	1.50	.80
641a	Checklist 1-50 (41 Hal McRae)	.10	.08	.04
641b	Checklist 1-50 (41 Hal McRae Double Threat)	.40	.30	.15
642	Checklist 51-109	.06	.05	.02
643	Checklist 110-168	.06	.05	.02
644a	Checklist 169-220 (202 George Foster)	.10	.08	.04
644b	Checklist 169-220 (202 George Foster "Slugger")	.40	.30	.15
645a	Triple Threat (Larry Bowa, Pete Rose, Mike Schmidt) (no number on back)	2.00	1.00	.50
645b	Larry Bowa, Pete Rose, Mike Schmidt (corrected)	2.00	1.50	.80
646	Checklist 221-267	.06	.05	.02
647	Checklist 268-315	.06	.05	.02
648	Checklist 316-359	.06	.05	.02
649	Checklist 360-408	.06	.05	.02
650	Reggie Jackson	3.25	2.50	1.25
651	Checklist 409-458	.06	.05	.02
652a	Checklist 459-509 (483 Aurelio Lopez)	.10	.08	.04
652b	Checklist 459-506 (no 483)	.40	.30	.15
653	Willie Wilson	1.00	.70	.40
654a	Checklist 507-550 (514 Jerry Augustine)	.10	.08	.04
654b	Checklist 507-550 (514 Billy Travers)	.40	.30	.15
655	George Brett	3.00	2.25	1.25
656	Checklist 551-593	.06	.05	.02
657	Tug McGraw	1.00	.70	.40
658	Checklist 594-637	.06	.05	.02
659a	Checklist 640-660 (last number on front is 551)	.10	.08	.04
659b	Checklist 640-660 (last number on front is 483)	.40	.30	.15
660a	Steve Carlton (date 1066 on back)	1.00	.70	.40
660b	Steve Carlton (date 1966 on back)	2.00	1.50	.80

1981 Fleer Star Stickers

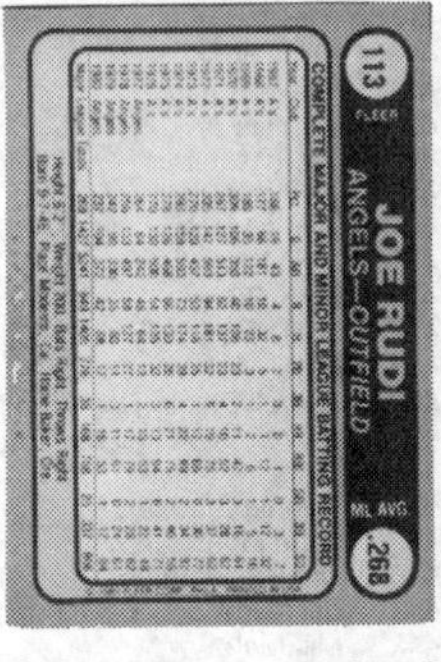

The 128-card 1981 Fleer Star Sticker set was designed for the card fronts to be peeled away from the cardboard backs. The card obverses feature color photos with blue and yellow trim. The card backs are identical in design to the regular 1981 Fleer set except for color and numbering. The set contains three unnumbered checklist cards whose fronts depict Reggie Jackson (#'s 1-42), George Brett (#'s 43-83) and Mike Schmidt (#'s 84-125). The cards, which are the standard 2-1/2" 3-1/2", were issued in gum wax packs.

		MT	NR MT	EX
Complete Set		65.00	49.00	26.00
Common Player		.10	.08	.04
1	Steve Garvey	1.00	.70	.40
2	Ron LeFlore	.10	.08	.04
3	Ron Cey	.25	.20	.10
4	Dave Revering	.10	.08	.04
5	Tony Armas	.15	.11	.06

		MT	NR MT	EX
6	Mike Norris	.10	.08	.04
7	Steve Kemp	.15	.11	.06
8	Bruce Bochte	.10	.08	.04
9	Mike Schmidt	4.00	3.00	1.50
10	Scott McGregor	.10	.08	.04
11	Buddy Bell	.20	.15	.08
12	Carney Lansford	.20	.15	.08
13	Carl Yastrzemski	4.00	3.00	1.50
14	Ben Oglivie	.10	.08	.04
15	Willie Stargell	4.00	3.00	1.50
16	Cecil Cooper	.15	.11	.06
17	Gene Richards	.10	.08	.04
18	Jim Kern	.10	.08	.04
19	Jerry Koosman	.15	.11	.06
20	Larry Bowa	.20	.15	.08
21	Kent Tekulve	.15	.11	.06
22	Dan Driessen	.10	.08	.04
23	Phil Niekro	1.00	.70	.40
24	Dan Quisenberry	.30	.25	.12
25	Dave Winfield	1.00	.70	.40
26	Dave Parker	1.00	.70	.40
27	Rick Langford	.10	.08	.04
28	Amos Otis	.15	.11	.06
29	Bill Buckner	.15	.11	.06
30	Al Bumbry	.10	.08	.04
31	Bake McBride	.10	.08	.04
32	Mickey Rivers	.10	.08	.04
33	Rick Burleson	.10	.08	.04
34	Dennis Eckersley	.60	.45	.25
35	Cesar Cedeno	.20	.15	.08
36	Enos Cabell	.10	.08	.04
37	Johnny Bench	4.00	3.00	1.50
38	Robin Yount	4.00	3.00	1.50
39	Mark Belanger	.10	.08	.04
40	Rod Carew	1.00	.70	.40
41	George Foster	.40	.30	.15
42	Lee Mazzilli	.15	.11	.06
43	Triple Threat (Larry Bowa, Pete Rose, Mike Schmidt)	2.00	1.50	.80
44	J.R. Richard	.15	.11	.06
45	Lou Piniella	.30	.25	.12
46	Ken Landreaux	.10	.08	.04
47	Rollie Fingers	1.00	.70	.40
48	Joaquin Andujar	.10	.08	.04
49	Tom Seaver	4.00	3.00	1.50
50	Bobby Grich	.20	.15	.08
51	Jon Matlack	.10	.08	.04
52	Jack Clark	.25	.20	.10
53	Jim Rice	.25	.20	.10
54	Rickey Henderson	4.00	3.00	1.50
55	Roy Smalley	.10	.08	.04
56	Mike Flanagan	.15	.11	.06
57	Steve Rogers	.10	.08	.04
58	Carlton Fisk	.60	.45	.25
59	Don Sutton	1.00	.70	.40
60	Ken Griffey	.20	.15	.08
61	Burt Hooton	.10	.08	.04
62	Dusty Baker	.20	.15	.08
63	Vida Blue	.25	.20	.10
64	Al Oliver	.30	.25	.12
65	Jim Bibby	.10	.08	.04
66	Tony Perez	1.00	.70	.40
67	Davy Lopes (Davey)	.15	.11	.06
68	Bill Russell	.15	.11	.06
69	Larry Parrish	.20	.15	.08
70	Garry Maddox	.15	.11	.06
71	Phil Garner	.15	.11	.06
72	Graig Nettles	.35	.25	.14
73	Gary Carter	1.00	.70	.40
74	Pete Rose	4.00	3.00	1.50
75	Greg Luzinski	.30	.25	.12
76	Ron Guidry	.25	.20	.10
77	Gorman Thomas	.15	.11	.06
78	Jose Cruz	.20	.15	.08
79	Bob Boone	.15	.11	.06
80	Bruce Sutter	.35	.25	.14
81	Chris Chambliss	.15	.11	.06
82	Paul Molitor	.60	.45	.25
83	Tug McGraw	.25	.20	.10
84	Ferguson Jenkins	.40	.30	.15
85	Steve Carlton	5.00	3.75	2.00
86	Miguel Dilone	.10	.08	.04
87	Reggie Smith	.20	.15	.08
88	Rick Cerone	.10	.08	.04
89	Alan Trammell	1.00	.70	.40
90	Doug DeCinces	.20	.15	.08
91	Sparky Lyle	.15	.11	.06
92	Warren Cromartie	.10	.08	.04
93	Rick Reuschel	.25	.20	.10
94	Larry Hisle	.10	.08	.04
95	Paul Splittorff	.10	.08	.04
96	Manny Trillo	.10	.08	.04
97	Frank White	.20	.15	.08
98	Fred Lynn	.25	.20	.10
99	Bob Horner	.15	.11	.06
100	Omar Moreno	.10	.08	.04
101	Dave Concepcion	.20	.15	.08
102	Larry Gura	.10	.08	.04
103	Ken Singleton	.20	.15	.08
104	Steve Stone	.15	.11	.06
105	Richie Zisk	.10	.08	.04
106	Willie Wilson	.40	.30	.15
107	Willie Randolph	.20	.15	.08
108	Nolan Ryan	6.00	4.50	2.50
109	Joe Morgan	1.00	.70	.40
110	Bucky Dent	.20	.15	.08
111	Dave Kingman	.40	.30	.15
112	John Castino	.10	.08	.04
113	Joe Rudi	.20	.15	.08
114	Ed Farmer	.10	.08	.04
115	Reggie Jackson	4.00	3.00	1.50
116	George Brett	1.00	.70	.40
117	Eddie Murray	.25	.20	.10
118	Rich Gossage	.25	.20	.10
119	Dale Murphy	1.00	.70	.40
120	Ted Simmons	.15	.11	.06
121	Tommy John	.25	.20	.10
122	Don Baylor	.30	.25	.12
123	Andre Dawson	1.00	.70	.40
124	Jim Palmer	4.00	3.00	1.50
125	Garry Templeton	.20	.15	.08
----	Reggie Jackson/Checklist 1-42	4.00	3.00	1.50
----	George Brett/Checklist 43-83	4.00	3.00	1.50
----	Mike Schmidt/Checklist 84-125	4.00	3.00	1.50

1982 Fleer

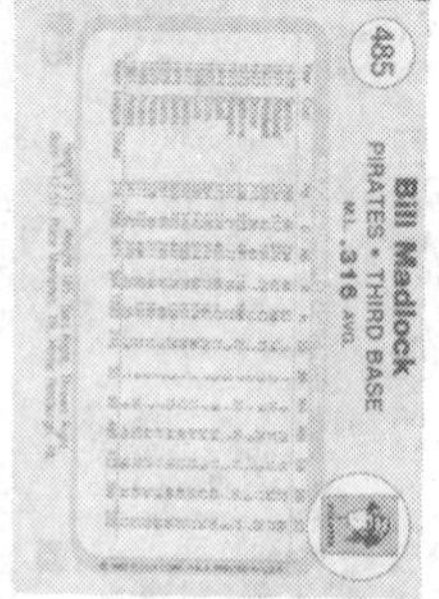

Fleer's 1982 set did not match the quality of the previous year's effort. Many of the photos in the set are blurred and have muddied backgrounds. The cards, which measure 2-1/2" by 3-1/2", feature color photos surrounded by a border frame which is color-coded by team. The card backs are blue, white, and yellow and contain the player's team logo plus the logos of Major League Baseball and the Major League Baseball Players Association. Due to a lawsuit by Topps, Fleer was forced to issue the set with team logo stickers rather than gum. The complete set price does not include the higher priced variations.

	MT	NR MT	EX
Complete Set (660):	100.00	75.00	40.00
Common Player:	.06	.05	.02

		MT	NR MT	EX
1	Dusty Baker	.10	.08	.04
2	Robert Castillo	.06	.05	.02
3	Ron Cey	.12	.09	.05
4	Terry Forster	.08	.06	.03
5	Steve Garvey	.50	.40	.20
6	Dave Goltz	.08	.06	.03
7	Pedro Guerrero(FC)	.10	.08	.04
8	Burt Hooton	.08	.06	.03
9	Steve Howe	.08	.06	.03
10	Jay Johnstone	.08	.06	.03
11	Ken Landreaux	.06	.05	.02
12	Davey Lopes	.10	.08	.04
13	*Mike Marshall*(FC)	.25	.20	.10
14	Bobby Mitchell	.06	.05	.02

		MT	NR MT	EX
15	Rick Monday	.10	.08	.04
16	*Tom Niedenfuer*(FC)	.08	.06	.03
17	*Ted Power*(FC)	.08	.06	.03
18	Jerry Reuss	.10	.08	.04
19	Ron Roenicke	.06	.05	.02
20	Bill Russell	.08	.06	.03
21	*Steve Sax*(FC)	2.00	1.50	.80
22	Mike Scioscia	.08	.06	.03
23	Reggie Smith	.10	.08	.04
24	*Dave Stewart*(FC)	3.00	2.25	1.25
25	Rick Sutcliffe	.15	.11	.06
26	Derrel Thomas	.06	.05	.02
27	Fernando Valenzuela	.60	.45	.25
28	Bob Welch	.12	.09	.05
29	Steve Yeager	.06	.05	.02
30	Bobby Brown	.06	.05	.02
31	Rick Cerone	.06	.05	.02
32	Ron Davis	.06	.05	.02
33	Bucky Dent	.10	.08	.04
34	Barry Foote	.06	.05	.02
35	George Frazier	.06	.05	.02
36	Oscar Gamble	.08	.06	.03
37	Rich Gossage	.20	.15	.08
38	Ron Guidry	.25	.20	.10
39	Reggie Jackson	2.00	1.50	.80
40	Tommy John	.20	.15	.08
41	Rudy May	.06	.05	.02
42	Larry Milbourne	.06	.05	.02
43	Jerry Mumphrey	.06	.05	.02
44	Bobby Murcer	.10	.08	.04
45	*Gene Nelson*	.12	.09	.05
46	Graig Nettles	.15	.11	.06
47	Johnny Oates	.06	.05	.02
48	Lou Piniella	.12	.09	.05
49	Willie Randolph	.10	.08	.04
50	Rick Reuschel	.10	.08	.04
51	Dave Revering	.06	.05	.02
52	*Dave Righetti*(FC)	.60	.45	.25
53	Aurelio Rodriguez	.08	.06	.03
54	Bob Watson	.08	.06	.03
55	Dennis Werth	.06	.05	.02
56	Dave Winfield	2.50	2.00	1.00
57	Johnny Bench	.80	.60	.30
58	Bruce Berenyi	.06	.05	.02
59	Larry Biittner	.06	.05	.02
60	Scott Brown	.06	.05	.02
61	Dave Collins	.08	.06	.03
62	Geoff Combe	.06	.05	.02
63	Dave Concepcion	.12	.09	.05
64	Dan Driessen	.08	.06	.03
65	Joe Edelen	.06	.05	.02
66	George Foster	.20	.15	.08
67	Ken Griffey	.12	.09	.05
68	Paul Householder	.06	.05	.02
69	Tom Hume	.06	.05	.02
70	Junior Kennedy	.06	.05	.02
71	Ray Knight	.10	.08	.04
72	Mike LaCoss	.06	.05	.02
73	Rafael Landestoy	.06	.05	.02
74	Charlie Leibrandt	.10	.08	.04
75	Sam Mejias	.06	.05	.02
76	Paul Moskau	.06	.05	.02
77	Joe Nolan	.06	.05	.02
78	Mike O'Berry	.06	.05	.02
79	Ron Oester	.06	.05	.02
80	Frank Pastore	.06	.05	.02
81	Joe Price	.06	.05	.02
82	Tom Seaver	1.50	1.25	.60
83	Mario Soto	.08	.06	.03
84	Mike Vail	.06	.05	.02
85	Tony Armas	.10	.08	.04
86	Shooty Babitt	.06	.05	.02
87	Dave Beard	.06	.05	.02
88	Rick Bosetti	.06	.05	.02
89	Keith Drumright	.06	.05	.02
90	Wayne Gross	.06	.05	.02
91	Mike Heath	.06	.05	.02
92	Rickey Henderson	4.00	3.00	1.50
93	Cliff Johnson	.06	.05	.02
94	Jeff Jones	.06	.05	.02
95	Matt Keough	.06	.05	.02
96	Brian Kingman	.06	.05	.02
97	Mickey Klutts	.06	.05	.02
98	Rick Langford	.06	.05	.02
99	Steve McCatty	.06	.05	.02
100	Dave McKay	.06	.05	.02
101	Dwayne Murphy	.08	.06	.03
102	Jeff Newman	.06	.05	.02
103	Mike Norris	.06	.05	.02
104	Bob Owchinko	.06	.05	.02
105	Mitchell Page	.06	.05	.02
106	Rob Picciolo	.06	.05	.02
107	Jim Spencer	.06	.05	.02
108	Fred Stanley	.06	.05	.02
109	Tom Underwood	.06	.05	.02
110	Joaquin Andujar	.08	.06	.03
111	Steve Braun	.06	.05	.02
112	Bob Forsch	.08	.06	.03
113	George Hendrick	.08	.06	.03
114	Keith Hernandez	.40	.30	.15
115	Tom Herr	.10	.08	.04
116	Dane Iorg	.06	.05	.02
117	Jim Kaat	.15	.11	.06
118	Tito Landrum	.06	.05	.02
119	Sixto Lezcano	.06	.05	.02
120	Mark Littell	.06	.05	.02
121	John Martin	.06	.05	.02
122	Silvio Martinez	.06	.05	.02
123	Ken Oberkfell	.06	.05	.02
124	Darrell Porter	.08	.06	.03
125	Mike Ramsey	.06	.05	.02
126	Orlando Sanchez	.06	.05	.02
127	Bob Shirley	.06	.05	.02
128	Lary Sorensen	.06	.05	.02
129	Bruce Sutter	.15	.11	.06
130	Bob Sykes	.06	.05	.02
131	Garry Templeton	.10	.08	.04
132	Gene Tenace	.08	.06	.03
133	Jerry Augustine	.06	.05	.02
134	Sal Bando	.08	.06	.03
135	Mark Brouhard	.06	.05	.02
136	Mike Caldwell	.06	.05	.02
137	Reggie Cleveland	.06	.05	.02
138	Cecil Cooper	.15	.11	.06
139	Jamie Easterly	.06	.05	.02
140	Marshall Edwards	.06	.05	.02
141	Rollie Fingers	.50	.40	.20
142	Jim Gantner	.08	.06	.03
143	Moose Haas	.06	.05	.02
144	Larry Hisle	.08	.06	.03
145	Roy Howell	.06	.05	.02
146	Rickey Keeton	.06	.05	.02
147	Randy Lerch	.06	.05	.02
148	Paul Molitor	3.00	2.25	1.25
149	Don Money	.06	.05	.02
150	Charlie Moore	.06	.05	.02
151	Ben Oglivie	.08	.06	.03
152	Ted Simmons	.12	.09	.05
153	Jim Slaton	.06	.05	.02
154	Gorman Thomas	.10	.08	.04
155	Robin Yount	3.00	2.25	1.25
156	Pete Vukovich	.08	.06	.03
157	Benny Ayala	.06	.05	.02
158	Mark Belanger	.08	.06	.03
159	Al Bumbry	.08	.06	.03
160	Terry Crowley	.06	.05	.02
161	Rich Dauer	.06	.05	.02
162	Doug DeCinces	.10	.08	.04
163	Rick Dempsey	.08	.06	.03
164	Jim Dwyer	.06	.05	.02
165	Mike Flanagan	.10	.08	.04
166	Dave Ford	.06	.05	.02
167	Dan Graham	.06	.05	.02
168	Wayne Krenchicki	.06	.05	.02
169	John Lowenstein	.06	.05	.02
170	Dennis Martinez	.08	.06	.03
171	Tippy Martinez	.06	.05	.02
172	Scott McGregor	.08	.06	.03
173	Jose Morales	.06	.05	.02
174	Eddie Murray	.80	.60	.30
175	Jim Palmer	.60	.45	.25
176	*Cal Ripken, Jr.*(FC)	50.00	37.00	20.00
177	Gary Roenicke	.06	.05	.02
178	Lenn Sakata	.06	.05	.02
179	Ken Singleton	.10	.08	.04
180	Sammy Stewart	.06	.05	.02
181	Tim Stoddard	.06	.05	.02
182	Steve Stone	.08	.06	.03
183	Stan Bahnsen	.06	.05	.02
184	Ray Burris	.06	.05	.02
185	Gary Carter	.35	.25	.14
186	Warren Cromartie	.06	.05	.02
187	Andre Dawson	2.00	1.50	.80
188	*Terry Francona*(FC)	.08	.06	.03
189	Woodie Fryman	.08	.06	.03
190	Bill Gullickson	.08	.06	.03
191	Grant Jackson	.06	.05	.02
192	Wallace Johnson	.06	.05	.02
193	Charlie Lea	.06	.05	.02
194	Bill Lee	.08	.06	.03
195	Jerry Manuel	.06	.05	.02
196	Brad Mills	.06	.05	.02

		MT	NR MT	EX
197	John Milner	.06	.05	.02
198	Rowland Office	.06	.05	.02
199	David Palmer	.06	.05	.02
200	Larry Parrish	.10	.08	.04
201	Mike Phillips	.06	.05	.02
202	Tim Raines	1.50	1.25	.60
203	Bobby Ramos	.06	.05	.02
204	Jeff Reardon	1.00	.70	.40
205	Steve Rogers	.08	.06	.03
206	Scott Sanderson	.06	.05	.02
207	Rodney Scott (photo actually Tim Raines)	.10	.08	.04
208	Elias Sosa	.06	.05	.02
209	Chris Speier	.06	.05	.02
210	*Tim Wallach*(FC)	2.00	1.50	.80
211	Jerry White	.06	.05	.02
212	Alan Ashby	.06	.05	.02
213	Cesar Cedeno	.12	.09	.05
214	Jose Cruz	.12	.09	.05
215	Kiko Garcia	.06	.05	.02
216	Phil Garner	.08	.06	.03
217	Danny Heep	.06	.05	.02
218	Art Howe	.06	.05	.02
219	Bob Knepper	.08	.06	.03
220	Frank LaCorte	.06	.05	.02
221	Joe Niekro	.12	.09	.05
222	Joe Pittman	.06	.05	.02
223	Terry Puhl	.06	.05	.02
224	Luis Pujols	.06	.05	.02
225	Craig Reynolds	.06	.05	.02
226	J.R. Richard	.10	.08	.04
227	Dave Roberts	.06	.05	.02
228	Vern Ruhle	.06	.05	.02
229	Nolan Ryan	9.00	6.75	3.50
230	Joe Sambito	.06	.05	.02
231	Tony Scott	.06	.05	.02
232	Dave Smith	.10	.08	.04
233	Harry Spilman	.06	.05	.02
234	Don Sutton	.30	.25	.12
235	Dickie Thon	.08	.06	.03
236	Denny Walling	.06	.05	.02
237	Gary Woods	.06	.05	.02
238	*Luis Aguayo*(FC)	.08	.06	.03
239	Ramon Aviles	.06	.05	.02
240	Bob Boone	.10	.08	.04
241	Larry Bowa	.15	.11	.06
242	Warren Brusstar	.06	.05	.02
243	Steve Carlton	1.00	.70	.40
244	Larry Christenson	.06	.05	.02
245	Dick Davis	.06	.05	.02
246	Greg Gross	.06	.05	.02
247	Sparky Lyle	.10	.08	.04
248	Garry Maddox	.10	.08	.04
249	Gary Matthews	.10	.08	.04
250	Bake McBride	.06	.05	.02
251	Tug McGraw	.12	.09	.05
252	Keith Moreland	.10	.08	.04
253	Dickie Noles	.06	.05	.02
254	Mike Proly	.06	.05	.02
255	Ron Reed	.06	.05	.02
256	Pete Rose	1.00	.70	.40
257	Dick Ruthven	.06	.05	.02
258	Mike Schmidt	2.00	1.50	.80
259	Lonnie Smith	.08	.06	.03
260	Manny Trillo	.08	.06	.03
261	Del Unser	.06	.05	.02
262	George Vukovich	.06	.05	.02
263	Tom Brookens	.06	.05	.02
264	George Cappuzzello	.06	.05	.02
265	Marty Castillo	.06	.05	.02
266	Al Cowens	.06	.05	.02
267	Kirk Gibson	.70	.50	.30
268	Richie Hebner	.06	.05	.02
269	Ron Jackson	.06	.05	.02
270	Lynn Jones	.06	.05	.02
271	Steve Kemp	.08	.06	.03
272	*Rick Leach*(FC)	.12	.09	.05
273	Aurelio Lopez	.06	.05	.02
274	Jack Morris	.30	.25	.12
275	Kevin Saucier	.06	.05	.02
276	Lance Parrish	.35	.25	.14
277	Rick Peters	.06	.05	.02
278	Dan Petry	.08	.06	.03
279	David Rozema	.06	.05	.02
280	Stan Papi	.06	.05	.02
281	Dan Schatzeder	.06	.05	.02
282	Champ Summers	.06	.05	.02
283	Alan Trammell	.40	.30	.15
284	Lou Whitaker	.40	.30	.15
285	Milt Wilcox	.06	.05	.02
286	John Wockenfuss	.06	.05	.02
287	Gary Allenson	.06	.05	.02
288	Tom Burgmeier	.06	.05	.02
289	Bill Campbell	.06	.05	.02
290	Mark Clear	.06	.05	.02
291	Steve Crawford	.06	.05	.02
292	Dennis Eckersley	1.50	1.25	.60
293	Dwight Evans	.15	.11	.06
294	*Rich Gedman*(FC)	.25	.20	.10
295	Garry Hancock	.06	.05	.02
296	Glenn Hoffman	.06	.05	.02
297	Bruce Hurst(FC)	.30	.25	.12
298	Carney Lansford	.08	.06	.03
299	Rick Miller	.06	.05	.02
300	Reid Nichols	.06	.05	.02
301	*Bob Ojeda*(FC)	.50	.40	.20
302	Tony Perez	.20	.15	.08
303	Chuck Rainey	.06	.05	.02
304	Jerry Remy	.06	.05	.02
305	Jim Rice	.40	.30	.15
306	Joe Rudi	.10	.08	.04
307	Bob Stanley	.06	.05	.02
308	Dave Stapleton	.06	.05	.02
309	Frank Tanana	.10	.08	.04
310	Mike Torrez	.08	.06	.03
311	John Tudor(FC)	.25	.20	.10
312	Carl Yastrzemski	1.00	.70	.40
313	Buddy Bell	.12	.09	.05
314	Steve Comer	.06	.05	.02
315	Danny Darwin	.06	.05	.02
316	John Ellis	.06	.05	.02
317	John Grubb	.06	.05	.02
318	Rick Honeycutt	.06	.05	.02
319	Charlie Hough	.10	.08	.04
320	Fergie Jenkins	.15	.11	.06
321	John Henry Johnson	.06	.05	.02
322	Jim Kern	.06	.05	.02
323	Jon Matlack	.08	.06	.03
324	Doc Medich	.06	.05	.02
325	Mario Mendoza	.06	.05	.02
326	Al Oliver	.15	.11	.06
327	Pat Putnam	.06	.05	.02
328	Mickey Rivers	.08	.06	.03
329	Leon Roberts	.06	.05	.02
330	Billy Sample	.06	.05	.02
331	Bill Stein	.06	.05	.02
332	Jim Sundberg	.08	.06	.03
333	Mark Wagner	.06	.05	.02
334	Bump Wills	.06	.05	.02
335	Bill Almon	.06	.05	.02
336	Harold Baines	.30	.25	.12
337	Ross Baumgarten	.06	.05	.02
338	Tony Bernazard	.06	.05	.02
339	Britt Burns	.06	.05	.02
340	Richard Dotson	.10	.08	.04
341	Jim Essian	.06	.05	.02
342	Ed Farmer	.06	.05	.02
343	Carlton Fisk	1.50	1.25	.60
344	Kevin Hickey	.06	.05	.02
345	Lamarr Hoyt (LaMarr)	.06	.05	.02
346	Lamar Johnson	.06	.05	.02
347	Jerry Koosman	.10	.08	.04
348	Rusty Kuntz	.06	.05	.02
349	Dennis Lamp	.06	.05	.02
350	Ron LeFlore	.08	.06	.03
351	Chet Lemon	.08	.06	.03
352	Greg Luzinski	.15	.11	.06
353	Bob Molinaro	.06	.05	.02
354	Jim Morrison	.06	.05	.02
355	Wayne Nordhagen	.06	.05	.02
356	Greg Pryor	.06	.05	.02
357	Mike Squires	.06	.05	.02
358	Steve Trout	.06	.05	.02
359	Alan Bannister	.06	.05	.02
360	Len Barker	.08	.06	.03
361	Bert Blyleven	.12	.09	.05
362	Joe Charboneau	.08	.06	.03
363	John Denny	.06	.05	.02
364	Bo Diaz	.08	.06	.03
365	Miguel Dilone	.06	.05	.02
366	Jerry Dybzinski	.06	.05	.02
367	Wayne Garland	.06	.05	.02
368	Mike Hargrove	.06	.05	.02
369	Toby Harrah	.08	.06	.03
370	Ron Hassey	.06	.05	.02
371	*Von Hayes*(FC)	.40	.30	.15
372	Pat Kelly	.06	.05	.02
373	Duane Kuiper	.06	.05	.02
374	Rick Manning	.06	.05	.02
375	Sid Monge	.06	.05	.02
376	Jorge Orta	.06	.05	.02
377	Dave Rosello	.06	.05	.02

		MT	NR MT	EX
378	Dan Spillner	.06	.05	.02
379	Mike Stanton	.06	.05	.02
380	Andre Thornton	.10	.08	.04
381	Tom Veryzer	.06	.05	.02
382	Rick Waits	.06	.05	.02
383	Doyle Alexander	.10	.08	.04
384	Vida Blue	.12	.09	.05
385	Fred Breining	.06	.05	.02
386	Enos Cabell	.06	.05	.02
387	Jack Clark	.25	.20	.10
388	Darrell Evans	.15	.11	.06
389	Tom Griffin	.06	.05	.02
390	Larry Herndon	.08	.06	.03
391	Al Holland	.06	.05	.02
392	Gary Lavelle	.06	.05	.02
393	Johnnie LeMaster	.06	.05	.02
394	Jerry Martin	.06	.05	.02
395	Milt May	.06	.05	.02
396	Greg Minton	.06	.05	.02
397	Joe Morgan	.50	.40	.20
398	Joe Pettini	.06	.05	.02
399	Alan Ripley	.06	.05	.02
400	Billy Smith	.06	.05	.02
401	Rennie Stennett	.06	.05	.02
402	Ed Whitson	.06	.05	.02
403	Jim Wohlford	.06	.05	.02
404	Willie Aikens	.06	.05	.02
405	George Brett	3.00	2.25	1.25
406	Ken Brett	.08	.06	.03
407	Dave Chalk	.06	.05	.02
408	Rich Gale	.06	.05	.02
409	Cesar Geronimo	.06	.05	.02
410	Larry Gura	.06	.05	.02
411	Clint Hurdle	.06	.05	.02
412	Mike Jones	.06	.05	.02
413	Dennis Leonard	.08	.06	.03
414	Renie Martin	.06	.05	.02
415	Lee May	.08	.06	.03
416	Hal McRae	.12	.09	.05
417	Darryl Motley	.06	.05	.02
418	Rance Mulliniks	.06	.05	.02
419	Amos Otis	.08	.06	.03
420	*Ken Phelps*(FC)	.10	.08	.04
421	Jamie Quirk	.06	.05	.02
422	Dan Quisenberry	.15	.11	.06
423	Paul Splittorff	.06	.05	.02
424	U.L. Washington	.06	.05	.02
425	John Wathan	.08	.06	.03
426	Frank White	.10	.08	.04
427	Willie Wilson	.15	.11	.06
428	Brian Asselstine	.06	.05	.02
429	Bruce Benedict	.06	.05	.02
430	Tom Boggs	.06	.05	.02
431	Larry Bradford	.06	.05	.02
432	Rick Camp	.06	.05	.02
433	Chris Chambliss	.08	.06	.03
434	Gene Garber	.06	.05	.02
435	Preston Hanna	.06	.05	.02
436	Bob Horner	.12	.09	.05
437	Glenn Hubbard	.08	.06	.03
438a	Al Hrabosky (All Hrabosky, 5'1" on back)	20.00	15.00	8.00
438b	Al Hrabosky (Al Hrabosky, 5'1" on back)	1.25	.90	.50
438c	Al Hrabosky (Al Hrabosky, 5'10" on back)	.35	.25	.14
439	Rufino Linares	.06	.05	.02
440	*Rick Mahler*(FC)	.25	.20	.10
441	Ed Miller	.06	.05	.02
442	John Montefusco	.08	.06	.03
443	Dale Murphy	.90	.70	.35
444	Phil Niekro	.30	.25	.12
445	Gaylord Perry	.40	.30	.15
446	Biff Pocoroba	.06	.05	.02
447	Rafael Ramirez	.08	.06	.03
448	Jerry Royster	.06	.05	.02
449	Claudell Washington	.08	.06	.03
450	Don Aase	.06	.05	.02
451	Don Baylor	.12	.09	.05
452	Juan Beniquez	.06	.05	.02
453	Rick Burleson	.08	.06	.03
454	Bert Campaneris	.10	.08	.04
455	Rod Carew	1.00	.70	.40
456	Bob Clark	.06	.05	.02
457	Brian Downing	.10	.08	.04
458	Dan Ford	.06	.05	.02
459	Ken Forsch	.06	.05	.02
460	Dave Frost	.06	.05	.02
461	Bobby Grich	.10	.08	.04
462	Larry Harlow	.06	.05	.02
463	John Harris	.06	.05	.02

		MT	NR MT	EX
464	Andy Hassler	.06	.05	.02
465	Butch Hobson	.06	.05	.02
466	Jesse Jefferson	.06	.05	.02
467	Bruce Kison	.06	.05	.02
468	Fred Lynn	.20	.15	.08
469	Angel Moreno	.06	.05	.02
470	Ed Ott	.06	.05	.02
471	Fred Patek	.06	.05	.02
472	Steve Renko	.06	.05	.02
473	*Mike Witt*(FC)	.35	.25	.12
474	Geoff Zahn	.06	.05	.02
475	Gary Alexander	.06	.05	.02
476	Dale Berra	.06	.05	.02
477	Kurt Bevacqua	.06	.05	.02
478	Jim Bibby	.06	.05	.02
479	John Candelaria	.10	.08	.04
480	Victor Cruz	.06	.05	.02
481	Mike Easler	.08	.06	.03
482	Tim Foli	.06	.05	.02
483	Lee Lacy	.06	.05	.02
484	Vance Law(FC)	.06	.05	.02
485	Bill Madlock	.12	.09	.05
486	Willie Montanez	.06	.05	.02
487	Omar Moreno	.06	.05	.02
488	Steve Nicosia	.06	.05	.02
489	Dave Parker	.30	.25	.12
490	Tony Pena(FC)	.25	.20	.10
491	Pascual Perez(FC)	.15	.11	.06
492	*Johnny Ray*(FC)	.10	.08	.04
493	Rick Rhoden	.10	.08	.04
494	Bill Robinson	.06	.05	.02
495	Don Robinson	.08	.06	.03
496	Enrique Romo	.06	.05	.02
497	Rod Scurry	.06	.05	.02
498	Eddie Solomon	.06	.05	.02
499	Willie Stargell	.40	.30	.15
500	Kent Tekulve	.08	.06	.03
501	Jason Thompson	.06	.05	.02
502	Glenn Abbott	.06	.05	.02
503	Jim Anderson	.06	.05	.02
504	Floyd Bannister	.10	.08	.04
505	Bruce Bochte	.06	.05	.02
506	Jeff Burroughs	.08	.06	.03
507	Bryan Clark	.06	.05	.02
508	Ken Clay	.06	.05	.02
509	Julio Cruz	.06	.05	.02
510	Dick Drago	.06	.05	.02
511	Gary Gray	.06	.05	.02
512	Dan Meyer	.06	.05	.02
513	Jerry Narron	.06	.05	.02
514	Tom Paciorek	.06	.05	.02
515	Casey Parsons	.06	.05	.02
516	Lenny Randle	.06	.05	.02
517	Shane Rawley	.10	.08	.04
518	Joe Simpson	.06	.05	.02
519	Richie Zisk	.08	.06	.03
520	Neil Allen	.06	.05	.02
521	Bob Bailor	.06	.05	.02
522	Hubie Brooks(FC)	.50	.40	.20
523	Mike Cubbage	.06	.05	.02
524	Pete Falcone	.06	.05	.02
525	Doug Flynn	.06	.05	.02
526	Tom Hausman	.06	.05	.02
527	Ron Hodges	.06	.05	.02
528	Randy Jones	.08	.06	.03
529	Mike Jorgensen	.06	.05	.02
530	Dave Kingman	.15	.11	.06
531	Ed Lynch	.06	.05	.02
532	Mike Marshall	.10	.08	.04
533	Lee Mazzilli	.08	.06	.03
534	Dyar Miller	.06	.05	.02
535	Mike Scott(FC)	.20	.15	.08
536	Rusty Staub	.10	.08	.04
537	John Stearns	.06	.05	.02
538	Craig Swan	.06	.05	.02
539	Frank Taveras	.06	.05	.02
540	Alex Trevino	.06	.05	.02
541	Ellis Valentine	.06	.05	.02
542	Mookie Wilson(FC)	.15	.11	.06
543	Joel Youngblood	.06	.05	.02
544	Pat Zachry	.06	.05	.02
545	Glenn Adams	.06	.05	.02
546	Fernando Arroyo	.06	.05	.02
547	John Verhoeven	.06	.05	.02
548	Sal Butera	.06	.05	.02
549	John Castino	.06	.05	.02
550	Don Cooper	.06	.05	.02
551	Doug Corbett	.06	.05	.02
552	Dave Engle	.06	.05	.02
553	Roger Erickson	.06	.05	.02
554	Danny Goodwin	.06	.05	.02

		MT	NR MT	EX
555a	Darrell Jackson (black cap)	1.00	.70	.40
555b	Darrell Jackson (red cap with emblem)	.10	.08	.04
555c	Darrell Jackson (red cap, no emblem)	.25	.20	.10
556	Pete Mackanin	.06	.05	.02
557	Jack O'Connor	.06	.05	.02
558	Hosken Powell	.06	.05	.02
559	Pete Redfern	.06	.05	.02
560	Roy Smalley	.06	.05	.02
561	Chuck Baker	.06	.05	.02
562	Gary Ward	.08	.06	.03
563	Rob Wilfong	.06	.05	.02
564	Al Williams	.06	.05	.02
565	Butch Wynegar	.06	.05	.02
566	Randy Bass	.06	.05	.02
567	Juan Bonilla	.06	.05	.02
568	Danny Boone	.06	.05	.02
569	John Curtis	.06	.05	.02
570	Juan Eichelberger	.06	.05	.02
571	Barry Evans	.06	.05	.02
572	Tim Flannery	.06	.05	.02
573	Ruppert Jones	.06	.05	.02
574	Terry Kennedy	.08	.06	.03
575	Joe Lefebvre	.06	.05	.02
576a	John Littlefield (pitching lefty)	200.00	150.00	80.00
576b	John Littlefield (pitching righty)	.08	.06	.03
577	Gary Lucas	.06	.05	.02
578	Steve Mura	.06	.05	.02
579	Broderick Perkins	.06	.05	.02
580	Gene Richards	.06	.05	.02
581	Luis Salazar	.06	.05	.02
582	Ozzie Smith	1.75	1.25	.70
583	John Urrea	.06	.05	.02
584	Chris Welsh	.06	.05	.02
585	Rick Wise	.08	.06	.03
586	Doug Bird	.06	.05	.02
587	Tim Blackwell	.06	.05	.02
588	Bobby Bonds	.10	.08	.04
589	Bill Buckner	.12	.09	.05
590	Bill Caudill	.06	.05	.02
591	Hector Cruz	.06	.05	.02
592	*Jody Davis*(FC)	.10	.08	.04
593	Ivan DeJesus	.06	.05	.02
594	Steve Dillard	.06	.05	.02
595	Leon Durham	.08	.06	.03
596	Rawly Eastwick	.06	.05	.02
597	Steve Henderson	.06	.05	.02
598	Mike Krukow	.08	.06	.03
599	Mike Lum	.06	.05	.02
600	Randy Martz	.06	.05	.02
601	Jerry Morales	.06	.05	.02
602	Ken Reitz	.06	.05	.02
603a	*Lee Smith* (Cubs logo reversed on back)	12.00	9.00	4.75
603b	*Lee Smith* (corrected)	9.00	6.75	3.50
604	Dick Tidrow	.06	.05	.02
605	Jim Tracy	.06	.05	.02
606	Mike Tyson	.06	.05	.02
607	Ty Waller	.06	.05	.02
608	Danny Ainge	1.25	.90	.50
609	*Jorge Bell*(FC)	6.00	4.50	2.50
610	Mark Bomback	.06	.05	.02
611	Barry Bonnell	.06	.05	.02
612	Jim Clancy	.08	.06	.03
613	Damaso Garcia	.06	.05	.02
614	Jerry Garvin	.06	.05	.02
615	Alfredo Griffin	.08	.06	.03
616	Garth Iorg	.06	.05	.02
617	Luis Leal	.06	.05	.02
618	Ken Macha	.06	.05	.02
619	John Mayberry	.08	.06	.03
620	Joey McLaughlin	.06	.05	.02
621	Lloyd Moseby	.12	.09	.05
622	Dave Stieb	.12	.09	.05
623	Jackson Todd	.06	.05	.02
624	Willie Upshaw(FC)	.08	.06	.03
625	Otto Velez	.06	.05	.02
626	Ernie Whitt	.08	.06	.03
627	Al Woods	.06	.05	.02
628	1981 All-Star Game	.08	.06	.03
629	All-Star Infielders (Bucky Dent, Frank White)	.10	.08	.04
630	Big Red Machine (Dave Concepcion, Dan Driessen, George Foster)	.15	.11	.06
631	Top N.L. Relief Pitcher (Bruce Sutter)	.15	.11	.06
632	Steve & Carlton (Steve Carlton, Carlton Fisk)	.25	.20	.10
633	3000th Game, May 25, 1981 (Carl Yastrzemski)	.35	.25	.14
634	Dynamic Duo (Johnny Bench, Tom Seaver)	.30	.25	.12
635	West Meets East (Gary Carter, Fernando Valenzuela)	.30	.25	.12
636a	N.L. Strikeout King (Fernando Valenzuela) ("...led he National League...")	1.00	.70	.40
636b	N.L. Strikeout King (Fernando Valenzuela) ("... led the National League)	.50	.40	.20
637	Home Run King (Mike Schmidt)	.40	.30	.15
638	N.L. All-Stars (Gary Carter, Dave Parker)	.25	.20	.10
639	Perfect Game! (Len Barker, Bo Diaz)	.08	.06	.03
640	Pete & Re-Pete (Pete Rose, Pete Rose, Jr.)	1.50	1.25	.60
641	Phillies' Finest (Steve Carlton, Mike Schmidt, Lonnie Smith)	.50	.40	.20
642	Red Sox Reunion (Dwight Evans, Fred Lynn)	.15	.11	.06
643	Most Hits and Runs (Rickey Henderson)	2.00	1.50	.75
644	Most Saves 1981 A.L. (Rollie Fingers)	.15	.11	.06
645	Most 1981 Wins (Tom Seaver)	.25	.20	.10
646a	Yankee Powerhouse (Reggie Jackson, Dave Winfield) (comma after "outfielder" on back)	2.00	1.50	.80
646b	Yankee Powerhouse (Reggie Jackson, Dave Winfield) (no comma)	2.00	1.50	.80
647	Checklist 1-56	.06	.05	.02
648	Checklist 57-109	.06	.05	.02
649	Checklist 110-156	.06	.05	.02
650	Checklist 157-211	.06	.05	.02
651	Checklist 212-262	.06	.05	.02
652	Checklist 263-312	.06	.05	.02
653	Checklist 313-358	.06	.05	.02
654	Checklist 359-403	.06	.05	.02
655	Checklist 404-449	.06	.05	.02
656	Checklist 450-501	.06	.05	.02
657	Checklist 502-544	.06	.05	.02
658	Checklist 545-585	.06	.05	.02
659	Checklist 586-627	.06	.05	.02
660	Checklist 628-646	.06	.05	.02

1982 Fleer Stamps

Issued by Fleer in 1982, this set consists of 242 player stamps, each measuring 2-1/2" by 1-13/16". Originally issued in perforated strips of 10, the full-color stamps are numbered in the lower left corner and were designed to be placed in an album. Six stamps feature two players each.

	MT	NR MT	EX
Complete Set:	12.00	9.00	4.75
Common Player:	.03	.02	.01
Stamp Album:	1.50	1.25	.60

		MT	NR MT	EX
1	Fernando Valenzuela	.15	.11	.06
2	Rick Monday	.04	.03	.02
3	Ron Cey	.06	.05	.02
4	Dusty Baker	.04	.03	.02
5	Burt Hooton	.04	.03	.02
6	Pedro Guerrero	.12	.09	.05
7	Jerry Reuss	.06	.05	.02
8	Bill Russell	.04	.03	.02
9	Steve Garvey	.20	.15	.08
10	Davey Lopes	.04	.03	.02
11	Tom Seaver	.25	.20	.10

		MT	NR MT	EX
12	George Foster	.08	.06	.03
13	Frank Pastore	.03	.02	.01
14	Dave Collins	.03	.02	.01
15	Dave Concepcion	.06	.05	.02
16	Ken Griffey	.08	.06	.03
17	Johnny Bench	.03	.02	.01
18	Ray Knight	.04	.03	.02
19	Mario Soto	.04	.03	.02
20	Ron Oester	.03	.02	.01
21	Ken Oberkfell	.03	.02	.01
22	Bob Forsch	.03	.02	.01
23	Keith Hernandez	.15	.11	.06
24	Dane Iorg	.03	.02	.01
25	George Hendrick	.04	.03	.02
26	Gene Tenace	.03	.02	.01
27	Garry Templeton	.06	.05	.02
28	Bruce Sutter	.08	.06	.03
29	Darrell Porter	.03	.02	.01
30	Tom Herr	.06	.05	.02
31	Tim Raines	.20	.15	.08
32	Chris Speier	.03	.02	.01
33	Warren Cromartie	.03	.02	.01
34	Larry Parrish	.04	.03	.02
35	Andre Dawson	.15	.11	.06
36	Steve Rogers	.03	.02	.01
37	Jeff Reardon	.08	.06	.03
38	Rodney Scott	.03	.02	.01
39	Gary Carter	.20	.15	.08
40	Scott Sanderson	.03	.02	.01
41	Cesar Cedeno	.06	.05	.02
42	Nolan Ryan	.20	.15	.08
43	Don Sutton	.12	.09	.05
44	Terry Puhl	.03	.02	.01
45	Joe Niekro	.06	.05	.02
46	Tony Scott	.03	.02	.01
47	Joe Sambito	.03	.02	.01
48	Art Howe	.03	.02	.01
49	Bob Knepper	.06	.05	.02
50	Jose Cruz	.04	.03	.02
51	Pete Rose	.40	.30	.15
52	Dick Ruthven	.03	.02	.01
53	Mike Schmidt	.30	.25	.12
54	Steve Carlton	.20	.15	.08
55	Tug McGraw	.08	.06	.03
56	Larry Bowa	.08	.06	.03
57	Garry Maddox	.04	.03	.02
58	Gary Matthews	.04	.03	.02
59	Manny Trillo	.04	.03	.02
60	Lonnie Smith	.03	.02	.01
61	Vida Blue	.08	.06	.03
62	Milt May	.03	.02	.01
63	Joe Morgan	.12	.09	.05
64	Enos Cabell	.03	.02	.01
65	Jack Clark	.10	.08	.04
66	Claudell Washington	.04	.03	.02
67	Gaylord Perry	.15	.11	.06
68	Phil Niekro	.15	.11	.06
69	Bob Horner	.08	.06	.03
70	Chris Chambliss	.04	.03	.02
71	Dave Parker	.12	.09	.05
72	Tony Pena	.06	.05	.02
73	Kent Tekulve	.04	.03	.02
74	Mike Easler	.04	.03	.02
75	Tim Foli	.03	.02	.01
76	Willie Stargell	.20	.15	.08
77	Bill Madlock	.06	.05	.02
78	Jim Bibby	.03	.02	.01
79	Omar Moreno	.03	.02	.01
80	Lee Lacy	.03	.02	.01
81	Hubie Brooks	.06	.05	.02
82	Rusty Staub	.06	.05	.02
83	Ellis Valentine	.03	.02	.01
84	Neil Allen	.03	.02	.01
85	Dave Kingman	.08	.06	.03
86	Mookie Wilson	.04	.03	.02
87	Doug Flynn	.03	.02	.01
88	Pat Zachry	.03	.02	.01
89	John Stearns	.03	.02	.01
90	Lee Mazzilli	.04	.03	.02
91	Ken Reitz	.03	.02	.01
92	Mike Krukow	.03	.02	.01
93	Jerry Morales	.03	.02	.01
94	Leon Durham	.06	.05	.02
95	Ivan DeJesus	.03	.02	.01
96	Bill Buckner	.06	.05	.02
97	Jim Tracy	.03	.02	.01
98	Steve Henderson	.03	.02	.01
99	Dick Tidrow	.03	.02	.01
100	Mike Tyson	.03	.02	.01
101	Ozzie Smith	.08	.06	.03
102	Ruppert Jones	.03	.02	.01

		MT	NR MT	EX
103	Broderick Perkins	.03	.02	.01
104	Gene Richrds	.03	.02	.01
105	Terry Kennedy	.04	.03	.02
106	Jim Bibby, Willie Stargell	.12	.09	.05
107	Larry Bowa, Pete Rose	.25	.20	.10
108	Warren Spahn, Fernando Valenzuela	.15	.11	.06
109	Dave Concepcion, Pete Rose	.25	.20	.10
110	Reggie Jackson, Dave Winfield	.20	.15	.08
111	Tom Lasorda, Fernando Valenzuela	.10	.08	.04
112	Reggie Jackson	.30	.25	.12
113	Dave Winfield	.20	.15	.08
114	Lou Piniella	.08	.06	.03
115	Tommy John	.10	.08	.04
116	Rich Gossage	.10	.08	.04
117	Ron Davis	.03	.02	.01
118	Rick Cerone	.03	.02	.01
119	Graig Nettles	.08	.06	.03
120	Ron Guidry	.08	.06	.03
121	Willie Randolph	.06	.05	.02
122	Dwayne Murphy	.03	.02	.01
123	Rickey Henderson	.25	.20	.10
124	Wayne Gross	.03	.02	.01
125	Mike Norris	.03	.02	.01
126	Rick Langford	.03	.02	.01
127	Jim Spencer	.03	.02	.01
128	Tony Armas	.03	.02	.01
129	Matt Keough	.03	.02	.01
130	Jeff Jones	.03	.02	.01
131	Steve McCatty	.03	.02	.01
132	Rollie Fingers	.10	.08	.04
133	Jim Gantner	.03	.02	.01
134	Gorman Thomas	.04	.03	.02
135	Robin Yount	.15	.11	.06
136	Paul Molitor	.10	.08	.04
137	Ted Simmons	.08	.06	.03
138	Ben Oglivie	.04	.03	.02
139	Moose Haas	.03	.02	.01
140	Cecil Cooper	.08	.06	.03
141	Pete Vuckovich	.04	.03	.02
142	Doug DeCinces	.04	.03	.02
143	Jim Palmer	.15	.11	.06
144	Steve Stone	.06	.05	.02
145	Mike Flanagan	.04	.03	.02
146	Rick Dempsey	.03	.02	.01
147	Al Bumbry	.03	.02	.01
148	Mark Belanger	.04	.03	.02
149	Scott McGregor	.04	.03	.02
150	Ken Singleton	.06	.05	.02
151	Eddie Murray	.25	.20	.10
152	Lance Parrish	.12	.09	.05
153	David Rozema	.03	.02	.01
154	Champ Summers	.03	.02	.01
155	Alan Trammell	.15	.11	.06
156	Lou Whitaker	.10	.08	.04
157	Milt Wilcox	.03	.02	.01
158	Kevin Saucier	.03	.02	.01
159	Jack Morris	.12	.09	.05
160	Steve Kemp	.04	.03	.02
161	Kirk Gibson	.12	.09	.05
162	Carl Yastrzemski	.35	.25	.14
163	Jim Rice	.20	.15	.08
164	Carney Lansford	.06	.05	.02
165	Dennis Eckersley	.06	.05	.02
166	Mike Torrez	.03	.02	.01
167	Dwight Evans	.08	.06	.03
168	Glenn Hoffman	.03	.02	.01
169	Bob Stanley	.03	.02	.01
170	Tony Perez	.08	.06	.03
171	Jerry Remy	.03	.02	.01
172	Buddy Bell	.06	.05	.02
173	Ferguson Jenkins	.08	.06	.03
174	Mickey Rivers	.04	.03	.02
175	Bump Wills	.03	.02	.01
176	Jon Matlack	.03	.02	.01
177	Steve Comer	.03	.02	.01
178	Al Oliver	.06	.05	.02
179	Bill Stein	.03	.02	.01
180	Pat Putnam	.03	.02	.01
181	Jim Sundberg	.03	.02	.01
182	Ron Leflore	.03	.02	.01
183	Carlton Fisk	.12	.09	.05
184	Harold Baines	.10	.08	.04
185	Bill Almon	.03	.02	.01
186	Richard Dotson	.04	.03	.02
187	Greg Luzinski	.08	.06	.03
188	Mike Squires	.03	.02	.01
189	Britt Burns	.03	.02	.01
190	Lamarr Hoyt	.03	.02	.01
191	Chet Lemon	.04	.03	.02
192	Joe Charboneau	.04	.03	.02

		MT	NR MT	EX
193	Toby Harrah	.03	.02	.01
194	John Denny	.03	.02	.01
195	Rick Manning	.03	.02	.01
196	Miguel Dilone	.03	.02	.01
197	Bo Diaz	.03	.02	.01
198	Mike Hargrove	.03	.02	.01
199	Bert Blyleven	.10	.08	.04
200	Len Barker	.03	.02	.01
201	Andre Thornton	.04	.03	.02
202	George Brett	.30	.25	.12
203	U.L. Washington	.03	.02	.01
204	Dan Quisenberry	.06	.05	.02
205	Larry Gura	.03	.02	.01
206	Willie Aikens	.03	.02	.01
207	Willie Wilson	.08	.06	.03
208	Dennis Leonard	.03	.02	.01
209	Frank White	.06	.05	.02
210	Hal McRae	.06	.05	.02
211	Amos Otis	.04	.03	.02
212	Don Aase	.03	.02	.01
213	Butch Hobson	.03	.02	.01
214	Fred Lynn	.10	.08	.04
215	Brian Downing	.04	.03	.02
216	Dan Ford	.03	.02	.01
217	Rod Carew	.25	.20	.10
218	Bobby Grich	.06	.05	.02
219	Rick Burleson	.03	.02	.01
220	Don Baylor	.10	.08	.04
221	Ken Forsch	.03	.02	.01
222	Bruce Bochte	.03	.02	.01
223	Richie Zisk	.03	.02	.01
224	Tom Paciorek	.03	.02	.01
225	Julio Cruz	.03	.02	.01
226	Jeff Burroughs	.03	.02	.01
227	Doug Corbett	.03	.02	.01
228	Roy Smalley	.03	.02	.01
229	Gary Ward	.03	.02	.01
230	John Castino	.03	.02	.01
231	Rob Wilfong	.03	.02	.01
232	Dave Stieb	.06	.05	.02
233	Otto Velez	.03	.02	.01
234	Damaso Garcia	.03	.02	.01
235	John Mayberry	.03	.02	.01
236	Alfredo Griffin	.06	.05	.02
237	Ted Williams, Carl Yastrzemski	.35	.25	.14
238	Rick Cerone, Graig Nettles	.04	.03	.02
239	Buddy Bell, George Brett	.15	.11	.06
240	Steve Carlton, Jim Kaat	.12	.09	.05
241	Steve Carlton, Dave Parker	.12	.09	.05
242	Ron Davis, Nolan Ryan	.10	.08	.04

1983 Fleer

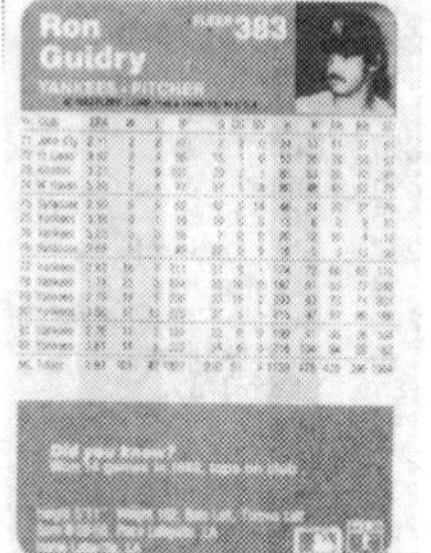

The 1983 Fleer set features color photos set inside a light brown border. The cards are the standard size of 2-1/2" by 3-1/2". A team logo is located at the card bottom and the word "Fleer" is found at the top. The card backs are designed on a vertical format and include a small black and white photo of the player along with biographical and statistical information. The reverses are done in two shades of brown on white stock. The set was issued with team logo stickers.

	MT	NR MT	EX
Complete Set (660):	125.00	90.00	50.00
Common Player:	.06	.05	.02

		MT	NR MT	EX
1	Joaquin Andujar	.08	.06	.03
2	Doug Bair	.06	.05	.02
3	Steve Braun	.06	.05	.02
4	Glenn Brummer	.06	.05	.02
5	Bob Forsch	.08	.06	.03
6	David Green	.06	.05	.02
7	George Hendrick	.08	.06	.03
8	Keith Hernandez	.40	.30	.15
9	Tom Herr	.10	.08	.04
10	Dane Iorg	.06	.05	.02
11	Jim Kaat	.15	.11	.06
12	Jeff Lahti	.06	.05	.02
13	Tito Landrum	.06	.05	.02
14	*Dave LaPoint*(FC)	.08	.06	.03
15	*Willie McGee*(FC)	3.00	2.25	1.25
16	Steve Mura	.06	.05	.02
17	Ken Oberkfell	.06	.05	.02
18	Darrell Porter	.08	.06	.03
19	Mike Ramsey	.06	.05	.02
20	Gene Roof	.06	.05	.02
21	Lonnie Smith	.08	.06	.03
22	Ozzie Smith	1.50	1.25	.60
23	John Stuper	.06	.05	.02
24	Bruce Sutter	.15	.11	.06
25	Gene Tenace	.08	.06	.03
26	Jerry Augustine	.06	.05	.02
27	Dwight Bernard	.06	.05	.02
28	Mark Brouhard	.06	.05	.02
29	Mike Caldwell	.06	.05	.02
30	Cecil Cooper	.15	.11	.06
31	Jamie Easterly	.06	.05	.02
32	Marshall Edwards	.06	.05	.02
33	Rollie Fingers	.60	.45	.25
34	Jim Gantner	.08	.06	.03
35	Moose Haas	.06	.05	.02
36	Roy Howell	.06	.05	.02
37	Peter Ladd	.06	.05	.02
38	Bob McClure	.06	.05	.02
39	Doc Medich	.06	.05	.02
40	Paul Molitor	2.00	1.50	1.00
41	Don Money	.06	.05	.02
42	Charlie Moore	.06	.05	.02
43	Ben Oglivie	.08	.06	.03
44	Ed Romero	.06	.05	.02
45	Ted Simmons	.12	.09	.05
46	Jim Slaton	.06	.05	.02
47	Don Sutton	.30	.25	.12
48	Gorman Thomas	.10	.08	.04
49	Pete Vuckovich	.08	.06	.03
50	Ned Yost	.06	.05	.02
51	Robin Yount	3.00	2.25	1.25
52	Benny Ayala	.06	.05	.02
53	Bob Bonner	.06	.05	.02
54	Al Bumbry	.08	.06	.03
55	Terry Crowley	.06	.05	.02
56	*Storm Davis*(FC)	.10	.08	.04
57	Rich Dauer	.06	.05	.02
58	Rick Dempsey	.08	.06	.03
59	Jim Dwyer	.06	.05	.02
60	Mike Flanagan	.10	.08	.04
61	Dan Ford	.06	.05	.02
62	Glenn Gulliver	.06	.05	.02
63	John Lowenstein	.06	.05	.02
64	Dennis Martinez	.08	.06	.03
65	Tippy Martinez	.06	.05	.02
66	Scott McGregor	.08	.06	.03
67	Eddie Murray	1.00	.70	.40
68	Joe Nolan	.06	.05	.02
69	Jim Palmer	.50	.40	.20
70	Cal Ripken, Jr.	15.00	11.00	6.00
71	Gary Roenicke	.06	.05	.02
72	Lenn Sakata	.06	.05	.02
73	Ken Singleton	.10	.08	.04
74	Sammy Stewart	.06	.05	.02
75	Tim Stoddard	.06	.05	.02
76	Don Aase	.06	.05	.02
77	Don Baylor	.12	.09	.05
78	Juan Beniquez	.06	.05	.02
79	Bob Boone	.10	.08	.04
80	Rick Burleson	.08	.06	.03
81	Rod Carew	1.00	.70	.40
82	Bobby Clark	.06	.05	.02
83	Doug Corbett	.06	.05	.02
84	John Curtis	.06	.05	.02
85	Doug DeCinces	.10	.08	.04
86	Brian Downing	.10	.08	.04
87	Joe Ferguson	.06	.05	.02
88	Tim Foli	.06	.05	.02
89	Ken Forsch	.06	.05	.02
90	Dave Goltz	.08	.06	.03
91	Bobby Grich	.10	.08	.04
92	Andy Hassler	.06	.05	.02

		MT	NR MT	EX
93	Reggie Jackson	.50	.40	.20
94	Ron Jackson	.06	.05	.02
95	Tommy John	.20	.15	.08
96	Bruce Kison	.06	.05	.02
97	Fred Lynn	.20	.15	.08
98	Ed Ott	.06	.05	.02
99	Steve Renko	.06	.05	.02
100	Luis Sanchez	.06	.05	.02
101	Rob Wilfong	.06	.05	.02
102	Mike Witt	.15	.11	.06
103	Geoff Zahn	.06	.05	.02
104	Willie Aikens	.06	.05	.02
105	Mike Armstrong	.06	.05	.02
106	Vida Blue	.12	.09	.05
107	*Bud Black*(FC)	.50	.40	.20
108	George Brett	3.00	2.25	1.25
109	Bill Castro	.06	.05	.02
110	Onix Concepcion	.06	.05	.02
111	Dave Frost	.06	.05	.02
112	Cesar Geronimo	.06	.05	.02
113	Larry Gura	.06	.05	.02
114	Steve Hammond	.06	.05	.02
115	Don Hood	.06	.05	.02
116	Dennis Leonard	.08	.06	.03
117	Jerry Martin	.06	.05	.02
118	Lee May	.08	.06	.03
119	Hal McRae	.12	.09	.05
120	Amos Otis	.08	.06	.03
121	Greg Pryor	.06	.05	.02
122	Dan Quisenberry	.15	.11	.06
123	*Don Slaught*(FC)	.20	.15	.08
124	Paul Splittorff	.06	.05	.02
125	U.L. Washington	.06	.05	.02
126	John Wathan	.08	.06	.03
127	Frank White	.10	.08	.04
128	Willie Wilson	.15	.11	.06
129	Steve Bedrosian(FC)	.25	.20	.10
130	Bruce Benedict	.06	.05	.02
131	Tommy Boggs	.06	.05	.02
132	Brett Butler(FC)	.15	.11	.06
133	Rick Camp	.06	.05	.02
134	Chris Chambliss	.08	.06	.03
135	Ken Dayley(FC)	.10	.08	.04
136	Gene Garber	.06	.05	.02
137	Terry Harper	.06	.05	.02
138	Bob Horner	.12	.09	.05
139	Glenn Hubbard	.08	.06	.03
140	Rufino Linares	.06	.05	.02
141	Rick Mahler	.08	.06	.03
142	Dale Murphy	.90	.70	.35
143	Phil Niekro	.30	.25	.12
144	Pascual Perez	.08	.06	.03
145	Biff Pocoroba	.06	.05	.02
146	Rafael Ramirez	.06	.05	.02
147	Jerry Royster	.06	.05	.02
148	Ken Smith	.06	.05	.02
149	Bob Walk	.08	.06	.03
150	Claudell Washington	.08	.06	.03
151	Bob Watson	.08	.06	.03
152	Larry Whisenton	.06	.05	.02
153	Porfirio Altamirano	.06	.05	.02
154	Marty Bystrom	.06	.05	.02
155	Steve Carlton	.50	.40	.20
156	Larry Christenson	.06	.05	.02
157	Ivan DeJesus	.06	.05	.02
158	John Denny	.06	.05	.02
159	Bob Dernier(FC)	.10	.08	.04
160	Bo Diaz	.08	.06	.03
161	Ed Farmer	.06	.05	.02
162	Greg Gross	.06	.05	.02
163	Mike Krukow	.08	.06	.03
164	Garry Maddox	.10	.08	.04
165	Gary Matthews	.10	.08	.04
166	Tug McGraw	.12	.09	.05
167	Bob Molinaro	.06	.05	.02
168	Sid Monge	.06	.05	.02
169	Ron Reed	.06	.05	.02
170	Bill Robinson	.06	.05	.02
171	Pete Rose	1.50	1.25	.60
172	Dick Ruthven	.06	.05	.02
173	Mike Schmidt	1.50	1.25	.60
174	Manny Trillo	.08	.06	.03
175	Ozzie Virgil(FC)	.10	.08	.04
176	George Vukovich	.06	.05	.02
177	Gary Allenson	.06	.05	.02
178	Luis Aponte	.06	.05	.02
179	*Wade Boggs*(FC)	25.00	18.00	10.00
180	Tom Burgmeier	.06	.05	.02
181	Mark Clear	.06	.05	.02
182	Dennis Eckersley	.12	.09	.05
183	Dwight Evans	.15	.11	.06

		MT	NR MT	EX
184	Rich Gedman	.08	.06	.03
185	Glenn Hoffman	.06	.05	.02
186	Bruce Hurst	.10	.08	.04
187	Carney Lansford	.08	.06	.03
188	Rick Miller	.06	.05	.02
189	Reid Nichols	.06	.05	.02
190	Bob Ojeda	.12	.09	.05
191	Tony Perez	.20	.15	.08
192	Chuck Rainey	.06	.05	.02
193	Jerry Remy	.06	.05	.02
194	Jim Rice	.40	.30	.15
195	Bob Stanley	.06	.05	.02
196	Dave Stapleton	.06	.05	.02
197	Mike Torrez	.08	.06	.03
198	John Tudor	.10	.08	.04
199	Julio Valdez	.06	.05	.02
200	Carl Yastrzemski	1.00	.70	.40
201	Dusty Baker	.10	.08	.04
202	Joe Beckwith	.06	.05	.02
203	*Greg Brock*(FC)	.06	.05	.02
204	Ron Cey	.12	.09	.05
205	Terry Forster	.08	.06	.03
206	Steve Garvey	.40	.30	.15
207	Pedro Guerrero	.25	.20	.10
208	Burt Hooton	.08	.06	.03
209	Steve Howe	.08	.06	.03
210	Ken Landreaux	.06	.05	.02
211	Mike Marshall	.20	.15	.08
212	*Candy Maldonado*(FC)	.20	.15	.08
213	Rick Monday	.10	.08	.04
214	Tom Niedenfuer	.10	.08	.04
215	Jorge Orta	.06	.05	.02
216	Jerry Reuss	.10	.08	.04
217	Ron Roenicke	.06	.05	.02
218	Vicente Romo	.06	.05	.02
219	Bill Russell	.08	.06	.03
220	Steve Sax	.30	.25	.12
221	Mike Scioscia	.08	.06	.03
222	Dave Stewart	.70	.50	.30
223	Derrel Thomas	.06	.05	.02
224	Fernando Valenzuela	.30	.25	.12
225	Bob Welch	.12	.09	.05
226	Ricky Wright	.06	.05	.02
227	Steve Yeager	.06	.05	.02
228	Bill Almon	.06	.05	.02
229	Harold Baines	.15	.11	.06
230	Salome Barojas	.06	.05	.02
231	Tony Bernazard	.06	.05	.02
232	Britt Burns	.06	.05	.02
233	Richard Dotson	.10	.08	.04
234	Ernesto Escarrega	.06	.05	.02
235	Carlton Fisk	1.00	.70	.40
236	Jerry Hairston	.06	.05	.02
237	Kevin Hickey	.06	.05	.02
238	LaMarr Hoyt	.06	.05	.02
239	Steve Kemp	.10	.08	.04
240	Jim Kern	.06	.05	.02
241	*Ron Kittle*(FC)	.08	.06	.03
242	Jerry Koosman	.10	.08	.04
243	Dennis Lamp	.06	.05	.02
244	Rudy Law	.06	.05	.02
245	Vance Law	.08	.06	.03
246	Ron LeFlore	.08	.06	.03
247	Greg Luzinski	.12	.09	.05
248	Tom Paciorek	.06	.05	.02
249	Aurelio Rodriguez	.08	.06	.03
250	Mike Squires	.06	.05	.02
251	Steve Trout	.06	.05	.02
252	Jim Barr	.06	.05	.02
253	Dave Bergman	.06	.05	.02
254	Fred Breining	.06	.05	.02
255	Bob Brenly(FC)	.08	.06	.03
256	Jack Clark	.25	.20	.10
257	Chili Davis(FC)	.20	.15	.08
258	Darrell Evans	.15	.11	.06
259	Alan Fowlkes	.06	.05	.02
260	Rich Gale	.06	.05	.02
261	Atlee Hammaker(FC)	.06	.05	.02
262	Al Holland	.06	.05	.02
263	Duane Kuiper	.06	.05	.02
264	Bill Laskey	.06	.05	.02
265	Gary Lavelle	.06	.05	.02
266	Johnnie LeMaster	.06	.05	.02
267	Renie Martin	.06	.05	.02
268	Milt May	.06	.05	.02
269	Greg Minton	.06	.05	.02
270	Joe Morgan	.50	.40	.20
271	Tom O'Malley	.06	.05	.02
272	Reggie Smith	.10	.08	.04
273	Guy Sularz	.06	.05	.02
274	Champ Summers	.06	.05	.02

		MT	NR MT	EX
275	Max Venable	.06	.05	.02
276	Jim Wohlford	.06	.05	.02
277	Ray Burris	.06	.05	.02
278	Gary Carter	.35	.25	.14
279	Warren Cromartie	.06	.05	.02
280	Andre Dawson	1.25	.90	.50
281	Terry Francona	.06	.05	.02
282	Doug Flynn	.06	.05	.02
283	Woody Fryman	.08	.06	.03
284	Bill Gullickson	.06	.05	.02
285	Wallace Johnson	.06	.05	.02
286	Charlie Lea	.06	.05	.02
287	Randy Lerch	.06	.05	.02
288	Brad Mills	.06	.05	.02
289	Dan Norman	.06	.05	.02
290	Al Oliver	.15	.11	.06
291	David Palmer	.06	.05	.02
292	Tim Raines	.35	.25	.14
293	Jeff Reardon	.80	.60	.30
294	Steve Rogers	.08	.06	.03
295	Scott Sanderson	.06	.05	.02
296	Dan Schatzeder	.06	.05	.02
297	Bryn Smith	.08	.06	.03
298	Chris Speier	.06	.05	.02
299	Tim Wallach	.20	.15	.08
300	Jerry White	.06	.05	.02
301	Joel Youngblood	.06	.05	.02
302	Ross Baumgarten	.06	.05	.02
303	Dale Berra	.06	.05	.02
304	John Candelaria	.10	.08	.04
305	Dick Davis	.06	.05	.02
306	Mike Easler	.08	.06	.03
307	Richie Hebner	.06	.05	.02
308	Lee Lacy	.06	.05	.02
309	Bill Madlock	.12	.09	.05
310	Larry McWilliams	.06	.05	.02
311	John Milner	.06	.05	.02
312	Omar Moreno	.06	.05	.02
313	Jim Morrison	.06	.05	.02
314	Steve Nicosia	.06	.05	.02
315	Dave Parker	.30	.25	.12
316	Tony Pena	.10	.08	.04
317	Johnny Ray	.06	.05	.02
318	Rick Rhoden	.10	.08	.04
319	Don Robinson	.08	.06	.03
320	Enrique Romo	.06	.05	.02
321	Manny Sarmiento	.06	.05	.02
322	Rod Scurry	.06	.05	.02
323	Jim Smith	.06	.05	.02
324	Willie Stargell	.40	.30	.15
325	Jason Thompson	.06	.05	.02
326	Kent Tekulve	.08	.06	.03
327a	Tom Brookens (narrow (1/4") brown box at bottom on back)	.30	.25	.12
327b	Tom Brookens (wide (1-1/4") brown box at bottom on back)	.08	.06	.03
328	Enos Cabell	.06	.05	.02
329	Kirk Gibson	.40	.30	.15
330	Larry Herndon	.08	.06	.03
331	Mike Ivie	.06	.05	.02
332	*Howard Johnson*(FC)	2.50	1.50	1.00
333	Lynn Jones	.06	.05	.02
334	Rick Leach	.06	.05	.02
335	Chet Lemon	.08	.06	.03
336	Jack Morris	.80	.60	.30
337	Lance Parrish	.35	.25	.14
338	Larry Pashnick	.06	.05	.02
339	Dan Petry	.08	.06	.03
340	Dave Rozema	.06	.05	.02
341	Dave Rucker	.06	.05	.02
342	Elias Sosa	.06	.05	.02
343	Dave Tobik	.06	.05	.02
344	Alan Trammell	.40	.30	.15
345	Jerry Turner	.06	.05	.02
346	Jerry Ujdur	.06	.05	.02
347	Pat Underwood	.06	.05	.02
348	Lou Whitaker	.40	.30	.15
349	Milt Wilcox	.06	.05	.02
350	*Glenn Wilson*(FC)	.08	.06	.03
351	John Wockenfuss	.06	.05	.02
352	Kurt Bevacqua	.06	.05	.02
353	Juan Bonilla	.06	.05	.02
354	Floyd Chiffer	.06	.05	.02
355	Luis DeLeon	.06	.05	.02
356	*Dave Dravecky*(FC)	.30	.25	.12
357	Dave Edwards	.06	.05	.02
358	Juan Eichelberger	.06	.05	.02
359	Tim Flannery	.06	.05	.02
360	*Tony Gwynn*(FC)	25.00	18.00	10.00
361	Ruppert Jones	.06	.05	.02
362	Terry Kennedy	.08	.06	.03
363	Joe Lefebvre	.06	.05	.02
364	Sixto Lezcano	.06	.05	.02
365	Tim Lollar	.06	.05	.02
366	Gary Lucas	.06	.05	.02
367	John Montefusco	.06	.05	.02
368	Broderick Perkins	.06	.05	.02
369	Joe Pittman	.06	.05	.02
370	Gene Richards	.06	.05	.02
371	Luis Salazar	.06	.05	.02
372	*Eric Show*(FC)	.15	.11	.06
373	Garry Templeton	.10	.08	.04
374	Chris Welsh	.06	.05	.02
375	Alan Wiggins	.06	.05	.02
376	Rick Cerone	.06	.05	.02
377	Dave Collins	.08	.06	.03
378	Roger Erickson	.06	.05	.02
379	George Frazier	.06	.05	.02
380	Oscar Gamble	.08	.06	.03
381	Goose Gossage	.20	.15	.08
382	Ken Griffey	.12	.09	.05
383	Ron Guidry	.25	.20	.10
384	Dave LaRoche	.06	.05	.02
385	Rudy May	.06	.05	.02
386	John Mayberry	.08	.06	.03
387	Lee Mazzilli	.08	.06	.03
388	Mike Morgan(FC)	.12	.09	.05
389	Jerry Mumphrey	.06	.05	.02
390	Bobby Murcer	.10	.08	.04
391	Graig Nettles	.15	.11	.06
392	Lou Piniella	.12	.09	.05
393	Willie Randolph	.10	.08	.04
394	Shane Rawley	.10	.08	.04
395	Dave Righetti	.25	.20	.10
396	Andre Robertson	.06	.05	.02
397	Roy Smalley	.06	.05	.02
398	Dave Winfield	2.50	2.00	1.00
399	Butch Wynegar	.06	.05	.02
400	Chris Bando	.06	.05	.02
401	Alan Bannister	.06	.05	.02
402	Len Barker	.08	.06	.03
403	Tom Brennan	.06	.05	.02
404	*Carmelo Castillo*(FC)	.06	.05	.02
405	Miguel Dilone	.06	.05	.02
406	Jerry Dybzinski	.06	.05	.02
407	Mike Fischlin	.06	.05	.02
408	Ed Glynn (photo actually Bud Anderson)	.06	.05	.02
409	Mike Hargrove	.06	.05	.02
410	Toby Harrah	.08	.06	.03
411	Ron Hassey	.06	.05	.02
412	Von Hayes	.15	.11	.06
413	Rick Manning	.06	.05	.02
414	Bake McBride	.06	.05	.02
415	Larry Milbourne	.06	.05	.02
416	Bill Nahorodny	.06	.05	.02
417	Jack Perconte	.06	.05	.02
418	Lary Sorensen	.06	.05	.02
419	Dan Spillner	.06	.05	.02
420	Rick Sutcliffe	.12	.09	.05
421	Andre Thornton	.10	.08	.04
422	Rick Waits	.06	.05	.02
423	Eddie Whitson	.06	.05	.02
424	Jesse Barfield(FC)	.60	.45	.25
425	Barry Bonnell	.06	.05	.02
426	Jim Clancy	.08	.06	.03
427	Damaso Garcia	.06	.05	.02
428	Jerry Garvin	.06	.05	.02
429	Alfredo Griffin	.08	.06	.03
430	Garth Iorg	.06	.05	.02
431	Roy Lee Jackson	.06	.05	.02
432	Luis Leal	.06	.05	.02
433	Buck Martinez	.06	.05	.02
434	Joey McLaughlin	.06	.05	.02
435	Lloyd Moseby	.12	.09	.05
436	Rance Mulliniks	.06	.05	.02
437	Dale Murray	.06	.05	.02
438	Wayne Nordhagen	.06	.05	.02
439	*Gene Petralli*(FC)	.08	.06	.03
440	Hosken Powell	.06	.05	.02
441	Dave Stieb	.12	.09	.05
442	Willie Upshaw	.08	.06	.03
443	Ernie Whitt	.08	.06	.03
444	Al Woods	.06	.05	.02
445	Alan Ashby	.06	.05	.02
446	Jose Cruz	.12	.09	.05
447	Kiko Garcia	.06	.05	.02
448	Phil Garner	.08	.06	.03
449	Danny Heep	.06	.05	.02
450	Art Howe	.06	.05	.02
451	Bob Knepper	.08	.06	.03
452	Alan Knicely	.06	.05	.02

		MT	NR MT	EX
453	Ray Knight	.10	.08	.04
454	Frank LaCorte	.06	.05	.02
455	Mike LaCoss	.06	.05	.02
456	Randy Moffitt	.06	.05	.02
457	Joe Niekro	.12	.09	.05
458	Terry Puhl	.06	.05	.02
459	Luis Pujols	.06	.05	.02
460	Craig Reynolds	.06	.05	.02
461	Bert Roberge	.06	.05	.02
462	Vern Ruhle	.06	.05	.02
463	Nolan Ryan	8.00	6.00	3.25
464	Joe Sambito	.06	.05	.02
465	Tony Scott	.06	.05	.02
466	Dave Smith	.08	.06	.03
467	Harry Spilman	.06	.05	.02
468	Dickie Thon	.08	.06	.03
469	Denny Walling	.06	.05	.02
470	Larry Andersen	.06	.05	.02
471	Floyd Bannister	.10	.08	.04
472	Jim Beattie	.06	.05	.02
473	Bruce Bochte	.06	.05	.02
474	Manny Castillo	.06	.05	.02
475	Bill Caudill	.06	.05	.02
476	Bryan Clark	.06	.05	.02
477	Al Cowens	.06	.05	.02
478	Julio Cruz	.06	.05	.02
479	Todd Cruz	.06	.05	.02
480	Gary Gray	.06	.05	.02
481	Dave Henderson(FC)	.20	.15	.08
482	*Mike Moore*(FC)	.50	.40	.20
483	Gaylord Perry	.40	.30	.15
484	Dave Revering	.06	.05	.02
485	Joe Simpson	.06	.05	.02
486	Mike Stanton	.06	.05	.02
487	Rick Sweet	.06	.05	.02
488	*Ed Vande Berg*(FC)	.06	.05	.02
489	Richie Zisk	.08	.06	.03
490	Doug Bird	.06	.05	.02
491	Larry Bowa	.12	.09	.05
492	Bill Buckner	.12	.09	.05
493	Bill Campbell	.06	.05	.02
494	Jody Davis	.10	.08	.04
495	Leon Durham	.08	.06	.03
496	Steve Henderson	.06	.05	.02
497	Willie Hernandez	.08	.06	.03
498	Fergie Jenkins	.15	.11	.06
499	Jay Johnstone	.08	.06	.03
500	Junior Kennedy	.06	.05	.02
501	Randy Martz	.06	.05	.02
502	Jerry Morales	.06	.05	.02
503	Keith Moreland	.08	.06	.03
504	Dickie Noles	.06	.05	.02
505	Mike Proly	.06	.05	.02
506	Allen Ripley	.06	.05	.02
507	*Ryne Sandberg*(FC)	30.00	22.00	12.00
508	Lee Smith	2.00	1.50	.80
509	Pat Tabler(FC)	.15	.11	.06
510	Dick Tidrow	.06	.05	.02
511	Bump Wills	.06	.05	.02
512	Gary Woods	.06	.05	.02
513	Tony Armas	.10	.08	.04
514	Dave Beard	.06	.05	.02
515	Jeff Burroughs	.08	.06	.03
516	John D'Acquisto	.06	.05	.02
517	Wayne Gross	.06	.05	.02
518	Mike Heath	.06	.05	.02
519	Rickey Henderson	3.00	2.25	1.25
520	Cliff Johnson	.06	.05	.02
521	Matt Keough	.06	.05	.02
522	Brian Kingman	.06	.05	.02
523	Rick Langford	.06	.05	.02
524	Davey Lopes	.10	.08	.04
525	Steve McCatty	.06	.05	.02
526	Dave McKay	.06	.05	.02
527	Dan Meyer	.06	.05	.02
528	Dwayne Murphy	.08	.06	.03
529	Jeff Newman	.06	.05	.02
530	Mike Norris	.06	.05	.02
531	Bob Owchinko	.06	.05	.02
532	Joe Rudi	.10	.08	.04
533	Jimmy Sexton	.06	.05	.02
534	Fred Stanley	.06	.05	.02
535	Tom Underwood	.06	.05	.02
536	Neil Allen	.06	.05	.02
537	Wally Backman	.08	.06	.03
538	Bob Bailor	.06	.05	.02
539	Hubie Brooks	.12	.09	.05
540	Carlos Diaz	.06	.05	.02
541	Pete Falcone	.06	.05	.02
542	George Foster	.15	.11	.06
543	Ron Gardenhire	.06	.05	.02
544	Brian Giles	.06	.05	.02
545	Ron Hodges	.06	.05	.02
546	Randy Jones	.08	.06	.03
547	Mike Jorgensen	.06	.05	.02
548	Dave Kingman	.15	.11	.06
549	Ed Lynch	.06	.05	.02
550	Jesse Orosco(FC)	.08	.06	.03
551	Rick Ownbey	.06	.05	.02
552	*Charlie Puleo*(FC)	.06	.05	.02
553	Gary Rajsich	.06	.05	.02
554	Mike Scott	.10	.08	.04
555	Rusty Staub	.10	.08	.04
556	John Stearns	.06	.05	.02
557	Craig Swan	.06	.05	.02
558	Ellis Valentine	.06	.05	.02
559	Tom Veryzer	.06	.05	.02
560	Mookie Wilson	.10	.08	.04
561	Pat Zachry	.06	.05	.02
562	Buddy Bell	.12	.09	.05
563	John Butcher	.06	.05	.02
564	Steve Comer	.06	.05	.02
565	Danny Darwin	.06	.05	.02
566	Bucky Dent	.10	.08	.04
567	John Grubb	.06	.05	.02
568	Rick Honeycutt	.06	.05	.02
569	Dave Hostetler	.06	.05	.02
570	Charlie Hough	.10	.08	.04
571	Lamar Johnson	.06	.05	.02
572	Jon Matlack	.08	.06	.03
573	Paul Mirabella	.06	.05	.02
574	Larry Parrish	.10	.08	.04
575	Mike Richardt	.06	.05	.02
576	Mickey Rivers	.08	.06	.03
577	Billy Sample	.06	.05	.02
578	*Dave Schmidt*(FC)	.10	.08	.04
579	Bill Stein	.06	.05	.02
580	Jim Sundberg	.08	.06	.03
581	Frank Tanana	.10	.08	.04
582	Mark Wagner	.06	.05	.02
583	George Wright	.06	.05	.02
584	Johnny Bench	1.00	.70	.40
585	Bruce Berenyi	.06	.05	.02
586	Larry Biittner	.06	.05	.02
587	Cesar Cedeno	.12	.09	.05
588	Dave Concepcion	.12	.09	.05
589	Dan Driessen	.08	.06	.03
590	Greg Harris(FC)	.08	.06	.03
591	Ben Hayes	.06	.05	.02
592	Paul Householder	.06	.05	.02
593	Tom Hume	.06	.05	.02
594	Wayne Krenchicki	.06	.05	.02
595	Rafael Landestoy	.06	.05	.02
596	Charlie Leibrandt	.08	.06	.03
597	*Eddie Milner*(FC)	.06	.05	.02
598	Ron Oester	.06	.05	.02
599	Frank Pastore	.06	.05	.02
600	Joe Price	.06	.05	.02
601	Tom Seaver	1.00	.70	.40
602	Bob Shirley	.06	.05	.02
603	Mario Soto	.08	.06	.03
604	Alex Trevino	.06	.05	.02
605	Mike Vail	.06	.05	.02
606	Duane Walker	.06	.05	.02
607	Tom Brunansky(FC)	.08	.06	.03
608	Bobby Castillo	.06	.05	.02
609	John Castino	.06	.05	.02
610	Ron Davis	.06	.05	.02
611	Lenny Faedo	.06	.05	.02
612	Terry Felton	.06	.05	.02
613	*Gary Gaetti*(FC)	.50	.40	.20
614	Mickey Hatcher	.08	.06	.03
615	Brad Havens	.06	.05	.02
616	Kent Hrbek(FC)	1.00	.70	.40
617	Randy S. Johnson	.06	.05	.02
618	Tim Laudner(FC)	.12	.09	.05
619	Jeff Little	.06	.05	.02
620	Bob Mitchell	.06	.05	.02
621	Jack O'Connor	.06	.05	.02
622	John Pacella	.06	.05	.02
623	Pete Redfern	.06	.05	.02
624	Jesus Vega	.06	.05	.02
625	*Frank Viola*(FC)	3.00	2.25	1.25
626	Ron Washington	.06	.05	.02
627	Gary Ward	.08	.06	.03
628	Al Williams	.06	.05	.02
629	Red Sox All-Stars (Mark Clear, Dennis Eckersley, Carl Yastrzemski)	.25	.20	.10
630	300 Career Wins (Terry Bulling, Gaylord Perry)	.15	.11	.06
631	Pride of Venezuela (Dave Concepcion, Manny Trillo)	.10	.08	.04

		MT	NR MT	EX
632	All-Star Infielders (Buddy Bell, Robin Yount)	.15	.11	.06
633	Mr. Vet & Mr. Rookie (Kent Hrbek, Dave Winfield)	.25	.20	.10
634	Fountain of Youth (Pete Rose, Willie Stargell)	.40	.30	.15
635	Big Chiefs (Toby Harrah, Andre Thornton)	.08	.06	.03
636	"Smith Bros." (Lonnie Smith, Ozzie Smith)	.10	.08	.04
637	Base Stealers' Threat (Gary Carter, Bo Diaz)	.15	.11	.06
638	All-Star Catchers (Gary Carter, Carlton Fisk)	.20	.15	.08
639	Rickey Henderson (IA)	2.00	1.50	.80
640	Home Run Threats (Reggie Jackson, Ben Oglivie)	.25	.20	.10
641	Two Teams - Same Day (Joel Youngblood)	.08	.06	.03
642	Last Perfect Game (Len Barker, Ron Hassey)	.08	.06	.03
643	Blue (Vida Blue)	.10	.08	.04
644	Black & (Bud Black)	.10	.08	.04
645	Power (Reggie Jackson)	.30	.25	.12
646	Speed & (Rickey Henderson)	.30	.25	.12
647	Checklist 1-51	.06	.05	.02
648	Checklist 52-103	.06	.05	.02
649	Checklist 104-152	.06	.05	.02
650	Checklist 153-200	.06	.05	.02
651	Checklist 201-251	.06	.05	.02
652	Checklist 252-301	.06	.05	.02
653	Checklist 302-351	.06	.05	.02
654	Checklist 352-399	.06	.05	.02
655	Checklist 400-444	.06	.05	.02
656	Checklist 445-489	.06	.05	.02
657	Checklist 490-535	.06	.05	.02
658	Checklist 536-583	.06	.05	.02
659	Checklist 584-628	.06	.05	.02
660	Checklist 629-646	.06	.05	.02

1983 Fleer Stamps

The 1983 Fleer Stamp set consists of 288 stamps, including 224 player stamps and 64 team logo stamps. They were originally issued on four different sheets of 72 stamps each (checklisted below) and in "Vend-A-Stamp" dispensers of 18 stamps each. Sixteen different dispenser strips were needed to complete the set (strips 1-4 comprise Sheet 1; strips 5-8 comprise Sheet 2; strips 9-12 comprise Sheet 3; and strips 13-16 comprise Sheet 4.)

	MT	NR MT	EX
Complete Sheet Set:	7.00	5.25	2.75
Complete Vend-A-Stamp Set:	7.00	5.25	2.75
Common Sheet:	1.75	1.25	.70
Common Stamp Dispenser:	.25	.20	.10
Common Single Stamp:	.01	.01	

		MT	NR MT	EX
1	Sheet 1 (A's Logo, Angels Logo, Astros Logo, Cardinals Logo, Cubs Logo, Dodgers Logo, Expos Logo, Giants Logo, Indians Logo, Mets Logo, Orioles Logo, Phillies Logo, Pirates Logo, Red Sox Logo, Twins Logo, White Sox Logo, Neil Allen, Harold Baines, Buddy Bell, Dale Berra, Wade Boggs, George Brett, Bill Buckner, Jack Clark, Dave Concepcion, Warren Cromartie, Doug DeCinces, Luis DeLeon, Brian Downing, Dan Driessen, Mike Flanagan, Bob Forsch, Ken Forsch, Toby Harrah, Keith Hernandez, Steve Howe, Reggie Jackson, Ruppert Jones, Ray Knight, Gary Lavelle, Ron LeFlore, Davey Lopes, Lee Mazzilli, Bob McClure, Tug McGraw, Paul Molitor, Rick Monday, John Montefusco, Gaylord Perry, Dan Quisenberry, Ron Reed, Rick Rhoden, Ron Roenicke, Jerry Royster, Mike Schmidt, Roy Smalley, Reggie Smith, Mario Soto, Chris Speier, Willie Stargell, Rick Sutcliffe, Don Sutton, Craig Swan, Kent Tekulve, Dick Tidrow, Willie Upshaw, Fernando Valenzuela, U.L. Washington, Bump Wills, Dave Winfield, Robin Yount, Pat Zachry)	1.75	1.25	.70
2	Sheet 2 (Angels Logo, Astros Logo, Braves Logo, Cardinals Logo, Dodgers Logo, Expos Logo, Indians Logo, Mariners Logo, Mets Logo, Phillies Logo, Pirates Logo, Rangers Logo, Reds Logo, Royals Logo, Tigers Logo, Yankees Logo, Willie Aikens, Bob Bailor, Dusty Baker, Floyd Bannister, Len Barker, Hubie Brooks, Tom Brunansky, Chris Chambliss, Mark Clear, Andre Dawson, Bo Diaz, Dennis Eckersley, Rollie Fingers, George Foster, Goose Gossage, Ken Griffey, Ron Guidry, Rickey Henderson, Bob Horner, Lamarr Hoyt (LaMarr), Tom Hume, Garth Iorg, Tommy John, Sixto Lezcano, Fred Lynn, John Matlack (Jon), Scott McGregor, Eddie Milner, Greg Minton, Joe Morgan, Steve Mura, Dwayne Murphy, Ken Oberkfell, Ben Oglivie, Al Oliver, Jim Palmer, Lance Parrish, Larry Parrish, Lou Piniella, Tim Raines, Rafael Ramirez, Jeff Reardon, Jerry Reuss, Jim Rice, Pete Rose, Tom Seaver, Eric Show, Jim Sundberg, Bruce Sutter, Gorman Thomas, Jason Thompson, Tom Underwood, Mookie Wilson, Willie Wilson, John Wockenfuss, Carl Yastrzemski)	1.75	1.25	.70
3	Sheet 3 (A's Logo, Angels Logo, Blue Jays Logo, Braves Logo, Brewers Logo, Dodgers Logo, Giants Logo, Indians Logo, Mariners Logo, Orioles Logo, Padres Logo, Reds Logo, Royals Logo, Tigers Logo, Twins Logo, White Sox Logo, Alan Ashby, Dave Beard, Jim Beattie, Johnny Bench, Larry Biittner, Bob Boone, Rod Carew, Gary Carter, Bobby Castillo, Bill Caudill, Cecil Cooper, Mike Easler, Dwight Evans, Carlton Fisk, Gene Garber, Damaso Garcia, Larry Herndon, Al Holland, Burt Hooton, Art Howe, Kent Hrbek, Jerry Koosman, Duane Kuiper, Bill Laskey, Dennis Leonard, Garry Maddox, Bill Madlock, Rick Manning, Hal McRae, Keith Moreland, Jerry Mumphrey, Eddie Murray, Joe Niekro, Phil Niekro, Amos Otis, Darrell Porter, Johnny Ray, Mike Richardt, Cal Ripken, Jr, Steve Rogers, Nolan Ryan, Manny Sarmiento, Steve Sax, Ted Simmons, Ken Singleton, Bob Stanley, Rusty Staub, Dave Stieb, Dickie Thon, Andre Thornton, Manny Trillo, John Tudor, Ed Vande Berg, Bob Watson, Frank White, Milt Wilcox)	1.75	1.25	.70
4	Sheet 4 (Blue Jays Logo, Braves Logo, Brewers Logo, Cubs Logo, Expos Logo, Giants Logo, Padres Logo, Phillies Logo, Pirates Logo, Rangers Logo, Red Sox Logo, Reds Logo, Royals Logo, Twins Logo, White Sox Logo, Yankees Logo, Joaquin Andujar, Don Baylor, Vida Blue, Bruce Bochte, Larry Bowa, Al Bumbry, Jeff Burroughs, Enos Cabell, Steve Carlton, Cesar Cedeno, Rick Cerone, Ron Cey, Larry Christenson, Jim Clancy, Jose Cruz, Danny Darwin, Rich Dauer, Ron Davis, Ivan DeJesus, Leon Durham, Phil Garner, Steve Garvey, John Grubb, Atlee Hammaker, Mike Hargrove, Tom Herr, Ferguson Jenkins, Steve Kemp, Bruce Kison, Ken Landreaux, Carney Lansford, Charlie Lea, John Lowenstein, Greg Luzinski, Dennis Martinez, Tippy Martinez, Randy Martz, Gary Matthews, Milt May, Dale Murphy, Graig Nettles, Tom Paciorek, Dave Parker, Tony Pena, Hosken Powell, Willie Randolph, Lonnie Smith, Ozzie Smith, Dan Spillner, Ellis Valentine, Pete Vuckovich, Gary Ward, Claudell Washington, Lou Whitaker, Al Williams, Richie Zisk)	1.75	1.25	.70

1983 Fleer Stickers

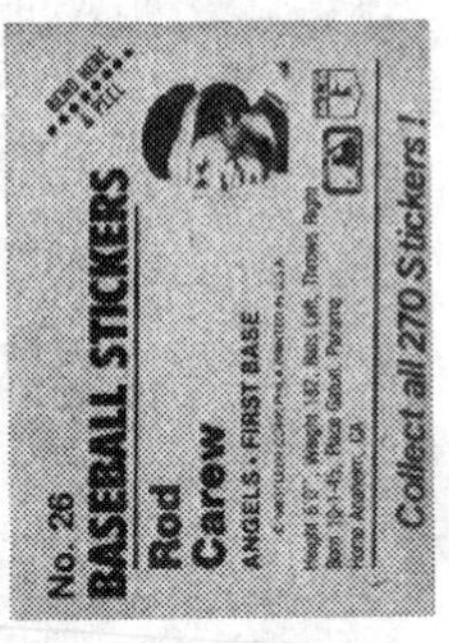

This 270-sticker set consists of both player stickers and team logo stickers, all measuring 1-13/16" by 2-1/2". The player stickers are numbered on the back. The front features a full-color photo surrounded by a blue border with two stars at the top. The 1983 Fleer stickers were issued in strips of ten player stickers plus two team logo stickers. The 26 logo stickers have been assigned numbers 271 through 296.

		MT	NR MT	EX
Complete Set:		18.00	13.50	7.25
Common Player:		.03	.02	.01
1	Bruce Sutter	.08	.06	.03
2	Willie McGee	.08	.06	.03
3	Darrell Porter	.03	.02	.01
4	Lonnie Smith	.03	.02	.01
5	Dane Iorg	.03	.02	.01
6	Keith Hernandez	.15	.11	.06
7	Joaquin Andujar	.04	.03	.02
8	Ken Oberkfell	.03	.02	.01
9	John Stuper	.03	.02	.01
10	Ozzie Smith	.10	.08	.04
11	Bob Forsch	.03	.02	.01
12	Jim Gantner	.03	.02	.01
13	Rollie Fingers	.10	.08	.04
14	Pete Vuckovich	.03	.02	.01
15	Ben Oglivie	.04	.03	.02
16	Don Sutton	.10	.08	.04
17	Bob McClure	.03	.02	.01
18	Robin Yount	.15	.11	.06
19	Paul Molitor	.10	.08	.04
20	Gorman Thomas	.06	.05	.02
21	Mike Caldwell	.03	.02	.01
22	Ted Simmons	.06	.05	.02
23	Cecil Cooper	.08	.06	.03
24	Steve Renko	.03	.02	.01
25	Tommy John	.08	.06	.03
26	Rod Carew	.25	.20	.10
27	Bruce Kison	.03	.02	.01
28	Ken Forsch	.03	.02	.01
29	Geoff Zahn	.03	.02	.01
30	Doug DiCinces	.06	.05	.02
31	Fred Lynn	.10	.08	.04
32	Reggie Jackson	.25	.20	.10
33	Don Baylor	.08	.06	.03
34	Bob Boone	.04	.03	.02
35	Brian Downing	.04	.03	.02
36	Goose Gossage	.08	.06	.03
37	Roy Smalley	.03	.02	.01
38	Graig Nettles	.06	.05	.02
39	Dave Winfield	.20	.15	.08
40	Lee Mazzilli	.04	.03	.02
41	Jerry Mumphrey	.03	.02	.01
42	Dave Collins	.03	.02	.01
43	Rick Cerone	.03	.02	.01
44	Willie Randolph	.06	.05	.02
45	Lou Piniella	.06	.05	.02
46	Ken Griffey	.06	.05	.02
47	Ron Guidry	.10	.08	.04
48	Jack Clark	.08	.06	.03
49	Reggie Smith	.06	.05	.02
50	Atlee Hammaker	.03	.02	.01
51	Fred Breining	.03	.02	.01
52	Gary Lavelle	.03	.02	.01
53	Chili Davis	.06	.05	.02
54	Greg Minton	.03	.02	.01
55	Joe Morgan	.12	.09	.05
56	Al Holland	.03	.02	.01
57	Bill Laskey	.03	.02	.01
58	Duane Kuiper	.03	.02	.01
59	Tom Burgmeier	.03	.02	.01
60	Carl Yastrzemski	.35	.25	.14
61	Mark Clear	.03	.02	.01
62	Mike Torrez	.03	.02	.01
63	Dennis Eckersley	.06	.05	.02
64	Wade Boggs	.75	.60	.30
65	Bob Stanley	.03	.02	.01
66	Jim Rice	.20	.15	.08
67	Carney Lansford	.06	.05	.02
68	Jerry Remy	.03	.02	.01
69	Dwight Evans	.08	.06	.03
70	John Candelaria	.06	.05	.02
71	Bill Madlock	.06	.05	.02
72	Dave Parker	.10	.08	.04
73	Kent Tekulve	.04	.03	.02
74	Tony Pena	.06	.05	.02
75	Manny Sarmiento	.03	.02	.01
76	Johnny Ray	.06	.05	.02
77	Dale Berra	.03	.02	.01
78	Lee Lacy	.03	.02	.01
79	Jason Thompson	.03	.02	.01
80	Mike Easler	.04	.03	.02
81	Willie Stargell	.20	.15	.08
82	Rick Camp	.03	.02	.01
83	Bob Watson	.03	.02	.01
84	Bob Horner	.08	.06	.03
85	Rafael Ramirez	.03	.02	.01
86	Chris Chambliss	.04	.03	.02
87	Gene Garber	.03	.02	.01
88	Claudell Washington	.04	.03	.02
89	Steve Bedrosian	.06	.05	.02
90	Dale Murphy	.30	.25	.12
91	Phil Niekro	.10	.08	.04
92	Jerry Royster	.03	.02	.01
93	Bob Walk	.03	.02	.01
94	Frank White	.06	.05	.02
95	Dennis Leonard	.03	.02	.01
96	Vida Blue	.06	.05	.02
97	U.L. Washington	.03	.02	.01
98	George Brett	.30	.25	.12
99	Amos Otis	.04	.03	.02
100	Dan Quisenberry	.06	.05	.02
101	Willie Aikens	.03	.02	.01
102	Hal McRae	.06	.05	.02
103	Larry Gura	.03	.02	.01
104	Willie Wilson	.06	.05	.02
105	Damaso Garcia	.03	.02	.01
106	Hosken Powell	.03	.02	.01
107	Joey McLaughlin	.03	.02	.01
108	Jim Clancy	.03	.02	.01
109	Barry Bonnell	.03	.02	.01
110	Garth Iorg	.03	.02	.01
111	Dave Stieb	.06	.05	.02
112	Fernando Valenzuela	.15	.11	.06
113	Steve Garvey	.20	.15	.08
114	Rick Monday	.04	.03	.02
115	Burt Hooton	.03	.02	.01
116	Bill Russell	.04	.03	.02
117	Pedro Guerrero	.12	.09	.05
118	Steve Sax	.08	.06	.03
119	Steve Howe	.04	.03	.02
120	Ken Landreaux	.03	.02	.01
121	Dusty Baker	.04	.03	.02
122	Ron Cey	.06	.05	.02
123	Jerry Reuss	.06	.05	.02
124	Bump Wills	.03	.02	.01
125	Keith Moreland	.06	.05	.02
126	Dick Tidrow	.03	.02	.01
127	Bill Campbell	.03	.02	.01
128	Larry Bowa	.06	.05	.02
129	Randy Martz	.03	.02	.01
130	Ferguson Jenkins	.06	.05	.02
131	Leon Durham	.04	.03	.02
132	Bill Buckner	.06	.05	.02
133	Ron Davis	.03	.02	.01
134	Jack O'Connor	.03	.02	.01
135	Kent Hrbek	.10	.08	.04
136	Gary Ward	.03	.02	.01
137	Al Williams	.03	.02	.01
138	Tom Brunansky	.06	.05	.02
139	Bobby Castillo	.03	.02	.01
140	Dusty Baker, Dale Murphy	.20	.15	.08
141	Nolan Ryan	.10	.08	.04
142	Lee Lacey, Omar Moreno	.03	.02	.01
143	Al Oliver, Pete Rose	.40	.30	.15
144	Ricky Henderson	.25	.20	.10
145	Ray Knight, Pete Rose, Mike Schmidt	.40	.30	.15
146	Hal McRae, Ben Oglivie	.06	.05	.02

		MT	NR MT	EX
147	Tom Hume, Ray Knight	.04	.03	.02
148	Buddy Bell, Carlton Fisk	.06	.05	.02
149	Steve Kemp	.04	.03	.02
150	Rudy Law	.03	.02	.01
151	Ron LeFlore	.04	.03	.02
152	Jerry Koosman	.04	.03	.02
153	Carlton Fisk	.12	.09	.05
154	Salome Barojas	.03	.02	.01
155	Harold Baines	.10	.08	.04
156	Britt Burns	.03	.02	.01
157	Tom Paciorek	.03	.02	.01
158	Greg Luzinski	.06	.05	.02
159	LaMarr Hoyt	.03	.02	.01
160	George Wright	.03	.02	.01
161	Danny Darwin	.03	.02	.01
162	Lamar Johnson	.03	.02	.01
163	Charlie Hough	.04	.03	.02
164	Buddy Bell	.06	.05	.02
165	John Matlack (Jon)	.04	.03	.02
166	Billy Sample	.03	.02	.01
167	John Grubb	.03	.02	.01
168	Larry Parrish	.06	.05	.02
169	Ivan DeJesus	.03	.02	.01
170	Mike Schmidt	.30	.25	.12
171	Tug McGraw	.06	.05	.02
172	Ron Reed	.03	.02	.01
173	Garry Maddox	.04	.03	.02
174	Pete Rose	.40	.30	.15
175	Manny Trillo	.04	.03	.02
176	Steve Carlton	.20	.15	.08
177	Bo Diaz	.04	.03	.02
178	Gary Matthews	.04	.03	.02
179	Bill Caudill	.03	.02	.01
180	Ed Vande Berg	.03	.02	.01
181	Gaylord Perry	.12	.09	.05
182	Floyd Bannister	.04	.03	.02
183	Richie Zisk	.04	.03	.02
184	Al Cowens	.03	.02	.01
185	Bruce Bochte	.03	.02	.01
186	Jeff Burroughs	.04	.03	.02
187	Dave Beard	.03	.02	.01
188	Davey Lopes	.04	.03	.02
189	Dwayne Murphy	.04	.03	.02
190	Rick Langford	.03	.02	.01
191	Tom Underwood	.03	.02	.01
192	Rickey Henderson	.25	.20	.10
193	Mike Flanagan	.06	.05	.02
194	Scott McGregor	.04	.03	.02
195	Ken Singleton	.06	.05	.02
196	Rich Dauer	.03	.02	.01
197	John Lowenstein	.03	.02	.01
198	Cal Ripken, Jr.	.25	.20	.10
199	Dennis Martinez	.04	.03	.02
200	Jim Palmer	.15	.11	.06
201	Tippy Martinez	.03	.02	.01
202	Eddie Murray	.25	.20	.10
203	Al Bumbry	.03	.02	.01
204	Dickie Thon	.03	.02	.01
205	Phil Garner	.03	.02	.01
206	Jose Cruz	.04	.03	.02
207	Nolan Ryan	.15	.11	.06
208	Ray Knight	.04	.03	.02
209	Terry Puhl	.03	.02	.01
210	Joe Niekro	.06	.05	.02
211	Art Howe	.03	.02	.01
212	Alan Ashby	.03	.02	.01
213	Tom Hume	.03	.02	.01
214	Johnny Bench	.25	.20	.10
215	Larry Biittner	.03	.02	.01
216	Mario Soto	.04	.03	.02
217	Dan Driessen	.04	.03	.02
218	Tom Seaver	.20	.15	.08
219	Dave Concepcion	.06	.05	.02
220	Wayne Krenchicki	.03	.02	.01
221	Cesar Cedeno	.06	.05	.02
222	Ruppert Jones	.03	.02	.01
223	Terry Kennedy	.04	.03	.02
224	Luis DeLeon	.03	.02	.01
225	Eric Show	.04	.03	.02
226	Tim Flannery	.03	.02	.01
227	Garry Templeton	.04	.03	.02
228	Tim Lollar	.03	.02	.01
229	Sixto Lezcano	.03	.02	.01
230	Bob Bailor	.03	.02	.01
231	Craig Swan	.03	.02	.01
232	Dave Kingman	.06	.05	.02
233	Mookie Wilson	.04	.03	.02
234	John Stearns	.03	.02	.01
235	Ellis Valentine	.03	.02	.01
236	Neil Allen	.03	.02	.01
237	Pat Zachry	.03	.02	.01
238	Rusty Staub	.06	.05	.02
239	George Foster	.06	.05	.02
240	Rick Sutcliffe	.06	.05	.02
241	Andre Thornton	.04	.03	.02
242	Mike Hargrove	.03	.02	.01
243	Dan Spillner	.03	.02	.01
244	Lary Sorensen	.03	.02	.01
245	Len Barker	.03	.02	.01
246	Rick Manning	.03	.02	.01
247	Toby Harrah	.04	.03	.02
248	Milt Wilcox	.03	.02	.01
249	Lou Whitaker	.10	.08	.04
250	Tom Brookens	.03	.02	.01
251	Chet Lemon	.04	.03	.02
252	Jack Morris	.12	.09	.05
253	Alan Trammell	.15	.11	.06
254	John Wockenfuss	.03	.02	.01
255	Lance Parrish	.12	.09	.05
256	Larry Herndon	.03	.02	.01
257	Chris Speier	.03	.02	.01
258	Woody Fryman	.03	.02	.01
259	Scott Sanderson	.03	.02	.01
260	Steve Rogers	.03	.02	.01
261	Warren Cromartie	.03	.02	.01
262	Gary Carter	.20	.15	.08
263	Bill Gullickson	.03	.02	.01
264	Andre Dawson	.15	.11	.06
265	Tim Raines	.20	.15	.08
266	Charlie Lea	.03	.02	.01
267	Jeff Reardon	.06	.05	.02
268	Al Oliver	.06	.05	.02
269	George Hendrick	.04	.03	.02
270	John Montefusco	.03	.02	.01
(271)	A's Logo	.03	.02	.01
(272)	Angels Logo	.03	.02	.01
(273)	Astros Logo	.03	.02	.01
(274)	Blue Jays Logo	.03	.02	.01
(275)	Braves Logo	.03	.02	.01
(276)	Brewers Logo	.03	.02	.01
(277)	Cardinals Logo	.03	.02	.01
(278)	Cubs Logo	.03	.02	.01
(279)	Dodgers Logo	.03	.02	.01
(280)	Expos Logo	.03	.02	.01
(281)	Giants Logo	.03	.02	.01
(282)	Indians Logo	.03	.02	.01
(283)	Mariners Logo	.03	.02	.01
(284)	Mets Logo	.03	.02	.01
(285)	Orioles Logo	.03	.02	.01
(286)	Padres Logo	.03	.02	.01
(287)	Phillies Logo	.03	.02	.01
(288)	Pirates Logo	.03	.02	.01
(289)	Rangers Logo	.03	.02	.01
(290)	Red Sox Logo	.03	.02	.01
(291)	Reds Logo	.03	.02	.01
(292)	Royals Logo	.03	.02	.01
(293)	Tigers Logo	.03	.02	.01
(294)	Twins Logo	.03	.02	.01
(295)	Yankees Logo	.03	.02	.01
(296)	White Sox Logo	.03	.02	.01

1984 Fleer

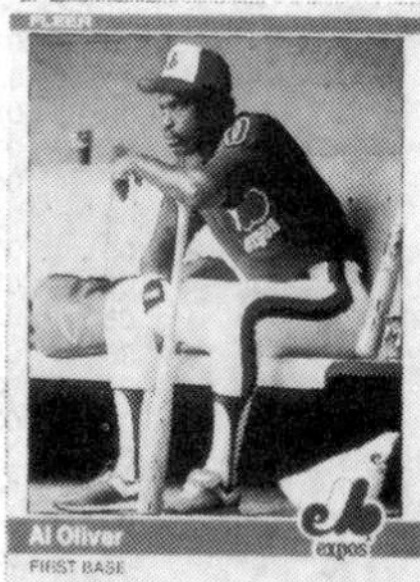

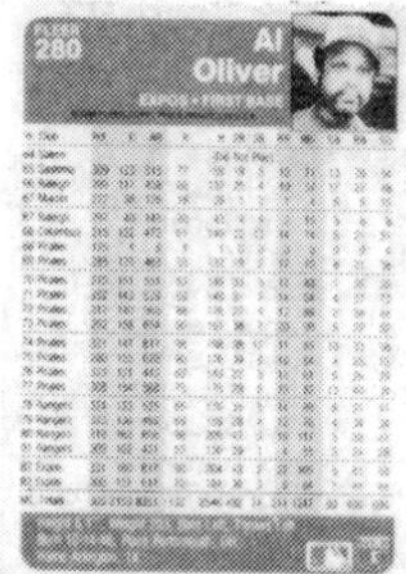

The 1984 Fleer set contained 660 cards for the fourth consecutive year. The cards, which measure 2-1/2" by 3-1/2", feature a color photo surrounded by four white borders and two blue stripes. The top stripe contains the word "Fleer" with the lower carrying the player's name. The card backs contain a small black and white photo of the player and are done in blue ink on white stock.

The set was issued with team logo stickers.

		MT	NR MT	EX
Complete Set (660):		200.00	150.00	80.00
Common Player:		.08	.06	.03
1	Mike Boddicker(FC)	.20	.15	.08
2	Al Bumbry	.10	.08	.04
3	Todd Cruz	.08	.06	.03
4	Rich Dauer	.08	.06	.03
5	Storm Davis	.12	.09	.05
6	Rick Dempsey	.10	.08	.04
7	Jim Dwyer	.08	.06	.03
8	Mike Flanagan	.12	.09	.05
9	Dan Ford	.08	.06	.03
10	John Lowenstein	.08	.06	.03
11	Dennis Martinez	.10	.08	.04
12	Tippy Martinez	.08	.06	.03
13	Scott McGregor	.10	.08	.04
14	Eddie Murray	3.00	2.25	1.25
15	Joe Nolan	.08	.06	.03
16	Jim Palmer	2.00	1.50	.80
17	Cal Ripken, Jr.	18.00	13.50	7.25
18	Gary Roenicke	.08	.06	.03
19	Lenn Sakata	.08	.06	.03
20	*John Shelby*(FC)	.08	.06	.03
21	Ken Singleton	.12	.09	.05
22	Sammy Stewart	.08	.06	.03
23	Tim Stoddard	.08	.06	.03
24	Marty Bystrom	.08	.06	.03
25	Steve Carlton	3.00	2.25	1.25
26	Ivan DeJesus	.08	.06	.03
27	John Denny	.08	.06	.03
28	Bob Dernier	.08	.06	.03
29	Bo Diaz	.10	.08	.04
30	Kiko Garcia	.08	.06	.03
31	Greg Gross	.08	.06	.03
32	*Kevin Gross*(FC)	.15	.11	.06
33	Von Hayes	.15	.11	.06
34	Willie Hernandez	.12	.09	.05
35	Al Holland	.08	.06	.03
36	*Charles Hudson*(FC)	.08	.06	.03
37	Joe Lefebvre	.08	.06	.03
38	Sixto Lezcano	.08	.06	.03
39	Garry Maddox	.10	.08	.04
40	Gary Matthews	.12	.09	.05
41	Len Matuszek	.08	.06	.03
42	Tug McGraw	.12	.09	.05
43	Joe Morgan	.40	.30	.15
44	Tony Perez	.20	.15	.08
45	Ron Reed	.08	.06	.03
46	Pete Rose	3.00	2.25	1.25
47	*Juan Samuel*(FC)	2.00	1.50	.80
48	Mike Schmidt	8.00	6.00	3.25
49	Ozzie Virgil	.08	.06	.03
50	*Juan Agosto*(FC)	.15	.11	.06
51	Harold Baines	.25	.20	.10
52	Floyd Bannister	.08	.06	.03
53	Salome Barojas	.08	.06	.03
54	Britt Burns	.08	.06	.03
55	Julio Cruz	.08	.06	.03
56	Richard Dotson	.08	.06	.03
57	Jerry Dybzinski	.08	.06	.03
58	Carlton Fisk	2.50	2.00	1.00
59	Scott Fletcher(FC)	.15	.11	.06
60	Jerry Hairston	.08	.06	.03
61	Kevin Hickey	.08	.06	.03
62	Marc Hill	.08	.06	.03
63	LaMarr Hoyt	.08	.06	.03
64	Ron Kittle	.15	.11	.06
65	Jerry Koosman	.12	.09	.05
66	Dennis Lamp	.08	.06	.03
67	Rudy Law	.08	.06	.03
68	Vance Law	.10	.08	.04
69	Greg Luzinski	.12	.09	.05
70	Tom Paciorek	.08	.06	.03
71	Mike Squires	.08	.06	.03
72	Dick Tidrow	.08	.06	.03
73	*Greg Walker*(FC)	.15	.11	.06
74	Glenn Abbott	.08	.06	.03
75	Howard Bailey	.08	.06	.03
76	Doug Bair	.08	.06	.03
77	Juan Berenguer	.08	.06	.03
78	Tom Brookens	.08	.06	.03
79	Enos Cabell	.08	.06	.03
80	Kirk Gibson	1.00	.70	.40
81	John Grubb	.08	.06	.03
82	Larry Herndon	.08	.06	.03
83	Wayne Krenchicki	.08	.06	.03
84	Rick Leach	.08	.06	.03
85	Chet Lemon	.10	.08	.04

		MT	NR MT	EX
86	Aurelio Lopez	.08	.06	.03
87	Jack Morris	2.00	1.50	.80
88	Lance Parrish	.15	.11	.06
89	Dan Petry	.08	.06	.03
90	Dave Rozema	.08	.06	.03
91	Alan Trammell	.40	.30	.15
92	Lou Whitaker	.40	.30	.15
93	Milt Wilcox	.08	.06	.03
94	Glenn Wilson	.08	.06	.03
95	John Wockenfuss	.08	.06	.03
96	Dusty Baker	.12	.09	.05
97	Joe Beckwith	.08	.06	.03
98	Greg Brock	.08	.06	.03
99	Jack Fimple	.08	.06	.03
100	Pedro Guerrero	.15	.11	.06
101	Rick Honeycutt	.08	.06	.03
102	Burt Hooton	.10	.08	.04
103	Steve Howe	.08	.06	.03
104	Ken Landreaux	.08	.06	.03
105	Mike Marshall	.15	.11	.06
106	Rick Monday	.10	.08	.04
107	Jose Morales	.08	.06	.03
108	Tom Niedenfuer	.10	.08	.04
109	*Alejandro Pena*(FC)	.10	.08	.04
110	Jerry Reuss	.12	.09	.05
111	Bill Russell	.10	.08	.04
112	Steve Sax	.20	.15	.08
113	Mike Scioscia	.10	.08	.04
114	Derrel Thomas	.08	.06	.03
115	Fernando Valenzuela	.40	.30	.15
116	Bob Welch	.15	.11	.06
117	Steve Yeager	.08	.06	.03
118	Pat Zachry	.08	.06	.03
119	Don Baylor	.15	.11	.06
120	Bert Campaneris	.12	.09	.05
121	Rick Cerone	.08	.06	.03
122	*Ray Fontenot*(FC)	.08	.06	.03
123	George Frazier	.08	.06	.03
124	Oscar Gamble	.10	.08	.04
125	Goose Gossage	.25	.20	.10
126	Ken Griffey	.12	.09	.05
127	Ron Guidry	.30	.25	.12
128	Jay Howell(FC)	.15	.11	.06
129	Steve Kemp	.10	.08	.04
130	Matt Keough	.08	.06	.03
131	*Don Mattingly*(FC)	30.00	15.00	8.00
132	John Montefusco	.08	.06	.03
133	Omar Moreno	.08	.06	.03
134	Dale Murray	.08	.06	.03
135	Graig Nettles	.20	.15	.08
136	Lou Piniella	.15	.11	.06
137	Willie Randolph	.12	.09	.05
138	Shane Rawley	.08	.06	.03
139	Dave Righetti	.25	.20	.10
140	Andre Robertson	.08	.06	.03
141	Bob Shirley	.08	.06	.03
142	Roy Smalley	.08	.06	.03
143	Dave Winfield	8.00	5.00	2.50
144	Butch Wynegar	.08	.06	.03
145	*Jim Acker*(FC)	.12	.09	.05
146	Doyle Alexander	.08	.06	.03
147	Jesse Barfield	.25	.20	.10
148	Jorge Bell	2.00	1.50	.80
149	Barry Bonnell	.08	.06	.03
150	Jim Clancy	.10	.08	.04
151	Dave Collins	.10	.08	.04
152	*Tony Fernandez*(FC)	5.00	3.00	1.50
153	Damaso Garcia	.08	.06	.03
154	Dave Geisel	.08	.06	.03
155	Jim Gott(FC)	.10	.08	.04
156	Alfredo Griffin	.10	.08	.04
157	Garth Iorg	.08	.06	.03
158	Roy Lee Jackson	.08	.06	.03
159	Cliff Johnson	.08	.06	.03
160	Luis Leal	.08	.06	.03
161	Buck Martinez	.08	.06	.03
162	Joey McLaughlin	.08	.06	.03
163	Randy Moffitt	.08	.06	.03
164	Lloyd Moseby	.08	.06	.03
165	Rance Mulliniks	.08	.06	.03
166	Jorge Orta	.08	.06	.03
167	Dave Stieb	.15	.11	.06
168	Willie Upshaw	.10	.08	.04
169	Ernie Whitt	.10	.08	.04
170	Len Barker	.08	.06	.03
171	Steve Bedrosian	.08	.06	.03
172	Bruce Benedict	.08	.06	.03
173	Brett Butler	.10	.08	.04
174	Rick Camp	.08	.06	.03
175	Chris Chambliss	.10	.08	.04
176	Ken Dayley	.08	.06	.03

		MT	NR MT	EX
177	Pete Falcone	.08	.06	.03
178	Terry Forster	.10	.08	.04
179	Gene Garber	.08	.06	.03
180	Terry Harper	.08	.06	.03
181	Bob Horner	.12	.09	.05
182	Glenn Hubbard	.10	.08	.04
183	Randy S. Johnson	.08	.06	.03
184	*Craig McMurtry*(FC)	.08	.06	.03
185	Donnie Moore(FC)	.10	.08	.04
186	Dale Murphy	1.00	.70	.40
187	Phil Niekro	.30	.25	.12
188	Pascual Perez	.10	.08	.04
189	Biff Pocoroba	.08	.06	.03
190	Rafael Ramirez	.08	.06	.03
191	Jerry Royster	.08	.06	.03
192	Claudell Washington	.10	.08	.04
193	Bob Watson	.10	.08	.04
194	Jerry Augustine	.08	.06	.03
195	Mark Brouhard	.08	.06	.03
196	Mike Caldwell	.08	.06	.03
197	*Tom Candiotti*(FC)	1.00	.70	.40
198	Cecil Cooper	.15	.11	.06
199	Rollie Fingers	.25	.20	.10
200	Jim Gantner	.10	.08	.04
201	Bob L. Gibson	.08	.06	.03
202	Moose Haas	.08	.06	.03
203	Roy Howell	.08	.06	.03
204	Pete Ladd	.08	.06	.03
205	Rick Manning	.08	.06	.03
206	Bob McClure	.08	.06	.03
207	Paul Molitor	4.00	3.00	1.50
208	Don Money	.08	.06	.03
209	Charlie Moore	.08	.06	.03
210	Ben Oglivie	.10	.08	.04
211	Chuck Porter	.08	.06	.03
212	Ed Romero	.08	.06	.03
213	Ted Simmons	.15	.11	.06
214	Jim Slaton	.08	.06	.03
215	Don Sutton	.30	.25	.12
216	Tom Tellmann	.08	.06	.03
217	Pete Vuckovich	.10	.08	.04
218	Ned Yost	.08	.06	.03
219	Robin Yount	6.00	4.50	2.50
220	Alan Ashby	.08	.06	.03
221	Kevin Bass(FC)	.20	.15	.08
222	Jose Cruz	.12	.09	.05
223	*Bill Dawley*(FC)	.08	.06	.03
224	Frank DiPino	.08	.06	.03
225	*Bill Doran*(FC)	1.00	.70	.50
226	Phil Garner	.10	.08	.04
227	Art Howe	.08	.06	.03
228	Bob Knepper	.10	.08	.04
229	Ray Knight	.12	.09	.05
230	Frank LaCorte	.08	.06	.03
231	Mike LaCoss	.08	.06	.03
232	Mike Madden	.08	.06	.03
233	Jerry Mumphrey	.08	.06	.03
235	Terry Puhl	.08	.06	.03
236	Luis Pujols	.08	.06	.03
237	Craig Reynolds	.08	.06	.03
238	Vern Ruhle	.08	.06	.03
239	Nolan Ryan	20.00	15.00	8.00
240	Mike Scott	.20	.15	.08
241	Tony Scott	.08	.06	.03
242	Dave Smith	.10	.08	.04
243	Dickie Thon	.10	.08	.04
244	Denny Walling	.08	.06	.03
245	Dale Berra	.08	.06	.03
246	Jim Bibby	.08	.06	.03
247	John Candelaria	.12	.09	.05
248	*Jose DeLeon*(FC)	.50	.40	.20
249	Mike Easler	.08	.06	.03
250	Cecilio Guante(FC)	.08	.06	.03
251	Richie Hebner	.08	.06	.03
252	Lee Lacy	.08	.06	.03
253	Bill Madlock	.12	.09	.05
254	Milt May	.08	.06	.03
255	Lee Mazzilli	.10	.08	.04
256	Larry McWilliams	.08	.06	.03
257	Jim Morrison	.08	.06	.03
258	Dave Parker	.30	.25	.12
259	Tony Pena	.12	.09	.05
260	Johnny Ray	.12	.09	.05
261	Rick Rhoden	.12	.09	.05
262	Don Robinson	.10	.08	.04
263	Manny Sarmiento	.08	.06	.03
264	Rod Scurry	.08	.06	.03
265	Kent Tekulve	.10	.08	.04
266	Gene Tenace	.10	.08	.04
267	Jason Thompson	.08	.06	.03
268	*Lee Tunnell*(FC)	.08	.06	.03
269	*Marvell Wynne*(FC)	.08	.06	.03
270	Ray Burris	.08	.06	.03
271	Gary Carter	.40	.30	.15
272	Warren Cromartie	.08	.06	.03
273	Andre Dawson	3.00	2.25	1.25
274	Doug Flynn	.08	.06	.03
275	Terry Francona	.08	.06	.03
276	Bill Gullickson	.08	.06	.03
277	Bob James	.08	.06	.03
278	Charlie Lea	.08	.06	.03
279	Bryan Little	.08	.06	.03
280	Al Oliver	.20	.15	.08
281	Tim Raines	.70	.50	.30
282	Bobby Ramos	.08	.06	.03
283	Jeff Reardon	.15	.11	.06
284	Steve Rogers	.10	.08	.04
285	Scott Sanderson	.08	.06	.03
286	Dan Schatzeder	.08	.06	.03
287	Bryn Smith	.08	.06	.03
288	Chris Speier	.08	.06	.03
289	Manny Trillo	.10	.08	.04
290	Mike Vail	.08	.06	.03
291	Tim Wallach	.15	.11	.06
292	Chris Welsh	.08	.06	.03
293	Jim Wohlford	.08	.06	.03
294	Kurt Bevacqua	.08	.06	.03
295	Juan Bonilla	.08	.06	.03
296	Bobby Brown	.08	.06	.03
297	Luis DeLeon	.08	.06	.03
298	Dave Dravecky	.10	.08	.04
299	Tim Flannery	.08	.06	.03
300	Steve Garvey	.50	.40	.20
301	Tony Gwynn	12.00	9.00	4.75
302	*Andy Hawkins*(FC)	.20	.15	.08
303	Ruppert Jones	.08	.06	.03
304	Terry Kennedy	.10	.08	.04
305	Tim Lollar	.08	.06	.03
306	Gary Lucas	.08	.06	.03
307	*Kevin McReynolds*(FC)	1.50	1.00	.50
308	Sid Monge	.08	.06	.03
309	Mario Ramirez	.08	.06	.03
310	Gene Richards	.08	.06	.03
311	Luis Salazar	.08	.06	.03
312	Eric Show	.12	.09	.05
313	Elias Sosa	.08	.06	.03
314	Garry Templeton	.12	.09	.05
315	*Mark Thurmond*(FC)	.10	.08	.04
316	Ed Whitson	.08	.06	.03
317	Alan Wiggins	.08	.06	.03
318	Neil Allen	.08	.06	.03
319	Joaquin Andujar	.10	.08	.04
320	Steve Braun	.08	.06	.03
321	Glenn Brummer	.08	.06	.03
322	Bob Forsch	.10	.08	.04
323	David Green	.08	.06	.03
324	George Hendrick	.10	.08	.04
325	Tom Herr	.12	.09	.05
326	Dane Iorg	.08	.06	.03
327	Jeff Lahti	.08	.06	.03
328	Dave LaPoint	.10	.08	.04
329	Willie McGee	.35	.25	.14
330	Ken Oberkfell	.08	.06	.03
331	Darrell Porter	.10	.08	.04
332	Jamie Quirk	.08	.06	.03
333	Mike Ramsey	.08	.06	.03
334	Floyd Rayford	.08	.06	.03
335	Lonnie Smith	.10	.08	.04
336	Ozzie Smith	1.50	1.25	.60
337	John Stuper	.08	.06	.03
338	Bruce Sutter	.20	.15	.08
339	*Andy Van Slyke*(FC)	7.00	5.25	2.75
340	Dave Von Ohlen	.08	.06	.03
341	Willie Aikens	.08	.06	.03
342	Mike Armstrong	.08	.06	.03
343	Bud Black	.10	.08	.04
344	George Brett	6.00	4.50	2.50
345	Onix Concepcion	.08	.06	.03
346	Keith Creel	.08	.06	.03
347	Larry Gura	.08	.06	.03
348	Don Hood	.08	.06	.03
349	Dennis Leonard	.10	.08	.04
350	Hal McRae	.12	.09	.05
351	Amos Otis	.12	.09	.05
352	Gaylord Perry	.60	.45	.25
353	Greg Pryor	.08	.06	.03
354	Dan Quisenberry	.12	.09	.05
355	Steve Renko	.08	.06	.03
356	Leon Roberts	.08	.06	.03
357	*Pat Sheridan*(FC)	.08	.06	.03
358	Joe Simpson	.08	.06	.03
359	Don Slaught	.08	.06	.03

		MT	NR MT	EX
360	Paul Splittorff	.08	.06	.03
361	U.L. Washington	.08	.06	.03
362	John Wathan	.10	.08	.04
363	Frank White	.12	.09	.05
364	Willie Wilson	.15	.11	.06
365	Jim Barr	.08	.06	.03
366	Dave Bergman	.08	.06	.03
367	Fred Breining	.08	.06	.03
368	Bob Brenly	.08	.06	.03
369	Jack Clark	.25	.20	.10
370	Chili Davis	.12	.09	.05
371	Mark Davis(FC)	.20	.15	.08
372	Darrell Evans	.15	.11	.06
373	Atlee Hammaker	.08	.06	.03
374	Mike Krukow	.10	.08	.04
375	Duane Kuiper	.08	.06	.03
376	Bill Laskey	.08	.06	.03
377	Gary Lavelle	.08	.06	.03
378	Johnnie LeMaster	.08	.06	.03
379	Jeff Leonard	.08	.06	.03
380	Randy Lerch	.08	.06	.03
381	Renie Martin	.08	.06	.03
382	Andy McGaffigan	.08	.06	.03
383	Greg Minton	.08	.06	.03
384	Tom O'Malley	.08	.06	.03
385	Max Venable	.08	.06	.03
386	Brad Wellman	.08	.06	.03
387	Joel Youngblood	.08	.06	.03
388	Gary Allenson	.08	.06	.03
389	Luis Aponte	.08	.06	.03
390	Tony Armas	.12	.09	.05
391	Doug Bird	.08	.06	.03
392	Wade Boggs	12.00	9.00	4.75
393	*Dennis Boyd*(FC)	.50	.40	.20
394	Mike Brown	.08	.06	.03
395	Mark Clear	.08	.06	.03
396	Dennis Eckersley	.15	.11	.06
397	Dwight Evans	.20	.15	.08
398	Rich Gedman	.10	.08	.04
399	Glenn Hoffman	.08	.06	.03
400	Bruce Hurst	.15	.11	.06
401	John Henry Johnson	.08	.06	.03
402	Ed Jurak	.08	.06	.03
403	Rick Miller	.08	.06	.03
404	Jeff Newman	.08	.06	.03
405	Reid Nichols	.08	.06	.03
406	Bob Ojeda	.12	.09	.05
407	Jerry Remy	.08	.06	.03
408	Jim Rice	.40	.30	.15
409	Bob Stanley	.08	.06	.03
410	Dave Stapleton	.08	.06	.03
411	John Tudor	.12	.09	.05
412	Carl Yastrzemski	.80	.60	.30
413	Buddy Bell	.12	.09	.05
414	Larry Biittner	.08	.06	.03
415	John Butcher	.08	.06	.03
416	Danny Darwin	.08	.06	.03
417	Bucky Dent	.12	.09	.05
418	Dave Hostetler	.08	.06	.03
419	Charlie Hough	.12	.09	.05
420	Bobby Johnson	.08	.06	.03
421	Odell Jones	.08	.06	.03
422	Jon Matlack	.10	.08	.04
423	*Pete O'Brien*(FC)	.80	.60	.30
424	Larry Parrish	.12	.09	.05
425	Mickey Rivers	.10	.08	.04
426	Billy Sample	.08	.06	.03
427	Dave Schmidt	.08	.06	.03
428	*Mike Smithson*(FC)	.08	.06	.03
429	Bill Stein	.08	.06	.03
430	Dave Stewart	.15	.11	.06
431	Jim Sundberg	.10	.08	.04
432	Frank Tanana	.12	.09	.05
433	Dave Tobik	.08	.06	.03
434	Wayne Tolleson(FC)	.08	.06	.03
435	George Wright	.08	.06	.03
436	Bill Almon	.08	.06	.03
437	*Keith Atherton*(FC)	.08	.06	.03
438	Dave Beard	.08	.06	.03
439	Tom Burgmeier	.08	.06	.03
440	Jeff Burroughs	.10	.08	.04
441	*Chris Codiroli*(FC)	.08	.06	.03
442	*Tim Conroy*(FC)	.08	.06	.03
443	Mike Davis	.08	.06	.03
444	Wayne Gross	.08	.06	.03
445	Garry Hancock	.08	.06	.03
446	Mike Heath	.08	.06	.03
447	Rickey Henderson	7.00	5.25	2.75
448	*Don Hill*(FC)	.08	.06	.03
449	Bob Kearney	.08	.06	.03
450	Bill Krueger	.08	.06	.03

		MT	NR MT	EX
451	Rick Langford	.08	.06	.03
452	Carney Lansford	.12	.09	.05
453	Davey Lopes	.10	.08	.04
454	Steve McCatty	.08	.06	.03
455	Dan Meyer	.08	.06	.03
456	Dwayne Murphy	.08	.06	.03
457	Mike Norris	.08	.06	.03
458	Ricky Peters	.08	.06	.03
459	*Tony Phillips*(FC)	2.50	2.00	1.00
460	Tom Underwood	.08	.06	.03
461	Mike Warren	.08	.06	.03
462	Johnny Bench	.80	.60	.30
463	Bruce Berenyi	.08	.06	.03
464	Dann Bilardello	.08	.06	.03
465	Cesar Cedeno	.12	.09	.05
466	Dave Concepcion	.15	.11	.06
467	Dan Driessen	.08	.06	.03
468	*Nick Esasky*(FC)	.08	.06	.03
469	Rich Gale	.08	.06	.03
470	Ben Hayes	.08	.06	.03
471	Paul Householder	.08	.06	.03
472	Tom Hume	.08	.06	.03
473	Alan Knicely	.08	.06	.03
474	Eddie Milner	.08	.06	.03
475	Ron Oester	.08	.06	.03
476	Kelly Paris	.08	.06	.03
477	Frank Pastore	.08	.06	.03
478	Ted Power	.10	.08	.04
479	Joe Price	.08	.06	.03
480	Charlie Puleo	.08	.06	.03
481	*Gary Redus*(FC)	.25	.20	.10
482	Bill Scherrer	.08	.06	.03
483	Mario Soto	.10	.08	.04
484	Alex Trevino	.08	.06	.03
485	Duane Walker	.08	.06	.03
486	Larry Bowa	.15	.11	.06
487	Warren Brusstar	.08	.06	.03
488	Bill Buckner	.15	.11	.06
489	Bill Campbell	.08	.06	.03
490	Ron Cey	.12	.09	.05
491	Jody Davis	.08	.06	.03
492	Leon Durham	.10	.08	.04
493	Mel Hall(FC)	.10	.08	.04
494	Fergie Jenkins	.20	.15	.08
495	Jay Johnstone	.10	.08	.04
496	*Craig Lefferts*(FC)	.20	.15	.08
497	*Carmelo Martinez*(FC)	.08	.06	.03
498	Jerry Morales	.08	.06	.03
499	Keith Moreland	.10	.08	.04
500	Dickie Noles	.08	.06	.03
501	Mike Proly	.08	.06	.03
502	Chuck Rainey	.08	.06	.03
503	Dick Ruthven	.08	.06	.03
504	Ryne Sandberg	18.00	13.50	7.25
505	Lee Smith	.15	.11	.06
506	Steve Trout	.08	.06	.03
507	Gary Woods	.08	.06	.03
508	Juan Beniquez	.08	.06	.03
509	Bob Boone	.10	.08	.04
510	Rick Burleson	.10	.08	.04
511	Rod Carew	1.25	.90	.50
512	Bobby Clark	.08	.06	.03
513	John Curtis	.08	.06	.03
514	Doug DeCinces	.12	.09	.05
515	Brian Downing	.12	.09	.05
516	Tim Foli	.08	.06	.03
517	Ken Forsch	.08	.06	.03
518	Bobby Grich	.12	.09	.05
519	Andy Hassler	.08	.06	.03
520	Reggie Jackson	1.50	1.25	.60
521	Ron Jackson	.08	.06	.03
522	Tommy John	.25	.20	.10
523	Bruce Kison	.08	.06	.03
524	Steve Lubratich	.08	.06	.03
525	Fred Lynn	.25	.20	.10
526	*Gary Pettis*(FC)	.15	.11	.06
527	Luis Sanchez	.08	.06	.03
528	Daryl Sconiers	.08	.06	.03
529	Ellis Valentine	.08	.06	.03
530	Rob Wilfong	.08	.06	.03
531	Mike Witt	.15	.11	.06
532	Geoff Zahn	.08	.06	.03
533	Bud Anderson	.08	.06	.03
534	Chris Bando	.08	.06	.03
535	Alan Bannister	.08	.06	.03
536	Bert Blyleven	.20	.15	.08
537	Tom Brennan	.08	.06	.03
538	Jamie Easterly	.08	.06	.03
539	Juan Eichelberger	.08	.06	.03
540	Jim Essian	.08	.06	.03
541	Mike Fischlin	.08	.06	.03

		MT	NR MT	EX
542	Julio Franco(FC)	2.00	1.50	.80
543	Mike Hargrove	.08	.06	.03
544	Toby Harrah	.10	.08	.04
545	Ron Hassey	.08	.06	.03
546	*Neal Heaton*(FC)	.15	.11	.06
547	Bake McBride	.08	.06	.03
548	Broderick Perkins	.08	.06	.03
549	Lary Sorensen	.08	.06	.03
550	Dan Spillner	.08	.06	.03
551	Rick Sutcliffe	.15	.11	.06
552	Pat Tabler	.10	.08	.04
553	Gorman Thomas	.10	.08	.04
554	Andre Thornton	.12	.09	.05
555	George Vukovich	.08	.06	.03
556	Darrell Brown	.08	.06	.03
557	Tom Brunansky	.20	.15	.08
558	*Randy Bush*(FC)	.15	.11	.06
559	Bobby Castillo	.08	.06	.03
560	John Castino	.08	.06	.03
561	Ron Davis	.08	.06	.03
562	Dave Engle	.08	.06	.03
563	Lenny Faedo	.08	.06	.03
564	Pete Filson	.08	.06	.03
565	Gary Gaetti	.30	.25	.12
566	Mickey Hatcher	.10	.08	.04
567	Kent Hrbek	.40	.30	.15
568	Rusty Kuntz	.08	.06	.03
569	Tim Laudner	.08	.06	.03
570	Rick Lysander	.08	.06	.03
571	Bobby Mitchell	.08	.06	.03
572	Ken Schrom	.08	.06	.03
573	Ray Smith	.08	.06	.03
574	*Tim Teufel*(FC)	.30	.25	.12
575	Frank Viola	1.00	.70	.40
576	Gary Ward	.10	.08	.04
577	Ron Washington	.08	.06	.03
578	Len Whitehouse	.08	.06	.03
579	Al Williams	.08	.06	.03
580	Bob Bailor	.08	.06	.03
581	Mark Bradley	.08	.06	.03
582	Hubie Brooks	.15	.11	.06
583	Carlos Diaz	.08	.06	.03
584	George Foster	.20	.15	.08
585	Brian Giles	.08	.06	.03
586	Danny Heep	.08	.06	.03
587	Keith Hernandez	.40	.30	.15
588	Ron Hodges	.08	.06	.03
589	Scott Holman	.08	.06	.03
590	Dave Kingman	.15	.11	.06
591	Ed Lynch	.08	.06	.03
592	*Jose Oquendo*(FC)	.15	.11	.06
593	Jesse Orosco	.10	.08	.04
594	*Junior Ortiz*(FC)	.10	.08	.04
595	Tom Seaver	4.00	3.00	1.50
596	*Doug Sisk*(FC)	.10	.08	.04
597	Rusty Staub	.12	.09	.05
598	John Stearns	.08	.06	.03
599	*Darryl Strawberry*(FC)	11.00	7.00	3.50
600	Craig Swan	.08	.06	.03
601	*Walt Terrell*(FC)	.25	.20	.10
602	Mike Torrez	.10	.08	.04
603	Mookie Wilson	.12	.09	.05
604	Jamie Allen	.08	.06	.03
605	Jim Beattie	.08	.06	.03
606	Tony Bernazard	.08	.06	.03
607	Manny Castillo	.08	.06	.03
608	Bill Caudill	.08	.06	.03
609	Bryan Clark	.08	.06	.03
610	Al Cowens	.08	.06	.03
611	Dave Henderson	.12	.09	.05
612	Steve Henderson	.08	.06	.03
613	Orlando Mercado	.08	.06	.03
614	Mike Moore	.10	.08	.04
615	Ricky Nelson	.08	.06	.03
616	*Spike Owen*(FC)	.20	.15	.08
617	Pat Putnam	.08	.06	.03
618	Ron Roenicke	.08	.06	.03
619	Mike Stanton	.08	.06	.03
620	Bob Stoddard	.08	.06	.03
621	Rick Sweet	.08	.06	.03
622	Roy Thomas	.08	.06	.03
623	Ed Vande Berg	.08	.06	.03
624	*Matt Young*(FC)	.15	.11	.06
625	Richie Zisk	.10	.08	.04
626	'83 All-Star Game Record Breaker (Fred Lynn)	.12	.09	.05
627	'83 All-Star Game Record Breaker (Manny Trillo)	.10	.08	.04
628	N.L. Iron Man (Steve Garvey)	.20	.15	.08
629	A.L. Batting Runner-Up (Rod Carew)	.25	.20	.10
630	Wade Boggs (AL Champ)	1.00	.70	.40
631	Letting Go Of The Raines (Tim Raines)	.20	.15	.08
632	Double Trouble (Al Oliver)	.10	.08	.04
633	All-Star Second Base (Steve Sax)	.15	.11	.06
634	All-Star Shortstop (Dickie Thon)	.10	.08	.04
635	Ace Firemen (Tippy Martinez, Dan Quisenberry)	.10	.08	.04
636	Reds Reunited (Joe Morgan, Tony Perez, Pete Rose)	.50	.40	.20
637	Backstop Stars (Bob Boone, Lance Parrish)	.15	.11	.06
638	The Pine Tar Incident, 7/24/83 (George Brett, Gaylord Perry) (G.Brett)	.30	.25	.12
639	1983 No-Hitters (Bob Forsch, Dave Righetti, Mike Warren)	.10	.08	.04
640	Retiring Superstars (Johnny Bench, Carl Yastrzemski)	2.00	1.50	.80
641	Going Out In Style (Gaylord Perry)	.15	.11	.06
642	300 Club & Strikeout Record (Steve Carlton)	.20	.15	.08
643	The Managers (Joe Altobelli, Paul Owens)	.10	.08	.04
644	The MVP (Rick Dempsey)	.10	.08	.04
645	The Rookie Winner (Mike Boddicker)	.12	.09	.05
646	The Clincher (Scott McGregor)	.10	.08	.04
647	Checklist: Orioles/Royals (Joe Altobelli)	.08	.06	.03
648	Checklist: Phillies/Giants (Paul Owens)	.08	.06	.03
649	Checklist: White Sox/Red Sox (Tony LaRussa)	.08	.06	.03
650	Checklist: Tigers/Rangers (Sparky Anderson)	.08	.06	.03
651	Checklist: Dodgers/A's (Tom Lasorda)	.08	.06	.03
652	Checklist: Yankees/Reds (Billy Martin)	.08	.06	.03
653	Checklist: Blue Jays/Cubs (Bobby Cox)	.08	.06	.03
654	Checklist: Braves/Angels (Joe Torre)	.08	.06	.03
655	Checklist: Brewers/Indians (Rene Lachemann)	.08	.06	.03
656	Checklist: Astros/Twins (Bob Lillis)	.08	.06	.03
657	Checklist: Pirates/Mets (Chuck Tanner)	.08	.06	.03
658	Checklist: Expos/Mariners (Bill Virdon)	.08	.06	.03
659	Checklist: Padres/Specials (Dick Williams)	.08	.06	.03
660	Checklist: Cardinals/Specials (Whitey Herzog)	.08	.06	.03

1984 Fleer Update

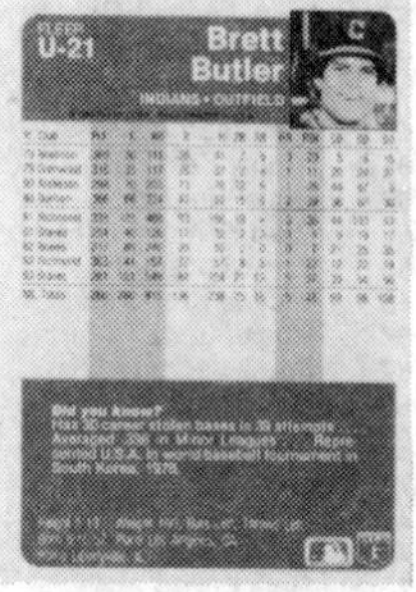

Following the lead of Topps, Fleer issued near the end of the baseball season a 132-card set to update player trades and include rookies not depicted in the regular issue. The cards, which measure 2-1/2" by 3-1/2", are identical in design to the regular issue but are numbered U-1 through U-132. Available to the collecting public only through hobby dealers, the set was printed in limited quantities and has escalated in price quite rapidly the past several years. The set was issued with team logo stickers in a specially designed box.

		MT	NR MT	EX
Complete Set (132):		850.00	625.00	300.00
Common Player:		.25	.20	.10
1	Willie Aikens	.25	.20	.10
2	Luis Aponte	.25	.20	.10
3	Mark Bailey(FC)	.25	.20	.10
4	Bob Bailor	.25	.20	.10
5	Dusty Baker	.25	.20	.10
6	Steve Balboni(FC)	.40	.30	.15
7	Alan Bannister	.25	.20	.10
8	Marty Barrett(FC)	.50	.40	.20
9	Dave Beard	.25	.20	.10
10	Joe Beckwith	.25	.20	.10
11	Dave Bergman	.25	.20	.10
12	Tony Bernazard	.25	.20	.10
13	Bruce Bochte	.25	.20	.10
14	Barry Bonnell	.25	.20	.10
15	Phil Bradley(FC)	.40	.30	.15
16	Fred Breining	.25	.20	.10
17	Mike Brown	.25	.20	.10
18	Bill Buckner	.50	.40	.20
19	Ray Burris	.25	.20	.10
20	John Butcher	.25	.20	.10
21	Brett Butler	.60	.45	.25
22	Enos Cabell	.25	.20	.10
23	Bill Campbell	.25	.20	.10
24	Bill Caudill	.25	.20	.10
25	Bobby Clark	.25	.20	.10
26	Bryan Clark	.25	.20	.10
27	Roger Clemens(FC)	400.00	300.00	150.00
28	Jaime Cocanower	.25	.20	.10
29	Ron Darling(FC)	7.00	5.25	2.75
30	Alvin Davis(FC)	.25	.20	.10
31	Bob Dernier	.25	.20	.10
32	Carlos Diaz	.25	.20	.10
33	Mike Easler	.25	.20	.10
34	Dennis Eckersley	10.00	7.50	4.50
35	Jim Essian	.25	.20	.10
36	Darrell Evans	.60	.45	.25
37	Mike Fitzgerald(FC)	.25	.20	.10
38	Tim Foli	.25	.20	.10
39	John Franco(FC)	6.00	4.50	2.25
40	George Frazier	.25	.20	.10
41	Rich Gale	.25	.20	.10
42	Barbaro Garbey	.25	.20	.10
43	Dwight Gooden(FC)	60.00	45.00	22.50
44	Goose Gossage	.50	.40	.20
45	Wayne Gross	.25	.20	.10
46	Mark Gubicza(FC)	3.00	2.25	1.25
47	Jackie Gutierrez	.25	.20	.10
48	Toby Harrah	.25	.20	.10
49	Ron Hassey	.25	.20	.10
50	Richie Hebner	.25	.20	.10
51	Willie Hernandez	.25	.20	.10
52	Ed Hodge	.25	.20	.10
53	Ricky Horton(FC)	.25	.20	.10
54	Art Howe	.25	.20	.10
55	Dane Iorg	.25	.20	.10
56	Brook Jacoby(FC)	2.00	1.50	.75
57	Dion James(FC)	.25	.20	.10
58	Mike Jeffcoat(FC)	.25	.20	.10
59	Ruppert Jones	.25	.20	.10
60	Bob Kearney	.25	.20	.10
61	Jimmy Key(FC)	15.00	9.00	4.50
62	Dave Kingman	.25	.20	.10
63	Brad Komminsk(FC)	.25	.20	.10
64	Jerry Koosman	.50	.40	.20
65	Wayne Krenchicki	.25	.20	.10
66	Rusty Kuntz	.25	.20	.10
67	Frank LaCorte	.25	.20	.10
68	Dennis Lamp	.25	.20	.10
69	Tito Landrum	.25	.20	.10
70	Mark Langston(FC)	25.00	18.00	10.00
71	Rick Leach	.25	.20	.10
72	Craig Lefferts(FC)	.25	.20	.10
73	Gary Lucas	.25	.20	.10
74	Jerry Martin	.25	.20	.10
75	Carmelo Martinez	.25	.20	.10
76	Mike Mason(FC)	.25	.20	.10
77	Gary Matthews	.25	.20	.10
78	Andy McGaffigan	.25	.20	.10
79	Joey McLaughlin	.25	.20	.10
80	Joe Morgan	6.00	4.50	2.50
81	Darryl Motley	.25	.20	.10
82	Graig Nettles	1.00	.70	.40
83	Phil Niekro	4.00	3.00	1.50
84	Ken Oberkfell	.25	.20	.10
85	Al Oliver	.80	.60	.30
86	Jorge Orta	.25	.20	.10
87	Amos Otis	.25	.20	.10
88	Bob Owchinko	.25	.20	.10
89	Dave Parker	4.00	3.00	1.50
90	Jack Perconte	.25	.20	.10
91	Tony Perez	7.00	5.25	2.75
92	Gerald Perry(FC)	1.00	.70	.40
93	Kirby Puckett(FC)	400.00	300.00	150.00
94	Shane Rawley	.25	.20	.10
95	Floyd Rayford	.25	.20	.10
96	Ron Reed	.25	.20	.10
97	R.J. Reynolds(FC)	.25	.20	.10
98	Gene Richards	.25	.20	.10
99	Jose Rijo(FC)	25.00	18.00	10.00
100	Jeff Robinson(FC)	.50	.40	.20
101	Ron Romanick(FC)	.25	.20	.10
102	Pete Rose	30.00	15.00	8.00
103	Bret Saberhagen(FC)	25.00	18.00	10.00
104	Scott Sanderson	.25	.20	.10
105	Dick Schofield(FC)	.40	.30	.15
106	Tom Seaver	25.00	18.00	10.00
107	Jim Slaton	.25	.20	.10
108	Mike Smithson	.25	.20	.10
109	Lary Sorensen	.25	.20	.10
110	Tim Stoddard	.25	.20	.10
111	Jeff Stone(FC)	.25	.20	.10
112	Champ Summers	.25	.20	.10
113	Jim Sundberg	.25	.20	.10
114	Rick Sutcliffe	.80	.60	.30
115	Craig Swan	.25	.20	.10
116	Derrel Thomas	.25	.20	.10
117	Gorman Thomas	.25	.20	.10
118	Alex Trevino	.25	.20	.10
119	Manny Trillo	.25	.20	.10
120	John Tudor	.25	.20	.10
121	Tom Underwood	.25	.20	.10
122	Mike Vail	.25	.20	.10
123	Tom Waddell(FC)	.25	.20	.10
124	Gary Ward	.25	.20	.10
125	Terry Whitfield	.25	.20	.10
126	Curtis Wilkerson	.25	.20	.10
127	Frank Williams(FC)	.25	.20	.10
128	Glenn Wilson	.25	.20	.10
129	John Wockenfuss	.25	.20	.10
130	Ned Yost	.25	.20	.10
131	Mike Young(FC)	.25	.20	.10
132	Checklist 1-132	.25	.20	.10

1984 Fleer Stickers

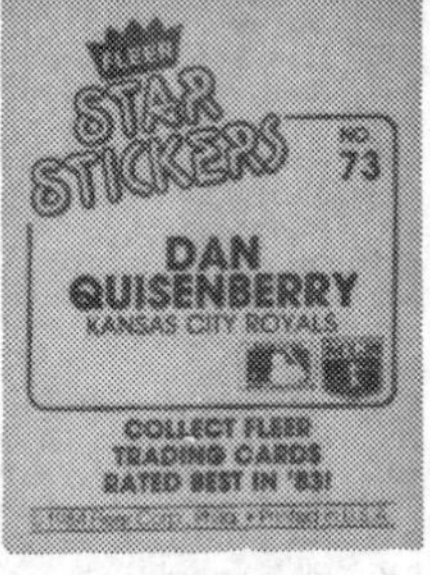

This 126-sticker set was designed to be housed in a special collector's album that was organized according to various league leader categories, resulting in some players being pictured on more than one sticker. Each full-color sticker measures 2-1/2" by 1-15/16" and is framed with a beige border. The stickers, which were sold in packs of six, are numbered on the back.

		MT	NR MT	EX
Complete Set:		12.00	9.00	4.75
Common Player:		.03	.02	.01
Sticker Album:		1.00	.70	.40
1	Dickie Thon	.03	.02	.01
2	Ken Landreaux	.03	.02	.01
3	Darrell Evans	.06	.05	.02
4	Harold Baines	.10	.08	.04
5	Dave Winfield	.20	.15	.08
6	Bill Madlock	.06	.05	.02
7	Lonnie Smith	.03	.02	.01

		MT	NR MT	EX
8	Jose Cruz	.04	.03	.02
9	George Hendrick	.04	.03	.02
10	Ray Knight	.04	.03	.02
11	Wade Boggs	.40	.30	.15
12	Rod Carew	.25	.20	.10
13	Lou Whitaker	.10	.08	.04
14	Alan Trammell	.15	.11	.06
15	Cal Ripken, Jr.	.50	.40	.20
16	Mike Schmidt	.40	.30	.15
17	Dale Murphy	.30	.25	.12
18	Andre Dawson	.15	.11	.06
19	Pedro Guerrero	.12	.09	.05
20	Jim Rice	.20	.15	.08
21	Tony Armas	.03	.02	.01
22	Ron Kittle	.04	.03	.02
23	Eddie Murray	.25	.20	.10
24	Jose Cruz	.04	.03	.02
25	Andre Dawson	.15	.11	.06
26	Rafael Ramirez	.03	.02	.01
27	Al Oliver	.06	.05	.02
28	Wade Boggs	.40	.30	.15
29	Cal Ripken, Jr.	.50	.40	.20
30	Lou Whitaker	.10	.08	.04
31	Cecil Cooper	.08	.06	.03
32	Dale Murphy	.30	.25	.12
33	Andre Dawson	.15	.11	.06
34	Pedro Guerrero	.12	.09	.05
35	Mike Schmidt	.40	.30	.15
36	George Brett	.30	.25	.12
37	Jim Rice	.20	.15	.08
38	Eddie Murray	.25	.20	.10
39	Carlton Fisk	.12	.09	.05
40	Rusty Staub	.06	.05	.02
41	Duane Walker	.03	.02	.01
42	Steve Braun	.03	.02	.01
43	Kurt Bevacqua	.03	.02	.01
44	Hal McRae	.06	.05	.02
45	Don Baylor	.10	.08	.04
46	Ken Singleton	.06	.05	.02
47	Greg Luzinski	.08	.06	.03
48	Mike Schmidt	.40	.30	.15
49	Keith Hernandez	.15	.11	.06
50	Dale Murphy	.30	.25	.12
51	Tim Raines	.20	.15	.08
52	Wade Boggs	.40	.30	.15
53	Rickey Henderson	.25	.20	.10
54	Rod Carew	.25	.20	.10
55	Ken Singleton	.06	.05	.02
56	John Denny	.03	.02	.01
57	John Candelaria	.04	.03	.02
58	Larry McWilliams	.03	.02	.01
59	Pascual Perez	.04	.03	.02
60	Jesse Orosco	.04	.03	.02
61	Moose Haas	.03	.02	.01
62	Richard Dotson	.04	.03	.02
63	Mike Flanagan	.04	.03	.02
64	Scott McGregor	.04	.03	.02
65	Atlee Hammaker	.03	.02	.01
66	Rick Honeycutt	.03	.02	.01
67	Lee Smith	.06	.05	.02
68	Al Holland	.03	.02	.01
69	Greg Minton	.03	.02	.01
70	Bruce Sutter	.08	.06	.03
71	Jeff Reardon	.08	.06	.03
72	Frank DiPino	.03	.02	.01
73	Dan Quisenberry	.06	.05	.02
74	Bob Stanley	.03	.02	.01
75	Ron Davis	.03	.02	.01
76	Bill Caudill	.03	.02	.01
77	Peter Ladd	.03	.02	.01
78	Steve Carlton	.20	.15	.08
79	Mario Soto	.04	.03	.02
80	Larry McWilliams	.03	.02	.01
81	Fernando Valenzuela	.15	.11	.06
82	Nolan Ryan	.75	.55	.30
83	Jack Morris	.12	.09	.05
84	Floyd Bannister	.04	.03	.02
85	Dave Stieb	.06	.05	.02
86	Dave Righetti	.12	.09	.05
87	Rick Sutcliffe	.08	.06	.03
88	Tim Raines	.20	.15	.08
89	Alan Wiggins	.03	.02	.01
90	Steve Sax	.10	.08	.04
91	Mookie Wilson	.04	.03	.02
92	Rickey Henderson	.25	.20	.10
93	Rudy Law	.03	.02	.01
94	Willie Wilson	.08	.06	.03
95	Julio Cruz	.03	.02	.01
96	Johnny Bench	.30	.25	.12
97	Carl Yastrzemski	.35	.25	.14
98	Gaylord Perry	.15	.11	.06

		MT	NR MT	EX
99	Pete Rose	.40	.30	.15
100	Joe Morgan	.12	.09	.05
101	Steve Carlton	.20	.15	.08
102	Jim Palmer	.15	.11	.06
103	Rod Carew	.25	.20	.10
104	Darryl Strawberry	.20	.15	.08
105	Craig McMurtry	.03	.02	.01
106	Mel Hall	.03	.02	.01
107	Lee Tunnell	.03	.02	.01
108	Bill Dawley	.03	.02	.01
109	Ron Kittle	.04	.03	.02
110	Mike Boddicker	.04	.03	.02
111	Julio Franco	.08	.06	.03
112	Daryl Sconiers	.03	.02	.01
113	Neal Heaton	.03	.02	.01
114	John Shelby	.03	.02	.01
115	Rick Dempsey	.03	.02	.01
116	John Lowenstein	.03	.02	.01
117	Jim Dwyer	.03	.02	.01
118	Bo Diaz	.03	.02	.01
119	Pete Rose	.40	.30	.15
120	Joe Morgan	.20	.15	.08
121	Gary Matthews	.04	.03	.02
122	Garry Maddox	.04	.03	.02
123	Paul Owens	.03	.02	.01
124	Tom Lasorda	.06	.05	.02
125	Joe Altobelli	.03	.02	.01
126	Tony LaRussa	.03	.02	.01

1985 Fleer

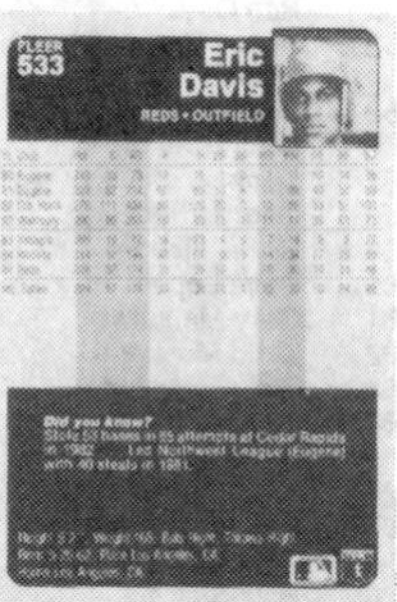

The 1985 Fleer set consists of 660 cards, each measuring 2-1/2" by 3-1/2" in size. The card fronts feature a color photo plus the player's team logo and the word "Fleer." The photos have a color-coded frame which corresponds to the player's team. A grey border surrounds the color-coded frame. The card backs are similar in design to the previous two years, but have two shades of red and black ink on white stock. For the fourth consecutive year, Fleer included special cards and team checklists in the set. Also incorporated in a set for the first time were ten "Major League Prospect" cards, each featuring two rookie hopefuls. The set was issued with team logo stickers.

		MT	NR MT	EX
Complete Set (660):		200.00	150.00	80.00
Common Player:		.06	.05	.02
1	Doug Bair	.06	.05	.02
2	Juan Berenguer	.06	.05	.02
3	Dave Bergman	.06	.05	.02
4	Tom Brookens	.06	.05	.02
5	Marty Castillo	.06	.05	.02
6	Darrell Evans	.12	.09	.05
7	Barbaro Garbey	.12	.09	.05
8	Kirk Gibson	.35	.25	.14
9	John Grubb	.06	.05	.02
10	Willie Hernandez	.08	.06	.03
11	Larry Herndon	.08	.06	.03
12	Howard Johnson	.50	.40	.20
13	Ruppert Jones	.06	.05	.02
14	Rusty Kuntz	.06	.05	.02
15	Chet Lemon	.08	.06	.03
16	Aurelio Lopez	.06	.05	.02
17	Sid Monge	.06	.05	.02
18	Jack Morris	.25	.20	.10

		MT	NR MT	EX
19	Lance Parrish	.10	.08	.04
20	Dan Petry	.08	.06	.03
21	Dave Rozema	.06	.05	.02
22	Bill Scherrer	.06	.05	.02
23	Alan Trammell	.35	.25	.14
24	Lou Whitaker	.35	.25	.14
25	Milt Wilcox	.06	.05	.02
26	Kurt Bevacqua	.06	.05	.02
27	*Greg Booker*(FC)	.06	.05	.02
28	Bobby Brown	.06	.05	.02
29	Luis DeLeon	.06	.05	.02
30	Dave Dravecky	.08	.06	.03
31	Tim Flannery	.06	.05	.02
32	Steve Garvey	.40	.30	.15
33	Goose Gossage	.20	.15	.08
34	Tony Gwynn	5.00	3.75	2.00
35	Greg Harris	.06	.05	.02
36	Andy Hawkins	.08	.06	.03
37	Terry Kennedy	.08	.06	.03
38	Craig Lefferts	.08	.06	.03
39	Tim Lollar	.06	.05	.02
40	Carmelo Martinez	.08	.06	.03
41	Kevin McReynolds	.25	.20	.10
42	Graig Nettles	.15	.11	.06
43	Luis Salazar	.06	.05	.02
44	Eric Show	.08	.06	.03
45	Garry Templeton	.08	.06	.03
46	Mark Thurmond	.06	.05	.02
47	Ed Whitson	.06	.05	.02
48	Alan Wiggins	.06	.05	.02
49	Rich Bordi	.06	.05	.02
50	Larry Bowa	.12	.09	.05
51	Warren Brusstar	.06	.05	.02
52	Ron Cey	.10	.08	.04
53	*Henry Cotto*(FC)	.15	.11	.06
54	Jody Davis	.10	.08	.04
55	Bob Dernier	.06	.05	.02
56	Leon Durham	.08	.06	.03
57	Dennis Eckersley	1.25	.90	.50
58	George Frazier	.06	.05	.02
59	Richie Hebner	.06	.05	.02
60	Dave Lopes	.08	.06	.03
61	Gary Matthews	.10	.08	.04
62	Keith Moreland	.08	.06	.03
63	Rick Reuschel	.10	.08	.04
64	Dick Ruthven	.06	.05	.02
65	Ryne Sandberg	8.00	6.00	3.25
66	Scott Sanderson	.06	.05	.02
67	Lee Smith	.10	.08	.04
68	Tim Stoddard	.06	.05	.02
69	Rick Sutcliffe	.12	.09	.05
70	Steve Trout	.06	.05	.02
71	Gary Woods	.06	.05	.02
72	Wally Backman	.08	.06	.03
73	Bruce Berenyi	.06	.05	.02
74	Hubie Brooks	.10	.08	.04
75	Kelvin Chapman	.06	.05	.02
76	Ron Darling	.30	.25	.12
77	Sid Fernandez(FC)	.50	.40	.20
78	Mike Fitzgerald	.08	.06	.03
79	George Foster	.15	.11	.06
80	Brent Gaff	.06	.05	.02
81	Ron Gardenhire	.06	.05	.02
82	*Dwight Gooden*	8.00	6.00	3.25
83	Tom Gorman	.06	.05	.02
84	Danny Heep	.06	.05	.02
85	Keith Hernandez	.30	.25	.12
86	Ray Knight	.10	.08	.04
87	Ed Lynch	.06	.05	.02
88	Jose Oquendo	.08	.06	.03
89	Jesse Orosco	.08	.06	.03
90	*Rafael Santana*(FC)	.06	.05	.02
91	Doug Sisk	.06	.05	.02
92	Rusty Staub	.12	.09	.05
93	Darryl Strawberry	3.00	2.25	1.25
94	Walt Terrell	.08	.06	.03
95	Mookie Wilson	.10	.08	.04
96	Jim Acker	.06	.05	.02
97	Willie Aikens	.06	.05	.02
98	Doyle Alexander	.10	.08	.04
99	Jesse Barfield	.25	.20	.10
100	George Bell	.50	.40	.20
101	Jim Clancy	.08	.06	.03
102	Dave Collins	.08	.06	.03
103	Tony Fernandez	.50	.40	.20
104	Damaso Garcia	.06	.05	.02
105	Jim Gott	.06	.05	.02
106	Alfredo Griffin	.08	.06	.03
107	Garth Iorg	.06	.05	.02
108	Roy Lee Jackson	.06	.05	.02
109	Cliff Johnson	.06	.05	.02

		MT	NR MT	EX
110	*Jimmy Key*	4.00	3.00	1.50
111	Dennis Lamp	.06	.05	.02
112	Rick Leach	.06	.05	.02
113	Luis Leal	.06	.05	.02
114	Buck Martinez	.06	.05	.02
115	Lloyd Moseby	.10	.08	.04
116	Rance Mulliniks	.06	.05	.02
117	Dave Stieb	.12	.09	.05
118	Willie Upshaw	.08	.06	.03
119	Ernie Whitt	.08	.06	.03
120	Mike Armstrong	.06	.05	.02
121	Don Baylor	.12	.09	.05
122	Marty Bystrom	.06	.05	.02
123	Rick Cerone	.06	.05	.02
124	Joe Cowley(FC)	.06	.05	.02
125	Brian Dayett(FC)	.06	.05	.02
126	Tim Foli	.06	.05	.02
127	Ray Fontenot	.06	.05	.02
128	Ken Griffey	.10	.08	.04
129	Ron Guidry	.25	.20	.10
130	Toby Harrah	.08	.06	.03
131	Jay Howell	.08	.06	.03
132	Steve Kemp	.08	.06	.03
133	Don Mattingly	6.00	4.50	2.50
134	Bobby Meacham	.06	.05	.02
135	John Montefusco	.06	.05	.02
136	Omar Moreno	.06	.05	.02
137	Dale Murray	.06	.05	.02
138	Phil Niekro	.25	.20	.10
139	*Mike Pagliarulo*(FC)	.70	.50	.30
140	Willie Randolph	.10	.08	.04
141	Dennis Rasmussen(FC)	.15	.11	.06
142	Dave Righetti	.20	.15	.08
143	*Jose Rijo*	3.00	2.25	1.25
144	Andre Robertson	.06	.05	.02
145	Bob Shirley	.06	.05	.02
146	Dave Winfield	4.00	3.00	1.50
147	Butch Wynegar	.06	.05	.02
148	Gary Allenson	.06	.05	.02
149	Tony Armas	.10	.08	.04
150	Marty Barrett	.20	.15	.08
151	Wade Boggs	4.00	3.00	1.50
152	Dennis Boyd	.10	.08	.04
153	Bill Buckner	.12	.09	.05
154	Mark Clear	.06	.05	.02
155	*Roger Clemens*	52.00	39.00	21.00
156	Steve Crawford	.06	.05	.02
157	Mike Easler	.08	.06	.03
158	Dwight Evans	.12	.09	.05
159	Rich Gedman	.10	.08	.04
160	Jackie Gutierrez	.06	.05	.02
161	Bruce Hurst	.12	.09	.05
162	John Henry Johnson	.06	.05	.02
163	Rick Miller	.06	.05	.02
164	Reid Nichols	.06	.05	.02
165	*Al Nipper*(FC)	.08	.06	.03
166	Bob Ojeda	.10	.08	.04
167	Jerry Remy	.06	.05	.02
168	Jim Rice	.35	.25	.14
169	Bob Stanley	.06	.05	.02
170	Mike Boddicker	.10	.08	.04
171	Al Bumbry	.08	.06	.03
172	Todd Cruz	.06	.05	.02
173	Rich Dauer	.06	.05	.02
174	Storm Davis	.10	.08	.04
175	Rick Dempsey	.08	.06	.03
176	Jim Dwyer	.06	.05	.02
177	Mike Flanagan	.10	.08	.04
178	Dan Ford	.06	.05	.02
179	Wayne Gross	.06	.05	.02
180	John Lowenstein	.06	.05	.02
181	Dennis Martinez	.08	.06	.03
182	Tippy Martinez	.06	.05	.02
183	Scott McGregor	.08	.06	.03
184	Eddie Murray	1.75	1.25	.70
185	Joe Nolan	.06	.05	.02
186	Floyd Rayford	.06	.05	.02
187	Cal Ripken, Jr.	10.00	7.50	4.00
188	Gary Roenicke	.06	.05	.02
189	Lenn Sakata	.06	.05	.02
190	John Shelby	.08	.06	.03
191	Ken Singleton	.08	.06	.03
192	Sammy Stewart	.06	.05	.02
193	Bill Swaggerty	.06	.05	.02
194	Tom Underwood	.06	.05	.02
195	Mike Young	.12	.09	.05
196	Steve Balboni	.08	.06	.03
197	Joe Beckwith	.06	.05	.02
198	Bud Black	.06	.05	.02
199	George Brett	4.00	3.00	1.50
200	Onix Concepcion	.06	.05	.02

		MT	NR MT	EX
201	*Mark Gubicza*	.80	.60	.30
202	Larry Gura	.06	.05	.02
203	Mark Huismann(FC)	.06	.05	.02
204	Dane Iorg	.06	.05	.02
205	Danny Jackson(FC)	.15	.11	.06
206	Charlie Leibrandt	.08	.06	.03
207	Hal McRae	.10	.08	.04
208	Darryl Motley	.06	.05	.02
209	Jorge Orta	.06	.05	.02
210	Greg Pryor	.06	.05	.02
211	Dan Quisenberry	.10	.08	.04
212	*Bret Saberhagen*	3.00	2.25	1.25
213	Pat Sheridan	.06	.05	.02
214	Don Slaught	.06	.05	.02
215	U.L. Washington	.06	.05	.02
216	John Wathan	.08	.06	.03
217	Frank White	.10	.08	.04
218	Willie Wilson	.12	.09	.05
219	Neil Allen	.06	.05	.02
220	Joaquin Andujar	.08	.06	.03
221	Steve Braun	.06	.05	.02
222	Danny Cox(FC)	.20	.15	.08
223	Bob Forsch	.08	.06	.03
224	David Green	.06	.05	.02
225	George Hendrick	.08	.06	.03
226	Tom Herr	.10	.08	.04
227	*Ricky Horton*	.15	.11	.06
228	Art Howe	.06	.05	.02
229	Mike Jorgensen	.06	.05	.02
230	Kurt Kepshire	.06	.05	.02
231	Jeff Lahti	.06	.05	.02
232	Tito Landrum	.06	.05	.02
233	Dave LaPoint	.08	.06	.03
234	Willie McGee	.30	.25	.12
235	*Tom Nieto*(FC)	.06	.05	.02
236	*Terry Pendleton*(FC)	7.00	5.25	2.75
237	Darrell Porter	.08	.06	.03
238	Dave Rucker	.06	.05	.02
239	Lonnie Smith	.08	.06	.03
240	Ozzie Smith	2.00	1.50	.80
241	Bruce Sutter	.12	.09	.05
242	Andy Van Slyke	1.75	1.25	.70
243	Dave Von Ohlen	.06	.05	.02
244	Larry Andersen	.06	.05	.02
245	Bill Campbell	.06	.05	.02
246	Steve Carlton	1.50	1.25	.60
247	Tim Corcoran	.06	.05	.02
248	Ivan DeJesus	.06	.05	.02
249	John Denny	.06	.05	.02
250	Bo Diaz	.08	.06	.03
251	Greg Gross	.06	.05	.02
252	Kevin Gross	.10	.08	.04
253	Von Hayes	.12	.09	.05
254	Al Holland	.06	.05	.02
255	Charles Hudson	.08	.06	.03
256	Jerry Koosman	.10	.08	.04
257	Joe Lefebvre	.06	.05	.02
258	Sixto Lezcano	.06	.05	.02
259	Garry Maddox	.10	.08	.04
260	Len Matuszek	.06	.05	.02
261	Tug McGraw	.10	.08	.04
262	Al Oliver	.12	.09	.05
263	Shane Rawley	.10	.08	.04
264	Juan Samuel	.20	.15	.08
265	Mike Schmidt	5.00	3.75	2.00
266	*Jeff Stone*	.06	.05	.02
267	Ozzie Virgil	.06	.05	.02
268	Glenn Wilson	.08	.06	.03
269	John Wockenfuss	.06	.05	.02
270	Darrell Brown	.06	.05	.02
271	Tom Brunansky	.12	.09	.05
272	Randy Bush	.06	.05	.02
273	John Butcher	.06	.05	.02
274	Bobby Castillo	.06	.05	.02
275	Ron Davis	.06	.05	.02
276	Dave Engle	.06	.05	.02
277	Pete Filson	.06	.05	.02
278	Gary Gaetti	.25	.20	.10
279	Mickey Hatcher	.06	.05	.02
280	Ed Hodge	.06	.05	.02
281	Kent Hrbek	.25	.20	.10
282	Houston Jimenez	.06	.05	.02
283	Tim Laudner	.06	.05	.02
284	Rick Lysander	.06	.05	.02
285	Dave Meier	.06	.05	.02
286	*Kirby Puckett*	55.00	41.00	22.00
287	Pat Putnam	.06	.05	.02
288	Ken Schrom	.06	.05	.02
289	Mike Smithson	.06	.05	.02
290	Tim Teufel	.08	.06	.03
291	Frank Viola	.20	.15	.08

		MT	NR MT	EX
292	Ron Washington	.06	.05	.02
293	Don Aase	.06	.05	.02
294	Juan Beniquez	.06	.05	.02
295	Bob Boone	.08	.06	.03
296	Mike Brown	.06	.05	.02
297	Rod Carew	1.50	1.25	.60
298	Doug Corbett	.06	.05	.02
299	Doug DeCinces	.10	.08	.04
300	Brian Downing	.10	.08	.04
301	Ken Forsch	.06	.05	.02
302	Bobby Grich	.10	.08	.04
303	Reggie Jackson	2.00	1.50	.80
304	Tommy John	.20	.15	.08
305	Curt Kaufman	.06	.05	.02
306	Bruce Kison	.06	.05	.02
307	Fred Lynn	.20	.15	.08
308	Gary Pettis	.08	.06	.03
309	*Ron Romanick*	.06	.05	.02
310	Luis Sanchez	.06	.05	.02
311	Dick Schofield	.12	.09	.05
312	Daryl Sconiers	.06	.05	.02
313	Jim Slaton	.06	.05	.02
314	Derrel Thomas	.06	.05	.02
315	Rob Wilfong	.06	.05	.02
316	Mike Witt	.12	.09	.05
317	Geoff Zahn	.06	.05	.02
318	Len Barker	.08	.06	.03
319	Steve Bedrosian	.12	.09	.05
320	Bruce Benedict	.06	.05	.02
321	Rick Camp	.06	.05	.02
322	Chris Chambliss	.08	.06	.03
323	*Jeff Dedmon*(FC)	.06	.05	.02
324	Terry Forster	.08	.06	.03
325	Gene Garber	.06	.05	.02
326	*Albert Hall*(FC)	.06	.05	.02
327	Terry Harper	.06	.05	.02
328	Bob Horner	.12	.09	.05
329	Glenn Hubbard	.06	.05	.02
330	Randy S. Johnson	.06	.05	.02
331	Brad Komminsk	.06	.05	.02
332	Rick Mahler	.06	.05	.02
333	Craig McMurtry	.06	.05	.02
334	Donnie Moore	.06	.05	.02
335	Dale Murphy	.60	.45	.25
336	Ken Oberkfell	.06	.05	.02
337	Pascual Perez	.08	.06	.03
338	Gerald Perry	.35	.25	.14
339	Rafael Ramirez	.06	.05	.02
340	Jerry Royster	.06	.05	.02
341	Alex Trevino	.06	.05	.02
342	Claudell Washington	.08	.06	.03
343	Alan Ashby	.06	.05	.02
344	*Mark Bailey*	.06	.05	.02
345	Kevin Bass	.06	.05	.02
346	Enos Cabell	.06	.05	.02
347	Jose Cruz	.10	.08	.04
348	Bill Dawley	.06	.05	.02
349	Frank DiPino	.06	.05	.02
350	Bill Doran	.12	.09	.05
351	Phil Garner	.08	.06	.03
352	Bob Knepper	.08	.06	.03
353	Mike LaCoss	.06	.05	.02
354	Jerry Mumphrey	.06	.05	.02
355	Joe Niekro	.10	.08	.04
356	Terry Puhl	.06	.05	.02
357	Craig Reynolds	.06	.05	.02
358	Vern Ruhle	.06	.05	.02
359	Nolan Ryan	10.00	7.50	4.00
360	Joe Sambito	.06	.05	.02
361	Mike Scott	.15	.11	.06
362	Dave Smith	.08	.06	.03
363	*Julio Solano*(FC)	.06	.05	.02
364	Dickie Thon	.08	.06	.03
365	Denny Walling	.06	.05	.02
366	Dave Anderson	.06	.05	.02
367	Bob Bailor	.06	.05	.02
368	Greg Brock	.08	.06	.03
369	Carlos Diaz	.06	.05	.02
370	Pedro Guerrero	.25	.20	.10
371	*Orel Hershiser*(FC)	3.00	2.25	1.25
372	Rick Honeycutt	.06	.05	.02
373	Burt Hooton	.08	.06	.03
374	*Ken Howell*(FC)	.15	.11	.06
375	Ken Landreaux	.08	.06	.03
376	Candy Maldonado	.10	.08	.04
377	Mike Marshall	.15	.11	.06
378	Tom Niedenfuer	.08	.06	.03
379	Alejandro Pena	.08	.06	.03
380	Jerry Reuss	.08	.06	.03
381	*R.J. Reynolds*	.06	.05	.02
382	German Rivera	.06	.05	.02

		MT	NR MT	EX
383	Bill Russell	.08	.06	.03
384	Steve Sax	.20	.15	.08
385	Mike Scioscia	.08	.06	.03
386	*Franklin Stubbs*(FC)	.06	.05	.02
387	Fernando Valenzuela	.10	.08	.04
388	Bob Welch	.12	.09	.05
389	Terry Whitfield	.06	.05	.02
390	Steve Yeager	.06	.05	.02
391	Pat Zachry	.06	.05	.02
392	Fred Breining	.06	.05	.02
393	Gary Carter	.35	.25	.14
394	Andre Dawson	2.00	1.50	.80
395	Miguel Dilone	.06	.05	.02
396	Dan Driessen	.08	.06	.03
397	Doug Flynn	.06	.05	.02
398	Terry Francona	.06	.05	.02
399	Bill Gullickson	.06	.05	.02
400	Bob James	.06	.05	.02
401	Charlie Lea	.06	.05	.02
402	Bryan Little	.06	.05	.02
403	Gary Lucas	.06	.05	.02
404	David Palmer	.06	.05	.02
405	Tim Raines	.35	.25	.14
406	Mike Ramsey	.06	.05	.02
407	Jeff Reardon	.12	.09	.05
408	Steve Rogers	.08	.06	.03
409	Dan Schatzeder	.06	.05	.02
410	Bryn Smith	.06	.05	.02
411	Mike Stenhouse	.06	.05	.02
412	Tim Wallach	.12	.09	.05
413	Jim Wohlford	.06	.05	.02
414	Bill Almon	.06	.05	.02
415	Keith Atherton	.06	.05	.02
416	Bruce Bochte	.06	.05	.02
417	Tom Burgmeier	.06	.05	.02
418	Ray Burris	.06	.05	.02
419	Bill Caudill	.06	.05	.02
420	Chris Codiroli	.06	.05	.02
421	Tim Conroy	.06	.05	.02
422	Mike Davis	.08	.06	.03
423	Jim Essian	.06	.05	.02
424	Mike Heath	.06	.05	.02
425	Rickey Henderson	4.00	3.00	1.50
426	Donnie Hill	.06	.05	.02
427	Dave Kingman	.15	.11	.06
428	Bill Krueger	.06	.05	.02
429	Carney Lansford	.10	.08	.04
430	Steve McCatty	.06	.05	.02
431	Joe Morgan	.40	.30	.15
432	Dwayne Murphy	.08	.06	.03
433	Tony Phillips	.30	.25	.12
434	Lary Sorensen	.06	.05	.02
435	Mike Warren	.06	.05	.02
436	*Curt Young*(FC)	.10	.08	.04
437	Luis Aponte	.06	.05	.02
438	Chris Bando	.06	.05	.02
439	Tony Bernazard	.06	.05	.02
440	Bert Blyleven	.15	.11	.06
441	Brett Butler	.10	.08	.04
442	Ernie Camacho	.06	.05	.02
443	Joe Carter(FC)	11.00	8.25	4.50
444	Carmelo Castillo	.06	.05	.02
445	Jamie Easterly	.06	.05	.02
446	*Steve Farr*(FC)	.40	.30	.15
447	Mike Fischlin	.06	.05	.02
448	Julio Franco	.60	.45	.25
449	Mel Hall	.08	.06	.03
450	Mike Hargrove	.06	.05	.02
451	Neal Heaton	.06	.05	.02
452	Brook Jacoby	.30	.25	.12
453	*Mike Jeffcoat*	.08	.06	.03
454	*Don Schulze*(FC)	.06	.05	.02
455	Roy Smith	.06	.05	.02
456	Pat Tabler	.08	.06	.03
457	Andre Thornton	.10	.08	.04
458	George Vukovich	.06	.05	.02
459	Tom Waddell	.06	.05	.02
460	Jerry Willard	.06	.05	.02
461	Dale Berra	.06	.05	.02
462	John Candelaria	.10	.08	.04
463	Jose DeLeon	.08	.06	.03
464	Doug Frobel	.06	.05	.02
465	Cecilio Guante	.06	.05	.02
466	Brian Harper	.06	.05	.02
467	Lee Lacy	.06	.05	.02
468	Bill Madlock	.12	.09	.05
469	Lee Mazzilli	.08	.06	.03
470	Larry McWilliams	.06	.05	.02
471	Jim Morrison	.06	.05	.02
472	Tony Pena	.10	.08	.04
473	Johnny Ray	.06	.05	.02
474	Rick Rhoden	.10	.08	.04
475	Don Robinson	.08	.06	.03
476	Rod Scurry	.06	.05	.02
477	Kent Tekulve	.08	.06	.03
478	Jason Thompson	.06	.05	.02
479	John Tudor	.10	.08	.04
480	Lee Tunnell	.06	.05	.02
481	Marvell Wynne	.06	.05	.02
482	Salome Barojas	.06	.05	.02
483	Dave Beard	.06	.05	.02
484	Jim Beattie	.06	.05	.02
485	Barry Bonnell	.06	.05	.02
486	*Phil Bradley*	.10	.08	.04
487	Al Cowens	.06	.05	.02
488	*Alvin Davis*	.10	.08	.04
489	Dave Henderson	.15	.11	.06
490	Steve Henderson	.06	.05	.02
491	Bob Kearney	.06	.05	.02
492	*Mark Langston*	4.00	3.00	1.50
493	Larry Milbourne	.06	.05	.02
494	Paul Mirabella	.06	.05	.02
495	Mike Moore	.20	.15	.08
496	Edwin Nunez(FC)	.08	.06	.03
497	Spike Owen	.08	.06	.03
498	Jack Perconte	.06	.05	.02
499	Ken Phelps	.10	.08	.04
500	*Jim Presley*(FC)	.06	.05	.02
501	Mike Stanton	.06	.05	.02
502	Bob Stoddard	.06	.05	.02
503	Gorman Thomas	.06	.05	.02
504	Ed Vande Berg	.06	.05	.02
505	Matt Young	.06	.05	.02
506	Juan Agosto	.06	.05	.02
507	Harold Baines	.15	.11	.06
508	Floyd Bannister	.10	.08	.04
509	Britt Burns	.06	.05	.02
510	Julio Cruz	.06	.05	.02
511	Richard Dotson	.10	.08	.04
512	Jerry Dybzinski	.06	.05	.02
513	Carlton Fisk	1.00	.70	.40
514	Scott Fletcher	.08	.06	.03
515	Jerry Hairston	.06	.05	.02
516	Marc Hill	.06	.05	.02
517	LaMarr Hoyt	.06	.05	.02
518	Ron Kittle	.06	.05	.02
519	Rudy Law	.06	.05	.02
520	Vance Law	.08	.06	.03
521	Greg Luzinski	.10	.08	.04
522	Gene Nelson	.06	.05	.02
523	Tom Paciorek	.06	.05	.02
524	Ron Reed	.06	.05	.02
525	Bert Roberge	.06	.05	.02
526	Tom Seaver	1.25	.90	.50
527	Roy Smalley	.06	.05	.02
528	Dan Spillner	.06	.05	.02
529	Mike Squires	.06	.05	.02
530	Greg Walker	.06	.05	.02
531	Cesar Cedeno	.10	.08	.04
532	Dave Concepcion	.12	.09	.05
533	*Eric Davis*(FC)	6.00	4.50	2.50
534	Nick Esasky	.08	.06	.03
535	Tom Foley	.06	.05	.02
536	*John Franco*	.75	.60	.30
537	Brad Gulden	.06	.05	.02
538	Tom Hume	.06	.05	.02
539	Wayne Krenchicki	.06	.05	.02
540	Andy McGaffigan	.06	.05	.02
541	Eddie Milner	.06	.05	.02
542	Ron Oester	.06	.05	.02
543	Bob Owchinko	.06	.05	.02
544	Dave Parker	.25	.20	.10
545	Frank Pastore	.06	.05	.02
546	Tony Perez	.15	.11	.06
547	Ted Power	.06	.05	.02
548	Joe Price	.06	.05	.02
549	Gary Redus	.08	.06	.03
550	Pete Rose	2.00	1.50	.80
551	Jeff Russell(FC)	.10	.08	.04
552	Mario Soto	.08	.06	.03
553	*Jay Tibbs*(FC)	.15	.11	.06
554	Duane Walker	.06	.05	.02
555	Alan Bannister	.06	.05	.02
556	Buddy Bell	.12	.09	.05
557	Danny Darwin	.06	.05	.02
558	Charlie Hough	.08	.06	.03
559	Bobby Jones	.06	.05	.02
560	Odell Jones	.06	.05	.02
561	*Jeff Kunkel*(FC)	.06	.05	.02
562	*Mike Mason*	.06	.05	.02
563	Pete O'Brien	.12	.09	.05
564	Larry Parrish	.10	.08	.04

		MT	NR MT	EX
565	Mickey Rivers	.08	.06	.03
566	Billy Sample	.06	.05	.02
567	Dave Schmidt	.06	.05	.02
568	Donnie Scott	.06	.05	.02
569	Dave Stewart	.12	.09	.05
570	Frank Tanana	.10	.08	.04
571	Wayne Tolleson	.06	.05	.02
572	Gary Ward	.08	.06	.03
573	Curtis Wilkerson	.08	.06	.03
574	George Wright	.06	.05	.02
575	Ned Yost	.06	.05	.02
576	Mark Brouhard	.06	.05	.02
577	Mike Caldwell	.06	.05	.02
578	Bobby Clark	.06	.05	.02
579	Jaime Cocanower	.06	.05	.02
580	Cecil Cooper	.15	.11	.06
581	Rollie Fingers	.20	.15	.08
582	Jim Gantner	.06	.05	.02
583	Moose Haas	.06	.05	.02
584	Dion James	.06	.05	.02
585	Pete Ladd	.06	.05	.02
586	Rick Manning	.06	.05	.02
587	Bob McClure	.06	.05	.02
588	Paul Molitor	2.00	1.50	.80
589	Charlie Moore	.06	.05	.02
590	Ben Oglivie	.08	.06	.03
591	Chuck Porter	.06	.05	.02
592	*Randy Ready*(FC)	.20	.15	.08
593	Ed Romero	.06	.05	.02
594	Bill Schroeder(FC)	.06	.05	.02
595	Ray Searage	.06	.05	.02
596	Ted Simmons	.12	.09	.05
597	Jim Sundberg	.08	.06	.03
598	Don Sutton	.30	.25	.12
599	Tom Tellmann	.06	.05	.02
600	Rick Waits	.06	.05	.02
601	Robin Yount	4.00	3.00	1.50
602	Dusty Baker	.08	.06	.03
603	Bob Brenly	.06	.05	.02
604	Jack Clark	.20	.15	.08
605	Chili Davis	.20	.15	.08
606	Mark Davis	.06	.05	.02
607	*Dan Gladden*(FC)	.50	.40	.20
608	Atlee Hammaker	.06	.05	.02
609	Mike Krukow	.08	.06	.03
610	Duane Kuiper	.06	.05	.02
611	Bob Lacey	.06	.05	.02
612	Bill Laskey	.06	.05	.02
613	Gary Lavelle	.06	.05	.02
614	Johnnie LeMaster	.06	.05	.02
615	Jeff Leonard	.06	.05	.02
616	Randy Lerch	.06	.05	.02
617	Greg Minton	.06	.05	.02
618	Steve Nicosia	.06	.05	.02
619	Gene Richards	.06	.05	.02
620	*Jeff Robinson*	.10	.08	.04
621	Scot Thompson	.06	.05	.02
622	Manny Trillo	.08	.06	.03
623	Brad Wellman	.06	.05	.02
624	*Frank Williams*	.15	.11	.06
625	Joel Youngblood	.06	.05	.02
626	Cal Ripken (IA)	3.50	2.75	1.50
627	Mike Schmidt (IA)	1.50	1.25	.60
628	Giving the Signs (Sparky Anderson)	.08	.06	.03
629	A.L. Pitcher's Nightmare (Rickey Henderson, Dave Winfield)	1.00	.70	.40
630	N.L. Pitcher's Nightmare (Ryne Sandberg, Mike Schmidt)	2.00	1.50	.80
631	N.L. All-Stars (Gary Carter, Steve Garvey, Ozzie Smith, Darryl Strawberry)	.30	.25	.12
632	All-Star Game Winning Battery (Gary Carter, Charlie Lea)	.15	.11	.06
633	N.L. Pennant Clinchers (Steve Garvey, Goose Gossage)	.20	.15	.08
634	N.L. Rookie Phenoms (Dwight Gooden, Juan Samuel)	.30	.25	.12
635	Toronto's Big Guns (Willie Upshaw)	.08	.06	.03
636	Toronto's Big Guns (Lloyd Moseby)	.08	.06	.03
637	Holland (Al Holland)	.08	.06	.03
638	Tunnell (Lee Tunnell)	.08	.06	.03
639	Reggie Jackson (IA)	.75	.60	.30
640	Pete Rose (IA)	.75	.60	.30
641	Father & Son (Cal Ripken, Jr., Cal Ripken, Sr.)	3.00	2.25	1.25
642	Cubs Team	.08	.06	.03
643	1984's Two Perfect Games & One No Hitter (Jack Morris, David Palmer, Mike Witt)	.15	.11	.06
644	Major League Prospect (Willie Lozado, Vic Mata)	.06	.05	.02
645	Major League Prospect (*Kelly Gruber, Randy O'Neal*)(FC)	.25	.20	.10
646	Major League Prospect (*Jose Roman, Joel Skinner*)(FC)	.06	.05	.02
647	Major League Prospect (*Steve Kiefer, Danny Tartabull*)	8.00	6.00	3.25
648	Major League Prospect (*Rob Deer, Alejandro Sanchez*)(FC)	1.00	.70	.40
649	Major League Prospect (*Shawon Dunston, Bill Hatcher*)	1.00	.70	.40
650	Major League Prospect (*Mike Bielecki, Ron Robinson*)(FC)	.30	.25	.12
651	Major League Prospect (*Zane Smith, Paul Zuvella*)(FC)	.60	.45	.25
652	Major League Prospect (*Glenn Davis, Joe Hesketh*)(FC)	.50	.40	.20
653	Major League Prospect (*Steve Jeltz, John Russell*)(FC)	.10	.08	.04
654	Checklist 1-95	.06	.05	.02
655	Checklist 96-195	.06	.05	.02
656	Checklist 196-292	.06	.05	.02
657	Checklist 293-391	.06	.05	.02
658	Checklist 392-481	.06	.05	.02
659	Checklist 482-575	.06	.05	.02
660	Checklist 576-660	.06	.05	.02

1985 Fleer Update

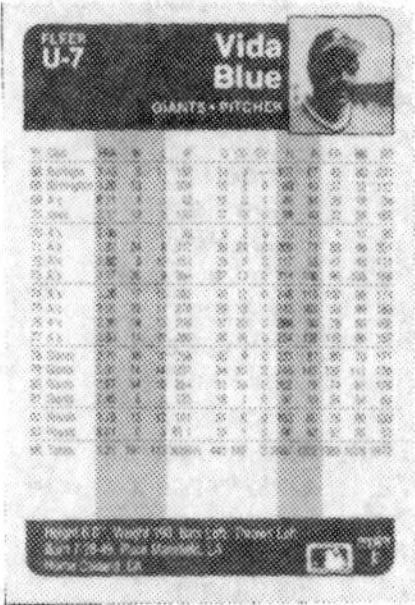

For the second straight year, Fleer issued a 132- card update set. The cards, which measure 2-1/2" by 3-1/2", portray players on their new teams and also includes rookies not depicted in the regular issue. The cards are identical in design to the 1985 Fleer set but are numbered U-1 through U-132. The set was issued with team logo stickers in a specially designed box and was available only through hobby dealers.

		MT	NR MT	EX
Complete Set (132):		30.00	22.00	12.00
Common Player:		.10	.08	.04
1	Don Aase	.10	.08	.04
2	Bill Almon	.10	.08	.04
3	Dusty Baker	.15	.11	.06
4	Dale Berra	.10	.08	.04
5	Karl Best(FC)	.10	.08	.04
6	Tim Birtsas(FC)	.20	.15	.08
7	Vida Blue	.20	.15	.08
8	Rich Bordi	.10	.08	.04
9	Daryl Boston(FC)	.20	.15	.08
10	Hubie Brooks	.20	.15	.08
11	Chris Brown(FC)	.10	.08	.04
12	Tom Browning(FC)	.35	.25	.12
13	Al Bumbry	.10	.08	.04
14	Tim Burke(FC)	.20	.12	.06
15	Ray Burris	.10	.08	.04
16	Jeff Burroughs	.15	.11	.06
17	Ivan Calderon(FC)	.25	.20	.10
18	Jeff Calhoun	.10	.08	.04
19	Bill Campbell	.10	.08	.04
20	Don Carman(FC)	.10	.08	.04
21	Gary Carter	.60	.40	.20
22	Bobby Castillo	.10	.08	.04
23	Bill Caudill	.10	.08	.04
24	Rick Cerone	.10	.08	.04
25	Jack Clark	.20	.15	.07
26	Pat Clements(FC)	.10	.08	.04
27	Stewart Cliburn(FC)	.10	.08	.04
28	Vince Coleman(FC)	1.75	1.00	.50
29	Dave Collins	.15	.11	.06

		MT	NR MT	EX
30	Fritz Connally	.10	.08	.04
31	Henry Cotto(FC)	.20	.15	.08
32	Danny Darwin	.15	.11	.06
33	Darren Daulton(FC)	20.00	12.00	6.00
34	Jerry Davis	.10	.08	.04
35	Brian Dayett	.10	.08	.04
36	Ken Dixon(FC)	.10	.08	.04
37	Tommy Dunbar	.10	.08	.04
38	Mariano Duncan(FC)	.80	.60	.30
39	Bob Fallon	.10	.08	.04
40	Brian Fisher(FC)	.15	.11	.06
41	Mike Fitzgerald	.10	.08	.04
42	Ray Fontenot	.10	.08	.04
43	Greg Gagne(FC)	.50	.40	.20
44	Oscar Gamble	.10	.08	.04
45	Jim Gott	.10	.08	.04
46	David Green	.10	.08	.04
47	Alfredo Griffin	.15	.11	.06
48	Ozzie Guillen(FC)	1.50	.90	.50
49	Toby Harrah	.15	.11	.06
50	Ron Hassey	.10	.08	.04
51	Rickey Henderson	5.00	3.75	2.00
52	Steve Henderson	.10	.08	.04
53	George Hendrick	.15	.11	.06
54	Teddy Higuera(FC)	.12	.08	.04
55	Al Holland	.10	.08	.04
56	Burt Hooton	.15	.11	.06
57	Jay Howell	.15	.11	.06
58	LaMarr Hoyt	.10	.08	.04
59	Tim Hulett(FC)	.20	.15	.08
60	Bob James	.10	.08	.04
61	Cliff Johnson	.10	.08	.04
62	Howard Johnson	1.25	.60	.30
63	Ruppert Jones	.10	.08	.04
64	Steve Kemp	.15	.11	.06
65	Bruce Kison	.10	.08	.04
66	Mike LaCoss	.10	.08	.04
67	Lee Lacy	.10	.08	.04
68	Dave LaPoint	.10	.08	.04
69	Gary Lavelle	.10	.08	.04
70	Vance Law	.10	.08	.04
71	Manny Lee(FC)	.10	.08	.04
72	Sixto Lezcano	.10	.08	.04
73	Tim Lollar	.10	.08	.04
74	Urbano Lugo(FC)	.10	.08	.04
75	Fred Lynn	.30	.25	.12
76	Steve Lyons(FC)	.15	.11	.06
77	Mickey Mahler	.10	.08	.04
78	Ron Mathis(FC)	.10	.08	.04
79	Len Matuszek	.10	.08	.04
80	Oddibe McDowell(FC)	.15	.11	.06
81	Roger McDowell(FC)	.50	.40	.20
82	Donnie Moore	.10	.08	.04
83	Ron Musselman	.10	.08	.04
84	Al Oliver	.25	.20	.10
85	Joe Orsulak(FC)	.20	.15	.08
86	Dan Pasqua(FC)	.60	.45	.25
87	Chris Pittaro(FC)	.10	.08	.04
88	Rick Reuschel	.10	.08	.04
89	Earnie Riles(FC)	.20	.15	.08
90	Jerry Royster	.10	.08	.04
91	Dave Rozema	.10	.08	.04
92	Dave Rucker	.10	.08	.04
93	Vern Ruhle	.10	.08	.04
94	Mark Salas(FC)	.10	.08	.04
95	Luis Salazar	.10	.08	.04
96	Joe Sambito	.10	.08	.04
97	Billy Sample	.10	.08	.04
98	Alex Sanchez	.10	.08	.04
99	Calvin Schiraldi(FC)	.25	.20	.10
100	Rick Schu(FC)	.20	.15	.08
101	Larry Sheets(FC)	.10	.08	.04
102	Ron Shepherd	.10	.08	.04
103	Nelson Simmons(FC)	.10	.08	.04
104	Don Slaught	.10	.08	.04
105	Roy Smalley	.10	.08	.04
106	Lonnie Smith	.15	.11	.06
107	Nate Snell(FC)	.10	.08	.04
108	Lary Sorensen	.10	.08	.04
109	Chris Speier	.10	.08	.04
110	Mike Stenhouse	.10	.08	.04
111	Tim Stoddard	.10	.08	.04
112	John Stuper	.10	.08	.04
113	Jim Sundberg	.10	.08	.04
114	Bruce Sutter	.15	.11	.06
115	Don Sutton	.60	.45	.25
116	Bruce Tanner(FC)	.10	.08	.04
117	Kent Tekulve	.10	.08	.04
118	Walt Terrell	.10	.08	.04
119	Mickey Tettleton(FC)	8.00	5.00	2.50
120	Rich Thompson	.10	.08	.04
121	Louis Thornton(FC)	.10	.08	.04
122	Alex Trevino	.10	.08	.04
123	John Tudor	.30	.25	.12
124	Jose Uribe(FC)	.10	.08	.04
125	Dave Valle(FC)	.20	.15	.08
126	Dave Von Ohlen	.10	.08	.04
127	Curt Wardle	.10	.08	.04
128	U.L. Washington	.10	.08	.04
129	Ed Whitson	.10	.08	.04
130	Herm Winningham(FC)	.10	.08	.04
131	Rich Yett(FC)	.10	.08	.04
132	Checklist	.10	.08	.04

1985 Fleer Stickers

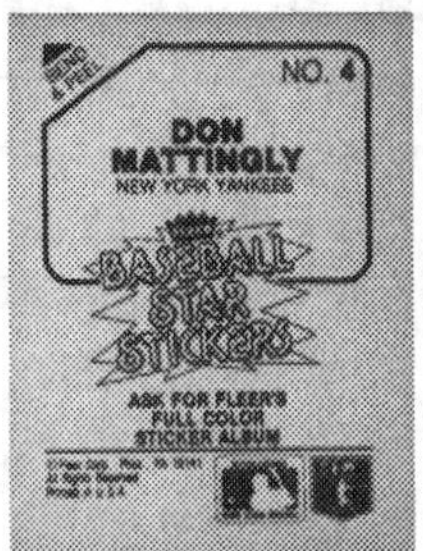

The 1985 Fleer sticker set consists of 126 player stickers, each measuring 2-1/2" by 1-15/16". Numbered on the back, the stickers were designed to be put in a special album.

		MT	NR MT	EX
Complete Set:		15.00	11.00	6.00
Common Player:		.03	.02	.01
Sticker Album:		1.00	.70	.40
1	Pete Rose	.40	.30	.15
2	Pete Rose	.30	.25	.12
3	Pete Rose	.30	.25	.12
4	Don Mattingly	.90	.70	.35
5	Dave Winfield	.20	.15	.08
6	Wade Boggs	.50	.40	.20
7	Buddy Bell	.06	.05	.02
8	Tony Gwynn	.25	.20	.10
9	Lee Lacy	.03	.02	.01
10	Chili Davis	.06	.05	.02
11	Ryne Sandberg	.50	.40	.20
12	Tony Armas	.04	.03	.02
13	Jim Rice	.20	.15	.08
14	Dave Kingman	.06	.05	.02
15	Alvin Davis	.12	.09	.05
16	Gary Carter	.20	.15	.08
17	Mike Schmidt	.30	.25	.12
18	Dale Murphy	.30	.25	.12
19	Ron Cey	.06	.05	.02
20	Eddie Murray	.25	.20	.10
21	Harold Baines	.10	.08	.04
22	Kirk Gibson	.15	.11	.06
23	Jim Rice	.20	.15	.08
24	Gary Matthews	.06	.05	.02
25	Keith Hernandez	.15	.11	.06
26	Gary Carter	.20	.15	.08
27	George Hendrick	.04	.03	.02
28	Tony Armas	.04	.03	.02
29	Dave Kingman	.06	.05	.02
30	Dwayne Murphy	.04	.03	.02
31	Lance Parrish	.12	.09	.05
32	Andre Thornton	.04	.03	.02
33	Dale Murphy	.30	.25	.12
34	Mike Schmidt	.30	.25	.12
35	Gary Carter	.20	.15	.08
36	Darryl Strawberry	.30	.25	.12
37	Don Mattingly	.90	.70	.35
38	Larry Parrish	.04	.03	.02
39	George Bell	.20	.15	.08
40	Dwight Evans	.06	.05	.02
41	Cal Ripken, Jr.	.25	.20	.10
42	Tim Raines	.20	.15	.08
43	Johnny Ray	.06	.05	.02

		MT	NR MT	EX
44	Juan Samuel	.08	.06	.03
45	Ryne Sandberg	.50	.40	.20
46	Mike Easler	.04	.03	.02
47	Andre Thornton	.04	.03	.02
48	Dave Kingman	.06	.05	.02
49	Don Baylor	.08	.06	.03
50	Rusty Staub	.06	.05	.02
51	Steve Braun	.03	.02	.01
52	Kevin Bass	.06	.05	.02
53	Greg Gross	.03	.02	.01
54	Rickey Henderson	.25	.20	.10
55	Dave Collins	.03	.02	.01
56	Brett Butler	.04	.03	.02
57	Gary Pettis	.04	.03	.02
58	Tim Raines	.20	.15	.08
59	Juan Samuel	.08	.06	.03
60	Alan Wiggins	.03	.02	.01
61	Lonnie Smith	.03	.02	.01
62	Eddie Murray	.25	.20	.10
63	Eddie Murray	.25	.20	.10
64	Eddie Murray	.25	.20	.10
65	Eddie Murray	.25	.20	.10
66	Eddie Murray	.25	.20	.10
67	Eddie Murray	.25	.20	.10
68	Tom Seaver	.20	.15	.08
69	Tom Seaver	.20	.15	.08
70	Tom Seaver	.20	.15	.08
71	Tom Seaver	.20	.15	.08
72	Tom Seaver	.20	.15	.08
73	Tom Seaver	.20	.15	.08
74	Mike Schmidt	.30	.25	.12
75	Mike Schmidt	.30	.25	.12
76	Mike Schmidt	.30	.25	.12
77	Mike Schmidt	.30	.25	.12
78	Mike Schmidt	.30	.25	.12
79	Mike Schmidt	.30	.25	.12
80	Mike Boddicker	.04	.03	.02
81	Bert Blyleven	.08	.06	.03
82	Jack Morris	.12	.09	.05
83	Dan Petry	.04	.03	.02
84	Frank Viola	.06	.05	.02
85	Joaquin Andujar	.04	.03	.02
86	Mario Soto	.04	.03	.02
87	Dwight Gooden	.60	.45	.25
88	Joe Niekro	.06	.05	.02
89	Rick Sutcliffe	.08	.06	.03
90	Mike Boddicker	.04	.03	.02
91	Dave Stieb	.06	.05	.02
92	Bert Blyleven	.08	.06	.03
93	Phil Niekro	.12	.09	.05
94	Alejandro Pena	.03	.02	.01
95	Dwight Gooden	.60	.45	.25
96	Orel Hershiser	.15	.11	.06
97	Rick Rhoden	.04	.03	.02
98	John Candelaria	.04	.03	.02
99	Dan Quisenberry	.06	.05	.02
100	Bil Caudill	.03	.02	.01
101	Willie Hernandez	.04	.03	.02
102	Dave Righetti	.10	.08	.04
103	Ron Davis	.03	.02	.01
104	Bruce Sutter	.08	.06	.03
105	Lee Smith	.06	.05	.02
106	Jesse Orosco	.04	.03	.02
107	Al Holland	.03	.02	.01
108	Goose Gossage	.08	.06	.03
109	Mark Langston	.10	.08	.04
110	Dave Stieb	.06	.05	.02
111	Mike Witt	.06	.05	.02
112	Bert Blyleven	.08	.06	.03
113	Dwight Gooden	.60	.45	.25
114	Fernando Valenzuela	.15	.11	.06
115	Nolan Ryan	.15	.11	.06
116	Mario Soto	.04	.03	.02
117	Ron Darling	.08	.06	.03
118	Dan Gladden	.04	.03	.02
119	Jeff Stone	.04	.03	.02
120	John Franco	.06	.05	.02
121	Barbaro Garbey	.03	.02	.01
122	Kirby Puckett	.20	.15	.08
123	Roger Clemens	.60	.45	.25
124	Bret Saberhagen	.20	.15	.08
125	Sparky Anderson	.03	.02	.01
126	Dick Williams	.03	.02	.01

1985 Fleer Limited Edition

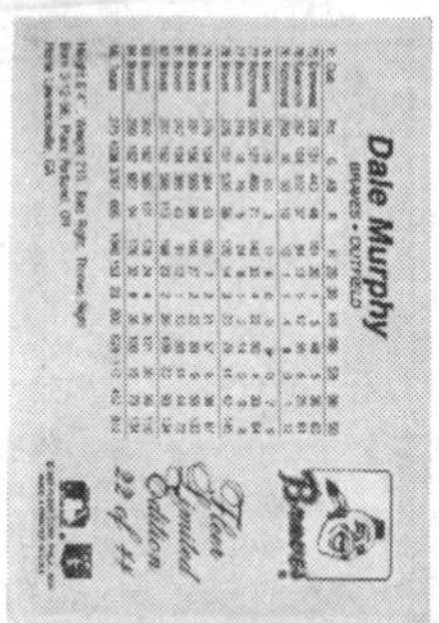

The 1985 Fleer Limited Edition 44-card set was distributed through McCrory's, J.J. Newbury, McClellan, Kress, YDC, and Green stores. The cards, which are the standard 2-1/2" by 3-1/2" size, have full-color photos inside a red and yellow frame. The card backs are set in black type against two different shades of yellow and contain the player's personal and statistical information. The set was issued in a specially designed box which carried the complete checklist for the set on the back. Six team logo stickers were also included with the set.

		MT	NR MT	EX
Complete Set:		6.00	4.50	2.50
Common Player:		.05	.04	.02
1	Buddy Bell	.07	.05	.03
2	Bert Blyleven	.10	.08	.04
3	Wade Boggs	.70	.50	.30
4	George Brett	.70	.50	.30
5	Rod Carew	.30	.25	.12
6	Steve Carlton	.25	.20	.10
7	Alvin Davis	.05	.04	.02
8	Andre Dawson	.15	.11	.06
9	Steve Garvey	.25	.20	.10
10	Goose Gossage	.07	.05	.03
11	Tony Gwynn	.20	.15	.07
12	Keith Hernandez	.07	.05	.02
13	Kent Hrbek	.15	.11	.06
14	Reggie Jackson	.30	.25	.12
15	Dave Kingman	.05	.04	.02
16	Ron Kittle	.05	.04	.02
17	Mark Langston	.10	.08	.04
18	Jeff Leonard	.05	.04	.02
19	Bill Madlock	.07	.05	.03
20	Don Mattingly	.70	.50	.30
21	Jack Morris	.15	.11	.06
22	Dale Murphy	.30	.25	.12
23	Eddie Murray	.25	.20	.10
24	Tony Pena	.07	.05	.03
25	Dan Quisenberry	.07	.05	.03
26	Tim Raines	.15	.11	.06
27	Jim Rice	.25	.20	.10
28	Cal Ripken, Jr.	.70	.50	.30
29	Pete Rose	.60	.45	.25
30	Nolan Ryan	1.25	.90	.50
31	Ryne Sandberg	.70	.50	.30
32	Steve Sax	.15	.11	.06
33	Mike Schmidt	.70	.50	.30
34	Tom Seaver	.50	.40	.20
35	Ozzie Smith	.20	.15	.07
36	Mario Soto	.05	.04	.02
37	Dave Stieb	.10	.08	.04
38	Darryl Strawberry	.30	.25	.12
39	Rick Sutcliffe	.10	.08	.04
40	Alan Trammell	.15	.11	.06
41	Willie Upshaw	.05	.04	.02
42	Fernando Valenzuela	.07	.05	.03
43	Dave Winfield	.25	.20	.10
44	Robin Yount	.50	.40	.20

Definitions for grading conditions are located in the Introduction of this price guide.

1986 Fleer

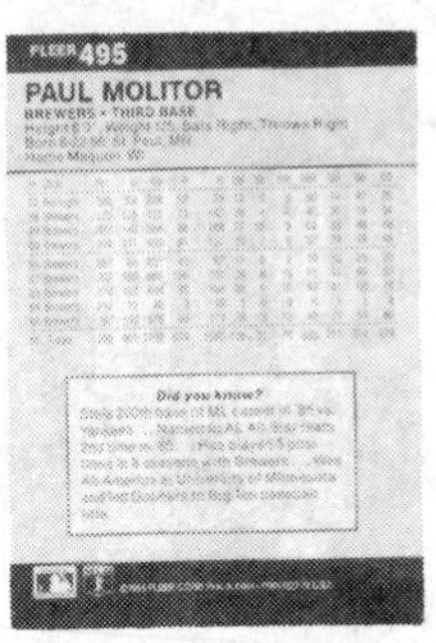

The 1986 Fleer set contains 660 color photos, with each card measuring 2-1/2" by 3-1/2" in size. The card fronts include the word "Fleer," the player's team logo, and a player picture enclosed by a dark blue border. The card reverses are minus the black and white photo that was included in past Fleer efforts. Player biographical and statistical information appear in black and yellow ink on white stock. As in 1985, Fleer devoted ten cards, entitled "Major League Prospects," to twenty promising rookie players. The 1986 set, as in the previous four years was issued with team logo stickers.

		MT	NR MT	EX
Complete Set (660):		125.00	94.00	50.00
Common Player:		.06	.05	.02
1	Steve Balboni	.08	.06	.03
2	Joe Beckwith	.06	.05	.02
3	Buddy Biancalana	.06	.05	.02
4	Bud Black	.06	.05	.02
5	George Brett	2.00	1.50	.80
6	Onix Concepcion	.06	.05	.02
7	Steve Farr	.08	.06	.03
8	Mark Gubicza	.12	.09	.05
9	Dane Iorg	.06	.05	.02
10	Danny Jackson	.20	.15	.08
11	Lynn Jones	.06	.05	.02
12	Mike Jones	.06	.05	.02
13	Charlie Leibrandt	.08	.06	.03
14	Hal McRae	.10	.08	.04
15	Omar Moreno	.06	.05	.02
16	Darryl Motley	.06	.05	.02
17	Jorge Orta	.06	.05	.02
18	Dan Quisenberry	.08	.06	.03
19	Bret Saberhagen	.50	.40	.20
20	Pat Sheridan	.06	.05	.02
21	Lonnie Smith	.08	.06	.03
22	Jim Sundberg	.08	.06	.03
23	John Wathan	.08	.06	.03
24	Frank White	.10	.08	.04
25	Willie Wilson	.12	.09	.05
26	Joaquin Andujar	.08	.06	.03
27	Steve Braun	.06	.05	.02
28	Bill Campbell	.06	.05	.02
29	Cesar Cedeno	.10	.08	.04
30	Jack Clark	.20	.15	.08
31	*Vince Coleman*	.90	.70	.35
32	Danny Cox	.10	.08	.04
33	Ken Dayley	.06	.05	.02
34	Ivan DeJesus	.06	.05	.02
35	Bob Forsch	.08	.06	.03
36	Brian Harper	.06	.05	.02
37	Tom Herr	.10	.08	.04
38	Ricky Horton	.08	.06	.03
39	Kurt Kepshire	.06	.05	.02
40	Jeff Lahti	.06	.05	.02
41	Tito Landrum	.06	.05	.02
42	Willie McGee	.15	.11	.06
43	Tom Nieto	.06	.05	.02
44	Terry Pendleton	.80	.60	.30
45	Darrell Porter	.08	.06	.03
46	Ozzie Smith	1.00	.70	.40
47	John Tudor	.10	.08	.04
48	Andy Van Slyke	.60	.45	.25
49	*Todd Worrell*(FC)	.40	.30	.15
50	Jim Acker	.06	.05	.02
51	Doyle Alexander	.10	.08	.04
52	Jesse Barfield	.20	.15	.08
53	George Bell	.30	.25	.12
54	Jeff Burroughs	.08	.06	.03
55	Bill Caudill	.06	.05	.02
56	Jim Clancy	.08	.06	.03
57	Tony Fernandez	.20	.15	.08
58	Tom Filer	.06	.05	.02
59	Damaso Garcia	.06	.05	.02
60	Tom Henke(FC)	.15	.11	.06
61	Garth Iorg	.06	.05	.02
62	Cliff Johnson	.06	.05	.02
63	Jimmy Key	.50	.40	.20
64	Dennis Lamp	.06	.05	.02
65	Gary Lavelle	.06	.05	.02
66	Buck Martinez	.06	.05	.02
67	Lloyd Moseby	.10	.08	.04
68	Rance Mulliniks	.06	.05	.02
69	Al Oliver	.10	.08	.04
70	Dave Stieb	.12	.09	.05
71	Louis Thornton	.06	.05	.02
72	Willie Upshaw	.08	.06	.03
73	Ernie Whitt	.08	.06	.03
74	*Rick Aguilera*(FC)	1.00	.70	.40
75	Wally Backman	.08	.06	.03
76	Gary Carter	.25	.20	.10
77	Ron Darling	.15	.11	.06
78	*Len Dykstra*(FC)	6.00	4.50	2.50
79	Sid Fernandez	.12	.09	.05
80	George Foster	.15	.11	.06
81	Dwight Gooden	1.50	1.25	.60
82	Tom Gorman	.06	.05	.02
83	Danny Heep	.06	.05	.02
84	Keith Hernandez	.30	.25	.12
85	Howard Johnson	.20	.15	.08
86	Ray Knight	.08	.06	.03
87	Terry Leach	.08	.06	.03
88	Ed Lynch	.06	.05	.02
89	*Roger McDowell*(FC)	.40	.30	.15
90	Jesse Orosco	.08	.06	.03
91	Tom Paciorek	.06	.05	.02
92	Ronn Reynolds	.06	.05	.02
93	Rafael Santana	.06	.05	.02
94	Doug Sisk	.06	.05	.02
95	Rusty Staub	.10	.08	.04
96	Darryl Strawberry	1.25	.90	.50
97	Mookie Wilson	.10	.08	.04
98	Neil Allen	.06	.05	.02
99	Don Baylor	.12	.09	.05
100	Dale Berra	.06	.05	.02
101	Rich Bordi	.06	.05	.02
102	Marty Bystrom	.06	.05	.02
103	Joe Cowley	.06	.05	.02
104	*Brian Fisher*	.15	.11	.06
105	Ken Griffey	.10	.08	.04
106	Ron Guidry	.20	.15	.08
107	Ron Hassey	.06	.05	.02
108	Rickey Henderson	2.00	1.50	.80
109	Don Mattingly	2.50	2.00	1.00
110	Bobby Meacham	.06	.05	.02
111	John Montefusco	.06	.05	.02
112	Phil Niekro	.25	.20	.10
113	Mike Pagliarulo	.20	.15	.08
114	Dan Pasqua	.08	.06	.03
115	Willie Randolph	.10	.08	.04
116	Dave Righetti	.08	.06	.03
117	Andre Robertson	.06	.05	.02
118	Billy Sample	.06	.05	.02
119	Bob Shirley	.06	.05	.02
120	Ed Whitson	.06	.05	.02
121	Dave Winfield	1.50	1.25	.60
122	Butch Wynegar	.06	.05	.02
123	Dave Anderson	.06	.05	.02
124	Bob Bailor	.06	.05	.02
125	Greg Brock	.08	.06	.03
126	Enos Cabell	.06	.05	.02
127	Bobby Castillo	.06	.05	.02
128	Carlos Diaz	.06	.05	.02
129	*Mariano Duncan*	.15	.11	.06
130	Pedro Guerrero	.08	.06	.03
131	Orel Hershiser	.30	.25	.12
132	Rick Honeycutt	.06	.05	.02
133	Ken Howell	.06	.05	.02
134	Ken Landreaux	.06	.05	.02
135	Bill Madlock	.12	.09	.05
136	Candy Maldonado	.10	.08	.04
137	Mike Marshall	.15	.11	.06
138	Len Matuszek	.06	.05	.02
139	Tom Niedenfuer	.08	.06	.03
140	Alejandro Pena	.08	.06	.03
141	Jerry Reuss	.08	.06	.03
142	Bill Russell	.08	.06	.03

		MT	NR MT	EX
143	Steve Sax	.20	.15	.08
144	Mike Scioscia	.08	.06	.03
145	Fernando Valenzuela	.10	.08	.04
146	Bob Welch	.12	.09	.05
147	Terry Whitfield	.06	.05	.02
148	Juan Beniquez	.06	.05	.02
149	Bob Boone	.08	.06	.03
150	John Candelaria	.10	.08	.04
151	Rod Carew	.70	.50	.30
152	*Stewart Cliburn*(FC)	.08	.06	.03
153	Doug DeCinces	.10	.08	.04
154	Brian Downing	.08	.06	.03
155	Ken Forsch	.06	.05	.02
156	Craig Gerber	.06	.05	.02
157	Bobby Grich	.10	.08	.04
158	George Hendrick	.08	.06	.03
159	Al Holland	.06	.05	.02
160	Reggie Jackson	1.25	.90	.50
161	Ruppert Jones	.06	.05	.02
162	*Urbano Lugo*	.08	.06	.03
163	*Kirk McCaskill*(FC)	.35	.25	.14
164	Donnie Moore	.06	.05	.02
165	Gary Pettis	.06	.05	.02
166	Ron Romanick	.06	.05	.02
167	Dick Schofield	.06	.05	.02
168	Daryl Sconiers	.06	.05	.02
169	Jim Slaton	.06	.05	.02
170	Don Sutton	.25	.20	.10
171	Mike Witt	.10	.08	.04
172	Buddy Bell	.10	.08	.04
173	Tom Browning	.30	.25	.12
174	Dave Concepcion	.12	.09	.05
175	Eric Davis	1.00	.70	.40
176	Bo Diaz	.08	.06	.03
177	Nick Esasky	.08	.06	.03
178	John Franco	.12	.09	.05
179	Tom Hume	.06	.05	.02
180	Wayne Krenchicki	.06	.05	.02
181	Andy McGaffigan	.06	.05	.02
182	Eddie Milner	.06	.05	.02
183	Ron Oester	.06	.05	.02
184	Dave Parker	.20	.15	.08
185	Frank Pastore	.06	.05	.02
186	Tony Perez	.15	.11	.06
187	Ted Power	.08	.06	.03
188	Joe Price	.06	.05	.02
189	Gary Redus	.06	.05	.02
190	Ron Robinson	.08	.06	.03
191	Pete Rose	.70	.50	.30
192	Mario Soto	.08	.06	.03
193	John Stuper	.06	.05	.02
194	Jay Tibbs	.06	.05	.02
195	Dave Van Gorder	.06	.05	.02
196	Max Venable	.06	.05	.02
197	Juan Agosto	.06	.05	.02
198	Harold Baines	.15	.11	.06
199	Floyd Bannister	.10	.08	.04
200	Britt Burns	.06	.05	.02
201	Julio Cruz	.06	.05	.02
202	*Joel Davis*(FC)	.08	.06	.03
203	Richard Dotson	.10	.08	.04
204	Carlton Fisk	.50	.40	.20
205	Scott Fletcher	.08	.06	.03
206	*Ozzie Guillen*	.80	.60	.30
207	Jerry Hairston	.06	.05	.02
208	Tim Hulett	.08	.06	.03
209	Bob James	.06	.05	.02
210	Ron Kittle	.10	.08	.04
211	Rudy Law	.06	.05	.02
212	Bryan Little	.06	.05	.02
213	Gene Nelson	.06	.05	.02
214	Reid Nichols	.06	.05	.02
215	Luis Salazar	.06	.05	.02
216	Tom Seaver	1.00	.70	.40
217	Dan Spillner	.06	.05	.02
218	Bruce Tanner	.06	.05	.02
219	Greg Walker	.10	.08	.04
220	Dave Wehrmeister	.06	.05	.02
221	Juan Berenguer	.06	.05	.02
222	Dave Bergman	.06	.05	.02
223	Tom Brookens	.06	.05	.02
224	Darrell Evans	.12	.09	.05
225	Barbaro Garbey	.06	.05	.02
226	Kirk Gibson	.30	.25	.12
227	John Grubb	.06	.05	.02
228	Willie Hernandez	.08	.06	.03
229	Larry Herndon	.08	.06	.03
230	Chet Lemon	.08	.06	.03
231	Aurelio Lopez	.06	.05	.02
232	Jack Morris	.20	.15	.08
233	Randy O'Neal	.06	.05	.02
234	Lance Parrish	.08	.06	.03
235	Dan Petry	.08	.06	.03
236	Alex Sanchez	.06	.05	.02
237	Bill Scherrer	.06	.05	.02
238	Nelson Simmons	.06	.05	.02
239	Frank Tanana	.10	.08	.04
240	Walt Terrell	.08	.06	.03
241	Alan Trammell	.30	.25	.12
242	Lou Whitaker	.30	.25	.12
243	Milt Wilcox	.06	.05	.02
244	Hubie Brooks	.10	.08	.04
245	*Tim Burke*(FC)	.30	.25	.12
246	Andre Dawson	.30	.25	.12
247	Mike Fitzgerald	.06	.05	.02
248	Terry Francona	.06	.05	.02
249	Bill Gullickson	.06	.05	.02
250	Joe Hesketh	.06	.05	.02
251	Bill Laskey	.06	.05	.02
252	Vance Law	.08	.06	.03
253	Charlie Lea	.06	.05	.02
254	Gary Lucas	.06	.05	.02
255	David Palmer	.06	.05	.02
256	Tim Raines	.30	.25	.12
257	Jeff Reardon	.12	.09	.05
258	Bert Roberge	.06	.05	.02
259	Dan Schatzeder	.06	.05	.02
260	Bryn Smith	.06	.05	.02
261	Randy St. Claire(FC)	.08	.06	.03
262	Scot Thompson	.06	.05	.02
263	Tim Wallach	.12	.09	.05
264	U.L. Washington	.06	.05	.02
265	*Mitch Webster*(FC)	.08	.06	.03
266	*Herm Winningham*	.06	.05	.02
267	*Floyd Youmans*(FC)	.06	.05	.02
268	Don Aase	.06	.05	.02
269	Mike Boddicker	.08	.06	.03
270	Rich Dauer	.06	.05	.02
271	Storm Davis	.10	.08	.04
272	Rick Dempsey	.08	.06	.03
273	Ken Dixon	.06	.05	.02
274	Jim Dwyer	.06	.05	.02
275	Mike Flanagan	.10	.08	.04
276	Wayne Gross	.06	.05	.02
277	Lee Lacy	.06	.05	.02
278	Fred Lynn	.10	.08	.04
279	Tippy Martinez	.06	.05	.02
280	Dennis Martinez	.08	.06	.03
281	Scott McGregor	.08	.06	.03
282	Eddie Murray	1.00	.70	.40
283	Floyd Rayford	.06	.05	.02
284	Cal Ripken, Jr.	5.00	3.75	2.00
285	Gary Roenicke	.06	.05	.02
286	Larry Sheets	.08	.06	.03
287	John Shelby	.06	.05	.02
288	Nate Snell	.06	.05	.02
289	Sammy Stewart	.06	.05	.02
290	Alan Wiggins	.06	.05	.02
291	Mike Young	.06	.05	.02
292	Alan Ashby	.06	.05	.02
293	Mark Bailey	.06	.05	.02
294	Kevin Bass	.10	.08	.04
295	Jeff Calhoun	.06	.05	.02
296	Jose Cruz	.10	.08	.04
297	Glenn Davis	.20	.15	.08
298	Bill Dawley	.06	.05	.02
299	Frank DiPino	.06	.05	.02
300	Bill Doran	.10	.08	.04
301	Phil Garner	.08	.06	.03
302	*Jeff Heathcock*(FC)	.06	.05	.02
303	*Charlie Kerfeld*(FC)	.06	.05	.02
304	Bob Knepper	.08	.06	.03
305	Ron Mathis	.06	.05	.02
306	Jerry Mumphrey	.06	.05	.02
307	Jim Pankovits	.06	.05	.02
308	Terry Puhl	.06	.05	.02
309	Craig Reynolds	.06	.05	.02
310	Nolan Ryan	6.00	4.50	2.50
311	Mike Scott	.15	.11	.06
312	Dave Smith	.08	.06	.03
313	Dickie Thon	.08	.06	.03
314	Denny Walling	.06	.05	.02
315	Kurt Bevacqua	.06	.05	.02
316	Al Bumbry	.06	.05	.02
317	Jerry Davis	.06	.05	.02
318	Luis DeLeon	.06	.05	.02
319	Dave Dravecky	.08	.06	.03
320	Tim Flannery	.06	.05	.02
321	Steve Garvey	.30	.25	.12
322	Goose Gossage	.20	.15	.08
323	Tony Gwynn	3.00	2.25	1.25
324	Andy Hawkins	.06	.05	.02

		MT	NR MT	EX
325	LaMarr Hoyt	.06	.05	.02
326	Roy Lee Jackson	.06	.05	.02
327	Terry Kennedy	.08	.06	.03
328	Craig Lefferts	.06	.05	.02
329	Carmelo Martinez	.08	.06	.03
330	*Lance McCullers*(FC)	.25	.20	.10
331	Kevin McReynolds	.12	.09	.05
332	Graig Nettles	.15	.11	.06
333	Jerry Royster	.06	.05	.02
334	Eric Show	.08	.06	.03
335	Tim Stoddard	.06	.05	.02
336	Garry Templeton	.08	.06	.03
337	Mark Thurmond	.06	.05	.02
338	Ed Wojna	.06	.05	.02
339	Tony Armas	.08	.06	.03
340	Marty Barrett	.10	.08	.04
341	Wade Boggs	2.25	1.75	.90
342	Dennis Boyd	.08	.06	.03
343	Bill Buckner	.12	.09	.05
344	Mark Clear	.06	.05	.02
345	Roger Clemens	9.00	6.75	3.50
346	Steve Crawford	.06	.05	.02
347	Mike Easler	.08	.06	.03
348	Dwight Evans	.12	.09	.05
349	Rich Gedman	.10	.08	.04
350	Jackie Gutierrez	.06	.05	.02
351	Glenn Hoffman	.06	.05	.02
352	Bruce Hurst	.12	.09	.05
353	Bruce Kison	.06	.05	.02
354	Tim Lollar	.06	.05	.02
355	Steve Lyons	.08	.06	.03
356	Al Nipper	.08	.06	.03
357	Bob Ojeda	.08	.06	.03
358	Jim Rice	.12	.09	.05
359	Bob Stanley	.06	.05	.02
360	Mike Trujillo	.06	.05	.02
361	Thad Bosley	.06	.05	.02
362	Warren Brusstar	.06	.05	.02
363	Ron Cey	.10	.08	.04
364	Jody Davis	.10	.08	.04
365	Bob Dernier	.06	.05	.02
366	Shawon Dunston	.15	.11	.06
367	Leon Durham	.08	.06	.03
368	Dennis Eckersley	.20	.15	.08
369	Ray Fontenot	.06	.05	.02
370	George Frazier	.06	.05	.02
371	Bill Hatcher	.10	.08	.04
372	Dave Lopes	.08	.06	.03
373	Gary Matthews	.10	.08	.04
374	Ron Meredith	.06	.05	.02
375	Keith Moreland	.08	.06	.03
376	Reggie Patterson	.06	.05	.02
377	Dick Ruthven	.06	.05	.02
378	Ryne Sandberg	4.00	3.00	1.50
379	Scott Sanderson	.06	.05	.02
380	Lee Smith	.50	.40	.20
381	Lary Sorensen	.06	.05	.02
382	Chris Speier	.06	.05	.02
383	Rick Sutcliffe	.12	.09	.05
384	Steve Trout	.06	.05	.02
385	Gary Woods	.06	.05	.02
386	Bert Blyleven	.15	.11	.06
387	Tom Brunansky	.12	.09	.05
388	Randy Bush	.06	.05	.02
389	John Butcher	.06	.05	.02
390	Ron Davis	.06	.05	.02
391	Dave Engle	.06	.05	.02
392	Frank Eufemia	.06	.05	.02
393	Pete Filson	.06	.05	.02
394	Gary Gaetti	.20	.15	.08
395	Greg Gagne	.10	.08	.04
396	Mickey Hatcher	.06	.05	.02
397	Kent Hrbek	.20	.15	.08
398	Tim Laudner	.06	.05	.02
399	Rick Lysander	.06	.05	.02
400	Dave Meier	.06	.05	.02
401	Kirby Puckett	10.00	7.50	4.00
402	Mark Salas	.08	.06	.03
403	Ken Schrom	.06	.05	.02
404	Roy Smalley	.06	.05	.02
405	Mike Smithson	.06	.05	.02
406	Mike Stenhouse	.06	.05	.02
407	Tim Teufel	.06	.05	.02
408	Frank Viola	.15	.11	.06
409	Ron Washington	.06	.05	.02
410	Keith Atherton	.06	.05	.02
411	Dusty Baker	.08	.06	.03
412	*Tim Birtsas*	.12	.09	.05
413	Bruce Bochte	.06	.05	.02
414	Chris Codiroli	.06	.05	.02
415	Dave Collins	.08	.06	.03

		MT	NR MT	EX
416	Mike Davis	.08	.06	.03
417	Alfredo Griffin	.08	.06	.03
418	Mike Heath	.06	.05	.02
419	Steve Henderson	.06	.05	.02
420	Donnie Hill	.06	.05	.02
421	Jay Howell	.08	.06	.03
422	Tommy John	.20	.15	.08
423	Dave Kingman	.15	.11	.06
424	Bill Krueger	.06	.05	.02
425	Rick Langford	.06	.05	.02
426	Carney Lansford	.10	.08	.04
427	Steve McCatty	.06	.05	.02
428	Dwayne Murphy	.06	.05	.02
429	*Steve Ontiveros*(FC)	.06	.05	.02
430	Tony Phillips	.06	.05	.02
431	Jose Rijo	.25	.20	.10
432	*Mickey Tettleton*	4.00	3.00	1.50
433	Luis Aguayo	.06	.05	.02
434	Larry Andersen	.06	.05	.02
435	Steve Carlton	.30	.25	.12
436	*Don Carman*	.10	.08	.04
437	Tim Corcoran	.06	.05	.02
438	*Darren Daulton*	5.00	3.75	2.00
439	John Denny	.06	.05	.02
440	Tom Foley	.06	.05	.02
441	Greg Gross	.06	.05	.02
442	Kevin Gross	.08	.06	.03
443	Von Hayes	.10	.08	.04
444	Charles Hudson	.06	.05	.02
445	Garry Maddox	.08	.06	.03
446	Shane Rawley	.10	.08	.04
447	Dave Rucker	.06	.05	.02
448	John Russell	.06	.05	.02
449	Juan Samuel	.12	.09	.05
450	Mike Schmidt	2.00	1.50	.80
451	Rick Schu	.08	.06	.03
452	Dave Shipanoff	.06	.05	.02
453	Dave Stewart	.12	.09	.05
454	Jeff Stone	.06	.05	.02
455	Kent Tekulve	.08	.06	.03
456	Ozzie Virgil	.06	.05	.02
457	Glenn Wilson	.08	.06	.03
458	Jim Beattie	.06	.05	.02
459	Karl Best	.06	.05	.02
460	Barry Bonnell	.06	.05	.02
461	Phil Bradley	.08	.06	.03
462	*Ivan Calderon*	.25	.20	.10
463	Al Cowens	.06	.05	.02
464	Alvin Davis	.06	.05	.02
465	Dave Henderson	.10	.08	.04
466	Bob Kearney	.06	.05	.02
467	Mark Langston	.30	.25	.12
468	Bob Long	.06	.05	.02
469	Mike Moore	.06	.05	.02
470	Edwin Nunez	.06	.05	.02
471	Spike Owen	.06	.05	.02
472	Jack Perconte	.06	.05	.02
473	Jim Presley	.06	.05	.02
474	Donnie Scott	.06	.05	.02
475	Bill Swift(FC)	.12	.09	.05
476	Danny Tartabull	2.00	1.50	.80
477	Gorman Thomas	.06	.05	.02
478	Roy Thomas	.06	.05	.02
479	Ed Vande Berg	.06	.05	.02
480	Frank Wills	.06	.05	.02
481	Matt Young	.06	.05	.02
482	Ray Burris	.06	.05	.02
483	Jaime Cocanower	.06	.05	.02
484	Cecil Cooper	.12	.09	.05
485	Danny Darwin	.06	.05	.02
486	Rollie Fingers	.20	.15	.08
487	Jim Gantner	.08	.06	.03
488	Bob L. Gibson	.06	.05	.02
489	Moose Haas	.06	.05	.02
490	*Teddy Higuera*	.10	.08	.04
491	Paul Householder	.06	.05	.02
492	Pete Ladd	.06	.05	.02
493	Rick Manning	.06	.05	.02
494	Bob McClure	.06	.05	.02
495	Paul Molitor	1.25	.90	.50
496	Charlie Moore	.06	.05	.02
497	Ben Oglivie	.08	.06	.03
498	Randy Ready	.06	.05	.02
499	*Earnie Riles*	.08	.06	.03
500	Ed Romero	.06	.05	.02
501	Bill Schroeder	.06	.05	.02
502	Ray Searage	.06	.05	.02
503	Ted Simmons	.12	.09	.05
504	Pete Vuckovich	.08	.06	.03
505	Rick Waits	.06	.05	.02
506	Robin Yount	2.00	1.50	.80

		MT	NR MT	EX
507	Len Barker	.08	.06	.03
508	Steve Bedrosian	.12	.09	.05
509	Bruce Benedict	.06	.05	.02
510	Rick Camp	.06	.05	.02
511	Rick Cerone	.06	.05	.02
512	Chris Chambliss	.08	.06	.03
513	Jeff Dedmon	.06	.05	.02
514	Terry Forster	.08	.06	.03
515	Gene Garber	.06	.05	.02
516	Terry Harper	.06	.05	.02
517	Bob Horner	.12	.09	.05
518	Glenn Hubbard	.06	.05	.02
519	*Joe Johnson*(FC)	.06	.05	.02
520	Brad Komminsk	.06	.05	.02
521	Rick Mahler	.06	.05	.02
522	Dale Murphy	.35	.25	.14
523	Ken Oberkfell	.06	.05	.02
524	Pascual Perez	.08	.06	.03
525	Gerald Perry	.12	.09	.05
526	Rafael Ramirez	.06	.05	.02
527	*Steve Shields*(FC)	.12	.09	.05
528	Zane Smith	.10	.08	.04
529	Bruce Sutter	.12	.09	.05
530	*Milt Thompson*(FC)	.15	.11	.06
531	Claudell Washington	.08	.06	.03
532	Paul Zuvella	.06	.05	.02
533	Vida Blue	.10	.08	.04
534	Bob Brenly	.06	.05	.02
535	*Chris Brown*	.06	.05	.02
536	Chili Davis	.10	.08	.04
537	Mark Davis	.06	.05	.02
538	Rob Deer	.12	.09	.05
539	Dan Driessen	.08	.06	.03
540	Scott Garrelts	.08	.06	.03
541	Dan Gladden	.08	.06	.03
542	Jim Gott	.06	.05	.02
543	David Green	.06	.05	.02
544	Atlee Hammaker	.06	.05	.02
545	Mike Jeffcoat	.06	.05	.02
546	Mike Krukow	.08	.06	.03
547	Dave LaPoint	.08	.06	.03
548	Jeff Leonard	.08	.06	.03
549	Greg Minton	.06	.05	.02
550	Alex Trevino	.06	.05	.02
551	Manny Trillo	.08	.06	.03
552	*Jose Uribe*	.06	.05	.02
553	Brad Wellman	.06	.05	.02
554	Frank Williams	.06	.05	.02
555	Joel Youngblood	.06	.05	.02
556	Alan Bannister	.06	.05	.02
557	Glenn Brummer	.06	.05	.02
558	*Steve Buechele*(FC)	.20	.15	.08
559	*Jose Guzman*(FC)	.20	.15	.08
560	Toby Harrah	.08	.06	.03
561	Greg Harris	.06	.05	.02
562	*Dwayne Henry*(FC)	.10	.08	.04
563	Burt Hooton	.08	.06	.03
564	Charlie Hough	.08	.06	.03
565	Mike Mason	.06	.05	.02
566	*Oddibe McDowell*	.10	.08	.04
567	Dickie Noles	.06	.05	.02
568	Pete O'Brien	.10	.08	.04
569	Larry Parrish	.10	.08	.04
570	Dave Rozema	.06	.05	.02
571	Dave Schmidt	.06	.05	.02
572	Don Slaught	.06	.05	.02
573	Wayne Tolleson	.06	.05	.02
574	Duane Walker	.06	.05	.02
575	Gary Ward	.08	.06	.03
576	Chris Welsh	.06	.05	.02
577	Curtis Wilkerson	.06	.05	.02
578	George Wright	.06	.05	.02
579	Chris Bando	.06	.05	.02
580	Tony Bernazard	.06	.05	.02
581	Brett Butler	.08	.06	.03
582	Ernie Camacho	.06	.05	.02
583	Joe Carter	3.00	2.25	1.25
584	Carmello Castillo (Carmelo)	.06	.05	.02
585	Jamie Easterly	.06	.05	.02
586	Julio Franco	.10	.08	.04
587	Mel Hall	.08	.06	.03
588	Mike Hargrove	.06	.05	.02
589	Neal Heaton	.06	.05	.02
590	Brook Jacoby	.10	.08	.04
591	*Otis Nixon*(FC)	.60	.45	.25
592	Jerry Reed	.06	.05	.02
593	Vern Ruhle	.06	.05	.02
594	Pat Tabler	.08	.06	.03
595	Rich Thompson	.06	.05	.02
596	Andre Thornton	.08	.06	.03
597	Dave Von Ohlen	.06	.05	.02

		MT	NR MT	EX
598	George Vukovich	.06	.05	.02
599	Tom Waddell	.06	.05	.02
600	Curt Wardle	.06	.05	.02
601	Jerry Willard	.06	.05	.02
602	Bill Almon	.06	.05	.02
603	Mike Bielecki	.08	.06	.03
604	Sid Bream	.10	.08	.04
605	Mike Brown	.06	.05	.02
606	*Pat Clements*	.12	.09	.05
607	Jose DeLeon	.08	.06	.03
608	Denny Gonzalez	.06	.05	.02
609	Cecilio Guante	.06	.05	.02
610	Steve Kemp	.08	.06	.03
611	Sam Khalifa	.06	.05	.02
612	Lee Mazzilli	.08	.06	.03
613	Larry McWilliams	.06	.05	.02
614	Jim Morrison	.06	.05	.02
615	*Joe Orsulak*	.25	.20	.10
616	Tony Pena	.10	.08	.04
617	Johnny Ray	.10	.08	.04
618	Rick Reuschel	.10	.08	.04
619	R.J. Reynolds	.08	.06	.03
620	Rick Rhoden	.10	.08	.04
621	Don Robinson	.08	.06	.03
622	Jason Thompson	.06	.05	.02
623	Lee Tunnell	.06	.05	.02
624	Jim Winn	.06	.05	.02
625	Marvell Wynne	.06	.05	.02
626	Dwight Gooden (IA)	.50	.40	.20
627	Don Mattingly (IA)	1.25	.90	.50
628	Pete Rose (4,192 hits)	.50	.40	.20
629	Rod Carew (3,000 Hits)	.50	.40	.20
630	Phil Niekro, Tom Seaver (300 Wins)	.20	.15	.08
631	Ouch! (Don Baylor)	.08	.06	.03
632	Instant Offense (Tim Raines, Darryl Strawberry)	.30	.25	.12
633	Shortstops Supreme (Cal Ripken, Jr., Alan Trammell)	1.00	.70	.40
634	Boggs & "Hero" (Wade Boggs, George Brett)	1.00	.70	.40
635	Braves Dynamic Duo (Bob Horner, Dale Murphy)	.30	.25	.12
636	Cardinal Ignitors (Vince Coleman, Willie McGee)	.35	.25	.14
637	Terror on the Basepaths (Vince Coleman)	.20	.15	.08
638	Charlie Hustle & Dr. K (Dwight Gooden, Pete Rose)	.70	.50	.30
639	1984 and 1985 A.L. Batting Champs (Wade Boggs, Don Mattingly)	1.00	.70	.40
640	N.L. West Sluggers (Steve Garvey, Dale Murphy, Dave Parker)	.30	.25	.12
641	Staff Aces (Dwight Gooden, Fernando Valenzuela)	.40	.30	.15
642	Blue Jay Stoppers (Jimmy Key, Dave Stieb)	.10	.08	.04
643	A.L. All-Star Backstops (Carlton Fisk, Rich Gedman)	.10	.08	.04
644	Major League Prospect *(Benito Santiago, Gene Walter)*(FC)	2.00	1.50	.80
645	Major League Prospect *(Colin Ward, Mike Woodard)*(FC)	.10	.08	.04
646	Major League Prospect *(Kal Daniels, Paul O'Neill)*	2.00	1.50	.80
647	Major League Prospect *(Andres Galarraga, Fred Toliver)*	4.00	3.00	1.50
648	Major League Prospect *(Curt Ford, Bob Kipper)*(FC)	.25	.20	.10
649	Major League Prospect *(Jose Canseco, Eric Plunk)*	18.00	13.50	7.25
650	Major League Prospect *(Mark McLemore, Gus Polidor)*(FC)	.15	.11	.06
651	Major League Prospect *(Mickey Brantley, Rob Woodward)*(FC)	.15	.11	.06
652	Major League Prospect *(Mark Funderburk, Billy Joe Robidoux)*(FC)	.10	.08	.04
653	Major League Prospect *(Cecil Fielder, Cory Snyder)*	21.00	15.50	8.50
654	Checklist 1-97	.06	.05	.02
655	Checklist 98-196	.06	.05	.02
656	Checklist 197-291	.06	.05	.02
657	Checklist 292-385	.06	.05	.02
658	Checklist 386-482	.06	.05	.02
659	Checklist 483-578	.06	.05	.02
660	Checklist 579-660	.06	.05	.02

A card number in parentheses () indicates the set is unnumbered.

1986 Fleer All Stars

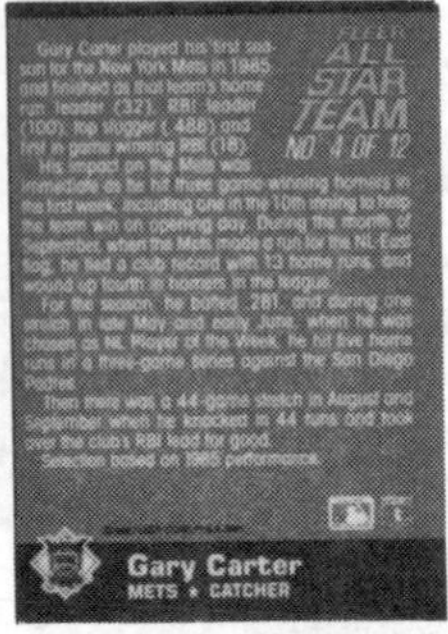

Fleer's choices for a major league All-Star team make up this 12-card set. The cards, which measure 2-1/2" by 3-1/2", were randomly inserted in 35¢ wax packs and 59¢ cello packs. The card fronts have a color photo set against a bright red background for A.L. players or a bright blue background for N.L. players. The card backs feature the player's career highlights set in white type against a red and blue background.

		MT	NR MT	EX
Complete Set (12):		22.00	15.00	8.00
Common Player:		.25	.15	.10
1	Don Mattingly	6.00	3.00	1.50
2	Tom Herr	.25	.15	.10
3	George Brett	4.00	3.00	1.50
4	Gary Carter	.75	.50	.25
5	Cal Ripken, Jr.	8.00	6.00	3.00
6	Dave Parker	.75	.60	.30
7	Rickey Henderson	3.00	2.25	1.25
8	Pedro Guerrero	.25	.15	.10
9	Dan Quisenberry	.60	.45	.25
10	Dwight Gooden	.75	.50	.25
11	Gorman Thomas	.25	.15	.10
12	John Tudor	.25	.15	.10

1986 Fleer Future Hall Of Famers

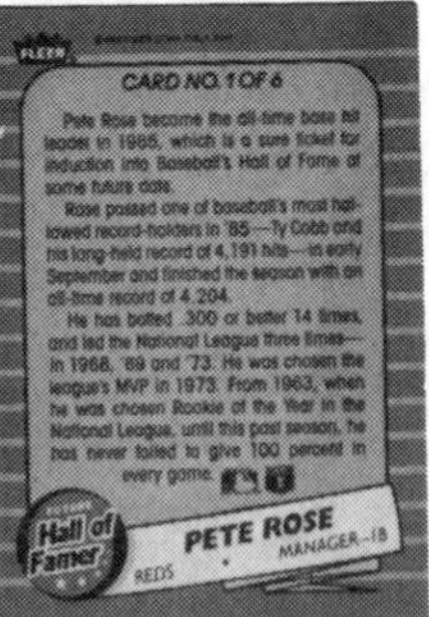

The 1986 Fleer Future Hall of Famers set is comprised of six players Fleer felt would gain eventual entrance into the Baseball Hall of Fame. The cards are the standard 2-1/2" by 3-1/2" in size and were randomly inserted in three-pack cello packs. The card fronts feature a player photo set against a blue background with horizontal light blue stripes. The card backs are printed in black on a blue background and feature player highlights in paragraph form.

		MT	NR MT	EX
Complete Set (6):		15.00	10.00	5.00
Common Player:		1.75	1.25	.70
1	Pete Rose	2.00	1.50	.75
2	Steve Carlton	1.75	1.25	.70
3	Tom Seaver	1.75	1.25	.70
4	Rod Carew	1.75	1.25	.70
5	Nolan Ryan	9.00	6.00	3.00
6	Reggie Jackson	1.75	1.25	.70

1986 Fleer Box Panels

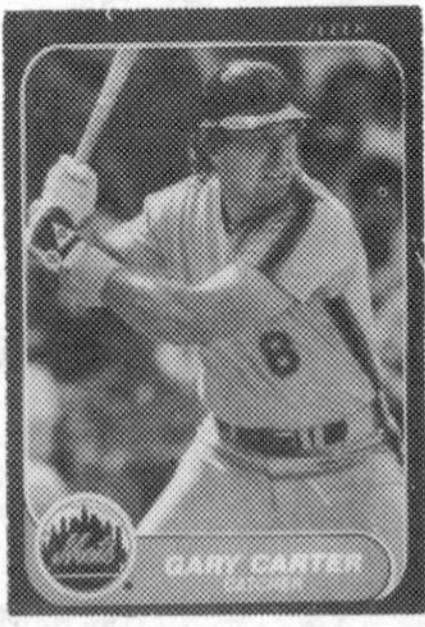

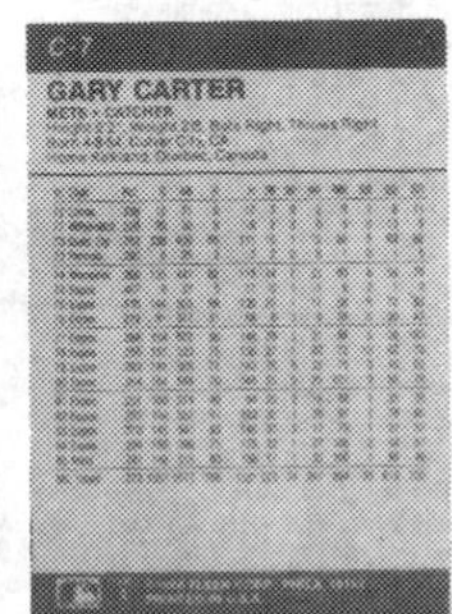

Picking up on a Donruss idea, Fleer issued eight cards in panels of four on the bottoms of the wax and cello pack boxes. The cards are numbered C-1 through C-8 and are 2-1/2" by 3-1/2", with a complete panel measuring 5" by 7-1/8" in size. Included in the eight cards are six player cards and two team logo/checklist cards.

		MT	NR MT	EX
Complete Panel Set:		3.50	2.75	1.50
Complete Singles Set:		1.75	1.25	.70
Common Single Player:		.20	.15	.08
	Panel	2.50	2.00	1.00
1	Royals Logo/Checklist	.05	.04	.02
2	George Brett	.90	.70	.35
3	Ozzie Guillen	.40	.30	.15
4	Dale Murphy	.40	.30	.15
	Panel	1.50	1.25	.60
5	Cardinals Logo/Checklist	.05	.04	.02
6	Tom Browning	.20	.15	.08
7	Gary Carter	.35	.25	.14
8	Carlton Fisk	.20	.15	.08

1986 Fleer Update

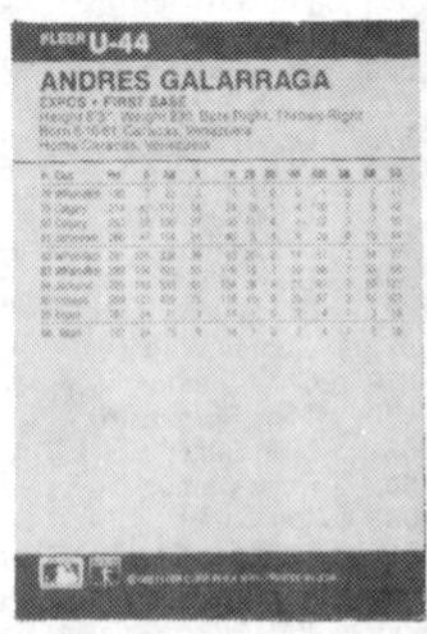

Issued near the end of the baseball season, the 1986 Fleer Update set consists of 132 cards numbered U-1 through U-132. The cards, which measure 2-1/2" by 3-1/2" in size, are identical in design to the regular 1986 Fleer set. The purpose of the set is to update player trades and include new players not depicted in the regular issue. The set was issued with team logo stickers in a specially designed box and was available only through hobby dealers.

		MT	NR MT	EX
Complete Set (132):		30.00	22.00	12.00
Common Player:		.08	.06	.03
1	Mike Aldrete(FC)	.08	.06	.03
2	Andy Allanson(FC)	.08	.06	.03
3	Neil Allen	.08	.06	.03
4	Joaquin Andujar	.08	.06	.03
5	Paul Assenmacher(FC)	.20	.15	.08
6	Scott Bailes(FC)	.08	.06	.03
7	Jay Baller(FC)	.08	.06	.03
8	Scott Bankhead(FC)	.20	.15	.08
9	Bill Bathe(FC)	.08	.06	.03
10	Don Baylor	.15	.11	.06
11	Billy Beane(FC)	.08	.06	.03
12	Steve Bedrosian	.15	.11	.06
13	Juan Beniquez	.08	.06	.03
14	Barry Bonds(FC)	15.00	11.00	6.00
15	Bobby Bonilla(FC)	3.00	2.25	1.25
16	Rich Bordi	.08	.06	.03
17	Bill Campbell	.08	.06	.03
18	Tom Candiotti	.08	.06	.03
19	John Cangelosi(FC)	.08	.06	.03
20	Jose Canseco	4.00	3.00	1.50
21	Chuck Cary(FC)	.08	.06	.03
22	Juan Castillo(FC)	.08	.06	.03
23	Rick Cerone	.08	.06	.03
24	John Cerutti(FC)	.10	.08	.04
25	Will Clark(FC)	8.00	6.00	3.25
26	Mark Clear	.08	.06	.03
27	Darnell Coles(FC)	.15	.11	.06
28	Dave Collins	.10	.08	.04
29	Tim Conroy	.08	.06	.03
30	Ed Correa(FC)	.08	.06	.03
31	Joe Cowley	.08	.06	.03
32	Bill Dawley	.08	.06	.03
33	Rob Deer	.08	.06	.03
34	John Denny	.08	.06	.03
35	Jim DeShaies	.25	.20	.10
36	Doug Drabek(FC)	1.25	.90	.50
37	Mike Easler	.12	.09	.05
38	Mark Eichhorn(FC)	.12	.09	.05
39	Dave Engle	.08	.06	.03
40	Mike Fischlin	.08	.06	.03
41	Scott Fletcher	.15	.11	.06
42	Terry Forster	.12	.09	.05
43	Terry Francona	.08	.06	.03
44	Andres Galarraga	2.50	2.00	1.00
45	Lee Guetterman(FC)	.20	.15	.08
46	Bill Gullickson	.08	.06	.03
47	Jackie Gutierrez	.08	.06	.03
48	Moose Haas	.08	.06	.03
49	Billy Hatcher	.15	.11	.06
50	Mike Heath	.08	.06	.03
51	Guy Hoffman(FC)	.08	.06	.03
52	Tom Hume	.08	.06	.03
53	Pete Incaviglia(FC)	1.00	.70	.40
54	Dane Iorg	.08	.06	.03
55	Chris James(FC)	.08	.06	.03
56	Stan Javier(FC)	.12	.09	.05
57	Tommy John	.20	.15	.08
58	Tracy Jones(FC)	.08	.06	.03
59	Wally Joyner(FC)	1.50	1.25	.60
60	Wayne Krenchicki	.08	.06	.03
61	John Kruk(FC)	2.00	1.50	.80
62	Mike LaCoss	.08	.06	.03
63	Pete Ladd	.08	.06	.03
64	Dave LaPoint	.08	.06	.03
65	Mike LaValliere(FC)	.20	.15	.08
66	Rudy Law	.08	.06	.03
67	Dennis Leonard	.10	.08	.04
68	Steve Lombardozzi(FC)	.08	.06	.03
69	Aurelio Lopez	.08	.06	.03
70	Mickey Mahler	.08	.06	.03
71	Candy Maldonado	.08	.06	.03
72	Roger Mason(FC)	.10	.08	.04
73	Greg Mathews(FC)	.10	.08	.04
74	Andy McGaffigan	.08	.06	.03
75	Joel McKeon(FC)	.08	.06	.03
76	Kevin Mitchell(FC)	2.00	1.50	.80
77	Bill Mooneyham(FC)	.08	.06	.03
78	Omar Moreno	.08	.06	.03
79	Jerry Mumphrey	.08	.06	.03
80	Al Newman(FC)	.12	.09	.05
81	Phil Niekro	.25	.20	.10
82	Randy Niemann	.08	.06	.03
83	Juan Nieves(FC)	.08	.06	.03
84	Bob Ojeda	.12	.09	.05
85	Rick Ownbey	.08	.06	.03
86	Tom Paciorek	.08	.06	.03
87	David Palmer	.08	.06	.03
88	Jeff Parrett(FC)	.08	.06	.03
89	Pat Perry(FC)	.08	.06	.03
90	Dan Plesac(FC)	.12	.09	.05
91	Darrell Porter	.12	.09	.05
92	Luis Quinones(FC)	.08	.06	.03
93	Rey Quinonez(FC)	.08	.06	.03
94	Gary Redus	.10	.08	.04
95	Jeff Reed(FC)	.08	.06	.03
96	Bip Roberts(FC)	.60	.45	.25
97	Billy Joe Robidoux	.12	.09	.05
98	Gary Roenicke	.08	.06	.03
99	Ron Roenicke	.08	.06	.03
100	Angel Salazar	.08	.06	.03
101	Joe Sambito	.08	.06	.03
102	Billy Sample	.08	.06	.03
103	Dave Schmidt	.08	.06	.03
104	Ken Schrom	.08	.06	.03
105	Ruben Sierra(FC)	5.00	3.75	2.00
106	Ted Simmons	.20	.15	.08
107	Sammy Stewart	.08	.06	.03
108	Kurt Stillwell(FC)	.08	.06	.03
109	Dale Sveum(FC)	.08	.06	.03
110	Tim Teufel	.08	.06	.03
111	Bob Tewksbury(FC)	.75	.60	.30
112	Andres Thomas(FC)	.08	.06	.03
113	Jason Thompson	.08	.06	.03
114	Milt Thompson	.12	.09	.05
115	Rob Thompson(FC)	1.50	1.25	.60
116	Jay Tibbs	.08	.06	.03
117	Fred Toliver	.12	.09	.05
118	Wayne Tolleson	.08	.06	.03
119	Alex Trevino	.08	.06	.03
120	Manny Trillo	.10	.08	.04
121	Ed Vande Berg	.08	.06	.03
122	Ozzie Virgil	.08	.06	.03
123	Tony Walker(FC)	.08	.06	.03
124	Gene Walter	.12	.09	.05
125	Duane Ward(FC)	1.00	.70	.40
126	Jerry Willard	.08	.06	.03
127	Mitch Williams(FC)	.40	.30	.15
128	Reggie Williams(FC)	.08	.06	.03
129	Bobby Witt(FC)	.30	.25	.12
130	Marvell Wynne	.08	.06	.03
131	Steve Yeager	.08	.06	.03
132	Checklist	.08	.06	.03

1986 Fleer Baseball's Best

The 1986 Fleer Baseball's Best set consists of 44 cards and was produced for the McCrory's store chain and their affiliated stores. Subtitled "Sluggers vs. Pitchers," the set contains 22 each of the game's best hitters and pitchers. The cards, which measure 2-1/2" by 3-1/2", have color photos depicting an action pose. The backs are done in blue and red ink on white stock and carry the player's personal and statistical information. The sets were issued in a specially designed box with six team logo stickers.

		MT	NR MT	EX
Complete Set:		7.00	5.25	2.75
Common Player:		.05	.04	.02
1	Bert Blyleven	.10	.08	.04

		MT	NR MT	EX
2	Wade Boggs	.70	.50	.30
3	George Brett	.70	.50	.30
4	Tom Browning	.15	.11	.06
5	Jose Canseco	2.00	1.50	.75
6	Will Clark	1.50	1.25	.60
7	Roger Clemens	.70	.50	.30
8	Alvin Davis	.10	.08	.04
9	Julio Franco	.10	.08	.04
10	Kirk Gibson	.20	.15	.08
11	Dwight Gooden	.50	.40	.20
12	Goose Gossage	.12	.09	.05
13	Pedro Guerrero	.15	.11	.06
14	Ron Guidry	.12	.09	.05
15	Tony Gwynn	.25	.20	.10
16	Orel Hershiser	.20	.15	.08
17	Kent Hrbek	.15	.11	.06
18	Reggie Jackson	.50	.40	.20
19	Wally Joyner	.50	.40	.20
20	Charlie Leibrandt	.05	.04	.02
21	Don Mattingly	.70	.50	.30
22	Willie McGee	.12	.09	.05
23	Jack Morris	.15	.11	.06
24	Dale Murphy	.30	.25	.12
25	Eddie Murray	.25	.20	.10
26	Jeff Reardon	.07	.05	.03
27	Rick Reuschel	.07	.05	.03
28	Cal Ripken, Jr	.80	.60	.30
29	Pete Rose	.60	.45	.25
30	Nolan Ryan	1.75	1.25	.70
31	Bret Saberhagen	.15	.11	.06
32	Ryne Sandberg	.80	.60	.30
33	Mike Schmidt	.50	.40	.20
34	Tom Seaver	.25	.20	.10
35	Bryn Smith	.05	.04	.02
36	Mario Soto	.05	.04	.02
37	Dave Stieb	.10	.08	.04
38	Darryl Strawberry	.35	.25	.14
39	Rick Sutcliffe	.10	.08	.04
40	John Tudor	.10	.08	.04
41	Fernando Valenzuela	.20	.15	.08
42	Bobby Witt	.15	.11	.06
43	Mike Witt	.07	.05	.03
44	Robin Yount	.35	.25	.14

1986 Fleer League Leaders

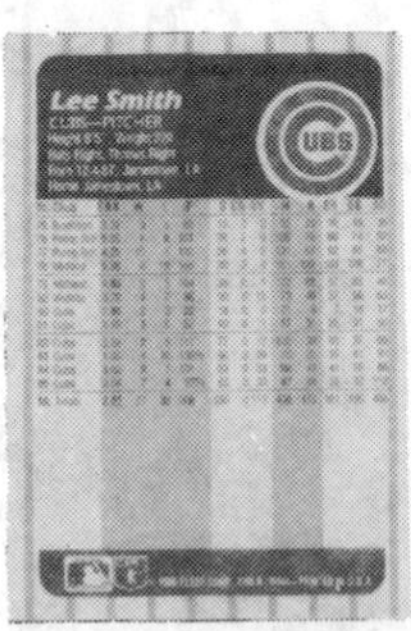

Fleer's 1986 "League Leaders" set features 44 of the game's top players and was issued through the Walgreens drug store chain. The card fronts contain a color photo and feature the player's name, team and postition in a blue band near the bottom of the card. The words "League Leaders" appear in a red band at the top of the card. The background for the card fronts is alternating blue and white stripes. The card backs are printed in blue, red and white and carry the player's statistical information and team logo. The cards are the standard 2-1/2" by 3-1/2" size. The set was issued in a special cardboard box, along with six team logo stickers.

		MT	NR MT	EX
Complete Set:		7.00	5.25	2.75
Common Player:		.05	.04	.02
1	Wade Boggs	.60	.45	.25

		MT	NR MT	EX
2	George Brett	.60	.45	.25
3	Jose Canseco	2.00	1.50	.75
4	Rod Carew	.30	.25	.12
5	Gary Carter	.25	.20	.10
6	Jack Clark	.12	.09	.05
7	Vince Coleman	.30	.25	.12
8	Jose Cruz	.05	.04	.02
9	Alvin Davis	.10	.08	.04
10	Mariano Duncan	.05	.04	.02
11	Leon Durham	.05	.04	.02
12	Carlton Fisk	.25	.20	.10
13	Julio Franco	.10	.08	.04
14	Scott Garrelts	.05	.04	.02
15	Steve Garvey	.25	.20	.10
16	Dwight Gooden	.40	.30	.15
17	Ozzie Guillen	.10	.08	.04
18	Willie Hernandez	.05	.04	.02
19	Bob Horner	.07	.05	.03
20	Kent Hrbek	.15	.11	.06
21	Charlie Leibrandt	.05	.04	.02
22	Don Mattingly	.60	.45	.25
23	Oddibe McDowell	.12	.09	.05
24	Willie McGee	.10	.08	.04
25	Keith Moreland	.05	.04	.02
26	Lloyd Moseby	.07	.05	.03
27	Dale Murphy	.30	.25	.12
28	Phil Niekro	.15	.11	.06
29	Joe Orsulak	.05	.04	.02
30	Dave Parker	.25	.20	.10
31	Lance Parrish	.15	.11	.06
32	Kirby Puckett	.70	.50	.30
33	Tim Raines	.25	.20	.10
34	Earnie Riles	.07	.05	.03
35	Cal Ripken, Jr.	.80	.60	.30
36	Pete Rose	.60	.45	.25
37	Bret Saberhagen	.15	.11	.06
38	Juan Samuel	.10	.08	.04
39	Ryne Sandberg	.80	.60	.30
40	Tom Seaver	.25	.20	.10
41	Lee Smith	.07	.05	.03
42	Ozzie Smith	.12	.09	.05
43	Dave Stieb	.10	.08	.04
44	Robin Yount	.35	.25	.12

1986 Fleer Limited Edition

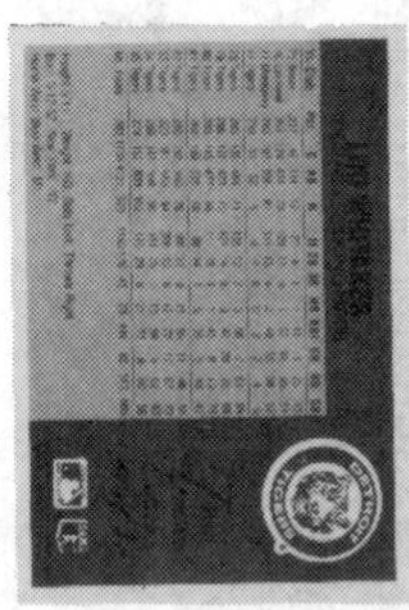

Produced for the McCrory's store chain and their affiliates for the second year in a row, the 1986 Fleer Limited Edition set contains 44 cards. The cards, which are the standard 2-1/2" by 3-1/2" size, have color photos enclosed by green, red and yellow trim. The card backs carry black print on two shades of red. The set was issued in a special cardboard box, along with six team logo stickers.

		MT	NR MT	EX
Complete Set:		6.00	4.50	2.50
Common Player:		.05	.04	.02
1	Doyle Alexander	.05	.04	.02
2	Joaquin Andujar	.05	.04	.02
3	Harold Baines	.12	.09	.05
4	Wade Boggs	.70	.50	.30
5	Phil Bradley	.05	.04	.02
6	George Brett	.70	.50	.30
7	Hubie Brooks	.07	.05	.03

		MT	NR MT	EX
8	Chris Brown	.05	.04	.02
9	Tom Brunansky	.05	.04	.02
10	Gary Carter	.25	.20	.10
11	Vince Coleman	.25	.20	.10
12	Cecil Cooper	.07	.05	.03
13	Jose Cruz	.05	.04	.02
14	Mike Davis	.05	.04	.02
15	Carlton Fisk	.15	.11	.06
16	Julio Franco	.07	.05	.03
17	Damaso Garcia	.05	.04	.02
18	Rich Gedman	.05	.04	.02
19	Kirk Gibson	.20	.15	.08
20	Dwight Gooden	.40	.30	.15
21	Pedro Guerrero	.07	.05	.03
22	Tony Gwynn	.25	.20	.10
23	Rickey Henderson	.50	.40	.20
24	Orel Hershiser	.20	.15	.08
25	LaMarr Hoyt	.05	.04	.02
26	Reggie Jackson	.30	.25	.12
27	Don Mattingly	.70	.50	.30
28	Oddibe McDowell	.05	.04	.02
29	Willie McGee	.10	.08	.04
30	Paul Molitor	.20	.15	.08
31	Dale Murphy	.30	.25	.12
32	Eddie Murray	.25	.20	.10
33	Dave Parker	.20	.15	.08
34	Tony Pena	.05	.04	.02
35	Jeff Reardon	.05	.04	.02
36	Cal Ripken, Jr.	.70	.50	.30
37	Pete Rose	.60	.45	.25
38	Bret Saberhagen	.15	.11	.06
39	Juan Samuel	.07	.05	.03
40	Ryne Sandberg	.70	.50	.30
41	Mike Schmidt	.60	.45	.25
42	Lee Smith	.07	.05	.03
43	Don Sutton	.12	.09	.05
44	Lou Whitaker	.15	.11	.06

1986 Fleer Mini

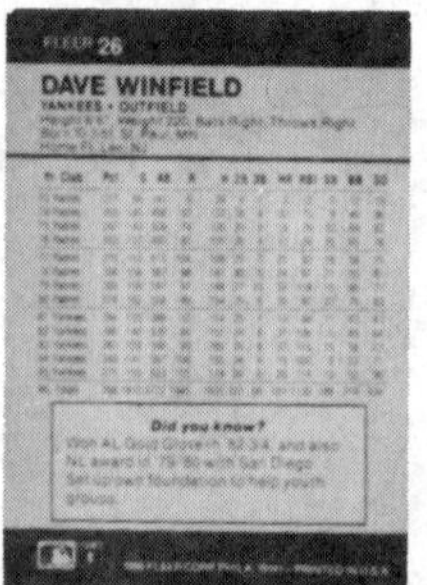

Fleer's 1986 "Classic Miniatures" set contains 120 cards that measure 1-13/16" by 2-9/16" in size. The design of the high-gloss cards is identical to the regular 1986 Fleer set but the player photos are entirely different. The set, which was issued in a specially designed box along with 18 team logo stickers, was available to the collecting public only through hobby dealers.

		MT	NR MT	EX
Complete Set:		15.00	11.00	6.00
Common Player:		.05	.04	.02
1	George Brett	.80	.60	.30
2	Dan Quisenberry	.07	.05	.03
3	Bret Saberhagen	.15	.11	.06
4	Lonnie Smith	.05	.04	.02
5	Willie Wilson	.10	.08	.04
6	Jack Clark	.12	.09	.05
7	Vince Coleman	.50	.40	.20
8	Tom Herr	.07	.05	.03
9	Willie McGee	.10	.08	.04
10	Ozzie Smith	.12	.09	.05
11	John Tudor	.07	.05	.03
12	Jesse Barfield	.12	.09	.05
13	George Bell	.20	.15	.08
14	Tony Fernandez	.10	.08	.04
15	Damaso Garcia	.05	.04	.02
16	Dave Stieb	.07	.05	.03
17	Gary Carter	.20	.15	.08
18	Ron Darling	.10	.08	.04
19	Dwight Gooden	.60	.45	.25
20	Keith Hernandez	.20	.15	.08
21	Darryl Strawberry	.50	.40	.20
22	Ron Guidry	.15	.11	.06
23	Rickey Henderson	.60	.45	.25
24	Don Mattingly	.90	.70	.35
25	Dave Righetti	.12	.09	.05
26	Dave Winfield	.20	.15	.08
27	Mariano Duncan	.07	.05	.03
28	Pedro Guerrero	.12	.09	.05
29	Bill Madlock	.10	.08	.04
30	Mike Marshall	.10	.08	.04
31	Fernando Valenzuela	.10	.08	.04
32	Reggie Jackson	.30	.25	.12
33	Gary Pettis	.05	.04	.02
34	Ron Romanick	.05	.04	.02
35	Don Sutton	.12	.09	.05
36	Mike Witt	.07	.05	.03
37	Buddy Bell	.07	.05	.03
38	Tom Browning	.10	.08	.04
39	Dave Parker	.12	.09	.05
40	Pete Rose	.60	.45	.25
41	Mario Soto	.05	.04	.02
42	Harold Baines	.12	.09	.05
43	Carlton Fisk	.15	.11	.06
44	Ozzie Guillen	.12	.09	.05
45	Ron Kittle	.07	.05	.03
46	Tom Seaver	.20	.15	.08
47	Kirk Gibson	.20	.15	.08
48	Jack Morris	.15	.11	.06
49	Lance Parrish	.15	.11	.06
50	Alan Trammell	.20	.15	.08
51	Lou Whitaker	.15	.11	.06
52	Hubie Brooks	.07	.05	.03
53	Andre Dawson	.15	.11	.06
54	Tim Raines	.20	.15	.08
55	Bryn Smith	.05	.04	.02
56	Tim Wallach	.10	.08	.04
57	Mike Boddicker	.05	.04	.02
58	Eddie Murray	.25	.20	.10
59	Cal Ripken	1.00	.70	.40
60	John Shelby	.05	.04	.02
61	Mike Young	.05	.04	.02
62	Jose Cruz	.07	.05	.03
63	Glenn Davis	.15	.11	.06
64	Phil Garner	.05	.04	.02
65	Nolan Ryan	2.00	1.50	.80
66	Mike Scott	.12	.09	.05
67	Steve Garvey	.20	.15	.08
68	Goose Gossage	.12	.09	.05
69	Tony Gwynn	.25	.20	.10
70	Andy Hawkins	.05	.04	.02
71	Garry Templeton	.05	.04	.02
72	Wade Boggs	.80	.60	.30
73	Roger Clemens	.80	.60	.30
74	Dwight Evans	.12	.09	.05
75	Rich Gedman	.05	.04	.02
76	Jim Rice	.20	.15	.08
77	Shawon Dunston	.10	.08	.04
78	Leon Durham	.05	.04	.02
79	Keith Moreland	.05	.04	.02
80	Ryne Sandberg	.20	.15	.08
81	Rick Sutcliffe	.10	.08	.04
82	Bert Blyleven	.12	.09	.05
83	Tom Brunansky	.10	.08	.04
84	Kent Hrbek	.15	.11	.06
85	Kirby Puckett	.70	.50	.30
86	Bruce Bochte	.05	.04	.02
87	Jose Canseco	1.00	.70	.40
88	Mike Davis	.05	.04	.02
89	Jay Howell	.07	.05	.03
90	Dwayne Murphy	.05	.04	.02
91	Steve Carlton	.20	.15	.08
92	Von Hayes	.10	.08	.04
93	Juan Samuel	.12	.09	.05
94	Mike Schmidt	.50	.40	.20
95	Glenn Wilson	.05	.04	.02
96	Phil Bradley	.10	.08	.04
97	Alvin Davis	.10	.08	.04
98	Jim Presley	.10	.08	.04
99	Danny Tartabull	.15	.11	.06
100	Cecil Cooper	.10	.08	.04
101	Paul Molitor	.12	.09	.05
102	Earnie Riles	.07	.05	.03
103	Robin Yount	.30	.25	.12
104	Bob Horner	.10	.08	.04
105	Dale Murphy	.30	.25	.12
106	Bruce Sutter	.10	.08	.04

		MT	NR MT	EX
107	Claudell Washington	.05	.04	.02
108	Chris Brown	.12	.09	.05
109	Chili Davis	.05	.04	.02
110	Scott Garrelts	.05	.04	.02
111	Oddibe McDowell	.12	.09	.05
112	Pete O'Brien	.07	.05	.03
113	Gary Ward	.05	.04	.02
114	Brett Butler	.05	.04	.02
115	Julio Franco	.10	.08	.04
116	Brook Jacoby	.10	.08	.04
117	Mike Brown	.05	.04	.02
118	Joe Orsulak	.05	.04	.02
119	Tony Pena	.07	.05	.03
120	R.J. Reynolds	.05	.04	.02

1986 Fleer Star Stickers

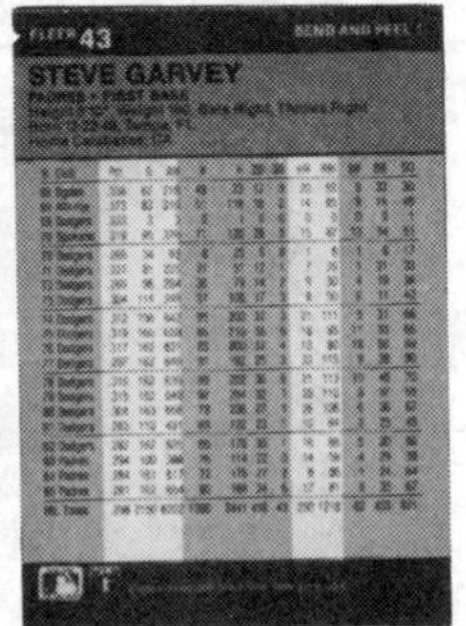

After a five-year layoff, Fleer once again produced a Star Sticker set. The cards, which measure 2-1/2" by 3-1/2", have color photos inside dark maroon borders. The card backs are identical to the 1986 regular issue except for the 1-132 numbering system and blue ink instead of yellow. The words "Bend and Peel" are found in the upper right corner of the card backs. Card #132 is a multi-player card featuring Dwight Gooden and Dale Murphy on the front and a complete checklist for the set on the reverse. The cards were sold in wax packs with team logo stickers.

		MT	NR MT	EX
Complete Set		30.00	22.00	12.00
Common Player		.05	.04	.02
1	Harold Baines	.20	.15	.08
2	Jesse Barfield	.20	.15	.08
3	Don Baylor	.12	.09	.05
4	Juan Beniquez	.05	.04	.02
5	Tim Birtsas	.08	.06	.03
6	Bert Blyleven	.15	.11	.06
7	Bruce Bochte	.05	.04	.02
8	Wade Boggs	1.00	.70	.40
9	Dennis Boyd	.12	.09	.05
10	Phil Bradley	.05	.04	.02
11	George Brett	1.00	.70	.40
12	Hubie Brooks	.10	.08	.04
13	Chris Brown	.05	.04	.02
14	Tom Browning	.10	.08	.04
15	Tom Brunansky	.05	.04	.02
16	Bill Buckner	.10	.08	.04
17	Britt Burns	.05	.04	.02
18	Brett Butler	.08	.06	.03
19	Jose Canseco	1.00	.70	.40
20	Rod Carew	.40	.30	.15
21	Steve Carlton	.40	.30	.15
22	Don Carman	.05	.04	.02
23	Gary Carter	.25	.20	.10
24	Jack Clark	.10	.08	.04
25	Vince Coleman	.25	.20	.10
26	Cecil Cooper	.10	.08	.04
27	Jose Cruz	.10	.08	.04
28	Ron Darling	.20	.15	.08
29	Alvin Davis	.05	.04	.02
30	Jody Davis	.05	.04	.02
31	Mike Davis	.05	.04	.02
32	Andre Dawson	.25	.20	.10
33	Mariano Duncan	.10	.08	.04
34	Shawon Dunston	.10	.08	.04
35	Leon Durham	.05	.04	.02
36	Darrell Evans	.10	.08	.04
37	Tony Fernandez	.10	.08	.04
38	Carlton Fisk	.20	.15	.08
39	John Franco	.10	.08	.04
40	Julio Franco	.10	.08	.04
41	Damaso Garcia	.05	.04	.02
42	Scott Garrelts	.05	.04	.02
43	Steve Garvey	.25	.20	.10
44	Rich Gedman	.05	.04	.02
45	Kirk Gibson	.25	.20	.10
46	Dwight Gooden	.50	.40	.20
47	Pedro Guerrero	.10	.08	.04
48	Ron Guidry	.10	.08	.04
49	Ozzie Guillen	.15	.11	.06
50	Tony Gwynn	.25	.20	.10
51	Andy Hawkins	.08	.06	.03
52	Von Hayes	.10	.08	.04
53	Rickey Henderson	.50	.40	.20
54	Tom Henke	.05	.04	.02
55	Keith Hernandez	.10	.08	.04
56	Willie Hernandez	.05	.04	.02
57	Tom Herr	.05	.04	.02
58	Orel Hershiser	.20	.15	.08
59	Teddy Higuera	.05	.04	.02
60	Bob Horner	.10	.08	.04
61	Charlie Hough	.08	.06	.03
62	Jay Howell	.08	.06	.03
63	LaMarr Hoyt	.05	.04	.02
64	Kent Hrbek	.20	.15	.08
65	Reggie Jackson	.50	.40	.20
66	Bob James	.05	.04	.02
67	Dave Kingman	.05	.04	.02
68	Ron Kittle	.05	.04	.02
69	Charlie Leibrandt	.05	.04	.02
70	Fred Lynn	.25	.20	.10
71	Mike Marshall	.05	.04	.02
72	Don Mattingly	1.00	.70	.40
73	Oddibe McDowell	.10	.08	.04
74	Willie McGee	.10	.08	.04
75	Scott McGregor	.05	.04	.02
76	Paul Molitor	.20	.15	.08
77	Donnie Moore	.05	.04	.02
78	Keith Moreland	.05	.04	.02
79	Jack Morris	.10	.08	.04
80	Dale Murphy	.40	.30	.15
81	Eddie Murray	.25	.20	.10
82	Phil Niekro	.25	.20	.10
83	Joe Orsulak	.10	.08	.04
84	Dave Parker	.25	.20	.10
85	Lance Parrish	.10	.08	.04
86	Larry Parrish	.05	.04	.02
87	Tony Pena	.10	.08	.04
88	Gary Pettis	.05	.04	.02
89	Jim Presley	.05	.04	.02
90	Kirby Puckett	.90	.70	.35
91	Dan Quisenberry	.10	.08	.04
92	Tim Raines	.20	.15	.08
93	Johnny Ray	.05	.04	.02
94	Jeff Reardon	.10	.08	.04
95	Rick Reuschel	.05	.04	.02
96	Jim Rice	.15	.11	.06
97	Dave Righetti	.10	.08	.04
98	Earnie Riles	.05	.04	.02
99	Cal Ripken, Jr.	1.00	.70	.40
100	Ron Romanick	.05	.04	.02
101	Pete Rose	.70	.50	.30
102	Nolan Ryan	2.00	1.50	.80
103	Bret Saberhagen	.20	.15	.08
104	Mark Salas	.05	.04	.02
105	Juan Samuel	.10	.08	.04
106	Ryne Sandberg	1.00	.70	.40
107	Mike Schmidt	.90	.70	.35
108	Mike Scott	.10	.08	.04
109	Tom Seaver	.30	.25	.12
110	Bryn Smith	.05	.04	.02
111	Dave Smith	.05	.04	.02
112	Lee Smith	.10	.08	.04
113	Ozzie Smith	.25	.20	.10
114	Mario Soto	.05	.04	.02
115	Dave Stieb	.10	.08	.04
116	Darryl Strawberry	.50	.40	.20
117	Bruce Sutter	.10	.08	.04
118	Garry Templeton	.05	.04	.02
119	Gorman Thomas	.05	.04	.02
120	Andre Thornton	.05	.04	.02
121	Alan Trammell	.20	.15	.08
122	John Tudor	.05	.04	.02
123	Fernando Valenzuela	.20	.15	.08
124	Frank Viola	.20	.15	.08
125	Gary Ward	.05	.04	.02

		MT	NR MT	EX
126	Lou Whitaker	.20	.15	.08
127	Frank White	.05	.04	.02
128	Glenn Wilson	.05	.04	.02
129	Willie Wilson	.10	.08	.04
130	Dave Winfield	.40	.30	.15
131	Robin Yount	.35	.25	.14
132	Dwight Gooden, Dale Murphy/Checklist	.50	.40	.20

1986 Fleer Star Stickers Box Panels

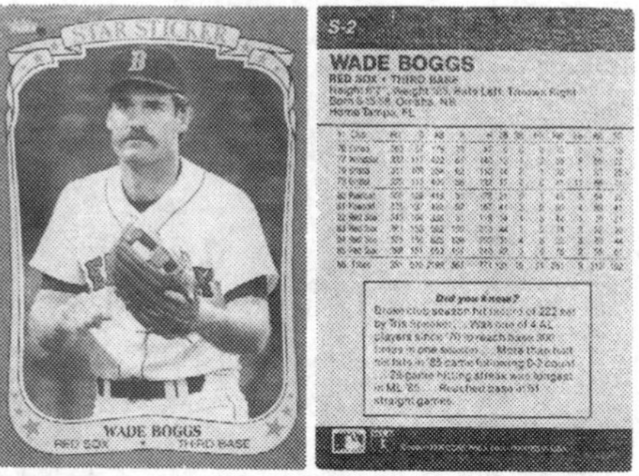

Four cards, numbered S-1 through S-4, were placed on the bottoms of 1986 Fleer Star Stickers wax pack boxes. The cards are nearly identical in format to the regular issue sticker cards. Individual cards measure 2-1/2" by 3-1/2" in size, while a complete panel of four measures 5" by 7-1/8".

	MT	NR MT	EX
Complete Panel Set:	2.00	1.50	.80
Complete Singles Set:	1.00	.70	.40
Common Single Player:	.30	.25	.12

		MT	NR MT	EX
	Panel	2.00	1.50	.80
1	Dodgers Logo	.05	.04	.02
2	Wade Boggs	1.00	.70	.40
3	Steve Garvey	.30	.25	.12
4	Dave Winfield	.30	.25	.12

1987 Fleer

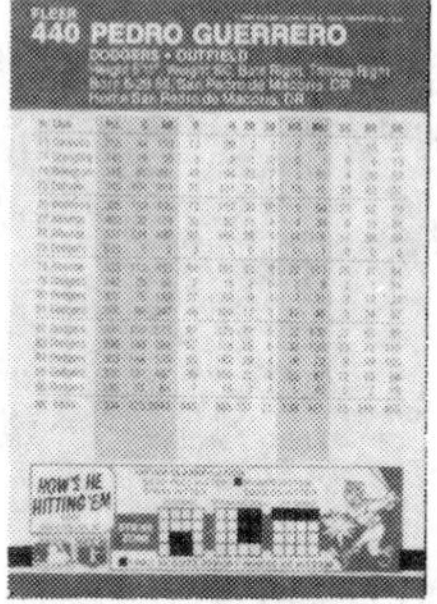

The 1987 Fleer set consists of 660 cards, each measuring 2-1/2" by 3-1/2". The card fronts feature an attractive blue and white border. The player's name and position appears in the upper left corner of the card. The player's team logo is located in the lower right corner. The card backs are done in blue, red and white and contain an innovative "Pro Scouts Report" feature which lists the hitter's or pitcher's batting and pitching strengths. For the third year in a row, Fleer included its "Major League Prospects" subset. Fleer produced a glossy-finish Collectors Edition set which came housed in a specially-designed tin box. It was speculated that 100,000 of the glossy sets were produced. After experiencing a dramatic drop in price during 1987, the glossy set now sells for only a few dollars more than the regular issue.

	MT	NR MT	EX
Complete Set (660):	110.00	82.00	40.00
Common Player:	.06	.05	.02

		MT	NR MT	EX
1	Rick Aguilera	.06	.05	.02
2	Richard Anderson	.06	.05	.02
3	Wally Backman	.08	.06	.03
4	Gary Carter	.25	.20	.10
5	Ron Darling	.15	.11	.06
6	Len Dykstra	.70	.50	.30
7	*Kevin Elster*(FC)	.10	.08	.04
8	Sid Fernandez	.12	.09	.05
9	Dwight Gooden	.40	.30	.15
10	*Ed Hearn*(FC)	.06	.05	.02
11	Danny Heep	.06	.05	.02
12	Keith Hernandez	.10	.08	.04
13	Howard Johnson	.10	.08	.04
14	Ray Knight	.08	.06	.03
15	Lee Mazzilli	.06	.05	.02
16	Roger McDowell	.12	.09	.05
17	*Kevin Mitchell*	1.50	1.25	.60
18	Randy Niemann	.06	.05	.02
19	Bob Ojeda	.08	.06	.03
20	Jesse Orosco	.08	.06	.03
21	Rafael Santana	.06	.05	.02
22	Doug Sisk	.06	.05	.02
23	Darryl Strawberry	.60	.45	.25
24	Tim Teufel	.06	.05	.02
25	Mookie Wilson	.10	.08	.04
26	Tony Armas	.08	.06	.03
27	Marty Barrett	.10	.08	.04
28	Don Baylor	.12	.09	.05
29	Wade Boggs	1.50	1.25	.60
30	Oil Can Boyd	.08	.06	.03
31	Bill Buckner	.10	.08	.04
32	Roger Clemens	3.00	2.25	1.25
33	Steve Crawford	.06	.05	.02
34	Dwight Evans	.12	.09	.05
35	Rich Gedman	.10	.08	.04
36	Dave Henderson	.10	.08	.04
37	Bruce Hurst	.10	.08	.04
38	Tim Lollar	.06	.05	.02
39	Al Nipper	.06	.05	.02
40	Spike Owen	.06	.05	.02
41	Jim Rice	.20	.15	.08
42	Ed Romero	.06	.05	.02
43	Joe Sambito	.06	.05	.02
44	Calvin Schiraldi	.06	.05	.02
45	Tom Seaver	1.25	.90	.50
46	*Jeff Sellers*(FC)	.06	.05	.02
47	Bob Stanley	.06	.05	.02
48	Sammy Stewart	.06	.05	.02
49	Larry Andersen	.06	.05	.02
50	Alan Ashby	.06	.05	.02
51	Kevin Bass	.10	.08	.04
52	Jeff Calhoun	.06	.05	.02
53	Jose Cruz	.10	.08	.04
54	Danny Darwin	.06	.05	.02
55	Glenn Davis	.08	.06	.03
56	*Jim Deshaies*	.25	.20	.10
57	Bill Doran	.10	.08	.04
58	Phil Garner	.06	.05	.02
59	Billy Hatcher	.08	.06	.03
60	Charlie Kerfeld	.06	.05	.02
61	Bob Knepper	.08	.06	.03
62	Dave Lopes	.08	.06	.03
63	Aurelio Lopez	.06	.05	.02
64	Jim Pankovits	.06	.05	.02
65	Terry Puhl	.06	.05	.02
66	Craig Reynolds	.06	.05	.02
67	Nolan Ryan	4.00	3.00	1.50
68	Mike Scott	.15	.11	.06
69	Dave Smith	.06	.05	.02
70	Dickie Thon	.06	.05	.02
71	Tony Walker	.06	.05	.02
72	Denny Walling	.06	.05	.02
73	Bob Boone	.08	.06	.03
74	Rick Burleson	.08	.06	.03
75	John Candelaria	.06	.05	.02
76	Doug Corbett	.06	.05	.02
77	Doug DeCinces	.08	.06	.03
78	Brian Downing	.08	.06	.03
79	*Chuck Finley*(FC)	1.50	1.25	.60
80	Terry Forster	.08	.06	.03
81	Bobby Grich	.10	.08	.04
82	George Hendrick	.08	.06	.03
83	Jack Howell(FC)	.10	.08	.04
84	Reggie Jackson	1.00	.70	.40
85	Ruppert Jones	.06	.05	.02

		MT	NR MT	EX
86	*Wally Joyner*	2.00	1.50	.80
87	Gary Lucas	.06	.05	.02
88	Kirk McCaskill	.08	.06	.03
89	Donnie Moore	.06	.05	.02
90	Gary Pettis	.06	.05	.02
91	Vern Ruhle	.06	.05	.02
92	Dick Schofield	.06	.05	.02
93	Don Sutton	.20	.15	.08
94	Rob Wilfong	.06	.05	.02
95	Mike Witt	.10	.08	.04
96	*Doug Drabek*	1.75	1.25	.70
97	Mike Easler	.08	.06	.03
98	Mike Fischlin	.06	.05	.02
99	Brian Fisher	.08	.06	.03
100	Ron Guidry	.15	.11	.06
101	Rickey Henderson	2.00	1.50	.80
102	Tommy John	.10	.08	.04
103	Ron Kittle	.06	.05	.02
104	Don Mattingly	1.50	1.25	.60
105	Bobby Meacham	.06	.05	.02
106	Joe Niekro	.10	.08	.04
107	Mike Pagliarulo	.10	.08	.04
108	Dan Pasqua	.10	.08	.04
109	Willie Randolph	.10	.08	.04
110	Dennis Rasmussen	.10	.08	.04
111	Dave Righetti	.15	.11	.06
112	Gary Roenicke	.06	.05	.02
113	Rod Scurry	.06	.05	.02
114	Bob Shirley	.06	.05	.02
115	Joel Skinner	.06	.05	.02
116	Tim Stoddard	.06	.05	.02
117	*Bob Tewksbury*	.80	.60	.30
118	Wayne Tolleson	.06	.05	.02
119	Claudell Washington	.06	.05	.02
120	Dave Winfield	1.00	.70	.40
121	Steve Buechele	.08	.06	.03
122	*Ed Correa*	.06	.05	.02
123	Scott Fletcher	.08	.06	.03
124	Jose Guzman	.10	.08	.04
125	Toby Harrah	.08	.06	.03
126	Greg Harris	.06	.05	.02
127	Charlie Hough	.08	.06	.03
128	*Pete Incaviglia*	1.50	1.25	.60
129	Mike Mason	.06	.05	.02
130	Oddibe McDowell	.10	.08	.04
131	*Dale Mohorcic*(FC)	.06	.05	.02
132	Pete O'Brien	.10	.08	.04
133	Tom Paciorek	.06	.05	.02
134	Larry Parrish	.08	.06	.03
135	Geno Petralli	.06	.05	.02
136	Darrell Porter	.08	.06	.03
137	Jeff Russell	.06	.05	.02
138	*Ruben Sierra*	9.00	6.75	3.50
139	Don Slaught	.06	.05	.02
140	Gary Ward	.08	.06	.03
141	Curtis Wilkerson	.06	.05	.02
142	*Mitch Williams*	.60	.45	.25
143	*Bobby Witt*	.40	.30	.15
144	Dave Bergman	.06	.05	.02
145	Tom Brookens	.06	.05	.02
146	Bill Campbell	.06	.05	.02
147	*Chuck Cary*	.10	.08	.04
148	Darnell Coles	.08	.06	.03
149	Dave Collins	.08	.06	.03
150	Darrell Evans	.12	.09	.05
151	Kirk Gibson	.15	.11	.06
152	John Grubb	.06	.05	.02
153	Willie Hernandez	.08	.06	.03
154	Larry Herndon	.08	.06	.03
155	*Eric King*	.10	.08	.04
156	Chet Lemon	.08	.06	.03
157	Dwight Lowry	.06	.05	.02
158	Jack Morris	.20	.15	.08
159	Randy O'Neal	.06	.05	.02
160	Lance Parrish	.08	.06	.03
161	Dan Petry	.08	.06	.03
162	Pat Sheridan	.06	.05	.02
163	Jim Slaton	.06	.05	.02
164	Frank Tanana	.08	.06	.03
165	Walt Terrell	.08	.06	.03
166	Mark Thurmond	.06	.05	.02
167	Alan Trammell	.25	.20	.10
168	Lou Whitaker	.25	.20	.10
169	Luis Aguayo	.06	.05	.02
170	Steve Bedrosian	.06	.05	.02
171	Don Carman	.06	.05	.02
172	Darren Daulton	1.50	1.25	.60
173	Greg Gross	.06	.05	.02
174	Kevin Gross	.08	.06	.03
175	Von Hayes	.10	.08	.04
176	Charles Hudson	.06	.05	.02

		MT	NR MT	EX
177	Tom Hume	.06	.05	.02
178	Steve Jeltz	.06	.05	.02
179	*Mike Maddux*(FC)	.20	.15	.08
180	Shane Rawley	.08	.06	.03
181	Gary Redus	.06	.05	.02
182	Ron Roenicke	.06	.05	.02
183	*Bruce Ruffin*(FC)	.06	.05	.02
184	John Russell	.06	.05	.02
185	Juan Samuel	.12	.09	.05
186	Dan Schatzeder	.06	.05	.02
187	Mike Schmidt	1.50	1.25	.60
188	Rick Schu	.06	.05	.02
189	Jeff Stone	.06	.05	.02
190	Kent Tekulve	.08	.06	.03
191	Milt Thompson	.08	.06	.03
192	Glenn Wilson	.08	.06	.03
193	Buddy Bell	.10	.08	.04
194	Tom Browning	.10	.08	.04
195	Sal Butera	.06	.05	.02
196	Dave Concepcion	.12	.09	.05
197	Kal Daniels	.06	.05	.02
198	Eric Davis	.50	.40	.20
199	John Denny	.06	.05	.02
200	Bo Diaz	.08	.06	.03
201	Nick Esasky	.08	.06	.03
202	John Franco	.10	.08	.04
203	Bill Gullickson	.06	.05	.02
204	*Barry Larkin*(FC)	6.00	4.50	2.50
205	Eddie Milner	.06	.05	.02
206	*Rob Murphy*(FC)	.20	.15	.08
207	Ron Oester	.06	.05	.02
208	Dave Parker	.20	.15	.08
209	Tony Perez	.15	.11	.06
210	Ted Power	.06	.05	.02
211	Joe Price	.06	.05	.02
212	Ron Robinson	.06	.05	.02
213	Pete Rose	.75	.60	.30
214	Mario Soto	.08	.06	.03
215	*Kurt Stillwell*	.06	.05	.02
216	Max Venable	.06	.05	.02
217	Chris Welsh	.06	.05	.02
218	*Carl Willis*(FC)	.06	.05	.02
219	Jesse Barfield	.15	.11	.06
220	George Bell	.25	.20	.10
221	Bill Caudill	.06	.05	.02
222	*John Cerutti*	.06	.05	.02
223	Jim Clancy	.08	.06	.03
224	*Mark Eichhorn*	.15	.11	.06
225	Tony Fernandez	.20	.15	.08
226	Damaso Garcia	.06	.05	.02
227	Kelly Gruber	.20	.15	.08
228	Tom Henke	.08	.06	.03
229	Garth Iorg	.06	.05	.02
230	Cliff Johnson	.06	.05	.02
231	Joe Johnson	.06	.05	.02
232	Jimmy Key	.25	.20	.10
233	Dennis Lamp	.06	.05	.02
234	Rick Leach	.06	.05	.02
235	Buck Martinez	.06	.05	.02
236	Lloyd Moseby	.06	.05	.02
237	Rance Mulliniks	.06	.05	.02
238	Dave Stieb	.12	.09	.05
239	Willie Upshaw	.08	.06	.03
240	Ernie Whitt	.08	.06	.03
241	*Andy Allanson*	.06	.05	.02
242	*Scott Bailes*	.06	.05	.02
243	Chris Bando	.06	.05	.02
244	Tony Bernazard	.06	.05	.02
245	John Butcher	.06	.05	.02
246	Brett Butler	.08	.06	.03
247	Ernie Camacho	.06	.05	.02
248	Tom Candiotti	.06	.05	.02
249	Joe Carter	2.00	1.50	.80
250	Carmen Castillo	.06	.05	.02
251	Julio Franco	.10	.08	.04
252	Mel Hall	.08	.06	.03
253	Brook Jacoby	.10	.08	.04
254	Phil Niekro	.20	.15	.08
255	Otis Nixon	.20	.15	.08
256	Dickie Noles	.06	.05	.02
257	Bryan Oelkers	.06	.05	.02
258	Ken Schrom	.06	.05	.02
259	Don Schulze	.06	.05	.02
260	Cory Snyder	.15	.11	.06
261	Pat Tabler	.08	.06	.03
262	Andre Thornton	.08	.06	.03
263	*Rich Yett*(FC)	.06	.05	.02
264	*Mike Aldrete*	.10	.08	.04
265	Juan Berenguer	.06	.05	.02
266	Vida Blue	.10	.08	.04
267	Bob Brenly	.06	.05	.02

		MT	NR MT	EX
268	Chris Brown	.08	.06	.03
269	*Will Clark*	20.00	15.00	8.00
270	Chili Davis	.08	.06	.03
271	Mark Davis	.06	.05	.02
272	*Kelly Downs*(FC)	.12	.09	.05
273	Scott Garrelts	.06	.05	.02
274	Dan Gladden	.06	.05	.02
275	Mike Krukow	.08	.06	.03
276	*Randy Kutcher*(FC)	.06	.05	.02
277	Mike LaCoss	.06	.05	.02
278	Jeff Leonard	.08	.06	.03
279	Candy Maldonado	.08	.06	.03
280	Roger Mason	.06	.05	.02
281	Bob Melvin(FC)	.06	.05	.02
282	Greg Minton	.06	.05	.02
283	Jeff Robinson	.08	.06	.03
284	Harry Spilman	.06	.05	.02
285	*Rob Thompson*	2.00	1.50	.80
286	Jose Uribe	.06	.05	.02
287	Frank Williams	.06	.05	.02
288	Joel Youngblood	.06	.05	.02
289	Jack Clark	.08	.06	.03
290	Vince Coleman	.20	.15	.08
291	Tim Conroy	.06	.05	.02
292	Danny Cox	.08	.06	.03
293	Ken Dayley	.06	.05	.02
294	Curt Ford	.06	.05	.02
295	Bob Forsch	.06	.05	.02
296	Tom Herr	.10	.08	.04
297	Ricky Horton	.08	.06	.03
298	Clint Hurdle	.06	.05	.02
299	Jeff Lahti	.06	.05	.02
300	Steve Lake	.06	.05	.02
301	Tito Landrum	.06	.05	.02
302	*Mike LaValliere*	.25	.20	.10
303	*Greg Mathews*(FC)	.20	.15	.08
304	Willie McGee	.12	.09	.05
305	Jose Oquendo	.06	.05	.02
306	Terry Pendleton	.50	.40	.20
307	Pat Perry	.08	.06	.03
308	Ozzie Smith	.80	.60	.30
309	Ray Soff	.06	.05	.02
310	John Tudor	.10	.08	.04
311	Andy Van Slyke	.50	.40	.20
312	Todd Worrell	.20	.15	.08
313	Dann Bilardello	.06	.05	.02
314	Hubie Brooks	.10	.08	.04
315	Tim Burke	.06	.05	.02
316	Andre Dawson	.75	.60	.30
317	Mike Fitzgerald	.06	.05	.02
318	Tom Foley	.06	.05	.02
319	Andres Galarraga	1.00	.70	.40
320	Joe Hesketh	.06	.05	.02
321	Wallace Johnson	.06	.05	.02
322	Wayne Krenchicki	.06	.05	.02
323	Vance Law	.06	.05	.02
324	Dennis Martinez	.08	.06	.03
325	Bob McClure	.06	.05	.02
326	Andy McGaffigan	.06	.05	.02
327	*Al Newman*	.08	.06	.03
328	Tim Raines	.30	.25	.12
329	Jeff Reardon	.10	.08	.04
330	*Luis Rivera*(FC)	.10	.08	.04
331	*Bob Sebra*(FC)	.06	.05	.02
332	Bryn Smith	.06	.05	.02
333	Jay Tibbs	.06	.05	.02
334	Tim Wallach	.12	.09	.05
335	Mitch Webster	.08	.06	.03
336	Jim Wohlford	.06	.05	.02
337	Floyd Youmans	.08	.06	.03
338	*Chris Bosio*(FC)	.70	.50	.30
339	*Glenn Braggs*(FC)	.20	.15	.08
340	Rick Cerone	.06	.05	.02
341	Mark Clear	.06	.05	.02
342	*Bryan Clutterbuck*(FC)	.06	.05	.02
343	Cecil Cooper	.12	.09	.05
344	Rob Deer	.10	.08	.04
345	Jim Gantner	.08	.06	.03
346	Ted Higuera	.06	.05	.02
347	John Henry Johnson	.06	.05	.02
348	Tim Leary(FC)	.08	.06	.03
349	Rick Manning	.06	.05	.02
350	Paul Molitor	.75	.60	.30
351	Charlie Moore	.06	.05	.02
352	Juan Nieves	.10	.08	.04
353	Ben Oglivie	.08	.06	.03
354	*Dan Plesac*	.15	.11	.06
355	Ernest Riles	.06	.05	.02
356	Billy Joe Robidoux	.06	.05	.02
357	Bill Schroeder	.06	.05	.02
358	*Dale Sveum*	.08	.06	.03
359	Gorman Thomas	.06	.05	.02
360	Bill Wegman(FC)	.10	.08	.04
361	Robin Yount	1.25	.90	.50
362	Steve Balboni	.08	.06	.03
363	*Scott Bankhead*	.08	.06	.03
364	Buddy Biancalana	.06	.05	.02
365	Bud Black	.06	.05	.02
366	George Brett	1.25	.90	.50
367	Steve Farr	.06	.05	.02
368	Mark Gubicza	.12	.09	.05
369	*Bo Jackson*	8.00	6.00	3.25
370	Danny Jackson	.15	.11	.06
371	*Mike Kingery*	.06	.05	.02
372	Rudy Law	.06	.05	.02
373	Charlie Leibrandt	.08	.06	.03
374	Dennis Leonard	.08	.06	.03
375	Hal McRae	.10	.08	.04
376	Jorge Orta	.06	.05	.02
377	Jamie Quirk	.06	.05	.02
378	Dan Quisenberry	.08	.06	.03
379	Bret Saberhagen	.20	.15	.08
380	Angel Salazar	.06	.05	.02
381	Lonnie Smith	.08	.06	.03
382	Jim Sundberg	.08	.06	.03
383	Frank White	.10	.08	.04
384	Willie Wilson	.12	.09	.05
385	Joaquin Andujar	.08	.06	.03
386	Doug Bair	.06	.05	.02
387	Dusty Baker	.08	.06	.03
388	Bruce Bochte	.06	.05	.02
389	Jose Canseco	5.00	3.75	2.00
390	Chris Codiroli	.06	.05	.02
391	Mike Davis	.08	.06	.03
392	Alfredo Griffin	.08	.06	.03
393	Moose Haas	.06	.05	.02
394	Donnie Hill	.06	.05	.02
395	Jay Howell	.08	.06	.03
396	Dave Kingman	.12	.09	.05
397	Carney Lansford	.10	.08	.04
398	*David Leiper*(FC)	.10	.08	.04
399	*Bill Mooneyham*	.10	.08	.04
400	Dwayne Murphy	.08	.06	.03
401	Steve Ontiveros	.06	.05	.02
402	Tony Phillips	.06	.05	.02
403	Eric Plunk	.08	.06	.03
404	Jose Rijo	.25	.20	.10
405	*Terry Steinbach*(FC)	.60	.45	.25
406	Dave Stewart	.25	.20	.10
407	Mickey Tettleton	.60	.45	.25
408	Dave Von Ohlen	.06	.05	.02
409	Jerry Willard	.06	.05	.02
410	Curt Young	.08	.06	.03
411	Bruce Bochy	.06	.05	.02
412	Dave Dravecky	.08	.06	.03
413	Tim Flannery	.06	.05	.02
414	Steve Garvey	.25	.20	.10
415	Goose Gossage	.15	.11	.06
416	Tony Gwynn	1.50	1.25	.60
417	Andy Hawkins	.06	.05	.02
418	LaMarr Hoyt	.06	.05	.02
419	Terry Kennedy	.08	.06	.03
420	*John Kruk*	7.00	5.25	2.75
421	Dave LaPoint	.06	.05	.02
422	Craig Lefferts	.06	.05	.02
423	Carmelo Martinez	.06	.05	.02
424	Lance McCullers	.06	.05	.02
425	Kevin McReynolds	.15	.11	.06
426	Graig Nettles	.12	.09	.05
427	*Bip Roberts*	.80	.60	.30
428	Jerry Royster	.06	.05	.02
429	Benito Santiago	.40	.30	.15
430	Eric Show	.08	.06	.03
431	Bob Stoddard	.06	.05	.02
432	Garry Templeton	.08	.06	.03
433	Gene Walter	.06	.05	.02
434	Ed Whitson	.06	.05	.02
435	Marvell Wynne	.06	.05	.02
436	Dave Anderson	.06	.05	.02
437	Greg Brock	.06	.05	.02
438	Enos Cabell	.06	.05	.02
439	Mariano Duncan	.06	.05	.02
440	Pedro Guerrero	.15	.11	.06
441	Orel Hershiser	.25	.20	.10
442	Rick Honeycutt	.06	.05	.02
443	Ken Howell	.06	.05	.02
444	Ken Landreaux	.06	.05	.02
445	Bill Madlock	.12	.09	.05
446	Mike Marshall	.12	.09	.05
447	Len Matuszek	.06	.05	.02
448	Tom Niedenfuer	.06	.05	.02
449	Alejandro Pena	.08	.06	.03

		MT	NR MT	EX
450	Dennis Powell(FC)	.06	.05	.02
451	Jerry Reuss	.08	.06	.03
452	Bill Russell	.08	.06	.03
453	Steve Sax	.15	.11	.06
454	Mike Scioscia	.08	.06	.03
455	Franklin Stubbs	.08	.06	.03
456	Alex Trevino	.06	.05	.02
457	Fernando Valenzuela	.10	.08	.04
458	Ed Vande Berg	.06	.05	.02
459	Bob Welch	.10	.08	.04
460	*Reggie Williams*	.06	.05	.02
461	Don Aase	.06	.05	.02
462	Juan Beniquez	.06	.05	.02
463	Mike Boddicker	.08	.06	.03
464	Juan Bonilla	.06	.05	.02
465	Rich Bordi	.06	.05	.02
466	Storm Davis	.10	.08	.04
467	Rick Dempsey	.08	.06	.03
468	Ken Dixon	.06	.05	.02
469	Jim Dwyer	.06	.05	.02
470	Mike Flanagan	.08	.06	.03
471	Jackie Gutierrez	.06	.05	.02
472	Brad Havens	.06	.05	.02
473	Lee Lacy	.06	.05	.02
474	Fred Lynn	.15	.11	.06
475	Scott McGregor	.08	.06	.03
476	Eddie Murray	.75	.60	.30
477	Tom O'Malley	.06	.05	.02
478	Cal Ripken, Jr.	3.00	2.25	1.25
479	Larry Sheets	.08	.06	.03
480	John Shelby	.06	.05	.02
481	Nate Snell	.06	.05	.02
482	Jim Traber(FC)	.06	.05	.02
483	Mike Young	.06	.05	.02
484	Neil Allen	.06	.05	.02
485	Harold Baines	.15	.11	.06
486	Floyd Bannister	.06	.05	.02
487	Daryl Boston	.06	.05	.02
488	Ivan Calderon	.06	.05	.02
489	*John Cangelosi*	.12	.09	.05
490	Steve Carlton	.25	.20	.10
491	Joe Cowley	.06	.05	.02
492	Julio Cruz	.06	.05	.02
493	Bill Dawley	.06	.05	.02
494	Jose DeLeon	.08	.06	.03
495	Richard Dotson	.08	.06	.03
496	Carlton Fisk	.60	.45	.25
497	Ozzie Guillen	.10	.08	.04
498	Jerry Hairston	.06	.05	.02
499	Ron Hassey	.06	.05	.02
500	Tim Hulett	.06	.05	.02
501	Bob James	.06	.05	.02
502	Steve Lyons	.06	.05	.02
503	*Joel McKeon*	.06	.05	.02
504	Gene Nelson	.06	.05	.02
505	Dave Schmidt	.06	.05	.02
506	Ray Searage	.06	.05	.02
507	*Bobby Thigpen*(FC)	.20	.15	.08
508	Greg Walker	.06	.05	.02
509	Jim Acker	.06	.05	.02
510	Doyle Alexander	.08	.06	.03
511	*Paul Assenmacher*	.15	.11	.06
512	Bruce Benedict	.06	.05	.02
513	Chris Chambliss	.08	.06	.03
514	Jeff Dedmon	.06	.05	.02
515	Gene Garber	.06	.05	.02
516	Ken Griffey	.10	.08	.04
517	Terry Harper	.06	.05	.02
518	Bob Horner	.10	.08	.04
519	Glenn Hubbard	.06	.05	.02
520	Rick Mahler	.06	.05	.02
521	Omar Moreno	.06	.05	.02
522	Dale Murphy	.40	.30	.15
523	Ken Oberkfell	.06	.05	.02
524	Ed Olwine	.06	.05	.02
525	David Palmer	.06	.05	.02
526	Rafael Ramirez	.06	.05	.02
527	Billy Sample	.06	.05	.02
528	Ted Simmons	.12	.09	.05
529	Zane Smith	.08	.06	.03
530	Bruce Sutter	.12	.09	.05
531	*Andres Thomas*	.06	.05	.02
532	Ozzie Virgil	.06	.05	.02
533	*Allan Anderson*(FC)	.06	.05	.02
534	Keith Atherton	.06	.05	.02
535	Billy Beane	.06	.05	.02
536	Bert Blyleven	.12	.09	.05
537	Tom Brunansky	.10	.08	.04
538	Randy Bush	.06	.05	.02
539	George Frazier	.06	.05	.02
540	Gary Gaetti	.15	.11	.06

		MT	NR MT	EX
541	Greg Gagne	.06	.05	.02
542	Mickey Hatcher	.06	.05	.02
543	Neal Heaton	.06	.05	.02
544	Kent Hrbek	.15	.11	.06
545	Roy Lee Jackson	.06	.05	.02
546	Tim Laudner	.06	.05	.02
547	Steve Lombardozzi	.06	.05	.02
548	*Mark Portugal*(FC)	.75	.60	.30
549	Kirby Puckett	4.00	3.00	1.50
550	Jeff Reed	.06	.05	.02
551	Mark Salas	.06	.05	.02
552	Roy Smalley	.06	.05	.02
553	Mike Smithson	.06	.05	.02
554	Frank Viola	.25	.20	.10
555	Thad Bosley	.06	.05	.02
556	Ron Cey	.10	.08	.04
557	Jody Davis	.08	.06	.03
558	Ron Davis	.06	.05	.02
559	Bob Dernier	.06	.05	.02
560	Frank DiPino	.06	.05	.02
561	Shawon Dunston	.15	.11	.06
562	Leon Durham	.08	.06	.03
563	Dennis Eckersley	.40	.30	.15
564	Terry Francona	.06	.05	.02
565	Dave Gumpert	.06	.05	.02
566	Guy Hoffman	.08	.06	.03
567	Ed Lynch	.06	.05	.02
568	Gary Matthews	.10	.08	.04
569	Keith Moreland	.08	.06	.03
570	*Jamie Moyer*(FC)	.06	.05	.02
571	Jerry Mumphrey	.06	.05	.02
572	Ryne Sandberg	3.00	2.25	1.25
573	Scott Sanderson	.06	.05	.02
574	Lee Smith	.10	.08	.04
575	Chris Speier	.06	.05	.02
576	Rick Sutcliffe	.12	.09	.05
577	Manny Trillo	.08	.06	.03
578	Steve Trout	.06	.05	.02
579	Karl Best	.06	.05	.02
580	Scott Bradley(FC)	.08	.06	.03
581	Phil Bradley	.12	.09	.05
582	Mickey Brantley	.08	.06	.03
583	Mike Brown	.06	.05	.02
584	Alvin Davis	.06	.05	.02
585	*Lee Guetterman*(FC)	.15	.11	.06
586	Mark Huismann	.06	.05	.02
587	Bob Kearney	.06	.05	.02
588	Pete Ladd	.06	.05	.02
589	Mark Langston	.30	.25	.12
590	Mike Moore	.06	.05	.02
591	Mike Morgan	.06	.05	.02
592	John Moses	.06	.05	.02
593	Ken Phelps	.08	.06	.03
594	Jim Presley	.10	.08	.04
595	*Rey Quinonez (Quinones)*	.06	.05	.02
596	Harold Reynolds	.15	.11	.06
597	Billy Swift	.30	.25	.12
598	Danny Tartabull	.50	.40	.20
599	Steve Yeager	.06	.05	.02
600	Matt Young	.06	.05	.02
601	Bill Almon	.06	.05	.02
602	*Rafael Belliard*(FC)	.12	.09	.05
603	Mike Bielecki	.06	.05	.02
604	*Barry Bonds*	35.00	26.00	14.00
605	*Bobby Bonilla*	4.50	3.50	1.75
606	Sid Bream	.08	.06	.03
607	Mike Brown	.06	.05	.02
608	Pat Clements	.06	.05	.02
609	*Mike Diaz*(FC)	.06	.05	.02
610	Cecillo Guante	.06	.05	.02
611	*Barry Jones*(FC)	.06	.05	.02
612	Bob Kipper	.06	.05	.02
613	Larry McWilliams	.06	.05	.02
614	Jim Morrison	.06	.05	.02
615	Joe Orsulak	.06	.05	.02
616	Junior Ortiz	.06	.05	.02
617	Tony Pena	.08	.06	.03
618	Johnny Ray	.06	.05	.02
619	Rick Reuschel	.06	.05	.02
620	R.J. Reynolds	.06	.05	.02
621	Rick Rhoden	.10	.08	.04
622	Don Robinson	.08	.06	.03
623	Bob Walk	.06	.05	.02
624	Jim Winn	.06	.05	.02
625	Youthful Power (Jose Canseco, Pete Incaviglia)	.70	.50	.30
626	300 Game Winners (Phil Niekro, Don Sutton)	.12	.09	.05
627	A.L. Firemen (Don Aase, Dave Righetti)	.08	.06	.03
628	Rookie All-Stars (Jose Canseco, Wally Joyner)	.75	.60	.30

		MT	NR MT	EX
629	Magic Mets (Gary Carter, Dwight Gooden, Keith Hernandez, Darryl Strawberry)	.20	.15	.08
630	N.L. Best Righties (Mike Krukow, Mike Scott)	.08	.06	.03
631	Sensational Southpaws (John Franco, Fernando Valenzuela)	.10	.08	.04
632	Count 'Em (Bob Horner)	.08	.06	.03
633	A.L. Pitcher's Nightmare (Jose Canseco, Kirby Puckett, Jim Rice)	.70	.50	.30
634	All Star Battery (Gary Carter, Roger Clemens)	.40	.30	.15
635	4,000 Strikeouts (Steve Carlton)	.12	.09	.05
636	Big Bats At First Sack (Glenn Davis, Eddie Murray)	.20	.15	.08
637	On Base (Wade Boggs, Keith Hernandez)	.35	.25	.14
638	Sluggers From Left Side (Don Mattingly, Darryl Strawberry)	.90	.70	.35
639	Former MVP's (Dave Parker, Ryne Sandberg)	.12	.09	.05
640	Dr. K. & Super K (Roger Clemens, Dwight Gooden)	.50	.40	.20
641	A.L. West Stoppers (Charlie Hough, Mike Witt)	.08	.06	.03
642	Doubles & Triples (Tim Raines, Juan Samuel)	.12	.09	.05
643	Outfielders With Punch (Harold Baines, Jesse Barfield)	.10	.08	.04
644	Major League Prospects *(Dave Clark, Greg Swindell)*	1.00	.70	.40
645	Major League Prospects *(Ron Karkovice, Russ Morman)*(FC)	.12	.09	.05
646	Major League Prospects *(Willie Fraser, Devon White)*(FC)	2.00	1.50	.80
647	Major League Prospects *(Jerry Browne, Mike Stanley)*	1.25	.90	.50
648	Major League Prospects *(Phil Lombardi, Dave Magadan)*	.80	.60	.30
649	Major League Prospects *(Ralph Bryant, Jose Gonzalez)*(FC)	.20	.15	.08
650	Major League Prospects *(Randy Asadoor, Jimmy Jones)*(FC)	.20	.15	.08
651	Major League Prospects *(Marvin Freeman, Tracy Jones)*	.25	.20	.10
652	Major League Prospects *(Kevin Seitzer,* John Stefero)(FC)	.25	.20	.10
653	Major League Prospects *(Steve Fireovid, Rob Nelson)*(FC)	.10	.08	.04
654	Checklist 1-95	.06	.05	.02
655	Checklist 96-192	.06	.05	.02
656	Checklist 193-288	.06	.05	.02
657	Checklist 289-384	.06	.05	.02
658	Checklist 385-483	.06	.05	.02
659	Checklist 484-578	.06	.05	.02
660	Checklist 579-660	.06	.05	.02

1987 Fleer All Stars

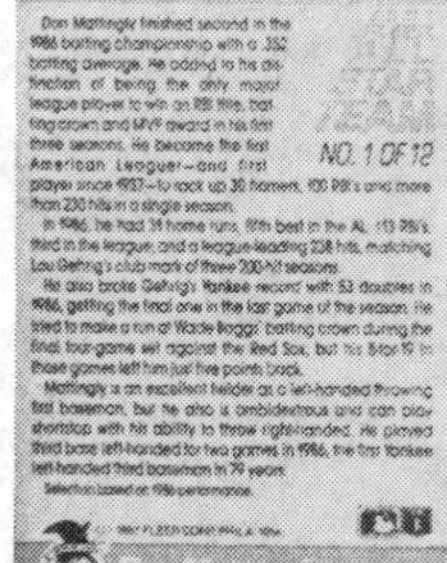

As in 1986, Fleer All Star Team cards were randomly inserted in Fleer wax and cello packs. Twelve cards, each measuring the standard 2-1/2" by 3-1/2", comprise the set. The card fronts feature a full-color player photo set against a gray background for American League players and a black background for National Leaguers. Card backs are printed in black, red and white and feature a lengthy player biography. Fleer's choices for a major league All-Star team is once again the theme for the set.

		MT	NR MT	EX
	Complete Set (12):	18.00	13.50	7.25
	Common Player:	.30	.20	.10
1	Don Mattingly	3.00	1.50	.80
2	Gary Carter	1.00	.70	.40
3	Tony Fernandez	.40	.30	.15
4	Steve Sax	.30	.20	.10
5	Kirby Puckett	6.00	4.00	2.00
6	Mike Schmidt	3.00	1.50	.80
7	Mike Easler	.30	.20	.10
8	Todd Worrell	.30	.20	.10
9	George Bell	.60	.45	.25
10	Fernando Valenzuela	.30	.20	.10
11	Roger Clemens	5.00	3.00	1.50
12	Tim Raines	1.00	.70	.40

1987 Fleer Headliners

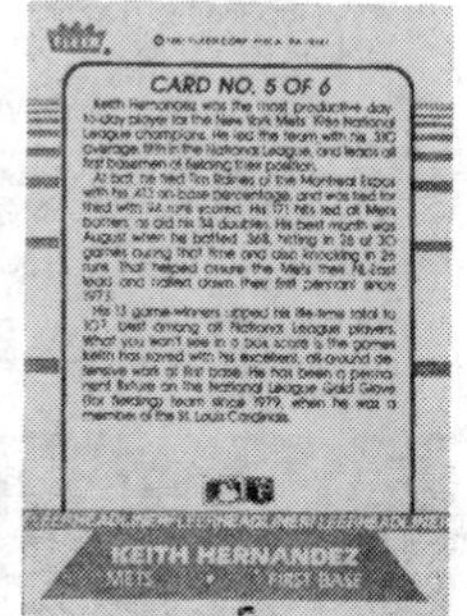

A continuation of the 1986 Future Hall of Famers idea, Fleer encountered legal problems with using the Hall of Fame name and abated them by entitling the set "Headliners." The cards, which are the standard 2-1/2" by 3-1/2" size, were randomly inserted in three-pack cello packs. Card fronts feature a player photo set against a beige background with bright red stripes. The card backs are printed in black, red and gray and offer a brief biography with an emphasis on the player's performance during the 1986 season.

		MT	NR MT	EX
	Complete Set (6):	5.00	3.75	1.75
	Common Player:	.30	.20	.10
1	Wade Boggs	1.50	1.00	.50
2	Jose Canseco	1.50	1.00	.50
3	Dwight Gooden	.40	.30	.15
4	Rickey Henderson	1.50	1.00	.50
5	Keith Hernandez	.50	.30	.15
6	Jim Rice	.50	.30	.15

1987 Fleer '86 World Series

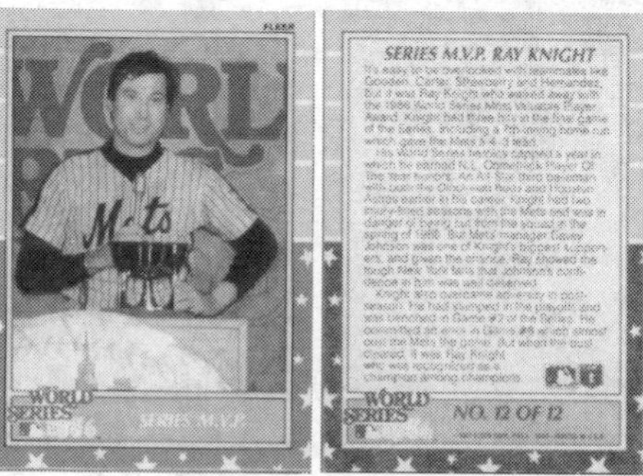

Fleer issued a set of 12 cards highlighting the 1986 World Series between the Boston Red Sox and New

York Mets. The sets were available only with Fleer factory-packaged sets of 660 regular issue cards. The cards, which are the standard 2-1/2" by 3-1/2" size, have either horizontal or vertical formats. The fronts are bordered in red, white and blue stars and stripes with a thin gold frame around the photo. The backs are printed in red and blue ink on white stock and include information regarding the photo on the card fronts.

		MT	NR MT	EX
Complete Set (12):		4.00	3.00	1.50
Common Player:		.25	.15	.10
1	Left-Hand Finesse Beats Mets (Bruce Hurst)	.25	.15	.10
2	Wade Boggs, Keith Hernandez	.70	.50	.30
3	Roger Clemens	1.50	1.00	.50
4	Gary Carter	.50	.40	.20
5	Ron Darling	.50	.40	.20
6	.433 Series Batting Average (Marty Barrett)	.50	.40	.20
7	Dwight Gooden	.50	.30	.15
8	Strategy At Work	.25	.15	.10
9	Dewey! (Dwight Evans)	.25	.15	.10
10	One Strike From Boston Victory (Dave Henderson, Spike Owen)	.50	.40	.20
11	Ray Knight, Darryl Strawberry	.40	.30	.20
12	Series M.V.P. (Ray Knight)	.50	.40	.20

1987 Fleer Box Panels

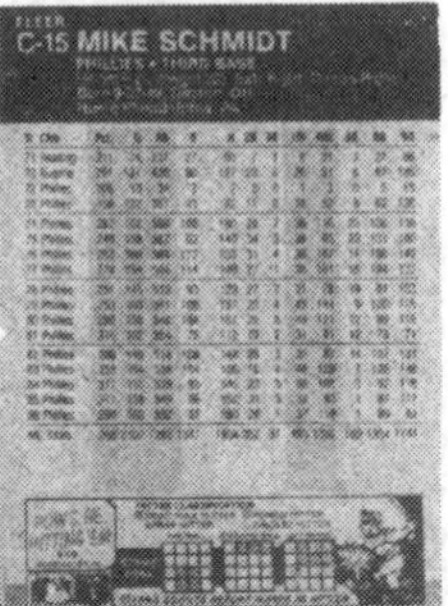

For the second straight year, Fleer produced a special set of cards designed to stimulate sales of their wax and cello pack boxes. In 1987, Fleer issued 16 cards in panels of four on the bottoms of retail boxes. The cards are numbered C-1 through C-16 and are 2-1/2" by 3-1/2" in size. The cards have the same design as the regular issue set with the player photos and card numbers being different.

		MT	NR MT	EX
Complete Panel Set:		8.00	6.00	3.25
Complete Singles Set:		3.50	2.75	1.50
Common Panel:		2.25	1.75	.90
Common Single Player:		.20	.15	.08
	Panel	2.50	2.00	1.00
1	Mets Logo	.05	.04	.02
6	Keith Hernandez	.30	.25	.12
8	Dale Murphy	.60	.45	.25
14	Ryne Sandberg	.80	.60	.30
	Panel	2.25	1.75	.90
2	Jesse Barfield	.20	.15	.08
3	George Brett	.80	.60	.30
5	Red Sox Logo	.05	.04	.02
11	Kirby Puckett	.60	.45	.25
	Panel	2.75	2.00	1.00
4	Dwight Gooden	.80	.60	.30
9	Astros Logo	.05	.04	.02
10	Dave Parker	.25	.20	.10
15	Mike Schmidt	.60	.45	.25
	Panel	2.75	2.00	1.00
7	Wally Joyner	.60	.45	.25
12	Dave Righetti	.20	.15	.08
13	Angels Logo	.05	.04	.02
16	Robin Yount	.60	.45	.25

1987 Fleer Update

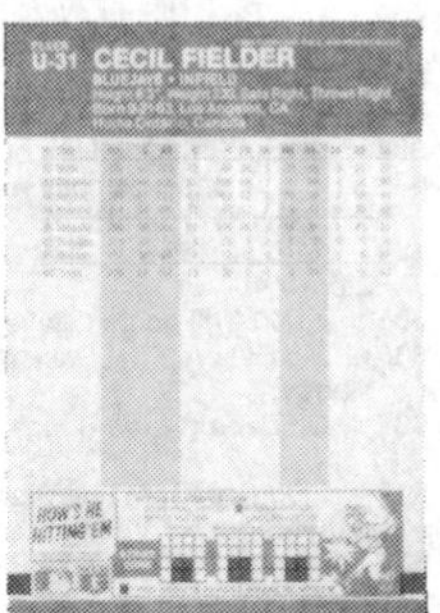

Fleer followed suit on a Topps idea in 1984 and began producing "Update" sets. The 1987 edition brings the regular Fleer set to date by including traded players and hot rookies. The cards measure 2-1/2" by 3-1/2" and are housed in a specially designed box with 25 team logo stickers. As a companion to the glossy-coated Fleer Collectors Edition set, Fleer produced a special edition Update set it its own tin box. Values of the glossy-coated cards are only a few dollars more than the regular Update cards.

		MT	NR MT	EX
Complete Set (132):		15.00	11.00	6.00
Common Player:		.06	.05	.02
1	Scott Bankhead	.08	.06	.03
2	Eric Bell(FC)	.06	.05	.02
3	Juan Beniquez	.06	.05	.02
4	Juan Berenguer	.06	.05	.02
5	Mike Birkbeck(FC)	.06	.05	.02
6	Randy Bockus(FC)	.06	.05	.02
7	Rod Booker(FC)	.06	.05	.02
8	Thad Bosley	.06	.05	.02
9	Greg Brock	.06	.05	.02
10	Bob Brower(FC)	.06	.05	.02
11	Chris Brown	.06	.05	.02
12	Jerry Browne	.06	.05	.02
13	Ralph Bryant	.06	.05	.02
14	DeWayne Buice(FC)	.06	.05	.02
15	Ellis Burks(FC)	.60	.45	.25
16	Casey Candaele(FC)	.10	.08	.04
17	Steve Carlton	.40	.30	.15
18	Juan Castillo	.06	.05	.02
19	Chuck Crim(FC)	.10	.08	.04
20	Mark Davidson(FC)	.20	.15	.08
21	Mark Davis	.06	.05	.02
22	Storm Davis	.06	.05	.02
23	Bill Dawley	.06	.05	.02
24	Andre Dawson	.40	.30	.15
25	Brian Dayett	.06	.05	.02
26	Rick Dempsey	.06	.05	.02
27	Ken Dowell(FC)	.06	.05	.02
28	Dave Dravecky	.08	.06	.03
29	Mike Dunne(FC)	.10	.08	.04
30	Dennis Eckersley	.30	.25	.12
31	Cecil Fielder	1.00	.70	.40
32	Brian Fisher	.10	.08	.04
33	Willie Fraser	.10	.08	.04
34	Ken Gerhart(FC)	.06	.05	.02
35	Jim Gott	.06	.05	.02
36	Dan Gladden	.06	.05	.02
37	Mike Greenwell(FC)	.80	.60	.30
38	Cecilio Guante	.06	.05	.02
39	Albert Hall	.06	.05	.02
40	Atlee Hammaker	.06	.05	.02
41	Mickey Hatcher	.06	.05	.02
42	Mike Heath	.06	.05	.02
43	Neal Heaton	.06	.05	.02
44	Mike Henneman(FC)	.30	.25	.12
45	Guy Hoffman	.06	.05	.02
46	Charles Hudson	.06	.05	.02
47	Chuck Jackson(FC)	.06	.05	.02
48	Mike Jackson(FC)	.06	.05	.02
49	Reggie Jackson	.60	.45	.25
50	Chris James	.06	.05	.02
51	Dion James	.06	.05	.02
52	Stan Javier	.06	.05	.02
53	Stan Jefferson(FC)	.06	.05	.02
54	Jimmy Jones	.10	.08	.04

		MT	NR MT	EX
55	Tracy Jones	.10	.08	.04
56	Terry Kennedy	.08	.06	.03
57	Mike Kingery	.06	.05	.02
58	Ray Knight	.10	.08	.04
59	Gene Larkin(FC)	.30	.25	.12
60	Mike LaValliere	.06	.05	.02
61	Jack Lazorko(FC)	.06	.05	.02
62	Terry Leach	.06	.05	.02
63	Rick Leach	.06	.05	.02
64	Craig Lefferts	.06	.05	.02
65	Jim Lindeman(FC)	.06	.05	.02
66	Bill Long(FC)	.06	.05	.02
67	Mike Loynd(FC)	.06	.05	.02
68	Greg Maddux(FC)	4.00	3.00	1.50
69	Bill Madlock	.15	.11	.06
70	Dave Magadan	.80	.60	.30
71	Joe Magrane(FC)	.60	.45	.25
72	Fred Manrique(FC)	.06	.05	.02
73	Mike Mason	.06	.05	.02
74	Lloyd McClendon(FC)	.06	.05	.02
75	Fred McGriff(FC)	4.00	3.00	1.50
76	Mark McGwire(FC)	4.00	3.00	1.50
77	Mark McLemore	.06	.05	.02
78	Kevin McReynolds	.08	.05	.02
79	Dave Meads(FC)	.06	.05	.02
80	Greg Minton	.06	.05	.02
81	John Mitchell(FC)	.06	.05	.02
82	Kevin Mitchell	.60	.45	.25
83	John Morris	.06	.05	.02
84	Jeff Musselman(FC)	.15	.11	.06
85	Randy Myers(FC)	.40	.30	.15
86	Gene Nelson	.06	.05	.02
87	Joe Niekro	.10	.08	.04
88	Tom Nieto	.06	.05	.02
89	Reid Nichols	.06	.05	.02
90	Matt Nokes(FC)	.40	.30	.15
91	Dickie Noles	.06	.05	.02
92	Edwin Nunez	.06	.05	.02
93	Jose Nunez(FC)	.06	.05	.02
94	Paul O'Neill	.50	.40	.20
95	Jim Paciorek(FC)	.06	.05	.02
96	Lance Parrish	.08	.05	.02
97	Bill Pecota(FC)	.08	.06	.03
98	Tony Pena	.08	.06	.03
99	Luis Polonia(FC)	.40	.30	.15
100	Randy Ready	.06	.05	.02
101	Jeff Reardon	.08	.06	.03
102	Gary Redus	.08	.06	.03
103	Rick Rhoden	.10	.08	.04
104	Wally Ritchie(FC)	.06	.05	.02
105	Jeff Robinson(FC)	.08	.05	.02
106	Mark Salas	.06	.05	.02
107	Dave Schmidt	.06	.05	.02
108	Kevin Seitzer	.06	.05	.02
109	John Shelby	.06	.05	.02
110	John Smiley(FC)	.30	.25	.12
111	Lary Sorenson	.06	.05	.02
112	Chris Speier	.06	.05	.02
113	Randy St. Claire	.06	.05	.02
114	Jim Sundberg	.08	.06	.03
115	B.J. Surhoff(FC)	.35	.25	.14
116	Greg Swindell	.40	.25	.15
117	Danny Tartabull	.40	.30	.15
118	Dorn Taylor(FC)	.06	.05	.02
119	Lee Tunnell	.06	.05	.02
120	Ed Vande Berg	.06	.05	.02
121	Andy Van Slyke	.20	.15	.08
122	Gary Ward	.06	.05	.02
123	Devon White	.40	.30	.15
124	Alan Wiggins	.06	.05	.02
125	Bill Wilkinson(FC)	.06	.05	.02
126	Jim Winn	.06	.05	.02
127	Frank Williams	.06	.05	.02
128	Ken Williams(FC)	.06	.05	.02
129	Matt Williams(FC)	4.00	3.00	1.50
130	Herm Winningham	.06	.05	.02
131	Matt Young	.06	.05	.02
132	Checklist 1-132	.06	.05	.02

1987 Fleer Baseball's Award Winners

The 1987 Fleer Award Winners boxed set was prepared by Fleer for distribution by 7-Eleven stores. The cards, which measure 2-1/2" by 3-1/2", feature players who have won various major league awards during their

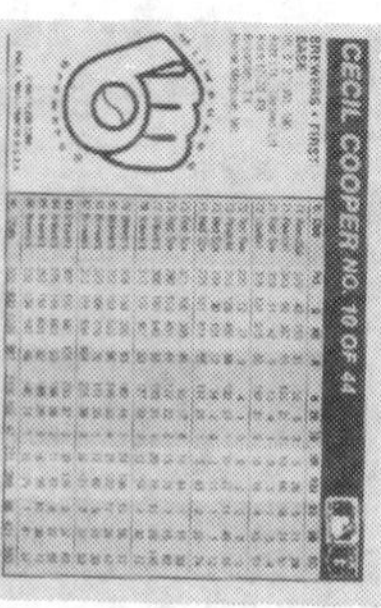

careers. The card fronts contain full-color photos surrounded by a yellow border. The name of the award the player won is printed at the bottom of the card in an oval-shaped band designed to resemble a metal nameplate on a trophy. Card backs, printed in black, yellow and white, include lifetime major and minor league statistics along with typical personal information. Each boxed set contained six team logo stickers.

		MT	NR MT	EX
Complete Set:		6.00	4.50	2.50
Common Player:		.05	.04	.02
1	Marty Barrett	.07	.05	.03
2	George Bell	.20	.15	.08
3	Bert Blyleven	.10	.08	.04
4	Bob Boone	.05	.04	.02
5	John Candelaria	.05	.04	.02
6	Jose Canseco	1.00	.70	.40
7	Gary Carter	.25	.20	.10
8	Joe Carter	.25	.20	.10
9	Roger Clemens	.50	.40	.20
10	Cecil Cooper	.10	.08	.04
11	Eric Davis	.60	.45	.25
12	Tony Fernandez	.10	.08	.04
13	Scott Fletcher	.05	.04	.02
14	Bob Forsch	.05	.04	.02
15	Dwight Gooden	.50	.40	.20
16	Ron Guidry	.12	.09	.05
17	Ozzie Guillen	.07	.05	.03
18	Bill Gullickson	.05	.04	.02
19	Tony Gwynn	.25	.20	.10
20	Bob Knepper	.05	.04	.02
21	Ray Knight	.05	.04	.02
22	Mark Langston	.20	.15	.08
23	Candy Maldonado	.05	.04	.02
24	Don Mattingly	1.00	.70	.40
25	Roger McDowell	.07	.05	.03
26	Dale Murphy	.30	.25	.12
27	Dave Parker	.12	.09	.05
28	Lance Parrish	.15	.11	.06
29	Gary Pettis	.05	.04	.02
30	Kirby Puckett	.70	.50	.40
31	Johnny Ray	.07	.05	.03
32	Dave Righetti	.12	.09	.05
33	Cal Ripken, Jr.	.60	.45	.25
34	Bret Saberhagen	.15	.11	.06
35	Ryne Sandberg	.20	.15	.08
36	Mike Schmidt	.30	.25	.12
37	Mike Scott	.12	.09	.05
38	Ozzie Smith	.12	.09	.05
39	Robbie Thompson	.10	.08	.04
40	Fernando Valenzuela	.20	.15	.08
41	Mitch Webster	.05	.04	.02
42	Frank White	.07	.05	.03
43	Mike Witt	.07	.05	.03
44	Todd Worrell	.15	.11	.06

1987 Fleer Baseball All Stars

Produced by Fleer for exclusive distribution through Ben Franklin stores, the "Baseball All Stars" set is comprised of 44 cards which are the standard 2-1/2" by 3-1/2" size. The cards have full-color photos surrounded by a bright red border with white pinstripes at the top and bottom. The card backs are printed in blue, white and dark

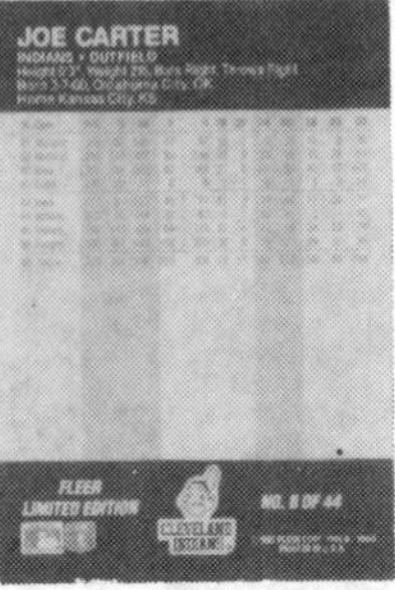

red and include complete major and minor league statistics. The set was issued in a special cardboard box.

		MT	NR MT	EX
	Complete Set:	6.00	4.00	2.00
	Common Player:	.10	.06	.03
1	Harold Baines	.10	.06	.03
2	Jesse Barfield	.12	.09	.05
3	Wade Boggs	.60	.45	.25
4	Dennis "Oil Can" Boyd	.05	.04	.02
5	Scott Bradley	.05	.04	.02
6	Jose Canseco	1.00	.70	.40
7	Gary Carter	.25	.20	.10
8	Joe Carter	.25	.20	.10
9	Mark Clear	.05	.04	.02
10	Roger Clemens	.50	.40	.20
11	Jose Cruz	.05	.04	.02
12	Chili Davis	.07	.05	.03
13	Jody Davis	.05	.04	.02
14	Rob Deer	.05	.04	.02
15	Brian Downing	.05	.04	.02
16	Sid Fernandez	.07	.05	.03
17	John Franco	.07	.05	.03
18	Andres Galarraga	.15	.11	.06
19	Dwight Gooden	.50	.40	.20
20	Tony Gwynn	.25	.20	.10
21	Charlie Hough	.05	.04	.02
22	Bruce Hurst	.10	.08	.04
23	Wally Joyner	.70	.50	.30
24	Carney Lansford	.05	.04	.02
25	Fred Lynn	.12	.09	.05
26	Don Mattingly	1.50	1.25	.60
27	Willie McGee	.10	.08	.04
28	Jack Morris	.15	.11	.06
29	Dale Murphy	.30	.25	.12
30	Bob Ojeda	.07	.05	.03
31	Tony Pena	.07	.05	.03
32	Kirby Puckett	.70	.50	.30
33	Dan Quisenberry	.07	.05	.03
34	Tim Raines	.25	.20	.10
35	Willie Randolph	.07	.05	.03
36	Cal Ripken, Jr.	.50	.40	.20
37	Pete Rose	.50	.40	.20
38	Nolan Ryan	1.00	.70	.40
39	Juan Samuel	.10	.08	.04
40	Mike Schmidt	.30	.25	.12
41	Ozzie Smith	.12	.09	.05
42	Andres Thomas	.10	.08	.04
43	Fernando Valenzuela	.20	.15	.08
44	Mike Witt	.07	.05	.03

1987 Fleer Baseball's Best

For a second straight baseball card season, Fleer produced for McCrory's stores and their affiliates a 44-card "Baseball's Best" set. Subtitled "Sluggers vs. Pitchers," 28 everyday players and 16 pitchers are featured. The card design is nearly identical to the previous year's effort. The cards, which measure 2-1/2" by 3-1/2", were housed in a specially designed box along with six team logo stickers.

		MT	NR MT	EX
	Complete Set:	6.00	4.50	2.50
	Common Player:	.05	.04	.02
1	Kevin Bass	.07	.05	.03
2	Jesse Barfield	.12	.09	.05
3	George Bell	.20	.15	.08
4	Wade Boggs	.60	.45	.25
5	Sid Bream	.05	.04	.02
6	George Brett	.30	.25	.12
7	Ivan Calderon	.10	.08	.04
8	Jose Canseco	1.00	.70	.40
9	Jack Clark	.12	.09	.05
10	Roger Clemens	.50	.40	.20
11	Eric Davis	.50	.40	.20
12	Andre Dawson	.15	.11	.06
13	Sid Fernandez	.07	.05	.03
14	John Franco	.07	.05	.03
15	Dwight Gooden	.50	.40	.20
16	Pedro Guerrero	.15	.11	.06
17	Tony Gwynn	.25	.20	.10
18	Rickey Henderson	.30	.25	.12
19	Tom Henke	.05	.04	.02
20	Ted Higuera	.10	.08	.04
21	Pete Incaviglia	.30	.25	.12
22	Wally Joyner	.50	.40	.20
23	Jeff Leonard	.05	.04	.02
24	Joe Magrane	.15	.11	.06
25	Don Mattingly	1.00	.70	.40
26	Mark McGwire	.60	.45	.25
27	Jack Morris	.15	.11	.06
28	Dale Murphy	.30	.25	.12
29	Dave Parker	.12	.09	.05
30	Ken Phelps	.05	.04	.02
31	Kirby Puckett	.70	.50	.30
32	Tim Raines	.25	.20	.10
33	Jeff Reardon	.10	.08	.04
34	Dave Righetti	.12	.09	.05
35	Cal Ripken, Jr.	.60	.45	.25
36	Bret Saberhagen	.15	.11	.06
37	Mike Schmidt	.30	.25	.12
38	Mike Scott	.12	.09	.05
39	Kevin Seitzer	.50	.40	.20
40	Darryl Strawberry	.40	.30	.15
41	Rick Sutcliffe	.10	.08	.04
42	Pat Tabler	.05	.04	.02
43	Fernando Valenzuela	.10	.08	.04
44	Mike Witt	.07	.05	.03

1987 Fleer Baseball's Exciting Stars

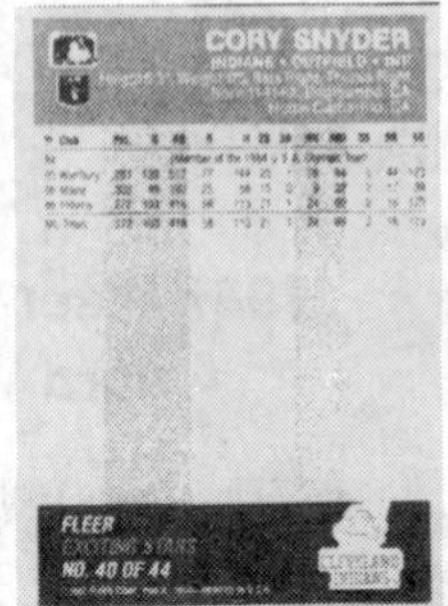

Another entry into the Fleer lineup of individual boxed sets, the "Baseball's Exciting Stars" set was produced by Fleer for Cumberland Farms stores. The card fronts feature a red, white and blue border with the words "Exciting Stars" printed in yellow at the top. The backs are printed in red and blue and carry complete major and minor league statistics. Included with the boxed set of 44 cards were six team logo stickers.

		MT	NR MT	EX
Complete Set:		6.00	4.50	2.50
Common Player:		.05	.04	.02
1	Don Aase	.05	.04	.02
2	Rick Aguilera	.07	.05	.03
3	Jesse Barfield	.12	.09	.05
4	Wade Boggs	.60	.45	.25
5	Dennis "Oil Can" Boyd	.05	.04	.02
6	Sid Bream	.07	.05	.03
7	Jose Canseco	1.00	.70	.40
8	Steve Carlton	.25	.20	.10
9	Gary Carter	.25	.20	.10
10	Will Clark	1.00	.70	.40
11	Roger Clemens	.40	.30	.15
12	Danny Cox	.07	.05	.03
13	Alvin Davis	.10	.08	.04
14	Eric Davis	.50	.40	.20
15	Rob Deer	.07	.05	.03
16	Brian Downing	.05	.04	.02
17	Gene Garber	.05	.04	.02
18	Steve Garvey	.25	.20	.10
19	Dwight Gooden	.50	.40	.20
20	Mark Gubicza	.10	.08	.04
21	Mel Hall	.05	.04	.02
22	Terry Harper	.05	.04	.02
23	Von Hayes	.10	.08	.04
24	Rickey Henderson	.60	.45	.25
25	Tom Henke	.05	.04	.02
26	Willie Hernandez	.05	.04	.02
27	Ted Higuera	.10	.08	.04
28	Rick Honeycutt	.05	.04	.02
29	Kent Hrbek	.15	.11	.06
30	Wally Joyner	.60	.45	.25
31	Charlie Kerfeld	.05	.04	.02
32	Fred Lynn	.12	.09	.05
33	Don Mattingly	1.50	1.25	.60
34	Tim Raines	.25	.20	.10
35	Dennis Rasmussen	.07	.05	.03
36	Johnny Ray	.07	.05	.03
37	Jim Rice	.20	.15	.08
38	Pete Rose	.50	.40	.20
39	Lee Smith	.07	.05	.03
40	Cory Snyder	.25	.20	.10
41	Darryl Strawberry	.40	.30	.15
42	Kent Tekulve	.05	.04	.02
43	Willie Wilson	.10	.08	.04
44	Bobby Witt	.12	.09	.05

1987 Fleer Baseball's Game Winners

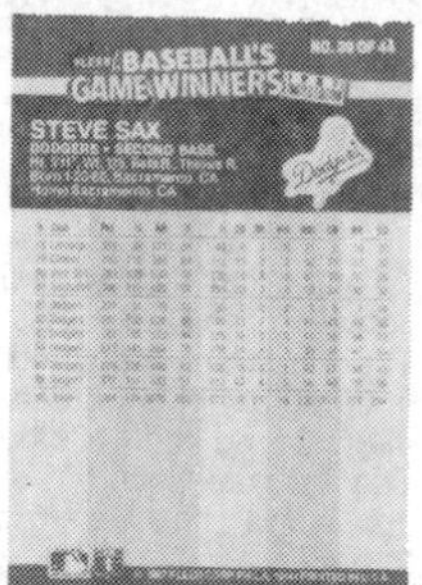

The 1987 Fleer "Baseball's Game Winners" boxed set of 44 cards was produced for distribution through Bi-Mart Discount Drug, Pay'n-Save, Mott's 5 & 10, M.E. Moses, and Winn's stores. The cards, which measure 2-1/2" by 3-1/2", have a light blue border with the player's name and game winning RBI or games won statistics in a yellow oval band at the top of the card. Below the full-color player photo is the name of the set in blue, yellow and red. Included with the boxed set were six team logo stickers.

		MT	NR MT	EX
Complete Set:		6.00	4.50	2.50
Common Player:		.05	.04	.02
1	Harold Baines	.10	.08	.04
2	Don Baylor	.10	.08	.04
3	George Bell	.20	.15	.08
4	Tony Bernazard	.05	.04	.02
5	Wade Boggs	.60	.45	.25
6	George Brett	.40	.30	.15
7	Hubie Brooks	.07	.05	.03
8	Jose Canseco	1.00	.70	.40
9	Gary Carter	.20	.15	.08
10	Roger Clemens	.40	.30	.15
11	Eric Davis	.50	.40	.20
12	Glenn Davis	.15	.11	.06
13	Shawon Dunston	.07	.05	.03
14	Mark Eichhorn	.10	.08	.04
15	Gary Gaetti	.12	.09	.05
16	Steve Garvey	.25	.20	.10
17	Kirk Gibson	.20	.15	.08
18	Dwight Gooden	.50	.40	.20
19	Von Hayes	.07	.05	.03
20	Willie Hernandez	.07	.05	.03
21	Ted Higuera	.10	.08	.04
22	Wally Joyner	.80	.60	.30
23	Bob Knepper	.05	.04	.02
24	Mike Krukow	.05	.04	.02
25	Jeff Leonard	.05	.04	.02
26	Don Mattingly	1.00	.70	.40
27	Kirk McCaskill	.07	.05	.03
28	Kevin McReynolds	.12	.09	.05
29	Jim Morrison	.05	.04	.02
30	Dale Murphy	.30	.25	.12
31	Pete O'Brien	.07	.05	.03
32	Bob Ojeda	.07	.05	.03
33	Larry Parrish	.05	.04	.02
34	Ken Phelps	.05	.04	.02
35	Dennis Rasmussen	.07	.05	.03
36	Ernest Riles	.07	.05	.03
37	Cal Ripken, Jr.	.60	.45	.25
38	Ron Robinson	.05	.04	.02
39	Steve Sax	.15	.11	.06
40	Mike Schmidt	.30	.25	.12
41	John Tudor	.07	.05	.03
42	Fernando Valenzuela	.20	.15	.08
43	Mike Witt	.07	.05	.03
44	Curt Young	.05	.04	.02

1987 Fleer Baseball's Hottest Stars

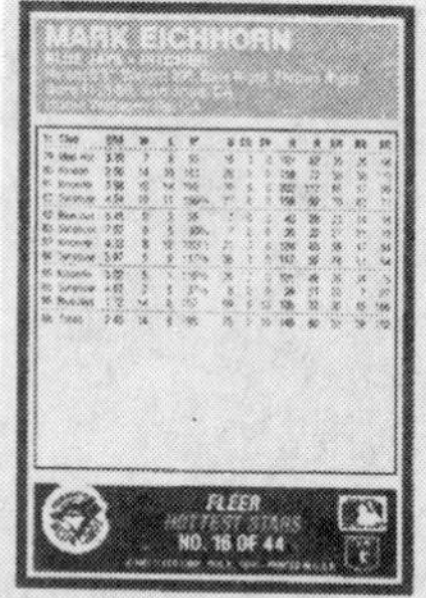

The "Baseball's Hottest Stars" 44-card set was produced by Fleer for the Revco Drug Store chain. Measuring the standard 2-1/2" by 3-1/2", the cards feature full-color photos surrounded by a red, white and blue border. The player's name, position and team appear in a blue band at the bottom of the card. Card backs are printed in red, white and black and contain the player's lifetime professional statistics. The set was housed in a special cardboard box with six team logo stickers.

		MT	NR MT	EX
Complete Set:		6.00	4.50	2.50
Common Player:		.05	.04	.02
1	Joaquin Andujar	.05	.04	.02
2	Harold Baines	.10	.08	.04
3	Kevin Bass	.07	.05	.03
4	Don Baylor	.10	.08	.04
5	Barry Bonds	.20	.15	.08
6	George Brett	.30	.25	.12
7	Tom Brunansky	.10	.08	.04
8	Brett Butler	.05	.04	.02
9	Jose Canseco	1.00	.70	.40
10	Roger Clemens	.50	.40	.20
11	Ron Darling	.10	.08	.04
12	Eric Davis	.50	.40	.20
13	Andre Dawson	.15	.11	.06
14	Doug DeCinces	.05	.04	.02
15	Leon Durham	.07	.05	.03
16	Mark Eichhorn	.10	.08	.04
17	Scott Garrelts	.05	.04	.02
18	Dwight Gooden	.50	.40	.20
19	Dave Henderson	.05	.04	.02
20	Rickey Henderson	.50	.40	.20
21	Keith Hernandez	.15	.11	.06
22	Ted Higuera	.10	.08	.04
23	Bob Horner	.07	.05	.03
24	Pete Incaviglia	.40	.30	.15
25	Wally Joyner	.50	.40	.20
26	Mark Langston	.07	.05	.03
27	Don Mattingly	1.00	.70	.40
28	Dale Murphy	.30	.25	.12
29	Kirk McCaskill	.07	.05	.03
30	Willie McGee	.10	.08	.04
31	Dave Righetti	.12	.09	.05
32	Pete Rose	.40	.30	.15
33	Bruce Ruffin	.15	.11	.06
34	Steve Sax	.15	.11	.06
35	Mike Schmidt	.30	.25	.12
36	Larry Sheets	.10	.08	.04
37	Eric Show	.07	.05	.03
38	Dave Smith	.05	.04	.02
39	Cory Snyder	.07	.05	.03
40	Frank Tanana	.05	.04	.02
41	Alan Trammell	.20	.15	.08
42	Reggie Williams	.07	.05	.03
43	Mookie Wilson	.07	.05	.03
44	Todd Worrell	.15	.11	.06

1987 Fleer League Leaders

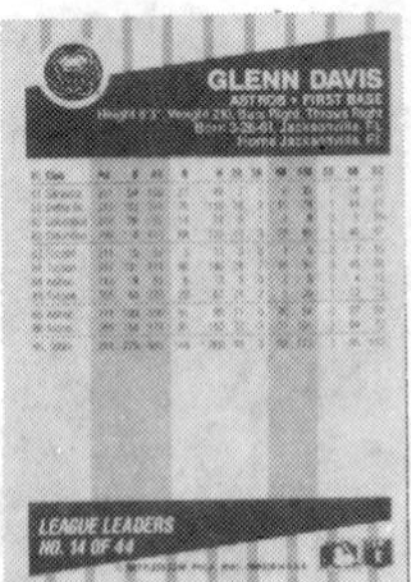

For the second year in a row, Fleer produced a 44- card "League Leaders" set for Walgreens. The card fronts feature a border style which is identical to that used in 1986. However, an elliptical shaped full-color player photo is placed diagonally on the front. "1987 Fleer League Leaders" appears in the upper left corner of the front although nowhere on the card does it state in which pitching, hitting or fielding department was the player a league leader. The card backs are printed in red and blue on white stock. The cards in the boxed set are the standard 2-1/2" by 3-1/2" size.

		MT	NR MT	EX
Complete Set:		5.00	3.75	2.00
Common Player:		.05	.04	.02
1	Jesse Barfield	.12	.09	.05
2	Mike Boddicker	.07	.05	.03
3	Wade Boggs	.60	.45	.25
4	Phil Bradley	.10	.08	.04
5	George Brett	.30	.25	.12
6	Hubie Brooks	.07	.05	.03
7	Chris Brown	.07	.05	.03
8	Jose Canseco	.70	.50	.30
9	Joe Carter	.12	.09	.05
10	Roger Clemens	.40	.30	.15
11	Vince Coleman	.15	.11	.06
12	Joe Cowley	.05	.04	.02
13	Kal Daniels	.20	.15	.08
14	Glenn Davis	.15	.11	.06
15	Jody Davis	.07	.05	.03
16	Darrell Evans	.07	.05	.03
17	Dwight Evans	.10	.08	.04
18	John Franco	.07	.05	.03
19	Julio Franco	.10	.08	.04
20	Dwight Gooden	.40	.30	.15
21	Goose Gossage	.12	.09	.05
22	Tom Herr	.07	.05	.03
23	Ted Higuera	.10	.08	.04
24	Bob Horner	.07	.05	.03
25	Pete Incaviglia	.40	.30	.15
26	Wally Joyner	.40	.30	.15
27	Dave Kingman	.10	.08	.04
28	Don Mattingly	1.00	.70	.40
29	Willie McGee	.10	.08	.04
30	Donnie Moore	.05	.04	.02
31	Keith Moreland	.05	.04	.02
32	Eddie Murray	.25	.20	.10
33	Mike Pagliarulo	.10	.08	.04
34	Larry Parrish	.05	.04	.02
35	Tony Pena	.07	.05	.03
36	Kirby Puckett	.50	.40	.20
37	Pete Rose	.50	.40	.20
38	Juan Samuel	.12	.09	.05
39	Ryne Sandberg	.20	.15	.08
40	Mike Schmidt	.30	.25	.12
41	Darryl Strawberry	.40	.30	.15
42	Greg Walker	.07	.05	.03
43	Bob Welch	.07	.05	.03
44	Todd Worrell	.12	.09	.05

1987 Fleer Limited Edition

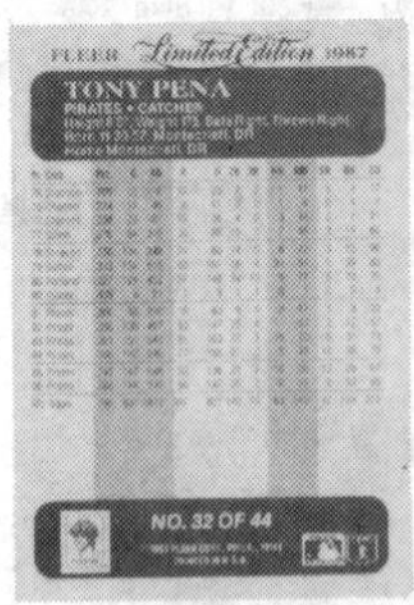

For the third straight year, Fleer produced a Limited Edition set for the McCrory's store chain and their affiliates. The cards are the standard 2-1/2" by 3-1/2" size and feature light blue borders at the top and bottom and a diagonal red and white border running along both sides. The set was issued in a specially prepared cardboard box, along with six team logo stickers.

		MT	NR MT	EX
Complete Set:		5.00	3.75	2.00
Common Player:		.05	.04	.02
1	Floyd Bannister	.05	.04	.02
2	Marty Barrett	.07	.05	.03
3	Steve Bedrosian	.10	.08	.04
4	George Bell	.20	.15	.08

		MT	NR MT	EX
5	George Brett	.30	.25	.12
6	Jose Canseco	1.00	.70	.40
7	Joe Carter	.12	.09	.05
8	Will Clark	1.00	.70	.40
9	Roger Clemens	.40	.30	.15
10	Vince Coleman	.15	.11	.06
11	Glenn Davis	.15	.11	.06
12	Mike Davis	.05	.04	.02
13	Len Dykstra	.07	.05	.03
14	John Franco	.07	.05	.03
15	Julio Franco	.10	.08	.04
16	Steve Garvey	.25	.20	.10
17	Kirk Gibson	.20	.15	.08
18	Dwight Gooden	.40	.30	.15
19	Tony Gwynn	.25	.20	.10
20	Keith Hernandez	.20	.15	.08
21	Teddy Higuera	.10	.08	.04
22	Kent Hrbek	.15	.11	.06
23	Wally Joyner	.50	.40	.20
24	Mike Krukow	.05	.04	.02
25	Mike Marshall	.10	.08	.04
26	Don Mattingly	1.00	.70	.40
27	Oddibe McDowell	.10	.08	.04
28	Jack Morris	.15	.11	.06
29	Lloyd Moseby	.07	.05	.03
30	Dale Murphy	.30	.25	.12
31	Eddie Murray	.25	.20	.10
32	Tony Pena	.07	.05	.03
33	Jim Presley	.10	.08	.04
34	Jeff Reardon	.10	.08	.04
35	Jim Rice	.20	.15	.08
36	Pete Rose	.40	.30	.15
37	Mike Schmidt	.30	.25	.12
38	Mike Scott	.12	.09	.05
39	Lee Smith	.07	.05	.03
40	Lonnie Smith	.05	.04	.02
41	Gary Ward	.05	.04	.02
42	Dave Winfield	.25	.20	.10
43	Todd Worrell	.12	.09	.05
44	Robin Yount	.20	.15	.08

1987 Fleer Mini

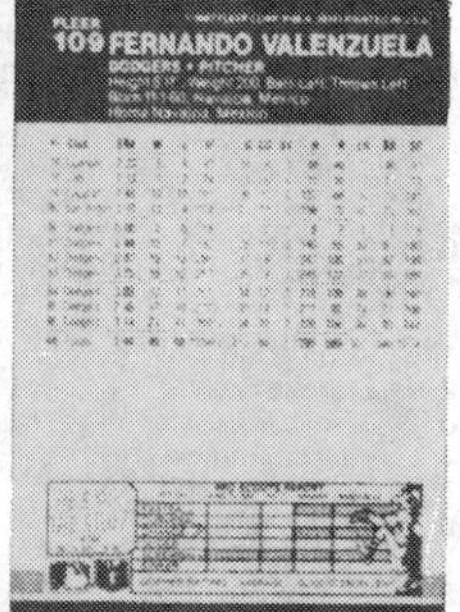

Continuing with an idea originated the previous year, the Fleer "Classic Miniatures" set consists of 120 cards that measure 1-13/16" by 2-9/16" in size. The cards are identical in design to the regular issue set produced by Fleer, but use completely different photos. The set was issued in a specially prepared collectors box along with 18 team logo stickers. The Fleer Mini set was available only through hobby dealers.

		MT	NR MT	EX
Complete Set:		9.00	6.75	3.50
Common Player:		.05	.04	.02
1	Don Aase	.05	.04	.02
2	Joaquin Andujar	.05	.04	.02
3	Harold Baines	.12	.09	.05
4	Jesse Barfield	.12	.09	.05
5	Kevin Bass	.05	.04	.02
6	Don Baylor	.10	.08	.04
7	George Bell	.20	.15	.08
8	Tony Bernazard	.05	.04	.02
9	Bert Blyleven	.12	.09	.05
10	Wade Boggs	.60	.45	.25
11	Phil Bradley	.10	.08	.04
12	Sid Bream	.05	.04	.02
13	George Brett	.60	.45	.25
14	Hubie Brooks	.07	.05	.03
15	Chris Brown	.07	.05	.03
16	Tom Candiotti	.05	.04	.02
17	Jose Canseco	1.00	.70	.40
18	Gary Carter	.20	.15	.08
19	Joe Carter	.12	.09	.05
20	Roger Clemens	.60	.45	.25
21	Vince Coleman	.15	.11	.06
22	Cecil Cooper	.10	.08	.04
23	Ron Darling	.10	.08	.04
24	Alvin Davis	.10	.08	.04
25	Chili Davis	.05	.04	.02
26	Eric Davis	.40	.30	.15
27	Glenn Davis	.15	.11	.06
28	Mike Davis	.05	.04	.02
29	Doug DeCinces	.05	.04	.02
30	Rob Deer	.07	.05	.03
31	Jim Deshaies	.10	.08	.04
32	Bo Diaz	.05	.04	.02
33	Richard Dotson	.07	.05	.03
34	Brian Downing	.05	.04	.02
35	Shawon Dunston	.07	.05	.03
36	Mark Eichhorn	.10	.08	.04
37	Dwight Evans	.12	.09	.05
38	Tony Fernandez	.10	.08	.04
39	Julio Franco	.10	.08	.04
40	Gary Gaetti	.12	.09	.05
41	Andres Galarraga	.15	.11	.06
42	Scott Garrelts	.05	.04	.02
43	Steve Garvey	.20	.15	.08
44	Kirk Gibson	.20	.15	.08
45	Dwight Gooden	.40	.30	.15
46	Ken Griffey	.07	.05	.03
47	Mark Gubicza	.10	.08	.04
48	Ozzie Guillen	.07	.05	.03
49	Bill Gullickson	.05	.04	.02
50	Tony Gwynn	.25	.20	.10
51	Von Hayes	.10	.08	.04
52	Rickey Henderson	.60	.45	.25
53	Keith Hernandez	.15	.11	.06
54	Willie Hernandez	.05	.04	.02
55	Ted Higuera	.10	.08	.04
56	Charlie Hough	.05	.04	.02
57	Kent Hrbek	.15	.11	.06
58	Pete Incaviglia	.20	.15	.08
59	Wally Joyner	.30	.25	.12
60	Bob Knepper	.07	.05	.03
61	Mike Krukow	.05	.04	.02
62	Mark Langston	.10	.08	.04
63	Carney Lansford	.07	.05	.03
64	Jim Lindeman	.12	.09	.05
65	Bill Madlock	.10	.08	.04
66	Don Mattingly	.80	.60	.30
67	Kirk McCaskill	.05	.04	.02
68	Lance McCullers	.10	.08	.04
69	Keith Moreland	.05	.04	.02
70	Jack Morris	.15	.11	.06
71	Jim Morrison	.05	.04	.02
72	Lloyd Moseby	.07	.05	.03
73	Jerry Mumphrey	.05	.04	.02
74	Dale Murphy	.30	.25	.12
75	Eddie Murray	.25	.20	.10
76	Pete O'Brien	.07	.05	.03
77	Bob Ojeda	.07	.05	.03
78	Jesse Orosco	.05	.04	.02
79	Dan Pasqua	.10	.08	.04
80	Dave Parker	.12	.09	.05
81	Larry Parrish	.05	.04	.02
82	Jim Presley	.05	.04	.02
83	Kirby Puckett	.60	.45	.25
84	Dan Quisenberry	.07	.05	.03
85	Tim Raines	.20	.15	.08
86	Dennis Rasmussen	.07	.05	.03
87	Johnny Ray	.07	.05	.03
88	Jeff Reardon	.07	.05	.03
89	Jim Rice	.20	.15	.08
90	Dave Righetti	.12	.09	.05
91	Earnest Riles	.05	.04	.02
92	Cal Ripken, Jr.	.80	.60	.30
93	Ron Robinson	.05	.04	.02
94	Juan Samuel	.12	.09	.05
95	Ryne Sandberg	.80	.60	.30
96	Steve Sax	.15	.11	.06
97	Mike Schmidt	.30	.25	.12
98	Ken Schrom	.05	.04	.02
99	Mike Scott	.12	.09	.05
100	Ruben Sierra	.75	.55	.30
101	Lee Smith	.07	.05	.03
102	Ozzie Smith	.12	.09	.05
103	Cory Snyder	.20	.15	.08

		MT	NR MT	EX
104	Kent Tekulve	.05	.04	.02
105	Andres Thomas	.10	.08	.04
106	Rob Thompson	.10	.08	.04
107	Alan Trammell	.20	.15	.08
108	John Tudor	.07	.05	.03
109	Fernando Valenzuela	.20	.15	.08
110	Greg Walker	.07	.05	.03
111	Mitch Webster	.05	.04	.02
112	Lou Whitaker	.15	.11	.06
113	Frank White	.07	.05	.03
114	Reggie Williams	.10	.08	.04
115	Glenn Wilson	.05	.04	.02
116	Willie Wilson	.10	.08	.04
117	Dave Winfield	.20	.15	.08
118	Mike Witt	.07	.05	.03
119	Todd Worrell	.12	.09	.05
120	Floyd Youmans	.05	.04	.02

1987 Fleer Baseball Record Setters

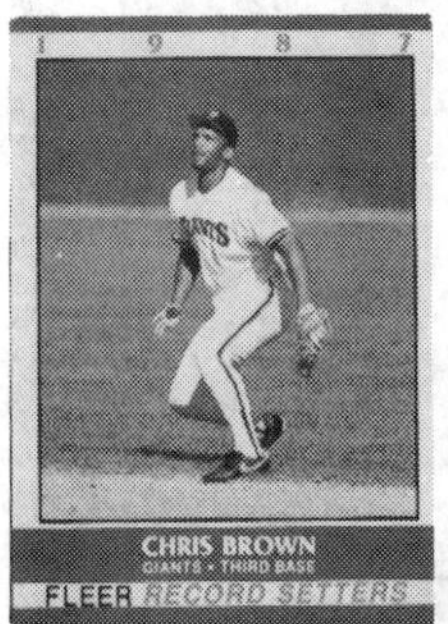

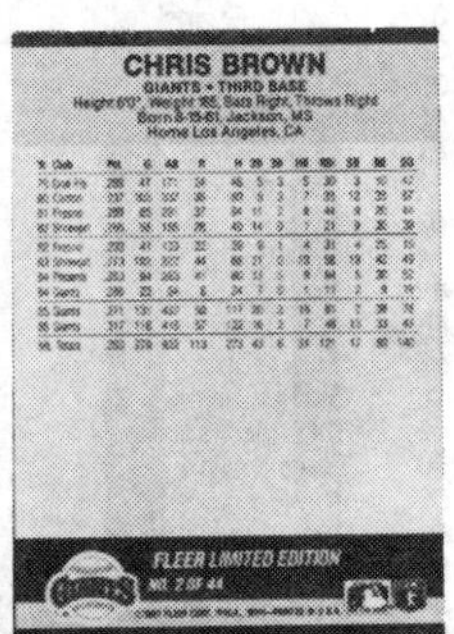

Produced by Fleer for the Eckerd Drug chain, the 1987 Fleer Record Setters set contains 44 cards that measure the standard 2-1/2" by 3-1/2" size. Although the set is titled "Record Setters," the actual records the players have set is not specified anywhere on the cards. Given that several players included in the set were young prospects, a better title for those cards might have been "Possible Record Setters". The set came housed in a special cardboard box with six team logo stickers.

		MT	NR MT	EX
	Complete Set:	5.00	3.75	2.00
	Common Player:	.05	.04	.02
1	George Brett	.30	.25	.12
2	Chris Brown	.07	.05	.03
3	Jose Canseco	1.00	.70	.40
4	Roger Clemens	.40	.30	.15
5	Alvin Davis	.10	.08	.04
6	Shawon Dunston	.07	.05	.03
7	Tony Fernandez	.10	.08	.04
8	Carlton Fisk	.12	.09	.05
9	Gary Gaetti	.10	.08	.04
10	Gene Garber	.05	.04	.02
11	Rich Gedman	.05	.04	.02
12	Dwight Gooden	.40	.30	.15
13	Ozzie Guillen	.07	.05	.03
14	Bill Gullickson	.05	.04	.02
15	Billy Hatcher	.07	.05	.03
16	Orel Hershiser	.20	.15	.08
17	Wally Joyner	.70	.50	.30
18	Ray Knight	.05	.04	.02
19	Craig Lefferts	.05	.04	.02
20	Don Mattingly	1.00	.70	.40
21	Kevin Mitchell	.70	.50	.30
22	Lloyd Moseby	.07	.05	.03
23	Dale Murphy	.30	.25	.12
24	Eddie Murray	.25	.20	.10
25	Phil Niekro	.15	.11	.06
26	Ben Oglivie	.05	.04	.02
27	Jesse Orosco	.05	.04	.02
28	Joe Orsulak	.05	.04	.02
29	Larry Parrish	.05	.04	.02
30	Tim Raines	.25	.20	.10
31	Shane Rawley	.07	.05	.03
32	Dave Righetti	.12	.09	.05
33	Pete Rose	.40	.30	.15
34	Steve Sax	.15	.11	.06
35	Mike Schmidt	.30	.25	.12
36	Mike Scott	.12	.09	.05
37	Don Sutton	.12	.09	.05
38	Alan Trammell	.20	.15	.08
39	John Tudor	.10	.08	.04
40	Gary Ward	.05	.04	.02
41	Lou Whitaker	.15	.11	.06
42	Willie Wilson	.10	.08	.04
43	Todd Worrell	.15	.11	.06
44	Floyd Youmans	.10	.08	.04

1987 Fleer Star Stickers

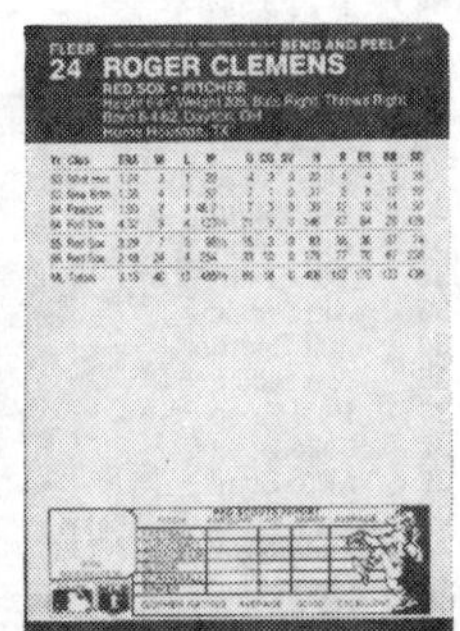

The 1987 Fleer Star Stickers set contains 132 cards which become stickers if the back is bent and peeled off. As in the previous year, the card backs are identical, save the numbering system, to the regular issue cards. The cards measure 2-1/2" by 3-1/2" and were sold in wax packs with team logo stickers. The fronts have a green border with a red and white banner wrapped across the upper left corner and the sides. The backs are printed in green and yellow.

		MT	NR MT	EX
	Complete Set:	20.00	15.00	8.00
	Common Player:	.05	.04	.02
1	Don Aase	.05	.04	.02
2	Harold Baines	.20	.15	.08
3	Floyd Bannister	.08	.06	.03
4	Jesse Barfield	.20	.15	.08
5	Marty Barrett	.10	.08	.04
6	Kevin Bass	.10	.08	.04
7	Don Baylor	.12	.09	.05
8	Steve Bedrosian	.15	.11	.06
9	George Bell	.35	.25	.14
10	Bert Blyleven	.15	.11	.06
11	Mike Boddicker	.08	.06	.03
12	Wade Boggs	1.00	.70	.40
13	Phil Bradley	.15	.11	.06
14	Sid Bream	.08	.06	.03
15	George Brett	.70	.50	.30
16	Hubie Brooks	.10	.08	.04
17	Tom Brunansky	.15	.11	.06
18	Tom Candiotti	.05	.04	.02
19	Jose Canseco	1.00	.70	.40
20	Gary Carter	.40	.30	.15
21	Joe Carter	.20	.15	.08
22	Will Clark	1.00	.70	.40
23	Mark Clear	.05	.04	.02
24	Roger Clemens	.90	.70	.35
25	Vince Coleman	.25	.20	.10
26	Jose Cruz	.10	.08	.04
27	Ron Darling	.20	.15	.08
28	Alvin Davis	.20	.15	.08
29	Chili Davis	.10	.08	.04
30	Eric Davis	.60	.45	.25
31	Glenn Davis	.20	.15	.08
32	Mike Davis	.05	.04	.02
33	Andre Dawson	.25	.20	.10
34	Doug DeCinces	.08	.06	.03
35	Brian Downing	.08	.06	.03
36	Shawon Dunston	.12	.09	.05
37	Mark Eichhorn	.12	.09	.05

		MT	NR MT	EX
38	Dwight Evans	.15	.11	.06
39	Tony Fernandez	.15	.11	.06
40	Bob Forsch	.05	.04	.02
41	John Franco	.10	.08	.04
42	Julio Franco	.12	.09	.05
43	Gary Gaetti	.20	.15	.08
44	Gene Garber	.05	.04	.02
45	Scott Garrelts	.05	.04	.02
46	Steve Garvey	.40	.30	.15
47	Kirk Gibson	.30	.25	.12
48	Dwight Gooden	.90	.70	.35
49	Ken Griffey	.10	.08	.04
50	Ozzie Guillen	.10	.08	.04
51	Bill Gullickson	.05	.04	.02
52	Tony Gwynn	.40	.30	.15
53	Mel Hall	.08	.06	.03
54	Greg Harris	.05	.04	.02
55	Von Hayes	.12	.09	.05
56	Rickey Henderson	1.00	.70	.40
57	Tom Henke	.10	.08	.04
58	Keith Hernandez	.35	.25	.14
59	Willie Hernandez	.05	.04	.02
60	Ted Higuera	.20	.15	.08
61	Bob Horner	.12	.09	.05
62	Charlie Hough	.08	.06	.03
63	Jay Howell	.08	.06	.03
64	Kent Hrbek	.30	.25	.12
65	Bruce Hurst	.12	.09	.05
66	Pete Incaviglia	.60	.45	.25
67	Bob James	.05	.04	.02
68	Wally Joyner	.50	.40	.20
69	Mike Krukow	.05	.04	.02
70	Mark Langston	.15	.11	.06
71	Carney Lansford	.08	.06	.03
72	Fred Lynn	.25	.20	.10
73	Bill Madlock	.12	.09	.05
74	Don Mattingly	1.00	.70	.40
75	Kirk McCaskill	.05	.04	.02
76	Lance McCullers	.12	.09	.05
77	Oddibe McDowell	.15	.11	.06
78	Paul Molitor	.20	.15	.08
79	Keith Moreland	.08	.06	.03
80	Jack Morris	.25	.20	.10
81	Jim Morrison	.05	.04	.02
82	Jerry Mumphrey	.05	.04	.02
83	Dale Murphy	.70	.50	.30
84	Eddie Murray	.50	.40	.20
85	Ben Oglivie	.05	.04	.02
86	Bob Ojeda	.10	.08	.04
87	Jesse Orosco	.08	.06	.03
88	Dave Parker	.25	.20	.10
89	Larry Parrish	.08	.06	.03
90	Tony Pena	.10	.08	.04
91	Jim Presley	.15	.11	.06
92	Kirby Puckett	.70	.50	.30
93	Dan Quisenberry	.12	.09	.05
94	Tim Raines	.35	.25	.14
95	Dennis Rasmussen	.10	.08	.04
96	Shane Rawley	.08	.06	.03
97	Johnny Ray	.10	.08	.04
98	Jeff Reardon	.10	.08	.04
99	Jim Rice	.35	.25	.14
100	Dave Righetti	.20	.15	.08
101	Cal Ripken, Jr.	1.00	.70	.40
102	Pete Rose	1.00	.70	.40
103	Nolan Ryan	2.00	1.50	.80
104	Juan Samuel	.15	.11	.06
105	Ryne Sandberg	.60	.45	.25
106	Steve Sax	.20	.15	.08
107	Mike Schmidt	1.25	.90	.50
108	Mike Scott	.15	.11	.06
109	Dave Smith	.05	.04	.02
110	Lee Smith	.10	.08	.04
111	Lonnie Smith	.05	.04	.02
112	Ozzie Smith	.20	.15	.08
113	Cory Snyder	.50	.40	.20
114	Darryl Strawberry	.70	.50	.30
115	Don Sutton	.25	.20	.10
116	Kent Tekulve	.08	.06	.03
117	Gorman Thomas	.08	.06	.03
118	Alan Trammell	.30	.25	.12
119	John Tudor	.12	.09	.05
120	Fernando Valenzuela	.12	.09	.05
121	Bob Welch	.12	.09	.05
122	Lou Whitaker	.25	.20	.10
123	Frank White	.10	.08	.04
124	Reggie Williams	.12	.09	.05
125	Willie Wilson	.15	.11	.06
126	Dave Winfield	.40	.30	.15
127	Mike Witt	.10	.08	.04
128	Todd Worrell	.25	.20	.10
129	Curt Young	.08	.06	.03
130	Robin Yount	.30	.25	.12
131	Jose Canseco, Don Mattingly/Checklist	2.50	2.00	1.00
132	Eric Davis, Bo Jackson/Checklist	1.25	.90	.50

1987 Fleer Star Sticker Box Panels

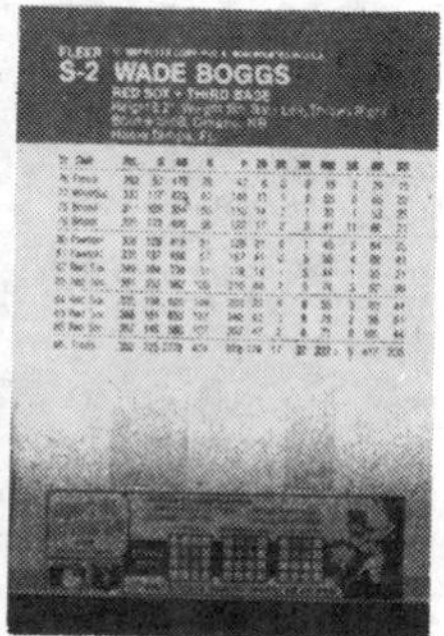

Fleer issued on the bottoms of their Fleer Star Stickers wax pack boxes six player cards plus two team logo/checklist cards. The cards, which measure 2-1/2" by 3-1/2", are numbered S-1 through S-8. The cards are identical in design to the Star Stickers.

		MT	NR MT	EX
Complete Panel Set:		6.00	4.50	2.50
Complete Singles Set:		3.25	2.50	1.25
Common Single Player:		.15	.11	.06
	Panel	5.00	3.75	2.00
2	Wade Boggs	1.00	.70	.40
3	Bert Blyleven	.20	.15	.08
6	Phillies Logo	.05	.04	.02
8	Don Mattingly	1.00	.70	.40
	Panel	1.00	.70	.40
1	Tigers Logo	.05	.04	.02
4	Jose Cruz	.15	.11	.06
5	Glenn Davis	.10	.08	.04
7	Bob Horner	.10	.08	.04

1988 Fleer

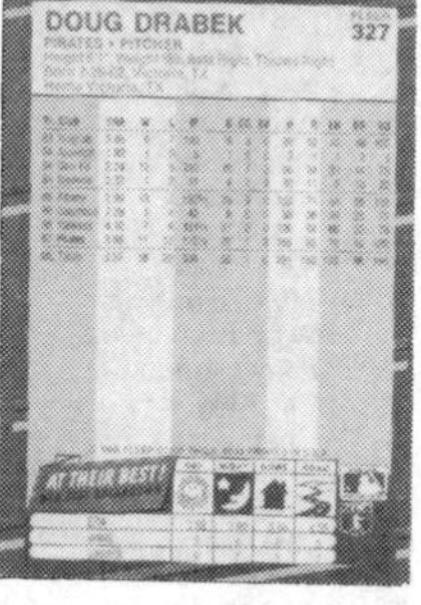

A clean, uncluttered look was the trademark of the 660-card 1988 Fleer set. The cards, which are the standard 2-1/2" by 3-1/2", feature blue and red diagonal lines set inside a white border. The player name and position are located on a slant in the upper left corner of the card. The player's team logo appears in the upper right corner. Below the player photo a blue and red band with the word "Fleer" appears. The backs of the cards include the card number, player personal information, and career statistics, plus a new feature called "At Their Best."

This feature graphically shows a player's pitching or hitting statistics for home and road games and how he fared during day games as opposed to night contests. The set includes 19 special cards (#'s 622-640) and 12 "Major League Prospects" cards (#'s 641-653).

		MT	NR MT	EX
Complete Set (660):		35.00	27.00	13.50
Common Player:		.06	.05	.02
1	Keith Atherton	.06	.05	.02
2	Don Baylor	.10	.08	.04
3	Juan Berenguer	.06	.05	.02
4	Bert Blyleven	.12	.09	.05
5	Tom Brunansky	.10	.08	.04
6	Randy Bush	.06	.05	.02
7	Steve Carlton	.30	.25	.12
8	*Mark Davidson*(FC)	.12	.09	.05
9	George Frazier	.06	.05	.02
10	Gary Gaetti	.15	.11	.06
11	Greg Gagne	.06	.05	.02
12	Dan Gladden	.06	.05	.02
13	Kent Hrbek	.15	.11	.06
14	*Gene Larkin*	.20	.15	.08
15	Tim Laudner	.06	.05	.02
16	Steve Lombardozzi	.06	.05	.02
17	Al Newman	.06	.05	.02
18	Joe Niekro	.08	.06	.03
19	Kirby Puckett	.60	.45	.25
20	Jeff Reardon	.10	.08	.04
21a	Dan Schatzader (incorrect spelling)	.20	.15	.08
21b	Dan Schatzeder (correct spelling)	.06	.05	.02
22	Roy Smalley	.06	.05	.02
23	Mike Smithson	.06	.05	.02
24	*Les Straker*(FC)	.06	.05	.02
25	Frank Viola	.15	.11	.06
26	Jack Clark	.15	.11	.06
27	Vince Coleman	.10	.08	.04
28	Danny Cox	.08	.06	.03
29	Bill Dawley	.06	.05	.02
30	Ken Dayley	.06	.05	.02
31	Doug DeCinces	.08	.06	.03
32	Curt Ford	.06	.05	.02
33	Bob Forsch	.08	.06	.03
34	David Green	.06	.05	.02
35	Tom Herr	.08	.06	.03
36	Ricky Horton	.08	.06	.03
37	*Lance Johnson*(FC)	.75	.60	.30
38	Steve Lake	.06	.05	.02
39	Jim Lindeman	.10	.08	.04
40	*Joe Magrane*	.10	.08	.04
41	Greg Mathews	.08	.06	.03
42	Willie McGee	.12	.09	.05
43	John Morris	.06	.05	.02
44	Jose Oquendo	.06	.05	.02
45	Tony Pena	.08	.06	.03
46	Terry Pendleton	.20	.15	.08
47	Ozzie Smith	.15	.11	.06
48	John Tudor	.10	.08	.04
49	Lee Tunnell	.06	.05	.02
50	Todd Worrell	.10	.08	.04
51	Doyle Alexander	.08	.06	.03
52	Dave Bergman	.06	.05	.02
53	Tom Brookens	.06	.05	.02
54	Darrell Evans	.10	.08	.04
55	Kirk Gibson	.08	.06	.03
56	Mike Heath	.06	.05	.02
57	*Mike Henneman*	.25	.20	.10
58	Willie Hernandez	.08	.06	.03
59	Larry Herndon	.06	.05	.02
60	Eric King	.08	.06	.03
61	Chet Lemon	.08	.06	.03
62	*Scott Lusader*(FC)	.06	.05	.02
63	Bill Madlock	.10	.08	.04
64	Jack Morris	.20	.15	.08
65	Jim Morrison	.06	.05	.02
66	*Matt Nokes*	.50	.40	.20
67	Dan Petry	.08	.06	.03
68a	*Jeff Robinson* (Born 12-13-60 on back)	.30	.25	.12
68b	*Jeff Robinson* (Born 12/14/61 on back)	.15	.11	.06
69	Pat Sheridan	.06	.05	.02
70	Nate Snell	.06	.05	.02
71	Frank Tanana	.08	.06	.03
72	Walt Terrell	.08	.06	.03
73	Mark Thurmond	.06	.05	.02
74	Alan Trammell	.10	.08	.04
75	Lou Whitaker	.10	.08	.04
76	Mike Aldrete	.08	.06	.03
77	Bob Brenly	.06	.05	.02
78	Will Clark	1.00	.70	.40
79	Chili Davis	.08	.06	.03
80	Kelly Downs	.10	.08	.04
81	Dave Dravecky	.08	.06	.03
82	Scott Garrelts	.06	.05	.02
83	Atlee Hammaker	.06	.05	.02
84	Dave Henderson	.10	.08	.04
85	Mike Krukow	.08	.06	.03
86	Mike LaCoss	.06	.05	.02
87	Craig Lefferts	.06	.05	.02
88	Jeff Leonard	.08	.06	.03
89	Candy Maldonado	.08	.06	.03
90	Ed Milner	.06	.05	.02
91	Bob Melvin	.06	.05	.02
92	Kevin Mitchell	.20	.15	.08
93	*Jon Perlman*(FC)	.06	.05	.02
94	Rick Reuschel	.10	.08	.04
95	Don Robinson	.08	.06	.03
96	Chris Speier	.06	.05	.02
97	Harry Spilman	.06	.05	.02
98	Robbie Thompson	.10	.08	.04
99	Jose Uribe	.06	.05	.02
100	*Mark Wasinger*(FC)	.06	.05	.02
101	*Matt Williams*	5.00	3.75	2.00
102	Jesse Barfield	.15	.11	.06
103	George Bell	.12	.09	.05
104	Juan Beniquez	.06	.05	.02
105	John Cerutti	.08	.06	.03
106	Jim Clancy	.08	.06	.03
107	*Rob Ducey*(FC)	.06	.05	.02
108	Mark Eichhorn	.08	.06	.03
109	Tony Fernandez	.12	.09	.05
110	Cecil Fielder	.75	.60	.30
111	Kelly Gruber	.08	.06	.03
112	Tom Henke	.08	.06	.03
113	Garth Iorq (Iorg)	.06	.05	.02
114	Jimmy Key	.10	.08	.04
115	Rick Leach	.06	.05	.02
116	Manny Lee	.08	.06	.03
117	*Nelson Liriano*(FC)	.15	.11	.06
118	*Fred McGriff*	2.25	1.75	.90
119	Lloyd Moseby	.08	.06	.03
120	Rance Mulliniks	.06	.05	.02
121	Jeff Musselman	.10	.08	.04
122	*Jose Nunez*	.06	.05	.02
123	Dave Stieb	.10	.08	.04
124	Willie Upshaw	.08	.06	.03
125	Duane Ward(FC)	.08	.06	.03
126	Ernie Whitt	.08	.06	.03
127	Rick Aguilera	.06	.05	.02
128	Wally Backman	.08	.06	.03
129	*Mark Carreon*(FC)	.12	.09	.05
130	Gary Carter	.10	.08	.04
131	David Cone(FC)	.80	.60	.30
132	Ron Darling	.12	.09	.05
133	Len Dykstra	.20	.15	.08
134	Sid Fernandez	.10	.08	.04
135	Dwight Gooden	.12	.09	.05
136	Keith Hernandez	.08	.06	.03
137	*Gregg Jefferies*(FC)	5.00	3.75	2.00
138	Howard Johnson	.10	.08	.04
139	Terry Leach	.06	.05	.02
140	*Barry Lyons*(FC)	.06	.05	.02
141	Dave Magadan	.10	.08	.04
142	Roger McDowell	.10	.08	.04
143	Kevin McReynolds	.15	.11	.06
144	*Keith Miller*(FC)	.06	.05	.02
145	*John Mitchell*(FC)	.06	.05	.02
146	Randy Myers	.15	.11	.06
147	Bob Ojeda	.08	.06	.03
148	Jesse Orosco	.08	.06	.03
149	Rafael Santana	.06	.05	.02
150	Doug Sisk	.06	.05	.02
151	Darryl Strawberry	.25	.20	.10
152	Tim Teufel	.06	.05	.02
153	Gene Walter	.06	.05	.02
154	Mookie Wilson	.08	.06	.03
155	*Jay Aldrich*(FC)	.06	.05	.02
156	Chris Bosio	.08	.06	.03
157	Glenn Braggs	.10	.08	.04
158	Greg Brock	.08	.06	.03
159	Juan Castillo	.06	.05	.02
160	Mark Clear	.06	.05	.02
161	Cecil Cooper	.10	.08	.04
162	*Chuck Crim*	.12	.09	.05
163	Rob Deer	.08	.06	.03
164	Mike Felder	.06	.05	.02
165	Jim Gantner	.06	.05	.02
166	Ted Higuera	.10	.08	.04
167	Steve Kiefer	.06	.05	.02

		MT	NR MT	EX
168	Rick Manning	.06	.05	.02
169	Paul Molitor	.30	.25	.12
170	Juan Nieves	.08	.06	.03
171	Dan Plesac	.10	.08	.04
172	Earnest Riles	.06	.05	.02
173	Bill Schroeder	.06	.05	.02
174	*Steve Stanicek*(FC)	.06	.05	.02
175	B.J. Surhoff	.10	.08	.04
176	Dale Sveum	.08	.06	.03
177	Bill Wegman	.06	.05	.02
178	Robin Yount	.40	.30	.15
179	Hubie Brooks	.10	.08	.04
180	Tim Burke	.06	.05	.02
181	Casey Candaele	.06	.05	.02
182	Mike Fitzgerald	.06	.05	.02
183	Tom Foley	.06	.05	.02
184	Andres Galarraga	.25	.20	.10
185	Neal Heaton	.06	.05	.02
186	Wallace Johnson	.06	.05	.02
187	Vance Law	.08	.06	.03
188	Dennis Martinez	.08	.06	.03
189	Bob McClure	.06	.05	.02
190	Andy McGaffigan	.06	.05	.02
191	Reid Nichols	.06	.05	.02
192	Pascual Perez	.08	.06	.03
193	Tim Raines	.10	.08	.04
194	Jeff Reed	.06	.05	.02
195	Bob Sebra	.06	.05	.02
196	Bryn Smith	.06	.05	.02
197	Randy St. Claire	.06	.05	.02
198	Tim Wallach	.10	.08	.04
199	Mitch Webster	.08	.06	.03
200	Herm Winningham	.06	.05	.02
201	Floyd Youmans	.06	.05	.02
202	*Brad Arnsberg*(FC)	.08	.06	.03
203	Rick Cerone	.06	.05	.02
204	Pat Clements	.06	.05	.02
205	Henry Cotto	.06	.05	.02
206	Mike Easler	.08	.06	.03
207	Ron Guidry	.15	.11	.06
208	Bill Gullickson	.06	.05	.02
209	Rickey Henderson	.60	.45	.25
210	Charles Hudson	.06	.05	.02
211	Tommy John	.15	.11	.06
212	*Roberto Kelly*(FC)	1.50	1.25	.60
213	Ron Kittle	.08	.06	.03
214	Don Mattingly	.60	.45	.25
215	Bobby Meacham	.06	.05	.02
216	Mike Pagliarulo	.10	.08	.04
217	Dan Pasqua	.10	.08	.04
218	Willie Randolph	.08	.06	.03
219	Rick Rhoden	.08	.06	.03
220	Dave Righetti	.15	.11	.06
221	Jerry Royster	.06	.05	.02
222	Tim Stoddard	.06	.05	.02
223	Wayne Tolleson	.06	.05	.02
224	Gary Ward	.08	.06	.03
225	Claudell Washington	.08	.06	.03
226	Dave Winfield	.40	.30	.15
227	Buddy Bell	.08	.06	.03
228	Tom Browning	.10	.08	.04
229	Dave Concepcion	.08	.06	.03
230	Kal Daniels	.08	.06	.03
231	Eric Davis	.15	.11	.06
232	Bo Diaz	.08	.06	.03
233	Nick Esasky	.08	.06	.03
234	John Franco	.10	.08	.04
235	Guy Hoffman	.06	.05	.02
236	Tom Hume	.06	.05	.02
237	Tracy Jones	.12	.09	.05
238	*Bill Landrum*(FC)	.10	.08	.04
239	Barry Larkin	.30	.25	.12
240	Terry McGriff(FC)	.06	.05	.02
241	Rob Murphy	.08	.06	.03
242	Ron Oester	.06	.05	.02
243	Dave Parker	.10	.08	.04
244	Pat Perry	.06	.05	.02
245	Ted Power	.06	.05	.02
246	Dennis Rasmussen	.10	.08	.04
247	Ron Robinson	.06	.05	.02
248	Kurt Stillwell	.10	.08	.04
249	*Jeff Treadway*(FC)	.12	.09	.05
250	Frank Williams	.06	.05	.02
251	Steve Balboni	.08	.06	.03
252	Bud Black	.06	.05	.02
253	Thad Bosley	.06	.05	.02
254	George Brett	.40	.30	.15
255	*John Davis*(FC)	.06	.05	.02
256	Steve Farr	.06	.05	.02
257	Gene Garber	.06	.05	.02
258	Jerry Gleaton	.06	.05	.02

		MT	NR MT	EX
259	Mark Gubicza	.12	.09	.05
260	Bo Jackson	.90	.70	.35
261	Danny Jackson	.12	.09	.05
262	*Ross Jones*(FC)	.06	.05	.02
263	Charlie Leibrandt	.06	.05	.02
264	*Bill Pecota*	.06	.05	.02
265	*Melido Perez*(FC)	.10	.08	.04
266	Jamie Quirk	.06	.05	.02
267	Dan Quisenberry	.08	.06	.03
268	Bret Saberhagen	.15	.11	.06
269	Angel Salazar	.06	.05	.02
270	Kevin Seitzer	.08	.06	.03
271	Danny Tartabull	.30	.25	.12
272	*Gary Thurman*(FC)	.08	.06	.03
273	Frank White	.08	.06	.03
274	Willie Wilson	.10	.08	.04
275	Tony Bernazard	.06	.05	.02
276	Jose Canseco	1.00	.70	.40
277	Mike Davis	.08	.06	.03
278	Storm Davis	.10	.08	.04
279	Dennis Eckersley	.12	.09	.05
280	Alfredo Griffin	.08	.06	.03
281	Rick Honeycutt	.06	.05	.02
282	Jay Howell	.08	.06	.03
283	Reggie Jackson	.50	.40	.20
284	Dennis Lamp	.06	.05	.02
285	Carney Lansford	.10	.08	.04
286	Mark McGwire	1.50	1.25	.60
287	Dwayne Murphy	.08	.06	.03
288	Gene Nelson	.06	.05	.02
289	Steve Ontiveros	.06	.05	.02
290	Tony Phillips	.06	.05	.02
291	Eric Plunk	.06	.05	.02
292	*Luis Polonia*	.40	.30	.15
293	*Rick Rodriguez*(FC)	.06	.05	.02
294	Terry Steinbach	.10	.08	.04
295	Dave Stewart	.10	.08	.04
296	Curt Young	.08	.06	.03
297	Luis Aguayo	.06	.05	.02
298	Steve Bedrosian	.12	.09	.05
299	Jeff Calhoun	.06	.05	.02
300	Don Carman	.08	.06	.03
301	*Todd Frohwirth*(FC)	.20	.15	.08
302	Greg Gross	.06	.05	.02
303	Kevin Gross	.08	.06	.03
304	Von Hayes	.08	.06	.03
305	*Keith Hughes*(FC)	.06	.05	.02
306	*Mike Jackson*	.06	.05	.02
307	Chris James	.20	.15	.08
308	Steve Jeltz	.06	.05	.02
309	Mike Maddux	.07	.05	.03
310	Lance Parrish	.15	.11	.06
311	Shane Rawley	.08	.06	.03
312	*Wally Ritchie*	.06	.05	.02
313	Bruce Ruffin	.08	.06	.03
314	Juan Samuel	.12	.09	.05
315	Mike Schmidt	.50	.40	.20
316	Rick Schu	.06	.05	.02
317	Jeff Stone	.06	.05	.02
318	Kent Tekulve	.08	.06	.03
319	Milt Thompson	.06	.05	.02
320	Glenn Wilson	.08	.06	.03
321	Rafael Belliard	.06	.05	.02
322	Barry Bonds	2.00	1.50	.80
323	Bobby Bonilla	.50	.40	.20
324	Sid Bream	.08	.06	.03
325	John Cangelosi	.06	.05	.02
326	Mike Diaz	.08	.06	.03
327	Doug Drabek	.08	.06	.03
328	*Mike Dunne*	.08	.06	.03
329	Brian Fisher	.08	.06	.03
330	*Brett Gideon*(FC)	.06	.05	.02
331	Terry Harper	.06	.05	.02
332	Bob Kipper	.06	.05	.02
333	Mike LaValliere	.08	.06	.03
334	*Jose Lind*(FC)	.30	.25	.12
335	Junior Ortiz	.06	.05	.02
336	*Vicente Palacios*(FC)	.12	.09	.05
337	*Bob Patterson*(FC)	.12	.09	.05
338	*Al Pedrique*(FC)	.06	.05	.02
339	R.J. Reynolds	.06	.05	.02
340	*John Smiley*	.20	.15	.08
341	Andy Van Slyke	.20	.15	.08
342	Bob Walk	.06	.05	.02
343	Marty Barrett	.08	.06	.03
344	*Todd Benzinger*(FC)	.12	.09	.05
345	Wade Boggs	.35	.25	.14
346	*Tom Bolton*(FC)	.06	.05	.02
347	Oil Can Boyd	.08	.06	.03
348	*Ellis Burks*	1.00	.70	.40
349	Roger Clemens	.80	.60	.30

		MT	NR MT	EX
350	Steve Crawford	.06	.05	.02
351	Dwight Evans	.12	.09	.05
352	*Wes Gardner*(FC)	.08	.06	.03
353	Rich Gedman	.08	.06	.03
354	Mike Greenwell	.30	.25	.12
355	*Sam Horn*(FC)	.15	.11	.06
356	Bruce Hurst	.10	.08	.04
357	*John Marzano*(FC)	.08	.06	.03
358	Al Nipper	.06	.05	.02
359	Spike Owen	.06	.05	.02
360	*Jody Reed*(FC)	.30	.25	.12
361	Jim Rice	.10	.08	.04
362	Ed Romero	.06	.05	.02
363	Kevin Romine(FC)	.08	.06	.03
364	Joe Sambito	.06	.05	.02
365	Calvin Schiraldi	.06	.05	.02
366	Jeff Sellers	.08	.06	.03
367	Bob Stanley	.06	.05	.02
368	Scott Bankhead	.06	.05	.02
369	Phil Bradley	.10	.08	.04
370	Scott Bradley	.06	.05	.02
371	Mickey Brantley	.06	.05	.02
372	*Mike Campbell*(FC)	.06	.05	.02
373	Alvin Davis	.06	.05	.02
374	Lee Guetterman	.06	.05	.02
375	*Dave Hengel*(FC)	.06	.05	.02
376	Mike Kingery	.06	.05	.02
377	Mark Langston	.12	.09	.05
378	*Edgar Martinez*(FC)	1.50	1.25	.60
379	Mike Moore	.06	.05	.02
380	Mike Morgan	.06	.05	.02
381	John Moses	.06	.05	.02
382	*Donnell Nixon*(FC)	.06	.05	.02
383	Edwin Nunez	.06	.05	.02
384	Ken Phelps	.08	.06	.03
385	Jim Presley	.10	.08	.04
386	Rey Quinones	.06	.05	.02
387	Jerry Reed	.06	.05	.02
388	Harold Reynolds	.08	.06	.03
389	Dave Valle	.08	.06	.03
390	*Bill Wilkinson*	.06	.05	.02
391	Harold Baines	.12	.09	.05
392	Floyd Bannister	.08	.06	.03
393	Daryl Boston	.06	.05	.02
394	Ivan Calderon	.08	.06	.03
395	Jose DeLeon	.08	.06	.03
396	Richard Dotson	.08	.06	.03
397	Carlton Fisk	.20	.15	.08
398	Ozzie Guillen	.08	.06	.03
399	Ron Hassey	.06	.05	.02
400	Donnie Hill	.06	.05	.02
401	Bob James	.06	.05	.02
402	Dave LaPoint	.08	.06	.03
403	*Bill Lindsey*(FC)	.06	.05	.02
404	*Bill Long*(FC)	.06	.05	.02
405	Steve Lyons	.06	.05	.02
406	*Fred Manrique*	.06	.05	.02
407	*Jack McDowell*(FC)	4.00	3.00	1.50
408	Gary Redus	.06	.05	.02
409	Ray Searage	.06	.05	.02
410	Bobby Thigpen	.06	.05	.02
411	Greg Walker	.08	.06	.03
412	*Kenny Williams*	.06	.05	.02
413	Jim Winn	.06	.05	.02
414	Jody Davis	.08	.06	.03
415	Andre Dawson	.20	.15	.08
416	Brian Dayett	.06	.05	.02
417	Bob Dernier	.06	.05	.02
418	Frank DiPino	.06	.05	.02
419	Shawon Dunston	.10	.08	.04
420	Leon Durham	.08	.06	.03
421	*Les Lancaster*(FC)	.10	.08	.04
422	Ed Lynch	.06	.05	.02
423	Greg Maddux	1.50	1.25	.60
424	Dave Martinez(FC)	.07	.05	.03
425a	Keith Moreland (bunting, photo actually Jody Davis)	3.00	2.25	1.25
425b	Keith Moreland (standing upright, correct photo)	.08	.06	.03
426	Jamie Moyer	.08	.06	.03
427	Jerry Mumphrey	.06	.05	.02
428	*Paul Noce*(FC)	.06	.05	.02
429	Rafael Palmeiro(FC)	1.75	1.25	.70
430	Wade Rowdon(FC)	.06	.05	.02
431	Ryne Sandberg	1.00	.70	.40
432	Scott Sanderson	.06	.05	.02
433	Lee Smith	.10	.08	.04
434	Jim Sundberg	.08	.06	.03
435	Rick Sutcliffe	.10	.08	.04
436	Manny Trillo	.08	.06	.03
437	Juan Agosto	.06	.05	.02
438	Larry Andersen	.06	.05	.02
439	Alan Ashby	.06	.05	.02
440	Kevin Bass	.08	.06	.03
441	*Ken Caminiti*(FC)	.60	.45	.25
442	*Rocky Childress*(FC)	.06	.05	.02
443	Jose Cruz	.08	.06	.03
444	Danny Darwin	.06	.05	.02
445	Glenn Davis	.06	.05	.02
446	Jim Deshaies	.08	.06	.03
447	Bill Doran	.08	.06	.03
448	Ty Gainey	.06	.05	.02
449	Billy Hatcher	.08	.06	.03
450	Jeff Heathcock	.06	.05	.02
451	Bob Knepper	.08	.06	.03
452	*Rob Mallicoat*(FC)	.06	.05	.02
453	*Dave Meads*	.06	.05	.02
454	Craig Reynolds	.06	.05	.02
455	Nolan Ryan	1.50	1.25	.60
456	Mike Scott	.12	.09	.05
457	Dave Smith	.08	.06	.03
458	Denny Walling	.06	.05	.02
459	*Robbie Wine*(FC)	.06	.05	.02
460	*Gerald Young*(FC)	.06	.05	.02
461	Bob Brower	.08	.06	.03
462a	Jerry Browne (white player, photo actually Bob Brower)	3.50	2.75	1.50
462b	Jerry Browne (black player, correct photo)	.08	.06	.03
463	Steve Buechele	.06	.05	.02
464	Edwin Correa	.06	.05	.02
465	*Cecil Espy*(FC)	.15	.11	.06
466	Scott Fletcher	.08	.06	.03
467	Jose Guzman	.08	.06	.03
468	Greg Harris	.06	.05	.02
469	Charlie Hough	.08	.06	.03
470	Pete Incaviglia	.10	.08	.04
471	*Paul Kilgus*(FC)	.06	.05	.02
472	Mike Loynd	.08	.06	.03
473	Oddibe McDowell	.08	.06	.03
474	Dale Mohorcic	.06	.05	.02
475	Pete O'Brien	.08	.06	.03
476	Larry Parrish	.08	.06	.03
477	Geno Petralli	.06	.05	.02
478	Jeff Russell	.06	.05	.02
479	Ruben Sierra	1.00	.70	.40
480	Mike Stanley	.12	.09	.05
481	Curtis Wilkerson	.06	.05	.02
482	Mitch Williams	.08	.06	.03
483	Bobby Witt	.10	.08	.04
484	Tony Armas	.08	.06	.03
485	Bob Boone	.08	.06	.03
486	Bill Buckner	.10	.08	.04
487	*DeWayne Buice*	.06	.05	.02
488	Brian Downing	.08	.06	.03
489	Chuck Finley	.06	.05	.02
490	Willie Fraser	.06	.05	.02
491	Jack Howell	.08	.06	.03
492	Ruppert Jones	.06	.05	.02
493	Wally Joyner	.15	.11	.06
494	Jack Lazorko	.06	.05	.02
495	Gary Lucas	.06	.05	.02
496	Kirk McCaskill	.08	.06	.03
497	Mark McLemore	.06	.05	.02
498	Darrell Miller	.06	.05	.02
499	Greg Minton	.06	.05	.02
500	Donnie Moore	.06	.05	.02
501	Gus Polidor	.06	.05	.02
502	Johnny Ray	.08	.06	.03
503	Mark Ryal(FC)	.06	.05	.02
504	Dick Schofield	.06	.05	.02
505	Don Sutton	.12	.09	.05
506	Devon White	.15	.11	.06
507	Mike Witt	.08	.06	.03
508	Dave Anderson	.06	.05	.02
509	Tim Belcher(FC)	.20	.15	.08
510	Ralph Bryant	.06	.05	.02
511	*Tim Crews*(FC)	.15	.11	.06
512	*Mike Devereaux*(FC)	1.25	.90	.50
513	Mariano Duncan	.06	.05	.02
514	Pedro Guerrero	.15	.11	.06
515	Jeff Hamilton(FC)	.12	.09	.05
516	Mickey Hatcher	.06	.05	.02
517	Brad Havens	.06	.05	.02
518	Orel Hershiser	.10	.08	.04
519	*Shawn Hillegas*(FC)	.06	.05	.02
520	Ken Howell	.06	.05	.02
521	Tim Leary	.08	.06	.03
522	Mike Marshall	.12	.09	.05
523	Steve Sax	.15	.11	.06
524	Mike Sciosscia	.08	.06	.03
525	Mike Sharperson(FC)	.06	.05	.02

		MT	NR MT	EX
526	John Shelby	.06	.05	.02
527	Franklin Stubbs	.08	.06	.03
528	Fernando Valenzuela	.08	.06	.03
529	Bob Welch	.10	.08	.04
530	Matt Young	.06	.05	.02
531	Jim Acker	.06	.05	.02
532	Paul Assenmacher	.06	.05	.02
533	*Jeff Blauser*(FC)	1.00	.70	.40
534	*Joe Boever*(FC)	.08	.06	.03
535	Martin Clary(FC)	.06	.05	.02
536	*Kevin Coffman*(FC)	.06	.05	.02
537	Jeff Dedmon	.06	.05	.02
538	*Ron Gant*(FC)	4.00	3.00	1.50
539	*Tom Glavine*(FC)	9.00	6.75	3.50
540	Ken Griffey	.08	.06	.03
541	Al Hall	.06	.05	.02
542	Glenn Hubbard	.06	.05	.02
543	Dion James	.08	.06	.03
544	Dale Murphy	.15	.11	.06
545	Ken Oberkfell	.06	.05	.02
546	David Palmer	.06	.05	.02
547	Gerald Perry	.10	.08	.04
548	Charlie Puleo	.06	.05	.02
549	Ted Simmons	.10	.08	.04
550	Zane Smith	.08	.06	.03
551	Andres Thomas	.08	.06	.03
552	Ozzie Virgil	.06	.05	.02
553	Don Aase	.06	.05	.02
554	*Jeff Ballard*(FC)	.06	.05	.02
555	Eric Bell	.08	.06	.03
556	Mike Boddicker	.08	.06	.03
557	Ken Dixon	.06	.05	.02
558	Jim Dwyer	.06	.05	.02
559	Ken Gerhart	.08	.06	.03
560	*Rene Gonzales*(FC)	.06	.05	.02
561	Mike Griffin	.06	.05	.02
562	John Hayban (Habyan)	.06	.05	.02
563	Terry Kennedy	.08	.06	.03
564	Ray Knight	.08	.06	.03
565	Lee Lacy	.06	.05	.02
566	Fred Lynn	.15	.11	.06
567	Eddie Murray	.35	.25	.14
568	Tom Niedenfuer	.08	.06	.03
569	*Bill Ripken*(FC)	.12	.09	.05
570	Cal Ripken, Jr.	1.00	.70	.40
571	Dave Schmidt	.06	.05	.02
572	Larry Sheets	.08	.06	.03
573	*Pete Stanicek*(FC)	.06	.05	.02
574	*Mark Williamson*(FC)	.06	.05	.02
575	Mike Young	.06	.05	.02
576	Shawn Abner(FC)	.08	.06	.03
577	Greg Booker	.06	.05	.02
578	Chris Brown	.08	.06	.03
579	*Keith Comstock*(FC)	.06	.05	.02
580	*Joey Cora*(FC)	.20	.15	.08
581	Mark Davis	.06	.05	.02
582	Tim Flannery	.06	.05	.02
583	Goose Gossage	.15	.11	.06
584	Mark Grant	.06	.05	.02
585	Tony Gwynn	.50	.40	.20
586	Andy Hawkins	.06	.05	.02
587	Stan Jefferson	.10	.08	.04
588	Jimmy Jones	.08	.06	.03
589	John Kruk	.10	.08	.04
590	*Shane Mack*(FC)	.50	.40	.20
591	Carmelo Martinez	.08	.06	.03
592	Lance McCullers	.08	.06	.03
593	*Eric Nolte*(FC)	.06	.05	.02
594	Randy Ready	.06	.05	.02
595	Luis Salazar	.06	.05	.02
596	Benito Santiago	.20	.15	.08
597	Eric Show	.08	.06	.03
598	Garry Templeton	.08	.06	.03
599	Ed Whitson	.06	.05	.02
600	Scott Bailes	.08	.06	.03
601	Chris Bando	.06	.05	.02
602	*Jay Bell*(FC)	1.50	1.25	.60
603	Brett Butler	.08	.06	.03
604	Tom Candiotti	.06	.05	.02
605	Joe Carter	.50	.40	.20
606	Carmen Castillo	.06	.05	.02
607	*Brian Dorsett*(FC)	.06	.05	.02
608	*John Farrell*(FC)	.06	.05	.02
609	Julio Franco	.10	.08	.04
610	Mel Hall	.08	.06	.03
611	*Tommy Hinzo*(FC)	.06	.05	.02
612	Brook Jacoby	.10	.08	.04
613	*Doug Jones*(FC)	.40	.30	.15
614	Ken Schrom	.06	.05	.02
615	Cory Snyder	.08	.06	.03
616	Sammy Stewart	.06	.05	.02
617	Greg Swindell	.25	.20	.10
618	Pat Tabler	.08	.06	.03
619	Ed Vande Berg	.06	.05	.02
620	*Eddie Williams*(FC)	.06	.05	.02
621	Rich Yett	.06	.05	.02
622	Slugging Sophomores (Wally Joyner, Cory Snyder)	.35	.25	.14
623	Dominican Dynamite (George Bell, Pedro Guerrero)	.12	.09	.05
624	Oakland's Power Team (Jose Canseco, Mark McGwire)	.50	.40	.20
625	Classic Relief (Dan Plesac, Dave Righetti)	.08	.06	.03
626	All Star Righties (Jack Morris, Bret Saberhagen, Mike Witt)	.10	.08	.04
627	Game Closers (Steve Bedrosian, John Franco)	.08	.06	.03
628	Masters of the Double Play (Ryne Sandberg, Ozzie Smith)	.35	.25	.14
629	Rookie Record Setter (Mark McGwire)	.35	.25	.14
630	Changing the Guard in Boston (Todd Benzinger, Ellis Burks, Mike Greenwell)	.20	.15	.08
631	N.L. Batting Champs (Tony Gwynn, Tim Raines)	.20	.15	.08
632	Pitching Magic (Orel Hershiser, Mike Scott)	.12	.09	.05
633	Big Bats At First (Mark McGwire, Pat Tabler)	.60	.45	.25
634	Hitting King and the Thief (Tony Gwynn, Vince Coleman)	.20	.15	.08
635	A.L. Slugging Shortstops (Tony Fernandez, Cal Ripken, Jr., Alan Trammell)	.15	.11	.06
636	Tried and True Sluggers (Gary Carter, Mike Schmidt)	.25	.20	.10
637	Crunch Time (Eric Davis, Darryl Strawberry)	.15	.11	.06
638	A.L. All Stars (Matt Nokes, Kirby Puckett)	.20	.15	.08
639	N.L. All Stars (Keith Hernandez, Dale Murphy)	.20	.15	.08
640	The "O's" Brothers (Bill Ripken, Cal Ripken, Jr.)	.50	.40	.20
641	Major League Prospects *(Mark Grace, Darrin Jackson)*	5.00	3.75	2.00
642	Major League Prospects *(Damon Berryhill, Jeff Montgomery)*	1.25	.90	.50
643	Major League Prospects *(Felix Fermin, Jessie Reid)*(FC)	.20	.15	.08
644	Major League Prospects *(Greg Myers, Greg Tabor)*(FC)	.20	.15	.08
645	Major League Prospects *(Jim Eppard,* Joey Meyer)(FC)	.20	.15	.08
646	Major League Prospects *(Adam Peterson, Randy Velarde)*(FC)	.20	.15	.08
647	Major League Prospects *(Chris Gwynn, Peter Smith)*(FC)	.25	.20	.10
648	Major League Prospects *(Greg Jelks, Tom Newell)*(FC)	.25	.20	.10
649	Major League Prospects *(Mario Diaz, Clay Parker)*(FC)	.25	.20	.10
650	Major League Prospects *(Jack Savage, Todd Simmons)*(FC)	.25	.20	.10
651	Major League Prospects *(John Burkett, Kirt Manwaring)*(FC)	2.50	2.00	1.00
652	Major League Prospects *(Dave Otto, Walt Weiss)*	.40	.30	.15
653	Major League Prospects *(Randell Byers (Randall), Jeff King)*	1.00	.70	.40
654a	Checklist 1-101 (21 is Schatzader)	.10	.08	.04
654b	Checklist 1-101 (21 is Schatzeder)	.06	.05	.02
655	Checklist 102-201	.06	.05	.02
656	Checklist 202-296	.06	.05	.02
657	Checklist 297-390	.06	.05	.02
658	Checklist 391-483	.06	.05	.02
659	Checklist 484-575	.06	.05	.02
660	Checklist 576-660	.06	.05	.02

1988 Fleer All Stars

For the third consecutive year, Fleer randomly inserted All Star Team cards in their wax and cello packs. Twelve cards make up the set, each card measuring 2-1/2" by 3-1/2" in size. Players chosen for the set are Fleer's choices for a major league All-Star team.

		MT	NR MT	EX
Complete Set (12):		8.00	6.00	3.00
Common Player:		.25	.15	.10
1	Matt Nokes	.40	.30	.15
2	Tom Henke	.25	.15	.10
3	Ted Higuera	.25	.15	.10
4	Roger Clemens	3.00	2.00	1.00
5	George Bell	.60	.45	.25
6	Andre Dawson	.60	.45	.25
7	Eric Davis	.60	.45	.25
8	Wade Boggs	1.00	.50	.30
9	Alan Trammell	.60	.45	.25
10	Juan Samuel	.25	.15	.10
11	Jack Clark	.25	.15	.10
12	Paul Molitor	1.00	.70	.40

1988 Fleer Headliners

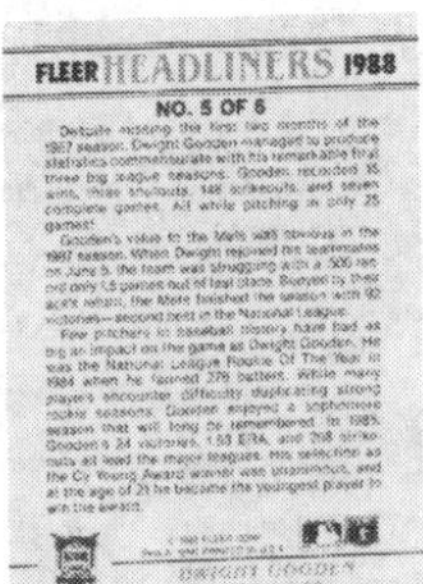

This six-card special set was inserted in Fleer three-packs, sold by retail outlets and hobby dealers nationwide. The card fronts feature crisp full-color player cut-outs printed on a grey and white USA Today-style sports page. "Fleer Headliners 1988" is printed in black and red on a white banner across the top of the card, both front and back. A similar white banner across the card bottom bears the black and white National or American League logo and a red player/team name. Card backs are black on grey with red accents and include the card number and a three-paragraph career summary.

		MT	NR MT	EX
Complete Set (6):		5.00	3.00	1.50
Common Player:		.50	.30	.15
1	Don Mattingly	2.00	1.50	.80
2	Mark McGwire	1.50	1.00	.50
3	Jack Morris	.50	.30	.15
4	Darryl Strawberry	.60	.40	.20
5	Dwight Gooden	.60	.40	.20
6	Tim Raines	.60	.40	.20

The values quoted are intended to reflect the market price.

1988 Fleer '87 World Series

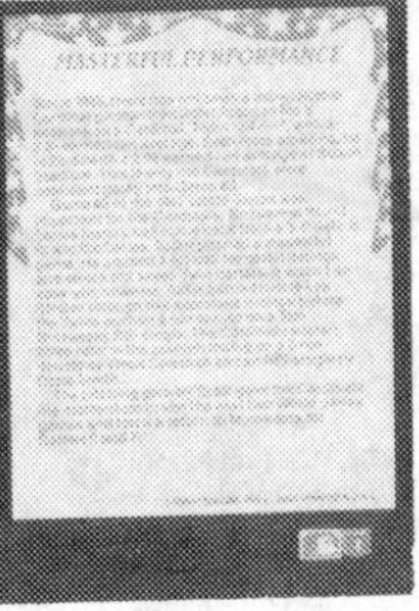

Highlights of the 1987 Series are captured in this full-color insert set found only in Fleer's regular 660-card factory sealed sets. This second World Series edition by Fleer features cards framed in red, with a blue and white starred bunting draped over the upper edges of the photo and a brief photo caption printed on a yellow band across the lower border. Numbered card backs are red, white and blue and include a description of the action pictured on the front, with stats for the Series.

		MT	NR MT	EX
Complete Set (12):		2.50	1.50	.75
Common Player:		.20	.12	.06
1	"Grand" Hero In Game 1 (Dan Gladden)	.30	.25	.12
2	The Cardinals "Bush" Whacked (Randy Bush, Tony Pena)	.30	.25	.12
3	Masterful Performance Turns Momentum (John Tudor)	.30	.25	.12
4	Ozzie Smith	.75	.50	.25
5	Throw Smoke! (Tony Pena, Todd Worrell)	.35	.25	.14
6	Cardinal Attack - Disruptive Speed (Vince Coleman)	.20	.12	.06
7	Herr's Wallop (Dan Driessen, Tom Herr)	.20	.12	.06
8	Kirby Puckett	1.00	.70	.40
9	Kent Hrbek	.30	.25	.12
10	Rich Hacker (coach), Tom Herr, Lee Weyer (umpire)	.20	.12	.06
11	Game 7's Play At The Plate (Don Baylor, Dave Phillips (umpire))	.30	.25	.12
12	Frank Viola	.35	.25	.14

1988 Fleer Box Panels

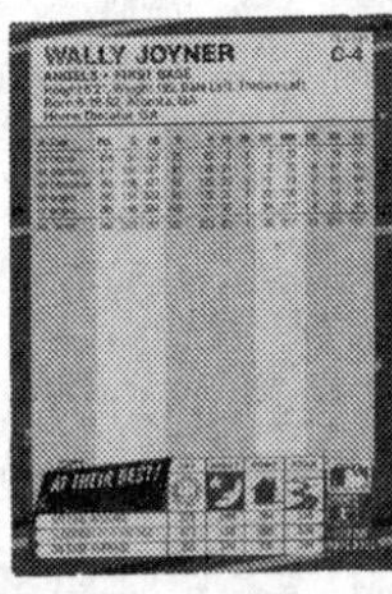

Fleer's third annual box-bottom issue once again included 16 full-color trading cards printed on the bottoms of four different wax and cello pack retail display boxes. Each box contains three player cards and one team logo card. Player cards follow the same design as the basic 1988 Fleer issue - full-color player photo, name upper left, team logo upper right, Fleer logo lower right. Card fronts feature a blue and red striped border, with a thin white line framing the photo. Card backs are printed in blue and red and include personal information and statistics. Standard- size, the cards are numbered C-1 through C-16.

		MT	NR MT	EX
Complete Panel Set:		6.25	4.75	2.50
Complete Singles Set:		2.50	2.00	1.00
Common Panel:		1.25	.90	.50
Common Single Player:		.15	.11	.06
	Panel	2.00	1.50	.80
1	Cardinals Logo	.05	.04	.02
11	Mike Schmidt	.60	.45	.25
14	Dave Stewart	.15	.11	.06
15	Tim Wallach	.20	.15	.08
	Panel	2.00	1.50	.80
2	Dwight Evans	.15	.11	.06
8	Shane Rawley	.15	.11	.06
10	Ryne Sandberg	.60	.45	.25
13	Tigers Logo	.05	.04	.02
	Panel	2.75	2.00	1.00
3	Andres Galarraga	.40	.30	.15
6	Dale Murphy	.60	.45	.25
9	Giants Logo	.05	.04	.02
12	Kevin Seitzer	.25	.20	.10
	Panel	2.25	1.75	.90
4	Wally Joyner	.40	.30	.15
5	Twins Logo	.05	.04	.02
7	Kirby Puckett	.50	.40	.20
16	Todd Worrell	.10	.08	.04

1988 Fleer Update

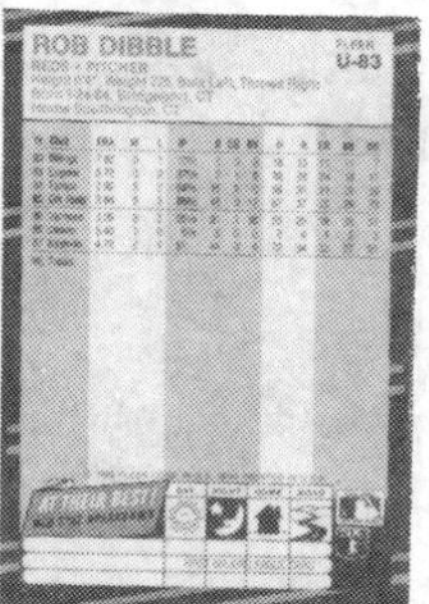

This 132-card update set (numbered U-1 through U-132 and 2-1/2" by 3-1/2") features traded veterans and rookies in a mixture of full-color action shots and close-ups, framed by white borders with red and blue stripes. Player name and position appear upper left, printed on an upward slant leading into the team logo, upper right. A bright stripe in a variety of colors (blue, red, green, yellow) edges the bottom of the photo and leads into the Fleer logo at lower right. The backs are red, white and blue-grey and include personal info, along with yearly and "At Their Best" (day, night, home, road) stats charts. The set was packaged in white cardboard boxes with red and blue stripes. A glossy-coated edition of the update set was issued in its own in box and is valued at two times greater than the regular issue.

		MT	NR MT	EX
Complete Set (132):		15.00	11.00	6.00
Common Player:		.06	.05	.02
1	Jose Bautista(FC)	.06	.05	.02
2	Joe Orsulak	.06	.05	.02
3	Doug Sisk	.06	.05	.02
4	Craig Worthington(FC)	.08	.05	.02
5	Mike Boddicker	.08	.06	.03
6	Rick Cerone	.06	.05	.02
7	Larry Parrish	.08	.06	.03
8	Lee Smith	.20	.12	.06
9	Mike Smithson	.06	.05	.02
10	John Trautwein(FC)	.06	.05	.02
11	Sherman Corbett(FC)	.06	.05	.02
12	Chili Davis	.10	.08	.04
13	Jim Eppard	.08	.06	.03
14	Bryan Harvey(FC)	1.50	.75	.40
15	John Davis	.08	.06	.03
16	Dave Gallagher(FC)	.10	.06	.03
17	Ricky Horton	.08	.06	.03
18	Dan Pasqua	.10	.08	.04
19	Melido Perez	.20	.12	.06
20	Jose Segura(FC)	.15	.11	.06
21	Andy Allanson	.08	.06	.03
22	Jon Perlman	.06	.05	.02
23	Domingo Ramos	.06	.05	.02
24	Rick Rodriguez	.08	.06	.03
25	Willie Upshaw	.10	.08	.04
26	Paul Gibson(FC)	.15	.11	.06
27	Don Heinkel(FC)	.15	.11	.06
28	Ray Knight	.08	.06	.03
29	Gary Pettis	.08	.06	.03
30	Luis Salazar	.06	.05	.02
31	Mike MacFarlane	.40	.30	.15
32	Jeff Montgomery	.35	.20	.10
33	Ted Power	.06	.05	.02
34	Israel Sanchez(FC)	.06	.05	.02
35	Kurt Stillwell	.06	.05	.02
36	Pat Tabler	.06	.05	.02
37	Don August(FC)	.06	.05	.02
38	Darryl Hamilton(FC)	.40	.30	.15
39	Jeff Leonard	.08	.06	.03
40	Joey Meyer	.15	.11	.06
41	Allan Anderson	.10	.08	.04
42	Brian Harper	.06	.05	.02
43	Tom Herr	.10	.08	.04
44	Charlie Lea	.06	.05	.02
45	John Moses	.06	.05	.02
46	John Candelaria	.10	.08	.04
47	Jack Clark	.15	.11	.06
48	Richard Dotson	.06	.05	.02
49	Al Leiter(FC)	.06	.05	.02
50	Rafael Santana	.06	.05	.02
51	Don Slaught	.06	.05	.02
52	Todd Burns(FC)	.06	.05	.02
53	Dave Henderson	.10	.08	.04
54	Doug Jennings(FC)	.10	.06	.03
55	Dave Parker	.12	.09	.05
56	Walt Weiss	.20	.15	.08
57	Bob Welch	.10	.08	.04
58	Henry Cotto	.06	.05	.02
59	Marion Diaz (Mario)	.06	.05	.02
60	Mike Jackson	.06	.05	.02
61	Bill Swift	.15	.10	.05
62	Jose Cecena(FC)	.06	.05	.02
63	Ray Hayward(FC)	.06	.05	.02
64	Jim Steels(FC)	.06	.05	.02
65	Pat Borders(FC)	.40	.25	.15
66	Sil Campusano(FC)	.08	.05	.02
67	Mike Flanagan	.06	.05	.02
68	Todd Stottlemyre(FC)	.30	.25	.12
69	David Wells(FC)	.30	.25	.12
70	Jose Alvarez(FC)	.06	.05	.02
71	Paul Runge	.06	.05	.02
72	Cesar Jimenez (German)(FC)	.06	.05	.02
73	Pete Smith	.20	.12	.06
74	John Smoltz(FC)	5.00	3.75	2.00
75	Damon Berryhill	.10	.08	.04
76	Goose Gossage	.10	.08	.04
77	Mark Grace	2.50	2.00	1.00
78	Darrin Jackson	.15	.10	.05
79	Vance Law	.06	.05	.02
80	Jeff Pico(FC)	.06	.05	.02
81	Gary Varsho(FC)	.06	.05	.02
82	Tim Birtsas	.06	.05	.02
83	Rob Dibble(FC)	.40	.25	.15
84	Danny Jackson	.15	.11	.06
85	Paul O'Neill	.15	.11	.06
86	Jose Rijo	.15	.10	.05
87	Chris Sabo(FC)	.80	.60	.30
88	John Fishel(FC)	.06	.05	.02
89	Craig Biggio(FC)	1.50	1.25	.60
90	Terry Puhl	.06	.05	.02
91	Rafael Ramirez	.06	.05	.02
92	Louie Meadows(FC)	.06	.05	.02
93	Kirk Gibson	.20	.15	.08
94	Alfredo Griffin	.08	.06	.03
95	Jay Howell	.08	.06	.03
96	Jesse Orosco	.06	.05	.02
97	Alejandro Pena	.06	.05	.02
98	Tracy Woodson(FC)	.06	.05	.02
99	John Dopson(FC)	.06	.05	.02
100	Brian Holman(FC)	.15	.10	.05
101	Rex Hudler(FC)	.08	.06	.03
102	Jeff Parrett(FC)	.06	.05	.02
103	Nelson Santovenia(FC)	.06	.05	.02
104	Kevin Elster	.06	.05	.02

		MT	NR MT	EX
105	Jeff Innis(FC)	.06	.05	.02
106	Mackey Sasser(FC)	.06	.05	.02
107	Phil Bradley	.06	.05	.02
108	Danny Clay(FC)	.06	.05	.02
109	Greg Harris	.06	.05	.02
110	Ricky Jordan(FC)	.06	.05	.02
111	David Palmer	.06	.05	.02
112	Jim Gott	.06	.05	.02
113	Tommy Gregg (photo actually Randy Milligan)(FC)	.10	.08	.04
114	Barry Jones	.06	.05	.02
115	Randy Milligan(FC)	.20	.12	.06
116	Luis Alicea(FC)	.15	.11	.06
117	Tom Brunansky	.06	.05	.02
118	John Costello(FC)	.15	.11	.06
119	Jose DeLeon	.08	.06	.03
120	Bob Horner	.10	.08	.04
121	Scott Terry(FC)	.06	.05	.02
122	Roberto Alomar(FC)	12.00	9.00	4.75
123	Dave Leiper	.06	.05	.02
124	Keith Moreland	.06	.05	.02
125	Mark Parent(FC)	.06	.05	.02
126	Dennis Rasmussen	.10	.08	.04
127	Randy Bockus	.06	.05	.02
128	Brett Butler	.10	.08	.04
129	Donell Nixon	.06	.05	.02
130	Earnest Riles	.06	.05	.02
131	Roger Samuels(FC)	.06	.05	.02
132	Checklist	.06	.05	.02

1988 Fleer Award Winners

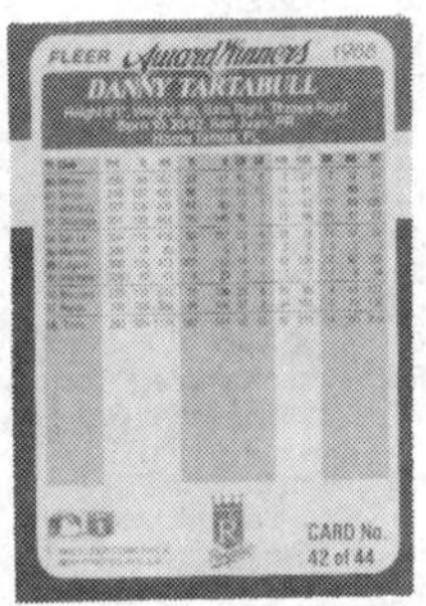

This limited edition 44-card boxed set of 1987 award-winning player cards also includes six team logo sticker cards. Red, white, blue and yellow bands border the sharp, full-color player photos printed below a "Fleer Award Winners 1988" banner. The player's name and award are printed beneath the photo. Flip sides are red, white and blue and list personal information, career data, team logo and card number. This set was sold exclusively at 7-11 stores nationwide.

		MT	NR MT	EX
Complete Set:		5.00	3.75	2.00
Common Player:		.05	.04	.02
1	Steve Bedrosian	.10	.08	.04
2	George Bell	.20	.15	.08
3	Wade Boggs	.70	.50	.30
4	Jose Canseco	.70	.50	.30
5	Will Clark	.50	.40	.20
6	Roger Clemens	.40	.30	.15
7	Kal Daniels	.20	.15	.08
8	Eric Davis	.50	.40	.20
9	Andre Dawson	.15	.11	.06
10	Mike Dunne	.10	.08	.04
11	Dwight Evans	.10	.08	.04
12	Carlton Fisk	.15	.11	.06
13	Julio Franco	.07	.05	.03
14	Dwight Gooden	.40	.30	.15
15	Pedro Guerrero	.15	.11	.06
16	Tony Gwynn	.25	.20	.10
17	Orel Hershiser	.20	.15	.08
18	Tom Henke	.05	.04	.02
19	Ted Higuera	.10	.08	.04
20	Charlie Hough	.05	.04	.02
21	Wally Joyner	.30	.25	.12
22	Jimmy Key	.07	.05	.03
23	Don Mattingly	.70	.50	.30
24	Mark McGwire	.70	.50	.30
25	Paul Molitor	.12	.09	.05
26	Jack Morris	.12	.09	.05
27	Dale Murphy	.30	.25	.12
28	Terry Pendleton	.05	.04	.02
29	Kirby Puckett	.70	.50	.30
30	Tim Raines	.25	.20	.10
31	Jeff Reardon	.07	.05	.03
32	Harold Reynolds	.05	.04	.02
33	Dave Righetti	.12	.09	.05
34	Benito Santiago	.25	.20	.10
35	Mike Schmidt	.30	.25	.12
36	Mike Scott	.10	.08	.04
37	Kevin Seitzer	.60	.45	.25
38	Larry Sheets	.07	.05	.03
39	Ozzie Smith	.15	.11	.06
40	Darryl Strawberry	.40	.30	.15
41	Rick Sutcliffe	.10	.08	.04
42	Danny Tartabull	.12	.09	.05
43	Alan Trammell	.15	.11	.06
44	Tim Wallach	.10	.08	.04

1988 Fleer Baseball All Stars

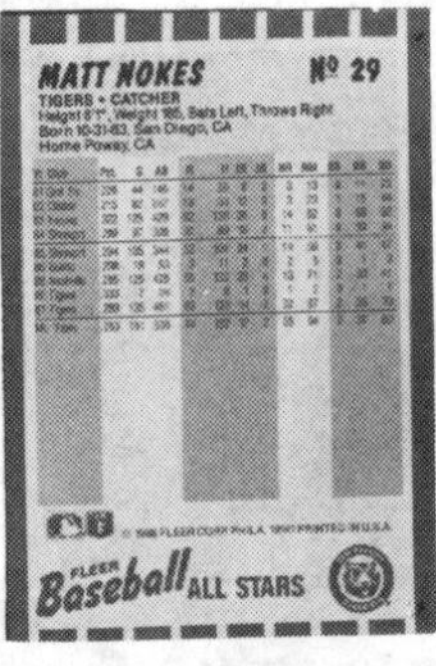

This limited edition 44-card boxed set features excellent photography of major league All-Stars. The standard-size cards feature a sporty bright blue- and yellow-striped background. The player name is printed in white across the upper left front corner. "Fleer Baseball 88 All Stars" appears on a yellow band beneath the photo. Card backs feature a blue- and white-striped design with a yellow highlighted section at the top that contains the player name, card number, team, position and personal data, followed by lifetime career stats. Fleer All Stars are cello-wrapped in blue and yellow striped boxes with checklist backs. The set includes six team logo sticker cards that feature black and white aerial shots of major league ballparks. The set was marketed exclusively by Ben Franklin stores.

		MT	NR MT	EX
Complete Set:		6.00	4.50	2.50
Common Player:		.05	.04	.02
1	George Bell	.20	.15	.08
2	Wade Boggs	.70	.50	.30
3	Bobby Bonilla	.12	.09	.05
4	George Brett	.30	.25	.12
5	Jose Canseco	.70	.50	.30
6	Jack Clark	.15	.11	.06
7	Will Clark	.70	.50	.30
8	Roger Clemens	.40	.30	.15
9	Eric Davis	.50	.40	.20
10	Andre Dawson	.15	.11	.06
11	Julio Franco	.07	.05	.03
12	Dwight Gooden	.40	.30	.15
13	Tony Gwynn	.25	.20	.10
14	Orel Hershiser	.20	.15	.08
15	Teddy Higuera	.10	.08	.04

		MT	NR MT	EX
16	Charlie Hough	.05	.04	.02
17	Kent Hrbek	.15	.11	.06
18	Bruce Hurst	.10	.08	.04
19	Wally Joyner	.30	.25	.12
20	Mark Langston	.10	.08	.04
21	Dave LaPoint	.05	.04	.02
22	Candy Maldonado	.05	.04	.02
23	Don Mattingly	.70	.50	.30
24	Roger McDowell	.07	.05	.03
25	Mark McGwire	.70	.50	.30
26	Jack Morris	.12	.09	.05
27	Dale Murphy	.30	.25	.12
28	Eddie Murray	.20	.15	.08
29	Matt Nokes	.30	.25	.12
30	Kirby Puckett	.70	.50	.30
31	Tim Raines	.25	.20	.10
32	Willie Randolph	.07	.05	.03
33	Jeff Reardon	.07	.05	.03
34	Nolan Ryan	1.50	1.25	.60
35	Juan Samuel	.10	.08	.04
36	Mike Schmidt	.30	.25	.12
37	Mike Scott	.10	.08	.04
38	Kevin Seitzer	.60	.45	.25
39	Ozzie Smith	.15	.11	.06
40	Darryl Strawberry	.40	.30	.15
41	Rick Sutcliffe	.10	.08	.04
42	Alan Trammell	.15	.11	.06
43	Tim Wallach	.10	.08	.04
44	Dave Winfield	.20	.15	.08

1988 Fleer Baseball MVP

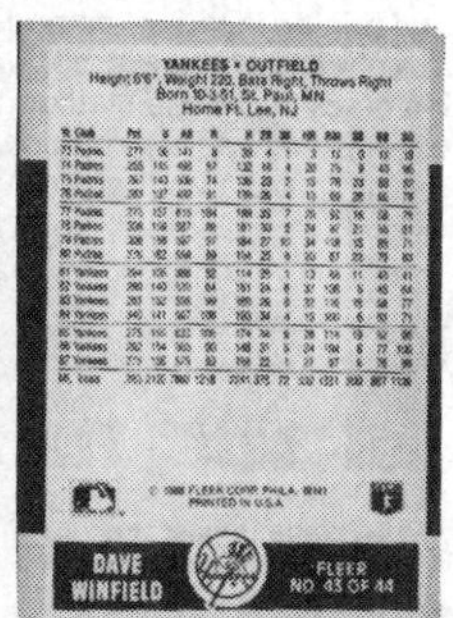

This boxed set of 44 standard-size cards and six team logo stickers was produced by Fleer for exclusive distribution at Toys "R" Us stores. This premiere edition features full-color player photos framed by a yellow and blue border. The player's name is printed in red below and to the left of the photo; team and position are printed in black in the lower right corner. The "Fleer Baseball MVP" logo appears bottom center. Card backs are yellow and blue on a white background. The player's team, position and personal data are followed by stats, logo and a blue banner bearing the player's name, team logo and card number. The six sticker cards feature black and white stadium photos on the backs.

		MT	NR MT	EX
Complete Set:		6.00	4.50	2.50
Common Player:		.05	.04	.02
1	George Bell	.20	.15	.08
2	Wade Boggs	.80	.60	.30
3	Jose Canseco	.80	.60	.30
4	Ivan Calderon	.07	.05	.03
5	Will Clark	.80	.60	.30
6	Roger Clemens	.40	.30	.15
7	Vince Coleman	.15	.11	.06
8	Eric Davis	.50	.40	.20
9	Andre Dawson	.15	.11	.06
10	Dave Dravecky	.05	.04	.02
11	Mike Dunne	.10	.08	.04
12	Dwight Evans	.10	.08	.04
13	Sid Fernandez	.07	.05	.03
14	Tony Fernandez	.10	.08	.04
15	Julio Franco	.07	.05	.03
16	Dwight Gooden	.40	.30	.15
17	Tony Gwynn	.25	.20	.10
18	Ted Higuera	.10	.08	.04
19	Charlie Hough	.05	.04	.02
20	Wally Joyner	.30	.25	.12
21	Mark Langston	.10	.08	.04
22	Don Mattingly	.80	.60	.30
23	Mark McGwire	.80	.60	.30
24	Jack Morris	.12	.09	.05
25	Dale Murphy	.30	.25	.12
26	Kirby Puckett	.50	.40	.20
27	Tim Raines	.25	.20	.10
28	Willie Randolph	.07	.05	.03
29	Ryne Sandberg	.20	.15	.08
30	Benito Santiago	.25	.20	.10
31	Mike Schmidt	.30	.25	.12
32	Mike Scott	.10	.08	.04
33	Kevin Seitzer	.60	.45	.25
34	Larry Sheets	.07	.05	.03
35	Ozzie Smith	.15	.11	.06
36	Dave Stewart	.10	.08	.04
37	Darryl Strawberry	.40	.30	.15
38	Rick Sutcliffe	.10	.08	.04
39	Alan Trammell	.15	.11	.06
40	Fernando Valenzuela	.20	.15	.08
41	Frank Viola	.12	.09	.05
42	Tim Wallach	.10	.08	.04
43	Dave Winfield	.20	.15	.08
44	Robin Yount	.25	.20	.10

1988 Fleer Baseball's Best

This boxed set of 44 standard-size cards (2-1/2" by 3-1/2") and six team logo stickers is the third annual issue from Fleer highlighting the best major league sluggers and pitchers. Five additional player cards were printed on retail display box bottoms, along with a checklist logo card (numbered C-1 through C-6). Full-color player photos are framed by a green border that fades to yellow. A red (slugger) or blue (pitcher) player name is printed beneath the photo. The card backs are printed in green on a white background with yellow highlights. Card number, player name and personal info appear in a green vertical box on the left-hand side of the card back with a yellow cartoon-style team logo overprinted across a stats chart on the right. This set was produced by Fleer for exclusive distribution by McCrory's stores (McCrory, McClellan, J.J. Newberry, H.L. Green, TG&Y).

		MT	NR MT	EX
Complete Set:		6.00	4.50	2.50
Common Player:		.05	.04	.02
1	George Bell	.20	.15	.08
2	Wade Boggs	.80	.60	.30
3	Bobby Bonilla	.12	.09	.05
4	Tom Brunansky	.10	.08	.04
5	Ellis Burks	.80	.60	.30
6	Jose Canseco	.80	.60	.30
7	Joe Carter	.12	.09	.05
8	Will Clark	.80	.60	.30
9	Roger Clemens	.40	.30	.15

		MT	NR MT	EX
10	Eric Davis	.50	.40	.20
11	Glenn Davis	.12	.09	.05
12	Andre Dawson	.15	.11	.06
13	Dennis Eckersley	.07	.05	.03
14	Andres Galarraga	.15	.11	.06
15	Dwight Gooden	.40	.30	.15
16	Pedro Guerrero	.15	.11	.06
17	Tony Gwynn	.25	.20	.10
18	Orel Hershiser	.20	.15	.08
19	Ted Higuera	.10	.08	.04
20	Pete Incaviglia	.12	.09	.05
21	Danny Jackson	.10	.08	.04
22	Doug Jennings	.07	.05	.03
23	Mark Langston	.10	.08	.04
24	Dave LaPoint	.05	.04	.02
25	Mike LaValliere	.07	.05	.03
26	Don Mattingly	.80	.60	.30
27	Mark McGwire	.80	.60	.30
28	Dale Murphy	.30	.25	.12
29	Ken Phelps	.05	.04	.02
30	Kirby Puckett	.50	.40	.20
31	Johnny Ray	.05	.04	.02
32	Jeff Reardon	.07	.05	.03
33	Dave Righetti	.12	.09	.05
34	Cal Ripkin, Jr. (Ripken)	.60	.45	.25
35	Chris Sabo	.90	.70	.35
36	Mike Schmidt	.30	.25	.12
37	Mike Scott	.10	.08	.04
38	Kevin Seitzer	.60	.45	.25
39	Dave Stewart	.10	.08	.04
40	Darryl Strawberry	.40	.30	.15
41	Greg Swindell	.10	.08	.04
42	Frank Tanana	.05	.04	.02
43	Dave Winfield	.20	.15	.08
44	Todd Worrell	.10	.08	.04

1988 Fleer Baseball's Best Box Panel

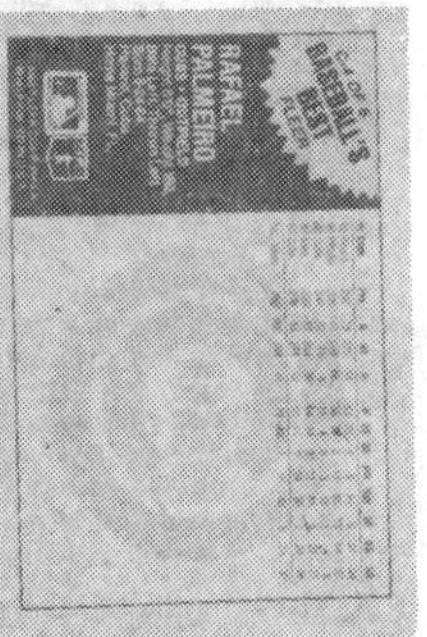

Six cards were placed on the bottoms of retail boxes of the Fleer 44-card Baseball's Best boxed sets in 1988. The cards, which measure 2-1/2" by 3-1/2", are identical in design to cards found in the 44-card set. The cards are numbered C-1 through C-6 and were produced by Fleer for distribution by McCrory stores and its affiliates.

		MT	NR MT	EX
Complete Panel Set:		1.50	1.25	.60
Complete Singles Set:		.90	.70	.35
Common Single Player:		.15	.11	.06
	Panel	1.50	1.25	.60
1	Ron Darling	.20	.15	.08
2	Rickey Henderson	.60	.45	.25
3	Carney Lansford	.15	.11	.06
4	Rafael Palmeiro	.20	.15	.08
5	Frank Viola	.20	.15	.08
6	Twins Logo	.05	.04	.02

The values quoted are intended to reflect the market price.

1988 Fleer Baseball's Exciting Stars

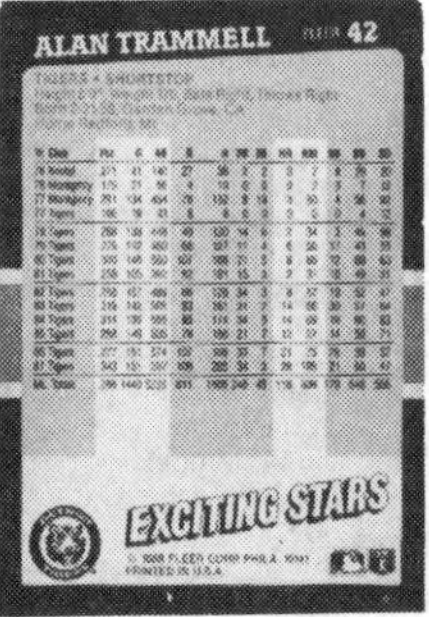

This 44-card limited-edition boxed set showcases star major leaguers. Player photos are slanted upwards to the right, framed by a blue border with a red and white bar stripe across the middle. The player's name is printed in white above the photo. "Baseball's Exciting Stars" is printed in red and yellow across the bottom margin, following the upward slant of the photo. Fleer's logo appears lower right intersecting a white baseball bearing the number "88". Card backs are numbered and printed in red, white and blue. The set was packaged in a checklist box, with six team logo sticker cards featuring black and white stadium photos on the flip sides. Exciting Stars was distributed via Cumberland Farm stores throughout the northeastern U.S. and Florida.

		MT	NR MT	EX
Complete Set:		5.00	3.75	2.00
Common Player:		.05	.04	.02
1	Harold Baines	.10	.08	.04
2	Kevin Bass	.07	.05	.03
3	George Bell	.20	.15	.08
4	Wade Boggs	.80	.60	.30
5	Mickey Brantley	.05	.04	.02
6	Sid Bream	.05	.04	.02
7	Jose Canseco	.80	.60	.30
8	Jack Clark	.15	.11	.06
9	Will Clark	.80	.60	.30
10	Roger Clemens	.40	.30	.15
11	Vince Coleman	.15	.11	.06
12	Eric Davis	.50	.40	.20
13	Andre Dawson	.15	.11	.06
14	Julio Franco	.07	.05	.03
15	Dwight Gooden	.40	.30	.15
16	Mike Greenwell	.40	.30	.15
17	Tony Gwynn	.25	.20	.10
18	Von Hayes	.07	.05	.03
19	Tom Henke	.05	.04	.02
20	Orel Hershiser	.20	.15	.08
21	Teddy Higuera	.10	.08	.04
22	Brook Jacoby	.07	.05	.03
23	Wally Joyner	.30	.25	.12
24	Jimmy Key	.07	.05	.03
25	Don Mattingly	.80	.60	.30
26	Mark McGwire	.80	.60	.30
27	Jack Morris	.12	.09	.05
28	Dale Murphy	.30	.25	.12
29	Matt Nokes	.30	.25	.12
30	Kirby Puckett	.50	.40	.20
31	Tim Raines	.25	.20	.10
32	Ryne Sandberg	.20	.15	.08
33	Benito Santiago	.25	.20	.10
34	Mike Schmidt	.30	.25	.12
35	Mike Scott	.10	.08	.04
36	Kevin Seitzer	.60	.45	.25
37	Larry Sheets	.07	.05	.03
38	Ruben Sierra	.12	.09	.05
39	Darryl Strawberry	.40	.30	.15
40	Ozzie Smith	.15	.11	.06
41	Danny Tartabull	.10	.08	.04
42	Alan Trammell	.15	.11	.06
43	Fernando Valenzuela	.20	.15	.08
44	Devon White	.20	.15	.08

1988 Fleer Baseball's Hottest Stars

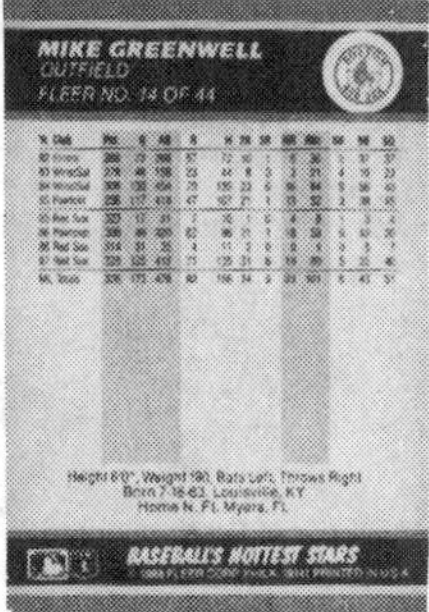

This boxed set of 44 standard-size player cards and six team logo sticker cards was produced by Fleer for exclusive distribution at Revco drug stores nation-wide. Card fronts feature full-color photos of players representing every major league team. Photos are framed in red, orange and yellow, with a blue and white player name printed across the bottom of the card front. A flaming baseball logo bearing the words "Hottest Stars" appears in the lower left corner of the player photo. Card backs are red, white and blue. The player's name, position, card number and team togo are printed across the top section, followed by a stats box, personal data, batting and throwing preferences. The set also includes a six team logo sticker cards with flipside stadium photos in black and white.

		MT	NR MT	EX
Complete Set:		6.00	4.50	2.50
Common Player:		.05	.04	.02
1	George Bell	.20	.15	.08
2	Wade Boggs	.80	.60	.30
3	Bobby Bonilla	.12	.09	.05
4	George Brett	.30	.25	.12
5	Jose Canseco	.80	.60	.30
6	Will Clark	.80	.60	.30
7	Roger Clemens	.40	.30	.15
8	Eric Davis	.50	.40	.20
9	Andre Dawson	.15	.11	.06
10	Tony Fernandez	.10	.08	.04
11	Julio Franco	.07	.05	.03
12	Gary Gaetti	.10	.08	.04
13	Dwight Gooden	.40	.30	.15
14	Mike Greenwell	.40	.30	.15
15	Tony Gwynn	.25	.20	.10
16	Rickey Henderson	.50	.40	.20
17	Keith Hernandez	.15	.11	.06
18	Tom Herr	.07	.05	.03
19	Orel Hershiser	.20	.15	.08
20	Ted Higuera	.10	.08	.04
21	Wally Joyner	.30	.25	.12
22	Jimmy Key	.07	.05	.03
23	Mark Langston	.10	.08	.04
24	Don Mattingly	.80	.60	.30
25	Jack McDowell	.20	.15	.08
26	Mark McGwire	.80	.60	.30
27	Kevin Mitchell	.50	.40	.20
28	Jack Morris	.12	.09	.05
29	Dale Murphy	.30	.25	.12
30	Kirby Puckett	.50	.40	.20
31	Tim Raines	.25	.20	.10
32	Shane Rawley	.05	.04	.02
33	Benito Santiago	.25	.20	.10
34	Mike Schmidt	.30	.25	.12
35	Mike Scott	.10	.08	.04
36	Kevin Seitzer	.60	.45	.25
37	Larry Sheets	.07	.05	.03
38	Ruben Sierra	.50	.40	.20
39	Dave Smith	.05	.04	.02
40	Ozzie Smith	.30	.25	.12
41	Darryl Strawberry	.40	.30	.15
42	Rick Sutcliffe	.10	.08	.04
43	Pat Tabler	.05	.04	.02
44	Alan Trammell	.15	.11	.06

1988 Fleer League Leaders

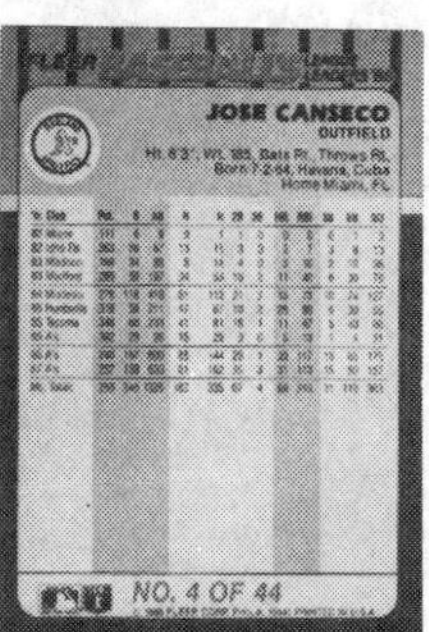

This 44-card boxed set is the third annual limited edition set from Fleer highlighting leading players. The 1988 edition contains the same type of information, front and back, as the previous sets, with a new color scheme and design. Card fronts have bright blue borders, solid on the lower portion, striped on the upper, with a gold bar separating the two sections. "Fleer's Baseball's League Leaders '88" headlines the card face. The full-color player photo is centered above a yellow player name banner. The numbered card backs are blue, pink and white, and contain player stats and personal notes. Six team logo sticker cards, with flipside black and white photos of ballparks, accompany this set which was marketed exclusively by Walgreen drug stores.

		MT	NR MT	EX
Complete Set:		6.00	4.50	2.50
Common Player:		.05	.04	.02
1	George Bell	.20	.15	.08
2	Wade Boggs	.80	.60	.30
3	Ivan Calderon	.07	.05	.03
4	Jose Canseco	.80	.60	.30
5	Will Clark	.80	.60	.30
6	Roger Clemens	.40	.30	.15
7	Vince Coleman	.15	.11	.06
8	Eric Davis	.50	.40	.20
9	Andre Dawson	.15	.11	.06
10	Bill Doran	.07	.05	.03
11	Dwight Evans	.10	.08	.04
12	Julio Franco	.07	.05	.03
13	Gary Gaetti	.10	.08	.04
14	Andres Galarraga	.15	.11	.06
15	Dwight Gooden	.40	.30	.15
16	Tony Gwynn	.25	.20	.10
17	Tom Henke	.05	.04	.02
18	Keith Hernandez	.20	.15	.08
19	Orel Hershiser	.20	.15	.08
20	Ted Higuera	.10	.08	.04
21	Kent Hrbek	.15	.11	.06
22	Wally Joyner	.30	.25	.12
23	Jimmy Key	.07	.05	.03
24	Mark Langston	.10	.08	.04
25	Don Mattingly	.80	.60	.30
26	Mark McGwire	.80	.60	.30
27	Paul Molitor	.12	.09	.05
28	Jack Morris	.12	.09	.05
29	Dale Murphy	.30	.25	.12
30	Kirby Puckett	.50	.40	.20
31	Tim Raines	.25	.20	.10
32	Rick Rueschel	.07	.05	.03
33	Bret Saberhagen	.15	.11	.06
34	Benito Santiago	.25	.20	.10
35	Mike Schmidt	.30	.25	.12
36	Mike Scott	.10	.08	.04
37	Kevin Seitzer	.60	.45	.25
38	Larry Sheets	.07	.05	.03
39	Ruben Sierra	.50	.40	.20
40	Darryl Strawberry	.40	.30	.15
41	Rick Sutcliffe	.10	.08	.04
42	Alan Trammell	.15	.11	.06
43	Andy Van Slyke	.10	.08	.04
44	Todd Worrell	.10	.08	.04

1988 Fleer Mini

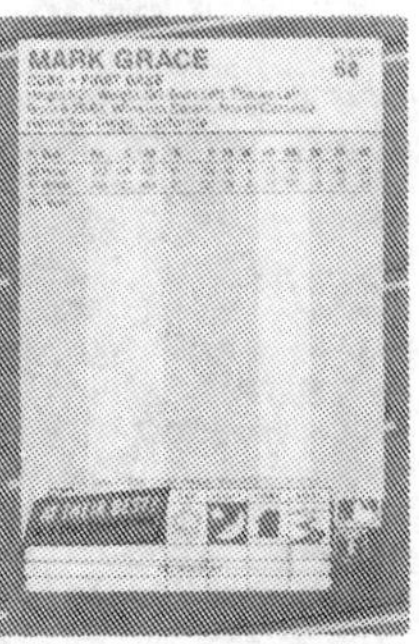

This third annual issue of miniatures (1-7/8" by 2-5/8") includes 120 high-gloss cards featuring new photos, not copies from the regular issue, although the card designs are identical. Card fronts have white borders, with red and blue striping and a bright color band beneath the photo leading to a blue Fleet logo lower right. The player name is printed upper left; the full-color team logo appears upper right. Card backs are red, white and blue and include personal data, yearly career stats and a stats breakdown of batting average, slugging percentage and on-base average, listed for day, night, home and road games. Card backs are numbered in alphabetical order by teams which are also listed alphabetically. The set includes 18 team logo stickers with black and white aerial stadium photos on the flip sides.

		MT	NR MT	EX
Complete Set:		12.00	9.00	4.75
Common Player:		.05	.04	.02
1	Eddie Murray	.25	.20	.10
2	Dave Schmidt	.05	.04	.02
3	Larry Sheets	.07	.05	.03
4	Wade Boggs	.70	.50	.30
5	Roger Clemens	.80	.60	.30
6	Dwight Evans	.12	.09	.05
7	Mike Greenwell	.40	.30	.15
8	Sam Horn	.20	.15	.08
9	Lee Smith	.07	.05	.03
10	Brian Downing	.05	.04	.02
11	Wally Joyner	.30	.25	.12
12	Devon White	.10	.08	.04
13	Mike Witt	.07	.05	.03
14	Ivan Calderon	.15	.11	.06
15	Ozzie Guillen	.07	.05	.03
16	Jack McDowell	.50	.40	.20
17	Kenny Williams	.12	.09	.05
18	Joe Carter	.20	.15	.08
19	Julio Franco	.20	.15	.08
20	Pat Tabler	.05	.04	.02
21	Doyle Alexander	.05	.04	.02
22	Jack Morris	.15	.11	.06
23	Matt Nokes	.30	.25	.12
24	Walt Terrell	.05	.04	.02
25	Alan Trammell	.20	.15	.08
26	Bret Saberhagen	.15	.11	.06
27	Kevin Seitzer	.20	.15	.08
28	Danny Tartabull	.15	.11	.06
29	Gary Thurman	.20	.15	.08
30	Ted Higuera	.10	.08	.04
31	Paul Molitor	.12	.09	.05
32	Dan Plesac	.10	.08	.04
33	Robin Yount	.25	.20	.10
34	Gary Gaetti	.12	.09	.05
35	Kent Hrbek	.15	.11	.06
36	Kirby Puckett	.50	.40	.20
37	Jeff Reardon	.07	.05	.03
38	Frank Viola	.12	.09	.05
39	Jack Clark	.12	.09	.05
40	Rickey Henderson	.80	.60	.30
41	Don Mattingly	.80	.60	.30
42	Willie Randolph	.05	.04	.02
43	Dave Righetti	.12	.09	.05
44	Dave Winfield	.20	.15	.08
45	Jose Canseco	.80	.60	.30
46	Mark McGwire	.60	.45	.25
47	Dave Parker	.12	.09	.05
48	Dave Stewart	.07	.05	.03
49	Walt Weiss	.60	.45	.25
50	Bob Welch	.07	.05	.03
51	Mickey Brantley	.05	.04	.02
52	Mark Langston	.10	.08	.04
53	Harold Reynolds	.07	.05	.03
54	Scott Fletcher	.05	.04	.02
55	Charlie Hough	.05	.04	.02
56	Pete Incaviglia	.12	.09	.05
57	Larry Parrish	.05	.04	.02
58	Ruben Sierra	.35	.25	.14
59	George Bell	.20	.15	.08
60	Mark Eichhorn	.05	.04	.02
61	Tony Fernandez	.10	.08	.04
62	Tom Henke	.05	.04	.02
63	Jimmy Key	.07	.05	.03
64	Dion James	.05	.04	.02
65	Dale Murphy	.30	.25	.12
66	Zane Smith	.05	.04	.02
67	Andre Dawson	.15	.11	.06
68	Mark Grace	1.00	.70	.40
69	Jerry Mumphrey	.05	.04	.02
70	Ryne Sandberg	.60	.45	.25
71	Rick Sutcliffe	.10	.08	.04
72	Kal Daniels	.12	.09	.05
73	Eric Davis	.40	.30	.15
74	John Franco	.07	.05	.03
75	Ron Robinson	.05	.04	.02
76	Jeff Treadway	.20	.15	.08
77	Kevin Bass	.07	.05	.03
78	Glenn Davis	.15	.11	.06
79	Nolan Ryan	1.00	.70	.40
80	Mike Scott	.12	.09	.05
81	Dave Smith	.05	.04	.02
82	Kirk Gibson	.20	.15	.08
83	Pedro Guerrero	.12	.09	.05
84	Orel Hershiser	.20	.15	.08
85	Steve Sax	.15	.11	.06
86	Fernando Valenzuela	.15	.11	.06
87	Tim Burke	.05	.04	.02
88	Andres Galarraga	.15	.11	.06
89	Neal Heaton	.05	.04	.02
90	Tim Raines	.20	.15	.08
91	Tim Wallach	.10	.08	.04
92	Dwight Gooden	.40	.30	.15
93	Keith Hernandez	.15	.11	.06
94	Gregg Jefferies	.70	.50	.30
95	Howard Johnson	.10	.08	.04
96	Roger McDowell	.05	.04	.02
97	Darryl Strawberry	.50	.40	.20
98	Steve Bedrosian	.10	.08	.04
99	Von Hayes	.10	.08	.04
100	Shane Rawley	.05	.04	.02
101	Juan Samuel	.12	.09	.05
102	Mike Schmidt	.30	.25	.12
103	Bobby Bonilla	.30	.25	.12
104	Mike Dunne	.07	.05	.03
105	Andy Van Slyke	.10	.08	.04
106	Vince Coleman	.15	.11	.06
107	Bob Horner	.07	.05	.03
108	Willie McGee	.10	.08	.04
109	Ozzie Smith	.12	.09	.05
110	John Tudor	.07	.05	.03
111	Todd Worrell	.10	.08	.04
112	Tony Gwynn	.25	.20	.10
113	John Kruk	.12	.09	.05
114	Lance McCullers	.05	.04	.02
115	Benito Santiago	.15	.11	.06
116	Will Clark	.40	.30	.15
117	Jeff Leonard	.05	.04	.02
118	Candy Maldonado	.05	.04	.02
119	Rick Rueschel	.07	.05	.03
120	Don Robinson	.05	.04	.02

1988 Fleer Record Setters

For the second consecutive year, Fleer Corp. issued this special limited-edition 44-card set for exclusive distribution by Eckerd Drug stores. Cards are standard size with red and blue borders framing the full-color player photos. A "1988 Fleer Record Setters" headline is printed on a yellow strip above the player's photo. The player's photo. The player's name, team and position appear

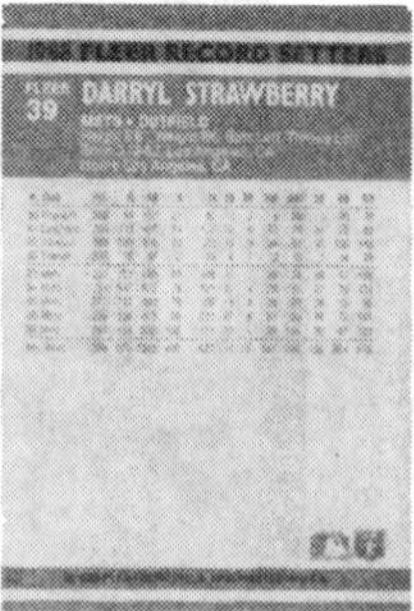

beneath the pose. Card backs list personal information and career stats in red and blue ink on a white background. Each 44-card set comes cello-wrapped in a checklist box that contains six additional cards with peel-off team logo stickers. The sticker cards feature black and white aerial photos of major league ballparks, along with stadium statistics such as field size, seating capacity and date of the first game played.

		MT	NR MT	EX
Complete Set:		5.00	3.75	2.00
Common Player:		.05	.04	.02
1	Jesse Barfield	.10	.08	.04
2	George Bell	.20	.15	.08
3	Wade Boggs	.80	.60	.30
4	Jose Canseco	.80	.60	.30
5	Jack Clark	.15	.11	.06
6	Will Clark	.80	.60	.30
7	Roger Clemens	.40	.30	.15
8	Alvin Davis	.10	.08	.04
9	Eric Davis	.50	.40	.20
10	Andre Dawson	.15	.11	.06
11	Mike Dunne	.10	.08	.04
12	John Franco	.07	.05	.03
13	Julio Franco	.07	.05	.03
14	Dwight Gooden	.40	.30	.15
15	Mark Gubicza	.07	.05	.03
16	Ozzie Guillen	.07	.05	.03
17	Tony Gwynn	.25	.20	.10
18	Orel Hershiser	.20	.15	.08
19	Teddy Higuera	.10	.08	.04
20	Howard Johnson	.07	.05	.03
21	Wally Joyner	.30	.25	.12
22	Jimmy Key	.07	.05	.03
23	Jeff Leonard	.05	.04	.02
24	Don Mattingly	.80	.60	.30
25	Mark McGwire	.80	.60	.30
26	Jack Morris	.12	.09	.05
27	Dale Murphy	.30	.25	.12
28	Larry Parrish	.05	.04	.02
29	Kirby Puckett	.50	.40	.20
30	Tim Raines	.25	.20	.10
31	Harold Reynolds	.07	.05	.03
32	Dave Righetti	.12	.09	.05
33	Cal Ripken, Jr.	.80	.60	.30
34	Benito Santiago	.25	.20	.10
35	Mike Schmidt	.70	.50	.25
36	Mike Scott	.10	.08	.04
37	Kevin Seitzer	.10	.08	.04
38	Ozzie Smith	.12	.09	.05
39	Darryl Strawberry	.40	.30	.15
40	Rick Sutcliffe	.10	.08	.04
41	Alan Trammell	.15	.11	.06
42	Frank Viola	.12	.09	.05
43	Mitch Williams	.05	.04	.02
44	Todd Worrell	.10	.08	.04

1988 Fleer Star Stickers

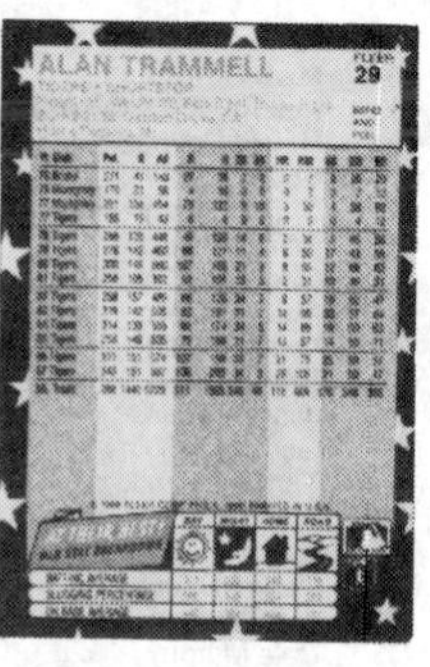

This set of 132 standard-size sticker cards (including a checklist card) features exclusive player photos, different from those in the Fleer regular issue. Card fronts have light gray borders sprinkled with multi-colored stars. The "Fleer Star Stickers" logo appears upper left, player names are printed beneath the photos. Card backs are printed in red, gray and black on white and include personal data and a breakdown of pitching and batting stats into day, night, home and road categories. Cards were marketed in two different display boxes that feature six players and two team logos from Fleer's 1988 Limited Edition box-bottom set.

		MT	NR MT	EX
Complete Set:		20.00	15.00	8.00
Common Player:		.05	.04	.02
1	Mike Boddicker	.08	.06	.03
2	Eddie Murray	.50	.40	.20
3	Cal Ripken, Jr.	1.00	.70	.40
4	Larry Sheets	.15	.11	.06
5	Wade Boggs	.80	.60	.30
6	Ellis Burks	.30	.25	.12
7	Roger Clemens	.70	.50	.25
8	Dwight Evans	.15	.11	.06
9	Mike Greenwell	.40	.30	.15
10	Bruce Hurst	.12	.09	.05
11	Brian Downing	.08	.06	.03
12	Wally Joyner	.40	.30	.15
13	Mike Witt	.10	.08	.04
14	Ivan Calderon	.12	.09	.05
15	Jose DeLeon	.05	.04	.02
16	Ozzie Guillen	.15	.11	.06
17	Bobby Thigpen	.10	.08	.04
18	Joe Carter	.20	.15	.08
19	Julio Franco	.12	.09	.05
20	Brook Jacoby	.12	.09	.05
21	Cory Snyder	.05	.04	.02
22	Pat Tabler	.10	.08	.04
23	Doyle Alexander	.08	.06	.03
24	Kirk Gibson	.30	.25	.12
25	Mike Henneman	.20	.15	.08
26	Jack Morris	.25	.20	.10
27	Matt Nokes	.30	.25	.12
28	Walt Terrell	.05	.04	.02
29	Alan Trammell	.30	.25	.12
30	George Brett	.70	.50	.30
31	Charlie Leibrandt	.05	.04	.02
32	Bret Saberhagen	.25	.20	.10
33	Kevin Seitzer	.15	.11	.06
34	Danny Tartabull	.25	.20	.10
35	Frank White	.10	.08	.04
36	Rob Deer	.10	.08	.04
37	Ted Higuera	.15	.11	.06
38	Paul Molitor	.20	.15	.08
39	Dan Plesac	.12	.09	.05
40	Robin Yount	.50	.40	.20
41	Bert Blyleven	.15	.11	.06
42	Tom Brunansky	.15	.11	.06
43	Gary Gaetti	.20	.15	.08
44	Kent Hrbek	.30	.25	.12
45	Kirby Puckett	.50	.40	.20
46	Jeff Reardon	.10	.08	.04
47	Frank Viola	.15	.11	.06
48	Don Mattingly	.90	.70	.35
49	Mike Pagliarulo	.12	.09	.05
50	Willie Randolph	.08	.06	.03
51	Rick Rhoden	.08	.06	.03
52	Dave Righetti	.20	.15	.08
53	Dave Winfield	.40	.30	.15
54	Jose Canseco	1.00	.70	.40
55	Carney Lansford	.08	.06	.03
56	Mark McGwire	.60	.45	.25
57	Dave Stewart	.12	.09	.05
58	Curt Young	.08	.06	.03
59	Alvin Davis	.15	.11	.06

		MT	NR MT	EX
60	Mark Langston	.15	.11	.06
61	Ken Phelps	.05	.04	.02
62	Harold Reynolds	.10	.08	.04
63	Scott Fletcher	.05	.04	.02
64	Charlie Hough	.08	.06	.03
65	Pete Incaviglia	.25	.20	.10
66	Oddibe McDowell	.10	.08	.04
67	Pete O'Brien	.10	.08	.04
68	Larry Parrish	.08	.06	.03
69	Ruben Sierra	.25	.20	.10
70	Jesse Barfield	.12	.09	.05
71	George Bell	.25	.20	.10
72	Tony Fernandez	.12	.09	.05
73	Tom Henke	.10	.08	.04
74	Jimmy Key	.12	.09	.05
75	Lloyd Moseby	.10	.08	.04
76	Dion James	.05	.04	.02
77	Dale Murphy	.35	.25	.12
78	Zane Smith	.08	.06	.03
79	Andre Dawson	.25	.20	.10
80	Ryne Sandberg	1.00	.70	.40
81	Rick Sutcliffe	.15	.11	.06
82	Kal Daniels	.10	.08	.04
83	Eric Davis	.30	.25	.12
84	John Franco	.10	.08	.04
85	Kevin Bass	.10	.08	.04
86	Glenn Davis	.20	.15	.08
87	Bill Doran	.10	.08	.04
88	Nolan Ryan	1.00	.70	.40
89	Mike Scott	.15	.11	.06
90	Dave Smith	.05	.04	.02
91	Pedro Guerrero	.20	.15	.08
92	Orel Hershiser	.35	.25	.14
93	Steve Sax	.20	.15	.08
94	Fernando Valenzuela	.25	.20	.10
95	Tim Burke	.05	.04	.02
96	Andres Galarraga	.20	.15	.08
97	Tim Raines	.25	.20	.10
98	Tim Wallach	.12	.09	.05
99	Mitch Webster	.05	.04	.02
100	Ron Darling	.20	.15	.08
101	Sid Fernandez	.10	.08	.04
102	Dwight Gooden	.60	.45	.25
103	Keith Hernandez	.10	.08	.04
104	Howard Johnson	.12	.09	.05
105	Roger McDowell	.10	.08	.04
106	Darryl Strawberry	.70	.50	.30
107	Steve Bedrosian	.12	.09	.05
108	Von Hayes	.12	.09	.05
109	Shane Rawley	.08	.06	.03
110	Juan Samuel	.15	.11	.06
111	Mike Schmidt	.70	.50	.30
112	Milt Thompson	.05	.04	.02
113	Sid Bream	.08	.06	.03
114	Bobby Bonilla	.35	.25	.14
115	Mike Dunne	.15	.11	.06
116	Andy Van Slyke	.12	.09	.05
117	Vince Coleman	.25	.20	.10
118	Willie McGee	.15	.11	.06
119	Terry Pendleton	.10	.08	.04
120	Ozzie Smith	.20	.15	.08
121	John Tudor	.12	.09	.05
122	Todd Worrell	.20	.15	.08
123	Tony Gwynn	.40	.30	.15
124	John Kruk	.20	.15	.08
125	Benito Santiago	.30	.25	.12
126	Will Clark	.60	.45	.25
127	Dave Dravecky	.05	.04	.02
128	Jeff Leonard	.05	.04	.02
129	Candy Maldonado	.05	.04	.02
130	Rick Rueschel	.10	.08	.04
131	Don Robinson	.05	.04	.02
132	Checklist	.05	.04	.02

1988 Fleer Star Stickers Box Panels

This set of eight box-bottom cards was printed on two different retail display boxes. Six players and two team logo sticker cards are included in the set, three player photos and one team photo per box. The full-color player photos are exclusively limited to the Fleer Star Sticker set. The cards, which measure 2-1/2" by 3-1/2", have a light gray border sprinkled with multi-color stars. The backs are printed in navy blue and red.

		MT	NR MT	EX
Complete Panel Set:		3.50	2.75	1.50
Complete Singles Set:		1.75	1.25	.70
Common Singles Player:		.15	.11	.06
	Panel	2.50	2.00	1.00
1	Eric Davis, Mark McGwire	.70	.50	.30
3	Kevin Mitchell	.25	.20	.10
5	Rickey Henderson	.50	.40	.20
7	Tigers Logo	.05	.04	.02
	Panel	1.00	.70	.40
2	Gary Carter	.35	.25	.14
4	Ron Guidry	.15	.11	.06
6	Don Baylor	.15	.11	.06
8	Giants Logo	.05	.04	.02

1988 Fleer Superstars

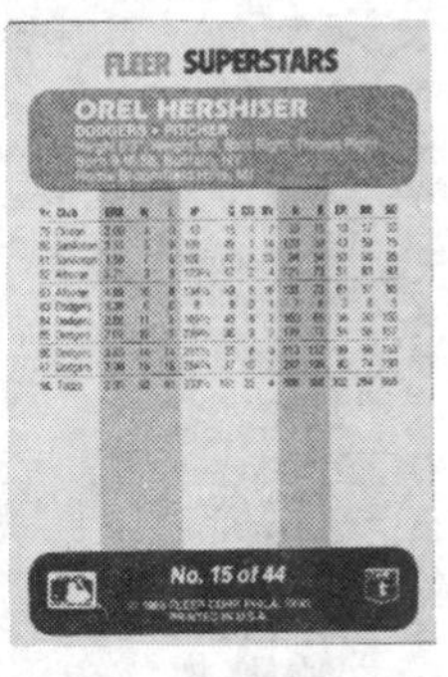

This is the fourth edition of Fleer's 44-card boxed set produced for distribution by McCrory's (1985-87 issues were simply titled "Fleer Limited Edition"). The Superstars standard-size card set features full-color player photos framed by red, white and blue striped top and bottom borders. "Fleer 1988" is printed in an elongated yellow oval banner above the photo. A pale yellow rectangle below the photo carries the player's name and team logo. Card fronts have a semi-glossy slightly textured finish. Card backs are red and blue on white and include card numbers, personal data and statistics. Six team logo sticker cards are also included in this set which was marketed in red, white and blue boxes with checklist backs. Boxed sets were sold exclusively at McCrory's stores and its affiliates.

		MT	NR MT	EX
Complete Set:		6.00	4.50	2.50
Common Player:		.05	.04	.02
1	Steve Bedrosian	.10	.08	.04
2	George Bell	.20	.15	.08
3	Wade Boggs	.80	.60	.30
4	Barry Bonds	.12	.09	.05
5	Jose Canseco	.80	.60	.30
6	Joe Carter	.12	.09	.05
7	Jack Clark	.15	.11	.06

		MT	NR MT	EX
8	Will Clark	.60	.45	.25
9	Roger Clemens	.40	.30	.15
10	Alvin Davis	.10	.08	.04
11	Eric Davis	.50	.40	.20
12	Glenn Davis	.12	.09	.05
13	Andre Dawson	.15	.11	.06
14	Dwight Gooden	.40	.30	.15
15	Orel Hershiser	.20	.15	.08
16	Teddy Higuera	.10	.08	.04
17	Kent Hrbek	.15	.11	.06
18	Wally Joyner	.30	.25	.12
19	Jimmy Key	.07	.05	.03
20	John Kruk	.10	.08	.04
21	Jeff Leonard	.05	.04	.02
22	Don Mattingly	.80	.60	.30
23	Mark McGwire	.60	.45	.25
24	Kevin McReynolds	.12	.09	.05
25	Dale Murphy	.30	.25	.12
26	Matt Nokes	.30	.25	.12
27	Terry Pendleton	.05	.04	.02
28	Kirby Puckett	.50	.40	.20
29	Tim Raines	.25	.20	.10
30	Rick Rhoden	.07	.05	.03
31	Cal Ripken, Jr.	.60	.45	.25
32	Benito Santiago	.25	.20	.10
33	Mike Schmidt	.30	.25	.12
34	Mike Scott	.10	.08	.04
35	Kevin Seitzer	.10	.08	.04
36	Ruben Sierra	.25	.20	.10
37	Cory Snyder	.12	.09	.05
38	Darryl Strawberry	.40	.30	.15
39	Rick Sutcliffe	.10	.08	.04
40	Danny Tartabull	.12	.09	.05
41	Alan Trammell	.15	.11	.06
42	Ken Williams	.07	.05	.03
43	Mike Witt	.07	.05	.03
44	Robin Yount	.30	.25	.12

1989 Fleer

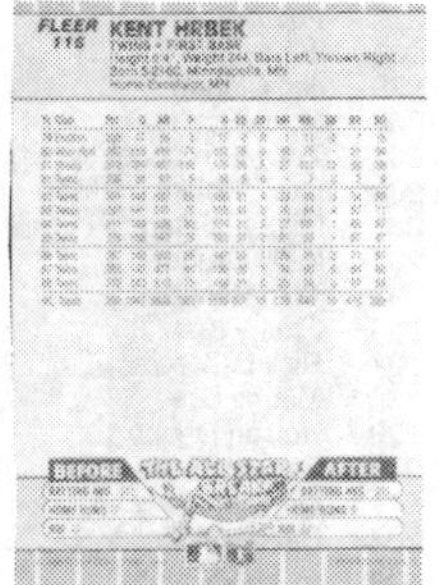

This set includes 660 standard-size cards and was issued with 45 team logo stickers. Individual card fronts feature a grey and white striped background with full-color player photos framed by a bright line of color that slants upward to the right. The set also includes two subsets: 15 Major League Prospects and 12 SuperStar Specials. A special bonus set of 12 All-Star Team cards was randomly inserted in individual wax packs of 15 cards. The last seven cards in the set are checklists, with players listed alphabetically by teams.

	MT	NR MT	EX
Complete Set (660):	18.00	12.00	6.00
Common Player:	.05	.04	.02

		MT	NR MT	EX
1	Don Baylor	.10	.08	.04
2	*Lance Blankenship*(FC)	.10	.08	.04
3	*Todd Burns*	.08	.06	.03
4	Greg Cadaret(FC)	.07	.05	.03
5	Jose Canseco	.30	.25	.12
6	Storm Davis	.10	.08	.04
7	Dennis Eckersley	.12	.09	.05
8	Mike Gallego(FC)	.05	.04	.02
9	Ron Hassey	.05	.04	.02
10	Dave Henderson	.10	.08	.04
11	Rick Honeycutt	.05	.04	.02
12	Glenn Hubbard	.05	.04	.02
13	Stan Javier	.05	.04	.02
14	*Doug Jennings*	.08	.06	.03
15	*Felix Jose*(FC)	.40	.30	.15
16	Carney Lansford	.07	.05	.03
17	Mark McGwire	.40	.30	.15
18	Gene Nelson	.05	.04	.02
19	Dave Parker	.12	.09	.05
20	Eric Plunk	.05	.04	.02
21	Luis Polonia	.07	.05	.03
22	Terry Steinbach	.10	.08	.04
23	Dave Stewart	.10	.08	.04
24	Walt Weiss	.10	.08	.04
25	Bob Welch	.10	.08	.04
26	Curt Young	.07	.05	.03
27	Rick Aguilera	.05	.04	.02
28	Wally Backman	.07	.05	.03
29	Mark Carreon	.07	.05	.03
30	Gary Carter	.08	.06	.03
31	David Cone	.10	.08	.04
32	Ron Darling	.12	.09	.05
33	Len Dykstra	.15	.11	.06
34	Kevin Elster	.10	.08	.04
35	Sid Fernandez	.10	.08	.04
36	Dwight Gooden	.12	.09	.05
37	Keith Hernandez	.08	.06	.03
38	Gregg Jefferies	.40	.30	.15
39	Howard Johnson	.10	.08	.04
40	Terry Leach	.05	.04	.02
41	Dave Magadan	.10	.08	.04
42	Bob McClure	.05	.04	.02
43	Roger McDowell	.10	.08	.04
44	Kevin McReynolds	.15	.11	.06
45	Keith Miller	.10	.08	.04
46	Randy Myers	.10	.08	.04
47	Bob Ojeda	.07	.05	.03
48	Mackey Sasser	.07	.05	.03
49	Darryl Strawberry	.20	.15	.08
50	Tim Teufel	.05	.04	.02
51	*Dave West*(FC)	.12	.09	.05
52	Mookie Wilson	.07	.05	.03
53	Dave Anderson	.05	.04	.02
54	Tim Belcher	.10	.08	.04
55	Mike Davis	.07	.05	.03
56	Mike Devereaux	.15	.11	.06
57	Kirk Gibson	.08	.06	.03
58	Alfredo Griffin	.07	.05	.03
59	Chris Gwynn	.12	.09	.05
60	Jeff Hamilton	.07	.05	.03
61a	Danny Heep (Home: San Antonio, TX)	.70	.50	.30
61b	Danny Heep (Home: Lake Hills, TX)	.05	.04	.02
62	Orel Hershiser	.08	.06	.03
63	Brian Holton(FC)	.07	.05	.03
64	Jay Howell	.07	.05	.03
65	Tim Leary	.07	.05	.03
66	Mike Marshall	.12	.09	.05
67	*Ramon Martinez*(FC)	.60	.45	.25
68	Jesse Orosco	.07	.05	.03
69	Alejandro Pena	.07	.05	.03
70	Steve Sax	.15	.11	.06
71	Mike Scioscia	.07	.05	.03
72	Mike Sharperson	.05	.04	.02
73	John Shelby	.05	.04	.02
74	Franklin Stubbs	.05	.04	.02
75	John Tudor	.10	.08	.04
76	Fernando Valenzuela	.08	.06	.03
77	Tracy Woodson	.10	.08	.04
78	Marty Barrett	.07	.05	.03
79	Todd Benzinger	.12	.09	.05
80	Mike Boddicker	.07	.05	.03
81	Wade Boggs	.25	.20	.10
82	"Oil Can" Boyd	.07	.05	.03
83	Ellis Burks	.10	.08	.04
84	Rick Cerone	.05	.04	.02
85	Roger Clemens	.40	.30	.15
86	*Steve Curry*(FC)	.06	.05	.02
87	Dwight Evans	.10	.08	.04
88	Wes Gardner	.07	.05	.03
89	Rich Gedman	.07	.05	.03
90	Mike Greenwell	.08	.06	.03
91	Bruce Hurst	.10	.08	.04
92	Dennis Lamp	.05	.04	.02
93	Spike Owen	.05	.04	.02
94	Larry Parrish	.07	.05	.03
95	*Carlos Quintana*(FC)	.12	.09	.05
96	Jody Reed	.12	.09	.05
97	Jim Rice	.08	.06	.03
98a	Kevin Romine (batting follow-thru, photo actually Randy Kutcher)	.50	.40	.20
98b	Kevin Romine (arms crossed on chest, correct photo)	.60	.45	.25

		MT	NR MT	EX
99	Lee Smith	.10	.08	.04
100	Mike Smithson	.05	.04	.02
101	Bob Stanley	.05	.04	.02
102	Allan Anderson	.07	.05	.03
103	Keith Atherton	.05	.04	.02
104	Juan Berenguer	.05	.04	.02
105	Bert Blyleven	.12	.09	.05
106	*Eric Bullock*(FC)	.15	.11	.06
107	Randy Bush	.05	.04	.02
108	John Christensen(FC)	.05	.04	.02
109	Mark Davidson	.07	.05	.03
110	Gary Gaetti	.15	.11	.06
111	Greg Gagne	.05	.04	.02
112	Dan Gladden	.05	.04	.02
113	*German Gonzalez*(FC)	.06	.05	.02
114	Brian Harper	.05	.04	.02
115	Tom Herr	.07	.05	.03
116	Kent Hrbek	.08	.06	.03
117	Gene Larkin	.10	.08	.04
118	Tim Laudner	.05	.04	.02
119	Charlie Lea	.05	.04	.02
120	Steve Lombardozzi	.05	.04	.02
121a	John Moses (Home: Phoenix, AZ)	1.00	.70	.40
121b	John Moses (Home: Tempe, AZ)	.05	.04	.02
122	Al Newman	.05	.04	.02
123	Mark Portugal	.05	.04	.02
124	Kirby Puckett	.35	.25	.14
125	Jeff Reardon	.10	.08	.04
126	Fred Toliver	.05	.04	.02
127	Frank Viola	.15	.11	.06
128	Doyle Alexander	.07	.05	.03
129	Dave Bergman	.05	.04	.02
130a	Tom Brookens (Mike Heath stats on back)	2.25	1.75	.90
130b	Tom Brookens (correct stats on back)	.30	.25	.12
131	*Paul Gibson*	.05	.04	.02
132a	Mike Heath (Tom Brookens stats on back)	2.25	1.75	.90
132b	Mike Heath (correct stats on back)	.30	.25	.12
133	*Don Heinkel*	.15	.11	.06
134	Mike Henneman	.10	.08	.04
135	Guillermo Hernandez	.07	.05	.03
136	Eric King	.05	.04	.02
137	Chet Lemon	.07	.05	.03
138	Fred Lynn	.10	.08	.04
139	Jack Morris	.15	.11	.06
140	Matt Nokes	.10	.08	.04
141	Gary Pettis	.05	.04	.02
142	Ted Power	.05	.04	.02
143	Jeff Robinson	.12	.09	.05
144	Luis Salazar	.05	.04	.02
145	*Steve Searcy*(FC)	.10	.08	.04
146	Pat Sheridan	.05	.04	.02
147	Frank Tanana	.07	.05	.03
148	Alan Trammell	.08	.06	.03
149	Walt Terrell	.07	.05	.03
150	Jim Walewander(FC)	.07	.05	.03
151	Lou Whitaker	.08	.06	.03
152	Tim Birtsas	.05	.04	.02
153	Tom Browning	.10	.08	.04
154	*Keith Brown*(FC)	.06	.05	.02
155	*Norm Charlton*(FC)	.30	.25	.12
156	Dave Concepcion	.10	.08	.04
157	Kal Daniels	.15	.11	.06
158	Eric Davis	.12	.09	.05
159	Bo Diaz	.07	.05	.03
160	*Rob Dibble*	.30	.25	.12
161	Nick Esasky	.07	.05	.03
162	John Franco	.10	.08	.04
163	Danny Jackson	.15	.11	.06
164	Barry Larkin	.15	.11	.06
165	Rob Murphy	.05	.04	.02
166	Paul O'Neill	.05	.04	.02
167	Jeff Reed	.05	.04	.02
168	Jose Rijo	.07	.05	.03
169	Ron Robinson	.05	.04	.02
170	*Chris Sabo*	.40	.30	.15
171	*Candy Sierra*(FC)	.15	.11	.06
172	*Van Snider*(FC)	.08	.06	.03
173	Jeff Treadway	.12	.09	.05
174	Frank Williams	.05	.04	.02
175	Herm Winningham	.05	.04	.02
176	Jim Adduci(FC)	.05	.04	.02
177	Don August	.10	.08	.04
178	Mike Birkbeck	.05	.04	.02
179	Chris Bosio	.05	.04	.02
180	Glenn Braggs	.07	.05	.03
181	Greg Brock	.07	.05	.03
182	Mark Clear	.05	.04	.02
183	Chuck Crim	.05	.04	.02
184	Rob Deer	.07	.05	.03
185	Tom Filer	.05	.04	.02
186	Jim Gantner	.05	.04	.02
187	*Darryl Hamilton*	.30	.25	.12
188	Ted Higuera	.10	.08	.04
189	Odell Jones	.05	.04	.02
190	Jeffrey Leonard	.07	.05	.03
191	Joey Meyer	.10	.08	.04
192	Paul Mirabella	.05	.04	.02
193	Paul Molitor	.20	.15	.08
194	Charlie O'Brien(FC)	.07	.05	.03
195	Dan Plesac	.10	.08	.04
196	*Gary Sheffield*(FC)	1.75	1.25	.70
197	B.J. Surhoff	.10	.08	.04
198	Dale Sveum	.07	.05	.03
199	Bill Wegman	.05	.04	.02
200	Robin Yount	.25	.20	.10
201	Rafael Belliard	.05	.04	.02
202	Barry Bonds	.50	.40	.20
203	Bobby Bonilla	.15	.11	.06
204	Sid Bream	.07	.05	.03
205	Benny Distefano(FC)	.05	.04	.02
206	Doug Drabek	.07	.05	.03
207	Mike Dunne	.10	.08	.04
208	Felix Fermin	.07	.05	.03
209	Brian Fisher	.07	.05	.03
210	Jim Gott	.05	.04	.02
211	Bob Kipper	.05	.04	.02
212	Dave LaPoint	.07	.05	.03
213	Mike LaValliere	.07	.05	.03
214	Jose Lind	.10	.08	.04
215	Junior Ortiz	.05	.04	.02
216	Vicente Palacios	.07	.05	.03
217	Tom Prince(FC)	.10	.08	.04
218	Gary Redus	.05	.04	.02
219	R.J. Reynolds	.05	.04	.02
220	Jeff Robinson	.07	.05	.03
221	John Smiley	.12	.09	.05
222	Andy Van Slyke	.12	.09	.05
223	Bob Walk	.05	.04	.02
224	Glenn Wilson	.07	.05	.03
225	Jesse Barfield	.10	.08	.04
226	George Bell	.10	.08	.04
227	*Pat Borders*	.30	.25	.12
228	John Cerutti	.07	.05	.03
229	Jim Clancy	.07	.05	.03
230	Mark Eichhorn	.07	.05	.03
231	Tony Fernandez	.12	.09	.05
232	Cecil Fielder	.25	.20	.10
233	Mike Flanagan	.07	.05	.03
234	Kelly Gruber	.05	.04	.02
235	Tom Henke	.07	.05	.03
236	Jimmy Key	.10	.08	.04
237	Rick Leach	.05	.04	.02
238	Manny Lee	.05	.04	.02
239	Nelson Liriano	.07	.05	.03
240	Fred McGriff	.35	.25	.14
241	Lloyd Moseby	.07	.05	.03
242	Rance Mulliniks	.05	.04	.02
243	Jeff Musselman	.07	.05	.03
244	Dave Stieb	.10	.08	.04
245	Todd Stottlemyre(FC)	.10	.08	.04
246	Duane Ward	.05	.04	.02
247	David Wells	.10	.08	.04
248	Ernie Whitt	.07	.05	.03
249	Luis Aguayo	.05	.04	.02
250a	Neil Allen (Home: Sarasota, FL)	1.50	1.25	.60
250b	Neil Allen (Home: Syosset, NY)	.05	.04	.02
251	John Candelaria	.07	.05	.03
252	Jack Clark	.15	.11	.06
253	Richard Dotson	.07	.05	.03
254	Rickey Henderson	.35	.25	.14
255	Tommy John	.12	.09	.05
256	Roberto Kelly	.20	.15	.08
257	Al Leiter	.15	.11	.06
258	Don Mattingly	.30	.25	.12
259	Dale Mohorcic	.05	.04	.02
260	*Hal Morris*(FC)	.50	.40	.20
261	Scott Nielsen(FC)	.10	.08	.04
262	Mike Pagliarulo	.10	.08	.04
263	*Hipolito Pena*(FC)	.15	.11	.06
264	Ken Phelps	.07	.05	.03
265	Willie Randolph	.07	.05	.03
266	Rick Rhoden	.07	.05	.03
267	Dave Righetti	.12	.09	.05
268	Rafael Santana	.05	.04	.02
269	Steve Shields(FC)	.07	.05	.03
270	Joel Skinner	.05	.04	.02
271	Don Slaught	.05	.04	.02
272	Claudell Washington	.07	.05	.03
273	Gary Ward	.07	.05	.03

		MT	NR MT	EX
274	Dave Winfield	.30	.25	.12
275	Luis Aquino(FC)	.05	.04	.02
276	Floyd Bannister	.07	.05	.03
277	George Brett	.25	.20	.10
278	Bill Buckner	.10	.08	.04
279	*Nick Capra*(FC)	.15	.11	.06
280	*Jose DeJesus*(FC)	.15	.11	.06
281	Steve Farr	.05	.04	.02
282	Jerry Gleaton	.05	.04	.02
283	Mark Gubicza	.10	.08	.04
284	*Tom Gordon*(FC)	.10	.08	.04
285	Bo Jackson	.35	.25	.14
286	Charlie Leibrandt	.07	.05	.03
287	*Mike Macfarlane*	.20	.15	.08
288	Jeff Montgomery	.12	.09	.05
289	Bill Pecota	.07	.05	.03
290	Jamie Quirk	.05	.04	.02
291	Bret Saberhagen	.15	.11	.06
292	Kevin Seitzer	.06	.05	.02
293	Kurt Stillwell	.07	.05	.03
294	Pat Tabler	.07	.05	.03
295	Danny Tartabull	.20	.15	.08
296	Gary Thurman	.12	.09	.05
297	Frank White	.07	.05	.03
298	Willie Wilson	.10	.08	.04
299	Roberto Alomar	1.00	.70	.40
300	*Sandy Alomar, Jr.*(FC)	.40	.30	.15
301	Chris Brown	.07	.05	.03
302	Mike Brumley(FC)	.07	.05	.03
303	Mark Davis	.05	.04	.02
304	Mark Grant	.05	.04	.02
305	Tony Gwynn	.35	.25	.14
306	*Greg Harris*(FC)	.10	.08	.04
307	Andy Hawkins	.05	.04	.02
308	Jimmy Jones	.05	.04	.02
309	John Kruk	.12	.09	.05
310	Dave Leiper	.05	.04	.02
311	Carmelo Martinez	.05	.04	.02
312	Lance McCullers	.07	.05	.03
313	Keith Moreland	.07	.05	.03
314	Dennis Rasmussen	.10	.08	.04
315	Randy Ready	.05	.04	.02
316	Benito Santiago	.15	.11	.06
317	Eric Show	.07	.05	.03
318	Todd Simmons	.10	.08	.04
319	Garry Templeton	.07	.05	.03
320	Dickie Thon	.05	.04	.02
321	Ed Whitson	.05	.04	.02
322	Marvell Wynne	.05	.04	.02
323	Mike Aldrete	.07	.05	.03
324	Brett Butler	.07	.05	.03
325	Will Clark	.40	.30	.15
326	Kelly Downs	.10	.08	.04
327	Dave Dravecky	.07	.05	.03
328	Scott Garrelts	.05	.04	.02
329	Atlee Hammaker	.05	.04	.02
330	*Charlie Hayes*(FC)	.60	.45	.25
331	Mike Krukow	.07	.05	.03
332	Craig Lefferts	.05	.04	.02
333	Candy Maldonado	.07	.05	.03
334	Kirt Manwaring	.10	.08	.04
335	Bob Melvin	.05	.04	.02
336	Kevin Mitchell	.10	.08	.04
337	Donell Nixon	.05	.04	.02
338	*Tony Perezchica*(FC)	.15	.11	.06
339	Joe Price	.05	.04	.02
340	Rick Reuschel	.10	.08	.04
341	Earnest Riles	.05	.04	.02
342	Don Robinson	.05	.04	.02
343	Chris Speier	.05	.04	.02
344	Robby Thompson	.07	.05	.03
345	Jose Uribe	.05	.04	.02
346	Matt Williams	.30	.25	.12
347	*Trevor Wilson*(FC)	.15	.11	.06
348	Juan Agosto	.05	.04	.02
349	Larry Andersen	.05	.04	.02
350	Alan Ashby	.05	.04	.02
351	Kevin Bass	.07	.05	.03
352	Buddy Bell	.07	.05	.03
353	*Craig Biggio*	.60	.45	.25
354	Danny Darwin	.05	.04	.02
355	Glenn Davis	.06	.05	.02
356	Jim Deshaies	.05	.04	.02
357	Bill Doran	.07	.05	.03
358	*John Fishel*	.20	.15	.08
359	Billy Hatcher	.07	.05	.03
360	Bob Knepper	.07	.05	.03
361	*Louie Meadows*	.15	.11	.06
362	Dave Meads	.05	.04	.02
363	Jim Pankovits	.05	.04	.02
364	Terry Puhl	.05	.04	.02

		MT	NR MT	EX
365	Rafael Ramirez	.05	.04	.02
366	Craig Reynolds	.05	.04	.02
367	Mike Scott	.12	.09	.05
368	Nolan Ryan	.50	.40	.20
369	Dave Smith	.07	.05	.03
370	Gerald Young	.12	.09	.05
371	Hubie Brooks	.10	.08	.04
372	Tim Burke	.05	.04	.02
373	*John Dopson*	.10	.08	.04
374	Mike Fitzgerald	.05	.04	.02
375	Tom Foley	.05	.04	.02
376	Andres Galarraga	.15	.11	.06
377	Neal Heaton	.05	.04	.02
378	Joe Hesketh	.05	.04	.02
379	*Brian Holman*	.10	.08	.04
380	Rex Hudler	.05	.04	.02
381	*Randy Johnson*(FC)	.75	.60	.30
382	Wallace Johnson	.05	.04	.02
383	Tracy Jones	.10	.08	.04
384	Dave Martinez	.07	.05	.03
385	Dennis Martinez	.07	.05	.03
386	Andy McGaffigan	.05	.04	.02
387	Otis Nixon	.05	.04	.02
388	*Johnny Paredes*(FC)	.12	.09	.05
389	Jeff Parrett	.10	.08	.04
390	Pascual Perez	.07	.05	.03
391	Tim Raines	.08	.06	.03
392	Luis Rivera	.05	.04	.02
393	*Nelson Santovenia*	.15	.11	.06
394	Bryn Smith	.05	.04	.02
395	Tim Wallach	.10	.08	.04
396	Andy Allanson	.05	.04	.02
397	*Rod Allen*	.15	.11	.06
398	Scott Bailes	.05	.04	.02
399	Tom Candiotti	.05	.04	.02
400	Joe Carter	.20	.15	.08
401	Carmen Castillo	.05	.04	.02
402	Dave Clark	.07	.05	.03
403	John Farrell	.10	.08	.04
404	Julio Franco	.10	.08	.04
405	Don Gordon	.05	.04	.02
406	Mel Hall	.07	.05	.03
407	Brad Havens	.05	.04	.02
408	Brook Jacoby	.10	.08	.04
409	Doug Jones	.12	.09	.05
410	*Jeff Kaiser*(FC)	.15	.11	.06
411	*Luis Medina*(FC)	.06	.05	.02
412	Cory Snyder	.15	.11	.06
413	Greg Swindell	.12	.09	.05
414	*Ron Tingley*(FC)	.15	.11	.06
415	Willie Upshaw	.07	.05	.03
416	Ron Washington	.05	.04	.02
417	Rich Yett	.05	.04	.02
418	Damon Berryhill	.12	.09	.05
419	Mike Bielecki	.05	.04	.02
420	*Doug Dascenzo*(FC)	.08	.06	.03
421	Jody Davis	.07	.05	.03
422	Andre Dawson	.20	.15	.08
423	Frank DiPino	.05	.04	.02
424	Shawon Dunston	.10	.08	.04
425	"Goose" Gossage	.12	.09	.05
426	Mark Grace	.40	.30	.15
427	*Mike Harkey*(FC)	.15	.11	.06
428	Darrin Jackson	.07	.05	.03
429	Les Lancaster	.07	.05	.03
430	Vance Law	.07	.05	.03
431	Greg Maddux	.20	.15	.08
432	Jamie Moyer	.05	.04	.02
433	Al Nipper	.05	.04	.02
434	Rafael Palmeiro	.30	.25	.12
435	Pat Perry	.05	.04	.02
436	*Jeff Pico*	.05	.04	.02
437	Ryne Sandberg	.40	.30	.15
438	Calvin Schiraldi	.05	.04	.02
439	Rick Sutcliffe	.10	.08	.04
440	Manny Trillo	.05	.04	.02
441	*Gary Varsho*	.08	.06	.03
442	Mitch Webster	.07	.05	.03
443	*Luis Alicea*	.15	.11	.06
444	Tom Brunansky	.12	.09	.05
445	Vince Coleman	.15	.11	.06
446	*John Costello*	.15	.11	.06
447	Danny Cox	.07	.05	.03
448	Ken Dayley	.05	.04	.02
449	Jose DeLeon	.07	.05	.03
450	Curt Ford	.05	.04	.02
451	Pedro Guerrero	.15	.11	.06
452	Bob Horner	.10	.08	.04
453	*Tim Jones*(FC)	.15	.11	.06
454	Steve Lake	.05	.04	.02
455	Joe Magrane	.10	.08	.04

		MT	NR MT	EX
456	Greg Mathews	.07	.05	.03
457	Willie McGee	.12	.09	.05
458	Larry McWilliams	.05	.04	.02
459	Jose Oquendo	.05	.04	.02
460	Tony Pena	.07	.05	.03
461	Terry Pendleton	.10	.08	.04
462	*Steve Peters*(FC)	.15	.11	.06
463	Ozzie Smith	.15	.11	.06
464	Scott Terry	.08	.06	.03
465	Denny Walling	.05	.04	.02
466	Todd Worrell	.10	.08	.04
467	Tony Armas	.07	.05	.03
468	*Dante Bichette*(FC)	.30	.25	.12
469	Bob Boone	.07	.05	.03
470	*Terry Clark*(FC)	.05	.04	.02
471	Stew Cliburn(FC)	.05	.04	.02
472	*Mike Cook*(FC)	.05	.04	.02
473	*Sherman Corbett*	.05	.04	.02
474	Chili Davis	.07	.05	.03
475	Brian Downing	.07	.05	.03
476	Jim Eppard	.07	.05	.03
477	Chuck Finley	.05	.04	.02
478	Willie Fraser	.05	.04	.02
479	*Bryan Harvey*	.30	.25	.12
480	Jack Howell	.07	.05	.03
481	Wally Joyner	.10	.08	.04
482	Jack Lazorko	.05	.04	.02
483	Kirk McCaskill	.07	.05	.03
484	Mark McLemore	.05	.04	.02
485	Greg Minton	.05	.04	.02
486	Dan Petry	.07	.05	.03
487	Johnny Ray	.07	.05	.03
488	Dick Schofield	.05	.04	.02
489	Devon White	.12	.09	.05
490	Mike Witt	.07	.05	.03
491	Harold Baines	.12	.09	.05
492	Daryl Boston	.05	.04	.02
493	Ivan Calderon	.07	.05	.03
494	Mike Diaz	.07	.05	.03
495	Carlton Fisk	.20	.15	.08
496	*Dave Gallagher*	.15	.11	.06
497	Ozzie Guillen	.07	.05	.03
498	Shawn Hillegas	.07	.05	.03
499	Lance Johnson	.07	.05	.03
500	Barry Jones	.05	.04	.02
501	Bill Long	.07	.05	.03
502	Steve Lyons	.05	.04	.02
503	Fred Manrique	.07	.05	.03
504	Jack McDowell	.15	.11	.06
505	*Donn Pall*	.15	.11	.06
506	Kelly Paris	.05	.04	.02
507	Dan Pasqua	.10	.08	.04
508	*Ken Patterson*	.15	.11	.06
509	Melido Perez	.10	.08	.04
510	Jerry Reuss	.07	.05	.03
511	Mark Salas	.05	.04	.02
512	Bobby Thigpen	.10	.08	.04
513	Mike Woodard	.05	.04	.02
514	Bob Brower	.05	.04	.02
515	Steve Buechele	.05	.04	.02
516	*Jose Cecena*	.15	.11	.06
517	Cecil Espy	.07	.05	.03
518	Scott Fletcher	.07	.05	.03
519	Cecilio Guante	.05	.04	.02
520	Jose Guzman	.10	.08	.04
521	Ray Hayward	.05	.04	.02
522	Charlie Hough	.07	.05	.03
523	Pete Incaviglia	.12	.09	.05
524	Mike Jeffcoat	.05	.04	.02
525	Paul Kilgus	.10	.08	.04
526	*Chad Kreuter*(FC)	.15	.11	.06
527	Jeff Kunkel	.05	.04	.02
528	Oddibe McDowell	.07	.05	.03
529	Pete O'Brien	.07	.05	.03
530	Geno Petralli	.05	.04	.02
531	Jeff Russell	.05	.04	.02
532	Ruben Sierra	.35	.25	.14
533	Mike Stanley	.05	.04	.02
534	Ed Vande Berg	.05	.04	.02
535	Curtis Wilkerson	.05	.04	.02
536	Mitch Williams	.07	.05	.03
537	Bobby Witt	.10	.08	.04
538	Steve Balboni	.07	.05	.03
539	Scott Bankhead	.05	.04	.02
540	Scott Bradley	.05	.04	.02
541	Mickey Brantley	.05	.04	.02
542	Jay Buhner	.15	.11	.06
543	Mike Campbell	.10	.08	.04
544	Darnell Coles	.07	.05	.03
545	Henry Cotto	.05	.04	.02
546	Alvin Davis	.12	.09	.05

		MT	NR MT	EX
547	Mario Diaz	.07	.05	.03
548	*Ken Griffey, Jr.*(FC)	7.00	5.25	2.75
549	*Erik Hanson*(FC)	.20	.15	.08
550	Mike Jackson	.07	.05	.03
551	Mark Langston	.10	.08	.04
552	Edgar Martinez	.15	.11	.06
553	*Bill McGuire*(FC)	.05	.04	.02
554	Mike Moore	.05	.04	.02
555	Jim Presley	.07	.05	.03
556	Rey Quinones	.05	.04	.02
557	Jerry Reed	.05	.04	.02
558	Harold Reynolds	.07	.05	.03
559	*Mike Schooler*(FC)	.10	.08	.04
560	Bill Swift	.05	.04	.02
561	Dave Valle	.05	.04	.02
562	Steve Bedrosian	.10	.08	.04
563	Phil Bradley	.10	.08	.04
564	Don Carman	.07	.05	.03
565	Bob Dernier	.05	.04	.02
566	Marvin Freeman	.05	.04	.02
567	Todd Frohwirth	.07	.05	.03
568	Greg Gross	.05	.04	.02
569	Kevin Gross	.07	.05	.03
570	Greg Harris	.05	.04	.02
571	Von Hayes	.10	.08	.04
572	Chris James	.10	.08	.04
573	Steve Jeltz	.05	.04	.02
574	*Ron Jones*(FC)	.05	.04	.02
575	*Ricky Jordan*	.10	.08	.04
576	Mike Maddux	.05	.04	.02
577	David Palmer	.05	.04	.02
578	Lance Parrish	.15	.11	.06
579	Shane Rawley	.07	.05	.03
580	Bruce Ruffin	.05	.04	.02
581	Juan Samuel	.12	.09	.05
582	Mike Schmidt	.35	.25	.14
583	Kent Tekulve	.07	.05	.03
584	Milt Thompson	.05	.04	.02
585	*Jose Alvarez*	.05	.04	.02
586	Paul Assenmacher	.05	.04	.02
587	Bruce Benedict	.05	.04	.02
588	Jeff Blauser	.10	.08	.04
589	*Terry Blocker*(FC)	.05	.04	.02
590	Ron Gant	.30	.25	.12
591	Tom Glavine	.40	.30	.15
592	Tommy Gregg	.10	.08	.04
593	Albert Hall	.05	.04	.02
594	Dion James	.05	.04	.02
595	Rick Mahler	.05	.04	.02
596	Dale Murphy	.10	.08	.04
597	Gerald Perry	.10	.08	.04
598	Charlie Puleo	.05	.04	.02
599	Ted Simmons	.10	.08	.04
600	Pete Smith	.10	.08	.04
601	Zane Smith	.07	.05	.03
602	*John Smoltz*	.80	.60	.30
603	Bruce Sutter	.10	.08	.04
604	Andres Thomas	.07	.05	.03
605	Ozzie Virgil	.05	.04	.02
606	*Brady Anderson*(FC)	.50	.40	.20
607	Jeff Ballard	.07	.05	.03
608	*Jose Bautista*	.08	.06	.03
609	Ken Gerhart	.07	.05	.03
610	Terry Kennedy	.07	.05	.03
611	Eddie Murray	.30	.25	.12
612	Carl Nichols(FC)	.05	.04	.02
613	Tom Niedenfuer	.07	.05	.03
614	Joe Orsulak	.05	.04	.02
615	*Oswaldo Peraza (Oswald)*(FC)	.15	.11	.06
616a	Bill Ripken (vulgarity on bat knob)	8.00	6.00	3.25
616b	Bill Ripken (sribble over vulgarity)	10.00	7.50	4.00
616c	Bill Ripken (black box over vulgarity)	.10	.08	.04
616d	Bill Ripken (vulgarity whited out)	30.00	22.00	12.00
617	Cal Ripken, Jr.	.40	.30	.15
618	Dave Schmidt	.05	.04	.02
619	Rick Schu	.05	.04	.02
620	Larry Sheets	.07	.05	.03
621	Doug Sisk	.05	.04	.02
622	Pete Stanicek	.05	.04	.02
623	Mickey Tettleton	.15	.11	.06
624	Jay Tibbs	.05	.04	.02
625	Jim Traber	.07	.05	.03
626	Mark Williamson	.07	.05	.03
627	*Craig Worthington*	.20	.15	.08
628	Speed and Power (Jose Canseco)	.20	.15	.08
629	Pitcher Perfect (Tom Browning)	.10	.08	.04
630	Like Father Like Sons (Roberto Alomar, Sandy Alomar, Jr.)	.50	.40	.20
631	N.L. All-Stars (Will Clark, Rafael Palmeiro)	.40	.30	.15

		MT	NR MT	EX
632	Homeruns Coast to Coast (Will Clark, Darryl Strawberry)	.30	.25	.12
633	Hot Corner's Hot Hitters (Wade Boggs, Carney Lansford)	.10	.08	.04
634	Triple A's (Jose Canseco, Mark McGwire, Terry Steinbach)	.30	.25	.12
635	Dual Heat (Mark Davis, Dwight Gooden)	.20	.15	.08
636	N.L. Pitching Power (David Cone, Danny Jackson)	.15	.11	.06
637	Cannon Arms (Bobby Bonilla, Chris Sabo)	.20	.15	.08
638	Double Trouble (Andres Galarraga, Gerald Perry)	.10	.08	.04
639	Power Center (Eric Davis, Kirby Puckett)	.15	.11	.06
640	Major League Prospects *(Cameron Drew, Steve Wilson)*(FC)	.15	.11	.06
641	Major League Prospects (Kevin Brown, *Kevin Reimer*)(FC)	.75	.60	.30
642	Major League Prospects *(Jerald Clark, Brad Pounders)*(FC)	.20	.15	.08
643	Major League Prospects *(Mike Capel, Drew Hall)*(FC)	.15	.11	.06
644	Major League Prospects *(Joe Girardi, Rolando Roomes)*(FC)	.15	.11	.06
645	Major League Prospects *(Marty Brown, Lenny Harris)*	.12	.09	.05
646	Major League Prospects *(Luis de los Santos, Jim Campbell)*(FC)	.20	.15	.08
647	Major League Prospects *(Miguel Garcia, Randy Kramer)*(FC)	.15	.11	.06
648	Major League Prospects *(Torey Lovullo, Robert Palacios)*(FC)	.15	.11	.06
649	Major League Prospects *(Jim Corsi, Bob Milacki)*(FC)	.12	.09	.05
650	Major League Prospects *(Grady Hall, Mike Rochford)*(FC)	.15	.11	.06
651	Major League Prospects *(Vance Lovelace, Terry Taylor)*(FC)	.15	.11	.06
652	Major League Prospects *(Dennis Cook, Ken Hill)*(FC)	.50	.40	.20
653	Major League Prospects *(Scott Service, Shane Turner)*(FC)	.15	.11	.06
654	Checklist 1-101	.05	.04	.02
655	Checklist 102-200	.05	.04	.02
656	Checklist 201-298	.05	.04	.02
657	Checklist 299-395	.05	.04	.02
658	Checklist 396-490	.05	.04	.02
659	Checklist 491-584	.05	.04	.02
660	Checklist 585-660	.05	.04	.02

1989 Fleer All Stars

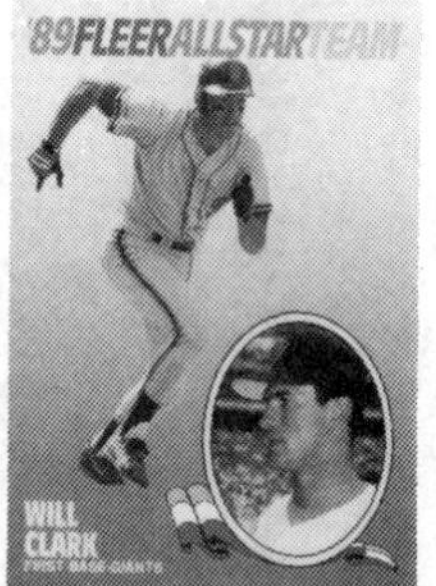

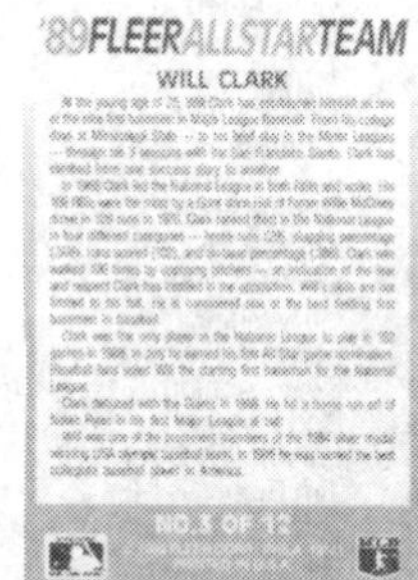

This special 12-card set represents Fleer's choices for its 1989 Major League All-Star Team. For the fourth consecutive year, Fleer inserted the special cards randomly inside their regular 1989 wax and cello packs. The cards feature two player photos set against a green background with the "1989 Fleer All Star Team" logo bannered across the top, and the player's name, position and team in the lower left corner. The backs contain a several-paragraph player profile.

	MT	NR MT	EX
Complete Set (12):	4.00	3.00	1.50
Common Player:	.15	.10	.05

1	Bobby Bonilla	.50	.40	.20
2	Jose Canseco	1.00	.70	.40
3	Will Clark	.90	.70	.35
4	Dennis Eckersley	.40	.30	.15
5	Julio Franco	.15	.11	.06
6	Mike Greenwell	.25	.20	.10
7	Orel Hershiser	.15	.11	.06
8	Paul Molitor	.90	.70	.35
9	Mike Scioscia	.15	.11	.06
10	Darryl Strawberry	.40	.30	.15
11	Alan Trammell	.25	.20	.10
12	Frank Viola	.25	.20	.10

1989 Fleer For The Record

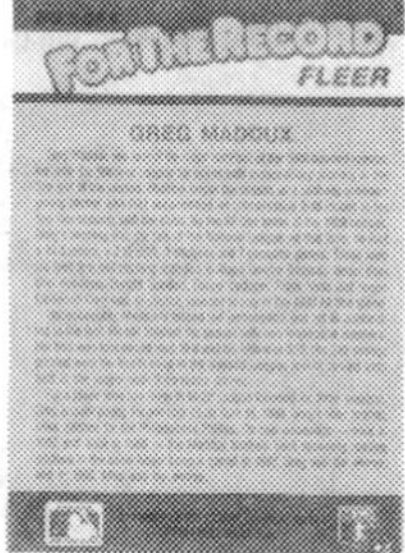

Fleer's "For the Record" set features six players and their achievements from 1988. Fronts of the standard 2-1/2" by 3-1/2" cards feature a full color photo of the player set against a red background. The words "For the Record" appear in blue script at the top of the card and the players name on the bottom, printed in white type. Card backs are grey and describe individual accomplishments. The cards were distributed randomly in rack packs.

		MT	NR MT	EX
Complete Set (6):		4.00	3.00	1.50
Common Player:		.25	.15	.10
1	Wade Boggs	1.00	.70	.40
2	Roger Clemens	1.00	.70	.40
3	Andres Galarraga	.80	.60	.30
4	Kirk Gibson	.25	.20	.10
5	Greg Maddux	.80	.60	.30
6	Don Mattingly	1.00	.70	.40

1989 Fleer World Series

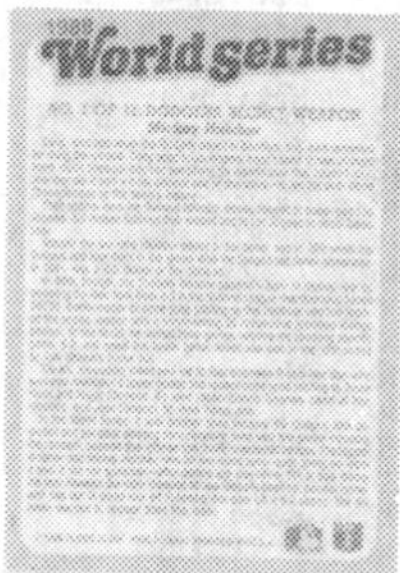

This 12-card set, which depicts highlights of the 1988 World Series, was included as a special sub-set with the regular factory-collated Fleer set. It was not available as individual cards in wax packs, cello packs or any other form.

	MT	NR MT	EX
Complete Set (12):	2.50	1.50	.75
Common Player:	.15	.10	.05

		MT	NR MT	EX
1	Dodgers' Secret Weapon (Mickey Hatcher)	.15	.10	.05
2	Rookie Starts Series (Tim Belcher)	.15	.10	.05
3	Jose Canseco	.40	.30	.20
4	Dramatic Comeback (Mike Scioscia)	.15	.10	.05
5	Kirk Gibson	.30	.20	.10
6	Orel Hershiser	.30	.25	.12
7	One Swing, Three RBI's (Mike Marshall)	.25	.20	.10
8	Mark McGwire	.40	.30	.15
9	Sax's Speed Wins Game 4 (Steve Sax)	.15	.10	.05
10	Series Caps Award-Winning Year (Walt Weiss)	.15	.10	.05
11	Orel Hershiser	.25	.15	.10
12	Dodger Blue, World Champs	.25	.20	.10

1989 Fleer Box Panels

For the fourth consecutive year, Fleer issued a series of cards on the bottom panels of its regular 1989 wax pack boxes. The 28-card set includes 20 players and eight team logo cards, all designed in the identical style of the regular 1989 Fleer set. The box-bottom cards were randomly printed, four cards (three player cards and one team logo) on each bottom panel. The cards were numbered from C-1 to C-28.

	MT	NR MT	EX
Complete Panel Set:	6.00	4.50	2.50
Complete Singles Set:	3.00	2.25	1.25
Common Single Player:	.15	.11	.06

		MT	NR MT	EX
1	Mets Logo	.05	.04	.02
2	Wade Boggs	.40	.30	.15
3	George Brett	.40	.30	.15
4	Jose Canseco	.50	.40	.20
5	A's Logo	.05	.04	.02
6	Will Clark	.40	.30	.15
7	David Cone	.25	.20	.10
8	Andres Galarraga	.25	.20	.10
9	Dodgers Logo	.05	.04	.02
10	Kirk Gibson	.15	.11	.06
11	Mike Greenwell	.25	.20	.10
12	Tony Gwynn	.25	.20	.10
13	Tigers Logo	.05	.04	.02
14	Orel Hershiser	.20	.15	.08
15	Danny Jackson	.15	.11	.06
16	Wally Joyner	.25	.20	.10
17	Red Sox Logo	.05	.04	.02
18	Yankees Logo	.05	.04	.02
19	Fred McGriff	.30	.25	.12
20	Kirby Puckett	.35	.25	.12
21	Chris Sabo	.15	.11	.06
22	Kevin Seitzer	.15	.11	.06
23	Pirates Logo	.05	.04	.02
24	Astros Logo	.05	.04	.02
25	Darryl Strawberry	.30	.25	.12
26	Alan Trammell	.20	.15	.08
27	Andy Van Slyke	.20	.15	.07
28	Frank Viola	.20	.15	.08

Regional interest may affect the value of a card.

1989 Fleer Update

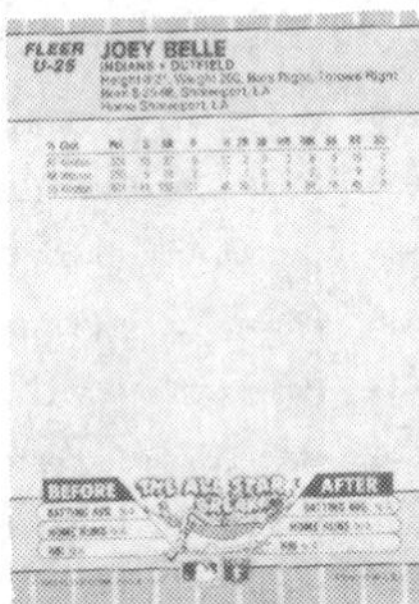

Fleer produced its sixth consecutive "Update" set in 1989 to supplement the company's regular set. As in the past, the set consisted of 132 cards (numbered U-1 through U-132) that were sold by hobby dealers in special collector's boxes.

	MT	NR MT	EX
Complete Set (132):	12.00	9.00	4.75
Common Player:	.06	.05	.02

		MT	NR MT	EX
1	Phil Bradley	.06	.05	.02
2	Mike Devereaux	.25	.20	.10
3	Steve Finley(FC)	.25	.20	.10
4	Kevin Hickey	.06	.05	.02
5	Brian Holton	.06	.05	.02
6	Bob Milacki	.20	.15	.08
7	Randy Milligan	.10	.08	.04
8	John Dopson	.15	.11	.06
9	Nick Esasky	.10	.08	.04
10	Rob Murphy	.06	.05	.02
11	Jim Abbott(FC)	1.25	.90	.50
12	Bert Blyleven	.06	.05	.02
13	Jeff Manto(FC)	.08	.06	.03
14	Bob McClure	.06	.05	.02
15	Lance Parrish	.06	.05	.02
16	Lee Stevens(FC)	.06	.05	.02
17	Claudell Washington	.06	.05	.02
18	Mark Davis	.06	.05	.02
19	Eric King	.06	.05	.02
20	Ron Kittle	.06	.05	.02
21	Matt Merullo(FC)	.15	.11	.06
22	Steve Rosenberg(FC)	.08	.06	.03
23	Robin Ventura(FC)	3.00	2.25	1.25
24	Keith Atherton	.06	.05	.02
25	Joey Belle(FC)	5.00	3.75	2.00
26	Jerry Browne	.06	.05	.02
27	Felix Fermin	.06	.05	.02
28	Brad Komminsk	.06	.05	.02
29	Pete O'Brien	.06	.05	.02
30	Mike Brumley	.06	.05	.02
31	Tracy Jones	.06	.05	.02
32	Mike Schwabe(FC)	.06	.05	.02
33	Gary Ward	.06	.05	.02
34	Frank Williams	.06	.05	.02
35	Kevin Appier(FC)	.90	.70	.35
36	Bob Boone	.06	.05	.02
37	Luis de los Santos	.06	.05	.02
38	Jim Eisenreich(FC)	.06	.05	.02
39	Jaime Navarro(FC)	.50	.40	.20
40	Bill Spiers(FC)	.06	.05	.02
41	Greg Vaughn(FC)	.90	.70	.35
42	Randy Veres(FC)	.06	.05	.02
43	Wally Backman	.06	.05	.02
44	Shane Rawley	.06	.05	.02
45	Steve Balboni	.06	.05	.02
46	Jesse Barfield	.06	.05	.02
47	Alvaro Espinoza(FC)	.06	.05	.02
48	Bob Geren(FC)	.20	.15	.08
49	Mel Hall	.06	.05	.02
50	Andy Hawkins	.06	.05	.02
51	Hensley Meulens(FC)	.06	.05	.02
52	Steve Sax	.10	.08	.04
53	Deion Sanders(FC)	2.50	2.00	1.00
54	Rickey Henderson	.20	.15	.08
55	Mike Moore	.10	.08	.04
56	Tony Phillips	.06	.05	.02
57	Greg Briley	.10	.08	.04
58	Gene Harris	.10	.08	.04

		MT	NR MT	EX
59	Randy Johnson	.75	.50	.25
60	Jeffrey Leonard	.06	.05	.02
61	Dennis Powell	.06	.05	.02
62	Omar Vizquel(FC)	.20	.15	.08
63	Kevin Brown	.08	.06	.03
64	Julio Franco	.08	.05	.02
65	Jamie Moyer	.06	.05	.02
66	Rafael Palmeiro	.15	.11	.06
67	Nolan Ryan	1.75	1.25	.70
68	Francisco Cabrera(FC)	.20	.15	.08
69	Junior Felix(FC)	.20	.12	.06
70	Al Leiter	.06	.05	.02
71	Alex Sanchez(FC)	.06	.09	.05
72	Geronimo Berroa(FC)	.06	.06	.03
73	Derek Lilliquist(FC)	.06	.11	.06
74	Lonnie Smith	.10	.08	.04
75	Jeff Treadway	.06	.05	.02
76	Paul Kilgus	.06	.05	.02
77	Lloyd McClendon	.15	.11	.06
78	Scott Sanderson	.06	.05	.02
79	Dwight Smith(FC)	.10	.08	.04
80	Jerome Walton(FC)	.06	.11	.06
81	Mitch Williams	.15	.11	.06
82	Steve Wilson	.08	.05	.02
83	Todd Benzinger	.06	.05	.02
84	Ken Griffey	.10	.06	.03
85	Rick Mahler	.06	.05	.02
86	Rolando Roomes	.15	.11	.06
87	Scott Scudder(FC)	.10	.08	.04
88	Jim Clancy	.06	.05	.02
89	Rick Rhoden	.06	.05	.02
90	Dan Schatzeder	.06	.05	.02
91	Mike Morgan	.06	.05	.02
92	Eddie Murray	.20	.15	.08
93	Willie Randolph	.06	.05	.02
94	Ray Searage	.06	.05	.02
95	Mike Aldrete	.06	.05	.02
96	Kevin Gross	.06	.05	.02
97	Mark Langston	.15	.11	.06
98	Spike Owen	.06	.05	.02
99	Zane Smith	.06	.05	.02
100	Don Aase	.06	.05	.02
101	Barry Lyons	.06	.05	.02
102	Juan Samuel	.06	.05	.02
103	Wally Whitehurst(FC)	.10	.08	.04
104	Dennis Cook	.15	.11	.06
105	Lenny Dykstra	.20	.12	.06
106	Charlie Hayes(FC)	.50	.40	.20
107	Tommy Herr	.06	.05	.02
108	Ken Howell	.06	.05	.02
109	John Kruk	.15	.10	.05
110	Roger McDowell	.06	.05	.02
111	Terry Mulholland(FC)	.10	.08	.04
112	Jeff Parrett	.06	.05	.02
113	Neal Heaton	.06	.05	.02
114	Jeff King	.10	.08	.04
115	Randy Kramer	.06	.05	.02
116	Bill Landrum	.06	.05	.02
117	Cris Carpenter(FC)	.06	.11	.06
118	Frank DiPino	.06	.05	.02
119	Ken Hill	.15	.11	.06
120	Dan Quisenberry	.06	.05	.02
121	Milt Thompson	.06	.05	.02
122	Todd Zeile(FC)	.80	.60	.30
123	Jack Clark	.10	.08	.04
124	Bruce Hurst	.06	.05	.02
125	Mark Parent	.06	.05	.02
126	Bip Roberts	.06	.05	.02
127	Jeff Brantley(FC)	.15	.11	.06
128	Terry Kennedy	.06	.05	.02
129	Mike LaCoss	.06	.05	.02
130	Greg Litton(FC)	.08	.06	.03
131	Mike Schmidt	.60	.45	.25
132	Checklist	.06	.05	.02

1989 Fleer Baseball All Stars

This specially-boxed set was produced by Fleer for the Ben Franklin store chain. The full-color player photos are surrounded by a border of pink and yellow vertical bands. "Fleer Baseball All-Stars" appears along the top in red, white and blue. The set was sold in a box with a checklist on the back.

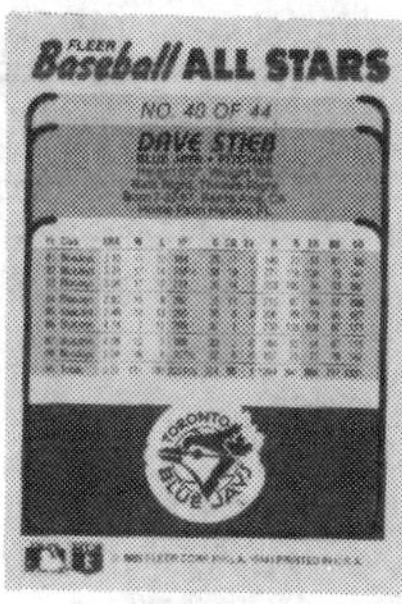

Complete Set (44):		4.00	3.00	1.50
Common Player:		.10	.06	.03
1	Doyle Alexander	.10	.08	.04
2	George Bell	.12	.09	.05
3	Wade Boggs	.50	.40	.20
4	Bobby Bonilla	.15	.11	.06
5	Jose Canseco	.50	.40	.20
6	Will Clark	.40	.30	.15
7	Roger Clemens	.30	.25	.12
8	Vince Coleman	.15	.11	.06
9	David Cone	.15	.11	.06
10	Mark Davis	.10	.08	.04
11	Andre Dawson	.15	.11	.06
12	Dennis Eckersley	.15	.11	.06
13	Andres Galarraga	.15	.11	.06
14	Kirk Gibson	.12	.09	.05
15	Dwight Gooden	.30	.25	.12
16	Mike Greenwell	.25	.20	.10
17	Mark Gubicza	.10	.08	.04
18	Ozzie Guillen	.10	.08	.04
19	Tony Gwynn	.20	.15	.08
20	Rickey Henderson	.25	.20	.10
21	Orel Hershiser	.20	.15	.08
22	Danny Jackson	.10	.08	.04
23	Doug Jones	.10	.08	.04
24	Ricky Jordan	.10	.08	.04
25	Bob Knepper	.10	.08	.04
26	Barry Larkin	.20	.15	.08
27	Vance Law	.10	.08	.04
28	Don Mattingly	.50	.40	.20
29	Mark McGwire	.40	.30	.15
30	Paul Molitor	.40	.30	.15
31	Gerald Perry	.10	.08	.04
32	Kirby Puckett	.40	.30	.15
33	Johnny Ray	.10	.08	.04
34	Harold Reynolds	.10	.08	.04
35	Cal Ripken, Jr.	.50	.40	.20
36	Don Robinson	.10	.08	.04
37	Ruben Sierra	.30	.25	.12
38	Dave Smith	.10	.08	.04
39	Darryl Strawberry	.30	.25	.12
40	Dave Steib	.10	.08	.04
41	Alan Trammell	.15	.11	.06
42	Andy Van Slyke	.15	.11	.06
43	Frank Viola	.12	.09	.05
44	Dave Winfield	.25	.20	.10

1989 Fleer Baseball MVP

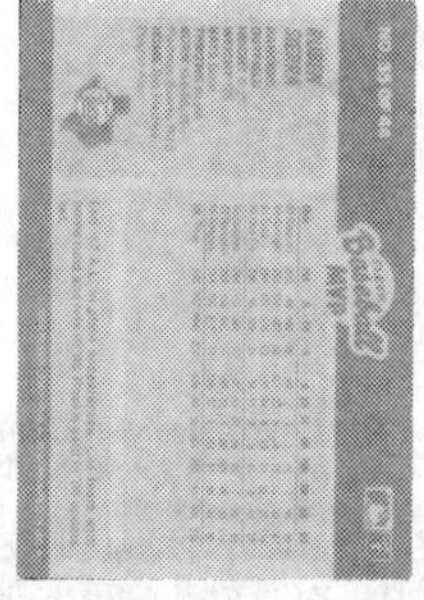

Filled with superstars, this 44-card boxed set

was produced by Fleer in 1989 for the Toys "R" Us chain. The fronts of the cards are designed in a yellow and green color scheme and include a "Fleer Baseball MVP" logo above the color player photo. The backs are printed in shades of green and yellow and include biographical notes and stats. The set was issued in a special box with a checklist on the back.

		MT	NR MT	EX
Complete Set:		3.75	2.75	1.50
Common Player:		.05	.04	.02
1	Steve Bedrosian	.05	.04	.02
2	George Bell	.10	.08	.04
3	Wade Boggs	.70	.50	.30
4	George Brett	.70	.50	.30
5	Hubie Brooks	.05	.04	.02
6	Jose Canseco	.90	.70	.35
7	Will Clark	.70	.50	.30
8	Roger Clemens	.30	.25	.12
9	Eric Davis	.20	.15	.08
10	Glenn Davis	.07	.05	.03
11	Andre Dawson	.12	.09	.05
12	Andres Galarraga	.12	.09	.05
13	Kirk Gibson	.10	.08	.04
14	Dwight Gooden	.20	.15	.08
15	Mark Grace	.20	.15	.08
16	Mike Greenwell	.15	.11	.06
17	Tony Gwynn	.20	.15	.08
18	Bryan Harvey	.10	.08	.04
19	Orel Hershiser	.15	.11	.06
20	Ted Higuera	.07	.05	.03
21	Danny Jackson	.05	.04	.02
22	Mike Jackson	.05	.04	.02
23	Doug Jones	.05	.04	.02
24	Greg Maddux	.15	.11	.06
25	Mike Marshall	.05	.04	.02
26	Don Mattingly	.70	.50	.30
27	Fred McGriff	.30	.25	.12
28	Mark McGwire	.50	.60	.30
29	Kevin McReynolds	.10	.08	.04
30	Jack Morris	.05	.04	.02
31	Gerald Perry	.05	.04	.02
32	Kirby Puckett	.35	.25	.12
33	Chris Sabo	.10	.08	.04
34	Mike Scott	.07	.05	.03
35	Ruben Sierra	.25	.20	.10
36	Darryl Strawberry	.35	.25	.12
37	Danny Tartabull	.09	.07	.04
38	Bobby Thigpen	.07	.05	.03
39	Alan Trammell	.15	.11	.06
40	Andy Van Slyke	.12	.09	.05
41	Frank Viola	.10	.08	.04
42	Walt Weiss	.15	.11	.06
43	Dave Winfield	.25	.11	.06
44	Todd Worrell	.07	.05	.03

1989 Fleer Baseball's Exciting Stars

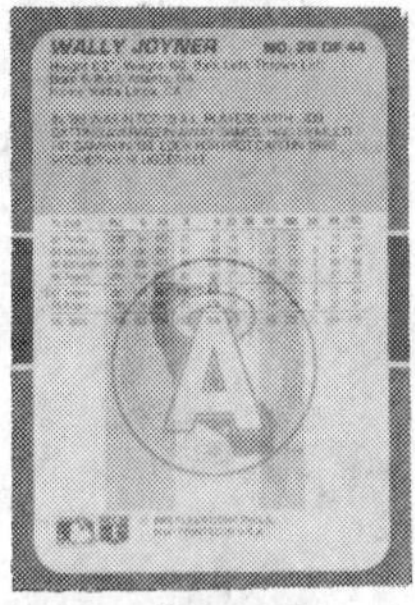

Sold exclusively in Cumberland Farm stores, this 44-card boxed set pictures the game's top stars. The card fronts feature a color player photo surrounded by a blue border with "Baseball's Exciting Stars" along the top. The cards were were numbered alphabetically and packed in a special box with a complete checklist on the back.

		MT	NR MT	EX
Complete Set:		3.50	2.75	1.50
Common Player:		.05	.04	.02
1	Harold Baines	.07	.05	.03
2	Wade Boggs	.70	.50	.30
3	Jose Canseco	.90	.70	.35
4	Joe Carter	.12	.09	.05
5	Will Clark	.70	.50	.30
6	Roger Clemens	.30	.25	.12
7	Vince Coleman	.15	.11	.06
8	David Cone	.15	.11	.06
9	Eric Davis	.20	.15	.08
10	Glenn Davis	.05	.04	.02
11	Andre Dawson	.12	.09	.05
12	Dwight Evans	.09	.07	.04
13	Andres Galarraga	.12	.09	.05
14	Kirk Gibson	.12	.09	.05
15	Dwight Gooden	.30	.25	.12
16	Jim Gott	.05	.04	.02
17	Mark Grace	.20	.15	.07
18	Mike Greenwell	.20	.15	.07
19	Mark Gibicza	.07	.05	.03
20	Tony Gwynn	.25	.20	.10
21	Rickey Henderson	.40	.30	.15
22	Tom Henke	.05	.04	.02
23	Mike Henneman	.05	.04	.02
24	Orel Hershiser	.20	.15	.07
25	Danny Jackson	.05	.04	.02
26	Gregg Jefferies	.20	.15	.07
27	Ricky Jordan	.05	.04	.02
28	Wally Joyner	.15	.11	.06
29	Mark Langston	.15	.11	.06
30	Tim Leary	.05	.04	.02
31	Don Mattingly	.70	.50	.30
32	Mark McGwire	.60	.45	.25
33	Dale Murphy	.15	.11	.06
34	Kirby Puckett	.35	.25	.14
35	Chris Sabo	.10	.08	.04
36	Kevin Seitzer	.05	.04	.02
37	Ruben Sierra	.30	.25	.12
38	Ozzie Smith	.15	.11	.06
39	Dave Stewart	.07	.05	.03
40	Darryl Strawberry	.35	.25	.14
41	Alan Trammell	.15	.11	.06
42	Frank Viola	.15	.11	.06
43	Dave Winfield	.30	.25	.12
44	Robin Yount	.30	.25	.12

1989 Fleer Heroes of Baseball

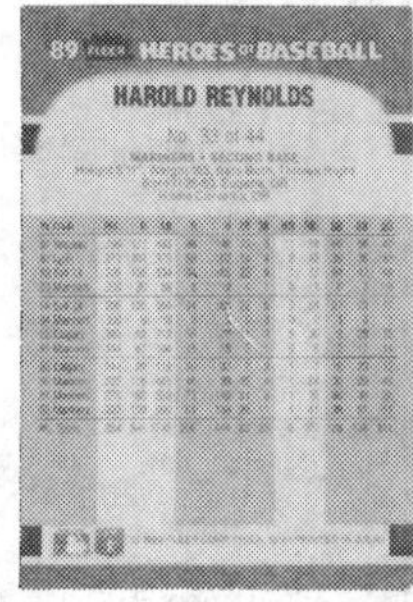

This 44-card boxed set was produced by Fleer for the Woolworth store chain. The fronts of the cards are designed in a red and blue color scheme and feature full-color photos that fade into a soft focus on all edges. "Fleer Heroes of Baseball" appears just above the player's name, team and position at the bottom of the card. The set is numbered alphabetically and was packaged in a special box with a checklist on the back.

		MT	NR MT	EX
Complete Set:		3.50	2.75	1.50
Common Player:		.05	.04	.02
1	George Bell	.12	.09	.05

		MT	NR MT	EX
2	Wade Boggs	.70	.50	.30
3	Barry Bonds	.40	.30	.15
4	Tom Brunansky	.08	.06	.03
5	Jose Canseco	.90	.70	.35
6	Joe Carter	.12	.09	.05
7	Will Clark	.50	.40	.20
8	Roger Clemens	.30	.25	.12
9	David Cone	.15	.11	.06
10	Eric Davis	.25	.20	.10
11	Glenn Davis	.05	.04	.02
12	Andre Dawson	.12	.09	.05
13	Dennis Eckersley	.12	.09	.05
14	John Franco	.05	.04	.02
15	Gary Gaetti	.12	.09	.05
16	Andres Galarraga	.15	.11	.06
17	Kirk Gibson	.12	.09	.05
18	Dwight Gooden	.30	.25	.12
19	Mike Greenwell	.20	.15	.07
20	Tony Gwynn	.25	.20	.10
21	Bryan Harvey	.07	.05	.03
22	Orel Hershiser	.20	.15	.08
23	Ted Higuera	.05	.04	.02
24	Danny Jackson	.05	.04	.02
25	Ricky Jordan	.05	.04	.02
26	Don Mattingly	.70	.50	.30
27	Fred McGriff	.30	.25	.12
28	Mark McGwire	.60	.45	.25
29	Kevin McReynolds	.15	.11	.06
30	Gerald Perry	.05	.04	.02
31	Kirby Puckett	.35	.25	.12
32	Johnny Ray	.05	.04	.02
33	Harold Reynolds	.05	.04	.02
34	Cal Ripken, Jr.	.70	.50	.30
35	Ryne Sandberg	.70	.50	.30
36	Kevin Seitzer	.05	.04	.02
37	Ruben Sierra	.20	.15	.07
38	Darryl Strawberry	.30	.25	.12
39	Bobby Thigpen	.05	.04	.02
40	Alan Trammell	.12	.09	.05
41	Andy Van Slyke	.10	.08	.04
42	Frank Viola	.10	.08	.04
43	Dave Winfield	.30	.25	.12
44	Robin Yount	.30	.25	.12

1989 Fleer League Leaders

Another of the various small, boxed sets issued by Fleer, the 44-card "League Leaders" set was produced for Walgreen stores. The standard-size cards feature color photos on the front surrounded by a red border with "Fleer League Leaders" across the top. The player's name, team and position appear in a yellow band at the bottom. The backs include player stats and data and the team logo. The cards are numbered alphabetically and packaged in a special box that includes the full checklist on the back.

		MT	NR MT	EX
Complete Set:		4.00	3.00	1.50
Common Player:		.05	.04	.02
1	Allan Anderson	.05	.04	.02
2	Wade Boggs	.70	.50	.30
3	Jose Canseco	.90	.70	.35
4	Will Clark	.60	.45	.25
5	Roger Clemens	.30	.25	.12
6	Vince Coleman	.15	.11	.06
7	David Cone	.15	.11	.06
8	Kal Daniels	.05	.04	.02
9	Chili Davis	.05	.04	.02
10	Eric Davis	.20	.15	.08
11	Glenn Davis	.05	.04	.02
12	Andre Dawson	.12	.09	.05
13	John Franco	.05	.04	.02
14	Andres Galarraga	.12	.09	.05
15	Kirk Gibson	.12	.09	.05
16	Dwight Gooden	.30	.25	.12
17	Mark Grace	.30	.25	.12
18	Mike Greenwell	.20	.15	.07
19	Tony Gwynn	.25	.20	.10
20	Orel Hershiser	.15	.11	.06
21	Pete Incaviglia	.10	.08	.04
22	Danny Jackson	.05	.04	.02
23	Gregg Jefferies	.30	.25	.12
24	Joe Magrane	.05	.04	.02
25	Don Mattingly	.70	.50	.30
26	Fred McGriff	.30	.25	.12
27	Mark McGwire	.60	.45	.25
28	Dale Murphy	.15	.11	.06
29	Dan Plesac	.05	.04	.02
30	Kirby Puckett	.40	.30	.15
31	Harold Reynolds	.12	.09	.05
32	Cal Ripken, Jr.	.70	.50	.30
33	Jeff Robinson	.05	.04	.02
34	Mike Scott	.12	.09	.05
35	Ozzie Smith	.15	.09	.05
36	Dave Stewart	.07	.05	.03
37	Darryl Strawberry	.30	.25	.12
38	Greg Swindell	.09	.07	.04
39	Bobby Thigpen	.05	.04	.02
40	Alan Trammell	.12	.09	.05
41	Andy Van Slyke	.12	.09	.05
42	Frank Viola	.12	.09	.05
43	Dave Winfield	.30	.25	.12
44	Robin Yount	.30	.25	.12

1989 Fleer Superstars

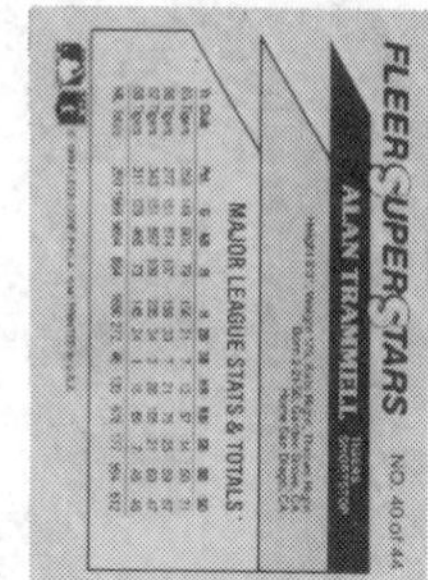

This 44-card boxed set was produced by Fleer for the McCrory store chain. The cards are the standard 2-1/2" by 3-1/2" and the full-color player photos are outlined in red with a tan-and-white striped border. The player's name, position and team logo appear at the bottom of the card. The backs carry yellow and white stripes and include the Fleer "SuperStars" logo, player stats and biographical information. The cards are numbered alphabetically and packaged in a special box that includes a checklist on the back.

		MT	NR MT	EX
Complete Set:		4.00	3.00	1.50
Common Player:		.05	.04	.02
1	Roberto Alomar	.30	.25	.12
2	Harold Baines	.12	.09	.05
3	Tim Belcher	.07	.05	.03
4	Wade Boggs	.70	.50	.30
5	George Brett	.70	.50	.30
6	Jose Canseco	.90	.70	.35
7	Gary Carter	.05	.04	.02

		MT	NR MT	EX
8	Will Clark	.60	.45	.25
9	Roger Clemens	.30	.25	.12
10	Kal Daniels	.05	.04	.02
11	Eric Davis	.20	.15	.08
12	Andre Dawson	.12	.09	.05
13	Tony Fernandez	.09	.07	.04
14	Scott Fletcher	.05	.04	.02
15	Andres Galarraga	.15	.11	.06
16	Kirk Gibson	.15	.11	.06
17	Dwight Gooden	.30	.25	.12
18	Jim Gott	.05	.04	.02
19	Mark Grace	.20	.15	.07
20	Mike Greenwell	.20	.15	.07
21	Tony Gwynn	.25	.20	.10
22	Rickey Henderson	.30	.25	.12
23	Orel Hershiser	.15	.11	.06
24	Ted Higuera	.05	.04	.02
25	Gregg Jefferies	.20	.15	.07
26	Wally Joyner	.15	.11	.06
27	Mark Langston	.15	.11	.06
28	Greg Maddux	.15	.11	.06
29	Don Mattingly	.70	.50	.30
30	Fred McGriff	.30	.25	.12
31	Mark McGwire	.60	.45	.25
32	Dan Plesac	.05	.04	.02
33	Kirby Puckett	.60	.45	.25
34	Jeff Reardon	.05	.04	.02
35	Chris Sabo	.07	.05	.03
36	Mike Schmidt	.50	.40	.20
37	Mike Scott	.07	.05	.03
38	Cory Snyder	.05	.04	.02
39	Darryl Strawberry	.30	.25	.12
40	Alan Trammell	.12	.09	.05
41	Frank Viola	.10	.08	.04
42	Walt Weiss	.10	.08	.04
43	Dave Winfield	.30	.25	.12
44	Todd Worrell	.05	.04	.02

1990 Fleer

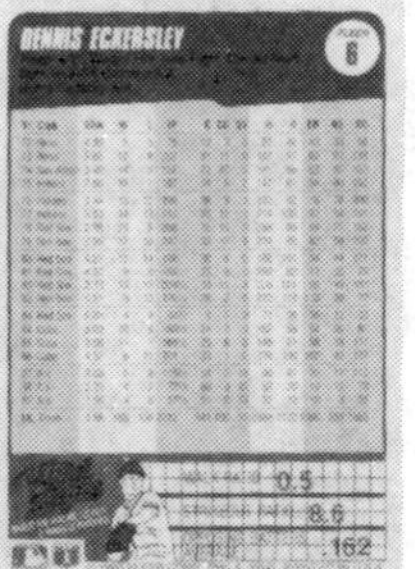

Fleer's 1990 set, its 10th consecutive baseball card offering, again consisted of 660 cards numbered by team. The front of the cards feature mostly action photos surrounded by one of several different color bands and a white border. The "Fleer '90" logo appears in the upper left corner, while the team logo is the upper right. The player's name and position are printed in a flowing banner below the photo. The set includes various special cards, including a series of "Major League Prospects," Players of the Decade, team checklist cards and a series of multi-player cards. The backs include complete career stats, player data, and a special "Vital Signs" section showing on-base percentage, slugging percentage, etc. for batters; and strikeout and walk ratios, opposing batting averages, etc. for pitchers.

	MT	NR MT	EX
Complete Set (660):	18.00	13.50	7.25
Common Player:	.05	.04	.02

		MT	NR MT	EX
1	Lance Blankenship	.07	.05	.03
2	Todd Burns	.06	.05	.02
3	Jose Canseco	.50	.40	.20
4	Jim Corsi	.09	.07	.04
5	Storm Davis	.06	.05	.02
6	Dennis Eckersley	.12	.09	.05
7	Mike Gallego	.06	.05	.02
8	Ron Hassey	.05	.04	.02
9	Dave Henderson	.10	.08	.06
10	Rickey Henderson	.30	.25	.12
11	Rick Honeycutt	.05	.04	.02
12	Stan Javier	.05	.04	.02
13	Felix Jose	.20	.15	.08
14	Carney Lansford	.07	.05	.03
15	Mark McGwire	.25	.20	.10
16	Mike Moore	.10	.08	.04
17	Gene Nelson	.05	.04	.02
18	Dave Parker	.12	.09	.05
19	Tony Phillips	.05	.04	.02
20	Terry Steinbach	.10	.08	.06
21	Dave Stewart	.10	.08	.06
22	Walt Weiss	.10	.08	.06
23	Bob Welch	.06	.05	.03
24	Curt Young	.05	.04	.02
25	Paul Assenmacher	.05	.04	.02
26	Damon Berryhill	.10	.08	.04
27	Mike Bielecki	.10	.08	.04
28	Kevin Blankenship	.07	.05	.03
29	Andre Dawson	.12	.09	.05
30	Shawon Dunston	.09	.07	.04
31	Joe Girardi	.12	.09	.05
32	Mark Grace	.25	.20	.10
33	Mike Harkey	.12	.09	.05
34	Paul Kilgus	.05	.04	.02
35	Les Lancaster	.06	.05	.02
36	Vance Law	.05	.04	.02
37	Greg Maddux	.10	.08	.04
38	Lloyd McClendon	.10	.08	.04
39	Jeff Pico	.05	.04	.02
40	Ryne Sandberg	.35	.25	.14
41	Scott Sanderson	.05	.04	.02
42	Dwight Smith	.25	.20	.10
43	Rick Sutcliffe	.08	.06	.03
44	*Jerome Walton*	.05	.04	.02
45	Mitch Webster	.05	.04	.02
46	Curt Wilkerson	.05	.04	.02
47	*Dean Wilkins*(FC)	.05	.04	.02
48	Mitch Williams	.08	.06	.03
49	Steve Wilson	.15	.11	.06
50	Steve Bedrosian	.06	.05	.02
51	*Mike Benjamin*(FC)	.15	.11	.06
52	*Jeff Brantley*	.10	.08	.04
53	Brett Butler	.07	.05	.03
54	Will Clark	.40	.30	.15
55	Kelly Downs	.05	.04	.02
56	Scott Garrelts	.09	.07	.04
57	Atlee Hammaker	.05	.04	.02
58	Terry Kennedy	.05	.04	.02
59	Mike LaCoss	.05	.04	.02
60	Craig Lefferts	.06	.05	.02
61	*Greg Litton*	.10	.08	.04
62	Candy Maldonado	.06	.05	.02
63	Kirt Manwaring	.09	.07	.04
64	*Randy McCament*(FC)	.05	.04	.02
65	Kevin Mitchell	.30	.25	.12
66	Donell Nixon	.05	.04	.02
67	Ken Oberkfell	.05	.04	.02
68	Rick Reuschel	.09	.07	.04
69	Ernest Riles	.05	.04	.02
70	Don Robinson	.05	.04	.02
71	Pat Sheridan	.05	.04	.02
72	Chris Speier	.05	.04	.02
73	Robby Thompson	.07	.05	.03
74	Jose Uribe	.06	.05	.02
75	Matt Williams	.20	.15	.08
76	George Bell	.10	.08	.04
77	Pat Borders	.07	.05	.03
78	John Cerutti	.05	.04	.02
79	*Junior Felix*	.20	.15	.08
80	Tony Fernandez	.09	.07	.04
81	Mike Flanagan	.05	.04	.02
82	*Mauro Gozzo*(FC)	.05	.04	.02
83	Kelly Gruber	.07	.05	.03
84	Tom Henke	.05	.04	.02
85	Jimmy Key	.07	.05	.03
86	Manny Lee	.05	.04	.02
87	Nelson Liriano	.05	.04	.02
88	Lee Mazzilli	.05	.04	.02
89	Fred McGriff	.25	.20	.10
90	Lloyd Moseby	.06	.05	.02
91	Rance Mulliniks	.05	.04	.02
92	Alex Sanchez	.15	.11	.06
93	Dave Steib	.09	.07	.05
94	Todd Stottlemyre	.09	.07	.05
95	Duane Ward	.05	.04	.02

		MT	NR MT	EX
96	David Wells	.05	.04	.02
97	Ernie Whitt	.06	.05	.02
98	Frank Wills	.05	.04	.02
99	Mookie Wilson	.09	.07	.04
100	*Kevin Appier*(FC)	.25	.20	.10
101	Luis Aquino	.05	.04	.02
102	Bob Boone	.07	.05	.03
103	George Brett	.15	.11	.06
104	Jose DeJesus	.08	.06	.03
105	Luis de los Santos	.08	.06	.03
106	Jim Eisenreich	.05	.04	.02
107	Steve Farr	.05	.04	.02
108	Tom Gordon	.25	.20	.10
109	Mark Gubicza	.09	.07	.04
110	Bo Jackson	.35	.25	.14
111	Terry Leach	.05	.04	.02
112	Charlie Leibrandt	.05	.04	.02
113	*Rick Luecken*(FC)	.10	.08	.04
114	Mike Macfarlane	.05	.04	.02
115	Jeff Montgomery	.06	.05	.03
116	Bret Saberhagen	.10	.08	.04
117	Kevin Seitzer	.10	.08	.04
118	Kurt Stillwell	.06	.05	.02
119	Pat Tabler	.05	.04	.02
121	Gary Thurman	.05	.04	.02
122	Frank White	.07	.05	.03
123	Willie Wilson	.06	.05	.03
124	*Matt Winters*(FC)	.05	.04	.02
125	Jim Abbott	.35	.25	.14
126	Tony Armas	.05	.04	.02
127	Dante Bichette	.09	.07	.04
128	Bert Blyleven	.09	.07	.04
129	Chili Davis	.06	.05	.02
130	Brian Downing	.06	.05	.02
131	*Mike Fetters*(FC)	.20	.15	.08
132	Chuck Finley	.06	.05	.02
133	Willie Fraser	.05	.04	.02
134	Bryan Harvey	.05	.04	.02
135	Jack Howell	.05	.04	.02
136	Wally Joyner	.10	.08	.04
137	*Jeff Manto*	.10	.08	.04
138	Kirk McCaskill	.06	.05	.02
139	Bob McClure	.05	.04	.02
140	Greg Minton	.05	.04	.02
141	Lance Parrish	.07	.05	.02
142	Dan Petry	.05	.04	.02
143	Johnny Ray	.05	.04	.02
144	Dick Schofield	.06	.05	.02
145	*Lee Stevens*	.20	.15	.08
146	Claudell Washington	.06	.05	.02
147	Devon White	.08	.06	.03
148	Mike Witt	.06	.05	.02
149	Roberto Alomar	.30	.25	.12
150	Sandy Alomar, Jr.	.25	.20	.10
151	Andy Benes(FC)	.30	.25	.12
152	Jack Clark	.06	.05	.02
153	Pat Clements	.05	.04	.02
154	Joey Cora	.15	.11	.06
155	Mark Davis	.09	.07	.04
156	Mark Grant	.05	.04	.02
157	Tony Gwynn	.25	.20	.10
158	Greg Harris	.10	.08	.04
159	Bruce Hurst	.06	.05	.02
160	Darrin Jackson	.05	.04	.02
161	Chris James	.06	.05	.02
162	Carmelo Martinez	.06	.05	.02
163	Mike Pagliarulo	.06	.05	.02
164	Mark Parent	.05	.04	.02
165	Dennis Rasmussen	.05	.04	.02
166	Bip Roberts	.08	.06	.03
167	Benito Santiago	.12	.09	.05
168	Calvin Schiraldi	.05	.04	.02
169	Eric Show	.06	.05	.02
170	Garry Templeton	.06	.05	.02
171	Ed Whitson	.06	.05	.02
172	Brady Anderson	.07	.05	.03
173	Jeff Ballard	.07	.05	.03
174	Phil Bradley	.07	.05	.03
175	Mike Devereaux	.07	.05	.03
176	*Steve Finley*	.20	.15	.08
177	Pete Harnisch(FC)	.10	.08	.04
178	Kevin Hickey	.10	.08	.04
179	Brian Holton	.05	.04	.02
180	*Ben McDonald*(FC)	.40	.30	.15
181	Bob Melvin	.05	.04	.02
182	Bob Milacki	.07	.05	.03
183	Randy Milligan	.06	.05	.02
184	Gregg Olson(FC)	.30	.25	.12
185	Joe Orsulak	.05	.04	.02
186	Bill Ripken	.05	.04	.02
187	Cal Ripken, Jr.	.30	.25	.12

		MT	NR MT	EX
188	Dave Schmidt	.05	.04	.02
189	Larry Sheets	.05	.04	.02
190	Mickey Tettleton	.08	.06	.03
191	Mark Thurmond	.05	.04	.02
192	Jay Tibbs	.05	.04	.02
193	Jim Traber	.05	.04	.02
194	Mark Williamson	.05	.04	.02
195	Craig Worthington	.15	.11	.06
196	Don Aase	.05	.04	.02
197	*Blaine Beatty*(FC)	.10	.08	.04
198	Mark Carreon	.10	.08	.04
199	Gary Carter	.06	.05	.02
200	David Cone	.10	.08	.04
201	Ron Darling	.07	.05	.03
202	Kevin Elster	.05	.04	.02
203	Sid Fernandez	.09	.07	.04
204	Dwight Gooden	.20	.15	.08
205	Keith Hernandez	.06	.05	.02
206	*Jeff Innis*	.10	.08	.04
207	Gregg Jefferies	.20	.15	.08
208	Howard Johnson	.15	.11	.06
209	Barry Lyons	.05	.04	.02
210	Dave Magadan	.06	.05	.02
211	Kevin McReynolds	.07	.05	.03
212	Jeff Musselman	.05	.04	.02
213	Randy Myers	.06	.05	.02
214	Bob Ojeda	.06	.05	.02
215	Juan Samuel	.06	.05	.02
216	Mackey Sasser	.05	.04	.02
217	Darryl Strawberry	.25	.20	.10
218	Tim Teufel	.05	.04	.02
219	Frank Viola	.10	.08	.04
220	Juan Agosto	.05	.04	.02
221	Larry Anderson	.05	.04	.02
222	*Eric Anthony*(FC)	.50	.40	.20
223	Kevin Bass	.08	.06	.03
224	Craig Biggio	.10	.08	.04
225	Ken Caminiti	.06	.05	.02
226	Jim Clancy	.05	.04	.02
227	Danny Darwin	.05	.04	.02
228	Glenn Davis	.09	.07	.04
229	Jim Deshaies	.07	.05	.02
230	Bill Doran	.06	.05	.02
231	Bob Forsch	.05	.04	.02
233	Terry Puhl	.05	.04	.02
234	Rafael Ramirez	.05	.04	.02
235	Rick Rhoden	.05	.04	.02
236	Dan Schatzeder	.05	.04	.02
237	Mike Scott	.08	.06	.03
238	Dave Smith	.06	.05	.02
239	Alex Trevino	.05	.04	.02
240	Glenn Wilson	.05	.04	.02
241	Gerald Young	.05	.04	.02
242	Tom Brunansky	.07	.05	.03
243	Cris Carpenter	.10	.08	.04
244	*Alex Cole*(FC)	.20	.15	.08
245	Vince Coleman	.10	.08	.04
246	John Costello	.05	.04	.02
247	Ken Dayley	.05	.04	.02
248	Jose DeLeon	.06	.05	.02
249	Frank DiPino	.05	.04	.02
250	Pedro Guerrero	.09	.07	.04
251	Ken Hill	.09	.07	.04
252	Joe Magrane	.09	.07	.04
253	Willie McGee	.06	.05	.02
254	John Morris	.05	.04	.02
255	Jose Oquendo	.06	.05	.02
256	Tony Pena	.06	.05	.02
257	Terry Pendleton	.06	.05	.02
258	Ted Power	.05	.04	.02
259	Dan Quisenberry	.05	.04	.02
260	Ozzie Smith	.09	.07	.04
261	Scott Terry	.06	.05	.02
262	Milt Thompson	.05	.04	.02
263	Denny Walling	.05	.04	.02
264	Todd Worrell	.06	.05	.02
265	*Todd Zeile*	.50	.40	.20
266	Marty Barrett	.05	.04	.02
267	Mike Boddicker	.05	.04	.02
268	Wade Boggs	.40	.30	.15
269	Ellis Burks	.35	.25	.12
270	Rick Cerone	.05	.04	.02
271	Roger Clemens	.25	.20	.10
272	John Dopson	.06	.05	.02
273	Nick Esasky	.07	.05	.03
274	Dwight Evans	.09	.07	.05
275	Wes Gardner	.05	.04	.02
276	Rich Gedman	.05	.04	.02
277	Mike Greenwell	.50	.40	.20
278	Danny Heep	.05	.04	.02
279	Eric Hetzel	.10	.08	.04

		MT	NR MT	EX
280	Dennis Lamp	.05	.04	.02
281	Rob Murphy	.05	.04	.02
282	Joe Price	.05	.04	.02
283	Carlos Quintana	.10	.07	.04
284	Jody Reed	.06	.05	.02
285	Luis Rivera	.05	.04	.02
286	Kevin Romine	.05	.04	.02
287	Lee Smith	.05	.04	.02
288	Mike Smithson	.05	.04	.02
289	Bob Stanley	.05	.04	.02
290	Harold Baines	.09	.07	.04
291	Kevin Brown	.09	.07	.04
292	Steve Buechele	.05	.04	.02
293	*Scott Coolbaugh*(FC)	.05	.04	.02
294	*Jack Daugherty*(FC)	.05	.04	.02
295	Cecil Espy	.06	.05	.02
296	Julio Franco	.07	.05	.03
297	*Juan Gonzalez*(FC)	2.00	1.50	.80
298	Cecilio Guante	.05	.04	.02
299	Drew Hall	.05	.04	.02
300	Charlie Hough	.06	.05	.02
301	Pete Incaviglia	.08	.06	.03
302	Mike Jeffcoat	.05	.04	.02
303	Chad Kreuter	.08	.06	.03
304	Jeff Kunkel	.05	.04	.02
305	Rick Leach	.05	.04	.02
306	Fred Manrique	.05	.04	.02
307	Jamie Moyer	.06	.05	.02
308	Rafael Palmeiro	.07	.05	.02
309	Geno Petralli	.05	.04	.02
310	Kevin Reimer	.10	.08	.06
311	*Kenny Rogers*(FC)	.20	.15	.08
312	Jeff Russell	.06	.05	.02
313	Nolan Ryan	.50	.40	.20
314	Ruben Sierra	.15	.11	.06
315	Bobby Witt	.05	.04	.02
316	Chris Bosio	.07	.05	.02
317	Glenn Braggs	.07	.05	.02
318	Greg Brock	.05	.04	.02
319	Chuck Crim	.05	.04	.02
320	Rob Deer	.06	.05	.02
321	Mike Felder	.05	.04	.02
322	Tom Filer	.05	.04	.02
323	*Tony Fossas*(FC)	.05	.04	.02
324	Jim Gantner	.05	.04	.02
325	Darryl Hamilton	.08	.06	.03
326	Ted Higuera	.08	.06	.03
327	Mark Knudson(FC)	.10	.08	.04
328	Bill Krueger	.05	.04	.02
329	*Tim McIntosh*(FC)	.05	.04	.02
330	Paul Molitor	.10	.08	.04
331	*Jaime Navarro*	.25	.20	.10
332	Charlie O'Brien	.05	.04	.02
333	*Jeff Peterek*(FC)	.05	.04	.02
334	Dan Plesac	.07	.05	.03
335	Jerry Reuss	.06	.05	.02
336	Gary Sheffield	.30	.25	.12
337	*Bill Spiers*	.10	.08	.04
338	B.J. Surhoff	.07	.05	.02
339	*Greg Vaughn*	.60	.45	.25
340	Robin Yount	.20	.15	.08
341	Hubie Brooks	.06	.05	.02
342	Tim Burke	.06	.05	.02
343	Mike Fitzgerald	.05	.04	.02
344	Tom Foley	.05	.04	.02
345	Andres Galarraga	.15	.11	.06
346	Damaso Garcia	.05	.04	.02
347	*Marquis Grissom*(FC)	.50	.40	.20
348	Kevin Gross	.06	.05	.02
349	Joe Hesketh	.05	.04	.02
350	*Jeff Huson*(FC)	.25	.20	.10
351	Wallace Johnson	.05	.04	.02
352	Mark Langston	.15	.11	.06
353	Dave Martinez	.06	.05	.02
354	Dennis Martinez	.06	.05	.02
355	Andy McGaffigan	.05	.04	.02
356	Otis Nixon	.05	.04	.02
357	Spike Owen	.05	.04	.02
358	Pascual Perez	.06	.05	.02
359	Tim Raines	.10	.08	.04
360	Nelson Santovenia	.10	.08	.04
361	Bryn Smith	.06	.05	.02
362	Zane Smith	.05	.04	.02
363	*Larry Walker*(FC)	1.00	.70	.40
364	Tim Wallach	.06	.05	.02
365	Rick Aguilera	.05	.04	.02
366	Allan Anderson	.06	.05	.02
367	Wally Backman	.06	.05	.02
368	Doug Baker(FC)	.05	.04	.02
369	Juan Berenguer	.05	.04	.02
370	Randy Bush	.05	.04	.02
371	Carmen Castillo	.05	.04	.02
372	*Mike Dyer*(FC)	.05	.04	.02
373	Gary Gaetti	.07	.05	.03
374	Greg Gagne	.05	.04	.02
375	Dan Gladden	.05	.04	.02
376	German Gonzalez	.05	.04	.02
377	Brian Harper	.06	.05	.02
378	Kent Hrbek	.10	.08	.04
379	Gene Larkin	.05	.04	.02
380	Tim Laudner	.05	.04	.02
381	John Moses	.05	.04	.02
382	Al Newman	.05	.04	.02
383	Kirby Puckett	.40	.30	.15
384	Shane Rawley	.06	.05	.02
385	Jeff Reardon	.06	.05	.02
386	Roy Smith	.05	.04	.02
387	*Gary Wayne*(FC)	.05	.04	.02
388	Dave West	.25	.20	.10
389	Tim Belcher	.12	.09	.05
390	Tim Crews	.05	.04	.02
391	Mike Davis	.05	.04	.02
392	Rick Dempsey	.05	.04	.02
393	Kirk Gibson	.09	.07	.04
394	Jose Gonzalez	.05	.04	.02
395	Alfredo Griffin	.06	.05	.02
396	Jeff Hamilton	.06	.05	.02
397	Lenny Harris	.10	.08	.06
398	Mickey Hatcher	.05	.04	.02
399	Orel Hershiser	.12	.09	.05
400	Jay Howell	.06	.05	.02
401	Mike Marshall	.06	.05	.02
402	Ramon Martinez	.25	.20	.10
403	Mike Morgan	.05	.04	.02
404	Eddie Murray	.10	.08	.04
405	Alejandro Pena	.05	.04	.02
406	Willie Randolph	.08	.06	.03
407	Mike Scioscia	.06	.05	.02
408	Ray Searage	.05	.04	.02
409	Fernando Valenzuela	.07	.05	.03
410	*Jose Vizcaino*(FC)	.25	.20	.10
411	*John Wetteland*(FC)	.25	.20	.10
412	Jack Armstrong	.05	.04	.02
413	Todd Benzinger	.07	.05	.03
414	Tim Birtsas	.05	.04	.02
415	Tom Browning	.07	.05	.03
416	Norm Charlton	.08	.06	.03
417	Eric Davis	.20	.15	.08
418	Rob Dibble	.15	.11	.06
419	John Franco	.07	.05	.03
420	Ken Griffey, Sr.	.07	.05	.03
421	*Chris Hammond*(FC)	.25	.20	.10
422	Danny Jackson	.06	.05	.02
423	Barry Larkin	.15	.11	.06
424	Tim Leary	.06	.05	.02
425	Rick Mahler	.05	.04	.02
426	*Joe Oliver*(FC)	.30	.25	.12
427	Paul O'Neill	.07	.05	.03
428	Luis Quinones	.05	.04	.02
429	Jeff Reed	.05	.04	.02
430	Jose Rijo	.07	.05	.03
431	Ron Robinson	.05	.04	.02
432	Rolando Roomes	.10	.08	.04
433	Chris Sabo	.15	.11	.06
434	*Scott Scudder*	.30	.25	.12
435	Herm Winningham	.05	.04	.02
436	Steve Balboni	.05	.04	.02
437	Jesse Barfield	.08	.06	.03
438	*Mike Blowers*(FC)	.20	.15	.08
439	Tom Brookens	.05	.04	.02
440	Greg Cadaret	.05	.04	.02
441	Alvaro Espinoza	.25	.20	.10
442	*Bob Geren*	.15	.11	.06
443	Lee Guetterman	.05	.04	.02
444	Mel Hall	.06	.05	.02
445	Andy Hawkins	.06	.05	.02
446	Roberto Kelly	.15	.11	.06
447	Don Mattingly	.35	.25	.14
448	Lance McCullers	.05	.04	.02
449	Hensley Meulens	.35	.25	.14
450	Dale Mohorcic	.05	.04	.02
451	Clay Parker	.10	.07	.04
452	Eric Plunk	.05	.04	.02
453	Dave Righetti	.07	.05	.03
454	*Deion Sanders*	.30	.25	.12
455	Steve Sax	.07	.05	.03
456	Don Slaught	.05	.04	.02
457	Walt Terrell	.05	.04	.02
458	Dave Winfield	.15	.11	.06
459	Jay Bell	.05	.04	.02
460	Rafael Belliard	.05	.04	.02
461	Barry Bonds	.10	.08	.04

		MT	NR MT	EX
462	Bobby Bonilla	.10	.08	.04
463	Sid Bream	.05	.04	.02
464	Benny Distefano	.06	.05	.02
465	Doug Drabek	.06	.05	.02
466	Jim Gott	.06	.05	.02
467	Billy Hatcher	.06	.05	.02
468	Neal Heaton	.06	.05	.02
469	Jeff King	.20	.15	.08
470	Bob Kipper	.05	.04	.02
471	Randy Kramer	.05	.04	.02
472	Bill Landrum	.06	.05	.02
473	Mike LaValliere	.06	.05	.02
474	Jose Lind	.06	.05	.02
475	Junior Ortiz	.05	.04	.02
476	Gary Redus	.05	.04	.02
477	*Rick Reed*(FC)	.05	.04	.02
478	R.J. Reynolds	.05	.04	.02
479	Jeff Robinson	.05	.04	.02
480	John Smiley	.07	.05	.03
481	Andy Van Slyke	.09	.07	.04
482	Bob Walk	.06	.05	.04
483	Andy Allanson	.05	.04	.02
484	Scott Bailes	.05	.04	.02
485	*Albert Belle*	1.00	.70	.40
486	Bud Black	.05	.04	.02
487	Jerry Browne	.07	.05	.03
488	Tom Candiotti	.05	.04	.02
489	Joe Carter	.08	.06	.03
490	David Clark	.06	.05	.02
491	John Farrell	.06	.05	.02
492	Felix Fermin	.05	.04	.02
493	Brook Jacoby	.06	.05	.02
494	Dion James	.06	.05	.02
495	Doug Jones	.06	.05	.02
496	Brad Komminsk	.05	.04	.02
497	Rod Nichols	.05	.04	.02
498	Pete O'Brien	.07	.05	.03
499	*Steve Olin*(FC)	.15	.11	.06
500	Jesse Orosco	.05	.04	.02
501	Joel Skinner	.05	.04	.02
502	Cory Snyder	.09	.07	.04
503	Greg Swindell	.10	.08	.04
504	Rich Yett	.05	.04	.02
505	Scott Bankhead	.07	.05	.03
506	Scott Bradley	.05	.04	.02
507	Greg Briley	.15	.11	.06
508	Jay Buhner	.07	.05	.03
509	Darnell Coles	.05	.04	.02
510	Keith Comstock	.05	.04	.02
511	Henry Cotto	.05	.04	.02
512	Alvin Davis	.12	.09	.05
513	Ken Griffey, Jr.	1.00	.70	.40
514	Erik Hanson	.20	.15	.08
515	Gene Harris	.15	.11	.06
516	Brian Holman	.07	.05	.03
517	Mike Jackson	.05	.04	.02
518	Randy Johnson	.15	.11	.06
519	Jeffrey Leonard	.08	.06	.03
520	Edgar Martinez	.10	.08	.04
521	Dennis Powell	.05	.04	.02
522	Jim Presley	.06	.05	.02
523	Jerry Reed	.05	.04	.02
524	Harold Reynolds	.07	.05	.03
525	Mike Schooler	.06	.05	.04
526	Bill Swift	.05	.04	.02
527	David Valle	.05	.04	.02
528	*Omar Vizquel*	.20	.15	.08
529	Ivan Calderon	.06	.05	.02
530	Carlton Fisk	.10	.08	.04
531	Scott Fletcher	.06	.05	.02
532	Dave Gallagher	.09	.07	.04
533	Ozzie Guillen	.07	.05	.03
534	*Greg Hibbard*(FC)	.20	.15	.08
535	Shawn Hillegas	.05	.04	.02
536	Lance Johnson	.07	.05	.03
537	Eric King	.05	.04	.02
538	Ron Kittle	.07	.05	.02
539	Steve Lyons	.05	.04	.02
540	Carlos Martinez	.15	.11	.06
541	*Tom McCarthy*(FC)	.10	.07	.04
542	*Matt Merullo*	.25	.20	.10
543	Donn Pall	.05	.04	.02
544	Dan Pasqua	.06	.05	.02
545	Ken Patterson	.06	.05	.02
546	Melido Perez	.07	.05	.03
547	Steve Rosenberg	.07	.05	.03
548	*Sammy Sosa*(FC)	.50	.40	.20
549	Bobby Thigpen	.07	.05	.03
550	Robin Ventura	.60	.45	.25
551	Greg Walker	.06	.05	.02
552	Don Carman	.05	.04	.02

		MT	NR MT	EX
553	*Pat Combs*(FC)	.10	.08	.04
554	Dennis Cook	.20	.15	.08
555	Darren Daulton	.05	.04	.02
556	Lenny Dykstra	.07	.05	.03
557	Curt Ford	.05	.04	.02
558	Charlie Hayes	.10	.08	.04
559	Von Hayes	.07	.05	.03
560	Tom Herr	.06	.05	.02
561	Ken Howell	.05	.04	.02
562	Steve Jeltz	.05	.04	.02
563	Ron Jones	.15	.11	.06
564	Ricky Jordan	.35	.25	.14
565	John Kruk	.07	.05	.03
566	Steve Lake	.05	.04	.02
567	Roger McDowell	.06	.05	.02
568	Terry Mulholland	.05	.04	.02
569	Dwayne Murphy	.05	.04	.02
570	Jeff Parrett	.06	.05	.02
571	Randy Ready	.05	.04	.02
572	Bruce Ruffin	.05	.04	.02
573	Dickie Thon	.05	.04	.02
574	Jose Alvarez	.05	.04	.02
575	Geronimo Berroa	.06	.05	.03
576	Jeff Blauser	.05	.04	.02
577	Joe Boever	.07	.05	.03
578	Marty Clary	.05	.04	.02
579	Jody Davis	.05	.04	.02
580	Mark Eichhorn	.05	.04	.02
581	Darrell Evans	.06	.05	.02
582	Ron Gant	.06	.05	.02
583	Tom Glavine	.09	.07	.04
584	*Tommy Greene*(FC)	.25	.20	.10
585	Tommy Gregg	.10	.07	.04
586	*David Justice*(FC)	1.50	1.25	.60
587	Mark Lemke(FC)	.10	.08	.04
588	Derek Lilliquist	.10	.08	.04
589	Oddibe McDowell	.07	.05	.03
590	*Kent Mercker*(FC)	.30	.25	.12
591	Dale Murphy	.15	.11	.06
592	Gerald Perry	.06	.05	.02
593	Lonnie Smith	.06	.05	.02
594	Pete Smith	.07	.05	.03
595	John Smoltz	.15	.11	.06
596	*Mike Stanton*(FC)	.30	.25	.12
597	Andres Thomas	.06	.05	.02
598	Jeff Treadway	.06	.05	.02
599	Doyle Alexander	.06	.05	.02
600	Dave Bergman	.05	.04	.02
601	*Brian Dubois*(FC)	.15	.11	.06
602	Paul Gibson	.06	.05	.02
603	Mike Heath	.05	.04	.02
604	Mike Henneman	.07	.05	.03
605	Guillermo Hernandez	.05	.04	.02
606	*Shawn Holman*(FC)	.05	.04	.02
607	Tracy Jones	.09	.07	.04
608	Chet Lemon	.06	.05	.02
609	Fred Lynn	.06	.05	.02
610	Jack Morris	.07	.05	.02
611	Matt Nokes	.10	.08	.04
612	Gary Pettis	.05	.04	.02
613	*Kevin Ritz*(FC)	.15	.11	.06
614	Jeff Robinson	.07	.05	.03
615	Steve Searcy	.10	.08	.04
616	Frank Tanana	.06	.05	.02
617	Alan Trammell	.09	.07	.04
618	Gary Ward	.05	.04	.02
619	Lou Whitaker	.09	.07	.04
620	Frank Williams	.05	.04	.02
621a	Players of the Decade - 1980 (George Brett) (... 10 .390 hitting ...)	2.25	1.75	.90
621b	Players of the Decade - 1980 (George Brett) (... 10 .300 hitting ...)	.50	.40	.20
622	Players Of The Decade - 1981 (Fernando Valenzuela)	.20	.15	.08
623	Players Of The Decade - 1982 (Dale Murphy)	.25	.20	.10
624a	Players of the Decade - 1983 (Cal Ripkin, Jr.) (Ripkin)	3.00	2.25	1.25
624b	Players of the Decade - 1983 (Cal Ripken, Jr.) (Ripken)	.25	.20	.10
625	Players of the Decade - 1984 (Ryne Sandberg)	.25	.20	.10
626	Players of the Decade - 1985 (Don Mattingly)	.50	.40	.20
627	Players of the Decade - 1986 (Roger Clemens)	.25	.20	.10
628	Players of the Decade - 1987 (George Bell)	.20	.15	.08
629	Players of the Decade - 1988 (Jose Canseco)	.60	.45	.25
630a	Players of the Decade - 1989 (Will Clark) (total bases 32)	1.50	1.25	.60

		MT	NR MT	EX
630b	Players of the Decade - 1989 (Will Clark) (total bases 321)	.60	.45	.25
631	Game Savers (Mark Davis/ Mitch Williams)	.10	.08	.04
632	Boston Igniters (Wade Boggs/ Mike Greenwell)	.10	.08	.04
633	Starter & Stopper (Mark Gubicza/ Jeff Russell)	.10	.08	.04
634	League's Best Shortstops (Tony Fernandez/ Cal Ripken, Jr.)	.10	.08	.04
635	Human Dynamos (Kirby Puckett/ Bo Jackson)	.10	.08	.04
636	300 Strikeout Club (Nolan Ryan/ Mike Scott)	.10	.08	.04
637	The Dymanic Duo (Will Clark/ Kevin Mitchell)	.10	.08	.04
638	A.L. All-Stars (Don Mattingly/ Mark McGwire)	.10	.08	.04
639	N.L. East Rivals (Howard Johnson/ Ryne Sandberg)	.10	.08	.04
640	Major League Prospects *(Rudy Seanez, Colin Charland)*(FC)	.15	.11	.06
641	Major League Prospects *(George Canale, Kevin Maas)*(FC)	.30	.25	.12
642	Major League Prospects *(Kelly Mann, Dave Hansen)*(FC)	.30	.25	.12
643	Major League Prospects *(Greg Smith, Stu Tate)*(FC)	.15	.11	.06
644	Major League Prospects *(Tom Drees, Dan Howitt)*(FC)	.15	.11	.06
645	Major League Prospects *(Mike Roesler, Derrick May)*(FC)	.60	.45	.25
646	Major League Prospects *(Scott Hemond, Mark Gardner)*(FC)	.35	.25	.14
647	Major League Prospects *(John Orton, Scott Leuis)*(FC)	.25	.20	.10
648	Major League Prospects *(Rich Monteleone, Dana Williams)*(FC)	.15	.11	.06
649	Major League Prospects *(Mike Huff, Steve Frey)*(FC)	.25	.20	.10
650	Major League Prospects *(Chuck McElroy, Moises Alou)*(FC)	.60	.45	.25
651	Major League Prospects *(Bobby Rose, Mike Hartley)*(FC)	.15	.11	.06
652	Major League Prospects *(Matt Kinzer, Wayne Edwards)*(FC)	.20	.15	.08
653	Major League Prospects *(Delino DeShields, Jason Grimsley)*(FC)	.80	.60	.30
654	Athletics, Cubs, Giants & Blue Jays (Checklist)	.05	.04	.02
655	Royals, Angels, Padres & Orioles (Checklist)	.05	.04	.02
656	Mets, Astros, Cardinals & Red Sox (Checklist)	.05	.04	.02
657	Rangers, Brewers, Expos & Twins (Checklist)	.05	.04	.02
658	Dodgers, Reds, Yankees & Pirates (Checklist)	.05	.04	.02
659	Indians, Mariners, White Sox & Phillies (Checklist)	.05	.04	.02
660	Braves, Tigers & Special Cards (Checklist)	.05	.04	.02

1990 Fleer All-Stars

The top players at each position, as selected by Fleer, are featured in this 12-card set. The cards were inserted in cello packs and some wax packs. The cards measure 2-1/2" by 3-1/2" and feature a unique two-photo format on the card fronts.

		MT	NR MT	EX
Complete Set (12):		5.00	4.00	2.00
Common Player:		.20	.15	.08
1	Harold Baines	.25	.20	.10
2	Will Clark	.80	.60	.30
3	Mark Davis	.20	.15	.08
4	Howard Johnson	.40	.30	.15
5	Joe Magrane	.25	.20	.10
6	Kevin Mitchell	.25	.15	.10
7	Kirby Puckett	1.00	.70	.40
8	Cal Ripken	1.50	1.00	.50
9	Ryne Sandberg	1.50	1.00	.50
10	Mike Scott	.20	.15	.08
11	Ruben Sierra	.50	.30	.15
12	Mickey Tettleton	.20	.15	.08

1990 Fleer League Standouts

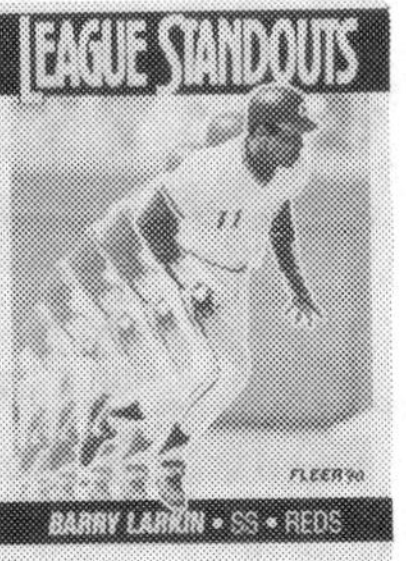

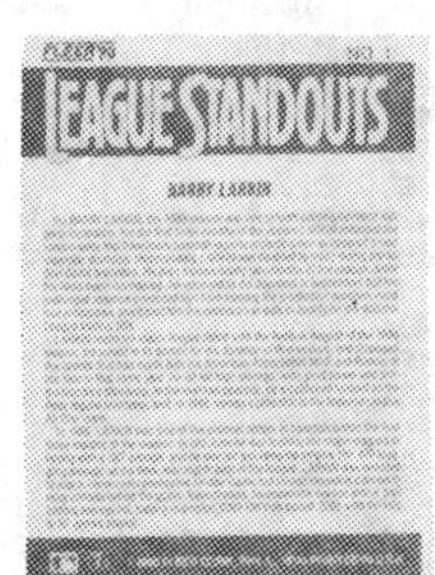

Fleer's "League Standouts" set features six of baseball's top players. The cards were distributed randomly in Fleer three-packs. The card fronts feature full color photos with a six dimensional effect. An attractive black and gold frame borders the photo. The card backs are yellow and describe the player's individual accomplishments. The cards measure 2-1/2" by 3-1/2" in size.

		MT	NR MT	EX
Complete Set (6):		4.00	3.00	1.50
Common Player:		.50	.40	.20
1	Barry Larkin	.50	.40	.20
2	Mark Grace	.60	.45	.25
3	Don Mattingly	1.00	.60	.30
4	Darryl Strawberry	.60	.45	.25
5	Jose Canseco	.75	.50	.25
6	Wade Boggs	1.00	.70	.40

1990 Fleer World Series

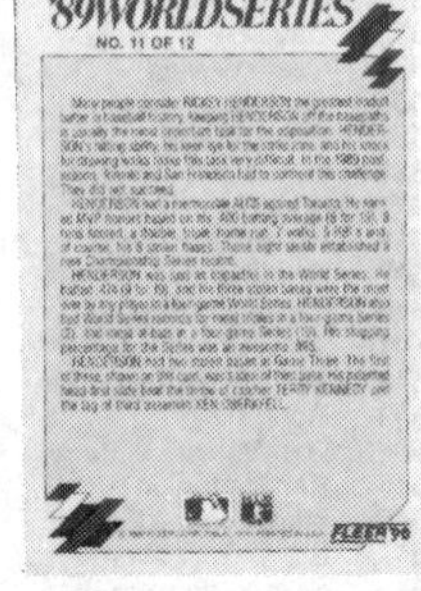

This 12-card set, which depicts highlights of the 1989 World Series, was included as a special sub-set with the regular factory-collated Fleer set. Ironically, single World

Series cards were discovered in cello and three-packs. This was not intended to happen. Fronts of the 2-1/2" by 3-1/2" cards feature full-color photos set against a white background with a red and blue "'89 World Series" banner. The card backs are pink and white and describe the events of the 1989 Fall Classic.

		MT	NR MT	EX
Complete Set (12):		2.50	1.50	.75
Common Player:		.10	.06	.03
1	The Final Piece To The Puzzle (Mike Moore)	.20	.15	.08
2	Kevin Mitchell	.30	.25	.12
3	Game Two's Crushing Blow	.20	.15	.08
4	Will Clark	.75	.50	.25
5	Jose Canseco	.40	.30	.15
6	Great leather In The Field	.20	.15	.08
7	Game One And A's Break Out On Top	.20	.15	.08
8	Dave Stewart	.25	.20	.10
9	Parker's Bat Produces Power (Dave Parker)	.20	.15	.08
10	World Series Record Book Game 3	.20	.15	.08
11	Rickey Henderson	.30	.20	.10
12	Oakland A's - Baseball's Best In '89	.25	.20	.10

1990 Fleer Box Panels

Photos not available at press time

For the fifth consecutive year, Fleer issued a series of cards on the bottom panels of its regular 1990 wax pack boxes. This 28-card set features both players and team logo cards. The cards were numbered C-1 to C-28.

		MT	NR MT	EX
Complete Set:		5.00	3.75	2.00
Common Player:		.05	.04	.02
1	Giants Logo	.05	.04	.02
2	Tim Belcher	.06	.05	.02
3	Roger Clemens	.35	.25	.14
4	Eric Davis	.35	.25	.14
5	Glenn Davis	.10	.08	.04
6	Cubs Logo	.05	.04	.02
7	Jon Franco	.06	.05	.02
8	Mike Greenwell	.20	.15	.07
9	Athletics Logo	.05	.04	.02
10	Ken Griffey, Jr.	1.50	1.25	.60
11	Pedro Guerrero	.05	.04	.02
12	Tony Gwynn	.20	.15	.08
13	Blue Jays Logo	.05	.04	.02
14	Orel Hershiser	.20	.15	.08
15	Bo Jackson	.70	.50	.30
16	Howard Johnson	.15	.11	.06
17	Mets Logo	.05	.04	.02
18	Cardinals Logo	.05	.04	.02
19	Don Mattingly	.60	.45	.25
20	Mark McGwire	.40	.30	.15
21	Kevin Mitchell	.25	.20	.10
22	Kirby Puckett	.35	.25	.14
23	Royals Logo	.05	.04	.02
24	Orioles Logo	.05	.04	.02
25	Ruben Sierra	.30	.25	.12
26	Dave Stewart	.20	.15	.08
27	Jerome Walton	.05	.04	.02
28	Robin Yount	.25	.20	.10

1990 Fleer Update

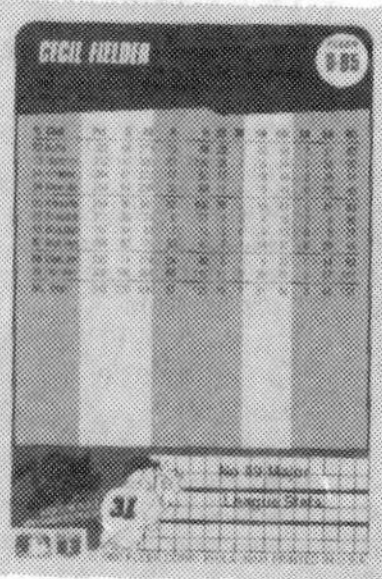

Fleer produced its seventh consecutive "Update" set in 1990 to supplement the company's regular set. As in the past, the set consists of 132 cards (numbered U-1 through U-132) that were sold by hobby dealers in special collectors boxes. The cards are designed in the exact same style as the regular issue. A special Nolan Ryan commemorative card is included in the 1990 Fleer Update set.

		MT	NR MT	EX
Complete Set (132):		10.00	7.50	4.00
Common Player:		.06	.05	.02
1	Steve Avery(FC)	1.00	.70	.40
2	Francisco Cabrera	.20	.15	.08
3	Nick Esasky	.06	.05	.02
4	Jim Kremers(FC)	.06	.05	.02
5	Greg Olson(FC)	.10	.08	.04
6	Jim Presley	.06	.05	.02
7	Shawn Boskie(FC)	.25	.20	.10
8	Joe Kraemer(FC)	.06	.05	.02
9	Luis Salazar	.06	.05	.02
10	Hector Villanueva(FC)	.30	.25	.12
11	Glenn Braggs	.06	.05	.02
12	Mariano Duncan	.06	.05	.02
13	Billy Hatcher	.06	.05	.02
14	Tim Layana(FC)	.20	.15	.08
15	Hal Morris	.40	.30	.15
16	Javier Ortiz(FC)	.20	.15	.08
17	Dave Rohde(FC)	.15	.11	.06
18	Eric Yelding(FC)	.20	.15	.08
19	Hubie Brooks	.08	.06	.03
20	Kal Daniels	.08	.06	.03
21	Dave Hansen	.15	.11	.06
22	Mike Hartley	.15	.11	.06
23	Stan Javier	.06	.05	.02
24	Jose Offerman(FC)	.12	.09	.05
25	Juan Samuel	.06	.05	.02
26	Dennis Boyd	.06	.05	.02
27	Delino DeShields	.70	.50	.30
28	Steve Frey	.12	.09	.05
29	Mark Gardner	.15	.11	.06
30	Chris Nabholz(FC)	.20	.15	.07
31	Bill Sampen(FC)	.15	.11	.06
32	Dave Schmidt	.06	.05	.02
33	Daryl Boston	.06	.05	.02
34	Chuck Carr(FC)	.35	.25	.14
35	John Franco	.08	.06	.03
36	Todd Hundley(FC)	.25	.20	.10
37	Julio Machado(FC)	.06	.05	.02
38	Alejandro Pena	.06	.05	.02
39	Darren Reed(FC)	.12	.09	.05
40	Kelvin Torve(FC)	.12	.09	.05
41	Darrel Akerfelds(FC)	.12	.09	.05
42	Jose DeJesus	.20	.15	.08
43	Dave Hollins(FC)	1.00	.70	.40
44	Carmelo Martinez	.06	.05	.02
45	Brad Moore(FC)	.10	.08	.04
46	Dale Murphy	.10	.08	.04
47	Wally Backman	.06	.05	.02
48	Stan Belinda(FC)	.20	.15	.08
49	Bob Patterson	.06	.05	.02
50	Ted Power	.06	.05	.02
51	Don Slaught	.06	.05	.02
52	Geronimo Pena(FC)	.25	.20	.10
53	Lee Smith	.08	.06	.03
54	John Tudor	.06	.05	.02
55	Joe Carter	.10	.08	.04
56	Tom Howard(FC)	.20	.15	.08

		MT	NR MT	EX
57	Craig Lefferts	.06	.05	.02
58	Rafael Valdez(FC)	.10	.08	.04
59	Dave Anderson	.06	.05	.02
60	Kevin Bass	.06	.05	.02
61	John Burkett	.25	.20	.10
62	Gary Carter	.10	.08	.04
63	Rick Parker(FC)	.10	.08	.04
64	Trevor Wilson	.10	.08	.04
65	Chris Hoiles(FC)	.25	.20	.10
66	Tim Hulett	.06	.05	.02
67	Dave Johnson(FC)	.10	.08	.04
68	Curt Schilling(FC)	.30	.25	.12
69	David Segui(FC)	.10	.08	.04
70	Tom Brunansky	.08	.06	.03
71	Greg Harris	.06	.05	.02
72	Dana Kiecker(FC)	.12	.09	.05
73	Tim Naehring(FC)	.40	.30	.15
74	Tony Pena	.06	.05	.02
75	Jeff Reardon	.08	.06	.03
76	Jerry Reed	.06	.05	.02
77	Mark Eichhorn	.06	.05	.02
78	Mark Langston	.08	.06	.03
79	John Orton	.12	.09	.05
80	Luis Polonia	.06	.05	.02
81	Dave Winfield	.12	.09	.05
82	Cliff Young(FC)	.10	.08	.04
83	Wayne Edwards	.10	.08	.04
84	Alex Fernandez(FC)	1.50	.40	.20
85	Craig Grebeck(FC)	.15	.11	.06
86	Scott Radinsky(FC)	.25	.20	.10
87	Frank Thomas(FC)	4.00	3.00	1.50
88	Beau Allred(FC)	.10	.08	.04
89	Sandy Alomar,Jr.	.35	.25	.14
90	Carlos Baerga(FC)	1.25	.90	.45
91	Kevin Bearse(FC)	.10	.08	.04
92	Chris James	.06	.05	.02
93	Candy Maldonado	.06	.05	.02
94	Jeff Manto	.12	.09	.05
95	Cecil Fielder	.40	.30	.15
96	Travis Fryman(FC)	1.50	1.25	.60
97	Lloyd Moseby	.06	.05	.02
98	Edwin Nunez	.06	.05	.02
99	Tony Phillips	.06	.05	.02
100	Larry Sheets	.06	.05	.02
101	Mark Davis	.06	.05	.02
102	Storm Davis	.06	.05	.02
103	Gerald Perry	.06	.05	.02
104	Terry Shumpert(FC)	.10	.08	.04
105	Edgar Diaz(FC)	.10	.08	.04
106	Dave Parker	.10	.08	.04
107	Tim Drummond(FC)	.10	.08	.04
108	Junior Ortiz	.06	.05	.02
109	Park Pittman(FC)	.10	.08	.04
110	Kevin Tapani(FC)	.25	.20	.10
111	Oscar Azocar(FC)	.15	.11	.06
112	Jim Leyritz(FC)	.15	.11	.06
113	Kevin Maas	.30	.25	.12
114	Alan Mills(FC)	.25	.20	.10
115	Matt Nokes	.06	.05	.02
116	Pascual Perez	.06	.05	.02
117	Ozzie Canseco(FC)	.10	.08	.04
118	Scott Sanderson	.06	.05	.02
119	Tino Martinez(FC)	.60	.45	.25
120	Jeff Schaefer(FC)	.10	.08	.04
121	Matt Young	.06	.05	.02
122	Brian Bohanon(FC)	.20	.15	.08
123	Jeff Huson	.15	.11	.06
124	Ramon Manon(FC)	.10	.08	.04
125	Gary Mielke(FC)	.10	.08	.04
126	Willie Blair(FC)	.15	.11	.06
127	Glenallen Hill(FC)	.10	.08	.04
128	John Olerud(FC)	1.50	1.25	.60
129	Luis Sojo(FC)	.15	.11	.06
130	Mark Whiten(FC)	.70	.50	.30
131	Three Decades of No Hitters (Nolan Ryan)	.70	.50	.30
132	Checklist	.06	.05	.02

Values quoted in this guide reflect the retail price of a card – the price a collector can expect to pay when buying a card from a dealer. The wholesale price – that which a collector can expect to receive from a dealer when selling cards – will be significantly lower, depending on desirability and condition.

1991 Fleer

Fleer expanded its 1991 set to include 720 cards. The cards feature yellow boders surrounding full- color action photos. The player's name appears above the photo, while the team and position is displayed below. The "Fleer 91" logo appears in the lower right corner of the photo. The card backs feature a circular player photo, biographical information, complete statistics, and career highlights. Five special Super Star cards are among the cards in the regular set. Once again the cards are numbered alphabetically within team. Because Fleer used more than one printer, many minor variations in photo cropping and typography can be found. The most notable are included in the checklist here.

		MT	NR MT	EX
Complete Set (720):		15.00	11.00	6.00
Common Player:		.05	.04	.02
1	*Troy Afenir*(FC)	.10	.08	.04
2	Harold Baines	.08	.06	.03
3	Lance Blankenship	.06	.05	.02
4	Todd Burns	.05	.04	.02
5	Jose Canseco	.15	.11	.06
6	Dennis Eckersley	.10	.08	.04
7	Mike Gallego	.05	.04	.02
8	Ron Hassey	.05	.04	.02
9	Dave Henderson	.08	.06	.03
10	Rickey Henderson	.15	.11	.06
11	Rick Honeycutt	.05	.04	.02
12	Doug Jennings	.06	.05	.02
13	*Joe Klink*(FC)	.10	.08	.04
14	Carney Lansford	.08	.06	.03
15	*Darren Lewis*(FC)	.20	.15	.08
16	Willie McGee	.08	.06	.03
17a	Mark McGwire (six-line career summary)	.20	.15	.08
17b	Mark McGwire (seven-line career summary)	.20	.15	.08
18	Mike Moore	.06	.05	.02
19	Gene Nelson	.05	.04	.02
20	Dave Otto	.05	.04	.02
21	Jamie Quirk	.05	.04	.02
22	Willie Randolph	.06	.05	.02
23	Scott Sanderson	.06	.05	.02
24	Terry Steinbach	.06	.05	.02
25	Dave Stewart	.10	.08	.04
26	Walt Weiss	.06	.05	.02
27	Bob Welch	.08	.06	.03
28	Curt Young	.05	.04	.02
29	Wally Backman	.05	.04	.02
30	*Stan Belinda*	.10	.08	.04
31	Jay Bell	.06	.05	.02
32	Rafael Belliard	.05	.04	.02

A player's name in italic indicates a rookie card. An (FC) indicates a player's first card for that particular card company.

		MT	NR MT	EX
30	*Stan Belinda*	.10	.08	.04
31	Jay Bell	.06	.05	.02
32	Rafael Belliard	.05	.04	.02
33	Barry Bonds	.25	.20	.10
34	Bobby Bonilla	.12	.09	.05
35	Sid Bream	.06	.05	.02
36	Doug Drabek	.10	.08	.04
37	*Carlos Garcia*(FC)	.60	.45	.25
38	Neal Heaton	.06	.05	.02
39	Jeff King	.08	.06	.03
40	Bob Kipper	.05	.04	.02
41	Bill Landrum	.06	.05	.02
42	Mike LaValliere	.06	.05	.02
43	Jose Lind	.06	.05	.02
44	Carmelo Martinez	.05	.04	.02
45	Bob Patterson	.05	.04	.02
46	Ted Power	.05	.04	.02
47	Gary Redus	.05	.04	.02
48	R.J. Reynolds	.05	.04	.02
49	Don Slaught	.05	.04	.02
50	John Smiley	.05	.04	.02
51	Zane Smith	.06	.05	.02
52	*Randy Tomlin*(FC)	.10	.08	.04
53	Andy Van Slyke	.08	.06	.03
54	Bob Walk	.05	.04	.02
55	Jack Armstrong	.08	.06	.03
56	Todd Benzinger	.06	.05	.02
57	Glenn Braggs	.06	.05	.02
58	Keith Brown	.06	.05	.02
59	Tom Browning	.06	.05	.02
60	Norm Charlton	.08	.06	.03
61	Eric Davis	.20	.15	.08
62	Rob Dibble	.10	.08	.04
63	Bill Doran	.08	.06	.03
64	Mariano Duncan	.06	.05	.02
65	Chris Hammond	.06	.05	.02
66	Billy Hatcher	.06	.05	.02
67	Danny Jackson	.06	.05	.02
68	Barry Larkin	.10	.08	.04
69	*Tim Layana*	.10	.08	.04
70	*Terry Lee*(FC)	.15	.11	.06
71	Rick Mahler	.05	.04	.02
72	Hal Morris	.15	.11	.06
73	Randy Myers	.08	.06	.03
74	Ron Oester	.05	.04	.02
75	Joe Oliver	.08	.06	.03
76	Paul O'Neill	.06	.05	.02
77	Luis Quinones	.05	.04	.02
78	Jeff Reed	.05	.04	.02
79	Jose Rijo	.08	.06	.03
80	Chris Sabo	.08	.06	.03
81	Scott Scudder	.06	.05	.02
82	Herm Winningham	.05	.04	.02
83	Larry Andersen	.05	.04	.02
84	Marty Barrett	.05	.04	.02
85	Mike Boddicker	.06	.05	.02
86	Wade Boggs	.12	.09	.05
87	Tom Bolton	.05	.04	.02
88	Tom Brunansky	.06	.05	.02
89	Ellis Burks	.15	.11	.06
90	Roger Clemens	.20	.15	.08
91	Scott Cooper(FC)	.20	.15	.08
92	John Dopson	.05	.04	.02
93	Dwight Evans	.06	.05	.02
94	Wes Gardner	.05	.04	.02
95	*Jeff Gray*(FC)	.10	.08	.04
96	Mike Greenwell	.10	.08	.04
97	Greg Harris	.05	.04	.02
98	*Daryl Irvine*(FC)	.08	.06	.03
99	*Dana Kiecker*	.10	.08	.04
100	Randy Kutcher	.05	.04	.02
101	Dennis Lamp	.05	.04	.02
102	Mike Marshall	.05	.04	.02
103	John Marzano	.05	.04	.02
104	Rob Murphy	.05	.04	.02
105	*Tim Naehring*	.08	.06	.03
106	Tony Pena	.06	.05	.02
107	*Phil Plantier*(FC)	.50	.40	.20
108	Carlos Quintana	.06	.05	.02
109	Jeff Reardon	.06	.05	.02
110	Jerry Reed	.05	.04	.02
111	Jody Reed	.06	.05	.02
112	Luis Rivera	.05	.04	.02
113	Kevin Romine	.05	.04	.02
114	Phil Bradley	.06	.05	.02
115	Ivan Calderon	.06	.05	.02
116	Wayne Edwards	.05	.04	.02
117	*Alex Fernandez*	.25	.20	.10
118	Carlton Fisk	.10	.08	.04
119	Scott Fletcher	.05	.04	.02
120	*Craig Grebeck*	.08	.06	.03

		MT	NR MT	EX
121	Ozzie Guillen	.08	.06	.03
122	Greg Hibbard	.06	.05	.02
123	Lance Johnson	.06	.05	.02
124	Barry Jones	.05	.04	.02
125	Ron Karkovice	.05	.04	.02
126	Eric King	.05	.04	.02
127	Steve Lyons	.05	.04	.02
128	Carlos Martinez	.06	.05	.02
129	Jack McDowell	.06	.05	.02
130	Donn Pall	.05	.04	.02
131	Dan Pasqua	.05	.04	.02
132	Ken Patterson	.05	.04	.02
133	Melido Perez	.06	.05	.02
134	Adam Peterson	.05	.04	.02
135	*Scott Radinsky*	.08	.06	.03
136	Sammy Sosa	.15	.11	.06
137	Bobby Thigpen	.08	.06	.03
138	Frank Thomas	1.25	.90	.50
139	Robin Ventura	.20	.15	.08
140	Daryl Boston	.05	.04	.02
141	*Chuck Carr*	.20	.15	.08
142	Mark Carreon	.05	.04	.02
143	David Cone	.06	.05	.02
144	Ron Darling	.06	.05	.02
145	Kevin Elster	.05	.04	.02
146	Sid Fernandez	.06	.05	.02
147	John Franco	.08	.06	.03
148	Dwight Gooden	.20	.15	.08
149	Tom Herr	.06	.05	.02
150	*Todd Hundley*	.08	.06	.03
151	Gregg Jefferies	.10	.08	.04
152	Howard Johnson	.08	.06	.03
153	Dave Magadan	.08	.06	.03
154	Kevin McReynolds	.08	.06	.03
155	Keith Miller	.06	.05	.02
156	Bob Ojeda	.05	.04	.02
157	Tom O'Malley	.05	.04	.02
158	Alejandro Pena	.05	.04	.02
159	*Darren Reed*	.08	.06	.03
160	Mackey Sasser	.06	.05	.02
161	Darryl Strawberry	.10	.08	.04
162	Tim Teufel	.05	.04	.02
163	Kelvin Torve	.08	.06	.03
164	Julio Valera	.10	.08	.04
165	Frank Viola	.12	.09	.05
166	Wally Whitehurst	.05	.04	.02
167	Jim Acker	.05	.04	.02
168	*Derek Bell*(FC)	.35	.25	.14
169	George Bell	.08	.06	.03
170	*Willie Blair*	.08	.06	.03
171	Pat Borders	.06	.05	.02
172	John Cerutti	.05	.04	.02
173	Junior Felix	.06	.05	.02
174	Tony Fernandez	.08	.06	.03
175	Kelly Gruber	.05	.04	.02
176	Tom Henke	.06	.05	.02
177	Glenallen Hill	.08	.06	.03
178	Jimmy Key	.06	.05	.02
179	Manny Lee	.05	.04	.02
180	Fred McGriff	.20	.15	.08
181	Rance Mulliniks	.05	.04	.02
182	Greg Myers	.05	.04	.02
183	John Olerud	.30	.25	.12
184	Luis Sojo	.08	.06	.03
185	Dave Steib	.08	.06	.03
186	Todd Stottlemyre	.06	.05	.02
187	Duane Ward	.05	.04	.02
188	David Wells	.05	.04	.02
189	*Mark Whiten*	.20	.15	.08
190	Ken Williams	.05	.04	.02
191	Frank Wills	.05	.04	.02
192	Mookie Wilson	.05	.04	.02
193	Don Aase	.05	.04	.02
194	Tim Belcher	.08	.06	.03
195	Hubie Brooks	.08	.06	.03
196	Dennis Cook	.06	.05	.02
197	Tim Crews	.05	.04	.02
198	Kal Daniels	.06	.05	.02
199	Kirk Gibson	.08	.06	.03
200	Jim Gott	.05	.04	.02
201	Alfredo Griffin	.05	.04	.02
202	Chris Gwynn	.06	.05	.02
203	Dave Hansen	.08	.06	.03
204	Lenny Harris	.06	.05	.02
205	Mike Hartley	.10	.08	.04
206	Mickey Hatcher	.05	.04	.02
207	*Carlos Hernandez*(FC)	.10	.08	.04
208	Orel Hershiser	.10	.08	.04
209	Jay Howell	.06	.05	.02
210	Mike Huff	.10	.08	.04
211	Stan Javier	.05	.04	.02

		MT	NR MT	EX
212	Ramon Martinez	.08	.06	.03
213	Mike Morgan	.05	.04	.02
214	Eddie Murray	.08	.06	.03
215	*Jim Neidlinger*(FC)	.08	.06	.03
216	Jose Offerman	.10	.08	.04
217	*Jim Poole*(FC)	.06	.05	.02
218	Juan Samuel	.06	.05	.02
219	Mike Scioscia	.06	.05	.02
220	Ray Searage	.05	.04	.02
221	Mike Sharperson	.06	.05	.02
222	Fernando Valenzuela	.06	.05	.02
223	Jose Vizcaino	.10	.08	.04
224	Mike Aldrete	.05	.04	.02
225	*Scott Anderson*(FC)	.10	.08	.04
226	Dennis Boyd	.06	.05	.02
227	Tim Burke	.06	.05	.02
228	Delino DeShields	.15	.11	.06
229	Mike Fitzgerald	.05	.04	.02
230	Tom Foley	.05	.04	.02
231	Steve Frey	.05	.04	.02
232	Andres Galarraga	.08	.06	.03
233	Mark Gardner	.10	.08	.04
234	Marquis Grissom(FC)	.20	.15	.08
235	Kevin Gross	.06	.05	.02
236	Drew Hall	.05	.04	.02
237	Dave Martinez	.06	.05	.02
238	Dennis Martinez	.06	.05	.02
239	Dale Mohorcic	.05	.04	.02
240	*Chris Nabholz*	.08	.06	.03
241	Otis Nixon	.05	.04	.02
242	Junior Noboa(FC)	.08	.06	.03
243	Spike Owen	.06	.05	.02
244	Tim Raines	.08	.06	.03
245	*Mel Rojas*(FC)	.12	.09	.05
246	*Scott Ruskin*(FC)	.08	.06	.03
247	*Bill Sampen*	.06	.05	.02
248	Nelson Santovenia	.05	.04	.02
249	Dave Schmidt	.05	.04	.02
250	Larry Walker	.15	.11	.06
251	Tim Wallach	.08	.06	.03
252	Dave Anderson	.05	.04	.02
253	Kevin Bass	.06	.05	.02
254	Steve Bedrosian	.06	.05	.02
255	Jeff Brantley	.08	.06	.03
256	John Burkett	.08	.06	.03
257	Brett Butler	.06	.05	.02
258	Gary Carter	.08	.06	.03
259	Will Clark	.25	.20	.10
260	*Steve Decker*(FC)	.10	.08	.04
261	Kelly Downs	.05	.04	.02
262	Scott Garrelts	.06	.05	.02
263	Terry Kennedy	.05	.04	.02
264	Mike LaCoss	.05	.04	.02
265	*Mark Leonard*(FC)	.10	.08	.04
266	Greg Litton	.06	.05	.02
267	Kevin Mitchell	.08	.06	.03
268	Randy O'Neal(FC)	.05	.04	.02
269	*Rick Parker*	.06	.05	.02
270	Rick Reuschel	.06	.05	.02
271	Ernest Riles	.05	.04	.02
272	Don Robinson	.05	.04	.02
273	Robby Thompson	.06	.05	.02
274	Mark Thurmond	.05	.04	.02
275	Jose Uribe	.05	.04	.02
276	Matt Williams	.15	.11	.06
277	Trevor Wilson	.06	.05	.02
278	*Gerald Alexander*(FC)	.15	.11	.06
279	Brad Arnsberg	.06	.05	.02
280	*Kevin Belcher*(FC)	.15	.11	.06
281	*Joe Bitker*(FC)	.08	.06	.03
282	Kevin Brown	.06	.05	.02
283	Steve Buechele	.05	.04	.02
284	Jack Daugherty	.06	.05	.02
285	Julio Franco	.10	.08	.04
286	Juan Gonzalez	.70	.50	.30
287	*Bill Haselman*(FC)	.15	.11	.06
288	Charlie Hough	.05	.04	.02
289	Jeff Huson	.06	.05	.02
290	Pete Incaviglia	.06	.05	.02
291	Mike Jeffcoat	.05	.04	.02
292	Jeff Kunkel	.05	.04	.02
293	Gary Mielke	.08	.06	.03
294	Jamie Moyer	.05	.04	.02
295	Rafael Palmeiro	.08	.06	.03
296	Geno Petralli	.05	.04	.02
297	Gary Pettis	.06	.05	.02
298	Kevin Reimer	.10	.08	.04
299	Kenny Rogers	.06	.05	.02
300	Jeff Russell	.06	.05	.02
301	John Russell	.05	.04	.02
302	Nolan Ryan	.40	.30	.15

		MT	NR MT	EX
303	Ruben Sierra	.12	.09	.05
304	Bobby Witt	.08	.06	.03
305	Jim Abbott	.08	.06	.03
306	Kent Anderson(FC)	.06	.05	.02
307	Dante Bichette	.06	.05	.02
308	Bert Blyleven	.08	.06	.03
309	Chili Davis	.06	.05	.02
310	Brian Downing	.05	.04	.02
311	Mark Eichhorn	.05	.04	.02
312	Mike Fetters	.08	.06	.03
313	Chuck Finley	.08	.06	.03
314	Willie Fraser	.05	.04	.02
315	Bryan Harvey	.06	.05	.02
316	Donnie Hill	.05	.04	.02
317	Wally Joyner	.10	.08	.04
318	Mark Langston	.10	.08	.04
319	Kirk McCaskill	.06	.05	.02
320	John Orton	.06	.05	.02
321	Lance Parrish	.08	.06	.03
322	Luis Polonia	.05	.04	.02
323	Johnny Ray	.05	.04	.02
324	Bobby Rose	.06	.05	.02
325	Dick Schofield	.05	.04	.02
326	Rick Schu	.05	.04	.02
327	Lee Stevens	.10	.08	.04
328	Devon White	.06	.05	.02
329	Dave Winfield	.12	.09	.05
330	*Cliff Young*	.15	.11	.06
331	Dave Bergman	.05	.04	.02
332	*Phil Clark*(FC)	.12	.09	.05
333	Darnell Coles	.05	.04	.02
334	Milt Cuyler(FC)	.08	.06	.03
335	Cecil Fielder	.15	.11	.06
336	*Travis Fryman*	.60	.45	.25
337	Paul Gibson	.05	.04	.02
338	Jerry Don Gleaton	.05	.04	.02
339	Mike Heath	.05	.04	.02
340	Mike Henneman	.06	.05	.02
341	Chet Lemon	.06	.05	.02
342	Lance McCullers	.05	.04	.02
343	Jack Morris	.08	.06	.03
344	lloyd Moseby	.06	.05	.02
345	Edwin Nunez	.05	.04	.02
346	Clay Parker	.05	.04	.02
347	Dan Petry	.05	.04	.02
348	Tony Phillips	.06	.05	.02
349	Jeff Robinson	.06	.05	.02
350	Mark Salas	.05	.04	.02
351	*Mike Schwabe*	.06	.05	.02
352	Larry Sheets	.05	.04	.02
353	John Shelby	.05	.04	.02
354	Frank Tanana	.06	.05	.02
355	Alan Trammell	.08	.06	.03
356	Gary Ward	.05	.04	.02
357	Lou Whitaker	.08	.06	.03
358	Beau Allred	.06	.05	.02
359	Sandy Alomar,Jr.	.08	.06	.03
360	*Carlos Baerga*	.25	.20	.10
361	*Kevin Bearse*	.06	.05	.02
362	Tom Brookens	.05	.04	.02
363	Jerry Browne	.06	.05	.02
364	Tom Candiotti	.05	.04	.02
365	Alex Cole	.06	.05	.02
366	John Farrell	.05	.04	.02
367	Felix Fermin	.05	.04	.02
368	Keith Hernandez	.08	.06	.03
369	Brook Jacoby	.08	.06	.03
370	Chris James	.06	.05	.02
371	Dion James	.05	.04	.02
372	Doug Jones	.08	.06	.03
373	Candy Maldonado	.08	.06	.03
374	Steve Olin	.06	.05	.02
375	Jesse Orosco	.05	.04	.02
376	Rudy Seanez	.06	.05	.02
377	Joel Skinner	.05	.04	.02
378	Cory Snyder	.08	.06	.03
379	Greg Swindell	.06	.05	.02
380	Sergio Valdez(FC)	.08	.06	.03
381	*Mike Walker*(FC)	.06	.05	.02
382	*Colby Ward*(FC)	.06	.05	.02
383	*Turner Ward*(FC)	.10	.08	.04
384	Mitch Webster	.05	.04	.02
385	Kevin Wickander(FC)	.06	.05	.02
386	Darrel Akerfelds	.06	.05	.02
387	Joe Boever	.05	.04	.02
388	Rod Booker	.05	.04	.02
389	Sil Campusano	.05	.04	.02
390	Don Carman	.05	.04	.02
391	*Wes Chamberlain*(FC)	.20	.15	.08
392	Pat Combs	.06	.05	.02
393	Darren Daulton	.06	.05	.02

		MT	NR MT	EX
394	Jose DeJesus	.06	.05	.02
395	Len Dykstra	.10	.08	.04
396	Jason Grimsley	.06	.05	.02
397	Charlie Hayes	.08	.06	.03
398	Von Hayes	.08	.06	.03
399	*David Hollins*	.30	.25	.12
400	Ken Howell	.06	.05	.02
401	Ricky Jordan	.10	.08	.04
402	John Kruk	.06	.05	.02
403	Steve Lake	.05	.04	.02
404	*Chuck Malone*(FC)	.08	.06	.03
405	Roger McDowell	.08	.06	.03
406	Chuck McElroy	.08	.06	.03
407	*Mickey Morandini*(FC)	.08	.06	.03
408	Terry Mulholland	.06	.05	.02
409	Dale Murphy	.10	.08	.04
410	Randy Ready	.05	.04	.02
411	Bruce Ruffin	.05	.04	.02
412	Dickie Thon	.05	.04	.02
413	Paul Assenmacher	.05	.04	.02
414	Damon Berryhill	.06	.05	.02
415	Mike Bielecki	.06	.05	.02
416	*Shawn Boskie*	.08	.06	.03
417	Dave Clark	.05	.04	.02
418	Doug Dascenzo	.05	.04	.02
419	Andre Dawson	.10	.08	.04
420	Shawon Dunston	.10	.08	.04
421	Joe Girardi	.06	.05	.02
422	Mark Grace	.10	.08	.04
423	Mike Harkey	.08	.06	.03
424	Les Lancaster	.05	.04	.02
425	Bill Long	.05	.04	.02
426	Greg Maddux	.08	.06	.03
427	Derrick May	.25	.20	.10
428	Jeff Pico	.05	.04	.02
429	Domingo Ramos	.05	.04	.02
430	Luis Salazar	.05	.04	.02
431	Ryne Sandberg	.20	.15	.08
432	Dwight Smith	.06	.05	.02
433	Greg Smith	.08	.06	.03
434	Rick Sutcliffe	.08	.06	.03
435	Gary Varsho	.05	.04	.02
436	*Hector Villanueva*	.08	.06	.03
437	Jerome Walton	.08	.06	.03
438	Curtis Wilkerson	.05	.04	.02
439	Mitch Williams	.08	.06	.03
440	Steve Wilson	.06	.05	.02
441	Marvell Wynne	.05	.04	.02
442	Scott Bankhead	.06	.05	.02
443	Scott Bradley	.05	.04	.02
444	Greg Briley	.06	.05	.02
445	Mike Brumley	.05	.04	.02
446	Jay Buhner	.06	.05	.02
447	*Dave Burba*(FC)	.10	.08	.04
448	Henry Cotto	.05	.04	.02
449	Alvin Davis	.08	.06	.03
450	Ken Griffey,Jr.	.70	.50	.30
451	Erik Hanson	.12	.09	.05
452	Gene Harris	.05	.04	.02
453	Brian Holman	.06	.05	.02
454	Mike Jackson	.06	.05	.02
455	Randy Johnson	.10	.08	.04
456	Jeffrey Leonard	.06	.05	.02
457	Edgar Martinez	.06	.05	.02
458	Tino Martinez	.10	.08	.04
459	Pete O'Brien	.05	.04	.02
460	Harold Reynolds	.08	.06	.03
461	Mike Schooler	.08	.06	.03
462	Bill Swift	.06	.05	.02
463	David Valle	.05	.04	.02
464	Omar Vizquel	.06	.05	.02
465	Matt Young	.06	.05	.02
466	Brady Anderson	.05	.04	.02
467	Jeff Ballard	.06	.05	.02
468	Juan Bell(FC)	.08	.06	.03
469	Mike Devereaux	.06	.05	.02
470	Steve Finley	.06	.05	.02
471	Dave Gallagher	.05	.04	.02
472	*Leo Gomez*(FC)	.10	.08	.04
473	Rene Gonzales	.05	.04	.02
474	Pete Harnisch	.06	.05	.02
475	Kevin Hickey	.05	.04	.02
476	*Chris Hoiles*	.10	.08	.04
477	Sam Horn	.06	.05	.02
478	Tim Hulett	.05	.04	.02
479	Dave Johnson	.05	.04	.02
480	Ron Kittle	.08	.06	.03
481	Ben McDonald	.10	.08	.04
482	Bob Melvin	.05	.04	.02
483	Bob Milacki	.06	.05	.02
484	Randy Milligan	.06	.05	.02

		MT	NR MT	EX
485	*John Mitchell*(FC)	.06	.05	.02
486	Gregg Olson	.08	.06	.03
487	Joe Orsulak	.05	.04	.02
488	Joe Price	.05	.04	.02
489	Bill Ripken	.05	.04	.02
490	Cal Ripken, Jr.	.20	.15	.08
491	Curt Schilling	.06	.05	.02
492	*David Segui*	.06	.05	.02
493	*Anthony Telford*(FC)	.06	.05	.02
494	Mickey Tettleton	.06	.05	.02
495	Mark Williamson	.05	.04	.02
496	Craig Worthington	.06	.05	.02
497	Juan Agosto	.05	.04	.02
498	Eric Anthony	.08	.06	.03
499	Craig Biggio	.08	.06	.03
500	Ken Caminiti	.06	.05	.02
501	Casey Candaele	.05	.04	.02
502	*Andujar Cedeno*(FC)	.25	.20	.10
503	Danny Darwin	.06	.05	.02
504	Mark Davidson	.05	.04	.02
505	Glenn Davis	.05	.04	.02
506	Jim Deshaies	.06	.05	.02
507	*Luis Gonzalez*(FC)	.40	.30	.15
508	Bill Gullickson	.05	.04	.02
509	Xavier Hernandez(FC)	.08	.06	.03
510	Brian Meyer	.06	.05	.02
511	Ken Oberkfell	.05	.04	.02
512	Mark Portugal	.05	.04	.02
513	Rafael Ramirez	.05	.04	.02
514	*Karl Rhodes*(FC)	.08	.06	.03
515	Mike Scott	.08	.06	.03
516	*Mike Simms*(FC)	.10	.08	.04
517	Dave Smith	.06	.05	.02
518	Franklin Stubbs	.06	.05	.02
519	Glenn Wilson	.06	.05	.02
520	Eric Yelding	.10	.08	.04
521	Gerald Young	.05	.04	.02
522	Shawn Abner	.05	.04	.02
523	Roberto Alomar	.15	.11	.06
524	Andy Benes	.10	.08	.04
525	Joe Carter	.10	.08	.04
526	Jack Clark	.08	.06	.03
527	Joey Cora	.06	.05	.02
528	*Paul Faries*(FC)	.06	.05	.02
529	Tony Gwynn	.15	.11	.06
530	Atlee Hammaker	.05	.04	.02
531	Greg Harris	.06	.05	.02
532	*Thomas Howard*	.06	.05	.02
533	Bruce Hurst	.06	.05	.02
534	Craig Lefferts	.06	.05	.02
535	Derek Lilliquist	.06	.05	.02
536	Fred Lynn	.06	.05	.02
537	Mike Pagliarulo	.06	.05	.02
538	Mark Parent	.05	.04	.02
539	Dennis Rasmussen	.05	.04	.02
540	Bip Roberts	.08	.06	.03
541	*Richard Rodriguez*(FC)	.06	.05	.02
542	Benito Santiago	.10	.08	.04
543	Calvin Schiraldi	.05	.04	.02
544	Eric Show	.06	.05	.02
545	Phil Stephenson	.05	.04	.02
546	Garry Templeton	.06	.05	.02
547	Ed Whitson	.06	.05	.02
548	Eddie Williams	.05	.04	.02
549	Kevin Appier	.10	.08	.04
550	Luis Aquino	.05	.04	.02
551	Bob Boone	.08	.06	.03
552	George Brett	.12	.09	.05
553	*Jeff Conine*(FC)	.30	.25	.12
554	Steve Crawford	.05	.04	.02
555	Mark Davis	.06	.05	.02
556	Storm Davis	.06	.05	.02
557	Jim Eisenreich	.06	.05	.02
558	Steve Farr	.05	.04	.02
559	Tom Gordon	.10	.08	.04
560	Mark Gubicza	.08	.06	.03
561	Bo Jackson	.20	.15	.08
562	Mike Macfarlane	.05	.04	.02
563	*Brian McRae*(FC)	.25	.20	.10
564	Jeff Montgomery	.06	.05	.02
565	Bill Pecota	.05	.04	.02
566	Gerald Perry	.06	.05	.02
567	Bret Saberhagen	.10	.08	.04
568	*Jeff Schulz*(FC)	.08	.06	.03
569	Kevin Seitzer	.08	.06	.03
570	*Terry Shumpert*	.06	.05	.02
571	Kurt Stillwell	.06	.05	.02
572	Danny Tartabull	.08	.06	.03
573	Gary Thurman	.05	.04	.02
574	Frank White	.06	.05	.02
575	Willie Wilson	.06	.05	.02

		MT	NR MT	EX
576	Chris Bosio	.06	.05	.02
577	Greg Brock	.06	.05	.02
578	George Canale	.06	.05	.02
579	Chuck Crim	.05	.04	.02
580	Rob Deer	.06	.05	.02
581	*Edgar Diaz*	.06	.05	.02
582	*Tom Edens*(FC)	.08	.06	.03
583	Mike Felder	.05	.04	.02
584	Jim Gantner	.06	.05	.02
585	Darryl Hamilton	.06	.05	.02
586	Ted Higuera	.08	.06	.03
587	Mark Knudson	.05	.04	.02
588	Bill Krueger	.05	.04	.02
589	Tim McIntosh	.08	.06	.03
590	Paul Mirabella	.05	.04	.02
591	Paul Molitor	.10	.08	.04
592	Jaime Navarro	.08	.06	.03
593	Dave Parker	.12	.09	.05
594	Dan Plesac	.06	.05	.02
595	Ron Robinson	.06	.05	.02
596	Gary Sheffield	.15	.11	.06
597	Bill Spiers	.06	.05	.02
598	B.J. Surhoff	.06	.05	.02
599	Greg Vaughn	.12	.09	.05
600	Randy Veres	.05	.04	.02
601	Robin Yount	.15	.11	.06
602	Rick Aguilera	.06	.05	.02
603	Allan Anderson	.05	.04	.02
604	Juan Berenguer	.05	.04	.02
605	Randy Bush	.05	.04	.02
606	Carmen Castillo	.05	.04	.02
607	Tim Drummond	.06	.05	.02
608	*Scott Erickson*(FC)	.10	.08	.04
609	Gary Gaetti	.08	.06	.03
610	Greg Gagne	.06	.05	.02
611	Dan Gladden	.06	.05	.02
612	Mark Guthrie(FC)	.06	.05	.02
613	Brian Harper	.06	.05	.02
614	Kent Hrbek	.08	.06	.03
615	Gene Larkin	.06	.05	.02
616	Terry Leach	.05	.04	.02
617	Nelson Liriano	.05	.04	.02
618	Shane Mack	.06	.05	.02
619	John Moses	.05	.04	.02
620	*Pedro Munoz*(FC)	.10	.08	.04
621	Al Newman	.05	.04	.02
622	Junior Ortiz	.05	.04	.02
623	Kirby Puckett	.15	.11	.06
624	Roy Smith	.05	.04	.02
625	Kevin Tapani	.10	.08	.04
626	Gary Wayne	.05	.04	.02
627	David West	.06	.05	.02
628	Cris Carpenter	.06	.05	.02
629	Vince Coleman	.08	.06	.03
630	Ken Dayley	.06	.05	.02
631	Jose DeLeon	.06	.05	.02
632	Frank DiPino	.05	.04	.02
633	*Bernard Gilkey*(FC)	.25	.20	.10
634	Pedro Guerrero	.08	.06	.03
635	Ken Hill	.06	.05	.02
636	Felix Jose	.08	.06	.03
637	*Ray Lankford*(FC)	.20	.15	.08
638	Joe Magrane	.08	.06	.03
639	Tom Niedenfuer	.05	.04	.02
640	Jose Oquendo	.05	.04	.02
641	Tom Pagnozzi	.05	.04	.02
642	Terry Pendleton	.06	.05	.02
643	*Mike Perez*(FC)	.12	.09	.05
644	Bryn Smith	.05	.04	.02
645	Lee Smith	.08	.06	.03
646	Ozzie Smith	.10	.08	.04
647	Scott Terry	.05	.04	.02
648	Bob Tewksbury	.05	.04	.02
649	Milt Thompson	.05	.04	.02
650	John Tudor	.06	.05	.02
651	Denny Walling	.05	.04	.02
652	*Craig Wilson*(FC)	.06	.05	.02
653	Todd Worrell	.06	.05	.02
654	Todd Zeile	.08	.06	.03
655	*Oscar Azocar*	.06	.05	.02
656	Steve Balboni	.05	.04	.02
657	Jesse Barfield	.08	.06	.03
658	Greg Cadaret	.05	.04	.02
659	Chuck Cary	.05	.04	.02
660	Rick Cerone	.05	.04	.02
661	Dave Eiland(FC)	.06	.05	.02
662	Alvaro Espinoza	.06	.05	.02
663	Bob Geren	.06	.05	.02
664	Lee Guetterman	.05	.04	.02
665	Mel Hall	.06	.05	.02
666	Andy Hawkins	.06	.05	.02

		MT	NR MT	EX
667	Jimmy Jones	.05	.04	.02
668	Roberto Kelly	.10	.08	.04
669	Dave LaPoint	.05	.04	.02
670	Tim Leary	.06	.05	.02
671	*Jim Leyritz*	.06	.05	.02
672	Kevin Maas	.06	.05	.02
673	Don Mattingly	.20	.15	.08
674	Matt Nokes	.06	.05	.02
675	Pascual Perez	.06	.05	.02
676	Eric Plunk	.05	.04	.02
677	Dave Righetti	.08	.06	.03
678	Jeff Robinson	.05	.04	.02
679	Steve Sax	.10	.08	.04
680	Mike Witt	.06	.05	.02
681	Steve Avery	.20	.15	.08
682	Mike Bell	.10	.08	.04
683	Jeff Blauser	.06	.05	.02
684	Francisco Cabrera	.10	.08	.04
685	Tony Castillo(FC)	.08	.06	.03
686	Marty Clary	.05	.04	.02
687	Nick Esasky	.08	.06	.03
688	Ron Gant	.10	.08	.04
689	Tom Glavine	.15	.11	.06
690	Mark Grant	.05	.04	.02
691	Tommy Gregg	.06	.05	.02
692	Dwayne Henry	.05	.04	.02
693	Dave Justice	.40	.30	.15
694	*Jimmy Kremers*	.08	.06	.03
695	Charlie Leibrandt	.06	.05	.02
696	Mark Lemke	.06	.05	.02
697	Oddibe McDowell	.06	.05	.02
698	*Greg Olson*	.08	.06	.03
699	Jeff Parrett	.06	.05	.02
700	Jim Presley	.06	.05	.02
701	*Victor Rosario*(FC)	.05	.04	.02
702	Lonnie Smith	.06	.05	.02
703	Pete Smith	.06	.05	.02
704	John Smoltz	.08	.06	.03
705	Mike Stanton	.08	.06	.03
706	Andres Thomas	.05	.04	.02
707	Jeff Treadway	.06	.05	.02
708	*Jim Vatcher*(FC)	.05	.04	.02
709	Home Run Kings (Ryne Sandberg, Cecil Fielder)	.15	.11	.06
710	Second Generation Superstars (Barry Bonds, Ken Griffey, Jr.)	.30	.25	.12
711	NLCS Team Leaders (Bobby Bonilla, Barry Larkin)	.15	.11	.06
712	Top Game Savers (Bobby Thigpen, John Franco)	.10	.08	.04
713	Chicago's 100 Club (Andre Dawson, Ryne Sandberg)	.15	.11	.06
714	Checklists (Athletics, Pirates, Reds, Red Sox)	.05	.04	.02
715	Checklists (White Sox, Mets Blue Jays, Dodgers)	.05	.04	.02
716	Checklists (Expos, Giants, Rangers, Angels)	.05	.04	.02
717	Checklists (Tigers, Indians, Phillies, Cubs)	.05	.04	.02
718	Checklists (Mariners, Orioles, Astros, Padres)	.05	.04	.02
719	Checklists (Royals, Brewers, Twins, Cardinals)	.05	.04	.02
720	Checklists (Yankees, Braves, Super Stars)	.05	.04	.02

1991 Fleer All Stars

Three player photos are featured on each card in

this special insert set. An action shot and portrait close-up are featured on the front, while a full-figure pose is showcased on the back. The cards are horizontal and were inserted into 1991 Fleer cello packs.

		MT	NR MT	EX
Complete Set (10):		18.00	13.50	7.25
Common Player:		.60	.45	.25
1	Ryne Sandberg	2.50	2.00	1.00
2	Barry Larkin	.60	.45	.25
3	Matt Williams	.60	.45	.25
4	Cecil Fielder	1.50	1.00	.50
5	Barry Bonds	2.50	2.00	1.00
6	Rickey Henderson	1.00	.75	.40
7	Ken Griffey, Jr.	6.00	4.00	2.00
8	Jose Canseco	1.00	.75	.40
9	Benito Santiago	.60	.45	.25
10	Roger Clemens	1.50	1.00	.50

1991 Fleer ProVisions

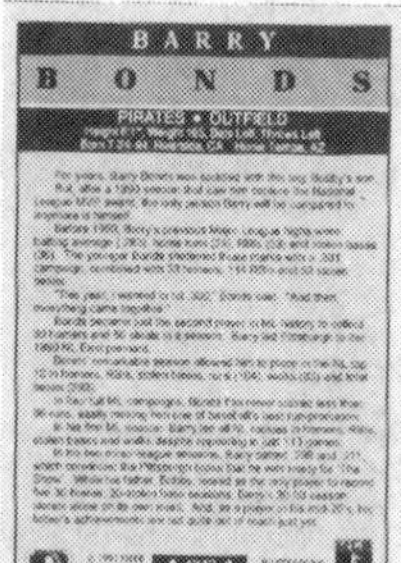

The illustrations of artist Terry Smith are showcased in this special set. Twelve fantasy portraits were produced for cards inserted into rack packs. Four other ProVision cards were inserted into factory sets. The rack pack cards feature black borders, while the factory set cards have white borders. Information on the card backs supports the manner in which Smith painted each player.

		MT	NR MT	EX
Complete Set (12):		4.00	3.00	1.50
Common Player:		.15	.10	.05
Complete Factory Set (4):		3.00	2.25	1.25
Common Player:		.40	.30	.15
1	Kirby Puckett	.40	.30	.15
2	Will Clark	.60	.45	.25
3	Ruben Sierra	.20	.15	.08
4	Mark McGwire	.20	.15	.08
5	Bo Jackson	.50	.40	.20
6	Jose Canseco	.50	.40	.20
7	Dwight Gooden	.25	.20	.10
8	Mike Greenwell	.25	.20	.10
9	Roger Clemens	.40	.30	.15
10	Eric Davis	.25	.20	.10
11	Don Mattingly	.90	.70	.35
12	Darryl Strawberry	.25	.20	.10
1F	Barry Bonds	1.00	.75	.40
2F	Rickey Henderson	.50	.40	.20
3F	Ryne Sandberg	1.00	.70	.40
4F	Dave Stewart	.40	.30	.15

1991 Fleer World Series

Once again Fleer released a set in honor of the World Series from the previous season. The 1991 issue features only eight cards compared to twelve in 1990. The cards feature white borders surrounding full-color action shots from the 1990 Fall Classic. The card backs feature an overview of the World Series action.

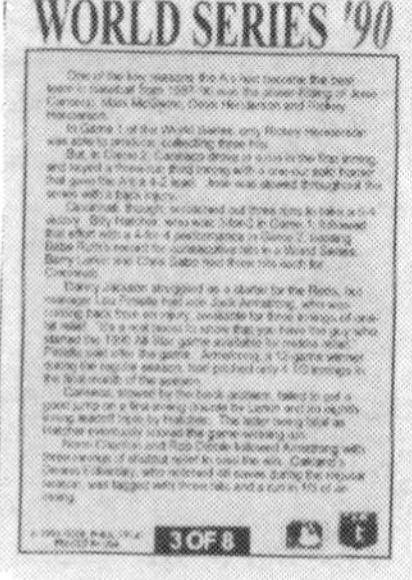

		MT	NR MT	EX
Complete Set (8):		1.50	1.00	.50
Common Player:		.20	.15	.08
1	Eric Davis	.25	.20	.10
2	Billy Hatcher	.20	.15	.08
3	Jose Canseco	.35	.25	.14
4	Rickey Henderson	.35	.25	.14
5	Chris Sabo/ Carney Lansford	.20	.15	.08
6	Dave Stewart	.25	.20	.10
7	Jose Rijo	.25	.20	.10
8	Reds Celebrate	.20	.15	.08

1991 Fleer Box Panels

Photos not available at press time

Unlike past box panel sets, the 1991 Fleer box panels feature a theme. 1990 no-hitters are celebrated on the three different boxes. The cards feature blank backs and are numbered in order of no-hitter on the front. A team logo was included on each box. The card fronts are styled after the 1991 Fleer cards. A special no-hitter logo appears in the lower left corner.

		MT	NR MT	EX
Complete Set:		2.00	1.50	.80
Common Player:		.10	.08	.04
1	Mark Langston/ Mike Witt	.10	.08	.04
2	Randy Johnson	.10	.08	.04
3	Nolan Ryan	.80	.60	.30
4	Dave Stewart	.15	.11	.06
5	Fernando Valenzuela	.15	.11	.06
6	Andy Hawkins	.10	.08	.04
7	Melido Perez	.10	.08	.04
8	Terry Mulholland	.10	.08	.04
9	Dave Steib	.15	.11	.06
----	Team Logos	.05	.04	.02

1991 Fleer Update

Fleer produced its eighth consecutive "Update" set in 1991 to supplement the company's regular set. As in the past, the set consists of 132 cards that were sold by hobby dealers in special collectors boxes. The cards are

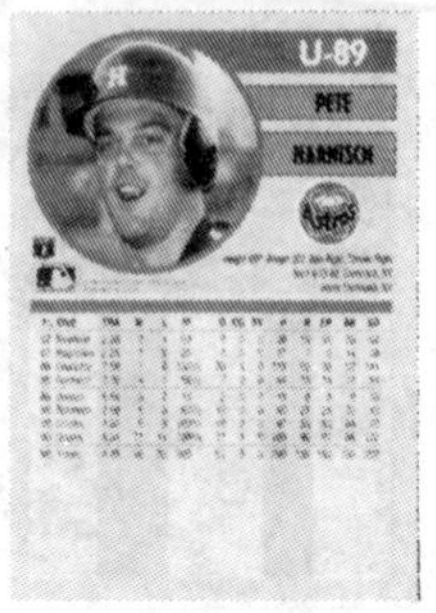

designed in the same style as the regular Fleer issue.

		MT	NR MT	EX
Complete Set (132):		6.00	4.50	2.50
Common Player:		.06	.05	.02
1	Glenn Davis	.06	.05	.02
2	Dwight Evans	.08	.06	.03
3	Jose Mesa(FC)	.08	.06	.03
4	Jack Clark	.12	.09	.05
5	Danny Darwin	.06	.05	.02
6	Steve Lyons	.06	.05	.02
7	Mo Vaughn(FC)	.35	.25	.14
8	Floyd Bannister	.06	.05	.02
9	Gary Gaetti	.08	.06	.03
10	Dave Parker	.35	.25	.14
11	Joey Cora	.06	.05	.02
12	Charlie Hough	.06	.05	.02
13	Matt Merullo	.08	.06	.03
14	Warren Newson(FC)	.10	.08	.04
15	Tim Raines	.15	.11	.06
16	Albert Belle	.30	.25	.12
17	Glenallen Hill	.08	.06	.03
18	Shawn Hillegas	.06	.05	.02
19	Mark Lewis(FC)	.15	.11	.06
20	Charles Nagy(FC)	.25	.20	.10
21	Mark Whiten	.20	.15	.08
22	John Cerutti	.06	.05	.02
23	Rob Deer	.06	.05	.02
24	Mickey Tettleton	.08	.06	.03
25	Warren Cromartie	.06	.05	.02
26	Kirk Gibson	.08	.06	.03
27	David Howard(FC)	.15	.11	.06
28	Brent Mayne(FC)	.25	.20	.10
29	Dante Bichette	.06	.05	.02
30	Mark Lee(FC)	.08	.06	.03
31	Julio Machado	.06	.05	.02
32	Edwin Nunez	.06	.05	.02
33	Willie Randolph	.08	.06	.03
34	Franklin Stubbs	.06	.05	.02
35	Bill Wegman	.06	.05	.02
36	Chili Davis	.08	.06	.03
37	Chuck Knoblauch(FC)	.50	.40	.20
38	Scott Leius	.15	.11	.06
39	Jack Morris	.10	.08	.04
40	Mike Pagliarulo	.06	.05	.02
41	Lenny Webster(FC)	.06	.05	.02
42	John Habyan(FC)	.12	.09	.05
43	Steve Howe	.08	.06	.03
44	Jeff Johnson(FC)	.10	.08	.04
45	Scott Kamieniecki(FC)	.10	.08	.04
46	Pat Kelly(FC)	.25	.20	.10
47	Hensley Meulens	.12	.09	.05
48	Wade Taylor(FC)	.20	.15	.08
49	Bernie Williams(FC)	.20	.15	.08
50	Kirk Dressendorfer(FC)	.20	.15	.08
51	Ernest Riles	.06	.05	.02
52	Rich DeLucia(FC)	.08	.06	.03
53	Tracy Jones	.06	.05	.02
54	Bill Krueger	.06	.05	.02
55	Alonzo Powell(FC)	.06	.05	.02
56	Jeff Schaefer	.06	.05	.02
57	Russ Swan(FC)	.06	.05	.02
58	John Barfield(FC)	.06	.05	.02
59	Rich Gossage	.08	.06	.03
60	Jose Guzman	.06	.05	.02
61	Dean Palmer(FC)	.40	.30	.15
62	Ivan Rodriguez(FC)	1.00	.70	.40
63	Roberto Alomar	.25	.20	.10
64	Tom Candiotti	.06	.05	.02
65	Joe Carter	.15	.11	.06
66	Ed Sprague(FC)	.20	.15	.08
67	Pat Tabler	.06	.05	.02
68	Mike Timlin(FC)	.20	.15	.08
69	Devon White	.08	.06	.03
70	Rafael Belliard	.06	.05	.02
71	Juan Berenguer	.06	.05	.02
72	Sid Bream	.08	.06	.03
73	Marvin Freeman	.06	.05	.02
74	Kent Mercker	.08	.06	.03
75	Otis Nixon	.06	.05	.02
76	Terry Pendleton	.08	.06	.03
77	George Bell	.10	.08	.04
78	Danny Jackson	.06	.05	.02
79	Chuck McElroy	.06	.05	.02
80	Gary Scott(FC)	.06	.05	.02
81	Heathcliff Slocumb(FC)	.15	.11	.06
82	Dave Smith	.06	.05	.02
83	Rick Wilkins(FC)	.30	.25	.12
84	Freddie Benavides(FC)	.20	.15	.08
85	Ted Power	.06	.05	.02
86	Mo Sanford(FC)	.30	.25	.12
87	Jeff Bagwell(FC)	1.25	.90	.50
88	Steve Finley	.08	.06	.03
89	Pete Harnisch	.08	.06	.03
90	Darryl Kile(FC)	.20	.15	.08
91	Brett Butler	.08	.06	.03
92	John Candelaria	.06	.05	.02
93	Gary Carter	.08	.06	.03
94	Kevin Gross	.06	.05	.02
95	Bob Ojeda	.06	.05	.02
96	Darryl Strawberry	.30	.25	.12
97	Ivan Calderon	.08	.06	.03
98	Ron Hassey	.06	.05	.02
99	Gilberto Reyes	.08	.06	.03
100	Hubie Brooks	.08	.06	.03
101	Rick Cerone	.06	.05	.02
102	Vince Coleman	.08	.06	.03
103	Jeff Innis	.08	.06	.03
104	Pete Schourek(FC)	.20	.15	.08
105	Andy Ashby(FC)	.12	.09	.05
106	Wally Backman	.06	.05	.02
107	Darrin Fletcher(FC)	.12	.09	.05
108	Tommy Greene	.08	.06	.03
109	John Morris	.06	.05	.02
110	Mitch Williams	.08	.06	.03
111	Lloyd McClendon	.06	.05	.02
112	Orlando Merced(FC)	.40	.30	.15
113	Vicente Palacios	.06	.05	.02
114	Gary Varsho	.06	.05	.02
115	John Wehner(FC)	.15	.11	.06
116	Rex Hudler	.06	.05	.02
117	Tim Jones	.06	.05	.02
118	Geronimo Pena(FC)	.15	.11	.06
119	Gerald Perry	.06	.05	.02
120	Larry Andersen	.06	.05	.02
121	Jerald Clark	.06	.05	.02
122	Scott Coolbaugh	.08	.06	.03
123	Tony Fernandez	.08	.06	.03
124	Darrin Jackson	.06	.05	.02
125	Fred McGriff	.15	.11	.06
126	Jose Mota(FC)	.06	.05	.02
127	Tim Teufel	.06	.05	.02
128	Bud Black	.06	.05	.02
129	Mike Felder	.06	.05	.02
130	Willie McGee	.08	.06	.03
131	Dave Righetti	.08	.06	.03
132	Checklist	.06	.05	.02

1991 Fleer Ultra

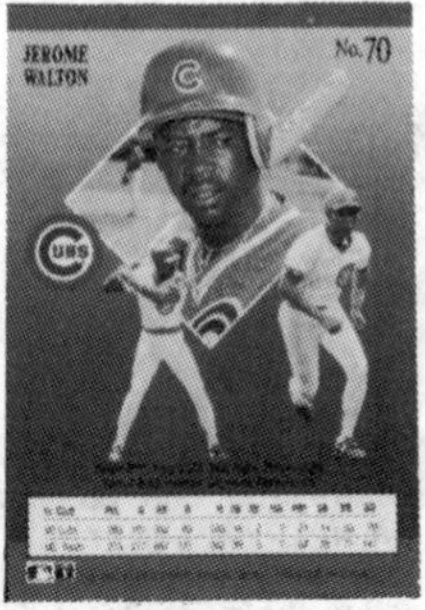

This 400-card set was originally going to be called the

Elite set, but Fleer chose to use the Ultra label. The card fronts feature gray borders surrounding full-color action photos. The backs feature three player photos and statistics. Hot Prospects and Great Performers are among the special cards featured within the set. This set is the premier release for Fleer Ultra.

		MT	NR MT	EX
Complete Set (400):		30.00	22.00	12.00
Common Player:		.06	.05	.02
1	Steve Avery	1.00	.70	.40
2	Jeff Blauser	.06	.05	.02
3	Francisco Cabrera	.08	.06	.03
4	Ron Gant	.45	.35	.20
5	Tom Glavine	.60	.45	.25
6	Tommy Gregg	.06	.05	.02
7	Dave Justice	1.25	.90	.50
8	Oddibe McDowell	.06	.05	.02
9	Greg Olson	.08	.06	.03
10	Terry Pendleton	.15	.11	.06
11	Lonnie Smith	.06	.05	.02
12	John Smoltz	.15	.11	.06
13	Jeff Treadway	.06	.05	.02
14	Glenn Davis	.10	.08	.04
15	Mike Devereaux	.08	.06	.03
16	Leo Gomez	.30	.25	.12
17	Chris Hoiles	.50	.40	.20
18	Dave Johnson	.06	.05	.02
19	Ben McDonald	.20	.15	.08
20	Randy Milligan	.08	.06	.03
21	Gregg Olson	.10	.08	.04
22	Joe Orsulak	.06	.05	.02
23	Bill Ripken	.06	.05	.02
24	Cal Ripken, Jr.	.60	.45	.25
25	David Segui	.15	.11	.06
26	Craig Worthington	.08	.06	.03
27	Wade Boggs	.25	.20	.10
28	Tom Bolton	.06	.05	.02
29	Tom Brunansky	.08	.06	.03
30	Ellis Burks	.12	.09	.05
31	Roger Clemens	.50	.40	.20
32	Mike Greenwell	.15	.11	.06
33	Greg Harris	.06	.05	.02
34	Daryl Irvine	.15	.11	.06
35	Mike Marshall	.06	.05	.02
36	Tim Naehring	.15	.11	.06
37	Tony Pena	.06	.05	.02
38	Phil Plantier	1.25	.90	.50
39	Carlos Quintana	.08	.06	.03
40	Jeff Reardon	.08	.06	.03
41	Jody Reed	.06	.05	.02
42	Luis Rivera	.06	.05	.02
43	Jim Abbott	.20	.15	.08
44	Chuck Finley	.15	.11	.06
45	Bryan Harvey	.08	.06	.03
46	Donnie Hill	.06	.05	.02
47	Jack Howell	.06	.05	.02
48	Wally Joyner	.15	.11	.06
49	Mark Langston	.12	.09	.05
50	Kirk McCaskill	.06	.05	.02
51	Lance Parrish	.08	.06	.03
52	Dick Schofield	.06	.05	.02
53	Lee Stevens	.15	.11	.06
54	Dave Winfield	.30	.25	.12
55	George Bell	.12	.09	.05
56	Damon Berryhill	.06	.05	.02
57	Mike Bielecki	.06	.05	.02
58	Andre Dawson	.20	.15	.08
59	Shawon Dunston	.10	.08	.04
60	Joe Girardi	.06	.05	.02
61	Mark Grace	.15	.11	.06
62	Mike Harkey	.08	.06	.03
63	Les Lancaster	.06	.05	.02
64	Greg Maddux	.30	.25	.12
65	Derrick May	.50	.40	.20
66	Ryne Sandberg	.60	.45	.25
67	Luis Salazar	.06	.05	.02
68	Dwight Smith	.06	.05	.02
69	Hector Villanueva	.08	.06	.03
70	Jerome Walton	.12	.09	.05
71	Mitch Williams	.08	.06	.03
72	Carlton Fisk	.20	.15	.08
73	Scott Fletcher	.06	.05	.02
74	Ozzie Guillen	.10	.08	.04
75	Greg Hibbard	.08	.06	.03
76	Lance Johnson	.06	.05	.02
77	Steve Lyons	.06	.05	.02
78	Jack McDowell	.12	.09	.05
79	Dan Pasqua	.06	.05	.02
80	Melido Perez	.06	.05	.02
81	Tim Raines	.10	.08	.04
82	Sammy Sosa	.60	.45	.25
83	Cory Snyder	.06	.05	.02
84	Bobby Thigpen	.08	.06	.03
85	Frank Thomas	6.00	4.50	2.50
86	Robin Ventura	.80	.60	.30
87	Todd Benzinger	.06	.05	.02
88	Glenn Braggs	.06	.05	.02
89	Tom Browning	.08	.06	.03
90	Norm Charlton	.08	.06	.03
91	Eric Davis	.15	.11	.06
92	Rob Dibble	.10	.08	.04
93	Bill Doran	.08	.06	.03
94	Mariano Duncan	.06	.05	.02
95	Billy Hatcher	.06	.05	.02
96	Barry Larkin	.15	.11	.06
97	Randy Myers	.08	.06	.03
98	Hal Morris	.20	.15	.08
99	Joe Oliver	.06	.05	.02
100	Paul O'Neill	.08	.06	.03
101	Jeff Reed	.06	.05	.02
102	Jose Rijo	.08	.06	.03
103	Chris Sabo	.10	.08	.04
104	Beau Allred	.06	.05	.02
105	Sandy Alomar,Jr.	.10	.08	.04
106	Carlos Baerga	1.50	1.25	.60
107	Albert Belle	.80	.60	.30
108	Jerry Browne	.06	.05	.02
109	Tom Candiotti	.06	.05	.02
110	Alex Cole	.06	.05	.02
111	John Farrell	.06	.05	.02
112	Felix Fermin	.06	.05	.02
113	Brook Jacoby	.06	.05	.02
114	Chris James	.06	.05	.02
115	Doug Jones	.06	.05	.02
116	Steve Olin	.06	.05	.02
117	Greg Swindell	.08	.06	.03
118	Turner Ward	.20	.15	.08
119	Mitch Webster	.06	.05	.02
120	Dave Bergman	.06	.05	.02
121	Cecil Fielder	.40	.30	.15
122	Travis Fryman	2.50	2.00	1.00
123	Mike Henneman	.08	.06	.03
124	Lloyd Moseby	.06	.05	.02
125	Dan Petry	.06	.05	.02
126	Tony Phillips	.06	.05	.02
127	Mark Salas	.06	.05	.02
128	Frank Tanana	.06	.05	.02
129	Alan Trammell	.15	.11	.06
130	Lou Whitaker	.08	.06	.03
131	Eric Anthony	.10	.08	.04
132	Craig Biggio	.15	.11	.06
133	Ken Caminiti	.08	.06	.03
134	Casey Candaele	.06	.05	.02
135	Andujar Cedeno	.50	.40	.20
136	Mark Davidson	.06	.05	.02
137	Jim Deshaies	.06	.05	.02
138	Mark Portugal	.06	.05	.02
139	Rafael Ramirez	.06	.05	.02
140	Mike Scott	.08	.06	.03
141	Eric Yelding	.06	.05	.02
142	Gerald Young	.06	.05	.02
143	Kevin Appier	.10	.08	.04
144	George Brett	.35	.25	.14
145	Jeff Conine	.50	.40	.20
146	Jim Eisenreich	.06	.05	.02
147	Tom Gordon	.10	.08	.04
148	Mark Gubicza	.08	.06	.03
149	Bo Jackson	.40	.30	.15
150	Brent Mayne	.15	.11	.06
151	Mike Macfarlane	.06	.05	.02
152	Brian McRae	.50	.40	.20
153	Jeff Montgomery	.08	.06	.03
154	Bret Saberhagen	.10	.08	.04
155	Kevin Seitzer	.06	.05	.02
156	Terry Shumpert	.06	.05	.02
157	Kurt Stillwell	.06	.05	.02
158	Danny Tartabull	.15	.11	.06
159	Tim Belcher	.08	.06	.03
160	Kal Daniels	.10	.08	.04
161	Alfredo Griffin	.06	.05	.02
162	Lenny Harris	.06	.05	.02
163	Jay Howell	.06	.05	.02
164	Ramon Martinez	.15	.11	.06
165	Mike Morgan	.06	.05	.02
166	Eddie Murray	.20	.15	.08
167	Jose Offerman	.15	.11	.06
168	Juan Samuel	.08	.06	.03
169	Mike Scioscia	.08	.06	.03
170	Mike Sharperson	.06	.05	.02
171	Darryl Strawberry	.15	.11	.06

		MT	NR MT	EX
172	Greg Brock	.06	.05	.02
173	Chuck Crim	.06	.05	.02
174	Jim Gantner	.08	.06	.03
175	Ted Higuera	.08	.06	.03
176	Mark Knudson	.06	.05	.02
177	Tim McIntosh	.08	.06	.03
178	Paul Molitor	.25	.20	.10
179	Dan Plesac	.06	.05	.02
180	Gary Sheffield	.60	.45	.25
181	Bill Spiers	.06	.05	.02
182	B.J. Surhoff	.06	.05	.02
183	Greg Vaughn	.20	.15	.08
184	Robin Yount	.20	.15	.08
185	Rick Aguilera	.08	.06	.03
186	Greg Gagne	.06	.05	.02
187	Dan Gladden	.06	.05	.02
188	Brian Harper	.06	.05	.02
189	Kent Hrbek	.08	.06	.03
190	Gene Larkin	.06	.05	.02
191	Shane Mack	.08	.06	.03
192	Pedro Munoz	.20	.15	.08
193	Al Newman	.06	.05	.02
194	Junior Ortiz	.06	.05	.02
195	Kirby Puckett	.75	.60	.30
196	Kevin Tapani	.08	.06	.03
197	Dennis Boyd	.06	.05	.02
198	Tim Burke	.06	.05	.02
199	Ivan Calderon	.08	.06	.03
200	Delino DeShields	.30	.25	.12
201	Mike Fitzgerald	.06	.05	.02
202	Steve Frey	.06	.05	.02
203	Andres Galarraga	.08	.06	.03
204	Marquis Grissom	.40	.30	.15
205	Dave Martinez	.06	.05	.02
206	Dennis Martinez	.08	.06	.03
207	Junior Noboa	.06	.05	.02
208	Spike Owen	.06	.05	.02
209	Scott Ruskin	.06	.05	.02
210	Tim Wallach	.08	.06	.03
211	Daryl Boston	.06	.05	.02
212	Vince Coleman	.10	.08	.04
213	David Cone	.10	.08	.04
214	Ron Darling	.08	.06	.03
215	Kevin Elster	.06	.05	.02
216	Sid Fernandez	.08	.06	.03
217	John Franco	.08	.06	.03
218	Dwight Gooden	.12	.09	.05
219	Tom Herr	.06	.05	.02
220	Todd Hundley	.15	.11	.06
221	Gregg Jefferies	.15	.11	.06
222	Howard Johnson	.15	.11	.06
223	Dave Magadan	.10	.08	.04
224	Kevin McReynolds	.10	.08	.04
225	Keith Miller	.06	.05	.02
226	Mackey Sasser	.06	.05	.02
227	Frank Viola	.10	.08	.04
228	Jesse Barfield	.08	.06	.03
229	Greg Cadaret	.06	.05	.02
230	Alvaro Espinoza	.06	.05	.02
231	Bob Geren	.06	.05	.02
232	Lee Guetterman	.06	.05	.02
233	Mel Hall	.08	.06	.03
234	Andy Hawkins	.06	.05	.02
235	Roberto Kelly	.10	.08	.04
236	Tim Leary	.06	.05	.02
237	Jim Leyritz	.06	.05	.02
238	Kevin Maas	.10	.08	.04
239	Don Mattingly	.30	.25	.12
240	Hensley Meulens	.10	.08	.04
241	Eric Plunk	.06	.05	.02
242	Steve Sax	.08	.06	.03
243	Todd Burns	.06	.05	.02
244	Jose Canseco	.40	.30	.15
245	Dennis Eckersley	.10	.08	.04
246	Mike Gallego	.06	.05	.02
247	Dave Henderson	.10	.08	.04
248	Rickey Henderson	.30	.25	.12
249	Rick Honeycutt	.06	.05	.02
250	Carney Lansford	.08	.06	.03
251	Mark McGwire	.30	.25	.12
252	Mike Moore	.06	.05	.02
253	Terry Steinbach	.06	.05	.02
254	Dave Stewart	.10	.08	.04
255	Walt Weiss	.06	.05	.02
256	Bob Welch	.08	.06	.03
257	Curt Young	.06	.05	.02
258	Wes Chamberlain	.30	.25	.12
259	Pat Combs	.08	.06	.03
260	Darren Daulton	.06	.05	.02
261	Jose DeJesus	.06	.05	.02
262	Len Dykstra	.15	.11	.06
263	Charlie Hayes	.08	.06	.03
264	Von Hayes	.08	.06	.03
265	Ken Howell	.06	.05	.02
266	John Kruk	.08	.06	.03
267	Roger McDowell	.08	.06	.03
268	Mickey Morandini	.15	.11	.06
269	Terry Mulholland	.08	.06	.03
270	Dale Murphy	.10	.08	.04
271	Randy Ready	.06	.05	.02
272	Dickie Thon	.06	.05	.02
273	Stan Belinda	.06	.05	.02
274	Jay Bell	.08	.06	.03
275	Barry Bonds	.75	.60	.30
276	Bobby Bonilla	.25	.20	.10
277	Doug Drabek	.10	.08	.04
278	Carlos Garcia	.75	.60	.30
279	Neal Heaton	.06	.05	.02
280	Jeff King	.08	.06	.03
281	Bill Landrum	.06	.05	.02
282	Mike LaValliere	.06	.05	.02
283	Jose Lind	.06	.05	.02
284	Orlando Merced	.70	.50	.30
285	Gary Redus	.06	.05	.02
286	Don Slaught	.06	.05	.02
287	Andy Van Slyke	.10	.08	.04
288	Jose DeLeon	.06	.05	.02
289	Pedro Guerrero	.10	.08	.04
290	Ray Lankford	.60	.45	.25
291	Joe Magrane	.08	.06	.03
292	Jose Oquendo	.06	.05	.02
293	Tom Pagnozzi	.06	.05	.02
294	Bryn Smith	.06	.05	.02
295	Lee Smith	.08	.06	.03
296	Ozzie Smith	.20	.15	.08
297	Milt Thompson	.06	.05	.02
298	Craig Wilson	.12	.09	.05
299	Todd Zeile	.20	.15	.08
300	Shawn Abner	.06	.05	.02
301	Andy Benes	.15	.11	.06
302	Paul Faries	.15	.11	.06
303	Tony Gwynn	.20	.15	.08
304	Greg Harris	.06	.05	.02
305	Thomas Howard	.10	.08	.04
306	Bruce Hurst	.08	.06	.03
307	Craig Lefferts	.06	.05	.02
308	Fred McGriff	.50	.40	.20
309	Dennis Rasmussen	.06	.05	.02
310	Bip Roberts	.08	.06	.03
311	Benito Santiago	.10	.08	.04
312	Garry Templeton	.06	.05	.02
313	Ed Whitson	.06	.05	.02
314	Dave Anderson	.06	.05	.02
315	Kevin Bass	.06	.05	.02
316	Jeff Brantley	.06	.05	.02
317	John Burkett	.08	.06	.03
318	Will Clark	.50	.40	.20
319	Steve Decker	.30	.25	.12
320	Scott Garrelts	.06	.05	.02
321	Terry Kennedy	.06	.05	.02
322	Mark Leonard	.20	.15	.08
323	Darren Lewis	.30	.25	.12
324	Greg Litton	.06	.05	.02
325	Willie McGee	.10	.08	.04
326	Kevin Mitchell	.15	.11	.06
327	Don Robinson	.06	.05	.02
328	Andres Santana	.25	.20	.10
329	Robby Thompson	.06	.05	.02
330	Jose Uribe	.06	.05	.02
331	Matt Williams	.25	.20	.10
332	Scott Bradley	.06	.05	.02
334	Alvin Davis	.08	.06	.03
335	Ken Griffey, Sr.	.08	.06	.03
336	Ken Griffey, Jr.	2.75	2.00	1.00
337	Erik Hanson	.10	.08	.04
338	Brian Holman	.06	.05	.02
339	Randy Johnson	.08	.06	.03
340	Edgar Martinez	.08	.06	.03
341	Tino Martinez	.20	.15	.08
342	Pete O'Brien	.06	.05	.02
343	Harold Reynolds	.08	.06	.03
344	David Valle	.06	.05	.02
345	Omar Vizquel	.06	.05	.02
346	Brad Arnsberg	.06	.05	.02
347	Kevin Brown	.06	.05	.02
348	Julio Franco	.10	.08	.04
349	Jeff Huson	.06	.05	.02
350	Rafael Palmeiro	.20	.15	.08
351	Geno Petralli	.06	.05	.02
352	Gary Pettis	.06	.05	.02
353	Kenny Rogers	.06	.05	.02
354	Jeff Russell	.06	.05	.02

		MT	NR MT	EX
355	Nolan Ryan	1.25	.90	.50
356	Ruben Sierra	.25	.20	.10
357	Bobby Witt	.08	.06	.03
358	Roberto Alomar	1.25	.90	.50
359	Pat Borders	.06	.05	.02
360	Joe Carter	.30	.25	.12
361	Kelly Gruber	.08	.06	.03
362	Tom Henke	.08	.06	.03
363	Glenallen Hill	.08	.06	.03
364	Jimmy Key	.08	.06	.03
365	Manny Lee	.06	.05	.02
366	Rance Mulliniks	.06	.05	.02
367	John Olerud	1.25	.90	.50
368	Dave Stieb	.08	.06	.03
369	Duane Ward	.06	.05	.02
370	David Wells	.06	.05	.02
371	Mark Whiten	.30	.25	.12
372	Mookie Wilson	.06	.05	.02
373	Willie Banks	.30	.25	.12
374	Steve Carter	.06	.05	.02
375	Scott Chiamparino	.10	.08	.04
376	Steve Chitren	.10	.08	.04
377	Darrin Fletcher	.10	.08	.04
378	Rich Garces	.10	.08	.04
379	Reggie Jefferson	.40	.30	.15
380	Eric Karros	1.50	1.25	.60
381	Pat Kelly	.70	.50	.30
382	Chuck Knoblauch	.80	.60	.30
383	Denny Neagle	.25	.20	.10
384	Dan Opperman	.20	.15	.08
385	John Ramos	.10	.08	.04
386	Henry Rodriguez	.30	.25	.12
387	Mo Vaughn	1.50	1.25	.60
388	Gerald Williams	.40	.30	.15
389	Mike York	.20	.15	.08
390	Eddie Zosky	.20	.15	.08
391	Great Performer (Barry Bonds)	.20	.15	.08
392	Great Performer (Cecil Fielder)	.20	.15	.08
393	Great Performer (Rickey Henderson)	.20	.15	.08
394	Great Performer (Dave Justice)	.40	.30	.15
395	Great Performer (Nolan Ryan)	.40	.30	.15
396	Great Performer (Bobby Thigpen)	.10	.08	.04
397	Checklist	.06	.05	.02
398	Checklist	.06	.05	.02
399	Checklist	.06	.05	.02
400	Checklist	.06	.05	.02

1991 Fleer Ultra Gold

Photos not available at press time

A three dimensional effect is presented on the front of the Fleer Ultra Gold cards. The flip sides feature career information. The cards are numbered on the back. The Puckett and Sandberg cards feature incorrect historical information on the backs.

		MT	NR MT	EX
Complete Set (10):		9.00	6.00	3.00
Common Player:		.40	.30	.15
1	Barry Bonds	1.50	.90	.50
2	Will Clark	1.25	.90	.50
3	Doug Drabek	.40	.30	.15
4	Ken Griffey, Jr.	3.00	2.25	1.25
5	Rickey Henderson	1.00	.75	.40
6	Bo Jackson	1.00	.75	.40
7	Ramon Martinez	.40	.30	.15
8	Kirby Puckett	1.25	.90	.50
9	Chris Sabo	.40	.30	.15
10	Ryne Sandberg	1.50	1.25	.60

1991 Fleer Ultra Update

Photos not available at press time

This 120-card set was produced as a supplement to the premier Fleer Ultra set. The cards feature the same style as the regular Fleer Ultra cards. The 4-photo Ultra look is featured on each card. The cards were sold in full color, shrinkwrapped boxes.

		MT	NR MT	EX
Complete Set (120):		75.00	56.00	30.00
Common Player:		.15	.11	.06
1	Dwight Evans	.15	.11	.06
2	Chito Martinez	.25	.20	.10
3	Bob Melvin	.15	.11	.06
4	Mike Mussina	8.00	6.00	3.25
5	Jack Clark	.15	.11	.06
6	Dana Kiecker	.15	.11	.06
7	Steve Lyons	.15	.11	.06
8	Gary Gaetti	.15	.11	.06
9	Dave Gallagher	.15	.11	.06
10	Dave Parker	.50	.40	.20
11	Luis Polonia	.15	.11	.06
12	Luis Sojo	.15	.11	.06
13	Wilson Alvarez	3.00	2.25	1.25
14	Alex Fernandez	7.00	5.25	2.75
15	Craig Grebeck	.15	.11	.06
16	Ron Karkovice	.15	.11	.06
17	Warren Newson	.15	.11	.06
18	Scott Radinsky	.15	.11	.06
19	Glenallen Hill	.15	.11	.06
20	Charles Nagy	1.00	.70	.40
21	Mark Whiten	1.75	1.25	.70
22	Milt Cuyler	.15	.11	.06
23	Paul Gibson	.15	.11	.06
24	Mickey Tettleton	.40	.30	.15
25	Todd Benzinger	.15	.11	.06
26	Storm Davis	.15	.11	.06
27	Kirk Gibson	.15	.11	.06
28	Bill Pecota	.15	.11	.06
29	Gary Thurman	.15	.11	.06
30	Darryl Hamilton	.35	.25	.14
31	Jaime Navarro	.15	.11	.06
32	Willie Randolph	.15	.11	.06
33	Bill Wegman	.15	.11	.06
34	Randy Bush	.15	.11	.06
35	Chili Davis	.15	.11	.06
36	Scott Erickson	.50	.40	.20
37	Chuck Knoblauch	1.50	1.25	.60
38	Scott Leius	.15	.11	.06
39	Jack Morris	.20	.15	.08
40	John Habyan	.15	.11	.06
41	Pat Kelly	.75	.60	.30
42	Matt Nokes	.15	.11	.06
43	Scott Sanderson	.15	.11	.06
44	Bernie Williams	1.50	1.25	.60
45	Harold Baines	.20	.15	.08
46	Brook Jacoby	.15	.11	.06
47	Ernest Riles	.15	.11	.06
48	Willie Wilson	.15	.11	.06
49	Jay Buhner	.75	.60	.30
50	Rich DeLucia	.15	.11	.06
51	Mike Jackson	.15	.11	.06
52	Bill Krueger	.15	.11	.06
53	Bill Swift	.15	.11	.06

		MT	NR MT	EX
54	Brian Downing	.15	.11	.06
55	Juan Gonzalez	40.00	30.00	16.00
56	Dean Palmer	5.00	3.75	2.00
57	Kevin Reimer	.15	.11	.06
58	Ivan Rodriguez	5.00	3.75	2.00
59	Tom Candiotti	.15	.11	.06
60	Juan Guzman	8.00	6.00	3.25
61	Bob MacDonald	.15	.11	.06
62	Greg Myers	.15	.11	.06
63	Ed Sprague	.75	.60	.30
64	Devon White	.30	.25	.12
65	Rafael Belliard	.15	.11	.06
66	Juan Berenguer	.15	.11	.06
67	Brian Hunter	.20	.15	.08
68	Kent Mercker	.15	.11	.06
69	Otis Nixon	.15	.11	.06
70	Danny Jackson	.15	.11	.06
71	Chuck McElroy	.15	.11	.06
72	Gary Scott	.15	.11	.06
73	Heathcliff Slocumb	.15	.11	.06
74	Chico Walker	.15	.11	.06
75	Rick Wilkins	3.00	2.25	1.25
76	Chris Hammond	.75	.60	.30
77	Luis Quinones	.15	.11	.06
78	Herm Winningham	.15	.11	.06
79	Jeff Bagwell	7.00	5.25	2.75
80	Jim Corsi	.15	.11	.06
81	Steve Finley	.15	.11	.06
82	Luis Gonzalez	2.50	2.00	1.00
83	Pete Harnisch	.15	.11	.06
84	Darryl Kile	3.50	2.75	1.50
85	Brett Butler	.15	.11	.06
86	Gary Carter	.30	.25	.12
87	Tim Crews	.15	.11	.06
88	Orel Hershiser	.15	.11	.06
89	Bob Ojeda	.15	.11	.06
90	Bret Barberie	.60	.45	.25
91	Barry Jones	.15	.11	.06
92	Gilberto Reyes	.15	.11	.06
93	Larry Walker	3.00	2.25	1.25
94	Hubie Brooks	.15	.11	.06
95	Tim Burke	.15	.11	.06
96	Rick Cerone	.15	.11	.06
97	Jeff Innis	.15	.11	.06
98	Wally Backman	.15	.11	.06
99	Tommy Greene	2.00	1.50	.80
100	Ricky Jordan	.15	.11	.06
101	Mitch Williams	.15	.11	.06
102	John Smiley	.15	.11	.06
103	Randy Tomlin	.40	.30	.15
104	Gary Varsho	.15	.11	.06
105	Cris Carpenter	.15	.11	.06
106	Ken Hill	.75	.60	.30
107	Felix Jose	.25	.20	.10
108	Omar Oliveras	.40	.30	.15
109	Gerald Perry	.15	.11	.06
110	Jerald Clark	.15	.11	.06
111	Tony Fernandez	.15	.11	.06
112	Darrin Jackson	.15	.11	.06
113	Mike Maddux	.15	.11	.06
114	Tim Teufel	.15	.11	.06
115	Bud Black	.15	.11	.06
116	Kelly Downs	.15	.11	.06
117	Mike Felder	.15	.11	.06
118	Willie McGee	.15	.11	.06
119	Trevor Wilson	.15	.11	.06
120	Checklist	.15	.11	.06

1992 Fleer

For the second consecutive year, Fleer produced a 720-card set. The standard card fronts feature full-color action photos bordered in blue with the player's name, position and team logo on the right border. The backs feature another full-color action photo, biographical information and statistics. A special twelve card Roger Clemens subset is also included in the 1992 Fleer set. Three more Clemens cards are available through a mail-in offer, and 2,000 Roger Clemens autographed cards were inserted in 1992 packs. Once again the cards are numbered according to team. Subsets in the issue included Major League Propects (#652-680), Record Setters (#681-687), League Leaders (#688-697), Superstar Specials (#698-707) and ProVisions (#708-713), which for the first time were part of the regular numbered set rather tham limited edition insert cards.

		MT	NR MT	EX
Complete Set (720):		20.00	15.00	8.00
Common Player:		.04	.03	.02
1	Brady Anderson	.04	.03	.02
2	Jose Bautista	.04	.03	.02
3	Juan Bell	.06	.05	.02
4	Glenn Davis	.08	.06	.03
5	Mike Devereaux	.05	.04	.02
6	Dwight Evans	.08	.06	.03
7	Mike Flanagan	.04	.03	.02
8	Leo Gomez	.15	.11	.06
9	Chris Hoiles	.10	.08	.04
10	Sam Horn	.05	.04	.02
11	Tim Hulett	.04	.03	.02
12	Dave Johnson	.04	.03	.02
13	*Chito Martinez*(FC)	.20	.15	.08
14	Ben McDonald	.10	.08	.04
15	Bob Melvin	.04	.03	.02
16	*Luis Mercedes*(FC)	.15	.11	.06
17	Jose Mesa	.05	.04	.02
18	Bob Milacki	.05	.04	.02
19	Randy Milligan	.06	.05	.02
20	Mike Mussina	.50	.40	.20
21	Gregg Olson	.08	.06	.03
22	Joe Orsulak	.04	.03	.02
23	Jim Poole	.05	.04	.02
24	*Arthur Rhodes*(FC)	.20	.15	.08
25	Billy Ripken	.04	.03	.02
26	Cal Ripken, Jr.	.20	.15	.08
27	David Segui	.08	.06	.03
28	Roy Smith	.04	.03	.02
29	Anthony Telford	.04	.03	.02
30	Mark Williamson	.04	.03	.02
31	Craig Worthington	.06	.05	.02
32	Wade Boggs	.15	.11	.06
33	Tom Bolton	.04	.03	.02
34	Tom Brunansky	.05	.04	.02
35	Ellis Burks	.08	.06	.03
36	Jack Clark	.08	.06	.03
37	Roger Clemens	.15	.11	.06
38	Danny Darwin	.04	.03	.02
39	Mike Greenwell	.08	.06	.03
40	Joe Hesketh	.04	.03	.02
41	Daryl Irvine	.05	.04	.02
42	Dennis Lamp	.04	.03	.02
43	Tony Pena	.05	.04	.02
44	Phil Plantier	.25	.20	.10
45	Carlos Quintana	.06	.05	.02
46	Jeff Reardon	.08	.06	.03
47	Jody Reed	.05	.04	.02
48	Luis Rivera	.04	.03	.02
49	Mo Vaughn	.30	.25	.12
50	Jim Abbott	.10	.08	.04
51	Kyle Abbott	.08	.06	.03
52	*Ruben Amaro, Jr.*(FC)	.15	.11	.06
53	Scott Bailes	.04	.03	.02
54	*Chris Beasley*(FC)	.12	.09	.05
55	Mark Eichhorn	.04	.03	.02
56	Mike Fetters	.04	.03	.02
57	Chuck Finley	.08	.06	.03
58	Gary Gaetti	.08	.06	.03
59	Dave Gallagher	.05	.04	.02
60	Donnie Hill	.04	.03	.02
61	Bryan Harvey	.06	.05	.02
62	Wally Joyner	.10	.08	.04
63	Mark Langston	.10	.08	.04
64	Kirk McCaskill	.05	.04	.02
65	John Orton	.04	.03	.02
66	Lance Parrish	.06	.05	.02
67	Luis Polonia	.05	.04	.02
68	Bobby Rose	.05	.04	.02
69	Dick Schofield	.04	.03	.02

		MT	NR MT	EX
70	Luis Sojo	.05	.04	.02
71	Lee Stevens	.08	.06	.03
72	Dave Winfield	.12	.09	.05
73	Cliff Young	.06	.05	.02
74	Wilson Alvarez	.08	.06	.03
75	*Esteban Beltre*(FC)	.20	.15	.08
76	Joey Cora	.04	.03	.02
77	*Brian Drahman*(FC)	.15	.11	.06
78	Alex Fernandez	.15	.11	.06
79	Carlton Fisk	.10	.08	.04
80	Scott Fletcher	.04	.03	.02
81	Craig Grebeck	.04	.03	.02
82	Ozzie Guillen	.06	.05	.02
83	Greg Hibbard	.06	.05	.02
84	Charlie Hough	.05	.04	.02
85	Mike Huff	.05	.04	.02
86	Bo Jackson	.40	.30	.15
87	Lance Johnson	.04	.03	.02
88	Ron Karkovice	.04	.03	.02
89	Jack McDowell	.08	.06	.03
90	Matt Merullo	.04	.03	.02
91	*Warren Newson*	.15	.11	.06
92	Donn Pall	.04	.03	.02
93	Dan Pasqua	.05	.04	.02
94	Ken Patterson	.04	.03	.02
95	Melido Perez	.05	.04	.02
96	Scott Radinsky	.04	.03	.02
97	Tim Raines	.10	.08	.04
98	Sammy Sosa	.08	.06	.03
99	Bobby Thigpen	.08	.06	.03
100	Frank Thomas	1.00	.70	.40
101	Robin Ventura	.20	.15	.08
102	Mike Aldrete	.04	.03	.02
103	Sandy Alomar, Jr.	.10	.08	.04
104	Carlos Baerga	.15	.11	.06
105	Albert Belle	.15	.11	.06
106	Willie Blair	.05	.04	.02
107	Jerry Browne	.04	.03	.02
108	Alex Cole	.06	.05	.02
109	Felix Fermin	.04	.03	.02
110	Glenallen Hill	.06	.05	.02
111	Shawn Hillegas	.04	.03	.02
112	Chris James	.05	.04	.02
113	Reggie Jefferson(FC)	.20	.15	.08
114	Doug Jones	.05	.04	.02
115	Eric King	.04	.03	.02
116	Mark Lewis	.15	.11	.06
117	Carlos Martinez	.05	.04	.02
118	Charles Nagy	.08	.06	.03
119	Rod Nichols	.04	.03	.02
120	Steve Olin	.04	.03	.02
121	Jesse Orosco	.04	.03	.02
122	Rudy Seanez	.04	.03	.02
123	Joel Skinner	.04	.03	.02
124	Greg Swindell	.08	.06	.03
125	*Jim Thome*(FC)	.20	.15	.08
126	Mark Whiten	.10	.08	.04
127	Scott Aldred	.10	.08	.04
128	Andy Allanson	.04	.03	.02
129	John Cerutti	.04	.03	.02
130	Milt Cuyler	.10	.08	.04
131	*Mike Dalton*(FC)	.15	.11	.06
132	Rob Deer	.05	.04	.02
133	Cecil Fielder	.15	.11	.06
134	Travis Fryman	.25	.20	.10
135	*Dan Gakeler*(FC)	.15	.11	.06
136	Paul Gibson	.04	.03	.02
137	Bill Gullickson	.05	.04	.02
138	Mike Henneman	.05	.04	.02
139	Pete Incaviglia	.05	.04	.02
140	*Mark Leiter*(FC)	.12	.09	.05
141	*Scott Livingstone*(FC)	.20	.15	.08
142	Lloyd Moseby	.04	.03	.02
143	Tony Phillips	.05	.04	.02
144	Mark Salas	.04	.03	.02
145	Frank Tanana	.05	.04	.02
146	Walt Terrell	.04	.03	.02
147	Mickey Tettleton	.06	.05	.02
148	Alan Trammell	.10	.08	.04
149	Lou Whitaker	.08	.06	.03
150	Kevin Appier	.06	.05	.02
151	Luis Aquino	.04	.03	.02
152	Todd Benzinger	.05	.04	.02
153	Mike Boddicker	.05	.04	.02
154	George Brett	.15	.11	.06
155	Storm Davis	.05	.04	.02
156	Jim Eisenreich	.04	.03	.02
157	Kirk Gibson	.08	.06	.03
158	Tom Gordon	.06	.05	.02
159	Mark Gubicza	.06	.05	.02
160	*David Howard*(FC)	.20	.15	.08
161	Mike Macfarlane	.05	.04	.02
162	Brent Mayne	.05	.04	.02
163	Brian McRae	.25	.20	.10
164	Jeff Montgomery	.05	.04	.02
165	Bill Pecota	.04	.03	.02
166	*Harvey Pulliam*(FC)	.15	.11	.06
167	Bret Saberhagen	.08	.06	.03
168	Kevin Seitzer	.05	.04	.02
169	Terry Shumpert	.05	.04	.02
170	Kurt Stillwell	.05	.04	.02
171	Danny Tartabull	.08	.06	.03
172	Gary Thurman	.04	.03	.02
173	Dante Bichette	.05	.04	.02
174	Kevin Brown	.04	.03	.02
175	Chuck Crim	.04	.03	.02
176	Jim Gantner	.05	.04	.02
177	Darryl Hamilton	.05	.04	.02
178	Ted Higuera	.06	.05	.02
179	Darren Holmes	.04	.03	.02
180	Mark Lee	.04	.03	.02
181	Julio Machado	.04	.03	.02
182	Paul Molitor	.15	.11	.06
183	Jaime Navarro	.06	.05	.02
184	Edwin Nunez	.04	.03	.02
185	Dan Plesac	.05	.04	.02
186	Willie Randolph	.05	.04	.02
187	Ron Robinson	.04	.03	.02
188	Gary Sheffield	.25	.20	.10
189	Bill Spiers	.05	.04	.02
190	B.J. Surhoff	.05	.04	.02
191	Dale Sveum	.04	.03	.02
192	Greg Vaughn	.10	.08	.04
193	Bill Wegman	.05	.04	.02
194	Robin Yount	.15	.11	.06
195	Rick Aguilera	.05	.04	.02
196	Allan Anderson	.04	.03	.02
197	Steve Bedrosian	.04	.03	.02
198	Randy Bush	.04	.03	.02
199	Larry Casian(FC)	.05	.04	.02
200	Chili Davis	.06	.05	.02
201	Scott Erickson	.20	.15	.08
202	Greg Gagne	.04	.03	.02
203	Dan Gladden	.04	.03	.02
204	Brian Harper	.05	.04	.02
205	Kent Hrbek	.06	.05	.02
206	Chuck Knoblauch	.20	.15	.08
207	Gene Larkin	.04	.03	.02
208	Terry Leach	.04	.03	.02
209	Scott Leius	.10	.08	.04
210	Shane Mack	.08	.06	.03
211	Jack Morris	.08	.06	.03
212	Pedro Munoz(FC)	.20	.15	.08
213	*Denny Neagle*(FC)	.20	.15	.08
214	Al Newman	.04	.03	.02
215	Junior Ortiz	.04	.03	.02
216	Mike Pagliarulo	.04	.03	.02
217	Kirby Puckett	.15	.11	.06
218	Paul Sorrento	.06	.05	.02
219	Kevin Tapani	.08	.06	.03
220	Lenny Webster	.06	.05	.02
221	Jesse Barfield	.06	.05	.02
222	Greg Cadaret	.04	.03	.02
223	Dave Eiland	.04	.03	.02
224	Alvaro Espinoza	.04	.03	.02
225	Steve Farr	.05	.04	.02
226	Bob Geren	.04	.03	.02
227	Lee Guetterman	.04	.03	.02
228	John Habyan	.04	.03	.02
229	Mel Hall	.06	.05	.02
230	Steve Howe	.06	.05	.02
231	*Mike Humphreys*(FC)	.20	.15	.08
232	*Scott Kamieniecki*	.15	.11	.06
233	Pat Kelly	.15	.11	.06
234	Roberto Kelly	.08	.06	.03
235	Tim Leary	.04	.03	.02
236	Kevin Maas	.15	.11	.06
237	Don Mattingly	.25	.20	.10
238	Hensley Meulens	.08	.06	.03
239	Matt Nokes	.06	.05	.02
240	Pascual Perez	.05	.04	.02
241	Eric Plunk	.04	.03	.02
242	*John Ramos*(FC)	.15	.11	.06
243	Scott Sanderson	.05	.04	.02
244	Steve Sax	.06	.05	.02
245	*Wade Taylor*	.15	.11	.06
246	Randy Velarde	.04	.03	.02
247	Bernie Williams	.20	.15	.08
248	Troy Afenir	.05	.04	.02
249	Harold Baines	.08	.06	.03
250	Lance Blankenship	.04	.03	.02
251	*Mike Bordick*(FC)	.10	.08	.04

		MT	NR MT	EX
252	Jose Canseco	.12	.09	.05
253	Steve Chitren	.06	.05	.02
254	Ron Darling	.06	.05	.02
255	Dennis Eckersley	.08	.06	.03
256	Mike Gallego	.04	.03	.02
257	Dave Henderson	.08	.06	.03
258	Rickey Henderson	.20	.15	.08
259	Rick Honeycutt	.04	.03	.02
260	Brook Jacoby	.06	.05	.02
261	Carney Lansford	.06	.05	.02
262	Mark McGwire	.15	.11	.06
263	Mike Moore	.05	.04	.02
264	Gene Nelson	.04	.03	.02
265	Jamie Quirk	.04	.03	.02
266	*Joe Slusarski*(FC)	.15	.11	.06
267	Terry Steinbach	.06	.05	.02
268	Dave Stewart	.08	.06	.03
269	Todd Van Poppel(FC)	.20	.15	.08
270	Walt Weiss	.06	.05	.02
271	Bob Welch	.06	.05	.02
272	Curt Young	.04	.03	.02
273	Scott Bradley	.04	.03	.02
274	Greg Briley	.04	.03	.02
275	Jay Buhner	.06	.05	.02
276	Henry Cotto	.04	.03	.02
277	Alvin Davis	.06	.05	.02
278	Rich DeLucia	.06	.05	.02
279	Ken Griffey, Jr.	.70	.50	.30
280	Erik Hanson	.08	.06	.03
281	Brian Holman	.05	.04	.02
282	Mike Jackson	.04	.03	.02
283	Randy Johnson	.08	.06	.03
284	Tracy Jones	.04	.03	.02
285	Bill Krueger	.04	.03	.02
286	Edgar Martinez	.06	.05	.02
287	Tino Martinez	.10	.08	.04
288	Rob Murphy	.04	.03	.02
289	Pete O'Brien	.04	.03	.02
290	Alonzo Powell	.06	.05	.02
291	Harold Reynolds	.06	.05	.02
292	Mike Schooler	.05	.04	.02
293	Russ Swan	.04	.03	.02
294	Bill Swift	.04	.03	.02
295	Dave Valle	.04	.03	.02
296	Omar Vizquel	.04	.03	.02
297	Gerald Alexander	.05	.04	.02
298	Brad Arnsberg	.05	.04	.02
299	Kevin Brown	.05	.04	.02
300	Jack Daugherty	.04	.03	.02
301	Mario Diaz	.04	.03	.02
302	Brian Downing	.05	.04	.02
303	Julio Franco	.08	.06	.03
304	Juan Gonzalez	.70	.50	.30
305	Rich Gossage	.05	.04	.02
306	Jose Guzman	.05	.04	.02
307	*Jose Hernandez*(FC)	.20	.15	.08
308	Jeff Huson	.05	.04	.02
309	Mike Jeffcoat	.04	.03	.02
310	*Terry Mathews*(FC)	.20	.15	.08
311	Rafael Palmeiro	.10	.08	.04
312	Dean Palmer	.20	.15	.08
313	Geno Petralli	.04	.03	.02
314	Gary Pettis	.04	.03	.02
315	Kevin Reimer	.05	.04	.02
316	*Ivan Rodriguez*	.30	.25	.12
317	Kenny Rogers	.05	.04	.02
318	*Wayne Rosenthal*(FC)	.10	.08	.04
319	Jeff Russell	.05	.04	.02
320	Nolan Ryan	.25	.20	.10
321	Ruben Sierra	.15	.11	.06
322	Jim Acker	.04	.03	.02
323	Roberto Alomar	.10	.08	.04
324	Derek Bell	.35	.25	.14
325	Pat Borders	.05	.04	.02
326	Tom Candiotti	.05	.04	.02
327	Joe Carter	.08	.06	.03
328	Rob Ducey	.05	.04	.02
329	Kelly Gruber	.08	.06	.03
330	*Juan Guzman*(FC)	.30	.25	.12
331	Tom Henke	.06	.05	.02
332	Jimmy Key	.06	.05	.02
333	Manny Lee	.05	.04	.02
334	Al Leiter	.04	.03	.02
335	*Bob MacDonald*(FC)	.10	.08	.04
336	Candy Maldonado	.05	.04	.02
337	Rance Mulliniks	.04	.03	.02
338	Greg Myers	.05	.04	.02
339	John Olerud	.30	.25	.12
340	*Ed Sprague*	.10	.08	.04
341	Dave Stieb	.08	.06	.03
342	Todd Stottlemyre	.05	.04	.02

		MT	NR MT	EX
343	*Mike Timlin*	.15	.11	.06
344	Duane Ward	.05	.04	.02
345	David Wells	.05	.04	.02
346	Devon White	.08	.06	.03
347	Mookie Wilson	.04	.03	.02
348	Eddie Zosky	.08	.06	.03
349	Steve Avery	.20	.15	.08
350	Mike Bell(FC)	.08	.06	.03
351	Rafael Belliard	.04	.03	.02
352	Juan Berenguer	.04	.03	.02
353	Jeff Blauser	.05	.04	.02
354	Sid Bream	.05	.04	.02
355	Francisco Cabrera	.05	.04	.02
356	Marvin Freeman	.04	.03	.02
357	Ron Gant	.15	.11	.06
358	Tom Glavine	.15	.11	.06
359	*Brian Hunter*(FC)	.25	.20	.10
360	Dave Justice	.30	.25	.12
361	Charlie Leibrandt	.04	.03	.02
362	Mark Lemke	.05	.04	.02
363	Kent Mercker	.05	.04	.02
364	*Keith Mitchell*(FC)	.20	.15	.08
365	Greg Olson	.05	.04	.02
366	Terry Pendleton	.08	.06	.03
367	*Armando Reynoso*(FC)	.15	.11	.06
368	Deion Sanders	.15	.11	.06
369	Lonnie Smith	.04	.03	.02
370	Pete Smith	.04	.03	.02
371	John Smoltz	.10	.08	.04
372	Mike Stanton	.05	.04	.02
373	Jeff Treadway	.05	.04	.02
374	*Mark Wohlers*(FC)	.25	.20	.10
375	Paul Assenmacher	.04	.03	.02
376	George Bell	.08	.06	.03
377	Shawn Boskie	.06	.05	.02
378	*Frank Castillo*(FC)	.25	.20	.10
379	Andre Dawson	.12	.09	.05
380	Shawon Dunston	.08	.06	.03
381	Mark Grace	.08	.06	.03
382	Mike Harkey	.05	.04	.02
383	Danny Jackson	.05	.04	.02
384	Les Lancaster	.04	.03	.02
385	*Cedric Landrum*(FC)	.15	.11	.06
386	Greg Maddux	.06	.05	.02
387	Derrick May	.15	.11	.06
388	Chuck McElroy	.04	.03	.02
389	Ryne Sandberg	.20	.15	.08
390	*Heathcliff Slocumb*	.10	.08	.04
391	Dave Smith	.05	.04	.02
392	Dwight Smith	.05	.04	.02
393	Rick Sutcliffe	.05	.04	.02
394	Hector Villanueva	.06	.05	.02
395	*Chico Walker*(FC)	.10	.08	.04
396	Jerome Walton	.06	.05	.02
397	*Rick Wilkins*	.15	.11	.06
398	Jack Armstrong	.06	.05	.02
399	*Freddie Benavides*	.10	.08	.04
400	Glenn Braggs	.05	.04	.02
401	Tom Browning	.06	.05	.02
402	Norm Charlton	.06	.05	.02
403	Eric Davis	.12	.09	.05
404	Rob Dibble	.08	.06	.03
405	Bill Doran	.05	.04	.02
406	Mariano Duncan	.05	.04	.02
407	*Kip Gross*(FC)	.10	.08	.04
408	Chris Hammond	.06	.05	.02
409	Billy Hatcher	.04	.03	.02
410	*Chris Jones*(FC)	.15	.11	.06
411	Barry Larkin	.10	.08	.04
412	Hal Morris	.10	.08	.04
413	Randy Myers	.05	.04	.02
414	Joe Oliver	.05	.04	.02
415	Paul O'Neill	.06	.05	.02
416	Ted Power	.04	.03	.02
417	Luis Quinones	.04	.03	.02
418	Jeff Reed	.04	.03	.02
419	Jose Rijo	.08	.06	.03
420	Chris Sabo	.08	.06	.03
421	Reggie Sanders(FC)	.15	.11	.06
422	Scott Scudder	.05	.04	.02
423	Glenn Sutko	.05	.04	.02
424	Eric Anthony	.08	.06	.03
425	*Jeff Bagwell*	.30	.25	.12
426	Craig Biggio	.08	.06	.03
427	Ken Caminiti	.05	.04	.02
428	Casey Candaele	.04	.03	.02
429	Mike Capel	.04	.03	.02
430	Andujar Cedeno	.15	.11	.06
431	Jim Corsi	.04	.03	.02
432	Mark Davidson	.04	.03	.02
433	Steve Finley	.06	.05	.02

		MT	NR MT	EX
434	Luis Gonzalez	.20	.15	.08
435	Pete Harnisch	.06	.05	.02
436	Dwayne Henry	.04	.03	.02
437	Xavier Hernandez	.04	.03	.02
438	Jimmy Jones	.04	.03	.02
439	*Darryl Kile*	.10	.08	.04
440	*Rob Mallicoat*(FC)	.15	.11	.06
441	*Andy Mota*(FC)	.15	.11	.06
442	Al Osuna	.05	.04	.02
443	Mark Portugal	.04	.03	.02
444	*Scott Servais*(FC)	.10	.08	.04
445	Mike Simms	.10	.08	.04
446	Gerald Young	.04	.03	.02
447	Tim Belcher	.06	.05	.02
448	Brett Butler	.08	.06	.03
449	John Candelaria	.04	.03	.02
450	Gary Carter	.08	.06	.03
451	Dennis Cook	.04	.03	.02
452	Tim Crews	.04	.03	.02
453	Kal Daniels	.08	.06	.03
454	Jim Gott	.04	.03	.02
455	Alfredo Griffin	.04	.03	.02
456	Kevin Gross	.04	.03	.02
457	Chris Gwynn	.04	.03	.02
458	Lenny Harris	.05	.04	.02
459	Orel Hershiser	.08	.06	.03
460	Jay Howell	.05	.04	.02
461	Stan Javier	.04	.03	.02
462	Eric Karros(FC)	.40	.30	.15
463	Ramon Martinez	.12	.09	.05
464	Roger McDowell	.05	.04	.02
465	Mike Morgan	.05	.04	.02
466	Eddie Murray	.12	.09	.05
467	Jose Offerman	.12	.09	.05
468	Bob Ojeda	.05	.04	.02
469	Juan Samuel	.06	.05	.02
470	Mike Scioscia	.06	.05	.02
471	Darryl Strawberry	.15	.11	.06
472	*Bret Barberie*(FC)	.15	.11	.06
473	Brian Barnes	.06	.05	.02
474	Eric Bullock	.04	.03	.02
475	Ivan Calderon	.08	.06	.03
476	Delino DeShields	.08	.06	.03
477	*Jeff Fassero*(FC)	.10	.08	.04
478	Mike Fitzgerald	.04	.03	.02
479	Steve Frey	.04	.03	.02
480	Andres Galarraga	.06	.05	.02
481	Mark Gardner	.06	.05	.02
482	Marquis Grissom	.12	.09	.05
483	*Chris Haney*(FC)	.20	.15	.08
484	Barry Jones	.04	.03	.02
485	Dave Martinez	.05	.04	.02
486	Dennis Martinez	.08	.06	.03
487	Chris Nabholz	.06	.05	.02
488	Spike Owen	.04	.03	.02
489	Gilberto Reyes	.05	.04	.02
490	Mel Rojas	.05	.04	.02
491	Scott Ruskin	.05	.04	.02
492	Bill Sampen	.05	.04	.02
493	Larry Walker	.10	.08	.04
494	Tim Wallach	.08	.06	.03
495	Daryl Boston	.04	.03	.02
496	Hubie Brooks	.06	.05	.02
497	Tim Burke	.05	.04	.02
498	Mark Carreon	.04	.03	.02
499	Tony Castillo	.04	.03	.02
500	Vince Coleman	.08	.06	.03
501	David Cone	.08	.06	.03
502	Kevin Elster	.04	.03	.02
503	Sid Fernandez	.06	.05	.02
504	John Franco	.06	.05	.02
505	Dwight Gooden	.12	.09	.05
506	Todd Hundley	.12	.09	.05
507	Jeff Innis	.04	.03	.02
508	Gregg Jefferies	.12	.09	.05
509	Howard Johnson	.12	.09	.05
510	Dave Magadan	.06	.05	.02
511	*Terry McDaniel*(FC)	.20	.15	.08
512	Kevin McReynolds	.08	.06	.03
513	Keith Miller	.04	.03	.02
514	Charlie O'Brien	.04	.03	.02
515	Mackey Sasser	.04	.03	.02
516	*Pete Schourek*	.10	.08	.04
517	Julio Valera	.06	.05	.02
518	Frank Viola	.10	.08	.04
519	Wally Whitehurst	.05	.04	.02
520	*Anthony Young*(FC)	.20	.15	.08
521	*Andy Ashby*	.10	.08	.04
522	*Kim Batiste*(FC)	.10	.08	.04
523	Joe Boever	.04	.03	.02
524	Wes Chamberlain	.20	.15	.08
525	Pat Combs	.05	.04	.02
526	Danny Cox	.04	.03	.02
527	Darren Daulton	.05	.04	.02
528	Jose DeJesus	.05	.04	.02
529	Lenny Dykstra	.08	.06	.03
530	Darrin Fletcher	.05	.04	.02
531	Tommy Greene	.06	.05	.02
532	Jason Grimsley	.05	.04	.02
533	Charlie Hayes	.05	.04	.02
534	Von Hayes	.06	.05	.02
535	Dave Hollins	.08	.06	.03
536	Ricky Jordan	.08	.06	.03
537	John Kruk	.06	.05	.02
538	Jim Lindeman	.04	.03	.02
539	Mickey Morandini	.08	.06	.03
540	Terry Mulholland	.06	.05	.02
541	Dale Murphy	.12	.09	.05
542	Randy Ready	.04	.03	.02
543	Wally Ritchie	.04	.03	.02
544	Bruce Ruffin	.04	.03	.02
545	Steve Searcy	.04	.03	.02
546	Dickie Thon	.04	.03	.02
547	Mitch Williams	.08	.06	.03
548	Stan Belinda	.04	.03	.02
549	Jay Bell	.06	.05	.02
550	Barry Bonds	.15	.11	.06
551	Bobby Bonilla	.12	.09	.05
552	Steve Buechele	.05	.04	.02
553	Doug Drabek	.08	.06	.03
554	Neal Heaton	.04	.03	.02
555	Jeff King	.05	.04	.02
556	Bob Kipper	.04	.03	.02
557	Bill Landrum	.04	.03	.02
558	Mike LaValliere	.05	.04	.02
559	Jose Lind	.04	.03	.02
560	Lloyd McClendon	.04	.03	.02
561	Orlando Merced	.25	.20	.10
562	Bob Patterson	.04	.03	.02
563	*Joe Redfield*(FC)	.10	.08	.04
564	Gary Redus	.04	.03	.02
565	Rosario Rodriguez	.04	.03	.02
566	Don Slaught	.04	.03	.02
567	John Smiley	.06	.05	.02
568	Zane Smith	.05	.04	.02
569	Randy Tomlin	.08	.06	.03
570	Andy Van Slyke	.08	.06	.03
571	Gary Varsho	.04	.03	.02
572	Bob Walk	.04	.03	.02
573	*John Wehner*(FC)	.25	.20	.10
574	Juan Agosto	.04	.03	.02
575	Cris Carpenter	.05	.04	.02
576	Jose DeLeon	.05	.04	.02
577	Rich Gedman	.04	.03	.02
578	Bernard Gilkey	.10	.08	.04
579	Pedro Guerrero	.08	.06	.03
580	Ken Hill	.05	.04	.02
581	Rex Hudler	.04	.03	.02
582	Felix Jose	.10	.08	.04
583	Ray Lankford	.15	.11	.06
584	Omar Olivares	.06	.05	.02
585	Jose Oquendo	.04	.03	.02
586	Tom Pagnozzi	.05	.04	.02
587	Geronimo Pena	.05	.04	.02
588	Mike Perez	.05	.04	.02
589	Gerald Perry	.04	.03	.02
590	Bryn Smith	.04	.03	.02
591	Lee Smith	.06	.05	.02
592	Ozzie Smith	.12	.09	.05
593	Scott Terry	.04	.03	.02
594	Bob Tewksbury	.04	.03	.02
595	Milt Thompson	.04	.03	.02
596	Todd Zeile	.12	.09	.05
597	Larry Andersen	.04	.03	.02
598	Oscar Azocar	.04	.03	.02
599	Andy Benes	.10	.08	.04
600	*Ricky Bones*(FC)	.10	.08	.04
601	Jerald Clark	.05	.04	.02
602	Pat Clements	.04	.03	.02
603	Paul Faries	.06	.05	.02
604	Tony Fernandez	.06	.05	.02
605	Tony Gwynn	.12	.09	.05
606	Greg Harris	.05	.04	.02
607	Thomas Howard	.05	.04	.02
608	Bruce Hurst	.06	.05	.02
609	Darrin Jackson	.04	.03	.02
610	Tom Lampkin	.04	.03	.02
611	Craig Lefferts	.04	.03	.02
612	*Jim Lewis*(FC)	.20	.15	.08
613	Mike Maddux	.04	.03	.02
614	Fred McGriff	.15	.11	.06
615	*Jose Melendez*(FC)	.20	.15	.08

		MT	NR MT	EX
616	*Jose Mota*	.15	.11	.06
617	Dennis Rasmussen	.04	.03	.02
618	Bip Roberts	.06	.05	.02
619	Rich Rodriguez	.04	.03	.02
620	Benito Santiago	.08	.06	.03
621	*Craig Shipley*(FC)	.10	.08	.04
622	Tim Teufel	.04	.03	.02
623	*Kevin Ward*(FC)	.15	.11	.06
624	Ed Whitson	.05	.04	.02
625	Dave Anderson	.04	.03	.02
626	Kevin Bass	.05	.04	.02
627	*Rod Beck*(FC)	.10	.08	.04
628	Bud Black	.05	.04	.02
629	Jeff Brantley	.05	.04	.02
630	John Burkett	.05	.04	.02
631	Will Clark	.25	.20	.10
632	Royce Clayton(FC)	.20	.15	.08
633	Steve Decker	.10	.08	.04
634	Kelly Downs	.04	.03	.02
635	Mike Felder	.04	.03	.02
636	Scott Garrelts	.04	.03	.02
637	Eric Gunderson	.08	.06	.03
638	*Bryan Hickerson*(FC)	.20	.15	.08
639	Darren Lewis	.15	.11	.06
640	Greg Litton	.04	.03	.02
641	Kirt Manwaring	.06	.05	.02
642	*Paul McClellan*(FC)	.10	.08	.04
643	Willie McGee	.08	.06	.03
644	Kevin Mitchell	.12	.09	.05
645	Francisco Olivares	.04	.03	.02
646	*Mike Remlinger*(FC)	.10	.08	.04
647	Dave Righetti	.06	.05	.02
648	Robby Thompson	.05	.04	.02
649	Jose Uribe	.04	.03	.02
650	Matt Williams	.12	.09	.05
651	Trevor Wilson	.06	.05	.02
652	Tom Goodwin (MLP)(FC)	.25	.20	.10
653	Terry Bross (MLP)(FC)	.08	.06	.03
654	*Mike Christopher* (MLP)(FC)	.20	.15	.08
655	*Kenny Lofton* (MLP)(FC)	.50	.40	.20
656	*Chris Cron* (MLP)(FC)	.20	.15	.08
657	Willie Banks (MLP)(FC)	.25	.20	.10
658	*Pat Rice* (MLP)(FC)	.25	.20	.10
659a	*Rob Mauer* (MLP, last name misspelled)(FC)	1.00	.70	.40
659b	*Rob Maurer* (MLP, corrected)(FC)	.25	.20	.10
660	Don Harris (MLP)(FC)	.20	.15	.08
661	Henry Rodriguez (MLP)(FC)	.10	.08	.04
662	*Cliff Brantley* (MLP)(FC)	.20	.15	.08
663	*Mike Linskey* (MLP)(FC)	.20	.15	.08
664	Gary Disarcina (MLP)(FC)	.08	.06	.03
665	*Gil Heredia* (MLP)(FC)	.20	.15	.08
666	*Vinny Castilla* (MLP)(FC)	.25	.20	.10
667	Paul Abbott (MLP)(FC)	.08	.06	.03
668	Monty Fariss (MLP)(FC)	.08	.06	.03
669	*Jarvis Brown* (MLP)(FC)	.10	.08	.04
670	*Wayne Kirby* (MLP)(FC)	.25	.20	.10
671	*Scott Brosius* (MLP)(FC)	.15	.11	.06
672	Bob Hamelin (MLP)(FC)	.10	.08	.04
673	*Joel Johnston* (MLP)(FC)	.20	.15	.08
674	*Tim Spehr* (MLP)(FC)	.15	.11	.06
675	*Jeff Gardner* (MLP)(FC)	.15	.11	.06
676	*Rico Rossy* (MLP)(FC)	.20	.15	.08
677	*Roberto Hernandez* (MLP)(FC)	.20	.15	.08
678	*Ted Wood* (MLP)(FC)	.25	.20	.10
679	Cal Eldred (MLP)(FC)	.20	.15	.08
680	Sean Berry (MLP)(FC)	.08	.06	.03
681	Rickey Henderson (Stolen Base Record)	.15	.11	.06
682	Nolan Ryan (Record 7th No-hitter)	.20	.15	.08
683	Dennis Martinez (Perfect Game)	.05	.04	.02
684	Wilson Alvarez (Rookie No-hitter)	.05	.04	.02
685	Joe Carter (3 100 RBI Seasons)	.06	.05	.02
686	Dave Winfield (400 Home Runs)	.10	.08	.04
687	David Cone (Ties NL Record Strikeouts)	.06	.05	.02
688	Jose Canseco (LL)	.15	.11	.06
689	Howard Johnson (LL)	.08	.06	.03
690	Julio Franco (LL)	.08	.06	.03
691	Terry Pendleton (LL)	.08	.06	.03
692	Cecil Fielder (LL)	.10	.08	.04
693	Scott Erickson (LL)	.10	.08	.04
694	Tom Glavine (LL)	.08	.06	.03
695	Dennis Martinez (LL)	.05	.04	.02
696	Bryan Harvey (LL)	.05	.04	.02
697	Lee Smith (LL)	.05	.04	.02
698	Super Siblings (Roberto & Sandy Alomar)	.08	.06	.03
699	The Indispensables (Bobby Bonilla/ Will Clark)	.10	.08	.04
700	Teamwork (Mark Wohlers/ Kent Mercker Alejandro Pena)	.06	.05	.02
701	Tiger Tandems (Chris Jones/ Bo Jackson Gregg Olson/ Frank Thomas)	.20	.15	.08
702	The Ignitors (Paul Molitor/ Brett Butler)	.06	.05	.02
703	The Indispensables II (Cal Ripken, Jr./ Joe Carter)	.15	.11	.06
704	Power Packs (Barry Larkin/ Kirby Puckett)	.10	.08	.04
705	Today and Tomorrow (Mo Vaughn/ Cecil Fielder)	.15	.11	.06
706	Teenage Sensations (Ramon Martinez/ Ozzie Guillen)	.08	.06	.03
707	Designated Hitters (Harold Baines/ Wade Boggs)	.08	.06	.03
708	Robin Yount (PV)	.20	.15	.08
709	Ken Griffey, Jr. (PV)	.80	.60	.30
710	Nolan Ryan (PV)	.80	.60	.30
711	Cal Ripken, Jr. (PV)	.25	.20	.10
712	Frank Thomas (PV)	1.00	.70	.40
713	Dave Justice (PV)	.70	.50	.30
714	Checklist	.04	.03	.02
715	Checklist	.04	.03	.02
716	Checklist	.04	.03	.02
717	Checklist	.04	.03	.02
718	Checklist	.04	.03	.02
719	Checklist	.04	.03	.02
720	Checklist (659 Rob Mauer)	.04	.03	.02
720	(659 Rob Maurer)	.04	.03	.02

1992 Fleer All-Stars

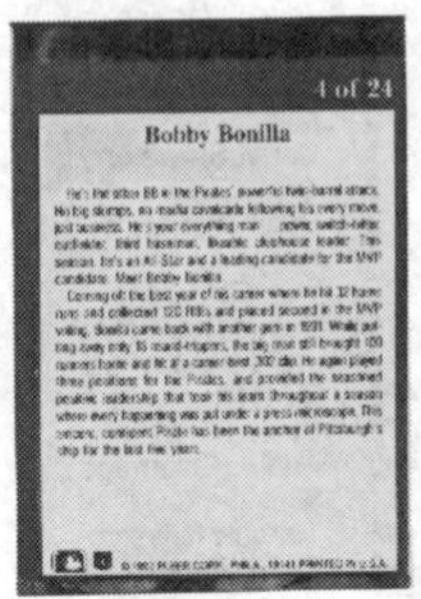

Black borders with gold highlights are featured on these special wax pack insert cards. The fronts feature glossy action photos with a portrait photo inset. The card backs feature career highlights and are numbered.

		MT	NR MT	EX
Complete Set (24):		30.00	22.00	12.00
Common Player:		.40	.30	.15
1	Felix Jose	.40	.30	.15
2	Tony Gwynn	1.50	1.25	.60
3	Barry Bonds	2.00	1.50	.80
4	Bobby Bonilla	1.25	.90	.50
5	Mike LaValliere	.40	.30	.15
6	Tom Glavine	.60	.45	.25
7	Ramon Martinez	.40	.30	.15
8	Lee Smith	.40	.30	.15
9	Mickey Tettleton	.50	.40	.20
10	Scott Erickson	.50	.40	.20
11	Frank Thomas	9.00	6.00	3.25
12	Danny Tartabull	.80	.60	.30
13	Will Clark	2.00	1.50	.80
14	Ryne Sandberg	3.00	2.00	1.00
15	Terry Pendleton	.60	.45	.25
16	Barry Larkin	.80	.60	.30
17	Rafael Palmeiro	.80	.60	.30
18	Julio Franco	.40	.30	.15
19	Robin Ventura	2.00	1.50	.80
20	Cal Ripken, Jr.	3.00	2.25	1.25
21	Joe Carter	1.00	.70	.40
22	Kirby Puckett	2.00	1.50	.80
23	Ken Griffey, Jr.	7.50	5.00	2.50
24	Jose Canseco	1.50	1.00	.50

Regional interest may affect the value of a card.

1992 Fleer Roger Clemens

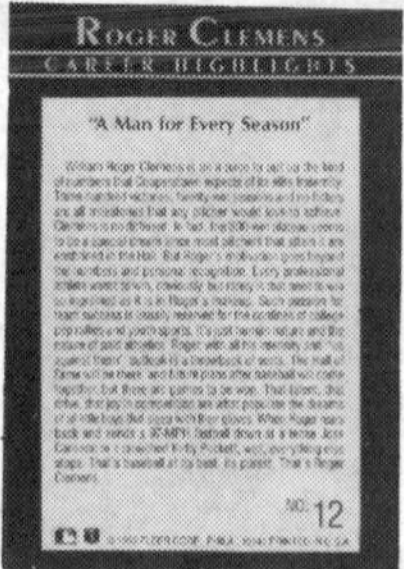

This 15-card set honors the career highlights of Roger Clemens. The initial 12 cards from the set were inserted in 1992 Fleer wax packs. A limited number of autographed cards were inserted as well. The additional three cards from the set were available through a mail-in offer. The card fronts feature black borders with metallic gold type. The flip side is yellow with black borders. Various career highlights are featured on the backs of the different cards.

	MT	NR MT	EX
Complete Set (15):	15.00	10.00	5.00
Common card:	1.00	.60	.30
Autographed card:	75.00	55.00	30.00

		MT	NR MT	EX
1	Quiet Storm	1.00	.75	.40
2	Courted by the Mets and Twins	1.00	.75	.40
3	The Show	1.00	.75	.40
4	Rocket Launched	1.00	.75	.40
5	Time of Trial	1.00	.75	.40
6	Break Through	1.00	.75	.40
7	Play it Again Roger	1.00	.75	.40
8	Business as Usual	1.00	.75	.40
9	Heee's Back	1.00	.75	.40
10	Blood, Sweat and Tears	1.00	.75	.45
11	Prime of Life	1.00	.75	.40
12	Man for Every Season	1.00	.75	.40
13	Cooperstown Bound	1.00	.75	.40
14	The Heat of the Moment	1.00	.75	.40
15	Final Words	1.00	.75	.40

1992 Fleer Lumber Co.

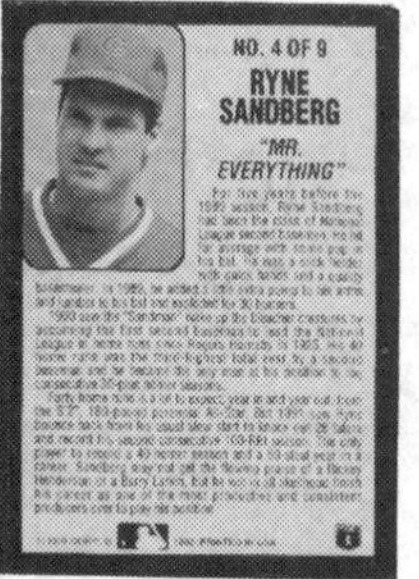

Baseball's top power hitters at each position are featured in this nine-card set. The card fronts feature full-color action photos bordered in black. "The Lumber Co." appears along the right border in the shape of a baseball bat. The card backs feature posed player photos and career highlights. The set was included only in factory sets released to the hobby trade.

	MT	NR MT	EX
Complete Set (9):	18.00	13.50	7.25
Common Player:	1.00	.60	.30

		MT	NR MT	EX
1	Cecil Fielder	2.50	2.00	1.00
2	Mickey Tettleton	1.00	.60	.30
3	Darryl Strawberry	1.25	.90	.50
4	Ryne Sandberg	4.00	3.00	1.50
5	Jose Canseco	2.00	1.50	.75
6	Matt Williams	1.50	.90	.50
7	Cal Ripken, Jr.	4.00	3.00	1.50
8	Barry Bonds	3.00	2.25	1.25
9	Ron Gant	1.25	.90	.50

1992 Fleer Rookie Sensations

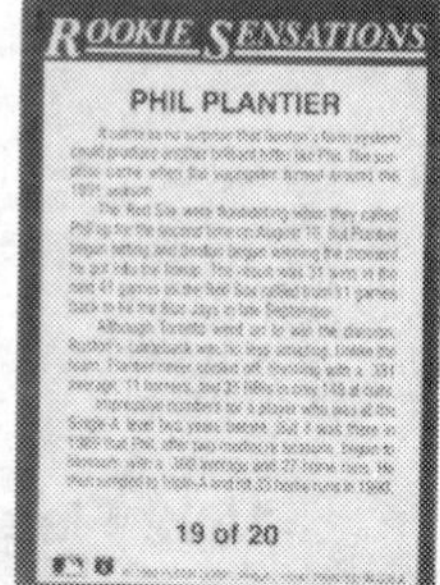

This 20-card set features the top rookies of 1991 and rookie prospects from 1992. The card fronts feature blue borders with "Rookie Sensations" in gold along the top border. A name plate is featured below the photo and also includes the team. The flip sides feature background information on the player. The cards were randomly inserted in 1992 Fleer cello packs. This issue saw very high prices when initially released then suffered long-term declines as the hobby became inundated with more and more insert sets.

	MT	NR MT	EX
Complete Set (20):	90.00	67.00	36.00
Common Player:	1.00	.70	.40

		MT	NR MT	EX
1	Frank Thomas	30.00	22.00	12.00
2	Todd Van Poppel	6.00	4.50	2.50
3	Orlando Merced	3.00	2.00	1.00
4	Jeff Bagwell	12.00	9.00	4.75
5	Jeff Fassero	1.00	.70	.40
6	Darren Lewis	2.50	1.50	.75
7	Milt Cuyler	1.00	.70	.40
8	Mike Timlin	1.00	.70	.40
9	Brian McRae	2.50	1.50	.75
10	Chuck Knoblauch	4.00	2.50	1.25
11	Rich DeLucia	1.00	.70	.40
12	Ivan Rodriguez	10.00	6.00	3.00
13	Juan Guzman	9.00	6.75	3.50
14	Steve Chitren	1.00	.70	.40
15	Mark Wohlers	1.50	1.25	.60
16	Wes Chamberlain	1.50	1.25	.60
17	Ray Lankford	5.00	3.00	1.50
18	Chito Martinez	1.00	.70	.40
19	Phil Plantier	6.00	4.50	2.50
20	Scott Leius	2.00	1.50	.80

1992 Fleer Smoke'n Heat

This 12-card set of top pitchers was included in factory sets designated for sale within the general retail trade. Card numbers have an S prefix.

	MT	NR MT	EX
Complete Set (12):	10.00	7.50	4.00
Common Player:	.50	.40	.20

		MT	NR MT	EX
1	Lee Smith	.60	.45	.25
2	Jack McDowell	.90	.70	.35
3	David Cone	.50	.40	.20
4	Roger Clemens	3.00	2.25	1.25
5	Nolan Ryan	6.00	4.50	2.50

6	Scott Erickson	.50	.30	.15
7	Tom Glavine	.90	.70	.35
8	Dwight Gooden	.75	.55	.30
9	Andy Benes	.60	.40	.20
10	Steve Avery	.90	.70	.35
11	Randy Johnson	.90	.70	.35
12	Jim Abbott	1.00	.60	.30

1992 Fleer 7-Eleven

The 1992 Performer Collection was a combined effort from Fleer and 7-11. Customers at 7-11 stores received a packet of five cards with gasoline purchases to build the 24-card set of major stars. The cards are standard size, with virtually the identical design to the regular issue Fleer set of 1992, with only the addition of "The Performer" logo on the lower corner of the card.

		MT	NR MT	EX
Complete Set (24):		6.00	4.50	2.25
Common Player:		.15	.11	.06
1	Nolan Ryan	1.00	.75	.40
2	Frank Thomas	1.00	.75	.40
3	Ryne Sandberg	.50	.40	.20
4	Ken Griffey Jr.	.75	.55	.30
5	Cal Ripken Jr.	.50	.40	.30
6	Roger Clemens	.30	.25	.12
7	Cecil Fielder	.30	.25	.12
8	Dave Justice	.20	.15	.07
9	Wade Boggs	.40	.30	.15
10	Tony Gwynn	.20	.15	.07
11	Kirby Puckett	.25	.20	.10
12	Darryl Strawberry	.20	.15	.07
13	Jose Canseco	.35	.25	.12
14	Barry Larkin	.15	.11	.06
15	Terry Pendleton	.15	.11	.06
16	Don Mattingly	.40	.30	.15
17	Rickey Henderson	.20	.15	.07
18	Ruben Sierra	.20	.15	.07
19	Jeff Bagwell	.20	.15	.07
20	Tom Glavine	.15	.11	.06
21	Ramon Martinez	.15	.11	.06
22	Will Clark	.25	.20	.10
23	Barry Bonds	.30	.25	.12
24	Roberto Alomar	.20	.15	.07

1992 Fleer Team Leaders

White and green borders highlight this insert set from Fleer. The card fronts also feature a special gold-foil "team leaders" logo beneath the full-color player photo. The card backs feature player information. The cards were randomly inserted in 1992 Fleer rack packs.

		MT	NR MT	EX
Complete Set (20):		28.00	21.00	11.00
Common Player:		.50	.40	.20
1	Don Mattingly	1.50	1.25	.60
2	Howard Johnson	.70	.50	.30
3	Chris Sabo	.50	.40	.20
4	Carlton Fisk	1.00	.70	.40
5	Kirby Puckett	1.50	1.25	.60
6	Cecil Fielder	1.00	.75	.40
7	Tony Gwynn	1.00	.75	.40
8	Will Clark	1.50	1.25	.60
9	Bobby Bonilla	1.00	.75	.40
10	Len Dykstra	1.00	.75	.40
11	Tom Glavine	.50	.40	.20
12	Rafael Palmeiro	1.00	.75	.40
13	Wade Boggs	1.50	1.25	.60
14	Joe Carter	1.00	.75	.40
15	Ken Griffey, Jr.	4.00	3.00	1.50
16	Darryl Strawberry	1.00	.75	.40
17	Cal Ripken, Jr.	2.50	2.00	1.00
18	Danny Tartabull	.90	.60	.30
19	Jose Canseco	1.25	.75	.40
20	Andre Dawson	1.00	.75	.40

1992 Fleer Update

Photos not available at press time

This 132-card set was released in boxed set form and features traded players, free agents and top rookies from 1992. The cards are styled after the regular 1992 Fleer and are numbered alphabetically according to team. This set marks the ninth year that Fleer has released an update set. The set includes four black-bordered "Headliner" cards.

	MT	NR MT	EX
Complete Set (136):	150.00	115.00	60.00
Common Player:	.10	.08	.04

		MT	NR MT	EX
H	1992 All-Star Game MVP (Ken Griffey, Jr.)	25.00	20.00	10.00
H	3000 Career Hits (Robin Yount)	7.00	5.25	2.75
H	Major League Career Saves Record (Jeff Reardon)	1.00	.70	.40
H	Record RBI Performance (Cecil Fielder)	4.00	3.00	1.50
1	Todd Frohwirth	.10	.08	.04
2	Alan Mills	.10	.08	.04
3	Rick Sutcliffe	.10	.08	.04
4	John Valentin(FC)	2.25	1.75	.90
5	Frank Viola	.10	.08	.04
6	Bob Zupcic(FC)	1.25	.90	.50
7	Mike Butcher(FC)	.10	.08	.04
8	Chad Curtis(FC)	8.00	6.00	3.25
9	Damion Easley(FC)	3.00	2.25	1.25
10	Tim Salmon(FC)	40.00	30.00	16.00
11	Julio Valera	.10	.08	.04
12	George Bell	.10	.08	.04
13	Roberto Hernandez(FC)	.10	.08	.04
14	Shawn Jeter(FC)	.70	.50	.30
15	Thomas Howard	.10	.08	.04
16	Jesse Levis(FC)	.70	.50	.30
17	Kenny Lofton	7.00	5.25	2.75
18	Paul Sorrento	.10	.08	.04
19	Rico Brogna(FC)	.70	.50	.30
20	John Doherty(FC)	.10	.08	.04
21	Dan Gladden	.10	.08	.04
22	Buddy Groom(FC)	.70	.50	.30
23	Shawn Hare(FC)	.70	.50	.30
24	John Kiely(FC)	.70	.50	.30
25	Kurt Knudsen(FC)	.30	.25	.12
26	Gregg Jefferies	.30	.25	.12
27	Wally Joyner	.30	.25	.12
28	Kevin Koslofski(FC)	.70	.50	.30
29	Kevin McReynolds	.10	.08	.04
30	Rusty Meacham	.10	.08	.04
31	Keith Miller	.10	.08	.04
32	Hipolito Pichardo(FC)	.70	.50	.30
33	James Austin(FC)	.10	.08	.04
34	Scott Fletcher	.10	.08	.04
35	John Jaha(FC)	1.25	.90	.50
36	Pat Listach(FC)	2.50	2.00	1.00
37	Dave Nilsson(FC)	.75	.60	.30
38	Kevin Seitzer	.10	.08	.04
39	Tom Edens	.10	.08	.04
40	Pat Mahomes(FC)	1.00	.70	.40
41	John Smiley	.10	.08	.04
42	Charlie Hayes	.75	.60	.30
43	Sam Militello(FC)	1.50	1.25	.60
44	Andy Stankiewicz(FC)	.60	.45	.25
45	Danny Tartabull	.10	.08	.04
46	Bob Wickman(FC)	5.00	3.75	2.00
47	Jerry Browne	.10	.08	.04
48	Kevin Campbell(FC)	.10	.08	.04
49	Vince Horsman(FC)	.10	.08	.04
50	Troy Neel(FC)	3.50	2.75	1.50
51	Ruben Sierra	1.00	.70	.40
52	Bruce Walton(FC)	.10	.08	.04
53	Willie Wilson	.10	.08	.04
54	Bret Boone(FC)	4.00	3.00	1.50
55	Dave Fleming(FC)	2.50	2.00	1.00
56	Kevin Mitchell	.10	.08	.04
57	Jeff Nelson(FC)	.10	.08	.04
58	Shane Turner(FC)	.70	.50	.30
59	Jose Canseco	1.25	.90	.50
60	Jeff Frye(FC)	.30	.25	.12
61	Damilo Leon(FC)	.70	.50	.30
62	Roger Pavlik(FC)	.60	.45	.25
63	David Cone	.10	.08	.04
64	Pat Hentgen(FC)	8.00	6.00	3.25
65	Randy Knorr(FC)	.10	.08	.04
66	Jack Morris	.10	.08	.04
67	Dave Winfield	2.50	2.00	1.00
68	David Nied(FC)	8.00	6.00	3.25
69	Otis Nixon	.10	.08	.04
70	Alejandro Pena	.10	.08	.04
71	Jeff Reardon	.10	.08	.04
72	Alex Arias(FC)	.80	.60	.30
73	Jim Bullinger(FC)	.30	.25	.12
74	Mike Morgan	.10	.08	.04
75	Rey Sanchez(FC)	.10	.08	.04
76	Bob Scanlan	.10	.08	.04
77	Sammy Sosa	2.00	1.50	.80
78	Scott Bankhead	.10	.08	.04
79	Tim Belcher	.10	.08	.04
80	Steve Foster(FC)	.80	.60	.30
81	Willie Greene(FC)	1.00	.70	.40
82	Bip Roberts	.10	.08	.04
83	Scott Ruskin	.10	.08	.04
84	Greg Swindell	.10	.08	.04
85	Juan Guerrero(FC)	.70	.50	.30
86	Butch Henry(FC)	.30	.25	.12
87	Doug Jones	.10	.08	.04
88	Brian Williams(FC)	1.00	.70	.40
89	Tom Candiotti	.10	.08	.04
90	Eric Davis	.75	.60	.30
91	Carlos Hernandez(FC)	.10	.08	.04
92	Mike Piazza(FC)	75.00	56.00	30.00
93	Mike Sharperson	.10	.08	.04
94	Eric Young(FC)	3.00	2.25	1.25
95	Moises Alou	3.00	2.25	1.25
96	Greg Colbrunn	.10	.08	.04
97	Wil Cordero(FC)	3.00	2.25	1.25
98	Ken Hill	.10	.08	.04
99	John Vander Wal(FC)	.40	.30	.15
100	John Wetteland	.10	.08	.04
101	Bobby Bonilla	.75	.60	.30
102	Eric Hilman(FC)	.60	.45	.25
103	Pat Howell(FC)	.60	.45	.25
104	Jeff Kent(FC)	2.00	1.50	.80
105	Dick Schofield	.10	.08	.04
106	Ryan Thompson(FC)	1.25	.90	.50
107	Chico Walker	.10	.08	.04
108	Juan Bell	.10	.08	.04
109	Mariano Duncan	.10	.08	.04
110	Jeff Grotewold(FC)	.70	.50	.30
111	Ben Rivera(FC)	.35	.25	.14
112	Curt Schilling	.10	.08	.04
113	Victor Cole(FC)	.70	.50	.30
114	Albert Martin(FC)	4.00	3.00	1.50
115	Roger Mason	.10	.08	.04
116	Blas Minor(FC)	.70	.50	.30
117	Tim Wakefield(FC)	2.50	2.00	1.00
118	Mark Clark(FC)	.35	.25	.14
119	Rheal Cormier(FC)	.40	.30	.15
120	Donovan Osborne(FC)	2.00	1.50	.80
121	Todd Worrell	.10	.08	.04
122	Jeremy Hernandez(FC)	.30	.25	.12
123	Randy Myers	.10	.08	.04
124	Frank Seminara(FC)	.30	.25	.12
125	Gary Sheffield	2.50	2.00	1.00
126	Dan Walters(FC)	.30	.25	.12
127	Steve Hosey(FC)	1.00	.70	.40
128	Mike Jackson	.10	.08	.04
129	Jim Pena(FC)	.70	.50	.30
130	Cory Snyder	.10	.08	.04
131	Bill Swift	.10	.08	.04
132	Checklist	.10	.08	.04

1992 Fleer Ultra

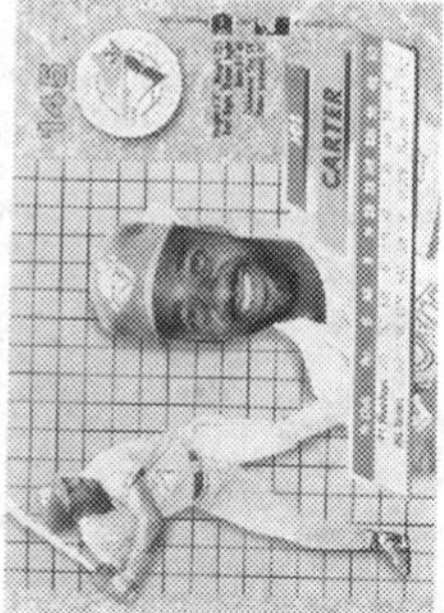

Fleer released its second consecutive Ultra set in 1992. The card fronts feature full-color action photos with a marble accent at the card bottom. The flip sides are horizontal with two additional player photos. Many insert sets were randomly included in foil packs as premiums. These included rookie, All-Star and award winners, among others. A two-card Tony Gwynn send-away set was also available through an offer from Fleer. For $1 and 10 Ultra wrappers, collectors could receive the Gwynn cards. The set is numbered by team; cards #1-300 comprise Series I, cards #301-600 are Series II.

		MT	NR MT	EX
Complete Set (600):		60.00	45.00	25.00
Common Player:		.12	.09	.05
1	Glenn Davis	.12	.09	.05

		MT	NR MT	EX
2	Mike Devereaux	.15	.11	.06
3	Dwight Evans	.12	.09	.05
4	Leo Gomez	.30	.25	.12
5	Chris Hoiles	.30	.25	.12
6	Sam Horn	.12	.09	.05
7	Chito Martinez	.15	.11	.06
8	Randy Milligan	.12	.09	.05
9	Mike Mussina	2.00	1.50	.80
10	Billy Ripken	.12	.09	.05
11	Cal Ripken, Jr.	1.00	.70	.40
12	Tom Brunansky	.12	.09	.05
13	Ellis Burks	.15	.11	.06
14	Jack Clark	.12	.09	.05
15	Roger Clemens	.75	.60	.30
16	Mike Greenwell	.12	.09	.05
17	Joe Hesketh	.12	.09	.05
18	Tony Pena	.12	.09	.05
19	Carlos Quintana	.12	.09	.05
20	Jeff Reardon	.12	.09	.05
21	Jody Reed	.12	.09	.05
22	Luis Rivera	.12	.09	.05
23	Mo Vaughn	1.00	.70	.40
24	Gary DiSarcina	.12	.09	.05
25	Chuck Finley	.15	.11	.06
26	Gary Gaetti	.12	.09	.05
27	Bryan Harvey	.15	.11	.06
28	Lance Parrish	.12	.09	.05
29	Luis Polonia	.12	.09	.05
30	Dick Schofield	.12	.09	.05
31	Luis Polonia	.12	.09	.05
32	Wilson Alvarez	.12	.09	.05
33	Carlton Fisk	.30	.25	.12
34	Craig Grebeck	.12	.09	.05
35	Ozzie Guillen	.12	.09	.05
36	Greg Hibbard	.12	.09	.05
37	Charlie Hough	.12	.09	.05
38	Lance Johnson	.12	.09	.05
39	Ron Karkovice	.12	.09	.05
40	Jack McDowell	.15	.11	.06
41	Donn Pall	.12	.09	.05
42	Melido Perez	.12	.09	.05
43	Tim Raines	.15	.11	.06
44	Frank Thomas	5.00	3.75	2.00
45	Sandy Alomar, Jr.	.15	.11	.06
46	Carlos Baerga	1.00	.70	.40
47	Albert Belle	1.00	.70	.40
48	Jerry Browne	.12	.09	.05
49	Felix Fermin	.12	.09	.05
50	Reggie Jefferson	.15	.11	.06
51	Mark Lewis	.20	.15	.08
52	Carlos Martinez	.12	.09	.05
53	Steve Olin	.12	.09	.05
54	Jim Thome	.50	.40	.20
55	Mark Whiten	.40	.30	.15
56	Dave Bergman	.12	.09	.05
57	Milt Cuyler	.12	.09	.05
58	Rob Deer	.12	.09	.05
59	Cecil Fielder	.80	.60	.30
60	Travis Fryman	1.75	1.25	.70
61	Scott Livingstone	.15	.11	.06
62	Tony Phillips	.15	.11	.06
63	Mickey Tettleton	.15	.11	.06
64	Alan Trammell	.15	.11	.06
65	Lou Whitaker	.15	.11	.06
66	Kevin Appier	.15	.11	.06
67	Mike Boddicker	.12	.09	.05
68	George Brett	.40	.30	.15
69	Jim Eisenreich	.12	.09	.05
70	Mark Gubicza	.12	.09	.05
71	David Howard	.12	.09	.05
72	Joel Johnston	.12	.09	.05
73	Mike Macfarlane	.12	.09	.05
74	Brent Mayne	.12	.09	.05
75	Brian McRae	.30	.25	.12
76	Jeff Montgomery	.12	.09	.05
77	Danny Tartabull	.15	.11	.06
78	Danny Tartabull	.30	.25	.12
79	Dante Bichette	.12	.09	.05
80	Ted Higuera	.12	.09	.05
81	Paul Molitor	.30	.25	.12
82	Jamie Navarro	.15	.11	.06
83	Gary Sheffield	.80	.60	.30
84	Bill Spiers	.12	.09	.05
85	B.J. Surhoff	.12	.09	.05
86	Greg Vaughn	.30	.25	.12
87	Robin Yount	.40	.30	.15
88	Rick Aguilera	.12	.09	.05
89	Chili Davis	.12	.09	.05
90	Scott Erickson	.15	.11	.06
91	Brian Harper	.12	.09	.05
92	Kent Hrbek	.12	.09	.05

		MT	NR MT	EX
93	Chuck Knoblauch	.40	.30	.15
94	Scott Leius	.12	.09	.05
95	Shane Mack	.15	.11	.06
96	Mike Pagliarulo	.12	.09	.05
97	Kirby Puckett	1.00	.70	.40
98	Kevin Tapani	.12	.09	.05
99	Jesse Barfield	.12	.09	.05
100	Alvaro Espinoza	.12	.09	.05
101	Mel Hall	.12	.09	.05
102	Pat Kelly	.12	.09	.05
103	Roberto Kelly	.10	.08	.04
104	Kevin Maas	.12	.09	.05
105	Don Mattingly	.50	.40	.20
106	Hensley Meulens	.12	.09	.05
107	Matt Nokes	.12	.09	.05
108	Steve Sax	.15	.11	.06
109	Harold Baines	.15	.11	.06
110	Jose Canseco	.50	.40	.20
111	Ron Darling	.12	.09	.05
112	Mike Gallego	.12	.09	.05
113	Dave Henderson	.12	.09	.05
114	Rickey Henderson	.40	.30	.15
115	Mark McGwire	.50	.40	.20
116	Terry Steinbach	.12	.09	.05
117	Dave Stewart	.15	.11	.06
118	Todd Van Poppel	1.00	.70	.40
119	Bob Welch	.12	.09	.05
120	Greg Briley	.12	.09	.05
121	Jay Buhner	.12	.09	.05
122	Rich DeLucia	.12	.09	.05
123	Ken Griffey, Jr.	4.00	3.00	1.50
124	Erik Hanson	.12	.09	.05
125	Randy Johnson	.12	.09	.05
126	Edgar Martinez	.15	.11	.06
127	Tino Martinez	.15	.11	.06
128	Pete O'Brien	.12	.09	.05
129	Harold Reynolds	.12	.09	.05
130	Dave Valle	.12	.09	.05
131	Julio Franco	.15	.11	.06
132	Juan Gonzalez	4.00	3.00	1.50
133	Jeff Huson	.12	.09	.05
134	Mike Jeffcoat	.12	.09	.05
135	Terry Mathews	.12	.09	.05
136	Rafael Palmeiro	.20	.15	.08
137	Dean Palmer	1.00	.70	.40
138	Geno Petralli	.12	.09	.05
139	Ivan Rodriguez	1.50	1.25	.60
140	Jeff Russell	.12	.09	.05
141	Nolan Ryan	3.00	2.25	1.25
142	Ruben Sierra	.50	.40	.20
143	Roberto Alomar	1.00	.70	.40
144	Pat Borders	.12	.09	.05
145	Joe Carter	.30	.25	.12
146	Kelly Gruber	.12	.09	.05
147	Jimmy Key	.12	.09	.05
148	Manny Lee	.12	.09	.05
149	Rance Mulliniks	.12	.09	.05
150	Greg Myers	.12	.09	.05
151	John Olerud	1.75	1.25	.70
152	Dave Stieb	.12	.09	.05
153	Todd Stottlemyre	.12	.09	.05
154	Duane Ward	.12	.09	.05
155	Devon White	.12	.09	.05
156	Eddie Zosky	.15	.11	.06
157	Steve Avery	1.00	.70	.40
158	Rafael Belliard	.12	.09	.05
159	Jeff Blauser	.12	.09	.05
160	Mark Lemke	.12	.09	.05
161	Ron Gant	.60	.45	.25
162	Tom Glavine	.50	.40	.20
163	Brian Hunter	.30	.25	.12
164	Dave Justice	1.00	.70	.40
166	Greg Olson	.12	.09	.05
167	Terry Pendleton	.15	.11	.06
168	Lonnie Smith	.12	.09	.05
169	John Smoltz	.15	.11	.06
170	Mike Stanton	.12	.09	.05
171	Jeff Treadway	.12	.09	.05
172	Paul Assenmacher	.12	.09	.05
173	George Bell	.15	.11	.06
174	Shawon Dunston	.12	.09	.05
175	Mark Grace	.30	.25	.12
176	Danny Jackson	.12	.09	.05
177	Les Lancaster	.12	.09	.05
178	Greg Maddux	.15	.11	.06
179	Luis Salazar	.12	.09	.05
180	Rey Sanchez	.15	.11	.06
181	Ryne Sandberg	1.00	.70	.40
182	Jose Vizcaino	.12	.09	.05
183	Chico Walker	.12	.09	.05
184	Jerome Walton	.12	.09	.05

No.	Player	MT	NR MT	EX
185	Glenn Braggs	.12	.09	.05
186	Tom Browning	.12	.09	.05
187	Rob Dibble	.15	.11	.06
188	Bill Doran	.12	.09	.05
189	Chris Hammond	.15	.11	.06
190	Billy Hatcher	.12	.09	.05
191	Barry Larkin	.40	.30	.15
192	Hal Morris	.15	.11	.06
193	Joe Oliver	.12	.09	.05
194	Paul O'Neill	.12	.09	.05
195	Jeff Reed	.12	.09	.05
196	Jose Rijo	.12	.09	.05
197	Chris Sabo	.15	.11	.06
198	Jeff Bagwell	1.50	1.25	.60
199	Craig Biggio	.15	.11	.06
200	Ken Caminiti	.12	.09	.05
201	Andujar Cedeno	.15	.11	.06
202	Steve Finley	.15	.11	.06
203	Luis Gonzalez	.15	.11	.06
204	Pete Harnisch	.15	.11	.06
205	Xavier Hernandez	.12	.09	.05
206	Darryl Kile	.12	.09	.05
207	Al Osuna	.12	.09	.05
208	Curt Schilling	.12	.09	.05
209	Brett Butler	.12	.09	.05
210	Kal Daniels	.12	.09	.05
211	Lenny Harris	.12	.09	.05
212	Stan Javier	.12	.09	.05
213	Ramon Martinez	.15	.11	.06
214	Roger McDowell	.12	.09	.05
215	Jose Offerman	.12	.09	.05
216	Juan Samuel	.12	.09	.05
217	Mike Scioscia	.12	.09	.05
218	Mike Sharperson	.12	.09	.05
219	Darryl Strawberry	.30	.25	.12
220	Delino DeShields	.15	.11	.06
221	Tom Foley	.12	.09	.05
222	Steve Frey	.12	.09	.05
223	Dennis Martinez	.12	.09	.05
224	Spike Owen	.12	.09	.05
225	Gilberto Reyes	.12	.09	.05
226	Tim Wallach	.12	.09	.05
227	Daryl Boston	.12	.09	.05
228	Tim Burke	.12	.09	.05
229	Vince Coleman	.12	.09	.05
230	David Cone	.15	.11	.06
231	Kevin Elster	.12	.09	.05
232	Dwight Gooden	.15	.11	.06
233	Todd Hundley	.15	.11	.06
234	Jeff Innis	.12	.09	.05
235	Howard Johnson	.15	.11	.06
236	Dave Magadan	.12	.09	.05
237	Mackey Sasser	.12	.09	.05
238	Anthony Young	.15	.11	.06
239	Wes Chamberlain	.30	.25	.12
240	Darren Daulton	.15	.11	.06
241	Lenny Dykstra	.15	.11	.06
242	Tommy Greene	.12	.09	.05
243	Charlie Hayes	.12	.09	.05
244	Dave Hollins	.15	.11	.06
245	Ricky Jordan	.15	.11	.06
246	John Kruk	.15	.11	.06
247	Mickey Morandini	.15	.11	.06
248	Terry Mulholland	.12	.09	.05
249	Dale Murphy	.15	.11	.06
250	Jay Bell	.15	.11	.06
251	Barry Bonds	1.50	1.25	.60
252	Steve Buechele	.12	.09	.05
253	Doug Drabek	.15	.11	.06
254	Mike LaValliere	.12	.09	.05
255	Jose Lind	.12	.09	.05
256	Lloyd McClendon	.12	.09	.05
257	Orlando Merced	.30	.25	.12
258	Don Slaught	.12	.09	.05
259	John Smiley	.12	.09	.05
260	Zane Smith	.12	.09	.05
261	Randy Tomlin	.15	.11	.06
262	Andy Van Slyke	.15	.11	.06
263	Pedro Guerrero	.15	.11	.06
264	Felix Jose	.12	.09	.05
265	Ray Lankford	.40	.30	.15
266	Omar Olivares	.12	.09	.05
267	Jose Oquendo	.12	.09	.05
268	Tom Pagnozzi	.12	.09	.05
269	Bryn Smith	.12	.09	.05
270	Lee Smith	.12	.09	.05
271	Ozzie Smith	.50	.40	.20
272	Milt Thompson	.12	.09	.05
273	Todd Zeile	.12	.09	.05
274	Andy Benes	.15	.11	.06
275	Jerald Clark	.12	.09	.05
276	Tony Fernandez	.12	.09	.05
277	Tony Gwynn	.50	.40	.20
278	Greg Harris	.12	.09	.05
279	Thomas Howard	.12	.09	.05
280	Bruce Hurst	.12	.09	.05
281	Mike Maddux	.12	.09	.05
282	Fred McGriff	.50	.40	.20
283	Benito Santiago	.15	.11	.06
284	Kevin Bass	.12	.09	.05
285	Jeff Brantley	.12	.09	.05
286	John Burkett	.12	.09	.05
287	Will Clark	.80	.60	.30
288	Royce Clayton	.60	.45	.25
289	Steve Decker	.12	.09	.05
290	Kelly Downs	.12	.09	.05
291	Mike Felder	.12	.09	.05
292	Darren Lewis	.15	.11	.06
293	Kirt Manwaring	.12	.09	.05
294	Willie McGee	.12	.09	.05
295	Robby Thompson	.12	.09	.05
296	Matt Williams	.40	.30	.15
297	Trevor Wilson	.12	.09	.05
298	Checklist	.10	.08	.04
299	Checklist	.10	.08	.04
300	Checklist	.10	.08	.04
301	Brady Anderson	.20	.15	.08
302	Todd Frohwirth	.12	.09	.05
303	Ben McDonald	.30	.25	.12
304	Mark McLemore	.12	.09	.05
305	Jose Mesa	.12	.09	.05
306	Bob Milacki	.12	.09	.05
307	Gregg Olson	.20	.15	.08
308	David Segui	.12	.09	.05
309	Rick Sutcliffe	.20	.15	.08
310	Jeff Tackett	.20	.15	.08
311	Wade Boggs	.50	.40	.20
312	Scott Cooper	.20	.15	.08
313	John Flaherty	.25	.20	.10
314	Wayne Housie	.20	.15	.08
315	Peter Hoy	.20	.15	.08
316	John Marzano	.12	.09	.05
317	Tim Naehring	.20	.15	.08
318	Phil Plantier	.60	.45	.25
319	Frank Viola	.40	.30	.15
320	Matt Young	.12	.09	.05
321	Jim Abbott	.40	.30	.15
322	Hubie Brooks	.12	.09	.05
323	Chad Curtis	1.50	1.25	.60
324	Alvin Davis	.12	.09	.05
325	Junior Felix	.20	.15	.08
326	Von Hayes	.12	.09	.05
327	Mark Langston	.30	.25	.12
328	Scott Lewis	.12	.09	.05
329	Don Robinson	.12	.09	.05
330	Bobby Rose	.12	.09	.05
331	Lee Stevens	.12	.09	.05
332	George Bell	.30	.25	.12
333	Esteban Beltre	.12	.09	.05
334	Joey Cora	.12	.09	.05
335	Alex Fernandez	.40	.30	.15
336	Roberto Hernandez	.15	.11	.06
337	Mike Huff	.12	.09	.05
338	Kirk McCaskill	.12	.09	.05
339	Dan Pasqua	.12	.09	.05
340	Scott Radinsky	.12	.09	.05
341	Steve Sax	.20	.15	.08
342	Bobby Thigpen	.30	.25	.12
343	Robin Ventura	.60	.45	.25
344	Jack Armstrong	.12	.09	.05
345	Alex Cole	.12	.09	.05
346	Dennis Cook	.12	.09	.05
347	Glenallen Hill	.12	.09	.05
348	Thomas Howard	.12	.09	.05
349	Brook Jacoby	.12	.09	.05
350	Kenny Lofton	1.25	.90	.50
351	Charles Nagy	.20	.15	.08
352	Rod Nichols	.12	.09	.05
353	Junior Ortiz	.12	.09	.05
354	Dave Otto	.12	.09	.05
355	Tony Perezchica	.12	.09	.05
356	Scott Scudder	.12	.09	.05
357	Paul Sorrento	.12	.09	.05
358	Skeeter Barnes	.12	.09	.05
359	Mark Carreon	.12	.09	.05
360	John Doherty	.12	.09	.05
361	Dan Gladden	.12	.09	.05
362	Bill Gullickson	.20	.15	.08
363	Shawn Hare	.15	.11	.06
364	Mike Henneman	.20	.15	.08
365	Chad Kreuter	.12	.09	.05
366	Mark Leiter	.12	.09	.05

		MT	NR MT	EX
367	Mike Munoz	.12	.09	.05
368	Kevin Ritz	.12	.09	.05
369	Mark Davis	.12	.09	.05
370	Tom Gordon	.12	.09	.05
371	Tony Gwynn	.12	.09	.05
372	Gregg Jefferies	.25	.20	.10
373	Wally Joyner	.15	.11	.06
374	Kevin McReynolds	.20	.15	.08
375	Keith Miller	.12	.09	.05
376	Rico Rossy	.15	.11	.06
377	Curtis Wilkerson	.12	.09	.05
378	Ricky Bones	.12	.09	.05
379	Chris Bosio	.12	.09	.05
380	Cal Eldred	.75	.60	.30
381	Scott Fletcher	.12	.09	.05
382	Jim Gantner	.12	.09	.05
383	Darryl Hamilton	.12	.09	.05
384	Doug Henry	.25	.20	.10
385	Pat Listach	.90	.70	.35
386	Tim McIntosh	.12	.09	.05
387	Edwin Nunez	.12	.09	.05
388	Dan Plesac	.12	.09	.05
389	Kevin Seitzer	.12	.09	.05
390	Franklin Stubbs	.12	.09	.05
391	William Suero	.15	.11	.06
392	Bill Wegman	.12	.09	.05
393	Willie Banks	.12	.09	.05
394	Jarvis Brown	.15	.11	.06
395	Greg Gagne	.12	.09	.05
396	Mark Guthrie	.12	.09	.05
397	Bill Krueger	.12	.09	.05
398	Pat Mahomes	.50	.40	.20
399	Pedro Munoz	.15	.11	.06
400	John Smiley	.12	.09	.05
401	Gary Wayne	.12	.09	.05
402	Lenny Webster	.12	.09	.05
403	Carl Willis	.12	.09	.05
404	Greg Cadaret	.12	.09	.05
405	Steve Farr	.12	.09	.05
406	Mike Gallego	.12	.09	.05
407	Charlie Hayes	.12	.09	.05
408	Steve Howe	.12	.09	.05
409	Dion James	.12	.09	.05
410	Jeff Johnson	.12	.09	.05
411	Tim Leary	.12	.09	.05
412	Jim Leyritz	.12	.09	.05
413	Melido Perez	.12	.09	.05
414	Scott Sanderson	.12	.09	.05
415	Andy Stankiewicz	.35	.25	.14
416	Mike Stanley	.12	.09	.05
417	Danny Tartabull	.15	.11	.06
418	Lance Blankenship	.12	.09	.05
419	Mike Bordick	.12	.09	.05
420	Scott Brosius	.12	.09	.05
421	Dennis Eckersley	.20	.15	.08
422	Scott Hemond	.12	.09	.05
423	Carney Lansford	.12	.09	.05
424	Henry Mercedes	.25	.20	.10
425	Mike Moore	.12	.09	.05
426	Gene Nelson	.12	.09	.05
427	Randy Ready	.12	.09	.05
428	Bruce Wilson	.12	.09	.05
429	Willie Wilson	.12	.09	.05
430	Rich Amaral	.12	.09	.05
431	Dave Cochrane	.12	.09	.05
432	Henry Cotto	.12	.09	.05
433	Calvin Jones	.20	.15	.08
434	Kevin Mitchell	.25	.20	.10
435	Clay Parker	.12	.09	.05
436	Omar Vizquel	.12	.09	.05
437	Floyd Bannister	.12	.09	.05
438	Kevin Brown	.12	.09	.05
439	John Cangelosi	.12	.09	.05
440	Brian Downing	.12	.09	.05
441	Monty Fariss	.12	.09	.05
443	Donald Harris	.25	.20	.10
444	Kevin Reimer	.12	.09	.05
445	Kenny Rogers	.12	.09	.05
446	Wayne Rosenthal	.12	.09	.05
447	Dickie Thon	.12	.09	.05
448	Derek Bell	.50	.40	.20
449	Juan Guzman	1.50	1.25	.60
450	Tom Henke	.12	.09	.05
451	Candy Maldonado	.12	.09	.05
452	Jack Morris	.20	.15	.08
453	David Wells	.12	.09	.05
454	Dave Winfield	.50	.40	.20
455	Juan Berenguer	.12	.09	.05
456	Damon Berryhill	.12	.09	.05
457	Mike Bielecki	.12	.09	.05
458	Marvin Freeman	.12	.09	.05
459	Charlie Leibrandt	.12	.09	.05
460	Kent Mercker	.12	.09	.05
461	Otis Nixon	.15	.11	.06
462	Alejandro Pena	.12	.09	.05
463	Ben Rivera	.15	.11	.06
464	Deion Sanders	.50	.40	.20
465	Mark Wohlers	.30	.25	.12
466	Shawn Boskie	.12	.09	.05
467	Frank Castillo	.12	.09	.05
468	Andre Dawson	.40	.30	.15
469	Joe Girardi	.12	.09	.05
470	Chuck McElroy	.12	.09	.05
471	Mike Morgan	.12	.09	.05
472	Ken Patterson	.12	.09	.05
473	Bob Scanlan	.12	.09	.05
474	Gary Scott	.25	.20	.10
475	Dave Smith	.12	.09	.05
476	Sammy Sosa	.50	.40	.20
477	Hector Villanueva	.12	.09	.05
478	Scott Bankhead	.12	.09	.05
479	Tim Belcher	.12	.09	.05
480	Freddie Benavides	.15	.11	.06
481	Jacob Brumfield	.25	.20	.10
482	Norm Charlton	.15	.11	.06
483	Dwayne Henry	.12	.09	.05
484	Dave Martinez	.12	.09	.05
485	Bip Roberts	.15	.11	.06
486	Reggie Sanders	.60	.45	.25
487	Greg Swindell	.15	.11	.06
488	Ryan Bowen	.25	.20	.10
489	Casey Candaele	.12	.09	.05
490	Juan Guerrero	.25	.20	.10
491	Pete Incaviglia	.12	.09	.05
492	Jeff Juden	.20	.15	.08
493	Rob Murphy	.12	.09	.05
494	Mark Portugal	.12	.09	.05
495	Rafael Ramirez	.12	.09	.05
496	Scott Servais	.12	.09	.05
497	Ed Taubensee	.35	.25	.14
498	Brian Williams	.30	.25	.12
499	Todd Benzinger	.12	.09	.05
500	John Candelaria	.12	.09	.05
501	Tom Candiotti	.12	.09	.05
502	Tim Crews	.12	.09	.05
503	Eric Davis	.40	.30	.15
504	Jim Gott	.12	.09	.05
505	Dave Hansen	.12	.09	.05
506	Carlos Hernandez	.12	.09	.05
507	Orel Hershiser	.12	.09	.05
508	Eric Karros	1.50	1.25	.60
509	Bob Ojeda	.12	.09	.05
510	Steve Wilson	.12	.09	.05
511	Moises Alou	.15	.11	.06
512	Bret Barberie	.20	.15	.08
513	Ivan Calderon	.25	.20	.10
514	Gary Carter	.25	.20	.10
515	Archi Cianfrocco	.60	.45	.25
516	Jeff Fassero	.12	.09	.05
517	Darrin Fletcher	.12	.09	.05
518	Marquis Grissom	.30	.25	.12
519	Chris Haney	.20	.15	.08
520	Ken Hill	.15	.11	.06
521	Chris Nabholz	.12	.09	.05
522	Bill Sampen	.12	.09	.05
523	John VanderWal	.30	.25	.12
524	David Wainhouse	.25	.20	.10
525	Larry Walker	.60	.45	.25
526	John Wetteland	.15	.11	.06
527	Bobby Bonilla	.25	.20	.10
528	Sid Fernandez	.15	.11	.06
529	John Franco	.12	.09	.05
530	Dave Gallagher	.12	.09	.05
531	Paul Gibson	.12	.09	.05
532	Eddie Murray	.25	.20	.10
533	Junior Noboa	.12	.09	.05
534	Charlie O'Brien	.12	.09	.05
535	Bill Pecota	.12	.09	.05
536	Willie Randolph	.12	.09	.05
537	Bret Saberhagen	.12	.09	.05
538	Dick Schofield	.12	.09	.05
539	Pete Schourek	.12	.09	.05
540	Ruben Amaro	.20	.15	.08
541	Andy Ashby	.12	.09	.05
542	Kim Batiste	.25	.20	.10
543	Cliff Brantley	.20	.15	.08
544	Mariano Duncan	.12	.09	.05
545	Jeff Grotewold	.20	.15	.08
546	Barry Jones	.12	.09	.05
547	Julio Peguero	.20	.15	.08
548	Curt Schilling	.12	.09	.05
549	Mitch Williams	.20	.15	.08

		MT	NR MT	EX
550	Stan Belinda	.12	.09	.05
551	Scott Bullett	.20	.15	.08
552	Cecil Espy	.12	.09	.05
553	Jeff King	.12	.09	.05
554	Roger Mason	.12	.09	.05
555	Paul Miller	.20	.15	.08
556	Denny Neagle	.20	.15	.08
557	Vocente Palacios	.12	.09	.05
558	Bob Patterson	.12	.09	.05
559	Tom Prince	.12	.09	.05
560	Gary Redus	.12	.09	.05
561	Gary Varsho	.12	.09	.05
562	Juan Agosto	.12	.09	.05
563	Cris Carpenter	.12	.09	.05
564	Mark Clark	.20	.15	.08
565	Jose DeLeon	.12	.09	.05
566	Rich Gedman	.12	.09	.05
567	Bernard Gilkey	.15	.11	.06
568	Rex Hudler	.12	.09	.05
569	Tim Jones	.12	.09	.05
570	Donovan Osborne	.60	.45	.25
571	Mike Perez	.12	.09	.05
572	Gerald Perry	.12	.09	.05
573	Bob Tewksbury	.15	.11	.06
574	Todd Worrell	.12	.09	.05
575	Dave Eiland	.12	.09	.05
576	Jeremy Hernandez	.20	.15	.08
577	Craig Lefferts	.12	.09	.05
578	Jose Melendez	.12	.09	.05
579	Randy Myers	.12	.09	.05
580	Gary Pettis	.12	.09	.05
581	Rich Rodriguez	.12	.09	.05
582	Gary Sheffield	1.00	.70	.40
583	Craig Shipley	.12	.09	.05
584	Kurt Stillwell	.12	.09	.05
585	Tim Teufel	.12	.09	.05
586	Rod Beck	.50	.40	.20
587	Dave Burba	.12	.09	.05
588	Craig Colbert	.20	.15	.08
589	Bryan Hickerson	.12	.09	.05
590	Mike Jackson	.12	.09	.05
591	Mark Leonard	.12	.09	.05
592	Jim McNamara	.25	.20	.10
593	John Patterson	.20	.15	.08
594	Dave Righetti	.12	.09	.05
595	Cory Snyder	.12	.09	.05
596	Bill Swift	.20	.15	.08
597	Ted Wood	.15	.11	.06
598	Checklist	.10	.08	.04
599	Checklist	.10	.08	.04
600	Checklist	.10	.08	.04

1992 Fleer Ultra Award Winners

The 25 cards in this insert issue were randomly packaged with Series I Ultra. One of the Cal Ripken cards (#21) can be found with a photo made from a reversed negative, as well as with the proper orientation. Neither version carries a premium.

		MT	NR MT	EX
Complete Set (25):		50.00	30.00	20.00
Common Player:		1.00	.60	.30
1	Jack Morris	1.00	.70	.40
2	Chuck Knoblauch	1.25	.90	.50
3	Jeff Bagwell	3.00	2.25	1.25
4	Terry Pendleton	1.00	.70	.40
5	Cal Ripken, Jr.	6.00	4.50	2.50
6	Roger Clemens	6.00	4.50	2.50
7	Tom Glavine	3.00	2.25	1.25
8	Tom Pagnozzi	1.00	.70	.40
9	Ozzie Smith	2.50	2.00	1.00
10	Andy Van Slyke	1.00	.70	.40
11	Barry Bonds	4.00	3.00	1.50
12	Tony Gwynn	2.50	2.00	1.00
13	Matt Williams	2.00	1.50	.80
14	Will Clark	4.00	3.00	1.50
15	Robin Ventura	2.50	2.00	1.00
16	Mark Langston	1.00	.70	.40
18	Devon White	1.00	.70	.40
19	Don Mattingly	3.00	2.25	1.25
20	Roberto Alomar	4.00	3.00	1.50
21a	Cal Ripken, Jr. (reversed negative)	5.00	3.75	2.00
21b	Cal Ripken, Jr. (correct)	5.00	3.75	2.00
22	Ken Griffey, Jr.	10.00	7.50	4.00
23	Kirby Puckett	5.00	3.75	2.00
24	Greg Maddux	3.00	2.25	1.25
25	Ryne Sandberg	5.00	3.75	2.00

1992 Fleer Ultra All-Rookies

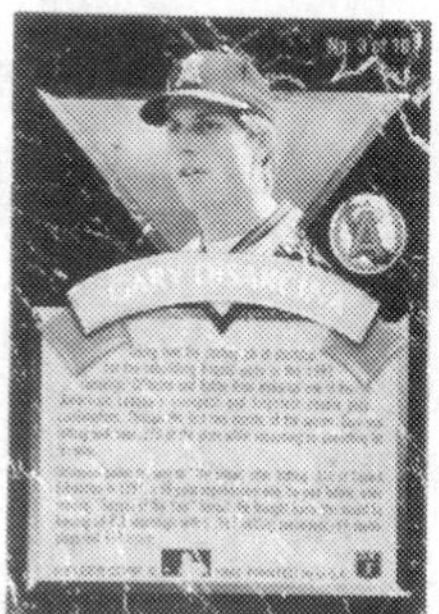

The 10 promising rookies in this set could be found on special cards inserted in Ultra Series II foil packs.

		MT	NR MT	EX
Complete Set (10):		15.00	12.00	6.00
Common Player:		.60	.40	.20
1	Eric Karros	3.50	2.50	1.25
2	Andy Stankiewicz	.60	.40	.20
3	Gary DiSarcina	.60	.40	.20
4	Archi Cianfrocco	1.00	.60	.30
5	Jim McNamara	.60	.40	.20
6	Chad Curtis	4.50	3.00	1.50
7	Kenny Lofton	7.50	5.00	2.50
8	Reggie Sanders	3.00	2.00	1.00
9	Pat Mahomes	.90	.70	.35
10	Donovan Osborne	.90	.70	.35

1992 Fleer Ultra All-Stars

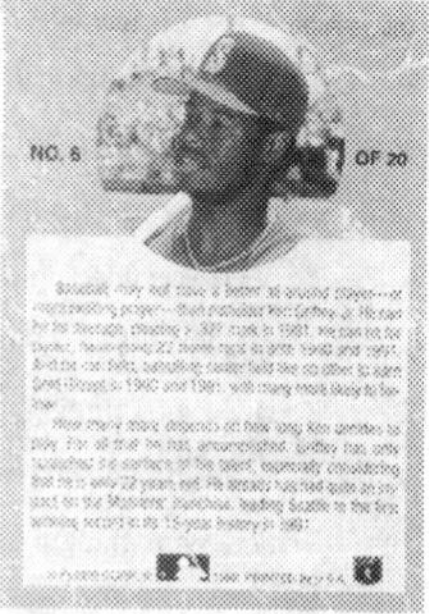

An All-Star team from each league, with two pitchers,

could be assembled by collecting these inserts from Ultra Series II foil packs.

		MT	NR MT	EX
Complete Set (20):		28.00	16.00	8.00
Common Player:		.60	.40	.20
1	Mark McGwire	1.00	.75	.40
2	Roberto Alomar	2.00	1.50	.75
3	Cal Ripken, Jr.	3.50	2.50	1.25
4	Wade Boggs	1.25	.75	.40
5	Mickey Tettleton	.60	.40	.20
6	Ken Griffey Jr.	9.00	6.00	3.00
7	Tom Glavine	.60	.40	.20
8	Kirby Puckett	3.00	2.00	1.00
9	Frank Thomas	11.00	6.00	3.00
10	Jack McDowell	.90	.70	.35
11	Will Clark	2.50	1.50	.75
12	Ryne Sandberg	3.50	2.50	1.25
13	Barry Larkin	.90	.70	.35
14	Gary Sheffield	.90	.70	.35
15	Tom Pagnozzi	.60	.40	.20
16	Barry Bonds	3.00	2.25	1.20
17	Deion Sanders	1.50	1.00	.50
18	Darryl Strawberry	.90	.60	.30
19	David Cone	.60	.40	.20
20	Tom Glavine	.90	.70	.35

1992 Fleer Ultra Tony Gwynn

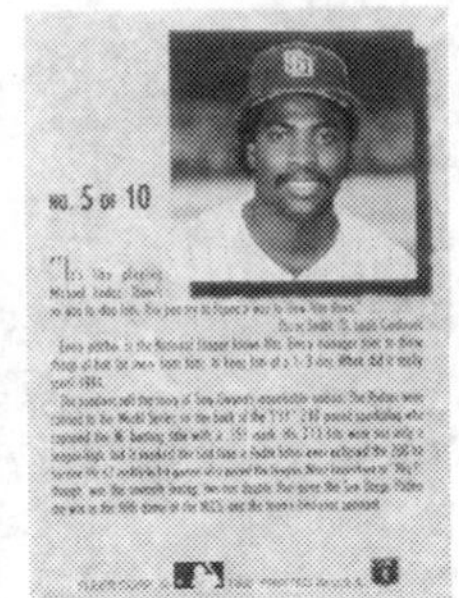

This 12-card subset of Ultra's spokesman features 10 cards which were available as inserts in Series I foil packs, plus two cards labeled "Special No. 1" and "Special No. 2" which could only be obtained in a send-away offer. Some 2,000 of these cards carry a "certified" Gwynn autograph.

		MT	NR MT	EX
Complete Set (12):		12.00	8.00	4.00
Common card:		1.00	.60	.30
Autograph:		90.00	70.00	35.00
	INSERT CARDS			
1	Tony Gwynn (leaping at outfield wall)	1.00	.75	.40
2	Tony Gwynn (batting in brown warm-up jersey)	1.00	.75	.40
3	Tony Gwynn (catching fly, glove over head)	1.00	.75	.40
4	Tony Gwynn (follow-through of swing)	1.00	.75	.40
5	Tony Gwynn (leading off first base)	1.00	.75	.40
6	Tony Gwynn (Silver Slugger/Gold Glove)	1.00	.75	.40
7	Tony Gwynn (bunting)	1.00	.75	.40
8	Tony Gwynn (swinging)	1.00	.75	.40
9	Tony Gwynn (leaving batter's box)	1.00	.75	.40
10	Tony Gwynn (batting, wearing sun glasses)	1.00	.75	.40
	SEND-AWAY CARDS			
1	Tony Gwynn (batting)	1.00	.75	.40
2	Tony Gwynn (fielding)	1.00	.75	.40

1993 Fleer

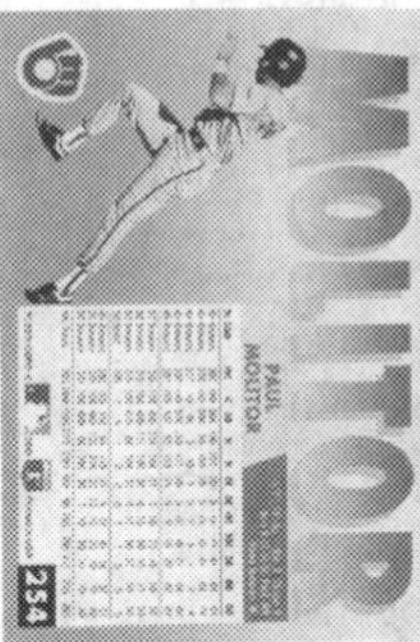

The card fronts feature silver borders with the player's name, team and position in a banner along the left side of the card. The Fleer logo appears in the lower right corner. The backs feature an action photo of the player with his name in bold behind him. A box featuring biographical information, statistics and player information is located to the right of the action photo. The cards are numbered alphabetically by team. The basic Fleer issue for 1993 was issued in two series of 360 cards each. The 720-card set included a number of subsets and could be found in many different types of packaging with an unprecedented number of inserts sets to spice up each offering.

		MT	NR MT	EX
Complete Set (720):		30.00	22.00	12.00
Common Player:		.04	.03	.02
1	Steve Avery	.10	.08	.04
2	Sid Bream	.04	.03	.02
3	Ron Gant	.08	.06	.03
4	Tom Glavine	.10	.08	.04
5	Brian Hunter	.08	.06	.03
6	Ryan Klesko(FC)	.25	.15	.08
7	Charlie Leibrandt	.04	.03	.02
8	Kent Mercker	.04	.03	.02
9	*David Nied*(FC)	.60	.30	.20
10	Otis Nixon	.06	.05	.02
11	Greg Olson	.04	.03	.02
12	Terry Pendleton	.08	.06	.03
13	Deion Sanders	.15	.11	.06
14	John Smoltz	.08	.06	.03
15	Mike Stanton	.04	.03	.02
16	Mark Wohlers	.08	.06	.03
17	Paul Assenmacher	.04	.03	.02
18	Steve Buechele	.04	.03	.02
19	Shawon Dunston	.06	.05	.02
20	Mark Grace	.08	.06	.03
21	Derrick May	.10	.08	.04
22	Chuck McElroy	.04	.03	.02
23	Mike Morgan	.06	.05	.02
24	Rey Sanchez	.10	.08	.04
25	Ryne Sandberg	.20	.12	.05
26	Bob Scanlan	.04	.03	.02
27	Sammy Sosa	.06	.05	.02
28	Rick Wilkins	.06	.05	.02
29	*Bobby Ayala*(FC)	.15	.11	.06
30	Tim Belcher	.06	.05	.02
31	*Jeff Branson*(FC)	.12	.09	.05
32	Norm Charlton	.08	.06	.03
33	*Steve Foster*(FC)	.12	.09	.05
34	Willie Greene(FC)	.12	.09	.05
35	Chris Hammond	.06	.05	.02
36	Milt Hill(FC)	.10	.08	.04
37	Hal Morris	.06	.05	.02
38	Joe Oliver	.06	.05	.02
39	Paul O'Neill	.06	.05	.02
40	*Tim Pugh*(FC)	.12	.09	.05
41	Jose Rijo	.08	.06	.03
42	Bip Roberts	.08	.06	.03
43	Chris Sabo	.08	.06	.03
44	Reggie Sanders	.15	.11	.06
45	Eric Anthony	.08	.06	.03
46	Jeff Bagwell	.20	.12	.05
47	Craig Biggio	.08	.06	.03
48	Joe Boever	.04	.03	.02
49	Casey Candaele	.04	.03	.02
50	Steve Finley	.06	.05	.02
51	Luis Gonzalez	.08	.06	.03

#	Player	MT	NR MT	EX
52	Pete Harnisch	.08	.06	.03
53	Xavier Hernandez	.04	.03	.02
54	Doug Jones	.05	.04	.02
55	Eddie Taubensee	.08	.06	.03
56	Brian Williams	.08	.06	.03
57	*Pedro Astacio*(FC)	.12	.09	.05
58	Todd Benzinger	.04	.03	.02
59	Brett Butler	.06	.05	.02
60	Tom Candiotti	.06	.05	.02
61	Lenny Harris	.04	.03	.02
62	Carlos Hernandez	.08	.06	.03
63	Orel Hershiser	.08	.06	.03
64	Eric Karros	.15	.11	.06
65	Ramon Martinez	.08	.06	.03
66	Jose Offerman	.06	.05	.02
67	Mike Scioscia	.04	.03	.02
68	Mike Sharperson	.04	.03	.02
69	*Eric Young*(FC)	.15	.11	.06
70	Moises Alou	.08	.06	.03
71	Ivan Calderon	.08	.06	.03
72	*Archi Cianfrocco*	.15	.11	.06
73	Wil Cordero	.10	.08	.04
74	Delino DeShields	.08	.06	.03
75	Mark Gardner	.05	.04	.02
76	Ken Hill	.08	.06	.03
77	*Tim Laker*(FC)	.15	.11	.06
78	Chris Nabholz	.06	.05	.02
79	Mel Rojas	.04	.03	.02
80	*John Vander Wal*	.12	.09	.05
81	Larry Walker	.10	.08	.04
82	Tim Wallach	.06	.05	.02
83	John Wetteland	.08	.06	.03
84	Bobby Bonilla	.12	.09	.05
85	Daryl Boston	.04	.03	.02
86	Sid Fernandez	.08	.06	.03
87	*Eric Hillman*(FC)	.12	.09	.05
88	Todd Hundley	.08	.06	.03
89	Howard Johnson	.08	.06	.03
90	*Jeff Kent*	.15	.11	.06
91	Eddie Murray	.10	.08	.04
92	Bill Pecota	.04	.03	.02
93	Bret Saberhagen	.08	.06	.03
94	Dick Schofield	.04	.03	.02
95	Pete Schourek	.04	.03	.02
96	Anthony Young	.06	.05	.02
97	Ruben Amaro Jr.	.06	.05	.02
98	Juan Bell	.06	.05	.02
99	Wes Chamberlain	.06	.05	.02
100	Darren Daulton	.08	.06	.03
101	Mariano Duncan	.04	.03	.02
102	Mike Hartley	.04	.03	.02
103	Ricky Jordan	.06	.05	.02
104	John Kruk	.08	.06	.03
105	Mickey Morandini	.08	.06	.03
106	Terry Mulholland	.06	.05	.02
107	*Ben Rivera*(FC)	.12	.09	.05
108	Curt Schilling	.08	.06	.03
109	*Keith Shepherd*(FC)	.12	.09	.05
110	Stan Belinda	.05	.04	.02
111	Jay Bell	.06	.05	.02
112	Barry Bonds	.20	.15	.08
113	Jeff King	.05	.04	.02
114	Mike LaValliere	.04	.03	.02
115	Jose Lind	.04	.03	.02
116	Roger Mason	.04	.03	.02
117	Orlando Merced	.06	.05	.02
118	Bob Patterson	.04	.03	.02
119	Don Slaught	.04	.03	.02
120	Zane Smith	.05	.04	.02
121	Randy Tomlin	.06	.05	.02
122	Andy Van Slyke	.08	.06	.03
123	*Tim Wakefield*	.10	.08	.04
124	Rheal Cormier	.08	.06	.03
125	Bernard Gilkey	.08	.06	.03
126	Felix Jose	.08	.06	.03
127	Ray Lankford	.12	.09	.05
128	Bob McClure	.04	.03	.02
129	Donovan Osborne	.10	.08	.04
130	Tom Pagnozzi	.06	.05	.02
131	Geronimo Pena	.06	.05	.02
132	Mike Perez	.06	.05	.02
133	Lee Smith	.06	.05	.02
134	Bob Tewksbury	.06	.05	.02
135	Todd Worrell	.06	.05	.02
136	Todd Zeile	.08	.06	.03
137	Jerald Clark	.05	.04	.02
138	Tony Gwynn	.12	.09	.05
139	Greg Harris	.05	.04	.02
140	Jeremy Hernandez	.05	.04	.02
141	Darrin Jackson	.05	.04	.02
142	Mike Maddux	.04	.03	.02
143	Fred McGriff	.15	.11	.06

#	Player	MT	NR MT	EX
144	Jose Melendez	.08	.06	.03
145	Rich Rodriguez	.04	.03	.02
146	Frank Seminara	.08	.06	.03
147	Gary Sheffield	.12	.09	.05
148	Kurt Stillwell	.05	.04	.02
149	*Dan Walters*	.10	.08	.04
150	Rod Beck	.06	.05	.02
151	Bud Black	.04	.03	.02
152	Jeff Brantley	.05	.04	.02
153	John Burkett	.05	.04	.02
154	Will Clark	.15	.11	.06
155	Royce Clayton	.08	.06	.03
156	Mike Jackson	.04	.03	.02
157	Darren Lewis	.08	.06	.03
158	Kirt Manwaring	.05	.04	.02
159	Willie McGee	.06	.05	.02
160	Cory Snyder	.06	.05	.02
161	Bill Swift	.06	.05	.02
162	Trevor Wilson	.05	.04	.02
163	Brady Anderson	.10	.08	.04
164	Glenn Davis	.06	.05	.02
165	Mike Devereaux	.08	.06	.03
166	Todd Frohwirth	.04	.03	.02
167	Leo Gomez	.06	.05	.02
168	Chris Hoiles	.08	.06	.03
169	Ben McDonald	.08	.06	.03
170	Randy Milligan	.04	.03	.02
171	Alan Mills	.04	.03	.02
172	Mike Mussina	.25	.20	.10
173	Gregg Olson	.08	.06	.03
174	Arthur Rhodes	.10	.08	.04
175	David Segui	.05	.04	.02
176	Ellis Burks	.08	.06	.03
177	Roger Clemens	.15	.11	.06
178	Scott Cooper	.08	.06	.03
179	Danny Darwin	.04	.03	.02
180	Tony Fossas	.04	.03	.02
181	*Paul Quantrill*(FC)	.12	.09	.05
182	Jody Reed	.05	.04	.02
183	*John Valentin*	.12	.09	.05
184	Mo Vaughn	.08	.06	.03
185	Frank Viola	.08	.06	.03
186	Bob Zupcic	.08	.06	.03
187	Jim Abbott	.08	.06	.03
188	Gary DiSarcina	.04	.03	.02
189	*Damion Easley*	.15	.11	.06
190	Junior Felix	.06	.05	.02
191	Chuck Finley	.06	.05	.02
192	Joe Grahe	.06	.05	.02
193	Bryan Harvey	.06	.05	.02
194	Mark Langston	.08	.06	.03
195	John Orton	.04	.03	.02
196	Luis Polonia	.05	.04	.02
197	*Tim Salmon*	1.50	.90	.60
198	Luis Sojo	.05	.04	.02
199	Wilson Alvarez	.05	.04	.02
200	George Bell	.08	.06	.03
201	Alex Fernandez	.08	.06	.03
202	Craig Grebeck	.04	.03	.02
203	Ozzie Guillen	.06	.05	.02
204	Lance Johnson	.06	.05	.02
205	Ron Karkovice	.04	.03	.02
206	Kirk McCaskill	.05	.04	.02
207	Jack McDowell	.10	.08	.04
208	Scott Radinsky	.04	.03	.02
209	Tim Raines	.08	.06	.03
210	Frank Thomas	.75	.40	.25
211	Robin Ventura	.12	.09	.05
212	Sandy Alomar Jr.	.10	.08	.04
213	Carlos Baerga	.20	.12	.08
214	Dennis Cook	.04	.03	.02
215	Thomas Howard	.06	.05	.02
216	Mark Lewis	.08	.06	.03
217	Derek Lilliquist	.04	.03	.02
218	Kenny Lofton	.20	.12	.06
219	Charles Nagy	.15	.11	.06
220	Steve Olin	.06	.05	.02
221	Paul Sorrento	.06	.05	.02
222	Jim Thome	.10	.08	.04
223	Mark Whiten	.10	.08	.04
224	Milt Cuyler	.06	.05	.02
225	Rob Deer	.06	.05	.02
226	*John Doherty*	.12	.09	.05
227	Cecil Fielder	.12	.09	.05
228	Travis Fryman	.20	.12	.06
229	Mike Henneman	.06	.05	.02
230	*John Kiely*	.12	.09	.05
231	*Kurt Knudsen*	.12	.09	.05
232	Scott Livingstone	.10	.08	.04
233	Tony Phillips	.08	.06	.03
234	Mickey Tettleton	.08	.06	.03

		MT	NR MT	EX
235	Kevin Appier	.08	.06	.03
236	George Brett	.12	.09	.05
237	Tom Gordon	.05	.04	.02
238	Gregg Jefferies	.10	.08	.04
239	Wally Joyner	.10	.08	.04
240	*Kevin Koslofski*	.12	.09	.05
241	Mike Macfarlane	.05	.04	.02
242	Brian McRae	.08	.06	.03
243	Rusty Meacham	.08	.06	.03
244	Keith Miller	.06	.05	.02
245	Jeff Montgomery	.06	.05	.02
246	*Hipolito Pichardo*	.10	.08	.04
247	Ricky Bones	.08	.06	.03
248	Cal Eldred	.15	.11	.06
249	Mike Fetters	.05	.04	.02
250	Darryl Hamilton	.08	.06	.03
251	Doug Henry	.06	.05	.02
252	John Jaha(FC)	.15	.11	.06
253	*Pat Listach*	.10	.08	.04
254	Paul Molitor	.12	.09	.05
255	Jaime Navarro	.08	.06	.03
256	Kevin Seitzer	.06	.05	.02
257	B.J. Surhoff	.06	.05	.02
258	Greg Vaughn	.06	.05	.02
259	Bill Wegman	.06	.05	.02
260	Robin Yount	.15	.11	.06
261	Rick Aguilera	.08	.06	.03
262	Chili Davis	.06	.05	.02
263	Scott Erickson	.06	.05	.02
264	Greg Gagne	.05	.04	.02
265	Mark Guthrie	.04	.03	.02
266	Brian Harper	.08	.06	.03
267	Kent Hrbek	.08	.06	.03
268	Terry Jorgensen	.08	.06	.03
269	Gene Larkin	.04	.03	.02
270	Scott Leius	.06	.05	.02
271	Pat Mahomes	.15	.11	.06
272	Pedro Munoz	.10	.08	.04
273	Kirby Puckett	.20	.12	.06
274	Kevin Tapani	.08	.06	.03
275	Carl Willis	.04	.03	.02
276	Steve Farr	.05	.04	.02
277	John Habyan	.04	.03	.02
278	Mel Hall	.06	.05	.02
279	Charlie Hayes	.06	.05	.02
280	Pat Kelly	.06	.05	.02
281	Don Mattingly	.12	.09	.05
282	Sam Militello	.10	.08	.04
283	Matt Nokes	.06	.05	.02
284	Melido Perez	.06	.05	.02
285	Andy Stankiewicz	.10	.08	.04
286	Danny Tartabull	.10	.08	.04
287	Randy Velarde	.04	.03	.02
288	Bob Wickman	.15	.11	.06
289	Bernie Williams	.10	.08	.04
290	Lance Blankenship	.05	.04	.02
291	Mike Bordick	.08	.06	.03
292	Jerry Browne	.04	.03	.02
293	Dennis Eckersley	.10	.08	.04
294	Rickey Henderson	.15	.11	.06
295	*Vince Horsman*	.12	.09	.05
296	Mark McGwire	.10	.08	.04
297	Jeff Parrett	.04	.03	.02
298	Ruben Sierra	.10	.08	.04
299	Terry Steinbach	.06	.05	.02
300	Walt Weiss	.05	.04	.02
301	Bob Welch	.06	.05	.02
302	Willie Wilson	.06	.05	.02
303	Bobby Witt	.06	.05	.02
304	*Bret Boone*	.20	.15	.10
305	Jay Buhner	.06	.05	.02
306	Dave Fleming	.12	.09	.05
307	Ken Griffey, Jr.	.50	.30	.15
308	Erik Hanson	.06	.05	.02
309	Edgar Martinez	.12	.09	.05
310	Tino Martinez	.08	.06	.03
311	Jeff Nelson	.12	.09	.05
312	Dennis Powell	.04	.03	.02
313	Mike Schooler	.05	.04	.02
314	Russ Swan	.04	.03	.02
315	Dave Valle	.04	.03	.02
316	Omar Vizquel	.04	.03	.02
317	Kevin Brown	.08	.06	.03
318	Todd Burns	.04	.03	.02
319	Jose Canseco	.10	.08	.04
320	Julio Franco	.08	.06	.03
321	*Jeff Frye*(FC)	.12	.09	.05
322	Juan Gonzalez	.50	.30	.20
323	Jose Guzman	.06	.05	.02
324	Jeff Huson	.05	.04	.02
325	Dean Palmer	.08	.06	.03

		MT	NR MT	EX
326	Kevin Reimer	.06	.05	.02
327	Ivan Rodriguez	.15	.11	.06
328	Kenny Rogers	.04	.03	.02
329	Dan Smith(FC)	.08	.06	.03
330	Roberto Alomar	.20	.15	.08
331	Derek Bell	.12	.09	.05
332	Pat Borders	.06	.05	.02
333	Joe Carter	.12	.09	.05
334	Kelly Gruber	.08	.06	.03
335	Tom Henke	.08	.06	.03
336	Jimmy Key	.08	.06	.03
337	Manuel Lee	.05	.04	.02
338	Candy Maldonado	.06	.05	.02
339	John Olerud	.25	.15	.08
340	Todd Stottlemyre	.05	.04	.02
341	Duane Ward	.05	.04	.02
342	Devon White	.08	.06	.03
343	Dave Winfield	.15	.11	.06
344	Edgar Martinez (League Leaders)	.08	.06	.03
345	Cecil Fielder (League Leaders)	.10	.08	.04
346	Kenny Lofton (League Leaders)	.15	.11	.06
347	Jack Morris (League Leaders)	.08	.06	.03
348	Roger Clemens (League Leaders)	.12	.09	.05
349	Fred McGriff (Round Trippers)	.15	.11	.06
350	Barry Bonds (Round Trippers)	.15	.11	.06
351	Gary Sheffield (Round Trippers)	.15	.11	.06
352	Darren Daulton (Round Trippers)	.10	.08	.04
353	Dave Hollins (Round Trippers)	.10	.08	.04
354	Brothers In Blue (Pedro Martinez, Ramon Martinez)	.15	.11	.06
355	Power Packs (Ivan Rodriguez, Kirby Puckett)	.15	.11	.06
356	Triple Threats (Ryne Sandberg, Gary Sheffield)	.15	.11	.06
357	Infield Trifecta (Roberto Alomar, Chuck Knoblauch, Carlos Baerga)	.15	.11	.06
358	Checklist	.04	.03	.02
359	Checklist	.04	.03	.02
360	Checklist	.04	.03	.02
361	Rafael Belliard	.05	.04	.02
362	Damon Berryhill	.05	.04	.02
363	Mike Bielecki	.05	.04	.02
364	Jeff Blauser	.05	.04	.02
365	Francisco Cabrera	.05	.04	.02
366	Marvin Freeman	.05	.04	.02
367	David Justice	.25	.15	.10
368	Mark Lemke	.06	.05	.02
369	Alejandro Pena	.06	.05	.02
370	Jeff Reardon	.05	.04	.02
371	Lonnie Smith	.06	.05	.02
372	Pete Smith	.06	.05	.02
373	Shawn Boskie	.05	.04	.02
374	Jim Bullinger	.05	.04	.02
375	Frank Castillo	.05	.04	.02
376	Doug Dascenzo	.06	.05	.02
377	Andre Dawson	.10	.08	.04
378	Mike Harkey	.06	.05	.02
379	Greg Hibbard	.05	.04	.02
380	Greg Maddux	.10	.08	.04
381	Ken Patterson	.05	.04	.02
382	Jeff Robinson	.05	.04	.02
383	Luis Salazar	.04	.03	.02
384	Dwight Smith	.06	.05	.02
385	Jose Vizcaino	.05	.04	.02
386	Scott Bankhead	.06	.05	.02
387	Tom Browning	.06	.05	.02
388	Darnell Coles	.06	.05	.02
389	Rob Dibble	.05	.04	.02
390	Bill Doran	.05	.04	.02
391	Dwayne Henry	.06	.05	.02
392	Cesar Hernandez	.07	.05	.02
393	Roberto Kelly	.08	.06	.03
394	Barry Larkin	.10	.08	.04
395	Dave Martinez	.05	.04	.02
396	Kevin Mitchell	.06	.05	.02
397	Jeff Reed	.06	.05	.02
398	Scott Ruskin	.05	.04	.02
399	Greg Swindell	.06	.05	.02
400	Dan Wilson	.08	.06	.03
401	Andy Ashby	.06	.05	.02
402	Freddie Benavides	.05	.04	.02
403	Dante Bichette	.06	.05	.02
404	Willie Blair	.05	.04	.02
405	Denis Boucher	.06	.05	.02
406	Vinny Castilla	.06	.05	.02
407	Braulio Castillo	.06	.05	.02
408	Alex Cole	.06	.05	.02
409	Andres Galarraga	.08	.06	.03
410	Joe Girardi	.05	.04	.02
411	Butch Henry	.05	.04	.02
412	Darren Holmes	.05	.04	.02

		MT	NR MT	EX
413	Calvin Jones	.06	.05	.02
414	*Steve Reed*	.15	.11	.06
415	Kevin Ritz	.05	.04	.02
416	*Jim Tatum*	.15	.11	.06
417	Jack Armstrong	.05	.04	.02
418	Bret Barberie	.05	.04	.02
419	Ryan Bowen	.06	.05	.02
420	Cris Carpenter	.06	.05	.02
421	Chuck Carr	.06	.05	.02
422	Scott Chiamparino	.06	.05	.02
423	Jeff Conine	.08	.06	.03
424	Jim Corsi	.06	.05	.02
425	Steve Decker	.05	.04	.02
426	Chris Donnels	.06	.05	.02
427	Monty Fariss	.06	.05	.02
428	Bob Natal	.06	.05	.02
429	*Pat Rapp*	.15	.11	.06
430	Dave Weathers	.06	.05	.02
431	*Nigel Wilson*	.60	.40	.20
432	Ken Caminiti	.05	.04	.02
433	Andujar Cedeno	.06	.05	.02
434	Tom Edens	.06	.05	.02
435	Juan Guerrero	.06	.05	.02
436	Pete Incaviglia	.06	.05	.02
437	Jimmy Jones	.05	.04	.02
438	Darryl Kile	.05	.04	.02
439	Rob Murphy	.05	.04	.02
440	Al Osuna	.04	.03	.02
441	Mark Portugal	.04	.03	.02
442	Scott Servais	.04	.03	.02
443	John Candelaria	.04	.03	.02
444	Tim Crews	.04	.03	.02
445	Eric Davis	.06	.05	.02
446	Tom Goodwin	.06	.05	.02
447	Jim Gott	.05	.04	.02
448	Kevin Gross	.05	.04	.02
449	Dave Hansen	.05	.04	.02
450	Jay Howell	.06	.05	.02
451	Roger McDowell	.05	.04	.02
452	Bob Ojeda	.05	.04	.02
453	Henry Rodriguez	.06	.05	.02
454	Darryl Strawberry	.08	.06	.03
455	Mitch Webster	.06	.05	.02
456	Steve Wilson	.04	.03	.02
457	Brian Barnes	.05	.04	.02
458	Sean Berry	.08	.06	.03
459	Jeff Fassero	.06	.05	.02
460	Darrin Fletcher	.05	.04	.02
461	Marquis Grissom	.10	.08	.04
462	Dennis Martinez	.06	.05	.02
463	Spike Owen	.05	.04	.02
464	Matt Stairs	.05	.04	.02
465	Sergio Valdez	.06	.05	.02
466	Kevin Bass	.05	.04	.02
467	Vince Coleman	.05	.04	.02
468	Mark Dewey	.05	.04	.02
469	Kevin Elster	.05	.04	.02
470	Tony Fernandez	.06	.05	.02
471	John Franco	.05	.04	.02
472	Dave Gallagher	.05	.04	.02
473	Paul Gibson	.06	.05	.02
474	Dwight Gooden	.08	.06	.03
475	Lee Guetterman	.05	.04	.02
476	Jeff Innis	.05	.04	.02
477	Dave Magadan	.06	.05	.02
478	Charlie O'Brien	.06	.05	.02
479	Willie Randolph	.06	.05	.02
480	Mackey Sasser	.06	.05	.02
481	Ryan Thompson	.20	.15	.08
482	Chico Walker	.06	.05	.02
483	Kyle Abbott	.05	.04	.02
484	Bob Ayrault	.06	.05	.02
485	Kim Batiste	.06	.05	.02
486	Cliff Brantley	.06	.05	.02
487	Jose DeLeon	.05	.04	.02
488	Lenny Dykstra	.10	.08	.04
489	Tommy Greene	.08	.06	.03
490	Jeff Grotewold	.06	.05	.02
491	Dave Hollins	.10	.08	.04
492	Danny Jackson	.05	.04	.02
493	Stan Javier	.05	.04	.02
494	Tom Marsh	.05	.04	.02
495	Greg Matthews	.05	.04	.02
496	Dale Murphy	.05	.04	.02
497	*Todd Pratt*(FC)	.15	.11	.06
498	Mitch Williams	.05	.04	.02
499	Danny Cox	.05	.04	.02
500	Doug Drabek	.05	.04	.02
501	Carlos Garcia	.12	.09	.05
502	Lloyd McClendon	.05	.04	.02
503	Denny Neagle	.05	.04	.02

		MT	NR MT	EX
504	Gary Redus	.05	.04	.02
505	Bob Walk	.05	.04	.02
506	John Wehner	.05	.04	.02
507	Luis Alicea	.05	.04	.02
508	Mark Clark	.05	.04	.02
509	Pedro Guerrero	.05	.04	.02
510	Rex Hudler	.05	.04	.02
511	Brian Jordan	.12	.09	.05
512	Omar Olivares	.05	.04	.02
513	Jose Oquendo	.05	.04	.02
514	Gerald Perry	.05	.04	.02
515	Bryn Smith	.05	.04	.02
516	Craig Wilson	.05	.04	.02
517	Tracy Woodson	.05	.04	.02
518	Larry Anderson	.05	.04	.02
519	Andy Benes	.05	.04	.02
520	Jim Deshaies	.05	.04	.02
521	Bruce Hurst	.05	.04	.02
522	Randy Myers	.05	.04	.02
523	Benito Santiago	.05	.04	.02
524	Tim Scott	.05	.04	.02
525	Tim Teufel	.05	.04	.02
526	Mike Benjamin	.05	.04	.02
527	Dave Burba	.05	.04	.02
528	Craig Colbert	.05	.04	.02
529	Mike Felder	.05	.04	.02
530	Bryan Hickerson	.05	.04	.02
531	Chris James	.05	.04	.02
532	Mark Leonard	.05	.04	.02
533	Greg Litton	.05	.04	.02
534	Francisco Oliveras	.05	.04	.02
535	John Patterson	.05	.04	.02
536	Jim Pena	.05	.04	.02
537	Dave Righetti	.05	.04	.02
538	Robby Thompson	.05	.04	.02
539	Jose Uribe	.05	.04	.02
540	Matt Williams	.05	.04	.02
541	Storm Davis	.05	.04	.02
542	Sam Horn	.05	.04	.02
543	Tim Hulett	.05	.04	.02
544	Craig Lefferts	.05	.04	.02
545	Chito Martinez	.05	.04	.02
546	Mark McLemore	.05	.04	.02
547	Luis Mercedes	.05	.04	.02
548	Bob Milacki	.05	.04	.02
549	Joe Orsulak	.05	.04	.02
550	Billy Ripken	.05	.04	.02
551	Cal Ripken, Jr.	.20	.15	.08
552	Rick Sutcliffe	.05	.04	.02
553	Jeff Tackett	.05	.04	.02
554	Wade Boggs	.10	.08	.04
555	Tom Brunansky	.05	.04	.02
556	Jack Clark	.05	.04	.02
557	John Dopson	.05	.04	.02
558	Mike Gardiner	.05	.04	.02
559	Mike Greenwell	.05	.04	.02
560	Greg Harris	.05	.04	.02
561	Billy Hatcher	.05	.04	.02
562	Joe Hesketh	.05	.04	.02
563	Tony Pena	.05	.04	.02
564	Phil Plantier	.05	.04	.02
565	Luis Riveria	.05	.04	.02
566	Herm Winningham	.05	.04	.02
567	Matt Young	.05	.04	.02
568	Bert Blyleven	.05	.04	.02
569	Mike Butcher	.05	.04	.02
570	Chuck Crim	.05	.04	.02
571	*Chad Curtis*	.12	.09	.05
572	Tim Fortugno	.05	.04	.02
573	Steve Frey	.05	.04	.02
574	Gary Gaetti	.05	.04	.02
575	Scott Lewis	.05	.04	.02
576	Lee Stevens	.05	.04	.02
577	Ron Tingley	.05	.04	.02
578	Julio Valera	.05	.04	.02
579	Shawn Abner	.05	.04	.02
580	Joey Cora	.05	.04	.02
581	Chris Cron	.05	.04	.02
582	Carlton Fisk	.05	.04	.02
583	Roberto Hernandez	.05	.04	.02
584	Charlie Hough	.05	.04	.02
585	Terry leach	.05	.04	.02
586	Donn Pall	.05	.04	.02
587	Dan Pasqua	.05	.04	.02
588	Steve Sax	.05	.04	.02
589	Bobby Thigpen	.05	.04	.02
590	Albert Belle	.10	.08	.04
591	Felix Fermin	.05	.04	.02
592	Glenallen Hill	.05	.04	.02
593	Brook Jacoby	.05	.04	.02
594	Reggie Jefferson	.05	.04	.02

		MT	NR MT	EX
595	Carlos Martinez	.05	.04	.02
596	Jose Mesa	.05	.04	.02
597	Rod Nichols	.05	.04	.02
598	Junior Ortiz	.05	.04	.02
599	Eric Plunk	.05	.04	.02
600	Ted Power	.05	.04	.02
601	Scott Scudder	.05	.04	.02
602	Kevin Wickander	.05	.04	.02
603	Skeeter Barnes	.05	.04	.02
604	Mark Carreon	.05	.04	.02
605	Dan Gladden	.05	.04	.02
606	Bill Gullickson	.05	.04	.02
607	Chad Kreuter	.05	.04	.02
608	Mark Leiter	.05	.04	.02
609	Mike Munoz	.05	.04	.02
610	Rich Rowland	.05	.04	.02
611	Frank Tanana	.05	.04	.02
612	Walt Terrell	.05	.04	.02
613	Alan Trammell	.05	.04	.02
614	Lou Whitaker	.05	.04	.02
615	Luis Aquino	.05	.04	.02
616	Mike Boddicker	.05	.04	.02
617	Jim Eisenreich	.05	.04	.02
618	Mark Gubicza	.05	.04	.02
619	David Howard	.05	.04	.02
620	Mike Magnante	.05	.04	.02
621	Brent Mayne	.05	.04	.02
622	Kevin McReynolds	.05	.04	.02
623	*Eddie Pierce*(FC)	.15	.11	.06
624	Bill Sampen	.05	.04	.02
625	Steve Shifflett	.05	.04	.02
626	Gary Thurman	.05	.04	.02
627	Curtis Wilkerson	.05	.04	.02
628	Chris Bosio	.05	.04	.02
629	Scott Fletcher	.05	.04	.02
630	Jim Gantner	.05	.04	.02
631	Dave Nilsson	.05	.04	.02
632	Jesse Orosco	.05	.04	.02
633	Dan Plesac	.05	.04	.02
634	Ron Robinson	.05	.04	.02
635	Bill Spiers	.05	.04	.02
636	Franklin Stubbs	.05	.04	.02
637	Willie Banks	.05	.04	.02
638	Randy Bush	.05	.04	.02
639	Chuck Knoblauch	.12	.09	.05
640	Shane Mack	.05	.04	.02
641	Mike Pagliarulo	.05	.04	.02
642	Jeff Reboulet	.05	.04	.02
643	John Smiley	.05	.04	.02
644	*Mike Trombley*(FC)	.15	.11	.06
645	Gary Wayne	.05	.04	.02
646	Lenny Webster	.05	.04	.02
647	Tim Burke	.05	.04	.02
648	Mike Gallego	.05	.04	.02
649	Dion James	.05	.04	.02
650	Jeff Johnson	.05	.04	.02
651	Scott Kamieniecki	.05	.04	.02
652	Kevin Maas	.05	.04	.02
653	Rich Monteleone	.05	.04	.02
654	Jerry Nielsen	.05	.04	.02
655	Scott Sanderson	.05	.04	.02
656	Mike Stanley	.05	.04	.02
657	Gerald Williams	.05	.04	.02
658	Curt Young	.05	.04	.02
659	Harold Baines	.05	.04	.02
660	Kevin Campbell	.05	.04	.02
661	Ron Darling	.05	.04	.02
662	Kelly Downs	.05	.04	.02
663	Eric Fox	.05	.04	.02
664	Dave Henderson	.05	.04	.02
665	Rick Honeycutt	.05	.04	.02
666	Mike Moore	.05	.04	.02
667	Jamie Quirk	.05	.04	.02
668	Jeff Russell	.05	.04	.02
669	Dave Stewart	.05	.04	.02
670	Greg Briley	.05	.04	.02
671	Dave Cochrane	.05	.04	.02
672	Henry Cotto	.05	.04	.02
673	Rich DeLucia	.05	.04	.02
674	Brian Fisher	.05	.04	.02
675	Mark Grant	.05	.04	.02
676	Randy Johnson	.05	.04	.02
677	Tim Leary	.05	.04	.02
678	Pete O'Brien	.05	.04	.02
679	Lance Parrish	.05	.04	.02
680	Harold Reynolds	.05	.04	.02
681	Shane Turner	.05	.04	.02
682	Jack Daugherty	.05	.04	.02
683	*David Hulse*(FC)	.15	.11	.06
684	Terry Mathews	.05	.04	.02
685	Al Newman	.05	.04	.02

		MT	NR MT	EX
686	Edwin Nunez	.05	.04	.02
687	Rafael Palmeiro	.10	.08	.04
688	Roger Pavlik	.05	.04	.02
689	Geno Petralli	.05	.04	.02
690	Nolan Ryan	.40	.30	.15
691	David Cone	.05	.04	.02
692	Alfredo Griffin	.05	.04	.02
693	Juan Guzman	.15	.11	.06
694	Pat Hentgen	.15	.11	.06
695	Randy Knorr	.05	.04	.02
696	Bob MacDonald	.05	.04	.02
697	Jack Morris	.05	.04	.02
698	Ed Sprague	.05	.04	.02
699	Dave Stieb	.05	.04	.02
700	Pat Tabler	.05	.04	.02
701	Mike Timlin	.05	.04	.02
702	David Wells	.05	.04	.02
703	Eddie Zosky	.05	.04	.02
704	Gary Sheffield (League Leaders)	.10	.08	.04
705	Darren Daulton (League Leaders)	.08	.06	.03
706	Marquis Grissom (League Leaders)	.08	.06	.03
707	Greg Maddux (League Leaders)	.08	.06	.03
708	Bill Swift (League Leaders)	.05	.04	.02
709	Juan Gonzales (Round Trippers)	.50	.30	.15
710	Mark McGwire (Round Trippers)	.10	.08	.04
711	Cecil Fielder (Round Trippers)	.12	.09	.05
712	Albert Belle (Round Trippers)	.12	.09	.05
713	Joe Carter (Round Trippers)	.10	.08	.04
714	Power Brokers (Frank Thomas, Cecil Fielder)	.10	.08	.04
715	Unsung Heroes (Larry Walker, Darren Daulton)	.10	.08	.04
716	Hot Corner Hammers (Edgar Martinez, Robin Ventura)	.10	.08	.04
717	Start to Finish (Roger Clemens, Dennis Eckersley)	.10	.08	.04
718	Checklist	.05	.04	.02
719	Checklist	.05	.04	.02
720	Checklist	.05	.04	.02

1993 Fleer Golden Moments I

This three-card insert set was available in Series I wax packs. Fronts feature black borders with gold-foil baseballs in the corners. The palyer's name appears in a "Golden Moments" banner at the bottom of the photo. Backs have a portrait photo of the player at top-center and a white box with information on the highlight. The cards are not numbered and are checklisted here alphabetically.

		MT	NR MT	EX
Complete Set (3):		5.00	3.75	2.00
Common Player:		.75	.60	.30
(1)	George Brett	3.00	2.25	1.20
(2)	Mickey Morandini	.75	.60	.30
(3)	Dave Winfield	2.00	1.50	.80

1993 Fleer Golden Moments II

A second three-card series of "Golden Moments" was randomly inserted into Fleer Series II wax packs.

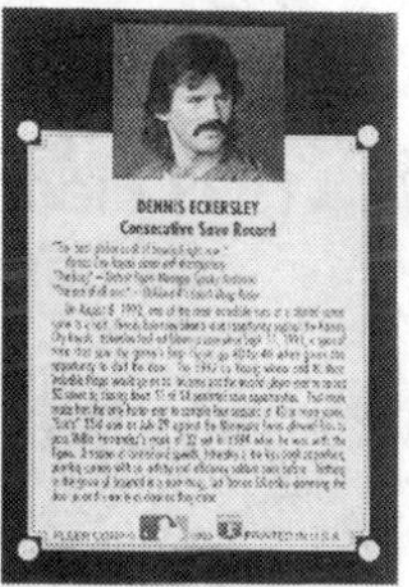

Complete Set (3):		7.00	5.50	3.00
Common Player:		.75	.60	.30
(1)	Dennis Eckersley	.75	.60	.30
(2)	Bip Roberts	.75	.60	.30
(3)	Frank Thomas/ Juan Gonzalez	6.00	4.50	2.25

1993 Fleer Major League Prospects I

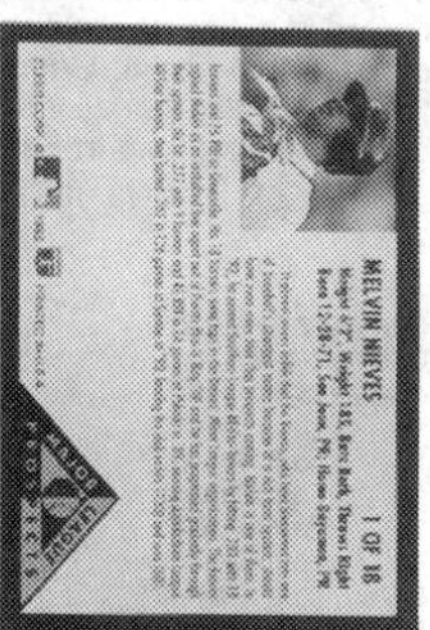

Yet another way to package currently hot rookies and future prospects to increase sales of the base product, there were 18 insert cards found in Series I wax packs.

		MT	NR MT	EX
Complete Set (18):		25.00	15.00	10.00
Common Player:		.75	.60	.30
1	Melvin Nieves	3.00	2.25	1.20
2	Sterling Hitchcock	1.50	1.00	.60
3	Tim Costo	1.00	.75	.40
4	Manny Alexander	.75	.60	.30
5	Alan Embree	.75	.60	.30
6	Kevin Young	2.00	1.50	.80
7	J.T. Snow	3.00	2.25	1.20
8	Russ Springer	.75	.60	.30
9	Billy Ashley	4.00	3.00	1.50
10	Kevin Rogers	.75	.60	.30
11	Steve Hosey	2.00	1.50	.80
12	Eric Wedge	.75	.60	.30
13	Mike Piazza	15.00	10.00	6.00
14	Jesse Levis	.75	.60	.30
15	Rico Brogna	.75	.60	.30
16	Alex Arias	.75	.60	.30
17	Rod Brewer	.75	.60	.30
18	Troy Neel	1.25	.95	.50

1993 Fleer Major League Prospects II

Photos not available at press time

Series II wax packs could be found with a second series of 18 potential future stars. Most of the players in the second series were still a few seasons away from everyday play in the majors.

		MT	NR MT	EX
Complete Set (18):		16.00	10.00	5.00
Common Player:		.75	.60	.30
1	Scooter Tucker	.75	.60	.30
2	Kerry Woodson	.75	.60	.30
3	Greg Colbrunn	.75	.60	.30
4	Pedro Martinez	1.50	1.00	.60
5	Dave Silvestri	.75	.60	.30
6	Kent Bottenfield	.75	.60	.30
7	Rafael Bournigal	.75	.60	.30
8	J.T. Bruett	.75	.60	.30
9	Dave Mlicki	.75	.60	.30
10	Paul Wagner	.75	.60	.30
11	Mike Williams	.75	.60	.30
12	Henry Mercedes	.75	.60	.30
13	Scott Taylor	.75	.60	.30
14	Dennis Moeller	.75	.60	.30
15	Javy Lopez	6.00	4.50	2.25
16	Steve Cooke	1.50	1.00	.60
17	Pete Young	.75	.60	.30
18	Ken Ryan	1.00	.75	.40

1993 Fleer All-Stars

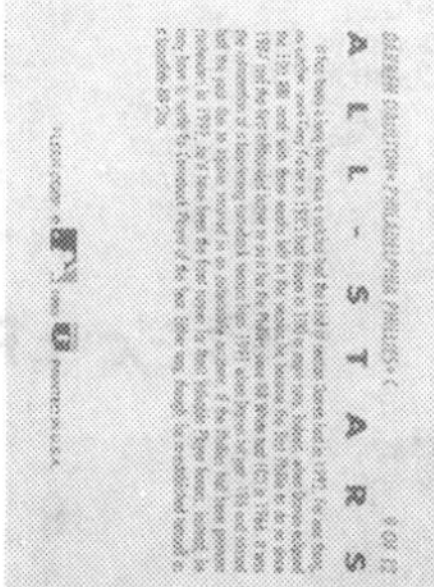

Attractive horizontal-format All-Star cards comprised another of the many 1993 Fleer insert issues. Twelve cards of National League All-Stars were included in Series I wax packs, while a dozen American League All-Stars were found in Series II packs. They are among the more popular and valuable of the '93 Fleer inserts.

		MT	NR MT	EX
Complete Set AL (12):		30.00	20.00	10.00
Complete Set NL (12):		16.00	10.00	6.00
Common Player:		.75	.60	.30
	AL All-Stars			
1	Frank Thomas	10.00	7.50	4.00
2	Roberto Alomar	4.00	3.00	1.50
3	Edgar Martinez	1.00	.75	.40
4	Pat Listach	.75	.60	.30
5	Cecil Fielder	1.75	1.25	.70
6	Juan Gonzalez	8.00	6.00	3.25
7	Ken Griffey Jr.	9.00	6.75	3.50
8	Joe Carter	3.00	2.25	1.20

		MT	NR MT	EX
9	Kirby Puckett	4.00	3.00	1.50
10	Brian Harper	.75	.60	.30
11	Dave Fleming	.75	.60	.30
12	Jack McDowell	2.00	1.50	.80
	NL All-Stars			
1	Fred McGriff	3.00	2.25	1.20
2	Delino DeShields	1.00	.75	.40
3	Gary Sheffield	1.50	1.00	.60
4	Barry Larkin	1.00	.75	.40
5	Felix Jose	1.00	.75	.40
6	Larry Walker	1.50	1.00	.60
7	Barry Bonds	4.50	3.50	1.75
8	Andy Van Slyke	2.00	1.50	.80
9	Darren Daulton	1.50	1.00	.60
10	Greg Maddux	2.50	2.00	1.00
11	Tom Glavine	2.00	1.50	.80
12	Lee Smith	2.00	1.50	.80

1993 Fleer ProVisions I

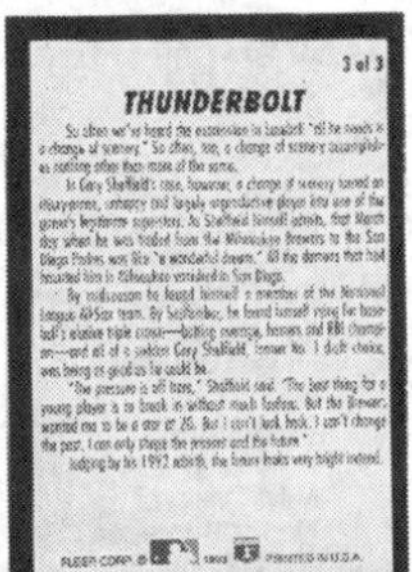

This three-card insert set in Series I wax packs features the baseball art of Wayne Still. Black-bordered fronts feature a player-fantasy painting at center, with the player's name gold-foil stamped beneath. Backs are also bordered in black and have a white box with a career summary.

		MT	NR MT	EX
Complete Set (3):		6.00	4.00	2.00
Common Player:		.75	.60	.30
1	Roberto Alomar	4.00	3.00	1.50
2	Dennis Eckersley	.75	.60	.30
3	Gary Sheffield	1.75	1.25	.70

1993 Fleer ProVisions II

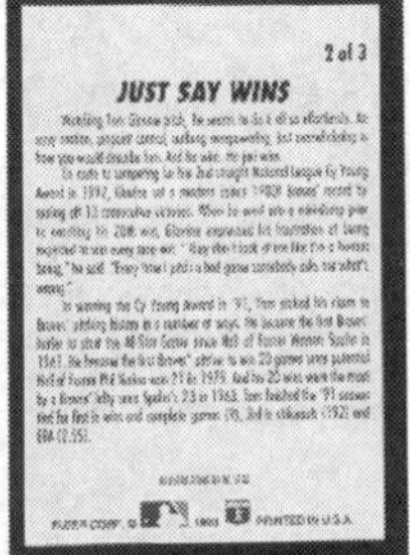

A second series of three cards based on Wayne Still's artwork was randomply inserted in Series II wax packs.

		MT	NR MT	EX
Complete Set (3):		4.00	3.00	1.50
Common Player:		.75	.60	.30
1	Andy Van Slyke	.75	.60	.30
2	Tom Glavine	1.75	1.25	.70

		MT	NR MT	EX
3	Cecil Fielder	2.00	1.50	.80

1993 Fleer Tom Glavine Career Highlights

This 15-card insert set spotlighted the career highlights of Fleer's 1993 spokesman, Tom Glavine. Twelve cards were available in Series I and Series II packs; cards #13-15 could be obtained only via a special mail offer. A limited number of certified autograph cards were also inserted into packs. Cards #1-4 and 7-10 can each be found with two variations of the writeups on the back. The versions found in Series II packaging are the "correct" backs. Neither version carries a premium value.

		MT	NR MT	EX
Complete set (15):		6.00	4.50	2.25
Common card:		.50	.40	.20
Autographed card:		60.00	45.00	22.50
1	Tom Glavine	.50	.40	.20
2	Tom Glavine	.50	.40	.20
3	Tom Glavine	.50	.40	.20
4	Tom Glavine	.50	.40	.20
5	Tom Glavine	.50	.40	.20
6	Tom Glavine	.50	.40	.20
7	Tom Glavine	.50	.40	.20
8	Tom Glavine	.50	.40	.20
9	Tom Glavine	.50	.40	.20
10	Tom Glavine	.50	.40	.20
11	Tom Glavine	.50	.40	.20
12	Tom Glavine	.50	.40	.20
13	Tom Glavine	.50	.40	.20
14	Tom Glavine	.50	.40	.20
15	Tom Glavine	.50	.40	.20

1993 Fleer Rookie Sensations I

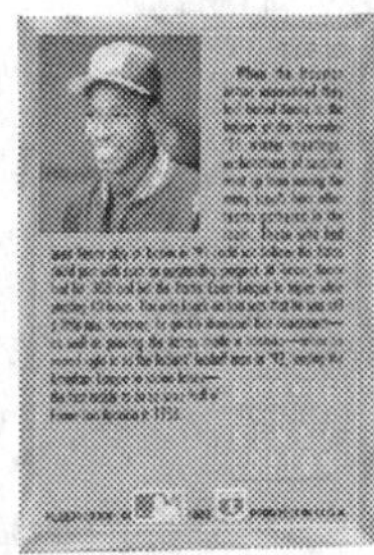

Ten rookie sensations - some of whom had not been true rookies for several seasons - were featured in this insert issue which was packaged exclusively in Series I cello packs. Card fronts have a player photo set against a silver background and surrounded by a blue border.

The player's name and other front printing are in gold foil. Backs are also printed in silver with a blue border. There is a player portrait photo and career summary.

		MT	NR MT	EX
Complete Set (10):		28.00	16.00	10.00
Common Player:		1.00	.60	.30
1	Kenny Lofton	8.00	6.00	3.00
2	Cal Eldred	4.50	3.00	1.50
3	Pat Listach	2.50	1.50	.75
4	Roberto Hernandez	1.25	.75	.40
5	Dave Fleming	4.00	3.00	1.50
6	Eric Karros	5.00	3.00	1.50
7	Reggie Sanders	4.50	3.00	1.50
8	Derrick May	3.00	2.00	1.00
9	Mike Perez	2.00	1.25	.60
10	Donovan Osborne	3.00	2.00	1.00

1993 Fleer Rookie Sensations II

A second, less formidable line-up, of 10 young players was randomly inserted in Series II cello packs. Format was the same as Series I cards.

		MT	NR MT	EX
Complete Set (10):		18.00	12.00	6.00
Common Player:		1.00	.60	.30
1	Moises Alou	3.50	2.50	1.25
2	Pedro Astacio	3.00	2.00	1.00
3	Jim Austin	2.50	1.50	.75
4	Chad Curtis	7.00	5.00	2.50
5	Gary DiSarcina	2.50	1.75	.75
6	Scott Livingstone	2.00	1.25	.60
7	Sam Militello	1.50	1.00	.50
8	Arthur Rhodes	1.50	1.00	.50
9	Tim Wakefield	2.00	1.50	.75
10	Bob Zupcic	1.25	.75	.40

1993 Fleer AL Team Leaders

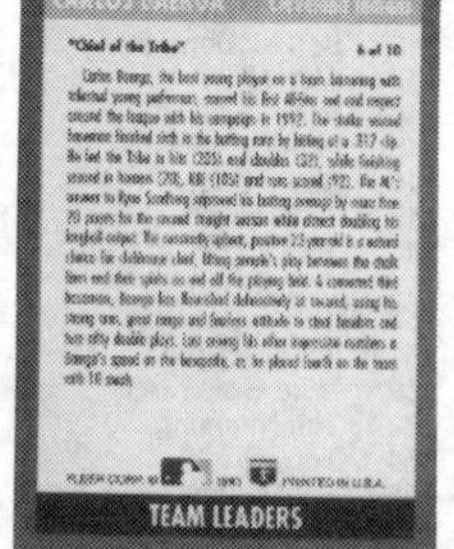

This 10-card insert issue was exclusive to Series I rack packs. Fronts have a portrait photo, with a small action photo superimposed. At the side is a red-and-blue bar with the player's name and "Team Leaders" printed vertically. On back is a career summary. Card borders are a light metallic green and both sides of the card are UV coated.

		MT	NR MT	EX
Complete Set (10):		20.00	12.00	6.00
Common Player:		.75	.50	.25
1	Kirby Puckett	3.00	2.00	1.00
2	Mark McGwire	1.25	.75	.40
3	Pat Listach	1.00	.60	.30
4	Roger Clemens	2.50	1.50	.75
5	Frank Thomas	7.50	5.00	2.50
6	Carlos Baerga	2.50	1.50	.75
7	Brady Anderson	.75	.50	.25
8	Juan Gonzalez	6.00	4.00	2.00
9	Roberto Alomar	3.00	2.00	1.00
10	Ken Griffey Jr.	7.00	5.00	2.50

1993 Fleer NL Team Leaders

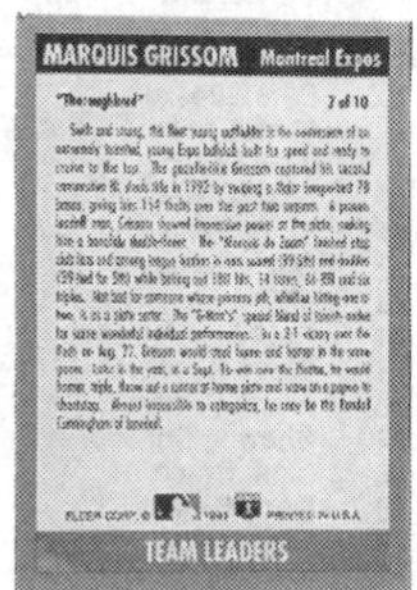

This 10-card insert issue was exclusive to Series II rack packs. Format is similar to the American League cards issued with Series I.

		MT	NR MT	EX
Complete Set (10):		10.00	6.00	3.00
Common Player:		.75	.50	.25
1	Will Clark	2.00	1.50	.75
2	Terry Pendleton	.75	.50	.25
3	Ray Lankford	.90	.60	.30
4	Eric Karros	1.50	1.00	.50
5	Gary sheffield	1.50	1.00	.50
6	Ryne Sandberg	3.00	2.00	1.00
7	Marquis Grissom	1.25	.75	.40
8	John Kruk	.75	.50	.25
9	Jeff Bagwell	2.00	1.50	.75
10	Andy Van Slyke	.75	.50	.25

1993 Fleer Ultra

The first series of 300 cards retains Fleer's successful features from 1992, including additional gold foil stamping, UV coating, and team color-coded marbled bars on the fronts. The backs feature a dimensionalized ballpark background, which creates a 3-D effect, stats and two photos, a portrait and an action shot. Dennis Eckersley is featured in a limited-edition "Career Highlights" set and has personally autographed more than 2,000 of his cards, to be randomly inserted into both series' packs. A 10-card Home Run Kings subset and 25-card Ultra Awards Winners subset were also randomly inserted in packs. These subsets' card have gold foil on both sides. Ultra Rookies cards are included in both series. Ultra's second series has three limited-edition subsets: Ultra All-Stars, Ultra All-Rookie Team, and Strikeout Kings, plus cards featuring Colorado Rockies and Florida Marlins players.

		MT	NR MT	EX
Complete Set (650):		25.00	18.00	10.00
Common Player:		.10	.08	.04
1	Steve Avery	.60	.45	.25
2	Rafael Belliard	.10	.08	.04
3	Damon Berryhill	.10	.08	.04
4	Sid Bream	.10	.08	.04
5	Ron Gant	.20	.15	.08
6	Tom Glavine	.30	.25	.12
7	Ryan Klesko	.80	.60	.30
8	Mark Lemke	.10	.08	.04
9	Javy Lopez	1.25	.90	.50
10	Greg Olson	.10	.08	.04
11	Terry Pendleton	.10	.08	.04
12	Deion Sanders	.30	.25	.12
13	Mike Stanton	.10	.08	.04
14	Paul Assenmacher	.10	.08	.04
15	Steve Buechele	.10	.08	.04
16	Frank Castillo	.10	.08	.04
17	Shawon Dunston	.10	.08	.04
18	Mark Grace	.20	.15	.08
19	Derrick May	.10	.08	.04
20	Chuck McElroy	.10	.08	.04
21	Mike Morgan	.10	.08	.04
22	Bob Scanlan	.10	.08	.04
23	Dwight Smith	.10	.08	.04
24	Sammy Sosa	.10	.08	.04
25	Rick Wilkins	.10	.08	.04
26	Tim Belcher	.10	.08	.04
27	Jeff Branson	.10	.08	.04
28	Bill Doran	.10	.08	.04
29	Chris Hammond	.10	.08	.04
30	Barry Larkin	.20	.15	.08
31	Hal Morris	.10	.08	.04
32	Joe Oliver	.10	.08	.04
33	Jose Rijo	.10	.08	.04
34	Bip Roberts	.10	.08	.04
35	Chris Sabo	.10	.08	.04
36	Reggie Sanders	.30	.25	.12
37	Craig Biggio	.10	.08	.04
38	Ken Caminiti	.10	.08	.04
39	Steve Finley	.10	.08	.04
40	Luis Gonzalez	.10	.08	.04
41	Juan Guerrero	.10	.08	.04
42	Pete Harnisch	.10	.08	.04
43	Xavier Hernandez	.10	.08	.04
44	Doug Jones	.10	.08	.04
45	Al Osuna	.10	.08	.04
46	Eddie Taubensee	.10	.08	.04
47	Scooter Tucker	.10	.08	.04
48	Brian Williams	.10	.08	.04
49	Pedro Astacio	.40	.30	.15
50	Rafael Bournigal	.25	.20	.10
51	Brett Butler	.10	.08	.04
52	Tom Candiotti	.10	.08	.04
53	Eric Davis	.10	.08	.04
54	Lenny Harris	.10	.08	.04
55	Orel Hershiser	.10	.08	.04
56	Eric Karros	.60	.45	.25
57	Pedro Martinez	.25	.20	.10
58	Roger McDowell	.10	.08	.04
59	Jose Offerman	.10	.08	.04
60	Mike Piazza	7.00	5.25	2.75
61	Moises Alou	.15	.11	.06
62	Kent Bottenfield	.10	.08	.04
63	Archi Cianfrocco	.10	.08	.04
64	Greg Colbrunn	.10	.08	.04
65	Wil Cordero	.35	.25	.14
66	Delino DeShields	.20	.15	.08
67	Darrin Fletcher	.10	.08	.04
68	Ken Hill	.10	.08	.04
69	Chris Nabholz	.10	.08	.04
70	Mel Rojas	.10	.08	.04
71	Larry Walker	.40	.30	.15
72	Sid Fernandez	.10	.08	.04
73	John Franco	.10	.08	.04
74	Dave Gallagher	.10	.08	.04
75	Todd Hundley	.10	.08	.04
76	Howard Johnson	.10	.08	.04
77	Jeff Kent	.20	.15	.08
78	Eddie Murray	.25	.20	.10
79	Bret Saberhagen	.10	.08	.04
80	Chico Walker	.10	.08	.04
81	Anthony Young	.10	.08	.04
82	Kyle Abbott	.10	.08	.04
83	Ruben Amaro Jr.	.10	.08	.04
84	Juan Bell	.10	.08	.04
85	Wes Chamberlain	.10	.08	.04
86	Darren Daulton	.20	.15	.08
87	Mariano Duncan	.10	.08	.04
88	Dave Hollins	.25	.20	.10
89	Ricky Jordan	.10	.08	.04
90	John Kruk	.20	.15	.08
91	Mickey Morandini	.10	.08	.04
92	Terry Mulholland	.10	.08	.04
93	Ben Rivera	.10	.08	.04
94	Mike Williams	.20	.15	.08
95	Stan Belinda	.10	.08	.04
96	Jay Bell	.10	.08	.04
97	Jeff King	.10	.08	.04
98	Mike LaValliere	.10	.08	.04
99	Lloyd McClendon	.10	.08	.04
100	Orlando Merced	.10	.08	.04
101	Zane Smith	.10	.08	.04
102	Randy Tomlin	.10	.08	.04
103	Andy Van Slyke	.10	.08	.04
104	Tim Wakefield	.20	.15	.08
105	John Wehner	.10	.08	.04
106	Bernard Gilkey	.10	.08	.04
107	Brian Jordan	.30	.25	.12
108	Ray Lankford	.30	.25	.12
109	Donovan Osborne	.30	.25	.12
110	Tom Pagnozzi	.10	.08	.04
111	Mike Perez	.10	.08	.04
112	Lee Smith	.10	.08	.04
113	Ozzie Smith	.30	.25	.12
114	Bob Tewksbury	.10	.08	.04
115	Todd Zeile	.10	.08	.04
116	Andy Benes	.15	.11	.06
117	Greg Harris	.10	.08	.04
118	Darrin Jackson	.10	.08	.04
119	Fred McGriff	.40	.25	.12
120	Rich Rodriguez	.10	.08	.04
121	Frank Seminara	.10	.08	.04
122	Gary Sheffield	.40	.30	.15
123	Craig Shipley	.10	.08	.04
124	Kurt Stillwell	.10	.08	.04
125	Dan Walters	.10	.08	.04
126	Rod Beck	.10	.08	.04
127	Mike Benjamin	.10	.08	.04
128	Jeff Brantley	.10	.08	.04
129	John Burkett	.10	.08	.04
130	Will Clark	.40	.30	.20
131	Royce Clayton	.30	.25	.12
132	Steve Hosey	.35	.25	.14
133	Mike Jackson	.10	.08	.04
134	Darren Lewis	.10	.08	.04
135	Kirt Manwaring	.10	.08	.04
136	Bill Swift	.10	.08	.04
137	Robby Thompson	.10	.08	.04
138	Brady Anderson	.15	.11	.06
139	Glenn Davis	.10	.08	.04
140	Leo Gomez	.10	.08	.04
141	Chito Martinez	.10	.08	.04
142	Ben McDonald	.10	.08	.04
143	Alan Mills	.10	.08	.04
144	Mike Mussina	.80	.60	.30
145	Gregg Olson	.10	.08	.04
146	David Segui	.10	.08	.04
147	Jeff Tackett	.10	.08	.04
148	Jack Clark	.10	.08	.04
149	Scott Cooper	.10	.08	.04
150	Danny Darwin	.10	.08	.04
151	John Dopson	.10	.08	.04
152	Mike Greenwell	.10	.08	.04
153	Tim Naehring	.10	.08	.04
154	Tony Pena	.10	.08	.04
155	Paul Quantrill	.10	.08	.04
156	Mo Vaughn	.50	.40	.20
157	Frank Viola	.10	.08	.04
158	Bob Zupcic	.10	.08	.04
159	Chad Curtis	.45	.25	.12
160	Gary Discarcina	.10	.08	.04

		MT	NR MT	EX
161	Damion Easley	.35	.20	.10
162	Chuck Finley	.10	.08	.04
163	Tim Fortugno	.10	.08	.04
164	Rene Gonzales	.10	.08	.04
165	Joe Grahe	.10	.08	.04
166	Mark Langston	.10	.08	.04
167	John Orton	.10	.08	.04
168	Luis Polonia	.10	.08	.04
169	Julio Valera	.10	.08	.04
170	Wilson Alvarez	.20	.15	.08
171	George Bell	.10	.08	.04
172	Joey Cora	.10	.08	.04
173	Alex Fernandez	.20	.15	.08
174	Lance Johnson	.10	.08	.04
175	Ron Karkovice	.10	.08	.04
176	Jack McDowell	.40	.30	.15
177	Scott Radinsky	.10	.08	.04
178	Tim Raines	.10	.08	.04
179	Steve Sax	.10	.08	.04
180	Bobby Thigpen	.10	.08	.04
181	Frank Thomas	3.00	2.25	1.25
182	Sandy Alomar Jr.	.10	.08	.04
183	Carlos Baerga	.70	.40	.20
184	Felix Fermin	.10	.08	.04
185	Thomas Howard	.10	.08	.04
186	Mark Lewis	.10	.08	.04
187	Derek Lilliquist	.10	.08	.04
188	Carlos Martinez	.10	.08	.04
189	Charles Nagy	.20	.15	.08
190	Scott Scudder	.10	.08	.04
191	Paul Sorrento	.10	.08	.04
192	Jim Thome	.20	.15	.08
193	Mark Whiten	.15	.11	.06
194	Milt Cuyler	.10	.08	.04
195	Rob Deer	.10	.08	.04
196	John Doherty	.10	.08	.04
197	Travis Fryman	.60	.45	.25
198	Dan Gladden	.10	.08	.04
199	Mike Henneman	.10	.08	.04
200	John Kiely	.10	.08	.04
201	Chad Kreuter	.10	.08	.04
202	Scott Livingstone	.10	.08	.04
203	Tony Phillips	.10	.08	.04
204	Alan Trammell	.10	.08	.04
205	Mike Boddicker	.10	.08	.04
206	George Brett	.30	.25	.12
207	Tom Gordon	.10	.08	.04
208	Mark Gubicza	.10	.08	.04
209	Gregg Jefferies	.20	.15	.08
210	Wally Joyner	.10	.08	.04
211	Kevin Koslofski	.10	.08	.04
212	Brent Mayne	.10	.08	.04
213	Brian McRae	.10	.08	.04
214	Kevin McReynolds	.10	.08	.04
215	Rusty Meacham	.10	.08	.04
216	Steve Shifflett	.10	.08	.04
217	James Austin	.10	.08	.04
218	Cal Eldred	.25	.20	.10
219	Darryl Hamilton	.10	.08	.04
220	Doug Henry	.10	.08	.04
221	John Jaha	.40	.30	.15
222	Dave Nilsson	.25	.20	.10
223	Jesse Orosco	.10	.08	.04
224	B.J. Surhoff	.10	.08	.04
225	Greg Vaughn	.10	.08	.04
226	Bill Wegman	.10	.08	.04
227	Robin Yount	.30	.25	.12
228	Rick Aguilera	.10	.08	.04
229	J.T. Bruett	.10	.08	.04
230	Scott Erickson	.10	.08	.04
231	Kent Hrbek	.10	.08	.04
232	Terry Jorgensen	.10	.08	.04
233	Scott Leius	.10	.08	.04
234	Pat Mahomes	.20	.15	.08
235	Pedro Munoz	.20	.15	.08
236	Kirby Puckett	.60	.45	.25
237	Kevin Tapani	.15	.11	.06
238	Lenny Webster	.10	.08	.04
239	Carl Willis	.10	.08	.04
240	Mike Gallego	.10	.08	.04
241	John Habyan	.10	.08	.04
242	Pat Kelly	.10	.08	.04
243	Kevin Maas	.10	.08	.04
244	Don Mattingly	.40	.30	.15
245	Hensley Meulens	.10	.08	.04
246	Sam Militello	.30	.25	.12
247	Matt Nokes	.10	.08	.04
248	Melido Perez	.10	.08	.04
249	Andy Stankiewicz	.10	.08	.04
250	Rany Velarde	.10	.08	.04
251	Bob Wickman	.50	.40	.20
252	Bernie Williams	.10	.08	.04
253	Lance Blankenship	.10	.08	.04
254	Mike Bordick	.10	.08	.04
255	Jerry Browne	.10	.08	.04
256	Ron Darling	.10	.08	.04
257	Dennis Eckersley	.20	.15	.08
258	Rickey Henderson	.30	.25	.12
259	Vince Horsman	.10	.08	.04
260	Troy Neel	.30	.25	.12
261	Jeff Parrett	.10	.08	.04
262	Terry Steinbach	.10	.08	.04
263	Bob Welch	.10	.08	.04
264	Bobby Witt	.10	.08	.04
265	Rich Amaral	.10	.08	.04
266	Bret Boone	.45	.35	.25
267	Jay Buhner	.10	.08	.04
268	Dave Fleming	.30	.25	.12
269	Randy Johnson	.20	.15	.08
270	Edgar Martinez	.10	.08	.04
271	Mike Schooler	.10	.08	.04
272	Russ Swan	.10	.08	.04
273	Dave Valle	.10	.08	.04
274	Omar Vizquel	.10	.08	.04
275	Kerry Woodson	.10	.08	.04
276	Kevin Brown	.10	.08	.04
277	Julio Franco	.10	.08	.04
278	Jeff Frye	.10	.08	.04
279	Juan Gonzalez	3.00	2.25	1.25
280	Jeff Huson	.10	.08	.04
281	Rafael Palmeiro	.15	.11	.06
282	Dean Palmer	.40	.25	.15
283	Roger Pavlik	.10	.08	.04
284	Ivan Rodriguez	.50	.40	.20
285	Kenny Rogers	.10	.08	.04
286	Derek Bell	.10	.08	.04
287	Pat Borders	.10	.08	.04
288	Joe Carter	.25	.20	.10
289	Bob MacDonald	.10	.08	.04
290	Jack Morris	.10	.08	.04
291	John Olerud	1.00	.70	.40
292	Ed Sprague	.20	.15	.08
293	Todd Stottlemyre	.10	.08	.04
294	Mike Timlin	.10	.08	.04
295	Duane Ward	.10	.08	.04
296	David Wells	.10	.08	.04
297	Devon White	.10	.08	.04
298	Checklist	.10	.08	.04
299	Checklist	.10	.08	.04
300	Checklist	.10	.08	.04
301	Steve Bedrosian	.10	.08	.04
302	Jeff Blauser	.10	.08	.04
303	Francisco Cabrera	.10	.08	.04
304	Marvin Freeman	.10	.08	.04
305	Brian Hunter	.10	.08	.04
306	David Justice	.75	.60	.30
307	Greg Maddux	.40	.30	.15
308	*Greg McMichael*	.70	.50	.25
309	Kent Mercker	.10	.08	.04
310	Otis Nixon	.10	.08	.04
311	Pete Smith	.10	.08	.04
312	John Smoltz	.20	.15	.08
313	Jose Guzman	.10	.08	.04
314	Mike Harkey	.10	.08	.04
315	Greg Hibbard	.10	.08	.04
316	Candy Maldonado	.10	.08	.04
317	Randy Myers	.10	.08	.04
318	Dan Plesac	.10	.08	.04
319	Rey Sanchez	.10	.08	.04
320	Ryne Sandberg	.90	.70	.35
321	*Tommy Shields*	.30	.25	.12
322	Jose Vizcaino	.10	.08	.04
323	*Matt Walbeck*	.25	.20	.10
324	Willie Wilson	.10	.08	.04
325	Tom Browning	.10	.08	.04
326	Tim Costo	.15	.11	.06
327	Rob Dibble	.10	.08	.04
328	Steve Foster	.10	.08	.04
329	Roberto Kelly	.10	.08	.04
330	Randy Milligan	.10	.08	.04
331	Kevin Mitchell	.10	.08	.04
332	*Tim Pugh*	.50	.40	.20
333	Jeff Reardon	.10	.08	.04
334	*John Roper*	.20	.15	.08
335	Juan Samuel	.10	.08	.04
336	John Smiley	.10	.08	.04
337	San Wilson	.10	.08	.04
338	Scott Aldred	.10	.08	.04
339	Andy Ashby	.10	.08	.04
340	Freddie Benavides	.10	.08	.04
341	Dante Bichette	.10	.08	.04
342	Willie Blair	.10	.08	.04

		MT	NR MT	EX
343	Daryl Boston	.10	.08	.04
344	*Vinny Castilla*	.15	.11	.06
345	Jerald Clark	.10	.08	.04
346	Alex Cole	.10	.08	.04
347	Andres Galarraga	.10	.08	.04
348	Joe Girardi	.10	.08	.04
349	*Ryan Hawblitzel*	.15	.11	.06
350	Charlie Hayes	.10	.08	.04
351	Butch Henry	.10	.08	.04
352	Darren Holmes	.10	.08	.04
353	Dale Murphy	.10	.08	.04
354	David Nied	1.25	.90	.50
355	Jeff Parrett	.10	.08	.04
356	*Steve Reed*	.20	.15	.08
357	Bruce Ruffin	.10	.08	.04
358	*Danny Sheaffer*	.15	.11	.06
359	Bryn Smith	.10	.08	.04
360	*Jim Tatum*	.30	.25	.12
361	Eric Young	.40	.30	.15
362	Gerald Young	.10	.08	.04
363	Luis Aquino	.10	.08	.04
364	*Alex Arias*	.10	.08	.04
365	Jack Armstrong	.10	.08	.04
366	Bret Barberie	.10	.08	.04
367	Ryan Bowen	.10	.08	.04
368	Greg Briley	.10	.08	.04
369	Cris Carpenter	.10	.08	.04
370	Chuck Carr	.10	.08	.04
371	*Jeff Conine*	.15	.11	.06
372	Steve Decker	.10	.08	.04
373	Orestes Destrade	.10	.08	.04
374	Monty Fariss	.10	.08	.04
375	Junior Felix	.10	.08	.04
376	Chris Hammond	.10	.08	.04
377	Bryan Harvey	.10	.08	.04
378	*Trevor Hoffman*	.15	.11	.06
379	Charlie Hough	.10	.08	.04
380	Joe Klink	.10	.08	.04
381	*Richie Lewis*	.40	.30	.15
382	Dave Magadan	.10	.08	.04
383	Bob McCLure	.10	.08	.04
384	*Scott Pose*	.40	.30	.15
385	*Rich Renteria*	.15	.11	.06
386	Benito Santiago	.10	.08	.04
387	Walt Weiss	.10	.08	.04
388	Nigel Wilson	1.00	.70	.40
389	Eric Anthony	.10	.08	.04
390	Jeff Bagwell	.50	.40	.20
391	Andujar Cedeno	.10	.08	.04
392	Doug Drabek	.10	.08	.04
393	Darryl Kile	.10	.08	.04
394	Mark Portugal	.10	.08	.04
395	Karl Rhodes	.10	.08	.04
396	Scott Servais	.10	.08	.04
397	Greg Swindell	.10	.08	.04
398	Tom Goodwin	.10	.08	.04
399	Kevin Gross	.10	.08	.04
400	Carlos Hernandez	.10	.08	.04
401	Ramon Martinez	.10	.08	.04
402	Raul Mondesi	.50	.40	.20
403	Jody Reed	.10	.08	.04
404	Mike Sharperson	.10	.08	.04
405	Cory Snyder	.10	.08	.04
406	Darryl Strawberry	.10	.08	.04
407	*Rick Trlicek*	.15	.11	.06
408	Tim Wallach	.10	.08	.04
409	Todd Worrell	.10	.08	.04
410	Tavo Alvarez	.25	.20	.10
411	*Sean Berry*	.15	.11	.06
412	*Frank Bolick*	.15	.11	.06
413	Cliff Floyd	3.50	2.75	1.50
414	Mike Gardiner	.10	.08	.04
415	Marquis Grissom	.20	.15	.08
416	*Tim Laker*	.30	.25	.12
417	*Mike Lansing*	1.25	.90	.50
418	Dennis Martinez	.10	.08	.04
419	John Vander Wal	.10	.08	.04
420	John Wetteland	.10	.08	.04
421	Rondell White	1.25	.90	.50
422	Bobby Bonilla	.15	.11	.06
423	Jeromy Burnitz	.50	.40	.20
424	*Vince Burnitz*	.15	.11	.06
425	*Mike Draper*	.15	.11	.06
426	Tony Fernandez	.10	.08	.04
427	Dwight Gooden	.10	.08	.04
428	Jeff Innis	.10	.08	.04
429	Bobby Jones	.75	.60	.30
430	Mike Maddux	.10	.08	.04
431	Charlie O'Brien	.10	.08	.04
432	Joe Orsulak	.10	.08	.04
433	Pete Schourek	.10	.08	.04
434	Frank Tanana	.10	.08	.04
435	*Ryan Thompson*	.40	.30	.15
436	Kim Batiste	.10	.08	.04
437	Mark Davis	.10	.08	.04
438	Jose DeLeon	.10	.08	.04
439	Lenny Dykstra	.20	.15	.08
440	Jim Eisenreich	.10	.08	.04
441	Tommy Greene	.10	.08	.04
442	Pete Incaviglia	.10	.08	.04
443	Danny Jackson	.10	.08	.04
444	Todd Pratt	.10	.08	.04
445	Curt Schilling	.10	.08	.04
446	Milt Thompson	.10	.08	.04
447	David West	.10	.08	.04
448	Mitch Williams	.10	.08	.04
449	Steve Cooke	.50	.40	.20
450	Carlos Garcia	.15	.11	.06
451	Al Martin	.50	.40	.20
452	*Blas Minor*	.15	.11	.06
453	Dennis Moeller	.15	.11	.06
454	Denny Neagle	.10	.08	.04
455	Don Slaught	.10	.08	.04
456	Lonnie Smith	.10	.08	.04
457	Paul Wagner	.15	.11	.06
458	Bob Walk	.10	.08	.04
459	Kevin Young	.60	.45	.25
460	*Rene Arocha*	.75	.60	.30
461	Brian Barber	.60	.45	.25
462	Rheal Cormier	.10	.08	.04
463	Gregg Jefferies	.15	.11	.06
464	Joe Magrane	.10	.08	.04
465	Omar Olivares	.10	.08	.04
466	Geronimo Pena	.10	.08	.04
467	Allen Watson	1.25	.90	.50
468	Mark Whiten	.15	.11	.06
469	Derek Bell	.25	.20	.10
470	Phil Clark	.10	.08	.04
471	*Pat Gomez*	.25	.20	.10
472	Tony Gwynn	.30	.25	.12
473	Jeremy Hernandez	.10	.08	.04
474	Bruce Hurst	.10	.08	.04
475	Phil Plantier	.20	.15	.08
476	*Scott Sanders*	.20	.15	.08
477	*Tim Scott*	.15	.11	.06
478	*Darrell Sherman*	.25	.20	.10
479	Guillermo Velasquez	.20	.15	.08
480	*Tim Worrell*	.20	.15	.08
481	Todd Benzinger	.10	.08	.04
482	Bud Black	.10	.08	.04
483	Barry Bonds	1.00	.70	.40
484	Dave Burba	.10	.08	.04
485	Bryan Hickerson	.10	.08	.04
486	Dave Martinez	.10	.08	.04
487	Willie McGee	.10	.08	.04
488	Jeff Reed	.10	.08	.04
489	Kevin Rogers	.15	.11	.06
490	Matt Williams	.15	.11	.06
491	Trevor Wilson	.10	.08	.04
492	Harold Baines	.10	.08	.04
493	Mike Devereaux	.10	.08	.04
494	Todd Frohwirth	.10	.08	.04
495	Chris Hoiles	.10	.08	.04
496	Luis Mercedes	.15	.11	.06
497	*Sherman Obando*	.30	.25	.12
498	*Brad Pennington*	.15	.11	.06
499	Harold Reynolds	.10	.08	.04
500	Arthur Rhodes	.15	.11	.06
501	Cal Ripken, Jr.	.75	.60	.30
502	Rick Sutcliffe	.10	.08	.04
503	Fernando Valenzuela	.10	.08	.04
504	Mark Williamson	.10	.08	.04
505	Scott Bankhead	.10	.08	.04
506	Greg Blosser	.40	.30	.15
507	Ivan Calderon	.10	.08	.04
508	Roger Clemens	.60	.45	.25
509	Andre Clemens	.10	.08	.04
510	Scott Fletcher	.10	.08	.04
511	Greg Harris	.10	.08	.04
512	Billy Hatcher	.10	.08	.04
513	Bob Melvin	.10	.08	.04
514	Carlos Quintana	.10	.08	.04
515	Luis Rivera	.10	.08	.04
516	Jeff Russell	.10	.08	.04
517	*Ken Ryan*	.30	.25	.12
518	Chili Davis	.10	.08	.04
519	*Jim Edmonds*	.30	.25	.12
520	Gary Gaetti	.10	.08	.04
521	Torey Lovullo	.10	.08	.04
522	*Tony Percival*	.15	.11	.06
523	Tim Salmon	3.50	2.75	1.50
524	Scott Sanderson	.10	.08	.04

		MT	NR MT	EX
525	*J.T. Snow*	1.75	1.25	.70
526	Jerome Walton	.10	.08	.04
527	Jason Bere	1.25	.90	.50
528	*Rod Bolton*	.15	.11	.06
529	Ellis Burks	.10	.08	.04
530	Carlton Fisk	.10	.08	.04
531	Craig Grebeck	.10	.08	.04
532	Ozzie Guillen	.10	.08	.04
533	Roberto Hernandez	.10	.08	.04
534	Bo Jackson	.25	.20	.10
535	Kirk McCaskill	.10	.08	.04
536	Dave Stieb	.10	.08	.04
537	Robin Ventura	.35	.20	.10
538	Albert Belle	.70	.50	.25
539	Mike Bielecki	.10	.08	.04
540	Glenallen Hill	.10	.08	.04
541	Reggie Jefferson	.10	.08	.04
542	Kenny Lofton	.40	.30	.15
543	*Jeff Mutis*	.15	.11	.06
544	Junior Ortiz	.10	.08	.04
545	Manny Ramirez	2.00	1.50	.80
546	Jeff Treadway	.10	.08	.04
547	Kevin Wickander	.10	.08	.04
548	Cecil Fielder	.35	.20	.10
549	Kirk Gibson	.10	.08	.04
550	*Greg Gohr*	.15	.11	.06
551	David Haas	.10	.08	.04
552	Bill Krueger	.10	.08	.04
553	Mike Moore	.10	.08	.04
554	Mickey Tettleton	.10	.08	.04
555	Lou Whitaker	.10	.08	.04
556	Kevin Appier	.10	.08	.04
557	*Billy Brewer*	.20	.15	.08
558	David Cone	.10	.08	.04
559	Greg Gagne	.10	.08	.04
560	Mark Gardner	.10	.08	.04
561	Phil Hiatt	.50	.40	.20
562	Felix Jose	.10	.08	.04
563	Jose Lind	.10	.08	.04
564	Mike Macfarlane	.10	.08	.04
565	Keith Miller	.10	.08	.04
566	Jeff Montgomery	.10	.08	.04
567	Hipolito Pechardo	.10	.08	.04
568	Ricky Bones	.10	.08	.04
569	Tom Brunansky	.10	.08	.04
570	*Joe Kmak*	.15	.11	.06
571	Pat Listach	.20	.15	.08
572	*Graeme Lloyd*	.20	.15	.08
573	*Carlos Maldonado*	.15	.11	.06
574	Josias Manzanillo	.15	.11	.06
575	Matt Mieske	.25	.20	.10
576	Kevin Reimer	.10	.08	.04
577	Bill Spiers	.10	.08	.04
578	Dickie Thon	.10	.08	.04
579	Willie Banks	.10	.08	.04
580	Jim Deshaies	.10	.08	.04
581	Mark Guthrie	.10	.08	.04
582	Brian Harper	.10	.08	.04
583	Chuck Knoblauch	.15	.11	.06
584	Gene Larkin	.10	.08	.04
585	Shane Mack	.10	.08	.04
586	David McCarty	.90	.70	.35
587	Mike Pagliarulo	.10	.08	.04
588	Mike Trombley	.10	.08	.04
589	Dave Winfield	.30	.25	.12
590	Jim Abbott	.20	.15	.08
591	Wade Boggs	.25	.20	.10
592	*Russ Davis*	.40	.30	.15
593	Steve Farr	.10	.08	.04
594	Steve Howe	.10	.08	.04
595	*Mike Humphreys*	.15	.11	.06
596	Jimmy Key	.10	.08	.04
597	Jim Leyritz	.10	.08	.04
598	*Bobby Munoz*	.15	.11	.06
599	Paul O'Neill	.10	.08	.04
600	Spike Owen	.10	.08	.04
601	Mike Stanley	.10	.08	.04
602	Danny Tartabull	.10	.08	.04
603	Scott Brosius	.10	.08	.04
604	Storm Davis	.10	.08	.04
605	Eric Fox	.10	.08	.04
606	Goose Gossage	.10	.08	.04
607	Scott Hammond	.10	.08	.04
608	Dave Henderson	.10	.08	.04
609	Mark McGwire	.20	.15	.08
610	*Mike Mohler*	.30	.25	.12
611	Edwin Nunez	.10	.08	.04
612	Kevin Seitzer	.10	.08	.04
613	Ruben Sierra	.15	.11	.06
614	Chris Bosio	.10	.08	.04
615	Norm Charlton	.10	.08	.04
616	*Jim Converse*	.25	.20	.10
617	*John Cummings*	.25	.20	.10
618	Mike Felder	.10	.08	.04
619	Ken Griffey Jr.	3.00	2.25	1.25
620	*Mike Hampton*	.15	.11	.06
621	Erik Hanson	.10	.08	.04
622	Bill Haselman	.10	.08	.04
623	Tino Martinez	.10	.08	.04
624	Lee Tinsley	.20	.15	.08
625	*Fernando Vina*	.25	.20	.10
626	*David Wainhouse*	.15	.11	.06
627	Jose Canseco	.20	.15	.08
628	Benji Gil	.75	.60	.30
629	Tom Henke	.10	.08	.04
630	*David Hulse*	.60	.45	.25
631	Manuel Lee	.10	.08	.04
632	Craig Lefferts	.10	.08	.04
633	*Robb Nen*	.15	.11	.06
634	Gary Redus	.10	.08	.04
635	Bill Ripken	.10	.08	.04
636	Nolan Ryan	2.00	1.50	.80
637	Dan Smith	.10	.08	.04
638	*Matt Whiteside*	.20	.15	.08
639	Roberto Alomar	.90	.70	.35
640	Juan Guzman	.40	.30	.15
641	Pat Hentgen	.90	.70	.35
642	Darrin Jackson	.10	.08	.04
643	Randy Knorr	.10	.08	.04
644	*Domingo Martinez*	.30	.25	.12
645	Paul Molitor	.20	.15	.08
646	Dick Schofield	.10	.08	.04
647	Dave Stewart	.10	.08	.04
648	Checklist	.10	.08	.04
649	Checklist	.10	.08	.04
650	Checklist	.10	.08	.04

1993 Fleer Ultra All-Rookies

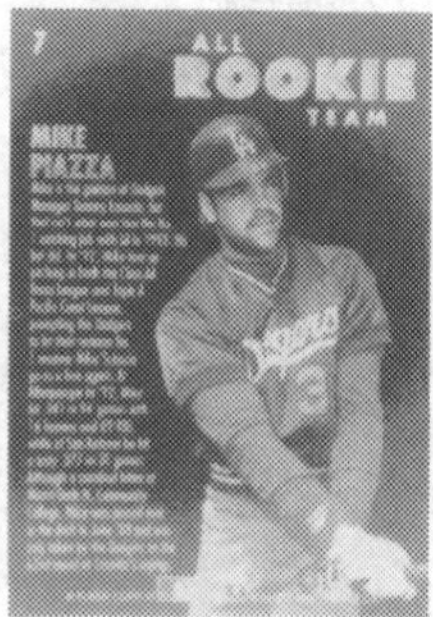

These insert cards are foil stamped on both sides and were randomly inserted into 1994 Series II packs. The cards have black fronts, with six different colors of type. The player's uniform number and position are located in the upper right-hand corner. The player's name and Ultra logo are gold-foil stamped. Backs have a black background on which are a player photo and a career summary.

		MT	NR MT	EX
Complete Set (10):		25.00	19.00	10.00
Common Player:		1.00	.70	.40
1	Rene Arocha	1.50	1.25	.60
2	Jeff Conine	1.50	1.25	.60
3	Phil Hiatt	1.50	1.25	.60
4	Mike Lansing	1.50	1.25	.60
5	Al Martin	1.00	.70	.40
6	David Nied	2.00	3.00	1.50
7	Mike Piazza	12.00	9.00	4.75
8	Tim Salmon	7.00	5.25	2.75
9	J.T. Snow	2.50	2.00	1.00
10	Kevin Young	1.00	.70	.40

Regional interest may affect the value of a card.

1993 Fleer Ultra All-Stars

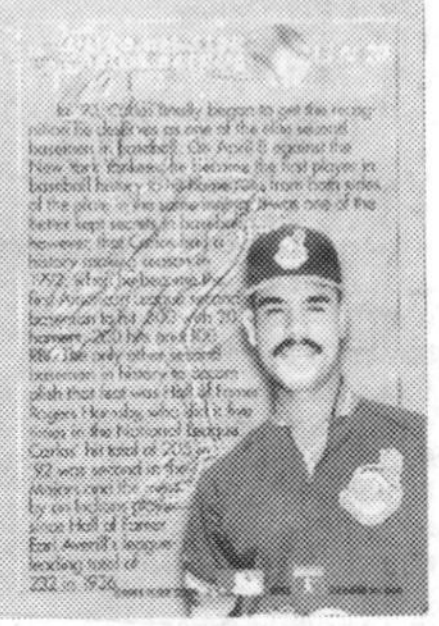

This 20-card set features 10 of the top players from each league. Cards were randomly inserted into Series II packs and are foil stamped on both sides.

		MT	NR MT	EX
Complete Set (20):		40.00	30.00	16.00
Common Player:		1.00	.75	.40
1	Darren Daulton	2.50	1.50	.75
2	Will Clark	3.00	2.25	1.20
3	Ryne Sandberg	6.00	4.50	2.25
4	Barry Larkin	1.25	.95	.50
5	Gary Sheffield	3.00	2.25	1.20
6	Barry Bonds	5.00	3.75	2.00
7	Ray Lankford	1.00	.75	.40
8	Larry Walker	1.00	.75	.40
9	Greg Maddux	2.00	1.50	.75
10	Lee Smith	1.50	1.00	.60
11	Ivan Rodriguez	2.50	2.00	1.00
12	Mark McGwire	3.00	2.25	1.20
13	Carlos Baerga	3.00	2.25	1.20
14	Cal Ripken, Jr.	6.00	4.50	2.25
15	Edgar Martinez	2.00	1.50	.75
16	Juan Gonzalez	5.00	3.75	2.00
17	Ken Griffey Jr.	10.00	8.00	4.00
18	Kirby Puckett	5.00	3.75	2.00
19	Frank Thomas	10.00	8.00	4.00
20	Mike Mussina	2.00	1.50	.75

1993 Fleer Ultra Award Winners

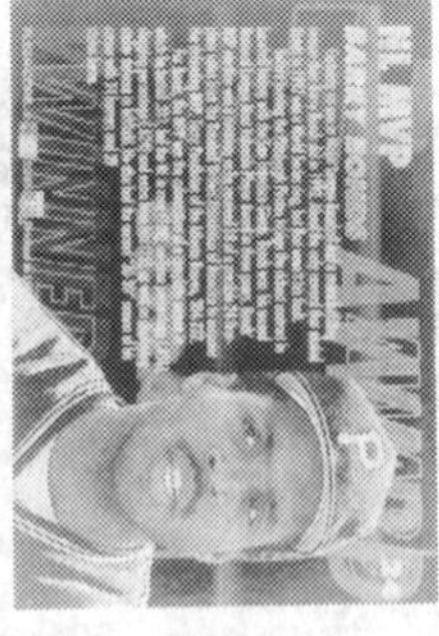

This 25-card insert set features 18 Top Glove players (nine from each league), two rookies of the year, three MVPs (both leagues and World Series), both Cy Young Award winners and one Player of the Year. All cards are UV coated and foil stamped on both sides and were found Series I packs. Fronts have a black background with "Fleer Ultra Award Winners" splashed around in trendy colors. The Ultra logo, player's name and his award are spelled out in gold foil. The horizontally arranged backs have much the same elements, plus a summary of the season's performance which led to the award. There is a close-up player photo, as well.

		MT	NR MT	EX
Complete Set (25):		50.00	35.00	20.00
Common Player:		1.00	.75	.40
1	Greg Maddux	2.00	1.50	.75
2	Tom Pagnozzi	1.00	.75	.40
3	Mark Grace	3.00	2.25	1.20
4	Jose Lind	1.00	.75	.40
5	Terry Pendleton	1.00	.75	.40
6	Ozzie Smith	2.00	1.50	.75
7	Barry Bonds	5.00	3.75	2.00
8	Andy Van Slyke	2.00	1.25	.60
9	Larry Walker	1.00	.75	.40
10	Mark Langston	1.00	.75	.40
11	Ivan Rodriguez	2.00	1.50	.75
12	Don Mattingly	5.00	3.75	2.00
13	Roberto Alomar	4.00	3.00	1.50
14	Robin Ventura	2.00	1.50	.75
15	Cal Ripken, Jr.	6.00	4.50	2.25
16	Ken Griffey Jr.	10.00	8.00	4.00
17	Kirby Puckett	4.00	3.00	1.50
18	Devon White	1.50	1.00	.60
19	Pat Listach	1.00	.75	.40
20	Eric Karros	2.50	1.50	.75
21	Pat Borders	1.50	1.00	.60
22	Greg Maddux	2.00	1.50	.80
23	Dennis Eckersley	2.00	1.50	.60
24	Barry Bonds	5.00	3.75	2.00
25	Gary Sheffield	2.00	1.50	.60

1993 Fleer Ultra Dennis Eckersley

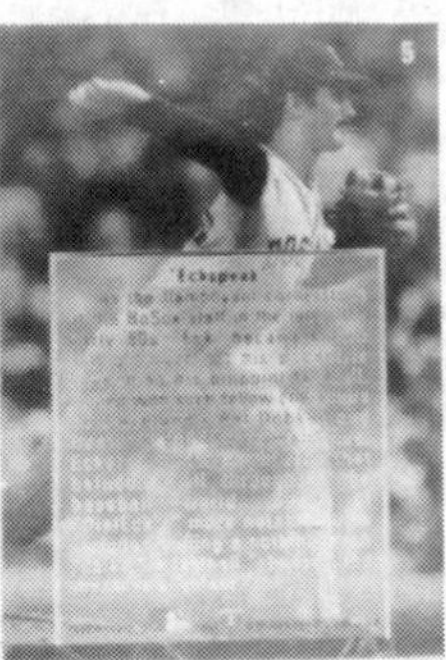

This 10-card, limited-edition "Career Highlights" subset commemorates Dennis Eckersley's illustrious career. Cards, which are UV coated and silver foil-stamped on both sides, were randomly inserted into both series' packs. Eckersley autographed more than 2,000 of the cards, which were also randomly inserted into packs. By sending in 10 Fleer Ultra wrappers plus $1, collectors could receive two additional Eckersley cards which were not available in regualr packs. Card fronts have a color action photo, the background of which has been colorized into shades of purple. A black marble strip at bottom has the city name and years he was with the team in silver foil. A large black marble box in one corner has the "Dennis Eckersley Career Highlights" logo in silver foil. On back, a purple box is dropped out of a color photo, and silver-foil typography describes some phrase of Eck's career.

		MT	NR MT	EX
Complete set (12):		7.50	5.50	3.00
Common card:		.75	.60	.30
Autographed card:		75.00	55.00	30.00
1	Dennis Eckersley	.75	.60	.30
2	Dennis Eckersley	.75	.60	.30
3	Dennis Eckersley	.75	.60	.30
4	Dennis Eckersley	.75	.60	.30
5	Dennis Eckersley	.75	.60	.30
6	Dennis Eckersley	.75	.60	.30
7	Dennis Eckersley	.75	.60	.30
8	Dennis Eckersley	.75	.60	.30
9	Dennis Eckersley	.75	.60	.30

		MT	NR MT	EX
10	Dennis Eckersley	.75	.60	.30
11	Dennis Eckersley	.75	.60	.30
12	Dennis Eckersley	.75	.60	.30

1993 Fleer Ultra Home Run Kings

This 10-card subset features top home run kings. Cards, which are UV coated and have gold foil stamping on both sides, were inserts in Series I packs.

		MT	NR MT	EX
Complete Set (10):		30.00	22.50	12.00
Common Player:		2.50	2.00	1.00
1	Juan Gonzalez	10.00	7.50	4.00
2	Mark McGwire	3.00	2.25	1.20
3	Cecil Fielder	3.50	2.50	1.25
4	Fred McGriff	3.00	2.25	1.20
5	Albert Belle	2.50	2.00	1.00
6	Barry Bonds	5.00	3.75	2.00
7	Joe Carter	3.00	2.25	1.20
8	Gary Sheffield	2.50	2.00	1.00
9	Darren Daulton	2.50	2.00	1.00
10	Dave Hollins	2.50	2.00	1.00

1993 Fleer Ultra Performers

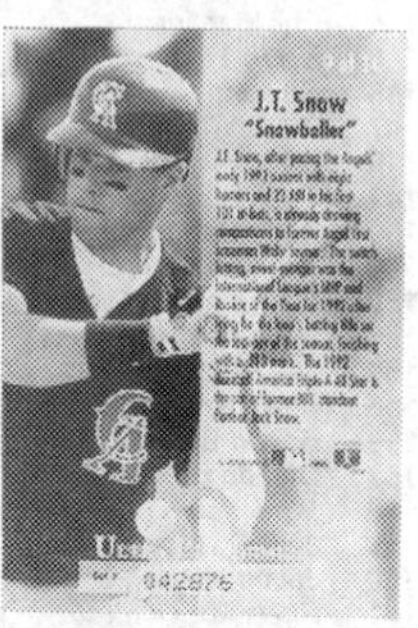

A 10-card Ultra Performers subset of Fleer Ultra baseball cards was offered directly to collectors in 1993. The subset, available only by mail, was limited to 150,000 sets. The cards featured gold-foil stamping and UV coating on both sides and a six-photo design, including five on the front of the card. Each card was identified on the back by set serial number jet-printed in black in a strip at bottom.

		MT	NR MT	EX
Complete Set (10):		15.00	11.25	6.00
Common Player:		1.00	.75	.40
1	Barry Bonds	4.00	3.00	1.50
2	Juan Gonzalez	4.00	3.00	1.50
3	Ken Griffey Jr.	6.00	4.50	2.25
4	Eric Karros	1.50	1.00	.60
5	Pat Listach	1.00	.75	.40
6	Greg Maddux	1.50	1.00	.60
7	David Nied	2.00	1.50	.75
8	Gary Sheffield	2.00	1.50	.75
9	J.T. Snow	2.50	2.00	1.00
10	Frank Thomas	6.00	4.50	2.25

1993 Fleer Ultra Strikeout Kings

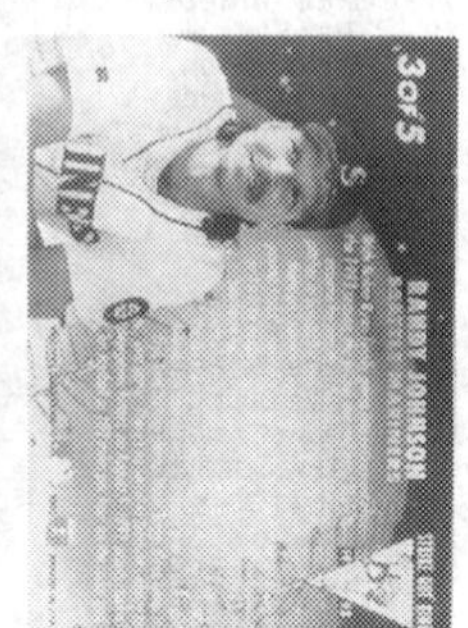

Five of baseball's top strikeout pitchers are featured in this second-series Ultra insert set. Cards are UV coated and foil stamped on both sides. Each card front has a picture of a pitcher winding up to throw. A baseball is in the background, with the pitcher in the forefront.

		MT	NR MT	EX
Complete Set (5):		15.00	11.25	6.00
Common player:		1.00	.75	.40
1	Roger Clemens	4.00	3.00	1.75
2	Juan Guzman	3.00	2.25	1.20
3	Randy Johnson	2.00	1.50	.80
4	Nolan Ryan	10.00	7.50	4.00
5	John Smoltz	2.00	1.50	.80

1993 Fleer Final Edition

This 310-card set was sold as a complete set in its own box. Cards have the prefix F included with their card numbers. The set also includes 10 Diamond Tribute cards, which are numbered DT1-DT10.

		MT	NR MT	EX
Complete Set (310):		20.00	15.00	8.00
Common Player:		.05	.04	.02
DT	Wade Boggs	.50	.40	.20
DT	George Brett	.50	.40	.20
DT	Andre Dawson	.20	.15	.08
DT	Carlton Fisk	.20	.15	.08
DT	Paul Molitor	.40	.30	.15
DT	Nolan Ryan	1.50	1.00	.60
DT	Lee Smith	.20	.15	.08

		MT	NR MT	EX
DT	Ozzie Smith	.40	.30	.15
DT	Dave Winfield	.50	.40	.20
DT	Robin Yount	.50	.40	.20
1	Steve Bedrosian	.05	.04	.02
2	Jay Howell	.05	.04	.02
3	Greg Maddux	.15	.11	.06
4	*Greg McMichael*	.25	.20	.10
5	*Tony Tarasco*	.40	.30	.15
6	Jose Bautista	.05	.04	.02
7	Jose Guzman	.05	.04	.02
8	Greg Hibbard	.05	.04	.02
9	Candy Maldonado	.05	.04	.02
10	Randy Myers	.05	.04	.02
11	*Matt Walbeck*	.10	.08	.04
12	Turk Wendell	.05	.04	.02
13	Willie Nelson	.05	.04	.02
14	Greg Cadaret	.05	.04	.02
15	Roberto Kelly	.05	.04	.02
16	Randy Milligan	.05	.04	.02
17	Kevin Mitchell	.05	.04	.02
18	Jeff Reardon	.05	.04	.02
19	John Roper	.05	.04	.02
20	John Smiley	.05	.04	.02
21	Andy Ashby	.05	.04	.02
22	Dante Bichette	.05	.04	.02
23	Willie Blair	.05	.04	.02
24	Pedro Castellano	.05	.04	.02
25	Vinny Castilla	.05	.04	.02
26	Jerald Clark	.05	.04	.02
27	Alex Cole	.05	.04	.02
28	*Scott Fredrickson*	.20	.15	.08
29	*Jay Gainer*	.20	.15	.08
30	Andres Galarraga	.15	.11	.06
31	Joe Girardi	.05	.04	.02
32	Ryan Hawblitzel	.05	.04	.02
33	Charlie Hayes	.05	.04	.02
34	Darren Holmes	.05	.04	.02
35	Chris Jones	.05	.04	.02
36	David Nied	.40	.30	.15
37	*J. Owens*	.20	.15	.08
38	*Lance Painter*	.10	.08	.04
39	Jeff Parrett	.05	.04	.02
40	Steve Reed	.05	.04	.02
41	Armando Reynoso	.05	.04	.02
42	Bruce Ruffin	.05	.04	.02
43	*Danny Sheaffer*	.10	.08	.04
44	Keith Shepherd	.05	.04	.02
45	Jim Tatum	.05	.04	.02
46	Gary Wayne	.05	.04	.02
47	Eric Young	.10	.08	.04
48	Luis Aquino	.05	.04	.02
49	Alex Arias	.05	.04	.02
50	Jack Armstrong	.05	.04	.02
51	Bret Barberie	.05	.04	.02
52	Geronimo Berroa	.05	.04	.02
53	Ryan Bowen	.05	.04	.02
54	Greg Briley	.05	.04	.02
55	Chris Carpenter	.05	.04	.02
56	Chuck Carr	.05	.04	.02
57	Jeff Conine	.05	.04	.02
58	Jim Corsi	.05	.04	.02
59	Orestes Destrade	.05	.04	.02
60	Junior Felix	.05	.04	.02
61	Chris Hammond	.05	.04	.02
62	Bryan Harvey	.05	.04	.02
63	Charlie Hough	.05	.04	.02
64	Joe Klink	.05	.04	.02
65	*Richie Lewis*	.20	.15	.08
66	*Mitch Lyden*	.15	.11	.06
67	Bob Natal	.05	.04	.02
68	*Scott Pose*	.10	.08	.04
69	Rich Renteria	.05	.04	.02
70	Benito Santiago	.05	.04	.02
71	Gary Sheffield	.10	.08	.04
72	*Matt Turner*	.15	.11	.06
73	Walt Weiss	.05	.04	.02
74	*Darrell Whitmore*	.30	.20	.10
75	Nigel Wilson	.50	.40	.20
76	Kevin Bass	.05	.04	.02
77	Doug Drabek	.05	.04	.02
78	Tom Edens	.05	.04	.02
79	Chris James	.05	.04	.02
80	Greg Swindell	.05	.04	.02
81	*Omar Daal*	.10	.08	.04
82	Raul Mondesi	.05	.04	.02
83	Jody Reed	.05	.04	.02
84	Cory Snyder	.05	.04	.02
85	Rick Trlicek	.05	.04	.02
86	Tim Wallach	.05	.04	.02
87	Todd Worrell	.05	.04	.02
88	Tavo Alvarez	.10	.08	.04
89	Frank Bolick	.05	.04	.02

		MT	NR MT	EX
90	Kent Bottenfield	.05	.04	.02
91	Greg Colbrynn	.05	.04	.02
92	Cliff Floyd	1.75	1.25	.70
93	*Lou Frazier*	.15	.11	.06
94	Mike Gardiner	.05	.04	.02
95	*Mike Lansing*	.15	.11	.06
96	Bill Risley	.05	.04	.02
97	Jeff Shaw	.05	.04	.02
98	Kevin Baez	.05	.04	.02
99	*Tim Bogar*	.10	.08	.04
100	Jeromy Burnitz	.10	.08	.04
101	Mike Draper	.10	.08	.04
102	Darrin Jackson	.05	.04	.02
103	Mike Maddux	.05	.04	.02
104	Joe Orsulak	.05	.04	.02
105	Doug Saunders	.10	.08	.04
106	Frank Tanana	.05	.04	.02
107	Dave Telgheder	.15	.11	.06
108	Larry Anderson	.05	.04	.02
109	Jim Eisenreich	.05	.04	.02
110	Pete Incaviglia	.05	.04	.02
111	Danny Jackson	.05	.04	.02
112	David West	.05	.04	.02
113	Al Martin	.20	.15	.08
114	Blas Minor	.05	.04	.02
115	Dennis Moeller	.05	.04	.02
116	Will Pennyfeather	.05	.04	.02
117	Rich Robertson	.05	.04	.02
118	Ben Shelton	.05	.04	.02
119	Lonnie Smith	.05	.04	.02
120	Freddie Toliver	.05	.04	.02
121	Paul Wagner	.05	.04	.02
122	Kevin Young	.15	.11	.06
123	*Rene Arocha*	.30	.20	.10
124	Greg Jefferies	.10	.08	.04
125	Paul Kilgus	.05	.04	.02
126	Les Lancaster	.05	.04	.02
127	Joe Magrane	.05	.04	.02
128	Rob Murphy	.05	.04	.02
129	Erik Pappas	.05	.04	.02
130	Stan Royer	.05	.04	.02
131	Ozzie Smith	.15	.11	.06
132	Tom Urbani	.05	.04	.02
133	Mark Whiten	.05	.04	.02
134	Derek Bell	.05	.04	.02
135	Doug Brocall	.05	.04	.02
136	Phil Clark	.05	.04	.02
137	*Mark Ettles*	.10	.08	.04
138	Jeff Gardner	.05	.04	.02
139	*Pat Gomez*	.10	.08	.04
140	Ricky Gutierrez	.10	.08	.04
141	Gene Harris	.05	.04	.02
142	*Kevin Higgins*	.15	.11	.06
143	Trevor Hoffman	.05	.04	.02
144	Phil Plantier	.10	.08	.04
145	*Kerry Taylor*	.10	.08	.04
146	Guillermo Velasquez	.05	.04	.02
147	Wally Whitehurst	.05	.04	.02
148	*Tim Worrell*	.10	.08	.04
149	Todd Benzinger	.05	.04	.02
150	Barry Bonds	.50	.40	.20
151	Greg Brummett	.05	.04	.02
152	Mark Carreon	.05	.04	.02
153	Dave Martinez	.05	.04	.02
154	Jeff Reed	.05	.04	.02
155	Kevin Rogers	.05	.04	.02
156	Harold Baines	.05	.04	.02
157	Damon Buford	.05	.04	.02
158	*Paul Carey*	.15	.11	.06
159	Jeffrey Hammonds	.75	.60	.30
160	Jaime Moyer	.05	.04	.02
161	*Sherman Obando*	.15	.11	.06
162	*John O'Donoghue*	.15	.11	.06
163	Brad Pennington	.05	.04	.02
164	Jim Poole	.05	.04	.02
165	Harold Reynolds	.05	.04	.02
166	Fernando Valenzuela	.05	.04	.02
167	*Jack Voight*	.15	.11	.06
168	Mark Williamson	.05	.04	.02
169	Scott Bankhead	.05	.04	.02
170	Greg Blosser	.05	.04	.02
171	*Jim Byrd*	.10	.08	.04
172	Ivan Calderon	.05	.04	.02
173	Andre Dawson	.05	.04	.02
174	Scott Fletcher	.05	.04	.02
175	Jose Melendez	.05	.04	.02
176	Carlos Quintana	.05	.04	.02
177	Jeff Russell	.05	.04	.02
178	Aaron Sele	.75	.60	.30
179	*Rod Correia*	.10	.08	.04
180	Chili Davis	.05	.04	.02

		MT	NR MT	EX
181	*Jim Edmonds*	.20	.15	.08
182	Rene Gonzales	.05	.04	.02
183	*Hilly Hathaway*	.15	.11	.06
184	Torey Lovullo	.05	.04	.02
185	Greg Myers	.05	.04	.02
186	Gene Nelson	.05	.04	.02
187	Troy Percival	.05	.04	.02
188	Scott Sanderson	.05	.04	.02
189	*Darryl Scott*	.15	.11	.06
190	*J.T. Snow*	.60	.40	.20
191	Russ Springer	.05	.04	.02
192	Jason Bere	1.00	.70	.40
193	Rodney Bolton	.05	.04	.02
194	Ellis Burks	.05	.04	.02
195	Bo Jackson	.15	.11	.06
196	Mike LaValliere	.05	.04	.02
197	Scott Ruffcorn	.25	.20	.10
198	*Jeff Schwartz*	.10	.08	.04
199	Jerry DiPoto	.05	.04	.02
200	Alvaro Espinoza	.05	.04	.02
201	Wayne Kirby	.05	.04	.02
202	*Tom Kramer*	.10	.08	.04
203	Jesse Levis	.05	.04	.02
204	Manny Rodriguez	.75	.60	.30
205	Jeff Treadway	.05	.04	.02
206	*Bill Wertz*	.10	.08	.04
207	Cliff Young	.05	.04	.02
208	Matt Young	.05	.04	.02
209	Kirk Gibson	.05	.04	.02
210	Greg Gohr	.05	.04	.02
211	Bill Krueger	.05	.04	.02
212	Bob MacDonald	.05	.04	.02
213	Mike Moore	.05	.04	.02
214	David Wells	.05	.04	.02
215	*Billy Brewer*	.10	.08	.04
216	David Cone	.05	.04	.02
217	Greg Gagne	.05	.04	.02
218	Mark Gardner	.05	.04	.02
219	Chis Haney	.05	.04	.02
220	Phil Hiatt	.15	.11	.06
221	Jose Lind	.05	.04	.02
222	Juan Bell	.05	.04	.02
223	Tom Brunansky	.05	.04	.02
224	Mike Ignasiak	.05	.04	.02
225	Joe Knak	.05	.04	.02
226	Tom Lampkin	.05	.04	.02
227	*Graeme Lloyd*	.10	.08	.04
228	Carlos Maldonado	.05	.04	.02
229	Matt Mieske	.05	.04	.02
230	Angel Miranda	.05	.04	.02
231	*Troy O'Leary*	.25	.20	.10
232	Kevin Reimer	.05	.04	.02
233	Larry Casian	.05	.04	.02
234	Jim Deshaies	.05	.04	.02
235	*Eddie Guardado*	.15	.11	.06
236	Chip Hale	.05	.04	.02
237	*Mike Maksudian*	.25	.20	.10
238	David McCarty	.25	.20	.10
239	*Pat Meares*	.10	.08	.04
240	*George Tsamis*	.10	.08	.04
241	Dave Winfield	.15	.11	.06
242	Jim Abbott	.10	.08	.04
243	Wade Boggs	.10	.08	.04
244	*Andy Cook*	.10	.08	.04
245	*Russ Davis*	.20	.15	.08
246	Mike Humphreys	.05	.04	.02
247	Jimmy Key	.05	.04	.02
248	Jim Leyritz	.05	.04	.02
249	Bobby Munoz	.05	.04	.02
250	Paul O'Neill	.05	.04	.02
251	Spike Owen	.05	.04	.02
252	Dave Silvestri	.05	.04	.02
253	*Marcos Armas*	.25	.20	.10
254	Brent Gates	.20	.15	.08
255	Goose Gossage	.05	.04	.02
256	*Scott Lydy*	.25	.20	.10
257	Henry Mercedes	.05	.04	.02
258	*Mike Mohler*	.10	.08	.04
259	Troy Neel	.25	.20	.10
260	Edwin Nunez	.05	.04	.02
261	Craig Paquette	.10	.08	.04
262	Kevin Seitzer	.05	.04	.02
263	Rich Amaral	.05	.04	.02
264	Mike Blowers	.05	.04	.02
265	Chris Bosio	.05	.04	.02
266	Norm Charlton	.05	.04	.02
267	*Jim Converse*	.10	.08	.04
268	*John Cummings*	.10	.08	.04
269	Mike Felder	.05	.04	.02
270	Mike Hampton	.05	.04	.02
271	Bill Haselman	.05	.04	.02
272	Dwayne Henry	.05	.04	.02
273	Greg Litton	.05	.04	.02
274	Mackey Sasser	.05	.04	.02
275	Lee Tinsley	.05	.04	.02
276	David Wainhouse	.05	.04	.02
277	*Jeff Bronkey*	.10	.08	.04
278	Benji Gil	.15	.11	.06
279	Tom Henke	.05	.04	.02
280	Charlie Leibrandt	.05	.04	.02
281	Robb Nen	.05	.04	.02
282	Bill Ripken	.05	.04	.02
283	*Jon Shave*	.10	.08	.04
284	Doug Strange	.05	.04	.02
285	*Matt Whiteside*	.10	.08	.04
286	*Scott Brow*	.15	.11	.06
287	*Willie Canate*	.15	.11	.06
288	Tony Castillo	.05	.04	.02
289	*Domingo Cedeno*	.10	.08	.04
290	Darnell Coles	.05	.04	.02
291	Danny Cox	.05	.04	.02
292	Mark Eichhorn	.05	.04	.02
293	Tony Fernandez	.05	.04	.02
294	Al Leiter	.05	.04	.02
295	Paul Molitor	.25	.20	.10
296	Dave Stewart	.05	.04	.02
297	*Woody Williams*	.15	.11	.06
298	Checklist	.05	.04	.02
299	Checklist	.05	.04	.02
300	Checklist	.05	.04	.02

1993 Fleer Flair

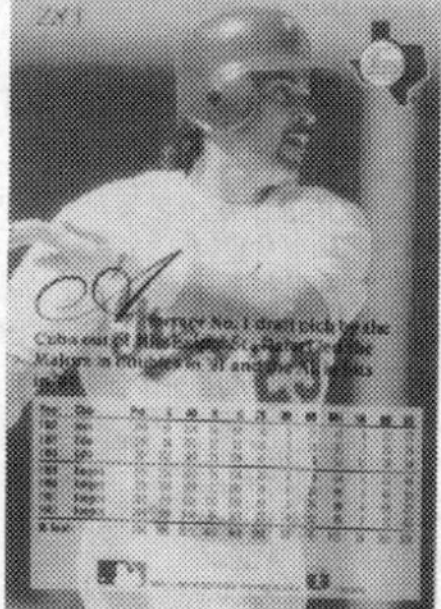

Designed as Fleer's super-premium card brand, this 300-card set contains extra-thick cards which feature gold stamping and UV coating front and back. Portrait and action photos are combined in a high-tech front picture and there is a muted photo on the back, as well.

		MT	NR MT	EX
Complete Set (300):		125.00	75.00	50.00
Common Player:		.25	.15	.08
1	Steve Avery	1.00	.70	.40
2	Jeff Blauser	.25	.15	.08
3	Ron Gant	.60	.45	.25
4	Tom Glavine	1.00	.70	.40
5	David Justice	2.75	2.00	1.00
6	Mark Lemke	.25	.15	.08
7	Greg Maddux	.75	.60	.30
8	Fred McGriff	1.25	.90	.50
9	Terry Pendleton	.40	.30	.15
10	Deion Sanders	.75	.60	.30
11	John Smoltz	.40	.30	.15
12	Mike Stanton	.25	.15	.08
13	Steve Buechele	.25	.15	.08
14	Mark Grace	.50	.30	.15
15	Greg Hibbard	.25	.15	.08
16	Derrick May	.40	.30	.15
17	Chuck McElroy	.25	.15	.08
18	Mike Morgan	.25	.15	.08
19	Randy Myers	.25	.15	.08
20	Ryne Sandberg	3.00	2.25	1.25
21	Dwight Smith	.25	.15	.08
22	Sammy Sosa	.75	.60	.30
23	Jose Vizcaino	.25	.15	.08
24	Tim Belcher	.25	.15	.08
25	Rob Dibble	.25	.15	.08
26	Roberto Kelly	.30	.25	.12

		MT	NR MT	EX
27	Barry Larkin	.40	.30	.15
28	Kevin Mitchell	.25	.15	.08
29	Hal Morris	.25	.15	.08
30	Joe Oliver	.25	.15	.08
31	Jose Rijo	.25	.15	.08
32	Bip Roberts	.25	.15	.08
33	Chris Sabo	.25	.15	.08
34	Reggie Sanders	.60	.45	.25
35	Dante Bichette	.25	.15	.08
36	Willie Blair	.25	.15	.08
37	Jerald Clark	.25	.15	.08
38	Alex Cole	.25	.15	.08
39	Andres Galarraga	.50	.30	.15
40	Joe Girardi	.25	.15	.08
41	Charlie Hayes	.25	.15	.08
42	Chris Jones	.25	.15	.08
43	David Nied	2.00	1.50	.80
44	Eric Young	.75	.60	.30
45	Alex Arias	.25	.15	.08
46	Jack Armstrong	.25	.15	.08
47	Bret Barberie	.25	.15	.08
48	Chuck Carr	.40	.30	.15
49	Jeff Conine	.40	.30	.15
50	Orestes Destrade	.25	.15	.08
51	Chris Hammond	.25	.15	.08
52	Bryan Harvey	.25	.15	.08
53	Benito Santiago	.25	.15	.08
54	Gary Sheffield	1.50	1.25	.60
55	Walt Weiss	.25	.15	.08
56	Eric Anthony	.25	.15	.08
57	Jeff Bagwell	1.50	1.25	.60
58	Craig Biggio	.25	.15	.08
59	Ken Caminiti	.25	.15	.08
60	Andujar Cedeno	.40	.30	.15
61	Doug Drabek	.25	.15	.08
62	Steve Finley	.25	.15	.08
63	Luis Gonzalez	.35	.20	.10
64	Pete Harnisch	.25	.15	.08
65	Doug Jones	.25	.15	.08
66	Darryl Kile	.25	.15	.08
67	Greg Swindell	.25	.15	.08
68	Brett Butler	.25	.15	.08
69	Jim Gott	.25	.15	.08
70	Orel Hershiser	.25	.15	.08
71	Eric Karros	1.25	.90	.50
72	Pedro Martinez	.50	.30	.15
73	Ramon Martinez	.25	.15	.08
74	Roger McDowell	.25	.15	.08
75	Mike Piazza	11.00	8.25	4.50
76	Jody Reed	.25	.15	.08
77	Tim Wallach	.25	.15	.08
78	Moises Alou	.75	.60	.30
79	Greg Colbrunn	.25	.15	.08
80	Wil Cordero	.40	.30	.15
81	Delino DeShields	.60	.45	.25
82	Jeff Fassero	.25	.15	.08
83	Marquis Grissom	.80	.60	.30
84	Ken Hill	.25	.15	.08
85	*Mike Lansing*	1.75	1.00	.50
86	Dennis Martinez	.25	.15	.08
87	Larry Walker	.60	.45	.25
88	John Wetteland	.25	.15	.08
89	Bobby Bonilla	.50	.30	.15
90	Vince Coleman	.25	.15	.08
91	Dwight Gooden	.25	.15	.08
92	Todd Hundley	.25	.15	.08
93	Howard Johnson	.25	.15	.08
94	Eddie Murray	.50	.30	.15
95	Joe Orsulak	.25	.15	.08
96	Bret Saberhagen	.25	.15	.08
97	Darren Daulton	.40	.30	.15
98	Mariano Duncan	.25	.15	.08
99	Len Dykstra	.60	.45	.25
100	Jim Eisenreich	.25	.15	.08
101	Tommy Greene	.35	.20	.10
102	Dave Hollins	.40	.30	.15
103	Pete Incaviglia	.25	.15	.08
104	Danny Jackson	.25	.15	.08
105	John Kruk	.40	.30	.15
106	Terry Mulholland	.25	.15	.08
107	Curt Schilling	.25	.15	.08
108	Mitch Williams	.25	.15	.08
109	Stan Belinda	.25	.15	.08
110	Jay Bell	.25	.15	.08
111	Steve Cooke	.25	.15	.08
112	Carlos Garcia	1.50	1.25	.60
113	Jeff King	.25	.15	.08
114	Al Martin	.50	.30	.15
115	Orlando Merced	.25	.15	.08
116	Don Slaught	.25	.15	.08
117	Andy Van Slyke	.40	.30	.15
118	Tim Wakefield	.25	.15	.08
119	*Rene Arocha*	1.25	.90	.50
120	Bernard Gilkey	.40	.30	.15
121	Greg Jefferies	.50	.30	.15
122	Ray Lankford	.25	.15	.08
123	Donovan Osborne	.25	.15	.08
124	Tom Pagnozzi	.25	.15	.08
125	Erik Pappas	.25	.15	.08
126	Geronimo Pena	.25	.15	.08
127	Lee Smith	.25	.15	.08
128	Ozzie Smith	1.00	.70	.40
129	Bob Tewksbury	.25	.15	8.00
130	Mark Whiten	.50	.30	.15
131	Derek Bell	.25	.15	.08
132	Andy Benes	.25	.15	.08
133	Tony Gwynn	2.00	1.50	.80
134	Gene Harris	.25	.15	.08
135	Trevor Hoffman	.25	.15	.08
136	Phil Plantier	1.00	.70	.40
137	Rod Beck	.25	.15	.08
138	Barry Bonds	4.00	3.00	1.50
139	John Burkett	.25	.15	.08
140	Will Clark	2.00	1.50	.80
141	Royce Clayton	.40	.30	.15
142	Mike Jackson	.25	.15	.08
143	Darren Lewis	.25	.15	.08
144	Kirt Manwaring	.25	.15	.08
145	Willie McGee	.25	.15	.08
146	Bill Swift	.25	.15	.08
147	Robby Thompson	.25	.15	.08
148	Matt Williams	.75	.60	.30
149	Brady Anderson	.25	.15	.08
150	Mike Devereaux	.25	.15	.08
151	Chris Hoiles	.25	.15	.08
152	Ben McDonald	.25	.15	.08
153	Mark McLemore	.25	.15	.08
154	Mike Mussina	4.00	2.50	1.25
155	Gregg Olson	.25	.15	.08
156	Harold Reynolds	.25	.15	.08
157	Cal Ripken Jr.	3.50	2.75	1.50
158	Rick Sutcliffe	.25	.15	.08
159	Fernando Valenzuela	.25	.15	.08
160	Roger Clemens	2.00	1.50	.80
161	Scott Cooper	.25	.15	.08
162	Andre Dawson	.75	.60	.30
163	Scott Fletcher	.25	.15	.08
164	Mike Greenwell	.25	.15	.08
165	Greg Harris	.25	.15	.08
166	Billy Hatcher	.25	.15	.08
167	Jeff Russell	.25	.15	.08
168	Mo Vaughn	1.25	.90	.50
169	Frank Viola	.25	.15	.08
170	Chad Curtis	1.50	1.25	.60
171	Chili Davis	.25	.15	.08
172	Gary DiSarcina	.25	.15	.08
173	Damion Easley	.75	.60	.30
174	Chuck Finley	.25	.15	.08
175	Mark Langston	.25	.15	.08
176	Luis Polonia	.25	.15	.08
177	Tim Salmon	7.00	5.25	2.75
178	Scott Sanderson	.25	.15	.08
179	J.T. Snow	2.00	1.50	.80
180	Wilson Alvarez	.35	.20	.10
181	Ellis Burks	.25	.15	.08
182	Joey Cora	.25	.15	.08
183	Alex Fernandez	.50	.30	.15
184	Ozzie Guillen	.25	.15	.08
185	Roberto Hernandez	.25	.15	.08
186	Bo Jackson	1.50	1.25	.60
187	Lance Johnson	.25	.15	.08
188	Jack McDowell	.60	.45	.25
189	Frank Thomas	8.00	6.00	3.25
190	Robin Ventura	1.00	.70	.40
191	Carlos Baerga	2.50	2.00	1.00
192	Albert Belle	2.00	1.50	.80
193	Wayne Kirby	.25	.15	.08
194	Derek Lilliquist	.25	.15	.08
195	Kenny Lofton	1.25	.90	.50
196	Carlos Martinez	.25	.15	.08
197	Jose Mesa	.25	.15	.08
198	Eric Plunk	.25	.15	.08
199	Paul Sorrento	.25	.15	.08
200	John Doherty	.25	.15	.08
201	Cecil Fielder	1.00	.70	.40
202	Travis Fryman	2.50	2.00	1.00
203	Kirk Gibson	.25	.15	.08
204	Mike Henneman	.25	.15	.08
205	Chad Kreuter	.25	.15	.08
206	Scott Livingstone	.25	.15	.08
207	Tony Phillips	.25	.15	.08
208	Mickey Tettleton	.25	.15	.08

		MT	NR MT	EX
209	Alan Trammell	.25	.15	.08
210	David Wells	.25	.15	.08
211	Lou Whitaker	.25	.15	.08
212	Kevin Appier	.25	.15	.08
213	George Brett	3.00	2.25	1.25
214	David Cone	.25	.15	.08
215	Tom Gordon	.25	.15	.08
216	Phil Hiatt	1.00	.70	.40
217	Felix Jose	.25	.15	.08
218	Wally Joyner	.25	.15	.08
219	Jose Lind	.25	.15	.08
220	Mike Macfarlane	.25	.15	.08
221	Brian McRae	.25	.15	.08
222	Jeff Montgomery	.25	.15	.08
223	Cal Eldred	.50	.30	.15
224	Darryl Hamilton	.25	.15	.08
225	John Jaha	.60	.45	.25
226	Pat Listach	.50	.30	.15
227	Graeme Lloyd	.25	.15	.08
228	Kevin Reimer	.25	.15	.08
229	Bill Spiers	.25	.15	.08
230	B.J. Surhoff	.25	.15	.08
231	Greg Vaughn	.40	.30	.15
232	Robin Yount	2.00	1.50	.80
233	Rick Aguilera	.25	.15	.08
234	Jim Deshaies	.25	.15	.08
235	Brian Harper	.25	.15	.08
236	Kent Hrbek	.25	.15	.08
237	Chuck Knoblauch	.40	.30	.15
238	Shane Mack	.25	.15	.08
239	David McCarty	2.25	1.25	.60
240	Pedro Munoz	.25	.15	.08
241	Mike Pagliarulo	.25	.15	.08
242	Kirby Puckett	3.50	2.75	1.50
243	Dave Winfield	1.00	.70	.40
244	Jim Abbott	.50	.30	.15
245	Wade Boggs	1.00	.70	.40
246	Pat Kelly	.25	.15	.08
247	Jimmy Key	.25	.15	.08
248	Jim Leyritz	.25	.15	.08
249	Don Mattingly	2.00	1.50	.80
250	Matt Nokes	.25	.15	.08
251	Paul O'Neill	.25	.15	.08
252	Mike Stanley	.25	.15	.08
253	Danny Tartabull	.25	.15	.08
254	Bob Wickman	.75	.60	.30
255	Bernie Williams	.25	.15	.08
256	Mike Bordick	.25	.15	.08
257	Dennis Eckersley	.25	.15	.08
258	Brent Gates	1.50	1.25	.60
259	Goose Gossage	.25	.15	.08
260	Rickey Henderson	1.00	.70	.40
261	Mark McGwire	.50	.30	.15
262	Ruben Sierra	.75	.60	.30
263	Terry Steinbach	.25	.15	.08
264	Bob Welch	.25	.15	.08
265	Bobby Witt	.25	.15	.08
266	Rich Amaral	.25	.15	.08
267	Chris Bosio	.25	.15	.08
268	Jay Buhner	.25	.15	.08
269	Norm Charlton	.25	.15	.08
270	Ken Griffey Jr.	6.00	4.50	2.50
271	Erik Hanson	.25	.15	.08
272	Randy Johnson	.60	.45	.25
273	Edgar Martinez	.25	.15	.08
274	Tino Martinez	.25	.15	.08
275	Dave Valle	.25	.15	.08
276	Omar Vizquel	.25	.15	.08
277	Kevin Brown	.25	.15	.08
278	Jose Canseco	.50	.30	.15
279	Julio Franco	.25	.15	.08
280	Juan Gonzalez	6.00	4.50	2.50
281	Tom Henke	.25	.15	.08
282	David Hulse	.25	.15	.08
283	Rafael Palmeiro	.60	.45	.25
284	Dean Palmer	.75	.60	.30
285	Ivan Rodriguez	1.25	.90	.50
286	Nolan Ryan	5.00	3.75	2.00
287	Roberto Alomar	2.50	2.00	1.00
288	Pat Borders	.25	.15	.08
289	Joe Carter	.60	.45	.25
290	Juan Guzman	1.50	1.25	.60
291	Pat Hentgen	3.00	2.25	1.25
292	Paul Molitor	1.50	1.25	.60
293	John Olerud	2.00	1.50	.80
294	Ed Sprague	.25	.15	.08
295	Dave Stewart	.25	.15	.08
296	Duane Ward	.25	.15	.08
297	Devon White	.25	.15	.08
298	Checklist	.25	.15	.08
299	Checklist	.25	.15	.08
300	Checklist	.25	.15	.08

1993 Fleer Flair Wave of the Future

Twenty of the game's top prospects were featured in this insert issue randomly packaged in Flair packs. Cards #19-20, Darrell Whitmore and Nigel Wilson, were printed with each other's back; no corrected version was made.

		MT	NR MT	EX
Complete Set (20):		100.00	75.00	45.00
Common Player:		3.00	2.25	1.25
1	Jason Bere	8.00	6.00	3.25
2	Jeremy Burnitz	4.00	3.00	1.50
3	Russ Davis	5.00	3.75	2.00
4	Jim Edmonds	3.00	2.25	1.25
5	Cliff Floyd	15.00	11.00	6.00
6	Jeffrey Hammonds	8.00	6.00	3.25
7	Trevor Hoffman	3.00	2.25	1.25
8	Domingo Jean	4.00	3.00	1.50
9	David McCarty	4.00	3.00	1.50
10	Bobby Munoz	3.00	2.25	1.25
11	Brad Pennington	3.00	2.25	1.25
12	Mike Piazza	15.00	11.00	6.00
13	Manny Ramirez	8.00	6.00	3.25
14	John Roper	3.00	2.25	1.25
15	Tim Salmon	8.00	6.00	3.25
16	Aaron Sele	8.00	6.00	3.25
17	Allen Watson	5.00	3.75	2.00
18	Rondell White	6.00	4.50	2.50
19	Darell Whitmore	5.00	3.75	2.00
20	Nigel Wilson	6.00	4.50	2.50

1994 Fleer

Fleer's 720-card 1994 set, released in one series, includes another 204 insert cards to be pusued by collectors. Every pack includes one of the cards, randomly inserted form among the 12 insert sets the company produced. Regular cards have action photos on front, with a team logo in one of the lower corners. The player's name and position is stamped in gold foil around the logo. On back, another color player photo is overprinted with color boxes and player data and stats, leaving a clear image of the player's face, 1-1/2" x 1-3/4" in size. Cards are UV coated on both sides. Insert sets are: Rookie Sensations (20 cards), Lumber Company (10), Smoke N' Heat (12), Team Leaders (28), League Leaders (28), Fleer Award Winners (6), Major League Prospects (35), ProVisions (9), American League All-Stars (25), National League All-Stars (25), Golden Moments (10), and Tim Salmon, Rookie of the Year (12). Salmon has autographed more than 2,000 cards. Three additional Salmon cards not available in regular card packs were available only through a mail-in program with Fleer. Collectors could receive the cards by cards by sending 10 wrappers and $1.50 to the company.

		MT	NR MT	EX
Complete Set (720):		35.00	26.00	14.00
Common Player:		.05	.04	.02
1	Brady Anderson	.05	.04	.02
2	Harold Baines	.05	.04	.02
3	Mike Devereaux	.05	.04	.02
4	Todd Frohwirth	.05	.04	.02
5	Jeffrey Hammonds	.75	.60	.30
6	Chris Hoiles	.05	.04	.02
7	Tim Hulett	.05	.04	.02
8	Ben McDonald	.05	.04	.02
9	Mark McLemore	.05	.04	.02
10	Alan Mills	.05	.04	.02
11	Jamie Moyer	.05	.04	.02
12	Mike Mussina	.25	.20	.10
13	Gregg Olson	.05	.04	.02
14	Mike Pagliarulo	.05	.04	.02
15	Brad Pennington	.05	.04	.02
16	Jim Poole	.05	.04	.02
17	Harold Reynolds	.05	.04	.02
18	Arthur Rhodes	.05	.04	.02
19	Cal Ripken, Jr.	.35	.25	.14
20	David Segui	.05	.04	.02
21	Rick Sutcliffe	.05	.04	.02
22	Fernando Valenzuela	.05	.04	.02
23	Jack Voigt	.05	.04	.02
24	Mark Williamson	.05	.04	.02
25	Scott Bankhead	.05	.04	.02
26	Roger Clemens	.20	.15	.08
27	Scott Cooper	.05	.04	.02
28	Danny Darwin	.05	.04	.02
29	Andre Dawson	.05	.04	.02
30	Rob Deer	.05	.04	.02
31	John Dopson	.05	.04	.02
32	Scott Fletcher	.05	.04	.02
33	Mike Greenwell	.05	.04	.02
34	Greg Harris	.05	.04	.02
35	Billy Hatcher	.05	.04	.02
36	Bob Melvin	.05	.04	.02
37	Tony Pena	.05	.04	.02
38	Paul Quantrill	.05	.04	.02
39	Carlos Quintana	.05	.04	.02
40	Ernest Riles	.05	.04	.02
41	Jeff Russell	.05	.04	.02
42	Ken Ryan	.05	.04	.02
43	Aaron Sele	1.00	.70	.40
44	John Valentin	.05	.04	.02
45	Mo Vaughn	.10	.08	.04
46	Frank Viola	.05	.04	.02
47	Bob Zupcic	.05	.04	.02
48	Mike Butcher	.05	.04	.02
49	Rod Correia	.05	.04	.02
50	Chad Curtis	.15	.11	.06
51	Chili Davis	.05	.04	.02
52	Gary DiSarcina	.05	.04	.02
53	Damion Easley	.15	.11	.06
54	Jim Edmonds	.05	.04	.02
55	Chuck Finley	.05	.04	.02
56	Steve Frey	.05	.04	.02
57	Rene Gonzales	.05	.04	.02
58	Joe Grahe	.05	.04	.02
59	Hilly Hathaway	.05	.04	.02
60	Stan Javier	.05	.04	.02
61	Mark Langston	.05	.04	.02
62	Phil Leftwich	.05	.04	.02
63	Torey Lovullo	.05	.04	.02
64	Joe Magrane	.05	.04	.02
65	Greg Myers	.05	.04	.02
66	Ken Patterson	.05	.04	.02
67	Eduardo Perez	.05	.04	.02
68	Luis Polonia	.05	.04	.02
69	Tim Salmon	1.25	.90	.50

		MT	NR MT	EX
70	J.T. Snow	.40	.30	.15
71	Ron Tingley	.05	.04	.02
72	Julio Valera	.05	.04	.02
73	Wilson Alvarez	.05	.04	.02
74	Tim Belcher	.05	.04	.02
75	George Bell	.05	.04	.02
76	Jason Bere	.75	.60	.30
77	Rod Bolton	.05	.04	.02
78	Ellis Burks	.05	.04	.02
79	Joey Cora	.05	.04	.02
80	Alex Fernandez	.05	.04	.02
81	Craig Grebeck	.05	.04	.02
82	Ozzie Guillen	.05	.04	.02
83	Roberto Hernandez	.05	.04	.02
84	Bo Jackson	.15	.11	.06
85	Lance Johnson	.05	.04	.02
86	Ron Karkovice	.05	.04	.02
87	Mike LaValliere	.05	.04	.02
88	Kirk McCaskill	.05	.04	.02
89	Jack McDowell	.15	.11	.06
90	Warren Newson	.05	.04	.02
91	Dan Pasqua	.05	.04	.02
92	Scott Radinsky	.05	.04	.02
93	Tim Raines	.05	.04	.02
94	Steve Sax	.05	.04	.02
95	Jeff Schwarz	.05	.04	.02
96	Frank Thomas	1.50	1.25	.60
97	Robin Ventura	.15	.11	.06
98	Sandy Alomar, Jr.	.05	.04	.02
99	Carlos Baerga	.25	.20	.10
100	Albert Belle	.25	.20	.10
101	Mark Clark	.05	.04	.02
102	Jerry DiPoto	.05	.04	.02
103	Alvaro Espinoza	.05	.04	.02
104	Felix Fermin	.05	.04	.02
105	Jeremy Hernandez	.05	.04	.02
106	Reggie Jefferson	.05	.04	.02
107	Wayne Kirby	.05	.04	.02
108	Tom Kramer	.05	.04	.02
109	Mark Lewis	.05	.04	.02
110	Derek Lilliquist	.05	.04	.02
111	Kenny Lofton	.15	.11	.06
112	Candy Maldonado	.05	.04	.02
113	Jose Mesa	.05	.04	.02
114	Jeff Mutis	.05	.04	.02
115	Charles Nagy	.05	.04	.02
116	Bob Ojeda	.05	.04	.02
117	Junior Ortiz	.05	.04	.02
118	Eric Plunk	.05	.04	.02
119	Manny Ramirez	.75	.60	.30
120	Paul Sorrento	.05	.04	.02
121	Jim Thome	.10	.08	.04
122	Jeff Treadway	.05	.04	.02
123	Bill Wertz	.05	.04	.02
124	Skeeter Barnes	.05	.04	.02
125	Milt Cuyler	.05	.04	.02
126	Eric Davis	.05	.04	.02
127	John Doherty	.05	.04	.02
128	Cecil Fielder	.10	.08	.04
129	Travis Fryman	.25	.20	.10
130	Kirk Gibson	.05	.04	.02
131	Dan Gladden	.05	.04	.02
132	Greg Gohr	.05	.04	.02
133	Chris Gomez	.05	.04	.02
134	Bill Gullickson	.05	.04	.02
135	Mike Henneman	.05	.04	.02
136	Kurt Knudsen	.05	.04	.02
137	Chad Kreuter	.05	.04	.02
138	Bill Krueger	.05	.04	.02
139	Scott Livingstone	.05	.04	.02
140	Bob MacDonald	.05	.04	.02
141	Mike Moore	.05	.04	.02
142	Tony Phillips	.05	.04	.02
143	Mickey Tettleton	.05	.04	.02
144	Alan Trammell	.05	.04	.02
145	David Wells	.05	.04	.02
146	Lou Whitaker	.05	.04	.02
147	Kevin Appier	.05	.04	.02
148	Stan Belinda	.05	.04	.02
149	George Brett	.20	.15	.08
150	Billy Brewer	.05	.04	.02
151	Hubie Brooks	.05	.04	.02
152	David Cone	.05	.04	.02
153	Gary Gaetti	.05	.04	.02
154	Greg Gagne	.05	.04	.02
155	Tom Gordon	.05	.04	.02
156	Mark Gubicza	.05	.04	.02
157	Chris Gwynn	.05	.04	.02
158	John Habyan	.05	.04	.02
159	Chris Haney	.05	.04	.02
160	Phil Hiatt	.15	.11	.06

		MT	NR MT	EX
161	Felix Jose	.05	.04	.02
162	Wally Joyner	.05	.04	.02
163	Jose Lind	.05	.04	.02
164	Mike Macfarlane	.05	.04	.02
165	Mike Magnante	.05	.04	.02
166	Brent Mayne	.05	.04	.02
167	Brian McRae	.05	.04	.02
168	Kevin McReynolds	.05	.04	.02
169	Keith Miller	.05	.04	.02
170	Jeff Montgomery	.05	.04	.02
171	Hipolito Pichardo	.05	.04	.02
172	Rico Rossy	.05	.04	.02
173	Juan Bell	.05	.04	.02
174	Ricky Bones	.05	.04	.02
175	Cal Eldred	.10	.08	.04
176	Mike Fetters	.05	.04	.02
177	Darryl Hamilton	.05	.04	.02
178	Doug Henry	.05	.04	.02
179	Mike Ignasiak	.05	.04	.02
180	John Jaha	.10	.08	.04
181	Pat Listach	.10	.08	.04
182	Graeme Lloyd	.10	.08	.04
183	Matt Mieske	.10	.08	.04
184	Angel Miranda	.05	.04	.02
185	Jaime Navarro	.05	.04	.02
186	Dave Nilsson	.05	.04	.02
187	Troy O'Leary	.05	.04	.02
188	Jesse Orosco	.05	.04	.02
189	Kevin Reimer	.05	.04	.02
190	Kevin Seitzer	.05	.04	.02
191	Bill Spiers	.05	.04	.02
192	B.J. Surhoff	.05	.04	.02
193	Dickie Thon	.05	.04	.02
194	Jose Valentin	.05	.04	.02
195	Greg Vaughn	.05	.04	.02
196	Bill Wegman	.05	.04	.02
197	Robin Yount	.15	.11	.06
198	Rick Aguilera	.05	.04	.02
199	Willie Banks	.05	.04	.02
200	Bernardo Brito	.05	.04	.02
201	Larry Casian	.05	.04	.02
202	Scott Erickson	.05	.04	.02
203	Eddie Guardado	.05	.04	.02
204	Mark Guthrie	.05	.04	.02
205	Chip Hale	.05	.04	.02
206	Brian Harper	.05	.04	.02
207	Mike Hartley	.05	.04	.02
208	Kent Hrbek	.05	.04	.02
209	Terry Jorgensen	.05	.04	.02
210	Chuck Knoblauch	.05	.04	.02
211	Gene Larkin	.05	.04	.02
212	Shane Mack	.05	.04	.02
213	David McCarty	.15	.11	.06
214	Pat Meares	.05	.04	.02
215	Pedro Munoz	.05	.04	.02
216	Derek Parks	.05	.04	.02
217	Kirby Puckett	.25	.20	.10
218	Jeff Reboulet	.05	.04	.02
219	Kevin Tapani	.05	.04	.02
220	Mike Trombley	.05	.04	.02
221	George Tsamis	.05	.04	.02
222	Carl Willis	.05	.04	.02
223	Dave Winfield	.10	.08	.04
224	Jim Abbott	.05	.04	.02
225	Paul Assenmacher	.05	.04	.02
226	Wade Boggs	.15	.11	.06
227	Russ Davis	.05	.04	.02
228	Steve Farr	.05	.04	.02
229	Mike Gallego	.05	.04	.02
230	Paul Gibson	.05	.04	.02
231	Steve Howe	.05	.04	.02
232	Dion James	.05	.04	.02
233	Domingo Jean	.05	.04	.02
234	Scott Kamieniecki	.05	.04	.02
235	Pat Kelly	.05	.04	.02
236	Jimmy Key	.05	.04	.02
237	Jim Leyritz	.05	.04	.02
238	Kevin Maas	.05	.04	.02
239	Don Mattingly	.15	.11	.06
240	Rich Monteleone	.05	.04	.02
241	Bobby Munoz	.05	.04	.02
242	Matt Nokes	.05	.04	.02
243	Paul O'Neill	.05	.04	.02
244	Spike Owen	.05	.04	.02
245	Melido Perez	.05	.04	.02
246	Lee Smith	.05	.04	.02
247	Mike Stanley	.05	.04	.02
248	Danny Tartabull	.05	.04	.02
249	Randy Velarde	.05	.04	.02
250	Bob Wickman	.05	.04	.02
251	Bernie Williams	.05	.04	.02

		MT	NR MT	EX
252	Mike Aldrete	.05	.04	.02
253	Marcos Armas	.15	.11	.06
254	Lance Blankenship	.05	.04	.02
255	Mike Bordick	.05	.04	.02
256	Scott Brosius	.05	.04	.02
257	Jerry Browne	.05	.04	.02
258	Ron Darling	.05	.04	.02
259	Kelly Downs	.05	.04	.02
260	Dennis Eckersley	.05	.04	.02
261	Brent Gates	.15	.11	.06
262	Goose Gossage	.05	.04	.02
263	Scott Hemond	.05	.04	.02
264	Dave Henderson	.05	.04	.02
265	Rick Honeycutt	.05	.04	.02
266	Vince Horsman	.05	.04	.02
267	Scott Lydy	.05	.04	.02
268	Mark McGwire	.10	.08	.04
269	Mike Mohler	.05	.04	.02
270	Troy Neel	.15	.11	.06
271	Edwin Nunez	.05	.04	.02
272	Craig Paquette	.05	.04	.02
273	Ruben Sierra	.10	.08	.04
274	Terry Steinbach	.05	.04	.02
275	Todd Van Poppel	.15	.11	.06
276	Bob Welch	.05	.04	.02
277	Bobby Witt	.05	.04	.02
278	Rich Amaral	.05	.04	.02
279	Mike Blowers	.05	.04	.02
280	Bret Boone	.10	.08	.04
281	Chris Bosio	.05	.04	.02
282	Jay Buhner	.05	.04	.02
283	Norm Charlton	.05	.04	.02
284	Mike Felder	.05	.04	.02
285	Dave Fleming	.05	.04	.02
286	Ken Griffey, Jr.	1.25	.90	.50
287	Erik Hanson	.05	.04	.02
288	Bill Haselman	.05	.04	.02
289	Brad Holman	.05	.04	.02
290	Randy Johnson	.15	.11	.06
291	Tim Leary	.05	.04	.02
292	Greg Litton	.05	.04	.02
293	Dave Magadan	.05	.04	.02
294	Edgar Martinez	.05	.04	.02
295	Tino Martinez	.05	.04	.02
296	Jeff Nelson	.05	.04	.02
297	Erik Plantenberg	.05	.04	.02
298	Mackey Sasser	.05	.04	.02
299	Brian Turang	.05	.04	.02
300	Dave Valle	.05	.04	.02
301	Omar Vizquel	.05	.04	.02
302	Brian Bohanon	.05	.04	.02
303	Kevin Brown	.05	.04	.02
304	Jose Canseco	.10	.08	.04
305	Mario Diaz	.05	.04	.02
306	Julio Franco	.05	.04	.02
307	Juan Gonzalez	1.25	.90	.50
308	Tom Henke	.05	.04	.02
309	David Hulse	.15	.11	.06
310	Manuel Lee	.05	.04	.02
311	Craig Lefferts	.05	.04	.02
312	Charlie Leibrandt	.05	.04	.02
313	Rafael Palmeiro	.10	.08	.04
314	Dean Palmer	.05	.04	.02
315	Roger Pavlik	.05	.04	.02
316	Dan Peltier	.15	.11	.06
317	Geno Petralli	.05	.04	.02
318	Gary Redus	.05	.04	.02
319	Ivan Rodriguez	.10	.08	.04
320	Kenny Rogers	.05	.04	.02
321	Nolan Ryan	1.00	.70	.40
322	Doug Strange	.05	.04	.02
323	Matt Whiteside	.05	.04	.02
324	Roberto Alomar	.40	.30	.15
325	Pat Borders	.05	.04	.02
326	Joe Carter	.15	.11	.06
327	Tony Castillo	.05	.04	.02
328	Darnell Coles	.05	.04	.02
329	Danny Cox	.05	.04	.02
330	Mark Eichhorn	.05	.04	.02
331	Tony Fernandez	.05	.04	.02
332	Alfredo Griffin	.05	.04	.02
333	Juan Guzman	.15	.11	.06
334	Rickey Hendereson	.15	.11	.06
335	Pat Hentgen	.30	.25	.12
336	Randy Knorr	.05	.04	.02
337	Al Leiter	.05	.04	.02
338	Paul Molitor	.25	.20	.10
339	Jack Morris	.05	.04	.02
340	John Olerud	.25	.20	.10
341	Dick Schofield	.05	.04	.02
342	Ed Sprague	.05	.04	.02

		MT	NR MT	EX
343	Dave Stewart	.05	.04	.02
344	Todd Stottlemyre	.05	.04	.02
345	Mike Timlin	.05	.04	.02
346	Duane Ward	.05	.04	.02
347	Turner Ward	.05	.04	.02
348	Devon White	.05	.04	.02
349	Woody Williams	.05	.04	.02
350	Steve Avery	.15	.11	.06
351	Steve Bedrosian	.05	.04	.02
352	Rafael Belliard	.05	.04	.02
353	Damon Berryhill	.05	.04	.02
354	Jeff Blauser	.05	.04	.02
355	Sid Bream	.05	.04	.02
356	Francisco Cabrera	.05	.04	.02
357	Marvin Freeman	.05	.04	.02
358	Ron Gant	.10	.08	.04
359	Tom Glavine	.15	.11	.06
360	Jay Howell	.05	.04	.02
361	David Justice	.25	.20	.10
362	Ryan Klesko	.25	.20	.10
363	Mark Lemke	.05	.04	.02
364	Javier Lopez	.60	.45	.25
365	Greg Maddux	.15	.11	.06
366	Fred McGriff	.20	.15	.08
367	Greg McMichael	.20	.15	.08
368	Kent Mercker	.05	.04	.02
369	Otis Nixon	.05	.04	.02
370	Greg Olson	.05	.04	.02
371	Bill Pecota	.05	.04	.02
372	Terry Pendleton	.05	.04	.02
373	Deion Sanders	.10	.08	.04
374	Pete Smith	.05	.04	.02
375	John Smoltz	.10	.08	.04
376	Mike Stanton	.05	.04	.02
377	Tony Tarasco	.25	.20	.10
378	Mark Wohlers	.05	.04	.02
379	Jose Bautista	.05	.04	.02
380	Shawn Boskie	.05	.04	.02
381	Steve Buechele	.05	.04	.02
382	Frank Castillo	.05	.04	.02
383	Mark Grace	.10	.08	.04
384	Jose Guzman	.05	.04	.02
385	Mike Harkey	.05	.04	.02
386	Greg Hibbard	.05	.04	.02
387	Glenallen Hill	.05	.04	.02
388	Steve Lake	.05	.04	.02
389	Derrick May	.05	.04	.02
390	Chuck McElroy	.05	.04	.02
391	Mike Morgan	.05	.04	.02
392	Randy Myers	.05	.04	.02
393	Dan Plesac	.05	.04	.02
394	Kevin Roberson	.15	.11	.06
395	Rey Sanchez	.05	.04	.02
396	Ryne Sandberg	.40	.30	.15
397	Bob Scanlan	.05	.04	.02
398	Dwight Smith	.05	.04	.02
399	Sammy Sosa	.10	.08	.04
400	Jose Vizcaino	.05	.04	.02
401	Rick Wilkins	.05	.04	.02
402	Willie Wilson	.05	.04	.02
403	Eric Yelding	.05	.04	.02
404	Bobby Ayala	.05	.04	.02
405	Jeff Branson	.05	.04	.02
406	Tom Browning	.05	.04	.02
407	Jacob Brumfield	.05	.04	.02
408	Tim Costo	.15	.11	.06
409	Rob Dibble	.05	.04	.02
410	Willie Greene	.05	.04	.02
411	Thomas Howard	.05	.04	.02
412	Roberto Kelly	.05	.04	.02
413	Bill Landrum	.05	.04	.02
414	Barry Larkin	.05	.04	.02
415	Larry Luebbers	.05	.04	.02
416	Kevin Mitchell	.05	.04	.02
417	Hal Morris	.05	.04	.02
418	Joe Oliver	.05	.04	.02
419	Tim Pugh	.05	.04	.02
420	Jeff Reardon	.05	.04	.02
421	Jose Rijo	.05	.04	.02
422	Bip Roberts	.05	.04	.02
423	John Roper	.05	.04	.02
424	Johnny Ruffin	.05	.04	.02
425	Chris Sabo	.05	.04	.02
426	Juan Samuel	.05	.04	.02
427	Reggie Sanders	.10	.08	.04
428	Scott Service	.05	.04	.02
429	John Smiley	.05	.04	.02
430	Jerry Spradlin	.05	.04	.02
431	Kevin Wickander	.05	.04	.02
432	Freddie Benavides	.05	.04	.02
433	Dante Bichette	.05	.04	.02

		MT	NR MT	EX
434	Willie Blair	.05	.04	.02
435	Daryl Boston	.05	.04	.02
436	Kent Bottenfield	.05	.04	.02
437	Vinny Castilla	.05	.04	.02
438	Jerald Clark	.05	.04	.02
439	Alex Cole	.05	.04	.02
440	Andres Galarraga	.05	.04	.02
441	Joe Girardi	.05	.04	.02
442	Greg Harris	.05	.04	.02
443	Charlie Hayes	.05	.04	.02
444	Darren Holmes	.05	.04	.02
445	Chris Jones	.05	.04	.02
446	Roberto Mejia	.30	.25	.12
447	David Nied	.25	.20	.10
448	J. Owens	.05	.04	.02
449	Jeff Parrett	.05	.04	.02
450	Steve Reed	.05	.04	.02
451	Armando Reynoso	.05	.04	.02
452	Bruce Ruffin	.05	.04	.02
453	Mo Sanford	.05	.04	.02
454	Danny Sheaffer	.05	.04	.02
455	Jim Tatum	.20	.15	.08
456	Gary Wayne	.05	.04	.02
457	Eric Young	.10	.08	.04
458	Luis Aquino	.05	.04	.02
459	Alex Arias	.05	.04	.02
460	Jack Armstrong	.05	.04	.02
461	Bret Barberie	.05	.04	.02
462	Ryan Bowen	.05	.04	.02
463	Chuck Carr	.05	.04	.02
464	Jeff Conine	.05	.04	.02
465	Henry Cotto	.05	.04	.02
466	Orestes Destrade	.05	.04	.02
467	Chris Hammond	.05	.04	.02
468	Bryan Harvey	.05	.04	.02
469	Charlie Hough	.05	.04	.02
470	Joe Klink	.05	.04	.02
471	Richie Lewis	.05	.04	.02
472	*Bob Natal*	.15	.11	.06
473	*Pat Rapp*	.15	.11	.06
474	*Rich Renteria*	.15	.11	.06
475	Rich Rodriguez	.05	.04	.02
476	Benito Santiago	.05	.04	.02
477	Gary Sheffield	.15	.11	.06
478	Matt Turner	.05	.04	.02
479	David Weathers	.05	.04	.02
480	Walt Weiss	.05	.04	.02
481	Darrell Whitmore	.40	.30	.15
482	Eric Anthony	.05	.04	.02
483	Jeff Bagwell	.15	.11	.06
484	Kevin Bass	.05	.04	.02
485	Craig Biggio	.05	.04	.02
486	Ken Caminiti	.05	.04	.02
487	Andujar Cedeno	.05	.04	.02
488	Chris Donnels	.05	.04	.02
489	Doug Drabek	.05	.04	.02
490	Steve Finley	.05	.04	.02
491	Luis Gonzalez	.05	.04	.02
492	Pete Harnisch	.05	.04	.02
493	Xavier Hernandez	.05	.04	.02
494	Doug Jones	.05	.04	.02
495	Todd Jones	.05	.04	.02
496	Darryl Kile	.05	.04	.02
497	Al Osuna	.05	.04	.02
498	Mark Portugal	.05	.04	.02
499	Scott Servais	.05	.04	.02
500	Greg Swindell	.05	.04	.02
501	Eddie Taubensee	.05	.04	.02
502	Jose Uribe	.05	.04	.02
503	Brian Williams	.05	.04	.02
504	Billy Ashley	.30	.25	.12
505	Pedro Astacio	.15	.11	.06
506	Brett Butler	.05	.04	.02
507	Tom Candiotti	.05	.04	.02
508	Omar Daal	.05	.04	.02
509	Jim Gott	.05	.04	.02
510	Kevin Gross	.05	.04	.02
511	Dave Hansen	.05	.04	.02
512	Carlos Hernandez	.05	.04	.02
513	Orel Hershiser	.05	.04	.02
514	Eric Karros	.15	.11	.06
515	Pedro Martinez	.20	.15	.08
516	Ramon Martinez	.05	.04	.02
517	Roger McDowell	.05	.04	.02
518	Raul Mondesi	.10	.08	.04
519	Jose Offerman	.05	.04	.02
520	Mike Piazza	2.75	2.00	1.00
521	Jody Reed	.05	.04	.02
522	Henry Rodriguez	.05	.04	.02
523	Mike Sharperson	.05	.04	.02
524	Cory Snyder	.05	.04	.02

		MT	NR MT	EX
525	Darryl Strawberry	.05	.04	.02
526	Rick Trlicek	.05	.04	.02
527	Tim Wallach	.05	.04	.02
528	Mitch Webster	.05	.04	.02
529	Steve Wilson	.05	.04	.02
530	Todd Worrell	.05	.04	.02
531	Moises Alou	.10	.08	.04
532	Brian Barnes	.05	.04	.02
533	Sean Berry	.05	.04	.02
534	Greg Colbrunn	.05	.04	.02
535	Delino DeShields	.10	.08	.04
536	Jeff Fassero	.15	.11	.06
537	Darrin Fletcher	.05	.04	.02
538	Cliff Floyd	1.25	.90	.50
539	Lou Frazier	.05	.04	.02
540	Marquis Grissom	.10	.08	.04
541	Butch Henry	.05	.04	.02
542	Ken Hill	.05	.04	.02
543	Mike Lansing	.15	.11	.06
544	Brian Looney	.05	.04	.02
545	Dennis Martinez	.05	.04	.02
546	Chris Nabholz	.05	.04	.02
547	Randy Ready	.05	.04	.02
548	Mel Rojas	.05	.04	.02
549	Kirk Rueter	.05	.04	.02
550	Tim Scott	.05	.04	.02
551	Jeff Shaw	.05	.04	.02
552	Tim Spehr	.05	.04	.02
553	John VanderWal	.05	.04	.02
554	Larry Walker	.10	.08	.04
555	John Wetteland	.05	.04	.02
556	Rondell White	.60	.45	.25
557	Tim Bogar	.15	.11	.06
558	Bobby Bonilla	.05	.04	.02
559	Jeremy Burnitz	.05	.04	.02
560	Sid Fernandez	.05	.04	.02
561	John Franco	.05	.04	.02
562	Dave Gallagher	.05	.04	.02
563	Dwight Gooden	.05	.04	.02
564	Eric Hillman	.05	.04	.02
565	Todd Hundley	.05	.04	.02
566	Jeff Innis	.05	.04	.02
567	Darrin Jackson	.05	.04	.02
568	Howard Johnson	.05	.04	.02
569	Bobby Jones	.05	.04	.02
570	Jeff Kent	.05	.04	.02
571	Mike Maddux	.05	.04	.02
572	Jeff McKnight	.05	.04	.02
573	Eddie Murray	.10	.08	.04
574	Charlie O'Brien	.05	.04	.02
575	Joe Orsulak	.05	.04	.02
576	Bret Saberhagen	.05	.04	.02
577	Pete Schourek	.05	.04	.02
578	Dave Telgheder	.05	.04	.02
579	Ryan Thompson	.05	.04	.02
580	Anthony Young	.05	.04	.02
581	Ruben Amaro	.05	.04	.02
582	Larry Andersen	.05	.04	.02
583	Kim Batiste	.05	.04	.02
584	Wes Chamberlain	.05	.04	.02
585	Darren Daulton	.10	.08	.04
586	Mariano Duncan	.05	.04	.02
587	Lenny Dykstra	.15	.11	.06
588	Jim Eisenreich	.05	.04	.02
589	Tommy Greene	.05	.04	.02
590	Dave Hollins	.10	.08	.04
591	Pete Incaviglia	.05	.04	.02
592	Danny Jackson	.05	.04	.02
593	Ricky Jordan	.05	.04	.02
594	John Kruk	.10	.08	.04
595	Roger Mason	.05	.04	.02
596	Mickey Morandini	.05	.04	.02
597	Terry Mulholland	.05	.04	.02
598	Todd Pratt	.05	.04	.02
599	Ben Rivera	.05	.04	.02
600	Curt Schilling	.05	.04	.02
601	Kevin Stocker	.75	.60	.30
602	Milt Thompson	.05	.04	.02
603	David West	.05	.04	.02
604	Mitch Williams	.05	.04	.02
605	Jay Bell	.05	.04	.02
606	Dave Clark	.05	.04	.02
607	Steve Cooke	.05	.04	.02
608	Tom Foley	.05	.04	.02
609	Carlos Garcia	.20	.15	.08
610	Joel Johnston	.05	.04	.02
611	Jeff King	.05	.04	.02
612	Al Martin	.20	.15	.08
613	Lloyd McClendon	.05	.04	.02
614	Orlando Merced	.05	.04	.02
615	Blas Minor	.20	.15	.08

		MT	NR MT	EX
616	Denny Neagle	.05	.04	.02
617	Mark Petkovsek	.05	.04	.02
618	Tom Prince	.05	.04	.02
619	Don Slaught	.05	.04	.02
620	Zane Smith	.05	.04	.02
621	Randy Tomlin	.05	.04	.02
622	Andy Van Slyke	.05	.04	.02
623	Paul Wagner	.05	.04	.02
624	Tim Wakefield	.05	.04	.02
625	Bob Walk	.05	.04	.02
626	Kevin Young	.20	.15	.08
627	Luis Alicea	.05	.04	.02
628	Rene Arocha	.25	.20	.10
629	Rod Brewer	.05	.04	.02
630	Rheal Cormier	.05	.04	.02
631	Bernard Gilkey	.10	.08	.04
632	Lee Guetterman	.05	.04	.02
633	Gregg Jefferies	.05	.04	.02
634	Brian Jordan	.05	.04	.02
635	Les Lancaster	.05	.04	.02
636	Ray Lankford	.05	.04	.02
637	Rob Murphy	.05	.04	.02
638	Omar Olivares	.05	.04	.02
639	Jose Oquendo	.05	.04	.02
640	Donovan Osborne	.05	.04	.02
641	Tom Pagnozzi	.05	.04	.02
642	Erik Pappas	.05	.04	.02
643	Geronimo Pena	.05	.04	.02
644	Mike Perez	.05	.04	.02
645	Gerald Perry	.05	.04	.02
646	Ozzie Smith	.15	.11	.06
647	Bob Tewksbury	.05	.04	.02
648	Allen Watson	.20	.15	.08
649	Mark Whiten	.10	.08	.04
650	Tracy Woodson	.15	.11	.06
651	Todd Zeile	.05	.04	.02
652	Andy Ashby	.05	.04	.02
653	Brad Ausmus	.05	.04	.02
654	Billy Bean	.05	.04	.02
655	Derek Bell	.05	.04	.02
656	Andy Benes	.05	.04	.02
657	Doug Brocail	.05	.04	.02
658	Jarvis Brown	.05	.04	.02
659	Archi Cianfrocco	.05	.04	.02
660	Phil Clark	.05	.04	.02
661	Mark Davis	.05	.04	.02
662	Jeff Gardner	.05	.04	.02
663	Pat Gomez	.05	.04	.02
664	Ricky Gutierrez	.05	.04	.02
665	Tony Gwynn	.20	.15	.08
666	Gene Harris	.05	.04	.02
667	Kevin Higgins	.05	.04	.02
668	Trevor Hoffman	.05	.04	.02
669	Pedro Martinez	.20	.15	.08
670	Tim Mauser	.05	.04	.02
671	Melvin Nieves	.10	.08	.04
672	Phil Plantier	.05	.04	.02
673	Frank Seminara	.05	.04	.02
674	Craig Shipley	.05	.04	.02
675	Kerry Taylor	.05	.04	.02
676	Tim Teufel	.05	.04	.02
677	Guillermo Velasquez	.05	.04	.02
678	Wally Whitehurst	.05	.04	.02
679	Tim Worrell	.10	.08	.04
680	Rod Beck	.05	.04	.02
681	Mike Benjamin	.05	.04	.02
682	Todd Benzinger	.05	.04	.02
683	Bud Black	.05	.04	.02
684	Barry Bonds	.50	.40	.20
685	Jeff Brantley	.05	.04	.02
686	Dave Burba	.05	.04	.02
687	John Burkett	.05	.04	.02
688	Mark Carreon	.05	.04	.02
689	Will Clark	.20	.15	.08
690	Royce Clayton	.10	.08	.04
691	Bryan Hickerson	.05	.04	.02
692	Mike Jackson	.05	.04	.02
693	Darren Lewis	.05	.04	.02
694	Kirt Manwaring	.05	.04	.02
695	Dave Martinez	.05	.04	.02
696	Willie McGee	.05	.04	.02
697	John Patterson	.05	.04	.02
698	Jeff Reed	.05	.04	.02
699	Kevin Rogers	.05	.04	.02
700	Scott Sanderson	.05	.04	.02
701	Steve Scarsone	.05	.04	.02
702	Billy Swift	.05	.04	.02
703	Robby Thompson	.05	.04	.02
704	Matt Williams	.10	.08	.04
705	Trevor Wilson	.05	.04	.02
706	"Brave New World" (Fred McGriff, Ron Gant, Dave Justice)	.05	.04	.02

		MT	NR MT	EX
707	"1-2 Punch" (Paul Molitor, John Olerud)	.15	.11	.06
708	"American Heat" (Mike Mussina, Jack McDowell)	.05	.04	.02
709	"Together Again" (Lou Whitaker, Alan Trammell)	.05	.04	.02
710	"Lone Star Lumber" (Rafael Palmeiro, Juan Gonzalez)	.40	.30	.15
711	"Batmen" (Brett Butler, Tony Gwynn)	.05	.04	.02
712	"Twin Peaks" (Kirby Puckett, Chuck Knoblauch)	.05	.04	.02
713	"Back to Back" (Mike Piazza, Eric Karros)	.60	.45	.25
714	Checklist	.05	.04	.02
715	Checklist	.05	.04	.02
716	Checklist	.05	.04	.02
717	Checklist	.05	.04	.02
718	Checklist	.05	.04	.02
719	Checklist	.05	.04	.02
720	Checklist	.05	.04	.02

1994 Fleer Rookie Sensations

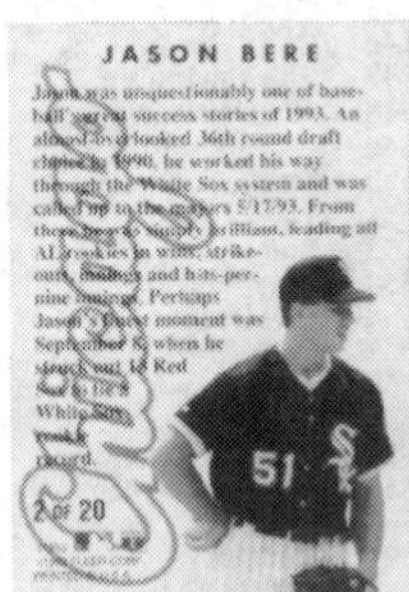

This 20-card insert set features the top rookies from 1993. Both Rookie of the Year award winners, Tim Salmon and Mike Piazza, are included. This insert was available only in 21-card jumbo packs, with stated odds of finding a Rookie Seasations card of one in four packs. Full-bleed fronts have a pair player photos - one highlighted by a neon outline - superimposed on a graduated background approximating the team colors. Team uniform logo details appear vertically at the right or left side. The player's name is gold-foil stamped in a banner at bottom. The Rookie Sensations and Fleer logos are also gold-imprinted. On back, the team uniform logo is repeated on a white background, along with another player photo and a short write-up.

		MT	NR MT	EX
	Complete Set (20):	30.00	22.00	12.00
	Common Player:	1.00	.70	.40
1	Rene Arocha	1.00	.70	.40
2	Jason Bere	5.00	3.75	2.00
3	Jeromy Burnitz	1.50	1.25	.60
4	Chuck Carr	1.50	1.25	.60
5	Jeff Conine	1.50	1.25	.60
6	Steve Cooke	1.50	1.25	.60
7	Cliff Floyd	9.00	6.75	3.50
8	Jeffrey Hammonds	5.00	3.75	2.00
9	Wayne Kirby	1.00	.70	.40
10	Mike Lansing	2.00	1.50	.80
11	Al Martin	1.50	1.25	.60
12	Greg McMichael	1.00	.70	.40
13	Troy Neel	1.50	1.25	.60
14	Mike Piazza	15.00	11.00	6.00
15	Armando Reynoso	1.00	.70	.40
16	Kirk Rueter	6.00	4.50	2.50
17	Tim Salmon	9.00	6.75	3.50
18	Aaron Sele	3.00	2.25	1.25
19	J.T. Snow	3.00	2.25	1.25
20	Kevin Stocker	3.00	2.25	1.25

1994 Fleer Lumber Co.

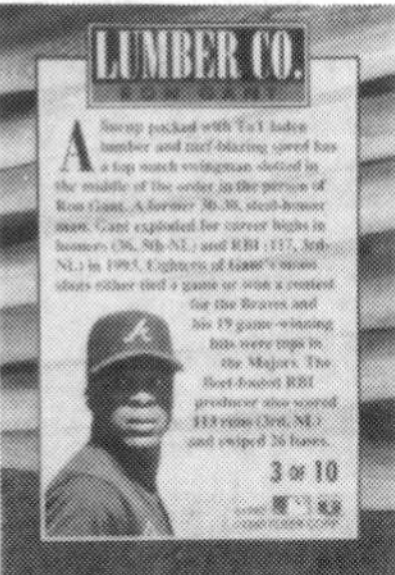

This 10-card insert set features the major leagues' top home run hitters. Inserted only in 21-card jumbo packs, odds of finding one were given as one per five packs. Card fronts feature player action photos against a background resembling the label area of a baseball bat. On back is a background photo of a row of bats on the dirt. A player write-up and close-up photo complete the design. Cards are UV coated on both sides.

		MT	NR MT	EX
	Complete Set (10):	12.00	9.00	4.75
	Common Player:	.50	.40	.20
1	Albert Belle	.75	.60	.30
2	Barry Bonds	2.00	1.50	.80
3	Ron Gant	.50	.40	.20
4	Juan Gonzalez	2.50	2.00	1.00
5	Ken Griffey, Jr.	3.00	2.25	1.25
6	David Justice	1.00	.70	.40
7	Fred McGriff	1.00	.70	.40
8	Rafael Palmeiro	.75	.60	.30
9	Frank Thomas	5.00	3.75	2.00
10	Matt Williams	.75	.60	.30

1994 Fleer Smoke N' Heat

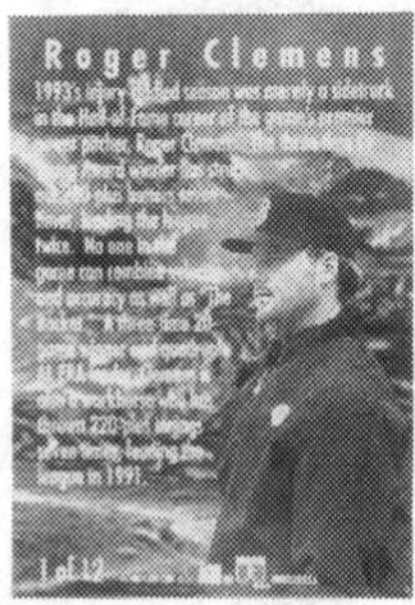

Among the scarcest of the '94 Fleer inserts, available at a stated rate of one per 30 packs, these feature 10 of the top strikeout pitchers in the major leagues. "Metallized" card fronts have a player photo set against an infernal background with large letters, "Smoke 'N Heat". The player's name is in gold foil at bottom. Backs have a similar choatic hot-red background, a player photo and career summary.

		MT	NR MT	EX
	Complete Set (12):	9.00	6.75	3.50
	Common Player:	.50	.40	.20
1	Roger Clemens	1.00	.70	.40
2	David Cone	.50	.40	.20
3	Juan Guzman	.75	.60	.30
4	Pete Harnisch	.50	.40	.20
5	Randy Johnson	1.00	.70	.40
6	Mark Langston	.50	.40	.20

		MT	NR MT	EX
7	Greg Maddux	1.25	.90	.50
8	Mike Mussina	1.50	1.25	.60
9	Jose Rijo	.50	.40	.20
10	Nolan Ryan	3.50	2.75	1.50
11	Curt Schilling	.50	.40	.20
12	John Smoltz	.75	.60	.30

1994 Fleer Team Leaders

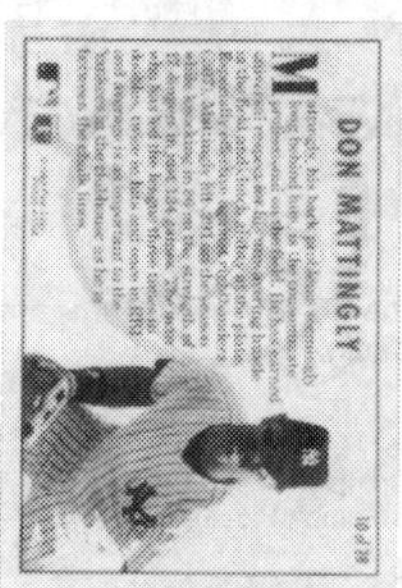

A player from each major league team has been chosen for this 28-card insert set. Fronts feature a team logo against a backgound of graduated team colors. Player portrait and action photos are superimposed. At bottom is the player name, team and position, all in gold foil. Backs have a team logo and player photo set against a white background, with a short write-up justifying the player's selection as a "Team Leader." Odds of finding one of these inserts were given as one in eight packs.

		MT	NR MT	EX
Complete Set (28):		22.00	16.50	8.75
Common Player:		.50	.40	.20
1	Cal Ripken, Jr.	2.00	1.50	.80
2	Mo Vaughn	.75	.60	.30
3	Tim Salmon	5.00	3.75	2.00
4	Frank Thomas	6.00	4.50	2.50
5	Carlos Baerga	2.00	1.50	.80
6	Cecil Fielder	1.00	.70	.40
7	Brian McRae	.50	.40	.20
8	Greg Vaughn	.50	.40	.20
9	Kirby Puckett	1.50	1.25	.60
10	Don Mattingly	1.50	1.25	.60
11	Mark McGwire	.75	.60	.30
12	Ken Griffey, Jr.	4.00	3.00	1.50
13	Juan Gonzalez	4.00	3.00	1.50
14	Paul Molitor	1.50	1.25	.60
15	David Justice	1.50	1.25	.60
16	Ryne Sandberg	2.00	1.50	.80
17	Barry Larkin	.75	.60	.30
18	Andres Galarraga	.50	.40	.20
19	Gary Sheffield	.75	.60	.30
20	Jeff Bagwell	1.00	.70	.40
21	Mike Piazza	7.00	5.25	2.75
22	Marquis Grissom	.75	.60	.30
23	Bobby Bonilla	.50	.40	.20
24	Lenny Dykstra	1.25	.90	.50
25	Jay Bell	.50	.40	.20
26	Gregg Jefferies	.75	.60	.30
27	Tony Gwynn	1.25	.90	.50
28	Will Clark	1.50	1.25	.60

1994 Fleer League Leaders

Twelve players who led the major leagues in various statistical categories in 1993 are featured in this insert set. Cards are UV coated and have gold-foil stamping on both sides. Within a light metallic green border, card fronts feature a color action photo superimposed over a similar photo in black-and-white. The category in which the player led his league is printed down the right border. Other printing is gold-foil. On back is a color photo and details of the league-leading performance. Cards are UV coated on each side. Stated odds of finding a League

Leaders card were one per 17 packs.

		MT	NR MT	EX
Complete Set (12):		8.00	6.00	3.25
Common Player:		.40	.30	.15
1	John Olerud	1.00	.70	.40
2	Albert Belle	1.00	.70	.40
3	Rafael Palmeiro	.50	.40	.20
4	Kenny Lofton	.60	.45	.25
5	Jack McDowell	.60	.45	.25
6	Kevin Appier	.40	.30	.15
7	Andres Galarraga	.40	.30	.15
8	Barry Bonds	2.50	2.00	1.00
9	Lenny Dykstra	1.50	1.25	.60
10	Chuck Carr	.40	.30	.15
11	Tom Glavine	1.00	.70	.40
12	Greg Maddux	1.00	.70	.40

1994 Fleer Award Winners

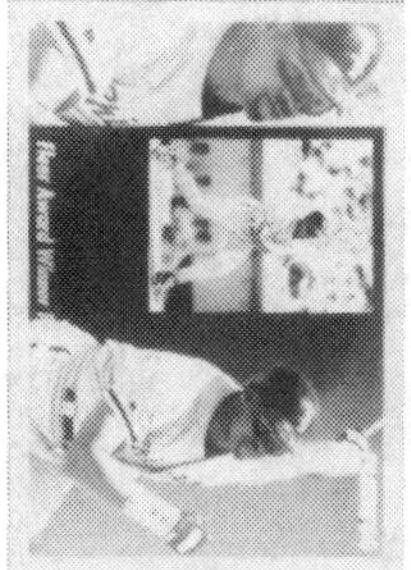

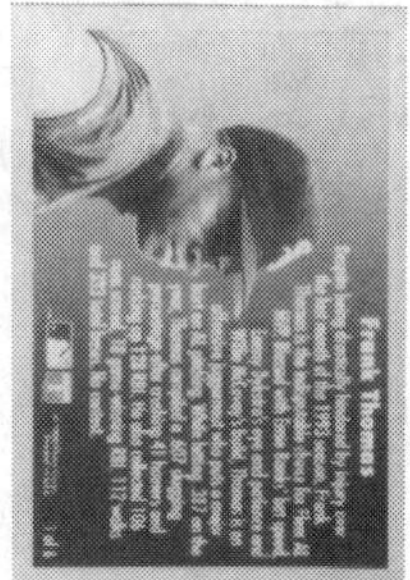

The 1993 MVP, Cy Young and Rookie of the Year award winners from both leagues are featured in this six-card insert set. Cards are UV coated on both sides. Three different croppings of the same player action photo are featured on the front, with the player's name and other printing in gold foil. Backs have a player potrait and short summary of his previous season's perormance. According to the company, odds of finding one of these horozontal-format inserts were one in 37 packs.

		MT	NR MT	EX
Complete Set (6):		13.00	9.75	5.25
Common Player:		1.00	.70	.40
1	Frank Thomas	3.50	2.75	1.50
2	Barry Bonds	2.00	1.50	.80
3	Jack McDowell	1.00	.70	.40
4	Greg Maddux	2.00	1.50	.80
5	Tim Salmon	4.00	3.00	1.50
6	Mike Piazza	6.00	4.50	2.50

The values quoted are intended to reflect the market price.

1994 Fleer Major League Prospects

Thirty-five of the game promising young stars are featured in this insert set. A light green metallic border frames a player photo, with his team logo lightly printed over the background. Most of the printing is gold-foil stamped. Backs have a player photo against a pinstriped background. A light blue box contains career details. Given odds of finding a "Major League Prospects" cards are one in six packs.

		MT	NR MT	EX
Complete Set (35):		28.00	21.00	11.00
Common Player:		.40	.30	.15
1	Kurt Abbott	.40	.30	.15
2	Brian Anderson	.40	.30	.15
3	Rich Aude	.40	.30	.15
4	Cory Bailey	.40	.30	.15
5	Danny Bautista	.40	.30	.15
6	Marty Cordova	.40	.30	.15
7	Tripp Cromer	1.00	.70	.40
8	Midre Cummings	1.50	1.25	.60
9	Carlos Delgado	5.00	3.75	2.00
10	Steve Dreyer	.75	.60	.30
11	Steve Dunn	.40	.30	.15
12	Jeff Granger	1.00	.70	.40
13	Tyrone Hill	.60	.45	.25
14	Denny Hocking	.60	.45	.25
15	John Hope	.60	.45	.25
16	Butch Huskey	.40	.30	.15
17	Miguel Jimenez	.60	.45	.25
18	Chipper Jones	4.00	3.00	1.50
19	Steve Karsay	1.00	.70	.40
20	Mike Kelly	1.50	1.25	.60
21	Mike Lieberthal	.75	.60	.30
22	Albie Lopez	.40	.30	.15
23	Jeff McNeely	2.50	2.00	1.00
24	Dan Miceli	.40	.30	.15
25	Nate Minchey	.40	.30	.15
26	Marc Newfield	2.00	1.50	.80
27	Darren Oliver	.40	.30	.15
28	Luis Ortiz	.40	.30	.15
29	Curtis Pride	3.00	2.25	1.25
30	Roger Salkeld	1.25	.90	.50
31	Scott Sanders	.40	.30	.15
32	Dave Staton	.40	.30	.15
33	Salomon Torres	1.50	1.25	.60
34	Steve Trachsel	.40	.30	.15
35	Chris Turner	.40	.30	.15

1994 Fleer All-Stars

Each league's 25 representatives for the 1993 All-Star Game are featured in this insert set. Fronts have a player action photo with a rippling American flag in the top half of the background. The '93 All-Star logo is featured at the bottom, along with a gold-foil impression of the player's name. The flag motif is repeated at top of the card back, along with a player potrait photo set against a red (American League) or blue (National League) background. The player's name, career summary and card number are printed in black. Odds of finding one of

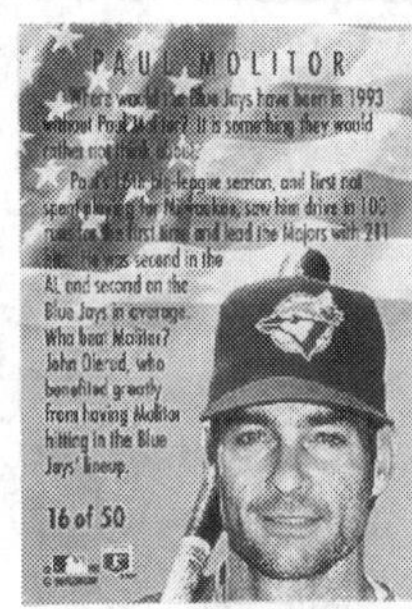

the 50 All-Star inserts are one in every two 15-card foil packs.

		MT	NR MT	EX
Complete Set (50):		38.00	28.00	15.00
Common Player:		.50	.40	.20
1	Roberto Alomar	1.50	1.25	.60
2	Carlos Baerga	1.50	1.25	.60
3	Albert Belle	1.25	.90	.50
4	Wade Boggs	.60	.45	.25
5	Joe Carter	1.00	.70	.40
6	Scott Cooper	.50	.40	.20
7	Cecil Fielder	.75	.60	.30
8	Travis Fryman	1.00	.70	.40
9	Juan Gonzalez	3.00	2.25	1.25
10	Ken Griffey, Jr.	4.00	3.00	1.50
11	Pat Hentgen	.75	.60	.30
12	Randy Johnson	1.00	.70	.40
13	Jimmy Key	.50	.40	.20
14	Mark Langston	.50	.40	.20
15	Jack McDowell	.75	.60	.30
16	Paul Molitor	1.25	.90	.50
17	Jeff Montgomery	.50	.40	.20
18	Mike Mussina	1.00	.70	.40
19	John Olerud	1.50	1.25	.60
20	Kirby Puckett	1.50	1.25	.60
21	Cal Ripken, Jr.	2.00	1.50	.80
22	Ivan Rodriguez	1.00	.70	.40
23	Frank Thomas	5.00	3.75	2.00
24	Greg Vaughn	.60	.45	.25
25	Duane Ward	.50	.40	.20
26	Steve Avery	1.00	.70	.40
27	Rod Beck	.50	.40	.20
28	Jay Bell	.50	.40	.20
29	Andy Benes	.50	.40	.20
30	Jeff Blauser	.50	.40	.20
31	Barry Bonds	2.50	2.00	1.00
32	Bobby Bonilla	.50	.40	.20
33	John Burkett	.50	.40	.20
34	Darren Daulton	1.00	.70	.40
35	Andres Galarraga	.60	.45	.25
36	Tom Glavine	1.00	.70	.40
37	Mark Grace	.75	.60	.30
38	Marquis Grissom	.75	.60	.30
39	Tony Gwynn	1.25	.90	.50
40	Bryan Harvey	.50	.40	.20
41	Dave Hollins	.75	.60	.30
42	David Justice	1.00	.70	.40
43	Darryl Kile	.50	.40	.20
44	John Kruk	.75	.60	.30
45	Barry Larkin	.60	.45	.25
46	Terry Mulholland	.50	.40	.20
47	Mike Piazza	7.50	5.75	3.00
48	Ryne Sandberg	2.00	1.50	.80
49	Gary Sheffield	1.00	.70	.40
50	John Smoltz	.75	.60	.30

1994 Fleer Tim Salmon A.L. Rookie of the Year

The popular Angels Rookie of the Year is featured in a 15-card set produced in what Fleer terms "metalized" format. The first 12 cards in the set were inserted into foil packs at the rate of about one card per box. Three additional cards could be obtained by sending $1.50 and 10

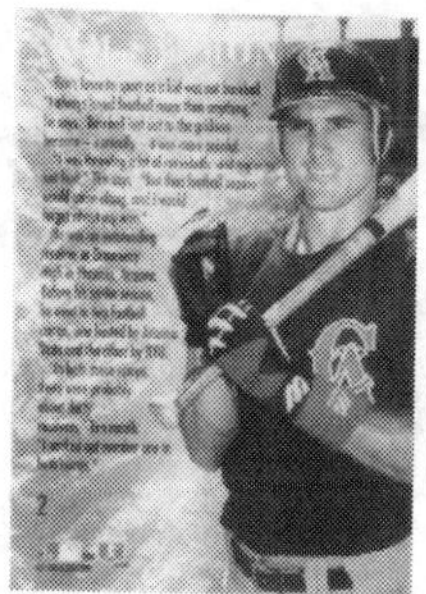

'94 Fleer wrappers to a mail-in offer. On both front and back, the cards have a color player photo set against a metallic-image background.

		MT	NR MT	EX
Complete set (15):		15.00	11.00	6.00
Common card:		1.00	.70	.40
1	Tim Salmon	1.00	.70	.40
2	Tim Salmon	1.00	.70	.40
3	Tim Salmon	1.00	.70	.40
4	Tim Salmon	1.00	.70	.40
5	Tim Salmon	1.00	.70	.40
6	Tim Salmon	1.00	.70	.40
7	Tim Salmon	1.00	.70	.40
8	Tim Salmon	1.00	.70	.40
9	Tim Salmon	1.00	.70	.40
10	Tim Salmon	1.00	.70	.40
11	Tim Salmon	1.00	.70	.40
12	Tim Salmon	1.00	.70	.40
13	Tim Salmon	1.00	.70	.40
14	Tim Salmon	1.00	.70	.40
15	Tim Salmon	1.00	.70	.40

1994 Fleer Golden Moments

Photos not available at press time

Ten highlights from the 1993 Major League baseball season are commemorated in this insert set. Each of the cards has a title which summarizes the historical moment. These inserts were available exclusively in Fleer cards packaged for large retail outlets.

		MT	NR MT	EX
Complete Set (10):		18.00	13.50	7.25
Common Player:		.50	.40	.20
1	"Four in One" (Mark Whiten)	.50	.40	.20
2	"Left and Right" (Carlos Baerga)	2.00	1.50	.80
3	"3,000 Hit Club" (Dave Winfield)	1.50	1.25	.60
4	"Eight Straight" (Ken Griffey, Jr.)	5.00	3.75	2.00
5	"Triumphant Return" (Bo Jackson)	1.50	1.25	.60
6	"Farewell to Baseball" (George Brett)	2.50	2.00	1.00
7	"Farewell to Baseball" (Nolan Ryan)	4.00	3.00	1.50
8	"Thirty Times Six" (Fred McGriff)	1.50	1.25	.60
9	"Enters 5th Dimension" (Frank Thomas)	6.00	4.50	2.50
10	"The No-Hit Parade" (Chris Bosio, Jim Abbott, Darryl Kile)	.50	.40	.20

1994 Fleer Golden Moments Super

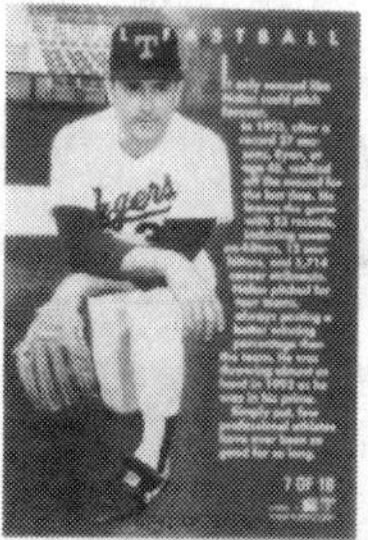

Super-size (3-1/2" x 5") versions of the Golden Moments insert set of 10 were included in hobby cases at the rate of one set, in a specially-printed folder, per 20-box case. Each card carries a serial number designating its position in an edition of 10,000.

		MT	NR MT	EX
Complete set (10):		75.00	56.00	30.00
Common player:		5.00	3.75	2.00
1	"Four in One" (Mark Whiten)	5.00	3.75	2.00
2	"Left and Right" (Carlos Baerga)	7.50	5.50	3.00
3	"3,000 Hit Club" (Dave Winfield)	7.50	5.50	3.00
4	"Eight Straight" (Ken Griffey, Jr.)	15.00	11.00	6.00
5	"Triumphant Return" (Bo Jackson)	7.50	5.50	3.00
6	"Farewell to Baseball" (George Brett)	10.00	7.50	4.00
7	"Farewell to Baseball" (Nolan Ryan)	12.50	9.50	5.00
8	"Thirty Times Six" (Fred McGriff)	7.50	5.50	3.00
9	"Enters 5th Dimension" (Frank Thomas)	15.00	11.00	6.00
10	"The No-Hit Parade (Chris Bosio, Jim Abbott, Darryl Kile)	5.00	3.75	2.00

1994 Fleer ProVisions

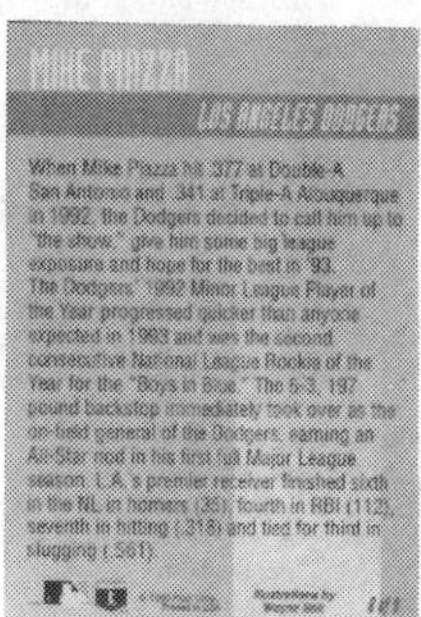

Nine players are featured in this ProVisions insert set. Cards feature the fantasy artwork of Wayne Still in a format that produces one large image when all nine cards are properly arranged. Besides the art, card fronts feature the player's name in gold-foil. Backs have a background in several shades of red, with the player's name and team at the top in white. A short career summary is printed in black. Cards are UV coated on both sides. Odds of finding this particular insert in a pack are one in 12.

		MT	NR MT	EX
Complete Set (9):		10.00	7.50	4.00
Common Player:		.60	.45	.25
1	Darren Daulton	.60	.45	.25
2	John Olerud	1.00	.70	.40
3	Matt Williams	.60	.45	.25
4	Carlos Baerga	1.50	1.25	.60
5	Ozzie Smith	.90	.70	.35
6	Juan Gonzalez	3.00	2.25	1.25
7	Jack McDowell	1.00	.70	.40
8	Mike Piazza	4.50	3.50	1.75
9	Tony Gwynn	.90	.70	.35

1975 Hostess

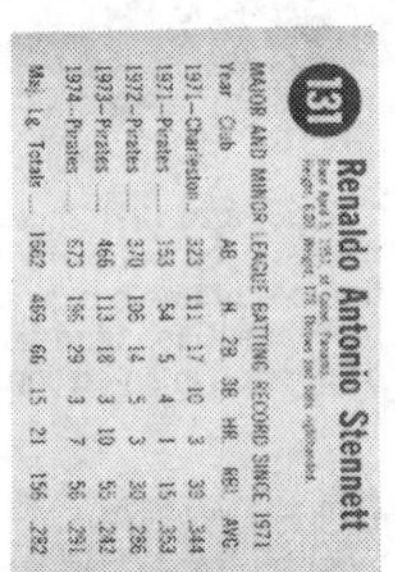

The first of what would become five annual issues, the 1975 Hostess set consists of 50 three-card panels which formed the bottom of boxes of family-size snack cake products. Unlike many similar issues, the Hostess cards do not share common borders, so it was possible to cut them neatly and evenly from the box. Well-cut single cards measure 2-1/4" by 3-1/4", while a three-card panel measures 7-1/4" by 3-1/4". Because some of the panels were issued on packages of less popular snack cakes, they are somewhat scarcer today. Since the hobby was quite well- developed when the Hostess cards were first issued, there is no lack of complete panels. Even unused complete boxes are available today. Some of the photos in this issue also appear on Topps cards of the era.

		NR MT	EX	VG
Complete Panel Set:		400.00	200.00	120.00
Complete Singles Set:		200.00	100.00	60.00
Common Panel:		2.50	1.25	.70
Common Single Player:		.40	.20	.12
	Panel 1	2.50	1.25	.70
1	Bobby Tolan	.40	.20	.12
2	Cookie Rojas	.40	.20	.12
3	Darrell Evans	.70	.35	.20
	Panel 2	5.50	2.75	1.75
4	Sal Bando	.50	.25	.15
5	Joe Morgan	2.00	1.00	.60
6	Mickey Lolich	.60	.30	.20
	Panel 3	4.00	2.00	1.25
7	Don Sutton	1.50	.70	.45
8	Bill Melton	.40	.20	.12
9	Tim Foli	.40	.20	.12
	Panel 4	5.00	2.50	1.50
10	Joe Lahoud	.40	.20	.12
11a	Bert Hooten (incorrect spelling)	1.50	.70	.45
11b	Burt Hooton (correct spelling)	1.50	.70	.45
12	Paul Blair	.40	.20	.12
	Panel 5	2.50	1.25	.70
13	Jim Barr	.40	.20	.12
14	Toby Harrah	.50	.25	.15
15	John Milner	.40	.20	.12
	Panel 6	3.50	1.75	1.00
16	Ken Holtzman	.50	.25	.15
17	Cesar Cedeno	.50	.25	.15
18	Dwight Evans	.90	.45	.25
	Panel 7	7.50	3.75	2.25
19	Willie McCovey	3.00	1.50	.90
20	Tony Oliva	.70	.35	.20
21	Manny Sanguillen	.40	.20	.12
	Panel 8	8.00	4.00	2.50
22	Mickey Rivers	.50	.25	.15
23	Lou Brock	3.00	1.50	.90
24	Craig Nettles	.90	.45	.25
	Panel 9	3.00	1.50	.90
25	Jimmy Wynn	.50	.25	.15
26	George Scott	.50	.25	.15
27	Greg Luzinski	.50	.25	.15
	Panel 10	20.00	10.00	6.00
28	Bert Campaneris	.50	.25	.15
29	Pete Rose	8.00	4.00	2.50
30	Buddy Bell	.50	.25	.15
	Panel 11	2.50	1.25	.70
31	Gary Matthews	.50	.25	.15
32	Fred Patek	.40	.20	.12
33	Mike Lum	.40	.20	.12
	Panel 12	2.50	1.25	.70
34	Ellie Rodriguez	.40	.20	.12
35	Milt May	.40	.20	.12
36	Willie Horton	.50	.25	.15
	Panel 13	10.00	5.00	3.00
37	Dave Winfield	4.50	2.25	1.25
38	Tom Grieve	.40	.20	.12
39	Barry Foote	.40	.20	.12
	Panel 14	2.50	1.25	.70
40	Joe Rudi	.50	.25	.15
41	Bake McBride	.40	.20	.12
42	Mike Cuellar	.50	.25	.15
	Panel 15	2.50	1.25	.70
43	Garry Maddox	.50	.25	.15
44	Carlos May	.40	.20	.12
45	Bud Harrelson	.40	.20	.12
	Panel 16	15.00	7.50	4.50
46	Dave Chalk	.40	.20	.12
47	Dave Concepcion	.50	.25	.15
48	Carl Yastrzemski	6.50	3.25	2.00
	Panel 17	9.00	4.50	2.75
49	Steve Garvey	4.00	2.00	1.25
50	Amos Otis	.50	.25	.15
51	Rickey Reuschel	.50	.25	.15
	Panel 18	3.75	2.00	1.25
52	Rollie Fingers	1.25	.60	.40
53	Bob Watson	.40	.20	.12
54	John Ellis	.40	.20	.12
	Panel 19	9.50	4.75	2.75
55	Bob Bailey	.40	.20	.12
56	Rod Carew	4.00	2.00	1.25
57	Richie Hebner	.40	.20	.12
	Panel 20	15.00	7.50	4.50
58	Nolan Ryan	10.00	5.00	3.00
59	Reggie Smith	.50	.25	.15
60	Joe Coleman	.40	.20	.12
	Panel 21	10.00	5.00	3.00
61	Ron Cey	.50	.25	.15
62	Darrell Porter	.50	.25	.15
63	Steve Carlton	4.00	2.00	1.25
	Panel 22	2.50	1.25	.70
64	Gene Tenace	.40	.20	.12
65	Jose Cardenal	.40	.20	.12
66	Bill Lee	.40	.20	.12
	Panel 23	2.50	1.25	.70
67	Dave Lopes	.50	.25	.15
68	Wilbur Wood	.50	.25	.15
69	Steve Renko	.40	.20	.12
	Panel 24	3.00	1.50	.90
70	Joe Torre	.50	.25	.15
71	Ted Sizemore	.40	.20	.12
72	Bobby Grich	.50	.25	.15
	Panel 25	11.00	5.50	3.25
73	Chris Speier	.40	.20	.12
74	Bert Blyleven	.70	.35	.20
75	Tom Seaver	4.50	2.25	1.25
	Panel 26	2.50	1.25	.70
76	Nate Colbert	.40	.20	.12
77	Don Kessinger	.40	.20	.12
78	George Medich	.40	.20	.12
	Panel 27	30.00	15.00	9.00
79	Andy Messersmith	.70	.35	.20
80	Robin Yount	20.00	10.00	6.00
81	Al Oliver	1.50	.70	.45
	Panel 28	18.00	9.00	5.50
82	Bill Singer	.50	.25	.15
83	Johnny Bench	6.00	3.00	1.75
84	Gaylord Perry	3.00	1.50	.90
	Panel 29	5.00	2.50	1.50
85	Dave Kingman	1.25	.60	.40

		NR MT	EX	VG
86	Ed Herrmann	.50	.25	.15
87	Ralph Garr	.60	.30	.20
	Panel 30	23.00	11.50	7.00
88	Reggie Jackson	9.00	4.50	2.75
89a	Doug Radar (incorrect spelling)	2.00	1.00	.60
89b	Doug Rader (correct spelling)	2.00	1.00	.60
90	Elliott Maddox	.50	.25	.15
	Panel 31	3.50	1.75	1.00
91	Bill Russell	.60	.30	.20
92	John Mayberry	.50	.25	.15
93	Dave Cash	.50	.25	.15
	Panel 32	5.00	2.50	1.50
94	Jeff Burroughs	.60	.30	.20
95	Ted Simmons	1.25	.60	.40
96	Joe Decker	.50	.25	.15
	Panel 33	10.00	5.00	3.00
97	Bill Buckner	1.00	.50	.30
98	Bobby Darwin	.50	.25	.15
99	Phil Niekro	3.50	1.75	1.00
	Panel 34	3.00	1.50	.90
100	Mike Sundberg (Jim)	.50	.25	.15
101	Greg Gross	.40	.20	.12
102	Luis Tiant	.70	.35	.20
	Panel 35	2.50	1.25	.70
103	Glenn Beckert	.40	.20	.12
104	Hal McRae	.50	.25	.15
105	Mike Jorgensen	.40	.20	.12
	Panel 36	2.50	1.25	.70
106	Mike Hargrove	.40	.20	.12
107	Don Gullett	.40	.20	.12
108	Tito Fuentes	.40	.20	.12
	Panel 37	3.50	1.75	1.00
109	John Grubb	.40	.20	.12
110	Jim Kaat	.90	.45	.25
111	Felix Millan	.40	.20	.12
	Panel 38	2.50	1.25	.70
112	Don Money	.40	.20	.12
113	Rick Monday	.50	.25	.15
114	Dick Bosman	.40	.20	.12
	Panel 39	3.50	1.75	1.00
115	Roger Metzger	.40	.20	.12
116	Fergie Jenkins	.90	.45	.25
117	Dusky Baker	.50	.25	.15
	Panel 40	10.00	5.00	3.00
118	Billy Champion	.50	.25	.15
119	Bob Gibson	3.50	1.75	1.00
120	Bill Freehan	.80	.40	.25
	Panel 41	2.50	1.25	.70
121	Cesar Geronimo	.40	.20	.12
122	Jorge Orta	.40	.20	.12
123	Cleon Jones	.40	.20	.12
	Panel 42	10.50	5.25	3.25
124	Steve Busby	.40	.20	.12
125a	Bill Madlock (Pitcher)	2.00	1.00	.60
125b	Bill Madlock (Third Base)	2.00	1.00	.60
126	Jim Palmer	2.75	1.50	.80
	Panel 43	4.25	2.25	1.25
127	Tony Perez	1.00	.50	.30
128	Larry Hisle	.40	.20	.12
129	Rusty Staub	.70	.35	.20
	Panel 44	20.00	10.00	6.00
130	Hank Aaron	9.00	4.50	2.75
131	Rennie Stennett	.50	.25	.15
132	Rico Petrocelli	.70	.35	.20
	Panel 45	16.00	8.00	4.75
133	Mike Schmidt	6.00	3.00	1.75
134	Sparky Lyle	.50	.25	.15
135	Willie Stargell	3.00	1.50	.90
	Panel 46	7.00	3.50	2.00
136	Ken Henderson	.40	.20	.12
137	Willie Montanez	.40	.20	.12
138	Thurman Munson	2.50	1.25	.70
	Panel 47	2.50	1.25	.70
139	Richie Zisk	.40	.20	.12
140	Geo. Hendricks (Hendrick)	.50	.25	.15
141	Bobby Murcer	.50	.25	.15
	Panel 48	10.00	5.00	3.00
142	Lee May	.50	.25	.15
143	Carlton Fisk	1.00	.50	.30
144	Brooks Robinson	3.50	1.75	1.00
	Panel 49	2.50	1.25	.70
145	Bobby Bonds	.50	.25	.15
146	Gary Sutherland	.40	.20	.12
147	Oscar Gamble	.40	.20	.12
	Panel 50	6.00	3.00	1.75
148	Jim Hunter	2.50	1.25	.70
149	Tug McGraw	.50	.25	.15
150	Dave McNally	.50	.25	.15

1975 Hostess Twinkies

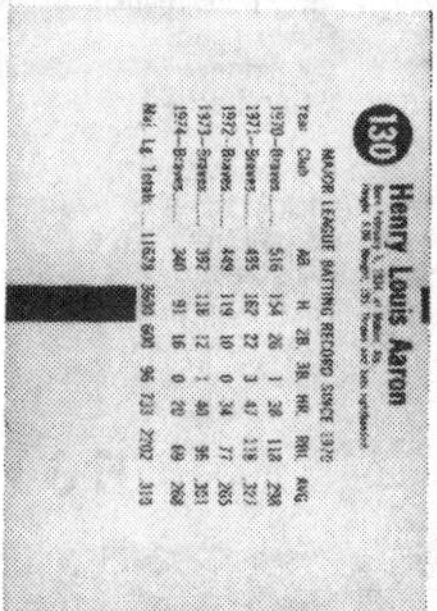

Believed to have been issued only in the Western states, and on a limited basis at that, the 1975 Hostess Twinkie set features 60 of the cards from the "regular" Hostess set of that year. The cards were issued one per pack with the popular snack cake. Card #'s 1-36 are a direct pick-up from the Hostess set, while the remaining 24 cards in the set were selected from the more popular names in the remainder of the Hostess issue - with an emphasis on West Coast players. Thus, after card #36, the '75 Twinkie cards are skip-numbered from 40-136. In identical 2-1/4" by 3-1/4" size, the Twinkie cards differ from the Hostess issue only in the presence of small black bars at top and bottom center of the back of the card. Values quoted are for full bottom panels.

		NR MT	EX	VG
Complete Set:		200.00	100.00	60.00
Common Player:		.90	.45	.25
1	Bobby Tolan	.90	.45	.25
2	Cookie Rojas	.90	.45	.25
3	Darrell Evans	2.00	1.00	.60
4	Sal Bando	1.25	.60	.40
5	Joe Morgan	5.00	2.50	1.50
6	Mickey Lolich	2.00	1.00	.60
7	Don Sutton	4.50	2.25	1.25
8	Bill Melton	.90	.45	.25
9	Tim Foli	.90	.45	.25
10	Joe Lahoud	.90	.45	.25
11	Bert Hooten (Burt Hooton)	1.25	.60	.40
12	Paul Blair	.90	.45	.25
13	Jim Barr	.90	.45	.25
14	Toby Harrah	.90	.45	.25
15	John Milner	.90	.45	.25
16	Ken Holtzman	1.00	.50	.30
17	Cesar Cedeno	1.25	.60	.40
18	Dwight Evans	3.00	1.50	.90
19	Willie McCovey	7.00	3.50	2.00
20	Tony Oliva	2.00	1.00	.60
21	Manny Sanguillen	.90	.45	.25
22	Mickey Rivers	.90	.45	.25
23	Lou Brock	6.50	3.25	2.00
24	Graig Nettles	3.00	1.50	.90
25	Jim Wynn	.90	.45	.25
26	George Scott	.90	.45	.25
27	Greg Luzinski	1.25	.60	.40
28	Bert Campaneris	1.25	.60	.40
29	Pete Rose	20.00	10.00	6.00
30	Buddy Bell	1.75	.90	.50
31	Gary Matthews	1.25	.60	.40
32	Fred Patek	.90	.45	.25
33	Mike Lum	.90	.45	.25
34	Ellie Rodriguez	.90	.45	.25
35	Milt May (photo actually Lee May)	1.25	.60	.40
36	Willie Horton	.90	.45	.25
40	Joe Rudi	1.25	.60	.40
43	Garry Maddox	.90	.45	.25
46	Dave Chalk	.90	.45	.25
49	Steve Garvey	10.00	5.00	3.00
52	Rollie Fingers	4.00	2.00	1.25
58	Nolan Ryan	12.00	6.00	3.50
61	Ron Cey	1.50	.70	.45
64	Gene Tenace	.90	.45	.25
65	Jose Cardenal	.90	.45	.25
67	Dave Lopes	1.25	.60	.40
68	Wilbur Wood	.90	.45	.25

		NR MT	EX	VG
73	Chris Speier	.90	.45	.25
77	Don Kessinger	.90	.45	.25
79	Andy Messersmith	.90	.45	.25
80	Robin Yount	20.00	10.00	6.00
82	Bill Singer	.90	.45	.25
103	Glenn Beckert	.90	.45	.25
110	Jim Kaat	2.50	1.25	.70
112	Don Money	.90	.45	.25
113	Rick Monday	1.25	.60	.40
122	Jorge Orta	.90	.45	.25
125	Bill Madlock	2.25	1.25	.70
130	Hank Aaron	15.00	7.50	4.50
136	Ken Henderson	.90	.45	.25

1976 Hostess

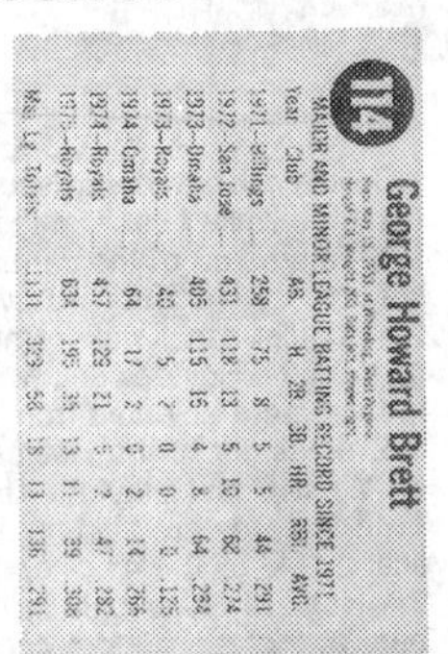

The second of five annual Hostess issues, the 1976 cards carried a "Bicentennial" color theme, with red, white and blue stripes at the bottom of the 2-1/4" by 3-1/4" cards. Like other Hostess issues, the cards were printed in panels of three as the bottom of family-size boxes of snack cake products. This leads to a degree of scarcity for some of the 150 cards in the set; those which were found on less-popular brands. A well-trimmed three-card panel measures 7-1/4" by 3-1/4" size. Some of the photos used in the 1976 Hostess set can also be found on Topps issues of the era.

	NR MT	EX	VG
Complete Panel Set:	400.00	200.00	120.00
Complete Singles Set:	225.00	112.00	67.00
Common Panel:	2.50	1.25	.70
Common Single Player:	.40	.20	.12

		NR MT	EX	VG
	Panel 1	11.75	6.00	3.50
1	Fred Lynn	1.25	.60	.40
2	Joe Morgan	2.00	1.00	.60
3	Phil Niekro	2.25	1.25	.70
	Panel 2	4.50	2.25	1.25
4	Gaylord Perry	1.75	.90	.50
5	Bob Watson	.40	.20	.12
6	Bill Freehan	.50	.25	.15
	Panel 3	6.50	3.25	2.00
7	Lou Brock	3.00	1.50	.90
8	Al Fitzmorris	.40	.20	.12
9	Rennie Stennett	.40	.20	.12
	Panel 4	9.00	4.50	2.75
10	Tony Oliva	.70	.35	.20
11	Robin Yount	10.00	5.00	3.00
12	Rick Manning	.40	.20	.12
	Panel 5	3.50	1.75	1.00
13	Bobby Grich	.50	.25	.15
14	Terry Forster	.40	.20	.12
15	Dave Kingman	.70	.35	.20
	Panel 6	7.00	3.50	2.00
16	Thurman Munson	2.50	1.25	.70
17	Rick Reuschel	.50	.25	.15
18	Bobby Bonds	.50	.25	.15
	Panel 7	9.50	4.75	2.75
19	Steve Garvey	4.00	2.00	1.25
20	Vida Blue	.50	.25	.15
21	Dave Rader	.40	.20	.12
	Panel 8	9.00	4.50	2.75
22	Johnny Bench	4.00	2.00	1.25
23	Luis Tiant	.50	.25	.15
24	Darrell Evans	.70	.35	.20
	Panel 9	2.50	1.25	.70
25	Larry Dierker	.40	.20	.12
26	Willie Horton	.50	.25	.15
27	John Ellis	.40	.20	.12
	Panel 10	3.00	1.50	.90
28	Al Cowens	.40	.20	.12
29	Jerry Reuss	.50	.25	.15
30	Reggie Smith	.50	.25	.15
	Panel 11	13.00	6.50	4.00
31	Bobby Darwin	.50	.25	.15
32	Fritz Peterson	.50	.25	.15
33	Rod Carew	6.00	3.00	1.75
	Panel 12	21.00	10.50	6.25
34	Carlos May	.50	.25	.15
35	Tom Seaver	6.00	3.00	1.75
36	Brooks Robinson	5.00	2.50	1.50
	Panel 13	2.50	1.25	.70
37	Jose Cardenal	.40	.20	.12
38	Ron Blomberg	.40	.20	.12
39	Lee Stanton	.40	.20	.12
	Panel 14	2.50	1.25	.70
40	Dave Cash	.40	.20	.12
41	John Montefusco	.40	.20	.12
42	Bob Tolan	.40	.20	.12
	Panel 15	2.50	1.25	.70
43	Carl Morton	.40	.20	.12
44	Rick Burleson	.50	.25	.15
45	Don Gullett	.40	.20	.12
	Panel 16	2.50	1.25	.70
46	Vern Ruhle	.40	.20	.12
47	Cesar Cedeno	.50	.25	.15
48	Toby Harrah	.50	.25	.15
	Panel 17	6.00	3.00	1.75
49	Willie Stargell	3.00	1.50	.90
50	Al Hrabosky	.40	.20	.12
51	Amos Otis	.50	.25	.15
	Panel 18	2.50	1.25	.70
52	Bud Harrelson	.50	.25	.15
53	Jim Hughes	.40	.20	.12
54	George Scott	.50	.25	.15
	Panel 19	9.50	4.75	2.75
55	Mike Vail	.50	.25	.15
56	Jim Palmer	4.00	2.00	1.25
57	Jorge Orta	.80	.40	.25
	Panel 20	3.50	1.75	1.00
58	Chris Chambliss	.80	.40	.25
59	Dave Chalk	.50	.25	.15
60	Ray Burris	.50	.25	.15
	Panel 21	14.00	7.00	4.25
61	Bert Campaneris	.80	.40	.25
62	Gary Carter	6.00	3.00	1.75
63	Ron Cey	.90	.45	.25
	Panel 22	28.00	14.00	8.50
64	Carlton Fisk	2.00	1.00	.60
65	Marty Perez	.50	.25	.15
66	Pete Rose	10.00	5.00	3.00
	Panel 23	3.50	1.75	1.00
67	Roger Metzger	.50	.25	.15
68	Jim Sundberg	.60	.30	.20
69	Ron LeFlore	.60	.30	.20
	Panel 24	3.50	1.75	1.00
70	Ted Sizemore	.50	.25	.15
71	Steve Busby	.50	.25	.15
72	Manny Sanguillen	.50	.25	.15
	Panel 25	5.00	2.50	1.50
73	Larry Hisle	.60	.30	.20
74	Pete Broberg	.50	.25	.15
75	Boog Powell	1.25	.60	.40
	Panel 26	6.50	3.25	2.00
76	Ken Singleton	.80	.40	.25
77	Rich Gossage	2.00	1.00	.60
78	Jerry Grote	.50	.25	.15
	Panel 27	16.00	8.00	4.75
79	Nolan Ryan	12.00	6.00	3.50
80	Rick Monday	.70	.35	.20
81	Graig Nettles	1.25	.60	.40
	Panel 28	18.00	9.00	5.50
82	Chris Speier	.40	.20	.12
83	Dave Winfield	4.00	2.00	1.25
84	Mike Schmidt	6.00	3.00	1.75
	Panel 29	4.00	2.00	1.25
85	Buzz Capra	.40	.20	.12
86	Tony Perez	1.00	.50	.30
87	Dwight Evans	.90	.45	.25
	Panel 30	2.50	1.25	.70
88	Mike Hargrove	.40	.20	.12
89	Joe Coleman	.40	.20	.12
90	Greg Gross	.40	.20	.12
	Panel 31	2.50	1.25	.70
91	John Mayberry	.40	.20	.12
92	John Candelaria	.50	.25	.15

		NR MT	EX	VG
93	Bake McBride	.40	.20	.12
	Panel 32	15.00	7.50	4.50
94	Hank Aaron	7.00	3.50	2.00
95	Buddy Bell	.50	.25	.15
96	Steve Braun	.40	.20	.12
	Panel 33	2.50	1.25	.70
97	Jon Matlack	.40	.20	.12
98	Lee May	.50	.25	.15
99	Wilbur Wood	.50	.25	.15
	Panel 34	4.00	2.00	1.25
100	Bill Madlock	.90	.45	.25
101	Frank Tanana	.50	.25	.15
102	Mickey Rivers	.50	.25	.15
	Panel 35	3.75	2.00	1.25
103	Mike Ivie	.40	.20	.12
104	Rollie Fingers	1.25	.60	.40
105	Dave Lopes	.50	.25	.15
	Panel 36	3.50	1.75	1.00
106	George Foster	.90	.45	.25
107	Denny Doyle	.40	.20	.12
108	Earl Williams	.40	.20	.12
	Panel 37	2.50	1.25	.70
109	Tom Veryzer	.40	.20	.12
110	J.R. Richard	.50	.25	.15
111	Jeff Burroughs	.40	.20	.12
	Panel 38	14.00	7.00	4.25
112	Al Oliver	.90	.45	.25
113	Ted Simmons	.80	.40	.25
114	George Brett	5.00	2.50	1.50
	Panel 39	3.00	1.50	.90
115	Frank Duffy	.40	.20	.12
116	Bert Blyleven	.80	.40	.25
117	Darrell Porter	.50	.25	.15
	Panel 40	2.50	1.25	.70
118	Don Baylor	.70	.35	.20
119	Bucky Dent	.50	.25	.15
120	Felix Millan	.40	.20	.12
	Panel 41	2.50	1.25	.70
121	Mike Cuellar	.50	.25	.15
122	Gene Tenace	.40	.20	.12
123	Bobby Murcer	.50	.25	.15
	Panel 42	7.00	3.50	2.00
124	Willie McCovey	3.00	1.50	.90
125	Greg Luzinski	.50	.25	.15
126	Larry Parrish	.50	.25	.15
	Panel 43	10.00	5.00	3.00
127	Jim Rice	4.00	2.00	1.25
128	Dave Concepcion	.50	.25	.15
129	Jim Wynn	.50	.25	.15
	Panel 44	2.50	1.25	.70
130	Tom Grieve	.40	.20	.12
131	Mike Cosgrove	.40	.20	.12
132	Dan Meyer	.40	.20	.12
	Panel 45	5.00	2.50	1.50
133	Dave Parker	1.50	.70	.45
134	Don Kessinger	.40	.20	.12
135	Hal McRae	.50	.25	.15
	Panel 46	4.00	2.00	1.25
136	Don Money	.70	.35	.20
137	Dennis	.90	.45	.25
138	Fergie Jenkins	.80	.40	.25
	Panel 47	4.00	2.00	1.25
139	Mike Torrez	.40	.20	.12
140	Jerry Morales	.40	.20	.12
141	Jim Hunter	1.25	.60	.40
	Panel 48	2.50	1.25	.70
142	Gary Matthews	.50	.25	.15
143	Randy Jones	.40	.20	.12
144	Mike Jorgensen	.40	.20	.12
	Panel 49	13.00	6.50	4.00
145	Larry Bowa	.60	.30	.20
146	Reggie Jackson	5.00	2.50	1.50
147	Steve Yeager	.40	.20	.12
	Panel 50	15.00	7.50	4.50
148	Dave May	.40	.20	.12
149	Carl Yastrzemski	6.50	3.25	2.00
150	Cesar Geronimo	.40	.20	.12

1976 Hostess Twinkies

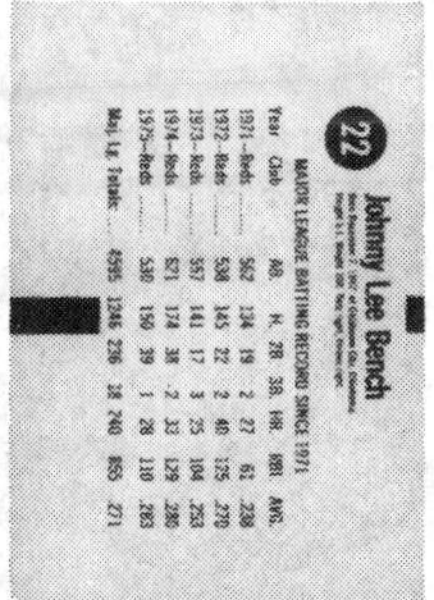

The 60 cards in this regionally-issued (West Coast only) set closely parallel the first 60 cards in the numerical sequence of the "regular" 1976 Hostess issue. The singular difference is the appearance on the back of a black band toward the center of the card at top and bottom. Also unlike the three-card panels of the regular Hostess issue, the 2-1/4" by 3-1/4" Twinkie cards were issued singly, as the cardboard stiffener for the cellophane-wrapped snack cakes. Values quoted are for complete bottom panels.

		NR MT	EX	VG
Complete Set:		200.00	100.00	60.00
Common Player:		.90	.45	.25
1	Fred Lynn	3.00	1.50	.90
2	Joe Morgan	5.00	2.50	1.50
3	Phil Niekro	4.50	2.25	1.25
4	Gaylord Perry	5.00	2.50	1.50
5	Bob Watson	.90	.45	.25
6	Bill Freehan	1.25	.60	.40
7	Lou Brock	7.00	3.50	2.00
8	Al Fitzmorris	.90	.45	.25
9	Rennie Stennett	.90	.45	.25
10	Tony Oliva	2.00	1.00	.60
11	Robin Yount	12.00	6.00	3.50
12	Rick Manning	.90	.45	.25
13	Bobby Grich	1.25	.60	.40
14	Terry Forster	.90	.45	.25
15	Dave Kingman	2.00	1.00	.60
16	Thurman Munson	6.50	3.25	2.00
17	Rick Reuschel	1.25	.60	.40
18	Bobby Bonds	1.25	.60	.40
19	Steve Garvey	10.00	5.00	3.00
20	Vida Blue	1.75	.90	.50
21	Dave Rader	.90	.45	.25
22	Johnny Bench	10.00	5.00	3.00
23	Luis Tiant	1.50	.70	.45
24	Darrell Evans	2.00	1.00	.60
25	Larry Dierker	.90	.45	.25
26	Willie Horton	.90	.45	.25
27	John Ellis	.90	.45	.25
28	Al Cowens	.90	.45	.25
29	Jerry Reuss	1.25	.60	.40
30	Reggie Smith	1.25	.60	.40
31	Bobby Darwin	.90	.45	.25
32	Fritz Peterson	.90	.45	.25
33	Rod Carew	10.00	5.00	3.00
34	Carlos May	.90	.45	.25
35	Tom Seaver	10.00	5.00	3.00
36	Brooks Robinson	9.00	4.50	2.75
37	Jose Cardenal	.90	.45	.25
38	Ron Blomberg	.90	.45	.25
39	Lee Stanton	.90	.45	.25
40	Dave Cash	.90	.45	.25
41	John Montefusco	.90	.45	.25
42	Bob Tolan	.90	.45	.25
43	Carl Morton	.90	.45	.25
44	Rick Burleson	.90	.45	.25
45	Don Gullett	.90	.45	.25
46	Vern Ruhle	.90	.45	.25
47	Cesar Cedeno	1.25	.60	.40
48	Toby Harrah	.90	.45	.25
49	Willie Stargell	7.00	3.50	2.00
50	Al Hrabosky	.90	.45	.25
51	Amos Otis	.90	.45	.25
52	Bud Harrelson	.90	.45	.25
53	Jim Hughes	.90	.45	.25
54	George Scott	.90	.45	.25
55	Mike Vail	.90	.45	.25
56	Jim Palmer	7.00	3.50	2.00
57	Jorge Orta	.90	.45	.25
58	Chris Chambliss	1.25	.60	.40
59	Dave Chalk	.90	.45	.25
60	Ray Burris	.90	.45	.25

1977 Hostess

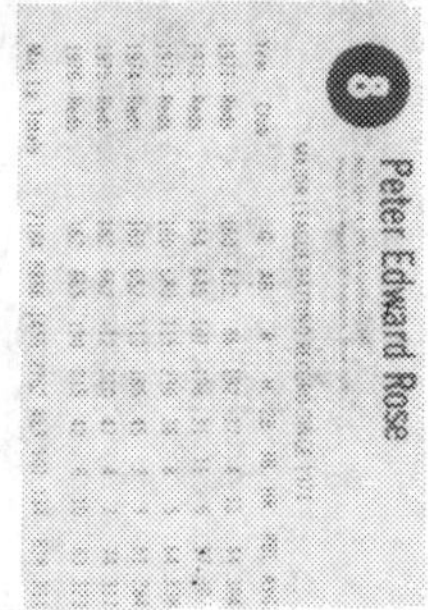

The third of five consecutive annual issues, the 1977 Hostess cards retained the same card size 2-1/4" by 3-1/4", set size - 150 cards, and mode of issue - three cards on a 7-1/4" by 3-1/4" panel, as the previous two efforts. Because they were issued as the bottom panel of snack cake boxes, and because some brands of Hostess products were more popular than others, certain cards in the set are scarcer than others.

		NR MT	EX	VG
Complete Panel Set:		350.00	175.00	105.00
Complete Singles Set:		225.00	112.00	70.00
Common Panel:		2.50	1.25	.70
Common Single Player:		.40	.20	.12
	Panel 1	20.00	10.00	6.00
1	Jim Palmer	3.00	1.50	.90
2	Joe Morgan	3.00	1.50	.90
3	Reggie Jackson	5.00	2.50	1.50
	Panel 2	23.00	11.50	7.00
4	Carl Yastrzemski	6.00	3.00	1.75
5	Thurman Munson	2.50	1.25	.70
6	Johnny Bench	4.00	2.00	1.25
	Panel 3	32.00	16.00	9.50
7	Tom Seaver	3.00	1.50	.90
8	Pete Rose	8.00	4.00	2.50
9	Rod Carew	4.00	2.00	1.25
	Panel 4	2.50	1.25	.70
10	Luis Tiant	.60	.30	.20
11	Phil Garner	.40	.20	.12
12	Sixto Lezcano	.40	.20	.12
	Panel 5	2.50	1.25	.70
13	Mike Torrez	.40	.20	.12
14	Dave Lopes	.50	.25	.15
15	Doug DeCinces	.40	.20	.12
	Panel 6	2.50	1.25	.70
16	Jim Spencer	.40	.20	.12
17	Hal McRae	.50	.25	.15
18	Mike Hargrove	.40	.20	.12
	Panel 7	3.50	1.75	1.00
19	Willie Montanez	.50	.25	.15
20	Roger Metzger	.50	.25	.15
21	Dwight Evans	.70	.35	.20
	Panel 8	6.00	3.00	1.75
22	Steve Rogers	.40	.20	.12
23	Jim Rice	2.00	1.00	.60
24	Pete Falcone	.40	.20	.12
	Panel 9	9.00	4.50	2.75
25	Greg Luzinski	.90	.45	.25
26	Randy Jones	.50	.25	.15
27	Willie Stargell	3.00	1.50	.90
	Panel 10	3.50	1.75	1.00
28	John Hiller	.50	.25	.15
29	Bobby Murcer	.70	.35	.20
30	Rick Monday	.70	.35	.20
	Panel 11	9.00	4.50	2.75
31	John Montefusco	.50	.25	.15
32	Lou Brock	4.00	2.00	1.25
33	Bill North	.50	.25	.15
	Panel 12	24.00	12.00	7.25
34	Robin Yount	6.00	3.00	1.75
35	Steve Garvey	3.00	1.50	.90
36	George Brett	6.00	3.00	1.75
	Panel 13	2.50	1.25	.70
37	Toby Harrah	.50	.25	.15
38	Jerry Royster	.50	.25	.15
39	Bob Watson	.50	.25	.15
	Panel 14	8.00	4.00	2.50
40	George Foster	.90	.45	.25
41	Gary Carter	3.50	1.75	1.00
42	John Denny	.40	.20	.12
	Panel 15	20.00	10.00	6.00
43	Mike Schmidt	7.00	3.50	2.00
44	Dave Winfield	4.00	2.00	1.25
45	Al Oliver	.90	.45	.25
	Panel 16	3.00	1.50	.90
46	Mark Fidrych	.60	.30	.20
47	Larry Herndon	.50	.25	.15
48	Dave Goltz	.40	.20	.12
	Panel 17	3.50	1.75	1.00
49	Jerry Morales	.40	.20	.12
50	Ron LeFlore	.50	.25	.15
51	Fred Lynn	.90	.45	.25
	Panel 18	3.50	1.75	1.00
52	Vida Blue	.50	.25	.15
53	Rick Manning	.40	.20	.12
54	Bill Buckner	.70	.35	.20
	Panel 19	2.50	1.25	.70
55	Lee May	.50	.25	.15
56	John Mayberry	.40	.20	.12
57	Darrel Chaney	.40	.20	.12
	Panel 20	2.50	1.25	.70
58	Cesar Cedeno	.50	.25	.15
59	Ken Griffey	.50	.25	.15
60	Dave Kingman	.40	.20	.12
	Panel 21	2.50	1.25	.70
61	Ted Simmons	.50	.25	.15
62	Larry Bowa	.50	.25	.15
63	Frank Tanana	.40	.20	.12
	Panel 22	2.50	1.25	.70
64	Jason Thompson	.40	.20	.12
65	Ken Brett	.40	.20	.12
66	Roy Smalley	.40	.20	.12
	Panel 23	2.50	1.25	.70
67	Ray Burris	.40	.20	.12
68	Rick Burleson	.40	.20	.12
69	Buddy Bell	.50	.25	.15
	Panel 24	4.50	2.25	1.25
70	Don Sutton	2.00	1.00	.60
71	Mark Belanger	.40	.20	.12
72	Dennis Leonard	.40	.20	.12
	Panel 25	5.00	2.50	1.50
73	Gaylord Perry	2.00	1.00	.60
74	Dick Ruthven	.40	.20	.12
75	Jose Cruz	.50	.25	.15
	Panel 26	2.50	1.25	.70
76	Cesar Geronimo	.40	.20	.12
77	Jerry Koosman	.50	.25	.15
78	Garry Templeton	.50	.25	.15
	Panel 27	20.00	10.00	6.00
79	Catfish Hunter	2.00	1.00	.60
80	John Candelaria	.50	.25	.15
81	Nolan Ryan	10.00	5.00	3.00
	Panel 28	2.50	1.25	.70
82	Rusty Staub	.50	.25	.15
83	Jim Barr	.40	.20	.12
84	Butch Wynegar	.50	.25	.15
	Panel 29	2.50	1.25	.70
85	Jose Cardenal	.40	.20	.12
86	Claudell Washington	.50	.25	.15
87	Bill Travers	.40	.20	.12
	Panel 30	2.50	1.25	.70
88	Rick Waits	.40	.20	.12
89	Ron Cey	.50	.25	.15
90	Al Bumbry	.40	.20	.12
	Panel 31	2.50	1.25	.70
91	Bucky Dent	.50	.25	.15
92	Amos Otis	.50	.25	.15
93	Tom Grieve	.40	.20	.12
	Panel 32	2.50	1.25	.70
94	Enos Cabell	.40	.20	.12
95	Dave Concepcion	.50	.25	.15
96	Felix Millan	.40	.20	.12
	Panel 33	2.50	1.25	.70
97	Bake McBride	.40	.20	.12
98	Chris Chambliss	.50	.25	.15
99	Butch Metzger	.40	.20	.12
	Panel 34	2.50	1.25	.70
100	Rennie Stennett	.40	.20	.12
101	Dave Roberts	.40	.20	.12
102	Lyman Bostock	.40	.20	.12
	Panel 35	3.50	1.75	1.00
103	Rick Reuschel	.50	.25	.15
104	Carlton Fisk	1.00	.50	.30
105	Jim Slaton	.40	.20	.12
	Panel 36	3.00	1.50	.90
106	Dennis Eckersley	1.00	.30	.20
107	Ken Singleton	.40	.20	.12
108	Ralph Garr	.40	.20	.12
	Panel 37	6.00	3.00	1.75

		NR MT	EX	VG
109	Freddie Patek	.50	.25	.15
110	Jim Sundberg	.50	.25	.15
111	Phil Niekro	2.50	1.25	.70
	Panel 38	3.00	1.50	.90
112	J.R. Richard	.50	.25	.15
113	Gary Nolan	.50	.25	.15
114	Jon Matlack	.60	.30	.20
	Panel 39	12.00	6.00	3.50
115	Keith Hernandez	.70	.35	.20
116	Graig Nettles	.70	.35	.20
117	Steve Carlton	5.00	2.25	1.25
	Panel 40	3.50	1.75	1.00
118	Bill Madlock	.80	.40	.25
119	Jerry Reuss	.50	.25	.15
120	Aurelio Rodriguez	.40	.20	.12
	Panel 41	2.50	1.25	.70
121	Dan Ford	.40	.20	.12
122	Ray Fosse	.40	.20	.12
123	George Hendrick	.40	.20	.12
	Panel 42	2.50	1.25	.70
124	Alan Ashby	.40	.20	.12
125	Joe Lis	.40	.20	.12
126	Sal Bando	.50	.25	.15
	Panel 43	4.00	2.00	1.25
127	Richie Zisk	.50	.25	.15
128	Rich Gossage	.90	.45	.25
129	Don Baylor	.60	.30	.20
	Panel 44	2.50	1.25	.70
130	Dave McKay	.40	.20	.12
131	Bob Grich	.50	.25	.15
132	Dave Pagan	.40	.20	.12
	Panel 45	2.50	1.25	.70
133	Dave Cash	.40	.20	.12
134	Steve Braun	.40	.20	.12
135	Dan Meyer	.40	.20	.12
	Panel 46	5.50	2.75	1.75
136	Bill Stein	.40	.20	.12
137	Rollie Fingers	2.00	1.00	.60
138	Brian Downing	.50	.25	.15
	Panel 47	2.50	1.25	.70
139	Bill Singer	.40	.20	.12
140	Doyle Alexander	.50	.25	.15
141	Gene Tenace	.40	.20	.12
	Panel 48	2.50	1.25	.70
142	Gary Matthews	.50	.25	.15
143	Don Gullett	.40	.20	.12
144	Wayne Garland	.40	.20	.12
	Panel 49	2.50	1.25	.70
145	Pete Broberg	.40	.20	.12
146	Joe Rudi	.50	.25	.15
147	Glenn Abbott	.40	.20	.12
	Panel 50	2.50	1.25	.70
148	George Scott	.50	.25	.15
149	Bert Campaneris	.50	.25	.15
150	Andy Messersmith	.40	.20	.12

1977 Hostess Twinkies

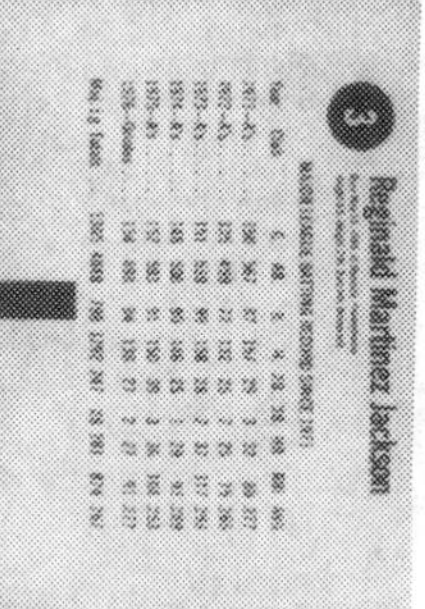

The 1977 Hostess Twinkie issue, at 150 different cards, is the largest of the single-panel Twinkie sets. It is also the most obscure. The cards, which measure 2-1/4" by 3-1/4", but are part of a larger panel, were found not only with Twinkies, but with Hostess Cupcakes as well. Card #'s 1-30 and 111-150 are Twinkies panels and #'s 31-135 are Cupcakes panels. Complete Cupcakes panels are approximately 2-1/4" by 4-1/2" in size, while complete Twinkies panels measure 3-1/8" by 4-1/4". The photos used in the set are identical to those in the 1977 Hostess three-card panel set. The main difference is the appearance of a black band at the center of the card back. The values quoted in the checklist that follows are for complete bottom panels.

		NR MT	EX	VG
	Complete Set:	300.00	150.00	90.00
	Common Player:	.80	.40	.25
1	Jim Palmer	6.00	3.00	1.75
2	Joe Morgan	4.00	2.00	1.25
3	Reggie Jackson	10.00	5.00	3.00
4	Carl Yastrzemski	12.00	6.00	3.50
5	Thurman Munson	5.00	2.50	1.50
6	Johnny Bench	8.00	4.00	2.50
7	Tom Seaver	7.00	3.50	2.00
8	Pete Rose	15.00	7.50	4.50
9	Rod Carew	8.00	4.00	2.50
10	Luis Tiant	1.00	.50	.30
11	Phil Garner	.80	.40	.25
12	Sixto Lezcano	.80	.40	.25
13	Mike Torrez	.80	.40	.25
14	Dave Lopes	1.00	.50	.30
15	Doug DeCinces	1.00	.50	.30
16	Jim Spencer	.80	.40	.25
17	Hal McRae	1.00	.50	.30
18	Mike Hargrove	.80	.40	.25
19	Willie Montanez	.80	.40	.25
20	Roger Metzger	.80	.40	.25
21	Dwight Evans	1.00	.50	.30
22	Steve Rogers	.80	.40	.25
23	Jim Rice	3.00	1.50	.90
24	Pete Falcone	.80	.40	.25
25	Greg Luzinski	1.50	.70	.45
26	Randy Jones	.80	.40	.25
27	Willie Stargell	6.00	3.00	1.75
28	John Hiller	.80	.40	.25
29	Bobby Murcer	1.25	.60	.40
30	Rick Monday	1.00	.50	.30
31	John Montefusco	.80	.40	.25
32	Lou Brock	6.00	3.00	1.75
33	Bill North	.80	.40	.25
34	Robin Yount	8.00	4.00	2.50
35	Steve Garvey	7.00	3.50	2.00
36	George Brett	8.00	4.00	2.50
37	Toby Harrah	.80	.40	.25
38	Jerry Royster	.80	.40	.25
39	Bob Watson	1.00	.50	.30
40	George Foster	1.75	.90	.50
41	Gary Carter	7.00	3.50	2.00
42	John Denny	.80	.40	.25
43	Mike Schmidt	9.00	4.50	2.75
44	Dave Winfield	6.00	3.00	1.75
45	Al Oliver	1.75	.90	.50
46	Mark Fidrych	1.50	.70	.45
47	Larry Herndon	.80	.40	.25
48	Dave Goltz	.80	.40	.25
49	Jerry Morales	.80	.40	.25
50	Ron LeFlore	1.00	.50	.30
51	Fred Lynn	1.75	.90	.50
52	Vida Blue	1.00	.50	.30
53	Rick Manning	.80	.40	.25
54	Bill Buckner	1.00	.50	.30
55	Lee May	.80	.40	.25
56	John Mayberry	.80	.40	.25
57	Darrel Chaney	.80	.40	.25
58	Cesar Cedeno	1.25	.60	.40
59	Ken Griffey	1.25	.60	.40
60	Dave Kingman	1.75	.90	.50
61	Ted Simmons	1.50	.70	.45
62	Larry Bowa	1.25	.60	.40
63	Frank Tanana	1.00	.50	.30
64	Jason Thompson	.80	.40	.25
65	Ken Brett	.80	.40	.25
66	Roy Smalley	.80	.40	.25
67	Ray Burris	.80	.40	.25
68	Rick Burleson	.80	.40	.25
69	Buddy Bell	1.25	.60	.40
70	Don Sutton	3.50	1.75	1.00
71	Mark Belanger	.80	.40	.25
72	Dennis Leonard	.80	.40	.25
73	Gaylord Perry	4.00	2.00	1.25
74	Dick Ruthven	.80	.40	.25
75	Jose Cruz	1.25	.60	.40
76	Cesar Geronimo	.80	.40	.25
77	Jerry Koosman	1.25	.60	.40
78	Garry Templeton	2.50	1.25	.70
79	Catfish Hunter	4.00	2.00	1.25
80	John Candelaria	1.00	.50	.30
81	Nolan Ryan	15.00	7.50	4.50

		NR MT	EX	VG
82	Rusty Staub	1.50	.70	.45
83	Jim Barr	.80	.40	.25
84	Butch Wynegar	1.00	.50	.30
85	Jose Cardenal	.80	.40	.25
86	Claudell Washington	1.00	.50	.30
87	Bill Travers	.80	.40	.25
88	Rick Waits	.80	.40	.25
89	Ron Cey	1.25	.60	.40
90	Al Bumbry	.80	.40	.25
91	Bucky Dent	1.00	.50	.30
92	Amos Otis	1.00	.50	.30
93	Tom Grieve	.80	.40	.25
94	Enos Cabell	.80	.40	.25
95	Dave Concepcion	1.25	.60	.40
96	Felix Millan	.80	.40	.25
97	Bake McBride	.80	.40	.25
98	Chris Chambliss	1.00	.50	.30
99	Butch Metzger	.80	.40	.25
100	Rennie Stennett	.80	.40	.25
101	Dave Roberts	.80	.40	.25
102	Lyman Bostock	1.00	.50	.30
103	Rick Reuschel	1.00	.50	.30
104	Carlton Fisk	2.25	1.25	.70
105	Jim Slaton	.80	.40	.25
106	Dennis Eckersley	1.25	.60	.40
107	Ken Singleton	1.00	.50	.30
108	Ralph Garr	.80	.40	.25
109	Freddie Patek	.80	.40	.25
110	Jim Sundberg	.80	.40	.25
111	Phil Niekro	3.50	1.75	1.00
112	J. R. Richard	1.00	.50	.30
113	Gary Nolan	.80	.40	.25
114	Jon Matlack	.80	.40	.25
115	Keith Hernandez	1.50	.70	.45
116	Graig Nettles	2.00	1.00	.60
117	Steve Carlton	7.00	3.50	2.00
118	Bill Madlock	1.50	.70	.45
119	Jerry Reuss	1.00	.50	.30
120	Aurelio Rodriguez	.80	.40	.25
121	Dan Ford	.80	.40	.25
122	Ray Fosse	.80	.40	.25
123	George Hendrick	1.00	.50	.30
124	Alan Ashby	.80	.40	.25
125	Joe Lis	.80	.40	.25
126	Sal Bando	1.00	.50	.30
127	Richie Zisk	1.00	.50	.30
128	Rich Gossage	1.75	.90	.50
129	Don Baylor	1.50	.70	.45
130	Dave McKay	.80	.40	.25
131	Bob Grich	1.00	.50	.30
132	Dave Pagan	.80	.40	.25
133	Dave Cash	.80	.40	.25
134	Steve Braun	.80	.40	.25
135	Dan Meyer	.80	.40	.25
136	Bill Stein	.80	.40	.25
137	Rollie Fingers	3.00	1.50	.90
138	Brian Downing	1.00	.50	.30
139	Bill Singer	.80	.40	.25
140	Doyle Alexander	1.00	.50	.30
141	Gene Tenace	1.00	.50	.30
142	Gary Matthews	1.00	.50	.30
143	Don Gullett	.80	.40	.25
144	Wayne Garland	.80	.40	.25
145	Pete Broberg	.80	.40	.25
146	Joe Rudi	1.00	.50	.30
147	Glenn Abbott	.80	.40	.25
148	George Scott	1.00	.50	.30
149	Bert Campaneris	1.25	.60	.40
150	Andy Messersmith	1.00	.50	.30

1978 Hostess

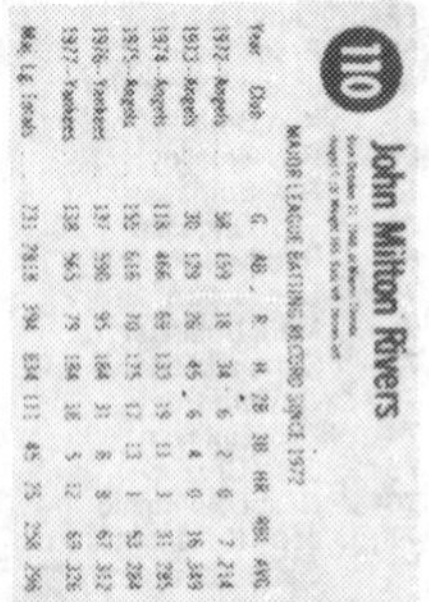

Other than the design on the front of the card, there was little different about the 1978 Hostess cards from the three years' issues which had preceded it, or the one which followed. The 2-1/4" by 3-1/4" cards were printed in panels of three (7-1/4" by 3-1/4") as the bottom of family-sized boxes of snake cakes. The 1978 set was again complete at 150 cards. Like other years of Hostess issues, there are scarcities within the 1978 set that are the result of those panels having been issued with less-popular brands of snack cakes.

	NR MT	EX	VG
Complete Panel:	325.00	162.00	97.00
Complete Singles Set:	225.00	112.00	70.00
Common Panel:	2.50	1.25	.70
Common Single Player:	.40	.20	.12

		NR MT	EX	VG
	Panel 1	4.00	2.00	1.25
1	Butch Hobson	.40	.20	.12
2	George Foster	.90	.45	.25
3	Bob Forsch	.50	.25	.15
	Panel 2	5.00	2.50	1.50
4	Tony Perez	1.00	.50	.30
5	Bruce Sutter	.90	.45	.25
6	Hal McRae	.50	.25	.15
	Panel 3	6.00	3.00	1.75
7	Tommy John	1.50	.70	.45
8	Greg Luzinski	.80	.40	.25
9	Enos Cabell	.40	.20	.12
	Panel 4	7.00	3.50	2.00
10	Doug DeCinces	.50	.25	.15
11	Willie Stargell	3.00	1.50	.90
12	Ed Halicki	.40	.20	.12
	Panel 5	2.50	1.25	.70
13	Larry Hisle	.40	.20	.12
14	Jim Slaton	.40	.20	.12
15	Buddy Bell	.50	.25	.15
	Panel 6	2.50	1.25	.70
16	Earl Williams	.40	.20	.12
17	Glenn Abbott	.40	.20	.12
18	Dan Ford	.40	.20	.12
	Panel 7	2.50	1.25	.70
19	Gary Mathews	.50	.25	.15
20	Eric Soderholm	.40	.20	.12
21	Bump Wills	.40	.20	.12
	Panel 8	3.50	1.75	1.00
22	Keith Hernandez	.70	.35	.20
23	Dave Cash	.40	.20	.12
24	George Scott	.50	.25	.15
	Panel 9	15.00	7.50	4.50
25	Ron Guidry	1.50	.70	.45
26	Dave Kingman	.80	.40	.25
27	George Brett	7.00	3.50	2.00
	Panel 10	3.50	1.75	1.00
28	Bob Watson	.50	.25	.15
29	Bob Boone	.70	.35	.20
30	Reggie Smith	.70	.35	.20
	Panel 11	12.00	6.00	3.50
31	Eddie Murray	6.00	3.00	1.75
32	Gary Lavelle	.40	.20	.12
33	Rennie Stennett	.40	.20	.12
	Panel 12	3.50	1.75	1.00
34	Duane Kuiper	.50	.25	.15
35	Sixto Lezcano	.50	.25	.15
36	Dave Rozema	.50	.25	.15
	Panel 13	3.50	1.75	1.00
37	Butch Wynegar	.50	.25	.15
38	Mitchell Page	.50	.25	.15
39	Bill Stein	.50	.25	.15
	Panel 14	2.50	1.25	.70
40	Elliott Maddox	.40	.20	.12
41	Mike Hargrove	.40	.20	.12
42	Bobby Bonds	.50	.25	.15
	Panel 15	15.00	7.50	4.50
43	Garry Templeton	.80	.40	.25
44	Johnny Bench	6.00	3.00	1.75
45	Jim Rice	2.00	1.00	.60
	Panel 16	13.00	6.50	4.00
46	Bill Buckner	.80	.40	.25
47	Reggie Jackson	5.00	2.50	1.50
48	Freddie Patek	.40	.20	.12
	Panel 17	8.50	4.25	2.50
49	Steve Carlton	3.50	1.75	1.00
50	Cesar Cedeno	.50	.25	.15
51	Steve Yeager	.40	.20	.12
	Panel 18	3.50	1.75	1.00
52	Phil Garner	.50	.25	.15
53	Lee May	.50	.25	.15
54	Darrell Evans	.70	.35	.20
	Panel 19	2.50	1.25	.70
55	Steve Kemp	.50	.25	.15

		NR MT	EX	VG
56	Dusty Baker	.50	.25	.15
57	Ray Fosse	.40	.20	.12
	Panel 20	2.50	1.25	.70
58	Manny Sanguillen	.40	.20	.12
59	Tom Johnson	.40	.20	.12
60	Lee Stanton	.40	.20	.12
	Panel 21	10.00	5.00	3.00
61	Jeff Burroughs	.40	.20	.12
62	Bobby Grich	.50	.25	.15
63	Dave Winfield	4.00	2.00	1.25
	Panel 22	3.50	1.75	1.00
64	Dan Driessen	.50	.25	.15
65	Ted Simmons	.80	.40	.25
66	Jerry Remy	.40	.20	.12
	Panel 23	2.50	1.25	.70
67	Al Cowens	.40	.20	.12
68	Sparky Lyle	.50	.25	.15
69	Manny Trillo	.50	.25	.15
	Panel 24	5.00	2.50	1.50
70	Don Sutton	1.50	.70	.45
71	Larry Bowa	.50	.25	.15
72	Jose Cruz	.50	.25	.15
	Panel 25	8.00	4.00	2.50
73	Willie McCovey	3.00	1.50	.90
74	Bert Blyleven	.70	.35	.20
75	Ken Singleton	.50	.25	.15
	Panel 26	3.50	1.75	1.00
76	Bill North	.40	.20	.12
77	Jason Thompson	.40	.20	.12
78	Dennis Eckersley	1.00	.50	.30
	Panel 27	2.50	1.25	.70
79	Jim Sundberg	.50	.25	.15
80	Jerry Koosman	.50	.25	.15
81	Bruce Bochte	.40	.20	.12
	Panel 28	17.00	8.50	5.00
82	George Hendrick	.40	.20	.12
83	Nolan Ryan	10.00	5.00	3.00
84	Roy Howell	.40	.20	.12
	Panel 29	5.50	2.75	1.75
85	Butch Metzger	.40	.20	.12
86	George Medich	.40	.20	.12
87	Joe Morgan	2.00	1.00	.60
	Panel 30	3.00	1.50	.90
88	Dennis Leonard	.50	.25	.15
89	Willie Randolph	.50	.25	.15
90	Bobby Murcer	.50	.25	.15
	Panel 31	3.00	1.50	.90
91	Rick Manning	.40	.20	.12
92	J.R. Richard	.50	.25	.15
93	Ron Cey	.60	.30	.20
	Panel 32	2.50	1.25	.70
94	Sal Bando	.50	.25	.15
95	Ron LeFlore	.50	.25	.15
96	Dave Goltz	.40	.20	.12
	Panel 33	2.50	1.25	.70
97	Dan Meyer	.40	.20	.12
98	Chris Chambliss	.50	.25	.15
99	Biff Pocoroba	.40	.20	.12
	Panel 34	2.50	1.25	.70
100	Oscar Gamble	.40	.20	.12
101	Frank Tanana	.50	.25	.15
102	Lenny Randle	.40	.20	.12
	Panel 35	2.50	1.25	.70
103	Tommy Hutton	.40	.20	.12
104	John Candelaria	.50	.25	.15
105	Jorge Orta	.40	.20	.12
	Panel 36	3.00	1.50	.90
106	Ken Reitz	.40	.20	.12
107	Bill Campbell	.40	.20	.12
108	Dave Concepcion	.70	.35	.20
	Panel 37	2.50	1.25	.70
109	Joe Ferguson	.40	.20	.12
110	Mickey Rivers	.50	.25	.15
111	Paul Splittorff	.40	.20	.12
	Panel 38	12.00	6.00	3.50
112	Davey Lopes	.50	.25	.15
113	Mike Schmidt	7.00	3.50	2.00
114	Joe Rudi	.50	.25	.15
	Panel 39	7.00	3.50	2.00
115	Milt May	.40	.20	.12
116	Jim Palmer	3.00	1.50	.90
117	Bill Madlock	.70	.35	.20
	Panel 40	2.50	1.25	.70
118	Roy Smalley	.40	.20	.12
119	Cecil Cooper	.50	.25	.15
120	Rick Langford	.40	.20	.12
	Panel 41	5.75	3.00	1.75
121	Ruppert Jones	.40	.20	.12
122	Phil Niekro	2.25	1.25	.70
123	Toby Harrah	.50	.25	.15
	Panel 42	2.50	1.25	.70

		NR MT	EX	VG
124	Chet Lemon	.50	.25	.15
125	Gene Tenace	.40	.20	.12
126	Steve Henderson	.40	.20	.12
	Panel 43	20.00	10.00	6.00
127	Mike Torrez	.40	.20	.12
128	Pete Rose	8.00	4.00	2.50
129	John Denny	.50	.25	.15
	Panel 44	4.00	2.00	1.25
130	Darrell Porter	.50	.25	.15
131	Rick Reuschel	.50	.25	.15
132	Graig Nettles	.90	.45	.25
	Panel 45	4.50	2.25	1.25
133	Garry Maddox	.50	.25	.15
134	Mike Flanagan	.50	.25	.15
135	Dave Parker	1.25	.60	.40
	Panel 46	12.00	6.00	3.50
136	Terry Whitfield	.40	.20	.12
137	Wayne Garland	.40	.20	.12
138	Robin Yount	6.00	3.00	1.75
	Panel 47	15.00	7.50	4.50
139	Gaylord Perry	2.50	1.25	.70
140	Rod Carew	6.00	3.00	1.75
141	Wayne Gross	.40	.20	.12
	Panel 48	5.00	2.50	1.50
142	Barry Bonnell	.40	.20	.12
143	Willie Montanez	.40	.20	.12
144	Rollie Fingers	2.00	1.00	.60
	Panel 49	12.00	6.00	3.50
145	Bob Bailor	.40	.20	.12
146	Tom Seaver	4.00	1.75	1.00
147	Thurman Munson	2.50	1.25	.70
	Panel 50	5.50	2.75	1.75
148	Lyman Bostock	.50	.25	.15
149	Gary Carter	2.00	1.00	.60
150	Ron Blomberg	.40	.20	.12

1979 Hostess

The last of five consecutive annual issues, the 1979 Hostess set retained the 150-card set size, 2-1/4" by 3-1/4" single-card size and 7-1/4" by 3-1/4" three-card panel format from the previous years. The cards were printed as the bottom panel on family-size boxes of Hostess snack cakes. Some panels, which were printed on less-popular brands, are somewhat scarcer today than the rest of the set. Like all Hostess issues, because the hobby was in a well-developed state at the time of issue, the 1979s survive today in complete panels and complete unused boxes, for collectors who like original packaging.

	NR MT	EX	VG
Complete Panel Set:	350.00	175.00	105.00
Complete Singles Set:	200.00	100.00	60.00
Common Panel:	2.50	1.25	.70
Common Single Player:	.40	.20	.12

		NR MT	EX	VG
	Panel 1	5.50	2.75	1.75
1	John Denny	.40	.20	.12
2	Jim Rice	2.00	1.00	.60
3	Doug Bair	.40	.20	.12
	Panel 2	2.50	1.25	.70
4	Darrell Porter	.50	.25	.15
5	Ross Grimsley	.40	.20	.12
6	Bobby Murcer	.50	.25	.15
	Panel 3	15.00	7.50	4.50

		NR MT	EX	VG
7	Lee Mazzilli	.50	.25	.15
8	Steve Garvey	3.00	1.50	.90
9	Mike Schmidt	5.00	2.50	1.50
	Panel 4	6.50	3.25	2.00
10	Terry Whitfield	.40	.20	.12
11	Jim Palmer	3.00	1.50	.90
12	Omar Moreno	.40	.20	.12
	Panel 5	2.50	1.25	.70
13	Duane Kuiper	.40	.20	.12
14	Mike Caldwell	.40	.20	.12
15	Steve Kemp	.50	.25	.15
	Panel 6	2.50	1.25	.70
16	Dave Goltz	.40	.20	.12
17	Mitchell Page	.40	.20	.12
18	Bill Stein	.40	.20	.12
	Panel 7	2.50	1.25	.70
19	Gene Tenace	.40	.20	.12
20	Jeff Burroughs	.40	.20	.12
21	Francisco Barrios	.40	.20	.12
	Panel 8	5.00	2.50	1.50
22	Mike Torrez	.40	.20	.12
23	Ken Reitz	.40	.20	.12
24	Gary Carter	2.00	1.00	.60
	Panel 9	8.00	4.00	2.50
25	Al Hrabosky	.50	.25	.15
26	Thurman Munson	2.50	1.25	.70
27	Bill Buckner	.80	.40	.25
	Panel 10	5.00	2.50	1.50
28	Ron Cey	.90	.45	.25
29	J.R. Richard	.70	.35	.20
30	Greg Luzinski	.90	.45	.25
	Panel 11	5.00	2.50	1.50
31	Ed Ott	.50	.25	.15
32	Denny Martinez	.50	.25	.15
33	Darrell Evans	1.25	.60	.40
	Panel 12	2.50	1.25	.70
34	Ron LeFlore	.50	.25	.15
35	Rick Waits	.40	.20	.12
36	Cecil Cooper	.50	.25	.15
	Panel 13	9.50	4.75	2.75
37	Leon Roberts	.40	.20	.12
38	Rod Carew	4.00	2.00	1.25
39	John Henry Johnson	.40	.20	.12
	Panel 14	2.50	1.25	.70
40	Chet Lemon	.50	.25	.15
41	Craig Swan	.40	.20	.12
42	Gary Matthews	.50	.25	.15
	Panel 15	3.50	1.75	1.00
43	Lamar Johnson	.40	.20	.12
44	Ted Simmons	.80	.40	.25
45	Ken Griffey	.50	.25	.15
	Panel 16	4.00	2.00	1.25
46	Freddie Patek	.40	.20	.12
47	Frank Tanana	.50	.25	.15
48	Rich Gossage	1.25	.60	.40
	Panel 17	2.50	1.25	.70
49	Burt Hooton	.40	.20	.12
50	Ellis Valentine	.40	.20	.12
51	Ken Forsch	.40	.20	.12
	Panel 18	5.00	2.50	1.50
52	Bob Knepper	.50	.25	.15
53	Dave Parker	1.50	.70	.45
54	Doug DeCinces	.50	.25	.15
	Panel 19	10.00	5.00	3.00
55	Robin Yount	4.00	2.00	1.25
56	Rusty Staub	.80	.40	.25
57	Gary Alexander	.40	.20	.12
	Panel 20	2.50	1.25	.70
58	Julio Cruz	.40	.20	.12
59	Matt Keough	.40	.20	.12
60	Roy Smalley	.40	.20	.12
	Panel 21	9.00	4.50	2.75
61	Joe Morgan	2.50	1.25	.70
62	Phil Niekro	2.00	1.00	.60
63	Don Baylor	.50	.25	.15
	Panel 22	10.00	5.00	3.00
64	Dwight Evans	.90	.45	.25
65	Tom Seaver	4.00	2.00	1.25
66	George Hendrick	.50	.25	.15
	Panel 23	12.00	6.00	3.50
67	Rick Reuschel	.40	.25	.15
68	George Brett	5.00	2.50	1.50
69	Lou Piniella	.80	.40	.25
	Panel 24	8.50	4.25	2.50
70	Enos Cabell	.40	.20	.12
71	Steve Carlton	3.50	1.75	1.00
72	Reggie Smith	.50	.25	.15
	Panel 25	4.00	2.00	1.25
73	Rick Dempsey	.50	.25	.15
74	Vida Blue	.80	.40	.25
75	Phil Garner	.70	.35	.20

		NR MT	EX	VG
	Panel 26	3.50	1.75	1.00
76	Rick Manning	.50	.25	.15
77	Mark Fidrych	.80	.40	.25
78	Mario Guerrero	.50	.25	.15
	Panel 27	5.00	2.50	1.50
79	Bob Stinson	.50	.25	.15
80	Al Oliver	1.25	.60	.40
81	Doug Flynn	.50	.25	.15
	Panel 28	6.00	3.00	1.75
82	John Mayberry	.40	.20	.12
83	Gaylord Perry	2.50	1.25	.70
84	Joe Rudi	.50	.25	.15
	Panel 29	3.50	1.75	1.00
85	Dave Concepcion	.70	.35	.20
86	John Candelaria	.50	.25	.15
87	Pete Vuckovich	.50	.25	.15
	Panel 30	5.00	2.50	1.50
88	Ivan DeJesus	.40	.20	.12
89	Ron Guidry	1.50	.70	.45
90	Hal McRae	.50	.25	.15
	Panel 31	5.50	2.75	1.75
91	Cesar Cedeno	.50	.25	.15
92	Don Sutton	2.00	1.00	.60
93	Andre Thornton	.50	.25	.15
	Panel 32	2.50	1.25	.70
94	Roger Erickson	.40	.20	.12
95	Larry Hisle	.40	.20	.12
96	Jason Thompson	.40	.20	.12
	Panel 33	3.00	1.50	.90
97	Jim Sundberg	.50	.25	.15
98	Bob Horner	.50	.25	.15
99	Ruppert Jones	.40	.20	.12
	Panel 34	20.00	10.00	6.00
100	Willie Montanez	.40	.20	.12
101	Nolan Ryan	8.00	4.00	2.50
102	Ozzie Smith	12.00	6.00	3.50
	Panel 35	7.50	3.75	2.25
103	Eric Soderholm	.40	.20	.12
104	Willie Stargell	3.00	1.50	.90
105	Bob Bailor	.40	.20	.12
	Panel 36	5.00	2.50	1.50
106	Carlton Fisk	1.25	.60	.40
107	George Foster	.70	.35	.20
108	Keith Hernandez	.50	.25	.15
	Panel 37	4.00	2.00	1.25
109	Dennis Leonard	.50	.25	.15
110	Graig Nettles	.90	.45	.25
111	Jose Cruz	.50	.25	.15
	Panel 38	3.50	1.75	1.00
112	Bobby Grich	.50	.25	.15
113	Bob Boone	.70	.35	.20
114	Dave Lopes	.50	.25	.15
	Panel 39	9.00	4.50	2.75
115	Eddie Murray	3.00	1.50	.90
116	Jack Clark	.50	.25	.15
117	Lou Whitaker	1.00	.50	.30
	Panel 40	10.00	5.00	3.00
118	Miguel Dilone	.40	.20	.12
119	Sal Bando	.50	.25	.15
120	Reggie Jackson	4.50	2.25	1.25
	Panel 41	8.00	4.00	2.50
121	Dale Murphy	4.00	2.00	1.25
122	Jon Matlack	.40	.20	.12
123	Bruce Bochte	.40	.20	.12
	Panel 42	9.00	4.50	2.75
124	John Stearns	.40	.20	.12
125	Dave Winfield	3.50	1.75	1.00
126	Jorge Orta	.40	.20	.12
	Panel 43	9.00	4.50	2.75
127	Garry Templeton	.70	.35	.20
128	Johnny Bench	4.00	2.00	1.25
129	Butch Hobson	.40	.20	.12
	Panel 44	4.50	2.25	1.25
130	Bruce Sutter	1.25	.60	.40
131	Bucky Dent	.50	.25	.15
132	Amos Otis	.50	.25	.15
	Panel 45	3.50	1.75	1.00
133	Bert Blyleven	.70	.35	.20
134	Larry Bowa	.50	.25	.15
135	Ken Singleton	.50	.25	.15
	Panel 46	3.50	1.75	1.00
136	Sixto Lezcano	.40	.20	.12
137	Roy Howell	.40	.20	.12
138	Bill Madlock	.80	.40	.25
	Panel 47	2.50	1.25	.70
139	Dave Revering	.40	.20	.12
140	Richie Zisk	.50	.25	.15
141	Butch Wynegar	.50	.25	.15
	Panel 48	18.00	9.00	5.50
142	Alan Ashby	.40	.20	.12
143	Sparky Lyle	.50	.25	.15

		NR MT	EX	VG
144	Pete Rose	8.00	4.00	2.50
	Panel 49	4.50	2.25	1.25
145	Dennis Eckersley	1.50	.70	.45
146	Dave Kingman	.50	.25	.15
147	Buddy Bell	.50	.25	.15
	Panel 50	2.50	1.25	.70
148	Mike Hargrove	.40	.20	.12
149	Jerry Koosman	.50	.25	.15
150	Toby Harrah	.50	.25	.15

1993 Hostess Twinkies

The Continental Baking Company, makers of Hostess Twinkies and cupcakes, returned to the baseball card market in 1993 with a 32-card set issued in two series. The promotion began around opening day with the first series; the second series was made available after the All-Star break. The cards were packaged in multi-packs with cupcakes that look like baseballs, with three cards in a box of eight cupcakes.

		NR MT	EX	VG
Complete Set:		12.00	9.00	4.75
Common Player:		.25	.20	.10
1	Andy Van Slyke	.25	.20	.10
2	Ryne Sandberg	1.00	.70	.40
3	Bobby Bonilla	.50	.40	.20
4	John Kruk	.35	.25	.14
5	Ray Lankford	.25	.20	.10
6	Gary Sheffield	.35	.25	.14
7	Darryl Strawberry	.35	.25	.14
8	Barry Larkin	.35	.25	.14
9	Terry Pendleton	.25	.20	.10
10	Jose Canseco	.75	.60	.30
11	Dennis Eckersley	.25	.20	.10
12	Brian McRae	.25	.20	.10
13	Frank Thomas	1.50	1.25	.60
14	Roberto Alomar	.40	.30	.15
15	Cecil Fielder	.40	.30	.15
16	Carlos Baerga	.35	.25	.14
17	Will Clark	.75	.60	.30
18	Andres Galaraga	.35	.25	.14
19	Jeff Bagwell	.25	.20	.10
20	Brett Butler	.25	.20	.10
21	Benito Santiago	.25	.20	.10
22	Tom Glavine	.30	.25	.12
23	Rickey Henderson	.60	.45	.25
24	Wally Joyner	.40	.30	.15
25	Ken Griffey, Jr.	1.00	.70	.40
26	Cal Ripken, Jr.	1.00	.70	.40
27	Roger Clemens	.60	.45	.25
28	Don Mattingly	.75	.60	.30
29	Kirby Puckett	.50	.40	.20
30	Larry Walker	.25	.20	.10
31	Jack McDowell	.25	.20	.10
32	Pat Listach	.25	.20	.10

A player's name in italic indicates a rookie card. An (FC) indicates a player's first card for that particular card company.

1970 Kellogg's

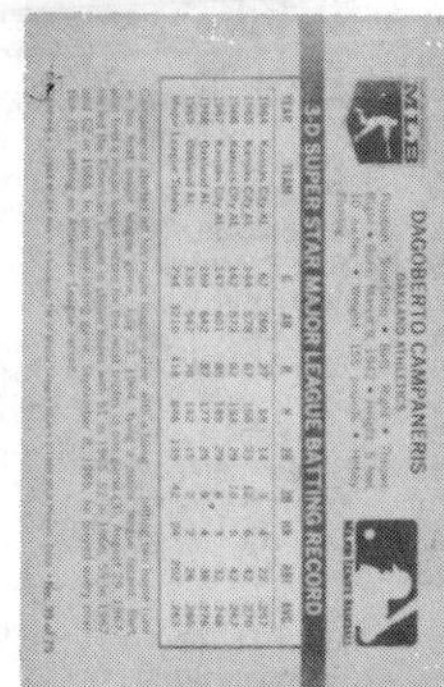

For 14 years in the 1970s and early 1980s, the Kellogg's cereal company provided Topps with virtually the only meaningful national competition in the baseball card market. Kellogg's kicked off its baseball card program in 1970 with a 75-player set of simulated 3-D cards. Single cards were available in selected brands of the company's cereal, while a mail-in program offered complete sets. The 3-D effect was achieved by the sandwiching of a clear color player photo between a purposely blurred stadium background scene and a layer of ribbed plastic. The relatively narrow dimension of the card, 2-1/4" by 3-1/2" and the nature of the plastic overlay seem to conspire to cause the cards to curl, often cracking the plastic layer, if not stored properly. Cards with major cracks in the plastic can be considered in Fair condition, at best.

		NR MT	EX	VG
Complete Set:		300.00	150.00	90.00
Common Player:		2.00	1.00	.60
1	Ed Kranepool	2.00	1.00	.60
2	Pete Rose	25.00	12.50	15.00
3	Cleon Jones	2.00	1.00	.60
4	Willie McCovey	8.00	4.00	2.50
5	Mel Stottlemyre	2.00	1.00	.60
6	Frank Howard	4.00	2.00	1.25
7	Tom Seaver	15.00	7.50	4.50
8	Don Sutton	4.00	2.00	1.25
9	Jim Wynn	2.00	1.00	.60
10	Jim Maloney	2.00	1.00	.60
11	Tommie Agee	2.00	1.00	.60
12	Willie Mays	20.00	10.00	6.00
13	Juan Marichal	8.00	4.00	2.50
14	Dave McNally	2.00	1.00	.60
15	Frank Robinson	12.00	6.00	3.50
16	Carlos May	2.00	1.00	.60
17	Bill Singer	2.00	1.00	.60
18	Rick Reichardt	2.00	1.00	.60
19	Boog Powell	4.00	2.00	1.25
20	Gaylord Perry	8.00	4.00	2.50
21	Brooks Robinson	12.00	6.00	3.50
22	Luis Aparicio	8.00	4.00	2.50
23	Joel Horlen	2.00	1.00	.60
24	Mike Epstein	2.00	1.00	.60
25	Tom Haller	2.00	1.00	.60
26	Willie Crawford	2.00	1.00	.60
27	Roberto Clemente	15.00	7.50	4.50
28	Matty Alou	2.00	1.00	.60
29	Willie Stargell	8.00	4.00	2.50
30	Tim Cullen	2.00	1.00	.60
31	Randy Hundley	2.00	1.00	.60
32	Reggie Jackson	15.00	7.50	4.50
33	Rich Allen	3.00	1.50	.90
34	Tim McCarver	3.00	1.50	.90
35	Ray Culp	2.00	1.00	.60
36	Jim Fregosi	3.00	1.50	.90
37	Billy Williams	8.00	4.00	2.50
38	Johnny Odom	2.00	1.00	.60
39	Bert Campaneris	3.00	1.50	.90
40	Ernie Banks	12.00	6.00	3.50
41	Chris Short	2.00	1.00	.60
42	Ron Santo	3.00	1.50	.90
43	Glenn Beckert	2.00	1.00	.60
44	Lou Brock	8.00	4.00	2.50

		NR MT	EX	VG
45	Larry Hisle	2.00	1.00	.60
46	Reggie Smith	2.00	1.00	.60
47	Rod Carew	8.00	4.00	2.50
48	Curt Flood	3.00	1.50	.90
49	Jim Lonborg	2.00	1.00	.60
50	Sam McDowell	2.00	1.00	.60
51	Sal Bando	2.00	1.00	.60
52	Al Kaline	12.00	6.00	3.50
53	Gary Nolan	2.00	1.00	.60
54	Rico Petrocelli	2.00	1.00	.60
55	Ollie Brown	2.00	1.00	.60
56	Luis Tiant	2.00	1.00	.60
57	Bill Freehan	2.00	1.00	.60
58	Johnny Bench	12.00	6.00	3.50
59	Joe Pepitone	2.00	1.00	.60
60	Bobby Murcer	2.00	1.00	.60
61	Harmon Killebrew	8.00	4.00	2.50
62	Don Wilson	2.00	1.00	.60
63	Tony Oliva	4.00	2.00	1.25
64	Jim Perry	2.00	1.00	.60
65	Mickey Lolich	3.00	1.50	.90
66	Coco Laboy	2.00	1.00	.60
67	Dean Chance	2.00	1.00	.60
68	Ken Harrelson	2.00	1.00	.60
69	Willie Horton	2.00	1.00	.60
70	Wally Bunker	2.00	1.00	.60
71a	Bob Gibson (1959 IP blank)	10.00	5.00	3.00
71b	Bob Gibson (1959 IP 76)	10.00	5.00	3.00
72	Joe Morgan	8.00	4.00	2.50
73	Denny McLain	3.00	1.50	.90
74	Tommy Harper	2.00	1.00	.60
75	Don Mincher	2.00	1.00	.60

1971 Kellogg's

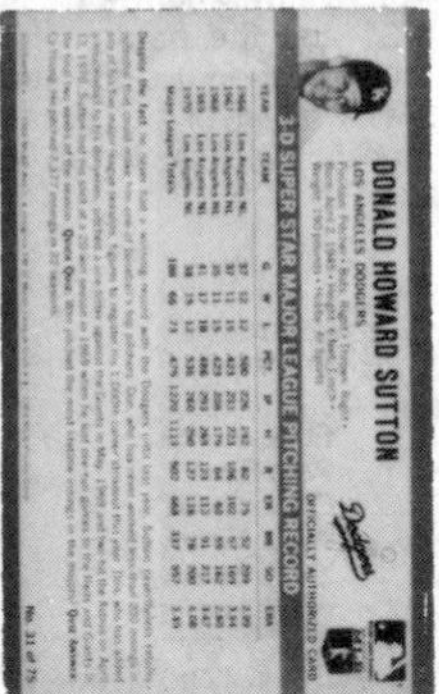

The scarcest and most valuable of the Kellogg's editions, the 75-card 1971 set was the only one not offered by the company on a mail-in basis; the only way to complete it was to buy ... and buy and buy ... boxes of cereal. Kellogg's again used the simulated 3-D effect in the cards' design, with the same result being many of the 2-1/4" by 3-1/2" cards are found today with cracks resulting from the cards' curling. A number of scarcer back variations are checklisted below. In addition, all 75 cards can be found with and without the 1970 date before the "Xograph" copyright line on the back; though there is no difference in value.

	NR MT	EX	VG
Complete Set:	950.00	475.00	285.00
Common Player:	12.00	6.00	3.50

		NR MT	EX	VG
1a	Wayne Simpson (SO 120)	12.00	6.00	3.50
1b	Wayne Simpson (SO 119)	15.00	7.50	4.50
2	Tom Seaver	35.00	17.50	10.50
3a	Jim Perry (IP 2238)	10.00	5.00	3.00
3b	Jim Perry (IP 2239)	15.00	7.50	4.50
4a	Bob Robertson (RBI 94)	12.00	6.00	3.50
4b	Bob Robertson (RBI 95)	12.00	6.00	3.50
5	Roberto Clemente	40.00	20.00	12.00
6a	Gaylord Perry (IP 2014)	20.00	10.00	6.00
6b	Gaylord Perry (IP 2015)	25.00	12.50	7.50
7a	Felipe Alou (1970 Oakland NL)	15.00	7.50	4.50
7b	Felipe Alou (1970 Oakland AL)	10.00	5.00	3.00
8	Denis Menke	12.00	6.00	3.50
9a	Don Kessinger (Hits 849)	10.00	5.00	3.00
9b	Don Kessinger (Hits 850)	15.00	7.50	4.50
10	Willie Mays	40.00	20.00	12.00
11	Jim Hickman	12.00	6.00	3.50
12	Tony Oliva	15.00	7.50	4.50
13	Manny Sanguillen	12.00	6.00	3.50
14a	Frank Howard (1968 Washington NL)	20.00	10.00	6.00
14b	Frank Howard (1968 Washington AL)	15.00	7.50	4.50
15	Frank Robinson	30.00	15.00	9.00
16	Willie Davis	10.00	5.00	3.00
17	Lou Brock	25.00	12.50	7.50
18	Cesar Tovar	12.00	6.00	3.50
19	Luis Aparicio	20.00	10.00	6.00
20	Boog Powell	15.00	7.50	4.50
21a	Dick Selma (SO 584)	12.00	6.00	3.50
21b	Dick Selma (SO 587)	12.00	6.00	3.50
22	Danny Walton	12.00	6.00	3.50
23	Carl Morton	12.00	6.00	3.50
24a	Sonny Siebert (SO 1054)	12.00	6.00	3.50
24b	Sonny Siebert (SO 1055)	12.00	6.00	3.50
25	Jim Merritt	12.00	6.00	3.50
26a	Jose Cardenal (Hits 828)	12.00	6.00	3.50
26b	Jose Cardenal (Hits 829)	12.00	6.00	3.50
27	Don Mincher	12.00	6.00	3.50
28a	Clyde Wright (California state logo)	12.00	6.00	3.50
28b	Clyde Wright (Angels crest logo)	12.00	6.00	3.50
29	Les Cain	12.00	6.00	3.50
30	Danny Cater	12.00	6.00	3.50
31	Don Sutton	15.00	7.50	4.50
32	Chuck Dobson	12.00	6.00	3.50
33	Willie McCovey	25.00	12.50	7.50
34	Mike Epstein	12.00	6.00	3.50
35a	Paul Blair (Runs 386)	12.00	6.00	3.50
35b	Paul Blair (Runs 385)	12.00	6.00	3.50
36a	Gary Nolan (SO 577)	12.00	6.00	3.50
36b	Gary Nolan (SO 581)	12.00	6.00	3.50
37	Sam McDowell	10.00	5.00	3.00
38	Amos Otis	10.00	5.00	3.00
39a	Ray Fosse (RBI 69)	12.00	6.00	3.50
39b	Ray Fosse (RBI 70)	12.00	6.00	3.50
40	Mel Stottlemyre	10.00	5.00	3.00
41	Cito Gaston	12.00	6.00	3.50
42	Dick Dietz	12.00	6.00	3.50
43	Roy White	10.00	5.00	3.00
44	Al Kaline	30.00	15.00	9.00
45	Carlos May	12.00	6.00	3.50
46a	Tommie Agee (RBI 313)	12.00	6.00	3.50
46b	Tommie Agee (RBI 314)	12.00	6.00	3.50
47	Tommy Harper	12.00	6.00	3.50
48	Larry Dierker	12.00	6.00	3.50
49	Mike Cuellar	10.00	5.00	3.00
50	Ernie Banks	30.00	15.00	9.00
51	Bob Gibson	25.00	12.50	7.50
52	Reggie Smith	10.00	5.00	3.00
53a	Matty Alou (RBI 273)	10.00	5.00	3.00
53b	Matty Alou (RBI 274)	15.00	7.50	4.50
54a	Alex Johnson (California state logo)	12.00	6.00	3.50
54b	Alex Johnson (Angels crest logo)	12.00	6.00	3.50
55	Harmon Killebrew	25.00	12.50	7.50
56	Billy Grabarkewitz	12.00	6.00	3.50
57	Rich Allen	15.00	7.50	4.50
58	Tony Perez	15.00	7.50	4.50
59a	Dave McNally (SO 1065)	10.00	5.00	3.00
59b	Dave McNally (SO 1067)	15.00	7.50	4.50
60a	Jim Palmer (SO 564)	20.00	10.00	6.00
60b	Jim Palmer (SO 567)	25.00	12.50	7.50
61	Billy Williams	20.00	10.00	6.00
62	Joe Torre	12.00	6.00	3.50
63a	Jim Northrup (AB 2773)	12.00	6.00	3.50
63b	Jim Northrup (AB 2772)	12.00	6.00	3.50
64a	Jim Fregosi (Calif. state logo - Hits 1326)	12.00	6.00	3.50
64b	Jim Fregosi (Calif. state logo - Hits 1327)	12.00	6.00	3.50
64c	Jim Fregosi (Angels crest logo)	12.00	6.00	3.50
65	Pete Rose	60.00	30.00	18.00
66a	Bud Harrelson (RBI 112)	12.00	6.00	3.50
66b	Bud Harrelson (RBI 113)	12.00	6.00	3.50
67	Tony Taylor	12.00	6.00	3.50
68	Willie Stargell	25.00	12.50	7.50
69	Tony Horton	8.50	4.25	2.50
70a	Claude Osteen (no number)	20.00	10.00	6.00
70b	Claude Osteen (#70 on back)	12.00	6.00	3.50
71	Glenn Beckert	10.00	5.00	3.00
72	Nate Colbert	12.00	6.00	3.50
73a	Rick Monday (AB 1705)	10.00	5.00	3.00
73b	Rick Monday (AB 1704)	15.00	7.50	4.50
74a	Tommy John (BB 444)	15.00	7.50	4.50
74b	Tommy John (BB 443)	20.00	10.00	6.00
75	Chris Short	12.00	6.00	3.50

1972 Kellogg's

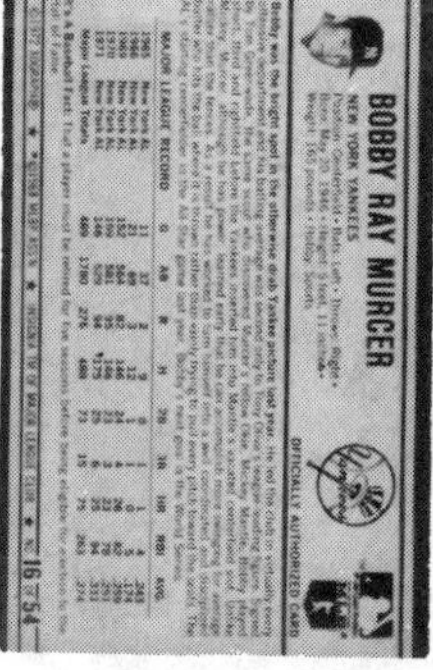

For 1972, Kellogg's reduced both the number of cards in its set and the dimensions of each card, moving to a 2-1/8" by 3-1/4" size and fixing the set at 54 cards. Once again, the cards were produced to simulate a 3-D effect (see description for 1970 Kellogg's). The set was available via a mail-in offer. The checklist includes variations which resulted from the correction of erroneous statistics on the backs of some cards. The complete set values quoted do not include the scarcer variations.

		NR MT	EX	VG
Complete Set:		75.00	37.00	22.00
Common Player:		.70	.35	.20
1a	Tom Seaver (1970 ERA 2.85)	9.00	4.50	2.75
1b	Tom Seaver (1970 ERA 2.81)	6.50	3.25	2.00
2	Amos Otis	.80	.40	.25
3a	Willie Davis (Runs 842)	1.25	.60	.40
3b	Willie Davis (Runs 841)	.80	.40	.25
4	Wilbur Wood	.80	.40	.25
5	Bill Parsons	.70	.35	.20
6	Pete Rose	20.00	10.00	6.00
7a	Willie McCovey (HR 360)	5.00	2.50	1.50
7b	Willie McCovey (HR 370)	3.50	1.75	1.00
8	Fergie Jenkins	3.00	1.50	.90
9a	Vida Blue (ERA 2.35)	1.50	.70	.45
9b	Vida Blue (ERA 2.31)	.90	.45	.25
10	Joe Torre	.90	.45	.25
11	Merv Rettenmund	.70	.35	.20
12	Bill Melton	.70	.35	.20
13a	Jim Palmer (Games 170)	4.75	2.50	1.50
13b	Jim Palmer (Games 168)	3.00	1.50	.90
14	Doug Rader	.70	.35	.20
15a	Dave Roberts (...Seaver, the NL leader...)	1.25	.60	.40
15b	Dave Roberts (...Seaver, the league leader...)	.70	.35	.20
16	Bobby Murcer	.80	.40	.25
17	Wes Parker	.70	.35	.20
18a	Joe Coleman (BB 394)	1.25	.60	.40
18b	Joe Coleman (BB 393)	.70	.35	.20
19	Manny Sanguillen	.70	.35	.20
20	Reggie Jackson	8.00	4.00	2.50
21	Ralph Garr	.70	.35	.20
22	Jim "Catfish" Hunter	3.00	1.50	.90
23	Rick Wise	.70	.35	.20
24	Glenn Beckert	.70	.35	.20
25	Tony Oliva	1.50	.70	.45
26a	Bob Gibson (SO 2577)	4.75	2.50	1.50
26b	Bob Gibson (SO 2578)	3.00	1.50	.90
27a	Mike Cuellar (1971 ERA 3.80)	1.25	.60	.40
27b	Mike Cuellar (1971 ERA 3.08)	.80	.40	.25
28	Chris Speier	.70	.35	.20
29a	Dave McNally (ERA 3.18)	1.25	.60	.40
29b	Dave McNally (ERA 3.15)	.80	.40	.25
30	Chico Cardenas	.70	.35	.20
31a	Bill Freehan (AVG. .263)	1.25	.60	.40
31b	Bill Freehan (AVG. .262)	.80	.40	.25
32a	Bud Harrelson (Hits 634)	1.25	.60	.40
32b	Bud Harrelson (Hits 624)	.70	.35	.20
33a	Sam McDowell (...less than 200 innings...)	1.25	.60	.40
33b	Sam McDowell (...less than 225 innings...)	.80	.40	.25
34a	Claude Osteen (1971 ERA 3.25)	1.25	.60	.40
34b	Claude Osteen (1971 ERA 3.51)	.70	.35	.20
35	Reggie Smith	.80	.40	.25
36	Sonny Siebert	.70	.35	.20
37	Lee May	.80	.40	.25
38	Mickey Lolich	.90	.45	.25
39a	Cookie Rojas (2B 149)	1.25	.60	.40
39b	Cookie Rojas (2B 150)	.70	.35	.20
40	Dick Drago	.70	.35	.20
41	Nate Colbert	.70	.35	.20
42	Andy Messersmith	.70	.35	.20
43a	Dave Johnson (AVG. .262)	1.50	.70	.45
43b	Dave Johnson (AVG. .264)	.90	.45	.25
44	Steve Blass	.70	.35	.20
45	Bob Robertson	.70	.35	.20
46a	Billy Williams (...missed only one last season...)	5.00	2.50	1.50
46b	Billy Williams (phrase omitted)	3.00	1.50	.90
47	Juan Marichal	3.00	1.50	.90
48	Lou Brock	3.50	1.75	1.00
49	Roberto Clemente	10.00	5.00	3.00
50	Mel Stottlemyre	.80	.40	.25
51	Don Wilson	.70	.35	.20
52a	Sal Bando (RBI 355)	1.25	.60	.40
52b	Sal Bando (RBI 356)	.80	.40	.25
53a	Willie Stargell (2B 197)	5.00	2.50	1.50
53b	Willie Stargell (2B 196)	3.00	1.50	.90
54a	Willie Mays (RBI 1855)	18.00	9.00	5.50
54b	Willie Mays (RBI 1856)	10.00	5.00	3.00

1972 Kellogg's All-Time Baseball Greats

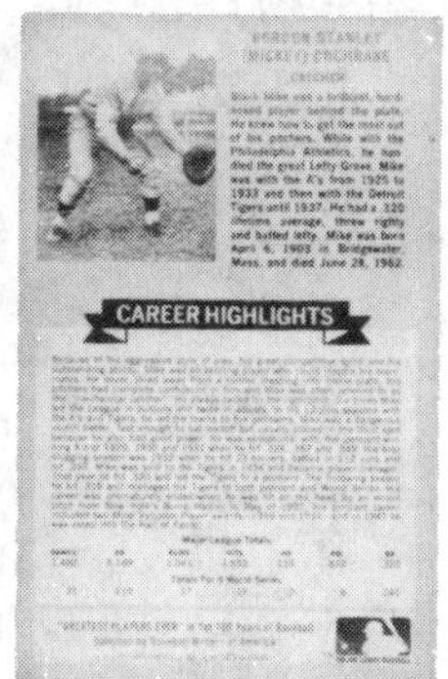

Kellogg's issued a second baseball card set in 1972, inserted into packages of breakfast rolls. The 2-1/4" by 3-1/2" cards also featured a simulated 3-D effect, but the 15 players in the set were "All-Time Baseball Greats", rather than current players. The set is virtually identical to a Rold Gold pretzel issue of 1970; the only difference being the 1972 copyright date on the back of the Kellog's cards, while the pretzel issue bears a 1970 date. The pretzel cards are considerably scarcer than the Kellogg's.

		NR MT	EX	VG
Complete Set:		15.00	7.50	4.50
Common Player:		.50	.25	.15
1	Walter Johnson	1.25	.60	.40
2	Rogers Hornsby	.80	.40	.25
3	John McGraw	.50	.25	.15
4	Mickey Cochrane	.50	.25	.15
5	George Sisler	.50	.25	.15
6	Babe Ruth	4.00	2.00	1.25
7	Robert "Lefty" Grove	.70	.35	.20
8	Harold "Pie" Traynor	.50	.25	.15
9	Honus Wagner	1.00	.50	.30
10	Eddie Collins	.50	.25	.15
11	Tris Speaker	.70	.35	.20
12	Cy Young	.80	.40	.25
13	Lou Gehrig	2.00	1.00	.60
14	Babe Ruth	4.00	2.00	1.25
15	Ty Cobb	2.00	1.00	.60

1973 Kellogg's

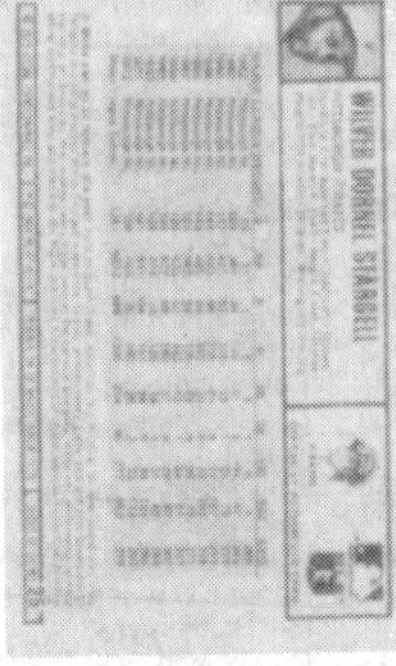

The lone exception to Kellogg's long run of simulated 3-D effect cards came in 1973, when the cereal company's 54-card set was produced by "normal" printing methods. In 2'1/4" by 3-1/2" size, the design was otherwise quite compatible with the issues which preceded and succeeded it. Because it was available via a mail-in offer, it is not as scarce as some other Kellogg's issues.

		NR MT	EX	VG
Complete Set:		75.00	37.00	22.00
Common Player:		.50	.25	.15
1	Amos Otis	.60	.30	.20
2	Ellie Rodriguez	.50	.25	.15
3	Mickey Lolich	.80	.40	.25
4	Tony Oliva	1.25	.60	.40
5	Don Sutton	1.25	.60	.40
6	Pete Rose	11.00	5.50	3.25
7	Steve Carlton	4.00	2.00	1.25
8	Bobby Bonds	.70	.35	.20
9	Wilbur Wood	.60	.30	.20
10	Billy Williams	2.50	1.25	.70
11	Steve Blass	.50	.25	.15
12	Jon Matlack	.50	.25	.15
13	Cesar Cedeno	.70	.35	.20
14	Bob Gibson	2.50	1.25	.70
15	Sparky Lyle	.60	.30	.20
16	Nolan Ryan	15.00	7.50	4.50
17	Jim Palmer	2.50	1.25	.70
18	Ray Fosse	.50	.25	.15
19	Bobby Murcer	.60	.30	.20
20	Jim "Catfish" Hunter	2.50	1.25	.70
21	Tug McGraw	.80	.40	.25
22	Reggie Jackson	7.00	3.50	2.00
23	Bill Stoneman	.50	.25	.15
24	Lou Piniella	.80	.40	.25
25	Willie Stargell	2.50	1.25	.70
26	Dick Allen	1.50	.70	.45
27	Carlton Fisk	1.25	.60	.40
28	Fergie Jenkins	2.50	1.25	.70
29	Phil Niekro	1.50	.70	.45
30	Gary Nolan	.50	.25	.15
31	Joe Torre	.80	.40	.25
32	Bobby Tolan	.50	.25	.15
33	Nate Colbert	.50	.25	.15
34	Joe Morgan	2.50	1.25	.70
35	Bert Blyleven	.90	.45	.25
36	Joe Rudi	.60	.30	.20
37	Ralph Garr	.50	.25	.15
38	Gaylord Perry	2.50	1.25	.70
39	Bobby Grich	.60	.30	.20
40	Lou Brock	2.50	1.25	.70
41	Pete Broberg	.50	.25	.15
42	Manny Sanguillen	.50	.25	.15
43	Willie Davis	.60	.30	.20
44	Dave Kingman	.60	.30	.20
45	Carlos May	.50	.25	.15
46	Tom Seaver	4.00	2.00	1.25
47	Mike Cuellar	.60	.30	.20
48	Joe Coleman	.50	.25	.15
49	Claude Osteen	.50	.25	.15
50	Steve Kline	.50	.25	.15
51	Rod Carew	4.00	2.00	1.25
52	Al Kaline	5.00	2.50	1.50
53	Larry Dierker	.50	.25	.15
54	Ron Santo	.70	.35	.20

1974 Kellogg's

For 1974, Kellogg's returned to the use of simulated 3-D for its 54-player baseball card issue (see 1970 Kellogg's listing for description). In 2-1/8" by 3-1/4" size, the cards were available as a complete set via a mail-in offer.

		NR MT	EX	VG
Complete Set:		65.00	32.00	19.50
Common Player:		.50	.25	.15
1	Bob Gibson	5.00	2.50	1.50
2	Rick Monday	.70	.35	.20
3	Joe Coleman	.50	.25	.15
4	Bert Campaneris	.70	.35	.20
5	Carlton Fisk	1.25	.60	.40
6	Jim Palmer	2.50	1.25	.70
7a	Ron Santo (Chicago Cubs)	1.50	.70	.45
7b	Ron Santo (Chicago White Sox)	.80	.40	.25
8	Nolan Ryan	10.00	5.00	3.00
9	Greg Luzinski	.80	.40	.25
10a	Buddy Bell (Runs 134)	1.50	.70	.45
10b	Buddy Bell (Runs 135)	.80	.40	.25
11	Bob Watson	.50	.25	.15
12	Bill Singer	.50	.25	.15
13	Dave May	.50	.25	.15
14	Jim Brewer	.50	.25	.15
15	Manny Sanguillen	.50	.25	.15
16	Jeff Burroughs	.50	.25	.15
17	Amos Otis	.50	.25	.15
18	Ed Goodson	.50	.25	.15
19	Nate Colbert	.50	.25	.15
20	Reggie Jackson	4.00	2.00	1.25
21	Ted Simmons	.90	.45	.25
22	Bobby Murcer	.60	.30	.20
23	Willie Horton	.60	.30	.20
24	Orlando Cepeda	2.50	1.25	.70
25	Ron Hunt	.50	.25	.15
26	Wayne Twitchell	.50	.25	.15
27	Ron Fairly	.50	.25	.15
28	Johnny Bench	5.00	2.50	1.50
29	John Mayberry	.50	.25	.15
30	Rod Carew	4.00	2.00	1.25
31	Ken Holtzman	.50	.25	.15
32	Billy Williams	2.50	1.25	.70
33	Dick Allen	1.50	.70	.45
34a	Wilbur Wood (SO 959)	1.25	.60	.40
34b	Wilbur Wood (SO 960)	.70	.35	.20
35	Danny Thompson	.50	.25	.15
36	Joe Morgan	2.50	1.25	.70
37	Willie Stargell	3.00	1.50	.90
38	Pete Rose	12.00	6.00	3.50
39	Bobby Bonds	.70	.35	.20
40	Chris Speier	.50	.25	.15
41	Sparky Lyle	.60	.30	.20
42	Cookie Rojas	.50	.25	.15
43	Tommy Davis	.60	.30	.20
44	Jim "Catfish" Hunter	2.50	1.25	.70
45	Willie Davis	.60	.30	.20
46	Bert Blyleven	.90	.45	.25
47	Pat Kelly	.50	.25	.15
48	Ken Singleton	.60	.30	.20
49	Manny Mota	.60	.30	.20
50	Dave Johnson	.90	.45	.25
51	Sal Bando	.60	.30	.20
52	Tom Seaver	5.00	2.50	1.50
53	Felix Millan	.50	.25	.15
54	Ron Blomberg	.80	.40	.25

1975 Kellogg's

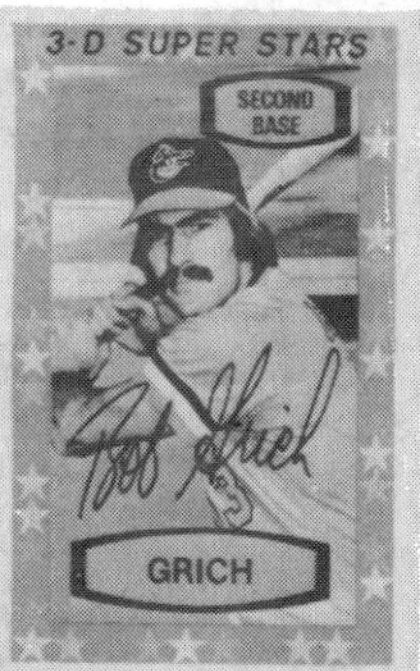

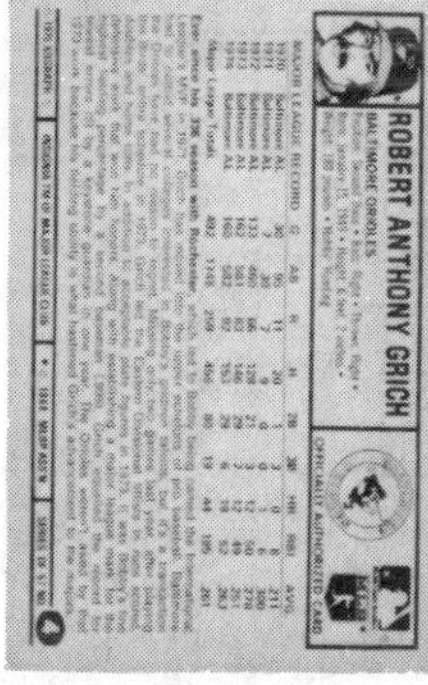

While the card size remained the same at 2-1/8" by 3-1/4", the size of the 1975 Kellogg's "3-D" set was increased by three, to 57 cards. Despite the fact cards could be obtained by a mail-in offer, as well as in cereal boxes, the '75 Kellogg's are noticeably scarcer than the company's other issues, with the exception of the 1971 set. Also helping to raise the value of the cards is the presence of an unusually large number of current and future Hall of Famers.

		NR MT	EX	VG
Complete Set:		150.00	75.00	45.00
Common Player:		2.00	1.00	.60
1	Roy White	3.50	1.75	1.00
2	Ross Grimsley	2.00	1.00	.60
3	Reggie Smith	2.50	1.25	.70
4a	Bob Grich ("...1973 work..." in last line)	4.00	2.00	1.25
4b	Bob Grich (no "...1973 work...")	2.50	1.25	.70
5	Greg Gross	2.00	1.00	.60
6	Bob Watson	2.00	1.00	.60
7	Johnny Bench	12.00	6.00	3.50
8	Jeff Burroughs	2.00	1.00	.60
9	Elliott Maddox	2.00	1.00	.60
10	Jon Matlack	2.00	1.00	.60
11	Pete Rose	18.00	9.00	5.50
12	Leroy Stanton	2.00	1.00	.60
13	Bake McBride	2.00	1.00	.60
14	Jorge Orta	2.00	1.00	.60
15	Al Oliver	2.50	1.25	.70
16	John Briggs	2.00	1.00	.60
17	Steve Garvey	9.00	4.50	2.75
18	Brooks Robinson	12.00	6.00	3.50
19	John Hiller	2.00	1.00	.60
20	Lynn McGlothen	2.00	1.00	.60
21	Cleon Jones	2.00	1.00	.60
22	Fergie Jenkins	6.50	3.25	2.00
23	Bill North	2.00	1.00	.60
24	Steve Busby	2.00	1.00	.60
25	Richie Zisk	2.00	1.00	.60
26	Nolan Ryan	20.00	10.00	6.00
27	Joe Morgan	6.50	3.25	2.00
28	Joe Rudi	2.50	1.25	.70
29	Jose Cardenal	2.00	1.00	.60
30	Andy Messersmith	2.00	1.00	.60
31	Willie Montanez	2.00	1.00	.60
32	Bill Buckner	2.50	1.25	.70
33	Rod Carew	10.00	5.00	3.00
34	Lou Piniella	2.50	1.25	.70
35	Ralph Garr	2.00	1.00	.60
36	Mike Marshall	2.00	1.00	.60
37	Garry Maddox	2.00	1.00	.60
38	Dwight Evans	3.00	1.50	.90
39	Lou Brock	9.00	4.50	2.75
40	Ken Singleton	2.50	1.25	.70
41	Steve Braun	2.00	1.00	.60
42	Dick Allen	3.00	1.50	.90
43	Johnny Grubb	2.00	1.00	.60
44a	Jim Hunter (Oakland)	12.00	6.00	3.50
44b	Jim Hunter (New York)	8.00	4.00	2.50
45	Gaylord Perry	6.50	3.25	2.00
46	George Hendrick	2.00	1.00	.60
47	Sparky Lyle	2.50	1.25	.70
48	Dave Cash	2.00	1.00	.60
49	Luis Tiant	2.50	1.25	.70
50	Cesar Geronimo	2.00	1.00	.60
51	Carl Yastrzemski	16.00	8.00	4.75
52	Ken Brett	2.00	1.00	.60
53	Hal McRae	2.50	1.25	.70
54	Reggie Jackson	16.00	8.00	4.75
55	Rollie Fingers	6.00	3.00	1.75
56	Mike Schmidt	14.00	7.00	4.25
57	Richie Hebner	2.50	1.25	.70

1976 Kellogg's

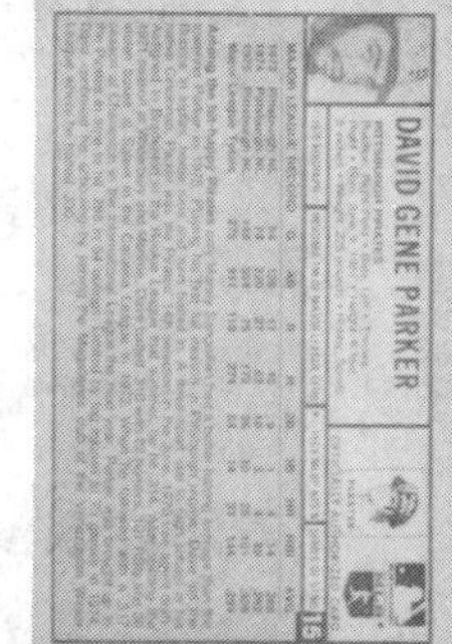

A sizeable list of corrected errors and other variation cards dots the checklist for the 57-card 1976 Kellogg's 3-D set. Again containing 57 cards, the first three cards in the set are found far less often than cards #4-57, indicating they were short-printed in relation to the rest of the set. The complete set values quoted below dot not include the scarcer variation cards. Card size remained at 2-1/8" by 3-1/4". Cards #1-3 were short-printed.

		NR MT	EX	VG
Complete Set:		80.00	40.00	24.00
Common Player:		1.25	.60	.40
1	Steve Hargan	8.00	4.00	2.50
2	Claudell Washington	8.00	4.00	2.50
3	Don Gullett	8.00	4.00	2.50
4	Randy Jones	1.25	.60	.40
5	Jim "Catfish" Hunter	6.50	3.25	2.00
6a	Clay Carroll (Cincinnati)	3.00	1.50	.90
6b	Clay Carroll (Chicago)	1.50	.70	.45
7	Joe Rudi	1.50	.70	.45
8	Reggie Jackson	10.00	5.00	3.00
9	Felix Millan	1.25	.60	.40
10	Jim Rice	5.00	2.50	1.50
11	Bert Blyleven	2.50	1.25	.70
12	Ken Singleton	1.50	.70	.45
13	Don Sutton	2.50	1.25	.70
14	Joe Morgan	6.00	3.00	1.75
15	Dave Parker	6.00	3.00	1.75
16	Dave Cash	1.25	.60	.40
17	Ron LeFlore	1.25	.60	.40
18	Greg Luzinski	2.00	1.00	.60
19	Dennis Eckersley	2.25	1.25	.70
20	Bill Madlock	2.25	1.25	.70
21	George Scott	1.25	.60	.40
22	Willie Stargell	6.50	3.25	2.00
23	Al Hrabosky	1.25	.60	.40
24	Carl Yastrzemski	13.00	6.50	4.00
25	Jim Kaat	2.50	1.25	.70
26	Marty Perez	1.25	.60	.40
27	Bob Watson	1.25	.60	.40
28	Eric Soderholm	1.25	.60	.40
29	Bill Lee	1.25	.60	.40
30a	Frank Tanana (1975 ERA 2.63)	2.50	1.25	.70
30b	Frank Tanana (1975 ERA 2.62)	1.50	.70	.45
31	Fred Lynn	3.50	1.75	1.00
32a	Tom Seaver (1967 PCT. 552)	10.00	5.00	3.00
32b	Tom Seaver (1967 Pct. .552)	8.00	4.00	2.50
33	Steve Busby	1.25	.60	.40
34	Gary Carter	10.00	5.00	3.00
35	Rick Wise	1.25	.60	.40
36	Johnny Bench	10.00	5.00	3.00
37	Jim Palmer	8.00	4.00	2.50
38	Bobby Murcer	2.00	1.00	.60
39	Von Joshua	1.25	.60	.40
40	Lou Brock	8.00	4.00	2.50
41a	Mickey Rivers (last line begins "In three...")	2.75	1.50	.80
41b	Mickey Rivers (last line begins "The Yankees...")	1.25	.60	.40

		NR MT	EX	VG
42	Manny Sanguillen	1.25	.60	.40
43	Jerry Reuss	1.50	.70	.45
44	Ken Griffey	1.50	.70	.45
45a	Jorge Orta (AB 1616)	2.25	1.25	.70
45b	Jorge Orta (AB 1615)	1.25	.60	.40
46	John Mayberry	1.25	.60	.40
47a	Vida Blue (2nd line reads "...pitched more innings...")	3.00	1.50	.90
47b	Vida Blue (2nd line reads "...struck out more...")	2.00	1.00	.60
48	Rod Carew	10.00	5.00	3.00
49a	Jon Matlack (1975 ER 87)	2.25	1.25	.70
49b	Jon Matlack (1975 ER 86)	1.25	.60	.40
50	Boog Powell	2.50	1.25	.70
51a	Mike Hargrove (AB 935)	2.25	1.25	.70
51b	Mike Hargrove (AB 934)	1.25	.60	.40
52a	Paul Lindblad (1975 ERA 2.72)	2.25	1.25	.70
52b	Paul Lindblad (1975 ERA 2.73)	1.25	.60	.40
53	Thurman Munson	6.50	3.25	2.00
54	Steve Garvey	6.00	3.00	1.75
55	Pete Rose	18.00	9.00	5.50
56a	Greg Gross (Games 302)	2.25	1.25	.70
56b	Greg Gross (Games 334)	1.25	.60	.40
57	Ted Simmons	2.50	1.25	.70

1977 Kellogg's

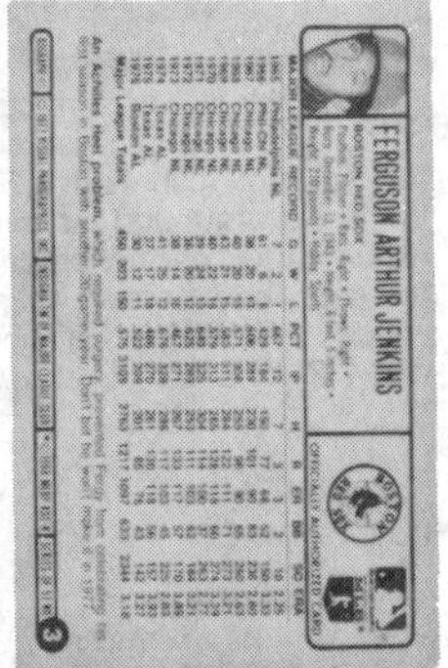

Other than another innovative card design to complement the simulated 3-D effect, there was little change in the 1977 Kellogg's issue. Set size remained at 57 cards, the set remained in the 2-1/8" by 3-1/4" format, and the cards were available either individually in boxes of cereal, or as a complete set via a mail-in box top offer. The 1977 set is the last in which Kellogg's used a player portrait photo on the back of the card.

		NR MT	EX	VG
	Complete Set:	55.00	28.00	16.50
	Common Player:	.40	.20	.12
1	George Foster	.90	.45	.25
2	Bert Campaneris	.60	.30	.20
3	Fergie Jenkins	2.00	1.00	.60
4	Dock Ellis	.40	.20	.12
5	John Montefusco	.40	.20	.12
6	George Brett	8.50	4.25	2.50
7	John Candelaria	.50	.25	.15
8	Fred Norman	.40	.20	.12
9	Bill Travers	.40	.20	.12
10	Hal McRae	.60	.30	.20
11	Doug Rau	.40	.20	.12
12	Greg Luzinski	.70	.35	.20
13	Ralph Garr	.40	.20	.12
14	Steve Garvey	4.50	2.25	1.25
15	Rick Manning	.40	.20	.12
16	Lyman Bostock	.50	.25	.15
17	Randy Jones	.40	.20	.12
18a	Ron Cey (58 homers in first sentence)	1.00	.50	.30
18b	Ron Cey (48 homers in first sentence)	.60	.30	.20
19	Dave Parker	1.25	.60	.40
20	Pete Rose	9.00	4.50	2.75
21a	Wayne Garland (last line begins "Prior to...")	.90	.45	.25
21b	Wayne Garland (last line begins "There he...")	.40	.20	.12
22	Bill North	.40	.20	.12
23	Thurman Munson	2.50	1.25	.70
24	Tom Poquette	.40	.20	.12
25	Ron LeFlore	.50	.25	.15
26	Mark Fidrych	.50	.25	.15
27	Sixto Lezcano	.40	.20	.12
28	Dave Winfield	4.00	2.00	1.25
29	Jerry Koosman	.50	.25	.15
30	Mike Hargrove	.40	.20	.12
31	Willie Montanez	.40	.20	.12
32	Don Stanhouse	.40	.20	.12
33	Jay Johnstone	.50	.25	.15
34	Bake McBride	.40	.20	.12
35	Dave Kingman	.70	.35	.20
36	Freddie Patek	.40	.20	.12
37	Garry Maddox	.50	.25	.15
38a	Ken Reitz (last line begins "The previous...")	.90	.45	.25
38b	Ken Reitz (last line begins "In late...")	.40	.20	.12
39	Bobby Grich	.60	.30	.20
40	Cesar Geronimo	.40	.20	.12
41	Jim Lonborg	.40	.20	.12
42	Ed Figueroa	.40	.20	.12
43	Bill Madlock	.80	.40	.25
44	Jerry Remy	.40	.20	.12
45	Frank Tanana	.50	.25	.15
46	Al Oliver	.90	.45	.25
47	Charlie Hough	.50	.25	.15
48	Lou Piniella	.70	.35	.20
49	Ken Griffey	.60	.30	.20
50	Jose Cruz	.60	.30	.20
51	Rollie Fingers	2.50	1.25	.70
52	Chris Chambliss	.50	.25	.15
53	Rod Carew	4.00	2.00	1.25
54	Andy Messersmith	.40	.20	.12
55	Mickey Rivers	.40	.20	.12
56	Butch Wynegar	.40	.20	.12
57	Steve Carlton	5.00	2.50	1.50

1978 Kellogg's

Besides the substitution of a Tony the Tiger drawing for a player portrait photo on the back of the card, the 1978 Kellogg's set offered no major changes from the previous few years issues. Cards were once again in the 2-1/8" by 3-1/4" format, with 57 cards comprising a complete set. Single cards were available in selected brands of the company's cereal, while complete sets could be obtained by a mail-in offer.

		NR MT	EX	VG
	Complete Set:	55.00	27.00	16.50
	Common Player:	.40	.20	.12
1	Steve Carlton	4.00	2.00	1.25
2	Bucky Dent	.50	.25	.15
3	Mike Schmidt	4.00	2.00	1.25
4	Ken Griffey	.50	.25	.15
5	Al Cowens	.40	.20	.12
6	George Brett	5.00	2.50	1.50
7	Lou Brock	3.00	1.50	.90
8	Rich Gossage	.70	.35	.20
9	Tom Johnson	.40	.20	.12
10	George Foster	.70	.35	.20
11	Dave Winfield	3.50	1.75	1.00
12	Dan Meyer	.40	.20	.12
13	Chris Chambliss	.50	.25	.15

		NR MT	EX	VG
14	Paul Dade	.40	.20	.12
15	Jeff Burroughs	.40	.20	.12
16	Jose Cruz	.60	.30	.20
17	Mickey Rivers	.40	.20	.12
18	John Candelaria	.50	.25	.15
19	Ellis Valentine	.40	.20	.12
20	Hal McRae	.50	.25	.15
21	Dave Rozema	.40	.20	.12
22	Lenny Randle	.40	.20	.12
23	Willie McCovey	3.00	1.50	.90
24	Ron Cey	.70	.35	.20
25	Eddie Murray	9.00	4.50	2.75
26	Larry Bowa	.60	.30	.20
27	Tom Seaver	3.50	1.75	1.00
28	Garry Maddox	.50	.25	.15
29	Rod Carew	3.00	1.50	.90
30	Thurman Munson	2.50	1.25	.70
31	Garry Templeton	.60	.30	.20
32	Eric Soderholm	.40	.20	.12
33	Greg Luzinski	.70	.35	.20
34	Reggie Smith	.50	.25	.15
35	Dave Goltz	.40	.20	.12
36	Tommy John	.90	.45	.25
37	Ralph Garr	.40	.20	.12
38	Alan Bannister	.40	.20	.12
39	Bob Bailor	.40	.20	.12
40	Reggie Jackson	5.00	2.50	1.50
41	Cecil Cooper	.80	.40	.25
42	Burt Hooton	.40	.20	.12
43	Sparky Lyle	.50	.25	.15
44	Steve Ontiveros	.40	.20	.12
45	Rick Reuschel	.60	.30	.20
46	Lyman Bostock	.50	.25	.15
47	Mitchell Page	.40	.20	.12
48	Bruce Sutter	.70	.35	.20
49	Jim Rice	2.00	1.00	.60
50	Bob Forsch	.40	.20	.12
51	Nolan Ryan	8.00	4.00	2.50
52	Dave Parker	1.25	.60	.40
53	Bert Blyleven	.90	.45	.25
54	Frank Tanana	.50	.25	.15
55	Ken Singleton	.50	.25	.15
56	Mike Hargrove	.40	.20	.12
57	Don Sutton	1.25	.60	.40

1979 Kellogg's

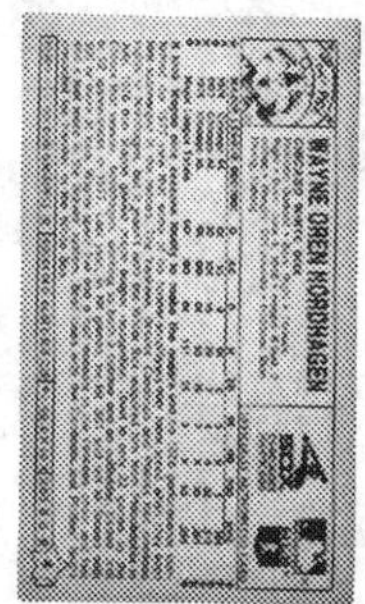

For its 1979 3-D issue, Kellogg's increased the size of the set to 60 cards, but reduced the width of the cards to 1-15/16". Depth stayed the same as in previous years, 3-1/4". The narrower card format seems to have compounded the problem of curling and subsequent cracking of the ribbed plastic surface which helps give the card a 3-D effect. Cards with major cracks can be graded no higher than VG. The complete set price in the checklist that follows does not include the scarcer variations. Numerous minor variations featuring copyright and trademark logos can be found in the set.

		NR MT	EX	VG
Complete Set:		35.00	17.50	10.50
Common Player:		.30	.15	.09
1	Bruce Sutter	.40	.20	.12
2	Ted Simmons	.40	.20	.12
3	Ross Grimsley	.30	.15	.09
4	Wayne Nordhagen	.30	.15	.09
5a	Jim Palmer (PCT. .649)	2.25	1.25	.70
5b	Jim Palmer (PCT. .650)	1.50	.70	.45
6	John Henry Johnson	.30	.15	.09
7	Jason Thompson	.30	.15	.09
8	Pat Zachry	.30	.15	.09
9	Dennis Eckersley	.75	.40	.25
10a	Paul Splittorff (IP 1665)	.60	.30	.20
10b	Paul Splittorff (IP 1666)	.30	.15	.09
11a	Ron Guidry (Hits 397)	1.00	.50	.30
11b	Ron Guidry (Hits 396)	.50	.25	.15
12	Jeff Burroughs	.30	.15	.09
13	Rod Carew	2.50	1.25	.70
14a	Buddy Bell (no trade line in bio)	1.25	.60	.40
14b	Buddy Bell (trade line in bio)	.30	.15	.09
15	Jim Rice	.60	.30	.20
16	Garry Maddox	.50	.25	.15
17	Willie McCovey	2.50	1.25	.70
18	Steve Carlton	2.50	1.25	.70
19a	J. R. Richard (stats begin with 1972)	.60	.30	.20
19b	J. R. Richard (stats begin with 1971)	.30	.15	.09
20	Paul Molitor	.90	.45	.25
21a	Dave Parker (AVG. .281)	2.00	1.00	.60
21b	Dave Parker (AVG. .318)	1.00	.50	.30
22a	Pete Rose (1978 3B 3)	6.00	6.00	3.50
22b	Pete Rose (1978 3B 33)	4.00	2.00	1.25
23a	Vida Blue (Runs 819)	.90	.45	.25
23b	Vida Blue (Runs 818)	.40	.20	.12
24	Richie Zisk	.30	.15	.09
25a	Darrell Porter (2B 101)	.80	.40	.25
25b	Darrell Porter (2B 111)	.40	.20	.12
26a	Dan Driessen (Games 642)	.80	.40	.25
26b	Dan Driessen (Games 742)	.40	.20	.12
27a	Geoff Zahn (1978 Minnessota)	.60	.30	.20
27b	Geoff Zahn (1978 Minnesota)	.30	.15	.09
28	Phil Niekro	1.25	.60	.40
29	Tom Seaver	2.50	1.25	.70
30	Fred Lynn	1.00	.50	.30
31	Bill Bonham	.30	.15	.09
32	George Foster	.40	.20	.12
33a	Terry Puhl (last line of bio begins "Terry...")	.60	.30	.20
33b	Terry Puhl (last line of bio begins "His...")	.30	.15	.09
34a	John Candelaria (age is 24)	.90	.45	.25
34b	John Candelaria (age is 25)	.50	.25	.15
35	Bob Knepper	.40	.20	.12
36	Freddie Patek	.30	.15	.09
37	Chris Chambliss	.40	.20	.12
38a	Bob Forsch (1977 Games 86)	.80	.40	.25
38b	Bob Forsch (1977 Games 35)	.40	.20	.12
39a	Ken Griffey (1978 AB 674)	.90	.45	.25
39b	Ken Griffey (1978 AB 614)	.50	.25	.15
40	Jack Clark	.40	.20	.12
41a	Dwight Evans (1978 Hits 13)	1.50	.70	.45
41b	Dwight Evans (1978 Hits 123)	.90	.45	.25
42	Lee Mazzilli	.30	.15	.09
43	Mario Guerrero	.30	.15	.09
44	Larry Bowa	.50	.25	.15
45a	Carl Yastrzemski (Games 9930)	6.00	3.00	1.75
45b	Carl Yastrzemski (Games 9929)	4.00	2.00	1.25
46a	Reggie Jackson (1978 Games 162)	5.00	2.50	1.50
46b	Reggie Jackson (1978 Games 139)	3.00	1.50	.90
47	Rick Reuschel	.60	.30	.20
48a	Mike Flanagan (1976 SO 57)	.90	.45	.25
48b	Mike Flanagan (1976 SO 56)	.50	.25	.15
49a	Gaylord Perry (1973 Hits 325)	2.00	1.00	.60
49b	Gaylord Perry (1973 Hits 315)	1.25	.60	.40
50	George Brett	3.50	1.75	1.00
51a	Craig Reynolds (last line of bio begins "He spent...")	.60	.30	.20
51b	Craig Reynolds (last line of bio begins "In those...")	.30	.15	.09
52	Davey Lopes	.40	.20	.12
53a	Bill Almon (2B 31)	.60	.30	.20
53b	Bill Almon (2B 41)	.30	.15	.09
54	Roy Howell	.30	.15	.09
55	Frank Tanana	.40	.20	.12
56a	Doug Rau (1978 PCT. .577)	.60	.30	.20
56b	Doug Rau (1978 PCT. .625)	.30	.15	.09
57a	Rick Monday (1976 Runs 197)	.90	.45	.25
57b	Rick Monday (1976 Runs 107)	.50	.25	.15
58	Jon Matlack	.30	.15	.09
59a	Ron Jackson (last line of bio begins "His best...")	.60	.30	.20
59b	Ron Jackson (last line of bio begins "The Twins...")	.30	.15	.09

		NR MT	EX	VG
60	Jim Sundberg	.50	.25	.15

1980 Kellogg's

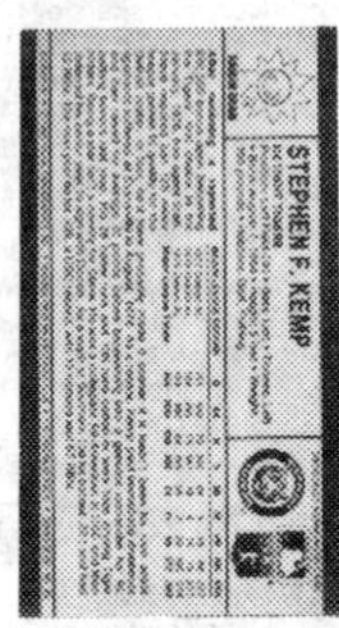

The 1980 cereal company issue featured the narrowest format of any Kellogg's card, 1-7/8" by 3-1/4". For the second straight year, set size remained at 60 cards, available either singly in boxes of cereal, or as complete sets by a mail-in offer.

		NR MT	EX	VG
Complete Set:		25.00	12.50	7.50
Common Player:		.30	.15	.09
1	Ross Grimsley	.30	.15	.09
2	Mike Schmidt	4.00	2.00	1.25
3	Mike Flanagan	.40	.20	.12
4	Ron Guidry	.40	.20	.12
5	Bert Blyleven	.80	.40	.25
6	Dave Kingman	.30	.15	.09
7	Jeff Newman	.30	.15	.09
8	Steve Rogers	.30	.15	.09
9	George Brett	4.00	2.00	1.25
10	Bruce Sutter	.60	.30	.20
11	Gorman Thomas	.30	.15	.09
12	Darrell Porter	.30	.15	.09
13	Roy Smalley	.30	.15	.09
14	Steve Carlton	1.50	.70	.45
15	Jim Palmer	1.50	.70	.45
16	Bob Bailor	.30	.15	.09
17	Jason Thompson	.30	.15	.09
18	Graig Nettles	.40	.20	.12
19	Ron Cey	.50	.25	.15
20	Nolan Ryan	5.00	2.50	1.50
21	Ellis Valentine	.30	.15	.09
22	Larry Hisle	.30	.15	.09
23	Dave Parker	.90	.45	.25
24	Eddie Murray	1.00	.50	.30
25	Willie Stargell	1.50	.70	.45
26	Reggie Jackson	2.50	1.25	.70
27	Carl Yastrzemski	3.50	1.75	1.00
28	Andre Thornton	.40	.20	.12
29	Davey Lopes	.40	.20	.12
30	Ken Singleton	.40	.20	.12
31	Steve Garvey	2.00	1.00	.60
32	Dave Winfield	2.50	1.25	.70
33	Steve Kemp	.40	.20	.12
34	Claudell Washington	.40	.20	.12
35	Pete Rose	5.00	2.50	1.50
36	Cesar Cedeno	.40	.20	.12
37	John Stearns	.30	.15	.09
38	Lee Mazzilli	.30	.15	.09
39	Larry Bowa	.40	.20	.12
40	Fred Lynn	.80	.40	.25
41	Carlton Fisk	.90	.45	.25
42	Vida Blue	.50	.25	.15
43	Keith Hernandez	.50	.25	.15
44	Jim Rice	.75	.40	.25
45	Ted Simmons	.50	.25	.15
46	Chet Lemon	.30	.15	.09
47	Fergie Jenkins	1.00	.50	.30
48	Gary Matthews	.40	.20	.12
49	Tom Seaver	2.50	1.25	.70
50	George Foster	.70	.35	.20
51	Phil Niekro	.75	.40	.25
52	Johnny Bench	2.50	1.25	.70
53	Buddy Bell	.50	.25	.15
54	Lance Parrish	.50	.25	.15
55	Joaquin Andujar	.30	.15	.09
56	Don Baylor	.50	.25	.15
57	Jack Clark	.40	.20	.12
58	J.R. Richard	.30	.15	.09
59	Bruce Bochte	.30	.15	.09
60	Rod Carew	2.50	1.25	.70

1981 Kellogg's

"Bigger" is the word to best describe Kellogg's 1981 card set. Not only were the cards themselves larger than ever before at 2-1/2" by 3-1/2", but the size of the set was increased to 66, the largest since the 75-card issues of 1970-71. The '81 Kellogg's set was available only as complete sets by mail. It is thought that the wider format of the 1981s may help prevent the problems of curling and cracking from which other years of Kellogg's issues suffer.

		MT	NR MT	EX
Complete Set:		12.00	9.00	4.75
Common Player:		.08	.06	.03
1	George Foster	.15	.11	.06
2	Jim Palmer	.60	.45	.25
3	Reggie Jackson	1.25	.90	.50
4	Al Oliver	.15	.11	.06
5	Mike Schmidt	1.25	.90	.50
6	Nolan Ryan	2.00	1.50	.80
7	Bucky Dent	.10	.08	.04
8	George Brett	1.25	.90	.50
9	Jim Rice	.35	.25	.14
10	Steve Garvey	.40	.30	.15
11	Willie Stargell	.60	.45	.25
12	Phil Niekro	.25	.20	.10
13	Dave Parker	.20	.15	.08
14	Cesar Cedeno	.10	.08	.04
15	Don Baylor	.10	.08	.04
16	J.R. Richard	.08	.06	.03
17	Tony Perez	.15	.11	.06
18	Eddie Murray	.60	.45	.25
19	Chet Lemon	.08	.06	.03
20	Ben Oglivie	.08	.06	.03
21	Dave Winfield	.60	.45	.25
22	Joe Morgan	.60	.45	.25
23	Vida Blue	.10	.08	.04
24	Willie Wilson	.15	.11	.06
25	Steve Henderson	.08	.06	.03
26	Rod Carew	1.00	.70	.40
27	Garry Templeton	.08	.06	.03
28	Dave Concepcion	.10	.08	.04
29	Davey Lopes	.08	.06	.03
30	Ken Landreaux	.08	.06	.03
31	Keith Hernandez	.20	.15	.08
32	Cecil Cooper	.10	.08	.04
33	Rickey Henderson	1.00	.70	.40
34	Frank White	.10	.08	.04
35	George Hendrick	.08	.06	.03
36	Reggie Smith	.10	.08	.04
37	Tug McGraw	.10	.08	.04
38	Tom Seaver	1.00	.70	.40
39	Ken Singleton	.10	.08	.04
40	Fred Lynn	.20	.15	.08
41	Rich "Goose" Gossage	.20	.15	.08
42	Terry Puhl	.08	.06	.03
43	Larry Bowa	.10	.08	.04
44	Phil Garner	.08	.06	.03
45	Ron Guidry	.20	.15	.08
46	Lee Mazzilli	.08	.06	.03

		MT	NR MT	EX
47	Dave Kingman	.15	.11	.06
48	Carl Yastrzemski	1.00	.70	.40
49	Rick Burleson	.08	.06	.03
50	Steve Carlton	.60	.45	.25
51	Alan Trammell	.30	.25	.12
52	Tommy John	.20	.15	.08
53	Paul Molitor	.20	.15	.08
54	Joe Charboneau	.08	.06	.03
55	Rick Langford	.08	.06	.03
56	Bruce Sutter	.10	.08	.04
57	Robin Yount	.60	.45	.25
58	Steve Stone	.08	.06	.03
59	Larry Gura	.08	.06	.03
60	Mike Flanagan	.10	.08	.04
61	Bob Horner	.15	.11	.06
62	Bruce Bochte	.08	.06	.03
63	Pete Rose	1.00	.70	.40
64	Buddy Bell	.15	.11	.06
65	Johnny Bench	1.00	.70	.40
66	Mike Hargrove	.08	.06	.03

1982 Kellogg's

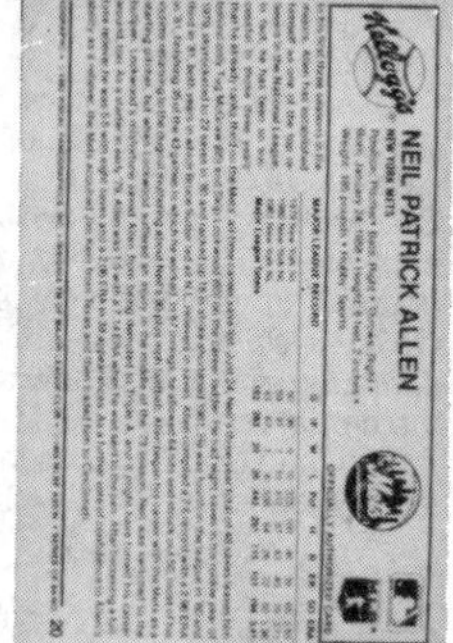

For the second straight year in 1982, Kellogg's cards were not inserted into cereal boxes, but had to be obtained by sending cash and box tops to the company for complete sets. The '82 cards were downsized both in number of cards in the set - 64 - and in physical dimensions, 2-1/8" by 3-1/4".

		MT	NR MT	EX
Complete Set:		16.00	12.00	6.50
Common Player:		.12	.09	.05
1	Richie Zisk	.12	.09	.05
2	Bill Buckner	.12	.09	.05
3	George Brett	1.00	.70	.40
4	Rickey Henderson	.90	.70	.35
5	Jack Morris	.30	.25	.12
6	Ozzie Smith	.25	.20	.10
7	Rollie Fingers	.25	.20	.10
8	Tom Seaver	.50	.25	.13
9	Fernando Valenzuela	.20	.15	.08
10	Hubie Brooks	.12	.09	.05
11	Nolan Ryan	1.50	1.25	.60
12	Dave Winfield	.60	.30	.15
13	Bob Horner	.20	.15	.08
14	Reggie Jackson	1.00	.70	.40
15	Burt Hooton	.12	.09	.05
16	Mike Schmidt	1.00	.70	.40
17	Bruce Sutter	.20	.15	.08
18	Pete Rose	1.00	.70	.40
19	Dave Kingman	.12	.09	.05
20	Neil Allen	.12	.09	.05
21	Don Sutton	.25	.20	.10
22	Dave Concepcion	.20	.15	.08
23	Keith Hernandez	.12	.09	.05
24	Gary Carter	.30	.25	.12
25	Carlton Fisk	.30	.25	.12
26	Ron Guidry	.25	.20	.10
27	Steve Carlton	.75	.60	.30
28	Robin Yount	.60	.45	.25
29	John Castino	.12	.09	.05
30	Johnny Bench	1.00	.70	.40
31	Bob Knepper	.12	.09	.05
32	Rich "Goose" Gossage	.20	.15	.08
33	Buddy Bell	.20	.15	.08
34	Art Howe	.12	.09	.05

		MT	NR MT	EX
35	Tony Armas	.12	.09	.05
36	Phil Niekro	.30	.25	.12
37	Len Barker	.12	.09	.05
38	Bobby Grich	.20	.15	.08
39	Steve Kemp	.12	.09	.05
40	Kirk Gibson	.35	.20	.09
41	Carney Lansford	.20	.15	.08
42	Jim Palmer	.60	.45	.25
43	Carl Yastrzemski	1.00	.50	.25
44	Rick Burleson	.12	.09	.05
45	Dwight Evans	.25	.20	.10
46	Ron Cey	.20	.15	.08
47	Steve Garvey	.70	.50	.30
48	Dave Parker	.30	.25	.12
49	Mike Easler	.12	.09	.05
50	Dusty Baker	.12	.09	.05
51	Rod Carew	.70	.50	.30
52	Chris Chambliss	.12	.09	.05
53	Tim Raines	.70	.50	.30
54	Chet Lemon	.12	.09	.05
55	Bill Madlock	.20	.15	.08
56	George Foster	.20	.15	.08
57	Dwayne Murphy	.12	.09	.05
58	Ken Singleton	.20	.15	.08
59	Mike Norris	.12	.09	.05
60	Cecil Cooper	.20	.15	.08
61	Al Oliver	.20	.15	.08
62	Willie Wilson	.25	.20	.10
63	Vida Blue	.20	.15	.08
64	Eddie Murray	1.00	.70	.40

1983 Kellogg's

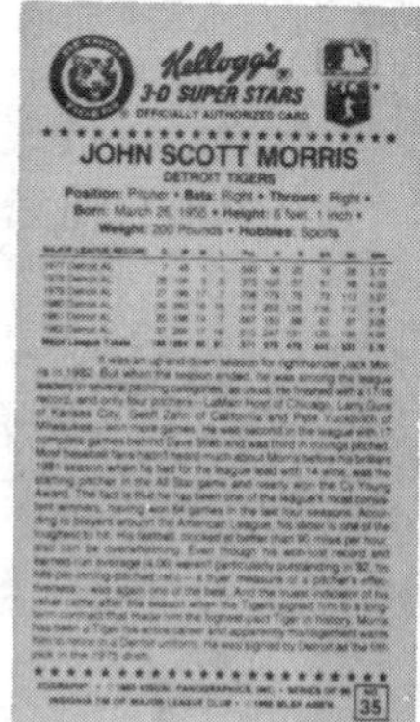

In its 14th consecutive year of baseball card issue, Kellogg's returned to the policy of inserting single cards into cereal boxes, as well as offering complete sets by a mail-in box top redemption offer. The 3-D cards themselves returned to a narrow 1-7/8" by 3-1/4" format, while the set size was reduced to 60 cards.

		MT	NR MT	EX
Complete Set:		15.00	11.00	6.00
Common Player:		.10	.08	.04
1	Rod Carew	.80	.60	.30
2	Rollie Fingers	.20	.15	.08
3	Reggie Jackson	.80	.60	.30
4	George Brett	.80	.60	.30
5	Hal McRae	.15	.11	.06
6	Pete Rose	.80	.60	.30
7	Fernando Valenzuela	.20	.15	.08
8	Rickey Henderson	.80	.60	.30
9	Carl Yastrzemski	.80	.60	.30
10	Rich "Goose" Gossage	.20	.15	.08
11	Eddie Murray	.50	.40	.20
12	Buddy Bell	.10	.08	.04
13	Jim Rice	.20	.15	.08
14	Robin Yount	.80	.60	.30
15	Dave Winfield	.80	.60	.30
16	Harold Baines	.20	.15	.08
17	Garry Templeton	.10	.08	.04
18	Bill Madlock	.10	.08	.04
19	Pete Vuckovich	.10	.08	.04
20	Pedro Guerrero	.10	.08	.04
21	Ozzie Smith	.20	.15	.08
22	George Foster	.10	.08	.04
23	Willie Wilson	.20	.15	.08

		MT	NR MT	EX
24	Johnny Ray	.10	.08	.04
25	George Hendrick	.10	.08	.04
26	Andre Thornton	.10	.08	.04
27	Leon Durham	.10	.08	.04
28	Cecil Cooper	.10	.08	.04
29	Don Baylor	.15	.11	.06
30	Lonnie Smith	.10	.08	.04
31	Nolan Ryan	1.25	.90	.50
32	Dan Quiesenberry (Quisenberry)	.10	.08	.04
33	Len Barker	.10	.08	.04
34	Neil Allen	.10	.08	.04
35	Jack Morris	.20	.15	.08
36	Dave Stieb	.15	.11	.06
37	Bruce Sutter	.15	.11	.06
38	Jim Sundberg	.10	.08	.04
39	Jim Palmer	.35	.25	.14
40	Lance Parrish	.20	.15	.08
41	Floyd Bannister	.10	.08	.04
42	Larry Gura	.10	.08	.04
43	Britt Burns	.10	.08	.04
44	Toby Harrah	.10	.08	.04
45	Steve Carlton	.50	.40	.20
46	Greg Minton	.10	.08	.04
47	Gorman Thomas	.10	.08	.04
48	Jack Clark	.15	.11	.06
49	Keith Hernandez	.20	.15	.08
50	Greg Luzinski	.15	.11	.06
51	Fred Lynn	.25	.20	.10
52	Dale Murphy	.70	.50	.30
53	Kent Hrbek	.20	.15	.08
54	Bob Horner	.10	.08	.04
55	Gary Carter	.30	.25	.12
56	Carlton Fisk	.25	.20	.10
57	Dave Concepcion	.15	.11	.06
58	Mike Schmidt	.80	.60	.30
59	Bill Buckner	.10	.08	.04
60	Bobby Grich	.10	.08	.04

1991 Kellogg's 3-D

In 1991, specially-marked packages of Kellogg's Corn Flakes included 3-D baseball cards, resuming a tradition that began in 1970 and continued without interruption until 1983. In the 1991 edition, there are 15 cards to collect, featuring many of the greatest living retired stars in the game. Most of the players are in the Hall of Fame. The card fronts show two pictures of the player, while the backs include career highlights and a portrait. The cards are 2-1/2" x 3-5/16", numbered and were made by Sportflics. A complete set was available via a mail-in offer for $4.95 plus proofs of purchase.

		MT	NR MT	EX
Complete Set:		6.00	4.50	2.50
Common Player:		.25	.20	.10
1	Gaylord Perry	.25	.20	.10
2	Hank Aaron	1.00	.70	.40
3	Willie Mays	1.00	.70	.40
4	Ernie Banks	.75	.60	.30
5	Bob Gibson	.50	.40	.20
6	Harmon Killebrew	.50	.40	.20
7	Rollie Fingers	.25	.20	.10
8	Steve Carlton	.25	.20	.10
9	Billy Williams	.25	.20	.10
10	Lou Brock	.25	.20	.10
11	Yogi Berra	.75	.60	.30
12	Warren Spahn	.50	.40	.20
13	Boog Powell	.25	.20	.10
14	Don Baylor	.25	.20	.10
15	Ralph Kiner	.25	.20	.10

1992 Kellogg's 3-D

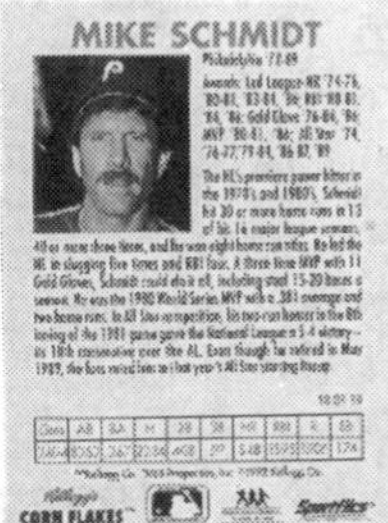

Kellogg's cereal company created a 10-card 1992 All Star set of retired stars, with one card inserted in specially-marked boxes of corn flakes, and complete sets available by mail. The cards, produced by Sportflics/ Optigraphics feature two sequential action images on each front. Red, white and blue designs comprise the border, with yellow bands above and beneath the photo. On back is a black-and-white portrait photo, plus a career summary and a MLB, few stats, along with the logos for the cereal company, the Major League Baseball Players Alumni and Sportflics. As in the previous year, cards are slightly longer, at 2-1/2" x 5/16", than standard size.

		MT	NR MT	EX
Complete Set:		3.00	2.25	1.25
Common Player:		.25	.20	.10
1	Willie Stargell	.50	.40	.20
2	Tony Perez	.25	.20	.10
3	Jim Palmer	.50	.40	.20
4	Rod Carew	.50	.40	.20
5	Tom Seaver	.50	.40	.20
6	Phil Niekro	.25	.20	.10
7	Bill Madlock	.25	.20	.10
8	Jim Rice	.25	.20	.10
9	Dan Quisenberry	.25	.20	.10
10	Mike Schmidt	.50	.40	.20

1988 Kenner Starting Lineup

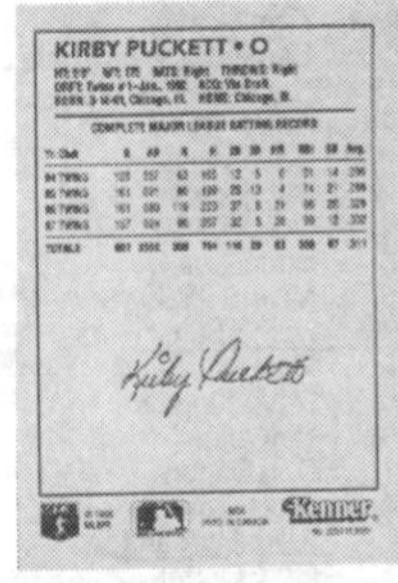

This massive three-sport set was distributed in conjuntion with Kenner's Starting Lineup sports figurines, one card per statue. Cards were not sold separately. Baseball, football and basketball stars were included in the lineup of full-color figurines, with 123 figure/card combinations devoted to baseball. Individual major league team assortments include one to seven players per team. The figurines are mildly reminiscent of the

1950s Hartland Statues, but Kenner's version features smaller (4" to 6") figures and a more extensive catalog which includes athletes other than baseball players. The Starting Lineup cards feature action photos framed in red and white, with the "Starting Lineup" logo in the upper left corner and the player's name printed along the bottom border. Colorful team logos are superimposed in the lower right corner of the player photos. Card backs were printed in blue and contain major league stats, a few biographical details, a facsimile autograph and the major league and Kenner logos. The values in the checklist that follows include both the statue and card for the 123 baseball players in the set. Several players which were included in the checklist printed on the package were never produced.

		MT	NR MT	EX
Complete Set:		2000.00	1500.00	800.00
Common Player:		9.00	6.75	3.50
(1)	Alan Ashby	11.00	8.25	4.50
(2)	Harold Baines	9.00	6.75	3.50
(3)	Kevin Bass	11.00	8.25	4.50
(4)	Steve Bedrosian	9.00	6.75	3.50
(5)	Buddy Bell	9.00	6.75	3.50
(6)	George Bell	9.00	6.75	3.50
(7)	Mike Boddicker	9.00	6.75	3.50
(8)	Wade Boggs	15.00	11.00	6.00
(9)	Barry Bonds	32.50	24.00	13.00
(10)	Bobby Bonilla	15.00	11.00	6.00
(11)	Sid Bream	15.00	11.00	6.00
(12)	George Brett	25.00	18.50	10.00
(13)	Chris Brown	11.00	8.25	4.50
(14)	Tom Brunansky	9.00	6.75	3.50
(15)	Ellis Burks	17.50	13.00	7.00
(16)	Jose Canseco	17.50	13.00	7.00
(17)	Gary Carter	9.00	6.75	3.50
(18)	Joe Carter	15.00	11.00	6.00
(19)	Jack Clark	15.00	11.00	6.00
(20)	Will Clark	17.50	13.00	7.00
(21)	Roger Clemens	17.50	13.00	7.00
(22)	Vince Coleman	9.00	6.75	3.50
(23)	Kal Daniels	9.00	6.75	3.50
(24)	Alvin Davis	9.00	6.75	3.50
(25)	Eric Davis	9.00	6.75	3.50
(26)	Glenn Davis	11.00	8.25	4.50
(27)	Jody Davis	9.00	6.75	3.50
(28)	Andre Dawson	13.00	9.75	5.25
(29)	Rob Deer	9.00	6.75	3.50
(30)	Brian Downing	9.00	6.75	3.50
(31)	Mike Dunne	9.00	6.75	3.50
(32)	Shawon Dunston	15.00	11.00	6.00
(33)	Leon Durham	9.00	6.75	3.50
(34)	Len Dykstra	17.50	13.00	7.00
(35)	Dwight Evans	9.00	6.75	3.50
(36)	Carlton Fisk	21.50	16.00	8.50
(37)	John Franco	9.00	6.75	3.50
(38)	Julio Franco	9.00	6.75	3.50
(39)	Gary Gaetti	9.00	6.75	3.50
(40)	Dwight Gooden	9.00	6.75	3.50
(41)	Ken Griffey, Sr.	15.00	11.00	6.00
(42)	Pedro Guerrero	9.00	6.75	3.50
(43)	Ozzie Guillen	11.00	8.25	4.50
(44)	Tony Gwynn	15.00	11.00	6.00
(45)	Mel Hall	9.00	6.75	3.50
(46)	Billy Hatcher	9.00	6.75	3.50
(47)	Von Hayes	11.00	8.25	4.50
(48)	Rickey Henderson	15.00	11.00	6.00
(49)	Keith Hernandez	9.00	6.75	3.50
(50)	Willie Hernandez	11.00	8.25	4.50
(51)	Tom Herr	9.00	6.75	3.50
(52)	Ted Higuera	11.00	8.25	4.50
(53)	Charlie Hough	9.00	6.75	3.50
(54)	Kent Hrbek	9.00	6.75	3.50
(55)	Pete Incaviglia	9.00	6.75	3.50
(56)	Howard Johnson	15.00	11.00	6.00
(57)	Wally Joyner	9.00	6.75	3.50
(58)	Terry Kennedy	11.00	8.25	4.50
(59)	John Kruk	20.00	15.00	8.00
(60)	Mark Langston	15.00	11.00	6.00
(61)	Carney Lansford	15.00	11.00	6.00
(62)	Jeffrey Leonard	9.00	6.75	3.50
(63)	Fred Lynn	13.00	9.75	5.25
(64)	Candy Maldonado	11.00	8.25	4.50
(65)	Mike Marshall	15.00	11.00	6.00
(66)	Don Mattingly	15.00	11.00	6.00
(67)	Willie McGee	9.00	6.75	3.50
(68)	Mark McGwire	25.00	18.50	10.00
(69)	Kevin McReynolds	11.00	8.25	4.50
(70)	Paul Molitor	21.50	16.00	8.50
(71)	Donnie Moore	11.00	8.25	4.50
(72)	Jack Morris	15.00	11.00	6.00
(73)	Dale Murphy	9.00	6.75	3.50
(74)	Eddie Murray	9.00	6.75	3.50
(75)	Matt Nokes	9.00	6.75	3.50
(76)	Pete O'Brien	9.00	6.75	3.50
(77)	Ken Oberkfell	9.00	6.75	3.50
(78)	Dave Parker	15.00	11.00	6.00
(79)	Larry Parrish	9.00	6.75	3.50
(80)	Ken Phelps	15.00	11.00	6.00
(81)	Jim Presley	9.00	6.75	3.50
(82)	Kirby Puckett	17.50	13.00	7.00
(83)	Dan Quisenberry	9.00	6.75	3.50
(84)	Tim Raines	9.00	6.75	3.50
(85)	Willie Randolph	9.00	6.75	3.50
(86)	Shane Rawley	9.00	6.75	3.50
(87)	Jeff Reardon	13.00	9.75	5.25
(88)	Gary Redus	11.00	8.25	4.50
(89)	Rick Reuschel	9.00	6.75	3.50
(90)	Jim Rice	11.00	8.25	4.50
(91)	Dave Righetti	9.00	6.75	3.50
(92)	Cal Ripken, Jr.	55.00	41.00	22.00
(93)	Pete Rose	15.00	11.00	6.00
(94)	Nolan Ryan	180.00	135.00	72.00
(95)	Bret Saberhagen	9.00	6.75	3.50
(96)	Juan Samuel	9.00	6.75	3.50
(97)	Ryne Sandberg	32.50	24.00	13.00
(98)	Benito Santiago	9.00	6.75	3.50
(99)	Steve Sax	9.00	6.75	3.50
(100)	Mike Schmidt	36.00	27.00	14.50
(101)	Mike Scott	9.00	6.75	3.50
(102)	Kevin Seitzer	15.00	11.00	6.00
(103)	Ruben Sierra	15.00	11.00	6.00
(104)	Ozzie Smith	15.00	11.00	6.00
(105)	Zane Smith	9.00	6.75	3.50
(106)	Cory Snyder	9.00	6.75	3.50
(107)	Darryl Strawberry	9.00	6.75	3.50
(108)	Franklin Stubbs	15.00	11.00	6.00
(109)	B.J. Surhoff	9.00	6.75	3.50
(110)	Rick Sutcliffe	9.00	6.75	3.50
(111)	Pat Tabler	9.00	6.75	3.50
(112)	Danny Tartabull	15.00	11.00	6.00
(113)	Alan Trammell	9.00	6.75	3.50
(114)	Fernando Valenzuela	9.00	6.75	3.50
(115)	Andy Van Slyke	17.50	13.00	7.00
(116)	Frank Viola	9.00	6.75	3.50
(117)	Ozzie Virgil	9.00	6.75	3.50
(118)	Greg Walker	9.00	6.75	3.50
(119)	Lou Whitaker	15.00	11.00	6.00
(120)	Devon White	13.00	9.75	5.25
(121)	Dave Winfield	17.50	13.00	7.00
(122)	Mike Witt	9.00	6.75	3.50
(123)	Todd Worrell	11.00	8.25	4.50
(124)	Robin Yount	32.50	24.00	13.00

1989 Kenner Starting Lineup

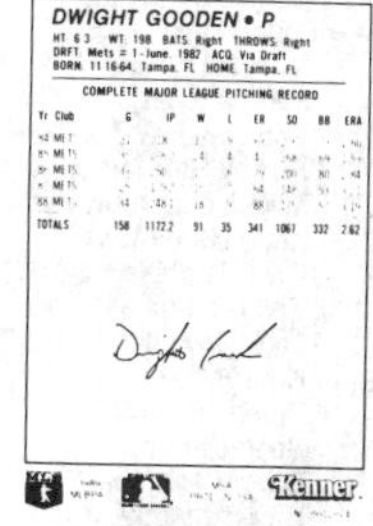

Kenner returned in 1989 with another set of sports figurines and accompanying trading cards. As in the previous year, the figurines were sold individually in a blister pack with one card packaged with each figure. No cards were sold separately. The 1989 cards have a green border with the "Starting Lineup" logo in the upper left, while the words "1989 Edition" and the player's name and uniform number appear at bottom. Backs are identical in format to the previous year. The values listed here are for complete, unopened packages of figure and card. Values are based on relative scarcity, resulting in some minor stars and common players being priced higher than superstars, whose cards and figures were produced in much greater numbers.

		MT	NR MT	EX
Complete Set:		1750.00	1312.00	700.00
Common Player:		8.00	6.00	3.25
(1)	Roberto Alomar	32.50	24.00	13.00
(2)	Brady Anderson	11.00	8.25	4.50
(3)	Harold Baines	11.00	8.25	4.50
(4)	Marty Barrett	9.00	6.75	3.50
(5)	Kevin Bass	9.00	6.75	3.50
(6)	Steve Bedrosian	9.00	6.75	3.50
(7)	George Bell	11.00	8.25	4.50
(8)	Damon Berryhill	9.00	6.75	3.50
(9)	Wade Boggs	13.00	9.75	5.25
(10)	Barry Bonds	25.00	18.50	10.00
(11)	Bobby Bonilla	9.00	6.75	3.50
(12)	Phil Bradley	9.00	6.75	3.50
(13)	Glenn Braggs	8.00	6.00	3.25
(14)	George Brett	18.00	13.50	7.25
(15)	Tom Brookens	9.00	6.75	3.50
(16)	Tom Brunansky	11.00	8.25	4.50
(17)	Steve Buechele	9.00	6.75	3.50
(18)	Ellis Burks	11.00	8.25	4.50
(19)	Brett Butler	11.00	8.25	4.50
(20)	Ivan Calderon	11.00	8.25	4.50
(21)	Jose Canseco	9.00	6.75	3.50
(22)	Gary Carter	8.00	6.00	3.25
(23)	Joe Carter	8.00	6.00	3.25
(24)	Will Clark	13.00	9.75	5.25
(25)	Roger Clemens	15.00	11.00	6.00
(26)	Vince Coleman	8.00	6.00	3.25
(27)	David Cone	11.00	8.25	4.50
(28)	Kal Daniels	8.00	6.00	3.25
(29)	Alvin Davis	8.00	6.00	3.25
(30)	Chili Davis	13.00	9.75	5.25
(31)	Eric Davis	9.00	6.75	3.50
(32)	Glenn Davis	8.00	6.00	3.25
(33)	Mark Davis	8.00	6.00	3.25
(34)	Andre Dawson	8.00	6.00	3.25
(35)	Rob Deer	9.00	6.75	3.50
(36)	Bo Diaz	9.00	6.75	3.50
(37)	Bill Doran	11.00	8.25	4.50
(38)	Doug Drabek	13.00	9.75	5.25
(39)	Shawon Dunston	9.00	6.75	3.50
(40)	Len Dykstra	13.00	9.75	5.25
(41)	Dennis Eckersley	22.00	16.50	8.75
(42)	Kevin Elster	8.00	6.00	3.25
(43)	Scott Fletcher	9.00	6.75	3.50
(44)	John Franco	8.00	6.00	3.25
(45)	Gary Gaetti	8.00	6.00	3.25
(46)	Ron Gant	30.00	22.00	12.00
(47)	Kirk Gibson	11.00	8.25	4.50
(48)	Dan Gladden	9.00	6.75	3.50
(49)	Dwight Gooden	11.00	8.25	4.50
(50)	Mark Grace	13.00	9.75	5.25
(51)	Mike Greenwell	9.00	6.75	3.50
(52)	Mark Gubicza	11.00	8.25	4.50
(53)	Pedro Guerrero	9.00	6.75	3.50
(54)	Ozzie Guillen	11.00	8.25	4.50
(55)	Tony Gwynn	18.00	13.50	7.25
(56)	Albert Hall	9.00	6.75	3.50
(57)	Mel Hall	9.00	6.75	3.50
(58)	Billy Hatcher	9.00	6.75	3.50
(59)	Von Hayes	9.00	6.75	3.50
(60)	Rickey Henderson	11.00	8.25	4.50
(61)	Mike Henneman	8.00	6.00	3.25
(62)	Keith Hernandez	8.00	6.00	3.25
(63)	Orel Hershiser	15.00	11.00	6.00
(64)	Ted Higuera	8.00	6.00	3.25
(65)	Jack Howell	13.00	9.75	5.25
(66)	Kent Hrbek	8.00	6.00	3.25
(67)	Pete Incaviglia	8.00	6.00	3.25
(68)	Bo Jackson	22.00	16.50	8.75
(69)	Danny Jackson	9.00	6.75	3.50
(70)	Brook Jacoby	8.00	6.00	3.25
(71)	Chris James	8.00	6.00	3.25
(72)	Dion James	8.00	6.00	3.25
(73)	Gregg Jefferies	15.00	11.00	6.00
(74)	Doug Jones	13.00	9.75	5.25
(75)	Wally Joyner	9.00	6.75	3.50
(76)	John Kruk	22.00	16.50	8.75
(77)	Mike LaValliere	9.00	6.75	3.50
(78)	Mark Langston	11.00	8.25	4.50
(79)	Carney Lansford	11.00	8.25	4.50
(80)	Barry Larkin	24.00	18.00	9.50
(81)	Tim Laudner	9.00	6.75	3.50
(82)	Al Leiter	9.00	6.75	3.50
(83)	Chet Lemon	9.00	6.75	3.50
(84)	Jose Lind	11.00	8.25	4.50
(85)	Greg Maddux	24.00	18.00	9.50
(86)	Candy Maldonado	9.00	6.75	3.50
(87)	Mike Marshall	9.00	6.75	3.50
(88)	Don Mattingly	13.00	9.75	5.25
(89)	Willie McGee	8.00	6.00	3.25
(90)	Mark McGwire	11.00	8.25	4.50
(91)	Kevin McReynolds	11.00	8.25	4.50
(92)	Kevin Mitchell	11.00	8.25	4.50
(93)	Paul Molitor	18.00	13.50	7.25
(94)	Jack Morris	11.00	8.25	4.50
(95)	Dale Murphy	9.00	6.75	3.50
(96)	Randy Myers	9.00	6.75	3.50
(97)	Matt Nokes	11.00	8.25	4.50
(98)	Mike Pagliarulo	9.00	6.75	3.50
(99)	Dave Parker	11.00	8.25	4.50
(100)	Dan Pasqua	9.00	6.75	3.50
(101)	Tony Pena	11.00	8.25	4.50
(102)	Terry Pendleton	11.00	8.25	4.50
(103)	Melido Perez	9.00	6.75	3.50
(104)	Gerald Perry	8.00	6.00	3.25
(105)	Dan Plesac	8.00	6.00	3.25
(106)	Kirby Puckett	22.00	16.50	8.75
(107)	Rey Quinones	9.00	6.75	3.50
(108)	Tim Raines	11.00	8.25	4.50
(109)	Johnny Ray	13.00	9.75	5.25
(110)	Jeff Reardon	13.00	9.75	5.25
(111)	Harold Reynolds	8.00	6.00	3.25
(112)	Jim Rice	9.00	6.75	3.50
(113)	Dave Righetti	11.00	8.25	4.50
(114)	Cal Ripken, Jr.	40.00	30.00	16.00
(115)	Jeff Russell	11.00	8.25	4.50
(116)	Bret Saberhagen	9.00	6.75	3.50
(117)	Chris Sabo	11.00	8.25	4.50
(118)	Luis Salazar	9.00	6.75	3.50
(119)	Juan Samuel	9.00	6.75	3.50
(120)	Ryne Sandberg	15.00	11.00	6.00
(121)	Benito Santiago	11.00	8.25	4.50
(122)	Mike Schmidt	32.50	24.00	13.00
(123)	Dick Schofield	13.00	9.75	5.25
(124)	Mike Scioscia	12.00	9.00	4.75
(125)	Mike Scott	9.00	6.75	3.50
(126)	Kevin Seitzer	13.00	9.75	5.25
(127)	Larry Sheets	9.00	6.75	3.50
(128)	John Shelby	9.00	6.75	3.50
(129)	Ruben Sierra	22.00	16.50	8.75
(130)	Don Slaught	9.00	6.75	3.50
(131)	Dave Smith	9.00	6.75	3.50
(132)	Lee Smith	11.00	8.25	4.50
(133)	Ozzie Smith	11.00	8.25	4.50
(134)	Zane Smith	9.00	6.75	3.50
(135)	Cory Snyder	8.00	6.00	3.25
(136)	Pete Stanicek	9.00	6.75	3.50
(137)	Terry Steinbach	11.00	8.25	4.50
(138)	Dave Stewart	13.00	9.75	5.25
(139)	Kurt Stillwell	8.00	6.00	3.25
(140)	Darryl Strawberry	9.00	6.75	3.50
(141)	B.J. Surhoff	8.00	6.00	3.25
(142)	Rick Sutcliffe	9.00	6.75	3.50
(143)	Bruce Sutter	11.50	8.75	4.50
(144)	Greg Swindell	9.00	6.75	3.50
(145)	Pat Tabler	8.00	6.00	3.25
(146)	Danny Tartabull	8.00	6.00	3.25
(147)	Bobby Thigpen	11.00	8.25	4.50
(148)	Milt Thompson	9.00	6.75	3.50
(149)	Robby Thompson	8.00	6.00	3.25
(150)	Alan Trammell	11.00	8.25	4.50
(151)	Jeff Treadway	13.00	9.75	5.25
(152)	Jose Uribe	9.00	6.75	3.50
(153)	Fernando Valenzuela	9.00	6.75	3.50
(154)	Andy Van Slyke	9.00	6.75	3.50
(155)	Frank Viola	9.00	6.75	3.50
(156)	Bob Walk	9.00	6.75	3.50
(157)	Greg Walker	13.00	9.75	5.25
(158)	Walt Weiss	13.00	9.75	5.25
(159)	Bob Welch	11.00	8.25	4.50
(160)	Lou Whitaker	11.00	8.25	4.50
(161)	Devon White	15.00	11.00	6.00
(162)	Dave Winfield	11.00	8.25	4.50
(163)	Mike Witt	9.00	6.75	3.50
(164)	Todd Worrell	10.00	7.50	4.00
(165)	Marvell Wynne	9.00	6.75	3.50
(166)	Gerald Young	9.00	6.75	3.50
(167)	Robin Yount	30.00	22.00	12.00

Regional interest may affect the value of a card.

1989 Kenner Starting Lineup Baseball Greats

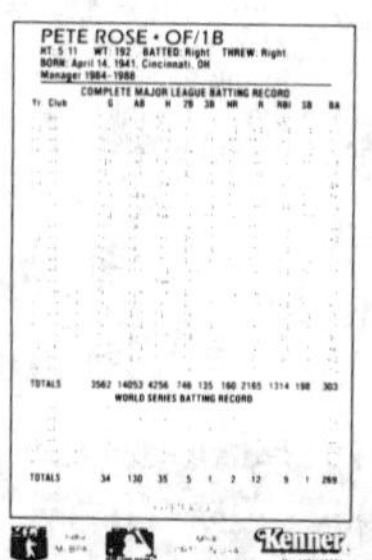

The "Baseball Greats" series of figurines and trading cards was an addition to the Kenner "Starting Lineup" series for 1989. The series features baseball greats of the past, and were packaged two figurines and two collector cards per package. The collector cards that accompany the figures feature an original action photo of the player done in a sepia-tone to enhance the historic nature of the set. The Starting Lineup logo and "Baseball Greats" heading appear at the top of the card. The player's name and a descriptive nickname, such as "Sultan of Swat" appear below the photo. The backs of the cards carry a blue-and- white color scheme and include career stats. The values listed below include both the figure and the card.

		MT	NR MT	EX
Complete Set:		150.00	112.00	60.00
Common Player:		15.00	11.00	6.00
(1)	Hank Aaron/ Eddie Mathews	20.00	15.00	8.00
(2)	Ernie Banks/ Billy Williams	15.00	11.00	6.00
(3)	Johnny Bench/ Pete Rose	20.00	15.00	8.00
(4)	Roberto Clemente/ Willie Stargell	15.00	11.00	6.00
(5)	Don Drysdale/ Reggie Jackson	20.00	15.00	8.00
(6)	Mickey Mantle/ Joe DiMaggio	30.00	22.00	12.00
(7)	Willie Mays/ Willie McCovey	15.00	11.00	6.00
(8)	Stan Musial/ Bob Gibson	20.00	15.00	8.00
(9)	Babe Ruth/ Lou Gehrig	22.00	16.50	8.75
(10)	Carl Yastrzemski/ Hank Aaron	22.00	16.50	8.75

1990 Kenner Starting Lineup

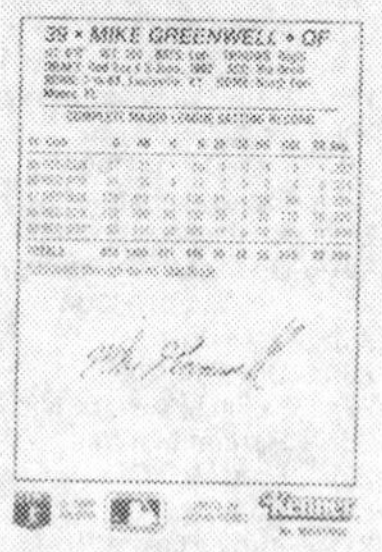

Kenner introduced special bonus rookie year cards with its regular card and statue in 1990. The cards follow designs much like the Kenner cards of 1988 and 1989. The values are based on relative scarcity. Esasky, Backman and Pettis Kenners were pulled when the players switched teams, thus making them rare. Five variations of figures are included in the 1990 set. Prices listed are for unopened packaged of statue and card.

		MT	NR MT	EX
Complete Set:		600.00	450.00	250.00
Common Player:		6.50	5.00	2.50
(1)	Jim Abbott	16.00	12.00	6.50
(2)	Sandy Alomar	11.00	8.25	4.50
(3)	Allan Anderson	9.00	6.75	3.50
(4)	Wally Backman	11.00	8.25	4.50
(5)	Jeff Ballard	6.50	5.00	2.50
(6)	Jesse Barfield	9.00	6.75	3.50
(7)	Steve Bedrosian	6.50	5.00	2.50
(8)	Todd Benzinger	9.00	6.75	3.50
(9)	Damon Berryhill	6.50	5.00	2.50
(10)	Wade Boggs	13.00	9.75	5.25
(11)	Barry Bonds	21.00	15.50	8.50
(12)	Bobby Bonilla	11.00	8.25	4.50
(13)	Chris Bosio	7.50	5.75	3.00
(14)	Ellis Burks	9.00	6.75	3.50
(15)	Jose Canseco	11.00	8.25	4.50
(16)	Joe Carter	16.00	12.00	6.50
(17a)	Will Clark (bat held in one hand)	11.00	8.25	4.50
(17b)	Will Clark (swinging)	15.00	11.00	6.00
(18)	Roger Clemens	13.00	9.75	5.25
(19)	Vince Coleman	6.50	5.00	2.50
(20)	Ron Darling	6.50	5.00	2.50
(21)	Eric Davis	6.50	5.00	2.50
(22)	Andre Dawson	11.00	8.25	4.50
(23)	Rob Dibble	9.00	6.75	3.50
(24)	Len Dykstra	15.00	11.00	6.00
(25)	Dennis Eckersley	15.00	11.00	6.00
(26)	Nick Esasky	15.00	11.00	6.00
(27)	Gary Gaetti	6.50	5.00	2.50
(28)	Andres Gallarraga	13.00	9.75	5.25
(29)	Kirk Gibson	6.50	5.00	2.50
(30)	Dwight Gooden	6.50	5.00	2.50
(31a)	Mark Grace (standing at bat)	15.00	11.00	6.00
(31b)	Mark Grace (swinging)	16.00	12.00	6.50
(32)	Mike Greenwell	6.50	5.00	2.50
(33a)	Ken Griffey, Jr. (sliding)	30.00	22.00	12.00
(33b)	Ken Griffey,Jr. (fielding)	21.00	15.50	8.50
(34)	Pedro Guerrero	6.50	5.00	2.50
(35)	Von Hayes	6.50	5.00	2.50
(36)	Dave Henderson	6.50	5.00	2.50
(37)	Rickey Henderson	11.00	8.25	4.50
(38)	Tom Herr	6.50	5.00	2.50
(39)	Orel Hershiser	11.00	8.25	4.50
(40)	Kent Hrbek	6.50	5.00	2.50
(41)	Bo Jackson	11.00	8.25	4.50
(42)	Gregg Jefferies	9.00	6.75	3.50
(43)	Howard Johnson	9.00	6.75	3.50
(44)	Ricky Jordan	6.50	5.00	2.50
(45)	Roberto Kelly	11.00	8.25	4.50
(46)	Barry Larkin	15.00	11.00	6.00
(47)	Greg Maddux	15.00	11.00	6.00
(48)	Joe Magrane	6.50	5.00	2.50
(49a)	Don Mattingly (bat held in one hand)	13.00	9.75	5.25
(49b)	Don Mattingly (swinging)	13.00	9.75	5.25
(50)	Kevin Mitchell	7.50	5.75	3.00
(51)	Ben McDonald	15.00	11.00	6.00
(52)	Fred McGriff	13.00	9.75	5.25
(53)	Mark McGwire	9.00	6.75	3.50
(54)	Kevin McReynolds	6.50	5.00	2.50
(55)	Paul Molitor	15.00	11.00	6.00
(56)	Eddie Murray	13.00	9.75	5.25
(57)	Matt Nokes	9.00	6.75	3.50
(58)	Paul O'Neill	11.00	8.25	4.50
(59)	Jose Oquendo	6.50	5.00	2.50
(60)	Gary Pettis	15.00	11.00	6.00
(61)	Kirby Puckett	15.00	11.00	6.00
(62)	Willie Randolph	9.00	6.75	3.50
(63)	Jody Reed	9.00	6.75	3.50
(64)	Rick Reuschel	6.50	5.00	2.50
(65)	Dave Righetti	7.50	5.75	3.00
(66)	Cal Ripken, Jr.	20.00	15.00	8.00
(67)	Nolan Ryan	20.00	15.00	8.00
(68)	Chris Sabo	6.50	5.00	2.50
(69)	Juan Samuel	9.00	6.75	3.50
(70)	Ryne Sandberg	15.00	11.00	6.00
(71)	Steve Sax	6.50	5.00	2.50
(72)	Mike Scott	9.00	6.75	3.50
(73)	Gary Sheffield	17.00	12.50	6.75
(74)	John Smiley	6.50	5.00	2.50
(75)	Ozzie Smith	11.00	8.25	4.50
(76)	Dave Stewart	9.00	6.75	3.50
(77a)	Darryl Strawberry (standing at bat)	9.00	6.75	3.50

		MT	NR MT	EX
(77b)	Darryl Strawberry (fielding)	13.00	9.75	5.25
(78)	Rick Sutcliffe	6.50	5.00	2.50
(79)	Mickey Tettleton	11.00	8.25	4.50
(80)	Alan Trammell	6.50	5.00	2.50
(81)	Andy Van Slyke	11.00	8.25	4.50
(82)	Frank Viola	9.00	6.75	3.50
(83)	Jerome Walton	7.50	5.75	3.00
(84)	Lou Whitaker	9.00	6.75	3.50
(85)	Mitch Williams	9.00	6.75	3.50
(86)	Dave Winfield	15.00	11.00	6.00
(87)	Robin Yount	25.00	18.50	10.00

1991 Kenner Starting Lineup

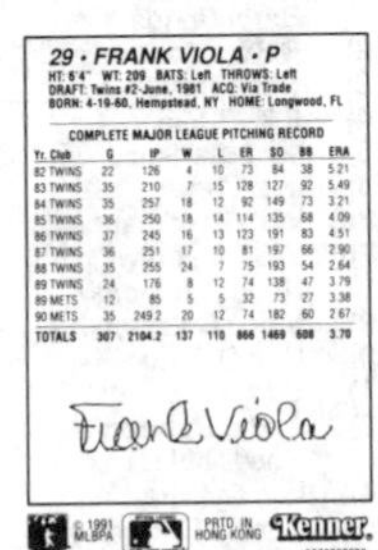

Kenner continued its Starting Lineup with 54 baseball figures for 1991. A bonus with the 1991 card and figure was an aluminum collector coin depicting the player. The 1991 cards featured a yellow border. The players are here alphabetically. Values are based on demand and relative scarcity for complete statue/card/coin unopened packages.

		MT	NR MT	EX
Complete Set:		500.00	375.00	200.00
Common Player:		6.50	5.00	2.50
(1)	Jim Abbott	11.00	8.25	4.50
(2)	Sandy Alomar, Jr.	7.50	5.75	3.00
(3)	Jack Armstrong	6.50	5.00	2.50
(4)	George Bell	7.50	5.75	3.00
(5)	Barry Bonds	15.00	11.00	6.00
(6)	Bobby Bonilla	9.00	6.75	3.50
(7)	Tom Browning	6.50	5.00	2.50
(8)	Jose Canseco	6.50	5.00	2.50
(9)	Will Clark	11.00	8.25	4.50
(10)	Vince Coleman	11.00	8.25	4.50
(11)	Eric Davis	7.50	5.75	3.00
(12)	Glenn Davis	7.50	5.75	3.00
(13)	Andre Dawson	11.00	8.25	4.50
(14)	Delino DeShields	11.00	8.25	4.50
(15)	Doug Drabek	11.00	8.25	4.50
(16)	Shawon Dunston	7.50	5.75	3.00
(17)	Len Dykstra	9.00	6.75	3.50
(18)	Cecil Fielder	9.00	6.75	3.50
(19)	John Franco	7.50	5.75	3.00
(20)	Dwight Gooden	6.50	5.00	2.50
(21)	Mark Grace	9.00	6.75	3.50
(22)	Ken Griffey, Jr.	11.00	8.25	4.50
(23)	Ken Griffey, Sr.	11.00	8.25	4.50
(24)	Kelly Gruber	7.50	5.75	3.00
(25)	Ozzie Guillen	9.00	6.75	3.50
(26)	Rickey Henderson	9.00	6.75	3.50
(27)	Bo Jackson (White Sox)	9.00	6.75	3.50
(28)	Bo Jackson (Royals)	6.50	5.00	2.50
(29)	Gregg Jefferies	6.50	5.00	2.50
(30)	Howard Johnson	9.00	6.75	3.50
(31)	Dave Justice	17.00	12.50	6.75
(32)	Roberto Kelly	7.50	5.75	3.00
(33)	Barry Larkin	7.50	5.75	3.00
(34)	Kevin Maas	6.50	5.00	2.50
(35)	Dave Magadan	9.00	6.75	3.50
(36)	Ramon Martinez	11.00	8.25	4.50
(37)	Don Mattingly	9.00	6.75	3.50
(38)	Ben McDonald	9.00	6.75	3.50
(39)	Mark McGwire	6.50	5.00	2.50
(40)	Kevin Mitchell	6.50	5.00	2.50
(41)	Kirby Puckett	11.00	8.25	4.50

		MT	NR MT	EX
(42)	Tim Raines	11.00	8.25	4.50
(43)	Nolan Ryan	17.00	12.50	6.75
(44)	Chris Sabo	7.50	5.75	3.00
(45)	Ryne Sandberg	11.00	8.25	4.50
(46)	Benito Santiago	9.00	6.75	3.50
(47)	Steve Sax	8.00	6.00	3.25
(48)	Dave Stewart	9.00	6.75	3.50
(49)	Darryl Strawberry (Dodgers)	9.00	6.75	3.50
(50)	Darryl Strawberry (Mets)	9.00	6.75	3.50
(51)	Alan Trammell	9.00	6.75	3.50
(52)	Frank Viola	7.50	5.75	3.00
(53)	Matt Williams	21.00	15.50	8.50
(54)	Todd Zeile	13.00	9.75	5.25

1992 Kenner Starting Lineup

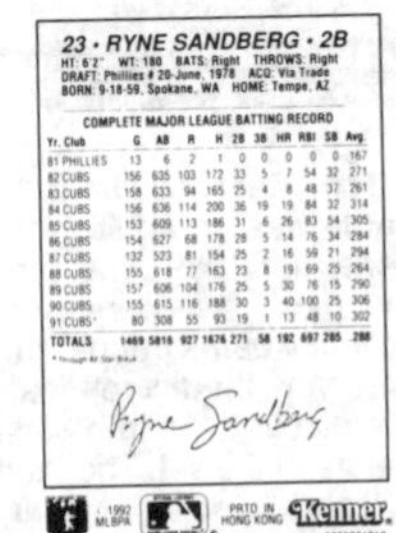

Kenner reduced its figurine/card set to 37 subjects in 1992. Unlike in past years, two cards were included with each figurine. A "rookie year" card and a regular card are featured. The players are listed here alphabetically. Values are based on demand and relative scarcity for complete unopened statue/card packages.

		MT	NR MT	EX
Complete Set:		400.00	300.00	150.00
Common Player:		5.00	3.75	2.00
(1)	Roberto Alomar	15.00	11.00	6.00
(2)	Steve Avery	15.00	11.00	6.00
(3)	George Bell	6.00	4.50	2.50
(4)	Albert Belle	11.00	8.25	4.50
(5)	Craig Biggio	9.00	6.75	3.50
(6)	Barry Bonds	11.00	8.25	4.50
(7)	Bobby Bonilla	6.00	4.50	2.50
(8)	Ivan Calderon	6.00	4.50	2.50
(9)	Jose Canseco	5.00	3.75	2.00
(10)	Will Clark	11.00	8.25	4.50
(11)	Roger Clemens	11.00	8.25	4.50
(12)	Eric Davis	5.00	3.75	2.00
(13)	Rob Dibble	5.00	3.75	2.00
(14)	Scott Erickson	6.00	4.50	2.50
(15)	Cecil Fielder	9.00	6.75	3.50
(16)	Chuck Finley	5.00	3.75	2.00
(17)	Tom Glavine	15.00	11.00	6.00
(18)	Juan Gonzalez	16.00	12.00	6.50
(19a)	Ken Griffey, Jr. (gray)	11.00	8.25	4.50
(19b)	Ken Griffey, Jr. (navy)	11.00	8.25	4.50
(20)	Tony Gwynn	9.00	6.75	3.50
(21)	Dave Henderson	5.00	3.75	2.00
(22)	Rickey Henderson	7.50	5.75	3.00
(23)	Bo Jackson (spring training)	9.00	6.75	3.50
(23)	Bo Jackson (running)	9.00	6.75	3.50
(24)	Howard Johnson	11.00	8.25	4.50
(25)	Felix Jose	11.00	8.25	4.50
(26)	Dave Justice	11.00	8.25	4.50
(27)	Kevin Maas	6.00	4.50	2.50
(28)	Ramon Martinez	5.00	3.75	2.00
(29)	Fred McGriff	11.00	8.25	4.50
(30)	Brian McRae	7.50	5.75	3.00
(31)	Kirby Puckett	11.00	8.25	4.50
(32)	Cal Ripken, Jr.			
(33)	Nolan Ryan	11.00	8.25	4.50
(34)	Bret Saberhagen	5.00	3.75	2.00
(35)	Chris Sabo	9.00	6.75	3.50
(36)	Ryne Sandberg	7.50	5.75	3.00
(37)	Tom Seaver	16.00	12.00	6.50
(38)	Ruben Sierra	13.00	9.75	5.25

		MT	NR MT	EX
(39)	Darryl Strawberry	7.50	5.75	3.00
(40)	Danny Tartabull	5.00	3.75	2.00
(41)	Frank Thomas			
(42)	Todd Van Poppel	9.00	6.75	3.50
(43)	Matt Williams	9.00	6.75	3.50

1993 Kenner Starting Lineup

In its sixth year, the roster of these popular little figurines continued with 43 players in 45 collectible poses. As before, the moveable figures were blister-packed with two baseball cards. The "regular" card features a player portrait wiht a wide white border at left and bottom, highlighted by green stripes. At top-left is a color team logo. The player's name is in black at bottom. Back is the same format used since 1988. Each 1993 figures also includes a "Special Series" card on which the player action photo is bordered in green with white accent stripes. The theme of the "Special Series" is printed at bottom, above the player's name. On back, printed in blue is a short career summary of the player, along logos of the toy company and major league baseball. As in the past, values of complete, unopened statue/cards packages listed alphabetically here are based on relative scarcity as well as demand.

		MT	NR MT	EX
Complete set:		150.00	110.00	60.00
Common player:		6.00	4.50	2.50
(1)	Roberto Alomar	8.00	6.00	3.25
(2)	Carlos Baerga	12.50	9.50	5.00
(3)	Jeff Bagwell	10.00	7.50	4.00
(4)	Barry Bonds (Pirates)	12.50	9.50	5.00
(4)	Barry Bonds (Giants)	12.50	9.50	5.00
(5)	Kevin Brown	6.00	4.50	2.50
(6)	Jose Canseco	8.00	6.00	3.25
(7)	Will Clark	8.00	6.00	3.25
(8)	Roger Clemens	7.50	5.75	3.00
(9)	David Cone	6.00	4.50	2.50
(10)	Carlton Fisk	10.00	7.50	4.00
(11)	Travis Fryman	6.00	4.50	2.50
(12)	Tom Glavine	10.00	7.50	4.00
(13)	Juan Gonzalez	12.50	9.50	5.00
(14)	Ken Griffey, Jr.	8.00	6.00	3.25
(15)	Marquis Grissom	6.00	4.50	2.50
(16)	Juan Guzman	6.00	4.50	2.50
(17)	Bo Jackson	7.50	5.75	3.00
(18)	Eric Karros	9.00	6.75	3.50
(19)	Roberto Kelly	6.00	4.50	2.50
(20)	John Kruk	10.00	7.50	4.00
(21)	Ray Lankford	6.00	4.50	2.50
(22)	Barry Larkin	6.00	4.50	2.50
(23)	Greg Maddux	8.00	6.00	3.25
(24)	Shane Mack	6.00	4.50	2.50
(25)	Jack McDowell	8.00	6.00	3.25
(26)	Fred McGriff	8.00	6.00	3.25
(27)	Mark McGwire	6.00	4.50	2.50
(28)	Mike Mussina	9.00	6.75	3.50
(29)	David Neid	12.50	9.50	5.00
(30)	Dean Palmer	6.00	4.50	2.50
(31)	Terry Pendleton	6.00	4.50	2.50
(32)	Kirby Puckett	9.00	6.75	3.50
(33)	Cal Ripken, Jr.	9.00	6.75	3.50
(34)	Bip Roberts	6.00	4.50	2.50
(35)	Nolan Ryan	12.50	9.50	5.00
(36)	Nolan Ryan (Retirement)	18.00	13.50	7.25

		MT	NR MT	EX
(37)	Ryne Sandberg	8.00	6.00	3.25
(38)	Benito Santiago	7.50	5.75	3.00
(39)	Gary Sheffield	9.00	6.75	3.50
(40)	John Smoltz	6.00	4.50	2.50
(41)	Frank Thomas	10.00	7.50	4.00
(42)	Andy Van Slyke	6.00	4.50	2.50
(43)	Robin Ventura	7.50	5.75	3.00
(44)	Larry Walker	6.00	4.50	2.50

1948 Leaf

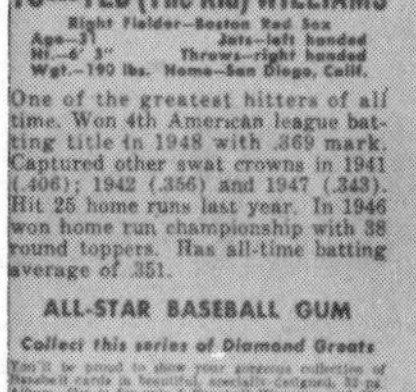

The first color baseball cards of the post-World War II era were the 98-card, 2-3/8" by 2-7/8", set produced by Chicago's Leaf Gum Company in 1948-1949. The color was crude, probably helping to make the set less popular than the Bowman issues of the same era. One of the toughest post-war sets to complete, exactly half of the Leaf issue - 49 of the cards - are significantly harder to find than the other 49. Probably intended to confound bubble gum buyers of the day, the set is skip-numbered between 1-168. Card backs contain offers of felt pennants, an album for the cards or 5-1/2" by 7-1/2" premium photos of Hall of Famers.

		NR MT	EX	VG
Complete Set (98):		30000.00	15000.00	9000.
Common Player:		25.00	12.50	7.50
Common short-print:		300.00	150.00	90.00
1	Joe DiMaggio	1750.00	875.00	525.00
3	Babe Ruth	2200.00	1100.00	660.00
4	*Stan Musial*	650.00	325.00	195.00
5	Virgil Trucks	400.00	200.00	120.00
8	*Satchel Paige*	2400.00	1200.00	720.00
10	Paul Trout	25.00	12.50	7.50
11	*Phil Rizzuto*	200.00	100.00	60.00
13	Casimer Michaels	300.00	150.00	90.00
14	Billy Johnson	30.00	15.00	9.00
17	Frank Overmire	25.00	12.50	7.50
19	John Wyrostek	300.00	150.00	90.00
20	*Hank Sauer*	400.00	200.00	120.00
22	Al Evans	25.00	12.50	7.50
26	Sam Chapman	25.00	12.50	7.50
27	Mickey Harris	25.00	12.50	7.50
28	*Jim Hegan*	30.00	15.00	9.00
29	*Elmer Valo*	30.00	15.00	9.00
30	*Bill Goodman*	300.00	150.00	90.00
31	Lou Brissie	25.00	12.50	7.50
32	*Warren Spahn*	300.00	150.00	90.00
33	Harry Lowrey	300.00	150.00	90.00
36	Al Zarilla	300.00	150.00	90.00
38	*Ted Kluszewski*	100.00	50.00	30.00
39	*Ewell Blackwell*	50.00	25.00	15.00
42	Kent Peterson	25.00	12.50	7.50
43	Eddie Stevens	300.00	150.00	90.00
45	Ken Keltner	300.00	150.00	90.00
46	Johnny Mize	90.00	45.00	27.00
47	George Vico	25.00	12.50	7.50
48	Johnny Schmitz	300.00	150.00	90.00
49	*Del Ennis*	40.00	20.00	12.00
50	Dick Wakefield	25.00	12.50	7.50
51	*Alvin Dark*	400.00	200.00	120.00

		NR MT	EX	VG
53	John Vandermeer	40.00	20.00	12.00
54	Bobby Adams	300.00	150.00	90.00
55	Tommy Henrich	400.00	200.00	120.00
56	*Larry Jensen*	30.00	15.00	9.00
57	Bob McCall	25.00	12.50	7.50
59	Luke Appling	80.00	40.00	24.00
61	Jake Early	25.00	12.50	7.50
62	Eddie Joost	300.00	150.00	90.00
63	Barney McCosky	300.00	150.00	90.00
65	Bob Elliot (Elliott)	25.00	12.50	7.50
66	Orval Grove	300.00	150.00	90.00
68	Ed Miller	300.00	150.00	90.00
70	Honus Wagner	250.00	125.00	75.00
72	Hank Edwards	25.00	12.50	7.50
73	Pat Seerey	25.00	12.50	7.50
75	Dom DiMaggio	500.00	250.00	150.00
76	Ted Williams	900.00	450.00	270.00
77	Roy Smalley	25.00	12.50	7.50
78	Walter Evers	300.00	150.00	90.00
79	*Jackie Robinson*	950.00	475.00	285.00
81	George Kurowski	300.00	150.00	90.00
82	Johnny Lindell	25.00	12.50	7.50
83	Bobby Doerr	100.00	50.00	30.00
84	Sid Hudson	25.00	12.50	7.50
85	*Dave Philley*	375.00	187.00	112.00
86	Ralph Weigel	25.00	12.50	7.50
88	Frank Gustine	300.00	150.00	90.00
91	*Ralph Kiner*	200.00	100.00	60.00
93	Bob Feller	1200.00	600.00	360.00
95	George Stirnweiss	25.00	12.50	7.50
97	*Martin Marion*	50.00	25.00	15.00
98	*Hal Newhouser*	600.00	300.00	180.00
102a	Gene Hermansk (incorrect spelling)	300.00	150.00	90.00
102b	Gene Hermanski (correct spelling)	25.00	12.50	7.50
104	Edward Stewart	300.00	150.00	90.00
106	Lou Boudreau	100.00	50.00	30.00
108	Matthew Batts	300.00	150.00	90.00
111	Gerald Priddy	25.00	12.50	7.50
113	Emil Leonard	300.00	150.00	90.00
117	Joe Gordon	25.00	12.50	7.50
120	*George Kell*	550.00	275.00	165.00
121	*John Pesky*	400.00	200.00	120.00
123	Clifford Fannin	300.00	150.00	90.00
125	*Andy Pafko*	30.00	15.00	9.00
127	Enos Slaughter	725.00	362.00	217.00
128	Warren Rosar	25.00	12.50	7.50
129	Kirby Higbe	300.00	150.00	90.00
131	Sid Gordon	300.00	150.00	90.00
133	Tommy Holmes	400.00	200.00	120.00
136a	Cliff Aberson (full sleeve)	25.00	12.50	7.50
136b	Cliff Aberson (short sleeve)	175.00	87.00	52.00
137	Harry Walker	300.00	150.00	90.00
138	*Larry Doby*	500.00	250.00	150.00
139	Johnny Hopp	25.00	12.50	7.50
142	*Danny Murtaugh*	400.00	200.00	120.00
143	Dick Sisler	300.00	150.00	90.00
144	Bob Dillinger	300.00	150.00	90.00
146	Harold Reiser	400.00	200.00	120.00
149	Henry Majeski	300.00	150.00	90.00
153	Floyd Baker	300.00	150.00	90.00
158	*Harry Brecheen*	400.00	200.00	120.00
159	Mizell Platt	25.00	12.50	7.50
160	Bob Scheffing	400.00	200.00	120.00
161	*Vernon Stephens*	400.00	200.00	120.00
163	*Freddy Hutchinson*	400.00	200.00	120.00
165	*Dale Mitchell*	400.00	200.00	120.00
168	Phil Cavaretta	400.00	200.00	120.00

1960 Leaf

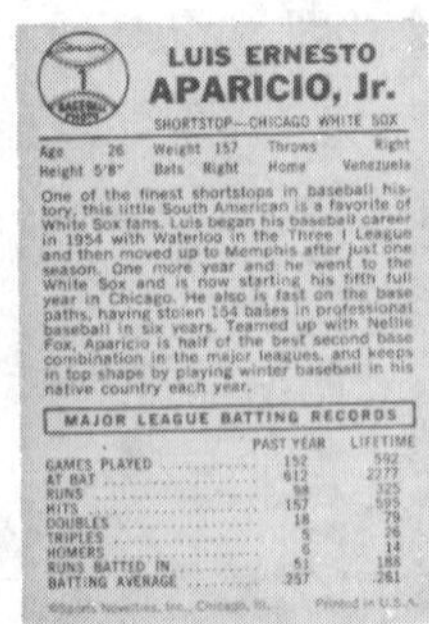

While known to the hobby as "Leaf" cards, this set of 144 cards carries the copyright of Sports Novelties Inc., Chicago. The 2-1/2" by 3-1/2" cards feature black and white player portrait photos, with background air-brushed away. Cards were sold in 5¢ wax packs with a marble, rather than a piece of bubble gum. The second half of the set, cards #73-144, are very scarce and make the set a real challenge for the collector. Card #25, Jim Grant, is found in two versions, with his own picture (black cap) and with a photo of Brooks Lawrence (white cap). Eight cards (#'s 1, 12, 17, 23, 35, 58, 61 and 72) exist with close-up photos that are much rarer than the normal cap to chest photos. It is believed the scarce "face only" cards are proof cards prepared by Leaf as only a handful are known to exist.

		NR MT	EX	VG
	Complete Set (145):	1400.00	700.00	420.00
	Common Player: 1-72	4.00	2.00	1.25
	Common Player: 73-145	15.00	7.50	4.50
1	Luis Aparicio	25.00	12.50	7.50
2	Woody Held	4.00	2.00	1.25
3	Frank Lary	4.00	2.00	1.25
4	Camilo Pascual	4.00	2.00	1.25
5	Frank Herrera	4.00	2.00	1.25
6	Felipe Alou	9.00	4.50	2.75
7	Bennie Daniels	4.00	2.00	1.25
8	Roger Craig	7.00	3.50	2.00
9	Eddie Kasko	4.00	2.00	1.25
10	Bob Grim	4.00	2.00	1.25
11	Jim Busby	4.00	2.00	1.25
12	Ken Boyer	8.00	4.00	2.50
13	Bob Boyd	4.00	2.00	1.25
14	Sam Jones	4.00	2.00	1.25
15	Larry Jackson	4.00	2.00	1.25
16	Roy Face	6.00	3.00	1.75
17	Walt Moryn	4.00	2.00	1.25
18	Jim Gilliam	6.00	3.00	1.75
19	Don Newcombe	4.00	2.00	1.25
20	Glen Hobbie	4.00	2.00	1.25
21	Pedro Ramos	4.00	2.00	1.25
22	Ryne Duren	5.00	2.50	1.50
23	Joe Jay	4.00	2.00	1.25
24	Lou Berberet	4.00	2.00	1.25
25a	Jim Grant (ERR)	14.00	7.00	4.25
25b	Jim Grant (COR)	20.00	10.00	6.00
26	Tom Borland	4.00	2.00	1.25
27	Brooks Robinson	40.00	20.00	12.00
28	Jerry Adair	4.00	2.00	1.25
29	Ron Jackson	4.00	2.00	1.25
30	George Strickland	4.00	2.00	1.25
31	Rocky Bridges	4.00	2.00	1.25
32	Bill Tuttle	4.00	2.00	1.25
33	Ken Hunt	4.00	2.00	1.25
34	Hal Griggs	4.00	2.00	1.25
35	Jim Coates	4.00	2.00	1.25
36	Brooks Lawrence	4.00	2.00	1.25
37	Duke Snider	50.00	25.00	15.00
38	Al Spangler	4.00	2.00	1.25
39	Jim Owens	4.00	2.00	1.25
40	Bill Virdon	4.00	2.00	1.25
41	Ernie Broglio	4.00	2.00	1.25
42	Andre Rodgers	4.00	2.00	1.25
43	Julio Becquer	4.00	2.00	1.25
44	Tony Taylor	4.00	2.00	1.25
45	Jerry Lynch	4.00	2.00	1.25
46	Clete Boyer	4.00	2.00	1.25
47	Jerry Lumpe	4.00	2.00	1.25
48	Charlie Maxwell	4.00	2.00	1.25
49	Jim Perry	4.00	2.00	1.25
50	Danny McDevitt	4.00	2.00	1.25
51	Juan Pizarro	4.00	2.00	1.25
52	*Dallas Green*	9.00	4.50	2.75
53	Bob Friend	4.00	2.00	1.25
54	Jack Sanford	4.00	2.00	1.25
55	Jim Rivera	4.00	2.00	1.25
56	Ted Wills	4.00	2.00	1.25
57	Milt Pappas	4.00	2.00	1.25
58a	Hal Smith (team & position on back)	4.00	2.00	1.25
58b	Hal Smith (team blackened out on back)	50.00	25.00	15.00
58c	Hal Smith (team missing on back)	50.00	25.00	15.00
59	Bob Avila	4.00	2.00	1.25
60	Clem Labine	4.00	2.00	1.25
61	Vic Rehm	4.00	2.00	1.25
62	John Gabler	4.00	2.00	1.25

#	Player	NR MT	EX	VG
63	John Tsitouris	4.00	2.00	1.25
64	Dave Sisler	4.00	2.00	1.25
65	Vic Power	4.00	2.00	1.25
66	Earl Battey	4.00	2.00	1.25
67	Bob Purkey	4.00	2.00	1.25
68	Moe Drabowsky	4.00	2.00	1.25
69	Hoyt Wilhelm	18.00	9.00	5.50
70	Humberto Robinson	4.00	2.00	1.25
71	Whitey Herzog	8.00	4.00	2.50
72	Dick Donovan	4.00	2.00	1.25
73	Gordon Jones	15.00	7.50	4.50
74	Joe Hicks	15.00	7.50	4.50
75	*Ray Culp*	18.00	9.00	5.50
76	Dick Drott	15.00	7.50	4.50
77	Bob Duliba	15.00	7.50	4.50
78	Art Ditmar	18.00	9.00	5.50
79	Steve Korcheck	15.00	7.50	4.50
80	Henry Mason	15.00	7.50	4.50
81	Harry Simpson	15.00	7.50	4.50
82	Gene Green	15.00	7.50	4.50
83	Bob Shaw	15.00	7.50	4.50
84	Howard Reed	15.00	7.50	4.50
85	Dick Stigman	15.00	7.50	4.50
86	Rip Repulski	15.00	7.50	4.50
87	Seth Morehead	15.00	7.50	4.50
88	Camilo Carreon	15.00	7.50	4.50
89	John Blanchard	18.00	9.00	5.50
90	Billy Hoeft	15.00	7.50	4.50
91	Fred Hopke	15.00	7.50	4.50
92	Joe Martin	15.00	7.50	4.50
93	Wally Shannon	15.00	7.50	4.50
94	Baseball's Two Hal Smiths (Hal Smith, Harold Wayne Smith)	20.00	10.00	6.00
95	Al Schroll	15.00	7.50	4.50
96	John Kucks	15.00	7.50	4.50
97	Tom Morgan	15.00	7.50	4.50
98	Willie Jones	15.00	7.50	4.50
99	Marshall Renfroe	18.00	9.00	5.50
100	Willie Tasby	15.00	7.50	4.50
101	Irv Noren	15.00	7.50	4.50
102	Russ Snyder	15.00	7.50	4.50
103	Bob Turley	20.00	10.00	6.00
104	Jim Woods	15.00	7.50	4.50
105	Ronnie Kline	15.00	7.50	4.50
106	Steve Bilko	15.00	7.50	4.50
107	Elmer Valo	15.00	7.50	4.50
108	Tom McAvoy	15.00	7.50	4.50
109	Stan Williams	15.00	7.50	4.50
110	Earl Averill	15.00	7.50	4.50
111	Lee Walls	15.00	7.50	4.50
112	Paul Richards	18.00	9.00	5.50
113	Ed Sadowski	15.00	7.50	4.50
114	Stover McIlwain	18.00	9.00	5.50
115	Chuck Tanner (photo actually Ken Kuhn)	20.00	10.00	6.00
116	Lou Klimchock	15.00	7.50	4.50
117	Neil Chrisley	15.00	7.50	4.50
118	John Callison	20.00	10.00	6.00
119	Hal Smith	15.00	7.50	4.50
120	Carl Sawatski	15.00	7.50	4.50
121	Frank Leja	15.00	7.50	4.50
122	Earl Torgeson	15.00	7.50	4.50
123	Art Schult	15.00	7.50	4.50
124	Jim Brosnan	18.00	9.00	5.50
125	Sparky Anderson	80.00	40.00	24.00
126	Joe Pignatano	15.00	7.50	4.50
127	Rocky Nelson	15.00	7.50	4.50
128	Orlando Cepeda	60.00	30.00	18.00
129	Daryl Spencer	15.00	7.50	4.50
130	Ralph Lumenti	15.00	7.50	4.50
131	Sam Taylor	15.00	7.50	4.50
132	Harry Brecheen	15.00	7.50	4.50
133	Johnny Groth	15.00	7.50	4.50
134	Wayne Terwilliger	15.00	7.50	4.50
135	Kent Hadley	15.00	7.50	4.50
136	Faye Throneberry	15.00	7.50	4.50
137	Jack Meyer	15.00	7.50	4.50
138	*Chuck Cottier*	15.00	7.50	4.50
139	Joe DeMaestri	15.00	7.50	4.50
140	Gene Freese	15.00	7.50	4.50
141	Curt Flood	35.00	17.50	10.50
142	Gino Cimoli	15.00	7.50	4.50
143	Clay Dalrymple	15.00	7.50	4.50
144	Jim Bunning	60.00	30.00	18.00

Definitions for grading conditions are located in the Introduction of this price guide.

1990 Leaf

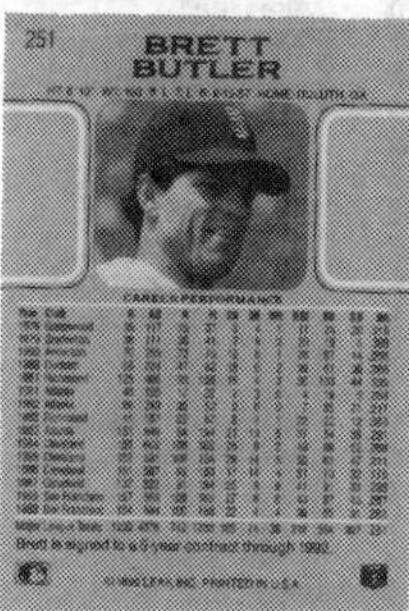

This 528-card set was issued in two 264-card series. The cards were printed on heavy quality stock and both the card fronts and backs have full color player photos. Cards also have an ultra-glossy finish on both the fronts and the backs. A high-tech foil Hall of Fame puzzle features former Yankee great Yogi Berra.

		MT	NR MT	EX
Complete Set (528):		275.00	200.00	125.00
Common Player:		.25	.20	.10
1	Introductory Card	.25	.20	.10
2	Mike Henneman	.25	.20	.10
3	Steve Bedrosian	.25	.20	.10
4	Mike Scott	.25	.20	.10
5	Allan Anderson	.25	.20	.10
6	Rick Sutcliffe	.35	.25	.14
7	Gregg Olson	1.00	.70	.40
8	Kevin Elster	.25	.20	.10
9	Pete O'Brien	.30	.25	.12
10	Carlton Fisk	1.00	.70	.40
11	Joe Magrane	.25	.20	.10
12	Roger Clemens	4.00	3.00	1.50
13	Tom Glavine	9.00	6.75	3.50
14	Tom Gordon	.25	.20	.10
15	Todd Benzinger	.25	.20	.10
16	Hubie Brooks	.25	.20	.10
17	Roberto Kelly	.35	.25	.14
18	Barry Larkin	.75	.60	.30
19	Mike Boddicker	.25	.20	.10
20	Roger McDowell	.25	.20	.10
21	Nolan Ryan	7.00	5.25	2.75
22	John Farrell	.25	.20	.10
23	Bruce Hurst	.25	.20	.10
24	Wally Joyner	.40	.30	.15
25	Greg Maddux	5.00	3.75	2.00
26	Chris Bosio	.30	.25	.12
27	John Cerutti	.25	.20	.10
28	Tim Burke	.25	.20	.10
29	Dennis Eckersley	.50	.40	.20
30	Glenn Davis	.25	.20	.10
31	Jim Abbott	4.00	3.00	1.50
32	Mike LaValliere	.25	.20	.10
33	Andres Thomas	.25	.20	.10
34	Lou Whitaker	.35	.25	.14
35	Alvin Davis	.25	.20	.10
36	Melido Perez	.25	.20	.10
37	Craig Biggio	.80	.60	.30
38	Rick Aguilera	.35	.25	.14
39	Pete Harnisch	.75	.60	.30
40	David Cone	.60	.45	.25
41	Scott Garrelts	.25	.20	.10
42	Jay Howell	.25	.20	.10
43	Eric King	.25	.20	.10
44	Pedro Guerrero	.35	.25	.14
45	Mike Bielecki	.25	.20	.10
46	Bob Boone	.35	.25	.14
47	Kevin Brown	.50	.40	.20
48	Jerry Browne	.25	.20	.10
49	Mike Scioscia	.25	.20	.10
50	Chuck Cary	.25	.20	.10
51	Wade Boggs	2.00	1.50	.80
52	Von Hayes	.25	.20	.10
53	Tony Fernandez	.35	.25	.14
54	Dennis Martinez	.35	.25	.14
55	Tom Candiotti	.30	.25	.12
56	Andy Benes	2.50	2.00	1.00
57	Rob Dibble	.40	.30	.15

#	Player	MT	NR MT	EX
58	Chuck Crim	.30	.25	.12
59	John Smoltz	4.50	3.50	1.75
60	Mike Heath	.25	.20	.10
61	Kevin Gross	.25	.20	.10
62	Mark McGwire	1.75	1.25	.70
63	Bert Blyleven	.35	.25	.14
64	Bob Walk	.30	.25	.12
65	Mickey Tettleton	.50	.40	.20
66	Sid Fernandez	.35	.25	.14
67	Terry Kennedy	.25	.20	.10
68	Fernando Valenzuela	.40	.30	.15
69	Don Mattingly	2.50	2.00	1.00
70	Paul O'Neill	.35	.25	.14
71	Robin Yount	2.00	1.50	.80
72	Bret Saberhagen	.30	.25	.12
73	Geno Petralli	.25	.20	.10
74	Brook Jacoby	.25	.20	.10
75	Roberto Alomar	8.00	6.00	3.25
76	Devon White	.35	.25	.14
77	Jose Lind	.30	.25	.12
78	Pat Combs	.25	.20	.10
79	Dave Steib	.35	.25	.14
80	Tim Wallach	.35	.25	.14
81	Dave Stewart	.35	.25	.14
82	Eric Anthony	2.00	1.50	.80
83	Randy Bush	.25	.20	.10
84	Checklist	.25	.20	.10
85	Jaime Navarro	.40	.30	.15
86	Tommy Gregg	.30	.25	.12
87	Frank Tanana	.25	.20	.10
88	Omar Vizquel	.30	.25	.12
89	Ivan Calderon	.30	.25	.12
90	Vince Coleman	.35	.25	.14
91	Barry Bonds	6.00	4.50	2.50
92	Randy Milligan	.35	.25	.14
93	Frank Viola	.35	.25	.14
94	Matt Williams	3.50	2.75	1.50
95	Alfredo Griffin	.30	.25	.12
96	Steve Sax	.35	.25	.14
97	Gary Gaetti	.35	.25	.14
98	Ryne Sandberg	4.00	3.00	1.50
99	Danny Tartabull	.35	.25	.14
100	Rafael Palmeiro	2.50	2.00	1.00
101	Jesse Orosco	.25	.20	.10
102	Garry Templeton	.25	.20	.10
103	Frank DiPino	.25	.20	.10
104	Tony Pena	.25	.20	.10
105	Dickie Thon	.25	.20	.10
106	Kelly Gruber	.30	.25	.12
107	Marquis Grissom	6.00	4.50	2.50
108	Jose Canseco	1.50	1.25	.60
109	Mike Blowers	.30	.25	.12
110	Tom Browning	.25	.20	.10
111	Greg Vaughn	2.00	1.50	.80
112	Oddibe McDowell	.25	.20	.10
113	Gary Ward	.25	.20	.10
114	Jay Buhner	1.00	.70	.40
115	Eric Show	.30	.25	.12
116	Bryan Harvey	1.00	.70	.40
117	Andy Van Slyke	.35	.25	.14
118	Jeff Ballard	.25	.20	.10
119	Barry Lyons	.25	.20	.10
120	Kevin Mitchell	.50	.40	.20
121	Mike Gallego	.30	.25	.12
122	Dave Smith	.25	.20	.10
123	Kirby Puckett	4.00	3.00	1.50
124	Jerome Walton	.25	.20	.10
125	Bo Jackson	3.00	2.25	1.25
126	Harold Baines	.35	.25	.14
127	Scott Bankhead	.25	.20	.10
128	Ozzie Guillen	.35	.25	.14
129	Jose Oquendo	.30	.25	.12
130	John Dopson	.30	.25	.12
131	Charlie Hayes	1.00	.70	.40
132	Fred McGriff	3.75	2.75	1.50
133	Chet Lemon	.25	.20	.10
134	Gary Carter	.35	.25	.14
135	Rafael Ramirez	.25	.20	.10
136	Shane Mack	.50	.40	.20
137	Mark Grace	.80	.60	.30
138	Phil Bradley	.25	.20	.10
139	Dwight Gooden	.40	.30	.15
140	Harold Reynolds	.35	.25	.14
141	Scott Fletcher	.30	.25	.12
142	Ozzie Smith	.80	.60	.30
143	Mike Greenwell	.80	.60	.30
144	Pete Smith	.30	.25	.12
145	Mark Gubicza	.30	.25	.12
146	Chris Sabo	.30	.25	.12
147	Ramon Martinez	.35	.25	.14
148	Dave Winfield	1.50	1.25	.60
149	Randy Myers	.35	.25	.14
150	Jody Reed	.25	.20	.10
151	Bruce Ruffin	.25	.20	.10
152	Jeff Russell	.35	.25	.14
153	Doug Jones	.25	.20	.10
154	Tony Gwynn	2.00	1.50	.80
155	Mark Langston	.50	.40	.20
156	Mitch Williams	.35	.25	.14
157	Gary Sheffield	6.00	4.50	2.50
158	Tom Henke	.25	.20	.10
159	Oil Can Boyd	.25	.20	.10
160	Rickey Henderson	1.75	1.25	.70
161	Bill Doran	.25	.20	.10
162	Chuck Finley	.40	.30	.15
163	Jeff King	.35	.25	.14
164	Nick Esasky	.25	.20	.10
165	Cecil Fielder	2.50	2.00	1.00
166	Dave Valle	.30	.25	.12
167	Robin Ventura	6.00	4.50	2.50
168	Jim Deshaies	.25	.20	.10
169	Juan Berenguer	.25	.20	.10
170	Craig Worthington	.25	.20	.10
171	Gregg Jefferies	4.50	3.50	1.75
172	Will Clark	3.00	2.25	1.25
173	Kirk Gibson	.35	.25	.14
174	Checklist	.25	.20	.10
175	Bobby Thigpen	.25	.20	.10
176	John Tudor	.25	.20	.10
177	Andre Dawson	.75	.60	.30
178	George Brett	2.00	1.50	.80
179	Steve Buechele	.30	.25	.12
180	Albert Belle	15.00	11.00	6.00
181	Eddie Murray	.80	.60	.30
182	Bob Geren	.25	.20	.10
183	Rob Murphy	.30	.25	.12
184	Tom Herr	.25	.20	.10
185	George Bell	.50	.40	.20
186	Spike Owen	.25	.20	.10
187	Cory Snyder	.25	.20	.10
188	Fred Lynn	.40	.30	.15
189	Eric Davis	.60	.45	.25
190	Dave Parker	.50	.40	.20
191	Jeff Blauser	.35	.25	.14
192	Matt Nokes	.30	.25	.12
193	Delino DeShields	6.00	4.50	2.50
194	Scott Sanderson	.25	.20	.10
195	Lance Parrish	.25	.20	.10
196	Bobby Bonilla	.60	.45	.25
197	Cal Ripken, Jr.	4.50	3.50	1.75
198	Kevin McReynolds	.35	.25	.14
199	Robby Thompson	.40	.30	.15
200	Tim Belcher	.25	.20	.10
201	Jesse Barfield	.25	.20	.10
202	Mariano Duncan	.25	.20	.10
203	Bill Spiers	.25	.20	.10
204	Frank White	.25	.20	.10
205	Julio Franco	.35	.25	.14
206	Greg Swindell	.25	.20	.10
207	Benito Santiago	.30	.25	.12
208	Johnny Ray	.25	.20	.10
209	Gary Redus	.30	.25	.12
210	Jeff Parrett	.30	.25	.12
211	Jimmy Key	.30	.25	.12
212	Tim Raines	.35	.25	.14
213	Carney Lansford	.25	.20	.10
214	Gerald Young	.25	.20	.10
215	Gene Larkin	.25	.20	.10
216	Dan Plesac	.25	.20	.10
217	Lonnie Smith	.25	.20	.10
218	Alan Trammell	.40	.30	.15
219	Jeffrey Leonard	.25	.20	.10
220	Sammy Sosa	5.00	3.75	2.00
221	Todd Zeile	1.75	1.25	.70
222	Bill Landrum	.25	.20	.10
223	Mike Devereaux	.60	.45	.25
224	Mike Marshall	.25	.20	.10
225	Jose Uribe	.25	.20	.10
226	Juan Samuel	.25	.20	.10
227	Mel Hall	.25	.20	.10
228	Kent Hrbek	.40	.30	.15
229	Shawon Dunston	.30	.25	.12
230	Kevin Seitzer	.25	.20	.10
231	Pete Incaviglia	.35	.25	.14
232	Sandy Alomar	.50	.40	.20
233	Bip Roberts	.30	.25	.12
234	Scott Terry	.25	.20	.10
235	Dwight Evans	.35	.25	.14
236	Ricky Jordan	.25	.20	.10
237	John Olerud	20.00	15.00	8.00
238	Zane Smith	.25	.20	.10
239	Walt Weiss	.30	.25	.12

		MT	NR MT	EX
240	Alvaro Espinoza	.25	.20	.10
241	Billy Hatcher	.30	.25	.12
242	Paul Molitor	1.50	1.25	.60
243	Dale Murphy	.80	.60	.30
244	Dave Bergman	.30	.25	.12
245	Ken Griffey, Jr.	25.00	18.50	10.00
246	Ed Whitson	.25	.20	.10
247	Kirk McCaskill	.25	.20	.10
248	Jay Bell	.50	.40	.20
249	Ben McDonald	3.00	2.25	1.25
250	Darryl Strawberry	.60	.45	.25
251	Brett Butler	.30	.25	.12
252	Terry Steinbach	.30	.25	.12
253	Ken Caminiti	.30	.25	.12
254	Dan Gladden	.25	.20	.10
255	Dwight Smith	.25	.20	.10
256	Kurt Stillwell	.25	.20	.10
257	Ruben Sierra	1.50	1.25	.60
258	Mike Schooler	.25	.20	.10
259	Lance Johnson	.35	.25	.14
260	Terry Pendleton	.50	.40	.20
261	Ellis Burks	.40	.30	.15
262	Len Dykstra	.90	.70	.35
263	Mookie Wilson	.25	.20	.10
264	Checklist (Nolan Ryan)	.50	.40	.20
265	No-Hit King (Nolan Ryan)	6.00	4.50	2.50
266	Brian DuBois	.35	.25	.14
267	Don Robinson	.30	.25	.12
268	Glenn Wilson	.25	.20	.10
269	Kevin Tapani	.75	.60	.30
270	Marvell Wynne	.25	.20	.10
271	Billy Ripken	.25	.20	.10
272	Howard Johnson	.50	.40	.20
273	Brian Holman	.35	.25	.14
274	Dan Pasqua	.30	.25	.12
275	Ken Dayley	.25	.20	.10
276	Jeff Reardon	.30	.25	.12
277	Jim Presley	.25	.20	.10
278	Jim Eisenreich	.30	.25	.12
279	Danny Jackson	.25	.20	.10
280	Orel Hershiser	.35	.25	.14
281	Andy Hawkins	.25	.20	.10
282	Jose Rijo	.40	.30	.15
283	Luis Rivera	.25	.20	.10
284	John Kruk	.60	.45	.25
285	Jeff Huson	.25	.20	.10
286	Joel Skinner	.25	.20	.10
287	Jack Clark	.35	.25	.14
288	Chili Davis	.35	.25	.14
289	Joe Girardi	.30	.25	.12
290	B.J. Surhoff	.25	.20	.10
291	Luis Sojo	.25	.20	.10
292	Tom Foley	.25	.20	.10
293	Mike Moore	.25	.20	.10
294	Ken Oberkfell	.25	.20	.10
295	Luis Polonia	.30	.25	.12
296	Doug Drabek	.35	.25	.14
297	Dave Justice	17.00	12.50	6.75
298	Paul Gibson	.25	.20	.10
299	Edgar Martinez	.60	.45	.25
300	Frank Thomas	62.00	46.00	25.00
301	Eric Yelding	.25	.20	.10
302	Greg Gagne	.30	.25	.12
303	Brad Komminsk	.25	.20	.10
304	Ron Darling	.25	.20	.10
305	Kevin Bass	.25	.20	.10
306	Jeff Hamilton	.25	.20	.10
307	Ron Karkovice	.25	.20	.10
308	Milt Thompson	.25	.20	.10
309	Mike Harkey	.25	.20	.10
310	Mel Stottlemyre	.25	.20	.10
311	Kenny Rogers	.35	.25	.14
312	Mitch Webster	.30	.25	.12
313	Kal Daniels	.25	.20	.10
314	Matt Nokes	.25	.20	.10
315	Dennis Lamp	.25	.20	.10
316	Ken Howell	.30	.25	.12
317	Glenallen Hill	.25	.20	.10
318	Dave Martinez	.30	.25	.12
319	Chris James	.25	.20	.10
320	Mike Pagliarulo	.30	.25	.12
321	Hal Morris	.40	.30	.15
322	Rob Deer	.25	.20	.10
323	Greg Olson	.30	.25	.12
324	Tony Phillips	.30	.25	.12
325	Larry Walker	9.00	6.75	3.50
326	Ron Hassey	.30	.25	.12
327	Jack Howell	.30	.25	.12
328	John Smiley	.25	.20	.10
329	Steve Finley	.50	.40	.20
330	Dave Magadan	.35	.25	.14

		MT	NR MT	EX
331	Greg Litton	.25	.20	.10
332	Mickey Hatcher	.30	.25	.12
333	Lee Guetterman	.25	.20	.10
334	Norm Charlton	.35	.25	.14
335	Edgar Diaz	.25	.20	.10
336	Willie Wilson	.30	.25	.12
337	Bobby Witt	.35	.25	.14
338	Candy Maldonado	.25	.20	.10
339	Craig Lefferts	.25	.20	.10
340	Dante Bichette	1.25	.90	.50
341	Wally Backman	.25	.20	.10
342	Dennis Cook	.25	.20	.10
343	Pat Borders	.40	.30	.15
344	Wallace Johnson	.25	.20	.10
345	Willie Randolph	.25	.20	.10
346	Danny Darwin	.25	.20	.10
347	Al Newman	.25	.20	.10
348	Mark Knudson	.25	.20	.10
349	Joe Boever	.25	.20	.10
350	Larry Sheets	.25	.20	.10
351	Mike Jackson	.25	.20	.10
352	Wayne Edwards	.25	.20	.10
353	Bernard Gilkey	3.00	2.25	1.25
354	Don Slaught	.30	.25	.12
355	Joe Orsulak	.30	.25	.12
356	John Franco	.35	.25	.14
357	Jeff Brantley	.25	.20	.10
358	Mike Morgan	.30	.25	.12
359	Deion Sanders	6.00	4.50	2.50
360	Terry Leach	.25	.20	.10
361	Les Lancaster	.25	.20	.10
362	Storm Davis	.25	.20	.10
363	Scott Coolbaugh	.25	.20	.10
364	Checklist	.25	.20	.10
365	Cecilio Guante	.25	.20	.10
366	Joey Cora	.25	.20	.10
367	Willie McGee	.35	.25	.14
368	Jerry Reed	.25	.20	.10
369	Darren Daulton	1.50	1.25	.60
370	Manny Lee	.25	.20	.10
371	Mark Gardner	.25	.20	.10
372	Rick Honeycutt	.25	.20	.10
373	Steve Balboni	.25	.20	.10
374	Jack Armstrong	.30	.25	.12
375	Charlie O'Brien	.25	.20	.10
376	Ron Gant	4.00	3.00	1.50
377	Lloyd Moseby	.25	.20	.10
378	Gene Harris	.30	.25	.12
379	Joe Carter	2.00	1.50	.80
380	Scott Bailes	.25	.20	.10
381	R.J. Reynolds	.25	.20	.10
382	Bob Melvin	.25	.20	.10
383	Tim Teufel	.30	.25	.12
384	John Burkett	2.00	1.50	.80
385	Felix Jose	1.00	.70	.40
386	Larry Andersen	.30	.25	.12
387	David West	.30	.25	.12
388	Luis Salazar	.20	.15	.08
389	Mike Macfarlane	.35	.25	.14
390	Charlie Hough	.30	.25	.12
391	Greg Briley	.35	.25	.14
392	Donn Pall	.30	.25	.12
393	Bryn Smith	.25	.20	.10
394	Carlos Quintana	.25	.20	.10
395	Steve Lake	.25	.20	.10
396	Mark Whiten	4.50	3.50	1.75
397	Edwin Nunez	.25	.20	.10
398	Rick Parker	.25	.20	.10
399	Mark Portugal	.25	.20	.10
400	Roy Smith	.25	.20	.10
401	Hector Villanueva	.25	.20	.10
402	Bob Milacki	.25	.20	.10
403	Alejandro Pena	.25	.20	.10
404	Scott Bradley	.25	.20	.10
405	Ron Kittle	.25	.20	.10
406	Bob Tewksbury	.30	.25	.12
407	Wes Gardner	.30	.25	.12
408	Ernie Whitt	.25	.20	.10
409	Terry Shumpert	.30	.25	.12
410	Tim Layana	.25	.20	.10
411	Chris Gwynn	.25	.20	.10
412	Jeff Robinson	.30	.25	.12
413	Scott Scudder	.25	.20	.10
414	Kevin Romine	.25	.20	.10
415	Jose DeJesus	.25	.20	.10
416	Mike Jeffcoat	.25	.20	.10
417	Rudy Seanez	.25	.20	.10
418	Mike Dunne	.25	.20	.10
419	Dick Schofield	.25	.20	.10
420	Steve Wilson	.35	.25	.14
421	Bill Krueger	.25	.20	.10

		MT	NR MT	EX
422	Junior Felix	.35	.25	.14
423	Drew Hall	.25	.20	.10
424	Curt Young	.25	.20	.10
425	Franklin Stubbs	.25	.20	.10
426	Dave Winfield	1.50	1.25	.60
427	Rick Reed	.25	.20	.10
428	Charlie Leibrandt	.25	.20	.10
429	Jeff Robinson	.30	.25	.12
430	Erik Hanson	.75	.60	.30
431	Barry Jones	.25	.20	.10
432	Alex Trevino	.25	.20	.10
433	John Moses	.25	.20	.10
434	Dave Johnson	.25	.20	.10
435	Mackey Sasser	.25	.20	.10
436	Rick Leach	.25	.20	.10
437	Lenny Harris	.25	.20	.10
438	Carlos Martinez	.25	.20	.10
439	Rex Hudler	.25	.20	.10
440	Domingo Ramos	.25	.20	.10
441	Gerald Perry	.25	.20	.10
442	John Russell	.25	.20	.10
443	Carlos Baerga	16.00	12.00	6.50
444	Checklist	.25	.20	.10
445	Stan Javier	.25	.20	.10
446	Kevin Maas	.35	.25	.14
447	Tom Brunansky	.25	.20	.10
448	Carmelo Martinez	.25	.20	.10
449	*Willie Blair*	.25	.20	.10
450	Andres Galarraga	1.00	.70	.40
451	Bud Black	.30	.25	.12
452	Greg Harris	.30	.25	.12
453	Joe Oliver	.40	.30	.15
454	Greg Brock	.25	.20	.10
455	Jeff Treadway	.25	.20	.10
456	Lance McCullers	.25	.20	.10
457	Dave Schmidt	.25	.20	.10
458	Todd Burns	.25	.20	.10
459	Max Venable	.25	.20	.10
460	Neal Heaton	.25	.20	.10
461	Mark Williamson	.25	.20	.10
462	Keith Miller	.25	.20	.10
463	Mike LaCoss	.25	.20	.10
464	Jose Offerman	.50	.40	.20
465	Jim Leyritz	.50	.40	.20
466	Glenn Braggs	.25	.20	.10
467	Ron Robinson	.25	.20	.10
468	Mark Davis	.25	.20	.10
469	Gary Pettis	.25	.20	.10
470	Keith Hernandez	.25	.20	.10
471	Dennis Rasmussen	.25	.20	.10
472	Mark Eichhorn	.25	.20	.10
473	Ted Power	.25	.20	.10
474	Terry Mulholland	.30	.25	.12
475	Todd Stottlemyre	.40	.30	.15
476	Jerry Goff	.25	.20	.10
477	Gene Nelson	.25	.20	.10
478	Rich Gedman	.25	.20	.10
479	Brian Harper	.25	.20	.10
480	Mike Felder	.25	.20	.10
481	Steve Avery	12.00	9.00	4.75
482	Jack Morris	.35	.25	.14
483	Randy Johnson	3.00	2.25	1.25
484	Scott Radinsky	.30	.25	.12
485	Jose DeLeon	.30	.25	.12
486	*Stan Belinda*	.40	.30	.15
487	Brain Holton	.30	.25	.12
488	Mark Carreon	.25	.20	.10
489	Trevor Wilson	.30	.25	.12
490	Mike Sharperson	.25	.20	.10
491	*Alan Mills*	.35	.25	.14
492	John Candelaria	.25	.20	.10
493	Paul Assenmacher	.25	.20	.10
494	Steve Crawford	.25	.20	.10
495	Brad Arnsberg	.25	.20	.10
496	Sergio Valdez	.25	.20	.10
497	Mark Parent	.25	.20	.10
498	Tom Pagnozzi	.25	.20	.10
499	Greg Harris	.30	.25	.12
500	Randy Ready	.25	.20	.10
501	Duane Ward	.30	.25	.12
502	Nelson Santovenia	.25	.20	.10
503	Joe Klink	.25	.20	.10
504	Eric Plunk	.25	.20	.10
505	Jeff Reed	.25	.20	.10
506	Ted Higuera	.25	.20	.10
507	Joe Hesketh	.25	.20	.10
508	Dan Petry	.25	.20	.10
509	Matt Young	.25	.20	.10
510	Jerald Clark	.50	.40	.20
511	*John Orton*	.40	.30	.15
512	Scott Ruskin	.30	.25	.12
513	Chris Hoiles	4.00	3.00	1.50
514	Daryl Boston	.25	.20	.10
515	Francisco Oliveras	.25	.20	.10
516	Ozzie Canseco	.30	.25	.12
517	Xavier Hernandez	.35	.25	.14
518	Fred Manrique	.25	.20	.10
519	Shawn Boskie	.30	.25	.12
520	Jeff Montgomery	.75	.60	.30
521	Jack Daugherty	.25	.20	.10
522	Keith Comstock	.25	.20	.10
523	*Greg Hibbard*	.30	.25	.12
524	Lee Smith	.40	.30	.15
525	Dana Kiecker	.25	.20	.10
526	Darrel Akerfelds	.25	.20	.10
527	Greg Myers	.25	.20	.10
528	Checklist	.25	.20	.10

1991 Leaf Previews

Cello packs of four cards previewing the 1991 Leaf set were included in each 1991 Donruss hobby factory set. The cards are identical in format to the regular 1991 Leafs, except there is a white notation, "1991 PREVIEW CARD" in white print beneath the statistics and career information on the back.

		MT	NR MT	EX
Complete Set (26):		30.00	22.00	12.00
Common Player:		.50	.40	.20
1	Dave Justice	1.00	.70	.40
2	Ryne Sandberg	3.00	2.25	1.25
3	Barry Larkin	.75	.60	.30
4	Craig Biggio	.50	.40	.20
5	Ramon Martinez	.50	.40	.20
6	Tim Wallach	.50	.40	.20
7	Dwight Gooden	.75	.60	.30
8	Len Dykstra	.75	.60	.30
9	Barry Bonds	2.00	1.50	.80
10	Ray Lankford	.60	.45	.25
11	Tony Gwynn	1.50	1.25	.60
12	Will Clark	2.00	1.50	.80
13	Leo Gomez	.50	.40	.20
14	Wade Boggs	1.50	1.25	.60
15	Chuck Finley	.50	.40	.20
16	Carlton Fisk	.75	.60	.30
17	Sandy Alomar, Jr.	.50	.40	.20
18	Cecil Fielder	2.00	1.50	.80
19	Bo Jackson	2.00	1.50	.80
20	Paul Molitor	1.50	1.25	.60
21	Kirby Puckett	2.00	1.50	.80
22	Don Mattingly	2.00	1.50	.80
23	Rickey Henderson	2.00	1.50	.80
24	Tino Martinez	.50	.40	.20
25	Nolan Ryan	5.00	3.75	2.00
26	Dave Steib	.50	.40	.20

1991 Leaf

Silver borders and black insets surround the full-color action photos on the 1991 Leaf cards. The set was once again released in two series. Series I consists of cards 1-264. Card backs feature an additional player photo, biographical information, statistics and career highlights.

The 1991 issue is not considered as scarce as the 1990 release. 1991 Leaf promo cards were first introduced in the 1991 Donruss factory sets.

		MT	NR MT	EX
Complete Set (528):		32.00	20.00	10.00
Common Player:		.08	.06	.03
1	The Leaf Card	.08	.06	.03
2	Kurt Stillwell	.08	.06	.03
3	Bobby Witt	.08	.06	.03
4	Tony Phillips	.08	.06	.03
5	Scott Garrelts	.08	.06	.03
6	Greg Swindell	.10	.08	.04
7	Billy Ripken	.08	.06	.03
8	Dave Martinez	.08	.06	.03
9	Kelly Gruber	.10	.08	.04
10	Juan Samuel	.10	.08	.04
11	Brian Holman	.08	.06	.03
12	Craig Biggio	.12	.09	.05
13	Lonnie Smith	.08	.06	.03
14	Ron Robinson	.08	.06	.03
15	Mike LaValliere	.08	.06	.03
16	Mark Davis	.08	.06	.03
17	Jack Daugherty	.08	.06	.03
18	Mike Henneman	.08	.06	.03
19	Mike Greenwell	.20	.15	.08
20	Dave Magadan	.12	.09	.05
21	Mark Williamson	.08	.06	.03
22	Marquis Grissom	.50	.40	.20
23	Pat Borders	.08	.06	.03
24	Mike Scioscia	.08	.06	.03
25	Shawon Dunston	.15	.11	.06
26	Randy Bush	.08	.06	.03
27	John Smoltz	.30	.25	.12
28	Chuck Crim	.08	.06	.03
29	Don Slaught	.08	.06	.03
30	Mike Macfarlane	.08	.06	.03
31	Wally Joyner	.20	.15	.08
32	Pat Combs	.10	.08	.04
33	Tony Pena	.10	.08	.04
34	Howard Johnson	.25	.20	.10
35	Leo Gomez	.35	.25	.14
36	Spike Owen	.08	.06	.03
37	Eric Davis	.15	.11	.06
38	Roberto Kelly	.10	.08	.04
39	Jerome Walton	.15	.11	.06
40	Shane Mack	.15	.11	.06
41	Kent Mercker	.10	.08	.04
42	B.J. Surhoff	.08	.06	.03
43	Jerry Browne	.08	.06	.03
44	Lee Smith	.10	.08	.04
45	Chuck Finley	.20	.15	.08
46	Terry Mulholland	.10	.08	.04
47	Tom Bolton	.08	.06	.03
48	Tom Herr	.08	.06	.03
49	Jim Deshaies	.08	.06	.03
50	Walt Weiss	.10	.08	.04
51	Hal Morris	.15	.11	.06
52	Lee Guetterman	.08	.06	.03
53	Paul Assenmacher	.08	.06	.03
54	Brian Harper	.10	.08	.04
55	Paul Gibson	.08	.06	.03
56	John Burkett	.08	.06	.03
57	Doug Jones	.08	.06	.03
58	Jose Oquendo	.08	.06	.03
59	Dick Schofield	.08	.06	.03
60	Dickie Thon	.08	.06	.03
61	Ramon Martinez	.12	.09	.05
62	Jay Buhner	.15	.11	.06
63	Mark Portugal	.08	.06	.03
64	Bob Welch	.10	.08	.04
65	Chris Sabo	.20	.15	.08
66	Chuck Cary	.08	.06	.03
67	Mark Langston	.15	.11	.06
68	Joe Boever	.08	.06	.03
69	Jody Reed	.10	.08	.04
70	Alejandro Pena	.08	.06	.03
71	Jeff King	.10	.08	.04
72	Tom Pagnozzi	.08	.06	.03
73	Joe Oliver	.08	.06	.03
74	Mike Witt	.08	.06	.03
75	Hector Villanueva	.15	.11	.06
76	Dan Gladden	.08	.06	.03
77	Dave Justice	1.25	.90	.50
78	Mike Gallego	.08	.06	.03
79	Tom Candiotti	.08	.06	.03
80	Ozzie Smith	.20	.15	.08
81	Luis Polonia	.08	.06	.03
82	Randy Ready	.08	.06	.03
83	Greg Harris	.08	.06	.03
84	Checklist (David Justice)	.25	.20	.10
85	Kevin Mitchell	.30	.25	.12
86	Mark McLemore	.08	.06	.03
87	Terry Steinbach	.08	.06	.03
88	Tom Browning	.10	.08	.04
89	Matt Nokes	.10	.08	.04
90	Mike Harkey	.12	.09	.05
91	Omar Vizquel	.08	.06	.03
92	Dave Bergman	.08	.06	.03
93	Matt Williams	.30	.25	.12
94	Steve Olin	.08	.06	.03
95	Craig Wilson	.20	.15	.08
96	Dave Stieb	.10	.08	.04
97	Ruben Sierra	.30	.25	.12
98	Jay Howell	.08	.06	.03
99	Scott Bradley	.08	.06	.03
100	Eric Yelding	.08	.06	.03
101	Rickey Henderson	.30	.25	.12
102	Jeff Reed	.08	.06	.03
103	Jimmy Key	.10	.08	.04
104	Terry Shumpert	.08	.06	.03
105	Kenny Rogers	.08	.06	.03
106	Cecil Fielder	.40	.30	.15
107	Robby Thompson	.08	.06	.03
108	Alex Cole	.10	.08	.04
109	Randy Milligan	.10	.08	.04
110	Andres Galarraga	.10	.08	.04
111	Bill Spiers	.08	.06	.03
112	Kal Daniels	.15	.11	.06
113	Henry Cotto	.08	.06	.03
114	Casy Candaele	.08	.06	.03
115	Jeff Blauser	.08	.06	.03
116	Robin Yount	.40	.30	.15
117	Ben McDonald	.20	.15	.08
118	Bret Saberhagen	.15	.11	.06
119	Juan Gonzalez	5.00	3.75	2.00
120	Lou Whitaker	.10	.08	.04
121	Ellis Burks	.20	.15	.08
122	Charlie O'Brien	.08	.06	.03
123	John Smiley	.10	.08	.04
124	Tim Burke	.08	.06	.03
125	John Olerud	1.25	.90	.50
126	Eddie Murray	.30	.25	.12
127	Greg Maddux	.30	.25	.12
128	Kevin Tapani	.12	.09	.05
129	Ron Gant	.50	.40	.20
130	Jay Bell	.10	.08	.04
131	Chris Hoiles	.20	.15	.08
132	Tom Gordon	.10	.08	.04
133	Kevin Seitzer	.08	.06	.03
134	Jeff Huson	.10	.08	.04
135	Jerry Don Gleaton	.08	.06	.03
136	Jeff Brantley	.08	.06	.03
137	Felix Fermin	.08	.06	.03
138	Mike Devereaux	.10	.08	.04
139	Delino DeShields	.20	.15	.08
140	David Wells	.08	.06	.03
141	Tim Crews	.08	.06	.03
142	Erik Hanson	.15	.11	.06
143	Mark Davidson	.08	.06	.03
144	Tommy Gregg	.08	.06	.03
145	Jim Gantner	.08	.06	.03
146	Jose Lind	.08	.06	.03
147	Danny Tartabull	.15	.11	.06
148	Geno Petralli	.08	.06	.03
149	Travis Fryman	3.00	2.25	1.25
150	Tim Naehring	.12	.09	.05
151	Kevin McReynolds	.12	.09	.05
152	Joe Orsulak	.08	.06	.03
153	Steve Frey	.15	.11	.06
154	Duane Ward	.08	.06	.03

		MT	NR MT	EX
155	Stan Javier	.08	.06	.03
156	Damon Berryhill	.08	.06	.03
157	Gene Larkin	.08	.06	.03
158	Greg Olson	.10	.08	.04
159	Mark Knudson	.08	.06	.03
160	Carmelo Martinez	.08	.06	.03
161	Storm Davis	.08	.06	.03
162	Jim Abbott	.20	.15	.08
163	Len Dykstra	.15	.11	.06
164	Tom Brunansky	.08	.06	.03
165	Dwight Gooden	.10	.08	.04
166	Jose Mesa	.08	.06	.03
167	Oil Can Boyd	.08	.06	.03
168	Barry Larkin	.15	.11	.06
169	Scott Sanderson	.08	.06	.03
170	Mark Grace	.20	.15	.08
171	Mark Guthrie	.08	.06	.03
172	Tom Glavine	.60	.45	.25
173	Gary Sheffield	1.00	.70	.40
174	Checklist (Roger Clemens)	.08	.06	.03
175	Chris James	.08	.06	.03
176	Milt Thompson	.08	.06	.03
177	Donnie Hill	.08	.06	.03
178	Wes Chamberlain	.40	.30	.15
179	John Marzano	.08	.06	.03
180	Frank Viola	.15	.11	.06
181	Eric Anthony	.15	.11	.06
182	Jose Canseco	.40	.30	.15
183	Scott Scudder	.10	.08	.04
184	Dave Eiland	.08	.06	.03
185	Luis Salazar	.08	.06	.03
186	Pedro Munoz	.20	.15	.08
187	Steve Searcy	.08	.06	.03
188	Don Robinson	.08	.06	.03
189	Sandy Alomar	.15	.11	.06
190	Jose DeLeon	.08	.06	.03
191	John Orton	.08	.06	.03
192	Darren Daulton	.08	.06	.03
193	Mike Morgan	.08	.06	.03
194	Greg Briley	.08	.06	.03
195	Karl Rhodes	.15	.11	.06
196	Harold Baines	.10	.08	.04
197	Bill Doran	.10	.08	.04
198	Alvaro Espinoza	.08	.06	.03
199	Kirk McCaskill	.10	.08	.04
200	Jose DeJesus	.10	.08	.04
201	Jack Clark	.10	.08	.04
202	Daryl Boston	.08	.06	.03
203	Randy Tomlin	.20	.15	.08
204	Pedro Guerrero	.15	.11	.06
205	Billy Hatcher	.08	.06	.03
206	Tim Leary	.08	.06	.03
207	Ryne Sandberg	.80	.60	.30
208	Kirby Puckett	.50	.40	.20
209	Charlie Leibrandt	.08	.06	.03
210	Rick Honeycutt	.08	.06	.03
211	Joel Skinner	.08	.06	.03
212	Rex Hudler	.08	.06	.03
213	Bryan Harvey	.10	.08	.04
214	Charlie Hayes	.10	.08	.04
215	Matt Young	.08	.06	.03
216	Terry Kennedy	.08	.06	.03
217	Carl Nichols	.08	.06	.03
218	Mike Moore	.08	.06	.03
219	Paul O'Neill	.10	.08	.04
220	Steve Sax	.10	.08	.04
221	Shawn Boskie	.10	.08	.04
222	Rich DeLucia	.30	.25	.12
223	Lloyd Moseby	.08	.06	.03
224	Mike Kingery	.08	.06	.03
225	Carlos Baerga	1.25	.90	.50
226	Bryn Smith	.08	.06	.03
227	Todd Stottlemyre	.10	.08	.04
228	Julio Franco	.10	.08	.04
229	Jim Gott	.08	.06	.03
230	Mike Schooler	.10	.08	.04
231	Steve Finley	.10	.08	.04
232	Dave Henderson	.10	.08	.04
233	Luis Quinones	.08	.06	.03
234	Mark Whiten	.40	.30	.15
235	Brian McRae	.50	.40	.20
236	Rich Gossage	.10	.08	.04
237	Rob Deer	.08	.06	.03
238	Will Clark	.50	.40	.20
239	Albert Belle	1.00	.70	.40
240	Bob Melvin	.08	.06	.03
241	Larry Walker	.50	.40	.20
242	Dante Bichette	.08	.06	.03
243	Orel Hershiser	.15	.11	.06
244	Pete O'Brien	.08	.06	.03
245	Pete Harnisch	.10	.08	.04
246	Jeff Treadway	.08	.06	.03
247	Julio Machado	.08	.06	.03
248	Dave Johnson	.08	.06	.03
249	Kirk Gibson	.12	.09	.05
250	Kevin Brown	.08	.06	.03
251	Milt Cuyler	.15	.11	.06
252	Jeff Reardon	.10	.08	.04
253	David Cone	.15	.11	.06
254	Gary Redus	.08	.06	.03
255	Junior Noboa	.08	.06	.03
256	Greg Myers	.08	.06	.03
257	Dennis Cook	.08	.06	.03
258	Joe Girardi	.08	.06	.03
259	Allan Anderson	.08	.06	.03
260	Paul Marak	.20	.15	.08
261	Barry Bonds	.70	.50	.30
262	Juan Bell	.10	.08	.04
263	Russ Morman	.08	.06	.03
264	Checklist (George Brett)	.20	.15	.08
265	Jerald Clark	.10	.08	.04
266	Dwight Evans	.10	.08	.04
267	Roberto Alomar	1.00	.70	.40
268	Danny Jackson	.08	.06	.03
269	Brian Downing	.08	.06	.03
270	John Cerutti	.08	.06	.03
271	Robin Ventura	.75	.60	.30
273	Wade Boggs	.20	.15	.08
274	Dennis Martinez	.15	.11	.06
275	Andy Benes	.20	.15	.08
276	Tony Fossas	.08	.06	.03
277	Franklin Stubbs	.08	.06	.03
278	John Kruk	.20	.15	.08
279	Kevin Gross	.10	.08	.04
280	Von Hayes	.10	.08	.04
281	Frank Thomas	6.00	4.50	2.50
282	Rob Dibble	.15	.11	.06
283	Mel Hall	.10	.08	.04
284	Rick Mahler	.08	.06	.03
285	Dennis Eckersley	.20	.15	.08
286	Bernard Gilkey	.25	.20	.10
287	Dan Plesac	.08	.06	.03
288	Jason Grimsley	.10	.08	.04
289	Mark Lewis	.20	.15	.08
290	Tony Gwynn	.40	.30	.15
291	Jeff Russell	.10	.08	.04
292	Curt Schilling	.10	.08	.04
293	Pascual Perez	.08	.06	.03
294	Jack Morris	.15	.11	.06
295	Hubie Brooks	.10	.08	.04
296	Alex Fernandez	1.00	.70	.40
297	Harold Reynolds	.10	.08	.04
298	Craig Worthington	.08	.06	.03
299	Willie Wilson	.08	.06	.03
300	Mike Maddux	.08	.06	.03
301	Dave Righetti	.10	.08	.04
302	Paul Molitor	.40	.30	.15
303	Gary Gaetti	.10	.08	.04
304	Terry Pendleton	.20	.15	.08
305	Kevin Elster	.08	.06	.03
306	Scott Fletcher	.08	.06	.03
307	Jeff Robinson	.08	.06	.03
308	Jesse Barfield	.10	.08	.04
309	Mike LaCoss	.08	.06	.03
310	Andy Van Slyke	.15	.11	.06
311	Glenallen Hill	.15	.11	.06
312	Bud Black	.08	.06	.03
313	Kent Hrbek	.15	.11	.06
314	Tim Teufel	.08	.06	.03
315	Tony Fernandez	.15	.11	.06
316	Beau Allred	.08	.06	.03
317	Curtis Wilkerson	.08	.06	.03
318	Bill Sampen	.08	.06	.03
319	Randy Johnson	.15	.11	.06
320	Mike Heath	.08	.06	.03
321	Sammy Sosa	.50	.40	.20
322	Mickey Tettleton	.15	.11	.06
323	Jose Vizcaino	.08	.06	.03
324	John Candelaria	.08	.06	.03
325	David Howard	.20	.15	.08
326	Jose Rijo	.10	.08	.04
327	Todd Zeile	.25	.20	.10
328	Gene Nelson	.08	.06	.03
329	Dwayne Henry	.08	.06	.03
330	Mike Boddicker	.08	.06	.03
331	Ozzie Guillen	.10	.08	.04
332	Sam Horn	.08	.06	.03
333	Wally Whitehurst	.08	.06	.03
334	Dave Parker	.10	.08	.04
335	George Brett	.25	.20	.10
336	Bobby Thigpen	.10	.08	.04
337	Ed Whitson	.08	.06	.03

		MT	NR MT	EX
338	Ivan Calderon	.10	.08	.04
339	Mike Pagliarulo	.08	.06	.03
340	Jack McDowell	.15	.11	.06
341	Dana Kiecker	.08	.06	.03
342	Fred McGriff	.40	.30	.15
343	Mark Lee	.08	.06	.03
344	Alfredo Griffin	.08	.06	.03
345	Scott Bankhead	.08	.06	.03
346	Darrin Jackson	.10	.08	.04
347	Rafael Palmeiro	.25	.20	.10
348	Steve Farr	.08	.06	.03
349	Hensley Meulens	.10	.08	.04
350	Danny Cox	.08	.06	.03
351	Alan Trammell	.15	.11	.06
352	Edwin Nunez	.08	.06	.03
353	Joe Carter	.25	.20	.10
354	Eric Show	.08	.06	.03
355	Vance Law	.08	.06	.03
356	Jeff Gray	.08	.06	.03
357	Bobby Bonilla	.20	.15	.08
358	Ernest Riles	.08	.06	.03
359	Ron Hassey	.08	.06	.03
360	Willie McGee	.12	.09	.05
361	Mackey Sasser	.08	.06	.03
362	Glenn Braggs	.08	.06	.03
363	Mario Diaz	.08	.06	.03
364	Checklist Barry Bonds	.08	.06	.03
365	Kevin Bass	.08	.06	.03
366	Pete Incaviglia	.10	.08	.04
367	Luis Sojo	.10	.08	.04
368	Lance Parrish	.10	.08	.04
369	Mark Leonard	.15	.11	.06
370	Heathcliff Slocumb	.10	.08	.04
371	Jimmy Jones	.08	.06	.03
372	Ken Griffey, Jr.	3.00	2.25	1.25
373	Chris Hammond	.20	.15	.08
374	Chili Davis	.10	.08	.04
375	Joey Cora	.08	.06	.03
376	Ken Hill	.15	.11	.06
377	Darryl Strawberry	.20	.15	.08
378	Ron Darling	.08	.06	.03
379	Sid Bream	.08	.06	.03
380	Bill Swift	.10	.08	.04
381	Shawn Abner	.08	.06	.03
382	Eric King	.08	.06	.03
383	Mickey Morandini	.15	.11	.06
384	Carlton Fisk	.30	.25	.12
385	Steve Lake	.08	.06	.03
386	Mike Jeffcoat	.08	.06	.03
387	Darren Holmes	.08	.06	.03
388	Tim Wallach	.10	.08	.04
389	George Bell	.15	.11	.06
390	Craig Lefferts	.08	.06	.03
391	Ernie Whitt	.08	.06	.03
392	Felix Jose	.25	.20	.10
393	Kevin Maas	.10	.08	.04
394	Devon White	.10	.08	.04
395	Otis Nixon	.10	.08	.04
396	Chuck Knoblauch	.75	.60	.30
397	Scott Coolbaugh	.08	.06	.03
398	Glenn Davis	.12	.09	.05
399	Manny Lee	.08	.06	.03
400	Andre Dawson	.20	.15	.08
401	Scott Chiamparino	.10	.08	.04
402	Bill Gullickson	.10	.08	.04
403	Lance Johnson	.08	.06	.03
404	Juan Agosto	.08	.06	.03
405	Danny Darwin	.08	.06	.03
406	Barry Jones	.08	.06	.03
407	Larry Andersen	.08	.06	.03
408	Luis Rivera	.08	.06	.03
409	Jaime Navarro	.12	.09	.05
410	Roger McDowell	.08	.06	.03
411	Brett Butler	.10	.08	.04
412	Dale Murphy	.15	.11	.06
413	Tim Raines	.15	.11	.06
414	Norm Charlton	.10	.08	.04
415	Greg Cadaret	.08	.06	.03
416	Chris Nabholz	.15	.11	.06
417	Dave Stewart	.10	.08	.04
418	Rich Gedman	.08	.06	.03
419	Willie Randolph	.10	.08	.04
420	Mitch Williams	.10	.08	.04
421	Brook Jacoby	.08	.06	.03
422	Greg Harris	.08	.06	.03
423	Nolan Ryan	3.00	2.25	1.25
424	Dave Rohde	.10	.08	.04
425	Don Mattingly	.50	.40	.20
426	Greg Gagne	.08	.06	.03
427	Vince Coleman	.10	.08	.04
428	Dan Pasqua	.08	.06	.03

		MT	NR MT	EX
429	Alvin Davis	.08	.06	.03
430	Cal Ripken	.75	.60	.30
431	Jamie Quirk	.08	.06	.03
432	Benito Santiago	.15	.11	.06
433	Jose Uribe	.08	.06	.03
434	Candy Maldonado	.08	.06	.03
435	Junior Felix	.10	.08	.04
436	Deion Sanders	.75	.60	.30
437	John Franco	.10	.08	.04
438	Greg Hibbard	.08	.06	.03
439	Floyd Bannister	.08	.06	.03
440	Steve Howe	.08	.06	.03
441	Steve Decker	.25	.20	.10
442	Vicente Palacios	.08	.06	.03
443	Pat Tabler	.08	.06	.03
444	Checklist Darryl Strawberry	.08	.06	.03
445	Mike Felder	.08	.06	.03
446	Al Newman	.08	.06	.03
447	Chris Donnels	.25	.20	.10
448	Rich Rodriguez	.10	.08	.04
449	Turner Ward	.15	.11	.06
450	Bob Walk	.08	.06	.03
451	Gilberto Reyes	.08	.06	.03
452	Mike Jackson	.08	.06	.03
453	Rafael Belliard	.08	.06	.03
454	Wayne Edwards	.08	.06	.03
455	Andy Allanson	.08	.06	.03
456	Dave Smith	.08	.06	.03
457	Gary Carter	.15	.11	.06
458	Warren Cromartie	.08	.06	.03
459	Jack Armstrong	.08	.06	.03
460	Bob Tewksbury	.10	.08	.04
461	Joe Klink	.08	.06	.03
462	Xavier Hernandez	.08	.06	.03
463	Scott Radinsky	.08	.06	.03
464	Jeff Robinson	.08	.06	.03
465	Gregg Jefferies	.40	.30	.15
466	Denny Neagle	.20	.15	.08
467	Carmelo Martinez	.08	.06	.03
468	Donn Pall	.08	.06	.03
469	Bruce Hurst	.10	.08	.04
470	Eric Bullock	.08	.06	.03
471	Rick Aguilera	.10	.08	.04
472	Charlie Hough	.08	.06	.03
473	Carlos Quintana	.08	.06	.03
474	Marty Barrett	.08	.06	.03
475	Kevin Brown	.10	.08	.04
476	Bobby Ojeda	.08	.06	.03
477	Edgar Martinez	.15	.11	.06
478	Bip Roberts	.08	.06	.03
479	Mike Flanagan	.08	.06	.03
480	John Habyan	.08	.06	.03
481	Larry Casian	.10	.08	.04
482	Wally Backman	.08	.06	.03
483	Doug Dascenzo	.08	.06	.03
484	Rick Dempsey	.08	.06	.03
485	Ed Sprague	.10	.08	.04
486	Steve Chitren	.10	.08	.04
487	Mark McGwire	.30	.25	.12
488	Roger Clemens	.50	.40	.20
489	Orlando Merced	.70	.50	.30
490	Rene Gonzales	.08	.06	.03
491	Mike Stanton	.08	.06	.03
492	Al Osuna	.15	.11	.06
493	Rick Cerone	.08	.06	.03
494	Mariano Duncan	.08	.06	.03
495	Zane Smith	.08	.06	.03
496	John Morris	.08	.06	.03
497	Frank Tanana	.08	.06	.03
498	Junior Ortiz	.08	.06	.03
499	Dave Winfield	.35	.25	.14
500	Gary Varsho	.08	.06	.03
501	Chico Walker	.08	.06	.03
502	Ken Caminiti	.08	.06	.03
503	Ken Griffey, Sr.	.10	.08	.04
504	Randy Myers	.10	.08	.04
505	Steve Bedrosian	.08	.06	.03
506	Cory Snyder	.10	.08	.04
507	Cris Carpenter	.08	.06	.03
508	Tim Belcher	.10	.08	.04
509	Jeff Hamilton	.08	.06	.03
510	Steve Avery	1.00	.70	.40
511	Dave Valle	.08	.06	.03
512	Tom Lampkin	.08	.06	.03
513	Shawn Hillegas	.08	.06	.03
514	Reggie Jefferson	.40	.30	.15
515	Ron Karkovice	.08	.06	.03
516	Doug Drabek	.10	.08	.04
517	Tom Henke	.10	.08	.04
518	Chris Bosio	.08	.06	.03
519	Gregg Olson	.12	.09	.05

		MT	NR MT	EX
520	Bob Scanlan	.10	.08	.04
521	Alonzo Powell	.10	.08	.04
522	Jeff Ballard	.08	.06	.03
523	Ray Lankford	.75	.60	.30
524	Tommy Greene	.15	.11	.06
525	Mike Timlin	.25	.20	.10
526	Juan Berenguer	.08	.06	.03
527	Scott Erickson	.20	.15	.08
528	Checklist Sandy Alomar, Jr.	.08	.06	.03

1991 Leaf Gold Rookies

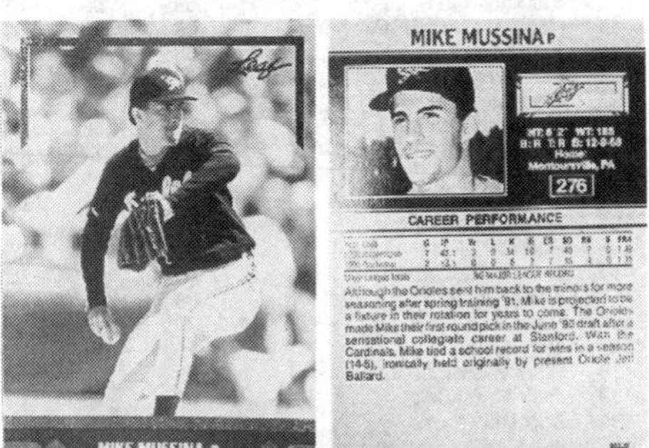

Special gold rookie and gold bonus cards were randomly inserted in 1991 Leaf packs. The card backs are designed in the same style as the regular Leaf cards with the exception of a gold back instead of silver. The card fronts feature a partial top inset with a banner on the bottom featuring the player's name and position. Variations of Series I cards exist. They can be found numbered 265-276 as an extension of the first series. The more common cards are numbered with a "BC" designation, BC1-BC12.

		MT	NR MT	EX
Complete Set (26):		60.00	45.00	24.00
Common Player:		1.00	.70	.40
1	Scott Leius	1.00	.70	.40
265	Scott Leius	8.00	6.00	3.25
2	Luis Gonzalez	3.00	2.25	1.25
266	Luis Gonzalez	25.00	18.50	10.00
3	Wil Cordero	3.00	2.25	1.25
267	Wil Cordero	25.00	18.50	10.00
4	Gary Scott	1.00	.70	.40
268	Gary Scott	8.00	6.00	3.25
5	Willie Banks	1.00	.70	.40
269	Willie Banks	8.00	6.00	3.25
6	Arthur Rhodes	2.00	1.50	.80
270	Arthur Rhodes	15.00	11.00	6.00
7	Mo Vaughn	6.00	4.50	2.50
271	Mo Vaughn	45.00	34.00	18.00
8	Henry Rodriguez	1.00	.70	.40
272	Henry Rodriguez	8.00	6.00	3.25
9	Todd Van Poppel	3.00	2.25	1.25
273	Todd Van Poppel	25.00	18.50	10.00
10	Reggie Sanders	3.00	2.25	1.25
274	Reggie Sanders	25.00	18.50	10.00
11	Rico Brogna	1.00	.70	.40
275	Rico Brogna	8.00	6.00	3.25
12	Mike Mussina	8.00	6.00	3.25
276	Mike Mussina	55.00	41.00	22.00
13	Kirk Dressendorfer	1.00	.70	.40
14	Jeff Bagwell	6.00	4.50	2.50
15	Pete Schourek	2.00	1.50	.80
16	Wade Taylor	1.00	.70	.40
17	Pat Kelly	2.00	1.50	.80
18	Tim Costo	2.00	1.50	.80
19	Roger Salkeld	2.00	1.50	.80
20	Andujar Cedeno	2.00	1.50	.80
21	Ryan Klesko	6.00	4.50	2.50
22	Mike Huff	1.00	.70	.40
23	Anthony Young	1.00	.70	.40
24	Eddie Zosky	2.00	1.50	.80
25	Nolan Ryan	3.00	2.25	1.25
26	Rickey Henderson (Record Steal)	1.50	1.25	.60

1992 Leaf Previews

Photos not available at press time

In a format identical to the regular-issue 1992 Leaf cards, this 26-card preview set was issued as a bonus in packs of four cards in each 1992 Donruss hobby factory set.

		MT	NR MT	EX
Complete Set (26):		80.00	60.00	32.00
Common Player:		1.00	.70	.40
1	Steve Avery	2.00	1.50	.80
2	Ryne Sandberg	5.00	3.75	2.00
3	Chris Sabo	1.50	1.25	.60
4	Jeff Bagwell	2.00	1.50	.80
5	Darryl Strawberry	2.00	1.50	.80
6	Bret Barberie	1.50	1.25	.60
7	Howard Johnson	1.50	1.25	.60
8	John Kruk	2.50	2.00	1.00
9	Andy Van Slyke	1.25	.90	.50
10	Felix Jose	1.50	1.25	.60
11	Fred McGriff	3.00	2.25	1.25
12	Will Clark	4.00	3.00	1.50
13	Cal Ripken, Jr.	5.00	3.75	2.00
14	Phil Plantier	2.00	1.50	.80
15	Lee Stevens	1.00	.70	.40
16	Frank Thomas	9.00	6.75	3.50
17	Mark Whiten	1.50	1.25	.60
18	Cecil Fielder	2.00	1.50	.80
19	George Brett	5.00	3.75	2.00
20	Robin Yount	4.00	3.00	1.50
21	Scott Erickson	1.00	.70	.40
22	Don Mattingly	4.00	3.00	1.50
23	Jose Canseco	3.00	2.25	1.25
24	Ken Griffey Jr.	9.00	6.75	3.50
25	Nolan Ryan	9.00	6.75	3.50
26	Joe Carter	2.50	2.00	1.00

1992 Leaf

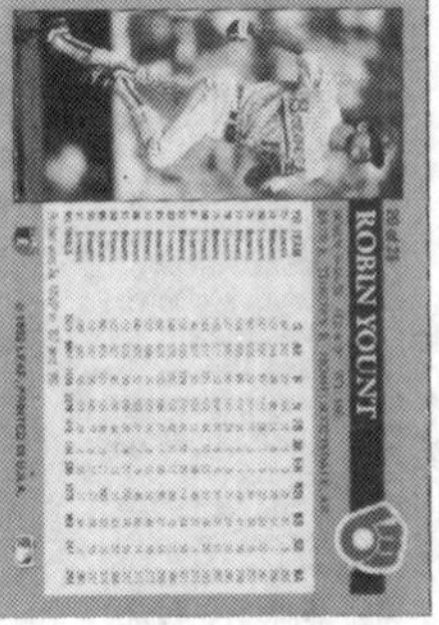

Two 264-card series comprise this 528-card set. The cards feature action photos on both the front and the back. Silver borders surround the photo on the card front. Each leaf card was also produced in a gold foil version. One gold card was issued per pack and a complete Leaf Gold Edition set can be assembled. Traded players and free agents are shown in uniform with their new teams.

		MT	NR MT	EX
Complete Set (528):		30.00	22.00	12.00
Common Player:		.08	.06	.03
1	Jim Abbott	.15	.10	.05
2	Cal Eldred	.40	.30	.15
3	Bud Black	.08	.06	.03
4	Dave Howard	.08	.06	.03
5	Luis Sojo	.08	.06	.03
6	Gary Scott	.12	.09	.05
7	Joe Oliver	.10	.08	.04
8	Chris Gardner	.10	.08	.04
9	Sandy Alomar	.10	.08	.04
10	Greg Harris	.10	.08	.04
11	Doug Drabek	.08	.06	.03
12	Darryl Hamilton	.15	.11	.06
13	Mike Mussina	1.00	.75	.40
14	Kevin Tapani	.15	.11	.06
15	Ron Gant	.20	.15	.08
16	Mark McGwire	.25	.15	.08
17	Robin Ventura	.25	.15	.08
18	Pedro Guerrero	.15	.11	.06
19	Roger Clemens	.40	.30	.15
20	Steve Farr	.08	.06	.03
21	Frank Tanana	.08	.06	.03
22	Joe Hesketh	.08	.06	.03
23	Erik Hanson	.12	.09	.05
24	Greg Cadaret	.08	.06	.03
25	Rex Hudler	.08	.06	.03
26	Mark Grace	.20	.15	.08
27	Kelly Gruber	.10	.08	.04
28	Jeff Bagwell	.80	.60	.30
29	Darryl Strawberry	.12	.09	.05
30	Dave Smith	.08	.06	.03
31	Kevin Appier	.15	.11	.06
32	Steve Chitren	.08	.06	.03
33	Kevin Gross	.08	.06	.03
34	Rick Aguilera	.10	.08	.04
35	Juan Guzman	.40	.30	.15
36	Joe Orsulak	.08	.06	.03
37	Tim Raines	.15	.11	.06
38	Harold Reynolds	.10	.08	.04
39	Charlie Hough	.08	.06	.03
40	Tony Phillips	.10	.08	.04
41	Nolan Ryan	1.25	.90	.50
42	Vince Coleman	.10	.08	.04
43	Andy Van Slyke	.15	.11	.06
44	Tim Burke	.08	.06	.03
45	Luis Polonia	.08	.06	.03
46	Tom Browning	.10	.08	.04
47	Willie McGee	.10	.08	.04
48	Gary DiSarcina	.10	.08	.04
49	Mark Lewis	.10	.08	.04
50	Phil Plantier	.25	.15	.08
51	Doug Dascenzo	.08	.06	.03
52	Cal Ripken, Jr.	.50	.30	.15
53	Pedro Munoz	.10	.08	.04
54	Carlos Hernandez	.15	.11	.06
55	Jerald Clark	.10	.08	.04
56	Jeff Brantley	.08	.06	.03
57	Don Mattingly	.25	.15	.08
58	Roger McDowell	.08	.06	.03
59	Steve Avery	.40	.30	.15
60	John Olerud	.75	.50	.25
61	Bill Gullickson	.08	.06	.03
62	Juan Gonzalez	2.00	1.50	.75
63	Felix Jose	.10	.08	.04
64	Robin Yount	.25	.20	.10
65	Greg Briley	.08	.06	.03
66	Steve Finley	.12	.09	.05
67	Checklist	.08	.06	.03
68	Tom Gordon	.08	.06	.03
69	Rob Dibble	.15	.11	.06
70	Glenallen Hill	.08	.06	.03
71	Calvin Jones	.08	.06	.03
72	Joe Girardi	.08	.06	.03
73	Barry Larkin	.15	.10	.05
74	Andy Benes	.20	.15	.08
75	Milt Cyler	.08	.06	.03
76	Kevin Bass	.08	.06	.03
77	Pete Harnisch	.10	.08	.04
78	Wilson Alvarez	.10	.08	.04
79	Mike Devereaux	.15	.11	.06
80	Doug Henry	.10	.08	.04
81	Orel Hershiser	.15	.11	.06
82	Shane Mack	.10	.08	.04
83	Mike Macfarlane	.10	.08	.04
84	Thomas Howard	.10	.08	.04
85	Alex Fernandez	.20	.15	.08
86	Reggie Jefferson	.30	.25	.12
87	Leo Gomez	.20	.15	.08
88	Mel Hall	.10	.08	.04
89	Mike Greenwell	.15	.11	.06
90	Jeff Russell	.10	.08	.04
91	Steve Buechele	.10	.08	.04
92	David Cone	.15	.11	.06
93	Kevin Reimer	.10	.08	.04
94	Mark Lemke	.10	.08	.04
95	Bob Tewksbury	.10	.08	.04
96	Zane Smith	.10	.08	.04
97	Mark Eichhorn	.08	.06	.03
98	Kirby Puckett	.50	.30	.15
99	Paul O'Neill	.12	.09	.05
100	Dennis Eckersley	.12	.09	.05
101	Duane Ward	.10	.08	.04
102	Matt Nokes	.10	.08	.04
103	Mo Vaughn	.30	.25	.12
104	Pat Kelly	.10	.08	.04
105	Ron Karkovice	.08	.06	.03
106	Bill Spiers	.08	.06	.03
107	Gary Gaetti	.10	.08	.04
108	Mackey Sasser	.08	.06	.03
109	Robby Thompson	.10	.08	.04
110	Marvin Freeman	.08	.06	.03
111	Jimmy Key	.10	.08	.04
112	Dwight Gooden	.12	.09	.05
113	Charlie Leibrandt	.08	.06	.03
114	Devon White	.10	.08	.04
115	Charles Nagy	.10	.08	.04
116	Rickey Henderson	.25	.15	.08
117	Paul Assenmacher	.08	.06	.03
118	Junior Felix	.10	.08	.04
119	Julio Franco	.20	.15	.08
120	Norm Charlton	.10	.08	.04
121	Scott Servais	.10	.08	.04
122	Gerald Perry	.08	.06	.03
123	Brian McRae	.12	.09	.05
124	Don Slaught	.08	.06	.03
125	Juan Samuel	.08	.06	.03
126	Harold Baines	.15	.11	.06
127	Scott Livingstone	.15	.11	.06
128	Jay Buhner	.10	.08	.04
129	Darrin Jackson	.10	.08	.04
130	Luis Mercedes	.20	.15	.08
131	Brian Harper	.10	.08	.04
132	Howard Johnson	.08	.06	.03
133	Checklist	.08	.06	.03
134	Dante Bichette	.08	.06	.03
135	Dave Righetti	.10	.08	.04
136	Jeff Montgomery	.10	.08	.04
137	Joe Grahe	.10	.08	.04
138	Delino DeShields	.25	.20	.10
139	Jose Rijo	.12	.09	.05
140	Ken Caminiti	.10	.08	.04
141	Steve Olin	.10	.08	.04
142	Kurt Stillwell	.10	.08	.04
143	Jay Bell	.12	.09	.05
144	Jaime Navarro	.12	.09	.05
145	Ben McDonald	.30	.25	.12
146	Greg Gagne	.08	.06	.03
147	Jeff Blauser	.10	.08	.04
148	Carney Lansford	.10	.08	.04
149	Ozzie Guillen	.10	.08	.04
150	Milt Thompson	.08	.06	.03
151	Jeff Reardon	.15	.11	.06
152	Scott Sanderson	.08	.06	.03
153	Cecil Fielder	.25	.15	.08
154	Greg Harris	.08	.06	.03
155	Rich DeLucia	.08	.06	.03
156	Roberto Kelly	.10	.08	.04
157	Bryn Smith	.08	.06	.03
158	Chuck McElroy	.08	.06	.03
159	Tom Henke	.12	.09	.05
160	Luis Gonzalez	.08	.06	.03
161	Steve Wilson	.08	.06	.03
162	Shawn Boskie	.08	.06	.03
163	Mark Davis	.08	.06	.03
164	Mike Moore	.10	.08	.04
165	Mike Scioscia	.10	.08	.04
166	Scott Erickson	.10	.08	.04
167	Todd Stottlemyre	.10	.08	.04
168	Alvin Davis	.10	.08	.04
169	Greg Hibbard	.10	.08	.04
170	David Valle	.08	.06	.03
171	Dave Winfield	.25	.15	.08
172	Alan Trammell	.12	.09	.05
173	Kenny Rogers	.08	.06	.03
174	John Franco	.10	.08	.04
175	Jose Lind	.08	.06	.03
176	Pete Schourek	.10	.08	.04
177	Von Hayes	.08	.06	.03
178	Chris Hammond	.10	.08	.04
179	John Burkett	.08	.06	.03
180	Dickie Thon	.08	.06	.03

		MT	NR MT	EX
181	Joel Skinner	.08	.06	.03
182	Scott Cooper	.12	.09	.05
183	Andre Dawson	.15	.10	.05
184	Billy Ripken	.08	.06	.03
185	Kevin Mitchell	.10	.08	.04
186	Brett Butler	.10	.08	.04
187	Tony Fernandez	.10	.08	.04
188	Cory Snyder	.10	.08	.04
189	John Habyan	.08	.06	.03
190	Dennis Martinez	.12	.09	.05
191	John Smoltz	.15	.11	.06
192	Greg Myers	.08	.06	.03
193	Rob Deer	.10	.08	.04
194	Ivan Rodriguez	.80	.60	.30
195	Ray Lankford	.25	.15	.08
196	Bill Wegman	.10	.08	.04
197	Edgar Martinez	.15	.11	.06
198	Darryl Kile	.10	.08	.04
199	Checklist	.08	.06	.03
200	Brent Mayne	.08	.06	.03
201	Larry Walker	.20	.15	.08
202	Carlos Baerga	.50	.30	.15
203	Russ Swan	.08	.06	.03
204	Mike Morgan	.10	.08	.04
205	Hal Morris	.10	.08	.04
206	Tony Gwynn	.20	.15	.08
207	Mark Leiter	.08	.06	.03
208	Kirt Manwaring	.08	.06	.03
209	Al Osuna	.08	.06	.03
210	Bobby Thigpen	.08	.06	.04
211	Chris Hoiles	.15	.10	.05
212	B.J. Surhoff	.10	.08	.04
213	Lenny Harris	.08	.06	.03
214	Scott Leius	.10	.08	.04
215	Gregg Jefferies	.25	.20	.10
216	Bruce Hurst	.10	.08	.04
217	Steve Sax	.12	.09	.05
218	Dave Otto	.08	.06	.03
219	Sam Horn	.08	.06	.03
220	Charlie Hayes	.10	.08	.04
221	Frank Viola	.10	.08	.04
222	Jose Guzman	.10	.08	.04
223	Gary Redus	.08	.06	.03
224	Dave Gallagher	.08	.06	.03
225	Dean Palmer	.60	.45	.25
226	Greg Olson	.10	.08	.04
227	Jose DeLeon	.08	.06	.03
228	Mike LaValliere	.08	.06	.03
229	Mark Langston	.15	.11	.06
230	Chuck Knoblauch	.25	.15	.08
231	Bill Doran	.10	.08	.04
232	Dave Henderson	.10	.08	.04
233	Roberto Alomar	.50	.40	.20
234	Scott Fletcher	.08	.06	.03
235	Tim Naehring	.08	.06	.03
236	Mike Gallego	.08	.06	.03
237	Lance Johnson	.10	.08	.04
238	Paul Molitor	.25	.15	.08
239	Dan Gladden	.08	.06	.03
240	Willie Randolph	.10	.08	.04
241	Will Clark	.30	.20	.10
242	Sid Bream	.08	.06	.03
243	Derek Bell	.50	.40	.20
244	Bill Pecota	.08	.06	.03
245	Terry Pendleton	.15	.11	.06
246	Randy Ready	.08	.06	.03
247	Jack Armstrong	.08	.06	.03
248	Todd Van Poppel	.40	.30	.15
249	Shawon Dunston	.10	.08	.04
250	Bobby Rose	.08	.06	.03
251	Jeff Huson	.08	.06	.03
252	Bip Roberts	.12	.09	.05
253	Doug Jones	.10	.08	.04
254	Lee Smith	.15	.11	.06
255	George Brett	.25	.20	.10
256	Randy Tomlin	.10	.08	.04
257	Todd Benzinger	.08	.06	.03
258	Dave Stewart	.15	.11	.06
259	Mark Carreon	.08	.06	.03
260	Pete O'Brien	.08	.06	.03
261	Tim Teufel	.08	.06	.03
262	Bob Milacki	.08	.06	.03
263	Mark Guthrie	.08	.06	.03
264	Darrin Fletcher	.08	.06	.03
265	Omar Vizquel	.08	.06	.03
266	Chris Bosio	.10	.08	.04
267	Jose Canseco	.25	.15	.08
268	Mike Boddicker	.08	.06	.03
269	Lance Parrish	.10	.08	.04
270	Jose Vizcaino	.08	.06	.03
271	Chris Sabo	.15	.11	.06

		MT	NR MT	EX
272	Royce Clayton	.20	.15	.08
273	Marquis Grissom	.20	.15	.08
274	Fred McGriff	.20	.15	.08
275	Barry Bonds	.60	.45	.25
276	Greg Vaughn	.15	.11	.06
277	Gregg Olson	.12	.09	.05
278	Dave Hollins	.20	.15	.08
279	Tom Glavine	.20	.15	.08
280	Bryan Hickerson	.15	.11	.06
281	Scott Radinsky	.08	.06	.03
282	Omar Olivares	.10	.08	.04
283	Ivan Calderon	.12	.09	.05
284	Kevin Maas	.15	.11	.06
285	Mickey Tettleton	.15	.11	.06
286	Wade Boggs	.20	.15	.08
287	Stan Belinda	.08	.06	.03
288	Bret Barberie	.10	.08	.04
289	Jose Oquendo	.08	.06	.03
290	Frank Castillo	.12	.09	.05
291	Dave Stieb	.10	.08	.04
292	Tommy Greene	.12	.09	.05
293	Eric Karros	.75	.50	.25
294	Greg Maddux	.25	.20	.10
295	Jim Eisenreich	.08	.06	.03
296	Rafael Palmeiro	.15	.11	.06
297	Ramon Martinez	.20	.15	.08
298	Tim Wallach	.10	.08	.04
299	Jim Thome	.50	.40	.20
300	Chito Martinez	.10	.08	.04
301	Mitch Williams	.12	.09	.05
302	Randy Johnson	.10	.08	.04
303	Carlton Fisk	.20	.15	.08
304	Travis Fryman	.80	.60	.30
305	Bobby Witt	.10	.08	.04
306	Dave Magadan	.10	.08	.04
307	Alex Cole	.08	.06	.03
308	Bobby Bonilla	.15	.10	.05
309	Bryan Harvey	.12	.09	.05
310	Rafael Belliard	.08	.06	.03
311	Mariano Duncan	.08	.06	.03
312	Chuck Crim	.08	.06	.03
313	John Kruk	.15	.11	.06
314	Ellis Burks	.15	.11	.06
315	Craig Biggio	.15	.11	.06
316	Glenn Davis	.10	.08	.04
317	Ryne Sandberg	.50	.30	.15
318	Mike Sharperson	.08	.06	.03
319	Rich Rodriguez	.08	.06	.03
320	Lee Guetterman	.08	.06	.03
321	Benito Santiago	.15	.11	.06
322	Jose Offerman	.12	.09	.05
323	Tony Pena	.10	.08	.04
324	Pat Borders	.10	.08	.04
325	Mike Henneman	.10	.08	.04
326	Kevin Brown	.15	.11	.06
327	Chris Nabholz	.10	.08	.04
328	Franklin Stubbs	.08	.06	.03
329	Tino Martinez	.15	.11	.06
330	Mickey Morandini	.15	.11	.06
331	Checklist	.08	.06	.03
332	Mark Gubicza	.10	.08	.04
333	Bill Landrum	.08	.06	.03
334	Mark Whiten	.15	.11	.06
335	Darren Daulton	.20	.15	.08
336	Rick Wilkins	.12	.09	.05
337	Brian Jordan	.50	.40	.20
338	Kevin Ward	.12	.09	.05
339	Ruben Amaro	.12	.09	.05
340	Trevor Wilson	.10	.08	.04
341	Andujar Cedeno	.15	.11	.06
342	Michael Huff	.08	.06	.03
343	Brady Anderson	.15	.11	.06
344	Craig Grebeck	.08	.06	.03
345	Bobby Ojeda	.08	.06	.03
346	Mike Pagliarulo	.08	.06	.03
347	Terry Shumpert	.08	.06	.03
348	Dann Bilardello	.08	.06	.03
349	Frank Thomas	3.50	2.25	1.25
350	Albert Belle	.50	.40	.20
351	Jose Mesa	.08	.06	.03
352	Rich Monteleone	.08	.06	.03
353	Bob Walk	.08	.06	.03
354	Monty Fariss	.10	.08	.04
355	Luis Rivera	.08	.06	.03
356	Anthony Young	.12	.09	.05
357	Geno Petralli	.08	.06	.03
358	Otis Nixon	.10	.08	.04
359	Tom Pagnozzi	.10	.08	.04
360	Reggie Sanders	.50	.40	.20
361	Lee Stevens	.08	.06	.03
362	Kent Hrbek	.15	.11	.06

		MT	NR MT	EX
363	Orlando Merced	.10	.08	.04
364	Mike Bordick	.20	.15	.08
365	Dion James	.08	.06	.03
366	Jack Clark	.10	.08	.04
367	Mike Stanley	.08	.06	.03
368	Randy Velarde	.08	.06	.03
369	Dan Pasqua	.08	.06	.03
370	Pat Listach	.50	.30	.15
371	Mike Fitzgerald	.08	.06	.03
372	Tom Foley	.08	.06	.03
373	Matt Williams	.20	.15	.06
374	Brian Hunter	.15	.11	.06
375	Joe Carter	.25	.20	.10
376	Bret Saberhagen	.15	.11	.06
377	Mike Stanton	.08	.06	.03
378	Hubie Brooks	.08	.06	.03
379	Eric Bell	.12	.09	.05
380	Walt Weiss	.10	.08	.04
381	Danny Jackson	.08	.06	.03
382	Manuel Lee	.08	.06	.03
383	Ruben Sierra	.15	.10	.05
384	Greg Swindell	.15	.11	.06
385	Ryan Bowen	.12	.09	.05
386	Kevin Ritz	.10	.08	.04
387	Curtis Wilkerson	.08	.06	.03
388	Gary Varsho	.08	.06	.03
389	Dave Hansen	.08	.06	.03
390	Bob Welch	.10	.08	.04
391	Lou Whitaker	.12	.09	.05
392	Ken Griffey, Jr.	2.00	1.25	.60
393	Mike Maddux	.08	.06	.03
394	Arthur Rhodes	.15	.11	.06
395	Chili Davis	.10	.08	.04
396	Eddie Murray	.15	.11	.06
397	Checklist	.08	.06	.03
398	Dave Cochrane	.08	.06	.03
399	Kevin Seitzer	.10	.08	.04
400	Ozzie Smith	.20	.15	.08
401	Paul Sorrento	.10	.08	.04
402	Les Lancaster	.08	.06	.03
403	Junior Noboa	.08	.06	.03
404	Dave Justice	.60	.40	.20
405	Andy Ashby	.12	.09	.05
406	Danny Tartabull	.15	.11	.06
407	Bill Swift	.10	.08	.04
408	Craig Lefferts	.10	.08	.04
409	Tom Candiotti	.10	.08	.04
410	Lance Blankenship	.08	.06	.03
411	Jeff Tackett	.15	.11	.06
412	Sammy Sosa	.25	.15	.08
413	Jody Reed	.10	.08	.04
414	Bruce Ruffin	.08	.06	.03
415	Gene Larkin	.08	.06	.03
416	John Vanderwal	.10	.08	.04
417	Tim Belcher	.10	.08	.04
418	Steve Frey	.08	.06	.03
419	Dick Schofield	.08	.06	.03
420	Jeff King	.10	.08	.04
421	Kim Batiste	.12	.09	.05
422	Jack McDowell	.15	.11	.06
423	Damon Berryhill	.08	.06	.03
424	Gary Wayne	.08	.06	.03
425	Jack Morris	.15	.11	.06
426	Moises Alou	.20	.15	.08
427	Mark McLemore	.08	.06	.03
428	Juan Guerrero	.15	.11	.06
429	Scott Scudder	.08	.06	.03
430	Eric Davis	.20	.15	.08
431	Joe Slusarski	.10	.08	.04
432	Todd Zeile	.15	.11	.06
433	Dwayne Henry	.08	.06	.03
434	Cliff Brantley	.15	.11	.06
435	Butch Henry	.15	.11	.06
436	Todd Worrell	.10	.08	.04
437	Bob Scanlan	.08	.06	.03
438	Wally Joyner	.15	.11	.06
439	John Flaherty	.12	.09	.05
440	Brian Downing	.08	.06	.03
441	Darren Lewis	.12	.09	.05
442	Gary Carter	.15	.11	.06
443	Wally Ritchie	.08	.06	.03
444	Chris Jones	.10	.08	.04
445	Jeff Kent	.15	.11	.06
446	Gary Sheffield	.30	.25	.12
447	Ron Darling	.10	.08	.04
448	Deion Sanders	.30	.25	.12
449	Andres Galarraga	.10	.08	.04
450	Chuck Finley	.10	.08	.04
451	Derek Lilliquist	.08	.06	.03
452	Carl Willis	.08	.06	.03
453	Wes Chamberlain	.10	.08	.04

		MT	NR MT	EX
454	Roger Mason	.08	.06	.03
455	Spike Owen	.08	.06	.03
456	Thomas Howard	.08	.06	.03
457	Dave Martinez	.08	.06	.03
458	Pete Incaviglia	.10	.08	.04
459	Keith Miller	.10	.08	.04
460	Mike Fetters	.08	.06	.03
461	Paul Gibson	.08	.06	.03
462	George Bell	.10	.08	.04
463	Checklist	.08	.06	.03
464	Terry Mulholland	.10	.08	.04
465	Storm Davis	.08	.06	.03
466	Gary Pettis	.08	.06	.03
467	Randy Bush	.08	.06	.03
468	Ken Hill	.12	.09	.05
469	Rheal Cormier	.12	.09	.05
470	Andy Stankiewicz	.10	.08	.04
471	Dave Burba	.08	.06	.03
472	Henry Cotto	.08	.06	.03
473	Dale Sveum	.08	.06	.03
474	Rich Gossage	.10	.08	.04
475	William Suero	.08	.06	.03
476	Doug Strange	.08	.06	.03
477	Bill Krueger	.10	.08	.04
478	John Wetteland	.15	.11	.06
479	Melido Perez	.10	.08	.04
480	Lonnie Smith	.10	.08	.04
481	Mike Jackson	.08	.06	.03
482	Mike Gardiner	.08	.06	.03
483	David Wells	.08	.06	.03
484	Barry Jones	.08	.06	.03
485	Scott Bankhead	.08	.06	.03
486	Terry Leach	.08	.06	.03
487	Vince Horseman	.15	.11	.06
488	Dave Eiland	.08	.06	.03
489	Alejandro Pena	.08	.06	.03
490	Julio Valera	.15	.11	.06
491	Joe Boever	.08	.06	.03
492	Paul Miller	.15	.11	.06
493	Arci Cianfrocco	.25	.20	.10
494	Dave Fleming	.50	.40	.20
495	Kyle Abbott	.12	.09	.05
496	Chad Kreuter	.08	.06	.03
497	Chris James	.08	.06	.03
498	Donnie Hill	.08	.06	.03
499	Jacob Brumfield	.15	.11	.06
500	Ricky Bones	.10	.08	.04
501	Terry Steinbach	.10	.08	.04
502	Bernard Gilkey	.10	.08	.04
503	Dennis Cook	.08	.06	.03
504	Lenny Dykstra	.15	.11	.06
505	Mike Bielecki	.08	.06	.03
506	Bob Kipper	.08	.06	.03
507	Jose Melendez	.15	.11	.06
508	Rick Sutcliffe	.12	.09	.05
509	Ken Patterson	.08	.06	.03
510	Andy Allanson	.08	.06	.03
511	Al Newman	.08	.06	.03
512	Mark Gardner	.08	.06	.03
513	Jeff Schaefer	.08	.06	.03
514	Jim McNamara	.15	.11	.06
515	Peter Hoy	.12	.09	.05
516	Curt Schilling	.12	.09	.05
517	Kirk McCaskill	.10	.08	.04
518	Chris Gwynn	.08	.06	.03
519	Sid Fernandez	.12	.09	.05
520	Jeff Parrett	.08	.06	.03
521	Scott Ruskin	.08	.06	.03
522	Kevin McReynolds	.12	.09	.05
523	Rick Cerone	.08	.06	.03
524	Jesse Orosco	.08	.06	.03
525	Troy Afenir	.08	.06	.03
526	John Smiley	.12	.09	.05
527	Dale Murphy	.12	.09	.05
528	Leaf Set Card	.08	.06	.03

1992 Leaf Gold Edition

This set is a gold foil version of Leaf's regular 1992 set. The cards do not use the traditional silver like the regular cards do; a gold metallic ink and gold foil are used instead. A Gold Edition card was inserted in each 15-card 1992 Leaf foil pack.

	MT	NR MT	EX
Complete Set (528):	300.00	225.00	125.00
Common Player:	.25	.20	.10

Gold stars: 5X to 7X regular Leaf card value

Values for recent cards and sets are listed in Mint (MT), Near Mint (NM) and Excellent (EX), reflecting the fact that many cards from recent years have been preserved in top condition. Recent cards and sets in less than Excellent condition have little collector interest.

1992 Leaf Gold Rookies

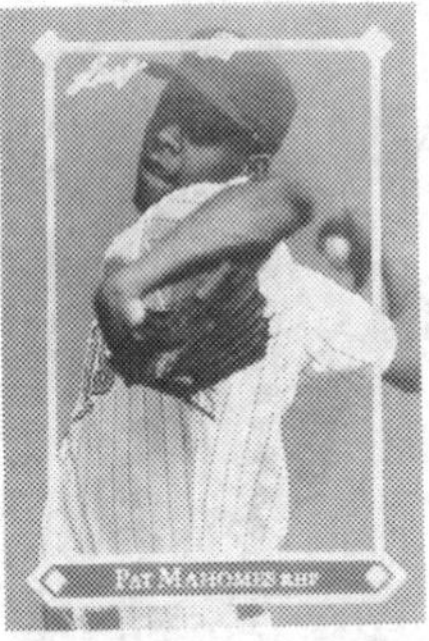

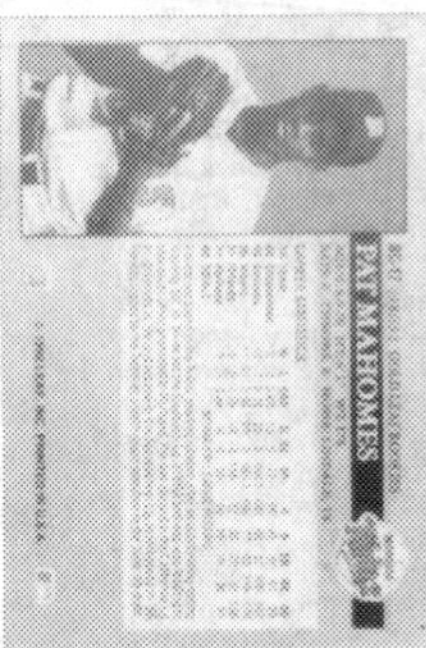

Two dozen of the major league's most promising players are featured in this insert set. Cards 1-12 were randomly included in Series I foil packs, while cards 13-24 were in Series II packs. Cards, numbered with a BC prefix, are standard size and enhanced with gold foil.

		MT	NR MT	EX
Complete Set (24):		34.00	25.00	13.50
Common Player:		.60	.45	.25
1	Chad Curtis	3.50	2.75	1.50
2	Brent Gates	3.00	2.25	1.25
3	Pedro Martinez	2.00	1.50	.80
4	Kenny Lofton	4.50	3.50	1.75
5	Turk Wendell	.90	.70	.35
6	Mark Hutton	1.00	.70	.40
7	Todd Hundley	.60	.45	.25
8	Matt Stairs	.75	.60	.30
9	Ed Taubensee	.75	.60	.30
10	David Nied	3.00	2.25	1.25
11	Salomon Torres	3.00	2.25	1.25
12	Bret Boone	1.50	1.25	.60
13	John Ruffin	1.25	.90	.50
14	Ed Martel	.75	.60	.30
15	Rick Tricek	.75	.60	.30
16	Raul Mondesi	1.75	1.25	.70
17	Pat Mahomes	1.25	.90	.50
18	Dan Wilson	.60	.45	.25
19	Donovan Osborne	1.75	1.25	.70
20	Dave Silvestri	1.00	.70	.40
21	Gary DiSarcina	.60	.45	.25
22	Denny Neagle	.60	.45	.25
23	Steve Hosey	2.00	1.50	.80
24	John Doherty	1.50	1.25	.60

1993 Leaf

Leaf issued this set in three series: two 220-card series and a 110-card update set. Card fronts have full-bleed action photos and players' names stamped in gold foil. Color-coded slate corners are used to differentiate teams. Backs have player photos against cityscapes or landmarks from the team's home city, a holographic embossed team logo and 1992 and career statistics. Cards are UV coated on both sides and are printed on premium

stock. Insert sets are titled Fasttrack, Gold All-Stars, Gold Rookies, Heading for the Hall, and Frank Thomas. Players from the National League's expansion teams, the Colorado Rockies and Florida Marlins, along with the Cincinnati Reds, California Angels and Seattle Mariners were featured in Series II packs so they could be pictured in their new uniforms. The Update series included a specially numbered "DW" insert card honoring Dave Winfield's 3,000-hit landmark, plus 3,500 special Frank Thomas autographed cards.

		MT	NR MT	EX
Complete Set (550):		70.00	50.00	25.00
Common Player:		.10	.08	.04
1	Ben McDonald	.10	.08	.04
2	Sid Fernandez	.10	.08	.04
3	Juan Guzman	.50	.40	.20
4	Curt Schilling	.10	.08	.04
5	Ivan Rodriguez	.50	.40	.20
6	Don Slaught	.10	.08	.04
7	Terry Steinbach	.10	.08	.04
8	Todd Zeile	.10	.08	.04
9	Andy Stankiewicz	.10	.08	.04
10	Tim Teufel	.10	.08	.04
11	Marvin Freeman	.10	.08	.04
12	Jim Austin	.10	.08	.04
13	Bob Scanlan	.10	.08	.04
14	Rusty Meacham	.10	.08	.04
15	Casey Candaele	.10	.08	.04
16	Travis Fryman	.80	.60	.30
17	Jose Offerman	.10	.08	.04
18	Albert Belle	.80	.60	.30
19	John Vander Wahl	.10	.08	.04
20	Dan Pasqua	.10	.08	.04
21	Frank Viola	.10	.08	.04
22	Terry Mulholland	.10	.08	.04
23	Gregg Olson	.10	.08	.04
24	Randy Tomlin	.10	.08	.04
25	Todd Stottlemyre	.10	.08	.04
26	Jose Oquendo	.10	.08	.04
27	Julio Franco	.10	.08	.04
28	Tony Gwynn	.25	.20	.10
29	Ruben Sierra	.20	.15	.08
30	Bobby Thigpen	.10	.08	.04
31	Jim Bullinger	.10	.08	.04
32	Rick Aguilera	.10	.08	.04
33	Scott Servais	.10	.08	.04
34	Cal Eldred	.35	.25	.14
35	Mike Piazza	5.00	3.75	2.00
36	Brent Mayne	.10	.08	.04
37	Wil Cordero	.30	.25	.12
38	Milt Cuyler	.10	.08	.04
39	Howard Johnson	.10	.08	.04
40	Kenny Lofton	.50	.40	.20
41	Alex Fernandez	.20	.15	.08
42	Denny Neagle	.10	.08	.04
43	Tony Pena	.10	.08	.04
44	Bob Tewksbury	.10	.08	.04
45	Glenn Davis	.10	.08	.04
46	Fred McGriff	.50	.40	.20
47	John Olerud	1.00	.70	.40
48	Steve Hosey	.25	.20	.10
49	Rafael Palmeiro	.20	.15	.08
50	David Justice	.75	.60	.30
51	Pete Harnisch	.10	.08	.04
52	Sam Militello	.10	.08	.04
53	Orel Hershisher	.10	.08	.04
54	Pat Mahomes	.10	.08	.04
55	Greg Colbrunn	.10	.08	.04
56	Greg Vaughn	.10	.08	.04

		MT	NR MT	EX
57	Vince Coleman	.10	.08	.04
58	Brian McRae	.10	.08	.04
59	Lenny Dykstra	.20	.15	.08
60	Dan Gladden	.10	.08	.04
61	Ted Power	.10	.08	.04
62	Donovan Osborne	.20	.15	.08
63	Ron Karkovice	.10	.08	.04
64	Frank Seminara	.10	.08	.04
65	Bob Zupcic	.10	.08	.04
66	Kirt Manwaring	.10	.08	.04
67	Mike Devereaux	.10	.08	.04
68	Mark Lemke	.10	.08	.04
69	Devon White	.10	.08	.04
70	Sammy Sosa	.15	.11	.06
71	Pedro Astacio	.30	.25	.12
72	Dennis Eckersley	.10	.08	.04
73	Chris Nabholz	.10	.08	.04
74	Melido Perez	.10	.08	.04
75	Todd Hundley	.10	.08	.04
76	Kent Hrbek	.10	.08	.04
77	Mickey Morandini	.10	.08	.04
78	Tim McIntosh	.10	.08	.04
79	Andy Van Slyke	.10	.08	.04
80	Kevin McReynolds	.10	.08	.04
81	Mike Henneman	.10	.08	.04
82	Greg Harris	.10	.08	.04
83	Sandy Alomar Jr.	.10	.08	.04
84	Mike Jackson	.10	.08	.04
85	Ozzie Guillen	.10	.08	.04
86	Jeff Blauser	.10	.08	.04
87	John Valentin	.40	.30	.15
88	Rey Sanchez	.10	.08	.04
89	Rick Sutcliffe	.10	.08	.04
90	Luis Gonzalez	.10	.08	.04
91	Jeff Fassero	.10	.08	.04
92	Kenny Rogers	.10	.08	.04
93	Bret Saberhagen	.10	.08	.04
94	Bob Welch	.10	.08	.04
95	Darren Daulton	.15	.11	.06
96	Mike Gallego	.10	.08	.04
97	Orlando Merced	.10	.08	.04
98	Chuck Knoblauch	.15	.11	.06
99	Bernard Gilkey	.10	.08	.04
100	Billy Ashley	.75	.60	.30
101	Kevin Appier	.10	.08	.04
102	Jeff Brantley	.10	.08	.04
103	Bill Gullickson	.10	.08	.04
104	John Smoltz	.10	.08	.04
105	Paul Sorrento	.10	.08	.04
106	Steve Buechele	.10	.08	.04
107	Steve Sax	.10	.08	.04
108	Andujar Cedeno	.10	.08	.04
109	Billy Hatcher	.10	.08	.04
110	Checklist	.10	.08	.04
111	Alan Mills	.10	.08	.04
112	John Franco	.10	.08	.04
113	Jack Morris	.10	.08	.04
114	Mitch Williams	.10	.08	.04
115	Nolan Ryan	2.00	1.50	.80
116	Jay Bell	.10	.08	.04
117	Mike Bordick	.10	.08	.04
118	Geronimo Pena	.10	.08	.04
119	Danny Tartabull	.10	.08	.04
120	Checklist	.10	.08	.04
121	Steve Avery	.50	.40	.20
122	Ricky Bones	.10	.08	.04
123	Mike Morgan	.10	.08	.04
124	Jeff Montgomery	.10	.08	.04
125	Jeff Bagwell	.50	.40	.20
126	Tony Phillips	.10	.08	.04
127	Lenny Harris	.10	.08	.04
128	Glenallen Hill	.10	.08	.04
129	Marquis Grissom	.40	.30	.15
130	Bernie Williams	.10	.08	.04
131	Greg Harris	.10	.08	.04
132	Tommy Greene	.10	.08	.04
133	Chris Hoiles	.10	.08	.04
134	Bob Walk	.10	.08	.04
135	Duane Ward	.10	.08	.04
136	Tom Pagnozzi	.10	.08	.04
137	Jeff Huson	.10	.08	.04
138	Kurt Stillwell	.10	.08	.04
139	Dave Henderson	.10	.08	.04
140	Darrin Jackson	.10	.08	.04
141	Frank Castillo	.10	.08	.04
142	Scott Erickson	.10	.08	.04
143	Darryl Kile	.10	.08	.04
144	Bill Wegman	.10	.08	.04
145	Steve Wilson	.10	.08	.04
146	George Brett	.50	.40	.20
147	Moises Alou	.15	.11	.06

		MT	NR MT	EX
148	Lou Whitaker	.10	.08	.04
149	Chico Walker	.10	.08	.04
150	Jerry Browne	.10	.08	.04
151	Kirk McCaskill	.10	.08	.04
152	Zane Smith	.10	.08	.04
153	Matt Young	.10	.08	.04
154	Lee Smith	.10	.08	.04
155	Leo Gomez	.10	.08	.04
156	Dan Walters	.10	.08	.04
157	Pat Borders	.10	.08	.04
158	Matt Williams	.20	.15	.08
159	Dean Palmer	.40	.30	.15
160	John Patterson	.10	.08	.04
161	Doug Jones	.10	.08	.04
162	John Habyan	.10	.08	.04
163	Pedro Martinez	.25	.20	.10
164	Carl Willis	.10	.08	.04
165	Darrin Fletcher	.10	.08	.04
166	B.J. Surhoff	.10	.08	.04
167	Eddie Murray	.20	.15	.08
168	Keith Miller	.10	.08	.04
169	Ricky Jordan	.10	.08	.04
170	Juan Gonzalez	3.25	2.50	1.25
171	Charles Nagy	.10	.08	.04
172	Mark Clark	.10	.08	.04
173	Bobby Thigpen	.10	.08	.04
174	Tim Scott	.10	.08	.04
175	Scott Cooper	.10	.08	.04
176	Royce Clayton	.10	.08	.04
177	Brady Anderson	.10	.08	.04
178	Sid Bream	.10	.08	.04
179	Derek Bell	.20	.15	.08
180	Otis Nixon	.10	.08	.04
181	Kevin Gross	.10	.08	.04
182	Ron Darling	.10	.08	.04
183	John Wetteland	.10	.08	.04
184	Mike Stanley	.10	.08	.04
185	Jeff Kent	.10	.08	.04
186	Brian Harper	.10	.08	.04
187	Mariano Duncan	.10	.08	.04
188	Robin Yount	.50	.40	.20
189	Al Martin	.70	.50	.30
190	Eddie Zosky	.10	.08	.04
191	Mike Munoz	.10	.08	.04
192	Andy Benes	.10	.08	.04
193	Dennis Cook	.10	.08	.04
194	Bill Swift	.10	.08	.04
195	Frank Thomas	4.00	3.00	1.50
196	Damon Berryhill	.10	.08	.04
197	Mike Greenwell	.10	.08	.04
198	Mark Grace	.20	.15	.08
199	Darryl Hamilton	.10	.08	.04
200	Derrick May	.10	.08	.04
201	Ken Hill	.10	.08	.04
202	Kevin Brown	.10	.08	.04
203	Dwight Gooden	.10	.08	.04
204	Bobby Witt	.10	.08	.04
205	Juan Bell	.10	.08	.04
206	Kevin Maas	.10	.08	.04
207	Jeff King	.10	.08	.04
208	Scott Leius	.10	.08	.04
209	Rheal Cormier	.10	.08	.04
210	Darryl Strawberry	.10	.08	.04
211	Tom Gordon	.10	.08	.04
212	Bud Black	.10	.08	.04
213	Mickey Tettleton	.10	.08	.04
214	Pete Smith	.10	.08	.04
215	Felix Fermin	.10	.08	.04
216	Rick Wilkins	.10	.08	.04
217	George Bell	.10	.08	.04
218	Eric Anthony	.10	.08	.04
219	Pedro Munoz	.10	.08	.04
220	Checklist	.10	.08	.04
221	Lance Blankenship	.10	.08	.04
222	Deion Sanders	.25	.20	.10
223	Craig Biggio	.10	.08	.04
224	Ryne Sandberg	.75	.60	.30
225	Ron Gant	.20	.15	.08
226	Tom Brunansky	.10	.08	.04
227	Chad Curtis	.30	.25	.12
228	Joe Carter	.30	.25	.12
229	Brian Jordan	.10	.08	.04
230	Brett Butler	.10	.08	.04
231	Frank Bolick	.10	.08	.04
232	Rod Beck	.10	.08	.04
233	Carlos Baerga	.80	.60	.30
234	Eric Karros	.40	.30	.15
235	Jack Armstrong	.10	.08	.04
236	Bobby Bonilla	.10	.08	.04
237	Don Mattingly	.30	.25	.12
238	Jeff Gardner	.10	.08	.04

		MT	NR MT	EX
239	Dave Hollins	.30	.25	.12
240	Steve Cooke	.30	.25	.12
241	Jose Canseco	.25	.20	.10
242	Ivan Calderon	.10	.08	.04
243	Tim Belcher	.10	.08	.04
244	Freddie Benavides	.10	.08	.04
245	Roberto Alomar	.80	.60	.30
246	Rob Deer	.10	.08	.04
247	Will Clark	.40	.30	.15
248	Mike Felder	.10	.08	.04
249	Harold Baines	.10	.08	.04
250	David Cone	.10	.08	.04
251	Mark Guthrie	.10	.08	.04
252	Ellis Burks	.10	.08	.04
253	Jim Abbott	.20	.15	.08
254	Chili Davis	.10	.08	.04
255	Chris Bosio	.10	.08	.04
256	Bret Barberie	.10	.08	.04
257	Hal Morris	.10	.08	.04
258	Dante Bichette	.10	.08	.04
259	Storm Davis	.10	.08	.04
260	Gary DiSarcina	.10	.08	.04
261	Ken Caminiti	.10	.08	.04
262	Paul Molitor	.20	.15	.08
263	Joe Oliver	.10	.08	.04
264	Pat Listach	.20	.15	.08
265	Gregg Jefferies	.15	.11	.06
266	Jose Guzman	.10	.08	.04
267	Eric Davis	.10	.08	.04
268	Delino DeShields	.15	.11	.06
269	Barry Bonds	1.00	.70	.40
270	Mike Bielecki	.10	.08	.04
271	Jay Buhner	.10	.08	.04
272	*Scott Pose*	.40	.30	.15
273	Tony Fernandez	.10	.08	.04
274	Chito Martinez	.10	.08	.04
275	Phil Plantier	.25	.20	.10
276	Pete Incaviglia	.10	.08	.04
277	Carlos Garcia	.25	.20	.10
278	Tom Henke	.10	.08	.04
279	Roger Clemens	.60	.45	.25
280	Rob Dibble	.10	.08	.04
281	Daryl Boston	.10	.08	.04
282	Greg Gagne	.10	.08	.04
283	Cecil Fielder	.40	.30	.15
284	Carlton Fisk	.10	.08	.04
285	Wade Boggs	.20	.15	.08
286	Damion Easley	.25	.20	.10
287	Norm Charlton	.10	.08	.04
288	Jeff Conine	.10	.08	.04
289	Roberto Kelly	.10	.08	.04
290	Jerald Clark	.10	.08	.04
291	Rickey Henderson	.25	.20	.10
292	Chuck Finley	.10	.08	.04
293	Doug Drabek	.10	.08	.04
294	Dave Stewart	.10	.08	.04
295	Tom Glavine	.50	.40	.20
296	Jaime Navarro	.10	.08	.04
297	Ray Lankford	.10	.08	.04
298	Greg Hibbard	.10	.08	.04
299	Jody Reed	.10	.08	.04
300	Dennis Martinez	.10	.08	.04
301	Dave Martinez	.10	.08	.04
302	Reggie Jefferson	.10	.08	.04
303	*John Cummings*	.30	.25	.12
304	Orestes Destrade	.10	.08	.04
305	Mike Maddux	.10	.08	.04
306	David Segui	.10	.08	.04
307	Gary Sheffield	.30	.25	.12
308	Danny Jackson	.10	.08	.04
309	Criag Lefferts	.10	.08	.04
310	Andre Dawson	.15	.11	.06
311	Barry Larkin	.10	.08	.04
312	Alex Cole	.10	.08	.04
313	Mark Gardner	.10	.08	.04
314	Kirk Gibson	.10	.08	.04
315	Shane Mack	.10	.08	.04
316	Bo Jackson	.25	.20	.10
317	Jimmy Key	.10	.08	.04
318	Greg Myers	.10	.08	.04
319	Ken Griffey Jr.	3.25	2.50	1.25
320	Monty Fariss	.10	.08	.04
321	Kevin Mitchell	.10	.08	.04
322	Andres Galarraga	.15	.11	.06
323	Mark McGwire	.25	.20	.10
324	Mark Langston	.10	.08	.04
325	Steve Finley	.10	.08	.04
326	Greg Maddux	.30	.25	.12
327	Dave Nilsson	.10	.08	.04
328	Ozzie Smith	.20	.15	.08
329	Candy Maldonado	.10	.08	.04

		MT	NR MT	EX
330	Checklist	.10	.08	.04
331	*Tim Pugh*	.40	.30	.15
332	Joe Girardi	.10	.08	.04
333	Junior Feliz	.10	.08	.04
334	Greg Swindell	.10	.08	.04
335	Ramon Martinez	.10	.08	.04
336	Sean Berry	.10	.08	.04
337	Joe Orsulak	.10	.08	.04
338	Wes Chamberlain	.10	.08	.04
339	Stan Belinda	.10	.08	.04
340	Checklist	.10	.08	.04
341	Bruce Hurst	.10	.08	.04
342	John Burkett	.10	.08	.04
343	Mike Mussina	.60	.45	.25
344	Scott Fletcher	.10	.08	.04
345	Rene Gonzales	.10	.08	.04
346	Roberto Hernandez	.10	.08	.04
347	Carlos Martinez	.10	.08	.04
348	Bill Krueger	.10	.08	.04
349	Felix Jose	.10	.08	.04
350	John Jaha	.20	.15	.08
351	Willie Banks	.10	.08	.04
352	Matt Nokes	.10	.08	.04
353	Kevin Seitzer	.10	.08	.04
354	Erik Hanson	.10	.08	.04
355	*David Hulse*	.30	.25	.12
356	*Domingo Martinez*	.30	.25	.12
357	Greg Olson	.10	.08	.04
358	Randy Myers	.10	.08	.04
359	Tom Browning	.10	.08	.04
360	Charlie Hayes	.10	.08	.04
361	Bryan Harvey	.10	.08	.04
362	Eddie Taubensee	.10	.08	.04
363	Tim Wallach	.10	.08	.04
364	Mel Rojas	.10	.08	.04
365	Frank Tanana	.10	.08	.04
366	John Kruk	.15	.11	.06
367	*Tim Laker*	.30	.25	.12
368	Rich Rodriguez	.10	.08	.04
369	Darren Lewis	.10	.08	.04
370	Harold Reynolds	.10	.08	.04
371	Jose Melendez	.10	.08	.04
372	Joe Grahe	.10	.08	.04
373	Lance Johnson	.10	.08	.04
374	Jose Mesa	.10	.08	.04
375	Scott Livingstone	.10	.08	.04
376	Wally Joyner	.10	.08	.04
377	Kevin Reimer	.10	.08	.04
378	Kirby Puckett	.60	.45	.25
379	Paul O'Neill	.10	.08	.04
380	Randy Johnson	.15	.11	.06
381	Manuel Lee	.10	.08	.04
382	Dick Schofield	.10	.08	.04
383	Darren Holmes	.10	.08	.04
384	Charlie Hough	.10	.08	.04
385	John Orton	.10	.08	.04
386	Edgar Martinez	.10	.08	.04
387	Terry Pendleton	.10	.08	.04
388	Dan Plesac	.10	.08	.04
389	Jeff Reardon	.10	.08	.04
390	David Nied	.75	.60	.30
391	Dave Magadan	.10	.08	.04
392	Larry Walker	.25	.20	.10
393	Ben Rivera	.10	.08	.04
394	Lonnie Smith	.10	.08	.04
395	Craig Shipley	.10	.08	.04
396	Willie McGee	.10	.08	.04
397	Arthur Rhodes	.10	.08	.04
398	Mike Stanton	.10	.08	.04
399	Luis Polonia	.10	.08	.04
400	Jack McDowell	.25	.20	.10
401	Mike Moore	.10	.08	.04
402	Jose Lind	.10	.08	.04
403	Bill Spiers	.10	.08	.04
404	Kevin Tapani	.10	.08	.04
405	Spike Owen	.10	.08	.04
406	Tino Martinez	.10	.08	.04
407	Charlie Leibrandt	.10	.08	.04
408	Ed Sprague	.10	.08	.04
409	Bryn Smith	.10	.08	.04
410	Benito Santiago	.10	.08	.04
411	Jose Rijo	.10	.08	.04
412	Pete O'Brien	.10	.08	.04
413	Willie Wilson	.10	.08	.04
414	Bip Roberts	.10	.08	.04
415	Eric Young	.40	.30	.15
416	Walt Weiss	.10	.08	.04
417	Milt Thompson	.10	.08	.04
418	Chris Sabo	.10	.08	.04
419	Scott Sanderson	.10	.08	.04
420	Tim Raines	.10	.08	.04

		MT	NR MT	EX
421	Alan Trammell	.10	.08	.04
422	Mike Macfarlane	.10	.08	.04
423	Dave Winfield	.40	.30	.15
424	Bob Wickman	.30	.25	.12
425	David Valie	.10	.08	.04
426	Gary Redus	.10	.08	.04
427	Turner Ward	.10	.08	.04
428	Reggie Sanders	.25	.20	.10
429	Todd Worrell	.10	.08	.04
430	Julio Valera	.10	.08	.04
431	Cal Ripken, Jr.	.80	.60	.30
432	Mo Vaughn	.40	.30	.15
433	John Smiley	.10	.08	.04
434	Omar Vizquel	.10	.08	.04
435	Billy Ripken	.10	.08	.04
436	Cory Snyder	.10	.08	.04
437	Carlos Quintana	.10	.08	.04
438	Omar Olivares	.10	.08	.04
439	Robin Ventura	.50	.40	.20
440	Checklist	.10	.08	.04
441	Kevin Higgins	.10	.08	.04
442	Carlos Hernandez	.10	.08	.04
443	Dan Peltier	.15	.11	.06
444	Derek Lilliquist	.10	.08	.04
445	Tim Salmon	2.50	2.00	1.00
446	Sherman Obando	.15	.11	.06
447	Pat Kelly	.15	.11	.06
448	Todd Van Poppel	.25	.20	.10
449	Mark Whiten	.10	.08	.04
450	Checklist	.10	.08	.04
451	Pat Meares	.15	.11	.06
452	Tony Tarasco	.20	.15	.08
453	Chris Gwynn	.10	.08	.04
454	Armando Reynoso	.15	.11	.06
455	Danny Darwin	.10	.08	.04
456	Willie Greene	.15	.11	.06
457	Mike Blowers	.10	.08	.04
458	Kevin Roberson	.20	.15	.08
459	Graeme Lloyd	.10	.08	.04
460	David West	.10	.08	.04
461	Joey Cora	.10	.08	.04
462	Alex Arias	.10	.08	.04
463	Chad Kreuter	.10	.08	.04
464	Mike Lansing	.50	.40	.20
465	Mike Timlin	.10	.08	.04
466	Paul Wagner	.10	.08	.04
467	Mark Portugal	.10	.08	.04
468	Jim Leyritz	.10	.08	.04
469	Ryan Klesko	.40	.30	.15
470	Mario Diaz	.10	.08	.04
471	Guillermo Velasquez	.15	.11	.06
472	Fernando Valenzuela	.15	.11	.06
473	Raul Mondesi	.20	.15	.08
474	Mike Pagliarulo	.10	.08	.04
475	Chris Hammond	.10	.08	.04
476	Torey Lovullo	.10	.08	.04
477	Trevor Wilson	.10	.08	.04
478	Marcos Armas	.20	.15	.08
479	Dave Gallagher	.10	.08	.04
480	Jeff Treadway	.10	.08	.04
481	Jeff Branson	.10	.08	.04
482	Dickie Thon	.10	.08	.04
483	Eduardo Perez	.60	.45	.25
484	David Wells	.10	.08	.04
485	Brian Williams	.10	.08	.04
486	Domingo Cedeno	.15	.11	.06
487	Tom Candiotti	.10	.08	.04
488	Steve Frey	.10	.08	.04
489	Greg McMichael	.25	.20	.10
490	Marc Newfield	.20	.15	.08
491	Larry Andersen	.10	.08	.04
492	Damon Buford	.15	.11	.06
493	Ricky Gutierrez	.10	.08	.04
494	Jeff Russell	.10	.08	.04
495	Vinny Castilla	.10	.08	.04
496	Wilson Alvarez	.15	.11	.06
497	Scott Bullett	.10	.08	.04
498	Larry Casian	.15	.11	.06
499	Jose Vizcaino	.10	.08	.04
500	J.T. Snow	.75	.60	.30
501	Bryan Hickerson	.10	.08	.04
502	Jeremy Hernandez	.20	.15	.08
503	Jeromy Burnitz	.25	.20	.10
504	Steve Farr	.10	.08	.04
505	J. Owens	.35	.25	.14
506	Craig Paquette	.10	.08	.04
507	Jim Eisenreich	.10	.08	.04
508	Matt Whiteside	.15	.11	.06
509	Luis Aquino	.10	.08	.04
510	Mike LaValliere	.10	.08	.04
511	Jim Gott	.10	.08	.04

		MT	NR MT	EX
512	Mark McLemore	.10	.08	.04
513	Randy Milligan	.10	.08	.04
514	Gary Gaetti	.15	.11	.06
515	Lou Frazier	.20	.15	.08
516	Rich Amaral	.10	.08	.04
517	Gene Harris	.10	.08	.04
518	Aaron Sele	2.00	1.50	.80
519	Mark Wohlers	.10	.08	.04
520	Scott Kamieniecki	.15	.11	.06
521	Kent Mercker	.10	.08	.04
522	Jim Deshaies	.10	.08	.04
523	Kevin Stocker	1.00	.70	.40
524	Jason Bere	1.50	1.25	.60
525	Tim Bogar	.15	.11	.06
526	Brad Pennington	.15	.11	.06
527	Curt Leskanic	.15	.11	.06
528	Wayne Kirby	.10	.08	.04
529	Tim Costo	.10	.08	.04
530	Doug Henry	.10	.08	.04
531	Trevor Hoffman	.20	.15	.08
532	Kelly Gruber	.10	.08	.04
533	Mike Harkey	.10	.08	.04
534	John Doherty	.10	.08	.04
535	Erik Pappas	.15	.11	.06
536	Brent Gates	.15	.11	.06
537	Roger McDowell	.10	.08	.04
538	Chris Haney	.10	.08	.04
539	Blas Minor	.10	.08	.04
540	Pat Hentgen	.20	.15	.08
541	Chuck Carr	.20	.15	.08
542	Doug Strange	.10	.08	.04
543	Xavier Hernandez	.10	.08	.04
544	Paul Quantrill	.10	.08	.04
545	Anthony Young	.15	.11	.06
546	Bret Boone	.15	.11	.06
547	Dwight Smith	.10	.08	.04
548	Bobby Munoz	.20	.15	.08
549	Russ Springer	.10	.08	.04
550	Roger Pavlik	.10	.08	.04
---	Dave Winfield (3000 Major League Career Hits)	3.00	2.25	1.25
---	Autographed Frank Thomas	300.00	225.00	125.00

1993 Leaf Fasttrack

This 20-card insert set was released in two series; cards 1-10 were randomly included in Leaf Series I retail packs, while 11-20 were in Series II packs. Card fronts and backs are similar with a player photo and a diagonal white strip with "on the Fasttrack" printed in black and red. Fronts have the gold embossed Leaf logo, backs have the silver holographic team logo.

		MT	NR MT	EX
Complete Set (20):		80.00	60.00	32.00
Common Player:		2.00	1.50	.80
1	Frank Thomas	20.00	15.00	8.00
2	Tim Wakefield	2.00	1.50	.80
3	Kenny Lofton	5.00	3.75	2.00
4	Mike Mussina	6.00	4.50	2.50
5	Juan Gonzalez	18.00	13.50	7.25
6	Chuck Knoblauch	2.00	1.50	.80
7	Eric Karros	6.00	4.50	2.50
8	Ray Lankford	3.00	2.25	1.25
9	Juan Guzman	3.00	2.25	1.25
10	Pat Listach	2.00	1.50	.80
11	Carlos Baerga	7.00	5.25	2.75

		MT	NR MT	EX
12	Felix Jose	2.00	1.50	.80
13	Steve Avery	3.00	2.25	1.25
14	Robin Ventura	3.00	2.25	1.25
15	Ivan Rodriguez	4.00	3.00	1.50
16	Cal Eldred	3.00	2.25	1.25
17	Jeff Bagwell	4.00	3.00	1.50
18	David Justice	5.00	3.75	2.00
19	Travis Fryman	5.00	3.75	2.00
20	Marquis Grissom	3.00	2.25	1.25

1993 Leaf Gold All-Stars

Photos not available at press time

Cards 1-10 in this insert set were randomly inserted one per Leaf Series I jumbo packs, while cards 11-20 were in Series II jumbo packs. Cards feature two players per card, one on each side. Only one side is numbered, but both sides have gold foil.

		MT	NR MT	EX
Complete Set (20):		35.00	26.00	14.00
Common Player:		1.00	.70	.40
1	Ivan Rodriquez, Darren Daulton	1.50	1.25	.60
2	Don Mattingly, Fred McGriff	3.00	2.25	1.25
3	Cecil Fielder, Jeff Bagwell	2.50	2.00	1.00
4	Carlos Baerga, Ryne Sandberg	4.00	3.00	1.50
5	Chuck Knoblauch, Delino DeShields	1.25	.90	.50
6	Robin Ventura, Terry Pendleton	1.50	1.25	.60
7	Ken Griffey Jr., Andy Van Slyke	6.00	4.50	2.50
8	Joe Carter, Dave Justice	3.00	2.25	1.25
9	Jose Canseco, Tony Gwynn	1.25	.90	.50
10	Dennis Eckersley, Rob Dibble	1.00	.70	.40
11	Mark McGwire, Will Clark	2.00	1.50	.80
12	Frank Thomas, Mark Grace	7.50	5.75	3.00
13	Roberto Alomar, Craig Biggio	2.50	2.00	1.00
14	Barry Larkin, Cal Ripken Jr.	3.00	2.25	1.25
15	Gary Sheffield, Edgar Martinez	1.25	.90	.50
16	Juan Gonzalez, Barry Bonds	8.00	6.00	3.25
17	Kirby Puckett, Marquis Grissom	3.00	2.25	1.25
18	Jim Abbott, Tom Glavine	1.50	1.25	.60
19	Nolan Ryan, Greg Maddux	5.00	3.75	2.00
20	Roger Clemens, Doug Drabek	2.00	1.50	.80

1993 Leaf Gold Rookies

These cards, numbered 1 of 20 etc., feature 20 1993 rookies. Cards were randomly inserted into hobby foil packs, 10 different cards per series. Card fronts feature action photos, while the backs show a player photo against a landmark from his team's city.

		MT	NR MT	EX
Complete Set (20):		60.00	45.00	24.00
Common Player:		1.25	.90	.50
1	Kevin Young	3.00	2.25	1.25
2	Wil Cordero	2.00	1.50	.80
3	Mark Kiefer	1.25	.90	.50
4	Gerald Williams	1.25	.90	.50
5	Brandon Wilson	1.25	.90	.50
6	Greg Gohr	1.25	.90	.50
7	Ryan Thompson	2.00	1.50	.80
8	Tim Wakefield	1.50	1.25	.60
9	Troy Neel	2.50	2.00	1.00
10	Tim Salmon	18.00	13.50	7.25
11	Kevin Rogers	1.50	1.25	.60
12	Rod Bolton	1.25	.90	.50
13	Ken Ryan	1.25	.90	.50
14	Phil Hiatt	2.50	2.00	1.00
15	Rene Arocha	2.50	2.00	1.00
16	Nigel Wilson	6.00	4.50	2.50
17	J.T. Snow	5.00	3.75	2.00
18	Benji Gil	2.50	2.00	1.00
19	Chipper Jones	7.50	5.75	3.00
20	Darrell Sherman	1.25	.90	.50

1993 Leaf Heading for the Hall

Ten players on the way to the Baseball Hall of Fame are featured in this insert set. Series I Leaf packs had cards 1-5 randomly included; Series II packs had cards 6-10. The front of the card states the player is Heading for the Hall.

		MT	NR MT	EX
Complete Set (10):		45.00	34.00	18.00
Common Player:		2.50	2.00	1.00
1	Nolan Ryan	15.00	11.00	6.00
2	Tony Gwynn	2.50	2.00	1.00
3	Robin Yount	4.00	3.00	1.50
4	Eddie Murray	2.50	2.00	1.00
5	Cal Ripken, Jr.	6.00	4.50	2.50
6	Roger Clemens	4.00	3.00	1.50
7	George Brett	5.00	3.75	2.00
8	Ryne Sandberg	6.00	4.50	2.50
9	Kirby Puckett	5.00	3.75	2.00
10	Ozzie Smith	2.50	2.00	1.00

1993 Leaf Frank Thomas

Leaf signed Frank Thomas as its spokesman for 1993, and honored him with a 10-card insert set. Cards 1-5 were randomly included in Series I packs; cards 6-10 were in Series II packs. A custom designed "Frank" logo in a holographic foil stamp is featured on each card front which includes a one-word character trait. On back is a color portrait photo of Thomas superimposed on a Chicago skyline. A paragraph on back describes how the charater trait on front applies to Thomas.

		MT	NR MT	EX
Complete Set (10):		50.00	35.00	20.00
Common Thomas:		5.00	3.00	1.50
Autographed Thomas:		300.00	225.00	125.00
1	Aggressive	5.00	3.75	2.00
2	Serious	5.00	3.75	2.00
3	Intense	5.00	3.75	2.00
4	Confident	5.00	3.75	2.00
5	Assertive	5.00	3.75	2.00
6	Power	5.00	3.75	2.00
7	Control	5.00	3.75	2.00
8	Strength	5.00	3.75	2.00
9	Concentration	5.00	3.75	2.00
10	Preparation	5.00	3.75	2.00

1993 Leaf Update Gold All-Stars

These 10 cards, featuring 20 all-stars, were randomly inserted in Leaf Update packs. Each card features two players, one on each side. Cards are distinguished from the regular Gold All-Stars by indicating on the front the card is number X of 10, with a tiny white "Update" in the red stripe above the card number.

		MT	NR MT	EX
Complete Set (10):		20.00	15.00	8.00
Common Player:		.75	.60	.30
1	Mark Langston/ Terry Mulholland	.75	.60	.30
2	Ivan Rodriguez/ Darren Daulton	1.50	1.25	.60
3	John Olerud/ John Kruk	3.00	2.25	1.25
4	Roberto Alomar/ Ryne Sandberg	4.00	3.00	1.50
5	Wade Boggs/ Gary Sheffield	1.25	.90	.50
6	Cal Ripken, Jr./ Barry Larkin	3.00	2.25	1.25
7	Kirby Puckett/ Barry Bonds	7.50	5.75	3.00
8	Ken Griffey, Jr./ Marquis Grissom	5.00	3.75	2.00
9	Joe Carter/ Dave Justice	3.00	2.25	1.25
10	Paul Molitor/ Mark Grace	3.00	2.25	1.25

A card number in parentheses () indicates the set is unnumbered.

1993 Leaf Update Gold Rookies

These five cards were randomly inserted in Leaf Update packs. Cards are similiar in design to the regular Gold Rookies cards, except the logo on the back indicates they are from the Update series.

		MT	NR MT	EX
Complete Set (5):		35.00	26.00	14.00
Common Player:		3.00	2.25	1.25
1	Allen Watson	5.00	3.75	2.00
2	Jeffrey Hammonds	7.50	5.75	3.00
3	David McCarty	4.00	3.00	1.50
4	Mike Piazza	25.00	18.50	10.00
5	Roberto Meija	3.00	2.25	1.25

1993 Leaf Update Frank Thomas Super

This 10-card insert set features Leaf's 1993 spokesman, Frank Thomas. Cards, which measure 5" by 7", were included one per every Leaf Update foil box and are identical to the inserts found in Series I and II except in size. Cards are individually numbered. Thomas autographed 3,500 cards.

		MT	NR MT	EX
Complete Set (10):		90.00	67.00	36.00
Common Thomas:		10.00	7.50	4.00
1	Aggressive	10.00	7.50	4.00
2	Serious	10.00	7.50	4.00
3	Intense	10.00	7.50	4.00
4	Confident	10.00	7.50	4.00
5	Assertive	10.00	7.50	4.00
6	Power	10.00	7.50	4.00
7	Control	10.00	7.50	4.00
8	Strength	10.00	7.50	4.00
9	Concentration	10.00	7.50	4.00
10	Preparation	10.00	7.50	4.00

1991 O-Pee-Chee Premier

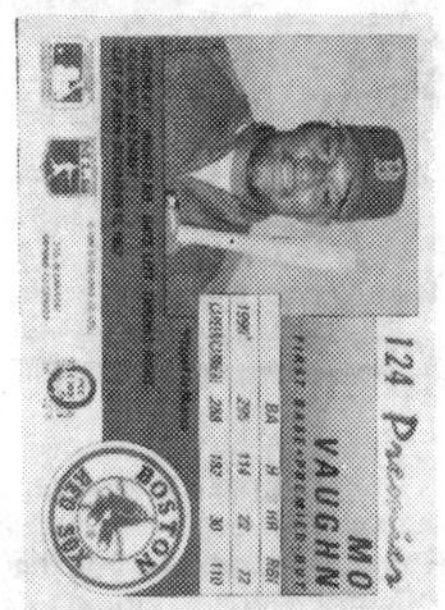

The O-Pee-Chee Co. of London, Ontario, Canada produced this 132-card set. The card fronts feature action photos, while the flip sides display a posed photo and career statistics. The cards were packaged seven cards per pack in a tamper-proof foil wrap. Several Expo and Blue Jay players are featured. Two special cards are included in this set. Card #62 honors Rickey Henderson's stolen base record, while card #102 commemorates Nolan Ryan's seventh no-hitter. Traded players and free agents are featured with their new teams.

		MT	NR MT	EX
Complete Set (132):		25.00	18.00	10.00
Common Player:		.10	.08	.04
1	Roberto Alomar	.70	.50	.30
2	Sandy Alomar	.20	.15	.08
3	Moises Alou	.12	.09	.05
4	Brian Barnes	.25	.20	.10
5	Steve Bedrosian	.10	.08	.04
6	George Bell	.20	.15	.08
7	Juan Bell	.12	.09	.05
8	Albert Belle	.70	.50	.30
9	Bud Black	.10	.08	.04
10	Mike Boddicker	.10	.08	.04
11	Wade Boggs	.60	.45	.25
12	Barry Bonds	.60	.45	.25
13	Denis Boucher	.25	.20	.10
14	George Brett	.40	.30	.15
15	Hubie Brooks	.10	.08	.04
16	Brett Butler	.12	.09	.05
17	Ivan Calderon	.15	.11	.06
18	Jose Canseco	1.50	1.25	.60
19	Gary Carter	.20	.15	.08
20	Joe Carter	.25	.20	.10
21	Jack Clark	.15	.11	.06
22	Will Clark	1.50	1.25	.60
23	Roger Clemens	1.50	1.25	.60
24	Alex Cole	.15	.11	.06
25	Vince Coleman	.15	.11	.06
26	Jeff Conine	.20	.15	.08
27	Milt Cuyler	.60	.45	.25
28	Danny Darwin	.10	.08	.04
29	Eric Davis	.30	.25	.12
30	Glenn Davis	.15	.11	.06
31	Andre Dawson	.30	.25	.12
32	Ken Dayley	.10	.08	.04
33	Steve Decker	.50	.40	.20
34	Delino DeShields	.30	.25	.12
35	Lance Dickson	.50	.40	.20
36	Kirk Dressendorfer	.80	.60	.30
37	Shawon Dunston	.15	.11	.06
38	Dennis Eckersley	.15	.11	.06
39	Dwight Evans	.12	.09	.05
40	Howard Farmer	.20	.15	.08
41	Junior Felix	.15	.11	.06
42	Alex Fernandez	.50	.40	.20
43	Tony Fernandez	.12	.09	.05
44	Cecil Fielder	1.00	.70	.40
45	Carlton Fisk	.50	.40	.20
46	Willie Fraser	.10	.08	.04
47	Gary Gaetti	.12	.09	.05
48	Andres Galarraga	.10	.08	.04
49	Ron Gant	.80	.60	.30
50	Kirk Gibson	.15	.11	.06
51	Bernard Gilkey	.30	.25	.12
52	Leo Gomez	.50	.40	.20
53	Rene Gonzalez	.10	.08	.04
54	Juan Gonzalez	3.00	2.25	1.25
55	Doc Gooden	.40	.30	.15
56	Ken Griffey,Jr.	3.00	2.25	1.25
57	Kelly Gruber	.20	.15	.08
58	Pedro Guerrero	.15	.11	.06
59	Tony Gwynn	.60	.45	.25
60	Chris Hammond	.20	.15	.08
61	Ron Hassey	.10	.08	.04
62	Rickey Henderson	1.00	.70	.40
63	Tom Henke	.12	.09	.05
64	Orel Hershiser	.20	.15	.08
65	Chris Hoiles	.20	.15	.08
66	Todd Hundley	.30	.25	.12
67	Pete Incaviglia	.10	.08	.04
68	Danny Jackson	.10	.08	.04
69	Barry Jones	.10	.08	.04
70	David Justice	3.00	2.25	1.25
71	Jimmy Key	.12	.09	.05
72	Ray Lankford	1.00	.70	.40
73	Darren Lewis	.80	.60	.30
74	Kevin Maas	.60	.45	.25
75	Denny Martinez	.12	.09	.05
76	Tino Martinez	.50	.40	.20
77	Don Mattingly	1.00	.70	.40
78	Willie McGee	.15	.11	.06
79	Fred McGriff	.30	.25	.12
80	Hensley Meulens	.20	.15	.08
81	Kevin Mitchell	.30	.25	.12
82	Paul Molitor	.25	.20	.10
83	Mickey Morandini	.25	.20	.10
84	Jack Morris	.25	.20	.10
85	Dale Murphy	.25	.20	.10
86	Eddie Murray	.30	.25	.12
87	Chris Nabholz	.15	.11	.06
88	Tim Naehring	.20	.15	.08
89	Otis Nixon	.12	.09	.05
90	Jose Offerman	.20	.15	.08
91	Bob Ojeda	.10	.08	.04
92	John Olerud	.50	.40	.20
93	Gregg Olson	.15	.11	.06
94	Dave Parker	.15	.11	.06
95	Terry Pendleton	.20	.15	.08
96	Kirby Puckett	1.00	.70	.40
97	Rock Raines	.15	.11	.06
98	Jeff Reardon	.12	.09	.05
99	Dave Righetti	.12	.09	.05
100	Cal Ripken	3.00	2.25	1.25
101	Mel Rojas	.15	.11	.06
102	Nolan Ryan	4.00	3.00	1.50
103	Ryne Sandberg	2.00	1.50	.80
104	Scott Sanderson	.10	.08	.04
105	Benito Santiago	.15	.11	.06
106	Pete Schourek	.25	.20	.10
107	Gary Scott	.25	.20	.10
108	Terry Shumpert	.10	.08	.04
109	Ruben Sierra	.80	.60	.30
110	Doug Simons	.20	.15	.08
111	Dave Smith	.10	.08	.04
112	Ozzie Smith	.35	.25	.14
113	Cory Snyder	.10	.08	.04
114	Luis Sojo	.10	.08	.04
115	Dave Stewart	.15	.11	.06
116	Dave Stieb	.12	.09	.05
117	Darryl Strawberry	1.25	.90	.50
118	Pat Tabler	.10	.08	.04
119	Wade Taylor	.30	.25	.12
120	Bobby Thigpen	.15	.11	.06
121	Frank Thomas	6.00	4.50	2.50
122	Mike Timlin	.30	.25	.12
123	Alan Trammell	.20	.15	.08
124	Mo Vaughn	2.00	1.50	.80
125	Tim Wallach	.12	.09	.05
126	Devon White	.12	.09	.05
127	Mark Whiten	.60	.45	.25
128	Bernie Williams	1.25	.90	.50
129	Willie Wilson	.10	.08	.04
130	Dave Winfield	.30	.25	.12
131	Robin Yount	.60	.45	.25
132	Checklist	.10	.08	.04

1992 O-Pee-Chee Premier

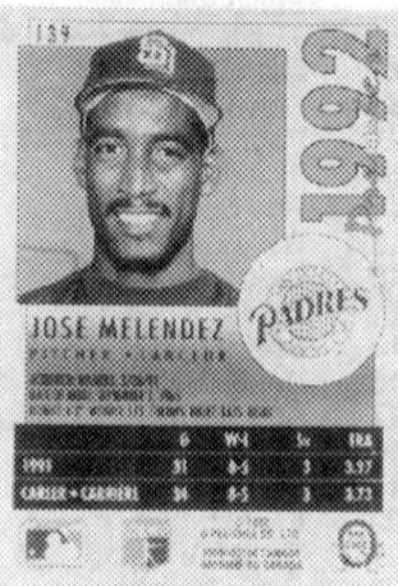

O-Pee-Chee increased the number of cards in its premier set to 198 for 1992. The cards feature white borders surrounding full-color player photos. The O-Pee-Chee banner appears at the top of the card and the player's name and position appear at the bottom. The backs feature an additional player photo, statistics and player information. Traded players and free agents are featured with their new teams.

		MT	NR MT	EX
Complete Set (198):		25.00	18.00	10.00
Common Player:		.08	.06	.03
1	Wade Boggs	.40	.30	.15
2	John Smiley	.10	.08	.04
3	Checklist	.08	.06	.03
4	Ron Gant	.20	.15	.08
5	Mike Bordick	.20	.15	.08
6	Charlie Hayes	.08	.06	.03
7	Kevin Morton	.08	.06	.03
8	Checklist	.08	.06	.03
9	Chris Gwynn	.08	.06	.03
10	Scott Bankhead	.08	.06	.03
11	Danny Gladden	.08	.06	.03
12	Brian McRae	.20	.15	.08
13	Denny Martinez	.10	.08	.04
14	Bob Scanlan	.15	.11	.06
15	Julio Franco	.10	.08	.04
16	Ruben Amaro	.15	.11	.06
17	Mo Sanford	.15	.11	.06
18	Melido Perez	.08	.06	.03
19	Dickie Thon	.08	.06	.03
20	Chris James	.08	.06	.03
21	Mike Huff	.08	.06	.03
22	Orlando Merced	.10	.08	.04
23	Chris Sabo	.15	.11	.06
24	Jose Canseco	.50	.40	.20
25	Reggie Sanders	.50	.40	.20
26	Chris Nabholz	.10	.08	.04
27	Kevin Seitzer	.08	.06	.03
28	Ryan Bowen	.15	.11	.06
29	Gary Carter	.15	.11	.06
30	Wayne Rosenthal	.08	.06	.03
31	Alan Trammell	.20	.15	.08
32	Doug Drabek	.20	.15	.08
33	Craig Shipley	.10	.08	.04
34	Ryne Sandberg	.30	.25	.12
35	Chuck Knoblauch	.25	.20	.10
36	Bret Barberie	.20	.15	.08
37	Tim Naehring	.12	.09	.05
38	Omar Olivares	.12	.09	.05
39	Royce Clayton	.25	.20	.10
40	Brent Mayne	.12	.09	.05
41	Darrin Fletcher	.08	.06	.03
42	Howard Johnson	.15	.11	.06
43	Steve Sax	.12	.09	.05
44	Greg Swindell	.20	.15	.08
45	Andre Dawson	.20	.15	.08
46	Kent Hrbek	.15	.11	.06
47	Doc Gooden	.35	.25	.14
48	Mark Leiter	.08	.06	.03
49	Tom Glavine	.20	.15	.08
50	Mo Vaughn	.20	.15	.08
51	Doug Jones	.08	.06	.03
52	Brian Barnes	.12	.09	.05
53	Rob Dibble	.15	.11	.06
54	Kevin McReynolds	.12	.09	.05
55	Ivan Rodriguez	.40	.30	.15
56	Scott Livingstone	.20	.15	.08
57	Mike Magnante	.12	.09	.05
58	Pete Schourek	.10	.08	.04
59	Frank Thomas	1.50	1.25	.60
60	Kirk McCaskill	.12	.09	.05
61	Wally Joyner	.15	.11	.06
62	Rick Aguilera	.15	.11	.06
63	Eric Karros	2.00	1.50	.80
64	Tino Martinez	.20	.15	.08
65	Bryan Hickerson	.20	.15	.08
66	Ruben Sierra	.30	.25	.12
67	Willie Randolph	.10	.08	.04
68	Bill Landrum	.08	.06	.03
69	Bip Roberts	.15	.11	.06
70	Cecil Fielder	.40	.30	.15
71	Pat Kelly	.15	.11	.06
72	Kenny Lofton	.50	.40	.20
73	John Franco	.10	.08	.04
74	Phil Plantier	.20	.15	.08
75	Dave Martinez	.08	.06	.03
76	Warren Newson	.08	.06	.03
77	Chito Martinez	.15	.11	.06
78	Brian Hunter	.15	.11	.06
79	Jack Morris	.20	.15	.08
80	Eric King	.08	.06	.03
81	Nolan Ryan	.60	.45	.25
82	Bret Saberhagen	.15	.11	.06
83	Roberto Kelly	.15	.11	.06
84	Ozzie Smith	.20	.15	.08
85	Chuck McElroy	.08	.06	.03
86	Carlton Fisk	.25	.20	.10
87	Mike Mussina	1.00	.70	.40
88	Mark Carreon	.08	.06	.03
89	Ken Hill	.15	.11	.06
90	Rick Cerone	.08	.06	.03
91	Deion Sanders	.40	.30	.15
92	Don Mattingly	.40	.30	.15
93	Danny Tartabull	.15	.11	.06
94	Keith Miller	.12	.09	.05
95	Gregg Jefferies	.15	.11	.06
96	Barry Larkin	.20	.15	.08
97	Kevin Mitchell	.15	.11	.06
98	Rick Sutcliffe	.15	.11	.06
99	Mark McGwire	.30	.25	.12
100	Albert Belle	.30	.25	.12
101	Gregg Olson	.15	.11	.06
102	Kirby Puckett	.50	.40	.20
103	Luis Gonzalez	.20	.15	.08
104	Randy Myers	.10	.08	.04
105	Roger Clmens	.50	.40	.20
106	Tony Gwynn	.40	.30	.15
107	Jeff Bagwell	.50	.40	.20
108	John Wetteland	.15	.11	.06
109	Bernie Williams	.15	.11	.06
110	Scott Kamieniecki	.15	.11	.06
111	Robin Yount	.25	.20	.10
112	Dean Palmer	.15	.11	.06
113	Tim Belcher	.10	.08	.04
114	George Brett	.25	.20	.10
115	Frank Viola	.20	.15	.08
116	Kelly Gruber	.10	.08	.04
117	David Justice	.25	.20	.10
118	Scott Leuis	.10	.08	.04
119	Jeff Fassero	.10	.08	.04
120	Sammy Sosa	.12	.09	.05
121	Al Osuna	.08	.06	.03
122	Wilson Alvarez	.10	.08	.04
123	Jose Offerman	.15	.11	.06
124	Mel Rojas	.10	.08	.04
125	Shawon Dunston	.10	.08	.04
126	Pete Incaviglia	.10	.08	.04
127	Von Hayes	.08	.06	.03
128	Dave Gallagher	.08	.06	.03
129	Eric Davis	.15	.11	.06
130	Roberto Alomar	.50	.40	.20
131	Mike Gallego	.08	.06	.03
132	Robin Ventura	.40	.30	.15
133	Bill Swift	.10	.08	.04
134	John Kruk	.15	.11	.06
135	Craig Biggio	.15	.11	.06
136	Eddie Taubensee	.25	.20	.10
137	Cal Ripken, Jr.	.75	.60	.30
138	Charles Nagy	.15	.11	.06
139	Jose Melendez	.20	.15	.08
140	Jim Abbott	.20	.15	.08
141	Paul Molitor	.20	.15	.08
142	Tom Candiotti	.08	.06	.03
143	Bobby Bonilla	.40	.30	.15
144	Matt Williams	.15	.11	.06
145	Brett Butler	.12	.09	.05
146	Will Clark	.50	.40	.20
147	Rickey Henderson	.30	.25	.12

		MT	NR MT	EX
148	Ray Lankford	.30	.25	.12
149	Bill Pecota	.08	.06	.03
150	Dave Winfield	.20	.15	.08
151	Darren Lewis	.10	.08	.04
152	Bob MacDonald	.10	.08	.04
153	David Segui	.10	.08	.04
154	Benny Santiago	.20	.15	.08
155	Chuck Finley	.12	.09	.05
156	Andujar Cedeno	.25	.20	.10
157	Barry Bonds	.50	.40	.20
158	Joe Grahe	.08	.06	.03
159	Frank Castillo	.15	.11	.06
160	Dave Burba	.08	.06	.03
161	Leo Gomez	.15	.11	.06
162	Orel Hershiser	.15	.11	.06
163	Delino DeShields	.20	.15	.08
164	Sandy Alomar	.30	.25	.12
165	Denny Neagle	.20	.15	.08
166	Fred McGriff	.25	.20	.10
167	Ken Griffey, Jr.	.80	.60	.30
168	Juan Guzman	.50	.40	.20
169	Bobby Rose	.08	.06	.03
170	Steve Avery	.15	.11	.06
171	Rich DeLucia	.10	.08	.04
172	Mike Timlin	.15	.11	.06
173	Randy Johnson	.10	.08	.04
174	Paul Gibson	.08	.06	.03
175	David Cone	.15	.11	.06
176	Marquis Grissom	.20	.15	.08
177	Kurt Stillwell	.08	.06	.03
178	Mark Whiten	.15	.11	.06
179	Darryl Strawberry	.25	.20	.10
180	Mike Morgan	.08	.06	.03
181	Scott Scudder	.08	.06	.03
182	George Bell	.15	.11	.06
183	Alvin Davis	.08	.06	.03
184	Len Dykstra	.15	.11	.06
185	Kyle Abbott	.15	.11	.06
186	Chris Haney	.15	.11	.06
187	Junior Noboa	.08	.06	.03
188	Dennis Eckersley	.20	.15	.08
189	Derek Bell	.35	.25	.14
190	Lee Smith	.12	.09	.05
191	Andres Galarraga	.10	.08	.04
192	Jack Armstrong	.08	.06	.03
193	Eddie Murray	.15	.11	.06
194	Joe Carter	.20	.15	.08
195	Terry Pendleton	.20	.15	.08
196	Darryl Kile	.15	.11	.06
197	Rod Beck	.15	.11	.06
198	Hubie Brooks	.08	.06	.03

1993 O-Pee-Chee

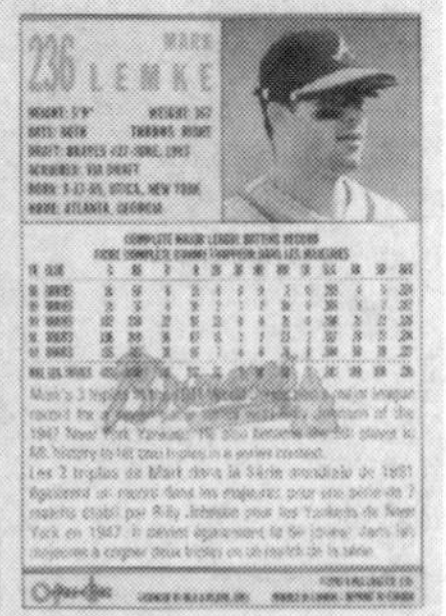

For the first time in history, the 1993 O-Pee-Chee set differed significantly from the Topps set; photographs and designs are entirely different. Team names are scripted across the top, but a yellow triangle with a new team name appears on the front for players who have been traded. Two insert sets honoring the 1992 World Champion Toronto Blue Jays were also produced.

		MT	NR MT	EX
Complete Set (396):		80.00	60.00	32.00
Common Player:		.15	.11	.06
1	Jim Abbott	.30	.25	.12
2	Eric Anthony	.15	.11	.06
3	Harold Baines	.15	.11	.06
4	Roberto Alomar	1.75	1.25	.70
5	Steve Avery	1.00	.70	.40
6	James Austin	.15	.11	.06
7	Mark Wohlers	.15	.11	.06
8	Steve Buechele	.15	.11	.06
9	Pedro Astacio	1.00	.70	.40
10	Moises Alou	.30	.25	.12
11	Rod Beck	.25	.20	.10
12	Sandy Alomar	.15	.11	.06
13	Brett Boone	.40	.30	.15
14	Bryan Harvey	.15	.11	.06
15	Bobby Bonilla	.20	.15	.08
16	Brady Anderson	.15	.11	.06
17	Andy Benes	.20	.15	.08
18	Ruben Amaro	.15	.11	.06
19	Jay Bell	.15	.11	.06
20	Kevin Brown	.15	.11	.06
21	Scott Bankhead	.15	.11	.06
22	Denis Boucher	.15	.11	.06
23	Kevin Appier	.20	.15	.08
24	Pat Kelly	.15	.11	.06
25	Rick Aguilera	.15	.11	.06
26	George Bell	.15	.11	.06
27	Steve Farr	.15	.11	.06
28	Chad Curtis	1.00	.70	.40
29	Jeff Bagwell	1.25	.90	.50
30	Lance Blankenship	.10	.08	.04
31	Derek Bell	.40	.30	.15
32	Damon Berryhill	.10	.08	.04
33	Ricky Bones	.15	.11	.06
34	Rheal Cormier	.15	.11	.06
35	Andre Dawson	.25	.20	.10
36	Brett Butler	.15	.11	.06
37	Sean Berry	.15	.11	.06
38	Bud Black	.15	.11	.06
39	Carlos Baerga	2.00	1.50	.80
40	Jay Buhner	.15	.11	.06
41	Charlie Hough	.15	.11	.06
42	Sid Fernandez	.15	.11	.06
43	Luis Mercedes	.15	.11	.06
44	Jerald Clark	.15	.11	.06
45	Wes Chamberlain	.15	.11	.06
46	Barry Bonds	2.50	2.00	1.00
47	Jose Canseco	.40	.30	.15
48	Tim Belcher	.15	.11	.06
49	David Nied	2.50	2.00	1.00
50	George Brett	1.00	.70	.40
51	Cecil Fielder	.80	.60	.30
52	Chili Davis	.15	.11	.06
53	Alex Fernandez	.50	.40	.20
54	Charlie Hayes	.15	.11	.06
55	Rob Ducey	.15	.11	.06
56	Craig Biggio	.15	.11	.06
57	Mike Bordick	.15	.11	.06
58	Pat Borders	.15	.11	.06
59	Jeff Blauser	.15	.11	.06
60	Chris Bosio	.15	.11	.06
61	Bernard Gilkey	.15	.11	.06
62	Shawon Dunston	.15	.11	.06
63	Tom Candiotti	.15	.11	.06
64	Darrin Fletcher	.15	.11	.06
65	Jeff Brantley	.15	.11	.06
66	Albert Belle	2.00	1.50	.80
67	Dave Fleming	.40	.30	.15
68	John Franco	.15	.11	.06
69	Glenn Davis	.15	.11	.06
70	Tony Fernandez	.15	.11	.06
71	Darren Daulton	.30	.25	.12
72	Doug Drabek	.15	.11	.06
73	Julio Franco	.15	.11	.06
74	Tom Browning	.15	.11	.06
75	Tom Gordon	.15	.11	.06
76	Travis Fryman	2.00	1.50	.80
77	Scott Erickson	.15	.11	.06
78	Carlton Fisk	.15	.11	.06
79	Roberto Kelly	.15	.11	.06
80	Gary DiSarcina	.15	.11	.06
81	Ken Caminiti	.15	.11	.06
82	Ron Darling	.15	.11	.06
83	Joe Carter	.90	.70	.35
84	Sid Bream	.15	.11	.06
85	Cal Eldred	.40	.30	.15
86	Mark Grace	.40	.30	.15
87	Eric Davis	.15	.11	.06
88	Ivan Calderon	.15	.11	.06
89	John Burkett	.15	.11	.06
90	Felix Fermin	.15	.11	.06
91	Ken Griffey Jr.	7.50	5.75	3.00
92	Doc Gooden	.15	.11	.06
93	Mike Devereaux	.15	.11	.06

		MT	NR MT	EX
94	Tony Gwynn	.50	.40	.20
95	Mariano Duncan	.15	.11	.06
96	Jeff King	.15	.11	.06
97	Juan Gonzalez	7.50	5.75	3.00
98	Norm Charlton	.15	.11	.06
99	Mark Gubicza	.15	.11	.06
100	Danny Gladden	.15	.11	.06
101	Greg Gagne	.15	.11	.06
102	Ozzie Guillen	.15	.11	.06
103	Don Mattingly	1.00	.70	.40
104	Damion Easley	.60	.45	.25
105	Casey Candaele	.15	.11	.06
106	Dennis Eckersley	.15	.11	.06
107	David Cone	.15	.11	.06
108	Ron Gant	.60	.45	.25
109	Mike Fetters	.15	.11	.06
110	Mike Harkey	.15	.11	.06
111	Kevin Gross	.15	.11	.06
112	Archi Cianfrocco	.15	.11	.06
113	Will Clark	1.00	.70	.40
114	Glenallen Hill	.15	.11	.06
115	Erik Hanson	.15	.11	.06
116	Todd Hundley	.15	.11	.06
117	Leo Gomez	.15	.11	.06
118	Bruce Hurst	.15	.11	.06
119	Len Dykstra	.40	.30	.15
120	Jose Lind	.15	.11	.06
121	Jose Guzman	.15	.11	.06
122	Rob Dibble	.15	.11	.06
123	Gregg Jefferies	.20	.15	.08
124	Bill Gulickson	.15	.11	.06
125	Brian Harper	.15	.11	.06
126	Roberto Hernandez	.15	.11	.06
127	Sam Millitello	.40	.30	.15
128	Junior Felix	.15	.11	.06
129	Andujar Cedeno	.15	.11	.06
130	Rickey Henderson	.40	.30	.15
131	Bob MacDonald	.15	.11	.06
132	Tom Glavine	1.00	.70	.40
133	Scott Fletcher	.15	.11	.06
134	Brian Jordan	.50	.40	.20
135	Greg Maddux	.60	.45	.25
136	Orel Hershiser	.15	.11	.06
137	Greg Colbrunn	.15	.11	.06
138	Royce Clayton	.15	.11	.06
139	Thomas Howard	.15	.11	.06
140	Randy Johnson	.30	.25	.12
141	Jeff Innis	.15	.11	.06
142	Chris Hoiles	.15	.11	.06
143	Darrin Jackson	.15	.11	.06
144	Tommy Greene	.15	.11	.06
145	Mike LaValliere	.15	.11	.06
146	*David Hulse*	1.25	.90	.50
147	Barry Larkin	.20	.15	.08
148	Wally Joyner	.15	.11	.06
149	Mike Henneman	.15	.11	.06
150	Kent Hrbek	.15	.11	.06
151	Bo Jackson	.50	.40	.20
152	Rich Monteleone	.15	.11	.06
153	Chuck Finley	.15	.11	.06
154	Steve Finley	.15	.11	.06
155	Dave Henderson	.15	.11	.06
156	Kelly Gruber	.15	.11	.06
157	Brian Hunter	.15	.11	.06
158	Darryl Hamilton	.15	.11	.06
159	Derrick May	.30	.25	.12
160	Jay Howell	.15	.11	.06
161	Wil Cordero	.50	.40	.20
162	Bryan Hickerson	.15	.11	.06
163	Reggie Jefferson	.15	.11	.06
164	Edgar Martinez	.15	.11	.06
165	Nigel Wilson	3.50	2.75	1.50
166	Howard Johnson	.15	.11	.06
167	Tim Hulett	.15	.11	.06
168	Mike Maddux	.15	.11	.06
169	Dave Hollins	.60	.45	.25
170	Zane Smith	.15	.11	.06
171	Rafael Palmeiro	.25	.20	.10
172	Dave Martinez	.15	.11	.06
173	Rusty Meacham	.15	.11	.06
174	Mark Leiter	.15	.11	.06
175	Chuck Knoblauch	.30	.25	.12
176	Lance Johnson	.15	.11	.06
177	Matt Nokes	.15	.11	.06
178	Luis Gonzalez	.15	.11	.06
179	Jack Morris	.15	.11	.06
180	David Justice	1.75	1.25	.70
181	Doug Henry	.15	.11	.06
182	Felix Jose	.15	.11	.06
183	Delino DeShields	.40	.30	.15
184	Rene Gonzales	.15	.11	.06
185	Pete Harnisch	.15	.11	.06
186	Mike Moore	.15	.11	.06
187	Juan Guzman	1.00	.70	.40
188	John Olerud	2.00	1.50	.80
189	Ryan Klesko	2.00	1.50	.80
190	John Jaha	.40	.30	.15
191	Ray Lankford	.50	.40	.20
192	Jeff Fassero	.15	.11	.06
193	Darren Lewis	.15	.11	.06
194	Mark Lewis	.15	.11	.06
195	Alan Mills	.15	.11	.06
196	Wade Boggs	.40	.30	.15
197	Hal Morris	.15	.11	.06
198	Ron Karkovice	.15	.11	.06
199	John Grahe	.15	.11	.06
200	Butch henry	.15	.11	.06
201	Mark McGwire	.60	.45	.25
202	Tom Henke	.15	.11	.06
203	Ed Sprague	.15	.11	.06
204	Charlie Leibrandt	.15	.11	.06
205	Pat Listach	.50	.40	.20
206	Omar Olivares	.15	.11	.06
207	Mike Morgan	.15	.11	.06
208	Eric Karros	1.00	.70	.40
209	Marquis Grissom	.75	.60	.30
210	Willie McGee	.15	.11	.06
211	Derek Lilliquist	.15	.11	.06
212	Tino Martinez	.15	.11	.06
213	Jeff Kent	.15	.11	.06
214	Mike Mussina	1.75	1.25	.70
215	Randy Myers	.15	.11	.06
216	John Kruk	.25	.20	.10
217	Tom Brunansky	.15	.11	.06
218	Paul O'Neill	.15	.11	.06
219	Scott Livingstone	.15	.11	.06
220	John Valentin	.60	.45	.25
221	Eddie Zosky	.15	.11	.06
222	Pete Smith	.15	.11	.06
223	Bill Wegman	.15	.11	.06
224	Todd Zeile	.30	.25	.12
225	Tim Wallach	.15	.11	.06
226	Mitch Williams	.15	.11	.06
227	Tim Wakefield	.30	.25	.12
228	Frank Viola	.15	.11	.06
229	Nolan Ryan	5.00	3.75	2.00
230	Kirk McCaskill	.15	.11	.06
231	Melido Perez	.15	.11	.06
232	Mark Langston	.15	.11	.06
233	Xavier Hernandez	.15	.11	.06
234	Jerry Browne	.15	.11	.06
235	Dave Stieb	.15	.11	.06
236	Mark Lemke	.15	.11	.06
237	Paul Molitor	.50	.40	.20
238	Geronimo Pena	.15	.11	.06
239	Ken Hill	.15	.11	.06
240	Jack Clark	.15	.11	.06
241	Greg Myers	.15	.11	.06
242	Pete Incaviglia	.15	.11	.06
243	Ruben Sierra	.40	.30	.15
244	Todd Stottlemyre	.15	.11	.06
245	Pat Hentgen	2.00	1.50	.80
246	Melvin Nieves	1.50	1.25	.60
247	Jaime Navarro	.15	.11	.06
248	Donovan Osborne	.40	.30	.15
249	Brian Barnes	.15	.11	.06
250	Cory Snyder	.15	.11	.06
251	Kenny Lofton	1.50	1.25	.60
252	Kevin Mitchell	.15	.11	.06
253	Dave Magadan	.15	.11	.06
254	Ben McDonald	.40	.30	.15
255	Fred McGriff	.80	.60	.30
256	Mickey Morandini	.15	.11	.06
257	Randy Tomlin	.15	.11	.06
258	Dean Palmer	.75	.60	.30
259	Roger Clemens	1.50	1.25	.60
260	Joe Oliver	.15	.11	.06
261	Jeff Montgomery	.15	.11	.06
262	Tony Phillips	.15	.11	.06
263	Shane Mack	.15	.11	.06
264	Jack McDowell	.75	.60	.30
265	Mike Macfarlane	.15	.11	.06
266	Luis Polonia	.15	.11	.06
267	Doug Jones	.15	.11	.06
268	Terry Steinbach	.15	.11	.06
269	Jimmy Key	.15	.11	.06
270	Pat Taber	.15	.11	.06
271	Otis Nixon	.15	.11	.06
272	Dave Nilsson	.30	.25	.12
273	Tom Pagnozzi	.15	.11	.06
274	Ryne Sandberg	2.00	1.50	.80
275	Ramon Martinez	.20	.15	.08

		MT	NR MT	EX
276	*Tim Laker*	.60	.45	.25
277	Bill Swift	.15	.11	.06
278	Charles Nagy	.15	.11	.06
279	Harold Reynolds	.15	.11	.06
280	Eddie Murray	.40	.30	.15
281	Gregg Olson	.15	.11	.06
282	Frank Seminara	.15	.11	.06
283	Terry Mulholland	.15	.11	.06
284	Kevin Palmer	.40	.30	.15
285	Mike Greenwell	.20	.15	.08
286	Jose Rijo	.15	.11	.06
287	Brian McRae	.15	.11	.06
288	Frank Tanana	.15	.11	.06
289	Pedro Munoz	.15	.11	.06
290	Tim Raines	.15	.11	.06
291	Andy Stankiewicz	.15	.11	.06
292	Tim Salmon	14.00	10.50	5.50
293	Jimmy Jones	.15	.11	.06
294	Dave Stewart	.15	.11	.06
295	Mike Timlin	.15	.11	.06
296	Greg Olson	.15	.11	.06
297	Dan Plesac	.15	.11	.06
298	Mike Perez	.15	.11	.06
299	Jose Offerman	.15	.11	.06
300	Denny Martinez	.15	.11	.06
301	Robby Thompson	.15	.11	.06
302	Bret Saberhagen	.15	.11	.06
303	Joe Orsulak	.15	.11	.06
304	Tim Naehring	.15	.11	.06
305	Bip Roberts	.15	.11	.06
306	Kirby Puckett	2.00	1.50	.80
307	Steve Sax	.15	.11	.06
308	Danny Tartabull	.15	.11	.06
309	Jeff Juden	.15	.11	.06
310	Duane Ward	.15	.11	.06
311	Alejandro Pena	.15	.11	.06
312	Kevin Seitzer	.15	.11	.06
313	Ozzie Smith	.90	.70	.35
314	Mike Piazza	22.00	16.50	8.75
315	Chris Nabholz	.15	.11	.06
316	Tony Pena	.15	.11	.06
317	Gary Sheffield	.75	.60	.30
318	Mark Portugal	.15	.11	.06
319	Walt Weiss	.15	.11	.06
320	Manuel Lee	.15	.11	.06
321	David Wells	.15	.11	.06
322	Terry Pendleton	.15	.11	.06
323	Billy Spiers	.15	.11	.06
324	Lee Smith	.15	.11	.06
325	Bob Scanlan	.15	.11	.06
326	Mike Scioscia	.15	.11	.06
327	Spike Owen	.15	.11	.06
328	Mackey Sasser	.15	.11	.06
329	Arthur Rhodes	.40	.30	.15
330	Ben Rivera	.15	.11	.06
331	Ivan Rodriguez	1.75	1.25	.70
332	Phil Plantier	.60	.45	.25
333	Chris Sabo	.15	.11	.06
334	Mickey Tettleton	.15	.11	.06
335	John Smiley	.15	.11	.06
336	Bobby Thigpen	.15	.11	.06
337	Randy Velarde	.15	.11	.06
338	Luis Sojo	.15	.11	.06
339	Scott Servais	.15	.11	.06
340	Bob Welch	.15	.11	.06
341	Devon White	.30	.25	.12
342	Jeff Reardon	.15	.11	.06
343	B.J. Surhoff	.15	.11	.06
344	Bob Tewksbury	.15	.11	.06
345	Jose Vizcaino	.15	.11	.06
346	Mike Sharperson	.15	.11	.06
347	Mel Rojas	.15	.11	.06
348	Matt Williams	.60	.45	.25
349	Steve Olin	.15	.11	.06
350	Mike Schooler	.15	.11	.06
351	Ryan Thompson	.75	.60	.30
352	Cal Ripken	2.00	1.50	.80
353	Benny Santiago	.15	.11	.06
354	Curt Schilling	.15	.11	.06
355	Andy Van Slyke	.30	.25	.12
356	Kenny Rogers	.15	.11	.06
357	Jody Reed	.15	.11	.06
358	Reggie Sanders	.90	.70	.35
359	Kevin McReynolds	.15	.11	.06
360	Alan Trammell	.15	.11	.06
361	Kevin Tapani	.15	.11	.06
362	Frank Thomas	9.00	6.75	3.50
363	Bernie Williams	.30	.25	.12
364	John Smoltz	.40	.30	.15
365	Robin Yount	.90	.70	.35
366	John Wetteland	.15	.11	.06
367	Bob Zupcic	.15	.11	.06
368	Julio Valera	.15	.11	.06
369	Brian Williams	.15	.11	.06
370	Willie Wilson	.15	.11	.06
371	Dave Winfield	1.00	.70	.40
372	Deion Sanders	.75	.60	.30
373	Greg Vaughn	.40	.30	.15
374	Todd Worrell	.15	.11	.06
375	Darryl Strawberry	.15	.11	.06
376	John Vander Wal	.15	.11	.06
377	Mike Benjamin	.15	.11	.06
378	Mark Whiten	.15	.11	.06
379	Omar Vizquel	.15	.11	.06
380	Anthony Young	.15	.11	.06
381	Rick Sutcliffe	.15	.11	.06
382	Candy Maldonado	.15	.11	.06
383	Francisco Cabrera	.15	.11	.06
384	Larry Walker	.75	.60	.30
385	Scott Cooper	.30	.25	.12
386	Gerald Williams	.15	.11	.06
387	Robin Ventura	1.00	.70	.40
388	Carl Willis	.15	.11	.06
389	Lou Whitaker	.15	.11	.06
390	Hipolito Pichardo	.15	.11	.06
391	Rudy Seanez	.15	.11	.06
392	Greg Swindell	.15	.11	.06
393	Mo Vaughn	1.25	.90	.50
394	Checklist (1 of 3)	.15	.11	.06
395	Checklist (2 of 3)	.15	.11	.06
396	Checklist (3 of 3)	.15	.11	.06

1993 O-Pee-Chee World Champs

Photos not available at press time

This 18-card insert set commemorates the Toronto Blue Jays' 1992 World Series victory; seventeen players and Manager Cito Gaston are featured. Cards were randomly inserted, one World Champs or World Series Heroes card per every 69-cent, eight-card pack.

		MT	NR MT	EX
Complete Set (18):		11.00	8.25	4.50
Common Player:		.25	.20	.10
1	Roberto Alomar	2.50	2.00	1.00
2	Pat Borders	.30	.25	.12
3	Joe Carter	2.00	1.50	.80
4	David Cone	.35	.25	.14
5	Kelly Gruber	.25	.20	.10
6	Juan Guzman	1.25	.90	.50
7	Tom Henke	.25	.20	.10
8	Jimmy Key	.60	.45	.25
9	Manuel Lee	.25	.20	.10
10	Candy Maldonado	.25	.20	.10
11	Jack Morris	.40	.30	.15
12	John Olerud	3.00	2.25	1.25
13	Ed Sprague	.30	.25	.12
14	Todd Stottlemyre	.25	.20	.10
15	Duane Ward	.35	.25	.14
16	Devon White	.75	.60	.30
17	Dave Winfield	1.25	.90	.50
18	Cito Gaston	.50	.40	.20

A card number in parentheses () indicates the set is unnumbered.

1993 O-Pee-Chee World Series Heroes

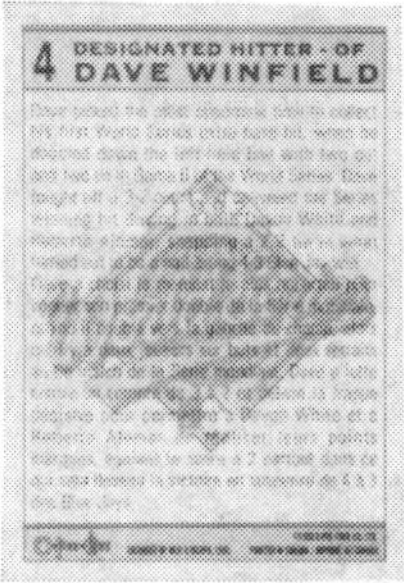

This insert set honors four of the Toronto Blue Jays' World Series stars. Cards were randomly inserted in every 69-cent, eight-card pack, one World Champs or World Series Heroes card per pack.

		MT	NR MT	EX
Complete Set (4):		2.00	1.50	.80
Common Player:		.50	.40	.20
1	Pat Borders	.50	.40	.20
2	Jimmy Key	.50	.40	.20
3	Ed Sprague	.50	.40	.20
4	Dave Winfield	1.00	.70	.40

1993 O-Pee-Chee Premier

For the third consecutive year, O-Pee-Chee produced a set under its Premier brand name. The regular set, issued in three series, has 132 cards and 48 insert cards. The insert sets are titled Star Performers (gold borders), Foil Star Performers (full-bleed photos and gold stamping), and Top Draft Picks (four cards, two each featuring the Toronto Blue Jays and Montreal Expos top picks). O-Pee-Chee announced it produced only 4,000 cases for this set.

		MT	NR MT	EX
Complete Set (132):		15.00	11.00	6.00
Common Player:		.10	.08	.04
1	Barry Bonds	1.00	.70	.40
2	Chad Curtis	.30	.25	.12
3	Chris Bosio	.10	.08	.04
4	Cal Eldred	.20	.15	.08
5	Dan Walter	.10	.08	.04
6	*Rene Arocha*	.70	.50	.30
7	Delino DeShields	.15	.11	.06
8	Spike Owen	.10	.08	.04
9	Jeff Russell	.10	.08	.04
10	Phil Plantier	.20	.15	.08
11	Mike Christopher	.10	.08	.04
12	Darren Daulton	.20	.15	.08
13	Scott Cooper	.10	.08	.04
14	Paul O'Neill	.10	.08	.04
15	Jimmy Key	.10	.08	.04
16	Dickie Thon	.10	.08	.04
17	Greg Gohr	.10	.08	.04
18	Andre Dawson	.15	.11	.06
19	Steve Cooke	.50	.40	.20
20	Tony Fernandez	.10	.08	.04
21	Mark Gardner	.10	.08	.04
22	Dave Martinez	.10	.08	.04
23	Jose Guzman	.10	.08	.04
24	Chili Davis	.10	.08	.04
25	Randy Knorr	.10	.08	.04
26	Mike Piazza	5.00	3.75	2.00
27	Benji Gil	.75	.60	.30
28	Dave Winfield	.30	.25	.12
29	Wil Cordero	.15	.11	.06
30	Butch Henry	.10	.08	.04
31	Eric Young	.50	.40	.20
32	Orestes Destrade	.10	.08	.04
33	Randy Myers	.10	.08	.04
34	Tom Brunansky	.10	.08	.04
35	Dan Wilson	.10	.08	.04
36	Juan Guzman	.40	.30	.15
37	Tim Salmon	3.50	2.75	1.50
38	Bill Krueger	.10	.08	.04
39	Larry Walker	.30	.25	.12
40	*David Hulse*	.50	.40	.20
41	*Ken Ryan*	.25	.20	.10
42	Jose Lind	.10	.08	.04
43	Benny Santiago	.10	.08	.04
44	Ray Lankford	.20	.15	.08
45	Dave Stewart	.10	.08	.04
46	Don Mattingly	.40	.30	.15
47	Fernando Valenzuela	.10	.08	.04
48	Scott Fletcher	.10	.08	.04
49	Wade Boggs	.20	.15	.08
50	Norm Charlton	.10	.08	.04
51	Carlos Baerga	.80	.60	.30
52	John Olerud	1.00	.70	.40
53	Willie Wilson	.10	.08	.04
54	Dennis Moeller	.10	.08	.04
55	Joe Orsulak	.10	.08	.04
56	John Smiley	.10	.08	.04
57	Al Martin	.60	.45	.25
58	Andres Galarraga	.10	.08	.04
59	Billy Ripken	.10	.08	.04
60	Dave Stieb	.10	.08	.04
61	Dave Magadan	.10	.08	.04
62	Todd Worrell	.10	.08	.04
63	*Sherman Obando*	.30	.25	.12
64	Kent Bottenfield	.10	.08	.04
65	Vinny Castilla	.10	.08	.04
66	Charlie Hayes	.10	.08	.04
67	Mike Hartley	.10	.08	.04
68	Harold Baines	.10	.08	.04
69	*John Cummings*	.25	.20	.10
70	*J.T. Snow*	1.75	1.25	.70
71	*Graeme Lloyd*	.40	.30	.15
72	Frank Bolick	.10	.08	.04
73	Doug Drabek	.10	.08	.04
74	Milt Thompson	.10	.08	.04
75	*Tim Pugh*	.50	.40	.20
76	John Kruk	.15	.11	.06
77	Tom Henke	.10	.08	.04
78	Kevin Young	.75	.60	.30
79	Ryan Thompson	.25	.20	.10
80	Mike Hampton	.10	.08	.04
81	Jose Canseco	.20	.15	.08
82	*Mike Lansing*	.60	.45	.25
83	Candy Maldonado	.10	.08	.04
84	Alex Arias	.10	.08	.04
85	Troy Neel	.50	.40	.20
86	Greg Swindell	.10	.08	.04
87	Tim Wallach	.10	.08	.04
88	Andy Van Slyke	.15	.11	.06
89	Harold Baines	.10	.08	.04
90	Bryan Harvey	.10	.08	.04
91	Jerald Clark	.10	.08	.04
92	David Cone	.10	.08	.04
93	Ellis Burks	.10	.08	.04
94	Scott Bankhead	.10	.08	.04
95	Pete Incaviglia	.10	.08	.04
96	Cecil Fielder	.35	.25	.14
97	Sean Berry	.10	.08	.04
98	Gregg Jefferies	.15	.11	.06
99	*Billy Brewer*	.40	.30	.15
100	Scott Sanderson	.10	.08	.04
101	Walt Weiss	.10	.08	.04
102	Travis Fryman	.80	.60	.30
103	Barry Larkin	.15	.11	.06
104	Darren Holmes	.10	.08	.04

		MT	NR MT	EX
105	Ivan Calderon	.10	.08	.04
106	Terry Jorgensen	.10	.08	.04
107	David Nied	1.25	.90	.50
108	*Tim Bogar*	.40	.30	.15
109	Roberto Kelly	.10	.08	.04
110	Mike Moore	.10	.08	.04
111	Carlos Garcia	.20	.15	.08
112	Mike Bielecki	.10	.08	.04
113	Trevor Hoffman	.10	.08	.04
114	Rich Amaral	.10	.08	.04
115	Jody Reed	.10	.08	.04
116	Charlie Leibrandt	.10	.08	.04
117	Greg Gagne	.10	.08	.04
118	*Darrell Sherman*	.80	.60	.30
119	Jeff Conine	.15	.11	.06
120	*Tim Laker*	.30	.25	.12
121	Kevin Seitzer	.10	.08	.04
122	Jeff Mutis	.10	.08	.04
123	Rico Rossy	.10	.08	.04
124	Paul Molitor	.20	.15	.08
125	Cal Ripken	.70	.50	.30
126	Greg Maddux	.25	.20	.10
127	*Greg McMichael*	.30	.25	.12
128	Felix Jose	.10	.08	.04
129	Dick Schofield	.10	.08	.04
130	Jim Abbott	.20	.15	.08
131	Kevin Reimer	.10	.08	.04
132	Checklist	.10	.08	.04

1993 O-Pee-Chee Premier Star Performers

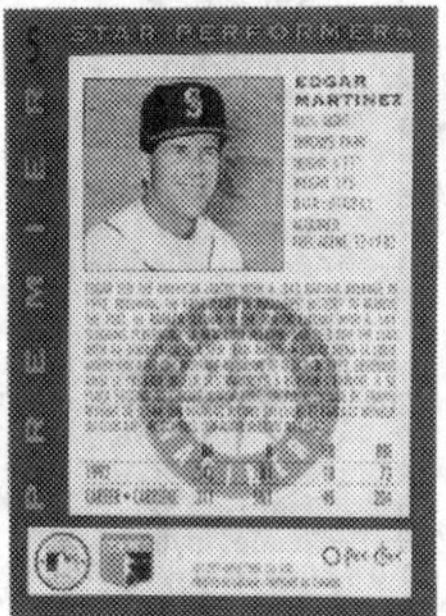

O-Pee-Chee released a 22-card insert set in two forms: Star Performers (featuring a gold border design) and Foil Star Performers (featuring full-bleed photos and gold stamping). The players are identical in both sets, but foil cards are generally worth more. There are 34 Star Performers per 36-card wax box and one Foil Star Performer card per box.

		MT	NR MT	EX
Complete Set (22):		15.00	11.00	6.00
Common Player:		.15	.11	.06
1	Frank Thomas	3.00	2.25	1.25
2	Fred McGriff	.35	.25	.14
3	Roberto Alomar	.60	.45	.25
4	Ryne Sandberg	.60	.45	.25
6	Gary Sheffield	.30	.25	.12
7	Juan Gonzalez	2.00	1.50	.80
8	Eric Karros	.30	.25	.12
9	Ken Griffey Jr.	2.00	1.50	.80
10	Deion Sanders	.20	.15	.08
11	Kirby Puckett	.60	.45	.25
12	Will Clark	.35	.25	.14
13	Joe Carter	.40	.30	.15
14	Barry Bonds	1.00	.70	.40
15	Pat Listach	.15	.11	.06
16	Mark McGwire	.25	.20	.10
17	Kenny Lofton	.40	.30	.15
18	Roger Clemens	.50	.40	.20
19	Greg Maddux	.25	.20	.10
20	Nolan Ryan	2.00	1.50	.80
21	Tom Glavine	.25	.20	.10

1993 O-Pee-Chee Premier Top Draft Picks

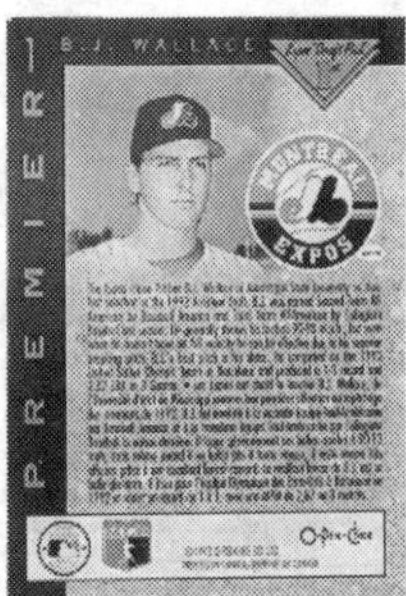

These randomly inserted cards feature four prospects; two each for Montreal and Toronto. Card fronts are foil-stamped and have a vertical banner with the player's name. The OPC Premier logo is in the corner. On back is another player photo, a team logo and a bi-lingual rationale for the player's draft status.

		MT	NR MT	EX
Complete Set (4):		14.00	10.50	5.50
Common Player:		3.50	2.75	1.50
1	B.J. Wallace	6.00	4.50	2.50
2	Shannon Stewart	3.50	2.75	1.50
3	Rod Henderson	5.00	3.75	2.00
4	Todd Steverson	4.50	3.50	1.75

1993 Pacific Spanish

This set marks the first time a major league set was designed entirely for the Spanish-speaking market. Distribution areas included retail markets in the United States, Mexico, South America and the Caribbean. The cards are glossy and are written in Spanish on both sides. Cards are numbered in alphabetical order by team, beginning with Atlanta. Insert sets are titled Prism (20 cards featuring Spanish players and their accomplishments), Beisbol De Estralla (Stars of Baseball), Hot Players and Amigos (a 30-card set which features two players per card).

		MT	NR MT	EX
Complete Set (660):		20.00	15.00	8.00
Complete Series 1 (330):		12.00	9.00	4.75
Complete Series 2 (330):		8.00	6.00	3.25
Common Player:		.05	.04	.02
1	Rafael Belliard	.05	.04	.02

		MT	NR MT	EX
2	Sid Bream	.05	.04	.02
3	Francisco Cabrera	.05	.04	.02
4	Marvin Freeman	.05	.04	.02
5	Ron Gant	.15	.11	.06
6	Tom Glavine	.15	.11	.06
7	Brian Hunter	.05	.04	.02
8	David Justice	.20	.15	.08
9	Ryan Klesko	.50	.40	.20
10	Melvin Nieves	.20	.15	.08
11	Deion Sanders	.20	.15	.08
12	John Smoltz	.15	.11	.06
13	Mark Wohlers	.05	.04	.02
14	Brady Anderson	.15	.11	.06
15	Glenn Davis	.05	.04	.02
16	Mike Devereaux	.05	.04	.02
17	Leo Gomez	.05	.04	.02
18	Chris Hoiles	.15	.11	.06
19	Chito Martinez	.05	.04	.02
20	Ben McDonald	.15	.11	.06
21	Mike Mussina	.40	.30	.15
22	Gregg Olson	.05	.04	.02
23	Joe Orsulak	.05	.04	.02
24	Cal Ripken,Jr.	.50	.40	.20
25	David Segui	.05	.04	.02
26	Rick Sutcliffe	.05	.04	.02
27	Wade Boggs	.20	.15	.08
28	Tom Brunansky	.05	.04	.02
29	Ellis Burks	.05	.04	.02
30	Roger Clemens	.50	.40	.20
31	John Dopson	.05	.04	.02
32	John Flaherty	.05	.04	.02
33	Mike Greenwell	.05	.04	.02
34	Tony Pena	.05	.04	.02
35	Carlos Quintana	.05	.04	.02
36	Luis Rivera	.05	.04	.02
37	Mo Vaughn	.05	.04	.02
38	Frank Viola	.05	.04	.02
39	Matt Young	.05	.04	.02
40	Scott Bailes	.05	.04	.02
41	Bert Blyleven	.05	.04	.02
42	Chad Curtis	.50	.40	.20
43	Gary DiSarcina	.05	.04	.02
44	Chuck Finley	.05	.04	.02
45	Mike Fitzgerald	.05	.04	.02
46	Gary Gaetti	.05	.04	.02
47	Rene Gonzales	.05	.04	.02
48	Mark Langston	.05	.04	.02
49	Scott Lewis	.05	.04	.02
50	Luis Polonia	.05	.04	.02
51	Tim Salmon	.50	.40	.20
52	Lee Stevens	.05	.04	.02
53	Steve Buechele	.05	.04	.02
54	Frank Castillo	.05	.04	.02
55	Doug Dascenzo			
56	Andre Dawson	.20	.15	.08
57	Shawon Dunston	.05	.04	.02
58	Mark Grace	.20	.15	.08
59	Mike Morgan	.05	.04	.02
60	Luis Salazar	.05	.04	.02
61	Rey Sanchez	.05	.04	.02
62	Ryne Sandberg	.50	.40	.20
63	Dwight Smith	.05	.04	.02
64	Jerome Walton	.05	.04	.02
65	Rick Wilkins	.05	.04	.02
66	Wilson Alvarez	.05	.04	.02
67	George Bell	.05	.04	.02
68	Joey Cora	.05	.04	.02
69	Alex Fernandez	.05	.04	.02
70	Carlton Fisk	.05	.04	.02
71	Craig Grebeck	.05	.04	.02
72	Ozzie Guillen	.05	.04	.02
73	Jack McDowell	.20	.15	.08
74	Scott Radinsky	.05	.04	.02
75	Tim Raines	.05	.04	.02
76	Bobby Thigpen	.05	.04	.02
77	Frank Thomas	2.00	1.50	.80
78	Robin Ventura	.30	.25	.12
79	Tom Browning	.05	.04	.02
80	Jacob Brumfield	.05	.04	.02
81	Rob Dibble	.05	.04	.02
82	Bill Doran	.05	.04	.02
83	Billy Hatcher	.05	.04	.02
84	Barry Larkin	.20	.15	.08
85	Hal Morris	.05	.04	.02
86	Joe Oliver	.05	.04	.02
87	Jeff Reed	.05	.04	.02
88	Jose Rijo	.05	.04	.02
89	Bip Roberts	.05	.04	.02
90	Chris Sabo	.05	.04	.02
91	Sandy Alomar, Jr.	.20	.15	.08
92	Brad Arnsberg	.05	.04	.02

		MT	NR MT	EX
93	Carlos Baerga	.30	.25	.12
94	Albert Belle	.30	.25	.12
95	Felix Fermin	.05	.04	.02
96	Mark Lewis	.05	.04	.02
97	Kenny Lofton	.50	.40	.20
98	Carlos Martinez	.05	.04	.02
99	Rod Nicholos	.05	.04	.02
100	Dave Rohde	.05	.04	.02
101	Scott Scudder			
102	Paul Sorrento	.05	.04	.02
103	Mark Whiten	.05	.04	.02
104	Mark Carreon	.05	.04	.02
105	Milt Cuyler	.05	.04	.02
106	Rob Deer	.05	.04	.02
107	Cecil Fielder	.25	.20	.10
108	Travis Fryman	.40	.30	.15
109	Dan Gladden	.05	.04	.02
110	Bill Gullickson	.05	.04	.02
111	Les Lancaster	.05	.04	.02
112	Mark Leiter	.05	.04	.02
113	Tony Phillips	.05	.04	.02
114	Mickey Tettleton	.05	.04	.02
115	Alan Trammell	.05	.04	.02
116	Lou Whitaker	.05	.04	.02
117	Jeff Bagwell	.30	.25	.12
118	Craig Biggio	.05	.04	.02
119	Joe Boever	.05	.04	.02
120	Casey Candaele	.05	.04	.02
121	Andujar Cedeno	.05	.04	.02
122	Steve Finley	.05	.04	.02
123	Luis Gonzalez	.05	.04	.02
124	Pete Harnisch	.05	.04	.02
125	Jimmy Jones	.05	.04	.02
126	Mark Portugal	.05	.04	.02
127	Rafael Ramirez	.05	.04	.02
128	Mike Simms	.05	.04	.02
129	Eric Yelding	.05	.04	.02
130	Luis Aquino	.05	.04	.02
131	Kevin Appier	.05	.04	.02
132	Mike Boddicker	.05	.04	.02
133	George Brett	.30	.25	.12
134	Tom Gordon	.05	.04	.02
135	Mark Gubicza	.05	.04	.02
136	David Howard	.05	.04	.02
137	Gregg Jefferies	.20	.15	.08
138	Wally Joyner	.20	.15	.08
139	Brian McRae	.05	.04	.02
140	Jeff Montgomery	.05	.04	.02
141	Terry Shumpert	.05	.04	.02
142	Curtis Wilkerson	.05	.04	.02
143	Brett Butler	.05	.04	.02
144	Eric Davis	.20	.15	.08
145	Kevin Gross	.05	.04	.02
146	Dave Hansen	.05	.04	.02
147	Lenny Harris	.05	.04	.02
148	Carlos Hernandez	.05	.04	.02
149	Orel Hershiser	.05	.04	.02
150	Jay Howell	.05	.04	.02
151	Eric Karros	.50	.40	.20
152	Ramon Martinez	.20	.15	.08
153	Jose Offerman	.05	.04	.02
154	Mike Sharperson	.05	.04	.02
155	Darryl Strawberry	.30	.25	.12
156	Jim Gantner	.05	.04	.02
157	Darryl Hamilton	.05	.04	.02
158	Doug Henry	.05	.04	.02
159	John Jaha	.20	.15	.08
160	Pat Listach	.50	.40	.20
161	Jaime Navarro	.05	.04	.02
162	Dave Nilsson	.25	.20	.10
163	Jesse Orosco	.05	.04	.02
164	Kevin Seitzer	.05	.04	.02
165	B.J. Surhoff	.05	.04	.02
166	Greg Vaughn	.05	.04	.02
167	Robin Yount	.30	.25	.12
168	Rick Aguilera	.05	.04	.02
169	Scott Erickson	.05	.04	.02
170	Mark Guthrie	.05	.04	.02
171	Kent Hrbek	.05	.04	.02
172	Chuck Knoblauch	.30	.25	.12
173	Gene Larkin	.05	.04	.02
174	Shane Mack	.15	.11	.06
175	Pedro Munoz	.05	.04	.02
176	Mike Pagliarulo	.05	.04	.02
177	Kirby Puckett	.50	.40	.20
178	Kevin Tapani	.05	.04	.02
179	Gary Wayne	.05	.04	.02
180	Moises Alou	.20	.15	.08
181	Brian Barnes	.05	.04	.02
182	Archie Cianfrocco	.05	.04	.02
183	Delino DeShields	.20	.15	.08

		MT	NR MT	EX
184	Darrin Fletcher	.05	.04	.02
185	Marquis Grissom	.30	.25	.12
186	Ken Hill	.05	.04	.02
187	Dennis Martinez	.05	.04	.02
188	Bill Sampen	.05	.04	.02
189	John VanderWal	.05	.04	.02
190	Larry Walker	.30	.25	.12
191	Tim Wallach	.05	.04	.02
192	Bobby Bonilla	.25	.20	.10
193	Daryl Boston	.05	.04	.02
194	Vince Coleman	.05	.04	.02
195	Kevin Elster	.05	.04	.02
196	Sid Fernandez	.05	.04	.02
197	John Franco	.05	.04	.02
198	Dwight Gooden	.25	.20	.10
199	Howard Johnson	.05	.04	.02
200	Willie Randolph	.05	.04	.02
201	Bret Saberhagen	.05	.04	.02
202	Dick Schofield	.05	.04	.02
203	Pete Schourek	.05	.04	.02
204	Greg Cadaret	.05	.04	.02
205	John Habyan	.05	.04	.02
206	Pat Kelly	.05	.04	.02
207	Kevin Maas	.05	.04	.02
208	Don Mattingly	.30	.25	.12
209	Matt Nokes	.05	.04	.02
210	Melido Perez	.05	.04	.02
211	Scott Sanderson	.05	.04	.02
212	Andy Stankiewicz	.05	.04	.02
213	Danny Tartabull	.05	.04	.02
215	Bernie Williams	.05	.04	.02
216	Harold Baines	.05	.04	.02
217	Mike Bordick	.05	.04	.02
218	Scott Brosius	.05	.04	.02
219	Jerry Browne	.05	.04	.02
220	Ron Darling	.05	.04	.02
221	Dennis Eckersley	.25	.20	.10
222	Rickey Henderson	.30	.25	.12
223	Rick Honeycutt	.05	.04	.02
224	Mark McGwire	.30	.25	.12
225	Ruben Sierra	.15	.11	.06
226	Terry Steinbach	.05	.04	.02
227	Bob Welch	.05	.04	.02
228	Willie Wilson	.05	.04	.02
229	Ruben Amaro	.05	.04	.02
230	Kim Batiste	.05	.04	.02
231	Juan Bell	.05	.04	.02
232	Wes Chamberlain	.05	.04	.02
233	Darren Daulton	.15	.11	.06
234	Mariano Duncan	.05	.04	.02
235	Lenny Dykstra	.05	.04	.02
236	Dave Hollins	.15	.11	.06
237	Stan Javier	.05	.04	.02
238	John Kruk	.05	.04	.02
239	Mickey Morandini	.05	.04	.02
240	Terry Mulholland	.05	.04	.02
241	Mitch Williams	.05	.04	.02
242	Stan Belinda	.05	.04	.02
243	Jay Bell	.05	.04	.02
244	Carlos Garcia	.30	.25	.12
245	Jeff King	.05	.04	.02
246	Mike LaValliere	.05	.04	.02
247	Lloyd McClendon	.05	.04	.02
248	Orlando Merced	.05	.04	.02
249	Paul Miller	.05	.04	.02
250	Gary Redus	.05	.04	.02
251	Don Slaught	.05	.04	.02
252	Zane Smith	.05	.04	.02
253	Andy Van Slyke	.15	.11	.06
254	Tim Wakefield	.60	.45	.25
255	Andy Benes	.05	.04	.02
256	Dann Bilardello	.05	.04	.02
257	Tony Gwynn	.25	.20	.10
258	Greg Harris	.05	.04	.02
259	Darrin Jackson	.05	.04	.02
260	Mike Maddux	.05	.04	.02
261	Fred McGriff	.25	.20	.10
262	Rich Rodriguez	.05	.04	.02
263	Benito Santiago	.05	.04	.02
264	Gary Sheffield	.50	.40	.20
265	Kurt Stillwell	.05	.04	.02
266	Tim Teufel	.05	.04	.02
267	Bud Black	.05	.04	.02
268	John Burkett	.05	.04	.02
269	Will Clark	.40	.30	.15
270	Royce Calyton	.15	.11	.06
271	Bryan Hickerson	.05	.04	.02
272	Chris James	.05	.04	.02
273	Darren Lewis	.05	.04	.02
274	Willie McGee	.05	.04	.02
275	Jim McNamara	.05	.04	.02
276	Francisco Oliveras	.05	.04	.02
277	Robby Thompson	.05	.04	.02
278	Matt Williams	.15	.11	.06
279	Trevor Wilson	.05	.04	.02
280	Bret Boone	.25	.20	.10
281	Greg Briley	.05	.04	.02
282	Jay Buhner	.05	.04	.02
283	Henry Cotto	.05	.04	.02
284	Rich DeLucia	.05	.04	.02
285	Dave Fleming	.25	.20	.10
286	Ken Griffey, Jr.	1.00	.70	.40
287	Erik Hanson	.05	.04	.02
288	Randy Johnson	.05	.04	.02
289	Tino Martinez,	.05	.04	.02
290	Edgar Martinez	.20	.15	.08
291	Dave Valle	.05	.04	.02
292	Omar Vizquel	.05	.04	.02
293	Luis Alicea	.05	.04	.02
294	Bernard Gilkey	.05	.04	.02
295	Felix Jose	.05	.04	.02
296	Ray Lankford	.30	.25	.12
297	Omar Olivares	.05	.04	.02
298	Jose Oquendo	.05	.04	.02
299	Tom Pagnozzi	.05	.04	.02
300	Geronimo Pena	.05	.04	.02
301	Gerald Perry	.05	.04	.02
302	Ozzie Smith	.30	.25	.12
303	Lee Smith	.05	.04	.02
304	Bob Tewksbury	.05	.04	.02
305	Todd Zeile	.15	.11	.06
306	Kevin Brown	.05	.04	.02
307	Todd Burns	.05	.04	.02
308	Jose Canseco	.50	.40	.20
309	Hector Fajardo	.05	.04	.02
310	Julio Franco	.05	.04	.02
311	Juan Gonzalez	.50	.40	.20
312	Jeff Huson	.05	.04	.02
313	Rob Maurer	.05	.04	.02
314	Rafael Palmeiro	.20	.15	.08
315	Dean Palmer	.20	.15	.08
316	Ivan Rodriguez	.30	.25	.12
317	Nolan Ryan	.60	.45	.25
318	Dickie Thon	.05	.04	.02
319	Roberto Alomar	.50	.40	.20
320	Derek Bell	.05	.04	.02
321	Pat Borders	.05	.04	.02
322	Joe Carter	.30	.25	.12
323	Kelly Gruber	.05	.04	.02
324	Juan Guzman	.25	.20	.10
325	Manny Lee	.05	.04	.02
326	Jack Morris	.05	.04	.02
327	John Olerud	.05	.04	.02
328	Ed Sprague	.05	.04	.02
329	Todd Stottlemyre	.05	.04	.02
330	Duane Ward	.05	.04	.02
331	Steve Avery	.20	.15	.08
332	Damon Berryhill	.05	.04	.02
333	Jeff Blauser	.05	.04	.02
334	Mark Lemke	.05	.04	.02
335	Greg Maddux	.20	.15	.08
336	Kent Mercker	.05	.04	.02
337	Otis Nixon	.07	.05	.03
338	Greg Olson	.05	.04	.02
339	Bill Pecota	.05	.04	.02
340	Terry Pendleton	.08	.06	.03
341	Mike Stanton	.05	.04	.02
342	Todd Frohwirth	.05	.04	.02
343	Tim Hulett	.05	.04	.02
344	Mark McLemore	.05	.04	.02
345	*Luis Mercedes*	.08	.06	.03
346	Alan Mills	.05	.04	.02
347	*Sherman Obando*	.10	.07	.04
348	Jim Poole	.05	.04	.02
349	Harold Reynolds	.05	.04	.02
350	Arthur Rhodes	.05	.04	.02
351	Jeff Tackett	.05	.04	.02
352	Fernando Valenzuela	.05	.04	.02
353	Scott Bankhead	.05	.04	.02
354	Ivan Calderon	.05	.04	.02
355	Scott Cooper	.08	.06	.03
356	Danny Darwin	.05	.04	.02
357	Scott Fletcher	.05	.04	.02
358	Tony Fossas	.05	.04	.02
359	Greg Harris	.05	.04	.02
360	Joe Hasketh	.05	.04	.02
361	Jose Melendez	.05	.04	.02
362	Paul Quantrill	.08	.06	.03
363	John Valentin	.07	.05	.03
364	*Mike Butcher*	.08	.06	.03
365	Chuck Crim	.05	.04	.02
366	Chili Davis	.05	.04	.02

		MT	NR MT	EX
367	Damion Easley	.10	.07	.04
368	Steve Frey	.05	.04	.02
369	Joe Grahe	.05	.04	.02
370	Greg Myers	.05	.04	.02
371	John Orton	.05	.04	.02
372	*J.T. Snow*	.60	.45	.25
373	Ron Tingley	.05	.04	.02
374	Julio Valera	.05	.04	.02
375	Paul Assenmacher	.05	.04	.02
376	Jose Bautista	.05	.04	.02
377	Jose Guzman	.05	.04	.02
378	Greg Hibbard	.05	.04	.02
379	Candy Maldonado	.05	.04	.02
380	Derrick May	.08	.06	.03
381	Dan Plesac	.05	.04	.02
382	*Tommy Shields*	.08	.06	.03
383	Sammy Sosa	.10	.07	.04
384	Jose Vizcaino	.05	.04	.02
385	*Greg Walbeck*	.08	.06	.03
386	Ellis Burks	.05	.04	.02
387	Roberto Hernandez	.05	.04	.02
388	Mike Huff	.08	.06	.03
389	Bo Jackson	.15	.11	.06
390	Lance Johnson	.05	.04	.02
391	Ron Karkovice	.05	.04	.02
392	Kirk McCaskill	.05	.04	.02
393	Donn Pall	.05	.04	.02
394	Dan Pasqua	.05	.04	.02
395	Steve Sax	.05	.04	.02
396	Dave Stieb	.05	.04	.02
397	*Bobby Ayala*	.07	.05	.03
398	Tim Belcher	.05	.04	.02
399	*Jeff Branson*	.08	.06	.03
400	Cesar Hernandez	.07	.05	.03
401	Roberto Kelly	.08	.06	.03
402	Randy Milligan	.05	.04	.02
403	Kevin Mitchell	.05	.04	.02
404	Juan Samuel	.05	.04	.02
405	Reggie Sanders	.10	.07	.04
406	John Smiley	.05	.04	.02
407	*Dan Wilson*	.15	.11	.06
408	Mike Christopher	.05	.04	.02
409	Dennis Cook	.05	.04	.02
410	Alvaro Espinoza	.05	.04	.02
411	Glenallen Hill	.05	.04	.02
412	Reggie Jefferson	.08	.06	.03
413	Derek Lilliquist	.05	.04	.02
414	Jose Mesa	.05	.04	.02
415	Charles Nagy	.05	.04	.02
416	Junior Ortiz	.05	.04	.02
417	Eric Plunk	.05	.04	.02
418	Ted Power	.05	.04	.02
419	Scott Aldred	.05	.04	.02
420	Andy Ashby	.05	.04	.02
421	Freddie Benavides	.05	.04	.02
422	Dante Bichette	.05	.04	.02
423	Willie Blair	.05	.04	.02
424	Vinny Castilla	.05	.04	.02
425	Jerald Clark	.05	.04	.02
426	Alex Cole	.05	.04	.02
427	Andres Galarraga	.08	.06	.03
428	Joe Girardi	.05	.04	.02
429	Charlie Hayes	.07	.05	.03
430	Butch Henry	.05	.04	.02
431	Darren Holmes	.05	.04	.02
432	Dale Murphy	.08	.06	.03
433	*David Nied*	.20	.15	.08
434	Jeff Parrett	.05	.04	.02
435	Steve Reed	.05	.04	.02
436	Armando Reynoso	.05	.04	.02
437	Bruce Ruffin	.05	.04	.02
438	Bryn Smith	.05	.04	.02
439	*Jim Tatum*	.10	.07	.04
440	Eric Young	.10	.07	.04
441	Skeeter Barnes	.05	.04	.02
442	Tom Bolton	.05	.04	.02
443	Kirk Gibson	.05	.04	.02
444	Chad Krueter	.05	.04	.02
445	Bill Krueger	.05	.04	.02
446	Scott Livingstone	.05	.04	.02
447	Bob MacDonald	.05	.04	.02
448	Mike Moore	.05	.04	.02
449	Mike Munoz	.05	.04	.02
450	Gary Thurman	.05	.04	.02
451	David Wells	.05	.04	.02
452	Alex Arias	.07	.05	.03
453	Jack Armstrong	.05	.04	.02
454	Bret Barberie	.05	.04	.02
455	Ryan Bowen	.08	.06	.03
456	Cris Carpenter	.05	.04	.02
457	Chuck Carr	.08	.06	.03

		MT	NR MT	EX
458	Jeff Conine	.08	.06	.03
459	Steve Decker	.08	.06	.03
460	Orestes Destrade	.07	.05	.03
461	Monty Fariss	.07	.05	.03
462	Junior Felix	.05	.04	.02
463	Bryan Harvey	.07	.05	.03
464	*Trevor Hoffman*	.08	.06	.03
465	Charlie Hough	.05	.04	.02
466	Dave Magadan	.05	.04	.02
467	Bob McClure	.05	.04	.02
468	*Rob Natal*	.07	.05	.03
469	*Scott Pose*	.07	.05	.03
470	Rich Renteria	.05	.04	.02
471	Benito Santiago	.05	.04	.02
472	*Matt Turner*	.08	.06	.03
473	Walt Weiss	.05	.04	.02
474	Eric Anthony	.08	.06	.03
475	Chris Donnels	.05	.04	.02
476	Doug Drabek	.05	.04	.02
477	Xavier Hernandez	.05	.04	.02
478	Doug Jones	.05	.04	.02
479	Darryl Kile	.05	.04	.02
480	Scott Servais	.05	.04	.02
481	Greg Swindell	.05	.04	.02
482	Eddie Taubensee	.05	.04	.02
483	Jose Uribe	.05	.04	.02
484	Brian Williams	.07	.05	.03
485	*Billy Brewer*	.08	.06	.03
486	David Cone	.05	.04	.02
487	Greg Gagne	.05	.04	.02
488	*Phil Hiatt*	.25	.20	.10
489	Jose Lind	.05	.04	.02
490	Brent Mayne	.05	.04	.02
491	Kevin Mcreynolds	.05	.04	.02
492	Keith Miller	.05	.04	.02
493	*Hipolito Pichardo*	.07	.05	.03
494	Harvey Pulliam	.05	.04	.02
495	Rico Rossay	.05	.04	.02
496	*Pedro Astacio*	.15	.11	.06
497	Tom Candiotti	.05	.04	.02
498	Tom Goodwin	.05	.04	.02
499	Jim Gott	.05	.04	.02
500	*Pedro Martinez*	.10	.07	.04
501	Roger McDowell	.05	.04	.02
502	*Mike Piazza*	2.00	1.50	.80
503	Jody Reed	.05	.04	.02
504	Rick Trlicek	.08	.06	.03
505	Mitch Weber	.08	.06	.03
506	Steve Wilson	.05	.04	.02
507	James Austin	.05	.04	.02
508	Ricky Bones	.05	.04	.02
509	*Alex Diaz*	.08	.06	.03
510	Mike Fetters	.05	.04	.02
511	Teddy Higuera	.05	.04	.02
512	*Graeme Lloyd*	.10	.07	.04
513	Carlos Maldonado	.05	.04	.02
514	*Josias Manzanillo*	.08	.06	.03
515	Kevin Reimer	.05	.04	.02
516	Bill Spiers	.05	.04	.02
517	Bill Wegman	.05	.04	.02
518	Willie Banks	.05	.04	.02
519	*J.T. Bruett*	.08	.06	.03
520	Brian Harper	.05	.04	.02
521	Terry Jorgensen	.05	.04	.02
522	Scott Leius	.05	.04	.02
523	Pat Mahomes	.08	.06	.03
524	Dave McCarty	.15	.11	.06
525	Jeff Reboulet	.08	.06	.03
526	Mike Trombley	.05	.04	.02
527	Carl Willis	.05	.04	.02
528	Dave Winfield	.10	.07	.04
529	Sean Berry	.05	.04	.02
530	Frank Bolick	.08	.06	.03
531	Kent Bottenfield	.05	.04	.02
532	Wil Cordero	.10	.07	.04
533	Jeff Fassero	.08	.06	.03
534	*Tim Laker*	.10	.07	.04
535	*Mike Lansing*	.20	.15	.08
536	Chris Nabholz	.05	.04	.02
537	Mel Rojas	.05	.04	.02
538	John Wetteland	.05	.04	.02
539	Ted Wood	.05	.04	.02
540	Mike Draper	.05	.04	.02
541	Tony Fernandez	.05	.04	.02
542	Todd Hundley	.05	.04	.02
543	Jeff Innis	.05	.04	.02
544	Jeff McKnight	.05	.04	.02
545	Eddie Murray	.10	.07	.04
546	Charlie O'Brien	.05	.04	.02
547	Frank Tanana	.05	.04	.02
548	*Ryan Thompson*	.08	.06	.03

		MT	NR MT	EX
549	*Chico Walker*	.10	.07	.04
550	Anthony Young	.05	.04	.02
551	Jim Abbott	.10	.07	.04
552	Wade Boggs	.10	.07	.04
553	Steve Farr	.05	.04	.02
554	Neal Heaton	.05	.04	.02
555	Steve Howe	.05	.04	.02
556	Dion James	.05	.04	.02
557	Scott Kamieniecki	.05	.04	.02
558	Jimmy Key	.05	.04	.02
559	Jim Leyritz	.05	.04	.02
560	Paul O'Neill	.07	.05	.03
561	Spike Owen	.05	.04	.02
562	Lance Blankenship	.05	.04	.02
563	Joe Boever	.05	.04	.02
564	Storm Davis	.05	.04	.02
565	Kelly Downs	.05	.04	.02
566	*Eric Fox*	.10	.07	.04
567	Rich Gossage	.05	.04	.02
568	Dave Henderson	.05	.04	.02
569	Shawn Hillegas	.05	.04	.02
570	Mike Mohler	.08	.06	.03
571	*Troy Neel*	.15	.11	.06
572	Dale Sveum	.05	.04	.02
573	Larry Anderson	.05	.04	.02
574	Bob Ayrault	.05	.04	.02
575	Jose DeLeon	.05	.04	.02
576	Jim Eisenreich	.05	.04	.02
577	Pete Incaviglia	.05	.04	.02
578	Danny Jackson	.05	.04	.02
579	Ricky Jordan	.05	.04	.02
580	Ben Rivera	.05	.04	.02
581	Curt Schilling	.05	.04	.02
582	Milt Thompson	.05	.04	.02
583	David West	.05	.04	.02
584	John Candelaria	.05	.04	.02
585	Steve Cooke	.05	.04	.02
586	Tom Foley	.05	.04	.02
587	*Al Martin*	.10	.07	.04
588	*Blas Minor*	.10	.07	.04
589	Dennis Moeller	.07	.05	.03
590	Denny Neagle	.05	.04	.02
591	Tom Prince	.05	.04	.02
592	Randy Tomlin	.05	.04	.02
593	Bob Walk	.05	.04	.02
594	*Kevin Young*	.10	.07	.04
595	Pat Gomez	.05	.04	.02
596	Ricky Gutierrez	.05	.04	.02
597	Gene Harris	.05	.04	.02
598	Jeremy Hernandez	.05	.04	.02
599	Phil Plantier	.10	.07	.04
600	Tim Scott	.07	.05	.03
601	Frank Seminara	.07	.05	.03
602	*Darrell Sherman*	.07	.05	.03
603	Craig Shipley	.05	.04	.02
604	Guillermo Velasquez	.05	.04	.02
605	Dan Walters	.08	.06	.03
606	Mike Benjamin	.05	.04	.02
607	Barry Bonds	.20	.15	.08
608	Jeff Brantley	.05	.04	.02
609	Dave Burba	.05	.04	.02
610	*Craig Colbert*	.08	.06	.03
611	Mike Jackson	.05	.04	.02
612	Kirt Manwaring	.05	.04	.02
613	Dave Martinez	.05	.04	.02
614	Dave Righetti	.05	.04	.02
615	Kevin Rogers	.05	.04	.02
616	Bill Swift	.05	.04	.02
617	Rich Amaral	.05	.04	.02
618	Mike Blowers	.05	.04	.02
619	Chris Bosio	.05	.04	.02
620	Norm Charlton	.05	.04	.02
621	*John Cummings*	.10	.07	.04
622	Mike Felder	.05	.04	.02
623	Bill Haselman	.05	.04	.02
624	Tim Leary	.05	.04	.02
625	Pete O'Brien	.05	.04	.02
626	Russ Swan	.05	.04	.02
627	*Fernando Vina*	.08	.06	.03
628	*Rene Arocha*	.10	.07	.04
629	Rod Brewer	.05	.04	.02
630	Ozzie Canseco	.05	.04	.02
631	Rheal Cormier	.08	.06	.03
632	Brian Jordan	.08	.06	.03
633	Joe Magrane	.05	.04	.02
634	Donovan Osborne	.05	.04	.02
635	Mike Perez	.05	.04	.02
636	Stan Royer	.05	.04	.02
637	Hector Villanueva	.05	.04	.02
638	Tracy Woodson	.05	.04	.02
639	*Benji Gil*	.35	.25	.14
640	Tom Henke	.05	.04	.02
641	*David Hulse*	.15	.11	.06
642	Charlie Leibrandt	.05	.04	.02
643	*Robb Nen*	.08	.06	.03
644	*Dan Peltier*	.10	.07	.04
645	Billy Ripken	.05	.04	.02
646	Kenny Rogers	.05	.04	.02
647	John Russell	.05	.04	.02
648	*Dan Smith*	.08	.06	.03
649	Matt Whiteside	.08	.06	.03
650	*William Canate*	.10	.07	.04
651	Darnell Coles	.05	.04	.02
652	Al Leiter	.05	.04	.02
653	*Dominigo Martinez*	.08	.06	.03
654	Paul Molitor	.10	.07	.04
655	Luis Sojo	.05	.04	.02
656	Dave Stewart	.05	.04	.02
657	Mike Timlin	.05	.04	.02
658	Turner Ward	.05	.04	.02
659	Devon White	.08	.06	.03
660	Eddie Zosky	.08	.06	.03

1993 Pacific Spanish Gold Foil Stars

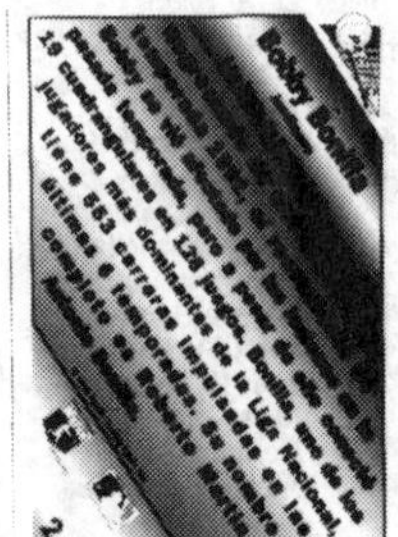

Pacific produced a Gold Foil Stars of Baseball set of 20 that was randomly inserted as part of the company's first-ever Spanish Language Major League set in 1993. Each card features a color action photo on the front surrounded by a gold-foil border. Both the Stars of Baseball and the Pacific Prism sets were limited to 10,000 of each.

		MT	NR MT	EX
Complete Set (20):		300.00	225.00	125.00
Common Player:		12.00	9.00	4.75
1	Moises Alou	18.00	13.50	7.25
2	Bobby Bonilla	15.00	11.00	6.00
3	Tony Fernandez	12.00	9.00	4.75
4	Felix Jose	12.00	9.00	4.75
5	Dennis Martinez	12.00	9.00	4.75
6	Orlando Merced	12.00	9.00	4.75
7	Jose Oquendo	12.00	9.00	4.75
8	Geronimo Pena	12.00	9.00	4.75
9	Jose Rijo	12.00	9.00	4.75
10	Benito Santiago	15.00	11.00	6.00
11	Sandy Alomar Jr.	15.00	11.00	6.00
12	Carlos Baerga	35.00	26.00	14.00
13	Jose Canseco	20.00	15.00	8.00
14	Juan "Igor" Gonzalez	45.00	34.00	18.00
15	Juan Guzman	18.00	13.50	7.25
16	Edgar Martinez	12.00	9.00	4.75
17	Rafael Palmerio	18.00	13.50	7.25
18	Ruben Sierra	18.00	13.50	7.25
19	Danny Tartabull	17.00	12.50	6.75
20	Omar Vizquel	12.00	9.00	4.75

1993 Pacific Prism Insert

Pacific also produced a Prism card that was randomly inserted in the Spanish Language Major League set in 1993. Each card in the 20-card set has a color photo of

the player on the front superimposed over a prismatic background. The card backs contain a color action photo and a brief player biography on a marbelized background.

		MT	NR MT	EX
Complete Set (20):		300.00	225.00	125.00
Common Player:		12.00	9.00	4.75
1	Francisco Cabrera	12.00	9.00	4.75
2	Jose Lind	12.00	9.00	4.75
3	Dennis Martinez	12.00	9.00	4.75
4	Ramon Martinez	14.00	10.50	5.50
5	Jose Rijo	12.00	9.00	4.75
6	Benito Santiago	12.00	9.00	4.75
7	Roberto Alomar	35.00	26.00	14.00
8	Sandy Alomar Jr.	12.00	9.00	4.75
9	Carlos Baerga	35.00	26.00	14.00
10	George Bell	14.00	10.50	5.50
11	Jose Canseco	20.00	15.00	8.00
12	Alex Fernandez	20.00	15.00	8.00
13	Julio Franco	15.00	11.00	6.00
14	Igor (Juan) Gonzalez	45.00	34.00	18.00
15	Ozzie Guillen	12.00	9.00	4.75
16	Teddy Higuera	12.00	9.00	4.75
17	Edgar Martinez	12.00	9.00	4.75
18	Hipolito Pichardo	12.00	9.00	4.75
19	Luis Polonia	12.00	9.00	4.75
20	Ivan Rodriguez	20.00	15.00	8.00

1994 Pacific Crown

Following its 1993 Spanish-language set, Pacific's 1994 "Crown Collection" offering is bi-lingual, featuring both English and Spanish for most of the back printing. Fronts have an action photo which is borderless at the top and sides. A gold-foil line separates the bottom of the photo from a marbled strip that is color-coded by team. The player's name appears in two lines at the left of the strip, a gold-foil crown logo is at left. A Pacific logo appears in one of the upper corners of the photo. Backs have a photo, again borderless at top and sides, with a Pacific logo in one upper corner and the card number and MLB logos in the lower corners. At bottom is a gray marble strip with a few biographical details, 1993 and career stats and a ghost-image color team logo. The 660 cards in the set were issued in a single series.

		MT	NR MT	EX
Complete Set (660):		30.00	22.00	12.00
Common Player:		.08	.06	.03
1	Steve Avery	.20	.15	.08
2	Steve Bedrosian	.08	.06	.03
3	Damion Beryhill	.08	.06	.03
4	Jeff Blauser	.08	.06	.03
5	Sid Bream	.08	.06	.03
6	Francisco Cabrera	.08	.06	.03
7	*Ramon Caraballo*	.15	.11	.06
8	Ron Gant	.15	.11	.06
9	Tom Glavine	.20	.15	.08
10	Chipper Jones	.40	.30	.15
11	Dave Justice	.20	.15	.08
12	Ryan Klesko	.15	.11	.06
13	Mark Lemke	.08	.06	.03
14	Javier Lopez	.50	.40	.20
15	Greg Maddux	.20	.15	.08
16	Fred McGriff	.15	.11	.06
17	Greg McMichael	.10	.07	.04
18	Kent Merker	.08	.06	.03
19	Otis Nixon	.08	.06	.03
20	Terry Pendleton	.10	.07	.04
21	Deion Sanders	.15	.11	.06
22	John Smoltz	.10	.07	.04
23	Tony Tarasco	.35	.25	.14
24	Manny Alexander	.15	.11	.06
25	Brady Anderson	.08	.06	.03
26	Harold Baines	.08	.06	.03
27	Damion Buford	.15	.11	.06
28	Paul Carey	.15	.11	.06
29	Mike Devereaux	.08	.06	.03
30	Todd Frohwirth	.08	.06	.03
31	Leo Gomez	.08	.06	.03
32	Jeffrey Hammonds	.35	.25	.14
33	Chris Hoiles	.08	.06	.03
34	Tim Hullett	.08	.06	.03
35	Ben McDonald	.10	.07	.04
36	Mark McLemore	.08	.06	.03
37	Alan Mills	.10	.07	.04
38	Mike Mussina	.20	.15	.08
39	Sherman Obando	.10	.07	.04
40	Gregg Olson	.08	.06	.03
41	Mike Pagliarulo	.08	.06	.03
42	Jim Poole	.10	.07	.04
43	Harold Reynolds	.08	.06	.03
44	Cal Ripken	.35	.25	.14
45	David Segui	.08	.06	.03
46	Fernando Valenzuela	.08	.06	.03
47	Jack Voight	.08	.06	.03
48	Scott Bankhead	.08	.06	.03
49	Roger Clemens	.15	.11	.06
50	Scott Cooper	.08	.06	.03
51	Danny Darwin	.08	.06	.03
52	Andre Dawson	.10	.07	.04
53	John Dopson	.08	.06	.03
54	Scott Fletcher	.08	.06	.03
55	Tony Fossas	.08	.06	.03
56	Mike Greenwell	.08	.06	.03
57	Billy Hatcher	.08	.06	.03
58	Jeff McNeely	.40	.30	.15
59	Jose Melendez	.08	.06	.03
60	Tim Neahring	.08	.06	.03
61	Tony Pena	.08	.06	.03
62	Carlos Quintana	.08	.06	.03
63	Paul Quantrill	.08	.06	.03
64	Luis Rivera	.08	.06	.03
65	Jeff Russell	.08	.06	.03
66	Aaron Sele	.60	.45	.25
67	John Valentin	.10	.07	.04
68	Mo Vaughn	.10	.07	.04
69	Frank Viola	.08	.06	.03
70	Bob Zupcic	.08	.06	.03
71	Mike Butcher	.08	.06	.03
72	Ron Correia	.08	.06	.03
73	Chad Curtis	.15	.11	.06
74	Chili Davis	.08	.06	.03
75	Gary DiSarcia	.08	.06	.03
76	Damion Easley	.15	.11	.06
77	John Farrell	.08	.06	.03
78	Chuck Finley	.08	.06	.03
79	Joe Grahe	.08	.06	.03
80	Stan Javier	.08	.06	.03
81	Mark Langston	.08	.06	.03
82	Phil Leftwich	.15	.11	.06
83	Torey Lovullo	.08	.06	.03
84	Joe Magrane	.08	.06	.03
85	Greg Myers	.08	.06	.03
86	Eduardo Perez	.08	.06	.03
87	Luis Polonia	.08	.06	.03
88	Tim Salmon	1.25	.90	.50

		MT	NR MT	EX
89	J.T. Snow	.75	.60	.30
90	Kurt Stillwell	.08	.06	.03
91	Ron Tingley	.08	.06	.03
92	Chris Turner	.15	.11	.06
93	Julio Valera	.08	.06	.03
94	Jose Bautista	.08	.06	.03
95	Shawn Boskie	.08	.06	.03
96	Steve Buechele	.08	.06	.03
97	Frank Castillo	.08	.06	.03
98	Mark Grace	.10	.07	.04
99	Jose Guzman	.08	.06	.03
100	Mike Harkey	.08	.06	.03
101	Greg Hibbard	.08	.06	.03
102	Doug Jennings	.10	.07	.04
103	Derrick May	.08	.06	.03
104	Mike Morgan	.08	.06	.03
105	Randy Myers	.08	.06	.03
106	Karl Rhodes	.08	.06	.03
107	Kevin Robinson	.15	.11	.06
108	Rey Sanchez	.08	.06	.03
109	Ryne Sandberg	.40	.30	.15
110	Tommy Shields	.08	.06	.03
111	Dwight Smith	.08	.06	.03
112	Sammy Sosa	.15	.11	.06
113	Jose Vizcaino	.08	.06	.03
114	Turk Wendell	.10	.07	.04
115	Rick Wilkins	.08	.06	.03
116	Willie Wilson	.08	.06	.03
117	Eddie Zambrano	.10	.07	.04
118	Wilson Alvarez	.08	.06	.03
119	Tim Belcher	.08	.06	.03
120	Jason Bere	1.00	.75	.40
121	Rodney Bolton	.08	.06	.03
122	Ellis Burks	.08	.06	.03
123	Joey Cora	.08	.06	.03
124	Alex Fernandez	.10	.07	.04
125	Ozzie Guillen	.08	.06	.03
126	Craig Grebeck	.08	.06	.03
127	Roberto Hernandez	.08	.06	.03
128	Bo Jackson	.15	.11	.06
129	Lance Johnson	.08	.06	.03
130	Ron Karkovice	.08	.06	.03
131	Mike Lavalliere	.08	.06	.03
132	Norberto Martin	.08	.06	.03
133	Kirk McCaskill	.08	.06	.03
134	Jack McDowell	.15	.11	.06
135	Scott Radinsky	.08	.06	.03
136	Tim Raines	.08	.06	.03
137	Steve Sax	.08	.06	.03
138	Frank Thomas	2.50	2.00	1.00
139	Dan Pasqua	.08	.06	.03
140	Robin Ventura	.20	.15	.08
141	Jeff Branson	.08	.06	.03
142	Tom Browning	.08	.06	.03
143	Jacob Brumfield	.15	.11	.06
144	Tim Costo	.10	.07	.04
145	Rob Dibble	.08	.06	.03
146	Brian Dorsett	.15	.11	.06
147	Steve Foster	.08	.06	.03
148	Cesar Hernandez	.08	.06	.03
149	Roberto Kelly	.08	.06	.03
150	Barry Larkin	.10	.07	.04
151	*Larry Luebbers*	.15	.11	.06
152	Kevin Mitchell	.08	.06	.03
153	Joe Oliver	.08	.06	.03
154	Tim Pugh	.08	.06	.03
155	Jeff Reardon	.08	.06	.03
156	Jose Rijo	.08	.06	.03
157	Bip Roberts	.08	.06	.03
158	Chris Sabo	.08	.06	.03
159	Juan Samuel	.08	.06	.03
160	Reggie Sanders	.10	.07	.04
161	John Smiley	.08	.06	.03
162	Jerry Spradlin	.10	.07	.04
163	Gary Varsho	.08	.06	.03
164	Sandy Alomar Jr.	.08	.06	.03
165	Carlos Baerga	.25	.20	.10
166	Albert Belle	.25	.20	.10
167	Mark Clark	.08	.06	.03
168	Alvaro Espinoza	.08	.06	.03
169	Felix Fermin	.08	.06	.03
170	Reggie Jefferson	.10	.07	.04
171	Wayne Kirby	.08	.06	.03
172	Tom Kramer	.08	.06	.03
173	Jesse Levis	.08	.06	.03
174	Kenny Lofton	.15	.11	.06
175	Candy Maldonado	.08	.06	.03
176	Carlos Martinez	.08	.06	.03
177	Jose Mesa	.08	.06	.03
178	Jeff Mutis	.10	.07	.04
179	Charles Nagy	.08	.06	.03

		MT	NR MT	EX
180	Bob Ojeda	.08	.06	.03
181	Junior Ortiz	.08	.06	.03
182	Eric Plunk	.08	.06	.03
183	Manny Ramirez	.15	.11	.06
184	Paul Sorrento	.08	.06	.03
185	Jeff Treadway	.08	.06	.03
186	Bill Wertz	.08	.06	.03
187	Freddie Benavides	.08	.06	.03
188	Dante Bichette	.08	.06	.03
189	Willie Blair	.08	.06	.03
190	Daryl Boston	.08	.06	.03
191	Pedro Castellano	.10	.07	.04
192	Vinny Castilla	.08	.06	.03
193	Jerald Clark	.08	.06	.03
194	Alex Cole	.08	.06	.03
195	Andre Galarraga	.10	.07	.04
196	Joe Girardi	.08	.06	.03
197	Charlie Hayes	.08	.06	.03
198	Darren Holmes	.08	.06	.03
199	Chris Jones	.10	.07	.04
200	Curt Leskanic	.10	.07	.04
201	Roberto Mejia	.10	.07	.04
202	David Nied	.35	.25	.14
203	*J. Owens*	.15	.11	.06
204	Steve Reed	.10	.07	.04
205	Armando Reynoso	.08	.06	.03
206	Bruce Ruffin	.08	.06	.03
207	Keith Shepherd	.08	.06	.03
208	Jim Tatum	.10	.07	.04
209	Eric Young	.15	.11	.06
210	Skeeter Barnes	.08	.06	.03
211	Danny Bautista	.08	.06	.03
212	Tom Bolton	.08	.06	.03
213	Eric Davis	.08	.06	.03
214	Storm Davis	.08	.06	.03
215	John Doherty	.08	.06	.03
216	Cecil Fielder	.15	.11	.06
217	Travis Fryman	.40	.30	.15
218	Kirk Gibson	.08	.06	.03
219	Dan Gladden	.08	.06	.03
220	Chris Gomez	.08	.06	.03
221	David Haas	.08	.06	.03
222	Bill Krueger	.08	.06	.03
223	Chad Kreuter	.08	.06	.03
224	Mark Leiter	.08	.06	.03
225	Bob MacDonald	.08	.06	.03
226	Mike Moore	.08	.06	.03
227	Tony Phillips	.08	.06	.03
228	Rich Rowland	.10	.07	.04
229	Mickey Tettleton	.08	.06	.03
230	Alan Trammell	.08	.06	.03
231	David Wells	.08	.06	.03
232	Lou Whitaker	.08	.06	.03
233	Luis Aquino	.08	.06	.03
234	Alex Arias	.10	.07	.04
235	Jack Armstrong	.08	.06	.03
236	Ryan Bowen	.10	.07	.04
237	Chuck Carr	.08	.06	.03
238	Matias Carrillo	.10	.07	.04
239	Jeff Conine	.08	.06	.03
240	Henry Cotto	.08	.06	.03
241	Orestes Destrade	.08	.06	.03
242	Chris Hammond	.08	.06	.03
243	Bryan Harvey	.08	.06	.03
244	Charlie Hough	.08	.06	.03
245	Richie Lewis	.10	.07	.04
246	Mitch Lyden	.10	.07	.04
247	Dave Magadan	.08	.06	.03
248	Bob Natal	.08	.06	.03
249	Benito Santiago	.08	.06	.03
250	Gary Sheffield	.15	.11	.06
251	Matt Turner	.08	.06	.03
252	Walt Weiss	.08	.06	.03
253	David Weathers	.10	.07	.04
254	Darrell Whitmore	.15	.11	.06
255	Nigel Wilson	.25	.20	.10
256	Eric Anthony	.10	.07	.04
257	Jeff Bagwell	.25	.20	.10
258	Kevin Bass	.08	.06	.03
259	Craig Biggio	.08	.06	.03
260	Ken Caminiti	.08	.06	.03
261	Andujar Cedeno	.10	.07	.04
262	Chris Donnels	.08	.06	.03
263	Doug Drabek	.08	.06	.03
264	Tom Edens	.08	.06	.03
265	Steve Finley	.08	.06	.03
266	Luis Gonzalez	.08	.06	.03
267	Pete Harnisch	.08	.06	.03
268	Xavier Hernandez	.08	.06	.03
269	Todd Jones	.08	.06	.03
270	Darryl Kile	.08	.06	.03

		MT	NR MT	EX
271	Al Osuna	.08	.06	.03
272	Rick Parker	.10	.07	.04
273	Mark Portugal	.08	.06	.03
274	Scott Servais	.08	.06	.03
275	Greg Swindell	.08	.06	.03
276	Eddie Taubensee	.08	.06	.03
277	Jose Uribe	.08	.06	.03
278	Brian Williams	.08	.06	.03
279	Kevin Appier	.08	.06	.03
280	Billy Brewer	.10	.07	.04
281	David Cone	.08	.06	.03
282	Greg Gagne	.08	.06	.03
283	Tom Gordon	.08	.06	.03
284	Chris Gwynn	.08	.06	.03
285	John Habyan	.08	.06	.03
286	Chris Haney	.08	.06	.03
287	Phil Hiatt	.20	.15	.08
288	David Howard	.08	.06	.03
289	Felix Jose	.08	.06	.03
290	Wally Joyner	.08	.06	.03
291	Kevin Koslofski	.10	.07	.04
292	Jose Lind	.08	.06	.03
293	Brent Mayne	.08	.06	.03
294	Mike Mcfarlane	.08	.06	.03
295	Brian McRae	.08	.06	.03
296	Kevin McReynolds	.08	.06	.03
297	Keith Miller	.08	.06	.03
298	Jeff Montgomery	.08	.06	.03
299	Hipolito Pichardo	.08	.06	.03
300	Rico Rossy	.08	.06	.03
301	Curtis Wilkerson	.08	.06	.03
302	Pedro Astacio	.15	.11	.06
303	Rafael Bournigal	.08	.06	.03
304	Brett Butler	.08	.06	.03
305	Tom Candiotti	.08	.06	.03
306	Omar Daal	.10	.07	.04
307	Jim Gott	.08	.06	.03
308	Kevin Gross	.08	.06	.03
309	Dave Hansen	.08	.06	.03
310	Carlos Hernandez	.08	.06	.03
311	Orel Hershiser	.08	.06	.03
312	Eric Karros	.25	.20	.10
313	Pedro Martinez	.15	.11	.06
314	Ramon Martinez	.10	.07	.04
315	Roger McDowell	.08	.06	.03
316	Raul Mondesi	.10	.07	.04
317	Jose Offerman	.08	.06	.03
318	Mike Piazza	3.00	2.25	1.25
319	Jody Reed	.08	.06	.03
320	Henry Rodriguez	.08	.06	.03
321	Cory Snyder	.08	.06	.03
322	Darryl Strawberry	.08	.06	.03
323	Tim Wallach	.08	.06	.03
324	Steve Wilson	.08	.06	.03
325	Juan Bell	.08	.06	.03
326	Ricky Bones	.08	.06	.03
327	Alex Diaz	.10	.07	.04
328	Cal Eldred	.15	.11	.06
329	Darryl Hamilton	.08	.06	.03
330	Doug Henry	.08	.06	.03
331	John Jaha	.15	.11	.06
332	Pat Listach	.10	.07	.04
333	Graeme Lloyd	.10	.07	.04
334	Carlos Maldonado	.08	.06	.03
335	Angel Miranda	.10	.07	.04
336	Jaime Navarro	.08	.06	.03
337	Dave Nilsson	.08	.06	.03
338	Rafael Novoa	.08	.06	.03
339	Troy O'Leary	.15	.11	.06
340	Jesse Orosco	.08	.06	.03
341	Kevin Seitzer	.08	.06	.03
342	Bill Spiers	.08	.06	.03
343	William Suero	.08	.06	.03
344	B.J. Surhoff	.08	.06	.03
345	Dickie Thon	.08	.06	.03
346	Jose Valentin	.08	.06	.03
347	Greg Vaughn	.10	.07	.04
348	Robin Yount	.20	.15	.08
349	Willie Banks	.08	.06	.03
350	Bernardo Brito	.10	.07	.04
351	Scott Erickson	.08	.06	.03
352	Mark Guthrie	.08	.06	.03
353	Chip Hale	.08	.06	.03
354	Brian Harper	.08	.06	.03
355	Kent Hrbek	.08	.06	.03
356	Terry Jorgenson	.08	.06	.03
357	Chuck Knoblauch	.10	.07	.04
358	Gene Larkin	.08	.06	.03
359	Scott Leius	.08	.06	.03
360	Shane Mack	.08	.06	.03
361	David McCarty	.10	.07	.04

		MT	NR MT	EX
362	Pat Meares	.10	.07	.04
363	Pedro Munoz	.08	.06	.03
364	Derek Parks	.10	.07	.04
365	Kirby Puckett	.25	.20	.10
366	Jeff Reboulet	.10	.07	.04
367	Kevin Tapani	.08	.06	.03
368	Mike Trombley	.08	.06	.03
369	George Tsamis	.10	.07	.04
370	Carl Willis	.08	.06	.03
371	Dave Winfield	.20	.15	.08
372	Moises Alou	.15	.11	.06
373	Brian Barnes	.08	.06	.03
374	Sean Berry	.08	.06	.03
375	Frank Bolick	.08	.06	.03
376	Wil Cordero	.15	.11	.06
377	Delino DeShields	.10	.07	.04
378	Jeff Fassero	.08	.06	.03
379	Darren Fletcher	.08	.06	.03
380	Cliff Floyd	2.00	1.50	.80
381	Lou Frazier	.10	.07	.04
382	Marquis Grissom	.15	.11	.06
383	Gil Heredia	.10	.07	.04
384	Mike Lansing	.20	.15	.08
385	Oreste Marrero	.10	.07	.04
386	Dennis Martinez	.08	.06	.03
387	Curtis Pride	1.00	.75	.40
388	Mel Rojas	.08	.06	.03
389	Kirk Rueter	2.00	1.50	.80
390	Joe Siddall	.10	.07	.04
391	John Vander Wal	.08	.06	.03
392	Larry Walker	.15	.11	.06
393	John Wetteland	.08	.06	.03
394	Rondell White	.40	.30	.15
395	Tom Bogar	.08	.06	.03
396	Bobby Bonilla	.10	.07	.04
397	Jeromy Burnitz	.10	.07	.04
398	Mike Draper	.08	.06	.03
399	Sid Fernandez	.08	.06	.03
400	John Franco	.08	.06	.03
401	Dave Gallagher	.08	.06	.03
402	Dwight Gooden	.08	.06	.03
403	Eric Hillman	.08	.06	.03
404	Todd Hundley	.08	.06	.03
405	Butch Huskey	.08	.06	.03
406	Jeff Innis	.08	.06	.03
407	Howard Johnson	.08	.06	.03
408	Jeff Kent	.08	.06	.03
409	Ced Landrum	.08	.06	.03
410	Mike Maddux	.08	.06	.03
411	Jeff McKnight	.08	.06	.03
412	Josias Manzanillo	.08	.06	.03
413	Eddie Murray	.10	.07	.04
414	Tito Navarro	.10	.07	.04
415	Joe Orlusak	.08	.06	.03
416	Bret Saberhagen	.08	.06	.03
417	Dave Telgheder	.08	.06	.03
418	Ryan Thompson	.15	.11	.06
419	Chico Walker	.15	.11	.06
420	Jim Abbott	.10	.07	.04
421	Wade Boggs	.15	.11	.06
422	Mike Gallego	.08	.06	.03
423	Mark Hutton	.08	.06	.03
424	Dion James	.08	.06	.03
425	Domingo Jean	.10	.07	.04
426	Pat Kelly	.08	.06	.03
427	Jimmy Key	.08	.06	.03
428	Jim Leyritz	.08	.06	.03
429	Kevin Maas	.08	.06	.03
430	Don Mattingly	.15	.11	.06
431	Bobby Munoz	.08	.06	.03
432	Matt Nokes	.08	.06	.03
433	Paul O'Neill	.08	.06	.03
434	Spike Owen	.08	.06	.03
435	Melido Perez	.08	.06	.03
436	Lee Smith	.08	.06	.03
437	Andy Stankiewicz	.08	.06	.03
438	Mike Stanley	.08	.06	.03
439	Danny Tartabull	.10	.07	.04
440	Randy Velarde	.08	.06	.03
441	Bernie Williams	.10	.07	.04
442	Gerald Williams	.10	.07	.04
443	Mike Witt	.08	.06	.03
444	Marcos Armas	.10	.07	.04
445	Lance Blankenship	.08	.06	.03
446	Mike Bordick	.08	.06	.03
447	Ron Darling	.08	.06	.03
448	Dennis Eckersley	.10	.07	.04
449	Brent Gates	.20	.15	.08
450	Goose Gossage	.08	.06	.03
451	Scott Hemond	.10	.07	.04
452	Dave Henderson	.08	.06	.03

		MT	NR MT	EX
453	Shawn Hillegas	.08	.06	.03
454	Rick Honeycutt	.08	.06	.03
455	Scott Lydy	.10	.07	.04
456	Mark McGwire	.10	.07	.04
457	Henry Mercedes	.10	.07	.04
458	Mike Mohler	.08	.06	.03
459	Troy Neel	.25	.20	.10
460	Edwin Nunez	.08	.06	.03
461	Craig Paquette	.08	.06	.03
462	Ruben Sierra	.15	.11	.06
463	Terry Steinbach	.08	.06	.03
464	Todd Van Poppel	.15	.11	.06
465	Bob Welch	.08	.06	.03
466	Bobby Witt	.08	.06	.03
467	Ruben Amaro	.10	.07	.04
468	Larry Anderson	.08	.06	.03
469	Kim Batiste	.08	.06	.03
470	Wes Chamberlain	.08	.06	.03
471	Darren Daulton	.10	.07	.04
472	Mariano Duncan	.08	.06	.03
473	Len Dykstra	.10	.07	.04
474	Jim Eisenreich	.08	.06	.03
475	Tommy Greene	.08	.06	.03
476	Dave Hollins	.10	.07	.04
477	Pete Incaviglia	.08	.06	.03
478	Danny Jackson	.08	.06	.03
479	John Kruk	.10	.07	.04
480	Tony Longmire	.10	.07	.04
481	Jeff Manto	.08	.06	.03
482	Mike Morandini	.08	.06	.03
483	Terry Mulholland	.08	.06	.03
484	Todd Pratt	.08	.06	.03
485	Ben Rivera	.08	.06	.03
486	Curt Shilling	.08	.06	.03
487	Kevin Stocker	1.00	.75	.40
488	Milt Thompson	.08	.06	.03
489	David West	.08	.06	.03
490	Mitch Williams	.08	.06	.03
491	Jeff Ballard	.08	.06	.03
492	Jay Bell	.08	.06	.03
493	Scott Bullett	.08	.06	.03
494	Dave Clark	.08	.06	.03
495	Steve Cooke	.10	.07	.04
496	Midre Cummings	.25	.20	.10
497	Mark Dewey	.10	.07	.04
498	Carlos Garcia	.15	.11	.06
499	Jeff King	.08	.06	.03
500	Al Martin	.10	.07	.04
501	Lloyd McClendon	.08	.06	.03
502	Orlando Merced	.08	.06	.03
503	Blas Minor	.10	.07	.04
504	Denny Neagle	.08	.06	.03
505	Tom Prince	.08	.06	.03
506	Don Slaught	.08	.06	.03
507	Zane Smith	.08	.06	.03
508	Randy Tomlin	.08	.06	.03
509	Andy Van Slyke	.10	.07	.04
510	Paul Wagner	.08	.06	.03
511	Tim Wakefield	.10	.07	.04
512	Bob Walk	.08	.06	.03
513	John Wehner	.08	.06	.03
514	Kevin Young	.10	.07	.04
515	Billy Bean	.08	.06	.03
516	Andy Benes	.10	.07	.04
517	Derek Bell	.08	.06	.03
518	Doug Brocail	.08	.06	.03
519	Jarvis Brown	.10	.07	.04
520	Phil Clark	.08	.06	.03
521	Mark Davis	.08	.06	.03
522	Jeff Gardner	.08	.06	.03
523	Pat Gomez	.08	.06	.03
524	Ricky Gutierrez	.08	.06	.03
525	Tony Gwynn	.15	.11	.06
526	Gene Harris	.08	.06	.03
527	Kevin Higgins	.08	.06	.03
528	Trevor Hoffman	.08	.06	.03
529	Luis Lopez	.08	.06	.03
530	Pedro A. Martinez	.10	.07	.04
531	Melvin Nieves	.08	.06	.03
532	Phil Plantier	.10	.07	.04
533	Frank Seminara	.08	.06	.03
534	Craig Shipley	.08	.06	.03
535	Tim Teufel	.08	.06	.03
536	Guillermo Velasquez	.08	.06	.03
537	Wally Whitehurst	.08	.06	.03
538	Rod Beck	.08	.06	.03
539	Todd Benzinger	.08	.06	.03
540	Barry Bonds	.40	.30	.15
541	Jeff Brantley	.08	.06	.03
542	Dave Burba	.08	.06	.03
543	John Burkett	.08	.06	.03

		MT	NR MT	EX
544	Will Clark	.20	.15	.08
545	Royce Clayton	.10	.07	.04
546	Brian Hickerson	.10	.07	.04
547	Mike Jackson	.08	.06	.03
548	Darren Lewis	.10	.07	.04
549	Kirt Manwaring	.08	.06	.03
550	Dave Martinez	.08	.06	.03
551	Willie McGee	.08	.06	.03
552	Jeff Reed	.08	.06	.03
553	Dave Righetti	.08	.06	.03
554	Kevin Rogers	.08	.06	.03
555	Steve Scarsone	.08	.06	.03
556	Bill Swift	.08	.06	.03
557	Robby Thompson	.08	.06	.03
558	Solomon Torres	.15	.11	.06
559	Matt Williams	.10	.07	.04
560	Trevor Wilson	.08	.06	.03
561	Rich Amaral	.10	.07	.04
562	Mike Blowers	.08	.06	.03
563	Chris Bosio	.08	.06	.03
564	Jay Buhner	.08	.06	.03
565	Norm Charlton	.08	.06	.03
566	Jim Converse	.08	.06	.03
567	Rich DeLucia	.08	.06	.03
568	Mike Felder	.08	.06	.03
569	Dave Fleming	.08	.06	.03
570	Ken Griffey Jr.	1.50	1.25	.60
571	Bill Haselman	.08	.06	.03
572	Dwayne Henry	.08	.06	.03
573	Brad Holman	.08	.06	.03
574	Randy Johnson	.10	.07	.04
575	Greg Litton	.08	.06	.03
576	Edgar Martinez	.08	.06	.03
577	Tino Martinez	.08	.06	.03
578	Jeff Nelson	.08	.06	.03
579	Mark Newfield	.20	.15	.08
580	Roger Salkeld	.15	.11	.06
581	Mackey Sasser	.08	.06	.03
582	Brian Turang	.15	.11	.06
583	Omar Vizquel	.08	.06	.03
584	Dave Valle	.08	.06	.03
585	Luis Alicea	.08	.06	.03
586	Rene Arocha	.10	.07	.04
587	Rheal Cormier	.08	.06	.03
588	Tripp Cromer	.10	.07	.04
589	Bernard Gilkey	.08	.06	.03
590	Lee Guetterman	.08	.06	.03
591	Gregg Jefferies	.10	.07	.04
592	Tim Jones	.08	.06	.03
593	Paul Kilgus	.08	.06	.03
594	Les Lancaster	.08	.06	.03
595	Omar Olivares	.08	.06	.03
596	Jose Oquendo	.08	.06	.03
597	Donovan Osborne	.08	.06	.03
598	Tom Pagnozzi	.08	.06	.03
599	Erik Pappas	.08	.06	.03
600	Geronimo Pena	.08	.06	.03
601	Mike Perez	.08	.06	.03
602	Gerald Perry	.08	.06	.03
603	Stan Royer	.08	.06	.03
604	Ozzie Smith	.15	.11	.06
605	Bob Tewksbury	.08	.06	.03
606	Allen Watson	1.00	.75	.40
607	Mark Whiten	.10	.07	.04
608	Todd Zeile	.08	.06	.03
609	Jeff Bronkey	.08	.06	.03
610	Kevin Brown	.08	.06	.03
611	Jose Canseco	.10	.07	.04
612	Doug Dascenzo	.08	.06	.03
613	Butch Davis	.10	.07	.04
614	Mario Diaz	.08	.06	.03
615	Julio Franco	.08	.06	.03
616	Benji Gil	.40	.30	.15
617	Juan Gonzalez	1.50	1.25	.60
618	Tom Henke	.08	.06	.03
619	Jeff Huson	.10	.07	.04
620	David Hulse	.15	.11	.06
621	Craig Lefferts	.08	.06	.03
622	Rafael Palmeiro	.10	.07	.04
623	Dean Palmer	.10	.07	.04
624	Bob Patterson	.08	.06	.03
625	Roger Pavlik	.10	.07	.04
626	Gary Redus	.08	.06	.03
627	Ivan Rodriguez	.15	.11	.06
628	Kenny Rogers	.08	.06	.03
629	Jon Shave	.08	.06	.03
630	Doug Strange	.08	.06	.03
631	Matt Whiteside	.08	.06	.03
632	Roberto Alomar	.35	.25	.14
633	Pat Borders	.08	.06	.03
634	Scott Brow	.15	.11	.06

		MT	NR MT	EX
635	Roberto Butler	.15	.11	.06
636	Joe Carter	.10	.07	.04
637	Tony Castillo	.08	.06	.03
638	Mark Eichhorn	.08	.06	.03
639	Tony Fernandez	.08	.06	.03
640	Huck Flener	.15	.11	.06
641	Alfredo Griffin	.08	.06	.03
642	Juan Guzman	.15	.11	.06
643	Rickey Henderson	.15	.11	.06
644	Pat Hentgen	.10	.07	.04
645	Randy Knorr	.08	.06	.03
646	Al Leiter	.08	.06	.03
647	Dominigo Martinez	.08	.06	.03
648	Paul Molitor	.15	.11	.06
649	Jack Morris	.08	.06	.03
650	John Olerud	.25	.20	.10
651	Ed Sprague	.08	.06	.03
652	Dave Stewart	.08	.06	.03
653	Devon White	.10	.07	.04
654	Woody Williams	.15	.11	.06
655	Barry Bonds	.40	.30	.15
656	Greg Maddux	.20	.15	.08
657	Jack McDowell	.10	.07	.04
658	Mike Piazza	3.00	2.25	1.25
659	Tim Salmon	1.50	1.25	.60
660	Frank Thomas	2.50	2.00	1.00

1994 Pacific Crown Jewels of the Crown

Photos not available at press time

		MT	NR MT	EX
Complete Set (36):		450.00	350.00	175.00
Common Player:		8.00	6.00	3.25
(1)	John Olerud	20.00	15.00	8.00
(2)	Paul Molitor	20.00	15.00	8.00
(3)	Carlos Baerga	20.00	15.00	8.00
(4)	Frank Thomas	40.00	30.00	16.00
(5)	Juan "Igor" Gonzalez	30.00	22.00	12.00
(6)	Ken Griffey Jr.	30.00	22.00	12.00
(7)	Tim Salmon	30.00	22.00	12.00
(8)	Rafael Palmeiro	10.00	7.50	4.00
(9)	Kenny Lofton	12.00	9.00	4.75
(10)	Randy Johnson	10.00	7.50	4.00
(11)	Cal Ripken	18.00	13.50	7.25
(12)	Cecil Fielder	12.00	9.00	4.75
(13)	Robin Yount	14.00	10.50	5.50
(14)	Don Mattingly	14.00	10.50	5.50
(15)	Wade Boggs	9.00	6.75	3.50
(16)	Kirby Puckett	15.00	11.00	6.00
(17)	Roberto Alomar	20.00	15.00	8.00
(18)	Fernando Valenzuela (Comeback Player)	8.00	6.00	3.25
(19)	Tony Gwynn	12.00	9.00	4.75
(20)	Orlando Merced	8.00	6.00	3.25
(21)	Bobby Bonds	25.00	18.50	10.00
(22)	Lenny Dykstra	12.00	9.00	4.75
(23)	Gregg Jefferies	8.00	6.00	3.25
(24)	Mike Piazza	40.00	30.00	16.00
(25)	Mark Grace	10.00	7.50	4.00
(26)	Jeff Conine	8.00	6.00	3.25
(27)	Charlie Hayes	8.00	6.00	3.25
(28)	John Burkett	8.00	6.00	3.25
(29)	Greg Maddux	12.00	9.00	4.75
(30)	Ryne Sandberg	18.00	13.50	7.25
(31)	Darren Dalton	9.00	6.75	3.50
(32)	Orestes Destrade	8.00	6.00	3.25
(33)	Robbie Thompson	8.00	6.00	3.25
(34)	Jeff Bagwell	12.00	9.00	4.75
(35)	John Kruk	9.00	6.75	3.50
(36)	Andres Galarraga (Comeback Player)	8.00	6.00	3.25

1994 Pacific Crown 1993 Homerun Leaders

Photos not available at press time

		MT	NR MT	EX
Complete Set (20):		250.00	185.00	100.00
Common Player:		8.00	6.00	3.25
(1)	Juan "Igor" Gonzalez	30.00	22.00	12.00
(2)	Ken Griffey Jr.	30.00	22.00	12.00
(3)	Frank Thomas	40.00	30.00	16.00
(4)	Albert Belle	20.00	15.00	8.00
(5)	Rafael Palmeiro	10.00	7.50	4.00
(6)	Joe Carter	12.00	9.00	4.75
(7)	Dean Palmer	8.00	6.00	3.25
(8)	Mickey Tettleton	8.00	6.00	3.25
(9)	Tim Salmon	30.00	22.00	12.00
(10)	Danny Tartabull	8.00	6.00	3.25
(11)	Barry Bonds	25.00	18.50	10.00
(12)	Dave Justice	16.00	12.00	6.50
(13)	Matt Williams	10.00	7.50	4.00
(14)	Fred McGriff	14.00	10.50	5.50
(15)	Ron Gant	10.00	7.50	4.00
(16)	Mike Piazza	40.00	30.00	16.00
(17)	Bobby Bonilla	9.00	6.75	3.50
(18)	Phil Plantier	9.00	6.75	3.50
(19)	Sammy Sosa	12.00	9.00	4.75
(20)	Rick Wilkins	8.00	6.00	3.25

1994 Pacific Crown All Latino All-Star Team

Photos not available at press time

		MT	NR MT	EX
Complete Set (20):		20.00	15.00	8.00
Common Player:		.75	.60	.30
(1)	Ivan Rodriguez	1.00	.75	.40

		MT	NR MT	EX
(2)	Alex Fernandez	1.00	.75	.40
(3)	Rafael Palmeiro	1.00	.75	.40
(4)	Roberto Alomar	3.50	2.75	1.50
(5)	Omar Vizquel	.75	.60	.30
(6)	Eduardo Perez	.75	.60	.30
(7)	Juan "Igor" Gonzalez	5.00	3.75	2.00
(8)	Jose Canseco	1.25	.90	.50
(9)	Ruben Sierra	1.00	.75	.40
(10)	Danny Tartabull	.75	.60	.30
(11)	Benito Santiago	.75	.60	.30
(12)	Dennis Martinez	.75	.60	.30
(13)	Andres Galarraga	1.00	.75	.40
(14)	Mariano Duncan	.75	.60	.30
(15)	Jose Offerman	.75	.60	.30
(16)	Dave Magadan	.75	.60	.30
(17)	Luis Gonzalez	.75	.60	.30
(18)	Bobby Bonilla	1.00	.75	.40
(19)	Orlando Merced	1.00	.75	.40
(20)	Jose Rijo	.75	.40	.30

1988 Score

A fifth member joined the group of nationally distributed baseball cards in 1988. Titled "Score," the cards are characterized by extremely sharp and excellent full-color photography and printing. Card backs are full-color also and carry a player head-shot, along with a brief biography and player personal and statistical information. The 660 cards in the set each measure 2-1/2" by 3-1/2" in size. The fronts come with one of six different border colors - blue, red, green, purple, orange and gold - which are equally divided at 110 cards per color. The Score set was produced by Major League Marketing, the same company that marketed the "triple-action" Sportflics card sets.

		MT	NR MT	EX
Complete Set (660):		20.00	15.00	8.00
Common Player:		.04	.03	.02
1	Don Mattingly	.30	.25	.12
2	Wade Boggs	.25	.15	.08
3	Tim Raines	.08	.06	.03
4	Andre Dawson	.20	.15	.08
5	Mark McGwire	.35	.20	.10
6	Kevin Seitzer	.08	.06	.03
7	Wally Joyner	.10	.08	.04
8	Jesse Barfield	.10	.08	.04
9	Pedro Guerrero	.15	.11	.06
10	Eric Davis	.12	.08	.04
11	George Brett	.30	.25	.12
12	Ozzie Smith	.12	.09	.05
13	Rickey Henderson	.25	.15	.08
14	Jim Rice	.08	.06	.03
15	*Matt Nokes*	.25	.15	.08
16	Mike Schmidt	.40	.30	.15
17	Dave Parker	.12	.09	.05
18	Eddie Murray	.25	.20	.10
19	Andres Galarraga	.15	.11	.06
20	Tony Fernandez	.10	.08	.04
21	Kevin McReynolds	.12	.09	.05
22	B.J. Surhoff	.10	.08	.04
23	Pat Tabler	.06	.05	.02
24	Kirby Puckett	.40	.25	.15
25	Benny Santiago	.12	.08	.04
26	Ryne Sandberg	.40	.30	.15
27	Kelly Downs	.08	.06	.03
28	Jose Cruz	.06	.05	.02
29	Pete O'Brien	.06	.05	.02
30	Mark Langston	.10	.08	.04
31	Lee Smith	.08	.06	.03
32	Juan Samuel	.10	.08	.04
33	Kevin Bass	.06	.05	.02
34	R.J. Reynolds	.04	.03	.02
35	Steve Sax	.12	.09	.05
36	John Kruk	.12	.08	.04
37	Alan Trammell	.08	.06	.03
38	Chris Bosio	.06	.05	.02
39	Brook Jacoby	.08	.06	.03
40	Willie McGee	.10	.08	.04
41	Dave Magadan	.10	.08	.04
42	Fred Lynn	.10	.08	.04
43	Kent Hrbek	.12	.09	.05
44	Brian Downing	.06	.05	.02
45	Jose Canseco	.35	.20	.10
46	Jim Presley	.08	.06	.03
47	Mike Stanley	.10	.08	.04
48	Tony Pena	.06	.05	.02
49	David Cone	.20	.15	.08
50	Rick Sutcliffe	.08	.06	.03
51	Doug Drabek	.10	.08	.04
52	Bill Doran	.06	.05	.02
53	Mike Scioscia	.06	.05	.02
54	Candy Maldonado	.06	.05	.02
55	Dave Winfield	.30	.20	.10
56	Lou Whitaker	.08	.06	.03
57	Tom Henke	.06	.05	.02
58	Ken Gerhart	.06	.05	.02
59	Glenn Braggs	.08	.06	.03
60	Julio Franco	.08	.06	.03
61	Charlie Leibrandt	.06	.05	.02
62	Gary Gaetti	.10	.08	.04
63	Bob Boone	.06	.05	.02
64	*Luis Polonia*	.20	.15	.08
65	Dwight Evans	.10	.08	.04
66	Phil Bradley	.08	.06	.03
67	Mike Boddicker	.06	.05	.02
68	Vince Coleman	.08	.06	.03
69	Howard Johnson	.08	.06	.03
70	Tim Wallach	.08	.06	.03
71	Keith Moreland	.06	.05	.02
72	Barry Larkin	.20	.15	.08
73	Alan Ashby	.04	.03	.02
74	Rick Rhoden	.06	.05	.02
75	Darrell Evans	.08	.06	.03
76	Dave Stieb	.08	.06	.03
77	Dan Plesac	.08	.06	.03
78	Will Clark	.40	.25	.15
79	Frank White	.06	.05	.02
80	Joe Carter	.25	.20	.10
81	Mike Witt	.06	.05	.02
82	Terry Steinbach	.10	.08	.04
83	Alvin Davis	.10	.08	.04
84	Tom Herr	.06	.05	.02
85	Vance Law	.06	.05	.02
86	Kal Daniels	.15	.11	.06
87	Rick Honeycutt	.04	.03	.02
88	Alfredo Griffin	.06	.05	.02
89	Bret Saberhagen	.10	.08	.04
90	Bert Blyleven	.10	.08	.04
91	Jeff Reardon	.08	.06	.03
92	Cory Snyder	.06	.05	.02
93	Greg Walker	.06	.05	.02
94	*Joe Magrane*	.10	.08	.04
95	Rob Deer	.06	.05	.02
96	Ray Knight	.06	.05	.02
97	Casey Candaele	.04	.03	.02
98	John Cerutti	.06	.05	.02
99	Buddy Bell	.08	.06	.03
100	Jack Clark	.12	.09	.05
101	Eric Bell	.06	.05	.02
102	Willie Wilson	.08	.06	.03
103	Dave Schmidt	.04	.03	.02
104	Dennis Eckersley	.10	.08	.04
105	Don Sutton	.12	.09	.05
106	Danny Tartabull	.10	.08	.04
107	Fred McGriff	.40	.25	.15
108	*Les Straker*	.15	.11	.06
109	Lloyd Moseby	.06	.05	.02
110	Roger Clemens	.35	.20	.10
111	Glenn Hubbard	.04	.03	.02
112	*Ken Williams*	.08	.06	.03
113	Ruben Sierra	.30	.20	.10

		MT	NR MT	EX
114	Stan Jefferson	.06	.05	.02
115	Milt Thompson	.04	.03	.02
116	Bobby Bonilla	.20	.15	.08
117	Wayne Tolleson	.04	.03	.02
118	*Matt Williams*	1.50	1.25	.60
119	Chet Lemon	.06	.05	.02
120	Dale Sveum	.06	.05	.02
121	Dennis Boyd	.06	.05	.02
122	Brett Butler	.06	.05	.02
123	Terry Kennedy	.06	.05	.02
124	Jack Howell	.06	.05	.02
125	Curt Young	.06	.05	.02
126a	Dale Valle (first name incorrect)	.25	.20	.10
126b	Dave Valle (correct spelling)	.06	.05	.02
127	Curt Wilkerson	.04	.03	.02
128	Tim Teufel	.04	.03	.02
129	Ozzie Virgil	.04	.03	.02
130	Brian Fisher	.06	.05	.02
131	Lance Parrish	.12	.09	.05
132	Tom Browning	.08	.06	.03
133a	Larry Anderson (incorrect spelling)	.25	.20	.10
133b	Larry Andersen (correct spelling)	.06	.05	.02
134a	Bob Brenley (incorrect spelling)	.25	.20	.10
134b	Bob Brenly (correct spelling)	.06	.05	.02
135	Mike Marshall	.10	.08	.04
136	Gerald Perry	.08	.06	.03
137	Bobby Meacham	.04	.03	.02
138	Larry Herndon	.04	.03	.02
139	*Fred Manrique*	.06	.05	.02
140	Charlie Hough	.06	.05	.02
141	Ron Darling	.10	.08	.04
142	Herm Winningham	.04	.03	.02
143	Mike Diaz	.06	.05	.02
144	*Mike Jackson*	.06	.05	.02
145	Denny Walling	.04	.03	.02
146	Rob Thompson	.06	.05	.02
147	Franklin Stubbs	.06	.05	.02
148	Albert Hall	.04	.03	.02
149	Bobby Witt	.08	.06	.03
150	Lance McCullers	.06	.05	.02
151	Scott Bradley	.04	.03	.02
152	Mark McLemore	.04	.03	.02
153	Tim Laudner	.04	.03	.02
154	Greg Swindell	.15	.11	.06
155	Marty Barrett	.06	.05	.02
156	Mike Heath	.04	.03	.02
157	Gary Ward	.06	.05	.02
158a	Lee Mazilli (incorrect spelling)	.25	.20	.10
158b	Lee Mazzilli (correct spelling)	.08	.06	.03
159	Tom Foley	.04	.03	.02
160	Robin Yount	.30	.25	.12
161	Steve Bedrosian	.10	.08	.04
162	Bob Walk	.04	.03	.02
163	Nick Esasky	.06	.05	.02
164	*Ken Caminiti*	.25	.20	.10
165	Jose Uribe	.04	.03	.02
166	Dave Anderson	.04	.03	.02
167	Ed Whitson	.04	.03	.02
168	Ernie Whitt	.06	.05	.02
169	Cecil Cooper	.08	.06	.03
170	Mike Pagliarulo	.08	.06	.03
171	Pat Sheridan	.04	.03	.02
172	Chris Bando	.04	.03	.02
173	Lee Lacy	.04	.03	.02
174	Steve Lombardozzi	.04	.03	.02
175	Mike Greenwell	.12	.08	.04
176	Greg Minton	.04	.03	.02
177	Moose Haas	.04	.03	.02
178	Mike Kingery	.04	.03	.02
179	Greg Harris	.04	.03	.02
180	Bo Jackson	.30	.20	.10
181	Carmelo Martinez	.06	.05	.02
182	Alex Trevino	.04	.03	.02
183	Ron Oester	.04	.03	.02
184	Danny Darwin	.04	.03	.02
185	Mike Krukow	.06	.05	.02
186	Rafael Palmeiro	.40	.25	.15
187	Tim Burke	.04	.03	.02
188	Roger McDowell	.08	.06	.03
189	Garry Templeton	.06	.05	.02
190	Terry Pendleton	.12	.08	.04
191	Larry Parrish	.06	.05	.02
192	Rey Quinones	.04	.03	.02
193	Joaquin Andujar	.06	.05	.02
194	Tom Brunansky	.08	.06	.03
195	Donnie Moore	.04	.03	.02
196	Dan Pasqua	.08	.06	.03
197	Jim Gantner	.04	.03	.02
198	Mark Eichhorn	.06	.05	.02
199	John Grubb	.04	.03	.02
200	*Bill Ripken*	.08	.06	.03
201	*Sam Horn*	.08	.06	.03
202	Todd Worrell	.08	.06	.03
203	Terry Leach	.04	.03	.02
204	Garth Iorg	.04	.03	.02
205	Brian Dayett	.04	.03	.02
206	Bo Diaz	.06	.05	.02
207	Craig Reynolds	.04	.03	.02
208	Brian Holton	.08	.06	.03
209	Marvelle Wynne (Marvell)	.04	.03	.02
210	Dave Concepcion	.06	.05	.02
211	Mike Davis	.06	.05	.02
212	Devon White	.15	.11	.06
213	Mickey Brantley	.04	.03	.02
214	Greg Gagne	.04	.03	.02
215	Oddibe McDowell	.06	.05	.02
216	Jimmy Key	.08	.06	.03
217	Dave Bergman	.04	.03	.02
218	Calvin Schiraldi	.04	.03	.02
219	Larry Sheets	.06	.05	.02
220	Mike Easler	.06	.05	.02
221	Kurt Stillwell	.08	.06	.03
222	*Chuck Jackson*	.06	.05	.02
223	Dave Martinez	.08	.06	.03
224	Tim Leary	.06	.05	.02
225	Steve Garvey	.12	.08	.04
226	Greg Mathews	.06	.05	.02
227	Doug Sisk	.04	.03	.02
228	Dave Henderson	.08	.06	.03
229	Jimmy Dwyer	.04	.03	.02
230	Larry Owen	.04	.03	.02
231	Andre Thornton	.06	.05	.02
232	Mark Salas	.04	.03	.02
233	Tom Brookens	.04	.03	.02
234	Greg Brock	.06	.05	.02
235	Rance Mulliniks	.04	.03	.02
236	Bob Brower	.06	.05	.02
237	Joe Niekro	.06	.05	.02
238	Scott Bankhead	.04	.03	.02
239	Doug DeCinces	.06	.05	.02
240	Tommy John	.12	.09	.05
241	Rich Gedman	.06	.05	.02
242	Ted Power	.04	.03	.02
243	*Dave Meads*	.12	.09	.05
244	Jim Sundberg	.06	.05	.02
245	Ken Oberkfell	.04	.03	.02
246	Jimmy Jones	.08	.06	.03
247	Ken Landreaux	.04	.03	.02
248	Jose Oquendo	.04	.03	.02
249	*John Mitchell*	.06	.05	.02
250	Don Baylor	.08	.06	.03
251	Scott Fletcher	.06	.05	.02
252	Al Newman	.04	.03	.02
253	Carney Lansford	.08	.06	.03
254	Johnny Ray	.06	.05	.02
255	Gary Pettis	.04	.03	.02
256	Ken Phelps	.06	.05	.02
257	Rick Leach	.04	.03	.02
258	Tim Stoddard	.04	.03	.02
259	Ed Romero	.04	.03	.02
260	Sid Bream	.06	.05	.02
261a	Tom Neidenfuer (incorrect spelling)	.25	.20	.10
261b	Tom Niedenfuer (correct spelling)	.06	.05	.02
262	Rick Dempsey	.06	.05	.02
263	Lonnie Smith	.06	.05	.02
264	Bob Forsch	.06	.05	.02
265	Barry Bonds	.60	.45	.25
266	Willie Randolph	.06	.05	.02
267	Mike Ramsey	.04	.03	.02
268	Don Slaught	.04	.03	.02
269	Mickey Tettleton	.10	.08	.04
270	Jerry Reuss	.06	.05	.02
271	Marc Sullivan	.04	.03	.02
272	Jim Morrison	.04	.03	.02
273	Steve Balboni	.06	.05	.02
274	Dick Schofield	.04	.03	.02
275	John Tudor	.08	.06	.03
276	*Gene Larkin*	.15	.11	.06
277	Harold Reynolds	.06	.05	.02
278	Jerry Browne	.06	.05	.02
279	Willie Upshaw	.06	.05	.02
280	Ted Higuera	.08	.06	.03
281	Terry McGriff	.04	.03	.02
282	Terry Puhl	.04	.03	.02
283	*Mark Wasinger*	.06	.05	.02
284	Luis Salazar	.04	.03	.02
285	Ted Simmons	.08	.06	.03
286	John Shelby	.04	.03	.02
287	*John Smiley*	.20	.15	.08
288	Curt Ford	.04	.03	.02
289	Steve Crawford	.04	.03	.02

		MT	NR MT	EX
290	Dan Quisenberry	.06	.05	.02
291	Alan Wiggins	.04	.03	.02
292	Randy Bush	.04	.03	.02
293	John Candelaria	.06	.05	.02
294	Tony Phillips	.04	.03	.02
295	Mike Morgan	.04	.03	.02
296	Bill Wegman	.04	.03	.02
297a	Terry Franconia (incorrect spelling)	.25	.20	.10
297b	Terry Francona (correct spelling)	.06	.05	.02
298	Mickey Hatcher	.04	.03	.02
299	Andres Thomas	.06	.05	.02
300	Bob Stanley	.04	.03	.02
301	*Alfredo Pedrique*	.06	.05	.02
302	Jim Lindeman	.06	.05	.02
303	Wally Backman	.06	.05	.02
304	Paul O'Neill	.06	.05	.02
305	Hubie Brooks	.08	.06	.03
306	Steve Buechele	.04	.03	.02
307	Bobby Thigpen	.08	.06	.03
308	George Hendrick	.06	.05	.02
309	John Moses	.04	.03	.02
310	Ron Guidry	.12	.09	.05
311	Bill Schroeder	.04	.03	.02
312	*Jose Nunez*	.06	.05	.02
313	Bud Black	.04	.03	.02
314	Joe Sambito	.04	.03	.02
315	Scott McGregor	.06	.05	.02
316	Rafael Santana	.04	.03	.02
317	Frank Williams	.04	.03	.02
318	Mike Fitzgerald	.04	.03	.02
319	Rick Mahler	.04	.03	.02
320	Jim Gott	.04	.03	.02
321	Mariano Duncan	.04	.03	.02
322	Jose Guzman	.06	.05	.02
323	Lee Guetterman	.04	.03	.02
324	Dan Gladden	.04	.03	.02
325	Gary Carter	.10	.08	.04
326	Tracy Jones	.10	.08	.04
327	Floyd Youmans	.04	.03	.02
328	Bill Dawley	.04	.03	.02
329	*Paul Noce*	.06	.05	.02
330	Angel Salazar	.04	.03	.02
331	Goose Gossage	.12	.09	.05
332	George Frazier	.04	.03	.02
333	Ruppert Jones	.04	.03	.02
334	Billy Jo Robidoux	.04	.03	.02
335	Mike Scott	.10	.08	.04
336	Randy Myers	.10	.08	.04
337	Bob Sebra	.04	.03	.02
338	Eric Show	.06	.05	.02
339	Mitch Williams	.06	.05	.02
340	Paul Molitor	.20	.15	.08
341	Gus Polidor	.04	.03	.02
342	Steve Trout	.04	.03	.02
343	Jerry Don Gleaton	.04	.03	.02
344	Bob Knepper	.06	.05	.02
345	Mitch Webster	.06	.05	.02
346	John Morris	.04	.03	.02
347	Andy Hawkins	.04	.03	.02
348	Dave Leiper	.04	.03	.02
349	Ernest Riles	.04	.03	.02
350	Dwight Gooden	.10	.08	.04
351	Dave Righetti	.12	.09	.05
352	Pat Dodson	.04	.03	.02
353	John Habyan	.04	.03	.02
354	Jim Deshaies	.06	.05	.02
355	Butch Wynegar	.04	.03	.02
356	Bryn Smith	.04	.03	.02
357	Matt Young	.04	.03	.02
358	*Tom Pagnozzi*	.10	.08	.04
359	Floyd Rayford	.04	.03	.02
360	Darryl Strawberry	.20	.15	.08
361	Sal Butera	.04	.03	.02
362	Domingo Ramos	.04	.03	.02
363	Chris Brown	.06	.05	.02
364	Jose Gonzalez	.04	.03	.02
365	Dave Smith	.06	.05	.02
366	Andy McGaffigan	.04	.03	.02
367	Stan Javier	.04	.03	.02
368	Henry Cotto	.04	.03	.02
369	Mike Birkbeck	.06	.05	.02
370	Len Dykstra	.15	.11	.06
371	Dave Collins	.06	.05	.02
372	Spike Owen	.04	.03	.02
373	Geno Petralli	.04	.03	.02
374	Ron Karkovice	.04	.03	.02
375	Shane Rawley	.06	.05	.02
376	*DeWayne Buice*	.06	.05	.02
377	*Bill Pecota*	.06	.05	.02
378	Leon Durham	.06	.05	.02
379	Ed Olwine	.04	.03	.02
380	Bruce Hurst	.08	.06	.03
381	Bob McClure	.04	.03	.02
382	Mark Thurmond	.04	.03	.02
383	Buddy Biancalana	.04	.03	.02
384	Tim Conroy	.04	.03	.02
385	Tony Gwynn	.25	.20	.10
386	Greg Gross	.04	.03	.02
387	*Barry Lyons*	.06	.05	.02
388	Mike Felder	.04	.03	.02
389	Pat Clements	.04	.03	.02
390	Ken Griffey	.06	.05	.02
391	Mark Davis	.04	.03	.02
392	Jose Rijo	.06	.05	.02
393	Mike Young	.04	.03	.02
394	Willie Fraser	.06	.05	.02
395	Dion James	.06	.05	.02
396	*Steve Shields*	.06	.05	.02
397	Randy St. Claire	.04	.03	.02
398	Danny Jackson	.12	.09	.05
399	Cecil Fielder	.20	.15	.08
400	Keith Hernandez	.15	.11	.06
401	Don Carman	.06	.05	.02
402	*Chuck Crim*	.08	.06	.03
403	Rob Woodward	.04	.03	.02
404	Junior Ortiz	.04	.03	.02
405	Glenn Wilson	.06	.05	.02
406	Ken Howell	.04	.03	.02
407	Jeff Kunkel	.04	.03	.02
408	Jeff Reed	.04	.03	.02
409	Chris James	.10	.08	.04
410	Zane Smith	.06	.05	.02
411	Ken Dixon	.04	.03	.02
412	Ricky Horton	.06	.05	.02
413	Frank DiPino	.04	.03	.02
414	*Shane Mack*	.25	.20	.10
415	Danny Cox	.06	.05	.02
416	Andy Van Slyke	.12	.08	.04
417	Danny Heep	.04	.03	.02
418	John Cangelosi	.04	.03	.02
419a	John Christiansen (incorrect spelling)	.25	.20	.10
419b	John Christensen (correct spelling)	.06	.05	.02
420	*Joey Cora*	.12	.09	.05
421	Mike LaValliere	.06	.05	.02
422	Kelly Gruber	.08	.06	.03
423	Bruce Benedict	.04	.03	.02
424	Len Matuszek	.04	.03	.02
425	Kent Tekulve	.06	.05	.02
426	Rafael Ramirez	.04	.03	.02
427	Mike Flanagan	.06	.05	.02
428	Mike Gallego	.04	.03	.02
429	Juan Castillo	.04	.03	.02
430	Neal Heaton	.04	.03	.02
431	Phil Garner	.04	.03	.02
432	*Mike Dunne*	.12	.09	.05
433	Wallace Johnson	.04	.03	.02
434	Jack O'Connor	.04	.03	.02
435	Steve Jeltz	.04	.03	.02
436	*Donnell Nixon*	.06	.05	.02
437	Jack Lazorko	.04	.03	.02
438	*Keith Comstock*	.06	.05	.02
439	Jeff Robinson	.04	.03	.02
440	Graig Nettles	.08	.06	.03
441	Mel Hall	.06	.05	.02
442	*Gerald Young*	.08	.06	.03
443	Gary Redus	.04	.03	.02
444	Charlie Moore	.04	.03	.02
445	Bill Madlock	.08	.06	.03
446	Mark Clear	.04	.03	.02
447	Greg Booker	.04	.03	.02
448	Rick Schu	.04	.03	.02
449	Ron Kittle	.06	.05	.02
450	Dale Murphy	.10	.08	.04
451	Bob Dernier	.04	.03	.02
452	Dale Mohorcic	.06	.05	.02
453	Rafael Belliard	.04	.03	.02
454	Charlie Puleo	.04	.03	.02
455	Dwayne Murphy	.06	.05	.02
456	Jim Eisenreich	.04	.03	.02
457	David Palmer	.04	.03	.02
458	Dave Stewart	.08	.06	.03
459	Pascual Perez	.06	.05	.02
460	Glenn Davis	.12	.09	.05
461	Dan Petry	.06	.05	.02
462	Jim Winn	.04	.03	.02
463	Darrell Miller	.04	.03	.02
464	Mike Moore	.04	.03	.02
465	Mike LaCoss	.04	.03	.02
466	Steve Farr	.04	.03	.02
467	Jerry Mumphrey	.04	.03	.02

		MT	NR MT	EX
468	Kevin Gross	.06	.05	.02
469	Bruce Bochy	.04	.03	.02
470	Orel Hershiser	.08	.06	.03
471	Eric King	.06	.05	.02
472	*Ellis Burks*	.30	.20	.10
473	Darren Daulton	.20	.15	.08
474	Mookie Wilson	.06	.05	.02
475	Frank Viola	.12	.09	.05
476	Ron Robinson	.04	.03	.02
477	Bob Melvin	.04	.03	.02
478	Jeff Musselman	.06	.05	.02
479	Charlie Kerfeld	.04	.03	.02
480	Richard Dotson	.06	.05	.02
481	Kevin Mitchell	.15	.11	.06
482	Gary Roenicke	.04	.03	.02
483	Tim Flannery	.04	.03	.02
484	Rich Yett	.04	.03	.02
485	Pete Incaviglia	.12	.09	.05
486	Rick Cerone	.04	.03	.02
487	Tony Armas	.06	.05	.02
488	Jerry Reed	.04	.03	.02
489	Davey Lopes	.06	.05	.02
490	Frank Tanana	.06	.05	.02
491	Mike Loynd	.04	.03	.02
492	Bruce Ruffin	.06	.05	.02
493	Chris Speier	.04	.03	.02
494	Tom Hume	.04	.03	.02
495	Jesse Orosco	.06	.05	.02
496	*Robby Wine, Jr.*	.06	.05	.02
497	*Jeff Montgomery*	.60	.40	.20
498	Jeff Dedmon	.04	.03	.02
499	Luis Aguayo	.04	.03	.02
500	Reggie Jackson (1968-75)	.20	.15	.08
501	Reggie Jackson (1976)	.20	.15	.08
502	Reggie Jackson (1977-81)	.20	.15	.08
503	Reggie Jackson (1982-86)	.20	.15	.08
504	Reggie Jackson (1987)	.20	.15	.08
505	Billy Hatcher	.06	.05	.02
506	Ed Lynch	.04	.03	.02
507	Willie Hernandez	.06	.05	.02
508	Jose DeLeon	.06	.05	.02
509	Joel Youngblood	.04	.03	.02
510	Bob Welch	.08	.06	.03
511	Steve Ontiveros	.04	.03	.02
512	Randy Ready	.04	.03	.02
513	Juan Nieves	.06	.05	.02
514	Jeff Russell	.04	.03	.02
515	Von Hayes	.06	.05	.02
516	Mark Gubicza	.10	.08	.04
517	Ken Dayley	.04	.03	.02
518	Don Aase	.04	.03	.02
519	Rick Reuschel	.08	.06	.03
520	*Mike Henneman*	.25	.20	.10
521	Rick Aguilera	.04	.03	.02
522	Jay Howell	.06	.05	.02
523	Ed Correa	.04	.03	.02
524	Manny Trillo	.06	.05	.02
525	Kirk Gibson	.15	.11	.06
526	*Wally Ritchie*	.06	.05	.02
527	Al Nipper	.04	.03	.02
528	Atlee Hammaker	.04	.03	.02
529	Shawon Dunston	.08	.06	.03
530	Jim Clancy	.06	.05	.02
531	Tom Paciorek	.04	.03	.02
532	Joel Skinner	.04	.03	.02
533	Scott Garrelts	.04	.03	.02
534	Tom O'Malley	.04	.03	.02
535	John Franco	.08	.06	.03
536	*Paul Kilgus*	.08	.06	.03
537	Darrell Porter	.06	.05	.02
538	Walt Terrell	.06	.05	.02
539	*Bill Long*	.06	.05	.02
540	George Bell	.12	.08	.04
541	Jeff Sellers	.06	.05	.02
542	*Joe Boever*	.08	.06	.03
543	Steve Howe	.06	.05	.02
544	Scott Sanderson	.04	.03	.02
545	Jack Morris	.10	.08	.04
546	*Todd Benzinger*	.20	.15	.08
547	Steve Henderson	.04	.03	.02
548	Eddie Milner	.04	.03	.02
549	*Jeff Robinson*	.10	.08	.04
550	Cal Ripken, Jr.	.40	.30	.15
551	Jody Davis	.06	.05	.02
552	Kirk McCaskill	.06	.05	.02
553	Craig Lefferts	.04	.03	.02
554	Darnell Coles	.06	.05	.02
555	Phil Niekro	.15	.11	.06
556	Mike Aldrete	.06	.05	.02
557	Pat Perry	.04	.03	.02
558	Juan Agosto	.04	.03	.02
559	Rob Murphy	.06	.05	.02
560	Dennis Rasmussen	.08	.06	.03
561	Manny Lee	.04	.03	.02
562	*Jeff Blauser*	.40	.25	.15
563	Bob Ojeda	.06	.05	.02
564	Dave Dravecky	.06	.05	.02
565	Gene Garber	.04	.03	.02
566	Ron Roenicke	.04	.03	.02
567	*Tommy Hinzo*	.06	.05	.02
568	*Eric Nolte*	.06	.05	.02
569	Ed Hearn	.04	.03	.02
570	*Mark Davidson*	.08	.06	.03
571	*Jim Walewander*	.06	.05	.02
572	Donnie Hill	.04	.03	.02
573	Jamie Moyer	.06	.05	.02
574	Ken Schrom	.04	.03	.02
575	Nolan Ryan	.60	.45	.25
576	Jim Acker	.04	.03	.02
577	Jamie Quirk	.04	.03	.02
578	*Jay Aldrich*	.06	.05	.02
579	Claudell Washington	.06	.05	.02
580	Jeff Leonard	.06	.05	.02
581	Carmen Castillo	.04	.03	.02
582	Daryl Boston	.04	.03	.02
583	*Jeff DeWillis*	.06	.05	.02
584	*John Marzano*	.08	.06	.03
585	Bill Gullickson	.06	.05	.02
586	Andy Allanson	.08	.06	.03
587	Lee Tunnell	.04	.03	.02
588	Gene Nelson	.04	.03	.02
589	Dave LaPoint	.04	.03	.02
590	Harold Baines	.10	.08	.04
591	Bill Buckner	.08	.06	.03
592	Carlton Fisk	.20	.15	.08
593	Rick Manning	.04	.03	.02
594	*Doug Jones*	.20	.15	.08
595	Tom Candiotti	.04	.03	.02
596	Steve Lake	.04	.03	.02
597	*Jose Lind*	.15	.11	.06
598	*Ross Jones*	.06	.05	.02
599	Gary Matthews	.06	.05	.02
600	Fernando Valezuela	.08	.06	.03
601	Dennis Martinez	.06	.05	.02
602	*Les Lancaster*	.15	.11	.06
603	Ozzie Guillen	.06	.05	.02
604	Tony Bernazard	.04	.03	.02
605	Chili Davis	.06	.05	.02
606	Roy Smalley	.04	.03	.02
607	Ivan Calderon	.08	.06	.03
608	Jay Tibbs	.04	.03	.02
609	Guy Hoffman	.04	.03	.02
610	Doyle Alexander	.06	.05	.02
611	Mike Bielecki	.04	.03	.02
612	*Shawn Hillegas*	.06	.05	.02
613	Keith Atherton	.04	.03	.02
614	Eric Plunk	.04	.03	.02
615	Sid Fernandez	.08	.06	.03
616	Dennis Lamp	.04	.03	.02
617	Dave Engle	.04	.03	.02
618	Harry Spilman	.04	.03	.02
619	Don Robinson	.06	.05	.02
620	*John Farrell*	.08	.06	.03
621	*Nelson Liriano*	.06	.05	.02
622	Floyd Bannister	.06	.05	.02
623	*Randy Milligan*	.25	.15	.08
624	*Kevin Elster*	.06	.05	.02
625	*Jody Reed*	.25	.15	.08
626	*Shawn Abner*	.08	.06	.03
627	*Kirt Manwaring*	.15	.11	.06
628	*Pete Stanicek*	.08	.06	.03
629	*Rob Ducey*	.08	.06	.03
630	Steve Kiefer	.04	.03	.02
631	*Gary Thurman*	.08	.06	.03
632	*Darrel Akerfelds*	.12	.09	.05
633	Dave Clark	.06	.05	.02
634	*Roberto Kelly*	.60	.40	.20
635	*Keith Hughes*	.08	.06	.03
636	*John Davis*	.08	.06	.03
637	*Mike Devereaux*	.80	.60	.30
638	*Tom Glavine*	2.50	2.00	1.00
639	*Keith Miller*	.20	.15	.08
640	*Chris Gwynn*	.20	.15	.08
641	*Tim Crews*	.08	.06	.03
642	*Mackey Sasser*	.08	.06	.03
643	*Vicente Palacios*	.08	.06	.03
644	Kevin Romine	.06	.05	.02
645	*Gregg Jefferies*	2.00	1.50	.80
646	*Jeff Treadway*	.10	.08	.04
647	*Ron Gant*	1.50	.90	.50
648	Rookie Sluggers (Mark McGwire, Matt Nokes)	.20	.15	.08

		MT	NR MT	EX
649	Speed and Power (Eric Davis, Tim Raines)	.25	.20	.10
650	Game Breakers (Jack Clark, Don Mattingly)	.20	.15	.08
651	Super Shortstops (Tony Fernandez, Cal Ripken, Jr., Alan Trammell)	.20	.15	.08
652	1987 Highlights (Vince Coleman)	.08	.06	.03
653	1987 Highlights (Kirby Puckett)	.20	.15	.08
654	1987 Highlights (Benito Santiago)	.10	.08	.04
655	1987 Highlights (Juan Nieves)	.06	.05	.02
656	1987 Highlights (Steve Bedrosian)	.06	.05	.02
657	1987 Highlights (Mike Schmidt)	.20	.15	.08
658	1987 Highlights (Don Mattingly)	.30	.25	.12
659	1987 Highlights (Mark McGwire)	.15	.11	.06
660	1987 Highlights (Paul Molitor)	.15	.11	.06

1988 Score Box Panels

This 18-card set, produced by Major League Marketing and manufactured by Optigraphics, is the premiere box-bottom set issued under the Score trademark. The set features 1987 major league All-star players in full-color action poses, framed by a white border. A "1987 All-Star" banner (red or purple) curves above an orange player name block beneath the player photo. Card backs are printed in red, blue, gold and black and carry the card number, player name and position and league logo. Six colorful "Great Moments in Baseball" trivia cards are also included in this set. Each trivia card highlights an historical event at a famous ballpark.

		MT	NR MT	EX
Complete Panel Set:		8.00	6.00	3.25
Complete Singles Set:		3.00	2.25	1.25
Common Panel:		1.50	1.25	.60
Common Single Player:		.15	.11	.06
	Panel	1.50	1.25	.60
1	Terry Kennedy	.15	.11	.06
3	Willie Randolph	.15	.11	.06
15	Eric Davis	.40	.30	.15
	Panel	1.75	1.25	.70
3	Don Mattingly	.60	.45	.25
5	Cal Ripken, Jr.	.50	.40	.20
11	Jack Clark	.25	.20	.10
	Panel	2.00	1.50	.80
4	Wade Boggs	.50	.40	.20
9	Bret Saberhagen	.20	.15	.08
12	Ryne Sandberg	.60	.45	.25
	Panel	1.50	1.25	.60
6	George Bell	.25	.20	.10
13	Mike Schmidt	.35	.25	.14
18	Mike Scott	.15	.11	.06
	Panel	2.00	1.50	.80
7	Rickey Henderson	.60	.45	.25
16	Andre Dawson	.25	.20	.10
17	Darryl Strawberry	.40	.30	.15
	Panel	1.50	1.25	.60
8	Dave Winfield	.25	.20	.10
10	Gary Carter	.20	.15	.08
14	Ozzie Smith	.25	.20	.10

Regional interest may affect the value of a card.

1988 Score Traded

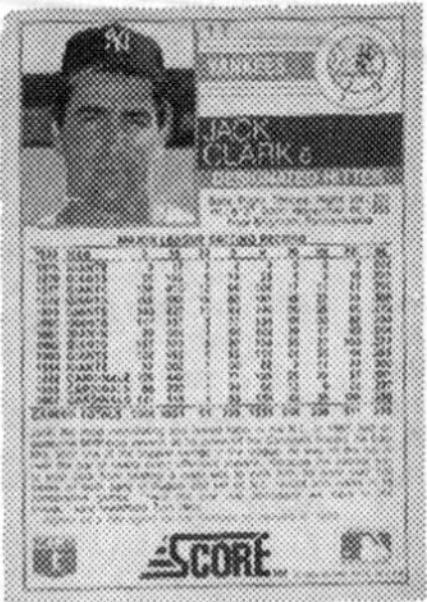

This 110-card set featuring new rookies and traded veterans is similar in design to the 1988 Score set, except for a change in border color. Individual standard-size player cards (2-1/2" by 3-1/2") feature a bright orange border framing full-figure action photos highlighted by a thin white outline. The player name (in white) is centered in the bottom margin, flanked by three yellow stars lower left and a yellow Score logo lower right. The backs carry full-color player close-ups on a cream-colored background, followed by card number, team name and logo, player personal information and a purple stats chart that lists year-by-year and major league totals. A brief player profile follows the stats chart and, on some cards, information is included about the player's trade or acquisition. The update set also includes 10 Magic Motion 3-D trivia cards.

		MT	NR MT	EX
Complete Set (110):		100.00	75.00	40.00
Common Player:		.08	.06	.03
1T	Jack Clark	.10	.08	.04
2T	Danny Jackson	.10	.08	.04
3T	Brett Butler	.25	.15	.08
4T	Kurt Stillwell	.12	.09	.05
5T	Tom Brunansky	.15	.11	.06
6T	Dennis Lamp	.08	.06	.03
7T	Jose DeLeon	.10	.08	.04
8T	Tom Herr	.12	.09	.05
9T	Keith Moreland	.10	.08	.04
10T	Kirk Gibson	.20	.15	.08
11T	Bud Black	.08	.06	.03
12T	Rafael Ramirez	.08	.06	.03
13T	Luis Salazar	.08	.06	.03
14T	Goose Gossage	.15	.11	.06
15T	Bob Welch	.15	.11	.06
16T	Vance Law	.10	.08	.04
17T	Ray Knight	.10	.08	.04
18T	Dan Quisenberry	.10	.08	.04
19T	Don Slaught	.08	.06	.03
20T	Lee Smith	1.00	.70	.40
21T	Rick Cerone	.08	.06	.03
22T	Pat Tabler	.10	.08	.04
23T	Larry McWilliams	.08	.06	.03
24T	Rick Horton	.10	.08	.04
25T	Graig Nettles	.12	.09	.05
26T	Dan Petry	.10	.08	.04
27T	Joe Rijo	.50	.30	.15
28T	Chili Davis	.10	.08	.04
29T	Dickie Thon	.10	.08	.04
30T	Mackey Sasser	.25	.15	.08
31T	Mickey Tettleton	.75	.60	.30
32T	Rick Dempsey	.08	.06	.03
33T	Ron Hassey	.08	.06	.03
34T	Phil Bradley	.12	.09	.05
35T	Jay Howell	.10	.08	.04
36T	Bill Buckner	.12	.09	.05
37T	Alfredo Griffin	.10	.08	.04
38T	Gary Pettis	.08	.06	.03
39T	Calvin Schiraldi	.08	.06	.03
40T	John Candelaria	.10	.08	.04
41T	Joe Orsulak	.08	.06	.03
42T	Willie Upshaw	.10	.08	.04
43T	Herm Winningham	.08	.06	.03
44T	Ron Kittle	.12	.09	.05

		MT	NR MT	EX
45T	Bob Dernier	.08	.06	.03
46T	Steve Balboni	.10	.08	.04
47T	Steve Shields	.08	.06	.03
48T	Henry Cotto	.08	.06	.03
49T	Dave Henderson	.10	.08	.04
50T	Dave Parker	.15	.11	.06
51T	Mike Young	.08	.06	.03
52T	Mark Salas	.08	.06	.03
53T	Mike Davis	.08	.06	.03
54T	Rafael Santana	.08	.06	.03
55T	Don Baylor	.15	.11	.06
56T	Dan Pasqua	.12	.09	.05
57T	Ernest Riles	.08	.06	.03
58T	Glenn Hubbard	.08	.06	.03
59T	Mike Smithson	.08	.06	.03
60T	Richard Dotson	.10	.08	.04
61T	Jerry Reuss	.10	.08	.04
62T	Mike Jackson	.10	.08	.04
63T	Floyd Bannister	.10	.08	.04
64T	Jesse Orosco	.10	.08	.04
65T	Larry Parrish	.10	.08	.04
66T	Jeff Bittiger(FC)	.10	.08	.04
67T	Ray Hayward(FC)	.10	.08	.04
68T	Ricky Jordan(FC)	.10	.08	.04
69T	Tommy Gregg(FC)	.12	.09	.05
70T	Brady Anderson(FC)	5.00	4.50	2.50
71T	Jeff Montgomery	4.00	1.50	.80
72T	Darryl Hamilton(FC)	3.00	2.25	1.25
73T	Cecil Espy(FC)	.10	.08	.04
74T	Greg Briley(FC)	.50	.40	.20
75T	Joey Meyer(FC)	.10	.08	.04
76T	Mike Macfarlane(FC)	.20	.15	.08
77T	Oswald Peraza(FC)	.10	.08	.04
78T	Jack Armstrong(FC)	.20	.15	.08
79T	Don Heinkel(FC)	.10	.08	.04
80T	Mark Grace(FC)	15.00	11.00	6.00
81T	Steve Curry(FC)	.10	.08	.04
82T	Damon Berryhill(FC)	.20	.15	.08
83T	Steve Ellsworth(FC)	.10	.08	.04
84T	Pete Smith(FC)	.20	.15	.08
85T	Jack McDowell	15.00	11.00	6.00
86T	Rob Dibble(FC)	1.50	1.25	.60
87T	Brian Harvey(FC)	6.00	3.00	1.50
88T	John Dopson(FC)	.25	.20	.10
89T	Dave Gallagher(FC)	.25	.20	.10
90T	Todd Stottlemyre(FC)	1.50	1.25	.60
91T	Mike Schooler(FC)	.20	.15	.08
92T	Don Gordon(FC)	.08	.06	.03
93T	Sil Campusano(FC)	.10	.08	.04
94T	Jeff Pico(FC)	.10	.08	.04
95T	Jay Buhner(FC)	7.00	3.00	1.50
96T	Nelson Santovenia(FC)	.10	.08	.04
97T	Al Leiter(FC)	.10	.08	.04
98T	Luis Alicea(FC)	.20	.15	.08
99T	Pat Borders(FC)	.75	.60	.30
100T	Chris Sabo(FC)	3.00	2.25	1.25
101T	Tim Belcher(FC)	.70	.50	.30
102T	Walt Weiss(FC)	.80	.60	.30
103T	Craig Biggio(FC)	6.00	3.75	2.00
104T	Don August(FC)	.10	.08	.04
105T	Roberto Alomar(FC)	65.00	48.00	26.00
106T	Todd Burns(FC)	.20	.15	.08
107T	John Costello(FC)	.20	.15	.08
108T	Melido Perez(FC)	1.00	.70	.40
109T	Darrin Jackson(FC)	2.00	1.50	.80
110T	Orestes Destrade(FC)	3.00	2.25	1.25

1989 Score

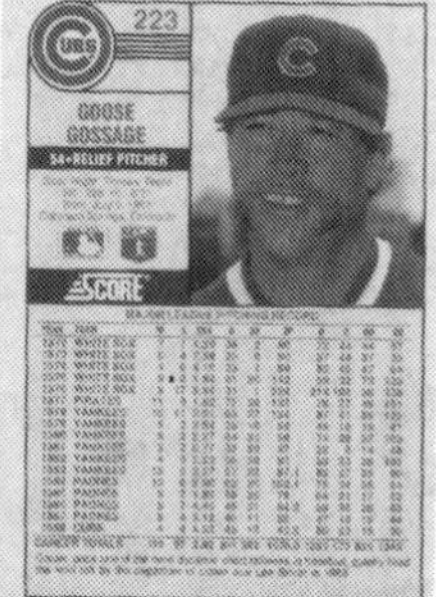

This set of 660 cards plus 56 Magic Motion trivia cards is the second annual basic issue from Score. Full-color player photos highlight 651 individual players and 9 season highlights, including the first Wrigley Field night game. Action photos are framed by thin brightly colored borders (green, cyan blue, purple, orange, red, royal blue) with a baseball diamond logo/player name beneath the photo. Full-color player close-ups (1-5/16" by 1-5/8") are printed on the pastel-colored backs, along with the card number, personal information, stats and career highlights. The cards measure 2-1/2" by 3-1/2" in size.

		MT	NR MT	EX
Complete Set (660):		15.00	11.00	6.00
Common Player:		.03	.02	.01
1	Jose Canseco	.35	.25	.14
2	Andre Dawson	.15	.11	.06
3	Mark McGwire	.30	.25	.12
4	Benny Santiago	.12	.09	.05
5	Rick Reuschel	.08	.06	.03
6	Fred McGriff	.35	.25	.14
7	Kal Daniels	.12	.09	.05
8	Gary Gaetti	.12	.09	.05
9	Ellis Burks	.08	.05	.02
10	Darryl Strawberry	.20	.12	.06
11	Julio Franco	.08	.06	.03
12	Lloyd Moseby	.06	.05	.02
13	*Jeff Pico*	.06	.05	.02
14	Johnny Ray	.06	.05	.02
15	Cal Ripken, Jr.	.40	.30	.15
16	Dick Schofield	.03	.02	.01
17	Mel Hall	.06	.05	.02
18	Bill Ripken	.06	.05	.02
19	Brook Jacoby	.08	.06	.03
20	Kirby Puckett	.35	.25	.14
21	Bill Doran	.06	.05	.02
22	Pete O'Brien	.06	.05	.02
23	Matt Nokes	.15	.11	.06
24	Brian Fisher	.06	.05	.02
25	Jack Clark	.12	.09	.05
26	Gary Pettis	.03	.02	.01
27	Dave Valle	.03	.02	.01
28	Willie Wilson	.08	.06	.03
29	Curt Young	.06	.05	.02
30	Dale Murphy	.10	.06	.03
31	Barry Larkin	.15	.10	.05
32	Dave Stewart	.08	.06	.03
33	Mike LaValliere	.06	.05	.02
34	Glen Hubbard	.03	.02	.01
35	Ryne Sandberg	.40	.30	.15
36	Tony Pena	.06	.05	.02
37	Greg Walker	.06	.05	.02
38	Von Hayes	.08	.06	.03
39	Kevin Mitchell	.08	.05	.02
40	Tim Raines	.08	.05	.02
41	Keith Hernandez	.20	.15	.08
42	Keith Moreland	.06	.05	.02
43	Ruben Sierra	.20	.12	.06
44	Chet Lemon	.06	.05	.02
45	Willie Randolph	.06	.05	.02
46	Andy Allanson	.03	.02	.01
47	Candy Maldonado	.06	.05	.02
48	Sid Bream	.06	.05	.02
49	Denny Walling	.03	.02	.01
50	Dave Winfield	.25	.20	.10
51	Alvin Davis	.10	.08	.04
52	Cory Snyder	.15	.11	.06
53	Hubie Brooks	.08	.06	.03
54	Chili Davis	.06	.05	.02
55	Kevin Seitzer	.12	.09	.05
56	Jose Uribe	.03	.02	.01
57	Tony Fernandez	.10	.08	.04
58	Tim Teufel	.03	.02	.01
59	Oddibe McDowell	.06	.05	.02
60	Les Lancaster	.06	.05	.02
61	Billy Hatcher	.06	.05	.02
62	Dan Gladden	.03	.02	.01
63	Marty Barrett	.06	.05	.02
64	Nick Esasky	.06	.05	.02
65	Wally Joyner	.08	.05	.02
66	Mike Greenwell	.08	.05	.02
67	Ken Williams	.06	.05	.02
68	Bob Horner	.08	.06	.03
69	Steve Sax	.12	.09	.05
70	Rickey Henderson	.20	.12	.06
71	Mitch Webster	.06	.05	.02
72	Rob Deer	.06	.05	.02
73	Jim Presley	.06	.05	.02

		MT	NR MT	EX
74	Albert Hall	.03	.02	.01
75a	George Brett (""At age 33 ...")	1.00	.70	.40
75b	George Brett ("At age 35 ...")	.30	.25	.12
76	Brian Downing	.06	.05	.02
77	Dave Martinez	.06	.05	.02
78	Scott Fletcher	.06	.05	.02
79	Phil Bradley	.08	.06	.03
80	Ozzie Smith	.12	.09	.05
81	Larry Sheets	.06	.05	.02
82	Mike Aldrete	.06	.05	.02
83	Darnell Coles	.06	.05	.02
84	Len Dykstra	.12	.08	.04
85	Jim Rice	.08	.05	.02
86	Jeff Treadway	.10	.08	.04
87	Jose Lind	.08	.06	.03
88	Willie McGee	.10	.08	.04
89	Mickey Brantley	.03	.02	.01
90	Tony Gwynn	.20	.15	.08
91	R.J. Reynolds	.03	.02	.01
92	Milt Thompson	.03	.02	.01
93	Kevin McReynolds	.12	.09	.05
94	Eddie Murray	.15	.10	.05
95	Lance Parrish	.12	.09	.05
96	Ron Kittle	.06	.05	.02
97	Gerald Young	.10	.08	.04
98	Ernie Whitt	.06	.05	.02
99	Jeff Reed	.03	.02	.01
100	Don Mattingly	.20	.12	.06
101	Gerald Perry	.08	.06	.03
102	Vance Law	.06	.05	.02
103	John Shelby	.03	.02	.01
104	*Chris Sabo*	.40	.30	.15
105	Danny Tartabull	.15	.11	.06
106	Glenn Wilson	.06	.05	.02
107	Mark Davidson	.06	.05	.02
108	Dave Parker	.10	.08	.04
109	Eric Davis	.08	.05	.02
110	Alan Trammell	.15	.11	.06
111	Ozzie Virgil	.03	.02	.01
112	Frank Tanana	.06	.05	.02
113	Rafael Ramirez	.03	.02	.01
114	Dennis Martinez	.06	.05	.02
115	Jose DeLeon	.06	.05	.02
116	Bob Ojeda	.06	.05	.02
117	Doug Drabek	.06	.05	.02
118	Andy Hawkins	.03	.02	.01
119	Greg Maddux(FC)	.25	.20	.10
120	Cecil Fielder (reversed negative)	.25	.15	.08
121	Mike Scioscia	.06	.05	.02
122	Dan Petry	.06	.05	.02
123	Terry Kennedy	.06	.05	.02
124	Kelly Downs	.08	.06	.03
125	Greg Gross	.20	.15	.08
126	Fred Lynn	.10	.08	.04
127	Barry Bonds	.50	.30	.15
128	Harold Baines	.10	.08	.04
129	Doyle Alexander	.06	.05	.02
130	Kevin Elster	.08	.06	.03
131	Mike Heath	.03	.02	.01
132	Teddy Higuera	.08	.06	.03
133	Charlie Leibrandt	.06	.05	.02
134	Tim Laudner	.03	.02	.01
135a	Ray Knight (photo reversed)	.60	.45	.25
135b	Ray Knight (correct photo)	.08	.06	.03
136	Howard Johnson	.08	.06	.03
137	Terry Pendleton	.12	.08	.04
138	Andy McGaffigan	.03	.02	.01
139	Ken Oberkfell	.03	.02	.01
140	Butch Wynegar	.03	.02	.01
141	Rob Murphy	.03	.02	.01
142	*Rich Renteria*(FC)	.06	.05	.02
143	Jose Guzman	.08	.06	.03
144	Andres Galarraga	.12	.09	.05
145	Rick Horton	.06	.05	.02
146	Frank DiPino	.03	.02	.01
147	Glenn Braggs	.06	.05	.02
148	John Kruk	.12	.08	.04
149	Mike Schmidt	.35	.25	.14
150	Lee Smith	.08	.06	.03
151	Robin Yount	.25	.20	.10
152	Mark Eichhorn	.06	.05	.02
153	DeWayne Buice	.04	.03	.02
154	B.J. Surhoff	.08	.06	.03
155	Vince Coleman	.12	.09	.05
156	Tony Phillips	.03	.02	.01
157	Willie Fraser	.03	.02	.01
158	Lance McCullers	.06	.05	.02
159	Greg Gagne	.03	.02	.01
160	Jesse Barfield	.08	.06	.03
161	Mark Langston	.08	.06	.03
162	Kurt Stillwell	.06	.05	.02

		MT	NR MT	EX
163	Dion James	.03	.02	.01
164	Glenn Davis	.12	.09	.05
165	Walt Weiss	.10	.06	.03
166	Dave Concepcion	.08	.06	.03
167	Alfredo Griffin	.06	.05	.02
168	*Don Heinkel*	.03	.02	.01
169	Luis Rivera(FC)	.03	.02	.01
170	Shane Rawley	.06	.05	.02
171	Darrell Evans	.08	.06	.03
172	Robby Thompson	.06	.05	.02
173	Jody Davis	.06	.05	.02
174	Andy Van Slyke	.12	.09	.05
175	Wade Boggs	.20	.12	.06
176	Garry Templeton	.06	.05	.02
177	Gary Redus	.03	.02	.01
178	Craig Lefferts	.03	.02	.01
179	Carney Lansford	.06	.05	.02
180	Ron Darling	.10	.08	.04
181	Kirk McCaskill	.06	.05	.02
182	Tony Armas	.06	.05	.02
183	Steve Farr	.03	.02	.01
184	Tom Brunansky	.10	.08	.04
185	*Bryan Harvey*	.30	.25	.12
186	Mike Marshall	.10	.08	.04
187	Bo Diaz	.06	.05	.02
188	Willie Upshaw	.06	.05	.02
189	Mike Pagliarulo	.08	.06	.03
190	Mike Krukow	.06	.05	.02
191	Tommy Herr	.06	.05	.02
192	Jim Pankovits	.03	.02	.01
193	Dwight Evans	.10	.08	.04
194	Kelly Gruber	.03	.02	.01
195	Bobby Bonilla	.15	.10	.05
196	Wallace Johnson	.03	.02	.01
197	Dave Stieb	.08	.06	.03
198	*Pat Borders*	.25	.20	.10
199	Rafael Palmeiro	.15	.11	.06
200	Doc Gooden	.08	.05	.02
201	Pete Incaviglia	.08	.06	.03
202	Chris James	.08	.06	.03
203	Marvell Wynne	.03	.02	.01
204	Pat Sheridan	.03	.02	.01
205	Don Baylor	.08	.06	.03
206	Paul O'Neill	.03	.02	.01
207	Pete Smith	.08	.06	.03
208	Mark McLemore	.03	.02	.01
209	Henry Cotto	.03	.02	.01
210	Kirk Gibson	.08	.05	.02
211	Claudell Washington	.06	.05	.02
212	Randy Bush	.03	.02	.01
213	Joe Carter	.25	.15	.08
214	Bill Buckner	.08	.06	.03
215	Bert Blyleven	.25	.20	.10
216	Brett Butler	.06	.05	.02
217	Lee Mazzilli	.06	.05	.02
218	Spike Owen	.03	.02	.01
219	Bill Swift	.03	.02	.01
220	Tim Wallach	.08	.06	.03
221	David Cone	.10	.06	.03
222	Don Carman	.06	.05	.02
223	Rich Gossage	.10	.08	.04
224	Bob Walk	.03	.02	.01
225	Dave Righetti	.10	.08	.04
226	Kevin Bass	.06	.05	.02
227	Kevin Gross	.06	.05	.02
228	Tim Burke	.03	.02	.01
229	Rick Mahler	.03	.02	.01
230	Lou Whitaker	.15	.11	.06
231	*Luis Alicea*	.10	.06	.03
232	Roberto Alomar	1.00	.70	.40
233	Bob Boone	.06	.05	.02
234	Dickie Thon	.03	.02	.01
235	Shawon Dunston	.08	.06	.03
236	Pete Stanicek	.08	.06	.03
237	*Craig Biggio*	.50	.40	.20
238	Dennis Boyd	.06	.05	.02
239	Tom Candiotti	.03	.02	.01
240	Gary Carter	.15	.11	.06
241	Mike Stanley	.03	.02	.01
242	Ken Phelps	.06	.05	.02
243	Chris Bosio	.03	.02	.01
244	Les Straker	.06	.05	.02
245	Dave Smith	.06	.05	.02
246	John Candelaria	.06	.05	.02
247	Joe Orsulak	.03	.02	.01
248	Storm Davis	.08	.06	.03
249	Floyd Bannister	.06	.05	.02
250	Jack Morris	.12	.09	.05
251	Bret Saberhagen	.12	.09	.05
252	Tom Niedenfuer	.06	.05	.02
253	Neal Heaton	.03	.02	.01

		MT	NR MT	EX
254	Eric Show	.06	.05	.02
255	Juan Samuel	.10	.08	.04
256	Dale Sveum	.06	.05	.02
257	Jim Gott	.03	.02	.01
258	Scott Garrelts	.03	.02	.01
259	Larry McWilliams	.03	.02	.01
260	Steve Bedrosian	.08	.06	.03
261	Jack Howell	.06	.05	.02
262	Jay Tibbs	.03	.02	.01
263	Jamie Moyer	.03	.02	.01
264	Doug Sisk	.03	.02	.01
265	Todd Worrell	.08	.06	.03
266	John Farrell	.08	.06	.03
267	Dave Collins	.06	.05	.02
268	Sid Fernandez	.08	.06	.03
269	Tom Brookens	.03	.02	.01
270	Shane Mack	.06	.05	.02
271	Paul Kilgus	.08	.06	.03
272	Chuck Crim	.03	.02	.01
273	Bob Knepper	.06	.05	.02
274	Mike Moore	.03	.02	.01
275	Guillermo Hernandez	.06	.05	.02
276	Dennis Eckersley	.10	.08	.04
277	Graig Nettles	.10	.08	.04
278	Rich Dotson	.06	.05	.02
279	Larry Herndon	.03	.02	.01
280	Gene Larkin	.08	.06	.03
281	Roger McDowell	.08	.06	.03
282	Greg Swindell	.10	.08	.04
283	Juan Agosto	.03	.02	.01
284	Jeff Robinson	.06	.05	.02
285	Mike Dunne	.08	.06	.03
286	Greg Mathews	.06	.05	.02
287	Kent Tekulve	.06	.05	.02
288	Jerry Mumphrey	.03	.02	.01
289	Jack McDowell(FC)	.40	.30	.15
290	Frank Viola	.12	.09	.05
291	Mark Gubicza	.08	.06	.03
292	Dave Schmidt	.03	.02	.01
293	Mike Henneman	.08	.06	.03
294	Jimmy Jones	.03	.02	.01
295	Charlie Hough	.06	.05	.02
296	Rafael Santana	.03	.02	.01
297	Chris Speier	.03	.02	.01
298	Mike Witt	.06	.05	.02
299	Pascual Perez	.06	.05	.02
300	Nolan Ryan	.50	.40	.20
301	Mitch Williams	.06	.05	.02
302	Mookie Wilson	.06	.05	.02
303	Mackey Sasser	.06	.05	.02
304	John Cerutti	.06	.05	.02
305	Jeff Reardon	.08	.06	.03
306	Randy Myers	.08	.06	.03
307	Greg Brock	.06	.05	.02
308	Bob Welch	.08	.06	.03
309	Jeff Robinson	.12	.09	.05
310	Harold Reynolds	.06	.05	.02
311	Jim Walewander	.03	.02	.01
312	Dave Magadan	.08	.06	.03
313	Jim Gantner	.03	.02	.01
314	Walt Terrell	.06	.05	.02
315	Wally Backman	.06	.05	.02
316	Luis Salazar	.03	.02	.01
317	Rick Rhoden	.06	.05	.02
318	Tom Henke	.06	.05	.02
319	*Mike Macfarlane*	.15	.10	.05
320	Dan Plesac	.08	.06	.03
321	Calvin Schiraldi	.03	.02	.01
322	Stan Javier	.03	.02	.01
323	Devon White	.10	.08	.04
324	Scott Bradley	.03	.02	.01
325	Bruce Hurst	.08	.06	.03
326	Manny Lee	.03	.02	.01
327	Rick Aguilera	.03	.02	.01
328	Bruce Ruffin	.03	.02	.01
329	Ed Whitson	.03	.02	.01
330	Bo Jackson	.30	.20	.10
331	Ivan Calderon	.06	.05	.02
332	Mickey Hatcher	.03	.02	.01
333	Barry Jones(FC)	.03	.02	.01
334	Ron Hassey	.03	.02	.01
335	Bill Wegman	.03	.02	.01
336	Damon Berryhill	.15	.11	.06
337	Steve Ontiverso	.03	.02	.01
338	Dan Pasqua	.08	.06	.03
339	Bill Pecota	.06	.05	.02
340	Greg Cadaret	.06	.05	.02
341	Scott Bankhead	.03	.02	.01
342	Ron Guidry	.12	.09	.05
343	Danny Heep	.03	.02	.01
344	Bob Brower	.03	.02	.01

		MT	NR MT	EX
345	Rich Gedman	.06	.05	.02
346	*Nelson Santovenia*	.06	.04	.02
347	George Bell	.08	.05	.02
348	Ted Power	.03	.02	.01
349	Mark Grant	.03	.02	.01
350a	Roger Clemens (778 wins)	3.00	2.25	1.25
350b	Roger Clemens (78 wins)	.40	.30	.15
351	Bill Long	.06	.05	.02
352	Jay Bell(FC)	.06	.05	.02
353	Steve Balboni	.06	.05	.02
354	Bob Kipper	.03	.02	.01
355	Steve Jeltz	.03	.02	.01
356	Jesse Orosco	.06	.05	.02
357	Bob Dernier	.03	.02	.01
358	Mickey Tettleton	.03	.02	.01
359	Duane Ward(FC)	.03	.02	.01
360	Darrin Jackson(FC)	.08	.06	.03
361	Rey Quinones	.03	.02	.01
362	Mark Grace(FC)	.80	.60	.30
363	Steve Lake	.03	.02	.01
364	Pat Perry	.03	.02	.01
365	Terry Steinbach	.08	.06	.03
366	Alan Ashby	.03	.02	.01
367	Jeff Montgomery	.06	.05	.02
368	Steve Buechele	.03	.02	.01
369	Chris Brown	.06	.05	.02
370	Orel Hershiser	.08	.05	.02
371	Todd Benzinger	.10	.08	.04
372	Ron Gant	.40	.30	.15
373	Paul Assenmacher(FC)	.03	.02	.01
374	Joey Meyer	.08	.06	.03
375	Neil Allen	.03	.02	.01
376	Mike Davis	.06	.05	.02
377	Jeff Parrett(FC)	.08	.06	.03
378	Jay Howell	.06	.05	.02
379	Rafael Belliard	.03	.02	.01
380	Luis Polonia	.06	.05	.02
381	Keith Atherton	.03	.02	.01
382	Kent Hrbek	.15	.11	.06
383	Bob Stanley	.03	.02	.01
384	Dave LaPoint	.06	.05	.02
385	Rance Mulliniks	.03	.02	.01
386	Melido Perez	.08	.06	.03
387	Doug Jones	.10	.08	.04
388	Steve Lyons	.03	.02	.01
389	Alejandro Pena	.06	.05	.02
390	Frank White	.06	.05	.02
391	Pat Tabler	.06	.05	.02
392	Eric Plunk(FC)	.03	.02	.01
393	Mike Maddux(FC)	.03	.02	.01
394	Allan Anderson(FC)	.06	.05	.02
395	Bob Brenly	.03	.02	.01
396	Rick Cerone	.03	.02	.01
397	Scott Terry(FC)	.08	.06	.03
398	Mike Jackson	.06	.05	.02
399	Bobby Thigpen	.08	.06	.03
400	Don Sutton	.08	.05	.02
401	Cecil Espy	.06	.05	.02
402	Junior Ortiz	.03	.02	.01
403	Mike Smithson	.03	.02	.01
404	Bud Black	.03	.02	.01
405	Tom Foley	.03	.02	.01
406	Andres Thomas	.06	.05	.02
407	Rick Sutcliffe	.08	.06	.03
408	Brian Harper	.03	.02	.01
409	John Smiley	.10	.08	.04
410	Juan Nieves	.06	.05	.02
411	Shawn Abner	.08	.06	.03
412	Wes Gardner(FC)	.06	.05	.02
413	Darren Daulton	.15	.10	.05
414	Juan Berenguer	.03	.02	.01
415	Charles Hudson	.03	.02	.01
416	Rick Honeycutt	.03	.02	.01
417	Greg Booker	.03	.02	.01
418	Tim Belcher	.08	.06	.03
419	Don August	.08	.06	.03
420	Dale Mohorcic	.03	.02	.01
421	Steve Lombardozzi	.03	.02	.01
422	Atlee Hammaker	.03	.02	.01
423	Jerry Don Gleaton	.03	.02	.01
424	Scott Bailes(FC)	.03	.02	.01
425	Bruce Sutter	.08	.06	.03
426	Randy Ready	.03	.02	.01
427	Jerry Reed	.03	.02	.01
428	Bryn Smith	.03	.02	.01
429	Tim Leary	.06	.05	.02
430	Mark Clear	.03	.02	.01
431	Terry Leach	.03	.02	.01
432	John Moses	.03	.02	.01
433	Ozzie Guillen	.06	.05	.02
434	Gene Nelson	.03	.02	.01

		MT	NR MT	EX
435	Gary Ward	.06	.05	.02
436	Luis Aguayo	.03	.02	.01
437	Fernando Valenzuela	.15	.11	.06
438	Jeff Russell	.03	.02	.01
439	Cecilio Guante	.03	.02	.01
440	Don Robinson	.03	.02	.01
441	Rick Anderson(FC)	.03	.02	.01
442	Tom Glavine	.60	.40	.15
443	Daryl Boston	.03	.02	.01
444	Joe Price	.03	.02	.01
445	Stewart Cliburn	.03	.02	.01
446	Manny Trillo	.03	.02	.01
447	Joel Skinner	.03	.02	.01
448	Charlie Puleo	.03	.02	.01
449	Carlton Fisk	.12	.09	.05
450	Will Clark	.50	.40	.20
451	Otis Nixon	.03	.02	.01
452	Rick Schu	.03	.02	.01
453	Todd Stottlemyre(FC)	.15	.11	.06
454	Tim Birtsas	.03	.02	.01
455	*Dave Gallagher*	.08	.05	.02
456	Barry Lyons	.03	.02	.01
457	Fred Manrique	.06	.05	.02
458	Ernest Riles	.03	.02	.01
459	*Doug Jennings*(FC)	.06	.04	.02
460	Joe Magrane	.08	.06	.03
461	Jamie Quirk	.03	.02	.01
462	*Jack Armstrong*	.10	.06	.03
463	Bobby Witt	.08	.06	.03
464	Keith Miller	.06	.05	.02
465	*Todd Burns*	.08	.06	.03
466	*John Dopson*	.08	.06	.03
467	Rich Yett	.03	.02	.01
468	Craig Reynolds	.03	.02	.01
469	Dave Bergman	.03	.02	.01
470	Rex Hudler	.03	.02	.01
471	Eric King	.03	.02	.01
472	Joaquin Andujar	.06	.05	.02
473	*Sil Campusano*	.06	.05	.02
474	Terry Mulholland(FC)	.03	.02	.01
475	Mike Flanagan	.06	.05	.02
476	Greg Harris	.03	.02	.01
477	Tommy John	.10	.08	.04
478	Dave Anderson	.03	.02	.01
479	Fred Toliver	.03	.02	.01
480	Jimmy Key	.08	.06	.03
481	Donell Nixon	.03	.02	.01
482	Mark Portugal(FC)	.03	.02	.01
483	Tom Pagnozzi	.06	.05	.02
484	Jeff Kunkel	.03	.02	.01
485	Frank Williams	.03	.02	.01
486	Jody Reed	.10	.08	.04
487	Roberto Kelly	.12	.08	.04
488	Shawn Hillegas	.06	.05	.02
489	Jerry Reuss	.06	.05	.02
490	Mark Davis	.03	.02	.01
491	Jeff Sellers	.03	.02	.01
492	Zane Smith	.06	.05	.02
493	Al Newman(FC)	.03	.02	.01
494	Mike Young	.03	.02	.01
495	Larry Parrish	.06	.05	.02
496	Herm Winningham	.03	.02	.01
497	Carmen Castillo	.03	.02	.01
498	Joe Hesketh	.03	.02	.01
499	Darrell Miller	.03	.02	.01
500	Mike LaCoss	.03	.02	.01
501	Charlie Lea	.03	.02	.01
502	Bruce Benedict	.03	.02	.01
503	Chuck Finley(FC)	.03	.02	.01
504	Brad Wellman(FC)	.03	.02	.01
505	Tim Crews	.06	.05	.02
506	Ken Gerhart	.06	.05	.02
507	Brian Holton (Born: 1/25/65, Denver)	.20	.15	.08
507	Brian Holton (Born: 11/29/59, McKeesport)			
508	Dennis Lamp	.03	.02	.01
509	Bobby Meacham	.20	.15	.08
510	Tracy Jones	.08	.06	.03
511	Mike Fitzgerald	.03	.02	.01
512	*Jeff Bittiger*	.06	.05	.02
513	Tim Flannery	.03	.02	.01
514	Ray Hayward(FC)	.03	.02	.01
515	Dave Leiper	.03	.02	.01
516	Rod Scurry	.03	.02	.01
517	Carmelo Martinez	.03	.02	.01
518	Curtis Wilkerson	.03	.02	.01
519	Stan Jefferson	.03	.02	.01
520	Dan Quisenberry	.06	.05	.02
521	Lloyd McClendon(FC)	.03	.02	.01
522	Steve Trout	.03	.02	.01

		MT	NR MT	EX
523	Larry Andersen	.03	.02	.01
524	Don Aase	.03	.02	.01
525	Bob Forsch	.06	.05	.02
526	Geno Petralli	.03	.02	.01
527	Angel Salazar	.03	.02	.01
528	*Mike Schooler*	.08	.06	.03
529	Jose Oquendo	.03	.02	.01
530	Jay Buhner(FC)	.15	.10	.05
531	Tom Bolton(FC)	.06	.05	.02
532	Al Nipper	.03	.02	.01
533	Dave Henderson	.08	.06	.03
534	*John Costello*(FC)	.06	.05	.02
535	Donnie Moore	.03	.02	.01
536	Mike Laga	.03	.02	.01
537	Mike Gallego	.03	.02	.01
538	Jim Clancy	.06	.05	.02
539	Joel Youngblood	.03	.02	.01
540	Rick Leach	.03	.02	.01
541	Kevin Romine	.03	.02	.01
542	Mark Salas	.03	.02	.01
543	Greg Minton	.03	.02	.01
544	Dave Palmer	.03	.02	.01
545	Dwayne Murphy	.06	.05	.02
546	Jim Deshaies	.03	.02	.01
547	Don Gordon(FC)	.03	.02	.01
548	*Ricky Jordan*	.10	.06	.03
549	Mike Boddicker	.06	.05	.02
550	Mike Scott	.10	.08	.04
551	Jeff Ballard(FC)	.08	.06	.03
552a	Jose Rijo (uniform number #24 on card back)	.20	.15	.08
552b	Jose Rijo (uniform number #27 on card back)	.08	.06	.03
553	Danny Darwin	.03	.02	.01
554	Tom Browning	.08	.06	.03
555	Danny Jackson	.12	.09	.05
556	Rick Dempsey	.06	.05	.02
557	Jeffrey Leonard	.06	.05	.02
558	Jeff Musselman	.06	.05	.02
559	Ron Robinson	.03	.02	.01
560	John Tudor	.08	.06	.03
561	Don Slaught	.03	.02	.01
562	Dennis Rasmussen	.08	.06	.03
563	*Brady Anderson*	.40	.30	.15
564	Pedro Guerrero	.12	.09	.05
565	Paul Molitor	.20	.12	.06
566	*Terry Clark*(FC)	.06	.05	.02
567	Terry Puhl	.03	.02	.01
568	Mike Campbell(FC)	.08	.06	.03
569	Paul Mirabella	.03	.02	.01
570	Jeff Hamilton(FC)	.06	.05	.02
571	*Oswald Peraza*	.08	.06	.03
572	Bob McClure	.03	.02	.01
573	*Jose Bautista*(FC)	.15	.11	.06
574	Alex Trevino	.03	.02	.01
575	John Franco	.08	.06	.03
576	*Mark Parent*(FC)	.06	.05	.02
577	Nelson Liriano	.06	.05	.02
578	Steve Shields	.03	.02	.01
579	Odell Jones	.03	.02	.01
580	Al Leiter	.15	.11	.06
581	Dave Stapleton(FC)	.06	.05	.02
582	1988 World Series (Jose Canseco, Kirk Gibson, Orel Hershiser, Dave Stewart)	.10	.06	.03
583	Donnie Hill	.03	.02	.01
584	Chuck Jackson	.06	.05	.02
585	Rene Gonzales(FC)	.06	.05	.02
586	Tracy Woodson(FC)	.08	.06	.03
587	Jim Adduci(FC)	.03	.02	.01
588	Mario Soto	.06	.05	.02
589	Jeff Blauser	.08	.06	.03
590	Jim Traber	.06	.05	.02
591	Jon Perlman(FC)	.03	.02	.01
592	Mark Williamson(FC)	.06	.05	.02
593	Dave Meads	.03	.02	.01
594	Jim Eisenreich	.03	.02	.01
595	*Paul Gibson*(FC)	.06	.05	.02
596	Mike Birkbeck	.03	.02	.01
597	Terry Francona	.03	.02	.01
598	Paul Zuvella(FC)	.03	.02	.01
599	Franklin Stubbs	.03	.02	.01
600	Gregg Jefferies	.30	.25	.12
601	John Cangelosi	.03	.02	.01
602	Mike Sharperson(FC)	.03	.02	.01
603	Mike Diaz	.06	.05	.02
604	*Gary Varsho*(FC)	.06	.04	.02
605	*Terry Blocker*(FC)	.08	.06	.03
606	Charlie O'Brien(FC)	.03	.02	.01
607	Jim Eppard(FC)	.06	.05	.02
608	John Davis	.03	.02	.01
609	Ken Griffey, Sr.	.08	.06	.03

		MT	NR MT	EX
610	Buddy Bell	.06	.05	.02
611	Ted Simmons	.08	.06	.03
612	Matt Williams	.25	.15	.08
613	Danny Cox	.06	.05	.02
614	Al Pedrique	.03	.02	.01
615	Ron Oester	.03	.02	.01
616	*John Smoltz*(FC)	.80	.60	.30
617	Bob Melvin	.03	.02	.01
618	*Rob Dibble*	.20	.12	.06
619	Kirt Manwaring	.10	.08	.04
620	Felix Fermin(FC)	.06	.05	.02
621	*Doug Dascenzo*(FC)	.08	.05	.02
622	*Bill Brennan*(FC)	.06	.05	.02
623	*Carlos Quintana*	.12	.08	.03
624	*Mike Harkey*	.25	.20	.10
625	*Gary Sheffield*	1.25	.75	.50
626	*Tom Prince*(FC)	.08	.06	.03
627	*Steve Searcy*(FC)	.15	.11	.06
628	*Charlie Hayes*	.50	.30	.15
629	*Felix Jose*	.35	.20	.10
630	*Sandy Alomar*	.30	.25	.12
631	*Derek Lilliquist*	.15	.11	.06
632	Geronimo Berroa(FC)	.06	.05	.02
633	*Luis Medina*	.06	.05	.02
634	*Tom Gordon*	.10	.06	.03
635	*Ramon Martinez*	.60	.45	.25
636	*Craig Worthington*(FC)	.08	.05	.02
637	Edgar Martinez(FC)	.20	.12	.06
638	*Chad Krueter*	.15	.11	.06
639	*Ron Jones*	.08	.05	.02
640	*Van Snider*	.06	.05	.02
641	*Lance Blankenship*	.15	.11	.06
642	*Dwight Smith*	.10	.08	.04
643	*Cameron Drew*	.03	.02	.01
644	*Jerald Clark*	.20	.12	.06
645	*Randy Johnson*	.75	.50	.25
646	*Norm Charlton*	.30	.25	.12
647	Todd Frohwirth(FC)	.08	.06	.03
648	*Luis de los Santos*	.06	.05	.02
649	*Tim Jones*(FC)	.06	.05	.02
650	*Dave West*	.20	.15	.08
651	*Bob Milacki*	.10	.06	.03
652	1988 HL (Wrigley Field)	.06	.05	.02
653	1988 HL (Orel Hershiser)	.10	.08	.04
654a	1988 HL (Wade Boggs) ("...sixth consecutive seaason..." on back)	3.00	2.25	1.25
654b	1988 HL (Wade Boggs) ("season" corrected)	.10	.06	.03
655	1988 HL (Jose Canseco)	.20	.15	.08
656	1988 HL (Doug Jones)	.06	.05	.02
657	1988 HL (Rickey Henderson)	.12	.09	.05
658	1988 HL (Tom Browning)	.06	.05	.02
659	1988 HL (Mike Greenwell)	.15	.11	.06
660	1988 HL (Joe Morgan) (A.L. Win Streak)	.06	.05	.02

1989 Score Traded

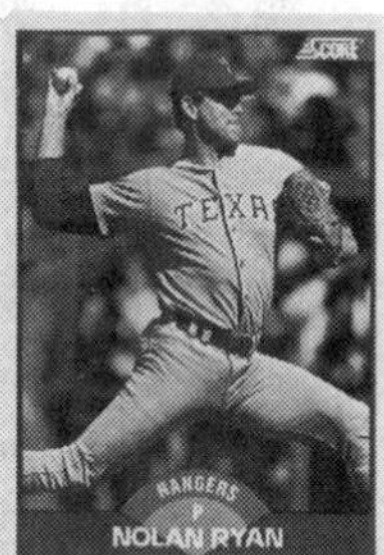

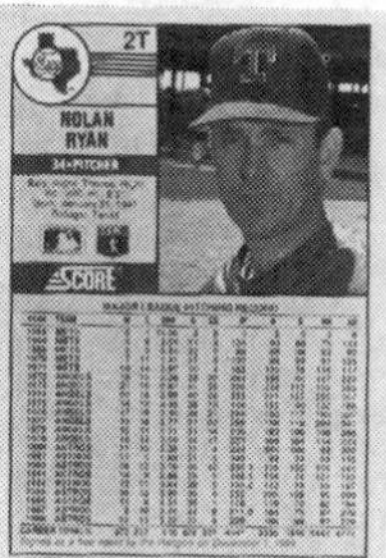

Score issued its second consecutive traded set in 1989 to supplement and update its regular set. The 110-card traded set features the same basic card design as the regular 1989 Score set. The set consists of rookies and traded players pictured with correct teams. The set was sold by hobby dealers in a special box that included an assortment of "Magic Motion" trivia cards.

		MT	NR MT	EX
	Complete Set (110):	10.00	6.00	3.00
	Common Player:	.06	.05	.02
1T	Rafael Palmeiro	.20	.12	.06
2T	Nolan Ryan	1.50	1.25	.60
3T	Jack Clark	.10	.08	.04
4T	Dave LaPoint	.06	.05	.02
5T	Mike Moore	.08	.06	.03
6T	Pete O'Brien	.06	.05	.02
7T	Jeffrey Leonard	.06	.05	.02
8T	Rob Murphy	.06	.05	.02
9T	Tom Herr	.06	.05	.02
10T	Claudell Washington	.06	.05	.02
11T	Mike Pagliarulo	.06	.05	.02
12T	Steve Lake	.06	.05	.02
13T	Spike Owen	.06	.05	.02
14T	Andy Hawkins	.06	.05	.02
15T	Todd Benzinger	.06	.05	.02
16T	Mookie Wilson	.06	.05	.03
17T	Bert Blyleven	.08	.06	.03
18T	Jeff Treadway	.06	.05	.02
19T	Bruce Hurst	.08	.06	.03
20T	Steve Sax	.12	.09	.05
21T	Juan Samuel	.06	.05	.02
22T	Jesse Barfield	.06	.05	.02
23T	Carmelo Castillo	.06	.05	.02
24T	Terry Leach	.06	.05	.02
25T	Mark Langston	.12	.09	.05
26T	Eric King	.06	.05	.02
27T	Steve Balboni	.06	.05	.02
28T	Len Dykstra	.15	.10	.05
29T	Keith Moreland	.06	.05	.02
30T	Terry Kennedy	.06	.05	.02
31T	Eddie Murray	.15	.10	.05
32T	Mitch Williams	.10	.08	.04
33T	Jeff Parrett	.06	.05	.02
34T	Wally Backman	.06	.05	.02
35T	Julio Franco	.10	.08	.04
36T	Lance Parrish	.06	.05	.02
37T	Nick Esasky	.06	.05	.02
38T	Luis Polonia	.06	.05	.02
39T	Kevin Gross	.06	.05	.02
40T	John Dopson	.06	.05	.02
41T	Willie Randolph	.08	.06	.03
42T	Jim Clancy	.06	.05	.02
43T	Tracy Jones	.06	.05	.02
44T	Phil Bradley	.06	.05	.02
45T	Milt Thompson	.06	.05	.02
46T	Chris James	.06	.05	.02
47T	Scott Fletcher	.06	.05	.02
48T	Kal Daniels	.08	.06	.03
49T	Steve Bedrosian	.06	.05	.02
50T	Rickey Henderson	.50	.40	.20
51T	Dion James	.06	.05	.02
52T	Tim Leary	.06	.05	.02
53T	Roger McDowell	.06	.05	.02
54T	Mel Hall	.06	.05	.02
55T	Dickie Thon	.06	.05	.02
56T	Zane Smith	.06	.05	.02
57T	Danny Heep	.06	.05	.02
58T	Bob McClure	.06	.05	.02
59T	Brian Holton	.06	.05	.02
60T	Randy Ready	.06	.05	.02
61T	Bob Melvin	.06	.05	.02
62T	Harold Baines	.08	.06	.03
63T	Lance McCullers	.06	.05	.02
64T	Jody Davis	.06	.05	.02
65T	Darrell Evans	.06	.05	.02
66T	Joel Youngblood	.08	.06	.03
67T	Frank Viola	.08	.06	.03
68T	Mike Aldrete	.06	.05	.02
69T	Greg Cadaret	.06	.05	.02
70T	John Kruk	.12	.08	.04
71T	Pat Sheridan	.06	.05	.02
72T	Oddibe McDowell	.06	.05	.02
73T	Tom Brookens	.06	.05	.02
74T	Bob Boone	.08	.06	.03
75T	Walt Terrell	.06	.05	.02
76T	Joel Skinner	.06	.05	.02
77T	Randy Johnson	.60	.40	.20
78T	Felix Fermin	.06	.05	.03
79T	Rick Mahler	.06	.05	.03
80T	Rich Dotson	.06	.05	.03
81T	Cris Carpenter(FC)	.20	.15	.08
82T	Bill Spiers(FC)	.12	.08	.04
83T	Junior Felix(FC)	.25	.20	.10
84T	Joe Girardi(FC)	.20	.15	.08
85T	Jerome Walton(FC)	.25	.20	.10
86T	Greg Litton(FC)	.25	.20	.10
87T	Greg Harris(FC)	.20	.15	.08
88T	Jim Abbott(FC)	1.50	1.25	.60

		MT	NR MT	EX
89T	Kevin Brown(FC)	.20	.15	.08
90T	John Wetteland(FC)	.20	.15	.08
91T	Gary Wayne(FC)	.15	.11	.06
92T	Rich Monteleone(FC)	.15	.11	.06
93T	Bob Geren(FC)	.20	.15	.08
94T	Clay Parker(FC)	.15	.11	.06
95T	Steve Finley(FC)	.30	.20	.10
96T	Gregg Olson(FC)	.35	.25	.14
97T	Ken Patterson(FC)	.15	.11	.06
98T	Ken Hill(FC)	.50	.40	.20
99T	Scott Scudder(FC)	.15	.10	.05
100T	Ken Griffey, Jr.(FC)	5.00	3.75	2.00
101T	Jeff Brantley(FC)	.25	.20	.10
102T	Donn Pall(FC)	.15	.11	.06
103T	Carlos Martinez(FC)	.20	.15	.08
104T	Joe Oliver(FC)	.30	.25	.12
105T	Omar Vizquel(FC)	.15	.11	.06
106T	Joey Belle(FC)	5.00	3.00	1.50
107T	Kenny Rogers(FC)	.20	.15	.08
108T	Mark Carreon(FC)	.15	.11	.06
109T	Rolando Roomes(FC)	.15	.11	.06
110T	Pete Harnsisch(FC)	.35	.25	.14

1990 Score

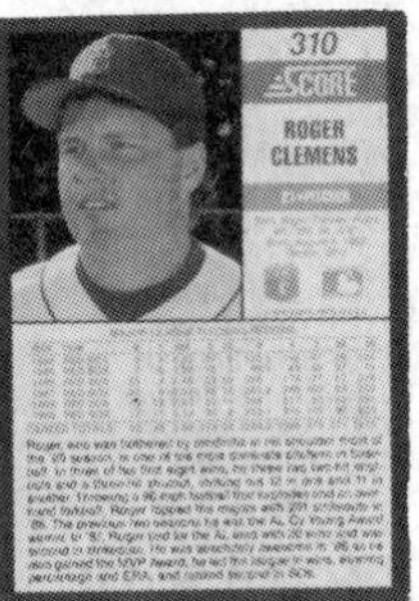

The regular Score set increased to 704 cards in 1990. Included were a series of cards picturing first-round draft picks, an expanded subset of rookie cards, four World Series specials, five Highlight cards, and a 13-card "Dream Team" series featuring the game's top players pictured on old tobacco-style cards. For the first time in a Score set, team logos are displayed on the card fronts in the lower right corner. Card backs again include a full-color portrait photo with player data. A one-paragraph write-up of each player was again provided by former Sports Illustrated editor Les Woodcock. The Score set was again distributed with "Magic Motion" triva cards, this year using "Baseball's Most Valuable Players" as its theme.

		MT	NR MT	EX
Complete Set (704):		20.00	15.00	8.00
Common Player:		.04	.03	.02
1	Don Mattingly	.35	.25	.14
2	Cal Ripken, Jr.	.40	.30	.15
3	Dwight Evans	.08	.06	.03
4	Barry Bonds	.12	.09	.05
5	Kevin McReynolds	.12	.09	.05
6	Ozzie Guillen	.05	.04	.02
7	Terry Kennedy	.04	.03	.02
8	Bryan Harvey	.06	.05	.02
9	Alan Trammell	.09	.07	.04
10	Cory Snyder	.09	.07	.04
11	Jody Reed	.05	.04	.02
12	Roberto Alomar	.30	.25	.12
13	Pedro Guerrero	.09	.07	.04
14	Gary Redus	.04	.03	.02
15	Marty Barrett	.05	.04	.02
16	Ricky Jordan	.20	.15	.08
17	Joe Magrane	.07	.05	.03
18	Sid Fernandez	.07	.05	.03
19	Rich Dotson	.04	.03	.02
20	Jack Clark	.09	.07	.04
21	Bob Walk	.05	.04	.02
22	Ron Karkovice	.04	.03	.02

		MT	NR MT	EX
23	Lenny Harris(FC)	.10	.08	.04
24	Phil Bradley	.06	.05	.02
25	Andres Galarraga	.15	.11	.06
26	Brian Downing	.06	.05	.02
27	Dave Martinez	.06	.05	.02
28	Eric King	.04	.03	.02
29	Barry Lyons	.04	.03	.02
30	Dave Schmidt	.04	.03	.02
31	Mike Boddicker	.06	.05	.02
32	Tom Foley	.04	.03	.02
33	Brady Anderson	.07	.05	.03
34	Jim Presley	.05	.04	.02
35	Lance Parrish	.06	.05	.02
36	Von Hayes	.09	.07	.03
37	Lee Smith	.06	.05	.02
38	Herm Winningham	.04	.03	.02
39	Alejandro Pena	.04	.03	.02
40	Mike Scott	.09	.07	.04
41	Joe Orsulak	.04	.03	.02
42	Rafael Ramirez	.05	.04	.02
43	Gerald Young	.05	.04	.02
44	Dick Schofield	.05	.04	.02
45	Dave Smith	.06	.05	.02
46	Dave Magadan	.07	.05	.03
47	Dennis Martinez	.06	.05	.02
48	Greg Minton	.04	.03	.02
49	Milt Thompson	.04	.03	.02
50	Orel Hershiser	.12	.09	.05
51	Bip Roberts(FC)	.20	.15	.08
52	Jerry Browne	.09	.07	.04
53	Bob Ojeda	.05	.04	.02
54	Fernando Valenzuela	.09	.07	.04
55	Matt Nokes	.09	.07	.04
56	Brook Jacoby	.08	.06	.03
57	Frank Tanana	.05	.04	.02
58	Scott Fletcher	.05	.04	.02
59	Ron Oester	.05	.04	.02
60	Bob Boone	.08	.06	.03
61	Dan Gladden	.08	.06	.03
62	Darnell Coles	.04	.03	.02
63	Gregg Olson	.25	.20	.10
64	Todd Burns	.05	.04	.02
65	Todd Benzinger	.07	.05	.03
66	Dale Murphy	.12	.09	.05
67	Mike Flanagan	.06	.05	.02
68	Jose Oquendo	.06	.05	.02
69	Cecil Espy	.08	.06	.03
70	Chris Sabo	.10	.08	.04
71	Shane Rawley	.05	.04	.02
72	Tom Brunansky	.08	.06	.03
73	Vance Law	.05	.04	.02
74	B.J. Surhoff	.08	.06	.03
75	Lou Whitaker	.09	.07	.04
76	Ken Caminiti	.09	.07	.04
77	Nelson Liriano	.04	.03	.02
78	Tommy Gregg	.09	.07	.04
79	Don Slaught	.05	.04	.02
80	Eddie Murray	.12	.09	.05
81	Joe Boever	.08	.06	.03
82	Charlie Leibrandt	.06	.05	.02
83	Jose Lind	.06	.05	.02
84	Tony Phillips	.05	.04	.02
85	Mitch Webster	.04	.03	.02
86	Dan Plesac	.07	.05	.02
87	Rick Mahler	.05	.04	.02
88	Steve Lyons	.05	.04	.02
89	Tony Fernandez	.09	.07	.04
90	Ryne Sandberg	.30	.25	.12
91	Nick Esasky	.09	.07	.04
92	Luis Salazar	.04	.03	.02
93	Pete Incaviglia	.08	.06	.03
94	Ivan Calderon	.06	.05	.02
95	Jeff Treadway	.06	.05	.02
96	Kurt Stillwell	.06	.05	.02
97	Gary Sheffield	.25	.20	.10
98	Jeffrey Leonard	.07	.05	.03
99	Andres Thomas	.05	.04	.02
100	Roberto Kelly	.15	.11	.06
101	Alvaro Espinoza(FC)	.06	.05	.02
102	Greg Gagne	.05	.04	.02
103	John Farrell	.05	.04	.02
104	Willie Wilson	.05	.04	.02
105	Glenn Braggs	.08	.06	.03
106	Chet Lemon	.06	.05	.02
107	Jamie Moyer	.06	.05	.02
108	Chuck Crim	.04	.03	.02
109	Dave Valle	.04	.03	.02
110	Walt Weiss	.10	.08	.04
111	Larry Sheets	.04	.03	.02
112	Don Robinson	.05	.04	.02
113	Danny Heep	.04	.03	.02
114	Carmelo Martinez	.06	.05	.02

		MT	NR MT	EX
115	Dave Gallagher	.08	.06	.03
116	Mike LaValliere	.05	.04	.02
117	Bob McClure	.04	.03	.02
118	Rene Gonzales	.04	.03	.02
119	Mark Parent	.05	.04	.02
120	Wally Joyner	.15	.11	.06
121	Mark Gubicza	.09	.07	.04
122	Tony Pena	.08	.06	.03
123	Carmen Castillo	.04	.03	.02
124	Howard Johnson	.10	.08	.04
125	Steve Sax	.10	.08	.04
126	Tim Belcher	.10	.08	.04
127	Tim Burke	.06	.05	.02
128	Al Newman	.04	.03	.02
129	Dennis Rasmussen	.05	.04	.02
130	Doug Jones	.06	.05	.02
131	Fred Lynn	.09	.07	.04
132	Jeff Hamilton	.06	.05	.02
133	German Gonzalez	.05	.04	.02
134	John Morris	.05	.04	.02
135	Dave Parker	.10	.08	.04
136	Gary Pettis	.05	.04	.02
137	Dennis Boyd	.07	.05	.02
138	Candy Maldonado	.06	.05	.02
139	Rick Cerone	.04	.03	.02
140	George Brett	.15	.11	.06
141	Dave Clark	.05	.04	.02
142	Dickie Thon	.05	.04	.02
143	Junior Ortiz	.04	.03	.02
144	Don August	.06	.05	.02
145	Gary Gaetti	.10	.08	.04
146	Kirt Manwaring	.12	.09	.05
147	Jeff Reed	.04	.03	.02
148	Jose Alvarez(FC)	.04	.03	.02
149	Mike Schooler	.08	.06	.03
150	Mark Grace	.25	.20	.10
151	Geronimo Berroa	.08	.06	.03
152	Barry Jones	.04	.03	.02
153	Geno Petralli	.05	.04	.02
154	Jim Deshaies	.08	.06	.03
155	Barry Larkin	.15	.11	.06
156	Alfredo Griffin	.05	.04	.02
157	Tom Henke	.06	.05	.02
158	Mike Jeffcoat(FC)	.04	.03	.02
159	Bob Welch	.09	.07	.04
160	Julio Franco	.10	.08	.04
161	Henry Cotto	.04	.03	.02
162	Terry Steinbach	.10	.08	.04
163	Damon Berryhill	.08	.06	.03
164	Tim Crews	.04	.03	.02
165	Tom Browning	.09	.07	.04
166	Frd Manrique	.04	.03	.02
167	Harold Reynolds	.09	.07	.04
168	Ron Hassey	.05	.04	.02
169	Shawon Dunston	.08	.06	.03
170	Bobby Bonilla	.15	.11	.06
171	Tom Herr	.07	.05	.03
172	Mike Heath	.04	.03	.02
173	Rich Gedman	.05	.04	.02
174	Bill Ripken	.05	.04	.02
175	Pete O'Brien	.07	.05	.03
176a	Lloyd McClendon (uniform number 1 on back)	1.00	.70	.40
176b	Lloyd McClendon (uniform number 10 on back)	.20	.15	.08
177	Brian Holton	.05	.04	.02
178	Jeff Blauser	.05	.04	.02
179	Jim Eisenreich	.05	.04	.02
180	Bert Blyleven	.09	.07	.04
181	Rob Murphy	.05	.04	.02
182	Bill Doran	.07	.05	.03
183	Curt Ford	.04	.03	.02
184	Mike Henneman	.06	.05	.02
185	Eric Davis	.12	.09	.05
186	Lance McCullers	.06	.05	.02
187	*Steve Davis*	.08	.06	.03
188	Bill Wegman	.05	.04	.02
189	Brian Harper	.06	.05	.02
190	Mike Moore	.09	.07	.04
191	Dale Mohorcic	.04	.03	.02
192	Tim Wallach	.09	.07	.04
193	Keith Hernandez	.09	.07	.04
194	Dave Righetti	.07	.05	.03
195a	Bret Saberhagen ("joke" on card back)	.25	.20	.10
195b	Bret Saberhagen ("joker" on card back)	.30	.25	.12
196	Paul Kilgus	.04	.03	.02
197	Bud Black	.05	.04	.02
198	Juan Samuel	.09	.07	.04
199	Kevin Seitzer	.15	.11	.06

		MT	NR MT	EX
200	Darryl Strawberry	.12	.09	.05
201	Dave Steib	.09	.07	.04
202	Charlie Hough	.06	.05	.02
203	Jack Morris	.08	.06	.03
204	Rance Mulliniks	.04	.03	.02
205	Alvin Davis	.10	.08	.04
206	Jack Howell	.06	.05	.02
207	Ken Patterson(FC)	.06	.05	.02
208	Terry Pendleton	.15	.10	.05
209	Craig Lefferts	.06	.05	.02
210	Kevin Brown(FC)	.10	.08	.04
211	Dan Petry	.04	.03	.02
212	Dave Leiper	.06	.05	.02
213	Daryl Boston	.04	.03	.02
214	Kevin Hickey(FC)	.04	.03	.02
215	Mike Krukow	.06	.05	.02
216	Terry Francona	.04	.03	.02
217	Kirk McCaskill	.08	.06	.03
218	Scott Bailes	.05	.04	.02
219	Bob Forsch	.04	.03	.02
220	Mike Aldrete	.05	.04	.02
221	Steve Buechele	.06	.05	.02
222	Jesse Barfield	.09	.07	.05
223	Juan Berenguer	.06	.05	.02
224	Andy McGaffigan	.06	.05	.02
225	Pete Smith	.09	.07	.04
226	Mike Witt	.06	.05	.02
227	Jay Howell	.08	.06	.03
228	Scott Bradley	.05	.04	.02
229	*Jerome Walton*	.08	.06	.03
230	Greg Swindell	.15	.11	.06
231	Atlee Hammaker	.04	.03	.02
232	Mike Devereaux	.09	.07	.04
233	Ken Hill(FC)	.20	.15	.08
234	Craig Worthington	.15	.11	.06
235	Scott Terry	.08	.06	.03
236	Brett Butler	.09	.07	.04
237	Doyle Alexander	.07	.05	.03
238	Dave Anderson	.04	.03	.02
239	Bob Milacki	.10	.08	.04
240	Dwight Smith	.08	.06	.03
241	Otis Nixon	.04	.03	.02
242	Pat Tabler	.06	.05	.02
243	Derek Lilliquist	.12	.09	.05
244	Danny Tartabull	.15	.11	.06
245	Wade Boggs	.30	.25	.12
246	Scott Garrelts	.08	.06	.03
247	Spike Owen	.04	.03	.02
248	Norm Charlton	.12	.09	.05
249	Gerald Perry	.06	.05	.02
250	Nolan Ryan	.50	.40	.20
251	Kevin Gross	.07	.05	.03
252	Randy Milligan	.07	.05	.03
253	Mike LaCoss	.05	.04	.02
254	Dave Bergman	.04	.03	.02
255	Tony Gwynn	.35	.25	.12
256	Felix Fermin	.04	.03	.02
257	Greg Harris	.10	.08	.04
258	*Junior Felix*	.10	.08	.04
259	Mark Davis	.09	.07	.04
260	Vince Coleman	.15	.11	.06
261	Paul Gibson	.10	.08	.04
262	Mitch Williams	.10	.08	.04
263	Jeff Russell	.08	.06	.03
264	*Omar Vizquel*	.20	.15	.08
265	Andre Dawson	.12	.09	.05
266	Storm Davis	.08	.06	.03
267	Guillermo Hernandez	.04	.03	.02
268	Mike Felder	.05	.04	.02
269	Tom Candiotti	.05	.04	.02
270	Bruce Hurst	.09	.07	.04
271	Fred McGriff	.30	.25	.12
272	Glenn Davis	.15	.11	.60
273	John Franco	.09	.07	.04
274	Rich Yett	.04	.03	.02
275	Craig Biggio	.15	.11	.06
276	Gene Larkin	.05	.04	.02
277	Rob Dibble	.15	.11	.06
278	Randy Bush	.05	.04	.02
279	Kevin Bass	.08	.06	.03
280a	Bo Jackson ("Watham" on back)	.60	.45	.25
280b	Bo Jackson ("Wathan" on back)	1.00	.70	.40
281	Wally Backman	.06	.05	.02
282	Larry Andersen	.04	.03	.02
283	Chris Bosio	.09	.07	.04
284	Juan Agosto	.04	.03	.02
285	Ozzie Smith	.12	.09	.05
286	George Bell	.10	.08	.04
287	Rex Hudler	.05	.04	.02
288	Pat Borders	.10	.08	.04
289	Danny Jackson	.07	.05	.03

		MT	NR MT	EX
290	Carlton Fisk	.09	.07	.04
291	Tracy Jones	.05	.04	.02
292	Allan Anderson	.07	.05	.03
293	Johnny Ray	.07	.05	.03
294	Lee Guetterman	.04	.03	.02
295	Paul O'Neill	.09	.07	.05
296	Carney Lansford	.08	.06	.03
297	Tom Brookens	.04	.03	.02
298	Claudell Washington	.08	.06	.03
299	Hubie Brooks	.08	.06	.03
300	Will Clark	.60	.45	.25
301	*Kenny Rogers*	.20	.15	.08
302	Darrell Evans	.07	.05	.03
303	Greg Briley	.08	.06	.03
304	Donn Pall	.09	.07	.04
305	Teddy Higuera	.09	.07	.04
306	Dan Pasqua	.07	.05	.02
307	Dave Winfield	.15	.11	.06
308	Dennis Powell	.04	.03	.02
309	Jose DeLeon	.08	.06	.03
310	Roger Clemens	.25	.20	.10
311	Melido Perez	.09	.07	.04
312	Devon White	.09	.07	.04
313	Doc Gooden	.10	.08	.04
314	*Carlos Martinez*	.08	.06	.03
315	Dennis Eckersley	.10	.08	.04
316	Clay Parker	.12	.09	.05
317	Rick Honeycutt	.05	.04	.02
318	Tim Laudner	.05	.04	.02
319	Joe Carter	.15	.08	.04
320	Robin Yount	.20	.15	.08
321	Felix Jose	.30	.25	.15
322	Mickey Tettleton	.09	.07	.04
323	Mike Gallego	.04	.03	.02
324	Edgar Martinez	.09	.07	.04
325	Dave Henderson	.09	.07	.04
326	Chili Davis	.09	.07	.04
327	Steve Balboni	.05	.04	.02
328	Jody Davis	.04	.03	.02
329	Shawn Hillegas	.04	.03	.02
330	Jim Abbott	.35	.25	.12
331	John Dopson	.10	.08	.04
332	Mark Williamson	.04	.03	.02
333	Jeff Robinson	.08	.06	.03
334	John Smiley	.09	.07	.04
335	Bobby Thigpen	.07	.05	.03
336	Garry Templeton	.05	.04	.02
337	Marvell Wynne	.05	.04	.02
338a	Ken Griffey, Sr. (uniform number 25 on card back)	.25	.20	.10
338b	Ken Griffey, Sr. (uniform number 30 on card back)	3.00	2.25	1.25
339	*Steve Finley*	.25	.20	.10
340	Ellis Burks	.08	.06	.03
341	Frank Williams	.04	.03	.02
342	Mike Morgan	.05	.04	.02
343	Kevin Mitchell	.08	.06	.03
344	Joel Youngblood	.04	.03	.02
345	Mike Greenwell	.10	.08	.04
346	Glenn Wilson	.05	.04	.02
347	John Costello	.05	.04	.02
348	Wes Gardner	.04	.03	.02
349	Jeff Ballard	.09	.07	.04
350	Mark Thurmond	.04	.03	.02
351	Randy Myers	.07	.05	.03
352	Shawn Abner	.07	.05	.03
353	Jesse Orosco	.04	.03	.02
354	Greg Walker	.05	.04	.02
355	Pete Harnisch	.15	.11	.06
356	Steve Farr	.05	.04	.02
357	Dave LaPoint	.05	.04	.02
358	Willie Fraser	.05	.04	.02
359	Mickey Hatcher	.04	.03	.02
360	Rickey Henderson	.30	.25	.12
361	Mike Fitzgerald	.04	.03	.02
362	Bill Schroeder	.04	.03	.02
363	Mark Carreon	.10	.08	.04
364	Ron Jones	.10	.08	.04
365	Jeff Montgomery	.06	.05	.02
366	Bill Krueger(FC)	.04	.03	.02
367	John Cangelosi	.04	.03	.02
368	Jose Gonzalez	.10	.08	.04
369	*Greg Hibbard*(FC)	.15	.11	.06
370	John Smoltz	.15	.11	.06
371	*Jeff Brantley*	.08	.06	.03
372	Frank White	.08	.06	.03
373	Ed Whitson	.06	.05	.02
374	Willie McGee	.09	.07	.04
375	Jose Canseco	.25	.20	.10
376	Randy Ready	.04	.03	.02
377	Don Aase	.04	.03	.02

		MT	NR MT	EX
378	Tony Armas	.05	.04	.02
379	Steve Bedrosian	.07	.05	.03
380	Chuck Finley	.07	.05	.03
381	Kent Hrbek	.12	.09	.05
382	Jim Gantner	.06	.05	.02
383	Mel Hall	.06	.05	.02
384	Mike Marshall	.07	.05	.03
385	Mark McGwire	.20	.15	.08
386	Wayne Tolleson	.04	.03	.02
387	Brian Holton	.05	.04	.02
388	*John Wetteland*	.20	.15	.08
389	Darren Daulton	.04	.03	.02
390	Rob Deer	.07	.05	.03
391	John Moses	.04	.03	.02
392	Todd Worrell	.07	.05	.03
393	Chuck Cary(FC)	.10	.08	.04
394	Stan Javier	.05	.04	.02
395	Willie Randolph	.09	.07	.04
396	Bill Buckner	.06	.05	.02
397	Robby Thompson	.07	.05	.02
398	Mike Scioscia	.07	.05	.03
399	Lonnie Smith	.09	.07	.04
400	Kirby Puckett	.40	.30	.15
401	Mark Langston	.15	.11	.06
402	Danny Darwin	.04	.03	.02
403	Greg Maddux	.15	.11	.06
404	Lloyd Moseby	.07	.05	.02
405	Rafael Palmeiro	.15	.07	.04
406	Chad Kreuter	.10	.08	.04
407	Jimmy Key	.09	.07	.05
408	Tim Birtsas	.04	.03	.02
409	Tim Raines	.10	.08	.04
410	Dave Stewart	.09	.07	.04
411	*Eric Yelding*	.15	.11	.06
412	*Kent Anderson*(FC)	.06	.05	.02
413	Les Lancaster	.05	.04	.02
414	Rick Dempsey	.04	.03	.02
415	Randy Johnson	.12	.09	.05
416	Gary Carter	.07	.05	.03
417	Rolando Roomes	.15	.11	.06
418	Dan Schatzeder	.04	.03	.02
419	Bryn Smith	.07	.05	.03
420	Ruben Sierra	.20	.15	.08
421	Steve Jeltz	.04	.03	.02
422	Ken Oberkfell	.04	.03	.02
423	Sid Bream	.04	.03	.02
424	Jim Clancy	.04	.03	.02
425	Kelly Gruber	.09	.07	.04
426	Rick Leach	.04	.03	.02
427	Lenny Dykstra	.07	.05	.03
428	Jeff Pico	.06	.05	.02
429	John Cerutti	.06	.05	.02
430	David Cone	.15	.11	.06
431	Jeff Kunkel	.04	.03	.02
432	Luis Aquino	.05	.04	.02
433	Ernie Whitt	.05	.04	.02
434	Bo Diaz	.05	.04	.02
435	Steve Lake	.04	.03	.02
436	Pat Perry	.04	.03	.02
437	Mike Davis	.05	.04	.02
438	Cecilio Guante	.04	.03	.02
439	Duane Ward	.04	.03	.02
440	Andy Van Slyke	.10	.08	.04
441	Gene Nelson	.04	.03	.02
442	Luis Polonia	.06	.05	.02
443	Kevin Elster	.06	.05	.02
444	Keith Moreland	.06	.05	.02
445	Roger McDowell	.06	.05	.02
446	Ron Darling	.08	.06	.03
447	Ernest Riles	.04	.03	.02
448	Mookie Wilson	.08	.06	.03
449a	*Bill Spiers* (66 missing for year of birth)	1.25	.90	.50
449b	*Bill Spiers* (1966 for birth year)	.30	.25	.12
450	Rick Sutcliffe	.07	.05	.03
451	Nelson Santovenia	.10	.08	.04
452	Andy Allanson	.04	.03	.02
453	Bob Melvin	.04	.03	.02
454	Benny Santiago	.12	.09	.05
455	Jose Uribe	.05	.04	.02
456	Bill Landrum(FC)	.08	.06	.03
457	Bobby Witt	.07	.05	.03
458	Kevin Romine	.07	.05	.03
459	Lee Mazzilli	.04	.03	.02
460	Paul Molitor	.15	.08	.04
461	*Ramon Martinez*	.15	.10	.05
462	Frank DiPino	.04	.03	.02
463	Walt Terrell	.06	.05	.02
464	*Bob Geren*	.10	.08	.04
465	Rick Reuchel	.09	.07	.04
466	Mark Grant	.06	.05	.02

		MT	NR MT	EX
467	John Kruk	.07	.05	.03
468	Gregg Jefferies	.25	.20	.10
469	R.J. Reynolds	.04	.03	.02
470	Harold Baines	.09	.07	.04
471	Dennis Lamp	.04	.03	.02
472	Tom Gordon	.20	.15	.08
473	Terry Puhl	.04	.03	.02
474	Curtis Wilkerson	.04	.03	.02
475	Dan Quisenberry	.05	.04	.02
476	Oddibe McDowell	.07	.05	.03
477	Zane Smith	.04	.03	.02
478	Franklin Stubbs	.04	.03	.02
479	Wallace Johnson	.04	.03	.02
480	Jay Tibbs	.04	.03	.02
481	Tom Glavine	.15	.07	.03
482	Manny Lee	.05	.04	.02
483	Joe Hesketh	.04	.03	.02
484	Mike Bielecki	.07	.05	.03
485	Greg Brock	.06	.05	.02
486	Pascual Perez	.06	.05	.02
487	Kirk Gibson	.09	.07	.04
488	Scott Sanderson	.05	.04	.02
489	Domingo Ramos	.04	.03	.02
490	Kal Daniels	.10	.08	.04
491a	David Wells (reversed negative on back photo)	3.00	2.25	1.25
491b	David Wells (corrected)	.05	.04	.02
492	Jerry Reed	.04	.03	.02
493	Eric Show	.06	.05	.02
494	Mike Pagliarulo	.06	.05	.02
495	Ron Robinson	.05	.04	.02
496	Brad Komminsk	.04	.03	.02
497	*Greg Litton*	.08	.06	.03
498	Chris James	.07	.05	.02
499	Luis Quinones(FC)	.05	.04	.02
500	Frank Viola	.10	.08	.04
501	Tim Teufel	.05	.04	.02
502	Terry Leach	.04	.03	.02
503	Matt Williams	.15	.10	.05
504	Tim Leary	.06	.05	.02
505	Doug Drabek	.06	.05	.02
506	Mariano Duncan	.06	.05	.02
507	Charlie Hayes	.10	.08	.04
508	*Albert Belle*	1.00	.70	.40
509	Pat Sheridan	.05	.04	.02
510	Mackey Sasser	.05	.04	.02
511	Jose Rijo	.09	.07	.04
512	Mike Smithson	.04	.03	.02
513	Gary Ward	.04	.03	.02
514	Dion James	.06	.05	.02
515	Jim Gott	.06	.05	.02
516	Drew Hall(FC)	.04	.03	.02
517	Doug Bair	.04	.03	.02
518	*Scott Scudder*	.10	.08	.04
519	Rick Aguilera	.06	.05	.02
520	Rafael Belliard	.05	.04	.02
521	Jay Buhner	.10	.08	.04
522	Jeff Reardon	.06	.05	.02
523	Steve Rosenberg(FC)	.06	.05	.02
524	Randy Velarde(FC)	.09	.07	.04
525	Jeff Musselman	.06	.05	.02
526	Bill Long	.06	.05	.02
527	*Gary Wayne*	.06	.05	.02
528	*Dave Johnson*(FC)	.06	.05	.02
529	Ron Kittle	.08	.06	.03
530	Erik Hanson(FC)	.20	.15	.08
531	Steve Wilson(FC)	.20	.15	.08
532	Joey Meyer	.04	.03	.02
533	Curt Young	.04	.03	.02
534	Kelly Downs	.06	.05	.02
535	Joe Girardi	.20	.15	.08
536	Lance Blankenship	.09	.07	.04
537	Greg Mathews	.05	.04	.02
538	Donell Nixon	.04	.03	.02
539	Mark Knudson(FC)	.06	.05	.02
540	*Jeff Wetherby*(FC)	.10	.08	.04
541	Darrin Jackson	.04	.03	.02
542	Terry Mulholland	.09	.07	.03
543	Eric Hetzel(FC)	.08	.06	.03
544	*Rick Reed*(FC)	.08	.06	.03
545	Dennis Cook(FC)	.10	.08	.04
546	Mike Jackson	.05	.04	.02
547	Brian Fisher	.06	.05	.02
548	*Gene Harris*(FC)	.10	.08	.04
549	Jeff King(FC)	.20	.15	.08
550	Dave Dravecky (Salute)	.10	.08	.04
551	Randy Kutcher(FC)	.08	.06	.03
552	Mark Portugal	.06	.05	.02
553	*Jim Corsi*(FC)	.12	.09	.05
554	Todd Stottlemyre	.12	.09	.05
555	Scott Bankhead	.09	.07	.04

		MT	NR MT	EX
556	Ken Dayley	.05	.04	.02
557	*Rick Wrona*(FC)	.15	.11	.06
558	*Sammy Sosa*	.60	.45	.25
559	Keith Miller	.08	.06	.03
560	Ken Griffey, Jr.	1.50	1.00	.50
561a	Ryne Sandberg (HL, 3B on front)	10.00	7.50	4.00
561b	Ryne Sandberg (HL, no position)	.50	.40	.20
562	Billy Hatcher	.06	.05	.02
563	Jay Bell(FC)	.09	.07	.04
564	*Jack Daugherty*	.06	.05	.02
565	*Rich Monteleone*	.08	.06	.03
566	Bo Jackson (AS-MVP)	.30	.25	.12
567	*Tony Fossas*(FC)	.06	.05	.02
568	*Roy Smith*(FC)	.06	.05	.02
569	*Jaime Navarro*	.15	.10	.05
570	Lance Johnson	.15	.11	.06
571	*Mike Dyer*	.06	.05	.02
572	*Kevin Ritz*(FC)	.10	.08	.04
573	Dave West	.15	.11	.06
574	*Gary Mielke*	.08	.06	.03
575	Scott Lusader(FC)	.09	.07	.04
576	*Joe Oliver*	.10	.08	.04
577	Sandy Alomar, Jr.	.10	.08	.04
578	Andy Benes	.30	.25	.12
579	Tim Jones	.07	.05	.03
580	*Randy McCament*(FC)	.06	.05	.02
581	Curt Schilling(FC)	.15	.11	.06
582	*John Orton*	.08	.06	.03
583a	*Milt Cuyler* (998 games)	2.00	1.50	.80
583b	*Milt Cuyler* (98 games)	.40	.30	.15
584	*Eric Anthony*(FC)	.25	.20	.10
585	*Greg Vaughn*	.40	.30	.15
586	*Deion Sanders*	.50	.40	.20
587	Jose DeJesus(FC)	.06	.05	.02
588	*Chip Hale*(FC)	.15	.11	.06
589	*John Olerud*	1.50	1.25	.60
590	*Steve Olin*	.08	.06	.03
591	*Marquis Grissom*	.60	.45	.25
592	*Moises Alou*	.60	.45	.25
593	Mark Lemke(FC)	.06	.05	.02
594	*Dean Palmer*	.60	.45	.25
595	*Robin Ventura*	.75	.50	.25
596	*Tino Martinez*	.15	.10	.05
597	*Mike Huff*	.08	.06	.03
598	*Scott Hemond*	.08	.06	.03
599	*Wally Whitehurst*(FC)	.20	.15	.08
600	*Todd Zeile*(FC)	.20	.15	.08
601	*Glenallen Hill*	.10	.08	.04
602	Hal Morris(FC)	.15	.11	.06
603	Juan Bell(FC)	.15	.11	.06
604	*Bobby Rose*	.08	.06	.03
605	*Matt Merullo*(FC)	.20	.15	.08
606	*Kevin Maas*	.12	.09	.05
607	*Randy Nosek*(FC)	.15	.11	.06
608	*Billy Bates*(FC)	.06	.05	.02
609	*Mike Stanton*	.30	.25	.12
610	*Goose Gozzo*(FC)	.10	.08	.04
611	*Charles Nagy*(FC)	.20	.15	.08
612	*Scott Coolbaugh*(FC)	.08	.06	.03
613	*Jose Vizcaino*(FC)	.25	.20	.10
614	*Greg Smith*(FC)	.08	.06	.03
615	*Jeff Huson*	.10	.08	.04
616	*Mickey Weston*(FC)	.08	.06	.03
617	*John Pawlowski*(FC)	.08	.06	.03
618a	*Joe Skalski* (uniform #27)(FC)	.15	.11	.06
618b	*Joe Skalski* (uniform #67)(FC)	2.00	1.50	.80
619	*Bernie Williams*	.25	.20	.10
620	*Shawn Holman*	.06	.05	.02
621	*Gary Eave*	.06	.05	.02
622	*Darrin Fletcher*	.25	.20	.10
623	*Pat Combs*	.10	.08	.04
624	*Mike Blowers*	.25	.20	.10
625	*Kevin Appier*	.30	.25	.12
626	*Pat Austin*	.08	.06	.03
627	*Kelly Mann*	.06	.05	.02
628	*Matt Kinzer*	.08	.06	.03
629	*Chris Hammond*	.25	.20	.10
630	*Dean Wilkins*(FC)	.08	.06	.03
631	*Larry Walker*	1.00	.45	.25
632	*Blaine Beatty*	.20	.15	.08
633a	Tom Barrett (uniform #29)(FC)	.15	.11	.06
633b	Tom Barrett (uniform #14)(FC)	4.00	3.00	1.50
634	*Stan Belinda*(FC)	.10	.08	.04
635	*Tex Smith*(FC)	.06	.05	.02
636	*Hensley Meulens*	.08	.06	.03
637	*Juan Gonzalez*	3.00	2.25	1.25
638	*Lenny Webster*	.10	.08	.04
639	*Mark Gardner*	.10	.08	.04
640	*Tommy Greene*(FC)	.35	.25	.14
641	*Mike Hartley*(FC)	.08	.06	.03

		MT	NR MT	EX
642	*Phil Stephenson*(FC)	.06	.05	.02
643	*Kevin Mmahat*(FC)	.15	.11	.06
644	*Ed Whited*(FC)	.08	.06	.03
645	*Delino DeShields*(FC)	.40	.30	.15
646	Kevin Blankenship(FC)	.15	.11	.06
647	*Paul Sorrento*	.20	.15	.08
648	*Mike Roesler*(FC)	.15	.11	.06
649	*Jason Grimsley*	.10	.08	.04
650	*Dave Justice*	2.00	1.50	.80
651	*Scott Cooper*	.40	.30	.15
652	Dave Eiland(FC)	.08	.06	.03
653	*Mike Munoz*(FC)	.08	.06	.03
654	*Jeff Fischer*(FC)	.08	.06	.03
655	*Terry Jorgenson*(FC)	.06	.05	.02
656	*George Canale*(FC)	.06	.05	.02
657	*Brian DuBois*	.08	.06	.03
658	Carlos Quintana	.10	.08	.04
659	Luis de los Santos	.06	.05	.02
660	Jerald Clark	.10	.08	.04
661	*Donald Harris* (1st Round Pick)	.20	.15	.08
662	*Paul Coleman* (1st Round Pick)	.20	.15	.08
663	*Frank Thomas* (1st Round Pick)	7.00	5.25	2.75
664	*Brent Mayne* (1st Round Pick)	.30	.25	.12
665	*Eddie Zosky* (1st Round Pick)	.25	.20	.10
666	*Steve Hosey* (1st Round Pick)	.20	.15	.08
667	*Scott Bryant* (1st Round Pick)	.20	.15	.08
668	*Tom Goodwin* (1st Round Pick)	.15	.10	.05
669	*Cal Eldred* (1st Round Pick)	.40	.30	.15
670	*Earl Cunningham* (1st Round Pick)	.15	.10	.05
671	*Alan Zinter* (1st Round Pick)	.25	.20	.10
672	*Chuck Knoblauch* (1st Round Pick)	.50	.30	.15
673	*Kyle Abbott* (1st Round Pick)	.25	.20	.10
674	*Roger Salkeld* (1st Round Pick)	.25	.20	.10
675	*Mo Vaughn* (1st Round Pick)	1.00	.70	.40
676	*Kiki Jones* (1st Round Pick)	.12	.09	.05
677	*Tyler Houston* (1st Round Pick)	.25	.20	.10
678	*Jeff Jackson* (1st Round Pick)	.15	.11	.06
679	*Greg Gohr* (1st Round Pick)	.25	.20	.10
680	*Ben McDonald* (1st Round Pick)	.60	.45	.25
681	*Greg Blosser* (1st Round Pick)	.25	.20	.10
682	*Willie Green* ((Greene) 1st Round Pick)	.15	.10	.05
683	Wade Boggs (Dream Team)	.20	.15	.08
684	Will Clark (Dream Team)	.20	.15	.08
685	Tony Gwynn (Dream Team)	.20	.15	.08
686	Rickey Henderson (Dream Team)	.20	.15	.08
687	Bo Jackson (Dream Team)	.30	.25	.12
688	Mark Langston (Dream Team)	.20	.15	.08
689	Barry Larkin (Dream Team)	.20	.15	.08
690	Kirby Puckett (Dream Team)	.20	.15	.08
691	Ryne Sandberg (Dream Team)	.30	.25	.12
692	Mike Scott (Dream Team)	.20	.15	.08
693	Terry Steinbach (Dream Team)	.20	.15	.08
694	Bobby Thigpen (Dream Team)	.20	.15	.08
695	Mitch Williams (Dream Team)	.20	.15	.08
696	Nolan Ryan (HL)	.50	.40	.20
697	Bo Jackson (FB/BB)	1.50	1.25	.60
698	Rickey Henderson (ALCS MVP)	.25	.20	.10
699	Will Clark (NLCS MVP)	.25	.20	.10
700	World Series Games 1-2 (Dave Stewart/ Mike Moore)	.30	.25	.12
701	Lights Out: Candlestick	.30	.25	.12
702	World Series Game 3	.30	.25	.12
703	World Series Wrap-up	.30	.25	.12
704	Wade Boggs (HL)	.25	.20	.10

1990 Score Dream Team

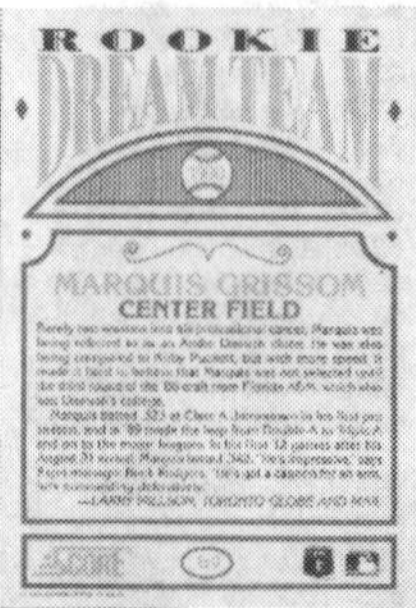

This 10 card "Dream Team" set, in the same format as those found in the regular issue 1990 Score, were available only in factory sets for the hobby trade. Factory sets for general retail outlets did not include these cards, nor were they available in Score packs. Cards carry a "B" prefix to their numbers.

		MT	NR MT	EX
Complete Set (10):		8.00	6.00	3.25
Common Player:		.25	.15	.10
1	A. Bartlett Giamatti	1.00	.75	.40
2	Pat Combs	.25	.15	.10
3	Todd Zeile	1.50	1.00	.60
4	Luis de los Santos	.25	.15	.10
5	Mark Lemke	.25	.20	.10
6	Robin Ventura	5.00	3.75	2.00
7	Jeff Huson	.25	.15	.10
8	Greg Vaughn	1.50	1.00	.60
9	Marquis Grissom	1.50	1.00	.60
10	Eric Anthony	.60	.45	.25

1990 Score Traded

This 110-card set features players with new teams as well as 1990 Major League rookies. The cards feature full-color action photos framed in yellow with an orange border. The player's name and position appear in green print below the photo. The team logo is displayed next to the player's name. The card backs feature posed player photos and follow the style of the regular 1990 Score issue. The cards are numbered 1T-110T. Young hockey phenom Eric Lindros is featured trying out for the Toronto Blue Jays.

		MT	NR MT	EX
Complete Set (110):		12.00	9.00	4.75
Common Player:		.06	.05	.02
1T	Dave Winfield	.15	.11	.06
2T	Kevin Bass	.06	.05	.02
3T	Nick Esasky	.06	.05	.02
4T	Mitch Webster	.06	.05	.02
5T	Pascual Perez	.06	.05	.02
6T	Gary Pettis	.06	.05	.02
7T	Tony Pena	.08	.06	.03
8T	Candy Maldonado	.08	.06	.03
9T	Cecil Fielder	.30	.25	.12
10T	Carmelo Martinez	.06	.05	.02
11T	Mark Langston	.08	.06	.03
12T	Dave Parker	.15	.11	.06
13T	Don Slaught	.06	.05	.02
14T	Tony Phillips	.06	.05	.02
15T	John Franco	.08	.06	.03
16T	Randy Myers	.08	.06	.03
17T	Jeff Reardon	.08	.06	.03
18T	Sandy Alomar, Jr.	.20	.15	.08
19T	Joe Carter	.10	.08	.04
20T	Fred Lynn	.06	.05	.02
21T	Storm Davis	.06	.05	.02
22T	Craig Lefferts	.06	.05	.02
23T	Pete O'Brien	.06	.05	.02
24T	Dennis Boyd	.06	.05	.02
25T	Lloyd Moseby	.06	.05	.02
26T	Mark Davis	.06	.05	.02
27T	Tim Leary	.06	.05	.02
28T	Gerald Perry	.06	.05	.02
29T	Don Aase	.06	.05	.02
30T	Ernie Whitt	.06	.05	.02

		MT	NR MT	EX
31T	Dale Murphy	.10	.08	.04
32T	Alejandro Pena	.06	.05	.02
33T	Juan Samuel	.08	.06	.03
34T	Hubie Brooks	.08	.06	.03
35T	Gary Carter	.10	.08	.04
36T	Jim Presley	.06	.05	.02
37T	Wally Backman	.06	.05	.02
38T	Matt Nokes	.06	.05	.02
39T	Dan Petry	.06	.05	.02
40T	Franklin Stubbs	.06	.05	.02
41T	Jeff Huson	.15	.11	.06
42T	Billy Hatcher	.06	.05	.02
43T	Terry Leach	.06	.05	.02
44T	Phil Bradley	.06	.05	.02
45T	Claudell Washington	.06	.05	.02
46T	Luis Polonia	.06	.05	.02
47T	Daryl Boston	.06	.05	.02
48T	Lee Smith	.08	.06	.03
49T	Tom Brunansky	.08	.06	.03
50T	Mike Witt	.06	.05	.02
51T	Willie Randolph	.08	.06	.03
52T	Stan Javier	.06	.05	.02
53T	Brad Komminsk	.06	.05	.02
54T	John Candelaria	.06	.05	.02
55T	Bryn Smith	.06	.05	.02
56T	Glenn Braggs	.06	.05	.02
57T	Keith Hernandez	.08	.06	.03
58T	Ken Oberkfell	.06	.05	.02
59T	Steve Jeltz	.06	.05	.02
60T	Chris James	.06	.05	.02
61T	Scott Sanderson	.06	.05	.02
62T	Bill Long	.06	.05	.02
63T	Rick Cerone	.06	.05	.02
64T	Scott Bailes	.06	.05	.02
65T	Larry Sheets	.06	.05	.02
66T	Junior Ortiz	.06	.05	.02
67T	Francisco Cabrera(FC)	.06	.05	.02
68T	Gary DiSarcina(FC)	.15	.11	.06
69T	Greg Olson(FC)	.08	.06	.03
70T	Beau Allred(FC)	.06	.05	.02
71T	Oscar Azocar(FC)	.15	.11	.06
72T	Kent Mercker(FC)	.25	.20	.10
73T	John Burkett(FC)	.40	.30	.15
74T	Carlos Baerga(FC)	2.00	1.50	.80
75T	Dave Hollins(FC)	1.00	.70	.40
76T	Todd Hundley(FC)	.20	.15	.08
77T	Rick Parker(FC)	.08	.06	.03
78T	Steve Cummings(FC)	.08	.06	.03
79T	Bill Sampen(FC)	.08	.06	.03
80T	Jerry Kutzler(FC)	.08	.06	.03
81T	Derek Bell(FC)	.15	.11	.06
82T	Kevin Tapani(FC)	.35	.25	.14
83T	Jim Leyritz(FC)	.25	.20	.10
84T	Ray Lankford(FC)	1.25	.90	.50
85T	Wayne Edwards(FC)	.15	.11	.06
86T	Frank Thomas	7.00	5.25	2.75
87T	Tim Naehring(FC)	.20	.15	.08
88T	Willie Blair(FC)	.15	.11	.06
89T	Alan Mills(FC)	.25	.20	.10
90T	Scott Radinsky(FC)	.25	.20	.10
91T	Howard Farmer(FC)	.10	.08	.04
92T	Julio Machado(FC)	.06	.05	.02
93T	Rafael Valdez(FC)	.06	.05	.02
94T	Shawn Boskie(FC)	.25	.20	.10
95T	David Segui(FC)	.20	.15	.08
96T	Chris Hoiles(FC)	.30	.25	.12
97T	D.J. Dozier(FC)	.20	.15	.08
98T	Hector Villanueva(FC)	.25	.20	.10
99T	Eric Gunderson(FC)	.10	.08	.04
100T	Eric Lindros(FC)	6.00	4.50	2.50
101T	Dave Otto(FC)	.12	.09	.05
102T	Dana Kiecker(FC)	.10	.08	.04
103T	Tim Drummond(FC)	.08	.06	.03
104T	Mickey Pina(FC)	.06	.05	.02
105T	Craig Grebeck(FC)	.10	.08	.04
106T	Bernard Gilkey(FC)	.50	.40	.20
107T	Tim Layana(FC)	.25	.20	.10
108T	Scott Chiamparino(FC)	.10	.08	.04
109T	Steve Avery(FC)	1.00	.70	.40
110T	Terry Shumpert(FC)	.10	.08	.04

1991 Score

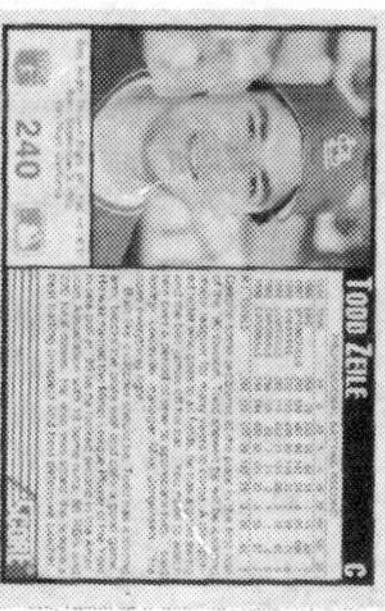

Score introduced a two series format in 1991. The first series includes cards 1-441. Score cards once again feature multiple border colors within the set, several subsets (Master Blaster, K-Man, Highlights and Rifleman), full-color action photos on the front, posed photos on the flip side. Score eliminated providing the player's uniform number on the 1991 cards. Card number 441 of Series I features a Jose Canseco Vanity Fair photo. All of the 1991 Dream Team cards feature this style. Prospects and #1 Draft Picks highlight the 1991 set. The second series was released in February of 1991.

		MT	NR MT	EX
Complete Set (893):		20.00	15.00	8.00
Common Player:		.04	.03	.02
1	Jose Canseco	.15	.10	.05
2	Ken Griffey, Jr.	.80	.60	.30
3	Ryne Sandberg	.20	.15	.08
4	Nolan Ryan	.30	.25	.12
5	Bo Jackson	.30	.25	.12
6	Bret Saberhagen	.12	.09	.05
7	Will Clark	.20	.15	.08
8	Ellis Burks	.15	.11	.06
9	Joe Carter	.15	.11	.06
10	Rickey Henderson	.25	.20	.10
11	Ozzie Guillen	.10	.08	.04
12	Wade Boggs	.20	.15	.08
13	Jerome Walton	.15	.11	.06
14	John Franco	.10	.08	.04
15	Ricky Jordan	.08	.06	.03
16	Wally Backman	.04	.03	.02
17	Rob Dibble	.10	.08	.04
18	Glenn Braggs	.05	.04	.02
19	Cory Snyder	.10	.08	.04
20	Kal Daniels	.10	.08	.04
21	Mark Langston	.10	.08	.04
22	Kevin Gross	.06	.05	.02
23	Don Mattingly	.25	.20	.10
24	Dave Righetti	.08	.06	.03
25	Roberto Alomar	.25	.20	.10
26	Robby Thompson	.06	.05	.02
27	Jack McDowell	.08	.06	.03
28	Bip Roberts	.08	.06	.03
29	Jay Howell	.05	.04	.02
30	Dave Steib	.08	.06	.03
31	Johnny Ray	.04	.03	.02
32	Steve Sax	.10	.08	.04
33	Terry Mulholland	.08	.06	.03
34	Lee Guetterman	.04	.03	.02
35	Tim Raines	.12	.09	.05
36	Scott Fletcher	.04	.03	.02
37	Lance Parrish	.08	.06	.03
38	Tony Phillips	.05	.04	.02
39	Todd Stottlemyre	.06	.05	.02
40	Alan Trammell	.12	.09	.05
41	Todd Burns	.04	.03	.02
42	Mookie Wilson	.06	.05	.02
43	Chris Bosio	.05	.04	.02
44	Jeffrey Leonard	.06	.05	.02
45	Doug Jones	.08	.06	.03
46	Mike Scott	.08	.06	.03
47	Andy Hawkins	.05	.04	.02
48	Harold Reynolds	.08	.06	.03
49	Paul Molitor	.12	.09	.05
50	John Farrell	.05	.04	.02
51	Danny Darwin	.06	.05	.02
52	Jeff Blauser	.04	.03	.02
53	John Tudor	.05	.04	.02
54	Milt Thompson	.04	.03	.02
55	Dave Justice	.30	.25	.12
56	*Greg Olson*	.12	.09	.05
57	*Willie Blair*	.12	.09	.05
58	*Rick Parker*	.10	.08	.04

		MT	NR MT	EX
59	*Shawn Boskie*	.15	.11	.06
60	Kevin Tapani	.10	.08	.04
61	*Dave Hollins*	.20	.15	.08
62	*Scott Radinsky*	.12	.09	.05
63	Francisco Cabrera	.10	.08	.04
64	*Tim Layana*	.12	.09	.05
65	*Jim Leyritz*	.12	.09	.05
66	Wayne Edwards	.08	.06	.03
67	Lee Stevens(FC)	.15	.11	.06
68	*Bill Sampen*	.15	.11	.06
69	*Craig Grebeck*	.10	.08	.04
70	John Burkett	.15	.11	.06
71	*Hector Villanueva*	.15	.11	.06
72	*Oscar Azocar*	.15	.11	.06
73	*Alan Mills*	.15	.11	.06
74	*Carlos Baerga*	.25	.20	.10
75	Charles Nagy	.08	.06	.03
76	Tim Drummond	.08	.06	.03
77	*Dana Kiecker*	.15	.11	.06
78	*Tom Edens*(FC)	.10	.08	.04
79	Kent Mercker	.10	.08	.04
80	Steve Avery	.20	.15	.08
81	Lee Smith	.08	.06	.03
82	Dave Martinez	.05	.04	.02
83	Dave Winfield	.12	.09	.05
84	Bill Spiers	.06	.05	.02
85	Dan Pasqua	.05	.04	.02
86	Randy Milligan	.06	.05	.02
87	Tracy Jones	.04	.03	.02
88	Greg Myers(FC)	.06	.05	.02
89	Keith Hernandez	.06	.05	.02
90	Todd Benzinger	.06	.05	.02
91	Mike Jackson	.05	.04	.02
92	Mike Stanley	.04	.03	.02
93	Candy Maldonado	.06	.05	.02
94	John Kruk	.05	.04	.02
95	Cal Ripken, Jr.	.30	.25	.12
96	Willie Fraser	.04	.03	.02
97	Mike Felder	.04	.03	.02
98	Bill Landrum	.05	.04	.02
99	Chuck Crim	.04	.03	.02
100	Chuck Finley	.08	.06	.03
101	Kirt Manwaring	.06	.05	.02
102	Jaime Navarro	.08	.06	.03
103	Dickie Thon	.04	.03	.02
104	Brian Downing	.05	.04	.02
105	Jim Abbott	.12	.09	.05
106	Tom Brookens	.04	.03	.02
107	Darryl Hamilton	.06	.05	.02
108	Bryan Harvey	.06	.05	.02
109	Greg Harris	.04	.03	.02
110	Greg Swindell	.08	.06	.03
111	Juan Berenguer	.04	.03	.02
112	Mike Heath	.04	.03	.02
113	Scott Bradley	.04	.03	.02
114	Jack Morris	.08	.06	.03
115	Barry Jones	.05	.04	.02
116	Kevin Romine	.04	.03	.02
117	Garry Templeton	.05	.04	.02
118	Scott Sanderson	.05	.04	.02
119	Roberto Kelly	.08	.06	.03
120	George Brett	.15	.11	.06
121	Oddibe McDowell	.05	.04	.02
122	Jim Acker	.04	.03	.02
123	Bill Swift	.05	.04	.02
124	Eric King	.05	.04	.02
125	Jay Buhner	.06	.05	.02
126	Matt Young	.04	.03	.02
127	Alvaro Espinoza	.05	.04	.02
128	Greg Hibbard	.08	.06	.03
129	Jeff Robinson	.05	.04	.02
130	Mike Greenwell	.15	.11	.06
131	Dion James	.04	.03	.02
132	Donn Pall	.04	.03	.02
133	Lloyd Moseby	.06	.05	.02
134	Randy Velarde	.04	.03	.02
135	Allan Anderson	.05	.04	.02
136	Mark Davis	.06	.05	.02
137	Eric Davis	.10	.08	.06
138	Phil Stephenson	.04	.03	.02
139	Felix Fermin	.04	.03	.02
140	Pedro Guerrero	.08	.06	.03
141	Charlie Hough	.05	.04	.02
142	Mike Henneman	.06	.05	.02
143	Jeff Montgomery	.06	.05	.02
144	Lenny Harris	.06	.05	.02
145	Bruce Hurst	.06	.05	.02
146	Eric Anthony	.15	.11	.06
147	Paul Assenmacher	.04	.03	.02
148	Jesse Barfield	.06	.05	.02
149	Carlos Quintana	.08	.06	.03

		MT	NR MT	EX
150	Dave Stewart	.12	.09	.05
151	Roy Smith	.04	.03	.02
152	Paul Gibson	.04	.03	.02
153	Mickey Hatcher	.04	.03	.02
154	Jim Eisenreich	.04	.03	.02
155	Kenny Rogers	.06	.05	.02
156	Dave Schmidt	.04	.03	.02
157	Lance Johnson	.06	.05	.02
158	Dave West	.05	.04	.02
159	Steve Balboni	.04	.03	.02
160	Jeff Brantley	.08	.06	.03
161	Craig Biggio	.06	.05	.02
162	Brook Jacoby	.06	.05	.02
163	Dan Gladden	.05	.04	.02
164	Jeff Reardon	.08	.06	.03
165	Mark Carreon	.05	.04	.02
166	Mel Hall	.05	.04	.02
167	Gary Mielke	.06	.05	.02
168	Cecil Fielder	.25	.20	.10
169	Darrin Jackson	.04	.03	.02
170	Rick Aguilera	.06	.05	.02
171	Walt Weiss	.06	.05	.02
172	Steve Farr	.05	.04	.02
173	Jody Reed	.06	.05	.02
174	Mike Jeffcoat	.04	.03	.02
175	Mark Grace	.15	.11	.06
176	Larry Sheets	.04	.03	.02
177	Bill Gullickson	.05	.04	.02
178	Chris Gwynn	.06	.05	.02
179	Melido Perez	.06	.05	.02
180	Sid Fernandez	.08	.06	.03
181	Tim Burke	.06	.05	.02
182	Gary Pettis	.05	.04	.02
183	Rob Murphy	.04	.03	.02
184	Craig Lefferts	.06	.05	.02
185	Howard Johnson	.10	.08	.04
186	Ken Caminiti	.05	.04	.02
187	Tim Belcher	.06	.05	.02
188	Greg Cadaret	.04	.03	.02
189	Matt Williams	.15	.11	.06
190	Dave Magadan	.08	.06	.03
191	Geno Petralli	.04	.03	.02
192	Jeff Robinson	.05	.04	.02
193	Jim Deshaies	.05	.04	.02
194	Willie Randolph	.06	.05	.02
195	George Bell	.10	.08	.04
196	Hubie Brooks	.10	.08	.04
197	Tom Gordon	.10	.08	.04
198	Mike Fitzgerald	.04	.03	.02
199	Mike Pagliarulo	.05	.04	.02
200	Kirby Puckett	.15	.11	.06
201	Shawon Dunston	.08	.06	.03
202	Dennis Boyd	.05	.04	.02
203	Junior Felix	.08	.06	.03
204	Alejandro Pena	.04	.03	.02
205	Pete Smith	.05	.04	.02
206	Tom Glavine	.06	.05	.02
207	Luis Salazar	.04	.03	.02
208	John Smoltz	.08	.06	.03
209	Doug Dascenzo	.05	.04	.02
210	Tim Wallach	.08	.06	.03
211	Greg Gagne	.05	.04	.02
212	Mark Gubicza	.08	.06	.03
213	Mark Parent	.04	.03	.02
214	Ken Oberkfell	.04	.03	.02
215	Gary Carter	.08	.06	.03
216	Rafael Palmeiro	.10	.08	.04
217	Tom Niedenfuer	.04	.03	.02
218	Dave LaPoint	.05	.04	.02
219	Jeff Treadway	.05	.04	.02
220	Mitch Williams	.06	.05	.02
221	Jose DeLeon	.05	.04	.02
222	Mike LaValliere	.05	.04	.02
223	Darrel Akerfelds	.04	.03	.02
224	Kent Anderson	.05	.04	.02
225	Dwight Evans	.08	.06	.03
226	Gary Redus	.04	.03	.02
227	Paul O'Neill	.06	.05	.02
228	Marty Barrett	.05	.04	.02
229	Tom Browning	.06	.05	.02
230	Terry Pendleton	.06	.05	.02
231	Jack Armstrong	.08	.06	.03
232	Mike Boddicker	.06	.05	.02
233	Neal Heaton	.05	.04	.02
234	Marquis Grissom	.10	.08	.04
235	Bert Blyleven	.08	.06	.03
236	Curt Young	.05	.04	.02
237	Don Carman	.05	.04	.02
238	Charlie Hayes	.06	.05	.02
239	Mark Knudson	.04	.03	.02
240	Todd Zeile	.10	.08	.04

		MT	NR MT	EX
241	Larry Walker	.10	.08	.04
242	Jerald Clark	.06	.05	.02
243	Jeff Ballard	.05	.04	.02
244	Jeff King	.06	.05	.02
245	Tom Brunansky	.08	.06	.03
246	Darren Daulton	.06	.05	.02
247	Scott Terry	.04	.03	.02
248	Rob Deer	.06	.05	.02
249	Brady Anderson	.04	.03	.02
250	Lenny Dykstra	.08	.06	.03
251	Greg Harris	.06	.05	.02
252	Mike Hartley	.08	.06	.03
253	Joey Cora	.04	.03	.02
254	Ivan Calderon	.08	.06	.03
255	Ted Power	.04	.03	.02
256	Sammy Sosa	.15	.11	.06
257	Steve Buechele	.05	.04	.02
258	Mike Devereaux	.05	.04	.02
259	Brad Komminsk	.04	.03	.02
260	Teddy Higuera	.08	.06	.03
261	Shawn Abner	.05	.04	.02
262	Dave Valle	.05	.04	.02
263	Jeff Huson	.06	.05	.02
264	Edgar Martinez	.06	.05	.02
265	Carlton Fisk	.10	.08	.04
266	Steve Finley	.06	.05	.02
267	John Wetteland	.06	.05	.02
268	Kevin Appier	.08	.06	.03
269	Steve Lyons	.04	.03	.02
270	Mickey Tettleton	.05	.04	.02
271	Luis Rivera	.04	.03	.02
272	Steve Jeltz	.04	.03	.02
273	R.J. Reynolds	.04	.03	.02
274	Carlos Martinez	.05	.04	.02
275	Dan Plesac	.06	.05	.02
276	Mike Morgan	.04	.03	.02
277	Jeff Russell	.06	.05	.02
278	Pete Incaviglia	.06	.05	.02
279	Kevin Seitzer	.08	.06	.03
280	Bobby Thigpen	.08	.06	.03
281	Stan Javier	.04	.03	.02
282	Henry Cotto	.04	.03	.02
283	Gary Wayne	.05	.04	.02
284	Shane Mack	.05	.04	.02
285	Brian Holman	.06	.05	.02
286	Gerald Perry	.05	.04	.02
287	Steve Crawford	.04	.03	.02
288	Nelson Liriano	.04	.03	.02
289	Don Aase	.04	.03	.02
290	Randy Johnson	.06	.05	.02
291	Harold Baines	.08	.06	.03
292	Kent Hrbek	.08	.06	.03
293	Les Lancaster	.04	.03	.02
294	Jeff Musselman	.04	.03	.02
295	Kurt Stillwell	.06	.05	.02
296	Stan Belinda	.06	.05	.02
297	Lou Whitaker	.08	.06	.03
298	Glenn Wilson	.05	.04	.02
299	Omar Vizquel	.04	.03	.02
300	Ramon Martinez	.20	.15	.08
301	Dwight Smith	.06	.05	.02
302	Tim Crews	.04	.03	.02
303	Lance Blankenship	.05	.04	.02
304	Sid Bream	.06	.05	.02
305	Rafael Ramirez	.04	.03	.02
306	Steve Wilson	.06	.05	.02
307	Mackey Sasser	.06	.05	.02
308	Franklin Stubbs	.06	.05	.02
309	Jack Daugherty	.06	.05	.02
310	Eddie Murray	.10	.08	.04
311	Bob Welch	.08	.06	.03
312	Brian Harper	.06	.05	.02
313	Lance McCullers	.04	.03	.02
314	Dave Smith	.06	.05	.02
315	Bobby Bonilla	.10	.08	.04
316	Jerry Don Gleaton	.04	.03	.02
317	Greg Maddux	.08	.06	.03
318	Keith Miller	.05	.04	.03
319	Mark Portugal	.04	.03	.02
320	Robin Ventura	.20	.15	.10
321	Bob Ojeda	.04	.03	.02
322	Mike Harkey	.08	.06	.03
323	Jay Bell	.06	.05	.02
324	Mark McGwire	.10	.08	.04
325	Gary Gaetti	.10	.08	.04
326	Jeff Pico	.04	.03	.02
327	Kevin McReynolds	.08	.06	.03
328	Frank Tanana	.05	.04	.02
329	Eric Yelding	.06	.05	.02
330	Barry Bonds	.20	.15	.08
331	*Brian McRae*(FC)	.10	.08	.04
332	*Pedro Munoz*(FC)	.08	.06	.03
333	*Daryl Irvine*(FC)	.08	.06	.03
334	*Chris Hoiles*	.20	.15	.10
335	*Thomas Howard*(FC)	.08	.06	.03
336	*Jeff Schulz*(FC)	.08	.06	.03
337	Jeff Manto(FC)	.08	.06	.03
338	Beau Allred	.10	.08	.04
339	*Mike Bordick*(FC)	.08	.06	.03
340	*Todd Hundley*	.06	.04	.02
341	*Jim Vatcher*(FC)	.06	.04	.02
342	Luis Sojo(FC)	.10	.08	.04
343	*Jose Offerman*	.30	.25	.12
344	*Pete Coachman*(FC)	.15	.11	.06
345	Mike Benjamin(FC)	.10	.08	.04
346	*Ozzie Canseco*(FC)	.08	.06	.03
347	Tim McIntosh(FC)	.08	.06	.03
348	*Phil Plantier*	.40	.30	.15
349	*Terry Shumpert*	.10	.08	.06
350	*Darren Lewis*	.30	.25	.12
351	*David Walsh*(FC)	.10	.08	.04
352	*Scott Chiamparino*	.15	.11	.06
353	*Julio Valera*(FC)	.08	.06	.03
354	*Anthony Telford*(FC)	.08	.06	.03
355	Kevin Wickander(FC)	.10	.08	.04
356	*Tim Naehring*	.08	.06	.03
357	*Jim Poole*(FC)	.08	.06	.03
358	*Mark Whiten*	.40	.30	.15
359	*Terry Wells*	.10	.08	.04
360	*Rafael Valdez*	.10	.08	.04
361	*Mel Stottlemyre*(FC)	.15	.11	.06
362	*David Segui*	.20	.15	.08
363	Paul Abbott	.15	.11	.06
364	*Steve Howard*(FC)	.15	.11	.06
365	*Karl Rhodes*(FC)	.10	.08	.04
366	*Rafael Novoa*	.10	.06	.03
367	*Joe Grahe*	.15	.11	.06
368	*Darren Reed*(FC)	.15	.11	.06
369	Jeff McKnight(FC)	.10	.08	.04
370	Scott Leius(FC)	.10	.08	.04
371	*Mark Dewey*	.10	.06	.03
372	*Mark Lee*	.10	.06	.03
373	*Rosario Rodriguez*	.15	.11	.06
374	Chuck McElroy(FC)	.10	.08	.04
375	*Mike Bell*	.10	.06	.03
376	Mickey Morandini(FC)	.10	.08	.04
377	*Bill Haselman*	.12	.10	.06
378	*Dave Pavlas*	.10	.06	.03
379	*Derrick May*	.25	.20	.10
380	*Jeromy Burnitz* (1st Draft Pick)	.60	.40	.30
381	*Donald Peters* (1st Draft Pick)	.10	.08	.04
382	*Alex Fernandez* (1st Draft Pick)	.40	.25	.12
383	*Michael Mussina* (1st Draft Pick)	1.50	1.25	.60
384	*Daniel Smith* (1st Draft Pick)	.12	.09	.05
385	*Lance Dickson* (1st Draft Pick)	.10	.08	.04
386	*Carl Everett* (1st Draft Pick)	.40	.30	.15
387	*Thomas Nevers* (1st Draft Pick)	.15	.10	.05
388	*Adam Hyzdu* (1st Draft Pick)	.15	.10	.05
389	*Todd Van Poppel* (1st Draft Pick)	.75	.50	.30
390	*Rondell White* (1st Draft Pick)	.75	.45	.25
391	*Marc Newfield* (1st Draft Pick)	.40	.30	.20
392	Julio Franco (AS)	.10	.08	.04
393	Wade Boggs (AS)	.12	.09	.05
394	Ozzie Guillen (AS)	.10	.08	.04
395	Cecil Fielder (AS)	.15	.10	.08
396	Ken Griffey,Jr. (AS)	.40	.30	.15
397	Rickey Henderson (AS)	.15	.10	.08
398	Jose Canseco (AS)	.10	.08	.04
399	Roger Clemens (AS)	.15	.11	.06
400	Sandy Alomar,Jr. (AS)	.10	.08	.04
401	Bobby Thigpen (AS)	.10	.08	.04
402	Bobby Bonilla (Master Blaster)	.10	.08	.04
403	Eric Davis (Master Blaster)	.10	.08	.04
404	Fred McGriff (Master Blaster)	.15	.08	.04
405	Glenn Davis (Master Blaster)	.10	.08	.04
406	Kevin Mitchell (Master Blaster)	.10	.08	.04
407	Rob Dibble (K-Man)	.10	.08	.04
408	Ramon Martinez (K-Man)	.15	.11	.06
409	David Cone (K-Man)	.10	.08	.04
410	Bobby Witt (K-Man)	.10	.08	.04
411	Mark Langston (K-Man)	.10	.08	.04
412	Bo Jackson (Rifleman)	.20	.15	.12
413	Shawon Dunston (Rifleman)	.10	.08	.04
414	Jesse Barfield (Rifleman)	.08	.06	.03
415	Ken Caminiti (Rifleman)	.08	.06	.03
416	Benito Santiago (Rifleman)	.10	.08	.04
417	Nolan Ryan (HL)	.30	.25	.12
418	Bobby Thigpen (HL)	.10	.08	.04
419	Ramon Martinez (HL)	.15	.11	.06
420	Bo Jackson (HL)	.20	.15	.08
421	Carlton Fisk (HL)	.10	.08	.04
422	Jimmy Key	.06	.05	.02

		MT	NR MT	EX
423	Junior Noboa(FC)	.05	.04	.02
424	Al Newman	.04	.03	.02
425	Pat Borders	.05	.04	.02
426	Von Hayes	.08	.06	.03
427	Tim Teufel	.04	.03	.02
428	Eric Plunk	.04	.03	.02
429	John Moses	.04	.03	.02
430	Mike Witt	.05	.04	.02
431	Otis Nixon	.04	.03	.02
432	Tony Fernandez	.08	.06	.03
433	Rance Mulliniks	.04	.03	.02
434	Dan Petry	.04	.03	.02
435	Bob Geren	.05	.04	.02
436	Steve Frey(FC)	.06	.05	.02
437	Jamie Moyer	.05	.04	.02
438	Junior Ortiz	.04	.03	.02
439	Tom O'Malley	.04	.03	.02
440	Pat Combs	.06	.05	.02
441	Jose Canseco (Dream Team)	.50	.30	.15
442	Alfredo Griffin	.04	.03	.02
443	Andres Galarraga	.08	.06	.03
444	Bryn Smith	.04	.03	.02
445	Andre Dawson	.12	.09	.05
446	Juan Samuel	.06	.05	.02
447	Mike Aldrete	.04	.03	.02
448	Ron Gant	.12	.09	.05
449	Fernando Valenzuela	.08	.06	.03
450	Vince Coleman	.08	.06	.03
451	Kevin Mitchell	.15	.11	.06
452	Spike Owen	.04	.03	.02
453	Mike Bielecki	.04	.03	.02
454	Dennis Martinez	.08	.06	.03
455	Brett Butler	.08	.06	.03
456	Ron Darling	.06	.05	.02
457	Dennis Rasmussen	.04	.03	.02
458	Ken Howell	.04	.03	.02
459	Steve Bedrosian	.05	.04	.02
460	Frank Viola	.12	.09	.05
461	Jose Lind	.04	.03	.02
462	Chris Sabo	.08	.06	.03
463	Dante Bichette	.05	.04	.02
464	Rick Mahler	.04	.03	.02
465	John Smiley	.06	.05	.02
466	Devon White	.06	.05	.02
467	John Orton	.04	.03	.02
468	Mike Stanton	.08	.06	.03
469	Billy Hatcher	.04	.03	.02
470	Wally Joyner	.12	.09	.05
471	Gene Larkin	.05	.04	.02
472	Doug Drabek	.08	.06	.03
473	Gary Sheffield	.15	.11	.06
474	David Wells	.04	.03	.02
475	Andy Van Slyke	.08	.06	.03
476	Mike Gallego	.05	.04	.02
477	B.J. Surhoff	.08	.06	.03
478	Gene Nelson	.04	.03	.02
479	Mariano Duncan	.05	.04	.02
480	Fred McGriff	.20	.15	.05
481	Jerry Browne	.04	.03	.02
482	Alvin Davis	.06	.05	.02
483	Bill Wegman	.05	.04	.02
484	Dave Parker	.08	.06	.03
485	Dennis Eckersley	.12	.09	.05
486	Erik Hanson	.12	.09	.05
487	Bill Ripken	.04	.03	.02
488	Tom Candiotti	.05	.04	.02
489	Mike Schooler	.06	.05	.02
490	Gregg Olson	.12	.09	.05
491	Chris James	.05	.04	.02
492	Pete Harnisch	.06	.05	.02
493	Julio Franco	.10	.08	.04
494	Greg Briley	.05	.04	.02
495	Ruben Sierra	.15	.11	.06
496	Steve Olin	.05	.04	.02
497	Mike Fetters	.05	.04	.02
498	Mark Williamson	.04	.03	.02
499	Bob Tewksbury	.04	.03	.02
500	Tony Gwynn	.15	.11	.06
501	Randy Myers	.08	.06	.03
502	Keith Comstock	.04	.03	.02
503	Craig Worthington	.08	.06	.03
504	Mark Eichhorn	.04	.03	.02
505	Barry Larkin	.12	.09	.05
506	Dave Johnson	.04	.03	.02
507	Bobby Witt	.06	.05	.02
508	Joe Orsulak	.04	.03	.02
509	Pete O'Brien	.04	.03	.02
510	Brad Arnsberg	.05	.04	.02
511	Storm Davis	.05	.04	.02
512	Bob Milacki	.05	.04	.02
513	Bill Pecota	.05	.04	.02
514	Glenallen Hill	.08	.06	.03
515	Danny Tartabull	.10	.08	.04
516	Mike Moore	.05	.04	.02
517	Ron Robinson	.04	.03	.02
518	Mark Gardner	.08	.06	.03
519	Rick Wrona	.04	.03	.02
520	Mike Scioscia	.06	.05	.02
521	Frank Wills	.04	.03	.02
522	Greg Brock	.04	.03	.02
523	Jack Clark	.08	.06	.03
524	Bruce Ruffin	.05	.04	.02
525	Robin Yount	.15	.11	.06
526	Tom Foley	.04	.03	.02
527	Pat Perry	.04	.03	.02
528	Greg Vaughn	.10	.08	.06
529	Wally Whitehurst	.06	.05	.02
530	Norm Charlton	.06	.05	.02
531	Marvell Wynne	.04	.03	.02
532	Jim Gantner	.05	.04	.02
533	Greg Litton	.04	.03	.02
534	Manny Lee	.05	.04	.02
535	Scott Bailes	.04	.03	.02
536	Charlie Leibrandt	.04	.03	.02
537	Roger McDowell	.05	.04	.02
538	Andy Benes	.12	.09	.06
539	Rick Honeycutt	.04	.03	.02
540	Doc Gooden	.15	.11	.06
541	Scott Garrelts	.04	.03	.02
542	Dave Clark	.04	.03	.02
543	Lonnie Smith	.04	.03	.02
544	Rick Rueschel	.05	.04	.02
545	Delino DeShields	.20	.15	.08
546	Mike Sharperson	.04	.03	.02
547	Mike Kingery	.04	.03	.02
548	Terry Kennedy	.04	.03	.02
549	David Cone	.08	.06	.03
550	Orel Hershiser	.12	.09	.05
551	Matt Nokes	.06	.05	.02
552	Eddie Williams	.04	.03	.02
553	Frank DiPino	.04	.03	.02
554	Fred Lynn	.05	.04	.02
555	Alex Cole(FC)	.10	.08	.06
556	Terry Leach	.04	.03	.02
557	Chet Lemon	.04	.03	.02
558	Paul Mirabella	.04	.03	.02
559	Bill Long	.04	.03	.02
560	Phil Bradley	.05	.04	.02
561	Duane Ward	.05	.04	.02
562	Dave Bergman	.04	.03	.02
563	Eric Show	.04	.03	.02
564	Xavier Hernandez(FC)	.08	.06	.03
565	Jeff Parrett	.04	.03	.02
566	Chuck Cary	.04	.03	.02
567	Ken Hill	.06	.05	.02
568	Bob Welch	.08	.06	.03
569	John Mitchell	.04	.03	.02
570	*Travis Fryman*(FC)	.60	.45	.25
571	Derek Lilliquist	.04	.03	.02
572	Steve Lake	.04	.03	.02
573	*John Barfield*(FC)	.10	.08	.04
574	Randy Bush	.04	.03	.02
575	Joe Magrane	.06	.05	.02
576	Edgar Diaz	.04	.03	.02
577	Casy Candaele	.04	.03	.02
578	Jesse Orosco	.04	.03	.02
579	Tom Henke	.06	.05	.02
580	Rick Cerone	.04	.03	.02
581	Drew Hall	.04	.03	.02
582	Tony Castillo	.04	.03	.02
583	Jimmy Jones	.04	.03	.02
584	Rick Reed	.04	.03	.02
585	Joe Girardi	.05	.04	.02
586	*Jeff Gray*(FC)	.15	.11	.06
587	Luis Polonia	.06	.05	.02
588	Joe Klink(FC)	.08	.06	.03
589	Rex Hudler	.05	.04	.02
590	Kirk McCaskill	.06	.05	.02
591	Juan Agosto	.04	.03	.02
592	Wes Gardner	.04	.03	.02
593	*Rich Rodriguez*(FC)	.12	.09	.05
594	Mitch Webster	.04	.03	.02
595	Kelly Gruber	.12	.09	.05
596	Dale Mohorcic	.04	.03	.02
597	Willie McGee	.08	.06	.03
598	Bill Krueger	.05	.04	.02
599	Bob Walk	.04	.03	.02
600	Kevin Maas	.10	.08	.04
601	Danny Jackson	.06	.05	.02
602	Craig McMurtry	.04	.03	.02
603	Curtis Wilkerson	.04	.03	.02
604	Adam Peterson	.04	.03	.02

		MT	NR MT	EX
605	Sam Horn	.06	.05	.02
606	Tommy Gregg	.04	.03	.02
607	Ken Dayley	.04	.03	.02
608	Carmelo Castillo	.04	.03	.02
609	John Shelby	.04	.03	.02
610	Don Slaught	.04	.03	.02
611	Calvin Schiraldi	.04	.03	.02
612	Dennis Lamp	.04	.03	.02
613	Andres Thomas	.04	.03	.02
614	Jose Gonzales	.04	.03	.02
615	Randy Ready	.04	.03	.02
616	Kevin Bass	.06	.05	.02
617	Mike Marshall	.05	.04	.02
618	Daryl Boston	.04	.03	.02
619	Andy McGaffigan	.04	.03	.02
620	Joe Oliver	.06	.05	.02
621	Jim Gott	.04	.03	.02
622	Jose Oquendo	.04	.03	.02
623	Jose DeJesus	.06	.05	.02
624	Mike Brumley	.04	.03	.02
625	John Olerud	.50	.40	.20
626	Ernest Riles	.04	.03	.02
627	Gene Harris	.05	.04	.02
628	Jose Uribe	.04	.03	.02
629	Darnell Coles	.04	.03	.02
630	Carney Lansford	.06	.05	.02
631	Tim Leary	.05	.04	.02
632	Tim Hulett	.04	.03	.02
633	Kevin Elster	.06	.05	.02
634	Tony Fossas	.04	.03	.02
635	Francisco Oliveras	.04	.03	.02
636	Bob Patterson	.04	.03	.02
637	Gary Ward	.04	.03	.02
638	Rene Gonzales	.04	.03	.02
639	Don Robinson	.04	.03	.02
640	Darryl Strawberry	.12	.10	.08
641	Dave Anderson	.04	.03	.02
642	Scott Scudder	.06	.05	.02
643	*Reggie Harris*(FC)	.20	.15	.08
644	Dave Henderson	.08	.06	.03
645	Ben McDonald	.10	.08	.04
646	Bob Kipper	.04	.03	.02
647	Hal Morris	.15	.11	.06
648	Tim Birtsas	.04	.03	.02
649	Steve Searcy	.04	.03	.02
650	Dale Murphy	.12	.09	.05
651	Ron Oester	.04	.03	.02
652	Mike LaCoss	.04	.03	.02
653	Ron Jones	.05	.04	.02
654	Kelly Downs	.04	.03	.02
655	Roger Clemens	.20	.15	.08
656	Herm Winningham	.04	.03	.02
657	Trevor Wilson	.06	.05	.02
658	Jose Rijo	.08	.06	.03
659	Dann Bilardello	.04	.03	.02
660	Gregg Jefferies	.15	.11	.06
661	Doug Drabek (AS)	.08	.06	.03
662	Randy Myers (AS)	.06	.05	.02
663	Benito Santiago (AS)	.08	.06	.03
664	Will Clark (AS)	.15	.11	.06
665	Ryne Sandberg (AS)	.15	.11	.06
666	Barry Larkin (AS)	.08	.06	.03
667	Matt Williams (AS)	.10	.06	.03
668	Barry Bonds (AS)	.20	.15	.05
669	Eric Davis	.12	.09	.05
670	Bobby Bonilla (AS)	.08	.06	.03
671	*Chipper Jones* (1st Draft Pick)	1.25	.90	.50
672	*Eric Christopherson* (1st Draft Pick)	.15	.11	.06
673	*Robbie Beckett* (1st Draft Pick)	.15	.11	.06
674	*Shane Andrews* (1st Draft Pick)	.20	.15	.08
675	*Steve Karsay* (1st Draft Pick)	.40	.30	.15
676	*Aaron Holbert* (1st Draft Pick)	.20	.15	.08
677	*Donovan Osborne* (1st Draft Pick)	.60	.45	.25
678	*Todd Ritchie* (1st Draft Pick)	.15	.11	.06
679	*Ron Walden* (1st Draft Pick)	.10	.08	.06
680	*Tim Costo* (1st Draft Pick)	.20	.15	.10
681	*Dan Wilson* (1st Draft Pick)	.15	.10	.05
682	*Kurt Miller* (1st Draft Pick)	.15	.11	.06
683	*Mike Lieberthal* (1st Draft Pick)	.25	.20	.10
684	*Roger Clemens* (K-Man)	.15	.11	.06
685	Doc Gooden (K-Man)	.15	.11	.06
686	Nolan Ryan (K-Man)	.25	.15	.08
687	Frank Viola (K-Man)	.08	.06	.03
688	Erik Hanson (K-Man)	.08	.06	.03
689	Matt Williams (Master Blaster)	.10	.08	.04
690	Jose Canseco (Master Blaster)	.10	.08	.04
691	Darryl Strawberry (Master Blaster)	.10	.08	.06
692	Bo Jackson (Master Blaster)	.20	.15	.12
693	Cecil Fielder (Master Blaster)	.20	.15	.08
694	Sandy Alomar, Jr. (Rifleman)	.08	.06	.03

		MT	NR MT	EX
695	Cory Snyder (Rifleman)	.05	.04	.02
696	Eric Davis, Eric Davis (Rifleman)	.08	.06	.03
697	Ken Griffey,Jr. (Rifleman)	.30	.25	.12
698	Andy Van Slyke (Rifleman)	.08	.06	.03
699	Langston/Witt (No-hitter)	.08	.06	.03
700	Randy Johnson (No-hitter)	.08	.06	.03
701	Nolan Ryan (No-hitter)	.25	.15	.08
702	Dave Stewart (No-hitter)	.08	.06	.03
703	Fernando Valenzuela (No-hitter)	.06	.05	.02
704	Andy Hawkins (No-hitter)	.04	.03	.02
705	Melido Perez (No-hitter)	.04	.03	.02
706	Terry Mulholland (No-hitter)	.06	.05	.02
707	Dave Stieb (No-hitter)	.06	.05	.02
708	*Brian Barnes*	.20	.15	.08
709	*Bernard Gilkey*	.30	.25	.12
710	*Steve Decker*(FC)	.10	.08	.04
711	*Paul Faries*(FC)	.12	.09	.05
712	*Paul Marak*(FC)	.10	.08	.04
713	*Wes Chamberlain*(FC)	.20	.10	.05
714	*Kevin Belcher*(FC)	.10	.08	.04
715	Dan Boone(FC)	.05	.04	.02
716	*Steve Adkins*(FC)	.10	.08	.04
717	*Geronimo Pena*(FC)	.10	.08	.04
718	*Howard Farmer*	.08	.06	.03
719	*Mark Leonard*(FC)	.10	.08	.04
720	Tom Lampkin	.04	.03	.02
721	*Mike Gardiner*(FC)	.10	.06	.03
722	*Jeff Conine*(FC)	.30	.15	.06
723	*Efrain Valdez*(FC)	.10	.08	.04
724	Chuck Malone(FC)	.08	.06	.03
725	*Leo Gomez*(FC)	.12	.09	.05
726	*Paul McClellan*(FC)	.15	.11	.06
727	*Mark Leiter*(FC)	.10	.08	.04
728	*Rich DeLucia*(FC)	.15	.11	.06
729	Mel Rojas(FC)	.08	.06	.03
730	*Hector Wagner*(FC)	.10	.08	.04
731	*Ray Lankford*	.25	.20	.15
732	*Turner Ward*(FC)	.10	.08	.04
733	*Gerald Alexander*(FC)	.10	.08	.04
734	*Scott Anderson*(FC)	.10	.08	.04
735	Tony Perezchica(FC)	.05	.04	.02
736	Jimmy Kremers(FC)	.08	.06	.03
737	American Flag	.30	.25	.12
738	*Mike York*(FC)	.10	.08	.04
739	Mike Rochford(FC)	.06	.05	.02
740	Scott Aldred(FC)	.08	.06	.03
741	*Rico Brogna*(FC)	.10	.08	.04
742	*Dave Burba*(FC)	.10	.08	.04
743	*Ray Stephens*(FC)	.10	.08	.04
744	*Eric Gunderson*	.08	.06	.03
745	*Troy Afenir*(FC)	.08	.06	.03
746	Jeff Shaw(FC)	.08	.06	.03
747	*Orlando Merced*(FC)	.20	.15	.08
748	*Omar Oliveras*(FC)	.10	.08	.04
749	Jerry Kutzler(FC)	.06	.05	.02
750	Maurice Vaughn	.45	.25	.12
751	*Matt Stark*(FC)	.10	.08	.04
752	*Randy Hennis*(FC)	.10	.08	.04
753	*Andujar Cedeno*(FC)	.30	.25	.12
754	Kelvin Torve(FC)	.08	.06	.03
755	Joe Kraemer(FC)	.08	.06	.03
756	*Phil Clark*(FC)	.15	.11	.06
757	*Ed Vosberg*(FC)	.10	.08	.04
758	*Mike Perez*(FC)	.10	.08	.04
759	*Scott Lewis*(FC)	.10	.08	.04
760	*Steve Chitren*(FC)	.10	.08	.04
761	*Ray Young*(FC)	.10	.08	.04
762	*Andres Santana*(FC)	.15	.11	.06
763	*Rodney McCray*(FC)	.10	.08	.04
764	*Sean Berry*(FC)	.10	.08	.04
765	Brent Mayne	.08	.06	.03
766	*Mike Simms*(FC)	.15	.11	.06
767	*Glenn Sutko*(FC)	.10	.08	.04
768	Gary Disarcina	.06	.05	.02
769	George Brett (HL)	.12	.10	.03
770	Cecil Fielder (HL)	.08	.06	.03
771	Jim Presley	.05	.04	.02
772	John Dopson	.05	.04	.02
773	Bo Jackson (Breaker)	.35	.25	.14
774	Brent Knackert(FC)	.08	.06	.03
775	Bill Doran	.06	.05	.02
776	Dick Schofield	.04	.03	.02
777	Nelson Santovenia	.04	.03	.02
778	Mark Guthrie(FC)	.08	.06	.03
779	Mark Lemke	.08	.06	.03
780	Terry Steinbach	.06	.05	.02
781	Tom Bolton	.05	.04	.02
782	*Randy Tomlin*(FC)	.10	.06	.03
783	Jeff Kunkel	.04	.03	.02
784	Felix Jose	.10	.08	.04
785	Rick Sutcliffe	.05	.04	.02

		MT	NR MT	EX
786	John Cerutti	.04	.03	.02
787	Jose Vizcaino	.05	.04	.02
788	Curt Schilling	.06	.05	.02
789	Ed Whitson	.05	.04	.02
790	Tony Pena	.06	.05	.02
791	John Candelaria	.04	.03	.02
792	Carmelo Martinez	.04	.03	.02
793	Sandy Alomar, Jr.	.08	.06	.03
794	*Jim Neidlinger*(FC)	.08	.06	.03
795	Red's October	.08	.06	.03
796	Paul Sorrento	.05	.04	.02
797	Tom Pagnozzi	.06	.05	.02
798	Tino Martinez	.10	.08	.06
799	Scott Ruskin(FC)	.08	.06	.03
800	Kirk Gibson	.08	.06	.03
801	Walt Terrell	.04	.03	.02
802	John Russell	.04	.03	.02
803	Chili Davis	.08	.06	.03
804	Chris Nabholz(FC)	.08	.06	.03
805	Juan Gonzalez	.50	.25	.12
806	Ron Hassey	.04	.03	.02
807	Todd Worrell	.06	.05	.02
808	Tommy Greene	.06	.05	.02
809	Joel Skinner	.04	.03	.02
810	Benito Santiago	.08	.06	.03
811	Pat Tabler	.04	.03	.02
812	*Scott Erickson*(FC)	.10	.08	.04
813	Moises Alou	.25	.15	.10
814	Dale Sveum	.04	.03	.02
815	Ryne Sandberg (Man of the Year)	.20	.15	.08
816	Rick Dempsey	.04	.03	.02
817	Scott Bankhead	.05	.04	.02
818	Jason Grimsley	.05	.04	.02
819	Doug Jennings	.04	.03	.02
820	Tom Herr	.05	.04	.02
821	Rob Ducey	.04	.03	.02
822	Luis Quinones	.04	.03	.02
823	Greg Minton	.04	.03	.02
824	Mark Grant	.04	.03	.02
825	Ozzie Smith	.10	.08	.04
826	Dave Eiland	.04	.03	.02
827	Danny Heep	.04	.03	.02
828	Hensley Meulens	.08	.06	.03
829	Charlie O'Brien	.04	.03	.02
830	Glenn Davis	.08	.06	.03
831	John Marzano	.04	.03	.02
832	Steve Ontiveros	.04	.03	.02
833	Ron Karkovice	.04	.03	.02
834	Jerry Goff(FC)	.08	.06	.03
835	Ken Griffey, Sr.	.08	.06	.03
836	Kevin Reimer(FC)	.10	.08	.04
837	Randy Kutcher	.04	.03	.02
838	Mike Blowers	.05	.04	.02
839	Mike Macfarlane	.05	.04	.02
840	Frank Thomas	1.25	.90	.50
841	Ken Griffey, Jr. & Sr.	.50	.30	.15
842	Jack Howell	.04	.03	.02
843	Mauro Gozzo(FC)	.06	.05	.02
844	Gerald Young	.04	.03	.02
845	Zane Smith	.05	.04	.02
846	Kevin Brown	.05	.04	.02
847	Sil Campusano	.04	.03	.02
848	Larry Andersen	.04	.03	.02
849	Cal Ripken, Jr. (Franchise)	.12	.09	.05
850	Roger Clemens (Franchise)	.12	.09	.05
851	Sandy Alomar, Jr. (Franchise)	.08	.06	.03
852	Alan Trammell (Franchise)	.08	.06	.03
853	George Brett (Franchise)	.10	.06	.03
854	Robin Yount (Franchise)	.10	.06	.03
855	Kirby Puckett (Franchise)	.12	.06	.03
856	Don Mattingly (Franchise)	.15	.11	.06
857	Rickey Henderson (Franchise)	.12	.10	.06
858	Ken Griffey, Jr. (Franchise)	.40	.30	.20
859	Ruben Sierra (Franchise)	.10	.08	.04
860	John Olerud (Franchise)	.20	.15	.08
861	Dave Justice (Franchise)	.15	.10	.05
862	Ryne Sandberg (Franchise)	.15	.11	.06
863	Eric Davis (Franchise)	.08	.06	.03
864	Darryl Strawberry (Franchise)	.10	.08	.04
865	Tim Wallach (Franchise)	.05	.04	.02
866	Doc Gooden (Franchise)	.08	.06	.03
867	Lenny Dykstra (Franchise)	.12	.08	.04
868	Barry Bonds (Franchise)	.25	.15	.10
869	Todd Zeile (Franchise)	.10	.08	.04
870	Benito Santiago (Franchise)	.08	.06	.03
871	Will Clark (Franchise)	.12	.10	.08
872	Craig Biggio (Franchise)	.08	.06	.03
873	Wally Joyner (Franchise)	.08	.06	.03
874	Frank Thomas (Franchise)	.75	.45	.25
875	Rickey Henderson (MVP)	.10	.08	.04
876	Barry Bonds (MVP)	.25	.08	.04
877	Bob Welch (Cy Young)	.05	.04	.02
878	Doug Drabek (Cy Young)	.06	.05	.03
879	Sandy Alomar, Jr. (ROY)	.08	.06	.03
880	Dave Justice (ROY)	.25	.20	.10
881	Damon Berryhill	.05	.04	.02
882	Frank Viola (Dream Team)	.10	.08	.04
883	Dave Stewart (Dream Team)	.10	.08	.04
884	Doug Jones (Dream Team)	.05	.04	.02
885	Randy Myers (Dream Team)	.06	.05	.02
886	Will Clark (Dream Team)	.30	.25	.12
887	Roberto Alomar (Dream Team)	.40	.30	.20
888	Barry Larkin (Dream Team)	.12	.09	.05
889	Wade Boggs (Dream Team)	.20	.15	.08
890	Rickey Henderson (Dream Team)	.20	.15	.08
891	Kirby Puckett (Dream Team)	.20	.15	.08
892	Ken Griffey,Jr. (Dream Team)	1.50	1.25	.60
893	Benito Santiago (Dream Team)	.10	.08	.04

1991 Score Cooperstown

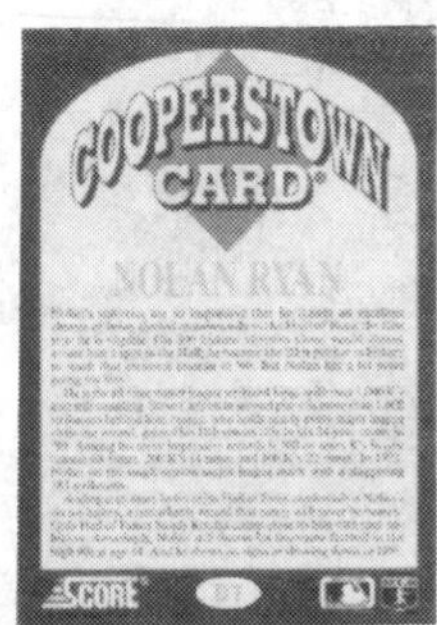

These standard-size cards were available as a seven-card set, one per every factory set. The card fronts are white, with a player portrait inside an oval. "Cooperstown Card" is written across the top in yellow along with a yellow stripe. A yellow stripe also appears at the bottom, along with the player's name in yellow. The backs have green borders surrounding a yellow background which contains a summary of the player's career. Cards are numbered B1-B7.

		MT	NR MT	EX
Complete Set (7):		8.00	6.00	3.25
Common Player		.50	.40	.20
1	Wade Boggs	1.00	.70	.40
2	Barry Larkin	.50	.40	.20
3	Ken Griffey Jr.	3.50	2.75	1.50
4	Rickey Henderson	1.00	.70	.40
5	George Brett	1.25	.90	.50
6	Will Clark	1.00	.70	.40
7	Nolan Ryan	3.00	2.25	1.25

1991 Score Hot Rookies

Photos not available at press time

These standard-size cards were inserted one per every 100-card 1991 Score blister pack. Action photos with white borders are featured on the front, and "Hot Rookie" is written in yellow at the top. The background is shaded from yellow to orange. The backs are numbered and each has a color mug shot and a career summary.

		MT	NR MT	EX
Complete Set (10):		22.00	16.50	8.75
Common Card:		.75	.60	.30
1	Dave Justice	3.00	2.25	1.25
2	Kevin Maas	.75	.60	.30
3	Hal Morris	.75	.60	.30
4	Frank Thomas	11.00	8.25	4.50
5	Jeff Conine	2.00	1.50	.80
6	Sandy Alomar Jr.	.75	.60	.30
7	Ray Lankford	1.25	.90	.50
8	Steve Decker	.75	.60	.30
9	Juan Gonzalez	11.00	8.25	4.50
10	Jose Offerman	.75	.60	.30

1991 Score Mickey Mantle

Photos not available at press time.

These standard-size cards recall Mickey Mantle's career as a Yankee. Card fronts are glossy and have red and white borders. The card's caption appears at the bottom in a blue stripe. The backs have a photo and a summary of the caption, plus the card number and serial number. Dealers and media members who were on Score's mailing list received the seven-card sets, which were limited to 5,000 sets produced.

	MT	NR MT	EX
Complete Set (7):	300.00	250.00	140.00
Common Card:	50.00	40.00	20.00
Autograph:	500.00	370.00	200.00

1991 Score Traded

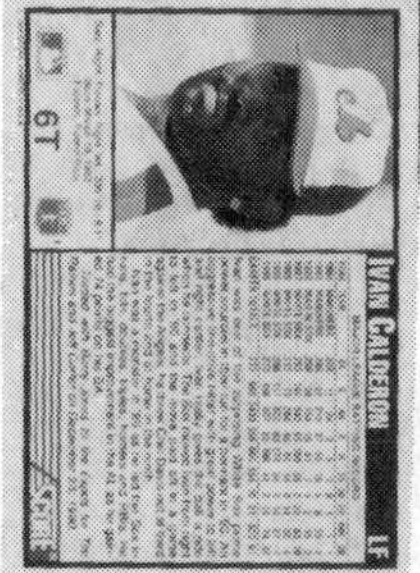

This 110-card set features players with new teams as well as 1991 Major League rookies. The cards are designed in the same style as the regular 1991 Score issue. The cards once again feature a "T" designation along with the card number. The complete set was sold at hobby shops in a special box.

		MT	NR MT	EX
Complete Set (110):		6.00	4.50	2.50
Common Player:		.06	.05	.02
1	Bo Jackson	.35	.25	.14
2	Mike Flanagan	.06	.05	.02
3	Pete Incaviglia	.08	.06	.03
4	Jack Clark	.10	.08	.04
5	Hubie Brooks	.08	.06	.03
6	Ivan Calderon	.12	.09	.05
7	Glenn Davis	.12	.09	.05
8	Wally Backman	.06	.05	.02
9	Dave Smith	.08	.06	.03
10	Tim Raines	.15	.11	.06
11	Joe Carter	.15	.11	.06
12	Sid Bream	.08	.06	.03
13	George Bell	.12	.09	.05
14	Steve Bedrosian	.06	.05	.02
15	Willie Wilson	.06	.05	.02
16	Darryl Strawberry	.12	.10	.05
17	Danny Jackson	.06	.05	.02
18	Kirk Gibson	.08	.06	.03
19	Willie McGee	.10	.08	.04
20	Junior Felix	.08	.06	.03
21	Steve Farr	.06	.05	.02
22	Pat Tabler	.06	.05	.02
23	Brett Butler	.10	.08	.04
24	Danny Darwin	.06	.05	.02
25	Mikey Tettleton	.08	.06	.03
26	Gary Carter	.10	.08	.04
27	Mitch Williams	.08	.06	.03
28	Candy Maldonado	.08	.06	.03
29	Otis Nixon	.08	.06	.03
30	Brian Downing	.06	.05	.02
31	Tom Candiotti	.06	.05	.02
32	John Candelaria	.06	.05	.02
33	Rob Murphy	.06	.05	.02
34	Deion Sanders	.20	.15	.08
35	Willie Randolph	.08	.06	.03
36	Pete Harnisch	.08	.06	.03
37	Dante Bichette	.06	.05	.02
38	Garry Templeton	.08	.06	.03
39	Gary Gaetti	.08	.06	.03
40	John Cerutti	.06	.05	.02
41	Rick Cerone	.06	.05	.02
42	Mike Pagliarulo	.06	.05	.02
43	Ron Hassey	.06	.05	.02
44	Roberto Alomar	.30	.25	.12
45	Mike Boddicker	.08	.06	.03
46	Bud Black	.06	.05	.02
47	Rob Deer	.06	.05	.02
48	Devon White	.08	.06	.03
49	Luis Sojo	.06	.05	.02
50	Terry Pendleton	.08	.06	.03
51	Kevin Gross	.06	.05	.02
52	Mike Huff	.08	.06	.03
53	Dave Righetti	.08	.06	.03
54	Matt Young	.06	.05	.02
55	Ernest Riles	.06	.05	.02
56	Bill Gullickson	.08	.06	.03
57	Vince Coleman	.10	.08	.04
58	Fred McGriff	.20	.15	.08
59	Franklin Stubbs	.06	.05	.02
60	Eric King	.06	.05	.02
61	Cory Snyder	.06	.05	.02
62	Dwight Evans	.08	.06	.03
63	Gerald Perry	.06	.05	.02
64	Eric Show	.06	.05	.02
65	Shawn Hillegas	.06	.05	.02
66	Tony Fernandez	.08	.06	.03
67	Tim Teufel	.06	.05	.02
68	Mitch Webster	.06	.05	.02
69	Mike Heath	.06	.05	.02
70	Chili Davis	.08	.06	.03
71	Larry Andersen	.06	.05	.02
72	Gary Varsho	.06	.05	.02
73	Juan Berenguer	.06	.05	.02
74	Jack Morris	.08	.06	.03
75	Barry Jones	.06	.05	.02
76	Rafael Belliard	.06	.05	.02
77	Steve Buechele	.06	.05	.02
78	Scott Sanderson	.06	.05	.02
79	Bob Ojeda	.06	.05	.02
80	Curt Schilling	.06	.05	.02
81	Brian Drahman(FC)	.15	.11	.06
82	Ivan Rodriguez(FC)	1.00	.70	.40
83	David Howard(FC)	.10	.08	.04
84	Heath Slocumb(FC)	.10	.08	.06
85	Mike Timlin(FC)	.20	.15	.08
86	Darruyl Kile(FC)	.25	.15	.08

		MT	NR MT	EX
87	Pete Schourek(FC)	.10	.08	.04
88	Bruce Walton(FC)	.12	.09	.05
89	Al Osuna(FC)	.15	.11	.06
90	Gary Scott(FC)	.10	.08	.04
91	Doug Simons(FC)	.15	.11	.06
92	Chris Jones(FC)	.10	.08	.04
93	Chuck Knoblauch	.25	.20	.15
94	Dana Allison(FC)	.15	.11	.06
95	Erik Pappas(FC)	.20	.15	.08
96	Jeff Bagwell(FC)	1.25	.90	.50
97	Kirk Dressendorfer(FC)	.10	.08	.04
98	Freddie Benavides(FC)	.20	.15	.08
99	Luis Gonzalez(FC)	.40	.30	.15
100	Wade Taylor(FC)	.20	.15	.08
101	Ed Sprague(FC)	.15	.11	.06
102	Bob Scanlan(FC)	.10	.08	.06
103	Rick Wilkins(FC)	.30	.25	.12
104	Chris Donnels(FC)	.10	.08	.04
105	Joe Slusarski(FC)	.10	.08	.04
106	Mark Lewis(FC)	.10	.08	.04
107	Pat Kelly(FC)	.25	.20	.10
108	John Briscoe(FC)	.15	.11	.06
109	Luis Lopez(FC)	.10	.08	.04
110	Jeff Johnson(FC)	.25	.20	.10

1992 Score

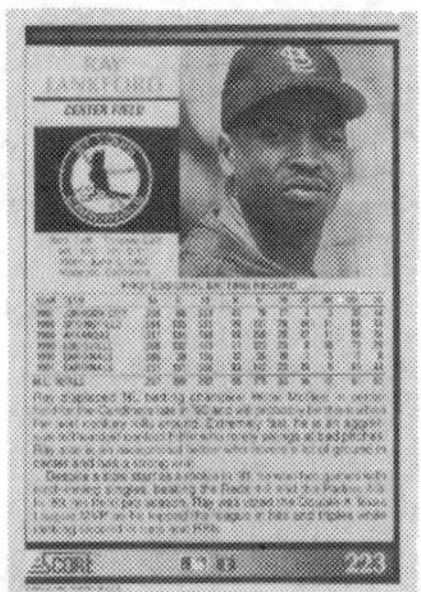

Score used a two series format for the second consecutive year in 1992. Cards 1-442 are featured in the first series. The card fronts feature full-color game action photos. The player's name, in white lettering, is across the top with the team logo on the upper-right corner. The player's position is across the bottom. Four-color borders are used. Card backs feature color head shots of the players, team logo and career stats on a vertical layout. Several subsets are included in 1992, including a five-card Joe DiMaggio set. DiMaggio autographed cards were also inserted into random packs. Cards 736-772 can be found with or without a "Rookie Prospects" banner on the card front.

	MT	NR MT	EX
Complete Set (893):	20.00	15.00	8.00
Common Player:	.04	.03	.02

		MT	NR MT	EX
1	Ken Griffey, Jr.	.75	.60	.30
2	Nolan Ryan	.50	.40	.20
3	Will Clark	.25	.20	.10
4	Dave Justice	.30	.25	.12
5	Dave Henderson	.08	.06	.03
6	Bret Saberhagen	.08	.06	.03
7	Fred McGriff	.15	.11	.06
8	Erik Hanson	.08	.06	.03
9	Darryl Strawberry	.10	.08	.04
10	Doc Gooden	.12	.09	.05
11	Juan Gonzalez	.75	.60	.30
12	Mark Langston	.08	.06	.03
13	Lonnie Smith	.04	.03	.02
14	Jeff Montgomery	.05	.04	.02
15	Roberto Alomar	.25	.20	.10
16	Delino DeShields	.08	.06	.03
17	Steve Bedrosian	.04	.03	.02
18	Terry Pendleton	.08	.06	.03
19	Mark Carreon	.04	.03	.02
20	Mark McGwire	.12	.09	.05
21	Roger Clemens	.15	.11	.06
22	Chuck Crim	.04	.03	.02
23	Don Mattingly	.15	.11	.06
24	Dickie Thon	.04	.03	.02
25	Ron Gant	.15	.11	.06
26	Milt Cuyler	.10	.08	.04
27	Mike Macfarlane	.05	.04	.02
28	Dan Gladden	.04	.03	.02
29	Melido Perez	.04	.03	.02
30	Willie Randolph	.05	.04	.02
31	Albert Belle	.20	.15	.08
32	Dave Winfield	.12	.09	.05
33	Jimmy Jones	.04	.03	.02
34	Kevin Gross	.04	.03	.02
35	Andres Galarraga	.06	.05	.02
36	Mike Devereaux	.05	.04	.02
37	Chris Bosio	.05	.04	.02
38	Mike LaValliere	.05	.04	.02
39	Gary Gaetti	.08	.06	.03
40	Felix Jose	.10	.08	.04
41	Alvaro Espinoza	.04	.03	.02
42	Rick Aguilera	.06	.05	.02
43	Mike Gallego	.04	.03	.02
44	Eric Davis	.12	.09	.05
45	George Bell	.08	.06	.03
46	Tom Brunansky	.06	.05	.02
47	Steve Farr	.04	.03	.02
48	Duane Ward	.05	.04	.02
49	David Wells	.04	.03	.02
50	Cecil Fielder	.20	.15	.08
51	Walt Weiss	.06	.05	.02
52	Todd Zeile	.10	.08	.04
53	Doug Jones	.04	.03	.02
54	Bob Walk	.04	.03	.02
55	Rafael Palmeiro	.08	.06	.03
56	Rob Deer	.04	.03	.02
57	Paul O'Neill	.08	.06	.03
58	Jeff Reardon	.08	.06	.03
59	Randy Ready	.04	.03	.02
60	Scott Erickson	.08	.06	.03
61	Paul Molitor	.12	.09	.05
62	Jack McDowell	.08	.06	.03
63	Jim Acker	.04	.03	.02
64	Jay Buhner	.06	.05	.02
65	Travis Fryman	.20	.15	.08
66	Marquis Grissom	.10	.08	.04
67	Mike Harkey	.05	.04	.02
68	Luis Polonia	.05	.04	.02
69	Ken Caminiti	.05	.04	.02
70	Chris Sabo	.08	.06	.03
71	Gregg Olson	.08	.06	.03
72	Carlton Fisk	.12	.09	.05
73	Juan Samuel	.06	.05	.02
74	Todd Stottlemyre	.06	.05	.02
75	Andre Dawson	.12	.09	.05
76	Alvin Davis	.06	.05	.02
77	Bill Doran	.06	.05	.02
78	B.J. Surhoff	.06	.05	.02
79	Kirk McCaskill	.06	.05	.02
80	Dale Murphy	.08	.06	.03
81	Jose DeLeon	.05	.04	.02
82	Alex Fernandez	.20	.15	.08
83	Ivan Calderon	.08	.06	.03
84	Brent Mayne	.06	.05	.02
85	Jody Reed	.06	.05	.02
86	Randy Tomlin	.06	.05	.02
87	Randy Milligan	.06	.05	.02
88	Pascual Perez	.04	.03	.02
89	Hensley Meulens	.08	.06	.03
90	Joe Carter	.10	.08	.04
91	Mike Moore	.05	.04	.02
92	Ozzie Guillen	.08	.06	.03
93	Shawn Hillegas	.04	.03	.02
94	Chili Davis	.08	.06	.03
95	Vince Coleman	.08	.06	.03
96	Jimmy Key	.06	.05	.02
97	Billy Ripken	.04	.03	.02
98	Dave Smith	.06	.05	.02
99	Tom Bolton	.04	.03	.02
100	Barry Larkin	.12	.09	.05
101	Kenny Rogers	.04	.03	.02
102	Mike Boddicker	.06	.05	.02
103	Kevin Elster	.04	.03	.02
104	Ken Hill	.06	.05	.02
105	Charlie Leibrandt	.04	.03	.02
106	Pat Combs	.06	.05	.02
107	Hubie Brooks	.06	.05	.02
108	Julio Franco	.10	.08	.04
109	Vicente Palacios	.04	.03	.02
110	Kal Daniels	.08	.06	.03
111	Bruce Hurst	.06	.05	.02
112	Willie McGee	.08	.06	.03
113	Ted Power	.04	.03	.02
114	Milt Thompson	.04	.03	.02

#	Player	MT	NR MT	EX
115	Doug Drabek	.08	.06	.03
116	Rafael Belliard	.04	.03	.02
117	Scott Garrelts	.04	.03	.02
118	Terry Mulholland	.06	.05	.02
119	Jay Howell	.05	.04	.02
120	Danny Jackson	.05	.04	.02
121	Scott Ruskin	.05	.04	.02
122	Robin Ventura	.15	.11	.06
123	Bip Roberts	.06	.05	.02
124	Jeff Russell	.05	.04	.02
125	Hal Morris	.08	.06	.03
126	Teddy Higuera	.06	.05	.02
127	Luis Sojo	.05	.04	.02
128	Carlos Baerga	.25	.20	.10
129	Jeff Ballard	.04	.03	.02
130	Tom Gordon	.08	.06	.03
131	Sid Bream	.06	.05	.02
132	Rance Mulliniks	.04	.03	.02
133	Andy Benes	.10	.08	.04
134	Mickey Tettleton	.08	.06	.03
135	Rich DeLucia	.06	.05	.02
136	Tom Pagnozzi	.06	.05	.02
137	Harold Baines	.08	.06	.03
138	Danny Darwin	.04	.03	.02
139	Kevin Bass	.06	.05	.02
140	Chris Nabholz	.06	.05	.02
141	Pete O'Brien	.04	.03	.02
142	Jeff Treadway	.05	.04	.02
143	Mickey Morandini	.08	.06	.03
144	Eric King	.04	.03	.02
145	Danny Tartabull	.08	.06	.03
146	Lance Johnson	.04	.03	.02
147	Casey Candaele	.04	.03	.02
148	Felix Fermin	.04	.03	.02
149	Rich Rodriguez	.06	.05	.02
150	Dwight Evans	.08	.06	.03
151	Joe Klink	.04	.03	.02
152	Kevin Reimer	.08	.06	.03
153	Orlando Merced	.10	.08	.04
154	Mel Hall	.05	.04	.02
155	Randy Myers	.06	.05	.02
156	Greg Harris	.04	.03	.02
157	Jeff Brantley	.05	.04	.02
158	Jim Eisenreich	.05	.04	.02
159	Luis Rivera	.04	.03	.02
160	Cris Carpenter	.05	.04	.02
161	Bruce Ruffin	.04	.03	.02
162	Omar Vizquel	.04	.03	.02
163	Gerald Alexander	.05	.04	.02
164	Mark Guthrie	.06	.05	.02
165	Scott Lewis	.06	.05	.02
166	Bill Sampen	.06	.05	.02
167	Dave Anderson	.04	.03	.02
168	Kevin McReynolds	.08	.06	.03
169	Jose Vizcaino	.04	.03	.02
170	Bob Geren	.04	.03	.02
171	Mike Morgan	.05	.04	.02
172	Jim Gott	.04	.03	.02
173	Mike Pagliarulo	.05	.04	.02
174	Mike Jeffcoat	.04	.03	.02
175	Craig Lefferts	.05	.04	.02
176	Steve Finley	.08	.06	.03
177	Wally Backman	.04	.03	.02
178	Kent Mercker	.06	.05	.02
179	John Cerutti	.04	.03	.02
180	Jay Bell	.06	.05	.02
181	Dale Sveum	.04	.03	.02
182	Greg Gagne	.04	.03	.02
183	Donnie Hill	.04	.03	.02
184	Rex Hudler	.04	.03	.02
185	Pat Kelly	.08	.06	.03
186	Jeff Robinson	.04	.03	.02
187	Jeff Gray	.08	.06	.03
188	Jerry Willard	.04	.03	.02
189	Carlos Quintana	.08	.06	.03
190	Dennis Eckersley	.08	.06	.03
191	Kelly Downs	.04	.03	.02
192	Gregg Jefferies	.12	.09	.05
193	Darrin Fletcher	.05	.04	.02
194	Mike Jackson	.05	.04	.02
195	Eddie Murray	.12	.09	.05
196	Billy Landrum	.04	.03	.02
197	Eric Yelding	.04	.03	.02
198	Devon White	.06	.05	.02
199	Larry Walker	.08	.06	.03
200	Ryne Sandberg	.20	.15	.08
201	Dave Magadan	.08	.06	.03
202	Steve Chitren	.06	.05	.02
203	Scott Fletcher	.04	.03	.02
204	Dwayne Henry	.04	.03	.02
205	Scott Coolbaugh	.06	.05	.02
206	Tracy Jones	.04	.03	.02
207	Von Hayes	.06	.05	.02
208	Bob Melvin	.04	.03	.02
209	Scott Scudder	.05	.04	.02
210	Luis Gonzalez	.08	.06	.03
211	Scott Sanderson	.05	.04	.02
212	*Chris Donnels*	.05	.04	.02
213	*Heath Slocumb*	.08	.06	.03
214	Mike Timlin	.12	.09	.05
215	Brian Harper	.06	.05	.02
216	Juan Berenguer	.04	.03	.02
217	Mike Henneman	.06	.05	.02
218	Bill Spiers	.04	.03	.02
219	Scott Terry	.04	.03	.02
220	Frank Viola	.12	.09	.05
221	Mark Eichhorn	.04	.03	.02
222	Ernest Riles	.04	.03	.02
223	Ray Lankford	.10	.08	.04
224	Pete Harnisch	.06	.05	.02
225	Bobby Bonilla	.12	.09	.05
226	Mike Scioscia	.05	.04	.02
227	Joel Skinner	.04	.03	.02
228	Brian Holman	.05	.04	.02
229	Gilberto Reyes(FC)	.06	.05	.02
230	Matt Williams	.15	.11	.06
231	Jaime Navarro	.06	.05	.02
232	Jose Rijo	.08	.06	.03
233	Atlee Hammaker	.04	.03	.02
234	Tim Teufel	.04	.03	.02
235	John Kruk	.08	.06	.03
236	Kurt Stillwell	.05	.04	.02
237	Dan Pasqua	.05	.04	.02
238	Tim Crews	.04	.03	.02
239	Dave Gallagher	.05	.04	.02
240	Leo Gomez	.08	.06	.03
241	Steve Avery	.25	.20	.10
242	Bill Gullickson	.06	.05	.02
243	Mark Portugal	.04	.03	.02
244	Lee Guetterman	.04	.03	.02
245	Benny Santiago	.08	.06	.03
246	Jim Gantner	.04	.03	.02
247	Robby Thompson	.05	.04	.02
248	Terry Shumpert	.04	.03	.02
249	*Mike Bell*(FC)	.15	.11	.06
250	Harold Reynolds	.06	.05	.02
251	Mike Felder	.04	.03	.02
252	Bill Pecota	.04	.03	.02
253	Bill Krueger	.04	.03	.02
254	Alfredo Griffin	.04	.03	.02
255	Lou Whitaker	.08	.06	.03
256	Roy Smith	.04	.03	.02
257	Jerald Clark	.05	.04	.02
258	Sammy Sosa	.08	.06	.03
259	Tim Naehring	.10	.08	.04
260	Dave Righetti	.08	.06	.03
261	Paul Gibson	.04	.03	.02
262	Chris James	.05	.04	.02
263	Larry Andersen	.04	.03	.02
264	Storm Davis	.05	.04	.02
265	Jose Lind	.04	.03	.02
266	Greg Hibbard	.06	.05	.02
267	Norm Charlton	.06	.05	.02
268	Paul Kilgus	.04	.03	.02
269	Greg Maddux	.06	.05	.02
270	Ellis Burks	.12	.09	.05
271	Frank Tanana	.05	.04	.02
272	Gene Larkin	.05	.04	.02
273	Ron Hassey	.04	.03	.02
274	Jeff Robinson	.04	.03	.02
275	Steve Howe	.05	.04	.02
276	Daryl Boston	.04	.03	.02
277	Mark Lee	.04	.03	.02
278	*Jose Segura*(FC)	.12	.09	.05
279	Lance Blankenship	.04	.03	.02
280	Don Slaught	.04	.03	.02
281	Russ Swan	.08	.06	.03
282	Bob Tewksbury	.04	.03	.02
283	Geno Petralli	.04	.03	.02
284	Shane Mack	.08	.06	.03
285	Bob Scanlan	.10	.08	.04
286	Tim Leary	.05	.04	.02
287	John Smoltz	.15	.11	.06
288	Pat Borders	.05	.04	.02
289	Mark Davidson	.04	.03	.02
290	Sam Horn	.06	.05	.02
291	Lenny Harris	.05	.04	.02
292	Franklin Stubbs	.04	.03	.02
293	Thomas Howard	.05	.04	.02
294	Steve Lyons	.04	.03	.02
295	Francisco Oliveras	.04	.03	.02
296	Terry Leach	.04	.03	.02

		MT	NR MT	EX
297	Barry Jones	.04	.03	.02
298	Lance Parrish	.08	.06	.03
299	Wally Whitehurst	.06	.05	.02
300	Bob Welch	.06	.05	.02
301	Charlie Hayes	.05	.04	.02
302	Charlie Hough	.05	.04	.02
303	Gary Redus	.04	.03	.02
304	Scott Bradley	.04	.03	.02
305	Jose Oquendo	.04	.03	.02
306	Pete Incaviglia	.06	.05	.02
307	Marvin Freeman	.04	.03	.02
308	Gary Pettis	.04	.03	.02
309	Joe Slusarski	.10	.08	.04
310	Kevin Seitzer	.05	.04	.02
311	Jeff Reed	.04	.03	.02
312	Pat Tabler	.04	.03	.02
313	Mike Maddux	.04	.03	.02
314	Bob Milacki	.04	.03	.02
315	Eric Anthony	.10	.08	.04
316	Dante Bichette	.05	.04	.02
317	Steve Decker	.10	.08	.04
318	Jack Clark	.08	.06	.03
319	Doug Dascenzo	.04	.03	.02
320	Scott Leius	.10	.08	.04
321	Jim Lindeman	.04	.03	.02
322	Bryan Harvey	.08	.06	.03
323	Spike Owen	.04	.03	.02
324	Roberto Kelly	.10	.08	.04
325	Stan Belinda	.05	.04	.02
326	Joey Cora	.04	.03	.02
327	Jeff Innis	.04	.03	.02
328	Willie Wilson	.05	.04	.02
329	Juan Agosto	.04	.03	.02
330	Charles Nagy	.10	.08	.04
331	Scott Bailes	.04	.03	.02
332	*Pete Schourek*	.08	.06	.03
333	Mike Flanagan	.04	.03	.02
334	Omar Olivares	.10	.08	.04
335	Dennis Lamp	.04	.03	.02
336	Tommy Greene	.06	.05	.02
337	Randy Velarde	.04	.03	.02
338	Tom Lampkin	.04	.03	.02
339	John Russell	.04	.03	.02
340	Bob Kipper	.04	.03	.02
341	Todd Burns	.04	.03	.02
342	Ron Jones	.05	.04	.02
343	Dave Valle	.04	.03	.02
344	Mike Heath	.04	.03	.02
345	John Olerud	.25	.20	.10
346	Gerald Young	.04	.03	.02
347	Ken Patterson	.04	.03	.02
348	Les Lancaster	.04	.03	.02
349	Steve Crawford	.04	.03	.02
350	John Candelaria	.04	.03	.02
351	Mike Aldrete	.04	.03	.02
352	Mariano Duncan	.05	.04	.02
353	Julio Machado	.04	.03	.02
354	Ken Williams	.04	.03	.02
355	Walt Terrell	.04	.03	.02
356	Mitch Williams	.08	.06	.03
357	Al Newman	.04	.03	.02
358	Bud Black	.05	.04	.02
359	Joe Hesketh	.04	.03	.02
360	Paul Assenmacher	.05	.04	.02
361	Bo Jackson	.25	.20	.10
362	Jeff Blauser	.04	.03	.02
363	Mike Brumley	.04	.03	.02
364	Jim Deshaies	.04	.03	.02
365	Brady Anderson	.04	.03	.02
366	Chuck McElroy	.04	.03	.02
367	Matt Merullo	.04	.03	.02
368	Tim Belcher	.06	.05	.02
369	Luis Aquino	.04	.03	.02
370	Joe Oliver	.05	.04	.02
371	Greg Swindell	.08	.06	.03
372	Lee Stevens	.10	.08	.04
373	Mark Knudson	.04	.03	.02
374	Bill Wegman	.05	.04	.02
375	Jerry Don Gleaton	.04	.03	.02
376	Pedro Guerrero	.10	.08	.04
377	Randy Bush	.04	.03	.02
378	Greg Harris	.04	.03	.02
379	Eric Plunk	.04	.03	.02
380	Jose DeJesus	.08	.06	.03
381	Bobby Witt	.06	.05	.02
382	Curtis Wilkerson	.04	.03	.02
383	Gene Nelson	.04	.03	.02
384	Wes Chamberlain	.10	.08	.04
385	Tom Henke	.06	.05	.02
386	Mark Lemke	.06	.05	.02
387	Greg Briley	.04	.03	.02
388	Rafael Ramirez	.04	.03	.02
389	Tony Fossas	.04	.03	.02
390	Henry Cotto	.04	.03	.02
391	Tim Hulett	.04	.03	.02
392	Dean Palmer	.25	.20	.10
393	Glenn Braggs	.05	.04	.02
394	Mark Salas	.04	.03	.02
395	*Rusty Meacham*(FC)	.08	.06	.03
396	*Andy Ashby*(FC)	.08	.06	.03
397	*Jose Melendez*(FC)	.10	.08	.04
398	*Warren Newson*(FC)	.08	.06	.03
399	*Frank Castillo*(FC)	.15	.11	.06
400	*Chito Martinez*(FC)	.10	.08	.04
401	Bernie Williams	.10	.08	.04
402	Derek Bell(FC)	.12	.09	.05
403	*Javier Ortiz*(FC)	.10	.08	.04
404	*Tim Sherrill*(FC)	.08	.06	.03
405	*Rob MacDonald*(FC)	.10	.08	.04
406	Phil Plantier	.15	.11	.06
407	Troy Afenir	.10	.08	.04
408	*Gino Minutelli*(FC)	.10	.08	.04
409	*Reggie Jefferson*(FC)	.10	.08	.04
410	*Mike Remlinger*(FC)	.15	.11	.06
411	*Carlos Rodriguez*(FC)	.10	.08	.04
412	*Joe Redfield*(FC)	.20	.15	.08
413	Alonzo Powell(FC)	.08	.06	.03
414	*Scott Livingstone*(FC)	.08	.06	.03
415	*Scott Kamieniecki*(FC)	.08	.06	.03
416	*Tim Spehr*(FC)	.10	.08	.04
417	*Brian Hunter*(FC)	.10	.08	.04
418	*Ced Landrum*(FC)	.10	.08	.04
419	*Bret Barberie*(FC)	.08	.06	.03
420	Kevin Morton(FC)	.08	.06	.03
421	*Doug Henry*(FC)	.10	.08	.04
422	*Doug Piatt*(FC)	.08	.06	.03
423	*Pat Rice*(FC)	.15	.11	.06
424	*Juan Guzman*(FC)	.20	.15	.08
425	Nolan Ryan (No-Hit)	.30	.25	.12
426	Tommy Greene (No-Hit)	.10	.08	.04
427	Bob Milacki, Mike Flanagan, Mark Williamson, Gregg Olson (No-Hit)	.10	.08	.04
428	Wilson Alvarez (No-Hit)	.08	.06	.03
429	Otis Nixon (Highlight)	.08	.06	.03
430	Rickey Henderson (Highlight)	.10	.08	.04
431	Cecil Fielder (AS)	.10	.08	.04
432	Julio Franco (AS)	.08	.06	.03
433	Cal Ripken, Jr. (AS)	.15	.11	.06
434	Wade Boggs (AS)	.10	.08	.04
435	Joe Carter (AS)	.10	.08	.04
436	Ken Griffey, Jr. (AS)	.40	.30	.15
437	Ruben Sierra (AS)	.10	.08	.04
438	Scott Erickson (AS)	.15	.11	.06
439	Tom Henke (AS)	.05	.04	.02
440	Terry Steinbach (AS)	.05	.04	.02
441	Rickey Henderson (Dream Team)	.25	.20	.10
442	Ryne Sandberg (Dream Team)	.35	.25	.14
443	Otis Nixon	.06	.05	.02
444	Scott Radinsky	.04	.03	.02
445	Mark Grace	.08	.06	.03
446	Tony Pena	.06	.05	.02
447	Billy Hatcher	.04	.03	.02
448	Glenallen Hill	.06	.05	.02
449	Chris Gwynn	.04	.03	.02
450	Tom Glavine	.08	.06	.03
451	John Habyan	.04	.03	.02
452	Al Osuna	.04	.03	.02
453	Tony Phillips	.06	.05	.02
454	Greg Cadaret	.04	.03	.02
455	Rob Dibble	.08	.06	.03
456	Rick Honeycutt	.04	.03	.02
457	Jerome Walton	.04	.03	.02
458	Mookie Wilson	.04	.03	.02
459	Mark Gubicza	.04	.03	.02
460	Craig Biggio	.08	.06	.03
461	Dave Cochrane	.04	.03	.02
462	Keith Miller	.04	.03	.02
463	Alex Cole	.06	.05	.02
464	Pete Smith	.04	.03	.02
465	Brett Butler	.06	.05	.02
466	Jeff Huson	.04	.03	.02
467	Steve Lake	.04	.03	.02
468	Lloyd Moseby	.04	.03	.02
469	Tim McIntosh	.04	.03	.02
470	Dennis Martinez	.06	.05	.02
471	Greg Myers	.04	.03	.02
472	Mackey Sasser	.04	.03	.02
473	Junior Ortiz	.04	.03	.02
474	Greg Olson	.04	.03	.02
475	Steve Sax	.06	.05	.02
476	Ricky Jordan	.06	.05	.02
477	Max Venable	.04	.03	.02

		MT	NR MT	EX
478	Brian McRae	.10	.08	.04
479	Doug Simons	.04	.03	.02
480	Rickey Henderson	.15	.11	.06
481	Gary Varsho	.04	.03	.02
482	Carl Willis	.04	.03	.02
483	*Rick Wilkins*	.10	.08	.04
484	Donn Pall	.04	.03	.02
485	Edgar Martinez	.08	.06	.03
486	Tom Foley	.08	.06	.03
487	Mark Williamson	.08	.06	.03
488	Jack Armstrong	.08	.06	.03
489	Gary Carter	.08	.06	.03
490	Ruben Sierra	.15	.11	.06
491	Gerald Perry	.04	.03	.02
492	Rob Murphy	.04	.03	.02
493	Zane Smith	.04	.03	.02
494	*Darryl Kile*	.10	.08	.04
495	Kelly Gruber	.06	.05	.02
496	Jerry Browne	.04	.03	.02
497	Darryl Hamilton	.06	.05	.02
498	Mike Stanton	.04	.03	.02
499	Mark Leonard	.04	.03	.02
500	Jose Canseco	.12	.09	.05
501	Dave Martinez	.04	.03	.02
502	Jose Guzman	.04	.03	.02
503	Terry Kennedy	.04	.03	.02
504	*Ed Sprague*	.08	.06	.03
505	Frank Thomas	1.00	.70	.40
506	Darren Daulton	.06	.05	.02
507	Kevin Tapani	.06	.05	.02
508	Luis Salazar	.04	.03	.02
509	Paul Faries	.04	.03	.02
510	Sandy Alomar, Jr.	.08	.06	.03
511	Jeff King	.04	.03	.02
512	Gary Thurman	.04	.03	.02
513	Chris Hammond	.06	.05	.02
514	*Pedro Munoz*	.15	.11	.06
515	Alan Trammell	.08	.06	.03
516	Geronimo Pena	.06	.05	.02
517	Rodney McCray	.04	.03	.02
518	Manny Lee	.04	.03	.02
519	Junior Felix	.06	.05	.02
520	Kirk Gibson	.06	.05	.02
521	Darrin Jackson	.06	.05	.02
522	John Burkett	.06	.05	.02
523	Jeff Johnson	.06	.05	.02
524	Jim Corsi	.04	.03	.02
525	Robin Yount	.12	.09	.05
526	Jamie Quirk	.04	.03	.02
527	Bob Ojeda	.04	.03	.02
528	Mark Lewis	.10	.08	.04
529	Bryn Smith	.04	.03	.02
530	Kent Hrbek	.06	.05	.02
531	Dennis Boyd	.04	.03	.02
532	Ron Karkovice	.04	.03	.02
533	Don August	.04	.03	.02
534	Todd Frohwirth	.04	.03	.02
535	Wally Joyner	.08	.06	.03
536	Dennis Rasmussen	.04	.03	.02
537	Andy Allanson	.04	.03	.02
538	Rich Gossage	.04	.03	.02
539	John Marzano	.04	.03	.02
540	Cal Ripken, Jr.	.20	.15	.08
541	Bill Swift	.06	.05	.02
542	Kevin Appier	.06	.05	.02
543	Dave Bergman	.04	.03	.02
544	Bernard Gilkey	.10	.08	.04
545	Mike Greenwell	.08	.06	.03
546	Jose Uribe	.04	.03	.02
547	Jesse Orosco	.04	.03	.02
548	Bob Patterson	.04	.03	.02
549	Mike Stanley	.04	.03	.02
550	Howard Johnson	.08	.06	.03
551	Joe Orsulak	.04	.03	.02
552	Dick Schofield	.04	.03	.02
553	Dave Hollins	.08	.06	.03
554	David Segui	.06	.05	.02
555	Barry Bonds	.30	.25	.12
556	Mo Vaughn	.20	.15	.08
557	Craig Wilson	.06	.05	.02
558	Bobby Rose	.04	.03	.02
559	Rod Nichols	.04	.03	.02
560	Len Dykstra	.12	.09	.05
561	Craig Grebeck	.04	.03	.02
562	Darren Lewis	.10	.08	.04
563	Todd Benzinger	.04	.03	.02
564	Ed Whitson	.04	.03	.02
565	Jesse Barfield	.04	.03	.02
566	Lloyd McClendon	.04	.03	.02
567	Dan Plesac	.04	.03	.02
568	Danny Cox	.04	.03	.02
569	Skeeter Barnes	.04	.03	.02
570	Bobby Thigpen	.08	.06	.03
571	Deion Sanders	.10	.08	.04
572	Chuck Knoblauch	.10	.08	.04
573	Matt Nokes	.06	.05	.02
574	Herm Winningham	.04	.03	.02
575	Tom Candiotti	.06	.05	.02
576	*Jeff Bagwell*	.25	.20	.10
577	Brook Jacoby	.04	.03	.02
578	Chico Walker	.04	.03	.02
579	Brian Downing	.04	.03	.02
580	Dave Stewart	.06	.05	.02
581	Francisco Cabrera	.04	.03	.02
582	Rene Gonzales	.04	.03	.02
583	Stan Javier	.04	.03	.02
584	Randy Johnson	.06	.05	.02
585	Chuck Finley	.06	.05	.02
586	Mark Gardner	.04	.03	.02
587	Mark Whiten	.10	.08	.04
588	Garry Templeton	.04	.03	.02
589	Gary Sheffield	.20	.15	.08
590	Ozzie Smith	.08	.06	.03
591	Candy Maldonado	.04	.03	.02
592	Mike Sharperson	.04	.03	.02
593	Carlos Martinez	.04	.03	.02
594	Scott Bankhead	.04	.03	.02
595	Tim Wallach	.06	.05	.02
596	Tino Martinez	.08	.06	.03
597	Roger McDowell	.04	.03	.02
598	Cory Snyder	.06	.05	.02
599	Andujar Cedeno	.10	.08	.04
600	Kirby Puckett	.15	.11	.06
601	Rick Parker	.04	.03	.02
602	Todd Hundley	.08	.06	.03
603	Greg Litton	.04	.03	.02
604	Dave Johnson	.04	.03	.02
605	John Franco	.04	.03	.02
606	Mike Fetters	.04	.03	.02
607	Luis Alicea	.04	.03	.02
608	Trevor Wilson	.04	.03	.02
609	Rob Ducey	.04	.03	.02
610	Ramon Martinez	.08	.06	.03
611	Dave Burba	.04	.03	.02
612	Dwight Smith	.04	.03	.02
613	Kevin Maas	.08	.06	.03
614	John Costello	.04	.03	.02
615	Glenn Davis	.06	.05	.02
616	Shawn Abner	.04	.03	.02
617	Scott Hemond	.04	.03	.02
618	Tom Prince	.04	.03	.02
619	Wally Ritchie	.04	.03	.02
620	Jim Abbott	.08	.06	.03
621	Charlie O'Brien	.04	.03	.02
622	Jack Daugherty	.04	.03	.02
623	Tommy Gregg	.04	.03	.02
624	Jeff Shaw	.04	.03	.02
625	Tony Gwynn	.15	.11	.06
626	Mark Leiter	.04	.03	.02
627	Jim Clancy	.04	.03	.02
628	Tim Layana	.04	.03	.02
629	Jeff Schaefer	.04	.03	.02
630	Lee Smith	.06	.05	.02
631	Wade Taylor	.06	.05	.02
632	Mike Simms	.06	.05	.02
633	Terry Steinbach	.04	.03	.02
634	Shawon Dunston	.06	.05	.02
635	Tim Raines	.06	.05	.02
636	Kirt Manwaring	.04	.03	.02
637	Warren Cromartie	.04	.03	.02
638	Luis Quinones	.04	.03	.02
639	Greg Vaughn	.08	.06	.03
640	Kevin Mitchell	.08	.06	.03
641	Chris Hoiles	.10	.08	.04
642	Tom Browning	.04	.03	.02
643	Mitch Webster	.04	.03	.02
644	Steve Olin	.06	.05	.02
645	Tony Fernandez	.06	.05	.02
646	Juan Bell	.04	.03	.02
647	Joe Boever	.04	.03	.02
648	Carney Lansford	.06	.05	.02
649	Mike Benjamin	.04	.03	.02
650	George Brett	.12	.09	.05
651	Tim Burke	.04	.03	.02
652	Jack Morris	.06	.05	.02
653	Orel Hershiser	.06	.05	.02
654	Mike Schooler	.04	.03	.02
655	Andy Van Slyke	.08	.06	.03
656	Dave Stieb	.06	.05	.02
657	Dave Clark	.04	.03	.02
658	Ben McDonald	.10	.08	.04
659	John Smiley	.06	.05	.02

		MT	NR MT	EX
660	Wade Boggs	.12	.09	.05
661	Eric Bullock	.04	.03	.02
662	Eric Show	.04	.03	.02
663	Lenny Webster	.06	.05	.02
664	Mike Huff	.04	.03	.02
665	Rick Sutcliffe	.06	.05	.02
666	Jeff Manto	.04	.03	.02
667	Mike Fitzgerald	.04	.03	.02
668	Matt Young	.04	.03	.02
669	Dave West	.04	.03	.02
670	Mike Hartley	.04	.03	.02
671	Curt Schilling	.06	.05	.02
672	Brian Bohanon	.04	.03	.02
673	Cecil Espy	.04	.03	.02
674	Joe Grahe	.04	.03	.02
675	Sid Fernandez	.06	.05	.02
676	Edwin Nunez	.04	.03	.02
677	Hector Villanueva	.04	.03	.02
678	Sean Berry	.06	.05	.02
679	Dave Eiland	.04	.03	.02
680	David Cone	.08	.06	.03
681	Mike Bordick	.06	.05	.02
682	Tony Castillo	.04	.03	.02
683	John Barfield	.04	.03	.02
684	Jeff Hamilton	.04	.03	.02
685	Ken Dayley	.04	.03	.02
686	Carmelo Martinez	.04	.03	.02
687	Mike Capel	.04	.03	.02
688	Scott Chiamparino	.04	.03	.02
689	Rich Gedman	.04	.03	.02
690	Rich Monteleone	.04	.03	.02
691	Alejandro Pena	.04	.03	.02
692	Oscar Azocar	.04	.03	.02
693	Jim Poole	.04	.03	.02
694	Mike Gardiner	.04	.03	.02
695	Steve Buechele	.04	.03	.02
696	Rudy Seanez	.04	.03	.02
697	Paul Abbott	.04	.03	.02
698	Steve Searcy	.04	.03	.02
699	Jose Offerman	.06	.05	.02
700	*Ivan Rodriguez*	.30	.25	.12
701	Joe Girardi	.04	.03	.02
702	Tony Perezchica	.04	.03	.02
703	Paul McClellan	.05	.04	.02
704	*David Howard*	.06	.05	.02
705	Dan Petry	.04	.03	.02
706	Jack Howell	.04	.03	.02
707	Jose Mesa	.04	.03	.02
708	Randy St. Claire	.04	.03	.02
709	Kevin Brown	.06	.05	.02
710	Ron Darling	.06	.05	.02
711	Jason Grimsley	.04	.03	.02
712	John Orton	.04	.03	.02
713	Shawn Boskie	.04	.03	.02
714	Pat Clements	.04	.03	.02
715	Brian Barnes	.06	.05	.02
716	*Luis Lopez*(FC)	.08	.06	.03
717	Bob McClure	.04	.03	.02
718	Mark Davis	.04	.03	.02
719	Dann Billardello	.04	.03	.02
720	Tom Edens	.04	.03	.02
721	Willie Fraser	.04	.03	.02
722	Curt Young	.04	.03	.02
723	Neal Heaton	.04	.03	.02
724	Craig Worthington	.04	.03	.02
725	Mel Rojas	.04	.03	.02
726	Daryl Irvine	.04	.03	.02
727	Roger Mason	.04	.03	.02
728	Kirk Dressendorfer	.08	.06	.03
729	Scott Aldred	.04	.03	.02
730	Willie Blair	.04	.03	.02
731	Allan Anderson	.04	.03	.02
732	Dana Kiecker	.04	.03	.02
733	Jose Gonzalez	.04	.03	.02
734	Brian Drahman	.04	.03	.02
735	Brad Komminsk	.04	.03	.02
736	*Arthur Rhodes*(FC)	.15	.11	.06
737	*Terry Mathews*(FC)	.10	.08	.04
738	*Jeff Fassero*(FC)	.08	.06	.03
739	*Mike Magnante*(FC)	.08	.06	.03
740	*Kip Gross*(FC)	.08	.06	.03
741	*Jim Hunter*(FC)	.06	.05	.02
742	*Jose Mota*(FC)	.08	.06	.03
743	Joe Bitker	.04	.03	.02
744	*Tim Mauser*(FC)	.08	.06	.03
745	*Ramon Garcia*(FC)	.08	.06	.03
746	*Rod Beck*(FC)	.10	.08	.04
747	*Jim Austin*(FC)	.08	.06	.03
748	*Keith Mitchell*(FC)	.10	.08	.04
749	*Wayne Rosenthal*(FC)	.06	.05	.02
750	*Bryan Hickerson*(FC)	.08	.06	.03

		MT	NR MT	EX
751	*Bruce Egloff*(FC)	.08	.06	.03
752	*John Wehner*(FC)	.08	.06	.03
753	Darren Holmes(FC)	.05	.04	.02
754	Dave Hansen	.06	.05	.02
755	Mike Mussina(FC)	.20	.15	.08
756	*Anthony Young*(FC)	.10	.08	.04
757	Ron Tingley	.04	.03	.02
758	*Ricky Bones*(FC)	.10	.08	.04
759	*Mark Wohlers*(FC)	.10	.08	.04
760	Wilson Alvarez(FC)	.08	.06	.03
761	*Harvey Pulliam*(FC)	.08	.06	.03
762	*Ryan Bowen*(FC)	.10	.08	.04
763	Terry Bross(FC)	.04	.03	.02
764	*Joel Johnston*(FC)	.08	.06	.03
765	*Terry McDaniel*(FC)	.10	.08	.04
766	*Esteban Beltre*(FC)	.08	.06	.03
767	*Rob Maurer*(FC)	.10	.08	.04
768	Ted Wood	.10	.08	.04
769	*Mo Sanford*(FC)	.10	.08	.04
770	*Jeff Carter*(FC)	.08	.06	.03
771	*Gil Heredia*(FC)	.08	.06	.03
772	Monty Fariss(FC)	.08	.06	.03
773	Will Clark (AS)	.10	.08	.04
774	Ryne Sandberg (AS)	.10	.08	.04
775	Barry Larkin (AS)	.08	.06	.03
776	Howard Johnson (AS)	.08	.06	.03
777	Barry Bonds (AS)	.15	.11	.06
778	Brett Butler (AS)	.06	.05	.02
779	Tony Gwynn (AS)	.10	.08	.04
780	Ramon Martinez (AS)	.06	.05	.02
781	Lee Smith (AS)	.06	.05	.02
782	Mike Scioscia (AS)	.04	.03	.02
783	Dennis Martinez (Highlight)	.04	.03	.02
784	Dennis Martinez (No-Hit)	.04	.03	.02
785	Mark Gardner (No-Hit)	.04	.03	.02
786	Bret Saberhagen (No-Hit)	.06	.05	.02
787	Kent Mercker, Mark Wohlers, Alejandro Pena (No-Hit)	.06	.05	.02
788	Cal Ripken (MVP)	.10	.08	.04
789	Terry Pendleton (MVP)	.08	.06	.03
790	Roger Clemens (CY)	.10	.08	.04
791	Tom Glavine (CY)	.08	.06	.03
792	Chuck Knoblauch (ROY)	.10	.08	.04
793	Jeff Bagwell (ROY)	.15	.11	.06
794	Cal Ripken, Jr. (Man of the Year)	.08	.06	.03
795	David Cone (Highlight)	.06	.05	.02
796	Kirby Puckett (Highlight)	.08	.06	.03
797	Steve Avery (Highlight)	.10	.08	.04
798	Jack Morris (Highlight)	.06	.05	.02
799	*Allen Watson*(FC)	.50	.40	.20
800	*Manny Ramirez*(FC)	1.00	.70	.40
801	Cliff Floyd	2.50	2.00	1.00
802	*Al Shirley*(FC)	.10	.08	.04
803	*Brian Barber*(FC)	.20	.15	.08
804	*John Farrell*(FC)	.20	.15	.08
805	*Brent Gates*(FC)	.50	.40	.20
806	*Scott Ruffcorn*(FC)	.20	.15	.08
807	*Tyrone Hill*(FC)	.30	.25	.12
808	*Benji Gill*(FC)	.30	.25	.12
809	*Aaron Sele*(FC)	1.25	.90	.50
810	*Tyler Green*(FC)	.30	.25	.12
811	Chris Jones	.04	.03	.02
812	Steve Wilson	.04	.03	.02
813	*Cliff Young*	.08	.06	.03
814	*Don Wakamatsu*	.08	.06	.03
815	*Mike Humphreys*	.08	.06	.03
816	*Scott Servais*	.08	.06	.03
817	*Rico Rossy*	.08	.06	.03
818	*John Ramos*	.08	.06	.03
819	Rob Mallicoat	.06	.05	.02
820	*Milt Hill*	.08	.06	.03
821	Carlos Carcia	.06	.05	.02
822	Stan Royer	.06	.05	.02
823	*Jeff Plympton*(FC)	.15	.11	.06
824	*Braulio Castillo*(FC)	.20	.15	.08
825	*David Haas*(FC)	.08	.06	.03
826	*Luis Mercedes*(FC)	.10	.08	.04
827	*Eric Karros*(FC)	.25	.20	.10
828	*Shawn Hare*(FC)	.10	.08	.04
829	*Reggie Sanders*(FC)	.30	.25	.12
830	Tom Goodwin	.10	.08	.04
831	*Dan Gakeler*(FC)	.08	.06	.03
832	*Stacy Jones*(FC)	.08	.06	.03
833	*Kim Batiste*	.08	.06	.03
834	Cal Eldred	.08	.06	.03
835	*Chris George*(FC)	.10	.08	.04
836	*Wayne Housie*(FC)	.10	.08	.04
837	*Mike Ignasiak*(FC)	.10	.08	.04
838	*Josias Manzanillo*(FC)	.10	.08	.04
839	*Jim Olander*(FC)	.10	.08	.04
840	*Gary Cooper*(FC)	.10	.08	.04

		MT	NR MT	EX
841	*Royce Clayton*(FC)	.20	.15	.08
842	*Hector Fajardo*(FC)	.20	.15	.08
843	Blaine Beatty	.04	.03	.02
844	*Jorge Pedre*(FC)	.10	.08	.04
845	*Kenny Lofton*(FC)	.40	.30	.15
846	*Scott Brosius*(FC)	.08	.06	.03
847	*Chris Cron*(FC)	.08	.06	.03
848	Denis Boucher	.06	.05	.02
849	Kyle Abbott	.10	.08	.04
850	*Bob Zupcic*(FC)	.30	.25	.12
851	*Rheal Cormier*(FC)	.15	.11	.06
852	*Jim Lewis*(FC)	.08	.06	.03
853	Anthony Telford	.04	.03	.02
854	*Cliff Brantley*(FC)	.10	.08	.04
855	*Kevin Campbell*(FC)	.10	.08	.04
856	*Craig Shipley*(FC)	.08	.06	.03
857	Chuck Carr	.04	.03	.02
858	*Tony Eusebio*(FC)	.10	.08	.04
859	*Jim Thome*(FC)	.20	.15	.08
860	*Vinny Castilla*(FC)	.10	.08	.04
861	Dann Howitt	.04	.03	.02
862	*Kevin Ward*(FC)	.10	.08	.04
863	*Steve Wapnick*(FC)	.08	.06	.03
864	Rod Brewer	.08	.06	.03
865	Todd Van Poppel	.20	.15	.08
866	*Jose Hernandez*(FC)	.10	.08	.04
867	*Amalio Carreno*(FC)	.10	.08	.04
868	*Calvin Jones*(FC)	.10	.08	.04
869	*Jeff Gardner*(FC)	.10	.08	.04
870	*Jarvis Brown*(FC)	.10	.08	.04
871	*Eddie Taubensee*(FC)	.20	.15	.08
872	*Andy Mota*(FC)	.08	.06	.03
873	Chris Haney	.06	.05	.02
874	Roberto Hernandez	.10	.08	.04
875	*Laddie Renfroe*(FC)	.10	.08	.04
876	Scott Cooper	.08	.06	.03
877	*Armando Reynoso*(FC)	.10	.08	.04
878	Ty Cobb (Memorabilia)	.30	.25	.12
879	Babe Ruth (Memorabilia)	.40	.30	.15
880	Honus Wagner (Memorabilia)	.20	.15	.08
881	Lou Gehrig (Memorabilia)	.30	.25	.12
882	Satchel Paige (Memorabilia)	.20	.15	.08
883	Will Clark (Dream Team)	.20	.15	.08
884	Cal Ripken, Jr. (Dream Team)	.30	.25	.12
885	Wade Boggs (Dream Team)	.20	.15	.08
886	Kirby Puckett (Dream Team)	.20	.15	.08
887	Tony Gwynn (Dream Team)	.20	.15	.08
889	Scott Erickson (Dream Team)	.08	.06	.03
890	Tom Glavine (Dream Team)	.15	.11	.06
891	Rob Dibble (Dream Team)	.08	.06	.03
892	Mitch Williams (Dream Team)	.06	.05	.02
893	Frank Thomas (Dream Team)	.80	.60	.30

1992 Score Joe DiMaggio

Photos not available at press time

Colorized vintage photos are featured on the front and back of each of five Joe DiMaggio tribute cards which were issued as random inserts in 1992 Score Series I packs. A limited number of each card were autographed.

	MT	NR MT	EX
Complete Set (5):	100.00	75.00	40.00
Common Card:	20.00	15.00	8.00
Autographed Card:	450.00	350.00	175.00

		MT	NR MT	EX
1	The Minors (Joe DiMaggio)	20.00	15.00	8.00
2	The Rookie (Joe DiMaggio)	20.00	15.00	8.00
3	The MVP (Joe DiMaggio)	20.00	15.00	8.00
4	The Streak (Joe DiMaggio)	20.00	15.00	8.00
5	The Legend (Joe DiMaggio)	20.00	15.00	8.00

1992 Score Factory Inserts

Photos not available at press time

Available exclusively in factory sets these 17 cards are divided into four subsets commemorating the 1991 World Series, potential future Hall of Famers, the career of Joe DiMaggio and Carl Yastrzemski's 1967 Triple Crown season. Cards carry a "B" prefix to the card number.

	MT	NR MT	EX
Complete Set (17):	12.00	9.00	4.75
Common World Series (1-7):	.20	.15	.08
Common Cooperstown (8-11):	1.00	.70	.40
Common DiMaggio (12-14):	1.25	.90	.50
Common Yastrzemski (15-17):	.60	.45	.25

		MT	NR MT	EX
1	World Series Game 1 (Greg Gagne)	.20	.15	.08
2	World Series Game 2 (Scott Leius)	.20	.15	.08
3	World Series Game 3 (Mark Lemke)	.20	.15	.08
4	World Series Game 4 (Lonnie Smith/ Brian Harper)	.20	.15	.08
5	World Series Game 5 (David Justice)	2.00	1.50	.80
6	World Series Game 6 (Kirby Puckett)	2.00	1.50	.80
7	World Series Game 7 (Gene Larkin)	.20	.15	.08
8	Carlton Fisk (Cooperstown)	1.00	.70	.40
9	Ozzie Smith (Cooperstown)	1.50	1.25	.60
10	Dave Winfield (Cooperstown)	2.00	1.50	.80
11	Robin Yount (Cooperstown)	2.50	2.00	1.00
12	The Hard Hitter (Joe DiMaggio)	1.25	.90	.50
13	The Stylish Fielder (Joe DiMaggio)	1.25	.90	.50
14	The Champion Player (Joe DiMaggio)	1.25	.90	.50
15	The Impossible Dream (Carl Yastrzemski)	.60	.45	.25
16	The Triple Crown (Carl Yastrzemski)	.60	.45	.25
17	The World Series (Carl Yastrzemski)	.60	.45	.25

1992 Score The Franchise

This four-card set, in both autographed and unautographed form, was a random insert in various premium packaging of Score's 1992 Series II cards. Each of the four cards was produced in an edition of 150,000, with 2,000 of each play's card being autographed and 500 of the triple-player card carrying the autographs of all three superstars.

	MT	NR MT	EX
Complete set (4):	30.00	22.50	12.00
Common player:	8.00	6.00	3.25
Musial autograph:	250.00	175.00	100.00
Mantle autograph:	500.00	375.00	200.00

Yastrzemski autograph:		150.00	110.00	60.00
Triple autograph:		1000.00	750.00	400.00
1	Stan Musial	8.00	6.00	3.25
2	Mickey Mantle	12.00	9.00	4.75
3	Carl Yastrzemski	8.00	6.00	3.25
4	Musial/Mantle/ Yastrzemski	9.00	6.75	3.50

1992 Score Hot Rookies

Photos not available at press time

This 10-card rookie issue was produced as an insert in special blister packs of 1992 Score cards sold at retail outlets. Action photos on front and portraits on back are set against white backgrounds with orange highlights. Cards are standard 2-1/2" x 3-1/2".

		MT	NR MT	EX
Complete Set (10):		10.00	7.50	4.00
Common Player:		.30	.25	.12
1	Cal Eldred	2.00	1.50	.75
2	Royce Clayton	1.50	1.00	.60
3	Kenny Lofton	4.00	3.00	1.50
4	Todd Van Poppel	1.50	1.00	.60
5	Scott Cooper	1.25	.95	.50
6	Todd Hundley	.30	.25	.12
7	Tino Martinez	.30	.25	.12
8	Anthony Telford	.30	.25	.12
9	Derek Bell	1.00	.75	.40
10	Reggie Jefferson	1.00	.75	.40

1992 Score Impact Players

Jumbo packs of 1992 Score Series I and II cards contained five of these special inserts labeled "90's Impact Players". The designation and the player's name and position are printed on team color-coated stripes at the left and bottom of the card front, along with a team logo. Front action photos contrast with portrait photos on the backs, which are again color-coded by team. Cards #1-

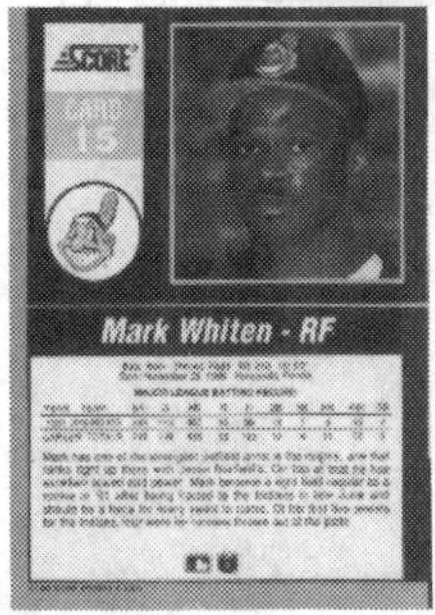

45 were packaged with Series I, cards 46-90 were included in Series II packs.

		MT	NR MT	EX
Complete Set (90):		22.00	15.00	10.00
Common Player:		.10	.08	.04
1	Chuck Knoblauch	.25	.20	.10
2	Jeff Bagwell	.40	.30	.15
3	Juan Guzman	.30	.25	.12
4	Milt Cuyler	.10	.08	.04
5	Ivan Rodriguez	.60	.45	.25
6	Rich DeLucia	.10	.08	.04
7	Orlando Merced	.20	.15	.08
8	Ray Lankford	.20	.15	.08
9	Brian Hunter	.10	.08	.04
10	Roberto Alomar	.60	.45	.25
11	Wes Chamberlain	.10	.08	.04
12	Steve Avery	.50	.40	.20
13	Scott Erickson	.10	.08	.04
14	Jim Abbott	.20	.15	.08
15	Mark Whiten	.10	.08	.04
16	Leo Gomez	.10	.08	.04
17	Doug Henry	.10	.08	.04
18	Brent Mayne	.10	.08	.04
19	Charles Nagy	.10	.08	.04
20	Phil Plantier	.20	.15	.08
21	Mo Vaughn	.40	.30	.15
22	Craig Biggio	.10	.08	.04
23	Derek Bell	.20	.15	.08
24	Royce Clayton	.20	.15	.08
25	Gary Cooper	.10	.08	.04
26	Scott Cooper	.25	.20	.10
27	Juan Gonzalez	2.50	2.00	1.00
28	Ken Griffey, Jr.	3.00	2.25	1.25
29	Larry Walker	.25	.20	.10
30	John Smoltz	.25	.20	.10
31	Todd Hundley	.10	.08	.04
32	Kenny Lofton	1.25	.90	.50
33	Andy Mota	.10	.08	.04
34	Todd Zeile	.10	.08	.04
35	Arthur Rhodes	.10	.08	.04
36	Jim Thome	.25	.20	.10
37	Todd Van Poppel	.20	.15	.08
38	Mark Wohlers	.10	.08	.04
39	Anthony Young	.10	.08	.04
40	Sandy Alomar Jr.	.10	.08	.04
41	John Olerud	1.25	.90	.50
42	Robin Ventura	.25	.20	.10
43	Frank Thomas	4.00	3.00	1.50
44	Dave Justice	.25	.20	.10
45	Hal Morris	.10	.08	.04
46	Ruben Sierra	.30	.25	.12
47	Travis Fryman	1.00	.70	.40
48	Mike Mussina	2.00	1.50	.80
49	Tom Glavine	.20	.15	.08
50	Barry Larkin	.20	.15	.08
51	Will Clark	.50	.40	.20
52	Jose Canseco	.30	.25	.12
53	Bo Jackson	.25	.20	.10
54	Dwight Gooden	.20	.15	.08
55	Barry Bonds	.50	.40	.20
56	Fred McGriff	.25	.20	.10
57	Roger Clemens	.30	.25	.12
58	Benito Santiago	.10	.08	.04
59	Darryl Strawberry	.20	.15	.08
60	Cecil Fielder	.30	.25	.12
61	John Franco	.10	.08	.04
62	Matt Williams	.20	.15	.08
63	Marquis Grissom	.10	.08	.04
64	Danny Tartabull	.10	.08	.04
65	Ron Gant	.20	.15	.08

		MT	NR MT	EX
66	Paul O'Neill	.10	.08	.04
67	Devon White	.10	.08	.04
68	Rafael Palmeiro	.20	.15	.08
69	Tom Gordon	.10	.08	.04
70	Shawon Dunston	.10	.08	.04
71	Rob Dibble	.10	.08	.04
72	Eddie Zosky	.10	.08	.04
73	Jack McDowell	.20	.15	.08
74	Len Dykstra	.20	.15	.08
75	Ramon Martinez	.10	.08	.04
76	Reggie Sanders	.30	.25	.12
77	Greg Maddux	.25	.20	.10
78	Ellis Burks	.10	.08	.04
79	John Smiley	.10	.08	.04
80	Roberto Kelly	.20	.15	.08
81	Ben McDonald	.10	.08	.04
82	Mark Lewis	.10	.08	.04
83	Jose Rijo	.10	.08	.04
84	Ozzie Guillen	.10	.08	.04
85	Lance Dickson	.10	.08	.04
86	Kim Batiste	.10	.08	.04
87	Gregg Olson	.10	.08	.04
88	Andy Benes	.20	.15	.08
89	Cal Eldred	.20	.15	.08
90	David Cone	.10	.08	.04

1992 Score Pinnacle

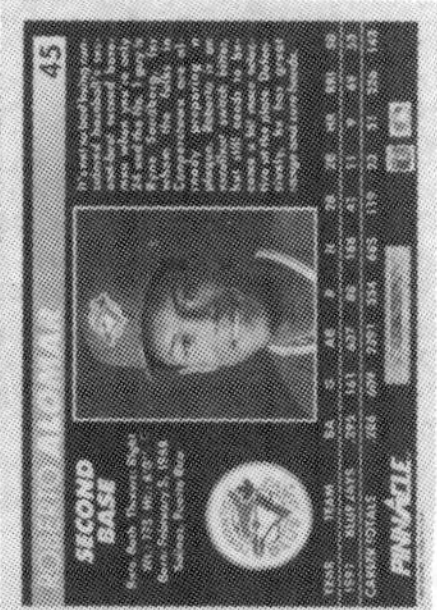

Score entered the high-end card market with the release of this 620-card set. The cards feature black borders surrounding a white frame with a full-color action photo inside. The player extends beyond the natural background. The backs are horizontal and feature a closeup photo, statistics, team logo, biographical information and player information. Several subsets can be found within the set including "Idols, Sidelines, Grips, Shades" and "Technicians". Score produced Pinnacle lines in football and hockey as well as in baseball.

		MT	NR MT	EX
Complete Set (620):		50.00	37.00	20.00
Common Player:		.10	.08	.04
1	Frank Thomas	4.00	3.00	1.50
2	Benito Santiago	.15	.11	.06
3	Carlos Baerga	.75	.60	.30
4	Cecil Fielder	.50	.40	.20
5	Barry Larkin	.30	.25	.12
6	Ozzie Smith	.30	.25	.12
7	Willie McGee	.12	.09	.05
8	Paul Moltior	.30	.25	.12
9	Andy Van Slyke	.12	.09	.05
10	Ryne Sandberg	.60	.45	.25
11	Kevin Seitzer	.10	.08	.04
12	Lenny Dykstra	.20	.15	.08
13	Edgar Martinez	.15	.11	.06
14	Ruben Sierra	.25	.20	.10
15	Howard Johnson	.20	.15	.08
16	Dave Henderson	.10	.08	.04
17	Devon White	.10	.08	.04
18	Terry Pendleton	.15	.11	.06
19	Steve Finley	.10	.08	.04
20	Kirby Puckett	.50	.40	.20
21	Orel Hershiser	.10	.08	.04
22	Hal Morris	.10	.08	.04
23	Don Mattingly	.20	.15	.08
24	Delino DeShields	.15	.11	.06
25	Dennis Eckersley	.15	.11	.06
26	Ellis Burks	.10	.08	.04

		MT	NR MT	EX
27	Jay Buhner	.10	.08	.04
28	Matt Williams	.20	.15	.08
29	Lou Whitaker	.10	.08	.04
30	Alex Fernandez	.12	.09	.05
31	Albert Belle	.50	.40	.20
32	Todd Zeile	.12	.09	.05
33	Tony Pena	.10	.08	.04
34	Jay Bell	.10	.08	.04
35	Rafael Palmeiro	.25	.20	.10
36	Wes Chamberlain	.10	.08	.04
37	George Bell	.12	.09	.05
38	Robin Yount	.50	.40	.20
39	Vince Coleman	.10	.08	.04
40	Bruce Hurst	.10	.08	.04
41	Harold Baines	.12	.09	.05
42	Chuck Finley	.12	.09	.05
43	Ken Caminiti	.10	.08	.04
44	Ben McDonald	.20	.15	.08
45	Roberto Alomar	.75	.60	.30
46	Chili Davis	.10	.08	.04
47	Bill Doran	.10	.08	.04
48	Jerald Clark	.10	.08	.04
49	Jose Lind	.10	.08	.04
50	Nolan Ryan	1.50	1.25	.60
51	Phil Plantier	.60	.45	.25
52	Gary DiSarcina	.10	.08	.04
53	Kevin Bass	.10	.08	.04
54	Pat Kelly	.10	.08	.04
55	Mark Wohlers	.10	.08	.04
56	Walt Weiss	.10	.08	.04
57	Lenny Harris	.10	.08	.04
58	Ivan Calderon	.10	.08	.04
59	Harold Reynolds	.10	.08	.04
60	George Brett	.40	.30	.15
61	Gregg Olson	.12	.09	.05
62	Orlando Merced	.10	.08	.04
63	Steve Decker	.10	.08	.04
64	John Franco	.10	.08	.04
65	Greg Maddux	.20	.15	.08
66	Alex Cole	.10	.08	.04
67	Dave Holins	.15	.11	.06
68	Kent Hrbek	.10	.08	.04
69	Tom Pagnozzi	.10	.08	.04
70	Jeff Bagwell	.60	.45	.25
71	Jim Gantner	.10	.08	.04
72	Matt Nokes	.10	.08	.04
73	Brian Harper	.10	.08	.04
74	Andy Benes	.20	.15	.08
75	Tom Glavine	.30	.25	.12
76	Terry Steinbach	.10	.08	.04
77	Dennis Martinez	.10	.08	.04
78	John Olerud	1.00	.70	.40
79	Ozzie Guillen	.10	.08	.04
80	Darryl Strawberry	.20	.15	.08
81	Gary Gaetti	.10	.08	.04
82	Dave Righetti	.10	.08	.04
83	Chris Hoiles	.15	.11	.06
84	Andujar Cedeno	.20	.15	.08
85	Jack Clark	.10	.08	.04
86	David Howard	.10	.08	.04
87	Bill Gullickson	.10	.08	.04
88	Bernard Gilkey	.15	.11	.06
89	Kevin Elster	.10	.08	.04
90	Kevin Maas	.15	.11	.06
91	Mark Lewis	.15	.11	.06
92	Greg Vaughn	.20	.15	.08
93	Bret Barberie	.15	.11	.06
94	Dave Smith	.10	.08	.04
95	Roger Clemens	.50	.40	.20
96	Doug Drabek	.15	.11	.06
97	Omar Vizquel	.10	.08	.04
98	Jose Guzman	.10	.08	.04
99	Juan Samuel	.10	.08	.04
100	Dave Justice	.75	.60	.30
101	Tom Browning	.10	.08	.04
102	Mark Gubicza	.10	.08	.04
103	Mickey Morandini	.10	.08	.04
104	Ed Whitson	.10	.08	.04
105	Lance Parrish	.10	.08	.04
106	Scott Erickson	.10	.08	.04
107	Jack McDowell	.30	.25	.12
108	Dave Stieb	.10	.08	.04
109	Mike Moore	.10	.08	.04
110	Travis Fryman	1.00	.70	.40
111	Doc Gooden	.15	.11	.06
112	Fred McGriff	.25	.20	.10
113	Alan Trammell	.10	.08	.04
114	Roberto Kelly	.15	.11	.06
115	Andre Dawson	.25	.20	.10
116	Bill Landrum	.10	.08	.04
117	Brian McRae	.10	.08	.04
119	Chuck Knoblauch	.30	.25	.12

		MT	NR MT	EX
120	Steve Olin	.12	.09	.05
121	Robin Ventura	.40	.30	.15
122	Will Clark	.50	.40	.20
123	Tino Martinez	.15	.11	.06
124	Dale Murphy	.15	.11	.06
125	Pete O'Brien	.10	.08	.04
126	Ray Lankford	.30	.25	.12
127	Juan Gonzalez	3.00	2.25	1.25
128	Ron Gant	.30	.25	.12
129	Marquis Grissom	.30	.25	.12
130	Jose Canseco	.25	.20	.10
131	Mike Greenwell	.20	.15	.08
132	Mark Langston	.12	.09	.05
133	Brett Butler	.12	.09	.05
134	Kelly Gruber	.10	.08	.04
135	Chris Sabo	.20	.15	.08
136	Mark Grace	.20	.15	.08
137	Tony Fernandez	.12	.09	.05
138	Glenn Davis	.12	.09	.05
139	Pedro Munoz	.15	.11	.06
140	Craig Biggio	.12	.09	.05
141	Pete Schourek	.10	.08	.04
142	Mike Boddicker	.10	.08	.04
143	Robby Thompson	.10	.08	.04
144	Mel Hall	.12	.09	.05
145	Bryan Harvey	.12	.09	.05
146	Mike LaValliere	.10	.08	.04
147	John Kruk	.12	.09	.05
148	Joe Carter	.30	.25	.12
149	Greg Olson	.10	.08	.04
150	Julio Franco	.12	.09	.05
151	Darryl Hamilton	.12	.09	.05
152	Felix Fermin	.10	.08	.04
153	Jose Offerman	.12	.09	.05
154	Paul O'Neill	.12	.09	.05
155	Tommy Greene	.12	.09	.05
156	Ivan Rodriguez	1.00	.70	.40
157	Dave Stewart	.12	.09	.05
158	Jeff Reardon	.12	.09	.05
159	Felix Jose	.15	.11	.06
160	Doug Dascenzo	.10	.08	.04
161	Tim Wallach	.10	.08	.04
162	Dan Plesac	.10	.08	.04
163	Luis Gonzalez	.12	.09	.05
164	Mike Henneman	.12	.09	.05
165	Mike Devereaux	.12	.09	.05
166	Luis Polonia	.10	.08	.04
167	Mike Sharperson	.10	.08	.04
168	Chris Donnels	.10	.08	.04
169	Greg Harris	.10	.08	.04
170	Deion Sanders	.60	.45	.25
171	Mike Schooler	.10	.08	.04
172	Jose DeJesus	.10	.08	.04
173	Jeff Montgomery	.10	.08	.04
174	Milt Cuyler	.10	.08	.04
175	Wade Boggs	.40	.30	.15
176	Kevin Tapani	.15	.11	.06
177	Bill Spiers	.10	.08	.04
178	Tim Raines	.15	.11	.06
179	Randy Milligan	.10	.08	.04
180	Rob Dibble	.15	.11	.06
181	Kirt Manwaring	.10	.08	.04
182	Pascual Perez	.10	.08	.04
183	Juan Guzman	1.00	.70	.40
184	John Smiley	.12	.09	.05
185	David Segui	.10	.08	.04
186	Omar Olivares	.10	.08	.04
187	Joe Slusarski	.10	.08	.04
188	Erik Hanson	.10	.08	.04
189	Mark Portugal	.10	.08	.04
190	Walt Terrell	.10	.08	.04
191	John Smoltz	.20	.15	.08
192	Wilson Alvarez	.10	.08	.04
193	Jimmy Key	.12	.09	.05
194	Larry Walker	.20	.15	.08
195	Lee Smith	.12	.09	.05
196	Pete Harnisch	.12	.09	.05
197	Mike Harkey	.10	.08	.04
198	Frank Tananna	.10	.08	.04
199	Terry Mulholland	.10	.08	.04
200	Cal Ripken, Jr.	1.00	.70	.40
201	Dave Magadan	.10	.08	.04
202	Bud Black	.10	.08	.04
203	Terry Shumpert	.10	.08	.04
204	Mike Mussina	1.75	1.25	.70
205	Mo Vaughn	.75	.60	.30
206	Steve Farr	.10	.08	.04
207	Darrin Jackson	.10	.08	.04
208	Jerry Browne	.10	.08	.04
209	Jeff Russell	.10	.08	.04
210	Mike Scioscia	.10	.08	.04

		MT	NR MT	EX
211	Rick Aguilera	.12	.09	.05
212	Jaime Navarro	.12	.09	.05
213	Randy Tomlin	.12	.09	.05
214	Bobby Thigpen	.10	.08	.04
215	Mark Gardner	.10	.08	.04
216	Norm Charlton	.12	.09	.05
217	Mark McGwire	.30	.25	.12
219	Bob Tewksbury	.12	.09	.05
220	Junior Felix	.10	.08	.04
221	Sam Horn	.10	.08	.04
222	Jody Reed	.10	.08	.04
223	Luis Sojo	.10	.08	.04
224	Jerome Walton	.10	.08	.04
225	Darryl Kile	.12	.09	.05
226	Mickey Tettleton	.15	.11	.06
227	Dan Pasqua	.10	.08	.04
228	Jim Gott	.10	.08	.04
229	Bernie Williams	.12	.09	.05
230	Shane Mack	.25	.20	.10
231	Steve Avery	.50	.40	.20
232	Dave Valle	.10	.08	.04
233	Mark Leonard	.10	.08	.04
234	Spike Owen	.10	.08	.04
235	Gary Sheffield	.40	.30	.15
236	Steve Chitren	.10	.08	.04
237	Zane Smith	.10	.08	.04
238	Tom Gordon	.10	.08	.04
239	Jose Oquendo	.10	.08	.04
240	Todd Stottlemyre	.10	.08	.04
241	Darren Daulton	.15	.11	.06
242	Tim Naehring	.12	.09	.05
243	Tony Phillips	.12	.09	.05
244	Shawon Dunston	.12	.09	.05
245	Manuel Lee	.10	.08	.04
246	Mike Pagliarulo	.10	.08	.04
247	Jim Thome (Rookie Prospect)	.50	.40	.20
248	Luis Mercedes (Rookie Prospect)	.25	.20	.10
249	Cal Eldred (Rookie Prospect)	.50	.40	.20
250	Derek Bell (Rookie Prospect)	.50	.40	.20
251	Arthur Rhodes (Rookie Prospect)	.15	.11	.06
252	Scott Cooper (Rookie Prospect)	.20	.15	.08
253	Roberto Hernandez (Rookie Prospect)	.20	.15	.08
254	Mo Sanford (Rookie Prospect)	.30	.25	.12
255	Scott Servais (Rookie Prospect)	.10	.08	.04
256	Eric Karros (Rookie Prospect)	1.50	1.25	.60
259	Joel Johnston (Rookie Prospect)	.12	.09	.05
260	John Wehner (Rookie Prospect)	.12	.09	.05
261	Gino Minutelli (Rookie Prospect)	.12	.09	.05
262	Greg Gagne	.10	.08	.04
263	Stan Royer (Rookie Prospect)	.15	.11	.06
264	Carlos Garcia (Rookie Prospect)	.15	.11	.06
265	Andy Ashby (Rookie Prospect)	.12	.09	.05
266	Kim Batiste (Rookie Prospect)	.10	.08	.04
267	Julio Valera (Rookie Prospect)	.12	.09	.05
268	Royce Clayton (Rookie Prospect)	.40	.30	.15
269	Gary Scott (Rookie Prospect)	.10	.08	.04
270	Kirk Dressendorfer (Rookie Prospect)	.10	.08	.04
271	Sean Berry (Rookie Prospect)	.12	.09	.05
272	Lance Dickson (Rookie Prospect)	.12	.09	.05
273	Rob Maurer (Rookie Prospect)	.20	.15	.08
274	Scott Brosius (Rookie Prospect)	.20	.15	.08
275	Dave Fleming (Rookie Prospect)	.50	.40	.20
276	Lenny Webster (Rookie Prospect)	.12	.09	.05
278	Freddie Benavides (Rookie Prospect)	.12	.09	.05
279	Harvey Pulliam (Rookie Prospect)	.12	.09	.05
280	Jeff Carter (Rookie Prospect)	.12	.09	.05
281	Jim Abbott/ Nolan Ryan (Idols)	.15	.11	.06
282	Wade Boggs/ George Brett (Idols)	.15	.11	.06
283	Ken Griffey, Jr./ Rickey Henderson (Idols)	.75	.60	.30
284	Wally Joyner/ Dale Murphy (Idols)	.15	.11	.06
285	Chuck Knoblauch/ Ozzie Smith (Idols)	.20	.15	.08
286	Robin Ventura/ Lou Gehrig (Idols)	.25	.20	.10
287	Robin Yount (Sidelines - Motocross)	.30	.25	.12
288	Bob Tewksbury (Sidelines - Cartoonist)	.12	.09	.05
289	Kirby Puckett (Sidelines - Pool Player)	.40	.30	.15
290	Kenny Lofton (Sidelines - Basketball Player)	.60	.45	.25
291	Jack McDowell (Sidelines - Cuitarist)	.30	.25	.12
292	John Burkett (Sidelines - Bowler)	.12	.09	.05
293	Dwight Smith (Sidelines - Singer)	.12	.09	.05
294	Nolan Ryan (Sidelines - Cattle Rancher)	1.00	.70	.40

		MT	NR MT	EX
295	Manny Ramirez (1st Round Draft Pick)	1.50	1.25	.60
296	Cliff Floyd (1st Round Draft Pick)	4.50	3.50	1.75
297	Al Shirley (1st Round Draft Pick)	.20	.15	.08
298	Brian Barber (1st Round Draft Pick)	.40	.30	.15
299	Jon Farrell (1st Round Draft Pick)	.30	.25	.12
300	Scott Ruffcorn (1st Round Draft Pick)	.90	.70	.35
301	Tyrone Hill (1st Round Draft Pick)	.40	.30	.15
302	Benji Gil (1st Round Draft Pick)	.80	.60	.30
303	Tyler Green (1st Round Draft Pick)	.30	.25	.12
304	Allen Watson (Shades)	.15	.11	.06
305	Jay Buhner (Shades)	.12	.09	.05
306	Roberto Alomar (Shades)	.30	.25	.12
307	Chuck Knoblauch (Shades)	.25	.20	.10
308	Darryl Strawberry (Shades)	.10	.08	.04
309	Danny Tartabull (Shades)	.12	.09	.05
310	Bobby Bonilla (Shades)	.10	.08	.04
311	Mike Felder	.10	.08	.04
312	Storm Davis	.10	.08	.04
313	Tim Teufel	.10	.08	.04
314	Tom Brunansky	.10	.08	.04
315	Rex Hudler	.10	.08	.04
316	Dave Otto	.10	.08	.04
317	Jeff King	.10	.08	.04
318	Dan Gladden	.10	.08	.04
319	Bill Pecota	.10	.08	.04
320	Franklin Stubbs	.10	.08	.04
321	Gary Carter	.15	.11	.06
322	Melido Perez	.10	.08	.04
323	Eric Davis	.20	.15	.08
324	Greg Myers	.10	.08	.04
325	Pete Incaviglia	.10	.08	.04
326	Von Hayes	.10	.08	.04
327	Greg Swindell	.15	.11	.06
328	Steve Sax	.10	.08	.04
329	Chuck McElroy	.10	.08	.04
330	Gregg Jefferies	.20	.15	.08
331	Joe Oliver	.10	.08	.04
332	Paul Faries	.10	.08	.04
333	David West	.10	.08	.04
334	Craig Grebeck	.10	.08	.04
335	Chris Hammond	.10	.08	.04
336	Billy Ripken	.10	.08	.04
337	Scott Sanderson	.10	.08	.04
338	Dick Schofield	.10	.08	.04
339	Bob Milacki	.10	.08	.04
340	Kevin Reimer	.10	.08	.04
341	Jose DeLeon	.10	.08	.04
342	Henry Cotto	.10	.08	.04
343	Daryl Boston	.10	.08	.04
344	Kevin Gross	.10	.08	.04
345	Milt Thompson	.10	.08	.04
346	Luis Rivera	.10	.08	.04
347	Al Osuna	.10	.08	.04
348	Rob Deer	.10	.08	.04
349	Tim Leary	.10	.08	.04
350	Mike Stanton	.10	.08	.04
351	Dean Palmer	.40	.30	.15
352	Trevor Wilson	.10	.08	.04
353	Mark Eichhorn	.10	.08	.04
354	Scott Aldred	.12	.09	.05
355	Mark Whiten	.20	.15	.08
356	Leo Gomez	.12	.09	.05
357	Rafael Belliard	.10	.08	.04
358	Carlos Quintana	.10	.08	.04
359	Mark Davis	.10	.08	.04
360	Chris Nabholz	.10	.08	.04
361	Carlton Fisk	.20	.15	.08
362	Joe Orsulak	.10	.08	.04
363	Eric Anthony	.12	.09	.05
364	Greg Hibbard	.12	.09	.05
365	Scott Leius	.12	.09	.05
366	Hensley Meulens	.12	.09	.05
367	Chris Bosio	.12	.09	.05
368	Brian Downing	.10	.08	.04
369	Sammy Sosa	.12	.09	.05
370	Stan Belinda	.10	.08	.04
371	Joe Grahe	.10	.08	.04
372	Luis Salazar	.10	.08	.04
373	Lance Johnson	.10	.08	.04
374	Kal Daniels	.10	.08	.04
375	Dave Winfield	.25	.20	.10
376	Brook Jacoby	.10	.08	.04
377	Mariano Duncan	.10	.08	.04
378	Ron Darling	.12	.09	.05
379	Randy Johnson	.12	.09	.05
380	Chito Martinez	.12	.09	.05
381	Andres Galarraga	.12	.09	.05
382	Willie Randolph	.12	.09	.05

		MT	NR MT	EX
383	Charles Nagy	.25	.20	.10
384	Tim Belcher	.12	.09	.05
385	Duane Ward	.10	.08	.04
386	Vicente Palacios	.10	.08	.04
387	Mike Gallego	.10	.08	.04
388	Rich DeLucia	.10	.08	.04
389	Scott Radinsky	.10	.08	.04
390	Damon Berryhill	.10	.08	.04
391	Kirk McCaskill	.10	.08	.04
392	Pedro Guerrero	.12	.09	.05
393	Kevin Mitchell	.10	.08	.04
394	Dickie Thon	.10	.08	.04
395	Bobby Bonilla	.30	.25	.12
396	Bill Wegman	.10	.08	.04
397	Dave Martinez	.10	.08	.04
398	Rick Sutcliffe	.12	.09	.05
399	Larry Andersen	.10	.08	.04
400	Tony Gwynn	.40	.30	.15
401	Rickey Henderson	.50	.40	.20
402	Greg Cadaret	.10	.08	.04
403	Keith Miller	.10	.08	.04
404	Bip Roberts	.12	.09	.05
405	Kevin Brown	.12	.09	.05
406	Mitch Williams	.10	.08	.04
407	Frank Viola	.10	.08	.04
408	Darren Lewis	.10	.08	.04
409	Bob Walk	.12	.09	.05
410	Bob Walk	.10	.08	.04
411	Todd Frohwirth	.10	.08	.04
412	Brian Hunter	.15	.11	.06
413	Ron Karkovice	.10	.08	.04
414	Mike Morgan	.10	.08	.04
415	Joe Hesketh	.10	.08	.04
416	Don Slaught	.10	.08	.04
417	Tom Henke	.12	.09	.05
418	Kurt Stillwell	.10	.08	.04
419	Hector Villanueva	.10	.08	.04
420	Glenallen Hill	.10	.08	.04
421	Pat Borders	.10	.08	.04
422	Charlie Hough	.10	.08	.04
423	Charlie Leibrandt	.10	.08	.04
424	Eddie Murray	.20	.15	.08
425	Jesse Barfield	.10	.08	.04
426	Mark Lemke	.10	.08	.04
427	Kevin McReynolds	.12	.09	.05
428	Gilberto Reyes	.10	.08	.04
429	Ramon Martinez	.10	.08	.04
430	Steve Buechele	.10	.08	.04
431	David Wells	.10	.08	.04
432	Kyle Abbott (Rookie Prospect)	.15	.11	.06
433	John Habyan	.10	.08	.04
434	Kevin Appier	.15	.11	.06
435	Gene Larkin	.10	.08	.04
436	Sandy Alomar, Jr.	.10	.08	.04
437	Mike Jackson	.10	.08	.04
438	Todd Benzinger	.10	.08	.04
439	Teddy Higuera	.10	.08	.04
440	Reggie Sanders (Rookie Prospect)	.40	.30	.15
441	Mark Carreon	.10	.08	.04
442	Bret Saberhagen	.10	.08	.04
443	Gene Nelson	.10	.08	.04
444	Jay Howell	.10	.08	.04
445	Roger McDowell	.10	.08	.04
446	Sid Bream	.10	.08	.04
447	Mackey Sasser	.10	.08	.04
448	Bill Swift	.10	.08	.04
449	Hubie Brooks	.10	.08	.04
450	David Cone	.10	.08	.04
451	Bobby Witt	.12	.09	.05
452	Brady Anderson	.10	.08	.04
453	Lee Stevens	.10	.08	.04
454	Luis Aquino	.10	.08	.04
455	Carney Lansford	.12	.09	.05
456	Carlos Hernandez (Rookie Prospect)	.15	.11	.06
457	Danny Jackson	.10	.08	.04
458	Gerald Young	.10	.08	.04
459	Tom Candiotti	.10	.08	.04
460	Billy Hatcher	.10	.08	.04
461	John Wetteland	.15	.11	.06
462	Mike Bordick	.15	.11	.06
463	Don Robinson	.10	.08	.04
464	Jeff Johnson	.12	.09	.05
465	Lonnie Smith	.10	.08	.04
466	Paul Assenmacher	.10	.08	.04
467	Alvin Davis	.10	.08	.04
468	Jim Eisenreich	.10	.08	.04
469	Brent Mayne	.10	.08	.04
470	Jeff Brantley	.10	.08	.04
471	Tim Burke	.10	.08	.04
472	Pat Mahomes (Rookie Prospect)	.40	.30	.15

		MT	NR MT	EX
473	Ryan Bowen	.20	.15	.08
474	Bryn Smith	.10	.08	.04
475	Mike Flanagan	.10	.08	.04
476	Reggie Jefferson (Rookie Prospect)	.15	.11	.06
477	Jeff Blauser	.10	.08	.04
478	Craig Lefferts	.10	.08	.04
479	Todd Worrell	.10	.08	.04
480	Scott Scudder	.10	.08	.04
481	Kirk Gibson	.10	.08	.04
482	Kenny Rogers	.10	.08	.04
483	Jack Morris	.20	.15	.08
484	Russ Swan	.10	.08	.04
485	Mike Huff	.10	.08	.04
486	Ken Hill	.15	.11	.06
487	Geronimo Pena	.12	.09	.05
488	Charlie O'Brien	.10	.08	.04
489	Mike Maddux	.10	.08	.04
490	Scott Livingstone (Rookie Prospect)	.12	.09	.05
491	Carl Willis	.10	.08	.04
492	Kelly Downs	.10	.08	.04
493	Dennis Cook	.10	.08	.04
494	Joe Magrane	.10	.08	.04
495	Bob Kipper	.10	.08	.04
496	Jose Mesa	.10	.08	.04
497	Charlie Hayes	.10	.08	.04
498	Joe Girardi	.10	.08	.04
499	Doug Jones	.10	.08	.04
500	Barry Bonds	1.00	.70	.40
501	Bill Krueger	.10	.08	.04
502	Glenn Braggs	.10	.08	.04
503	Eric King	.10	.08	.04
504	Frank Castillo	.10	.08	.04
505	Mike Gardiner	.10	.08	.04
506	Cory Snyder	.10	.08	.04
507	Steve Howe	.10	.08	.04
508	Jose Rijo	.12	.09	.05
509	Sid Fernandez	.12	.09	.05
510	Archi Cianfrocco (Rookie Prospect)	.40	.30	.15
511	Mark Guthrie	.10	.08	.04
512	Bob Ojeda	.10	.08	.04
513	John Doherty (Rookie Prospect)	.15	.11	.06
514	Dante Bichette	.10	.08	.04
515	Juan Berenguer	.10	.08	.04
516	Jeff Robinson	.10	.08	.04
517	Mike MacFarlane	.10	.08	.04
518	Matt Young	.10	.08	.04
519	Otis Nixon	.12	.09	.05
520	Brian Holman	.10	.08	.04
521	Chris Haney	.20	.15	.08
522	Jeff Kent (Rookie Prospect)	.15	.11	.06
523	Chad Curtis (Rookie Prospect)	1.25	.90	.50
524	Vince Horsman	.12	.09	.05
525	Rod Nichols	.10	.08	.04
526	Peter Hoy (Rookie Prospect)	.15	.11	.06
527	Shawn Boskie	.12	.09	.05
528	Alejandro Pena	.10	.08	.04
529	Dave Burba (Rookie Prospect)	.10	.08	.04
530	Ricky Jordan	.15	.11	.06
531	David Silvestri (Rookie Prospect)	.20	.15	.08
532	John Patterson (Rookie Prospect)	.20	.15	.08
533	Jeff Branson (Rookie Prospect)	.12	.09	.05
534	Derrick May (Rookie Prospect)	.20	.15	.08
535	Esteban Beltre (Rookie Prospect)	.20	.15	.08
536	Jose Melendez	.15	.11	.06
537	Wally Joyner	.12	.09	.05
538	Eddie Taubensee (Rookie Prospect)	.25	.20	.10
539	Jim Abbott	.20	.15	.08
540	Brian Williams (Rookie Prospect)	.15	.11	.06
541	Donovan Osborne (Rookie Prospect)	.40	.30	.15
542	Patrick Lennon (Rookie Prospect)	.20	.15	.08
543	Mike Groppuso (Rookie Prospect)	.12	.09	.05
544	Jarvis Brown (Rookie Prospect)	.12	.09	.05
545	Shawn Livesy (1st Round Draft Pick)	.20	.15	.08
546	Jeff Ware (1st Round Draft Pick)	.15	.11	.06
547	Danny Tartabull	.12	.09	.05
548	Bobby Jones (1st Round Draft Pick)	1.25	.90	.50
549	Ken Griffey, Jr.	3.00	2.25	1.25
550	Rey Sanchez (Rookie Prospect)	.25	.20	.10
551	Eric Wedge (Rookie Prospect)	.20	.15	.08
552	Juan Guerrero (Rookie Prospect)	.20	.15	.08
553	Jacob Brumfield (Rookie Prospect)	.25	.20	.10
554	Ben Rivera (Rookie Prospect)	.20	.15	.08
555	Brian Jordan (Rookie Prospect)	.50	.40	.20
556	Denny Neagle (Rookie Prospect)	.12	.09	.05

		MT	NR MT	EX
557	Cliff Brantley (Rookie Prospect)	.12	.09	.05
558	Anthony Young (Rookie Prospect)	.10	.08	.04
559	John VanderWal (Rookie Prospect)	.30	.25	.12
560	Monty Fariss (Rookie Prospect)	.20	.15	.08
561	Russ Springer (Rookie Prospect)	.20	.15	.08
562	Pat Listach (Rookie Prospect)	.50	.40	.20
563	Pat Hentgen (Rookie Prospect)	.70	.50	.30
564	Andy Stankiewicz (Rookie Prospect)	.12	.09	.05
565	Mike Perez (Rookie Prospect)	.15	.11	.06
566	Mike Bielecki	.10	.08	.04
567	Butch Henry (Rookie Prospect)	.12	.09	.05
568	Dave Nilsson (Rookie Prospect)	.20	.15	.08
569	Scott Hatteberg (1st Round Draft Pick)	.20	.15	.08
570	Ruben Amaro, Jr. (Rookie Prospect)	.12	.09	.05
571	Todd Hundley (Rookie Prospect)	.15	.11	.06
572	Moises Alou (Rookie Prospect)	.15	.11	.06
573	Hector Fajardo (Rookie Prospect)	.15	.11	.06
574	Todd Van Poppel (Rookie Prospect)	.60	.45	.25
575	Willie Banks (Rookie Prospect)	.15	.11	.06
576	Bob Zupcic (Rookie Prospect)	.15	.11	.06
577	J.J. Johnson (1st Round Draft Pick)	.30	.25	.12
578	John Burkett	.10	.08	.04
579	Trever Miller (1st Round Draft Pick)	.25	.20	.10
580	Scott Bankhead	.10	.08	.04
581	Rich Amaral (Rookie Prospect)	.10	.08	.04
582	Kenny Lofton (Rookie Prospect)	.80	.60	.30
583	Matt Stairs (Rookie Prospect)	.20	.15	.08
584	Don Mattingly/ Rod Carew (Idols)	.40	.30	.15
585	Steve Avery/ Jack Morris (Idols)	.30	.25	.12
586	Roberto Alomar/ Sandy Alomar (Idols)	.50	.40	.20
587	Scott Sanderson/ Catfish Hunter (Idols)	.10	.08	.04
588	Dave Justice/ Willie Stargell (Idols)	.30	.25	.12
589	Rex Hudler/ Roger Staubach (Idols)	.10	.08	.04
590	David Cone/ Jackie Gleason (Idols)	.20	.15	.08
591	Tony Gwynn/ Willie Davis (Idols)	.25	.20	.10
592	Orel Hershiser (Sidelines - Golfer)	.15	.11	.06
593	John Wetteland (Sidelines - Musician)	.15	.11	.06
594	Tom Glavine (Sidelines - Hockey Player)	.20	.15	.08
595	Randy Johnson (Sidelines — Photographer)	.15	.11	.06
596	Jim Gott (Sidelines - Black Belt)	.10	.08	.04
597	Donald Harris	.10	.08	.04
598	Shawn Hare	.35	.25	.14
599	Chris Gardner	.25	.20	.10
600	Rusty Meacham	.10	.08	.04
601	Benito Santiago (Shades)	.10	.08	.04
602	Eric Davis (Shades)	.20	.15	.08
603	Jose Lind (Shades)	.10	.08	.04
604	Dave Justice (Shades)	.30	.25	.12
605	Tim Raines (Shades)	.15	.11	.06
606	Randy Tomlin (Grips -Vulcan Change)	.15	.11	.06
607	Jack McDowell (Grips - Split-finger)	.20	.15	.08
608	Greg Maddux (Grips - Circle change)	.20	.15	.08
609	Charles Nagy (Grips - Slider)	.12	.09	.05
610	Tom Candiotti (Grips - Knuckleball)	.10	.08	.04
611	David Cone (Grips - Curveball)	.10	.08	.04
612	Steve Avery (Grips - Fastball)	.25	.20	.10
613	Rod Beck	.10	.08	.04
614	Rickey Henderson (Technician - Base Stealing)	.25	.20	.10
615	Benito Santiago (Technician - Catching)	.10	.08	.04
616	Ruben Sierra (Technician - Outfield)	.20	.15	.08
617	Ryne Sandberg (Technician - Infield)	.40	.30	.15
618	Nolan Ryan (Technician - Pitching)	.40	.30	.15
619	Brett Butler (Technician - Bunting)	.10	.08	.04
620	Dave Justice (Technician - Hitting)	.30	.25	.12

Definitions for grading conditions are located in the Introduction of this price guide.

1992 Score Pinnacle Rookies

Photos not available at press time

Styled after the regular 1992 Score Pinnacle cards, this 30-card boxed set features the top rookies of 1992. The cards feature black borders surrounding full-color player photos. The flip sides feature an additional player photo and background information.

		MT	NR MT	EX
Complete Set (30):		10.00	7.50	4.00
Common Player:		.20	.15	.08
1	Luis Mercedes	.25	.20	.10
2	Scott Cooper	.25	.20	.10
3	Kenny Lofton	1.50	1.25	.60
4	John Doherty	.25	.20	.10
5	Pat Listach	1.00	.75	.40
6	Andy Stankiewicz	.50	.40	.20
7	Derek Bell	.30	.25	.12
8	Gary DiSarcina	.20	.15	.08
9	Roberto Hernandez	.30	.25	.12
10	Joel Johnston	.25	.20	.10
11	Pat Mahomes	1.00	.70	.40
12	Todd Van Poppel	.50	.40	.20
13	Dave Fleming	1.00	.70	.40
14	Monty Fariss	.25	.20	.10
15	Gary Scott	.25	.20	.10
16	Moises Alou	.35	.25	.14
17	Todd Hundley	.25	.20	.10
18	Kim Batiste	.20	.15	.08
19	Denny Neagle	.25	.20	.10
20	Donovan Osborne	.35	.25	.14
21	Mark Wohlers	.20	.15	.08
22	Reggie Sanders	1.00	.70	.40
23	Brian Williams	.20	.15	.08
24	Eric Karros	2.50	2.00	1.00
25	Frank Seminara	.25	.20	.10
26	Royce Clayton	.30	.25	.12
27	Dave Nilsson	.35	.25	.14
28	Matt Stairs	.20	.15	.08
29	Chad Curtis	.35	.25	.14
30	Carlos Hernandez	.25	.20	.10

1992 Score Pinnacle Team 2000

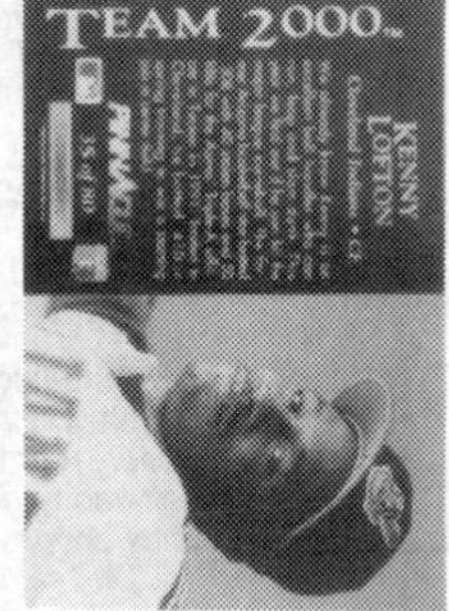

Young stars who were projected to be the game's superstars in the year 2000 were chosen for this 80-card insert set found three at a time in jumbo packs. Cards #1-40 were included in Series I packaging, while cards 41-80 were inserted with Series II Pinnacle. Cards feature gold foil stamping on both front and back.

		MT	NR MT	EX
Complete Set (80):		45.00	34.00	18.00
Common Player:		.10	.08	.04
1	Mike Mussina	1.50	1.25	.60
2	Phil Plantier	.60	.45	.25
3	Frank Thomas	6.00	4.50	2.25
4	Travis Fryman	1.50	1.25	.60
5	Kevin Appier	.10	.08	.04
6	Chuck Knoblauch	.30	.25	.12
7	Pat Kelly	.10	.08	.04
8	Ivan Rodriguez	1.50	1.25	.60
9	David Justice	1.50	1.25	.60
10	Jeff Bagwell	1.50	1.25	.60
11	Marquis Grissom	.40	.30	.15
12	Andy Benes	.10	.08	.04
13	Gregg Olson	.10	.08	.04
14	Kevin Morton	.10	.08	.04
15	Tim Naehring	.10	.08	.04
16	Dave Hollins	1.00	.70	.40
17	Sandy Alomar Jr.	.10	.08	.04
18	Albert Belle	1.00	.70	.40
19	Charles Nagy	.10	.08	.04
20	Brian McRae	.10	.08	.04
21	Larry Walker	.50	.40	.20
22	Delino DeShields	.25	.15	.10
23	Jeff Johnson	.10	.08	.04
24	Bernie Williams	.20	.15	.08
25	Jose Offerman	.10	.08	.04
26	Juan Gonzalez	3.00	2.00	1.00
27	Juan Guzman	1.00	.70	.40
28	Eric Anthony	.10	.08	.04
29	Brian Hunter	.10	.08	.04
30	John Smoltz	.30	.25	.12
31	Deion Sanders	.80	.60	.30
32	Greg Maddux	.10	.08	.04
33	Andujar Cedeno	.10	.08	.04
34	Royce Clayton	.50	.40	.20
35	Kenny Lofton	1.00	.70	.40
36	Cal Eldred	.75	.60	.30
37	Jim Thome	.10	.08	.04
38	Gary DiSarcina	.10	.08	.04
39	Brian Jordan	.80	.60	.30
40	Chad Curtis	1.00	.70	.40
41	Ben McDonald	.10	.08	.04
42	Jim Abbott	.30	.25	.12
43	Robin Ventura	.80	.60	.30
44	Milt Cuyler	.10	.08	.04
45	Gregg Jefferies	.40	.30	.15
46	Scott Radinsky	.10	.08	.04
47	Ken Griffey, Jr.	4.00	3.00	1.50
48	Roberto Alomar	1.25	.95	.50
49	Ramon Martinez	.10	.08	.04
50	Bret Barberie	.10	.08	.04
51	Ray Lankford	.20	.15	.08
52	Leo Gomez	.10	.08	.04
53	Tommy Greene	.30	.25	.12
54	Mo Vaughn	1.00	.70	.40
55	Sammy Sosa	1.00	.70	.40
56	Carlos Baerga	.10	.08	.04
57	Mark Lewis	.10	.08	.04
58	Carlos Baerga	1.25	.90	.50
59	Gary Sheffield	.60	.45	.25
60	Scott Erickson	.10	.08	.04
61	Pedro Munoz	.10	.08	.04
62	Tino Martinez	.10	.08	.04
63	Darren Lewis	.10	.08	.04
64	Dean Palmer	1.00	.70	.40
65	John Olerud	1.50	1.25	.60
66	Steve Avery	.80	.60	.30
67	Pete Harnisch	.10	.08	.04
68	Luis Gonzalez	.10	.08	.04
69	Kim Batiste	.10	.08	.04
70	Reggie Sanders	.80	.60	.30
71	Luis Mercedes	.10	.08	.04
72	Todd Van Poppel	.50	.40	.20
73	Gary Scott	.10	.08	.04
74	Monty Fariss	.10	.08	.04
75	Kyle Abbott	.10	.08	.04
76	Eric Karros	.75	.60	.30
77	Mo Sanford	.10	.08	.04
78	Todd Hundley	.10	.08	.04
79	Reggie Jefferson	.20	.15	.08
80	Pat Mahomes	.30	.25	.12

1992 Score Pinnacle Slugfest

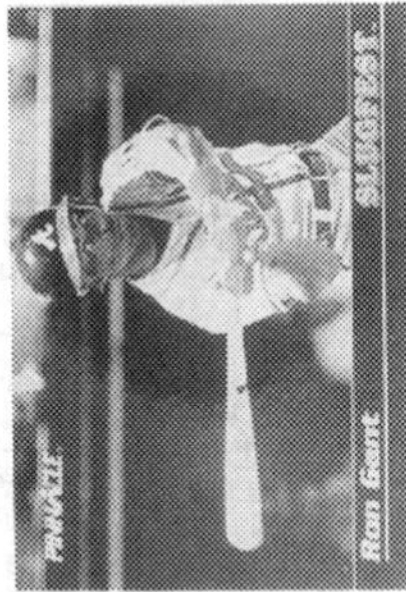

Each specially marked Slugfest jumbo pack of '92 Pinnacle contained one of these horizontal-format cards of the game's top hitters. The player's name is printed in gold foil at the bottom of the card, along with a red and white Slugfest logo. Backs, which are vertical in orientation have a color player photo, a career summary and a few lifetime stats.

		MT	NR MT	EX
Complete Set (15):		30.00	22.00	12.00
Common Player:		1.00	.70	.40
1	Cecil Fielder	1.50	1.25	.60
2	Mark McGwire	2.00	1.50	.80
3	Jose Canseco	2.00	1.50	.80
4	Barry Bonds	3.00	2.25	1.25
5	Dave Justice	2.00	1.50	.80
6	Bobby Bonilla	1.00	.70	.40
7	Ken Griffey Jr.	6.00	4.50	2.50
8	Ron Gant	1.00	.70	.40
9	Ryne Sandberg	5.00	3.75	2.00
10	Ruben Sierra	1.50	1.25	.60
11	Frank Thomas	9.00	6.75	3.50
12	Will Clark	3.00	2.25	1.25
13	Kirby Puckett	4.00	3.00	1.50
14	Cal Ripken, Jr.	5.00	3.75	2.00
15	Jeff Bagwell	2.00	1.50	.80

1992 Score Pinnacle Team Pinnacle

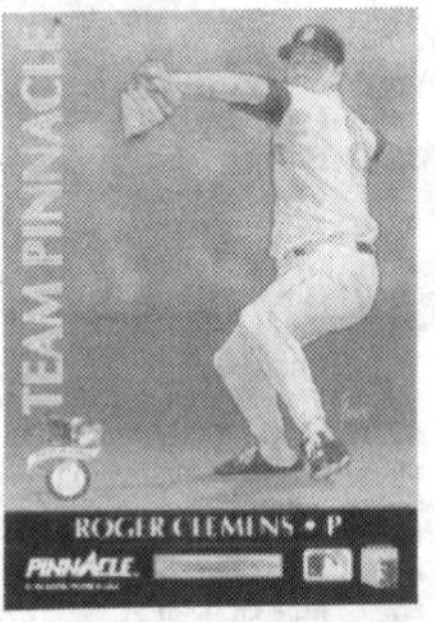

The most sought-after and valuable of the 1992 Pinnacle insert cards is this 12-piece set of "two-headed" cards. An American and a National League superstar at each position are featured on each card, with two cards each for starting and relief pitchers. The ultra-realistic artwork of Chris Greco is featured on the cards, which were inserted into Series I foil packs.

		MT	NR MT	EX
Complete Set (12):		250.00	185.00	100.00
Common Card:		7.50	5.75	3.00
1	Roger Clemens/ Ramon Martinez	15.00	11.00	6.00
2	Jim Abbott/ Steve Avery	15.00	11.00	6.00
3	Ivan Rodriguez/ Benito Santiago	10.00	7.50	4.00
4	Frank Thomas/ Will Clark	45.00	35.00	18.00
5	Roberto Alomar/ Ryne Sandberg	40.00	30.00	16.00
6	Robin Ventura/ Matt Williams	15.00	11.00	6.00
7	Cal Ripken, Jr./ Barry Larkin	35.00	26.00	14.00
8	Danny Tartabull/ Barry Bonds	25.00	18.50	10.00
9	Ken Griffey, Jr./ Brett Butler	35.00	26.00	14.00
10	Ruben Sierra/ Dave Justice	20.00	15.00	8.00
11	Dennis Eckersley/ Rob Dibble	7.50	5.75	3.00
12	Scott Radinsky/ John Franco	7.50	5.75	3.00

1992 Score Pinnacle Rookie Idols

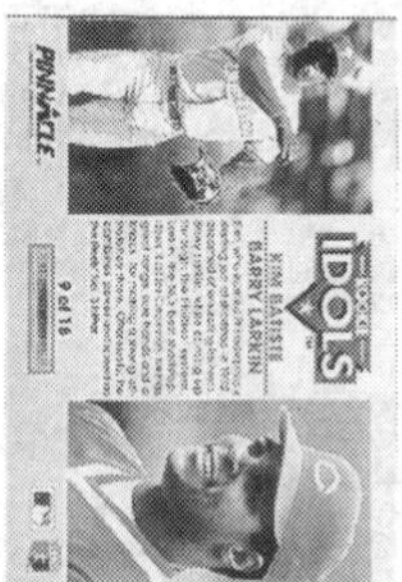

Carrying on with the Idols subset theme in the regular issue, these Series II foil-pack inserts feature 18 of the year's rookie prospects sharing cards with their baseball heroes. Both front and back are horizontal in format and include photos of both the rookie and his idol.

		MT	NR MT	EX
Complete Set (18):		125.00	90.00	50.00
Common Card:		5.00	3.75	2.00
1	Reggie Sanders/ Eric Davis	5.00	3.75	2.00
2	Hector Fajardo/ Jim Abbott	5.00	3.75	2.00
3	Gary Cooper/ George Brett	10.00	7.50	4.00
4	Mark Wohlers/ Roger Clemens	8.00	6.00	3.25
5	Luis Mercedes/ Julio Franco	5.00	3.75	2.00
6	Willie Banks/ Dwight Gooden	5.00	3.75	2.00
7	Kenny Lofton/ Rickey Henderson	16.00	12.00	6.50
8	Keith Mitchell/ Dave Henderson	5.00	3.75	2.00
9	Kim Batiste/ Barry Larkin	5.00	3.75	2.00
10	Todd Hundley/ Thurman Munson	7.50	5.50	3.00
11	Eddie Zosky/ Cal Ripken, Jr.	20.00	15.00	8.00
12	Todd Van Poppel/ Nolan Ryan	25.00	19.00	10.00
13	Jim Thome/ Ryne Sandberg	20.00	15.00	8.00
14	Dave Fleming/ Bobby Murcer	5.00	3.75	2.00
15	Royce Clayton/ Ozzie Smith	8.00	6.00	3.25
16	Don Harris/ Darryl Strawberry	5.00	3.75	2.00
17	Chad Curtis/ Alan Trammell	8.00	6.00	3.25
18	Derek Bell/ Dave Winfield	8.00	6.00	3.25

1992 Score Rookie & Traded

This 110-card set features traded players, free agents and top rookies from 1992. The cards are styled after the regular 1992 Score cards. Cards 80-110 feature the rookies. The set was released as a boxed set and was available at hobby shops and through hobby dealers.

	MT	NR MT	EX
Complete Set (110):	30.00	22.00	12.00
Common Player:	.05	.04	.02

Photos not available at press time

		MT	NR MT	EX
1	Gary Sheffield	.60	.45	.25
2	Kevin Seitzer	.05	.04	.02
3	Danny Tartabull	.08	.06	.03
4	Steve Sax	.06	.05	.02
5	Bobby Bonilla	.50	.40	.20
6	Frank Viola	.08	.06	.03
7	Dave Winfield	1.00	.70	.40
8	Rick Sutcliffe	.08	.06	.03
9	Jose Canseco	1.00	.70	.40
10	Greg Swindell	.08	.06	.03
11	Eddie Murray	1.00	.70	.40
12	Randy Myers	.06	.05	.02
13	Wally Joyner	.08	.06	.03
14	Kenny Lofton	3.00	2.25	1.25
15	Jack Morris	.25	.15	.08
16	Charlie Hayes	.60	.45	.25
17	Pete Incaviglia	.06	.05	.02
18	Kevin Mitchell	.08	.06	.03
19	Kurt Stillwell	.05	.04	.02
20	Bret Saberhagen	.08	.06	.03
21	Steve Buechele	.05	.04	.02
22	John Smiley	.06	.05	.02
23	Sammy Sosa	.60	.45	.25
24	George Bell	.08	.06	.03
25	Curt Schilling	.08	.06	.03
26	Dick Schofield	.05	.04	.02
27	David Cone	.08	.06	.03
28	Dan Gladden	.05	.04	.02
29	Kirk McCaskill	.05	.04	.02
30	Mike Gallego	.05	.04	.02
31	Kevin McReynolds	.06	.05	.02
32	Bill Swift	.06	.05	.02
33	Dave Martinez	.05	.04	.02
34	Storm Davis	.05	.04	.02
35	Willie Randolph	.06	.05	.02
36	Melido Perez	.05	.04	.02
37	Mark Carreon	.05	.04	.02
38	Doug Jones	.05	.04	.02
39	Gregg Jefferies	.60	.45	.25
40	Mike Jackson	.05	.04	.02
41	Dickie Thon	.05	.04	.02
42	Eric King	.05	.04	.02
43	Herm Winningham	.05	.04	.02
44	Derek Lilliquist	.05	.04	.02
45	Dave Anderson	.05	.04	.02
46	Jeff Reardon	.08	.06	.03
47	Scott Bankhead	.05	.04	.02
48	Cory Snyder	.05	.04	.02
49	Al Newman	.05	.04	.02
50	Keith Miller	.05	.04	.02
51	Dave Burba	.05	.04	.02
52	Bill Pecota	.05	.04	.02
53	Chuck Crim	.05	.04	.02
54	Mariano Duncan	.08	.06	.03
55	Dave Gallagher	.05	.04	.02
56	Chris Gwynn	.05	.04	.02
57	Scott Ruskin	.05	.04	.02
58	Jack Armstrong	.05	.04	.02
59	Gary Carter	.12	.09	.05
60	Andres Galarraga	.60	.45	.25
61	Ken Hill	.20	.15	.08
62	Eric Davis	.50	.40	.20
63	Ruben Sierra	.60	.45	.25
64	Darrin Fletcher	.05	.04	.02
65	Tim Belcher	.06	.05	.02
66	Mike Morgan	.06	.05	.02
67	Scott Scudder	.05	.04	.02
68	Tom Candiotti	.05	.04	.02
69	Hubie Brooks	.05	.04	.02
70	Kal Daniels	.05	.04	.02
71	Bruce Ruffin	.05	.04	.02
72	Billy Hatcher	.08	.06	.03
73	Bob Melvin	.05	.04	.02
74	Lee Guetterman	.05	.04	.02
75	Rene Gonzales	.05	.04	.02
76	Kevin Bass	.05	.04	.02
77	Tom Bolton	.05	.04	.02
78	John Wetteland	.08	.06	.03
79	Bip Roberts	.08	.06	.03
80	Pat Listach(FC)	1.25	.90	.50
81	John Doherty(FC)	.50	.40	.20
82	Sam Militello(FC)	.75	.60	.30
83	Brian Jordan(FC)	3.00	2.25	1.25
84	Jeff Kent(FC)	1.50	1.25	.60
85	Dave Fleming(FC)	1.50	1.25	.60
86	Jeff Tackett(FC)	.12	.09	.05
87	Chad Curtis(FC)	3.00	2.25	1.25
88	Eric Fox	.12	.09	.05
89	Denny Neagle(FC)	.12	.09	.05
90	Donovan Osborne(FC)	1.00	.70	.40
91	Carlos Hernandez(FC)	.12	.09	.05
92	Tim Wakefield(FC)	.75	.60	.30
93	Tim Salmon(FC)	20.00	24.00	15.00
94	Dave Nilsson(FC)	.20	.15	.08
95	Mike Perez(FC)	.12	.09	.05
96	Pat Hentgen(FC)	2.00	1.50	.80
97	Frank Seminara(FC)	.12	.09	.05
98	Ruben Amaro, Jr.(FC)	.12	.09	.05
99	Archi Cianfrocco(FC)	.35	.25	.14
100	Andy Stankiewicz(FC)	.35	.25	.14
101	Jim Bullinger(FC)	.12	.09	.05
102	Pat Mahomes(FC)	.50	.40	.20
103	Hipolito Pichardo(FC)	.12	.09	.05
104	Bret Boone(FC)	2.00	1.50	.80
105	John Vander Wal(FC)	.12	.09	.05
106	Vince Horsman(FC)	.10	.08	.04
107	James Austin(FC)	.10	.08	.04
108	Brian Williams(FC)	.12	.09	.05
109	Dan Walters(FC)	.12	.09	.05
110	Wil Cordero(FC)	1.00	.70	.40

1993 Score

Score's 1993 cards have white borders surrounding color action photographs. The player's name is at the bottom of the card, while his team's name and position appears on the left side in a color band. Score's logo is in the upper right. Backs have color portraits, statistics and text. Subsets feature rookies, award winners, draft picks, highlights, World Series highlights, all-star caricatures, dream team players, and the Man of the Year (Kirby Puckett). Insert sets include: Boys of Summer, the Franchise and Stat Leaders, which feature Select's card design.

	MT	NR MT	EX
Complete Set (660):	20.00	15.00	8.00
Common Player:	.04	.03	.02

		MT	NR MT	EX
1	Ken Griffey, Jr.	.50	.40	.20
2	Gary Sheffield	.15	.11	.06
3	Frank Thomas	.80	.60	.30
4	Ryne Sandberg	.20	.15	.08
5	Larry Walker	.10	.08	.04
6	Cal Ripken, Jr.	.25	.20	.10
7	Roger Clemens	.10	.08	.04
8	Bobby Bonilla	.08	.06	.03
9	Carlos Baerga	.20	.15	.08
10	Darren Daulton	.08	.06	.03
11	Travis Fryman	.10	.08	.04
12	Andy Van Slyke	.08	.06	.03

		MT	NR MT	EX
13	Jose Canseco	.15	.11	.06
14	Roberto Alomar	.20	.15	.08
15	Tom Glavine	.10	.08	.04
16	Barry Larkin	.08	.06	.03
17	Gregg Jefferies	.08	.06	.03
18	Craig Biggio	.04	.03	.02
19	Shane Mack	.04	.03	.02
20	Brett Butler	.04	.03	.02
21	Dennis Eckersley	.08	.06	.03
22	Will Clark	.20	.15	.08
23	Don Mattingly	.20	.15	.08
24	Tony Gwynn	.15	.11	.06
25	Ivan Rodriguez	.15	.11	.06
26	Shawon Dunston	.04	.03	.02
27	Mike Mussina	.10	.08	.04
28	Marquis Grissom	.10	.08	.04
29	Charles Nagy	.04	.03	.02
30	Lenny Dykstra	.10	.08	.04
31	Cecil Fielder	.20	.15	.08
32	Jay Bell	.08	.06	.03
33	B.J. Surhoff	.04	.03	.02
34	Bob Tewksbury	.04	.03	.02
35	Danny Tartabull	.04	.03	.02
36	Terry Pendleton	.08	.06	.03
37	Jack Morris	.04	.03	.02
38	Hal Morris	.04	.03	.02
39	Luis Polonia	.04	.03	.02
40	Ken Caminiti	.04	.03	.02
41	Robin Ventura	.15	.11	.06
42	Darryl Strawberry	.15	.11	.06
43	Wally Joyner	.10	.08	.04
44	Fred McGriff	.15	.11	.06
45	Kevin Tapani	.04	.03	.02
46	Matt Williams	.10	.08	.04
47	Robin Yount	.15	.11	.06
48	Ken Hill	.04	.03	.02
49	Edgar Martinez	.08	.06	.03
50	Mark Grace	.08	.06	.03
51	Juan Gonzalez	.50	.40	.20
52	Curt Schilling	.04	.03	.02
53	Dwight Gooden	.08	.06	.03
54	Chris Hoiles	.04	.03	.02
55	Frank Viola	.04	.03	.02
56	Ray Lankford	.04	.03	.02
57	George Brett	.25	.20	.10
58	Kenny Lofton	.15	.11	.06
59	Nolan Ryan	.50	.40	.20
60	Mickey Tettleton	.04	.03	.02
61	John Smoltz	.04	.03	.02
62	Howard Johnson	.08	.06	.03
63	Eric Karros	.20	.15	.08
64	Rick Aguilera	.04	.03	.02
65	Steve Finley	.04	.03	.02
66	Mark Langston	.04	.03	.02
67	Bill Swift	.04	.03	.02
68	John Olerud	.15	.11	.06
69	Kevin McReynolds	.04	.03	.02
70	Jack McDowell	.08	.06	.03
71	Rickey Henderson	.20	.15	.08
72	Brian Harper	.04	.03	.02
73	Mike Morgan	.04	.03	.02
74	Rafael Palmeiro	.10	.08	.04
75	Dennis Martinez	.04	.03	.02
76	Tino Martinez	.04	.03	.02
77	Eddie Murray	.12	.09	.05
78	Ellis Burks	.08	.06	.03
79	John Kruk	.08	.06	.03
80	Gregg Olson	.04	.03	.02
81	Bernard Gilkey	.04	.03	.02
82	Milt Cuyler	.04	.03	.02
83	Mike LaValliere	.04	.03	.02
84	Albert Belle	.10	.08	.04
85	Bip Roberts	.08	.06	.03
86	Melido Perez	.04	.03	.02
87	Otis Nixon	.06	.05	.02
88	Bill Spiers	.04	.03	.02
89	Jeff Bagwell	.15	.11	.06
90	Orel Hershiser	.10	.08	.04
91	Andy Benes	.10	.08	.04
92	Devon White	.08	.06	.03
93	Willie McGee	.06	.05	.02
94	Ozzie Guillen	.06	.05	.02
95	Ivan Calderon	.04	.03	.02
96	Keith Miller	.04	.03	.02
97	Steve Buechele	.04	.03	.02
98	Kent Hrbek	.10	.08	.04
99	Dave Hollins	.04	.03	.02
100	Mike Bordick	.04	.03	.02
101	Randy Tomlin	.04	.03	.02
102	Omar Vizquel	.04	.03	.02
103	Lee Smith	.08	.06	.03
104	Leo Gomez	.04	.03	.02

		MT	NR MT	EX
105	Jose Rijo	.08	.06	.03
106	Mark Whiten	.06	.05	.02
107	Dave Justice	.20	.15	.08
108	Eddie Taubensee	.04	.03	.02
109	Lance Johnson	.08	.06	.03
110	Felix Jose	.04	.03	.02
111	Mike Harkey	.04	.03	.02
112	Randy Milligan	.06	.05	.02
113	Anthony Young	.04	.03	.02
114	Rico Brogna	.04	.03	.02
115	Bret Saberhagen	.08	.06	.03
116	Sandy Alomar, Jr.	.04	.03	.02
117	Terry Mulholland	.04	.03	.02
118	Darryl Hamilton	.04	.03	.02
119	Todd Zeile	.08	.06	.03
120	Bernie Williams	.04	.03	.02
121	Zane Smith	.04	.03	.02
122	Derek Bell	.04	.03	.02
123	Deion Sanders	.10	.08	.04
124	Luis Sojo	.04	.03	.02
125	Joe Oliver	.06	.05	.02
126	Craig Grebeck	.04	.03	.02
127	Andujar Cedeno	.04	.03	.02
128	Brian McRae	.06	.05	.02
129	Jose Offerman	.04	.03	.02
130	Pedro Munoz	.04	.03	.02
131	Bud Black	.04	.03	.02
132	Mo Vaughn	.08	.06	.03
133	Bruce Hurst	.04	.03	.02
134	Dave Henderson	.04	.03	.02
135	Tom Pagnozzi	.04	.03	.02
136	Erik Hanson	.04	.03	.02
137	Orlando Merced	.04	.03	.02
138	Dean Palmer	.08	.06	.03
139	John Franco	.04	.03	.02
140	Brady Anderson	.06	.05	.02
141	Ricky Jordan	.04	.03	.02
142	Jeff Blauser	.04	.03	.02
143	Sammy Sosa	.08	.06	.03
144	Bob Walk	.04	.03	.02
145	Delino DeShields	.08	.06	.03
146	Kevin Brown	.04	.03	.02
147	Mark Lemke	.04	.03	.02
148	Chuck Knoblauch	.08	.06	.03
149	Chris Sabo	.06	.05	.02
150	Bobby Witt	.04	.03	.02
151	Luis Gonzalez	.04	.03	.02
152	Ron Karkovice	.04	.03	.02
153	Jeff Brantley	.04	.03	.02
154	Kevin Appier	.04	.03	.02
155	Darrin Jackson	.04	.03	.02
156	Kelly Gruber	.04	.03	.02
157	Royce Clayton	.08	.06	.03
158	Chuck Finley	.04	.03	.02
159	Jeff King	.04	.03	.02
160	Greg Vaughn	.08	.06	.03
161	Geronimo Pena	.04	.03	.02
162	Steve Farr	.04	.03	.02
163	Jose Oquendo	.04	.03	.02
164	Mark Lewis	.04	.03	.02
165	John Wetteland	.06	.05	.02
166	Mike Henneman	.04	.03	.02
167	Todd Hundley	.04	.03	.02
168	Wes Chamberlain	.04	.03	.02
169	Steve Avery	.10	.08	.04
170	Mike Devereaux	.04	.03	.02
171	Reggie Sanders	.08	.06	.03
172	Jay Buhner	.08	.06	.03
173	Eric Anthony	.04	.03	.02
175	Tom Candiotti	.04	.03	.02
176	Phil Plantier	.08	.06	.03
177	Doug Henry	.04	.03	.02
178	Scott Leius	.04	.03	.02
179	Kirt Manwaring	.04	.03	.02
180	Jeff Parrett	.04	.03	.02
181	Don Slaught	.04	.03	.02
182	Scott Radinsky	.04	.03	.02
183	Luis Alicea	.04	.03	.02
184	Tom Gordon	.04	.03	.02
185	Rick Wilkins	.04	.03	.02
186	Todd Stottlemyre	.04	.03	.02
187	Moises Alou	.08	.06	.03
188	Joe Grahe	.04	.03	.02
189	Jeff Kent	.04	.03	.02
190	Bill Wegman	.04	.03	.02
191	Kim Batiste	.04	.03	.02
192	Matt Nokes	.04	.03	.02
193	Mark Wohlers	.04	.03	.02
194	Paul Sorrento	.04	.03	.02
195	Chris Hammond	.04	.03	.02
196	Scott Livingstone	.04	.03	.02

		MT	NR MT	EX
197	Doug Jones	.04	.03	.02
198	Scott Cooper	.04	.03	.02
199	Ramon Martinez	.04	.03	.02
200	Dave Valle	.04	.03	.02
201	Mariano Duncan	.04	.03	.02
202	Ben McDonald	.10	.08	.04
203	Darren Lewis	.04	.03	.02
204	Kenny Rogers	.04	.03	.02
205	Manuel Lee	.04	.03	.02
206	Scott Erickson	.06	.05	.02
207	Dan Gladden	.04	.03	.02
208	Bob Welch	.04	.03	.02
209	Greg Olson	.04	.03	.02
210	Dan Pasqua	.04	.03	.02
211	Tim Wallach	.04	.03	.02
212	Jeff Montgomery	.04	.03	.02
213	Derrick May	.04	.03	.02
214	Ed Sprague	.04	.03	.02
215	David Haas	.04	.03	.02
216	Darrin Fletcher	.04	.03	.02
217	Brian Jordan	.08	.06	.03
218	Jaime Navarro	.04	.03	.02
219	Randy Velarde	.04	.03	.02
220	Ron Gant	.10	.08	.04
221	Paul Quantrill	.04	.03	.02
222	*Damion Easley*	.15	.11	.06
223	Charlie Hough	.04	.03	.02
224	*Brad Brink*	.04	.03	.02
225	*Barry Manual*	.08	.06	.03
226	*Kevin Koslofski*	.04	.03	.02
227	*Ryan Thompson*	.15	.11	.06
228	*Mike Munoz*	.04	.03	.02
229	*Dan Wilson*	.08	.06	.03
230	*Peter Hoy*	.08	.06	.03
231	*Pedro Astacio*	.15	.11	.06
232	*Matt Stairs*	.04	.03	.02
233	*Jeff Reboulet*	.04	.03	.02
234	*Manny Alexander*	.08	.06	.03
235	*Willie Banks*	.08	.06	.03
236	*John Jaha*	.10	.08	.04
237	*Scooter Tucker*	.06	.05	.02
238	*Russ Springer*	.06	.05	.02
239	*Paul Miller*	.06	.05	.02
240	*Dan Peltier*	.06	.05	.02
241	*Ozzie Canseco*	.06	.05	.02
242	*Ben Rivera*	.06	.05	.02
243	*John Valentin*	.10	.08	.04
244	*Henry Rodriguez*	.08	.06	.03
245	*Derek Parks*	.08	.06	.03
246	*Carlos Garcia*	.10	.08	.04
247	*Tim Pugh*(FC)	.15	.11	.06
248	*Melvin Nieves*	.35	.25	.14
249	*Rich Amaral*	.08	.06	.03
250	*Willie Greene*	.08	.06	.03
251	*Tim Scott*	.08	.06	.03
252	*Dave Silvestri*	.08	.06	.03
253	*Rob Mallicoat*	.08	.06	.03
254	*Donald Harris*	.10	.08	.04
255	*Craig Colbert*	.08	.06	.03
256	Jose Guzman	.04	.03	.02
257	*Domingo Martinez*(FC)	.25	.20	.10
258	*William Suero*	.06	.05	.02
259	*Juan Guerrero*	.06	.05	.02
260	*J.T. Snow*(FC)	.75	.45	.30
261	Tony Pena	.04	.03	.02
262	*Tim Fortugno*	.06	.05	.02
263	*Tom Marsh*	.06	.05	.02
264	*Kurt Knudsen*	.08	.06	.03
265	*Tim Costo*	.08	.06	.03
266	*Steve Shifflett*	.06	.05	.02
267	*Billy Ashley*	.20	.15	.08
268	Jerry Nielsen	.06	.05	.02
269	*Pete Young*	.04	.03	.02
270	*Johnny Guzman*	.08	.06	.03
271	*Greg Colbrunn*	.08	.06	.03
272	*Jeff Nelson*	.08	.06	.03
273	*Kevin Young*	.20	.15	.08
274	*Jeff Frye*	.08	.06	.03
275	*J.T. Bruett*	.08	.06	.03
276	*Todd Pratt*	.08	.06	.03
277	*Mike Butcher*	.08	.06	.03
278	*John Flaherty*	.10	.08	.04
279	*John Patterson*	.08	.06	.03
280	*Eric Hillman*	.08	.06	.03
281	*Bien Figueros*	.08	.06	.03
282	*Shane Reynolds*	.10	.08	.04
283	*Rich Rowland*	.08	.06	.03
284	*Steve Foster*	.08	.06	.03
285	*Dave Mlicki*	.08	.06	.03
286	*Mike Piazza*	2.50	2.00	1.00
287	*Mike Trombley*	.08	.06	.03

		MT	NR MT	EX
288	*Jim Pena*	.08	.06	.03
289	*Bob Ayrault*	.08	.06	.03
290	*Henry Meroedee*	.06	.05	.02
291	Bob Wickman	.30	.25	.12
292	*Jacob Brumfield*	.08	.06	.03
293	*David Hulse*	.10	.08	.04
294	Ryan Klesko	.40	.25	.12
295	Doug Linton	.08	.06	.03
296	Steve Cooke	.04	.03	.02
297	Eddie Zosky	.04	.03	.02
298	*Gerald Williams*	.08	.06	.03
299	*Jonathan Hurst*	.08	.06	.03
300	*Larry Carter*	.06	.05	.02
301	*William Pennyfeather*	.06	.05	.02
302	*Cesar Hernandez*	.06	.05	.02
303	*Steve Hosey*	.15	.11	.06
304	*Blas Minor*	.10	.08	.04
305	*Jeff Grotewold*	.06	.05	.02
306	*Bernardo Brito*	.06	.05	.02
307	*Rafael Bournigal*	.08	.06	.03
308	*Jeff Branson*	.06	.05	.02
309	*Tom Quinlan*	.06	.05	.02
310	*Pat Gomez*	.08	.06	.03
311	*Sterling Hitchcock*	.30	.25	.12
312	*Kent Bottenfield*	.06	.05	.02
313	Alan Trammell	.04	.03	.02
314	*Cris Colon*	.06	.05	.02
315	*Paul Wagner*	.06	.05	.02
316	*Matt Maysey*	.06	.05	.02
317	Mike Stanton	.04	.03	.02
318	*Rick Tricek*	.06	.05	.02
319	*Kevin Rogers*	.06	.05	.02
320	*Mark Clark*	.06	.05	.02
321	*Pedro Martinez*	.12	.09	.05
322	*Al Martin*(FC)	.30	.25	.12
323	Mike Macfarlane	.04	.03	.02
324	*Rey Sanchez*	.06	.05	.02
325	*Roger Pavlik*	.06	.05	.02
326	*Troy Neel*	.20	.15	.08
327	*Kerry Woodson*	.06	.05	.02
328	*Wayne Kirby*	.08	.06	.03
329	*Ken Ryan*(FC)	.20	.15	.08
330	*Jesse Levis*	.06	.05	.02
331	James Austin	.04	.03	.02
332	Dan Walters	.04	.03	.02
333	Brian Williams	.04	.03	.02
334	Wil Cordero	.12	.09	.05
335	*Bret Boone*	.20	.15	.08
336	Hipolito Pichardo	.04	.03	.02
337	Pat Mahomes	.06	.05	.02
338	Andy Stankiewicz	.06	.05	.02
339	Jim Bullinger	.04	.03	.02
341	Ruben Amaro, Jr.	.06	.05	.02
342	Frank Seminara	.04	.03	.02
343	Pat Hentgen	.08	.06	.03
344	Dave Nilsson	.04	.03	.02
345	Mike Perez	.04	.03	.02
346	*Tim Salmon*	1.50	1.25	.60
347	*Tim Wakefield*	.10	.08	.04
348	Carlos Hernandez	.04	.03	.02
349	Donovan Osborne	.06	.05	.02
350	Denny Naegle	.04	.03	.02
351	Sam Militello	.06	.05	.02
352	Eric Fox	.04	.03	.02
353	John Doherty	.04	.03	.02
354	Chad Curtis	.08	.06	.03
355	Jeff Tackett	.04	.03	.02
356	Dave Fleming	.06	.05	.02
357	*Pat Listach*	.12	.09	.05
358	Kevin Wickander	.04	.03	.02
359	John VanderWal	.04	.03	.02
360	Arthur Rhodes	.06	.05	.02
361	Bob Scanlan	.04	.03	.02
362	Bob Zupcic	.04	.03	.02
363	Mel Rojas	.04	.03	.02
364	Jim Thome	.10	.08	.04
365	Bill Pecota	.04	.03	.02
366	Mark Carreon	.04	.03	.02
367	Mitch Williams	.04	.03	.02
368	Cal Eldred	.08	.06	.03
369	Stan Belinda	.04	.03	.02
370	Pat Kelly	.04	.03	.02
371	Pheal Cormier	.04	.03	.02
372	Juan Guzman	.10	.08	.04
373	Damon Berryhill	.04	.03	.02
374	Gary DiSarcina	.04	.03	.02
375	Norm Charlton	.04	.03	.02
376	Roberto Hernandez	.04	.03	.02
377	Scott Kamieniecki	.04	.03	.02
378	Rusty Meacham	.04	.03	.02
379	Kurt Stillwell	.04	.03	.02

#	Player	MT	NR MT	EX
380	Lloyd McClendon	.04	.03	.02
381	Mark Leonard	.04	.03	.02
382	Jerry Browne	.04	.03	.02
383	Glenn Davis	.04	.03	.02
384	Randy Johnson	.06	.05	.02
385	Mike Greenwell	.08	.06	.03
386	Scott Chiamparino	.04	.03	.02
387	George Bell	.06	.05	.02
388	Steve Olin	.04	.03	.02
389	Chuck McElroy	.04	.03	.02
390	Mark Gardner	.04	.03	.02
391	Rod Beck	.06	.05	.02
392	Dennis Rasmussen	.04	.03	.02
393	Charlie Leibrandt	.04	.03	.02
394	Julio Franco	.04	.03	.02
395	Pete Harnisch	.04	.03	.02
396	Sid Bream	.04	.03	.02
397	Milt Thompson	.04	.03	.02
398	Glenallen Hill	.04	.03	.02
399	Chico Walker	.04	.03	.02
400	Alex Cole	.04	.03	.02
401	Trevor Wilson	.04	.03	.02
402	Jeff Conine	.06	.05	.02
403	Kyle Abbott	.06	.05	.02
404	Tom Browning	.04	.03	.02
405	Jerald Clark	.04	.03	.02
406	Vince Horsman	.04	.03	.02
407	Kevin Mitchell	.08	.06	.03
408	Pete Smith	.04	.03	.02
409	Jeff Innis	.04	.03	.02
410	Mike Timlin	.04	.03	.02
411	Charlie Hayes	.06	.05	.02
412	Alex Fernandez	.06	.05	.02
413	Jeff Russell	.04	.03	.02
414	Jody Reed	.04	.03	.02
415	Mickey Morandini	.04	.03	.02
416	Darnell Coles	.04	.03	.02
417	Xavier Hernandez	.04	.03	.02
418	Steve Sax	.04	.03	.02
419	Joe Girardi	.04	.03	.02
420	Mike Fetters	.04	.03	.02
421	Danny Jackson	.04	.03	.02
422	Jim Gott	.04	.03	.02
423	Tim Belcher	.04	.03	.02
424	Jose Mesa	.04	.03	.02
425	Junior Felix	.04	.03	.02
426	Thomas Howard	.04	.03	.02
427	Julio Valera	.04	.03	.02
428	Dante Bichette	.06	.05	.02
429	Mike Sharperson	.04	.03	.02
430	Darryl Kile	.06	.05	.02
431	Lonnie Smith	.04	.03	.02
432	Monty Fariss	.06	.05	.02
433	Reggie Jefferson	.04	.03	.02
434	Bob McClure	.04	.03	.02
435	Craig lefferts	.04	.03	.02
436	Duane Ward	.04	.03	.02
437	Shawn Abner	.04	.03	.02
438	Roberto Kelly	.06	.05	.02
439	Paul O'Neill	.08	.06	.03
440	Alan Mills	.06	.05	.02
441	Roger Mason	.04	.03	.02
442	Gary Pettis	.04	.03	.02
443	Steve Lake	.04	.03	.02
444	Gene Larkin	.04	.03	.02
445	Larry Anderson	.04	.03	.02
446	Doug Dascenzo	.04	.03	.02
447	Daryl Boston	.04	.03	.02
448	John Candelaria	.04	.03	.02
449	Storm Davis	.04	.03	.02
450	Tom Edens	.04	.03	.02
451	Mike Maddux	.04	.03	.02
452	Tim Naehring	.04	.03	.02
453	John Orton	.04	.03	.02
454	Joey Cora	.04	.03	.02
455	Chuck Crim	.04	.03	.02
456	Dan Plesac	.04	.03	.02
457	Mike Bielecki	.04	.03	.02
458	*Terry Jorgensen*	.04	.03	.02
459	John Habyan	.04	.03	.02
460	Pete O'Brien	.04	.03	.02
461	Jeff Treadway	.04	.03	.02
462	Frank Castillo	.04	.03	.02
463	Jimmy Jones	.04	.03	.02
464	Tommy Greene	.04	.03	.02
465	Tracy Woodson	.06	.05	.02
466	Rich Rodriguez	.04	.03	.02
467	Joe Hesketh	.04	.03	.02
468	Greg Myers	.04	.03	.02
469	Kirk McCaskill	.04	.03	.02
470	Ricky Bones	.04	.03	.02
471	Lenny Webster	.04	.03	.02
472	Francisco Cabrera	.04	.03	.02
473	Turner Ward	.04	.03	.02
474	Dwayne Henry	.04	.03	.02
475	Al Osuna	.04	.03	.02
476	Craig Wilson	.04	.03	.02
477	Chris Nabholz	.04	.03	.02
478	Rafael Belliard	.04	.03	.02
479	Terry Leach	.04	.03	.02
480	Tim Teufel	.04	.03	.02
481	Dennis Eckersley (Award Winner)	.06	.05	.02
482	Barry Bonds (Award Winner)	.10	.08	.04
483	Dennis Eckersley (Award Winner)	.06	.05	.02
484	Greg Maddux (Award Winner)	.08	.06	.03
485	Pat Listach (ROY)	.10	.08	.04
486	Eric Karros (ROY)	.12	.09	.05
487	*Jamie Arnold*(FC)	.20	.15	.08
488	*B.J. Wallace*(FC)	.35	.25	.14
489	*Derek Jeter*(FC)	.45	.35	.20
490	*Jason Kendall*(FC)	.25	.20	.10
491	*Rick Helling*(FC)	.20	.15	.08
492	*Derek Wallace*(FC)	.20	.15	.08
493	*Sean Lowe*(FC)	.20	.15	.08
494	*Shannon Stewart*(FC)	.20	.15	.08
495	*Benji Grigsby*(FC)	.20	.15	.08
496	*Todd Steverson*(FC)	.20	.15	.08
497	*Dan Serafini*(FC)	.25	.20	.10
498	*Michael Tucker*(FC)	.50	.40	.20
499	Chris Roberts (Draft Pick)	.08	.06	.03
500	Pete Janicki (Draft Pick)	.08	.06	.03
501	*Jeff Schmidt*(FC)	.20	.15	.08
502	Edgar Martinez (Draft Pick)	.04	.03	.02
503	Omar Vizquel (AS)	.04	.03	.02
504	Ken Griffey, Jr. (AS)	.30	.25	.12
505	Kirby Puckett (AS)	.10	.08	.04
506	Joe Carter (AS)	.10	.08	.04
507	Ivan Rodriguez (AS)	.06	.05	.02
508	Jack Morris (AS)	.04	.03	.02
509	Dennis Eckersley (AS)	.04	.03	.02
510	Frank Thomas (AS)	.35	.25	.14
511	Roberto Alomar (AS)	.10	.08	.04
512	Mickey Morandini (Highlight)	.04	.03	.02
513	Dennis Eckersley (Highlight)	.06	.05	.02
514	Jeff Reardon (Highlight)	.04	.03	.02
515	Danny Tartabull (Hightlight)	.04	.03	.02
516	Bip Roberts (Highlight)	.04	.03	.02
517	George Brett (Highlight)	.08	.06	.03
518	Robin Yount (Highlight)	.08	.06	.03
519	Kevin Gross (Highlight)	.04	.03	.02
520	Ed Sprague (World Series Highlight)	.04	.03	.02
521	Dave Winfield (World Series Highlight)	.08	.06	.03
522	Ozzie Smith (AS)	.06	.05	.02
523	Barry Bonds (AS)	.10	.08	.04
524	Andy Van Slyke (AS)	.04	.03	.02
525	Tony Gwynn (AS)	.08	.06	.03
526	Darren Daulton (AS)	.06	.05	.02
527	Greg Maddux (AS)	.08	.06	.03
528	Fred McGriff (AS)	.08	.06	.03
529	Lee Smith (AS)	.04	.03	.02
530	Ryne Sandberg (AS)	.10	.08	.04
531	Gary Sheffield (AS)	.08	.06	.03
532	Ozzie Smith (Dream Team)	.06	.05	.02
533	Kirby Puckett (Dream Team)	.08	.06	.03
534	Gary Sheffield (Dream Team)	.06	.05	.02
535	Andy Van Slyke (Dream Team)	.04	.03	.02
536	Ken Griffey, Jr. (Dream Team)	.25	.20	.10
537	Ivan Rodriguez (Dream Team)	.08	.06	.03
538	Charles Nagy (Dream Team)	.04	.03	.02
539	Tom Glavine (Dream Team)	.10	.08	.04
540	Dennis Eckersley (Dream Team)	.06	.05	.02
541	Frank Thomas (Dream Team)	.40	.30	.15
542	Roberto Alomar (Dream Team)	.10	.08	.04
543	Sean Barry	.04	.03	.02
544	Mike Schooler	.04	.03	.02
545	Chuck Carr	.04	.03	.02
546	Lenny Harris	.04	.03	.02
547	Gary Scott	.04	.03	.02
548	Derek Lilliquist	.04	.03	.02
549	Brian Hunter	.04	.03	.02
550	Kirby Puckett (MOY)	.10	.08	.04
551	Jim Eisenreich	.04	.03	.02
552	Andre Dawson	.06	.05	.02
553	*David Nied*	.80	.60	.30
554	Spike Owen	.04	.03	.02
555	Greg Gagne	.06	.05	.02
556	Sid Fernandez	.04	.03	.02
557	Mark McGwire	.20	.15	.08
558	Bryan Harvey	.06	.05	.02
559	Harold Reynolds	.04	.03	.02

		MT	NR MT	EX
560	Barry Bonds	.30	.25	.12
561	*Eric Wedge*(FC)	.25	.20	.10
562	Ozzie Smith	.12	.09	.05
563	Rick Sutcliffe	.04	.03	.02
564	Jeff Reardon	.04	.03	.02
565	*Alex Arias*	.04	.03	.02
566	Greg Swindell	.04	.03	.02
567	Brook Jacoby	.04	.03	.02
568	Pete Incaviglia	.04	.03	.02
569	*Butch Henry*	.06	.05	.02
570	Eric Davis	.08	.06	.03
571	Kevin Seitzer	.04	.03	.02
572	Tony Fernandez	.04	.03	.02
573	*Steve Reed*	.08	.06	.03
574	Cory Snyder	.04	.03	.02
575	Joe Carter	.12	.09	.05
576	Greg Maddux	.15	.11	.06
577	Bert Blyleven	.08	.06	.03
578	Kevin Bass	.04	.03	.02
579	Carlton Fisk	.12	.09	.05
580	Doug Drabek	.08	.06	.03
581	Mark Gubicza	.06	.05	.02
582	Bobby Thigpen	.04	.03	.02
583	Chili Davis	.08	.06	.03
584	Scott Bankhead	.04	.03	.02
585	Harold Baines	.06	.05	.02
586	*Eric Young*	.06	.05	.02
587	Lance Parrish	.04	.03	.02
588	Juan Bell	.04	.03	.02
589	Bob Ojeda	.04	.03	.02
590	Joe Orsulak	.04	.03	.02
591	Benito Santiago	.06	.05	.02
592	Wade Boggs	.20	.15	.08
593	Robby Thompson	.06	.05	.02
594	Erik Plunk	.04	.03	.02
595	Hensley Meulens	.04	.03	.02
596	Lou Whitaker	.10	.08	.04
597	Dale Murphy	.20	.15	.08
598	Paul Molitor	.20	.15	.08
599	Greg W. Harris	.04	.03	.02
600	Darren Holmes	.04	.03	.02
601	Dave Martinez	.04	.03	.02
602	Tom Henke	.04	.03	.02
603	Mike Benjamin	.04	.03	.02
604	Rene Gonzales	.04	.03	.02
605	Roger McDowell	.04	.03	.02
606	Kirby Puckett	.20	.15	.08
607	Randy Myers	.04	.03	.02
608	Ruben Sierra	.10	.08	.04
609	Wilson Alvarez	.04	.03	.02
610	Dave Segui	.04	.03	.02
611	Juan Samuel	.04	.03	.02
612	Tom Brunansky	.04	.03	.02
613	Willie Randolph	.04	.03	.02
614	Tony Phillips	.04	.03	.02
615	Candy Maldonado	.04	.03	.02
616	Chris Bosio	.04	.03	.02
617	Bret Barberie	.06	.05	.02
618	Scott Sanderson	.04	.03	.02
619	Ron Darling	.04	.03	.02
620	Dave Winfield	.15	.11	.06
621	Mike Felder	.04	.03	.02
622	Greg Hibbard	.04	.03	.02
623	Mike Scioscia	.04	.03	.02
624	John Smiley	.04	.03	.02
625	Alejandro Pena	.04	.03	.02
626	Terry Steinbach	.08	.06	.03
627	Freddie Benavides	.04	.03	.02
628	Kevin Reimer	.04	.03	.02
629	Braulio Castillo	.04	.03	.02
630	Dave Stieb	.04	.03	.02
631	Dave Magadan	.08	.06	.03
632	Scott Fletcher	.04	.03	.02
633	Cris Carpenter	.04	.03	.02
634	Kevin Maas	.06	.05	.02
635	Todd Worrell	.04	.03	.02
636	Rob Deer	.04	.03	.02
637	Dwight Smith	.04	.03	.02
638	Chito Martinez	.04	.03	.02
639	Jimmy Key	.04	.03	.02
640	Greg Harris	.04	.03	.02
641	Mike Moore	.04	.03	.02
642	Pat Borders	.04	.03	.02
643	Bill Gullickson	.06	.05	.02
644	Gary Gaetti	.04	.03	.02
645	David Howard	.04	.03	.02
646	Jim Abbott	.10	.08	.04
647	Willie Wilson	.04	.03	.02
648	David Wells	.04	.03	.02
649	Andres Galarraga	.08	.06	.03
650	Vince Coleman	.06	.05	.02
651	Rob Dibble	.06	.05	.02
652	Frank Tanana	.04	.03	.02
653	Steve Decker	.04	.03	.02
654	David Cone	.06	.05	.02
655	Jack Armstrong	.04	.03	.02
656	Dave Stewart	.08	.06	.03
657	Billy Hatcher	.06	.05	.02
658	Tim Raines	.08	.06	.03
659	Walt Weiss	.06	.05	.02
660	Jose Lind	.06	.05	.02

1993 Score Boys of Summer

These cards were available as inserts only in Score 35-card Super Packs, about one in every four packs. Borderless fronts have a color action photo of the player superimposed over the sun. The player's name is in black script in a green strip at bottom, along with a subset logo. On back is a player portrait, again with the sun as a background. Subset, company, team and major league logos are in color on the right, and there is a short career summary on the green background at bottom.

		MT	NR MT	EX
Complete Set (30):		75.00	56.00	30.00
Common Player:		.75	.60	.30
1	Billy Ashley	4.00	3.00	1.50
2	Tim Salmon	18.00	13.50	7.25
3	Pedro Martinez	1.25	.90	.50
4	Luis Mercedes	.75	.60	.30
5	Mike Piazza	25.00	18.50	10.00
6	Troy Neel	1.50	1.25	.60
7	Melvin Nieves	2.50	2.00	1.00
8	Ryan Klesko	4.50	3.50	1.75
9	Ryan Thompson	.90	.70	.35
10	Kevin Young	2.00	1.50	.80
11	Gerald Williams	.75	.60	.30
12	Willie Greene	1.50	1.25	.60
13	John Patterson	.75	.60	.30
14	Carlos Garcia	1.50	1.25	.60
15	Eddie Zosky	.75	.60	.30
16	Sean Berry	.75	.60	.30
17	Rico Brogna	1.25	.90	.50
18	Larry Carter	1.00	.70	.40
19	Bobby Ayala	1.00	.70	.40
20	Alan Embree	1.00	.70	.40
21	Donald Harris	.75	.60	.30
22	Sterling Hitchcock	2.00	1.50	.80
23	David Nied	3.50	2.75	1.50
24	Henry Mercedes	1.00	.70	.40
25	Ozzie Canseco	.75	.60	.30
26	David Hulse	1.50	1.25	.60
27	Al Martin	3.00	2.25	1.25
28	Dan Wilson	.75	.60	.30
29	Paul Miller	1.00	.70	.40
30	Rich Rowland	.75	.60	.30

Definitions for grading conditions are located in the Introduction of this price guide.

1993 Score The Franchise

These glossy inserts have full-bleed color action photos against a darkened background so that the player stands out. Cards could be found in 16-card packs only; odds of finding one are 1 in every 24 packs. The fronts have a gold foil stamping which says Franchise.

		MT	NR MT	EX
Complete Set (28):		80.00	60.00	32.00
Common Player:		1.00	.70	.40
1	Cal Ripken, Jr.	7.00	5.25	2.75
2	Roger Clemens	5.00	3.75	2.00
3	Mark Langston	1.00	.70	.40
4	Frank Thomas	18.00	13.50	7.25
5	Carlos Baerga	5.00	3.75	2.00
6	Cecil Fielder	3.50	2.75	1.50
7	Gregg Jefferies	1.00	.70	.40
8	Robin Yount	4.00	3.00	1.50
9	Kirby Puckett	6.00	4.50	2.50
10	Don Mattingly	3.00	2.25	1.25
11	Dennis Eckersley	1.00	.70	.40
12	Ken Griffey Jr.	14.00	10.50	5.50
13	Juan Gonzalez	14.00	10.50	5.50
14	Roberto Alomar	6.00	4.50	2.50
15	Terry Pendleton	1.00	.70	.40
16	Ryne Sandberg	6.00	4.50	2.50
17	Barry Larkin	1.00	.70	.40
18	Jeff Bagwell	3.00	2.25	1.25
19	Brett Butler	1.00	.70	.40
20	Larry Walker	1.50	1.25	.60
21	Bobby Bonilla	1.00	.70	.40
22	Darren Daulton	2.00	1.50	.80
23	Andy Van Slyke	1.00	.70	.40
24	Ray Lankford	1.00	.70	.40
25	Gary Sheffield	2.00	1.50	.80
26	Will Clark	2.50	2.00	1.00
27	Bryan Harvey	1.00	.70	.40
28	David Nied	3.50	2.75	1.50

1993 Score Gold Dream Team

Photos not available at press time

This 11-player insert set consists of the same players in the regular set's Dream Team subset, except the cards are gold foil stamped. There is an unnumbered header card in the set, which was available only via a mail-in offer.

		MT	NR MT	EX
Complete Set (12):		15.00	10.00	5.00
Common Player:		.50	.30	.15
1	Ozzie Smith	1.00	.60	.30
2	Kirby Puckett	2.00	1.50	.75
3	Gary Sheffield	1.50	1.00	.50
4	Andy Van Slyke	.50	.40	.20
5	Ken Griffey, Jr.	4.00	3.00	1.50
6	Ivan Rodriguez	1.00	.60	.30
7	Charles Nagy	.50	.40	.20
8	Tom Glavine	1.50	1.00	.60
9	Dennis Eckersley	.75	.60	.30
10	Frank Thomas	5.00	3.00	1.50
11	Roberto Alomar	2.50	1.50	.75
---	Header card	.05	.04	.02

1993 Score Select

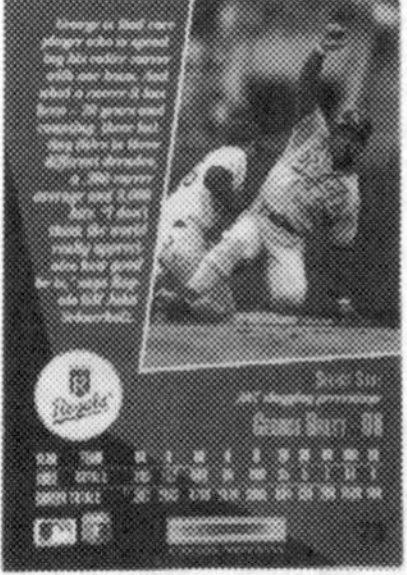

This 400-card set from Score is designed for the mid-priced card market. The card fronts feature green borders on two sides of the card with the photo filling the remaining portion of the card front. "Score Select" appears within the photo. The backs feature an additional photo, player information and statistics. Cards numbered 271-360 are devoted to rookies and draft picks. Several cards from this set are printed horizontally. The cards are UV coated on both sides.

		MT	NR MT	EX
Complete Set (405):		32.00	24.00	15.00
Common Player:		.06	.05	.02
1	Barry Bonds	.50	.40	.20
2	Ken Griffey Jr.	.75	.60	.30
3	Will Clark	.20	.15	.08
4	Kirby Puckett	.25	.20	.10
5	Tony Gwynn	.20	.15	.08
6	Frank Thomas	1.00	.70	.40
7	Tom Glavine	.20	.15	.08
8	Roberto Alomar	.25	.20	.10
9	Andre Dawson	.15	.11	.06
10	Ron Darling	.08	.06	.03
11	Bobby Bonilla	.15	.11	.06
12	Danny Tartabull	.15	.11	.06
13	Darren Daulton	.12	.09	.05
14	Roger Clemens	.25	.20	.10
15	Ozzie Smith	.12	.09	.05
16	Mark McGwire	.15	.11	.06
17	Terry Pendleton	.15	.11	.06
18	Cal Ripken, Jr.	.50	.40	.20
19	Fred McGriff	.20	.15	.08
20	Cecil Fielder	.25	.20	.10
21	Darryl Strawberry	.12	.09	.05
22	Robin Yount	.25	.20	.10
23	Barry Larkin	.20	.15	.08
24	Don Mattingly	.20	.15	.08
25	Craig Biggio	.10	.08	.04
26	Sandy Alomar Jr.	.15	.11	.06
27	Larry Walker	.15	.11	.06
28	Junior Felix	.06	.05	.02
29	Eddie Murray	.15	.11	.06
30	Robin Ventura	.15	.11	.06
31	Greg Maddux	.15	.11	.06
32	Dave Winfield	.20	.15	.08
33	John Kruk	.12	.09	.05

		MT	NR MT	EX
34	Wally Joyner	.12	.09	.05
35	Andy Van Slyke	.12	.09	.05
36	Chuck Knoblauch	.15	.11	.06
37	Tom Pagnozzi	.08	.06	.03
38	Dennis Eckersley	.15	.11	.06
39	Dave Justice	.30	.25	.12
40	Juan Gonzalez	.75	.60	.30
41	Gary Sheffield	.20	.15	.08
42	Paul Molitor	.15	.11	.06
43	Delino DeShields	.12	.09	.05
44	Travis Fryman	.25	.20	.10
45	Hal Morris	.10	.08	.04
46	Gregg Olson	.10	.08	.04
47	Ken Caminiti	.08	.06	.03
48	Wade Boggs	.15	.11	.06
49	Orel Hershiser	.12	.09	.05
50	Albert Belle	.15	.11	.06
51	Bill Swift	.08	.06	.03
52	Mark Langston	.12	.09	.05
53	Joe Girardi	.06	.05	.02
54	Keith Miller	.06	.05	.02
55	Gary Carter	.12	.09	.05
56	Brady Anderson	.15	.11	.06
57	Doc Gooden	.15	.11	.06
58	Julio Franco	.10	.08	.04
59	Lenny Dykstra	.10	.08	.04
60	Mickey Tettleton	.10	.08	.04
61	Randy Tomlin	.10	.08	.04
62	B.J. Surhoff	.08	.06	.03
63	Todd Zeile	.08	.06	.03
64	Roberto Kelly	.10	.08	.04
65	Rob Dibble	.10	.08	.04
66	Leo Gomez	.10	.08	.04
67	Doug Jones	.06	.05	.02
68	Ellis Burks	.12	.09	.05
69	Mike Scioscia	.06	.05	.02
70	Charles Nagy	.20	.15	.08
71	Cory Snyder	.06	.05	.02
72	Devon White	.08	.06	.03
73	Mark Grace	.12	.09	.05
74	Luis Polonia	.06	.05	.02
75	John Smiley	.08	.06	.03
76	Carlton Fisk	.15	.11	.06
77	Luis Sojo	.06	.05	.02
78	George Brett	.20	.15	.08
79	Mitch Williams	.10	.08	.04
80	Kent Hrbek	.10	.08	.04
81	Jay Bell	.10	.08	.04
82	Edgar Martinez	.15	.11	.06
83	Lee Smith	.10	.08	.04
84	Deion Sanders	.20	.15	.08
85	Bill Gullickson	.08	.06	.03
86	Paul O'Neill	.08	.06	.03
87	Kevin Seitzer	.08	.06	.03
88	Steve Finley	.08	.06	.03
89	Mel Hall	.08	.06	.03
90	Nolan Ryan	.60	.45	.25
91	Eric Davis	.15	.11	.06
92	Mike Mussina	.50	.40	.20
93	Tony Fernandez	.08	.06	.03
94	Frank Viola	.12	.09	.05
95	Matt Williams	.12	.09	.05
96	Joe Carter	.15	.11	.06
97	Ryne Sandberg	.35	.25	.14
98	Jim Abbott	.15	.11	.06
99	Marquis Grissom	.15	.11	.06
100	George Bell	.15	.11	.06
101	Howard Johnson	.10	.08	.04
102	Kevin Appier	.12	.09	.05
103	Dale Murphy	.12	.09	.05
104	Shane Mack	.10	.08	.04
105	Jose Lind	.08	.06	.03
106	Rickey Henderson	.30	.25	.12
107	Bob Tewksbury	.08	.06	.03
108	Kevin Mitchell	.12	.09	.05
109	Steve Avery	.15	.11	.06
110	Candy Maldonado	.08	.06	.03
111	Bip Roberts	.10	.08	.04
112	Lou Whitaker	.10	.08	.04
113	Jeff Bagwell	.25	.20	.10
114	Dante Bichette	.06	.05	.02
115	Brett Butler	.10	.08	.04
116	Melldo Perez	.06	.05	.02
117	Andy Benes	.12	.09	.05
118	Randy Johnson	.08	.06	.03
119	Willie McGee	.08	.06	.03
120	Jody Reed	.08	.06	.03
121	Shawon Dunston	.08	.06	.03
122	Carlos Baerga	.30	.25	.12
123	Bret Saberhagen	.12	.09	.05
124	John Olerud	.35	.25	.14
125	Ivan Calderon	.08	.06	.03

		MT	NR MT	EX
126	Bryan Harvey	.10	.08	.04
127	Terry Mulholland	.08	.06	.03
128	Ozzie Guillen	.10	.08	.04
129	Steve Buechele	.08	.06	.03
130	Kevin Tapani	.08	.06	.03
131	Felix Jose	.12	.09	.05
132	Terry Steinbach	.08	.06	.03
133	Ron Gant	.12	.09	.05
134	Harold Reynolds	.08	.06	.03
135	Chris Sabo	.10	.08	.04
136	Ivan Rodriguez	.20	.15	.08
137	Eric Anthony	.08	.06	.03
138	Mike Henneman	.08	.06	.03
139	Robby Thompson	.08	.06	.03
140	Scott Fletcher	.06	.05	.02
141	Bruce Hurst	.08	.06	.03
142	Kevin Maas	.08	.06	.03
143	Tom Candiotti	.08	.06	.03
144	Chris Hoiles	.20	.15	.08
145	Mike Morgan	.08	.06	.03
146	Mark Whiten	.15	.11	.06
147	Dennis Martinez	.10	.08	.04
148	Tony Pena	.08	.06	.03
149	Dave Magadan	.08	.06	.03
150	Mark Lewis	.10	.08	.04
151	Mariano Duncan	.06	.05	.02
152	Gregg Jefferies	.15	.11	.06
153	Doug Drabek	.12	.09	.05
154	Brian Harper	.12	.09	.05
155	Ray Lankford	.20	.15	.08
156	Carney Lansford	.08	.06	.03
157	Mike Sharperson	.08	.06	.03
158	Jack Morris	.15	.11	.06
159	Otis Nixon	.10	.08	.04
160	Steve Sax	.10	.08	.04
161	Mark Lemke	.08	.06	.03
162	Rafael Palmeiro	.12	.09	.05
163	Jose Rijo	.12	.09	.05
164	Omar Vizquel	.06	.05	.02
165	Sammy Sosa	.08	.06	.03
166	Milt Cuyler	.08	.06	.03
167	John Franco	.08	.06	.03
168	Darryl Hamilton	.08	.06	.03
169	Ken Hill	.10	.08	.04
170	Mike Devereaux	.10	.08	.04
171	Don Slaught	.06	.05	.02
172	Steve Farr	.06	.05	.02
173	Bernard Gilkey	.10	.08	.04
174	Mike Fetters	.06	.05	.02
175	Vince Coleman	.08	.06	.03
176	Kevin McReynolds	.10	.08	.04
177	John Smoltz	.15	.11	.06
178	Greg Gagne	.08	.06	.03
179	Greg Swindell	.15	.11	.06
180	Juan Guzman	.20	.15	.08
181	Kal Daniels	.08	.06	.03
182	Rick Sutcliffe	.12	.09	.05
183	Orlando Merced	.12	.09	.05
184	Bill Wegman	.08	.06	.03
185	Mark Gardner	.08	.06	.03
186	Rob Deer	.08	.06	.03
187	Dave Hollins	.15	.11	.06
188	Jack Clark	.08	.06	.03
189	Brian Hunter	.10	.08	.04
190	Tim Wallach	.08	.06	.03
191	Tim Belcher	.08	.06	.03
192	Walt Weiss	.08	.06	.03
193	Kurt Stillwell	.06	.05	.02
194	Charlie Hayes	.08	.06	.03
195	Willie Randolph	.08	.06	.03
196	Jack McDowell	.15	.11	.06
197	Jose Offerman	.10	.08	.04
198	Chuck Finley	.10	.08	.04
199	Darrin Jackson	.08	.06	.03
200	Kelly Gruber	.08	.06	.03
201	John Wetteland	.12	.09	.05
202	Jay Buhner	.08	.06	.03
203	Mike LaValliere	.06	.05	.02
204	Kevin Brown	.12	.09	.05
205	Luis Gonzalez	.12	.09	.05
206	Rick Aguilera	.12	.09	.05
207	Norm Charlton	.12	.09	.05
208	Mike Bordick	.12	.09	.05
209	Charlie Leibrandt	.06	.05	.02
210	Tom Brunansky	.08	.06	.03
211	Tom Henke	.10	.08	.04
212	Randy Milligan	.06	.05	.02
213	Ramon Martinez	.15	.11	.06
214	Mo Vaughn	.08	.06	.03
215	Randy Myers	.08	.06	.03
216	Greg Hibbard	.08	.06	.03

		MT	NR MT	EX
217	Wes Chamberlain	.10	.08	.04
218	Tony Phillips	.10	.08	.04
219	Pete Harnisch	.10	.08	.04
220	Mike Gallego	.06	.05	.02
221	Bud Black	.06	.05	.02
222	Greg Vaughn	.10	.08	.04
223	Milt Thompson	.06	.05	.02
224	Ben McDonald	.15	.11	.06
225	Billy Hatcher	.06	.05	.02
226	Paul Sorrento	.08	.06	.03
227	Mark Gubicza	.08	.06	.03
228	Mike Greenwell	.08	.06	.03
229	Curt Schilling	.08	.06	.03
230	Alan Trammell	.10	.08	.04
231	Zane Smith	.08	.06	.03
232	Bobby Thigpen	.10	.08	.04
233	Greg Olson	.06	.05	.02
234	Joe Orsulak	.06	.05	.02
235	Joe Oliver	.06	.05	.02
236	Tim Raines	.12	.09	.05
237	Juan Samuel	.06	.05	.02
238	Chili Davis	.08	.06	.03
239	Spike Owen	.06	.05	.02
240	Dave Stewart	.12	.09	.05
241	Jim Eisenreich	.06	.05	.02
242	Phil Plantier	.20	.15	.08
243	Sid Fernandez	.10	.08	.04
244	Dan Gladden	.06	.05	.02
245	Mickey Morandini	.12	.09	.05
246	Tino Martinez	.12	.09	.05
247	Kirt Manwaring	.06	.05	.02
248	Dean Palmer	.12	.09	.05
249	Tom Browning	.08	.06	.03
250	Brian McRae	.12	.09	.05
251	Scott Leius	.08	.06	.03
252	Bert Blyleven	.08	.06	.03
253	Scott Erickson	.10	.08	.04
254	Bob Welch	.10	.08	.04
255	Pat Kelly	.10	.08	.04
256	Felix Fermin	.06	.05	.02
257	Harold Baines	.12	.09	.05
258	Duane Ward	.08	.06	.03
259	Bill Spiers	.08	.06	.03
260	Jaime Navarro	.10	.08	.04
261	Scott Sanderson	.08	.06	.03
262	Gary Gaetti	.08	.06	.03
263	Bob Ojeda	.06	.05	.02
264	Jeff Montgomery	.08	.06	.03
265	Scott Bankhead	.08	.06	.03
266	Lance Johnson	.08	.06	.03
267	Rafael Belliard	.06	.05	.02
268	Kevin Reimer	.08	.06	.03
269	Benito Santiago	.12	.09	.05
270	Mike Moore	.08	.06	.03
271	Dave Fleming	.15	.11	.06
272	Moises Alou	.15	.11	.06
273	Pat Listach	.12	.09	.05
274	Reggie Sanders	.30	.25	.12
275	Kenny Lofton	.40	.30	.15
276	Donovan Osborne	.20	.15	.08
277	Rusty Meacham	.20	.15	.08
278	Eric Karros	.30	.25	.12
279	Andy Stankiewicz	.15	.11	.06
280	Brian Jordan	.15	.11	.06
281	Gary DiSarcina	.08	.06	.03
282	Mark Wohlers	.08	.06	.03
283	Dave Nilsson	.20	.15	.08
284	Anthony Young	.10	.08	.04
285	Jim Bullinger	.12	.09	.05
286	Derek Bell	.20	.15	.08
287	Brian Williams	.15	.11	.06
288	Julio Valera	.15	.11	.06
289	Dan Walters	.15	.11	.06
290	Chad Curtis	.25	.20	.10
291	Michael Tucker	.80	.60	.30
292	Bob Zupcic	.15	.11	.06
293	Todd Hundley	.15	.11	.06
294	Jeff Tackett	.15	.11	.06
295	Greg Colbrunn	.15	.11	.06
296	Cal Eldred	.40	.30	.15
297	Chris Roberts	.20	.15	.08
298	John Doherty	.20	.15	.08
299	Denny Neagle	.12	.09	.05
300	Arthur Rhodes	.20	.15	.08
301	Mark Clark	.20	.15	.08
302	Scott Cooper	.20	.15	.08
303	Jamie Arnold	.20	.15	.08
304	Jim Thome	.15	.11	.06
305	Frank Seminara	.15	.11	.06
306	Kurt Knudsen	.15	.11	.06
307	Tim Wakefield	.15	.11	.06

		MT	NR MT	EX
308	John Jaha	.20	.15	.08
309	Pat Hentgen	.15	.11	.06
310	B.J. Wallace	.20	.15	.08
311	Roberto Hernandez	.20	.15	.08
312	Hipolito Pichardo	.20	.15	.08
313	Eric Fox	.15	.11	.06
314	Willie Banks	.15	.11	.06
315	Sam Millitello	.20	.15	.08
316	Vince Horsman	.15	.11	.06
317	Carlos Hernandez	.15	.11	.06
318	Jeff Kent	.20	.15	.08
319	Mike Perez	.12	.09	.05
320	Scott Livingstone	.12	.09	.05
321	Jeff Conine	.15	.11	.06
322	James Austin	.15	.11	.06
323	John Vander Wal	.15	.11	.06
324	Pat Mahomes	.10	.08	.04
325	Pedro Astacio	.25	.20	.10
326	Bret Boone	.25	.20	.10
327	Matt Stairs	.15	.11	.06
328	Damion Easley	.20	.15	.08
329	Ben Rivera	.20	.15	.08
330	Reggie Jefferson	.20	.15	.08
331	Luis Mercedes	.20	.15	.08
332	Kyle Abbott	.20	.15	.08
333	Eddie Taubensee	.20	.15	.08
334	Tim McIntosh	.10	.08	.04
335	Phil Clark	.10	.08	.04
336	Will Cordero	.20	.15	.08
337	Russ Springer	.15	.11	.06
338	Craig Colbert	.10	.08	.04
339	Tim Salmon	3.00	2.25	1.25
340	Braulio Castillo	.20	.15	.08
341	Donald Harris	.12	.09	.05
342	Eric Young	.20	.15	.08
343	Bob Wickman	.25	.20	.10
344	John Valentin	.15	.11	.06
345	Dan Wilson	.15	.11	.06
346	Steve Hosey	.15	.11	.06
347	Mike Piazza	4.00	3.00	1.50
348	Willie Greene	.20	.15	.08
349	Tom Goodwin	.10	.08	.04
350	Eric Hillman	.15	.11	.06
351	Steve Reed	.15	.11	.06
352	Dan Serafini	.25	.20	.10
353	Todd Steverson	.25	.20	.10
354	Benji Grigsby	.25	.20	.10
355	Shannon Stewart	.25	.20	.10
356	Sean Lowe	.25	.20	.10
357	Derek Wallace	.25	.20	.10
358	Rick Helling	.25	.20	.10
359	Jason Kendall	.25	.20	.10
360	Derek Jeter	1.00	.70	.40
361	David Cone	.15	.11	.06
362	Jeff Reardon	.15	.11	.06
363	Bobby Witt	.08	.06	.03
364	Jose Canseco	.15	.11	.06
365	Jeff Russell	.08	.06	.03
366	Ruben Sierra	.25	.20	.10
367	Alan Mills	.06	.05	.02
368	Matt Nokes	.08	.06	.03
369	Pat Borders	.08	.06	.03
370	Pedro Munoz	.12	.09	.05
371	Danny Jackson	.06	.05	.02
372	Geronimo Pena	.10	.08	.04
373	Craig Lefferts	.08	.06	.03
374	Joe Grahe	.08	.06	.03
375	Roger McDowell	.06	.05	.02
376	Jimmy Key	.10	.08	.04
377	Steve Olin	.10	.08	.04
378	Glenn Davis	.10	.08	.04
379	Rene Gonzales	.06	.05	.02
380	Manuel Lee	.06	.05	.02
381	Ron Karkovice	.06	.05	.02
382	Sid Bream	.06	.05	.02
383	Gerald Williams	.12	.09	.05
384	Lenny Harris	.06	.05	.02
385	J.T. Snow	1.50	1.25	.60
386	Dave Stieb	.08	.06	.03
387	Kirk McCaskill	.08	.06	.03
388	Lance Parrish	.08	.06	.03
389	Craig Greback	.06	.05	.02
390	Rick Wilkins	.12	.09	.05
391	Manny Alexander	.25	.20	.10
392	Mike Schooler	.06	.05	.02
393	Bernie Williams	.12	.09	.05
394	Kevin Koslofski	.20	.15	.08
395	Willie Wilson	.08	.06	.03
396	Jeff Parrett	.06	.05	.02
397	Mike Harkey	.08	.06	.03
398	Frank Tanana	.08	.06	.03

		MT	NR MT	EX
399	Doug Henry	.08	.06	.03
400	Royce Clayton	.25	.20	.10
401	Eric Wedge	.12	.09	.05
402	Derrick May	.12	.09	.05
403	Carlos Garcia	.25	.20	.10
404	Henry Rodriguez	.12	.09	.05
405	Ryan Klesko	.20	.15	.08

1993 Score Select Aces

Cards from this set feature 24 of the top pitchers from 1992 and were included one per every 27-card Super Pack. The fronts have a picture of the player in action against an Ace card background. Backs have text and a portrait in the middle of a card suit for an Ace.

		MT	NR MT	EX
Complete Set (24):		70.00	52.00	28.00
Common Player:		3.00	2.25	1.25
1	Roger Clemens	10.00	7.50	4.00
2	Tom Glavine	6.00	4.50	2.50
3	Jack McDowell	6.00	4.50	2.50
4	Greg Maddux	7.50	5.75	3.00
5	Jack Morris	3.00	2.25	1.25
6	Dennis Martinez	3.00	2.25	1.25
7	Kevin Brown	3.00	2.25	1.25
8	Dwight Gooden	3.00	2.25	1.25
9	Kevin Appier	3.50	2.75	1.50
10	Mike Morgan	3.00	2.25	1.25
11	Juan Guzman	7.00	5.25	2.75
12	Charles Nagy	3.00	2.25	1.25
13	John Smiley	3.00	2.25	1.25
14	Ken Hill	3.00	2.25	1.25
15	Bob Tewksbury	3.00	2.25	1.25
16	Doug Drabek	3.00	2.25	1.25
17	John Smoltz	4.00	3.00	1.50
18	Greg Swindell	3.00	2.25	1.25
19	Bruce Hurst	3.00	2.25	1.25
20	Mike Mussina	9.00	6.75	3.50
21	Cal Eldred	6.00	4.50	2.50
22	Melido Perez	3.00	2.25	1.25
23	Dave Fleming	5.00	3.75	2.00
24	Kevin Tapani	3.00	2.25	1.25

1993 Score Select Chase Rookies

Top newcomers in 1992 are featured in this 21-card insert set. Cards were randomly inserted in 15-card hobby packs. The fronts have a Score Select Rookies logo on the front. The backs have text and a player portrait.

		MT	NR MT	EX
Complete Set (21):		245.00	184.00	98.00
Common Player:		6.00	4.50	2.50
1	Pat Listach	6.00	4.50	2.50
2	Moises Alou	9.00	6.75	3.50
3	Reggie Sanders	15.00	11.00	6.00
4	Kenny Lofton	29.00	22.00	11.50
5	Eric Karros	18.00	13.50	7.25
6	Brian Williams	6.00	4.50	2.50
7	Donovan Osborne	10.00	7.50	4.00
8	Sam Militello	6.00	4.50	2.50
9	Chad Curtis	22.00	16.50	8.75
10	Bob Zupcic	6.00	4.50	2.50
11	Tim Salmon	60.00	45.00	24.00
12	Jeff Conine	9.00	6.75	3.50
13	Pedro Astacio	15.00	11.00	6.00
14	Arthur Rhodes	6.00	4.50	2.50
15	Cal Eldred	15.00	11.00	6.00
16	Tim Wakefield	6.00	4.50	2.50
17	Andy Stankiewicz	6.00	4.50	2.50
18	Wil Cordero	9.00	6.75	3.50
19	Todd Hundley	6.00	4.50	2.50
20	Dave Fleming	13.00	9.75	5.25
21	Bret Boone	13.00	9.75	5.25

1993 Score Select Chase Stars

The top 24 players from 1992 are featured in this insert set. Cards were randomly inserted in 15-card retail packs.

		MT	NR MT	EX
Complete Set (24):		115.00	86.00	46.00
Common Player:		2.00	1.50	.80
1	Fred McGriff	6.00	4.50	2.50
2	Ryne Sandberg	10.00	7.50	4.00
3	Ozzie Smith	4.00	3.00	1.50
4	Gary Sheffield	4.00	3.00	1.50
5	Darren Daulton	6.00	4.50	2.50
6	Andy Van Slyke	2.00	1.50	.80
7	Barry Bonds	13.00	3.00	12.00
8	Tony Gwynn	3.50	2.75	1.50
9	Greg Maddux	6.00	4.50	2.50
10	Tom Glavine	5.50	4.25	2.25
11	John Franco	2.00	1.50	.80
12	Lee Smith	2.00	1.50	.80
13	Cecil Fielder	4.00	3.00	1.50
14	Roberto Alomar	11.00	8.25	4.50
15	Cal Ripken, Jr.	10.00	7.50	4.00
16	Edgar Martinez	2.00	1.50	.80
17	Ivan Rodriguez	4.00	3.00	1.50
18	Kirby Puckett	10.00	7.50	4.00
19	Ken Griffey Jr.	18.00	13.50	7.25
20	Joe Carter	6.00	4.50	2.50
21	Roger Clemens	8.00	6.00	3.25
22	Dave Fleming	3.50	2.75	1.50
23	Paul Molitor	6.00	4.50	2.50
24	Dennis Eckersley	2.00	1.50	.80

1993 Score Select Stat Leaders

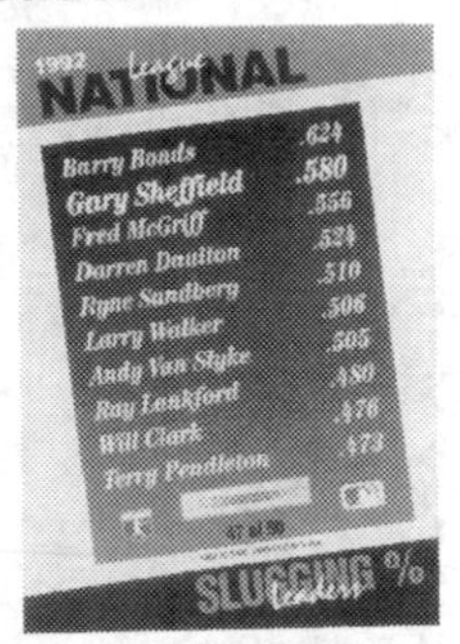

This 90-card set features 1992 American League and National League leaders in various statistical categories. Each card front indicates the league and the category the player finished at or near the top in. The backs have a list of the leaders; the pictured player's name is in larger type size. Backs use the special Dufex foil printing process. Cards were inserted one per foil pack.

		MT	NR MT	EX
Complete Set (90):		12.00	9.00	4.75
Common Player:		.10	.08	.04
1	Edgar Martinez	.20	.15	.08
2	Kirby Puckett	.50	.40	.20
3	Frank Thomas	1.00	.70	.40
4	Gary Sheffield	.20	.15	.08
5	Andy Van Slyke	.10	.08	.04
6	John Kruk	.20	.15	.08
7	Kirby Puckett	.50	.40	.20
8	Carlos Baerga	.35	.25	.14
9	Paul Molitor	.25	.20	.10
10	Terry Pendleton/ Andy Van Slyke	.10	.08	.04
11	Ryne Sandberg	.90	.30	.15
12	Mark Grace	.20	.15	.08
13	Frank Thomas	1.00	.70	.40
14	Don Mattingly	.75	.60	.30
15	Ken Griffey, Jr.	1.00	.70	.40
16	Andy Van Slyke	.10	.08	.04
17	Mariano Duncan/ Jerald Clark/ Ray Lankford	.10	.08	.04
18	Marquis Grissom/ Terry Pendleton	.10	.08	.04
19	Lance Johnson	.10	.08	.04
20	Mike Devereaux	.10	.08	.04
21	Brady Anderson	.10	.08	.04
22	Deion Sanders	.20	.15	.08
23	Steve Finley	.10	.08	.04
24	Andy Van Slyke	.10	.08	.04
25	Juan Gonzalez	.50	.40	.20
26	Mark McGwire	.40	.30	.15
27	Cecil Fielder	.30	.25	.12
28	Fred McGriff	.20	.15	.08
29	Barry Bonds	.40	.30	.15
30	Gary Sheffield	.20	.15	.08
31	Cecil Fielder	.30	.25	.12
32	Joe Carter	.20	.15	.08
33	Frank Thomas	1.00	.70	.40
34	Darren Daulton	.10	.08	.04
35	Terry Pendleton	.10	.08	.04
36	Fred McGriff	.20	.15	.08
37	Tony Phillips	.10	.08	.04
38	Frank Thomas	1.00	.70	.40
39	Roberto Alomar	.35	.25	.14
40	Barry Bonds	.40	.30	.15
41	Dave Hollins	.10	.08	.04
42	Andy Van Slyke	.10	.08	.04
43	Mark McGwire	.40	.30	.15
44	Edgar Martinez	.20	.15	.08
45	Frank Thomas	1.00	.70	.40
46	Barry Bonds	.40	.30	.15
47	Gary Sheffield	.20	.15	.08
48	Fred McGriff	.20	.15	.08
49	Frank Thomas	1.00	.70	.40
50	Danny Tartabull	.10	.08	.04
51	Roberto Alomar	.35	.25	.14
52	Barry Bonds	.40	.30	.15
53	John Kruk	.15	.11	.06
54	Brett Butler	.10	.08	.04
55	Kenny Lofton	.10	.08	.04
56	Pat Listach	.10	.08	.04
57	Brady Anderson	.10	.08	.04
58	Marquis Grissom	.10	.08	.04
59	Delino DeShields	.15	.11	.06
60	Steve Finley	.10	.08	.04
61	Jack McDowell	.10	.08	.04
62	Kevin Brown	.10	.08	.04
63	Melido Perez	.10	.08	.04
64	Terry Mulholland	.10	.08	.04
65	Curt Schilling	.10	.08	.04
66	Doug Drabek/ Greg Maddux/ John Smoltz	.10	.08	.04
67	Dennis Eckersley	.15	.11	.06
68	Rick Aguilera	.10	.08	.04
69	Jeff Montgomery	.10	.08	.04
70	Lee Smith	.15	.11	.06
71	Randy Myers	.10	.08	.04
72	John Wetteland	.10	.08	.04
73	Randy Johnson	.10	.08	.04
74	Melido Perez	.10	.08	.04
75	Roger Clemens	.30	.25	.12
76	John Smoltz	.10	.08	.04
77	David Cone	.10	.08	.04
78	Greg Maddux	.15	.11	.06
79	Roger Clemens	.30	.25	.12
80	Kevin Appier	.10	.08	.04
81	Mike Mussina	.10	.08	.04
82	Bill Swift	.10	.08	.04
83	Bob Tewksbury	.10	.08	.04
84	Greg Maddux	.15	.11	.06
85	Kevin Brown	.10	.08	.04
86	Jack McDowell	.10	.08	.04
87	Roger Clemens	.30	.25	.12
88	Tom Glavine	.10	.08	.04
89	Ken Hill/ Bob Tewksbury	.10	.08	.04
90	Mike Morgan/ Ramon Martinez	.10	.08	.04

1993 Score Select Triple Crown

This three-card set commemorates the Triple Crown seasons of Hall of Famers: Mickey Mantle, Frank Robinson and Carl Yastrzemski. Cards were randomly inserted in 15-card hobby packs. Card fronts have a green metallic-look textured border, with the player's name at top in gold, and "Triple Crown" in gold at bottom. There are other silver and green highlights around the photo, which features the player set against a metallized background. Dark green backs have a player photo and information on his Triple Crown season.

		MT	NR MT	EX
Complete Set (3):		100.00	75.00	40.00
Common Player:		30.00	22.00	12.00
1	Mickey Mantle	75.00	56.00	30.00
2	Frank Robinson	30.00	22.00	12.00
3	Carl Yastrzemski	30.00	22.00	12.00

Definitions for grading conditions are located in the Introduction of this price guide.

1993 Score Rookie/Traded

Production of this 150-card set was limited to 1,950 numbered cases. Several future Hall of Famers and six dozen top rookies are featured in the set. Cards were available in packs rather than collated sets and include randomly inserted FX cards, which feature Nolan Ryan (two per 24-box case), Tim Salmon and Mike Piazza (one per 576 packs) and All-Star Rookie Team members (one per 36 packs).

		MT	NR MT	EX
Complete Set (150):		80.00	60.00	32.00
Common Player:		.25	.20	.10
1	Rickey Henderson	1.50	1.25	.60
2	Rob Deer	.25	.20	.10
3	Tim Belcher	.25	.20	.10
4	Gary Sheffield	.75	.60	.30
5	Fred McGriff	1.75	1.25	.70
6	Mark Whiten	.25	.20	.10
7	Jeff Russell	.25	.20	.10
8	Harold Baines	.25	.20	.10
9	Dave Winfield	1.50	1.25	.60
10	Ellis Burks	.25	.20	.10
11	Andre Dawson	.25	.20	.10
12	Gregg Jefferies	.60	.45	.25
13	Jimmy Key	.25	.20	.10
14	Harold Reynolds	.25	.20	.10
15	Tom Henke	.25	.20	.10
16	Paul Molitor	1.50	1.25	.60
17	Wade Boggs	.75	.60	.30
18	David Cone	.25	.20	.10
19	Tony Fernandez	.25	.20	.10
20	Roberto Kelly	.25	.20	.10
21	Paul O'Neill	.25	.20	.10
22	Jose Lind	.25	.20	.10
23	Barry Bonds	3.00	2.25	1.25
24	Dave Stewart	.25	.20	.10
25	Randy Myers	.25	.20	.10
26	Benito Santiago	.25	.20	.10
27	Tim Wallach	.25	.20	.10
28	Greg Gagne	.25	.20	.10
29	Kevin Mitchell	.25	.20	.10
30	Jim Abbott	.50	.40	.20
31	Lee Smith	.25	.20	.10
32	*Bobby Munoz*	.75	.60	.30
33	*Mo Sanford*	.75	.60	.30
34	John Roper	.75	.60	.30
35	*David Hulse*	1.00	.70	.40
36	Pedro Martinez	2.00	1.50	.80
37	*Chuck Carr*	.50	.40	.20
38	*Armando Reynoso*	.75	.60	.30
39	Ryan Thompson	1.00	.70	.40
40	*Carlos Garcia*	1.00	.70	.40
41	Matt Whiteside	.25	.20	.10
42	*Benji Gil*	3.00	2.25	1.25
43	*Rodney Bolton*	.50	.40	.20
44	J.T. Snow	3.00	2.25	1.25
45	David McCarty	2.00	1.50	.80
46	*Paul Quantrill*	.40	.30	.15
47	Al Martin	1.75	1.25	.70
48	*Lance Painter*	.60	.45	.25
49	*Lou Frazier*	.50	.40	.20
50	*Eduardo Perez*	3.00	2.25	1.25
51	*Kevin Young*	1.25	.90	.50
52	Mike Trombley	.25	.20	.10
53	*Sterling Hitchcock*	1.50	1.25	.60
54	*Tim Bogar*	.40	.30	.15
55	*Hilly Hathaway*	1.00	.70	.40

		MT	NR MT	EX
56	*Wayne Kirby*	.60	.45	.25
57	*Craig Paquette*	.40	.30	.15
58	Bret Boone	1.50	1.25	.60
59	*Greg McMichael*	1.00	.70	.40
60	*Mike Lansing*	1.50	1.25	.60
61	*Brent Gates*	2.50	2.00	1.00
62	*Rene Arocha*	1.25	.90	.50
63	*Ricky Gutierrez*	.60	.45	.25
64	*Kevin Rogers*	.40	.30	.15
65	*Ken Ryan*	.60	.45	.25
66	*Phil Hiatt*	1.25	.90	.50
67	*Pat Meares*	.60	.45	.25
68	*Troy Neel*	1.50	1.25	.60
69	*Steve Cooke*	.60	.45	.25
70	*Sherman Obando*	1.00	.70	.40
71	*Blas Minor*	.75	.60	.30
72	*Angel Miranda*	.40	.30	.15
73	*Tom Kramer*	.40	.30	.15
74	*Chip Hale*	.60	.45	.25
75	*Brad Pennington*	.40	.30	.15
76	*Graeme Lloyd*	.60	.45	.25
77	*Darrell Whitmore*	1.25	.90	.50
78	David Nied	2.00	1.50	.80
79	Todd Van Poppel	1.00	.70	.40
80	*Chris Gomez*	.40	.30	.15
81	*Jason Bere*	4.00	3.00	1.50
82	Jeffrey Hammonds	4.00	3.00	1.50
83	*Brad Ausmus*	.40	.30	.15
84	*Kevin Stocker*	4.00	3.00	1.50
85	*Jeromy Burnitz*	1.00	.70	.40
86	*Aaron Sele*	5.00	3.50	2.00
87	*Roberto Mejia*	1.50	1.25	.60
88	*Kirk Rueter*	6.00	4.50	2.50
89	*Kevin Roberson*	2.50	2.00	1.00
90	*Allen Watson*	1.50	1.25	.60
91	Charlie Leibrandt	.25	.20	.10
92	Eric Davis	.25	.20	.10
93	Jody Reed	.25	.20	.10
94	Danny Jackson	.25	.20	.10
95	Gary Gaetti	.25	.20	.10
96	Norm Charlton	.25	.20	.10
97	Doug Drabek	.25	.20	.10
98	Scott Fletcher	.25	.20	.10
99	Greg Swindell	.25	.20	.10
100	John Smiley	.25	.20	.10
101	Kevin Reimer	.25	.20	.10
102	Andres Galarraga	.25	.20	.10
103	Greg Hibbard	.25	.20	.10
104	Chris Hammond	.25	.20	.10
105	Darnell Coles	.25	.20	.10
106	Mike Felder	.25	.20	.10
107	Jose Guzman	.25	.20	.10
108	Chris Bosio	.25	.20	.10
109	Spike Owen	.25	.20	.10
110	Felix Jose	.25	.20	.10
111	Cory Snyder	.25	.20	.10
112	Craig Lefferts	.25	.20	.10
113	David Wells	.25	.20	.10
114	Pete Incaviglia	.25	.20	.10
115	Mike Pagliarulo	.25	.20	.10
116	Dave Magadan	.25	.20	.10
117	Charlie Hough	.25	.20	.10
118	Ivan Calderon	.25	.20	.10
119	Manuel Lee	.25	.20	.10
120	Bob Patterson	.25	.20	.10
121	Bob Ojeda	.25	.20	.10
122	Scott Bankhead	.25	.20	.10
123	Greg Maddux	1.00	.70	.40
124	Chili Davis	.25	.20	.10
125	Milt Thompson	.25	.20	.10
126	Dave Martinez	.25	.20	.10
127	Frank Tanana	.25	.20	.10
128	Phil Plantier	.60	.45	.25
129	Juan Samuel	.25	.20	.10
130	Eric Young	.75	.60	.30
131	Joe Orsulak	.25	.20	.10
132	Derek Bell	.40	.30	.15
133	Darrin Jackson	.25	.20	.10
134	Tom Brunansky	.25	.20	.10
135	Jeff Reardon	.25	.20	.10
136	*Kevin Higgins*	.40	.30	.15
137	*Joel Johnston*	.40	.30	.15
138	*Rick Trlicek*	.40	.30	.15
139	*Richie Lewis*	1.00	.70	.40
140	*Jeff Gardner*	.40	.30	.15
141	*Jack Voigt*	.50	.40	.20
142	*Rod Correia*	.60	.45	.25
143	*Billy Brewer*	.50	.40	.20
144	*Terry Jorgensen*	.30	.25	.12
145	*Rich Amaral*	.40	.30	.15
146	*Sean Berry*	.40	.30	.15
147	*Dan Peltier*	.40	.30	.15

		MT	NR MT	EX
148	*Paul Wagner*	.50	.40	.20
149	*Damon Buford*	.40	.30	.15
150	Wil Cordero	1.00	.70	.40

1993 Score Select All-Star Rookies

These cards were randomly inserted into the Score Select Rookie/Traded packs, making them among the scarcest of the year's many "chase" cards.

		MT	NR MT	EX
Complete Set (10):		350.00	260.00	140.00
Common Player:		20.00	15.00	8.00
1	Jeff Conine	20.00	15.00	8.00
2	Brent Gates	20.00	15.00	8.00
3	Mike Lansing	40.00	30.00	15.00
4	Kevin Stocker	45.00	35.00	15.00
5	Mike Piazza	100.00	75.00	40.00
6	Jeffrey Hammonds	55.00	40.00	22.00
7	David Hulse	30.00	22.50	12.00
8	Tim Salmon	80.00	60.00	30.00
9	Rene Arocha	35.00	25.00	12.00
10	Greg McMichael	20.00	15.00	8.00

1993 Score Select Rookie/Traded Inserts

Photos not available at press time

Three cards honoring the 1993 Rookies of the Year and retiring superstar Nolan Ryan were issued as random inserts in the Select Rookie/Traded packs.

		MT	NR MT	EX
1NR	Nolan Ryan	150.00	110.00	60.00
1RO	Tim Salmon	100.00	75.00	40.00
2RO	Mike Piazza	200.00	150.00	80.00

Regional interest may affect the value of a card.

1993 Score Pinnacle

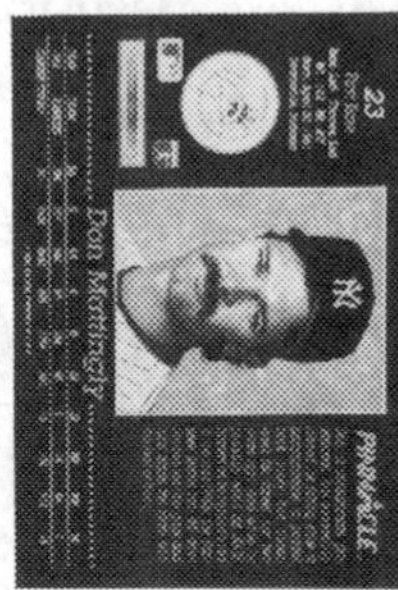

This 620-card set offers many of the same features which made the first Pinnacle set so popular in 1992. Subsets are titled Rookies, Now & Then (which shows the player as he looks now and as a rookie), Idols (active players and their heroes on the same card), Hometown Heroes (players who are playing with their hometown team), Draft Picks and Rookies. More than 100 rookies and 10 draft picks are featured. All regular cards have an action photo, a black border and the Pinnacle name stamped on in gold. Series I cards feature portraits of players on the two new expansion teams; Series II cards feature action shots of them. Team Pinnacle insert cards return, while Rookie Team Pinnacle cards make their debut. Other insert sets are titled Team 2001, Slugfest and Tribute, which features five cards each of Nolan Ryan and George Brett.

		MT	NR MT	EX
Complete Set (620):		60.00	45.00	24.00
Common Player:		.06	.05	.02
1	Gary Sheffield	.40	.30	.15
2	Cal Eldred	.25	.20	.10
3	Larry Walker	.20	.15	.08
4	Deion Sanders	.20	.15	.08
5	Dave Fleming	.15	.11	.06
6	Carlos Baerga	.50	.40	.20
7	Bernie Williams	.12	.09	.05
8	John Kruk	.06	.05	.02
9	Jimmy Key	.06	.05	.02
10	Jeff Bagwell	.20	.15	.08
11	Jim Abbott	.06	.05	.02
12	Terry Steinbach	.06	.05	.02
13	Bob Tewksbury	.06	.05	.02
14	Eric Karros	.40	.30	.15
15	Ryne Sandberg	.60	.45	.25
16	Will Clark	.25	.20	.10
17	Edgar Martinez	.06	.05	.02
18	Eddie Murray	.06	.05	.02
19	Andy Van Slyke	.06	.05	.02
20	Cal Ripken, Jr.	.50	.40	.20
21	Ivan Rodriguez	.50	.40	.20
22	Barry Larkin	.15	.11	.06
23	Don Mattingly	.20	.15	.08
24	Gregg Jefferies	.06	.05	.02
25	Roger Clemens	.50	.40	.20
26	Cecil Fielder	.20	.15	.08
27	Kent Hrbek	.06	.05	.02
28	Robin Ventura	.20	.15	.08
29	Rickey Henderson	.20	.15	.08
30	Roberto Alomar	.50	.40	.20
31	Luis Polonia	.06	.05	.02
32	Andujar Cedeno	.06	.05	.02
33	Pat Listach	.25	.20	.10
34	Mark Grace	.06	.05	.02
35	Otis Nixon	.06	.05	.02
36	Felix Jose	.06	.05	.02
37	Mike Sharperson	.06	.05	.02
38	Dennis Martinez	.06	.05	.02
39	Willie McGee	.06	.05	.02
40	Kenny Lofton	.60	.45	.25
41	Randy Johnson	.06	.05	.02
42	Andy Benes	.06	.05	.02
43	Bobby Bonilla	.06	.05	.02
44	Mike Mussina	.80	.60	.30
45	Lenny Dykstra	.15	.11	.06
46	Ellis Burks	.06	.05	.02
47	Chris Sabo	.06	.05	.02
48	Jay Bell	.06	.05	.02

		MT	NR MT	EX
49	Jose Canseco	.25	.20	.10
50	Craig Biggio	.06	.05	.02
51	Wally Joyner	.06	.05	.02
52	Mickey Tettleton	.06	.05	.02
53	Tim Raines	.06	.05	.02
54	Brian Harper	.06	.05	.02
55	Rene Gonzales	.06	.05	.02
56	Mark Langston	.06	.05	.02
57	Jack Morris	.06	.05	.02
58	Mark McGwire	.25	.20	.10
59	Ken Caminiti	.06	.05	.02
60	Terry Pendleton	.06	.05	.02
61	Dave Nilsson	.06	.05	.02
62	Tom Pagnozzi	.06	.05	.02
63	Mike Morgan	.06	.05	.02
64	Darryl Strawberry	.10	.08	.04
65	Charles Nagy	.06	.05	.02
66	Ken Hill	.06	.05	.02
67	Matt Williams	.06	.05	.02
68	Jay Buhner	.06	.05	.02
69	Vince Coleman	.06	.05	.02
70	Brady Anderson	.06	.05	.02
71	Fred McGriff	.25	.20	.10
72	Ben McDonald	.06	.05	.02
73	Terry Mulholland	.06	.05	.02
74	Randy Tomlin	.06	.05	.02
75	Nolan Ryan	1.75	1.25	.70
76	Frank Viola	.06	.05	.02
77	Jose Rijo	.06	.05	.02
78	Shane Mack	.06	.05	.02
79	Travis Fryman	.50	.40	.20
80	Jack McDowell	.06	.05	.02
81	Mark Gubicza	.06	.05	.02
82	Matt Nokes	.06	.05	.02
83	Bert Blyleven	.06	.05	.02
84	Eric Anthony	.06	.05	.02
85	Mike Bordick	.06	.05	.02
86	John Olerud	.30	.25	.12
87	B.J. Surhoff	.06	.05	.02
88	Bernard Gilkey	.06	.05	.02
89	Shawon Dunston	.06	.05	.02
90	Tom Glavine	.25	.20	.10
91	Brett Butler	.06	.05	.02
92	Moises Alou	.06	.05	.02
93	Albert Belle	.60	.45	.25
94	Darren Lewis	.06	.05	.02
95	Omar Vizquel	.06	.05	.02
96	Doc Gooden	.06	.05	.02
97	Gregg Olson	.06	.05	.02
98	Tony Gwynn	.15	.11	.06
99	Darren Daulton	.06	.05	.02
100	Dennis Eckersley	.06	.05	.02
101	Rob Dibble	.06	.05	.02
102	Mike Greenwell	.06	.05	.02
103	Jose Lind	.06	.05	.02
104	Julio Franco	.06	.05	.02
105	Tom Gordon	.06	.05	.02
106	Scott Livingstone	.06	.05	.02
107	Chuck Knoblauch	.25	.20	.10
108	Frank Thomas	3.50	2.75	1.50
110	Ken Griffey, Jr.	3.00	2.25	1.25
111	Harold Baines	.06	.05	.02
112	Gary Gaetti	.06	.05	.02
113	Pete Harnisch	.06	.05	.02
114	David Wells	.06	.05	.02
115	Charlie Leibrandt	.06	.05	.02
116	Ray Lankford	.35	.25	.14
117	Kevin Seitzer	.06	.05	.02
118	Robin Yount	.20	.15	.08
119	Lenny Harris	.06	.05	.02
120	Chris James	.06	.05	.02
121	Delino DeShields	.06	.05	.02
122	Kirt Manwaring	.06	.05	.02
123	Glenallen Hill	.06	.05	.02
124	Hensley Meulens	.06	.05	.02
125	Darrin Jackson	.06	.05	.02
126	Todd Hundley	.06	.05	.02
127	Dave Hollins	.20	.15	.08
128	Sam Horn	.06	.05	.02
129	Roberto Hernandez	.06	.05	.02
130	Vicente Palacios	.06	.05	.02
131	George Brett	.25	.20	.10
132	Dave Martinez	.06	.05	.02
133	Kevin Appier	.06	.05	.02
134	Pat Kelly	.06	.05	.02
135	Pedro Munoz	.06	.05	.02
136	Mark Carreon	.06	.05	.02
137	Lance Johnson	.06	.05	.02
138	Devon White	.06	.05	.02
139	Julio Valera	.06	.05	.02
140	Eddie Taubensee	.06	.05	.02
141	Willie Wilson	.06	.05	.02

		MT	NR MT	EX
142	Stan Belinda	.06	.05	.02
143	John Smoltz	.06	.05	.02
144	Darryl Hamilton	.06	.05	.02
145	Sammy Sosa	.06	.05	.02
146	Carlos Hernandez	.06	.05	.02
147	Tom Candiotti	.06	.05	.02
148	Mike Felder	.06	.05	.02
149	Rusty Meacham	.06	.05	.02
150	Ivan Calderon	.06	.05	.02
151	Pete O'Brien	.06	.05	.02
152	Erik Hanson	.06	.05	.02
153	Billy Ripken	.06	.05	.02
154	Kurt Stillwell	.06	.05	.02
155	Jeff Kent	.06	.05	.02
156	Mickey Morandini	.06	.05	.02
157	Randy Milligan	.06	.05	.02
158	Reggie Sanders	.20	.15	.08
159	Luis Rivera	.06	.05	.02
160	Orlando Merced	.06	.05	.02
161	Dean Palmer	.06	.05	.02
162	Mike Perez	.06	.05	.02
163	Scott Erikson	.06	.05	.02
164	Kevin McReynolds	.06	.05	.02
165	Kevin Maas	.06	.05	.02
166	Ozzie Guillen	.06	.05	.02
167	Rob Deer	.06	.05	.02
168	Danny Tartabull	.06	.05	.02
169	Lee Stevens	.06	.05	.02
170	Dave Henderson	.06	.05	.02
171	Derek Bell	.06	.05	.02
172	Steve Finley	.06	.05	.02
173	Greg Olson	.06	.05	.02
174	Geronimo Pena	.06	.05	.02
175	Paul Quantrill	.06	.05	.02
176	Steve Buechele	.06	.05	.02
177	Kevin Gross	.06	.05	.02
178	Tim Wallach	.06	.05	.02
179	Dave Valle	.06	.05	.02
180	Dave Silvestri	.06	.05	.02
181	Bud Black	.06	.05	.02
182	Henry Rodriguez	.06	.05	.02
183	Tim Teufel	.06	.05	.02
184	Mark McLemore	.06	.05	.02
185	Bret Saberhagen	.06	.05	.02
186	Chris Hoiles	.06	.05	.02
187	Ricky Jordan	.06	.05	.02
188	Don Slaught	.06	.05	.02
189	Mo Vaughn	.06	.05	.02
190	Joe Oliver	.06	.05	.02
191	Juan Gonzalez	.90	.70	.35
192	Scott Leius	.06	.05	.02
193	Milt Cuyler	.06	.05	.02
194	Chris Haney	.06	.05	.02
195	Ron Karkovice	.06	.05	.02
196	Steve Farr	.06	.05	.02
197	John Orton	.06	.05	.02
198	Kelly Gruber	.06	.05	.02
199	Ron Darling	.06	.05	.02
200	Ruben Sierra	.25	.20	.10
201	Chuck Finley	.06	.05	.02
202	Mike Moore	.06	.05	.02
203	Pat Borders	.06	.05	.02
204	Sid Bream	.06	.05	.02
205	Todd Zeile	.06	.05	.02
206	Rick Wilkins	.06	.05	.02
207	Jim Gantner	.06	.05	.02
208	Frank Castillo	.06	.05	.02
209	Dave Hansen	.06	.05	.02
210	Trevor Wilson	.06	.05	.02
211	Sandy Alomar Jr.	.06	.05	.02
212	Sean Berry	.06	.05	.02
213	Tino Martinez	.06	.05	.02
214	Chito Martinez	.06	.05	.02
215	Dan Walters	.06	.05	.02
216	John Franco	.06	.05	.02
217	Glenn Davis	.06	.05	.02
218	Mariano Duncan	.06	.05	.02
219	Mike LaValliere	.06	.05	.02
220	Rafael Palmeiro	.06	.05	.02
221	Jack Clark	.06	.05	.02
222	Hal Morris	.06	.05	.02
223	Ed Sprague	.06	.05	.02
224	John Valentin	.06	.05	.02
225	Sam Militello	.20	.15	.08
226	Bob Wickman	.35	.25	.14
227	Damion Easley	.35	.25	.14
228	John Jaha	.20	.15	.08
229	Bob Ayrault	.06	.05	.02
230	Mo Sanford	.06	.05	.02
231	Walt Weiss	.06	.05	.02
232	Dante Bichette	.06	.05	.02

		MT	NR MT	EX
233	Steve Decker	.06	.05	.02
234	Jerald Clark	.06	.05	.02
235	Bryan Harvey	.06	.05	.02
236	Joe Girardi	.06	.05	.02
237	Dave Magadan	.06	.05	.02
238	David Nied	1.25	.90	.50
239	Eric Wedge	.30	.25	.12
240	Rico Brogna	.06	.05	.02
241	J.T. Bruett	.06	.05	.02
242	Jonathan Hurst	.06	.05	.02
243	Bret Boone	.30	.25	.12
244	Manny Alexander	.20	.15	.08
245	Scooter Tucker	.06	.05	.02
246	Troy Neel	.30	.25	.12
247	Eddie Zosky	.06	.05	.02
248	Melvin Nieves	.30	.25	.12
249	Ryan Thompson	.30	.25	.12
250	Shawn Barton	.15	.11	.06
251	Ryan Klesko	.60	.45	.25
252	Mike Piazza	6.50	5.00	2.50
253	Steve Hosey	.20	.15	.08
254	Shane Reynolds	.06	.05	.02
255	Dan Wilson	.06	.05	.02
256	Tom Marsh	.06	.05	.02
257	Barry Manuel	.06	.05	.02
258	Paul Miller	.06	.05	.02
259	Pedro Martinez	.20	.15	.08
260	Steve Cooke	.30	.25	.12
261	Johnny Guzman	.06	.05	.02
262	Mike Butcher	.06	.05	.02
263	Bien Figueroa	.06	.05	.02
264	Rich Rowland	.06	.05	.02
265	Shawn Jeter	.06	.05	.02
266	Gerald Williams	.06	.05	.02
267	Derek Parks	.06	.05	.02
268	Henry Mercedes	.06	.05	.02
269	David Hulse	.20	.15	.08
270	Tim Pugh	.30	.25	.12
271	William Suero	.06	.05	.02
272	Ozzie Canseco	.06	.05	.02
273	Fernando Ramsey	.15	.11	.06
274	Bernardo Brito	.06	.05	.02
275	Dave Milcki	.06	.05	.02
276	Tim Salmon	3.25	2.50	1.25
277	Mike Raczka	.06	.05	.02
278	Ken Ryan	.45	.35	.20
279	Rafael Boumigal	.25	.20	.10
280	Wil Cordero	.25	.20	.10
281	Billy Ashley	.35	.25	.14
282	Paul Wagner	.06	.05	.02
283	Blas Minor	.06	.05	.02
284	Rick Trlicek	.06	.05	.02
285	Willie Greene	.20	.15	.08
286	Ted Wood	.06	.05	.02
287	Phil Clark	.06	.05	.02
288	Jesse Levis	.06	.05	.02
289	Tony Gwynn	.20	.15	.08
290	Nolan Ryan (N&T)	.60	.45	.25
291	Dennis Martinez	.06	.05	.02
292	Eddie Murray	.06	.05	.02
293	Robin Yount (N&T)	.20	.15	.08
294	George Brett (N&T)	.20	.15	.08
295	Dave Winfield (N&T)	.15	.11	.06
296	Bert Blyleven	.06	.05	.02
297	Jeff Bagwell	.15	.11	.06
298	John Smoltz	.06	.05	.02
299	Larry Walker	.06	.05	.02
300	Gary Sheffield	.06	.05	.02
301	Ivan Rodriguez	.06	.05	.02
302	Delino DeShields	.06	.05	.02
303	Tim Salmon (I)	.80	.60	.30
304	Bernard Gilkey	.06	.05	.02
305	Cal Ripken, Jr. (HH)	.25	.20	.10
306	Barry Larkin	.06	.05	.02
307	Kent Hrbek	.06	.05	.02
308	Rickey Henderson	.06	.05	.02
309	Darryl Strawberry	.06	.05	.02
310	John Franco	.06	.05	.02
311	Todd Stottlemyre	.06	.05	.02
312	Luis Gonzalez	.06	.05	.02
313	Tommy Greene	.20	.15	.08
314	Randy Velarde	.06	.05	.02
315	Steve Avery	.20	.15	.08
316	Jose Oquendo	.06	.05	.02
317	Rey Sanchez	.06	.05	.02
318	Greg Vaughn	.20	.15	.08
319	Orel Hershiser	.06	.05	.02
320	Paul Sorrento	.06	.05	.02
321	Royce Clayton	.15	.11	.06
322	John Vander Wal	.06	.05	.02
323	Henry Cotto	.06	.05	.02

		MT	NR MT	EX
324	Pete Schourek	.06	.05	.02
325	David Segui	.06	.05	.02
326	Arthur Rhodes	.06	.05	.02
327	Bruce Hurst	.06	.05	.02
328	Wes Chamberlain	.06	.05	.02
329	Ozzie Smith	.15	.11	.06
330	Scott Cooper	.15	.11	.06
331	Felix Fermin	.06	.05	.02
332	Mike Macfarlane	.06	.05	.02
333	Dan Gladden	.06	.05	.02
334	Kevin Tapani	.06	.05	.02
335	Steve Sax	.06	.05	.02
336	Jeff Montgomery	.06	.05	.02
337	Gary DiSarcina	.06	.05	.02
338	Lance Blankenship	.06	.05	.02
339	Brian Williams	.06	.05	.02
340	Duane Ward	.06	.05	.02
341	Chuck McElroy	.06	.05	.02
342	Joe Magrane	.06	.05	.02
343	Jaime Navarro	.06	.05	.02
344	Dave Justice	.60	.45	.25
345	Jose Offerman	.06	.05	.02
346	Marquis Grissom	.20	.15	.08
347	Bill Swift	.06	.05	.02
348	Jim Thome	.06	.05	.02
349	Archi Cianfrocco	.06	.05	.02
350	Anthony Young	.06	.05	.02
351	Leo Gomez	.06	.05	.02
352	Bill Gullickson	.06	.05	.02
353	Alan Trammell	.06	.05	.02
354	Dan Pasqua	.06	.05	.02
355	Jeff King	.06	.05	.02
356	Kevin Brown	.06	.05	.02
357	Tim Belcher	.06	.05	.02
358	Bip Roberts	.06	.05	.02
359	Brent Mayne	.06	.05	.02
360	Rheal Cormier	.06	.05	.02
361	Mark Guthrie	.06	.05	.02
362	Craig Grebeck	.06	.05	.02
363	Andy Stankiewicz	.06	.05	.02
364	Juan Guzman	.20	.15	.08
365	Bobby Witt	.06	.05	.02
366	Mark Portugal	.06	.05	.02
367	Brian McRae	.06	.05	.02
368	Mark Lemke	.06	.05	.02
369	Bill Wegman	.06	.05	.02
370	Donovan Osborne	.25	.20	.10
371	Derrick May	.20	.15	.08
372	Carl Willis	.06	.05	.02
373	Chris Nabholz	.06	.05	.02
374	Mark Lewis	.06	.05	.02
375	John Burkett	.06	.05	.02
376	Luis Mercedes	.06	.05	.02
377	Ramon Martinez	.20	.15	.08
378	Kyle Abbott	.06	.05	.02
379	Mark Wohlers	.06	.05	.02
380	Bob Walk	.06	.05	.02
381	Kenny Rogers	.06	.05	.02
382	Tim Naehring	.06	.05	.02
383	Alex Fernandez	.06	.05	.02
384	Keith Miller	.06	.05	.02
385	Mike Henneman	.06	.05	.02
386	Rick Aguilera	.06	.05	.02
387	George Bell	.06	.05	.02
388	Mike Gallego	.06	.05	.02
389	Howard Johnson	.06	.05	.02
390	Kim Batiste	.06	.05	.02
391	Jerry Browne	.06	.05	.02
392	Damon Berryhill	.06	.05	.02
393	Ricky Bones	.06	.05	.02
394	Omar Olivares	.06	.05	.02
395	Mike Harkey	.06	.05	.02
396	Pedro Astacio	.35	.25	.14
397	John Wetteland	.06	.05	.02
398	Rod Beck	.15	.11	.06
399	Thomas Howard	.06	.05	.02
400	Mike Devereaux	.06	.05	.02
401	Tim Wakefield	.15	.11	.06
402	Curt Schilling	.20	.15	.08
403	Zane Smith	.06	.05	.02
404	Bob Zupcic	.06	.05	.02
405	Tom Browning	.06	.05	.02
406	Tony Phillips	.06	.05	.02
407	John Doherty	.06	.05	.02
408	Pat Mahomes	.06	.05	.02
409	John Habyan	.06	.05	.02
410	Steve Olin	.06	.05	.02
411	Chad Curtis	.60	.45	.25
412	Joe Grahe	.06	.05	.02
413	John Patterson	.06	.05	.02
414	Brian Hunter	.06	.05	.02

		MT	NR MT	EX
415	Doug Henry	.06	.05	.02
416	Lee Smith	.06	.05	.02
417	Bob Scanlan	.06	.05	.02
418	Kent Mercker	.06	.05	.02
419	Mel Rojas	.06	.05	.02
420	Mark Whiten	.06	.05	.02
421	Carlton Fisk	.20	.15	.08
422	Candy Maldonado	.06	.05	.02
423	Doug Drabek	.06	.05	.02
424	Wade Boggs	.20	.15	.08
425	Mark Davis	.06	.05	.02
426	Kirby Puckett	.40	.30	.15
427	Joe Carter	.40	.30	.15
428	Paul Molitor	.35	.25	.14
429	Eric Davis	.15	.11	.06
430	Darryl Kile	.06	.05	.02
431	Jeff Parrett	.06	.05	.02
432	Jeff Blauser	.06	.05	.02
433	Dan Plesac	.06	.05	.02
434	Andres Galarraga	.15	.11	.06
435	Jim Gott	.06	.05	.02
436	Jose Mesa	.06	.05	.02
437	Ben Rivera	.06	.05	.02
438	Dave Winfield	.25	.20	.10
439	Norm Charlton	.06	.05	.02
440	Chris Bosio	.06	.05	.02
441	Wilson Alvarez	.06	.05	.02
442	Dave Stewart	.06	.05	.02
443	Doug Jones	.06	.05	.02
444	Jeff Russell	.06	.05	.02
445	Ron Gant	.15	.11	.06
446	Paul O'Neill	.06	.05	.02
447	Charlie Hayes	.06	.05	.02
448	Joe Hesketh	.06	.05	.02
449	Chris Hammond	.06	.05	.02
450	Hipolito Richardo	.06	.05	.02
451	Scott Radinsky	.06	.05	.02
452	Bobby Thigpen	.06	.05	.02
453	Xavier Hernandez	.06	.05	.02
454	Lonnie Smith	.06	.05	.02
455	Jamie Arnold (DP)	.40	.30	.15
456	B.J. Wallace (DP)	.70	.50	.30
457	Derek Jeter (DP)	1.25	.90	.50
458	Jason Kendall (DP)	.40	.30	.15
459	Rick Helling (DP)	.60	.45	.25
460	Derek Wallace (DP)	.60	.45	.25
461	Sean Lowe (DP)	.50	.40	.20
462	Shannon Stewart (DP)	.50	.40	.20
463	Benji Grigsby (DP)	.50	.40	.20
464	Todd Steverson (DP)	.80	.60	.30
465	Dan Serafini (DP)	.40	.30	.15
466	Michael Tucker (DP)	.80	.60	.30
467	Chris Roberts (DP)	.50	.40	.20
468	Pete Janicki (DP)	.40	.30	.15
469	Jeff Schmidt (DP)	.40	.30	.15
470	Don Mattingly (NT)	.25	.20	.10
471	Cal Ripken, Jr. (NT)	.30	.25	.12
472	Jack Morris (NT)	.06	.05	.02
473	Terry Pendleton (NT)	.06	.05	.02
474	Dennis Eckersley (NT)	.20	.15	.08
475	Carlton Fisk (NT)	.20	.15	.08
476	Wade Boggs (NT)	.20	.15	.08
477	Lenny Dykstra (I)	.10	.08	.04
478	Danny Tartabull (I)	.10	.08	.04
479	Jeff Conine (I)	.10	.08	.04
480	Gregg Jefferies (I)	.20	.15	.08
481	Paul Molitor (I)	.20	.15	.08
482	John Valentin (I)	.10	.08	.04
483	Alex Arias (I)	.10	.08	.04
484	Barry Bonds (HH)	.50	.40	.20
485	Doug Drabek (HH)	.10	.08	.04
486	Dave Winfield (HH)	.10	.08	.04
487	Brett Butler (HH)	.10	.08	.04
488	Harold Baines (HH)	.10	.08	.04
489	David Cone (HH)	.10	.08	.04
490	Willie McGee (HH)	.10	.08	.04
491	Robby Thompson	.08	.06	.04
492	Pete Incaviglia	.06	.05	.02
493	Manuel Lee	.06	.05	.02
494	Rafael Belliard	.06	.05	.02
495	Scott Fletcher	.06	.05	.02
496	Jeff Frye	.06	.05	.02
497	Andre Dawson	.25	.20	.10
498	Mike Scioscia	.06	.05	.02
499	Spike Owen	.06	.05	.02
500	Sid Fernandez	.06	.05	.02
501	Joe Orsulak	.06	.05	.02
502	Benito Santiago	.06	.05	.02
503	Dale Murphy	.06	.05	.02
504	Barry Bonds	.50	.40	.20
505	Jose Guzman	.06	.05	.02

		MT	NR MT	EX
506	TOny Pena	.06	.05	.02
507	Greg Swindell	.06	.05	.02
508	Mike Pagliarulo	.06	.05	.02
509	Lou Whitaker	.06	.05	.02
510	Greg Gagne	.06	.05	.02
511	Butch Henry	.06	.05	.02
512	Jeff Brantley	.06	.05	.02
513	Jack Armstrong	.06	.05	.02
514	Danny Jackson	.06	.05	.02
515	Junior Felix	.06	.05	.02
516	Milt Thompson	.06	.05	.02
517	Greg Maddux	.25	.20	.10
518	Eric Young	.06	.05	.02
519	Jody Reed	.06	.05	.02
520	Roberto Kelly	.06	.05	.02
521	Darren Holmes	.06	.05	.02
522	Craig Lefferts	.06	.05	.02
523	Charlie Hough	.06	.05	.02
524	Bo Jackson	.25	.20	.10
525	Bill Spiers	.06	.05	.02
526	Orestes Destrade	.30	.25	.12
527	Greg Hibbard	.06	.05	.02
528	Roger McDowell	.06	.05	.02
529	Cory Snyder	.06	.05	.02
530	Harold Reynolds	.06	.05	.02
531	Kevin Reimer	.06	.05	.02
532	Rick Sutcliffe	.06	.05	.02
533	Tony Fernandez	.06	.05	.02
534	Tom Brunansky	.06	.05	.02
535	Jeff Reardon	.06	.05	.02
536	Chili Davis	.06	.05	.02
537	Bob Ojeda	.06	.05	.02
538	Greg Colbrunn	.06	.05	.02
539	Phil Plantier	.30	.25	.12
540	Brian Jordan	.30	.25	.12
541	Pete Smith	.06	.05	.02
542	Frank Tanana	.06	.05	.02
543	John Smiley	.06	.05	.02
544	David Cone	.06	.05	.02
545	Daryl Boston	.06	.05	.02
546	Tom Henke	.06	.05	.02
547	Bill Krueger	.06	.05	.02
548	Freddie Benavides	.06	.05	.02
549	Randy Myers	.06	.05	.02
550	Reggie Jefferson	.06	.05	.02
551	Kevin Mitchell	.06	.05	.02
552	Dave Stieb	.06	.05	.02
553	Bret Barberie	.06	.05	.02
554	Tim Crews	.06	.05	.02
555	Doug Dascenzo	.06	.05	.02
556	Alex Cole	.06	.05	.02
557	Jeff Innis	.06	.05	.02
558	Carlos Garcia	.25	.20	.10
559	Steve Howe	.06	.05	.02
560	Kirk McCaskill	.06	.05	.02
561	Frank Seminara	.06	.05	.02
562	Cris Carpenter	.06	.05	.02
563	Mike Stanley	.06	.05	.02
564	Carlos Quintana	.06	.05	.02
565	Mitch Williams	.06	.05	.02
566	Juan Bell	.06	.05	.02
567	Eric Fox	.06	.05	.02
568	Al Leiter	.06	.05	.02
569	Mike Stanton	.06	.05	.02
570	Scott Kamieniecki	.06	.05	.02
571	Ryan Bowen	.06	.05	.02
572	Andy Ashby	.06	.05	.02
573	Bob Welch	.06	.05	.02
574	Scott Sanderson	.06	.05	.02
575	Joe Kmak	.20	.15	.08
576	Scott Pose	.30	.25	.12
577	Ricky Gutierrez	.20	.15	.08
578	Mike Trombley	.20	.15	.08
579	Sterling Hitchcock	.25	.20	.10
580	Rodney Bolton	.20	.15	.08
581	Tyler Green	.20	.15	.08
582	Tim Costo	.20	.15	.08
583	Tim Laker	.20	.15	.08
584	Steve Reed	.20	.15	.08
585	Tom Kramer	.40	.30	.15
586	Robb Nen	.25	.20	.10
587	Jim Tatum	.20	.15	.08
588	Frank Bolick	.25	.20	.10
589	Kevin Young	.70	.50	.30
590	Matt Whiteside	.25	.20	.10
591	Cesar Hernandez	.15	.11	.06
592	Mike Mohler	.20	.15	.08
593	Alan Embree	.30	.25	.12
594	Terry Jorgensen	.15	.11	.06
595	John Cummings	.15	.11	.06
596	Domingo Martinez	.25	.20	.10

		MT	NR MT	EX
597	Benji Gil	.50	.40	.20
598	Todd Pratt	.50	.40	.20
599	Rene Arocha	.80	.60	.30
600	Dennis Moeller	.20	.15	.08
601	Jeff Conine	.40	.30	.15
602	Trevor Hoffman	.30	.25	.12
603	Daniel Smith	.30	.25	.12
604	Lee Tinsley	.25	.20	.10
605	Dan Peltier	.20	.15	.08
606	Billy Brewer	.20	.15	.08
607	Matt Walbeck	.30	.25	.12
608	Richie Lewis	.50	.40	.20
609	J.T. Snow	.80	.60	.30
610	Pat Gomez	.20	.15	.08
611	Phil Hiatt	.60	.45	.25
612	Alex Arias	.30	.25	.12
613	Kevin Rogers	.30	.25	.12
614	Al Martin	.80	.60	.30
615	Greg Gohr	.20	.15	.08
616	Grame Lloyd	.20	.15	.08
617	Kent Bottenfield	.20	.15	.08
618	Chuck Carr	.30	.25	.12
619	Darrell Sherman	.50	.40	.20
620	Mike Lansing	.75	.60	.30

1993 Score Pinnacle Expansion Opening Day

This nine-card set features 18 players for the two new expansion teams: the Florida Marlins and Colorado Rockies; each card side shows a projected Opening Day starter for each team. Cards were available one per every Series II hobby box. Complete sets were available through a special mail-in offer.

		MT	NR MT	EX
Complete Set (9):		10.00	7.50	4.00
Common Player:		.75	.60	.30
1	Charlie Hough/ David Nied	2.00	1.50	.80
2	Benito Santiago/ Joe Girardi	.90	.70	.35
3	Orestes Destrade/ Andres Galarraga	3.00	2.25	1.20
4	Bret Barberie/ Eric Young	.75	.60	.30
5	Dave Magadan/ Charlie Hayes	1.50	1.00	.80
6	Walt Weiss/ Freddie Benevides	.75	.60	.30
7	Jeff Conine/ Jerald Clark	1.00	.75	.40
8	Scott Pose/ Alex Cole	.75	.60	.30
9	Junior Felix/ Dante Bichette	1.50	1.00	.80

1993 Score Pinnacle Rookie Team Pinnacle

These 10 cards were randomly inserted into Score Pinnacle Series II packs. Rookie Team Pinnacle is written in gold foil on both sides of the card. Cards are numbered 1 of 10, etc., and use the special Dufex process. Each card shows two players painted by artist Christopher Greco. Stated odds of finding a Rookie Team Pinnacle insert were given as one in 90 packs.

		MT	NR MT	EX
Complete Set (10):		275.00	175.00	100.00
Common Player:		12.00	8.00	5.00
1	Pedro Martinez/ Mike Trombley	12.00	8.00	4.00
2	Kevin Rogers/ Sterling Hitchcock	12.00	8.00	4.00
3	Mike Piazza/ Jesse Levis	125.00	75.00	40.00
4	Ryan Klesko/ J.T. Snow	45.00	30.00	20.00
5	John Patterson/ Bret Boone	16.00	10.00	6.00
6	Kevin Young/ Domingo Martinez	20.00	12.00	8.00
7	Wil Cordero/ Manny Alexander	18.00	10.00	6.00
8	Steve Hosey/ Tim Salmon	90.00	60.00	30.00
9	Ryan Thompson/ Gerald Williams	12.00	8.00	5.00
10	Melvin Nieves/ David Hulse	24.00	16.00	10.00

1993 Score Pinnacle Slugfest

Baseball's top sluggers are featured in this 30-card insert set. Cards were available one per Series II jumbo packs. Slugfest is written in gold foil on the card front.

		MT	NR MT	EX
Complete Set (30):		40.00	30.00	16.00
Common Player:		.50	.40	.20
1	Juan Gonzalez	5.00	3.75	2.00
2	Mark McGwire	1.00	.70	.40
3	Cecil Fielder	1.25	.90	.50
4	Joe Carter	2.00	1.50	.80
5	Fred McGriff	2.00	1.50	.80
6	Barry Bonds	3.50	2.75	1.50
7	Gary Sheffield	1.25	.90	.50
8	Dave Hollins	1.50	1.25	.60
9	Frank Thomas	7.50	5.75	3.00
11	Albert Belle	2.00	1.50	.80
12	Ruben Sierra	.75	.60	.30
13	Larry Walker	.90	.70	.35
14	Jeff Bagwell	1.50	1.25	.60
15	David Justice	2.50	2.00	1.00
16	Kirby Puckett	2.50	2.00	1.00
20	Will Clark	1.25	.90	.50
23	Don Mattingly	2.00	1.50	.80
24	Jose Canseco	1.00	.70	.40
26	Andre Dawson	.75	.60	.30
27	Ryne Sandberg	2.75	2.00	1.00
28	Ken Griffey, Jr.	6.00	4.50	2.50

		MT	NR MT	EX
29	Carlos Baerga	2.50	2.00	1.00
30	Travis Fryman	2.50	2.00	1.00

1993 Score Pinnacle Team Pinnacle

These cards were randomly inserted in Pinnacle Series I packs; cards were included one in about every 24 packs. Each card features two players painted by artist Christopher Greco. An eleventh card, featuring relief pitchers, was available only via a mail-in offer.

		MT	NR MT	EX
Complete Set (11):		150.00	110.00	60.00
Common Player:		10.00	7.50	4.00
1	Greg Maddux/ Mike Mussina	15.00	11.25	6.00
2	Tom Glavine/ John Smiley	10.00	7.50	4.00
3	Darren Daulton/ Ivan Rodriguez	12.50	9.00	5.00
4	Fred McGriff/ Frank Thomas	45.00	32.50	18.00
5	Delino DeShields/ Carlos Baerga	12.50	9.00	5.00
6	Gary Sheffield/ Edgar Martinez	10.00	7.50	4.00
7	Ozzie Smith/ Pat Listach	10.00	7.50	4.00
8	Barry Bonds/ Juan Gonzalez	45.00	30.00	18.00
9	Andy Van Slyke/ Kirby Puckett	15.00	11.25	6.00
10	Larry Walker/ Joe Carter	10.00	7.50	4.00
11	Rob Dibble/ Rick Aguilera	10.00	7.50	4.00

1993 Score Pinnacle Team 2001

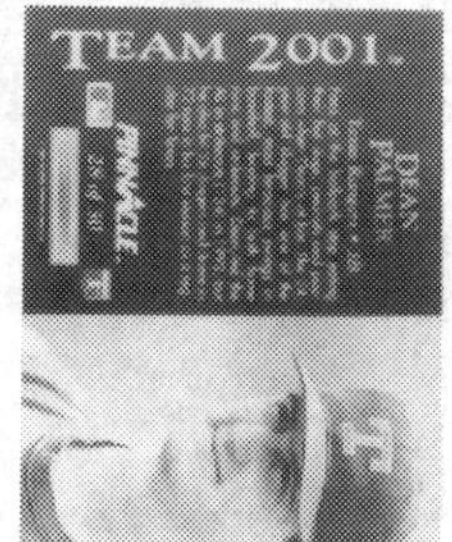

This insert set features 30 players who are expected to be stars in the year 2001. Cards were randomly inserted into 27-card jumbo packs from Series I.

		MT	NR MT	EX
Complete Set (30):		32.00	24.00	13.00
Common Player:		.50	.40	.20
1	Wil Cordero	.60	.45	.25
2	Cal Eldred	.75	.60	.30
3	Mike Mussina	2.00	1.50	.80
4	Chuck Knoblauch	.50	.40	.20
5	Melvin Nieves	1.50	1.25	.60
6	Tim Wakefield	.60	.45	.25
7	Carlos Baerga	2.50	2.00	1.00
8	Bret Boone	.75	.60	.30
9	Jeff Bagwell	1.75	1.25	.70
10	Travis Fryman	2.00	1.50	.80
11	Royce Clayton	.75	.60	.30
12	Delino DeSheilds	.50	.40	.20
13	Juan Gonzalez	4.00	3.00	1.50
14	Pedro Martinez	.75	.60	.30
15	Bernie Williams	.50	.40	.20
16	Billy Ashley	2.50	2.00	1.00
17	Marquis Grissom	.90	.70	.35
18	Kenny Lofton	1.50	1.25	.60
19	Ray Lankford	.50	.40	.20
20	Tim Salmon	7.50	5.75	3.00
21	Steve Hosey	.75	.60	.30
22	Charles Nagy	.50	.40	.20
23	Dave Fleming	.50	.40	.20
24	Reggie Sanders	.75	.60	.30
25	Sam Millitello	.50	.40	.20
26	Eric Karros	1.00	.70	.40
27	Ryan Klesko	2.00	1.50	.80
28	Dean Palmer	.75	.60	.30
29	Ivan Rodriguez	1.25	.90	.50
30	Sterling Hitchcock	1.50	1.25	.60

1993 Score Pinnacle Tribute

These two future Hall of Famers each have five-card sets devoted to their career achievements. Each card commemorates a milestone reached by George Brett or Nolan Ryan. Cards were random inserts in 1993 Score Pinnacle Series II packs, about one per every 24 packs. Fronts have a gold-foil stamped "Tribute" vertically at right.

		MT	NR MT	EX
Complete Set (10):		60.00	45.00	25.00
George Brett card (1-5):		5.00	3.75	2.00
Nolan Ryan card (6-10):		10.00	7.50	4.00
1	Kansas City Royalty (George Brett)	6.00	4.50	2.50
2	The Chase for .400 (George Brett)	6.00	4.50	2.50
3	Pine Tar Pandemonium ("The bat")	6.00	4.50	2.50
4	MVP and a World Series, Too (George Brett)	6.00	4.50	2.50
5	3,000 or Bust (George Brett)	6.00	4.50	2.50
6	The Rookie (Nolan Ryan)	10.00	7.50	4.00
7	Angel of No Mercy (Nolan Ryan)	10.00	7.50	4.00
8	Astronomical Success (Nolan Ryan)	10.00	7.50	4.00
9	5,000 Ks (Nolan Ryan)	10.00	7.50	4.00
10	No-Hitter No. 7 (Nolan Ryan)	10.00	7.50	4.00

Definitions for grading conditions are located in the Introduction of this price guide.

1993 Score Pinnacle Home Run Club

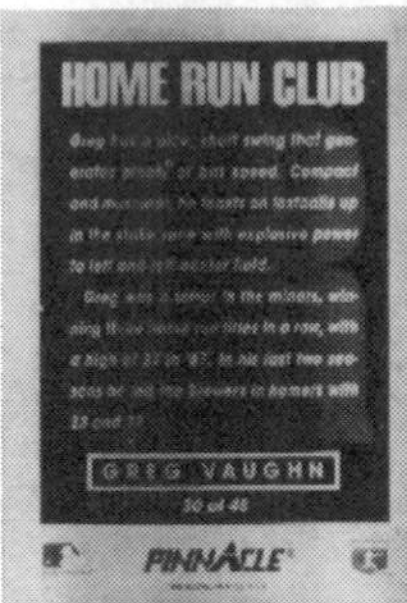

Pinnacle Brands Inc. released a 48-card boxed set in 1993 done in a special printing process called "Dufex," which gives the cards a 3-D metallic appearance. Limited to 200,000 numbered sets, the cards are UV coated and gold-foil stamped. The checklist includes 28 American League and 20 National League sluggers.

		MT	NR MT	EX
Complete Set (30):		25.00	19.00	10.00
Common Player:		.25	.20	.10
1	Juan Gonzalez	2.00	1.50	.80
2	Fred McGriff	.50	.40	.20
3	Cecil Fielder	.75	.60	.30
4	Barry Bonds	2.00	1.50	.80
5	Albert Belle	1.00	.70	.40
6	Gary Sheffield	.50	.40	.20
7	Joe Carter	.50	.40	.20
8	Mark McGwire	.75	.60	.30
9	Darren Daulton	.35	.25	.14
10	Jose Canseco	1.00	.70	.40
11	Dave Hollins	.35	.25	.14
12	Ryne Sandberg	3.00	2.25	1.25
13	Ken Griffey Jr.	3.00	2.25	1.25
14	Larry Walker	.25	.20	.10
15	Rob Deer	.25	.20	.10
16	Andre Dawson	.35	.25	.14
17	Frank Thomas	3.00	2.25	1.25
18	Mickey Tettleton	.25	.20	.10
19	Charlie Hayes	.25	.20	.10
20	Ron Gant	.35	.25	.14
21	Rickey Henderson	.50	.40	.20
22	Matt Williams	.35	.25	.14
23	Kevin Mitchell	.25	.20	.10
24	Robin Ventura	.35	.25	.14
25	Dean Palmer	.25	.20	.10
26	Mike Piazza	2.00	1.50	.80
27	J.T. Snow	.75	.60	.30
28	Jeff Bagwell	.50	.40	.20
29	John Olerud	.50	.40	.20
30	Greg Vaughn	.25	.20	.10
31	Dave Justice	.60	.45	.25
32	Dave Winfield	.75	.60	.30
33	Danny Tartabull	.25	.20	.10
34	Eric Anthony	.25	.20	.10
35	Eddie Murray	.50	.40	.20
36	Jay Buhner	.25	.20	.10
37	Derek Bell	.25	.20	.10
38	Will Clark	.75	.60	.30
39	Carlos Baerga	.50	.40	.20
40	Mo Vaughn	.50	.40	.20
41	Bobby Bonilla	.35	.25	.14
42	Tim Salmon	2.00	1.50	.80
43	Bo Jackson	.75	.60	.30
44	Howard Johnson	.35	.25	.14
45	Kent Hrbek	.25	.20	.10
46	Ruben Sierra	.35	.25	.14
47	Cal Ripken, Jr.	3.00	2.25	1.25
48	Travis Fryman	.35	.25	.14

Regional interest may affect the value of a card.

1993 Score Pinnacle Cooperstown

This 30-card boxed set features "today's superstar players bound to become Cooperstown inductees." In standard 2-1/2" x 3-1/2" format, the cards feature on both front and back an action photo which is borderless at the top and sides. At bottom-center of each photo is a half-moon green and gold-foil "Cooperstown Card" logo. The Pinnacle logo appears in black or white in one of the upper corners of each side. On front, the player's name is gold-foil stamped in a black bar at bottom. Om back is a black box, again with the player's name in gold-foil, plus a few stats justifying the player's Hall of Fame potential. Pinnacle's trademark optical-variable anti-counterfeiting device is at the bottom, flanked by the card number in red and the licensors' logos. Cards are UV coated on both sides.

		MT	NR MT	EX
Complete set (30):		9.00	6.75	3.50
Common player:		.25	.20	.10
1	Nolan Ryan	1.00	.75	.40
2	George Brett	.50	.40	.20
3	Robin Yount	.50	.40	.20
4	Carlton Fisk	.30	.25	.12
5	Dale Murphy	.30	.25	.12
6	Dennis Eckserley	.25	.20	.10
7	Rickey Henderson	.30	.25	.12
8	Ryne Sandberg	.50	.40	.20
9	Ozzie Smith	.30	.25	.12
10	Dave Winfield	.35	.25	.14
11	Andre Dawson	.25	.20	.10
12	Kirby Puckett	.35	.25	.14
13	Wade Boggs	.35	.25	.14
14	Don Mattingly	.45	.35	.20
15	Barry Bonds	.35	.25	.14
16	Will Clark	.35	.25	.14
17	Cal Ripken, Jr.	.50	.40	.20
18	Roger Clemens	.30	.25	.12
19	Dwight Gooden	.25	.20	.10
20	Tony Gwynn	.30	.25	.12
21	Joe Carter	.25	.20	.10
22	Ken Griffey, Jr.	.75	.60	.30
23	Paul Molitor	.30	.25	.12
24	Frank Thomas	1.00	.75	.40
25	Juan Gonzalez	.50	.40	.20
26	Barry Larkin	.25	.20	.10
27	Eddie Murray	.25	.20	.10
28	Cecil Fielder	.30	.25	.12
29	Roberto Alomar	.30	.25	.12
30	Mark McGwire	.35	.25	.14

Values quoted in this guide reflect the retail price of a card – the price a collector can expect to pay when buying a card from a dealer. The wholesale price – that which a collector can expect to receive from a dealer when selling cards – will be significantly lower, depending on desirability and condition.

1994 Score

Score's 1994 set, with a new design and UV coating, was issued in two series of 330 cards each. The cards, which use more action photos than before, have dark blue borders with the player's name in a team color-coded strip at the bottom. A special Gold Rush card, done for each card in the set, is included in every pack. These cards are actually printed on foil, rather than simply being foil stamped. Series I includes American League checklists, which are printed on the backs of cards depicting panoramic views of each team's ballpark. Series II has the National League team checklists. Insert sets include Dream Team players, and National (Series I packs) and American League Gold Stars (Series II packs), which use the Gold Rush process and appear once every 18 packs.

		MT	NR MT	EX
Complete Series I (330):		15.00	11.00	6.00
Common Player:		.04	.03	.02
1	Barry Bonds	.50	.40	.20
2	John Olerud	.25	.20	.10
3	Ken Griffey, Jr.	.75	.60	.30
4	Jeff Bagwell	.20	.15	.08
5	John Burkett	.04	.03	.02
6	Jack McDowell	.10	.08	.04
7	Albert Belle	.20	.15	.08
8	Andres Galarraga	.08	.06	.03
9	Mike Mussina	.15	.11	.06
10	Will Clark	.20	.15	.08
11	Travis Fryman	.20	.15	.08
12	Tony Gwynn	.20	.15	.08
13	Robin Yount	.20	.15	.08
14	Dave Magadan	.04	.03	.02
15	Paul O'Neill	.04	.03	.02
16	Ray Lankford	.04	.03	.02
17	Damion Easley	.04	.03	.02
18	Andy Van Slyke	.04	.03	.02
19	Brian McRae	.04	.03	.02
20	Ryne Sandberg	.25	.20	.10
21	Kirby Puckett	.25	.20	.10
22	Doc Gooden	.04	.03	.02
23	Don Mattingly	.20	.15	.08
24	Kevin Mitchell	.04	.03	.02
25	Roger Clemens	.15	.11	.06
26	Eric Karros	.15	.11	.06
27	Juan Gonzalez	.75	.60	.30
28	John Kruk	.10	.08	.04
29	Gregg Jefferies	.04	.03	.02
30	Tom Glavine	.15	.11	.06
31	Ivan Rodriguez	.15	.11	.06
32	Jay Bell	.04	.03	.02
33	Randy Johnson	.04	.03	.02
34	Darren Daulton	.04	.03	.02
35	Rickey Henderson	.10	.08	.04
36	Eddie Murray	.04	.03	.02
37	Brian Harper	.04	.03	.02
38	Delino DeShields	.08	.06	.03
39	Jose Lind	.04	.03	.02
40	Benito Santiago	.04	.03	.02
41	Frank Thomas	1.00	.70	.40
42	Mark Grace	.10	.08	.04
43	Roberto Alomar	.15	.11	.06
44	Andy Benes	.04	.03	.02
45	Luis Polonia	.04	.03	.02
46	Brett Butler	.04	.03	.02
47	Terry Steinbach	.04	.03	.02
48	Craig Biggio	.04	.03	.02
49	Greg Vaughn	.04	.03	.02
50	Charlie Hayes	.04	.03	.02
51	Mickey Tettleton	.04	.03	.02
52	Jose Rijo	.04	.03	.02
53	Carlos Baerga	.15	.11	.06
54	Jeff Blauser	.04	.03	.02
55	Leo Gomez	.04	.03	.02
56	Bob Tewksbury	.04	.03	.02
57	Mo Vaughn	.04	.03	.02
58	Orlando Merced	.04	.03	.02
59	Tino Martinez	.04	.03	.02
60	Lenny Dykstra	.10	.08	.04
61	Jose Canseco	.10	.08	.04
62	Tony Fernandez	.04	.03	.02
63	Donovan Osborne	.04	.03	.02
64	Ken Hill	.04	.03	.02
65	Kent Hrbek	.04	.03	.02
66	Bryan Harvey	.04	.03	.02
67	Wally Joyner	.04	.03	.02
68	Derrick May	.04	.03	.02
69	Lance Johnson	.04	.03	.02
70	Willie McGee	.04	.03	.02
71	Mark Langston	.04	.03	.02
72	Terry Pendleton	.04	.03	.02
73	Joe Carter	.10	.08	.04
74	Barry Larkin	.04	.03	.02
75	Jimmy Key	.04	.03	.02
76	Joe Girardi	.04	.03	.02
77	B.J. Surhoff	.04	.03	.02
78	Pete Harnisch	.04	.03	.02
79	Lou Whitaker	.04	.03	.02
80	Cory Snyder	.04	.03	.02
81	Kenny Lofton	.10	.08	.04
82	Fred McGriff	.10	.08	.04
83	Mike Greenwell	.04	.03	.02
84	Mike Perez	.04	.03	.02
85	Cal Ripken, Jr.	.25	.20	.10
86	Don Slaught	.04	.03	.02
87	Omar Vizquel	.04	.03	.02
88	Curt Schilling	.04	.03	.02
89	Chuck Knoblauch	.04	.03	.02
90	Moises Alou	.04	.03	.02
91	Greg Gagne	.04	.03	.02
92	Bret Saberhagen	.04	.03	.02
93	Ozzie Guillen	.04	.03	.02
94	Matt Williams	.04	.03	.02
95	Chad Curtis	.04	.03	.02
96	Mike Harkey	.04	.03	.02
97	Devon White	.04	.03	.02
98	Walt Weiss	.04	.03	.02
99	Kevin Brown	.04	.03	.02
100	Gary Sheffield	.10	.08	.04
101	Wade Boggs	.10	.08	.04
102	Orel Hershiser	.04	.03	.02
103	Tony Phillips	.04	.03	.02
104	Andujar Cedeno	.04	.03	.02
105	Bill Spiers	.04	.03	.02
106	Otis Nixon	.04	.03	.02
107	Felix Fermin	.04	.03	.02
108	Bip Roberts	.04	.03	.02
109	Dennis Eckersley	.04	.03	.02
110	Dante Bichette	.04	.03	.02
111	Ben McDonald	.04	.03	.02
112	Jim Poole	.04	.03	.02
113	John Dopson	.04	.03	.02
114	Rob Dibble	.04	.03	.02
115	Jeff Treadway	.04	.03	.02
116	Ricky Jordan	.04	.03	.02
117	Mike Henneman	.04	.03	.02
118	Willie Blair	.04	.03	.02
119	Doug Henry	.04	.03	.02
120	Gerald Perry	.04	.03	.02
121	Greg Myers	.04	.03	.02
122	John Franco	.04	.03	.02
123	Roger Mason	.04	.03	.02
124	Chris Hammond	.04	.03	.02
125	Hubie Brooks	.04	.03	.02
126	Kent Mercker	.04	.03	.02
127	Jim Abbott	.04	.03	.02
128	Kevin Bass	.04	.03	.02
129	Rick Aguilera	.04	.03	.02
130	Mitch Webster	.04	.03	.02
131	Eric Plunk	.04	.03	.02
132	Mark Carreon	.04	.03	.02
133	Dave Stewart	.04	.03	.02
134	Willie Wilson	.04	.03	.02
135	Dave Fleming	.04	.03	.02
136	Jeff Tackett	.04	.03	.02
137	Geno Petralli	.04	.03	.02
138	Gene Harris	.04	.03	.02
139	Scott Bankhead	.04	.03	.02
140	Trevor Wilson	.04	.03	.02
141	Alvaro Espinoza	.04	.03	.02

		MT	NR MT	EX
142	Ryan Bowen	.04	.03	.02
143	Mike Moore	.04	.03	.02
144	Bill Pecota	.04	.03	.02
145	Jaime Navarro	.04	.03	.02
146	Jack Daugherty	.04	.03	.02
147	Bob Wickman	.04	.03	.02
148	Chris Jones	.04	.03	.02
149	Todd Stottlemyre	.04	.03	.02
150	Brian Williams	.04	.03	.02
151	Chuck Finley	.04	.03	.02
152	Lenny Harris	.04	.03	.02
153	Alex Fernandez	.08	.06	.03
154	Candy Maldonado	.04	.03	.02
155	Jeff Montgomery	.04	.03	.02
156	David West	.04	.03	.02
157	Mark Williamson	.04	.03	.02
158	Milt Thompson	.04	.03	.02
159	Ron Darling	.04	.03	.02
160	Stan Belinda	.04	.03	.02
161	Henry Cotto	.04	.03	.02
162	Mel Rojas	.04	.03	.02
163	Doug Strange	.04	.03	.02
164	Rene Arocha (1993 Rookie)	.10	.08	.04
165	Tim Hulett	.04	.03	.02
166	Steve Avery	.10	.08	.04
167	Jim Thome	.10	.08	.04
168	Tom Browning	.04	.03	.02
169	Mario Diaz	.04	.03	.02
170	Steve Reed (1993 Rookie)	.04	.03	.02
171	Scott Livingstone	.04	.03	.02
172	Chris Donnels	.04	.03	.02
173	John Jaha	.10	.08	.04
174	Carlos Hernandez	.04	.03	.02
175	Dion James	.04	.03	.02
176	Bud Black	.04	.03	.02
177	Tony Castillo	.04	.03	.02
178	Jose Guzman	.04	.03	.02
179	Torey Lovullo	.04	.03	.02
180	John Vander Wal	.04	.03	.02
181	Mike LaValliere	.04	.03	.02
182	Sid Fernandez	.04	.03	.02
183	Brent Mayne	.04	.03	.02
184	Terry Mulholland	.04	.03	.02
185	Willie Banks	.04	.03	.02
186	Steve Cooke (1993 Rookie)	.04	.03	.02
187	Brent Gates (1993 Rookie)	.15	.11	.06
188	Erik Pappas (1993 Rookie)	.15	.11	.06
189	Bill Haselman (1993 Rookie)	.04	.03	.02
190	Fernando Valenzuela	.04	.03	.02
191	Gary Redus	.04	.03	.02
192	Danny Darwin	.04	.03	.02
193	Mark Portugal	.04	.03	.02
194	Derek Lilliquist	.04	.03	.02
195	Charlie O'Brien	.04	.03	.02
196	Matt Nokes	.04	.03	.02
197	Danny Sheaffer	.04	.03	.02
198	Bill Gullickson	.04	.03	.02
199	Alex Arias (1993 Rookie)	.10	.08	.04
200	Mike Fetters	.04	.03	.02
201	Brian Jordan	.04	.03	.02
202	Joe Grahe	.04	.03	.02
203	Tom Candiotti	.04	.03	.02
204	Jeremy Stanton	.04	.03	.02
205	Mike Stanton	.04	.03	.02
206	David Howard	.04	.03	.02
207	Darren Holmes	.04	.03	.02
208	Rick Honeycutt	.04	.03	.02
209	Danny Jackson	.04	.03	.02
210	Rich Amaral (1993 Rookie)	.04	.03	.02
211	Blas Minor (1993 Rookie)	.10	.08	.04
212	Kenny Rogers	.04	.03	.02
213	Jim Leyritz	.04	.03	.02
214	Mike Morgan	.04	.03	.02
215	Dan Gladden	.04	.03	.02
216	Randy Velarde	.04	.03	.02
217	Mitch Williams	.04	.03	.02
218	Hipolito Pichardo	.04	.03	.02
219	Dave Burba	.04	.03	.02
220	Wilson Alvarez	.04	.03	.02
221	Bob Zupcic	.04	.03	.02
222	Francisco Cabrera	.04	.03	.02
223	Julio Valera	.04	.03	.02
224	Paul Assenmacher	.04	.03	.02
225	Jeff Branson	.04	.03	.02
226	Todd Frohwirth	.04	.03	.02
227	Armando Reynoso	.04	.03	.02
228	Rich Rowland (1993 Rookie)	.04	.03	.02
229	Freddie Benavides	.04	.03	.02
230	Wayne Kirby (1993 Rookie)	.04	.03	.02
231	Darryl Kile	.04	.03	.02
232	Skeeter Barnes	.04	.03	.02
233	Ramon Martinez	.04	.03	.02
234	Tom Gordon	.04	.03	.02
235	Dave Gallagher	.04	.03	.02
236	Ricky Bones	.04	.03	.02
237	Larry Andersen	.04	.03	.02
238	Pat Meares (1993 Rookie)	.08	.06	.03
239	Zane Smith	.04	.03	.02
240	Tim Leary	.04	.03	.02
241	Phil Clark	.08	.06	.03
242	Danny Cox	.04	.03	.02
243	Mike Jackson	.04	.03	.02
244	Mike Gallego	.04	.03	.02
245	Lee Smith	.04	.03	.02
246	Todd Jones (1993 Rookie)	.04	.03	.02
247	Steve Bedrosian	.04	.03	.02
248	Troy Neel	.10	.08	.04
249	Jose Bautista	.04	.03	.02
250	Steve Frey	.04	.03	.02
251	Jeff Reardon	.04	.03	.02
252	Stan Javier	.04	.03	.02
253	Mo Sanford (1993 Rookie)	.04	.03	.02
254	Steve Sax	.04	.03	.02
255	Luis Aquino	.04	.03	.02
256	Domingo Jean (1993 Rookie)	.10	.08	.04
257	Scott Servais	.04	.03	.02
258	Brad Pennington (1993 Rookie)	.08	.06	.03
259	Dave Hansen	.04	.03	.02
260	Goose Gossage	.04	.03	.02
261	Jeff Fassero	.04	.03	.02
262	Junior Ortiz	.04	.03	.02
263	Anthony Young	.04	.03	.02
264	Chris Bosio	.04	.03	.02
265	Ruben Amaro, Jr.	.04	.03	.02
266	Mark Eichhorn	.04	.03	.02
267	Dave Clark	.04	.03	.02
268	Gary Thurman	.04	.03	.02
269	Les Lancaster	.04	.03	.02
270	Jamie Moyer	.04	.03	.02
271	Ricky Gutierrez (1993 Rookie)	.04	.03	.02
272	Greg Harris	.04	.03	.02
273	Mike Benjamin	.04	.03	.02
274	Gene Nelson	.04	.03	.02
275	Damon Berryhill	.04	.03	.02
276	Scott Radinsky	.04	.03	.02
277	Mike Aldrete	.04	.03	.02
278	Jerry DiPoto (1993 Rookie)	.04	.03	.02
279	Chris Haney	.04	.03	.02
280	Richie Lewis (1993 Rookie)	.04	.03	.02
281	Jarvis Brown	.04	.03	.02
282	Juan Bell	.04	.03	.02
283	Joe Klink	.04	.03	.02
284	Graeme Lloyd (1993 Rookie)	.08	.06	.03
285	Casey Candaele	.04	.03	.02
286	Bob MacDonald	.04	.03	.02
287	Mike Sharperson	.04	.03	.02
288	Gene Larkin	.04	.03	.02
289	Brian Barnes	.04	.03	.02
290	David McCarty (1993 Rookie)	.08	.06	.03
291	Jeff Innis	.04	.03	.02
292	Bob Patterson	.04	.03	.02
293	Ben Rivera	.04	.03	.02
294	John Habyan	.04	.03	.02
295	Rich Rodriguez	.04	.03	.02
296	Edwin Nunez	.04	.03	.02
297	Rod Brewer	.04	.03	.02
298	Mike Timlin	.04	.03	.02
299	Jesse Orosco	.04	.03	.02
300	Gary Gaetti	.04	.03	.02
301	Todd Benzinger	.04	.03	.02
302	Jeff Nelson	.04	.03	.02
303	Rafael Belliard	.04	.03	.02
304	Matt Whiteside (1994 Rookie)	.04	.03	.02
305	Vinny Castilla (1993 Rookie)	.04	.03	.02
306	Matt Turner (1993 Rookie)	.04	.03	.02
307	Eduardo Perez (1993 Rookie)	.04	.03	.02
308	Joel Johnston (1993 Rookie)	.04	.03	.02
309	Chris Gomez (1993 Rookie)	.04	.03	.02
310	Pat Rapp (1993 Rookie)	.04	.03	.02
311	Jim Tatum (1993 Rookie)	.10	.08	.04
312	*Kirk Rueter* (1993 Rookie)	.75	.60	.30
313	John Flaherty (1993 Rookie)	.10	.08	.04
314	Tom Kramer (1993 Rookie)	.04	.03	.02
315	Mark Whiten (Highligths)	.04	.03	.02
316	Chris Bosio (Highlights)	.04	.03	.02
317	Orioles Checklist	.04	.03	.02
318	Red Sox Checklist	.04	.03	.02
319	Angels Checklist	.04	.03	.02
320	White Sox Checklist	.04	.03	.02
321	Indians Checklist	.04	.03	.02
322	Tigers Checklist	.04	.03	.02
323	Royals Checklist	.04	.03	.02

		MT	NR MT	EX
324	Brewers Checklist	.04	.03	.02
325	Twins Checklist	.04	.03	.02
326	Yankees Checklist	.04	.03	.02
327	Athletics Checklist	.04	.03	.02
328	Mariners Checklist	.04	.03	.02
329	Rangers Checklist	.04	.03	.02
330	Blue Jays Checklist	.04	.03	.02

1994 Score Dream Team

Score's 1994 "Dream Team," one top player at each position, was featured in a 10-card insert set. The stars were decked out in vintage uniforms and equipment for the photos. Green and black bars at top and bottom frame the photo, and all printing on the front is in gold foil. Backs have a white background with green highlights. A color player portrait photo is featured, along with a brief justification for the player's selection to the squad. Cards are UV coated on both sides. Stated odds of finding a Dream Team insert were given as one per 72 packs.

		MT	NR MT	EX
Complete set (10):		45.00	34.00	18.00
Common player:		5.00	3.75	2.00
1	Mike Mussina	7.50	5.75	3.00
2	Tom Glavine	5.00	3.75	2.00
3	Don Mattingly	9.00	6.75	3.50
4	Carlos Baerga	7.50	5.75	3.00
5	Barry Larkin	5.00	3.75	2.00
6	Matt Williams	5.00	3.75	2.00
7	Juan Gonzalez	12.00	9.00	4.75
8	Andy Van Slyke	5.00	3.75	2.00
9	Larry Walker	5.00	3.75	2.00
10	Mike Stanley	5.00	3.75	2.00

1994 Score Gold Stars

Limited to inclusion in hobby packs, Score 60-card "Gold Stars" insert set features 30 National League players, found in Series I packs, and 30 American Leaguers inserted with Series II. Stated odds of finding a Gold Stars card were listed on the wrapper as one in 18 packs. A notation on the cards' back indicates that no more than 6,500 sets of Gold Stars were produced. The high-tech cards feature a color player action photo, the full-bleed background of which has been converted to metallic tones. Backs have a graduated gold background with a portrait-style color player photo.

		MT	NR MT	EX
Complete set (60):		160.00	120.00	65.00
Common player:		2.00	1.50	.80
1	Barry Bonds	8.00	6.00	3.25
2	Orlando Merced	2.00	1.50	.80
3	Mark Grace	4.00	3.00	1.50
4	Darren Daulton	2.00	1.50	.80
5	Jeff Blauser	2.00	1.50	.80
6	Deion Sanders	5.00	3.75	2.00
7	John Kruk	3.00	2.25	1.25
8	Jeff Bagwell	2.00	1.50	.80
9	Gregg Jefferies	3.00	2.25	1.25
10	Matt Williams	3.00	2.25	1.25
11	Andres Galarraga	3.00	2.25	1.25
12	Jay Bell	2.00	1.50	.80
13	Mike Piazza	6.00	4.50	2.50
14	Ron Gant	3.00	2.25	1.25
15	Barry Larkin	2.50	2.00	1.00
16	Tom Glavine	2.00	1.50	.80
17	Lenny Dykstra	3.00	2.25	1.25
18	Fred McGriff	3.00	2.25	1.25
19	Andy Van Slyke	2.00	1.50	.80
20	Gary Sheffield	2.50	2.00	1.00
21	John Burkett	2.00	1.50	.80
22	Dante Bichette	2.00	1.50	.80
23	Tony Gwynn	3.00	2.25	1.25
24	Dave Justice	3.00	2.25	1.25
25	Marquis Grissom	2.00	1.50	.80
26	Bobby Bonilla	2.50	2.00	1.00
27	Larry Walker	2.00	1.50	.80
28	Brett Butler	2.00	1.50	.80
29	Robby Thompson	2.00	1.50	.80
30	Jeff Conine	2.50	2.00	1.00
31	Joe Carter	2.50	2.00	1.00
32	Ken Griffey, Jr.	12.00	9.00	4.75
33	Juan Gonzalez	9.00	6.75	3.50
34	Rickey Henderson	4.00	3.00	1.50
35	Bo Jackson	4.00	3.00	1.50
36	Cal Ripken, Jr.	10.00	7.50	4.00
37	John Olerud	3.00	2.25	1.25
38	Carlos Baerga	4.00	3.00	1.50
39	Jack McDowell	2.50	2.00	1.00
40	Cecil Fielder	4.00	3.00	1.50
41	Kenny Lofton	2.50	2.00	1.00
42	Roberto Alomar	4.00	3.00	1.50
43	Randy Johnson	2.00	1.50	.80
44	Tim Salmon	4.00	3.00	1.50
45	Frank Thomas	12.00	9.00	4.75
46	Albert Belle	4.00	3.00	1.50
47	Greg Vaughn	2.00	1.50	.80
48	Travis Fryman	3.00	2.25	1.25
49	Don Mattingly	6.00	4.50	2.50
50	Wade Boggs	6.00	4.50	2.50
51	Mo Vaughn	4.00	3.00	1.50
52	Kirby Puckett	6.00	4.50	2.50
53	Devon White	2.50	2.00	1.00
54	Tony Phillips	2.00	1.50	.80
55	Brian Harper	2.00	1.50	.80
56	Chad Curtis	3.00	2.25	1.25
57	Paul Molitor	4.00	3.00	1.50
58	Ivan Rodriguez	3.00	2.25	1.25
59	Rafael Palmeiro	4.00	3.00	1.50
60	Brian McRae	2.00	1.50	.80

1994 Score Boys of Summer

Photos not available at press time

A heavy emphasis on rookies and recent rookies is noted in this 1994 Score insert set, released in two series, cards #1-30 with Score's Series I and 31-60 packaged with Series II.

		MT	NR MT	EX
Complete set (60):		95.00	71.00	38.00
Common player:		2.00	1.50	.80
1	Jeff Conine	2.50	2.00	1.00
2	Aaron Sele	4.00	3.00	1.50
3	Kevin Stocker	3.00	2.25	1.25
4	Pat Meares	2.50	2.00	1.00
5	Jeromy Burnitz	2.00	1.50	.80
6	Mike Piazza	6.00	4.50	2.50
7	Allen Watson	3.00	2.25	1.25
8	Jeffrey Hammonds	2.50	2.00	1.00
9	Kevin Roberson	2.50	2.00	1.00
10	Hilly Hathaway	2.00	1.50	.80
11	Kirk Reuter	3.00	2.25	1.25
12	Eduardo Perez	2.50	2.00	1.00
13	Ricky Gutierrez	3.50	2.75	1.50
14	Domingo Jean	2.50	2.00	1.00
15	David Nied	2.50	2.00	1.00
16	Wayne Kirby	2.50	2.00	1.00
17	Mike Lansing	2.50	2.00	1.00
18	Jason Bere	2.50	2.00	1.00
19	Brent Gates	2.00	1.50	.80
20	Javier Lopez	2.50	2.00	1.00
21	Greg McMichael	2.50	2.00	1.00
22	David Hulse	2.00	1.50	.80
23	Roberto Mejia	2.00	1.50	.80
24	Tim Salmon	5.00	3.75	2.00
25	Rene Arocha	2.50	2.00	1.00
26	Bret Boone	2.00	1.50	.80
27	David McCarty	2.50	2.00	1.00
28	Todd Van Poppel	2.00	1.50	.80
29	Lance Painter	2.00	1.50	.80
30	Erik Pappas	2.00	1.50	.80
31	Chuck Carr	2.50	2.00	1.00
32	Mark Hutton	2.00	1.50	.80
33	Jeff McNeely	2.00	1.50	.80
34	Willie Greene	2.00	1.50	.80
35	Nigel Wilson	2.50	2.00	1.00
36	Rondell White	2.50	2.00	1.00
37	Brian Turang	2.00	1.50	.80
38	Manny Ramirez	3.00	2.25	1.25
39	Salomon Torres	2.00	1.50	.80
40	Melvin Nieves	3.00	2.25	1.25
41	Ryan Klesko	2.50	2.00	1.00
42	Keith Kessinger	2.50	2.00	1.00
43	Eric Wedge	2.50	2.00	1.00
44	Bob Hamelin	2.00	1.50	.80
45	Carlos Delgado	4.00	3.00	1.50
46	Marc Newfield	2.00	1.50	.80
47	Raul Mondesi	2.50	2.00	1.00
48	Tim Costo	2.50	2.00	1.00
49	Pedro Martinez	2.00	1.50	.80
50	Steve Karsay	2.00	1.50	.80
51	Danny Bautista	2.00	1.50	.80
52	Butch Huskey	2.50	2.00	1.00
53	Kurt Abbott	2.00	1.50	.80
54	Darrell Sherman	2.00	1.50	.80
55	Damon Buford	2.00	1.50	.80
56	Ross Powell	2.00	1.50	.80
57	Darrell Whitmore	2.50	2.00	1.00
58	Chipper Jones	3.00	2.25	1.25
59	Jeff Granger	2.00	1.50	.80
60	Cliff Floyd	4.00	3.00	1.50

1994 Score Gold Rush

Opting to include one insert card in each pack of its 1994 product, Score created a "Gold Rush" version of each card in its regular set. Gold Rush cards are basically the same as their counterparts with a few enhancements. Card fronts are printed on foil with a gold border and a Score Gold Rush logo in one of the upper corners. The background of the photo has been metaliized, allowing the color player portion to stand out in sharp contrast. Backs are identical to the regular cards except for the appearance of a large Gold Rush logo under the typography at left.

	MT	NR MT	EX
Complete Series I (330):	125.00	95.00	50.00
Common player:	.25	.20	.10

Gold Rush cards valued at 5X same card in 1994 Score

1991 Studio Preview

Each 1991 Donruss set packaged for the retail trade included a pack of four cards previewing the debut Studio set. The cards are in the same format as the regular set, 2-1/2" x 3-1/2" with evocative black-and-white photos bordered in marron on front, and abiographical write-up on the back.

		MT	NR MT	EX
Complete Set (18):		12.00	9.00	4.75
Common Card:		.50	.40	.20
1	Juan Bell	.50	.40	.20
2	Roger Clemens	2.00	1.50	.80
3	Dave Parker	1.00	.70	.40
4	Tim Raines	.75	.60	.30
5	Kevin Seitzer	.50	.40	.20
6	Teddy Higuera	.50	.40	.20
7	Bernie Williams	.75	.60	.30
8	Harold Baines	.60	.45	.25
9	Gary Pettis	.50	.40	.20
10	Dave Justice	2.00	1.50	.80
11	Eric Davis	.75	.60	.30
12	Andujar Cedeno	.75	.60	.30
13	Tom Foley	.50	.40	.20
14	Dwight Gooden	1.00	.70	.40
15	Doug Drabek	.60	.45	.25
16	Steve Decker	.50	.40	.20
17	Joe Torre	.50	.40	.20
18	Header card	.50	.40	.20

1991 Studio

Donruss introduced this 264-card set in 1991. The cards feature maroon borders surrounding black and white posed player photos. The card backs are printed in black and white and feature personal data, career highlights, hobbies and interests and the player's hero. The cards were released in foil packs only and feature a special Rod Carew puzzle.

	MT	NR MT	EX
Complete Set (264):	15.00	11.00	6.00
Common Player:	.12	.09	.05

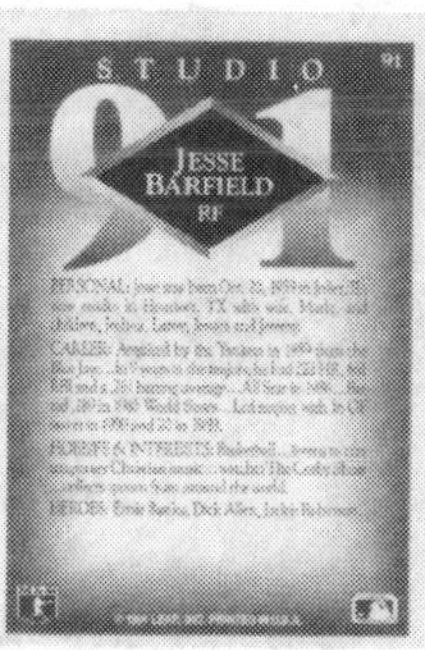

		MT	NR MT	EX
1	Glenn Davis	.15	.11	.06
2	Dwight Evans	.15	.11	.06
3	Leo Gomez	.30	.25	.12
4	Chris Hoiles	.25	.20	.10
5	Sam Horn	.12	.09	.05
6	Ben McDonald	.20	.15	.08
7	Randy Milligan	.12	.09	.05
8	Gregg Olson	.15	.11	.06
9	Cal Ripken, Jr.	.80	.60	.30
10	David Segui	.20	.15	.08
11	Wade Boggs	.30	.25	.12
12	Ellis Burks	.25	.20	.10
13	Jack Clark	.12	.09	.05
14	Roger Clemens	.75	.60	.30
15	Mike Greenwell	.20	.15	.08
16	Tim Naehring	.15	.11	.06
17	Tony Pena	.12	.09	.05
18	Phil Plantier	.60	.45	.25
19	Jeff Reardon	.15	.11	.06
20	Mo Vaughn	.75	.60	.30
21	Jimmy Reese	.15	.11	.06
22	Jim Abbott	.30	.25	.12
23	Bert Blyleven	.15	.11	.06
24	Chuck Finley	.20	.15	.08
25	Gary Gaetti	.12	.09	.05
26	Wally Joyner	.30	.25	.12
27	Mark Langston	.25	.20	.10
28	Kirk McCaskill	.12	.09	.05
29	Lance Parrish	.15	.11	.06
30	Dave Winfield	.25	.20	.10
31	Alex Fernandez	.30	.25	.12
32	Carlton Fisk	.20	.15	.08
33	Scott Fletcher	.12	.09	.05
34	Greg Hibbard	.12	.09	.05
35	Charlie Hough	.12	.09	.05
36	Jack McDowell	.25	.20	.10
37	Tim Raines	.25	.20	.10
38	Sammy Sosa	.75	.60	.30
39	Bobby Thigpen	.25	.20	.10
40	Frank Thomas	6.00	4.50	2.50
41	Sandy Alomar	.30	.25	.12
42	John Farrell	.12	.09	.05
43	Glenallen Hill	.15	.11	.06
44	Brook Jacoby	.12	.09	.05
45	Chris James	.12	.09	.05
46	Doug Jones	.12	.09	.05
47	Eric King	.12	.09	.05
48	Mark Lewis	.25	.20	.10
49	Greg Swindell	.15	.11	.06
50	Mark Whiten	.50	.40	.20
51	Milt Cuyler	.15	.11	.06
52	Rob Deer	.12	.09	.05
53	Cecil Fielder	.35	.25	.14
54	Travis Fryman	.75	.60	.30
55	Bill Gullickson	.12	.09	.05
56	Lloyd Moseby	.12	.09	.05
57	Frank Tanana	.12	.09	.05
58	Mickey Tettleton	.20	.15	.08
59	Alan Trammell	.25	.20	.10
60	Lou Whitaker	.20	.15	.08
61	Mike Boddicker	.12	.09	.05
62	George Brett	.40	.30	.15
63	Jeff Conine	.60	.45	.25
64	Warren Cromartie	.12	.09	.05
65	Storm Davis	.12	.09	.05
66	Kirk Gibson	.20	.15	.08
67	Mark Gubicza	.15	.11	.06
68	Brian McRae	.40	.30	.15
69	Bret Saberhagen	.15	.11	.06
70	Kurt Stillwell	.12	.09	.05
71	Tim McIntosh	.15	.11	.06
72	Candy Maldonado	.12	.09	.05
73	Paul Molitor	.50	.40	.20
74	Willie Randolph	.12	.09	.05
75	Ron Robinson	.12	.09	.05
76	Gary Sheffield	.30	.25	.12
77	Franklin Stubbs	.12	.09	.05
78	B.J. Surhoff	.12	.09	.05
79	Greg Vaughn	.20	.15	.08
80	Robin Yount	.60	.45	.25
81	Rick Aguilera	.12	.09	.05
82	Steve Bedrosian	.12	.09	.05
83	Scott Erickson	.20	.15	.08
84	Greg Gagne	.12	.09	.05
85	Dan Gladden	.12	.09	.05
86	Brian Harper	.15	.11	.06
87	Kent Hrbek	.15	.11	.06
88	Shane Mack	.25	.20	.10
89	Jack Morris	.20	.15	.08
90	Kirby Puckett	.30	.25	.12
91	Jesse Barfield	.12	.09	.05
92	Steve Farr	.12	.09	.05
93	Steve Howe	.12	.09	.05
94	Roberto Kelly	.20	.15	.08
95	Tim Leary	.12	.09	.05
96	Kevin Maas	.15	.11	.06
97	Don Mattingly	.30	.25	.12
98	Hensley Meulens	.20	.15	.08
99	Scott Sanderson	.12	.09	.05
100	Steve Sax	.15	.11	.06
101	Jose Canseco	.25	.20	.10
102	Dennis Eckersley	.15	.11	.06
103	Dave Henderson	.15	.11	.06
104	Rickey Henderson	.30	.25	.12
105	Rick Honeycutt	.12	.09	.05
106	Mark McGwire	.30	.25	.12
107	Dave Stewart	.20	.15	.08
108	Eric Show	.12	.09	.05
109	Todd Van Poppel	1.00	.70	.40
110	Bob Welch	.15	.11	.06
111	Alvin Davis	.12	.09	.05
112	Ken Griffey, Jr.	2.75	2.00	1.00
113	Ken Griffey, Sr.	.12	.09	.05
114	Erik Hanson	.15	.11	.06
115	Brian Holman	.12	.09	.05
116	Randy Johnson	.25	.20	.10
117	Edgar Martinez	.15	.11	.06
118	Tino Martinez	.15	.11	.06
119	Harold Reynolds	.15	.11	.06
120	David Valle	.12	.09	.05
121	Kevin Belcher	.12	.09	.05
122	Scott Chiamparino	.12	.09	.05
123	Julio Franco	.20	.15	.08
124	Juan Gonzalez	.80	.60	.30
125	Rich Gossage	.15	.11	.06
126	Jeff Kunkel	.12	.09	.05
127	Rafael Palmeiro	.25	.20	.10
128	Nolan Ryan	2.00	1.50	.80
129	Ruben Sierra	.15	.11	.06
130	Bobby Witt	.15	.11	.06
131	Roberto Alomar	.25	.20	.10
132	Tom Candiotti	.12	.09	.05
133	Joe Carter	.20	.15	.08
134	Ken Dayley	.12	.09	.05
135	Kelly Gruber	.15	.11	.06
136	John Olerud	.80	.60	.30
137	Dave Stieb	.15	.11	.06
138	Turner Ward	.15	.11	.06
139	Devon White	.15	.11	.06
140	Mookie Wilson	.12	.09	.05
141	Steve Avery	.25	.20	.10
142	Sid Bream	.12	.09	.05
143	Nick Esasky	.12	.09	.05
144	Ron Gant	.30	.25	.12
145	Tom Glavine	.20	.15	.08
146	David Justice	.60	.45	.25
147	Kelly Mann	.12	.09	.05
148	Terry Pendleton	.15	.11	.06
149	John Smoltz	.20	.15	.08
150	Jeff Treadway	.12	.09	.05
151	George Bell	.20	.15	.08
152	Shawn Boskie	.12	.09	.05
153	Andre Dawson	.20	.15	.08
154	Lance Dickson	.12	.09	.05
155	Shawon Dunston	.12	.09	.05
156	Joe Girardi	.12	.09	.05
157	Mark Grace	.25	.20	.10
158	Ryne Sandberg	.80	.60	.30
159	Gary Scott	.15	.11	.06
160	Dave Smith	.12	.09	.05
161	Tom Browning	.15	.11	.06
162	Eric Davis	.30	.25	.12
163	Rob Dibble	.20	.15	.08

		MT	NR MT	EX
164	Mariano Duncan	.12	.09	.05
165	Chris Hammond	.12	.09	.05
166	Billy Hatcher	.12	.09	.05
167	Barry Larkin	.20	.15	.08
168	Hal Morris	.15	.11	.06
169	Paul O'Neill	.15	.11	.06
170	Chris Sabo	.15	.11	.06
171	Eric Anthony	.15	.11	.06
172	Jeff Bagwell	.80	.60	.30
173	Craig Biggio	.20	.15	.08
174	Ken Caminitti	.15	.11	.06
175	Jim Deshaies	.12	.09	.05
176	Steve Finley	.15	.11	.06
177	Pete Harnisch	.15	.11	.06
178	Darryl Kile	.20	.15	.08
179	Curt Schilling	.12	.09	.05
180	Mike Scott	.12	.09	.05
181	Brett Butler	.15	.11	.06
182	Gary Carter	.15	.11	.06
183	Orel Hershiser	.20	.15	.08
184	Ramon Martinez	.15	.11	.06
185	Eddie Murray	.30	.25	.12
186	Jose Offerman	.15	.11	.06
187	Bob Ojeda	.12	.09	.05
188	Juan Samuel	.12	.09	.05
189	Mike Scioscia	.12	.09	.05
190	Darryl Strawberry	.20	.15	.08
191	Moises Alou	.50	.40	.20
192	Brian Barnes	.12	.09	.05
193	Oil Can Boyd	.12	.09	.05
194	Ivan Calderon	.12	.09	.05
195	Delino DeShields	.20	.15	.08
196	Mike Fitzgerald	.12	.09	.05
197	Andres Galarraga	.15	.11	.06
198	Marquis Grissom	.20	.15	.08
199	Bill Sampen	.12	.09	.05
200	Tim Wallach	.12	.09	.05
201	Daryl Boston	.12	.09	.05
202	Vince Coleman	.15	.11	.06
203	John Franco	.15	.11	.06
204	Dwight Gooden	.30	.25	.12
205	Tom Herr	.12	.09	.05
206	Gregg Jefferies	.25	.20	.10
207	Howard Johnson	.20	.15	.08
208	Dave Magadan	.20	.15	.08
209	Kevin McReynolds	.15	.11	.06
210	Frank Viola	.15	.11	.06
211	Wes Chamberlain	.30	.25	.12
212	Darren Daulton	.12	.09	.05
213	Lenny Dykstra	.20	.15	.08
214	Charlie Hayes	.15	.11	.06
215	Ricky Jordan	.15	.11	.06
216	Steve Lake	.12	.09	.05
217	Roger McDowell	.12	.09	.05
218	Mickey Morandini	.15	.11	.06
219	Terry Mulholland	.15	.11	.06
220	Dale Murphy	.20	.15	.08
221	Jay Bell	.15	.11	.06
222	Barry Bonds	.60	.45	.25
223	Bobby Bonilla	.20	.15	.08
224	Doug Drabek	.15	.11	.06
225	Bill Landrum	.12	.09	.05
226	Mike LaValliere	.12	.09	.05
227	Jose Lind	.12	.09	.05
228	Don Slaught	.12	.09	.05
229	John Smiley	.15	.11	.06
230	Andy Van Slyke	.15	.11	.06
231	Bernard Gilkey	.30	.25	.12
232	Pedro Guerrero	.20	.15	.08
233	Rex Hudler	.12	.09	.05
234	Ray Lankford	.30	.25	.12
235	Joe Magrane	.12	.09	.05
236	Jose Oquendo	.12	.09	.05
237	Lee Smith	.15	.11	.06
238	Ozzie Smith	.25	.20	.10
239	Milt Thompson	.12	.09	.05
240	Todd Zeile	.15	.11	.06
241	Larry Andersen	.12	.09	.05
242	Andy Benes	.15	.11	.06
243	Paul Faries	.12	.09	.05
244	Tony Fernandez	.12	.09	.05
245	Tony Gwynn	.20	.15	.08
246	Atlee Hammaker	.12	.09	.05
247	Fred McGriff	.20	.15	.08
248	Bip Roberts	.12	.09	.05
249	Benito Santiago	.15	.11	.06
250	Ed Whitson	.12	.09	.05
251	Dave Anderson	.12	.09	.05
252	Mike Benjamin	.15	.11	.06
253	John Burkett	.15	.11	.06
254	Will Clark	.40	.30	.15
255	Scott Garrelts	.12	.09	.05
256	Willie McGee	.15	.11	.06
257	Kevin Mitchell	.15	.11	.06
258	Dave Righetti	.15	.11	.06
259	Matt Williams	.30	.25	.12
260	Black & Decker	.20	.15	.08
261	Checklist	.10	.08	.04
262	Checklist	.10	.08	.04
263	Checklist	.10	.08	.04
264	Checklist	.10	.08	.04

1992 Studio

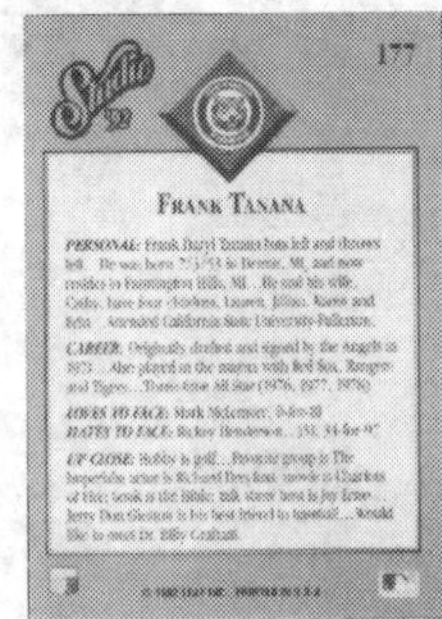

Donruss introduced the Studio line in 1991 and released another 264-card set entitled Leaf Studio for 1992. The cards feature a color player closeup with a large black and white photo behind the player. Tan borders surround the photos. The cards were only released in foil packs. Special Heritage insert cards featuring top players could be found in foil packs. Eight Heritage cards were released.

		MT	NR MT	EX
Complete Set:		15.00	15.00	8.00
Common Player:		.10	.08	.04
1	Steve Avery	.20	.15	.08
2	Sid Bream	.10	.08	.04
3	Ron Gant	.20	.15	.08
4	Tom Glavine	.20	.15	.08
5	David Justice	.25	.20	.10
6	Mark Lemke	.10	.08	.04
7	Greg Olson	.10	.08	.04
8	Terry Pendleton	.15	.11	.06
9	Deion Sanders	.30	.25	.12
10	John Smoltz	.15	.11	.06
11	Doug Dascenzo	.10	.08	.04
12	Andre Dawson	.20	.15	.08
13	Joe Girardi	.10	.08	.04
14	Mark Grace	.15	.11	.06
15	Greg Maddux	.20	.15	.08
16	Chuck McElroy	.10	.08	.04
17	Mike Morgan	.10	.08	.04
18	Ryne Sandberg	.50	.40	.20
19	Gary Scott	.10	.08	.04
20	Sammy Sosa	.25	.20	.10
21	Norm Charlton	.12	.09	.05
22	Rob Dibble	.15	.11	.06
23	Barry Larkin	.25	.20	.10
24	Hal Morris	.10	.08	.04
25	Paul O'Neill	.15	.11	.06
26	Jose Rijo	.12	.09	.05
27	Bip Roberts	.15	.11	.06
28	Chris Sabo	.15	.11	.06
29	Reggie Sanders	.20	.15	.08
30	Greg Swindell	.15	.11	.06
31	Jeff Bagwell	.20	.15	.08
32	Craig Biggio	.15	.11	.06
33	Ken Caminiti	.10	.08	.04
34	Andujar Cedeno	.15	.11	.06
35	Steve Finley	.15	.11	.06
36	Pete Harnisch	.12	.09	.05
37	Butch Henry	.10	.08	.04
38	Doug Jones	.10	.08	.04
39	Darryl Kile	.15	.11	.06
40	Eddie Taubensee	.10	.08	.04
41	Brett Butler	.12	.09	.05
42	Tom Candiotti	.10	.08	.04
43	Eric Davis	.15	.11	.06

#	Player	MT	NR MT	EX
44	Orel Hershiser	.15	.11	.06
45	Eric Karros	.75	.60	.30
46	Ramon Martinez	.15	.11	.06
47	Jose Offerman	.15	.11	.06
48	Mike Scioscia	.10	.08	.04
49	Mike Sharperson	.10	.08	.04
50	Darryl Strawberry	.20	.15	.08
51	Bret Barbarie	.15	.11	.06
52	Ivan Calderon	.10	.08	.04
53	Gary Carter	.15	.11	.06
54	Delino DeShields	.15	.11	.06
55	Marquis Grissom	.20	.15	.08
56	Ken Hill	.10	.08	.04
57	Dennis Martinez	.12	.09	.05
58	Spike Owen	.10	.08	.04
59	Larry Walker	.15	.11	.06
60	Tim Wallach	.12	.09	.05
61	Bobby Bonilla	.15	.11	.06
62	Tim Burke	.10	.08	.04
63	Vince Coleman	.15	.11	.06
64	John Franco	.10	.08	.04
65	Dwight Gooden	.25	.20	.10
66	Todd Hundley	.10	.08	.04
67	Howard Johnson	.15	.11	.06
68	Eddie Murray	.15	.11	.06
69	Bret Saberhagen	.15	.11	.06
70	Anthony Young	.10	.08	.04
71	Kim Batiste	.10	.08	.04
72	Wes Chamberlain	.10	.08	.04
73	Darren Daulton	.15	.11	.06
74	Mariano Duncan	.10	.08	.04
75	Lenny Dykstra	.15	.11	.06
76	John Kruk	.15	.11	.06
77	Mickey Morandini	.15	.11	.06
78	Terry Mulholland	.10	.08	.04
79	Dale Murphy	.20	.15	.08
80	Mitch Williams	.15	.11	.06
81	Jay Bell	.15	.11	.06
82	Barry Bonds	.60	.45	.25
83	Steve Buechele	.10	.08	.04
84	Doug Drabek	.15	.11	.06
85	Mike LaValliere	.10	.08	.04
86	Jose Lind	.10	.08	.04
87	Denny Neagle	.10	.08	.04
88	Randy Tomlin	.10	.08	.04
89	Andy Van Slyke	.10	.08	.04
90	Gary Varsho	.10	.08	.04
91	Pedro Guererro	.10	.08	.04
92	Rex Hudler	.10	.08	.04
93	Brian Jordan	.25	.20	.10
94	Felix Jose	.12	.09	.05
95	Donovan Osborne	.20	.15	.08
96	Tom Pagnozzi	.10	.08	.04
97	Lee Smith	.15	.11	.06
98	Ozzie Smith	.25	.20	.10
99	Todd Worrell	.10	.08	.04
100	Todd Zeile	.15	.11	.06
101	Andy Benes	.15	.11	.06
102	Jerald Clark	.10	.08	.04
103	Tony Fernandez	.10	.08	.04
104	Tony Gwynn	.20	.15	.08
105	Greg Harris	.10	.08	.04
106	Fred McGriff	.25	.20	.10
107	Benito Santiago	.15	.11	.06
108	Gary Sheffield	.30	.25	.12
109	Kurt Stillwell	.10	.08	.04
110	Tim Teufel	.10	.08	.04
111	Kevin Bass	.10	.08	.04
112	Jeff Brantley	.10	.08	.04
113	John Burkett	.10	.08	.04
114	Will Clark	.30	.25	.12
115	Royce Clayton	.15	.11	.06
116	Mike Jackson	.10	.08	.04
117	Darren Lewis	.12	.09	.05
118	Bill Swift	.10	.08	.04
119	Robby Thompson	.10	.08	.04
120	Matt Williams	.15	.11	.06
121	Brady Anderson	.20	.15	.08
122	Glenn Davis	.10	.08	.04
123	Mike Devereaux	.10	.08	.04
124	Chris Hoiles	.15	.11	.06
125	Sam Horn	.10	.08	.04
126	Ben McDonald	.15	.11	.06
127	Mike Mussina	.30	.25	.12
128	Gregg Olson	.15	.11	.06
129	Cal Ripken, Jr.	.50	.40	.20
130	Rick Sutcliffe	.15	.11	.06
131	Wade Boggs	.30	.25	.12
132	Roger Clemens	.40	.30	.15
133	Greg Harris	.10	.08	.04
134	Tim Naehring	.10	.08	.04

#	Player	MT	NR MT	EX
135	Tony Pena	.10	.08	.04
136	Phil Plantier	.15	.11	.06
137	Jeff Reardon	.15	.11	.06
138	Jody Reed	.10	.08	.04
139	Mo Vaughn	.35	.25	.14
140	Frank Viola	.20	.15	.08
141	Jim Abbott	.20	.15	.08
142	Hubie Brooks	.10	.08	.04
143	Chad Curtis	.60	.45	.25
144	Gary DiSarcina	.10	.08	.04
145	Chuck Finley	.15	.11	.06
146	Bryan Harvey	.15	.11	.06
147	Von Hayes	.10	.08	.04
148	Mark Langston	.15	.11	.06
149	Lance Parrish	.10	.08	.04
150	Lee Stevens	.10	.08	.04
151	George Bell	.15	.11	.06
152	Alex Fernandez	.15	.11	.06
153	Greg Hibbard	.10	.08	.04
154	Lance Johnson	.10	.08	.04
155	Kirk McCaskill	.10	.08	.04
156	Tim Raines	.15	.11	.06
157	Steve Sax	.10	.08	.04
158	Bobby Thigpen	.10	.08	.04
159	Frank Thomas	3.00	2.25	1.25
160	Robin Ventura	.25	.20	.10
161	Sandy Alomar, Jr.	.15	.11	.06
162	Jack Armstrong	.10	.08	.04
163	Carlos Baerga	.50	.40	.20
164	Albert Belle	.50	.40	.20
165	Alex Cole	.10	.08	.04
166	Glenallen Hill	.10	.08	.04
167	Mark Lewis	.15	.11	.06
168	Kenny Lofton	.30	.25	.12
169	Paul Sorrento	.10	.08	.04
170	Mark Whiten	.15	.11	.06
171	Milt Cuyler (color photo actually Lou Whitaker)	.10	.08	.04
172	Rob Deer	.10	.08	.04
173	Cecil Fielder	.30	.25	.12
174	Travis Fryman	.30	.25	.12
175	Mike Henneman	.10	.08	.04
176	Tony Phillips	.10	.08	.04
177	Frank Tanana	.10	.08	.04
178	Mickey Tettleton	.15	.11	.06
179	Alan Trammell	.20	.15	.08
180	Lou Whitaker	.15	.11	.06
181	George Brett	.40	.30	.15
182	Tom Gordon	.10	.08	.04
183	Mark Gubicza	.10	.08	.04
184	Gregg Jefferies	.20	.15	.08
185	Wally Joyner	.20	.15	.08
186	Brent Mayne	.10	.08	.04
187	Brian McRae	.15	.11	.06
188	Kevin McReynolds	.15	.11	.06
189	Keith Miller	.10	.08	.04
190	Jeff Montgomery	.10	.08	.04
191	Dante Bichette	.10	.08	.04
192	Ricky Bones	.10	.08	.04
193	Scott Fletcher	.10	.08	.04
194	Paul Molitor	.30	.25	.12
195	Jaime Navarro	.15	.11	.06
196	Franklin Stubbs	.10	.08	.04
197	B.J. Surhoff	.10	.08	.04
198	Greg Vaughn	.10	.08	.04
199	Bill Wegman	.10	.08	.04
200	Robin Yount	.40	.30	.15
201	Rick Aguilera	.10	.08	.04
202	Scott Erickson	.15	.11	.06
203	Greg Gagne	.10	.08	.04
204	Brian Harper	.10	.08	.04
205	Kent Hrbek	.15	.11	.06
206	Scott Leius	.10	.08	.04
207	Shane Mack	.15	.11	.06
208	Pat Mahomes	.10	.08	.04
209	Kirby Puckett	.50	.40	.20
210	John Smiley	.10	.08	.04
211	Mike Gallego	.10	.08	.04
212	Charlie Hayes	.10	.08	.04
213	Pat Kelly	.12	.09	.05
214	Roberto Kelly	.15	.11	.06
215	Kevin Maas	.10	.08	.04
216	Don Mattingly	.30	.25	.12
217	Matt Nokes	.10	.08	.04
218	Melido Perez	.10	.08	.04
219	Scott Sanderson	.10	.08	.04
220	Danny Tartabull	.15	.11	.06
221	Harold Baines	.15	.11	.06
222	Jose Canseco	.25	.20	.10
223	Dennis Eckersley	.20	.15	.08
224	Dave Henderson	.10	.08	.04

#	Player	MT	NR MT	EX
225	Carney Lansford	.10	.08	.04
226	Mark McGwire	.30	.25	.12
227	Mike Moore	.10	.08	.04
228	Randy Ready	.10	.08	.04
229	Terry Steinbach	.10	.08	.04
230	Dave Stewart	.15	.11	.06
231	Jay Buhner	.10	.08	.04
232	Ken Griffey, Jr.	2.00	1.50	.80
233	Erik Hanson	.10	.08	.04
234	Randy Johnson	.15	.11	.06
235	Edgar Martinez	.15	.11	.06
236	Tino Martinez	.10	.08	.04
237	Kevin Mitchell	.15	.11	.06
238	Pete O'Brien	.10	.08	.04
239	Harold Reynolds	.15	.11	.06
240	David Valle	.10	.08	.04
241	Julio Franco	.15	.11	.06
242	Juan Gonzalez	.60	.45	.25
243	Jose Guzman	.15	.11	.06
244	Rafael Palmeiro	.25	.20	.10
245	Dean Palmer	.20	.15	.08
246	Ivan Rodriguez	.30	.25	.12
247	Jeff Russell	.10	.08	.04
248	Nolan Ryan	1.50	1.25	.60
249	Ruben Sierra	.15	.11	.06
250	Dickie Thon	.10	.08	.04
251	Roberto Alomar	.30	.25	.12
252	Derek Bell	.20	.15	.08
253	Pat Borders	.10	.08	.04
254	Joe Carter	.25	.20	.10
255	Kelly Gruber	.10	.08	.04
256	Juan Guzman	.15	.11	.06
257	Jack Morris	.15	.11	.06
258	John Olerud	.40	.30	.15
259	Devon White	.15	.11	.06
260	Dave Winfield	.30	.25	.12
261	Checklist	.10	.08	.04
262	Checklist	.10	.08	.04
263	Checklist	.10	.08	.04
264	History Card	.10	.08	.04

1992 Studio Heritage

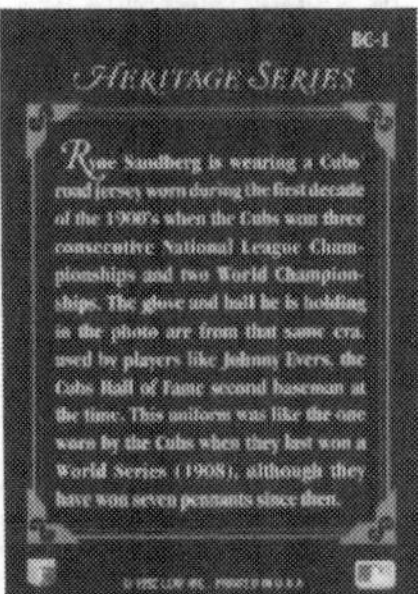

Superstars of 1992 were photographed in vintage-style uniforms in this 14-card insert set found in packages of Studio's 1992 issue. Cards #1-8 could be found in standard foil packs while 9-14 were inserted in Studio jumbos. Cards featured a sepia-tone photo bordered in turquoise and highlighted with copper foil. Cards carry a BC prefix to the card number on back.

		MT	NR MT	EX
Complete Set (14):		26.00	19.50	10.50
Common Player:		1.00	.70	.40
1	Ryne Sandberg	4.00	3.00	1.50
2	Carlton Fisk	1.25	.90	.50
3	Wade Boggs	3.00	2.25	1.25
4	Jose Canseco	1.50	1.25	.60
5	Don Mattingly	3.00	2.25	1.25
6	Darryl Strawberry	1.00	.70	.40
7	Cal Ripken, Jr.	4.00	3.00	1.50
8	Will Clark	3.00	2.25	1.25
9	Andre Dawson	1.00	.70	.40
10	Andy Van Slyke	1.00	.70	.40
11	Paul Molitor	2.50	2.00	1.00
12	Jeff Bagwell	2.00	1.50	.80
13	Darren Daulton	1.75	1.25	.70
14	Kirby Puckett	3.00	2.25	1.25

1993 Studio

This 220-card set features full-bleed photos. The player's portrait appears against one of several backgrounds featuring his team's uniform. His signature and the Studio logo are also stamped on in gold foil. Backs have a partial portrait of the player and insights into his personality.

		MT	NR MT	EX
Complete Set:		30.00	22.00	12.00
Common Player:		.10	.08	.04
1	Dennis Eckersley	.10	.08	.04
2	Chad Curtis	.50	.40	.20
3	Eric Anthony	.10	.08	.04
4	Roberto Alomar	.60	.45	.25
5	Steve Avery	.50	.40	.20
6	Cal Eldred	.15	.11	.06
7	Bernard Gilkey	.10	.08	.04
8	Steve Buechele	.08	.06	.03
9	Brett Butler	.08	.06	.03
10	Terry Mulholland	.08	.06	.03
11	Moises Alou	.15	.11	.06
12	Barry Bonds	1.00	.70	.40
13	Sandy Alomar Jr.	.08	.06	.03
14	Chris Bosio	.08	.06	.03
15	Scott Sanderson	.08	.06	.03
16	Bobby Bonilla	.15	.11	.06
17	Brady Anderson	.10	.08	.04
18	Derek Bell	.15	.11	.06
19	Wes Chamberlain	.08	.06	.03
20	Jay Bell	.08	.06	.03
21	Kevin Brown	.08	.06	.03
22	Roger Clemens	.60	.45	.25
23	Roberto Kelly	.10	.08	.04
24	Dante Bichette	.10	.08	.04
25	George Brett	.40	.30	.15
26	Rob Deer	.08	.06	.03
27	Brian Harper	.10	.08	.04
28	George Bell	.10	.08	.04
29	Jim Abbott	.12	.09	.05
30	Dave Henderson	.08	.06	.03
31	Wade Boggs	.20	.15	.08
32	Chili Davis	.08	.06	.03
33	Ellis Burks	.08	.06	.03
34	Jeff Bagwell	.40	.30	.15
35	Kent Hrbek	.08	.06	.03
36	Pat Borders	.08	.06	.03
37	Cecil Fielder	.30	.25	.12
38	Sid Bream	.08	.06	.03
39	Greg Gagne	.08	.06	.03
40	Darryl Hamilton	.10	.08	.04
41	Jerald Clark	.08	.06	.03
42	Mark Grace	.15	.11	.06
43	Barry Larkin	.20	.15	.08
44	John Burkett	.08	.06	.03
45	Scott Cooper	.08	.06	.03
46	*Mike Lansing*	.50	.40	.20
47	Jose Canseco	.25	.20	.10
48	Will Clark	.40	.30	.15
49	Carlos Garcia	.15	.11	.06
50	Carlos Baerga	.70	.50	.30
51	Darren Daulton	.30	.25	.12
52	Jay Buhner	.10	.08	.04
53	Andy Benes	.10	.08	.04
54	Jeff Conine	.08	.06	.03
55	Mike Devereaux	.08	.06	.03
56	Vince Coleman	.08	.06	.03
57	Terry Steinbach	.08	.06	.03
58	*J.T. Snow*	1.50	1.25	.60
59	Greg Swindell	.08	.06	.03

		MT	NR MT	EX
60	Devon White	.10	.08	.04
61	John Smoltz	.15	.11	.06
62	Todd Zeile	.10	.08	.04
63	Rick Wilkins	.10	.08	.04
64	Tim Wallach	.08	.06	.03
65	John Wetteland	.08	.06	.03
66	Matt Williams	.40	.30	.15
67	Paul Sorrento	.10	.08	.04
68	David Valle	.08	.06	.03
69	Walt Weiss	.08	.06	.03
70	John Franco	.08	.06	.03
71	Nolan Ryan	2.00	1.50	.80
72	Frank Viola	.08	.06	.03
73	Chris Sabo	.08	.06	.03
74	David Nied	.75	.60	.30
75	Kevin McReynolds	.08	.06	.03
76	Lou Whitaker	.10	.08	.04
77	Dave Winfield	.40	.30	.15
78	Robin Ventura	.50	.40	.20
79	Spike Owen	.08	.06	.03
80	Cal Ripken, Jr.	.80	.60	.30
81	Dan Walter	.08	.06	.03
82	Mitch Williams	.10	.08	.04
83	Tim Wakefield	.15	.11	.06
84	Rickey Henderson	.20	.15	.08
85	Gary DiSarcina	.10	.08	.04
86	Craig Biggio	.10	.08	.04
87	Joe Carter	.30	.25	.12
88	Ron Gant	.15	.11	.06
89	John Jaha	.15	.11	.06
90	Gregg Jefferies	.10	.08	.04
91	Jose Guzman	.10	.08	.04
92	Eric Karros	.25	.20	.10
93	Wil Cordero	.15	.11	.06
94	Royce Clayton	.10	.08	.04
95	Albert Belle	.80	.60	.30
96	Ken Griffey, Jr.	2.75	2.00	1.00
97	Orestes Destrade	.10	.08	.04
98	Tony Fernandez	.08	.06	.03
99	Leo Gomez	.08	.06	.03
100	Tony Gwynn	.20	.15	.08
101	Lenny Dykstra	.15	.11	.06
102	Jeff King	.10	.08	.04
103	Julio Franco	.08	.06	.03
104	Andre Dawson	.15	.11	.06
105	Randy Milligan	.08	.06	.03
106	Alex Cole	.08	.06	.03
107	Phil Hiatt	.50	.40	.20
108	Travis Fryman	.50	.40	.20
109	Chuck Knoblauch	.12	.09	.05
110	Bo Jackson	.50	.40	.20
111	Pat Kelly	.08	.06	.03
112	Bret Saberhagen	.08	.06	.03
113	Ruben Sierra	.15	.11	.06
114	Tim Salmon	3.00	2.25	1.25
115	Doug Jones	.08	.06	.03
116	Ed Sprague	.08	.06	.03
117	Terry Pendleton	.12	.09	.05
118	Robin Yount	.40	.30	.15
119	Mark Whiten	.10	.08	.04
120	Checklist	.08	.06	.03
121	Sammy Sosa	.12	.09	.05
122	Darryl Strawberry	.12	.09	.05
123	Larry Walker	.30	.25	.12
124	Robby Thompson	.10	.08	.04
125	Carlos Martinez	.08	.06	.03
126	Edgar Martinez	.10	.08	.04
127	Benito Santiago	.10	.08	.04
128	Howard Johnson	.08	.06	.03
129	Harold Reynolds	.08	.06	.03
130	Craig Shipley	.08	.06	.03
131	Curt Schilling	.10	.08	.04
132	Andy Van Slyke	.12	.09	.05
133	Ivan Rodriguez	.40	.30	.15
134	Mo Vaughn	.30	.25	.12
135	Bip Roberts	.08	.06	.03
136	Charlie Hayes	.12	.09	.05
137	Brian McRae	.10	.08	.04
138	Mickey Tettleton	.10	.08	.04
139	Frank Thomas	3.50	2.75	1.50
140	Paul O'Neill	.08	.06	.03
141	Mark McGwire	.25	.20	.10
142	Damion Easley	.25	.20	.10
143	Ken Caminiti	.08	.06	.03
144	Juan Guzman	.30	.25	.12
145	Tom Glavine	.40	.30	.15
146	Pat Listach	.20	.15	.08
147	Lee Smith	.10	.08	.04
148	Derrick May	.10	.08	.04
149	Ramon Martinez	.10	.08	.04
150	Delino DeShields	.15	.11	.06

		MT	NR MT	EX
151	Kirt Manwaring	.08	.06	.03
152	Reggie Jefferson	.08	.06	.03
153	Randy Johnson	.15	.11	.06
154	Dave Magadan	.08	.06	.03
155	Dwight Gooden	.10	.08	.04
156	Chris Hoiles	.10	.08	.04
157	Fred McGriff	.30	.25	.12
158	Dave Hollins	.20	.15	.08
159	Al Martin	.50	.40	.20
160	Juan Gonzalez	2.75	2.00	1.00
161	Mike Greenwell	.08	.06	.03
162	Kevin Mitchell	.10	.08	.04
163	Andres Galarraga	.20	.15	.08
164	Wally Joyner	.08	.06	.03
165	Kirk Gibson	.08	.06	.03
166	Pedro Munoz	.08	.06	.03
167	Ozzie Guillen	.08	.06	.03
168	Jimmy Key	.10	.08	.04
169	Kevin Seitzer	.08	.06	.03
170	Luis Polonia	.08	.06	.03
171	Luis Gonzalez	.10	.08	.04
172	Paul Molitor	.20	.15	.08
173	David Justice	.75	.60	.30
174	B.J. Surhoff	.08	.06	.03
175	Ray Lankford	.20	.15	.08
176	Ryne Sandberg	.80	.60	.30
177	Jody Reed	.08	.06	.03
178	Marquis Grissom	.25	.20	.10
179	Willie McGee	.10	.08	.04
180	Kenny Lofton	.80	.60	.30
181	Junior Felix	.08	.06	.03
182	Jose Offerman	.10	.08	.04
183	John Kruk	.20	.15	.08
184	Orlando Merced	.12	.09	.05
185	Rafael Palmeiro	.20	.15	.08
186	Billy Hatcher	.08	.06	.03
187	Joe Oliver	.08	.06	.03
188	Joe Girardi	.08	.06	.03
189	Jose Lind	.08	.06	.03
190	Harold Baines	.10	.08	.04
191	Mike Pagliarulo	.08	.06	.03
192	Lance Johnson	.08	.06	.03
193	Don Mattingly	.30	.25	.12
194	Doug Drabek	.10	.08	.04
195	John Olerud	.40	.30	.15
196	Greg Maddux	.20	.15	.08
197	Greg Vaughn	.12	.09	.05
198	Tom Pagnozzi	.08	.06	.03
199	Willie Wilson	.08	.06	.03
200	Jack McDowell	.30	.25	.12
201	Mike Piazza	6.00	4.50	2.50
202	Mike Mussina	.60	.45	.25
203	Charles Nagy	.08	.06	.03
204	Tino Martinez	.08	.06	.03
205	Charlie Hough	.08	.06	.03
206	Todd Hundley	.08	.06	.03
207	Gary Sheffield	.30	.25	.12
208	Mickey Morandini	.08	.06	.03
209	Don Slaught	.08	.06	.03
210	Dean Palmer	.30	.25	.12
211	Jose Rijo	.10	.08	.04
212	Vinny Castilla	.08	.06	.03
213	Tony Phillips	.08	.06	.03
214	Kirby Puckett	.70	.50	.30
215	Tim Raines	.12	.09	.05
216	Otis Nixon	.10	.08	.04
217	Ozzie Smith	.25	.20	.10
218	Jose Vizcaino	.08	.06	.03
220	Checklist	.08	.06	.03

1993 Studio Heritage

All types of 1993 Leaf Studio packs were candidates for having one of 12 Heritage cards inserted in them. The fronts feature the player posing in an old-time uniform. The picture has a frame and says Heritage Series at the top. The backs have a mug shot surrounded by an ornate frame and tell what year the uniform on the front is from. Team trivia is also included.

		MT	NR MT	EX
Complete Set (12):		30.00	22.00	12.00
Common Player:		1.50	1.25	.60
1	George Brett	4.00	3.00	1.50
2	Juan Gonzalez	7.50	5.75	3.00
3	Roger Clemens	3.50	2.75	1.50
4	Mark McGwire	2.00	1.50	.80
5	Mark Grace	1.75	1.25	.70
6	Ozzie Smith	2.50	2.00	1.00
7	Barry Larkin	1.50	1.25	.60
8	Frank Thomas	9.00	6.75	3.50
9	Carlos Baerga	2.00	1.50	.80
10	Eric Karros	2.00	1.50	.80
11	J.T. Snow	2.00	1.50	.80
12	John Kruk	2.00	1.50	.80

1993 Studio Silhouettes

These insert cards were randomly included in jumbo packs only. The card fronts feature a ghosted image of the player against an action silhouette on a gray background. The player's name is in bronze foil at bottom. Backs have a player action photo and description of a career highlights.

		MT	NR MT	EX
Complete Set (10):		40.00	30.00	16.00
Common Player:		1.00	.70	.40
1	Frank Thomas	10.00	7.50	4.00
2	Barry Bonds	6.00	4.50	2.50
3	Jeff Bagwell	2.50	2.00	1.00
4	Juan Gonzalez	8.00	6.00	3.25
5	Travis Fryman	4.00	3.00	1.50
6	J.T. Snow	3.00	2.25	1.25
7	John Kruk	2.50	2.00	1.00
8	Jeff Blauser	1.00	.70	.40
9	Mike Piazza	12.00	9.00	4.75
10	Nolan Ryan	9.00	6.75	3.50

1993 Studio Superstars on Canvas

Ten players are featured on these insert cards, which were availalbe in hobby and retail packs. The cards show player portraits which mix photography and artwork.

		MT	NR MT	EX
Complete Set (10):		30.00	22.00	12.00
Common Player:		1.50	1.25	.60
1	Ken Griffey Jr.	9.00	6.75	3.50
2	Jose Canseco	2.00	1.50	.80
3	Mark McGwire	2.00	1.50	.80
4	Mike Mussina	2.00	1.50	.80

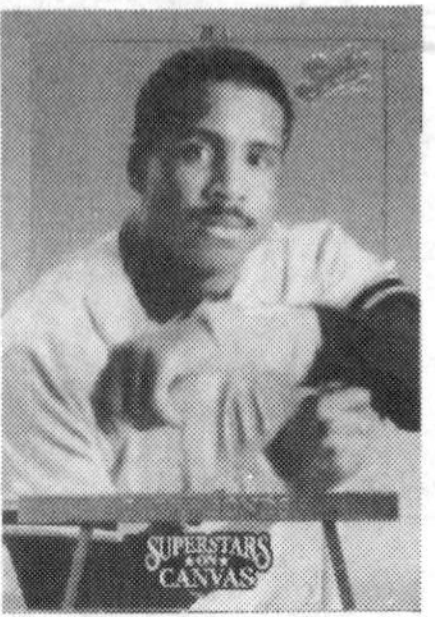

5	Joe Carter	2.00	1.50	.80
6	Frank Thomas	9.00	6.75	3.50
7	Darren Daulton	2.50	2.00	1.00
8	Mark Grace	1.50	1.25	.60
9	Andres Galarraga	1.50	1.25	.60
10	Barry Bonds	5.00	3.75	2.00

1993 Studio Frank Thomas

This five-card set is devoted to Frank Thomas. Cards were randomly included in all types of 1993 Leaf Studio packs. Topics covered on the cards include Thomas' childhood, his baseball memories, his family, his performance and being a role model.

	MT	NR MT	EX
Complete Set (5):	25.00	15.00	10.00
Common Player:	5.00	3.00	1.50

1993 Ted Williams Card Co. Premier Edition

		MT	NR MT	EX
Complete Set (160):		32.00	24.00	12.00
Common Player:		.10	.06	.04
1	Ted Williams	3.00	2.00	1.00
2	Rick Ferrell	.25	.15	.10
3	Jim Lonborg	.10	.06	.04
4	Mel Parnell	.10	.06	.04
5	Jim Piersall	.25	.15	.10
6	Luis Tiant	.10	.06	.04
7	Carl Yastrzemski	.75	.50	.25
8	Ralph Branca	.10	.06	.04
9	Roy Campanella	.50	.30	.15
10	Ron Cey	.10	.06	.04
11	Tommy Davis	.10	.06	.04

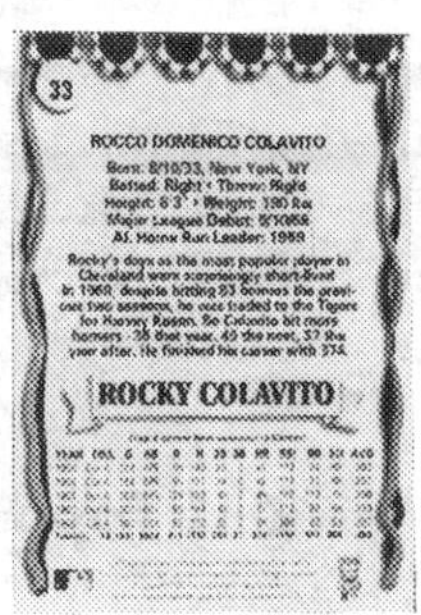

		MT	NR MT	EX
12	Don Drysdale	.75	.50	.25
13	Carl Erskine	.10	.06	.04
14	Steve Garvey	.20	.12	.06
15	Don Newcombe	.10	.06	.04
16	Duke Snider	.50	.30	.15
17	Maury Wills	.40	.30	.15
18	Jim Fregosi	.10	.06	.04
19	Bobby Grich	.10	.06	.04
20	Bill Buckner	.10	.06	.04
21	Billy Herman	.10	.06	.04
22	Ferguson Jenkins	.20	.12	.06
23	Ron Santo	.10	.06	.04
24	Billy Williams	.30	.20	.10
25	Luis Aparicio	.25	.15	.10
26	Luke Appling	.25	.15	.10
27	Minnie Minoso	.10	.06	.04
28	Johnny Bench	1.00	.60	.30
29	George Foster	.10	.06	.04
30	Joe Morgan	.60	.40	.20
31	Buddy Bell	.10	.06	.04
32	Lou Boudreau	.40	.30	.15
33	Rocky Colavito	.25	.15	.10
34	Jim "Mudcat" Grant	.10	.06	.04
35	Tris Speaker	.40	.30	.15
36	Ray Boone	.10	.06	.04
37	Darrell Evans	.10	.06	.04
38	Al Kaline	.50	.30	.15
39	George Kell	.25	.15	.10
40	Mickey Lolich	.10	.06	.04
41	Cesar Cedeno	.10	.06	.04
42	Sal Bando	.10	.06	.04
43	Vida Blue	.10	.06	.04
44	Bert Campaneris	.10	.06	.04
45	Ken Holtzman	.10	.06	.04
46	Lou Burdette	.10	.06	.04
47	Bob Horner	.10	.06	.04
48	Warren Spahn	.75	.50	.25
49	Cecil Cooper	.10	.06	.04
50	Tony Oliva	.30	.20	.10
51	Bobby Bonds	.25	.15	.10
52	Alvin Dark	.10	.06	.04
53	Dave Dravecky	.10	.06	.04
54	Monte Irvin	.10	.06	.04
55	Willie Mays	1.25	.75	.40
56	Bud Harrelson	.10	.06	.04
57	Dave Kingman	.10	.06	.04
58	Yogi Berra	.60	.40	.20
59	Don Baylor	.10	.06	.04
60	Jim Bouton	.10	.06	.04
61	Bobby Brown	.10	.06	.04
62	Whitey Ford	.50	.30	.15
63	Lou Gehrig	1.00	.60	.30
64	Charlie Keller	.10	.06	.04
65	Eddie Lopat	.10	.06	.04
66	Johnny Mize	.40	.30	.15
67	Bobby Mercer	.10	.06	.04
68	Graig Nettles	.20	.12	.06
69	Bobby Shantz	.10	.06	.04
70	Richie Ashburn	.10	.06	.04
71	Larry Bowa	.10	.06	.04
72	Steve Carlton	.40	.30	.15
73	Robin Roberts	.30	.20	.10
74	Matty Alou	.10	.06	.04
75	Harvey Haddix	.10	.06	.04
76	Ralph Kiner	.40	.30	.15
77	Bill Madlock	.10	.06	.04
78	Bill Mazeroski	.20	.12	.06
79	Al Oliver	.10	.06	.04
80	Manny Sanguillen	.10	.06	.04
81	Willie Stargell	.25	.15	.10
82	Al Brumbry	.10	.06	.04
83	Davey Johnson	.10	.06	.04
84	Boog Powell	.10	.06	.04
85	Earl Weaver	.10	.06	.04
86	Lou Brock	.50	.30	.15
87	Orlando Cepeda	.10	.06	.04
88	Curt Flood	.10	.06	.04
89	Joe Garagiola	.10	.06	.04
90	Bob Gibson	.50	.30	.15
91	Rogers Hornsby	.50	.30	.15
92	Enos Slaughter	.25	.15	.10
93	Joe Torre	.10	.06	.04
94	Gaylord Perry	.10	.06	.04
95	First half of teams	.10	.06	.04
96	Second half of teams	.10	.06	.04
97	Papa Bell	.25	.15	.10
98	George E. Blair Sr.	.10	.06	.04
99	Gene Benson	.10	.06	.04
100	Lyman Bostock Sr.	.25	.15	.10
101	Marlin Carter	.10	.06	.04
102	Oscar Charleston	.10	.06	.04
103	Ray Dandridge	.10	.06	.04
104	Mahlon Duckett	.10	.06	.04
105	Josh Gibson	.50	.30	.15
106	Cowan Hyde	.10	.06	.04
107	William Johnson	.25	.15	.10
108	Buck Leonard	.25	.15	.10
109	John Lloyd	.25	.15	.10
110	Lester Lockett	.10	.06	.04
111	Max Manning	.10	.06	.04
112	Satchel Paige	1.00	.60	.30
113	Armando Vazquez	.10	.06	.04
114	Joe Williams	.50	.30	.15
115	"Negro Leaguers" (CL)	.10	.06	.04
116	Alice "Lefty" Hohlmeyer	.10	.06	.04
117	Dorothy "Kammie" Kamenshek	.10	.06	.04
118	Lavonne "Pepper" Martin	.10	.06	.04
119	Marge Wenzell	.10	.06	.04
120	All-American Women's Prof. Baseball Leag (Checklist)	.10	.06	.04
121	Babe Ruth	1.00	.60	.30
122	Lou Gehrig	.75	.50	.25
123	Jimmie Foxx	.50	.30	.15
124	Rogers Hornsby	.50	.30	.15
125	Ty Cobb	.75	.50	.25
126	Willie Mays	.75	.50	.25
127	Tris Speaker	.30	.20	.10
128	Johnny Mize	.30	.20	.10
129	Ralph Kiner	.30	.20	.10
130	Ted's Greatest Hitters (Checklist)	.10	.06	.04
131	Joe Black	.10	.06	.04
132	Roy Campanella	.75	.50	.25
133	Larry Doby	.10	.06	.04
134	Jim Gilliam	.10	.06	.04
135	Monte Irvin	.25	.15	.10
136	Sam Jethro	.10	.06	.04
137	Willie Mays	.75	.50	.25
138	Don Newcombe	.10	.06	.04
139	Satchel Paige	.75	.50	.25
140	"Barrier Breakers" (Checklist)	.10	.06	.04
141	Roy Campanella	.50	.30	.15
142	Bob Gibson	.50	.30	.15
143	Boog Powell	.10	.06	.04
144	Willie Mays	.50	.30	.15
145	Johnny Mize	.25	.15	.10
146	Monte Irvin	.10	.06	.04
147	Earl Weaver	.10	.06	.04
148	Ted Williams	1.50	1.00	.60
149	Jim Gilliam	.10	.06	.04
150	"Goin North" (Checklist)	.10	.06	.04
151	Juan Gonzalez	1.50	1.00	.60
152	Juan Gonzalez	1.50	1.00	.60
153	Juan Gonzalez	1.50	1.00	.60
154	Juan Gonzalez	1.50	1.00	.60
155	"Dawning of a Legacy" (Checklist)	.10	.06	.04
156	Jeff Bagwell	.40	.30	.15
157	Jeff Bagwell	.40	.30	.15
158	Jeff Bagwell	.40	.30	.15
159	Jeff Bagwell	.40	.30	.15
160	"Dawning of a Legacy" (Checklist)	.10	.06	.04
	BOSTON RED SOX	.10	.06	.04
	BROOKLYN/LA DODGERS	.10	.06	.04
	CALIFORNIA ANGELS	.10	.06	.04
	CHICAGO CUBS	.10	.06	.04
	CHICAGO WHITE SOX	.10	.06	.04
	CINCINNATI REDS	.10	.06	.04
	CLEVELAND INDIANS	.10	.06	.04
	DETROIT TIGERS	.10	.06	.04
	HOUSTON ASTROS	.10	.06	.04
	K.C./OAKLAND ATHLETICS	.10	.06	.04
	MILWAUKEE/ATLANTA BRAVES	.10	.06	.04
	MILWAUKEE BREWERS	.10	.06	.04
	MINNESOTA TWINS	.10	.06	.04
	N.Y./S.F. GIANTS	.10	.06	.04

		MT	NR MT	EX
	NEW YORK METS	.10	.06	.04
	NEW YORK YANKEES	.10	.06	.04
	PHILADELPHIA PHILLIES	.10	.06	.04
	PITTSBURGH PIRATES	.10	.06	.04
	BALTIMORE ORIOLES	.10	.06	.04
	ST. LOUIS CARDINALS	.10	.06	.04
	SAN DIEGO PADRES	.10	.06	.04
	Checklist	.10	.06	.04
1	Locklear Collection			
2	Complete Set (10):	65.00	45.00	30.00
3	Common Player:	4.00	3.00	1.50
1	Yogi Berra	6.00	4.00	2.00
2	Lou Brock	5.00	3.00	1.50
3	Willie Mays	9.00	6.00	3.00
4	Johnny Mize	4.00	3.00	1.50
5	Satchel Paige	9.00	6.00	3.00
6	Babe Ruth	12.00	8.00	4.00
7	Enos Slaughter	4.00	3.00	1.50
8	Carl Yastrzemski	6.00	4.00	2.00
9	Ted Williams	15.00	10.00	5.00
10	Checklist	6.00	4.00	2.00
1	Roberto Clemente "Etched in Stone" (Roberto Clemente)	.10	.06	.04
2	Roberto Clemente "Etched in Stone" (Roberto Clemente)	.10	.06	.04
3	Roberto Clemente "Etched in Stone" (Roberto Clemente)	.10	.06	.04
4	Roberto Clemente "Etched in Stone" (Roberto Clemente)	.10	.06	.04
5	Roberto Clemente "Etched in Stone" (Roberto Clemente)	.10	.06	.04
6	Roberto Clemente "Etched in Stone" (Roberto Clemente)	.10	.06	.04
7	Roberto Clemente "Etched in Stone" (Roberto Clemente)	.10	.06	.04
8	Roberto Clemente "Etched in Stone" (Roberto Clemente)	.10	.06	.04
9	Roberto Clemente "Etched in Stone" (Roberto Clemente)	.10	.06	.04
10	Roberto Clemente "Etched in Stone" (Checklist)	.10	.06	.04
1	Mass Mrkt Spl Insert Set "Robinson Coll" (Brooks Robinson)	.10	.06	.04
2	Mass Mrkt Spl Insert Set "Robinson Coll" (Brooks Robinson)	.10	.06	.04
3	Mass Mrkt Spl Insert Set "Robinson Coll" (Brooks Robinson)	.10	.06	.04
4	Mass Mrkt Spl Insert Set "Robinson Coll" (Brooks Robinson)	.10	.06	.04
5	Mass Mrkt Spl Insert Set "Robinson Coll" (Brooks Robinson)	.10	.06	.04
6	Mass Mrkt Spl Insert Set "Robinson Coll" (Brooks Robinson)	.10	.06	.04
7	Mass Mrkt Spl Insert Set "Robinson Coll" (Brooks Robinson)	.10	.06	.04
8	Mass Mrkt Spl Insert Set "Robinson Coll" (Brooks Robinson)	.10	.06	.04
9	Mass Mrkt Spl Insert Set "Robinson Coll" (Brooks Robinson)	.10	.06	.04
10	Mass Mrkt Spl Insert Set "Robinson Coll" (Checklist)	.10	.06	.04
1	"Memories" (1955 Brooklyn Dodgers)	.10	.06	.04
2	"Memories" (1955 Brooklyn Dodgers)	.10	.06	.04
3	"Memories" (1955 Brooklyn Dodgers)	.10	.06	.04
4	"Memories" (1955 Brooklyn Dodgers)	.10	.06	.04
5	"Memories" (1955 Brooklyn Dodgers) (Checklist)	.10	.06	.04
6	"Memories" (1963 Los Angeles Dodgers)	.10	.06	.04
7	"Memories" (1963 Los Angeles Dodgers)	.10	.06	.04
8	"Memories" (1963 Los Angeles Dodgers)	.10	.06	.04
9	"Memories" (1963 Los Angeles Dodgers)	.10	.06	.04
10	"Memories" (1963 Los Angeles Dodgers) (Checklist)	.10	.06	.04
11	"Memories" (1971 Pittsburgh Pirates)	.10	.06	.04
12	"Memories" (1971 Pittsburgh Pirates)	.10	.06	.04
13	"Memories" (1971 Pittsburgh Pirates)	.10	.06	.04
14	"Memories" (1971 Pittsburgh Pirates)	.10	.06	.04
15	"Memories" (1971 Pittsburgh Pirates) (Checklist)	.10	.06	.04
16	"Memories" (1975 Cincinnati Reds)	.10	.06	.04
17	"Memories" (1975 Cincinnati Reds)	.10	.06	.04
18	"Memories" (1975 Cincinnati Reds)	.10	.06	.04
19	"Memories" (1975 Cincinnati Reds)	.10	.06	.04
20	"Memories" (1975 Cincinnati Reds) (Checklist)	.10	.06	.04

1951 Topps Red Backs

Like the Blue Backs, the Topps Red Backs which were sold at the same time, came two to a package for 1¢. Their black and white photographs appear on a red, white, blue and yellow background. The back printing is red on white. Their 2" by 2-5/8" size is the same as Blue Backs. Also identical is the set size (52 cards) and the game situations to be found on the fronts of the cards, for use in playing a card game of baseball. Red Backs are more common than the Blue Backs by virtue of a recent discovery of a large hoard of unopened boxes.

		NR MT	EX	VG
	Complete Set:	650.00	325.00	195.00
	Common Player:	10.00	5.00	3.00
1	Yogi Berra	75.00	38.00	23.50
2	Sid Gordon	11.00	5.50	3.25
3	Ferris Fain	10.00	5.00	3.00
4	Vern Stephens	10.00	5.00	3.00
5	Phil Rizzuto	30.00	15.00	9.00
6	Allie Reynolds	15.00	7.50	4.50
7	Howie Pollet	10.00	5.00	3.00
8	Early Wynn	25.00	12.50	7.50
9	Roy Sievers	10.00	5.00	3.00
10	Mel Parnell	10.00	5.00	3.00
11	Gene Hermanski	10.00	5.00	3.00
12	Jim Hegan	10.00	5.00	3.00
13	Dale Mitchell	10.00	5.00	3.00
14	Wayne Terwilliger	10.00	5.00	3.00
15	Ralph Kiner	25.00	12.50	7.50
16	Preacher Roe	12.00	6.00	3.50
17	Gus Bell	10.00	5.00	3.00
18	Gerry Coleman	12.50	6.25	3.75
19	Dick Kokos	10.00	5.00	3.00
20	Dom DiMaggio	12.50	6.25	3.75
21	Larry Jansen	10.00	5.00	3.00
22	Bob Feller	25.00	12.50	7.50
23	Ray Boone	10.00	5.00	3.00
24	Hank Bauer	12.50	6.25	3.75
25	Cliff Chambers	10.00	5.00	3.00
26	Luke Easter	10.00	5.00	3.00
27	Wally Westlake	10.00	5.00	3.00
28	Elmer Valo	10.00	5.00	3.00
29	Bob Kennedy	10.00	5.00	3.00
30	Warren Spahn	25.00	12.50	7.50
31	Gil Hodges	20.00	10.00	6.00
32	Henry Thompson	10.00	5.00	3.00
33	William Werle	10.00	5.00	3.00
34	Grady Hatton	10.00	5.00	3.00
35	Al Rosen	11.00	5.50	3.25
36a	Gus Zernial (Chicago in bio)	20.00	10.00	6.00
36b	Gus Zernial (Philadelphia in bio)	12.00	6.00	3.50
37	Wes Westrum	10.00	5.00	3.00

		NR MT	EX	VG
38	Duke Snider	30.00	15.00	9.00
39	Ted Kluszewski	12.00	6.00	3.50
40	Mike Garcia	10.00	5.00	3.00
41	Whitey Lockman	10.00	5.00	3.00
42	Ray Scarborough	10.00	5.00	3.00
43	Maurice McDermott	10.00	5.00	3.00
44	Sid Hudson	10.00	5.00	3.00
45	Andy Seminick	10.00	5.00	3.00
46	Billy Goodman	10.00	5.00	3.00
47	Tommy Glaviano	10.00	5.00	3.00
48	Eddie Stanky	11.00	5.50	3.25
49	Al Zarilla	10.00	5.00	3.00
50	Monte Irvin	25.00	12.50	7.50
51	Eddie Robinson	10.00	5.00	3.00
52a	Tommy Holmes (Boston in bio)	20.00	10.00	6.00
52b	Tommy Holmes (Hartford in bio)	20.00	10.00	6.00

1951 Topps Blue Backs

Sold two cards in a package with a piece of candy for 1¢, the Topps Blue Backs are considerably scarcer than their Red Back counterparts. The 2" by 2-5/8" cards carry a black and white player photograph on a red, white, yellow and green background along with the player's name and other information including their 1950 record on the front. The back is printed in blue on a white background. The 52-card set has varied baseball situations on them, making the playing of a rather elementary game of baseball possible. Although scarce, Blue Backs were printed on thick cardboard and have survived quite well over the years. There are, however, few stars (- Johnny Mize and Enos Slaughter are two) in the set. Despite being a Topps product, Blue Backs do not currently enjoy great popularity.

		NR MT	EX	VG
Complete Set:		1950.00	975.00	575.00
Common Player:		40.00	20.00	12.00
1	Eddie Yost	40.00	20.00	12.00
2	Henry Majeski	40.00	20.00	12.00
3	Richie Ashburn	50.00	25.00	15.00
4	Del Ennis	40.00	20.00	12.00
5	Johnny Pesky	40.00	20.00	12.00
6	Red Schoendienst	60.00	30.00	18.00
7	Gerry Staley	40.00	20.00	12.00
8	Dick Sisler	40.00	20.00	12.00
9	Johnny Sain	42.50	21.00	12.50
10	Joe Page	45.00	22.50	13.50
11	Johnny Groth	40.00	20.00	12.00
12	Sam Jethroe	40.00	20.00	12.00
13	Mickey Vernon	40.00	20.00	12.00
14	Red Munger	40.00	20.00	12.00
15	Eddie Joost	40.00	20.00	12.00
16	Murry Dickson	40.00	20.00	12.00
17	Roy Smalley	40.00	20.00	12.00
18	Ned Garver	40.00	20.00	12.00
19	Phil Masi	40.00	20.00	12.00
20	Ralph Branca	45.00	22.50	13.50
21	Billy Johnson	40.00	20.00	12.00
22	Bob Kuzava	40.00	20.00	12.00
23	Dizzy Trout	40.00	20.00	12.00
24	Sherman Lollar	40.00	20.00	12.00
25	Sam Mele	40.00	20.00	12.00
26	Chico Carrasquel	40.00	20.00	12.00
27	Andy Pafko	40.00	20.00	12.00
28	Harry (The Cat) Brecheen	40.00	20.00	12.00
29	Granny Hamner	40.00	20.00	12.00
30	Enos Slaughter	60.00	30.00	18.00
31	Lou Brissie	40.00	20.00	12.00
32	Bob Elliott	40.00	20.00	12.00
33	Don Lenhardt	40.00	20.00	12.00
34	Earl Torgeson	40.00	20.00	12.00
35	Tommy Byrne	42.50	21.00	12.50
36	Cliff Fannin	40.00	20.00	12.00
37	Bobby Doerr	60.00	30.00	18.00
38	Irv Noren	40.00	20.00	12.00
39	Ed Lopat	42.50	21.00	12.50
40	Vic Wertz	40.00	20.00	12.00
41	Johnny Schmitz	40.00	20.00	12.00
42	Bruce Edwards	40.00	20.00	12.00
43	Willie Jones	40.00	20.00	12.00
44	Johnny Wyrostek	40.00	20.00	12.00
45	Bill Pierce	40.00	20.00	12.00
46	Gerry Priddy	40.00	20.00	12.00
47	Herman Wehmeier	40.00	20.00	12.00
48	Billy Cox	42.50	21.00	12.50
49	Hank Sauer	40.00	20.00	12.00
50	Johnny Mize	60.00	30.00	18.00
51	Eddie Waitkus	40.00	20.00	12.00
52	Sam Chapman	40.00	20.00	12.00

1952 Topps

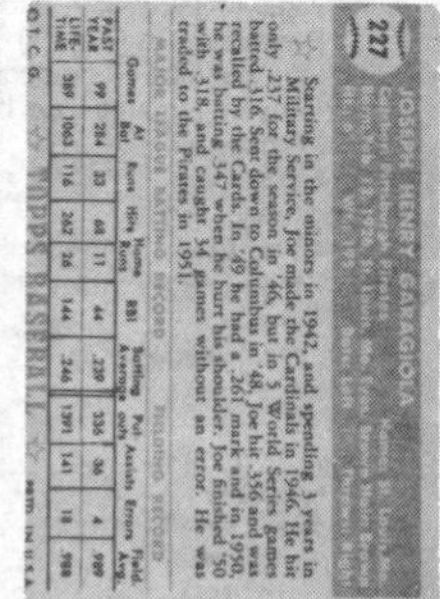

At 407 cards, the 1952 Topps set was the largest set of its day, both in number of cards and physical dimensions of the cards. Cards are 2-5/8" by 3-3/4" with a hand-colored black and white photo on front. Major baseball card innovations presented in the set include the first-ever use of color team logos as part of the design, and the inclusion of stats for the previous season and overall career on the backs. A major variety in the set is that first 80 cards can be found with backs printed entirely in black or black and red. Backs entirely in black command a $10-15 premium. Card numbers 311-407 were printed in limited supplies and are extremely rare.

		NR MT	EX	VG
Complete Set (407):		54250.00	25000.00	14500.
Common Player: 1-80		55.00	27.00	16.50
Common Player: 81-250		30.00	15.00	9.00
Common Player: 251-280		50.00	25.00	15.00
Common Player: 281-300		55.00	27.00	16.50
Common Player: 301-310		50.00	25.00	15.00
Common Player: 311-407		225.00	112.00	67.00
1	Andy Pafko	1200.00	100.00	25.00
2	*Pete Runnels*	60.00	20.00	16.50
3	Hank Thompson	55.00	27.00	16.50
4	Don Lenhardt	55.00	27.00	16.50
5	Larry Jansen	55.00	27.00	16.50
6	Grady Hatton	55.00	27.00	16.50
7	Wayne Terwilliger	60.00	30.00	18.00
8	Fred Marsh	55.00	27.00	16.50
9	Bobby Hogue	65.00	32.00	19.50
10	Al Rosen	80.00	40.00	24.00
11	Phil Rizzuto	225.00	112.00	67.00
12	Monty Basgall	55.00	27.00	16.50
13	Johnny Wyrostek	55.00	27.00	16.50
14	Bob Elliott	55.00	27.00	16.50
15	Johnny Pesky	55.00	27.00	16.50
16	Gene Hermanski	55.00	27.00	16.50

		NR MT	EX	VG
17	Jim Hegan	55.00	27.00	16.50
18	Merrill Combs	55.00	27.00	16.50
19	Johnny Bucha	55.00	27.00	16.50
20	*Billy Loes*	110.00	55.00	33.00
21	Ferris Fain	55.00	27.00	16.50
22	Dom DiMaggio	100.00	50.00	30.00
23	Billy Goodman	55.00	27.00	16.50
24	Luke Easter	55.00	27.00	16.50
25	Johnny Groth	55.00	27.00	16.50
26	Monte Irvin	100.00	50.00	30.00
27	Sam Jethroe	55.00	27.00	16.50
28	Jerry Priddy	55.00	27.00	16.50
29	Ted Kluszewski	100.00	50.00	30.00
30	Mel Parnell	55.00	27.00	16.50
31	Gus Zernial	55.00	27.00	16.50
32	Eddie Robinson	55.00	27.00	16.50
33	Warren Spahn	250.00	125.00	75.00
34	Elmer Valo	55.00	27.00	16.50
35	Hank Sauer	55.00	27.00	16.50
36	Gil Hodges	150.00	75.00	45.00
37	Duke Snider	300.00	150.00	90.00
38	Wally Westlake	55.00	27.00	16.50
39	"Dizzy" Trout	55.00	27.00	16.50
40	Irv Noren	55.00	27.00	16.50
41	Bob Wellman	55.00	27.00	16.50
42	Lou Kretlow	55.00	27.00	16.50
43	Ray Scarborough	55.00	27.00	16.50
44	Con Dempsey	55.00	27.00	16.50
45	Eddie Joost	55.00	27.00	16.50
46	Gordon Goldsberry	55.00	27.00	16.50
47	Willie Jones	55.00	27.00	16.50
48a	Joe Page (Johnny Sain back)	225.00	112.00	67.00
48b	Joe Page (Joe Page back)	80.00	40.00	24.00
49a	Johnny Sain (Joe Page back)	250.00	125.00	75.00
49b	Johnny Sain (Johnny Sain back)	80.00	40.00	24.00
50	Marv Rickert	55.00	27.00	16.50
51	Jim Russell	60.00	30.00	18.00
52	Don Mueller	55.00	27.00	16.50
53	Chris Van Cuyk	60.00	30.00	18.00
54	Leo Kiely	55.00	27.00	16.50
55	Ray Boone	60.00	30.00	18.00
56	Tommy Glaviano	55.00	27.00	16.50
57	Ed Lopat	75.00	37.50	22.50
58	Bob Mahoney	55.00	27.00	16.50
59	Robin Roberts	125.00	62.00	37.00
60	Sid Hudson	55.00	27.00	16.50
61	"Tookie" Gilbert	55.00	27.00	16.50
62	Chuck Stobbs	55.00	27.00	16.50
63	Howie Pollet	55.00	27.00	16.50
64	Roy Sievers	55.00	27.00	16.50
65	Enos Slaughter	100.00	50.00	30.00
66	Preacher Roe	90.00	45.00	27.00
67	Allie Reynolds	90.00	45.00	27.00
68	Cliff Chambers	55.00	27.00	16.50
69	Virgil Stallcup	55.00	27.00	16.50
70	Al Zarilla	55.00	27.00	16.50
71	Tom Upton	55.00	27.00	16.50
72	Karl Olson	55.00	27.00	16.50
73	William Werle	55.00	27.00	16.50
74	Andy Hansen	55.00	27.00	16.50
75	Wes Westrum	55.00	27.00	16.50
76	Eddie Stanky	55.00	27.00	16.50
77	Bob Kennedy	55.00	27.00	16.50
78	Ellis Kinder	55.00	27.00	16.50
79	Gerald Staley	55.00	27.00	16.50
80	Herman Wehmeier	55.00	27.00	16.50
81	Vernon Law	30.00	15.00	9.00
82	Duane Pillette	30.00	15.00	9.00
83	Billy Johnson	30.00	15.00	9.00
84	Vern Stephens	30.00	15.00	9.00
85	Bob Kuzava	40.00	20.00	12.00
86	Ted Gray	30.00	15.00	9.00
87	Dale Coogan	30.00	15.00	9.00
88	Bob Feller	225.00	112.00	67.00
89	Johnny Lipon	30.00	15.00	9.00
90	Mickey Grasso	30.00	15.00	9.00
91	Red Schoendienst	80.00	40.00	24.00
92	Dale Mitchell	30.00	15.00	9.00
93	Al Sima	30.00	15.00	9.00
94	Sam Mele	30.00	15.00	9.00
95	Ken Holcombe	30.00	15.00	9.00
96	Willard Marshall	30.00	15.00	9.00
97	Earl Torgeson	30.00	15.00	9.00
98	Bill Pierce	30.00	15.00	9.00
99	Gene Woodling	55.00	27.00	16.50
100	Del Rice	30.00	15.00	9.00
101	Max Lanier	30.00	15.00	9.00
102	Bill Kennedy	30.00	15.00	9.00
103	Cliff Mapes	30.00	15.00	9.00
104	Don Kolloway	30.00	15.00	9.00
105	John Pramesa	30.00	15.00	9.00

		NR MT	EX	VG
106	Mickey Vernon	30.00	15.00	9.00
107	Connie Ryan	30.00	15.00	9.00
108	Jim Konstanty	30.00	15.00	9.00
109	Ted Wilks	30.00	15.00	9.00
110	Dutch Leonard	30.00	15.00	9.00
111	Harry Lowrey	30.00	15.00	9.00
112	Henry Majeski	30.00	15.00	9.00
113	Dick Sisler	30.00	15.00	9.00
114	Willard Ramsdell	30.00	15.00	9.00
115	George Munger	30.00	15.00	9.00
116	Carl Scheib	30.00	15.00	9.00
117	Sherman Lollar	30.00	15.00	9.00
118	Ken Raffensberger	30.00	15.00	9.00
119	Maurice McDermott	30.00	15.00	9.00
120	Bob Chakales	30.00	15.00	9.00
121	Gus Niarhos	30.00	15.00	9.00
122	Jack Jensen	70.00	35.00	21.00
123	Eddie Yost	30.00	15.00	9.00
124	Monte Kennedy	30.00	15.00	9.00
125	Bill Rigney	30.00	15.00	9.00
126	Fred Hutchinson	30.00	15.00	9.00
127	Paul Minner	30.00	15.00	9.00
128	Don Bollweg	40.00	20.00	12.00
129	Johnny Mize	80.00	40.00	24.00
130	Sheldon Jones	30.00	15.00	9.00
131	Morrie Martin	30.00	15.00	9.00
132	Clyde Kluttz	30.00	15.00	9.00
133	Al Widmar	30.00	15.00	9.00
134	Joe Tipton	30.00	15.00	9.00
135	Dixie Howell	30.00	15.00	9.00
136	Johnny Schmitz	35.00	17.50	10.50
137	*Roy McMillan*	30.00	15.00	9.00
138	Bill MacDonald	30.00	15.00	9.00
139	Ken Wood	30.00	15.00	9.00
140	John Antonelli	30.00	15.00	9.00
141	Clint Hartung	30.00	15.00	9.00
142	Harry Perkowski	30.00	15.00	9.00
143	Les Moss	30.00	15.00	9.00
144	Ed Blake	30.00	15.00	9.00
145	Joe Haynes	30.00	15.00	9.00
146	Frank House	30.00	15.00	9.00
147	Bob Young	30.00	15.00	9.00
148	Johnny Klippstein	30.00	15.00	9.00
149	Dick Kryhoski	30.00	15.00	9.00
150	Ted Beard	30.00	15.00	9.00
151	Wally Post	30.00	15.00	9.00
152	Al Evans	30.00	15.00	9.00
153	Bob Rush	30.00	15.00	9.00
154	Joe Muir	30.00	15.00	9.00
155	Frank Overmire	40.00	20.00	12.00
156	Frank Hiller	30.00	15.00	9.00
157	Bob Usher	30.00	15.00	9.00
158	Eddie Waitkus	30.00	15.00	9.00
159	Saul Rogovin	30.00	15.00	9.00
160	Owen Friend	30.00	15.00	9.00
161	Bud Byerly	30.00	15.00	9.00
162	Del Crandall	30.00	15.00	9.00
163	Stan Rojek	30.00	15.00	9.00
164	Walt Dubiel	30.00	15.00	9.00
165	Eddie Kazak	30.00	15.00	9.00
166	Paul LaPalme	30.00	15.00	9.00
167	Bill Howerton	30.00	15.00	9.00
168	*Charlie Silvera*	40.00	20.00	12.00
169	Howie Judson	30.00	15.00	9.00
170	Gus Bell	30.00	15.00	9.00
171	Ed Erautt	30.00	15.00	9.00
172	Eddie Miksis	30.00	15.00	9.00
173	Roy Smalley	30.00	15.00	9.00
174	Clarence Marshall	30.00	15.00	9.00
175	*Billy Martin*	300.00	150.00	90.00
176	Hank Edwards	30.00	15.00	9.00
177	Bill Wight	30.00	15.00	9.00
178	Cass Michaels	30.00	15.00	9.00
179	Frank Smith	30.00	15.00	9.00
180	*Charley Maxwell*	30.00	15.00	9.00
181	Bob Swift	30.00	15.00	9.00
182	Billy Hitchcock	30.00	15.00	9.00
183	Erv Dusak	30.00	15.00	9.00
184	Bob Ramazzotti	30.00	15.00	9.00
185	Bill Nicholson	30.00	15.00	9.00
186	Walt Masterson	30.00	15.00	9.00
187	Bob Miller	30.00	15.00	9.00
188	Clarence Podbielan	35.00	17.50	10.50
189	Pete Reiser	30.00	15.00	9.00
190	Don Johnson	30.00	15.00	9.00
191	Yogi Berra	350.00	175.00	105.00
192	Myron Ginsberg	30.00	15.00	9.00
193	Harry Simpson	30.00	15.00	9.00
194	Joe Hatten	30.00	15.00	9.00
195	*Minnie Minoso*	150.00	75.00	45.00
196	Solly Hemus	30.00	15.00	9.00

		NR MT	EX	VG
197	George Strickland	30.00	15.00	9.00
198	Phil Haugstad	35.00	17.50	10.50
199	George Zuverink	30.00	15.00	9.00
200	Ralph Houk	60.00	30.00	18.00
201	Alex Kellner	30.00	15.00	9.00
202	Joe Collins	40.00	20.00	12.00
203	Curt Simmons	30.00	15.00	9.00
204	Ron Northey	30.00	15.00	9.00
205	Clyde King	35.00	17.50	10.50
206	Joe Ostrowski	40.00	20.00	12.00
207	Mickey Harris	30.00	15.00	9.00
208	Marlin Stuart	30.00	15.00	9.00
209	Howie Fox	30.00	15.00	9.00
210	Dick Fowler	30.00	15.00	9.00
211	Ray Coleman	30.00	15.00	9.00
212	Ned Garver	30.00	15.00	9.00
213	Nippy Jones	30.00	15.00	9.00
214	Johnny Hopp	40.00	20.00	12.00
215	Hank Bauer	50.00	25.00	15.00
216	Richie Ashburn	110.00	55.00	33.00
217	George Stirnweiss	30.00	15.00	9.00
218	Clyde McCullough	30.00	15.00	9.00
219	Bobby Shantz	30.00	15.00	9.00
220	Joe Presko	30.00	15.00	9.00
221	Granny Hamner	30.00	15.00	9.00
222	"Hoot" Evers	30.00	15.00	9.00
223	Del Ennis	30.00	15.00	9.00
224	Bruce Edwards	30.00	15.00	9.00
225	Frank Baumholtz	30.00	15.00	9.00
226	Dave Philley	30.00	15.00	9.00
227	Joe Garagiola	80.00	40.00	24.00
228	Al Brazle	30.00	15.00	9.00
229	Gene Bearden	30.00	15.00	9.00
230	Matt Batts	30.00	15.00	9.00
231	Sam Zoldak	30.00	15.00	9.00
232	Billy Cox	45.00	22.50	13.50
233	*Bob Friend*	30.00	15.00	9.00
234	Steve Souchock	30.00	15.00	9.00
235	Walt Dropo	30.00	15.00	9.00
236	Ed Fitz Gerald	30.00	15.00	9.00
237	Jerry Coleman	40.00	20.00	12.00
238	Art Houtteman	30.00	15.00	9.00
239	*Rocky Bridges*	35.00	17.50	10.50
240	Jack Phillips	30.00	15.00	9.00
241	Tommy Byrne	30.00	15.00	9.00
242	Tom Poholsky	30.00	15.00	9.00
243	Larry Doby	50.00	25.00	15.00
244	Vic Wertz	30.00	15.00	9.00
245	Sherry Robertson	30.00	15.00	9.00
246	George Kell	80.00	40.00	24.00
247	Randy Gumpert	30.00	15.00	9.00
248	Frank Shea	30.00	15.00	9.00
249	Bobby Adams	30.00	15.00	9.00
250	Carl Erskine	60.00	30.00	18.00
251	Chico Carrasquel	50.00	25.00	15.00
252	Vern Bickford	50.00	25.00	15.00
253	Johnny Berardino	60.00	30.00	18.00
254	Joe Dobson	50.00	25.00	15.00
255	Clyde Vollmer	50.00	25.00	15.00
256	Pete Suder	50.00	25.00	15.00
257	Bobby Avila	60.00	30.00	18.00
258	Steve Gromek	50.00	25.00	15.00
259	Bob Addis	50.00	25.00	15.00
260	Pete Castiglione	50.00	25.00	15.00
261	Willie Mays	2800.00	1400.00	840.00
262	Virgil Trucks	50.00	25.00	15.00
263	Harry Brecheen	50.00	25.00	15.00
264	Roy Hartsfield	50.00	25.00	15.00
265	Chuck Diering	50.00	25.00	15.00
266	Murry Dickson	50.00	25.00	15.00
267	Sid Gordon	50.00	25.00	15.00
268	Bob Lemon	150.00	75.00	45.00
269	Willard Nixon	50.00	25.00	15.00
270	Lou Brissie	50.00	25.00	15.00
271	Jim Delsing	50.00	25.00	15.00
272	Mike Garcia	50.00	25.00	15.00
273	Erv Palica	55.00	27.00	16.50
274	Ralph Branca	70.00	35.00	21.00
275	Pat Mullin	50.00	25.00	15.00
276	Jim Wilson	50.00	25.00	15.00
277	Early Wynn	200.00	100.00	60.00
278	Al Clark	50.00	25.00	15.00
279	Ed Stewart	50.00	25.00	15.00
280	Cloyd Boyer	50.00	25.00	15.00
281	Tommy Brown	55.00	27.00	16.50
282	Birdie Tebbetts	55.00	27.00	16.50
283	Phil Masi	55.00	27.00	16.50
284	Hank Arft	55.00	27.00	16.50
285	Cliff Fannin	55.00	27.00	16.50
286	Joe DeMaestri	55.00	27.00	16.50
287	Steve Bilko	55.00	27.00	16.50

		NR MT	EX	VG
288	Chet Nichols	55.00	27.00	16.50
289	Tommy Holmes	55.00	27.00	16.50
290	Joe Astroth	55.00	27.00	16.50
291	Gil Coan	55.00	27.00	16.50
292	Floyd Baker	55.00	27.00	16.50
293	Sibby Sisti	55.00	27.00	16.50
294	Walker Cooper	55.00	27.00	16.50
295	Phil Cavarretta	55.00	27.00	16.50
296	"Red" Rolfe	55.00	27.00	16.50
297	Andy Seminick	55.00	27.00	16.50
298	Bob Ross	55.00	27.00	16.50
299	Ray Murray	55.00	27.00	16.50
300	Barney McCosky	55.00	27.00	16.50
301	Bob Porterfield	50.00	25.00	15.00
302	Max Surkont	50.00	25.00	15.00
303	Harry Dorish	50.00	25.00	15.00
304	Sam Dente	50.00	25.00	15.00
305	Paul Richards	50.00	25.00	15.00
306	Lou Sleator	50.00	25.00	15.00
307	Frank Campos	50.00	25.00	15.00
308	Luis Aloma	50.00	25.00	15.00
309	Jim Busby	50.00	25.00	15.00
310	George Metkovich	50.00	25.00	15.00
311	Mickey Mantle	18000.00	8000.00	4500.
312	Jackie Robinson	1300.00	650.00	390.00
313	Bobby Thomson	250.00	125.00	75.00
314	Roy Campanella	1800.00	900.00	540.00
315	Leo Durocher	350.00	175.00	105.00
316	Davey Williams	225.00	112.00	67.00
317	Connie Marrero	225.00	112.00	67.00
318	Hal Gregg	225.00	112.00	67.00
319	Al Walker	240.00	120.00	72.00
320	John Rutherford	250.00	125.00	75.00
321	*Joe Black*	275.00	137.00	82.00
322	Randy Jackson	225.00	112.00	67.00
323	Bubba Church	225.00	112.00	67.00
324	Warren Hacker	225.00	112.00	67.00
325	Bill Serena	225.00	112.00	67.00
326	George Shuba	240.00	120.00	72.00
327	Archie Wilson	225.00	112.00	67.00
328	Bob Borkowski	225.00	112.00	67.00
329	Ike Delock	225.00	112.00	67.00
330	Turk Lown	225.00	112.00	67.00
331	Tom Morgan	250.00	125.00	75.00
332	Tony Bartirome	225.00	112.00	67.00
333	Pee Wee Reese	1200.00	600.00	360.00
334	Wilmer Mizell	225.00	112.00	67.00
335	Ted Lepcio	225.00	112.00	67.00
336	Dave Koslo	225.00	112.00	67.00
337	Jim Hearn	225.00	112.00	67.00
338	Sal Yvars	225.00	112.00	67.00
339	Russ Meyer	225.00	112.00	67.00
340	Bob Hooper	225.00	112.00	67.00
341	Hal Jeffcoat	225.00	112.00	67.00
342	*Clem Labine*	250.00	125.00	75.00
343	Dick Gernert	225.00	112.00	67.00
344	Ewell Blackwell	225.00	112.00	67.00
345	Sam White	225.00	112.00	67.00
346	George Spencer	225.00	112.00	67.00
347	Joe Adcock	225.00	112.00	67.00
348	Bob Kelly	225.00	112.00	67.00
349	Bob Cain	225.00	112.00	67.00
350	Cal Abrams	225.00	112.00	67.00
351	Al Dark	225.00	112.00	67.00
352	Karl Drews	225.00	112.00	67.00
353	Bob Del Greco	225.00	112.00	67.00
354	Fred Hatfield	225.00	112.00	67.00
355	Bobby Morgan	225.00	112.00	67.00
356	Toby Atwell	225.00	112.00	67.00
357	Smoky Burgess	225.00	112.00	67.00
358	John Kucab	225.00	112.00	67.00
359	Dee Fondy	225.00	112.00	67.00
360	George Crowe	225.00	112.00	67.00
361	Bill Posedel	225.00	112.00	67.00
362	Ken Heintzelman	225.00	112.00	67.00
363	Dick Rozek	225.00	112.00	67.00
364	Clyde Sukeforth	225.00	112.00	67.00
365	"Cookie" Lavagetto	240.00	120.00	72.00
366	Dave Madison	225.00	112.00	67.00
367	Bob Thorpe	225.00	112.00	67.00
368	Ed Wright	225.00	112.00	67.00
369	*Dick Groat*	350.00	175.00	105.00
370	Billy Hoeft	225.00	112.00	67.00
371	Bob Hofman	225.00	112.00	67.00
372	*Gil McDougald*	350.00	175.00	105.00
373	Jim Turner	250.00	125.00	75.00
374	Al Benton	225.00	112.00	67.00
375	Jack Merson	225.00	112.00	67.00
376	Faye Throneberry	225.00	112.00	67.00
377	Chuck Dressen	240.00	120.00	72.00
378	Les Fusselman	225.00	112.00	67.00

		NR MT	EX	VG
379	Joe Rossi	225.00	112.00	67.00
380	Clem Koshorek	225.00	112.00	67.00
381	Milton Stock	225.00	112.00	67.00
382	Sam Jones	225.00	112.00	67.00
383	Del Wilber	225.00	112.00	67.00
384	Frank Crosetti	265.00	132.00	79.00
385	Herman Franks	225.00	112.00	67.00
386	Eddie Yuhas	225.00	112.00	67.00
387	Billy Meyer	225.00	112.00	67.00
388	Bob Chipman	225.00	112.00	67.00
389	Ben Wade	240.00	120.00	72.00
390	Rocky Nelson	240.00	120.00	72.00
391	Ben Chapman (photo actually Sam Chapman)	225.00	112.00	67.00
392	*Hoyt Wilhelm*	700.00	350.00	210.00
393	Ebba St. Claire	225.00	112.00	67.00
394	Billy Herman	265.00	132.00	79.00
395	Jake Pitler	240.00	120.00	72.00
396	*Dick Williams*	260.00	130.00	78.00
397	Forrest Main	225.00	112.00	67.00
398	Hal Rice	225.00	112.00	67.00
399	Jim Fridley	225.00	112.00	67.00
400	Bill Dickey	650.00	325.00	195.00
401	Bob Schultz	225.00	112.00	67.00
402	Earl Harrist	225.00	112.00	67.00
403	Bill Miller	250.00	125.00	75.00
404	Dick Brodowski	225.00	112.00	67.00
405	Eddie Pellagrini	225.00	112.00	67.00
406	*Joe Nuxhall*	250.00	125.00	75.00
407	*Eddie Mathews*	3000.00	750.00	450.00

1953 Topps

The 1953 Topps set reflects the company's continuing legal battles with Bowman. The set, originally intended to consist of 280 cards, is lacking six numbers (#'s 253, 261, 267, 268, 271 and 275) which probably represent players whose contracts were lost to the competition. The 2-5/8" by 3-3/4" cards feature painted player pictures. A color team logo appears at a bottom panel (red for American Leauge and black for National.) Card backs contain the first baseball trivia questions along with brief statistics and player biographies. In the red panel at the top which lists the player's personal data, cards from the 2nd Series (#'s 86-165 plus 10, 44, 61, 72 and 81) can be found with that data printed in either black or white, black being the scarcer variety. Cards 221-280 are the scarce high numbers, with even scarcer short-printed cards interspersed in the series.

	NR MT	EX	VG
Complete Set (274):	15500.00	7500.00	4500.
Common Player: 1-165	25.00	12.50	7.50
Common Player: 166-220	20.00	10.00	6.00
Common Player: 221-280	50.00	25.00	15.00
Short-print Player: 221-280	90.00	45.00	27.00

		NR MT	EX	VG
1	Jackie Robinson	650.00	275.00	175.00
2	Luke Easter	25.00	12.50	7.50
3	George Crowe	25.00	12.50	7.50
4	Ben Wade	30.00	15.00	9.00
5	Joe Dobson	25.00	12.50	7.50
6	Sam Jones	25.00	12.50	7.50
7	Bob Borkowski	25.00	12.50	7.50
8	Clem Koshorek	25.00	12.50	7.50
9	Joe Collins	35.00	17.50	10.50
10	Smoky Burgess	40.00	20.00	12.00
11	Sal Yvars	25.00	12.50	7.50
12	Howie Judson	25.00	12.50	7.50
13	Connie Marrero	25.00	12.50	7.50
14	Clem Labine	30.00	15.00	9.00
15	Bobo Newsom	25.00	12.50	7.50
16	Harry Lowrey	25.00	12.50	7.50
17	Billy Hitchcock	25.00	12.50	7.50
18	Ted Lepcio	25.00	12.50	7.50
19	Mel Parnell	25.00	12.50	7.50
20	Hank Thompson	25.00	12.50	7.50
21	Billy Johnson	25.00	12.50	7.50
22	Howie Fox	25.00	12.50	7.50
23	Toby Atwell	25.00	12.50	7.50
24	Ferris Fain	25.00	12.50	7.50
25	Ray Boone	25.00	12.50	7.50
26	Dale Mitchell	25.00	12.50	7.50
27	Roy Campanella	225.00	112.00	67.00
28	Eddie Pellagrini	25.00	12.50	7.50
29	Hal Jeffcoat	25.00	12.50	7.50
30	Willard Nixon	25.00	12.50	7.50
31	Ewell Blackwell	40.00	20.00	12.00
32	Clyde Vollmer	25.00	12.50	7.50
33	Bob Kennedy	25.00	12.50	7.50
34	George Shuba	30.00	15.00	9.00
35	Irv Noren	35.00	17.50	10.50
36	Johnny Groth	25.00	12.50	7.50
37	Eddie Mathews	115.00	57.50	34.50
38	Jim Hearn	25.00	12.50	7.50
39	Eddie Miksis	25.00	12.50	7.50
40	John Lipon	25.00	12.50	7.50
41	Enos Slaughter	80.00	40.00	24.00
42	Gus Zernial	25.00	12.50	7.50
43	Gil McDougald	40.00	20.00	12.00
44	Ellis Kinder	30.00	15.00	9.00
45	Grady Hatton	25.00	12.50	7.50
46	Johnny Klippstein	25.00	12.50	7.50
47	Bubba Church	25.00	12.50	7.50
48	Bob Del Greco	25.00	12.50	7.50
49	Faye Throneberry	25.00	12.50	7.50
50	Chuck Dressen	30.00	15.00	9.00
51	Frank Campos	25.00	12.50	7.50
52	Ted Gray	25.00	12.50	7.50
53	Sherman Lollar	25.00	12.50	7.50
54	Bob Feller	125.00	67.00	37.00
55	Maurice McDermott	25.00	12.50	7.50
56	Gerald Staley	25.00	12.50	7.50
57	Carl Scheib	25.00	12.50	7.50
58	George Metkovich	25.00	12.50	7.50
59	Karl Drews	25.00	12.50	7.50
60	Cloyd Boyer	25.00	12.50	7.50
61	Early Wynn	80.00	40.00	25.00
62	Monte Irvin	80.00	40.00	24.00
63	Gus Niarhos	25.00	12.50	7.50
64	Dave Philley	25.00	12.50	7.50
65	Earl Harrist	25.00	12.50	7.50
66	Minnie Minoso	40.00	20.00	12.00
67	Roy Sievers	25.00	12.50	7.50
68	Del Rice	25.00	12.50	7.50
69	Dick Brodowski	25.00	12.50	7.50
70	Ed Yuhas	25.00	12.50	7.50
71	Tony Bartirome	25.00	12.50	7.50
72	Fred Hutchinson	25.00	12.50	7.50
73	Eddie Robinson	25.00	12.50	7.50
74	Joe Rossi	25.00	12.50	7.50
75	Mike Garcia	25.00	12.50	7.50
76	Pee Wee Reese	175.00	87.00	52.00
77	Johnny Mize	80.00	40.00	24.00
78	Red Schoendienst	80.00	40.00	24.00
79	Johnny Wyrostek	25.00	12.50	7.50
80	Jim Hegan	25.00	12.50	7.50
81	Joe Black	60.00	30.00	18.00
82	Mickey Mantle	3500.00	1750.00	1050.
83	Howie Pollet	25.00	12.50	7.50
84	Bob Hooper	25.00	12.50	7.50
85	Bobby Morgan	30.00	15.00	9.00
86	Billy Martin	100.00	50.00	30.00
87	Ed Lopat	35.00	17.50	10.50
88	Willie Jones	25.00	12.50	7.50
89	Chuck Stobbs	25.00	12.50	7.50
90	Hank Edwards	25.00	12.50	7.50
91	Ebba St. Claire	25.00	12.50	7.50
92	Paul Minner	25.00	12.50	7.50
93	Hal Rice	25.00	12.50	7.50
94	William Kennedy	25.00	12.50	7.50
95	Willard Marshall	25.00	12.50	7.50
96	Virgil Trucks	25.00	12.50	7.50
97	Don Kolloway	25.00	12.50	7.50
98	Cal Abrams	25.00	12.50	7.50
99	Dave Madison	25.00	12.50	7.50
100	Bill Miller	35.00	17.50	10.50
101	Ted Wilks	25.00	12.50	7.50
102	Connie Ryan	25.00	12.50	7.50

#	Player	NR MT	EX	VG
103	Joe Astroth	25.00	12.50	7.50
104	Yogi Berra	250.00	125.00	75.00
105	Joe Nuxhall	25.00	12.50	7.50
106	Johnny Antonelli	25.00	12.50	7.50
107	Danny O'Connell	25.00	12.50	7.50
108	Bob Porterfield	25.00	12.50	7.50
109	Alvin Dark	25.00	12.50	7.50
110	Herman Wehmeier	25.00	12.50	7.50
111	Hank Sauer	25.00	12.50	7.50
112	Ned Garver	25.00	12.50	7.50
113	Jerry Priddy	25.00	12.50	7.50
114	Phil Rizzuto	125.00	62.00	37.00
115	George Spencer	25.00	12.50	7.50
116	Frank Smith	25.00	12.50	7.50
117	Sid Gordon	25.00	12.50	7.50
118	Gus Bell	25.00	12.50	7.50
119	Johnny Sain	40.00	20.00	12.00
120	Davey Williams	25.00	12.50	7.50
121	Walt Dropo	25.00	12.50	7.50
122	Elmer Valo	25.00	12.50	7.50
123	Tommy Byrne	25.00	12.50	7.50
124	Sibby Sisti	25.00	12.50	7.50
125	Dick Williams	30.00	15.00	9.00
126	Bill Connelly	25.00	12.50	7.50
127	Clint Courtney	25.00	12.50	7.50
128	Wilmer Mizell	25.00	12.50	7.50
129	Keith Thomas	25.00	12.50	7.50
130	Turk Lown	25.00	12.50	7.50
131	Harry Byrd	25.00	12.50	7.50
132	Tom Morgan	35.00	17.50	10.50
133	Gil Coan	25.00	12.50	7.50
134	Rube Walker	30.00	15.00	9.00
135	Al Rosen	30.00	15.00	9.00
136	Ken Heintzelman	25.00	12.50	7.50
137	John Rutherford	30.00	15.00	9.00
138	George Kell	80.00	40.00	24.00
139	Sammy White	25.00	12.50	7.50
140	Tommy Glaviano	25.00	12.50	7.50
141	Allie Reynolds	40.00	20.00	12.00
142	Vic Wertz	25.00	12.50	7.50
143	Billy Pierce	25.00	12.50	7.50
144	Bob Schultz	25.00	12.50	7.50
145	Harry Dorish	25.00	12.50	7.50
146	Granny Hamner	25.00	12.50	7.50
147	Warren Spahn	150.00	75.00	45.00
148	Mickey Grasso	25.00	12.50	7.50
149	Dom DiMaggio	35.00	17.50	10.50
150	Harry Simpson	25.00	12.50	7.50
151	Hoyt Wilhelm	80.00	40.00	24.00
152	Bob Adams	25.00	12.50	7.50
153	Andy Seminick	25.00	12.50	7.50
154	Dick Groat	30.00	15.00	9.00
155	Dutch Leonard	25.00	12.50	7.50
156	Jim Rivera	25.00	12.50	7.50
157	Bob Addis	25.00	12.50	7.50
158	*Johnny Logan*	30.00	15.00	9.00
159	Wayne Terwilliger	25.00	12.50	7.50
160	Bob Young	25.00	12.50	7.50
161	Vern Bickford	25.00	12.50	7.50
162	Ted Kluszewski	50.00	25.00	15.00
163	Fred Hatfield	25.00	12.50	7.50
164	Frank Shea	25.00	12.50	7.50
165	Billy Hoeft	25.00	12.50	7.50
166	Bill Hunter	25.00	12.50	7.50
167	Art Schult	30.00	15.00	9.00
168	Willard Schmidt	20.00	10.00	6.00
169	Dizzy Trout	20.00	10.00	6.00
170	Bill Werle	20.00	10.00	6.00
171	Bill Glynn	20.00	10.00	6.00
172	Rip Repulski	20.00	10.00	6.00
173	Preston Ward	20.00	10.00	6.00
174	Billy Loes	25.00	12.50	7.50
175	Ron Kline	20.00	10.00	6.00
176	*Don Hoak*	30.00	15.00	9.00
177	Jim Dyck	20.00	10.00	6.00
178	Jim Waugh	20.00	10.00	6.00
179	Gene Hermanski	20.00	10.00	6.00
180	Virgil Stallcup	20.00	10.00	6.00
181	Al Zarilla	20.00	10.00	6.00
182	Bob Hofman	20.00	10.00	6.00
183	*Stu Miller*	20.00	10.00	6.00
184	*Hal Brown*	20.00	10.00	6.00
185	*Jim Pendleton*	20.00	10.00	6.00
186	Charlie Bishop	20.00	10.00	6.00
187	Jim Fridley	20.00	10.00	6.00
188	*Andy Carey*	30.00	15.00	9.00
189	Ray Jablonski	20.00	10.00	6.00
190	Dixie Walker	20.00	10.00	6.00
191	Ralph Kiner	70.00	35.00	21.00
192	Wally Westlake	20.00	10.00	6.00
193	Mike Clark	20.00	10.00	6.00
194	Eddie Kazak	20.00	10.00	6.00
195	Ed McGhee	20.00	10.00	6.00
196	Bob Keegan	20.00	10.00	6.00
197	Del Crandall	20.00	10.00	6.00
198	Forrest Main	20.00	10.00	6.00
199	Marion Fricano	20.00	10.00	6.00
200	Gordon Goldsberry	20.00	10.00	6.00
201	Paul LaPalme	20.00	10.00	6.00
202	Carl Sawatski	20.00	10.00	6.00
203	Cliff Fannin	20.00	10.00	6.00
204	Dick Bokelmann	20.00	10.00	6.00
205	Vern Benson	20.00	10.00	6.00
206	*Ed Bailey*	20.00	10.00	6.00
207	Whitey Ford	150.00	75.00	45.00
208	Jim Wilson	20.00	10.00	6.00
209	Jim Greengrass	20.00	10.00	6.00
210	*Bob Cerv*	30.00	15.00	9.00
211	J.W. Porter	20.00	10.00	6.00
212	Jack Dittmer	20.00	10.00	6.00
213	Ray Scarborough	20.00	10.00	6.00
214	*Bill Bruton*	20.00	10.00	6.00
215	*Gene Conley*	20.00	10.00	6.00
216	Jim Hughes	25.00	12.50	7.50
217	Murray Wall	20.00	10.00	6.00
218	Les Fusselman	20.00	10.00	6.00
219	Pete Runnels (picture actually Don Johnson)	20.00	10.00	6.00
220	Satchel Paige	450.00	225.00	135.00
221	Bob Milliken	95.00	47.50	28.50
222	Vic Janowicz	55.00	27.50	16.50
223	John O'Brien	50.00	25.00	15.00
224	Lou Sleater	50.00	25.00	15.00
225	Bobby Shantz	100.00	50.00	30.00
226	Ed Erautt	90.00	45.00	27.00
227	Morris Martin	50.00	25.00	15.00
228	Hal Newhouser	150.00	75.00	45.00
229	Rocky Krsnich	90.00	45.00	27.00
230	Johnny Lindell	50.00	25.00	15.00
231	Solly Hemus	50.00	25.00	15.00
232	Dick Kokos	90.00	45.00	27.00
233	Al Aber	90.00	45.00	27.00
234	Ray Murray	50.00	25.00	15.00
235	John Hetki	50.00	25.00	15.00
236	Harry Perkowski	50.00	25.00	15.00
237	Clarence Podbielan	50.00	25.00	15.00
238	Cal Hogue	50.00	25.00	15.00
239	Jim Delsing	90.00	45.00	27.00
240	Freddie Marsh	50.00	25.00	15.00
241	Al Sima	50.00	25.00	15.00
242	*Charlie Silvera*	100.00	50.00	30.00
243	Carlos Bernier	50.00	25.00	15.00
244	Willie Mays	2600.00	1300.00	800.00
245	Bill Norman	90.00	45.00	27.00
246	*Roy Face*	70.00	35.00	21.50
247	Mike Sandlock	50.00	25.00	15.00
248	Gene Stephens	50.00	25.00	15.00
249	Ed O'Brien	90.00	45.00	27.00
250	Bob Wilson	90.00	45.00	27.00
251	Sid Hudson	90.00	45.00	27.00
252	Henry Foiles	90.00	45.00	27.00
253	Not Issued			
254	Preacher Roe	80.00	40.00	24.00
255	Dixie Howell	95.00	47.50	28.50
256	Les Peden	90.00	45.00	27.00
257	Bob Boyd	90.00	45.00	27.00
258	*Jim Gilliam*	300.00	150.00	90.00
259	Roy McMillan	50.00	25.00	15.00
260	Sam Calderone	90.00	45.00	27.00
261	Not Issued			
262	Bob Oldis	90.00	45.00	27.00
263	*Johnny Podres*	250.00	125.00	70.00
264	Gene Woodling	70.00	35.00	20.00
265	Jackie Jensen	125.00	67.00	37.00
266	Bob Cain	90.00	45.00	27.00
267	Not Issued			
268	Not Issued			
269	Duane Pillette	90.00	45.00	27.00
270	Vern Stephens	90.00	45.00	27.00
271	Not Issued			
272	Bill Antonello	95.00	47.50	28.50
273	*Harvey Haddix*	150.00	75.00	40.00
274	John Riddle	90.00	45.00	27.00
275	Not Issued			
276	Ken Raffensberger	90.00	45.00	27.00
277	Don Lund	90.00	45.00	27.00
278	Willie Miranda	90.00	45.00	27.00
279	Joe Coleman	50.00	25.00	15.00
280	Milt Bolling	300.00	45.00	27.00

1954 Topps

The first issue to use two player pictures on the front, the 1954 Topps set is very popular today. Solid color backgrounds frame both color head- and-shoulders and black and white action pictures of the player. The player's name, position, team and team logo appear at the top. Backs include an "Inside Baseball" cartoon regarding the player as well as statistics and biography. The 250-card, 2-5/8" by 3-3/4", set includes manager and coaches cards, and the first use by Topps of two players together on a card; the players were, appropriately, the O'Brien twins.

	NR MT	EX	VG
Complete Set (250):	9050.00	4500.00	2700.
Common Player: 1-50	15.00	7.50	4.50
Common Player: 51-75	30.00	15.00	9.00
Common Player: 76-250	15.00	7.50	4.50

		NR MT	EX	VG
1	Ted Williams	650.00	200.00	125.00
2	Gus Zernial	15.00	7.50	4.50
3	Monte Irvin	35.00	17.50	10.50
4	Hank Sauer	15.00	7.50	4.50
5	Ed Lopat	20.00	10.00	6.00
6	Pete Runnels	15.00	7.50	4.50
7	Ted Kluszewski	30.00	15.00	9.00
8	Bobby Young	15.00	7.50	4.50
9	Harvey Haddix	15.00	7.50	4.50
10	Jackie Robinson	275.00	137.50	82.50
11	Paul Smith	15.00	7.50	4.50
12	Del Crandall	15.00	7.50	4.50
13	Billy Martin	75.00	37.50	22.50
14	Preacher Roe	30.00	15.00	9.00
15	Al Rosen	18.00	9.00	5.50
16	Vic Janowicz	18.00	9.00	5.50
17	Phil Rizzuto	70.00	35.00	20.00
18	Walt Dropo	15.00	7.50	4.50
19	Johnny Lipon	15.00	7.50	4.50
20	Warren Spahn	110.00	55.00	33.00
21	Bobby Shantz	18.00	9.00	5.50
22	Jim Greengrass	15.00	7.50	4.50
23	Luke Easter	15.00	7.50	4.50
24	Granny Hamner	15.00	7.50	4.50
25	*Harvey Kuenn*	35.00	17.50	10.50
26	Ray Jablonski	15.00	7.50	4.50
27	Ferris Fain	15.00	7.50	4.50
28	Paul Minner	15.00	7.50	4.50
29	Jim Hegan	15.00	7.50	4.50
30	Eddie Mathews	100.00	50.00	30.00
31	Johnny Klippstein	15.00	7.50	4.50
32	Duke Snider	135.00	67.50	40.00
33	Johnny Schmitz	15.00	7.50	4.50
34	Jim Rivera	15.00	7.50	4.50
35	Junior Gilliam	25.00	12.50	7.50
36	Hoyt Wilhelm	45.00	27.50	16.50
37	Whitey Ford	110.00	55.00	33.00
38	Eddie Stanky	15.00	7.50	4.50
39	Sherm Lollar	15.00	7.50	4.50
40	Mel Parnell	15.00	7.50	4.50
41	Willie Jones	15.00	7.50	4.50
42	Don Mueller	15.00	7.50	4.50
43	Dick Groat	15.00	7.50	4.50
44	Ned Garver	15.00	7.50	4.50
45	Richie Ashburn	40.00	20.00	12.00
46	Ken Raffensberger	15.00	7.50	4.50
47	Ellis Kinder	15.00	7.50	4.50
48	Billy Hunter	15.00	7.50	4.50
49	Ray Murray	15.00	7.50	4.50
50	Yogi Berra	240.00	120.00	72.00
51	Johnny Lindell	30.00	15.00	9.00
52	Vic Power	30.00	15.00	9.00
53	Jack Dittmer	30.00	15.00	9.00
54	Vern Stephens	30.00	15.00	9.00
55	Phil Cavarretta	30.00	15.00	9.00
56	Willie Miranda	35.00	17.50	10.50
57	Luis Aloma	30.00	15.00	9.00
58	Bob Wilson	30.00	15.00	9.00
59	Gene Conley	30.00	15.00	9.00
60	Frank Baumholtz	30.00	15.00	9.00
61	Bob Cain	30.00	15.00	9.00
62	Eddie Robinson	35.00	17.50	10.50
63	Johnny Pesky	30.00	15.00	9.00
64	Hank Thompson	30.00	15.00	9.00
65	Bob Swift	30.00	15.00	9.00
66	Ted Lepcio	30.00	15.00	9.00
67	Jim Willis	30.00	15.00	9.00
68	Sam Calderone	30.00	15.00	9.00
69	Bud Podbielan	30.00	15.00	9.00
70	Larry Doby	60.00	30.00	18.00
71	Frank Smith	30.00	15.00	9.00
72	Preston Ward	30.00	15.00	9.00
73	Wayne Terwilliger	30.00	15.00	9.00
74	Bill Taylor	30.00	15.00	9.00
75	Fred Haney	30.00	15.00	9.00
76	Bob Scheffing	15.00	7.50	4.50
77	Ray Boone	15.00	7.50	4.50
78	Ted Kazanski	15.00	7.50	4.50
79	Andy Pafko	15.00	7.50	4.50
80	Jackie Jensen	18.00	9.00	5.50
81	Dave Hoskins	15.00	7.50	4.50
82	Milt Bolling	15.00	7.50	4.50
83	Joe Collins	20.00	10.00	6.00
84	Dick Cole	15.00	7.50	4.50
85	*Bob Turley*	15.00	7.50	4.50
86	Billy Herman	40.00	20.00	12.00
87	Roy Face	15.00	7.50	4.50
88	Matt Batts	15.00	7.50	4.50
89	Howie Pollet	15.00	7.50	4.50
90	Willie Mays	600.00	300.00	175.00
91	Bob Oldis	15.00	7.50	4.50
92	Wally Westlake	15.00	7.50	4.50
93	Sid Hudson	15.00	7.50	4.50
94	*Ernie Banks*	800.00	400.00	250.00
95	Hal Rice	15.00	7.50	4.50
96	Charlie Silvera	20.00	10.00	6.00
97	Jerry Lane	15.00	7.50	4.50
98	Joe Black	20.00	10.00	6.00
99	Bob Hofman	15.00	7.50	4.50
100	Bob Keegan	15.00	7.50	4.50
101	Gene Woodling	20.00	10.00	6.00
102	Gil Hodges	75.00	38.00	23.00
103	*Jim Lemon*	18.00	9.00	4.50
104	Mike Sandlock	15.00	7.50	4.50
105	Andy Carey	20.00	10.00	6.00
106	Dick Kokos	15.00	7.50	4.50
107	Duane Pillette	15.00	7.50	4.50
108	Thornton Kipper	15.00	7.50	4.50
109	Bill Bruton	15.00	7.50	4.50
110	Harry Dorish	15.00	7.50	4.50
111	Jim Delsing	15.00	7.50	4.50
112	Bill Renna	15.00	7.50	4.50
113	Bob Boyd	15.00	7.50	4.50
114	Dean Stone	15.00	7.50	4.50
115	"Rip" Repulski	15.00	7.50	4.50
116	Steve Bilko	15.00	7.50	4.50
117	Solly Hemus	15.00	7.50	4.50
118	Carl Scheib	15.00	7.50	4.50
119	Johnny Antonelli	15.00	7.50	4.50
120	Roy McMillan	15.00	7.50	4.50
121	Clem Labine	20.00	10.00	6.00
122	Johnny Logan	15.00	7.50	4.50
123	Bobby Adams	15.00	7.50	4.50
124	Marion Fricano	15.00	7.50	4.50
125	Harry Perkowski	15.00	7.50	4.50
126	Ben Wade	18.00	9.00	4.50
127	Steve O'Neill	15.00	7.50	4.50
128	*Hank Aaron*	2000.00	1000.00	600.00
129	Forrest Jacobs	15.00	7.50	4.50
130	Hank Bauer	30.00	15.00	9.00
131	Reno Bertoia	15.00	7.50	4.50
132	*Tom Lasorda*	175.00	87.00	52.00
133	Del Baker	15.00	7.50	4.50
134	Cal Hogue	15.00	7.50	4.50
135	Joe Presko	15.00	7.50	4.50
136	Connie Ryan	15.00	7.50	4.50
137	*Wally Moon*	25.00	12.50	7.50
138	Bob Borkowski	15.00	7.50	4.50
139	Ed & Johnny O'Brien	45.00	22.50	13.50

		NR MT	EX	VG
140	Tom Wright	15.00	7.50	4.50
141	*Joe Jay*	15.00	7.50	4.50
142	Tom Poholsky	15.00	7.50	4.50
143	Rollie Hemsley	15.00	7.50	4.50
144	Bill Werle	15.00	7.50	4.50
145	Elmer Valo	15.00	7.50	4.50
146	Don Johnson	15.00	7.50	4.50
147	John Riddle	15.00	7.50	4.50
148	Bob Trice	15.00	7.50	4.50
149	Jim Robertson	15.00	7.50	4.50
150	Dick Kryhoski	15.00	7.50	4.50
151	Alex Grammas	15.00	7.50	4.50
152	Mike Blyzka	15.00	7.50	4.50
153	"Rube" Walker	18.00	9.00	4.50
154	Mike Fornieles	15.00	7.50	4.50
155	Bob Kennedy	15.00	7.50	4.50
156	Joe Coleman	15.00	7.50	4.50
157	Don Lenhardt	15.00	7.50	4.50
158	"Peanuts" Lowrey	15.00	7.50	4.50
159	Dave Philley	15.00	7.50	4.50
160	"Red" Kress	15.00	7.50	4.50
161	John Hetki	15.00	7.50	4.50
162	Herman Wehmeier	15.00	7.50	4.50
163	Frank House	15.00	7.50	4.50
164	Stu Miller	15.00	7.50	4.50
165	Jim Pendleton	15.00	7.50	4.50
166	Johnny Podres	30.00	15.00	9.00
167	Don Lund	15.00	7.50	4.50
168	Morrie Martin	15.00	7.50	4.50
169	Jim Hughes	18.00	9.00	4.50
170	*Dusty Rhodes*	15.00	7.50	4.50
171	Leo Kiely	15.00	7.50	4.50
172	Hal Brown	15.00	7.50	4.50
173	Jack Harshman	15.00	7.50	4.50
174	Tom Qualters	15.00	7.50	4.50
175	Frank Leja	20.00	10.00	6.00
176	Bob Keely	15.00	7.50	4.50
177	Bob Milliken	18.00	9.00	5.50
178	Bill Gylnn (Glynn)	15.00	7.50	4.50
179	Gair Allie	15.00	7.50	4.50
180	Wes Westrum	15.00	7.50	4.50
181	Mel Roach	15.00	7.50	4.50
182	Chuck Harmon	15.00	7.50	4.50
183	Earle Combs	35.00	17.50	10.50
184	Ed Bailey	15.00	7.50	4.50
185	Chuck Stobbs	15.00	7.50	4.50
186	Karl Olson	15.00	7.50	4.50
187	"Heinie" Manush	35.00	17.50	10.50
188	Dave Jolly	15.00	7.50	4.50
189	Bob Ross	15.00	7.50	4.50
190	Ray Herbert	15.00	7.50	4.50
191	*Dick Schofield*	18.00	9.00	5.50
192	"Cot" Deal	15.00	7.50	4.50
193	Johnny Hopp	15.00	7.50	4.50
194	Bill Sarni	15.00	7.50	4.50
195	Bill Consolo	15.00	7.50	4.50
196	Stan Jok	15.00	7.50	4.50
197	"Schoolboy" Rowe	15.00	7.50	4.50
198	Carl Sawatski	15.00	7.50	4.50
199	"Rocky" Nelson	15.00	7.50	4.50
200	Larry Jansen	15.00	7.50	4.50
201	*Al Kaline*	850.00	425.00	255.00
202	*Bob Purkey*	15.00	7.50	4.50
203	Harry Brecheen	15.00	7.50	4.50
204	Angel Scull	15.00	7.50	4.50
205	Johnny Sain	30.00	15.00	9.00
206	Ray Crone	15.00	7.50	4.50
207	Tom Oliver	15.00	7.50	4.50
208	Grady Hatton	15.00	7.50	4.50
209	Charlie Thompson	18.00	9.00	5.50
210	*Bob Buhl*	15.00	7.50	4.50
211	Don Hoak	18.00	9.00	5.50
212	Mickey Micelotta	15.00	7.50	4.50
213	John Fitzpatrick	15.00	7.50	4.50
214	Arnold Portocarrero	15.00	7.50	4.50
215	Ed McGhee	15.00	7.50	4.50
216	Al Sima	15.00	7.50	4.50
217	Paul Schreiber	15.00	7.50	4.50
218	Fred Marsh	15.00	7.50	4.50
219	Charlie Kress	15.00	7.50	4.50
220	Ruben Gomez	15.00	7.50	4.50
221	Dick Brodowski	15.00	7.50	4.50
222	Bill Wilson	15.00	7.50	4.50
223	Joe Haynes	15.00	7.50	4.50
224	Dick Weik	15.00	7.50	4.50
225	Don Liddle	15.00	7.50	4.50
226	Jehosie Heard	15.00	7.50	4.50
227	Buster Mills	15.00	7.50	4.50
228	Gene Hermanski	15.00	7.50	4.50
229	Bob Talbot	15.00	7.50	4.50
230	Bob Kuzava	20.00	10.00	6.00

		NR MT	EX	VG
231	Roy Smalley	15.00	7.50	4.50
232	Lou Limmer	15.00	7.50	4.50
233	Augie Galan	15.00	7.50	4.50
234	*Jerry Lynch*	15.00	7.50	4.50
235	Vern Law	15.00	7.50	4.50
236	Paul Penson	15.00	7.50	4.50
237	Mike Ryba	15.00	7.50	4.50
238	Al Aber	15.00	7.50	4.50
239	*Bill Skowron*	90.00	45.00	27.00
240	Sam Mele	15.00	7.50	4.50
241	Bob Miller	15.00	7.50	4.50
242	Curt Roberts	15.00	7.50	4.50
243	Ray Blades	15.00	7.50	4.50
244	Leroy Wheat	15.00	7.50	4.50
245	Roy Sievers	15.00	7.50	4.50
246	Howie Fox	15.00	7.50	4.50
247	Eddie Mayo	15.00	7.50	4.50
248	*Al Smith*	15.00	7.50	4.50
249	Wilmer Mizell	15.00	7.50	4.50
250	Ted Williams	700.00	225.00	110.00

1955 Topps

The 1955 Topps set is numerically the smallest of the regular issue Topps sets. The 3-3/4" by 2-5/8" cards mark the first time that Topps used a horizontal format. While that format was new, the design was not; they are very similar to the 1954 cards to the point many pictures appeared in both years. Although it was slated for a 210-card set, the 1955 Topps set turned out to be only 206 cards with numbers 175, 186, 203 and 209 never being released. The scarce high numbers in this set begin with #161.

	NR MT	EX	VG
Complete Set (206):	7750.00	3825.00	2300.
Common Player: 1-150	9.00	4.50	2.75
Common Player: 151-160	18.00	9.00	5.50
Common Player: 161-210	29.00	14.50	8.75

		NR MT	EX	VG
1	Dusty Rhodes	50.00	15.00	9.00
2	Ted Williams	360.00	180.00	100.00
3	Art Fowler	9.00	4.50	2.75
4	Al Kaline	250.00	125.00	75.00
5	Jim Gilliam	12.00	6.00	3.50
6	Stan Hack	9.00	4.50	2.75
7	Jim Hegan	9.00	4.50	2.75
8	Hal Smith	9.00	4.50	2.75
9	Bob Miller	9.00	4.50	2.75
10	Bob Keegan	9.00	4.50	2.75
11	Ferris Fain	9.00	4.50	2.75
12	"Jake" Thies	9.00	4.50	2.75
13	Fred Marsh	9.00	4.50	2.75
14	Jim Finigan	9.00	4.50	2.75
15	Jim Pendleton	9.00	4.50	2.75
16	Roy Sievers	8.00	4.00	2.25
17	Bobby Hofman	9.00	4.50	2.75
18	Russ Kemmerer	9.00	4.50	2.75
19	Billy Herman	12.00	6.00	3.50
20	Andy Carey	15.00	7.50	4.50
21	Alex Grammas	9.00	4.50	2.75
22	Bill Skowron	20.00	10.00	6.00
23	Jack Parks	9.00	4.50	2.75
24	Hal Newhouser	30.00	15.00	9.00
25	Johnny Podres	15.00	7.50	4.50
26	Dick Groat	12.00	6.00	3.50
27	Billy Gardner	9.00	4.50	2.75

		NR MT	EX	VG
28	Ernie Banks	250.00	125.00	75.00
29	Herman Wehmeier	9.00	4.50	2.75
30	Vic Power	9.00	4.50	2.75
31	Warren Spahn	90.00	45.00	27.00
32	Ed McGhee	9.00	4.50	2.75
33	Tom Qualters	9.00	4.50	2.75
34	Wayne Terwilliger	9.00	4.50	2.75
35	Dave Jolly	9.00	4.50	2.75
36	Leo Kiely	9.00	4.50	2.75
37	*Joe Cunningham*	9.00	4.50	2.75
38	Bob Turley	15.00	7.50	4.50
39	Bill Glynn	9.00	4.50	2.75
40	Don Hoak	12.00	6.00	3.50
41	Chuck Stobbs	9.00	4.50	2.75
42	"Windy" McCall	9.00	4.50	2.75
43	Harvey Haddix	9.00	4.50	2.75
44	"Corky" Valentine	9.00	4.50	2.75
45	Hank Sauer	9.00	4.50	2.75
46	Ted Kazanski	9.00	4.50	2.75
47	Hank Aaron	350.00	175.00	105.00
48	Bob Kennedy	9.00	4.50	2.75
49	J.W. Porter	9.00	4.50	2.75
50	Jackie Robinson	225.00	112.50	67.50
51	Jim Hughes	12.00	6.00	3.50
52	Bill Tremel	9.00	4.50	2.75
53	Bill Taylor	9.00	4.50	2.75
54	Lou Limmer	9.00	4.50	2.75
55	"Rip" Repulski	9.00	4.50	2.75
56	Ray Jablonski	9.00	4.50	2.75
57	*Billy O'Dell*	9.00	4.50	2.75
58	Jim Rivera	9.00	4.50	2.75
59	Gair Allie	9.00	4.50	2.75
60	Dean Stone	9.00	4.50	2.75
61	"Spook" Jacobs	9.00	4.50	2.75
62	Thornton Kipper	9.00	4.50	2.75
63	Joe Collins	15.00	7.50	4.50
64	*Gus Triandos*	10.00	5.00	3.00
65	Ray Boone	9.00	4.50	2.75
66	Ron Jackson	9.00	4.50	2.75
67	Wally Moon	9.00	4.50	2.75
68	Jim Davis	9.00	4.50	2.75
69	Ed Bailey	9.00	4.50	2.75
70	Al Rosen	12.00	6.00	3.50
71	Ruben Gomez	9.00	4.50	2.75
72	Karl Olson	9.00	4.50	2.75
73	Jack Shepard	9.00	4.50	2.75
74	Bob Borkowski	9.00	4.50	2.75
75	*Sandy Amoros*	15.00	7.50	4.50
76	Howie Pollet	9.00	4.50	2.75
77	Arnold Portocarrero	9.00	4.50	2.75
78	Gordon Jones	9.00	4.50	2.75
79	Danny Schell	9.00	4.50	2.75
80	Bob Grim	15.00	7.50	4.50
81	Gene Conley	9.00	4.50	2.75
82	Chuck Harmon	9.00	4.50	2.75
83	Tom Brewer	9.00	4.50	2.75
84	*Camilo Pascual*	9.00	4.50	2.75
85	*Don Mossi*	9.00	4.50	2.75
86	Bill Wilson	9.00	4.50	2.75
87	Frank House	9.00	4.50	2.75
88	*Bob Skinner*	9.00	4.50	2.75
89	*Joe Frazier*	9.00	4.50	2.75
90	*Karl Spooner*	12.00	6.00	3.50
91	Milt Bolling	9.00	4.50	2.75
92	*Don Zimmer*	40.00	20.00	12.00
93	Steve Bilko	9.00	4.50	2.75
94	Reno Bertoia	9.00	4.50	2.75
95	Preston Ward	9.00	4.50	2.75
96	Charlie Bishop	9.00	4.50	2.75
97	Carlos Paula	9.00	4.50	2.75
98	Johnny Riddle	9.00	4.50	2.75
99	Frank Leja	15.00	7.50	4.50
100	Monte Irvin	30.00	15.00	9.00
101	Johnny Gray	9.00	4.50	2.75
102	Wally Westlake	9.00	4.50	2.75
103	Charlie White	9.00	4.50	2.75
104	Jack Harshman	9.00	4.50	2.75
105	Chuck Diering	9.00	4.50	2.75
106	*Frank Sullivan*	9.00	4.50	2.75
107	Curt Roberts	9.00	4.50	2.75
108	"Rube" Walker	12.00	6.00	3.50
109	Ed Lopat	15.00	7.50	4.50
110	Gus Zernial	9.00	4.50	2.75
111	Bob Milliken	12.00	6.00	3.50
112	Nelson King	9.00	4.50	2.75
113	Harry Brecheen	9.00	4.50	2.75
114	Lou Ortiz	9.00	4.50	2.75
115	Ellis Kinder	9.00	4.50	2.75
116	Tom Hurd	9.00	4.50	2.75
117	Mel Roach	9.00	4.50	2.75
118	Bob Purkey	9.00	4.50	2.75
119	Bob Lennon	9.00	4.50	2.75
120	Ted Kluszewski	25.00	12.50	7.50
121	Bill Renna	9.00	4.50	2.75
122	Carl Sawatski	9.00	4.50	2.75
123	*Sandy Koufax*	1150.00	575.00	345.00
124	*Harmon Killebrew*	350.00	175.00	105.00
125	*Ken Boyer*	75.00	38.00	23.00
126	*Dick Hall*	9.00	4.50	2.75
127	*Dale Long*	9.00	4.50	2.75
128	Ted Lepcio	9.00	4.50	2.75
129	Elvin Tappe	9.00	4.50	2.75
130	Mayo Smith	9.00	4.50	2.75
131	Grady Hatton	9.00	4.50	2.75
132	Bob Trice	9.00	4.50	2.75
133	Dave Hoskins	9.00	4.50	2.75
134	Joe Jay	9.00	4.50	2.75
135	Johnny O'Brien	9.00	4.50	2.75
136	"Bunky" Stewart	9.00	4.50	2.75
137	Harry Elliott	9.00	4.50	2.75
138	Ray Herbert	9.00	4.50	2.75
139	Steve Kraly	15.00	7.50	4.50
140	Mel Parnell	9.00	4.50	2.75
141	Tom Wright	9.00	4.50	2.75
142	Jerry Lynch	9.00	4.50	2.75
143	Dick Schofield	9.00	4.50	2.75
144	Joe Amalfitano	9.00	4.50	2.75
145	Elmer Valo	9.00	4.50	2.75
146	*Dick Donovan*	9.00	4.50	2.75
147	Laurin Pepper	9.00	4.50	2.75
148	Hal Brown	9.00	4.50	2.75
149	Ray Crone	9.00	4.50	2.75
150	Mike Higgins	9.00	4.50	2.75
151	"Red" Kress	18.00	9.00	5.50
152	*Harry Agganis*	65.00	32.50	19.50
153	"Bud" Podbielan	18.00	9.00	5.50
154	Willie Miranda	18.00	9.00	5.50
155	Eddie Mathews	105.00	52.50	31.50
156	Joe Black	20.00	10.00	6.00
157	Bob Miller	18.00	9.00	5.50
158	Tom Carroll	22.50	11.25	6.75
159	Johnny Schmitz	18.00	9.00	5.50
160	Ray Narleski	18.00	9.00	5.50
161	*Chuck Tanner*	30.00	15.00	9.00
162	Joe Coleman	29.00	14.50	8.75
163	Faye Throneberry	29.00	14.50	8.75
164	*Roberto Clemente*	1500.00	750.00	450.00
165	Don Johnson	29.00	14.50	8.75
166	Hank Bauer	40.00	20.00	12.00
167	Tom Casagrande	29.00	14.50	8.75
168	Duane Pillette	29.00	14.50	8.75
169	Bob Oldis	29.00	14.50	8.75
170	Jim Pearce	29.00	14.50	8.75
171	Dick Brodowski	29.00	14.50	8.75
172	Frank Baumholtz	29.00	14.50	8.75
173	Bob Kline	29.00	14.50	8.75
174	Rudy Minarcin	29.00	14.50	8.75
175	Not Issued			
176	Norm Zauchin	29.00	14.50	8.75
177	Jim Robertson	29.00	14.50	8.75
178	Bobby Adams	29.00	14.50	8.75
179	Jim Bolger	29.00	14.50	8.75
180	Clem Labine	35.00	17.50	10.50
181	Roy McMillan	29.00	14.50	8.75
182	Humberto Robinson	29.00	14.50	8.75
183	Tony Jacobs	29.00	14.50	8.75
184	Harry Perkowski	29.00	14.50	8.75
185	Don Ferrarese	29.00	14.50	8.75
186	Not Issued			
187	Gil Hodges	135.00	67.50	40.00
188	Charlie Silvera	35.00	17.50	10.50
189	Phil Rizzuto	150.00	75.00	45.00
190	Gene Woodling	29.00	14.50	8.75
191	Ed Stanky	29.00	14.50	8.75
192	Jim Delsing	29.00	14.50	8.75
193	Johnny Sain	40.00	20.00	12.00
194	Willie Mays	550.00	275.00	165.00
195	Ed Roebuck	32.50	16.00	9.75
196	Gale Wade	29.00	14.50	8.75
197	Al Smith	29.00	14.50	8.75
198	Yogi Berra	200.00	100.00	60.00
199	Bert Hamric	32.50	16.00	9.75
200	Jack Jensen	40.00	20.00	12.00
201	Sherm Lollar	29.00	14.50	8.75
202	Jim Owens	29.00	14.50	8.75
203	Not Issued			
204	Frank Smith	29.00	14.50	8.75
205	Gene Freese	29.00	14.50	8.75
206	Pete Daley	29.00	14.50	8.75
207	Bill Consolo	29.00	14.50	8.75
208	Ray Moore	29.00	14.50	8.75
209	Not Issued			

		NR MT	EX	VG
210	Duke Snider	500.00	125.00	50.00

1956 Topps

This 340-card set is quite similar in design to the 1955 Topps set, again using both a portrait and an "action" picture. Some portraits are the same as those used in 1955 (and even 1954). Innovations found in the 1956 Topps set of 2-5/8" by 3-3/4" cards include team cards introduced as part of a regular set. Additionally, there are two unnumbered checklist cards (the complete set price quoted below does not include the checklist cards). Finally, there are cards of the two league presidents, William Harridge and Warren Giles. On the backs, a three-panel cartoon depicts big moments from the player's career while biographical information appears above the cartoon and the statistics below. Card backs for numbers 1-180 can be found with either white or grey cardboard. Some dealers charge a premium for grey backs (#'s 1-100) and white backs (#'s 101-180).

	NR MT	EX	VG
Complete Set (340):	7500.00	3750.00	2250.
Common Player: 1-100	8.50	4.25	2.50
Common Player: 101-180	12.50	6.25	3.75
Common Player: 181-260	17.50	8.75	5.25
Common Player: 261-340	15.00	7.50	4.50

		NR MT	EX	VG
1	William Harridge	100.00	50.00	30.00
2	Warren Giles	18.00	9.00	5.50
3	Elmer Valo	8.50	4.25	2.50
4	Carlos Paula	8.50	4.25	2.50
5	Ted Williams	335.00	167.00	100.00
6	Ray Boone	9.00	4.50	2.75
7	Ron Negray	8.50	4.25	2.50
8	Walter Alston	40.00	20.00	12.00
9	Ruben Gomez	8.50	4.25	2.50
10	Warren Spahn	75.00	37.00	22.00
11a	Cubs Team (with date)	50.00	25.00	15.00
11b	Cubs Team (no date, name centered)	25.00	12.50	7.50
11c	Cubs Team (no date, name at left)	25.00	12.50	7.50
12	Andy Carey	10.00	5.00	3.00
13	Roy Face	9.00	4.50	2.75
14	Ken Boyer	14.00	7.00	4.25
15	Ernie Banks	90.00	45.00	27.00
16	*Hector Lopez*	10.00	5.00	3.00
17	Gene Conley	12.50	6.25	3.75
18	Dick Donovan	8.50	4.25	2.50
19	Chuck Diering	8.50	4.25	2.50
20	Al Kaline	105.00	52.00	31.00
21	Joe Collins	10.00	5.00	3.00
22	Jim Finigan	8.50	4.25	2.50
23	Freddie Marsh	8.50	4.25	2.50
24	Dick Groat	10.50	5.25	3.25
25	Ted Kluszewski	20.00	10.00	6.00
26	Grady Hatton	8.50	4.25	2.50
27	Nelson Burbrink	8.50	4.25	2.50
28	Bobby Hofman	8.50	4.25	2.50
29	Jack Harshman	8.50	4.25	2.50
30	Jackie Robinson	137.50	69.00	41.00
31	Hank Aaron	225.00	112.00	67.00
32	Frank House	8.50	4.25	2.50
33	Roberto Clemente	400.00	200.00	120.00
34	Tom Brewer	8.50	4.25	2.50
35	Al Rosen	12.00	6.00	3.50
36	Rudy Minarcin	8.50	4.25	2.50
37	Alex Grammas	8.50	4.25	2.50
38	Bob Kennedy	8.50	4.25	2.50
39	Don Mossi	12.50	6.25	3.75
40	Bob Turley	13.00	6.50	4.00
41	Hank Sauer	8.50	4.25	2.50
42	Sandy Amoros	9.50	4.75	2.75
43	Ray Moore	8.50	4.25	2.50
44	"Windy" McCall	8.50	4.25	2.50
45	Gus Zernial	12.50	6.25	3.75
46	Gene Freese	8.50	4.25	2.50
47	Art Fowler	8.50	4.25	2.50
48	Jim Hegan	8.50	4.25	2.50
49	*Pedro Ramos*	12.50	6.25	3.75
50	"Dusty" Rhodes	12.50	6.25	3.75
51	Ernie Oravetz	8.50	4.25	2.50
52	Bob Grim	10.00	5.00	3.00
53	Arnold Portocarrero	8.50	4.25	2.50
54	Bob Keegan	8.50	4.25	2.50
55	Wally Moon	12.50	6.25	3.75
56	Dale Long	12.50	6.25	3.75
57	"Duke" Maas	8.50	4.25	2.50
58	Ed Roebuck	12.50	6.25	3.75
59	Jose Santiago	8.50	4.25	2.50
60	Mayo Smith	8.50	4.25	2.50
61	Bill Skowron	15.00	7.50	4.50
62	Hal Smith	8.50	4.25	2.50
63	*Roger Craig*	30.00	15.00	9.00
64	Luis Arroyo	8.50	4.25	2.50
65	Johnny O'Brien	8.50	4.25	2.50
66	Bob Speake	8.50	4.25	2.50
67	Vic Power	8.50	4.25	2.50
68	Chuck Stobbs	8.50	4.25	2.50
69	Chuck Tanner	9.00	4.50	2.75
70	Jim Rivera	8.50	4.25	2.50
71	Frank Sullivan	8.50	4.25	2.50
72a	Phillies Team (with date)	50.00	25.00	15.00
72b	Phillies Team (no date, name centered)	24.00	12.00	7.25
72c	Philadelphia Phillies (no date, name at left)	24.00	12.00	7.25
73	Wayne Terwilliger	8.50	4.25	2.50
74	Jim King	8.50	4.25	2.50
75	Roy Sievers	12.50	6.25	3.75
76	Ray Crone	8.50	4.25	2.50
77	Harvey Haddix	12.50	6.25	3.75
78	Herman Wehmeier	8.50	4.25	2.50
79	Sandy Koufax	350.00	175.00	105.00
80	Gus Triandos	9.50	4.75	2.75
81	Wally Westlake	8.50	4.25	2.50
82	Bill Renna	8.50	4.25	2.50
83	Karl Spooner	9.00	4.50	2.75
84	"Babe" Birrer	8.50	4.25	2.50
85a	Indians Team (with date)	50.00	25.00	15.00
85b	Indians Team (no date, name centered)	21.00	10.50	6.25
85c	Indians Team (no date, name at left)	21.00	10.50	6.25
86	Ray Jablonski	8.50	4.25	2.50
87	Dean Stone	8.50	4.25	2.50
88	Johnny Kucks	10.00	5.00	3.00
89	Norm Zauchin	8.50	4.25	2.50
90a	Redlegs Team (with date)	50.00	25.00	15.00
90b	Redlegs Team (no date, name centered)	24.00	12.00	7.25
90c	Redlegs Team (no date, name at left)	24.00	12.00	7.25
91	Gail Harris	8.50	4.25	2.50
92	"Red" Wilson	8.50	4.25	2.50
93	George Susce, Jr.	8.50	4.25	2.50
94	Ronnie Kline	8.50	4.25	2.50
95a	Braves Team (with date)	50.00	25.00	15.00
95b	Braves Team (no date, name centered)	35.00	17.50	10.50
95c	Braves Team (no date, name at left)	35.00	17.50	10.50
96	Bill Tremel	8.50	4.25	2.50
97	Jerry Lynch	8.50	4.25	2.50
98	Camilo Pascual	9.00	4.50	2.75
99	Don Zimmer	15.00	7.50	4.50
100a	Orioles Team (with date)	40.00	20.00	12.00
100b	Orioles Team (no date, name centered)	21.00	10.50	6.25
100c	Orioles Team (no date, name at left)	21.00	10.50	6.25
101	Roy Campanella	140.00	70.00	42.00
102	Jim Davis	12.50	6.25	3.75

		NR MT	EX	VG
103	Willie Miranda	12.50	6.25	3.75
104	Bob Lennon	12.50	6.25	3.75
105	Al Smith	12.50	6.25	3.75
106	Joe Astroth	12.50	6.25	3.75
107	Eddie Mathews	60.00	30.00	18.00
108	Laurin Pepper	12.50	6.25	3.75
109	Enos Slaughter	30.00	15.00	9.00
110	Yogi Berra	130.00	65.00	39.00
111	Red Sox Team	27.00	13.50	8.00
112	Dee Fondy	12.50	6.25	3.75
113	Phil Rizzuto	50.00	25.00	15.00
114	Jim Owens	12.50	6.25	3.75
115	Jackie Jensen	15.00	7.50	4.50
116	Eddie O'Brien	12.50	6.25	3.75
117	Virgil Trucks	12.50	6.25	3.75
118	Nellie Fox	30.00	15.00	9.00
119	*Larry Jackson*	12.50	6.25	3.75
120	Richie Ashburn	35.00	17.50	10.50
121	Pirates Team	27.00	13.50	8.00
122	Willard Nixon	12.50	6.25	3.75
123	Roy McMillan	12.50	6.25	3.75
124	Don Kaiser	12.50	6.25	3.75
125	"Minnie" Minoso	20.00	10.00	6.00
126	Jim Brady	12.50	6.25	3.75
127	Willie Jones	12.50	6.25	3.75
128	Eddie Yost	12.50	6.25	3.75
129	"Jake" Martin	12.50	6.25	3.75
130	Willie Mays	345.00	172.00	103.00
131	Bob Roselli	12.50	6.25	3.75
132	Bobby Avila	12.50	6.25	3.75
133	Ray Narleski	12.50	6.25	3.75
134	Cardinals Team	27.00	13.50	8.00
135	Mickey Mantle	1100.00	550.00	330.00
136	Johnny Logan	12.50	6.25	3.75
137	Al Silvera	12.50	6.25	3.75
138	Johnny Antonelli	12.50	6.25	3.75
139	Tommy Carroll	12.50	6.25	3.75
140	*Herb Score*	32.50	16.00	9.75
141	Joe Frazier	12.50	6.25	3.75
142	Gene Baker	12.50	6.25	3.75
143	Jim Piersall	12.50	6.25	3.75
144	Leroy Powell	12.50	6.25	3.75
145	Gil Hodges	45.00	22.00	13.50
146	Senators Team	24.00	12.00	7.25
147	Earl Torgeson	12.50	6.25	3.75
148	Alvin Dark	12.50	6.25	3.75
149	"Dixie" Howell	12.50	6.25	3.75
150	Duke Snider	125.00	62.00	37.00
151	"Spook" Jacobs	12.50	6.25	3.75
152	Billy Hoeft	12.50	6.25	3.75
153	Frank J. Thomas	12.50	6.25	3.75
154	Dave Pope	12.50	6.25	3.75
155	Harvey Kuenn	16.50	8.25	5.00
156	Wes Westrum	12.50	6.25	3.75
157	Dick Brodowski	12.50	6.25	3.75
158	Wally Post	12.50	6.25	3.75
159	Clint Courtney	12.50	6.25	3.75
160	Billy Pierce	15.00	7.50	4.50
161	Joe DeMaestri	12.50	6.25	3.75
162	"Gus" Bell	12.50	6.25	3.75
163	Gene Woodling	14.00	7.00	4.25
164	Harmon Killebrew	125.00	62.00	37.00
165	Red Schoendienst	27.00	13.50	8.00
166	Dodgers Team	175.00	87.00	52.00
167	Harry Dorish	12.50	6.25	3.75
168	Sammy White	12.50	6.25	3.75
169	Bob Nelson	12.50	6.25	3.75
170	Bill Virdon	15.00	7.50	4.50
171	Jim Wilson	12.50	6.25	3.75
172	*Frank Torre*	12.50	6.25	3.75
173	Johnny Podres	17.50	8.75	5.25
174	Glen Gorbous	12.50	6.25	3.75
175	Del Crandall	15.00	7.50	4.50
176	Alex Kellner	12.50	6.25	3.75
177	Hank Bauer	15.00	7.50	4.50
178	Joe Black	12.50	6.25	3.75
179	Harry Chiti	12.50	6.25	3.75
180	Robin Roberts	30.00	15.00	9.00
181	Billy Martin	95.00	47.00	28.00
182	Paul Minner	17.50	8.75	5.25
183	Stan Lopata	17.50	8.75	5.25
184	Don Bessent	20.00	10.00	6.00
185	Bill Bruton	17.50	8.75	5.25
186	Ron Jackson	17.50	8.75	5.25
187	Early Wynn	35.00	17.50	10.50
188	White Sox Team	32.50	16.00	9.75
189	Ned Garver	17.50	8.75	5.25
190	Carl Furillo	22.00	11.00	6.50
191	Frank Lary	17.50	8.75	5.25
192	"Smoky" Burgess	17.50	8.75	5.25
193	Wilmer Mizell	17.50	8.75	5.25
194	Monte Irvin	30.00	15.00	9.00
195	George Kell	30.00	15.00	9.00
196	Tom Poholsky	17.50	8.75	5.25
197	Granny Hamner	17.50	8.75	5.25
198	Ed Fitzgerald (Fitz Gerald)	17.50	8.75	5.25
199	Hank Thompson	17.50	8.75	5.25
200	Bob Feller	125.00	62.00	37.00
201	"Rip" Repulski	17.50	8.75	5.25
202	Jim Hearn	17.50	8.75	5.25
203	Bill Tuttle	17.50	8.75	5.25
204	Art Swanson	17.50	8.75	5.25
205	"Whitey" Lockman	17.50	8.75	5.25
206	Erv Palica	17.50	8.75	5.25
207	Jim Small	17.50	8.75	5.25
208	Elston Howard	35.00	17.50	10.50
209	Max Surkont	17.50	8.75	5.25
210	Mike Garcia	17.50	8.75	5.25
211	Murry Dickson	17.50	8.75	5.25
212	Johnny Temple	17.50	8.75	5.25
213	Tigers Team	50.00	25.00	15.00
214	Bob Rush	17.50	8.75	5.25
215	Tommy Byrne	20.00	10.00	6.00
216	Jerry Schoonmaker	17.50	8.75	5.25
217	Billy Klaus	17.50	8.75	5.25
218	Joe Nuxall (Nuxhall)	19.00	9.50	5.75
219	Lew Burdette	17.50	8.75	5.25
220	Del Ennis	17.50	8.75	5.25
221	Bob Friend	17.50	8.75	5.25
222	Dave Philley	17.50	8.75	5.25
223	Randy Jackson	20.00	10.00	6.00
224	"Bud" Podbielan	17.50	8.75	5.25
225	Gil McDougald	25.00	12.50	7.50
226	Giants Team	60.00	30.00	18.00
227	Russ Meyer	17.50	8.75	5.25
228	"Mickey" Vernon	17.50	8.75	5.25
229	Harry Brecheen	17.50	8.75	5.25
230	"Chico" Carrasquel	17.50	8.75	5.25
231	Bob Hale	17.50	8.75	5.25
232	"Toby" Atwell	17.50	8.75	5.25
233	Carl Erskine	24.00	12.00	7.25
234	"Pete" Runnels	17.50	8.75	5.25
235	Don Newcombe	45.00	22.00	13.50
236	Athletics Team	30.00	15.00	9.00
237	Jose Valdivielso	17.50	8.75	5.25
238	Walt Dropo	17.50	8.75	5.25
239	Harry Simpson	17.50	8.75	5.25
240	Whitey Ford	135.00	67.00	40.00
241	Don Mueller	17.50	8.75	5.25
242	Hershell Freeman	17.50	8.75	5.25
243	Sherm Lollar	17.50	8.75	5.25
244	Bob Buhl	17.50	8.75	5.25
245	Billy Goodman	17.50	8.75	5.25
246	Tom Gorman	17.50	8.75	5.25
247	Bill Sarni	17.50	8.75	5.25
248	Bob Porterfield	17.50	8.75	5.25
249	Johnny Klippstein	17.50	8.75	5.25
250	Larry Doby	24.00	12.00	7.25
251	Yankees Team	185.00	92.00	55.00
252	Vernon Law	17.50	8.75	5.25
253	Irv Noren	22.00	11.00	6.50
254	George Crowe	17.50	8.75	5.25
255	Bob Lemon	30.00	15.00	9.00
256	Tom Hurd	17.50	8.75	5.25
257	Bobby Thomson	19.00	9.50	5.75
258	Art Ditmar	17.50	8.75	5.25
259	Sam Jones	17.50	8.75	5.25
260	Pee Wee Reese	135.00	67.00	40.00
261	Bobby Shantz	15.00	7.50	4.50
262	Howie Pollet	15.00	7.50	4.50
263	Bob Miller	15.00	7.50	4.50
264	Ray Monzant	15.00	7.50	4.50
265	Sandy Consuegra	15.00	7.50	4.50
266	Don Ferrarese	15.00	7.50	4.50
267	Bob Nieman	15.00	7.50	4.50
268	Dale Mitchell	15.00	7.50	4.50
269	Jack Meyer	15.00	7.50	4.50
270	Billy Loes	17.50	8.75	5.25
271	Foster Castleman	15.00	7.50	4.50
272	Danny O'Connell	15.00	7.50	4.50
273	Walker Cooper	15.00	7.50	4.50
274	Frank Baumholtz	15.00	7.50	4.50
275	Jim Greengrass	15.00	7.50	4.50
276	George Zuverink	15.00	7.50	4.50
277	Daryl Spencer	15.00	7.50	4.50
278	Chet Nichols	15.00	7.50	4.50
279	Johnny Groth	15.00	7.50	4.50
280	Jim Gilliam	24.00	12.00	7.25
281	Art Houtteman	15.00	7.50	4.50
282	Warren Hacker	15.00	7.50	4.50
283	Hal Smith	15.00	7.50	4.50
284	Ike Delock	15.00	7.50	4.50

		NR MT	EX	VG
285	Eddie Miksis	15.00	7.50	4.50
286	Bill Wight	15.00	7.50	4.50
287	Bobby Adams	15.00	7.50	4.50
288	Bob Cerv	29.00	14.50	8.75
289	Hal Jeffcoat	15.00	7.50	4.50
290	Curt Simmons	15.00	7.50	4.50
291	Frank Kellert	15.00	7.50	4.50
292	*Luis Aparicio*	125.00	62.00	37.00
293	Stu Miller	15.00	7.50	4.50
294	Ernie Johnson	15.00	7.50	4.50
295	Clem Labine	20.00	10.00	6.00
296	Andy Seminick	15.00	7.50	4.50
297	Bob Skinner	15.00	7.50	4.50
298	Johnny Schmitz	15.00	7.50	4.50
299	Charley Neal	25.00	12.50	7.50
300	Vic Wertz	15.00	7.50	4.50
301	Marv Grissom	15.00	7.50	4.50
302	Eddie Robinson	20.00	10.00	6.00
303	Jim Dyck	15.00	7.50	4.50
304	Frank Malzone	15.00	7.50	4.50
305	Brooks Lawrence	15.00	7.50	4.50
306	Curt Roberts	15.00	7.50	4.50
307	Hoyt Wilhelm	32.50	16.00	9.75
308	"Chuck" Harmon	15.00	7.50	4.50
309	*Don Blasingame*	15.00	7.50	4.50
310	Steve Gromek	15.00	7.50	4.50
311	Hal Naragon	15.00	7.50	4.50
312	Andy Pafko	15.00	7.50	4.50
313	Gene Stephens	15.00	7.50	4.50
314	Hobie Landrith	15.00	7.50	4.50
315	Milt Bolling	15.00	7.50	4.50
316	Jerry Coleman	22.50	11.00	6.75
317	Al Aber	15.00	7.50	4.50
318	Fred Hatfield	15.00	7.50	4.50
319	Jack Crimian	15.00	7.50	4.50
320	Joe Adcock	15.00	7.50	4.50
321	Jim Konstanty	20.00	10.00	6.00
322	Karl Olson	15.00	7.50	4.50
323	Willard Schmidt	15.00	7.50	4.50
324	"Rocky" Bridges	15.00	7.50	4.50
325	Don Liddle	15.00	7.50	4.50
326	Connie Johnson	15.00	7.50	4.50
327	Bob Wiesler	15.00	7.50	4.50
328	Preston Ward	15.00	7.50	4.50
329	Lou Berberet	15.00	7.50	4.50
330	Jim Busby	15.00	7.50	4.50
331	Dick Hall	15.00	7.50	4.50
332	Don Larsen	42.50	21.00	12.50
333	Rube Walker	20.00	10.00	6.00
334	Bob Miller	15.00	7.50	4.50
335	Don Hoak	15.00	7.50	4.50
336	Ellis Kinder	15.00	7.50	4.50
337	Bobby Morgan	15.00	7.50	4.50
338	Jim Delsing	15.00	7.50	4.50
339	Rance Pless	15.00	7.50	4.50
340	Mickey McDermott	42.50	21.00	12.50
—	Checklist 1/3	200.00	100.00	60.00
—	Checklist 2/4	200.00	100.00	60.00

1956 Topps Pins

One of Topps first specialty issues, the 60-pin set of ballplayers issued in 1956 contains a high percentage of big-name stars which, combined with the scarcity of the pins, makes collecting a complete set extremely challenging. Compounding the situation is the fact that some pins are seen far less often than others, though the reason is unknown. Chuck Stobbs, Hector Lopez and Chuck Diering are unaccountably scarce. Measuring 1-1/8" in diameter, the pins utilize the same portraits found on 1956 Topps baseball cards. The photos are set against a solid color background.

		NR MT	EX	VG
Complete Set:		2750.00	1350.00	825.00
Common Player:		17.50	8.75	5.25
(1)	Hank Aaron	120.00	60.00	35.00
(2)	Sandy Amoros	17.50	8.75	5.25
(3)	Luis Arroyo	17.50	8.75	5.25
(4)	Ernie Banks	60.00	30.00	18.00
(5)	Yogi Berra	75.00	37.00	22.00
(6)	Joe Black	17.50	8.75	5.25
(7)	Ray Boone	17.50	8.75	5.25
(8)	Ken Boyer	20.00	10.00	6.00
(9)	Joe Collins	17.50	8.75	5.25
(10)	Gene Conley	17.50	8.75	5.25
(11)	Chuck Diering	225.00	112.00	67.00
(12)	Dick Donovan	17.50	8.75	5.25
(13)	Jim Finigan	17.50	8.75	5.25
(14)	Art Fowler	17.50	8.75	5.25
(15)	Ruben Gomez	17.50	8.75	5.25
(16)	Dick Groat	20.00	10.00	6.00
(17)	Harvey Haddix	17.50	8.75	5.25
(18)	Jack Harshman	17.50	8.75	5.25
(19)	Grady Hatton	17.50	8.75	5.25
(20)	Jim Hegan	17.50	8.75	5.25
(21)	Gil Hodges	40.00	20.00	12.00
(22)	Bobby Hofman	17.50	8.75	5.25
(23)	Frank House	17.50	8.75	5.25
(24)	Jackie Jensen	20.00	10.00	6.00
(25)	Al Kaline	65.00	32.00	19.50
(26)	Bob Kennedy	17.50	8.75	5.25
(27)	Ted Kluszewski	25.00	12.50	7.50
(28)	Dale Long	17.50	8.75	5.25
(29)	Hector Lopez	200.00	100.00	60.00
(30)	Ed Mathews	50.00	25.00	15.00
(31)	Willie Mays	120.00	60.00	35.00
(32)	Roy McMillan	17.50	8.75	5.25
(33)	Willie Miranda	17.50	8.75	5.25
(34)	Wally Moon	17.50	8.75	5.25
(35)	Don Mossi	17.50	8.75	5.25
(36)	Ron Negray	17.50	8.75	5.25
(37)	Johnny O'Brien	17.50	8.75	5.25
(38)	Carlos Paula	17.50	8.75	5.25
(39)	Vic Power	17.50	8.75	5.25
(40)	Jim Rivera	17.50	8.75	5.25
(41)	Phil Rizzuto	40.00	20.00	12.00
(42)	Jackie Robinson	100.00	50.00	30.00
(43)	Al Rosen	25.00	12.50	7.50
(44)	Hank Sauer	17.50	8.75	5.25
(45)	Roy Sievers	17.50	8.75	5.25
(46)	Bill Skowron	20.00	10.00	6.00
(47)	Al Smith	17.50	8.75	5.25
(48)	Hal Smith	17.50	8.75	5.25
(49)	Mayo Smith	17.50	8.75	5.25
(50)	Duke Snider	75.00	37.00	22.00
(51)	Warren Spahn	60.00	30.00	18.00
(52)	Karl Spooner	17.50	8.75	5.25
(53)	Chuck Stobbs	175.00	87.00	52.00
(54)	Frank Sullivan	17.50	8.75	5.25
(55)	Bill Tremel	17.50	8.75	5.25
(56)	Gus Triandos	17.50	8.75	5.25
(57)	Bob Turley	20.00	10.00	6.00
(58)	Herman Wehmeier	17.50	8.75	5.25
(59)	Ted Williams	125.00	62.50	37.50
(60)	Gus Zernial	17.50	8.75	5.25

1957 Topps

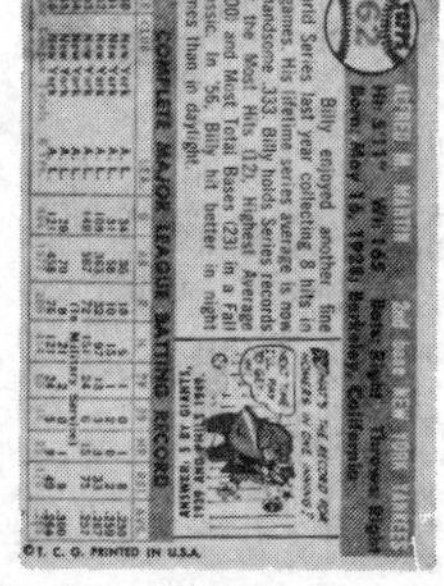

For 1957, Topps reduced the size of its cards to the

now-standard 2-1/2" by 3-1/2." Set size was increased to 407 cards. Another change came in the form of the use of real color photographs as opposed to the hand-colored black and whites of previous years. For the first time since 1954, there were also cards with more than one player. The two, "Dodger Sluggers" and "Yankees' Power Hitters" began a trend toward the increased use of mulitple-player cards. Another first-time innovation, found on the backs, is complete players statistics. The scarce cards in the set are not the highest numbers, but rather numbers 265-352. Four unnumbered checklist cards were issued along with the set. They are quite expensive and are not included in the complete set prices quoted below.

		NR MT	EX	VG
Complete Set (407):		7500.00	3750.00	2250.
Common Player: 1-264		7.00	3.50	2.00
Common Player: 265-352		18.00	9.00	5.50
Common Player: 353-407		7.00	3.50	2.00
1	Ted Williams	425.00	212.00	127.00
2	Yogi Berra	135.00	67.00	40.00
3	Dale Long	7.00	3.50	2.00
4	Johnny Logan	7.00	3.50	2.00
5	Sal Maglie	9.00	4.50	2.75
6	Hector Lopez	7.00	3.50	2.00
7	Luis Aparicio	30.00	15.00	9.00
8	Don Mossi	7.00	3.50	2.00
9	Johnny Temple	7.00	3.50	2.00
10	Willie Mays	215.00	107.00	64.00
11	George Zuverink	7.00	3.50	2.00
12	Dick Groat	8.00	4.00	2.50
13	Wally Burnette	7.00	3.50	2.00
14	Bob Nieman	7.00	3.50	2.00
15	Robin Roberts	21.00	10.50	6.25
16	Walt Moryn	7.00	3.50	2.00
17	Billy Gardner	7.00	3.50	2.00
18	*Don Drysdale*	225.00	112.00	67.00
19	Bob Wilson	7.00	3.50	2.00
20	Hank Aaron (negative reversed)	200.00	100.00	60.00
21	Frank Sullivan	7.00	3.50	2.00
22	Jerry Snyder (photo actually Ed Fitz Gerald)	7.00	3.50	2.00
23	Sherm Lollar	7.00	3.50	2.00
24	*Bill Mazeroski*	65.00	32.00	19.50
25	Whitey Ford	55.00	27.00	16.50
26	Bob Boyd	7.00	3.50	2.00
27	Ted Kazanski	7.00	3.50	2.00
28	Gene Conley	7.00	3.50	2.00
29	*Whitey Herzog*	25.00	12.50	7.50
30	Pee Wee Reese	65.00	32.00	19.50
31	Ron Northey	7.00	3.50	2.00
32	Hersh Freeman	7.00	3.50	2.00
33	Jim Small	7.00	3.50	2.00
34	Tom Sturdivant	8.00	4.00	2.50
35	*Frank Robinson*	275.00	137.00	82.00
36	Bob Grim	8.00	4.00	2.50
37	Frank Torre	7.00	3.50	2.00
38	Nellie Fox	20.00	10.00	6.00
39	Al Worthington	7.00	3.50	2.00
40	Early Wynn	22.00	11.00	6.50
41	Hal Smith	7.00	3.50	2.00
42	Dee Fondy	7.00	3.50	2.00
43	Connie Johnson	7.00	3.50	2.00
44	Joe DeMaestri	7.00	3.50	2.00
45	Carl Furillo	12.50	6.25	3.75
46	Bob Miller	7.00	3.50	2.00
47	Don Blasingame	7.00	3.50	2.00
48	Bill Bruton	7.00	3.50	2.00
49	Daryl Spencer	7.00	3.50	2.00
50	Herb Score	7.00	3.50	2.00
51	Clint Courtney	7.00	3.50	2.00
52	Lee Walls	7.00	3.50	2.00
53	Clem Labine	8.00	4.00	2.50
54	Elmer Valo	7.00	3.50	2.00
55	Ernie Banks	115.00	57.00	34.00
56	Dave Sisler	7.00	3.50	2.00
57	Jim Lemon	7.00	3.50	2.00
58	Ruben Gomez	7.00	3.50	2.00
59	Dick Williams	8.00	4.00	2.50
60	Billy Hoeft	7.00	3.50	2.00
61	Dusty Rhodes	7.00	3.50	2.00
62	Billy Martin	45.00	22.00	13.50
63	Ike Delock	7.00	3.50	2.00
64	Pete Runnels	7.00	3.50	2.00
65	Wally Moon	7.00	3.50	2.00
66	Brooks Lawrence	7.00	3.50	2.00

		NR MT	EX	VG
67	Chico Carrasquel	7.00	3.50	2.00
68	Ray Crone	7.00	3.50	2.00
69	Roy McMillan	7.00	3.50	2.00
70	Richie Ashburn	25.00	12.50	7.50
71	Murry Dickson	7.00	3.50	2.00
72	Bill Tuttle	7.00	3.50	2.00
73	George Crowe	7.00	3.50	2.00
74	Vito Valentinetti	7.00	3.50	2.00
75	Jim Piersall	8.00	4.00	2.50
76	Roberto Clemente	215.00	107.00	64.00
77	Paul Foytack	7.00	3.50	2.00
78	Vic Wertz	7.00	3.50	2.00
79	*Lindy McDaniel*	8.00	4.00	2.50
80	Gil Hodges	47.50	24.00	14.00
81	Herm Wehmeier	7.00	3.50	2.00
82	Elston Howard	20.00	10.00	6.00
83	Lou Skizas	7.00	3.50	2.00
84	Moe Drabowsky	7.00	3.50	2.00
85	Larry Doby	10.00	5.00	3.00
86	Bill Sarni	7.00	3.50	2.00
87	Tom Gorman	7.00	3.50	2.00
88	Harvey Kuenn	8.00	4.00	2.50
89	Roy Sievers	7.00	3.50	2.00
90	Warren Spahn	65.00	32.00	19.50
91	Mack Burk	7.00	3.50	2.00
92	Mickey Vernon	7.00	3.50	2.00
93	Hal Jeffcoat	7.00	3.50	2.00
94	Bobby Del Greco	7.00	3.50	2.00
95	Mickey Mantle	1050.00	525.00	315.00
96	*Hank Aguirre*	7.00	3.50	2.00
97	Yankees Team	60.00	30.00	18.00
98	Al Dark	8.00	4.00	2.50
99	Bob Keegan	7.00	3.50	2.00
100	League Presidents (Warren Giles, William Harridge)	9.00	4.50	2.75
101	Chuck Stobbs	7.00	3.50	2.00
102	Ray Boone	7.00	3.50	2.00
103	Joe Nuxhall	9.00	4.50	2.75
104	Hank Foiles	7.00	3.50	2.00
105	Johnny Antonelli	7.00	3.50	2.00
106	Ray Moore	7.00	3.50	2.00
107	Jim Rivera	7.00	3.50	2.00
108	Tommy Byrne	8.00	4.00	2.50
109	Hank Thompson	7.00	3.50	2.00
110	Bill Virdon	8.00	4.00	2.50
111	Hal Smith	7.00	3.50	2.00
112	Tom Brewer	7.00	3.50	2.00
113	Wilmer Mizell	7.00	3.50	2.00
114	Braves Team	15.00	7.50	4.50
115	Jim Gilliam	12.00	6.00	3.50
116	Mike Fornieles	7.00	3.50	2.00
117	Joe Adcock	7.00	3.50	2.00
118	Bob Porterfield	7.00	3.50	2.00
119	Stan Lopata	7.00	3.50	2.00
120	Bob Lemon	15.00	7.50	4.50
121	*Cletis Boyer*	15.00	7.50	4.50
122	Ken Boyer	8.00	4.00	2.50
123	Steve Ridzik	7.00	3.50	2.00
124	Dave Philley	7.00	3.50	2.00
125	Al Kaline	85.00	42.00	25.00
126	Bob Wiesler	7.00	3.50	2.00
127	Bob Buhl	7.00	3.50	2.00
128	Ed Bailey	7.00	3.50	2.00
129	Saul Rogovin	7.00	3.50	2.00
130	Don Newcombe	12.50	6.25	3.75
131	Milt Bolling	7.00	3.50	2.00
132	Art Ditmar	8.00	4.00	2.50
133	Del Crandall	8.00	4.00	2.50
134	Don Kaiser	7.00	3.50	2.00
135	Bill Skowron	13.50	6.75	4.00
136	Jim Hegan	7.00	3.50	2.00
137	Bob Rush	7.00	3.50	2.00
138	Minnie Minoso	8.00	4.00	2.50
139	Lou Kretlow	7.00	3.50	2.00
140	Frank J. Thomas	7.00	3.50	2.00
141	Al Aber	7.00	3.50	2.00
142	Charley Thompson	7.00	3.50	2.00
143	Andy Pafko	7.00	3.50	2.00
144	Ray Narleski	7.00	3.50	2.00
145	Al Smith	7.00	3.50	2.00
146	Don Ferrarese	7.00	3.50	2.00
147	Al Walker	8.00	4.00	2.50
148	Don Mueller	7.00	3.50	2.00
149	Bob Kennedy	7.00	3.50	2.00
150	Bob Friend	7.00	3.50	2.00
151	Willie Miranda	7.00	3.50	2.00
152	Jack Harshman	7.00	3.50	2.00
153	Karl Olson	7.00	3.50	2.00
154	Red Schoendienst	20.00	10.00	6.00
155	Jim Brosnan	7.00	3.50	2.00
156	Gus Triandos	7.00	3.50	2.00

		NR MT	EX	VG
157	Wally Post	7.00	3.50	2.00
158	Curt Simmons	7.00	3.50	2.00
159	Solly Drake	7.00	3.50	2.00
160	Billy Pierce	8.00	4.00	2.50
161	Pirates Team	12.50	6.25	3.75
162	Jack Meyer	7.00	3.50	2.00
163	Sammy White	7.00	3.50	2.00
164	Tommy Carroll	8.00	4.00	2.50
165	Ted Kluszewski	25.00	12.50	7.50
166	Roy Face	7.00	3.50	2.00
167	Vic Power	7.00	3.50	2.00
168	Frank Lary	7.00	3.50	2.00
169	Herb Plews	7.00	3.50	2.00
170	Duke Snider	100.00	50.00	30.00
171	Red Sox Team	12.00	6.00	3.50
172	Gene Woodling	7.00	3.50	2.00
173	Roger Craig	12.50	6.25	3.75
174	Willie Jones	7.00	3.50	2.00
175	Don Larsen	15.00	7.50	4.50
176	Gene Baker	7.00	3.50	2.00
177	Eddie Yost	7.00	3.50	2.00
178	Don Bessent	8.00	4.00	2.50
179	Ernie Oravetz	7.00	3.50	2.00
180	Gus Bell	7.00	3.50	2.00
181	Dick Donovan	7.00	3.50	2.00
182	Hobie Landrith	7.00	3.50	2.00
183	Cubs Team	15.00	7.50	4.50
184	*Tito Francona*	7.00	3.50	2.00
185	Johnny Kucks	8.00	4.00	2.50
186	Jim King	7.00	3.50	2.00
187	Virgil Trucks	7.00	3.50	2.00
188	Felix Mantilla	7.00	3.50	2.00
189	Willard Nixon	7.00	3.50	2.00
190	Randy Jackson	8.00	4.00	2.50
191	Joe Margoneri	7.00	3.50	2.00
192	Jerry Coleman	9.00	4.50	2.75
193	Del Rice	7.00	3.50	2.00
194	Hal Brown	7.00	3.50	2.00
195	Bobby Avila	7.00	3.50	2.00
196	Larry Jackson	7.00	3.50	2.00
197	Hank Sauer	7.00	3.50	2.00
198	Tigers Team	15.00	7.50	4.50
199	Vernon Law	7.00	3.50	2.00
200	Gil McDougald	15.00	7.50	4.50
201	Sandy Amoros	9.00	4.50	2.75
202	Dick Gernert	7.00	3.50	2.00
203	Hoyt Wilhelm	20.00	10.00	6.00
204	Athletics Team	15.00	7.50	4.50
205	Charley Maxwell	7.00	3.50	2.00
206	Willard Schmidt	7.00	3.50	2.00
207	Billy Hunter	7.00	3.50	2.00
208	Lew Burdette	7.00	3.50	2.00
209	Bob Skinner	7.00	3.50	2.00
210	Roy Campanella	115.00	57.00	34.00
211	Camilo Pascual	7.00	3.50	2.00
212	*Rocco Colavito*	135.00	67.00	40.00
213	Les Moss	7.00	3.50	2.00
214	Phillies Team	12.00	6.00	3.50
215	Enos Slaughter	22.00	11.00	6.50
216	Marv Grissom	7.00	3.50	2.00
217	Gene Stephens	7.00	3.50	2.00
218	Ray Jablonski	7.00	3.50	2.00
219	Tom Acker	7.00	3.50	2.00
220	Jackie Jensen	8.00	4.00	2.50
221	Dixie Howell	7.00	3.50	2.00
222	Alex Grammas	7.00	3.50	2.00
223	Frank House	7.00	3.50	2.00
224	Marv Blaylock	7.00	3.50	2.00
225	Harry Simpson	7.00	3.50	2.00
226	Preston Ward	7.00	3.50	2.00
227	Jerry Staley	7.00	3.50	2.00
228	Smoky Burgess	7.00	3.50	2.00
229	George Susce	7.00	3.50	2.00
230	George Kell	18.00	9.00	5.50
231	Solly Hemus	7.00	3.50	2.00
232	Whitey Lockman	7.00	3.50	2.00
233	Art Fowler	7.00	3.50	2.00
234	Dick Cole	7.00	3.50	2.00
235	Tom Poholsky	7.00	3.50	2.00
236	Joe Ginsberg	7.00	3.50	2.00
237	Foster Castleman	7.00	3.50	2.00
238	Eddie Robinson	7.00	3.50	2.00
239	Tom Morgan	7.00	3.50	2.00
240	Hank Bauer	10.00	5.00	3.00
241	Joe Lonnett	7.00	3.50	2.00
242	Charley Neal	8.00	4.00	2.50
243	Cardinals Team	15.00	7.50	4.50
244	Billy Loes	7.00	3.50	2.00
245	Rip Repulski	7.00	3.50	2.00
246	Jose Valdivielso	7.00	3.50	2.00
247	Turk Lown	7.00	3.50	2.00

		NR MT	EX	VG
248	Jim Finigan	7.00	3.50	2.00
249	Dave Pope	7.00	3.50	2.00
250	Eddie Mathews	40.00	20.00	12.00
251	Orioles Team	15.00	7.50	4.50
252	Carl Erskine	12.00	6.00	3.50
253	Gus Zernial	7.00	3.50	2.00
254	Ron Negray	7.00	3.50	2.00
255	Charlie Silvera	7.00	3.50	2.00
256	Ronnie Kline	7.00	3.50	2.00
257	Walt Dropo	7.00	3.50	2.00
258	Steve Gromek	7.00	3.50	2.00
259	Eddie O'Brien	7.00	3.50	2.00
260	Del Ennis	7.00	3.50	2.00
261	Bob Chakales	7.00	3.50	2.00
262	Bobby Thomson	7.00	3.50	2.00
263	George Strickland	7.00	3.50	2.00
264	Bob Turley	8.00	4.00	2.50
265	Harvey Haddix	20.00	10.00	6.00
266	Ken Kuhn	18.00	9.00	5.50
267	Danny Kravitz	18.00	9.00	5.50
268	Jackie Collum	18.00	9.00	5.50
269	Bob Cerv	18.00	9.00	5.50
270	Senators Team	30.00	15.00	9.00
271	Danny O'Connell	18.00	9.00	5.50
272	Bobby Shantz	27.50	13.50	8.25
273	Jim Davis	18.00	9.00	5.50
274	Don Hoak	18.00	9.00	5.50
275	Indians Team	40.00	20.00	12.00
276	Jim Pyburn	18.00	9.00	5.50
277	Johnny Podres	50.00	25.00	15.00
278	Fred Hatfield	18.00	9.00	5.50
279	Bob Thurman	18.00	9.00	5.50
280	Alex Kellner	18.00	9.00	5.50
281	Gail Harris	18.00	9.00	5.50
282	Jack Dittmer	18.00	9.00	5.50
283	*Wes Covington*	18.00	9.00	5.50
284	Don Zimmer	25.00	12.50	7.50
285	Ned Garver	18.00	9.00	5.50
286	*Bobby Richardson*	115.00	57.00	34.00
287	Sam Jones	18.00	9.00	5.50
288	Ted Lepcio	18.00	9.00	5.50
289	Jim Bolger	18.00	9.00	5.50
290	Andy Carey	22.00	11.00	6.50
291	Windy McCall	18.00	9.00	5.50
292	Billy Klaus	18.00	9.00	5.50
293	Ted Abernathy	18.00	9.00	5.50
294	Rocky Bridges	18.00	9.00	5.50
295	Joe Collins	22.00	11.00	6.50
296	Johnny Klippstein	18.00	9.00	5.50
297	Jack Crimian	18.00	9.00	5.50
298	Irv Noren	18.00	9.00	5.50
299	Chuck Harmon	18.00	9.00	5.50
300	Mike Garcia	18.00	9.00	5.50
301	Sam Esposito	18.00	9.00	5.50
302	Sandy Koufax	350.00	175.00	105.00
303	Billy Goodman	18.00	9.00	5.50
304	Joe Cunningham	18.00	9.00	5.50
305	Chico Fernandez	18.00	9.00	5.50
306	Darrell Johnson	22.00	11.00	6.50
307	Jack Phillips	18.00	9.00	5.50
308	Dick Hall	18.00	9.00	5.50
309	Jim Busby	18.00	9.00	5.50
310	Max Surkont	18.00	9.00	5.50
311	Al Pilarcik	18.00	9.00	5.50
312	*Tony Kubek*	95.00	47.00	28.00
313	Mel Parnell	18.00	9.00	5.50
314	Ed Bouchee	18.00	9.00	5.50
315	Lou Berberet	18.00	9.00	5.50
316	Billy O'Dell	18.00	9.00	5.50
317	Giants Team	60.00	30.00	18.00
318	Mickey McDermott	18.00	9.00	5.50
319	Gino Cimoli	20.00	10.00	6.00
320	Neil Chrisley	18.00	9.00	5.50
321	Red Murff	18.00	9.00	5.50
322	Redlegs Team	50.00	25.00	15.00
323	Wes Westrum	18.00	9.00	5.50
324	Dodgers Team	120.00	60.00	36.00
325	Frank Bolling	18.00	9.00	5.50
326	Pedro Ramos	18.00	9.00	5.50
327	Jim Pendleton	18.00	9.00	5.50
328	*Brooks Robinson*	375.00	187.00	112.00
329	White Sox Team	45.00	22.00	13.50
330	Jim Wilson	18.00	9.00	5.50
331	Ray Katt	18.00	9.00	5.50
332	Bob Bowman	18.00	9.00	5.50
333	Ernie Johnson	18.00	9.00	5.50
334	Jerry Schoonmaker	18.00	9.00	5.50
335	Granny Hamner	18.00	9.00	5.50
336	*Haywood Sullivan*	18.00	9.00	5.50
337	Rene Valdes	20.00	10.00	6.00
338	*Jim Bunning*	125.00	62.00	37.00

		NR MT	EX	VG
339	Bob Speake	18.00	9.00	5.50
340	Bill Wight	18.00	9.00	5.50
341	Don Gross	18.00	9.00	5.50
342	Gene Mauch	20.00	10.00	6.00
343	Taylor Phillips	18.00	9.00	5.50
344	Paul LaPalme	18.00	9.00	5.50
345	Paul Smith	18.00	9.00	5.50
346	Dick Littlefield	18.00	9.00	5.50
347	Hal Naragon	18.00	9.00	5.50
348	Jim Hearn	18.00	9.00	5.50
349	Nelson King	18.00	9.00	5.50
350	Eddie Miksis	18.00	9.00	5.50
351	Dave Hillman	18.00	9.00	5.50
352	Ellis Kinder	18.00	9.00	5.50
353	Cal Neeman	7.00	3.50	2.00
354	Rip Coleman	7.00	3.50	2.00
355	Frank Malzone	7.00	3.50	2.00
356	Faye Throneberry	7.00	3.50	2.00
357	Earl Torgeson	7.00	3.50	2.00
358	Jerry Lynch	7.00	3.50	2.00
359	Tom Cheney	7.00	3.50	2.00
360	Johnny Groth	7.00	3.50	2.00
361	Curt Barclay	7.00	3.50	2.00
362	Roman Mejias	7.00	3.50	2.00
363	Eddie Kasko	7.00	3.50	2.00
364	Cal McLish	7.00	3.50	2.00
365	Ossie Virgil	7.00	3.50	2.00
366	Ken Lehman	8.00	4.00	2.50
367	Ed Fitz Gerald	7.00	3.50	2.00
368	Bob Purkey	7.00	3.50	2.00
369	Milt Graff	7.00	3.50	2.00
370	Warren Hacker	7.00	3.50	2.00
371	Bob Lennon	7.00	3.50	2.00
372	Norm Zauchin	7.00	3.50	2.00
373	Pete Whisenant	7.00	3.50	2.00
374	Don Cardwell	7.00	3.50	2.00
375	*Jim Landis*	7.00	3.50	2.00
376	Don Elston	8.00	4.00	2.50
377	Andre Rodgers	7.00	3.50	2.00
378	Elmer Singleton	7.00	3.50	2.00
379	Don Lee	7.00	3.50	2.00
380	Walker Cooper	7.00	3.50	2.00
381	Dean Stone	7.00	3.50	2.00
382	Jim Brideweser	7.00	3.50	2.00
383	*Juan Pizarro*	7.00	3.50	2.00
384	Bobby Gene Smith	7.00	3.50	2.00
385	Art Houtteman	7.00	3.50	2.00
386	Lyle Luttrell	7.00	3.50	2.00
387	*Jack Sanford*	7.00	3.50	2.00
388	Pete Daley	7.00	3.50	2.00
389	Dave Jolly	7.00	3.50	2.00
390	Reno Bertoia	7.00	3.50	2.00
391	*Ralph Terry*	10.00	5.00	3.00
392	Chuck Tanner	7.00	3.50	2.00
393	Raul Sanchez	7.00	3.50	2.00
394	Luis Arroyo	7.00	3.50	2.00
395	Bubba Phillips	7.00	3.50	2.00
396	Casey Wise	7.00	3.50	2.00
397	Roy Smalley	7.00	3.50	2.00
398	Al Cicotte	7.00	3.50	2.00
399	Billy Consolo	7.00	3.50	2.00
400	Dodgers' Sluggers (Roy Campanella, Carl Furillo, Gil Hodges, Duke Snider)	200.00	100.00	60.00
401	*Earl Battey*	8.00	4.00	2.50
402	Jim Pisoni	7.00	3.50	2.00
403	Dick Hyde	7.00	3.50	2.00
404	Harry Anderson	7.00	3.50	2.00
405	Duke Maas	7.00	3.50	2.00
406	Bob Hale	7.00	3.50	2.00
407	Yankees' Power Hitters (Mickey Mantle, Yogi Berra)	350.00	175.00	105.00
---a	Checklist Series 1-2 (Big Blony ad on back)	175.00	87.00	52.00
---b	Checklist Series 1-2 (Bazooka ad on back)	175.00	87.00	52.00
---a	Checklist Series 2-3 (Big Blony ad on back)	300.00	150.00	90.00
---b	Checklist Series 2-3 (Bazooka ad on back)	300.00	150.00	90.00
---a	Checklist Series 3-4 (Big Blony ad on back)	500.00	250.00	150.00
---b	Checklist Series 3-4 (Bazooka ad on back)	500.00	250.00	150.00
---a	Checklist Series 4-5 (Big Blony ad on back)	750.00	325.00	225.00
---b	Checklist Series 4-5 (Bazooka ad on back)	750.00	325.00	225.00
——	Contest May 4	40.00	30.00	15.00
——	Contest May 25	40.00	30.00	15.00
——	Contest June 22	50.00	35.00	20.00
——	Contest July 19	60.00	40.00	20.00
——	Lucky Penny Insert Card	15.00	7.50	4.50

1958 Topps

Topps continued to expand its set size in 1958 with the release of a 494-card set. One card (#145) was not issued after Ed Bouchee was suspended from baseball. Cards retained the 2-1/2" by 3-1/2" size. There are a number of variations, including yellow or white lettering on 33 cards between numbers 2-108 (higher priced yellow letter variations checklisted below are not included in the complete set prices). The number of multiple-player cards was increased. A major innovation is the addition of 20 "All-Star" cards. For the first time, checklists were incorporated into the numbered series, as the backs of team cards.

		NR MT	EX	VG
Complete Set (494):		5500.00	2750.00	1650.
Common Player: 1-110		7.50	3.75	2.25
Common Player: 111-440		5.50	2.75	1.75
Common Player: 441-495		4.00	2.00	1.25
1	Ted Williams	375.00	187.00	112.00
2a	Bob Lemon (yellow team letters)	35.00	17.50	10.50
2b	Bob Lemon (white team letters)	12.00	6.00	3.50
3	Alex Kellner	7.50	3.75	2.25
4	Hank Foiles	7.50	3.75	2.25
5	Willie Mays	180.00	90.00	54.00
6	George Zuverink	7.50	3.75	2.25
7	Dale Long	7.50	3.75	2.25
8a	Eddie Kasko (yellow name)	20.00	10.00	6.00
8b	Eddie Kasko (white name)	7.50	3.75	2.25
9	Hank Bauer	12.00	6.00	3.50
10	Lou Burdette	7.50	3.75	2.25
11a	Jim Rivera (yellow team letters)	20.00	10.00	6.00
11b	Jim Rivera (white team letters)	7.50	3.75	2.25
12	George Crowe	7.50	3.75	2.25
13a	Billy Hoeft (yellow name)	20.00	10.00	6.00
13b	Billy Hoeft (white name, orange triangle by foot)	7.50	3.75	2.25
13c	Billy Hoeft (white name, red triangle by foot)	7.50	3.75	2.25
14	Rip Repulski	7.50	3.75	2.25
15	Jim Lemon	7.50	3.75	2.25
16	Charley Neal	7.50	3.75	2.25
17	Felix Mantilla	7.50	3.75	2.25
18	Frank Sullivan	7.50	3.75	2.25
19	Giants Team/Checklist 1-88	20.00	10.00	6.00
20a	Gil McDougald (yellow name)	30.00	15.00	9.00
20b	Gil McDougald (white name)	9.00	4.50	2.75
21	Curt Barclay	7.50	3.75	2.25
22	Hal Naragon	7.50	3.75	2.25
23a	Bill Tuttle (yellow name)	20.00	10.00	6.00
23b	Bill Tuttle (white name)	7.50	3.75	2.25
24a	Hobie Landrith (yellow name)	20.00	10.00	6.00
24b	Hobie Landrith (white name)	7.50	3.75	2.25
25	Don Drysdale	80.00	40.00	24.00
26	Ron Jackson	7.50	3.75	2.25
27	Bud Freeman	7.50	3.75	2.25
28	Jim Busby	7.50	3.75	2.25
29	Ted Lepcio	7.50	3.75	2.25
30a	Hank Aaron (yellow name)	350.00	175.00	105.00
30b	Hank Aaron (white name)	175.00	87.00	52.00
31	Tex Clevenger	7.50	3.75	2.25
32a	J.W. Porter (yellow name)	20.00	10.00	6.00

		NR MT	EX	VG
32b	J.W. Porter (white name)	7.50	3.75	2.25
33a	Cal Neeman (yellow team letters)	20.00	10.00	6.00
33b	Cal Neeman (white team letters)	7.50	3.75	2.25
34	Bob Thurman	7.50	3.75	2.25
35a	Don Mossi (yellow team letters)	20.00	10.00	6.00
35b	Don Mossi (white team letters)	7.50	3.75	2.25
36	Ted Kazanski	7.50	3.75	2.25
37	*Mike McCormick* (photo actually Ray Monzant)	7.50	3.75	2.25
38	Dick Gernert	7.50	3.75	2.25
39	Bob Martyn	7.50	3.75	2.25
40	George Kell	15.00	7.50	4.50
41	Dave Hillman	7.50	3.75	2.25
42	*John Roseboro*	9.00	4.50	2.75
43	Sal Maglie	10.00	5.00	3.00
44	Senators Team/Checklist 1-88	15.00	7.50	4.50
45	Dick Groat	7.50	3.75	2.25
46a	Lou Sleater (yellow name)	20.00	10.00	6.00
46b	Lou Sleater (white name)	7.50	3.75	2.25
47	*Roger Maris*	400.00	200.00	120.00
48	Chuck Harmon	7.50	3.75	2.25
49	Smoky Burgess	7.50	3.75	2.25
50a	Billy Pierce (yellow team letters)	20.00	10.00	6.00
50b	Billy Pierce (white team letters)	7.50	3.75	2.25
51	Del Rice	7.50	3.75	2.25
52a	Roberto Clemente (yellow team letters)	350.00	175.00	105.00
52b	Roberto Clemente (white team letters)	225.00	112.00	67.00
53a	Morrie Martin (yellow name)	20.00	10.00	6.00
53b	Morrie Martin (white name)	7.50	3.75	2.25
54	*Norm Siebern*	9.00	4.50	2.75
55	Chico Carrasquel	7.50	3.75	2.25
56	Bill Fischer	7.50	3.75	2.25
57a	Tim Thompson (yellow name)	20.00	10.00	6.00
57b	Tim Thompson (white name)	7.50	3.75	2.25
58a	Art Schult (yellow team letters)	20.00	10.00	6.00
58b	Art Schult (white team letters)	7.50	3.75	2.25
59	Dave Sisler	7.50	3.75	2.25
60a	Del Ennis (yellow name)	20.00	10.00	6.00
60b	Del Ennis (white name)	7.50	3.75	2.25
61a	Darrell Johnson (yellow name)	24.00	12.00	7.25
61b	Darrell Johnson (white name)	9.00	4.50	2.75
62	Joe DeMaestri	7.50	3.75	2.25
63	Joe Nuxhall	7.50	3.75	2.25
64	Joe Lonnett	7.50	3.75	2.25
65a	Von McDaniel (yellow name)	20.00	10.00	6.00
65b	Von McDaniel (white name)	7.50	3.75	2.25
66	Lee Walls	7.50	3.75	2.25
67	Joe Ginsberg	7.50	3.75	2.25
68	Daryl Spencer	7.50	3.75	2.25
69	Wally Burnette	7.50	3.75	2.25
70a	Al Kaline (yellow name)	175.00	87.00	52.00
70b	Al Kaline (white name)	70.00	35.00	21.00
71	Dodgers Team	30.00	15.00	9.00
72	Bud Byerly	7.50	3.75	2.25
73	Pete Daley	7.50	3.75	2.25
74	Roy Face	7.50	3.75	2.25
75	Gus Bell	7.50	3.75	2.25
76a	Dick Farrell (yellow team letters)	20.00	10.00	6.00
76b	Dick Farrell (white team letters)	7.50	3.75	2.25
77a	Don Zimmer (yellow team letters)	22.00	11.00	6.50
77b	Don Zimmer (white team letters)	9.00	4.50	2.75
78a	Ernie Johnson (yellow name)	20.00	10.00	6.00
78b	Ernie Johnson (white name)	7.50	3.75	2.25
79a	Dick Williams (yellow team name)	20.00	10.00	6.00
79b	Dick Williams (white team name)	7.50	3.75	2.25
80	Dick Drott	7.50	3.75	2.25
81a	*Steve Boros* (yellow team letters)	20.00	10.00	6.00
81b	*Steve Boros* (white team letters)	7.50	3.75	2.25
82	Ronnie Kline	7.50	3.75	2.25
83	*Bob Hazle*	7.50	3.75	2.25
84	Billy O'Dell	7.50	3.75	2.25
85a	Luis Aparicio (yellow team letters)	50.00	25.00	15.00
85b	Luis Aparicio (white team letters)	20.00	10.00	6.00
86	Valmy Thomas	7.50	3.75	2.25
87	Johnny Kucks	8.00	4.00	2.50
88	Duke Snider	75.00	37.00	22.00
89	Billy Klaus	7.50	3.75	2.25
90	Robin Roberts	21.00	10.50	6.25
91	Chuck Tanner	7.50	3.75	2.25
92a	Clint Courtney (yellow name)	20.00	10.00	6.00
92b	Clint Courtney (white name)	7.50	3.75	2.25
93	Sandy Amoros	7.50	3.75	2.25

		NR MT	EX	VG
94	Bob Skinner	7.50	3.75	2.25
95	Frank Bolling	7.50	3.75	2.25
96	Joe Durham	7.50	3.75	2.25
97a	Larry Jackson (yellow name)	20.00	10.00	6.00
97b	Larry Jackson (white name)	7.50	3.75	2.25
98a	Billy Hunter (yellow name)	20.00	10.00	6.00
98b	Billy Hunter (white name)	7.50	3.75	2.25
99	Bobby Adams	7.50	3.75	2.25
100a	Early Wynn (yellow team letters)	30.00	15.00	9.00
100b	Early Wynn (white team letters)	17.50	8.75	5.25
101a	Bobby Richardson (yellow name)	40.00	20.00	12.00
101b	Bobby Richardson (white name)	15.00	7.50	4.50
102	George Strickland	7.50	3.75	2.25
103	Jerry Lynch	7.50	3.75	2.25
104	Jim Pendleton	7.50	3.75	2.25
105	Billy Gardner	7.50	3.75	2.25
106	Dick Schofield	7.50	3.75	2.25
107	Ossie Virgil	7.50	3.75	2.25
108a	Jim Landis (yellow team letters)	20.00	10.00	6.00
108b	Jim Landis (white team letters)	7.50	3.75	2.25
109	Herb Plews	7.50	3.75	2.25
110	Johnny Logan	7.50	3.75	2.25
111	Stu Miller	5.50	2.75	1.75
112	Gus Zernial	5.50	2.75	1.75
113	Jerry Walker	5.50	2.75	1.75
114	Irv Noren	5.50	2.75	1.75
115	Jim Bunning	20.00	10.00	6.00
116	Dave Philley	5.50	2.75	1.75
117	Frank Torre	5.50	2.75	1.75
118	Harvey Haddix	5.50	2.75	1.75
119	Harry Chiti	5.50	2.75	1.75
120	Johnny Podres	7.50	3.75	2.25
121	Eddie Miksis	5.50	2.75	1.75
122	Walt Moryn	5.50	2.75	1.75
123	Dick Tomanek	5.50	2.75	1.75
124	Bobby Usher	5.50	2.75	1.75
125	Al Dark	6.50	3.25	2.00
126	Stan Palys	5.50	2.75	1.75
127	Tom Sturdivant	7.50	3.75	2.25
128	*Willie Kirkland*	5.50	2.75	1.75
129	Jim Derrington	5.50	2.75	1.75
130	Jackie Jensen	7.50	3.75	2.25
131	Bob Henrich	5.50	2.75	1.75
132	Vernon Law	5.50	2.75	1.75
133	Russ Nixon	5.50	2.75	1.75
134	Phillies Team/Checklist 89-176	12.00	6.00	3.50
135	Mike Drabowsky	5.50	2.75	1.75
136	Jim Finigan	5.50	2.75	1.75
137	Russ Kemmerer	5.50	2.75	1.75
138	Earl Torgeson	5.50	2.75	1.75
139	George Brunet	5.50	2.75	1.75
140	Wes Covington	5.50	2.75	1.75
141	Ken Lehman	5.50	2.75	1.75
142	Enos Slaughter	20.00	10.00	6.00
143	Billy Muffett	5.50	2.75	1.75
144	Bobby Morgan	5.50	2.75	1.75
145	Not Issued			
146	Dick Gray	5.50	2.75	1.75
147	*Don McMahon*	6.00	3.00	1.75
148	Billy Consolo	5.50	2.75	1.75
149	Tom Acker	5.50	2.75	1.75
150	Mickey Mantle	650.00	325.00	195.00
151	Buddy Pritchard	5.50	2.75	1.75
152	Johnny Antonelli	5.50	2.75	1.75
153	Les Moss	5.50	2.75	1.75
154	Harry Byrd	5.50	2.75	1.75
155	Hector Lopez	5.50	2.75	1.75
156	Dick Hyde	5.50	2.75	1.75
157	Dee Fondy	5.50	2.75	1.75
158	Indians Team/Checklist 177-264	12.50	6.25	3.75
159	Taylor Phillips	5.50	2.75	1.75
160	Don Hoak	5.50	2.75	1.75
161	Don Larsen	9.00	4.50	2.75
162	Gil Hodges	25.00	12.50	7.50
163	Jim Wilson	5.50	2.75	1.75
164	Bob Taylor	5.50	2.75	1.75
165	Bob Nieman	5.50	2.75	1.75
166	Danny O'Connell	5.50	2.75	1.75
167	Frank Baumann	5.50	2.75	1.75
168	Joe Cunningham	5.50	2.75	1.75
169	Ralph Terry	5.50	2.75	1.75
170	Vic Wertz	5.50	2.75	1.75
171	Harry Anderson	5.50	2.75	1.75
172	Don Gross	5.50	2.75	1.75
173	Eddie Yost	5.50	2.75	1.75
174	A's Team/Checklist 89-176	12.00	6.00	3.50
175	*Marv Throneberry*	12.00	6.00	3.50
176	Bob Buhl	5.50	2.75	1.75
177	Al Smith	5.50	2.75	1.75

		NR MT	EX	VG
178	Ted Kluszewski	9.00	4.50	2.75
179	Willy Miranda	5.50	2.75	1.75
180	Lindy McDaniel	5.50	2.75	1.75
181	Willie Jones	5.50	2.75	1.75
182	Joe Caffie	5.50	2.75	1.75
183	Dave Jolly	5.50	2.75	1.75
184	Elvin Tappe	5.50	2.75	1.75
185	Ray Boone	5.50	2.75	1.75
186	Jack Meyer	5.50	2.75	1.75
187	Sandy Koufax	175.00	87.00	52.00
188	Milt Bolling (photo actually Lou Berberet)	5.50	2.75	1.75
189	George Susce	5.50	2.75	1.75
190	Red Schoendienst	17.50	8.75	5.25
191	Art Ceccarelli	5.50	2.75	1.75
192	Milt Graff	5.50	2.75	1.75
193	*Jerry Lumpe*	7.00	3.50	2.00
194	Roger Craig	8.00	4.00	2.50
195	Whitey Lockman	5.50	2.75	1.75
196	Mike Garcia	5.50	2.75	1.75
197	Haywood Sullivan	5.50	2.75	1.75
198	Bill Virdon	5.50	2.75	1.75
199	Don Blasingame	5.50	2.75	1.75
200	Bob Keegan	5.50	2.75	1.75
201	Jim Bolger	5.50	2.75	1.75
202	*Woody Held*	5.50	2.75	1.75
203	Al Walker	5.50	2.75	1.75
204	Leo Kiely	5.50	2.75	1.75
205	Johnny Temple	5.50	2.75	1.75
206	Bob Shaw	5.50	2.75	1.75
207	Solly Hemus	5.50	2.75	1.75
208	Cal McLish	5.50	2.75	1.75
209	Bob Anderson	5.50	2.75	1.75
210	Wally Moon	5.50	2.75	1.75
211	Pete Burnside	5.50	2.75	1.75
212	Bubba Phillips	5.50	2.75	1.75
213	Red Wilson	5.50	2.75	1.75
214	Willard Schmidt	5.50	2.75	1.75
215	Jim Gilliam	7.50	3.75	2.25
216	Cards Team/Checklist 177-264	13.50	6.75	4.00
217	Jack Harshman	5.50	2.75	1.75
218	Dick Rand	5.50	2.75	1.75
219	Camilo Pascual	5.50	2.75	1.75
220	Tom Brewer	5.50	2.75	1.75
221	Jerry Kindall	5.50	2.75	1.75
222	Bud Daley	5.50	2.75	1.75
223	Andy Pafko	5.50	2.75	1.75
224	Bob Grim	8.00	4.00	2.50
225	Billy Goodman	5.50	2.75	1.75
226	Bob Smith (photo actually Bobby Gene Smith)	5.50	2.75	1.75
227	Gene Stephens	5.50	2.75	1.75
228	Duke Maas	5.50	2.75	1.75
229	Frank Zupo	5.50	2.75	1.75
230	Richie Ashburn	12.00	6.00	3.50
231	Lloyd Merritt	5.50	2.75	1.75
232	Reno Bertoia	5.50	2.75	1.75
233	Mickey Vernon	5.50	2.75	1.75
234	Carl Sawatski	5.50	2.75	1.75
235	Tom Gorman	5.50	2.75	1.75
236	Ed Fitz Gerald	5.50	2.75	1.75
237	Bill Wight	5.50	2.75	1.75
238	Bill Mazeroski	15.00	7.50	4.50
239	Chuck Stobbs	5.50	2.75	1.75
240	Moose Skowron	10.00	5.00	3.00
241	Dick Littlefield	5.50	2.75	1.75
242	Johnny Klippstein	5.50	2.75	1.75
243	Larry Raines	5.50	2.75	1.75
244	*Don Demeter*	5.50	2.75	1.75
245	*Frank Lary*	5.50	2.75	1.75
246	Yankees Team	45.00	22.00	13.50
247	Casey Wise	5.50	2.75	1.75
248	Herm Wehmeier	5.50	2.75	1.75
249	Ray Moore	5.50	2.75	1.75
250	Roy Sievers	5.50	2.75	1.75
251	Warren Hacker	5.50	2.75	1.75
252	Bob Trowbridge	5.50	2.75	1.75
253	Don Mueller	5.50	2.75	1.75
254	Alex Grammas	5.50	2.75	1.75
255	Bob Turley	7.00	3.50	2.00
256	White Sox Team/Checklist 265-352	12.00	6.00	3.50
257	Hal Smith	5.50	2.75	1.75
258	Carl Erskine	7.00	3.50	2.00
259	Al Pilarcik	5.50	2.75	1.75
260	Frank Malzone	5.50	2.75	1.75
261	Turk Lown	5.50	2.75	1.75
262	Johnny Groth	5.50	2.75	1.75
263	Eddie Bressoud	5.50	2.75	1.75
264	Jack Sanford	5.50	2.75	1.75
265	Pete Runnels	5.50	2.75	1.75

		NR MT	EX	VG
266	Connie Johnson	5.50	2.75	1.75
267	Sherm Lollar	5.50	2.75	1.75
268	Granny Hamner	5.50	2.75	1.75
269	Paul Smith	5.50	2.75	1.75
270	Warren Spahn	50.00	25.00	15.00
271	Billy Martin	12.00	6.00	3.50
272	Ray Crone	5.50	2.75	1.75
273	Hal Smith	5.50	2.75	1.75
274	Rocky Bridges	5.50	2.75	1.75
275	Elston Howard	8.00	4.00	2.50
276	Bobby Avila	5.50	2.75	1.75
277	Virgil Trucks	5.50	2.75	1.75
278	Mack Burk	5.50	2.75	1.75
279	Bob Boyd	5.50	2.75	1.75
280	Jim Piersall	6.00	3.00	1.75
281	Sam Taylor	5.50	2.75	1.75
282	Paul Foytack	5.50	2.75	1.75
283	Ray Shearer	5.50	2.75	1.75
284	Ray Katt	5.50	2.75	1.75
285	Frank Robinson	75.00	37.00	22.00
286	Gino Cimoli	5.50	2.75	1.75
287	Sam Jones	5.50	2.75	1.75
288	Harmon Killebrew	60.00	30.00	18.00
289	Series Hurling Rivals (Lou Burdette, Bobby Shantz)	8.00	4.00	2.50
290	Dick Donovan	5.50	2.75	1.75
291	Don Landrum	5.50	2.75	1.75
292	Ned Garver	5.50	2.75	1.75
293	Gene Freese	5.50	2.75	1.75
294	Hal Jeffcoat	5.50	2.75	1.75
295	Minnie Minoso	7.00	3.50	2.00
296	*Ryne Duren*	12.00	6.00	3.50
297	Don Buddin	5.50	2.75	1.75
298	Jim Hearn	5.50	2.75	1.75
299	Harry Simpson	7.00	3.50	2.00
300	League Presidents (Warren Giles, William Harridge)	9.00	4.50	2.75
301	Randy Jackson	5.50	2.75	1.75
302	Mike Baxes	5.50	2.75	1.75
303	Neil Chrisley	5.50	2.75	1.75
304	Tigers' Big Bats (Al Kaline, Harvey Kuenn)	17.50	8.75	5.25
305	Clem Labine	7.00	3.50	2.00
306	Whammy Douglas	5.50	2.75	1.75
307	Brooks Robinson	100.00	50.00	30.00
308	Paul Giel	5.50	2.75	1.75
309	Gail Harris	5.50	2.75	1.75
310	Ernie Banks	90.00	45.00	27.00
311	Bob Purkey	5.50	2.75	1.75
312	Red Sox Team	12.00	6.00	3.50
313	Bob Rush	5.50	2.75	1.75
314	Dodgers' Boss & Power (Duke Snider, Walter Alston)	17.50	8.75	5.25
315	Bob Friend	5.50	2.75	1.75
316	Tito Francona	5.50	2.75	1.75
317	*Albie Pearson*	6.00	3.00	1.75
318	Frank House	5.50	2.75	1.75
319	Lou Skizas	5.50	2.75	1.75
320	Whitey Ford	35.00	17.50	10.50
321	Sluggers Supreme (Ted Kluszewski, Ted Williams)	40.00	20.00	12.00
322	Harding Peterson	5.50	2.75	1.75
323	Elmer Valo	5.50	2.75	1.75
324	Hoyt Wilhelm	15.00	7.50	4.50
325	Joe Adcock	5.50	2.75	1.75
326	Bob Miller	5.50	2.75	1.75
327	Cubs Team/Checklist 265-352	12.50	6.25	3.75
328	Ike Delock	5.50	2.75	1.75
329	Bob Cerv	5.50	2.75	1.75
330	Ed Bailey	5.50	2.75	1.75
331	Pedro Ramos	5.50	2.75	1.75
332	Jim King	5.50	2.75	1.75
333	Andy Carey	7.50	3.75	2.25
334	Mound Aces (Bob Friend, Billy Pierce)	9.00	4.50	2.75
335	Ruben Gomez	5.50	2.75	1.75
336	Bert Hamric	5.50	2.75	1.75
337	Hank Aguirre	5.50	2.75	1.75
338	Walt Dropo	5.50	2.75	1.75
339	Fred Hatfield	5.50	2.75	1.75
340	Don Newcombe	7.50	3.75	2.25
341	Pirates Team/Checklist 265-352	12.50	6.25	3.75
342	Jim Brosnan	5.50	2.75	1.75
343	*Orlando Cepeda*	80.00	40.00	24.00
344	Bob Porterfield	5.50	2.75	1.75
345	Jim Hegan	5.50	2.75	1.75
346	Steve Bilko	5.50	2.75	1.75
347	Don Rudolph	5.50	2.75	1.75
348	Chico Fernandez	5.50	2.75	1.75
349	Murry Dickson	5.50	2.75	1.75

		NR MT	EX	VG
350	Ken Boyer	5.50	2.75	1.75
351	Braves Fence Busters (Hank Aaron, Joe Adcock, Del Crandall, Eddie Mathews)	30.00	15.00	9.00
352	Herb Score	5.50	2.75	1.75
353	Stan Lopata	5.50	2.75	1.75
354	Art Ditmar	7.50	3.75	2.25
355	Bill Bruton	5.50	2.75	1.75
356	Bob Malkmus	5.50	2.75	1.75
357	Danny McDevitt	5.50	2.75	1.75
358	Gene Baker	5.50	2.75	1.75
359	Billy Loes	5.50	2.75	1.75
360	Roy McMillan	5.50	2.75	1.75
361	Mike Fornieles	5.50	2.75	1.75
362	Ray Jablonski	5.50	2.75	1.75
363	Don Elston	5.50	2.75	1.75
364	Earl Battey	5.50	2.75	1.75
365	Tom Morgan	5.50	2.75	1.75
366	Gene Green	5.50	2.75	1.75
367	Jack Urban	5.50	2.75	1.75
368	Rocky Colavito	30.00	15.00	9.00
369	Ralph Lumenti	5.50	2.75	1.75
370	Yogi Berra	100.00	50.00	30.00
371	Marty Keough	5.50	2.75	1.75
372	Don Cardwell	5.50	2.75	1.75
373	Joe Pignatano	5.50	2.75	1.75
374	Brooks Lawrence	5.50	2.75	1.75
375	Pee Wee Reese	55.00	27.00	16.50
376	Charley Rabe	5.50	2.75	1.75
377a	Braves Team (alphabetical checklist on back)	15.00	7.50	4.50
377b	Braves Team (numerical checklist on back)	60.00	30.00	18.00
378	Hank Sauer	5.50	2.75	1.75
379	Ray Herbert	5.50	2.75	1.75
380	Charley Maxwell	5.50	2.75	1.75
381	Hal Brown	5.50	2.75	1.75
382	Al Cicotte	7.00	3.50	2.00
383	Lou Berberet	5.50	2.75	1.75
384	John Goryl	5.50	2.75	1.75
385	Wilmer Mizell	5.50	2.75	1.75
386	Birdie's Young Sluggers (Ed Bailey, Frank Robinson, Birdie Tebbetts)	12.00	6.00	3.50
387	Wally Post	5.50	2.75	1.75
388	Billy Moran	5.50	2.75	1.75
389	Bill Taylor	5.50	2.75	1.75
390	Del Crandall	6.00	3.00	1.75
391	Dave Melton	5.50	2.75	1.75
392	Bennie Daniels	5.50	2.75	1.75
393	Tony Kubek	15.00	7.50	4.50
394	*Jim Grant*	6.00	3.00	1.75
395	Willard Nixon	5.50	2.75	1.75
396	Dutch Dotterer	5.50	2.75	1.75
397a	Tigers Team (alphabetical checklist on back)	15.00	7.50	4.50
397b	Tigers Team (numerical checklist on back)	60.00	30.00	18.00
398	Gene Woodling	5.50	2.75	1.75
399	Marv Grissom	5.50	2.75	1.75
400	Nellie Fox	15.00	7.50	4.50
401	Don Bessent	5.50	2.75	1.75
402	Bobby Gene Smith	5.50	2.75	1.75
403	Steve Korcheck	5.50	2.75	1.75
404	Curt Simmons	5.50	2.75	1.75
405	Ken Aspromonte	5.50	2.75	1.75
406	Vic Power	5.50	2.75	1.75
407	Carlton Willey	5.50	2.75	1.75
408a	Orioles Team (alphabetical checklist on back)	12.00	6.00	3.50
408b	Orioles Team (numerical checklist on back)	60.00	30.00	18.00
409	Frank J. Thomas	5.50	2.75	1.75
410	Murray Wall	5.50	2.75	1.75
411	*Tony Taylor*	5.50	2.75	1.75
412	Jerry Staley	5.50	2.75	1.75
413	*Jim Davenport*	5.50	2.75	1.75
414	Sammy White	5.50	2.75	1.75
415	Bob Bowman	5.50	2.75	1.75
416	Foster Castleman	5.50	2.75	1.75
417	Carl Furillo	9.00	4.50	2.75
418	World Series Batting Foes (Hank Aaron, Mickey Mantle)	150.00	75.00	45.00
419	Bobby Shantz	7.50	3.75	2.25
420	*Vada Pinson*	30.00	15.00	9.00
421	Dixie Howell	5.50	2.75	1.75
422	Norm Zauchin	5.50	2.75	1.75
423	Phil Clark	5.50	2.75	1.75
424	Larry Doby	5.50	2.75	1.75
425	Sam Esposito	5.50	2.75	1.75
426	Johnny O'Brien	5.50	2.75	1.75
427	Al Worthington	5.50	2.75	1.75

		NR MT	EX	VG
428a	Redlegs Team (alphabetical checklist on back)	13.50	6.75	4.00
428b	Redlegs Team (numerical checklist on back)	50.00	25.00	15.00
429	Gus Triandos	5.50	2.75	1.75
430	Bobby Thomson	6.00	3.00	1.75
431	Gene Conley	5.50	2.75	1.75
432	John Powers	5.50	2.75	1.75
433	Pancho Herrera	5.50	2.75	1.75
434	Harvey Kuenn	6.00	3.00	1.75
435	Ed Roebuck	5.50	2.75	1.75
436	Rival Fence Busters (Willie Mays, Duke Snider)	60.00	30.00	18.00
437	Bob Speake	5.50	2.75	1.75
438	Whitey Herzog	7.50	3.75	2.25
439	Ray Narleski	5.50	2.75	1.75
440	Eddie Mathews	30.00	15.00	9.00
441	Jim Marshall	4.00	2.00	1.25
442	Phil Paine	4.00	2.00	1.25
443	Billy Harrell	7.50	3.75	2.25
444	Danny Kravitz	4.00	2.00	1.25
445	Bob Smith	4.00	2.00	1.25
446	Carroll Hardy	7.50	3.75	2.25
447	Ray Monzant	4.00	2.00	1.25
448	*Charlie Lau*	5.50	2.75	1.75
449	Gene Fodge	4.00	2.00	1.25
450	Preston Ward	7.50	3.75	2.25
451	Joe Taylor	4.00	2.00	1.25
452	Roman Mejias	4.00	2.00	1.25
453	Tom Qualters	4.00	2.00	1.25
454	Harry Hanebrink	4.00	2.00	1.25
455	Hal Griggs	4.00	2.00	1.25
456	Dick Brown	4.00	2.00	1.25
457	*Milt Pappas*	5.50	2.75	1.75
458	Julio Becquer	4.00	2.00	1.25
459	Ron Blackburn	4.00	2.00	1.25
460	Chuck Essegian	4.00	2.00	1.25
461	Ed Mayer	4.00	2.00	1.25
462	Gary Geiger	7.50	3.75	2.25
463	Vito Valentinetti	4.00	2.00	1.25
464	*Curt Flood*	25.00	12.50	7.50
465	Arnie Portocarrero	4.00	2.00	1.25
466	Pete Whisenant	4.00	2.00	1.25
467	Glen Hobbie	4.00	2.00	1.25
468	Bob Schmidt	4.00	2.00	1.25
469	Don Ferrarese	4.00	2.00	1.25
470	R.C. Stevens	4.00	2.00	1.25
471	Lenny Green	4.00	2.00	1.25
472	Joe Jay	4.00	2.00	1.25
473	Bill Renna	4.00	2.00	1.25
474	Roman Semproch	4.00	2.00	1.25
475	All-Star Managers (Fred Haney, Casey Stengel)	18.00	9.00	5.50
476	Stan Musial (All-Star)	40.00	20.00	12.00
477	Bill Skowron (All-Star)	6.00	3.00	1.75
478	Johnny Temple (All-Star)	7.00	3.50	2.00
479	Nellie Fox (All-Star)	10.00	5.00	3.00
480	Eddie Mathews (All-Star)	13.50	6.75	4.00
481	Frank Malzone (All-Star)	7.00	3.50	2.00
482	Ernie Banks (All-Star)	25.00	12.50	7.50
483	Luis Aparicio (All-Star)	12.00	6.00	3.50
484	Frank Robinson (All-Star)	25.00	12.50	7.50
485	Ted Williams (All-Star)	65.00	32.00	19.50
486	Willie Mays (All-Star)	50.00	25.00	15.00
487	Mickey Mantle (All-Star)	115.00	57.00	34.00
488	Hank Aaron (All-Star)	50.00	25.00	15.00
489	Jackie Jensen (All-Star)	7.00	3.50	2.00
490	Ed Bailey (All-Star)	7.00	3.50	2.00
491	Sherm Lollar (All-Star)	7.00	3.50	2.00
492	Bob Friend (All-Star)	7.00	3.50	2.00
493	Bob Turley (All-Star)	7.50	3.75	2.25
494	Warren Spahn (All-Star)	17.50	8.75	5.25
495	Herb Score (All-Star)	7.50	3.75	2.25
----	Contest Card (All-Star Game, July 8)	15.00	7.50	4.50
----	Felt Emblems Insert Card	15.00	7.50	4.50

1959 Topps

These 2-1/2" by 3-1/2" cards have a round photograph at the center of the front with a solid-color background and white border. A facsimile autograph is found across the photo. The 572- card set marks the largest set issued to that time. Card numbers below 507 have red and green printing with the card number in white in a green box. On high number cards beginning with #507, the printing is black and red and the card number is in a black

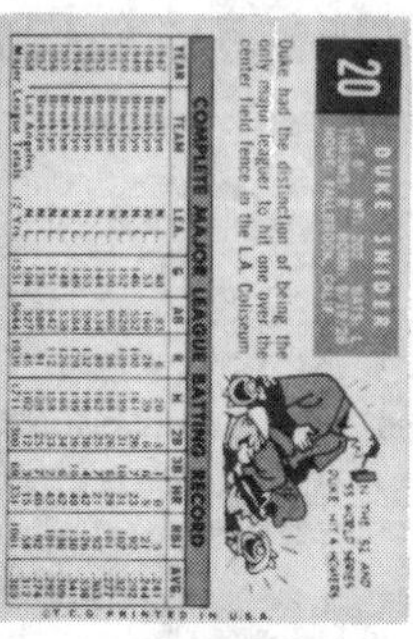

box. Specialty cards include multiple-player cards, team cards with checklists, "All-Star" cards, highlights from previous season, and 31 "Rookie Stars." There is also a card of the commissioner, Ford Frick, and one of Roy Campanella in a wheelchair. A handful of cards can be found with and without lines added to the biographies on back indicating trades or demotions; those without the added lines are considerably more rare and valuable and are not included in the complete set price. Card numbers 199-286 can be found with either white or grey backs, with the grey stock being the less common.

		NR MT	EX	VG
Complete Set (572):		5000.00	2500.00	1500.
Common Player: 1-110		6.00	3.00	1.75
Common Player: 111-506		4.00	2.00	1.25
Common Player: 507-572		15.00	7.50	4.50
1	Ford Frick	70.00	35.00	21.00
2	Eddie Yost	6.00	3.00	1.75
3	Don McMahon	6.00	3.00	1.75
4	Albie Pearson	6.00	3.00	1.75
5	Dick Donovan	6.00	3.00	1.75
6	Alex Grammas	6.00	3.00	1.75
7	Al Pilarcik	6.00	3.00	1.75
8	Phillies Team	30.00	15.00	9.00
9	Paul Giel	6.00	3.00	1.75
10	Mickey Mantle	500.00	250.00	150.00
11	Billy Hunter	6.00	3.00	1.75
12	Vern Law	6.00	3.00	1.75
13	Dick Gernert	6.00	3.00	1.75
14	Pete Whisenant	6.00	3.00	1.75
15	Dick Drott	6.00	3.00	1.75
16	Joe Pignatano	6.00	3.00	1.75
17	Danny's All-Stars (Ted Kluszewski, Danny Murtaugh, Frank J. Thomas)	9.00	4.50	2.75
18	Jack Urban	6.00	3.00	1.75
19	Ed Bressoud	6.00	3.00	1.75
20	Duke Snider	60.00	30.00	18.00
21	Connie Johnson	6.00	3.00	1.75
22	Al Smith	6.00	3.00	1.75
23	Murry Dickson	7.00	3.50	2.00
24	Red Wilson	6.00	3.00	1.75
25	Don Hoak	6.00	3.00	1.75
26	Chuck Stobbs	6.00	3.00	1.75
27	Andy Pafko	6.00	3.00	1.75
28	Red Worthington	6.00	3.00	1.75
29	Jim Bolger	6.00	3.00	1.75
30	Nellie Fox	20.00	10.00	6.00
31	Ken Lehman	6.00	3.00	1.75
32	Don Buddin	6.00	3.00	1.75
33	Ed Fitz Gerald	6.00	3.00	1.75
34	Pitchers Beware (Al Kaline, Charlie Maxwell)	12.00	6.00	3.50
35	Ted Kluszewski	10.00	5.00	3.00
36	Hank Aguirre	6.00	3.00	1.75
37	Gene Green	6.00	3.00	1.75
38	Morrie Martin	6.00	3.00	1.75
39	Ed Bouchee	6.00	3.00	1.75
40	Warren Spahn	50.00	25.00	15.00
41	Bob Martyn	6.00	3.00	1.75
42	Murray Wall	6.00	3.00	1.75
43	Steve Bilko	6.00	3.00	1.75
44	Vito Valentinetti	6.00	3.00	1.75
45	Andy Carey	7.00	3.50	2.00
46	Bill Henry	6.00	3.00	1.75
47	Jim Finigan	6.00	3.00	1.75

		NR MT	EX	VG
48	Orioles Team/Checklist 1-88	20.00	10.00	6.00
49	Bill Hall	6.00	3.00	1.75
50	Willie Mays	160.00	80.00	48.00
51	Rip Coleman	6.00	3.00	1.75
52	Coot Veal	6.00	3.00	1.75
53	Stan Williams	6.00	3.00	1.75
54	Mel Roach	6.00	3.00	1.75
55	Tom Brewer	6.00	3.00	1.75
56	Carl Sawatski	6.00	3.00	1.75
57	Al Cicotte	6.00	3.00	1.75
58	Eddie Miksis	6.00	3.00	1.75
59	Irv Noren	6.00	3.00	1.75
60	Bob Turley	7.00	3.50	2.00
61	Dick Brown	6.00	3.00	1.75
62	Tony Taylor	6.00	3.00	1.75
63	Jim Hearn	6.00	3.00	1.75
64	Joe DeMaestri	6.00	3.00	1.75
65	Frank Torre	6.00	3.00	1.75
66	Joe Ginsberg	6.00	3.00	1.75
67	Brooks Lawrence	6.00	3.00	1.75
68	Dick Schofield	6.00	3.00	1.75
69	Giants Team/Checklist 89-176	24.00	12.00	7.25
70	Harvey Kuenn	9.00	4.50	2.75
71	Don Bessent	6.00	3.00	1.75
72	Bill Renna	6.00	3.00	1.75
73	Ron Jackson	6.00	3.00	1.75
74	Directing the Power (Cookie Lavagetto, Jim Lemon, Roy Sievers)	9.00	4.50	2.75
75	Sam Jones	6.00	3.00	1.75
76	Bobby Richardson	17.50	8.75	5.25
77	John Goryl	6.00	3.00	1.75
78	Pedro Ramos	6.00	3.00	1.75
79	Harry Chiti	6.00	3.00	1.75
80	Minnie Minoso	7.50	3.75	2.25
81	Hal Jeffcoat	6.00	3.00	1.75
82	Bob Boyd	6.00	3.00	1.75
83	Bob Smith	6.00	3.00	1.75
84	Reno Bertoia	6.00	3.00	1.75
85	Harry Anderson	6.00	3.00	1.75
86	Bob Keegan	6.00	3.00	1.75
87	Danny O'Connell	6.00	3.00	1.75
88	Herb Score	6.00	3.00	1.75
89	Billy Gardner	6.00	3.00	1.75
90	Bill Skowron	12.50	6.25	3.75
91	Herb Moford	6.00	3.00	1.75
92	Dave Philley	6.00	3.00	1.75
93	Julio Becquer	6.00	3.00	1.75
94	W. Sox Team	20.00	10.00	6.00
95	Carl Willey	6.00	3.00	1.75
96	Lou Berberet	6.00	3.00	1.75
97	Jerry Lynch	6.00	3.00	1.75
98	Arnie Portocarrero	6.00	3.00	1.75
99	Ted Kazanski	6.00	3.00	1.75
100	Bob Cerv	6.00	3.00	1.75
101	Alex Kellner	6.00	3.00	1.75
102	*Felipe Alou*	30.00	15.00	9.00
103	Billy Goodman	6.00	3.00	1.75
104	Del Rice	6.00	3.00	1.75
105	Lee Walls	6.00	3.00	1.75
106	Hal Woodeshick	6.00	3.00	1.75
107	Norm Larker	6.00	3.00	1.75
108	Zack Monroe	7.00	3.50	2.00
109	Bob Schmidt	6.00	3.00	1.75
110	George Witt	6.00	3.00	1.75
111	Redlegs Team/Checklist 89-176	17.50	8.75	5.25
112	Billy Consolo	4.00	2.00	1.25
113	Taylor Phillips	4.00	2.00	1.25
114	Earl Battey	4.00	2.00	1.25
115	Mickey Vernon	4.00	2.00	1.25
116	*Bob Allison*	7.00	3.50	2.00
117	*John Blanchard*	5.00	2.50	1.50
118	John Buzhardt	4.00	2.00	1.25
119	*John Callison*	6.00	3.00	1.75
120	Chuck Coles	4.00	2.00	1.25
121	Bob Conley	4.00	2.00	1.25
122	Bennie Daniels	4.00	2.00	1.25
123	Don Dillard	4.00	2.00	1.25
124	Dan Dobbek	4.00	2.00	1.25
125	*Ron Fairly*	5.00	2.50	1.50
126	Eddie Haas	4.00	2.00	1.25
127	Kent Hadley	4.00	2.00	1.25
128	Bob Hartman	4.00	2.00	1.25
129	Frank Herrera	4.00	2.00	1.25
130	Lou Jackson	4.00	2.00	1.25
131	*Deron Johnson*	5.00	2.50	1.50
132	Don Lee	4.00	2.00	1.25
133	*Bob Lillis*	5.00	2.50	1.50
134	Jim McDaniel	4.00	2.00	1.25
135	Gene Oliver	4.00	2.00	1.25
136	*Jim O'Toole*	5.00	2.50	1.50

		NR MT	EX	VG
137	Dick Ricketts	4.00	2.00	1.25
138	John Romano	4.00	2.00	1.25
139	Ed Sadowski	4.00	2.00	1.25
140	Charlie Secrest	4.00	2.00	1.25
141	Joe Shipley	4.00	2.00	1.25
142	Dick Stigman	4.00	2.00	1.25
143	Willie Tasby	4.00	2.00	1.25
144	Jerry Walker	4.00	2.00	1.25
145	Dom Zanni	4.00	2.00	1.25
146	Jerry Zimmerman	4.00	2.00	1.25
147	Cubs' Clubbers (Ernie Banks, Dale Long, Walt Moryn)	12.00	6.00	3.50
148	Mike McCormick	4.00	2.00	1.25
149	Jim Bunning	15.00	7.50	4.50
150	Stan Musial	150.00	75.00	45.00
151	Bob Malkmus	4.00	2.00	1.25
152	Johnny Klippstein	4.00	2.00	1.25
153	Jim Marshall	4.00	2.00	1.25
154	Ray Herbert	4.00	2.00	1.25
155	Enos Slaughter	18.00	9.00	5.50
156	Ace Hurlers (Billy Pierce, Robin Roberts)	5.00	2.50	1.50
157	Felix Mantilla	4.00	2.00	1.25
158	Walt Dropo	4.00	2.00	1.25
159	Bob Shaw	4.00	2.00	1.25
160	Dick Groat	4.00	2.00	1.25
161	Frank Baumann	4.00	2.00	1.25
162	Bobby G. Smith	4.00	2.00	1.25
163	Sandy Koufax	160.00	80.00	48.00
164	Johnny Groth	4.00	2.00	1.25
165	Bill Bruton	4.00	2.00	1.25
166	Destruction Crew (Rocky Colavito, Larry Doby, Minnie Minoso)	5.00	2.50	1.50
167	Duke Maas	5.00	2.50	1.50
168	Carroll Hardy	4.00	2.00	1.25
169	Ted Abernathy	4.00	2.00	1.25
170	Gene Woodling	4.00	2.00	1.25
171	Willard Schmidt	4.00	2.00	1.25
172	A's Team/Checklist 177-242	12.00	6.00	3.50
173	*Bill Monbouquette*	4.00	2.00	1.25
174	Jim Pendleton	4.00	2.00	1.25
175	Dick Farrell	4.00	2.00	1.25
176	Preston Ward	4.00	2.00	1.25
177	Johnny Briggs	4.00	2.00	1.25
178	Ruben Amaro	4.00	2.00	1.25
179	Don Rudolph	4.00	2.00	1.25
180	Yogi Berra	80.00	40.00	24.00
181	Bob Porterfield	4.00	2.00	1.25
182	Milt Graff	4.00	2.00	1.25
183	Stu Miller	4.00	2.00	1.25
184	Harvey Haddix	4.00	2.00	1.25
185	Jim Busby	4.00	2.00	1.25
186	Mudcat Grant	4.00	2.00	1.25
187	Bubba Phillips	4.00	2.00	1.25
188	Juan Pizarro	4.00	2.00	1.25
189	Neil Chrisley	4.00	2.00	1.25
190	Bill Virdon	4.00	2.00	1.25
191	Russ Kemmerer	4.00	2.00	1.25
192	Charley Beamon	4.00	2.00	1.25
193	Sammy Taylor	4.00	2.00	1.25
194	Jim Brosnan	4.00	2.00	1.25
195	Rip Repulski	4.00	2.00	1.25
196	Billy Moran	4.00	2.00	1.25
197	Ray Semproch	4.00	2.00	1.25
198	Jim Davenport	4.00	2.00	1.25
199	Leo Kiely	4.00	2.00	1.25
200	Warren Giles	5.00	2.50	1.50
201	Tom Acker	4.00	2.00	1.25
202	Roger Maris	150.00	75.00	45.00
203	Ozzie Virgil	4.00	2.00	1.25
204	Casey Wise	4.00	2.00	1.25
205	Don Larsen	7.00	3.50	2.00
206	Carl Furillo	7.00	3.50	2.00
207	George Strickland	4.00	2.00	1.25
208	Willie Jones	4.00	2.00	1.25
209	Lenny Green	4.00	2.00	1.25
210	Ed Bailey	4.00	2.00	1.25
211	Bob Blaylock	4.00	2.00	1.25
212	Fence Busters (Hank Aaron, Eddie Mathews)	55.00	27.00	16.50
213	Jim Rivera	4.00	2.00	1.25
214	Marcelino Solis	4.00	2.00	1.25
215	Jim Lemon	4.00	2.00	1.25
216	Andre Rodgers	4.00	2.00	1.25
217	Carl Erskine	6.00	3.00	1.75
218	Roman Mejias	4.00	2.00	1.25
219	George Zuverink	4.00	2.00	1.25
220	Frank Malzone	4.00	2.00	1.25
221	Bob Bowman	4.00	2.00	1.25
222	Bobby Shantz	6.00	3.00	1.75
223	Cards Team/Checklist 265-352	12.00	6.00	3.50

		NR MT	EX	VG
224	*Claude Osteen*	4.00	2.00	1.25
225	Johnny Logan	4.00	2.00	1.25
226	Art Ceccarelli	4.00	2.00	1.25
227	Hal Smith	4.00	2.00	1.25
228	Don Gross	4.00	2.00	1.25
229	Vic Power	4.00	2.00	1.25
230	Bill Fischer	4.00	2.00	1.25
231	Ellis Burton	4.00	2.00	1.25
232	Eddie Kasko	4.00	2.00	1.25
233	Paul Foytack	4.00	2.00	1.25
234	Chuck Tanner	4.00	2.00	1.25
235	Valmy Thomas	4.00	2.00	1.25
236	Ted Bowsfield	4.00	2.00	1.25
237	Run Preventers (Gil McDougald, Bobby Richardson, Bob Turley)	9.00	4.50	2.75
238	Gene Baker	4.00	2.00	1.25
239	Bob Trowbridge	4.00	2.00	1.25
240	Hank Bauer	7.00	3.50	2.00
241	Billy Muffett	4.00	2.00	1.25
242	Ron Samford	4.00	2.00	1.25
243	Marv Grissom	4.00	2.00	1.25
244	Dick Gray	4.00	2.00	1.25
245	Ned Garver	4.00	2.00	1.25
246	J.W. Porter	4.00	2.00	1.25
247	Don Ferrarese	4.00	2.00	1.25
248	Red Sox Team/Checklist 177-264	12.50	6.25	3.75
249	Bobby Adams	4.00	2.00	1.25
250	Billy O'Dell	4.00	2.00	1.25
251	Cletis Boyer	6.00	3.00	1.75
252	Ray Boone	4.00	2.00	1.25
253	Seth Morehead	4.00	2.00	1.25
254	Zeke Bella	4.00	2.00	1.25
255	Del Ennis	4.00	2.00	1.25
256	Jerry Davie	4.00	2.00	1.25
257	*Leon Wagner*	4.00	2.00	1.25
258	Fred Kipp	4.00	2.00	1.25
259	Jim Pisoni	4.00	2.00	1.25
260	Early Wynn	15.00	7.50	4.50
261	Gene Stephens	4.00	2.00	1.25
262	Hitters' Foes (Don Drysdale, Clem Labine, Johnny Podres)	12.00	6.00	3.50
263	Buddy Daley	4.00	2.00	1.25
264	Chico Carrasquel	4.00	2.00	1.25
265	Ron Kline	4.00	2.00	1.25
266	Woody Held	4.00	2.00	1.25
267	John Romonosky	4.00	2.00	1.25
268	Tito Francona	4.00	2.00	1.25
269	Jack Meyer	4.00	2.00	1.25
270	Gil Hodges	20.00	10.00	6.00
271	*Orlando Pena*	4.00	2.00	1.25
272	Jerry Lumpe	5.00	2.50	1.50
273	Joe Jay	4.00	2.00	1.25
274	Jerry Kindall	4.00	2.00	1.25
275	Jack Sanford	4.00	2.00	1.25
276	Pete Daley	4.00	2.00	1.25
277	Turk Lown	4.00	2.00	1.25
278	Chuck Essegian	4.00	2.00	1.25
279	Ernie Johnson	4.00	2.00	1.25
280	Frank Bolling	4.00	2.00	1.25
281	Walt Craddock	4.00	2.00	1.25
282	R.C. Stevens	4.00	2.00	1.25
283	Russ Heman	4.00	2.00	1.25
284	Steve Korcheck	4.00	2.00	1.25
285	Joe Cunningham	4.00	2.00	1.25
286	Dean Stone	4.00	2.00	1.25
287	Don Zimmer	5.00	2.50	1.50
288	Dutch Dotterer	4.00	2.00	1.25
289	Johnny Kucks	5.00	2.50	1.50
290	Wes Covington	4.00	2.00	1.25
291	Pitching Partners (Camilo Pascual, Pedro Ramos)	5.00	2.50	1.50
292	Dick Williams	4.00	2.00	1.25
293	Ray Moore	4.00	2.00	1.25
294	Hank Foiles	4.00	2.00	1.25
295	Billy Martin	12.50	6.25	3.75
296	*Ernie Broglio*	4.00	2.00	1.25
297	*Jackie Brandt*	4.00	2.00	1.25
298	Tex Clevenger	4.00	2.00	1.25
299	Billy Klaus	4.00	2.00	1.25
300	Richie Ashburn	20.00	10.00	6.00
301	Earl Averill	4.00	2.00	1.25
302	Don Mossi	4.00	2.00	1.25
303	Marty Keough	4.00	2.00	1.25
304	Cubs Team/Checklist 265-352	12.00	6.00	3.50
305	Curt Raydon	4.00	2.00	1.25
306	Jim Gilliam	6.00	3.00	1.75
307	Curt Barclay	4.00	2.00	1.25
308	Norm Siebern	5.00	2.50	1.50
309	Sal Maglie	4.00	2.00	1.25
310	Luis Aparicio	15.00	7.50	4.50

		NR MT	EX	VG
311	Norm Zauchin	4.00	2.00	1.25
312	Don Newcombe	6.00	3.00	1.75
313	Frank House	4.00	2.00	1.25
314	Don Cardwell	4.00	2.00	1.25
315	Joe Adcock	4.00	2.00	1.25
316a	Ralph Lumenti (no optioned statement)	80.00	40.00	24.00
316b	Ralph Lumenti (optioned statement)	4.00	2.00	1.25
317	N.L. Hitting Kings (Richie Ashburn, Willie Mays)	25.00	12.50	7.50
318	Rocky Bridges	4.00	2.00	1.25
319	Dave Hillman	4.00	2.00	1.25
320	Bob Skinner	4.00	2.00	1.25
321a	Bob Giallombardo (no optioned statement)	80.00	40.00	24.00
321b	Bob Giallombardo (optioned statement)	4.00	2.00	1.25
322a	Harry Hanebrink (no trade statement)	65.00	32.00	19.50
322b	Harry Hanebrink (trade statement)	4.00	2.00	1.25
323	Frank Sullivan	4.00	2.00	1.25
324	Don Demeter	4.00	2.00	1.25
325	Ken Boyer	5.00	2.50	1.50
326	Marv Throneberry	6.00	3.00	1.75
327	*Gary Bell*	4.00	2.00	1.25
328	Lou Skizas	4.00	2.00	1.25
329	Tigers Team/Checklist 353-429	12.50	6.25	3.75
330	Gus Triandos	4.00	2.00	1.25
331	Steve Boros	4.00	2.00	1.25
332	Ray Monzant	4.00	2.00	1.25
333	Harry Simpson	4.00	2.00	1.25
334	Glen Hobbie	4.00	2.00	1.25
335	Johnny Temple	4.00	2.00	1.25
336a	Billy Loes (no trade statement)	65.00	32.00	19.50
336b	Billy Loes (trade statement)	4.00	2.00	1.25
337	George Crowe	4.00	2.00	1.25
338	*George (Sparky) Anderson*	55.00	27.00	16.50
339	Roy Face	4.00	2.00	1.25
340	Roy Sievers	4.00	2.00	1.25
341	Tom Qualters	4.00	2.00	1.25
342	Ray Jablonski	4.00	2.00	1.25
343	Billy Hoeft	4.00	2.00	1.25
344	Russ Nixon	4.00	2.00	1.25
345	Gil McDougald	7.00	3.50	2.00
346	Batter Bafflers (Tom Brewer, Dave Sisler)	5.00	2.50	1.50
347	Bob Buhl	5.00	2.50	1.50
348	Ted Lepcio	4.00	2.00	1.25
349	Hoyt Wilhelm	15.00	7.50	4.50
350	Ernie Banks	65.00	32.00	19.50
351	Earl Torgeson	4.00	2.00	1.25
352	Robin Roberts	15.00	7.50	4.50
353	Curt Flood	4.00	2.00	1.25
354	Pete Burnside	4.00	2.00	1.25
355	Jim Piersall	4.00	2.00	1.25
356	Bob Mabe	4.00	2.00	1.25
357	*Dick Stuart*	6.00	3.00	1.75
358	Ralph Terry	4.00	2.00	1.25
359	*Bill White*	30.00	15.00	9.00
360	Al Kaline	65.00	32.00	19.50
361	Willard Nixon	4.00	2.00	1.25
362a	Dolan Nichols (no optioned statement)	80.00	40.00	24.00
362b	Dolan Nichols (optioned statement)	4.00	2.00	1.25
363	Bobby Avila	4.00	2.00	1.25
364	Danny McDevitt	4.00	2.00	1.25
365	Gus Bell	4.00	2.00	1.25
366	Humberto Robinson	4.00	2.00	1.25
367	Cal Neeman	4.00	2.00	1.25
368	Don Mueller	4.00	2.00	1.25
369	Dick Tomanek	4.00	2.00	1.25
370	Pete Runnels	4.00	2.00	1.25
371	Dick Brodowski	4.00	2.00	1.25
372	Jim Hegan	4.00	2.00	1.25
373	Herb Plews	4.00	2.00	1.25
374	Art Ditmar	4.00	2.00	1.25
375	Bob Nieman	4.00	2.00	1.25
376	Hal Naragon	4.00	2.00	1.25
377	Johnny Antonelli	4.00	2.00	1.25
378	Gail Harris	4.00	2.00	1.25
379	Bob Miller	4.00	2.00	1.25
380	Hank Aaron	125.00	62.00	37.00
381	Mike Baxes	4.00	2.00	1.25
382	Curt Simmons	4.00	2.00	1.25
383	Words of Wisdom (Don Larsen, Casey Stengel)	9.00	4.50	2.75
384	Dave Sisler	4.00	2.00	1.25
385	Sherm Lollar	4.00	2.00	1.25

		NR MT	EX	VG
386	Jim Delsing	4.00	2.00	1.25
387	Don Drysdale	35.00	17.50	10.50
388	Bob Will	4.00	2.00	1.25
389	Joe Nuxhall	4.00	2.00	1.25
390	Orlando Cepeda	18.00	9.00	5.50
391	Milt Pappas	4.00	2.00	1.25
392	Whitey Herzog	6.00	3.00	1.75
393	Frank Lary	4.00	2.00	1.25
394	Randy Jackson	4.00	2.00	1.25
395	Elston Howard	7.00	3.50	2.00
396	Bob Rush	4.00	2.00	1.25
397	Senators Team/Checklist 430-495	12.00	6.00	3.50
398	Wally Post	4.00	2.00	1.25
399	Larry Jackson	4.00	2.00	1.25
400	Jackie Jensen	4.00	2.00	1.25
401	Ron Blackburn	4.00	2.00	1.25
402	Hector Lopez	4.00	2.00	1.25
403	Clem Labine	4.00	2.00	1.25
404	Hank Sauer	4.00	2.00	1.25
405	Roy McMillan	4.00	2.00	1.25
406	Solly Drake	4.00	2.00	1.25
407	Moe Drabowsky	4.00	2.00	1.25
408	Keystone Combo (Luis Aparicio, Nellie Fox)	12.00	6.00	3.50
409	Gus Zernial	4.00	2.00	1.25
410	Billy Pierce	4.00	2.00	1.25
411	Whitey Lockman	4.00	2.00	1.25
412	Stan Lopata	4.00	2.00	1.25
413	Camillo (Camilo) Pascual	4.00	2.00	1.25
414	Dale Long	4.00	2.00	1.25
415	Bill Mazeroski	5.00	2.50	1.50
416	Haywood Sullivan	4.00	2.00	1.25
417	Virgil Trucks	4.00	2.00	1.25
418	Gino Cimoli	4.00	2.00	1.25
419	Braves Team/Checklist 353-429	12.50	6.25	3.75
420	Rocco Colavito	25.00	12.50	7.50
421	Herm Wehmeier	4.00	2.00	1.25
422	Hobie Landrith	4.00	2.00	1.25
423	Bob Grim	4.00	2.00	1.25
424	Ken Aspromonte	4.00	2.00	1.25
425	Del Crandall	4.00	2.00	1.25
426	Jerry Staley	4.00	2.00	1.25
427	Charlie Neal	4.00	2.00	1.25
428	Buc Hill Aces (Roy Face, Bob Friend, Ron Kline, Vern Law)	5.00	2.50	1.50
429	Bobby Thomson	4.00	2.00	1.25
430	Whitey Ford	35.00	17.50	10.50
431	Whammy Douglas	4.00	2.00	1.25
432	Smoky Burgess	4.00	2.00	1.25
433	Billy Harrell	4.00	2.00	1.25
434	Hal Griggs	4.00	2.00	1.25
435	Frank Robinson	50.00	25.00	15.00
436	Granny Hamner	4.00	2.00	1.25
437	Ike Delock	4.00	2.00	1.25
438	Sam Esposito	4.00	2.00	1.25
439	Brooks Robinson	50.00	25.00	15.00
440	Lou Burdette	6.00	3.00	1.75
441	John Roseboro	4.00	2.00	1.25
442	Ray Narleski	4.00	2.00	1.25
443	Daryl Spencer	4.00	2.00	1.25
444	*Ronnie Hansen*	5.00	2.50	1.50
445	Cal McLish	4.00	2.00	1.25
446	Rocky Nelson	4.00	2.00	1.25
447	Bob Anderson	4.00	2.00	1.25
448	Vada Pinson	6.00	3.00	1.75
449	Tom Gorman	4.00	2.00	1.25
450	Eddie Mathews	30.00	15.00	9.00
451	Jimmy Constable	4.00	2.00	1.25
452	Chico Fernandez	4.00	2.00	1.25
453	Les Moss	4.00	2.00	1.25
454	Phil Clark	4.00	2.00	1.25
455	Larry Doby	4.00	2.00	1.25
456	Jerry Casale	4.00	2.00	1.25
457	Dodgers Team	20.00	10.00	6.00
458	Gordon Jones	4.00	2.00	1.25
459	Bill Tuttle	4.00	2.00	1.25
460	Bob Friend	4.00	2.00	1.25
461	Mantle Hits 42nd Homer For Crown	40.00	20.00	12.00
462	Colavito's Great Catch Saves Game	10.00	5.00	3.00
463	Kaline Becomes Youngest Batting Champ	12.00	6.00	3.50
464	Mays' Catch Makes Series History	25.00	12.50	7.50
465	Sievers Sets Homer Mark	5.00	2.50	1.50
466	Pierce All-Star Starter	5.00	2.50	1.50
467	Aaron Clubs World Series Homer	20.00	10.00	6.00
468	Snider's Play Brings L.A. Victory	12.50	6.25	3.75

		NR MT	EX	VG
469	Hustler Banks Wins M.V.P. Award	10.00	5.00	3.00
470	Musial Raps Out 3,000th Hit	18.00	9.00	5.50
471	Tom Sturdivant	5.00	2.50	1.50
472	Gene Freese	4.00	2.00	1.25
473	Mike Fornieles	4.00	2.00	1.25
474	Moe Thacker	4.00	2.00	1.25
475	Jack Harshman	4.00	2.00	1.25
476	Indians Team/Checklist 496-572	12.00	6.00	3.50
477	Barry Latman	4.00	2.00	1.25
478	Roberto Clemente	115.00	57.00	34.00
479	Lindy McDaniel	4.00	2.00	1.25
480	Red Schoendienst	15.00	7.50	4.50
481	Charley Maxwell	4.00	2.00	1.25
482	Russ Meyer	4.00	2.00	1.25
483	Clint Courtney	4.00	2.00	1.25
484	Willie Kirkland	4.00	2.00	1.25
485	Ryne Duren	6.00	3.00	1.75
486	Sammy White	4.00	2.00	1.25
487	Hal Brown	4.00	2.00	1.25
488	Walt Moryn	4.00	2.00	1.25
489	John C. Powers	4.00	2.00	1.25
490	Frank J. Thomas	4.00	2.00	1.25
491	Don Blasingame	4.00	2.00	1.25
492	Gene Conley	4.00	2.00	1.25
493	Jim Landis	4.00	2.00	1.25
494	Don Pavletich	4.00	2.00	1.25
495	Johnny Podres	6.00	3.00	1.75
496	Wayne Terwilliger	4.00	2.00	1.25
497	Hal R. Smith	4.00	2.00	1.25
498	Dick Hyde	4.00	2.00	1.25
499	Johnny O'Brien	4.00	2.00	1.25
500	Vic Wertz	4.00	2.00	1.25
501	Bobby Tiefenauer	4.00	2.00	1.25
502	Al Dark	4.00	2.00	1.25
503	Jim Owens	4.00	2.00	1.25
504	Ossie Alvarez	4.00	2.00	1.25
505	Tony Kubek	8.00	4.00	2.50
506	Bob Purkey	4.00	2.00	1.25
507	Bob Hale	15.00	7.50	4.50
508	Art Fowler	15.00	7.50	4.50
509	*Norm Cash*	60.00	30.00	18.00
510	Yankees Team	70.00	35.00	21.00
511	George Susce	15.00	7.50	4.50
512	George Altman	15.00	7.50	4.50
513	Tom Carroll	15.00	7.50	4.50
514	*Bob Gibson*	420.00	210.00	126.00
515	Harmon Killebrew	160.00	80.00	48.00
516	Mike Garcia	15.00	7.50	4.50
517	Joe Koppe	15.00	7.50	4.50
518	*Mike Cueller*	15.00	7.50	4.50
519	Infield Power (Dick Gernert, Frank Malzone, Pete Runnels)	18.00	9.00	5.50
520	Don Elston	15.00	7.50	4.50
521	Gary Geiger	15.00	7.50	4.50
522	Gene Snyder	15.00	7.50	4.50
523	Harry Bright	15.00	7.50	4.50
524	Larry Osborne	15.00	7.50	4.50
525	Jim Coates	16.00	8.00	4.75
526	Bob Speake	15.00	7.50	4.50
527	Solly Hemus	15.00	7.50	4.50
528	Pirates Team	45.00	22.00	13.50
529	*George Bamberger*	16.00	8.00	4.75
530	Wally Moon	16.00	8.00	4.75
531	Ray Webster	15.00	7.50	4.50
532	Mark Freeman	15.00	7.50	4.50
533	Darrell Johnson	16.00	8.00	4.75
534	Faye Throneberry	15.00	7.50	4.50
535	Ruben Gomez	15.00	7.50	4.50
536	Dan Kravitz	15.00	7.50	4.50
537	Rodolfo Arias	15.00	7.50	4.50
538	Chick King	15.00	7.50	4.50
539	Gary Blaylock	15.00	7.50	4.50
540	Willy Miranda	15.00	7.50	4.50
541	Bob Thurman	15.00	7.50	4.50
542	*Jim Perry*	20.00	10.00	6.00
543	Corsair Outfield Trio (Roberto Clemente, Bob Skinner, Bill Virdon)	50.00	25.00	15.00
544	Lee Tate	15.00	7.50	4.50
545	Tom Morgan	15.00	7.50	4.50
546	Al Schroll	15.00	7.50	4.50
547	Jim Baxes	15.00	7.50	4.50
548	Elmer Singleton	15.00	7.50	4.50
549	Howie Nunn	15.00	7.50	4.50
550	Roy Campanella	150.00	75.00	45.00
551	Fred Haney (All-Star)	20.00	10.00	6.00
552	Casey Stengel (All-Star)	30.00	15.00	9.00
553	Orlando Cepeda (All-Star)	24.00	12.00	7.25
554	Bill Skowron (All-Star)	20.00	10.00	6.00
555	Bill Mazeroski (All-Star)	24.00	12.00	7.25
556	Nellie Fox (All-Star)	20.00	10.00	6.00
557	Ken Boyer (All-Star)	20.00	10.00	6.00
558	Frank Malzone (All-Star)	18.00	9.00	5.50
559	Ernie Banks (All-Star)	50.00	25.00	15.00
560	Luis Aparicio (All-Star)	20.00	10.00	6.00
561	Hank Aaron (All-Star)	125.00	62.00	37.00
562	Al Kaline (All-Star)	50.00	25.00	15.00
563	Willie Mays (All-Star)	135.00	67.00	40.00
564	Mickey Mantle (All-Star)	300.00	150.00	90.00
565	Wes Covington (All-Star)	18.00	9.00	5.50
566	Roy Sievers (All-Star)	18.00	9.00	5.50
567	Del Crandall (All-Star)	18.00	9.00	5.50
568	Gus Triandos (All-Star)	18.00	9.00	5.50
569	Bob Friend (All-Star)	18.00	9.00	5.50
570	Bob Turley (All-Star)	18.00	9.00	5.50
571	Warren Spahn (All-Star)	30.00	15.00	9.00
572	Billy Pierce (All-Star)	25.00	12.50	7.50
---	Elect Your Favorite Rookie Insert (paper stock, September 29 date on back)	15.00	7.50	4.50
---	Felt Pennants Insert (paper stock)	15.00	7.50	4.50

1960 Topps

In 1960, Topps returned to a horizontal format (3-1/2" by 2-1/2") with a color portrait and a black and white "action" photograph on the front. The backs returned to the use of just the previous year and lifetime statistics along with a cartoon and short career summary or previous season highlights. Specialty cards in the 572-card set are multi-player cards, managers and coaches cards, and highlights of the 1959 World Series. Two groups of rookie cards are included. The first are numbers 117-148, which are the Sport Magazine rookies. The second group is called "Topps All-Star Rookies." Finally, there is a continuation of the All-Star cards to close out the set in the scarcer high numbers. Card #'s 375-440 can be found with backs printed on either white or grey cardboard, with the white stock being the less common.

	NR MT	EX	VG
Complete Set (572):	4250.00	2125.00	1275.
Common Player: 1-286	3.50	1.75	1.00
Common Player: 287-440	4.00	2.00	1.25
Common Player: 441-506	5.50	2.75	1.75
Common Player: 507-572	12.00	6.00	3.50

		NR MT	EX	VG
1	Early Wynn	35.00	17.50	10.50
2	Roman Mejias	3.50	1.75	1.00
3	Joe Adcock	3.50	1.75	1.00
4	Bob Purkey	3.50	1.75	1.00
5	Wally Moon	3.50	1.75	1.00
6	Lou Berberet	3.50	1.75	1.00
7	Master and Mentor (Willie Mays, Bill Rigney)	15.00	7.50	4.50
8	Bud Daley	3.50	1.75	1.00
9	Faye Throneberry	3.50	1.75	1.00
10	Ernie Banks	50.00	25.00	15.00
11	Norm Siebern	3.50	1.75	1.00
12	Milt Pappas	3.50	1.75	1.00
13	Wally Post	3.50	1.75	1.00
14	Jim Grant	3.50	1.75	1.00
15	Pete Runnels	3.50	1.75	1.00
16	Ernie Broglio	3.50	1.75	1.00

		NR MT	EX	VG
17	Johnny Callison	3.50	1.75	1.00
18	Dodgers Team/ Checklist 1-88	15.00	7.50	4.50
19	Felix Mantilla	3.50	1.75	1.00
20	Roy Face	3.50	1.75	1.00
21	Dutch Dotterer	3.50	1.75	1.00
22	Rocky Bridges	3.50	1.75	1.00
23	Eddie Fisher	3.50	1.75	1.00
24	Dick Gray	3.50	1.75	1.00
25	Roy Sievers	3.50	1.75	1.00
26	Wayne Terwilliger	3.50	1.75	1.00
27	Dick Drott	3.50	1.75	1.00
28	Brooks Robinson	45.00	22.00	13.50
29	Clem Labine	3.50	1.75	1.00
30	Tito Francona	3.50	1.75	1.00
31	Sammy Esposito	3.50	1.75	1.00
32	Sophomore Stalwarts (Jim O'Toole, Vada Pinson)	6.00	3.00	1.75
33	Tom Morgan	3.50	1.75	1.00
34	George (Sparky) Anderson	15.00	7.50	4.50
35	Whitey Ford	40.00	20.00	12.00
36	Russ Nixon	3.50	1.75	1.00
37	Bill Bruton	3.50	1.75	1.00
38	Jerry Casale	3.50	1.75	1.00
39	Earl Averill	3.50	1.75	1.00
40	Joe Cunningham	3.50	1.75	1.00
41	Barry Latman	3.50	1.75	1.00
42	Hobie Landrith	3.50	1.75	1.00
43	Senators Team/Checklist 1-88	10.00	5.00	3.00
44	Bobby Locke	3.50	1.75	1.00
45	Roy McMillan	3.50	1.75	1.00
46	Jack Fisher	3.50	1.75	1.00
47	Don Zimmer	3.50	1.75	1.00
48	Hal Smith	3.50	1.75	1.00
49	Curt Raydon	3.50	1.75	1.00
50	Al Kaline	50.00	25.00	15.00
51	Jim Coates	3.50	1.75	1.00
52	Dave Philley	3.50	1.75	1.00
53	Jackie Brandt	3.50	1.75	1.00
54	Mike Fornieles	3.50	1.75	1.00
55	Bill Mazeroski	5.00	2.50	1.50
56	Steve Korcheck	3.50	1.75	1.00
57	Win - Savers (Turk Lown, Gerry Staley)	4.50	2.25	1.25
58	Gino Cimoli	3.50	1.75	1.00
59	Juan Pizarro	3.50	1.75	1.00
60	Gus Triandos	3.50	1.75	1.00
61	Eddie Kasko	3.50	1.75	1.00
62	Roger Craig	3.50	1.75	1.00
63	George Strickland	3.50	1.75	1.00
64	Jack Meyer	3.50	1.75	1.00
65	Elston Howard	6.00	3.00	1.75
66	Bob Trowbridge	3.50	1.75	1.00
67	*Jose Pagan*	3.50	1.75	1.00
68	Dave Hillman	3.50	1.75	1.00
69	Billy Goodman	3.50	1.75	1.00
70	Lou Burdette	3.50	1.75	1.00
71	Marty Keough	3.50	1.75	1.00
72	Tigers Team/Checklist 89-176	12.00	6.00	3.50
73	Bob Gibson	60.00	30.00	18.00
74	Walt Moryn	3.50	1.75	1.00
75	Vic Power	3.50	1.75	1.00
76	Bill Fischer	3.50	1.75	1.00
77	Hank Foiles	3.50	1.75	1.00
78	Bob Grim	3.50	1.75	1.00
79	Walt Dropo	3.50	1.75	1.00
80	Johnny Antonelli	3.50	1.75	1.00
81	Russ Snyder	3.50	1.75	1.00
82	Ruben Gomez	3.50	1.75	1.00
83	Tony Kubek	4.50	2.25	1.25
84	Hal Smith	3.50	1.75	1.00
85	Frank Lary	3.50	1.75	1.00
86	Dick Gernert	3.50	1.75	1.00
87	John Romonosky	3.50	1.75	1.00
88	John Roseboro	3.50	1.75	1.00
89	Hal Brown	3.50	1.75	1.00
90	Bobby Avila	3.50	1.75	1.00
91	Bennie Daniels	3.50	1.75	1.00
92	Whitey Herzog	4.50	2.25	1.25
93	Art Schult	3.50	1.75	1.00
94	Leo Kiely	3.50	1.75	1.00
95	Frank J. Thomas	3.50	1.75	1.00
96	Ralph Terry	3.50	1.75	1.00
97	Ted Lepcio	3.50	1.75	1.00
98	Gordon Jones	3.50	1.75	1.00
99	Lenny Green	3.50	1.75	1.00
100	Nellie Fox	7.00	3.50	2.00
101	Bob Miller	3.50	1.75	1.00
102	Kent Hadley	3.50	1.75	1.00
103	Dick Farrell	3.50	1.75	1.00
104	Dick Schofield	3.50	1.75	1.00
105	Larry Sherry	3.50	1.75	1.00
106	Billy Gardner	3.50	1.75	1.00
107	Carl Willey	3.50	1.75	1.00
108	Pete Daley	3.50	1.75	1.00
109	Cletis Boyer	3.50	1.75	1.00
110	Cal McLish	3.50	1.75	1.00
111	Vic Wertz	3.50	1.75	1.00
112	Jack Harshman	3.50	1.75	1.00
113	Bob Skinner	3.50	1.75	1.00
114	Ken Aspromonte	3.50	1.75	1.00
115	Fork and Knuckler (Roy Face, Hoyt Wilhelm)	6.00	3.00	1.75
116	Jim Rivera	3.50	1.75	1.00
117	Tom Borland	3.50	1.75	1.00
118	Bob Bruce	3.50	1.75	1.00
119	*Chico Cardenas*	3.50	1.75	1.00
120	Duke Carmel	3.50	1.75	1.00
121	Camilo Carreon	3.50	1.75	1.00
122	Don Dillard	3.50	1.75	1.00
123	Dan Dobbek	3.50	1.75	1.00
124	Jim Donohue	3.50	1.75	1.00
125	*Dick Ellsworth*	3.50	1.75	1.00
126	*Chuck Estrada*	3.50	1.75	1.00
127	Ronnie Hansen	3.50	1.75	1.00
128	Bill Harris	3.50	1.75	1.00
129	Bob Hartman	3.50	1.75	1.00
130	Frank Herrera	3.50	1.75	1.00
131	Ed Hobaugh	3.50	1.75	1.00
132	*Frank Howard*	18.00	9.00	5.50
133	*Manuel Javier*	3.50	1.75	1.00
134	Deron Johnson	5.00	2.50	1.50
135	Ken Johnson	3.50	1.75	1.00
136	*Jim Kaat*	35.00	17.50	10.50
137	Lou Klimchock	3.50	1.75	1.00
138	*Art Mahaffey*	3.50	1.75	1.00
139	Carl Mathias	3.50	1.75	1.00
140	Julio Navarro	3.50	1.75	1.00
141	Jim Proctor	3.50	1.75	1.00
142	Bill Short	5.00	2.50	1.50
143	Al Spangler	3.50	1.75	1.00
144	Al Stieglitz	3.50	1.75	1.00
145	Jim Umbricht	3.50	1.75	1.00
146	Ted Wieand	3.50	1.75	1.00
147	Bob Will	3.50	1.75	1.00
148	*Carl Yastrzemski*	250.00	125.00	75.00
149	Bob Nieman	3.50	1.75	1.00
150	Billy Pierce	3.50	1.75	1.00
151	Giants Team/Checklist 177-264	9.00	4.50	2.75
152	Gail Harris	3.50	1.75	1.00
153	Bobby Thomson	3.50	1.75	1.00
154	Jim Davenport	3.50	1.75	1.00
155	Charlie Neal	3.50	1.75	1.00
156	Art Ceccarelli	3.50	1.75	1.00
157	Rocky Nelson	3.50	1.75	1.00
158	Wes Covington	3.50	1.75	1.00
159	Jim Piersall	3.50	1.75	1.00
160	Rival All-Stars (Ken Boyer, Mickey Mantle)	52.50	26.00	15.50
161	Ray Narleski	3.50	1.75	1.00
162	Sammy Taylor	3.50	1.75	1.00
163	Hector Lopez	3.50	1.75	1.00
164	Reds Team/Checklist 89-176	9.00	4.50	2.75
165	Jack Sanford	3.50	1.75	1.00
166	Chuck Essegian	3.50	1.75	1.00
167	Valmy Thomas	3.50	1.75	1.00
168	Alex Grammas	3.50	1.75	1.00
169	Jake Striker	3.50	1.75	1.00
170	Del Crandall	3.50	1.75	1.00
171	Johnny Groth	3.50	1.75	1.00
172	Willie Kirkland	3.50	1.75	1.00
173	Billy Martin	10.00	5.00	3.00
174	Indians Team/Checklist 89-176	9.00	4.50	2.75
175	Pedro Ramos	3.50	1.75	1.00
176	Vada Pinson	3.50	1.75	1.00
177	Johnny Kucks	3.50	1.75	1.00
178	Woody Held	3.50	1.75	1.00
179	Rip Coleman	3.50	1.75	1.00
180	Harry Simpson	3.50	1.75	1.00
181	Billy Loes	3.50	1.75	1.00
182	Glen Hobbie	3.50	1.75	1.00
183	Eli Grba	3.50	1.75	1.00
184	Gary Geiger	3.50	1.75	1.00
185	Jim Owens	3.50	1.75	1.00
186	Dave Sisler	3.50	1.75	1.00
187	Jay Hook	3.50	1.75	1.00
188	Dick Williams	3.50	1.75	1.00
189	Don McMahon	3.50	1.75	1.00
190	Gene Woodling	3.50	1.75	1.00
191	Johnny Klippstein	3.50	1.75	1.00
192	Danny O'Connell	3.50	1.75	1.00
193	Dick Hyde	3.50	1.75	1.00
194	Bobby Gene Smith	3.50	1.75	1.00

		NR MT	EX	VG
195	Lindy McDaniel	3.50	1.75	1.00
196	Andy Carey	3.50	1.75	1.00
197	Ron Kline	3.50	1.75	1.00
198	Jerry Lynch	3.50	1.75	1.00
199	Dick Donovan	3.50	1.75	1.00
200	Willie Mays	125.00	62.00	37.00
201	Larry Osborne	3.50	1.75	1.00
202	Fred Kipp	3.50	1.75	1.00
203	Sammy White	3.50	1.75	1.00
204	Ryne Duren	4.50	2.25	1.25
205	Johnny Logan	3.50	1.75	1.00
206	Claude Osteen	3.50	1.75	1.00
207	Bob Boyd	3.50	1.75	1.00
208	White Sox Team/Checklist 177-264	9.00	4.50	2.75
209	Ron Blackburn	3.50	1.75	1.00
210	Harmon Killebrew	25.00	12.50	7.50
211	Taylor Phillips	3.50	1.75	1.00
212	Walt Alston	9.00	4.50	2.75
213	Chuck Dressen	3.50	1.75	1.00
214	Jimmie Dykes	3.50	1.75	1.00
215	Bob Elliott	3.50	1.75	1.00
216	Joe Gordon	3.50	1.75	1.00
217	Charley Grimm	3.50	1.75	1.00
218	Solly Hemus	3.50	1.75	1.00
219	Fred Hutchinson	3.50	1.75	1.00
220	Billy Jurges	3.50	1.75	1.00
221	Cookie Lavagetto	3.50	1.75	1.00
222	Al Lopez	5.50	2.75	1.75
223	Danny Murtaugh	3.50	1.75	1.00
224	Paul Richards	3.50	1.75	1.00
225	Bill Rigney	3.50	1.75	1.00
226	Eddie Sawyer	3.50	1.75	1.00
227	Casey Stengel	15.00	7.50	4.50
228	Ernie Johnson	3.50	1.75	1.00
229	Joe M. Morgan	3.50	1.75	1.00
230	Mound Magicians (Bob Buhl, Lou Burdette, Warren Spahn)	9.00	4.50	2.75
231	Hal Naragon	3.50	1.75	1.00
232	Jim Busby	3.50	1.75	1.00
233	Don Elston	3.50	1.75	1.00
234	Don Demeter	3.50	1.75	1.00
235	Gus Bell	3.50	1.75	1.00
236	Dick Ricketts	3.50	1.75	1.00
237	Elmer Valo	3.50	1.75	1.00
238	Danny Kravitz	3.50	1.75	1.00
239	Joe Shipley	3.50	1.75	1.00
240	Luis Aparicio	12.00	6.00	3.50
241	Albie Pearson	3.50	1.75	1.00
242	Cards Team/Checklist 265-352	9.00	4.50	2.75
243	Bubba Phillips	3.50	1.75	1.00
244	Hal Griggs	3.50	1.75	1.00
245	Eddie Yost	3.50	1.75	1.00
246	Lee Maye	3.50	1.75	1.00
247	Gil McDougald	5.00	2.50	1.50
248	Del Rice	3.50	1.75	1.00
249	*Earl Wilson*	3.50	1.75	1.00
250	Stan Musial	110.00	55.00	33.00
251	Bobby Malkmus	3.50	1.75	1.00
252	Ray Herbert	3.50	1.75	1.00
253	Eddie Bressoud	3.50	1.75	1.00
254	Arnie Portocarrero	3.50	1.75	1.00
255	Jim Gilliam	5.00	2.50	1.50
256	Dick Brown	3.50	1.75	1.00
257	Gordy Coleman	3.50	1.75	1.00
258	Dick Groat	4.50	2.25	1.25
259	George Altman	3.50	1.75	1.00
260	Power Plus (Rocky Colavito, Tito Francona)	6.00	3.00	1.75
261	Pete Burnside	3.50	1.75	1.00
262	Hank Bauer	3.50	1.75	1.00
263	Darrell Johnson	3.50	1.75	1.00
264	Robin Roberts	12.00	6.00	3.50
265	Rip Repulski	3.50	1.75	1.00
266	Joe Jay	3.50	1.75	1.00
267	Jim Marshall	3.50	1.75	1.00
268	Al Worthington	3.50	1.75	1.00
269	Gene Green	3.50	1.75	1.00
270	Bob Turley	4.50	2.25	1.25
271	Julio Becquer	3.50	1.75	1.00
272	Fred Green	3.50	1.75	1.00
273	Neil Chrisley	3.50	1.75	1.00
274	Tom Acker	3.50	1.75	1.00
275	Curt Flood	3.50	1.75	1.00
276	Ken McBride	3.50	1.75	1.00
277	Harry Bright	3.50	1.75	1.00
278	Stan Williams	3.50	1.75	1.00
279	Chuck Tanner	3.50	1.75	1.00
280	Frank Sullivan	3.50	1.75	1.00
281	Ray Boone	3.50	1.75	1.00
282	Joe Nuxhall	3.50	1.75	1.00

		NR MT	EX	VG
283	John Blanchard	4.50	2.25	1.25
284	Don Gross	3.50	1.75	1.00
285	Harry Anderson	3.50	1.75	1.00
286	Ray Semproch	3.50	1.75	1.00
287	Felipe Alou	6.00	3.00	1.75
288	Bob Mabe	4.00	2.00	1.25
289	Willie Jones	4.00	2.00	1.25
290	Jerry Lumpe	4.00	2.00	1.25
291	Bob Keegan	4.00	2.00	1.25
292	Dodger Backstops (Joe Pignatano, John Roseboro)	6.00	3.00	1.75
293	Gene Conley	4.00	2.00	1.25
294	Tony Taylor	4.00	2.00	1.25
295	Gil Hodges	18.00	9.00	5.50
296	Nelson Chittum	4.00	2.00	1.25
297	Reno Bertoia	4.00	2.00	1.25
298	George Witt	4.00	2.00	1.25
299	Earl Torgeson	4.00	2.00	1.25
300	Hank Aaron	125.00	62.00	37.00
301	Jerry Davie	4.00	2.00	1.25
302	Phillies Team/Checklist 353-429	10.00	5.00	3.00
303	Billy O'Dell	4.00	2.00	1.25
304	Joe Ginsberg	4.00	2.00	1.25
305	Richie Ashburn	10.00	5.00	3.00
306	Frank Baumann	4.00	2.00	1.25
307	Gene Oliver	4.00	2.00	1.25
308	Dick Hall	4.00	2.00	1.25
309	Bob Hale	4.00	2.00	1.25
310	Frank Malzone	4.00	2.00	1.25
311	Raul Sanchez	4.00	2.00	1.25
312	Charlie Lau	4.50	2.25	1.25
313	Turk Lown	4.00	2.00	1.25
314	Chico Fernandez	4.00	2.00	1.25
315	Bobby Shantz	5.00	2.50	1.50
316	*Willie McCovey*	210.00	105.00	63.00
317	Pumpsie Green	4.00	2.00	1.25
318	Jim Baxes	4.00	2.00	1.25
319	Joe Koppe	4.00	2.00	1.25
320	Bob Allison	4.00	2.00	1.25
321	Ron Fairly	4.00	2.00	1.25
322	Willie Tasby	4.00	2.00	1.25
323	Johnny Romano	4.00	2.00	1.25
324	Jim Perry	4.00	2.00	1.25
325	Jim O'Toole	4.00	2.00	1.25
326	Roberto Clemente	125.00	62.00	37.00
327	*Ray Sadecki*	4.00	2.00	1.25
328	Earl Battey	4.00	2.00	1.25
329	Zack Monroe	4.00	2.00	1.25
330	Harvey Kuenn	4.50	2.25	1.25
331	Henry Mason	4.00	2.00	1.25
332	Yankees Team/ Checklist 265-352	25.00	12.50	7.50
333	Danny McDevitt	4.00	2.00	1.25
334	Ted Abernathy	4.00	2.00	1.25
335	Red Schoendienst	12.50	6.25	3.75
336	Ike Delock	4.00	2.00	1.25
337	Cal Neeman	4.00	2.00	1.25
338	Ray Monzant	4.00	2.00	1.25
339	Harry Chiti	4.00	2.00	1.25
340	Harvey Haddix	4.00	2.00	1.25
341	Carroll Hardy	4.00	2.00	1.25
342	Casey Wise	4.00	2.00	1.25
343	Sandy Koufax	125.00	62.00	37.00
344	Clint Courtney	4.00	2.00	1.25
345	Don Newcombe	4.00	2.00	1.25
346	J.C. Martin (photo actually Gary Peters)	4.00	2.00	1.25
347	Ed Bouchee	4.00	2.00	1.25
348	Barry Shetrone	4.00	2.00	1.25
349	Moe Drabowsky	4.00	2.00	1.25
350	Mickey Mantle	400.00	200.00	120.00
351	Don Nottebart	4.00	2.00	1.25
352	Cincy Clouters (Gus Bell, Jerry Lynch, Frank Robinson)	9.00	4.50	2.75
353	Don Larsen	4.50	2.25	1.25
354	Bob Lillis	4.00	2.00	1.25
355	Bill White	4.50	2.25	1.25
356	Joe Amalfitano	4.00	2.00	1.25
357	Al Schroll	4.00	2.00	1.25
358	Joe DeMaestri	4.00	2.00	1.25
359	Buddy Gilbert	4.00	2.00	1.25
360	Herb Score	4.00	2.00	1.25
361	Bob Oldis	4.00	2.00	1.25
362	Russ Kemmerer	4.00	2.00	1.25
363	Gene Stephens	4.00	2.00	1.25
364	Paul Foytack	4.00	2.00	1.25
365	Minnie Minoso	4.50	2.25	1.25
366	*Dallas Green*	4.50	2.25	1.25
367	Bill Tuttle	4.00	2.00	1.25
368	Daryl Spencer	4.00	2.00	1.25

		NR MT	EX	VG
369	Billy Hoeft	4.00	2.00	1.25
370	Bill Skowron	6.00	3.00	1.75
371	Bud Byerly	4.00	2.00	1.25
372	Frank House	4.00	2.00	1.25
373	Don Hoak	4.00	2.00	1.25
374	Bob Buhl	4.00	2.00	1.25
375	Dale Long	4.00	2.00	1.25
376	Johnny Briggs	4.00	2.00	1.25
377	Roger Maris	120.00	60.00	36.00
378	Stu Miller	4.00	2.00	1.25
379	Red Wilson	4.00	2.00	1.25
380	Bob Shaw	4.00	2.00	1.25
381	Braves Team/Checklist 353-429	10.00	5.00	3.00
382	Ted Bowsfield	4.00	2.00	1.25
383	Leon Wagner	4.00	2.00	1.25
384	Don Cardwell	4.00	2.00	1.25
385	World Series Game 1 (Neal Steals Second)	6.00	3.00	1.75
386	World Series Game 2 (Neal Belts 2nd Homer)	6.00	3.00	1.75
387	World Series Game 3 (Furillo Breaks Up Game)	8.00	4.00	2.50
388	World Series Game 4 (Hodges' Winning Homer)	8.00	4.00	2.50
389	World Series Game 5 (Luis Swipes Base)	8.00	4.00	2.50
390	World Series Game 6 (Scrambling After Ball)	6.00	3.00	1.75
391	World Series Summary (The Champs Celebrate)	7.00	3.50	2.00
392	Tex Clevenger	4.00	2.00	1.25
393	Smoky Burgess	4.00	2.00	1.25
394	Norm Larker	4.00	2.00	1.25
395	Hoyt Wilhelm	15.00	7.50	4.50
396	Steve Bilko	4.00	2.00	1.25
397	Don Blasingame	4.00	2.00	1.25
398	Mike Cuellar	4.00	2.00	1.25
399	Young Hill Stars (Jack Fisher, Milt Pappas, Jerry Walker)	5.00	2.50	1.50
400	Rocky Colavito	15.00	7.50	4.50
401	Bob Duliba	4.00	2.00	1.25
402	Dick Stuart	4.50	2.25	1.25
403	Ed Sadowski	4.00	2.00	1.25
404	Bob Rush	4.00	2.00	1.25
405	Bobby Richardson	6.00	3.00	1.75
406	Billy Klaus	4.00	2.00	1.25
407	*Gary Peters* (photo actually J.C. Martin)	4.00	2.00	1.25
408	Carl Furillo	7.50	3.75	2.25
409	Ron Samford	4.00	2.00	1.25
410	Sam Jones	4.00	2.00	1.25
411	Ed Bailey	4.00	2.00	1.25
412	Bob Anderson	4.00	2.00	1.25
413	A's Team/Checklist 430-495	10.00	5.00	3.00
414	Don Williams	4.00	2.00	1.25
415	Bob Cerv	4.00	2.00	1.25
416	Humberto Robinson	4.00	2.00	1.25
417	Chuck Cottier	4.00	2.00	1.25
418	Don Mossi	4.00	2.00	1.25
419	George Crowe	4.00	2.00	1.25
420	Eddie Mathews	35.00	17.50	10.50
421	Duke Maas	4.00	2.00	1.25
422	Johnny Powers	4.00	2.00	1.25
423	Ed Fitz Gerald	4.00	2.00	1.25
424	Pete Whisenant	4.00	2.00	1.25
425	Johnny Podres	4.50	2.25	1.25
426	Ron Jackson	4.00	2.00	1.25
427	Al Grunwald	4.00	2.00	1.25
428	Al Smith	4.00	2.00	1.25
429	American League Kings (Nellie Fox, Harvey Kuenn)	6.00	3.00	1.75
430	Art Ditmar	4.00	2.00	1.25
431	Andre Rodgers	4.00	2.00	1.25
432	Chuck Stobbs	4.00	2.00	1.25
433	Irv Noren	4.00	2.00	1.25
434	Brooks Lawrence	4.00	2.00	1.25
435	Gene Freese	4.00	2.00	1.25
436	Marv Throneberry	4.00	2.00	1.25
437	Bob Friend	4.00	2.00	1.25
438	Jim Coker	4.00	2.00	1.25
439	Tom Brewer	4.00	2.00	1.25
440	Jim Lemon	4.00	2.00	1.25
441	Gary Bell	5.50	2.75	1.75
442	Joe Pignatano	5.50	2.75	1.75
443	Charlie Maxwell	5.50	2.75	1.75
444	Jerry Kindall	5.50	2.75	1.75
445	Warren Spahn	50.00	25.00	15.00
446	Ellis Burton	5.50	2.75	1.75
447	Ray Moore	5.50	2.75	1.75
448	*Jim Gentile*	5.50	2.75	1.75

		NR MT	EX	VG
449	Jim Brosnan	5.50	2.75	1.75
450	Orlando Cepeda	15.00	7.50	4.50
451	Curt Simmons	5.50	2.75	1.75
452	Ray Webster	5.50	2.75	1.75
453	Vern Law	5.50	2.75	1.75
454	Hal Woodeshick	5.50	2.75	1.75
455	Orioles Coaches (Harry Brecheen, Lum Harris, Eddie Robinson)	5.50	2.75	1.75
456	Red Sox Coaches (Del Baker, Billy Herman, Sal Maglie, Rudy York)	6.50	3.25	2.00
457	Cubs Coaches (Lou Klein, Charlie Root, Elvin Tappe)	5.50	2.75	1.75
458	White Sox Coaches (Ray Berres, Johnny Cooney, Tony Cuccinello, Don Gutteridge)	5.50	2.75	1.75
459	Reds Coaches (Cot Deal, Wally Moses, Reggie Otero)	5.50	2.75	1.75
460	Indians Coaches (Mel Harder, Red Kress, Bob Lemon, Jo-Jo White)	6.50	3.25	2.00
461	Tigers Coaches (Luke Appling, Tom Ferrick, Billy Hitchcock)	6.50	3.25	2.00
462	A's Coaches (Walker Cooper, Fred Fitzsimmons, Don Heffner)	5.50	2.75	1.75
463	Dodgers Coaches (Joe Becker, Bobby Bragan, Greg Mulleavy, Pete Reiser)	5.50	2.75	1.75
464	Braves Coaches (George Myatt, Andy Pafko, Bob Scheffing, Whitlow Wyatt)	5.50	2.75	1.75
465	Yankees Coaches (Frank Crosetti, Bill Dickey, Ralph Houk, Ed Lopat)	12.00	6.00	3.50
466	Phillies Coaches (Dick Carter, Andy Cohen, Ken Silvestri)	5.50	2.75	1.75
467	Pirates Coaches (Bill Burwell, Sam Narron, Frank Oceak, Mickey Vernon)	5.50	2.75	1.75
468	Cardinals Coaches (Ray Katt, Johnny Keane, Howie Pollet, Harry Walker)	5.50	2.75	1.75
469	Giants Coaches (Salty Parker, Bill Posedel, Wes Westrum)	5.50	2.75	1.75
470	Senators Coaches (Ellis Clary, Sam Mele, Bob Swift)	5.50	2.75	1.75
471	Ned Garver	5.50	2.75	1.75
472	Al Dark	5.50	2.75	1.75
473	Al Cicotte	5.50	2.75	1.75
474	Haywood Sullivan	5.50	2.75	1.75
475	Don Drysdale	35.00	17.50	10.50
476	Lou Johnson	5.50	2.75	1.75
477	Don Ferrarese	5.50	2.75	1.75
478	Frank Torre	5.50	2.75	1.75
479	Georges Maranda	5.50	2.75	1.75
480	Yogi Berra	80.00	40.00	24.00
481	Wes Stock	5.50	2.75	1.75
482	Frank Bolling	5.50	2.75	1.75
483	Camilo Pascual	5.50	2.75	1.75
484	Pirates Team/Checklist 430-495	25.00	12.50	7.50
485	Ken Boyer	6.00	3.00	1.75
486	Bobby Del Greco	5.50	2.75	1.75
487	Tom Sturdivant	5.50	2.75	1.75
488	Norm Cash	6.00	3.00	1.75
489	Steve Ridzik	5.50	2.75	1.75
490	Frank Robinson	50.00	25.00	15.00
491	Mel Roach	5.50	2.75	1.75
492	Larry Jackson	5.50	2.75	1.75
493	Duke Snider	50.00	25.00	15.00
494	Orioles Team/Checklist 496-572	10.00	5.00	3.00
495	Sherm Lollar	5.50	2.75	1.75
496	Bill Virdon	5.50	2.75	1.75
497	John Tsitouris	5.50	2.75	1.75
498	Al Pilarcik	5.50	2.75	1.75
499	Johnny James	5.50	2.75	1.75
500	Johnny Temple	5.50	2.75	1.75
501	Bob Schmidt	5.50	2.75	1.75
502	Jim Bunning	12.00	6.00	3.50
503	Don Lee	5.50	2.75	1.75
504	Seth Morehead	5.50	2.75	1.75
505	Ted Kluszewski	9.00	4.50	2.75
506	Lee Walls	5.50	2.75	1.75
507	Dick Stigman	12.00	6.00	3.50
508	Billy Consolo	12.00	6.00	3.50
509	*Tommy Davis*	25.00	12.50	7.50
510	Jerry Staley	12.00	6.00	3.50
511	Ken Walters	12.00	6.00	3.50
512	Joe Gibbon	12.00	6.00	3.50
513	Cubs Team/Checklist 496-572	30.00	15.00	9.00
514	*Steve Barber*	12.00	6.00	3.50
515	Stan Lopata	12.00	6.00	3.50
516	Marty Kutyna	12.00	6.00	3.50
517	Charley James	12.00	6.00	3.50
518	*Tony Gonzalez*	12.00	6.00	3.50
519	Ed Roebuck	12.00	6.00	3.50

		NR MT	EX	VG
520	Don Buddin	12.00	6.00	3.50
521	Mike Lee	12.00	6.00	3.50
522	Ken Hunt	12.00	6.00	3.50
523	*Clay Dalrymple*	12.00	6.00	3.50
524	Bill Henry	12.00	6.00	3.50
525	Marv Breeding	12.00	6.00	3.50
526	Paul Giel	12.00	6.00	3.50
527	Jose Valdivielso	12.00	6.00	3.50
528	Ben Johnson	12.00	6.00	3.50
529	Norm Sherry	12.00	6.00	3.50
530	Mike McCormick	12.00	6.00	3.50
531	Sandy Amoros	12.00	6.00	3.50
532	Mike Garcia	12.00	6.00	3.50
533	Lu Clinton	12.00	6.00	3.50
534	Ken MacKenzie	12.00	6.00	3.50
535	Whitey Lockman	12.00	6.00	3.50
536	Wynn Hawkins	12.00	6.00	3.50
537	Red Sox Team/Checklist 496-572	30.00	15.00	9.00
538	Frank Barnes	12.00	6.00	3.50
539	Gene Baker	12.00	6.00	3.50
540	Jerry Walker	12.00	6.00	3.50
541	Tony Curry	12.00	6.00	3.50
542	Ken Hamlin	12.00	6.00	3.50
543	Elio Chacon	12.00	6.00	3.50
544	Bill Monbouquette	12.00	6.00	3.50
545	Carl Sawatski	12.00	6.00	3.50
546	Hank Aguirre	12.00	6.00	3.50
547	*Bob Aspromonte*	12.00	6.00	3.50
548	*Don Mincher*	12.00	6.00	3.50
549	John Buzhardt	12.00	6.00	3.50
550	Jim Landis	12.00	6.00	3.50
551	Ed Rakow	12.00	6.00	3.50
552	Walt Bond	12.00	6.00	3.50
553	Bill Skowron (All-Star)	15.00	7.50	4.50
554	Willie McCovey (All-Star)	60.00	30.00	18.00
555	Nellie Fox (All-Star)	20.00	10.00	6.00
556	Charlie Neal (All-Star)	15.00	7.50	4.50
557	Frank Malzone (All-Star)	15.00	7.50	4.50
558	Eddie Mathews (All-Star)	30.00	15.00	9.00
559	Luis Aparicio (All-Star)	20.00	10.00	6.00
560	Ernie Banks (All-Star)	45.00	22.00	13.50
561	Al Kaline (All-Star)	45.00	22.00	13.50
562	Joe Cunningham (All-Star)	15.00	7.50	4.50
563	Mickey Mantle (All-Star)	275.00	137.00	82.00
564	Willie Mays (All-Star)	120.00	60.00	36.00
565	Roger Maris (All-Star)	115.00	57.00	34.00
566	Hank Aaron (All-Star)	120.00	60.00	36.00
567	Sherm Lollar (All-Star)	15.00	7.50	4.50
568	Del Crandall (All-Star)	15.00	7.50	4.50
569	Camilo Pascual (All-Star)	15.00	7.50	4.50
570	Don Drysdale (All-Star)	24.00	12.00	7.25
571	Billy Pierce (All-Star)	15.00	7.50	4.50
572	Johnny Antonelli (All-Star)	24.00	12.00	7.25
----	Elect Your Favorite Rookie Insert (paper stock, no date on back)	15.00	7.50	4.50
----	Hot Iron Transfer Insert (paper stock)	15.00	7.50	4.50

1960 Topps Baseball Tattoos

Probably the least popular of all Topps products among parents and teachers, the Topps Tattoos were delightful little items on the reverse of the wrappers of Topps "Tattoo Bubble Gum." The entire wrapper was 1-9/16" by 3-1/2." The happy owner simply moistened his skin and applied the back of the wrapper to the wet spot. Presto, out came a "tattoo" in color (although often blurred by running colors).

The set offered 96 tattoo possibilities of which 55 were players, 16 teams, 15 action shots and 10 autographed balls. Surviving specimens are very rare today.

		NR MT	EX	VG
Complete Set:		675.00	337.00	202.00
Common Player:		4.50	2.25	1.25
(1)	Hank Aaron	25.00	12.50	7.50
(2)	Bob Allison	10.00	5.00	3.00
(3)	John Antonelli	10.00	5.00	3.00
(4)	Richie Ashburn	10.00	5.00	3.00
(5)	Ernie Banks	15.00	7.50	4.50
(6)	Yogi Berra	18.00	9.00	5.50
(7)	Lew Burdette	9.00	4.50	2.75
(8)	Orlando Cepeda	10.00	5.00	3.00
(9)	Rocky Colavito	9.00	4.50	2.75
(10)	Joe Cunningham	4.50	2.25	1.25
(11)	Buddy Daley	4.50	2.25	1.25
(12)	Don Drysdale	12.00	6.00	3.50
(13)	Ryne Duren	10.00	5.00	3.00
(14)	Roy Face	10.00	5.00	3.00
(15)	Whitey Ford	15.00	7.50	4.50
(16)	Nellie Fox	10.00	5.00	3.00
(17)	Tito Francona	4.50	2.25	1.25
(18)	Gene Freese	4.50	2.25	1.25
(19)	Jim Gilliam	9.00	4.50	2.75
(20)	Dick Groat	9.00	4.50	2.75
(21)	Ray Herbert	4.50	2.25	1.25
(22)	Glen Hobbie	4.50	2.25	1.25
(23)	Jackie Jensen	9.00	4.50	2.75
(24)	Sam Jones	4.50	2.25	1.25
(25)	Al Kaline	15.00	7.50	4.50
(26)	Harmon Killebrew	12.00	6.00	3.50
(27)	Harvy Kuenn (Harvey)	9.00	4.50	2.75
(28)	Frank Lary	4.50	2.25	1.25
(29)	Vernon Law	10.00	5.00	3.00
(30)	Frank Malzone	4.50	2.25	1.25
(31)	Mickey Mantle	75.00	37.00	22.00
(32)	Roger Maris	15.00	7.50	4.50
(33)	Ed Mathews	12.00	6.00	3.50
(34)	Willie Mays	25.00	12.50	7.50
(35)	Cal Mclish	4.50	2.25	1.25
(36)	Wally Moon	10.00	5.00	3.00
(37)	Walt Moryn	4.50	2.25	1.25
(38)	Don Mossi	4.50	2.25	1.25
(39)	Stan Musial	25.00	12.50	7.50
(40)	Charlie Neal	4.50	2.25	1.25
(41)	Don Newcombe	10.00	5.00	3.00
(42)	Milt Pappas	10.00	5.00	3.00
(43)	Camilo Pascual	10.00	5.00	3.00
(44)	Billie Pierce (Billy)	10.00	5.00	3.00
(45)	Robin Roberts	12.00	6.00	3.50
(46)	Frank Robinson	15.00	7.50	4.50
(47)	Pete Runnels	10.00	5.00	3.00
(48)	Herb Score	10.00	5.00	3.00
(49)	Warren Spahn	12.00	6.00	3.50
(50)	Johnny Temple	4.50	2.25	1.25
(51)	Gus Triandos	4.50	2.25	1.25
(52)	Jerry Walker	4.50	2.25	1.25
(53)	Bill White	10.00	5.00	3.00
(54)	Gene Woodling	10.00	5.00	3.00
(55)	Early Wynn	12.00	6.00	3.50
(56)	Chicago Cubs Logo	4.50	2.25	1.25
(57)	Cincinnati Reds Logo	4.50	2.25	1.25
(58)	Los Angeles Dodgers Logo	4.50	2.25	1.25
(59)	Milwaukee Braves Logo	4.50	2.25	1.25
(60)	Philadelphia Phillies Logo	4.50	2.25	1.25
(61)	Pittsburgh Pirates Logo	10.00	5.00	3.00
(62)	San Francisco Giants Logo	4.50	2.25	1.25
(63)	St. Louis Cardinals Logo	4.50	2.25	1.25
(64)	Baltimore Orioles Logo	4.50	2.25	1.25
(65)	Boston Red Sox Logo	4.50	2.25	1.25
(66)	Chicago White Sox Logo	4.50	2.25	1.25
(67)	Cleveland Indians Logo	4.50	2.25	1.25
(68)	Detroit Tigers Logo	4.50	2.25	1.25
(69)	Kansas City Athletics Logo	4.50	2.25	1.25
(70)	New York Yankees Logo	9.00	4.50	2.75
(71)	Washington Senators Logo	4.50	2.25	1.25
(72)	Autograph (Richie Ashburn)	4.50	2.25	1.25
(73)	Autograph (Rocky Colavito)	4.50	2.25	1.25
(74)	Autograph (Roy Face)	4.50	2.25	1.25
(75)	Autograph (Jackie Jensen)	4.50	2.25	1.25
(76)	Autograph (Harmon Killebrew)	10.00	5.00	3.00
(77)	Autograph (Mickey Mantle)	25.00	12.50	7.50
(78)	Autograph (Willie Mays)	10.00	5.00	3.00
(79)	Autograph (Stan Musial)	10.00	5.00	3.00
(80)	Autograph (Billy Pierce)	4.50	2.25	1.25
(81)	Autograph (Jerry Walker)	4.50	2.25	1.25
(82)	Run-Down	4.50	2.25	1.25

		NR MT	EX	VG
(83)	Out At First	4.50	2.25	1.25
(84)	The Final Word	4.50	2.25	1.25
(85)	Twisting Foul	4.50	2.25	1.25
(86)	Out At Home	4.50	2.25	1.25
(87)	Circus Catch	4.50	2.25	1.25
(88)	Great Catch	4.50	2.25	1.25
(89)	Stolen Base	4.50	2.25	1.25
(90)	Grand Slam Homer	4.50	2.25	1.25
(91)	Double Play	4.50	2.25	1.25
(92)	Right-Handed Follow-Thru (no caption)	4.50	2.25	1.25
(93)	Right-Handed High Leg Kick (no caption)	4.50	2.25	1.25
(94)	Left-Handed Pitcher (no caption)	4.50	2.25	1.25
(95)	Right-Handed Batter (no caption)	4.50	2.25	1.25
(96)	Left-Handed Batter (no caption)	4.50	2.25	1.25

1961 Topps

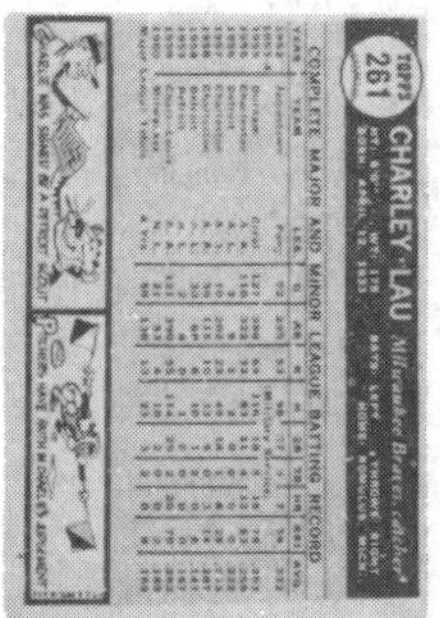

Except for some of the specialty cards, Topps returned to a vertical format with their 1961 cards. The set is numbered through 598, however only 587 cards were printed. No numbers 426, 587 and 588 were issued. Two cards numbered 463 exist (one a Braves team card and one a player card of Jack Fisher). Actually, the Braves team card is checklisted as #426. Designs for 1961 are basically large color portraits; the backs return to extensive statistics. A three-panel cartoon highlighting the player's career appears on the card backs. Innovations include numbered checklists, cards for statistical leaders, and 10 "Baseball Thrills" cards. The scarce high numbers are card numbers 523-589.

	NR MT	EX	VG
Complete Set (587):	6000.00	2850.00	1700.
Common Player: 1-370	2.50	1.25	.70
Common Player: 371-522	4.50	2.25	1.25
Common Player: 523-589	35.00	17.50	10.50

		NR MT	EX	VG
1	Dick Groat	20.00	5.00	3.00
2	Roger Maris	150.00	75.00	45.00
3	John Buzhardt	2.50	1.25	.70
4	Lenny Green	2.50	1.25	.70
5	Johnny Romano	2.50	1.25	.70
6	Ed Roebuck	2.50	1.25	.70
7	White Sox Team	6.00	3.00	1.75
8	Dick Williams	4.50	2.25	1.25
9	Bob Purkey	2.50	1.25	.70
10	Brooks Robinson	27.50	13.50	8.25
11	Curt Simmons	2.50	1.25	.70
12	Moe Thacker	2.50	1.25	.70
13	Chuck Cottier	2.50	1.25	.70
14	Don Mossi	2.50	1.25	.70
15	Willie Kirkland	2.50	1.25	.70
16	Billy Muffett	2.50	1.25	.70
17	Checklist 1-88	5.00	2.50	1.50
18	Jim Grant	2.50	1.25	.70
19	Cletis Boyer	2.50	1.25	.70
20	Robin Roberts	10.00	5.00	3.00
21	*Zorro Versalles*	3.50	1.75	1.00
22	Clem Labine	2.50	1.25	.70
23	Don Demeter	2.50	1.25	.70
24	Ken Johnson	2.50	1.25	.70
25	Reds' Heavy Artillery (Gus Bell, Vada Pinson, Frank Robinson)	8.00	4.00	2.50
26	Wes Stock	2.50	1.25	.70
27	Jerry Kindall	2.50	1.25	.70
28	Hector Lopez	2.50	1.25	.70
29	Don Nottebart	2.50	1.25	.70
30	Nellie Fox	6.00	3.00	1.75
31	Bob Schmidt	2.50	1.25	.70
32	Ray Sadecki	2.50	1.25	.70
33	Gary Geiger	2.50	1.25	.70
34	Wynn Hawkins	2.50	1.25	.70
35	*Ron Santo*	60.00	30.00	18.00
36	Jack Kralick	2.50	1.25	.70
37	Charlie Maxwell	2.50	1.25	.70
38	Bob Lillis	2.50	1.25	.70
39	Leo Posada	2.50	1.25	.70
40	Bob Turley	3.00	1.50	.90
41	N.L. Batting Leaders (Roberto Clemente, Dick Groat, Norm Larker, Willie Mays)	8.00	4.00	2.50
42	A.L. Batting Leaders (Minnie Minoso, Pete Runnels, Bill Skowron, Al Smith)	6.00	3.00	1.75
43	N.L. Home Run Leaders (Hank Aaron, Ernie Banks, Ken Boyer, Eddie Mathews)	8.00	4.00	2.50
44	A.L. Home Run Leaders (Rocky Colavito, Jim Lemon, Mickey Mantle, Roger Maris)	35.00	17.50	10.50
45	N.L. E.R.A. Leaders (Ernie Broglio, Don Drysdale, Bob Friend, Mike McCormick, Stan Williams)	6.00	3.00	1.75
46	A.L. E.R.A. Leaders (Frank Baumann, Hal Brown, Jim Bunning, Art Ditmar)	6.00	3.00	1.75
47	N.L. Pitching Leaders (Ernie Broglio, Lou Burdette, Vern Law, Warren Spahn)	6.00	3.00	1.75
48	A.L. Pitching Leaders (Bud Daley, Art Ditmar, Chuck Estrada, Frank Lary, Milt Pappas, Jim Perry)	6.00	3.00	1.75
49	N.L. Strikeout Leaders (Ernie Broglio, Don Drysdale, Sam Jones, Sandy Koufax)	8.00	4.00	2.50
50	A.L. Strikeout Leaders (Jim Bunning, Frank Lary, Pedro Ramos, Early Wynn)	6.00	3.00	1.75
51	Tigers Team	7.50	3.75	2.25
52	George Crowe	2.50	1.25	.70
53	Russ Nixon	2.50	1.25	.70
54	Earl Francis	2.50	1.25	.70
55	Jim Davenport	2.50	1.25	.70
56	Russ Kemmerer	2.50	1.25	.70
57	Marv Throneberry	2.50	1.25	.70
58	Joe Schaffernoth	2.50	1.25	.70
59	Jim Woods	2.50	1.25	.70
60	Woodie Held	2.50	1.25	.70
61	Ron Piche	2.50	1.25	.70
62	Al Pilarcik	2.50	1.25	.70
63	Jim Kaat	7.50	3.75	2.25
64	Alex Grammas	2.50	1.25	.70
65	Ted Kluszewski	7.50	3.75	2.25
66	Bill Henry	2.50	1.25	.70
67	Ossie Virgil	2.50	1.25	.70
68	Deron Johnson	2.50	1.25	.70
69	Earl Wilson	2.50	1.25	.70
70	Bill Virdon	2.50	1.25	.70
71	Jerry Adair	2.50	1.25	.70
72	Stu Miller	2.50	1.25	.70
73	Al Spangler	2.50	1.25	.70
74	Joe Pignatano	2.50	1.25	.70
75	Lindy Shows Larry (Larry Jackson, Lindy McDaniel)	5.00	2.50	1.50
76	Harry Anderson	2.50	1.25	.70
77	Dick Stigman	2.50	1.25	.70
78	Lee Walls	2.50	1.25	.70
79	Joe Ginsberg	2.50	1.25	.70
80	Harmon Killebrew	25.00	12.50	7.50
81	Tracy Stallard	2.50	1.25	.70
82	Joe Christopher	2.50	1.25	.70
83	Bob Bruce	2.50	1.25	.70
84	Lee Maye	2.50	1.25	.70
85	Jerry Walker	2.50	1.25	.70
86	Dodgers Team	7.50	3.75	2.25
87	Joe Amalfitano	2.50	1.25	.70
88	Richie Ashburn	8.00	4.00	2.50
89	Billy Martin	8.00	4.00	2.50
90	Jerry Staley	2.50	1.25	.70
91	Walt Moryn	2.50	1.25	.70
92	Hal Naragon	2.50	1.25	.70
93	Tony Gonzalez	2.50	1.25	.70
94	Johnny Kucks	2.50	1.25	.70
95	Norm Cash	3.50	1.75	1.00
96	Billy O'Dell	2.50	1.25	.70
97	Jerry Lynch	2.50	1.25	.70
98a	Checklist 89-176 (word "Checklist" in red on front)	7.00	3.50	2.00
98b	Checklist 89-176 ("Checklist" in yellow, 98 on back in black)	5.00	2.50	1.50

#	Card	NR MT	EX	VG
98c	Checklist 89-176 ("Checklist" in yellow, 98 on back in white)	7.00	3.50	2.00
99	Don Buddin	2.50	1.25	.70
100	Harvey Haddix	2.50	1.25	.70
101	Bubba Phillips	2.50	1.25	.70
102	Gene Stephens	2.50	1.25	.70
103	Ruben Amaro	2.50	1.25	.70
104	John Blanchard	2.50	1.25	.70
105	Carl Willey	2.50	1.25	.70
106	Whitey Herzog	4.00	2.00	1.25
107	Seth Morehead	2.50	1.25	.70
108	Dan Dobbek	2.50	1.25	.70
109	Johnny Podres	3.50	1.75	1.00
110	Vada Pinson	6.00	3.00	1.75
111	Jack Meyer	2.50	1.25	.70
112	Chico Fernandez	2.50	1.25	.70
113	Mike Fornieles	2.50	1.25	.70
114	Hobie Landrith	2.50	1.25	.70
115	Johnny Antonelli	2.50	1.25	.70
116	Joe DeMaestri	2.50	1.25	.70
117	Dale Long	2.50	1.25	.70
118	Chris Cannizzaro	2.50	1.25	.70
119	A's Big Armor (Hank Bauer, Jerry Lumpe, Norm Siebern)	5.00	2.50	1.50
120	Eddie Mathews	30.00	15.00	9.00
121	Eli Grba	2.50	1.25	.70
122	Cubs Team	6.00	3.00	1.75
123	Billy Gardner	2.50	1.25	.70
124	J.C. Martin	2.50	1.25	.70
125	Steve Barber	2.50	1.25	.70
126	Dick Stuart	3.00	1.50	.90
127	Ron Kline	2.50	1.25	.70
128	Rip Repulski	2.50	1.25	.70
129	Ed Hobaugh	2.50	1.25	.70
130	Norm Larker	2.50	1.25	.70
131	Paul Richards	2.50	1.25	.70
132	Al Lopez	5.00	2.50	1.50
133	Ralph Houk	5.00	2.50	1.50
134	Mickey Vernon	2.50	1.25	.70
135	Fred Hutchinson	2.50	1.25	.70
136	Walt Alston	5.00	2.50	1.50
137	Chuck Dressen	2.50	1.25	.70
138	Danny Murtaugh	2.50	1.25	.70
139	Solly Hemus	2.50	1.25	.70
140	Gus Triandos	2.50	1.25	.70
141	*Billy Williams*	100.00	50.00	30.00
142	Luis Arroyo	2.50	1.25	.70
143	Russ Snyder	2.50	1.25	.70
144	Jim Coker	2.50	1.25	.70
145	Bob Buhl	2.50	1.25	.70
146	Marty Keough	2.50	1.25	.70
147	Ed Rakow	2.50	1.25	.70
148	Julian Javier	2.50	1.25	.70
149	Bob Oldis	2.50	1.25	.70
150	Willie Mays	120.00	60.00	36.00
151	Jim Donohue	2.50	1.25	.70
152	Earl Torgeson	2.50	1.25	.70
153	Don Lee	2.50	1.25	.70
154	Bobby Del Greco	2.50	1.25	.70
155	Johnny Temple	2.50	1.25	.70
156	Ken Hunt	2.50	1.25	.70
157	Cal McLish	2.50	1.25	.70
158	Pete Daley	2.50	1.25	.70
159	Orioles Team	6.00	3.00	1.75
160	Whitey Ford	35.00	17.50	10.50
161	Sherman Jones (photo actually Eddie Fisher)	2.50	1.25	.70
162	Jay Hook	2.50	1.25	.70
163	Ed Sadowski	2.50	1.25	.70
164	Felix Mantilla	2.50	1.25	.70
165	Gino Cimoli	2.50	1.25	.70
166	Danny Kravitz	2.50	1.25	.70
167	Giants Team	6.00	3.00	1.75
168	Tommy Davis	5.00	2.50	1.50
169	Don Elston	2.50	1.25	.70
170	Al Smith	2.50	1.25	.70
171	Paul Foytack	2.50	1.25	.70
172	Don Dillard	2.50	1.25	.70
173	Beantown Bombers (Jackie Jensen, Frank Malzone, Vic Wertz)	6.00	3.00	1.75
174	Ray Semproch	2.50	1.25	.70
175	Gene Freese	2.50	1.25	.70
176	Ken Aspromonte	2.50	1.25	.70
177	Don Larsen	2.50	1.25	.70
178	Bob Nieman	2.50	1.25	.70
179	Joe Koppe	2.50	1.25	.70
180	Bobby Richardson	6.00	3.00	1.75
181	Fred Green	2.50	1.25	.70
182	Dave Nicholson	2.50	1.25	.70
183	Andre Rodgers	2.50	1.25	.70
184	Steve Bilko	2.50	1.25	.70

#	Card	NR MT	EX	VG
185	Herb Score	2.50	1.25	.70
186	Elmer Valo	2.50	1.25	.70
187	Billy Klaus	2.50	1.25	.70
188	Jim Marshall	2.50	1.25	.70
189	Checklist 177-264	5.00	2.50	1.50
190	Stan Williams	2.50	1.25	.70
191	Mike de la Hoz	2.50	1.25	.70
192	Dick Brown	2.50	1.25	.70
193	Gene Conley	2.50	1.25	.70
194	Gordy Coleman	2.50	1.25	.70
195	Jerry Casale	2.50	1.25	.70
196	Ed Bouchee	2.50	1.25	.70
197	Dick Hall	2.50	1.25	.70
198	Carl Sawatski	2.50	1.25	.70
199	Bob Boyd	2.50	1.25	.70
200	Warren Spahn	30.00	15.00	9.00
201	Pete Whisenant	2.50	1.25	.70
202	Al Neiger	2.50	1.25	.70
203	Eddie Bressoud	2.50	1.25	.70
204	Bob Skinner	2.50	1.25	.70
205	Bill Pierce	2.50	1.25	.70
206	Gene Green	2.50	1.25	.70
207	Dodger Southpaws (Sandy Koufax, Johnny Podres)	22.00	11.00	6.50
208	Larry Osborne	2.50	1.25	.70
209	Ken McBride	2.50	1.25	.70
210	Pete Runnels	2.50	1.25	.70
211	Bob Gibson	40.00	20.00	12.00
212	Haywood Sullivan	2.50	1.25	.70
213	*Bill Stafford*	4.50	2.25	1.25
214	Danny Murphy	2.50	1.25	.70
215	Gus Bell	2.50	1.25	.70
216	Ted Bowsfield	2.50	1.25	.70
217	Mel Roach	2.50	1.25	.70
218	Hal Brown	2.50	1.25	.70
219	Gene Mauch	2.50	1.25	.70
220	Al Dark	2.50	1.25	.70
221	Mike Higgins	2.50	1.25	.70
222	Jimmie Dykes	2.50	1.25	.70
223	Bob Scheffing	2.50	1.25	.70
224	Joe Gordon	2.50	1.25	.70
225	Bill Rigney	2.50	1.25	.70
226	Harry Lavagetto	2.50	1.25	.70
227	Juan Pizarro	2.50	1.25	.70
228	Yankees Team	35.00	17.50	10.50
229	Rudy Hernandez	2.50	1.25	.70
230	Don Hoak	2.50	1.25	.70
231	Dick Drott	2.50	1.25	.70
232	Bill White	4.50	2.25	1.25
233	Joe Jay	2.50	1.25	.70
234	Ted Lepcio	2.50	1.25	.70
235	Camilo Pascual	2.50	1.25	.70
236	Don Gile	2.50	1.25	.70
237	Billy Loes	2.50	1.25	.70
238	Jim Gilliam	4.50	2.25	1.25
239	Dave Sisler	2.50	1.25	.70
240	Ron Hansen	2.50	1.25	.70
241	Al Cicotte	2.50	1.25	.70
242	Hal W. Smith	2.50	1.25	.70
243	Frank Lary	2.50	1.25	.70
244	Chico Cardenas	2.50	1.25	.70
245	Joe Adcock	2.50	1.25	.70
246	Bob Davis	2.50	1.25	.70
247	Billy Goodman	2.50	1.25	.70
248	Ed Keegan	2.50	1.25	.70
249	Reds Team	6.00	3.00	1.75
250	Buc Hill Aces (Roy Face, Vern Law)	6.00	3.00	1.75
251	Bill Bruton	2.50	1.25	.70
252	Bill Short	2.50	1.25	.70
253	Sammy Taylor	2.50	1.25	.70
254	Ted Sadowski	2.50	1.25	.70
255	Vic Power	2.50	1.25	.70
256	Billy Hoeft	2.50	1.25	.70
257	Carroll Hardy	2.50	1.25	.70
258	Jack Sanford	2.50	1.25	.70
259	John Schaive	2.50	1.25	.70
260	Don Drysdale	25.00	12.50	7.50
261	Charlie Lau	2.50	1.25	.70
262	Tony Curry	2.50	1.25	.70
263	Ken Hamlin	2.50	1.25	.70
264	Glen Hobbie	2.50	1.25	.70
265	Tony Kubek	5.00	2.50	1.50
266	Lindy McDaniel	2.50	1.25	.70
267	Norm Siebern	2.50	1.25	.70
268	Ike DeLock (Delock)	2.50	1.25	.70
269	Harry Chiti	2.50	1.25	.70
270	Bob Friend	2.50	1.25	.70
271	Jim Landis	2.50	1.25	.70
272	Tom Morgan	2.50	1.25	.70
273	Checklist 265-352	5.00	2.50	1.50

#	Player	NR MT	EX	VG
274	Gary Bell	2.50	1.25	.70
275	Gene Woodling	2.50	1.25	.70
276	Ray Rippelmeyer	2.50	1.25	.70
277	Hank Foiles	2.50	1.25	.70
278	Don McMahon	2.50	1.25	.70
279	Jose Pagan	2.50	1.25	.70
280	Frank Howard	4.00	2.00	1.25
281	Frank Sullivan	2.50	1.25	.70
282	Faye Throneberry	2.50	1.25	.70
283	Bob Anderson	2.50	1.25	.70
284	Dick Gernert	2.50	1.25	.70
285	Sherm Lollar	2.50	1.25	.70
286	George Witt	2.50	1.25	.70
287	Carl Yastrzemski	90.00	45.00	27.00
288	Albie Pearson	2.50	1.25	.70
289	Ray Moore	2.50	1.25	.70
290	Stan Musial	100.00	50.00	30.00
291	Tex Clevenger	2.50	1.25	.70
292	Jim Baumer	2.50	1.25	.70
293	Tom Sturdivant	2.50	1.25	.70
294	Don Blasingame	2.50	1.25	.70
295	Milt Pappas	2.50	1.25	.70
296	Wes Covington	2.50	1.25	.70
297	Athletics Team	6.00	3.00	1.75
298	Jim Golden	2.50	1.25	.70
299	Clay Dalrymple	2.50	1.25	.70
300	Mickey Mantle	400.00	200.00	120.00
301	Chet Nichols	2.50	1.25	.70
302	Al Heist	2.50	1.25	.70
303	Gary Peters	2.50	1.25	.70
304	Rocky Nelson	2.50	1.25	.70
305	Mike McCormick	2.50	1.25	.70
306	World Series Game 1 (Virdon Saves Game)	7.50	3.75	2.25
307	World Series Game 2 (Mantle Slams 2 Homers)	40.00	20.00	12.00
308	World Series Game 3 (Richardson is Hero)	7.50	3.75	2.25
309	World Series Game 4 (Cimoli is Safe in Crucial Play)	7.50	3.75	2.25
310	World Series Game 5 (Face Saves the Day)	7.50	3.75	2.25
311	World Series Game 6 (Ford Pitches Second Shutout)	7.50	3.75	2.25
312	World Series Game 7 (Mazeroski's Homer Wins It')	12.00	6.00	3.50
313	World Series Summary (The Winners Celebrate)	7.50	3.75	2.25
314	Bob Miller	2.50	1.25	.70
315	Earl Battey	2.50	1.25	.70
316	Bobby Gene Smith	2.50	1.25	.70
317	*Jim Brewer*	2.50	1.25	.70
318	Danny O'Connell	2.50	1.25	.70
319	Valmy Thomas	2.50	1.25	.70
320	Lou Burdette	2.50	1.25	.70
321	Marv Breeding	2.50	1.25	.70
322	Bill Kunkel	2.50	1.25	.70
323	Sammy Esposito	2.50	1.25	.70
324	Hank Aguirre	2.50	1.25	.70
325	Wally Moon	2.50	1.25	.70
326	Dave Hillman	2.50	1.25	.70
327	*Matty Alou*	4.00	2.00	1.25
328	Jim O'Toole	2.50	1.25	.70
329	Julio Becquer	2.50	1.25	.70
330	Rocky Colavito	5.00	2.50	1.50
331	Ned Garver	2.50	1.25	.70
332	Dutch Dotterer (photo actually Tommy Dotterer)	2.50	1.25	.70
333	Fritz Brickell	3.00	1.50	.90
334	Walt Bond	2.50	1.25	.70
335	Frank Bolling	2.50	1.25	.70
336	Don Mincher	2.50	1.25	.70
337	Al's Aces (Al Lopez, Herb Score, Early Wynn)	7.50	3.75	2.25
338	Don Landrum	2.50	1.25	.70
339	Gene Baker	2.50	1.25	.70
340	Vic Wertz	2.50	1.25	.70
341	Jim Owens	2.50	1.25	.70
342	Clint Courtney	2.50	1.25	.70
343	Earl Robinson	2.50	1.25	.70
344	Sandy Koufax	85.00	42.00	25.00
345	Jim Piersall	2.50	1.25	.70
346	Howie Nunn	2.50	1.25	.70
347	Cardinals Team	6.00	3.00	1.75
348	Steve Boros	2.50	1.25	.70
349	Danny McDevitt	2.50	1.25	.70
350	Ernie Banks	40.00	20.00	12.00
351	Jim King	2.50	1.25	.70
352	Bob Shaw	2.50	1.25	.70
353	Howie Bedell	2.50	1.25	.70
354	Billy Harrell	2.50	1.25	.70

#	Player	NR MT	EX	VG
355	Bob Allison	2.50	1.25	.70
356	Ryne Duren	3.50	1.75	1.00
357	Daryl Spencer	2.50	1.25	.70
358	Earl Averill	2.50	1.25	.70
359	Dallas Green	3.50	1.75	1.00
360	Frank Robinson	30.00	15.00	9.00
361a	Checklist 353-429 ("Topps Baseball" in black on front)	5.00	2.50	1.50
361b	Checklist 353-429 ("Topps Baseball" in yellow)	6.00	3.00	1.75
362	Frank Funk	2.50	1.25	.70
363	John Roseboro	2.50	1.25	.70
364	Moe Drabowsky	2.50	1.25	.70
365	Jerry Lumpe	2.50	1.25	.70
366	Eddie Fisher	2.50	1.25	.70
367	Jim Rivera	2.50	1.25	.70
368	Bennie Daniels	2.50	1.25	.70
369	Dave Philley	2.50	1.25	.70
370	Roy Face	2.50	1.25	.70
371	Bill Skowron	5.00	2.50	1.50
372	Bob Hendley	4.50	2.25	1.25
373	Red Sox Team	8.00	4.00	2.50
374	Paul Giel	4.50	2.25	1.25
375	Ken Boyer	6.00	3.00	1.75
376	Mike Roarke	4.50	2.25	1.25
377	Ruben Gomez	4.50	2.25	1.25
378	Wally Post	4.50	2.25	1.25
379	Bobby Shantz	5.00	2.50	1.50
380	Minnie Minoso	6.00	3.00	1.75
381	Dave Wickersham	4.50	2.25	1.25
382	Frank J. Thomas	4.50	2.25	1.25
383	Frisco First Liners (Mike McCormick, Billy O'Dell, Jack Sanford)	6.00	3.00	1.75
384	Chuck Essegian	4.50	2.25	1.25
385	Jim Perry	4.50	2.25	1.25
386	Joe Hicks	4.50	2.25	1.25
387	Duke Maas	4.50	2.25	1.25
388	Roberto Clemente	100.00	50.00	30.00
389	Ralph Terry	5.00	2.50	1.50
390	Del Crandall	4.50	2.25	1.25
391	Winston Brown	4.50	2.25	1.25
392	Reno Bertoia	4.50	2.25	1.25
393	Batter Bafflers (Don Cardwell, Glen Hobbie)	4.50	2.25	1.25
394	Ken Walters	4.50	2.25	1.25
395	Chuck Estrada	4.50	2.25	1.25
396	Bob Aspromonte	4.50	2.25	1.25
397	Hal Woodeshick	4.50	2.25	1.25
398	Hank Bauer	4.50	2.25	1.25
399	Cliff Cook	4.50	2.25	1.25
400	Vern Law	4.50	2.25	1.25
401	Babe Ruth Hits 60th Homer	35.00	17.50	10.50
402	Larsen Pitches Perfect Game	15.00	7.50	4.50
403	Brooklyn-Boston Play 26-Inning Tie	4.50	2.25	1.25
404	Hornsby Tops N.L. with .424 Average	8.00	4.00	2.50
405	Gehrig Benched After 2,130 Games	27.50	13.50	8.25
406	Mantle Blasts 565 ft. Home Run	45.00	22.00	13.50
407	Jack Chesbro Wins 41st Game	4.50	2.25	1.25
408	Mathewson Strikes Out 267 Batters	6.00	3.00	1.75
409	Johnson Hurls 3rd Shutout in 4 Days	5.00	2.50	1.50
410	Haddix Pitches 12 Perfect Innings	6.00	3.00	1.75
411	Tony Taylor	4.50	2.25	1.25
412	Larry Sherry	4.50	2.25	1.25
413	Eddie Yost	4.50	2.25	1.25
414	Dick Donovan	4.50	2.25	1.25
415	Hank Aaron	120.00	60.00	36.00
416	*Dick Howser*	6.00	3.00	1.75
417	*Juan Marichal*	125.00	62.00	37.00
418	Ed Bailey	4.50	2.25	1.25
419	Tom Borland	4.50	2.25	1.25
420	Ernie Broglio	4.50	2.25	1.25
421	Ty Cline	4.50	2.25	1.25
422	Bud Daley	4.50	2.25	1.25
423	Charlie Neal	4.50	2.25	1.25
424	Turk Lown	4.50	2.25	1.25
425	Yogi Berra	60.00	30.00	18.00
426	Not Issued			
427	Dick Ellsworth	4.50	2.25	1.25
428	Ray Barker	4.50	2.25	1.25
429	Al Kaline	40.00	20.00	12.00
430	Bill Mazeroski	35.00	17.50	10.50
431	Chuck Stobbs	4.50	2.25	1.25
432	Coot Veal	4.50	2.25	1.25
433	Art Mahaffey	4.50	2.25	1.25
434	Tom Brewer	4.50	2.25	1.25
435	Orlando Cepeda	10.00	5.00	3.00

		NR MT	EX	VG
436	*Jim Maloney*	4.50	2.25	1.25
437a	Checklist 430-506 (#440 is Louis Aparicio)	6.00	3.00	1.75
437b	Checklist 430-506 (#440 is Luis Aparicio)	6.50	3.25	2.00
438	Curt Flood	4.50	2.25	1.25
439	*Phil Regan*	4.50	2.25	1.25
440	Luis Aparicio	14.00	7.00	4.25
441	Dick Bertell	4.50	2.25	1.25
442	Gordon Jones	4.50	2.25	1.25
443	Duke Snider	40.00	20.00	12.00
444	Joe Nuxhall	4.50	2.25	1.25
445	Frank Malzone	4.50	2.25	1.25
446	Bob "Hawk" Taylor	4.50	2.25	1.25
447	Harry Bright	4.50	2.25	1.25
448	Del Rice	4.50	2.25	1.25
449	*Bobby Bolin*	4.50	2.25	1.25
450	Jim Lemon	4.50	2.25	1.25
451	Power For Ernie (Ernie Broglio, Daryl Spencer, Bill White)	5.00	2.50	1.50
452	Bob Allen	4.50	2.25	1.25
453	Dick Schofield	4.50	2.25	1.25
454	Pumpsie Green	4.50	2.25	1.25
455	Early Wynn	15.00	7.50	4.50
456	Hal Bevan	4.50	2.25	1.25
457	Johnny James	4.50	2.25	1.25
458	Willie Tasby	4.50	2.25	1.25
459	Terry Fox	4.50	2.25	1.25
460	Gil Hodges	18.00	9.00	5.50
461	Smoky Burgess	4.50	2.25	1.25
462	Lou Klimchock	4.50	2.25	1.25
463a	Braves Team (should be card #426)	8.00	4.00	2.50
463b	Jack Fisher	4.50	2.25	1.25
464	*Leroy Thomas*	4.50	2.25	1.25
465	Roy McMillan	4.50	2.25	1.25
466	Ron Moeller	4.50	2.25	1.25
467	Indians Team	8.00	4.00	2.50
468	Johnny Callison	4.50	2.25	1.25
469	Ralph Lumenti	4.50	2.25	1.25
470	Roy Sievers	4.50	2.25	1.25
471	Phil Rizzuto (MVP)	12.00	6.00	3.50
472	Yogi Berra (MVP)	50.00	25.00	15.00
473	Bobby Shantz (MVP)	7.50	3.75	2.25
474	Al Rosen (MVP)	7.50	3.75	2.25
475	Mickey Mantle (MVP)	125.00	62.00	37.00
476	Jackie Jensen (MVP)	7.50	3.75	2.25
477	Nellie Fox (MVP)	9.00	4.50	2.75
478	Roger Maris (MVP)	45.00	22.00	13.50
479	Jim Konstanty	7.50	3.75	2.25
480	Roy Campanella (MVP)	35.00	17.50	10.50
481	Hank Sauer	7.50	3.75	2.25
482	Willie Mays	40.00	20.00	12.00
483	Don Newcombe (MVP)	9.00	4.50	2.75
484	Hank Aaron (MVP)	40.00	20.00	12.00
485	Ernie Banks (MVP)	35.00	17.50	10.50
486	Dick Groat (MVP)	7.50	3.75	2.25
487	Gene Oliver	4.50	2.25	1.25
488	Joe McClain	4.50	2.25	1.25
489	Walt Dropo	4.50	2.25	1.25
490	Jim Bunning	8.00	4.00	2.50
491	Phillies Team	9.00	4.50	2.75
492	Ron Fairly	4.50	2.25	1.25
493	Don Zimmer	4.50	2.25	1.25
494	Tom Cheney	4.50	2.25	1.25
495	Elston Howard	6.00	3.00	1.75
496	Ken MacKenzie	4.50	2.25	1.25
497	Willie Jones	4.50	2.25	1.25
498	Ray Herbert	4.50	2.25	1.25
499	Chuck Schilling	4.50	2.25	1.25
500	Harvey Kuenn	5.00	2.50	1.50
501	John DeMerit	4.50	2.25	1.25
502	Clarence Coleman	4.50	2.25	1.25
503	Tito Francona	4.50	2.25	1.25
504	Billy Consolo	4.50	2.25	1.25
505	Red Schoendienst	12.50	6.25	3.75
506	*Willie Davis*	12.00	6.00	3.50
507	Pete Burnside	4.50	2.25	1.25
508	Rocky Bridges	4.50	2.25	1.25
509	Camilo Carreon	4.50	2.25	1.25
510	Art Ditmar	4.50	2.25	1.25
511	Joe M. Morgan	4.50	2.25	1.25
512	Bob Will	4.50	2.25	1.25
513	Jim Brosnan	4.50	2.25	1.25
514	Jake Wood	4.50	2.25	1.25
515	Jackie Brandt	4.50	2.25	1.25
516	Checklist 507-587	10.00	5.00	3.00
517	Willie McCovey	55.00	27.00	16.50
518	Andy Carey	4.50	2.25	1.25
519	Jim Pagliaroni	4.50	2.25	1.25
520	Joe Cunningham	4.50	2.25	1.25

		NR MT	EX	VG
521	Brother Battery (Larry Sherry, Norm Sherry)	6.00	3.00	1.75
522	Dick Farrell	4.50	2.25	1.25
523	Joe Gibbon	35.00	17.50	10.50
524	Johnny Logan	35.00	17.50	10.50
525	*Ron Perranoski*	35.00	17.50	10.50
526	R.C. Stevens	35.00	17.50	10.50
527	Gene Leek	35.00	17.50	10.50
528	Pedro Ramos	35.00	17.50	10.50
529	Bob Roselli	35.00	17.50	10.50
530	Bobby Malkmus	35.00	17.50	10.50
531	Jim Coates	35.00	17.50	10.50
532	Bob Hale	35.00	17.50	10.50
533	Jack Curtis	35.00	17.50	10.50
534	Eddie Kasko	35.00	17.50	10.50
535	Larry Jackson	35.00	17.50	10.50
536	Bill Tuttle	35.00	17.50	10.50
537	Bobby Locke	35.00	17.50	10.50
538	Chuck Hiller	35.00	17.50	10.50
539	Johnny Klippstein	35.00	17.50	10.50
540	Jackie Jensen	35.00	17.50	10.50
541	Roland Sheldon	35.00	17.50	10.50
542	Twins Team	70.00	35.00	21.00
543	Roger Craig	40.00	20.00	12.00
544	George Thomas	35.00	17.50	10.50
545	Hoyt Wilhelm	65.00	32.00	19.50
546	Marty Kutyna	35.00	17.50	10.50
547	Leon Wagner	35.00	17.50	10.50
548	Ted Wills	35.00	17.50	10.50
549	Hal R. Smith	35.00	17.50	10.50
550	Frank Baumann	35.00	17.50	10.50
551	George Altman	35.00	17.50	10.50
552	Jim Archer	35.00	17.50	10.50
553	Bill Fischer	35.00	17.50	10.50
554	Pirates Team	60.00	30.00	18.00
555	Sam Jones	35.00	17.50	10.50
556	Ken R. Hunt	35.00	17.50	10.50
557	Jose Valdivielso	35.00	17.50	10.50
558	Don Ferrarese	35.00	17.50	10.50
559	Jim Gentile	35.00	17.50	10.50
560	Barry Latman	35.00	17.50	10.50
561	Charley James	35.00	17.50	10.50
562	Bill Monbouquette	35.00	17.50	10.50
563	Bob Cerv	35.00	17.50	10.50
564	Don Cardwell	35.00	17.50	10.50
565	Felipe Alou	45.00	22.00	13.50
566	Paul Richards (All-Star)	35.00	17.50	10.50
567	Danny Murtaugh (All-Star)	35.00	17.50	10.50
568	Bill Skowron (All-Star)	45.00	22.00	13.50
569	Frank Herrera (All-Star)	35.00	17.50	10.50
570	Nellie Fox (All-Star)	50.00	25.00	15.00
571	Bill Mazeroski (All-Star)	45.00	22.00	13.50
572	Brooks Robinson (All-Star)	75.00	37.00	22.00
573	Ken Boyer (All-Star)	40.00	20.00	12.00
574	Luis Aparicio (All-Star)	47.50	24.00	14.00
575	Ernie Banks (All-Star)	90.00	45.00	27.00
576	Roger Maris (All-Star)	125.00	62.00	37.00
577	Hank Aaron (All-Star)	150.00	75.00	45.00
578	Mickey Mantle (All-Star)	400.00	200.00	120.00
579	Willie Mays (All-Star)	150.00	75.00	45.00
580	Al Kaline (All-Star)	90.00	45.00	27.00
581	Frank Robinson (All-Star)	85.00	42.00	25.00
582	Earl Battey (All-Star)	35.00	17.50	10.50
583	Del Crandall (All-Star)	35.00	17.50	10.50
584	Jim Perry (All-Star)	35.00	17.50	10.50
585	Bob Friend (All-Star)	35.00	17.50	10.50
586	Whitey Ford (All-Star)	90.00	45.00	27.00
587	Not Issued			
588	Not Issued			
589	Warren Spahn (All-Star)	125.00	56.00	35.00

1961 Topps Dice Game

One of the more obscure Topps test issues that

may have never actually been issued is the 1961 Topps Dice Game. Eighteen black and white cards, each measuring 2-1/2" by 3-1/2" in size, comprise the set. Interestingly, there are no identifying marks, such as copyrights or trademarks, to indicate the set was produced by Topps. The card backs contain various baseball plays that occur when a certain pitch is called and a specific number of the dice is rolled.

		NR MT	EX	VG
Complete Set:		7500.00	3750.00	2250.
Common Player:		100.00	50.00	30.00
(1)	Earl Battey	100.00	50.00	30.00
(2)	Del Crandall	100.00	50.00	30.00
(3)	Jim Davenport	100.00	50.00	30.00
(4)	Don Drysdale	350.00	175.00	105.00
(5)	Dick Groat	150.00	75.00	45.00
(6)	Al Kaline	600.00	300.00	175.00
(7)	Tony Kubek	150.00	75.00	45.00
(8)	Mickey Mantle	2500.00	1250.00	750.00
(9)	Willie Mays	1000.00	500.00	300.00
(10)	Bill Mazeroski	150.00	75.00	45.00
(11)	Stan Musial	800.00	400.00	240.00
(12)	Camilo Pascual	100.00	50.00	30.00
(13)	Bobby Richardson	150.00	75.00	45.00
(14)	Brooks Robinson	400.00	200.00	120.00
(15)	Frank Robinson	350.00	175.00	105.00
(16)	Norm Siebern	100.00	50.00	30.00
(17)	Leon Wagner	100.00	50.00	30.00
(18)	Bill White	100.00	50.00	30.00

1961 Topps Magic Rub-Offs

Not too different in concept from the tattoos of the previous year, the Topps Magic Rub-Off was designed to leave impressions of team themes or individual players when properly applied. Measuring 2-1/16" by 3-1/16," the Magic Rub-Off was not designed specifically for application to the owner's skin. The set of 36 Rub-Offs seems to almost be a tongue-in-cheek product as the team themes were a far cry from official logos, and the players seem to have been included for their nicknames. Among the players (one representing each team) the best known and most valuable are Yogi Berra and Ernie Banks.

		NR MT	EX	VG
Complete Set:		85.00	42.00	25.00
Common Player:		2.00	1.00	.60
(1)	Baltimore Orioles Pennant	2.00	1.00	.60
(2)	Ernie "Bingo" Banks	12.00	6.00	3.50
(3)	Yogi Berra	20.00	10.00	6.00
(4)	Boston Red Sox Pennant	2.00	1.00	.60
(5)	Jackie "Ozark" Brandt	2.00	1.00	.60
(6)	Jim "Professor" Brosnan	2.00	1.00	.60
(7)	Chicago Cubs Pennant	2.00	1.00	.60
(8)	Chicago White Sox Pennant	2.00	1.00	.60
(9)	Cincinnati Red Legs Pennant	2.00	1.00	.60
(10)	Cleveland Indians Pennant	2.00	1.00	.60
(11)	Detroit Tigers Pennant	2.00	1.00	.60
(12)	Henry "Dutch" Dotterer	2.00	1.00	.60
(13)	Joe "Flash" Gordon	2.00	1.00	.60
(14)	Harvey "The Kitten" Haddix	2.00	1.00	.60
(15)	Frank "Pancho" Hererra	2.00	1.00	.60
(16)	Frank "Tower" Howard	3.50	1.75	1.00
(17)	"Sad" Sam Jones	2.00	1.00	.60
(18)	Kansas City Athletics Pennant	2.00	1.00	.60
(19)	Los Angeles Angels Pennant	2.00	1.00	.60
(20)	Los Angeles Dodgers Pennant	2.00	1.00	.60
(21)	Omar "Turk" Lown	2.00	1.00	.60
(22)	Billy "The Kid" Martin	6.00	3.00	1.75
(23)	Duane "Duke" Mass (Maas)	2.00	1.00	.60
(24)	Charlie "Paw Paw" Maxwell	2.00	1.00	.60
(25)	Milwaukee Braves Pennant	2.00	1.00	.60
(26)	Minnesota Twins Pennant	2.00	1.00	.60
(27)	"Farmer" Ray Moore	2.00	1.00	.60
(28)	Walt "Moose" Moryn	2.00	1.00	.60
(29)	New York Yankees Pennant	2.50	1.25	.70
(30)	Philadelphia Phillies Pennant	2.00	1.00	.60
(31)	Pittsburgh Pirates Pennant	2.00	1.00	.60
(32)	John "Honey" Romano	2.00	1.00	.60
(33)	"Pistol Pete" Runnels	2.00	1.00	.60
(34)	St. Louis Cardinals Pennant	2.00	1.00	.60
(35)	San Francisco Giants Pennant	2.00	1.00	.60
(36)	Washington Senators Pennant	2.00	1.00	.60

1961 Topps Stamps

Issued as an added insert to 1961 Topps wax packs these 1-3/8" by 1-3/16" stamps were desigend to be collected and placed in an album which could be bought for an additional 10¢. Packs of cards contained two stamps. There are 208 stamps in a complete set which depict 207 different players (Al Kaline appears twice). There are 104 players on brown stamps and 104 on green. While there are many Hall of Famers on the stamps, prices remain low because there is relatively little interest in what is a non-card set.

		NR MT	EX	VG
Complete Set:		225.00	112.00	67.00
Stamp Album:		35.00	17.50	10.50
Common Player:		1.00	.50	.30
(1)	Hank Aaron	10.00	5.00	3.00
(2)	Joe Adcock	1.00	.50	.30
(3)	Hank Aguirre	1.00	.50	.30
(4)	Bob Allison	1.00	.50	.30
(5)	George Altman	1.00	.50	.30
(6)	Bob Anderson	1.00	.50	.30
(7)	Johnny Antonelli	1.00	.50	.30
(8)	Luis Aparicio	3.00	1.50	.90
(9)	Luis Arroyo	1.00	.50	.30
(10)	Richie Ashburn	3.00	1.50	.90
(11)	Ken Aspromonte	1.00	.50	.30
(12)	Ed Bailey	1.00	.50	.30
(13)	Ernie Banks	6.00	3.00	1.75
(14)	Steve Barber	1.00	.50	.30
(15)	Earl Battey	1.00	.50	.30
(16)	Hank Bauer	1.00	.50	.30
(17)	Gus Bell	1.00	.50	.30
(18)	Yogi Berra	8.00	4.00	2.50
(19)	Reno Bertoia	1.00	.50	.30
(20)	John Blanchard	1.00	.50	.30
(21)	Don Blasingame	1.00	.50	.30
(22)	Frank Bolling	1.00	.50	.30
(23)	Steve Boros	1.00	.50	.30
(24)	Ed Bouchee	1.00	.50	.30
(25)	Bob Boyd	1.00	.50	.30
(26)	Cletis Boyer	1.00	.50	.30

		NR MT	EX	VG
(27)	Ken Boyer	1.50	.70	.45
(28)	Jackie Brandt	1.00	.50	.30
(29)	Marv Breeding	1.00	.50	.30
(30)	Eddie Bressoud	1.00	.50	.30
(31)	Jim Brewer	1.00	.50	.30
(32)	Tom Brewer	1.00	.50	.30
(33)	Jim Brosnan	1.00	.50	.30
(34)	Bill Bruton	1.00	.50	.30
(35)	Bob Buhl	1.00	.50	.30
(36)	Jim Bunning	1.50	.70	.45
(37)	Smoky Burgess	1.00	.50	.30
(38)	John Buzhardt	1.00	.50	.30
(39)	Johnny Callison	1.00	.50	.30
(40)	Chico Cardenas	1.00	.50	.30
(41)	Andy Carey	1.00	.50	.30
(42)	Jerry Casale	1.00	.50	.30
(43)	Norm Cash	1.50	.70	.45
(44)	Orlando Cepeda	2.00	1.00	.60
(45)	Bob Cerv	1.00	.50	.30
(46)	Harry Chiti	1.00	.50	.30
(47)	Gene Conley	1.00	.50	.30
(48)	Wes Covington	1.00	.50	.30
(49)	Del Crandall	1.00	.50	.30
(50)	Tony Curry	1.00	.50	.30
(51)	Bud Daley	1.00	.50	.30
(52)	Pete Daley	1.00	.50	.30
(53)	Clay Dalrymple	1.00	.50	.30
(54)	Jim Davenport	1.00	.50	.30
(55)	Tommy Davis	1.00	.50	.30
(56)	Bobby Del Greco	1.00	.50	.30
(57)	Ike Delock	1.00	.50	.30
(58)	Art Ditmar	1.00	.50	.30
(59)	Dick Donovan	1.00	.50	.30
(60)	Don Drysdale	6.00	3.00	1.75
(61)	Dick Ellsworth	1.00	.50	.30
(62)	Don Elston	1.00	.50	.30
(63)	Chuck Estrada	1.00	.50	.30
(64)	Roy Face	1.00	.50	.30
(65)	Dick Farrell	1.00	.50	.30
(66)	Chico Fernandez	1.00	.50	.30
(67)	Curt Flood	1.00	.50	.30
(68)	Whitey Ford	5.00	2.50	1.50
(69)	Tito Francona	1.00	.50	.30
(70)	Gene Freese	1.00	.50	.30
(71)	Bob Friend	1.00	.50	.30
(72)	Billy Gardner	1.00	.50	.30
(73)	Ned Garver	1.00	.50	.30
(74)	Gary Geiger	1.00	.50	.30
(75)	Jim Gentile	1.00	.50	.30
(76)	Dick Gernert	1.00	.50	.30
(77)	Tony Gonzalez	1.00	.50	.30
(78)	Alex Grammas	1.00	.50	.30
(79)	Jim Grant	1.00	.50	.30
(80)	Dick Groat	1.00	.50	.30
(81)	Dick Hall	1.00	.50	.30
(82)	Ron Hansen	1.00	.50	.30
(83)	Bob Hartman	1.00	.50	.30
(84)	Woodie Held	1.00	.50	.30
(85)	Ray Herbert	1.00	.50	.30
(86)	Frank Herrera	1.00	.50	.30
(87)	Whitey Herzog	1.50	.70	.45
(88)	Don Hoak	1.00	.50	.30
(89)	Elston Howard	2.00	1.00	.60
(90)	Frank Howard	2.00	1.00	.60
(91)	Ken Hunt	1.00	.50	.30
(92)	Larry Jackson	1.00	.50	.30
(93)	Julian Javier	1.00	.50	.30
(94)	Joe Jay	1.00	.50	.30
(95)	Jackie Jensen	1.00	.50	.30
(96)	Jim Kaat	1.50	.70	.45
(97a)	Al Kaline (green)	7.00	3.50	2.00
(97b)	Al Kaline (brown)	7.00	3.50	2.00
(98)	Eddie Kasko	1.00	.50	.30
(99)	Russ Kemmerer	1.00	.50	.30
(100)	Harmon Killebrew	5.00	2.50	1.50
(101)	Billy Klaus	1.00	.50	.30
(102)	Ron Kline	1.00	.50	.30
(103)	Johnny Klippstein	1.00	.50	.30
(104)	Ted Kluszewski	3.00	1.50	.90
(105)	Tony Kubek	2.00	1.00	.60
(106)	Harvey Kuenn	1.50	.70	.45
(107)	Jim Landis	1.00	.50	.30
(108)	Hobie Landrith	1.00	.50	.30
(109)	Norm Larker	1.00	.50	.30
(110)	Frank Lary	1.00	.50	.30
(111)	Barry Latman	1.00	.50	.30
(112)	Vern Law	1.00	.50	.30
(113)	Jim Lemon	1.00	.50	.30
(114)	Sherm Lollar	1.00	.50	.30
(115)	Dale Long	1.00	.50	.30
(116)	Jerry Lumpe	1.00	.50	.30

		NR MT	EX	VG
(117)	Jerry Lynch	1.00	.50	.30
(118)	Art Mahaffey	1.00	.50	.30
(119)	Frank Malzone	1.00	.50	.30
(120)	Felix Mantilla	1.00	.50	.30
(121)	Mickey Mantle	50.00	25.00	15.00
(122)	Juan Marichal	5.00	2.50	1.50
(123)	Roger Maris	12.00	6.00	3.50
(124)	Billy Martin	2.00	1.00	.60
(125)	J.C. Martin	1.00	.50	.30
(126)	Ed Mathews	6.00	3.00	1.75
(127)	Charlie Maxwell	1.00	.50	.30
(128)	Willie Mays	12.00	6.00	3.50
(129)	Bill Mazeroski	4.00	2.00	1.25
(130)	Mike McCormick	1.00	.50	.30
(131)	Willie McCovey	5.00	2.50	1.50
(132)	Lindy McDaniel	1.00	.50	.30
(133)	Roy McMillan	1.00	.50	.30
(134)	Minnie Minoso	1.50	.70	.45
(135)	Bill Monbouquette	1.00	.50	.30
(136)	Wally Moon	1.00	.50	.30
(137)	Stan Musial	12.00	6.00	3.50
(138)	Charlie Neal	1.00	.50	.30
(139)	Rocky Nelson	1.00	.50	.30
(140)	Russ Nixon	1.00	.50	.30
(141)	Billy O'Dell	1.00	.50	.30
(142)	Jim O'Toole	1.00	.50	.30
(143)	Milt Pappas	1.00	.50	.30
(144)	Camilo Pascual	1.00	.50	.30
(145)	Jim Perry	1.00	.50	.30
(146)	Bubba Phillips	1.00	.50	.30
(147)	Bill Pierce	1.00	.50	.30
(148)	Jim Piersall	1.00	.50	.30
(149)	Vada Pinson	1.50	.70	.45
(150)	Johnny Podres	1.50	.70	.45
(151)	Wally Post	1.00	.50	.30
(152)	Vic Powers (Power)	1.00	.50	.30
(153)	Pedro Ramos	1.00	.50	.30
(154)	Robin Roberts	3.00	1.50	.90
(155)	Brooks Robinson	6.00	3.00	1.75
(156)	Frank Robinson	6.00	3.00	1.75
(157)	Ed Roebuck	1.00	.50	.30
(158)	John Romano	1.00	.50	.30
(159)	John Roseboro	1.00	.50	.30
(160)	Pete Runnels	1.00	.50	.30
(161)	Ed Sadowski	1.00	.50	.30
(162)	Jack Sanford	1.00	.50	.30
(163)	Ron Santo	1.00	.50	.30
(164)	Ray Semproch	1.00	.50	.30
(165)	Bobby Shantz	1.50	.70	.45
(166)	Bob Shaw	1.00	.50	.30
(167)	Larry Sherry	1.00	.50	.30
(168)	Norm Siebern	1.00	.50	.30
(169)	Roy Sievers	1.00	.50	.30
(170)	Curt Simmons	1.00	.50	.30
(171)	Dave Sisler	1.00	.50	.30
(172)	Bob Skinner	1.00	.50	.30
(173)	Al Smith	1.00	.50	.30
(174)	Hal Smith	1.00	.50	.30
(175)	Hal Smith	1.00	.50	.30
(176)	Duke Snider	6.00	3.00	1.75
(177)	Warren Spahn	6.00	3.00	1.75
(178)	Daryl Spencer	1.00	.50	.30
(179)	Bill Stafford	1.00	.50	.30
(180)	Jerry Staley	1.00	.50	.30
(181)	Gene Stephens	1.00	.50	.30
(182)	Chuck Stobbs	1.00	.50	.30
(183)	Dick Stuart	1.00	.50	.30
(184)	Willie Tasby	1.00	.50	.30
(185)	Sammy Taylor	1.00	.50	.30
(186)	Tony Taylor	1.00	.50	.30
(187)	Johnny Temple	1.00	.50	.30
(188)	Marv Throneberry	1.00	.50	.30
(189)	Gus Triandos	1.00	.50	.30
(190)	Bob Turley	1.00	.50	.30
(191)	Bill Tuttle	1.00	.50	.30
(192)	Zorro Versalles	1.00	.50	.30
(193)	Bill Virdon	1.00	.50	.30
(194)	Lee Walls	1.00	.50	.30
(195)	Vic Wertz	1.00	.50	.30
(196)	Pete Whisenant	1.00	.50	.30
(197)	Bill White	1.50	.70	.45
(198)	Hoyt Wilhelm	3.00	1.50	.90
(199)	Bob Will	1.00	.50	.30
(200)	Carl Willey	1.00	.50	.30
(201)	Billy Williams	4.50	2.25	1.25
(202)	Dick Williams	1.00	.50	.30
(203)	Stan Williams	1.00	.50	.30
(204)	Gene Woodling	1.00	.50	.30
(205)	Early Wynn	3.00	1.50	.90
(206)	Carl Yastrzemski	7.00	3.50	2.00
(207)	Eddie Yost	1.00	.50	.30

1962 Topps

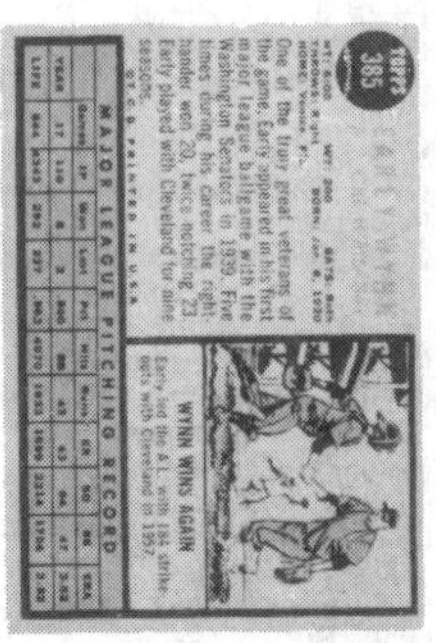

The 1962 Topps set established another plateau for set size with 598 cards. The 2-1/2" by 3-1/2" cards feature a photograph set against a woodgrain background. The lower righthand corner has been made to look like it is curling away. Many established specialty cards dot the set including statistical leaders, multi-player cards, team cards, checklists, World Series cards and All-Stars. Of note is that 1962 was the first year of the multi-player rookie card. There is a 9-card "In Action" subset and a 10-card run of special Babe Ruth cards. Photo variations of several cards in the 2nd Series (#'s 110-196) exist. All cards in the 2nd Series can be found with two distinct printing variations, an early printing with the cards containing a very noticeable greenish tint, having been corrected to clear photos in subsequent print runs. The complete set price in the checklist that follows does not include the higher-priced variations. Among the high numbers (#523-598) certain cards were "short-printed," produced in lesser quantities. These cards carry a higher value and are indicated in the checklist by the notation (SP) after the player name.

		NR MT	EX	VG
Complete Set (598):		5000.00	2500.00	1500.
Common Player: 1-370		3.50	1.75	1.00
Common Player: 371-522		5.00	2.50	1.50
Common Player: 523-598		20.00	10.00	6.00
1	Roger Maris	225.00	112.00	67.00
2	Jim Brosnan	3.50	1.75	1.00
3	Pete Runnels	3.50	1.75	1.00
4	John DeMerit	3.50	1.75	1.00
5	Sandy Koufax	115.00	57.00	34.00
6	Marv Breeding	3.50	1.75	1.00
7	Frank J. Thomas	3.50	1.75	1.00
8	Ray Herbert	3.50	1.75	1.00
9	Jim Davenport	3.50	1.75	1.00
10	Roberto Clemente	125.00	62.00	37.00
11	Tom Morgan	3.50	1.75	1.00
12	Harry Craft	3.50	1.75	1.00
13	Dick Howser	3.50	1.75	1.00
14	Bill White	4.50	2.25	1.25
15	Dick Donovan	3.50	1.75	1.00
16	Darrell Johnson	3.50	1.75	1.00
17	Johnny Callison	3.50	1.75	1.00
18	Managers' Dream (Mickey Mantle, Willie Mays)	100.00	50.00	30.00
19	*Ray Washburn*	3.50	1.75	1.00
20	Rocky Colavito	8.00	4.00	2.50
21	Jim Kaat	5.00	2.50	1.50
22a	Checklist 1-88 (numbers 121-176 on back)	5.00	2.50	1.50
22b	Checklist 1-88 (numbers 33-88 on back)	5.00	2.50	1.50
23	Norm Larker	3.50	1.75	1.00
24	Tigers Team	7.50	3.75	2.25
25	Ernie Banks	45.00	22.00	13.50
26	Chris Cannizzaro	3.50	1.75	1.00
27	Chuck Cottier	3.50	1.75	1.00
28	Minnie Minoso	5.00	2.50	1.50
29	Casey Stengel	20.00	10.00	6.00
30	Eddie Mathews	20.00	10.00	6.00
31	*Tom Tresh*	15.00	7.50	4.50
32	John Roseboro	3.50	1.75	1.00
33	Don Larsen	3.50	1.75	1.00
34	Johnny Temple	3.50	1.75	1.00
35	*Don Schwall*	3.50	1.75	1.00
36	Don Leppert	3.50	1.75	1.00
37	Tribe Hill Trio (Barry Latman, Jim Perry, Dick Stigman)	5.00	2.50	1.50
38	Gene Stephens	3.50	1.75	1.00
39	Joe Koppe	3.50	1.75	1.00
40	Orlando Cepeda	9.00	4.50	2.75
41	Cliff Cook	3.50	1.75	1.00
42	Jim King	3.50	1.75	1.00
43	Dodgers Team	7.50	3.75	2.25
44	Don Taussig	3.50	1.75	1.00
45	Brooks Robinson	35.00	17.50	10.50
46	*Jack Baldschun*	3.50	1.75	1.00
47	Bob Will	3.50	1.75	1.00
48	Ralph Terry	4.00	2.00	1.25
49	Hal Jones	3.50	1.75	1.00
50	Stan Musial	100.00	50.00	30.00
51	A.L. Batting Leaders (Norm Cash, Elston Howard, Al Kaline, Jim Piersall)	8.00	4.00	2.50
52	N.L. Batting Leaders (Ken Boyer, Bob Clemente, Wally Moon, Vada Pinson)	8.00	4.00	2.50
53	A.L. Home Run Leaders (Jim Gentile, Harmon Killebrew, Mickey Mantle, Roger Maris)	55.00	27.00	16.50
54	N.L. Home Run Leaders (Orlando Cepeda, Willie Mays, Frank Robinson)	12.00	6.00	3.50
55	A.L. E.R.A. Leaders (Dick Donovan, Don Mossi, Milt Pappas, Bill Stafford)	8.00	4.00	2.50
56	N.L. E.R.A. Leaders (Mike McCormick, Jim O'Toole, Curt Simmons, Warren Spahn)	8.00	4.00	2.50
57	A.L. Win Leaders (Steve Barber, Jim Bunning, Whitey Ford, Frank Lary)	8.00	4.00	2.50
58	N.L. Win Leaders (Joe Jay, Jim O'Toole, Warren Spahn)	8.00	4.00	2.50
59	A.L. Strikeout Leaders (Jim Bunning, Whitey Ford, Camilo Pascual, Juan Pizzaro)	8.00	4.00	2.50
60	N.L. Strikeout Leaders (Don Drysdale, Sandy Koufax, Jim O'Toole, Stan Williams)	9.00	4.50	2.75
61	Cardinals Team	7.50	3.75	2.25
62	Steve Boros	3.50	1.75	1.00
63	*Tony Cloninger*	3.50	1.75	1.00
64	Russ Snyder	3.50	1.75	1.00
65	Bobby Richardson	6.00	3.00	1.75
66	Cuno Barragon (Barragan)	3.50	1.75	1.00
67	Harvey Haddix	3.50	1.75	1.00
68	Ken L. Hunt	3.50	1.75	1.00
69	Phil Ortega	3.50	1.75	1.00
70	Harmon Killebrew	20.00	10.00	6.00
71	Dick LeMay	3.50	1.75	1.00
72	Bob's Pupils (Steve Boros, Bob Scheffing, Jake Wood)	4.50	2.25	1.25
73	Nellie Fox	8.00	4.00	2.50
74	Bob Lillis	3.50	1.75	1.00
75	Milt Pappas	3.50	1.75	1.00
76	Howie Bedell	3.50	1.75	1.00
77	Tony Taylor	3.50	1.75	1.00
78	Gene Green	3.50	1.75	1.00
79	Ed Hobaugh	3.50	1.75	1.00
80	Vada Pinson	5.00	2.50	1.50
81	Jim Pagliaroni	3.50	1.75	1.00
82	Deron Johnson	3.50	1.75	1.00
83	Larry Jackson	3.50	1.75	1.00
84	Lenny Green	3.50	1.75	1.00
85	Gil Hodges	17.50	8.75	5.25
86	*Donn Clendenon*	3.50	1.75	1.00
87	Mike Roarke	3.50	1.75	1.00
88	Ralph Houk	3.50	1.75	1.00
89	Barney Schultz	3.50	1.75	1.00
90	Jim Piersall	3.50	1.75	1.00
91	J.C. Martin	3.50	1.75	1.00
92	Sam Jones	3.50	1.75	1.00
93	John Blanchard	3.50	1.75	1.00
94	Jay Hook	3.50	1.75	1.00
95	Don Hoak	3.50	1.75	1.00
96	Eli Grba	3.50	1.75	1.00
97	Tito Francona	3.50	1.75	1.00
98	Checklist 89-176	5.00	2.50	1.50
99	*Boog Powell*	15.00	7.50	4.50
100	Warren Spahn	25.00	12.50	7.50
101	Carroll Hardy	3.50	1.75	1.00
102	Al Schroll	3.50	1.75	1.00
103	Don Blasingame	3.50	1.75	1.00
104	Ted Savage	3.50	1.75	1.00
105	Don Mossi	3.50	1.75	1.00
106	Carl Sawatski	3.50	1.75	1.00
107	Mike McCormick	3.50	1.75	1.00

		NR MT	EX	VG
108	Willie Davis	5.00	2.50	1.50
109	Bob Shaw	3.50	1.75	1.00
110	Bill Skowron	5.00	2.50	1.50
111	Dallas Green	4.50	2.25	1.25
112	Hank Foiles	3.50	1.75	1.00
113	White Sox Team	7.50	3.75	2.25
114	Howie Koplitz	3.50	1.75	1.00
115	Bob Skinner	3.50	1.75	1.00
116	Herb Score	3.50	1.75	1.00
117	Gary Geiger	3.50	1.75	1.00
118	Julian Javier	3.50	1.75	1.00
119	Danny Murphy	3.50	1.75	1.00
120	Bob Purkey	3.50	1.75	1.00
121	Billy Hitchcock	3.50	1.75	1.00
122	Norm Bass	3.50	1.75	1.00
123	Mike de la Hoz	3.50	1.75	1.00
124	Bill Pleis	3.50	1.75	1.00
125	Gene Woodling	3.50	1.75	1.00
126	Al Cicotte	3.50	1.75	1.00
127	Pride of the A's (Hank Bauer, Jerry Lumpe, Norm Siebern)	3.50	1.75	1.00
128	Art Fowler	3.50	1.75	1.00
129a	Lee Walls (facing left)	20.00	10.00	6.00
129b	Lee Walls (facing right)	3.50	1.75	1.00
130	Frank Bolling	3.50	1.75	1.00
131	*Pete Richert*	3.50	1.75	1.00
132a	Angels Team (with inset photos)	22.00	11.00	6.50
132b	Angels Team (no inset photos)	8.00	4.00	2.50
133	Felipe Alou	5.00	2.50	1.50
134a	Billy Hoeft (green sky)	20.00	10.00	6.00
134b	Billy Hoeft (blue sky)	3.50	1.75	1.00
135	Babe As A Boy	11.00	5.50	3.25
136	Babe Joins Yanks	15.00	7.50	4.50
137	Babe and Mgr. Huggins	15.00	7.50	4.50
138	The Famous Slugger	15.00	7.50	4.50
139a	Hal Reniff (pitching)	40.00	20.00	12.00
139b	Hal Reniff (portrait)	20.00	10.00	6.00
139c	Babe Hits 60	20.00	10.00	6.00
140	Gehrig and Ruth	20.00	10.00	6.00
141	Twilight Years	11.00	5.50	3.25
142	Coaching for the Dodgers	11.00	5.50	3.25
143	Greatest Sports Hero	11.00	5.50	3.25
144	Farewell Speech	11.00	5.50	3.25
145	Barry Latman	3.50	1.75	1.00
146	Don Demeter	3.50	1.75	1.00
147a	Bill Kunkel (pitching)	20.00	10.00	6.00
147b	Bill Kunkel (portrait)	3.50	1.75	1.00
148	Wally Post	3.50	1.75	1.00
149	Bob Duliba	3.50	1.75	1.00
150	Al Kaline	30.00	15.00	9.00
151	Johnny Klippstein	3.50	1.75	1.00
152	Mickey Vernon	3.50	1.75	1.00
153	Pumpsie Green	3.50	1.75	1.00
154	Lee Thomas	3.50	1.75	1.00
155	Stu Miller	3.50	1.75	1.00
156	Merritt Ranew	3.50	1.75	1.00
157	Wes Covington	3.50	1.75	1.00
158	Braves Team	7.50	3.75	2.25
159	Hal Reniff	3.50	1.75	1.00
160	Dick Stuart	3.50	1.75	1.00
161	Frank Baumann	3.50	1.75	1.00
162	Sammy Drake	3.50	1.75	1.00
163	Hot Corner Guardians (Cletis Boyer, Billy Gardner)	5.00	2.50	1.50
164	Hal Naragon	3.50	1.75	1.00
165	Jackie Brandt	3.50	1.75	1.00
166	Don Lee	3.50	1.75	1.00
167	*Tim McCarver*	30.00	15.00	9.00
168	Leo Posada	3.50	1.75	1.00
169	Bob Cerv	3.50	1.75	1.00
170	Ron Santo	12.00	6.00	3.50
171	Dave Sisler	3.50	1.75	1.00
172	Fred Hutchinson	3.50	1.75	1.00
173	Chico Fernandez	3.50	1.75	1.00
174a	Carl Willey (with cap)	20.00	10.00	6.00
174b	Carl Willey (no cap)	3.50	1.75	1.00
175	Frank Howard	5.00	2.50	1.50
176a	Eddie Yost (batting)	20.00	10.00	6.00
176b	Eddie Yost (portrait)	3.50	1.75	1.00
177	Bobby Shantz	4.50	2.25	1.25
178	Camilo Carreon	3.50	1.75	1.00
179	Tom Sturdivant	3.50	1.75	1.00
180	Bob Allison	3.50	1.75	1.00
181	Paul Brown	3.50	1.75	1.00
182	Bob Nieman	3.50	1.75	1.00
183	Roger Craig	5.00	2.50	1.50
184	Haywood Sullivan	3.50	1.75	1.00
185	Roland Sheldon	3.50	1.75	1.00
186	*Mack Jones*	3.50	1.75	1.00
187	Gene Conley	3.50	1.75	1.00
188	Chuck Hiller	3.50	1.75	1.00

		NR MT	EX	VG
189	Dick Hall	3.50	1.75	1.00
190a	Wally Moon (with cap)	22.00	11.00	6.50
190b	Wally Moon (no cap)	3.50	1.75	1.00
191	Jim Brewer	3.50	1.75	1.00
192a	Checklist 177-264 (192 is Check List, 3)	6.00	3.00	1.75
192b	Checklist 177-264 (192 is Check List 3)	5.00	2.50	1.50
193	Eddie Kasko	3.50	1.75	1.00
194	*Dean Chance*	5.00	2.50	1.50
195	Joe Cunningham	3.50	1.75	1.00
196	Terry Fox	3.50	1.75	1.00
197	Daryl Spencer	3.50	1.75	1.00
198	Johnny Keane	3.50	1.75	1.00
199	*Gaylord Perry*	150.00	75.00	45.00
200	Mickey Mantle	550.00	275.00	165.00
201	Ike Delock	3.50	1.75	1.00
202	Carl Warwick	3.50	1.75	1.00
203	Jack Fisher	3.50	1.75	1.00
204	Johnny Weekly	3.50	1.75	1.00
205	Gene Freese	3.50	1.75	1.00
206	Senators Team	7.50	3.75	2.25
207	Pete Burnside	3.50	1.75	1.00
208	Billy Martin	6.00	3.00	1.75
209	*Jim Fregosi*	10.00	5.00	3.00
210	Roy Face	3.50	1.75	1.00
211	Midway Masters (Frank Bolling, Roy McMillan)	3.50	1.75	1.00
212	Jim Owens	3.50	1.75	1.00
213	Richie Ashburn	6.00	3.00	1.75
214	Dom Zanni	3.50	1.75	1.00
215	Woody Held	3.50	1.75	1.00
216	Ron Kline	3.50	1.75	1.00
217	Walt Alston	5.00	2.50	1.50
218	*Joe Torre*	25.00	12.50	7.50
219	*Al Downing*	4.50	2.25	1.25
220	Roy Sievers	3.50	1.75	1.00
221	Bill Short	3.50	1.75	1.00
222	Jerry Zimmerman	3.50	1.75	1.00
223	Alex Grammas	3.50	1.75	1.00
224	Don Rudolph	3.50	1.75	1.00
225	Frank Malzone	3.50	1.75	1.00
226	Giants Team	7.50	3.75	2.25
227	Bobby Tiefenauer	3.50	1.75	1.00
228	Dale Long	3.50	1.75	1.00
229	Jesus McFarlane	3.50	1.75	1.00
230	Camlio Pascual	3.50	1.75	1.00
231	Ernie Bowman	3.50	1.75	1.00
232	World Series Game 1 (Yanks Win Opener)	7.00	3.50	2.00
233	World Series Game 2 (Jay Ties It Up)	7.00	3.50	2.00
234	World Series Game 3 (Maris Wins It In The 9th)	12.00	6.00	3.50
235	World Series Game 4 (Ford Sets New Mark)	9.00	4.50	2.75
236	World Series Game 5 (Yanks Crush Reds In Finale)	9.00	4.50	2.75
237	World Series Summary (The Winners Celebrate)	7.00	3.50	2.00
238	Norm Sherry	3.50	1.75	1.00
239	Cecil Butler	3.50	1.75	1.00
240	George Altman	3.50	1.75	1.00
241	Johnny Kucks	3.50	1.75	1.00
242	Mel McGaha	3.50	1.75	1.00
243	Robin Roberts	15.00	7.50	4.50
244	Don Gile	3.50	1.75	1.00
245	Ron Hansen	3.50	1.75	1.00
246	Art Ditmar	3.50	1.75	1.00
247	Joe Pignatano	3.50	1.75	1.00
248	Bob Aspromonte	3.50	1.75	1.00
249	Ed Keegan	3.50	1.75	1.00
250	Norm Cash	7.00	3.50	2.00
251	Yankees Team	25.00	12.50	7.50
252	Earl Francis	3.50	1.75	1.00
253	Harry Chiti	3.50	1.75	1.00
254	Gordon Windhorn	3.50	1.75	1.00
255	Juan Pizarro	3.50	1.75	1.00
256	Elio Chacon	3.50	1.75	1.00
257	Jack Spring	3.50	1.75	1.00
258	Marty Keough	3.50	1.75	1.00
259	Lou Klimchock	3.50	1.75	1.00
260	Bill Pierce	3.50	1.75	1.00
261	George Alusik	3.50	1.75	1.00
262	Bob Schmidt	3.50	1.75	1.00
263	The Right Pitch (Joe Jay, Bob Purkey, Jim Turner)	4.50	2.25	1.25
264	Dick Ellsworth	3.50	1.75	1.00
265	Joe Adcock	3.50	1.75	1.00
266	John Anderson	3.50	1.75	1.00
267	Dan Dobbek	3.50	1.75	1.00

		NR MT	EX	VG
268	Ken McBride	3.50	1.75	1.00
269	Bob Oldis	3.50	1.75	1.00
270	Dick Groat	3.50	1.75	1.00
271	Ray Rippelmeyer	3.50	1.75	1.00
272	Earl Robinson	3.50	1.75	1.00
273	Gary Bell	3.50	1.75	1.00
274	Sammy Taylor	3.50	1.75	1.00
275	Norm Siebern	3.50	1.75	1.00
276	Hal Kostad	3.50	1.75	1.00
277	Checklist 265-352	5.00	2.50	1.50
278	Ken Johnson	3.50	1.75	1.00
279	Hobie Landrith	3.50	1.75	1.00
280	Johnny Podres	4.50	2.25	1.25
281	*Jake Gibbs*	3.50	1.75	1.00
282	Dave Hillman	3.50	1.75	1.00
283	Charlie Smith	3.50	1.75	1.00
284	Ruben Amaro	3.50	1.75	1.00
285	Curt Simmons	3.50	1.75	1.00
286	Al Lopez	5.00	2.50	1.50
287	George Witt	3.50	1.75	1.00
288	Billy Williams	30.00	15.00	9.00
289	Mike Krsnich	3.50	1.75	1.00
290	Jim Gentile	3.50	1.75	1.00
291	Hal Stowe	3.50	1.75	1.00
292	Jerry Kindall	3.50	1.75	1.00
293	Bob Miller	3.50	1.75	1.00
294	Phillies Team	7.50	3.75	2.25
295	Vern Law	3.50	1.75	1.00
296	Ken Hamlin	3.50	1.75	1.00
297	Ron Perranoski	3.50	1.75	1.00
298	Bill Tuttle	3.50	1.75	1.00
299	*Don Wert*	3.50	1.75	1.00
300	Willie Mays	160.00	80.00	48.00
301	Galen Cisco	3.50	1.75	1.00
302	*John Edwards*	3.50	1.75	1.00
303	Frank Torre	3.50	1.75	1.00
304	Dick Farrell	3.50	1.75	1.00
305	Jerry Lumpe	3.50	1.75	1.00
306	Redbird Rippers (Larry Jackson, Lindy McDaniel)	3.50	1.75	1.00
307	Jim Grant	3.50	1.75	1.00
308	Neil Chrisley	3.50	1.75	1.00
309	Moe Morhardt	3.50	1.75	1.00
310	Whitey Ford	25.00	12.50	7.50
311	Kubek Makes The Double Play	6.00	3.00	1.75
312	Spahn Show No-Hit Form	8.00	4.00	2.50
313	Maris Blasts 61st	20.00	10.00	6.00
314	Colavito's Power	6.00	3.00	1.75
315	Ford Tosses a Curve	8.00	4.00	2.50
316	Killebrew Send One into Orbit	20.00	10.00	6.00
317	Musial Plays 21st Season	30.00	15.00	9.00
318	The Switch Hitter Connects (Mickey Mantle)	60.00	30.00	18.00
319	McCormick Shows His Stuff	5.00	2.50	1.50
320	Hank Aaron	145.00	72.00	43.00
321	Lee Stange	3.50	1.75	1.00
322	Al Dark	3.50	1.75	1.00
323	Don Landrum	3.50	1.75	1.00
324	Joe McClain	3.50	1.75	1.00
325	Luis Aparicio	20.00	10.00	6.00
326	Tom Parsons	3.50	1.75	1.00
327	Ozzie Virgil	3.50	1.75	1.00
328	Ken Walters	3.50	1.75	1.00
329	Bob Bolin	3.50	1.75	1.00
330	Johnny Romano	3.50	1.75	1.00
331	Moe Drabowsky	3.50	1.75	1.00
332	Don Buddin	3.50	1.75	1.00
333	Frank Cipriani	3.50	1.75	1.00
334	Red Sox Team	7.50	3.75	2.25
335	Bill Bruton	3.50	1.75	1.00
336	Billy Muffett	3.50	1.75	1.00
337	Jim Marshall	3.50	1.75	1.00
338	Billy Gardner	3.50	1.75	1.00
339	Jose Valdivielso	3.50	1.75	1.00
340	Don Drysdale	35.00	17.50	10.50
341	Mike Hershberger	3.50	1.75	1.00
342	Ed Rakow	3.50	1.75	1.00
343	Albie Pearson	3.50	1.75	1.00
344	Ed Bauta	3.50	1.75	1.00
345	Chuck Schilling	3.50	1.75	1.00
346	Jack Kralick	3.50	1.75	1.00
347	Chuck Hinton	3.50	1.75	1.00
348	Larry Burright	3.50	1.75	1.00
349	Paul Foytack	3.50	1.75	1.00
350	Frank Robinson	50.00	25.00	15.00
351	Braves' Backstops (Del Crandall, Joe Torre)	5.00	2.50	1.50
352	Frank Sullivan	3.50	1.75	1.00
353	Bill Mazeroski	8.00	4.00	2.50
354	Roman Mejias	3.50	1.75	1.00
355	Steve Barber	3.50	1.75	1.00

		NR MT	EX	VG
356	Tom Haller	3.50	1.75	1.00
357	Jerry Walker	3.50	1.75	1.00
358	Tommy Davis	5.00	2.50	1.50
359	Bobby Locke	3.50	1.75	1.00
360	Yogi Berra	70.00	35.00	21.00
361	Bob Hendley	3.50	1.75	1.00
362	Ty Cline	3.50	1.75	1.00
363	Bob Roselli	3.50	1.75	1.00
364	Ken Hunt	3.50	1.75	1.00
365	Charley Neal	3.50	1.75	1.00
366	Phil Regan	3.50	1.75	1.00
367	Checklist 353-429	5.00	2.50	1.50
368	Bob Tillman	3.50	1.75	1.00
369	Ted Bowsfield	3.50	1.75	1.00
370	Ken Boyer	5.00	2.50	1.50
371	Earl Battey	5.00	2.50	1.50
372	Jack Curtis	5.00	2.50	1.50
373	Al Heist	5.00	2.50	1.50
374	Gene Mauch	5.00	2.50	1.50
375	Ron Fairly	5.00	2.50	1.50
376	Bud Daley	5.00	2.50	1.50
377	Johnny Orsino	5.00	2.50	1.50
378	Bennie Daniels	5.00	2.50	1.50
379	Chuck Essegian	5.00	2.50	1.50
380	Lou Burdette	5.00	2.50	1.50
381	Chico Cardenas	5.00	2.50	1.50
382	Dick Williams	6.00	3.00	1.75
383	Ray Sadecki	5.00	2.50	1.50
384	Athletics Team	9.00	4.50	2.75
385	Early Wynn	20.00	10.00	6.00
386	Don Mincher	5.00	2.50	1.50
387	*Lou Brock*	200.00	100.00	60.00
388	Ryne Duren	5.00	2.50	1.50
389	Smoky Burgess	5.00	2.50	1.50
390	Orlando Cepeda (All-Star)	9.00	4.50	2.75
391	Bill Mazeroski (All-Star)	8.00	4.00	2.50
392	Ken Boyer (All-Star)	8.00	4.00	2.50
393	Roy McMillan (All-Star)	6.00	3.00	1.75
394	Hank Aaron (All-Star)	40.00	20.00	12.00
395	Willie Mays (All-Star)	40.00	20.00	12.00
396	Frank Robinson (All-Star)	25.00	12.50	7.50
397	John Roseboro (All-Star)	6.00	3.00	1.75
398	Don Drysdale (All-Star)	15.00	7.50	4.50
399	Warren Spahn (All-Star)	15.00	7.50	4.50
400	Elston Howard	7.00	3.50	2.00
401	AL & NL Homer Kings (Roger Maris, Orlando Cepeda)	35.00	17.50	10.50
402	Gino Cimoli	5.00	2.50	1.50
403	Chet Nichols	5.00	2.50	1.50
404	Tim Harkness	5.00	2.50	1.50
405	Jim Perry	5.00	2.50	1.50
406	Bob Taylor	5.00	2.50	1.50
407	Hank Aguirre	5.00	2.50	1.50
408	Gus Bell	5.00	2.50	1.50
409	Pirates Team	9.00	4.50	2.75
410	Al Smith	5.00	2.50	1.50
411	Danny O'Connell	5.00	2.50	1.50
412	Charlie James	5.00	2.50	1.50
413	Matty Alou	5.00	2.50	1.50
414	Joe Gaines	5.00	2.50	1.50
415	Bill Virdon	5.00	2.50	1.50
416	Bob Scheffing	5.00	2.50	1.50
417	Joe Azcue	5.00	2.50	1.50
418	Andy Carey	5.00	2.50	1.50
419	Bob Bruce	5.00	2.50	1.50
420	Gus Triandos	5.00	2.50	1.50
421	Ken MacKenzie	5.00	2.50	1.50
422	Steve Bilko	5.00	2.50	1.50
423	Rival League Relief Aces (Roy Face, Hoyt Wilhelm)	7.50	3.75	2.25
424	Al McBean	5.00	2.50	1.50
425	Carl Yastrzemski	175.00	87.00	52.00
426	Bob Farley	5.00	2.50	1.50
427	Jake Wood	5.00	2.50	1.50
428	Joe Hicks	5.00	2.50	1.50
429	Bill O'Dell	5.00	2.50	1.50
430	Tony Kubek	8.00	4.00	2.50
431	*Bob Rodgers*	7.00	3.50	2.00
432	Jim Pendleton	5.00	2.50	1.50
433	Jim Archer	5.00	2.50	1.50
434	Clay Dalrymple	5.00	2.50	1.50
435	Larry Sherry	5.00	2.50	1.50
436	Felix Mantilla	5.00	2.50	1.50
437	Ray Moore	5.00	2.50	1.50
438	Dick Brown	5.00	2.50	1.50
439	Jerry Buchek	5.00	2.50	1.50
440	Joe Jay	5.00	2.50	1.50
441	Checklist 430-506	8.00	4.00	2.50
442	Wes Stock	5.00	2.50	1.50
443	Del Crandall	5.00	2.50	1.50
444	Ted Wills	5.00	2.50	1.50

		NR MT	EX	VG
445	Vic Power	5.00	2.50	1.50
446	Don Elston	5.00	2.50	1.50
447	Willie Kirkland	5.00	2.50	1.50
448	Joe Gibbon	5.00	2.50	1.50
449	Jerry Adair	5.00	2.50	1.50
450	Jim O'Toole	5.00	2.50	1.50
451	*Jose Tartabull*	5.00	2.50	1.50
452	Earl Averill	5.00	2.50	1.50
453	Cal McLish	5.00	2.50	1.50
454	Floyd Robinson	5.00	2.50	1.50
455	Luis Arroyo	5.00	2.50	1.50
456	Joe Amalfitano	5.00	2.50	1.50
457	Lou Clinton	5.00	2.50	1.50
458a	Bob Buhl ("M" on cap)	5.00	2.50	1.50
458b	Bob Buhl (plain cap)	60.00	30.00	18.00
459	Ed Bailey	5.00	2.50	1.50
460	Jim Bunning	9.00	4.50	2.75
461	*Ken Hubbs*	20.00	10.00	6.00
462a	Willie Tasby ("W" on cap)	5.00	2.50	1.50
462b	Willie Tasby (plain cap)	60.00	30.00	18.00
463	Hank Bauer	5.00	2.50	1.50
464	*Al Jackson*	5.00	2.50	1.50
465	Reds Team	5.00	2.50	1.50
466	Norm Cash (All-Star)	8.00	4.00	2.50
467	Chuck Schilling (All-Star)	6.00	3.00	1.75
468	Brooks Robinson (All-Star)	20.00	10.00	6.00
469	Luis Aparicio (All-Star)	9.00	4.50	2.75
470	Al Kaline (All-Star)	20.00	10.00	6.00
471	Mickey Mantle (All-Star)	145.00	72.00	43.00
472	Rocky Colavito (All-Star)	12.00	6.00	3.50
473	Elston Howard (All-Star)	8.00	4.00	2.50
474	Frank Lary (All-Star)	6.00	3.00	1.75
475	Whitey Ford (All-Star)	10.00	5.00	3.00
476	Orioles Team	9.00	4.50	2.75
477	Andre Rodgers	6.00	3.00	1.75
478	Don Zimmer	5.00	2.50	1.50
479	*Joel Horlen*	6.00	3.00	1.75
480	Harvey Kuenn	5.00	2.50	1.50
481	Vic Wertz	5.00	2.50	1.50
482	Sam Mele	5.00	2.50	1.50
483	Don McMahon	5.00	2.50	1.50
484	Dick Schofield	5.00	2.50	1.50
485	Pedro Ramos	5.00	2.50	1.50
486	Jim Gilliam	6.00	3.00	1.75
487	Jerry Lynch	5.00	2.50	1.50
488	Hal Brown	5.00	2.50	1.50
489	Julio Gotay	5.00	2.50	1.50
490	Clete Boyer	5.00	2.50	1.50
491	Leon Wagner	5.00	2.50	1.50
492	Hal Smith	5.00	2.50	1.50
493	Danny McDevitt	5.00	2.50	1.50
494	Sammy White	5.00	2.50	1.50
495	Don Cardwell	5.00	2.50	1.50
496	Wayne Causey	5.00	2.50	1.50
497	Ed Bouchee	5.00	2.50	1.50
498	Jim Donohue	5.00	2.50	1.50
499	Zoilo Versalles	5.00	2.50	1.50
500	Duke Snider	45.00	22.00	13.50
501	Claude Osteen	5.00	2.50	1.50
502	Hector Lopez	5.00	2.50	1.50
503	Danny Murtaugh	5.00	2.50	1.50
504	Eddie Bressoud	5.00	2.50	1.50
505	Juan Marichal	37.50	18.50	11.00
506	Charley Maxwell	5.00	2.50	1.50
507	Ernie Broglio	5.00	2.50	1.50
508	Gordy Coleman	5.00	2.50	1.50
509	*Dave Giusti*	5.00	2.50	1.50
510	Jim Lemon	5.00	2.50	1.50
511	Bubba Phillips	5.00	2.50	1.50
512	Mike Fornieles	5.00	2.50	1.50
513	Whitey Herzog	6.00	3.00	1.75
514	Sherm Lollar	5.00	2.50	1.50
515	Stan Williams	5.00	2.50	1.50
516	Checklist 507-598	8.00	4.00	2.50
517	Dave Wickersham	5.00	2.50	1.50
518	Lee Maye	5.00	2.50	1.50
519	Bob Johnson	5.00	2.50	1.50
520	Bob Friend	5.00	2.50	1.50
521	Jacke Davis	5.00	2.50	1.50
522	Lindy McDaniel	5.00	2.50	1.50
523	Russ Nixon (SP)	24.00	12.00	7.25
524	Howie Nunn (SP)	24.00	12.00	7.25
525	George Thomas	20.00	10.00	6.00
526	Hal Woodeshick (SP)	24.00	12.00	7.25
527	*Dick McAuliffe*	20.00	10.00	6.00
528	Turk Lown	20.00	10.00	6.00
529	John Schaive (SP)	24.00	12.00	7.25
530	Bob Gibson	175.00	87.00	52.00
531	Bobby G. Smith	20.00	10.00	6.00
532	Dick Stigman	20.00	10.00	6.00
533	Charley Lau (SP)	24.00	12.00	7.25

		NR MT	EX	VG
534	Tony Gonzalez (SP)	24.00	12.00	7.25
535	Ed Roebuck	20.00	10.00	6.00
536	Dick Gernert	20.00	10.00	6.00
537	Indians Team	40.00	20.00	12.00
538	Jack Sanford	20.00	10.00	6.00
539	Billy Moran	20.00	10.00	6.00
540	Jim Landis (SP)	24.00	12.00	7.25
541	Don Nottebart (SP)	24.00	12.00	7.25
542	Dave Philley	20.00	10.00	6.00
543	Bob Allen (SP)	24.00	12.00	7.25
544	Willie McCovey	130.00	65.00	39.00
545	Hoyt Wilhelm	55.00	27.00	16.50
546	Moe Thacker (SP)	24.00	12.00	7.25
547	Don Ferrarese	20.00	10.00	6.00
548	Bobby Del Greco	20.00	10.00	6.00
549	Bill Rigney (SP)	26.00	13.00	7.75
550	Art Mahaffey (SP)	24.00	12.00	7.25
551	Harry Bright	20.00	10.00	6.00
552	Cubs Team	30.00	15.00	9.00
553	Jim Coates	20.00	10.00	6.00
554	Bubba Morton (SP)	24.00	12.00	7.25
555	John Buzhardt (SP)	24.00	12.00	7.25
556	Al Spangler	20.00	10.00	6.00
557	Bob Anderson (SP)	24.00	12.00	7.25
558	John Goryl	20.00	10.00	6.00
559	Mike Higgins	20.00	10.00	6.00
560	Chuck Estrada (SP)	24.00	12.00	7.25
561	Gene Oliver (SP)	24.00	12.00	7.25
562	Bill Henry	20.00	10.00	6.00
563	Ken Aspromonte	20.00	10.00	6.00
564	Bob Grim	20.00	10.00	6.00
565	Jose Pagan	20.00	10.00	6.00
566	Marty Kutyna (SP)	24.00	12.00	7.25
567	Tracy Stallard (SP)	24.00	12.00	7.25
568	Jim Golden	20.00	10.00	6.00
569	Ed Sadowski (SP)	24.00	12.00	7.25
570	Bill Stafford	20.00	10.00	6.00
571	Billy Klaus (SP)	24.00	12.00	7.25
572	Bob Miller	20.00	10.00	6.00
573	Johnny Logan	20.00	10.00	6.00
574	Dean Stone	20.00	10.00	6.00
575	Red Schoendienst	35.00	17.50	10.50
576	Russ Kemmerer (SP)	24.00	12.00	7.25
577	Dave Nicholson (SP)	24.00	12.00	7.25
578	Jim Duffalo	20.00	10.00	6.00
579	Jim Schaffer (SP)	24.00	12.00	7.25
580	Bill Monbouquette	20.00	10.00	6.00
581	Mel Roach	20.00	10.00	6.00
582	Ron Piche	20.00	10.00	6.00
583	Larry Osborne	20.00	10.00	6.00
584	Twins Team	35.00	17.50	10.50
585	Glen Hobbie (SP)	24.00	12.00	7.25
586	Sammy Esposito (SP)	24.00	12.00	7.25
587	Frank Funk (SP)	24.00	12.00	7.25
588	Birdie Tebbetts	20.00	10.00	6.00
589	Bob Turley	20.00	10.00	6.00
590	Curt Flood	20.00	10.00	6.00
591	Rookie Parade Pitchers (*Sam McDowell, Ron Nischwitz,* Art Quirk, *Dick Radatz, Ron Taylor*)	60.00	30.00	18.00
592	Rookie Parade Pitchers (*Bo Belinsky,* Joe Bonikowski, *Jim Bouton,* Dan Pfister, Dave Stenhouse)	60.00	30.00	18.00
593	Rookie Parade Pitchers (Craig Anderson, *Jack Hamilton,* Jack Lamabe, Bob Moorhead, *Bob Veale*)	25.00	12.50	7.50
594	Rookie Parade Catchers (Doug Camilli, *Doc Edwards,* Don Pavletich, Ken Retzer, *Bob Uecker*)	85.00	42.00	25.00
595	Rookie Parade Infielders (*Ed Charles,* Marlin Coughtry, Bob Sadowski, Felix Torres)	30.00	15.00	9.00
596	Rookie Parade Infielders (*Bernie Allen, Phil Linz, Joe Pepitone, Rich Rollins*)	65.00	32.00	19.50
597	Rookie Parade Infielders (Rod Kanehl, Jim McKnight, *Denis Menke,* Amado Samuel)	30.00	15.00	9.00
598	Rookie Parade Outfielders (Howie Goss, *Jim Hickman,* Manny Jimenez, Al Luplow, Ed Olivares)	65.00	33.00	20.00

1962 Topps Baseball Bucks

Issued in their own 1¢ package, the 1962 Topps "Baseball Bucks" were another in the growing list of specialty Topps items. The 96 Baseball Bucks in the set measure 4-1/8" by 1-3/4," and were designed to look

vaguely like dollar bills. The center player portrait has a banner underneath with the player's name. His home park is shown on the right and there is some biographical information on the left. The back features a large denomination, with the player's league and team logo on either side.

		NR MT	EX	VG
Complete Set:		750.00	375.00	225.00
Common Player:		3.00	1.50	.90
(1)	Hank Aaron	30.00	15.00	9.00
(2)	Joe Adcock	3.00	1.50	.90
(3)	George Altman	3.00	1.50	.90
(4)	Jim Archer	3.00	1.50	.90
(5)	Richie Ashburn	6.00	3.00	1.75
(6)	Ernie Banks	20.00	10.00	6.00
(7)	Earl Battey	3.00	1.50	.90
(8)	Gus Bell	3.00	1.50	.90
(9)	Yogi Berra	20.00	10.00	6.00
(10)	Ken Boyer	3.00	1.50	.90
(11)	Jackie Brandt	3.00	1.50	.90
(12)	Jim Bunning	4.00	2.00	1.25
(13)	Lou Burdette	3.00	1.50	.90
(14)	Don Cardwell	3.00	1.50	.90
(15)	Norm Cash	3.00	1.50	.90
(16)	Orlando Cepeda	6.00	3.00	1.75
(17)	Roberto Clemente	30.00	15.00	9.00
(18)	Rocky Colavito	6.00	3.00	1.75
(19)	Chuck Cottier	3.00	1.50	.90
(20)	Roger Craig	4.00	2.00	1.25
(21)	Bennie Daniels	3.00	1.50	.90
(22)	Don Demeter	3.00	1.50	.90
(23)	Don Drysdale	15.00	7.50	4.50
(24)	Chuck Estrada	3.00	1.50	.90
(25)	Dick Farrell	3.00	1.50	.90
(26)	Whitey Ford	15.00	7.50	4.50
(27)	Nellie Fox	6.00	3.00	1.75
(28)	Tito Francona	3.00	1.50	.90
(29)	Bob Friend	3.00	1.50	.90
(30)	Jim Gentile	3.00	1.50	.90
(31)	Dick Gernert	3.00	1.50	.90
(32)	Lenny Green	3.00	1.50	.90
(33)	Dick Groat	3.00	1.50	.90
(34)	Woody Held	3.00	1.50	.90
(35)	Don Hoak	3.00	1.50	.90
(36)	Gil Hodges	8.00	4.00	2.50
(37)	Frank Howard	4.00	2.00	1.25
(38)	Elston Howard	4.00	2.00	1.25
(39)	Dick Howser	3.00	1.50	.90
(40)	Ken Hunt	3.00	1.50	.90
(41)	Larry Jackson	3.00	1.50	.90
(42)	Joe Jay	3.00	1.50	.90
(43)	Al Kaline	15.00	7.50	4.50
(44)	Harmon Killebrew	15.00	7.50	4.50
(45)	Sandy Koufax	20.00	10.00	6.00
(46)	Harvey Kuenn	4.00	2.00	1.25
(47)	Jim Landis	3.00	1.50	.90
(48)	Norm Larker	3.00	1.50	.90
(49)	Frank Lary	3.00	1.50	.90
(50)	Jerry Lumpe	3.00	1.50	.90
(51)	Art Mahaffey	3.00	1.50	.90
(52)	Frank Malzone	3.00	1.50	.90
(53)	Felix Mantilla	3.00	1.50	.90
(54)	Mickey Mantle	125.00	62.00	37.00
(55)	Roger Maris	12.00	6.00	3.50
(56)	Ed Mathews	15.00	7.50	4.50
(57)	Willie Mays	30.00	15.00	9.00
(58)	Ken McBride	3.00	1.50	.90
(59)	Mike McCormick	3.00	1.50	.90
(60)	Minnie Minoso	4.00	2.00	1.25
(61)	Wally Moon	3.00	1.50	.90
(62)	Stu Miller	3.00	1.50	.90
(63)	Stan Musial	30.00	15.00	9.00
(64)	Danny O'Connell	3.00	1.50	.90
(65)	Jim O'Toole	3.00	1.50	.90
(66)	Camilo Pascual	3.00	1.50	.90
(67)	Jim Perry	3.00	1.50	.90
(68)	Jimmy Piersall	3.00	1.50	.90
(69)	Vada Pinson	5.00	2.50	1.50
(70)	Juan Pizarro	3.00	1.50	.90
(71)	Johnny Podres	3.00	1.50	.90
(72)	Vic Power	3.00	1.50	.90
(73)	Bob Purkey	3.00	1.50	.90
(74)	Pedro Ramos	3.00	1.50	.90
(75)	Brooks Robinson	15.00	7.50	4.50
(76)	Floyd Robinson	3.00	1.50	.90
(77)	Frank Robinson	15.00	7.50	4.50
(78)	Johnny Romano	3.00	1.50	.90
(79)	Pete Runnels	3.00	1.50	.90
(80)	Don Schwall	3.00	1.50	.90
(81)	Bobby Shantz	3.00	1.50	.90
(82)	Norm Siebern	3.00	1.50	.90
(83)	Roy Sievers	3.00	1.50	.90
(84)	Hal (W.) Smith	3.00	1.50	.90
(85)	Warren Spahn	15.00	7.50	4.50
(86)	Dick Stuart	3.00	1.50	.90
(87)	Tony Taylor	3.00	1.50	.90
(88)	Lee Thomas	3.00	1.50	.90
(89)	Gus Triandos	3.00	1.50	.90
(90)	Leon Wagner	3.00	1.50	.90
(91)	Jerry Walker	3.00	1.50	.90
(92)	Bill White	3.00	1.50	.90
(93)	Billy Williams	12.00	6.00	3.50
(94)	Gene Woodling	3.00	1.50	.90
(95)	Early Wynn	12.00	6.00	3.50
(96)	Carl Yastrzemski	15.00	7.50	4.50

1962 Topps Stamps

An artistic improvement over the somewhat drab Topps stamps of the previous year, the 1962 stamps, 1-3/8" by 1-7/8," had color player photographs set on red or yellow backgrounds. As in 1961, they were issued in two-stamp panels as insert with Topps baseball cards. A change from 1961 was the inclusion of team emblems in the set. A complete set consists of 201 stamps; Roy Sievers was originally portrayed on the wrong team - Athletics - and was later corrected to the Phillies.

		NR MT	EX	VG
Complete Set:		220.00	110.00	66.00
Stamp Album:		35.00	17.50	10.50
Common Player:		1.00	.50	.30
(1)	Hank Aaron	10.00	5.00	3.00
(2)	Jerry Adair	1.00	.50	.30
(3)	Joe Adcock	1.00	.50	.30
(4)	Bob Allison	1.00	.50	.30
(5)	Felipe Alou	2.00	1.00	.60
(6)	George Altman	1.00	.50	.30
(7)	Joe Amalfitano	1.00	.50	.30
(8)	Ruben Amaro	1.00	.50	.30
(9)	Luis Aparicio	3.00	1.50	.90
(10)	Jim Archer	1.00	.50	.30
(11)	Bob Aspromonte	1.00	.50	.30

		NR MT	EX	VG
(12)	Ed Bailey	1.00	.50	.30
(13)	Jack Baldschun	1.00	.50	.30
(14)	Ernie Banks	6.00	3.00	1.75
(15)	Earl Battey	1.00	.50	.30
(16)	Gus Bell	1.00	.50	.30
(17)	Yogi Berra	6.00	3.00	1.75
(18)	Dick Bertell	1.00	.50	.30
(19)	Steve Bilko	1.00	.50	.30
(20)	Frank Bolling	1.00	.50	.30
(21)	Steve Boros	1.00	.50	.30
(22)	Ted Bowsfield	1.00	.50	.30
(23)	Clete Boyer	1.00	.50	.30
(24)	Ken Boyer	1.50	.70	.45
(25)	Jackie Brandt	1.00	.50	.30
(26)	Bill Bruton	1.00	.50	.30
(27)	Jim Bunning	1.50	.70	.45
(28)	Lou Burdette	1.00	.50	.30
(29)	Smoky Burgess	1.00	.50	.30
(30)	Johnny Callizon (Callison)	1.00	.50	.30
(31)	Don Cardwell	1.00	.50	.30
(32)	Camilo Carreon	1.00	.50	.30
(33)	Norm Cash	1.50	.70	.45
(34)	Orlando Cepeda	2.00	1.00	.60
(35)	Roberto Clemente	10.00	5.00	3.00
(36)	Ty Cline	1.00	.50	.30
(37)	Rocky Colavito	2.50	1.25	.70
(38)	Gordon Coleman	1.00	.50	.30
(39)	Chuck Cottier	1.00	.50	.30
(40)	Roger Craig	1.50	.70	.45
(41)	Del Crandall	1.00	.50	.30
(42)	Pete Daley	1.00	.50	.30
(43)	Clay Dalrymple	1.00	.50	.30
(44)	Bennie Daniels	1.00	.50	.30
(45)	Jim Davenport	1.00	.50	.30
(46)	Don Demeter	1.00	.50	.30
(47)	Dick Donovan	1.00	.50	.30
(48)	Don Drysdale	7.00	3.50	2.00
(49)	John Edwards	1.00	.50	.30
(50)	Dick Ellsworth	1.00	.50	.30
(51)	Chuck Estrada	1.00	.50	.30
(52)	Roy Face	1.00	.50	.30
(53)	Ron Fairly	1.00	.50	.30
(54)	Dick Farrell	1.00	.50	.30
(55)	Whitey Ford	7.00	3.50	2.00
(56)	Mike Fornieles	1.00	.50	.30
(57)	Nellie Fox	3.00	1.50	.90
(58)	Tito Francona	1.00	.50	.30
(59)	Gene Freese	1.00	.50	.30
(60)	Bob Friend	1.00	.50	.30
(61)	Gary Geiger	1.00	.50	.30
(62)	Jim Gentile	1.00	.50	.30
(63)	Tony Gonzalez	1.00	.50	.30
(64)	Lenny Green	1.00	.50	.30
(65)	Dick Groat	1.00	.50	.30
(66)	Ron Hansen	1.00	.50	.30
(67)	Al Heist	1.00	.50	.30
(68)	Woody Held	1.00	.50	.30
(69)	Ray Herbert	1.00	.50	.30
(70)	Chuck Hinton	1.00	.50	.30
(71)	Don Hoak	1.00	.50	.30
(72)	Glen Hobbie	1.00	.50	.30
(73)	Gil Hodges	5.00	2.50	1.50
(74)	Jay Hook	1.00	.50	.30
(75)	Elston Howard	3.00	1.50	.90
(76)	Frank Howard	1.50	.70	.45
(77)	Dick Howser	1.00	.50	.30
(78)	Ken Hunt	1.00	.50	.30
(79)	Larry Jackson	1.00	.50	.30
(80)	Julian Javier	1.00	.50	.30
(81)	Joe Jay	1.00	.50	.30
(82)	Bob Johnson	1.00	.50	.30
(83)	Sam Jones	1.00	.50	.30
(84)	Al Kaline	7.00	3.50	2.00
(85)	Eddie Kasko	1.00	.50	.30
(86)	Harmon Killebrew	6.00	3.00	1.75
(87)	Sandy Koufax	10.00	5.00	3.00
(88)	Jack Kralick	1.00	.50	.30
(89)	Tony Kubek	2.00	1.00	.60
(90)	Harvey Kuenn	1.50	.70	.45
(91)	Jim Landis	1.00	.50	.30
(92)	Hobie Landrith	1.00	.50	.30
(93)	Frank Lary	1.00	.50	.30
(94)	Barry Latman	1.00	.50	.30
(95)	Jerry Lumpe	1.00	.50	.30
(96)	Art Mahaffey	1.00	.50	.30
(97)	Frank Malzone	1.00	.50	.30
(98)	Felix Mantilla	1.00	.50	.30
(99)	Mickey Mantle	45.00	22.00	13.50
(100)	Juan Marichal	5.00	2.50	1.50
(101)	Roger Maris	5.00	2.50	1.50
(102)	J.C. Martin	1.00	.50	.30

		NR MT	EX	VG
(103)	Ed Mathews	6.00	3.00	1.75
(104)	Willie Mays	10.00	5.00	3.00
(105)	Bill Mazeroski	2.00	1.00	.60
(106)	Ken McBride	1.00	.50	.30
(107)	Tim McCarver	1.50	.70	.45
(108)	Joe McClain	1.00	.50	.30
(109)	Mike McCormick	1.00	.50	.30
(110)	Lindy McDaniel	1.00	.50	.30
(111)	Roy McMillan	1.00	.50	.30
(112)	Bob L. Miller	1.00	.50	.30
(113)	Stu Miller	1.00	.50	.30
(114)	Minnie Minoso	1.50	.70	.45
(115)	Bill Monbouquette	1.00	.50	.30
(116)	Wally Moon	1.00	.50	.30
(117)	Don Mossi	1.00	.50	.30
(118)	Stan Musial	8.00	4.00	2.50
(119)	Russ Nixon	1.00	.50	.30
(120)	Danny O'Connell	1.00	.50	.30
(121)	Jim O'Toole	1.00	.50	.30
(122)	Milt Pappas	1.00	.50	.30
(123)	Camilo Pascual	1.00	.50	.30
(124)	Albie Pearson	1.00	.50	.30
(125)	Jim Perry	1.00	.50	.30
(126)	Bubba Phillips	1.00	.50	.30
(127)	Jimmy Piersall	1.00	.50	.30
(128)	Vada Pinson	1.50	.70	.45
(129)	Juan Pizarro	1.00	.50	.30
(130)	Johnny Podres	1.00	.50	.30
(131)	Leo Posada	1.00	.50	.30
(132)	Vic Power	1.00	.50	.30
(133)	Bob Purkey	1.00	.50	.30
(134)	Pedro Ramos	1.00	.50	.30
(135)	Bobby Richardson	1.50	.70	.45
(136)	Brooks Robinson	7.00	3.50	2.00
(137)	Floyd Robinson	1.00	.50	.30
(138)	Frank Robinson	7.00	3.50	2.00
(139)	Bob Rodgers	1.00	.50	.30
(140)	Johnny Romano	1.00	.50	.30
(141)	John Roseboro	1.00	.50	.30
(142)	Pete Runnels	1.00	.50	.30
(143)	Ray Sadecki	1.00	.50	.30
(144)	Ron Santo	1.50	.70	.45
(145)	Chuck Schilling	1.00	.50	.30
(146)	Barney Schultz	1.00	.50	.30
(147)	Don Schwall	1.00	.50	.30
(148)	Bobby Shantz	1.50	.70	.45
(149)	Bob Shaw	1.00	.50	.30
(150)	Norm Siebern	1.00	.50	.30
(151a)	Roy Sievers (Kansas City)	1.00	.50	.30
(151b)	Roy Sievers (Philadelphia)	1.00	.50	.30
(152)	Bill Skowron	1.50	.70	.45
(153)	Hal (W.) Smith	1.00	.50	.30
(154)	Duke Snider	7.00	3.50	2.00
(155)	Warren Spahn	2.00	1.00	.60
(156)	Al Spangler	1.00	.50	.30
(157)	Daryl Spencer	1.00	.50	.30
(158)	Gene Stephens	1.00	.50	.30
(159)	Dick Stuart	1.00	.50	.30
(160)	Haywood Sullivan	1.00	.50	.30
(161)	Tony Taylor	1.00	.50	.30
(162)	George Thomas	1.00	.50	.30
(163)	Lee Thomas	1.00	.50	.30
(164)	Bob Tiefenauer	1.00	.50	.30
(165)	Joe Torre	1.00	.50	.30
(166)	Gus Triandos	1.00	.50	.30
(167)	Bill Tuttle	1.00	.50	.30
(168)	Zoilo Versalles	1.00	.50	.30
(169)	Bill Virdon	1.00	.50	.30
(170)	Leon Wagner	1.00	.50	.30
(171)	Jerry Walker	1.00	.50	.30
(172)	Lee Walls	1.00	.50	.30
(173)	Bill White	1.50	.70	.45
(174)	Hoyt Wilhelm	4.00	2.00	1.25
(175)	Billy Williams	6.00	3.00	1.75
(176)	Jake Wood	1.00	.50	.30
(177)	Gene Woodling	1.00	.50	.30
(178)	Early Wynn	4.00	2.00	1.25
(179)	Carl Yastrzemski	7.00	3.50	2.00
(180)	Don Zimmer	1.00	.50	.30
(181)	Baltimore Orioles Logo	1.00	.50	.30
(182)	Boston Red Sox Logo	1.00	.50	.30
(183)	Chicago Cubs Logo	1.00	.50	.30
(184)	Chicago White Sox Logo	1.00	.50	.30
(185)	Cincinnati Reds Logo	1.00	.50	.30
(186)	Cleveland Indians Logo	1.00	.50	.30
(187)	Detroit Tigers Logo	1.00	.50	.30
(188)	Houston Colts Logo	1.00	.50	.30
(189)	Kansas City Athletics Logo	1.00	.50	.30
(190)	Los Angeles Angels Logo	1.00	.50	.30
(191)	Los Angeles Dodgers Logo	1.00	.50	.30
(192)	Milwaukee Braves Logo	1.00	.50	.30

		NR MT	EX	VG
(193)	Minnesota Twins Logo	1.00	.50	.30
(194)	New York Mets Logo	1.00	.50	.30
(195)	New York Yankees Logo	2.00	1.00	.60
(196)	Philadelphia Phillies Logo	1.00	.50	.30
(197)	Pittsburgh Pirates Logo	1.00	.50	.30
(198)	St. Louis Cardinals Logo	1.00	.50	.30
(199)	San Francisco Giants Logo	1.00	.50	.30
(200)	Washington Senators Logo	1.00	.50	.30

1963 Topps

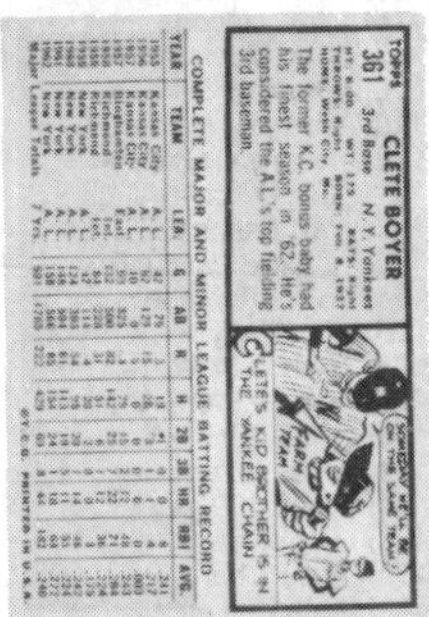

Although the number of cards dropped to 576, the 1963 Topps set is among the most popular of the 1960s. A color photo dominates the 2-1/2" by 3-1/2" card, but a colored circle at the bottom carries a black and white portrait as well. A colored band gives the player's name, team and position. The backs again feature career statistics and a cartoon, career summary and brief biographical details. The set is somewhat unlike those immediately preceding it in that there are fewer specialty cards. The major groupings are statistical leaders, World Series highlights and rookies. It is one rookie which makes the set special - Pete Rose. As one of most avidly sought cards in history and a high-numbered card at that, the Rose rookie card accounts for much of the value of a complete set.

	NR MT	EX	VG
Complete Set (576):	5250.00	2625.00	1575.
Common Player: 1-283	3.00	1.50	.90
Common Player: 284-446	3.75	2.00	1.25
Common Player: 447-506	15.00	7.50	4.50
Common Player: 507-576	11.00	5.50	3.25

		NR MT	EX	VG
1	N.L. Batting Leaders (Hank Aaron, Bill White, Frank Robinson, Tommy Davis, Stan Musial)	40.00	20.00	12.00
2	A.L. Batting Leaders (Chuck Hinton, Mickey Mantle, Floyd Robinson, Pete Runnels, Norm Siebern)	30.00	15.00	9.00
3	N.L. Home Run Leaders (Hank Aaron, Ernie Banks, Orlando Cepeda, Willie Mays, Frank Robinson)	20.00	10.00	6.00
4	A.L. Home Run Leaders (Norm Cash, Rocky Colavito, Harmon Killebrew, Roger Maris, Leon Wagner)	8.00	4.00	2.50
5	N.L. E.R.A. Leaders (Don Drysdale, Bob Gibson, Sandy Koufax)	8.00	4.00	2.50
6	A.L. E.R.A. Leaders (Whitey Ford, Hank Aguirre, Dean Chance, Eddie Fisher, Robin Roberts)	7.00	3.50	2.00
7	N.L. Pitching Leaders (Don Drysdale, Joe Jay, Art Mahaffey, Billy O'Dell, Bob Purkey, Jack Sanford)	7.00	3.50	2.00
8	A.L. Pitching Leaders (Jim Bunning, Dick Donovan, Ray Herbert, Camilo Pascual, Ralph Terry)	6.00	3.00	1.75
9	N.L. Strikeout Leaders (Don Drysdale, Dick Farrell, Bob Gibson, Sandy Koufax, Billy O'Dell)	7.00	3.50	2.00
10	A.L. Strikeout Leaders (Jim Bunning, Jim Kaat, Camilo Pascual, Ralph Terry)	6.00	3.00	1.75
11	Lee Walls	3.00	1.50	.90
12	Steve Barber	3.00	1.50	.90
13	Phillies Team	5.00	2.50	1.50
14	Pedro Ramos	3.00	1.50	.90
15	Ken Hubbs	3.75	2.00	1.25
16	Al Smith	3.00	1.50	.90
17	Ryne Duren	3.00	1.50	.90
18	Buc Blasters (Smoky Burgess, Roberto Clemente, Bob Skinner, Dick Stuart)	15.00	7.50	4.50
19	Pete Burnside	3.00	1.50	.90
20	Tony Kubek	6.00	3.00	1.75
21	Marty Keough	3.00	1.50	.90
22	Curt Simmons	3.00	1.50	.90
23	Ed Lopat	3.00	1.50	.90
24	Bob Bruce	3.00	1.50	.90
25	Al Kaline	35.00	17.50	10.50
26	Ray Moore	3.00	1.50	.90
27	Choo Choo Coleman	3.00	1.50	.90
28	Mike Fornieles	3.00	1.50	.90
29a	1962 Rookie Stars (Sammy Ellis, Ray Culp, *John Boozer,* Jesse Gonder)	7.00	3.50	2.00
29b	1963 Rookie Stars (Sammy Ellis, *Ray Culp,* John Boozer, Jesse Gonder)	3.00	1.50	.90
30	Harvey Kuenn	3.50	1.75	1.00
31	Cal Koonce	3.00	1.50	.90
32	Tony Gonzalez	3.00	1.50	.90
33	Bo Belinsky	3.00	1.50	.90
34	Dick Schofield	3.00	1.50	.90
35	John Buzhardt	3.00	1.50	.90
36	Jerry Kindall	3.00	1.50	.90
37	Jerry Lynch	3.00	1.50	.90
38	Bud Daley	3.00	1.50	.90
39	Angels Team	5.00	2.50	1.50
40	Vic Power	3.00	1.50	.90
41	Charlie Lau	3.00	1.50	.90
42	Stan Williams	3.00	1.50	.90
43	Veteran Masters (Casey Stengel, Gene Woodling)	4.00	2.00	1.25
44	Terry Fox	3.00	1.50	.90
45	Bob Aspromonte	3.00	1.50	.90
46	*Tommie Aaron*	3.00	1.50	.90
47	Don Lock	3.00	1.50	.90
48	Birdie Tebbetts	3.00	1.50	.90
49	*Dal Maxvill*	3.00	1.50	.90
50	Bill Pierce	3.00	1.50	.90
51	George Alusik	3.00	1.50	.90
52	Chuck Schilling	3.00	1.50	.90
53	Joe Moeller	3.00	1.50	.90
54a	1962 Rookie Stars *(Nelson Mathews, Harry Fanok, Jack Cullen, Dave DeBusschere)*	15.00	7.50	4.50
54b	1963 Rookie Stars *(Jack Cullen, Dave DeBusschere,* Harry Fanok, Nelson Mathews)	4.00	2.00	1.25
55	Bill Virdon	3.00	1.50	.90
56	Dennis Bennett	3.00	1.50	.90
57	Billy Moran	3.00	1.50	.90
58	Bob Will	3.00	1.50	.90
59	Craig Anderson	3.00	1.50	.90
60	Elston Howard	6.00	3.00	1.75
61	Ernie Bowman	3.00	1.50	.90
62	Bob Hendley	3.00	1.50	.90
63	Reds Team	5.00	2.50	1.50
64	Dick McAuliffe	3.00	1.50	.90
65	Jackie Brandt	3.00	1.50	.90
66	Mike Joyce	3.00	1.50	.90
67	Ed Charles	3.00	1.50	.90
68	Friendly Foes (Gil Hodges, Duke Snider)	12.50	6.25	3.75
69	Bud Zipfel	3.00	1.50	.90
70	Jim O'Toole	3.00	1.50	.90
71	*Bobby Wine*	3.00	1.50	.90
72	Johnny Romano	3.00	1.50	.90
73	Bobby Bragan	3.00	1.50	.90
74	*Denver Lemaster*	3.00	1.50	.90
75	Bob Allison	3.00	1.50	.90
76	Earl Wilson	3.00	1.50	.90
77	Al Spangler	3.00	1.50	.90
78	Marv Throneberry	3.00	1.50	.90
79	Checklist 1-88	5.00	2.50	1.50
80	Jim Gilliam	3.75	2.00	1.25
81	Jimmie Schaffer	3.00	1.50	.90
82	Ed Rakow	3.00	1.50	.90
83	Charley James	3.00	1.50	.90
84	Ron Kline	3.00	1.50	.90
85	Tom Haller	3.00	1.50	.90
86	Charley Maxwell	3.00	1.50	.90
87	Bob Veale	3.00	1.50	.90
88	Ron Hansen	3.00	1.50	.90
89	Dick Stigman	3.00	1.50	.90
90	Gordy Coleman	3.00	1.50	.90
91	Dallas Green	3.00	1.50	.90
92	Hector Lopez	3.00	1.50	.90
93	Galen Cisco	3.00	1.50	.90
94	Bob Schmidt	3.00	1.50	.90

		NR MT	EX	VG
95	Larry Jackson	3.00	1.50	.90
96	Lou Clinton	3.00	1.50	.90
97	Bob Duliba	3.00	1.50	.90
98	George Thomas	3.00	1.50	.90
99	Jim Umbricht	3.00	1.50	.90
100	Joe Cunningham	3.00	1.50	.90
101	Joe Gibbon	3.00	1.50	.90
102a	Checklist 89-176 ("Checklist" in red on front)	5.00	2.50	1.50
102b	Checklist 89-176 ("Checklist" in white)	10.00	5.00	3.00
103	Chuck Essegian	3.00	1.50	.90
104	Lew Krausse	3.00	1.50	.90
105	Ron Fairly	3.00	1.50	.90
106	Bob Bolin	3.00	1.50	.90
107	Jim Hickman	3.00	1.50	.90
108	Hoyt Wilhelm	10.00	5.00	3.00
109	Lee Maye	3.00	1.50	.90
110	Rich Rollins	3.00	1.50	.90
111	Al Jackson	3.00	1.50	.90
112	Dick Brown	3.00	1.50	.90
113	Don Landrum (photo actally Ron Santo)	3.00	1.50	.90
114	Dan Osinski	3.00	1.50	.90
115	Carl Yastrzemski	60.00	30.00	18.00
116	Jim Brosnan	3.00	1.50	.90
117	Jacke Davis	3.00	1.50	.90
118	Sherm Lollar	3.00	1.50	.90
119	Bob Lillis	3.00	1.50	.90
120	Roger Maris	65.00	32.00	19.50
121	Jim Hannan	3.00	1.50	.90
122	Julio Gotay	3.00	1.50	.90
123	Frank Howard	3.50	1.75	1.00
124	Dick Howser	3.00	1.50	.90
125	Robin Roberts	10.00	5.00	3.00
126	Bob Uecker	25.00	12.50	7.50
127	Bill Tuttle	3.00	1.50	.90
128	Matty Alou	3.00	1.50	.90
129	Gary Bell	3.00	1.50	.90
130	Dick Groat	3.00	1.50	.90
131	Senators Team	5.00	2.50	1.50
132	Jack Hamilton	3.00	1.50	.90
133	Gene Freese	3.00	1.50	.90
134	Bob Scheffing	3.00	1.50	.90
135	Richie Ashburn	10.00	5.00	3.00
136	Ike Delock	3.00	1.50	.90
137	Mack Jones	3.00	1.50	.90
138	Pride of N.L. (Willie Mays, Stan Musial)	35.00	17.50	10.50
139	Earl Averill	3.00	1.50	.90
140	Frank Lary	3.00	1.50	.90
141	*Manny Mota*	7.00	3.50	2.00
142	World Series Game 1 (Yanks' Ford Wins Series Opener)	7.00	3.50	2.00
143	World Series Game 2 (Sanford Flashes Shutout Magic)	5.00	2.50	1.50
144	World Series Game 3 (Maris Sparks Yankee Rally)	7.00	3.50	2.00
145	World Series Game 4 (Hiller Blasts Grand Slammer)	5.00	2.50	1.50
146	World Series Game 5 (Tresh's Homer Defeats Giants)	6.00	3.00	1.75
147	World Series Game 6 (Pierce Stars In 3 Hit Victory)	5.00	2.50	1.50
148	World Series Game 7 (Yanks Celebrate As Terry Wins)	6.00	3.00	1.75
149	Marv Breeding	3.00	1.50	.90
150	Johnny Podres	3.75	2.00	1.25
151	Pirates Team	5.00	2.50	1.50
152	Ron Nischwitz	3.00	1.50	.90
153	Hal Smith	3.00	1.50	.90
154	Walt Alston	5.00	2.50	1.50
155	Bill Stafford	3.00	1.50	.90
156	Roy McMillan	3.00	1.50	.90
157	*Diego Segui*	3.00	1.50	.90
158	1963 Rookie Stars (Rogelio Alvarez, *Tommy Harper*, Dave Roberts, Bob Saverine)	3.00	1.50	.90
159	Jim Pagliaroni	3.00	1.50	.90
160	Juan Pizarro	3.00	1.50	.90
161	Frank Torre	3.00	1.50	.90
162	Twins Team	5.00	2.50	1.50
163	Don Larsen	3.00	1.50	.90
164	Bubba Morton	3.00	1.50	.90
165	Jim Kaat	7.00	3.50	2.00
166	Johnny Keane	3.00	1.50	.90
167	Jim Fregosi	3.00	1.50	.90
168	Russ Nixon	3.00	1.50	.90
169	1963 Rookie Stars (Dick Egan, Julio Navarro, Gaylord Perry, Tommie Sisk)	30.00	15.00	9.00
170	Joe Adcock	3.00	1.50	.90
171	Steve Hamilton	3.00	1.50	.90
172	Gene Oliver	3.00	1.50	.90
173	Bombers' Best (Tom Tresh, Mickey Mantle, Bobby Richardson)	80.00	40.00	24.00
174	Larry Burright	3.00	1.50	.90
175	Bob Buhl	3.00	1.50	.90
176	Jim King	3.00	1.50	.90
177	Bubba Phillips	3.00	1.50	.90
178	Johnny Edwards	3.00	1.50	.90
179	Ron Piche	3.00	1.50	.90
180	Bill Skowron	4.50	2.25	1.25
181	Sammy Esposito	3.00	1.50	.90
182	Albie Pearson	3.00	1.50	.90
183	Joe Pepitone	4.00	2.00	1.25
184	Vern Law	3.00	1.50	.90
185	Chuck Hiller	3.00	1.50	.90
186	Jerry Zimmerman	3.00	1.50	.90
187	Willie Kirkland	3.00	1.50	.90
188	Eddie Bressoud	3.00	1.50	.90
189	Dave Giusti	3.00	1.50	.90
190	Minnie Minoso	4.00	2.00	1.25
191	Checklist 177-264	3.75	2.00	1.25
192	Clay Dalrymple	3.00	1.50	.90
193	Andre Rodgers	3.00	1.50	.90
194	Joe Nuxhall	3.00	1.50	.90
195	Manny Jimenez	3.00	1.50	.90
196	Doug Camilli	3.00	1.50	.90
197	Roger Craig	3.75	2.00	1.25
198	Lenny Green	3.00	1.50	.90
199	Joe Amalfitano	3.00	1.50	.90
200	Mickey Mantle	500.00	250.00	150.00
201	Cecil Butler	3.00	1.50	.90
202	Red Sox Team	5.00	2.50	1.50
203	Chico Cardenas	3.00	1.50	.90
204	Don Nottebart	3.00	1.50	.90
205	Luis Aparicio	15.00	7.50	4.50
206	Ray Washburn	3.00	1.50	.90
207	Ken Hunt	3.00	1.50	.90
208	1963 Rookie Stars (Ron Herbel, John Miller, Ron Taylor, Wally Wolf)	3.00	1.50	.90
209	Hobie Landrith	3.00	1.50	.90
210	Sandy Koufax	160.00	80.00	48.00
211	Fred Whitfield	3.00	1.50	.90
212	Glen Hobbie	3.00	1.50	.90
213	Billy Hitchcock	3.00	1.50	.90
214	Orlando Pena	3.00	1.50	.90
215	Bob Skinner	3.00	1.50	.90
216	Gene Conley	3.00	1.50	.90
217	Joe Christopher	3.00	1.50	.90
218	Tiger Twirlers (Jim Bunning, Frank Lary, Don Mossi)	3.75	2.00	1.25
219	Chuck Cottier	3.00	1.50	.90
220	Camilo Pascual	3.00	1.50	.90
221	*Cookie Rojas*	3.00	1.50	.90
222	Cubs Team	5.00	2.50	1.50
223	Eddie Fisher	3.00	1.50	.90
224	Mike Roarke	3.00	1.50	.90
225	Joe Jay	3.00	1.50	.90
226	Julian Javier	3.00	1.50	.90
227	Jim Grant	3.00	1.50	.90
228	1963 Rookie Stars (Max Alvis, *Bob Bailey, Ed Kranepool, Pedro Oliva*)	40.00	20.00	12.00
229	Willie Davis	3.50	1.75	1.00
230	Pete Runnels	3.00	1.50	.90
231	Eli Grba (photo actually Ryne Duren)	3.00	1.50	.90
232	Frank Malzone	3.00	1.50	.90
233	Casey Stengel	15.00	7.50	4.50
234	Dave Nicholson	3.00	1.50	.90
235	Billy O'Dell	3.00	1.50	.90
236	Bill Bryan	3.00	1.50	.90
237	Jim Coates	3.00	1.50	.90
238	Lou Johnson	3.00	1.50	.90
239	Harvey Haddix	3.00	1.50	.90
240	Rocky Colavito	15.00	7.50	4.50
241	Billy Smith	3.00	1.50	.90
242	Power Plus (Hank Aaron, Ernie Banks)	35.00	17.50	10.50
243	Don Leppert	3.00	1.50	.90
244	John Tsitouris	3.00	1.50	.90
245	Gil Hodges	12.50	6.25	3.75
246	Lee Stange	3.00	1.50	.90
247	Yankees Team	15.00	7.50	4.50
248	Tito Francona	3.00	1.50	.90
249	Leo Burke	3.00	1.50	.90
250	Stan Musial	100.00	50.00	30.00
251	Jack Lamabe	3.00	1.50	.90
252	Ron Santo	3.75	2.00	1.25
253	1963 Rookie Stars (Len Gabrielson, Pete Jernigan, Deacon Jones, John Wojcik)	3.00	1.50	.90

		NR MT	EX	VG
254	Mike Hershberger	3.00	1.50	.90
255	Bob Shaw	3.00	1.50	.90
256	Jerry Lumpe	3.00	1.50	.90
257	Hank Aguirre	3.00	1.50	.90
258	Alvin Dark	3.00	1.50	.90
259	Johnny Logan	3.00	1.50	.90
260	Jim Gentile	3.00	1.50	.90
261	Bob Miller	3.00	1.50	.90
262	Ellis Burton	3.00	1.50	.90
263	Dave Stenhouse	3.00	1.50	.90
264	Phil Linz	3.00	1.50	.90
265	Vada Pinson	3.50	1.75	1.00
266	Bob Allen	3.00	1.50	.90
267	Carl Sawatski	3.00	1.50	.90
268	Don Demeter	3.00	1.50	.90
269	Don Mincher	3.00	1.50	.90
270	Felipe Alou	3.50	1.75	1.00
271	Dean Stone	3.00	1.50	.90
272	Danny Murphy	3.00	1.50	.90
273	Sammy Taylor	3.00	1.50	.90
274	Checklist 265-352	3.75	2.00	1.25
275	Eddie Mathews	20.00	10.00	6.00
276	Barry Shetrone	3.00	1.50	.90
277	Dick Farrell	3.00	1.50	.90
278	Chico Fernandez	3.00	1.50	.90
279	Wally Moon	3.00	1.50	.90
280	Bob Rodgers	3.00	1.50	.90
281	Tom Sturdivant	3.00	1.50	.90
282	Bob Del Greco	3.00	1.50	.90
283	Roy Sievers	3.00	1.50	.90
284	Dave Sisler	3.75	2.00	1.25
285	Dick Stuart	3.75	2.00	1.25
286	Stu Miller	3.75	2.00	1.25
287	Dick Bertell	3.75	2.00	1.25
288	White Sox Team	5.00	2.50	1.50
289	Hal Brown	3.75	2.00	1.25
290	Bill White	4.50	2.25	1.25
291	Don Rudolph	3.75	2.00	1.25
292	Pumpsie Green	3.75	2.00	1.25
293	Bill Pleis	3.75	2.00	1.25
294	Bill Rigney	3.75	2.00	1.25
295	Ed Roebuck	3.75	2.00	1.25
296	Doc Edwards	3.75	2.00	1.25
297	Jim Golden	3.75	2.00	1.25
298	Don Dillard	3.75	2.00	1.25
299	1963 Rookie Stars (Tom Butters, Bob Dustal, Dave Morehead, Dan Schneider)	3.75	2.00	1.25
300	Willie Mays	175.00	87.00	52.00
301	Bill Fischer	3.75	2.00	1.25
302	Whitey Herzog	4.50	2.25	1.25
303	Earl Francis	3.75	2.00	1.25
304	Harry Bright	3.75	2.00	1.25
305	Don Hoak	3.75	2.00	1.25
306	Star Receivers (Earl Battey, Elston Howard)	4.50	2.25	1.25
307	Chet Nichols	3.75	2.00	1.25
308	Camilo Carreon	3.75	2.00	1.25
309	Jim Brewer	3.75	2.00	1.25
310	Tommy Davis	3.75	2.00	1.25
311	Joe McClain	3.75	2.00	1.25
312	Colt .45s Team	12.00	6.00	3.50
313	Ernie Broglio	3.75	2.00	1.25
314	John Goryl	3.75	2.00	1.25
315	Ralph Terry	3.75	2.00	1.25
316	Norm Sherry	3.75	2.00	1.25
317	Sam McDowell	3.75	2.00	1.25
318	Gene Mauch	3.75	2.00	1.25
319	Joe Gaines	3.75	2.00	1.25
320	Warren Spahn	35.00	17.50	10.50
321	Gino Cimoli	3.75	2.00	1.25
322	Bob Turley	3.75	2.00	1.25
323	Bill Mazeroski	6.00	3.00	1.75
324	1963 Rookie Stars (*Vic Davalillo,* Phil Roof, *Pete Ward,* George Williams)	4.50	2.25	1.25
325	Jack Sanford	3.75	2.00	1.25
326	Hank Foiles	3.75	2.00	1.25
327	Paul Foytack	3.75	2.00	1.25
328	Dick Williams	4.00	2.00	1.25
329	Lindy McDaniel	3.75	2.00	1.25
330	Chuck Hinton	3.75	2.00	1.25
331	Series Foes (Bill Pierce, Bill Stafford)	4.00	2.00	1.25
332	Joel Horlen	3.75	2.00	1.25
333	Carl Warwick	3.75	2.00	1.25
334	Wynn Hawkins	3.75	2.00	1.25
335	Leon Wagner	3.75	2.00	1.25
336	Ed Bauta	3.75	2.00	1.25
337	Dodgers Team	15.00	7.50	4.50
338	Russ Kemmerer	3.75	2.00	1.25
339	Ted Bowsfield	3.75	2.00	1.25

		NR MT	EX	VG
340	Yogi Berra	65.00	32.00	19.50
341	Jack Baldschun	3.75	2.00	1.25
342	Gene Woodling	3.75	2.00	1.25
343	Johnny Pesky	3.75	2.00	1.25
344	Don Schwall	3.75	2.00	1.25
345	Brooks Robinson	50.00	25.00	15.00
346	Billy Hoeft	3.75	2.00	1.25
347	Joe Torre	6.00	3.00	1.75
348	Vic Wertz	3.75	2.00	1.25
349	Zoilo Versalles	3.75	2.00	1.25
350	Bob Purkey	3.75	2.00	1.25
351	Al Luplow	3.75	2.00	1.25
352	Ken Johnson	3.75	2.00	1.25
353	Billy Williams	25.00	12.50	7.50
354	Dom Zanni	3.75	2.00	1.25
355	Dean Chance	3.75	2.00	1.25
356	John Schaive	3.75	2.00	1.25
357	George Altman	3.75	2.00	1.25
358	Milt Pappas	3.75	2.00	1.25
359	Haywood Sullivan	3.75	2.00	1.25
360	Don Drysdale	35.00	17.50	10.50
361	Clete Boyer	3.75	2.00	1.25
362	Checklist 353-429	4.50	2.25	1.25
363	Dick Radatz	2.75	1.50	.80
364	Howie Goss	3.75	2.00	1.25
365	Jim Bunning	10.00	5.00	3.00
366	Tony Taylor	3.75	2.00	1.25
367	Tony Cloninger	3.75	2.00	1.25
368	Ed Bailey	3.75	2.00	1.25
369	Jim Lemon	3.75	2.00	1.25
370	Dick Donovan	3.75	2.00	1.25
371	Rod Kanehl	3.75	2.00	1.25
372	Don Lee	3.75	2.00	1.25
373	Jim Campbell	3.75	2.00	1.25
374	Claude Osteen	3.75	2.00	1.25
375	Ken Boyer	4.00	2.00	1.25
376	Johnnie Wyatt	3.75	2.00	1.25
377	Orioles Team	7.50	3.75	2.25
378	Bill Henry	3.75	2.00	1.25
379	Bob Anderson	3.75	2.00	1.25
380	Ernie Banks	50.00	25.00	15.00
381	Frank Baumann	3.75	2.00	1.25
382	Ralph Houk	3.75	2.00	1.25
383	Pete Richert	3.75	2.00	1.25
384	Bob Tillman	3.75	2.00	1.25
385	Art Mahaffey	3.75	2.00	1.25
386	1963 Rookie Stars (*John Bateman,* Larry Bearnarth, *Ed Kirkpatrick,* Garry Roggenburk)	3.75	2.00	1.25
387	Al McBean	3.75	2.00	1.25
388	Jim Davenport	3.75	2.00	1.25
389	Frank Sullivan	3.75	2.00	1.25
390	Hank Aaron	150.00	75.00	45.00
391	Bill Dailey	3.75	2.00	1.25
392	Tribe Thumpers (Tito Francona, Johnny Romano)	4.00	2.00	1.25
393	Ken MacKenzie	3.75	2.00	1.25
394	Tim McCarver	4.00	2.00	1.25
395	Don McMahon	3.75	2.00	1.25
396	Joe Koppe	3.75	2.00	1.25
397	Athletics Team	7.50	3.75	2.25
398	Boog Powell	7.00	3.50	2.00
399	Dick Ellsworth	3.75	2.00	1.25
400	Frank Robinson	45.00	22.00	13.50
401	Jim Bouton	10.00	5.00	3.00
402	Mickey Vernon	3.75	2.00	1.25
403	Ron Perranoski	3.75	2.00	1.25
404	Bob Oldis	3.75	2.00	1.25
405	Floyd Robinson	3.75	2.00	1.25
406	Howie Koplitz	3.75	2.00	1.25
407	1963 Rookie Stars (Larry Elliot, Frank Kostro, Chico Ruiz, Dick Simpson)	3.75	2.00	1.25
408	Billy Gardner	3.75	2.00	1.25
409	Roy Face	3.75	2.00	1.25
410	Earl Battey	3.75	2.00	1.25
411	Jim Constable	3.75	2.00	1.25
412	Dodgers' Big Three (Johnny Podres, Don Drysdale, Sandy Koufax)	30.00	15.00	9.00
413	Jerry Walker	3.75	2.00	1.25
414	Ty Cline	3.75	2.00	1.25
415	Bob Gibson	35.00	17.50	10.50
416	Alex Grammas	3.75	2.00	1.25
417	Giants Team	7.50	3.75	2.25
418	Johnny Orsino	3.75	2.00	1.25
419	Tracy Stallard	3.75	2.00	1.25
420	Bobby Richardson	12.50	6.25	3.75
421	Tom Morgan	3.75	2.00	1.25
422	Fred Hutchinson	3.75	2.00	1.25
423	Ed Hobaugh	3.75	2.00	1.25
424	Charley Smith	3.75	2.00	1.25
425	Smoky Burgess	3.75	2.00	1.25

		NR MT	EX	VG
426	Barry Latman	3.75	2.00	1.25
427	Bernie Allen	3.75	2.00	1.25
428	Carl Boles	3.75	2.00	1.25
429	Lou Burdette	3.75	2.00	1.25
430	Norm Siebern	3.75	2.00	1.25
431a	Checklist 430-506 ("Checklist" in black on front)	4.50	2.25	1.25
431b	Checklist 430-506 ("Checklist" in white)	7.50	3.75	2.25
432	Roman Mejias	3.75	2.00	1.25
433	Denis Menke	3.75	2.00	1.25
434	Johnny Callison	3.75	2.00	1.25
435	Woody Held	3.75	2.00	1.25
436	Tim Harkness	3.75	2.00	1.25
437	Bill Bruton	3.75	2.00	1.25
438	Wes Stock	3.75	2.00	1.25
439	Don Zimmer	4.00	2.00	1.25
440	Juan Marichal	25.00	12.50	7.50
441	Lee Thomas	3.75	2.00	1.25
442	J.C. Hartman	3.75	2.00	1.25
443	Jim Piersall	3.75	2.00	1.25
444	Jim Maloney	3.75	2.00	1.25
445	Norm Cash	3.75	2.00	1.25
446	Whitey Ford	35.00	17.50	10.50
447	Felix Mantilla	15.00	7.50	4.50
448	Jack Kralick	15.00	7.50	4.50
449	Jose Tartabull	15.00	7.50	4.50
450	Bob Friend	15.00	7.50	4.50
451	Indians Team	22.00	11.00	6.50
452	Barney Schultz	15.00	7.50	4.50
453	Jake Wood	15.00	7.50	4.50
454a	Art Fowler (card # on orange background)	15.00	7.50	4.50
454b	Art Fowler (card # on white background)	15.00	7.50	4.50
455	Ruben Amaro	15.00	7.50	4.50
456	Jim Coker	15.00	7.50	4.50
457	Tex Clevenger	15.00	7.50	4.50
458	Al Lopez	17.50	8.75	5.25
459	Dick LeMay	15.00	7.50	4.50
460	Del Crandall	15.00	7.50	4.50
461	Norm Bass	15.00	7.50	4.50
462	Wally Post	15.00	7.50	4.50
463	Joe Schaffernoth	15.00	7.50	4.50
464	Ken Aspromonte	15.00	7.50	4.50
465	Chuck Estrada	15.00	7.50	4.50
466	1963 Rookie Stars (*Bill Freehan*, Tony Martinez, Nate Oliver, Jerry Robinson)	30.00	15.00	9.00
467	Phil Ortega	15.00	7.50	4.50
468	Carroll Hardy	15.00	7.50	4.50
469	Jay Hook	15.00	7.50	4.50
470	Tom Tresh	20.00	10.00	6.00
471	Ken Retzer	15.00	7.50	4.50
472	Lou Brock	125.00	62.00	37.00
473	Mets Team	100.00	50.00	30.00
474	Jack Fisher	15.00	7.50	4.50
475	Gus Triandos	15.00	7.50	4.50
476	Frank Funk	15.00	7.50	4.50
477	Donn Clendenon	15.00	7.50	4.50
478	Paul Brown	15.00	7.50	4.50
479	*Ed Brinkman*	15.00	7.50	4.50
480	Bill Monbouquette	15.00	7.50	4.50
481	Bob Taylor	15.00	7.50	4.50
482	Felix Torres	15.00	7.50	4.50
483	Jim Owens	15.00	7.50	4.50
484	Dale Long	15.00	7.50	4.50
485	Jim Landis	15.00	7.50	4.50
486	Ray Sadecki	15.00	7.50	4.50
487	John Roseboro	15.00	7.50	4.50
488	Jerry Adair	15.00	7.50	4.50
489	Paul Toth	15.00	7.50	4.50
490	Willie McCovey	135.00	67.00	40.00
491	Harry Craft	15.00	7.50	4.50
492	Dave Wickersham	15.00	7.50	4.50
493	Walt Bond	15.00	7.50	4.50
494	Phil Regan	15.00	7.50	4.50
495	Frank J. Thomas	15.00	7.50	4.50
496	1963 Rookie Stars (Carl Bouldin, *Steve Dalkowski, Fred Newman,* Jack Smith)	15.00	7.50	4.50
497	Bennie Daniels	15.00	7.50	4.50
498	Eddie Kasko	15.00	7.50	4.50
499	J.C. Martin	15.00	7.50	4.50
500	Harmon Killebrew	130.00	65.00	39.00
501	Joe Azcue	15.00	7.50	4.50
502	Daryl Spencer	15.00	7.50	4.50
503	Braves Team	22.00	11.00	6.50
504	Bob Johnson	15.00	7.50	4.50
505	Curt Flood	15.00	7.50	4.50
506	Gene Green	15.00	7.50	4.50

		NR MT	EX	VG
507	Roland Sheldon	11.00	5.50	3.25
508	Ted Savage	11.00	5.50	3.25
509a	Checklist 507-576 (copyright centered)	15.00	7.50	4.50
509b	Checklist 509-576 (copyright to right)	15.00	7.50	4.50
510	Ken McBride	11.00	5.50	3.25
511	Charlie Neal	11.00	5.50	3.25
512	Cal McLish	11.00	5.50	3.25
513	Gary Geiger	11.00	5.50	3.25
514	Larry Osborne	11.00	5.50	3.25
515	Don Elston	11.00	5.50	3.25
516	Purnal Goldy	11.00	5.50	3.25
517	Hal Woodeshick	11.00	5.50	3.25
518	Don Blasingame	11.00	5.50	3.25
519	Claude Raymond	11.00	5.50	3.25
520	Orlando Cepeda	25.00	12.50	7.50
521	Dan Pfister	11.00	5.50	3.25
522	1963 Rookie Stars (Mel Nelson, Gary Peters, Art Quirk, Jim Roland)	11.00	5.50	3.25
523	Bill Kunkel	11.00	5.50	3.25
524	Cardinals Team	17.50	8.75	5.25
525	Nellie Fox	25.00	12.50	7.50
526	Dick Hall	11.00	5.50	3.25
527	Ed Sadowski	11.00	5.50	3.25
528	Carl Willey	11.00	5.50	3.25
529	Wes Covington	11.00	5.50	3.25
530	Don Mossi	11.00	5.50	3.25
531	Sam Mele	11.00	5.50	3.25
532	Steve Boros	11.00	5.50	3.25
533	Bobby Shantz	12.50	6.25	3.75
534	Ken Walters	11.00	5.50	3.25
535	Jim Perry	11.00	5.50	3.25
536	Norm Larker	11.00	5.50	3.25
537	1963 Rookie Stars (Pedro Gonzalez, *Ken McMullen, Pete Rose, Al Weis*)	800.00	400.00	240.00
538	George Brunet	11.00	5.50	3.25
539	Wayne Causey	11.00	5.50	3.25
540	Roberto Clemente	250.00	125.00	75.00
541	Ron Moeller	11.00	5.50	3.25
542	Lou Klimchock	11.00	5.50	3.25
543	Russ Snyder	11.00	5.50	3.25
544	1963 Rookie Stars (Duke Carmel, Bill Haas, Dick Phillips, *Rusty Staub*)	40.00	20.00	12.00
545	Jose Pagan	11.00	5.50	3.25
546	Hal Reniff	11.00	5.50	3.25
547	Gus Bell	11.00	5.50	3.25
548	Tom Satriano	11.00	5.50	3.25
549	1963 Rookie Stars (*Marcelino Lopez,* Pete Lovrich, Elmo Plaskett, Paul Ratliff)	11.00	5.50	3.25
550	Duke Snider	75.00	37.00	22.00
551	Billy Klaus	11.00	5.50	3.25
552	Tigers Team	35.00	17.50	10.50
553	1963 Rookie Stars (Brock Davis, Jim Gosger, John Hermstein, *Willie Stargell*)	250.00	125.00	75.00
554	Hank Fischer	11.00	5.50	3.25
555	John Blanchard	11.00	5.50	3.25
556	Al Worthington	11.00	5.50	3.25
557	Cuno Barragan	11.00	5.50	3.25
558	1963 Rookie Stars (Bill Faul, *Ron Hunt,* Bob Lipski, Al Moran)	12.50	6.25	3.75
559	Danny Murtaugh	11.00	5.50	3.25
560	Ray Herbert	11.00	5.50	3.25
561	Mike de la Hoz	11.00	5.50	3.25
562	1963 Rookie Stars (Randy Cardinal, *Dave McNally,* Don Rowe, Ken Rowe)	18.00	9.00	5.50
563	Mike McCormick	11.00	5.50	3.25
564	George Banks	11.00	5.50	3.25
565	Larry Sherry	11.00	5.50	3.25
566	Cliff Cook	11.00	5.50	3.25
567	Jim Duffalo	11.00	5.50	3.25
568	Bob Sadowski	11.00	5.50	3.25
569	Luis Arroyo	11.00	5.50	3.25
570	Frank Bolling	11.00	5.50	3.25
571	Johnny Klippstein	11.00	5.50	3.25
572	Jack Spring	11.00	5.50	3.25
573	Coot Veal	11.00	5.50	3.25
574	Hal Kolstad	11.00	5.50	3.25
575	Don Cardwell	11.00	5.50	3.25
576	Johnny Temple	15.00	5.50	3.25

1963 Topps Peel-Offs

Measuring 1-1/4" by 2-3/4," Topps Peel-Offs were an insert with 1963 Topps baseball cards. There are 46 players in the unnumbered set, each pictured in a color photo inside an oval with the player's name, team and

position in a band below. The back of the Peel-Off is removable, leaving a sticky surface that made the Peel-Off a popular decorative item among youngsters of the day. Naturally, that makes them quite scarce today, but as a non-card Topps issue, demand is not particularly strong.

		NR MT	EX	VG
Complete Set:		175.00	87.00	52.00
Common Player:		2.00	1.00	.60
(1)	Hank Aaron	10.00	5.00	3.00
(2)	Luis Aparicio	4.00	2.00	1.25
(3)	Richie Ashburn	3.00	1.50	.90
(4)	Bob Aspromonte	2.00	1.00	.60
(5)	Ernie Banks	5.00	2.50	1.50
(6)	Ken Boyer	2.50	1.25	.70
(7)	Jim Bunning	3.00	1.50	.90
(8)	Johnny Callison	2.00	1.00	.60
(9)	Orlando Cepeda	3.00	1.50	.90
(10)	Roberto Clemente	8.00	4.00	2.50
(11)	Rocky Colavito	4.00	2.00	1.25
(12)	Tommy Davis	2.50	1.25	.70
(13)	Dick Donovan	2.00	1.00	.60
(14)	Don Drysdale	5.00	2.50	1.50
(15)	Dick Farrell	2.00	1.00	.60
(16)	Jim Gentile	2.00	1.00	.60
(17)	Ray Herbert	2.00	1.00	.60
(18)	Chuck Hinton	2.00	1.00	.60
(19)	Ken Hubbs	2.50	1.25	.70
(20)	Al Jackson	2.00	1.00	.60
(21)	Al Kaline	5.00	2.50	1.50
(22)	Harmon Killebrew	5.00	2.50	1.50
(23)	Sandy Koufax	8.00	4.00	2.50
(24)	Jerry Lumpe	2.00	1.00	.60
(25)	Art Mahaffey	2.00	1.00	.60
(26)	Mickey Mantle	50.00	25.00	15.00
(27)	Willie Mays	10.00	5.00	3.00
(28)	Bill Mazeroski	3.00	1.50	.90
(29)	Bill Monbouquette	2.00	1.00	.60
(30)	Stan Musial	10.00	5.00	3.00
(31)	Camilo Pascual	2.00	1.00	.60
(32)	Bob Purkey	2.00	1.00	.60
(33)	Bobby Richardson	3.00	1.50	.90
(34)	Brooks Robinson	6.00	3.00	1.75
(35)	Floyd Robinson	2.00	1.00	.60
(36)	Frank Robinson	6.00	3.00	1.75
(37)	Bob Rodgers	2.00	1.00	.60
(38)	Johnny Romano	2.00	1.00	.60
(39)	Jack Sanford	2.00	1.00	.60
(40)	Norm Siebern	2.00	1.00	.60
(41)	Warren Spahn	5.00	2.50	1.50
(42)	Dave Stenhouse	2.00	1.00	.60
(43)	Ralph Terry	2.00	1.00	.60
(44)	Lee Thomas	2.00	1.00	.60
(45)	Bill White	2.00	1.00	.60
(46)	Carl Yastrzemski	8.00	4.00	2.50

1964 Topps

The 1964 Topps set is a 587-card issue of 2-1/2" by 3-1/2" cards which is considered by many as being among the company's best efforts. Card fronts feature a large color photo which blends into a top panel which contains the team name, while a panel below the picture carries the player's name and position. An interesting innovation

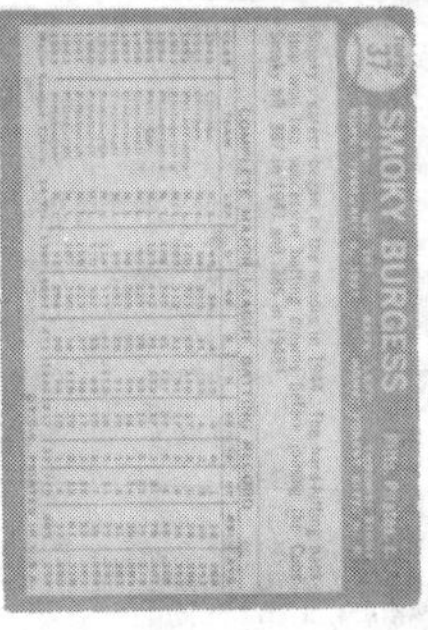

on the back is a baseball quiz question which required the rubbing of a white panel to reveal the answer. As in 1963, specialty cards remained modest in number with a 12-card set of statistical leaders, a few multi-player cards, rookies and World Series highlights. An interesting card is an "In Memoriam" card for Ken Hubbs who was killed in an airplane crash.

		NR MT	EX	VG
Complete Set (587):		3000.00	1500.00	900.00
Common Player: 1-370		2.50	1.25	.70
Common Player: 371-522		5.00	2.50	1.50
Common Player: 523-587		9.50	4.75	2.75
1	N.L. E.R.A. Leaders (Dick Ellsworth, Bob Friend, Sandy Koufax)	20.00	12.00	6.00
2	A.L. E.R.A. Leaders (Camilo Pascual, Gary Peters, Juan Pizarro)	5.00	2.50	1.50
3	N.L. Pitching Leaders (Sandy Koufax, Jim Maloney, Juan Marichal, Warren Spahn)	12.00	6.00	3.50
4a	A.L. Pitching Leaders (Jim Bouton, Whitey Ford, Camilo Pascual) (apostrophe after "Pitching" on back)	9.50	4.75	2.75
4b	A.L. Pitching Leaders (Jim Bouton, Whitey Ford, Camilo Pascual) (no apostrophe)	5.00	2.50	1.50
5	N.L. Strikeout Leaders (Don Drysdale, Sandy Koufax, Jim Maloney)	10.00	5.00	3.00
6	A.L. Strikeout Leaders (Jim Bunning, Camilo Pascual, Dick Stigman)	5.00	2.50	1.50
7	N.L. Batting Leaders (Hank Aaron, Roberto Clemente, Tommy Davis, Dick Groat)	11.00	5.50	3.25
8	A.L. Batting Leaders (Al Kaline, Rich Rollins, Carl Yastrzemski)	9.50	4.75	2.75
9	N.L. Home Run Leaders (Hank Aaron, Orlando Cepeda, Willie Mays, Willie McCovey)	16.00	8.00	4.75
10	A.L. Home Run Leaders (Bob Allison, Harmon Killebrew, Dick Stuart)	5.00	2.50	1.50
11	N.L. R.B.I. Leaders (Hank Aaron, Ken Boyer, Bill White)	8.00	4.00	2.50
12	A.L. R.B.I. Leaders (Al Kaline, Harmon Killebrew, Dick Stuart)	8.00	4.00	2.50
13	Hoyt Wilhelm	8.50	4.25	2.50
14	Dodgers Rookies (Dick Nen, Nick Willhite)	2.50	1.25	.70
15	Zoilo Versalles	2.50	1.25	.70
16	John Boozer	2.50	1.25	.70
17	Willie Kirkland	2.50	1.25	.70
18	Billy O'Dell	2.50	1.25	.70
19	Don Wert	2.50	1.25	.70
20	Bob Friend	2.50	1.25	.70
21	Yogi Berra	37.50	18.50	11.00
22	Jerry Adair	2.50	1.25	.70
23	Chris Zachary	2.50	1.25	.70
24	Carl Sawatski	2.50	1.25	.70
25	Bill Monbouquette	2.50	1.25	.70
26	Gino Cimoli	2.50	1.25	.70
27	Mets Team	5.00	2.50	1.50
28	Claude Osteen	2.50	1.25	.70
29	Lou Brock	35.00	17.50	10.50
30	Ron Perranoski	2.50	1.25	.70
31	Dave Nicholson	2.50	1.25	.70
32	Dean Chance	3.00	1.50	.90
33	Reds Rookies (Sammy Ellis, Mel Queen)	2.50	1.25	.70
34	Jim Perry	2.50	1.25	.70

		NR MT	EX	VG
35	Eddie Mathews	20.00	10.00	6.00
36	Hal Reniff	2.50	1.25	.70
37	Smoky Burgess	2.50	1.25	.70
38	*Jim Wynn*	5.00	2.50	1.50
39	Hank Aguirre	2.50	1.25	.70
40	Dick Groat	3.00	1.50	.90
41	Friendly Foes (Willie McCovey, Leon Wagner)	5.00	2.50	1.50
42	Moe Drabowsky	2.50	1.25	.70
43	Roy Sievers	2.50	1.25	.70
44	Duke Carmel	2.50	1.25	.70
45	Milt Pappas	2.50	1.25	.70
46	Ed Brinkman	2.50	1.25	.70
47	Giants Rookies (*Jesus Alou,* Ron Herbel)	3.50	1.75	1.00
48	Bob Perry	2.50	1.25	.70
49	Bill Henry	2.50	1.25	.70
50	Mickey Mantle	310.00	155.00	93.00
51	Pete Richert	2.50	1.25	.70
52	Chuck Hinton	2.50	1.25	.70
53	Denis Menke	2.50	1.25	.70
54	Sam Mele	2.50	1.25	.70
55	Ernie Banks	32.50	16.00	9.75
56	Hal Brown	2.50	1.25	.70
57	Tim Harkness	2.50	1.25	.70
58	Don Demeter	2.50	1.25	.70
59	Ernie Broglio	2.50	1.25	.70
60	Frank Malzone	2.50	1.25	.70
61	Angel Backstops (Bob Rodgers, Ed Sadowski)	3.50	1.75	1.00
62	Ted Savage	2.50	1.25	.70
63	Johnny Orsino	2.50	1.25	.70
64	Ted Abernathy	2.50	1.25	.70
65	Felipe Alou	5.50	2.75	1.75
66	Eddie Fisher	2.50	1.25	.70
67	Tigers Team	5.00	2.50	1.50
68	Willie Davis	3.50	1.75	1.00
69	Clete Boyer	3.50	1.75	1.00
70	Joe Torre	2.50	1.25	.70
71	Jack Spring	2.50	1.25	.70
72	Chico Cardenas	2.50	1.25	.70
73	*Jimmie Hall*	2.50	1.25	.70
74	Pirates Rookies (Tom Butters, Bob Priddy)	2.50	1.25	.70
75	Wayne Causey	2.50	1.25	.70
76	Checklist 1-88	5.00	2.50	1.50
77	Jerry Walker	2.50	1.25	.70
78	Merritt Ranew	2.50	1.25	.70
79	Bob Heffner	2.50	1.25	.70
80	Vada Pinson	3.50	1.75	1.00
81	All-Star Vets (Nellie Fox, Harmon Killebrew)	9.50	4.75	2.75
82	Jim Davenport	2.50	1.25	.70
83	Gus Triandos	2.50	1.25	.70
84	Carl Willey	2.50	1.25	.70
85	Pete Ward	2.50	1.25	.70
86	Al Downing	3.00	1.50	.90
87	Cardinals Team	9.50	4.75	2.75
88	John Roseboro	2.50	1.25	.70
89	Boog Powell	5.00	2.50	1.50
90	Earl Battey	2.50	1.25	.70
91	Bob Bailey	2.50	1.25	.70
92	Steve Ridzik	2.50	1.25	.70
93	Gary Geiger	2.50	1.25	.70
94	Braves Rookies (Jim Britton, Larry Maxie)	2.50	1.25	.70
95	George Altman	2.50	1.25	.70
96	Bob Buhl	2.50	1.25	.70
97	Jim Fregosi	3.00	1.50	.90
98	Bill Bruton	2.50	1.25	.70
99	Al Stanek	2.50	1.25	.70
100	Elston Howard	4.50	2.25	1.25
101	Walt Alston	5.00	2.50	1.50
102	Checklist 89-176	5.00	2.50	1.50
103	Curt Flood	3.50	1.75	1.00
104	Art Mahaffey	2.50	1.25	.70
105	Woody Held	2.50	1.25	.70
106	Joe Nuxhall	2.50	1.25	.70
107	White Sox Rookies (Bruce Howard, Frank Kreutzer)	2.50	1.25	.70
108	John Wyatt	2.50	1.25	.70
109	Rusty Staub	9.00	4.50	2.75
110	Albie Pearson	2.50	1.25	.70
111	Don Elston	2.50	1.25	.70
112	Bob Tillman	2.50	1.25	.70
113	Grover Powell	2.50	1.25	.70
114	Don Lock	2.50	1.25	.70
115	Frank Bolling	2.50	1.25	.70
116	Twins Rookies (Tony Oliva, Jay Ward)	15.00	7.50	4.50
117	Earl Francis	2.50	1.25	.70

		NR MT	EX	VG
118	John Blanchard	2.50	1.25	.70
119	Gary Kolb	2.50	1.25	.70
120	Don Drysdale	20.00	10.00	6.00
121	Pete Runnels	2.50	1.25	.70
122	Don McMahon	2.50	1.25	.70
123	Jose Pagan	2.50	1.25	.70
124	Orlando Pena	2.50	1.25	.70
125	Pete Rose	160.00	80.00	48.00
126	Russ Snyder	2.50	1.25	.70
127	Angels Rookies (Aubrey Gatewood, Dick Simpson)	2.50	1.25	.70
128	*Mickey Lolich*	14.00	7.00	4.25
129	Amado Samuel	2.50	1.25	.70
130	Gary Peters	2.50	1.25	.70
131	Steve Boros	2.50	1.25	.70
132	Braves Team	5.50	2.75	1.75
133	Jim Grant	2.50	1.25	.70
134	Don Zimmer	3.50	1.75	1.00
135	Johnny Callison	2.50	1.25	.70
136	World Series Game 1 (Koufax Strikes Out 15)	15.00	7.50	4.50
137	World Series Game 2 (Davis Sparks Rally)	3.50	1.75	1.00
138	World Series Game 3 (L.A. Takes 3rd Straight)	3.50	1.75	1.00
139	World Series Game 4 (Sealing Yanks' Doom)	3.50	1.75	1.00
140	World Series Summary (The Dodgers Celebrate)	3.50	1.75	1.00
141	Danny Murtaugh	2.50	1.25	.70
142	John Bateman	2.50	1.25	.70
143	Bubba Phillips	2.50	1.25	.70
144	Al Worthington	2.50	1.25	.70
145	Norm Siebern	2.50	1.25	.70
146	Indians Rookies (Bob Chance, *Tommy John*)	55.00	27.00	16.50
147	Ray Sadecki	2.50	1.25	.70
148	J.C. Martin	2.50	1.25	.70
149	Paul Foytack	2.50	1.25	.70
150	Willie Mays	95.00	47.00	28.00
151	Athletics Team	5.50	2.75	1.75
152	Denver Lemaster	2.50	1.25	.70
153	Dick Williams	3.00	1.50	.90
154	Dick Tracewski	2.50	1.25	.70
155	Duke Snider	27.50	13.50	8.25
156	Bill Dailey	2.50	1.25	.70
157	Gene Mauch	2.50	1.25	.70
158	Ken Johnson	2.50	1.25	.70
159	Charlie Dees	2.50	1.25	.70
160	Ken Boyer	6.00	3.00	1.75
161	Dave McNally	2.50	1.25	.70
162	Hitting Area (Vada Pinson, Dick Sisler)	3.50	1.75	1.00
163	Donn Clendenon	2.50	1.25	.70
164	Bud Daley	2.50	1.25	.70
165	Jerry Lumpe	2.50	1.25	.70
166	Marty Keough	2.50	1.25	.70
167	Mike Brumley, *Lou Piniella*	27.50	13.50	8.25
168	Al Weis	2.50	1.25	.70
169	Del Crandall	2.50	1.25	.70
170	Dick Radatz	2.50	1.25	.70
171	Ty Cline	2.50	1.25	.70
172	Indians Team	5.50	2.75	1.75
173	Ryne Duren	2.50	1.25	.70
174	Doc Edwards	2.50	1.25	.70
175	Billy Williams	15.00	7.50	4.50
176	Tracy Stallard	2.50	1.25	.70
177	Harmon Killebrew	25.00	12.50	7.50
178	Hank Bauer	2.50	1.25	.70
179	Carl Warwick	2.50	1.25	.70
180	Tommy Davis	5.00	2.50	1.50
181	Dave Wickersham	2.50	1.25	.70
182	Sox Sockers (Chuck Schilling, Carl Yastrzemski)	10.00	5.00	3.00
183	Ron Taylor	2.50	1.25	.70
184	Al Luplow	2.50	1.25	.70
185	Jim O'Toole	2.50	1.25	.70
186	Roman Mejias	2.50	1.25	.70
187	Ed Roebuck	2.50	1.25	.70
188	Checklist 177-264	5.00	2.50	1.50
189	Bob Hendley	2.50	1.25	.70
190	Bobby Richardson	7.50	3.75	2.25
191	Clay Dalrymple	2.50	1.25	.70
192	Cubs Rookies (John Boccabella, Billy Cowan)	2.50	1.25	.70
193	Jerry Lynch	2.50	1.25	.70
194	John Goryl	2.50	1.25	.70
195	Floyd Robinson	2.50	1.25	.70
196	Jim Gentile	2.50	1.25	.70
197	Frank Lary	2.50	1.25	.70
198	Len Gabrielson	2.50	1.25	.70

		NR MT	EX	VG
199	Joe Azcue	2.50	1.25	.70
200	Sandy Koufax	100.00	50.00	30.00
201	Orioles Rookies (Sam Bowens, *Wally Bunker*)	2.50	1.25	.70
202	Galen Cisco	2.50	1.25	.70
203	John Kennedy	2.50	1.25	.70
204	Matty Alou	2.50	1.25	.70
205	Nellie Fox	7.00	3.50	2.00
206	Steve Hamilton	2.50	1.25	.70
207	Fred Hutchinson	2.50	1.25	.70
208	Wes Covington	2.50	1.25	.70
209	Bob Allen	2.50	1.25	.70
210	Carl Yastrzemski	60.00	30.00	18.00
211	Jim Coker	2.50	1.25	.70
212	Pete Lovrich	2.50	1.25	.70
213	Angels Team	5.50	2.75	1.75
214	Ken McMullen	2.50	1.25	.70
215	Ray Herbert	2.50	1.25	.70
216	Mike de la Hoz	2.50	1.25	.70
217	Jim King	2.50	1.25	.70
218	Hank Fischer	2.50	1.25	.70
219	Young Aces (Jim Bouton, Al Downing)	5.00	2.50	1.50
220	Dick Ellsworth	2.50	1.25	.70
221	Bob Saverine	2.50	1.25	.70
222	Bill Pierce	2.50	1.25	.70
223	George Banks	2.50	1.25	.70
224	Tommie Sisk	2.50	1.25	.70
225	Roger Maris	60.00	30.00	18.00
226	Colts Rookies (*Gerald Grote,* Larry Yellen)	3.50	1.75	1.00
227	Barry Latman	2.50	1.25	.70
228	Felix Mantilla	2.50	1.25	.70
229	Charley Lau	2.50	1.25	.70
230	Brooks Robinson	32.50	16.00	9.75
231	Dick Calmus	2.50	1.25	.70
232	Al Lopez	5.00	2.50	1.50
233	Hal Smith	2.50	1.25	.70
234	Gary Bell	2.50	1.25	.70
235	Ron Hunt	2.50	1.25	.70
236	Bill Faul	2.50	1.25	.70
237	Cubs Team	5.50	2.75	1.75
238	Roy McMillan	2.50	1.25	.70
239	Herm Starrette	2.50	1.25	.70
240	Bill White	3.50	1.75	1.00
241	Jim Owens	2.50	1.25	.70
242	Harvey Kuenn	3.50	1.75	1.00
243	Phillies Rookies (*Richie Allen,* John Hermstein)	25.00	12.50	7.50
244	*Tony LaRussa*	22.50	11.00	6.75
245	Dick Stigman	2.50	1.25	.70
246	Manny Mota	3.00	1.50	.90
247	Dave DeBusschere	5.00	2.50	1.50
248	Johnny Pesky	2.50	1.25	.70
249	Doug Camilli	2.50	1.25	.70
250	Al Kaline	30.00	15.00	9.00
251	Choo Choo Coleman	2.50	1.25	.70
252	Ken Aspromonte	2.50	1.25	.70
253	Wally Post	2.50	1.25	.70
254	Don Hoak	2.50	1.25	.70
255	Lee Thomas	2.50	1.25	.70
256	Johnny Weekly	2.50	1.25	.70
257	Giants Team	5.50	2.75	1.75
258	Garry Roggenburk	2.50	1.25	.70
259	Harry Bright	2.50	1.25	.70
260	Frank Robinson	27.50	13.50	8.25
261	Jim Hannan	2.50	1.25	.70
262	Cardinals Rookie Stars (Harry Fanok, *Mike Shannon*)	3.00	1.50	.90
263	Chuck Estrada	2.50	1.25	.70
264	Jim Landis	2.50	1.25	.70
265	Jim Bunning	7.00	3.50	2.00
266	Gene Freese	2.50	1.25	.70
267	*Wilbur Wood*	5.00	2.50	1.50
268	Bill's Got It (Danny Murtaugh, Bill Virdon)	3.00	1.50	.90
269	Ellis Burton	2.50	1.25	.70
270	Rich Rollins	2.50	1.25	.70
271	Bob Sadowski	2.50	1.25	.70
272	Jake Wood	2.50	1.25	.70
273	Mel Nelson	2.50	1.25	.70
274	Checklist 265-352	5.00	2.50	1.50
275	John Tsitouris	2.50	1.25	.70
276	Jose Tartabull	2.50	1.25	.70
277	Ken Retzer	2.50	1.25	.70
278	Bobby Shantz	3.00	1.50	.90
279	Joe Koppe	2.50	1.25	.70
280	Juan Marichal	12.50	6.25	3.75
281	Yankees Rookies (Jake Gibbs, Tom Metcalf)	5.00	2.50	1.50
282	Bob Bruce	2.50	1.25	.70
283	*Tommy McCraw*	2.50	1.25	.70
284	Dick Schofield	2.50	1.25	.70
285	Robin Roberts	10.00	5.00	3.00
286	Don Landrum	2.50	1.25	.70
287	Red Sox Rookies (*Tony Conigliaro,* Bill Spanswick)	30.00	15.00	9.00
288	Al Moran	2.50	1.25	.70
289	Frank Funk	2.50	1.25	.70
290	Bob Allison	2.50	1.25	.70
291	Phil Ortega	2.50	1.25	.70
292	Mike Roarke	2.50	1.25	.70
293	Phillies Team	5.50	2.75	1.75
294	Ken Hunt	2.50	1.25	.70
295	Roger Craig	3.50	1.75	1.00
296	Ed Kirkpatrick	2.50	1.25	.70
297	Ken MacKenzie	2.50	1.25	.70
298	Harry Craft	2.50	1.25	.70
299	Bill Stafford	2.50	1.25	.70
300	Hank Aaron	115.00	57.00	34.00
301	Larry Brown	2.50	1.25	.70
302	Dan Pfister	2.50	1.25	.70
303	Jim Campbell	2.50	1.25	.70
304	Bob Johnson	2.50	1.25	.70
305	Jack Lamabe	2.50	1.25	.70
306	Giant Gunners (Orlando Cepeda, Willie Mays)	18.00	9.00	5.50
307	Joe Gibbon	2.50	1.25	.70
308	Gene Stephens	2.50	1.25	.70
309	Paul Toth	2.50	1.25	.70
310	Jim Gilliam	3.50	1.75	1.00
311	Tom Brown	2.50	1.25	.70
312	Tigers Rookies (Fritz Fisher, Fred Gladding)	2.50	1.25	.70
313	Chuck Hiller	2.50	1.25	.70
314	Jerry Buchek	2.50	1.25	.70
315	Bo Belinsky	2.50	1.25	.70
316	Gene Oliver	2.50	1.25	.70
317	Al Smith	2.50	1.25	.70
318	Twins Team	5.50	2.75	1.75
319	Paul Brown	2.50	1.25	.70
320	Rocky Colavito	7.00	3.50	2.00
321	Bob Lillis	2.50	1.25	.70
322	George Brunet	2.50	1.25	.70
323	John Buzhardt	2.50	1.25	.70
324	Casey Stengel	17.50	8.75	5.25
325	Hector Lopez	2.50	1.25	.70
326	Ron Brand	2.50	1.25	.70
327	Don Blasingame	2.50	1.25	.70
328	Bob Shaw	2.50	1.25	.70
329	Russ Nixon	2.50	1.25	.70
330	Tommy Harper	2.50	1.25	.70
331	A.L. Bombers (Norm Cash, Al Kaline, Mickey Mantle, Roger Maris)	120.00	60.00	36.00
332	Ray Washburn	2.50	1.25	.70
333	Billy Moran	2.50	1.25	.70
334	Lew Krausse	2.50	1.25	.70
335	Don Mossi	2.50	1.25	.70
336	Andre Rodgers	2.50	1.25	.70
337	Dodgers Rookies (*Al Ferrara, Jeff Torborg*)	3.50	1.75	1.00
338	Jack Kralick	2.50	1.25	.70
339	Walt Bond	2.50	1.25	.70
340	Joe Cunningham	2.50	1.25	.70
341	Jim Roland	2.50	1.25	.70
342	Willie Stargell	40.00	20.00	12.00
343	Senators Team	5.50	2.75	1.75
344	Phil Linz	3.00	1.50	.90
345	Frank J. Thomas	2.50	1.25	.70
346	Joe Jay	2.50	1.25	.70
347	Bobby Wine	2.50	1.25	.70
348	Ed Lopat	2.50	1.25	.70
349	Art Fowler	2.50	1.25	.70
350	Willie McCovey	22.50	11.00	6.75
351	Dan Schneider	2.50	1.25	.70
352	Eddie Bressoud	2.50	1.25	.70
353	Wally Moon	2.50	1.25	.70
354	Dave Giusti	2.50	1.25	.70
355	Vic Power	2.50	1.25	.70
356	Reds Rookies (Bill McCool, Chico Ruiz)	2.50	1.25	.70
357	Charley James	2.50	1.25	.70
358	Ron Kline	2.50	1.25	.70
359	Jim Schaffer	2.50	1.25	.70
360	Joe Pepitone	3.00	1.50	.90
361	Jay Hook	2.50	1.25	.70
362	Checklist 353-429	5.00	2.50	1.50
363	Dick McAuliffe	2.50	1.25	.70
364	Joe Gaines	2.50	1.25	.70
365	Cal McLish	2.50	1.25	.70
366	Nelson Mathews	2.50	1.25	.70
367	Fred Whitfield	2.50	1.25	.70

		NR MT	EX	VG
368	White Sox Rookies (Fritz Ackley, *Don Buford*)	2.50	1.25	.70
369	Jerry Zimmerman	2.50	1.25	.70
370	Hal Woodeshick	2.50	1.25	.70
371	Frank Howard	6.00	3.00	1.75
372	Howie Koplitz	5.00	2.50	1.50
373	Pirates Team	9.00	4.50	2.75
374	Bobby Bolin	5.00	2.50	1.50
375	Ron Santo	7.00	3.50	2.00
376	Dave Morehead	5.00	2.50	1.50
377	Bob Skinner	5.00	2.50	1.50
378	Braves Rookies (Jack Smith, *Woody Woodward*)	5.00	2.50	1.50
379	Tony Gonzalez	5.00	2.50	1.50
380	Whitey Ford	30.00	15.00	9.00
381	Bob Taylor	5.00	2.50	1.50
382	Wes Stock	5.00	2.50	1.50
383	Bill Rigney	5.00	2.50	1.50
384	Ron Hansen	5.00	2.50	1.50
385	Curt Simmons	5.00	2.50	1.50
386	Lenny Green	5.00	2.50	1.50
387	Terry Fox	5.00	2.50	1.50
388	Athletics Rookies (John O'Donoghue, George Williams)	5.00	2.50	1.50
389	Jim Umbricht	5.00	2.50	1.50
390	Orlando Cepeda	9.00	4.50	2.75
391	Sam McDowell	6.00	3.00	1.75
392	Jim Pagliaroni	5.00	2.50	1.50
393	Casey Teaches (Ed Kranepool, Casey Stengel)	9.50	4.75	2.75
394	Bob Miller	5.00	2.50	1.50
395	Tom Tresh	6.00	3.00	1.75
396	Dennis Bennett	5.00	2.50	1.50
397	Chuck Cottier	5.00	2.50	1.50
398	Mets Rookies (Bill Haas, Dick Smith)	5.00	2.50	1.50
399	Jackie Brandt	5.00	2.50	1.50
400	Warren Spahn	35.00	17.50	10.50
401	Charlie Maxwell	5.00	2.50	1.50
402	Tom Sturdivant	5.00	2.50	1.50
403	Reds Team	9.00	4.50	2.75
404	Tony Martinez	5.00	2.50	1.50
405	Ken McBride	5.00	2.50	1.50
406	Al Spangler	5.00	2.50	1.50
407	Bill Freehan	5.00	2.50	1.50
408	Cubs Rookies (Fred Burdette, Jim Stewart)	5.00	2.50	1.50
409	Bill Fischer	5.00	2.50	1.50
410	Dick Stuart	5.50	2.75	1.75
411	Lee Walls	5.00	2.50	1.50
412	Ray Culp	5.00	2.50	1.50
413	Johnny Keane	5.00	2.50	1.50
414	Jack Sanford	5.00	2.50	1.50
415	Tony Kubek	7.00	3.50	2.00
416	Lee Maye	5.00	2.50	1.50
417	Don Cardwell	5.00	2.50	1.50
418	Orioles Rookies (*Darold Knowles*, Les Narum)	5.50	2.75	1.75
419	*Ken Harrelson*	7.00	3.50	2.00
420	Jim Maloney	5.00	2.50	1.50
421	Camilo Carreon	5.00	2.50	1.50
422	Jack Fisher	5.00	2.50	1.50
423	Tops in NL (Hank Aaron, Willie Mays)	110.00	55.00	33.00
424	Dick Bertell	5.00	2.50	1.50
425	Norm Cash	6.00	3.00	1.75
426	Bob Rodgers	5.00	2.50	1.50
427	Don Rudolph	5.00	2.50	1.50
428	Red Sox Rookies (Archie Skeen, Pete Smith)	5.00	2.50	1.50
429	Tim McCarver	6.00	3.00	1.75
430	Juan Pizarro	5.00	2.50	1.50
431	George Alusik	5.00	2.50	1.50
432	Ruben Amaro	5.00	2.50	1.50
433	Yankees Team	10.00	5.00	3.00
434	Don Nottebart	5.00	2.50	1.50
435	Vic Davalillo	5.00	2.50	1.50
436	Charlie Neal	5.00	2.50	1.50
437	Ed Bailey	5.00	2.50	1.50
438	Checklist 430-506	9.50	4.75	2.75
439	Harvey Haddix	5.00	2.50	1.50
440	Roberto Clemente	150.00	75.00	45.00
441	Bob Duliba	5.00	2.50	1.50
442	Pumpsie Green	5.00	2.50	1.50
443	Chuck Dressen	5.00	2.50	1.50
444	Larry Jackson	5.00	2.50	1.50
445	Bill Skowron	6.00	3.00	1.75
446	Julian Javier	5.00	2.50	1.50
447	Ted Bowsfield	5.00	2.50	1.50
448	Cookie Rojas	5.00	2.50	1.50
449	Deron Johnson	5.00	2.50	1.50

		NR MT	EX	VG
450	Steve Barber	5.00	2.50	1.50
451	Joe Amalfitano	5.00	2.50	1.50
452	Giants Rookies (Gil Garrido, *Jim Hart*)	5.50	2.75	1.75
453	Frank Baumann	5.00	2.50	1.50
454	Tommie Aaron	5.50	2.75	1.75
455	Bernie Allen	5.00	2.50	1.50
456	Dodgers Rookies (*Wes Parker*, John Werhas)	5.00	2.50	1.50
457	Jesse Gonder	5.00	2.50	1.50
458	Ralph Terry	5.00	2.50	1.50
459	Red Sox Rookies (Pete Charton, Dalton Jones)	5.00	2.50	1.50
460	Bob Gibson	30.00	15.00	9.00
461	George Thomas	5.00	2.50	1.50
462	Birdie Tebbetts	5.00	2.50	1.50
463	Don Leppert	5.00	2.50	1.50
464	Dallas Green	5.50	2.75	1.75
465	Mike Hershberger	5.00	2.50	1.50
466	Athletics Rookies (*Dick Green*, Aurelio Monteagudo)	5.50	2.75	1.75
467	Bob Aspromonte	5.00	2.50	1.50
468	Gaylord Perry	35.00	17.50	10.50
469	Cubs Rookies (Fred Norman, Sterling Slaughter)	5.00	2.50	1.50
470	Jim Bouton	6.00	3.00	1.75
471	*Gates Brown*	5.50	2.75	1.75
472	Vern Law	5.00	2.50	1.50
473	Orioles Team	9.00	4.50	2.75
474	Larry Sherry	5.00	2.50	1.50
475	Ed Charles	5.00	2.50	1.50
476	Braves Rookies (*Rico Carty*, Dick Kelley)	9.50	4.75	2.75
477	Mike Joyce	5.00	2.50	1.50
478	Dick Howser	5.00	2.50	1.50
479	Cardinals Rookies (Dave Bakenhaster, Johnny Lewis)	5.00	2.50	1.50
480	Bob Purkey	5.00	2.50	1.50
481	Chuck Schilling	5.00	2.50	1.50
482	Phillies Rookies (*John Briggs, Danny Cater*)	5.50	2.75	1.75
483	Fred Valentine	5.00	2.50	1.50
484	Bill Pleis	5.00	2.50	1.50
485	Tom Haller	5.00	2.50	1.50
486	Bob Kennedy	5.00	2.50	1.50
487	Mike McCormick	5.00	2.50	1.50
488	Yankees Rookies (Bob Meyer, Pete Mikkelsen)	5.00	2.50	1.50
489	Julio Navarro	5.00	2.50	1.50
490	Ron Fairly	5.00	2.50	1.50
491	Ed Rakow	5.00	2.50	1.50
492	Colts Rookies (Jim Beauchamp, Mike White)	5.00	2.50	1.50
493	Don Lee	5.00	2.50	1.50
494	Al Jackson	5.00	2.50	1.50
495	Bill Virdon	5.00	2.50	1.50
496	White Sox Team	9.00	4.50	2.75
497	Jeoff Long	5.00	2.50	1.50
498	Dave Stenhouse	5.00	2.50	1.50
499	Indians Rookies (Chico Salmon, Gordon Seyfried)	5.00	2.50	1.50
500	Camilo Pascual	5.00	2.50	1.50
501	Bob Veale	5.00	2.50	1.50
502	Angels Rookies (*Bobby Knoop*, Bob Lee)	5.50	2.75	1.75
503	Earl Wilson	5.00	2.50	1.50
504	Claude Raymond	5.00	2.50	1.50
505	Stan Williams	5.00	2.50	1.50
506	Bobby Bragan	5.00	2.50	1.50
507	John Edwards	5.00	2.50	1.50
508	Diego Segui	5.00	2.50	1.50
509	Pirates Rookies (*Gene Alley*, Orlando McFarlane)	5.50	2.75	1.75
510	Lindy McDaniel	5.00	2.50	1.50
511	Lou Jackson	5.00	2.50	1.50
512	Tigers Rookies (*Willie Horton, Joe Sparma*)	7.00	3.50	2.00
513	Don Larsen	5.00	2.50	1.50
514	Jim Hickman	5.00	2.50	1.50
515	Johnny Romano	5.00	2.50	1.50
516	Twins Rookies (Jerry Arrigo, Dwight Siebler)	5.00	2.50	1.50
517a	Checklist 507-587 (wrong numbering on back)	9.50	4.75	2.75
517b	Checklist 507-587 (correct numbering on back)	9.50	4.75	2.75
518	Carl Bouldin	5.00	2.50	1.50
519	Charlie Smith	5.00	2.50	1.50
520	Jack Baldschun	5.00	2.50	1.50
521	Tom Satriano	5.00	2.50	1.50
522	Bobby Tiefenauer	5.00	2.50	1.50

		NR MT	EX	VG
523	Lou Burdette	9.50	4.75	2.75
524	Reds Rookies (Jim Dickson, Bobby Klaus)	9.50	4.75	2.75
525	Al McBean	9.50	4.75	2.75
526	Lou Clinton	9.50	4.75	2.75
527	Larry Bearnarth	9.50	4.75	2.75
528	Athletics Rookies (*Dave Duncan*, Tom Reynolds)	9.50	4.75	2.75
529	Al Dark	9.50	4.75	2.75
530	Leon Wagner	9.50	4.75	2.75
531	Dodgers Team	20.00	10.00	6.00
532	Twins Rookies (Bud Bloomfield, Joe Nossek)	9.50	4.75	2.75
533	Johnny Klippstein	9.50	4.75	2.75
534	Gus Bell	9.50	4.75	2.75
535	Phil Regan	9.50	4.75	2.75
536	Mets Rookies (Larry Elliot, John Stephenson)	9.50	4.75	2.75
537	Dan Osinski	9.50	4.75	2.75
538	Minnie Minoso	11.00	5.50	3.25
539	Roy Face	9.50	4.75	2.75
540	Luis Aparicio	15.00	7.50	4.50
541	Braves Rookies (*Phil Niekro*, Phil Roof)	200.00	100.00	60.00
542	Don Mincher	9.50	4.75	2.75
543	Bob Uecker	50.00	25.00	15.00
544	Colts Rookies (Steve Hertz, Joe Hoerner)	9.50	4.75	2.75
545	Max Alvis	9.50	4.75	2.75
546	Joe Christopher	9.50	4.75	2.75
547	Gil Hodges	12.00	6.00	3.50
548	N.L. Rookies (Wayne Schurr, Paul Speckenbach)	9.50	4.75	2.75
549	Joe Moeller	9.50	4.75	2.75
550	Ken Hubbs	15.00	7.50	4.50
551	Billy Hoeft	9.50	4.75	2.75
552	Indians Rookies (Tom Kelley, *Sonny Siebert*)	9.50	4.75	2.75
553	Jim Brewer	9.50	4.75	2.75
554	Hank Foiles	9.50	4.75	2.75
555	Lee Stange	9.50	4.75	2.75
556	Mets Rookies (Steve Dillon, Ron Locke)	9.50	4.75	2.75
557	Leo Burke	9.50	4.75	2.75
558	Don Schwall	9.50	4.75	2.75
559	Dick Phillips	9.50	4.75	2.75
560	Dick Farrell	9.50	4.75	2.75
561	Phillies Rookies (Dave Bennett, *Rick Wise*)	9.50	4.75	2.75
562	Pedro Ramos	9.50	4.75	2.75
563	Dal Maxvill	9.50	4.75	2.75
564	A.L. Rookies (Joe McCabe, Jerry McNertney)	9.50	4.75	2.75
565	Stu Miller	9.50	4.75	2.75
566	Ed Kranepool	9.50	4.75	2.75
567	Jim Kaat	12.00	6.00	3.50
568	N.L. Rookies (Phil Gagliano, Cap Peterson)	9.50	4.75	2.75
569	Fred Newman	9.50	4.75	2.75
570	Bill Mazeroski	12.00	6.00	3.50
571	Gene Conley	9.50	4.75	2.75
572	A.L. Rookies (Dick Egan, Dave Gray)	9.50	4.75	2.75
573	Jim Duffalo	9.50	4.75	2.75
574	Manny Jimenez	9.50	4.75	2.75
575	Tony Cloninger	9.50	4.75	2.75
576	Mets Rookies (Jerry Hinsley, Bill Wakefield)	9.50	4.75	2.75
577	Gordy Coleman	9.50	4.75	2.75
578	Glen Hobbie	9.50	4.75	2.75
579	Red Sox Team	18.00	9.00	5.50
580	Johnny Podres	11.00	5.50	3.25
581	Yankees Rookies (Pedro Gonzalez, Archie Moore)	9.50	4.75	2.75
582	Rod Kanehl	9.50	4.75	2.75
583	Tito Francona	9.50	4.75	2.75
584	Joel Horlen	9.50	4.75	2.75
585	Tony Taylor	9.50	4.75	2.75
586	Jim Piersall	9.00	4.50	2.75
587	Bennie Daniels	12.00	2.50	1.25

1964 Topps Coins

The 164 metal coins in this set were issued by Topps as inserts in the company's baseball card wax packs. The series is divided into two principal types, 120 "regular" coins and 44 All-Star coins. The 1 1/2" diameter coins feature a full-color background for the player photos in the "regular" series, while the players in the All-Star series are featured against plain red or blue backgrounds. There are two variations each of the Mantle, Causey and Hinton coins among the All-Star subset.

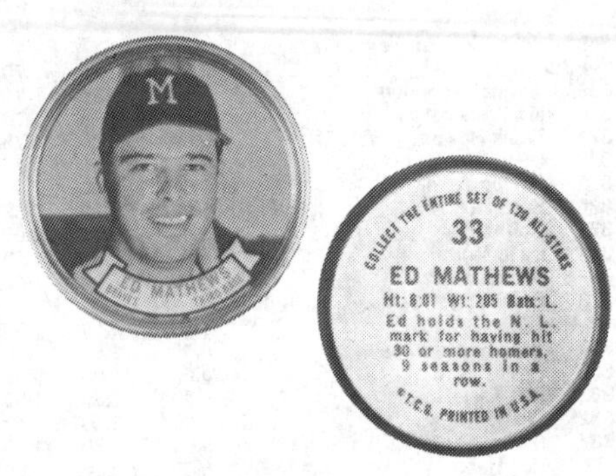

		NR MT	EX	VG
Complete Set:		700.00	350.00	210.00
Common Player:		2.00	1.00	.60
1	Don Zimmer	2.00	1.00	.60
2	Jim Wynn	2.00	1.00	.60
3	Johnny Orsino	2.00	1.00	.60
4	Jim Bouton	2.00	1.00	.60
5	Dick Groat	2.00	1.00	.60
6	Leon Wagner	2.00	1.00	.60
7	Frank Malzone	2.00	1.00	.60
8	Steve Barber	2.00	1.00	.60
9	Johnny Romano	2.00	1.00	.60
10	Tom Tresh	2.00	1.00	.60
11	Felipe Alou	2.00	1.00	.60
12	Dick Stuart	2.00	1.00	.60
13	Claude Osteen	2.00	1.00	.60
14	Juan Pizarro	2.00	1.00	.60
15	Donn Clendenon	2.00	1.00	.60
16	Jimmie Hall	2.00	1.00	.60
17	Larry Jackson	2.00	1.00	.60
18	Brooks Robinson	12.00	6.00	3.50
19	Bob Allison	2.00	1.00	.60
20	Ed Roebuck	2.00	1.00	.60
21	Pete Ward	2.00	1.00	.60
22	Willie McCovey	8.00	4.00	2.50
23	Elston Howard	2.50	1.25	.70
24	Diego Segui	2.00	1.00	.60
25	Ken Boyer	2.50	1.25	.70
26	Carl Yastrzemski	15.00	7.50	4.50
27	Bill Mazeroski	2.50	1.25	.70
28	Jerry Lumpe	2.00	1.00	.60
29	Woody Held	2.00	1.00	.60
30	Dick Radatz	2.00	1.00	.60
31	Luis Aparicio	5.00	2.50	1.50
32	Dave Nicholson	2.00	1.00	.60
33	Ed Mathews	12.00	6.00	3.50
34	Don Drysdale	10.00	5.00	3.00
35	Ray Culp	2.00	1.00	.60
36	Juan Marichal	8.00	4.00	2.50
37	Frank Robinson	12.00	6.00	3.50
38	Chuck Hinton	2.00	1.00	.60
39	Floyd Robinson	2.00	1.00	.60
40	Tommy Harper	2.00	1.00	.60
41	Ron Hansen	2.00	1.00	.60
42	Ernie Banks	15.00	7.50	4.50
43	Jesse Gonder	2.00	1.00	.60
44	Billy Williams	8.00	4.00	2.50
45	Vada Pinson	2.50	1.25	.70
46	Rocky Colavito	3.00	1.50	.90
47	Bill Monbouquette	2.00	1.00	.60
48	Max Alvis	2.00	1.00	.60
49	Norm Siebern	2.00	1.00	.60
50	John Callison	2.00	1.00	.60
51	Rich Rollins	2.00	1.00	.60
52	Ken McBride	2.00	1.00	.60
53	Don Lock	2.00	1.00	.60
54	Ron Fairly	2.00	1.00	.60
55	Roberto Clemente	20.00	10.00	6.00
56	Dick Ellsworth	2.00	1.00	.60
57	Tommy Davis	2.00	1.00	.60
58	Tony Gonzalez	2.00	1.00	.60
59	Bob Gibson	10.00	5.00	3.00
60	Jim Maloney	2.00	1.00	.60

		NR MT	EX	VG
61	Frank Howard	2.50	1.25	.70
62	Jim Pagliaroni	2.00	1.00	.60
63	Orlando Cepeda	3.00	1.50	.90
64	Ron Perranoski	2.00	1.00	.60
65	Curt Flood	2.00	1.00	.60
66	Al McBean	2.00	1.00	.60
67	Dean Chance	2.00	1.00	.60
68	Ron Santo	2.50	1.25	.70
69	Jack Baldschun	2.00	1.00	.60
70	Milt Pappas	2.00	1.00	.60
71	Gary Peters	2.00	1.00	.60
72	Bobby Richardson	2.50	1.25	.70
73	Lee Thomas	2.00	1.00	.60
74	Hank Aguirre	2.00	1.00	.60
75	Carl Willey	2.00	1.00	.60
76	Camilo Pascual	2.00	1.00	.60
77	Bob Friend	2.00	1.00	.60
78	Bill White	2.00	1.00	.60
79	Norm Cash	2.50	1.25	.70
80	Willie Mays	20.00	10.00	6.00
81	Duke Carmel	2.00	1.00	.60
82	Pete Rose	20.00	10.00	6.00
83	Hank Aaron	20.00	10.00	6.00
84	Bob Aspromonte	2.00	1.00	.60
85	Jim O'Toole	2.00	1.00	.60
86	Vic Davalillo	2.00	1.00	.60
87	Bill Freehan	2.00	1.00	.60
88	Warren Spahn	8.00	4.00	2.50
89	Ron Hunt	2.00	1.00	.60
90	Denis Menke	2.00	1.00	.60
91	Turk Farrell	2.00	1.00	.60
92	Jim Hickman	2.00	1.00	.60
93	Jim Bunning	3.00	1.50	.90
94	Bob Hendley	2.00	1.00	.60
95	Ernie Broglio	2.00	1.00	.60
96	Rusty Staub	2.50	1.25	.70
97	Lou Brock	8.00	4.00	2.50
98	Jim Fregosi	2.00	1.00	.60
99	Jim Grant	2.00	1.00	.60
100	Al Kaline	15.00	7.50	4.50
101	Earl Battey	2.00	1.00	.60
102	Wayne Causey	2.00	1.00	.60
103	Chuck Schilling	2.00	1.00	.60
104	Boog Powell	2.50	1.25	.70
105	Dave Wickersham	2.00	1.00	.60
106	Sandy Koufax	15.00	7.50	4.50
107	John Bateman	2.00	1.00	.60
108	Ed Brinkman	2.00	1.00	.60
109	Al Downing	2.00	1.00	.60
110	Joe Azcue	2.00	1.00	.60
111	Albie Pearson	2.00	1.00	.60
112	Harmon Killebrew	10.00	5.00	3.00
113	Tony Taylor	2.00	1.00	.60
114	Alvin Jackson	2.00	1.00	.60
115	Billy O'Dell	2.00	1.00	.60
116	Don Demeter	2.00	1.00	.60
117	Ed Charles	2.00	1.00	.60
118	Joe Torre	2.00	1.00	.60
119	Don Nottebart	2.00	1.00	.60
120	Mickey Mantle	40.00	20.00	12.00
121	Joe Pepitone	2.00	1.00	.60
122	Dick Stuart	2.00	1.00	.60
123	Bobby Richardson	2.50	1.25	.70
124	Jerry Lumpe	2.00	1.00	.60
125	Brooks Robinson	12.00	6.00	3.50
126	Frank Malzone	2.00	1.00	.60
127	Luis Aparicio	5.00	2.50	1.50
128	Jim Fregosi	2.00	1.00	.60
129	Al Kaline	15.00	7.50	4.50
130	Leon Wagner	2.00	1.00	.60
131a	Mickey Mantle (batting lefthanded)	45.00	22.00	13.50
131b	Mickey Mantle (batting righthanded)	45.00	22.00	13.50
132	Albie Pearson	2.00	1.00	.60
133	Harmon Killebrew	10.00	5.00	3.00
134	Carl Yastrzemski	15.00	7.50	4.50
135	Elston Howard	2.50	1.25	.70
136	Earl Battey	2.00	1.00	.60
137	Camilo Pascual	2.00	1.00	.60
138	Jim Bouton	2.00	1.00	.60
139	Whitey Ford	8.00	4.00	2.50
140	Gary Peters	2.00	1.00	.60
141	Bill White	2.00	1.00	.60
142	Orlando Cepeda	2.50	1.25	.70
143	Bill Mazeroski	3.00	1.50	.90
144	Tony Taylor	2.00	1.00	.60
145	Ken Boyer	2.50	1.25	.70
146	Ron Santo	2.00	1.00	.60
147	Dick Groat	2.00	1.00	.60
148	Roy McMillan	2.00	1.00	.60

		NR MT	EX	VG
149	Hank Aaron	20.00	10.00	6.00
150	Roberto Clemente	20.00	10.00	6.00
151	Willie Mays	20.00	10.00	6.00
152	Vada Pinson	2.50	1.25	.70
153	Tommy Davis	2.00	1.00	.60
154	Frank Robinson	15.00	7.50	4.50
155	Joe Torre	2.50	1.25	.70
156	Tim McCarver	2.00	1.00	.60
157	Juan Marichal	8.00	4.00	2.50
158	Jim Maloney	2.00	1.00	.60
159	Sandy Koufax	15.00	7.50	4.50
160	Warren Spahn	8.00	4.00	2.50
161a	Wayne Causey (N.L. on back)	15.00	7.50	4.50
161b	Wayne Causey (A.L. on back)	2.00	1.00	.60
162a	Chuck Hinton (N.L. on back)	15.00	7.50	4.50
162b	Chuck Hinton (A.L. on back)	2.00	1.00	.60
163	Bob Aspromonte	2.00	1.00	.60
164	Ron Hunt	2.00	1.00	.60

1964 Topps Giants

Measuring 3-1/8" by 5-1/4" the Topps Giants were the company's first postcard-size issue. The cards feature large color photographs surrounded by white borders with a white baseball containing the player's name, position and team. Card backs carry another photo of the player surrounded by a newspaper-style explanation of the depicted career highlight. The 60- card set contains primarily stars which means it's an excellent place to find inexpensive cards of Hall of Famers. The '64 Giants were not printed in equal quantity and seven of the cards, including Sandy Koufax and Willie Mays, are significantly scarcer than the remainder of the set.

		NR MT	EX	VG
Complete Set:		110.00	55.00	33.00
Common Player:		1.00	.50	.30
1	Gary Peters	1.00	.50	.30
2	Ken Johnson	1.00	.50	.30
3	Sandy Koufax	18.00	9.00	5.50
4	Bob Bailey	1.00	.50	.30
5	Milt Pappas	1.00	.50	.30
6	Ron Hunt	1.00	.50	.30
7	Whitey Ford	3.00	1.50	.90
8	Roy McMillan	1.00	.50	.30
9	Rocky Colavito	2.00	1.00	.60
10	Jim Bunning	1.50	.70	.45
11	Roberto Clemente	5.00	2.50	1.50
12	Al Kaline	3.00	1.50	.90
13	Nellie Fox	2.00	1.00	.60
14	Tony Gonzalez	1.00	.50	.30
15	Jim Gentile	1.00	.50	.30
16	Dean Chance	1.00	.50	.30
17	Dick Ellsworth	1.00	.50	.30
18	Jim Fregosi	1.00	.50	.30
19	Dick Groat	1.00	.50	.30
20	Chuck Hinton	1.00	.50	.30
21	Elston Howard	1.50	.70	.45
22	Dick Farrell	1.00	.50	.30
23	Albie Pearson	1.00	.50	.30
24	Frank Howard	1.50	.70	.45
25	Mickey Mantle	18.00	9.00	5.50
26	Joe Torre	1.00	.50	.30
27	Ed Brinkman	1.00	.50	.30
28	Bob Friend	4.00	2.00	1.25

		NR MT	EX	VG
29	Frank Robinson	3.00	1.50	.90
30	Bill Freehan	1.00	.50	.30
31	Warren Spahn	3.00	1.50	.90
32	Camilo Pascual	1.00	.50	.30
33	Pete Ward	1.00	.50	.30
34	Jim Maloney	1.00	.50	.30
35	Dave Wickersham	1.00	.50	.30
36	Johnny Callison	1.00	.50	.30
37	Juan Marichal	3.00	1.50	.90
38	Harmon Killebrew	3.00	1.50	.90
39	Luis Aparicio	3.00	1.50	.90
40	Dick Radatz	1.00	.50	.30
41	Bob Gibson	3.00	1.50	.90
42	Dick Stuart	4.00	2.00	1.25
43	Tommy Davis	1.00	.50	.30
44	Tony Oliva	1.50	.70	.45
45	Wayne Causey	4.00	2.00	1.25
46	Max Alvis	1.00	.50	.30
47	Galen Cisco	4.00	2.00	1.25
48	Carl Yastrzemski	3.00	1.50	.90
49	Hank Aaron	5.00	2.50	1.50
50	Brooks Robinson	3.00	1.50	.90
51	Willie Mays	18.00	9.00	5.50
52	Billy Williams	3.00	1.50	.90
53	Juan Pizarro	1.00	.50	.30
54	Leon Wagner	1.00	.50	.30
55	Orlando Cepeda	2.00	1.00	.60
56	Vada Pinson	1.50	.70	.45
57	Ken Boyer	1.50	.70	.45
58	Ron Santo	1.50	.70	.45
59	John Romano	1.00	.50	.30
60	Bill Skowron	4.00	2.00	1.25

1964 Topps Stand-Ups

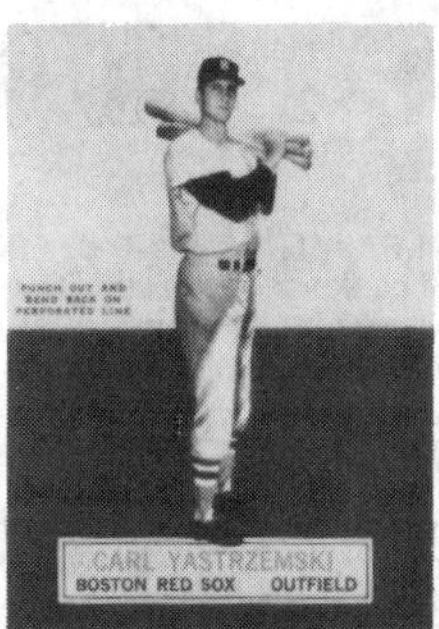

These 2-1/2" by 3-1/2" cards were the first since the All-Star sets of 1951 to be die-cut. This made it possible for a folded card to stand on display. The 77-cards in the set feature color photographs of the player with yellow and green backgrounds. Directions for folding are on the yellow top background, and when folded only the green background remains. Of the 77 cards, 55 were double-printed while 22 were single-printed, making them twice as scarce. Included in the single-printed group are Warren Spahn, Don Drysdale, Juan Marichal, Willie McCovey and Carl Yastrzemski.

		NR MT	EX	VG
Complete Set:		2400.00	1200.00	720.00
Common Player:		7.50	3.75	2.25
(1)	Hank Aaron	120.00	60.00	36.00
(2)	Hank Aguirre	7.50	3.75	2.25
(3)	George Altman	7.50	3.75	2.25
(4)	Max Alvis	7.50	3.75	2.25
(5)	Bob Aspromonte	7.50	3.75	2.25
(6)	Jack Baldschun	25.00	12.50	7.50
(7)	Ernie Banks	45.00	22.00	13.50
(8)	Steve Barber	7.50	3.75	2.25
(9)	Earl Battey	7.50	3.75	2.25
(10)	Ken Boyer	9.00	4.50	2.75
(11)	Ernie Broglio	7.50	3.75	2.25
(12)	Johnny Callison	7.50	3.75	2.25
(13)	Norm Cash	25.00	12.50	7.50
(14)	Wayne Causey	7.50	3.75	2.25
(15)	Orlando Cepeda	12.00	6.00	3.50
(16)	Ed Charles	7.50	3.75	2.25
(17)	Roberto Clemente	55.00	27.00	16.50
(18)	Donn Clendenon	25.00	12.50	7.50
(19)	Rocky Colavito	9.00	4.50	2.75
(20)	Ray Culp	25.00	12.50	7.50
(21)	Tommy Davis	9.00	4.50	2.75
(22)	Don Drysdale	125.00	62.00	37.00
(23)	Dick Ellsworth	7.50	3.75	2.25
(24)	Dick Farrell	7.50	3.75	2.25
(25)	Jim Fregosi	7.50	3.75	2.25
(26)	Bob Friend	7.50	3.75	2.25
(27)	Jim Gentile	7.50	3.75	2.25
(28)	Jesse Gonder	25.00	12.50	7.50
(29)	Tony Gonzalez	25.00	12.50	7.50
(30)	Dick Groat	9.00	4.50	2.75
(31)	Woody Held	7.50	3.75	2.25
(32)	Chuck Hinton	7.50	3.75	2.25
(33)	Elston Howard	9.00	4.50	2.75
(34)	Frank Howard	25.00	12.50	7.50
(35)	Ron Hunt	7.50	3.75	2.25
(36)	Al Jackson	7.50	3.75	2.25
(37)	Ken Johnson	7.50	3.75	2.25
(38)	Al Kaline	40.00	20.00	12.00
(39)	Harmon Killebrew	40.00	20.00	12.00
(40)	Sandy Koufax	45.00	22.00	13.50
(41)	Don Lock	25.00	12.50	7.50
(42)	Jerry Lumpe	25.00	12.50	7.50
(43)	Jim Maloney	7.50	3.75	2.25
(44)	Frank Malzone	7.50	3.75	2.25
(45)	Mickey Mantle	350.00	175.00	105.00
(46)	Juan Marichal	125.00	62.00	37.00
(47)	Ed Mathews	125.00	62.00	37.00
(48)	Willie Mays	120.00	60.00	36.00
(49)	Bill Mazeroski	9.00	4.50	2.75
(50)	Ken McBride	7.50	3.75	2.25
(51)	Willie McCovey	125.00	62.00	37.00
(52)	Claude Osteen	7.50	3.75	2.25
(53)	Jim O'Toole	7.50	3.75	2.25
(54)	Camilo Pascual	7.50	3.75	2.25
(55)	Albie Pearson	25.00	12.50	7.50
(56)	Gary Peters	7.50	3.75	2.25
(57)	Vada Pinson	9.00	4.50	2.75
(58)	Juan Pizarro	7.50	3.75	2.25
(59)	Boog Powell	9.00	4.50	2.75
(60)	Bobby Richardson	9.00	4.50	2.75
(61)	Brooks Robinson	50.00	25.00	15.00
(62)	Floyd Robinson	7.50	3.75	2.25
(63)	Frank Robinson	50.00	25.00	15.00
(64)	Ed Roebuck	25.00	12.50	7.50
(65)	Rich Rollins	7.50	3.75	2.25
(66)	Johnny Romano	7.50	3.75	2.25
(67)	Ron Santo	25.00	12.50	7.50
(68)	Norm Siebern	7.50	3.75	2.25
(69)	Warren Spahn	125.00	62.00	37.00
(70)	Dick Stuart	25.00	12.50	7.50
(71)	Lee Thomas	7.50	3.75	2.25
(72)	Joe Torre	7.50	3.75	2.25
(73)	Pete Ward	7.50	3.75	2.25
(74)	Bill White	25.00	12.50	7.50
(75)	Billy Williams	125.00	62.00	37.00
(76)	Hal Woodeshick	25.00	12.50	7.50
(77)	Carl Yastrzemski	400.00	200.00	120.00

1965 Topps

The 1965 Topps set features a large color photograph of the player which was surrounded by a colored, round-cornered frame and a white border. The bottom of the 2-1/2" by 3-1/2" cards include a pennant with a color team logo and name over the left side of a rectangle which features the player's name and position. Backs feature statistics and, if space allowed, a cartoon and headline about the player. There are no multi-player cards in the 1965 set other than the usual team cards and World Series highlights. Rookie cards include team, as well as league groupings from two to four players per card. Also present in the 598-card set are statistical leaders. Certain cards in the high-number series (#523-598) were produced in lesser quantities than the rest of the series. Known as "short-rpints," and valued somewhat higher than the other high numbers, they are indicated in the checklist by an (SP) after the player name.

		NR MT	EX	VG
Complete Set (598):		3750.00	1875.00	1125.
Common Player: 1-446		3.50	1.75	1.00
Common Player: 447-522		4.00	2.00	1.25
Common Player: 523-598		7.00	3.50	2.00
1	A.L. Batting Leaders (Elston Howard, Tony Oliva, Brooks Robinson)	12.00	6.00	3.50
2	N.L. Batting Leaders (Hank Aaron, Rico Carty, Roberto Clemente)	15.00	7.50	4.50
3	A.L. Home Run Leaders (Harmon Killebrew, Mickey Mantle, Boog Powell)	25.00	12.50	7.50
4	N.L. Home Run Leaders (Johnny Callison, Orlando Cepeda, Jim Hart, Willie Mays, Billy Williams)	15.00	7.50	4.50
5	A.L. RBI Leaders (Harmon Killebrew, Mickey Mantle, Brooks Robinson, Dick Stuart)	25.00	12.50	7.50
6	N.L. RBI Leaders (Ken Boyer, Willie Mays, Ron Santo)	12.00	6.00	3.50
7	A.L. ERA Leaders (Dean Chance, Joel Horlen)	7.00	3.50	2.00
8	N.L. ERA Leaders (Don Drysdale, Sandy Koufax)	9.00	4.50	2.75
9	A.L. Pitching Leaders (Wally Bunker, Dean Chance, Gary Peters, Juan Pizarro, Dave Wickersham)	6.00	3.00	1.75
10	N.L. Pitching Leaders (Larry Jackson, Juan Marichal, Ray Sadecki)	6.00	3.00	1.75
11	A.L. Strikeout Leaders (Dean Chance, Al Downing, Camilo Pascual)	6.00	3.00	1.75
12	N.L. Strikeout Leaders (Don Drysdale, Bob Gibson, Bob Veale)	7.00	3.50	2.00
13	Pedro Ramos	3.50	1.75	1.00
14	Len Gabrielson	3.50	1.75	1.00
15	Robin Roberts	9.00	4.50	2.75
16	Astros Rookies *(Sonny Jackson, Joe Morgan)*	125.00	62.00	37.00
17	Johnny Romano	3.50	1.75	1.00
18	Bill McCool	3.50	1.75	1.00
19	Gates Brown	3.50	1.75	1.00
20	Jim Bunning	5.00	2.50	1.50
21	Don Blasingame	3.50	1.75	1.00
22	Charlie Smith	3.50	1.75	1.00
23	Bob Tiefenauer	3.50	1.75	1.00
24	Twins Team	5.00	2.50	1.50
25	Al McBean	3.50	1.75	1.00
26	Bobby Knoop	3.50	1.75	1.00
27	Dick Bertell	3.50	1.75	1.00
28	Barney Schultz	3.50	1.75	1.00
29	Felix Mantilla	3.50	1.75	1.00
30	Jim Bouton	5.00	2.50	1.50
31	Mike White	3.50	1.75	1.00
32	Herman Franks	3.50	1.75	1.00
33	Jackie Brandt	3.50	1.75	1.00
34	Cal Koonce	3.50	1.75	1.00
35	Ed Charles	3.50	1.75	1.00
36	Bobby Wine	3.50	1.75	1.00
37	Fred Gladding	3.50	1.75	1.00
38	Jim King	3.50	1.75	1.00
39	Gerry Arrigo	3.50	1.75	1.00
40	Frank Howard	5.00	2.50	1.50
41	White Sox Rookies (Bruce Howard, Marv Staehle)	3.50	1.75	1.00
42	Earl Wilson	3.50	1.75	1.00
43	Mike Shannon	3.50	1.75	1.00
44	Wade Blasingame	3.50	1.75	1.00
45	Roy McMillan	3.50	1.75	1.00
46	Bob Lee	3.50	1.75	1.00
47	Tommy Harper	3.50	1.75	1.00
48	Claude Raymond	3.50	1.75	1.00
49	Orioles Rookies *(Curt Blefary,* John Miller)	4.50	2.25	1.25

		NR MT	EX	VG
50	Juan Marichal	11.00	5.50	3.25
51	Billy Bryan	3.50	1.75	1.00
52	Ed Roebuck	3.50	1.75	1.00
53	Dick McAuliffe	3.50	1.75	1.00
54	Joe Gibbon	3.50	1.75	1.00
55	Tony Conigliaro	5.00	2.50	1.50
56	Ron Kline	3.50	1.75	1.00
57	Cardinals Team	5.00	2.50	1.50
58	Fred Talbot	3.50	1.75	1.00
59	Nate Oliver	3.50	1.75	1.00
60	Jim O'Toole	3.50	1.75	1.00
61	Chris Cannizzaro	3.50	1.75	1.00
62	Jim Katt (Kaat)	5.00	2.50	1.50
63	Ty Cline	3.50	1.75	1.00
64	Lou Burdette	3.50	1.75	1.00
65	Tony Kubek	4.50	2.25	1.25
66	Bill Rigney	3.50	1.75	1.00
67	Harvey Haddix	3.50	1.75	1.00
68	Del Crandall	3.50	1.75	1.00
69	Bill Virdon	3.50	1.75	1.00
70	Bill Skowron	3.50	1.75	1.00
71	John O'Donoghue	3.50	1.75	1.00
72	Tony Gonzalez	3.50	1.75	1.00
73	Dennis Ribant	3.50	1.75	1.00
74	Red Sox Rookies *(Rico Petrocelli,* Jerry Stephenson)	7.00	3.50	2.00
75	Deron Johnson	3.50	1.75	1.00
76	Sam McDowell	3.50	1.75	1.00
77	Doug Camilli	3.50	1.75	1.00
78	Dal Maxvill	3.50	1.75	1.00
79a	Checklist 1-88 (61 is C. Cannizzaro)	4.50	2.25	1.25
79b	Checklist 1-88 (61 is Cannizzaro)	7.00	3.50	2.00
80	Turk Farrell	3.50	1.75	1.00
81	Don Buford	3.50	1.75	1.00
82	Braves Rookies *(Santos Alomar,* John Braun)	3.50	1.75	1.00
83	George Thomas	3.50	1.75	1.00
84	Ron Herbel	3.50	1.75	1.00
85	Willie Smith	3.50	1.75	1.00
86	Les Narum	3.50	1.75	1.00
87	Nelson Mathews	3.50	1.75	1.00
88	Jack Lamabe	3.50	1.75	1.00
89	Mike Hershberger	3.50	1.75	1.00
90	Rich Rollins	3.50	1.75	1.00
91	Cubs Team	5.00	2.50	1.50
92	Dick Howser	3.50	1.75	1.00
93	Jack Fisher	3.50	1.75	1.00
94	Charlie Lau	3.50	1.75	1.00
95	Bill Mazeroski	7.00	3.50	2.00
96	Sonny Siebert	3.50	1.75	1.00
97	Pedro Gonzalez	3.50	1.75	1.00
98	Bob Miller	3.50	1.75	1.00
99	Gil Hodges	7.50	3.75	2.25
100	Ken Boyer	5.00	2.50	1.50
101	Fred Newman	3.50	1.75	1.00
102	Steve Boros	3.50	1.75	1.00
103	Harvey Kuenn	4.00	2.00	1.25
104	Checklist 89-176	4.50	2.25	1.25
105	Chico Salmon	3.50	1.75	1.00
106	Gene Oliver	3.50	1.75	1.00
107	Phillies Rookies *(Pat Corrales,* Costen Shockley)	4.50	2.25	1.25
108	Don Mincher	3.50	1.75	1.00
109	Walt Bond	3.50	1.75	1.00
110	Ron Santo	4.50	2.25	1.25
111	Lee Thomas	3.50	1.75	1.00
112	Derrell Griffith	3.50	1.75	1.00
113	Steve Barber	3.50	1.75	1.00
114	Jim Hickman	3.50	1.75	1.00
115	Bobby Richardson	5.00	2.50	1.50
116	Cardinals Rookies (Dave Dowling, *Bob Tolan*)	3.50	1.75	1.00
117	Wes Stock	3.50	1.75	1.00
118	*Hal Lanier*	3.50	1.75	1.00
119	John Kennedy	3.50	1.75	1.00
120	Frank Robinson	25.00	12.50	7.50
121	Gene Alley	3.50	1.75	1.00
122	Bill Pleis	3.50	1.75	1.00
123	Frank J. Thomas	3.50	1.75	1.00
124	Tom Satriano	3.50	1.75	1.00
125	Juan Pizarro	3.50	1.75	1.00
126	Dodgers Team	7.00	3.50	2.00
127	Frank Lary	3.50	1.75	1.00
128	Vic Davalillo	3.50	1.75	1.00
129	Bennie Daniels	3.50	1.75	1.00
130	Al Kaline	25.00	12.50	7.50
131	Johnny Keane	3.50	1.75	1.00
132	World Series Game 1 (Cards Take Opener)	5.00	2.50	1.50
133	World Series Game 2 (Stottlemyre Wins)	5.00	2.50	1.50

		NR MT	EX	VG
134	World Series Game 3 (Mantle's Clutch HR)	35.00	17.50	10.50
135	World Series Game 4 (Boyer's Grand Slam)	7.00	3.50	2.00
136	World Series Game 5 (10th Inning Triumph)	5.00	2.50	1.50
137	World Series Game 6 (Bouton Wins Again)	5.00	2.50	1.50
138	World Series Game 7 (Gibson Wins Finale)	7.00	3.50	2.00
139	World Series Summary (The Cards Celebrate)	5.00	2.50	1.50
140	Dean Chance	3.50	1.75	1.00
141	Charlie James	3.50	1.75	1.00
142	Bill Monbouquette	3.50	1.75	1.00
143	Pirates Rookies (John Gelnar, Jerry May)	3.50	1.75	1.00
144	Ed Kranepool	3.50	1.75	1.00
145	*Luis Tiant*	15.00	7.50	4.50
146	Ron Hansen	3.50	1.75	1.00
147	Dennis Bennett	3.50	1.75	1.00
148	Willie Kirkland	3.50	1.75	1.00
149	Wayne Schurr	3.50	1.75	1.00
150	Brooks Robinson	25.00	12.50	7.50
151	Athletics Team	5.00	2.50	1.50
152	Phil Ortega	3.50	1.75	1.00
153	Norm Cash	4.00	2.00	1.25
154	Bob Humphreys	3.50	1.75	1.00
155	Roger Maris	60.00	30.00	18.00
156	Bob Sadowski	3.50	1.75	1.00
157	Zoilo Versalles	3.50	1.75	1.00
158	Dick Sisler	3.50	1.75	1.00
159	Jim Duffalo	3.50	1.75	1.00
160	Roberto Clemente	85.00	42.00	25.00
161	Frank Baumann	3.50	1.75	1.00
162	Russ Nixon	3.50	1.75	1.00
163	John Briggs	3.50	1.75	1.00
164	Al Spangler	3.50	1.75	1.00
165	Dick Ellsworth	3.50	1.75	1.00
166	Indians Rookies (*Tommie Agee,* George Culver)	4.50	2.25	1.25
167	Bill Wakefield	3.50	1.75	1.00
168	Dick Green	3.50	1.75	1.00
169	Dave Vineyard	3.50	1.75	1.00
170	Hank Aaron	95.00	47.00	28.00
171	Jim Roland	3.50	1.75	1.00
172	Jim Piersall	3.50	1.75	1.00
173	Tigers Team	5.00	2.50	1.50
174	Joe Jay	3.50	1.75	1.00
175	Bob Aspromonte	3.50	1.75	1.00
176	Willie McCovey	20.00	10.00	6.00
177	Pete Mikkelsen	3.50	1.75	1.00
178	Dalton Jones	3.50	1.75	1.00
179	Hal Woodeshick	3.50	1.75	1.00
180	Bob Allison	3.50	1.75	1.00
181	Senators Rookies (Don Loun, Joe McCabe)	3.50	1.75	1.00
182	Mike de la Hoz	3.50	1.75	1.00
183	Dave Nicholson	3.50	1.75	1.00
184	John Boozer	3.50	1.75	1.00
185	Max Alvis	3.50	1.75	1.00
186	Billy Cowan	3.50	1.75	1.00
187	Casey Stengel	18.00	9.00	5.50
188	Sam Bowens	3.50	1.75	1.00
189	Checklist 177-264	4.50	2.25	1.25
190	Bill White	4.00	2.00	1.25
191	Phil Regan	3.50	1.75	1.00
192	Jim Coker	3.50	1.75	1.00
193	Gaylord Perry	20.00	10.00	6.00
194	Angels Rookies (Bill Kelso, *Rick Reichardt*)	3.50	1.75	1.00
195	Bob Veale	3.50	1.75	1.00
196	Ron Fairly	3.50	1.75	1.00
197	Diego Segui	3.50	1.75	1.00
198	Smoky Burgess	3.50	1.75	1.00
199	Bob Heffner	3.50	1.75	1.00
200	Joe Torre	4.50	2.25	1.25
201	Twins Rookies (*Cesar Tovar,* Sandy Valdespino)	3.50	1.75	1.00
202	Leo Burke	3.50	1.75	1.00
203	Dallas Green	4.00	2.00	1.25
204	Russ Snyder	3.50	1.75	1.00
205	Warren Spahn	20.00	10.00	6.00
206	Willie Horton	3.50	1.75	1.00
207	Pete Rose	150.00	75.00	45.00
208	Tommy John	10.00	5.00	3.00
209	Pirates Team	5.00	2.50	1.50
210	Jim Fregosi	3.50	1.75	1.00
211	Steve Ridzik	3.50	1.75	1.00
212	Ron Brand	3.50	1.75	1.00
213	Jim Davenport	3.50	1.75	1.00
214	Bob Purkey	3.50	1.75	1.00
215	Pete Ward	3.50	1.75	1.00
216	Al Worthington	3.50	1.75	1.00
217	Walt Alston	5.00	2.50	1.50
218	Dick Schofield	3.50	1.75	1.00
219	Bob Meyer	3.50	1.75	1.00
220	Billy Williams	12.50	6.25	3.75
221	John Tsitouris	3.50	1.75	1.00
222	Bob Tillman	3.50	1.75	1.00
223	Dan Osinski	3.50	1.75	1.00
224	Bob Chance	3.50	1.75	1.00
225	Bo Belinsky	3.50	1.75	1.00
226	Yankees Rookies (Jake Gibbs, Elvio Jimenez)	3.50	1.75	1.00
227	Bobby Klaus	3.50	1.75	1.00
228	Jack Sanford	3.50	1.75	1.00
229	Lou Clinton	3.50	1.75	1.00
230	Ray Sadecki	3.50	1.75	1.00
231	Jerry Adair	3.50	1.75	1.00
232	*Steve Blass*	3.50	1.75	1.00
233	Don Zimmer	3.50	1.75	1.00
234	White Sox Team	5.00	2.50	1.50
235	Chuck Hinton	3.50	1.75	1.00
236	*Dennis McLain*	20.00	10.00	6.00
237	Bernie Allen	3.50	1.75	1.00
238	Joe Moeller	3.50	1.75	1.00
239	Doc Edwards	3.50	1.75	1.00
240	Bob Bruce	3.50	1.75	1.00
241	Mack Jones	3.50	1.75	1.00
242	George Brunet	3.50	1.75	1.00
243	Reds Rookies (Ted Davidson, *Tommy Helms*)	3.50	1.75	1.00
244	Lindy McDaniel	3.50	1.75	1.00
245	Joe Pepitone	3.50	1.75	1.00
246	Tom Butters	3.50	1.75	1.00
247	Wally Moon	3.50	1.75	1.00
248	Gus Triandos	3.50	1.75	1.00
249	Dave McNally	3.50	1.75	1.00
250	Willie Mays	100.00	50.00	30.00
251	Billy Herman	5.00	2.50	1.50
252	Pete Richert	3.50	1.75	1.00
253	Danny Cater	3.50	1.75	1.00
254	Roland Sheldon	3.50	1.75	1.00
255	Camilo Pascual	3.50	1.75	1.00
256	Tito Francona	3.50	1.75	1.00
257	Jim Wynn	3.50	1.75	1.00
258	Larry Bearnarth	3.50	1.75	1.00
259	Tigers Rookies (*Jim Northrup, Ray Oyler*)	3.50	1.75	1.00
260	Don Drysdale	20.00	10.00	6.00
261	Duke Carmel	3.50	1.75	1.00
262	Bud Daley	3.50	1.75	1.00
263	Marty Keough	3.50	1.75	1.00
264	Bob Buhl	3.50	1.75	1.00
265	Jim Pagliaroni	3.50	1.75	1.00
266	*Bert Campaneris*	7.00	3.50	2.00
267	Senators Team	5.00	2.50	1.50
268	Ken McBride	3.50	1.75	1.00
269	Frank Bolling	3.50	1.75	1.00
270	Milt Pappas	3.50	1.75	1.00
271	Don Wert	3.50	1.75	1.00
272	Chuck Schilling	3.50	1.75	1.00
273	Checklist 265-352	3.50	1.75	1.00
274	Lum Harris	3.50	1.75	1.00
275	Dick Groat	3.25	1.75	1.00
276	Hoyt Wilhelm	8.00	4.00	2.50
277	Johnny Lewis	3.50	1.75	1.00
278	Ken Retzer	3.50	1.75	1.00
279	Dick Tracewski	3.50	1.75	1.00
280	Dick Stuart	3.50	1.75	1.00
281	Bill Stafford	3.50	1.75	1.00
282	Giants Rookies (Dick Estelle, *Masanori Murakami*)	5.00	2.50	1.50
283	Fred Whitfield	3.50	1.75	1.00
284	Nick Willhite	3.50	1.75	1.00
285	Ron Hunt	3.50	1.75	1.00
286	Athletics Rookies (Jim Dickson, Aurelio Monteagudo)	3.50	1.75	1.00
287	Gary Kolb	3.50	1.75	1.00
288	Jack Hamilton	3.50	1.75	1.00
289	Gordy Coleman	3.50	1.75	1.00
290	Wally Bunker	3.50	1.75	1.00
291	Jerry Lynch	3.50	1.75	1.00
292	Larry Yellen	3.50	1.75	1.00
293	Angels Team	5.00	2.50	1.50
294	Tim McCarver	4.50	2.25	1.25
295	Dick Radatz	3.50	1.75	1.00
296	Tony Taylor	3.50	1.75	1.00
297	Dave DeBusschere	5.00	2.50	1.50
298	Jim Stewart	3.50	1.75	1.00
299	Jerry Zimmerman	3.50	1.75	1.00

		NR MT	EX	VG
300	Sandy Koufax	130.00	65.00	39.00
301	Birdie Tebbetts	3.50	1.75	1.00
302	Al Stanek	3.50	1.75	1.00
303	Johnny Orsino	3.50	1.75	1.00
304	Dave Stenhouse	3.50	1.75	1.00
305	Rico Carty	3.50	1.75	1.00
306	Bubba Phillips	3.50	1.75	1.00
307	Barry Latman	3.50	1.75	1.00
308	Mets Rookies (*Cleon Jones,* Tom Parsons)	3.50	1.75	1.00
309	Steve Hamilton	3.50	1.75	1.00
310	Johnny Callison	3.50	1.75	1.00
311	Orlando Pena	3.50	1.75	1.00
312	Joe Nuxhall	3.50	1.75	1.00
313	Jimmie Schaffer	3.50	1.75	1.00
314	Sterling Slaughter	3.50	1.75	1.00
315	Frank Malzone	3.50	1.75	1.00
316	Reds Team	5.00	2.50	1.50
317	Don McMahon	3.50	1.75	1.00
318	Matty Alou	3.50	1.75	1.00
319	Ken McMullen	3.50	1.75	1.00
320	Bob Gibson	30.00	15.00	9.00
321	Rusty Staub	5.00	2.50	1.50
322	Rick Wise	3.50	1.75	1.00
323	Hank Bauer	3.50	1.75	1.00
324	Bobby Locke	3.50	1.75	1.00
325	Donn Clendenon	3.50	1.75	1.00
326	Dwight Siebler	3.50	1.75	1.00
327	Denis Menke	3.50	1.75	1.00
328	Eddie Fisher	3.50	1.75	1.00
329	Hawk Taylor	3.50	1.75	1.00
330	Whitey Ford	30.00	15.00	9.00
331	Dodgers Rookies (Al Ferrara, John Purdin)	3.50	1.75	1.00
332	Ted Abernathy	3.50	1.75	1.00
333	Tommie Reynolds	3.50	1.75	1.00
334	Vic Roznovsky	3.50	1.75	1.00
335	Mickey Lolich	4.50	2.25	1.25
336	Woody Held	3.50	1.75	1.00
337	Mike Cuellar	3.50	1.75	1.00
338	Phillies Team	5.00	2.50	1.50
339	Ryne Duren	3.50	1.75	1.00
340	Tony Oliva	4.50	2.25	1.25
341	Bobby Bolin	3.50	1.75	1.00
342	Bob Rodgers	3.50	1.75	1.00
343	Mike McCormick	3.50	1.75	1.00
344	Wes Parker	3.50	1.75	1.00
345	Floyd Robinson	3.50	1.75	1.00
346	Bobby Bragan	3.50	1.75	1.00
347	Roy Face	3.50	1.75	1.00
348	George Banks	3.50	1.75	1.00
349	Larry Miller	3.50	1.75	1.00
350	Mickey Mantle	500.00	250.00	150.00
351	Jim Perry	3.50	1.75	1.00
352	*Alex Johnson*	3.50	1.75	1.00
353	Jerry Lumpe	3.50	1.75	1.00
354	Cubs Rookies (Billy Ott, Jack Warner)	3.50	1.75	1.00
355	Vada Pinson	6.00	3.00	1.75
356	Bill Spanswick	3.50	1.75	1.00
357	Carl Warwick	3.50	1.75	1.00
358	Albie Pearson	3.50	1.75	1.00
359	Ken Johnson	3.50	1.75	1.00
360	Orlando Cepeda	7.50	3.75	2.25
361	Checklist 353-429	4.50	2.25	1.25
362	Don Schwall	3.50	1.75	1.00
363	Bob Johnson	3.50	1.75	1.00
364	Galen Cisco	3.50	1.75	1.00
365	Jim Gentile	3.50	1.75	1.00
366	Dan Schneider	3.50	1.75	1.00
367	Leon Wagner	3.50	1.75	1.00
368	White Sox Rookies (*Ken Berry,* Joel Gibson)	3.50	1.75	1.00
369	Phil Linz	3.50	1.75	1.00
370	Tommy Davis	4.00	2.00	1.25
371	Frank Kreutzer	3.50	1.75	1.00
372	Clay Dalrymple	3.50	1.75	1.00
373	Curt Simmons	3.50	1.75	1.00
374	Angels Rookies (*Jose Cardenal,* Dick Simpson)	4.50	2.25	1.25
375	Dave Wickersham	3.50	1.75	1.00
376	Jim Landis	3.50	1.75	1.00
377	Willie Stargell	25.00	12.50	7.50
378	Chuck Estrada	3.50	1.75	1.00
379	Giants Team	5.00	2.50	1.50
380	Rocky Colavito	7.50	3.75	2.25
381	Al Jackson	3.50	1.75	1.00
382	J.C. Martin	3.50	1.75	1.00
383	Felipe Alou	5.00	2.50	1.50
384	Johnny Klippstein	3.50	1.75	1.00
385	Carl Yastrzemski	70.00	35.00	21.00

		NR MT	EX	VG
386	Cubs Rookies (Paul Jaeckel, Fred Norman)	3.50	1.75	1.00
387	Johnny Podres	4.00	2.00	1.25
388	John Blanchard	3.50	1.75	1.00
389	Don Larsen	3.50	1.75	1.00
390	Bill Freehan	3.50	1.75	1.00
391	Mel McGaha	3.50	1.75	1.00
392	Bob Friend	3.50	1.75	1.00
393	Ed Kirkpatrick	3.50	1.75	1.00
394	Jim Hannan	3.50	1.75	1.00
395	Jim Hart	3.50	1.75	1.00
396	Frank Bertaina	3.50	1.75	1.00
397	Jerry Buchek	3.50	1.75	1.00
398	Reds Rookies (Dan Neville, *Art Shamsky*)	3.50	1.75	1.00
399	Ray Herbert	3.50	1.75	1.00
400	Harmon Killebrew	30.00	15.00	9.00
401	Carl Willey	3.50	1.75	1.00
402	Joe Amalfitano	3.50	1.75	1.00
403	Red Sox Team	7.50	3.75	2.25
404	Stan Williams	3.50	1.75	1.00
405	John Roseboro	3.50	1.75	1.00
406	Ralph Terry	3.50	1.75	1.00
407	Lee Maye	3.50	1.75	1.00
408	Larry Sherry	3.50	1.75	1.00
409	Astros Rookies (Jim Beauchamp, *Larry Dierker*)	4.00	2.00	1.25
410	Luis Aparicio	9.00	4.50	2.75
411	Roger Craig	3.50	1.75	1.00
412	Bob Bailey	3.50	1.75	1.00
413	Hal Reniff	3.50	1.75	1.00
414	Al Lopez	6.00	3.00	1.75
415	Curt Flood	3.50	1.75	1.00
416	Jim Brewer	3.50	1.75	1.00
417	Ed Brinkman	3.50	1.75	1.00
418	Johnny Edwards	3.50	1.75	1.00
419	Ruben Amaro	3.50	1.75	1.00
420	Larry Jackson	3.50	1.75	1.00
421	Twins Rookies (Gary Dotter, Jay Ward)	3.50	1.75	1.00
422	Aubrey Gatewood	3.50	1.75	1.00
423	Jesse Gonder	3.50	1.75	1.00
424	Gary Bell	3.50	1.75	1.00
425	Wayne Causey	3.50	1.75	1.00
426	Braves Team	5.00	2.50	1.50
427	Bob Saverine	3.50	1.75	1.00
428	Bob Shaw	3.50	1.75	1.00
429	Don Demeter	3.50	1.75	1.00
430	Gary Peters	3.50	1.75	1.00
431	Cardinals Rookies (*Nelson Briles,* Wayne Spiezio)	3.50	1.75	1.00
432	Jim Grant	3.50	1.75	1.00
433	John Bateman	3.50	1.75	1.00
434	Dave Morehead	3.50	1.75	1.00
435	Willie Davis	3.50	1.75	1.00
436	Don Elston	3.50	1.75	1.00
437	Chico Cardenas	3.50	1.75	1.00
438	Harry Walker	3.50	1.75	1.00
439	Moe Drabowsky	3.50	1.75	1.00
440	Tom Tresh	5.00	2.50	1.50
441	Denver Lemaster	3.50	1.75	1.00
442	Vic Power	3.50	1.75	1.00
443	Checklist 430-506	4.50	2.25	1.25
444	Bob Hendley	3.50	1.75	1.00
445	Don Lock	3.50	1.75	1.00
446	Art Mahaffey	3.50	1.75	1.00
447	Julian Javier	4.00	2.00	1.25
448	Lee Stange	4.00	2.00	1.25
449	Mets Rookies (Jerry Hinsley, Gary Kroll)	4.00	2.00	1.25
450	Elston Howard	6.00	3.00	1.75
451	Jim Owens	4.00	2.00	1.25
452	Gary Geiger	4.00	2.00	1.25
453	Dodgers Rookies (*Willie Crawford,* John Werhas)	4.00	2.00	1.25
454	Ed Rakow	4.00	2.00	1.25
455	Norm Siebern	4.00	2.00	1.25
456	Bill Henry	4.00	2.00	1.25
457	Bob Kennedy	4.00	2.00	1.25
458	John Buzhardt	4.00	2.00	1.25
459	Frank Kostro	4.00	2.00	1.25
460	Richie Allen	10.00	5.00	3.00
461	Braves Rookies (*Clay Carroll,* Phil Niekro)	45.00	22.00	13.50
462	Lew Krausse (photo actually Pete Lovrich)	4.00	2.00	1.25
463	Manny Mota	4.00	2.00	1.25
464	Ron Piche	4.00	2.00	1.25
465	Tom Haller	4.00	2.00	1.25
466	Senators Rookies (Pete Craig, Dick Nen)	4.00	2.00	1.25

		NR MT	EX	VG
467	Ray Washburn	4.00	2.00	1.25
468	Larry Brown	4.00	2.00	1.25
469	Don Nottebart	4.00	2.00	1.25
470	Yogi Berra	50.00	25.00	15.00
471	Billy Hoeft	4.00	2.00	1.25
472	Don Pavletich	4.00	2.00	1.25
473	Orioles Rookies *(Paul Blair, Dave Johnson)*	15.00	7.50	4.50
474	Cookie Rojas	4.00	2.00	1.25
475	Clete Boyer	4.50	2.25	1.25
476	Billy O'Dell	4.00	2.00	1.25
477	Cardinals Rookies (Fritz Ackley, *Steve Carlton)*	500.00	250.00	150.00
478	Wilbur Wood	4.00	2.00	1.25
479	Ken Harrelson	5.00	2.50	1.50
480	Joel Horlen	4.00	2.00	1.25
481	Indians Team	7.50	3.75	2.25
482	Bob Priddy	4.00	2.00	1.25
483	George Smith	4.00	2.00	1.25
484	Ron Perranoski	4.00	2.00	1.25
485	Nellie Fox	11.00	5.50	3.25
486	Angels Rookies (Tom Egan, Pat Rogan)	4.00	2.00	1.25
487	Woody Woodward	4.00	2.00	1.25
488	Ted Wills	4.00	2.00	1.25
489	Gene Mauch	4.00	2.00	1.25
490	Earl Battey	4.00	2.00	1.25
491	Tracy Stallard	4.00	2.00	1.25
492	Gene Freese	4.00	2.00	1.25
493	Tigers Rookies (Bruce Brubaker, Bill Roman)	4.00	2.00	1.25
494	Jay Ritchie	4.00	2.00	1.25
495	Joe Christopher	4.00	2.00	1.25
496	Joe Cunningham	4.00	2.00	1.25
497	Giants Rookies *(Ken Henderson,* Jack Hiatt)	4.00	2.00	1.25
498	Gene Stephens	4.00	2.00	1.25
499	Stu Miller	4.00	2.00	1.25
500	Eddie Mathews	32.50	16.00	9.75
501	Indians Rookies (Ralph Gagliano, Jim Rittwage)	4.00	2.00	1.25
502	Don Cardwell	4.00	2.00	1.25
503	Phil Gagliano	4.00	2.00	1.25
504	Jerry Grote	4.00	2.00	1.25
505	Ray Culp	4.00	2.00	1.25
506	Sam Mele	4.00	2.00	1.25
507	Sammy Ellis	4.00	2.00	1.25
508a	Checklist 507-598 (large print on front)	7.50	3.75	2.25
508b	Checklist 507-598 (small print on front)	7.00	3.50	2.00
509	Red Sox Rookies (Bob Guindon, Gerry Vezendy)	4.00	2.00	1.25
510	Ernie Banks	75.00	37.00	22.00
511	Ron Locke	4.00	2.00	1.25
512	Cap Peterson	4.00	2.00	1.25
513	Yankees Team	18.00	9.00	5.50
514	Joe Azcue	4.00	2.00	1.25
515	Vern Law	4.00	2.00	1.25
516	Al Weis	4.00	2.00	1.25
517	Angels Rookies (Paul Schaal, Jack Warner)	4.00	2.00	1.25
518	Ken Rowe	4.00	2.00	1.25
519	Bob Uecker	40.00	20.00	12.00
520	Tony Cloninger	4.00	2.00	1.25
521	Phillies Rookies (Dave Bennett, Morrie Stevens)	4.00	2.00	1.25
522	Hank Aguirre	4.00	2.00	1.25
523	Mike Brumley (SP)	10.00	5.00	3.00
524	Dave Giusti (SP)	10.00	5.00	3.00
525	Eddie Bressoud	7.00	3.50	2.00
526	Athletics Rookies *(Catish Hunter, Rene Lachemann, Skip Lockwood, Johnny Odom)*	100.00	50.00	30.00
527	Jeff Torborg	7.50	3.75	2.25
528	George Altman	7.00	3.50	2.00
529	Jerry Fosnow (SP)	10.00	5.00	3.00
530	Jim Maloney	7.00	3.50	2.00
531	Chuck Hiller	7.00	3.50	2.00
532	Hector Lopez	7.00	3.50	2.00
533	Mets Rookies (Jim Bethke, *Tug McGraw,* Dan Napolean, *Ron Swoboda)*	20.00	10.00	6.00
534	John Herrnstein	7.00	3.50	2.00
535	Jack Kralick (SP)	10.00	5.00	3.00
536	Andre Rodgers (SP)	10.00	5.00	3.00
537	Angels Rookies (Marcelino Lopez, *Rudy May,* Phil Roof)	7.00	3.50	2.00
538	Chuck Dressen (SP)	10.00	5.00	3.00
539	Herm Starrette	7.00	3.50	2.00
540	Lou Brock	50.00	25.00	15.00
541	White Sox Rookies (Greg Bollo, Bob Locker)	7.00	3.50	2.00
542	Lou Klimchock	7.00	3.50	2.00
543	Ed Connolly (SP)	10.00	5.00	3.00
544	Howie Reed	7.00	3.50	2.00
545	Jesus Alou (SP)	10.00	5.00	3.00
546	Indians Rookies (Ray Barker, Bill Davis, Mike Hedlund, Floyd Weaver)	7.00	3.50	2.00
547	Jake Wood (SP)	10.00	5.00	3.00
548	Dick Stigman	7.00	3.50	2.00
549	Cubs Rookies *(Glenn Beckert,* Roberto Pena)	12.00	6.00	3.50
550	*Mel Stottlemyre*	20.00	10.00	6.00
551	Mets Team	20.00	10.00	6.00
552	Julio Gotay	7.00	3.50	2.00
553	Hosuton Rookies (Dan Coombs, Jack McClure, Gene Ratliff)	7.00	3.50	2.00
554	Chico Ruiz (SP)	10.00	5.00	3.00
555	Jack Baldschun (SP)	10.00	5.00	3.00
556	Red Schoendienst	15.00	7.50	4.50
557	Jose Santiago	7.00	3.50	2.00
558	Tommie Sisk	7.00	3.50	2.00
559	Ed Bailey (SP)	10.00	5.00	3.00
560	Boog Powell	12.00	6.00	3.50
561	Dodgers Rookies (Dennis Daboll, *Mike Kekich, Jim Lefebvre,* Hector Valle)	12.00	6.00	3.50
562	Billy Moran	7.00	3.50	2.00
563	Julio Navarro	7.00	3.50	2.00
564	Mel Nelson	7.00	3.50	2.00
565	Ernie Broglio (SP)	10.00	5.00	3.00
566	Yankees Rookies (Gil Blanco, Art Lopez, Ross Moschitto) (SP)	12.00	6.00	3.50
567	Tommie Aaron	7.00	3.50	2.00
568	Ron Taylor (SP)	10.00	5.00	3.00
569	Gino Cimoli (SP)	10.00	5.00	3.00
570	Claude Osteen (SP)	10.00	5.00	3.00
571	Ossie Virgil (SP)	10.00	5.00	3.00
572	Orioles Team	15.00	7.50	4.50
573	Red Sox Rookies *(Jim Lonborg,* Gerry Moses, Mike Ryan, Bill Schlesinger)	10.00	5.00	3.00
574	Roy Sievers	7.00	3.50	2.00
575	Jose Pagan	7.00	3.50	2.00
576	Terry Fox (SP)	10.00	5.00	3.00
577	A.L. Rookies (Jim Buschhorn, Darold Knowles, Richie Scheinblum) (SP)	10.00	5.00	3.00
578	Camilo Carreon (SP)	10.00	5.00	3.00
579	Dick Smith (SP)	10.00	5.00	3.00
580	Jimmie Hall (SP)	10.00	5.00	3.00
581	N.L. Rookies (Kevin Collins, *Tony Perez,* Dave Ricketts)	125.00	62.00	37.00
582	Bob Schmidt (SP)	10.00	5.00	3.00
583	Wes Covington (SP)	10.00	5.00	3.00
584	Harry Bright	7.00	3.50	2.00
585	Hank Fischer	7.00	3.50	2.00
586	Tommy McCraw (SP)	10.00	5.00	3.00
587	Joe Sparma	7.00	3.50	2.00
588	Lenny Green	7.00	3.50	2.00
589	Giants Rookies (Frank Linzy, Bob Schroder) (SP)	10.00	5.00	3.00
590	Johnnie Wyatt	7.00	3.50	2.00
591	Bob Skinner (SP)	10.00	5.00	3.00
592	Frank Bork (SP)	10.00	5.00	3.00
593	Tigers Rookies (Jackie Moore, John Sullivan)	7.00	3.50	2.00
594	Joe Gaines	7.00	3.50	2.00
595	Don Lee	7.00	3.50	2.00
596	Don Landrum (SP)	10.00	5.00	3.00
597	Twins Rookies (Joe Nossek, Dick Reese, John Sevcik)	7.50	3.75	2.25
598	Al Downing	10.00	3.50	2.00

1965 Topps Embossed

Inserted in regular packs, the 2-1/8" by 3-1/2"

Topps Embossed cards are one of the more fascinating issues of the company. The fronts feature an embossed profile portrait on gold foil-like cardboard (some collectors report finding the cards with silver cardboard). The player's name, team and position are below the portrait - which is good, because most of the embossed portraits are otherwise unrecognizeable. There is a gold border with American players framed in blue and National Leaguers in red. The set contains 72 cards divided equally bewteen the leagues. The set provides an inexpensive way to add some interesting cards to a collection. Being special cards, many stars appear in the set.

		NR MT	EX	VG
Complete Set:		200.00	100.00	60.00
Common Player:		2.00	1.00	.60
1	Carl Yastrzemski	5.00	2.50	1.50
2	Ron Fairly	2.00	1.00	.60
3	Max Alvis	2.00	1.00	.60
4	Jim Ray Hart	2.00	1.00	.60
5	Bill Skowron	3.00	1.50	.90
6	Ed Kranepool	2.00	1.00	.60
7	Tim McCarver	3.00	1.50	.90
8	Sandy Koufax	5.00	2.50	1.50
9	Donn Clendenon	2.00	1.00	.60
10	John Romano	2.00	1.00	.60
11	Mickey Mantle	20.00	10.00	6.00
12	Joe Torre	2.50	1.25	.70
13	Al Kaline	5.00	2.50	1.50
14	Al McBean	2.00	1.00	.60
15	Don Drysdale	5.00	2.50	1.50
16	Brooks Robinson	5.00	2.50	1.50
17	Jim Bunning	2.50	1.25	.70
18	Gary Peters	2.00	1.00	.60
19	Roberto Clemente	7.50	3.75	2.25
20	Milt Pappas	2.00	1.00	.60
21	Wayne Causey	2.00	1.00	.60
22	Frank Robinson	5.00	2.50	1.50
23	Bill Mazeroski	3.00	1.50	.90
24	Diego Segui	2.00	1.00	.60
25	Jim Bouton	2.50	1.25	.70
26	Ed Mathews	5.00	2.50	1.50
27	Willie Mays	7.50	3.75	2.25
28	Ron Santo	2.50	1.25	.70
29	Boog Powell	2.50	1.25	.70
30	Ken McBride	2.00	1.00	.60
31	Leon Wagner	2.00	1.00	.60
32	John Callison	2.00	1.00	.60
33	Zoilo Versalles	2.00	1.00	.60
34	Jack Baldschun	2.00	1.00	.60
35	Ron Hunt	2.00	1.00	.60
36	Richie Allen	2.50	1.25	.70
37	Frank Malzone	2.00	1.00	.60
38	Bob Allison	2.00	1.00	.60
39	Jim Fregosi	2.00	1.00	.60
40	Billy Williams	5.00	2.50	1.50
41	Bill Freehan	2.00	1.00	.60
42	Vada Pinson	2.50	1.25	.70
43	Bill White	2.50	1.25	.70
44	Roy McMillan	2.00	1.00	.60
45	Orlando Cepeda	3.00	1.50	.90
46	Rocky Colavito	3.00	1.50	.90
47	Ken Boyer	2.50	1.25	.70
48	Dick Radatz	2.00	1.00	.60
49	Tommy Davis	2.00	1.00	.60
50	Walt Bond	2.00	1.00	.60
51	John Orsino	2.00	1.00	.60
52	Joe Christopher	2.00	1.00	.60
53	Al Spangler	2.00	1.00	.60
54	Jim King	2.00	1.00	.60
55	Mickey Lolich	2.50	1.25	.70
56	Harmon Killebrew	5.00	2.50	1.50
57	Bob Shaw	2.00	1.00	.60
58	Ernie Banks	5.00	2.50	1.50
59	Hank Aaron	7.50	3.75	2.25
60	Chuck Hinton	2.00	1.00	.60
61	Bob Aspromonte	2.00	1.00	.60
62	Lee Maye	2.00	1.00	.60
63	Joe Cunningham	2.00	1.00	.60
64	Pete Ward	2.00	1.00	.60
65	Bobby Richardson	2.50	1.25	.70
66	Dean Chance	2.00	1.00	.60
67	Dick Ellsworth	2.00	1.00	.60
68	Jim Maloney	2.00	1.00	.60
69	Bob Gibson	5.00	2.50	1.50
70	Earl Battey	2.00	1.00	.60
71	Tony Kubek	2.50	1.25	.70
72	Jack Kralick	2.00	1.00	.60

1965 Topps Transfers

Issued as strips of three players each as inserts in 1965, the Topps Transfers were 2" by 3" portraits of players. The transfers have blue or red bands at the top and bottom with the team name and position in the top band and the player's name in the bottom. As is so often the case, the superstars in the transfer set can be quite expensive, but like many of Topps non-card products, the transfers are neither terribly expensive or popular today.

		NR MT	EX	VG
Complete Set:		225.00	112.00	67.00
Common Player:		2.00	1.00	.60
(1)	Hank Aaron	15.00	7.50	4.50
(2)	Richie Allen	2.50	1.25	.70
(3)	Bob Allison	2.00	1.00	.60
(4)	Max Alvis	2.00	1.00	.60
(5)	Luis Aparicio	3.00	1.50	.90
(6)	Bob Aspromonte	2.00	1.00	.60
(7)	Walt Bond	2.00	1.00	.60
(8)	Jim Bouton	2.50	1.25	.70
(9)	Ken Boyer	2.50	1.25	.70
(10)	Jim Bunning	2.50	1.25	.70
(11)	John Callison	2.00	1.00	.60
(12)	Rico Carty	2.00	1.00	.60
(13)	Wayne Causey	2.00	1.00	.60
(14)	Orlando Cepeda	3.00	1.50	.90
(15)	Bob Chance	2.00	1.00	.60
(16)	Dean Chance	2.00	1.00	.60
(17)	Joe Christopher	2.00	1.00	.60
(18)	Roberto Clemente	15.00	7.50	4.50
(19)	Rocky Colavito	3.00	1.50	.90
(20)	Tony Conigliaro	2.00	1.00	.60
(21)	Tommy Davis	2.00	1.00	.60
(22)	Don Drysdale	6.00	3.00	1.75
(23)	Bill Freehan	2.00	1.00	.60
(24)	Jim Fregosi	2.00	1.00	.60
(25)	Bob Gibson	6.00	3.00	1.75
(26)	Dick Groat	2.00	1.00	.60
(27)	Tom Haller	2.00	1.00	.60
(28)	Chuck Hinton	2.00	1.00	.60
(29)	Elston Howard	2.50	1.25	.70
(30)	Ron Hunt	2.00	1.00	.60
(31)	Al Jackson	2.00	1.00	.60
(32)	Al Kaline	6.00	3.00	1.75
(33)	Harmon Killebrew	6.00	3.00	1.75
(34)	Jim King	2.00	1.00	.60
(35)	Ron Kline	2.00	1.00	.60
(36)	Bobby Knoop	2.00	1.00	.60
(37)	Sandy Koufax	6.00	3.00	1.75
(38)	Ed Kranepool	2.00	1.00	.60
(39)	Jim Maloney	2.00	1.00	.60
(40)	Mickey Mantle	60.00	30.00	18.00
(41)	Juan Marichal	6.00	3.00	1.75
(42)	Lee Maye	2.00	1.00	.60
(43)	Willie Mays	15.00	7.50	4.50
(44)	Bill Mazeroski	3.00	1.50	.90
(45)	Tony Oliva	3.00	1.50	.90
(46)	Jim O'Toole	2.00	1.00	.60
(47)	Milt Pappas	2.00	1.00	.60
(48)	Camilo Pascual	2.00	1.00	.60
(49)	Gary Peters	2.00	1.00	.60

		NR MT	EX	VG
(50)	Vada Pinson	2.50	1.25	.70
(51)	Juan Pizarro	2.00	1.00	.60
(52)	Boog Powell	2.50	1.25	.70
(53)	Dick Radatz	2.00	1.00	.60
(54)	Bobby Richardson	2.50	1.25	.70
(55)	Brooks Robinson	6.00	3.00	1.75
(56)	Frank Robinson	6.00	3.00	1.75
(57)	Bob Rodgers	2.00	1.00	.60
(58)	John Roseboro	2.00	1.00	.60
(59)	Ron Santo	2.50	1.25	.70
(60)	Diego Segui	2.00	1.00	.60
(61)	Bill Skowron	2.50	1.25	.70
(62)	Al Spangler	2.00	1.00	.60
(63)	Dick Stuart	2.00	1.00	.60
(64)	Luis Tiant	2.50	1.25	.70
(65)	Joe Torre	2.00	1.00	.60
(66)	Bob Veale	2.00	1.00	.60
(67)	Leon Wagner	2.00	1.00	.60
(68)	Pete Ward	2.00	1.00	.60
(69)	Bill White	2.50	1.25	.70
(70)	Dave Wickersham	2.00	1.00	.60
(71)	Billy Williams	6.00	3.00	1.75
(72)	Carl Yastrzemski	12.50	6.25	3.75

1966 Topps

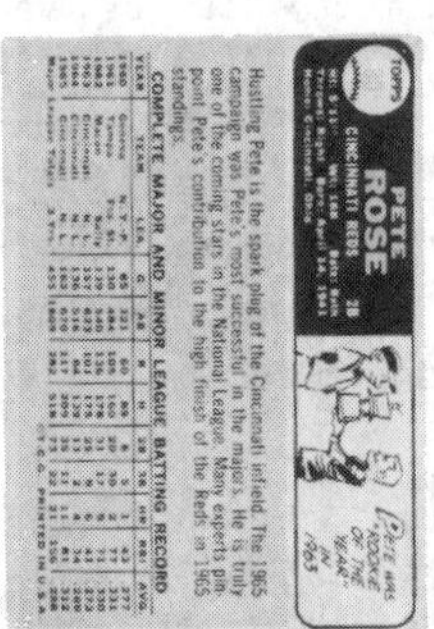

In 1966, Topps produced another 598-card set. The 2-1/2" by 3-1/2" cards feature the almost traditional color photograph with a diagonal strip in the upper left-hand corner carrying the team name. A band at the bottom carries the player's name and position. Multi-player cards returned in 1966 after having had a year's hiatus. The statistical leader cards feature the categorical leader and two runners-up. Most team managers have cards as well. The 1966 set features a handful of cards found with without a notice of the player's sale or trade to another team. Cards without the notice bring higher prices not included in the complete set prices below. Some cards in the high series (#523-598) were short-printed - produced in lesser quantities than the rest of the series. They are valued somewhat higher than the others and are indicated in the checklist by a (SP) notation following the player name.

	NR MT	EX	VG
Complete Set (598):	4750.00	2375.00	1425.
Common Player: 1-110	1.50	.70	.45
Common Player: 111-446	2.00	1.00	.60
Common Player: 447-522	7.50	3.75	2.25
Common Player: 523-598	21.00	10.50	6.25

		NR MT	EX	VG
1	Willie Mays	145.00	72.00	43.00
2	Ted Abernathy	1.50	.70	.45
3	Sam Mele	1.50	.70	.45
4	Ray Culp	1.50	.70	.45
5	Jim Fregosi	1.50	.70	.45
6	Chuck Schilling	1.50	.70	.45
7	Tracy Stallard	1.50	.70	.45
8	Floyd Robinson	1.50	.70	.45
9	Clete Boyer	2.00	1.00	.60
10	Tony Cloninger	1.50	.70	.45
11	Senators Rookies (Brant Alyea, Pete Craig)	1.50	.70	.45
12	John Tsitouris	1.50	.70	.45
13	Lou Johnson	1.50	.70	.45
14	Norm Siebern	1.50	.70	.45
15	Vern Law	1.50	.70	.45
16	Larry Brown	1.50	.70	.45
17	Johnny Stephenson	1.50	.70	.45
18	Roland Sheldon	1.50	.70	.45
19	Giants Team	5.00	2.50	1.50
20	Willie Horton	1.50	.70	.45
21	Don Nottebart	1.50	.70	.45
22	Joe Nossek	1.50	.70	.45
23	Jack Sanford	1.50	.70	.45
24	*Don Kessinger*	2.00	1.00	.60
25	Pete Ward	1.50	.70	.45
26	Ray Sadecki	1.50	.70	.45
27	Orioles Rookies *(Andy Etchebarren,* Darold Knowles)	2.00	1.00	.60
28	Phil Niekro	15.00	7.50	4.50
29	Mike Brumley	1.50	.70	.45
30	Pete Rose	45.00	22.00	13.50
31	Jack Cullen	1.50	.70	.45
32	Adolfo Phillips	1.50	.70	.45
33	Jim Pagliaroni	1.50	.70	.45
34	Checklist 1-88	5.00	2.50	1.50
35	Ron Swoboda	1.50	.70	.45
36	Jim Hunter	25.00	12.50	7.50
37	Billy Herman	5.00	2.50	1.50
38	Ron Nischwitz	1.50	.70	.45
39	Ken Henderson	1.50	.70	.45
40	Jim Grant	1.50	.70	.45
41	Don LeJohn	1.50	.70	.45
42	Aubrey Gatewood	1.50	.70	.45
43	Don Landrum	1.50	.70	.45
44	Indians Rookies (Bill Davis, Tom Kelley)	1.50	.70	.45
45	Jim Gentile	1.50	.70	.45
46	Howie Koplitz	1.50	.70	.45
47	J.C. Martin	1.50	.70	.45
48	Paul Blair	1.50	.70	.45
49	Woody Woodward	1.50	.70	.45
50	Mickey Mantle	225.00	112.00	67.00
51	Gordon Richardson	1.50	.70	.45
52	Power Plus (Johnny Callison, Wes Covington)	2.50	1.25	.70
53	Bob Duliba	1.50	.70	.45
54	Jose Pagan	1.50	.70	.45
55	Ken Harrelson	1.50	.70	.45
56	Sandy Valdespino	1.50	.70	.45
57	Jim Lefebvre	2.00	1.00	.60
58	Dave Wickersham	1.50	.70	.45
59	Reds Team	5.00	2.50	1.50
60	Curt Flood	1.50	.70	.45
61	Bob Bolin	1.50	.70	.45
62a	Merritt Ranew (no sold statement)	21.00	10.50	6.25
62b	Merritt Ranew (with sold statement)	1.50	.70	.45
63	Jim Stewart	1.50	.70	.45
64	Bob Bruce	1.50	.70	.45
65	Leon Wagner	1.50	.70	.45
66	Al Weis	1.50	.70	.45
67	Mets Rookies (Cleon Jones, Dick Selma)	1.50	.70	.45
68	Hal Reniff	1.50	.70	.45
69	Ken Hamlin	1.50	.70	.45
70	Carl Yastrzemski	40.00	20.00	12.00
71	Frank Carpin	1.50	.70	.45
72	Tony Perez	30.00	15.00	9.00
73	Jerry Zimmerman	1.50	.70	.45
74	Don Mossi	1.50	.70	.45
75	Tommy Davis	2.50	1.25	.70
76	Red Schoendienst	5.00	2.50	1.50
77	Johnny Orsino	1.50	.70	.45
78	Frank Linzy	1.50	.70	.45
79	Joe Pepitone	2.00	1.00	.60
80	Richie Allen	2.50	1.25	.70
81	Ray Oyler	1.50	.70	.45
82	Bob Hendley	1.50	.70	.45
83	Albie Pearson	1.50	.70	.45
84	Braves Rookies (Jim Beauchamp, Dick Kelley)	1.50	.70	.45
85	Eddie Fisher	1.50	.70	.45
86	John Bateman	1.50	.70	.45
87	Dan Napoleon	1.50	.70	.45
88	Fred Whitfield	1.50	.70	.45
89	Ted Davidson	1.50	.70	.45
90	Luis Aparicio	7.50	3.75	2.25
91a	Bob Uecker (no trade statement)	50.00	25.00	15.00
91b	Bob Uecker (with trade statement)	20.00	10.00	6.00
92	Yankees Team	7.50	3.75	2.25
93	Jim Lonborg	1.50	.70	.45

		NR MT	EX	VG
94	Matty Alou	1.50	.70	.45
95	Pete Richert	1.50	.70	.45
96	Felipe Alou	2.50	1.25	.70
97	Jim Merritt	1.50	.70	.45
98	Don Demeter	1.50	.70	.45
99	Buc Belters (Donn Clendenon, Willie Stargell)	5.00	2.50	1.50
100	Sandy Koufax	100.00	50.00	30.00
101a	Checklist 89-176 (115 is Spahn)	9.00	4.50	2.75
101b	Checklist 89-176 (115 is Henry)	4.00	2.00	1.25
102	Ed Kirkpatrick	1.50	.70	.45
103a	Dick Groat (no trade statement)	20.00	10.00	6.00
103b	Dick Groat (with trade statement)	3.00	1.50	.90
104a	Alex Johnson (no trade statement)	20.00	10.00	6.00
104b	Alex Johnson (with trade statement)	1.50	.70	.45
105	Milt Pappas	1.50	.70	.45
106	Rusty Staub	2.50	1.25	.70
107	Athletics Rookies (Larry Stahl, Ron Tompkins)	1.50	.70	.45
108	Bobby Klaus	1.50	.70	.45
109	Ralph Terry	1.50	.70	.45
110	Ernie Banks	25.00	12.50	7.50
111	Gary Peters	2.00	1.00	.60
112	Manny Mota	2.00	1.00	.60
113	Hank Aguirre	2.00	1.00	.60
114	Jim Gosger	2.00	1.00	.60
115	Bill Henry	2.00	1.00	.60
116	Walt Alston	5.00	2.50	1.50
117	Jake Gibbs	2.00	1.00	.60
118	Mike McCormick	2.00	1.00	.60
119	Art Shamsky	2.00	1.00	.60
120	Harmon Killebrew	20.00	10.00	6.00
121	Ray Herbert	2.00	1.00	.60
122	Joe Gaines	2.00	1.00	.60
123	Pirates Rookies (Frank Bork, Jerry May)	2.00	1.00	.60
124	Tug McGraw	2.00	1.00	.60
125	Lou Brock	20.00	10.00	6.00
126	*Jim Palmer*	175.00	87.00	52.00
127	Ken Berry	2.00	1.00	.60
128	Jim Landis	2.00	1.00	.60
129	Jack Kralick	2.00	1.00	.60
130	Joe Torre	2.25	1.25	.70
131	Angels Team	2.25	1.25	.70
132	Orlando Cepeda	6.00	3.00	1.75
133	Don McMahon	2.00	1.00	.60
134	Wes Parker	2.00	1.00	.60
135	Dave Morehead	2.00	1.00	.60
136	Woody Held	2.00	1.00	.60
137	Pat Corrales	2.00	1.00	.60
138	Roger Repoz	2.00	1.00	.60
139	Cubs Rookies (Byron Browne, Don Young)	2.00	1.00	.60
140	Jim Maloney	2.00	1.00	.60
141	Tom McCraw	2.00	1.00	.60
142	Don Dennis	2.00	1.00	.60
143	Jose Tartabull	2.00	1.00	.60
144	Don Schwall	2.00	1.00	.60
145	Bill Freehan	2.00	1.00	.60
146	George Altman	2.00	1.00	.60
147	Lum Harris	2.00	1.00	.60
148	Bob Johnson	2.00	1.00	.60
149	Dick Nen	2.00	1.00	.60
150	Rocky Colavito	4.00	2.00	1.25
151	Gary Wagner	2.00	1.00	.60
152	Frank Malzone	2.00	1.00	.60
153	Rico Carty	2.50	1.25	.70
154	Chuck Hiller	2.00	1.00	.60
155	Marcelino Lopez	2.00	1.00	.60
156	D P Combo (Hal Lanier, Dick Schofield)	2.50	1.25	.70
157	Rene Lachemann	2.00	1.00	.60
158	Jim Brewer	2.00	1.00	.60
159	Chico Ruiz	2.00	1.00	.60
160	Whitey Ford	25.00	12.50	7.50
161	Jerry Lumpe	2.00	1.00	.60
162	Lee Maye	2.00	1.00	.60
163	Tito Francona	2.00	1.00	.60
164	White Sox Rookies (Tommie Agee, Marv Staehle)	2.00	1.00	.60
165	Don Lock	2.00	1.00	.60
166	Chris Krug	2.00	1.00	.60
167	Boog Powell	2.50	1.25	.70
168	Dan Osinski	2.00	1.00	.60
169	Duke Sims	2.00	1.00	.60
170	Cookie Rojas	2.00	1.00	.60
171	Nick Willhite	2.00	1.00	.60
172	Mets Team	7.00	3.50	2.00
173	Al Spangler	2.00	1.00	.60

		NR MT	EX	VG
174	Ron Taylor	2.00	1.00	.60
175	Bert Campaneris	3.00	1.50	.90
176	Jim Davenport	2.00	1.00	.60
177	Hector Lopez	2.00	1.00	.60
178	Bob Tillman	2.00	1.00	.60
179	Cardinals Rookies (Dennis Aust, Bob Tolan)	2.00	1.00	.60
180	Vada Pinson	2.50	1.25	.70
181	Al Worthington	2.00	1.00	.60
182	Jerry Lynch	2.00	1.00	.60
183a	Checklist 177-264 (large print on front)	4.00	2.00	1.25
183b	Checklist 177-264 (small print on front)	6.00	3.00	1.75
184	Denis Menke	2.00	1.00	.60
185	Bob Buhl	2.00	1.00	.60
186	Ruben Amaro	2.00	1.00	.60
187	Chuck Dressen	2.00	1.00	.60
188	Al Luplow	2.00	1.00	.60
189	John Roseboro	2.00	1.00	.60
190	Jimmie Hall	2.00	1.00	.60
191	Darrell Sutherland	2.00	1.00	.60
192	Vic Power	2.00	1.00	.60
193	Dave McNally	2.00	1.00	.60
194	Senators Team	6.00	3.00	1.75
195	Joe Morgan	40.00	20.00	12.00
196	Don Pavletich	2.00	1.00	.60
197	Sonny Siebert	2.00	1.00	.60
198	*Mickey Stanley*	2.00	1.00	.60
199	Chisox Clubbers (Floyd Robinson, Johnny Romano, Bill Skowron)	2.50	1.25	.70
200	Eddie Mathews	20.00	10.00	6.00
201	Jim Dickson	2.00	1.00	.60
202	Clay Dalrymple	2.00	1.00	.60
203	Jose Santiago	2.00	1.00	.60
204	Cubs Team	6.00	3.00	1.75
205	Tom Tresh	5.00	2.50	1.50
206	Alvin Jackson	2.00	1.00	.60
207	Frank Quilici	2.00	1.00	.60
208	Bob Miller	2.00	1.00	.60
209	Tigers Rookies (Fritz Fisher, *John Hiller*)	2.00	1.00	.60
210	Bill Mazeroski	3.50	1.75	1.00
211	Frank Kreutzer	2.00	1.00	.60
212	Ed Kranepool	2.00	1.00	.60
213	Fred Newman	2.00	1.00	.60
214	Tommy Harper	2.00	1.00	.60
215	N.L. Batting Leaders (Hank Aaron, Roberto Clemente, Willie Mays)	20.00	10.00	6.00
216	A.L. Batting Leaders (Vic Davalillo, Tony Oliva, Carl Yastrzemski)	6.00	3.00	1.75
217	N.L. Home Run Leaders (Willie Mays, Willie McCovey, Billy Williams)	7.50	3.75	2.25
218	A.L. Home Run Leaders (Norm Cash, Tony Conigliaro, Willie Horton)	3.50	1.75	1.00
219	N.L. RBI Leaders (Deron Johnson, Willie Mays, Frank Robinson)	6.00	3.00	1.75
220	A.L. RBI Leaders (Rocky Colavito, Willie Horton, Tony Oliva)	3.50	1.75	1.00
221	N.L. ERA Leaders (Sandy Koufax, Vern Law, Juan Marichal)	6.00	3.00	1.75
222	A.L. ERA Leaders (Eddie Fisher, Sam McDowell, Sonny Siebert)	3.50	1.75	1.00
223	N.L. Pitching Leaders (Tony Cloninger, Don Drysdale, Sandy Koufax)	6.00	3.00	1.75
224	A.L. Pitching Leaders (Jim Grant, Jim Kaat, Mel Stottlemyre)	3.50	1.75	1.00
225	N.L. Strikeout Leaders (Bob Gibson, Sandy Koufax, Bob Veale)	6.00	3.00	1.75
226	A.L. Strikeout Leaders (Mickey Lolich, Sam McDowell, Denny McLain, Sonny Siebert)	3.50	1.75	1.00
227	Russ Nixon	2.00	1.00	.60
228	Larry Dierker	2.00	1.00	.60
229	Hank Bauer	2.00	1.00	.60
230	Johnny Callison	2.00	1.00	.60
231	Floyd Weaver	2.00	1.00	.60
232	Glenn Beckert	2.00	1.00	.60
233	Dom Zanni	2.00	1.00	.60
234	Yankees Rookies (Rich Beck, *Roy White*)	7.50	3.75	2.25
235	Don Cardwell	2.00	1.00	.60
236	Mike Hershberger	2.00	1.00	.60
237	Billy O'Dell	2.00	1.00	.60
238	Dodgers Team	6.00	3.00	1.75
239	Orlando Pena	2.00	1.00	.60
240	Earl Battey	2.00	1.00	.60
241	Dennis Ribant	2.00	1.00	.60
242	Jesus Alou	2.00	1.00	.60
243	Nelson Briles	2.00	1.00	.60
244	Astros Rookies (Chuck Harrison, Sonny Jackson)	2.00	1.00	.60

		NR MT	EX	VG
245	John Buzhardt	2.00	1.00	.60
246	Ed Bailey	2.00	1.00	.60
247	Carl Warwick	2.00	1.00	.60
248	Pete Mikkelsen	2.00	1.00	.60
249	Bill Rigney	2.00	1.00	.60
250	Sam Ellis	2.00	1.00	.60
251	Ed Brinkman	2.00	1.00	.60
252	Denver Lemaster	2.00	1.00	.60
253	Don Wert	2.00	1.00	.60
254	Phillies Rookies *(Fergie Jenkins,* Bill Sorrell)	135.00	67.00	40.00
255	Willie Stargell	18.00	9.00	5.50
256	Lew Krausse	2.00	1.00	.60
257	Jeff Torborg	2.00	1.00	.60
258	Dave Giusti	2.00	1.00	.60
259	Red Sox Team	6.00	3.00	1.75
260	Bob Shaw	2.00	1.00	.60
261	Ron Hansen	2.00	1.00	.60
262	Jack Hamilton	2.00	1.00	.60
263	Tom Egan	2.00	1.00	.60
264	Twins Rookies (Andy Kosco, Ted Uhlaender)	2.00	1.00	.60
265	Stu Miller	2.00	1.00	.60
266	Pedro Gonzalez	2.00	1.00	.60
267	Joe Sparma	2.00	1.00	.60
268	John Blanchard	2.00	1.00	.60
269	Don Heffner	2.00	1.00	.60
270	Claude Osteen	2.00	1.00	.60
271	Hal Lanier	2.00	1.00	.60
272	Jack Baldschun	2.00	1.00	.60
273	Astro Aces (Bob Aspromonte, Rusty Staub)	4.50	2.25	1.25
274	Buster Narum	2.00	1.00	.60
275	Tim McCarver	2.50	1.25	.70
276	Jim Bouton	2.50	1.25	.70
277	George Thomas	2.00	1.00	.60
278	Calvin Koonce	2.00	1.00	.60
279a	Checklist 265-352 (player's cap black)	6.00	3.00	1.75
279b	Checklist 265-352 (player's cap red)	4.00	2.00	1.25
280	Bobby Knoop	2.00	1.00	.60
281	Bruce Howard	2.00	1.00	.60
282	Johnny Lewis	2.00	1.00	.60
283	Jim Perry	2.00	1.00	.60
284	Bobby Wine	2.00	1.00	.60
285	Luis Tiant	2.50	1.25	.70
286	Gary Geiger	2.00	1.00	.60
287	Jack Aker	2.00	1.00	.60
288	Dodgers Rookies *(Bill Singer, Don Sutton)*	125.00	62.00	37.00
289	Larry Sherry	2.00	1.00	.60
290	Ron Santo	4.50	2.25	1.25
291	Moe Drabowsky	2.00	1.00	.60
292	Jim Coker	2.00	1.00	.60
293	Mike Shannon	2.00	1.00	.60
294	Steve Ridzik	2.00	1.00	.60
295	Jim Hart	2.00	1.00	.60
296	Johnny Keane	2.00	1.00	.60
297	Jim Owens	2.00	1.00	.60
298	Rico Petrocelli	2.00	1.00	.60
299	Lou Burdette	2.00	1.00	.60
300	Roberto Clemente	100.00	50.00	30.00
301	Greg Bollo	2.00	1.00	.60
302	Ernie Bowman	2.00	1.00	.60
303	Indians Team	6.00	3.00	1.75
304	John Herrnstein	2.00	1.00	.60
305	Camilo Pascual	2.00	1.00	.60
306	Ty Cline	2.00	1.00	.60
307	Clay Carroll	2.00	1.00	.60
308	Tom Haller	2.00	1.00	.60
309	Diego Segui	2.00	1.00	.60
310	Frank Robinson	35.00	17.50	10.50
311	Reds Rookies (Tommy Helms, Dick Simpson)	2.00	1.00	.60
312	Bob Saverine	2.00	1.00	.60
313	Chris Zachary	2.00	1.00	.60
314	Hector Valle	2.00	1.00	.60
315	Norm Cash	4.00	2.00	1.25
316	Jack Fisher	2.00	1.00	.60
317	Dalton Jones	2.00	1.00	.60
318	Harry Walker	2.00	1.00	.60
319	Gene Freese	2.00	1.00	.60
320	Bob Gibson	25.00	12.50	7.50
321	Rick Reichardt	2.00	1.00	.60
322	Bill Faul	2.00	1.00	.60
323	Ray Barker	2.00	1.00	.60
324	John Boozer	2.00	1.00	.60
325	Vic Davalillo	2.00	1.00	.60
326	Braves Team	6.00	3.00	1.75
327	Bernie Allen	2.00	1.00	.60
328	Jerry Grote	2.00	1.00	.60
329	Pete Charton	2.00	1.00	.60
330	Ron Fairly	2.00	1.00	.60
331	Ron Herbel	2.00	1.00	.60
332	Billy Bryan	2.00	1.00	.60
333	Senators Rookies *(Joe Coleman,* Jim French)	2.00	1.00	.60
334	Marty Keough	2.00	1.00	.60
335	Juan Pizarro	2.00	1.00	.60
336	Gene Alley	2.00	1.00	.60
337	Fred Gladding	2.00	1.00	.60
338	Dal Maxvill	2.00	1.00	.60
339	Del Crandall	2.00	1.00	.60
340	Dean Chance	2.00	1.00	.60
341	Wes Westrum	2.00	1.00	.60
342	Bob Humphreys	2.00	1.00	.60
343	Joe Christopher	2.00	1.00	.60
344	Steve Blass	2.00	1.00	.60
345	Bob Allison	2.00	1.00	.60
346	Mike de la Hoz	2.00	1.00	.60
347	Phil Regan	2.00	1.00	.60
348	Orioles Team	6.00	3.00	1.75
349	Cap Peterson	2.00	1.00	.60
350	Mel Stottlemyre	2.50	1.25	.70
351	Fred Valentine	2.00	1.00	.60
352	Bob Aspromonte	2.00	1.00	.60
353	Al McBean	2.00	1.00	.60
354	Smoky Burgess	2.00	1.00	.60
355	Wade Blasingame	2.00	1.00	.60
356	Red Sox Rookies (Owen Johnson, Ken Sanders)	2.00	1.00	.60
357	Gerry Arrigo	2.00	1.00	.60
358	Charlie Smith	2.00	1.00	.60
359	Johnny Briggs	2.00	1.00	.60
360	Ron Hunt	2.00	1.00	.60
361	Tom Satriano	2.00	1.00	.60
362	Gates Brown	2.00	1.00	.60
363	Checklist 353-429	4.00	2.00	1.25
364	Nate Oliver	2.00	1.00	.60
365	Roger Maris	60.00	30.00	18.00
366	Wayne Causey	2.00	1.00	.60
367	Mel Nelson	2.00	1.00	.60
368	Charlie Lau	2.00	1.00	.60
369	Jim King	2.00	1.00	.60
370	Chico Cardenas	2.00	1.00	.60
371	Lee Stange	2.00	1.00	.60
372	Harvey Kuenn	3.50	1.75	1.00
373	Giants Rookies (Dick Estelle, Jack Hiatt)	2.00	1.00	.60
374	Bob Locker	2.00	1.00	.60
375	Donn Clendenon	2.00	1.00	.60
376	Paul Schaal	2.00	1.00	.60
377	Turk Farrell	2.00	1.00	.60
378	Dick Tracewski	2.00	1.00	.60
379	Cardinals Team	6.00	3.00	1.75
380	Tony Conigliaro	4.50	2.25	1.25
381	Hank Fischer	2.00	1.00	.60
382	Phil Roof	2.00	1.00	.60
383	Jackie Brandt	2.00	1.00	.60
384	Al Downing	2.50	1.25	.70
385	Ken Boyer	2.50	1.25	.70
386	Gil Hodges	6.00	3.00	1.75
387	Howie Reed	2.00	1.00	.60
388	Don Mincher	2.00	1.00	.60
389	Jim O'Toole	2.00	1.00	.60
390	Brooks Robinson	30.00	15.00	9.00
391	Chuck Hinton	2.00	1.00	.60
392	Cubs Rookies *(Bill Hands, Randy Hundley)*	2.50	1.25	.70
393	George Brunet	2.00	1.00	.60
394	Ron Brand	2.00	1.00	.60
395	Len Gabrielson	2.00	1.00	.60
396	Jerry Stephenson	2.00	1.00	.60
397	Bill White	2.50	1.25	.70
398	Danny Cater	2.00	1.00	.60
399	Ray Washburn	2.00	1.00	.60
400	Zoilo Versalles	2.00	1.00	.60
401	Ken McMullen	2.00	1.00	.60
402	Jim Hickman	2.00	1.00	.60
403	Fred Talbot	2.00	1.00	.60
404	Pirates Team	6.00	3.00	1.75
405	Elston Howard	6.00	3.00	1.75
406	Joe Jay	2.00	1.00	.60
407	John Kennedy	2.00	1.00	.60
408	Lee Thomas	2.00	1.00	.60
409	Billy Hoeft	2.00	1.00	.60
410	Al Kaline	25.00	12.50	7.50
411	Gene Mauch	2.00	1.00	.60
412	Sam Bowens	2.00	1.00	.60
413	John Romano	2.00	1.00	.60
414	Dan Coombs	2.00	1.00	.60

		NR MT	EX	VG
415	Max Alvis	2.00	1.00	.60
416	Phil Ortega	2.00	1.00	.60
417	Angels Rookies (Jim McGlothlin, Ed Sukla)	2.00	1.00	.60
418	Phil Gagliano	2.00	1.00	.60
419	Mike Ryan	2.00	1.00	.60
420	Juan Marichal	8.00	4.00	2.50
421	Roy McMillan	2.00	1.00	.60
422	Ed Charles	2.00	1.00	.60
423	Ernie Broglio	2.00	1.00	.60
424	Reds Rookies (*Lee May,* Darrell Osteen)	2.25	1.25	.70
425	Bob Veale	2.00	1.00	.60
426	White Sox Team	6.00	3.00	1.75
427	John Miller	2.00	1.00	.60
428	Sandy Alomar	2.00	1.00	.60
429	Bill Monbouquette	2.00	1.00	.60
430	Don Drysdale	22.00	11.00	6.50
431	Walt Bond	2.00	1.00	.60
432	Bob Heffner	2.00	1.00	.60
433	Alvin Dark	2.00	1.00	.60
434	Willie Kirkland	2.00	1.00	.60
435	Jim Bunning	6.00	3.00	1.75
436	Julian Javier	2.00	1.00	.60
437	Al Stanek	2.00	1.00	.60
438	Willie Smith	2.00	1.00	.60
439	Pedro Ramos	2.00	1.00	.60
440	Deron Johnson	2.00	1.00	.60
441	Tommie Sisk	2.00	1.00	.60
442	Orioles Rookies (Ed Barnowski, Eddie Watt)	2.00	1.00	.60
443	Bill Wakefield	2.00	1.00	.60
444a	Checklist 430-506 (456 is R. Sox Rookies)	4.00	2.00	1.25
444b	Checklist 430-506 (456 is Red Sox Rookies)	6.00	3.00	1.75
445	Jim Kaat	6.00	3.00	1.75
446	Mack Jones	2.00	1.00	.60
447	Dick Ellsworth (photo actually Ken Hubbs)	7.50	3.75	2.25
448	Eddie Stanky	7.50	3.75	2.25
449	Joe Moeller	7.50	3.75	2.25
450	Tony Oliva	9.00	4.50	2.75
451	Barry Latman	7.50	3.75	2.25
452	Joe Azcue	7.50	3.75	2.25
453	Ron Kline	7.50	3.75	2.25
454	Jerry Buchek	7.50	3.75	2.25
455	Mickey Lolich	9.00	4.50	2.75
456	Red Sox Rookies (Darrell Brandon, Joe Foy)	7.50	3.75	2.25
457	Joe Gibbon	7.50	3.75	2.25
458	Manny Jiminez (Jimenez)	7.50	3.75	2.25
459	Bill McCool	7.50	3.75	2.25
460	Curt Blefary	7.50	3.75	2.25
461	Roy Face	7.50	3.75	2.25
462	Bob Rodgers	7.50	3.75	2.25
463	Phillies Team	11.00	5.50	3.25
464	Larry Bearnarth	7.50	3.75	2.25
465	Don Buford	7.50	3.75	2.25
466	Ken Johnson	7.50	3.75	2.25
467	Vic Roznovsky	7.50	3.75	2.25
468	Johnny Podres	8.00	4.00	2.50
469	Yankees Rookies (*Bobby Murcer,* Dooley Womack)	15.00	7.50	4.50
470	Sam McDowell	7.50	3.75	2.25
471	Bob Skinner	7.50	3.75	2.25
472	Terry Fox	7.50	3.75	2.25
473	Rich Rollins	7.50	3.75	2.25
474	Dick Schofield	7.50	3.75	2.25
475	Dick Radatz	7.50	3.75	2.25
476	Bobby Bragan	7.50	3.75	2.25
477	Steve Barber	7.50	3.75	2.25
478	Tony Gonzalez	7.50	3.75	2.25
479	Jim Hannan	7.50	3.75	2.25
480	Dick Stuart	7.50	3.75	2.25
481	Bob Lee	7.50	3.75	2.25
482	Cubs Rookies (John Boccabella, Dave Dowling)	7.50	3.75	2.25
483	Joe Nuxhall	7.50	3.75	2.25
484	Wes Covington	7.50	3.75	2.25
485	Bob Bailey	7.50	3.75	2.25
486	Tommy John	15.00	7.50	4.50
487	Al Ferrara	7.50	3.75	2.25
488	George Banks	7.50	3.75	2.25
489	Curt Simmons	7.50	3.75	2.25
490	Bobby Richardson	12.00	6.00	3.50
491	Dennis Bennett	7.50	3.75	2.25
492	Athletics Team	11.00	5.50	3.25
493	Johnny Klippstein	7.50	3.75	2.25
494	Gordon Coleman	7.50	3.75	2.25
495	Dick McAuliffe	7.50	3.75	2.25

		NR MT	EX	VG
496	Lindy McDaniel	7.50	3.75	2.25
497	Chris Cannizzaro	7.50	3.75	2.25
498	Pirates Rookies (*Woody Fryman,* Luke Walker)	7.50	3.75	2.25
499	Wally Bunker	7.50	3.75	2.25
500	Hank Aaron	125.00	62.00	37.00
501	John O'Donoghue	7.50	3.75	2.25
502	Lenny Green	7.50	3.75	2.25
503	Steve Hamilton	7.50	3.75	2.25
504	Grady Hatton	7.50	3.75	2.25
505	Jose Cardenal	7.50	3.75	2.25
506	Bo Belinsky	7.50	3.75	2.25
507	John Edwards	7.50	3.75	2.25
508	*Steve Hargan*	7.50	3.75	2.25
509	Jake Wood	7.50	3.75	2.25
510	Hoyt Wilhelm	15.00	7.50	4.50
511	Giants Rookies (Bob Barton, *Tito Fuentes*)	7.50	3.75	2.25
512	Dick Stigman	7.50	3.75	2.25
513	Camilo Carreon	7.50	3.75	2.25
514	Hal Woodeshick	7.50	3.75	2.25
515	Frank Howard	9.00	4.50	2.75
516	Eddie Bressoud	7.50	3.75	2.25
517a	Checklist 507-598 (529 is W. Sox Rookies)	9.00	4.50	2.75
517b	Checklist 506-598 (529 is White Sox Rookies)	10.00	5.00	3.00
518	Braves Rookies (Herb Hippauf, Arnie Umbach)	7.50	3.75	2.25
519	Bob Friend	7.50	3.75	2.25
520	Jim Wynn	7.50	3.75	2.25
521	John Wyatt	7.50	3.75	2.25
522	Phil Linz	7.50	3.75	2.25
523	Bob Sadowski	21.00	10.50	6.25
524	Giants Rookies (Ollie Brown, Don Mason) (SP)	24.00	12.00	7.25
525	Gary Bell (SP)	24.00	12.00	7.25
526	Twins Team	65.00	32.00	19.50
527	Julio Navarro	21.00	10.50	6.25
528	Jesse Gonder (SP)	24.00	12.00	7.25
529	White Sox Rookies (*Lee Elia,* Dennis Higgins, Bill Voss)	21.00	10.50	6.25
530	Robin Roberts	45.00	22.00	13.50
531	Joe Cunningham	21.00	10.50	6.25
532	Aurelio Monteagudo (SP)	24.00	12.00	7.25
533	Jerry Adair (SP)	24.00	12.00	7.25
534	Mets Rookies (Dave Eilers, Rob Gardner)	21.00	10.50	6.25
535	Willie Davis	40.00	20.00	12.00
536	Dick Egan	21.00	10.50	6.25
537	Herman Franks	21.00	10.50	6.25
538	Bob Allen (SP)	24.00	12.00	7.25
539	Astros Rookies (Bill Heath, Carroll Sembera)	21.00	10.50	6.25
540	Denny McLain	40.00	20.00	12.00
541	Gene Oliver (SP)	24.00	12.00	7.25
542	George Smith	21.00	10.50	6.25
543	Roger Craig	50.00	25.00	15.00
544	Cardinals Rookies (Joe Hoerner, George Kernek, Jimmy Williams) (SP)	24.00	12.00	7.25
545	Dick Green (SP)	24.00	12.00	7.25
546	Dwight Siebler	21.00	10.50	6.25
547	*Horace Clarke*	21.00	10.50	6.25
548	Gary Kroll (SP)	24.00	12.00	7.25
549	Senators Rookies (Al Closter, Casey Cox)	21.00	10.50	6.25
550	Willie McCovey	125.00	62.00	37.00
551	Bob Purkey (SP)	24.00	12.00	7.25
552	Birdie Tebbetts (SP)	24.00	12.00	7.25
553	Major League Rookies (Pat Garrett, Jackie Warner)	21.00	10.50	6.25
554	Jim Northrup (SP)	24.00	12.00	7.25
555	Ron Perranoski (SP)	24.00	12.00	7.25
556	Mel Queen (SP)	24.00	12.00	7.25
557	Felix Mantilla (SP)	24.00	12.00	7.25
558	Red Sox Rookies (Guido Grilli, Pete Magrini, *George Scott*)	30.00	15.00	9.00
559	Roberto Pena (SP)	24.00	12.00	7.25
560	Joel Horlen	21.00	10.50	6.25
561	Choo Choo Coleman	21.00	10.50	6.25
562	Russ Snyder	21.00	10.50	6.25
563	Twins Rookies (Pete Cimino, Cesar Tovar)	21.00	10.50	6.25
564	Bob Chance (SP)	24.00	12.00	7.25
565	Jimmy Piersall	35.00	17.50	10.50
566	Mike Cuellar	21.00	10.50	6.25
567	Dick Howser	21.00	10.50	6.25
568	Athletics Rookies (Paul Lindblad, Ron Stone)	21.00	10.50	6.25
569	Orlando McFarlane (SP)	24.00	12.00	7.25
570	Art Mahaffey (SP)	24.00	12.00	7.25

		NR MT	EX	VG
571	Dave Roberts (SP)	24.00	12.00	7.25
572	Bob Priddy	21.00	10.50	6.25
573	Derrell Griffith	21.00	10.50	6.25
574	Mets Rookies (Bill Hepler, Bill Murphy)	21.00	10.50	6.25
575	Earl Wilson	21.00	10.50	6.25
576	Dave Nicholson (SP)	24.00	12.00	7.25
577	Jack Lamabe (SP)	24.00	12.00	7.25
578	Chi Chi Olivo (SP)	24.00	12.00	7.25
579	Orioles Rookies (Frank Bertaina, Gene Brabender, Dave Johnson)	21.00	10.50	6.25
580	Billy Williams	100.00	50.00	30.00
581	Tony Martinez	21.00	10.50	6.25
582	Garry Roggenburk	21.00	10.50	6.25
583	Tigers Team	150.00	75.00	45.00
584	Yankees Rookies (Frank Fernandez, *Fritz Peterson*)	21.00	10.50	6.25
585	Tony Taylor	21.00	10.50	6.25
586	Claude Raymond (SP)	24.00	12.00	7.25
587	Dick Bertell	21.00	10.50	6.25
588	Athletics Rookies (Chuck Dobson, Ken Suarez)	21.00	10.50	6.25
589	Lou Klimchock	21.00	10.50	6.25
590	Bill Skowron	35.00	17.50	10.50
591	N.L. Rookies (*Grant Jackson,* Bart Shirley)	21.00	10.50	6.25
592	Andre Rodgers	21.00	10.50	6.25
593	Doug Camilli (SP)	24.00	12.00	7.25
594	Chico Salmon	21.00	10.50	6.25
595	Larry Jackson	21.00	10.50	6.25
596	Astros Rookies (*Nate Colbert,* Greg Sims)	21.00	10.50	6.25
597	John Sullivan	21.00	10.50	6.25
598	Gaylord Perry	250.00	80.00	50.00

1966 Topps Rub-Offs

Returning to a concept last tried in 1961, Topps tried an expanded version of Rub-Offs in 1966. Measuring 2-1/16" by 3," the Rub-Offs are in vertical format for the 100 players and horizontal for the 20 team pennants. The player Rub-Offs feature a color photo.

		NR MT	EX	VG
Complete Set:		400.00	200.00	120.00
Common Player:		2.00	1.00	.60
(1)	Hank Aaron	10.00	5.00	3.00
(2)	Jerry Adair	2.00	1.00	.60
(3)	Richie Allen	2.50	1.25	.70
(4)	Jesus Alou	2.00	1.00	.60
(5)	Max Alvis	2.00	1.00	.60
(6)	Bob Aspromonte	2.00	1.00	.60
(7)	Ernie Banks	6.00	3.00	1.75
(8)	Earl Battey	2.00	1.00	.60
(9)	Curt Blefary	2.00	1.00	.60
(10)	Ken Boyer	2.50	1.25	.70
(11)	Bob Bruce	2.00	1.00	.60
(12)	Jim Bunning	3.50	1.75	1.00
(13)	Johnny Callison	2.00	1.00	.60
(14)	Bert Campaneris	2.50	1.25	.70
(15)	Jose Cardenal	2.00	1.00	.60
(16)	Dean Chance	2.00	1.00	.60
(17)	Ed Charles	2.00	1.00	.60
(18)	Bob Clemente	10.00	5.00	3.00
(19)	Tony Cloninger	2.00	1.00	.60
(20)	Rocky Colavito	4.00	2.00	1.25
(21)	Tony Conigliaro	2.50	1.25	.70
(22)	Vic Davalillo	2.00	1.00	.60
(23)	Willie Davis	2.00	1.00	.60
(24)	Don Drysdale	5.00	2.50	1.50
(25)	Sammy Ellis	2.00	1.00	.60
(26)	Dick Ellsworth	2.00	1.00	.60
(27)	Ron Fairly	2.00	1.00	.60
(28)	Dick Farrell	2.00	1.00	.60
(29)	Eddie Fisher	2.00	1.00	.60
(30)	Jack Fisher	2.00	1.00	.60
(31)	Curt Flood	2.00	1.00	.60
(32)	Whitey Ford	5.00	2.50	1.50
(33)	Bill Freehan	2.00	1.00	.60
(34)	Jim Fregosi	2.00	1.00	.60
(35)	Bob Gibson	5.00	2.50	1.50
(36)	Jim Grant	2.00	1.00	.60
(37)	Jimmie Hall	2.00	1.00	.60
(38)	Ken Harrelson	2.00	1.00	.60
(39)	Jim Hart	2.00	1.00	.60
(40)	Joel Horlen	2.00	1.00	.60
(41)	Willie Horton	2.00	1.00	.60
(42)	Frank Howard	2.50	1.25	.70
(43)	Deron Johnson	2.00	1.00	.60
(44)	Al Kaline	6.00	3.00	1.75
(45)	Harmon Killebrew	5.00	2.50	1.50
(46)	Bobby Knoop	2.00	1.00	.60
(47)	Sandy Koufax	7.00	3.50	2.00
(48)	Ed Kranepool	2.00	1.00	.60
(49)	Gary Kroll	2.00	1.00	.60
(50)	Don Landrum	2.00	1.00	.60
(51)	Vernon Law	2.00	1.00	.60
(52)	Johnny Lewis	2.00	1.00	.60
(53)	Don Lock	2.00	1.00	.60
(54)	Mickey Lolich	2.50	1.25	.70
(55)	Jim Maloney	2.00	1.00	.60
(56)	Felix Mantilla	2.00	1.00	.60
(57)	Mickey Mantle	40.00	20.00	12.00
(58)	Juan Marichal	5.00	2.50	1.50
(59)	Ed Mathews	6.00	3.00	1.75
(60)	Willie Mays	10.00	5.00	3.00
(61)	Bill Mazeroski	3.00	1.50	.90
(62)	Dick McAuliffe	2.00	1.00	.60
(63)	Tim McCarver	2.50	1.25	.70
(64)	Willie McCovey	6.00	3.00	1.75
(65)	Sammy McDowell	2.00	1.00	.60
(66)	Ken McMullen	2.00	1.00	.60
(67)	Denis Menke	2.00	1.00	.60
(68)	Bill Monbouquette	2.00	1.00	.60
(69)	Joe Morgan	5.00	2.50	1.50
(70)	Fred Newman	2.00	1.00	.60
(71)	John O'Donoghue	2.00	1.00	.60
(72)	Tony Oliva	2.50	1.25	.70
(73)	Johnny Orsino	2.00	1.00	.60
(74)	Phil Ortega	2.00	1.00	.60
(75)	Milt Pappas	2.00	1.00	.60
(76)	Dick Radatz	2.00	1.00	.60
(77)	Bobby Richardson	2.50	1.25	.70
(78)	Pete Richert	2.00	1.00	.60
(79)	Brooks Robinson	6.00	3.00	1.75
(80)	Floyd Robinson	2.00	1.00	.60
(81)	Frank Robinson	6.00	3.00	1.75
(82)	Cookie Rojas	2.00	1.00	.60
(83)	Pete Rose	20.00	10.00	6.00
(84)	John Roseboro	2.00	1.00	.60
(85)	Ron Santo	2.50	1.25	.70
(86)	Bill Skowron	2.50	1.25	.70
(87)	Willie Stargell	6.00	3.00	1.75
(88)	Mel Stottlemyre	2.00	1.00	.60
(89)	Dick Stuart	2.00	1.00	.60
(90)	Ron Swoboda	2.00	1.00	.60
(91)	Fred Talbot	2.00	1.00	.60
(92)	Ralph Terry	2.00	1.00	.60
(93)	Joe Torre	2.00	1.00	.60
(94)	Tom Tresh	2.00	1.00	.60
(95)	Bob Veale	2.00	1.00	.60
(96)	Pete Ward	2.00	1.00	.60
(97)	Bill White	2.50	1.25	.70
(98)	Billy Williams	5.00	2.50	1.50
(99)	Jim Wynn	2.00	1.00	.60
(100)	Carl Yastrzemski	6.00	3.00	1.75
(101)	Angels Pennant	2.00	1.00	.60
(102)	Astros Pennant	2.00	1.00	.60
(103)	Athletics Pennant	2.00	1.00	.60
(104)	Braves Pennant	2.00	1.00	.60
(105)	Cards Pennant	2.00	1.00	.60
(106)	Cubs Pennant	2.00	1.00	.60
(107)	Dodgers Pennant	2.00	1.00	.60
(108)	Giants Pennant	2.00	1.00	.60
(109)	Indians Pennant	2.00	1.00	.60
(110)	Mets Pennant	2.00	1.00	.60
(111)	Orioles Pennant	2.00	1.00	.60

		NR MT	EX	VG
(112)	Phillies Pennant	2.00	1.00	.60
(113)	Pirates Pennant	2.00	1.00	.60
(114)	Red Sox Pennant	2.00	1.00	.60
(115)	Reds Pennant	2.00	1.00	.60
(116)	Senators Pennant	2.00	1.00	.60
(117)	Tigers Pennant	2.00	1.00	.60
(118)	Twins Pennant	2.00	1.00	.60
(119)	White Sox Pennant	2.00	1.00	.60
(120)	Yankees Pennant	2.00	1.00	.60

1967 Topps

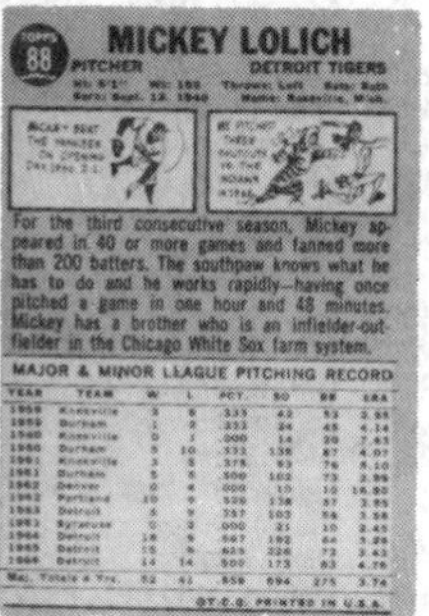

This 609-card set of 2-1/2" by 3-1/2" cards marked the largest set up to that time for Topps. Card fronts feature large color photographs bordered by white. The player's name and position are printed at the top with the team at the bottom. Across the front of the card with the exception of #254 (Milt Pappas) there is a facsimile autograph. The backs were the first to be done vertically, although they continued to carry familiar statistical and biographical information. The only subsets are statistical leaders and World Series highlights. Rookie cards are done by team or league with two players per card. The high numbers (#'s 534-609) in '67 are quite scarce, and while it is known that some are even scarcer, by virtue of having been short-printed in relation to the rest of the series, there is no general agreement on which cards are involved. Cards in the high series which are generally believed to have been double-printed - and thus worth somewhat less than the other cards in the series - and indicated in the checklist by a (DP) notation following the player name.

	NR MT	EX	VG
Complete Set (609):	5500.00	2750.00	1650.
Common Player: 1-110	1.50	.70	.45
Common Player: 111-457	2.50	1.25	.70
Common Player: 458-533	7.50	3.75	2.25
Common Player: 534-609	12.00	6.00	3.50

		NR MT	EX	VG
1	The Champs (Hank Bauer, Brooks Robinson, Frank Robinson)	20.00	10.00	6.00
2	Jack Hamilton	1.50	.70	.45
3	Duke Sims	1.50	.70	.45
4	Hal Lanier	1.50	.70	.45
5	Whitey Ford	17.50	8.75	5.25
6	Dick Simpson	1.50	.70	.45
7	Don McMahon	1.50	.70	.45
8	Chuck Harrison	1.50	.70	.45
9	Ron Hansen	1.50	.70	.45
10	Matty Alou	1.50	.70	.45
11	Barry Moore	1.50	.70	.45
12	Dodgers Rookies (Jimmy Campanis, Bill Singer)	2.50	1.25	.70
13	Joe Sparma	1.50	.70	.45
14	Phil Linz	1.50	.70	.45
15	Earl Battey	1.50	.70	.45
16	Bill Hands	1.50	.70	.45
17	Jim Gosger	1.50	.70	.45
18	Gene Oliver	1.50	.70	.45
19	Jim McGlothlin	1.50	.70	.45
20	Orlando Cepeda	10.00	5.00	3.00
21	Dave Bristol	1.50	.70	.45
22	Gene Brabender	1.50	.70	.45
23	Larry Elliot	1.50	.70	.45
24	Bob Allen	1.50	.70	.45
25	Elston Howard	4.00	2.00	1.25
26a	Bob Priddy (no trade statement)	15.00	7.50	4.50
26b	Bob Priddy (with trade statement)	1.50	.70	.45
27	Bob Saverine	1.50	.70	.45
28	Barry Latman	1.50	.70	.45
29	Tommy McCraw	1.50	.70	.45
30	Al Kaline	17.50	8.75	5.25
31	Jim Brewer	1.50	.70	.45
32	Bob Bailey	1.50	.70	.45
33	Athletics Rookies (*Sal Bando,* Randy Schwartz)	2.00	1.00	.60
34	Pete Cimino	1.50	.70	.45
35	Rico Carty	1.50	.70	.45
36	Bob Tillman	1.50	.70	.45
37	Rick Wise	1.50	.70	.45
38	Bob Johnson	1.50	.70	.45
39	Curt Simmons	1.50	.70	.45
40	Rick Reichardt	1.50	.70	.45
41	Joe Hoerner	1.50	.70	.45
42	Mets Team	5.00	2.50	1.50
43	Chico Salmon	1.50	.70	.45
44	Joe Nuxhall	1.50	.70	.45
45a	Roger Maris (Cards on fronts)	40.00	20.00	12.00
45b	Roger Maris (Yankees on front, blank back proof)	250.00	125.00	75.00
46	Lindy McDaniel	1.50	.70	.45
47	Ken McMullen	1.50	.70	.45
48	Bill Freehan	1.50	.70	.45
49	Roy Face	1.50	.70	.45
50	Tony Oliva	4.00	2.00	1.25
51	Astros Rookies (Dave Adlesh, Wes Bales)	1.50	.70	.45
52	Dennis Higgins	1.50	.70	.45
53	Clay Dalrymple	1.50	.70	.45
54	Dick Green	1.50	.70	.45
55	Don Drysdale	12.50	6.25	3.75
56	Jose Tartabull	1.50	.70	.45
57	*Pat Jarvis*	1.50	.70	.45
58	Paul Schaal	1.50	.70	.45
59	Ralph Terry	1.50	.70	.45
60	Luis Aparicio	7.50	3.75	2.25
61	Gordy Coleman	1.50	.70	.45
62	Checklist 1-109 (Frank Robinson)	5.00	2.50	1.50
63	Cards Clubbers (Lou Brock, Curt Flood)	13.00	6.50	4.00
64	Fred Valentine	1.50	.70	.45
65	Tom Haller	1.50	.70	.45
66	Manny Mota	1.50	.70	.45
67	Ken Berry	1.50	.70	.45
68	Bob Buhl	1.50	.70	.45
69	Vic Davalillo	1.50	.70	.45
70	Ron Santo	2.00	1.00	.60
71	Camilo Pascual	1.50	.70	.45
72	Tigers Rookies (George Korince, John Matchick)	1.50	.70	.45
73	Rusty Staub	2.50	1.25	.70
74	Wes Stock	1.50	.70	.45
75	George Scott	2.50	1.25	.70
76	Jim Barbieri	1.50	.70	.45
77	Dooley Womack	1.50	.70	.45
78	Pat Corrales	1.50	.70	.45
79	Bubba Morton	1.50	.70	.45
80	Jim Maloney	1.50	.70	.45
81	Eddie Stanky	1.50	.70	.45
82	Steve Barber	1.50	.70	.45
83	Ollie Brown	1.50	.70	.45
84	Tommie Sisk	1.50	.70	.45
85	Johnny Callison	1.50	.70	.45
86a	Mike McCormick (no trade statement)	15.00	7.50	4.50
86b	Mike McCormick (with trade statement)	1.50	.70	.45
87	George Altman	1.50	.70	.45
88	Mickey Lolich	2.25	1.25	.70
89	*Felix Millan*	1.50	.70	.45
90	Jim Nash	1.50	.70	.45
91	Johnny Lewis	1.50	.70	.45
92	Ray Washburn	1.50	.70	.45
93	Yankees Rookies (*Stan Bahnsen,* Bobby Murcer)	2.50	1.25	.70
94	Ron Fairly	1.50	.70	.45
95	Sonny Siebert	1.50	.70	.45
96	Art Shamsky	1.50	.70	.45
97	Mike Cuellar	1.50	.70	.45
98	Rich Rollins	1.50	.70	.45
99	Lee Stange	1.50	.70	.45
100	Frank Robinson	17.50	8.75	5.25
101	Ken Johnson	1.50	.70	.45
102	Phillies Team	5.00	2.50	1.50

		NR MT	EX	VG
103a	Checklist 110-196 (Mickey Mantle) (170 is D McAuliffe)	15.00	7.50	4.50
103b	Checklist 110-196 (Mickey Mantle) (170 is D. McAuliffe)	12.00	6.00	3.50
104	Minnie Rojas	1.50	.70	.45
105	Ken Boyer	2.00	1.00	.60
106	Randy Hundley	1.50	.70	.45
107	Joel Horlen	1.50	.70	.45
108	Alex Johnson	1.50	.70	.45
109	Tribe Thumpers (Rocky Colavito, Leon Wagner)	2.50	1.25	.70
110	Jack Aker	1.50	.70	.45
111	John Kennedy	2.50	1.25	.70
112	Dave Wickersham	2.50	1.25	.70
113	Dave Nicholson	2.50	1.25	.70
114	Jack Baldschun	2.50	1.25	.70
115	Paul Casanova	2.50	1.25	.70
116	Herman Franks	2.50	1.25	.70
117	Darrell Brandon	2.50	1.25	.70
118	Bernie Allen	2.50	1.25	.70
119	Wade Blasingame	2.50	1.25	.70
120	Floyd Robinson	2.50	1.25	.70
121	Ed Bressoud	2.50	1.25	.70
122	George Brunet	2.50	1.25	.70
123	Pirates Rookies (Jim Price, Luke Walker)	2.50	1.25	.70
124	Jim Stewart	2.50	1.25	.70
125	Moe Drabowsky	2.50	1.25	.70
126	Tony Taylor	2.50	1.25	.70
127	John O'Donoghue	2.50	1.25	.70
128	Ed Spiezio	2.50	1.25	.70
129	Phil Roof	2.50	1.25	.70
130	Phil Regan	2.50	1.25	.70
131	Yankees Team	7.50	3.75	2.25
132	Ozzie Virgil	2.50	1.25	.70
133	Ron Kline	2.50	1.25	.70
134	Gates Brown	2.50	1.25	.70
135	Deron Johnson	2.50	1.25	.70
136	Carroll Sembera	2.50	1.25	.70
137	Twins Rookies (Ron Clark, Jim Ollom)	2.50	1.25	.70
138	Dick Kelley	2.50	1.25	.70
139	Dalton Jones	2.50	1.25	.70
140	Willie Stargell	20.00	10.00	6.00
141	John Miller	2.50	1.25	.70
142	Jackie Brandt	2.50	1.25	.70
143	Sox Sockers (Don Buford, Pete Ward)	3.00	1.50	.90
144	Bill Hepler	2.50	1.25	.70
145	Larry Brown	2.50	1.25	.70
146	Steve Carlton	110.00	55.00	33.00
147	Tom Egan	2.50	1.25	.70
148	Adolfo Phillips	2.50	1.25	.70
149	Joe Moeller	2.50	1.25	.70
150	Mickey Mantle	275.00	137.00	82.00
151	World Series Game 1 (Moe Mows Down 11)	3.50	1.75	1.00
152	World Series Game 2 (Palmer Blanks Dodgers)	5.00	2.50	1.50
153	World Series Game 3 (Blair's Homer Defeats L.A.)	3.50	1.75	1.00
154	World Series Game 4 (Orioles Win 4th Straight)	3.50	1.75	1.00
155	World Series Summary (The Winners Celebrate)	3.50	1.75	1.00
156	Ron Herbel	2.50	1.25	.70
157	Danny Cater	2.50	1.25	.70
158	Jimmy Coker	2.50	1.25	.70
159	Bruce Howard	2.50	1.25	.70
160	Willie Davis	2.50	1.25	.70
161	Dick Williams	2.50	1.25	.70
162	Billy O'Dell	2.50	1.25	.70
163	Vic Roznovsky	2.50	1.25	.70
164	Dwight Siebler	2.50	1.25	.70
165	Cleon Jones	2.50	1.25	.70
166	Eddie Mathews	12.00	6.00	3.50
167	Senators Rookies (Joe Coleman, Tim Cullen)	2.50	1.25	.70
168	Ray Culp	2.50	1.25	.70
169	Horace Clarke	2.50	1.25	.70
170	Dick McAuliffe	2.50	1.25	.70
171	Calvin Koonce	2.50	1.25	.70
172	Bill Heath	2.50	1.25	.70
173	Cardinals Team	5.00	2.50	1.50
174	Dick Radatz	2.50	1.25	.70
175	Bobby Knoop	2.50	1.25	.70
176	Sammy Ellis	2.50	1.25	.70
177	Tito Fuentes	2.50	1.25	.70
178	John Buzhardt	2.50	1.25	.70
179	Braves Rookies (Cecil Upshaw, Chas. Vaughn)	2.50	1.25	.70

		NR MT	EX	VG
180	Curt Blefary	2.50	1.25	.70
181	Terry Fox	2.50	1.25	.70
182	Ed Charles	2.50	1.25	.70
183	Jim Pagliaroni	2.50	1.25	.70
184	George Thomas	2.50	1.25	.70
185	*Ken Holtzman*	2.50	1.25	.70
186	Mets Maulers (Ed Kranepool, Ron Swoboda)	3.00	1.50	.90
187	Pedro Ramos	2.50	1.25	.70
188	Ken Harrelson	2.50	1.25	.70
189	Chuck Hinton	2.50	1.25	.70
190	Turk Farrell	2.50	1.25	.70
191a	Checklist 197-283 (Willie Mays) (214 is Dick Kelley)	12.00	6.00	3.50
191b	Checklist 197-283 (Willie Mays) (214 is Tom Kelley)	12.00	6.00	3.50
192	Fred Gladding	2.50	1.25	.70
193	Jose Cardenal	2.50	1.25	.70
194	Bob Allison	2.50	1.25	.70
195	Al Jackson	2.50	1.25	.70
196	Johnny Romano	2.50	1.25	.70
197	Ron Perranoski	2.50	1.25	.70
198	Chuck Hiller	2.50	1.25	.70
199	Billy Hitchcock	2.50	1.25	.70
200	Willie Mays	100.00	50.00	30.00
201	Hal Reniff	2.50	1.25	.70
202	Johnny Edwards	2.50	1.25	.70
203	Al McBean	2.50	1.25	.70
204	Orioles Rookies (*Mike Epstein*, Tom Phoebus)	2.50	1.25	.70
205	Dick Groat	2.50	1.25	.70
206	Dennis Bennett	2.50	1.25	.70
207	John Orsino	2.50	1.25	.70
208	Jack Lamabe	2.50	1.25	.70
209	Joe Nossek	2.50	1.25	.70
210	Bob Gibson	18.00	9.00	5.50
211	Twins Team	5.00	2.50	1.50
212	Chris Zachary	2.50	1.25	.70
213	*Jay Johnstone*	1.75	.90	.50
214	Tom Kelley	3.00	1.50	.90
215	Ernie Banks	20.00	10.00	6.00
216	Bengal Belters (Norm Cash, Al Kaline)	7.50	3.75	2.25
217	Rob Gardner	2.50	1.25	.70
218	Wes Parker	2.50	1.25	.70
219	Clay Carroll	2.50	1.25	.70
220	Jim Hart	2.50	1.25	.70
221	Woody Fryman	2.50	1.25	.70
222	Reds Rookies (Lee May, Darrell Osteen)	2.50	1.25	.70
223	Mike Ryan	2.50	1.25	.70
224	Walt Bond	2.50	1.25	.70
225	Mel Stottlemyre	2.50	1.25	.70
226	Julian Javier	2.50	1.25	.70
227	Paul Lindblad	2.50	1.25	.70
228	Gil Hodges	5.00	2.50	1.50
229	Larry Jackson	2.50	1.25	.70
230	Boog Powell	2.50	1.25	.70
231	John Bateman	2.50	1.25	.70
232	Don Buford	2.50	1.25	.70
233	A.L. ERA Leaders (Steve Hargan, Joel Horlen, Gary Peters)	3.00	1.50	.90
234	N.L. ERA Leaders (Mike Cuellar, Sandy Koufax, Juan Marichal)	12.00	6.00	3.50
235	A.L. Pitching Leaders (Jim Kaat, Denny McLain, Earl Wilson)	3.00	1.50	.90
236	N.L. Pitching Leaders (Bob Gibson, Sandy Koufax, Juan Marichal, Gaylord Perry)	12.00	6.00	3.50
237	A.L. Strikeout Leaders (Jim Kaat, Sam McDowell, Earl Wilson)	3.00	1.50	.90
238	N.L. Strikeout Leaders (Jim Bunning, Sandy Koufax, Bob Veale)	12.00	6.00	3.50
239	A.L. Batting Leaders (Al Kaline, Tony Oliva, Frank Robinson)	12.00	6.00	3.50
240	N.L. Batting Leaders (Felipe Alou, Matty Alou, Rico Carty)	3.00	1.50	.90
241	A.L. RBI Leaders (Harmon Killebrew, Boog Powell, Frank Robinson)	4.50	2.25	1.25
242	N.L. RBI Leaders (Hank Aaron, Richie Allen, Bob Clemente)	12.00	6.00	3.50
243	A.L. Home Run Leaders (Harmon Killebrew, Boog Powell, Frank Robinson)	6.00	3.00	1.75
244	N.L. Home Run Leaders (Hank Aaron, Richie Allen, Willie Mays)	12.00	6.00	3.50
245	Curt Flood	2.50	1.25	.70
246	Jim Perry	2.50	1.25	.70
247	Jerry Lumpe	2.50	1.25	.70
248	Gene Mauch	2.50	1.25	.70
249	Nick Willhite	2.50	1.25	.70

		NR MT	EX	VG
250	Hank Aaron	100.00	50.00	30.00
251	Woody Held	2.50	1.25	.70
252	Bob Bolin	2.50	1.25	.70
253	Indians Rookies (Bill Davis, Gus Gil)	2.50	1.25	.70
254	Milt Pappas	2.50	1.25	.70
255	Frank Howard	3.00	1.50	.90
256	Bob Hendley	2.50	1.25	.70
257	Charley Smith	2.50	1.25	.70
258	Lee Maye	2.50	1.25	.70
259	Don Dennis	2.50	1.25	.70
260	Jim Lefebvre	2.50	1.25	.70
261	John Wyatt	2.50	1.25	.70
262	Athletics Team	5.00	2.50	1.50
263	Hank Aguirre	2.50	1.25	.70
264	Ron Swoboda	2.50	1.25	.70
265	Lou Burdette	2.50	1.25	.70
266	Pitt Power (Donn Clendenon, Willie Stargell)	5.00	2.50	1.50
267	Don Schwall	2.50	1.25	.70
268	John Briggs	2.50	1.25	.70
269	Don Nottebart	2.50	1.25	.70
270	Zoilo Versalles	2.50	1.25	.70
271	Eddie Watt	2.50	1.25	.70
272	Cubs Rookies (Bill Connors, Dave Dowling)	2.50	1.25	.70
273	Dick Lines	2.50	1.25	.70
274	Bob Aspromonte	2.50	1.25	.70
275	Fred Whitfield	2.50	1.25	.70
276	Bruce Brubaker	2.50	1.25	.70
277	Steve Whitaker	2.50	1.25	.70
278	Checklist 284-370 (Jim Kaat)	5.00	2.50	1.50
279	Frank Linzy	2.50	1.25	.70
280	Tony Conigliaro	3.50	1.75	1.00
281	Bob Rodgers	2.50	1.25	.70
282	Johnny Odom	2.50	1.25	.70
283	Gene Alley	2.50	1.25	.70
284	Johnny Podres	3.50	1.75	1.00
285	Lou Brock	20.00	10.00	6.00
286	Wayne Causey	2.50	1.25	.70
287	Mets Rookies (Greg Goossen, Bart Shirley)	2.50	1.25	.70
288	Denver Lemaster	2.50	1.25	.70
289	Tom Tresh	3.50	1.75	1.00
290	Bill White	2.50	1.25	.70
291	Jim Hannan	2.50	1.25	.70
292	Don Pavletich	2.50	1.25	.70
293	Ed Kirkpatrick	2.50	1.25	.70
294	Walt Alston	5.00	2.50	1.50
295	Sam McDowell	2.50	1.25	.70
296	Glenn Beckert	2.50	1.25	.70
297	Dave Morehead	2.50	1.25	.70
298	Ron Davis	2.50	1.25	.70
299	Norm Siebern	2.50	1.25	.70
300	Jim Kaat	9.00	4.50	2.75
301	Jesse Gonder	2.50	1.25	.70
302	Orioles Team	5.00	2.50	1.50
303	Gil Blanco	2.50	1.25	.70
304	Phil Gagliano	2.50	1.25	.70
305	Earl Wilson	2.50	1.25	.70
306	*Bud Harrelson*	2.50	1.25	.70
307	Jim Beauchamp	2.50	1.25	.70
308	Al Downing	2.50	1.25	.70
309	Hurlers Beware (Richie Allen, Johnny Callison)	2.00	1.00	.60
310	Gary Peters	2.50	1.25	.70
311	Ed Brinkman	2.50	1.25	.70
312	Don Mincher	2.50	1.25	.70
313	Bob Lee	2.50	1.25	.70
314	Red Sox Rookies (*Mike Andrews, Reggie Smith*)	7.50	3.75	2.25
315	Billy Williams	12.00	6.00	3.50
316	Jack Kralick	2.50	1.25	.70
317	Cesar Tovar	2.50	1.25	.70
318	Dave Giusti	2.50	1.25	.70
319	Paul Blair	2.50	1.25	.70
320	Gaylord Perry	12.50	6.25	3.75
321	Mayo Smith	2.50	1.25	.70
322	Jose Pagan	2.50	1.25	.70
323	Mike Hershberger	2.50	1.25	.70
324	Hal Woodeshick	2.50	1.25	.70
325	Chico Cardenas	2.50	1.25	.70
326	Bob Uecker	20.00	10.00	6.00
327	Angels Team	5.00	2.50	1.50
328	Clete Boyer	2.50	1.25	.70
329	Charlie Lau	2.50	1.25	.70
330	Claude Osteen	2.50	1.25	.70
331	Joe Foy	2.50	1.25	.70
332	Jesus Alou	2.50	1.25	.70
333	Fergie Jenkins	25.00	12.50	7.50
334	Twin Terrors (Bob Allison, Harmon Killebrew)	4.50	2.25	1.25

		NR MT	EX	VG
335	Bob Veale	2.50	1.25	.70
336	Joe Azcue	2.50	1.25	.70
337	Joe Morgan	22.00	11.00	6.50
338	Bob Locker	2.50	1.25	.70
339	Chico Ruiz	2.50	1.25	.70
340	Joe Pepitone	2.50	1.25	.70
341	Giants Rookies (*Dick Dietz,* Bill Sorrell)	2.50	1.25	.70
342	Hank Fischer	2.50	1.25	.70
343	Tom Satriano	2.50	1.25	.70
344	Ossie Chavarria	2.50	1.25	.70
345	Stu Miller	2.50	1.25	.70
346	Jim Hickman	2.50	1.25	.70
347	Grady Hatton	2.50	1.25	.70
348	Tug McGraw	2.50	1.25	.70
349	Bob Chance	2.50	1.25	.70
350	Joe Torre	2.50	1.25	.70
351	Vern Law	2.50	1.25	.70
352	Ray Oyler	2.50	1.25	.70
353	Bill McCool	2.50	1.25	.70
354	Cubs Team	5.00	2.50	1.50
355	Carl Yastrzemski	75.00	37.00	22.00
356	Larry Jaster	2.50	1.25	.70
357	Bill Skowron	3.50	1.75	1.00
358	Ruben Amaro	2.50	1.25	.70
359	Dick Ellsworth	2.50	1.25	.70
360	Leon Wagner	2.50	1.25	.70
361	Checklist 371-457 (Roberto Clemente)	13.00	6.50	4.00
362	Darold Knowles	2.50	1.25	.70
363	Dave Johnson	2.50	1.25	.70
364	Claude Raymond	2.50	1.25	.70
365	John Roseboro	2.50	1.25	.70
366	Andy Kosco	2.50	1.25	.70
367	Angels Rookies (Bill Kelso, Don Wallace)	2.50	1.25	.70
368	Jack Hiatt	2.50	1.25	.70
369	Catfish Hunter	18.00	9.00	5.50
370	Tommy Davis	2.50	1.25	.70
371	Jim Lonborg	2.50	1.25	.70
372	Mike de la Hoz	2.50	1.25	.70
373	White Sox Rookies (Duane Josephson, Fred Klages)	2.50	1.25	.70
374	Mel Queen	2.50	1.25	.70
375	Jake Gibbs	2.50	1.25	.70
376	Don Lock	2.50	1.25	.70
377	Luis Tiant	3.00	1.50	.90
378	Tigers Team	5.00	2.50	1.50
379	Jerry May	2.50	1.25	.70
380	Dean Chance	2.50	1.25	.70
381	Dick Schofield	2.50	1.25	.70
382	Dave McNally	2.50	1.25	.70
383	Ken Henderson	2.50	1.25	.70
384	Cardinals Rookies (Jim Cosman, Dick Hughes)	2.50	1.25	.70
385	Jim Fregosi	2.50	1.25	.70
386	Dick Selma	2.50	1.25	.70
387	Cap Peterson	2.50	1.25	.70
388	Arnold Earley	2.50	1.25	.70
389	Al Dark	2.50	1.25	.70
390	Jim Wynn	2.50	1.25	.70
391	Wilbur Wood	2.50	1.25	.70
392	Tommy Harper	2.50	1.25	.70
393	Jim Bouton	2.50	1.25	.70
394	Jake Wood	2.50	1.25	.70
395	Chris Short	2.50	1.25	.70
396	Atlanta Aces (Tony Cloninger, Denis Menke)	3.00	1.50	.90
397	Willie Smith	2.50	1.25	.70
398	Jeff Torborg	2.50	1.25	.70
399	Al Worthington	2.50	1.25	.70
400	Roberto Clemente	85.00	42.00	25.00
401	Jim Coates	2.50	1.25	.70
402	Phillies Rookies (Grant Jackson, Billy Wilson)	2.50	1.25	.70
403	Dick Nen	2.50	1.25	.70
404	Nelson Briles	2.50	1.25	.70
405	Russ Snyder	2.50	1.25	.70
406	Lee Elia	2.50	1.25	.70
407	Reds Team	5.00	2.50	1.50
408	Jim Northrup	2.50	1.25	.70
409	Ray Sadecki	2.50	1.25	.70
410	Lou Johnson	2.50	1.25	.70
411	Dick Howser	2.50	1.25	.70
412	Astros Rookies (Norm Miller, *Doug Rader*)	3.00	1.50	.90
413	Jerry Grote	2.50	1.25	.70
414	Casey Cox	2.50	1.25	.70
415	Sonny Jackson	2.50	1.25	.70
416	Roger Repoz	2.50	1.25	.70
417	Bob Bruce	2.50	1.25	.70

		NR MT	EX	VG
418	Sam Mele	2.50	1.25	.70
419	Don Kessinger	2.50	1.25	.70
420	Denny McLain	5.00	2.50	1.50
421	Dal Maxvill	2.50	1.25	.70
422	Hoyt Wilhelm	15.00	7.50	4.50
423	Fence Busters (Willie Mays, Willie McCovey)	25.00	12.50	7.50
424	Pedro Gonzalez	2.50	1.25	.70
425	Pete Mikkelsen	2.50	1.25	.70
426	Lou Clinton	2.50	1.25	.70
427	Ruben Gomez	2.50	1.25	.70
428	Dodgers Rookies (Tom Hutton, *Gene Michael*)	2.50	1.25	.70
429	Garry Roggenburk	2.50	1.25	.70
430	Pete Rose	75.00	37.00	22.00
431	Ted Uhlaender	2.50	1.25	.70
432	Jimmie Hall	2.50	1.25	.70
433	Al Luplow	2.50	1.25	.70
434	Eddie Fisher	2.50	1.25	.70
435	Mack Jones	2.50	1.25	.70
436	Pete Ward	2.50	1.25	.70
437	Senators Team	5.00	2.50	1.50
438	Chuck Dobson	2.50	1.25	.70
439	Byron Browne	2.50	1.25	.70
440	Steve Hargan	2.50	1.25	.70
441	Jim Davenport	2.50	1.25	.70
442	Yankees Rookies (*Bill Robinson,* Joe Verbanic)	2.50	1.25	.70
443	Tito Francona	2.50	1.25	.70
444	George Smith	2.50	1.25	.70
445	Don Sutton	25.00	12.50	7.50
446	Russ Nixon	2.50	1.25	.70
447	Bo Belinsky	2.50	1.25	.70
448	Harry Walker	2.50	1.25	.70
449	Orlando Pena	2.50	1.25	.70
450	Richie Allen	5.00	2.50	1.50
451	Fred Newman	2.50	1.25	.70
452	Ed Kranepool	2.50	1.25	.70
453	Aurelio Monteagudo	2.50	1.25	.70
454a	Checklist 458-533 (Juan Marichal) (left ear shows)	12.00	6.00	3.50
454b	Checklist 458-533 (Juan Marichal) (no left ear)	12.00	6.00	3.50
455	Tommie Agee	2.50	1.25	.70
456	Phil Niekro	12.00	6.00	3.50
457	Andy Etchebarren	2.50	1.25	.70
458	Lee Thomas	7.50	3.75	2.25
459	Senators Rookies (*Dick Bosman,* Pete Craig)	7.50	3.75	2.25
460	Harmon Killebrew	35.00	17.50	10.50
461	Bob Miller	7.50	3.75	2.25
462	Bob Barton	7.50	3.75	2.25
463	Hill Aces (Sam McDowell, Sonny Siebert)	11.00	5.50	3.25
464	Dan Coombs	7.50	3.75	2.25
465	Willie Horton	9.00	4.50	2.75
466	Bobby Wine	7.50	3.75	2.25
467	Jim O'Toole	7.50	3.75	2.25
468	Ralph Houk	9.00	4.50	2.75
469	Len Gabrielson	7.50	3.75	2.25
470	Bob Shaw	7.50	3.75	2.25
471	Rene Lachemann	7.50	3.75	2.25
472	Pirates Rookies (John Gelnar, George Spriggs)	7.50	3.75	2.25
473	Jose Santiago	7.50	3.75	2.25
474	Bob Tolan	7.50	3.75	2.25
475	Jim Palmer	100.00	50.00	30.00
476	Tony Perez	75.00	37.00	22.00
477	Braves Team	12.00	6.00	3.50
478	Bob Humphreys	7.50	3.75	2.25
479	Gary Bell	7.50	3.75	2.25
480	Willie McCovey	35.00	17.50	10.50
481	Leo Durocher	13.00	6.50	4.00
482	Bill Monbouquette	7.50	3.75	2.25
483	Jim Landis	7.50	3.75	2.25
484	Jerry Adair	7.50	3.75	2.25
485	Tim McCarver	13.00	6.50	4.00
486	Twins Rookies (Rich Reese, Bill Whitby)	7.50	3.75	2.25
487	Tom Reynolds	7.50	3.75	2.25
488	Gerry Arrigo	7.50	3.75	2.25
489	Doug Clemens	7.50	3.75	2.25
490	Tony Cloninger	7.50	3.75	2.25
491	Sam Bowens	7.50	3.75	2.25
492	Pirates Team	12.00	6.00	3.50
493	Phil Ortega	7.50	3.75	2.25
494	Bill Rigney	7.50	3.75	2.25
495	Fritz Peterson	9.00	4.50	2.75
496	Orlando McFarlane	7.50	3.75	2.25
497	Ron Campbell	7.50	3.75	2.25
498	Larry Dierker	7.50	3.75	2.25
499	Indians Rookies (George Culver, Jose Vidal)	7.50	3.75	2.25
500	Juan Marichal	24.00	12.00	7.25
501	Jerry Zimmerman	7.50	3.75	2.25
502	Derrell Griffith	7.50	3.75	2.25
503	Dodgers Team	13.00	6.50	4.00
504	Orlando Martinez	7.50	3.75	2.25
505	Tommy Helms	7.50	3.75	2.25
506	Smoky Burgess	7.50	3.75	2.25
507	Orioles Rookies (Ed Barnowski, Larry Haney)	7.50	3.75	2.25
508	Dick Hall	7.50	3.75	2.25
509	Jim King	7.50	3.75	2.25
510	Bill Mazeroski	13.00	6.50	4.00
511	Don Wert	7.50	3.75	2.25
512	Red Schoendienst	15.00	7.50	4.50
513	Marcelino Lopez	7.50	3.75	2.25
514	John Werhas	7.50	3.75	2.25
515	Bert Campaneris	9.00	4.50	2.75
516	Giants Team	12.00	6.00	3.50
517	Fred Talbot	7.50	3.75	2.25
518	Denis Menke	7.50	3.75	2.25
519	Ted Davidson	7.50	3.75	2.25
520	Max Alvis	7.50	3.75	2.25
521	Bird Bombers (Curt Blefary, Boog Powell)	13.00	6.50	4.00
522	John Stephenson	7.50	3.75	2.25
523	Jim Merritt	7.50	3.75	2.25
524	Felix Mantilla	7.50	3.75	2.25
525	Ron Hunt	7.50	3.75	2.25
526	Tigers Rookies (*Pat Dobson,* George Korince)	9.00	4.50	2.75
527	Dennis Ribant	7.50	3.75	2.25
528	Rico Petrocelli	9.00	4.50	2.75
529	Gary Wagner	7.50	3.75	2.25
530	Felipe Alou	12.00	6.00	3.50
531	Checklist 534-609 (Brooks Robinson)	12.00	6.00	3.50
532	Jim Hicks	7.50	3.75	2.25
533	Jack Fisher	7.50	3.75	2.25
534	Hank Bauer	9.00	4.50	2.75
535	Donn Clendenon	15.00	7.50	4.50
536	Cubs Rookies (*Joe Niekro,* Paul Popovich)	35.00	17.50	10.50
537	Chuck Estrada	9.00	4.50	2.75
538	J.C. Martin	15.00	7.50	4.50
539	Dick Egan	9.00	4.50	2.75
540	Norm Cash	35.00	17.50	10.50
541	Joe Gibbon	15.00	7.50	4.50
542	Athletics Rookies (*Rick Monday,* Tony Pierce)	15.00	7.50	4.50
543	Dan Schneider	15.00	7.50	4.50
544	Indians Team	22.00	11.00	6.50
545	Jim Grant	15.00	7.50	4.50
546	Woody Woodward	15.00	7.50	4.50
547	Red Sox Rookies (Russ Gibson, Bill Rohr)	9.00	4.50	2.75
548	Tony Gonzalez	9.00	4.50	2.75
549	Jack Sanford	15.00	7.50	4.50
550	Vada Pinson	18.00	9.00	5.50
551	Doug Camilli	9.00	4.50	2.75
552	Ted Savage	15.00	7.50	4.50
553	Yankees Rookies (Mike Hegan, Thad Tillotson)	18.00	9.00	5.50
554	Andre Rodgers	9.00	4.50	2.75
555	Don Cardwell	15.00	7.50	4.50
556	Al Weis	9.00	4.50	2.75
557	Al Ferrara	15.00	7.50	4.50
558	Orioles Rookies (*Mark Belanger,* Bill Dillman)	35.00	17.50	10.50
559	Dick Tracewski	9.00	4.50	2.75
560	Jim Bunning	50.00	25.00	15.00
561	Sandy Alomar	15.00	7.50	4.50
562	Steve Blass	9.00	4.50	2.75
563	Joe Adcock	15.00	7.50	4.50
564	Astros Rookies (Alonzo Harris, Aaron Pointer)	9.00	4.50	2.75
565	Lew Krausse	15.00	7.50	4.50
566	Gary Geiger	9.00	4.50	2.75
567	Steve Hamilton	15.00	7.50	4.50
568	John Sullivan	15.00	7.50	4.50
569	A.L. Rookies (Hank Allen, *Rod Carew*)	450.00	225.00	135.00
570	Maury Wills	80.00	40.00	24.00
571	Larry Sherry	15.00	7.50	4.50
572	Don Demeter	15.00	7.50	4.50
573	White Sox Team	22.00	11.00	6.50
574	Jerry Buchek	15.00	7.50	4.50
575	*Dave Boswell*	15.00	7.50	4.50
576	N.L. Rookies (Norm Gigon, Ramon Hernandez)	15.00	7.50	4.50

		NR MT	EX	VG
577	Bill Short	15.00	7.50	4.50
578	John Boccabella	15.00	7.50	4.50
579	Bill Henry	15.00	7.50	4.50
580	Rocky Colavito	75.00	37.00	22.00
581	Mets Rookies (Bill Denehy, *Tom Seaver*)	1200.00	600.00	360.00
582	Jim Owens	9.00	4.50	2.75
583	Ray Barker	15.00	7.50	4.50
584	Jim Piersall	20.00	10.00	6.00
585	Wally Bunker	15.00	7.50	4.50
586	Manny Jimenez	15.00	7.50	4.50
587	N.L. Rookies (Don Shaw, Gary Sutherland)	15.00	7.50	4.50
588	Johnny Klippstein	9.00	4.50	2.75
589	Dave Ricketts	9.00	4.50	2.75
590	Pete Richert	15.00	7.50	4.50
591	Ty Cline	15.00	7.50	4.50
592	N.L. Rookies (Jim Shellenback, Ron Willis)	15.00	7.50	4.50
593	Wes Westrum	15.00	7.50	4.50
594	Dan Osinski	15.00	7.50	4.50
595	Cookie Rojas	15.00	7.50	4.50
596	Galen Cisco	9.00	4.50	2.75
597	Ted Abernathy	15.00	7.50	4.50
598	White Sox Rookies (Ed Stroud, Walt Williams)	15.00	7.50	4.50
599	Bob Duliba	9.00	4.50	2.75
600	Brooks Robinson	225.00	112.00	67.00
601	Bill Bryan	9.00	4.50	2.75
602	Juan Pizarro	15.00	7.50	4.50
603	Athletics Rookies (Tim Talton, Ramon Webster)	15.00	7.50	4.50
604	Red Sox Team	100.00	50.00	30.00
605	Mike Shannon	35.00	17.50	10.50
606	Ron Taylor	15.00	7.50	4.50
607	Mickey Stanley	15.00	7.50	4.50
608	Cubs Rookies (Rich Nye, John Upham)	9.00	4.50	2.75
609	Tommy John	100.00	35.00	15.00

1967 Topps Pin-Ups

The 5" by 7" "All Star Pin-ups" were inserts to regular 1967 Topps baseball cards. They feature a full color picture with the player's name, position and team in a circle on the lower left side of the front. The numbered set consists of 32 players (generally big names). Even so, they are rather inexpensive. Because the large paper pin-ups had to be folded several times to fit into the wax packs, they are almost never found in true "Mint" condition.

		NR MT	EX	VG
Complete Set:		80.00	40.00	24.00
Common Player:		1.00	.50	.30
1	Boog Powell	1.50	.70	.45
2	Bert Campaneris	1.50	.70	.45
3	Brooks Robinson	6.00	3.00	1.75
4	Tommie Agee	1.00	.50	.30
5	Carl Yastrzemski	6.00	3.00	1.75
6	Mickey Mantle	20.00	10.00	6.00
7	Frank Howard	1.50	.70	.45
8	Sam McDowell	1.00	.50	.30
9	Orlando Cepeda	2.50	1.25	.70
10	Chico Cardenas	1.00	.50	.30
11	Roberto Clemente	10.00	5.00	3.00
12	Willie Mays	10.00	5.00	3.00
13	Cleon Jones	1.00	.50	.30
14	John Callison	1.00	.50	.30
15	Hank Aaron	10.00	5.00	3.00
16	Don Drysdale	6.00	3.00	1.75
17	Bobby Knoop	1.00	.50	.30
18	Tony Oliva	1.50	.70	.45
19	Frank Robinson	6.00	3.00	1.75
20	Denny McLain	1.50	.70	.45
21	Al Kaline	6.00	3.00	1.75
22	Joe Pepitone	1.00	.50	.30
23	Harmon Killebrew	5.00	2.50	1.50
24	Leon Wagner	1.00	.50	.30
25	Joe Morgan	4.00	2.00	1.25
26	Ron Santo	1.00	.50	.30
27	Joe Torre	1.00	.50	.30
28	Juan Marichal	4.00	2.00	1.25
29	Matty Alou	1.00	.50	.30
30	Felipe Alou	2.00	1.00	.60
31	Ron Hunt	1.00	.50	.30
32	Willie McCovey	5.00	2.50	1.50

1967 Topps Stand-Ups

Never actually issued, no more than a handful of each of these rare test issues has made their way into the hobby market. Designed so that the color photo of the player's head could be popped out of the black background, and the top folded over to create a stand-up display, examples of these 3-1/8" by 5-1/4" cards can be found either die-cut around the portrait or without the cutting. Blank-backed, there are 24 cards in the set, numbered on the front at bottom left. The cards are popular with advanced superstar collectors.

		NR MT	EX	VG
Complete Set:		6750.00	3375.00	2025.
Common Player:		65.00	32.00	19.50
1	Pete Rose	700.00	350.00	210.00
2	Gary Peters	65.00	32.00	19.50
3	Frank Robinson	200.00	100.00	60.00
4	Jim Lonborg	65.00	32.00	19.50
5	Ron Swoboda	65.00	32.00	19.50
6	Harmon Killebrew	200.00	100.00	60.00
7	Roberto Clemente	800.00	400.00	240.00
8	Mickey Mantle	1500.00	750.00	450.00
9	Jim Fregosi	75.00	37.00	22.00
10	Al Kaline	300.00	150.00	90.00
11	Don Drysdale	250.00	125.00	75.00
12	Dean Chance	65.00	32.00	19.50
13	Orlando Cepeda	75.00	37.00	22.00
14	Tim McCarver	75.00	37.00	22.00
15	Frank Howard	75.00	37.00	22.00
16	Max Alvis	65.00	32.00	19.50
17	Rusty Staub	75.00	37.00	22.00
18	Richie Allen	75.00	37.00	22.00
19	Willie Mays	800.00	400.00	240.00
20	Hank Aaron	800.00	400.00	240.00
21	Carl Yastrzemski	400.00	200.00	120.00
22	Ron Santo	75.00	37.00	22.00
23	Catfish Hunter	200.00	100.00	60.00
24	Jim Wynn	65.00	32.00	19.50

1967 Topps Stickers Pirates

Considered a "test" issue, this 33-sticker set of 2-1/2" by 3-1/2" stickers is very similar to the Red Sox stickers which were produced the same year. Player stickers have a color picture (often just the player's head) and the player's name in large "comic book" letters. Besides the players, there are other topics such as "I Love the Pirates," "Bob Clemente for Mayor," and a number of similar sentiments. The stickers have blank backs and are rather scarce.

		NR MT	EX	VG
Complete Set:		225.00	112.00	67.00
Common Player:		3.00	1.50	.90
1	Gene Alley	3.00	1.50	.90
2	Matty Alou	7.00	3.50	2.00
3	Dennis Ribant	3.00	1.50	.90
4	Steve Blass	3.00	1.50	.90
5	Juan Pizarro	3.00	1.50	.90
6	Bob Clemente	75.00	37.00	22.00
7	Donn Clendenon	5.00	2.50	1.50
8	Roy Face	5.00	2.50	1.50
9	Woody Fryman	3.00	1.50	.90
10	Jesse Gonder	3.00	1.50	.90
11	Vern Law	5.00	2.50	1.50
12	Al McBean	3.00	1.50	.90
13	Jerry May	3.00	1.50	.90
14	Bill Mazeroski	12.00	6.00	3.50
15	Pete Mikkelsen	3.00	1.50	.90
16	Manny Mota	5.00	2.50	1.50
17	Billy O'Dell	3.00	1.50	.90
18	Jose Pagan	3.00	1.50	.90
19	Jim Pagliaroni	3.00	1.50	.90
20	Johnny Pesky	3.00	1.50	.90
21	Tommie Sisk	3.00	1.50	.90
22	Willie Stargell	40.00	20.00	12.00
23	Bob Veale	3.00	1.50	.90
24	Harry Walker	3.00	1.50	.90
25	I Love The Pirates	3.00	1.50	.90
26	Let's Go Pirates	3.00	1.50	.90
27	Bob Clemente For Mayor	25.00	12.50	7.50
28	National League Batting Champion (Matty Alou)	4.00	2.00	1.25
29	Happiness Is A Pirate Win	3.00	1.50	.90
30	Donn Clendenon Is My Hero	4.00	2.00	1.25
31	Pirates' Home Run Champion (Willie Stargell)	15.00	7.50	4.50
32	Pirates Logo	3.00	1.50	.90
33	Pirates Pennant	3.00	1.50	.90

1967 Topps Stickers Red Sox

Like the 1967 Pirates Stickers, the Red Sox Stickers were part of the same test procedure. The Red Sox Stickers have the same 2-1/2" by 3-1/2" dimensions, color picture and large player's name on the front. A set is complete at 33 stickers. The majority are players, but themes such as "Let's Go Red Sox" are also included.

		NR MT	EX	VG
Complete Set:		225.00	112.00	67.00
Common Player:		3.00	1.50	.90
1	Dennis Bennett	3.00	1.50	.90
2	Darrell Brandon	3.00	1.50	.90
3	Tony Conigliaro	15.00	7.50	4.50
4	Don Demeter	3.00	1.50	.90
5	Hank Fischer	3.00	1.50	.90
6	Joe Foy	3.00	1.50	.90
7	Mike Andrews	3.00	1.50	.90
8	Dalton Jones	3.00	1.50	.90
9	Jim Lonborg	9.00	4.50	2.75
10	Don McMahon	3.00	1.50	.90
11	Dave Morehead	3.00	1.50	.90
12	George Smith	3.00	1.50	.90
13	Rico Petrocelli	6.00	3.00	1.75
14	Mike Ryan	3.00	1.50	.90
15	Jose Santiago	3.00	1.50	.90
16	George Scott	6.00	3.00	1.75
17	Sal Maglie	5.00	2.50	1.50
18	Reggie Smith	10.00	5.00	3.00
19	Lee Stange	3.00	1.50	.90
20	Jerry Stephenson	3.00	1.50	.90
21	Jose Tartabull	3.00	1.50	.90
22	George Thomas	3.00	1.50	.90
23	Bob Tillman	3.00	1.50	.90
24	Johnnie Wyatt	3.00	1.50	.90
25	Carl Yastrzemski	75.00	37.00	22.00
26	Dick Williams	6.00	3.00	1.75
27	I Love The Red Sox	3.00	1.50	.90
28	Let's Go Red Sox	3.00	1.50	.90
29	Carl Yastrzemski For Mayor	25.00	12.50	7.50
30	Tony Conigliaro Is My Hero	7.00	3.50	2.00
31	Happiness Is A Boston Win	3.00	1.50	.90
32	Red Sox Logo	3.00	1.50	.90
33	Red Sox Pennant	3.00	1.50	.90

1968 Topps

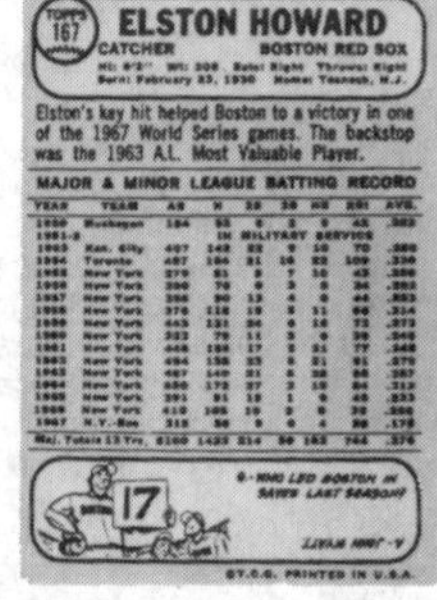

In 1968, Topps returned to a 598-card set of 2-1/2" by 3-1/2" cards. It is not, however, more of the same by way of appearance as the cards feature a color photograph on a background of what appears to be a burlap fabric. The player's name is below the photo but on the unusual background. A colored circle on the lower right carries the team and position. Backs were also changed. While retaining the vertical format introduced the previous year, with stats in the middle and cartoon at the bottom. The set features many of the old favorite subsets, including statistical leaders, World Series highlights, multi-player cards, checklists, rookie cards and the return of All-Star cards.

	NR MT	EX	VG
Complete Set (598):	3500.00	1750.00	1050.
Common Player: 1-533	1.50	.70	.45
Common Player: 534-598	3.00	1.50	.90

No.	Card	NR MT	EX	VG
1	N.L. Batting Leaders (Matty Alou, Roberto Clemente, Tony Gonzalez)	17.50	8.75	5.25
2	A.L. Batting Leaders (Al Kaline, Frank Robinson, Carl Yastrzemski)	8.00	4.00	2.50
3	N.L. RBI Leaders (Hank Aaron, Orlando Cepeda, Roberto Clemente)	9.00	4.50	2.75
4	A.L. RBI Leaders (Harmon Killebrew, Frank Robinson, Carl Yastrzemski)	8.00	4.00	2.50
5	N.L. Home Run Leaders (Hank Aaron, Willie McCovey, Ron Santo, Jim Wynn)	8.00	4.00	2.50
6	A.L. Home Run Leaders (Frank Howard, Harmon Killebrew, Carl Yastrzemski)	8.00	4.00	2.50
7	N.L. ERA Leaders (Jim Bunning, Phil Niekro, Chris Short)	3.50	1.75	1.00
8	A.L. ERA Leaders (Joe Horlen, Gary Peters, Sonny Siebert)	3.00	1.50	.90
9	N.L. Pitching Leaders (Jim Bunning, Fergie Jenkins, Mike McCormick, Claude Osteen)	3.50	1.75	1.00
10a	A.L. Pitching Leaders (Dean Chance, Jim Lonborg, Earl Wilson) ("Lonberg" on back)	3.50	1.75	1.00
10b	A.L. Pitching Leaders (Dean Chance, Jim Lonborg, Earl Wilson) ("Lonborg" on back)	3.00	1.50	.90
11	N.L. Strikeout Leaders (Jim Bunning, Fergie Jenkins, Gaylord Perry)	4.50	2.25	1.25
12	A.L. Strikeout Leaders (Dean Chance, Jim Lonborg, Sam McDowell)	3.00	1.50	.90
13	Chuck Hartenstein	1.50	.70	.45
14	Jerry McNertney	1.50	.70	.45
15	Ron Hunt	1.50	.70	.45
16	Indians Rookies (Lou Piniella, Richie Scheinblum)	2.50	1.25	.70
17	Dick Hall	1.50	.70	.45
18	Mike Hershberger	1.50	.70	.45
19	Juan Pizarro	1.50	.70	.45
20	Brooks Robinson	25.00	12.50	7.50
21	Ron Davis	1.50	.70	.45
22	Pat Dobson	1.50	.70	.45
23	Chico Cardenas	1.50	.70	.45
24	Bobby Locke	1.50	.70	.45
25	Julian Javier	1.50	.70	.45
26	Darrell Brandon	1.50	.70	.45
27	Gil Hodges	6.00	3.00	1.75
28	Ted Uhlaender	1.50	.70	.45
29	Joe Verbanic	1.50	.70	.45
30	Joe Torre	1.50	.70	.45
31	Ed Stroud	1.50	.70	.45
32	Joe Gibbon	1.50	.70	.45
33	Pete Ward	1.50	.70	.45
34	Al Ferrara	1.50	.70	.45
35	Steve Hargan	1.50	.70	.45
36	Pirates Rookies (Bob Moose, *Bob Robertson*)	1.50	.70	.45
37	Billy Williams	7.00	3.50	2.00
38	Tony Pierce	1.50	.70	.45
39	Cookie Rojas	1.50	.70	.45
40	Denny McLain	3.00	1.50	.90
41	Julio Gotay	1.50	.70	.45
42	Larry Haney	1.50	.70	.45
43	Gary Bell	1.50	.70	.45
44	Frank Kostro	1.50	.70	.45
45	Tom Seaver	175.00	87.00	52.00
46	Dave Ricketts	1.50	.70	.45
47	Ralph Houk	1.50	.70	.45
48	Ted Davidson	1.50	.70	.45
49a	Ed Brinkman (yellow team)	60.00	30.00	18.00
49b	Ed Brinkman (white team)	1.50	.70	.45
50	Willie Mays	65.00	32.00	19.50
51	Bob Locker	1.50	.70	.45
52	Hawk Taylor	1.50	.70	.45
53	Gene Alley	1.50	.70	.45
54	Stan Williams	1.50	.70	.45
55	Felipe Alou	2.50	1.25	.70
56	Orioles Rookies (Dave Leonhard, Dave May)	1.50	.70	.45
57	Dan Schneider	1.50	.70	.45
58	Eddie Mathews	10.00	5.00	3.00
59	Don Lock	1.50	.70	.45
60	Ken Holtzman	1.50	.70	.45
61	Reggie Smith	2.50	1.25	.70
62	Chuck Dobson	1.50	.70	.45
63	Dick Kenworthy	1.50	.70	.45
64	Jim Merritt	1.50	.70	.45
65	John Roseboro	1.50	.70	.45
66a	Casey Cox (yellow team)	60.00	30.00	18.00
66b	Casey Cox (white team)	1.50	.70	.45
67	Checklist 1-109 (Jim Kaat)	3.00	1.50	.90
68	Ron Willis	1.50	.70	.45
69	Tom Tresh	2.50	1.25	.70
70	Bob Veale	1.50	.70	.45
71	Vern Fuller	1.50	.70	.45
72	Tommy John	5.00	2.50	1.50
73	Jim Hart	1.50	.70	.45
74	Milt Pappas	1.50	.70	.45
75	Don Mincher	1.50	.70	.45
76	Braves Rookies (Jim Britton, *Ron Reed*)	2.50	1.25	.70
77	*Don Wilson*	1.50	.70	.45
78	Jim Northrup	1.50	.70	.45
79	Ted Kubiak	1.50	.70	.45
80	Rod Carew	115.00	57.00	34.00
81	Larry Jackson	1.50	.70	.45
82	Sam Bowens	1.50	.70	.45
83	John Stephenson	1.50	.70	.45
84	Bob Tolan	1.50	.70	.45
85	Gaylord Perry	12.00	6.00	3.50
86	Willie Stargell	8.00	4.00	2.50
87	Dick Williams	2.00	1.00	.60
88	Phil Regan	1.50	.70	.45
89	Jake Gibbs	1.50	.70	.45
90	Vada Pinson	3.00	1.50	.90
91	Jim Ollom	1.50	.70	.45
92	Ed Kranepool	1.50	.70	.45
93	Tony Cloninger	1.50	.70	.45
94	Lee Maye	1.50	.70	.45
95	Bob Aspromonte	1.50	.70	.45
96	Senators Rookies (Frank Coggins, Dick Nold)	1.50	.70	.45
97	Tom Phoebus	1.50	.70	.45
98	Gary Sutherland	1.50	.70	.45
99	Rocky Colavito	3.00	1.50	.90
100	Bob Gibson	20.00	10.00	6.00
101	Glenn Beckert	1.50	.70	.45
102	Jose Cardenal	1.50	.70	.45
103	Don Sutton	8.00	4.00	2.50
104	Dick Dietz	1.50	.70	.45
105	Al Downing	2.00	1.00	.60
106	Dalton Jones	1.50	.70	.45
107	Checklist 110-196 (Juan Marichal)	3.50	1.75	1.00
108	Don Pavletich	1.50	.70	.45
109	Bert Campaneris	2.00	1.00	.60
110	Hank Aaron	65.00	32.00	19.50
111	Rich Reese	1.50	.70	.45
112	Woody Fryman	1.50	.70	.45
113	Tigers Rookies (Tom Matchick, Daryl Patterson)	1.50	.70	.45
114	Ron Swoboda	1.50	.70	.45
115	Sam McDowell	1.50	.70	.45
116	Ken McMullen	1.50	.70	.45
117	Larry Jaster	1.50	.70	.45
118	Mark Belanger	2.00	1.00	.60
119	Ted Savage	1.50	.70	.45
120	Mel Stottlemyre	2.00	1.00	.60
121	Jimmie Hall	1.50	.70	.45
122	Gene Mauch	1.50	.70	.45
123	Jose Santiago	1.50	.70	.45
124	Nate Oliver	1.50	.70	.45
125	Joe Horlen	1.50	.70	.45
126	Bobby Etheridge	1.50	.70	.45
127	Paul Lindblad	1.50	.70	.45
128	Astros Rookies (Tom Dukes, Alonzo Harris)	1.50	.70	.45
129	Mickey Stanley	1.50	.70	.45
130	Tony Perez	5.00	2.50	1.50
131	Frank Bertaina	1.50	.70	.45
132	Bud Harrelson	1.50	.70	.45
133	Fred Whitfield	1.50	.70	.45
134	Pat Jarvis	1.50	.70	.45
135	Paul Blair	1.50	.70	.45
136	Randy Hundley	1.50	.70	.45
137	Twins Team	4.00	2.00	1.25
138	Ruben Amaro	1.50	.70	.45
139	Chris Short	1.50	.70	.45
140	Tony Conigliaro	3.00	1.50	.90
141	Dal Maxvill	1.50	.70	.45
142	White Sox Rookies (Buddy Bradford, Bill Voss)	1.50	.70	.45
143	Pete Cimino	1.50	.70	.45
144	Joe Morgan	15.00	7.50	4.50
145	Don Drysdale	12.00	6.00	3.50

		NR MT	EX	VG
146	Sal Bando	1.50	.70	.45
147	Frank Linzy	1.50	.70	.45
148	Dave Bristol	1.50	.70	.45
149	Bob Saverine	1.50	.70	.45
150	Roberto Clemente	65.00	32.00	19.50
151	World Series Game 1 (Brock Socks 4-Hits in Opener)	3.50	1.75	1.00
152	World Series Game 2 (Yaz Smashes Two Homers)	5.00	2.50	1.50
153	World Series Game 3 (Briles Cools Off Boston)	3.00	1.50	.90
154	World Series Game 4 (Gibson Hurls Shutout')	8.00	4.00	2.50
155	World Series Game 5 (Lonborg Wins Again')	3.00	1.50	.90
156	World Series Game 6 (Petrocelli Socks Two Homers)	3.00	1.50	.90
157	World Series Game 7 (St. Louis Wins It')	3.00	1.50	.90
158	World Series Summary (The Cardinals Celebrate')	3.00	1.50	.90
159	Don Kessinger	1.50	.70	.45
160	Earl Wilson	1.50	.70	.45
161	Norm Miller	1.50	.70	.45
162	Cardinals Rookies (Hal Gilson, *Mike Torrez*)	2.00	1.00	.60
163	Gene Brabender	1.50	.70	.45
164	Ramon Webster	1.50	.70	.45
165	Tony Oliva	2.50	1.25	.70
166	Claude Raymond	1.50	.70	.45
167	Elston Howard	2.50	1.25	.70
168	Dodgers Team	4.00	2.00	1.25
169	Bob Bolin	1.50	.70	.45
170	Jim Fregosi	2.00	1.00	.60
171	Don Nottebart	1.50	.70	.45
172	Walt Williams	1.50	.70	.45
173	John Boozer	1.50	.70	.45
174	Bob Tillman	1.50	.70	.45
175	Maury Wills	2.50	1.25	.70
176	Bob Allen	1.50	.70	.45
177	Mets Rookies *(Jerry Koosman, Nolan Ryan)*	1600.00	800.00	480.00
178	Don Wert	1.50	.70	.45
179	Bill Stoneman	1.50	.70	.45
180	Curt Flood	1.50	.70	.45
181	Jerry Zimmerman	1.50	.70	.45
182	Dave Giusti	1.50	.70	.45
183	Bob Kennedy	1.50	.70	.45
184	Lou Johnson	1.50	.70	.45
185	Tom Haller	1.50	.70	.45
186	Eddie Watt	1.50	.70	.45
187	Sonny Jackson	1.50	.70	.45
188	Cap Peterson	1.50	.70	.45
189	Bill Landis	1.50	.70	.45
190	Bill White	2.50	1.25	.70
191	Dan Frisella	1.50	.70	.45
192a	Checklist 197-283 (Carl Yastrzemski) ("To increase the..." on back)	4.50	2.25	1.25
192b	Checklist 197-283 (Carl Yastrzemski) ("To increase your..." on back)	6.00	3.00	1.75
193	Jack Hamilton	1.50	.70	.45
194	Don Buford	1.50	.70	.45
195	Joe Pepitone	1.50	.70	.45
196	Gary Nolan	1.50	.70	.45
197	Larry Brown	1.50	.70	.45
198	Roy Face	1.50	.70	.45
199	A's Rookies (Darrell Osteen, Roberto Rodriguez)	1.50	.70	.45
200	Orlando Cepeda	4.00	2.00	1.25
201	*Mike Marshall*	3.00	1.50	.90
202	Adolfo Phillips	1.50	.70	.45
203	Dick Kelley	1.50	.70	.45
204	Andy Etchebarren	1.50	.70	.45
205	Juan Marichal	8.00	4.00	2.50
206	Cal Ermer	1.50	.70	.45
207	Carroll Sembera	1.50	.70	.45
208	Willie Davis	1.50	.70	.45
209	Tim Cullen	1.50	.70	.45
210	Gary Peters	1.50	.70	.45
211	J.C. Martin	1.50	.70	.45
212	Dave Morehead	1.50	.70	.45
213	Chico Ruiz	1.50	.70	.45
214	Yankees Rookies (Stan Bahnsen, Frank Fernandez)	2.00	1.00	.60
215	Jim Bunning	4.00	2.00	1.25
216	Bubba Morton	1.50	.70	.45
217	Turk Farrell	1.50	.70	.45
218	Ken Suarez	1.50	.70	.45
219	Rob Gardner	1.50	.70	.45
220	Harmon Killebrew	12.50	6.25	3.75
221	Braves Team	4.00	2.00	1.25

		NR MT	EX	VG
222	Jim Hardin	1.50	.70	.45
223	Ollie Brown	1.50	.70	.45
224	Jack Aker	1.50	.70	.45
225	Richie Allen	2.50	1.25	.70
226	Jimmie Price	1.50	.70	.45
227	Joe Hoerner	1.50	.70	.45
228	Dodgers Rookies *(Jack Billingham,* Jim Fairey)	1.50	.70	.45
229	Fred Klages	1.50	.70	.45
230	Pete Rose	40.00	20.00	12.00
231	Dave Baldwin	1.50	.70	.45
232	Denis Menke	1.50	.70	.45
233	George Scott	1.50	.70	.45
234	Bill Monbouquette	1.50	.70	.45
235	Ron Santo	2.50	1.25	.70
236	Tug McGraw	1.50	.70	.45
237	Alvin Dark	1.50	.70	.45
238	Tom Satriano	1.50	.70	.45
239	Bill Henry	1.50	.70	.45
240	Al Kaline	20.00	10.00	6.00
241	Felix Millan	1.50	.70	.45
242	Moe Drabowsky	1.50	.70	.45
243	Rich Rollins	1.50	.70	.45
244	John Donaldson	1.50	.70	.45
245	Tony Gonzalez	1.50	.70	.45
246	Fritz Peterson	1.50	.70	.45
247	Reds Rookies *(Johnny Bench,* Ron Tompkins)	225.00	112.00	67.00
248	Fred Valentine	1.50	.70	.45
249	Bill Singer	1.50	.70	.45
250	Carl Yastrzemski	30.00	15.00	9.00
251	*Manny Sanguillen*	1.50	.70	.45
252	Angels Team	4.00	2.00	1.25
253	Dick Hughes	1.50	.70	.45
254	Cleon Jones	1.50	.70	.45
255	Dean Chance	1.50	.70	.45
256	Norm Cash	2.50	1.25	.70
257	Phil Niekro	5.00	2.50	1.50
258	Cubs Rookies (Jose Arcia, Bill Schlesinger)	2.50	1.25	.70
259	Ken Boyer	3.00	1.50	.90
260	Jim Wynn	1.50	.70	.45
261	Dave Duncan	1.50	.70	.45
262	Rick Wise	1.50	.70	.45
263	Horace Clarke	1.50	.70	.45
264	Ted Abernathy	1.50	.70	.45
265	Tommy Davis	1.50	.70	.45
266	Paul Popovich	1.50	.70	.45
267	Herman Franks	1.50	.70	.45
268	Bob Humphreys	1.50	.70	.45
269	Bob Tiefenauer	1.50	.70	.45
270	Matty Alou	1.50	.70	.45
271	Bobby Knoop	1.50	.70	.45
272	Ray Culp	1.50	.70	.45
273	Dave Johnson	1.50	.70	.45
274	Mike Cuellar	1.50	.70	.45
275	Tim McCarver	2.50	1.25	.70
276	Jim Roland	1.50	.70	.45
277	Jerry Buchek	1.50	.70	.45
278a	Checklist 284-370 (Orlando Cepeda) (copyright at right)	3.00	1.50	.90
278b	Checklist 284-370 (Orlando Cepeda) (copyright at left)	5.00	2.50	1.50
279	Bill Hands	1.50	.70	.45
280	Mickey Mantle	250.00	125.00	75.00
281	Jim Campanis	1.50	.70	.45
282	Rick Monday	1.50	.70	.45
283	Mel Queen	1.50	.70	.45
284	John Briggs	1.50	.70	.45
285	Dick McAuliffe	1.50	.70	.45
286	Cecil Upshaw	1.50	.70	.45
287	White Sox Rookies (Mickey Abarbanel, Cisco Carlos)	1.50	.70	.45
288	Dave Wickersham	1.50	.70	.45
289	Woody Held	1.50	.70	.45
290	Willie McCovey	10.00	5.00	3.00
291	Dick Lines	1.50	.70	.45
292	Art Shamsky	1.50	.70	.45
293	Bruce Howard	1.50	.70	.45
294	Red Schoendienst	4.00	2.00	1.25
295	Sonny Siebert	1.50	.70	.45
296	Byron Browne	1.50	.70	.45
297	Russ Gibson	1.50	.70	.45
298	Jim Brewer	1.50	.70	.45
299	Gene Michael	1.50	.70	.45
300	Rusty Staub	2.00	1.00	.60
301	Twins Rookies (George Mitterwald, Rick Renick)	1.50	.70	.45
302	Gerry Arrigo	1.50	.70	.45
303	Dick Green	1.50	.70	.45
304	Sandy Valdespino	1.50	.70	.45

		NR MT	EX	VG
305	Minnie Rojas	1.50	.70	.45
306	Mike Ryan	1.50	.70	.45
307	John Hiller	1.50	.70	.45
308	Pirates Team	4.00	2.00	1.25
309	Ken Henderson	1.50	.70	.45
310	Luis Aparicio	5.00	2.50	1.50
311	Jack Lamabe	1.50	.70	.45
312	Curt Blefary	1.50	.70	.45
313	Al Weis	1.50	.70	.45
314	Red Sox Rookies (Bill Rohr, George Spriggs)	1.50	.70	.45
315	Zoilo Versalles	1.50	.70	.45
316	Steve Barber	1.50	.70	.45
317	Ron Brand	1.50	.70	.45
318	Chico Salmon	1.50	.70	.45
319	George Culver	1.50	.70	.45
320	Frank Howard	2.50	1.25	.70
321	Leo Durocher	2.25	1.25	.70
322	Dave Boswell	1.50	.70	.45
323	Deron Johnson	1.50	.70	.45
324	Jim Nash	1.50	.70	.45
325	Manny Mota	1.50	.70	.45
326	Dennis Ribant	1.50	.70	.45
327	Tony Taylor	1.50	.70	.45
328	Angels Rookies (Chuck Vinson, Jim Weaver)	1.50	.70	.45
329	Duane Josephson	1.50	.70	.45
330	Roger Maris	40.00	20.00	12.00
331	Dan Osinski	1.50	.70	.45
332	Doug Rader	1.50	.70	.45
333	Ron Herbel	1.50	.70	.45
334	Orioles Team	4.00	2.00	1.25
335	Bob Allison	1.50	.70	.45
336	John Purdin	1.50	.70	.45
337	Bill Robinson	1.50	.70	.45
338	Bob Johnson	1.50	.70	.45
339	Rich Nye	1.50	.70	.45
340	Max Alvis	1.50	.70	.45
341	Jim Lemon	1.50	.70	.45
342	Ken Johnson	1.50	.70	.45
343	Jim Gosger	1.50	.70	.45
344	Donn Clendenon	1.50	.70	.45
345	Bob Hendley	1.50	.70	.45
346	Jerry Adair	1.50	.70	.45
347	George Brunet	1.50	.70	.45
348	Phillies Rookies (Larry Colton, Dick Thoenen)	1.50	.70	.45
349	Ed Spiezio	1.50	.70	.45
350	Hoyt Wilhelm	6.00	3.00	1.75
351	Bob Barton	1.50	.70	.45
352	Jackie Hernandez	1.50	.70	.45
353	Mack Jones	1.50	.70	.45
354	Pete Richert	1.50	.70	.45
355	Ernie Banks	24.00	12.00	7.25
356	Checklist 371-457 (Ken Holtzman)	3.00	1.50	.90
357	Len Gabrielson	1.50	.70	.45
358	Mike Epstein	1.50	.70	.45
359	Joe Moeller	1.50	.70	.45
360	Willie Horton	1.50	.70	.45
361	Harmon Killebrew (All-Star)	5.00	2.50	1.50
362	Orlando Cepeda (All-Star)	2.75	1.50	.80
363	Rod Carew (All-Star)	7.00	3.50	2.00
364	Joe Morgan (All-Star)	3.00	1.50	.90
365	Brooks Robinson (All-Star)	6.00	3.00	1.75
366	Ron Santo (All-Star)	3.50	1.75	1.00
367	Jim Fregosi (All-Star)	3.00	1.50	.90
368	Gene Alley (All-Star)	3.00	1.50	.90
369	Carl Yastrzemski (All-Star)	7.00	3.50	2.00
370	Hank Aaron (All-Star)	15.00	7.50	4.50
371	Tony Oliva (All-Star)	3.50	1.75	1.00
372	Lou Brock (All-Star)	6.00	3.00	1.75
373	Frank Robinson (All-Star)	8.00	4.00	2.50
374	Roberto Clemente (All-Star)	15.00	7.50	4.50
375	Bill Freehan (All-Star)	3.00	1.50	.90
376	Tim McCarver (All-Star)	3.50	1.75	1.00
377	Joe Horlen (All-Star)	3.00	1.50	.90
378	Bob Gibson (All-Star)	7.00	3.50	2.00
379	Gary Peters (All-Star)	3.00	1.50	.90
380	Ken Holtzman (All-Star)	3.00	1.50	.90
381	Boog Powell	3.00	1.50	.90
382	Ramon Hernandez	1.50	.70	.45
383	Steve Whitaker	1.50	.70	.45
384	Red Rookies (Bill Henry, *Hal McRae*)	12.00	6.00	3.50
385	Catfish Hunter	10.00	5.00	3.00
386	Greg Goossen	1.50	.70	.45
387	Joe Foy	1.50	.70	.45
388	Ray Washburn	1.50	.70	.45
389	Jay Johnstone	1.50	.70	.45
390	Bill Mazeroski	4.00	2.00	1.25

		NR MT	EX	VG
391	Bob Priddy	1.50	.70	.45
392	Grady Hatton	1.50	.70	.45
393	Jim Perry	1.50	.70	.45
394	Tommie Aaron	1.50	.70	.45
395	Camilo Pascual	1.50	.70	.45
396	Bobby Wine	1.50	.70	.45
397	Vic Davalillo	1.50	.70	.45
398	Jim Grant	1.50	.70	.45
399	Ray Oyler	1.50	.70	.45
400a	Mike McCormick (white team)	40.00	20.00	12.00
400b	Mike McCormick (yellow team)	1.50	.70	.45
401	Mets Team	4.50	2.25	1.25
402	Mike Hegan	1.50	.70	.45
403	John Buzhardt	1.50	.70	.45
404	Floyd Robinson	1.50	.70	.45
405	Tommy Helms	1.50	.70	.45
406	Dick Ellsworth	1.50	.70	.45
407	Gary Kolb	1.50	.70	.45
408	Steve Carlton	50.00	25.00	15.00
409	Orioles Rookies (Frank Peters, Ron Stone)	1.50	.70	.45
410	Fergie Jenkins	20.00	10.00	6.00
411	Ron Hansen	1.50	.70	.45
412	Clay Carroll	1.50	.70	.45
413	Tommy McCraw	1.50	.70	.45
414	Mickey Lolich	2.75	1.50	.80
415	Johnny Callison	1.50	.70	.45
416	Bill Rigney	1.50	.70	.45
417	Willie Crawford	1.50	.70	.45
418	Eddie Fisher	1.50	.70	.45
419	Jack Hiatt	1.50	.70	.45
420	Cesar Tovar	1.50	.70	.45
421	Ron Taylor	1.50	.70	.45
422	Rene Lachemann	1.50	.70	.45
423	Fred Gladding	1.50	.70	.45
424	White Sox Team	4.00	2.00	1.25
425	Jim Maloney	1.50	.70	.45
426	Hank Allen	1.50	.70	.45
427	Dick Calmus	1.50	.70	.45
428	Vic Roznovsky	1.50	.70	.45
429	Tommie Sisk	1.50	.70	.45
430	Rico Petrocelli	1.50	.70	.45
431	Dooley Womack	1.50	.70	.45
432	Indians Rookies (Bill Davis, Jose Vidal)	1.50	.70	.45
433	Bob Rodgers	1.50	.70	.45
434	Ricardo Joseph	1.50	.70	.45
435	Ron Perranoski	1.50	.70	.45
436	Hal Lanier	1.50	.70	.45
437	Don Cardwell	1.50	.70	.45
438	Lee Thomas	1.50	.70	.45
439	Luman Harris	1.50	.70	.45
440	Claude Osteen	1.50	.70	.45
441	Alex Johnson	1.50	.70	.45
442	Dick Bosman	1.50	.70	.45
443	Joe Azcue	1.50	.70	.45
444	Jack Fisher	1.50	.70	.45
445	Mike Shannon	1.50	.70	.45
446	Ron Kline	1.50	.70	.45
447	Tigers Rookies (George Korince, Fred Lasher)	1.50	.70	.45
448	Gary Wagner	1.50	.70	.45
449	Gene Oliver	1.50	.70	.45
450	Jim Kaat	6.00	3.00	1.75
451	Al Spangler	1.50	.70	.45
452	Jesus Alou	1.50	.70	.45
453	Sammy Ellis	1.50	.70	.45
454	Checklist 458-533 (Frank Robinson)	4.00	2.00	1.25
455	Rico Carty	1.50	.70	.45
456	John O'Donoghue	1.50	.70	.45
457	Jim Lefebvre	1.50	.70	.45
458	Lew Krausse	1.50	.70	.45
459	Dick Simpson	1.50	.70	.45
460	Jim Lonborg	2.00	1.00	.60
461	Chuck Hiller	1.50	.70	.45
462	Barry Moore	1.50	.70	.45
463	Jimmie Schaffer	1.50	.70	.45
464	Don McMahon	1.50	.70	.45
465	Tommie Agee	1.50	.70	.45
466	Bill Dillman	1.50	.70	.45
467	Dick Howser	1.50	.70	.45
468	Larry Sherry	1.50	.70	.45
469	Ty Cline	1.50	.70	.45
470	Bill Freehan	1.50	.70	.45
471	Orlando Pena	1.50	.70	.45
472	Walt Alston	4.00	2.00	1.25
473	Al Worthington	1.50	.70	.45
474	Paul Schaal	1.50	.70	.45
475	Joe Niekro	2.25	1.25	.70
476	Woody Woodward	1.50	.70	.45

		NR MT	EX	VG
477	Phillies Team	4.00	2.00	1.25
478	Dave McNally	1.50	.70	.45
479	Phil Gagliano	1.50	.70	.45
480	Manager's Dream (Chico Cardenas, Roberto Clemente, Tony Oliva)	25.00	12.50	7.50
481	John Wyatt	1.50	.70	.45
482	Jose Pagan	1.50	.70	.45
483	Darold Knowles	1.50	.70	.45
484	Phil Roof	1.50	.70	.45
485	Ken Berry	1.50	.70	.45
486	Cal Koonce	1.50	.70	.45
487	Lee May	1.50	.70	.45
488	Dick Tracewski	1.50	.70	.45
489	Wally Bunker	1.50	.70	.45
490	Superstars (Harmon Killebrew, Mickey Mantle, Willie Mays)	100.00	50.00	30.00
491	Denny Lemaster	1.50	.70	.45
492	Jeff Torborg	1.50	.70	.45
493	Jim McGlothlin	1.50	.70	.45
494	Ray Sadecki	1.50	.70	.45
495	Leon Wagner	1.50	.70	.45
496	Steve Hamilton	1.50	.70	.45
497	Cards Team	4.00	2.00	1.25
498	Bill Bryan	1.50	.70	.45
499	Steve Blass	1.50	.70	.45
500	Frank Robinson	22.00	11.00	6.50
501	John Odom	1.50	.70	.45
502	Mike Andrews	1.50	.70	.45
503	Al Jackson	1.50	.70	.45
504	Russ Snyder	1.50	.70	.45
505	Joe Sparma	1.50	.70	.45
506	Clarence Jones	1.50	.70	.45
507	Wade Blasingame	1.50	.70	.45
508	Duke Sims	1.50	.70	.45
509	Dennis Higgins	1.50	.70	.45
510	Ron Fairly	1.50	.70	.45
511	Bill Kelso	1.50	.70	.45
512	Grant Jackson	1.50	.70	.45
513	Hank Bauer	1.50	.70	.45
514	Al McBean	1.50	.70	.45
515	Russ Nixon	1.50	.70	.45
516	Pete Mikkelsen	1.50	.70	.45
517	Diego Segui	1.50	.70	.45
518a	Checklist 534-598 (Clete Boyer) (539 is Maj. L. Rookies)	3.00	1.50	.90
518b	Checklist 534-598 (Clete Boyer) (539 is Amer. L. Rookies)	5.00	2.50	1.50
519	Jerry Stephenson	1.50	.70	.45
520	Lou Brock	20.00	10.00	6.00
521	Don Shaw	1.50	.70	.45
522	Wayne Causey	1.50	.70	.45
523	John Tsitouris	1.50	.70	.45
524	Andy Kosco	1.50	.70	.45
525	Jim Davenport	1.50	.70	.45
526	Bill Denehy	1.50	.70	.45
527	Tito Francona	1.50	.70	.45
528	Tigers Team	60.00	30.00	18.00
529	Bruce Von Hoff	1.50	.70	.45
530	Bird Belters (Brooks Robinson, Frank Robinson)	10.00	5.00	3.00
531	Chuck Hinton	1.50	.70	.45
532	Luis Tiant	2.00	1.00	.60
533	Wes Parker	1.50	.70	.45
534	Bob Miller	3.00	1.50	.90
535	Danny Cater	3.00	1.50	.90
536	Bill Short	3.00	1.50	.90
537	Norm Siebern	3.00	1.50	.90
538	Manny Jimenez	3.00	1.50	.90
539	Major League Rookies (Mike Ferraro, Jim Ray)	3.00	1.50	.90
540	Nelson Briles	3.00	1.50	.90
541	Sandy Alomar	3.00	1.50	.90
542	John Boccabella	3.00	1.50	.90
543	Bob Lee	3.00	1.50	.90
544	Mayo Smith	3.00	1.50	.90
545	Lindy McDaniel	3.00	1.50	.90
546	Roy White	3.00	1.50	.90
547	Dan Coombs	3.00	1.50	.90
548	Bernie Allen	3.00	1.50	.90
549	Orioles Rookies (Curt Motton, Roger Nelson)	3.00	1.50	.90
550	Clete Boyer	3.00	1.50	.90
551	Darrell Sutherland	3.00	1.50	.90
552	Ed Kirkpatrick	3.00	1.50	.90
553	Hank Aguirre	3.00	1.50	.90
554	A's Team	6.00	3.00	1.75
555	Jose Tartabull	3.00	1.50	.90
556	Dick Selma	3.00	1.50	.90
557	Frank Quilici	3.00	1.50	.90
558	John Edwards	3.00	1.50	.90
559	Pirates Rookies (Carl Taylor, Luke Walker)	3.00	1.50	.90
560	Paul Casanova	3.00	1.50	.90
561	Lee Elia	3.00	1.50	.90
562	Jim Bouton	3.50	1.75	1.00
563	Ed Charles	3.00	1.50	.90
564	Eddie Stanky	3.00	1.50	.90
565	Larry Dierker	3.00	1.50	.90
566	Ken Harrelson	3.00	1.50	.90
567	Clay Dalrymple	3.00	1.50	.90
568	Willie Smith	3.00	1.50	.90
569	N.L. Rookies (Ivan Murrell, Les Rohr)	3.00	1.50	.90
570	Rick Reichardt	3.00	1.50	.90
571	Tony LaRussa	4.00	2.00	1.25
572	Don Bosch	3.00	1.50	.90
573	Joe Coleman	3.00	1.50	.90
574	Reds Team	6.00	3.00	1.75
575	Jim Palmer	50.00	25.00	15.00
576	Dave Adlesh	3.00	1.50	.90
577	Fred Talbot	3.00	1.50	.90
578	Orlando Martinez	3.00	1.50	.90
579	N.L. Rookies *(Larry Hisle, Mike Lum)*	3.00	1.50	.90
580	Bob Bailey	3.00	1.50	.90
581	Garry Roggenburk	3.00	1.50	.90
582	Jerry Grote	3.00	1.50	.90
583	Gates Brown	3.00	1.50	.90
584	Larry Shepard	3.00	1.50	.90
585	Wilbur Wood	3.00	1.50	.90
586	Jim Pagliaroni	3.00	1.50	.90
587	Roger Repoz	3.00	1.50	.90
588	Dick Schofield	3.00	1.50	.90
589	Twins Rookies (Ron Clark, Moe Ogier)	3.00	1.50	.90
590	Tommy Harper	3.00	1.50	.90
591	Dick Nen	3.00	1.50	.90
592	John Bateman	3.00	1.50	.90
593	Lee Stange	3.00	1.50	.90
594	Phil Linz	3.00	1.50	.90
595	Phil Ortega	3.00	1.50	.90
596	Charlie Smith	3.00	1.50	.90
597	Bill McCool	3.00	1.50	.90
598	Jerry May	9.00	1.50	.90

1968 Topps Action All-Star Stickers

Still another of the many Topps test issues of the late 1960s, the Action All-Star stickers were sold in a strip of three, with bubblegum, for 10¢. The strip is comprised of three 3-1/4" by 5-1/4" panels, perforated at the joints for separation. The central panel which is numbered, contains a large color picture of a star player. The top and bottom panels contains smaller pictures of three players each. While there are 16 numbered center panels, only 12 of them are different; panels 13-16 show players previously used. Similarly, the triple-player panels at top and bottom of stickers 13-16 repeat panels from #'s 1-4. Prices below are for stickers which have all three panels still joined. Individual panels are priced signicantly lower.

		NR MT	EX	VG
Complete Set:		1300.00	650.00	390.00
Common Player:		18.00	9.00	5.50
1	Orlando Cepeda, Joe Horlen, Al Kaline, Bill Mazeroski, Claude Osteen, Mel Stottlemyre, Carl Yastrzemski	100.00	50.00	30.00
2	Don Drysdale, Harmon Killebrew, Mike McCormick, Tom Phoebus, George Scott, Ron Swoboda, Pete Ward	30.00	15.00	9.00
3	Hank Aaron, Paul Casanova, Jim Maloney, Joe Pepitone, Rick Reichardt, Frank Robinson, Tom Seaver	35.00	17.50	10.50
4	Bob Aspromonte, Johnny Callison, Dean Chance, Jim Lefebvre, Jim Lonborg, Frank Robinson, Ron Santo	25.00	12.50	7.50
5	Bert Campaneris, Al Downing, Willie Horton, Ed Kranepool, Willie Mays, Pete Rose, Ron Santo	200.00	100.00	60.00
6	Max Alvis, Ernie Banks, Al Kaline, Tim McCarver, Rusty Staub, Walt Williams, Carl Yastrzemski	70.00	35.00	21.00
7	Rod Carew, Tony Gonzalez, Steve Hargan, Mickey Mantle, Willie McCovey, Rick Monday, Billy Williams	300.00	150.00	90.00
8	Clete Boyer, Jim Bunning, Tony Conigliaro, Mike Cuellar, Joe Horlen, Ken McMullen, Don Mincher	18.00	9.00	5.50
9	Orlando Cepeda, Bob Clemente, Jim Fregosi, Harmon Killebrew, Willie Mays, Chris Short, Earl Wilson	40.00	20.00	12.00
10	Hank Aaron, Bob Gibson, Bud Harrelson, Jim Hunter, Mickey Mantle, Gary Peters, Vada Pinson	100.00	50.00	30.00
11	Don Drysdale, Bill Freehan, Frank Howard, Ferguson Jenkins, Tony Oliva, Bob Veale, Jim Wynn	30.00	15.00	9.00
12	Richie Allen, Bob Clemente, Sam McDowell, Jim McGlothlin, Tony Perez, Brooks Robinson, Joe Torre	100.00	50.00	30.00
13	Dean Chance, Don Drysdale, Jim Lefebvre, Tom Phoebus, Frank Robinson, George Scott, Carl Yastrzemski	100.00	50.00	30.00
14	Paul Casanova, Orlando Cepeda, Joe Horlen, Harmon Killebrew, Bill Mazeroski, Rick Reichardt, Tom Seaver	35.00	17.50	10.50
15	Bob Aspromonte, Johnny Callison, Jim Lonborg, Mike McCormick, Frank Robinson, Ron Swoboda, Pete Ward	30.00	15.00	9.00
16	Hank Aaron, Al Kaline, Jim Maloney, Claude Osteen, Joe Pepitone, Ron Santo, Mel Stottlemyre	30.00	15.00	9.00

1968 Topps Discs

One of the scarcest of all Topps collectibles, this 28-player set was apparently a never-completed test issue. These full-color, cardboard discs, which measure approximately 2-1/8" in diameter, were apparantly intended to be made into a "pin" set, but for some reason, production was never completed and no actual "pins" are known to exist. Uncut sheets of the player discs have been found, however. The discs include a player portrait photo with the name beneath and the city and team nickname along the sides. The set includes eight Hall of Famers.

		NR MT	EX	VG
Complete Set:		3250.00	1750.00	1050.
Common Player:		35.00	17.50	10.50
(1)	Hank Aaron	300.00	150.00	90.00
(2)	Richie Allen	45.00	22.00	13.50
(3)	Gene Alley	35.00	17.50	10.50
(4)	Rod Carew	300.00	150.00	90.00
(5)	Orlando Cepeda	60.00	30.00	18.00
(6)	Dean Chance	35.00	17.50	10.50
(7)	Roberto Clemente	300.00	150.00	90.00
(8)	Tommy Davis	35.00	17.50	10.50
(9)	Bill Freehan	35.00	17.50	10.50
(10)	Jim Fregosi	35.00	17.50	10.50
(11)	Steve Hargan	35.00	17.50	10.50
(12)	Frank Howard	45.00	22.00	13.50
(13)	Al Kaline	200.00	100.00	60.00
(14)	Harmon Killebrew	150.00	75.00	45.00
(15)	Mickey Mantle	600.00	300.00	180.00
(16)	Willie Mays	300.00	150.00	90.00
(17)	Mike McCormick	35.00	17.50	10.50
(18)	Rick Monday	35.00	17.50	10.50
(19)	Claude Osteen	35.00	17.50	10.50
(20)	Gary Peters	35.00	17.50	10.50
(21)	Brooks Robinson	200.00	100.00	60.00
(22)	Frank Robinson	200.00	100.00	60.00
(23)	Pete Rose	350.00	175.00	105.00
(24)	Ron Santo	60.00	30.00	18.00
(25)	Rusty Staub	60.00	30.00	18.00
(26)	Joe Torre	35.00	17.50	10.50
(27)	Carl Yastrzemski	200.00	100.00	60.00
(28)	Bob Veale	35.00	17.50	10.50

1968 Topps Game

A throwback to the Red and Blue Back sets of 1951, the 33-cards in the 1968 Topps Game set, inserted into packs of regular '68 Topps cards or purchases as a complete boxed set, enable the owner to play a game of baseball based on the game situations on each card. Also on the 2-1/4" by 3-1/4" cards were a color photograph of a player and his facsimile autograph. One redeeming social value of the set (assuming you're not mesmerized by the game) is that it affords an inexpensive way to get big-name cards as the set is loaded with stars, but not at all popular with collectors.

		NR MT	EX	VG
Complete Set:		70.00	35.00	21.00
Common Player:		1.00	.50	.30
1	Mateo Alou	1.00	.50	.30
2	Mickey Mantle	25.00	12.50	7.50
3	Carl Yastrzemski	3.00	1.50	.90
4	Henry Aaron	5.00	2.50	1.50
5	Harmon Killebrew	2.00	1.00	.60
6	Roberto Clemente	5.00	2.50	1.50
7	Frank Robinson	3.00	1.50	.90
8	Willie Mays	5.00	2.50	1.50
9	Brooks Robinson	3.00	1.50	.90
10	Tommy Davis	1.00	.50	.30
11	Bill Freehan	1.00	.50	.30
12	Claude Osteen	1.00	.50	.30
13	Gary Peters	1.00	.50	.30
14	Jim Lonborg	1.00	.50	.30
15	Steve Hargan	1.00	.50	.30
16	Dean Chance	1.00	.50	.30
17	Mike McCormick	1.00	.50	.30
18	Tim McCarver	1.50	.70	.45
19	Ron Santo	1.50	.70	.45

		NR MT	EX	VG
20	Tony Gonzalez	1.00	.50	.30
21	Frank Howard	1.50	.70	.45
22	George Scott	1.00	.50	.30
23	Rich Allen	1.50	.70	.45
24	Jim Wynn	1.00	.50	.30
25	Gene Alley	1.00	.50	.30
26	Rick Monday	1.00	.50	.30
27	Al Kaline	3.00	1.50	.90
28	Rusty Staub	1.50	.70	.45
29	Rod Carew	3.00	1.50	.90
30	Pete Rose	6.00	3.00	1.75
31	Joe Torre	1.00	.50	.30
32	Orlando Cepeda	2.00	1.00	.60
33	Jim Fregosi	1.00	.50	.30

1968 Topps Plaks

Among the scarcest of the Topps test issues of the late 1960s, the "All Star Baseball Plaks" were plastic busts of two dozen stars of the era which came packaged like model airplane parts. The busts had to be snapped off a sprue and could be inserted into a base which carried the player's name. Packed with the plastic plaks was one of two checklist cards which featured six color photos per side. The 2-1/8" by 4" checklist cards are popular with superstar collectors and are considerably easier to find today than the actual plaks.

		NR MT	EX	VG
Complete Set:		2300.00	1150.00	690.00
Common Player:		20.00	10.00	6.00
1	Max Alvis	20.00	10.00	6.00
2	Frank Howard	30.00	15.00	9.00
3	Dean Chance	20.00	10.00	6.00
4	Catfish Hunter	50.00	25.00	15.00
5	Jim Fregosi	25.00	12.50	7.50
6	Al Kaline	60.00	30.00	18.00
7	Harmon Killebrew	60.00	30.00	18.00
8	Gary Peters	20.00	10.00	6.00
9	Jim Lonborg	20.00	10.00	6.00
10	Frank Robinson	60.00	30.00	18.00
11	Mickey Mantle	800.00	400.00	240.00
12	Carl Yastrzemski	75.00	37.00	22.00
13	Hank Aaron	100.00	50.00	30.00
14	Roberto Clemente	100.00	50.00	30.00
15	Richie Allen	30.00	15.00	9.00
16	Tommy Davis	25.00	12.50	7.50
17	Orlando Cepeda	40.00	20.00	12.00
18	Don Drysdale	60.00	30.00	18.00
19	Willie Mays	100.00	50.00	30.00
20	Rusty Staub	30.00	15.00	9.00
21	Tim McCarver	30.00	15.00	9.00
22	Pete Rose	200.00	100.00	60.00
23	Ron Santo	30.00	15.00	9.00
24	Jim Wynn	20.00	10.00	6.00
---	Checklist Card 1-12	250.00	125.00	75.00
---	Checklist Card 13-24	250.00	125.00	75.00

A player's name in italic indicates a rookie card. An (FC) indicates a player's first card for that particular card company.

1968 Topps Posters

Yet another innovation from the creative minds at Topps appeared in 1968; a set of color player posters. Measuring 9-3/4" by 18-1/8," each poster was sold separately with its own piece of gum, rather than as an insert. The posters feature a large color photograph with a star at the bottom containing the player's name, position and team. There are 24 different posters which were folded numerous times to fit into the package they were sold in.

		NR MT	EX	VG
Complete Set:		350.00	175.00	105.00
Common Player:		6.00	3.00	1.75
1	Dean Chance	6.00	3.00	1.75
2	Max Alvis	6.00	3.00	1.75
3	Frank Howard	8.00	4.00	2.50
4	Jim Fregosi	6.00	3.00	1.75
5	Catfish Hunter	12.00	6.00	3.50
6	Roberto Clemente	30.00	15.00	9.00
7	Don Drysdale	15.00	7.50	4.50
8	Jim Wynn	6.00	3.00	1.75
9	Al Kaline	20.00	10.00	6.00
10	Harmon Killebrew	20.00	10.00	6.00
11	Jim Lonborg	6.00	3.00	1.75
12	Orlando Cepeda	8.00	4.00	2.50
13	Gary Peters	6.00	3.00	1.75
14	Hank Aaron	30.00	15.00	9.00
15	Richie Allen	8.00	4.00	2.50
16	Carl Yastrzemski	20.00	10.00	6.00
17	Ron Swoboda	6.00	3.00	1.75
18	Mickey Mantle	60.00	30.00	18.00
19	Tim McCarver	8.00	4.00	2.50
20	Willie Mays	30.00	15.00	9.00
21	Ron Santo	8.00	4.00	2.50
22	Rusty Staub	8.00	4.00	2.50
23	Pete Rose	40.00	20.00	12.00
24	Frank Robinson	20.00	10.00	6.00

1968 Topps Punch-outs

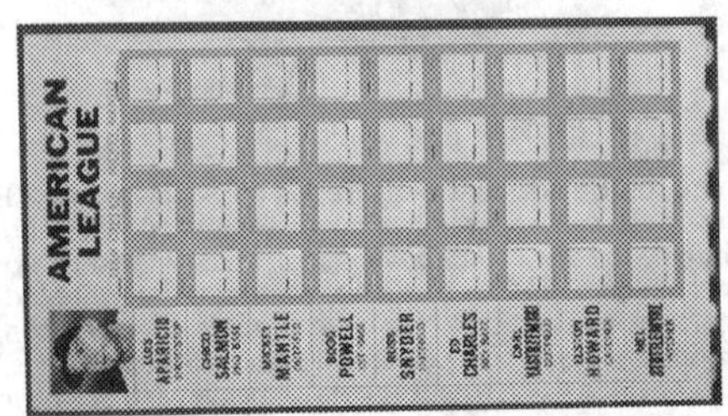

This little-known Topps test issue was reportedly issued around Maryland in cello packs containing two perforated strips of three game cards each. Cards are printed in black, white and red and measure 2-1/2x4-2/3". Backs have instructions on how to play a baseball game by punching out the small squares. Only the "Team Captain" is pictured on the card, and the same captain can be found with different line-ups on his team, creating a large number of collectible variations. Cropping variations in some player photos have been noted, also. The unnumbered issue is checklisted here in alphabetical order.

		NR MT	EX	VG
Complete Set:		2000.00	1000.00	600.00
Common Player:		15.00	7.50	4.50
(1)	Hank Aaron	100.00	50.00	30.00
(2)	Richie Allen	15.00	7.50	4.00
(3)	Gene Alley	15.00	7.50	4.50
(4)	Felipe Alou	15.00	7.50	4.50
(5)	Matty Alou	15.00	7.50	4.50
(6)	Max Alvis	15.00	7.50	4.50
(7)	Luis Aparicio	25.00	12.50	7.50
(8)	Steve Barber	15.00	7.50	4.50
(9)	Earl Battey	15.00	7.50	4.50
(10)	Clete Boyer	15.00	7.50	4.50
(11)	Ken Boyer	20.00	10.00	6.00
(12)	Lou Brock	25.00	12.50	7.50
(13)	Jim Bunning	20.00	10.00	6.00
(14)	Johnny Callison	15.00	7.50	4.50
(15)	Bert Campaneris	15.00	7.50	4.50
(16)	Leo Cardenas	15.00	7.50	4.50
(17)	Rico Carty	15.00	7.50	4.50
(18)	Norm Cash	15.00	7.50	4.50
(19)	Orlando Cepeda	20.00	10.00	6.00
(20)	Ed Charles	15.00	7.50	4.50
(21)	Roberto Clemente	100.00	50.00	30.00
(22)	Donn Clendenon	15.00	7.50	4.50
(23)	Rocky Colavito	20.00	10.00	6.00
(24)	Tony Conigliaro	20.00	10.00	6.00
(25)	Willie Davis	15.00	7.50	4.50
(26)	Johnny Edwards	15.00	7.50	4.50
(27)	Andy Etchebarren	15.00	7.50	4.50
(28)	Curt Flood	15.00	7.50	4.50
(29)	Bill Freehan	15.00	7.50	4.50
(30)	Jim Fregosi	15.00	7.50	4.50
(31)	Bob Gibson	30.00	15.00	9.00
(32)	Dick Green	15.00	7.50	4.50
(33)	Dick Groat	15.00	7.50	4.50
(34)	Tom Haller	15.00	7.50	4.50
(35)	Jim Ray Hart	15.00	7.50	4.50
(36)	Mike Hershberger	15.00	7.50	4.50
(37)	Elston Howard	15.00	7.50	4.50
(38)	Frank Howard	15.00	7.50	4.50
(39)	Ron Hunt	15.00	7.50	4.50
(40)	Sonny Jackson	15.00	7.50	4.50
(41)	Cleon Jones	15.00	7.50	4.50
(42)	Jim Kaat	20.00	10.00	6.00
(43)	Al Kaline	60.00	30.00	18.00
(44)	Harmon Killebrew	25.00	12.50	7.50
(45)	Bobby Knoop	15.00	7.50	4.50
(46)	Sandy Koufax	75.00	37.50	22.50
(47)	Ed Kranepool	15.00	7.50	4.50
(48)	Jim Lefebvre	15.00	7.50	4.50
(49)	Don Lock	15.00	7.50	4.50
(50)	Jerry Lumpe	15.00	7.50	4.50
(51)	Mickey Mantle	200.00	100.00	60.00
(52)	Juan Marichal	25.00	12.50	7.50
(53)	Willie Mays	100.00	50.00	30.00
(54)	Bill Mazeroski	20.00	10.00	6.00
(55)	Dick McAuliffe	15.00	7.50	4.50
(56)	Tim McCarver	20.00	10.00	6.00
(57)	Denny McLain	15.00	7.50	4.50
(58)	Roy McMillan	15.00	7.50	4.50
(59)	Denis Menke	15.00	7.50	4.50
(60)	Joe Morgan	25.00	12.50	7.50
(61)	Tony Oliva	20.00	10.00	6.00
(62)	Joe Pepitone	15.00	7.50	4.50
(63)	Gaylord Perry	20.00	10.00	6.00
(64)	Vada Pinson	15.00	7.50	4.50
(65)	Boog Powell	20.00	10.00	6.00
(66)	Rick Reichardt	15.00	7.50	4.50
(67)	Brooks Robinson	60.00	30.00	18.00
(68)	Floyd Robinson	15.00	7.50	4.50
(69)	Frank Robinson	50.00	25.00	15.00
(70)	Johnny Romano	15.00	7.50	4.50
(71)	Pete Rose	75.00	37.50	22.50
(72)	John Roseboro	15.00	7.50	4.50
(73)	Ron Santo	15.00	7.50	4.50
(74)	Chico Salmon	15.00	7.50	4.50
(75)	George Scott	15.00	7.50	4.50
(76)	Sonny Siebert	15.00	7.50	4.50
(77)	Russ Snyder	15.00	7.50	4.50
(78)	Willie Stargell	30.00	15.00	9.00
(79)	Mel Stottlemyre	15.00	7.50	4.50
(80)	Joe Torre	15.00	7.50	4.50
(81)	Cesar Tovar	15.00	7.50	4.50
(82)	Tom Tresh	15.00	7.50	4.50
(83)	Zoilo Versalles	15.00	7.50	4.50
(84)	Leon Wagner	15.00	7.50	4.50
(85)	Bill White	20.00	10.00	6.00
(86)	Fred Whitfield	15.00	7.50	4.50
(87)	Billy Williams	30.00	15.00	9.00
(88)	Jimmy Wynn	15.00	7.50	4.50
(89)	Carl Yastrzemski	75.00	37.50	22.50

1968 Topps 3-D

These are very rare pioneer issues on the part of Topps. The cards measure 2-1/4" by 3-1/2" and were specially printed to simulate a three- dimensional effect. Backgrounds are a purposely blurred stadium scene, in front of which was a normally sharp color player photograph. The outer layer is a thin coating of ribbed plastic. The special process gives the picture the illusion of depth when the card is moved or tilted. As this was done two years before Kellogg's began its 3-D cards, this 12-card test issue really was breaking new ground. Unfortunately, production and distribution were limited making the cards very tough to find.

		NR MT	EX	VG
Complete Set:		9000.00	4500.00	2500.
Common Player:		350.00	175.00	105.00
(1)	Bob Clemente	2500.00	1250.00	750.00
(2)	Willie Davis	400.00	200.00	125.00
(3)	Ron Fairly	400.00	200.00	125.00
(4)	Curt Flood	400.00	200.00	125.00
(5)	Jim Lonborg	400.00	200.00	125.00
(6)	Jim Maloney	350.00	175.00	105.00
(7)	Tony Perez	600.00	300.00	175.00
(8)	Boog Powell	500.00	250.00	150.00
(9)	Bill Robinson	350.00	175.00	105.00
(10)	Rusty Staub	450.00	230.00	135.00
(11)	Mel Stottlemyre	400.00	200.00	120.00
(12)	Ron Swoboda	350.00	175.00	105.00

1969 Topps

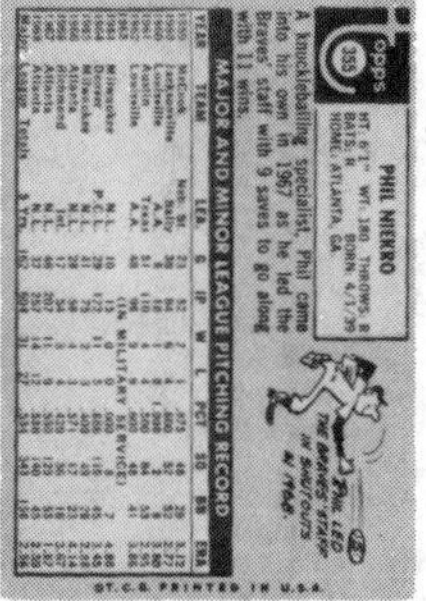

The 1969 Topps set broke yet another record for quantity as the issue is officially a whopping 664 cards. With substantial numbers of variations, the number of possible cards runs closer to 700. The design of the 2-1/2" by 3-1/2" cards in the set feature a color photo with the team name printed in block letters underneath. A circle contains the player's name and position. Card backs returned to a horizontal format. Despite the size of the set, it contains no teamcards. It does, however, have multi-player cards, All-Stars, statistical leaders, and World Series highlights. Most significant among the varieties are white and yellow letter cards from the run of #'s 440-511. The complete set prices below do not include the scarcer and more expensive "white letter" variations.

	NR MT	EX	VG
Complete Set (664):	2750.00	1375.00	825.00
Common Player: 1-218	1.00	.50	.30
Common Player: 219-327	1.50	.70	.45
Common Player: 328-664	1.00	.50	.30

		NR MT	EX	VG
1	A.L. Batting Leaders (Danny Cater, Tony Oliva, Carl Yastrzemski)	10.00	5.00	3.00
2	N.L. Batting Leaders (Felipe Alou, Matty Alou, Pete Rose)	6.00	3.00	1.75
3	A.L. RBI Leaders (Ken Harrelson, Frank Howard, Jim Northrup)	2.00	1.00	.60
4	N.L. RBI Leaders (Willie McCovey, Ron Santo, Billy Williams)	4.00	2.00	1.25
5	A.L. Home Run Leaders (Ken Harrelson, Willie Horton, Frank Howard)	2.00	1.00	.60
6	N.L. Home Run Leaders (Richie Allen, Ernie Banks, Willie McCovey)	4.00	2.00	1.25
7	A.L. ERA Leaders (Sam McDowell, Dave McNally, Luis Tiant)	2.00	1.00	.60
8	N.L. ERA Leaders (Bobby Bolin, Bob Gibson, Bob Veale)	3.00	1.50	.90
9	A.L. Pitching Leaders (Denny McLain, Dave McNally, Mel Stottlemyre, Luis Tiant)	2.50	1.25	.70
10	N.L. Pitching Leaders (Bob Gibson, Fergie Jenkins, Juan Marichal)	3.50	1.75	1.00
11	A.L. Strikeout Leaders (Sam McDowell, Denny McLain, Luis Tiant)	2.50	1.25	.70
12	N.L. Strikeout Leaders (Bob Gibson, Fergie Jenkins, Bill Singer)	3.00	1.50	.90
13	Mickey Stanley	1.00	.50	.30
14	Al McBean	1.00	.50	.30
15	Boog Powell	2.00	1.00	.60
16	Giants Rookies (Cesar Gutierrez, Rich Robertson)	1.00	.50	.30
17	Mike Marshall	1.00	.50	.30
18	Dick Schofield	1.00	.50	.30
19	Ken Suarez	1.00	.50	.30
20	Ernie Banks	20.00	10.00	6.00
21	Jose Santiago	1.00	.50	.30
22	Jesus Alou	1.00	.50	.30
23	Lew Krausse	1.00	.50	.30
24	Walt Alston	3.00	1.50	.90
25	Roy White	1.00	.50	.30
26	Clay Carroll	1.00	.50	.30
27	Bernie Allen	1.00	.50	.30
28	Mike Ryan	1.00	.50	.30
29	Dave Morehead	1.00	.50	.30
30	Bob Allison	1.00	.50	.30
31	Mets Rookies *(Gary Gentry, Amos Otis)*	1.50	.70	.45
32	Sammy Ellis	1.00	.50	.30
33	Wayne Causey	1.00	.50	.30
34	Gary Peters	1.00	.50	.30
35	Joe Morgan	12.00	6.00	3.50
36	Luke Walker	1.00	.50	.30
37	Curt Motton	1.00	.50	.30
38	Zoilo Versalles	1.00	.50	.30
39	Dick Hughes	1.00	.50	.30
40	Mayo Smith	1.00	.50	.30
41	Bob Barton	1.00	.50	.30
42	Tommy Harper	1.00	.50	.30
43	Joe Niekro	1.50	.70	.45
44	Danny Cater	1.00	.50	.30
45	Maury Wills	2.00	1.00	.60
46	Fritz Peterson	1.00	.50	.30
47a	Paul Popovich (emblem visible thru airbrush)	4.00	2.00	1.25
47b	Paul Popovich (helmet emblem completely airbrushed)	1.00	.50	.30
48	Brant Alyea	1.00	.50	.30
49a	Royals Rookies (Steve Jones, Eliseo Rodriquez) (Rodriquez on front)	6.00	3.00	1.75
49b	Royals Rookies (Steve Jones, Eliseo Rodriguez) (Rodriguez on front)	1.00	.50	.30
50	Roberto Clemente	45.00	22.00	13.50
51	Woody Fryman	1.00	.50	.30
52	Mike Andrews	1.00	.50	.30
53	Sonny Jackson	1.00	.50	.30
54	Cisco Carlos	1.00	.50	.30
55	Jerry Grote	1.00	.50	.30
56	Rich Reese	1.00	.50	.30
57	Checklist 1-109 (Denny McLain)	3.00	1.50	.90
58	Fred Gladding	1.00	.50	.30
59	Jay Johnstone	1.00	.50	.30
60	Nelson Briles	1.00	.50	.30
61	Jimmie Hall	1.00	.50	.30
62	Chico Salmon	1.00	.50	.30
63	Jim Hickman	1.00	.50	.30
64	Bill Monbouquette	1.00	.50	.30
65	Willie Davis	1.00	.50	.30
66	Orioles Rookies (Mike Adamson, *Merv Rettenmund)*	1.00	.50	.30
67	Bill Stoneman	1.00	.50	.30
68	Dave Duncan	1.00	.50	.30
69	Steve Hamilton	1.00	.50	.30
70	Tommy Helms	1.00	.50	.30
71	Steve Whitaker	1.00	.50	.30
72	Ron Taylor	1.00	.50	.30
73	Johnny Briggs	1.00	.50	.30
74	Preston Gomez	1.00	.50	.30
75	Luis Aparicio	5.00	2.50	1.50
76	Norm Miller	1.00	.50	.30
77a	Ron Perranoski (LA visible thru airbrush)	4.50	2.25	1.25
77b	Ron Perranoski (cap emblem completely airbrushed)	1.00	.50	.30
78	Tom Satriano	1.00	.50	.30
79	Milt Pappas	1.00	.50	.30
80	Norm Cash	1.75	.90	.50
81	Mel Queen	1.00	.50	.30
82	Pirates Rookies *(Rich Hebner, Al Oliver)*	12.00	6.00	3.50
83	Mike Ferraro	1.00	.50	.30
84	Bob Humphreys	1.00	.50	.30
85	Lou Brock	20.00	10.00	6.00
86	Pete Richert	1.00	.50	.30
87	Horace Clarke	1.00	.50	.30
88	Rich Nye	1.00	.50	.30
89	Russ Gibson	1.00	.50	.30
90	Jerry Koosman	2.00	1.00	.60
91	Al Dark	1.00	.50	.30
92	Jack Billingham	1.00	.50	.30
93	Joe Foy	1.00	.50	.30
94	Hank Aguirre	1.00	.50	.30
95	Johnny Bench	125.00	62.00	37.00
96	Denver Lemaster	1.00	.50	.30
97	Buddy Bradford	1.00	.50	.30
98	Dave Giusti	1.00	.50	.30
99a	Twins Rookies (Danny Morris, *Graig Nettles*) (black loop above "Twins")	20.00	10.00	6.00
99b	Twins Rookies (Danny Morris, *Graig Nettles*) (no black loop)	12.00	6.00	3.50
100	Hank Aaron	65.00	32.00	19.50
101	Daryl Patterson	1.00	.50	.30
102	Jim Davenport	1.00	.50	.30
103	Roger Repoz	1.00	.50	.30
104	Steve Blass	1.00	.50	.30
105	Rick Monday	1.00	.50	.30
106	Jim Hannan	1.00	.50	.30
107a	Checklist 110-218 (Bob Gibson) (161 is Jim Purdin)	3.00	1.50	.90
107b	Checklist 110-218 (Bob Gibson) (161 is John Purdin)	6.00	3.00	1.75
108	Tony Taylor	1.00	.50	.30
109	Jim Lonborg	1.25	.60	.40
110	Mike Shannon	1.00	.50	.30
111	Johnny Morris	1.00	.50	.30
112	J.C. Martin	1.00	.50	.30
113	Dave May	1.00	.50	.30
114	Yankees Rookies (Alan Closter, John Cumberland)	1.00	.50	.30
115	Bill Hands	1.00	.50	.30
116	Chuck Harrison	1.00	.50	.30
117	Jim Fairey	1.00	.50	.30
118	Stan Williams	1.00	.50	.30
119	Doug Rader	1.00	.50	.30
120	Pete Rose	35.00	17.50	10.50
121	Joe Grzenda	1.00	.50	.30
122	Ron Fairly	1.00	.50	.30
123	Wilbur Wood	1.25	.60	.40
124	Hank Bauer	1.00	.50	.30
125	Ray Sadecki	1.00	.50	.30
126	Dick Tracewski	1.00	.50	.30

		NR MT	EX	VG
127	Kevin Collins	1.00	.50	.30
128	Tommie Aaron	1.00	.50	.30
129	Bill McCool	1.00	.50	.30
130	Carl Yastrzemski	25.00	12.50	7.50
131	Chris Cannizzaro	1.00	.50	.30
132	Dave Baldwin	1.00	.50	.30
133	Johnny Callison	1.00	.50	.30
134	Jim Weaver	1.00	.50	.30
135	Tommy Davis	1.00	.50	.30
136	Cards Rookies (Steve Huntz, Mike Torrez)	1.00	.50	.30
137	Wally Bunker	1.00	.50	.30
138	John Bateman	1.00	.50	.30
139	Andy Kosco	1.00	.50	.30
140	Jim Lefebvre	1.00	.50	.30
141	Bill Dillman	1.00	.50	.30
142	Woody Woodward	1.00	.50	.30
143	Joe Nossek	1.00	.50	.30
144	Bob Hendley	1.00	.50	.30
145	Max Alvis	1.00	.50	.30
146	Jim Perry	1.00	.50	.30
147	Leo Durocher	2.00	1.00	.60
148	Lee Stange	1.00	.50	.30
149	Ollie Brown	1.00	.50	.30
150	Denny McLain	2.00	1.00	.60
151a	Clay Dalrymple (Phillies)	9.00	4.50	2.75
151b	Clay Dalrymple (Orioles)	1.00	.50	.30
152	Tommie Sisk	1.00	.50	.30
153	Ed Brinkman	1.00	.50	.30
154	Jim Britton	1.00	.50	.30
155	Pete Ward	1.00	.50	.30
156	Astros Rookies (Hal Gilson, Leon McFadden)	1.00	.50	.30
157	Bob Rodgers	1.00	.50	.30
158	Joe Gibbon	1.00	.50	.30
159	Jerry Adair	1.00	.50	.30
160	Vada Pinson	2.00	1.00	.60
161	John Purdin	1.00	.50	.30
162	World Series Game 1 (Gibson Fans 17; Sets New Record)	4.00	2.00	1.25
163	World Series Game 2 (Tiger Homers Deck The Cards)	3.00	1.50	.90
164	World Series Game 3 (McCarver's Homer Puts St. Louis Ahead)	3.50	1.75	1.00
165	World Series Game 4 (Brock's Lead-Off HR Starts Cards' Romp)	3.50	1.75	1.00
166	World Series Game 5 (Kaline's Key Hit Sparks Tiger Rally)	4.00	2.00	1.25
167	World Series Game 6 (Tiger 10-Run Inning Ties Mark)	3.50	1.75	1.00
168	World Series Game 7 (Lolich Series Hero Outduels Gibson)	3.50	1.75	1.00
169	World Series Summary (Tigers Celebrate Their Victory)	3.50	1.75	1.00
170	Frank Howard	1.50	.70	.45
171	Glenn Beckert	1.00	.50	.30
172	Jerry Stephenson	1.00	.50	.30
173	White Sox Rookies (Bob Christian, Gerry Nyman)	1.00	.50	.30
174	Grant Jackson	1.00	.50	.30
175	Jim Bunning	4.00	2.00	1.25
176	Joe Azcue	1.00	.50	.30
177	Ron Reed	1.00	.50	.30
178	Ray Oyler	1.00	.50	.30
179	Don Pavletich	1.00	.50	.30
180	Willie Horton	1.00	.50	.30
181	Mel Nelson	1.00	.50	.30
182	Bill Rigney	1.00	.50	.30
183	Don Shaw	1.00	.50	.30
184	Roberto Pena	1.00	.50	.30
185	Tom Phoebus	1.00	.50	.30
186	John Edwards	1.00	.50	.30
187	Leon Wagner	1.00	.50	.30
188	Rick Wise	1.00	.50	.30
189	Red Sox Rookies (Joe Lahoud, John Thibdeau)	1.00	.50	.30
190	Willie Mays	65.00	32.00	19.50
191	Lindy McDaniel	1.00	.50	.30
192	Jose Pagan	1.00	.50	.30
193	Don Cardwell	1.00	.50	.30
194	Ted Uhlaender	1.00	.50	.30
195	John Odom	1.00	.50	.30
196	Lum Harris	1.00	.50	.30
197	Dick Selma	1.00	.50	.30
198	Willie Smith	1.00	.50	.30
199	Jim French	1.00	.50	.30
200	Bob Gibson	12.50	6.25	3.75
201	Russ Snyder	1.00	.50	.30
202	Don Wilson	1.00	.50	.30
203	Dave Johnson	1.00	.50	.30
204	Jack Hiatt	1.00	.50	.30

		NR MT	EX	VG
205	Rick Reichardt	1.00	.50	.30
206	Phillies Rookies (Larry Hisle, Barry Lersch)	1.00	.50	.30
207	Roy Face	1.00	.50	.30
208a	Donn Clendenon (Expos)	7.00	3.50	2.00
208b	Donn Clendenon (Houston)	1.00	.50	.30
209	Larry Haney (photo reversed)	1.00	.50	.30
210	Felix Millan	1.00	.50	.30
211	Galen Cisco	1.00	.50	.30
212	Tom Tresh	1.50	.70	.45
213	Gerry Arrigo	1.00	.50	.30
214	Checklist 219-327	2.50	1.25	.70
215	Rico Petrocelli	1.25	.60	.40
216	Don Sutton	4.00	2.00	1.25
217	John Donaldson	1.00	.50	.30
218	John Roseboro	1.00	.50	.30
219	*Freddie Patek*	2.00	1.00	.60
220	Sam McDowell	1.50	.70	.45
221	Art Shamsky	1.50	.70	.45
222	Duane Josephson	1.50	.70	.45
223	Tom Dukes	1.50	.70	.45
224	Angels Rookies (Bill Harrelson, Steve Kealey)	1.50	.70	.45
225	Don Kessinger	1.50	.70	.45
226	Bruce Howard	1.50	.70	.45
227	Frank Johnson	1.50	.70	.45
228	Dave Leonhard	1.50	.70	.45
229	Don Lock	1.50	.70	.45
230	Rusty Staub	2.50	1.25	.70
231	Pat Dobson	1.50	.70	.45
232	Dave Ricketts	1.50	.70	.45
233	Steve Barber	1.50	.70	.45
234	Dave Bristol	1.50	.70	.45
235	Catfish Hunter	10.00	5.00	3.00
236	Manny Mota	1.50	.70	.45
237	*Bobby Cox*	1.50	.70	.45
238	Ken Johnson	1.50	.70	.45
239	Bob Taylor	1.50	.70	.45
240	Ken Harrelson	2.00	1.00	.60
241	Jim Brewer	1.50	.70	.45
242	Frank Kostro	1.50	.70	.45
243	Ron Kline	1.50	.70	.45
244	Indians Rookies (*Ray Fosse*, George Woodson)	1.50	.70	.45
245	Ed Charles	1.50	.70	.45
246	Joe Coleman	1.50	.70	.45
247	Gene Oliver	1.50	.70	.45
248	Bob Priddy	1.50	.70	.45
249	Ed Spiezio	1.50	.70	.45
250	Frank Robinson	27.50	13.50	8.25
251	Ron Herbel	1.50	.70	.45
252	Chuck Cottier	1.50	.70	.45
253	Jerry Johnson	1.50	.70	.45
254	Joe Schultz	1.50	.70	.45
255	Steve Carlton	50.00	25.00	15.00
256	Gates Brown	1.50	.70	.45
257	Jim Ray	1.50	.70	.45
258	Jackie Hernandez	1.50	.70	.45
259	Bill Short	1.50	.70	.45
260	*Reggie Jackson*	800.00	400.00	240.00
261	Bob Johnson	1.50	.70	.45
262	Mike Kekich	1.50	.70	.45
263	Jerry May	1.50	.70	.45
264	Bill Landis	1.50	.70	.45
265	Chico Cardenas	1.50	.70	.45
266	Dodgers Rookies (Alan Foster, Tom Hutton)	1.50	.70	.45
267	Vicente Romo	1.50	.70	.45
268	Al Spangler	1.50	.70	.45
269	Al Weis	1.50	.70	.45
270	Mickey Lolich	3.50	1.75	1.00
271	Larry Stahl	1.50	.70	.45
272	Ed Stroud	1.50	.70	.45
273	Ron Willis	1.50	.70	.45
274	Clyde King	1.50	.70	.45
275	Vic Davalillo	1.50	.70	.45
276	Gary Wagner	1.50	.70	.45
277	*Rod Hendricks*	1.50	.70	.45
278	Gary Geiger	1.50	.70	.45
279	Roger Nelson	1.50	.70	.45
280	Alex Johnson	1.50	.70	.45
281	Ted Kubiak	1.50	.70	.45
282	Pat Jarvis	1.50	.70	.45
283	Sandy Alomar	1.50	.70	.45
284	Expos Rookies (Jerry Robertson, Mike Wegener)	1.50	.70	.45
285	Don Mincher	1.50	.70	.45
286	*Dock Ellis*	1.50	.70	.45
287	Jose Tartabull	1.50	.70	.45
288	Ken Holtzman	1.50	.70	.45
289	Bart Shirley	1.50	.70	.45

		NR MT	EX	VG
290	Jim Kaat	4.50	2.25	1.25
291	Vern Fuller	1.50	.70	.45
292	Al Downing	1.50	.70	.45
293	Dick Dietz	1.50	.70	.45
294	Jim Lemon	1.50	.70	.45
295	Tony Perez	10.00	5.00	3.00
296	*Andy Messersmith*	1.50	.70	.45
297	Deron Johnson	1.50	.70	.45
298	Dave Nicholson	1.50	.70	.45
299	Mark Belanger	1.50	.70	.45
300	Felipe Alou	2.50	1.25	.70
301	Darrell Brandon	1.50	.70	.45
302	Jim Pagliaroni	1.50	.70	.45
303	Cal Koonce	1.50	.70	.45
304	Padres Rookies (Bill Davis, *Cito Gaston*)	15.00	7.50	4.50
305	Dick McAuliffe	1.50	.70	.45
306	Jim Grant	1.50	.70	.45
307	Gary Kolb	1.50	.70	.45
308	Wade Blasingame	1.50	.70	.45
309	Walt Williams	1.50	.70	.45
310	Tom Haller	1.50	.70	.45
311	*Sparky Lyle*	10.00	5.00	3.00
312	Lee Elia	1.50	.70	.45
313	Bill Robinson	1.50	.70	.45
314	Checklist 328-425 (Don Drysdale)	3.50	1.75	1.00
315	Eddie Fisher	1.50	.70	.45
316	Hal Lanier	1.50	.70	.45
317	Bruce Look	1.50	.70	.45
318	Jack Fisher	1.50	.70	.45
319	Ken McMullen	1.50	.70	.45
320	Dal Maxvill	1.50	.70	.45
321	Jim McAndrew	1.50	.70	.45
322	Jose Vidal	1.50	.70	.45
323	Larry Miller	1.50	.70	.45
324	Tigers Rookies (Les Cain, Dave Campbell)	1.50	.70	.45
325	Jose Cardenal	1.50	.70	.45
326	Gary Sutherland	1.50	.70	.45
327	Willie Crawford	1.50	.70	.45
328	Joe Horlen	1.00	.50	.30
329	Rick Joseph	1.00	.50	.30
330	Tony Conigliaro	1.50	.70	.45
331	Braves Rookies (Gil Garrido, *Tom House*)	1.00	.50	.30
332	Fred Talbot	1.00	.50	.30
333	Ivan Murrell	1.00	.50	.30
334	Phil Roof	1.00	.50	.30
335	Bill Mazeroski	2.50	1.25	.70
336	Jim Roland	1.00	.50	.30
337	Marty Martinez	1.00	.50	.30
338	*Del Unser*	1.00	.50	.30
339	Reds Rookies (Steve Mingori, Jose Pena)	1.00	.50	.30
340	Dave McNally	1.00	.50	.30
341	Dave Adlesh	1.00	.50	.30
342	Bubba Morton	1.00	.50	.30
343	Dan Frisella	1.00	.50	.30
344	Tom Matchick	1.00	.50	.30
345	Frank Linzy	1.00	.50	.30
346	Wayne Comer	1.00	.50	.30
347	Randy Hundley	1.00	.50	.30
348	Steve Hargan	1.00	.50	.30
349	Dick Williams	1.25	.60	.40
350	Richie Allen	2.00	1.00	.60
351	Carroll Sembera	1.00	.50	.30
352	Paul Schaal	1.00	.50	.30
353	Jeff Torborg	1.00	.50	.30
354	Nate Oliver	1.00	.50	.30
355	Phil Niekro	7.00	3.50	2.00
356	Frank Quilici	1.00	.50	.30
357	Carl Taylor	1.00	.50	.30
358	Athletics Rookies (George Lauzerique, Roberto Rodriguez)	1.00	.50	.30
359	Dick Kelley	1.00	.50	.30
360	Jim Wynn	1.00	.50	.30
361	Gary Holman	1.00	.50	.30
362	Jim Maloney	1.00	.50	.30
363	Russ Nixon	1.00	.50	.30
364	Tommie Agee	1.00	.50	.30
365	Jim Fregosi	1.00	.50	.30
366	Bo Belinsky	1.00	.50	.30
367	Lou Johnson	1.00	.50	.30
368	Vic Roznovsky	1.00	.50	.30
369	Bob Skinner	1.00	.50	.30
370	Juan Marichal	7.00	3.50	2.00
371	Sal Bando	1.25	.60	.40
372	Adolfo Phillips	1.00	.50	.30
373	Fred Lasher	1.00	.50	.30
374	Bob Tillman	1.00	.50	.30
375	Harmon Killebrew	20.00	10.00	6.00

		NR MT	EX	VG
376	Royals Rookies (Mike Fiore, *Jim Rooker*)	1.00	.50	.30
377	Gary Bell	1.00	.50	.30
378	Jose Herrera	1.00	.50	.30
379	Ken Boyer	1.50	.70	.45
380	Stan Bahnsen	1.00	.50	.30
381	Ed Kranepool	1.00	.50	.30
382	Pat Corrales	1.00	.50	.30
383	Casey Cox	1.00	.50	.30
384	Larry Shepard	1.00	.50	.30
385	Orlando Cepeda	4.00	2.00	1.25
386	Jim McGlothlin	1.00	.50	.30
387	Bobby Klaus	1.00	.50	.30
388	Tom McCraw	1.00	.50	.30
389	Dan Coombs	1.00	.50	.30
390	Bill Freehan	1.00	.50	.30
391	Ray Culp	1.00	.50	.30
392	Bob Burda	1.00	.50	.30
393	Gene Brabender	1.00	.50	.30
394	Pilots Rookies (Lou Piniella, Marv Staehle)	2.00	1.00	.60
395	Chris Short	1.00	.50	.30
396	Jim Campanis	1.00	.50	.30
397	Chuck Dobson	1.00	.50	.30
398	Tito Francona	1.00	.50	.30
399	Bob Bailey	1.00	.50	.30
400	Don Drysdale	10.00	5.00	3.00
401	Jake Gibbs	1.00	.50	.30
402	Ken Boswell	1.00	.50	.30
403	Bob Miller	1.00	.50	.30
404	Cubs Rookies (Vic LaRose, Gary Ross)	1.00	.50	.30
405	Lee May	1.00	.50	.30
406	Phil Ortega	1.00	.50	.30
407	Tom Egan	1.00	.50	.30
408	Nate Colbert	1.00	.50	.30
409	Bob Moose	1.00	.50	.30
410	Al Kaline	18.00	9.00	5.50
411	Larry Dierker	1.00	.50	.30
412	Checklist 426-512 (Mickey Mantle)	9.00	4.50	2.75
413	Roland Sheldon	1.00	.50	.30
414	Duke Sims	1.00	.50	.30
415	Ray Washburn	1.00	.50	.30
416	Willie McCovey (All-Star)	3.50	1.75	1.00
417	Ken Harrelson (All-Star)	1.00	.50	.30
418	Tommy Helms (All-Star)	1.00	.50	.30
419	Rod Carew (All-Star)	8.00	4.00	2.50
420	Ron Santo (All-Star)	1.50	.70	.45
421	Brooks Robinson (All-Star)	4.00	2.00	1.25
422	Don Kessinger (All-Star)	1.00	.50	.30
423	Bert Campaneris (All-Star)	1.00	.50	.30
424	Pete Rose (All-Star)	12.00	6.00	3.50
425	Carl Yastrzemski (All-Star)	8.00	4.00	2.50
426	Curt Flood (All-Star)	1.00	.50	.30
427	Tony Oliva (All-Star)	1.50	.70	.45
428	Lou Brock (All-Star)	5.00	2.50	1.50
429	Willie Horton (All-Star)	1.00	.50	.30
430	Johnny Bench (All-Star)	12.00	6.00	3.50
431	Bill Freehan (All-Star)	1.00	.50	.30
432	Bob Gibson (All-Star)	5.00	2.50	1.50
433	Denny McLain (All-Star)	1.50	.70	.45
434	Jerry Koosman (All-Star)	1.00	.50	.30
435	Sam McDowell (All-Star)	1.00	.50	.30
436	Gene Alley	1.00	.50	.30
437	Luis Alcaraz	1.00	.50	.30
438	Gary Waslewski	1.00	.50	.30
439	White Sox Rookies (Ed Herrmann, Dan Lazar)	1.00	.50	.30
440a	Willie McCovey (last name in white)	90.00	45.00	27.00
440b	Willie McCovey (last name in yellow)	18.00	9.00	5.50
441a	Dennis Higgins (last name in white)	10.00	5.00	3.00
441b	Dennis Higgins (last name in yellow)	1.00	.50	.30
442	Ty Cline	1.00	.50	.30
443	Don Wert	1.00	.50	.30
444a	Joe Moeller (last name in white)	10.00	5.00	3.00
444b	Joe Moeller (last name in yellow)	1.00	.50	.30
445	Bobby Knoop	1.00	.50	.30
446	Claude Raymond	1.00	.50	.30
447a	Ralph Houk (last name in white)	12.00	6.00	3.50
447b	Ralph Houk (last name in yellow)	1.50	.70	.45
448	Bob Tolan	1.00	.50	.30
449	Paul Lindblad	1.00	.50	.30
450	Billy Williams	6.00	3.00	1.75
451a	Rich Rollins (first name in white)	10.00	5.00	3.00
451b	Rich Rollins (first name in yellow)	1.25	.60	.40
452a	Al Ferrara (first name in white)	10.00	5.00	3.00

		NR MT	EX	VG
452b	Al Ferrara (first name in yellow)	1.00	.50	.30
453	Mike Cuellar	1.00	.50	.30
454a	Phillies Rookies (Larry Colton, *Don Money*) (names in white)	10.00	5.00	3.00
454b	Phillies Rookies (Larry Colton, *Don Money*) (names in yellow)	1.25	.60	.40
455	Sonny Siebert	1.00	.50	.30
456	Bud Harrelson	1.00	.50	.30
457	Dalton Jones	1.00	.50	.30
458	Curt Blefary	1.00	.50	.30
459	Dave Boswell	1.00	.50	.30
460	Joe Torre	1.00	.50	.30
461a	Mike Epstein (last name in white)	10.00	5.00	3.00
461b	Mike Epstein (last name in yellow)	1.00	.50	.30
462	Red Schoendienst	3.00	1.50	.90
463	Dennis Ribant	1.00	.50	.30
464a	Dave Marshall (last name in white)	10.00	5.00	3.00
464b	Dave Marshall (last name in yellow)	1.00	.50	.30
465	Tommy John	4.00	2.00	1.25
466	John Boccabella	1.00	.50	.30
467	Tom Reynolds	1.00	.50	.30
468a	Pirates Rookies (Bruce Dal Canton, Bob Robertson) (names in white)	10.00	5.00	3.00
468b	Pirates Rookies (Bruce Dal Canton, Bob Robertson) (names in yellow)	1.00	.50	.30
469	Chico Ruiz	1.00	.50	.30
470a	Mel Stottlemyre (last name in white)	12.00	6.00	3.50
470b	Mel Stottlemyre (last name in yellow)	1.50	.70	.45
471a	Ted Savage (last name in white)	10.00	5.00	3.00
471b	Ted Savage (last name in yellow)	1.00	.50	.30
472	Jim Price	1.00	.50	.30
473a	Jose Arcia (first name in white)	10.00	5.00	3.00
473b	Jose Arcia (first name in yellow)	1.00	.50	.30
474	Tom Murphy	1.00	.50	.30
475	Tim McCarver	1.50	.70	.45
476a	Red Sox Rookies *(Ken Brett,* Gerry Moses) (names in white)	10.00	5.00	3.00
476b	Red Sox Rookies *(Ken Brett,* Gerry Moses) (names in yellow)	1.00	.50	.30
477	Jeff James	1.00	.50	.30
478	Don Buford	1.00	.50	.30
479	Richie Scheinblum	1.00	.50	.30
480	Tom Seaver	100.00	50.00	30.00
481	*Bill Melton*	1.25	.60	.40
482a	Jim Gosger (first name in white)	10.00	5.00	3.00
482b	Jim Gosger (first name in yellow)	1.25	.60	.40
483	Ted Abernathy	1.00	.50	.30
484	Joe Gordon	1.00	.50	.30
485a	Gaylord Perry (last name in white)	75.00	37.00	22.00
485b	Gaylord Perry (last name in yellow)	10.00	5.00	3.00
486a	Paul Casanova (last name in white)	10.00	5.00	3.00
486b	Paul Casanova (last name in yellow)	1.00	.50	.30
487	Denis Menke	1.00	.50	.30
488	Joe Sparma	1.00	.50	.30
489	Clete Boyer	1.00	.50	.30
490	Matty Alou	1.00	.50	.30
491a	Twins Rookies (Jerry Crider, George Mitterwald) (names in white)	10.00	5.00	3.00
491b	Twins Rookies (Jerry Crider, George Mitterwald) (names in yellow)	1.00	.50	.30
492	Tony Cloninger	1.00	.50	.30
493a	Wes Parker (last name in white)	10.00	5.00	3.00
493b	Wes Parker (last name in yellow)	1.00	.50	.30
494	Ken Berry	1.00	.50	.30
495	Bert Campaneris	1.00	.50	.30
496	Larry Jaster	1.00	.50	.30
497	Julian Javier	1.00	.50	.30
498	Juan Pizarro	1.00	.50	.30
499	Astros Rookies (Don Bryant, Steve Shea)	1.00	.50	.30
500a	Mickey Mantle (last name in white)	500.00	250.00	150.00
500b	Mickey Mantle (last name in yellow)	250.00	125.00	75.00
501a	Tony Gonzalez (first name in white)	10.00	5.00	3.00
501b	Tony Gonzalez (first name in yellow)	1.00	.50	.30
502	Minnie Rojas	1.00	.50	.30
503	Larry Brown	1.00	.50	.30
504	Checklist 513-588 (Brooks Robinson)	4.00	2.00	1.25

		NR MT	EX	VG
505a	Bobby Bolin (last name in white)	10.00	5.00	3.00
505b	Bobby Bolin (last name in yellow)	1.00	.50	.30
506	Paul Blair	1.00	.50	.30
507	Cookie Rojas	1.00	.50	.30
508	Moe Drabowsky	1.00	.50	.30
509	Manny Sanguillen	1.00	.50	.30
510	Rod Carew	60.00	30.00	18.00
511a	Diego Segui (first name in white)	10.00	5.00	3.00
511b	Diego Segui (first name in yellow)	1.00	.50	.30
512	Cleon Jones	1.00	.50	.30
513	Camilo Pascual	1.00	.50	.30
514	Mike Lum	1.00	.50	.30
515	Dick Green	1.00	.50	.30
516	Earl Weaver	5.00	2.50	1.50
517	Mike McCormick	1.00	.50	.30
518	Fred Whitfield	1.00	.50	.30
519	Yankees Rookies (Len Boehmer, Gerry Kenney)	1.00	.50	.30
520	Bob Veale	1.00	.50	.30
521	George Thomas	1.00	.50	.30
522	Joe Hoerner	1.00	.50	.30
523	Bob Chance	1.00	.50	.30
524	Expos Rookies (Jose Laboy, Floyd Wicker)	1.00	.50	.30
525	Earl Wilson	1.00	.50	.30
526	Hector Torres	1.00	.50	.30
527	Al Lopez	3.00	1.50	.90
528	Claude Osteen	1.00	.50	.30
529	Ed Kirkpatrick	1.00	.50	.30
530	Cesar Tovar	1.00	.50	.30
531	Dick Farrell	1.00	.50	.30
532	Bird Hill Aces (Mike Cuellar, Jim Hardin, Dave McNally, Tom Phoebus)	1.50	.70	.45
533	Nolan Ryan	550.00	275.00	165.00
534	Jerry McNertney	1.00	.50	.30
535	Phil Regan	1.00	.50	.30
536	Padres Rookies (Danny Breeden, *Dave Roberts*)	1.25	.60	.40
537	Mike Paul	1.00	.50	.30
538	Charlie Smith	1.00	.50	.30
539	Ted Shows How (Mike Epstein, Ted Williams)	3.25	1.75	1.00
540	Curt Flood	1.50	.70	.45
541	Joe Verbanic	1.00	.50	.30
542	Bob Aspromonte	1.00	.50	.30
543	Fred Newman	1.00	.50	.30
544	Tigers Rookies (Mike Kilkenny, Ron Woods)	1.00	.50	.30
545	Willie Stargell	10.00	5.00	3.00
546	Jim Nash	1.00	.50	.30
547	Billy Martin	5.00	2.50	1.50
548	Bob Locker	1.00	.50	.30
549	Ron Brand	1.00	.50	.30
550	Brooks Robinson	15.00	7.50	4.50
551	Wayne Granger	1.00	.50	.30
552	Dodgers Rookies *(Ted Sizemore, Bill Sudakis)*	1.25	.60	.40
553	Ron Davis	1.00	.50	.30
554	Frank Bertaina	1.00	.50	.30
555	Jim Hart	1.00	.50	.30
556	A's Stars (Sal Bando, Bert Campaneris, Danny Cater)	1.50	.70	.45
557	Frank Fernandez	1.00	.50	.30
558	*Tom Burgmeier*	1.00	.50	.30
559	Cards Rookies (Joe Hague, Jim Hicks)	1.00	.50	.30
560	Luis Tiant	1.50	.70	.45
561	Ron Clark	1.00	.50	.30
562	*Bob Watson*	1.00	.50	.30
563	Marty Pattin	1.00	.50	.30
564	Gil Hodges	6.00	3.00	1.75
565	Hoyt Wilhelm	7.00	3.50	2.00
566	Ron Hansen	1.00	.50	.30
567	Pirates Rookies (Elvio Jimenez, Jim Shellenback)	1.00	.50	.30
568	Cecil Upshaw	1.00	.50	.30
569	Billy Harris	1.00	.50	.30
570	Ron Santo	1.50	.70	.45
571	Cap Peterson	1.00	.50	.30
572	Giants Heroes (Juan Marichal, Willie McCovey)	7.00	3.50	2.00
573	Jim Palmer	40.00	20.00	12.00
574	George Scott	1.00	.50	.30
575	Bill Singer	1.00	.50	.30
576	Phillies Rookies (Ron Stone, Bill Wilson)	1.00	.50	.30
577	Mike Hegan	1.00	.50	.30
578	Don Bosch	1.00	.50	.30
579	*Dave Nelson*	1.00	.50	.30
580	Jim Northrup	1.00	.50	.30
581	Gary Nolan	1.00	.50	.30

		NR MT	EX	VG
582a	Checklist 589-664 (Tony Oliva) (red circle on back)	3.50	1.75	1.00
582b	Checklist 589-664 (Tony Oliva) (white circle on back)	2.50	1.25	.70
583	*Clyde Wright*	1.00	.50	.30
584	Don Mason	1.00	.50	.30
585	Ron Swoboda	1.00	.50	.30
586	Tim Cullen	1.00	.50	.30
587	*Joe Rudi*	1.75	.90	.50
588	Bill White	1.50	.70	.45
589	Joe Pepitone	1.00	.50	.30
590	Rico Carty	1.00	.50	.30
591	Mike Hedlund	1.00	.50	.30
592	Padres Rookies (Rafael Robles, Al Santorini)	1.00	.50	.30
593	Don Nottebart	1.00	.50	.30
594	Dooley Womack	1.00	.50	.30
595	Lee Maye	1.00	.50	.30
596	Chuck Hartenstein	1.00	.50	.30
597	A.L. Rookies (Larry Burchart, *Rollie Fingers,* Bob Floyd)	125.00	62.00	37.00
598	Ruben Amaro	1.00	.50	.30
599	John Boozer	1.00	.50	.30
600	Tony Oliva	4.00	2.00	1.25
601	Tug McGraw	1.00	.50	.30
602	Cubs Rookies (Alec Distaso, Jim Qualls, Don Young)	1.00	.50	.30
603	Joe Keough	1.00	.50	.30
604	Bobby Etheridge	1.00	.50	.30
605	Dick Ellsworth	1.00	.50	.30
606	Gene Mauch	1.00	.50	.30
607	Dick Bosman	1.00	.50	.30
608	Dick Simpson	1.00	.50	.30
609	Phil Gagliano	1.00	.50	.30
610	Jim Hardin	1.00	.50	.30
611	Braves Rookies (Bob Didier, Walt Hriniak, Gary Neibauer)	1.00	.50	.30
612	Jack Aker	1.00	.50	.30
613	Jim Beauchamp	1.00	.50	.30
614	Astros Rookies (Tom Griffin, Skip Guinn)	1.00	.50	.30
615	Len Gabrielson	1.00	.50	.30
616	Don McMahon	1.00	.50	.30
617	Jesse Gonder	1.00	.50	.30
618	Ramon Webster	1.00	.50	.30
619	Royals Rookies (Bill Butler, *Pat Kelly,* Juan Rios)	1.00	.50	.30
620	Dean Chance	1.00	.50	.30
621	Bill Voss	1.00	.50	.30
622	Dan Osinski	1.00	.50	.30
623	Hank Allen	1.00	.50	.30
624	N.L. Rookies (Darrel Chaney, Duffy Dyer, Terry Harmon)	1.00	.50	.30
625	Mack Jones	1.00	.50	.30
626	Gene Michael	1.00	.50	.30
627	George Stone	1.00	.50	.30
628	Red Sox Rookies *(Bill Conigliaro,* Syd O'Brien, Fred Wenz)	1.00	.50	.30
629	Jack Hamilton	1.00	.50	.30
630	*Bobby Bonds*	30.00	15.00	9.00
631	John Kennedy	1.00	.50	.30
632	Jon Warden	1.00	.50	.30
633	Harry Walker	1.00	.50	.30
634	Andy Etchebarren	1.00	.50	.30
635	George Culver	1.00	.50	.30
636	Woodie Held	1.00	.50	.30
637	Padres Rookies (Jerry DaVanon, *Clay Kirby,* Frank Reberger)	1.00	.50	.30
638	Ed Sprague	1.00	.50	.30
639	Barry Moore	1.00	.50	.30
640	Fergie Jenkins	20.00	10.00	6.00
641	N.L. Rookies (Bobby Darwin, Tommy Dean, John Miller)	1.00	.50	.30
642	John Hiller	1.00	.50	.30
643	Billy Cowan	1.00	.50	.30
644	Chuck Hinton	1.00	.50	.30
645	George Brunet	1.00	.50	.30
646	Expos Rookies (Dan McGinn, *Carl Morton*)	1.00	.50	.30
647	Dave Wickersham	1.00	.50	.30
648	Bobby Wine	1.00	.50	.30
649	Al Jackson	1.00	.50	.30
650	Ted Williams	12.00	6.00	3.50
651	Gus Gil	1.00	.50	.30
652	Eddie Watt	1.00	.50	.30
653	*Aurelio Rodriguez* (photo actually batboy Leonard Garcia)	1.50	.70	.45
654	White Sox Rookies *(Carlos May,* Rich Morales, Don Secrist)	1.00	.50	.30
655	Mike Hershberger	1.00	.50	.30
656	Dan Schneider	1.00	.50	.30
657	Bobby Murcer	1.50	.70	.45
658	A.L. Rookies (Bill Burbach, Tom Hall, Jim Miles)	1.00	.50	.30
659	Johnny Podres	1.50	.70	.45
660	Reggie Smith	1.50	.70	.45
661	Jim Merritt	1.00	.50	.30
662	Royals Rookies (Dick Drago, Bob Oliver, George Spriggs)	1.00	.50	.30
663	Dick Radatz	1.00	.50	.30
664	Ron Hunt	3.00	1.50	.90

1969 Topps Decals

Designed as an insert for 1969 regular issue card packs, these decals are virtually identical in format to the '69 cards. The 48 decals in the set measure 1" by 2-1/2," although they are mounted on white paper backing which measures 1-3/4" by 2-1/8."

		NR MT	EX	VG
Complete Set:		650.00	325.00	195.00
Common Player:		5.00	2.50	1.50
(1)	Hank Aaron	50.00	25.00	15.00
(2)	Richie Allen	9.00	4.50	2.75
(3)	Felipe Alou	9.00	4.50	2.75
(4)	Matty Alou	5.00	2.50	1.50
(5)	Luis Aparicio	12.00	6.00	3.50
(6)	Bob Clemente	50.00	25.00	15.00
(7)	Donn Clendenon	5.00	2.50	1.50
(8)	Tommy Davis	5.00	2.50	1.50
(9)	Don Drysdale	12.00	6.00	3.50
(10)	Joe Foy	5.00	2.50	1.50
(11)	Jim Fregosi	5.00	2.50	1.50
(12)	Bob Gibson	12.00	6.00	3.50
(13)	Tony Gonzalez	5.00	2.50	1.50
(14)	Tom Haller	5.00	2.50	1.50
(15)	Ken Harrelson	5.00	2.50	1.50
(16)	Tommy Helms	5.00	2.50	1.50
(17)	Willie Horton	5.00	2.50	1.50
(18)	Frank Howard	6.00	3.00	1.75
(19)	Reggie Jackson	125.00	62.00	37.00
(20)	Fergie Jenkins	12.00	6.00	3.50
(21)	Harmon Killebrew	12.00	6.00	3.50
(22)	Jerry Koosman	5.00	2.50	1.50
(23)	Mickey Mantle	95.00	47.00	28.00
(24)	Willie Mays	50.00	25.00	15.00
(25)	Tim McCarver	7.50	3.75	2.25
(26)	Willie McCovey	12.00	6.00	3.50
(27)	Sam McDowell	5.00	2.50	1.50
(28)	Denny McLain	6.00	3.00	1.75
(29)	Dave McNally	5.00	2.50	1.50
(30)	Don Mincher	5.00	2.50	1.50
(31)	Rick Monday	5.00	2.50	1.50
(32)	Tony Oliva	6.00	3.00	1.75
(33)	Camilo Pascual	5.00	2.50	1.50
(34)	Rick Reichardt	5.00	2.50	1.50
(35)	Frank Robinson	12.00	6.00	3.50
(36)	Pete Rose	30.00	15.00	9.00
(37)	Ron Santo	6.00	3.00	1.75
(38)	Tom Seaver	50.00	25.00	15.00
(39)	Dick Selma	5.00	2.50	1.50
(40)	Chris Short	5.00	2.50	1.50
(41)	Rusty Staub	6.00	3.00	1.75
(42)	Mel Stottlemyre	5.00	2.50	1.50
(43)	Luis Tiant	6.00	3.00	1.75
(44)	Pete Ward	5.00	2.50	1.50
(45)	Hoyt Wilhelm	10.00	5.00	3.00

		NR MT	EX	VG
(46)	Maury Wills	6.00	3.00	1.75
(47)	Jim Wynn	5.00	2.50	1.50
(48)	Carl Yastrzemski	20.00	10.00	6.00

1969 Topps Deckle Edge

These 2-1/4" by 3-1/4" inch cards take their name from their interesting borders which have a scalloped effect. The fronts have a black and white picture of the player along with a blue facsimile autograph. Backs have the player's name and the card number in light blue ink in a small box at the bottom of the card. Technically, there are only 33 numbered cards, but there are actually 35 possible players; both Jim Wynn and Hoyt Wilhelm cards are found as #11 while cards of Joe Foy and Rusty Staub can be found as #22. Many of the players in the set are stars.

		NR MT	EX	VG
Complete Set:		160.00	80.00	48.00
Common Player:		1.50	.70	.45
1	Brooks Robinson	15.00	7.50	4.50
2	Boog Powell	2.50	1.25	.70
3	Ken Harrelson	1.50	.70	.45
4	Carl Yastrzemski	15.00	7.50	4.50
5	Jim Fregosi	1.50	.70	.45
6	Luis Aparicio	5.00	2.50	1.50
7	Luis Tiant	2.00	1.00	.60
8	Denny McLain	2.50	1.25	.70
9	Willie Horton	1.50	.70	.45
10	Bill Freehan	1.50	.70	.45
11a	Hoyt Wilhelm	10.00	5.00	3.00
11b	Jim Wynn	10.00	5.00	3.00
12	Rod Carew	15.00	7.50	4.50
13	Mel Stottlemyre	1.50	.70	.45
14	Rick Monday	1.50	.70	.45
15	Tommy Davis	1.50	.70	.45
16	Frank Howard	2.00	1.00	.60
17	Felipe Alou	2.50	1.25	.70
18	Don Kessinger	1.50	.70	.45
19	Ron Santo	2.50	1.25	.70
20	Tommy Helms	1.50	.70	.45
21	Pete Rose	10.00	5.00	3.00
22a	Rusty Staub	2.25	1.25	.70
22b	Joe Foy	7.00	3.50	2.00
23	Tom Haller	1.50	.70	.45
24	Maury Wills	2.00	1.00	.60
25	Jerry Koosman	1.50	.70	.45
26	Richie Allen	2.00	1.00	.60
27	Roberto Clemente	25.00	12.50	7.50
28	Curt Flood	1.50	.70	.45
29	Bob Gibson	10.00	5.00	3.00
30	Al Ferrara	1.50	.70	.45
31	Willie McCovey	10.00	5.00	3.00
32	Juan Marichal	7.00	3.50	2.00
33	Willie Mays, Willie Mays	15.00	7.50	4.50

1969 Topps 4-On-1 Mini Stickers

Another in the long line of Topps test issues, the 4-on-1s are 2-1/2" by 3-1/2" cards with blank backs featuring a quartet of miniature stickers in the design of the same cards from the 1969 Topps regular set.

There are 25 different cards, for a total of 100 different stickers. As they are not common, Mint cards bring fairly strong prices on today's market. As the set was drawn from the 3rd Series of the regular cards, it includes some rookie stickers and World Series highlight stickers.

		NR MT	EX	VG
Complete Set:		950.00	475.00	285.00
Common Player:		15.00	7.50	4.50
(1)	Jerry Adair, Willie Mays, Johnny Morris, Don Wilson	100.00	50.00	30.00
(2)	Tommie Aaron, Jim Britton, Donn Clendenon, Woody Woodward	15.00	7.50	4.50
(3)	World Series Game 4, Tommy Davis, Don Pavletich, Vada Pinson	20.00	10.00	6.00
(4)	Max Alvis, Glenn Beckert, Ron Fairly, Rick Wise	15.00	7.50	4.50
(5)	Johnny Callison, Jim French, Lum Harris, Dick Selma	15.00	7.50	4.50
(6)	World Series Game 3, Bob Gibson, Larry Haney, Rick Reichardt	40.00	20.00	12.00
(7)	Houston Rookie Stars, Wally Bunker, Don Cardwell, Joe Gibbon	15.00	7.50	4.50
(8)	Ollie Brown, Jim Bunning, Andy Kosco, Ron Reed	20.00	10.00	6.00
(9)	Bill Dillman, Jim Lefebvre, John Purdin, John Roseboro	15.00	7.50	4.50
(10)	Bill Hands, Chuck Harrison, Lindy McDaniel, Felix Millan	15.00	7.50	4.50
(11)	Jack Hiatt, Dave Johnson, Mel Nelson, Tommie Sisk	18.00	9.00	5.50
(12)	Clay Dalrymple, Leo Durocher, John Odom, Wilbur Wood	18.00	9.00	5.50
(13)	Hank Bauer, Kevin Collins, Ray Oyler, Russ Snyder	15.00	7.50	4.50
(14)	Red Sox Rookie Stars, World Series Game 7, Gerry Arrigo, Jim Perry	18.00	9.00	5.50
(15)	World Series Game 2, Bill McCool, Roberto Pena, Doug Rader	15.00	7.50	4.50
(16)	Ed Brinkman, Roy Face, Willie Horton, Bob Rodgers	18.00	9.00	5.50
(17)	Dave Baldwin, J.C. Martin, Dave May, Ray Sadecki	15.00	7.50	4.50
(18)	World Series Game 1, Jose Pagan, Tom Phoebus, Mike Shannon	15.00	7.50	4.50
(19)	Pete Rose, Lee Stange, Don Sutton, Ted Uhlaender	275.00	137.00	82.00
(20)	Joe Grzenda, Frank Howard, Dick Tracewski, Jim Weaver	20.00	10.00	6.00
(21)	White Sox Rookie Stars, Joe Azcue, Grant Jackson, Denny McLain	20.00	10.00	6.00
(22)	John Edwards, Jim Fairey, Phillies Rookies, Stan Williams	15.00	7.50	4.50
(23)	World Series Summary, John Bateman, Willie Smith, Leon Wagner	15.00	7.50	4.50
(24)	World Series Game 5, Yankees Rookies, Chris Cannizzaro, Bob Hendley	15.00	7.50	4.50
(25)	Cardinals Rookie Stars, Joe Nossek, Rico Petrocelli, Carl Yastrzemski	175.00	87.00	52.00

1969 Topps Stamps

Topps continued to refine its efforts at baseball stamps in 1969 with the release of 240 player stamps, each measuring 1" by 1-7/16." Each stamp has a color photo along with the player's name, position and team. Unlike prior stamp issues, the 1969 stamps have 24 separate albums (one per team). The stamps were issued in strips of 12.

	NR MT	EX	VG
Complete Sheet Set:	250.00	125.00	75.00
Common Sheet:	1.25	.60	.40
Complete Stamp Album Set:	14.00	7.00	4.25
Single Stamp Album:	.50	.25	.15

	NR MT	EX	VG
(1) Tommie Agee, Sandy Alomar, Jose Cardenal, Dean Chance, Joe Foy, Jim Grant, Don Kessinger, Mickey Mantle, Jerry May, Bob Rodgers, Cookie Rojas, Gary Sutherland	18.00	9.00	5.50
(2) Jesus Alou, Mike Andrews, Larry Brown, Moe Drabowsky, Alex Johnson, Lew Krausse, Jim Lefebvre, Dal Maxvill, John Odom, Claude Osteen, Rick Reichardt, Luis Tiant	1.50	.70	.45
(3) Hank Aaron, Matty Alou, Max Alvis, Nelson Briles, Eddie Fisher, Bud Harrelson, Willie Horton, Randy Hundley, Larry Jaster, Jim Kaat, Gary Peters, Pete Ward	7.00	3.50	2.00
(4) Don Buford, John Callison, Tommy Davis, Jackie Hernandez, Fergie Jenkins, Lee May, Denny McLain, Bob Oliver, Roberto Pena, Tony Perez, Joe Torre, Tom Tresh	3.00	1.50	.90
(5) Jim Bunning, Dean Chance, Joe Foy, Sonny Jackson, Don Kessinger, Rick Monday, Gaylord Perry, Roger Repoz, Cookie Rojas, Mel Stottlemyre, Leon Wagner, Jim Wynn	3.00	1.50	.90
(6) Felipe Alou, Gerry Arrigo, Bob Aspromonte, Gary Bell, Clay Dalrymple, Jim Fregosi, Tony Gonzalez, Duane Josephson, Dick McAuliffe, Tony Oliva, Brooks Robinson, Willie Stargell	6.00	3.00	1.75
(7) Steve Barber, Donn Clendenon, Joe Coleman, Vic Davalillo, Russ Gibson, Jerry Grote, Tom Haller, Andy Kosco, Willie McCovey, Don Mincher, Joe Morgan, Don Wilson	4.00	2.00	1.25
(8) George Brunet, Don Buford, John Callison, Danny Cater, Tommy Davis, Willie Davis, John Edwards, Jim Hart, Mickey Lolich, Willie Mays, Roberto Pena, Mickey Stanley	7.00	3.50	2.00
(9) Ernie Banks, Glenn Beckert, Ken Berry, Horace Clarke, Bob Clemente, Larry Dierker, Len Gabrielson, Jake Gibbs, Jerry Koosman, Sam McDowell, Tom Satriano, Bill Singer	3.50	1.75	1.00
(10) Gene Alley, Lou Brock, Larry Brown, Moe Drabowsky, Frank Howard, Tommie John, Roger Nelson, Claude Osteen, Phil Regan, Rick Reichardt, Tony Taylor, Roy White	4.00	2.00	1.25
(11) Bob Allison, John Bateman, Don Drysdale, Dave Johnson, Harmon Killebrew, Jim Maloney, Bill Mazeroski, Gerry McNertney, Ron Perranoski, Rico Petrocelli, Pete Rose, Billy Williams	18.00	9.00	5.50
(12) Bernie Allen, Jose Arcia, Stan Bahnsen, Sal Bando, Jim Davenport, Tito Francona, Dick Green, Ron Hunt, Mack Jones, Vada Pinson, George Scott, Don Wert	1.50	.70	.45
(13) Gerry Arrigo, Bob Aspromonte, Joe Azcue, Curt Blefary, Orlando Cepeda, Bill Freehan, Jim Fregosi, Dave Giusti, Duane Josephson, Tim McCarver, Jose Santiago, Bob Tolan	2.00	1.00	.60
(14) Jerry Adair, Johnny Bench, Clete Boyer, John Briggs, Bert Campaneris, Woody Fryman, Ron Kline, Bobby Knoop, Ken McMullen, Adolfo Phillips, John Roseboro, Tom Seaver	7.00	3.50	2.00
(15) Norm Cash, Ron Fairly, Bob Gibson, Bill Hands, Cleon Jones, Al Kaline, Paul Schaal, Mike Shannon, Duke Sims, Reggie Smith, Steve Whitaker, Carl Yastrzemski	12.00	6.00	3.50
(16) Steve Barber, Paul Casanova, Dick Dietz, Russ Gibson, Jerry Grote, Tom Haller, Ed Kranepool, Juan Marichal, Denis Menke, Jim Nash, Bill Robinson, Frank Robinson	4.00	2.00	1.25
(17) Bobby Bolin, Ollie Brown, Rod Carew, Mike Epstein, Bud Harrelson, Larry Jaster, Dave McNally, Willie Norton, Milt Pappas, Gary Peters, Paul Popovich, Stan Williams	6.00	3.00	1.75
(18) Ted Abernathy, Bob Allison, Ed Brinkman, Don Drysdale, Jim Hardin, Julian Javier, Hal Lanier, Jim McGlothlin, Ron Perranoski, Rich Rollins, Ron Santo, Billy Williams	3.00	1.50	.90
(19) Richie Allen, Luis Aparicio, Wally Bunker, Curt Flood, Ken Harrelson, Jim Hunter, Denver Lemaster, Felix Millan, Jim Northrop (Northrup), Art Shamsky, Larry Stahl, Ted Uhlaender	3.00	1.50	.90
(20) Bob Bailey, Johnny Bench, Woody Fryman, Jim Hannan, Ron Kline, Al McBean, Camilo Pascual, Joe Pepitone, Doug Rader, Ron Reed, John Roseboro, Sonny Siebert	3.00	1.50	.90
(21) Jack Aker, Tommy Harper, Tommy Helms, Dennis Higgins, Jim Hunter, Don Lock, Lee Maye, Felix Millan, Jim Northrop (Northrup), Larry Stahl, Don Sutton, Zoilo Versalles	3.00	1.50	.90
(22) Norm Cash, Ed Charles, Joe Horlen, Pat Jarvis, Jim Lonborg, Manny Mota, Boog Powell, Dick Selma, Mike Shannon, Duke Sims, Steve Whitaker, Hoyt Wilhelm	3.00	1.50	.90
(23) Bernie Allen, Ray Culp, Al Ferrara, Tito Francona, Dick Green, Ron Hunt, Ray Oyler, Tom Phoebus, Rusty Staub, Bob Veale, Maury Wills, Wilbur Wood	2.00	1.00	.60
(24) Ernie Banks, Mark Belanger, Steve Blass, Horace Clarke, Bob Clemente, Larry Dierker, Dave Duncan, Chico Salmon, Chris Short, Ron Swoboda, Cesar Tovar, Rick Wise	3.50	1.75	1.00

1969 Topps Super

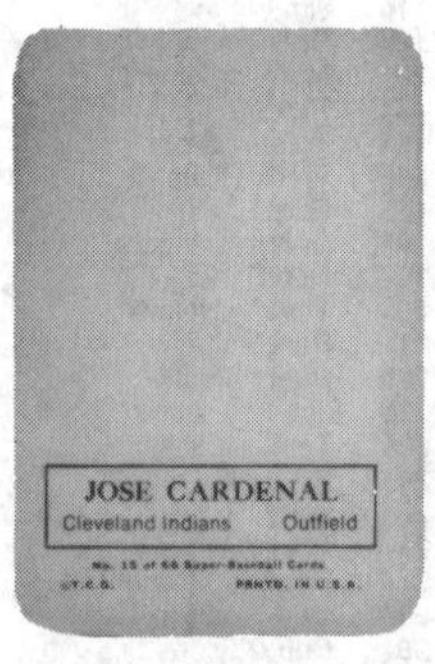

These 2-1/4" by 3-1/4" cards are not the bigger "Super" cards which would be seen in following years. Rather, what enabled Topps to dub them "Super Baseball Cards" is their high-gloss finish which enhances the bright color photograph used on their fronts. The only other design element on the front is a facsimile autograph. The backs contain a box at the the bottom which carries the player's name, team, position, a copyright line and the card number. Another unusual feature is that the cards have rounded corners. The 66-card set saw limited production, meaning supplies are tight today. Considering the quality of the cards and the fact that many big names are represented, it's easy to understand why the set is quite expensive and desirable.

		NR MT	EX	VG
Complete Set:		6500.00	3250.00	1950.
Common Player:		25.00	12.50	7.50
1	Dave McNally	25.00	12.50	7.50
2	Frank Robinson	350.00	175.00	105.00
3	Brooks Robinson	350.00	175.00	105.00
4	Ken Harrelson	25.00	12.50	7.50
5	Carl Yastrzemski	600.00	300.00	180.00
6	Ray Culp	25.00	12.50	7.50
7	James Fregosi	25.00	12.50	7.50
8	Rick Reichardt	25.00	12.50	7.50
9	Vic Davalillo	25.00	12.50	7.50
10	Luis Aparicio	100.00	50.00	30.00
11	Pete Ward	25.00	12.50	7.50
12	Joe Horlen	25.00	12.50	7.50
13	Luis Tiant	30.00	15.00	9.00
14	Sam McDowell	25.00	12.50	7.50
15	Jose Cardenal	25.00	12.50	7.50
16	Willie Horton	25.00	12.50	7.50
17	Denny McLain	30.00	15.00	9.00
18	Bill Freehan	25.00	12.50	7.50
19	Harmon Killebrew	275.00	137.00	82.00
20	Tony Oliva	30.00	15.00	9.00
21	Dean Chance	25.00	12.50	7.50
22	Joe Foy	25.00	12.50	7.50
23	Roger Nelson	25.00	12.50	7.50
24	Mickey Mantle	1250.00	625.00	375.00
25	Mel Stottlemyre	25.00	12.50	7.50
26	Roy White	25.00	12.50	7.50
27	Rick Monday	25.00	12.50	7.50
28	Reggie Jackson	750.00	375.00	225.00
29	Bert Campaneris	25.00	12.50	7.50
30	Frank Howard	30.00	15.00	9.00
31	Camilo Pascual	25.00	12.50	7.50
32	Tommy Davis	25.00	12.50	7.50
33	Don Mincher	25.00	12.50	7.50
34	Henry Aaron	600.00	300.00	180.00
35	Felipe Alou	45.00	22.00	13.50
36	Joe Torre	25.00	12.50	7.50
37	Fergie Jenkins	100.00	50.00	30.00
38	Ronald Santo	25.00	12.50	7.50
39	Billy Williams	100.00	50.00	30.00
40	Tommy Helms	25.00	12.50	7.50
41	Pete Rose	500.00	250.00	150.00
42	Joe Morgan	150.00	75.00	45.00
43	Jim Wynn	25.00	12.50	7.50
44	Curt Blefary	25.00	12.50	7.50
45	Willie Davis	25.00	12.50	7.50
46	Don Drysdale	250.00	125.00	75.00
47	Tom Haller	25.00	12.50	7.50
48	Rusty Staub	25.00	12.50	7.50
49	Maurice Wills	25.00	12.50	7.50
50	Cleon Jones	25.00	12.50	7.50
51	Jerry Koosman	25.00	12.50	7.50
52	Tom Seaver	700.00	350.00	210.00
53	Rich Allen	40.00	20.00	12.00
54	Chris Short	25.00	12.50	7.50
55	Cookie Rojas	25.00	12.50	7.50
56	Mateo Alou	25.00	12.50	7.50
57	Steve Blass	25.00	12.50	7.50
58	Roberto Clemente	600.00	300.00	180.00
59	Curt Flood	25.00	12.50	7.50
60	Bob Gibson	150.00	75.00	45.00
61	Tim McCarver	40.00	20.00	12.00
62	Dick Selma	25.00	12.50	7.50
63	Ollie Brown	25.00	12.50	7.50
64	Juan Marichal	150.00	75.00	45.00
65	Willie Mays	600.00	300.00	180.00
66	Willie McCovey	150.00	75.00	45.00

1969 Topps Team Posters

Picking up where the 1968 posters left off, the 1969 poster is larger at about 12" by 20." The posters, 24 in number like the previous year, are very different in style. Each has a team focus with a large pennant carrying the team name, along with nine or ten photos of players. Each of the photos carries a name and a facsimile autograph. Unfortunately, the bigger size of 1969 posters meant they had to be folded to fit in their packages as was the case in 1968. That means that collectors today will have a tough job finding them without fairly heavy creases from the folding.

		NR MT	EX	VG
Complete Set:		900.00	450.00	270.00
Common Poster:		20.00	10.00	6.00
1	Detroit Tigers (Norm Cash, Bill Freehan, Willie Horton, Al Kaline, Mickey Lolich, Dick McAuliffe, Denny McLain, Jim Northrup, Mickey Stanley, Don Wert, Earl Wilson)	40.00	20.00	12.00
2	Atlanta Braves (Hank Aaron, Felipe Alou, Clete Boyer, Rico Carty, Tito Francona, Sonny Jackson, Pat Jarvis, Felix Millan, Phil Niekro, Milt Pappas, Joe Torre)	40.00	20.00	12.00
3	Boston Red Sox (Mike Andrews, Tony Conigliaro, Ray Culp, Russ Gibson, Ken Harrelson, Jim Lonborg, Rico Petrocelli, Jose Santiago, George Scott, Reggie Smith, Carl Yastrzemski)	60.00	30.00	18.00
4	Chicago Cubs (Ernie Banks, Glenn Beckert, Bill Hands, Jim Hickman, Ken Holtzman, Randy Hundley, Fergie Jenkins, Don Kessinger, Adolfo Phillips, Ron Santo, Billy Williams)	40.00	20.00	12.00
5	Baltimore Orioles (Mark Belanger, Paul Blair, Don Buford, Andy Etchebarren, Jim Hardin, Dave Johnson, Dave McNally, Tom Phoebus, Boog Powell, Brooks Robinson, Frank Robinson)	40.00	20.00	12.00
6	Houston Astros (Curt Blefary, Donn Clendenon, Larry Dierker, John Edwards, Denny Lemaster, Denis Menke, Norm Miller, Joe Morgan, Doug Rader, Don Wilson, Jim Wynn)	20.00	10.00	6.00
7	Kansas City Royals (Jerry Adair, Wally Bunker, Mike Fiore, Joe Foy, Jackie Hernandez, Pat Kelly, Dave Morehead, Roger Nelson, Dave Nicholson, Eliseo Rodriguez, Steve Whitaker)	20.00	10.00	6.00
8	Philadelphia Phillies (Richie Allen, Johnny Callison, Woody Fryman, Larry Hisle, Don Money, Cookie Rojas, Mike Ryan, Chris Short, Tony Taylor, Bill White, Rick Wise)	20.00	10.00	6.00
9	Seattle Pilots (Jack Aker, Steve Barber, Gary Bell, Tommy Davis, Jim Gosger, Tommy Harper, Gerry McNertney, Don Mincher, Ray Oyler, Rich Rollins, Chico Salmon)	45.00	22.00	13.50
10	Montreal Expos (Bob Bailey, John Bateman, Jack Billingham, Jim Grant, Larry Jaster, Mack Jones, Manny Mota, Rusty Staub, Gary Sutherland, Jim Williams, Maury Wills)	20.00	10.00	6.00
11	Chicago White Sox (Sandy Alomar, Luis Aparicio, Ken Berry, Buddy Bradford, Joe Horlen, Tommy John, Duane Josephson, Tom McCraw, Bill Melton, Pete Ward, Wilbur Wood)	25.00	12.50	7.50
12	San Diego Padres (Jose Arcia, Danny Breeden, Ollie Brown, Bill Davis, Ron Davis, Tony Gonzalez, Dick Kelley, Al McBean, Roberto Pena, Dick Selma, Ed Spiezio)	20.00	10.00	6.00
13	Cleveland Indians (Max Alvis, Joe Azcue, Jose Cardenal, Vern Fuller, Lou Johnson, Sam McDowell, Sonny Siebert, Duke Sims, Russ Snyder, Luis Tiant, Zoilo Versalles)	20.00	10.00	6.00
14	San Francisco Giants (Bobby Bolin, Jim Davenport, Dick Dietz, Jim Hart, Ron Hunt, Hal Lanier, Juan Marichal, Willie Mays, Willie McCovey, Gaylord Perry, Charlie Smith)	40.00	20.00	12.00
15	Minnesota Twins (Bob Allison, Chico Cardenas, Rod Carew, Dean Chance, Jim Kaat, Harmon Killebrew, Tony Oliva, Jim Perry, John Roseboro, Cesar Tovar, Ted Uhlaender)	40.00	20.00	12.00

		NR MT	EX	VG
16	Pittsburgh Pirates (Gene Alley, Matty Alou, Steve Blass, Jim Bunning, Bob Clemente, Rich Hebner, Jerry May, Bill Mazeroski, Bob Robertson, Willie Stargell, Bob Veale)	40.00	20.00	12.00
17	California Angels (Ruben Amaro, George Brunet, Bob Chance, Vic Davalillo, Jim Fregosi, Bobby Knoop, Jim McGlothlin, Rick Reichardt, Roger Repoz, Bob Rodgers, Hoyt Wilhelm)	20.00	10.00	6.00
18	St. Louis Cardinals (Nelson Briles, Lou Brock, Orlando Cepeda, Curt Flood, Bob Gibson, Julian Javier, Dal Maxvill, Tim McCarver, Vada Pinson, Mike Shannon, Ray Washburn)	35.00	17.50	10.50
19	New York Yankees (Stan Bahnsen, Horace Clarke, Bobby Cox, Jake Gibbs, Mickey Mantle, Joe Pepitone, Fritz Peterson, Bill Robinson, Mel Stottlemyre, Tom Tresh, Roy White)	90.00	45.00	27.00
20	Cincinnati Reds (Gerry Arrigo, Johnny Bench, Tommy Helms, Alex Johnson, Jim Maloney, Lee May, Gary Nolan, Tony Perez, Pete Rose, Bob Tolan, Woody Woodward)	60.00	30.00	18.00
21	Oakland Athletics (Sal Bando, Bert Campaneris, Danny Cater, Dick Green, Mike Hershberger, Jim Hunter, Reggie Jackson, Rick Monday, Jim Nash, John Odom, Jim Pagliaroni)	60.00	30.00	18.00
22	Los Angeles Dodgers (Willie Crawford, Willie Davis, Don Drysdale, Ron Fairly, Tom Haller, Andy Kosco, Jim Lefebvre, Claude Osteen, Paul Popovich, Bill Singer, Bill Sudakis)	35.00	17.50	10.50
23	Washington Senators (Bernie Allen, Brant Alyea, Ed Brinkman, Paul Casanova, Joe Coleman, Mike Epstein, Jim Hannan, Frank Howard, Ken McMullen, Camilo Pascual, Del Unser)	20.00	10.00	6.00
24	New York Mets (Tommie Agee, Ken Boswell, Ed Charles, Jerry Grote, Bud Harrelson, Cleon Jones, Jerry Koosman, Ed Kranepool, Jim McAndrew, Tom Seaver, Ron Swoboda)	100.00	50.00	30.00

1970 Topps

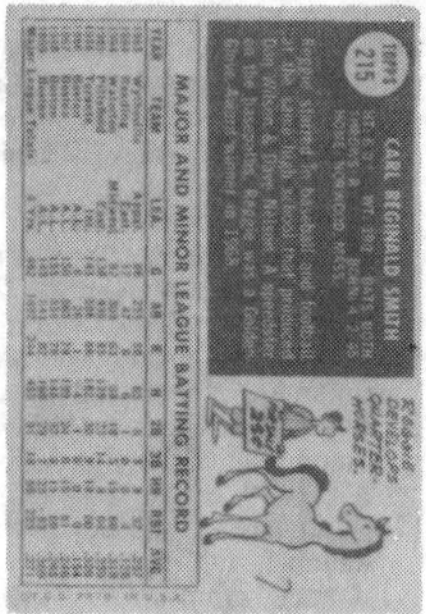

Topps established another set size record by coming out with 720 cards in 1970. The 2-1/2" by 3-1/2" cards have a color photo with a thin white frame. The photo have the player's team overprinted at the top, while the player's name in script and his position are at the bottom. A gray border surrounds the front. Card backs follows the normal design pattern, although they are more readable than some issues of the past. Team cards returned and were joined with many of the usual specialty cards. The World Series highlights were joined by cards with playoff highlights. Statistical leaders and All-Stars are also included in the set. High-numbered cards provide the most expensive cards in the set.

	NR MT	EX	VG
Complete Set (720):	2200.00	1100.00	660.00
Common Player: 1-546	.80	.40	.25
Common Player: 547-633	2.50	1.25	.70
Common Player: 634-720	5.00	2.50	1.50

		NR MT	EX	VG
1	World Champions (Mets Team)	12.00	6.00	3.50
2	Diego Segui	.80	.40	.25
3	Darrel Chaney	.80	.40	.25
4	Tom Egan	.80	.40	.25
5	Wes Parker	.80	.40	.25
6	Grant Jackson	.80	.40	.25
7	Indians Rookies (Gary Boyd, Russ Nagelson)	.80	.40	.25
8	Jose Martinez	.80	.40	.25
9	Checklist 1-132	3.50	1.75	1.00
10	Carl Yastrzemski	25.00	12.50	7.50
11	Nate Colbert	.80	.40	.25
12	John Hiller	.80	.40	.25
13	Jack Hiatt	.80	.40	.25
14	Hank Allen	.80	.40	.25
15	Larry Dierker	.80	.40	.25
16	Charlie Metro	.80	.40	.25
17	Hoyt Wilhelm	4.00	2.00	1.25
18	Carlos May	.80	.40	.25
19	John Boccabella	.80	.40	.25
20	Dave McNally	.80	.40	.25
21	Athletics Rookies *(Vida Blue, Gene Tenace)*	6.00	3.00	1.75
22	Ray Washburn	.80	.40	.25
23	Bill Robinson	.80	.40	.25
24	Dick Selma	.80	.40	.25
25	Cesar Tovar	.80	.40	.25
26	Tug McGraw	.80	.40	.25
27	Chuck Hinton	.80	.40	.25
28	Billy Wilson	.80	.40	.25
29	Sandy Alomar	.80	.40	.25
30	Matty Alou	.80	.40	.25
31	Marty Pattin	.80	.40	.25
32	Harry Walker	.80	.40	.25
33	Don Wert	.80	.40	.25
34	Willie Crawford	.80	.40	.25
35	Joe Horlen	.80	.40	.25
36	Reds Rookies (Danny Breeden, *Bernie Carbo)*	.80	.40	.25
37	Dick Drago	.80	.40	.25
38	Mack Jones	.80	.40	.25
39	Mike Nagy	.80	.40	.25
40	Rich Allen	2.00	1.00	.60
41	George Lauzerique	.80	.40	.25
42	Tito Fuentes	.80	.40	.25
43	Jack Aker	.80	.40	.25
44	Roberto Pena	.80	.40	.25
45	Dave Johnson	.80	.40	.25
46	Ken Rudolph	.80	.40	.25
47	Bob Miller	.80	.40	.25
48	Gill Garrido (Gil)	.80	.40	.25
49	Tim Cullen	.80	.40	.25
50	Tommie Agee	.80	.40	.25
51	Bob Christian	.80	.40	.25
52	Bruce Dal Canton	.80	.40	.25
53	John Kennedy	.80	.40	.25
54	Jeff Torborg	.80	.40	.25
55	John Odom	.80	.40	.25
56	Phillies Rookies (Joe Lis, Scott Reid)	.80	.40	.25
57	Pat Kelly	.80	.40	.25
58	Dave Marshall	.80	.40	.25
59	Dick Ellsworth	.80	.40	.25
60	Jim Wynn	.80	.40	.25
61	N.L. Batting Leaders (Roberto Clemente, Cleon Jones, Pete Rose)	5.00	2.50	1.50
62	A.L. Batting Leaders (Rod Carew, Tony Oliva, Reggie Smith)	3.50	1.75	1.00
63	N.L. RBI Leaders (Willie McCovey, Tony Perez, Ron Santo)	3.50	1.75	1.00
64	A.L. RBI Leaders (Reggie Jackson, Harmon Killebrew, Boog Powell)	5.00	2.50	1.50
65	N.L. Home Run Leaders (Hank Aaron, Lee May, Willie McCovey)	5.00	2.50	1.50
66	A.L. Home Run Leaders (Frank Howard, Reggie Jackson, Harmon Killebrew)	4.00	2.00	1.25
67	N.L. ERA Leaders (Steve Carlton, Bob Gibson, Juan Marichal)	4.00	2.00	1.25
68	A.L. ERA Leaders (Dick Bosman, Mike Cuellar, Jim Palmer)	3.50	1.75	1.00
69	N.L. Pitching Leaders (Fergie Jenkins, Juan Marichal, Phil Niekro, Tom Seaver)	4.00	2.00	1.25
70	A.L. Pitching Leaders (Dave Boswell, Mike Cuellar, Dennis McLain, Dave McNally, Jim Perry, Mel Stottlemyre)	3.50	1.75	1.00
71	N.L. Strikeout Leaders (Bob Gibson, Fergie Jenkins, Bill Singer)	4.00	2.00	1.25
72	A.L. Strikeout Leaders (Mickey Lolich, Sam McDowell, Andy Messersmith)	3.50	1.75	1.00

#	Card	NR MT	EX	VG
73	Wayne Granger	.80	.40	.25
74	Angels Rookies (Greg Washburn, Wally Wolf)	.80	.40	.25
75	Jim Kaat	3.00	1.50	.90
76	Carl Taylor	.80	.40	.25
77	Frank Linzy	.80	.40	.25
78	Joe Lahoud	.80	.40	.25
79	Clay Kirby	.80	.40	.25
80	Don Kessinger	.80	.40	.25
81	Dave May	.80	.40	.25
82	Frank Fernandez	.80	.40	.25
83	Don Cardwell	.80	.40	.25
84	Paul Casanova	.80	.40	.25
85	Max Alvis	.80	.40	.25
86	Lum Harris	.80	.40	.25
87	Steve Renko	.80	.40	.25
88	Pilots Rookies (Dick Baney, Miguel Fuentes)	.80	.40	.25
89	Juan Rios	.80	.40	.25
90	Tim McCarver	1.00	.50	.30
91	Rich Morales	.80	.40	.25
92	George Culver	.80	.40	.25
93	Rick Renick	.80	.40	.25
94	Fred Patek	.80	.40	.25
95	Earl Wilson	.80	.40	.25
96	Cards Rookies (Leron Lee, *Jerry Reuss*)	3.00	1.50	.90
97	Joe Moeller	.80	.40	.25
98	Gates Brown	.80	.40	.25
99	Bobby Pfeil	.80	.40	.25
100	Mel Stottlemyre	.80	.40	.25
101	Bobby Floyd	.80	.40	.25
102	Joe Rudi	.80	.40	.25
103	Frank Reberger	.80	.40	.25
104	Gerry Moses	.80	.40	.25
105	Tony Gonzalez	.80	.40	.25
106	Darold Knowles	.80	.40	.25
107	Bobby Etheridge	.80	.40	.25
108	Tom Burgmeier	.80	.40	.25
109	Expos Rookies (Garry Jestadt, Carl Morton)	.80	.40	.25
110	Bob Moose	.80	.40	.25
111	Mike Hegan	.80	.40	.25
112	Dave Nelson	.80	.40	.25
113	Jim Ray	.80	.40	.25
114	Gene Michael	.80	.40	.25
115	Alex Johnson	.80	.40	.25
116	Sparky Lyle	1.50	.70	.45
117	Don Young	.80	.40	.25
118	George Mitterwald	.80	.40	.25
119	Chuck Taylor	.80	.40	.25
120	Sal Bando	.80	.40	.25
121	Orioles Rookies (Fred Beene, *Terry Crowley*)	.80	.40	.25
122	George Stone	.80	.40	.25
123	Don Gutteridge	.80	.40	.25
124	Larry Jaster	.80	.40	.25
125	Deron Johnson	.80	.40	.25
126	Marty Martinez	.80	.40	.25
127	Joe Coleman	.80	.40	.25
128a	Checklist 133-263 (226 is R Perranoski)	3.00	1.50	.90
128b	Checklist 133-263 (226 is R. Perranoski)	3.50	1.75	1.00
129	Jimmie Price	.80	.40	.25
130	Ollie Brown	.80	.40	.25
131	Dodgers Rookies (Ray Lamb, Bob Stinson)	.80	.40	.25
132	Jim McGlothlin	.80	.40	.25
133	Clay Carroll	.80	.40	.25
134	Danny Walton	.80	.40	.25
135	Dick Dietz	.80	.40	.25
136	Steve Hargan	.80	.40	.25
137	Art Shamsky	.80	.40	.25
138	Joe Foy	.80	.40	.25
139	Rich Nye	.80	.40	.25
140	Reggie Jackson	200.00	100.00	60.00
141	Pirates Rookies (*Dave Cash*, Johnny Jeter)	.80	.40	.25
142	Fritz Peterson	.80	.40	.25
143	Phil Gagliano	.80	.40	.25
144	Ray Culp	.80	.40	.25
145	Rico Carty	.80	.40	.25
146	Danny Murphy	.80	.40	.25
147	Angel Hermoso	.80	.40	.25
148	Earl Weaver	1.75	.90	.50
149	Billy Champion	.80	.40	.25
150	Harmon Killebrew	8.00	4.00	2.50
151	Dave Roberts	.80	.40	.25
152	Ike Brown	.80	.40	.25
153	Gary Gentry	.80	.40	.25

#	Card	NR MT	EX	VG
154	Senators Rookies (Jan Dukes, Jim Miles)	.80	.40	.25
155	Denis Menke	.80	.40	.25
156	Eddie Fisher	.80	.40	.25
157	Manny Mota	.80	.40	.25
158	Jerry McNertney	.80	.40	.25
159	Tommy Helms	.80	.40	.25
160	Phil Niekro	3.50	1.75	1.00
161	Richie Scheinblum	.80	.40	.25
162	Jerry Johnson	.80	.40	.25
163	Syd O'Brien	.80	.40	.25
164	Ty Cline	.80	.40	.25
165	Ed Kirkpatrick	.80	.40	.25
166	Al Oliver	2.50	1.25	.70
167	Bill Burbach	.80	.40	.25
168	Dave Watkins	.80	.40	.25
169	Tom Hall	.80	.40	.25
170	Billy Williams	6.00	3.00	1.75
171	Jim Nash	.80	.40	.25
172	Braves Rookies (*Ralph Garr*, Garry Hill)	2.50	1.25	.70
173	Jim Hicks	.80	.40	.25
174	Ted Sizemore	.80	.40	.25
175	Dick Bosman	.80	.40	.25
176	Jim Hart	.80	.40	.25
177	Jim Northrup	.80	.40	.25
178	Denny Lemaster	.80	.40	.25
179	Ivan Murrell	.80	.40	.25
180	Tommy John	3.00	1.50	.90
181	Sparky Anderson	1.75	.90	.50
182	Dick Hall	.80	.40	.25
183	Jerry Grote	.80	.40	.25
184	Ray Fosse	.80	.40	.25
185	Don Mincher	.80	.40	.25
186	Rick Joseph	.80	.40	.25
187	Mike Hedlund	.80	.40	.25
188	Manny Sanguillen	.80	.40	.25
189	Yankees Rookies (Dave McDonald, *Thurman Munson*)	100.00	50.00	30.00
190	Joe Torre	.80	.40	.25
191	Vicente Romo	.80	.40	.25
192	Jim Qualls	.80	.40	.25
193	Mike Wegener	.80	.40	.25
194	Chuck Manuel	.80	.40	.25
195	N.L.C.S. Game 1 (Seaver Wins Opener')	10.00	5.00	3.00
196	N.L.C.S. Game 2 (Mets Show Muscle')	4.00	2.00	1.25
197	N.L.C.S. Game 3 (Ryan Saves the Day')	20.00	10.00	6.00
198	N.L. Playoffs Summary (We're Number One')	4.00	2.00	1.25
199	A.L.C.S. Game 1 (Orioles Win A Squeaker')	5.00	2.50	1.50
200	A.L.C.S. Game 2 (Powell Scores Winning Run')	5.00	2.50	1.50
201	A.L.C.S. Game 3 (Birds Wrap It Up')	5.00	2.50	1.50
202	A.L.C.S. Summary (Sweep Twins In Three')	5.00	2.50	1.50
203	Rudy May	.80	.40	.25
204	Len Gabrielson	.80	.40	.25
205	Bert Campaneris	.80	.40	.25
206	Clete Boyer	.80	.40	.25
207	Tigers Rookies (Norman McRae, Bob Reed)	.80	.40	.25
208	Fred Gladding	.80	.40	.25
209	Ken Suarez	.80	.40	.25
210	Juan Marichal	8.00	4.00	2.50
211	Ted Williams	10.00	5.00	3.00
212	Al Santorini	.80	.40	.25
213	Andy Etchebarren	.80	.40	.25
214	Ken Boswell	.80	.40	.25
215	Reggie Smith	1.00	.50	.30
216	Chuck Hartenstein	.80	.40	.25
217	Ron Hansen	.80	.40	.25
218	Ron Stone	.80	.40	.25
219	Jerry Kenney	.80	.40	.25
220	Steve Carlton	32.50	16.00	9.75
221	Ron Brand	.80	.40	.25
222	Jim Rooker	.80	.40	.25
223	Nate Oliver	.80	.40	.25
224	Steve Barber	.80	.40	.25
225	Lee May	.80	.40	.25
226	Ron Perranoski	.80	.40	.25
227	Astros Rookies (*John Mayberry*, Bob Watkins)	1.50	.70	.45
228	Aurelio Rodriguez	.80	.40	.25
229	Rich Robertson	.80	.40	.25
230	Brooks Robinson	12.00	6.00	3.50
231	Luis Tiant	1.25	.60	.40

		NR MT	EX	VG
232	Bob Didier	.80	.40	.25
233	Lew Krausse	.80	.40	.25
234	Tommy Dean	.80	.40	.25
235	Mike Epstein	.80	.40	.25
236	Bob Veale	.80	.40	.25
237	Russ Gibson	.80	.40	.25
238	Jose Laboy	.80	.40	.25
239	Ken Berry	.80	.40	.25
240	Fergie Jenkins	10.00	5.00	3.00
241	Royals Rookies (Al Fitzmorris, Scott Northey)	.80	.40	.25
242	Walter Alston	3.50	1.75	1.00
243	Joe Sparma	.80	.40	.25
244a	Checklist 264-372 (red bat on front)	3.00	1.50	.90
244b	Checklist 264-372 (brown bat on front)	3.50	1.75	1.00
245	Leo Cardenas	.80	.40	.25
246	Jim McAndrew	.80	.40	.25
247	Lou Klimchock	.80	.40	.25
248	Jesus Alou	.80	.40	.25
249	Bob Locker	.80	.40	.25
250	Willie McCovey	8.00	4.00	2.50
251	Dick Schofield	.80	.40	.25
252	Lowell Palmer	.80	.40	.25
253	Ron Woods	.80	.40	.25
254	Camilo Pascual	.80	.40	.25
255	*Jim Spencer*	.80	.40	.25
256	Vic Davalillo	.80	.40	.25
257	Dennis Higgins	.80	.40	.25
258	Paul Popovich	.80	.40	.25
259	Tommie Reynolds	.80	.40	.25
260	Claude Osteen	.80	.40	.25
261	Curt Motton	.80	.40	.25
262	Padres Rookies (Jerry Morales, Jim Williams)	.80	.40	.25
263	Duane Josephson	.80	.40	.25
264	Rich Hebner	.80	.40	.25
265	Randy Hundley	.80	.40	.25
266	Wally Bunker	.80	.40	.25
267	Twins Rookies (Herman Hill, Paul Ratliff)	.80	.40	.25
268	Claude Raymond	.80	.40	.25
269	Cesar Gutierrez	.80	.40	.25
270	Chris Short	.80	.40	.25
271	Greg Goossen	.80	.40	.25
272	Hector Torres	.80	.40	.25
273	Ralph Houk	1.00	.50	.30
274	Gerry Arrigo	.80	.40	.25
275	Duke Sims	.80	.40	.25
276	Ron Hunt	.80	.40	.25
277	Paul Doyle	.80	.40	.25
278	Tommie Aaron	.80	.40	.25
279	*Bill Lee*	.80	.40	.25
280	Donn Clendenon	.80	.40	.25
281	Casey Cox	.80	.40	.25
282	Steve Huntz	.80	.40	.25
283	Angel Bravo	.80	.40	.25
284	Jack Baldschun	.80	.40	.25
285	Paul Blair	.80	.40	.25
286	Dodgers Rookies (*Bill Buckner*, Jack Jenkins)	9.00	4.50	2.75
287	Fred Talbot	.80	.40	.25
288	Larry Hisle	.80	.40	.25
289	Gene Brabender	.80	.40	.25
290	Rod Carew	35.00	17.50	10.50
291	Leo Durocher	1.75	.90	.50
292	Eddie Leon	.80	.40	.25
293	Bob Bailey	.80	.40	.25
294	Jose Azcue	.80	.40	.25
295	Cecil Upshaw	.80	.40	.25
296	Woody Woodward	.80	.40	.25
297	Curt Blefary	.80	.40	.25
298	Ken Henderson	.80	.40	.25
299	Buddy Bradford	.80	.40	.25
300	Tom Seaver	90.00	45.00	27.00
301	Chico Salmon	.80	.40	.25
302	Jeff James	.80	.40	.25
303	Brant Alyea	.80	.40	.25
304	*Bill Russell*	3.00	1.50	.90
305	World Series Game 1 (Buford Belts Leadoff Homer')	4.00	2.00	1.25
306	World Series Game 2 (Clendenon's HR Breaks Ice')	4.00	2.00	1.25
307	World Series Game 3 (Agee's Catch Saves The Day')	4.00	2.00	1.25
308	World Series Game 4 (Martin's Bunt Ends Deadlock')	4.00	2.00	1.25
309	World Series Game 5 (Koosman Shuts The Door')	4.00	2.00	1.25
310	World Series Summary (Mets Whoop It Up')	4.00	2.00	1.25

		NR MT	EX	VG
311	Dick Green	.80	.40	.25
312	Mike Torrez	.80	.40	.25
313	Mayo Smith	.80	.40	.25
314	Bill McCool	.80	.40	.25
315	Luis Aparicio	4.50	2.25	1.25
316	Skip Guinn	.80	.40	.25
317	Red Sox Rookies (Luis Alvarado, Billy Conigliaro)	.80	.40	.25
318	Willie Smith	.80	.40	.25
319	Clayton Dalrymple	.80	.40	.25
320	Jim Maloney	.80	.40	.25
321	Lou Piniella	1.50	.70	.45
322	Luke Walker	.80	.40	.25
323	Wayne Comer	.80	.40	.25
324	Tony Taylor	.80	.40	.25
325	Dave Boswell	.80	.40	.25
326	Bill Voss	.80	.40	.25
327	Hal King	.80	.40	.25
328	George Brunet	.80	.40	.25
329	Chris Cannizzaro	.80	.40	.25
330	Lou Brock	10.00	5.00	3.00
331	Chuck Dobson	.80	.40	.25
332	Bobby Wine	.80	.40	.25
333	Bobby Murcer	.80	.40	.25
334	Phil Regan	.80	.40	.25
335	Bill Freehan	.80	.40	.25
336	Del Unser	.80	.40	.25
337	Mike McCormick	.80	.40	.25
338	Paul Schaal	.80	.40	.25
339	Johnny Edwards	.80	.40	.25
340	Tony Conigliaro	1.75	.90	.50
341	Bill Sudakis	.80	.40	.25
342	Wilbur Wood	.80	.40	.25
343a	Checklist 373-459 (red bat on front)	3.50	1.75	1.00
343b	Checklist 373-459 (brown bat on front)	3.00	1.50	.90
344	Marcelino Lopez	.80	.40	.25
345	Al Ferrara	.80	.40	.25
346	Red Schoendienst	1.75	.90	.50
347	Russ Snyder	.80	.40	.25
348	Mets Rookies (Jesse Hudson, Mike Jorgensen)	.80	.40	.25
349	Steve Hamilton	.80	.40	.25
350	Roberto Clemente	50.00	25.00	15.00
351	Tom Murphy	.80	.40	.25
352	Bob Barton	.80	.40	.25
353	Stan Williams	.80	.40	.25
354	Amos Otis	.80	.40	.25
355	Doug Rader	.80	.40	.25
356	Fred Lasher	.80	.40	.25
357	Bob Burda	.80	.40	.25
358	*Pedro Borbon*	1.00	.50	.30
359	Phil Roof	.80	.40	.25
360	Curt Flood	.80	.40	.25
361	Ray Jarvis	.80	.40	.25
362	Joe Hague	.80	.40	.25
363	Tom Shopay	.80	.40	.25
364	Dan McGinn	.80	.40	.25
365	Zoilo Versalles	.80	.40	.25
366	Barry Moore	.80	.40	.25
367	Mike Lum	.80	.40	.25
368	Ed Herrmann	.80	.40	.25
369	Alan Foster	.80	.40	.25
370	Tommy Harper	.80	.40	.25
371	Rod Gaspar	.80	.40	.25
372	Dave Giusti	.80	.40	.25
373	Roy White	.80	.40	.25
374	Tommie Sisk	.80	.40	.25
375	Johnny Callison	.80	.40	.25
376	Lefty Phillips	.80	.40	.25
377	Bill Butler	.80	.40	.25
378	Jim Davenport	.80	.40	.25
379	Tom Tischinski	.80	.40	.25
380	Tony Perez	3.00	1.50	.90
381	Athletics Rookies (Bobby Brooks, Mike Olivo)	.80	.40	.25
382	Jack DiLauro	.80	.40	.25
383	Mickey Stanley	.80	.40	.25
384	Gary Neibauer	.80	.40	.25
385	George Scott	.80	.40	.25
386	Bill Dillman	.80	.40	.25
387	Orioles Team	3.00	1.50	.90
388	Byron Browne	.80	.40	.25
389	Jim Shellenback	.80	.40	.25
390	Willie Davis	.80	.40	.25
391	Larry Brown	.80	.40	.25
392	Walt Hriniak	.80	.40	.25
393	John Gelnar	.80	.40	.25
394	Gil Hodges	4.00	2.00	1.25
395	Walt Williams	.80	.40	.25

		NR MT	EX	VG
396	Steve Blass	.80	.40	.25
397	Roger Repoz	.80	.40	.25
398	Bill Stoneman	.80	.40	.25
399	Yankees Team	5.00	2.50	1.50
400	Denny McLain	1.50	.70	.45
401	Giants Rookies (John Harrell, Bernie Williams)	.80	.40	.25
402	Ellie Rodriguez	.80	.40	.25
403	Jim Bunning	3.25	1.75	1.00
404	Rich Reese	.80	.40	.25
405	Bill Hands	.80	.40	.25
406	Mike Andrews	.80	.40	.25
407	Bob Watson	.80	.40	.25
408	Paul Lindblad	.80	.40	.25
409	Bob Tolan	.80	.40	.25
410	Boog Powell	1.50	.70	.45
411	Dodgers Team	4.00	2.00	1.25
412	Larry Burchart	.80	.40	.25
413	Sonny Jackson	.80	.40	.25
414	Paul Edmondson	.80	.40	.25
415	Julian Javier	.80	.40	.25
416	Joe Verbanic	.80	.40	.25
417	John Bateman	.80	.40	.25
418	John Donaldson	.80	.40	.25
419	Ron Taylor	.80	.40	.25
420	Ken McMullen	.80	.40	.25
421	Pat Dobson	.80	.40	.25
422	Royals Team	3.00	1.50	.90
423	Jerry May	.80	.40	.25
424	Mike Kilkenny	.80	.40	.25
425	Bobby Bonds	1.75	.90	.50
426	Bill Rigney	.80	.40	.25
427	Fred Norman	.80	.40	.25
428	Don Buford	.80	.40	.25
429	Cubs Rookies (Randy Bobb, Jim Cosman)	.80	.40	.25
430	Andy Messersmith	.80	.40	.25
431	Ron Swoboda	.80	.40	.25
432a	Checklist 460-546 ("Baseball" on front in yellow)	4.00	2.00	1.25
432b	Checklist 460-546 ("Baseball" on front in white)	3.50	1.75	1.00
433	Ron Bryant	.80	.40	.25
434	Felipe Alou	.70	.35	.20
435	Nelson Briles	.80	.40	.25
436	Phillies Team	3.00	1.50	.90
437	Danny Cater	.80	.40	.25
438	Pat Jarvis	.80	.40	.25
439	Lee Maye	.80	.40	.25
440	Bill Mazeroski	2.50	1.25	.70
441	John O'Donoghue	.80	.40	.25
442	Gene Mauch	.70	.35	.20
443	Al Jackson	.80	.40	.25
444	White Sox Rookies (Bill Farmer, John Matias)	.80	.40	.25
445	Vada Pinson	1.50	.70	.45
446	*Billy Grabarkewitz*	.80	.40	.25
447	Lee Stange	.80	.40	.25
448	Astros Team	3.00	1.50	.90
449	Jim Palmer	20.00	10.00	6.00
450	Willie McCovey (All-Star)	5.00	2.50	1.50
451	Boog Powell (All-Star)	1.50	.70	.45
452	Felix Millan (All-Star)	.80	.40	.25
453	Rod Carew (All-Star)	6.00	3.00	1.75
454	Ron Santo (All-Star)	1.50	.70	.45
455	Brooks Robinson (All-Star)	8.00	4.00	2.50
456	Don Kessinger (All-Star)	.80	.40	.25
457	Rico Petrocelli (All-Star)	.80	.40	.25
458	Pete Rose (All-Star)	12.00	6.00	3.50
459	Reggie Jackson (All-Star)	35.00	17.50	10.50
460	Matty Alou (All-Star)	.80	.40	.25
461	Carl Yastrzemski (All-Star)	8.00	4.00	2.50
462	Hank Aaron (All-Star)	15.00	7.50	4.50
463	Frank Robinson (All-Star)	8.00	4.00	2.50
464	Johnny Bench (All-Star)	10.00	5.00	3.00
465	Bill Freehan (All-Star)	.80	.40	.25
466	Juan Marichal (All-Star)	5.00	2.50	1.50
467	Denny McLain (All-Star)	1.50	.70	.45
468	Jerry Koosman (All-Star)	1.00	.50	.30
469	Sam McDowell (All-Star)	1.00	.50	.30
470	Willie Stargell	7.00	3.50	2.00
471	Chris Zachary	.80	.40	.25
472	Braves Team	3.00	1.50	.90
473	Don Bryant	.80	.40	.25
474	Dick Kelley	.80	.40	.25
475	Dick McAuliffe	.80	.40	.25
476	Don Shaw	.80	.40	.25
477	Orioles Rookies (Roger Freed, Al Severinsen)	.80	.40	.25
478	Bob Heise	.80	.40	.25
479	Dick Woodson	.80	.40	.25

		NR MT	EX	VG
480	Glenn Beckert	.80	.40	.25
481	Jose Tartabull	.80	.40	.25
482	Tom Hilgendorf	.80	.40	.25
483	Gail Hopkins	.80	.40	.25
484	Gary Nolan	.80	.40	.25
485	Jay Johnstone	.80	.40	.25
486	Terry Harmon	.80	.40	.25
487	Cisco Carlos	.80	.40	.25
488	J.C. Martin	.80	.40	.25
489	Eddie Kasko	.80	.40	.25
490	Bill Singer	.80	.40	.25
491	Graig Nettles	3.00	1.50	.90
492	Astros Rookies (Keith Lampard, Scipio Spinks)	.80	.40	.25
493	Lindy McDaniel	.80	.40	.25
494	Larry Stahl	.80	.40	.25
495	Dave Morehead	.80	.40	.25
496	Steve Whitaker	.80	.40	.25
497	Eddie Watt	.80	.40	.25
498	Al Weis	.80	.40	.25
499	Skip Lockwood	.80	.40	.25
500	Hank Aaron	60.00	30.00	18.00
501	White Sox Team	3.00	1.50	.90
502	Rollie Fingers	35.00	17.50	10.50
503	Dal Maxvill	.80	.40	.25
504	Don Pavletich	.80	.40	.25
505	Ken Holtzman	.80	.40	.25
506	Ed Stroud	.80	.40	.25
507	Pat Corrales	.80	.40	.25
508	Joe Niekro	.70	.35	.20
509	Expos Team	3.00	1.50	.90
510	Tony Oliva	1.50	.70	.45
511	Joe Hoerner	.80	.40	.25
512	Billy Harris	.80	.40	.25
513	Preston Gomez	.80	.40	.25
514	Steve Hovley	.80	.40	.25
515	Don Wilson	.80	.40	.25
516	Yankees Rookies (John Ellis, Jim Lyttle)	.80	.40	.25
517	Joe Gibbon	.80	.40	.25
518	Bill Melton	.80	.40	.25
519	Don McMahon	.80	.40	.25
520	Willie Horton	.70	.35	.20
521	Cal Koonce	.80	.40	.25
522	Angels Team	3.00	1.50	.90
523	Jose Pena	.80	.40	.25
524	Alvin Dark	.80	.40	.25
525	Jerry Adair	.80	.40	.25
526	Ron Herbel	.80	.40	.25
527	Don Bosch	.80	.40	.25
528	Elrod Hendricks	.80	.40	.25
529	Bob Aspromonte	.80	.40	.25
530	Bob Gibson	10.00	5.00	3.00
531	Ron Clark	.80	.40	.25
532	Danny Murtaugh	.80	.40	.25
533	Buzz Stephen	.80	.40	.25
534	Twins Team	3.00	1.50	.90
535	Andy Kosco	.80	.40	.25
536	Mike Kekich	.80	.40	.25
537	Joe Morgan	10.00	5.00	3.00
538	Bob Humphreys	.80	.40	.25
539	Phillies Rookies (*Larry Bowa,* Dennis Doyle)	3.00	1.50	.90
540	Gary Peters	.80	.40	.25
541	Bill Heath	.80	.40	.25
542a	Checklist 547-633 (grey bat on front)	3.50	1.75	1.00
542b	Checklist 547-633 (brown bat on front)	3.50	1.75	1.00
543	Clyde Wright	.80	.40	.25
544	Reds Team	3.00	1.50	.90
545	Ken Harrelson	.80	.40	.25
546	Ron Reed	.80	.40	.25
547	Rick Monday	2.50	1.25	.70
548	Howie Reed	2.50	1.25	.70
549	Cardinals Team	7.00	3.50	2.00
550	Frank Howard	3.50	1.75	1.00
551	Dock Ellis	2.50	1.25	.70
552	Royals Rookies (Don O'Riley, Dennis Paepke, Fred Rico)	2.50	1.25	.70
553	Jim Lefebvre	2.50	1.25	.70
554	Tom Timmermann	2.50	1.25	.70
555	Orlando Cepeda	4.50	2.25	1.25
556	Dave Bristol	2.50	1.25	.70
557	Ed Kranepool	2.50	1.25	.70
558	Vern Fuller	2.50	1.25	.70
559	Tommy Davis	2.50	1.25	.70
560	Gaylord Perry	10.00	5.00	3.00
561	Tom McCraw	2.50	1.25	.70
562	Ted Abernathy	2.50	1.25	.70
563	Red Sox Team	7.00	3.50	2.00

		NR MT	EX	VG
564	Johnny Briggs	2.50	1.25	.70
565	Catfish Hunter	9.00	4.50	2.75
566	Gene Alley	2.50	1.25	.70
567	Bob Oliver	2.50	1.25	.70
568	Stan Bahnsen	2.50	1.25	.70
569	Cookie Rojas	2.50	1.25	.70
570	Jim Fregosi	2.50	1.25	.70
571	Jim Brewer	2.50	1.25	.70
572	Frank Quilici	2.50	1.25	.70
573	Padres Rookies (Mike Corkins, Rafael Robles, Ron Slocum)	2.50	1.25	.70
574	Bobby Bolin	2.50	1.25	.70
575	Cleon Jones	2.50	1.25	.70
576	Milt Pappas	2.50	1.25	.70
577	Bernie Allen	2.50	1.25	.70
578	Tom Griffin	2.50	1.25	.70
579	Tigers Team	7.00	3.50	2.00
580	Pete Rose	70.00	35.00	21.00
581	Tom Satriano	2.50	1.25	.70
582	Mike Paul	2.50	1.25	.70
583	Hal Lanier	2.50	1.25	.70
584	Al Downing	2.50	1.25	.70
585	Rusty Staub	3.00	1.50	.90
586	Rickey Clark	2.50	1.25	.70
587	Jose Arcia	2.50	1.25	.70
588a	Checklist 634-720 (666 is Adolpho Phillips)	4.50	2.25	1.25
588b	Checklist 634-720 (666 is Adolfo Phillips)	3.00	1.50	.90
589	Joe Keough	2.50	1.25	.70
590	Mike Cuellar	2.50	1.25	.70
591	Mike Ryan	2.50	1.25	.70
592	Daryl Patterson	2.50	1.25	.70
593	Cubs Team	7.00	3.50	2.00
594	Jake Gibbs	2.50	1.25	.70
595	Maury Wills	3.00	1.50	.90
596	Mike Hershberger	2.50	1.25	.70
597	Sonny Siebert	2.50	1.25	.70
598	Joe Pepitone	2.50	1.25	.70
599	Senators Rookies (Gene Martin, Dick Stelmaszek, Dick Such)	2.50	1.25	.70
600	Willie Mays	80.00	40.00	24.00
601	Pete Richert	2.50	1.25	.70
602	Ted Savage	2.50	1.25	.70
603	Ray Oyler	2.50	1.25	.70
604	Cito Gaston	3.50	1.75	1.00
605	Rick Wise	2.50	1.25	.70
606	Chico Ruiz	2.50	1.25	.70
607	Gary Waslewski	2.50	1.25	.70
608	Pirates Team	7.00	3.50	2.00
609	*Buck Martinez*	2.50	1.25	.70
610	Jerry Koosman	2.50	1.25	.70
611	Norm Cash	3.00	1.50	.90
612	Jim Hickman	2.50	1.25	.70
613	Dave Baldwin	2.50	1.25	.70
614	Mike Shannon	2.50	1.25	.70
615	Mark Belanger	2.50	1.25	.70
616	Jim Merritt	2.50	1.25	.70
617	Jim French	2.50	1.25	.70
618	Billy Wynne	2.50	1.25	.70
619	Norm Miller	2.50	1.25	.70
620	Jim Perry	2.50	1.25	.70
621	Braves Rookies *(Darrell Evans,* Rick Kester, Mike McQueen)	20.00	10.00	6.00
622	Don Sutton	7.00	3.50	2.00
623	Horace Clarke	2.50	1.25	.70
624	Clyde King	2.50	1.25	.70
625	Dean Chance	2.50	1.25	.70
626	Dave Ricketts	2.50	1.25	.70
627	Gary Wagner	2.50	1.25	.70
628	Wayne Garrett	2.50	1.25	.70
629	Merv Rettenmund	2.50	1.25	.70
630	Ernie Banks	30.00	15.00	9.00
631	Athletics Team	7.00	3.50	2.00
632	Gary Sutherland	2.50	1.25	.70
633	Roger Nelson	2.50	1.25	.70
634	Bud Harrelson	2.50	1.25	.70
635	Bob Allison	2.50	1.25	.70
636	Jim Stewart	5.00	2.50	1.50
637	Indians Team	9.00	4.50	2.75
638	Frank Bertaina	5.00	2.50	1.50
639	Dave Campbell	5.00	2.50	1.50
640	Al Kaline	50.00	25.00	15.00
641	Al McBean	5.00	2.50	1.50
642	Angels Rookies (Greg Garrett, Gordon Lund, Jarvis Tatum)	5.00	2.50	1.50
643	Jose Pagan	5.00	2.50	1.50
644	Gerry Nyman	5.00	2.50	1.50
645	Don Money	5.00	2.50	1.50
646	Jim Britton	5.00	2.50	1.50
647	Tom Matchick	5.00	2.50	1.50
648	Larry Haney	5.00	2.50	1.50
649	Jimmie Hall	5.00	2.50	1.50
650	Sam McDowell	5.00	2.50	1.50
651	Jim Gosger	5.00	2.50	1.50
652	Rich Rollins	5.00	2.50	1.50
653	Moe Drabowsky	5.00	2.50	1.50
654	N.L. Rookies (Boots Day, *Oscar Gamble,* Angel Mangual)	5.00	2.50	1.50
655	John Roseboro	5.00	2.50	1.50
656	Jim Hardin	5.00	2.50	1.50
657	Padres Team	9.00	4.50	2.75
658	Ken Tatum	5.00	2.50	1.50
659	Pete Ward	5.00	2.50	1.50
660	Johnny Bench	150.00	75.00	45.00
661	Jerry Robertson	5.00	2.50	1.50
662	Frank Lucchesi	5.00	2.50	1.50
663	Tito Francona	5.00	2.50	1.50
664	Bob Robertson	5.00	2.50	1.50
665	Jim Lonborg	6.00	3.00	1.75
666	Adolfo Phillips	5.00	2.50	1.50
667	Bob Meyer	5.00	2.50	1.50
668	Bob Tillman	5.00	2.50	1.50
669	White Sox Rookies (Bart Johnson, Dan Lazar, Mickey Scott)	5.00	2.50	1.50
670	Ron Santo	6.00	3.00	1.75
671	Jim Campanis	5.00	2.50	1.50
672	Leon McFadden	5.00	2.50	1.50
673	Ted Uhlaender	5.00	2.50	1.50
674	Dave Leonhard	5.00	2.50	1.50
675	Jose Cardenal	5.00	2.50	1.50
676	Senators Team	9.00	4.50	2.75
677	Woodie Fryman	5.00	2.50	1.50
678	Dave Duncan	5.00	2.50	1.50
679	Ray Sadecki	5.00	2.50	1.50
680	Rico Petrocelli	6.00	3.00	1.75
681	Bob Garibaldi	5.00	2.50	1.50
682	Dalton Jones	5.00	2.50	1.50
683	Reds Rookies (Vern Geishert, Hal McRae, Wayne Simpson)	5.00	2.50	1.50
684	Jack Fisher	5.00	2.50	1.50
685	Tom Haller	5.00	2.50	1.50
686	Jackie Hernandez	5.00	2.50	1.50
687	Bob Priddy	5.00	2.50	1.50
688	Ted Kubiak	5.00	2.50	1.50
689	Frank Tepedino	5.00	2.50	1.50
690	Ron Fairly	5.00	2.50	1.50
691	Joe Grzenda	5.00	2.50	1.50
692	Duffy Dyer	5.00	2.50	1.50
693	Bob Johnson	5.00	2.50	1.50
694	Gary Ross	5.00	2.50	1.50
695	Bobby Knoop	5.00	2.50	1.50
696	Giants Team	9.00	4.50	2.75
697	Jim Hannan	5.00	2.50	1.50
698	Tom Tresh	6.00	3.00	1.75
699	Hank Aguirre	5.00	2.50	1.50
700	Frank Robinson	50.00	25.00	15.00
701	Jack Billingham	5.00	2.50	1.50
702	A.L. Rookies (Bob Johnson, Ron Klimkowski, Bill Zepp)	5.00	2.50	1.50
703	Lou Marone	5.00	2.50	1.50
704	Frank Baker	5.00	2.50	1.50
705	Tony Cloninger	5.00	2.50	1.50
706	John McNamara	5.00	2.50	1.50
707	Kevin Collins	5.00	2.50	1.50
708	Jose Santiago	5.00	2.50	1.50
709	Mike Fiore	5.00	2.50	1.50
710	Felix Millan	5.00	2.50	1.50
711	Ed Brinkman	5.00	2.50	1.50
712	Nolan Ryan	550.00	275.00	165.00
713	Pilots Team	20.00	10.00	6.00
714	Al Spangler	5.00	2.50	1.50
715	Mickey Lolich	5.00	2.50	1.50
716	Cards Rookies (Sal Campisi, *Reggie Cleveland,* Santiago Guzman)	5.00	2.50	1.50
717	Tom Phoebus	5.00	2.50	1.50
718	Ed Spiezio	5.00	2.50	1.50
719	Jim Roland	5.00	2.50	1.50
720	Rick Reichardt	5.00	2.50	1.50

1970 Topps Candy Lids

The 1970 Topps Candy Lids are a test issue that was utilized again in 1973. The set is made up of 24 lids that measure 1-7/8" in diameter and were the tops of small 1.1 oz. tubs of "Baseball Stars Candy." Unlike the 1973 versions, the 1970 lids have no border surrounding the full-color photos. Frank Howard, Tom Seaver and Carl

Yastrzemski photos are found on the bottom (inside) of the candy lid.

		NR MT	EX	VG
Complete Set:		2000.00	1000.00	600.00
Common Player:		30.00	15.00	9.00
(1)	Hank Aaron	200.00	100.00	60.00
(2)	Rich Allen	50.00	25.00	15.00
(3)	Luis Aparicio	80.00	40.00	24.00
(4)	Johnny Bench	200.00	100.00	60.00
(5)	Ollie Brown	30.00	15.00	9.00
(6)	Willie Davis	30.00	15.00	9.00
(7)	Jim Fregosi	30.00	15.00	9.00
(8)	Mike Hegan	30.00	15.00	9.00
(9)	Frank Howard	50.00	25.00	15.00
(10)	Reggie Jackson	200.00	100.00	60.00
(11)	Fergie Jenkins	60.00	30.00	18.00
(12)	Harmon Killebrew	100.00	50.00	30.00
(13)	Juan Marichal	100.00	50.00	30.00
(14)	Bill Mazeroski	50.00	25.00	15.00
(15)	Tim McCarver	50.00	25.00	15.00
(16)	Sam McDowell	30.00	15.00	9.00
(17)	Denny McLain	50.00	25.00	15.00
(18)	Lou Piniella	50.00	25.00	15.00
(19)	Frank Robinson	100.00	50.00	30.00
(20)	Tom Seaver	175.00	87.00	52.00
(21)	Rusty Staub	50.00	25.00	15.00
(22)	Mel Stottlemyre	50.00	25.00	15.00
(23)	Jim Wynn	30.00	15.00	9.00
(24)	Carl Yastrzemski	150.00	75.00	45.00

1970 Topps Cloth Stickers

The earliest and rarest of the Topps cloth sticker test issues, only 15 subjects are known, and only a single specimen apiece is known for many of them. In the same 2-1/2" x 3-1/2" size, and with the same design as the 1970 Topps baseball cards, the stickers are blank-backed. The stickers of Denny Lemaster, Dennis Higgins and Rich Nye use photos that are different from their '70 Topps cards. It is quite likely that the checklist presented here is incomplete. The stickers are unnumbered and are checklisted alphabetically.

		NR MT	EX	VG
Common player:		50.00	25.00	15.00
(1)	A.L. Playoff Game 2 (Boog Powell)	50.00	25.00	15.00
(2)	Bill Burbach	50.00	25.00	15.00
(3)	Chuck Hartenstein	50.00	25.00	15.00
(4)	Dennis Higgins	50.00	25.00	15.00
(5)	Jose Laboy	50.00	25.00	15.00
(6)	Denny Lemaster	50.00	25.00	15.00
(7)	Juan Marichal	150.00	75.00	45.00
(8)	Jerry McNertney	50.00	25.00	15.00
(9)	Ivan Murrell	50.00	25.00	15.00
(10)	N.L. Playoff Game 3 (Nolan Ryan)	300.00	150.00	90.00
(11)	Phil Niekro	60.00	30.00	18.00
(12)	Jim Northrup	50.00	25.00	15.00
(13)	Rich Nye	50.00	25.00	15.00
(14)	Ron Perranoski	50.00	25.00	15.00
(15)	Al Santorini	50.00	25.00	15.00

1970 Topps Posters

Helping to ease a price increase, Topps included extremely fragile 8-11/16" by 9-5/8" posters in packs of regular cards. The posters feature color portraits and a smaller black and white "action" pose as well as the player's name, team and position at the top. Although there are Hall of Famers in the 24-poster set, all the top names are not represented. Once again, due to folding, heavy creases are a fact of life for today's collector.

		NR MT	EX	VG
Complete Set:		30.00	15.00	9.00
Common Player:		.75	.40	.25
1	Joe Horlen	.75	.40	.25
2	Phil Niekro	1.50	.70	.45
3	Willie Davis	1.00	.50	.30
4	Lou Brock	2.00	1.00	.60
5	Ron Santo	1.25	.60	.40
6	Ken Harrelson	1.00	.50	.30
7	Willie McCovey	3.00	1.50	.90
8	Rick Wise	.75	.40	.25
9	Andy Messersmith	.75	.40	.25
10	Ron Fairly	.75	.40	.25
11	Johnny Bench	4.00	2.00	1.25
12	Frank Robinson	3.00	1.50	.90
13	Tommie Agee	.75	.40	.25
14	Roy White	1.00	.50	.30
15	Larry Dierker	.75	.40	.25
16	Rod Carew	3.00	1.50	.90
17	Don Mincher	.75	.40	.25
18	Ollie Brown	.75	.40	.25
19	Ed Kirkpatrick	.75	.40	.25
20	Reggie Smith	.75	.40	.25
21	Roberto Clemente	5.00	2.50	1.50
22	Frank Howard	1.25	.60	.40
23	Bert Campaneris	.75	.40	.25
24	Denny McLain	1.25	.60	.40

1970 Topps Scratch-Offs

Needing inserts, and having not given up on the idea of a game which could be played with baseball cards, Topps provided a new game - the baseball scratch-off.

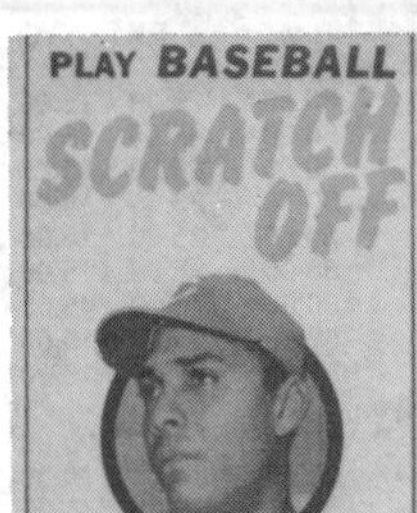

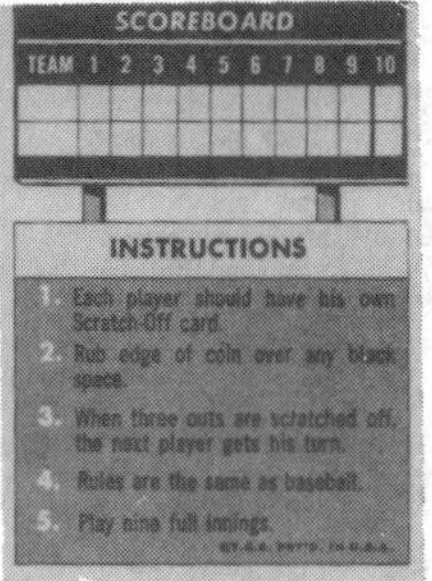

The set consists of 24 cards. Unfolded, they measure 3-3/8" by 5," and reveal a baseball game of sorts which was played by rubbing the black ink off playing squares which then determined the "action." Fronts of the cards have a player picture as "captain," while backs have instructions and a scoreboard. Inserts with white centers are from 1970 while those with red centers are from 1971.

		NR MT	EX	VG
Complete Set:		35.00	17.50	10.50
Common Player:		1.00	.50	.30
(1)	Hank Aaron	5.00	2.50	1.50
(2)	Rich Allen	1.50	.70	.45
(3)	Luis Aparicio	2.50	1.25	.70
(4)	Sal Bando	1.00	.50	.30
(5)	Glenn Beckert	1.00	.50	.30
(6)	Dick Bosman	1.00	.50	.30
(7)	Nate Colbert	1.00	.50	.30
(8)	Mike Hegan	1.00	.50	.30
(9)	Mack Jones	1.00	.50	.30
(10)	Al Kaline	3.00	1.50	.90
(11)	Harmon Killebrew	3.00	1.50	.90
(12)	Juan Marichal	2.00	1.00	.60
(13)	Tim McCarver	1.50	.70	.45
(14)	Sam McDowell	1.00	.50	.30
(15)	Claude Osteen	1.00	.50	.30
(16)	Tony Perez	1.25	.60	.40
(17)	Lou Piniella	1.00	.50	.30
(18)	Boog Powell	1.25	.60	.40
(19)	Tom Seaver	3.00	1.50	.90
(20)	Jim Spencer	1.00	.50	.30
(21)	Willie Stargell	3.00	1.50	.90
(22)	Mel Stottlemyre	1.00	.50	.30
(23)	Jim Wynn	1.00	.50	.30
(24)	Carl Yastrzemski	4.00	2.00	1.25

1970 Topps Story Booklets

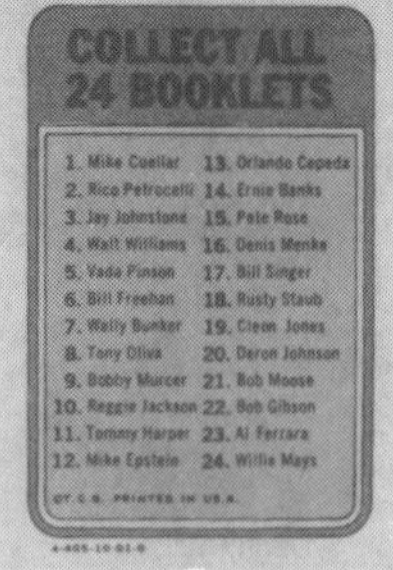

Measuring 2-1/2" by 3-7/16," the Topps Story Booklet was a 1970 regular pack insert. The booklet feature a photo, title and booklet number on the "cover." Inside are six pages of comic book story. The backs give a checklist of other available booklets. Not every star had a booklet as the set is only 24 in number.

		NR MT	EX	VG
Complete Set:		40.00	20.00	12.00
Common Player:		1.00	.50	.30
1	Mike Cuellar	1.00	.50	.30
2	Rico Petrocelli	1.00	.50	.30
3	Jay Johnstone	1.00	.50	.30
4	Walt Williams	1.00	.50	.30
5	Vada Pinson	1.50	.70	.45
6	Bill Freehan	1.00	.50	.30
7	Wally Bunker	1.00	.50	.30
8	Tony Oliva	1.50	.70	.45
9	Bobby Murcer	1.00	.50	.30
10	Reggie Jackson	5.00	2.50	1.50
11	Tommy Harper	6.00	3.00	1.75
12	Mike Epstein	1.00	.50	.30
13	Orlando Cepeda	2.00	1.00	.60
14	Ernie Banks	4.00	2.00	1.25
15	Pete Rose	8.00	4.00	2.50
16	Denis Menke	1.00	.50	.30
17	Bill Singer	1.00	.50	.30
18	Rusty Staub	1.50	.70	.45
19	Cleon Jones	1.00	.50	.30
20	Deron Johnson	1.00	.50	.30
21	Bob Moose	1.00	.50	.30
22	Bob Gibson	4.00	2.00	1.25
23	Al Ferrara	1.00	.50	.30
24	Willie Mays	7.00	3.50	2.00

1970 Topps Super

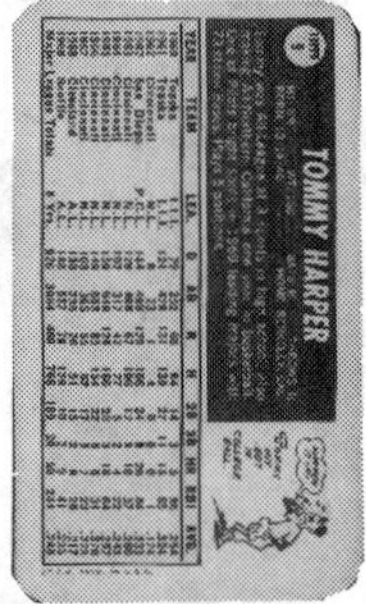

Representing a refinement of the concept begun in 1969, the 1970 Topps Supers had a new 3-1/8" by 5-1/4" postcard size. Printed on heavy stock with rounded corners, card fronts feature a borderless color photograph and facsimile autograph. Card backs are simply an enlarged back from the player's regular 1970 Topps card. The Topps Supers set numbers 42 cards. Probably due to the press sheet configuration eight of the 42 had smaller printings. The most elusive is card #38 (Boog Powell). The set was more widely produced than was the case in 1969, meaning collectors stand a much better chance of affording it.

		NR MT	EX	VG
Complete Set:		40.00	20.00	12.00
Common Player:		2.00	1.00	.60
1	Claude Osteen	3.00	1.50	.90
2	Sal Bando	3.50	1.75	1.00
3	Luis Aparicio	4.00	2.00	1.25
4	Harmon Killebrew	6.00	3.00	1.75
5	Tom Seaver	25.00	12.50	7.50
6	Larry Dierker	2.00	1.00	.60
7	Bill Freehan	2.00	1.00	.60
8	Johnny Bench	15.00	7.50	4.50
9	Tommy Harper	2.00	1.00	.60
10	Sam McDowell	2.00	1.00	.60
11	Lou Brock	6.00	3.00	1.75
12	Roberto Clemente	15.00	7.50	4.50
13	Willie McCovey	6.00	3.00	1.75
14	Rico Petrocelli	2.00	1.00	.60
15	Phil Niekro	3.00	1.50	.90
16	Frank Howard	2.50	1.25	.70
17	Denny McLain	2.50	1.25	.70

		NR MT	EX	VG
18	Willie Mays	15.00	7.50	4.50
19	Willie Stargell	6.00	3.00	1.75
20	Joe Horlen	2.00	1.00	.60
21	Ron Santo	2.50	1.25	.70
22	Dick Bosman	2.00	1.00	.60
23	Tim McCarver	2.50	1.25	.70
24	Henry Aaron	15.00	7.50	4.50
25	Andy Messersmith	2.00	1.00	.60
26	Tony Oliva	2.50	1.25	.70
27	Mel Stottlemyre	2.00	1.00	.60
28	Reggie Jackson	25.00	12.50	7.50
29	Carl Yastrzemski	12.00	6.00	3.50
30	James Fregosi	2.00	1.00	.60
31	Vada Pinson	2.50	1.25	.70
32	Lou Piniella	2.00	1.00	.60
33	Robert Gibson	6.00	3.00	1.75
34	Pete Rose	25.00	12.50	7.50
35	Jim Wynn	2.00	1.00	.60
36	Ollie Brown	5.00	2.50	1.50
37	Frank Robinson	18.00	9.00	5.50
38	Boog Powell	65.00	32.00	19.50
39	Willie Davis	5.00	2.50	1.50
40	Billy Williams	12.00	6.00	3.50
41	Rusty Staub	2.00	1.00	.60
42	Tommie Agee	2.00	1.00	.60

1971 Topps

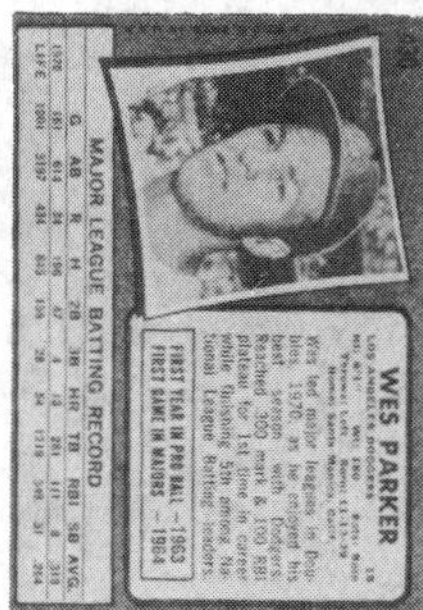

In 1971, Topps again increased the size of its set to 752 cards. These well-liked cards, measuring 2-1/2" by 3-1/2," feature a large color photo which has a thin white frame. Above the picture, in the card's overall black border, is the player's name, team and position. A facsimile autograph completes the front. Backs feature a major change as a black and white "snapshot" of the player appears. Abbreviated statistics, a line giving the player's first pro and major league games and a short biography complete the back of these innovative cards. Specialty cards in this issue are limited. There are statistical leaders as well as World Series and playoff highlights. High numbered cards #644-752 are scarce, with about half of the cards being short-printed.

	NR MT	EX	VG
Complete Set (752):	2200.00	1100.00	660.00
Common Player: 1-523	1.00	.50	.30
Common Player: 524-643	3.00	1.50	.90
Common Player: 644-752	3.00	1.50	.90

		NR MT	EX	VG
1	World Champions (Orioles Team)	12.00	6.00	3.50
2	Dock Ellis	1.00	.50	.30
3	Dick McAuliffe	1.00	.50	.30
4	Vic Davalillo	1.00	.50	.30
5	Thurman Munson	30.00	15.00	9.00
6	Ed Spiezio	1.00	.50	.30
7	Jim Holt	1.00	.50	.30
8	Mike McQueen	1.00	.50	.30
9	George Scott	1.00	.50	.30
10	Claude Osteen	1.00	.50	.30
11	*Elliott Maddox*	1.00	.50	.30
12	Johnny Callison	1.00	.50	.30
13	White Sox Rookies (Charlie Brinkman, Dick Moloney)	1.00	.50	.30
14	*Dave Concepcion*	20.00	10.00	6.00
15	Andy Messersmith	1.00	.50	.30
16	*Ken Singleton*	3.00	1.50	.90
17	Billy Sorrell	1.00	.50	.30
18	Norm Miller	1.00	.50	.30
19	Skip Pitlock	1.00	.50	.30
20	Reggie Jackson	100.00	50.00	30.00
21	Dan McGinn	1.00	.50	.30
22	Phil Roof	1.00	.50	.30
23	Oscar Gamble	1.00	.50	.30
24	Rich Hand	1.00	.50	.30
25	Cito Gaston	2.50	1.25	.70
26	*Bert Blyleven*	20.00	10.00	6.00
27	Pirates Rookies (Fred Cambria, Gene Clines)	1.00	.50	.30
28	Ron Klimkowski	1.00	.50	.30
29	Don Buford	1.00	.50	.30
30	Phil Niekro	3.25	1.75	1.00
31	Eddie Kasko	1.00	.50	.30
32	Jerry DaVanon	1.00	.50	.30
33	Del Unser	1.00	.50	.30
34	Sandy Vance	1.00	.50	.30
35	Lou Piniella	1.00	.50	.30
36	Dean Chance	1.00	.50	.30
37	Rich McKinney	1.00	.50	.30
38	*Jim Colborn*	1.00	.50	.30
39	Tigers Rookies (Gene Lamont, *Lerrin LaGrow*)	1.00	.50	.30
40	Lee May	1.00	.50	.30
41	Rick Austin	1.00	.50	.30
42	Boots Day	1.00	.50	.30
43	Steve Kealey	1.00	.50	.30
44	Johnny Edwards	1.00	.50	.30
45	Catfish Hunter	5.00	2.50	1.50
46	Dave Campbell	1.00	.50	.30
47	Johnny Jeter	1.00	.50	.30
48	Dave Baldwin	1.00	.50	.30
49	Don Money	1.00	.50	.30
50	Willie McCovey	7.00	3.50	2.00
51	Steve Kline	1.00	.50	.30
52	Braves Rookies (Oscar Brown, *Earl Williams*)	1.00	.50	.30
53	Paul Blair	1.00	.50	.30
54	Checklist 1-132	3.25	1.75	1.00
55	Steve Carlton	25.00	12.50	7.50
56	Duane Josephson	1.00	.50	.30
57	Von Joshua	1.00	.50	.30
58	Bill Lee	1.00	.50	.30
59	Gene Mauch	1.00	.50	.30
60	Dick Bosman	1.00	.50	.30
61	A.L. Batting Leaders (Alex Johnson, Tony Oliva, Carl Yastrzemski)	3.00	1.50	.90
62	N.L. Batting Leaders (Rico Carty, Manny Sanguillen, Joe Torre)	1.50	.70	.45
63	A.L. RBI Leaders (Tony Conigliaro, Frank Howard, Boog Powell)	1.50	.70	.45
64	N.L. RBI Leaders (Johnny Bench, Tony Perez, Billy Williams)	3.00	1.50	.90
65	A.L. Home Run Leaders (Frank Howard, Harmon Killebrew, Carl Yastrzemski)	3.00	1.50	.90
66	N.L. Home Run Leaders (Johnny Bench, Tony Perez, Billy Williams)	3.00	1.50	.90
67	A.L. ERA Leaders (Jim Palmer, Diego Segui, Clyde Wright)	1.50	.70	.45
68	N.L. ERA Leaders (Tom Seaver, Wayne Simpson, Luke Walker)	1.50	.70	.45
69	A.L. Pitching Leaders (Mike Cuellar, Dave McNally, Jim Perry)	1.50	.70	.45
70	N.L. Pitching Leaders (Bob Gibson, Fergie Jenkins, Gaylord Perry)	3.00	1.50	.90
71	A.L. Strikeout Leaders (Bob Johnson, Mickey Lolich, Sam McDowell)	1.50	.70	.45
72	N.L. Strikeout Leaders (Bob Gibson, Fergie Jenkins, Tom Seaver)	3.00	1.50	.90
73	George Brunet	1.00	.50	.30
74	Twins Rookies (Pete Hamm, Jim Nettles)	1.00	.50	.30
75	Gary Nolan	1.00	.50	.30
76	Ted Savage	1.00	.50	.30
77	Mike Compton	1.00	.50	.30
78	Jim Spencer	1.00	.50	.30
79	Wade Blasingame	1.00	.50	.30
80	Bill Melton	1.00	.50	.30
81	Felix Millan	1.00	.50	.30
82	Casey Cox	1.00	.50	.30
83	Mets Rookies (Randy Bobb, *Tim Foli*)	1.00	.50	.30
84	Marcel Lachemann	1.00	.50	.30
85	Billy Grabarkewitz	1.00	.50	.30
86	Mike Kilkenny	1.00	.50	.30
87	Jack Heidemann	1.00	.50	.30
88	Hal King	1.00	.50	.30
89	Ken Brett	1.00	.50	.30
90	Joe Pepitone	1.00	.50	.30

#	Player	NR MT	EX	VG
91	Bob Lemon	3.00	1.50	.90
92	Fred Wenz	1.00	.50	.30
93	Senators Rookies (Norm McRae, Denny Riddleberger)	1.00	.50	.30
94	Don Hahn	1.00	.50	.30
95	Luis Tiant	1.50	.70	.45
96	Joe Hague	1.00	.50	.30
97	Floyd Wicker	1.00	.50	.30
98	Joe Decker	1.00	.50	.30
99	Mark Belanger	1.00	.50	.30
100	Pete Rose	35.00	17.50	10.50
101	Les Cain	1.00	.50	.30
102	Astros Rookies (*Ken Forsch*, Larry Howard)	1.00	.50	.30
103	Rich Severson	1.00	.50	.30
104	Dan Frisella	1.00	.50	.30
105	Tony Conigliaro	1.25	.60	.40
106	Tom Dukes	1.00	.50	.30
107	Roy Foster	1.00	.50	.30
108	John Cumberland	1.00	.50	.30
109	Steve Hovley	1.00	.50	.30
110	Bill Mazeroski	2.50	1.25	.70
111	Yankees Rookies (Loyd Colson, Bobby Mitchell)	1.00	.50	.30
112	Manny Mota	1.00	.50	.30
113	Jerry Crider	1.00	.50	.30
114	Billy Conigliaro	1.00	.50	.30
115	Donn Clendenon	1.00	.50	.30
116	Ken Sanders	1.00	.50	.30
117	*Ted Simmons*	15.00	7.50	4.50
118	Cookie Rojas	1.00	.50	.30
119	Frank Lucchesi	1.00	.50	.30
120	Willie Horton	1.00	.50	.30
121	1971 Rookie Stars (Jim Dunegan, Roe Skidmore)	1.00	.50	.30
122	Eddie Watt	1.00	.50	.30
123a	Checklist 133-263 (card # on right, orange helmet)	3.25	1.75	1.00
123b	Checklist 133-263 (card # on right, red helmet)	3.25	1.75	1.00
123c	Checklist 133-263 (card # centered)	3.50	1.75	1.00
124	*Don Gullett*	1.00	.50	.30
125	Ray Fosse	1.00	.50	.30
126	Danny Coombs	1.00	.50	.30
127	*Danny Thompson*	1.00	.50	.30
128	Frank Johnson	1.00	.50	.30
129	Aurelio Monteagudo	1.00	.50	.30
130	Denis Menke	1.00	.50	.30
131	Curt Blefary	1.00	.50	.30
132	Jose Laboy	1.00	.50	.30
133	Mickey Lolich	1.25	.60	.40
134	Jose Arcia	1.00	.50	.30
135	Rick Monday	1.00	.50	.30
136	Duffy Dyer	1.00	.50	.30
137	Marcelino Lopez	1.00	.50	.30
138	Phillies Rookies (Joe Lis, *Willie Montanez*)	1.00	.50	.30
139	Paul Casanova	1.00	.50	.30
140	Gaylord Perry	6.00	3.00	1.75
141	Frank Quilici	1.00	.50	.30
142	Mack Jones	1.00	.50	.30
143	Steve Blass	1.00	.50	.30
144	Jackie Hernandez	1.00	.50	.30
145	Bill Singer	1.00	.50	.30
146	Ralph Houk	1.00	.50	.30
147	Bob Priddy	1.00	.50	.30
148	John Mayberry	1.00	.50	.30
149	Mike Hershberger	1.00	.50	.30
150	Sam McDowell	1.00	.50	.30
151	Tommy Davis	1.00	.50	.30
152	Angels Rookies (Lloyd Allen, Winston Llenas)	1.00	.50	.30
153	Gary Ross	1.00	.50	.30
154	Cesar Gutierrez	1.00	.50	.30
155	Ken Henderson	1.00	.50	.30
156	Bart Johnson	1.00	.50	.30
157	Bob Bailey	1.00	.50	.30
158	Jerry Reuss	1.00	.50	.30
159	Jarvis Tatum	1.00	.50	.30
160	Tom Seaver	45.00	22.00	13.50
161	Coins Checklist	3.25	1.75	1.00
162	Jack Billingham	1.00	.50	.30
163	Buck Martinez	1.00	.50	.30
164	Reds Rookies (Frank Duffy, *Milt Wilcox*)	1.00	.50	.30
165	Cesar Tovar	1.00	.50	.30
166	Joe Hoerner	1.00	.50	.30
167	Tom Grieve	1.00	.50	.30
168	Bruce Dal Canton	1.00	.50	.30
169	Ed Herrmann	1.00	.50	.30

#	Player	NR MT	EX	VG
170	Mike Cuellar	1.00	.50	.30
171	Bobby Wine	1.00	.50	.30
172	Duke Sims	1.00	.50	.30
173	Gil Garrido	1.00	.50	.30
174	*Dave LaRoche*	1.00	.50	.30
175	Jim Hickman	1.00	.50	.30
176	Red Sox Rookies (Doug Griffin, Bob Montgomery)	1.00	.50	.30
177	Hal McRae	2.00	1.00	.60
178	Dave Duncan	1.00	.50	.30
179	Mike Corkins	1.00	.50	.30
180	Al Kaline	15.00	7.50	4.50
181	Hal Lanier	1.00	.50	.30
182	Al Downing	1.00	.50	.30
183	Gil Hodges	4.00	2.00	1.25
184	Stan Bahnsen	1.00	.50	.30
185	Julian Javier	1.00	.50	.30
186	Bob Spence	1.00	.50	.30
187	Ted Abernathy	1.00	.50	.30
188	Dodgers Rookies (Mike Strahler, *Bob Valentine*)	3.00	1.50	.90
189	George Mitterwald	1.00	.50	.30
190	Bob Tolan	1.00	.50	.30
191	Mike Andrews	1.00	.50	.30
192	Billy Wilson	1.00	.50	.30
193	*Bob Grich*	3.00	1.50	.90
194	Mike Lum	1.00	.50	.30
195	A.L. Playoff Game 1 (Powell Muscles Twins!)	2.00	1.00	.60
196	A.L. Playoff Game 2 (McNally Makes It Two Straight!)	2.00	1.00	.60
197	A.L. Playoff Game 3 (Palmer Mows 'Em Down!)	3.00	1.50	.90
198	A.L. Playoffs Summary (A Team Effort!)	2.00	1.00	.60
199	N.L. Playoff Game 1 (Cline Pinch-Triple Decides It!)	2.00	1.00	.60
200	N.L. Playoff Game 2 (Tolan Scores For Third Time!)	2.00	1.00	.60
201	N.L. Playoff Game 3 (Cline Scores Winning Run!)	2.00	1.00	.60
202	N.L. Playoffs Summary (World Series Bound!)	2.00	1.00	.60
203	*Larry Gura*	1.00	.50	.30
204	Brewers Rookies (George Kopacz, Bernie Smith)	1.00	.50	.30
205	Gerry Moses	1.00	.50	.30
206a	Checklist 264-393 (orange helmet)	3.25	1.75	1.00
206b	Checklist 264-393 (red helmet)	3.25	1.75	1.00
207	Alan Foster	1.00	.50	.30
208	Billy Martin	3.00	1.50	.90
209	Steve Renko	1.00	.50	.30
210	Rod Carew	30.00	15.00	9.00
211	Phil Hennigan	1.00	.50	.30
212	Rich Hebner	1.00	.50	.30
213	Frank Baker	1.00	.50	.30
214	Al Ferrara	1.00	.50	.30
215	Diego Segui	1.00	.50	.30
216	Cards Rookies (Reggie Cleveland, Luis Melendez)	1.00	.50	.30
217	Ed Stroud	1.00	.50	.30
218	Tony Cloninger	1.00	.50	.30
219	Elrod Hendricks	1.00	.50	.30
220	Ron Santo	2.50	1.25	.70
221	Dave Morehead	1.00	.50	.30
222	Bob Watson	1.00	.50	.30
223	Cecil Upshaw	1.00	.50	.30
224	Alan Gallagher	1.00	.50	.30
225	Gary Peters	1.00	.50	.30
226	Bill Russell	2.00	1.00	.60
227	Floyd Weaver	1.00	.50	.30
228	Wayne Garrett	1.00	.50	.30
229	Jim Hannan	1.00	.50	.30
230	Willie Stargell	8.00	4.00	2.50
231	Indians Rookies (Vince Colbert, *John Lowenstein*)	1.00	.50	.30
232	John Strohmayer	1.00	.50	.30
233	Larry Bowa	2.00	1.00	.60
234	Jim Lyttle	1.00	.50	.30
235	Nate Colbert	1.00	.50	.30
236	Bob Humphreys	1.00	.50	.30
237	*Cesar Cedeno*	3.00	1.50	.90
238	Chuck Dobson	1.00	.50	.30
239	Red Schoendienst	3.00	1.50	.90
240	Clyde Wright	1.00	.50	.30
241	Dave Nelson	1.00	.50	.30
242	Jim Ray	1.00	.50	.30
243	Carlos May	1.00	.50	.30
244	Bob Tillman	1.00	.50	.30
245	Jim Kaat	2.50	1.25	.70

		NR MT	EX	VG
246	Tony Taylor	1.00	.50	.30
247	Royals Rookies (Jerry Cram, *Paul Splittorff*)	1.00	.50	.30
248	Hoyt Wilhelm	3.75	2.00	1.25
249	Chico Salmon	1.00	.50	.30
250	Johnny Bench	35.00	17.50	10.50
251	Frank Reberger	1.00	.50	.30
252	Eddie Leon	1.00	.50	.30
253	Bill Sudakis	1.00	.50	.30
254	Cal Koonce	1.00	.50	.30
255	Bob Robertson	1.00	.50	.30
256	Tony Gonzalez	1.00	.50	.30
257	Nelson Briles	1.00	.50	.30
258	Dick Green	1.00	.50	.30
259	Dave Marshall	1.00	.50	.30
260	Tommy Harper	1.00	.50	.30
261	Darold Knowles	1.00	.50	.30
262	Padres Rookies (Dave Robinson, Jim Williams)	1.00	.50	.30
263	John Ellis	1.00	.50	.30
264	Joe Morgan	10.00	5.00	3.00
265	Jim Northrup	1.00	.50	.30
266	Bill Stoneman	1.00	.50	.30
267	Rich Morales	1.00	.50	.30
268	Phillies Team	3.00	1.50	.90
269	Gail Hopkins	1.00	.50	.30
270	Rico Carty	1.00	.50	.30
271	Bill Zepp	1.00	.50	.30
272	Tommy Helms	1.00	.50	.30
273	Pete Richert	1.00	.50	.30
274	Ron Slocum	1.00	.50	.30
275	Vada Pinson	2.00	1.00	.60
276	Giants Rookies (Mike Davison, *George Foster*)	6.00	3.00	1.75
277	Gary Waslewski	1.00	.50	.30
278	Jerry Grote	1.00	.50	.30
279	Lefty Phillips	1.00	.50	.30
280	Fergie Jenkins	8.00	4.00	2.50
281	Danny Walton	1.00	.50	.30
282	Jose Pagan	1.00	.50	.30
283	Dick Such	1.00	.50	.30
284	Jim Gosger	1.00	.50	.30
285	Sal Bando	1.00	.50	.30
286	Jerry McNertney	1.00	.50	.30
287	Mike Fiore	1.00	.50	.30
288	Joe Moeller	1.00	.50	.30
289	White Sox Team	3.00	1.50	.90
290	Tony Oliva	1.50	.70	.45
291	George Culver	1.00	.50	.30
292	Jay Johnstone	1.00	.50	.30
293	Pat Corrales	1.00	.50	.30
294	Steve Dunning	1.00	.50	.30
295	Bobby Bonds	1.25	.60	.40
296	Tom Timmermann	1.00	.50	.30
297	Johnny Briggs	1.00	.50	.30
298	Jim Nelson	1.00	.50	.30
299	Ed Kirkpatrick	1.00	.50	.30
300	Brooks Robinson	20.00	10.00	6.00
301	Earl Wilson	1.00	.50	.30
302	Phil Gagliano	1.00	.50	.30
303	Lindy McDaniel	1.00	.50	.30
304	Ron Brand	1.00	.50	.30
305	Reggie Smith	1.50	.70	.45
306	Jim Nash	1.00	.50	.30
307	Don Wert	1.00	.50	.30
308	Cards Team	3.00	1.50	.90
309	Dick Ellsworth	1.00	.50	.30
310	Tommie Agee	1.00	.50	.30
311	Lee Stange	1.00	.50	.30
312	Harry Walker	1.00	.50	.30
313	Tom Hall	1.00	.50	.30
314	Jeff Torborg	1.00	.50	.30
315	Ron Fairly	1.00	.50	.30
316	Fred Scherman	1.00	.50	.30
317	Athletics Rookies (Jim Driscoll, Angel Mangual)	1.00	.50	.30
318	Rudy May	1.00	.50	.30
319	Ty Cline	1.00	.50	.30
320	Dave McNally	1.00	.50	.30
321	Tom Matchick	1.00	.50	.30
322	Jim Beauchamp	1.00	.50	.30
323	Billy Champion	1.00	.50	.30
324	Graig Nettles	2.00	1.00	.60
325	Juan Marichal	6.00	3.00	1.75
326	Richie Scheinblum	1.00	.50	.30
327	World Series Game 1 (Powell Homers To Opposite Field!)	3.00	1.50	.90
328	World Series Game 2 (Buford Goes 2-For 4!)	2.00	1.00	.60
329	World Series Game 3 (F. Robinson Shows Muscle!)	3.00	1.50	.90
330	World Series Game 4 (Reds Stay Alive!)	2.00	1.00	.60
331	World Series Game 5 (B. Robinson Commits Robbery!)	3.00	1.50	.90
332	World Series Summary (Convincing Performance!)	2.00	1.00	.60
333	Clay Kirby	1.00	.50	.30
334	Roberto Pena	1.00	.50	.30
335	Jerry Koosman	1.00	.50	.30
336	Tigers Team	3.00	1.50	.90
337	Jesus Alou	1.00	.50	.30
338	Gene Tenace	1.00	.50	.30
339	Wayne Simpson	1.00	.50	.30
340	Rico Petrocelli	1.00	.50	.30
341	*Steve Garvey*	60.00	30.00	18.00
342	Frank Tepedino	1.00	.50	.30
343	Pirates Rookies (Ed Acosta, *Milt May*)	1.00	.50	.30
344	Ellie Rodriguez	1.00	.50	.30
345	Joe Horlen	1.00	.50	.30
346	Lum Harris	1.00	.50	.30
347	Ted Uhlaender	1.00	.50	.30
348	Fred Norman	1.00	.50	.30
349	Rich Reese	1.00	.50	.30
350	Billy Williams	8.00	4.00	2.50
351	Jim Shellenback	1.00	.50	.30
352	Denny Doyle	1.00	.50	.30
353	Carl Taylor	1.00	.50	.30
354	Don McMahon	1.00	.50	.30
355	Bud Harrelson	1.00	.50	.30
356	Bob Locker	1.00	.50	.30
357	Reds Team	3.00	1.50	.90
358	Danny Cater	1.00	.50	.30
359	Ron Reed	1.00	.50	.30
360	Jim Fregosi	1.00	.50	.30
361	Don Sutton	3.50	1.75	1.00
362	Orioles Rookies (Mike Adamson, Roger Freed)	1.00	.50	.30
363	Mike Nagy	1.00	.50	.30
364	Tommy Dean	1.00	.50	.30
365	Bob Johnson	1.00	.50	.30
366	Ron Stone	1.00	.50	.30
367	Dalton Jones	1.00	.50	.30
368	Bob Veale	1.00	.50	.30
369a	Checklist 394-523 (orange helmet)	3.25	1.75	1.00
369b	Checklist 394-523 (red helmet, black line above ear)	3.25	1.75	1.00
369c	Checklist 394-523 (red helmet, no line)	3.25	1.75	1.00
370	Joe Torre	1.00	.50	.30
371	Jack Hiatt	1.00	.50	.30
372	Lew Krausse	1.00	.50	.30
373	Tom McCraw	1.00	.50	.30
374	Clete Boyer	1.00	.50	.30
375	Steve Hargan	1.00	.50	.30
376	Expos Rookies (Clyde Mashore, Ernie McAnally)	1.00	.50	.30
377	Greg Garrett	1.00	.50	.30
378	Tito Fuentes	1.00	.50	.30
379	Wayne Granger	1.00	.50	.30
380	Ted Williams	10.00	5.00	3.00
381	Fred Gladding	1.00	.50	.30
382	Jake Gibbs	1.00	.50	.30
383	Rod Gaspar	1.00	.50	.30
384	Rollie Fingers	7.50	3.75	2.25
385	Maury Wills	1.25	.60	.40
386	Red Sox Team	3.00	1.50	.90
387	Ron Herbel	1.00	.50	.30
388	Al Oliver	1.50	.70	.45
389	Ed Brinkman	1.00	.50	.30
390	Glenn Beckert	1.00	.50	.30
391	Twins Rookies (Steve Brye, Cotton Nash)	1.00	.50	.30
392	Grant Jackson	1.00	.50	.30
393	Merv Rettenmund	1.00	.50	.30
394	Clay Carroll	1.00	.50	.30
395	Roy White	1.00	.50	.30
396	Dick Schofield	1.00	.50	.30
397	Alvin Dark	1.00	.50	.30
398	Howie Reed	1.00	.50	.30
399	Jim French	1.00	.50	.30
400	Hank Aaron	45.00	22.00	13.50
401	Tom Murphy	1.00	.50	.30
402	Dodgers Team	3.00	1.50	.90
403	Joe Coleman	1.00	.50	.30
404	Astros Rookies (Buddy Harris, Roger Metzger)	1.00	.50	.30
405	Leo Cardenas	1.00	.50	.30
406	Ray Sadecki	1.00	.50	.30
407	Joe Rudi	1.00	.50	.30

		NR MT	EX	VG
408	Rafael Robles	1.00	.50	.30
409	Don Pavletich	1.00	.50	.30
410	Ken Holtzman	1.00	.50	.30
411	George Spriggs	1.00	.50	.30
412	Jerry Johnson	1.00	.50	.30
413	Pat Kelly	1.00	.50	.30
414	Woodie Fryman	1.00	.50	.30
415	Mike Hegan	1.00	.50	.30
416	Gene Alley	1.00	.50	.30
417	Dick Hall	1.00	.50	.30
418	Adolfo Phillips	1.00	.50	.30
419	Ron Hansen	1.00	.50	.30
420	Jim Merritt	1.00	.50	.30
421	John Stephenson	1.00	.50	.30
422	Frank Bertaina	1.00	.50	.30
423	Tigers Rookies (Tim Marting, Dennis Saunders)	1.00	.50	.30
424	Roberto Rodriquez (Rodriguez)	1.00	.50	.30
425	Doug Rader	1.00	.50	.30
426	Chris Cannizzaro	1.00	.50	.30
427	Bernie Allen	1.00	.50	.30
428	Jim McAndrew	1.00	.50	.30
429	Chuck Hinton	1.00	.50	.30
430	Wes Parker	1.00	.50	.30
431	Tom Burgmeier	1.00	.50	.30
432	Bob Didier	1.00	.50	.30
433	Skip Lockwood	1.00	.50	.30
434	Gary Sutherland	1.00	.50	.30
435	Jose Cardenal	1.00	.50	.30
436	Wilbur Wood	1.00	.50	.30
437	Danny Murtaugh	1.00	.50	.30
438	Mike McCormick	1.00	.50	.30
439	Phillies Rookies *(Greg Luzinski,* Scott Reid)	5.00	2.50	1.50
440	Bert Campaneris	1.00	.50	.30
441	Milt Pappas	1.00	.50	.30
442	Angels Team	3.00	1.50	.90
443	Rich Robertson	1.00	.50	.30
444	Jimmie Price	1.00	.50	.30
445	Art Shamsky	1.00	.50	.30
446	Bobby Bolin	1.00	.50	.30
447	*Cesar Geronimo*	1.00	.50	.30
448	Dave Roberts	1.00	.50	.30
449	Brant Alyea	1.00	.50	.30
450	Bob Gibson	10.00	5.00	3.00
451	Joe Keough	1.00	.50	.30
452	John Boccabella	1.00	.50	.30
453	Terry Crowley	1.00	.50	.30
454	Mike Paul	1.00	.50	.30
455	Don Kessinger	1.00	.50	.30
456	Bob Meyer	1.00	.50	.30
457	Willie Smith	1.00	.50	.30
458	White Sox Rookies (Dave Lemonds, Ron Lolich)	1.00	.50	.30
459	Jim Lefebvre	1.00	.50	.30
460	Fritz Peterson	1.00	.50	.30
461	Jim Hart	1.00	.50	.30
462	Senators Team	3.00	1.50	.90
463	Tom Kelley	1.00	.50	.30
464	Aurelio Rodriguez	1.00	.50	.30
465	Tim McCarver	1.50	.70	.45
466	Ken Berry	1.00	.50	.30
467	Al Santorini	1.00	.50	.30
468	Frank Fernandez	1.00	.50	.30
469	Bob Aspromonte	1.00	.50	.30
470	Bob Oliver	1.00	.50	.30
471	Tom Griffin	1.00	.50	.30
472	Ken Rudolph	1.00	.50	.30
473	Gary Wagner	1.00	.50	.30
474	Jim Fairey	1.00	.50	.30
475	Ron Perranoski	1.00	.50	.30
476	Dal Maxvill	1.00	.50	.30
477	Earl Weaver	3.00	1.50	.90
478	Bernie Carbo	1.00	.50	.30
479	Dennis Higgins	1.00	.50	.30
480	Manny Sanguillen	1.00	.50	.30
481	Daryl Patterson	1.00	.50	.30
482	Padres Team	3.00	1.50	.90
483	Gene Michael	1.00	.50	.30
484	Don Wilson	1.00	.50	.30
485	Ken McMullen	1.00	.50	.30
486	Steve Huntz	1.00	.50	.30
487	Paul Schaal	1.00	.50	.30
488	Jerry Stephenson	1.00	.50	.30
489	Luis Alvarado	1.00	.50	.30
490	Deron Johnson	1.00	.50	.30
491	Jim Hardin	1.00	.50	.30
492	Ken Boswell	1.00	.50	.30
493	Dave May	1.00	.50	.30
494	Braves Rookies (Ralph Garr, Rick Kester)	1.00	.50	.30

		NR MT	EX	VG
495	Felipe Alou	3.00	1.50	.90
496	Woody Woodward	1.00	.50	.30
497	Horacio Pina	1.00	.50	.30
498	John Kennedy	1.00	.50	.30
499	Checklist 524-643	3.25	1.75	1.00
500	Jim Perry	1.00	.50	.30
501	Andy Etchebarren	1.00	.50	.30
502	Cubs Team	3.00	1.50	.90
503	Gates Brown	1.00	.50	.30
504	Ken Wright	1.00	.50	.30
505	Ollie Brown	1.00	.50	.30
506	Bobby Knoop	1.00	.50	.30
507	George Stone	1.00	.50	.30
508	Roger Repoz	1.00	.50	.30
509	Jim Grant	1.00	.50	.30
510	Ken Harrelson	1.00	.50	.30
511	Chris Short	1.00	.50	.30
512	Red Sox Rookies (Mike Garman, Dick Mills)	1.00	.50	.30
513	Nolan Ryan	250.00	125.00	75.00
514	Ron Woods	1.00	.50	.30
515	Carl Morton	1.00	.50	.30
516	Ted Kubiak	1.00	.50	.30
517	Charlie Fox	1.00	.50	.30
518	Joe Grzenda	1.00	.50	.30
519	Willie Crawford	1.00	.50	.30
520	Tommy John	3.00	1.50	.90
521	Leron Lee	1.00	.50	.30
522	Twins Team	3.00	1.50	.90
523	John Odom	1.00	.50	.30
524	Mickey Stanley	3.00	1.50	.90
525	Ernie Banks	30.00	15.00	9.00
526	Ray Jarvis	3.00	1.50	.90
527	Cleon Jones	3.00	1.50	.90
528	Wally Bunker	3.00	1.50	.90
529	N.L. Rookies (Bill Buckner, Enzo Hernandez, Marty Perez)	4.00	2.00	1.25
530	Carl Yastrzemski	30.00	15.00	9.00
531	Mike Torrez	3.00	1.50	.90
532	Bill Rigney	3.00	1.50	.90
533	Mike Ryan	3.00	1.50	.90
534	Luke Walker	3.00	1.50	.90
535	Curt Flood	3.00	1.50	.90
536	Claude Raymond	3.00	1.50	.90
537	Tom Egan	3.00	1.50	.90
538	Angel Bravo	3.00	1.50	.90
539	Larry Brown	3.00	1.50	.90
540	Larry Dierker	3.00	1.50	.90
541	Bob Burda	3.00	1.50	.90
542	Bob Miller	3.00	1.50	.90
543	Yankees Team	7.50	3.75	2.25
544	Vida Blue	3.50	1.75	1.00
545	Dick Dietz	3.00	1.50	.90
546	John Matias	3.00	1.50	.90
547	Pat Dobson	3.00	1.50	.90
548	Don Mason	3.00	1.50	.90
549	Jim Brewer	3.00	1.50	.90
550	Harmon Killebrew	20.00	10.00	6.00
551	Frank Linzy	3.00	1.50	.90
552	Buddy Bradford	3.00	1.50	.90
553	Kevin Collins	3.00	1.50	.90
554	Lowell Palmer	3.00	1.50	.90
555	Walt Williams	3.00	1.50	.90
556	Jim McGlothlin	3.00	1.50	.90
557	Tom Satriano	3.00	1.50	.90
558	Hector Torres	3.00	1.50	.90
559	A.L. Rookies (Terry Cox, Bill Gogolewski, Gary Jones)	3.00	1.50	.90
560	Rusty Staub	4.00	2.00	1.25
561	Syd O'Brien	3.00	1.50	.90
562	Dave Giusti	3.00	1.50	.90
563	Giants Team	6.00	3.00	1.75
564	Al Fitzmorris	3.00	1.50	.90
565	Jim Wynn	3.00	1.50	.90
566	Tim Cullen	3.00	1.50	.90
567	Walt Alston	4.00	2.00	1.25
568	Sal Campisi	3.00	1.50	.90
569	Ivan Murrell	3.00	1.50	.90
570	Jim Palmer	24.00	12.00	7.25
571	Ted Sizemore	3.00	1.50	.90
572	Jerry Kenney	3.00	1.50	.90
573	Ed Kranepool	3.00	1.50	.90
574	Jim Bunning	4.00	2.00	1.25
575	Bill Freehan	3.00	1.50	.90
576	Cubs Rookies (Brock Davis, Adrian Garrett, Garry Jestadt)	3.00	1.50	.90
577	Jim Lonborg	4.00	2.00	1.25
578	Ron Hunt	3.00	1.50	.90
579	Marty Pattin	3.00	1.50	.90
580	Tony Perez	6.00	3.00	1.75
581	Roger Nelson	3.00	1.50	.90

#	Player	NR MT	EX	VG
582	Dave Cash	3.00	1.50	.90
583	Ron Cook	3.00	1.50	.90
584	Indians Team	6.00	3.00	1.75
585	Willie Davis	3.00	1.50	.90
586	Dick Woodson	3.00	1.50	.90
587	Sonny Jackson	3.00	1.50	.90
588	Tom Bradley	3.00	1.50	.90
589	Bob Barton	3.00	1.50	.90
590	Alex Johnson	3.00	1.50	.90
591	Jackie Brown	3.00	1.50	.90
592	Randy Hundley	3.00	1.50	.90
593	Jack Aker	3.00	1.50	.90
594	Cards Rookies (Bob Chlupsa, *Al Hrabosky*, Bob Stinson)	3.00	1.50	.90
595	Dave Johnson	3.00	1.50	.90
596	Mike Jorgensen	3.00	1.50	.90
597	Ken Suarez	3.00	1.50	.90
598	Rick Wise	3.00	1.50	.90
599	Norm Cash	4.00	2.00	1.25
600	Willie Mays	80.00	40.00	24.00
601	Ken Tatum	3.00	1.50	.90
602	Marty Martinez	3.00	1.50	.90
603	Pirates Team	7.50	3.75	2.25
604	John Gelnar	3.00	1.50	.90
605	Orlando Cepeda	6.00	3.00	1.75
606	Chuck Taylor	3.00	1.50	.90
607	Paul Ratliff	3.00	1.50	.90
608	Mike Wegener	3.00	1.50	.90
609	Leo Durocher	3.50	1.75	1.00
610	Amos Otis	3.00	1.50	.90
611	Tom Phoebus	3.00	1.50	.90
612	Indians Rookies (Lou Camilli, Ted Ford, Steve Mingori)	3.00	1.50	.90
613	Pedro Borbon	3.00	1.50	.90
614	Billy Cowan	3.00	1.50	.90
615	Mel Stottlemyre	3.00	1.50	.90
616	Larry Hisle	3.00	1.50	.90
617	Clay Dalrymple	3.00	1.50	.90
618	Tug McGraw	3.00	1.50	.90
619a	Checklist 644-752 (no copyright on back)	4.50	2.25	1.25
619b	Checklist 644-752 (with copyright, no wavy line on helmet brim)	3.00	1.50	.90
619c	Checklist 644-752 (with copyright, wavy line on helmet brim)	3.00	1.50	.90
620	Frank Howard	4.00	2.00	1.25
621	Ron Bryant	3.00	1.50	.90
622	Joe Lahoud	3.00	1.50	.90
623	Pat Jarvis	3.00	1.50	.90
624	Athletics Team	6.00	3.00	1.75
625	Lou Brock	20.00	10.00	6.00
626	Freddie Patek	3.00	1.50	.90
627	Steve Hamilton	3.00	1.50	.90
628	John Bateman	3.00	1.50	.90
629	John Hiller	3.00	1.50	.90
630	Roberto Clemente	80.00	40.00	24.00
631	Eddie Fisher	3.00	1.50	.90
632	Darrel Chaney	3.00	1.50	.90
633	A.L. Rookies (Bobby Brooks, Pete Koegel, Scott Northey)	3.00	1.50	.90
634	Phil Regan	3.00	1.50	.90
635	Bobby Murcer	4.00	2.00	1.25
636	Denny Lemaster	3.00	1.50	.90
637	Dave Bristol	3.00	1.50	.90
638	Stan Williams	3.00	1.50	.90
639	Tom Haller	3.00	1.50	.90
640	Frank Robinson	35.00	17.50	10.50
641	Mets Team	8.00	4.00	2.50
642	Jim Roland	3.00	1.50	.90
643	Rick Reichardt	3.00	1.50	.90
644	Jim Stewart	6.00	3.00	1.75
645	Jim Maloney	6.00	3.00	1.75
646	Bobby Floyd	6.00	3.00	1.75
647	Juan Pizarro	3.00	1.50	.90
648	Mets Rookies (Rich Folkers, Ted Martinez, *Jon Matlack*)	8.00	4.00	2.50
649	Sparky Lyle	8.00	4.00	2.50
650	Rich Allen	15.00	7.50	4.50
651	Jerry Robertson	6.00	3.00	1.75
652	Braves Team	3.25	1.75	1.00
653	Russ Snyder	6.00	3.00	1.75
654	Don Shaw	6.00	3.00	1.75
655	Mike Epstein	6.00	3.00	1.75
656	Gerry Nyman	6.00	3.00	1.75
657	Jose Azcue	3.00	1.50	.90
658	Paul Lindblad	6.00	3.00	1.75
659	Byron Browne	6.00	3.00	1.75
660	Ray Culp	3.00	1.50	.90
661	Chuck Tanner	6.00	3.00	1.75
662	Mike Hedlund	6.00	3.00	1.75
663	Marv Staehle	3.00	1.50	.90

#	Player	NR MT	EX	VG
664	Major League Rookies (Archie Reynolds, Bob Reynolds, Ken Reynolds)	6.00	3.00	1.75
665	Ron Swoboda	8.00	4.00	2.50
666	Gene Brabender	6.00	3.00	1.75
667	Pete Ward	3.25	1.75	1.00
668	Gary Neibauer	3.00	1.50	.90
669	Ike Brown	6.00	3.00	1.75
670	Bill Hands	3.00	1.50	.90
671	Bill Voss	6.00	3.00	1.75
672	Ed Crosby	6.00	3.00	1.75
673	Gerry Janeski	6.00	3.00	1.75
674	Expos Team	3.25	1.75	1.00
675	Dave Boswell	3.00	1.50	.90
676	Tommie Reynolds	3.00	1.50	.90
677	Jack DiLauro	6.00	3.00	1.75
678	George Thomas	3.00	1.50	.90
679	Don O'Riley	3.00	1.50	.90
680	Don Mincher	6.00	3.00	1.75
681	Bill Butler	3.00	1.50	.90
682	Terry Harmon	3.00	1.50	.90
683	Bill Burbach	6.00	3.00	1.75
684	Curt Motton	3.00	1.50	.90
685	Moe Drabowsky	3.00	1.50	.90
686	Chico Ruiz	6.00	3.00	1.75
687	Ron Taylor	6.00	3.00	1.75
688	Sparky Anderson	20.00	10.00	6.00
689	Frank Baker	3.00	1.50	.90
690	Bob Moose	3.00	1.50	.90
691	Bob Heise	3.00	1.50	.90
692	A.L. Rookies (Hal Haydel, Rogelio Moret, Wayne Twitchell)	6.00	3.00	1.75
693	Jose Pena	6.00	3.00	1.75
694	Rick Renick	6.00	3.00	1.75
695	Joe Niekro	3.00	1.50	.90
696	Jerry Morales	3.00	1.50	.90
697	Rickey Clark	6.00	3.00	1.75
698	Brewers Team	15.00	7.50	4.50
699	Jim Britton	3.00	1.50	.90
700	Boog Powell	12.00	6.00	3.50
701	Bob Garibaldi	3.00	1.50	.90
702	Milt Ramirez	3.00	1.50	.90
703	Mike Kekich	3.00	1.50	.90
704	J.C. Martin	6.00	3.00	1.75
705	Dick Selma	6.00	3.00	1.75
706	Joe Foy	6.00	3.00	1.75
707	Fred Lasher	3.00	1.50	.90
708	Russ Nagelson	6.00	3.00	1.75
709	Major League Rookies (*Dusty Baker, Don Baylor, Tom Paciorek*)	60.00	30.00	18.00
710	Sonny Siebert	3.00	1.50	.90
711	Larry Stahl	6.00	3.00	1.75
712	Jose Martinez	3.00	1.50	.90
713	Mike Marshall	6.00	3.00	1.75
714	Dick Williams	7.00	3.50	2.00
715	Horace Clarke	6.00	3.00	1.75
716	Dave Leonhard	3.00	1.50	.90
717	Tommie Aaron	6.00	3.00	1.75
718	Billy Wynne	3.00	1.50	.90
719	Jerry May	6.00	3.00	1.75
720	Matty Alou	3.50	1.75	1.00
721	John Morris	3.00	1.50	.90
722	Astros Team	9.00	4.50	2.75
723	Vicente Romo	6.00	3.00	1.75
724	Tom Tischinski	6.00	3.00	1.75
725	Gary Gentry	6.00	3.00	1.75
726	Paul Popovich	3.00	1.50	.90
727	Ray Lamb	6.00	3.00	1.75
728	N.L. Rookies (Keith Lampard, Wayne Redmond, Bernie Williams)	3.00	1.50	.90
729	Dick Billings	3.00	1.50	.90
730	Jim Rooker	3.00	1.50	.90
731	Jim Qualls	6.00	3.00	1.75
732	Bob Reed	3.00	1.50	.90
733	Lee Maye	6.00	3.00	1.75
734	Rob Gardner	6.00	3.00	1.75
735	Mike Shannon	6.00	3.00	1.75
736	Mel Queen	6.00	3.00	1.75
737	Preston Gomez	6.00	3.00	1.75
738	Russ Gibson	6.00	3.00	1.75
739	Barry Lersch	6.00	3.00	1.75
740	Luis Aparicio	15.00	7.50	4.50
741	Skip Guinn	3.00	1.50	.90
742	Royals Team	9.00	4.50	2.75
743	John O'Donoghue	6.00	3.00	1.75
744	Chuck Manuel	6.00	3.00	1.75
745	Sandy Alomar	6.00	3.00	1.75
746	Andy Kosco	3.00	1.50	.90
747	N.L. Rookies (Balor Moore, Al Severinsen, Scipio Spinks)	3.00	1.50	.90
748	John Purdin	6.00	3.00	1.75
749	Ken Szotkiewicz	3.00	1.50	.90

		NR MT	EX	VG
750	Denny McLain	15.00	7.50	4.50
751	Al Weis	6.00	3.00	1.75
752	Dick Drago	6.00	3.00	1.75

1971 Topps Coins

Measuring 1 1/2" in diameter, the latest edition of the Topps coins was a 153-piece set. The coins feature a color photograph surrounded by a colored band on the front. The band carries the player's name, team, position and several stars. Backs have a short biography, the coin number and encouragement to collect the entire set. Back colors differ, with #s 1-51 having a brass back, #s 52-102 chrome backs, and the rest have blue backs. Most of the stars of the period are included in the set.

		NR MT	EX	VG
Complete Set:		400.00	200.00	120.00
Common Player:		.90	.45	.25
1	Clarence Gaston	.90	.45	.25
2	Dave Johnson	1.25	.60	.40
3	Jim Bunning	2.00	1.00	.60
4	Jim Spencer	.90	.45	.25
5	Felix Millan	.90	.45	.25
6	Gerry Moses	.90	.45	.25
7	Fergie Jenkins	2.00	1.00	.60
8	Felipe Alou	1.00	.50	.30
9	Jim McGlothlin	.90	.45	.25
10	Dick McAuliffe	.90	.45	.25
11	Joe Torre	1.50	.70	.45
12	Jim Perry	1.25	.60	.40
13	Bobby Bonds	1.25	.60	.40
14	Danny Cater	.90	.45	.25
15	Bill Mazeroski	1.50	.70	.45
16	Luis Aparicio	5.00	2.50	1.50
17	Doug Rader	.90	.45	.25
18	Vada Pinson	1.50	.70	.45
19	John Bateman	.90	.45	.25
20	Lew Krausse	.90	.45	.25
21	Billy Grabarkewitz	.90	.45	.25
22	Frank Howard	1.50	.70	.45
23	Jerry Koosman	1.25	.60	.40
24	Rod Carew	8.00	4.00	2.50
25	Al Ferrara	.90	.45	.25
26	Dave McNally	1.00	.50	.30
27	Jim Hickman	.90	.45	.25
28	Sandy Alomar	.90	.45	.25
29	Lee May	1.00	.50	.30
30	Rico Petrocelli	1.00	.50	.30
31	Don Money	.90	.45	.25
32	Jim Rooker	.90	.45	.25
33	Dick Dietz	.90	.45	.25
34	Roy White	1.00	.50	.30
35	Carl Morton	.90	.45	.25
36	Walt Williams	.90	.45	.25
37	Phil Niekro	3.25	1.75	1.00
38	Bill Freehan	1.00	.50	.30
39	Julian Javier	.90	.45	.25
40	Rick Monday	1.00	.50	.30
41	Don Wilson	.90	.45	.25
42	Ray Fosse	.90	.45	.25
43	Art Shamsky	.90	.45	.25
44	Ted Savage	.90	.45	.25
45	Claude Osteen	1.00	.50	.30
46	Ed Brinkman	.90	.45	.25
47	Matty Alou	1.00	.50	.30
48	Bob Oliver	.90	.45	.25
49	Danny Coombs	.90	.45	.25

		NR MT	EX	VG
50	Frank Robinson	7.00	3.50	2.00
51	Randy Hundley	.90	.45	.25
52	Cesar Tovar	.90	.45	.25
53	Wayne Simpson	.90	.45	.25
54	Bobby Murcer	1.25	.60	.40
55	Tony Taylor	.90	.45	.25
56	Tommy John	2.50	1.25	.70
57	Willie McCovey	7.00	3.50	2.00
58	Carl Yastrzemski	15.00	7.50	4.50
59	Bob Bailey	.90	.45	.25
60	Clyde Wright	.90	.45	.25
61	Orlando Cepeda	2.00	1.00	.60
62	Al Kaline	7.00	3.50	2.00
63	Bob Gibson	7.00	3.50	2.00
64	Bert Campaneris	1.25	.60	.40
65	Ted Sizemore	.90	.45	.25
66	Duke Sims	.90	.45	.25
67	Bud Harrelson	.90	.45	.25
68	Jerry McNertney	.90	.45	.25
69	Jim Wynn	1.00	.50	.30
70	Dick Bosman	.90	.45	.25
71	Roberto Clemente	15.00	7.50	4.50
72	Rich Reese	.90	.45	.25
73	Gaylord Perry	4.00	2.00	1.25
74	Boog Powell	1.50	.70	.45
75	Billy Williams	5.00	2.50	1.50
76	Bill Melton	.90	.45	.25
77	Nate Colbert	.90	.45	.25
78	Reggie Smith	1.25	.60	.40
79	Deron Johnson	.90	.45	.25
80	Jim Hunter	5.00	2.50	1.50
81	Bob Tolan	.90	.45	.25
82	Jim Northrup	.90	.45	.25
83	Ron Fairly	1.00	.50	.30
84	Alex Johnson	.90	.45	.25
85	Pat Jarvis	.90	.45	.25
86	Sam McDowell	1.00	.50	.30
87	Lou Brock	7.00	3.50	2.00
88	Danny Walton	.90	.45	.25
89	Denis Menke	.90	.45	.25
90	Jim Palmer	7.00	3.50	2.00
91	Tommie Agee	.90	.45	.25
92	Duane Josephson	.90	.45	.25
93	Willie Davis	1.00	.50	.30
94	Mel Stottlemyre	1.00	.50	.30
95	Ron Santo	1.25	.60	.40
96	Amos Otis	1.00	.50	.30
97	Ken Henderson	.90	.45	.25
98	George Scott	1.00	.50	.30
99	Dock Ellis	.90	.45	.25
100	Harmon Killebrew	7.00	3.50	2.00
101	Pete Rose	30.00	15.00	9.00
102	Rick Reichardt	.90	.45	.25
103	Cleon Jones	.90	.45	.25
104	Ron Perranoski	.90	.45	.25
105	Tony Perez	2.50	1.25	.70
106	Mickey Lolich	1.25	.60	.40
107	Tim McCarver	1.25	.60	.40
108	Reggie Jackson	12.00	6.00	3.50
109	Chris Cannizzaro	.90	.45	.25
110	Steve Hargan	.90	.45	.25
111	Rusty Staub	2.50	1.25	.70
112	Andy Messersmith	1.00	.50	.30
113	Rico Carty	1.25	.60	.40
114	Brooks Robinson	7.00	3.50	2.00
115	Steve Carlton	7.00	3.50	2.00
116	Mike Hegan	.90	.45	.25
117	Joe Morgan	4.50	2.25	1.25
118	Thurman Munson	5.00	2.50	1.50
119	Don Kessinger	1.00	.50	.30
120	Joe Horlen	.90	.45	.25
121	Wes Parker	1.00	.50	.30
122	Sonny Siebert	.90	.45	.25
123	Willie Stargell	5.00	2.50	1.50
124	Ellie Rodriguez	.90	.45	.25
125	Juan Marichal	5.00	2.50	1.50
126	Mike Epstein	.90	.45	.25
127	Tom Seaver	8.00	4.00	2.50
128	Tony Oliva	2.50	1.25	.70
129	Jim Merritt	.90	.45	.25
130	Willie Horton	1.00	.50	.30
131	Rick Wise	.90	.45	.25
132	Sal Bando	1.00	.50	.30
133	Ollie Brown	.90	.45	.25
134	Ken Harrelson	1.00	.50	.30
135	Mack Jones	.90	.45	.25
136	Jim Fregosi	1.00	.50	.30
137	Hank Aaron	15.00	7.50	4.50
138	Fritz Peterson	.90	.45	.25
139	Joe Hague	.90	.45	.25
140	Tommy Harper	.90	.45	.25
141	Larry Dierker	.90	.45	.25

		NR MT	EX	VG
142	Tony Conigliaro	1.50	.70	.45
143	Glenn Beckert	1.00	.50	.30
144	Carlos May	.90	.45	.25
145	Don Sutton	3.25	1.75	1.00
146	Paul Casanova	.90	.45	.25
147	Bob Moose	.90	.45	.25
148	Leo Cardenas	.90	.45	.25
149	Johnny Bench	8.00	4.00	2.50
150	Mike Cuellar	1.00	.50	.30
151	Donn Clendenon	.90	.45	.25
152	Lou Piniella	1.25	.60	.40
153	Willie Mays	15.00	7.50	4.50

1971 Topps Greatest Moments

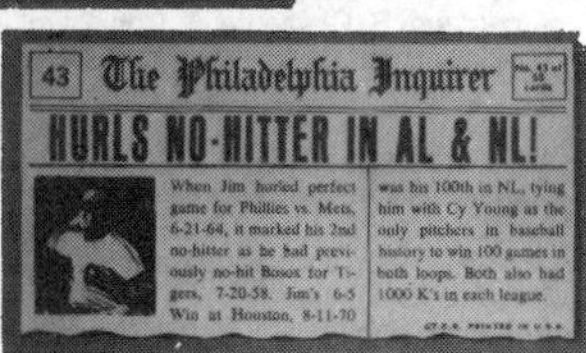

This 55-card set features a great moment from the careers of top players at the time. The front of the 2-1/2" by 4-3/4" cards features a portrait photo of the player at the left and deckle-edge action photo at the right. There is a small headline on the white border of the action photo. The player's name and "One of Baseball's Greatest Moments" along with a black border complete the front. The back features a detail from the front photo and the story of the event. The newspaper style presentation includes the name of real newspapers. Relatively scarce, virtually every card in this set is a star or at least an above-average player.

		NR MT	EX	VG
Complete Set:		1650.00	825.00	495.00
Common Player:		4.00	2.00	1.25
1	Thurman Munson	60.00	30.00	18.00
2	Hoyt Wilhelm	30.00	15.00	9.00
3	Rico Carty	15.00	7.50	4.50
4	Carl Morton	4.00	2.00	1.25
5	Sal Bando	5.00	2.50	1.50
6	Bert Campaneris	5.00	2.50	1.50
7	Jim Kaat	20.00	10.00	6.00
8	Harmon Killebrew	60.00	30.00	18.00
9	Brooks Robinson	75.00	37.00	22.00
10	Jim Perry	15.00	7.50	4.50
11	Tony Oliva	20.00	10.00	6.00
12	Vada Pinson	20.00	10.00	6.00
13	Johnny Bench	175.00	87.00	52.00
14	Tony Perez	25.00	12.50	7.50
15	Pete Rose	90.00	45.00	27.00
16	Jim Fregosi	4.00	2.00	1.25
17	Alex Johnson	4.00	2.00	1.25
18	Clyde Wright	4.00	2.00	1.25
19	Al Kaline	25.00	12.50	7.50
20	Denny McLain	20.00	10.00	6.00
21	Jim Northrup	15.00	7.50	4.50
22	Bill Freehan	15.00	7.50	4.50
23	Mickey Lolich	20.00	10.00	6.00
24	Bob Gibson	18.00	9.00	5.50
25	Tim McCarver	5.00	2.50	1.50
26	Orlando Cepeda	7.00	3.50	2.00
27	Lou Brock	18.00	9.00	5.50
28	Nate Colbert	4.00	2.00	1.25
29	Maury Wills	20.00	10.00	6.00
30	Wes Parker	15.00	7.50	4.50
31	Jim Wynn	15.00	7.50	4.50
32	Larry Dierker	15.00	7.50	4.50
33	Bill Melton	15.00	7.50	4.50
34	Joe Morgan	40.00	20.00	12.00
35	Rusty Staub	20.00	10.00	6.00
36	Ernie Banks	25.00	12.50	7.50
37	Billy Williams	50.00	25.00	15.00
38	Lou Piniella	20.00	10.00	6.00
39	Rico Petrocelli	4.00	2.00	1.25
40	Carl Yastrzemski	60.00	30.00	18.00
41	Willie Mays	45.00	22.00	13.50
42	Tommy Harper	15.00	7.50	4.50
43	Jim Bunning	7.00	3.50	2.00
44	Fritz Peterson	15.00	7.50	4.50
45	Roy White	15.00	7.50	4.50
46	Bobby Murcer	15.00	7.50	4.50
47	Reggie Jackson	250.00	125.00	75.00
48	Frank Howard	20.00	10.00	6.00
49	Dick Bosman	15.00	7.50	4.50
50	Sam McDowell	4.00	2.00	1.25
51	Luis Aparicio	12.00	6.00	3.50
52	Willie McCovey	15.00	7.50	4.50
53	Joe Pepitone	15.00	7.50	4.50
54	Jerry Grote	15.00	7.50	4.50
55	Bud Harrelson	15.00	7.50	4.50

1971 Topps Super

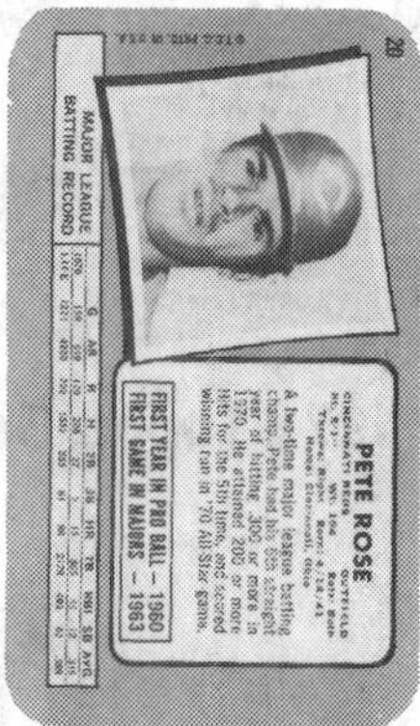

Topps continued to produce its special oversized cards in 1971. The cards, measuring 3-1/8" by 5-1/4," carry a large color photograph with a facsimile autograph on the front. Backs are basically enlargements of the player's regular Topps card. The set size was enlarged to 63 cards in 1971, so there are no short-printed cards as in 1970. Again, Topps included almost every major star who was active at the time, so the set of oversized cards with rounded corners remains an interesting source for those seeking the big names of the era.

		NR MT	EX	VG
Complete Set:		200.00	100.00	60.00
Common Player:		.80	.40	.25
1	Reggie Smith	1.00	.50	.30
2	Gaylord Perry	3.00	1.50	.90
3	Ted Savage	.80	.40	.25
4	Donn Clendenon	.80	.40	.25
5	John "Boog" Powell	1.25	.60	.40
6	Tony Perez	1.75	.90	.50
7	Dick Bosman	.80	.40	.25
8	Alex Johnson	.80	.40	.25
9	Rusty Staub	1.25	.60	.40
10	Mel Stottlemyre	1.00	.50	.30
11	Tony Oliva	1.50	.70	.45
12	Bill Freehan	1.00	.50	.30
13	Fritz Peterson	.80	.40	.25
14	Wes Parker	.80	.40	.25
15	Cesar Cedeno	1.25	.60	.40
16	Sam McDowell	1.00	.50	.30
17	Frank Howard	1.50	.70	.45
18	Dave McNally	1.00	.50	.30
19	Rico Petrocelli	.80	.40	.25
20	Pete Rose	25.00	12.50	7.50
21	Luke Walker	.80	.40	.25
22	Nate Colbert	.80	.40	.25
23	Luis Aparicio	2.50	1.25	.70
24	Jim Perry	1.00	.50	.30
25	Louis Brock	4.50	2.25	1.25
26	Roy White	1.00	.50	.30
27	Claude Osteen	.80	.40	.25

		NR MT	EX	VG
28	Carl W. Morton	.80	.40	.25
29	Ricardo A. Jacabo Carty	1.00	.50	.30
30	Larry Dierker	.80	.40	.25
31	Dagoberto Campaneris	1.00	.50	.30
32	Johnny Bench	8.00	4.00	2.50
33	Felix Millan	.80	.40	.25
34	Tim McCarver	1.25	.60	.40
35	Ronald Santo	1.25	.60	.40
36	Tommie Agee	.80	.40	.25
37	Roberto Clemente	10.00	5.00	3.00
38	Reggie Jackson	15.00	7.50	4.50
39	Clyde Wright	.80	.40	.25
40	Rich Allen	1.50	.70	.45
41	Curt Flood	1.25	.60	.40
42	Fergie Jenkins	1.75	.90	.50
43	Willie Stargell	3.00	1.50	.90
44	Henry Aaron	10.00	5.00	3.00
45	Amos Otis	1.00	.50	.30
46	Willie McCovey	4.50	2.25	1.25
47	William Melton	.80	.40	.25
48	Robert Gibson	3.50	1.75	1.00
49	Carl Yastrzemski	15.00	7.50	4.50
50	Glenn Beckert	1.00	.50	.30
51	Ray Fosse	.80	.40	.25
52	Clarence Gaston	.80	.40	.25
53	Tom Seaver	8.00	4.00	2.50
54	Al Kaline	6.00	3.00	1.75
55	Jim Northrup	.80	.40	.25
56	Willie Mays	10.00	5.00	3.00
57	Sal Bando	1.00	.50	.30
58	Deron Johnson	.80	.40	.25
59	Brooks Robinson	7.00	3.50	2.00
60	Harmon Killebrew	6.00	3.00	1.75
61	Joseph Torre	1.75	.90	.50
62	Lou Piniella	1.25	.60	.40
63	Tommy Harper	.80	.40	.25

1971 Topps Baseball Tattoos

Topps once again produced baseball tattoos in 1971. This time, the tattoos came in a variety of sizes, shapes and themes. The sheets of tattoos measure 3-1/2" by 14-1/4." Each sheet contains an assortment of tattoos in two sizes, 1-3/4" by 2-3/8," or 1-3/16" by 1-3/4." There are players, facsimile autographed baseballs, team pennants and assorted baseball cartoon figures carried on the 16 different sheets. Listings below are for complete sheets; with the exception of the biggest-name stars, individual tattoos have little or no collector value.

		NR MT	EX	VG
	Complete Sheet Set:	175.00	87.00	52.00
	Common Sheet:	4.00	2.00	1.25
1	Brooks Robinson Autograph, Montreal Expos Pennant, San Francisco Giants Pennant, Sal Bando, Dick Bosman, Nate Colbert, Cleon Jones, Juan Marichal, B. Robinson	10.00	5.00	3.00
2	Boston Red Sox Pennant, Carl Yastrzemski Autograph, New York Mets Pennant, Glenn Beckert, Tommy Harper, Ken Henderson, Fritz Peterson, Bob Robertson, C. Yastrzemski	18.00	9.00	5.50
3	Jim Fregosi Autograph, New York Yankees Pennant, Philadelphia Phillies Pennant, Orlando Cepeda, Jim Fregosi, Randy Hundley, Reggie Jackson, Jerry Koosman, Jim Palmer	15.00	7.50	4.50
4	Kansas City Royals Pennant, Oakland Athletics Pennant, Sam McDowell Autograph, Dick Dietz, C. Gaston, Dave Johnson, Sam McDowell, Gary Nolan, Amos Otis	3.50	1.75	1.00
5	Al Kaline Autograph, Atlanta Braves Pennant, L.A. Dodgers Pennant, B. Grabarkewitz, Al Kaline, Lee May, Tom Murphy, Vada Pinson, M. Sanguillen	10.00	5.00	3.00
6	Chicago Cubs Pennant, Cincinnati Reds Pennant, Harmon Killebrew Autograph, Luis Aparicio, Paul Blair, C. Cannizzaro, D. Clendenon, Larry Dieker, H. Killebrew	10.00	5.00	3.00
7	Boog Powell Autograph, Cleveland Indians Pennant, Milwaukee Brewers Pennant, Rich Allen, B. Campaneris, Don Money, Boog Powell, Ted Savage, Rusty Staub	5.00	2.50	1.50
8	Chicago White Sox Pennant, Frank Howard Autograph, San Diego Padres Pennant, Leo Cardenas, Bill Hands, Frank Howard, Wes Parker, Reggie Smith, W. Stargell	5.00	2.50	1.50
9	Detroit Tigers Pennant, Henry Aaron Autograph, Hank Aaron, Tommy Agee, Jim Hunter, Dick McAuliffe, Tony Perez, Lou Piniella	15.00	7.50	4.50
10	Baltimore Orioles Pennant, Fergie Jenkins Autograph, R. Clemente, T. Conigliaro, Fergie Jenkins, T. Munson, Gary Peters, Joe Torre	12.00	6.00	3.50
11	Johnny Bench Autograph, Washington Senators Pennant, Johnny Bench, Rico Carty, B. Mazeroski, Bob Oliver, R. Petrocelli, F. Robinson	10.00	5.00	3.00
12	Billy Williams Autograph, Houston Astros Pennant, Bill Freehan, Dave McNally, Felix Millan, M. Stottlemyre, Bob Tolan, Billy Williams	6.00	3.00	1.75
13	Pittsburgh Pirates Pennant, Willie McCovey Autograph, Ray Culp, Bud Harrelson, Mickey Lolich, W. McCovey, Ron Santo, Roy White	9.00	4.50	2.75
14	Minnesota Twins Pennant, Tom Seaver Autograph, Bill Melton, Jim Perry, Pete Rose, Tom Seaver, Maury Wills, Clyde Wright	25.00	12.50	7.50
15	Robert Gibson Autograph, St. Louis Cardinals Pennant, Rod Carew, Bob Gibson, Alex Johnson, Don Kessinger, Jim Merritt, Rick Monday	9.00	4.50	2.75
16	California Angels Pennant, Willie Mays Autograph, Larry Bowa, Mike Cuellar, Ray Fosse, Willie Mays, Carl Morton, Tony Oliva	15.00	7.50	4.50

1972 Topps

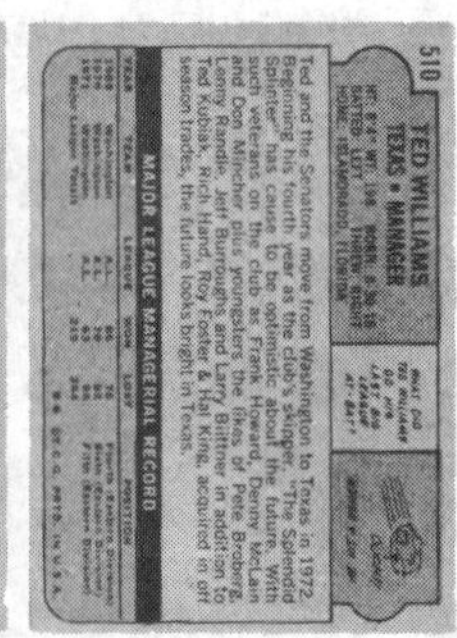

The largest Topps issue of its time appeared in 1972, with the set size reaching the 787 mark. The 2-1/2" by 3-1/2" cards are something special as well. Their fronts have a color photo which is shaped into an arch and surrounded by two different color borders, all of which is inside the overall white border. The player's name is in a white panel below the picture while the team name is above the picture in what might best be described as "superhero" type in a variety of colors. No mention of the player's position appears on the front. Cards backs are tame by comparison, featuring statistics and a trivia question. The set features a record number of specialty cards including more than six dozen "In Action" (shown as "IA" in checklists below) cards featuring action shots of popular players. There are the usual statistical leaders, playoff and World Series highlights. Other innovations are 16 "Boyhood Photo" cards which depict scrapbook black and white photos of 1972's top players, and a group of cards depicting the trophies which comprise baseball's major awards. Finally, a group of seven "Traded" cards was included which feature a large "Traded" across the front of the card.

	NR MT	EX	VG
Complete Set (787):	2500.00	1250.00	750.00
Common Player: 1-394	.75	.40	.25
Common Player: 395-525	1.00	.50	.30
Common Player: 526-656	2.00	1.00	.60
Common Player: 657-787	6.00	3.00	1.75

No.	Card	NR MT	EX	VG
1	World Champions (Pirates Team)	8.00	4.00	2.50
2	Ray Culp	.75	.40	.25
3	Bob Tolan	.75	.40	.25
4	Checklist 1-132	4.00	2.00	1.25
5	John Bateman	.75	.40	.25
6	Fred Scherman	.75	.40	.25
7	Enzo Hernandez	.75	.40	.25
8	Ron Swoboda	.75	.40	.25
9	Stan Williams	.75	.40	.25
10	Amos Otis	.75	.40	.25
11	Bobby Valentine	.75	.40	.25
12	Jose Cardenal	.75	.40	.25
13	Joe Grzenda	.75	.40	.25
14	Phillies Rookiess (Mike Anderson, Pete Koegel, Wayne Twitchell)	.75	.40	.25
15	Walt Williams	.75	.40	.25
16	Mike Jorgensen	.75	.40	.25
17	Dave Duncan	.75	.40	.25
18a	Juan Pizarro (green under "C" and "S")	3.50	1.75	1.00
18b	Juan Pizarro (yellow under "C" and "S")	.75	.40	.25
19	Billy Cowan	.75	.40	.25
20	Don Wilson	.75	.40	.25
21	Braves Team	3.50	1.75	1.00
22	Rob Gardner	.75	.40	.25
23	Ted Kubiak	.75	.40	.25
24	Ted Ford	.75	.40	.25
25	Bill Singer	.75	.40	.25
26	Andy Etchebarren	.75	.40	.25
27	Bob Johnson	.75	.40	.25
28	Twins Rookies (Steve Brye, Bob Gebhard, Hal Haydel)	.75	.40	.25
29a	Bill Bonham (green under "C" and "S")	3.50	1.75	1.00
29b	Bill Bonham (yellow under "C" and "S")	.75	.40	.25
30	Rico Petrocelli	.90	.45	.25
31	Cleon Jones	.75	.40	.25
32	Cleon Jones (In Action)	.75	.40	.25
33	Billy Martin	4.50	2.25	1.25
34	Billy Martin (In Action)	1.50	.70	.45
35	Jerry Johnson	.75	.40	.25
36	Jerry Johnson (In Action)	.75	.40	.25
37	Carl Yastrzemski	10.00	5.00	3.00
38	Carl Yastrzemski (In Action)	6.00	3.00	1.75
39	Bob Barton	.75	.40	.25
40	Bob Barton (In Action)	.75	.40	.25
41	Tommy Davis	.80	.40	.25
42	Tommy Davis (In Action)	.75	.40	.25
43	Rick Wise	.75	.40	.25
44	Rick Wise (In Action)	.75	.40	.25
45a	Glenn Beckert (green under "C" and "S")	3.50	1.75	1.00
45b	Glenn Beckert (yellow under "C" and "S")	.75	.40	.25
46	Glenn Beckert (In Action)	.75	.40	.25
47	John Ellis	.75	.40	.25
48	John Ellis (In Action)	.75	.40	.25
49	Willie Mays	30.00	15.00	9.00
50	Willie Mays (In Action)	15.00	7.50	4.50
51	Harmon Killebrew	6.00	3.00	1.75
52	Harmon Killebrew (In Action)	4.00	2.00	1.25
53	Bud Harrelson	.75	.40	.25
54	Bud Harrelson (In Action)	.75	.40	.25
55	Clyde Wright	.75	.40	.25
56	Rich Chiles	.75	.40	.25
57	Bob Oliver	.75	.40	.25
58	Ernie McAnally	.75	.40	.25
59	*Fred Stanley*	.90	.45	.25
60	Manny Sanguillen	.75	.40	.25
61	Cubs Rookies (Gene Hiser, *Burt Hooton,* Earl Stephenson)	1.00	.50	.30
62	Angel Mangual	.75	.40	.25
63	Duke Sims	.75	.40	.25
64	Pete Broberg	.75	.40	.25
65	Cesar Cedeno	1.00	.50	.30
66	Ray Corbin	.75	.40	.25
67	Red Schoendienst	3.00	1.50	.90
68	Jim York	.75	.40	.25
69	Roger Freed	.75	.40	.25
70	Mike Cuellar	.75	.40	.25
71	Angels Team	3.00	1.50	.90
72	*Bruce Kison*	.75	.40	.25
73	Steve Huntz	.75	.40	.25
74	Cecil Upshaw	.75	.40	.25
75	Bert Campaneris	.90	.45	.25
76	Don Carrithers	.75	.40	.25
77	Ron Theobald	.75	.40	.25
78	Steve Arlin	.75	.40	.25
79	Red Sox Rookies *(Cecil Cooper, Carlton Fisk,* Mike Garman)	100.00	50.00	30.00
80	Tony Perez	4.00	2.00	1.25
81	Mike Hedlund	.75	.40	.25
82	Ron Woods	.75	.40	.25
83	Dalton Jones	.75	.40	.25
84	Vince Colbert	.75	.40	.25
85	N.L. Batting Leaders (Glenn Beckert, Ralph Garr, Joe Torre)	2.00	1.00	.60
86	A.L. Batting Leaders (Bobby Murcer, Tony Oliva, Merv Rettenmund)	2.00	1.00	.60
87	N.L. R.B.I. Leaders (Hank Aaron, Willie Stargell, Joe Torre)	4.50	2.25	1.25
88	A.L. R.B.I. Leaders (Harmon Killebrew, Frank Robinson, Reggie Smith)	3.50	1.75	1.00
89	N.L. Home Run Leaders (Hank Aaron, Lee May, Willie Stargell)	4.50	2.25	1.25
90	A.L. Home Run Leaders (Norm Cash, Reggie Jackson, Bill Melton)	3.50	1.75	1.00
91	N.L. E.R.A. Leaders (Dave Roberts, Tom Seaver, Don Wilson)	3.00	1.50	.90
92	A.L. E.R.A. Leaders (Vida Blue, Jim Palmer, Wilbur Wood)	3.00	1.50	.90
93	N.L. Pitching Leaders (Steve Carlton, Al Downing, Fergie Jenkins, Tom Seaver)	3.50	1.75	1.00
94	A.L. Pitching Leaders (Vida Blue, Mickey Lolich, Wilbur Wood)	2.00	1.00	.60
95	N.L. Strikeout Leaders (Fergie Jenkins, Tom Seaver, Bill Stoneman)	3.00	1.50	.90
96	A.L. Strikeout Leaders (Vida Blue, Joe Coleman, Mickey Lolich)	2.00	1.00	.60
97	Tom Kelley	.75	.40	.25
98	Chuck Tanner	.70	.35	.20
99	*Ross Grimsley*	.80	.40	.25
100	Frank Robinson	6.00	3.00	1.75
101	Astros Rookies (Ray Busse, Bill Grief, *J.R. Richard)*	1.00	.50	.30
102	Lloyd Allen	.75	.40	.25
103	Checklist 133-263	3.00	1.50	.90
104	*Toby Harrah*	1.50	.70	.45
105	Gary Gentry	.75	.40	.25
106	Brewers Team	3.00	1.50	.90
107	*Jose Cruz*	2.50	1.25	.70
108	Gary Waslewski	.75	.40	.25
109	Jerry May	.75	.40	.25
110	Ron Hunt	.75	.40	.25
111	Jim Grant	.75	.40	.25
112	Greg Luzinski	1.00	.50	.30
113	Rogelio Moret	.75	.40	.25
114	Bill Buckner	1.25	.60	.40
115	Jim Fregosi	.75	.40	.25
116	*Ed Farmer*	.75	.40	.25
117a	Cleo James (green under "C" and "S")	3.50	1.75	1.00
117b	Cleo James (yellow under "C" and "S")	.75	.40	.25
118	Skip Lockwood	.75	.40	.25
119	Marty Perez	.75	.40	.25
120	Bill Freehan	.75	.40	.25
121	Ed Sprague	.75	.40	.25
122	Larry Biittner	.75	.40	.25
123	Ed Acosta	.75	.40	.25
124	Yankees (Alan Closter, Roger Hambright, Rusty Torres)	.75	.40	.25
125	Dave Cash	.75	.40	.25
126	Bart Johnson	.75	.40	.25
127	Duffy Dyer	.75	.40	.25
128	Eddie Watt	.75	.40	.25
129	Charlie Fox	.75	.40	.25
130	Bob Gibson	6.00	3.00	1.75

		NR MT	EX	VG
131	Jim Nettles	.75	.40	.25
132	Joe Morgan	5.00	2.50	1.50
133	Joe Keough	.75	.40	.25
134	Carl Morton	.75	.40	.25
135	Vada Pinson	1.00	.50	.30
136	Darrel Chaney	.75	.40	.25
137	Dick Williams	.75	.40	.25
138	Mike Kekich	.75	.40	.25
139	Tim McCarver	1.00	.50	.30
140	Pat Dobson	.75	.40	.25
141	Mets Rookies (Buzz Capra, Jon Matlack, Leroy Stanton)	.75	.40	.25
142	*Chris Chambliss*	1.25	.60	.40
143	Garry Jestadt	.75	.40	.25
144	Marty Pattin	.75	.40	.25
145	Don Kessinger	.75	.40	.25
146	Steve Kealey	.75	.40	.25
147	*Dave Kingman*	4.00	2.00	1.25
148	Dick Billings	.75	.40	.25
149	Gary Neibauer	.75	.40	.25
150	Norm Cash	1.00	.50	.30
151	Jim Brewer	.75	.40	.25
152	Gene Clines	.75	.40	.25
153	Rick Auerbach	.75	.40	.25
154	Ted Simmons	1.00	.50	.30
155	Larry Dierker	.75	.40	.25
156	Twins Team	3.00	1.50	.90
157	Don Gullett	.75	.40	.25
158	Jerry Kenney	.75	.40	.25
159	John Boccabella	.75	.40	.25
160	Andy Messersmith	.75	.40	.25
161	Brock Davis	.75	.40	.25
162	Brewers Rookies (Jerry Bell, *Darrell Porter,* Bob Reynolds) (Bell & Porter photos transposed)	.75	.40	.25
163	Tug McGraw	.75	.40	.25
164	Tug McGraw (In Action)	.75	.40	.25
165	*Chris Speier*	1.00	.50	.30
166	Chris Speier (In Action)	.75	.40	.25
167	Deron Johnson	.75	.40	.25
168	Deron Johnson (In Action)	.75	.40	.25
169	Vida Blue	1.00	.50	.30
170	Vida Blue (In Action)	.75	.40	.25
171	Darrell Evans	1.00	.50	.30
172	Darrell Evans (In Action)	.75	.40	.25
173	Clay Kirby	.75	.40	.25
174	Clay Kirby (In Action)	.75	.40	.25
175	Tom Haller	.75	.40	.25
176	Tom Haller (In Action)	.75	.40	.25
177	Paul Schaal	.75	.40	.25
178	Paul Schaal (In Action)	.75	.40	.25
179	Dock Ellis	.75	.40	.25
180	Dock Ellis (In Action)	.75	.40	.25
181	Ed Kranepool	.75	.40	.25
182	Ed Kranepool (In Action)	.75	.40	.25
183	Bill Melton	.75	.40	.25
184	Bill Melton (In Action)	.75	.40	.25
185	Ron Bryant	.75	.40	.25
186	Ron Bryant (In Action)	.75	.40	.25
187	Gates Brown	.75	.40	.25
188	Frank Lucchesi	.75	.40	.25
189	Gene Tenace	.75	.40	.25
190	Dave Giusti	.75	.40	.25
191	*Jeff Burroughs*	1.00	.50	.30
192	Cubs Team	3.00	1.50	.90
193	*Kurt Bevacqua*	.75	.40	.25
194	Fred Norman	.75	.40	.25
195	Orlando Cepeda	2.00	1.00	.60
196	Mel Queen	.75	.40	.25
197	Johnny Briggs	.75	.40	.25
198	Dodgers Rookies *(Charlie Hough,* Bob O'Brien, Mike Strahler)	6.00	3.00	1.75
199	Mike Fiore	.75	.40	.25
200	Lou Brock	6.00	3.00	1.75
201	Phil Roof	.75	.40	.25
202	Scipio Spinks	.75	.40	.25
203	*Ron Blomberg*	.75	.40	.25
204	Tommy Helms	.75	.40	.25
205	Dick Drago	.75	.40	.25
206	Dal Maxvill	.75	.40	.25
207	Tom Egan	.75	.40	.25
208	Milt Pappas	.75	.40	.25
209	Joe Rudi	.75	.40	.25
210	Denny McLain	1.00	.50	.30
211	Gary Sutherland	.75	.40	.25
212	Grant Jackson	.75	.40	.25
213	Angels Rookies (Art Kusnyer, Billy Parker, Tom Silverio)	.75	.40	.25
214	Mike McQueen	.75	.40	.25
215	Alex Johnson	.75	.40	.25
216	Joe Niekro	.75	.40	.25

		NR MT	EX	VG
217	Roger Metzger	.75	.40	.25
218	Eddie Kasko	.75	.40	.25
219	*Rennie Stennett*	.75	.40	.25
220	Jim Perry	.75	.40	.25
221	N.L. Playoffs (Bucs Champs!)	2.00	1.00	.60
222	A.L. Playoffs (Orioles Champs!)	2.00	1.00	.60
223	World Series Game 1	2.00	1.00	.60
224	World Series Game 2	2.00	1.00	.60
225	World Series Game 3	2.00	1.00	.60
226	World Series Game 4	2.00	1.00	.60
227	World Series Game 5	2.00	1.00	.60
228	World Series Game 6	2.00	1.00	.60
229	World Series Game 7	2.00	1.00	.60
230	World Series Summary (Series Celebration)	2.00	1.00	.60
231	Casey Cox	.75	.40	.25
232	Giants Rookies (Chris Arnold, Jim Barr, Dave Rader)	.75	.40	.25
233	Jay Johnstone	.75	.40	.25
234	Ron Taylor	.75	.40	.25
235	Merv Rettenmund	.75	.40	.25
236	Jim McGlothlin	.75	.40	.25
237	Yankees Team	4.50	2.25	1.25
238	Leron Lee	.75	.40	.25
239	Tom Timmermann	.75	.40	.25
240	Rich Allen	2.00	1.00	.60
241	Rollie Fingers	6.00	3.00	1.75
242	Don Mincher	.75	.40	.25
243	Frank Linzy	.75	.40	.25
244	Steve Braun	.75	.40	.25
245	Tommie Agee	.75	.40	.25
246	Tom Burgmeier	.75	.40	.25
247	Milt May	.75	.40	.25
248	Tom Bradley	.75	.40	.25
249	Harry Walker	.75	.40	.25
250	Boog Powell	1.25	.60	.40
251a	Checklist 264-394 (small print on front)	3.00	1.50	.90
251b	Checklist 264-394 (large print on front)	3.00	1.50	.90
252	Ken Reynolds	.75	.40	.25
253	Sandy Alomar	.75	.40	.25
254	Boots Day	.75	.40	.25
255	Jim Lonborg	.90	.45	.25
256	George Foster	1.00	.50	.30
257	Tigers Rookies (Jim Foor, Tim Hosley, Paul Jata)	.75	.40	.25
258	Randy Hundley	.75	.40	.25
259	Sparky Lyle	1.00	.50	.30
260	Ralph Garr	.75	.40	.25
261	Steve Mingori	.75	.40	.25
262	Padres Team	3.00	1.50	.90
263	Felipe Alou	2.00	1.00	.60
264	Tommy John	2.00	1.00	.60
265	Wes Parker	.75	.40	.25
266	Bobby Bolin	.75	.40	.25
267	Dave Concepcion	1.75	.90	.50
268	A's Rookies (Dwain Anderson, Chris Floethe)	.75	.40	.25
269	Don Hahn	.75	.40	.25
270	Jim Palmer	10.00	5.00	3.00
271	Ken Rudolph	.75	.40	.25
272	*Mickey Rivers*	1.00	.50	.30
273	Bobby Floyd	.75	.40	.25
274	Al Severinsen	.75	.40	.25
275	Cesar Tovar	.75	.40	.25
276	Gene Mauch	.75	.40	.25
277	Elliott Maddox	.75	.40	.25
278	Dennis Higgins	.75	.40	.25
279	Larry Brown	.75	.40	.25
280	Willie McCovey	6.00	3.00	1.75
281	Bill Parsons	.75	.40	.25
282	Astros Team	3.00	1.50	.90
283	Darrell Brandon	.75	.40	.25
284	Ike Brown	.75	.40	.25
285	Gaylord Perry	6.00	3.00	1.75
286	Gene Alley	.75	.40	.25
287	Jim Hardin	.75	.40	.25
288	Johnny Jeter	.75	.40	.25
289	Syd O'Brien	.75	.40	.25
290	Sonny Siebert	.75	.40	.25
291	Hal McRae	1.00	.50	.30
292	Hal McRae (In Action)	.75	.40	.25
293	Danny Frisella	.75	.40	.25
294	Danny Frisella (In Action)	.75	.40	.25
295	Dick Dietz	.75	.40	.25
296	Dick Dietz (In Action)	.75	.40	.25
297	Claude Osteen	.75	.40	.25
298	Claude Osteen (In Action)	.75	.40	.25
299	Hank Aaron	25.00	12.50	7.50
300	Hank Aaron (In Action)	15.00	7.50	4.50

		NR MT	EX	VG
301	George Mitterwald	.75	.40	.25
302	George Mitterwald (In Action)	.75	.40	.25
303	Joe Pepitone	.75	.40	.25
304	Joe Pepitone (In Action)	.75	.40	.25
305	Ken Boswell	.75	.40	.25
306	Ken Boswell (In Action)	.75	.40	.25
307	Steve Renko	.75	.40	.25
308	Steve Renko (In Action)	.75	.40	.25
309	Roberto Clemente	25.00	12.50	7.50
310	Roberto Clemente (In Action)	15.00	7.50	4.50
311	Clay Carroll	.75	.40	.25
312	Clay Carroll (In Action)	.75	.40	.25
313	Luis Aparicio	4.00	2.00	1.25
314	Luis Aparicio (In Action)	2.00	1.00	.60
315	Paul Splittorff	.75	.40	.25
316	Cardinals Rookies (*Jim Bibby,* Santiago Guzman, Jorge Roque)	.75	.40	.25
317	Rich Hand	.75	.40	.25
318	Sonny Jackson	.75	.40	.25
319	Aurelio Rodriguez	.75	.40	.25
320	Steve Blass	.75	.40	.25
321	Joe Lahoud	.75	.40	.25
322	Jose Pena	.75	.40	.25
323	Earl Weaver	1.00	.50	.30
324	Mike Ryan	.75	.40	.25
325	Mel Stottlemyre	.75	.40	.25
326	Pat Kelly	.75	.40	.25
327	*Steve Stone*	2.00	1.00	.60
328	Red Sox Team	4.00	2.00	1.25
329	Roy Foster	.75	.40	.25
330	Catfish Hunter	3.50	1.75	1.00
331	Stan Swanson	.75	.40	.25
332	Buck Martinez	.75	.40	.25
333	Steve Barber	.75	.40	.25
334	Rangers Rookies (Bill Fahey, Jim Mason, Tom Ragland)	.75	.40	.25
335	Bill Hands	.75	.40	.25
336	Marty Martinez	.75	.40	.25
337	Mike Kilkenny	.75	.40	.25
338	Bob Grich	.75	.40	.25
339	Ron Cook	.75	.40	.25
340	Roy White	.75	.40	.25
341	Boyhood Photo (Joe Torre)	.75	.40	.25
342	Boyhood Photo (Wilbur Wood)	.75	.40	.25
343	Boyhood Photo (Willie Stargell)	1.50	.70	.45
344	Boyhood Photo (Dave McNally)	.75	.40	.25
345	Boyhood Photo (Rick Wise)	.75	.40	.25
346	Boyhood Photo (Jim Fregosi)	.75	.40	.25
347	Boyhood Photo (Tom Seaver)	4.00	2.00	1.25
348	Boyhood Photo (Sal Bando)	.75	.40	.25
349	Al Fitzmorris	.75	.40	.25
350	Frank Howard	1.00	.50	.30
351	Braves Rookies (Jimmy Britton, Tom House, Rick Kester)	.75	.40	.25
352	Dave LaRoche	.75	.40	.25
353	Art Shamsky	.75	.40	.25
354	Tom Murphy	.75	.40	.25
355	Bob Watson	.75	.40	.25
356	Gerry Moses	.75	.40	.25
357	Woodie Fryman	.75	.40	.25
358	Sparky Anderson	1.50	.70	.45
359	Don Pavletich	.75	.40	.25
360	Dave Roberts	.75	.40	.25
361	Mike Andrews	.75	.40	.25
362	Mets Team	4.00	2.00	1.25
363	Ron Klimkowski	.75	.40	.25
364	Johnny Callison	.75	.40	.25
365	Dick Bosman	.75	.40	.25
366	Jimmy Rosario	.75	.40	.25
367	Ron Perranoski	.75	.40	.25
368	Danny Thompson	.75	.40	.25
369	Jim Lefebvre	.75	.40	.25
370	Don Buford	.75	.40	.25
371	Denny Lemaster	.75	.40	.25
372	Royals Rookies (Lance Clemons, Monty Montgomery)	.75	.40	.25
373	Royals Rookies (John Mayberry)	.75	.40	.25
374	Jack Heidemann	.75	.40	.25
375	Reggie Cleveland	.75	.40	.25
376	Andy Kosco	.75	.40	.25
377	Terry Harmon	.75	.40	.25
378	Checklist 395-525	3.00	1.50	.90
379	Ken Berry	.75	.40	.25
380	Earl Williams	.75	.40	.25
381	White Sox Team	3.00	1.50	.90
382	Joe Gibbon	.75	.40	.25
383	Brant Alyea	.75	.40	.25
384	Dave Campbell	.75	.40	.25
385	Mickey Stanley	.75	.40	.25
386	Jim Colborn	.75	.40	.25
387	Horace Clarke	.75	.40	.25

		NR MT	EX	VG
388	Charlie Williams	.75	.40	.25
389	Bill Rigney	.75	.40	.25
390	Willie Davis	.75	.40	.25
391	Ken Sanders	.75	.40	.25
392	Pirates Rookies (Fred Cambria, *Richie Zisk*)	1.00	.50	.30
393	Curt Motton	.75	.40	.25
394	Ken Forsch	.75	.40	.25
395	Matty Alou	1.00	.50	.30
396	Paul Lindblad	1.00	.50	.30
397	Phillies Team	4.00	2.00	1.25
398	Larry Hisle	1.00	.50	.30
399	Milt Wilcox	1.00	.50	.30
400	Tony Oliva	1.50	.70	.45
401	Jim Nash	1.00	.50	.30
402	Bobby Heise	1.00	.50	.30
403	John Cumberland	1.00	.50	.30
404	Jeff Torborg	1.00	.50	.30
405	Ron Fairly	1.00	.50	.30
406	*George Hendrick*	1.50	.70	.45
407	Chuck Taylor	1.00	.50	.30
408	Jim Northrup	1.00	.50	.30
409	Frank Baker	1.00	.50	.30
410	Fergie Jenkins	6.00	3.00	1.75
411	Bob Montgomery	1.00	.50	.30
412	Dick Kelley	1.00	.50	.30
413	White Sox Rookies (Don Eddy, Dave Lemonds)	1.00	.50	.30
414	Bob Miller	1.00	.50	.30
415	Cookie Rojas	1.00	.50	.30
416	Johnny Edwards	1.00	.50	.30
417	Tom Hall	1.00	.50	.30
418	Tom Shopay	1.00	.50	.30
419	Jim Spencer	1.00	.50	.30
420	Steve Carlton	15.00	7.50	4.50
421	Ellie Rodriguez	1.00	.50	.30
422	Ray Lamb	1.00	.50	.30
423	Oscar Gamble	1.00	.50	.30
424	Bill Gogolewski	1.00	.50	.30
425	Ken Singleton	1.00	.50	.30
426	Ken Singleton (In Action)	1.00	.50	.30
427	Tito Fuentes	1.00	.50	.30
428	Tito Fuentes (In Action)	1.00	.50	.30
429	Bob Robertson	1.00	.50	.30
430	Bob Robertson (In Action)	1.00	.50	.30
431	Cito Gaston	2.50	1.25	.70
432	Cito Gaston (In Action)	1.75	.90	.50
433	Johnny Bench	25.00	12.50	7.50
434	Johnny Bench (In Action)	15.00	7.50	4.50
435	Reggie Jackson	40.00	20.00	12.00
436	Reggie Jackson (In Action)	20.00	10.00	6.00
437	Maury Wills	1.50	.70	.45
438	Maury Wills (In Action)	1.00	.50	.30
439	Billy Williams	6.00	3.00	1.75
440	Billy Williams (In Action)	4.00	2.00	1.25
441	Thurman Munson	12.00	6.00	3.50
442	Thurman Munson (In Action)	7.00	3.50	2.00
443	Ken Henderson	1.00	.50	.30
444	Ken Henderson (In Action)	1.00	.50	.30
445	Tom Seaver	20.00	10.00	6.00
446	Tom Seaver (In Action)	12.00	6.00	3.50
447	Willie Stargell	6.00	3.00	1.75
448	Willie Stargell (In Action)	4.00	2.00	1.25
449	Bob Lemon	3.00	1.50	.90
450	Mickey Lolich	1.25	.60	.40
451	Tony LaRussa	1.25	.60	.40
452	Ed Herrmann	1.00	.50	.30
453	Barry Lersch	1.00	.50	.30
454	A's Team	4.00	2.00	1.25
455	Tommy Harper	1.00	.50	.30
456	Mark Belanger	1.00	.50	.30
457	Padres Rookies (Darcy Fast, Mike Ivie, *Derrel Thomas*)	1.00	.50	.30
458	Aurelio Monteagudo	1.00	.50	.30
459	Rick Renick	1.00	.50	.30
460	Al Downing	1.00	.50	.30
461	Tim Cullen	1.00	.50	.30
462	Rickey Clark	1.00	.50	.30
463	Bernie Carbo	1.00	.50	.30
464	Jim Roland	1.00	.50	.30
465	Gil Hodges	3.00	1.50	.90
466	Norm Miller	1.00	.50	.30
467	Steve Kline	1.00	.50	.30
468	Richie Scheinblum	1.00	.50	.30
469	Ron Herbel	1.00	.50	.30
470	Ray Fosse	1.00	.50	.30
471	Luke Walker	1.00	.50	.30
472	Phil Gagliano	1.00	.50	.30
473	Dan McGinn	1.00	.50	.30
474	Orioles Rookies (Don Baylor, Roric Harrison, Johnny Oates)	8.00	4.00	2.50

		NR MT	EX	VG
475	Gary Nolan	1.00	.50	.30
476	Lee Richard	1.00	.50	.30
477	Tom Phoebus	1.00	.50	.30
478a	Checklist 526-656 (small print on front)	3.00	1.50	.90
478b	Checklist 526-656 (large printing on front)	3.00	1.50	.90
479	Don Shaw	1.00	.50	.30
480	Lee May	1.00	.50	.30
481	Billy Conigliaro	1.00	.50	.30
482	Joe Hoerner	1.00	.50	.30
483	Ken Suarez	1.00	.50	.30
484	Lum Harris	1.00	.50	.30
485	Phil Regan	1.00	.50	.30
486	John Lowenstein	1.00	.50	.30
487	Tigers Team	4.00	2.00	1.25
488	Mike Nagy	1.00	.50	.30
489	Expos Rookies (Terry Humphrey, Keith Lampard)	1.00	.50	.30
490	Dave McNally	1.00	.50	.30
491	Boyhood Photo (Lou Piniella)	1.00	.50	.30
492	Boyhood Photo (Mel Stottlemyre)	1.00	.50	.30
493	Boyhood Photo (Bob Bailey)	1.00	.50	.30
494	Boyhood Photo (Willie Horton)	1.00	.50	.30
495	Boyhood Photo (Bill Melton)	1.00	.50	.30
496	Boyhood Photo (Bud Harrelson)	1.00	.50	.30
497	Boyhood Photo (Jim Perry)	1.00	.50	.30
498	Boyhood Photo (Brooks Robinson)	2.00	1.00	.60
499	Vicente Romo	1.00	.50	.30
500	Joe Torre	1.00	.50	.30
501	Pete Hamm	1.00	.50	.30
502	Jackie Hernandez	1.00	.50	.30
503	Gary Peters	1.00	.50	.30
504	Ed Spiezio	1.00	.50	.30
505	Mike Marshall	1.00	.50	.30
506	Indians Rookies (Terry Ley, Jim Moyer, *Dick Tidrow*)	1.00	.50	.30
507	Fred Gladding	1.00	.50	.30
508	Ellie Hendricks	1.00	.50	.30
509	Don McMahon	1.00	.50	.30
510	Ted Williams	6.00	3.00	1.75
511	Tony Taylor	1.00	.50	.30
512	Paul Popovich	1.00	.50	.30
513	Lindy McDaniel	1.00	.50	.30
514	Ted Sizemore	1.00	.50	.30
515	Bert Blyleven	7.00	3.50	2.00
516	Oscar Brown	1.00	.50	.30
517	Ken Brett	1.00	.50	.30
518	Wayne Garrett	1.00	.50	.30
519	Ted Abernathy	1.00	.50	.30
520	Larry Bowa	1.25	.60	.40
521	Alan Foster	1.00	.50	.30
522	Dodgers Team	4.00	2.00	1.25
523	Chuck Dobson	1.00	.50	.30
524	Reds Rookies (Ed Armbrister, Mel Behney)	1.00	.50	.30
525	Carlos May	1.00	.50	.30
526	Bob Bailey	2.00	1.00	.60
527	Dave Leonhard	2.00	1.00	.60
528	Ron Stone	2.00	1.00	.60
529	Dave Nelson	2.00	1.00	.60
530	Don Sutton	4.00	2.00	1.25
531	Freddie Patek	2.00	1.00	.60
532	Fred Kendall	2.00	1.00	.60
533	Ralph Houk	2.00	1.00	.60
534	Jim Hickman	2.00	1.00	.60
535	Ed Brinkman	2.00	1.00	.60
536	Doug Rader	2.00	1.00	.60
537	Bob Locker	2.00	1.00	.60
538	Charlie Sands	2.00	1.00	.60
539	*Terry Forster*	2.00	1.00	.60
540	Felix Millan	2.00	1.00	.60
541	Roger Repoz	2.00	1.00	.60
542	Jack Billingham	2.00	1.00	.60
543	Duane Josephson	2.00	1.00	.60
544	Ted Martinez	2.00	1.00	.60
545	Wayne Granger	2.00	1.00	.60
546	Joe Hague	2.00	1.00	.60
547	Indians Team	6.00	3.00	1.75
548	Frank Reberger	2.00	1.00	.60
549	Dave May	2.00	1.00	.60
550	Brooks Robinson	20.00	10.00	6.00
551	Ollie Brown	2.00	1.00	.60
552	Ollie Brown (In Action)	2.00	1.00	.60
553	Wilbur Wood	2.00	1.00	.60
554	Wilbur Wood (In Action)	2.00	1.00	.60
555	Ron Santo	3.00	1.50	.90
556	Ron Santo (In Action)	2.00	1.00	.60
557	John Odom	2.00	1.00	.60

		NR MT	EX	VG
558	John Odom (In Action)	2.00	1.00	.60
559	Pete Rose	35.00	17.50	10.50
560	Pete Rose (In Action)	19.00	9.50	5.75
561	Leo Cardenas	2.00	1.00	.60
562	Leo Cardenas (In Action)	2.00	1.00	.60
563	Ray Sadecki	2.00	1.00	.60
564	Ray Sadecki (In Action)	2.00	1.00	.60
565	Reggie Smith	2.00	1.00	.60
566	Reggie Smith (In Action)	2.00	1.00	.60
567	Juan Marichal	6.00	3.00	1.75
568	Juan Marichal (In Action)	4.00	2.00	1.25
569	Ed Kirkpatrick	2.00	1.00	.60
570	Ed Kirkpatrick (In Action)	2.00	1.00	.60
571	Nate Colbert	2.00	1.00	.60
572	Nate Colbert (In Action)	2.00	1.00	.60
573	Fritz Peterson	2.00	1.00	.60
574	Fritz Peterson (In Action)	2.00	1.00	.60
575	Al Oliver	3.00	1.50	.90
576	Leo Durocher	2.50	1.25	.70
577	Mike Paul	2.00	1.00	.60
578	Billy Grabarkewitz	2.00	1.00	.60
579	*Doyle Alexander*	2.00	1.00	.60
580	Lou Piniella	2.50	1.25	.70
581	Wade Blasingame	2.00	1.00	.60
582	Expos Team	5.00	2.50	1.50
583	Darold Knowles	2.00	1.00	.60
584	Jerry McNertney	2.00	1.00	.60
585	George Scott	2.00	1.00	.60
586	Denis Menke	2.00	1.00	.60
587	Billy Wilson	2.00	1.00	.60
588	Jim Holt	2.00	1.00	.60
589	Hal Lanier	2.00	1.00	.60
590	Graig Nettles	3.00	1.50	.90
591	Paul Casanova	2.00	1.00	.60
592	Lew Krausse	2.00	1.00	.60
593	Rich Morales	2.00	1.00	.60
594	Jim Beauchamp	2.00	1.00	.60
595	Nolan Ryan	250.00	125.00	75.00
596	Manny Mota	2.00	1.00	.60
597	Jim Magnuson	2.00	1.00	.60
598	Hal King	2.00	1.00	.60
599	Billy Champion	2.00	1.00	.60
600	Al Kaline	20.00	10.00	6.00
601	George Stone	2.00	1.00	.60
602	Dave Bristol	2.00	1.00	.60
603	Jim Ray	2.00	1.00	.60
604a	Checklist 657-787 (copyright on right)	3.50	1.75	1.00
604b	Checklist 657-787 (copyright on left)	5.00	2.50	1.50
605	Nelson Briles	2.00	1.00	.60
606	Luis Melendez	2.00	1.00	.60
607	Frank Duffy	2.00	1.00	.60
608	Mike Corkins	2.00	1.00	.60
609	Tom Grieve	2.00	1.00	.60
610	Bill Stoneman	2.00	1.00	.60
611	Rich Reese	2.00	1.00	.60
612	Joe Decker	2.00	1.00	.60
613	Mike Ferraro	2.00	1.00	.60
614	Ted Uhlaender	2.00	1.00	.60
615	Steve Hargan	2.00	1.00	.60
616	*Joe Ferguson*	2.00	1.00	.60
617	Royals Team	5.00	2.50	1.50
618	Rich Robertson	2.00	1.00	.60
619	Rich McKinney	2.00	1.00	.60
620	Phil Niekro	4.50	2.25	1.25
621	Commissioners Award	2.00	1.00	.60
622	MVP Award	2.00	1.00	.60
623	Cy Young Award	2.00	1.00	.60
624	Minor League Player Of The Year Award	2.00	1.00	.60
625	Rookie Of The Year Award	2.00	1.00	.60
626	Babe Ruth Award	2.00	1.00	.60
627	Moe Drabowsky	2.00	1.00	.60
628	Terry Crowley	2.00	1.00	.60
629	Paul Doyle	2.00	1.00	.60
630	Rich Hebner	2.00	1.00	.60
631	John Strohmayer	2.00	1.00	.60
632	Mike Hegan	2.00	1.00	.60
633	Jack Hiatt	2.00	1.00	.60
634	Dick Woodson	2.00	1.00	.60
635	Don Money	2.00	1.00	.60
636	Bill Lee	2.00	1.00	.60
637	Preston Gomez	2.00	1.00	.60
638	Ken Wright	2.00	1.00	.60
639	J.C. Martin	2.00	1.00	.60
640	Joe Coleman	2.00	1.00	.60
641	Mike Lum	2.00	1.00	.60
642	Denny Riddleberger	2.00	1.00	.60
643	Russ Gibson	2.00	1.00	.60
644	Bernie Allen	2.00	1.00	.60

		NR MT	EX	VG
645	Jim Maloney	2.00	1.00	.60
646	Chico Salmon	2.00	1.00	.60
647	Bob Moose	2.00	1.00	.60
648	Jim Lyttle	2.00	1.00	.60
649	Pete Richert	2.00	1.00	.60
650	Sal Bando	2.00	1.00	.60
651	Reds Team	6.00	3.00	1.75
652	Marcelino Lopez	2.00	1.00	.60
653	Jim Fairey	2.00	1.00	.60
654	Horacio Pina	2.00	1.00	.60
655	Jerry Grote	2.00	1.00	.60
656	Rudy May	2.00	1.00	.60
657	Bobby Wine	6.00	3.00	1.75
658	Steve Dunning	6.00	3.00	1.75
659	Bob Aspromonte	6.00	3.00	1.75
660	Paul Blair	6.00	3.00	1.75
661	Bill Virdon	6.00	3.00	1.75
662	Stan Bahnsen	6.00	3.00	1.75
663	Fran Healy	6.00	3.00	1.75
664	Bobby Knoop	6.00	3.00	1.75
665	Chris Short	6.00	3.00	1.75
666	Hector Torres	6.00	3.00	1.75
667	Ray Newman	6.00	3.00	1.75
668	Rangers Team	9.00	4.50	2.75
669	Willie Crawford	6.00	3.00	1.75
670	Ken Holtzman	6.00	3.00	1.75
671	Donn Clendenon	6.00	3.00	1.75
672	Archie Reynolds	6.00	3.00	1.75
673	Dave Marshall	6.00	3.00	1.75
674	John Kennedy	6.00	3.00	1.75
675	Pat Jarvis	6.00	3.00	1.75
676	Danny Cater	6.00	3.00	1.75
677	Ivan Murrell	6.00	3.00	1.75
678	Steve Luebber	6.00	3.00	1.75
679	Astros Rookies (Bob Fenwick, Bob Stinson)	6.00	3.00	1.75
680	Dave Johnson	6.00	3.00	1.75
681	Bobby Pfeil	6.00	3.00	1.75
682	Mike McCormick	6.00	3.00	1.75
683	Steve Hovley	6.00	3.00	1.75
684	Hal Breeden	6.00	3.00	1.75
685	Joe Horlen	6.00	3.00	1.75
686	Steve Garvey	45.00	22.00	13.50
687	Del Unser	6.00	3.00	1.75
688	Cardinals Team	12.00	6.00	3.50
689	Eddie Fisher	6.00	3.00	1.75
690	Willie Montanez	6.00	3.00	1.75
691	Curt Blefary	6.00	3.00	1.75
692	Curt Blefary (In Action)	6.00	3.00	1.75
693	Alan Gallagher	6.00	3.00	1.75
694	Alan Gallagher (In Action)	6.00	3.00	1.75
695	Rod Carew	75.00	37.00	22.00
696	Rod Carew (In Action)	35.00	17.50	10.50
697	Jerry Koosman	6.00	3.00	1.75
698	Jerry Koosman (In Action)	6.00	3.00	1.75
699	Bobby Murcer	6.00	3.00	1.75
700	Bobby Murcer (In Action)	6.00	3.00	1.75
701	Jose Pagan	6.00	3.00	1.75
702	Jose Pagan (In Action)	6.00	3.00	1.75
703	Doug Griffin	6.00	3.00	1.75
704	Doug Griffin (In Action)	6.00	3.00	1.75
705	Pat Corrales	6.00	3.00	1.75
706	Pat Corrales (In Action)	6.00	3.00	1.75
707	Tim Foli	6.00	3.00	1.75
708	Tim Foli (In Action)	6.00	3.00	1.75
709	Jim Kaat	9.00	4.50	2.75
710	Jim Kaat (In Action)	6.00	3.00	1.75
711	Bobby Bonds	12.00	6.00	3.50
712	Bobby Bonds (In Action)	7.00	3.50	2.00
713	Gene Michael	6.00	3.00	1.75
714	Gene Michael (In Action)	6.00	3.00	1.75
715	Mike Epstein	6.00	3.00	1.75
716	Jesus Alou	6.00	3.00	1.75
717	Bruce Dal Canton	6.00	3.00	1.75
718	Del Rice	6.00	3.00	1.75
719	Cesar Geronimo	6.00	3.00	1.75
720	Sam McDowell	6.00	3.00	1.75
721	Eddie Leon	6.00	3.00	1.75
722	Bill Sudakis	6.00	3.00	1.75
723	Al Santorini	6.00	3.00	1.75
724	A.L. Rookies (John Curtis, Rich Hinton, Mickey Scott)	6.00	3.00	1.75
725	Dick McAuliffe	6.00	3.00	1.75
726	Dick Selma	6.00	3.00	1.75
727	Jose Laboy	6.00	3.00	1.75
728	Gail Hopkins	6.00	3.00	1.75
729	Bob Veale	6.00	3.00	1.75
730	Rick Monday	6.00	3.00	1.75
731	Orioles Team	12.00	6.00	3.50
732	George Culver	6.00	3.00	1.75
733	Jim Hart	6.00	3.00	1.75
734	Bob Burda	6.00	3.00	1.75
735	Diego Segui	6.00	3.00	1.75
736	Bill Russell	6.00	3.00	1.75
737	*Lenny Randle*	6.00	3.00	1.75
738	Jim Merritt	6.00	3.00	1.75
739	Don Mason	6.00	3.00	1.75
740	Rico Carty	6.00	3.00	1.75
741	Major League Rookies (Tom Hutton, *Rick Miller, John Milner*)	6.00	3.00	1.75
742	Jim Rooker	6.00	3.00	1.75
743	Cesar Gutierrez	6.00	3.00	1.75
744	*Jim Slaton*	6.00	3.00	1.75
745	Julian Javier	6.00	3.00	1.75
746	Lowell Palmer	6.00	3.00	1.75
747	Jim Stewart	6.00	3.00	1.75
748	Phil Hennigan	6.00	3.00	1.75
749	Walter Alston	12.00	6.00	3.50
750	Willie Horton	6.00	3.00	1.75
751	Steve Carlton (Traded)	50.00	25.00	15.00
752	Joe Morgan (Traded)	30.00	15.00	9.00
753	Denny McLain (Traded)	10.00	5.00	3.00
754	Frank Robinson (Traded)	35.00	17.50	10.50
755	Jim Fregosi (Traded)	6.00	3.00	1.75
756	Rick Wise (Traded)	6.00	3.00	1.75
757	Jose Cardenal (Traded)	6.00	3.00	1.75
758	Gil Garrido	6.00	3.00	1.75
759	Chris Cannizzaro	6.00	3.00	1.75
760	Bill Mazeroski	12.00	6.00	3.50
761	A.L.-N.L. Rookies *(Ron Cey, Ben Oglivie,* Bernie Williams)	20.00	10.00	6.00
762	Wayne Simpson	6.00	3.00	1.75
763	Ron Hansen	6.00	3.00	1.75
764	Dusty Baker	9.00	4.50	2.75
765	Ken McMullen	6.00	3.00	1.75
766	Steve Hamilton	6.00	3.00	1.75
767	Tom McCraw	6.00	3.00	1.75
768	Denny Doyle	6.00	3.00	1.75
769	Jack Aker	6.00	3.00	1.75
770	Jim Wynn	6.00	3.00	1.75
771	Giants Team	9.00	4.50	2.75
772	Ken Tatum	6.00	3.00	1.75
773	Ron Brand	6.00	3.00	1.75
774	Luis Alvarado	6.00	3.00	1.75
775	Jerry Reuss	6.00	3.00	1.75
776	Bill Voss	6.00	3.00	1.75
777	Hoyt Wilhelm	16.00	8.00	4.75
778	Twins Rookies (Vic Albury, *Rick Dempsey,* Jim Strickland)	6.00	3.00	1.75
779	Tony Cloninger	6.00	3.00	1.75
780	Dick Green	6.00	3.00	1.75
781	Jim McAndrew	6.00	3.00	1.75
782	Larry Stahl	6.00	3.00	1.75
783	Les Cain	6.00	3.00	1.75
784	Ken Aspromonte	6.00	3.00	1.75
785	Vic Davalillo	6.00	3.00	1.75
786	Chuck Brinkman	6.00	3.00	1.75
787	Ron Reed	6.00	3.00	1.75

1972 Topps Cloth Stickers

Despite the fact they were never actually issued, examples of this test issue can readily be found within the hobby. The set of 33 contains stickers with designs identical to cards found in three contiguous rows of a regular Topps card sheet that year; thus the inclusion of a meaningless checklist card. Sometimes found in complete 33-sticker strips, individual stickers nominally measure 2-1/2" by 3-1/2," though dimensions vary according to the care with which they were cut. Stickers are unnumbered and blank-backed, and do not contain glue.

		NR MT	EX	VG
Complete Set:		200.00	100.00	60.00
Common Player:		3.00	1.50	.90
(1)	Hank Aaron	50.00	25.00	15.00
(2)	Luis Aparicio IA	10.00	5.00	3.00
(3)	Ike Brown	3.00	1.50	.90
(4)	Johnny Callison	5.00	2.50	1.50
(5)	Checklist 264-319	3.00	1.50	.90
(6)	Roberto Clemente IA	25.00	12.50	7.50
(7)	Dave Concepcion	8.00	4.00	2.50
(8)	Ron Cook	3.00	1.50	.90
(9)	Willie Davis	5.00	2.50	1.50
(10)	Al Fitzmorris	3.00	1.50	.90
(11)	Bobby Floyd	3.00	1.50	.90
(12)	Roy Foster	3.00	1.50	.90
(13)	Jim Fregosi Boyhood Photo	4.00	2.00	1.25
(14)	Danny Frisella IA	3.00	1.50	.90
(15)	Woody Fryman	3.50	1.75	1.00
(16)	Terry Harmon	3.00	1.50	.90
(17)	Frank Howard	7.00	3.50	2.00
(18)	Ron Klimkowski	3.00	1.50	.90
(19)	Joe Lahoud	3.00	1.50	.90
(20)	Jim Lefebvre	3.50	1.75	1.00
(21)	Elliott Maddox	3.00	1.50	.90
(22)	Marty Martinez	3.00	1.50	.90
(23)	Willie McCovey	25.00	12.50	7.50
(24)	Hal McRae	6.00	3.00	1.75
(25)	Syd O'Brien	3.00	1.50	.90
(26)	Red Sox Team	4.00	2.00	1.25
(27)	Aurelio Rodriguez	3.50	1.75	1.00
(28)	Al Severinsen	3.00	1.50	.90
(29)	Art Shamsky	3.00	1.50	.90
(30)	Steve Stone	4.00	2.00	1.25
(31)	Stan Swanson	3.00	1.50	.90
(32)	Bob Watson	3.50	1.75	1.00
(33)	Roy White	6.00	3.00	1.75

1972 Topps Posters

Issued as a separate set, rather than as a wax pack insert, the twenty-four 9-7/16" by 18" posters of 1972 feature a borderless full-color picture on the front with the player's name, team and position. Printed on very thin paper, the posters, as happened with earlier issues, were folded for packaging, causing large creases which cannot be removed. Even so, they are good display items for they feature many of stars of the period.

		NR MT	EX	VG
Complete Set:		300.00	150.00	90.00
Common Player:		5.00	2.50	1.50
1	Dave McNally	5.00	2.50	1.50
2	Carl Yastrzemski	30.00	15.00	9.00
3	Bill Melton	5.00	2.50	1.50
4	Ray Fosse	5.00	2.50	1.50
5	Mickey Lolich	6.00	3.00	1.75
6	Amos Otis	5.00	2.50	1.50
7	Tony Oliva	6.00	3.00	1.75
8	Vida Blue	6.00	3.00	1.75
9	Hank Aaron	20.00	10.00	6.00
10	Fergie Jenkins	8.00	4.00	2.50
11	Pete Rose	50.00	25.00	15.00
12	Willie Davis	6.00	3.00	1.75
13	Tom Seaver	20.00	10.00	6.00
14	Rick Wise	5.00	2.50	1.50
15	Willie Stargell	12.00	6.00	3.50
16	Joe Torre	7.00	3.50	2.00
17	Willie Mays	20.00	10.00	6.00
18	Andy Messersmith	5.00	2.50	1.50
19	Wilbur Wood	5.00	2.50	1.50
20	Harmon Killebrew	15.00	7.50	4.50
21	Billy Williams	12.00	6.00	3.50
22	Bud Harrelson	5.00	2.50	1.50
23	Roberto Clemente	20.00	10.00	6.00
24	Willie McCovey	15.00	7.50	4.50

1973 Topps

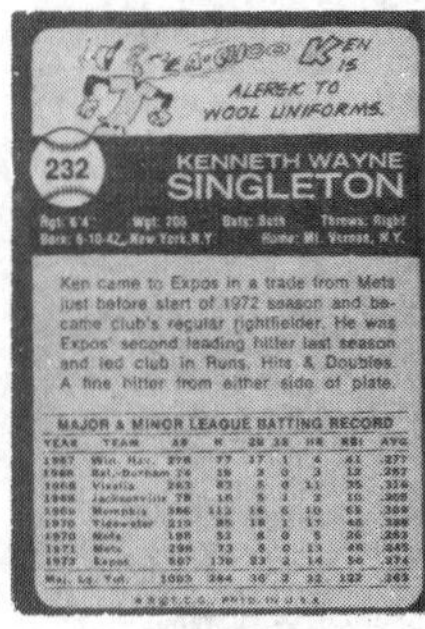

Topps cut back to 660 cards in 1973. The set is interesting for it marks the last time cards were issued by series, a procedure which had produced many a scarce high number card over the years. These 2-1/2" by 3-1/2" cards have a color photo, accented by a silhouette of a player on the front, indicative of his position. Card backs are vertical for the first time since 1968, with the usual statistical and biographical information. Specialty cards begin with card number 1, which depicted Ruth, Mays and Aaron as the all-time home run leaders. It was followed by statistical leaders, although there also were additional all-time leader cards. Also present are playoff and World Series highlights. From the age-and-youth department, the 1973 Topps set has coaches and managers as well as more "Boyhood Photos."

		NR MT	EX	VG
Complete Set (660):		1200.00	600.00	360.00
Common Player: 1-396		.40	.20	.12
Common Player: 397-528		.70	.35	.20
Common Player: 529-660		2.00	1.00	.60
1	All Time Home Run Leaders (Hank Aaron, Willie Mays, Babe Ruth)	30.00	15.00	9.00
2	Rich Hebner	.40	.20	.12
3	Jim Lonborg	.50	.25	.15
4	John Milner	.40	.20	.12
5	Ed Brinkman	.40	.20	.12
6	Mac Scarce	.40	.20	.12
7	Rangers Team	3.00	1.50	.90
8	Tom Hall	.40	.20	.12
9	Johnny Oates	.40	.20	.12
10	Don Sutton	2.00	1.00	.60
11	Chris Chambliss	.40	.20	.12
12a	Padres Mgr./Coaches (Dave Garcia, Johnny Podres, Bob Skinner, Whitey Wietelmann, Don Zimmer) (Coaches background brown)	.75	.40	.25
12b	Padres Mgr./Coaches (Dave Garcia, Johnny Podres, Bob Skinner, Whitey Wietelmann, Don Zimmer) (Coaches background orange)	.75	.40	.25
13	George Hendrick	.40	.20	.12
14	Sonny Siebert	.40	.20	.12
15	Ralph Garr	.40	.20	.12
16	Steve Braun	.40	.20	.12
17	Fred Gladding	.40	.20	.12
18	Leroy Stanton	.40	.20	.12
19	Tim Foli	.40	.20	.12

		NR MT	EX	VG
20a	Stan Bahnsen (small gap in left border)	.70	.35	.20
20b	Stan Bahnsen (no gap)	.40	.20	.12
21	Randy Hundley	.40	.20	.12
22	Ted Abernathy	.40	.20	.12
23	Dave Kingman	.75	.40	.25
24	Al Santorini	.40	.20	.12
25	Roy White	.50	.25	.15
26	Pirates Team	3.00	1.50	.90
27	Bill Gogolewski	.40	.20	.12
28	Hal McRae	.75	.40	.25
29	Tony Taylor	.40	.20	.12
30	Tug McGraw	.40	.20	.12
31	*Buddy Bell*	4.00	2.00	1.25
32	Fred Norman	.40	.20	.12
33	Jim Breazeale	.40	.20	.12
34	Pat Dobson	.40	.20	.12
35	Willie Davis	.40	.20	.12
36	Steve Barber	.40	.20	.12
37	Bill Robinson	.40	.20	.12
38	Mike Epstein	.40	.20	.12
39	Dave Roberts	.40	.20	.12
40	Reggie Smith	.40	.20	.12
41	Tom Walker	.40	.20	.12
42	Mike Andrews	.40	.20	.12
43	*Randy Moffitt*	.40	.20	.12
44	Rick Monday	.40	.20	.12
45	Ellie Rodriguez (photo actually Paul Ratliff)	.40	.20	.12
46	Lindy McDaniel	.40	.20	.12
47	Luis Melendez	.40	.20	.12
48	Paul Splittorff	.40	.20	.12
49a	Twins Mgr./Coaches (Vern Morgan, Frank Quilici, Bob Rodgers, Ralph Rowe, Al Worthington) (Coaches background brown)	.50	.25	.15
49b	Twins Mgr./Coaches (Vern Morgan, Frank Quilici, Bob Rodgers, Ralph Rowe, Al Worthington) (Coaches background orange)	.50	.25	.15
50	Roberto Clemente	35.00	17.50	10.50
51	Chuck Seelbach	.40	.20	.12
52	Denis Menke	.40	.20	.12
53	Steve Dunning	.40	.20	.12
54	Checklist 1-132	2.00	1.00	.60
55	Jon Matlack	.40	.20	.12
56	Merv Rettenmund	.40	.20	.12
57	Derrel Thomas	.40	.20	.12
58	Mike Paul	.40	.20	.12
59	*Steve Yeager*	.80	.40	.25
60	Ken Holtzman	.40	.20	.12
61	Batting Leaders (Rod Carew, Billy Williams)	2.25	1.25	.70
62	Home Run Leaders (Dick Allen, Johnny Bench)	2.25	1.25	.70
63	Runs Batted In Leaders (Dick Allen, Johnny Bench)	2.25	1.25	.70
64	Stolen Base Leaders (Lou Brock, Bert Campaneris)	2.00	1.00	.60
65	Earned Run Average Leaders (Steve Carlton, Luis Tiant)	2.00	1.00	.60
66	Victory Leaders (Steve Carlton, Gaylord Perry, Wilbur Wood)	2.00	1.00	.60
67	Strikeout Leaders (Steve Carlton, Nolan Ryan)	15.00	7.50	4.50
68	Leading Firemen (Clay Carroll, Sparky Lyle)	.75	.40	.25
69	Phil Gagliano	.40	.20	.12
70	Milt Pappas	.40	.20	.12
71	Johnny Briggs	.40	.20	.12
72	Ron Reed	.40	.20	.12
73	Ed Herrmann	.40	.20	.12
74	Billy Champion	.40	.20	.12
75	Vada Pinson	.75	.40	.25
76	Doug Rader	.40	.20	.12
77	Mike Torrez	.40	.20	.12
78	Richie Scheinblum	.40	.20	.12
79	Jim Willoughby	.40	.20	.12
80	Tony Oliva	.75	.40	.25
81a	Cubs Mgr./Coaches (Hank Aguirre, Ernie Banks, Larry Jansen, Whitey Lockman, Pete Reiser) (trees in Coaches background)	.90	.45	.25
81b	Cubs Mgr./Coaches (Hank Aguirre, Ernie Banks, Larry Jansen, Whitey Lockman, Pete Reiser) (orange, solid background)	.70	.35	.20
82	Fritz Peterson	.40	.20	.12
83	Leron Lee	.40	.20	.12
84	Rollie Fingers	5.00	2.50	1.50
85	Ted Simmons	1.50	.70	.45
86	Tom McCraw	.40	.20	.12
87	Ken Boswell	.40	.20	.12
88	Mickey Stanley	.40	.20	.12
89	Jack Billingham	.40	.20	.12
90	Brooks Robinson	7.50	3.75	2.25
91	Dodgers Team	4.00	2.00	1.25
92	Jerry Bell	.40	.20	.12
93	Jesus Alou	.40	.20	.12
94	Dick Billings	.40	.20	.12
95	Steve Blass	.40	.20	.12
96	Doug Griffin	.40	.20	.12
97	Willie Montanez	.40	.20	.12
98	Dick Woodson	.40	.20	.12
99	Carl Taylor	.40	.20	.12
100	Hank Aaron	25.00	12.50	7.50
101	Ken Henderson	.40	.20	.12
102	Rudy May	.40	.20	.12
103	Celerino Sanchez	.40	.20	.12
104	Reggie Cleveland	.40	.20	.12
105	Carlos May	.40	.20	.12
106	Terry Humphrey	.40	.20	.12
107	Phil Hennigan	.40	.20	.12
108	Bill Russell	.60	.30	.20
109	Doyle Alexander	.40	.20	.12
110	Bob Watson	.40	.20	.12
111	Dave Nelson	.40	.20	.12
112	Gary Ross	.40	.20	.12
113	Jerry Grote	.40	.20	.12
114	Lynn McGlothen	.40	.20	.12
115	Ron Santo	.75	.40	.25
116a	Yankees Mgr./Coaches (Jim Hegan, Ralph Houk, Elston Howard, Dick Howser, Jim Turner) (Coaches background brown)	2.25	1.25	.70
116b	Yankees Mgr./Coaches (Jim Hegan, Ralph Houk, Elston Howard, Dick Howser, Jim Turner) (Coaches background orange)	.90	.45	.25
117	Ramon Hernandez	.40	.20	.12
118	John Mayberry	.40	.20	.12
119	Larry Bowa	.75	.40	.25
120	Joe Coleman	.40	.20	.12
121	Dave Rader	.40	.20	.12
122	Jim Strickland	.40	.20	.12
123	Sandy Alomar	.40	.20	.12
124	Jim Hardin	.40	.20	.12
125	Ron Fairly	.40	.20	.12
126	Jim Brewer	.40	.20	.12
127	Brewers Team	3.00	1.50	.90
128	Ted Sizemore	.40	.20	.12
129	Terry Forster	.40	.20	.12
130	Pete Rose	20.00	10.00	6.00
131a	Red Sox Mgr./Coaches (Doug Camilli, Eddie Kasko, Don Lenhardt, Eddie Popowski, Lee Stange) (Coaches background brown)	.70	.35	.20
131b	Red Sox Mgr./Coaches (Doug Camilli, Eddie Kasko, Don Lenhardt, Eddie Popowski, Lee Stange) (Coaches background orange)	.50	.25	.15
132	Matty Alou	.40	.20	.12
133	Dave Roberts	.40	.20	.12
134	Milt Wilcox	.40	.20	.12
135	Lee May	.40	.20	.12
136a	Orioles Mgr./Coaches (George Bamberger, Jim Frey, Billy Hunter, George Staller, Earl Weaver) (Coaches background brown)	2.25	1.25	.70
136b	Orioles Mgr./Coaches (George Bamberger, Jim Frey, Billy Hunter, George Staller, Earl Weaver) (Coaches background orange)	.90	.45	.25
137	Jim Beauchamp	.40	.20	.12
138	Horacio Pina	.40	.20	.12
139	Carmen Fanzone	.40	.20	.12
140	Lou Piniella	.60	.30	.20
141	Bruce Kison	.40	.20	.12
142	Thurman Munson	10.00	5.00	3.00
143	John Curtis	.40	.20	.12
144	Marty Perez	.40	.20	.12
145	Bobby Bonds	.90	.45	.25
146	Woodie Fryman	.40	.20	.12
147	Mike Anderson	.40	.20	.12
148	*Dave Goltz*	.40	.20	.12
149	Ron Hunt	.40	.20	.12
150	Wilbur Wood	.40	.20	.12
151	Wes Parker	.40	.20	.12
152	Dave May	.40	.20	.12
153	Al Hrabosky	.40	.20	.12
154	Jeff Torborg	.40	.20	.12
155	Sal Bando	.40	.20	.12
156	Cesar Geronimo	.40	.20	.12
157	Denny Riddleberger	.40	.20	.12
158	Astros Team	3.00	1.50	.90

		NR MT	EX	VG
159	Cito Gaston	.75	.40	.25
160	Jim Palmer	10.00	5.00	3.00
161	Ted Martinez	.40	.20	.12
162	Pete Broberg	.40	.20	.12
163	Vic Davalillo	.40	.20	.12
164	Monty Montgomery	.40	.20	.12
165	Luis Aparicio	2.75	1.50	.80
166	Terry Harmon	.40	.20	.12
167	Steve Stone	.40	.20	.12
168	Jim Northrup	.40	.20	.12
169	Ron Schueler	.40	.20	.12
170	Harmon Killebrew	5.00	2.50	1.50
171	Bernie Carbo	.40	.20	.12
172	Steve Kline	.40	.20	.12
173	Hal Breeden	.40	.20	.12
174	*Rich Gossage*	15.00	7.50	4.50
175	Frank Robinson	10.00	5.00	3.00
176	Chuck Taylor	.40	.20	.12
177	Bill Plummer	.40	.20	.12
178	Don Rose	.40	.20	.12
179a	A's Mgr./Coaches (Jerry Adair, Vern Hoscheit, Irv Noren, Wes Stock, Dick Williams) (Coaches background brown)	1.00	.50	.30
179b	A's Mgr./Coaches (Jerry Adair, Vern Hoscheit, Irv Noren, Wes Stock, Dick Williams) (Coaches background orange)	.70	.35	.20
180	Fergie Jenkins	4.00	2.00	1.25
181	Jack Brohamer	.40	.20	.12
182	*Mike Caldwell*	.40	.20	.12
183	Don Buford	.40	.20	.12
184	Jerry Koosman	.40	.20	.12
185	Jim Wynn	.40	.20	.12
186	Bill Fahey	.40	.20	.12
187	Luke Walker	.40	.20	.12
188	Cookie Rojas	.40	.20	.12
189	Greg Luzinski	.90	.45	.25
190	Bob Gibson	5.00	2.50	1.50
191	Tigers Team	3.00	1.50	.90
192	Pat Jarvis	.40	.20	.12
193	Carlton Fisk	30.00	15.00	9.00
194	*Jorge Orta*	.40	.20	.12
195	Clay Carroll	.40	.20	.12
196	Ken McMullen	.40	.20	.12
197	Ed Goodson	.40	.20	.12
198	Horace Clarke	.40	.20	.12
199	Bert Blyleven	3.00	1.50	.90
200	Billy Williams	4.00	2.00	1.25
201	A.L. Playoffs (Hendrick Scores Winning Run.)	2.25	1.25	.70
202	N.L. Playoffs (Foster's Run Decides It.)	2.25	1.25	.70
203	World Series Game 1 (Tenace The Menace.)	2.25	1.25	.70
204	World Series Game 2 (A's Make It Two Straight.)	2.25	1.25	.70
205	World Series Game 3 (Reds Win Squeeker.)	2.25	1.25	.70
206	World Series Game 4 (Tenace Singles In Ninth.)	2.25	1.25	.70
207	World Series Game 5 (Odom Out At Plate.)	2.25	1.25	.70
208	World Series Game 6 (Reds' Slugging Ties Series.)	2.25	1.25	.70
209	World Series Game 7 (Campy Starts Winning Rally.)	2.25	1.25	.70
210	World Series Summary (World Champions.)	2.25	1.25	.70
211	Balor Moore	.40	.20	.12
212	Joe Lahoud	.40	.20	.12
213	Steve Garvey	7.50	3.75	2.25
214	Dave Hamilton	.40	.20	.12
215	Dusty Baker	.75	.40	.25
216	Toby Harrah	.40	.20	.12
217	Don Wilson	.40	.20	.12
218	Aurelio Rodriguez	.40	.20	.12
219	Cardinals Team	3.00	1.50	.90
220	Nolan Ryan	90.00	45.00	27.00
221	Fred Kendall	.40	.20	.12
222	Rob Gardner	.40	.20	.12
223	Bud Harrelson	.40	.20	.12
224	Bill Lee	.40	.20	.12
225	Al Oliver	.75	.40	.25
226	Ray Fosse	.40	.20	.12
227	Wayne Twitchell	.40	.20	.12
228	Bobby Darwin	.40	.20	.12
229	Roric Harrison	.40	.20	.12
230	Joe Morgan	5.00	2.50	1.50
231	Bill Parsons	.40	.20	.12
232	Ken Singleton	.40	.20	.12

		NR MT	EX	VG
233	Ed Kirkpatrick	.40	.20	.12
234	*Bill North*	.40	.20	.12
235	Catfish Hunter	4.00	2.00	1.25
236	Tito Fuentes	.40	.20	.12
237a	Braves Mgr./Coaches (Lew Burdette, Jim Busby, Roy Hartsfield, Eddie Mathews, Ken Silvestri) (Coaches background brown)	2.50	1.25	.70
237b	Braves Mgr./Coaches (Lew Burdette, Jim Busby, Roy Hartsfield, Eddie Mathews, Ken Silvestri) (Coaches background orange)	2.25	1.25	.70
238	Tony Muser	.40	.20	.12
239	Pete Richert	.40	.20	.12
240	Bobby Murcer	.60	.30	.20
241	Dwain Anderson	.40	.20	.12
242	George Culver	.40	.20	.12
243	Angels Team	3.00	1.50	.90
244	Ed Acosta	.40	.20	.12
245	Carl Yastrzemski	15.00	7.50	4.50
246	Ken Sanders	.40	.20	.12
247	Del Unser	.40	.20	.12
248	Jerry Johnson	.40	.20	.12
249	Larry Biittner	.40	.20	.12
250	Manny Sanguillen	.40	.20	.12
251	Roger Nelson	.40	.20	.12
252a	Giants Mgr./Coaches (Joe Amalfitano, Charlie Fox, Andy Gilbert, Don McMahon, John McNamara) (Coaches background brown)	.70	.35	.20
252b	Giants Mgr./Coaches (Joe Amalfitano, Charlie Fox, Andy Gilbert, Don McMahon, John McNamara) (Coaches background orange)	.50	.25	.15
253	Mark Belanger	.40	.20	.12
254	Bill Stoneman	.40	.20	.12
255	Reggie Jackson	30.00	15.00	9.00
256	Chris Zachary	.40	.20	.12
257a	Mets Mgr./Coaches (Yogi Berra, Roy McMillan, Joe Pignatano, Rube Walker, Eddie Yost) (Coaches background brown)	3.00	1.50	.90
257b	Mets Mgr./Coaches (Yogi Berra, Roy McMillan, Joe Pignatano, Rube Walker, Eddie Yost) (Coaches background orange)	2.50	1.25	.70
258	Tommy John	2.00	1.00	.60
259	Jim Holt	.40	.20	.12
260	Gary Nolan	.40	.20	.12
261	Pat Kelly	.40	.20	.12
262	Jack Aker	.40	.20	.12
263	George Scott	.40	.20	.12
264a	Checklist 133-264	2.00	1.00	.60
265	Gene Michael	.40	.20	.12
266	Mike Lum	.40	.20	.12
267	Lloyd Allen	.40	.20	.12
268	Jerry Morales	.40	.20	.12
269	Tim McCarver	.75	.40	.25
270	Luis Tiant	.75	.40	.25
271	Tom Hutton	.40	.20	.12
272	Ed Farmer	.40	.20	.12
273	Chris Speier	.40	.20	.12
274	Darold Knowles	.40	.20	.12
275	Tony Perez	3.00	1.50	.90
276	Joe Lovitto	.40	.20	.12
277	Bob Miller	.40	.20	.12
278	Orioles Team	3.00	1.50	.90
279	Mike Strahler	.40	.20	.12
280	Al Kaline	8.00	4.00	2.50
281	Mike Jorgensen	.40	.20	.12
282	Steve Hovley	.40	.20	.12
283	Ray Sadecki	.40	.20	.12
284	Glenn Borgmann	.40	.20	.12
285	Don Kessinger	.40	.20	.12
286	Frank Linzy	.40	.20	.12
287	Eddie Leon	.40	.20	.12
288	Gary Gentry	.40	.20	.12
289	Bob Oliver	.40	.20	.12
290	Cesar Cedeno	.40	.20	.12
291	Rogelio Moret	.40	.20	.12
292	Jose Cruz	.60	.30	.20
293	Bernie Allen	.40	.20	.12
294	Steve Arlin	.40	.20	.12
295	Bert Campaneris	.75	.40	.25
296	Reds Mgr./Coaches (Sparky Anderson, Alex Grammas, Ted Kluszewski, George Scherger, Larry Shepard)	2.00	1.00	.60
297	Walt Williams	.40	.20	.12
298	Ron Bryant	.40	.20	.12
299	Ted Ford	.40	.20	.12
300	Steve Carlton	15.00	7.50	4.50
301	Billy Grabarkewitz	.40	.20	.12
302	Terry Crowley	.40	.20	.12

		NR MT	EX	VG
303	Nelson Briles	.40	.20	.12
304	Duke Sims	.40	.20	.12
305	Willie Mays	35.00	17.50	10.50
306	Tom Burgmeier	.40	.20	.12
307	Boots Day	.40	.20	.12
308	Skip Lockwood	.40	.20	.12
309	Paul Popovich	.40	.20	.12
310	Dick Allen	.75	.40	.25
311	Joe Decker	.40	.20	.12
312	Oscar Brown	.40	.20	.12
313	Jim Ray	.40	.20	.12
314	Ron Swoboda	.40	.20	.12
315	John Odom	.40	.20	.12
316	Padres Team	3.00	1.50	.90
317	Danny Cater	.40	.20	.12
318	Jim McGlothlin	.40	.20	.12
319	Jim Spencer	.40	.20	.12
320	Lou Brock	6.00	3.00	1.75
321	Rich Hinton	.40	.20	.12
322	*Garry Maddox*	1.00	.50	.30
323	Tigers Mgr./Coaches (Art Fowler, Billy Martin, Joe Schultz, Charlie Silvera, Dick Tracewski)	1.50	.70	.45
324	Al Downing	.40	.20	.12
325	Boog Powell	.75	.40	.25
326	Darrell Brandon	.40	.20	.12
327	John Lowenstein	.40	.20	.12
328	Bill Bonham	.40	.20	.12
329	Ed Kranepool	.40	.20	.12
330	Rod Carew	15.00	7.50	4.50
331	Carl Morton	.40	.20	.12
332	*John Felske*	.40	.20	.12
333	Gene Clines	.40	.20	.12
334	Freddie Patek	.40	.20	.12
335	Bob Tolan	.40	.20	.12
336	Tom Bradley	.40	.20	.12
337	Dave Duncan	.40	.20	.12
338	Checklist 265-396	2.00	1.00	.60
339	Dick Tidrow	.40	.20	.12
340	Nate Colbert	.40	.20	.12
341	Boyhood Photo (Jim Palmer)	2.00	1.00	.60
342	Boyhood Photo (Sam McDowell)	.40	.20	.12
343	Boyhood Photo (Bobby Murcer)	.40	.20	.12
344	Boyhood Photo (Catfish Hunter)	1.50	.70	.45
345	Boyhood Photo (Chris Speier)	.40	.20	.12
346	Boyhood Photo (Gaylord Perry)	1.50	.70	.45
347	Royals Team	3.00	1.50	.90
348	Rennie Stennett	.40	.20	.12
349	Dick McAuliffe	.40	.20	.12
350	Tom Seaver	20.00	10.00	6.00
351	Jimmy Stewart	.40	.20	.12
352	*Don Stanhouse*	.40	.20	.12
353	Steve Brye	.40	.20	.12
354	Billy Parker	.40	.20	.12
355	Mike Marshall	.40	.20	.12
356	White Sox Mgr./Coaches (Joe Lonnett, Jim Mahoney, Al Monchak, Johnny Sain, Chuck Tanner)	.60	.30	.20
357	Ross Grimsley	.40	.20	.12
358	Jim Nettles	.40	.20	.12
359	Cecil Upshaw	.40	.20	.12
360	Joe Rudi (photo actually Gene Tenace)	.40	.20	.12
361	Fran Healy	.40	.20	.12
362	Eddie Watt	.40	.20	.12
363	Jackie Hernandez	.40	.20	.12
364	Rick Wise	.40	.20	.12
365	Rico Petrocelli	.40	.20	.12
366	Brock Davis	.40	.20	.12
367	Burt Hooton	.40	.20	.12
368	Bill Buckner	.60	.30	.20
369	Lerrin LaGrow	.40	.20	.12
370	Willie Stargell	6.00	3.00	1.75
371	Mike Kekich	.40	.20	.12
372	Oscar Gamble	.40	.20	.12
373	Clyde Wright	.40	.20	.12
374	Darrell Evans	.40	.20	.12
375	Larry Dierker	.40	.20	.12
376	Frank Duffy	.40	.20	.12
377	Expos Mgr./Coaches (Dave Bristol, Larry Doby, Gene Mauch, Cal McLish, Jerry Zimmerman)	.60	.30	.20
378	Lenny Randle	.40	.20	.12
379	Cy Acosta	.40	.20	.12
380	Johnny Bench	20.00	10.00	6.00
381	Vicente Romo	.40	.20	.12
382	Mike Hegan	.40	.20	.12
383	Diego Segui	.40	.20	.12
384	Don Baylor	2.00	1.00	.60
385	Jim Perry	.40	.20	.12
386	Don Money	.40	.20	.12
387	Jim Barr	.40	.20	.12
388	Ben Oglivie	.40	.20	.12
389	Mets Team	3.00	1.50	.90
390	Mickey Lolich	.75	.40	.25
391	*Lee Lacy*	.40	.20	.12
392	Dick Drago	.40	.20	.12
393	Jose Cardenal	.40	.20	.12
394	Sparky Lyle	.40	.20	.12
395	Roger Metzger	.40	.20	.12
396	Grant Jackson	.40	.20	.12
397	Dave Cash	.70	.35	.20
398	Rich Hand	.70	.35	.20
399	George Foster	1.50	.70	.45
400	Gaylord Perry	6.00	3.00	1.75
401	Clyde Mashore	.70	.35	.20
402	Jack Hiatt	.70	.35	.20
403	Sonny Jackson	.70	.35	.20
404	Chuck Brinkman	.70	.35	.20
405	Cesar Tovar	.70	.35	.20
406	Paul Lindblad	.70	.35	.20
407	Felix Millan	.70	.35	.20
408	Jim Colborn	.70	.35	.20
409	Ivan Murrell	.70	.35	.20
410	Willie McCovey	6.00	3.00	1.75
411	Ray Corbin	.70	.35	.20
412	Manny Mota	.70	.35	.20
413	Tom Timmermann	.70	.35	.20
414	Ken Rudolph	.70	.35	.20
415	Marty Pattin	.70	.35	.20
416	Paul Schaal	.70	.35	.20
417	Scipio Spinks	.70	.35	.20
418	Bobby Grich	.70	.35	.20
419	Casey Cox	.70	.35	.20
420	Tommie Agee	.70	.35	.20
421	Angels Mgr./Coaches (Tom Morgan, Salty Parker, Jimmie Reese, John Roseboro, Bobby Winkles)	.70	.35	.20
422	Bob Robertson	.70	.35	.20
423	Johnny Jeter	.70	.35	.20
424	Denny Doyle	.70	.35	.20
425	Alex Johnson	.70	.35	.20
426	Dave LaRoche	.70	.35	.20
427	Rick Auerbach	.70	.35	.20
428	Wayne Simpson	.70	.35	.20
429	Jim Fairey	.70	.35	.20
430	Vida Blue	1.00	.50	.30
431	Gerry Moses	.70	.35	.20
432	Dan Frisella	.70	.35	.20
433	Willie Horton	.70	.35	.20
434	Giants Team	4.00	2.00	1.25
435	Rico Carty	.70	.35	.20
436	Jim McAndrew	.70	.35	.20
437	John Kennedy	.70	.35	.20
438	Enzo Hernandez	.70	.35	.20
439	Eddie Fisher	.70	.35	.20
440	Glenn Beckert	.70	.35	.20
441	Gail Hopkins	.70	.35	.20
442	Dick Dietz	.70	.35	.20
443	Danny Thompson	.70	.35	.20
444	Ken Brett	.70	.35	.20
445	Ken Berry	.70	.35	.20
446	Jerry Reuss	.70	.35	.20
447	Joe Hague	.70	.35	.20
448	John Hiller	.70	.35	.20
449a	Indians Mgr./Coaches (Ken Aspromonte, Rocky Colavito, Joe Lutz, Warren Spahn) (Spahn's ear pointed)	1.50	.70	.45
449b	Indians Mgr./Coaches (Ken Aspromonte, Rocky Colavito, Joe Lutz, Warren Spahn) (Spahn's ear round)	2.00	1.00	.60
450	Joe Torre	.70	.35	.20
451	John Vukovich	.70	.35	.20
452	Paul Casanova	.70	.35	.20
453	Checklist 397-528	2.25	1.25	.70
454	Tom Haller	.70	.35	.20
455	Bill Melton	.70	.35	.20
456	Dick Green	.70	.35	.20
457	John Strohmayer	.70	.35	.20
458	Jim Mason	.70	.35	.20
459	Jimmy Howarth	.70	.35	.20
460	Bill Freehan	.70	.35	.20
461	Mike Corkins	.70	.35	.20
462	Ron Blomberg	.70	.35	.20
463	Ken Tatum	.70	.35	.20
464	Cubs Team	4.00	2.00	1.25
465	Dave Giusti	.70	.35	.20
466	Jose Arcia	.70	.35	.20
467	Mike Ryan	.70	.35	.20
468	Tom Griffin	.70	.35	.20
469	Dan Monzon	.70	.35	.20
470	Mike Cuellar	.70	.35	.20

		NR MT	EX	VG
471	All-Time Hit Leader (Ty Cobb)	5.00	2.50	1.50
472	All-Time Grand Slam Leader (Lou Gehrig)	5.00	2.50	1.50
473	All-Time Total Base Leader (Hank Aaron)	5.00	2.50	1.50
474	All-Time RBI Leader (Babe Ruth)	8.00	4.00	2.50
475	All-Time Batting Leader (Ty Cobb)	5.00	2.50	1.50
476	All-Time Shutout Leader (Walter Johnson)	2.00	1.00	.60
477	All-Time Victory Leader (Cy Young)	2.00	1.00	.60
478	All-Time Strikeout Leader (Walter Johnson)	2.00	1.00	.60
479	Hal Lanier	.70	.35	.20
480	Juan Marichal	6.00	3.00	1.75
481	White Sox Team	4.00	2.00	1.25
482	*Rick Reuschel*	1.50	.70	.45
483	Dal Maxvill	.70	.35	.20
484	Ernie McAnally	.70	.35	.20
485	Norm Cash	1.00	.50	.30
486a	Phillies Mgr./Coaches (Carroll Berringer, Billy DeMars, Danny Ozark, Ray Rippelmeyer, Bobby Wine) (Coaches background brown red)	.90	.45	.25
486b	Phillies Mgr./Coaches (Carroll Beringer, Billy DeMars, Danny Ozark, Ray Rippelmeyer, Bobby Wine) (Coaches background orange)	.70	.35	.20
487	Bruce Dal Canton	.70	.35	.20
488	Dave Campbell	.70	.35	.20
489	Jeff Burroughs	.70	.35	.20
490	Claude Osteen	.70	.35	.20
491	Bob Montgomery	.70	.35	.20
492	Pedro Borbon	.70	.35	.20
493	Duffy Dyer	.70	.35	.20
494	Rich Morales	.70	.35	.20
495	Tommy Helms	.70	.35	.20
496	Ray Lamb	.70	.35	.20
497	Cardinals Mgr./Coaches (Vern Benson, George Kissell, Red Schoendienst, Barney Schultz)	1.25	.60	.40
498	Graig Nettles	1.00	.50	.30
499	Bob Moose	.70	.35	.20
500	A's Team	4.00	2.00	1.25
501	Larry Gura	.70	.35	.20
502	Bobby Valentine	.70	.35	.20
503	Phil Niekro	5.00	2.50	1.50
504	Earl Williams	.70	.35	.20
505	Bob Bailey	.70	.35	.20
506	Bart Johnson	.70	.35	.20
507	Darrel Chaney	.70	.35	.20
508	Gates Brown	.70	.35	.20
509	Jim Nash	.70	.35	.20
510	Amos Otis	.70	.35	.20
511	Sam McDowell	.70	.35	.20
512	Dalton Jones	.70	.35	.20
513	Dave Marshall	.70	.35	.20
514	Jerry Kenney	.70	.35	.20
515	Andy Messersmith	.70	.35	.20
516	Danny Walton	.70	.35	.20
517a	Pirates Mgr./Coaches (Don Leppert, Bill Mazeroski, Dave Ricketts, Bill Virdon, Mel Wright) (Coaches background brown)	2.00	1.00	.60
517b	Pirates Mgr./Coaches (Don Leppert, Bill Mazeroski, Dave Ricketts, Bill Virdon, Mel Wright) (Coaches background orange)	.70	.35	.20
518	Bob Veale	.70	.35	.20
519	John Edwards	.70	.35	.20
520	Mel Stottlemyre	.70	.35	.20
521	Braves Team	4.00	2.00	1.25
522	Leo Cardenas	.70	.35	.20
523	Wayne Granger	.70	.35	.20
524	Gene Tenace	.70	.35	.20
525	Jim Fregosi	.70	.35	.20
526	Ollie Brown	.70	.35	.20
527	Dan McGinn	.70	.35	.20
528	Paul Blair	.70	.35	.20
529	Milt May	2.00	1.00	.60
530	Jim Kaat	4.00	2.00	1.25
531	Ron Woods	2.00	1.00	.60
532	Steve Mingori	2.00	1.00	.60
533	Larry Stahl	2.00	1.00	.60
534	Dave Lemonds	2.00	1.00	.60
535	John Callison	2.00	1.00	.60
536	Phillies Team	6.00	3.00	1.75
537	Bill Slayback	2.00	1.00	.60
538	Jim Hart	2.00	1.00	.60
539	Tom Murphy	2.00	1.00	.60
540	Cleon Jones	2.00	1.00	.60
541	Bob Bolin	2.00	1.00	.60

		NR MT	EX	VG
542	Pat Corrales	2.00	1.00	.60
543	Alan Foster	2.00	1.00	.60
544	Von Joshua	2.00	1.00	.60
545	Orlando Cepeda	4.00	2.00	1.25
546	Jim York	2.00	1.00	.60
547	Bobby Heise	2.00	1.00	.60
548	Don Durham	2.00	1.00	.60
549	Rangers Mgr./Coaches (Chuck Estrada, Whitey Herzog, Chuck Hiller, Jackie Moore)	2.50	1.25	.70
550	Dave Johnson	2.00	1.00	.60
551	Mike Kilkenny	2.00	1.00	.60
552	J.C. Martin	2.00	1.00	.60
553	Mickey Scott	2.00	1.00	.60
554	Dave Concepcion	2.50	1.25	.70
555	Bill Hands	2.00	1.00	.60
556	Yankees Team	7.50	3.75	2.25
557	Bernie Williams	2.00	1.00	.60
558	Jerry May	2.00	1.00	.60
559	Barry Lersch	2.00	1.00	.60
560	Frank Howard	2.00	1.00	.60
561	Jim Geddes	2.00	1.00	.60
562	Wayne Garrett	2.00	1.00	.60
563	Larry Haney	2.00	1.00	.60
564	Mike Thompson	2.00	1.00	.60
565	Jim Hickman	2.00	1.00	.60
566	Lew Krausse	2.00	1.00	.60
567	Bob Fenwick	2.00	1.00	.60
568	Ray Newman	2.00	1.00	.60
569	Dodgers Mgr./Coaches (Red Adams, Walt Alston, Monty Basgall, Jim Gillam, Tom Lasorda)	4.00	2.00	1.25
570	Bill Singer	2.00	1.00	.60
571	Rusty Torres	2.00	1.00	.60
572	Gary Sutherland	2.00	1.00	.60
573	Fred Beene	2.00	1.00	.60
574	Bob Didier	2.00	1.00	.60
575	Dock Ellis	2.00	1.00	.60
576	Expos Team	5.00	2.50	1.50
577	*Eric Soderholm*	2.00	1.00	.60
578	Ken Wright	2.00	1.00	.60
579	Tom Grieve	2.00	1.00	.60
580	Joe Pepitone	2.00	1.00	.60
581	Steve Kealey	2.00	1.00	.60
582	Darrell Porter	2.00	1.00	.60
583	Bill Greif	2.00	1.00	.60
584	Chris Arnold	2.00	1.00	.60
585	Joe Niekro	2.00	1.00	.60
586	Bill Sudakis	2.00	1.00	.60
587	Rich McKinney	2.00	1.00	.60
588	Checklist 529-660	2.00	1.00	.60
589	Ken Forsch	2.00	1.00	.60
590	Deron Johnson	2.00	1.00	.60
591	Mike Hedlund	2.00	1.00	.60
592	John Boccabella	2.00	1.00	.60
593	Royals Mgr./Coaches (Galen Cisco, Harry Dunlop, Charlie Lau, Jack McKeon)	2.25	1.25	.70
594	Vic Harris	2.00	1.00	.60
595	Don Gullett	2.00	1.00	.60
596	Red Sox Team	6.00	3.00	1.75
597	Mickey Rivers	2.00	1.00	.60
598	Phil Roof	2.00	1.00	.60
599	Ed Crosby	2.00	1.00	.60
600	Dave McNally	2.00	1.00	.60
601	Rookie Catchers (George Pena, Sergio Robles, Rick Stelmaszek)	2.00	1.00	.60
602	Rookie Pitchers (Mel Behney, Ralph Garcia, *Doug Rau*)	2.00	1.00	.60
603	Rookie Third Basemen (Terry Hughes, Bill McNulty, *Ken Reitz*)	2.00	1.00	.60
604	Rookie Pitchers (Jesse Jefferson, Dennis O'Toole, Bob Strampe)	2.00	1.00	.60
605	Rookie First Basemen (Pat Bourque, *Enos Cabell,* Gonzalo Marquez)	2.00	1.00	.60
606	Rookie Outfielders *(Gary Matthews,* Tom Paciorek, Jorge Roque)	2.25	1.25	.70
607	Rookie Shortstops (Ray Busse, Pepe Frias, Mario Guerrero)	2.00	1.00	.60
608	Rookie Pitchers *(Steve Busby,* Dick Colpaert, *George Medich)*	2.25	1.25	.70
609	Rookie Second Basemen (Larvell Blanks, Pedro Garcia, *Dave Lopes)*	4.00	2.00	1.25
610	Rookie Pitchers (Jimmy Freeman, Charlie Hough, Hank Webb)	2.25	1.25	.70
611	Rookie Outfielders (Rich Coggins, Jim Wohlford, Richie Zisk)	2.25	1.25	.70
612	Rookie Pitchers (Steve Lawson, Bob Reynolds, Brent Strom)	2.00	1.00	.60
613	Rookie Catchers *(Bob Boone,* Mike Ivie, Skip Jutze)	30.00	15.00	9.00
614	Rookie Outfielders *(Alonza Bumbry, Dwight Evans,* Charlie Spikes)	30.00	15.00	9.00

		NR MT	EX	VG
615	Rookie Third Basemen (Ron Cey, John Hilton, *Mike Schmidt*)	450.00	225.00	135.00
616	Rookie Pitchers (Norm Angelini, Steve Blateric, Mike Garman)	2.00	1.00	.60
617	Rich Chiles	2.00	1.00	.60
618	Andy Etchebarren	2.00	1.00	.60
619	Billy Wilson	2.00	1.00	.60
620	Tommy Harper	2.00	1.00	.60
621	Joe Ferguson	2.00	1.00	.60
622	Larry Hisle	2.00	1.00	.60
623	Steve Renko	2.00	1.00	.60
624	Astros Mgr./Coaches (Leo Durocher, Preston Gomez, Grady Hatton, Hub Kittle, Jim Owens)	2.25	1.25	.70
625	Angel Mangual	2.00	1.00	.60
626	Bob Barton	2.00	1.00	.60
627	Luis Alvarado	2.00	1.00	.60
628	Jim Slaton	2.00	1.00	.60
629	Indians Team	5.00	2.50	1.50
630	Denny McLain	3.00	1.50	.90
631	Tom Matchick	2.00	1.00	.60
632	Dick Selma	2.00	1.00	.60
633	Ike Brown	2.00	1.00	.60
634	Alan Closter	2.00	1.00	.60
635	Gene Alley	2.00	1.00	.60
636	Rick Clark	2.00	1.00	.60
637	Norm Niller	2.00	1.00	.60
638	Ken Reynolds	2.00	1.00	.60
639	Willie Crawford	2.00	1.00	.60
640	Dick Bosman	2.00	1.00	.60
641	Reds Team	6.00	3.00	1.75
642	Jose Laboy	2.00	1.00	.60
643	Al Fitzmorris	2.00	1.00	.60
644	Jack Heidemann	2.00	1.00	.60
645	Bob Locker	2.00	1.00	.60
646	Brewers Mgr./Coaches (Del Crandall, Harvey Kuenn, Joe Nossek, Bob Shaw, Jim Walton)	2.25	1.25	.70
647	George Stone	2.00	1.00	.60
648	Tom Egan	2.00	1.00	.60
649	Rich Folkers	2.00	1.00	.60
650	Felipe Alou	3.00	1.50	.90
651	Don Carrithers	2.00	1.00	.60
652	Ted Kubiak	2.00	1.00	.60
653	Joe Hoerner	2.00	1.00	.60
654	Twins Team	6.00	3.00	1.75
655	Clay Kirby	2.00	1.00	.60
656	John Ellis	2.00	1.00	.60
657	Bob Johnson	2.00	1.00	.60
658	Elliott Maddox	2.00	1.00	.60
659	Jose Pagan	2.00	1.00	.60
660	Fred Scherman	2.00	1.00	.60

1973 Topps Candy Lids

A bit out of the ordinary, the Topps Candy Lids were the top of a product called "Baseball Stars Bubble Gum." The bottom (inside) of the lids carry a color photo of a player with a ribbon which contains the name, position and team. The lids are 1-7/8" in diameter. A total of 55 different lids were made, featuring most of the stars of the day.

		NR MT	EX	VG
Complete Set:		450.00	225.00	135.00
Common Player:		2.00	1.00	.60
(1)	Hank Aaron	30.00	15.00	9.00
(2)	Dick Allen	4.00	2.00	1.25
(3)	Dusty Baker	2.00	1.00	.60
(4)	Sal Bando	3.00	1.50	.90
(5)	Johnny Bench	20.00	10.00	6.00
(6)	Bobby Bonds	3.00	1.50	.90
(7)	Dick Bosman	2.00	1.00	.60
(8)	Lou Brock	15.00	7.50	4.50
(9)	Rod Carew	20.00	10.00	6.00
(10)	Steve Carlton	20.00	10.00	6.00
(11)	Nate Colbert	2.00	1.00	.60
(12)	Willie Davis	3.00	1.50	.90
(13)	Larry Dierker	2.00	1.00	.60
(14)	Mike Epstein	2.00	1.00	.60
(15)	Carlton Fisk	7.00	3.50	2.00
(16)	Tim Foli	2.00	1.00	.60
(17)	Ray Fosse	2.00	1.00	.60
(18)	Bill Freehan	3.00	1.50	.90
(19)	Bob Gibson	15.00	7.50	4.50
(20)	Bud Harrelson	2.00	1.00	.60
(21)	Jim Hunter	12.00	6.00	3.50
(22)	Reggie Jackson	25.00	12.50	7.50
(23)	Fergie Jenkins	7.00	3.50	2.00
(24)	Al Kaline	15.00	7.50	4.50
(25)	Harmon Killebrew	15.00	7.50	4.50
(26)	Clay Kirby	2.00	1.00	.60
(27)	Mickey Lolich	4.00	2.00	1.25
(28)	Greg Luzinski	3.00	1.50	.90
(29)	Mike Marshall	2.00	1.00	.60
(30)	Lee May	2.00	1.00	.60
(31)	John Mayberry	2.00	1.00	.60
(32)	Willie Mays	30.00	15.00	9.00
(33)	Willie McCovey	15.00	7.50	4.50
(34)	Thurman Munson	15.00	7.50	4.50
(35)	Bobby Murcer	3.00	1.50	.90
(36)	Gary Nolan	2.00	1.00	.60
(37)	Amos Otis	2.00	1.00	.60
(38)	Jim Palmer	12.00	6.00	3.50
(39)	Gaylord Perry	12.00	6.00	3.50
(40)	Lou Piniella	3.00	1.50	.90
(41)	Brooks Robinson	18.00	9.00	5.50
(42)	Frank Robinson	15.00	7.50	4.50
(43)	Ellie Rodriguez	2.00	1.00	.60
(44)	Pete Rose	65.00	32.00	19.50
(45)	Nolan Ryan	18.00	9.00	5.50
(46)	Manny Sanguillen	2.00	1.00	.60
(47)	George Scott	2.00	1.00	.60
(48)	Tom Seaver	20.00	10.00	6.00
(49)	Chris Speier	2.00	1.00	.60
(50)	Willie Stargell	15.00	7.50	4.50
(51)	Don Sutton	12.00	6.00	3.50
(52)	Joe Torre	4.00	2.00	1.25
(53)	Billy Williams	12.00	6.00	3.50
(54)	Wilbur Wood	2.00	1.00	.60
(55)	Carl Yastrzemski	25.00	12.50	7.50

1973 Topps Comics

Strictly a test issue, if ever publicly distributed at all (most are found without any folding which would have occurred had they actually been used to wrap a piece of bubblegum), the 24 players in the 1973 Topps Comics issue appear on 4-5/8" by 3-7/16" waxed paper wrappers. The inside of the wrapper combines a color photo and facsimile autograph with a comic-style presentation of the player's career highlights. The Comics share a checklist with the 1973 Topps Pin-Ups, virtually all star players.

		NR MT	EX	VG
Complete Set:		3000.00	1500.00	900.00
Common Player:		70.00	35.00	21.00
(1)	Hank Aaron	200.00	100.00	60.00
(2)	Dick Allen	80.00	40.00	24.00
(3)	Johnny Bench	150.00	75.00	45.00
(4)	Steve Carlton	125.00	62.00	37.00
(5)	Nate Colbert	70.00	35.00	21.00
(6)	Willie Davis	80.00	40.00	24.00
(7)	Mike Epstein	70.00	35.00	21.00
(8)	Reggie Jackson	200.00	100.00	60.00
(9)	Harmon Killebrew	125.00	62.00	37.00
(10)	Mickey Lolich	80.00	40.00	24.00
(11)	Mike Marshall	70.00	35.00	21.00
(12)	Lee May	70.00	35.00	21.00
(13)	Willie McCovey	125.00	62.00	37.00
(14)	Bobby Murcer	80.00	40.00	24.00
(15)	Gaylord Perry	100.00	50.00	30.00
(16)	Lou Piniella	80.00	40.00	24.00
(17)	Brooks Robinson	125.00	62.00	37.00
(18)	Nolan Ryan	125.00	62.00	37.00
(19)	George Scott	70.00	35.00	21.00
(20)	Tom Seaver	150.00	75.00	45.00
(21)	Willie Stargell	100.00	50.00	30.00
(22)	Joe Torre	80.00	40.00	24.00
(23)	Billy Williams	100.00	50.00	30.00
(24)	Carl Yastrzemski	250.00	125.00	75.00

1973 Topps 1953 Reprints

Long before Topps reprinted virtually the entire 1953 set in its "Archives" program in 1991, selected cards from the '53 set had been reprinted in a rare eight-card issue. Some sources say the cards were produced as table favors at a Topps banquet, while at least one contemporary hobby periodical said they were sold on a test-issue basis in Brooklyn. It was said only 300 of the sets were made. Unlike the original cards in 2-5/8" x 3-3/4" format, the test issue cards are modern standard 2-1/2" x 3-1/2". Three of the players in the issue were misidentified. Card backs feature a career summary written as though in 1953; the backs are formatted differently than original 1953 Topps cards and are printed in black-and-white.

		NR MT	EX	VG
Complete set (8):		400.00	200.00	120.00
Common player:		15.00	7.50	4.50
1	Satchell Paige	150.00	75.00	45.00
2	Jackie Robinson	100.00	50.00	30.00
3	Carl Furillo (picture actually Bill Antonello)	25.00	12.50	7.50
4	Al Rosen (picture actually Jim Fridley)	20.00	10.00	6.00
5	Hal Newhouser	25.00	12.50	7.50
6	Clyde McCullough (picture actually Vic Janowicz)	15.00	7.50	4.50
7	"Peanuts Lowrey	15.00	7.50	4.50
8	Johnny Mize	50.00	25.00	15.00

The values quoted are intended to reflect the market price.

1973 Topps Pin-Ups

Another test issue of 1973, the 24 Topps Pin-Ups include the same basic format and the same checklist of star-caliber players as the Comics test issue of the same year. The 3-7/16" by 4-5/8" Pin-Ups are actually the inside of a wrapper for a piece of bubblegum. The color player photo features a decorative lozenge inserted at bottom with the player's name, team and position. There is also a facsimile autograph. Curiously, neither the Pin-Ups nor the Comics of 1973 bear team logos on the players' caps.

		NR MT	EX	VG
Complete Set:		1250.00	625.00	375.00
Common Player:		30.00	15.00	9.00
(1)	Hank Aaron	90.00	45.00	27.00
(2)	Dick Allen	35.00	17.50	10.50
(3)	Johnny Bench	70.00	35.00	21.00
(4)	Steve Carlton	60.00	30.00	18.00
(5)	Nate Colbert	30.00	15.00	9.00
(6)	Willie Davis	35.00	17.50	10.50
(7)	Mike Epstein	30.00	15.00	9.00
(8)	Reggie Jackson	90.00	45.00	27.00
(9)	Harmon Killebrew	50.00	25.00	15.00
(10)	Mickey Lolich	35.00	17.50	10.50
(11)	Mike Marshall	30.00	15.00	9.00
(12)	Lee May	30.00	15.00	9.00
(13)	Willie McCovey	50.00	25.00	15.00
(14)	Bobby Murcer	35.00	17.50	10.50
(15)	Gaylord Perry	45.00	22.00	13.50
(16)	Lou Piniella	35.00	17.50	10.50
(17)	Brooks Robinson	55.00	27.00	16.50
(18)	Nolan Ryan	55.00	27.00	16.50
(19)	George Scott	30.00	15.00	9.00
(20)	Tom Seaver	75.00	37.00	22.00
(21)	Willie Stargell	45.00	22.00	13.50
(22)	Joe Torre	35.00	17.50	10.50
(23)	Billy Williams	45.00	22.00	13.50
(24)	Carl Yastrzemski	110.00	55.00	33.00

1973 Topps Team Checklists

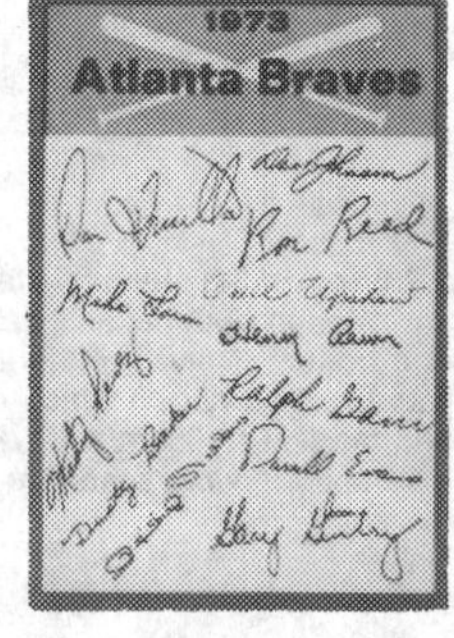

This is a 24-card unnumbered set of 2-1/2" by 3-1/2" cards that is generally believed to have been included with the high-numbered series in 1973, while also being made available in a mail-in offer. The front of the cards have the team name at the top and a white panel with various facsimile autographs takes up the rest of the space except for a blue border. Backs feature the team name and checklist. Relatively scarce, these somewhat mysterious cards are not included by many in their collections despite their obvious relationship to the regular set.

		NR MT	EX	VG
Complete Set:		75.00	37.00	22.00
Common Checklist:		3.00	1.50	.90
(1)	Atlanta Braves	3.00	1.50	.90
(2)	Baltimore Orioles	3.00	1.50	.90
(3)	Boston Red Sox	3.00	1.50	.90
(4)	California Angels	3.00	1.50	.90
(5)	Chicago Cubs	3.00	1.50	.90
(6)	Chicago White Sox	3.00	1.50	.90
(7)	Cincinnati Reds	3.00	1.50	.90
(8)	Cleveland Indians	3.00	1.50	.90
(9)	Detroit Tigers	3.50	1.75	1.00
(10)	Houston Astros	3.00	1.50	.90
(11)	Kansas City Royals	3.00	1.50	.90
(12)	Los Angeles Dodgers	3.00	1.50	.90
(13)	Milwaukee Brewers	3.00	1.50	.90
(14)	Minnesota Twins	3.00	1.50	.90
(15)	Montreal Expos	3.00	1.50	.90
(16)	New York Mets	3.50	1.75	1.00
(17)	New York Yankees	3.50	1.75	1.00
(18)	Oakland A's	3.50	1.75	1.00
(19)	Philadelphia Phillies	3.00	1.50	.90
(20)	Pittsburgh Pirates	3.00	1.50	.90
(21)	St. Louis Cardinals	3.00	1.50	.90
(22)	San Diego Padres	3.00	1.50	.90
(23)	San Francisco Giants	3.00	1.50	.90
(24)	Texas Rangers	3.00	1.50	.90

1974 Topps

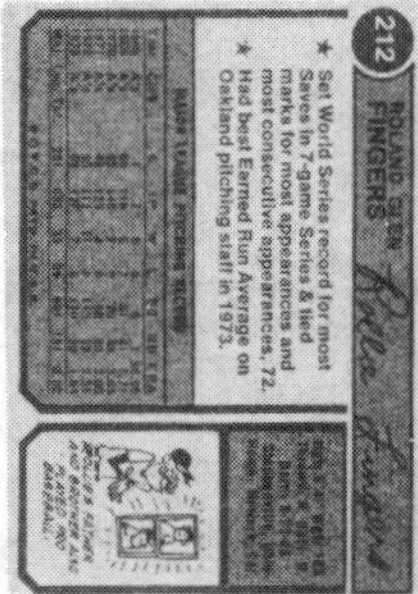

Issued all at once at the beginning of the year, rather than by series throughout the baseball season as had been done since 1952, this 660-card '74 Topps set features a famous group of error cards. At the time the cards were printed, it was uncertain whether the San Diego Padres would move to Washington, D.C., and by the time a decision was made some Padres cards had appeared with a "Washington, Nat'l League" designation on the front. A total of 15 cards were affected, and those with the Washington designation bring prices well in excess of regular cards of the same players (the Washington variations are not included in the complete set prices quoted below). The 2-1/2" by 3-1/2" cards feature color photos (frequently game-action shots) along with the player's name, team and position. Specialty cards abound, starting with a Hank Aaron tribute and running through the usual managers, statistical leaders, playoff and World Series highlights, multi-player rookie cards and All-Stars.

	NR MT	EX	VG
Complete Set (660):	650.00	325.00	195.00
Common Player:	.30	.15	.09

1	Hank Aaron (All-Time Home Run King)	24.00	12.00	7.25
2	Aaron Special 1954-57	3.00	1.50	.90
3	Aaron Special 1958-61	3.00	1.50	.90
4	Aaron Special 1962-65	3.00	1.50	.90
5	Aaron Special 1966-69	3.00	1.50	.90
6	Aaron Special 1970-73	3.00	1.50	.90
7	Catfish Hunter	4.00	2.00	1.25
8	George Theodore	.30	.15	.09
9	Mickey Lolich	.60	.30	.20
10	Johnny Bench	15.00	7.50	4.50
11	Jim Bibby	.30	.15	.09
12	Dave May	.30	.15	.09
13	Tom Hilgendorf	.30	.15	.09
14	Paul Popovich	.30	.15	.09
15	Joe Torre	.30	.15	.09
16	Orioles Team	2.00	1.00	.60
17	Doug Bird	.30	.15	.09
18	Gary Thomasson	.30	.15	.09
19	Gerry Moses	.30	.15	.09
20	Nolan Ryan	80.00	40.00	24.00
21	Bob Gallagher	.30	.15	.09
22	Cy Acosta	.30	.15	.09
23	Craig Robinson	.30	.15	.09
24	John Hiller	.30	.15	.09
25	Ken Singleton	.30	.15	.09
26	*Bill Campbell*	.30	.15	.09
27	George Scott	.30	.15	.09
28	Manny Sanguillen	.30	.15	.09
29	Phil Niekro	2.00	1.00	.60
30	Bobby Bonds	.50	.25	.15
31	Astros Mgr./Coaches (Roger Craig, Preston Gomez, Grady Hatton, Hub Kittle, Bob Lillis)	.75	.40	.25
32a	John Grubb (Washington)	3.50	1.75	1.00
32b	John Grubb (San Diego)	.30	.15	.09
33	Don Newhauser	.30	.15	.09
34	Andy Kosco	.30	.15	.09
35	Gaylord Perry	4.00	2.00	1.25
36	Cardinals Team	2.00	1.00	.60
37	Dave Sells	.30	.15	.09
38	Don Kessinger	.30	.15	.09
39	Ken Suarez	.30	.15	.09
40	Jim Palmer	9.00	4.50	2.75
41	Bobby Floyd	.30	.15	.09
42	Claude Osteen	.30	.15	.09
43	Jim Wynn	.30	.15	.09
44	Mel Stottlemyre	.30	.15	.09
45	Dave Johnson	.30	.15	.09
46	Pat Kelly	.30	.15	.09
47	*Dick Ruthven*	.30	.15	.09
48	Dick Sharon	.30	.15	.09
49	Steve Renko	.30	.15	.09
50	Rod Carew	12.00	6.00	3.50
51	Bobby Heise	.30	.15	.09
52	Al Oliver	.75	.40	.25
53a	Fred Kendall (Washington)	3.50	1.75	1.00
53b	Fred Kendall (San Diego)	.30	.15	.09
54	*Elias Sosa*	.30	.15	.09
55	Frank Robinson	9.00	4.50	2.75
56	Mets Team	2.00	1.00	.60
57	Darold Knowles	.30	.15	.09
58	Charlie Spikes	.30	.15	.09
59	Ross Grimsley	.30	.15	.09
60	Lou Brock	5.00	2.50	1.50
61	Luis Aparicio	2.50	1.25	.70
62	Bob Locker	.30	.15	.09
63	Bill Sudakis	.30	.15	.09
64	Doug Rau	.30	.15	.09
65	Amos Otis	.30	.15	.09
66	Sparky Lyle	.30	.15	.09
67	Tommy Helms	.30	.15	.09
68	Grant Jackson	.30	.15	.09
69	Del Unser	.30	.15	.09
70	Dick Allen	.50	.25	.15
71	Danny Frisella	.30	.15	.09
72	Aurleio Rodriguez	.30	.15	.09
73	Mike Marshall	.30	.15	.09
74	Twins Team	2.00	1.00	.60
75	Jim Colborn	.30	.15	.09
76	Mickey Rivers	.30	.15	.09
77a	Rich Troedson (Washington)	3.50	1.75	1.00
77b	Rich Troedson (San Diego)	.30	.15	.09
78	Giants Mgr./Coaches (Joe Amalfitano, Charlie Fox, Andy Gilbert, Don McMahon, John McNamara)	.30	.15	.09
79	Gene Tenace	.30	.15	.09
80	Tom Seaver	15.00	7.50	4.50
81	Frank Duffy	.30	.15	.09
82	Dave Giusti	.30	.15	.09
83	Orlando Cepeda	2.00	1.00	.60
84	Rick Wise	.30	.15	.09

		NR MT	EX	VG
85	Joe Morgan	5.00	2.50	1.50
86	Joe Ferguson	.30	.15	.09
87	Fergie Jenkins	4.00	2.00	1.25
88	Freddie Patek	.30	.15	.09
89	Jackie Brown	.30	.15	.09
90	Bobby Murcer	.40	.20	.12
91	Ken Forsch	.30	.15	.09
92	Paul Blair	.30	.15	.09
93	Rod Gilbreath	.30	.15	.09
94	Tigers Team	2.00	1.00	.60
95	Steve Carlton	9.00	4.50	2.75
96	*Jerry Hairston*	.30	.15	.09
97	Bob Bailey	.30	.15	.09
98	Bert Blyleven	1.00	.50	.30
99	Brewers Mgr./Coaches (Del Crandall, Harvey Kuenn, Joe Nossek, Jim Walton, Al Widmar)	.30	.15	.09
100	Willie Stargell	6.00	3.00	1.75
101	Bobby Valentine	.30	.15	.09
102a	Bill Greif (Washington)	3.50	1.75	1.00
102b	Bill Greif (San Diego)	.30	.15	.09
103	Sal Bando	.30	.15	.09
104	Ron Bryant	.30	.15	.09
105	Carlton Fisk	12.50	6.25	3.75
106	Harry Parker	.30	.15	.09
107	Alex Johnson	.30	.15	.09
108	Al Hrabosky	.30	.15	.09
109	Bob Grich	.40	.20	.12
110	Billy Williams	6.00	3.00	1.75
111	Clay Carroll	.30	.15	.09
112	Dave Lopes	.40	.20	.12
113	Dick Drago	.30	.15	.09
114	Angels Team	2.00	1.00	.60
115	Willie Horton	.30	.15	.09
116	Jerry Reuss	.30	.15	.09
117	Ron Blomberg	.30	.15	.09
118	Bill Lee	.30	.15	.09
119	Phillies Mgr./Coaches (Carroll Beringer, Bill DeMars, Danny Ozark, Ray Ripplemeyer, Bobby Wine)	.30	.15	.09
120	Wilbur Wood	.30	.15	.09
121	Larry Lintz	.30	.15	.09
122	Jim Holt	.30	.15	.09
123	Nelson Briles	.30	.15	.09
124	Bob Coluccio	.30	.15	.09
125a	Nate Colbert (Washington)	3.50	1.75	1.00
125b	Nate Colbert (San Diego)	.30	.15	.09
126	Checklist 1-132	1.50	.70	.45
127	Tom Paciorek	.30	.15	.09
128	John Ellis	.30	.15	.09
129	Chris Speier	.30	.15	.09
130	Reggie Jackson	30.00	15.00	9.00
131	Bob Boone	2.50	1.25	.70
132	Felix Millan	.30	.15	.09
133	*David Clyde*	.30	.15	.09
134	Denis Menke	.30	.15	.09
135	Roy White	.40	.20	.12
136	Rick Reuschel	.30	.15	.09
137	Al Bumbry	.30	.15	.09
138	Ed Brinkman	.30	.15	.09
139	Aurelio Monteagudo	.30	.15	.09
140	Darrell Evans	.60	.30	.20
141	Pat Bourque	.30	.15	.09
142	Pedro Garcia	.30	.15	.09
143	Dick Woodson	.30	.15	.09
144	Dodgers Mgr./Coaches (Red Adams, Walter Alston, Monty Basgall, Jim Gilliam, Tom Lasorda)	1.50	.70	.45
145	Dock Ellis	.30	.15	.09
146	Ron Fairly	.30	.15	.09
147	Bart Johnson	.30	.15	.09
148a	Dave Hilton (Washington)	3.50	1.75	1.00
148b	Dave Hilton (San Diego)	.30	.15	.09
149	Mac Scarce	.30	.15	.09
150	John Mayberry	.30	.15	.09
151	Diego Segui	.30	.15	.09
152	Oscar Gamble	.30	.15	.09
153	Jon Matlack	.30	.15	.09
154	Astros Team	2.00	1.00	.60
155	Bert Campaneris	.30	.15	.09
156	Randy Moffitt	.30	.15	.09
157	Vic Harris	.30	.15	.09
158	Jack Billingham	.30	.15	.09
159	Jim Ray Hart	.30	.15	.09
160	Brooks Robinson	9.00	4.50	2.75
161	*Ray Burris*	.30	.15	.09
162	Bill Freehan	.30	.15	.09
163	Ken Berry	.30	.15	.09
164	Tom House	.30	.15	.09
165	Willie Davis	.30	.15	.09
166	Royals Mgr./Coaches (Galen Cisco, Harry Dunlop, Charlie Lau, Jack McKeon)	.45	.25	.14

		NR MT	EX	VG
167	Luis Tiant	.50	.25	.15
168	Danny Thompson	.30	.15	.09
169	*Steve Rogers*	.30	.15	.09
170	Bill Melton	.30	.15	.09
171	Eduardo Rodriguez	.30	.15	.09
172	Gene Clines	.30	.15	.09
173a	*Randy Jones* (Washington)	3.50	1.75	1.00
173b	*Randy Jones* (San Diego)	.30	.15	.09
174	Bill Robinson	.30	.15	.09
175	Reggie Cleveland	.30	.15	.09
176	John Lowenstein	.30	.15	.09
177	Dave Roberts	.30	.15	.09
178	Garry Maddox	.30	.15	.09
179	Mets Mgr./Coaches (Yogi Berra, Roy McMillan, Joe Pignatano, Rube Walker, Eddie Yost)	2.00	1.00	.60
180	Ken Holtzman	.30	.15	.09
181	Cesar Geronimo	.30	.15	.09
182	Lindy McDaniel	.30	.15	.09
183	Johnny Oates	.30	.15	.09
184	Rangers Team	2.00	1.00	.60
185	Jose Cardenal	.30	.15	.09
186	Fred Scherman	.30	.15	.09
187	Don Baylor	.50	.25	.15
188	Rudy Meoli	.30	.15	.09
189	Jim Brewer	.30	.15	.09
190	Tony Oliva	.50	.25	.15
191	Al Fitzmorris	.30	.15	.09
192	Mario Guerrero	.30	.15	.09
193	Tom Walker	.30	.15	.09
194	Darrell Porter	.30	.15	.09
195	Carlos May	.30	.15	.09
196	Jim Fregosi	.30	.15	.09
197a	Vicente Romo (Washington)	3.50	1.75	1.00
197b	Vicente Romo (San Diego)	.30	.15	.09
198	Dave Cash	.30	.15	.09
199	Mike Kekich	.30	.15	.09
200	Cesar Cedeno	.30	.15	.09
201	Batting Leaders (Rod Carew, Pete Rose)	4.00	2.00	1.25
202	Home Run Leaders (Reggie Jackson, Willie Stargell)	5.00	2.50	1.50
203	Runs Batted In Leaders (Reggie Jackson, Willie Stargell)	5.00	2.50	1.50
204	Stolen Base Leaders (Lou Brock, Tommy Harper)	1.50	.70	.45
205	Victory Leaders (Ron Bryant, Wilbur Wood)	.50	.25	.15
206	Earned Run Average Leaders (Jim Palmer, Tom Seaver)	2.00	1.00	.60
207	Strikeout Leaders (Nolan Ryan, Tom Seaver)	15.00	7.50	4.50
208	Leading Firemen (John Hiller, Mike Marshall)	.50	.25	.15
209	Ted Sizemore	.30	.15	.09
210	Bill Singer	.30	.15	.09
211	Cubs Team	2.00	1.00	.60
212	Rollie Fingers	5.00	2.50	1.50
213	Dave Rader	.30	.15	.09
214	Billy Grabarkewitz	.30	.15	.09
215	Al Kaline	8.00	4.00	2.50
216	Ray Sadecki	.30	.15	.09
217	Tim Foli	.30	.15	.09
218	Johnny Briggs	.30	.15	.09
219	Doug Griffin	.30	.15	.09
220	Don Sutton	2.00	1.00	.60
221	White Sox Mgr./Coaches (Joe Lonnett, Jim Mahoney, Alex Monchak, Johnny Sain, Chuck Tanner)	.45	.25	.14
222	Ramon Hernandez	.30	.15	.09
223	Jeff Burroughs	.30	.15	.09
224	Roger Metzger	.30	.15	.09
225	Paul Splittorff	.30	.15	.09
226a	Washington Nat'l. Team	6.00	3.00	1.75
226b	Padres Team	2.00	1.00	.60
227	Mike Lum	.30	.15	.09
228	Ted Kubiak	.30	.15	.09
229	Fritz Peterson	.30	.15	.09
230	Tony Perez	1.25	.60	.40
231	Dick Tidrow	.30	.15	.09
232	Steve Brye	.30	.15	.09
233	Jim Barr	.30	.15	.09
234	John Milner	.30	.15	.09
235	Dave McNally	.30	.15	.09
236	Cardinals Mgr./Coaches (Vern Benson, George Kissell, Johnny Lewis, Red Schoendienst, Barney Schultz)	.75	.40	.25
237	Ken Brett	.30	.15	.09
238	Fran Healy	.30	.15	.09
239	Bill Russell	.30	.15	.09
240	Joe Coleman	.30	.15	.09

		NR MT	EX	VG
241a	Glenn Beckert (Washington)	3.50	1.75	1.00
241b	Glenn Beckert (San Diego)	3.50	1.75	1.00
242	Bill Gogolewski	.30	.15	.09
243	Bob Oliver	.30	.15	.09
244	Carl Morton	.30	.15	.09
245	Cleon Jones	.30	.15	.09
246	A's Team	2.00	1.00	.60
247	Rick Miller	.30	.15	.09
248	Tom Hall	.30	.15	.09
249	George Mitterwald	.30	.15	.09
250a	Willie McCovey (Washington)	25.00	12.50	7.50
250b	Willie McCovey (San Diego)	5.00	2.50	1.50
251	Graig Nettles	.30	.15	.09
252	*Dave Parker*	20.00	10.00	6.00
253	John Boccabella	.30	.15	.09
254	Stan Bahnsen	.30	.15	.09
255	Larry Bowa	.40	.20	.12
256	Tom Griffin	.30	.15	.09
257	Buddy Bell	.40	.20	.12
258	Jerry Morales	.30	.15	.09
259	Bob Reynolds	.30	.15	.09
260	Ted Simmons	.50	.25	.15
261	Jerry Bell	.30	.15	.09
262	Ed Kirkpatrick	.30	.15	.09
263	Checklist 133-264	1.50	.70	.45
264	Joe Rudi	.30	.15	.09
265	Tug McGraw	.30	.15	.09
266	Jim Northrup	.30	.15	.09
267	Andy Messersmith	.30	.15	.09
268	Tom Grieve	.30	.15	.09
269	Bob Johnson	.30	.15	.09
270	Ron Santo	.50	.25	.15
271	Bill Hands	.30	.15	.09
272	Paul Casanova	.30	.15	.09
273	Checklist 265-396	1.50	.70	.45
274	Fred Beene	.30	.15	.09
275	Ron Hunt	.30	.15	.09
276	Angels Mgr./Coaches (Tom Morgan, Salty Parker, Jimmie Reese, John Roseboro, Bobby Winkles)	.30	.15	.09
277	Gary Nolan	.30	.15	.09
278	Cookie Rojas	.30	.15	.09
279	Jim Crawford	.30	.15	.09
280	Carl Yastrzemski	15.00	7.50	4.50
281	Giants Team	2.00	1.00	.60
282	Doyle Alexander	.30	.15	.09
283	Mike Schmidt	75.00	37.00	22.00
284	Dave Duncan	.30	.15	.09
285	Reggie Smith	.30	.15	.09
286	Tony Muser	.30	.15	.09
287	Clay Kirby	.30	.15	.09
288	*Gorman Thomas*	.50	.25	.15
289	Rick Auerbach	.30	.15	.09
290	Vida Blue	.40	.20	.12
291	Don Hahn	.30	.15	.09
292	Chuck Seelbach	.30	.15	.09
293	Milt May	.30	.15	.09
294	Steve Foucault	.30	.15	.09
295	Rick Monday	.30	.15	.09
296	Ray Corbin	.30	.15	.09
297	Hal Breeden	.30	.15	.09
298	Roric Harrison	.30	.15	.09
299	Gene Michael	.30	.15	.09
300	Pete Rose	15.00	7.50	4.50
301	Bob Montgomery	.30	.15	.09
302	Rudy May	.30	.15	.09
303	George Hendrick	.30	.15	.09
304	Don Wilson	.30	.15	.09
305	Tito Fuentes	.30	.15	.09
306	Orioles Mgr./Coaches (George Bamberger, Jim Frey, Billy Hunter, George Staller, Earl Weaver)	1.50	.70	.45
307	Luis Melendez	.30	.15	.09
308	Bruce Dal Canton	.30	.15	.09
309a	Dave Roberts (Washington)	3.50	1.75	1.00
309b	Dave Roberts (San Diego)	.30	.15	.09
310	Terry Forster	.30	.15	.09
311	Jerry Grote	.30	.15	.09
312	Deron Johnson	.30	.15	.09
313	Berry Lersch	.30	.15	.09
314	Brewers Team	2.00	1.00	.60
315	Ron Cey	.60	.30	.20
316	Jim Perry	.30	.15	.09
317	Richie Zisk	.30	.15	.09
318	Jim Merritt	.30	.15	.09
319	Randy Hundley	.30	.15	.09
320	Dusty Baker	.40	.20	.12
321	Steve Braun	.30	.15	.09
322	Ernie McAnally	.30	.15	.09
323	Richie Scheinblum	.30	.15	.09
324	Steve Kline	.30	.15	.09
325	Tommy Harper	.30	.15	.09
326	Reds Mgr./Coaches (Sparky Anderson, Alex Grammas, Ted Kluszewski, George Scherger, Larry Shepard)	1.50	.70	.45
327	Tom Timmermann	.30	.15	.09
328	Skip Jutze	.30	.15	.09
329	Mark Belanger	.30	.15	.09
330	Juan Marichal	4.00	2.00	1.25
331	All-Star Catchers (Johnny Bench, Carlton Fisk)	5.00	2.50	1.50
332	All-Star First Basemen (Hank Aaron, Dick Allen)	5.00	2.50	1.50
333	All-Star Second Basemen (Rod Carew, Joe Morgan)	3.00	1.50	.90
334	All-Star Third Basemen (Brooks Robinson, Ron Santo)	3.00	1.50	.90
335	All-Star Shortstops (Bert Campaneris, Chris Speier)	.40	.20	.12
336	All-Star Left Fielders (Bobby Murcer, Pete Rose)	2.50	1.25	.70
337	All-Star Center Fielders (Cesar Cedeno, Amos Otis)	.40	.20	.12
338	All-Star Right Fielders (Reggie Jackson, Billy Williams)	5.00	2.50	1.50
339	All-Star Pitchers (Catfish Hunter, Rick Wise)	.80	.40	.25
340	Thurman Munson	5.00	2.50	1.50
341	*Dan Driessen*	.30	.15	.09
342	Jim Lonborg	.30	.15	.09
343	Royals Team	2.00	1.00	.60
344	Mike Caldwell	.30	.15	.09
345	Bill North	.30	.15	.09
346	Ron Reed	.30	.15	.09
347	Sandy Alomar	.30	.15	.09
348	Pete Richert	.30	.15	.09
349	John Vukovich	.30	.15	.09
350	Bob Gibson	6.00	3.00	1.75
351	Dwight Evans	5.00	2.50	1.50
352	Bill Stoneman	.30	.15	.09
353	Rich Coggins	.30	.15	.09
354	Cubs Mgr./Coaches (Hank Aguirre, Whitey Lockman, Jim Marshall, J.C. Martin, Al Spangler)	.30	.15	.09
355	Dave Nelson	.30	.15	.09
356	Jerry Koosman	.30	.15	.09
357	Buddy Bradford	.30	.15	.09
358	Dal Maxvill	.30	.15	.09
359	Brent Strom	.30	.15	.09
360	Greg Luzinski	.50	.25	.15
361	Don Carrithers	.30	.15	.09
362	Hal King	.30	.15	.09
363	Yankees Team	3.00	1.50	.90
364a	Cito Gaston (Washington)	4.50	2.25	1.25
364b	Cito Gaston (San Diego)	.75	.40	.25
365	Steve Busby	.30	.15	.09
366	Larry Hisle	.30	.15	.09
367	Norm Cash	.50	.25	.15
368	Manny Mota	.30	.15	.09
369	Paul Lindblad	.30	.15	.09
370	Bob Watson	.30	.15	.09
371	Jim Slaton	.30	.15	.09
372	Ken Reitz	.30	.15	.09
373	John Curtis	.30	.15	.09
374	Marty Perez	.30	.15	.09
375	Earl Williams	.30	.15	.09
376	Jorge Orta	.30	.15	.09
377	Ron Woods	.30	.15	.09
378	Burt Hooton	.30	.15	.09
379	Rangers Mgr./Coaches (Art Fowler, Frank Lucchesi, Billy Martin, Jackie Moore, Charlie Silvera)	1.00	.50	.30
380	Bud Harrelson	.30	.15	.09
381	Charlie Sands	.30	.15	.09
382	Bob Moose	.30	.15	.09
383	Phillies Team	2.00	1.00	.60
384	Chris Chambliss	.30	.15	.09
385	Don Gullett	.30	.15	.09
386	Gary Matthews	.30	.15	.09
387a	Rich Morales (Washington)	3.50	1.75	1.00
387b	Rich Morales (San Diego)	.30	.15	.09
388	Phil Roof	.30	.15	.09
389	Gates Brown	.30	.15	.09
390	Lou Piniella	.30	.15	.09
391	Billy Champion	.30	.15	.09
392	Dick Green	.30	.15	.09
393	Orlando Pena	.30	.15	.09
394	Ken Henderson	.30	.15	.09
395	Doug Rader	.30	.15	.09
396	Tommy Davis	.30	.15	.09
397	George Stone	.30	.15	.09
398	Duke Sims	.30	.15	.09

		NR MT	EX	VG
399	Mike Paul	.30	.15	.09
400	Harmon Killebrew	5.00	2.50	1.50
401	Elliott Maddox	.30	.15	.09
402	Jim Rooker	.30	.15	.09
403	Red Sox Mgr./Coaches (Don Bryant, Darrell Johnson, Eddie Popowski, Lee Stange, Don Zimmer)	.45	.25	.14
404	Jim Howarth	.30	.15	.09
405	Ellie Rodriguez	.30	.15	.09
406	Steve Arlin	.30	.15	.09
407	Jim Wohlford	.30	.15	.09
408	Charlie Hough	.40	.20	.12
409	Ike Brown	.30	.15	.09
410	Pedro Borbon	.30	.15	.09
411	Frank Baker	.30	.15	.09
412	Chuck Taylor	.30	.15	.09
413	Don Money	.30	.15	.09
414	Checklist 397-528	1.50	.70	.45
415	Gary Gentry	.30	.15	.09
416	White Sox Team	2.00	1.00	.60
417	Rich Folkers	.30	.15	.09
418	Walt Williams	.30	.15	.09
419	Wayne Twitchell	.30	.15	.09
420	Ray Fosse	.30	.15	.09
421	Dan Fife	.30	.15	.09
422	Gonzalo Marquez	.30	.15	.09
423	Fred Stanley	.30	.15	.09
424	Jim Beauchamp	.30	.15	.09
425	Pete Broberg	.30	.15	.09
426	Rennie Stennett	.30	.15	.09
427	Bobby Bolin	.30	.15	.09
428	Gary Sutherland	.30	.15	.09
429	Dick Lange	.30	.15	.09
430	Matty Alou	.30	.15	.09
431	*Gene Garber*	.30	.15	.09
432	Chris Arnold	.30	.15	.09
433	Lerrin LaGrow	.30	.15	.09
434	Ken McMullen	.30	.15	.09
435	Dave Concepcion	.50	.25	.15
436	Don Hood	.30	.15	.09
437	Jim Lyttle	.30	.15	.09
438	Ed Herrmann	.30	.15	.09
439	Norm Miller	.30	.15	.09
440	Jim Kaat	1.25	.60	.40
441	Tom Ragland	.30	.15	.09
442	Alan Foster	.30	.15	.09
443	Tom Hutton	.30	.15	.09
444	Vic Davalillo	.30	.15	.09
445	George Medich	.30	.15	.09
446	Len Randle	.30	.15	.09
447	Twins Mgr./Coaches (Vern Morgan, Frank Quilici, Bob Rodgers, Ralph Rowe)	.30	.15	.09
448	Ron Hodges	.30	.15	.09
449	Tom McCraw	.30	.15	.09
450	Rich Hebner	.30	.15	.09
451	Tommy John	1.00	.50	.30
452	Gene Hiser	.30	.15	.09
453	Balor Moore	.30	.15	.09
454	Kurt Bevacqua	.30	.15	.09
455	Tom Bradley	.30	.15	.09
456	*Dave Winfield*	225.00	112.00	67.00
457	Chuck Goggin	.30	.15	.09
458	Jim Ray	.30	.15	.09
459	Reds Team	.90	.45	.25
460	Boog Powell	.75	.40	.25
461	John Odom	.30	.15	.09
462	Luis Alvarado	.30	.15	.09
463	Pat Dobson	.30	.15	.09
464	Jose Cruz	.60	.30	.20
465	Dick Bosman	.30	.15	.09
466	Dick Billings	.30	.15	.09
467	Winston Llenas	.30	.15	.09
468	Pepe Frias	.30	.15	.09
469	Joe Decker	.30	.15	.09
470	A.L. Playoffs (Reggie Jackson)	6.00	3.00	1.75
471	N.L. Playoffs	.80	.40	.25
472	World Series Game 1	.80	.40	.25
473	World Series Game 2 (Willie Mays)	5.00	2.50	1.50
474	World Series Game 3	.80	.40	.25
475	World Series Game 4	.80	.40	.25
476	World Series Game 5	.80	.40	.25
477	World Series Game 6 (Reggie Jackson)	8.00	4.00	2.50
478	World Series Game 7	.80	.40	.25
479	World Series Summary (A's Celebrate)	.80	.40	.25
480	Willie Crawford	.30	.15	.09
481	Jerry Terrell	.30	.15	.09
482	Bob Didier	.30	.15	.09
483	Braves Team	2.00	1.00	.60

		NR MT	EX	VG
484	Carmen Fanzone	.30	.15	.09
485	Felipe Alou	.90	.45	.25
486	Steve Stone	.30	.15	.09
487	Ted Martinez	.30	.15	.09
488	Andy Etchebarren	.30	.15	.09
489	Pirates Mgr./Coaches (Don Leppert, Bill Mazeroski, Danny Murtaugh, Don Osborn, Bob Skinner)	.75	.40	.25
490	Vada Pinson	.60	.30	.20
491	Roger Nelson	.30	.15	.09
492	Mike Rogodzinski	.30	.15	.09
493	Joe Hoerner	.30	.15	.09
494	Ed Goodson	.30	.15	.09
495	Dick McAuliffe	.30	.15	.09
496	Tom Murphy	.30	.15	.09
497	Bobby Mitchell	.30	.15	.09
498	Pat Corrales	.30	.15	.09
499	Rusty Torres	.30	.15	.09
500	Lee May	.30	.15	.09
501	Eddie Leon	.30	.15	.09
502	Dave LaRoche	.30	.15	.09
503	Eric Soderholm	.30	.15	.09
504	Joe Niekro	.30	.15	.09
505	Bill Buckner	.30	.15	.09
506	Ed Farmer	.30	.15	.09
507	Larry Stahl	.30	.15	.09
508	Expos Team	2.00	1.00	.60
509	Jesse Jefferson	.30	.15	.09
510	Wayne Garrett	.30	.15	.09
511	Toby Harrah	.30	.15	.09
512	Joe Lahoud	.30	.15	.09
513	Jim Campanis	.30	.15	.09
514	Paul Schaal	.30	.15	.09
515	Willie Montanez	.30	.15	.09
516	Horacio Pina	.30	.15	.09
517	Mike Hegan	.30	.15	.09
518	Derrel Thomas	.30	.15	.09
519	Bill Sharp	.30	.15	.09
520	Tim McCarver	.45	.25	.14
521	Indians Mgr./Coaches (Ken Aspromonte, Clay Bryant, Tony Pacheco)	.30	.15	.09
522	J.R. Richard	.30	.15	.09
523	Cecil Cooper	.50	.25	.15
524	Bill Plummer	.30	.15	.09
525	Clyde Wright	.30	.15	.09
526	Frank Tepedino	.30	.15	.09
527	Bobby Darwin	.30	.15	.09
528	Bill Bonham	.30	.15	.09
529	Horace Clarke	.30	.15	.09
530	Mickey Stanley	.30	.15	.09
531	Expos Mgr./Coaches (Dave Bristol, Larry Doby, Gene Mauch, Cal McLish, Jerry Zimmerman)	.40	.20	.12
532	Skip Lockwood	.30	.15	.09
533	Mike Phillips	.30	.15	.09
534	Eddie Watt	.30	.15	.09
535	Bob Tolan	.30	.15	.09
536	Duffy Dyer	.30	.15	.09
537	Steve Mingori	.30	.15	.09
538	Cesar Tovar	.30	.15	.09
539	Lloyd Allen	.30	.15	.09
540	Bob Robertson	.30	.15	.09
541	Indians Team	2.00	1.00	.60
542	Rich Gossage	2.00	1.00	.60
543	Danny Cater	.30	.15	.09
544	Ron Schueler	.30	.15	.09
545	Billy Conigliaro	.30	.15	.09
546	Mike Corkins	.30	.15	.09
547	Glenn Borgmann	.30	.15	.09
548	Sonny Siebert	.30	.15	.09
549	Mike Jorgensen	.30	.15	.09
550	Sam McDowell	.30	.15	.09
551	Von Joshua	.30	.15	.09
552	Denny Doyle	.30	.15	.09
553	Jim Willoughby	.30	.15	.09
554	Tim Johnson	.30	.15	.09
555	Woodie Fryman	.30	.15	.09
556	Dave Campbell	.30	.15	.09
557	Jim McGlothlin	.30	.15	.09
558	Bill Fahey	.30	.15	.09
559	Darrel Chaney	.30	.15	.09
560	Mike Cuellar	.30	.15	.09
561	Ed Kranepool	.30	.15	.09
562	Jack Aker	.30	.15	.09
563	Hal McRae	.40	.20	.12
564	Mike Ryan	.30	.15	.09
565	Milt Wilcox	.30	.15	.09
566	Jackie Hernandez	.30	.15	.09
567	Red Sox Team	3.00	1.50	.90
568	Mike Torrez	.30	.15	.09
569	Rick Dempsey	.30	.15	.09

No.	Player	NR MT	EX	VG
570	Ralph Garr	.30	.15	.09
571	Rich Hand	.30	.15	.09
572	Enzo Hernandez	.30	.15	.09
573	Mike Adams	.30	.15	.09
574	Bill Parsons	.30	.15	.09
575	Steve Garvey	8.00	4.00	2.50
576	Scipio Spinks	.30	.15	.09
577	Mike Sadek	.30	.15	.09
578	Ralph Houk	.30	.15	.09
579	Cecil Upshaw	.30	.15	.09
580	Jim Spencer	.30	.15	.09
581	Fred Norman	.30	.15	.09
582	*Bucky Dent*	.50	.25	.15
583	Marty Pattin	.30	.15	.09
584	Ken Rudolph	.30	.15	.09
585	Merv Rettenmund	.30	.15	.09
586	Jack Brohamer	.30	.15	.09
587	*Larry Christenson*	.30	.15	.09
588	Hal Lanier	.30	.15	.09
589	Boots Day	.30	.15	.09
590	Rogelio Moret	.30	.15	.09
591	Sonny Jackson	.30	.15	.09
592	Ed Bane	.30	.15	.09
593	Steve Yeager	.30	.15	.09
594	Leroy Stanton	.30	.15	.09
595	Steve Blass	.30	.15	.09
596	Rookie Pitchers (*Wayne Garland,* Fred Holdsworth, *Mark Littell,* Dick Pole)	.30	.15	.09
597	Rookie Shortstops (Dave Chalk, John Gamble, Pete Mackanin, *Manny Trillo*)	.80	.40	.25
598	Rookie Outfielders (Dave Augustine, *Ken Griffey,* Steve Ontiveros, Jim Tyrone)	15.00	7.50	4.50
599a	Rookie Pitchers (Ron Diorio, Dave Freisleben, Frank Riccelli, Greg Shanahan) (Freisleben- Washington)	.80	.40	.25
599b	Rookie Pitchers (Ron Diorio, Dave Freisleben, Frank Riccelli, Greg Shanahan) (Freisleben- San Diego large print)	3.50	1.75	1.00
599c	Rookie Pitchers (Ron Diorio, Dave Freisleben, Frank Riccelli, Greg Shanahan) (Freisleben- San Diego small print)	6.00	3.00	1.75
600	Rookie Infielders (Ron Cash, Jim Cox, *Bill Madlock,* Reggie J. Sanders)	2.50	1.25	.70
601	Rookie Outfielders (Ed Armbrister, Rich Bladt, *Brian Downing, Bake McBride*)	3.00	1.50	.90
602	Rookie Pitchers (Glenn Abbott, Rick Henninger, Craig Swan, Dan Vossler)	.30	.15	.09
603	Rookie Catchers (Barry Foote, Tom Lundstedt, *Charlie Moore,* Sergio Robles)	.30	.15	.09
604	Rookie Infielders (Terry Hughes, John Knox, *Andy Thornton, Frank White*)	4.00	2.00	1.25
605	Rookie Pitchers (Vic Albury, Ken Frailing, Kevin Kobel, *Frank Tanana*)	4.00	2.00	1.25
606	Rookie Outfielders (Jim Fuller, Wilbur Howard, Tommy Smith, Otto Velez)	.30	.15	.09
607	Rookie Shortstops (Leo Foster, Tom Heintzelman, Dave Rosello, *Frank Taveras*)	.30	.15	.09
608a	Rookie Pitchers (Bob Apodaco, Dick Baney, John D'Acquisto, Mike Wallace)	2.00	1.00	.60
608b	Rookie Pitchers (Bob Apodaca, Dick Baney, John D'Acquisto, Mike Wallace)	.30	.15	.09
609	Rico Petrocelli	.30	.15	.09
610	Dave Kingman	.45	.25	.14
611	Rick Stelmaszek	.30	.15	.09
612	Luke Walker	.30	.15	.09
613	Dan Monzon	.30	.15	.09
614	Adrian Devine	.30	.15	.09
615	Johnny Jeter	.30	.15	.09
616	Larry Gura	.30	.15	.09
617	Ted Ford	.30	.15	.09
618	Jim Mason	.30	.15	.09
619	Mike Anderson	.30	.15	.09
620	Al Downing	.30	.15	.09
621	Bernie Carbo	.30	.15	.09
622	Phil Gagliano	.30	.15	.09
623	Celerino Sanchez	.30	.15	.09
624	Bob Miller	.30	.15	.09
625	Ollie Brown	.30	.15	.09
626	Pirates Team	2.00	1.00	.60
627	Carl Taylor	.30	.15	.09
628	Ivan Murrell	.30	.15	.09
629	Rusty Staub	.60	.30	.20
630	Tommie Agee	.30	.15	.09
631	Steve Barber	.30	.15	.09
632	George Culver	.30	.15	.09
633	Dave Hamilton	.30	.15	.09
634	Braves Mgr./Coaches (Jim Busby, Eddie Mathews, Connie Ryan, Ken Silvestri, Herm Starrette)	1.50	.70	.45
635	John Edwards	.30	.15	.09
636	Dave Goltz	.30	.15	.09
637	Checklist 529-660	1.50	.70	.45
638	Ken Sanders	.30	.15	.09
639	Joe Lovitto	.30	.15	.09
640	Milt Pappas	.30	.15	.09
641	Chuck Brinkman	.30	.15	.09
642	Terry Harmon	.30	.15	.09
643	Dodgers Team	3.00	1.50	.90
644	Wayne Granger	.30	.15	.09
645	Ken Boswell	.30	.15	.09
646	George Foster	.75	.40	.25
647	*Juan Beniquez*	.30	.15	.09
648	Terry Crowley	.30	.15	.09
649	Fernando Gonzalez	.30	.15	.09
650	Mike Epstein	.30	.15	.09
651	Leron Lee	.30	.15	.09
652	Gail Hopkins	.30	.15	.09
653	Bob Stinson	.30	.15	.09
654a	Jesus Alou (no position)	5.00	2.50	1.50
654b	Jesus Alou ("Outfield")	.30	.15	.09
655	Mike Tyson	.30	.15	.09
656	Adrian Garrett	.30	.15	.09
657	Jim Shellenback	.30	.15	.09
658	Lee Lacy	.30	.15	.09
659	Joe Lis	.30	.15	.09
660	Larry Dierker	.30	.15	.09

1974 Topps Deckle Edge

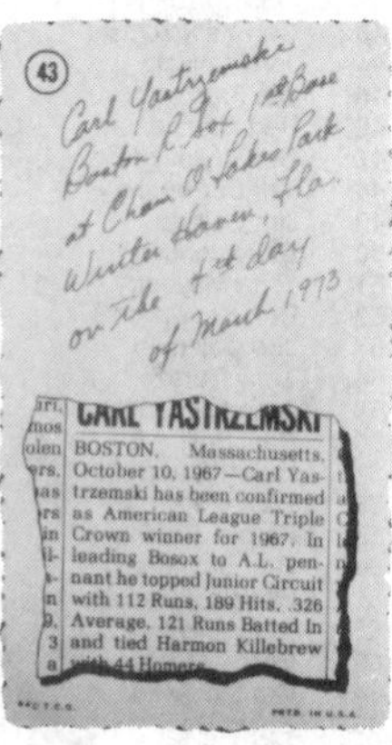

These borderless 2-7/8" by 5" cards feature a black and white photograph with a blue facsimile autograph on the front. The backs have in handwritten script the player's name, team, position and the date and location of the picture. Below is a mock newspaper clipping providing a detail from the player's career. The cards take their names from their specially cut edges which give them a scalloped appearance. The 72-card set was a test issue and received rather limited distribution around Massachusetts. The cards were sold three per pack for five cents, without gum.

		NR MT	EX	VG
Complete Set:		2000.00	1000.00	600.00
Common Player:		10.00	5.00	3.00
1	Amos Otis	10.00	5.00	3.00
2	Darrell Evans	15.00	7.50	4.50
3	Bob Gibson	50.00	25.00	15.00
4	David Nelson	10.00	5.00	3.00
5	Steve Carlton	80.00	40.00	25.00
6	Catfish Hunter	40.00	20.00	12.00

A card number in parentheses () indicates the set is unnumbered.

		NR MT	EX	VG
7	Thurman Munson	50.00	25.00	15.00
8	Bob Grich	15.00	7.50	4.50
9	Tom Seaver	50.00	25.00	15.00
10	Ted Simmons	15.00	7.50	4.50
11	Bobby Valentine	10.00	5.00	3.00
12	Don Sutton	25.00	12.50	7.50
13	Wilbur Wood	10.00	5.00	3.00
14	Doug Rader	10.00	5.00	3.00
15	Chris Chambliss	10.00	5.00	3.00
16	Pete Rose	150.00	75.00	45.00
17	John Hiller	10.00	5.00	3.00
18	Burt Hooton	10.00	5.00	3.00
19	Tim Foli	10.00	5.00	3.00
20	Lou Brock	50.00	25.00	15.00
21	Ron Bryant	10.00	5.00	3.00
22	Manuel Sanguillen	10.00	5.00	3.00
23	Bobby Tolan	10.00	5.00	3.00
24	Greg Luzinski	15.00	7.50	4.50
25	Brooks Robinson	60.00	30.00	18.00
26	Felix Millan	10.00	5.00	3.00
27	Luis Tiant	15.00	7.50	4.50
28	Willie McCovey	60.00	30.00	20.00
29	Chris Speier	10.00	5.00	3.00
30	George Scott	10.00	5.00	3.00
31	Willie Stargell	50.00	25.00	15.00
32	Rod Carew	50.00	25.00	15.00
33	Charlie Spikes	10.00	5.00	3.00
34	Nate Colbert	10.00	5.00	3.00
35	Richie Hebner	10.00	5.00	3.00
36	Bobby Bonds	20.00	10.00	6.00
37	Buddy Bell	15.00	7.50	4.50
38	Claude Osteen	10.00	5.00	3.00
39	Rich Allen	15.00	7.50	4.50
40	Bill Russell	10.00	5.00	3.00
41	Nolan Ryan	200.00	100.00	60.00
42	Willie Davis	15.00	7.50	4.50
43	Carl Yastrzemski	60.00	30.00	18.00
44	Jon Matlack	10.00	5.00	3.00
45	Jim Palmer	60.00	30.00	18.00
46	Bert Campaneris	15.00	7.50	4.50
47	Bert Blyleven	20.00	10.00	6.00
48	Jeff Burroughs	10.00	5.00	3.00
49	Jim Colborn	10.00	5.00	3.00
50	Dave Johnson	15.00	7.50	4.50
51	John Mayberry	10.00	5.00	3.00
52	Don Kessinger	10.00	5.00	3.00
53	Joe Coleman	10.00	5.00	3.00
54	Tony Perez	30.00	15.00	9.00
55	Jose Cardenal	10.00	5.00	3.00
56	Paul Splittorff	10.00	5.00	3.00
57	Henry Aaron	150.00	75.00	45.00
58	David May	10.00	5.00	3.00
59	Fergie Jenkins	50.00	25.00	15.00
60	Ron Blomberg	10.00	5.00	3.00
61	Reggie Jackson	175.00	90.00	55.00
62	Tony Oliva	25.00	12.50	7.50
63	Bobby Murcer	15.00	7.50	4.50
64	Carlton Fisk	25.00	12.50	7.50
65	Steve Rogers	10.00	5.00	3.00
66	Frank Robinson	60.00	30.00	18.00
67	Joe Ferguson	10.00	5.00	3.00
68	Bill Melton	10.00	5.00	3.00
69	Bob Watson	10.00	5.00	3.00
70	Larry Bowa	15.00	7.50	4.50
71	Johnny Bench	90.00	45.00	27.00
72	Willie Horton	10.00	5.00	3.00

1974 Topps Puzzles

One of many test issues by Topps in the mid-1970s, the 12-player jigsaw puzzle set was an innovation which never caught on with collectors. The 40-piece puzzles (4-3/4" by 7-1/2") feature color photos with a decorative lozenge at bottom naming the player, team and position. The puzzles came in individual wrappers.

		NR MT	EX	VG
Complete Set:		600.00	300.00	200.00
Common Player:		12.00	6.00	3.50
(1)	Hank Aaron	80.00	40.00	25.00
(2)	Dick Allen	20.00	10.00	6.00
(3)	Johnny Bench	75.00	38.00	23.00
(4)	Bobby Bonds	20.00	10.00	6.00
(5)	Bob Gibson	35.00	17.50	10.50
(6)	Reggie Jackson	60.00	30.00	18.00
(7)	Bobby Murcer	12.00	6.00	3.50
(8)	Jim Palmer	50.00	25.00	15.00
(9)	Nolan Ryan	80.00	40.00	24.00
(10)	Tom Seaver	45.00	22.00	13.50
(11)	Willie Stargell	40.00	20.00	12.00
(12)	Carl Yastrzemski	60.00	30.00	18.00

1974 Topps Stamps

Topps continued to market baseball stamps in 1974 through the release of 240 unnumbered stamps featuring color player portraits. The player's name, team and position are found in an oval at the bottom of the 1" by 1-1/2" stamps. The stamps, sold separately rather than issued as an insert, came in strips of six which were then pasted in an appropriate team album designed to hold 10 stamps.

		NR MT	EX	VG
Complete Sheet Set:		100.00	50.00	30.00
Common Sheet:		1.00	.50	.30
Complete Stamp Album Set:		75.00	37.00	22.00
Single Stamp Album:		2.50	1.25	.70
(1)	Hank Aaron, Luis Aparicio, Bob Bailey, Johnny Bench, Ron Blomberg, Bob Boone, Lou Brock, Bud Harrelson, Randy Jones, Dave Rader, Nolan Ryan, Joe Torre	6.00	3.00	1.75
(2)	Buddy Bell, Steve Braun, Jerry Grote, Tommy Helms, Bill Lee, Mike Lum, Dave May, Brooks Robinson, Bill Russell, Del Unser, Wilbur Wood, Carl Yastrzemski	10.00	5.00	3.00
(3)	Jerry Bell, Jerry Bell, Jim Colborn, Toby Harrah, Ken Henderson, John Hiller, Randy Hundley, Don Kessinger, Jerry Koosman, Dave Lopes, Felix Millan, Thurman Munson, Ted Simmons	3.50	1.75	1.00
(4)	Jerry Bell, Bill Buckner, Jim Colborn, Ken Henderson, Don Kessinger, Felix Millan, George Mitterwald, Dave Roberts, Ted Simmons, Jim Slaton, Charlie Spikes, Paul Splittorff	1.00	.50	.30
(5)	Glenn Beckert, Jim Bibby, Bill Buckner, Jim Lonborg, George Mitterwald, Dave Parker, Dave Roberts, Jim Slaton, Reggie Smith, Charlie Spikes, Paul Splittorff, Bob Watson	3.50	1.75	1.00
(6)	Paul Blair, Bobby Bonds, Ed Brinkman, Norm Cash, Mike Epstein, Tommy Harper, Mike Marshall, Phil Niekro, Cookie Rojas, George Scott, Mel Stottlemyre, Jim Wynn			

	NR MT	EX	VG
	3.50	1.75	1.00
(7) Jack Billingham, Reggie Cleveland, Bobby Darwin, Dave Duncan, Tim Foli, Ed Goodson, Cleon Jones, Mickey Lolich, George Medich, John Milner, Rick Monday, Bobby Murcer	1.00	.50	.30
(8) Steve Carlton, Orlando Cepeda, Joe Decker, Reggie Jackson, Dave Johnson, John Mayberry, Bill Melton, Roger Metzger, Dave Nelson, Jerry Reuss, Jim Spencer, Bobby Valentine	6.00	3.00	1.75
(9) Dan Driessen, Pedro Garcia, Grant Jackson, Al Kaline, Clay Kirby, Carlos May, Willie Montanez, Rogelio Moret, Jim Palmer, Doug Rader, J. R. Richard, Frank Robinson	3.50	1.75	1.00
(10) Pedro Garcia, Ralph Garr, Wayne Garrett, Ron Hunt, Al Kaline, Fred Kendall, Carlos May, Jim Palmer, Doug Rader, Frank Robinson, Rick Wise, Richie Zisk	3.50	1.75	1.00
(11) Dusty Baker, Larry Bowa, Steve Busby, Chris Chambliss, Dock Ellis, Cesar Geronimo, Fran Healy, Deron Johnson, Jorge Orta, Joe Rudi, Mickey Stanley, Rennie Stennett	3.50	1.75	1.00
(12) Bob Coluccio, Ray Corbin, John Ellis, Oscar Gamble, Dave Giusti, Bill Greif, Alex Johnson, Mike Jorgensen, Andy Messersmith, Elias Sosa, Willie Stargell	3.50	1.75	1.00
(13) Ron Bryant, Nate Colbert, Jose Cruz, Dan Driessen, Billy Grabarkewitz, Don Gullett, Willie Horton, Grant Jackson, Clay Kirby, Willie Montanez, Rogelio Moret, J. R. Richard	1.00	.50	.30
(14) Carlton Fisk, Bill Freehan, Bobby Grich, Vic Harris, George Hendrick, Ed Herrmann, Jim Holt, Ken Holtzman, Fergie Jenkins, Lou Piniella, Steve Rogers, Ken Singleton	3.50	1.75	1.00
(15) Stan Bahnsen, Sal Bando, Mark Belanger, David Clyde, Willie Crawford, Burt Hooton, Jon Matlack, Tim McCarver, Joe Morgan, Gene Tenace, Dick Tidrow, Dave Winfield	5.00	2.50	1.50
(16) Hank Aaron, Stan Bahnsen, Bob Bailey, Johnny Bench, Bob Boone, Joe Matlack, Tim McCarver, Joe Morgan, Dave Rader, Gene Tenace, Dick Tidrow, Joe Torre	5.00	2.50	1.50
(17) John Boccabella, Frank Duffy, Darrell Evans, Sparky Lyle, Lee May, Don Money, Bill North, Ted Sizemore, Chris Speier, Wayne Twitchell, Billy Williams, Earl Williams	1.00	.50	.30
(18) John Boccabella, Bobby Darwin, Frank Duffy, Dave Duncan, Tim Foli, Cleon Jones, Mickey Lolich, Sparky Lyle, Lee May, Rick Monday, Bill North, Billy Williams	1.00	.50	.30
(19) Don Baylor, Vida Blue, Tom Bradley, Jose Cardenal, Ron Cey, Greg Luzinski, Johnny Oates, Tony Oliva, Al Oliver, Tony Perez, Darrell Porter, Roy White	3.50	1.75	1.00
(20) Pedro Borbon, Rod Carew, Roric Harrison, Jim Hunter, Ed Kirkpatrick, Garry Maddox, Gene Michael, Rick Miller, Claude Osteen, Amos Otis, Rich Reuschel, Mike Tyson	5.00	2.50	1.50
(21) Sandy Alomar, Bert Campaneris, Tommy Davis, Joe Ferguson, Tito Fuentes, Jerry Morales, Carl Morton, Gaylord Perry, Vada Pinson, Dave Roberts, Ellie Rodriguez	3.50	1.75	1.00
(22) Dick Allen, Jeff Burroughs, Joe Coleman, Terry Forster, Bob Gibson, Harmon Killebrew, Tug McGraw, Bob Oliver, Steve Renko, Pete Rose, Luis Tiant, Otto Velez	13.00	6.50	4.00
(23) Johnny Briggs, Willie Davis, Jim Fregosi, Rich Hebner, Pat Kelly, Dave Kingman, Willie McCovey, Graig Nettles, Freddie Patek, Marty Pattin, Manny Sanguillen, Richie Scheinblum	5.00	2.50	1.50
(24) Bert Blyleven, Nelson Briles, Cesar Cedeno, Ron Fairly, Johnny Grubb, Dave McNally, Aurelio Rodriguez, Ron Santo, Tom Seaver, Bill Singer, Bill Sudakis, Don Sutton	6.00	3.00	1.75

Regional interest may affect the value of a card.

1974 Topps Team Checklists

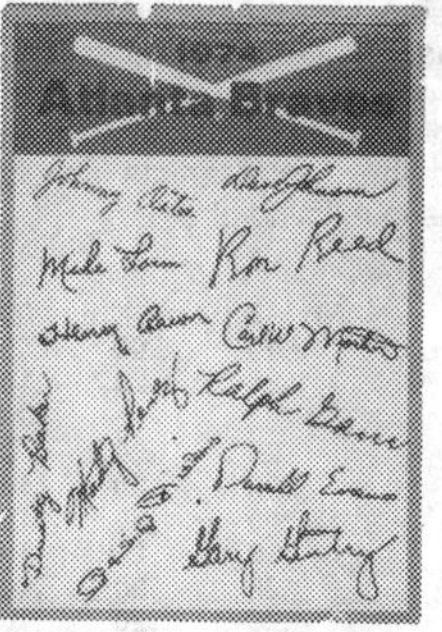

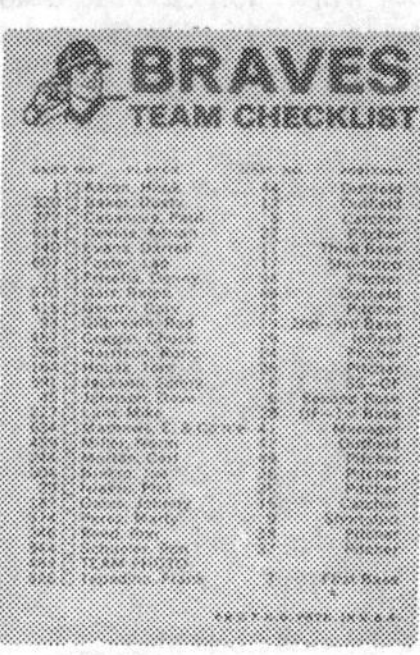

This set is a repeat of the 1973 mystery set in the form of 24 unnumbered 2-1/2" by 3-1/2" checklist cards. As with the 1973 set, the 1974s feature a team name on the front at the top with a white panel and a number of facsimile autographs below. Backs feature the team name and a checklist. The big difference between the 1973 and 1974 checklists is that the 1973s have blue borders while the 1974s have a red border. The 1974s were inserted into packages of the regular issue Topps cards.

	NR MT	EX	VG
Complete Set:	12.00	6.00	3.50
Common Checklist:	.50	.25	.15
(1) Atlanta Braves	.50	.25	.15
(2) Baltimore Orioles	.50	.25	.15
(3) Boston Red Sox	.50	.25	.15
(4) California Angels	.50	.25	.15
(5) Chicago Cubs	.50	.25	.15
(6) Chicago White Sox	.50	.25	.15
(7) Cincinnati Reds	.50	.25	.15
(8) Cleveland Indians	.50	.25	.15
(9) Detroit Tigers	.50	.25	.15
(10) Houston Astros	.50	.25	.15
(11) Kansas City Royals	.50	.25	.15
(12) Los Angeles Dodgers	.50	.25	.15
(13) Milwaukee Brewers	.50	.25	.15
(14) Minnesota Twins	.50	.25	.15
(15) Montreal Expos	.50	.25	.15
(16) New York Mets	.50	.25	.15
(17) New York Yankees	.50	.25	.15
(18) Oakland A's	.50	.25	.15
(19) Philadelphia Phillies	.50	.25	.15
(20) Pittsburgh Pirates	.50	.25	.15
(21) St. Louis Cardinals	.50	.25	.15
(22) San Diego Padres	.50	.25	.15
(23) San Francisco Giants	.50	.25	.15
(24) Texas Rangers	.50	.25	.15

1974 Topps Traded

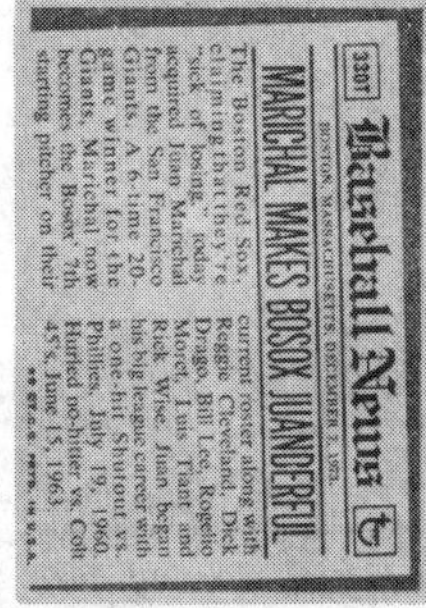

Appearing late in the season, these 2-1/2" by 3-1/2" cards are basically the same as the regular issue Topps cards. The major change was that a big red panel with the word "Traded" was added below the player photo. Backs feature a "Baseball News" newspaper which contains the details of the trade. Card numbers correspond to the player's regular card number in 1974 except that the suffix "T" is added after the number. The set consists of 43 player cards and a checklist. In most cases, Topps did not obtain pictures of the players in their new uniforms. Instead the Topps artists simply provided the needed changes to existing photos.

		NR MT	EX	VG
Complete Set (44):		12.00	6.00	3.50
Common Player:		.25	.20	.10
23T	Craig Robinson	.25	.20	.10
42T	Claude Osteen	.25	.20	.10
43T	Jim Wynn	.40	.30	.15
51T	Bobby Heise	.25	.20	.10
59T	Ross Grimsley	.25	.20	.10
62T	Bob Locker	.25	.20	.10
63T	Bill Sudakis	.25	.20	.10
73T	Mike Marshall	.60	.45	.25
123T	Nelson Briles	.25	.20	.10
139T	Aurelio Monteagudo	.25	.20	.10
151T	Diego Segui	.25	.20	.10
165T	Willie Davis	.40	.30	.15
175T	Reggie Cleveland	.25	.20	.10
182T	Lindy McDaniel	.25	.20	.10
186T	Fred Scherman	.25	.20	.10
249T	George Mitterwald	.25	.20	.10
262T	Ed Kirkpatrick	.25	.20	.10
269T	Bob Johnson	.25	.20	.10
270T	Ron Santo	2.00	1.50	.80
313T	Barry Lersch	.12	.09	.05
319T	Randy Hundley	.25	.20	.10
330T	Juan Marichal	3.00	2.25	1.25
348T	Pete Richert	.25	.20	.10
373T	John Curtis	.25	.20	.10
390T	Lou Piniella	1.00	.70	.40
428T	Gary Sutherland	.25	.20	.10
454T	Kurt Bevacqua	.25	.20	.10
458T	Jim Ray	.25	.20	.10
485T	Felipe Alou	1.00	.70	.40
486T	Steve Stone	.40	.30	.15
496T	Tom Murphy	.25	.20	.10
516T	Horacio Pina	.25	.20	.10
534T	Eddie Watt	.25	.20	.10
538T	Cesar Tovar	.25	.20	.10
544T	Ron Schueler	.25	.20	.10
579T	Cecil Upshaw	.25	.20	.10
585T	Merv Rettenmund	.25	.20	.10
612T	Luke Walker	.25	.20	.10
616T	Larry Gura	.25	.20	.10
618T	Jim Mason	.25	.20	.10
630T	Tommie Agee	.25	.20	.10
648T	Terry Crowley	.25	.20	.10
649T	Fernando Gonzalez	.25	.20	.10
----	Traded Checklist	.70	.35	.20

1975 Topps

This year Topps produced another 660-card set, one which collectors either seem to like or despise. The 2-1/2" by 3-1/2" cards have a color photo which is framed by a round-cornered white frame. Around that is an eye-catching two-color border in bright colors. The team name appears at the top in bright letters while the player name is at the bottom and his position a baseball at the lower right. A facsimile autograph runs across the picture. The card backs are vertical feature normal statistical and biographical information along with a trivia quiz. Specialty cards include a new 24-card series on MVP winners going back to 1951. Other specialty cards include statistical leaders and post-season highlights. The real highlight of the set, however, are the rookie cards which include their numbers such names as George Brett, Gary Carter, Robin Yount, Jim Rice, Keith Hernandez and Fred Lynn. While the set was released at one time, card numbers 1-132 were printed in somewhat shorter supply than the remainder of the issue.

		NR MT	EX	VG
Complete Set (660):		900.00	450.00	275.00
Common Player: 1-132		.35	.20	.11
Common Player: 133-660		.30	.15	.09
Complete Mini Set:		1000.00	500.00	300.00
Common Mini Player:		.40	.20	.12
1	'74 Highlights (Hank Aaron)	22.00	11.00	6.50
2	'74 Highlights (Lou Brock)	2.00	1.00	.60
3	'74 Highlights (Bob Gibson)	1.75	.90	.50
4	'74 Highlights (Al Kaline)	2.00	1.00	.60
5	;74 Highlights (Nolan Ryan)	25.00	12.50	7.50
6	'74 Highlights (Mike Marshall)	.40	.20	.12
7	'74 Highlights (Dick Bosman, Steve Busby, Nolan Ryan)	1.00	.50	.30
8	Rogelio Moret	.35	.20	.11
9	Frank Tepedino	.35	.20	.11
10	Willie Davis	.35	.20	.11
11	Bill Melton	.35	.20	.11
12	David Clyde	.35	.20	.11
13	Gene Locklear	.35	.20	.11
14	Milt Wilcox	.35	.20	.11
15	Jose Cardenal	.35	.20	.11
16	Frank Tanana	.35	.20	.11
17	Dave Concepcion	.45	.25	.14
18	Tigers Team (Ralph Houk)	2.00	1.00	.60
19	Jerry Koosman	.35	.20	.11
20	Thurman Munson	7.00	3.50	2.00
21	Rollie Fingers	5.00	2.50	1.50
22	Dave Cash	.35	.20	.11
23	Bill Russell	.35	.20	.11
24	Al Fitzmorris	.35	.20	.11
25	Lee May	.35	.20	.11
26	Dave McNally	.35	.20	.11
27	Ken Reitz	.35	.20	.11
28	Tom Murphy	.35	.20	.11
29	Dave Parker	8.00	4.00	2.50
30	Bert Blyleven	1.00	.50	.30
31	Dave Rader	.35	.20	.11
32	Reggie Cleveland	.35	.20	.11
33	Dusty Baker	.40	.20	.12
34	Steve Renko	.35	.20	.11
35	Ron Santo	.50	.25	.15
36	Joe Lovitto	.35	.20	.11
37	Dave Freisleben	.35	.20	.11
38	Buddy Bell	.35	.20	.11
39	Andy Thornton	.40	.20	.12
40	Bill Singer	.35	.20	.11
41	Cesar Geronimo	.35	.20	.11
42	Joe Coleman	.35	.20	.11
43	Cleon Jones	.35	.20	.11
44	Pat Dobson	.35	.20	.11
45	Joe Rudi	.40	.20	.12
46	Phillies Team (Danny Ozark)	2.00	1.00	.60
47	Tommy John	1.25	.60	.40
48	Freddie Patek	.35	.20	.11
49	Larry Dierker	.35	.20	.11
50	Brooks Robinson	6.00	3.00	1.75
51	*Bob Forsch*	.80	.40	.25
52	Darrell Porter	.35	.20	.11
53	Dave Giusti	.35	.20	.11
54	Eric Soderholm	.35	.20	.11
55	Bobby Bonds	.35	.20	.11
56	Rick Wise	.35	.20	.11
57	Dave Johnson	.35	.20	.11
58	Chuck Taylor	.35	.20	.11
59	Ken Henderson	.35	.20	.11
60	Fergie Jenkins	4.00	2.00	1.25
61	Dave Winfield	70.00	35.00	21.00
62	Fritz Peterson	.35	.20	.11
63	Steve Swisher	.35	.20	.11
64	Dave Chalk	.35	.20	.11
65	Don Gullett	.35	.20	.11

		NR MT	EX	VG
66	Willie Horton	.35	.20	.11
67	Tug McGraw	.35	.20	.11
68	Ron Blomberg	.35	.20	.11
69	John Odom	.35	.20	.11
70	Mike Schmidt	70.00	35.00	21.00
71	Charlie Hough	.35	.20	.11
72	Royals Team (Jack McKeon)	2.00	1.00	.60
73	J.R. Richard	.35	.20	.11
74	Mark Belanger	.35	.20	.11
75	Ted Simmons	.35	.20	.11
76	Ed Sprague	.35	.20	.11
77	Richie Zisk	.35	.20	.11
78	Ray Corbin	.35	.20	.11
79	Gary Matthews	.35	.20	.11
80	Carlton Fisk	15.00	7.50	4.50
81	Ron Reed	.35	.20	.11
82	Pat Kelly	.35	.20	.11
83	Jim Merritt	.35	.20	.11
84	Enzo Hernandez	.35	.20	.11
85	Bill Bonham	.35	.20	.11
86	Joe Lis	.35	.20	.11
87	George Foster	.75	.40	.25
88	Tom Egan	.35	.20	.11
89	Jim Ray	.35	.20	.11
90	Rusty Staub	.60	.30	.20
91	Dick Green	.35	.20	.11
92	Cecil Upshaw	.35	.20	.11
93	Dave Lopes	.40	.20	.12
94	Jim Lonborg	.35	.20	.11
95	John Mayberry	.35	.20	.11
96	Mike Cosgrove	.35	.20	.11
97	Earl Williams	.35	.20	.11
98	Rich Folkers	.35	.20	.11
99	Mike Hegan	.35	.20	.11
100	Willie Stargell	6.00	3.00	1.75
101	Expos Team (Gene Mauch)	2.00	1.00	.60
102	Joe Decker	.35	.20	.11
103	Rick Miller	.35	.20	.11
104	Bill Madlock	1.25	.60	.40
105	Buzz Capra	.35	.20	.11
106	*Mike Hargrove*	.35	.20	.11
107	Jim Barr	.35	.20	.11
108	Tom Hall	.35	.20	.11
109	George Hendrick	.35	.20	.11
110	Wilbur Wood	.35	.20	.11
111	Wayne Garrett	.35	.20	.11
112	Larry Hardy	.35	.20	.11
113	Elliott Maddox	.35	.20	.11
114	Dick Lange	.35	.20	.11
115	Joe Ferguson	.35	.20	.11
116	Lerrin LaGrow	.35	.20	.11
117	Orioles Team (Earl Weaver)	2.50	1.25	.70
118	Mike Anderson	.35	.20	.11
119	Tommy Helms	.35	.20	.11
120	Steve Busby (photo actually Fran Healy)	.35	.20	.11
121	Bill North	.35	.20	.11
122	Al Hrabosky	.35	.20	.11
123	Johnny Briggs	.35	.20	.11
124	Jerry Reuss	.35	.20	.11
125	Ken Singleton	.35	.20	.11
126	Checklist 1-132	1.50	.70	.45
127	Glen Borgmann	.35	.20	.11
128	Bill Lee	.35	.20	.11
129	Rick Monday	.35	.20	.11
130	Phil Niekro	1.50	.70	.45
131	Toby Harrah	.35	.20	.11
132	Randy Moffitt	.35	.20	.11
133	Dan Driessen	.35	.20	.11
134	Ron Hodges	.30	.15	.09
135	Charlie Spikes	.30	.15	.09
136	Jim Mason	.30	.15	.09
137	Terry Forster	.30	.15	.09
138	Del Unser	.30	.15	.09
139	Horacio Pina	.30	.15	.09
140	Steve Garvey	5.00	2.50	1.50
141	Mickey Stanley	.30	.15	.09
142	Bob Reynolds	.30	.15	.09
143	*Cliff Johnson*	.30	.15	.09
144	Jim Wohlford	.30	.15	.09
145	Ken Holtzman	.30	.15	.09
146	Padres Team (John McNamara)	2.00	1.00	.60
147	Pedro Garcia	.30	.15	.09
148	Jim Rooker	.30	.15	.09
149	Tim Foli	.30	.15	.09
150	Bob Gibson	5.00	2.50	1.50
151	Steve Brye	.30	.15	.09
152	Mario Guerrero	.30	.15	.09
153	Rick Reuschel	.30	.15	.09
154	Mike Lum	.30	.15	.09
155	Jim Bibby	.30	.15	.09

		NR MT	EX	VG
156	Dave Kingman	.45	.25	.14
157	Pedro Borbon	.30	.15	.09
158	Jerry Grote	.30	.15	.09
159	Steve Arlin	.30	.15	.09
160	Graig Nettles	.45	.25	.14
161	Stan Bahnsen	.30	.15	.09
162	Willie Montanez	.30	.15	.09
163	Jim Brewer	.30	.15	.09
164	Mickey Rivers	.30	.15	.09
165	Doug Rader	.30	.15	.09
166	Woodie Fryman	.30	.15	.09
167	Rich Coggins	.30	.15	.09
168	Bill Greif	.30	.15	.09
169	Cookie Rojas	.30	.15	.09
170	Bert Campaneris	.40	.20	.12
171	Ed Kirkpatrick	.30	.15	.09
172	Red Sox Team (Darrell Johnson)	2.00	1.00	.60
173	Steve Rogers	.30	.15	.09
174	Bake McBride	.30	.15	.09
175	Don Money	.30	.15	.09
176	Burt Hooton	.30	.15	.09
177	Vic Correll	.30	.15	.09
178	Cesar Tovar	.30	.15	.09
179	Tom Bradley	.30	.15	.09
180	Joe Morgan	5.00	2.50	1.50
181	Fred Beene	.30	.15	.09
182	Don Hahn	.30	.15	.09
183	Mel Stottlemyre	.30	.15	.09
184	Jorge Orta	.30	.15	.09
185	Steve Carlton	10.00	5.00	3.00
186	Willie Crawford	.30	.15	.09
187	Denny Doyle	.30	.15	.09
188	Tom Griffin	.30	.15	.09
189	Yogi Berra, Roy Campanella (MVP)	3.00	1.50	.90
190	Hank Sauer, Bobby Shantz (MVP)	.40	.20	.12
191	Roy Campanella, Al Rosen (MVP)	.90	.45	.25
192	Yogi Berra, Willie Mays (MVP)	2.00	1.00	.60
193	Yogi Berra, Roy Campanella (MVP)	2.00	1.00	.60
194	Mickey Mantle, Don Newcombe (MVP)	6.00	3.00	1.75
195	Hank Aaron, Mickey Mantle (MVP)	10.00	5.00	3.00
196	Ernie Banks, Jackie Jensen (MVP)	.90	.45	.25
197	Ernie Banks, Nellie Fox (MVP)	.90	.45	.25
198	Dick Groat, Roger Maris (MVP)	1.25	.60	.40
199	Roger Maris, Frank Robinson (MVP)	1.50	.70	.45
200	Mickey Mantle, Maury Wills (MVP)	6.00	3.00	1.75
201	Elston Howard, Sandy Koufax (MVP)	1.50	.70	.45
202	Ken Boyer, Brooks Robinson (MVP)	1.25	.60	.40
203	Willie Mays, Zoilo Versalles (MVP)	1.25	.60	.40
204	Roberto Clemente, Frank Robinson (MVP)	1.50	.70	.45
205	Orlando Cepeda, Carl Yastrzemski (MVP)	1.25	.60	.40
206	Bob Gibson, Denny McLain (MVP)	1.25	.60	.40
207	Harmon Killebrew, Willie McCovey (MVP)	1.50	.70	.45
208	Johnny Bench, Boog Powell (MVP)	1.25	.60	.40
209	Vida Blue, Joe Torre (MVP)	.50	.25	.15
210	Rich Allen, Johnny Bench (MVP)	1.25	.60	.40
211	Reggie Jackson, Pete Rose (MVP)	6.00	3.00	1.75
212	Jeff Burroughs, Steve Garvey (MVP)	.75	.40	.25
213	Oscar Gamble	.30	.15	.09
214	Harry Parker	.30	.15	.09
215	Bobby Valentine	.30	.15	.09
216	Giants Team (Wes Westrum)	2.00	1.00	.60
217	Lou Piniella	.30	.15	.09
218	Jerry Johnson	.30	.15	.09
219	Ed Herrmann	.30	.15	.09
220	Don Sutton	1.50	.70	.45
221	Aurelio Rodriquez (Rodriguez)	.30	.15	.09
222	Dan Spillner	.30	.15	.09
223	*Robin Yount*	200.00	100.00	60.00
224	Ramon Hernandez	.30	.15	.09
225	Bob Grich	.30	.15	.09
226	Bill Campbell	.30	.15	.09
227	Bob Watson	.30	.15	.09
228	*George Brett*	250.00	125.00	75.00
229	Barry Foote	.30	.15	.09
230	Catfish Hunter	2.00	1.00	.60
231	Mike Tyson	.30	.15	.09
232	Diego Segui	.30	.15	.09
233	Billy Grabarkewitz	.30	.15	.09
234	Tom Grieve	.30	.15	.09

#	Card	NR MT	EX	VG
235	Jack Billingham	.30	.15	.09
236	Angels Team (Dick Williams)	2.00	1.00	.60
237	Carl Morton	.30	.15	.09
238	Dave Duncan	.30	.15	.09
239	George Stone	.30	.15	.09
240	Garry Maddox	.30	.15	.09
241	Dick Tidrow	.30	.15	.09
242	Jay Johnstone	.30	.15	.09
243	Jim Kaat	1.25	.60	.40
244	Bill Buckner	.30	.15	.09
245	Mickey Lolich	.40	.20	.12
246	Cardinals Team (Red Schoendienst)	2.00	1.00	.60
247	Enos Cabell	.30	.15	.09
248	Randy Jones	.30	.15	.09
249	Danny Thompson	.30	.15	.09
250	Ken Brett	.30	.15	.09
251	Fran Healy	.30	.15	.09
252	Fred Scherman	.30	.15	.09
253	Jesus Alou	.30	.15	.09
254	Mike Torrez	.30	.15	.09
255	Dwight Evans	4.00	2.00	1.25
256	Billy Champion	.30	.15	.09
257	Checklist 133-264	1.50	.70	.45
258	Dave LaRoche	.30	.15	.09
259	Len Randle	.30	.15	.09
260	Johnny Bench	12.00	6.00	3.50
261	Andy Hassler	.30	.15	.09
262	Rowland Office	.30	.15	.09
263	Jim Perry	.30	.15	.09
264	John Milner	.30	.15	.09
265	Ron Bryant	.30	.15	.09
266	Sandy Alomar	.30	.15	.09
267	Dick Ruthven	.30	.15	.09
268	Hal McRae	.40	.20	.12
269	Doug Rau	.30	.15	.09
270	Ron Fairly	.30	.15	.09
271	Jerry Moses	.30	.15	.09
272	Lynn McGlothen	.30	.15	.09
273	Steve Braun	.30	.15	.09
274	Vicente Romo	.30	.15	.09
275	Paul Blair	.30	.15	.09
276	White Sox Team (Chuck Tanner)	2.00	1.00	.60
277	Frank Taveras	.30	.15	.09
278	Paul Lindblad	.30	.15	.09
279	Milt May	.30	.15	.09
280	Carl Yastrzemski	12.00	6.00	3.50
281	Jim Slaton	.30	.15	.09
282	Jerry Morales	.30	.15	.09
283	Steve Foucault	.30	.15	.09
284	Ken Griffey	.70	.35	.20
285	Ellie Rodriguez	.30	.15	.09
286	Mike Jorgensen	.30	.15	.09
287	Roric Harrison	.30	.15	.09
288	Bruce Ellingsen	.30	.15	.09
289	Ken Rudolph	.30	.15	.09
290	Jon Matlack	.30	.15	.09
291	Bill Sudakis	.30	.15	.09
292	Ron Schueler	.30	.15	.09
293	Dick Sharon	.30	.15	.09
294	*Geoff Zahn*	.30	.15	.09
295	Vada Pinson	.45	.25	.14
296	Alan Foster	.30	.15	.09
297	Craig Kusick	.30	.15	.09
298	Johnny Grubb	.30	.15	.09
299	Bucky Dent	.40	.20	.12
300	Reggie Jackson	35.00	17.50	10.50
301	Dave Roberts	.30	.15	.09
302	*Rick Burleson*	.30	.15	.09
303	Grant Jackson	.30	.15	.09
304	Pirates Team (Danny Murtaugh)	2.00	1.00	.60
305	Jim Colborn	.30	.15	.09
306	Batting Leaders (Rod Carew, Ralph Garr)	.80	.40	.25
307	Home Run Leaders (Dick Allen, Mike Schmidt)	.90	.45	.25
308	Runs Batted In Leaders (Johnny Bench, Jeff Burroughs)	.80	.40	.25
309	Stolen Base Leaders (Lou Brock, Bill North)	.75	.40	.25
310	Victory Leaders (Jim Hunter, Fergie Jenkins, Andy Messersmith, Phil Niekro)	.80	.40	.25
311	Earned Run Average Leaders (Buzz Capra, Catfish Hunter)	.50	.25	.15
312	Strikeout Leaders (Steve Carlton, Nolan Ryan)	9.00	4.50	2.75
313	Leading Firemen (Terry Forster, Mike Marshall)	.50	.25	.15
314	Buck Martinez	.30	.15	.09
315	Don Kessinger	.30	.15	.09
316	Jackie Brown	.30	.15	.09
317	Joe Lahoud	.30	.15	.09
318	Ernie McAnally	.30	.15	.09
319	Johnny Oates	.30	.15	.09
320	Pete Rose	20.00	10.00	6.00
321	Rudy May	.30	.15	.09
322	Ed Goodson	.30	.15	.09
323	Fred Holdsworth	.30	.15	.09
324	Ed Kranepool	.35	.20	.11
325	Tony Oliva	.45	.25	.14
326	Wayne Twitchell	.30	.15	.09
327	Jerry Hairston	.30	.15	.09
328	Sonny Siebert	.30	.15	.09
329	Ted Kubiak	.30	.15	.09
330	Mike Marshall	.30	.15	.09
331	Indians Team (Frank Robinson)	2.00	1.00	.60
332	Fred Kendall	.30	.15	.09
333	Dick Drago	.30	.15	.09
334	*Greg Gross*	.30	.15	.09
335	Jim Palmer	8.00	4.00	2.50
336	Rennie Stennett	.30	.15	.09
337	Kevin Kobel	.30	.15	.09
338	Rick Stelmaszek	.30	.15	.09
339	Jim Fregosi	.30	.15	.09
340	Paul Splittorff	.30	.15	.09
341	Hal Breeden	.30	.15	.09
342	Leroy Stanton	.30	.15	.09
343	Danny Frisella	.30	.15	.09
344	Ben Oglivie	.30	.15	.09
345	Clay Carroll	.30	.15	.09
346	Bobby Darwin	.30	.15	.09
347	Mike Caldwell	.30	.15	.09
348	Tony Muser	.30	.15	.09
349	Ray Sadecki	.30	.15	.09
350	Bobby Murcer	.30	.15	.09
351	Bob Boone	.40	.20	.12
352	Darold Knowles	.30	.15	.09
353	Luis Melendez	.30	.15	.09
354	Dick Bosman	.30	.15	.09
355	Chris Cannizzaro	.30	.15	.09
356	Rico Petrocelli			
357	Ken Forsch	.30	.15	.09
358	Al Bumbry	.30	.15	.09
359	Paul Popovich	.30	.15	.09
360	George Scott	.30	.15	.09
361	Dodgers Team (Walter Alston)	3.00	1.50	.90
362	Steve Hargan	.30	.15	.09
363	Carmen Fanzone	.30	.15	.09
364	Doug Bird	.30	.15	.09
365	Bob Bailey	.30	.15	.09
366	Ken Sanders	.30	.15	.09
367	Craig Robinson	.30	.15	.09
368	Vic Albury	.30	.15	.09
369	Merv Rettenmund	.30	.15	.09
370	Tom Seaver	15.00	7.50	4.50
371	Gates Brown	.30	.15	.09
372	John D'Acquisto	.30	.15	.09
373	Bill Sharp	.30	.15	.09
374	Eddie Watt	.30	.15	.09
375	Roy White	.30	.15	.09
376	Steve Yeager	.30	.15	.09
377	Tom Hilgendorf	.30	.15	.09
378	Derrel Thomas	.30	.15	.09
379	Bernie Carbo	.30	.15	.09
380	Sal Bando	.30	.15	.09
381	John Curtis	.30	.15	.09
382	Don Baylor	.45	.25	.14
383	Jim York	.30	.15	.09
384	Brewers Team (Del Crandall)	2.00	1.00	.60
385	Dock Ellis	.30	.15	.09
386	Checklist 265-396	1.50	.70	.45
387	Jim Spencer	.30	.15	.09
388	Steve Stone	.30	.15	.09
389	Tony Solaita	.30	.15	.09
390	Ron Cey	.30	.15	.09
391	Don DeMola	.30	.15	.09
392	Bruce Bochte	.30	.15	.09
393	Gary Gentry	.30	.15	.09
394	Larvell Blanks	.30	.15	.09
395	Bud Harrelson	.30	.15	.09
396	Fred Norman	.30	.15	.09
397	Bill Freehan	.30	.15	.09
398	Elias Sosa	.30	.15	.09
399	Terry Harmon	.30	.15	.09
400	Dick Allen	.80	.40	.25
401	Mike Wallace	.30	.15	.09
402	Bob Tolan	.30	.15	.09
403	Tom Buskey	.30	.15	.09
404	Ted Sizemore	.30	.15	.09
405	John Montague	.30	.15	.09
406	Bob Gallagher	.30	.15	.09

		NR MT	EX	VG
407	*Herb Washington*	.35	.20	.11
408	Clyde Wright	.30	.15	.09
409	Bob Robertson	.30	.15	.09
410	Mike Cueller (Cuellar)	.30	.15	.09
411	George Mitterwald	.30	.15	.09
412	Bill Hands	.30	.15	.09
413	Marty Pattin	.30	.15	.09
414	Manny Mota	.30	.15	.09
415	John Hiller	.30	.15	.09
416	Larry Lintz	.30	.15	.09
417	Skip Lockwood	.30	.15	.09
418	Leo Foster	.30	.15	.09
419	Dave Goltz	.30	.15	.09
420	Larry Bowa	.40	.20	.12
421	Mets Team (Yogi Berra)	2.50	1.25	.70
422	Brian Downing	.30	.15	.09
423	Clay Kirby	.30	.15	.09
424	John Lowenstein	.30	.15	.09
425	Tito Fuentes	.30	.15	.09
426	George Medich	.30	.15	.09
427	Clarence Gaston	.30	.15	.09
428	Dave Hamilton	.30	.15	.09
429	*Jim Dwyer*	.30	.15	.09
430	Luis Tiant	.40	.20	.12
431	Rod Gilbreath	.30	.15	.09
432	Ken Berry	.30	.15	.09
433	Larry Demery	.30	.15	.09
434	Bob Locker	.30	.15	.09
435	Dave Nelson	.30	.15	.09
436	Ken Frailing	.30	.15	.09
437	*Al Cowens*	.30	.15	.09
438	Don Carrithers	.30	.15	.09
439	Ed Brinkman	.30	.15	.09
440	Andy Messersmith	.30	.15	.09
441	Bobby Heise	.30	.15	.09
442	Maximino Leon	.30	.15	.09
443	Twins Team (Frank Quilici)	2.00	1.00	.60
444	Gene Garber	.30	.15	.09
445	Felix Millan	.30	.15	.09
446	Bart Johnson	.30	.15	.09
447	Terry Crowley	.30	.15	.09
448	Frank Duffy	.30	.15	.09
449	Charlie Williams	.30	.15	.09
450	Willie McCovey	4.00	2.00	1.25
451	Rick Dempsey	.30	.15	.09
452	Angel Mangual	.30	.15	.09
453	Claude Osteen	.30	.15	.09
454	Doug Griffin	.30	.15	.09
455	Don Wilson	.30	.15	.09
456	Bob Coluccio	.30	.15	.09
457	Mario Mendoza	.30	.15	.09
458	Ross Grimsley	.30	.15	.09
459	A.L. Championships	.80	.40	.25
460	N.L. Championships (Steve Garvey)	.80	.40	.25
461	World Series Game 1 (Reggie Jackson)	2.00	1.00	.60
462	World Series Game 2	.80	.40	.25
463	World Series Game 3 (Rollie Fingers)	1.00	.50	.30
464	World Series Game 4	.80	.40	.25
465	World Series Game 5	.80	.40	.25
466	World Series Summary (A's Do It Again)	.80	.40	.25
467	Ed Halicki	.30	.15	.09
468	Bobby Mitchell	.30	.15	.09
469	Tom Dettore	.30	.15	.09
470	Jeff Burroughs	.30	.15	.09
471	Bob Stinson	.30	.15	.09
472	Bruce Dal Canton	.30	.15	.09
473	Ken McMullen	.30	.15	.09
474	Luke Walker	.30	.15	.09
475	Darrell Evans	.45	.25	.14
476	*Ed Figueroa*	.30	.15	.09
477	Tom Hutton	.30	.15	.09
478	Tom Burgmeier	.30	.15	.09
479	Ken Boswell	.30	.15	.09
480	Carlos May	.30	.15	.09
481	*Will McEnaney*	.30	.15	.09
482	Tom McCraw	.30	.15	.09
483	Steve Ontiveros	.30	.15	.09
484	Glenn Beckert	.30	.15	.09
485	Sparky Lyle	.30	.15	.09
486	Ray Fosse	.30	.15	.09
487	Astros Team (Preston Gomez)	2.00	1.00	.60
488	Bill Travers	.30	.15	.09
489	Cecil Cooper	.45	.25	.14
490	Reggie Smith	.30	.15	.09
491	Doyle Alexander	.30	.15	.09
492	Rich Hebner	.30	.15	.09
493	Don Stanhouse	.30	.15	.09
494	*Pete LaCock*	.30	.15	.09
495	Nelson Briles	.30	.15	.09
496	Pepe Frias	.30	.15	.09
497	Jim Nettles	.30	.15	.09
498	Al Downing	.30	.15	.09
499	Marty Perez	.30	.15	.09
500	Nolan Ryan	80.00	40.00	24.00
501	Bill Robinson	.30	.15	.09
502	Pat Bourque	.30	.15	.09
503	Fred Stanley	.30	.15	.09
504	Buddy Bradford	.30	.15	.09
505	Chris Speier	.30	.15	.09
506	Leron Lee	.30	.15	.09
507	Tom Carroll	.30	.15	.09
508	Bob Hansen	.30	.15	.09
509	Dave Hilton	.30	.15	.09
510	Vida Blue	.50	.25	.15
511	Rangers Team (Billy Martin)	2.00	1.00	.60
512	Larry Milbourne	.30	.15	.09
513	Dick Pole	.30	.15	.09
514	Jose Cruz	.30	.15	.09
515	Manny Sanguillen	.30	.15	.09
516	Don Hood	.30	.15	.09
517	Checklist 397-528	1.25	.60	.40
518	Leo Cardenas	.30	.15	.09
519	Jim Todd	.30	.15	.09
520	Amos Otis	.30	.15	.09
521	Dennis Blair	.30	.15	.09
522	Gary Sutherland	.30	.15	.09
523	Tom Paciorek	.30	.15	.09
524	John Doherty	.30	.15	.09
525	Tom House	.30	.15	.09
526	Larry Hisle	.30	.15	.09
527	Mac Scarce	.30	.15	.09
528	Eddie Leon	.30	.15	.09
529	Gary Thomasson	.30	.15	.09
530	Gaylord Perry	3.00	1.50	.90
531	Reds Team (Sparky Anderson)	3.00	1.50	.90
532	Gorman Thomas	.30	.15	.09
533	Rudy Meoli	.30	.15	.09
534	Alex Johnson	.30	.15	.09
535	Gene Tenace	.30	.15	.09
536	Bob Moose	.30	.15	.09
537	Tommy Harper	.30	.15	.09
538	Duffy Dyer	.30	.15	.09
539	Jesse Jefferson	.30	.15	.09
540	Lou Brock	4.00	2.00	1.25
541	Roger Metzger	.30	.15	.09
542	Pete Broberg	.30	.15	.09
543	Larry Biittner	.30	.15	.09
544	Steve Mingori	.30	.15	.09
545	Billy Williams	3.00	1.50	.90
546	John Knox	.30	.15	.09
547	Von Joshua	.30	.15	.09
548	Charlie Sands	.30	.15	.09
549	Bill Butler	.30	.15	.09
550	Ralph Garr	.30	.15	.09
551	Larry Christenson	.30	.15	.09
552	Jack Brohamer	.30	.15	.09
553	John Boccabella	.30	.15	.09
554	Rich Gossage	.45	.25	.14
555	Al Oliver	.60	.30	.20
556	Tim Johnson	.30	.15	.09
557	Larry Gura	.30	.15	.09
558	Dave Roberts	.30	.15	.09
559	Bob Montgomery	.30	.15	.09
560	Tony Perez	2.00	1.00	.60
561	A's Team (Alvin Dark)	2.00	1.00	.60
562	Gary Nolan	.30	.15	.09
563	Wilbur Howard	.30	.15	.09
564	Tommy Davis	.30	.15	.09
565	Joe Torre	.70	.35	.20
566	Ray Burris	.30	.15	.09
567	*Jim Sundberg*	.30	.15	.09
568	Dale Murray	.30	.15	.09
569	Frank White	.40	.20	.12
570	Jim Wynn	.35	.20	.11
571	Dave Lemanczyk	.30	.15	.09
572	Roger Nelson	.30	.15	.09
573	Orlando Pena	.30	.15	.09
574	Tony Taylor	.30	.15	.09
575	Gene Clines	.30	.15	.09
576	Phil Roof	.30	.15	.09
577	John Morris	.30	.15	.09
578	Dave Tomlin	.30	.15	.09
579	Skip Pitlock	.30	.15	.09
580	Frank Robinson	6.00	3.00	1.75
581	Darrel Chaney	.30	.15	.09
582	Eduardo Rodriguez	.30	.15	.09
583	Andy Etchebarren	.30	.15	.09
584	Mike Garman	.30	.15	.09

		NR MT	EX	VG
585	Chris Chambliss	.30	.15	.09
586	Tim McCarver	.45	.25	.14
587	Chris Ward	.30	.15	.09
588	Rick Auerbach	.30	.15	.09
589	Braves Team (Clyde King)	2.00	1.00	.60
590	Cesar Cedeno	.30	.15	.09
591	Glenn Abbott	.30	.15	.09
592	Balor Moore	.30	.15	.09
593	Gene Lamont	.30	.15	.09
594	Jim Fuller	.30	.15	.09
595	Joe Niekro	.30	.15	.09
596	Ollie Brown	.30	.15	.09
597	Winston Llenas	.30	.15	.09
598	Bruce Kison	.30	.15	.09
599	Nate Colbert	.30	.15	.09
600	Rod Carew	9.00	4.50	2.75
601	Juan Beniquez	.30	.15	.09
602	John Vukovich	.30	.15	.09
603	Lew Krausse	.30	.15	.09
604	Oscar Zamora	.30	.15	.09
605	John Ellis	.30	.15	.09
606	Bruce Miller	.30	.15	.09
607	Jim Holt	.30	.15	.09
608	Gene Michael	.30	.15	.09
609	Ellie Hendricks	.30	.15	.09
610	Ron Hunt	.30	.15	.09
611	Yankees Team (Bill Virdon)	3.00	1.50	.90
612	Terry Hughes	.30	.15	.09
613	Bill Parsons	.30	.15	.09
614	Rookie Pitchers (Jack Kucek, Dyar Miller, Vern Ruhle, Paul Siebert)	.30	.15	.09
615	Rookie Pitchers (Pat Darcy, *Dennis Leonard, Tom Underwood,* Hank Webb)	.30	.15	.09
616	Rookie Outfielders (Dave Augustine, Pepe Mangual, *Jim Rice,* John Scott)	15.00	7.50	4.50
617	Rookie Infielders (Mike Cubbage, *Doug DeCinces,* Reggie J. Sanders, Manny Trillo)	1.25	.60	.40
618	Rookie Pitchers *(Jamie Easterly,* Tom Johnson, *Scott McGregor, Rick Rhoden)*	2.25	1.25	.70
619	Rookie Outfielders (Benny Ayala, Nyls Nyman, Tommy Smith, Jerry Turner)	.30	.15	.09
620	Rookie Catchers-Outfielders *(Gary Carter,* Marc Hill, Danny Meyer, Leon Roberts)	35.00	17.50	10.50
621	Rookie Pitchers *(John Denny, Rawly Eastwick, Jim Kern,* Juan Veintidos)	.60	.30	.20
622	Rookie Outfielders (Ed Armbrister, *Fred Lynn,* Tom Poquette, Terry Whitfield)	10.00	5.00	3.00
623	Rookie Infielders *(Phil Garner, Keith Hernandez,* Bob Sheldon, Tom Veryzer)	10.00	5.00	3.00
624	Rookie Pitchers (Doug Konieczny, *Gary Lavelle,* Jim Otten, Eddie Solomon)	.30	.15	.09
625	Boog Powell	.45	.25	.14
626	Larry Haney	.30	.15	.09
627	Tom Walker	.30	.15	.09
628	*Ron LeFlore*	.80	.40	.25
629	Joe Hoerner	.30	.15	.09
630	Greg Luzinski	.45	.25	.14
631	Lee Lacy	.30	.15	.09
632	Morris Nettles	.30	.15	.09
633	Paul Casanova	.30	.15	.09
634	Cy Acosta	.30	.15	.09
635	Chuck Dobson	.30	.15	.09
636	Charlie Moore	.30	.15	.09
637	Ted Martinez	.30	.15	.09
638	Cubs Team (Jim Marshall)	2.00	1.00	.60
639	Steve Kline	.30	.15	.09
640	Harmon Killebrew	5.00	2.50	1.50
641	Jim Northrup	.30	.15	.09
642	Mike Phillips	.30	.15	.09
643	Brent Strom	.30	.15	.09
644	Bill Fahey	.30	.15	.09
645	Danny Cater	.30	.15	.09
646	Checklist 529-660	1.50	.70	.45
647	*Claudell Washington*	1.00	.50	.30
648	Dave Pagan	.30	.15	.09
649	Jack Heidemann	.30	.15	.09
650	Dave May	.30	.15	.09
651	John Morlan	.30	.15	.09
652	Lindy McDaniel	.30	.15	.09
653	Lee Richards	.30	.15	.09
654	Jerry Terrell	.30	.15	.09
655	Rico Carty	.30	.15	.09
656	Bill Plummer	.30	.15	.09
657	Bob Oliver	.30	.15	.09
658	Vic Harris	.30	.15	.09
659	Bob Apodaca	.30	.15	.09
660	Hank Aaron	30.00	15.00	9.00

1975 Topps Mini

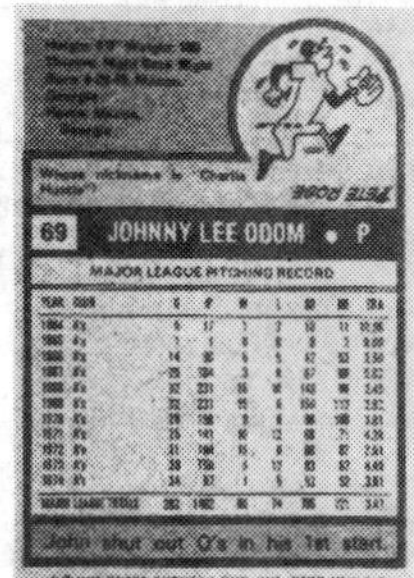

One of the most popular Topps sets of the 1970s is really a test issue. The Topps Minis measure 2-1/4" by 3-1/8," exactly 20 percent smaller than the regular card size. Other than their size, the Minis are in every way the same as the regular cards. The experiment primarily took place in parts of Michigan and the West Coast, where the Minis were snapped up quickly by collectors.

		NR MT	EX	VG
Complete Set:		1200.00	600.00	350.00
Common Player:		.40	.20	.12
1	'74 Highlights (Hank Aaron)	25.00	12.50	7.50
2	'74 Highlights (Lou Brock)	3.50	1.75	1.00
3	'74 Highlights (Bob Gibson)	3.25	1.75	1.00
4	'74 Highlights (Al Kaline)	3.25	1.75	1.00
5	'74 Highlights (Nolan Ryan)	15.00	7.50	4.50
6	'74 Highlights (Mike Marshall)	.60	.30	.20
7	'74 Highlights (Dick Bosman, Steve Busby, Nolan Ryan)	3.00	1.50	.90
8	Rogelio Moret	.40	.20	.12
9	Frank Tepedino	.40	.20	.12
10	Willie Davis	.60	.30	.20
11	Bill Melton	.40	.20	.12
12	David Clyde	.40	.20	.12
13	Gene Locklear	.40	.20	.12
14	Milt Wilcox	.40	.20	.12
15	Jose Cardenal	.40	.20	.12
16	Frank Tanana	.60	.30	.20
17	Dave Concepcion	.90	.45	.25
18	Tigers Team (Ralph Houk)	1.25	.60	.40
19	Jerry Koosman	.40	.20	.12
20	Thurman Munson	10.00	5.00	3.00
21	Rollie Fingers	6.00	3.00	1.75
22	Dave Cash	.40	.20	.12
23	Bill Russell	.60	.30	.20
24	Al Fitzmorris	.40	.20	.12
25	Lee May	.60	.30	.20
26	Dave McNally	.60	.30	.20
27	Ken Reitz	.40	.20	.12
28	Tom Murphy	.40	.20	.12
29	Dave Parker	10.00	5.00	3.00
30	Bert Blyleven	2.00	1.00	.60
31	Dave Rader	.40	.20	.12
32	Reggie Cleveland	.40	.20	.12
33	Dusty Baker	.90	.45	.25
34	Steve Renko	.40	.20	.12
35	Ron Santo	.80	.40	.25
36	Joe Lovitto	.40	.20	.12
37	Dave Freisleben	.40	.20	.12
38	Buddy Bell	.75	.40	.25
39	Andy Thornton	.60	.30	.20
40	Bill Singer	.40	.20	.12
41	Cesar Geronimo	.40	.20	.12
42	Joe Coleman	.40	.20	.12
43	Cleon Jones	.40	.20	.12
44	Pat Dobson	.40	.20	.12
45	Joe Rudi	.60	.30	.20
46	Phillies Team (Danny Ozark)	1.25	.60	.40
47	Tommy John	2.50	1.25	.70
48	Freddie Patek	.40	.20	.12
49	Larry Dierker	.40	.20	.12

		NR MT	EX	VG
50	Brooks Robinson	10.00	5.00	3.00
51	Bob Forsch	1.25	.60	.40
52	Darrell Porter	.60	.30	.20
53	Dave Giusti	.40	.20	.12
54	Eric Soderholm	.40	.20	.12
55	Bobby Bonds	.80	.40	.25
56	Rick Wise	.60	.30	.20
57	Dave Johnson	1.25	.60	.40
58	Chuck Taylor	.40	.20	.12
59	Ken Henderson	.40	.20	.12
60	Fergie Jenkins	3.00	1.50	.90
61	Dave Winfield	60.00	30.00	18.00
62	Fritz Peterson	.40	.20	.12
63	Steve Swisher	.40	.20	.12
64	Dave Chalk	.40	.20	.12
65	Don Gullett	.40	.20	.12
66	Willie Horton	.60	.30	.20
67	Tug McGraw	.60	.30	.20
68	Ron Blomberg	.40	.20	.12
69	John Odom	.40	.20	.12
70	Mike Schmidt	60.00	30.00	18.00
71	Charlie Hough	.60	.30	.20
72	Royals Team (Jack McKeon)	1.25	.60	.40
73	J.R. Richard	.60	.30	.20
74	Mark Belanger	.60	.30	.20
75	Ted Simmons	.60	.30	.20
76	Ed Sprague	.40	.20	.12
77	Richie Zisk	.40	.20	.12
78	Ray Corbin	.40	.20	.12
79	Gary Matthews	.60	.30	.20
80	Carlton Fisk	12.00	6.00	3.50
81	Ron Reed	.40	.20	.12
82	Pat Kelly	.40	.20	.12
83	Jim Merritt	.40	.20	.12
84	Enzo Hernandez	.40	.20	.12
85	Bill Bonham	.40	.20	.12
86	Joe Lis	.40	.20	.12
87	George Foster	1.75	.90	.50
88	Tom Egan	.40	.20	.12
89	Jim Ray	.40	.20	.12
90	Rusty Staub	.90	.45	.25
91	Dick Green	.40	.20	.12
92	Cecil Upshaw	.40	.20	.12
93	Dave Lopes	.60	.30	.20
94	Jim Lonborg	.75	.40	.25
95	John Mayberry	.40	.20	.12
96	Mike Cosgrove	.40	.20	.12
97	Earl Williams	.40	.20	.12
98	Rich Folkers	.40	.20	.12
99	Mike Hegan	.40	.20	.12
100	Willie Stargell	7.00	3.50	2.00
101	Expos Team (Gene Mauch)	1.25	.60	.40
102	Joe Decker	.40	.20	.12
103	Rick Miller	.40	.20	.12
104	Bill Madlock	1.00	.50	.30
105	Buzz Capra	.40	.20	.12
106	Mike Hargrove	.60	.30	.20
107	Jim Barr	.40	.20	.12
108	Tom Hall	.40	.20	.12
109	George Hendrick	.40	.20	.12
110	Wilbur Wood	.40	.20	.12
111	Wayne Garrett	.40	.20	.12
112	Larry Hardy	.40	.20	.12
113	Elliott Maddox	.40	.20	.12
114	Dick Lange	.40	.20	.12
115	Joe Ferguson	.40	.20	.12
116	Lerrin LaGrow	.40	.20	.12
117	Orioles Team (Earl Weaver)	1.25	.60	.40
118	Mike Anderson	.40	.20	.12
119	Tommy Helms	.40	.20	.12
120	Steve Busby (photo actually Fran Healy)	.40	.20	.12
121	Bill North	.40	.20	.12
122	Al Hrabosky	.40	.20	.12
123	Johnny Briggs	.40	.20	.12
124	Jerry Reuss	.60	.30	.20
125	Ken Singleton	.60	.30	.20
126	Checklist 1-132	2.25	1.25	.70
127	Glen Borgmann	.40	.20	.12
128	Bill Lee	.60	.30	.20
129	Rick Monday	.60	.30	.20
130	Phil Niekro	4.00	2.00	1.25
131	Toby Harrah	.40	.20	.12
132	Randy Moffitt	.40	.20	.12
133	Dan Driessen	.60	.30	.20
134	Ron Hodges	.40	.20	.12
135	Charlie Spikes	.40	.20	.12
136	Jim Mason	.40	.20	.12
137	Terry Forster	.40	.20	.12
138	Del Unser	.40	.20	.12
139	Horacio Pina	.40	.20	.12

		NR MT	EX	VG
140	Steve Garvey	9.00	4.50	2.75
141	Mickey Stanley	.40	.20	.12
142	Bob Reynolds	.40	.20	.12
143	Cliff Johnson	.40	.20	.12
144	Jim Wohlford	.40	.20	.12
145	Ken Holtzman	.60	.30	.20
146	Padres Team (John McNamara)	1.25	.60	.40
147	Pedro Garcia	.40	.20	.12
148	Jim Rooker	.40	.20	.12
149	Tim Foli	.40	.20	.12
150	Bob Gibson	7.00	3.50	2.00
151	Steve Brye	.40	.20	.12
152	Mario Guerrero	.40	.20	.12
153	Rick Reuschel	.60	.30	.20
154	Mike Lum	.40	.20	.12
155	Jim Bibby	.40	.20	.12
156	Dave Kingman	.90	.45	.25
157	Pedro Borbon	.40	.20	.12
158	Jerry Grote	.40	.20	.12
159	Steve Arlin	.40	.20	.12
160	Graig Nettles	2.00	1.00	.60
161	Stan Bahnsen	.40	.20	.12
162	Willie Montanez	.40	.20	.12
163	Jim Brewer	.40	.20	.12
164	Mickey Rivers	.60	.30	.20
165	Doug Rader	.60	.30	.20
166	Woodie Fryman	.40	.20	.12
167	Rich Coggins	.40	.20	.12
168	Bill Greif	.40	.20	.12
169	Cookie Rojas	.40	.20	.12
170	Bert Campaneris	.60	.30	.20
171	Ed Kirkpatrick	.40	.20	.12
172	Red Sox Team (Darrell Johnson)	1.25	.60	.40
173	Steve Rogers	.40	.20	.12
174	Bake McBride	.40	.20	.12
175	Don Money	.40	.20	.12
176	Burt Hooton	.40	.20	.12
177	Vic Correll	.40	.20	.12
178	Cesar Tovar	.40	.20	.12
179	Tom Bradley	.40	.20	.12
180	Joe Morgan	10.00	5.00	3.00
181	Fred Beene	.40	.20	.12
182	Don Hahn	.40	.20	.12
183	Mel Stottlemyre	.60	.30	.20
184	Jorge Orta	.40	.20	.12
185	Steve Carlton	15.00	7.50	4.50
186	Willie Crawford	.40	.20	.12
187	Denny Doyle	.40	.20	.12
188	Tom Griffin	.40	.20	.12
189	1951-MVPs (Larry (Yogi) Berra, Roy Campanella)	4.00	2.00	1.25
190	1952-MVPs (Hank Sauer, Bobby Shantz)	.60	.30	.20
191	1953-MVPs (Roy Campanella, Al Rosen)	2.00	1.00	.60
192	1954-MVPs (Yogi Berra, Willie Mays)	7.00	3.50	2.00
193	1955-MVPs (Yogi Berra, Roy Campanella)	4.00	2.00	1.25
194	1956-MVPs (Mickey Mantle, Don Newcombe)	9.00	4.50	2.75
195	1957-MVPs (Hank Aaron, Mickey Mantle)	15.00	7.50	4.50
196	1958-MVPs (Ernie Banks, Jackie Jensen)	4.00	2.00	1.25
197	1959-MVPs (Ernie Banks, Nellie Fox)	6.00	3.00	1.75
198	1960-MVPs (Dick Groat, Roger Maris)	6.00	3.00	1.75
199	1961-MVPs (Roger Maris, Frank Robinson)	6.00	3.00	1.75
200	1962-MVPs (Mickey Mantle, Maury Wills)	9.00	4.50	2.75
201	1963-MVPs (Elston Howard, Sandy Koufax)	4.00	2.00	1.25
202	1964-MVPs (Ken Boyer, Brooks Robinson)	3.50	1.75	1.00
203	1965-MVPs (Willie Mays, Zoilo Versalles)	3.00	1.50	.90
204	1966-MVPs (Roberto Clemente, Frank Robinson)	7.00	3.50	2.00
205	1967-MVPs (Orlando Cepeda, Carl Yastrzemski)	5.00	2.50	1.50
206	1968-MVPs (Bob Gibson, Denny McLain)	3.00	1.50	.90
207	1969-MVPs (Harmon Killebrew, Willie McCovey)	3.00	1.50	.90
208	1970-MVPs (Johnny Bench, Boog Powell)	2.50	1.25	.70
209	1971-MVPs (Vida Blue, Joe Torre)	.80	.40	.25
210	1972-MVPs (Rich Allen, Johnny Bench)	1.75	.90	.50

		NR MT	EX	VG
211	1973-MVPs (Reggie Jackson, Pete Rose)	7.00	3.50	2.00
212	1974-MVPs (Jeff Burroughs, Steve Garvey)	1.25	.60	.40
213	Oscar Gamble	.40	.20	.12
214	Harry Parker	.40	.20	.12
215	Bobby Valentine	.40	.20	.12
216	Giants Team (Wes Westrum)	1.25	.60	.40
217	Lou Piniella	.80	.40	.25
218	Jerry Johnson	.40	.20	.12
219	Ed Herrmann	.40	.20	.12
220	Don Sutton	3.00	1.50	.90
221	Aurelio Rodriquez (Rodriguez)	.40	.20	.12
222	Dan Spillner	.40	.20	.12
223	Robin Yount	200.00	100.00	60.00
224	Ramon Hernandez	.40	.20	.12
225	Bob Grich	.60	.30	.20
226	Bill Campbell	.40	.20	.12
227	Bob Watson	.40	.20	.12
228	George Brett	250.00	125.00	75.00
229	Barry Foote	.40	.20	.12
230	Catfish Hunter	4.00	2.00	1.25
231	Mike Tyson	.40	.20	.12
232	Diego Segui	.40	.20	.12
233	Billy Grabarkewitz	.40	.20	.12
234	Tom Grieve	.40	.20	.12
235	Jack Billingham	.40	.20	.12
236	Angels Team (Dick Williams)	1.25	.60	.40
237	Carl Morton	.40	.20	.12
238	Dave Duncan	.40	.20	.12
239	George Stone	.40	.20	.12
240	Garry Maddox	.60	.30	.20
241	Dick Tidrow	.40	.20	.12
242	Jay Johnstone	.60	.30	.20
243	Jim Kaat	2.00	1.00	.60
244	Bill Buckner	.80	.40	.25
245	Mickey Lolich	.80	.40	.25
246	Cardinals Team (Red Schoendienst)	1.25	.60	.40
247	Enos Cabell	.40	.20	.12
248	Randy Jones	.40	.20	.12
249	Danny Thompson	.40	.20	.12
250	Ken Brett	.40	.20	.12
251	Fran Healy	.40	.20	.12
252	Fred Scherman	.40	.20	.12
253	Jesus Alou	.40	.20	.12
254	Mike Torrez	.40	.20	.12
255	Dwight Evans	1.50	.70	.45
256	Billy Champion	.40	.20	.12
257	Checklist 133-264	2.25	1.25	.70
258	Dave LaRoche	.40	.20	.12
259	Len Randle	.40	.20	.12
260	Johnny Bench	15.00	7.50	4.50
261	Andy Hassler	.40	.20	.12
262	Rowland Office	.40	.20	.12
263	Jim Perry	.60	.30	.20
264	John Milner	.40	.20	.12
265	Ron Bryant	.40	.20	.12
266	Sandy Alomar	.40	.20	.12
267	Dick Ruthven	.40	.20	.12
268	Hal McRae	.60	.30	.20
269	Doug Rau	.40	.20	.12
270	Ron Fairly	.60	.30	.20
271	Jerry Moses	.40	.20	.12
272	Lynn McGlothen	.40	.20	.12
273	Steve Braun	.40	.20	.12
274	Vicente Romo	.40	.20	.12
275	Paul Blair	.60	.30	.20
276	White Sox Team (Chuck Tanner)	1.25	.60	.40
277	Frank Taveras	.40	.20	.12
278	Paul Lindblad	.40	.20	.12
279	Milt May	.40	.20	.12
280	Carl Yastrzemski	10.00	5.00	3.00
281	Jim Slaton	.40	.20	.12
282	Jerry Morales	.40	.20	.12
283	Steve Foucault	.40	.20	.12
284	Ken Griffey	3.00	1.50	.90
285	Ellie Rodriguez	.40	.20	.12
286	Mike Jorgensen	.40	.20	.12
287	Roric Harrison	.40	.20	.12
288	Bruce Ellingsen	.40	.20	.12
289	Ken Rudolph	.40	.20	.12
290	Jon Matlack	.40	.20	.12
291	Bill Sudakis	.40	.20	.12
292	Ron Schueler	.40	.20	.12
293	Dick Sharon	.40	.20	.12
294	Geoff Zahn	.40	.20	.12
295	Vada Pinson	1.50	.70	.45
296	Alan Foster	.40	.20	.12
297	Craig Kusick	.40	.20	.12
298	Johnny Grubb	.40	.20	.12

		NR MT	EX	VG
299	Bucky Dent	.60	.30	.20
300	Reggie Jackson	30.00	15.00	9.00
301	Dave Roberts	.40	.20	.12
302	Rick Burleson	.80	.40	.25
303	Grant Jackson	.40	.20	.12
304	Pirates Team (Danny Murtaugh)	1.25	.60	.40
305	Jim Colborn	.40	.20	.12
306	Batting Leaders (Rod Carew, Ralph Garr)	1.25	.60	.40
307	Home Run Leaders (Dick Allen, Mike Schmidt)	1.25	.60	.40
308	Runs Batted In Leaders (Johnny Bench, Jeff Burroughs)	1.25	.60	.40
309	Stole Base Leaders (Lou Brock, Bill North)	1.25	.60	.40
310	Victory Leaders (Catfish Hunter, Fergie Jenkins, Andy Messersmith, Phil Niekro)	1.25	.60	.40
311	Earned Run Average Leaders (Buzz Capra, Catfish Hunter)	.80	.40	.25
312	Strikeout Leaders (Steve Carlton, Nolan Ryan)	15.00	7.50	4.50
313	Leading Firemen (Terry Forster, Mike Marshall)	.80	.40	.25
314	Buck Martinez	.40	.20	.12
315	Don Kessinger	.40	.20	.12
316	Jackie Brown	.40	.20	.12
317	Joe Lahoud	.40	.20	.12
318	Ernie McAnally	.40	.20	.12
319	Johnny Oates	.40	.20	.12
320	Pete Rose	25.00	12.50	7.50
321	Rudy May	.40	.20	.12
322	Ed Goodson	.40	.20	.12
323	Fred Holdsworth	.40	.20	.12
324	Ed Kranepool	.40	.20	.12
325	Tony Oliva	2.50	1.25	.70
326	Wayne Twitchell	.40	.20	.12
327	Jerry Hairston	.40	.20	.12
328	Sonny Siebert	.40	.20	.12
329	Ted Kubiak	.40	.20	.12
330	Mike Marshall	.60	.30	.20
331	Indians Team (Frank Robinson)	1.25	.60	.40
332	Fred Kendall	.40	.20	.12
333	Dick Drago	.40	.20	.12
334	Greg Gross	.40	.20	.12
335	Jim Palmer	10.00	5.00	3.00
336	Rennie Stennett	.40	.20	.12
337	Kevin Kobel	.40	.20	.12
338	Rick Stelmaszek	.40	.20	.12
339	Jim Fregosi	.60	.30	.20
340	Paul Splittorff	.40	.20	.12
341	Hal Breeden	.40	.20	.12
342	Leroy Stanton	.40	.20	.12
343	Danny Frisella	.40	.20	.12
344	Ben Oglivie	.60	.30	.20
345	Clay Carroll	.40	.20	.12
346	Bobby Darwin	.40	.20	.12
347	Mike Caldwell	.40	.20	.12
348	Tony Muser	.40	.20	.12
349	Ray Sadecki	.40	.20	.12
350	Bobby Murcer	.60	.30	.20
351	Bob Boone	2.00	1.00	.60
352	Darold Knowles	.40	.20	.12
353	Luis Melendez	.40	.20	.12
354	Dick Bosman	.40	.20	.12
355	Chris Cannizzaro	.40	.20	.12
356	Rico Petrocelli	.40	.20	.12
357	Ken Forsch	.40	.20	.12
358	Al Bumbry	.40	.20	.12
359	Paul Popovich	.40	.20	.12
360	George Scott	.40	.20	.12
361	Dodgers Team (Walter Alston)	1.50	.70	.45
362	Steve Hargan	.40	.20	.12
363	Carmen Fanzone	.40	.20	.12
364	Doug Bird	.40	.20	.12
365	Bob Bailey	.40	.20	.12
366	Ken Sanders	.40	.20	.12
367	Craig Robinson	.40	.20	.12
368	Vic Albury	.40	.20	.12
369	Merv Rettenmund	.40	.20	.12
370	Tom Seaver	20.00	10.00	6.00
371	Gates Brown	.40	.20	.12
372	John D'Acquisto	.40	.20	.12
373	Bill Sharp	.40	.20	.12
374	Eddie Watt	.40	.20	.12
375	Roy White	.60	.30	.20
376	Steve Yeager	.40	.20	.12
377	Tom Hilgendorf	.40	.20	.12
378	Derrel Thomas	.40	.20	.12
379	Bernie Carbo	.40	.20	.12
380	Sal Bando	.60	.30	.20

		NR MT	EX	VG
381	John Curtis	.40	.20	.12
382	Don Baylor	.90	.45	.25
383	Jim York	.40	.20	.12
384	Brewers Team (Del Crandall)	1.25	.60	.40
385	Dock Ellis	.40	.20	.12
386	Checklist 265-396	2.25	1.25	.70
387	Jim Spencer	.40	.20	.12
388	Steve Stone	.60	.30	.20
389	Tony Solaita	.40	.20	.12
390	Ron Cey	.60	.30	.20
391	Don DeMola	.40	.20	.12
392	Bruce Bochte	.40	.20	.12
393	Gary Gentry	.40	.20	.12
394	Larvell Blanks	.40	.20	.12
395	Bud Harrelson	.40	.20	.12
396	Fred Norman	.40	.20	.12
397	Bill Freehan	.60	.30	.20
398	Elias Sosa	.40	.20	.12
399	Terry Harmon	.40	.20	.12
400	Dick Allen	1.25	.60	.40
401	Mike Wallace	.40	.20	.12
402	Bob Tolan	.40	.20	.12
403	Tom Buskey	.40	.20	.12
404	Ted Sizemore	.40	.20	.12
405	John Montague	.40	.20	.12
406	Bob Gallagher	.40	.20	.12
407	Herb Washington	.80	.40	.25
408	Clyde Wright	.40	.20	.12
409	Bob Robertson	.40	.20	.12
410	Mike Cueller (Cuellar)	.60	.30	.20
411	George Mitterwald	.40	.20	.12
412	Bill Hands	.40	.20	.12
413	Marty Pattin	.40	.20	.12
414	Manny Mota	.60	.30	.20
415	John Hiller	.40	.20	.12
416	Larry Lintz	.40	.20	.12
417	Skip Lockwood	.40	.20	.12
418	Leo Foster	.40	.20	.12
419	Dave Goltz	.40	.20	.12
420	Larry Bowa	.60	.30	.20
421	Mets Team (Yogi Berra)	1.50	.70	.45
422	Brian Downing	.60	.30	.20
423	Clay Kirby	.40	.20	.12
424	John Lowenstein	.40	.20	.12
425	Tito Fuentes	.40	.20	.12
426	George Medich	.40	.20	.12
427	Cito Gaston	.75	.40	.25
428	Dave Hamilton	.40	.20	.12
429	Jim Dwyer	.40	.20	.12
430	Luis Tiant	.80	.40	.25
431	Rod Gilbreath	.40	.20	.12
432	Ken Berry	.40	.20	.12
433	Larry Demery	.40	.20	.12
434	Bob Locker	.40	.20	.12
435	Dave Nelson	.40	.20	.12
436	Ken Frailing	.40	.20	.12
437	Al Cowens	.40	.20	.12
438	Don Carrithers	.40	.20	.12
439	Ed Brinkman	.40	.20	.12
440	Andy Messersmith	.60	.30	.20
441	Bobby Heise	.40	.20	.12
442	Maximino Leon	.40	.20	.12
443	Twins Team (Frank Quilici)	1.25	.60	.40
444	Gene Garber	.40	.20	.12
445	Felix Millan	.40	.20	.12
446	Bart Johnson	.40	.20	.12
447	Terry Crowley	.40	.20	.12
448	Frank Duffy	.40	.20	.12
449	Charlie Williams	.40	.20	.12
450	Willie McCovey	7.00	3.50	2.00
451	Rick Dempsey	.60	.30	.20
452	Angel Mangual	.40	.20	.12
453	Claude Osteen	.40	.20	.12
454	Doug Griffin	.40	.20	.12
455	Don Wilson	.40	.20	.12
456	Bob Coluccio	.40	.20	.12
457	Mario Mendoza	.40	.20	.12
458	Ross Grimsley	.40	.20	.12
459	A.L. Championships	1.25	.60	.40
460	N.L. Championships	1.25	.60	.40
461	World Series Game 1	2.25	1.25	.70
462	World Series Game 2	1.50	.70	.45
463	World Series Game 3	1.50	.70	.45
464	World Series Game 4	1.25	.60	.40
465	World Series Game 5	1.25	.60	.40
466	World Series Summary	1.25	.60	.40
467	Ed Halicki	.40	.20	.12
468	Bobby Mitchell	.40	.20	.12
469	Tom Dettore	.40	.20	.12
470	Jeff Burroughs	.40	.20	.12
471	Bob Stinson	.40	.20	.12

		NR MT	EX	VG
472	Bruce Dal Canton	.40	.20	.12
473	Ken McMullen	.40	.20	.12
474	Luke Walker	.40	.20	.12
475	Darrell Evans	.90	.45	.25
476	Ed Figueroa	.40	.20	.12
477	Tom Hutton	.40	.20	.12
478	Tom Burgmeier	.40	.20	.12
479	Ken Boswell	.40	.20	.12
480	Carlos May	.40	.20	.12
481	Will McEnaney	.40	.20	.12
482	Tom McCraw	.40	.20	.12
483	Steve Ontiveros	.40	.20	.12
484	Glenn Beckert	.40	.20	.12
485	Sparky Lyle	.60	.30	.20
486	Ray Fosse	.40	.20	.12
487	Astros Team (Preston Gomez)	1.25	.60	.40
488	Bill Travers	.40	.20	.12
489	Cecil Cooper	.75	.40	.25
490	Reggie Smith	.60	.30	.20
491	Doyle Alexander	.60	.30	.20
492	Rich Hebner	.40	.20	.12
493	Doug Stanhouse	.40	.20	.12
494	Pete LaCock	.40	.20	.12
495	Nelson Briles	.40	.20	.12
496	Pepe Frias	.40	.20	.12
497	Jim Nettles	.40	.20	.12
498	Al Downing	.40	.20	.12
499	Marty Perez	.40	.20	.12
500	Nolan Ryan	90.00	45.00	27.00
501	Bill Robinson	.40	.20	.12
502	Pat Bourque	.40	.20	.12
503	Fred Stanley	.40	.20	.12
504	Buddy Bradford	.40	.20	.12
505	Chris Speier	.40	.20	.12
506	Leron Lee	.40	.20	.12
507	Tom Carroll	.40	.20	.12
508	Bob Hansen	.40	.20	.12
509	Dave Hilton	.40	.20	.12
510	Vida Blue	.80	.40	.25
511	Rangers Team (Billy Martin)	1.25	.60	.40
512	Larry Milbourne	.40	.20	.12
513	Dick Pole	.40	.20	.12
514	Jose Cruz	.80	.40	.25
515	Manny Sanguillen	.40	.20	.12
516	Don Hood	.40	.20	.12
517	Checklist 397-528	2.25	1.25	.70
518	Leo Cardenas	.40	.20	.12
519	Jim Todd	.40	.20	.12
520	Amos Otis	.40	.20	.12
521	Dennis Blair	.40	.20	.12
522	Gary Sutherland	.40	.20	.12
523	Tom Paciorek	.40	.20	.12
524	John Doherty	.40	.20	.12
525	Tom House	.40	.20	.12
526	Larry Hisle	.40	.20	.12
527	Mac Scarce	.40	.20	.12
528	Eddie Leon	.40	.20	.12
529	Gary Thomasson	.40	.20	.12
530	Gaylord Perry	6.00	3.00	1.75
531	Reds Team (Sparky Anderson)	1.50	.70	.45
532	Gorman Thomas	.40	.20	.12
533	Rudy Meoli	.40	.20	.12
534	Alex Johnson	.40	.20	.12
535	Gene Tenace	.40	.20	.12
536	Bob Moose	.40	.20	.12
537	Tommy Harper	.40	.20	.12
538	Duffy Dyer	.40	.20	.12
539	Jesse Jefferson	.40	.20	.12
540	Lou Brock	7.00	3.50	2.00
541	Roger Metzger	.40	.20	.12
542	Pete Broberg	.40	.20	.12
543	Larry Biittner	.40	.20	.12
544	Steve Mingori	.40	.20	.12
545	Billy Williams	6.00	3.00	1.75
546	John Knox	.40	.20	.12
547	Von Joshua	.40	.20	.12
548	Charlie Sands	.40	.20	.12
549	Bill Butler	.40	.20	.12
550	Ralph Garr	.40	.20	.12
551	Larry Christenson	.40	.20	.12
552	Jack Brohamer	.40	.20	.12
553	John Boccabella	.40	.20	.12
554	Rich Gossage	1.75	.90	.50
555	Al Oliver	1.25	.60	.40
556	Tim Johnson	.40	.20	.12
557	Larry Gura	.40	.20	.12
558	Dave Roberts	.40	.20	.12
559	Bob Montgomery	.40	.20	.12
560	Tony Perez	4.00	2.00	1.25
561	A's Team (Alvin Dark)	1.25	.60	.40
562	Gary Nolan	.40	.20	.12

		NR MT	EX	VG
563	Wilbur Howard	.40	.20	.12
564	Tommy Davis	.60	.30	.20
565	Joe Torre	1.00	.50	.30
566	Ray Burris	.40	.20	.12
567	Jim Sundberg	.60	.30	.20
568	Dale Murray	.40	.20	.12
569	Frank White	.60	.30	.20
570	Jim Wynn	.60	.30	.20
571	Dave Lemanczyk	.40	.20	.12
572	Roger Nelson	.40	.20	.12
573	Orlando Pena	.40	.20	.12
574	Tony Taylor	.40	.20	.12
575	Gene Clines	.40	.20	.12
576	Phil Roof	.40	.20	.12
577	John Morris	.40	.20	.12
578	Dave Tomlin	.40	.20	.12
579	Skip Pitlock	.40	.20	.12
580	Frank Robinson	7.00	3.50	2.00
581	Darrel Chaney	.40	.20	.12
582	Eduardo Rodriguez	.40	.20	.12
583	Andy Etchebarren	.40	.20	.12
584	Mike Garman	.40	.20	.12
585	Chris Chambliss	.60	.30	.20
586	Tim McCarver	1.25	.60	.40
587	Chris Ward	.40	.20	.12
588	Rick Auerbach	.40	.20	.12
589	Braves Team (Clyde King)	1.25	.60	.40
590	Cesar Cedeno	.60	.30	.20
591	Glenn Abbott	.40	.20	.12
592	Balor Moore	.40	.20	.12
593	Gene Lamont	.40	.20	.12
594	Jim Fuller	.40	.20	.12
595	Joe Niekro	.60	.30	.20
596	Ollie Brown	.40	.20	.12
597	Winston Llenas	.40	.20	.12
598	Bruce Kison	.40	.20	.12
599	Nate Colbert	.40	.20	.12
600	Rod Carew	12.00	6.00	3.50
601	Juan Beniquez	.40	.20	.12
602	John Vukovich	.40	.20	.12
603	Lew Krausse	.40	.20	.12
604	Oscar Zamora	.40	.20	.12
605	John Ellis	.40	.20	.12
606	Bruce Miller	.40	.20	.12
607	Jim Holt	.40	.20	.12
608	Gene Michael	.40	.20	.12
609	Ellie Hendricks	.40	.20	.12
610	Ron Hunt	.40	.20	.12
611	Yankees Team (Bill Virdon)	1.75	.90	.50
612	Terry Hughes	.40	.20	.12
613	Bill Parsons	.40	.20	.12
614	Rookie Pitchers (Jack Kucek, Dyar Miller, Vern Ruhle, Paul Siebert)	.40	.20	.12
615	Rookie Pitchers (Pat Darcy, Dennis Leonard, Tom Underwood, Hank Webb)	.90	.45	.25
616	Rookie Outfielders (Dave Augustine, Pepe Mangual, Jim Rice, John Scott)	15.00	7.50	4.50
617	Rookie Infielders (Mike Cubbage, Doug DeCinces, Reggie Sanders, Manny Trillo)	2.50	1.25	.70
618	Rookie Pitchers (Jamie Easterly, Tom Johnson, Scott McGregor, Rick Rhoden)	5.00	2.50	1.50
619	Rookie Outfielders (Benny Ayala, Nyls Nyman, Tommy Smith, Jerry Turner)	.40	.20	.12
620	Rookie Catchers-Outfielders (Gary Carter, Marc Hill, Danny Meyer, Leon Roberts)	40.00	20.00	12.00
621	Rookie Pitchers (John Denny, Rawly Eastwick, Jim Kern, Juan Veintidos)	.90	.45	.25
622	Rookie Outfielders (Ed Armbrister, Fred Lynn, Tom Poquette, Terry Whitfield)	15.00	7.50	4.50
623	Rookie Infielders (Phil Garner, Keith Hernandez, Bob Sheldon, Tom Veryzer)	20.00	10.00	6.00
624	Rookie Pitchers (Doug Konieczny, Gary Lavelle, Jim Otten, Eddie Solomon)	.40	.20	.12
625	Boog Powell	2.00	1.00	.60
626	Larry Haney	.40	.20	.12
627	Tom Walker	.40	.20	.12
628	Ron LeFlore	1.25	.60	.40
629	Joe Hoerner	.40	.20	.12
630	Greg Luzinski	2.00	1.00	.60
631	Lee Lacy	.40	.20	.12
632	Morris Nettles	.40	.20	.12
633	Paul Casanova	.40	.20	.12
634	Cy Acosta	.40	.20	.12
635	Chuck Dobson	.40	.20	.12
636	Charlie Moore	.40	.20	.12
637	Ted Martinez	.40	.20	.12
638	Cubs Team (Jim Marshall)	1.25	.60	.40
639	Steve Kline	.40	.20	.12
640	Harmon Killebrew	6.00	3.00	1.75
641	Jim Northrup	.40	.20	.12
642	Mike Phillips	.40	.20	.12
643	Brent Strom	.40	.20	.12
644	Bill Fahey	.40	.20	.12
645	Danny Cater	.40	.20	.12
646	Checklist 529-660	2.25	1.25	.70
647	Claudell Washington	2.00	1.00	.60
648	Dave Pagan	.40	.20	.12
649	Jack Heidemann	.40	.20	.12
650	Dave May	.40	.20	.12
651	John Morlan	.40	.20	.12
652	Lindy McDaniel	.40	.20	.12
653	Lee Richards	.40	.20	.12
654	Jerry Terrell	.40	.20	.12
655	Rico Carty	.60	.30	.20
656	Bill Plummer	.40	.20	.12
657	Bob Oliver	.40	.20	.12
658	Vic Harris	.40	.20	.12
659	Bob Apodaca	.40	.20	.12
660	Hank Aaron	35.00	17.50	10.50

1976 Topps

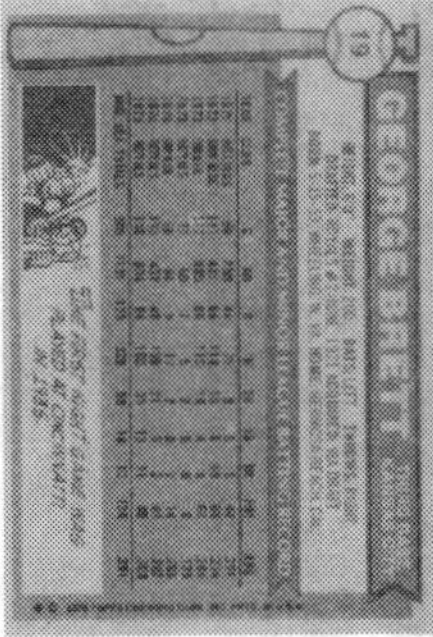

These 2-1/2" by 3-1/2" cards begin a design trend for Topps. The focus was more on the photo quality than in past years with a corresponding trend toward simplicity in the borders. The front of the cards has the player's name and team in two strips while his position is in the lower left corner under a drawing of a player representing that position. The backs have a bat and ball with the card number on the left; statistics and personal information and career highlights on the right. The 660-card set features a number of specialty sets including record-setting performances, statistical leaders, playoff and World Series highlights, the Sporting News All-Time All-Stars and father and son combinations.

		NR MT	EX	VG
Complete Set (660):		450.00	225.00	135.00
Commmon Player:		.25	.13	.08
1	Record Breaker (Hank Aaron)	15.00	7.50	4.50
2	Record Breaker (Bobby Bonds)	.40	.20	.12
3	Record Breaker (Mickey Lolich)	.35	.20	.11
4	Record Breaker (Dave Lopes)	.25	.13	.08
5	Record Breaker (Tom Seaver)	4.00	2.00	1.25
6	Record Breaker (Rennie Stennett)	.25	.13	.08
7	Jim Umbarger	.25	.13	.08
8	Tito Fuentes	.25	.13	.08
9	Paul Lindblad	.25	.13	.08
10	Lou Brock	4.00	2.00	1.25
11	Jim Hughes	.25	.13	.08
12	Richie Zisk	.25	.13	.08
13	Johnny Wockenfuss	.25	.13	.08
14	Gene Garber	.25	.13	.08
15	George Scott	.25	.13	.08
16	Bob Apodaca	.25	.13	.08
17	Yankees Team (Billy Martin)	1.25	.60	.40
18	Dale Murray	.25	.13	.08
19	George Brett	60.00	30.00	18.00
20	Bob Watson	.25	.13	.08
21	Dave LaRoche	.25	.13	.08

		NR MT	EX	VG
22	Bill Russell	.25	.13	.08
23	Brian Downing	.25	.13	.08
24	Cesar Geronimo	.25	.13	.08
25	Mike Torrez	.25	.13	.08
26	Andy Thornton	.25	.13	.08
27	Ed Figueroa	.25	.13	.08
28	Dusty Baker	.25	.13	.08
29	Rick Burleson	.25	.13	.08
30	*John Montefusco*	.25	.13	.08
31	Len Randle	.25	.13	.08
32	Danny Frisella	.25	.13	.08
33	Bill North	.25	.13	.08
34	Mike Garman	.25	.13	.08
35	Tony Oliva	.40	.20	.12
36	Frank Taveras	.25	.13	.08
37	John Hiller	.25	.13	.08
38	Garry Maddox	.25	.13	.08
39	Pete Broberg	.25	.13	.08
40	Dave Kingman	.25	.13	.08
41	*Tippy Martinez*	.25	.13	.08
42	Barry Foote	.25	.13	.08
43	Paul Splittorff	.25	.13	.08
44	Doug Rader	.25	.13	.08
45	Boog Powell	.25	.13	.08
46	Dodgers Team (Walter Alston)	1.00	.50	.30
47	Jesse Jefferson	.25	.13	.08
48	Dave Concepcion	.40	.20	.12
49	Dave Duncan	.25	.13	.08
50	Fred Lynn	2.00	1.00	.60
51	Ray Burris	.25	.13	.08
52	Dave Chalk	.25	.13	.08
53	Mike Beard	.25	.13	.08
54	Dave Rader	.25	.13	.08
55	Gaylord Perry	3.00	1.50	.90
56	Bob Tolan	.25	.13	.08
57	Phil Garner	.25	.13	.08
58	Ron Reed	.25	.13	.08
59	Larry Hisle	.25	.13	.08
60	Jerry Reuss	.25	.13	.08
61	Ron LeFlore	.25	.13	.08
62	Johnny Oates	.25	.13	.08
63	Bobby Darwin	.25	.13	.08
64	Jerry Koosman	.25	.13	.08
65	Chris Chambliss	.25	.13	.08
66	Father & Son (Buddy Bell, Gus Bell)	.25	.13	.08
67	Father & Son (Bob Boone, Ray Boone)	.40	.20	.12
68	Father & Son (Joe Coleman, Joe Coleman, Jr.)	.25	.13	.08
69	Father & Son (Jim Hegan, Mike Hegan)	.25	.13	.08
70	Father & Son (Roy Smalley, Roy Smalley, Jr.)	.25	.13	.08
71	Steve Rogers	.25	.13	.08
72	Hal McRae	.40	.20	.12
73	Orioles Team (Earl Weaver)	1.00	.50	.30
74	Oscar Gamble	.25	.13	.08
75	Larry Dierker	.25	.13	.08
76	Willie Crawford	.25	.13	.08
77	Pedro Borbon	.25	.13	.08
78	Cecil Cooper	.50	.25	.15
79	Jerry Morales	.25	.13	.08
80	Jim Kaat	.90	.45	.25
81	Darrell Evans	.40	.20	.12
82	Von Joshua	.25	.13	.08
83	Jim Spencer	.25	.13	.08
84	Brent Strom	.25	.13	.08
85	Mickey Rivers	.25	.13	.08
86	Mike Tyson	.25	.13	.08
87	Tom Burgmeier	.25	.13	.08
88	Duffy Dyer	.25	.13	.08
89	Vern Ruhle	.25	.13	.08
90	Sal Bando	.25	.13	.08
91	Tom Hutton	.25	.13	.08
92	Eduardo Rodriguez	.25	.13	.08
93	Mike Phillips	.25	.13	.08
94	Jim Dwyer	.25	.13	.08
95	Brooks Robinson	5.00	2.50	1.50
96	Doug Bird	.25	.13	.08
97	Wilbur Howard	.25	.13	.08
98	*Dennis Eckersley*	50.00	25.00	15.00
99	Lee Lacy	.25	.13	.08
100	Catfish Hunter	3.00	1.50	.90
101	Pete LaCock	.25	.13	.08
102	Jim Willoughby	.25	.13	.08
103	Biff Pocoroba	.25	.13	.08
104	Reds Team (Sparky Anderson)	1.00	.50	.30
105	Gary Lavelle	.25	.13	.08
106	Tom Grieve	.25	.13	.08
107	Dave Roberts	.25	.13	.08

		NR MT	EX	VG
108	Don Kirkwood	.25	.13	.08
109	Larry Lintz	.25	.13	.08
110	Carlos May	.25	.13	.08
111	Danny Thompson	.25	.13	.08
112	*Kent Tekulve*	.75	.40	.25
113	Gary Sutherland	.25	.13	.08
114	Jay Johnstone	.25	.13	.08
115	Ken Holtzman	.25	.13	.08
116	Charlie Moore	.25	.13	.08
117	Mike Jorgensen	.25	.13	.08
118	Red Sox Team (Darrell Johnson)	.90	.45	.25
119	Checklist 1-132	1.25	.60	.40
120	Rusty Staub	.35	.20	.11
121	Tony Solaita	.25	.13	.08
122	Mike Cosgrove	.25	.13	.08
123	Walt Williams	.25	.13	.08
124	Doug Rau	.25	.13	.08
125	Don Baylor	.40	.20	.12
126	Tom Dettore	.25	.13	.08
127	Larvell Blanks	.25	.13	.08
128	Ken Griffey	.40	.20	.12
129	Andy Etchebarren	.25	.13	.08
130	Luis Tiant	.40	.20	.12
131	Bill Stein	.25	.13	.08
132	Don Hood	.25	.13	.08
133	Gary Matthews	.25	.13	.08
134	Mike Ivie	.25	.13	.08
135	Bake McBride	.25	.13	.08
136	Dave Goltz	.25	.13	.08
137	Bill Robinson	.25	.13	.08
138	Lerrin LaGrow	.25	.13	.08
139	Gorman Thomas	.25	.13	.08
140	Vida Blue	.40	.20	.12
141	*Larry Parrish*	.80	.40	.25
142	Dick Drago	.25	.13	.08
143	Jerry Grote	.25	.13	.08
144	Al Fitzmorris	.25	.13	.08
145	Larry Bowa	.35	.20	.11
146	George Medich	.25	.13	.08
147	Astros Team (Bill Virdon)	.80	.40	.25
148	Stan Thomas	.25	.13	.08
149	Tommy Davis	.25	.13	.08
150	Steve Garvey	4.00	2.00	1.25
151	Bill Bonham	.25	.13	.08
152	Leroy Stanton	.25	.13	.08
153	Buzz Capra	.25	.13	.08
154	Bucky Dent	.25	.13	.08
155	Jack Billingham	.25	.13	.08
156	Rico Carty	.25	.13	.08
157	Mike Caldwell	.25	.13	.08
158	Ken Reitz	.25	.13	.08
159	Jerry Terrell	.25	.13	.08
160	Dave Winfield	50.00	25.00	15.00
161	Bruce Kison	.25	.13	.08
162	Jack Pierce	.25	.13	.08
163	Jim Slaton	.25	.13	.08
164	Pepe Mangual	.25	.13	.08
165	Gene Tenace	.25	.13	.08
166	Skip Lockwood	.25	.13	.08
167	Freddie Patek	.25	.13	.08
168	Tom Hilgendorf	.25	.13	.08
169	Graig Nettles	.50	.25	.15
170	Rick Wise	.25	.13	.08
171	Greg Gross	.25	.13	.08
172	Rangers Team (Frank Lucchesi)	.80	.40	.25
173	Steve Swisher	.25	.13	.08
174	Charlie Hough	.25	.13	.08
175	Ken Singleton	.25	.13	.08
176	Dick Lange	.25	.13	.08
177	Marty Perez	.25	.13	.08
178	Tom Buskey	.25	.13	.08
179	George Foster	.50	.25	.15
180	Rich Gossage	.50	.25	.15
181	Willie Montanez	.25	.13	.08
182	Harry Rasmussen	.25	.13	.08
183	Steve Braun	.25	.13	.08
184	Bill Greif	.25	.13	.08
185	Dave Parker	5.00	2.50	1.50
186	Tom Walker	.25	.13	.08
187	Pedro Garcia	.25	.13	.08
188	Fred Scherman	.25	.13	.08
189	Claudell Washington	.25	.13	.08
190	Jon Matlack	.25	.13	.08
191	N.L. Batting Leaders (Bill Madlock, Manny Sanguillen, Ted Simmons)	.60	.30	.20
192	A.L. Batting Leaders (Rod Carew, Fred Lynn, Thurman Munson)	2.00	1.00	.60
193	N.L. Home Run Leaders (Dave Kingman, Greg Luzinski, Mike Schmidt)	2.00	1.00	.60
194	A.L. Home Run Leaders (Reggie Jackson, John Mayberry, George Scott)	2.00	1.00	.60

		NR MT	EX	VG
195	N.L. RBI Leaders (Johnny Bench, Greg Luzinski, Tony Perez)	2.00	1.00	.60
196	A.L. RBI Leaders (Fred Lynn, John Mayberry, George Scott)	.60	.30	.20
197	N.L. Stolen Base Leaders (Lou Brock, Dave Lopes, Joe Morgan)	.90	.45	.25
198	A.L. Stolen Base Leaders (Amos Otis, Mickey Rivers, Claudell Washington)	.40	.20	.12
199	N.L. Victory Leaders (Randy Jones, Andy Messersmith, Tom Seaver)	.80	.40	.25
200	A.L. Victory Leaders (Vida Blue, Catfish Hunter, Jim Palmer)	.90	.45	.25
201	N.L. ERA Leaders (Randy Jones, Andy Messersmith, Tom Seaver)	.80	.40	.25
202	A.L. ERA Leaders (Dennis Eckersley, Catfish Hunter, Jim Palmer)	.90	.45	.25
203	N.L. Strikeout Leaders (Andy Messersmith, John Montefusco, Tom Seaver)	.80	.40	.25
204	A.L. Strikeout Leaders (Bert Blyleven, Gaylord Perry, Frank Tanana)	.70	.35	.20
205	Major League Leading Firemen (Rich Gossage, Al Hrabosky)	.40	.20	.12
206	Manny Trillo	.25	.13	.08
207	Andy Hassler	.25	.13	.08
208	Mike Lum	.25	.13	.08
209	Alan Ashby	.25	.13	.08
210	Lee May	.25	.13	.08
211	Clay Carroll	.25	.13	.08
212	Pat Kelly	.25	.13	.08
213	Dave Heaverlo	.25	.13	.08
214	Eric Soderholm	.25	.13	.08
215	Reggie Smith	.25	.13	.08
216	Expos Team (Karl Kuehl)	.80	.40	.25
217	Dave Freisleben	.25	.13	.08
218	John Knox	.25	.13	.08
219	Tom Murphy	.25	.13	.08
220	Manny Sanguillen	.25	.13	.08
221	Jim Todd	.25	.13	.08
222	Wayne Garrett	.25	.13	.08
223	Ollie Brown	.25	.13	.08
224	Jim York	.25	.13	.08
225	Roy White	.25	.13	.08
226	Jim Sundberg	.25	.13	.08
227	Oscar Zamora	.25	.13	.08
228	John Hale	.25	.13	.08
229	*Jerry Remy*	.25	.13	.08
230	Carl Yastrzemski	8.00	4.00	2.50
231	Tom House	.25	.13	.08
232	Frank Duffy	.25	.13	.08
233	Grant Jackson	.25	.13	.08
234	Mike Sadek	.25	.13	.08
235	Bert Blyleven	.50	.25	.15
236	Royals Team (Whitey Herzog)	.80	.40	.25
237	Dave Hamilton	.25	.13	.08
238	Larry Biittner	.25	.13	.08
239	John Curtis	.25	.13	.08
240	Pete Rose	12.00	6.00	3.50
241	Hector Torres	.25	.13	.08
242	Dan Meyer	.25	.13	.08
243	Jim Rooker	.25	.13	.08
244	Bill Sharp	.25	.13	.08
245	Felix Millan	.25	.13	.08
246	Cesar Tovar	.25	.13	.08
247	Terry Harmon	.25	.13	.08
248	Dick Tidrow	.25	.13	.08
249	Cliff Johnson	.25	.13	.08
250	Fergie Jenkins	2.00	1.00	.60
251	Rick Monday	.25	.13	.08
252	Tim Nordbrook	.25	.13	.08
253	Bill Buckner	.25	.13	.08
254	Rudy Meoli	.25	.13	.08
255	Fritz Peterson	.25	.13	.08
256	Rowland Office	.25	.13	.08
257	Ross Grimsley	.25	.13	.08
258	Nyls Nyman	.25	.13	.08
259	Darrel Chaney	.25	.13	.08
260	Steve Busby	.25	.13	.08
261	Gary Thomasson	.25	.13	.08
262	Checklist 133-264	1.50	.70	.45
263	*Lyman Bostock*	.80	.40	.25
264	Steve Renko	.25	.13	.08
265	Willie Davis	.25	.13	.08
266	Alan Foster	.25	.13	.08
267	Aurelio Rodriguez	.25	.13	.08
268	Del Unser	.25	.13	.08
269	Rick Austin	.25	.13	.08
270	Willie Stargell	3.00	1.50	.90
271	Jim Lonborg	.25	.13	.08
272	Rick Dempsey	.25	.13	.08
273	Joe Niekro	.25	.13	.08

		NR MT	EX	VG
274	Tommy Harper	.25	.13	.08
275	*Rick Manning*	.40	.20	.12
276	Mickey Scott	.25	.13	.08
277	Cubs Team (Jim Marshall)	.80	.40	.25
278	Bernie Carbo	.25	.13	.08
279	Roy Howell	.25	.13	.08
280	Burt Hooton	.25	.13	.08
281	Dave May	.25	.13	.08
282	Dan Osborn	.25	.13	.08
283	Merv Rettenmund	.25	.13	.08
284	Steve Ontiveros	.25	.13	.08
285	Mike Cuellar	.25	.13	.08
286	Jim Wohlford	.25	.13	.08
287	Pete Mackanin	.25	.13	.08
288	Bill Campbell	.25	.13	.08
289	Enzo Hernandez	.25	.13	.08
290	Ted Simmons	.25	.13	.08
291	Ken Sanders	.25	.13	.08
292	Leon Roberts	.25	.13	.08
293	Bill Castro	.25	.13	.08
294	Ed Kirkpatrick	.25	.13	.08
295	Dave Cash	.25	.13	.08
296	Pat Dobson	.25	.13	.08
297	Roger Metzger	.25	.13	.08
298	Dick Bosman	.25	.13	.08
299	Champ Summers	.25	.13	.08
300	Johnny Bench	10.00	5.00	3.00
301	Jackie Brown	.25	.13	.08
302	Rick Miller	.25	.13	.08
303	Steve Foucault	.25	.13	.08
304	Angels Team (Dick Williams)	.80	.40	.25
305	Andy Messersmith	.25	.13	.08
306	Rod Gilbreath	.25	.13	.08
307	Al Bumbry	.25	.13	.08
308	Jim Barr	.25	.13	.08
309	Bill Melton	.25	.13	.08
310	Randy Jones	.25	.13	.08
311	Cookie Rojas	.25	.13	.08
312	Don Carrithers	.25	.13	.08
313	*Dan Ford*	.25	.13	.08
314	Ed Kranepool	.25	.13	.08
315	Al Hrabosky	.25	.13	.08
316	Robin Yount	60.00	30.00	18.00
317	*John Candelaria*	2.00	1.00	.60
318	Bob Boone	.25	.13	.08
319	Larry Gura	.25	.13	.08
320	Willie Horton	.25	.13	.08
321	Jose Cruz	.25	.13	.08
322	Glenn Abbott	.25	.13	.08
323	Rob Sperring	.25	.13	.08
324	Jim Bibby	.25	.13	.08
325	Tony Perez	1.50	.70	.45
326	Dick Pole	.25	.13	.08
327	Dave Moates	.25	.13	.08
328	Carl Morton	.25	.13	.08
329	Joe Ferguson	.25	.13	.08
330	Nolan Ryan	70.00	35.00	21.00
331	Padres Team (John McNamara)	.80	.40	.25
332	Charlie Williams	.25	.13	.08
333	Bob Coluccio	.25	.13	.08
334	Dennis Leonard	.25	.13	.08
335	Bob Grich	.25	.13	.08
336	Vic Albury	.25	.13	.08
337	Bud Harrelson	.25	.13	.08
338	Bob Bailey	.25	.13	.08
339	John Denny	.25	.13	.08
340	Jim Rice	6.00	3.00	1.75
341	Lou Gehrig (All Time 1B)	5.00	2.50	1.50
342	Rogers Hornsby (All Time 2B)	1.25	.60	.40
343	Pie Traynor (All Time 3B)	.80	.40	.25
344	Honus Wagner (All Time SS)	1.25	.60	.40
345	Babe Ruth (All Time OF)	10.00	5.00	3.00
346	Ty Cobb (All Time OF)	5.00	2.50	1.50
347	Ted Williams (All Time OF)	5.00	2.50	1.50
348	Mickey Cochrane (All Time C)	.80	.40	.25
349	Walter Johnson (All Time RHP)	1.25	.60	.40
350	Lefty Grove (All Time LHP)	1.00	.50	.30
351	Randy Hundley	.25	.13	.08
352	Dave Giusti	.25	.13	.08
353	*Sixto Lezcano*	.25	.13	.08
354	Ron Blomberg	.25	.13	.08
355	Steve Carlton	7.00	3.50	2.00
356	Ted Martinez	.25	.13	.08
357	Ken Forsch	.25	.13	.08
358	Buddy Bell	.25	.13	.08
359	Rick Reuschel	.30	.15	.09
360	Jeff Burroughs	.25	.13	.08
361	Tigers Team (Ralph Houk)	1.00	.50	.30
362	Will McEnaney	.25	.13	.08
363	*Dave Collins*	.40	.20	.12
364	Elias Sosa	.25	.13	.08

		NR MT	EX	VG
365	Carlton Fisk	9.00	4.50	2.75
366	Bobby Valentine	.25	.13	.08
367	Bruce Miller	.25	.13	.08
368	Wilbur Wood	.25	.13	.08
369	Frank White	.25	.13	.08
370	Ron Cey	.25	.13	.08
371	Ellie Hendricks	.25	.13	.08
372	Rick Baldwin	.25	.13	.08
373	Johnny Briggs	.25	.13	.08
374	Dan Warthen	.25	.13	.08
375	Ron Fairly	.25	.13	.08
376	Rich Hebner	.25	.13	.08
377	Mike Hegan	.25	.13	.08
378	Steve Stone	.25	.13	.08
379	Ken Boswell	.25	.13	.08
380	Bobby Bonds	.25	.13	.08
381	Denny Doyle	.25	.13	.08
382	Matt Alexander	.25	.13	.08
383	John Ellis	.25	.13	.08
384	Phillies Team (Danny Ozark)	.80	.40	.25
385	Mickey Lolich	.40	.20	.12
386	Ed Goodson	.25	.13	.08
387	Mike Miley	.25	.13	.08
388	Stan Perzanowski	.25	.13	.08
389	Glenn Adams	.25	.13	.08
390	Don Gullett	.25	.13	.08
391	Jerry Hairston	.25	.13	.08
392	Checklist 265-396	1.50	.70	.45
393	Paul Mitchell	.25	.13	.08
394	Fran Healy	.25	.13	.08
395	Jim Wynn	.25	.13	.08
396	Bill Lee	.25	.13	.08
397	Tim Foli	.25	.13	.08
398	Dave Tomlin	.25	.13	.08
399	Luis Melendez	.25	.13	.08
400	Rod Carew	8.00	4.00	2.50
401	Ken Brett	.25	.13	.08
402	Don Money	.25	.13	.08
403	Geoff Zahn	.25	.13	.08
404	Enos Cabell	.25	.13	.08
405	Rollie Fingers	5.00	2.50	1.50
406	Ed Herrmann	.25	.13	.08
407	Tom Underwood	.25	.13	.08
408	Charlie Spikes	.25	.13	.08
409	Dave Lemanczyk	.25	.13	.08
410	Ralph Garr	.25	.13	.08
411	Bill Singer	.25	.13	.08
412	Toby Harrah	.25	.13	.08
413	Pete Varney	.25	.13	.08
414	Wayne Garland	.25	.13	.08
415	Vada Pinson	.40	.20	.12
416	Tommy John	1.00	.50	.30
417	Gene Clines	.25	.13	.08
418	Jose Morales	.25	.13	.08
419	Reggie Cleveland	.25	.13	.08
420	Joe Morgan	6.00	3.00	1.75
421	A's Team	.80	.40	.25
422	Johnny Grubb	.25	.13	.08
423	Ed Halicki	.25	.13	.08
424	Phil Roof	.25	.13	.08
425	Rennie Stennett	.25	.13	.08
426	Bob Forsch	.25	.13	.08
427	Kurt Bevacqua	.25	.13	.08
428	Jim Crawford	.25	.13	.08
429	Fred Stanley	.25	.13	.08
430	Jose Cardenal	.25	.13	.08
431	Dick Ruthven	.25	.13	.08
432	Tom Veryzer	.25	.13	.08
433	Rick Waits	.25	.13	.08
434	Morris Nettles	.25	.13	.08
435	Phil Niekro	1.50	.70	.45
436	Bill Fahey	.25	.13	.08
437	Terry Forster	.25	.13	.08
438	Doug DeCinces	.25	.13	.08
439	Rick Rhoden	.25	.13	.08
440	John Mayberry	.25	.13	.08
441	Gary Carter	10.00	5.00	3.00
442	Hank Webb	.25	.13	.08
443	Giants Team	.80	.40	.25
444	Gary Nolan	.25	.13	.08
445	Rico Petrocelli	.25	.13	.08
446	Larry Haney	.25	.13	.08
447	Gene Locklear	.25	.13	.08
448	Tom Johnson	.25	.13	.08
449	Bob Robertson	.25	.13	.08
450	Jim Palmer	6.00	3.00	1.75
451	Buddy Bradford	.25	.13	.08
452	Tom Hausman	.25	.13	.08
453	Lou Piniella	.25	.13	.08
454	Tom Griffin	.25	.13	.08
455	Dick Allen	.40	.20	.12

		NR MT	EX	VG
456	Joe Coleman	.25	.13	.08
457	Ed Crosby	.25	.13	.08
458	Earl Williams	.25	.13	.08
459	Jim Brewer	.25	.13	.08
460	Cesar Cedeno	.25	.13	.08
461	NL & AL Championships	.80	.40	.25
462	1975 World Series	.80	.40	.25
463	Steve Hargan	.25	.13	.08
464	Ken Henderson	.25	.13	.08
465	Mike Marshall	.25	.13	.08
466	Bob Stinson	.25	.13	.08
467	Woodie Fryman	.25	.13	.08
468	Jesus Alou	.25	.13	.08
469	Rawly Eastwick	.25	.13	.08
470	Bobby Murcer	.25	.13	.08
471	Jim Burton	.25	.13	.08
472	Bob Davis	.25	.13	.08
473	Paul Blair	.25	.13	.08
474	Ray Corbin	.25	.13	.08
475	Joe Rudi	.25	.13	.08
476	Bob Moose	.25	.13	.08
477	Indians Team (Frank Robinson)	.80	.40	.25
478	Lynn McGlothen	.25	.13	.08
479	Bobby Mitchell	.25	.13	.08
480	Mike Schmidt	30.00	15.00	9.00
481	Rudy May	.25	.13	.08
482	Tim Hosley	.25	.13	.08
483	Mickey Stanley	.25	.13	.08
484	Eric Raich	.25	.13	.08
485	Mike Hargrove	.25	.13	.08
486	Bruce Dal Canton	.25	.13	.08
487	Leron Lee	.25	.13	.08
488	Claude Osteen	.25	.13	.08
489	Skip Jutze	.25	.13	.08
490	Frank Tanana	.25	.13	.08
491	Terry Crowley	.25	.13	.08
492	Marty Pattin	.25	.13	.08
493	Derrel Thomas	.25	.13	.08
494	Craig Swan	.25	.13	.08
495	Nate Colbert	.25	.13	.08
496	Juan Beniquez	.25	.13	.08
497	Joe McIntosh	.25	.13	.08
498	Glenn Borgmann	.25	.13	.08
499	Mario Guerrero	.25	.13	.08
500	Reggie Jackson	30.00	15.00	9.00
501	Billy Champion	.25	.13	.08
502	Tim McCarver	.40	.20	.12
503	Elliott Maddox	.25	.13	.08
504	Pirates Team (Danny Murtaugh)	.80	.40	.25
505	Mark Belanger	.25	.13	.08
506	George Mitterwald	.25	.13	.08
507	Ray Bare	.25	.13	.08
508	*Duane Kuiper*	.25	.13	.08
509	Bill Hands	.25	.13	.08
510	Amos Otis	.25	.13	.08
511	Jamie Easterly	.25	.13	.08
512	Ellie Rodriguez	.25	.13	.08
513	Bart Johnson	.25	.13	.08
514	Dan Driessen	.25	.13	.08
515	Steve Yeager	.25	.13	.08
516	Wayne Granger	.25	.13	.08
517	John Milner	.25	.13	.08
518	*Doug Flynn*	.25	.13	.08
519	Steve Brye	.25	.13	.08
520	Willie McCovey	3.00	1.50	.90
521	Jim Colborn	.25	.13	.08
522	Ted Sizemore	.25	.13	.08
523	Bob Montgomery	.25	.13	.08
524	Pete Falcone	.25	.13	.08
525	Billy Williams	2.25	1.25	.70
526	Checklist 397-528	1.50	.70	.45
527	Mike Anderson	.25	.13	.08
528	Dock Ellis	.25	.13	.08
529	Deron Johnson	.25	.13	.08
530	Don Sutton	1.50	.70	.45
531	Mets Team (Joe Frazier)	.90	.45	.25
532	Milt May	.25	.13	.08
533	Lee Richard	.25	.13	.08
534	Stan Bahnsen	.25	.13	.08
535	Dave Nelson	.25	.13	.08
536	Mike Thompson	.25	.13	.08
537	Tony Muser	.25	.13	.08
538	Pat Darcy	.25	.13	.08
539	John Balaz	.25	.13	.08
540	Bill Freehan	.25	.13	.08
541	Steve Mingori	.25	.13	.08
542	Keith Hernandez	3.00	1.50	.90
543	Wayne Twitchell	.25	.13	.08
544	Pepe Frias	.25	.13	.08
545	Sparky Lyle	.25	.13	.08
546	Dave Rosello	.25	.13	.08

		NR MT	EX	VG
547	Roric Harrison	.25	.13	.08
548	Manny Mota	.25	.13	.08
549	Randy Tate	.25	.13	.08
550	Hank Aaron	25.00	12.50	7.50
551	Jerry DaVanon	.25	.13	.08
552	Terry Humphrey	.25	.13	.08
553	Randy Moffitt	.25	.13	.08
554	Ray Fosse	.25	.13	.08
555	Dyar Miller	.25	.13	.08
556	Twins Team (Gene Mauch)	.80	.40	.25
557	Dan Spillner	.25	.13	.08
558	Cito Gaston	.40	.20	.12
559	Clyde Wright	.25	.13	.08
560	Jorge Orta	.25	.13	.08
561	Tom Carroll	.25	.13	.08
562	Adrian Garrett	.25	.13	.08
563	Larry Demery	.25	.13	.08
564	Bubble Gum Blowing Champ (Kurt Bevacqua)	.30	.15	.09
565	Tug McGraw	.25	.13	.08
566	Ken McMullen	.25	.13	.08
567	George Stone	.25	.13	.08
568	Rob Andrews	.25	.13	.08
569	Nelson Briles	.25	.13	.08
570	George Hendrick	.25	.13	.08
571	Don DeMola	.25	.13	.08
572	Rich Coggins	.25	.13	.08
573	Bill Travers	.25	.13	.08
574	Don Kessinger	.25	.13	.08
575	Dwight Evans	2.00	1.00	.60
576	Maximino Leon	.25	.13	.08
577	Marc Hill	.25	.13	.08
578	Ted Kubiak	.25	.13	.08
579	Clay Kirby	.25	.13	.08
580	Bert Campaneris	.25	.13	.08
581	Cardinals Team (Red Schoendienst)	.80	.40	.25
582	Mike Kekich	.25	.13	.08
583	Tommy Helms	.25	.13	.08
584	Stan Wall	.25	.13	.08
585	Joe Torre	.25	.13	.08
586	Ron Schueler	.25	.13	.08
587	Leo Cardenas	.25	.13	.08
588	Kevin Kobel	.25	.13	.08
589	Rookie Pitchers (Santo Alcala, *Mike Flanagan,* Joe Pactwa, Pablo Torrealba)	1.00	.50	.30
590	Rookie Outfielders (Henry Cruz, *Chet Lemon, Ellis Valentine,* Terry Whitfield)	.60	.30	.20
591	Rookie Pitchers (Steve Grilli, Craig Mitchell, Jose Sosa, George Throop)	.25	.13	.08
592	Rookie Infielders (Dave McKay, *Willie Randolph, Jerry Royster,* Roy Staiger)	6.00	3.00	1.75
593	Rookie Pitchers (Larry Anderson, Ken Crosby, Mark Littell, *Butch Metzger*)	.25	.13	.08
594	Rookie Catchers & Outfielders (Andy Merchant, Ed Ott, Royle Stillman, Jerry White)	.25	.13	.08
595	Rookie Pitchers (Steve Barr, Art DeFilippis, Randy Lerch, Sid Monge)	.25	.13	.08
596	Rookie Infielders (Lamar Johnson, *Johnny LeMaster,* Jerry Manuel, *Craig Reynolds*)	.25	.13	.08
597	Rookie Pitchers *(Don Aase,* Jack Kucek, Frank LaCorte, Mike Pazik)	.25	.13	.08
598	Rookie Outfielders (Hector Cruz, *Jamie Quirk,* Jerry Turner, Joe Wallis)	.25	.13	.08
599	Rookie Pitchers (Rob Dressler, *Ron Guidry, Bob McClure,* Pat Zachry)	6.00	3.00	1.75
600	Tom Seaver	15.00	7.50	4.50
601	Ken Rudolph	.25	.13	.08
602	Doug Konieczny	.25	.13	.08
603	Jim Holt	.25	.13	.08
604	Joe Lovitto	.25	.13	.08
605	Al Downing	.25	.13	.08
606	Brewers Team (Alex Grammas)	.80	.40	.25
607	Rich Hinton	.25	.13	.08
608	Vic Correll	.25	.13	.08
609	Fred Norman	.25	.13	.08
610	Greg Luzinski	.40	.20	.12
611	Rich Folkers	.25	.13	.08
612	Joe Lahoud	.25	.13	.08
613	Tim Johnson	.25	.13	.08
614	Fernando Arroyo	.25	.13	.08
615	Mike Cubbage	.25	.13	.08
616	Buck Martinez	.25	.13	.08
617	Darold Knowles	.25	.13	.08
618	Jack Brohamer	.25	.13	.08
619	Bill Butler	.25	.13	.08
620	Al Oliver	.40	.20	.12

		NR MT	EX	VG
621	Tom Hall	.25	.13	.08
622	Rick Auerbach	.25	.13	.08
623	Bob Allietta	.25	.13	.08
624	Tony Taylor	.25	.13	.08
625	J.R. Richard	.25	.13	.08
626	Bob Sheldon	.25	.13	.08
627	Bill Plummer	.25	.13	.08
628	John D'Acquisto	.25	.13	.08
629	Sandy Alomar	.25	.13	.08
630	Chris Speier	.25	.13	.08
631	Braves Team (Dave Bristol)	.80	.40	.25
632	Rogelio Moret	.25	.13	.08
633	*John Stearns*	.25	.13	.08
634	Larry Christenson	.25	.13	.08
635	Jim Fregosi	.25	.13	.08
636	Joe Decker	.25	.13	.08
637	Bruce Bochte	.25	.13	.08
638	Doyle Alexander	.25	.13	.08
639	Fred Kendall	.25	.13	.08
640	Bill Madlock	.50	.25	.15
641	Tom Paciorek	.25	.13	.08
642	Dennis Blair	.25	.13	.08
643	Checklist 529-660	1.50	.70	.45
644	Tom Bradley	.25	.13	.08
645	Darrell Porter	.25	.13	.08
646	John Lowenstein	.25	.13	.08
648	Al Cowens	.25	.13	.08
649	Dave Roberts	.25	.13	.08
650	Thurman Munson	6.00	3.00	1.75
651	John Odom	.25	.13	.08
652	Ed Armbrister	.25	.13	.08
653	*Mike Norris*	.25	.13	.08
654	Doug Griffin	.25	.13	.08
655	Mike Vail	.25	.13	.08
656	White Sox Team (Chuck Tanner)	.80	.40	.25
657	*Roy Smalley*	.25	.13	.08
658	Jerry Johnson	.25	.13	.08
659	Ben Oglivie	.25	.13	.08
660	Dave Lopes	.25	.13	.08

1976 Topps Traded

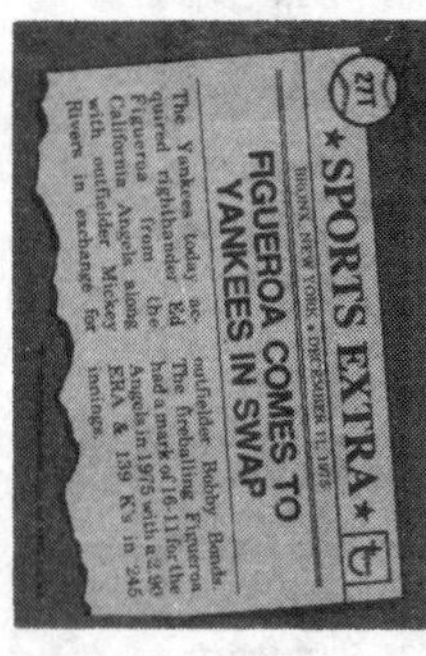

Similar to the Topps Traded set of 1974, the 2-1/2" by 3-1/2" cards feature photos of players traded after the printing deadline. The style of the cards is essentially the same as the regular issue but with a large "Sports Extra" headline announcing the trade and its date. The backs continue in newspaper style to detail the specifics of the trade. There are 43 player cards and one checklist in the set. Numbers remain the same as the player's regular card, with the addition of a "T" suffix.

		NR MT	EX	VG
Complete Set (44):		12.00	6.00	3.50
Common Player:		.25	.13	.08
27T	Ed Figueroa	.25	.13	.08
28T	Dusty Baker	1.25	.60	.40
44T	Doug Rader	.25	.13	.08
58T	Ron Reed	.25	.13	.08
74T	Oscar Gamble	.25	.13	.08
80T	Jim Kaat	1.00	.50	.30
83T	Jim Spencer	.25	.13	.08
85T	Mickey Rivers	.25	.13	.08
99T	Lee Lacy	.25	.13	.08
120T	Rusty Staub	.40	.20	.12

		NR MT	EX	VG
127T	Larvell Blanks	.25	.13	.08
146T	George Medich	.25	.13	.08
158T	Ken Reitz	.25	.13	.08
208T	Mike Lum	.25	.13	.08
211T	Clay Carroll	.25	.13	.08
231T	Tom House	.25	.13	.08
250T	Fergie Jenkins	3.00	1.50	.90
259T	Darrel Chaney	.25	.13	.08
292T	Leon Roberts	.25	.13	.08
296T	Pat Dobson	.25	.13	.08
309T	Bill Melton	.25	.13	.08
338T	Bob Bailey	.25	.13	.08
380T	Bobby Bonds	.90	.45	.25
383T	John Ellis	.25	.13	.08
385T	Mickey Lolich	.90	.45	.25
401T	Ken Brett	.25	.13	.08
410T	Ralph Garr	.25	.13	.08
411T	Bill Singer	.25	.13	.08
428T	Jim Crawford	.25	.13	.08
434T	Morris Nettles	.25	.13	.08
464T	Ken Henderson	.25	.13	.08
497T	Joe McIntosh	.25	.13	.08
524T	Pete Falcone	.25	.13	.08
527T	Mike Anderson	.25	.13	.08
528T	Dock Ellis	.25	.13	.08
532T	Milt May	.25	.13	.08
554T	Ray Fosse	.25	.13	.08
579T	Clay Kirby	.25	.13	.08
583T	Tommy Helms	.25	.13	.08
592T	Willie Randolph	2.00	1.00	.60
618T	Jack Brohamer	.25	.13	.08
632T	Rogelio Moret	.25	.13	.08
649T	Dave Roberts	.25	.13	.08
----	Traded Checklist	.80	.40	.25

1977 Topps

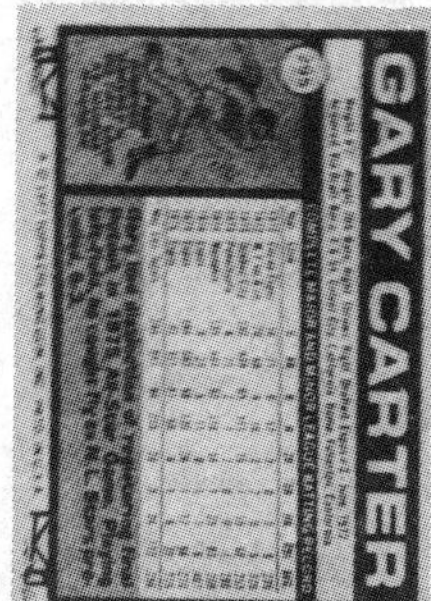

The 1977 Topps Set is a 660-card effort featuring front designs dominated by a color photograph on which there is a facsimile autograph. Above the picture are the player's name, team and position. The backs of the 2-1/2" by 3-1/2" cards include personal and career statistics along with newspaper-style highlights and a cartoon. Specialty cards include statistical leaders, record performances, a new "Turn Back The Clock" feature which highlighted great past moments and a "Big League Brothers" feature.

	NR MT	EX	VG
Complete Set (660):	400.00	200.00	120.00
Common Player:	.20	.10	.06

		NR MT	EX	VG
1	Batting Leaders (George Brett, Bill Madlock)	5.00	2.50	1.50
2	Home Run Leaders (Graig Nettles, Mike Schmidt)	1.50	.70	.45
3	RBI Leaders (George Foster, Lee May)	.20	.10	.06
4	Stolen Base Leaders (Dave Lopes, Bill North)	.20	.10	.06
5	Victory Leaders (Randy Jones, Jim Palmer)	.80	.40	.25
6	Strikeout Leaders (Nolan Ryan, Tom Seaver)	9.00	4.50	2.75
7	ERA Leaders (John Denny, Mark Fidrych)	.20	.10	.06
8	Leading Firemen (Bill Campbell, Rawly Eastwick)	.20	.10	.06
9	Doug Rader	.20	.10	.06
10	Reggie Jackson	20.00	10.00	6.00
11	Rob Dressler	.20	.10	.06
12	Larry Haney	.20	.10	.06
13	Luis Gomez	.20	.10	.06
14	Tommy Smith	.20	.10	.06
15	Don Gullett	.20	.10	.06
16	Bob Jones	.20	.10	.06
17	Steve Stone	.25	.13	.08
18	Indians Team (Frank Robinson)	2.00	1.00	.60
19	John D'Acquisto	.20	.10	.06
20	Graig Nettles	.45	.25	.14
21	Ken Forsch	.20	.10	.06
22	Bill Freehan	.25	.13	.08
23	Dan Driessen	.20	.10	.06
24	Carl Morton	.20	.10	.06
25	Dwight Evans	1.50	.70	.45
26	Ray Sadecki	.20	.10	.06
27	Bill Buckner	.30	.15	.09
28	Woodie Fryman	.20	.10	.06
29	Bucky Dent	.25	.13	.08
30	Greg Luzinski	.40	.20	.12
31	Jim Todd	.20	.10	.06
32	Checklist 1-132	1.25	.60	.40
33	Wayne Garland	.20	.10	.06
34	Angels Team (Norm Sherry)	.70	.35	.20
35	Rennie Stennett	.20	.10	.06
36	John Ellis	.20	.10	.06
37	Steve Hargan	.20	.10	.06
38	Craig Kusick	.20	.10	.06
39	Tom Griffin	.20	.10	.06
40	Bobby Murcer	.30	.15	.09
41	Jim Kern	.20	.10	.06
42	Jose Cruz	.30	.15	.09
43	Ray Bare	.20	.10	.06
44	Bud Harrelson	.20	.10	.06
45	Rawly Eastwick	.20	.10	.06
46	Buck Martinez	.20	.10	.06
47	Lynn McGlothen	.20	.10	.06
48	Tom Paciorek	.20	.10	.06
49	Grant Jackson	.20	.10	.06
50	Ron Cey	.35	.20	.11
51	Brewers Team (Alex Grammas)	1.25	.60	.40
52	Ellis Valentine	.20	.10	.06
53	Paul Mitchell	.20	.10	.06
54	Sandy Alomar	.20	.10	.06
55	Jeff Burroughs	.20	.10	.06
56	Rudy May	.20	.10	.06
57	Marc Hill	.20	.10	.06
58	Chet Lemon	.20	.10	.06
59	Larry Christenson	.20	.10	.06
60	Jim Rice	4.00	2.00	1.25
61	Manny Sanguillen	.20	.10	.06
62	Eric Raich	.20	.10	.06
63	Tito Fuentes	.20	.10	.06
64	Larry Biittner	.20	.10	.06
65	Skip Lockwood	.20	.10	.06
66	Roy Smalley	.20	.10	.06
67	*Joaquin Andujar*	.20	.10	.06
68	Bruce Bochte	.20	.10	.06
69	Jim Crawford	.20	.10	.06
70	Johnny Bench	10.00	5.00	3.00
71	Dock Ellis	.20	.10	.06
72	Mike Anderson	.20	.10	.06
73	Charlie Williams	.20	.10	.06
74	A's Team (Jack McKeon)	1.25	.60	.40
75	Dennis Leonard	.20	.10	.06
76	Tim Foli	.20	.10	.06
77	Dyar Miller	.20	.10	.06
78	Bob Davis	.20	.10	.06
79	Don Money	.20	.10	.06
80	Andy Messersmith	.20	.10	.06
81	Juan Beniquez	.20	.10	.06
82	Jim Rooker	.20	.10	.06
83	Kevin Bell	.20	.10	.06
84	Ollie Brown	.20	.10	.06
85	Duane Kuiper	.20	.10	.06
86	Pat Zachry	.20	.10	.06
87	Glenn Borgmann	.20	.10	.06
88	Stan Wall	.20	.10	.06
89	*Butch Hobson*	.20	.10	.06
90	Cesar Cedeno	.20	.10	.06
91	John Verhoeven	.20	.10	.06
92	Dave Rosello	.20	.10	.06
93	Tom Poquette	.20	.10	.06
94	Craig Swan	.20	.10	.06
95	Keith Hernandez	1.00	.50	.30
96	Lou Piniella	.30	.15	.09
97	Dave Heaverlo	.20	.10	.06
98	Milt May	.20	.10	.06
99	Tom Hausman	.20	.10	.06
100	Joe Morgan	6.00	3.00	1.75

		NR MT	EX	VG
101	Dick Bosman	.20	.10	.06
102	Jose Morales	.20	.10	.06
103	Mike Bacsik	.20	.10	.06
104	*Omar Moreno*	.20	.10	.06
105	Steve Yeager	.20	.10	.06
106	Mike Flanagan	.20	.10	.06
107	Bill Melton	.20	.10	.06
108	Alan Foster	.20	.10	.06
109	Jorge Orta	.20	.10	.06
110	Steve Carlton	8.00	4.00	2.50
111	Rico Petrocelli	.20	.10	.06
112	Bill Greif	.20	.10	.06
113	Blue Jays Mgr./Coaches (Roy Hartsfield, Don Leppert, Bob Miller, Jackie Moore, Harry Warner)	1.25	.60	.40
114	Bruce Dal Canton	.20	.10	.06
115	Rick Manning	.20	.10	.06
116	Joe Niekro	.30	.15	.09
117	Frank White	.25	.13	.08
118	Rick Jones	.20	.10	.06
119	John Stearns	.20	.10	.06
120	Rod Carew	8.00	4.00	2.50
121	Gary Nolan	.20	.10	.06
122	Ben Oglivie	.20	.10	.06
123	Fred Stanley	.20	.10	.06
124	George Mitterwald	.20	.10	.06
125	Bill Travers	.20	.10	.06
126	Rod Gilbreath	.20	.10	.06
127	Ron Fairly	.20	.10	.06
128	Tommy John	1.25	.60	.40
129	Mike Sadek	.20	.10	.06
130	Al Oliver	.60	.30	.20
131	Orlando Ramirez	.20	.10	.06
132	Chip Lang	.20	.10	.06
133	Ralph Garr	.20	.10	.06
134	Padres Team (John McNamara)	1.25	.60	.40
135	Mark Belanger	.20	.10	.06
136	*Jerry Mumphrey*	.20	.10	.06
137	Jeff Terpko	.20	.10	.06
138	Bob Stinson	.20	.10	.06
139	Fred Norman	.20	.10	.06
140	Mike Schmidt	15.00	7.50	4.50
141	Mark Littell	.20	.10	.06
142	Steve Dillard	.20	.10	.06
143	Ed Herrmann	.20	.10	.06
144	*Bruce Sutter*	3.00	1.50	.90
145	Tom Veryzer	.20	.10	.06
146	Dusty Baker	.25	.13	.08
147	Jackie Brown	.20	.10	.06
148	Fran Healy	.20	.10	.06
149	Mike Cubbage	.20	.10	.06
150	Tom Seaver	9.00	4.50	2.75
151	Johnnie LeMaster	.20	.10	.06
152	Gaylord Perry	3.00	1.50	.90
153	Ron Jackson	.20	.10	.06
154	Dave Giusti	.20	.10	.06
155	Joe Rudi	.25	.13	.08
156	Pete Mackanin	.20	.10	.06
157	Ken Brett	.20	.10	.06
158	Ted Kubiak	.20	.10	.06
159	Bernie Carbo	.20	.10	.06
160	Will McEnaney	.20	.10	.06
161	*Garry Templeton*	.90	.45	.25
162	Mike Cuellar	.20	.10	.06
163	Dave Hilton	.20	.10	.06
164	Tug McGraw	.20	.10	.06
165	Jim Wynn	.20	.10	.06
166	Bill Campbell	.20	.10	.06
167	Rich Hebner	.20	.10	.06
168	Charlie Spikes	.20	.10	.06
169	Darold Knowles	.20	.10	.06
170	Thurman Munson	5.00	2.50	1.50
171	Ken Sanders	.20	.10	.06
172	John Milner	.20	.10	.06
173	Chuck Scrivener	.20	.10	.06
174	Nelson Briles	.20	.10	.06
175	*Butch Wynegar*	.20	.10	.06
176	Bob Robertson	.20	.10	.06
177	Bart Johnson	.20	.10	.06
178	Bombo Rivera	.20	.10	.06
179	Paul Hartzell	.20	.10	.06
180	Dave Lopes	.25	.13	.08
181	Ken McMullen	.20	.10	.06
182	Dan Spillner	.20	.10	.06
183	Cardinals Team (Vern Rapp)	1.25	.60	.40
184	Bo McLaughlin	.20	.10	.06
185	Sixto Lezcano	.20	.10	.06
186	Doug Flynn	.20	.10	.06
187	Dick Pole	.20	.10	.06
188	Bob Tolan	.20	.10	.06
189	Rick Dempsey	.20	.10	.06
190	Ray Burris	.20	.10	.06
191	Doug Griffin	.20	.10	.06
192	Clarence Gaston	.20	.10	.06
193	Larry Gura	.20	.10	.06
194	Gary Matthews	.20	.10	.06
195	Ed Figueroa	.20	.10	.06
196	Len Randle	.20	.10	.06
197	Ed Ott	.20	.10	.06
198	Wilbur Wood	.20	.10	.06
199	Pepe Frias	.20	.10	.06
200	Frank Tanana	.30	.15	.09
201	Ed Kranepool	.20	.10	.06
202	Tom Johnson	.20	.10	.06
203	Ed Armbrister	.20	.10	.06
204	Jeff Newman	.20	.10	.06
205	Pete Falcone	.20	.10	.06
206	Boog Powell	.50	.25	.15
207	Glenn Abbott	.20	.10	.06
208	Checklist 133-264	1.25	.60	.40
209	Rob Andrews	.20	.10	.06
210	Fred Lynn	1.50	.70	.45
211	Giants Team (Joe Altobelli)	1.25	.60	.40
212	Jim Mason	.20	.10	.06
213	Maximino Leon	.20	.10	.06
214	Darrell Porter	.20	.10	.06
215	Butch Metzger	.20	.10	.06
216	Doug DeCinces	.25	.13	.08
217	Tom Underwood	.20	.10	.06
218	*John Wathan*	.60	.30	.20
219	Joe Coleman	.20	.10	.06
220	Chris Chambliss	.20	.10	.06
221	Bob Bailey	.20	.10	.06
222	Francisco Barrios	.20	.10	.06
223	Earl Williams	.20	.10	.06
224	Rusty Torres	.20	.10	.06
225	Bob Apodaca	.20	.10	.06
226	Leroy Stanton	.20	.10	.06
227	*Joe Sambito*	.25	.13	.08
228	Twins Team (Gene Mauch)	1.25	.60	.40
229	Don Kessinger	.20	.10	.06
230	Vida Blue	.40	.20	.12
231	George Brett (RB)	6.00	3.00	1.75
232	Minnie Minoso (RB)	.35	.20	.11
233	Jose Morales (RB)	.20	.10	.06
234	Nolan Ryan (RB)	12.00	6.00	3.50
235	Cecil Cooper	.20	.10	.06
236	Tom Buskey	.20	.10	.06
237	Gene Clines	.20	.10	.06
238	Tippy Martinez	.20	.10	.06
239	Bill Plummer	.20	.10	.06
240	Ron LeFlore	.20	.10	.06
241	Dave Tomlin	.20	.10	.06
242	Ken Henderson	.20	.10	.06
243	Ron Reed	.20	.10	.06
244	John Mayberry	.20	.10	.06
245	Rick Rhoden	.20	.10	.06
246	Mike Vail	.20	.10	.06
247	Chris Knapp	.20	.10	.06
248	Wilbur Howard	.20	.10	.06
249	Pete Redfern	.20	.10	.06
250	Bill Madlock	.40	.20	.12
251	Tony Muser	.20	.10	.06
252	Dale Murray	.20	.10	.06
253	John Hale	.20	.10	.06
254	Doyle Alexander	.20	.10	.06
255	George Scott	.20	.10	.06
256	Joe Hoerner	.20	.10	.06
257	Mike Miley	.20	.10	.06
258	Luis Tiant	.35	.20	.11
259	Mets Team (Joe Frazier)	1.25	.60	.40
260	J.R. Richard	.25	.13	.08
261	Phil Garner	.20	.10	.06
262	Al Cowens	.20	.10	.06
263	Mike Marshall	.20	.10	.06
264	Tom Hutton	.20	.10	.06
265	*Mark Fidrych*	.70	.35	.20
266	Derrel Thomas	.20	.10	.06
267	Ray Fosse	.20	.10	.06
268	Rick Sawyer	.20	.10	.06
269	Joe Lis	.20	.10	.06
270	Dave Parker	4.00	2.00	1.25
271	Terry Forster	.20	.10	.06
272	Lee Lacy	.20	.10	.06
273	Eric Soderholm	.20	.10	.06
274	Don Stanhouse	.20	.10	.06
275	Mike Hargrove	.20	.10	.06
276	A.L. Championship (Chambliss' Dramatic Homer Decides It)	.70	.35	.20
277	N.L. Championship (Reds Sweep Phillies 3 In Row)	.70	.35	.20
278	Danny Frisella	.20	.10	.06

		NR MT	EX	VG
279	Joe Wallis	.20	.10	.06
280	Catfish Hunter	2.00	1.00	.60
281	Roy Staiger	.20	.10	.06
282	Sid Monge	.20	.10	.06
283	Jerry DaVanon	.20	.10	.06
284	Mike Norris	.20	.10	.06
285	Brooks Robinson	6.00	3.00	1.75
286	Johnny Grubb	.20	.10	.06
287	Reds Team (Sparky Anderson)	2.00	1.00	.60
288	Bob Montgomery	.20	.10	.06
289	Gene Garber	.20	.10	.06
290	Amos Otis	.20	.10	.06
291	*Jason Thompson*	.20	.10	.06
292	Rogelio Moret	.20	.10	.06
293	Jack Brohamer	.20	.10	.06
294	George Medich	.20	.10	.06
295	Gary Carter	4.00	2.00	1.25
296	Don Hood	.20	.10	.06
297	Ken Reitz	.20	.10	.06
298	Charlie Hough	.25	.13	.08
299	Otto Velez	.20	.10	.06
300	Jerry Koosman	.20	.10	.06
301	Toby Harrah	.20	.10	.06
302	Mike Garman	.20	.10	.06
303	Gene Tenace	.20	.10	.06
304	Jim Hughes	.20	.10	.06
305	Mickey Rivers	.20	.10	.06
306	Rick Waits	.20	.10	.06
307	Gary Sutherland	.20	.10	.06
308	Gene Pentz	.20	.10	.06
309	Red Sox Team (Don Zimmer)	1.25	.60	.40
310	Larry Bowa	.30	.15	.09
311	Vern Ruhle	.20	.10	.06
312	Rob Belloir	.20	.10	.06
313	Paul Blair	.20	.10	.06
314	Steve Mingori	.20	.10	.06
315	Dave Chalk	.20	.10	.06
316	Steve Rogers	.20	.10	.06
317	Kurt Bevacqua	.20	.10	.06
318	Duffy Dyer	.20	.10	.06
319	Rich Gossage	.60	.30	.20
320	Ken Griffey	.30	.15	.09
321	Dave Goltz	.20	.10	.06
322	Bill Russell	.20	.10	.06
323	Larry Lintz	.20	.10	.06
324	John Curtis	.20	.10	.06
325	Mike Ivie	.20	.10	.06
326	Jesse Jefferson	.20	.10	.06
327	Astros Team (Bill Virdon)	1.25	.60	.40
328	Tommy Boggs	.20	.10	.06
329	Ron Hodges	.20	.10	.06
330	George Hendrick	.20	.10	.06
331	Jim Colborn	.20	.10	.06
332	Elliott Maddox	.20	.10	.06
333	Paul Reuschel	.20	.10	.06
334	Bill Stein	.20	.10	.06
335	Bill Robinson	.20	.10	.06
336	Denny Doyle	.20	.10	.06
337	Ron Schueler	.20	.10	.06
338	Dave Duncan	.20	.10	.06
339	Adrian Devine	.20	.10	.06
340	Hal McRae	.40	.20	.12
341	Joe Kerrigan	.20	.10	.06
342	Jerry Remy	.20	.10	.06
343	Ed Halicki	.20	.10	.06
344	Brian Downing	.25	.13	.08
345	Reggie Smith	.25	.13	.08
346	Bill Singer	.20	.10	.06
347	George Foster	.60	.30	.20
348	Brent Strom	.20	.10	.06
349	Jim Holt	.20	.10	.06
350	Larry Dierker	.20	.10	.06
351	Jim Sundberg	.20	.10	.06
352	Mike Phillips	.20	.10	.06
353	Stan Thomas	.20	.10	.06
354	Pirates Team (Chuck Tanner)	1.25	.60	.40
355	Lou Brock	4.00	2.00	1.25
356	Checklist 265-396	1.25	.60	.40
357	Tim McCarver	.40	.20	.12
358	Tom House	.20	.10	.06
359	Willie Randolph	.60	.30	.20
360	Rick Monday	.25	.13	.08
361	Eduardo Rodriguez	.20	.10	.06
362	Tommy Davis	.30	.15	.09
363	Dave Roberts	.20	.10	.06
364	Vic Correll	.20	.10	.06
365	Mike Torrez	.20	.10	.06
366	Ted Sizemore	.20	.10	.06
367	Dave Hamliton	.20	.10	.06
368	Mike Jorgensen	.20	.10	.06
369	Terry Humphrey	.20	.10	.06

		NR MT	EX	VG
370	John Montefusco	.20	.10	.06
371	Royals Team (Whitey Herzog)	2.00	1.00	.60
372	Rich Folkers	.20	.10	.06
373	Bert Campaneris	.30	.15	.09
374	Kent Tekulve	.70	.35	.20
375	Larry Hisle	.20	.10	.06
376	Nino Espinosa	.20	.10	.06
377	Dave McKay	.20	.10	.06
378	Jim Umbarger	.20	.10	.06
379	Larry Cox	.20	.10	.06
380	Lee May	.20	.10	.06
381	Bob Forsch	.20	.10	.06
382	Charlie Moore	.20	.10	.06
383	Stan Bahnsen	.20	.10	.06
384	Darrel Chaney	.20	.10	.06
385	Dave LaRoche	.20	.10	.06
386	Manny Mota	.20	.10	.06
387	Yankees Team (Billy Martin)	2.00	1.00	.60
388	Terry Harmon	.20	.10	.06
389	Ken Kravec	.20	.10	.06
390	Dave Winfield	24.00	12.00	7.25
391	Dan Warthen	.20	.10	.06
392	Phil Roof	.20	.10	.06
393	John Lowenstein	.20	.10	.06
394	Bill Laxton	.20	.10	.06
395	Manny Trillo	.20	.10	.06
396	Tom Murphy	.20	.10	.06
397	*Larry Herndon*	.40	.20	.12
398	Tom Burgmeier	.20	.10	.06
399	Bruce Boisclair	.20	.10	.06
400	Steve Garvey	3.50	1.75	1.00
401	Mickey Scott	.20	.10	.06
402	Tommy Helms	.20	.10	.06
403	Tom Grieve	.20	.10	.06
404	Eric Rasmussen	.20	.10	.06
405	Claudell Washington	.20	.10	.06
406	Tim Johnson	.20	.10	.06
407	Dave Freisleben	.20	.10	.06
408	Cesar Tovar	.20	.10	.06
409	Pete Broberg	.20	.10	.06
410	Willie Montanez	.20	.10	.06
411	World Series Games 1 & 2 (Joe Morgan/ Johnny Bench)	1.50	.70	.45
412	World Series Games 3 & 4 (Johnny Bench)	1.50	.70	.45
413	World Series Summary	.90	.45	.25
414	Tommy Harper	.20	.10	.06
415	Jay Johnstone	.20	.10	.06
416	Chuck Hartenstein	.20	.10	.06
417	Wayne Garrett	.20	.10	.06
418	White Sox Team (Bob Lemon)	1.25	.60	.40
419	Steve Swisher	.20	.10	.06
420	Rusty Staub	.35	.20	.11
421	Doug Rau	.20	.10	.06
422	Freddie Patek	.20	.10	.06
423	Gary Lavelle	.20	.10	.06
424	Steve Brye	.20	.10	.06
425	Joe Torre	.20	.10	.06
426	Dick Drago	.20	.10	.06
427	Dave Rader	.20	.10	.06
428	Rangers Team (Frank Lucchesi)	1.25	.60	.40
429	Ken Boswell	.20	.10	.06
430	Fergie Jenkins	3.00	1.50	.90
431	Dave Collins	.25	.13	.08
432	Buzz Capra	.20	.10	.06
433	Nate Colbert (Turn Back The Clock)	.20	.10	.06
434	Carl Yastrzemski (Turn Back The Clock)	1.50	.70	.45
435	Maury Wills (Turn Back The Clock)	.35	.20	.11
436	Bob Keegan (Turn Back The Clock)	.20	.10	.06
437	Ralph Kiner (Turn Back The Clock)	.35	.20	.11
438	Marty Perez	.20	.10	.06
439	Gorman Thomas	.20	.10	.06
440	Jon Matlack	.20	.10	.06
441	Larvell Blanks	.20	.10	.06
442	Braves Team (Dave Bristol)	1.25	.60	.40
443	Lamar Johnson	.20	.10	.06
444	Wayne Twitchell	.20	.10	.06
445	Ken Singleton	.25	.13	.08
446	Bill Bonham	.20	.10	.06
447	Jerry Turner	.20	.10	.06
448	Ellie Rodriguez	.20	.10	.06
449	Al Fitzmorris	.20	.10	.06
450	Pete Rose	9.00	4.50	2.75
451	Checklist 397-528	1.25	.60	.40
452	Mike Caldwell	.20	.10	.06
453	Pedro Garcia	.20	.10	.06
454	Andy Etchebarren	.20	.10	.06
455	Rick Wise	.20	.10	.06
456	Leon Roberts	.20	.10	.06

		NR MT	EX	VG
457	Steve Luebber	.20	.10	.06
458	Leo Foster	.20	.10	.06
459	Steve Foucault	.20	.10	.06
460	Willie Stargell	4.00	2.00	1.25
461	Dick Tidrow	.20	.10	.06
462	Don Baylor	.35	.20	.11
463	Jamie Quirk	.20	.10	.06
464	Randy Moffitt	.20	.10	.06
465	Rico Carty	.20	.10	.06
466	Fred Holdsworth	.20	.10	.06
467	Phillies Team (Danny Ozark)	1.25	.60	.40
468	Ramon Hernandez	.20	.10	.06
469	Pat Kelly	.20	.10	.06
470	Ted Simmons	.35	.20	.11
471	Del Unser	.20	.10	.06
472	Rookie Pitchers (Don Aase, Bob McClure, Gil Patterson, Dave Wehrmeister)	.20	.10	.06
473	Rookie Outfielders *(Andre Dawson, Gene Richards, John Scott, Denny Walling)*	75.00	37.00	22.00
474	Rookie Shortstops (Bob Bailor, Kiko Garcia, Craig Reynolds, Alex Taveras)	.20	.10	.06
475	Rookie Pitchers (Chris Batton, Rick Camp, Scott McGregor, Manny Sarmiento)	.20	.10	.06
476	Rookie Catchers (Gary Alexander, *Rick Cerone, Dale Murphy,* Kevin Pasley)	22.00	11.00	6.50
477	Rookie Infielders (Doug Ault, *Rich Dauer,* Orlando Gonzalez, Phil Mankowski)	.20	.10	.06
478	Rookie Pitchers (Jim Gideon, Leon Hooten, Dave Johnson, Mark Lemongello)	.20	.10	.06
479	Rookie Outfielders (Brian Asselstine, *Wayne Gross,* Sam Mejias, Alvis Woods)	.20	.10	.06
480	Carl Yastrzemski	6.00	3.00	1.75
481	Roger Metzger	.20	.10	.06
482	Tony Solaita	.20	.10	.06
483	Richie Zisk	.20	.10	.06
484	Burt Hooton	.20	.10	.06
485	Roy White	.30	.15	.09
486	Ed Bane	.20	.10	.06
487	Rookie Pitchers (Larry Anderson, Ed Glynn, Joe Henderson, Greg Terlecky)	.20	.10	.06
488	Rookie Outfielders *(Jack Clark, Ruppert Jones, Lee Mazzilli, Dan Thomas)*	3.00	1.50	.90
489	Rookie Pitchers *(Len Barker,* Randy Lerch, *Greg Minton,* Mike Overy)	.40	.20	.12
490	Rookie Shortstops *(Billy Almon,* Mickey Klutts, Tommy McMillan, Mark Wagner)	.20	.10	.06
491	Rookie Pitchers (Mike Dupree, *Denny Martinez,* Craig Mitchell, Bob Sykes)	6.00	3.00	1.75
492	Rookie Outfielders *(Tony Armas, Steve Kemp, Carlos Lopez, Gary Woods)*	1.00	.50	.30
493	Rookie Pitchers *(Mike Krukow,* Jim Otten, Gary Wheelock, Mike Willis)	.35	.20	.11
494	Rookie Infielders (Juan Bernhardt, Mike Champion, *Jim Gantner, Bump Wills)*	.35	.20	.11
495	Al Hrabosky	.20	.10	.06
496	Gary Thomasson	.20	.10	.06
497	Clay Carroll	.20	.10	.06
498	Sal Bando	.20	.10	.06
499	Pablo Torrealba	.20	.10	.06
500	Dave Kingman	.30	.15	.09
501	Jim Bibby	.20	.10	.06
502	Randy Hundley	.20	.10	.06
503	Bill Lee	.20	.10	.06
504	Dodgers Team (Tom Lasorda)	2.00	1.00	.60
505	Oscar Gamble	.20	.10	.06
506	Steve Grilli	.20	.10	.06
507	Mike Hegan	.20	.10	.06
508	Dave Pagan	.20	.10	.06
509	Cookie Rojas	.20	.10	.06
510	John Candelaria	.35	.20	.11
511	Bill Fahey	.20	.10	.06
512	Jack Billingham	.20	.10	.06
513	Jerry Terrell	.20	.10	.06
514	Cliff Johnson	.20	.10	.06
515	Chris Speier	.20	.10	.06
516	Bake McBride	.20	.10	.06
517	*Pete Vuckovich*	.50	.25	.15
518	Cubs Team (Herman Franks)	1.25	.60	.40
519	Don Kirkwood	.20	.10	.06
520	Garry Maddox	.20	.10	.06
521	Bob Grich	.25	.13	.08
522	Enzo Hernandez	.20	.10	.06
523	Rollie Fingers	3.00	1.50	.90
524	Rowland Office	.20	.10	.06
525	Dennis Eckersley	15.00	7.50	4.50
526	Larry Parrish	.20	.10	.06
527	Dan Meyer	.20	.10	.06
528	Bill Castro	.20	.10	.06
529	Jim Essian	.20	.10	.06
530	Rick Reuschel	.20	.10	.06
531	Lyman Bostock	.20	.10	.06
532	Jim Willoughby	.20	.10	.06
533	Mickey Stanley	.20	.10	.06
534	Paul Splittorff	.20	.10	.06
535	Cesar Geronimo	.20	.10	.06
536	Vic Albury	.20	.10	.06
537	Dave Roberts	.20	.10	.06
538	Frank Taveras	.20	.10	.06
539	Mike Wallace	.20	.10	.06
540	Bob Watson	.20	.10	.06
541	John Denny	.20	.10	.06
542	Frank Duffy	.20	.10	.06
543	Ron Blomberg	.20	.10	.06
544	Gary Ross	.20	.10	.06
545	Bob Boone	.35	.20	.11
546	Orioles Team (Earl Weaver)	2.00	1.00	.60
547	Willie McCovey	3.00	1.50	.90
548	*Joel Youngblood*	.20	.10	.06
549	Jerry Royster	.20	.10	.06
550	Randy Jones	.20	.10	.06
551	Bill North	.20	.10	.06
552	Pepe Mangual	.20	.10	.06
553	Jack Heidemann	.20	.10	.06
554	Bruce Kimm	.20	.10	.06
555	Dan Ford	.20	.10	.06
556	Doug Bird	.20	.10	.06
557	Jerry White	.20	.10	.06
558	Elias Sosa	.20	.10	.06
559	Alan Bannister	.20	.10	.06
560	Dave Concepcion	.35	.20	.11
561	Pete LaCock	.20	.10	.06
562	Checklist 529-660	1.25	.60	.40
563	Bruce Kison	.20	.10	.06
564	Alan Ashby	.20	.10	.06
565	Mickey Lolich	.35	.20	.11
566	Rick Miller	.20	.10	.06
567	Enos Cabell	.20	.10	.06
568	Carlos May	.20	.10	.06
569	Jim Lonborg	.20	.10	.06
570	Bobby Bonds	.35	.20	.11
571	Darrell Evans	.35	.20	.11
572	Ross Grimsley	.20	.10	.06
573	Joe Ferguson	.20	.10	.06
574	Aurelio Rodriguez	.20	.10	.06
575	Dick Ruthven	.20	.10	.06
576	Fred Kendall	.20	.10	.06
577	Jerry Augustine	.20	.10	.06
578	Bob Randall	.20	.10	.06
579	Don Carrithers	.20	.10	.06
580	George Brett	30.00	15.00	9.00
581	Pedro Borbon	.20	.10	.06
582	Ed Kirkpatrick	.20	.10	.06
583	Paul Lindblad	.20	.10	.06
584	Ed Goodson	.20	.10	.06
585	Rick Burleson	.20	.10	.06
586	Steve Renko	.20	.10	.06
587	Rick Baldwin	.20	.10	.06
588	Dave Moates	.20	.10	.06
589	Mike Cosgrove	.20	.10	.06
590	Buddy Bell	.20	.10	.06
591	Chris Arnold	.20	.10	.06
592	Dan Briggs	.20	.10	.06
593	Dennis Blair	.20	.10	.06
594	Biff Pocoroba	.20	.10	.06
595	John Hiller	.20	.10	.06
596	*Jerry Martin*	.20	.10	.06
597	Mariners Mgr./Coaches (Don Bryant, Jim Busby, Darrell Johnson, Vada Pinson, Wes Stock)	1.25	.60	.40
598	Sparky Lyle	.35	.20	.11
599	Mike Tyson	.20	.10	.06
600	Jim Palmer	4.00	2.00	1.25
601	Mike Lum	.20	.10	.06
602	Andy Hassler	.20	.10	.06
603	Willie Davis	.25	.13	.08
604	Jim Slaton	.20	.10	.06
605	Felix Millan	.20	.10	.06
606	Steve Braun	.20	.10	.06
607	Larry Demery	.20	.10	.06
608	Roy Howell	.20	.10	.06
609	Jim Barr	.20	.10	.06
610	Jose Cardenal	.20	.10	.06
611	Dave Lemanczyk	.20	.10	.06
612	Barry Foote	.20	.10	.06
613	Reggie Cleveland	.20	.10	.06
614	Greg Gross	.20	.10	.06

		NR MT	EX	VG
615	Phil Niekro	1.50	.70	.45
616	Tommy Sandt	.20	.10	.06
617	Bobby Darwin	.20	.10	.06
618	Pat Dobson	.20	.10	.06
619	Johnny Oates	.20	.10	.06
620	Don Sutton	1.50	.70	.45
621	Tigers Team (Ralph Houk)	1.50	.70	.45
622	Jim Wohlford	.20	.10	.06
623	Jack Kucek	.20	.10	.06
624	Hector Cruz	.20	.10	.06
625	Ken Holtzman	.20	.10	.06
626	Al Bumbry	.20	.10	.06
627	Bob Myrick	.20	.10	.06
628	Mario Guerrero	.20	.10	.06
629	Bobby Valentine	.25	.13	.08
630	Bert Blyleven	.90	.45	.25
631	Big League Brothers (George Brett, Ken Brett)	5.00	2.50	1.50
632	Big League Brothers (Bob Forsch, Ken Forsch)	.30	.15	.09
633	Big League Brothers (Carlos May, Lee May)	.30	.15	.09
634	Big League Brothers (Paul Reuschel, Rick Reuschel) (names switched)	.30	.15	.09
635	Robin Yount	30.00	15.00	9.00
636	Santo Alcala	.20	.10	.06
637	Alex Johnson	.20	.10	.06
638	Jim Kaat	.80	.40	.25
639	Jerry Morales	.20	.10	.06
640	Carlton Fisk	4.00	2.00	1.25
641	Dan Larson	.20	.10	.06
642	Willie Crawford	.20	.10	.06
643	Mike Pazik	.20	.10	.06
644	Matt Alexander	.20	.10	.06
645	Jerry Reuss	.25	.13	.08
646	Andres Mora	.20	.10	.06
647	Expos Team (Dick Williams)	1.25	.60	.40
648	Jim Spencer	.20	.10	.06
649	Dave Cash	.20	.10	.06
650	Nolan Ryan	40.00	20.00	12.00
651	Von Joshua	.20	.10	.06
652	Tom Walker	.20	.10	.06
653	Diego Segui	.20	.10	.06
654	Ron Pruitt	.20	.10	.06
655	Tony Perez	1.50	.70	.45
656	Ron Guidry	.90	.45	.25
657	Mick Kelleher	.20	.10	.06
658	Marty Pattin	.20	.10	.06
659	Merv Rettenmund	.20	.10	.06
660	Willie Horton	.20	.10	.06

1977 Topps Cloth Stickers

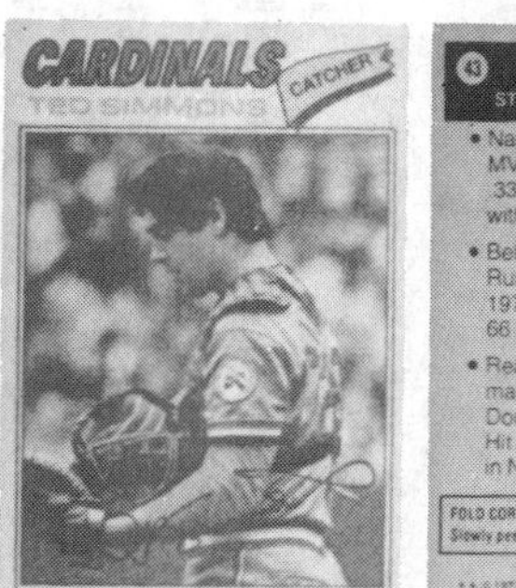

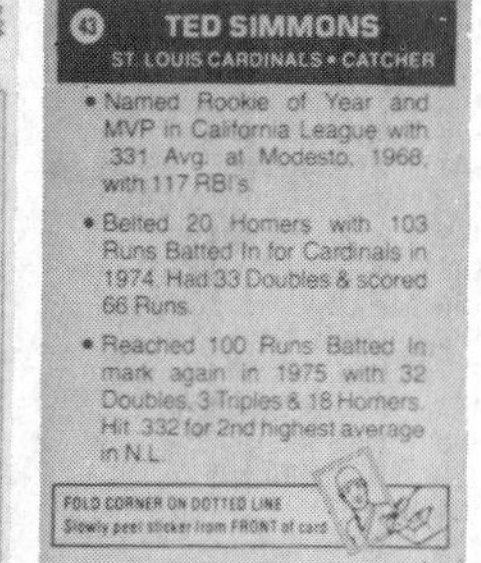

One of the few Topps specialty issues of the late 1970s, the 73-piece set of cloth stickers issued in 1977 includes 55 player stickers and 18 puzzle cards which could be joined to form a photo of the American League or National League All-Star teams. Issued as a separate issue, the 2-1/2" by 3-1/2" stickers have a paper backing which could be removed to allow the cloth to be adhered to a jacket, notebook, etc.

		NR MT	EX	VG
Complete Set:		300.00	150.00	90.00
Common Player:		1.00	.50	.30
1	Alan Ashby	1.00	.50	.30
2	Buddy Bell	1.00	.50	.30
3	Johnny Bench	10.00	5.00	3.00
4	Vida Blue	1.50	.70	.45
5	Bert Blyleven	1.50	.70	.45
6	Steve Braun	1.00	.50	.30
7	George Brett	15.00	7.50	4.50
8	Lou Brock	6.00	3.00	1.75
9	Jose Cardenal	1.00	.50	.30
10	Rod Carew	9.00	4.50	2.75
11	Steve Carlton	9.00	4.50	2.75
12	Dave Cash	1.00	.50	.30
13	Cesar Cedeno	1.00	.50	.30
14	Ron Cey	1.50	.70	.45
15	Mark Fidrych	1.50	.70	.45
16	Dan Ford	1.00	.50	.30
17	Wayne Garland	1.00	.50	.30
18	Ralph Garr	1.00	.50	.30
19	Steve Garvey	4.00	2.00	1.25
20	Mike Hargrove	1.00	.50	.30
21	Catfish Hunter	6.00	3.00	1.75
22	Reggie Jackson	12.00	6.00	3.50
23	Randy Jones	1.00	.50	.30
24	Dave Kingman	1.00	.50	.30
25	Bill Madlock	1.50	.70	.45
26	Lee May	1.00	.50	.30
27	John Mayberry	1.00	.50	.30
28	Andy Messersmith	1.00	.50	.30
29	Willie Montanez	1.00	.50	.30
30	John Montefusco	1.00	.50	.30
31	Joe Morgan	6.00	3.00	1.75
32	Thurman Munson	6.00	3.00	1.75
33	Bobby Murcer	1.50	.70	.45
34	Al Oliver	1.50	.70	.45
35	Dave Pagan	1.00	.50	.30
36	Jim Palmer	9.00	4.50	2.75
37	Tony Perez	3.00	1.50	.90
38	Pete Rose	15.00	7.50	4.50
39	Joe Rudi	1.50	.70	.45
40	Nolan Ryan	40.00	20.00	12.00
41	Mike Schmidt	30.00	15.00	9.00
42	Tom Seaver	20.00	10.00	6.00
43	Ted Simmons	1.50	.70	.45
44	Bill Singer	1.00	.50	.30
45	Willie Stargell	6.00	3.00	1.75
46	Rusty Staub	2.00	1.00	.60
47	Don Sutton	2.00	1.00	.60
48	Luis Tiant	1.50	.70	.45
49	Bill Travers	1.00	.50	.30
50	Claudell Washington	1.00	.50	.30
51	Bob Watson	1.00	.50	.30
52	Dave Winfield	12.00	6.00	3.50
53	Carl Yastrzemski	9.00	4.50	2.75
54	Robin Yount	12.00	6.00	3.50
55	Richie Zisk	1.00	.50	.30
---	American League 9-piece puzzle	15.00	7.50	4.50
---	National League 9-piece puzzle	15.00	7.50	4.50

1978 Topps

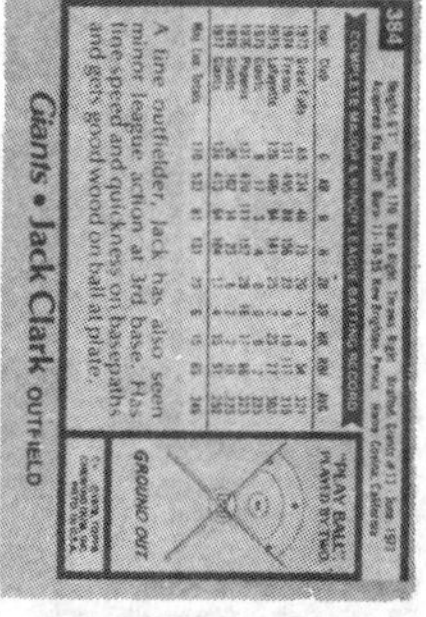

At 726 cards, this was the largest issue from Topps since 1972. In design, the color player photo is slightly larger than usual, with the player's name and team at the bottom. In the upper right-hand corner of the 2-1/2" by 3-1/2" cards there is a small white baseball with the player's position. Most of the starting All-Stars from the previous year had a red, white and blue shield instead of the baseball. Backs feature statistics and a baseball situation which made a card game of baseball possible. Specialty cards include baseball records, statistical leaders and the World Series and playoffs. As one row of cards per sheet had to be double-printed to accommodate the 726-card set size, some cards are more common, yet that seems to have no serious impact on their prices.

		NR MT	EX	VG
Complete Set (726):		350.00	175.00	105.00
Common Player:		.20	.10	.06
1	Lou Brock (Record Breaker)	2.00	1.00	.60
2	Sparky Lyle (Record Breaker)	.25	.13	.08
3	Willie McCovey (Record Breaker)	.70	.35	.20
4	Brooks Robinson (Record Breaker)	.90	.45	.25
5	Pete Rose (Record Breaker)	3.00	1.50	.90
6	Nolan Ryan (Record Breaker)	12.00	6.00	3.50
7	Reggie Jackson (Record Breaker)	6.00	3.00	1.75
8	Mike Sadek	.20	.10	.06
9	Doug DeCinces	.25	.13	.08
10	Phil Niekro	1.25	.60	.40
11	Rick Manning	.20	.10	.06
12	Don Aase	.20	.10	.06
13	Art Howe	.20	.10	.06
14	Lerrin LaGrow	.20	.10	.06
15	Tony Perez	.25	.13	.08
16	Roy White	.20	.10	.06
17	Mike Krukow	.20	.10	.06
18	Bob Grich	.25	.13	.08
19	Darrell Porter	.20	.10	.06
20	Pete Rose	.20	.10	.06
21	Steve Kemp	.30	.15	.09
22	Charlie Hough	.20	.10	.06
23	Bump Wills	.20	.10	.06
24	Don Money	.20	.10	.06
25	Jon Matlack	.20	.10	.06
26	Rich Hebner	.20	.10	.06
27	Geoff Zahn	.20	.10	.06
28	Ed Ott	.20	.10	.06
29	Bob Lacey	.20	.10	.06
30	George Hendrick	.20	.10	.06
31	Glenn Abbott	.20	.10	.06
32	Garry Templeton	.20	.10	.06
33	Dave Lemanczyk	.20	.10	.06
34	Willie McCovey	3.00	1.50	.90
35	Sparky Lyle	.30	.15	.09
36	*Eddie Murray*	80.00	40.00	24.00
37	Rick Waits	.20	.10	.06
38	Willie Montanez	.20	.10	.06
39	*Floyd Bannister*	.70	.35	.20
40	Carl Yastrzemski	5.00	2.50	1.50
41	Burt Hooton	.20	.10	.06
42	Jorge Orta	.20	.10	.06
43	Bill Atkinson	.20	.10	.06
44	Toby Harrah	.20	.10	.06
45	Mark Fidrych	.25	.13	.08
46	Al Cowens	.20	.10	.06
47	Jack Billingham	.20	.10	.06
48	Don Baylor	.35	.20	.11
49	Ed Kranepool	.20	.10	.06
50	Rick Reuschel	.20	.10	.06
51	Charlie Moore	.20	.10	.06
52	Jim Lonborg	.20	.10	.06
53	Phil Garner	.20	.10	.06
54	Tom Johnson	.20	.10	.06
55	Mitchell Page	.20	.10	.06
56	Randy Jones	.20	.10	.06
57	Dan Meyer	.20	.10	.06
58	Bob Forsch	.20	.10	.06
59	Otto Velez	.20	.10	.06
60	Thurman Munson	5.00	2.50	1.50
61	Larvell Blanks	.20	.10	.06
62	Jim Barr	.20	.10	.06
63	Don Zimmer	.20	.10	.06
64	Gene Pentz	.20	.10	.06
65	Ken Singleton	.20	.10	.06
66	White Sox Team	.50	.25	.15
67	Claudell Washington	.20	.10	.06
68	Steve Foucault	.20	.10	.06
69	Mike Vail	.20	.10	.06
70	Rich Gossage	.40	.20	.12
71	Terry Humphrey	.20	.10	.06
72	Andre Dawson	25.00	12.50	7.50
73	Andy Hassler	.20	.10	.06
74	Checklist 1-121	.90	.45	.25
75	Dick Ruthven	.20	.10	.06
76	Steve Ontiveros	.20	.10	.06
77	Ed Kirkpatrick	.20	.10	.06
78	Pablo Torrealba	.20	.10	.06
79	Darrell Johnson	.20	.10	.06
80	Ken Griffey	.25	.13	.08
81	Pete Redfern	.20	.10	.06
82	Giants Team	.50	.25	.15
83	Bob Montgomery	.20	.10	.06
84	Kent Tekulve	.20	.10	.06
85	Ron Fairly	.20	.10	.06
86	Dave Tomlin	.20	.10	.06
87	John Lowenstein	.20	.10	.06
88	Mike Phillips	.20	.10	.06
89	Ken Clay	.20	.10	.06
90	Larry Bowa	.30	.15	.09
91	Oscar Zamora	.20	.10	.06
92	Adrian Devine	.20	.10	.06
93	Bobby Cox	.20	.10	.06
94	Chuck Scrivener	.20	.10	.06
95	Jamie Quirk	.20	.10	.06
96	Orioles Team	.50	.25	.15
97	Stan Bahnsen	.20	.10	.06
98	Jim Essian	.20	.10	.06
99	*Willie Hernandez*	.30	.15	.09
100	George Brett	25.00	12.50	7.50
101	Sid Monge	.20	.10	.06
102	Matt Alexander	.20	.10	.06
103	Tom Murphy	.20	.10	.06
104	Lee Lacy	.20	.10	.06
105	Reggie Cleveland	.20	.10	.06
106	Bill Plummer	.20	.10	.06
107	Ed Halicki	.20	.10	.06
108	Von Joshua	.20	.10	.06
109	Joe Torre	.20	.10	.06
110	Richie Zisk	.20	.10	.06
111	Mike Tyson	.20	.10	.06
112	Astros Team	.50	.25	.15
113	Don Carrithers	.20	.10	.06
114	Paul Blair	.20	.10	.06
115	Gary Nolan	.20	.10	.06
116	Tucker Ashford	.20	.10	.06
117	John Montague	.20	.10	.06
118	Terry Harmon	.20	.10	.06
119	Denny Martinez	.25	.13	.08
120	Gary Carter	3.00	1.50	.90
121	Alvis Woods	.20	.10	.06
122	Dennis Eckersley	9.00	4.50	2.75
123	Manny Trillo	.20	.10	.06
124	*Dave Rozema*	.20	.10	.06
125	George Scott	.20	.10	.06
126	Paul Moskau	.20	.10	.06
127	Chet Lemon	.20	.10	.06
128	Bill Russell	.20	.10	.06
129	Jim Colborn	.20	.10	.06
130	Jeff Burroughs	.20	.10	.06
131	Bert Blyleven	.60	.30	.20
132	Enos Cabell	.20	.10	.06
133	Jerry Augustine	.20	.10	.06
134	*Steve Henderson*	.20	.10	.06
135	Ron Guidry	.30	.15	.09
136	Ted Sizemore	.20	.10	.06
137	Craig Kusick	.20	.10	.06
138	Larry Demery	.20	.10	.06
139	Wayne Gross	.20	.10	.06
140	Rollie Fingers	3.00	1.50	.90
141	Ruppert Jones	.20	.10	.06
142	John Montefusco	.20	.10	.06
143	Keith Hernandez	1.00	.50	.30
144	Jesse Jefferson	.20	.10	.06
145	Rick Monday	.20	.10	.06
146	Doyle Alexander	.20	.10	.06
147	Lee Mazzilli	.20	.10	.06
148	Andre Thornton	.25	.13	.08
149	Dale Murray	.20	.10	.06
150	Bobby Bonds	.20	.10	.06
151	Milt Wilcox	.20	.10	.06
152	*Ivan DeJesus*	.20	.10	.06
153	Steve Stone	.20	.10	.06
154	Cecil Cooper	.20	.10	.06
155	Butch Hobson	.20	.10	.06
156	Andy Messersmith	.20	.10	.06
157	Pete LaCock	.20	.10	.06
158	Joaquin Andujar	.20	.10	.06
159	Lou Piniella	.35	.20	.11
160	Jim Palmer	4.00	2.00	1.25
161	Bob Boone	.25	.13	.08
162	Paul Thormodsgard	.20	.10	.06
163	Bill North	.20	.10	.06
164	Bob Owchinko	.20	.10	.06
165	Rennie Stennett	.20	.10	.06
166	Carlos Lopez	.20	.10	.06
167	Tim Foli	.20	.10	.06
168	Reggie Smith	.25	.13	.08
169	Jerry Johnson	.20	.10	.06
170	Lou Brock	3.00	1.50	.90
171	Pat Zachry	.20	.10	.06

		NR MT	EX	VG
172	Mike Hargrove	.20	.10	.06
173	Robin Yount	25.00	12.50	7.50
174	Wayne Garland	.20	.10	.06
175	Jerry Morales	.20	.10	.06
176	Milt May	.20	.10	.06
177	Gene Garber	.20	.10	.06
178	Dave Chalk	.20	.10	.06
179	Dick Tidrow	.20	.10	.06
180	Dave Concepcion	.35	.20	.11
181	Ken Forsch	.20	.10	.06
182	Jim Spencer	.20	.10	.06
183	Doug Bird	.20	.10	.06
184	Checklist 122-242	.90	.45	.25
185	Ellis Valentine	.20	.10	.06
186	*Bob Stanley*	.20	.10	.06
187	Jerry Royster	.20	.10	.06
188	Al Bumbry	.20	.10	.06
189	Tom Lasorda	.50	.25	.15
190	John Candelaria	.25	.13	.08
191	Rodney Scott	.20	.10	.06
192	Padres Team	.50	.25	.15
193	Rich Chiles	.20	.10	.06
194	Derrel Thomas	.20	.10	.06
195	Larry Dierker	.20	.10	.06
196	Bob Bailor	.20	.10	.06
197	Nino Espinosa	.20	.10	.06
198	Ron Pruitt	.20	.10	.06
199	Craig Reynolds	.20	.10	.06
200	Reggie Jackson	15.00	7.50	4.50
201	Batting Leaders (Rod Carew, Dave Parker)	1.00	.50	.30
202	Home Run Leaders (George Foster, Jim Rice)	.25	.13	.08
203	RBI Leaders (George Foster, Larry Hisle)	.25	.13	.08
204	Stolen Base Leaders (Freddie Patek, Frank Taveras)	.20	.10	.06
205	Victory Leader (Steve Carlton, Dave Goltz, Dennis Leonard, Jim Palmer)	1.50	.70	.45
206	Strikeout Leaders (Phil Niekro, Nolan Ryan)	2.50	1.25	.70
207	ERA Leaders (John Candelaria, Frank Tanana)	.20	.10	.06
208	Leading Firemen (Bill Campbell, Rollie Fingers)	.50	.25	.15
209	Dock Ellis	.20	.10	.06
210	Jose Cardenal	.20	.10	.06
211	Earl Weaver	.50	.25	.15
212	Mike Caldwell	.20	.10	.06
213	Alan Bannister	.20	.10	.06
214	Angels Team	.50	.25	.15
215	Darrell Evans	.35	.20	.11
216	Mike Paxton	.20	.10	.06
217	Rod Gilbreath	.20	.10	.06
218	Marty Pattin	.20	.10	.06
219	Mike Cubbage	.20	.10	.06
220	Pedro Borbon	.20	.10	.06
221	Chris Speier	.20	.10	.06
222	Jerry Martin	.20	.10	.06
223	Bruce Kison	.20	.10	.06
224	Jerry Tabb	.20	.10	.06
225	Don Gullett	.20	.10	.06
226	Joe Ferguson	.20	.10	.06
227	Al Fitzmorris	.20	.10	.06
228	Manny Mota	.20	.10	.06
229	Leo Foster	.20	.10	.06
230	Al Hrabosky	.20	.10	.06
231	Wayne Nordhagen	.20	.10	.06
232	Mickey Stanley	.20	.10	.06
233	Dick Pole	.20	.10	.06
234	Herman Franks	.20	.10	.06
235	Tim McCarver	.30	.15	.09
236	Terry Whitfield	.20	.10	.06
237	Rich Dauer	.20	.10	.06
238	Juan Beniquez	.20	.10	.06
239	Dyar Miller	.20	.10	.06
240	Gene Tenace	.20	.10	.06
241	Pete Vuckovich	.20	.10	.06
242	Barry Bonnell	.20	.10	.06
243	Bob McClure	.20	.10	.06
244	Expos Team	.20	.10	.06
245	Rick Burleson	.20	.10	.06
246	Dan Driessen	.20	.10	.06
247	Larry Christenson	.20	.10	.06
248	Frank White	.20	.10	.06
249	Dave Goltz	.20	.10	.06
250	Graig Nettles	.30	.15	.09
251	Don Kirkwood	.20	.10	.06
252	Steve Swisher	.20	.10	.06
253	Jim Kern	.20	.10	.06
254	Dave Collins	.20	.10	.06

		NR MT	EX	VG
255	Jerry Reuss	.20	.10	.06
256	Joe Altobelli	.20	.10	.06
257	Hector Cruz	.20	.10	.06
258	John Hiller	.20	.10	.06
259	Dodgers Team	.80	.40	.25
260	Bert Campaneris	.25	.13	.08
261	Tim Hosley	.20	.10	.06
262	Rudy May	.20	.10	.06
263	Danny Walton	.20	.10	.06
264	Jamie Easterly	.20	.10	.06
265	Sal Bando	.20	.10	.06
266	*Bob Shirley*	.20	.10	.06
267	Doug Ault	.20	.10	.06
268	Gil Flores	.20	.10	.06
269	Wayne Twitchell	.20	.10	.06
270	Carlton Fisk	5.00	2.50	1.50
271	Randy Lerch	.20	.10	.06
272	Royle Stillman	.20	.10	.06
273	Fred Norman	.20	.10	.06
274	Freddie Patek	.20	.10	.06
275	Dan Ford	.20	.10	.06
276	Bill Bonham	.20	.10	.06
277	Bruce Boisclair	.20	.10	.06
278	Enrique Romo	.20	.10	.06
279	Bill Virdon	.20	.10	.06
280	Buddy Bell	.20	.10	.06
281	Eric Rasmussen	.20	.10	.06
282	Yankees Team	1.00	.50	.30
283	Omar Moreno	.20	.10	.06
284	Randy Moffitt	.20	.10	.06
285	Steve Yeager	.20	.10	.06
286	Ben Oglivie	.20	.10	.06
287	Kiko Garcia	.20	.10	.06
288	Dave Hamilton	.20	.10	.06
289	Checklist 243-363	.90	.45	.25
290	Willie Horton	.20	.10	.06
291	Gary Ross	.20	.10	.06
292	Gene Richard	.20	.10	.06
293	Mike Willis	.20	.10	.06
294	Larry Parrish	.25	.13	.08
295	Bill Lee	.20	.10	.06
296	Biff Pocoroba	.20	.10	.06
297	Warren Brusstar	.20	.10	.06
298	Tony Armas	.20	.10	.06
299	Whitey Herzog	.30	.15	.09
300	Joe Morgan	3.00	1.50	.90
301	Buddy Schultz	.20	.10	.06
302	Cubs Team	.50	.25	.15
303	Sam Hinds	.20	.10	.06
304	John Milner	.20	.10	.06
305	Rico Carty	.20	.10	.06
306	Joe Niekro	.20	.10	.06
307	Glenn Borgmann	.20	.10	.06
308	Jim Rooker	.20	.10	.06
309	Cliff Johnson	.20	.10	.06
310	Don Sutton	2.00	1.00	.60
311	Jose Baez	.20	.10	.06
312	Greg Minton	.20	.10	.06
313	Andy Etchebarren	.20	.10	.06
314	Paul Lindblad	.20	.10	.06
315	Mark Belanger	.20	.10	.06
316	Henry Cruz	.20	.10	.06
317	Dave Johnson	.30	.15	.09
318	Tom Griffin	.20	.10	.06
319	Alan Ashby	.20	.10	.06
320	Fred Lynn	.90	.45	.25
321	Santo Alcala	.20	.10	.06
322	Tom Paciorek	.20	.10	.06
323	Jim Fregosi	.20	.10	.06
324	Vern Rapp	.20	.10	.06
325	Bruce Sutter	.50	.25	.15
326	Mike Lum	.20	.10	.06
327	Rick Langford	.20	.10	.06
328	Brewers Team	.50	.25	.15
329	John Verhoeven	.20	.10	.06
330	Bob Watson	.20	.10	.06
331	Mark Littell	.20	.10	.06
332	Duane Kuiper	.20	.10	.06
333	Jim Todd	.20	.10	.06
334	John Stearns	.20	.10	.06
335	Bucky Dent	.30	.15	.09
336	Steve Busby	.20	.10	.06
337	Tom Grieve	.20	.10	.06
338	Dave Heaverlo	.20	.10	.06
339	Mario Guerrero	.20	.10	.06
340	Bake McBride	.20	.10	.06
341	Mike Flanagan	.20	.10	.06
342	Aurelio Rodriguez	.20	.10	.06
343	John Wathan	.20	.10	.06
344	Sam Ewing	.20	.10	.06
345	Luis Tiant	.35	.20	.11

		NR MT	EX	VG
346	Larry Biittner	.20	.10	.06
347	Terry Forster	.20	.10	.06
348	Del Unser	.20	.10	.06
349	Rick Camp	.20	.10	.06
350	Steve Garvey	4.00	2.00	1.25
351	Jeff Torborg	.20	.10	.06
352	Tony Scott	.20	.10	.06
353	Doug Bair	.20	.10	.06
354	Cesar Geronimo	.20	.10	.06
355	Bill Travers	.20	.10	.06
356	Mets Team	.70	.35	.20
357	Tom Poquette	.20	.10	.06
358	Mark Lemongello	.20	.10	.06
359	Marc Hill	.20	.10	.06
360	Mike Schmidt	15.00	7.50	4.50
361	Chris Knapp	.20	.10	.06
362	Dave May	.20	.10	.06
363	Bob Randall	.20	.10	.06
364	Jerry Turner	.20	.10	.06
365	Ed Figueroa	.20	.10	.06
366	Larry Milbourne	.20	.10	.06
367	Rick Dempsey	.20	.10	.06
368	Balor Moore	.20	.10	.06
369	Tim Nordbrook	.20	.10	.06
370	Rusty Staub	.30	.15	.09
371	Ray Burris	.20	.10	.06
372	Brian Asselstine	.20	.10	.06
373	Jim Willoughby	.20	.10	.06
374	Jose Morales	.20	.10	.06
375	Tommy John	.90	.45	.25
376	Jim Wohlford	.20	.10	.06
377	Manny Sarmiento	.20	.10	.06
378	Bobby Winkles	.20	.10	.06
379	Skip Lockwood	.20	.10	.06
380	Ted Simmons	.40	.20	.12
381	Phillies Team	.70	.35	.20
382	Joe Lahoud	.20	.10	.06
383	Mario Mendoza	.20	.10	.06
384	Jack Clark	2.00	1.00	.60
385	Tito Fuentes	.20	.10	.06
386	Bob Gorinski	.20	.10	.06
387	Ken Holtzman	.20	.10	.06
388	Bill Fahey	.20	.10	.06
389	Julio Gonzalez	.20	.10	.06
390	Oscar Gamble	.20	.10	.06
391	Larry Haney	.20	.10	.06
392	Billy Almon	.20	.10	.06
393	Tippy Martinez	.20	.10	.06
394	Roy Howell	.20	.10	.06
395	Jim Hughes	.20	.10	.06
396	Bob Stinson	.20	.10	.06
397	Greg Gross	.20	.10	.06
398	Don Hood	.20	.10	.06
399	Pete Mackanin	.20	.10	.06
400	Nolan Ryan	40.00	20.00	12.00
401	Sparky Anderson	.50	.25	.15
402	Dave Campbell	.20	.10	.06
403	Bud Harrelson	.20	.10	.06
404	Tigers Team	.60	.30	.20
405	Rawly Eastwick	.20	.10	.06
406	Mike Jorgensen	.20	.10	.06
407	Odell Jones	.20	.10	.06
408	Joe Zdeb	.20	.10	.06
409	Ron Schueler	.20	.10	.06
410	Bill Madlock	.50	.25	.15
411	A.L. Championships (Yankees Rally To Defeat Royals)	.70	.35	.20
412	N.L. Championships (Dodgers Overpower Phillies In Four)	.50	.25	.15
413	Reggie Jackson (WS)	3.00	1.50	.90
414	Darold Knowles	.20	.10	.06
415	Ray Fosse	.20	.10	.06
416	Jack Brohamer	.20	.10	.06
417	Mike Garman	.20	.10	.06
418	Tony Muser	.20	.10	.06
419	Jerry Garvin	.20	.10	.06
420	Greg Luzinski	.35	.20	.11
421	Junior Moore	.20	.10	.06
422	Steve Braun	.20	.10	.06
423	Dave Rosello	.20	.10	.06
424	Red Sox Team	.70	.35	.20
425	Steve Rogers	.20	.10	.06
426	Fred Kendall	.20	.10	.06
427	*Mario Soto*	.40	.20	.12
428	Joel Youngblood	.20	.10	.06
429	Mike Barlow	.20	.10	.06
430	Al Oliver	.40	.20	.12
431	Butch Metzger	.20	.10	.06
432	Terry Bulling	.20	.10	.06
433	Fernando Gonzalez	.20	.10	.06
434	Mike Norris	.20	.10	.06

		NR MT	EX	VG
435	Checklist 364-484	.90	.45	.25
436	Vic Harris	.20	.10	.06
437	Bo McLaughlin	.20	.10	.06
438	John Ellis	.20	.10	.06
439	Ken Kravec	.20	.10	.06
440	Dave Lopes	.25	.13	.08
441	Larry Gura	.20	.10	.06
442	Elliott Maddox	.20	.10	.06
443	Darrel Chaney	.20	.10	.06
444	Roy Hartsfield	.20	.10	.06
445	Mike Ivie	.20	.10	.06
446	Tug McGraw	.20	.10	.06
447	Leroy Stanton	.20	.10	.06
448	Bill Castro	.20	.10	.06
449	Tim Blackwell	.20	.10	.06
450	Tom Seaver	8.00	4.00	2.50
451	Twins Team	.50	.25	.15
452	Jerry Mumphrey	.20	.10	.06
453	Doug Flynn	.20	.10	.06
454	Dave LaRoche	.20	.10	.06
455	Bill Robinson	.20	.10	.06
456	Vern Ruhle	.20	.10	.06
457	Bob Bailey	.20	.10	.06
458	Jeff Newman	.20	.10	.06
459	Charlie Spikes	.20	.10	.06
460	Catfish Hunter	2.00	1.00	.60
461	Rob Andrews	.20	.10	.06
462	Rogelio Moret	.20	.10	.06
463	Kevin Bell	.20	.10	.06
464	Jerry Grote	.20	.10	.06
465	Hal McRae	.30	.15	.09
466	Dennis Blair	.20	.10	.06
467	Alvin Dark	.20	.10	.06
468	*Warren Cromartie*	.20	.10	.06
469	Rick Cerone	.20	.10	.06
470	J.R. Richard	.25	.13	.08
471	Roy Smalley	.20	.10	.06
472	Ron Reed	.20	.10	.06
473	Bill Buckner	.30	.15	.09
474	Jim Slaton	.20	.10	.06
475	Gary Matthews	.20	.10	.06
476	Bill Stein	.20	.10	.06
477	Doug Capilla	.20	.10	.06
478	Jerry Remy	.20	.10	.06
479	Cardinals Team	.50	.25	.15
480	Ron LeFlore	.20	.10	.06
481	Jackson Todd	.20	.10	.06
482	Rick Miller	.20	.10	.06
483	Ken Macha	.20	.10	.06
484	Jim Norris	.20	.10	.06
485	Chris Chambliss	.20	.10	.06
486	John Curtis	.20	.10	.06
487	Jim Tyrone	.20	.10	.06
488	Dan Spillner	.20	.10	.06
489	Rudy Meoli	.20	.10	.06
490	Amos Otis	.20	.10	.06
491	Scott McGregor	.20	.10	.06
492	Jim Sundberg	.20	.10	.06
493	Steve Renko	.20	.10	.06
494	Chuck Tanner	.20	.10	.06
495	Dave Cash	.20	.10	.06
496	*Jim Clancy*	.20	.10	.06
497	Glenn Adams	.20	.10	.06
498	Joe Sambito	.20	.10	.06
499	Mariners Team	.50	.25	.15
500	George Foster	.50	.25	.15
501	Dave Roberts	.20	.10	.06
502	Pat Rockett	.20	.10	.06
503	Ike Hampton	.20	.10	.06
504	Roger Freed	.20	.10	.06
505	Felix Millan	.20	.10	.06
506	Ron Blomberg	.20	.10	.06
507	Willie Crawford	.20	.10	.06
508	Johnny Oates	.20	.10	.06
509	Brent Strom	.20	.10	.06
510	Willie Stargell	3.00	1.50	.90
511	Frank Duffy	.20	.10	.06
512	Larry Herndon	.20	.10	.06
513	Barry Foote	.20	.10	.06
514	Rob Sperring	.20	.10	.06
515	Tim Corcoran	.20	.10	.06
516	Gary Beare	.20	.10	.06
517	Andres Mora	.20	.10	.06
518	Tommy Boggs	.20	.10	.06
519	Brian Downing	.25	.13	.08
520	Larry Hisle	.20	.10	.06
521	Steve Staggs	.20	.10	.06
522	Dick Williams	.20	.10	.06
523	*Donnie Moore*	.20	.10	.06
524	Bernie Carbo	.20	.10	.06
525	Jerry Terrell	.20	.10	.06

		NR MT	EX	VG
526	Reds Team	.60	.30	.20
527	Vic Correll	.20	.10	.06
528	Rob Picciolo	.20	.10	.06
529	Paul Hartzell	.20	.10	.06
530	Dave Winfield	24.00	12.00	7.25
531	Tom Underwood	.20	.10	.06
532	Skip Jutze	.20	.10	.06
533	Sandy Alomar	.20	.10	.06
534	Wilbur Howard	.20	.10	.06
535	Checklist 485-605	.90	.45	.25
536	Roric Harrison	.20	.10	.06
537	Bruce Bochte	.20	.10	.06
538	Johnnie LeMaster	.20	.10	.06
539	Vic Davalillo	.20	.10	.06
540	Steve Carlton	5.00	2.50	1.50
541	Larry Cox	.20	.10	.06
542	Tim Johnson	.20	.10	.06
543	Larry Harlow	.20	.10	.06
544	Len Randle	.20	.10	.06
545	Bill Campbell	.20	.10	.06
546	Ted Martinez	.20	.10	.06
547	John Scott	.20	.10	.06
548	Billy Hunter	.20	.10	.06
549	Joe Kerrigan	.20	.10	.06
550	John Mayberry	.20	.10	.06
551	Braves Team	.50	.25	.15
552	Francisco Barrios	.20	.10	.06
553	*Terry Puhl*	.35	.20	.11
554	Joe Coleman	.20	.10	.06
555	Butch Wynegar	.20	.10	.06
556	Ed Armbrister	.20	.10	.06
557	Tony Solaita	.20	.10	.06
558	Paul Mitchell	.20	.10	.06
559	Phil Mankowski	.20	.10	.06
560	Dave Parker	3.00	1.50	.90
561	Charlie Williams	.20	.10	.06
562	Glenn Burke	.20	.10	.06
563	Dave Rader	.20	.10	.06
564	Mick Kelleher	.20	.10	.06
565	Jerry Koosman	.20	.10	.06
566	Merv Rettenmund	.20	.10	.06
567	Dick Drago	.20	.10	.06
568	Tom Hutton	.20	.10	.06
569	*Lary Sorensen*	.20	.10	.06
570	Dave Kingman	.30	.15	.09
571	Buck Martinez	.20	.10	.06
572	Rick Wise	.20	.10	.06
573	Luis Gomez	.20	.10	.06
574	Bob Lemon	.30	.15	.09
575	Pat Dobson	.20	.10	.06
576	Sam Mejias	.20	.10	.06
577	A's Team	.50	.25	.15
578	Buzz Capra	.20	.10	.06
579	*Rance Mulliniks*	.35	.20	.11
580	Rod Carew	6.00	3.00	1.75
581	Lynn McGlothen	.20	.10	.06
582	Fran Healy	.20	.10	.06
583	George Medich	.20	.10	.06
584	John Hale	.20	.10	.06
585	Woodie Fryman	.20	.10	.06
586	Ed Goodson	.20	.10	.06
587	John Urrea	.20	.10	.06
588	Jim Mason	.20	.10	.06
589	*Bob Knepper*	.40	.20	.12
590	Bobby Murcer	.20	.10	.06
591	George Zeber	.20	.10	.06
592	Bob Apodaca	.20	.10	.06
593	Dave Skaggs	.20	.10	.06
594	Dave Freisleben	.20	.10	.06
595	Sixto Lezcano	.20	.10	.06
596	Gary Wheelock	.20	.10	.06
597	Steve Dillard	.20	.10	.06
598	Eddie Solomon	.20	.10	.06
599	Gary Woods	.20	.10	.06
600	Frank Tanana	.25	.13	.08
601	Gene Mauch	.20	.10	.06
602	Eric Soderholm	.20	.10	.06
603	Will McEnaney	.20	.10	.06
604	Earl Williams	.20	.10	.06
605	Rick Rhoden	.20	.10	.06
606	Pirates Team	.50	.25	.15
607	Fernando Arroyo	.20	.10	.06
608	Johnny Grubb	.20	.10	.06
609	John Denny	.20	.10	.06
610	Garry Maddox	.20	.10	.06
611	Pat Scanlon	.20	.10	.06
612	Ken Henderson	.20	.10	.06
613	Marty Perez	.20	.10	.06
614	Joe Wallis	.20	.10	.06
615	Clay Carroll	.20	.10	.06
616	Pat Kelly	.20	.10	.06

		NR MT	EX	VG
617	Joe Nolan	.20	.10	.06
618	Tommy Helms	.20	.10	.06
619	*Thad Bosley*	.20	.10	.06
620	Willie Randolph	.30	.15	.09
621	Craig Swan	.20	.10	.06
622	Champ Summers	.20	.10	.06
623	Eduardo Rodriguez	.20	.10	.06
624	Gary Alexander	.20	.10	.06
625	Jose Cruz	.25	.13	.08
626	Blue Jays Team	.25	.13	.08
627	Dave Johnson	.20	.10	.06
628	Ralph Garr	.20	.10	.06
629	Don Stanhouse	.20	.10	.06
630	Ron Cey	.25	.13	.08
631	Danny Ozark	.20	.10	.06
632	Rowland Office	.20	.10	.06
633	Tom Veryzer	.20	.10	.06
634	Len Barker	.20	.10	.06
635	Joe Rudi	.20	.10	.06
636	Jim Bibby	.20	.10	.06
637	Duffy Dyer	.20	.10	.06
638	Paul Splittorff	.20	.10	.06
639	Gene Clines	.20	.10	.06
640	Lee May	.20	.10	.06
641	Doug Rau	.20	.10	.06
642	Denny Doyle	.20	.10	.06
643	Tom House	.20	.10	.06
644	Jim Dwyer	.20	.10	.06
645	Mike Torrez	.20	.10	.06
646	Rick Auerbach	.20	.10	.06
647	Steve Dunning	.20	.10	.06
648	Gary Thomasson	.20	.10	.06
649	*Moose Haas*	.20	.10	.06
650	Cesar Cedeno	.25	.13	.08
651	Doug Rader	.20	.10	.06
652	Checklist 606-726	.90	.45	.25
653	Ron Hodges	.20	.10	.06
654	Pepe Frias	.20	.10	.06
655	Lyman Bostock	.20	.10	.06
656	Dave Garcia	.20	.10	.06
657	Bombo Rivera	.20	.10	.06
658	Manny Sanguillen	.20	.10	.06
659	Rangers Team	.50	.25	.15
660	Jason Thompson	.20	.10	.06
661	Grant Jackson	.20	.10	.06
662	Paul Dade	.20	.10	.06
663	Paul Reuschel	.20	.10	.06
664	Fred Stanley	.20	.10	.06
665	Dennis Leonard	.20	.10	.06
666	Billy Smith	.20	.10	.06
667	Jeff Byrd	.20	.10	.06
668	Dusty Baker	.25	.13	.08
669	Pete Falcone	.20	.10	.06
670	Jim Rice	2.50	1.25	.70
671	Gary Lavelle	.20	.10	.06
672	Don Kessinger	.20	.10	.06
673	Steve Brye	.20	.10	.06
674	*Ray Knight*	1.50	.70	.45
675	Jay Johnstone	.20	.10	.06
676	Bob Myrick	.20	.10	.06
677	Ed Herrmann	.20	.10	.06
678	Tom Burgmeier	.20	.10	.06
679	Wayne Garrett	.20	.10	.06
680	Vida Blue	.30	.15	.09
681	Rob Belloir	.20	.10	.06
682	Ken Brett	.20	.10	.06
683	Mike Champion	.20	.10	.06
684	Ralph Houk	.20	.10	.06
685	Frank Taveras	.20	.10	.06
686	Gaylord Perry	2.00	1.00	.60
687	*Julio Cruz*	.25	.13	.08
688	George Mitterwald	.20	.10	.06
689	Indians Team	.50	.25	.15
690	Mickey Rivers	.25	.13	.08
691	Ross Grimsley	.20	.10	.06
692	Ken Reitz	.20	.10	.06
693	Lamar Johnson	.20	.10	.06
694	Elias Sosa	.20	.10	.06
695	Dwight Evans	1.00	.50	.30
696	Steve Mingori	.20	.10	.06
697	Roger Metzger	.20	.10	.06
698	Juan Bernhardt	.20	.10	.06
699	Jackie Brown	.20	.10	.06
700	Johnny Bench	5.00	2.50	1.50
701	Rookie Pitchers (*Tom Hume,* Larry Landreth, *Steve McCatty,* Bruce Taylor)	.20	.10	.06
702	Rookie Catchers (Bill Nahorodny, Kevin Pasley, Rick Sweet, Don Werner)	.20	.10	.06
703	Rookie Pitchers (Larry Andersen, Tim Jones, Mickey Mahler, *Jack Morris*)	6.00	3.00	1.75

		NR MT	EX	VG
704	Rookie 2nd Basemen (*Garth Iorg*, Dave Oliver, Sam Perlozzo, *Lou Whitaker*)	20.00	10.00	6.00
705	Rookie Outfielders (*Dave Bergman*, Miguel Dilone, *Clint Hurdle*, Willie Norwood)	.20	.10	.06
706	Rookie 1st Basemen (Wayne Cage, Ted Cox, *Pat Putnam, Dave Revering*)	.20	.10	.06
707	Rookie Shortstops (Mickey Klutts, *Paul Molitor, Alan Trammell, U.L. Washington*)	90.00	45.00	27.00
708	Rookie Catchers (*Bo Diaz*, Dale Murphy, *Lance Parrish, Ernie Whitt*)	12.00	6.00	3.50
709	Rookie Pitchers (Steve Burke, *Matt Keough*, Lance Rautzhan, *Dan Schatzeder*)	.20	.10	.06
710	Rookie Outfielders (Dell Alston, Rick Bosetti, *Mike Easler*, Keith Smith)	.20	.10	.06
711	Rookie Pitchers (Cardell Camper, Dennis Lamp, Craig Mitchell, Roy Thomas)	.20	.10	.06
712	Bobby Valentine	.25	.13	.08
713	Bob Davis	.20	.10	.06
714	Mike Anderson	.20	.10	.06
715	Jim Kaat	.60	.30	.20
716	Cito Gaston	.35	.20	.11
717	Nelson Briles	.20	.10	.06
718	Ron Jackson	.20	.10	.06
719	Randy Elliott	.20	.10	.06
720	Fergie Jenkins	2.00	1.00	.60
721	Billy Martin	.50	.25	.15
722	Pete Broberg	.20	.10	.06
723	Johnny Wockenfuss	.20	.10	.06
724	Royals Team	.70	.35	.20
725	Kurt Bevacqua	.20	.10	.06
726	Wilbur Wood	.20	.10	.06

1979 Topps

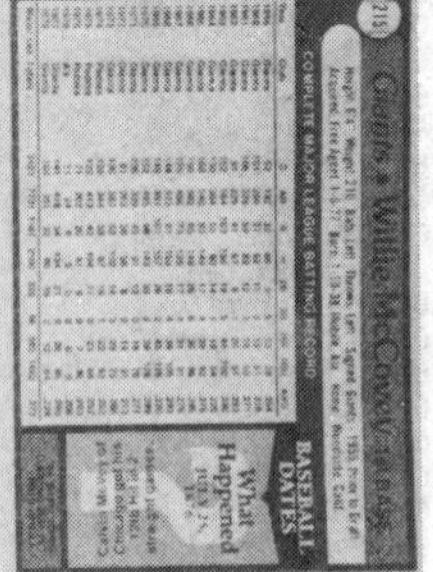

The size of this issue remained the same as in 1978 with 726 cards making their appearance. Actually, the 2-1/2" by 3-1/2" cards have a relatively minor design change from the previous year. The large color photo still dominates the front, with the player's name, team and position below it. The baseball with the player's position was moved to the lower left and the position replaced by a Topps logo. On the back, the printing color was changed and the game situation was replaced by a quiz called "Baseball Dates". Specialty cards include statistical leaders, major league records set during the season and eight cards devoted to career records. For the first time, rookies were arranged by teams under the heading of "Prospects."

	NR MT	EX	VG
Complete Set (726):	250.00	125.00	75.00
Common Player:	.15	.08	.05

		NR MT	EX	VG
1	Batting Leaders (Rod Carew, Dave Parker)	3.00	1.50	.90
2	Home Run Leaders (George Foster, Jim Rice)	.30	.15	.09
3	RBI Leaders (George Foster, Jim Rice)	.30	.15	.09
4	Stolen Base Leaders (Ron LeFlore, Omar Moreno)	.15	.08	.05
5	Victory Leaders (Ron Guidry, Gaylord Perry)	.30	.15	.09
6	Strikeout Leaders (J.R. Richard, Nolan Ryan)	4.00	2.00	1.25
7	ERA Leaders (Ron Guidry, Craig Swan)	.25	.13	.08
8	Leading Firemen (Rollie Fingers, Rich Gossage)	.40	.20	.12
9	Dave Campbell	.15	.08	.05
10	Lee May	.20	.10	.06
11	Marc Hill	.15	.08	.05
12	Dick Drago	.15	.08	.05
13	Paul Dade	.15	.08	.05
14	Rafael Landestoy	.15	.08	.05
15	Ross Grimsley	.20	.10	.06
16	Fred Stanley	.20	.10	.06
17	Donnie Moore	.20	.10	.06
18	Tony Solaita	.15	.08	.05
19	Larry Gura	.15	.08	.05
20	Joe Morgan	.40	.20	.12
21	Kevin Kobel	.15	.08	.05
22	Mike Jorgensen	.15	.08	.05
23	Terry Forster	.20	.10	.06
24	Paul Molitor	30.00	15.00	9.00
25	Steve Carlton	4.00	2.00	1.25
26	Jamie Quirk	.15	.08	.05
27	Dave Goltz	.20	.10	.06
28	Steve Brye	.15	.08	.05
29	Rick Langford	.15	.08	.05
30	Dave Winfield	14.00	7.00	4.25
31	Tom House	.15	.08	.05
32	Jerry Mumphrey	.15	.08	.05
33	Dave Rozema	.15	.08	.05
34	Rob Andrews	.15	.08	.05
35	Ed Figueroa	.20	.10	.06
36	Alan Ashby	.15	.08	.05
37	Joe Kerrigan	.15	.08	.05
38	Bernie Carbo	.15	.08	.05
39	Dale Murphy	6.00	3.00	1.75
40	Dennis Eckersley	8.00	4.00	2.50
41	Twins Team (Gene Mauch)	.50	.25	.15
42	Ron Blomberg	.15	.08	.05
43	Wayne Twitchell	.15	.08	.05
44	Kurt Bevacqua	.15	.08	.05
45	Al Hrabosky	.20	.10	.06
46	Ron Hodges	.15	.08	.05
47	Fred Norman	.15	.08	.05
48	Merv Rettenmund	.15	.08	.05
49	Vern Ruhle	.15	.08	.05
50	Steve Garvey	.90	.45	.25
51	Ray Fosse	.15	.08	.05
52	Randy Lerch	.15	.08	.05
53	Mick Kelleher	.15	.08	.05
54	Dell Alston	.15	.08	.05
55	Willie Stargell	2.00	1.00	.60
56	John Hale	.15	.08	.05
57	Eric Rasmussen	.15	.08	.05
58	Bob Randall	.15	.08	.05
59	John Denny	.15	.08	.05
60	Mickey Rivers	.20	.10	.06
61	Bo Diaz	.20	.10	.06
62	Randy Moffitt	.15	.08	.05
63	Jack Brohamer	.15	.08	.05
64	Tom Underwood	.15	.08	.05
65	Mark Belanger	.20	.10	.06
66	Tigers Team (Les Moss)	.60	.30	.20
67	Jim Mason	.15	.08	.05
68	Joe Niekro	.15	.08	.05
69	Elliott Maddox	.15	.08	.05
70	John Candelaria	.25	.13	.08
71	Brian Downing	.20	.10	.06
72	Steve Mingori	.15	.08	.05
73	Ken Henderson	.15	.08	.05
74	*Shane Rawley*	.15	.08	.05
75	Steve Yeager	.15	.08	.05
76	Warren Cromartie	.15	.08	.05
77	Dan Briggs	.15	.08	.05
78	Elias Sosa	.15	.08	.05
79	Ted Cox	.15	.08	.05
80	Jason Thompson	.20	.10	.06
81	Roger Erickson	.15	.08	.05
82	Mets Team (Joe Torre)	.60	.30	.20
83	Fred Kendall	.15	.08	.05
84	Greg Minton	.15	.08	.05
85	Gary Matthews	.20	.10	.06
86	Rodney Scott	.15	.08	.05
87	Pete Falcone	.15	.08	.05
88	Bob Molinaro	.15	.08	.05
89	Dick Tidrow	.20	.10	.06
90	Bob Boone	.25	.13	.08
91	Terry Crowley	.15	.08	.05
92	Jim Bibby	.15	.08	.05

		NR MT	EX	VG
93	Phil Mankowski	.15	.08	.05
94	Len Barker	.15	.08	.05
95	Robin Yount	15.00	7.50	4.50
96	Indians Team (Jeff Torborg)	.50	.25	.15
97	Sam Mejias	.15	.08	.05
98	Ray Burris	.15	.08	.05
99	John Wathan	.20	.10	.06
100	Tom Seaver	4.00	2.00	1.25
101	Roy Howell	.15	.08	.05
102	Mike Anderson	.15	.08	.05
103	Jim Todd	.15	.08	.05
104	Johnny Oates	.15	.08	.05
105	Rick Camp	.15	.08	.05
106	Frank Duffy	.15	.08	.05
107	Jesus Alou	.20	.10	.06
108	Eduardo Rodriguez	.15	.08	.05
109	Joel Youngblood	.15	.08	.05
110	Vida Blue	.30	.15	.09
111	Roger Freed	.15	.08	.05
112	Phillies Team (Danny Ozark)	.50	.25	.15
113	Pete Redfern	.15	.08	.05
114	Cliff Johnson	.20	.10	.06
115	Nolan Ryan	30.00	15.00	9.00
116	*Ozzie Smith*	90.00	45.00	27.00
117	Grant Jackson	.15	.08	.05
118	Bud Harrelson	.20	.10	.06
119	Don Stanhouse	.15	.08	.05
120	Jim Sundberg	.20	.10	.06
121	Checklist 1-121	.25	.13	.08
122	Mike Paxton	.15	.08	.05
123	Lou Whitaker	6.00	3.00	1.75
124	Dan Schatzeder	.15	.08	.05
125	Rick Burleson	.20	.10	.06
126	Doug Bair	.15	.08	.05
127	Thad Bosley	.15	.08	.05
128	Ted Martinez	.15	.08	.05
129	Marty Pattin	.15	.08	.05
130	Bob Watson	.15	.08	.05
131	Jim Clancy	.25	.13	.08
132	Rowland Office	.15	.08	.05
133	Bill Castro	.15	.08	.05
134	Alan Bannister	.15	.08	.05
135	Bobby Murcer	.25	.13	.08
136	Jim Kaat	.60	.30	.20
137	Larry Wolfe	.15	.08	.05
138	Mark Lee	.15	.08	.05
139	Luis Pujols	.15	.08	.05
140	Don Gullett	.20	.10	.06
141	Tom Paciorek	.15	.08	.05
142	Charlie Williams	.15	.08	.05
143	Tony Scott	.15	.08	.05
144	Sandy Alomar	.15	.08	.05
145	Rick Rhoden	.25	.13	.08
146	Duane Kuiper	.15	.08	.05
147	Dave Hamilton	.15	.08	.05
148	Bruce Boisclair	.15	.08	.05
149	Manny Sarmiento	.15	.08	.05
150	Wayne Cage	.15	.08	.05
151	John Hiller	.20	.10	.06
152	Rick Cerone	.20	.10	.06
153	Dennis Lamp	.15	.08	.05
154	Jim Gantner	.15	.08	.05
155	Dwight Evans	.75	.40	.25
156	Buddy Solomon	.15	.08	.05
157	U.L. Washington	.15	.08	.05
158	Joe Sambito	.15	.08	.05
159	Roy White	.25	.13	.08
160	Mike Flanagan	.30	.15	.09
161	Barry Foote	.15	.08	.05
162	Tom Johnson	.15	.08	.05
163	Glenn Burke	.15	.08	.05
164	Mickey Lolich	.30	.15	.09
165	Frank Taveras	.15	.08	.05
166	Leon Roberts	.15	.08	.05
167	Roger Metzger	.15	.08	.05
168	Dave Freisleben	.15	.08	.05
169	Bill Nahorodny	.15	.08	.05
170	Don Sutton	1.25	.60	.40
171	Gene Clines	.15	.08	.05
172	Mike Bruhert	.15	.08	.05
173	John Lowenstein	.15	.08	.05
174	Rick Auerbach	.15	.08	.05
175	George Hendrick	.20	.10	.06
176	Aurelio Rodriguez	.20	.10	.06
177	Ron Reed	.20	.10	.06
178	Alvis Woods	.15	.08	.05
179	Jim Beattie	.15	.08	.05
180	Larry Hisle	.20	.10	.06
181	Mike Garman	.15	.08	.05
182	Tim Johnson	.15	.08	.05
183	Paul Splittorff	.20	.10	.06

		NR MT	EX	VG
184	Darrel Chaney	.15	.08	.05
185	Mike Torrez	.20	.10	.06
186	Eric Soderholm	.15	.08	.05
187	Mark Lemongello	.15	.08	.05
188	Pat Kelly	.15	.08	.05
189	*Eddie Whitson*	.25	.13	.08
190	Ron Cey	.25	.13	.08
191	Mike Norris	.15	.08	.05
192	Cardinals Team (Ken Boyer)	.50	.25	.15
193	Glenn Adams	.15	.08	.05
194	Randy Jones	.20	.10	.06
195	Bill Madlock	.40	.20	.12
196	Steve Kemp	.15	.08	.05
197	Bob Apodaca	.15	.08	.05
198	Johnny Grubb	.15	.08	.05
199	Larry Milbourne	.15	.08	.05
200	Johnny Bench	2.00	1.00	.60
201	Mike Edwards (Record Breaker)	.15	.08	.05
202	Ron Guidry (Record Breaker)	.35	.20	.11
203	J.R. Richard (Record Breaker)	.20	.10	.06
204	Pete Rose (Record Breaker)	1.50	.70	.45
205	John Stearns (Record Breaker)	.15	.08	.05
206	Sammy Stewart (Record Breaker)	.15	.08	.05
207	Dave Lemanczyk	.15	.08	.05
208	Citoence Gaston	.30	.15	.09
209	Reggie Cleveland	.15	.08	.05
210	Larry Bowa	.30	.15	.09
211	Denny Martinez	.20	.10	.06
212	*Carney Lansford*	2.00	1.00	.60
213	Bill Travers	.15	.08	.05
214	Red Sox Team (Don Zimmer)	.60	.30	.20
215	Willie McCovey	2.00	1.00	.60
216	Wilbur Wood	.20	.10	.06
217	Steve Dillard	.15	.08	.05
218	Dennis Leonard	.20	.10	.06
219	Roy Smalley	.20	.10	.06
220	Cesar Geronimo	.20	.10	.06
221	Jesse Jefferson	.15	.08	.05
222	Bob Beall	.15	.08	.05
223	Kent Tekulve	.25	.13	.08
224	Dave Revering	.15	.08	.05
225	Rich Gossage	.40	.20	.12
226	Ron Pruitt	.15	.08	.05
227	Steve Stone	.20	.10	.06
228	Vic Davalillo	.15	.08	.05
229	Doug Flynn	.15	.08	.05
230	Bob Forsch	.20	.10	.06
231	Johnny Wockenfuss	.15	.08	.05
232	Jimmy Sexton	.15	.08	.05
233	Paul Mitchell	.15	.08	.05
234	Toby Harrah	.20	.10	.06
235	Steve Rogers	.20	.10	.06
236	Jim Dwyer	.15	.08	.05
237	Billy Smith	.15	.08	.05
238	Balor Moore	.15	.08	.05
239	Willie Horton	.20	.10	.06
240	Rick Reuschel	.25	.13	.08
241	Checklist 122-242	.25	.13	.08
242	Pablo Torrealba	.15	.08	.05
243	Buck Martinez	.15	.08	.05
244	Pirates Team (Chuck Tanner)	.80	.40	.25
245	Jeff Burroughs	.20	.10	.06
246	Darrell Jackson	.15	.08	.05
247	Tucker Ashford	.15	.08	.05
248	Pete LaCock	.15	.08	.05
249	Paul Thormodsgard	.15	.08	.05
250	Willie Randolph	.30	.15	.09
251	Jack Morris	3.00	1.50	.90
252	Bob Stinson	.15	.08	.05
253	Rick Wise	.20	.10	.06
254	Luis Gomez	.15	.08	.05
255	Tommy John	.80	.40	.25
256	Mike Sadek	.15	.08	.05
257	Adrian Devine	.15	.08	.05
258	Mike Phillips	.15	.08	.05
259	Reds Team (Sparky Anderson)	.60	.30	.20
260	Richie Zisk	.20	.10	.06
261	Mario Guerrero	.15	.08	.05
262	Nelson Briles	.15	.08	.05
263	Oscar Gamble	.20	.10	.06
264	*Don Robinson*	.15	.08	.05
265	Don Money	.15	.08	.05
266	Jim Willoughby	.15	.08	.05
267	Joe Rudi	.20	.10	.06
268	Julio Gonzalez	.15	.08	.05
269	Woodie Fryman	.20	.10	.06
270	Butch Hobson	.15	.08	.05
271	Rawly Eastwick	.15	.08	.05
272	Tim Corcoran	.15	.08	.05
273	Jerry Terrell	.15	.08	.05
274	Willie Norwood	.15	.08	.05

		NR MT	EX	VG
275	Junior Moore	.15	.08	.05
276	Jim Colborn	.15	.08	.05
277	Tom Grieve	.15	.08	.05
278	Andy Messersmith	.25	.13	.08
279	Jerry Grote	.15	.08	.05
280	Andre Thornton	.25	.13	.08
281	Vic Correll	.15	.08	.05
282	Blue Jays Team (Roy Hartsfield)	.50	.25	.15
283	Ken Kravec	.15	.08	.05
284	Johnnie LeMaster	.15	.08	.05
285	Bobby Bonds	.30	.15	.09
286	Duffy Dyer	.15	.08	.05
287	Andres Mora	.15	.08	.05
288	Milt Wilcox	.20	.10	.06
289	Jose Cruz	.25	.13	.08
290	Dave Lopes	.25	.13	.08
291	Tom Griffin	.15	.08	.05
292	Don Reynolds	.15	.08	.05
293	Jerry Garvin	.15	.08	.05
294	Pepe Frias	.15	.08	.05
295	Mitchell Page	.15	.08	.05
296	Preston Hanna	.15	.08	.05
297	Ted Sizemore	.15	.08	.05
298	Rich Gale	.15	.08	.05
299	Steve Ontiveros	.15	.08	.05
300	Rod Carew	4.00	2.00	1.25
301	Tom Hume	.15	.08	.05
302	Braves Team (Bobby Cox)	.50	.25	.15
303	Lary Sorensen	.15	.08	.05
304	Steve Swisher	.15	.08	.05
305	Willie Montanez	.15	.08	.05
306	Floyd Bannister	.15	.08	.05
307	Larvell Blanks	.15	.08	.05
308	Bert Blyleven	.30	.15	.09
309	Ralph Garr	.20	.10	.06
310	Thurman Munson	4.00	2.00	1.25
311	Gary Lavelle	.15	.08	.05
312	Bob Robertson	.15	.08	.05
313	Dyar Miller	.15	.08	.05
314	Larry Harlow	.15	.08	.05
315	Jon Matlack	.20	.10	.06
316	Milt May	.15	.08	.05
317	Jose Cardenal	.15	.08	.05
318	*Bob Welch*	2.50	1.25	.70
319	Wayne Garrett	.15	.08	.05
320	Carl Yastrzemski	4.00	2.00	1.25
321	Gaylord Perry	2.00	1.00	.60
322	Danny Goodwin	.15	.08	.05
323	Lynn McGlothen	.15	.08	.05
324	Mike Tyson	.15	.08	.05
325	Cecil Cooper	.20	.10	.06
326	Pedro Borbon	.15	.08	.05
327	Art Howe	.15	.08	.05
328	A's Team (Jack McKeon)	.50	.25	.15
329	Joe Coleman	.20	.10	.06
330	George Brett	18.00	9.00	5.50
331	Mickey Mahler	.15	.08	.05
332	Gary Alexander	.15	.08	.05
333	Chet Lemon	.20	.10	.06
334	Craig Swan	.15	.08	.05
335	Chris Chambliss	.25	.13	.08
336	Bobby Thompson	.15	.08	.05
337	John Montague	.15	.08	.05
338	Vic Harris	.15	.08	.05
339	Ron Jackson	.15	.08	.05
340	Jim Palmer	4.00	2.00	1.25
341	*Willie Upshaw*	.20	.10	.06
342	Dave Roberts	.15	.08	.05
343	Ed Glynn	.15	.08	.05
344	Jerry Royster	.15	.08	.05
345	Tug McGraw	.30	.15	.09
346	Bill Buckner	.30	.15	.09
347	Doug Rau	.15	.08	.05
348	Andre Dawson	12.00	6.00	3.50
349	Jim Wright	.15	.08	.05
350	Garry Templeton	.20	.10	.06
351	Wayne Nordhagen	.15	.08	.05
352	Steve Renko	.15	.08	.05
353	Checklist 243-363	.60	.30	.20
354	Bill Bonham	.15	.08	.05
355	Lee Mazzilli	.20	.10	.06
356	Giants Team (Joe Altobelli)	.50	.25	.15
357	Jerry Augustine	.15	.08	.05
358	Alan Trammell	10.00	5.00	3.00
359	Dan Spillner	.15	.08	.05
360	Amos Otis	.20	.10	.06
361	Tom Dixon	.15	.08	.05
362	Mike Cubbage	.15	.08	.05
363	Craig Skok	.15	.08	.05
364	Gene Richards	.15	.08	.05
365	Sparky Lyle	.30	.15	.09

		NR MT	EX	VG
366	Juan Bernhardt	.15	.08	.05
367	Dave Skaggs	.15	.08	.05
368	Don Aase	.20	.10	.06
369a	Bump Wills (Blue Jays)	2.00	1.00	.60
369b	Bump Wills (Rangers)	2.50	1.25	.70
370	Dave Kingman	.35	.20	.11
371	Jeff Holly	.15	.08	.05
372	Lamar Johnson	.15	.08	.05
373	Lance Rautzhan	.15	.08	.05
374	Ed Herrmann	.15	.08	.05
375	Bill Campbell	.15	.08	.05
376	Gorman Thomas	.25	.13	.08
377	Paul Moskau	.15	.08	.05
378	Rob Picciolo	.15	.08	.05
379	Dale Murray	.15	.08	.05
380	John Mayberry	.20	.10	.06
381	Astros Team (Bill Virdon)	.50	.25	.15
382	Jerry Martin	.15	.08	.05
383	Phil Garner	.20	.10	.06
384	Tommy Boggs	.15	.08	.05
385	Dan Ford	.15	.08	.05
386	Francisco Barrios	.15	.08	.05
387	Gary Thomasson	.15	.08	.05
388	Jack Billingham	.15	.08	.05
389	Joe Zdeb	.15	.08	.05
390	Rollie Fingers	2.50	1.25	.70
391	Al Oliver	.40	.20	.12
392	Doug Ault	.15	.08	.05
393	Scott McGregor	.20	.10	.06
394	Randy Stein	.15	.08	.05
395	Dave Cash	.15	.08	.05
396	Bill Plummer	.15	.08	.05
397	Sergio Ferrer	.15	.08	.05
398	Ivan DeJesus	.15	.08	.05
399	David Clyde	.15	.08	.05
400	Jim Rice	1.00	.50	.30
401	Ray Knight	.25	.13	.08
402	Paul Hartzell	.15	.08	.05
403	Tim Foli	.15	.08	.05
404	White Sox Team (Don Kessinger)	.50	.25	.15
405	Butch Wynegar	.20	.10	.06
406	Joe Wallis	.15	.08	.05
407	Pete Vuckovich	.20	.10	.06
408	Charlie Moore	.15	.08	.05
409	*Willie Wilson*	2.00	1.00	.60
410	Darrell Evans	.30	.15	.09
411	All-Time Hits Leaders (Ty Cobb, George Sisler) ((season))	.70	.35	.20
412	All-Time RBI Leaders (Hank Aaron, Hack Wilson) (season)	.70	.35	.20
413	All-Time Home Run Leaders (Hank Aaron, Roger Maris) (season)	1.00	.50	.30
414	All-Time Batting Average Leaders (Ty Cobb, Roger Hornsby) (season)	.70	.35	.20
415	All-Time Stolen Bases Leader (Lou Brock)	.50	.25	.15
416	All-Time Wins Leaders (Jack Chesbro, Cy Young) (career)	.40	.20	.12
417	All-Time Strikeout Leaders (Walter Johnson, Nolan Ryan) (season)	2.00	1.00	.60
418	All-Time ERA Leaders (Walter Johnson, Dutch Leonard) (season)	.20	.10	.06
419	Dick Ruthven	.15	.08	.05
420	Ken Griffey	.25	.13	.08
421	Doug DeCinces	.25	.13	.08
422	Ruppert Jones	.15	.08	.05
423	Bob Montgomery	.15	.08	.05
424	Angels Team (Jim Fregosi)	.60	.30	.20
425	Rick Manning	.15	.08	.05
426	Chris Speier	.20	.10	.06
427	Andy Replogle	.15	.08	.05
428	Bobby Valentine	.25	.13	.08
429	John Urrea	.15	.08	.05
430	Dave Parker	2.00	1.00	.60
431	Glenn Borgmann	.15	.08	.05
432	Dave Heaverlo	.15	.08	.05
433	Larry Biittner	.15	.08	.05
434	Ken Clay	.20	.10	.06
435	Gene Tenace	.20	.10	.06
436	Hector Cruz	.15	.08	.05
437	Rick Williams	.15	.08	.05
438	Horace Speed	.15	.08	.05
439	Frank White	.25	.13	.08
440	Rusty Staub	.30	.15	.09
441	Lee Lacy	.15	.08	.05
442	Doyle Alexander	.25	.13	.08
443	Bruce Bochte	.15	.08	.05
444	*Aurelio Lopez*	.20	.10	.06
445	Steve Henderson	.15	.08	.05
446	Jim Lonborg	.20	.10	.06
447	Manny Sanguillen	.15	.08	.05

No.	Player	NR MT	EX	VG
448	Moose Haas	.15	.08	.05
449	Bombo Rivera	.15	.08	.05
450	Dave Concepcion	.30	.15	.09
451	Royals Team (Whitey Herzog)	.50	.25	.15
452	Jerry Morales	.15	.08	.05
453	Chris Knapp	.15	.08	.05
454	Len Randle	.15	.08	.05
455	Bill Lee	.15	.08	.05
456	Chuck Baker	.15	.08	.05
457	Bruce Sutter	.40	.20	.12
458	Jim Essian	.15	.08	.05
459	Sid Monge	.15	.08	.05
460	Graig Nettles	.25	.13	.08
461	Jim Barr	.15	.08	.05
462	Otto Velez	.15	.08	.05
463	Steve Comer	.15	.08	.05
464	Joe Nolan	.15	.08	.05
465	Reggie Smith	.25	.13	.08
466	Mark Littell	.15	.08	.05
467	Don Kessinger	.15	.08	.05
468	Stan Bahnsen	.15	.08	.05
469	Lance Parrish	2.00	1.00	.60
470	Garry Maddox	.15	.08	.05
471	Joaquin Andujar	.20	.10	.06
472	Craig Kusick	.15	.08	.05
473	Dave Roberts	.15	.08	.05
474	Dick Davis	.15	.08	.05
475	Dan Driessen	.20	.10	.06
476	Tom Poquette	.15	.08	.05
477	Bob Grich	.25	.13	.08
478	Juan Beniquez	.15	.08	.05
479	Padres Team (Roger Craig)	.50	.25	.15
480	Fred Lynn	.70	.35	.20
481	Skip Lockwood	.15	.08	.05
482	Craig Reynolds	.15	.08	.05
483	Checklist 364-484	.25	.13	.08
484	Rick Waits	.15	.08	.05
485	Bucky Dent	.25	.13	.08
486	Bob Knepper	.25	.13	.08
487	Miguel Dilone	.15	.08	.05
488	Bob Owchinko	.15	.08	.05
489	Larry Cox (photo actually Dave Rader)	.15	.08	.05
490	Al Cowens	.15	.08	.05
491	Tippy Martinez	.15	.08	.05
492	Bob Bailor	.15	.08	.05
493	Larry Christenson	.15	.08	.05
494	Jerry White	.15	.08	.05
495	Tony Perez	.40	.20	.12
496	Barry Bonnell	.15	.08	.05
497	Glenn Abbott	.15	.08	.05
498	Rich Chiles	.15	.08	.05
499	Rangers Team (Pat Corrales)	.50	.25	.15
500	Ron Guidry	.30	.15	.09
501	Junior Kennedy	.15	.08	.05
502	Steve Braun	.15	.08	.05
503	Terry Humphrey	.15	.08	.05
504	*Larry McWilliams*	.20	.10	.06
505	Ed Kranepool	.20	.10	.06
506	John D'Acquisto	.15	.08	.05
507	Tony Armas	.20	.10	.06
508	Charlie Hough	.20	.10	.06
509	Mario Mendoza	.15	.08	.05
510	Ted Simmons	.20	.10	.06
511	Paul Reuschel	.15	.08	.05
512	Jack Clark	.60	.30	.20
513	Dave Johnson	.30	.15	.09
514	Mike Proly	.15	.08	.05
515	Enos Cabell	.15	.08	.05
516	Champ Summers	.15	.08	.05
517	Al Bumbry	.20	.10	.06
518	Jim Umbarger	.15	.08	.05
519	Ben Oglivie	.20	.10	.06
520	Gary Carter	2.00	1.00	.60
521	Sam Ewing	.15	.08	.05
522	Ken Holtzman	.20	.10	.06
523	John Milner	.15	.08	.05
524	Tom Burgmeier	.15	.08	.05
525	Freddie Patek	.15	.08	.05
526	Dodgers Team (Tom Lasorda)	.60	.30	.20
527	Lerrin LaGrow	.15	.08	.05
528	Wayne Gross	.15	.08	.05
529	Brian Asselstine	.15	.08	.05
530	Frank Tanana	.25	.13	.08
531	Fernando Gonzalez	.15	.08	.05
532	Buddy Schultz	.15	.08	.05
533	Leroy Stanton	.15	.08	.05
534	Ken Forsch	.15	.08	.05
535	Ellis Valentine	.15	.08	.05
536	Jerry Reuss	.20	.10	.06
537	Tom Veryzer	.15	.08	.05
538	Mike Ivie	.15	.08	.05
539	John Ellis	.15	.08	.05
540	Greg Luzinski	.30	.15	.09
541	Jim Slaton	.15	.08	.05
542	Rick Bosetti	.15	.08	.05
543	Kiko Garcia	.15	.08	.05
544	Fergie Jenkins	1.50	.70	.45
545	John Stearns	.15	.08	.05
546	Bill Russell	.20	.10	.06
547	Clint Hurdle	.15	.08	.05
548	Enrique Romo	.15	.08	.05
549	Bob Bailey	.15	.08	.05
550	Sal Bando	.20	.10	.06
551	Cubs Team (Herman Franks)	.50	.25	.15
552	Jose Morales	.15	.08	.05
553	Denny Walling	.15	.08	.05
554	Matt Keough	.15	.08	.05
555	Biff Pocoroba	.15	.08	.05
556	Mike Lum	.15	.08	.05
557	Ken Brett	.20	.10	.06
558	Jay Johnstone	.20	.10	.06
559	Greg Pryor	.15	.08	.05
560	John Montefusco	.15	.08	.05
561	Ed Ott	.15	.08	.05
562	Dusty Baker	.25	.13	.08
563	Roy Thomas	.15	.08	.05
564	Jerry Turner	.15	.08	.05
565	Rico Carty	.25	.13	.08
566	Nino Espinosa	.15	.08	.05
567	Rich Hebner	.15	.08	.05
568	Carlos Lopez	.15	.08	.05
569	Bob Sykes	.15	.08	.05
570	Cesar Cedeno	.25	.13	.08
571	Darrell Porter	.20	.10	.06
572	Rod Gilbreath	.15	.08	.05
573	Jim Kern	.15	.08	.05
574	Claudell Washington	.20	.10	.06
575	Luis Tiant	.20	.10	.06
576	Mike Parrott	.15	.08	.05
577	Brewers Team (George Bamberger)	.50	.25	.15
578	Pete Broberg	.15	.08	.05
579	Greg Gross	.15	.08	.05
580	Ron Fairly	.20	.10	.06
581	Darold Knowles	.15	.08	.05
582	Paul Blair	.20	.10	.06
583	Julio Cruz	.15	.08	.05
584	Jim Rooker	.15	.08	.05
585	Hal McRae	.25	.13	.08
586	*Bob Horner*	.90	.45	.25
587	Ken Reitz	.15	.08	.05
588	Tom Murphy	.15	.08	.05
589	Terry Whitfield	.15	.08	.05
590	J.R. Richard	.20	.10	.06
591	Mike Hargrove	.20	.10	.06
592	Mike Krukow	.20	.10	.06
593	Rick Dempsey	.20	.10	.06
594	Bob Shirley	.15	.08	.05
595	Phil Niekro	1.25	.60	.40
596	Jim Wohlford	.15	.08	.05
597	Bob Stanley	.20	.10	.06
598	Mark Wagner	.15	.08	.05
599	Jim Spencer	.20	.10	.06
600	George Foster	.30	.15	.09
601	Dave LaRoche	.15	.08	.05
602	Checklist 485-605	.60	.30	.20
603	Rudy May	.15	.08	.05
604	Jeff Newman	.15	.08	.05
605	Rick Monday	.15	.08	.05
606	Expos Team (Dick Williams)	.50	.25	.15
607	Omar Moreno	.15	.08	.05
608	Dave McKay	.15	.08	.05
609	Silvio Martinez	.15	.08	.05
610	Mike Schmidt	10.00	5.00	3.00
611	Jim Norris	.15	.08	.05
612	*Rick Honeycutt*	.15	.08	.05
613	Mike Edwards	.15	.08	.05
614	Willie Hernandez	.20	.10	.06
615	Ken Singleton	.20	.10	.06
616	Billy Almon	.15	.08	.05
617	Terry Puhl	.15	.08	.05
618	Jerry Remy	.15	.08	.05
619	*Ken Landreaux*	.15	.08	.05
620	Bert Campaneris	.25	.13	.08
621	Pat Zachry	.15	.08	.05
622	Dave Collins	.20	.10	.06
623	Bob McClure	.15	.08	.05
624	Larry Herndon	.20	.10	.06
625	Mark Fidrych	.25	.13	.08
626	Yankees Team (Bob Lemon)	.80	.40	.25
627	Gary Serum	.15	.08	.05

		NR MT	EX	VG
628	Del Unser	.15	.08	.05
629	Gene Garber	.15	.08	.05
630	Bake McBride	.15	.08	.05
631	Jorge Orta	.15	.08	.05
632	Don Kirkwood	.15	.08	.05
633	Rob Wilfong	.15	.08	.05
634	Paul Lindblad	.20	.10	.06
635	Don Baylor	.40	.20	.12
636	Wayne Garland	.15	.08	.05
637	Bill Robinson	.15	.08	.05
638	Al Fitzmorris	.15	.08	.05
639	Manny Trillo	.20	.10	.06
640	Eddie Murray	21.00	10.50	6.25
641	*Bobby Castillo*	.15	.08	.05
642	Wilbur Howard	.15	.08	.05
643	Tom Hausman	.15	.08	.05
644	Manny Mota	.20	.10	.06
645	George Scott	.15	.08	.05
646	Rick Sweet	.15	.08	.05
647	Bob Lacey	.15	.08	.05
648	Lou Piniella	.35	.20	.11
649	John Curtis	.15	.08	.05
650	Pete Rose	5.00	2.50	1.50
651	Mike Caldwell	.15	.08	.05
652	Stan Papi	.15	.08	.05
653	Warren Brusstar	.15	.08	.05
654	Rick Miller	.15	.08	.05
655	Jerry Koosman	.15	.08	.05
656	Hosken Powell	.15	.08	.05
657	George Medich	.15	.08	.05
658	Taylor Duncan	.15	.08	.05
659	Mariners Team (Darrell Johnson)	.50	.25	.15
660	Ron LeFlore	.15	.08	.05
661	Bruce Kison	.15	.08	.05
662	Kevin Bell	.15	.08	.05
663	Mike Vail	.15	.08	.05
664	Doug Bird	.15	.08	.05
665	Lou Brock	2.00	1.00	.60
666	Rich Dauer	.15	.08	.05
667	Don Hood	.15	.08	.05
668	Bill North	.15	.08	.05
669	Checklist 606-726	.60	.30	.20
670	Catfish Hunter	1.25	.60	.40
671	Joe Ferguson	.15	.08	.05
672	Ed Halicki	.15	.08	.05
673	Tom Hutton	.15	.08	.05
674	Dave Tomlin	.15	.08	.05
675	Tim McCarver	.30	.15	.09
676	Johnny Sutton	.15	.08	.05
677	Larry Parrish	.15	.08	.05
678	Geoff Zahn	.15	.08	.05
679	Derrel Thomas	.15	.08	.05
680	Carlton Fisk	3.00	1.50	.90
681	*John Henry Johnson*	.15	.08	.05
682	Dave Chalk	.15	.08	.05
683	Dan Meyer	.15	.08	.05
684	Jamie Easterly	.15	.08	.05
685	Sixto Lezcano	.15	.08	.05
686	Ron Schueler	.15	.08	.05
687	Rennie Stennett	.15	.08	.05
688	Mike Willis	.15	.08	.05
689	Orioles Team (Earl Weaver)	.70	.35	.20
690	Buddy Bell	.15	.08	.05
691	Dock Ellis	.15	.08	.05
692	Mickey Stanley	.20	.10	.06
693	Dave Rader	.15	.08	.05
694	Burt Hooton	.20	.10	.06
695	Keith Hernandez	1.00	.50	.30
696	Andy Hassler	.15	.08	.05
697	Dave Bergman	.15	.08	.05
698	Bill Stein	.15	.08	.05
699	Hal Dues	.15	.08	.05
700	Reggie Jackson	5.00	2.50	1.50
701	Orioles Prospects (Mark Corey, John Flinn, *Sammy Stewart*)	.15	.08	.05
702	Red Sox Prospects (Joel Finch, Garry Hancock, Allen Ripley)	.15	.08	.05
703	Angels Prospects (Jim Anderson, Dave Frost, Bob Slater)	.15	.08	.05
704	White Sox Prospects (Ross Baumgarten, Mike Colbern, *Mike Squires*)	.15	.08	.05
705	Indians Prospects (*Alfredo Griffin*, Tim Norrid, Dave Oliver)	.70	.35	.20
706	Tigers Prospects (Dave Stegman, Dave Tobik, Kip Young)	.15	.08	.05
707	Royals Prospects (Randy Bass, Jim Gaudet, Randy McGilberry)	.15	.08	.05
708	Brewers Prospects (*Kevin Bass, Eddie Romero*, Ned Yost)	.50	.25	.15
709	Twins Prospects (Sam Perlozzo, Rick Sofield, Kevin Stanfield)	.15	.08	.05
710	Yankees Prospects (Brian Doyle, *Mike Heath*, Dave Rajsich)	.30	.15	.09
711	A's Prospects (*Dwayne Murphy*, Bruce Robinson, Alan Wirth)	.30	.15	.09
712	Mariners Prospects (Bud Anderson, Greg Biercevicz, Byron McLaughlin)	.15	.08	.05
713	Rangers Prospects (*Danny Darwin*, Pat Putnam, *Billy Sample*)	.35	.20	.11
714	Blue Jays Prospects (Victor Cruz, Pat Kelly, Ernie Whitt)	.20	.10	.06
715	Braves Prospects (*Bruce Benedict, Glenn Hubbard*, Larry Whisenton)	.40	.20	.12
716	Cubs Prospects (Dave Geisel, Karl Pagel, *Scot Thompson*)	.15	.08	.05
717	Reds Prospects (*Mike LaCoss, Ron Oester, Harry Spilman*)	.15	.08	.05
718	Astros Prospects (Bruce Bochy, Mike Fischlin, Don Pisker)	.15	.08	.05
719	Dodgers Prospects (*Pedro Guerrero, Rudy Law*, Joe Simpson)	2.50	1.25	.70
720	Expos Prospects (*Jerry Fry, Jerry Pirtle, Scott Sanderson*)	.90	.45	.25
721	Mets Prospects (*Juan Berenguer*, Dwight Bernard, Dan Norman)	.15	.08	.05
722	Phillies Prospects (*Jim Morrison, Lonnie Smith, Jim Wright*)	.75	.40	.25
723	Pirates Prospects (*Dale Berra*, Eugenio Cotes, Ben Wiltbank)	.15	.08	.05
724	Cardinals Prospects (Tom Bruno, *George Frazier, Terry Kennedy*)	.20	.10	.06
725	Padres Prospects (Jim Beswick, Steve Mura, Broderick Perkins)	.15	.08	.05
726	Giants Prospects (Greg Johnston, Joe Strain, John Tamargo)	.15	.08	.05

1979 Topps Comics

Issued as the 3" by 3-3/4" wax wrapper for a piece of bubblegum, this "test" issue was bought up in great quantities by speculators and remains rather common. It is also inexpensive, because the comic-style player representations were not popular with collectors. The set is complete at 33 pieces.

		NR MT	EX	VG
Complete Set:		12.00	6.00	3.50
Common Player:		.10	.05	.03
1	Eddie Murray	.40	.20	.12
2	Jim Rice	.30	.15	.09
3	Carl Yastrzemski	.60	.30	.20
4	Nolan Ryan	2.00	1.00	.60
5	Chet Lemon	.10	.05	.03
6	Andre Thornton	.10	.05	.03
7	Rusty Staub	.15	.08	.05
8	Ron LeFlore	.10	.05	.03
9	George Brett	.90	.45	.25
10	Larry Hisle	.10	.05	.03
11	Rod Carew	.35	.20	.11
12	Reggie Jackson	.50	.25	.15
13	Ron Guidry	.20	.10	.06
14	Mitchell Page	.10	.05	.03
15	Leon Roberts	.10	.05	.03
16	Al Oliver	.15	.08	.05
17	John Mayberry	.10	.05	.03
18	Bob Horner	.20	.10	.06
19	Phil Niekro	.25	.13	.08
20	Dave Kingman	.15	.08	.05

		NR MT	EX	VG
21	John Bench	.40	.20	.12
22	Tom Seaver	.40	.20	.12
23	J.R. Richard	.10	.05	.03
24	Steve Garvey	.35	.20	.11
25	Reggie Smith	.15	.08	.05
26	Ross Grimsley	.10	.05	.03
27	Craig Swan	.10	.05	.03
28	Pete Rose	.90	.45	.25
29	Dave Parker	.40	.20	.12
30	Ted Simmons	.15	.08	.05
31	Dave Winfield	.60	.30	.20
32	Jack Clark	.20	.10	.06
33	Vida Blue	.15	.08	.05

1980 Topps

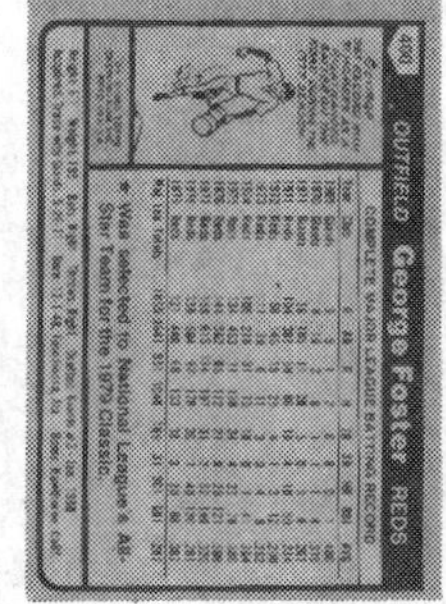

Again numbering 726 cards measuring 2-1/2" by 3-1/2", Topps did make some design changes in 1980. Fronts have the usual color picture with a facsimile autograph. The player's name appears above the picture, while his position is on a pennant at the upper left and his team on another pennant in the lower right. Backs no longer feature games, returning instead to statistics, personal information, a few headlines and a cartoon about the player. Specialty cards include statistical leaders, and previous season highlights. Many rookies again appear in team threesomes.

		NR MT	EX	VG
Complete Set (726):		275.00	137.00	82.00
Common Player:		.12	.06	.04
1	Lou Brock, Carl Yastrzemski (Highlights)	1.00	.50	.30
2	Willie McCovey (Highlights)	.50	.25	.15
3	Manny Mota (Highlights)	.15	.08	.05
4	Highlights (Pete Rose)	2.00	1.00	.60
5	Highlights (Garry Templeton)	.15	.08	.05
6	Highlights (Del Unser)	.12	.06	.04
7	Mike Lum	.12	.06	.04
8	Craig Swan	.12	.06	.04
9	Steve Braun	.12	.06	.04
10	Denny Martinez	.20	.10	.06
11	Jimmy Sexton	.12	.06	.04
12	John Curtis	.12	.06	.04
13	Ron Pruitt	.12	.06	.04
14	Dave Cash	.12	.06	.04
15	Bill Campbell	.12	.06	.04
16	Jerry Narron	.20	.10	.06
17	Bruce Sutter	.20	.10	.06
18	Ron Jackson	.12	.06	.04
19	Balor Moore	.12	.06	.04
20	Dan Ford	.12	.06	.04
21	Manny Sarmiento	.12	.06	.04
22	Pat Putnam	.12	.06	.04
23	Derrel Thomas	.12	.06	.04
24	Jim Slaton	.12	.06	.04
25	Lee Mazzilli	.20	.10	.06
26	Marty Pattin	.12	.06	.04
27	Del Unser	.12	.06	.04
28	Bruce Kison	.12	.06	.04
29	Mark Wagner	.12	.06	.04
30	Vida Blue	.15	.08	.05
31	Jay Johnstone	.20	.10	.06
32	Julio Cruz	.12	.06	.04
33	Tony Scott	.12	.06	.04
34	Jeff Newman	.12	.06	.04
35	Luis Tiant	.15	.08	.05
36	Rusty Torres	.12	.06	.04
37	Kiko Garcia	.12	.06	.04
38	Dan Spillner	.12	.06	.04
39	Rowland Office	.12	.06	.04
40	Carlton Fisk	3.00	1.50	.90
41	Rangers Team (Pat Corrales)	.50	.25	.15
42	*Dave Palmer*	.20	.10	.06
43	Bombo Rivera	.12	.06	.04
44	Bill Fahey	.12	.06	.04
45	Frank White	.15	.08	.05
46	Rico Carty	.12	.06	.04
47	Bill Bonham	.12	.06	.04
48	Rick Miller	.12	.06	.04
49	Mario Guerrero	.12	.06	.04
50	J.R. Richard	.20	.10	.06
51	Joe Ferguson	.12	.06	.04
52	Warren Brusstar	.12	.06	.04
53	Ben Oglivie	.20	.10	.06
54	Dennis Lamp	.12	.06	.04
55	Bill Madlock	.20	.10	.06
56	Bobby Valentine	.20	.10	.06
57	Pete Vuckovich	.12	.06	.04
58	Doug Flynn	.12	.06	.04
59	Eddy Putman	.12	.06	.04
60	Bucky Dent	.15	.08	.05
61	Gary Serum	.12	.06	.04
62	Mike Ivie	.12	.06	.04
63	Bob Stanley	.20	.10	.06
64	Joe Nolan	.12	.06	.04
65	Al Bumbry	.20	.10	.06
66	Royals Team (Jim Frey)	.60	.30	.20
67	Doyle Alexander	.25	.13	.08
68	Larry Harlow	.12	.06	.04
69	Rick Williams	.12	.06	.04
70	Gary Carter	1.25	.60	.40
71	John Milner	.12	.06	.04
72	Fred Howard	.12	.06	.04
73	Dave Collins	.20	.10	.06
74	Sid Monge	.12	.06	.04
75	Bill Russell	.20	.10	.06
76	John Stearns	.12	.06	.04
77	*Dave Stieb*	1.00	.50	.30
78	Ruppert Jones	.12	.06	.04
79	Bob Owchinko	.12	.06	.04
80	Ron LeFlore	.20	.10	.06
81	Ted Sizemore	.12	.06	.04
82	Astros Team (Bill Virdon)	.50	.25	.15
83	*Steve Trout*	.30	.15	.09
84	Gary Lavelle	.12	.06	.04
85	Ted Simmons	.15	.08	.05
86	Dave Hamilton	.12	.06	.04
87	Pepe Frias	.12	.06	.04
88	Ken Landreaux	.20	.10	.06
89	Don Hood	.20	.10	.06
90	Manny Trillo	.20	.10	.06
91	Rick Dempsey	.20	.10	.06
92	Rick Rhoden	.12	.06	.04
93	Dave Roberts	.12	.06	.04
94	*Neil Allen*	.12	.06	.04
95	Cecil Cooper	.35	.20	.11
96	A's Team (Jim Marshall)	.50	.25	.15
97	Bill Lee	.15	.08	.05
98	Jerry Terrell	.12	.06	.04
99	Victor Cruz	.12	.06	.04
100	Johnny Bench	4.00	2.00	1.25
101	Aurelio Lopez	.12	.06	.04
102	Rich Dauer	.12	.06	.04
103	*Bill Caudill*	.20	.10	.06
104	Manny Mota	.20	.10	.06
105	Frank Tanana	.20	.10	.06
106	*Jeff Leonard*	.40	.20	.12
107	Francisco Barrios	.12	.06	.04
108	Bob Horner	.15	.08	.05
109	Bill Travers	.12	.06	.04
110	Fred Lynn	.35	.20	.11
111	Bob Knepper	.20	.10	.06
112	White Sox Team (Tony LaRussa)	.50	.25	.15
113	Geoff Zahn	.12	.06	.04
114	Juan Beniquez	.12	.06	.04
115	Sparky Lyle	.15	.08	.05
116	Larry Cox	.12	.06	.04
117	Dock Ellis	.12	.06	.04
118	Phil Garner	.20	.10	.06
119	Sammy Stewart	.12	.06	.04
120	Greg Luzinski	.20	.10	.06
121	Checklist 1-121	.50	.25	.15
122	Dave Rosello	.12	.06	.04
123	Lynn Jones	.12	.06	.04
124	Dave Lemanczyk	.12	.06	.04

		NR MT	EX	VG
125	Tony Perez	.30	.15	.09
126	Dave Tomlin	.12	.06	.04
127	Gary Thomasson	.12	.06	.04
128	Tom Burgmeier	.12	.06	.04
129	Craig Reynolds	.12	.06	.04
130	Amos Otis	.20	.10	.06
131	Paul Mitchell	.12	.06	.04
132	Biff Pocoroba	.12	.06	.04
133	Jerry Turner	.12	.06	.04
134	Matt Keough	.12	.06	.04
135	Bill Buckner	.15	.08	.05
136	Dick Ruthven	.12	.06	.04
137	*John Castino*	.20	.10	.06
138	Ross Baumgarten	.12	.06	.04
139	*Dane Iorg*	.20	.10	.06
140	Rich Gossage	.30	.15	.09
141	Gary Alexander	.12	.06	.04
142	Phil Huffman	.12	.06	.04
143	Bruce Bochte	.12	.06	.04
144	Steve Comer	.12	.06	.04
145	Darrell Evans	.30	.15	.09
146	Bob Welch	1.00	.50	.30
147	Terry Puhl	.12	.06	.04
148	Manny Sanguillen	.12	.06	.04
149	Tom Hume	.12	.06	.04
150	Jason Thompson	.20	.10	.06
151	Tom Hausman	.12	.06	.04
152	John Fulgham	.12	.06	.04
153	Tim Blackwell	.12	.06	.04
154	Lary Sorensen	.12	.06	.04
155	Jerry Remy	.12	.06	.04
156	Tony Brizzolara	.12	.06	.04
157	Willie Wilson	.20	.10	.06
158	Rob Picciolo	.12	.06	.04
159	Ken Clay	.20	.10	.06
160	Eddie Murray	10.00	5.00	3.00
161	Larry Christenson	.12	.06	.04
162	Bob Randall	.12	.06	.04
163	Steve Swisher	.12	.06	.04
164	Greg Pryor	.12	.06	.04
165	Omar Moreno	.12	.06	.04
166	Glenn Abbott	.12	.06	.04
167	Jack Clark	.50	.25	.15
168	Rick Waits	.12	.06	.04
169	Luis Gomez	.12	.06	.04
170	Burt Hooton	.20	.10	.06
171	Fernando Gonzalez	.12	.06	.04
172	Ron Hodges	.12	.06	.04
173	John Henry Johnson	.12	.06	.04
174	Ray Knight	.15	.08	.05
175	Rick Reuschel	.12	.06	.04
176	Champ Summers	.12	.06	.04
177	Dave Heaverlo	.12	.06	.04
178	Tim McCarver	.15	.08	.05
179	*Ron Davis*	.20	.10	.06
180	Warren Cromartie	.12	.06	.04
181	Moose Haas	.12	.06	.04
182	Ken Reitz	.12	.06	.04
183	Jim Anderson	.12	.06	.04
184	Steve Renko	.12	.06	.04
185	Hal McRae	.25	.13	.08
186	Junior Moore	.12	.06	.04
187	Alan Ashby	.12	.06	.04
188	Terry Crowley	.12	.06	.04
189	Kevin Kobel	.12	.06	.04
190	Buddy Bell	.25	.13	.08
191	Ted Martinez	.12	.06	.04
192	Braves Team (Bobby Cox)	.50	.25	.15
193	Dave Goltz	.20	.10	.06
194	Mike Easler	.20	.10	.06
195	John Montefusco	.20	.10	.06
196	Lance Parrish	.40	.20	.12
197	Byron McLaughlin	.12	.06	.04
198	Dell Alston	.12	.06	.04
199	Mike LaCoss	.20	.10	.06
200	Jim Rice	1.00	.50	.30
201	Batting Leaders (Keith Hernandez, Fred Lynn)	.50	.25	.15
202	Home Run Leaders (Dave Kingman, Gorman Thomas)	.25	.13	.08
203	Runs Batted In Leaders (Don Baylor, Dave Winfield)	.50	.25	.15
204	Stolen Base Leaders (Omar Moreno, Willie Wilson)	.20	.10	.06
205	Victory Leaders (Mike Flanagan, Joe Niekro, Phil Niekro)	.40	.20	.12
206	Strikeout Leaders (J.R. Richard, Nolan Ryan)	2.00	1.00	.60
207	ERA Leaders (Ron Guidry, J.R. Richard)	.25	.13	.08
208	Wayne Cage	.12	.06	.04
209	Von Joshua	.12	.06	.04
210	Steve Carlton	4.00	2.00	1.25
211	Dave Skaggs	.12	.06	.04
212	Dave Roberts	.12	.06	.04
213	Mike Jorgensen	.12	.06	.04
214	Angels Team (Jim Fregosi)	.50	.25	.15
215	Sixto Lezcano	.12	.06	.04
216	Phil Mankowski	.12	.06	.04
217	Ed Halicki	.12	.06	.04
218	Jose Morales	.12	.06	.04
219	Steve Mingori	.12	.06	.04
220	Dave Concepcion	.30	.15	.09
221	Joe Cannon	.12	.06	.04
222	*Ron Hassey*	.25	.13	.08
223	Bob Sykes	.12	.06	.04
224	Willie Montanez	.12	.06	.04
225	Lou Piniella	.15	.08	.05
226	Bill Stein	.12	.06	.04
227	Len Barker	.12	.06	.04
228	Johnny Oates	.12	.06	.04
229	Jim Bibby	.12	.06	.04
230	Dave Winfield	10.00	5.00	3.00
231	Steve McCatty	.12	.06	.04
232	Alan Trammell	4.00	2.00	1.25
233	LaRue Washington	.12	.06	.04
234	Vern Ruhle	.12	.06	.04
235	Andre Dawson	9.00	4.50	2.75
236	Marc Hill	.12	.06	.04
237	Scott McGregor	.20	.10	.06
238	Rob Wilfong	.12	.06	.04
239	Don Aase	.12	.06	.04
240	Dave Kingman	.15	.08	.05
241	Checklist 122-242	.50	.25	.15
242	Lamar Johnson	.12	.06	.04
243	Jerry Augustine	.12	.06	.04
244	Cardinals Team (Ken Boyer)	.50	.25	.15
245	Phil Niekro	.80	.40	.25
246	Tim Foli	.12	.06	.04
247	Frank Riccelli	.12	.06	.04
248	Jamie Quirk	.12	.06	.04
249	Jim Clancy	.20	.10	.06
250	Jim Kaat	.50	.25	.15
251	Kip Young	.12	.06	.04
252	Ted Cox	.12	.06	.04
253	John Montague	.12	.06	.04
254	Paul Dade	.12	.06	.04
255	Dusty Baker	.12	.06	.04
256	Roger Erickson	.12	.06	.04
257	Larry Herndon	.20	.10	.06
258	Paul Moskau	.12	.06	.04
259	Mets Team (Joe Torre)	.60	.30	.20
260	Al Oliver	.20	.10	.06
261	Dave Chalk	.12	.06	.04
262	Benny Ayala	.12	.06	.04
263	Dave LaRoche	.12	.06	.04
264	Bill Robinson	.12	.06	.04
265	Robin Yount	12.00	6.00	3.50
266	Bernie Carbo	.12	.06	.04
267	Dan Schatzeder	.12	.06	.04
268	Rafael Landestoy	.12	.06	.04
269	Dave Tobik	.12	.06	.04
270	Mike Schmidt	6.00	3.00	1.75
271	Dick Drago	.12	.06	.04
272	Ralph Garr	.20	.10	.06
273	Eduardo Rodriguez	.12	.06	.04
274	Dale Murphy	4.00	2.00	1.25
275	Jerry Koosman	.25	.13	.08
276	Tom Veryzer	.12	.06	.04
277	Rick Bosetti	.12	.06	.04
278	Jim Spencer	.20	.10	.06
279	Rob Andrews	.12	.06	.04
280	Gaylord Perry	1.50	.70	.45
281	Paul Blair	.20	.10	.06
282	Mariners Team (Darrell Johnson)	.50	.25	.15
283	John Ellis	.12	.06	.04
284	Larry Murray	.12	.06	.04
285	Don Baylor	.35	.20	.11
286	Darold Knowles	.12	.06	.04
287	John Lowenstein	.12	.06	.04
288	Dave Rozema	.12	.06	.04
289	Bruce Bochy	.12	.06	.04
290	Steve Garvey	1.25	.60	.40
291	Randy Scarbery	.12	.06	.04
292	Dale Berra	.12	.06	.04
293	Elias Sosa	.12	.06	.04
294	Charlie Spikes	.12	.06	.04
295	Larry Gura	.12	.06	.04
296	Dave Rader	.12	.06	.04
297	Tim Johnson	.12	.06	.04
298	Ken Holtzman	.20	.10	.06
299	Steve Henderson	.12	.06	.04

		NR MT	EX	VG
300	Ron Guidry	.30	.15	.09
301	Mike Edwards	.12	.06	.04
302	Dodgers Team (Tom Lasorda)	.60	.30	.20
303	Bill Castro	.12	.06	.04
304	Butch Wynegar	.20	.10	.06
305	Randy Jones	.20	.10	.06
306	Denny Walling	.12	.06	.04
307	Rick Honeycutt	.20	.10	.06
308	Mike Hargrove	.20	.10	.06
309	Larry McWilliams	.12	.06	.04
310	Dave Parker	2.00	1.00	.60
311	Roger Metzger	.12	.06	.04
312	Mike Barlow	.12	.06	.04
313	Johnny Grubb	.12	.06	.04
314	*Tim Stoddard*	.12	.06	.04
315	Steve Kemp	.15	.08	.05
316	Bob Lacey	.12	.06	.04
317	Mike Anderson	.12	.06	.04
318	Jerry Reuss	.20	.10	.06
319	Chris Speier	.12	.06	.04
320	Dennis Eckersley	2.00	1.00	.60
321	Keith Hernandez	.90	.45	.25
322	Claudell Washington	.20	.10	.06
323	Mick Kelleher	.12	.06	.04
324	Tom Underwood	.12	.06	.04
325	Dan Driessen	.20	.10	.06
326	Bo McLaughlin	.12	.06	.04
327	Ray Fosse	.12	.06	.04
328	Twins Team (Gene Mauch)	.50	.25	.15
329	Bert Roberge	.12	.06	.04
330	Al Cowens	.12	.06	.04
331	Rich Hebner	.12	.06	.04
332	Enrique Romo	.12	.06	.04
333	Jim Norris	.12	.06	.04
334	Jim Beattie	.20	.10	.06
335	Willie McCovey	1.50	.70	.45
336	George Medich	.12	.06	.04
337	Carney Lansford	.30	.15	.09
338	Johnny Wockenfuss	.12	.06	.04
339	John D'Acquisto	.12	.06	.04
340	Ken Singleton	.20	.10	.06
341	Jim Essian	.12	.06	.04
342	Odell Jones	.12	.06	.04
343	Mike Vail	.12	.06	.04
344	Randy Lerch	.12	.06	.04
345	Larry Parrish	.20	.10	.06
346	Buddy Solomon	.12	.06	.04
347	*Harry Chappas*	.20	.10	.06
348	Checklist 243-363	.50	.25	.15
349	Jack Brohamer	.12	.06	.04
350	George Hendrick	.20	.10	.06
351	Bob Davis	.12	.06	.04
352	Dan Briggs	.12	.06	.04
353	Andy Hassler	.12	.06	.04
354	Rick Auerbach	.12	.06	.04
355	Gary Matthews	.15	.08	.05
356	Padres Team (Jerry Coleman)	.50	.25	.15
357	Bob McClure	.12	.06	.04
358	Lou Whitaker	1.25	.60	.40
359	Randy Moffitt	.12	.06	.04
360	Darrell Porter	.12	.06	.04
361	Wayne Garland	.12	.06	.04
362	Danny Goodwin	.12	.06	.04
363	Wayne Gross	.12	.06	.04
364	Ray Burris	.12	.06	.04
365	Bobby Murcer	.25	.13	.08
366	Rob Dressler	.12	.06	.04
367	Billy Smith	.12	.06	.04
368	*Willie Aikens*	.20	.10	.06
369	Jim Kern	.12	.06	.04
370	Cesar Cedeno	.25	.13	.08
371	Jack Morris	1.50	.70	.45
372	Joel Youngblood	.12	.06	.04
373	*Dan Petry*	.30	.15	.09
374	Jim Gantner	.20	.10	.06
375	Ross Grimsley	.12	.06	.04
376	Gary Allenson	.12	.06	.04
377	Junior Kennedy	.12	.06	.04
378	Jerry Mumphrey	.12	.06	.04
379	Kevin Bell	.12	.06	.04
380	Garry Maddox	.20	.10	.06
381	Cubs Team (Preston Gomez)	.50	.25	.15
382	Dave Freisleben	.12	.06	.04
383	Ed Ott	.12	.06	.04
384	Joey McLaughlin	.12	.06	.04
385	Enos Cabell	.12	.06	.04
386	Darrell Jackson	.12	.06	.04
387a	Fred Stanley (name in red)	.20	.10	.06
387b	Fred Stanley (name in yellow)	3.00	1.50	.90
388	Mike Paxton	.12	.06	.04
389	Pete LaCock	.12	.06	.04

		NR MT	EX	VG
390	Fergie Jenkins	.40	.20	.12
391	Tony Armas	.12	.06	.04
392	Milt Wilcox	.12	.06	.04
393	Ozzie Smith	20.00	10.00	6.00
394	Reggie Cleveland	.12	.06	.04
395	Ellis Valentine	.12	.06	.04
396	Dan Meyer	.12	.06	.04
397	Roy Thomas	.12	.06	.04
398	Barry Foote	.12	.06	.04
399	Mike Proly	.12	.06	.04
400	George Foster	.25	.13	.08
401	Pete Falcone	.12	.06	.04
402	Merv Rettenmund	.12	.06	.04
403	Pete Redfern	.12	.06	.04
404	Orioles Team (Earl Weaver)	.60	.30	.20
405	Dwight Evans	.90	.45	.25
406	Paul Molitor	15.00	7.50	4.50
407	Tony Solaita	.12	.06	.04
408	Bill North	.12	.06	.04
409	Paul Splittorff	.12	.06	.04
410	Bobby Bonds	.25	.13	.08
411	Frank LaCorte	.12	.06	.04
412	Thad Bosley	.12	.06	.04
413	Allen Ripley	.12	.06	.04
414	George Scott	.12	.06	.04
415	Bill Atkinson	.12	.06	.04
416	*Tom Brookens*	.15	.08	.05
417	Craig Chamberlain	.12	.06	.04
418	Roger Freed	.12	.06	.04
419	Vic Correll	.12	.06	.04
420	Butch Hobson	.12	.06	.04
421	Doug Bird	.12	.06	.04
422	Larry Milbourne	.12	.06	.04
423	Dave Frost	.12	.06	.04
424	Yankees Team (Dick Howser)	.70	.35	.20
425	Mark Belanger	.20	.10	.06
426	Grant Jackson	.12	.06	.04
427	Tom Hutton	.12	.06	.04
428	Pat Zachry	.12	.06	.04
429	Duane Kuiper	.12	.06	.04
430	Larry Hisle	.12	.06	.04
431	Mike Krukow	.20	.10	.06
432	Willie Norwood	.12	.06	.04
433	Rich Gale	.12	.06	.04
434	Johnnie LeMaster	.12	.06	.04
435	Don Gullett	.20	.10	.06
436	Billy Almon	.12	.06	.04
437	Joe Niekro	.20	.10	.06
438	Dave Revering	.12	.06	.04
439	Mike Phillips	.12	.06	.04
440	Don Sutton	1.00	.50	.30
441	Eric Soderholm	.12	.06	.04
442	Jorge Orta	.12	.06	.04
443	Mike Parrott	.12	.06	.04
444	Alvis Woods	.12	.06	.04
445	Mark Fidrych	.20	.10	.06
446	Duffy Dyer	.12	.06	.04
447	Nino Espinosa	.12	.06	.04
448	Jim Wohlford	.12	.06	.04
449	Doug Bair	.12	.06	.04
450	George Brett	12.00	6.00	3.50
451	Indians Team (Dave Garcia)	.50	.25	.15
452	Steve Dillard	.12	.06	.04
453	Mike Bacsik	.12	.06	.04
454	Tom Donohue	.12	.06	.04
455	Mike Torrez	.20	.10	.06
456	Frank Taveras	.12	.06	.04
457	Bert Blyleven	.50	.25	.15
458	Billy Sample	.12	.06	.04
459	Mickey Lolich	.12	.06	.04
460	Willie Randolph	.15	.08	.05
461	Dwayne Murphy	.20	.10	.06
462	Mike Sadek	.12	.06	.04
463	Jerry Royster	.12	.06	.04
464	John Denny	.12	.06	.04
465	Rick Monday	.20	.10	.06
466	Mike Squires	.12	.06	.04
467	Jesse Jefferson	.12	.06	.04
468	Aurelio Rodriguez	.20	.10	.06
469	Randy Niemann	.12	.06	.04
470	Bob Boone	.20	.10	.06
471	Hosken Powell	.12	.06	.04
472	Willie Hernandez	.20	.10	.06
473	Bump Wills	.12	.06	.04
474	Steve Busby	.12	.06	.04
475	Cesar Geronimo	.12	.06	.04
476	Bob Shirley	.12	.06	.04
477	Buck Martinez	.12	.06	.04
478	Gil Flores	.12	.06	.04
479	Expos Team (Dick Williams)	.50	.25	.15
480	Bob Watson	.20	.10	.06

		NR MT	EX	VG
481	Tom Paciorek	.12	.06	.04
482	*Rickey Henderson*	80.00	40.00	24.00
483	Bo Diaz	.20	.10	.06
484	Checklist 364-484	.50	.25	.15
485	Mickey Rivers	.20	.10	.06
486	Mike Tyson	.12	.06	.04
487	Wayne Nordhagen	.12	.06	.04
488	Roy Howell	.12	.06	.04
489	Preston Hanna	.12	.06	.04
490	Lee May	.20	.10	.06
491	Steve Mura	.12	.06	.04
492	Todd Cruz	.12	.06	.04
493	Jerry Martin	.12	.06	.04
494	Craig Minetto	.12	.06	.04
495	Bake McBride	.12	.06	.04
496	Silvio Martinez	.12	.06	.04
497	Jim Mason	.12	.06	.04
498	Danny Darwin	.20	.10	.06
499	Giants Team (Dave Bristol)	.50	.25	.15
500	Tom Seaver	3.00	1.50	.90
501	Rennie Stennett	.12	.06	.04
502	Rich Wortham	.12	.06	.04
503	Mike Cubbage	.12	.06	.04
504	Gene Garber	.12	.06	.04
505	Bert Campaneris	.20	.10	.06
506	Tom Buskey	.12	.06	.04
507	Leon Roberts	.12	.06	.04
508	U.L. Washington	.12	.06	.04
509	Ed Glynn	.12	.06	.04
510	Ron Cey	.25	.13	.08
511	Eric Wilkins	.12	.06	.04
512	Jose Cardenal	.12	.06	.04
513	Tom Dixon	.12	.06	.04
514	Steve Ontiveros	.12	.06	.04
515	Mike Caldwell	.12	.06	.04
516	Hector Cruz	.12	.06	.04
517	Don Stanhouse	.12	.06	.04
518	Nelson Norman	.12	.06	.04
519	Steve Nicosia	.12	.06	.04
520	Steve Rogers	.20	.10	.06
521	Ken Brett	.12	.06	.04
522	Jim Morrison	.12	.06	.04
523	Ken Henderson	.12	.06	.04
524	Jim Wright	.12	.06	.04
525	Clint Hurdle	.12	.06	.04
526	Phillies Team (Dallas Green)	.70	.35	.20
527	Doug Rau	.12	.06	.04
528	Adrian Devine	.12	.06	.04
529	Jim Barr	.12	.06	.04
530	Jim Sundberg	.12	.06	.04
531	Eric Rasmussen	.12	.06	.04
532	Willie Horton	.20	.10	.06
533	Checklist 485-605	.50	.25	.15
534	Andre Thornton	.25	.13	.08
535	Bob Forsch	.20	.10	.06
536	Lee Lacy	.12	.06	.04
537	*Alex Trevino*	.20	.10	.06
538	Joe Strain	.12	.06	.04
539	Rudy May	.12	.06	.04
540	Pete Rose	4.00	2.00	1.25
541	Miguel Dilone	.12	.06	.04
542	Joe Coleman	.12	.06	.04
543	Pat Kelly	.12	.06	.04
544	*Rick Sutcliffe*	2.00	1.00	.60
545	Jeff Burroughs	.20	.10	.06
546	Rick Langford	.12	.06	.04
547	John Wathan	.20	.10	.06
548	Dave Rajsich	.12	.06	.04
549	Larry Wolfe	.12	.06	.04
550	Ken Griffey	.25	.13	.08
551	Pirates Team (Chuck Tanner)	.50	.25	.15
552	Bill Nahorodny	.12	.06	.04
553	Dick Davis	.12	.06	.04
554	Art Howe	.12	.06	.04
555	Ed Figueroa	.20	.10	.06
556	Joe Rudi	.20	.10	.06
557	Mark Lee	.12	.06	.04
558	Alfredo Griffin	.15	.08	.05
559	Dale Murray	.12	.06	.04
560	Dave Lopes	.25	.13	.08
561	Eddie Whitson	.20	.10	.06
562	Joe Wallis	.12	.06	.04
563	Will McEnaney	.12	.06	.04
564	Rick Manning	.12	.06	.04
565	Dennis Leonard	.20	.10	.06
566	Bud Harrelson	.20	.10	.06
567	Skip Lockwood	.12	.06	.04
568	*Gary Roenicke*	.12	.06	.04
569	Terry Kennedy	.12	.06	.04
570	Roy Smalley	.12	.06	.04
571	Joe Sambito	.12	.06	.04

		NR MT	EX	VG
572	Jerry Morales	.12	.06	.04
573	Kent Tekulve	.12	.06	.04
574	Scot Thompson	.12	.06	.04
575	Ken Kravec	.12	.06	.04
576	Jim Dwyer	.12	.06	.04
577	Blue Jays Team (Bobby Mattick)	.50	.25	.15
578	Scott Sanderson	.20	.10	.06
579	Charlie Moore	.12	.06	.04
580	Nolan Ryan	25.00	12.50	7.50
581	Bob Bailor	.12	.06	.04
582	Brian Doyle	.20	.10	.06
583	Bob Stinson	.12	.06	.04
584	Kurt Bevacqua	.12	.06	.04
585	Al Hrabosky	.20	.10	.06
586	Mitchell Page	.12	.06	.04
587	Garry Templeton	.20	.10	.06
588	Greg Minton	.12	.06	.04
589	Chet Lemon	.20	.10	.06
590	Jim Palmer	3.00	1.50	.90
591	Rick Cerone	.12	.06	.04
592	Jon Matlack	.20	.10	.06
593	Jesus Alou	.12	.06	.04
594	Dick Tidrow	.12	.06	.04
595	Don Money	.12	.06	.04
596	Rick Matula	.12	.06	.04
597	Tom Poquette	.12	.06	.04
598	Fred Kendall	.12	.06	.04
599	Mike Norris	.12	.06	.04
600	Reggie Jackson	8.00	4.00	2.50
601	Buddy Schultz	.12	.06	.04
602	Brian Downing	.20	.10	.06
603	Jack Billingham	.12	.06	.04
604	Glenn Adams	.12	.06	.04
605	Terry Forster	.20	.10	.06
606	Reds Team (John McNamara)	.50	.25	.15
607	Woodie Fryman	.20	.10	.06
608	Alan Bannister	.12	.06	.04
609	Ron Reed	.20	.10	.06
610	Willie Stargell	1.50	.70	.45
611	Jerry Garvin	.12	.06	.04
612	Cliff Johnson	.12	.06	.04
613	Randy Stein	.12	.06	.04
614	John Hiller	.20	.10	.06
615	Doug DeCinces	.20	.10	.06
616	Gene Richards	.12	.06	.04
617	Joaquin Andujar	.20	.10	.06
618	Bob Montgomery	.12	.06	.04
619	Sergio Ferrer	.12	.06	.04
620	Richie Zisk	.20	.10	.06
621	Bob Grich	.20	.10	.06
622	Mario Soto	.12	.06	.04
623	Gorman Thomas	.12	.06	.04
624	Lerrin LaGrow	.12	.06	.04
625	Chris Chambliss	.12	.06	.04
626	Tigers Team (Sparky Anderson)	.60	.30	.20
627	Pedro Borbon	.12	.06	.04
628	Doug Capilla	.12	.06	.04
629	Jim Todd	.12	.06	.04
630	Larry Bowa	.25	.13	.08
631	Mark Littell	.12	.06	.04
632	Barry Bonnell	.12	.06	.04
633	Bob Apodaca	.12	.06	.04
634	Glenn Borgmann	.12	.06	.04
635	John Candelaria	.20	.10	.06
636	Toby Harrah	.20	.10	.06
637	Joe Simpson	.12	.06	.04
638	*Mark Clear*	.20	.10	.06
639	Larry Biittner	.12	.06	.04
640	Mike Flanagan	.15	.08	.05
641	Ed Kranepool	.20	.10	.06
642	Ken Forsch	.12	.06	.04
643	John Mayberry	.20	.10	.06
644	Charlie Hough	.20	.10	.06
645	Rick Burleson	.20	.10	.06
646	Checklist 606-726	.50	.25	.15
647	Milt May	.12	.06	.04
648	Roy White	.20	.10	.06
649	Tom Griffin	.12	.06	.04
650	Joe Morgan	2.00	1.00	.60
651	Rollie Fingers	1.00	.50	.30
652	Mario Mendoza	.12	.06	.04
653	Stan Bahnsen	.12	.06	.04
654	Bruce Boisclair	.12	.06	.04
655	Tug McGraw	.15	.08	.05
656	Larvell Blanks	.12	.06	.04
657	Dave Edwards	.12	.06	.04
658	Chris Knapp	.12	.06	.04
659	Brewers Team (George Bamberger)	.50	.25	.15
660	Rusty Staub	.20	.10	.06
661	Orioles Future Stars (Mark Corey, Dave Ford, Wayne Krenchicki)	.12	.06	.04

		NR MT	EX	VG
662	Red Sox Future Stars (Joel Finch, Mike O'Berry, Chuck Rainey)	.12	.06	.04
663	Angels Future Stars (Ralph Botting, Bob Clark, *Dickie Thon*)	.30	.15	.09
664	White Sox Future Stars (Mike Colbern, *Guy Hoffman*, Dewey Robinson)	.12	.06	.04
665	Indians Future Stars (Larry Andersen, Bobby Cuellar, Sandy Wihtol)	.12	.06	.04
666	Tigers Future Stars (Mike Chris, Al Greene, Bruce Robbins)	.12	.06	.04
667	Royals Future Stars (Renie Martin, Bill Paschall, *Dan Quisenberry*)	1.50	.70	.45
668	Brewers Future Stars (Danny Boitano, Willie Mueller, Lenn Sakata)	.12	.06	.04
669	Twins Future Stars (Dan Graham, Rick Sofield, *Gary Ward*)	.35	.20	.11
670	Yankees Future Stars (Bobby Brown, Brad Gulden, Darryl Jones)	.12	.06	.04
671	A's Future Stars (Derek Bryant, Brian Kingman, *Mike Morgan*)	1.00	.50	.30
672	Mariners Future Stars (Charlie Beamon, Rodney Craig, Rafael Vasquez)	.12	.06	.04
673	Rangers Future Stars (Brian Allard, Jerry Don Gleaton, Greg Mahlberg)	.12	.06	.04
674	Blue Jays Future Stars (Butch Edge, Pat Kelly, Ted Wilborn)	.12	.06	.04
675	Braves Future Stars (Bruce Benedict, Larry Bradford, Eddie Miller)	.12	.06	.04
676	Cubs Future Stars (Dave Geisel, Steve Macko, Karl Pagel)	.12	.06	.04
677	Reds Future Stars (Art DeFreites, *Frank Pastore*, Harry Spilman)	.12	.06	.04
678	Astros Future Stars (Reggie Baldwin, Alan Knicely, *Pete Ladd*)	.12	.06	.04
679	Dodgers Future Stars (Joe Beckwith, *Mickey Hatcher*, Dave Patterson)	.25	.13	.08
680	Expos Future Stars (*Tony Bernazard*, Randy Miller, John Tamargo)	.20	.10	.06
681	Mets Future Stars (Dan Norman, *Jesse Orosco, Mike Scott*)	1.50	.70	.45
682	Phillies Future Stars (Ramon Aviles, *Dickie Noles*, Kevin Saucier)	.12	.06	.04
683	Pirates Future Stars (Dorian Boyland, Alberto Lois, Harry Saferight)	.12	.06	.04
684	Cardinals Future Stars (George Frazier, *Tom Herr*, Dan O'Brien)	.30	.15	.09
685	Padres Future Stars (Tim Flannery, Brian Greer, Jim Wilhelm)	.12	.06	.04
686	Giants Future Stars (Greg Johnston, Dennis Littlejohn, Phil Nastu)	.12	.06	.04
687	Mike Heath	.12	.06	.04
688	Steve Stone	.20	.10	.06
689	Red Sox Team (Don Zimmer)	.60	.30	.20
690	Tommy John	.60	.30	.20
691	Ivan DeJesus	.12	.06	.04
692	Rawly Eastwick	.12	.06	.04
693	Craig Kusick	.12	.06	.04
694	Jim Rooker	.12	.06	.04
695	Reggie Smith	.20	.10	.06
696	Julio Gonzalez	.12	.06	.04
697	David Clyde	.12	.06	.04
698	Oscar Gamble	.20	.10	.06
699	Floyd Bannister	.20	.10	.06
700	Rod Carew	1.50	.70	.45
701	*Ken Oberkfell*	.12	.06	.04
702	Ed Farmer	.12	.06	.04
703	Otto Velez	.12	.06	.04
704	Gene Tenace	.20	.10	.06
705	Freddie Patek	.12	.06	.04
706	Tippy Martinez	.12	.06	.04
707	Elliott Maddox	.12	.06	.04
708	Bob Tolan	.12	.06	.04
709	Pat Underwood	.12	.06	.04
710	Graig Nettles	.15	.08	.05
711	Bob Galasso	.12	.06	.04
712	Rodney Scott	.12	.06	.04
713	Terry Whitfield	.12	.06	.04
714	Fred Norman	.12	.06	.04
715	Sal Bando	.20	.10	.06
716	Lynn McGlothen	.12	.06	.04
717	Mickey Klutts	.12	.06	.04
718	Greg Gross	.12	.06	.04
719	Don Robinson	.20	.10	.06
720	Carl Yastrzemski	1.50	.70	.45
721	Paul Hartzell	.12	.06	.04
722	Jose Cruz	.20	.10	.06
723	Shane Rawley	.20	.10	.06
724	Jerry White	.12	.06	.04
725	Rick Wise	.20	.10	.06
726	Steve Yeager	.20	.10	.06

1980 Topps Superstar 5X7 Photos

In actuality, these cards measure 4-7/8" by 6-7/8". These were another Topps "test" issue that was bought out almost entirely by investors. The 60 cards have a color photo on the front and a blue ink facsimile autograph. Backs have the player's name, team position and card number. The issue was printed on different cardboard stocks, with the first on thick cardboard with a white back and the second on thinner cardboard with a gray back. Prices below are for the more common gray backs; white backs are valued about three times the figures shown. The issue was distributed in selected geographical areas, but they were hoarded quickly. Those who hoarded them still probably have much of their supply as the set has never taken off, despite the presence of many big-name stars.

		NR MT	EX	VG
Complete Set:		9.00	4.50	2.75
Common Player:		.50	.25	.15
1	Willie Stargell	2.00	1.00	.60
2	Mike Schmidt	4.00	2.00	1.25
3	Johnny Bench	3.00	1.50	.90
4	Jim Palmer	2.00	1.00	.60
5	Jim Rice	1.00	.50	.30
6	Reggie Jackson	4.00	2.00	1.25
7	Ron Guidry	.75	.40	.25
8	Lee Mazzilli	.50	.25	.15
9	Don Baylor	.75	.40	.25
10	Fred Lynn	.75	.40	.25
11	Ken Singleton	.50	.25	.15
12	Rod Carew	2.00	1.00	.60
13	Steve Garvey	1.50	.70	.45
14	George Brett	4.00	2.00	1.25
15	Tom Seaver	3.00	1.50	.90
16	Dave Kingman	.50	.25	.15
17	Dave Parker	2.00	1.00	.60
18	Dave Winfield	3.00	1.50	.90
19	Pete Rose	4.00	2.00	1.25
20	Nolan Ryan	4.00	2.00	1.25
21	Graig Nettles	.50	.25	.15
22	Carl Yastrzemski	3.00	1.50	.90
23	Tommy John	1.00	.50	.30
24	George Foster	.50	.25	.15
25	J.R. Richard	.50	.25	.15
26	Keith Hernandez	.50	.25	.15
27	Bob Horner	.50	.25	.15
28	Eddie Murray	2.00	1.00	.60
29	Steve Kemp	.50	.25	.15
30	Gorman Thomas	.50	.25	.15
31	Sixto Lezcano	.50	.25	.15
32	Bruce Sutter	.50	.25	.15
33	Cecil Cooper	.50	.25	.15
34	Larry Bowa	.50	.25	.15
35	Al Oliver	1.00	.50	.30
36	Ted Simmons	.50	.25	.15
37	Garry Templeton	.50	.25	.15
38	Jerry Koosman	.50	.25	.15
39	Darrell Porter	.50	.25	.15
40	Roy Smalley	.50	.25	.15
41	Craig Swan	.50	.25	.15
42	Jason Thompson	.50	.25	.15
43	Andre Thornton	.50	.25	.15

		NR MT	EX	VG
44	Rick Manning	.50	.25	.15
45	Kent Tekulve	.50	.25	.15
46	Phil Niekro	1.50	.70	.45
47	Buddy Bell	.50	.25	.15
48	Randy Jones	.50	.25	.15
49	Brian Downing	.50	.25	.15
50	Amos Otis	.50	.25	.15
51	Rick Bosetti	.50	.25	.15
52	Gary Carter	1.50	.70	.45
53	Larry Parrish	.50	.25	.15
54	Jack Clark	.50	.25	.15
55	Bruce Bochte	.50	.25	.15
56	Cesar Cedeno	.50	.25	.15
57	Chet Lemon	.50	.25	.15
58	Dave Revering	.50	.25	.15
59	Vida Blue	.50	.25	.15
60	Davey Lopes	.50	.25	.15

1981 Topps

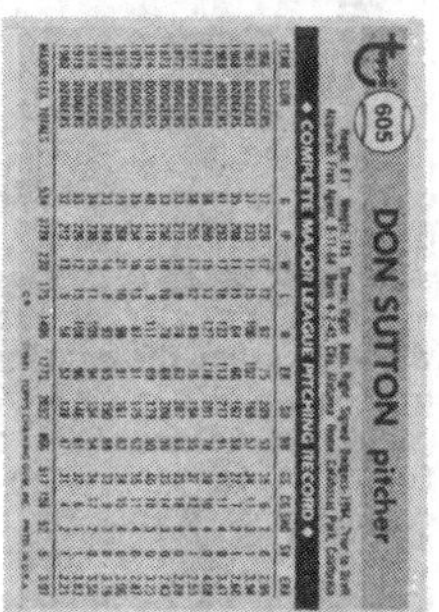

This is another 726-card set of 2-1/2" by 3-1/2" cards from Topps. The cards have the usual color photo with all cards from the same team sharing the same color borders. The player's name appears under the photo with his team and position appearing on a baseball cap at the lower left. The Topps logo returned in a small baseball in the lower right corner. Card backs include the usual stats along with a headline and a cartoon if there was room. Specialty cards include previous season record-breakers, highlights of the playoffs and World Series, along with the final appearance of team cards.

	MT	NR MT	EX
Complete Set (726):	75.00	56.00	30.00
Common Player:	.08	.06	.03

		MT	NR MT	EX
1	Batting Leaders (George Brett, Bill Buckner)	1.00	.70	.40
2	Home Run Leaders (Reggie Jackson, Ben Oglivie, Mike Schmidt)	.80	.60	.30
3	RBI Leaders (Cecil Cooper, Mike Schmidt)	.30	.25	.12
4	Stolen Base Leaders (Rickey Henderson, Ron LeFlore)	.50	.40	.20
5	Victory Leaders (Steve Carlton, Steve Stone)	.20	.15	.08
6	Strikeout Leaders (Len Barker, Steve Carlton)	.20	.15	.08
7	ERA Leaders (Rudy May, Don Sutton)	.15	.11	.06
8	Leading Firemen (Rollie Fingers, Tom Hume, Dan Quisenberry)	.10	.08	.04
9	Pete LaCock	.08	.06	.03
10	Mike Flanagan	.12	.09	.05
11	Jim Wohlford	.08	.06	.03
12	Mark Clear	.08	.06	.03
13	*Joe Charboneau*	.15	.11	.06
14	*John Tudor*	.20	.15	.08
15	Larry Parrish	.15	.11	.06
16	Ron Davis	.10	.08	.04
17	Cliff Johnson	.08	.06	.03
18	Glenn Adams	.08	.06	.03
19	Jim Clancy	.12	.09	.05
20	Jeff Burroughs	.10	.08	.04
21	Ron Oester	.08	.06	.03
22	Danny Darwin	.08	.06	.03
23	Alex Trevino	.08	.06	.03
24	Don Stanhouse	.08	.06	.03
25	Sixto Lezcano	.08	.06	.03
26	U.L. Washington	.08	.06	.03
27	Champ Summers	.08	.06	.03
28	Enrique Romo	.08	.06	.03
29	Gene Tenace	.10	.08	.04
30	Jack Clark	.20	.15	.08
31	Checklist 1-121	.08	.06	.03
32	Ken Oberkfell	.08	.06	.03
33	Rick Honeycutt	.08	.06	.03
34	Aurelio Rodriguez	.10	.08	.04
35	Mitchell Page	.08	.06	.03
36	Ed Farmer	.08	.06	.03
37	Gary Roenicke	.08	.06	.03
38	Win Remmerswaal	.08	.06	.03
39	Tom Veryzer	.08	.06	.03
40	Tug McGraw	.10	.08	.04
41	Rangers Future Stars (Bob Babcock, John Butcher, Jerry Don Gleaton)	.10	.08	.04
42	Jerry White	.08	.06	.03
43	Jose Morales	.08	.06	.03
44	Larry McWilliams	.08	.06	.03
45	Enos Cabell	.08	.06	.03
46	Rick Bosetti	.08	.06	.03
47	Ken Brett	.10	.08	.04
48	Dave Skaggs	.08	.06	.03
49	Bob Shirley	.08	.06	.03
50	Dave Lopes	.12	.09	.05
51	Bill Robinson	.08	.06	.03
52	Hector Cruz	.08	.06	.03
53	Kevin Saucier	.08	.06	.03
54	Ivan DeJesus	.08	.06	.03
55	Mike Norris	.08	.06	.03
56	Buck Martinez	.08	.06	.03
57	Dave Roberts	.08	.06	.03
58	Joel Youngblood	.08	.06	.03
59	Dan Petry	.12	.09	.05
60	Willie Randolph	.15	.11	.06
61	Butch Wynegar	.08	.06	.03
62	Joe Pettini	.08	.06	.03
63	Steve Renko	.08	.06	.03
64	Brian Asselstine	.08	.06	.03
65	Scott McGregor	.10	.08	.04
66	Royals Future Stars (Manny Castillo, Tim Ireland, Mike Jones)	.08	.06	.03
67	Ken Kravec	.08	.06	.03
68	Matt Alexander	.08	.06	.03
69	Ed Halicki	.08	.06	.03
70	Al Oliver	.15	.11	.06
71	Hal Dues	.08	.06	.03
72	Barry Evans	.08	.06	.03
73	Doug Bair	.08	.06	.03
74	Mike Hargrove	.08	.06	.03
75	Reggie Smith	.15	.11	.06
76	Mario Mendoza	.08	.06	.03
77	Mike Barlow	.08	.06	.03
78	Steve Dillard	.08	.06	.03
79	Bruce Robbins	.08	.06	.03
80	Rusty Staub	.15	.11	.06
81	Dave Stapleton	.08	.06	.03
82	Astros Future Stars (Danny Heep, Alan Knicely, Bobby Sprowl)	.08	.06	.03
83	Mike Proly	.08	.06	.03
84	Johnnie LeMaster	.08	.06	.03
85	Mike Caldwell	.08	.06	.03
86	Wayne Gross	.08	.06	.03
87	Rick Camp	.08	.06	.03
88	Joe Lefebvre	.08	.06	.03
89	Darrell Jackson	.08	.06	.03
90	Bake McBride	.08	.06	.03
91	Tim Stoddard	.08	.06	.03
92	Mike Easler	.10	.08	.04
93	Ed Glynn	.08	.06	.03
94	Harry Spilman	.08	.06	.03
95	Jim Sundberg	.10	.08	.04
96	A's Future Stars (Dave Beard, *Ernie Camacho,* Pat Dempsey)	.12	.09	.05
97	Chris Speier	.08	.06	.03
98	Clint Hurdle	.08	.06	.03
99	Eric Wilkins	.08	.06	.03
100	Rod Carew	2.00	1.50	.80
101	Benny Ayala	.08	.06	.03
102	Dave Tobik	.08	.06	.03
103	Jerry Martin	.08	.06	.03
104	Terry Forster	.10	.08	.04
105	Jose Cruz	.15	.11	.06
106	Don Money	.08	.06	.03
107	Rich Wortham	.08	.06	.03
108	Bruce Benedict	.08	.06	.03
109	Mike Scott	.80	.60	.30

		MT	NR MT	EX
110	Carl Yastrzemski	2.00	1.50	.80
111	Greg Minton	.08	.06	.03
112	White Sox Future Stars (Rusty Kuntz, Fran Mullins, Leo Sutherland)	.08	.06	.03
113	Mike Phillips	.08	.06	.03
114	Tom Underwood	.08	.06	.03
115	Roy Smalley	.08	.06	.03
116	Joe Simpson	.08	.06	.03
117	Pete Falcone	.08	.06	.03
118	Kurt Bevacqua	.08	.06	.03
119	Tippy Martinez	.08	.06	.03
120	Larry Bowa	.20	.15	.08
121	Larry Harlow	.08	.06	.03
122	John Denny	.08	.06	.03
123	Al Cowens	.08	.06	.03
124	Jerry Garvin	.08	.06	.03
125	Andre Dawson	2.00	1.50	.80
126	*Charlie Leibrandt*	.50	.40	.20
127	Rudy Law	.08	.06	.03
128	Gary Allenson	.08	.06	.03
129	Art Howe	.08	.06	.03
130	Larry Gura	.08	.06	.03
131	*Keith Moreland*	.35	.25	.14
132	Tommy Boggs	.08	.06	.03
133	Jeff Cox	.08	.06	.03
134	Steve Mura	.08	.06	.03
135	Gorman Thomas	.12	.09	.05
136	Doug Capilla	.08	.06	.03
137	Hosken Powell	.08	.06	.03
138	*Rich Dotson*	.20	.15	.08
139	Oscar Gamble	.10	.08	.04
140	Bob Forsch	.10	.08	.04
141	Miguel Dilone	.08	.06	.03
142	Jackson Todd	.08	.06	.03
143	Dan Meyer	.08	.06	.03
144	Allen Ripley	.08	.06	.03
145	Mickey Rivers	.10	.08	.04
146	Bobby Castillo	.08	.06	.03
147	Dale Berra	.08	.06	.03
148	Randy Niemann	.08	.06	.03
149	Joe Nolan	.08	.06	.03
150	Mark Fidrych	.12	.09	.05
151	Claudell Washington	.12	.09	.05
152	John Urrea	.08	.06	.03
153	Tom Poquette	.08	.06	.03
154	Rick Langford	.08	.06	.03
155	Chris Chambliss	.12	.09	.05
156	Bob McClure	.08	.06	.03
157	John Wathan	.12	.09	.05
158	Fergie Jenkins	.90	.70	.35
159	Brian Doyle	.08	.06	.03
160	Garry Maddox	.12	.09	.05
161	Dan Graham	.08	.06	.03
162	Doug Corbett	.08	.06	.03
163	Billy Almon	.08	.06	.03
164	*Lamarr Hoyt (LaMarr)*	.20	.15	.08
165	Tony Scott	.08	.06	.03
166	Floyd Bannister	.12	.09	.05
167	Terry Whitfield	.08	.06	.03
168	Don Robinson	.08	.06	.03
169	John Mayberry	.10	.08	.04
170	Ross Grimsley	.08	.06	.03
171	Gene Richards	.08	.06	.03
172	Gary Woods	.08	.06	.03
173	Bump Wills	.08	.06	.03
174	Doug Rau	.08	.06	.03
175	Dave Collins	.10	.08	.04
176	Mike Krukow	.10	.08	.04
177	Rick Peters	.08	.06	.03
178	Jim Essian	.08	.06	.03
179	Rudy May	.08	.06	.03
180	Pete Rose	3.00	2.25	1.25
181	Elias Sosa	.08	.06	.03
182	Bob Grich	.15	.11	.06
183	Dick Davis	.08	.06	.03
184	Jim Dwyer	.08	.06	.03
185	Dennis Leonard	.10	.08	.04
186	Wayne Nordhagen	.08	.06	.03
187	Mike Parrott	.08	.06	.03
188	Doug DeCinces	.15	.11	.06
189	Craig Swan	.08	.06	.03
190	Cesar Cedeno	.15	.11	.06
191	Rick Sutcliffe	.20	.15	.08
192	Braves Future Stars (*Terry Harper*, Ed Miller, *Rafael Ramirez*)	.10	.08	.04
193	Pete Vuckovich	.10	.08	.04
194	*Rod Scurry*	.10	.08	.04
195	Rich Murray	.08	.06	.03
196	Duffy Dyer	.08	.06	.03
197	Jim Kern	.08	.06	.03
198	Jerry Dybzinski	.08	.06	.03
199	Chuck Rainey	.08	.06	.03
200	George Foster	.25	.20	.10
201	Johnny Bench (Record Breaker)	.40	.30	.15
202	Steve Carlton (Record Breaker)	.40	.30	.15
203	Bill Gullickson (Record Breaker)	.08	.06	.03
204	Ron LeFlore, Rodney Scott (Record Breaker)	.10	.08	.04
205	Pete Rose (Record Breaker)	.70	.50	.30
206	Mike Schmidt (Record Breaker)	.60	.45	.25
207	Ozzie Smith (Record Breaker)	.20	.15	.08
208	Willie Wilson (Record Breaker)	.20	.15	.08
209	Dickie Thon	.10	.08	.04
210	Jim Palmer	2.00	1.50	.80
211	Derrel Thomas	.08	.06	.03
212	Steve Nicosia	.08	.06	.03
213	*Al Holland*	.10	.08	.04
214	Angels Future Stars (Ralph Botting, Jim Dorsey, John Harris)	.08	.06	.03
215	Larry Hisle	.10	.08	.04
216	John Henry Johnson	.08	.06	.03
217	Rich Hebner	.08	.06	.03
218	Paul Splittorff	.08	.06	.03
219	Ken Landreaux	.08	.06	.03
220	Tom Seaver	3.00	2.25	1.25
221	Bob Davis	.08	.06	.03
222	Jorge Orta	.08	.06	.03
223	Roy Lee Jackson	.08	.06	.03
224	Pat Zachry	.08	.06	.03
225	Ruppert Jones	.08	.06	.03
226	Manny Sanguillen	.08	.06	.03
227	Fred Martinez	.08	.06	.03
228	Tom Paciorek	.08	.06	.03
229	Rollie Fingers	.90	.70	.35
230	George Hendrick	.10	.08	.04
231	Joe Beckwith	.08	.06	.03
232	Mickey Klutts	.08	.06	.03
233	Skip Lockwood	.08	.06	.03
234	Lou Whitaker	.60	.45	.25
235	Scott Sanderson	.08	.06	.03
236	Mike Ivie	.08	.06	.03
237	Charlie Moore	.08	.06	.03
238	Willie Hernandez	.12	.09	.05
239	Rick Miller	.08	.06	.03
240	Nolan Ryan	12.00	9.00	4.75
241	Checklist 122-242	.08	.06	.03
242	Chet Lemon	.10	.08	.04
243	Sal Butera	.08	.06	.03
244	Cardinals Future Stars (*Tito Landrum*, Al Olmsted, Andy Rincon)	.15	.11	.06
245	Ed Figueroa	.08	.06	.03
246	Ed Ott	.08	.06	.03
247	Glenn Hubbard	.10	.08	.04
248	Joey McLaughlin	.08	.06	.03
249	Larry Cox	.08	.06	.03
250	Ron Guidry	.20	.15	.08
251	Tom Brookens	.10	.08	.04
252	Victor Cruz	.08	.06	.03
253	Dave Bergman	.08	.06	.03
254	Ozzie Smith	4.00	3.00	1.50
255	Mark Littell	.08	.06	.03
256	Bombo Rivera	.08	.06	.03
257	Rennie Stennett	.08	.06	.03
258	*Joe Price*	.12	.09	.05
259	Mets Future Stars (Juan Berenguer, *Hubie Brooks, Mookie Wilson*)	1.50	1.25	.60
260	Ron Cey	.15	.11	.06
261	Rickey Henderson	9.00	6.75	3.50
262	Sammy Stewart	.08	.06	.03
263	Brian Downing	.12	.09	.05
264	Jim Norris	.08	.06	.03
265	John Candelaria	.12	.09	.05
266	Tom Herr	.15	.11	.06
267	Stan Bahnsen	.08	.06	.03
268	Jerry Royster	.08	.06	.03
269	Ken Forsch	.08	.06	.03
270	Greg Luzinski	.20	.15	.08
271	Bill Castro	.08	.06	.03
272	Bruce Kimm	.08	.06	.03
273	Stan Papi	.08	.06	.03
274	Craig Chamberlain	.08	.06	.03
275	Dwight Evans	.15	.11	.06
276	Dan Spillner	.08	.06	.03
277	Alfredo Griffin	.12	.09	.05
278	Rick Sofield	.08	.06	.03
279	Bob Knepper	.12	.09	.05
280	Ken Griffey	.15	.11	.06
281	Fred Stanley	.08	.06	.03
282	Mariners Future Stars (Rick Anderson, Greg Biercevicz, Rodney Craig)	.08	.06	.03
283	Billy Sample	.08	.06	.03
284	Brian Kingman	.08	.06	.03

		MT	NR MT	EX
285	Jerry Turner	.08	.06	.03
286	Dave Frost	.08	.06	.03
287	Lenn Sakata	.08	.06	.03
288	Bob Clark	.08	.06	.03
289	Mickey Hatcher	.10	.08	.04
290	Bob Boone	.08	.06	.03
291	Aurelio Lopez	.08	.06	.03
292	Mike Squires	.08	.06	.03
293	*Charlie Lea*	.15	.11	.06
294	Mike Tyson	.08	.06	.03
295	Hal McRae	.15	.11	.06
296	Bill Nahorodny	.08	.06	.03
297	Bob Bailor	.08	.06	.03
298	Buddy Solomon	.08	.06	.03
299	Elliott Maddox	.08	.06	.03
300	Paul Molitor	5.00	3.75	2.00
301	Matt Keough	.08	.06	.03
302	Dodgers Future Stars (Jack Perconte, *Mike Scioscia, Fernando Valenzuela*)	2.50	2.00	1.00
303	Johnny Oates	.08	.06	.03
304	John Castino	.08	.06	.03
305	Ken Clay	.08	.06	.03
306	Juan Beniquez	.08	.06	.03
307	Gene Garber	.08	.06	.03
308	Rick Manning	.08	.06	.03
309	*Luis Salazar*	.08	.06	.03
310	Vida Blue	.08	.06	.03
311	Freddie Patek	.08	.06	.03
312	Rick Rhoden	.12	.09	.05
313	Luis Pujols	.08	.06	.03
314	Rich Dauer	.08	.06	.03
315	*Kirk Gibson*	3.00	2.25	1.25
316	Craig Minetto	.08	.06	.03
317	Lonnie Smith	.10	.08	.04
318	Steve Yeager	.08	.06	.03
319	Rowland Office	.08	.06	.03
320	Tom Burgmeier	.08	.06	.03
321	*Leon Durham*	.25	.20	.10
322	Neil Allen	.10	.08	.04
323	Jim Morrison	.08	.06	.03
324	Mike Willis	.08	.06	.03
325	Ray Knight	.12	.09	.05
326	Biff Pocoroba	.08	.06	.03
327	Moose Haas	.08	.06	.03
328	Twins Future Stars (*Dave Engle,* Greg Johnston, Gary Ward)	.12	.09	.05
329	Joaquin Andujar	.12	.09	.05
330	Frank White	.12	.09	.05
331	Dennis Lamp	.08	.06	.03
332	Lee Lacy	.08	.06	.03
333	Sid Monge	.08	.06	.03
334	Dane Iorg	.08	.06	.03
335	Rick Cerone	.08	.06	.03
336	Eddie Whitson	.08	.06	.03
337	Lynn Jones	.08	.06	.03
338	Checklist 243-363	.25	.20	.10
339	John Ellis	.08	.06	.03
340	Bruce Kison	.08	.06	.03
341	Dwayne Murphy	.10	.08	.04
342	Eric Rasmussen	.08	.06	.03
343	Frank Taveras	.08	.06	.03
344	Byron McLaughlin	.08	.06	.03
345	Warren Cromartie	.08	.06	.03
346	Larry Christenson	.08	.06	.03
347	*Harold Baines*	2.50	2.00	1.00
348	Bob Sykes	.08	.06	.03
349	Glenn Hoffman	.08	.06	.03
350	J.R. Richard	.12	.09	.05
351	Otto Velez	.08	.06	.03
352	Dick Tidrow	.08	.06	.03
353	Terry Kennedy	.12	.09	.05
354	Mario Soto	.10	.08	.04
355	Bob Horner	.25	.20	.10
356	Padres Future Stars (George Stablein, Craig Stimac, Tom Tellmann)	.08	.06	.03
357	Jim Slaton	.08	.06	.03
358	Mark Wagner	.08	.06	.03
359	Tom Hausman	.08	.06	.03
360	Willie Wilson	.15	.11	.06
361	Joe Strain	.08	.06	.03
362	Bo Diaz	.10	.08	.04
363	Geoff Zahn	.08	.06	.03
364	*Mike Davis*	.25	.20	.10
365	Graig Nettles	.12	.09	.05
366	Mike Ramsey	.08	.06	.03
367	Denny Martinez	.10	.08	.04
368	Leon Roberts	.08	.06	.03
369	Frank Tanana	.12	.09	.05
370	Dave Winfield	5.00	3.75	2.00
371	Charlie Hough	.15	.11	.06

		MT	NR MT	EX
372	Jay Johnstone	.10	.08	.04
373	Pat Underwood	.08	.06	.03
374	Tom Hutton	.08	.06	.03
375	Dave Concepcion	.20	.15	.08
376	Ron Reed	.08	.06	.03
377	Jerry Morales	.08	.06	.03
378	Dave Rader	.08	.06	.03
379	Lary Sorensen	.08	.06	.03
380	Willie Stargell	1.00	.70	.40
381	Cubs Future Stars (Carlos Lezcano, Steve Macko, Randy Martz)	.08	.06	.03
382	*Paul Mirabella*(FC)	.12	.09	.05
383	Eric Soderholm	.08	.06	.03
384	Mike Sadek	.08	.06	.03
385	Joe Sambito	.08	.06	.03
386	Dave Edwards	.08	.06	.03
387	Phil Niekro	.80	.60	.30
388	Andre Thornton	.12	.09	.05
389	Marty Pattin	.08	.06	.03
390	Cesar Geronimo	.08	.06	.03
391	Dave Lemanczyk	.08	.06	.03
392	Lance Parrish	.15	.11	.06
393	Broderick Perkins	.08	.06	.03
394	Woodie Fryman	.10	.08	.04
395	Scot Thompson	.08	.06	.03
396	Bill Campbell	.08	.06	.03
397	Julio Cruz	.08	.06	.03
398	Ross Baumgarten	.08	.06	.03
399	Orioles Future Stars (*Mike Boddicker,* Mark Corey, *Floyd Rayford*)	.50	.40	.20
400	Reggie Jackson	3.25	2.50	1.25
401	A.L. Championships (Royals Sweep Yankees)	.50	.40	.20
402	N.L. Championships (Phillies Squeak Past Astros)	.40	.30	.15
403	World Series (Phillies Beat Royals In 6)	.25	.20	.10
404	World Series Summary (Phillies Win First World Series)	.25	.20	.10
405	Nino Espinosa	.08	.06	.03
406	Dickie Noles	.08	.06	.03
407	Ernie Whitt	.10	.08	.04
408	Fernando Arroyo	.08	.06	.03
409	Larry Herndon	.10	.08	.04
410	Bert Campaneris	.12	.09	.05
411	Terry Puhl	.08	.06	.03
412	*Britt Burns*	.12	.09	.05
413	Tony Bernazard	.08	.06	.03
414	John Pacella	.08	.06	.03
415	Ben Oglivie	.10	.08	.04
416	Gary Alexander	.08	.06	.03
417	Dan Schatzeder	.08	.06	.03
418	Bobby Brown	.08	.06	.03
419	Tom Hume	.08	.06	.03
420	Keith Hernandez	.25	.20	.10
421	Bob Stanley	.08	.06	.03
422	Dan Ford	.08	.06	.03
423	Shane Rawley	.15	.11	.06
424	Yankees Future Stars (Tim Lollar, Bruce Robinson, Dennis Werth)	.08	.06	.03
425	Al Bumbry	.10	.08	.04
426	Warren Brusstar	.08	.06	.03
427	John D'Acquisto	.08	.06	.03
428	John Stearns	.08	.06	.03
429	Mick Kelleher	.08	.06	.03
430	Jim Bibby	.08	.06	.03
431	Dave Roberts	.08	.06	.03
432	Len Barker	.10	.08	.04
433	Rance Mulliniks	.08	.06	.03
434	Roger Erickson	.08	.06	.03
435	Jim Spencer	.08	.06	.03
436	Gary Lucas	.08	.06	.03
437	Mike Heath	.08	.06	.03
438	John Montefusco	.10	.08	.04
439	Denny Walling	.08	.06	.03
440	Jerry Reuss	.12	.09	.05
441	Ken Reitz	.08	.06	.03
442	Ron Pruitt	.08	.06	.03
443	Jim Beattie	.08	.06	.03
444	Garth Iorg	.08	.06	.03
445	Ellis Valentine	.08	.06	.03
446	Checklist 364-484	.25	.20	.10
447	Junior Kennedy	.08	.06	.03
448	Tim Corcoran	.08	.06	.03
449	Paul Mitchell	.08	.06	.03
450	Dave Kingman	.10	.08	.04
451	Indians Future Stars (Chris Bando, Tom Brennan, Sandy Wihtol)	.12	.09	.05
452	Renie Martin	.08	.06	.03
453	Rob Wilfong	.08	.06	.03
454	Andy Hassler	.08	.06	.03

No.	Player	MT	NR MT	EX
455	Rick Burleson	.10	.08	.04
456	*Jeff Reardon*	3.50	2.75	1.50
457	Mike Lum	.08	.06	.03
458	Randy Jones	.10	.08	.04
459	Greg Gross	.08	.06	.03
460	Rich Gossage	.20	.15	.08
461	Dave McKay	.08	.06	.03
462	Jack Brohamer	.08	.06	.03
463	Milt May	.08	.06	.03
464	Adrian Devine	.08	.06	.03
465	Bill Russell	.12	.09	.05
466	Bob Molinaro	.08	.06	.03
467	Dave Stieb	.35	.25	.14
468	Johnny Wockenfuss	.08	.06	.03
469	Jeff Leonard	.20	.15	.08
470	Manny Trillo	.10	.08	.04
471	Mike Vail	.08	.06	.03
472	Dyar Miller	.08	.06	.03
473	Jose Cardenal	.08	.06	.03
474	Mike LaCoss	.08	.06	.03
475	Buddy Bell	.15	.11	.06
476	Jerry Koosman	.15	.11	.06
477	Luis Gomez	.08	.06	.03
478	Juan Eichelberger	.08	.06	.03
479	Expos Future Stars (Bobby Pate, *Tim Raines,* Roberto Ramos)	9.00	6.75	3.50
480	Carlton Fisk	1.50	1.25	.60
481	Bob Lacey	.08	.06	.03
482	Jim Gantner	.10	.08	.04
483	Mike Griffin	.08	.06	.03
484	Max Venable	.08	.06	.03
485	Garry Templeton	.12	.09	.05
486	Marc Hill	.08	.06	.03
487	Dewey Robinson	.08	.06	.03
488	*Damaso Garcia*	.12	.09	.05
489	John Littlefield (photo actually Mark Riggins)	.08	.06	.03
490	Eddie Murray	2.00	1.50	.80
491	Gordy Pladson	.08	.06	.03
492	Barry Foote	.08	.06	.03
493	Dan Quisenberry	.20	.15	.08
494	*Bob Walk*	.20	.15	.08
495	Dusty Baker	.12	.09	.05
496	Paul Dade	.08	.06	.03
497	Fred Norman	.08	.06	.03
498	Pat Putnam	.08	.06	.03
499	Frank Pastore	.08	.06	.03
500	Jim Rice	.35	.25	.14
501	Tim Foli	.08	.06	.03
502	Giants Future Stars (Chris Bourjos, Al Hargesheimer, Mike Rowland)	.08	.06	.03
503	Steve McCatty	.08	.06	.03
504	Dale Murphy	.90	.70	.35
505	Jason Thompson	.08	.06	.03
506	Phil Huffman	.08	.06	.03
507	Jamie Quirk	.08	.06	.03
508	Rob Dressler	.08	.06	.03
509	Pete Mackanin	.08	.06	.03
510	Lee Mazzilli	.10	.08	.04
511	Wayne Garland	.08	.06	.03
512	Gary Thomasson	.08	.06	.03
513	Frank LaCorte	.08	.06	.03
514	George Riley	.08	.06	.03
515	Robin Yount	6.00	4.50	2.50
516	Doug Bird	.08	.06	.03
517	Richie Zisk	.10	.08	.04
518	Grant Jackson	.08	.06	.03
519	John Tamargo	.08	.06	.03
520	Steve Stone	.12	.09	.05
521	Sam Mejias	.08	.06	.03
522	Mike Colbern	.08	.06	.03
523	John Fulgham	.08	.06	.03
524	Willie Aikens	.08	.06	.03
525	Mike Torrez	.10	.08	.04
526	Phillies Future Stars (Marty Bystrom, Jay Loviglio, Jim Wright)	.08	.06	.03
527	Danny Goodwin	.08	.06	.03
528	Gary Matthews	.12	.09	.05
529	Dave LaRoche	.08	.06	.03
530	Steve Garvey	.90	.70	.35
531	John Curtis	.08	.06	.03
532	Bill Stein	.08	.06	.03
533	Jesus Figueroa	.08	.06	.03
534	*Dave Smith*	.60	.45	.25
535	Omar Moreno	.08	.06	.03
536	Bob Owchinko	.08	.06	.03
537	Ron Hodges	.08	.06	.03
538	Tom Griffin	.08	.06	.03
539	Rodney Scott	.08	.06	.03
540	Mike Schmidt	4.00	3.00	1.50
541	Steve Swisher	.08	.06	.03
542	Larry Bradford	.08	.06	.03
543	Terry Crowley	.08	.06	.03
544	Rich Gale	.08	.06	.03
545	Johnny Grubb	.08	.06	.03
546	Paul Moskau	.08	.06	.03
547	Mario Guerrero	.08	.06	.03
548	Dave Goltz	.10	.08	.04
549	Jerry Remy	.08	.06	.03
550	Tommy John	.50	.40	.20
551	Pirates Future Stars *(Vance Law, Tony Pena, Pascual Perez)*	.75	.60	.30
552	Steve Trout	.08	.06	.03
553	Tim Blackwell	.08	.06	.03
554	Bert Blyleven	.15	.11	.06
555	Cecil Cooper	.10	.08	.04
556	Jerry Mumphrey	.08	.06	.03
557	Chris Knapp	.08	.06	.03
558	Barry Bonnell	.08	.06	.03
559	Willie Montanez	.08	.06	.03
560	Joe Morgan	.90	.70	.35
561	Dennis Littlejohn	.08	.06	.03
562	Checklist 485-605	.25	.20	.10
563	Jim Kaat	.30	.25	.12
564	Ron Hassey	.08	.06	.03
565	Burt Hooton	.10	.08	.04
566	Del Unser	.08	.06	.03
567	Mark Bomback	.08	.06	.03
568	Dave Revering	.08	.06	.03
569	Al Williams	.08	.06	.03
570	Ken Singleton	.12	.09	.05
571	Todd Cruz	.08	.06	.03
572	Jack Morris	.75	.60	.30
573	Phil Garner	.10	.08	.04
574	Bill Caudill	.08	.06	.03
575	Tony Perez	.35	.25	.14
576	Reggie Cleveland	.08	.06	.03
577	Blue Jays Future Stars (Luis Leal, Brian Milner, *Ken Schrom)*	.20	.15	.08
578	*Bill Gullickson*	.20	.15	.08
579	Tim Flannery	.08	.06	.03
580	Don Baylor	.15	.11	.06
581	Roy Howell	.08	.06	.03
582	Gaylord Perry	.70	.50	.30
583	Larry Milbourne	.08	.06	.03
584	Randy Lerch	.08	.06	.03
585	Amos Otis	.10	.08	.04
586	Silvio Martinez	.08	.06	.03
587	Jeff Newman	.08	.06	.03
588	Gary Lavelle	.08	.06	.03
589	Lamar Johnson	.08	.06	.03
590	Bruce Sutter	.15	.11	.06
591	John Lowenstein	.08	.06	.03
592	Steve Comer	.08	.06	.03
593	Steve Kemp	.12	.09	.05
594	Preston Hanna	.08	.06	.03
595	Butch Hobson	.08	.06	.03
596	Jerry Augustine	.08	.06	.03
597	Rafael Landestoy	.08	.06	.03
598	George Vukovich	.08	.06	.03
599	Dennis Kinney	.08	.06	.03
600	Johnny Bench	2.00	1.50	.80
601	Don Aase	.08	.06	.03
602	Bobby Murcer	.15	.11	.06
603	John Verhoeven	.08	.06	.03
604	Rob Picciolo	.08	.06	.03
605	Don Sutton	.70	.50	.30
606	Reds Future Stars (Bruce Berenyi, Geoff Combe, Paul Householder)	.08	.06	.03
607	Dave Palmer	.08	.06	.03
608	Greg Pryor	.08	.06	.03
609	Lynn McGlothen	.08	.06	.03
610	Darrell Porter	.10	.08	.04
611	Rick Matula	.08	.06	.03
612	Duane Kuiper	.08	.06	.03
613	Jim Anderson	.08	.06	.03
614	Dave Rozema	.08	.06	.03
615	Rick Dempsey	.12	.09	.05
616	Rick Wise	.10	.08	.04
617	Craig Reynolds	.08	.06	.03
618	John Milner	.08	.06	.03
619	Steve Henderson	.08	.06	.03
620	Dennis Eckersley	1.50	1.25	.60
621	Tom Donohue	.08	.06	.03
622	Randy Moffitt	.08	.06	.03
623	Sal Bando	.12	.09	.05
624	Bob Welch	.30	.25	.12
625	Bill Buckner	.15	.11	.06
626	Tigers Future Stars (Dave Steffen, Jerry Ujdur, Roger Weaver)	.08	.06	.03
627	Luis Tiant	.10	.08	.04
628	Vic Correll	.08	.06	.03

		MT	NR MT	EX
629	Tony Armas	.12	.09	.05
630	Steve Carlton	3.00	2.25	1.25
631	Ron Jackson	.08	.06	.03
632	Alan Bannister	.08	.06	.03
633	Bill Lee	.10	.08	.04
634	Doug Flynn	.08	.06	.03
635	Bobby Bonds	.15	.11	.06
636	Al Hrabosky	.10	.08	.04
637	Jerry Narron	.08	.06	.03
638	Checklist 606	.25	.20	.10
639	Carney Lansford	.15	.11	.06
640	Dave Parker	.60	.45	.25
641	Mark Belanger	.10	.08	.04
642	Vern Ruhle	.08	.06	.03
643	*Lloyd Moseby*	.40	.30	.15
644	Ramon Aviles	.08	.06	.03
645	Rick Reuschel	.15	.11	.06
646	Marvis Foley	.08	.06	.03
647	Dick Drago	.08	.06	.03
648	Darrell Evans	.15	.11	.06
649	Manny Sarmiento	.08	.06	.03
650	Bucky Dent	.12	.09	.05
651	Pedro Guerrero	.20	.15	.08
652	John Montague	.08	.06	.03
653	Bill Fahey	.08	.06	.03
654	Ray Burris	.08	.06	.03
655	Dan Driessen	.12	.09	.05
656	Jon Matlack	.10	.08	.04
657	Mike Cubbage	.08	.06	.03
658	Milt Wilcox	.08	.06	.03
659	Brewers Future Stars (John Flinn, Ed Romero, Ned Yost)	.08	.06	.03
660	Gary Carter	.80	.60	.30
661	Orioles Team (Earl Weaver)	.30	.25	.12
662	Red Sox Team (Ralph Houk)	.30	.25	.12
663	Angels Team (Jim Fregosi)	.25	.20	.10
664	White Sox Team (Tony LaRussa)	.25	.20	.10
665	Indians Team (Dave Garcia)	.25	.20	.10
666	Tigers Team (Sparky Anderson)	.30	.25	.12
667	Royals Team (Jim Frey)	.25	.20	.10
668	Brewers Team (Bob Rodgers)	.25	.20	.10
669	Twins Team (John Goryl)	.25	.20	.10
670	Yankees Team (Gene Michael)	.35	.25	.14
671	A's Team (Billy Martin)	.30	.25	.12
672	Mariners Team (Maury Wills)	.25	.20	.10
673	Rangers Team (Don Zimmer)	.25	.20	.10
674	Blue Jays Team (Bobby Mattick)	.25	.20	.10
675	Braves Team (Bobby Cox)	.25	.20	.10
676	Cubs Team (Joe Amalfitano)	.25	.20	.10
677	Reds Team (John McNamara)	.25	.20	.10
678	Astros Team (Bill Virdon)	.25	.20	.10
679	Dodgers Team (Tom Lasorda)	.35	.25	.14
680	Expos Team (Dick Williams)	.25	.20	.10
681	Mets Team (Joe Torre)	.30	.25	.12
682	Phillies Team (Dallas Green)	.25	.20	.10
683	Pirates Team (Chuck Tanner)	.25	.20	.10
684	Cardinals Team (Whitey Herzog)	.30	.25	.12
685	Padres Team (Frank Howard)	.25	.20	.10
686	Giants Team (Dave Bristol)	.25	.20	.10
687	Jeff Jones	.08	.06	.03
688	Kiko Garcia	.08	.06	.03
689	Red Sox Future Stars (*Bruce Hurst*, Keith MacWhorter, *Reid Nichols*)	1.50	1.25	.60
690	Bob Watson	.10	.08	.04
691	Dick Ruthven	.08	.06	.03
692	Lenny Randle	.08	.06	.03
693	*Steve Howe*	.20	.15	.08
694	Bud Harrelson	.08	.06	.03
695	Kent Tekulve	.10	.08	.04
696	Alan Ashby	.08	.06	.03
697	Rick Waits	.08	.06	.03
698	Mike Jorgensen	.08	.06	.03
699	Glenn Abbott	.08	.06	.03
700	George Brett	6.00	4.50	2.50
701	Joe Rudi	.12	.09	.05
702	George Medich	.08	.06	.03
703	Alvis Woods	.08	.06	.03
704	Bill Travers	.08	.06	.03
705	Ted Simmons	.25	.20	.10
706	Dave Ford	.08	.06	.03
707	Dave Cash	.08	.06	.03
708	Doyle Alexander	.12	.09	.05
709	Alan Trammell	.70	.50	.30
710	Ron LeFlore	.08	.06	.03
711	Joe Ferguson	.08	.06	.03
712	Bill Bonham	.08	.06	.03
713	Bill North	.08	.06	.03
714	Pete Redfern	.08	.06	.03
715	Bill Madlock	.15	.11	.06
716	Glenn Borgmann	.08	.06	.03
717	Jim Barr	.08	.06	.03
718	Larry Biittner	.08	.06	.03
719	Sparky Lyle	.12	.09	.05
720	Fred Lynn	.35	.25	.14
721	Toby Harrah	.10	.08	.04
722	Joe Niekro	.20	.15	.08
723	Bruce Bochte	.08	.06	.03
724	Lou Piniella	.20	.15	.08
725	Steve Rogers	.10	.08	.04
726	Rick Monday	.15	.11	.06

1981 Topps Traded

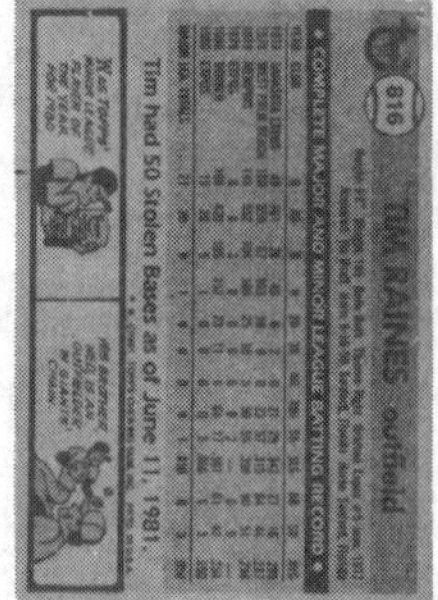

The 132 cards in this extension set are numbered from 727 to 858, technically making them a high-numbered series of the regular Topps set. The set was not packaged in gum packs, but rather placed in a specially designed red box and sold through baseball card dealers only. While many complained about the method, the fact remains, even at higher prices, the set has done well for its owners as it features not only mid-season trades, but also single-player rookie cards of some of the hottest prospects. The cards measure 2-1/2" by 3-1/2".

		MT	NR MT	EX
Complete Set (132):		45.00	35.00	18.00
Common Player:		.20	.15	.08
727	Danny Ainge(FC)	6.00	4.50	2.50
728	Doyle Alexander	.20	.15	.08
729	Gary Alexander	.20	.15	.08
730	Billy Almon	.20	.15	.08
731	Joaquin Andujar	.20	.15	.08
732	Bob Bailor	.20	.15	.08
733	Juan Beniquez	.20	.15	.08
734	Dave Bergman	.20	.15	.08
735	Tony Bernazard	.20	.15	.08
736	Larry Biittner	.20	.15	.08
737	Doug Bird	.20	.15	.08
738	Bert Blyleven	1.00	.70	.40
739	Mark Bomback	.20	.15	.08
740	Bobby Bonds	.20	.15	.08
741	Rick Bosetti	.20	.15	.08
742	Hubie Brooks	1.00	.70	.40
743	Rick Burleson	.20	.15	.08
744	Ray Burris	.20	.15	.08
745	Jeff Burroughs	.20	.15	.08
746	Enos Cabell	.20	.15	.08
747	Ken Clay	.20	.15	.08
748	Mark Clear	.20	.15	.08
749	Larry Cox	.20	.15	.08
750	Hector Cruz	.20	.15	.08
751	Victor Cruz	.20	.15	.08
752	Mike Cubbage	.20	.15	.08
753	Dick Davis	.20	.15	.08
754	Brian Doyle	.20	.15	.08
755	Dick Drago	.20	.15	.08
756	Leon Durham	.20	.15	.08
757	Jim Dwyer	.20	.15	.08
758	Dave Edwards	.20	.15	.08
759	Jim Essian	.20	.15	.08
760	Bill Fahey	.20	.15	.08
761	Rollie Fingers	5.00	3.75	2.00
762	Carlton Fisk	5.00	3.75	2.00
763	Barry Foote	.20	.15	.08
764	Ken Forsch	.20	.15	.08
765	Kiko Garcia	.20	.15	.08

		MT	NR MT	EX
766	Cesar Geronimo	.20	.15	.08
767	Gary Gray	.20	.15	.08
768	Mickey Hatcher	.20	.15	.08
769	Steve Henderson	.20	.15	.08
770	Marc Hill	.20	.15	.08
771	Butch Hobson	.20	.15	.08
772	Rick Honeycutt	.20	.15	.08
773	Roy Howell	.20	.15	.08
774	Mike Ivie	.20	.15	.08
775	Roy Lee Jackson	.20	.15	.08
776	Cliff Johnson	.20	.15	.08
777	Randy Jones	.20	.15	.08
778	Ruppert Jones	.20	.15	.08
779	Mick Kelleher	.20	.15	.08
780	Terry Kennedy	.20	.15	.08
781	Dave Kingman	.20	.15	.08
782	Bob Knepper	.20	.15	.08
783	Ken Kravec	.20	.15	.08
784	Bob Lacey	.20	.15	.08
785	Dennis Lamp	.20	.15	.08
786	Rafael Landestoy	.20	.15	.08
787	Ken Landreaux	.20	.15	.08
788	Carney Lansford	.20	.15	.08
789	Dave LaRoche	.20	.15	.08
790	Joe Lefebvre	.20	.15	.08
791	Ron LeFlore	.20	.15	.08
792	Randy Lerch	.20	.15	.08
793	Sixto Lezcano	.20	.15	.08
794	John Littlefield	.20	.15	.08
795	Mike Lum	.20	.15	.08
796	Greg Luzinski	.50	.40	.20
797	Fred Lynn	.50	.40	.20
798	Jerry Martin	.20	.15	.08
799	Buck Martinez	.20	.15	.08
800	Gary Matthews	.20	.15	.08
801	Mario Mendoza	.20	.15	.08
802	Larry Milbourne	.20	.15	.08
803	Rick Miller	.20	.15	.08
804	John Montefusco	.20	.15	.08
805	Jerry Morales	.20	.15	.08
806	Jose Morales	.20	.15	.08
807	Joe Morgan	3.00	2.25	1.25
808	Jerry Mumphrey	.20	.15	.08
809	Gene Nelson(FC)	.20	.15	.08
810	Ed Ott	.20	.15	.08
811	Bob Owchinko	.20	.15	.08
812	Gaylord Perry	2.50	2.00	1.00
813	Mike Phillips	.20	.15	.08
814	Darrell Porter	.20	.15	.08
815	Mike Proly	.20	.15	.08
816	Tim Raines	12.00	9.00	4.75
817	Lenny Randle	.20	.15	.08
818	Doug Rau	.20	.15	.08
819	Jeff Reardon	6.00	4.50	2.50
820	Ken Reitz	.20	.15	.08
821	Steve Renko	.20	.15	.08
822	Rick Reuschel	.20	.15	.08
823	Dave Revering	.20	.15	.08
824	Dave Roberts	.20	.15	.08
825	Leon Roberts	.20	.15	.08
826	Joe Rudi	.20	.15	.08
827	Kevin Saucier	.20	.15	.08
828	Tony Scott	.20	.15	.08
829	Bob Shirley	.20	.15	.08
830	Ted Simmons	.20	.15	.08
831	Lary Sorensen	.20	.15	.08
832	Jim Spencer	.20	.15	.08
833	Harry Spilman	.20	.15	.08
834	Fred Stanley	.20	.15	.08
835	Rusty Staub	.30	.25	.12
836	Bill Stein	.20	.15	.08
837	Joe Strain	.20	.15	.08
838	Bruce Sutter	.50	.40	.20
839	Don Sutton	1.50	1.25	.60
840	Steve Swisher	.20	.15	.08
841	Frank Tanana	.20	.15	.08
842	Gene Tenace	.20	.15	.08
843	Jason Thompson	.20	.15	.08
844	Dickie Thon	.20	.15	.08
845	Bill Travers	.20	.15	.08
846	Tom Underwood	.20	.15	.08
847	John Urrea	.20	.15	.08
848	Mike Vail	.20	.15	.08
849	Ellis Valentine	.20	.15	.08
850	Fernando Valenzuela	2.00	1.50	.80
851	Pete Vuckovich	.20	.15	.08
852	Mark Wagner	.20	.15	.08
853	Bob Walk	.20	.15	.08
854	Claudell Washington	.20	.15	.08
855	Dave Winfield	15.00	11.00	6.00
856	Geoff Zahn	.20	.15	.08
857	Richie Zisk	.20	.15	.08
858	Checklist 727-858	.20	.15	.08

1981 Topps Home Team 5X7 Photos

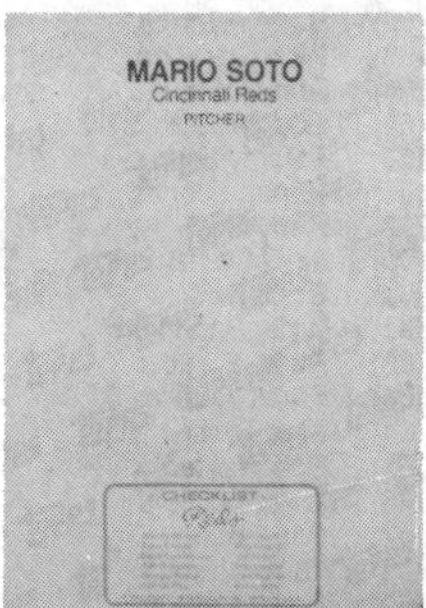

Once again testing the popularity of large cards, Topps issued 4-7/8" by 6-7/8" cards in two different sets. The Home Team cards feature a large color photo, facsimile autograph and white border on the front. Backs have the player's name, team, position and a checklist at the bottom. The 102 cards were sold in limited areas corresponding to the teams' geographic home. It was also possible to order the whole set by mail. Eleven teams are involved in the issue, with the number of players from each team ranging from 6 to 12. Although it is an attractive set featuring many stars, ready availability and many collectors' aversion to large cards keep prices relatively low today.

		MT	NR MT	EX
Complete Set:		40.00	30.00	16.00
Common Player:		.20	.15	.08
(1)	Dusty Baker	.25	.20	.10
(2)	Don Baylor	.40	.30	.15
(3)	Rick Burleson	.20	.15	.08
(4)	Rod Carew	.90	.70	.35
(5)	Ron Cey	.30	.25	.12
(6)	Steve Garvey	.40	.30	.15
(7)	Bobby Grich	.30	.25	.12
(8)	Butch Hobson	.20	.15	.08
(9)	Burt Hooton	.20	.15	.08
(10)	Steve Howe	.20	.15	.08
(11)	Dave Lopes	.25	.20	.10
(12)	Fred Lynn	.50	.40	.20
(13)	Rick Monday	.25	.20	.10
(14)	Jerry Reuss	.25	.20	.10
(15)	Bill Russell	.25	.20	.10
(16)	Reggie Smith	.30	.25	.12
(17)	Bob Welch	.40	.30	.15
(18)	Steve Yeager	.20	.15	.08
(19)	Buddy Bell	.30	.25	.12
(20)	Cesar Cedeno	.30	.25	.12
(21)	Jose Cruz	.30	.25	.12
(22)	Art Howe	.20	.15	.08
(23)	Jon Matlack	.20	.15	.08
(24)	Al Oliver	.40	.30	.15
(25)	Terry Puhl	.20	.15	.08
(26)	Mickey Rivers	.25	.20	.10
(27)	Nolan Ryan	2.00	1.50	.80
(28)	Jim Sundberg	.25	.20	.10
(29)	Don Sutton	.60	.45	.25
(30)	Bump Wills	.20	.15	.08
(31)	Tim Blackwell	.20	.15	.08
(32)	Bill Buckner	.40	.30	.15
(33)	Britt Burns	.20	.15	.08
(34)	Ivan DeJesus	.20	.15	.08
(35)	Rich Dotson	.25	.20	.10
(36)	Leon Durham	.25	.20	.10
(37)	Ed Farmer	.20	.15	.08
(38)	Lamar Johnson	.20	.15	.08
(39)	Dave Kingman	.40	.30	.15
(40)	Mike Krukow	.25	.20	.10
(41)	Ron LeFlore	.25	.20	.10

		MT	NR MT	EX
(42)	Chet Lemon	.25	.20	.10
(43)	Bob Molinaro	.20	.15	.08
(44)	Jim Morrison	.20	.15	.08
(45)	Wayne Nordhagen	.20	.15	.08
(46)	Ken Reitz	.20	.15	.08
(47)	Rick Reuschel	.30	.25	.12
(48)	Mike Tyson	.20	.15	.08
(49)	Neil Allen	.20	.15	.08
(50)	Rick Cerone	.20	.15	.08
(51)	Bucky Dent	.25	.20	.10
(52)	Doug Flynn	.20	.15	.08
(53)	Rich Gossage	.60	.45	.25
(54)	Ron Guidry	.60	.45	.25
(55)	Reggie Jackson	.90	.70	.35
(56)	Tommy John	.50	.40	.20
(57)	Ruppert Jones	.20	.15	.08
(58)	Rudy May	.20	.15	.08
(59)	Lee Mazzilli	.25	.20	.10
(60)	Graig Nettles	.40	.30	.15
(61)	Willie Randolph	.30	.25	.12
(62)	Rusty Staub	.40	.30	.15
(63)	Frank Taveras	.20	.15	.08
(64)	Alex Trevino	.20	.15	.08
(65)	Bob Watson	.25	.20	.10
(66)	Dave Winfield	.90	.70	.35
(67)	Bob Boone	.40	.30	.15
(68)	Larry Bowa	.40	.30	.15
(69)	Steve Carlton	.70	.50	.30
(70)	Greg Luzinski	.40	.30	.15
(71)	Garry Maddox	.25	.20	.10
(72)	Bake McBride	.20	.15	.08
(73)	Tug McGraw	.40	.30	.15
(74)	Pete Rose	1.50	1.25	.60
(75)	Dick Ruthven	.20	.15	.08
(76)	Mike Schmidt	.90	.70	.35
(77)	Manny Trillo	.25	.20	.10
(78)	Del Unser	.20	.15	.08
(79)	Tom Burgmeier	.20	.15	.08
(80)	Dennis Eckersley	.40	.30	.15
(81)	Dwight Evans	.25	.20	.10
(82)	Carlton Fisk	.60	.45	.25
(83)	Glenn Hoffman	.20	.15	.08
(84)	Carney Lansford	.30	.25	.12
(85)	Tony Perez	.50	.40	.20
(86)	Jim Rice	.50	.40	.20
(87)	Bob Stanley	.20	.15	.08
(88)	Dave Stapleton	.20	.15	.08
(89)	Frank Tanana	.25	.20	.10
(90)	Carl Yastrzemski	.90	.70	.35
(91)	Johnny Bench	.90	.70	.35
(92)	Dave Collins	.25	.20	.10
(93)	Dave Concepcion	.40	.30	.15
(94)	Dan Driessen	.25	.20	.10
(95)	George Foster	.40	.30	.15
(96)	Ken Griffey	.40	.30	.15
(97)	Tom Hume	.20	.15	.08
(98)	Ray Knight	.25	.20	.10
(99)	Joe Nolan	.20	.15	.08
(100)	Ron Oester	.20	.15	.08
(101)	Tom Seaver	.90	.70	.35
(102)	Mario Soto	.25	.20	.10

1981 Topps National 5X7 Photos

This set is the other half of Topps' efforts with large cards in 1981. Measuring 4-7/8" by 6-7/8", the National photo issue was limited to 15 cards. They were sold in areas not covered by the Home Team sets and feature ten cards which carry the same photos as found in the Home Team set, but with no checklist on the backs. Five cards are unique to the National set: George Brett, Cecil Cooper, Jim Palmer, Dave Parker and Ted Simmons. With their wide distribution and a limited demand, there are currently plenty of these cards to meet the demand, thus keeping prices fairly low.

		MT	NR MT	EX
Complete Set:		8.00	6.00	3.25
Common Player:		.30	.25	.12
(1)	Buddy Bell	.30	.25	.12
(2)	Johnny Bench	.60	.45	.25
(3)	George Brett	.90	.70	.35
(4)	Rod Carew	.60	.45	.25
(5)	Cecil Cooper	.40	.30	.15
(6)	Steve Garvey	.60	.45	.25
(7)	Rich Gossage	.40	.30	.15
(8)	Reggie Jackson	.70	.50	.30
(9)	Jim Palmer	.60	.45	.25
(10)	Dave Parker	.60	.45	.25
(11)	Jim Rice	.40	.30	.15
(12)	Pete Rose	.90	.70	.35
(13)	Mike Schmidt	.70	.50	.30
(14)	Tom Seaver	.60	.45	.25
(15)	Ted Simmons	.40	.30	.15

1981 Topps Scratchoffs

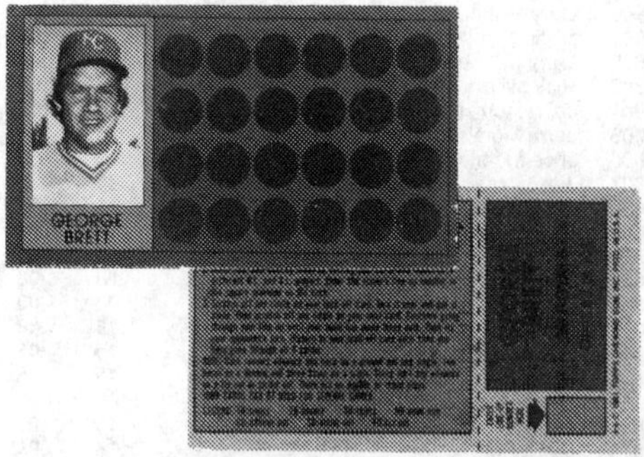

Sold as a separate issue with bubble gum, this 108-card set was issued in three-card panels that measure 3-1/4" by 5-1/4". Each individual card measures 1-13/16" by 3-1/4" and contains a small player photo alongside a series of black dots designed to be scratched off as part of a baseball game. Cards of National League players have a green backgrounds, while American League players have a red background. While there are 108 different players in the set, there are 144 possible panel combinations. An intact panel of three cards is valued approximately 20-25 percent more the sum of the individual cards.

		MT	NR MT	EX
Complete Set:		4.00	3.00	1.50
Common Player:		.02	.02	.01
1	George Brett	.12	.09	.05
2	Cecil Cooper	.04	.03	.02
3	Reggie Jackson	.12	.09	.05
4	Al Oliver	.04	.03	.02
5	Fred Lynn	.06	.05	.02
6	Tony Armas	.02	.02	.01
7	Ben Oglivie	.02	.02	.01
8	Tony Perez	.06	.05	.02
9	Eddie Murray	.10	.08	.04
10	Robin Yount	.08	.06	.03
11	Steve Kemp	.04	.03	.02
12	Joe Charboneau	.04	.03	.02
13	Jim Rice	.10	.08	.04
14	Lance Parrish	.08	.06	.03
15	John Mayberry	.02	.02	.01
16	Richie Zisk	.02	.02	.01
17	Ken Singleton	.04	.03	.02

		MT	NR MT	EX
18	Rod Carew	.10	.08	.04
19	Rick Manning	.02	.02	.01
20	Willie Wilson	.04	.03	.02
21	Buddy Bell	.04	.03	.02
22	Dave Revering	.02	.02	.01
23	Tom Paciorek	.02	.02	.01
24	Champ Summers	.02	.02	.01
25	Carney Lansford	.04	.03	.02
26	Lamar Johnson	.02	.02	.01
27	Willie Aikens	.02	.02	.01
28	Rick Cerone	.02	.02	.01
29	Al Bumbry	.02	.02	.01
30	Bruce Bochte	.02	.02	.01
31	Mickey Rivers	.02	.02	.01
32	Mike Hargrove	.02	.02	.01
33	John Castino	.02	.02	.01
34	Chet Lemon	.04	.03	.02
35	Paul Molitor	.06	.05	.02
36	Willie Randolph	.04	.03	.02
37	Rick Burleson	.02	.02	.01
38	Alan Trammell	.08	.06	.03
39	Rickey Henderson	.10	.08	.04
40	Dan Meyer	.02	.02	.01
41	Ken Landreaux	.02	.02	.01
42	Damaso Garcia	.02	.02	.01
43	Roy Smalley	.02	.02	.01
44	Otto Velez	.02	.02	.01
45	Sixto Lezcano	.02	.02	.01
46	Toby Harrah	.02	.02	.01
47	Frank White	.04	.03	.02
48	Dave Stapleton	.02	.02	.01
49	Steve Stone	.04	.03	.02
50	Jim Palmer	.08	.06	.03
51	Larry Gura	.02	.02	.01
52	Tommy John	.06	.05	.02
53	Mike Norris	.02	.02	.01
54	Ed Farmer	.02	.02	.01
55	Bill Buckner	.04	.03	.02
56	Steve Garvey	.10	.08	.04
57	Reggie Smith	.04	.03	.02
58	Bake McBride	.02	.02	.01
59	Dave Parker	.06	.05	.02
60	Mike Schmidt	.12	.09	.05
61	Bob Horner	.04	.03	.02
62	Pete Rose	.20	.15	.08
63	Ted Simmons	.06	.05	.02
64	Johnny Bench	.12	.09	.05
65	George Foster	.06	.05	.02
66	Gary Carter	.10	.08	.04
67	Keith Hernandez	.08	.06	.03
68	Ozzie Smith	.06	.05	.02
69	Dave Kingman	.06	.05	.02
70	Jack Clark	.06	.05	.02
71	Dusty Baker	.04	.03	.02
72	Dale Murphy	.12	.09	.05
73	Ron Cey	.04	.03	.02
74	Greg Luzinski	.04	.03	.02
75	Lee Mazzilli	.02	.02	.01
76	Gary Matthews	.04	.03	.02
77	Cesar Cedeno	.04	.03	.02
78	Warren Cromartie	.02	.02	.01
79	Steve Henderson	.02	.02	.01
80	Ellis Valentine	.02	.02	.01
81	Mike Easler	.02	.02	.01
82	Garry Templeton	.04	.03	.02
83	Jose Cruz	.04	.03	.02
84	Dave Collins	.02	.02	.01
85	George Hendrick	.02	.02	.01
86	Gene Richards	.02	.02	.01
87	Terry Whitfield	.02	.02	.01
88	Terry Puhl	.02	.02	.01
89	Larry Parrish	.04	.03	.02
90	Andre Dawson	.08	.06	.03
91	Ken Griffey	.04	.03	.02
92	Dave Lopes	.02	.02	.01
93	Doug Flynn	.02	.02	.01
94	Ivan DeJesus	.02	.02	.01
95	Dave Concepcion	.04	.03	.02
96	John Stearns	.02	.02	.01
97	Jerry Mumphrey	.02	.02	.01
98	Jerry Martin	.02	.02	.01
99	Art Howe	.02	.02	.01
100	Omar Moreno	.02	.02	.01
101	Ken Reitz	.02	.02	.01
102	Phil Garner	.02	.02	.01
103	Jerry Reuss	.04	.03	.02
104	Steve Carlton	.10	.08	.04
105	Jim Bibby	.02	.02	.01
106	Steve Rogers	.02	.02	.01
107	Tom Seaver	.10	.08	.04
108	Vida Blue	.04	.03	.02

1981 Topps Stickers

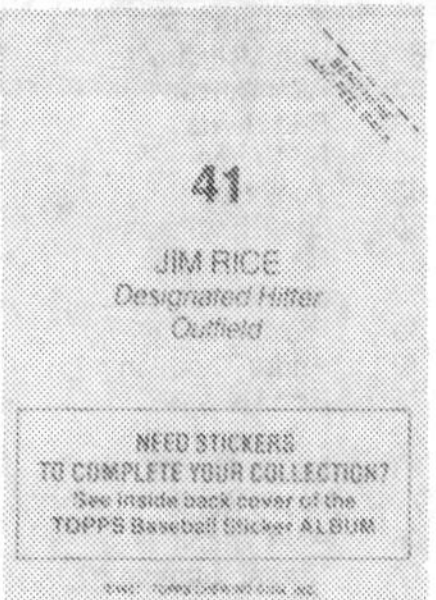

The 262 stickers in this full-color set measure 1-15/16" by 2-9/16" and are numbered on both the front and back. They were produced for Topps by the Panini Company of Italy. The set includes a series of "All-Star" stickers printed on silver or gold "foil". An album to house the stickers was also available.

	MT	NR MT	EX
Complete Set:	17.00	12.50	6.75
Common Player:	.03	.02	.01
Sticker Album:	.80	.60	.30

		MT	NR MT	EX
1	Steve Stone	.06	.05	.02
2	Tommy John, Mike Norris	.06	.05	.02
3	Rudy May	.03	.02	.01
4	Mike Norris	.03	.02	.01
5	Len Barker	.03	.02	.01
6	Mike Norris	.03	.02	.01
7	Dan Quisenberry	.06	.05	.02
8	Rich Gossage	.10	.08	.04
9	George Brett	.25	.20	.10
10	Cecil Cooper	.08	.06	.03
11	Reggie Jackson, Ben Oglivie	.06	.05	.02
12	Gorman Thomas	.06	.05	.02
13	Cecil Cooper	.08	.06	.03
14	George Brett, Ben Oglivie	.20	.15	.08
15	Rickey Henderson	.25	.20	.10
16	Willie Wilson	.08	.06	.03
17	Bill Buckner	.06	.05	.02
18	Keith Hernandez	.12	.09	.05
19	Mike Schmidt	.25	.20	.10
20	Bob Horner	.10	.08	.04
21	Mike Schmidt	.25	.20	.10
22	George Hendrick	.06	.05	.02
23	Ron LeFlore	.04	.03	.02
24	Omar Moreno	.03	.02	.01
25	Steve Carlton	.20	.15	.08
26	Joe Niekro	.06	.05	.02
27	Don Sutton	.10	.08	.04
28	Steve Carlton	.20	.15	.08
29	Steve Carlton	.20	.15	.08
30	Nolan Ryan	.20	.15	.08
31	Rollie Fingers, Tom Hume	.08	.06	.03
32	Bruce Sutter	.08	.06	.03
33	Ken Singleton	.06	.05	.02
34	Eddie Murray	.20	.15	.08
35	Al Bumbry	.03	.02	.01
36	Rich Dauer	.03	.02	.01
37	Scott McGregor	.04	.03	.02
38	Rick Dempsey	.04	.03	.02
39	Jim Palmer	.15	.11	.06
40	Steve Stone	.06	.05	.02
41	Jim Rice	.20	.15	.08
42	Fred Lynn	.10	.08	.04
43	Carney Lansford	.06	.05	.02
44	Tony Perez	.10	.08	.04
45	Carl Yastrzemski	.30	.25	.12
46	Carlton Fisk	.12	.09	.05
47	Dave Stapleton	.03	.02	.01
48	Dennis Eckersley	.06	.05	.02
49	Rod Carew	.20	.15	.08
50	Brian Downing	.04	.03	.02
51	Don Baylor	.08	.06	.03
52	Rick Burleson	.04	.03	.02
53	Bobby Grich	.06	.05	.02
54	Butch Hobson	.03	.02	.01
55	Andy Hassler	.03	.02	.01
56	Frank Tanana	.04	.03	.02

		MT	NR MT	EX
57	Chet Lemon	.04	.03	.02
58	Lamar Johnson	.03	.02	.01
59	Wayne Nordhagen	.03	.02	.01
60	Jim Morrison	.03	.02	.01
61	Bob Molinaro	.03	.02	.01
62	Rich Dotson	.04	.03	.02
63	Britt Burns	.03	.02	.01
64	Ed Farmer	.03	.02	.01
65	Toby Harrah	.04	.03	.02
66	Joe Charboneau	.04	.03	.02
67	Miguel Dilone	.03	.02	.01
68	Mike Hargrove	.04	.03	.02
69	Rick Manning	.03	.02	.01
70	Andre Thornton	.06	.05	.02
71	Ron Hassey	.03	.02	.01
72	Len Barker	.03	.02	.01
73	Lance Parrish	.12	.09	.05
74	Steve Kemp	.04	.03	.02
75	Alan Trammell	.15	.11	.06
76	Champ Summers	.03	.02	.01
77	Rick Peters	.03	.02	.01
78	Kirk Gibson	.15	.11	.06
79	Johnny Wockenfuss	.03	.02	.01
80	Jack Morris	.12	.09	.05
81	Willie Wilson	.08	.06	.03
82	George Brett	.25	.20	.10
83	Frank White	.06	.05	.02
84	Willie Aikens	.03	.02	.01
85	Clint Hurdle	.03	.02	.01
86	Hal McRae	.06	.05	.02
87	Dennis Leonard	.04	.03	.02
88	Larry Gura	.03	.02	.01
89	American League Pennant Winner (Kansas City Royals Team)	.04	.03	.02
90	American League Pennant Winner (Kansas City Royals Team)	.04	.03	.02
91	Paul Molitor	.10	.08	.04
92	Ben Oglivie	.04	.03	.02
93	Cecil Cooper	.08	.06	.03
94	Ted Simmons	.08	.06	.03
95	Robin Yount	.15	.11	.06
96	Gorman Thomas	.06	.05	.02
97	Mike Caldwell	.03	.02	.01
98	Moose Haas	.03	.02	.01
99	John Castino	.03	.02	.01
100	Roy Smalley	.03	.02	.01
101	Ken Landreaux	.03	.02	.01
102	Butch Wynegar	.04	.03	.02
103	Ron Jackson	.03	.02	.01
104	Jerry Koosman	.04	.03	.02
105	Roger Erickson	.03	.02	.01
106	Doug Corbett	.03	.02	.01
107	Reggie Jackson	.25	.20	.10
108	Willie Randolph	.04	.03	.02
109	Rick Cerone	.03	.02	.01
110	Bucky Dent	.04	.03	.02
111	Dave Winfield	.20	.15	.08
112	Ron Guidry	.12	.09	.05
113	Rich Gossage	.10	.08	.04
114	Tommy John	.10	.08	.04
115	Rickey Henderson	.25	.20	.10
116	Tony Armas	.04	.03	.02
117	Dave Revering	.03	.02	.01
118	Wayne Gross	.03	.02	.01
119	Dwayne Murphy	.04	.03	.02
120	Jeff Newman	.03	.02	.01
121	Rick Langford	.03	.02	.01
122	Mike Norris	.03	.02	.01
123	Bruce Bochte	.03	.02	.01
124	Tom Paciorek	.03	.02	.01
125	Dan Meyer	.03	.02	.01
126	Julio Cruz	.03	.02	.01
127	Richie Zisk	.04	.03	.02
128	Floyd Bannister	.04	.03	.02
129	Shane Rawley	.04	.03	.02
130	Buddy Bell	.06	.05	.02
131	Al Oliver	.06	.05	.02
132	Mickey Rivers	.04	.03	.02
133	Jim Sundberg	.03	.02	.01
134	Bump Wills	.03	.02	.01
135	Jon Matlack	.04	.03	.02
136	Danny Darwin	.03	.02	.01
137	Damaso Garcia	.04	.03	.02
138	Otto Velez	.03	.02	.01
139	John Mayberry	.04	.03	.02
140	Alfredo Griffin	.04	.03	.02
141	Alvis Woods	.03	.02	.01
142	Dave Stieb	.06	.05	.02
143	Jim Clancy	.04	.03	.02
144	Gary Matthews	.06	.05	.02
145	Bob Horner	.08	.06	.03

		MT	NR MT	EX
146	Dale Murphy	.25	.20	.10
147	Chris Chambliss	.04	.03	.02
148	Phil Niekro	.12	.09	.05
149	Glenn Hubbard	.03	.02	.01
150	Rick Camp	.03	.02	.01
151	Dave Kingman	.08	.06	.03
152	Bill Caudill	.03	.02	.01
153	Bill Buckner	.06	.05	.02
154	Barry Foote	.03	.02	.01
155	Mike Tyson	.03	.02	.01
156	Ivan DeJesus	.03	.02	.01
157	Rick Reuschel	.06	.05	.02
158	Ken Reitz	.03	.02	.01
159	George Foster	.08	.06	.03
160	Johnny Bench	.25	.20	.10
161	Dave Concepcion	.06	.05	.02
162	Dave Collins	.04	.03	.02
163	Ken Griffey	.06	.05	.02
164	Dan Driessen	.04	.03	.02
165	Tom Seaver	.20	.15	.08
166	Tom Hume	.03	.02	.01
167	Cesar Cedeno	.06	.05	.02
168	Rafael Landestoy	.03	.02	.01
169	Jose Cruz	.06	.05	.02
170	Art Howe	.03	.02	.01
171	Terry Puhl	.03	.02	.01
172	Joe Sambito	.03	.02	.01
173	Nolan Ryan	.20	.15	.08
174	Joe Niekro	.06	.05	.02
175	Dave Lopes	.04	.03	.02
176	Steve Garvey	.20	.15	.08
177	Ron Cey	.06	.05	.02
178	Reggie Smith	.06	.05	.02
179	Bill Russell	.04	.03	.02
180	Burt Hooton	.03	.02	.01
181	Jerry Reuss	.06	.05	.02
182	Dusty Baker	.04	.03	.02
183	Larry Parrish	.04	.03	.02
184	Gary Carter	.20	.15	.08
185	Rodney Scott	.03	.02	.01
186	Ellis Valentine	.03	.02	.01
187	Andre Dawson	.12	.09	.05
188	Warren Cromartie	.03	.02	.01
189	Chris Speier	.03	.02	.01
190	Steve Rogers	.03	.02	.01
191	Lee Mazzilli	.04	.03	.02
192	Doug Flynn	.03	.02	.01
193	Steve Henderson	.03	.02	.01
194	John Stearns	.03	.02	.01
195	Joel Youngblood	.03	.02	.01
196	Frank Taveras	.03	.02	.01
197	Pat Zachry	.03	.02	.01
198	Neil Allen	.03	.02	.01
199	Mike Schmidt	.25	.20	.10
200	Pete Rose	.40	.30	.15
201	Larry Bowa	.06	.05	.02
202	Bake McBride	.03	.02	.01
203	Bob Boone	.04	.03	.02
204	Garry Maddox	.04	.03	.02
205	Tug McGraw	.06	.05	.02
206	Steve Carlton	.20	.15	.08
207	National League Pennant Winner (Philadelphia Phillies Team)	.04	.03	.02
208	National League Pennant Winner (Philadelphia Phillies Team)	.04	.03	.02
209	Phil Garner	.04	.03	.02
210	Dave Parker	.12	.09	.05
211	Omar Moreno	.03	.02	.01
212	Mike Easler	.04	.03	.02
213	Bill Madlock	.06	.05	.02
214	Ed Ott	.03	.02	.01
215	Willie Stargell	.20	.15	.08
216	Jim Bibby	.03	.02	.01
217	Garry Templeton	.06	.05	.02
218	Sixto Lezcano	.03	.02	.01
219	Keith Hernandez	.12	.09	.05
220	George Hendrick	.04	.03	.02
221	Bruce Sutter	.08	.06	.03
222	Ken Oberkfell	.03	.02	.01
223	Tony Scott	.03	.02	.01
224	Darrell Porter	.04	.03	.02
225	Gene Richards	.03	.02	.01
226	Broderick Perkins	.03	.02	.01
227	Jerry Mumphrey	.03	.02	.01
228	Luis Salazar	.03	.02	.01
229	Jerry Turner	.03	.02	.01
230	Ozzie Smith	.10	.08	.04
231	John Curtis	.03	.02	.01
232	Rick Wise	.03	.02	.01
233	Terry Whitfield	.03	.02	.01
234	Jack Clark	.10	.08	.04

		MT	NR MT	EX
235	Darrell Evans	.08	.06	.03
236	Larry Herndon	.03	.02	.01
237	Milt May	.03	.02	.01
238	Greg Minton	.03	.02	.01
239	Vida Blue	.06	.05	.02
240	Eddie Whitson	.03	.02	.01
241	Cecil Cooper	.20	.15	.08
242	Willie Randolph	.20	.15	.08
243	George Brett	.40	.30	.15
244	Robin Yount	.30	.25	.12
245	Reggie Jackson	.40	.30	.15
246	Al Oliver	.20	.15	.08
247	Willie Wilson	.20	.15	.08
248	Rick Cerone	.15	.11	.06
249	Steve Stone	.15	.11	.06
250	Tommy John	.25	.20	.10
251	Rich Gossage	.25	.20	.10
252	Steve Garvey	.30	.25	.12
253	Phil Garner	.15	.11	.06
254	Mike Schmidt	.40	.30	.15
255	Garry Templeton	.20	.15	.08
256	George Hendrick	.15	.11	.06
257	Dave Parker	.25	.20	.10
258	Cesar Cedeno	.20	.15	.08
259	Gary Carter	.30	.25	.12
260	Jim Bibby	.15	.11	.06
261	Steve Carlton	.30	.25	.12
262	Tug McGraw	.20	.15	.08

1982 Topps

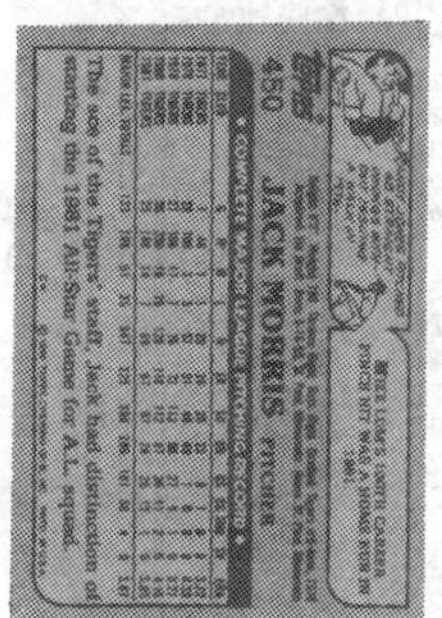

At 792 cards, this was the largest issue produced up to that time, eliminating the need for double- printed cards. The 2-1/2" by 3-1/2" cards feature a front color photo with a pair of stripes down the left side. Under the player's photo are found his name, team and position. A facsimile autograph runs across the front of the picture. Specialty cards include great performances of the previous season, All-Stars, statistical leaders and "In Action" cards (indicated by "IA" in listings below). Managers and hitting/pitching leaders have cards, while rookies are shown as "Future Stars" on group cards.

	MT	NR MT	EX
Complete Set (792):	150.00	112.00	60.00
Common Player:	.08	.06	.03

		MT	NR MT	EX
1	Steve Carlton (1981 Highlight)	.50	.40	.20
2	Ron Davis (1981 Highlight)	.08	.06	.03
3	Tim Raines (1981 Highlight)	.30	.25	.12
4	Pete Rose (1981 Highlight)	.70	.50	.30
5	Nolan Ryan (1981 Highlight)	3.00	2.25	1.25
6	Fernando Valenzuela (1981 Highlight)	.30	.25	.12
7	Scott Sanderson	.08	.06	.03
8	Rich Dauer	.08	.06	.03
9	Ron Guidry	.15	.11	.06
10	Ron Guidry (In Action)	.15	.11	.06
11	Gary Alexander	.08	.06	.03
12	Moose Haas	.08	.06	.03
13	Lamar Johnson	.08	.06	.03
14	Steve Howe	.10	.08	.04
15	Ellis Valentine	.08	.06	.03
16	Steve Comer	.08	.06	.03
17	Darrell Evans	.15	.11	.06
18	Fernando Arroyo	.08	.06	.03
19	Ernie Whitt	.10	.08	.04
20	Garry Maddox	.12	.09	.05
21	Orioles Future Stars *(Bob Bonner, Cal Ripken, Jr., Jeff Schneider)*	70.00	52.00	28.00
22	Jim Beattie	.08	.06	.03
23	Willie Hernandez	.10	.08	.04
24	Dave Frost	.08	.06	.03
25	Jerry Remy	.08	.06	.03
26	Jorge Orta	.08	.06	.03
27	Tom Herr	.12	.09	.05
28	John Urrea	.08	.06	.03
29	Dwayne Murphy	.10	.08	.04
30	Tom Seaver	2.00	1.50	.80
31	Tom Seaver (In Action)	1.00	.70	.40
32	Gene Garber	.08	.06	.03
33	Jerry Morales	.08	.06	.03
34	Joe Sambito	.08	.06	.03
35	Willie Aikens	.08	.06	.03
36	Rangers Batting/Pitching Leaders (George Medich, Al Oliver)	.12	.09	.05
37	Dan Graham	.08	.06	.03
38	Charlie Lea	.08	.06	.03
39	Lou Whitaker	.40	.30	.15
40	Dave Parker	.35	.25	.14
41	Dave Parker (In Action)	.15	.11	.06
42	Rick Sofield	.08	.06	.03
43	Mike Cubbage	.08	.06	.03
44	Britt Burns	.08	.06	.03
45	Rick Cerone	.08	.06	.03
46	Jerry Augustine	.08	.06	.03
47	Jeff Leonard	.08	.06	.03
48	Bobby Castillo	.08	.06	.03
49	Alvis Woods	.08	.06	.03
50	Buddy Bell	.08	.06	.03
51	Cubs Future Stars *(Jay Howell, Carlos Lezcano, Ty Waller)*	.40	.30	.15
52	Larry Andersen	.08	.06	.03
53	Greg Gross	.08	.06	.03
54	Ron Hassey	.08	.06	.03
55	Rick Burleson	.10	.08	.04
56	Mark Littell	.08	.06	.03
57	Craig Reynolds	.08	.06	.03
58	John D'Acquisto	.08	.06	.03
59	*Rich Gedman*(FC)	.15	.11	.06
60	Tony Armas	.12	.09	.05
61	Tommy Boggs	.08	.06	.03
62	Mike Tyson	.08	.06	.03
63	Mario Soto	.10	.08	.04
64	Lynn Jones	.08	.06	.03
65	Terry Kennedy	.12	.09	.05
66	Astros Batting/Pitching Leaders (Art Howe, Nolan Ryan)	.50	.40	.20
67	Rich Gale	.08	.06	.03
68	Roy Howell	.08	.06	.03
69	Al Williams	.08	.06	.03
70	Tim Raines	1.00	.70	.40
71	Roy Lee Jackson	.08	.06	.03
72	Rick Auerbach	.08	.06	.03
73	Buddy Solomon	.08	.06	.03
74	Bob Clark	.08	.06	.03
75	Tommy John	.30	.25	.12
76	Greg Pryor	.08	.06	.03
77	Miguel Dilone	.08	.06	.03
78	George Medich	.08	.06	.03
79	Bob Bailor	.08	.06	.03
80	Jim Palmer	1.00	.70	.40
81	Jim Palmer (In Action)	.30	.25	.12
82	Bob Welch	.25	.20	.10
83	Yankees Future Stars *(Steve Balboni, Andy McGaffigan, Andre Robertson)*(FC)	.15	.11	.06
84	Rennie Stennett	.08	.06	.03
85	Lynn McGlothen	.08	.06	.03
86	Dane Iorg	.08	.06	.03
87	Matt Keough	.08	.06	.03
88	Biff Pocoroba	.08	.06	.03
89	Steve Henderson	.08	.06	.03
90	Nolan Ryan	12.00	9.00	4.75
91	Carney Lansford	.12	.09	.05
92	Brad Havens	.08	.06	.03
93	Larry Hisle	.10	.08	.04
94	Andy Hassler	.08	.06	.03
95	Ozzie Smith	2.50	2.00	1.00
96	Royals Batting/Pitching Leaders (George Brett, Larry Gura)	.35	.25	.14
97	Paul Moskau	.08	.06	.03
98	Terry Bulling	.08	.06	.03
99	Barry Bonnell	.08	.06	.03
100	Mike Schmidt	3.00	2.25	1.25
101	Mike Schmidt (In Action)	1.25	.90	.50
102	Dan Briggs	.08	.06	.03

		MT	NR MT	EX
103	Bob Lacey	.08	.06	.03
104	Rance Mulliniks	.08	.06	.03
105	Kirk Gibson	.50	.40	.20
106	Enrique Romo	.08	.06	.03
107	Wayne Krenchicki	.08	.06	.03
108	Bob Sykes	.08	.06	.03
109	Dave Revering	.08	.06	.03
110	Carlton Fisk	1.00	.70	.40
111	Carlton Fisk (In Action)	.65	.50	.25
112	Billy Sample	.08	.06	.03
113	Steve McCatty	.08	.06	.03
114	Ken Landreaux	.08	.06	.03
115	Gaylord Perry	.50	.40	.20
116	Jim Wohlford	.08	.06	.03
117	Rawly Eastwick	.08	.06	.03
118	Expos Future Stars *(Terry Francona, Brad Mills, Bryn Smith)*	.20	.15	.08
119	Joe Pittman	.08	.06	.03
120	Gary Lucas	.08	.06	.03
121	Ed Lynch	.08	.06	.03
122	Jamie Easterly	.08	.06	.03
123	Danny Goodwin	.08	.06	.03
124	Reid Nichols	.08	.06	.03
125	Danny Ainge	2.00	1.50	.80
126	Braves Batting/Pitching Leaders (Rick Mahler, Claudell Washington)	.10	.08	.04
127	Lonnie Smith	.10	.08	.04
128	Frank Pastore	.08	.06	.03
129	Checklist 1-132	.12	.09	.05
130	Julio Cruz	.08	.06	.03
131	Stan Bahnsen	.08	.06	.03
132	Lee May	.10	.08	.04
133	Pat Underwood	.08	.06	.03
134	Dan Ford	.08	.06	.03
135	Andy Rincon	.08	.06	.03
136	Lenn Sakata	.08	.06	.03
137	George Cappuzzello	.08	.06	.03
138	Tony Pena	.10	.08	.04
139	Jeff Jones	.08	.06	.03
140	Ron LeFlore	.10	.08	.04
141	Indians Future Stars (Chris Bando, Tom Brennan, *Von Hayes*)(FC)	.20	.15	.08
142	Dave LaRoche	.08	.06	.03
143	Mookie Wilson	.12	.09	.05
144	Fred Breining	.08	.06	.03
145	Bob Horner	.10	.08	.04
146	Mike Griffin	.08	.06	.03
147	Denny Walling	.08	.06	.03
148	Mickey Klutts	.08	.06	.03
149	Pat Putnam	.08	.06	.03
150	Ted Simmons	.10	.08	.04
151	Dave Edwards	.08	.06	.03
152	Ramon Aviles	.08	.06	.03
153	Roger Erickson	.08	.06	.03
154	Dennis Werth	.08	.06	.03
155	Otto Velez	.08	.06	.03
156	A's Batting/Pitching Leaders (Rickey Henderson, Steve McCatty)	.25	.20	.10
157	Steve Crawford	.08	.06	.03
158	Brian Downing	.12	.09	.05
159	Larry Biittner	.08	.06	.03
160	Luis Tiant	.10	.08	.04
161	Batting Leaders (Carney Lansford, Bill Madlock)	.10	.08	.04
162	Home Run Leaders (Tony Armas, Dwight Evans, Bobby Grich, Eddie Murray, Mike Schmidt)	.25	.20	.10
163	Runs Batted In Leaders (Eddie Murray, Mike Schmidt)	.50	.40	.20
164	Stolen Base Leaders (Rickey Henderson, Tim Raines)	.90	.70	.35
165	Victory Leaders (Denny Martinez, Steve McCatty, Jack Morris, Tom Seaver, Pete Vuckovich)	.20	.15	.08
166	Strikeout Leaders (Len Barker, Fernando Valenzuela)	.20	.15	.08
167	ERA Leaders (Steve McCatty, Nolan Ryan)	1.50	1.25	.60
168	Leading Relievers (Rollie Fingers, Bruce Sutter)	.20	.15	.08
169	Charlie Leibrandt	.12	.09	.05
170	Jim Bibby	.08	.06	.03
171	Giants Future Stars *(Bob Brenly, Chili Davis,* Bob Tufts)	1.75	1.25	.70
172	Bill Gullickson	.10	.08	.04
173	Jamie Quirk	.08	.06	.03
174	Dave Ford	.08	.06	.03
175	Jerry Mumphrey	.08	.06	.03
176	Dewey Robinson	.08	.06	.03
177	John Ellis	.08	.06	.03
178	Dyar Miller	.08	.06	.03

		MT	NR MT	EX
179	Steve Garvey	.80	.60	.30
180	Steve Garvey (In Action)	.40	.30	.15
181	Silvio Martinez	.08	.06	.03
182	Larry Herndon	.10	.08	.04
183	Mike Proly	.08	.06	.03
184	Mick Kelleher	.08	.06	.03
185	Phil Niekro	.50	.40	.20
186	Cardinals Batting/Pitching Leaders (Bob Forsch, Keith Hernandez)	.15	.11	.06
187	Jeff Newman	.08	.06	.03
188	Randy Martz	.08	.06	.03
189	Glenn Hoffman	.08	.06	.03
190	J.R. Richard	.12	.09	.05
191	*Tim Wallach*(FC)	2.00	1.50	.80
192	Broderick Perkins	.08	.06	.03
193	Darrell Jackson	.08	.06	.03
194	Mike Vail	.08	.06	.03
195	Paul Molitor	4.00	3.00	1.50
196	Willie Upshaw	.12	.09	.05
197	Shane Rawley	.15	.11	.06
198	Chris Speier	.08	.06	.03
199	Don Aase	.08	.06	.03
200	George Brett	3.00	2.25	1.25
201	George Brett (In Action)	1.50	1.25	.60
202	Rick Manning	.08	.06	.03
203	Blue Jays Future Stars *(Jesse Barfield,* Brian Milner, Boomer Wells)	.50	.40	.20
204	Gary Roenicke	.08	.06	.03
205	Neil Allen	.08	.06	.03
206	Tony Bernazard	.08	.06	.03
207	Rod Scurry	.08	.06	.03
208	Bobby Murcer	.10	.08	.04
209	Gary Lavelle	.08	.06	.03
210	Keith Hernandez	.15	.11	.06
211	Dan Petry	.10	.08	.04
212	Mario Mendoza	.08	.06	.03
213	*Dave Stewart*(FC)	4.00	3.00	1.50
214	Brian Asselstine	.08	.06	.03
215	Mike Krukow	.10	.08	.04
216	White Sox Batting/Pitching Leaders (Dennis Lamp, Chet Lemon)	.10	.08	.04
217	Bo McLaughlin	.08	.06	.03
218	Dave Roberts	.08	.06	.03
219	John Curtis	.08	.06	.03
220	Manny Trillo	.10	.08	.04
221	Jim Slaton	.08	.06	.03
222	Butch Wynegar	.08	.06	.03
223	Lloyd Moseby	.10	.08	.04
224	Bruce Bochte	.08	.06	.03
225	Mike Torrez	.10	.08	.04
226	Checklist 133-264	.12	.09	.05
227	Ray Burris	.08	.06	.03
228	Sam Mejias	.08	.06	.03
229	Geoff Zahn	.08	.06	.03
230	Willie Wilson	.20	.15	.08
231	Phillies Future Stars *(Mark Davis, Bob Dernier, Ozzie Virgil)*(FC)	.20	.15	.08
232	Terry Crowley	.08	.06	.03
233	Duane Kuiper	.08	.06	.03
234	Ron Hodges	.08	.06	.03
235	Mike Easler	.10	.08	.04
236	John Martin	.08	.06	.03
237	Rusty Kuntz	.08	.06	.03
238	Kevin Saucier	.08	.06	.03
239	Jon Matlack	.10	.08	.04
240	Bucky Dent	.12	.09	.05
241	Bucky Dent (In Action)	.10	.08	.04
242	Milt May	.08	.06	.03
243	Bob Owchinko	.08	.06	.03
244	Rufino Linares	.08	.06	.03
245	Ken Reitz	.08	.06	.03
246	Mets Batting/Pitching Leaders (Hubie Brooks, Mike Scott)	.20	.15	.08
247	Pedro Guerrero	.20	.15	.08
248	Frank LaCorte	.08	.06	.03
249	Tim Flannery	.08	.06	.03
250	Tug McGraw	.15	.11	.06
251	Fred Lynn	.30	.25	.12
252	Fred Lynn (In Action)	.15	.11	.06
253	Chuck Baker	.08	.06	.03
254	*Jorge Bell*(FC)	3.00	2.25	1.25
255	Tony Perez	.30	.25	.12
256	Tony Perez (In Action)	.15	.11	.06
257	Larry Harlow	.08	.06	.03
258	Bo Diaz	.10	.08	.04
259	Rodney Scott	.08	.06	.03
260	Bruce Sutter	.10	.08	.04
261	Tigers Future Stars (Howard Bailey, Marty Castillo, Dave Rucker)	.08	.06	.03
262	Doug Bair	.08	.06	.03
263	Victor Cruz	.08	.06	.03

		MT	NR MT	EX
264	Dan Quisenberry	.10	.08	.04
265	Al Bumbry	.10	.08	.04
266	Rick Leach	.10	.08	.04
267	Kurt Bevacqua	.08	.06	.03
268	Rickey Keeton	.08	.06	.03
269	Jim Essian	.08	.06	.03
270	Rusty Staub	.15	.11	.06
271	Larry Bradford	.08	.06	.03
272	Bump Wills	.08	.06	.03
273	Doug Bird	.08	.06	.03
274	*Bob Ojeda*(FC)	.70	.50	.30
275	Bob Watson	.10	.08	.04
276	Angels Batting/Pitching Leaders (Rod Carew, Ken Forsch)	.25	.20	.10
277	Terry Puhl	.08	.06	.03
278	John Littlefield	.08	.06	.03
279	Bill Russell	.10	.08	.04
280	Ben Oglivie	.10	.08	.04
281	John Verhoeven	.08	.06	.03
282	Ken Macha	.08	.06	.03
283	Brian Allard	.08	.06	.03
284	Bob Grich	.15	.11	.06
285	Sparky Lyle	.12	.09	.05
286	Bill Fahey	.08	.06	.03
287	Alan Bannister	.08	.06	.03
288	Garry Templeton	.12	.09	.05
289	Bob Stanley	.08	.06	.03
290	Ken Singleton	.12	.09	.05
291	Pirates Future Stars (Vance Law, Bob Long, *Johnny Ray*)(FC)	.60	.45	.25
292	Dave Palmer	.08	.06	.03
293	Rob Picciolo	.08	.06	.03
294	Mike LaCoss	.08	.06	.03
295	Jason Thompson	.08	.06	.03
296	Bob Walk	.12	.09	.05
297	Clint Hurdle	.08	.06	.03
298	Danny Darwin	.08	.06	.03
299	Steve Trout	.08	.06	.03
300	Reggie Jackson	3.50	2.75	1.50
301	Reggie Jackson (In Action)	2.50	2.00	1.00
302	Doug Flynn	.08	.06	.03
303	Bill Caudill	.08	.06	.03
304	Johnnie LeMaster	.08	.06	.03
305	Don Sutton	.50	.40	.20
306	Don Sutton (In Action)	.25	.20	.10
307	Randy Bass	.08	.06	.03
308	Charlie Moore	.08	.06	.03
309	Pete Redfern	.08	.06	.03
310	Mike Hargrove	.08	.06	.03
311	Dodgers Batting/Pitching Leaders (Dusty Baker, Burt Hooton)	.12	.09	.05
312	Lenny Randle	.08	.06	.03
313	John Harris	.08	.06	.03
314	Buck Martinez	.08	.06	.03
315	Burt Hooton	.10	.08	.04
316	Steve Braun	.08	.06	.03
317	Dick Ruthven	.08	.06	.03
318	Mike Heath	.08	.06	.03
319	Dave Rozema	.08	.06	.03
320	Chris Chambliss	.10	.08	.04
321	Chris Chambliss (In Action)	.10	.08	.04
322	Garry Hancock	.08	.06	.03
323	Bill Lee	.10	.08	.04
324	Steve Dillard	.08	.06	.03
325	Jose Cruz	.15	.11	.06
326	Pete Falcone	.08	.06	.03
327	Joe Nolan	.08	.06	.03
328	Ed Farmer	.08	.06	.03
329	U.L. Washington	.08	.06	.03
330	Rick Wise	.10	.08	.04
331	Benny Ayala	.08	.06	.03
332	Don Robinson	.10	.08	.04
333	Brewers Future Stars *(Frank DiPino,* Marshall Edwards, Chuck Porter)	.12	.09	.05
334	Aurelio Rodriguez	.10	.08	.04
335	Jim Sundberg	.10	.08	.04
336	Mariners Batting/Pitching Leaders (Glenn Abbott, Tom Paciorek)	.10	.08	.04
337	Pete Rose (All-Star)	1.00	.70	.40
338	Dave Lopes (All-Star)	.12	.09	.05
339	Mike Schmidt (All-Star)	.75	.60	.30
340	Dave Concepcion (All-Star)	.12	.09	.05
341	Andre Dawson (All-Star)	.45	.35	.20
342a	George Foster (All-Star no autograph)	2.25	1.75	.90
342b	George Foster (All-Star autograph on front)	.20	.15	.08
343	Dave Parker (All-Star)	.20	.15	.08
344	Gary Carter (All-Star)	.20	.15	.08
345	Fernando Valenzuela (All-Star)	.20	.15	.08
346	Tom Seaver (All-Star)	.75	.60	.30

		MT	NR MT	EX
347	Bruce Sutter (All-Star)	.12	.09	.05
348	Derrel Thomas	.08	.06	.03
349	George Frazier	.08	.06	.03
350	Thad Bosley	.08	.06	.03
351	Reds Future Stars (Scott Brown, Geoff Combe, Paul Householder)	.08	.06	.03
352	Dick Davis	.08	.06	.03
353	Jack O'Connor	.08	.06	.03
354	Roberto Ramos	.08	.06	.03
355	Dwight Evans	.15	.11	.06
356	Denny Lewallyn	.08	.06	.03
357	Butch Hobson	.08	.06	.03
358	Mike Parrott	.08	.06	.03
359	Jim Dwyer	.08	.06	.03
360	Len Barker	.10	.08	.04
361	Rafael Landestoy	.08	.06	.03
362	Jim Wright	.08	.06	.03
363	Bob Molinaro	.08	.06	.03
364	Doyle Alexander	.12	.09	.05
365	Bill Madlock	.10	.08	.04
366	Padres Batting/Pitching Leaders (Juan Eichelberger, Luis Salazar)	.10	.08	.04
367	Jim Kaat	.25	.20	.10
368	Alex Trevino	.08	.06	.03
369	Champ Summers	.08	.06	.03
370	Mike Norris	.08	.06	.03
371	Jerry Don Gleaton	.08	.06	.03
372	Luis Gomez	.08	.06	.03
373	*Gene Nelson*	.10	.08	.04
374	Tim Blackwell	.08	.06	.03
375	Dusty Baker	.12	.09	.05
376	Chris Welsh	.08	.06	.03
377	Kiko Garcia	.08	.06	.03
378	Mike Caldwell	.08	.06	.03
379	Rob Wilfong	.08	.06	.03
380	Dave Stieb	.25	.20	.10
381	Red Sox Future Stars (Bruce Hurst, Dave Schmidt, Julio Valdez)	.25	.20	.10
382	Joe Simpson	.08	.06	.03
383a	Pascual Perez (no position on front)	18.00	13.50	7.25
383b	Pascual Perez ("Pitcher" on front)	.12	.09	.05
384	Keith Moreland	.12	.09	.05
385	Ken Forsch	.08	.06	.03
386	Jerry White	.08	.06	.03
387	Tom Veryzer	.08	.06	.03
388	Joe Rudi	.12	.09	.05
389	George Vukovich	.08	.06	.03
390	Eddie Murray	1.25	.90	.50
391	Dave Tobik	.08	.06	.03
392	Rick Bosetti	.08	.06	.03
393	Al Hrabosky	.10	.08	.04
394	Checklist 265-396	.12	.09	.05
395	Omar Moreno	.08	.06	.03
396	Twins Batting/Pitching Leaders (Fernando Arroyo, John Castino)	.10	.08	.04
397	Ken Brett	.10	.08	.04
398	Mike Squires	.08	.06	.03
399	Pat Zachry	.08	.06	.03
400	Johnny Bench	1.50	1.25	.60
401	Johnny Bench (In Action)	.40	.30	.15
402	Bill Stein	.08	.06	.03
403	Jim Tracy	.08	.06	.03
404	Dickie Thon	.10	.08	.04
405	Rick Reuschel	.15	.11	.06
406	Al Holland	.08	.06	.03
407	Danny Boone	.08	.06	.03
408	Ed Romero	.08	.06	.03
409	Don Cooper	.08	.06	.03
410	Ron Cey	.15	.11	.06
411	Ron Cey (In Action)	.10	.08	.04
412	Luis Leal	.08	.06	.03
413	Dan Meyer	.08	.06	.03
414	Elias Sosa	.08	.06	.03
415	Don Baylor	.15	.11	.06
416	Marty Bystrom	.08	.06	.03
417	Pat Kelly	.08	.06	.03
418	Rangers Future Stars (John Butcher, Bobby Johnson, *Dave Schmidt*)(FC)	.08	.06	.03
419	Steve Stone	.12	.09	.05
420	George Hendrick	.10	.08	.04
421	Mark Clear	.08	.06	.03
422	Cliff Johnson	.08	.06	.03
423	Stan Papi	.08	.06	.03
424	Bruce Benedict	.08	.06	.03
425	John Candelaria	.12	.09	.05
426	Orioles Batting/Pitching Leaders (Eddie Murray, Sammy Stewart)	.25	.20	.10
427	Ron Oester	.08	.06	.03
428	Lamarr Hoyt (LaMarr)	.08	.06	.03
429	John Wathan	.10	.08	.04

		MT	NR MT	EX
430	Vida Blue	.15	.11	.06
431	Vida Blue (In Action)	.10	.08	.04
432	Mike Scott	.25	.20	.10
433	Alan Ashby	.08	.06	.03
434	Joe Lefebvre	.08	.06	.03
435	Robin Yount	4.00	3.00	1.50
436	Joe Strain	.08	.06	.03
437	Juan Berenguer	.08	.06	.03
438	Pete Mackanin	.08	.06	.03
439	*Dave Righetti*(FC)	1.00	.70	.40
440	Jeff Burroughs	.10	.08	.04
441	Astros Future Stars (Danny Heep, Billy Smith, Bobby Sprowl)	.08	.06	.03
442	Bruce Kison	.08	.06	.03
443	Mark Wagner	.08	.06	.03
444	Terry Forster	.10	.08	.04
445	Larry Parrish	.12	.09	.05
446	Wayne Garland	.08	.06	.03
447	Darrell Porter	.10	.08	.04
448	Darrell Porter (In Action)	.10	.08	.04
449	*Luis Aguayo*(FC)	.12	.09	.05
450	Jack Morris	.60	.45	.25
451	Ed Miller	.08	.06	.03
452	*Lee Smith*(FC)	9.00	6.75	3.50
453	Art Howe	.08	.06	.03
454	Rick Langford	.08	.06	.03
455	Tom Burgmeier	.08	.06	.03
456	Cubs Batting/Pitching Leaders (Bill Buckner, Randy Martz)	.08	.06	.03
457	Tim Stoddard	.08	.06	.03
458	Willie Montanez	.08	.06	.03
459	Bruce Berenyi	.08	.06	.03
460	Jack Clark	.10	.08	.04
461	Rich Dotson	.10	.08	.04
462	Dave Chalk	.08	.06	.03
463	Jim Kern	.08	.06	.03
464	Juan Bonilla	.08	.06	.03
465	Lee Mazzilli	.10	.08	.04
466	Randy Lerch	.08	.06	.03
467	Mickey Hatcher	.10	.08	.04
468	Floyd Bannister	.12	.09	.05
469	Ed Ott	.08	.06	.03
470	John Mayberry	.10	.08	.04
471	Royals Future Stars *(Atlee Hammaker,* Mike Jones, Darryl Motley)	.25	.20	.10
472	Oscar Gamble	.10	.08	.04
473	Mike Stanton	.08	.06	.03
474	Ken Oberkfell	.08	.06	.03
475	Alan Trammell	.60	.45	.25
476	Brian Kingman	.08	.06	.03
477	Steve Yeager	.08	.06	.03
478	Ray Searage	.08	.06	.03
479	Rowland Office	.08	.06	.03
480	Steve Carlton	1.00	.70	.40
481	Steve Carlton (In Action)	.40	.30	.15
482	Glenn Hubbard	.10	.08	.04
483	Gary Woods	.08	.06	.03
484	Ivan DeJesus	.08	.06	.03
485	Kent Tekulve	.10	.08	.04
486	Yankees Batting/Pitching Leaders (Tommy John, Jerry Mumphrey)	.20	.15	.08
487	Bob McClure	.08	.06	.03
488	Ron Jackson	.08	.06	.03
489	Rick Dempsey	.10	.08	.04
490	Dennis Eckersley	.20	.15	.08
491	Checklist 397-528	.12	.09	.05
492	Joe Price	.08	.06	.03
493	Chet Lemon	.10	.08	.04
494	Hubie Brooks	.20	.15	.08
495	Dennis Leonard	.10	.08	.04
496	Johnny Grubb	.08	.06	.03
497	Jim Anderson	.08	.06	.03
498	Dave Bergman	.08	.06	.03
499	Paul Mirabella	.08	.06	.03
500	Rod Carew	1.00	.70	.40
501	Rod Carew (In Action)	.40	.30	.15
502	Braves Future Stars *(Steve Bedrosian, Brett Butler,* Larry Owen)	2.00	1.50	.80
503	Julio Gonzalez	.08	.06	.03
504	Rick Peters	.08	.06	.03
505	Graig Nettles	.15	.11	.06
506	Graig Nettles (In Action)	.12	.09	.05
507	Terry Harper	.08	.06	.03
508	*Jody Davis*(FC)	.15	.11	.06
509	Harry Spilman	.08	.06	.03
510	Fernando Valenzuela	.40	.30	.15
511	Ruppert Jones	.08	.06	.03
512	Jerry Dybzinski	.08	.06	.03
513	Rick Rhoden	.12	.09	.05
514	Joe Ferguson	.08	.06	.03
515	Larry Bowa	.20	.15	.08

		MT	NR MT	EX
516	Larry Bowa (In Action)	.12	.09	.05
517	Mark Brouhard	.08	.06	.03
518	Garth Iorg	.08	.06	.03
519	Glenn Adams	.08	.06	.03
520	Mike Flanagan	.12	.09	.05
521	Billy Almon	.08	.06	.03
522	Chuck Rainey	.08	.06	.03
523	Gary Gray	.08	.06	.03
524	Tom Hausman	.08	.06	.03
525	Ray Knight	.12	.09	.05
526	Expos Batting/Pitching Leaders (Warren Cromartie, Bill Gullickson)	.10	.08	.04
527	John Henry Johnson	.08	.06	.03
528	Matt Alexander	.08	.06	.03
529	Allen Ripley	.08	.06	.03
530	Dickie Noles	.08	.06	.03
531	A's Future Stars (Rich Bordi, Mark Budaska, Kelvin Moore)	.08	.06	.03
532	Toby Harrah	.10	.08	.04
533	Joaquin Andujar	.10	.08	.04
534	Dave McKay	.08	.06	.03
535	Lance Parrish	.15	.11	.06
536	Rafael Ramirez	.10	.08	.04
537	Doug Capilla	.08	.06	.03
538	Lou Piniella	.15	.11	.06
539	Vern Ruhle	.08	.06	.03
540	Andre Dawson	.80	.60	.30
541	Barry Evans	.08	.06	.03
542	Ned Yost	.08	.06	.03
543	Bill Robinson	.08	.06	.03
544	Larry Christenson	.08	.06	.03
545	Reggie Smith	.15	.11	.06
546	Reggie Smith (In Action)	.10	.08	.04
547	Rod Carew (All-Star)	.35	.25	.14
548	Willie Randolph (All-Star)	.12	.09	.05
549	George Brett (All-Star)	1.00	.70	.40
550	Bucky Dent (All-Star)	.12	.09	.05
551	Reggie Jackson (All-Star)	1.00	.70	.40
552	Ken Singleton (All-Star)	.12	.09	.05
553	Dave Winfield (All-Star)	.90	.70	.35
554	Carlton Fisk (All-Star)	.20	.15	.08
555	Scott McGregor (All-Star)	.12	.09	.05
556	Jack Morris (All-Star)	.20	.15	.08
557	Rich Gossage (All-Star)	.20	.15	.08
558	John Tudor	.15	.11	.06
559	Indians Batting/Pitching Leaders (Bert Blyleven, Mike Hargrove)	.15	.11	.06
560	Doug Corbett	.08	.06	.03
561	Cardinals Future Stars (Glenn Brummer, Luis DeLeon, Gene Roof)	.08	.06	.03
562	Mike O'Berry	.08	.06	.03
563	Ross Baumgarten	.08	.06	.03
564	Doug DeCinces	.15	.11	.06
565	Jackson Todd	.08	.06	.03
566	Mike Jorgensen	.08	.06	.03
567	Bob Babcock	.08	.06	.03
568	Joe Pettini	.08	.06	.03
569	Willie Randolph	.15	.11	.06
570	Willie Randolph (In Action)	.10	.08	.04
571	Glenn Abbott	.08	.06	.03
572	Juan Beniquez	.08	.06	.03
573	Rick Waits	.08	.06	.03
574	Mike Ramsey	.08	.06	.03
575	Al Cowens	.08	.06	.03
576	Giants Batting/Pitching Leaders (Vida Blue, Milt May)	.15	.11	.06
577	Rick Monday	.12	.09	.05
578	Shooty Babitt	.08	.06	.03
579	*Rick Mahler*(FC)	.08	.06	.03
580	Bobby Bonds	.15	.11	.06
581	Ron Reed	.08	.06	.03
582	Luis Pujols	.08	.06	.03
583	Tippy Martinez	.08	.06	.03
584	Hosken Powell	.08	.06	.03
585	Rollie Fingers	.30	.25	.12
586	Rollie Fingers (In Action)	.15	.11	.06
587	Tim Lollar	.08	.06	.03
588	Dale Berra	.08	.06	.03
589	Dave Stapleton	.08	.06	.03
590	Al Oliver	.20	.15	.08
591	Al Oliver (In Action)	.10	.08	.04
592	Craig Swan	.08	.06	.03
593	Billy Smith	.08	.06	.03
594	Renie Martin	.08	.06	.03
595	Dave Collins	.10	.08	.04
596	Damaso Garcia	.08	.06	.03
597	Wayne Nordhagen	.08	.06	.03
598	Bob Galasso	.08	.06	.03
599	White Sox Future Stars (Jay Loviglio, Reggie Patterson, Leo Sutherland)	.08	.06	.03
600	Dave Winfield	4.00	3.00	1.50

		MT	NR MT	EX
601	Sid Monge	.08	.06	.03
602	Freddie Patek	.08	.06	.03
603	Rich Hebner	.08	.06	.03
604	Orlando Sanchez	.08	.06	.03
605	Steve Rogers	.10	.08	.04
606	Blue Jays Batting/Pitching Leaders (John Mayberry, Dave Stieb)	.15	.11	.06
607	Leon Durham	.10	.08	.04
608	Jerry Royster	.08	.06	.03
609	Rick Sutcliffe	.25	.20	.10
610	Rickey Henderson	4.00	3.00	1.50
611	Joe Niekro	.08	.06	.03
612	Gary Ward	.10	.08	.04
613	Jim Gantner	.10	.08	.04
614	Juan Eichelberger	.08	.06	.03
615	Bob Boone	.12	.09	.05
616	Bob Boone (In Action)	.10	.08	.04
617	Scott McGregor	.10	.08	.04
618	Tim Foli	.08	.06	.03
619	Bill Campbell	.08	.06	.03
620	Ken Griffey	.15	.11	.06
621	Ken Griffey (In Action)	.10	.08	.04
622	Dennis Lamp	.08	.06	.03
623	Mets Future Stars (Ron Gardenhire, *Terry Leach, Tim Leary*)(FC)	.25	.20	.10
624	Fergie Jenkins	.60	.45	.25
625	Hal McRae	.15	.11	.06
626	Randy Jones	.10	.08	.04
627	Enos Cabell	.08	.06	.03
628	Bill Travers	.08	.06	.03
629	Johnny Wockenfuss	.08	.06	.03
630	Joe Charboneau	.10	.08	.04
631	Gene Tenace	.10	.08	.04
632	Bryan Clark	.08	.06	.03
633	Mitchell Page	.08	.06	.03
634	Checklist 529-660	.12	.09	.05
635	Ron Davis	.10	.08	.04
636	Phillies Batting/Pitching Leaders (Steve Carlton, Pete Rose)	.50	.40	.20
637	Rick Camp	.08	.06	.03
638	John Milner	.08	.06	.03
639	Ken Kravec	.08	.06	.03
640	Cesar Cedeno	.15	.11	.06
641	Steve Mura	.08	.06	.03
642	Mike Scioscia	.10	.08	.04
643	Pete Vuckovich	.10	.08	.04
644	John Castino	.08	.06	.03
645	Frank White	.12	.09	.05
646	Frank White (In Action)	.10	.08	.04
647	Warren Brusstar	.08	.06	.03
648	Jose Morales	.08	.06	.03
649	Ken Clay	.08	.06	.03
650	Carl Yastrzemski	1.50	1.25	.60
651	Carl Yastrzemski (In Action)	.60	.45	.25
652	Steve Nicosia	.08	.06	.03
653	Angels Rookies *(Tom Brunansky, Luis Sanchez, Daryl Sconiers)*	.50	.40	.20
654	Jim Morrison	.08	.06	.03
655	Joel Youngblood	.08	.06	.03
656	Eddie Whitson	.08	.06	.03
657	Tom Poquette	.08	.06	.03
658	Tito Landrum	.08	.06	.03
659	Fred Martinez	.08	.06	.03
660	Dave Concepcion	.15	.11	.06
661	Dave Concepcion (In Action)	.10	.08	.04
662	Luis Salazar	.08	.06	.03
663	Hector Cruz	.08	.06	.03
664	Dan Spillner	.08	.06	.03
665	Jim Clancy	.12	.09	.05
666	Tigers Batting/Pitching Leaders (Steve Kemp, Dan Petry)	.15	.11	.06
667	Jeff Reardon	1.00	.70	.40
668	Dale Murphy	1.25	.90	.50
669	Larry Milbourne	.08	.06	.03
670	Steve Kemp	.12	.09	.05
671	Mike Davis	.10	.08	.04
672	Bob Knepper	.12	.09	.05
673	Keith Drumright	.08	.06	.03
674	Dave Goltz	.10	.08	.04
675	Cecil Cooper	.08	.06	.03
676	Sal Butera	.08	.06	.03
677	Alfredo Griffin	.12	.09	.05
678	Tom Paciorek	.08	.06	.03
679	Sammy Stewart	.08	.06	.03
680	Gary Matthews	.12	.09	.05
681	Dodgers Future Stars *(Mike Marshall, Ron Roenicke, Steve Sax)*	1.00	.70	.40
682	Jesse Jefferson	.08	.06	.03
683	Phil Garner	.10	.08	.04
684	Harold Baines	.25	.20	.10
685	Bert Blyleven	.20	.15	.08

		MT	NR MT	EX
686	Gary Allenson	.08	.06	.03
687	Greg Minton	.08	.06	.03
688	Leon Roberts	.08	.06	.03
689	Lary Sorensen	.08	.06	.03
690	Dave Kingman	.10	.08	.04
691	Dan Schatzeder	.08	.06	.03
692	Wayne Gross	.08	.06	.03
693	Cesar Geronimo	.08	.06	.03
694	Dave Wehrmeister	.08	.06	.03
695	Warren Cromartie	.08	.06	.03
696	Pirates Batting/Pitching Leaders (Bill Madlock, Buddy Solomon)	.15	.11	.06
697	John Montefusco	.08	.06	.03
698	Tony Scott	.08	.06	.03
699	Dick Tidrow	.08	.06	.03
700	George Foster	.25	.20	.10
701	George Foster (In Action)	.12	.09	.05
702	Steve Renko	.08	.06	.03
703	Brewers Batting/Pitching Leaders (Cecil Cooper, Pete Vuckovich)	.15	.11	.06
704	Mickey Rivers	.10	.08	.04
705	Mickey Rivers (In Action)	.10	.08	.04
706	Barry Foote	.08	.06	.03
707	Mark Bomback	.08	.06	.03
708	Gene Richards	.08	.06	.03
709	Don Money	.08	.06	.03
710	Jerry Reuss	.12	.09	.05
711	Mariners Future Stars *(Dave Edler, Dave Henderson, Reggie Walton)*	1.00	.70	.40
712	Denny Martinez	.10	.08	.04
713	Del Unser	.08	.06	.03
714	Jerry Koosman	.12	.09	.05
715	Willie Stargell	.80	.60	.30
716	Willie Stargell (In Action)	.30	.25	.12
717	Rick Miller	.08	.06	.03
718	Charlie Hough	.12	.09	.05
719	Jerry Narron	.08	.06	.03
720	Greg Luzinski	.20	.15	.08
721	Greg Luzinski (In Action)	.12	.09	.05
722	Jerry Martin	.08	.06	.03
723	Junior Kennedy	.08	.06	.03
724	Dave Rosello	.08	.06	.03
725	Amos Otis	.10	.08	.04
726	Amos Otis (In Action)	.10	.08	.04
727	Sixto Lezcano	.08	.06	.03
728	Aurelio Lopez	.08	.06	.03
729	Jim Spencer	.08	.06	.03
730	Gary Carter	.80	.60	.30
731	Padres Future Stars (Mike Armstrong, Doug Gwosdz, Fred Kuhaulua)	.08	.06	.03
732	Mike Lum	.08	.06	.03
733	Larry McWilliams	.08	.06	.03
734	Mike Ivie	.08	.06	.03
735	Rudy May	.08	.06	.03
736	Jerry Turner	.08	.06	.03
737	Reggie Cleveland	.08	.06	.03
738	Dave Engle	.08	.06	.03
739	Joey McLaughlin	.08	.06	.03
740	Dave Lopes	.12	.09	.05
741	Dave Lopes (In Action)	.10	.08	.04
742	Dick Drago	.08	.06	.03
743	John Stearns	.08	.06	.03
744	*Mike Witt*(FC)	.50	.40	.20
745	Bake McBride	.08	.06	.03
746	Andre Thornton	.12	.09	.05
747	John Lowenstein	.08	.06	.03
748	Marc Hill	.08	.06	.03
749	Bob Shirley	.08	.06	.03
750	Jim Rice	.35	.25	.14
751	Rick Honeycutt	.08	.06	.03
752	Lee Lacy	.08	.06	.03
753	Tom Brookens	.08	.06	.03
754	Joe Morgan	.70	.50	.30
755	Joe Morgan (In Action)	.20	.15	.08
756	Reds Batting/Pitching Leaders (Ken Griffey, Tom Seaver)	.30	.25	.12
757	Tom Underwood	.08	.06	.03
758	Claudell Washington	.12	.09	.05
759	Paul Splittorff	.08	.06	.03
760	Bill Buckner	.15	.11	.06
761	Dave Smith	.12	.09	.05
762	Mike Phillips	.08	.06	.03
763	Tom Hume	.08	.06	.03
764	Steve Swisher	.08	.06	.03
765	Gorman Thomas	.12	.09	.05
766	Twins Future Stars *(Lenny Faedo, Kent Hrbek, Tim Laudner)*	2.50	2.00	1.00
767	Roy Smalley	.08	.06	.03
768	Jerry Garvin	.08	.06	.03
769	Richie Zisk	.10	.08	.04
770	Rich Gossage	.15	.11	.06

		MT	NR MT	EX
771	Rich Gossage (In Action)	.08	.06	.03
772	Bert Campaneris	.12	.09	.05
773	John Denny	.08	.06	.03
774	Jay Johnstone	.10	.08	.04
775	Bob Forsch	.10	.08	.04
776	Mark Belanger	.10	.08	.04
777	Tom Griffin	.08	.06	.03
778	Kevin Hickey	.08	.06	.03
779	Grant Jackson	.08	.06	.03
780	Pete Rose	2.25	1.75	.90
781	Pete Rose (In Action)	1.00	.70	.40
782	Frank Taveras	.08	.06	.03
783	*Greg Harris*(FC)	.15	.11	.06
784	Milt Wilcox	.08	.06	.03
785	Dan Driessen	.10	.08	.04
786	Red Sox Batting/Pitching Leaders (Carney Lansford, Mike Torrez)	.12	.09	.05
787	Fred Stanley	.08	.06	.03
788	Woodie Fryman	.10	.08	.04
789	Checklist 661-792	.12	.09	.05
790	Larry Gura	.08	.06	.03
791	Bobby Brown	.08	.06	.03
792	Frank Tanana	.12	.09	.05

1982 Topps Traded

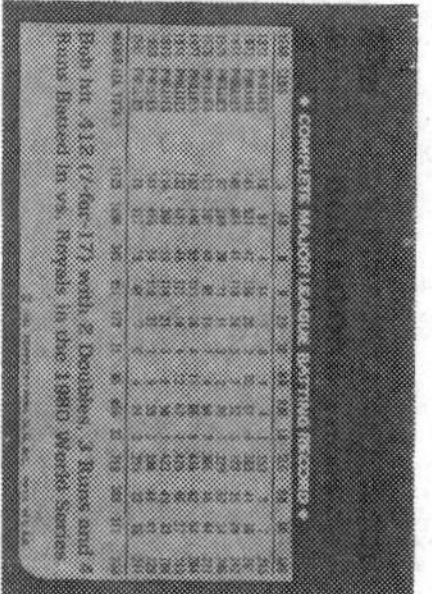

Topps released its second straight 132-card Traded set in September of 1982. Again, the 2-1/2" by 3-1/2" cards feature not only players who had been traded during the season, but also promising rookies who were given their first individual cards. The cards follow the basic design of the regular issues, but have their backs printed in red rather than the regular-issue green. As in 1981, the cards were not available in normal retail outlets and could only be purchased through regular baseball card dealers. Unlike the previous year, the cards are numbered 1-132 with the letter "T" following the number.

		MT	NR MT	EX
Complete Set (132):		275.00	206.00	110.00
Common Player:		.20	.15	.08
1T	Doyle Alexander	.20	.15	.08
2T	Jesse Barfield	.20	.15	.08
3T	Ross Baumgarten	.20	.15	.08
4T	Steve Bedrosian	.20	.15	.08
5T	Mark Belanger	.20	.15	.08
6T	Kurt Bevacqua	.20	.15	.08
7T	Tim Blackwell	.20	.15	.08
8T	Vida Blue	.25	.20	.10
9T	Bob Boone	.20	.15	.08
10T	Larry Bowa	.25	.20	.10
11T	Dan Briggs	.20	.15	.08
12T	Bobby Brown	.20	.15	.08
13T	Tom Brunansky	1.00	.70	.40
14T	Jeff Burroughs	.20	.15	.08
15T	Enos Cabell	.20	.15	.08
16T	Bill Campbell	.20	.15	.08
17T	Bobby Castillo	.20	.15	.08
18T	Bill Caudill	.20	.15	.08
19T	Cesar Cedeno	.20	.15	.08
20T	Dave Collins	.20	.15	.08
21T	Doug Corbett	.20	.15	.08
22T	Al Cowens	.20	.15	.08
23T	Chili Davis	2.00	1.50	.80
24T	Dick Davis	.20	.15	.08

		MT	NR MT	EX
25T	Ron Davis	.20	.15	.08
26T	Doug DeCinces	.20	.15	.08
27T	Ivan DeJesus	.20	.15	.08
28T	Bob Dernier	.20	.15	.08
29T	Bo Diaz	.20	.15	.08
30T	Roger Erickson	.20	.15	.08
31T	Jim Essian	.20	.15	.08
32T	Ed Farmer	.20	.15	.08
33T	Doug Flynn	.20	.15	.08
34T	Tim Foli	.20	.15	.08
35T	Dan Ford	.20	.15	.08
36T	George Foster	.40	.30	.15
37T	Dave Frost	.20	.15	.08
38T	Rich Gale	.20	.15	.08
39T	Ron Gardenhire	.20	.15	.08
40T	Ken Griffey	.25	.20	.10
41T	Greg Harris	.20	.15	.08
42T	Von Hayes	.20	.15	.08
43T	Larry Herndon	.20	.15	.08
44T	Kent Hrbek	5.00	3.75	2.00
45T	Mike Ivie	.20	.15	.08
46T	Grant Jackson	.20	.15	.08
47T	Reggie Jackson	15.00	11.00	6.00
48T	Ron Jackson	.20	.15	.08
49T	Fergie Jenkins	2.00	1.50	.80
50T	Lamar Johnson	.20	.15	.08
51T	Randy S. Johnson	.20	.15	.08
52T	Jay Johnstone	.20	.15	.08
53T	Mick Kelleher	.20	.15	.08
54T	Steve Kemp	.20	.15	.08
55T	Junior Kennedy	.20	.15	.08
56T	Jim Kern	.20	.15	.08
57T	Ray Knight	.20	.15	.08
58T	Wayne Krenchicki	.20	.15	.08
59T	Mike Krukow	.20	.15	.08
60T	Duane Kuiper	.20	.15	.08
61T	Mike LaCoss	.20	.15	.08
62T	Chet Lemon	.20	.15	.08
63T	Sixto Lezcano	.20	.15	.08
64T	Dave Lopes	.20	.15	.08
65T	Jerry Martin	.20	.15	.08
66T	Renie Martin	.20	.15	.08
67T	John Mayberry	.20	.15	.08
68T	Lee Mazzilli	.20	.15	.08
69T	Bake McBride	.20	.15	.08
70T	Dan Meyer	.20	.15	.08
71T	Larry Milbourne	.20	.15	.08
72T	Eddie Milner(FC)	.20	.15	.08
73T	Sid Monge	.20	.15	.08
74T	Jose Morales	.20	.15	.08
75T	Keith Moreland	.20	.15	.08
76T	John Montefusco	.20	.15	.08
77T	Jim Morrison	.20	.15	.08
78T	Rance Mulliniks	.20	.15	.08
79T	Steve Mura	.20	.15	.08
80T	Gene Nelson	.20	.15	.08
81T	Joe Nolan	.20	.15	.08
82T	Dickie Noles	.20	.15	.08
83T	Al Oliver	.30	.25	.12
84T	Jorge Orta	.20	.15	.08
85T	Tom Paciorek	.20	.15	.08
86T	Larry Parrish	.20	.15	.08
87T	Jack Perconte	.20	.15	.08
88T	Gaylord Perry	2.00	1.50	.80
89T	Rob Picciolo	.20	.15	.08
90T	Joe Pittman	.20	.15	.08
91T	Hosken Powell	.20	.15	.08
92T	Mike Proly	.20	.15	.08
93T	Greg Pryor	.20	.15	.08
94T	Charlie Puleo(FC)	.20	.15	.08
95T	Shane Rawley	.20	.15	.08
96T	Johnny Ray	.20	.15	.08
97T	Dave Revering	.20	.15	.08
98T	Cal Ripken, Jr.	235.00	176.00	94.00
99T	Allen Ripley	.20	.15	.08
100T	Bill Robinson	.20	.15	.08
101T	Aurelio Rodriguez	.20	.15	.08
102T	Joe Rudi	.20	.15	.08
103T	Steve Sax	3.00	2.25	1.25
104T	Dan Schatzeder	.20	.15	.08
105T	Bob Shirley	.20	.15	.08
106T	Eric Show(FC)	.20	.15	.08
107T	Roy Smalley	.20	.15	.08
108T	Lonnie Smith	.20	.15	.08
109T	Ozzie Smith	30.00	22.00	12.00
110T	Reggie Smith	.20	.15	.08
111T	Lary Sorensen	.20	.15	.08
112T	Elias Sosa	.20	.15	.08
113T	Mike Stanton	.20	.15	.08
114T	Steve Stroughter	.20	.15	.08
115T	Champ Summers	.20	.15	.08

		MT	NR MT	EX
116T	Rick Sutcliffe	.50	.40	.20
117T	Frank Tanana	.20	.15	.08
118T	Frank Taveras	.20	.15	.08
119T	Garry Templeton	.20	.15	.08
120T	Alex Trevino	.20	.15	.08
121T	Jerry Turner	.20	.15	.08
122T	Ed Vande Berg(FC)	.20	.15	.08
123T	Tom Veryzer	.20	.15	.08
124T	Ron Washington	.20	.15	.08
125T	Bob Watson	.20	.15	.08
126T	Dennis Werth	.20	.15	.08
127T	Eddie Whitson	.20	.15	.08
128T	Rob Wilfong	.20	.15	.08
129T	Bump Wills	.20	.15	.08
130T	Gary Woods	.20	.15	.08
131T	Butch Wynegar	.20	.15	.08
132T	Checklist 1-132	.20	.15	.08

1982 Topps Insert Stickers

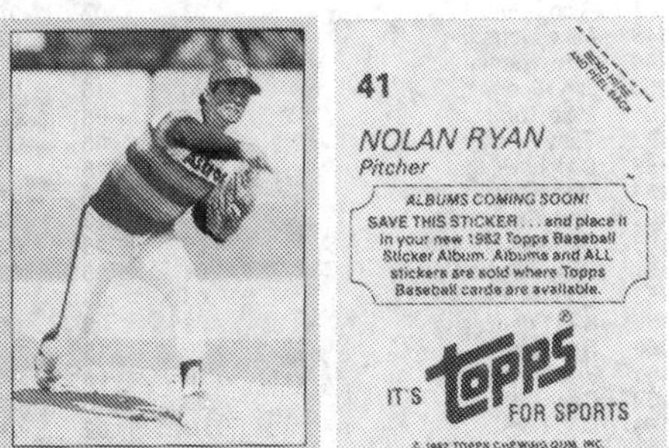

This 48-player set is actually an abbreviated version of the regular 1982 Topps sticker set with different backs. Used to promote the 1982 sticker set, Topps inserted these stickers in its baseball card wax packs. They are identical to the regular 1982 stickers, except for the backs, which advertise that the Topps sticker album will be "Coming Soon." The 48 stickers retain the same numbers used in the regular sticker set, resulting in the smaller set being skip-numbered.

		MT	NR MT	EX
Complete Set:		2.00	1.50	.80
Common Player:		.03	.02	.01
17	Chris Chambliss	.04	.03	.02
21	Bruce Benedict	.03	.02	.01
25	Leon Durham	.06	.05	.02
29	Bill Buckner	.06	.05	.02
33	Dave Collins	.04	.03	.02
37	Dave Concepcion	.06	.05	.02
41	Nolan Ryan	.15	.11	.06
45	Bob Knepper	.04	.03	.02
49	Ken Landreaux	.03	.02	.01
53	Burt Hooton	.03	.02	.01
57	Andre Dawson	.12	.09	.05
61	Gary Carter	.20	.15	.08
65	Joel Youngblood	.03	.02	.01
69	Ellis Valentine	.03	.02	.01
73	Garry Maddox	.04	.03	.02
77	Bob Boone	.04	.03	.02
81	Omar Moreno	.03	.02	.01
85	Willie Stargell	.20	.15	.08
89	Ken Oberkfell	.03	.02	.01
93	Darrell Porter	.04	.03	.02
97	Juan Eichelberger	.03	.02	.01
101	Luis Salazar	.03	.02	.01
105	Enos Cabell	.03	.02	.01
109	Larry Herndon	.03	.02	.01
143	Scott McGregor	.04	.03	.02
148	Mike Flanagan	.06	.05	.02
151	Mike Torrez	.04	.03	.02
156	Carney Lansford	.06	.05	.02
161	Fred Lynn	.10	.08	.04
166	Rich Dotson	.04	.03	.02
171	Tony Bernazard	.03	.02	.01
176	Bo Diaz	.04	.03	.02
181	Alan Trammell	.15	.11	.06
186	Milt Wilcox	.03	.02	.01
191	Dennis Leonard	.04	.03	.02
196	Willie Aikens	.03	.02	.01
201	Ted Simmons	.08	.06	.03
206	Hosken Powell	.03	.02	.01
211	Roger Erickson	.03	.02	.01
215	Graig Nettles	.06	.05	.02
216	Reggie Jackson	.25	.20	.10
221	Rickey Henderson	.25	.20	.10
226	Cliff Johnson	.03	.02	.01
231	Jeff Burroughs	.04	.03	.02
236	Tom Paciorek	.03	.02	.01
241	Pat Putnam	.03	.02	.01
246	Lloyd Moseby	.06	.05	.02
251	Barry Bonnell	.03	.02	.01

1982 Topps Stickers

The 1982 Topps sticker set is complete at 260 stickers and includes another series of "foil" All-Stars. The stickers measure 1-15/16" by 2-9/16" and feature full-color photos surrounded by a red border for American League players or a blue border for National League players. They are numbered on both the front and back and were designed to be mounted in a special album.

		MT	NR MT	EX
Complete Set:		15.00	11.00	6.00
Common Player:		.03	.02	.01
Sticker Album:		.80	.60	.30
1	Bill Madlock	.06	.05	.02
2	Carney Lansford	.06	.05	.02
3	Mike Schmidt	.25	.20	.10
4	Tony Armas, Dwight Evans, Bobby Grich, Eddie Murray	.12	.09	.05
5	Mike Schmidt	.25	.20	.10
6	Eddie Murray	.20	.15	.08
7	Tim Raines	.03	.02	.01
8	Rickey Henderson	.25	.20	.10
9	Tom Seaver	.20	.15	.08
10	Denny Martinez, Steve McCatty, Jack Morris, Pete Vuckovich	.06	.05	.02
11	Fernando Valenzuela	.15	.11	.06
12	Len Barker	.03	.02	.01
13	Nolan Ryan	.20	.15	.08
14	Steve McCatty	.03	.02	.01
15	Bruce Sutter	.08	.06	.03
16	Rollie Fingers	.10	.08	.04
17	Chris Chambliss	.04	.03	.02
18	Bob Horner	.08	.06	.03
19	Dale Murphy	.25	.20	.10
20	Phil Niekro	.12	.09	.05
21	Bruce Benedict	.03	.02	.01
22	Claudell Washington	.04	.03	.02
23	Glenn Hubbard	.03	.02	.01
24	Rick Camp	.03	.02	.01
25	Leon Durham	.06	.05	.02
26	Ken Reitz	.03	.02	.01
27	Dick Tidrow	.03	.02	.01
28	Tim Blackwell	.03	.02	.01
29	Bill Buckner	.06	.05	.02
30	Steve Henderson	.03	.02	.01
31	Mike Krukow	.04	.03	.02
32	Ivan DeJesus	.03	.02	.01
33	Dave Collins	.04	.03	.02

		MT	NR MT	EX
34	Ron Oester	.03	.02	.01
35	Johnny Bench	.25	.20	.10
36	Tom Seaver	.20	.15	.08
37	Dave Concepcion	.06	.05	.02
38	Ken Griffey	.06	.05	.02
39	Ray Knight	.06	.05	.02
40	George Foster	.08	.06	.03
41	Nolan Ryan	.20	.15	.08
42	Terry Puhl	.03	.02	.01
43	Art Howe	.03	.02	.01
44	Jose Cruz	.06	.05	.02
45	Bob Knepper	.06	.05	.02
46	Craig Reynolds	.03	.02	.01
47	Cesar Cedeno	.06	.05	.02
48	Alan Ashby	.03	.02	.01
49	Ken Landreaux	.03	.02	.01
50	Fernando Valenzuela	.15	.11	.06
51	Ron Cey	.06	.05	.02
52	Dusty Baker	.04	.03	.02
53	Burt Hooton	.04	.03	.02
54	Steve Garvey	.20	.15	.08
55	Pedro Guerrero	.12	.09	.05
56	Jerry Reuss	.06	.05	.02
57	Andre Dawson	.12	.09	.05
58	Chris Speier	.03	.02	.01
59	Steve Rogers	.03	.02	.01
60	Warren Cromartie	.03	.02	.01
61	Gary Carter	.20	.15	.08
62	Tim Raines	.20	.15	.08
63	Scott Sanderson	.03	.02	.01
64	Larry Parrish	.06	.05	.02
65	Joel Youngblood	.03	.02	.01
66	Neil Allen	.03	.02	.01
67	Lee Mazzilli	.04	.03	.02
68	Hubie Brooks	.06	.05	.02
69	Ellis Valentine	.03	.02	.01
70	Doug Flynn	.03	.02	.01
71	Pat Zachry	.03	.02	.01
72	Dave Kingman	.08	.06	.03
73	Garry Maddox	.04	.03	.02
74	Mike Schmidt	.25	.20	.10
75	Steve Carlton	.20	.15	.08
76	Manny Trillo	.04	.03	.02
77	Bob Boone	.04	.03	.02
78	Pete Rose	.40	.30	.15
79	Gary Matthews	.04	.03	.02
80	Larry Bowa	.06	.05	.02
81	Omar Moreno	.03	.02	.01
82	Rick Rhoden	.04	.03	.02
83	Bill Madlock	.06	.05	.02
84	Mike Easler	.04	.03	.02
85	Willie Stargell	.20	.15	.08
86	Jim Bibby	.03	.02	.01
87	Dave Parker	.12	.09	.05
88	Tim Foli	.03	.02	.01
89	Ken Oberkfell	.03	.02	.01
90	Bob Forsch	.04	.03	.02
91	George Hendrick	.04	.03	.02
92	Keith Hernandez	.12	.09	.05
93	Darrell Porter	.04	.03	.02
94	Bruce Sutter	.08	.06	.03
95	Sixto Lezcano	.03	.02	.01
96	Garry Templeton	.04	.03	.02
97	Juan Eichelberger	.03	.02	.01
98	Broderick Perkins	.03	.02	.01
99	Ruppert Jones	.03	.02	.01
100	Terry Kennedy	.04	.03	.02
101	Luis Salazar	.03	.02	.01
102	Gary Lucas	.03	.02	.01
103	Gene Richards	.03	.02	.01
104	Ozzie Smith	.10	.08	.04
105	Enos Cabell	.03	.02	.01
106	Jack Clark	.10	.08	.04
107	Greg Minton	.03	.02	.01
108	Johnnie LeMaster	.03	.02	.01
109	Larry Herndon	.03	.02	.01
110	Milt May	.03	.02	.01
111	Vida Blue	.06	.05	.02
112	Darrell Evans	.08	.06	.03
113	Len Barker	.03	.02	.01
114	Julio Cruz	.03	.02	.01
115	Billy Martin	.08	.06	.03
116	Tim Raines	.20	.15	.08
117	Pete Rose	.40	.30	.15
118	Bill Stein	.03	.02	.01
119	Fernando Valenzuela	.15	.11	.06
120	Carl Yastrzemski	.25	.20	.10
121	Pete Rose	.50	.40	.20
122	Manny Trillo	.15	.11	.06
123	Mike Schmidt	.40	.30	.15
124	Dave Concepcion	.20	.15	.08
125	Andre Dawson	.25	.20	.10
126	George Foster	.20	.15	.08
127	Dave Parker	.25	.20	.10
128	Gary Carter	.30	.25	.12
129	Steve Carlton	.30	.25	.12
130	Bruce Sutter	.25	.20	.10
131	Rod Carew	.40	.30	.15
132	Jerry Remy	.15	.11	.06
133	George Brett	.40	.30	.15
134	Rick Burleson	.15	.11	.06
135	Dwight Evans	.25	.20	.10
136	Ken Singleton	.20	.15	.08
137	Dave Winfield	.30	.25	.12
138	Carlton Fisk	.25	.20	.10
139	Jack Morris	.25	.20	.10
140	Rich Gossage	.25	.20	.10
141	Al Bumbry	.04	.03	.02
142	Doug DeCinces	.06	.05	.02
143	Scott McGregor	.04	.03	.02
144	Ken Singleton	.06	.05	.02
145	Eddie Murray	.20	.15	.08
146	Jim Palmer	.15	.11	.06
147	Rich Dauer	.03	.02	.01
148	Mike Flanagan	.04	.03	.02
149	Jerry Remy	.03	.02	.01
150	Jim Rice	.20	.15	.08
151	Mike Torrez	.04	.03	.02
152	Tony Perez	.10	.08	.04
153	Dwight Evans	.10	.08	.04
154	Mark Clear	.03	.02	.01
155	Carl Yastrzemski	.25	.20	.10
156	Carney Lansford	.06	.05	.02
157	Rick Burleson	.04	.03	.02
158	Don Baylor	.08	.06	.03
159	Ken Forsch	.03	.02	.01
160	Rod Carew	.20	.15	.08
161	Fred Lynn	.10	.08	.04
162	Bob Grich	.06	.05	.02
163	Dan Ford	.03	.02	.01
164	Butch Hobson	.03	.02	.01
165	Greg Luzinski	.08	.06	.03
166	Rich Dotson	.04	.03	.02
167	Billy Almon	.03	.02	.01
168	Chet Lemon	.04	.03	.02
169	Steve Trout	.03	.02	.01
170	Carlton Fisk	.12	.09	.05
171	Tony Bernazard	.03	.02	.01
172	Ron LeFlore	.04	.03	.02
173	Bert Blyleven	.08	.06	.03
174	Andre Thornton	.06	.05	.02
175	Jorge Orta	.03	.02	.01
176	Bo Diaz	.04	.03	.02
177	Toby Harrah	.04	.03	.02
178	Len Barker	.03	.02	.01
179	Rick Manning	.03	.02	.01
180	Mike Hargrove	.04	.03	.02
181	Alan Trammell	.15	.11	.06
182	Al Cowens	.03	.02	.01
183	Jack Morris	.12	.09	.05
184	Kirk Gibson	.15	.11	.06
185	Steve Kemp	.04	.03	.02
186	Milt Wilcox	.03	.02	.01
187	Lou Whitaker	.12	.09	.05
188	Lance Parrish	.12	.09	.05
189	Willie Wilson	.08	.06	.03
190	George Brett	.25	.20	.10
191	Dennis Leonard	.04	.03	.02
192	John Wathan	.04	.03	.02
193	Frank White	.06	.05	.02
194	Amos Otis	.04	.03	.02
195	Larry Gura	.03	.02	.01
196	Willie Aikens	.03	.02	.01
197	Ben Oglivie	.06	.05	.02
198	Rollie Fingers	.10	.08	.04
199	Cecil Cooper	.08	.06	.03
200	Paul Molitor	.10	.08	.04
201	Ted Simmons	.08	.06	.03
202	Pete Vuckovich	.04	.03	.02
203	Robin Yount	.15	.11	.06
204	Gorman Thomas	.04	.03	.02
205	Rob Wilfong	.03	.02	.01
206	Hosken Powell	.03	.02	.01
207	Roy Smalley	.03	.02	.01
208	Butch Wynegar	.04	.03	.02
209	John Castino	.03	.02	.01
210	Doug Corbett	.03	.02	.01
211	Roger Erickson	.03	.02	.01
212	Mickey Hatcher	.03	.02	.01
213	Dave Winfield	.20	.15	.08
214	Tommy John	.10	.08	.04
215	Graig Nettles	.06	.05	.02

		MT	NR MT	EX
216	Reggie Jackson	.25	.20	.10
217	Rich Gossage	.10	.08	.04
218	Rick Cerone	.03	.02	.01
219	Willie Randolph	.06	.05	.02
220	Jerry Mumphrey	.03	.02	.01
221	Rickey Henderson	.20	.15	.08
222	Mike Norris	.03	.02	.01
223	Jim Spencer	.03	.02	.01
224	Tony Armas	.04	.03	.02
225	Matt Keough	.03	.02	.01
226	Cliff Johnson	.03	.02	.01
227	Dwayne Murphy	.04	.03	.02
228	Steve McCatty	.03	.02	.01
229	Richie Zisk	.04	.03	.02
230	Lenny Randle	.03	.02	.01
231	Jeff Burroughs	.04	.03	.02
232	Bruce Bochte	.03	.02	.01
233	Gary Gray	.03	.02	.01
234	Floyd Bannister	.04	.03	.02
235	Julio Cruz	.03	.02	.01
236	Tom Paciorek	.03	.02	.01
237	Danny Darwin	.03	.02	.01
238	Buddy Bell	.06	.05	.02
239	Al Oliver	.06	.05	.02
240	Jim Sundberg	.04	.03	.02
241	Pat Putnam	.03	.02	.01
242	Steve Comer	.03	.02	.01
243	Mickey Rivers	.04	.03	.02
244	Bump Wills	.03	.02	.01
245	Damaso Garcia	.04	.03	.02
246	Lloyd Moseby	.06	.05	.02
247	Ernie Whitt	.03	.02	.01
248	John Mayberry	.03	.02	.01
249	Otto Velez	.03	.02	.01
250	Dave Stieb	.06	.05	.02
251	Barry Bonnell	.03	.02	.01
252	Alfredo Griffin	.04	.03	.02
253	1981 N.L. Championship (Gary Carter)	.10	.08	.04
254	1981 A.L. Championship (Mike Heath, Larry Milbourne)	.03	.02	.01
255	1981 World Champions (Los Angeles Dodgers Team)	.04	.03	.02
256	1981 World Champions (Los Angeles Dodgers Team)	.04	.03	.02
257	1981 World Series - Game 3 (Fernando Valenzuela)	.10	.08	.04
258	1981 World Series - Game 4 (Steve Garvey)	.10	.08	.04
259	1981 World Series - Game 5 (Jerry Reuss, Steve Yeager)	.03	.02	.01
260	1981 World Series - Game 6 (Pedro Guerrero)	.08	.06	.03

1983 Topps

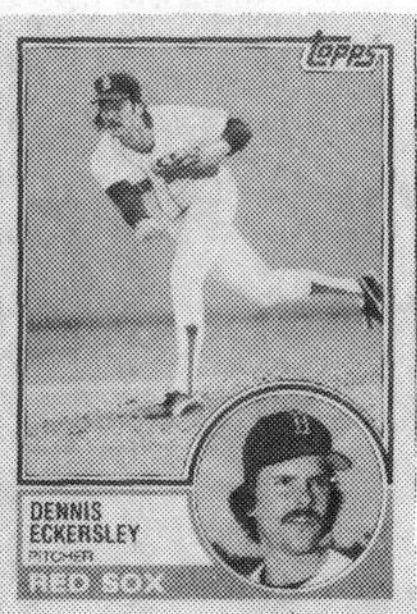

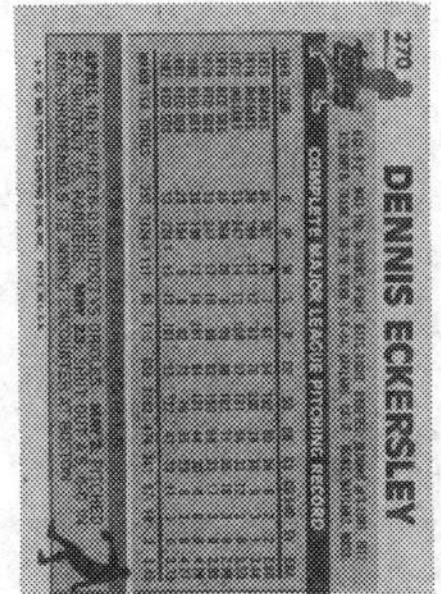

The 1983 Topps set totals 792 cards. Missing among the regular 2-1/2" by 3-1/2" cards are some form of future stars cards, as Topps was saving them for the now-established late season "Traded" set. The 1983 cards carry a large color photo as well as a smaller color photo on the front, quite similar in design to the 1963 set. Team colors frame the card, which, at the bottom, have the player's name, position and team. At the upper right-hand corner is a Topps Logo. The backs are horizontal and include statistics, personal information and 1982 highlights. Specialty cards include record-breaking perfor- mances, league leaders, All-Stars, numbered check- lists "Team Leaders" and "Super Veteran" cards which are horizontal with a current and first-season picture of the honored player.

		MT	NR MT	EX
	Complete Set (792):	175.00	125.00	75.00
	Common Player:	.08	.06	.03
1	Tony Armas (Record Breaker)	.12	.09	.05
2	Rickey Henderson (Record Breaker)	.50	.40	.20
3	Greg Minton (Record Breaker)	.08	.06	.03
4	Lance Parrish (Record Breaker)	.08	.06	.03
5	Manny Trillo (Record Breaker)	.08	.06	.03
6	John Wathan (Record Breaker)	.08	.06	.03
7	Gene Richards	.08	.06	.03
8	Steve Balboni	.10	.08	.04
9	Joey McLaughlin	.08	.06	.03
10	Gorman Thomas	.12	.09	.05
11	Billy Gardner	.08	.06	.03
12	Paul Mirabella	.08	.06	.03
13	Larry Herndon	.10	.08	.04
14	Frank LaCorte	.08	.06	.03
15	Ron Cey	.15	.11	.06
16	George Vukovich	.08	.06	.03
17	Kent Tekulve	.10	.08	.04
18	Kent Tekulve (Super Veteran)	.10	.08	.04
19	Oscar Gamble	.10	.08	.04
20	Carlton Fisk	1.00	.70	.40
21	Orioles Batting/Pitching Leaders (Eddie Murray, Jim Palmer)	.25	.20	.10
22	Randy Martz	.08	.06	.03
23	Mike Heath	.08	.06	.03
24	Steve Mura	.08	.06	.03
25	Hal McRae	.15	.11	.06
26	Jerry Royster	.08	.06	.03
27	Doug Corbett	.08	.06	.03
28	Bruce Bochte	.08	.06	.03
29	Randy Jones	.10	.08	.04
30	Jim Rice	.35	.25	.14
31	Bill Gullickson	.08	.06	.03
32	Dave Bergman	.08	.06	.03
33	Jack O'Connor	.08	.06	.03
34	Paul Householder	.08	.06	.03
35	Rollie Fingers	.60	.45	.25
36	Rollie Fingers (Super Veteran)	.15	.11	.06
37	Darrell Johnson	.08	.06	.03
38	Tim Flannery	.08	.06	.03
39	Terry Puhl	.08	.06	.03
40	Fernando Valenzuela	.25	.20	.10
41	Jerry Turner	.08	.06	.03
42	Dale Murray	.08	.06	.03
43	Bob Dernier	.08	.06	.03
44	Don Robinson	.10	.08	.04
45	John Mayberry	.10	.08	.04
46	Richard Dotson	.12	.09	.05
47	Dave McKay	.08	.06	.03
48	Lary Sorensen	.08	.06	.03
49	*Willie McGee*(FC)	2.00	1.50	.80
50	Bob Horner	.20	.15	.08
51	Cubs Batting/Pitching Leaders (Leon Durham, Fergie Jenkins)	.15	.11	.06
52	*Onix Concepcion*(FC)	.08	.06	.03
53	Mike Witt	.15	.11	.06
54	Jim Maler	.08	.06	.03
55	Mookie Wilson	.12	.09	.05
56	Chuck Rainey	.08	.06	.03
57	Tim Blackwell	.08	.06	.03
58	Al Holland	.08	.06	.03
59	Benny Ayala	.08	.06	.03
60	Johnny Bench	1.50	1.25	.60
61	Johnny Bench (Super Veteran)	.30	.25	.12
62	Bob McClure	.08	.06	.03
63	Rick Monday	.12	.09	.05
64	Bill Stein	.08	.06	.03
65	Jack Morris	.50	.40	.20
66	Bob Lillis	.08	.06	.03
67	Sal Butera	.08	.06	.03
68	*Eric Show*	.15	.11	.06
69	Lee Lacy	.08	.06	.03
70	Steve Carlton	1.25	.90	.50
71	Steve Carlton (Super Veteran)	.30	.25	.12
72	Tom Paciorek	.08	.06	.03
73	Allen Ripley	.08	.06	.03
74	Julio Gonzalez	.08	.06	.03
75	Amos Otis	.10	.08	.04
76	Rick Mahler	.12	.09	.05
77	Hosken Powell	.08	.06	.03
78	Bill Caudill	.08	.06	.03
79	Mick Kelleher	.08	.06	.03

		MT	NR MT	EX
80	George Foster	.12	.09	.05
81	Yankees Batting/Pitching Leaders (Jerry Mumphrey, Dave Righetti)	.15	.11	.06
82	Bruce Hurst	.15	.11	.06
83	*Ryne Sandberg*(FC)	40.00	30.00	16.00
84	Milt May	.08	.06	.03
85	Ken Singleton	.12	.09	.05
86	Tom Hume	.08	.06	.03
87	Joe Rudi	.12	.09	.05
88	Jim Gantner	.10	.08	.04
89	Leon Roberts	.08	.06	.03
90	Jerry Reuss	.12	.09	.05
91	Larry Milbourne	.08	.06	.03
92	Mike LaCoss	.08	.06	.03
93	John Castino	.08	.06	.03
94	Dave Edwards	.08	.06	.03
95	Alan Trammell	.50	.40	.20
96	Dick Howser	.08	.06	.03
97	Ross Baumgarten	.08	.06	.03
98	Vance Law	.10	.08	.04
99	Dickie Noles	.08	.06	.03
100	Pete Rose	1.75	1.25	.70
101	Pete Rose (Super Veteran)	.80	.60	.30
102	Dave Beard	.08	.06	.03
103	Darrell Porter	.10	.08	.04
104	Bob Walk	.08	.06	.03
105	Don Baylor	.15	.11	.06
106	Gene Nelson	.08	.06	.03
107	Mike Jorgensen	.08	.06	.03
108	Glenn Hoffman	.08	.06	.03
109	Luis Leal	.08	.06	.03
110	Ken Griffey	.15	.11	.06
111	Expos Batting/Pitching Leaders (Al Oliver, Steve Rogers)	.15	.11	.06
112	Bob Shirley	.08	.06	.03
113	Ron Roenicke	.08	.06	.03
114	Jim Slaton	.08	.06	.03
115	Chili Davis	.20	.15	.08
116	Dave Schmidt	.10	.08	.04
117	Alan Knicely	.08	.06	.03
118	Chris Welsh	.08	.06	.03
119	Tom Brookens	.08	.06	.03
120	Len Barker	.10	.08	.04
121	Mickey Hatcher	.10	.08	.04
122	Jimmy Smith	.08	.06	.03
123	George Frazier	.08	.06	.03
124	Marc Hill	.08	.06	.03
125	Leon Durham	.10	.08	.04
126	Joe Torre	.10	.08	.04
127	Preston Hanna	.08	.06	.03
128	Mike Ramsey	.08	.06	.03
129	Checklist 1-132	.12	.09	.05
130	Dave Stieb	.20	.15	.08
131	Ed Ott	.08	.06	.03
132	Todd Cruz	.08	.06	.03
133	Jim Barr	.08	.06	.03
134	Hubie Brooks	.15	.11	.06
135	Dwight Evans	.15	.11	.06
136	Willie Aikens	.08	.06	.03
137	Woodie Fryman	.10	.08	.04
138	Rick Dempsey	.10	.08	.04
139	Bruce Berenyi	.08	.06	.03
140	Willie Randolph	.12	.09	.05
141	Indians Batting/Pitching Leaders (Toby Harrah, Rick Sutcliffe)	.12	.09	.05
142	Mike Caldwell	.08	.06	.03
143	Joe Pettini	.08	.06	.03
144	Mark Wagner	.08	.06	.03
145	Don Sutton	.40	.30	.15
146	Don Sutton (Super Veteran)	.20	.15	.08
147	Rick Leach	.08	.06	.03
148	Dave Roberts	.08	.06	.03
149	Johnny Ray	.15	.11	.06
150	Bruce Sutter	.20	.15	.08
151	Bruce Sutter (Super Veteran)	.12	.09	.05
152	Jay Johnstone	.10	.08	.04
153	Jerry Koosman	.12	.09	.05
154	Johnnie LeMaster	.08	.06	.03
155	Dan Quisenberry	.20	.15	.08
156	Billy Martin	.12	.09	.05
157	Steve Bedrosian	.12	.09	.05
158	Rob Wilfong	.08	.06	.03
159	Mike Stanton	.08	.06	.03
160	Dave Kingman	.10	.08	.04
161	Dave Kingman (Super Veteran)	.10	.08	.04
162	Mark Clear	.08	.06	.03
163	Cal Ripken, Jr.	20.00	15.00	8.00
164	Dave Palmer	.08	.06	.03
165	Dan Driessen	.10	.08	.04
166	John Pacella	.08	.06	.03
167	Mark Brouhard	.08	.06	.03

		MT	NR MT	EX
168	Juan Eichelberger	.08	.06	.03
169	Doug Flynn	.08	.06	.03
170	Steve Howe	.10	.08	.04
171	Giants Batting/Pitching Leaders (Bill Laskey, Joe Morgan)	.15	.11	.06
172	Vern Ruhle	.08	.06	.03
173	Jim Morrison	.08	.06	.03
174	Jerry Ujdur	.08	.06	.03
175	Bo Diaz	.10	.08	.04
176	Dave Righetti	.15	.11	.06
177	Harold Baines	.25	.20	.10
178	Luis Tiant	.15	.11	.06
179	Luis Tiant (Super Veteran)	.10	.08	.04
180	Rickey Henderson	3.00	2.25	1.25
181	Terry Felton	.08	.06	.03
182	Mike Fischlin	.08	.06	.03
183	*Ed Vande Berg*	.12	.09	.05
184	Bob Clark	.08	.06	.03
185	Tim Lollar	.08	.06	.03
186	Whitey Herzog	.10	.08	.04
187	Terry Leach	.12	.09	.05
188	Rick Miller	.08	.06	.03
189	Dan Schatzeder	.08	.06	.03
190	Cecil Cooper	.10	.08	.04
191	Joe Price	.08	.06	.03
192	Floyd Rayford	.08	.06	.03
193	Harry Spilman	.08	.06	.03
194	Cesar Geronimo	.08	.06	.03
195	Bob Stoddard	.08	.06	.03
196	Bill Fahey	.08	.06	.03
197	*Jim Eisenreich*(FC)	.50	.40	.20
198	Kiko Garcia	.08	.06	.03
199	Marty Bystrom	.08	.06	.03
200	Rod Carew	.70	.50	.30
201	Rod Carew (Super Veteran)	.35	.25	.14
202	Blue Jays Batting/Pitching Leaders (Damaso Garcia, Dave Stieb)	.12	.09	.05
203	Mike Morgan	.15	.11	.06
204	Junior Kennedy	.08	.06	.03
205	Dave Parker	.40	.30	.15
206	Ken Oberkfell	.08	.06	.03
207	Rick Camp	.08	.06	.03
208	Dan Meyer	.08	.06	.03
209	*Mike Moore*(FC)	.70	.50	.30
210	Jack Clark	.15	.11	.06
211	John Denny	.08	.06	.03
212	John Stearns	.08	.06	.03
213	Tom Burgmeier	.08	.06	.03
214	Jerry White	.08	.06	.03
215	Mario Soto	.10	.08	.04
216	Tony LaRussa	.10	.08	.04
217	Tim Stoddard	.08	.06	.03
218	Roy Howell	.08	.06	.03
219	Mike Armstrong	.08	.06	.03
220	Dusty Baker	.12	.09	.05
221	Joe Niekro	.15	.11	.06
222	Damaso Garcia	.08	.06	.03
223	John Montefusco	.08	.06	.03
224	Mickey Rivers	.10	.08	.04
225	Enos Cabell	.08	.06	.03
226	Enrique Romo	.08	.06	.03
227	Chris Bando	.08	.06	.03
228	Joaquin Andujar	.10	.08	.04
229	Phillies Batting/Pitching Leaders (Steve Carlton, Bo Diaz)	.20	.15	.08
230	Fergie Jenkins	.60	.45	.25
231	Fergie Jenkins (Super Veteran)	.12	.09	.05
232	Tom Brunansky	.12	.09	.05
233	Wayne Gross	.08	.06	.03
234	Larry Andersen	.08	.06	.03
235	Claudell Washington	.10	.08	.04
236	Steve Renko	.08	.06	.03
237	Dan Norman	.08	.06	.03
238	*Bud Black*(FC)	.70	.50	.30
239	Dave Stapleton	.08	.06	.03
240	Rich Gossage	.20	.15	.08
241	Rich Gossage (Super Veteran)	.15	.11	.06
242	Joe Nolan	.08	.06	.03
243	Duane Walker	.08	.06	.03
244	Dwight Bernard	.08	.06	.03
245	Steve Sax	.15	.11	.06
246	George Bamberger	.08	.06	.03
247	Dave Smith	.12	.09	.05
248	Bake McBride	.08	.06	.03
249	Checklist 133-264	.12	.09	.05
250	Bill Buckner	.15	.11	.06
251	*Alan Wiggins*(FC)	.08	.06	.03
252	Luis Aguayo	.08	.06	.03
253	Larry McWilliams	.08	.06	.03
254	Rick Cerone	.08	.06	.03
255	Gene Garber	.08	.06	.03

		MT	NR MT	EX
256	Gene Garber (Super Veteran)	.08	.06	.03
257	Jesse Barfield	.20	.15	.08
258	Manny Castillo	.08	.06	.03
259	Jeff Jones	.08	.06	.03
260	Steve Kemp	.12	.09	.05
261	Tigers Batting/Pitching Leaders (Larry Herndon, Dan Petry)	.10	.08	.04
262	Ron Jackson	.08	.06	.03
263	Renie Martin	.08	.06	.03
264	Jamie Quirk	.08	.06	.03
265	Joel Youngblood	.08	.06	.03
266	Paul Boris	.08	.06	.03
267	Terry Francona	.08	.06	.03
268	*Storm Davis*(FC)	.30	.25	.12
269	Ron Oester	.08	.06	.03
270	Dennis Eckersley	1.50	1.25	.60
271	Ed Romero	.08	.06	.03
272	Frank Tanana	.12	.09	.05
273	Mark Belanger	.10	.08	.04
274	Terry Kennedy	.12	.09	.05
275	Ray Knight	.12	.09	.05
276	Gene Mauch	.10	.08	.04
277	Rance Mulliniks	.08	.06	.03
278	Kevin Hickey	.08	.06	.03
279	Greg Gross	.08	.06	.03
280	Bert Blyleven	.20	.15	.08
281	Andre Robertson	.08	.06	.03
282	Reggie Smith	.12	.09	.05
283	Reggie Smith (Super Veteran)	.10	.08	.04
284	Jeff Lahti	.08	.06	.03
285	Lance Parrish	.12	.09	.05
286	Rick Langford	.08	.06	.03
287	Bobby Brown	.08	.06	.03
288	*Joe Cowley*(FC)	.08	.06	.03
289	Jerry Dybzinski	.08	.06	.03
290	Jeff Reardon	.60	.45	.25
291	Pirates Batting/Pitching Leaders (John Candelaria, Bill Madlock)	.15	.11	.06
292	Craig Swan	.08	.06	.03
293	Glenn Gulliver	.08	.06	.03
294	Dave Engle	.08	.06	.03
295	Jerry Remy	.08	.06	.03
296	Greg Harris	.08	.06	.03
297	Ned Yost	.08	.06	.03
298	Floyd Chiffer	.08	.06	.03
299	George Wright	.08	.06	.03
300	Mike Schmidt	3.00	2.25	1.25
301	Mike Schmidt (Super Veteran)	1.00	.70	.40
302	Ernie Whitt	.10	.08	.04
303	Miguel Dilone	.08	.06	.03
304	Dave Rucker	.08	.06	.03
305	Larry Bowa	.15	.11	.06
306	Tom Lasorda	.12	.09	.05
307	Lou Piniella	.15	.11	.06
308	Jesus Vega	.08	.06	.03
309	Jeff Leonard	.12	.09	.05
310	Greg Luzinski	.15	.11	.06
311	Glenn Brummer	.08	.06	.03
312	Brian Kingman	.08	.06	.03
313	Gary Gray	.08	.06	.03
314	Ken Dayley(FC)	.15	.11	.06
315	Rick Burleson	.10	.08	.04
316	Paul Splittorff	.08	.06	.03
317	Gary Rajsich	.08	.06	.03
318	John Tudor	.15	.11	.06
319	Lenn Sakata	.08	.06	.03
320	Steve Rogers	.10	.08	.04
321	Brewers Batting/Pitching Leaders (Pete Vuckovich, Robin Yount)	.20	.15	.08
322	Dave Van Gorder	.08	.06	.03
323	Luis DeLeon	.08	.06	.03
324	Mike Marshall	.12	.09	.05
325	Von Hayes	.20	.15	.08
326	Garth Iorg	.08	.06	.03
327	Bobby Castillo	.08	.06	.03
328	Craig Reynolds	.08	.06	.03
329	Randy Niemann	.08	.06	.03
330	Buddy Bell	.15	.11	.06
331	Mike Krukow	.10	.08	.04
332	*Glenn Wilson*(FC)	.12	.09	.05
333	Dave LaRoche	.08	.06	.03
334	Dave LaRoche (Super Veteran)	.08	.06	.03
335	Steve Henderson	.08	.06	.03
336	Rene Lachemann	.08	.06	.03
337	Tito Landrum	.08	.06	.03
338	Bob Owchinko	.08	.06	.03
339	Terry Harper	.08	.06	.03
340	Larry Gura	.08	.06	.03
341	Doug DeCinces	.15	.11	.06
342	Atlee Hammaker	.10	.08	.04
343	Bob Bailor	.08	.06	.03
344	Roger LaFrancois	.08	.06	.03
345	Jim Clancy	.10	.08	.04
346	Joe Pittman	.08	.06	.03
347	Sammy Stewart	.08	.06	.03
348	Alan Bannister	.08	.06	.03
349	Checklist 265-396	.12	.09	.05
350	Robin Yount	4.00	3.00	1.50
351	Reds Batting/Pitching Leaders (Cesar Cedeno, Mario Soto)	.12	.09	.05
352	Mike Scioscia	.10	.08	.04
353	Steve Comer	.08	.06	.03
354	Randy S. Johnson	.08	.06	.03
355	Jim Bibby	.08	.06	.03
356	Gary Woods	.08	.06	.03
357	*Len Matuszek*(FC)	.08	.06	.03
358	Jerry Garvin	.08	.06	.03
359	Dave Collins	.10	.08	.04
360	Nolan Ryan	14.00	10.50	5.50
361	Nolan Ryan (Super Veteran)	5.00	3.75	2.00
362	Bill Almon	.08	.06	.03
363	*John Stuper*(FC)	.08	.06	.03
364	Brett Butler	.20	.15	.08
365	Dave Lopes	.12	.09	.05
366	Dick Williams	.08	.06	.03
367	Bud Anderson	.08	.06	.03
368	Richie Zisk	.10	.08	.04
369	Jesse Orosco	.15	.11	.06
370	Gary Carter	.25	.20	.10
371	Mike Richardt	.08	.06	.03
372	Terry Crowley	.08	.06	.03
373	Kevin Saucier	.08	.06	.03
374	Wayne Krenchicki	.08	.06	.03
375	Pete Vuckovich	.10	.08	.04
376	Ken Landreaux	.08	.06	.03
377	Lee May	.10	.08	.04
378	Lee May (Super Veteran)	.10	.08	.04
379	Guy Sularz	.08	.06	.03
380	Ron Davis	.08	.06	.03
381	Red Sox Batting/Pitching Leaders (Jim Rice, Bob Stanley)	.15	.11	.06
382	Bob Knepper	.12	.09	.05
383	Ozzie Virgil	.10	.08	.04
384	*Dave Dravecky*(FC)	.50	.40	.20
385	Mike Easler	.10	.08	.04
386	Rod Carew (All-Star)	.50	.40	.20
387	Bob Grich (All-Star)	.10	.08	.04
388	George Brett (All-Star)	.75	.60	.30
389	Robin Yount (All-Star)	.75	.60	.30
390	Reggie Jackson (All-Star)	.75	.60	.30
391	Rickey Henderson (All-Star)	.50	.40	.20
392	Fred Lynn (All-Star)	.15	.11	.06
393	Carlton Fisk (All-Star)	.15	.11	.06
394	Pete Vuckovich (All-Star)	.10	.08	.04
395	Larry Gura (All-Star)	.08	.06	.03
396	Dan Quisenberry (All-Star)	.12	.09	.05
397	Pete Rose (All-Star)	.75	.60	.30
398	Manny Trillo (All-Star)	.10	.08	.04
399	Mike Schmidt (All-Star)	.75	.60	.30
400	Dave Concepcion (All-Star)	.12	.09	.05
401	Dale Murphy (All-Star)	.40	.30	.15
402	Andre Dawson (All-Star)	.30	.25	.12
403	Tim Raines (All-Star)	.25	.20	.10
404	Gary Carter (All-Star)	.20	.15	.08
405	Steve Rogers (All-Star)	.10	.08	.04
406	Steve Carlton (All-Star)	.35	.25	.14
407	Bruce Sutter (All-Star)	.12	.09	.05
408	Rudy May	.08	.06	.03
409	Marvis Foley	.08	.06	.03
410	Phil Niekro	.40	.30	.15
411	Phil Niekro (Super Veteran)	.20	.15	.08
412	Rangers Batting/Pitching Leaders (Buddy Bell, Charlie Hough)	.15	.11	.06
413	Matt Keough	.08	.06	.03
414	Julio Cruz	.08	.06	.03
415	Bob Forsch	.10	.08	.04
416	Joe Ferguson	.08	.06	.03
417	Tom Hausman	.08	.06	.03
418	Greg Pryor	.08	.06	.03
419	Steve Crawford	.08	.06	.03
420	Al Oliver	.20	.15	.08
421	Al Oliver (Super Veteran)	.12	.09	.05
422	George Cappuzzello	.08	.06	.03
423	*Tom Lawless*(FC)	.10	.08	.04
424	Jerry Augustine	.08	.06	.03
425	Pedro Guerrero	.15	.11	.06
426	Earl Weaver	.10	.08	.04
427	Roy Lee Jackson	.08	.06	.03
428	Champ Summers	.08	.06	.03
429	Eddie Whitson	.08	.06	.03
430	Kirk Gibson	.25	.20	.10
431	*Gary Gaetti*(FC)	.70	.50	.30

		MT	NR MT	EX
432	Porfirio Altamirano	.08	.06	.03
433	Dale Berra	.08	.06	.03
434	Dennis Lamp	.08	.06	.03
435	Tony Armas	.12	.09	.05
436	Bill Campbell	.08	.06	.03
437	Rick Sweet	.08	.06	.03
438	*Dave LaPoint*(FC)	.10	.08	.04
439	Rafael Ramirez	.08	.06	.03
440	Ron Guidry	.30	.25	.12
441	Astros Batting/Pitching Leaders (Ray Knight, Joe Niekro)	.12	.09	.05
442	Brian Downing	.12	.09	.05
443	Don Hood	.08	.06	.03
444	Wally Backman(FC)	.25	.20	.10
445	Mike Flanagan	.12	.09	.05
446	Reid Nichols	.08	.06	.03
447	Bryn Smith	.10	.08	.04
448	Darrell Evans	.20	.15	.08
449	*Eddie Milner*	.12	.09	.05
450	Ted Simmons	.15	.11	.06
451	Ted Simmons (Super Veteran)	.08	.06	.03
452	Lloyd Moseby	.15	.11	.06
453	Lamar Johnson	.08	.06	.03
454	Bob Welch	.15	.11	.06
455	Sixto Lezcano	.08	.06	.03
456	Lee Elia	.08	.06	.03
457	Milt Wilcox	.08	.06	.03
458	Ron Washington	.08	.06	.03
459	Ed Farmer	.08	.06	.03
460	Roy Smalley	.08	.06	.03
461	Steve Trout	.08	.06	.03
462	Steve Nicosia	.08	.06	.03
463	Gaylord Perry	.40	.30	.15
464	Gaylord Perry (Super Veteran)	.20	.15	.08
465	Lonnie Smith	.10	.08	.04
466	Tom Underwood	.08	.06	.03
467	Rufino Linares	.08	.06	.03
468	Dave Goltz	.10	.08	.04
469	Ron Gardenhire	.08	.06	.03
470	Greg Minton	.08	.06	.03
471	Royals Batting/Pitching Leaders (Vida Blue, Willie Wilson)	.15	.11	.06
472	Gary Allenson	.08	.06	.03
473	John Lowenstein	.08	.06	.03
474	Ray Burris	.08	.06	.03
475	Cesar Cedeno	.12	.09	.05
476	Rob Picciolo	.08	.06	.03
477	Tom Niedenfuer(FC)	.15	.11	.06
478	Phil Garner	.10	.08	.04
479	Charlie Hough	.12	.09	.05
480	Toby Harrah	.10	.08	.04
481	Scot Thompson	.08	.06	.03
482	*Tony Gwynn*(FC)	30.00	22.00	12.00
483	Lynn Jones	.08	.06	.03
484	Dick Ruthven	.08	.06	.03
485	Omar Moreno	.08	.06	.03
486	Clyde King	.08	.06	.03
487	Jerry Hairston	.08	.06	.03
488	Alfredo Griffin	.10	.08	.04
489	Tom Herr	.12	.09	.05
490	Jim Palmer	1.00	.70	.40
491	Jim Palmer (Super Veteran)	.20	.15	.08
492	Paul Serna	.08	.06	.03
493	Steve McCatty	.08	.06	.03
494	Bob Brenly	.10	.08	.04
495	Warren Cromartie	.08	.06	.03
496	Tom Veryzer	.08	.06	.03
497	Rick Sutcliffe	.20	.15	.08
498	*Wade Boggs*(FC)	35.00	26.00	14.00
499	Jeff Little	.10	.08	.04
500	Reggie Jackson	2.50	2.00	1.00
501	Reggie Jackson (Super Veteran)	.50	.40	.20
502	Braves Batting & Pitching Ldrs. (Dale Murphy, Phil Niekro)	.25	.20	.10
503	Moose Haas	.08	.06	.03
504	Don Werner	.08	.06	.03
505	Garry Templeton	.12	.09	.05
506	*Jim Gott*(FC)	.25	.20	.10
507	Tony Scott	.08	.06	.03
508	Tom Filer	.15	.11	.06
509	Lou Whitaker	.40	.30	.15
510	Tug McGraw	.15	.11	.06
511	Tug McGraw (Super Veteran)	.10	.08	.04
512	Doyle Alexander	.12	.09	.05
513	Fred Stanley	.08	.06	.03
514	Rudy Law	.08	.06	.03
515	Gene Tenace	.10	.08	.04
516	Bill Virdon	.08	.06	.03
517	Gary Ward	.10	.08	.04
518	Bill Laskey	.08	.06	.03
519	Terry Bulling	.08	.06	.03

		MT	NR MT	EX
520	Fred Lynn	.25	.20	.10
521	Bruce Benedict	.08	.06	.03
522	Pat Zachry	.08	.06	.03
523	Carney Lansford	.12	.09	.05
524	Tom Brennan	.08	.06	.03
525	Frank White	.12	.09	.05
526	Checklist 397-528	.12	.09	.05
527	Larry Biittner	.08	.06	.03
528	Jamie Easterly	.08	.06	.03
529	Tim Laudner	.10	.08	.04
530	Eddie Murray	.80	.60	.30
531	Athletics Batting/Pitching Leaders (Rickey Henderson, Rick Langford)	.30	.25	.12
532	Dave Stewart	.75	.60	.30
533	Luis Salazar	.08	.06	.03
534	John Butcher	.08	.06	.03
535	Manny Trillo	.10	.08	.04
536	Johnny Wockenfuss	.08	.06	.03
537	Rod Scurry	.08	.06	.03
538	Danny Heep	.08	.06	.03
539	Roger Erickson	.08	.06	.03
540	Ozzie Smith	2.00	1.50	.80
541	Britt Burns	.08	.06	.03
542	Jody Davis	.12	.09	.05
543	Alan Fowlkes	.08	.06	.03
544	Larry Whisenton	.08	.06	.03
545	Floyd Bannister	.12	.09	.05
546	Dave Garcia	.08	.06	.03
547	Geoff Zahn	.08	.06	.03
548	Brian Giles	.08	.06	.03
549	*Charlie Puleo*	.15	.11	.06
550	Carl Yastrzemski	1.00	.70	.40
551	Carl Yastrzemski (Super Veteran)	.40	.30	.15
552	Tim Wallach	.30	.25	.12
553	Denny Martinez	.10	.08	.04
554	Mike Vail	.08	.06	.03
555	Steve Yeager	.08	.06	.03
556	Willie Upshaw	.10	.08	.04
557	Rick Honeycutt	.08	.06	.03
558	Dickie Thon	.10	.08	.04
559	Pete Redfern	.08	.06	.03
560	Ron LeFlore	.10	.08	.04
561	Cardinals Batting/Pitching Leaders (Joaquin Andujar, Lonnie Smith)	.12	.09	.05
562	Dave Rozema	.08	.06	.03
563	Juan Bonilla	.08	.06	.03
564	Sid Monge	.08	.06	.03
565	Bucky Dent	.12	.09	.05
566	Manny Sarmiento	.08	.06	.03
567	Joe Simpson	.08	.06	.03
568	Willie Hernandez	.12	.09	.05
569	Jack Perconte	.08	.06	.03
570	Vida Blue	.15	.11	.06
571	Mickey Klutts	.08	.06	.03
572	Bob Watson	.10	.08	.04
573	Andy Hassler	.08	.06	.03
574	Glenn Adams	.08	.06	.03
575	Neil Allen	.08	.06	.03
576	Frank Robinson	.12	.09	.05
577	Luis Aponte	.08	.06	.03
578	David Green	.08	.06	.03
579	Rich Dauer	.08	.06	.03
580	Tom Seaver	2.00	1.50	.80
581	Tom Seaver (Super Veteran)	.50	.40	.20
582	Marshall Edwards	.08	.06	.03
583	Terry Forster	.10	.08	.04
584	Dave Hostetler	.08	.06	.03
585	Jose Cruz	.15	.11	.06
586	*Frank Viola*(FC)	3.50	2.75	1.50
587	Ivan DeJesus	.08	.06	.03
588	Pat Underwood	.08	.06	.03
589	Alvis Woods	.08	.06	.03
590	Tony Pena	.12	.09	.05
591	White Sox Batting/Pitching Leaders (LaMarr Hoyt, Greg Luzinski)	.15	.11	.06
592	Shane Rawley	.12	.09	.05
593	Broderick Perkins	.08	.06	.03
594	Eric Rasmussen	.08	.06	.03
595	Tim Raines	.60	.45	.25
596	Randy S. Johnson	.08	.06	.03
597	Mike Proly	.08	.06	.03
598	Dwayne Murphy	.10	.08	.04
599	Don Aase	.08	.06	.03
600	George Brett	4.00	3.00	1.50
601	Ed Lynch	.08	.06	.03
602	Rich Gedman	.12	.09	.05
603	Joe Morgan	.60	.45	.25
604	Joe Morgan (Super Veteran)	.15	.11	.06
605	Gary Roenicke	.08	.06	.03
606	Bobby Cox	.08	.06	.03
607	Charlie Leibrandt	.10	.08	.04

		MT	NR MT	EX
608	Don Money	.08	.06	.03
609	Danny Darwin	.08	.06	.03
610	Steve Garvey	.50	.40	.20
611	Bert Roberge	.08	.06	.03
612	Steve Swisher	.08	.06	.03
613	Mike Ivie	.08	.06	.03
614	Ed Glynn	.08	.06	.03
615	Garry Maddox	.12	.09	.05
616	Bill Nahorodny	.08	.06	.03
617	Butch Wynegar	.08	.06	.03
618	LaMarr Hoyt	.08	.06	.03
619	Keith Moreland	.10	.08	.04
620	Mike Norris	.08	.06	.03
621	Mets Batting/Pitching Leaders (Craig Swan, Mookie Wilson)	.12	.09	.05
622	Dave Edler	.08	.06	.03
623	Luis Sanchez	.08	.06	.03
624	Glenn Hubbard	.10	.08	.04
625	Ken Forsch	.08	.06	.03
626	Jerry Martin	.08	.06	.03
627	Doug Bair	.08	.06	.03
628	Julio Valdez	.08	.06	.03
629	Charlie Lea	.08	.06	.03
630	Paul Molitor	3.00	2.25	1.25
631	Tippy Martinez	.08	.06	.03
632	Alex Trevino	.08	.06	.03
633	Vicente Romo	.08	.06	.03
634	Max Venable	.08	.06	.03
635	Graig Nettles	.20	.15	.08
636	Graig Nettles (Super Veteran)	.12	.09	.05
637	Pat Corrales	.08	.06	.03
638	Dan Petry	.10	.08	.04
639	Art Howe	.08	.06	.03
640	Andre Thornton	.12	.09	.05
641	Billy Sample	.08	.06	.03
642	Checklist 529-660	.12	.09	.05
643	Bump Wills	.08	.06	.03
644	Joe Lefebvre	.08	.06	.03
645	Bill Madlock	.15	.11	.06
646	Jim Essian	.08	.06	.03
647	Bobby Mitchell	.08	.06	.03
648	Jeff Burroughs	.10	.08	.04
649	Tommy Boggs	.08	.06	.03
650	George Hendrick	.10	.08	.04
651	Angels Batting/Pitching Leaders (Rod Carew, Mike Witt)	.30	.25	.12
652	Butch Hobson	.08	.06	.03
653	Ellis Valentine	.08	.06	.03
654	Bob Ojeda	.15	.11	.06
655	Al Bumbry	.10	.08	.04
656	Dave Frost	.08	.06	.03
657	Mike Gates	.08	.06	.03
658	Frank Pastore	.08	.06	.03
659	Charlie Moore	.08	.06	.03
660	Mike Hargrove	.08	.06	.03
661	Bill Russell	.10	.08	.04
662	Joe Sambito	.08	.06	.03
663	Tom O'Malley	.08	.06	.03
664	Bob Molinaro	.08	.06	.03
665	Jim Sundberg	.10	.08	.04
666	Sparky Anderson	.12	.09	.05
667	Dick Davis	.08	.06	.03
668	Larry Christenson	.08	.06	.03
669	Mike Squires	.08	.06	.03
670	Jerry Mumphrey	.08	.06	.03
671	Lenny Faedo	.08	.06	.03
672	Jim Kaat	.20	.15	.08
673	Jim Kaat (Super Veteran)	.12	.09	.05
674	Kurt Bevacqua	.08	.06	.03
675	Jim Beattie	.08	.06	.03
676	Biff Pocoroba	.08	.06	.03
677	Dave Revering	.08	.06	.03
678	Juan Beniquez	.08	.06	.03
679	Mike Scott	.20	.15	.08
680	Andre Dawson	1.75	1.25	.70
681	Dodgers Batting/Pitching Leaders (Pedro Guerrero, Fernando Valenzuela)	.25	.20	.10
682	Bob Stanley	.08	.06	.03
683	Dan Ford	.08	.06	.03
684	Rafael Landestoy	.08	.06	.03
685	Lee Mazzilli	.10	.08	.04
686	Randy Lerch	.08	.06	.03
687	U.L. Washington	.08	.06	.03
688	Jim Wohlford	.08	.06	.03
689	Ron Hassey	.08	.06	.03
690	Kent Hrbek	.70	.50	.30
691	Dave Tobik	.08	.06	.03
692	Denny Walling	.08	.06	.03
693	Sparky Lyle	.12	.09	.05
694	Sparky Lyle (Super Veteran)	.10	.08	.04
695	Ruppert Jones	.08	.06	.03

		MT	NR MT	EX
696	Chuck Tanner	.08	.06	.03
697	Barry Foote	.08	.06	.03
698	Tony Bernazard	.08	.06	.03
699	Lee Smith	2.00	1.50	.80
700	Keith Hernandez	.50	.40	.20
701	Batting Leaders (Al Oliver, Willie Wilson)	.15	.11	.06
702	Home Run Leaders (Reggie Jackson, Dave Kingman, Gorman Thomas)	.25	.20	.10
703	Runs Batted In Leaders (Hal McRae, Dale Murphy, Al Oliver)	.35	.25	.14
704	Stolen Base Leaders (Rickey Henderson, Tim Raines)	.35	.25	.14
705	Victory Leaders (Steve Carlton, LaMarr Hoyt)	.20	.15	.08
706	Strikeout Leaders (Floyd Bannister, Steve Carlton)	.20	.15	.08
707	Earned Run Average Leaders (Steve Rogers, Rick Sutcliffe)	.12	.09	.05
708	Leading Firemen (Dan Quisenberry, Bruce Sutter)	.15	.11	.06
709	Jimmy Sexton	.08	.06	.03
710	Willie Wilson	.20	.15	.08
711	Mariners Batting/Pitching Leaders (Jim Beattie, Bruce Bochte)	.12	.09	.05
712	Bruce Kison	.08	.06	.03
713	Ron Hodges	.08	.06	.03
714	Wayne Nordhagen	.08	.06	.03
715	Tony Perez	.25	.20	.10
716	Tony Perez (Super Veteran)	.12	.09	.05
717	Scott Sanderson	.08	.06	.03
718	Jim Dwyer	.08	.06	.03
719	Rich Gale	.08	.06	.03
720	Dave Concepcion	.15	.11	.06
721	John Martin	.08	.06	.03
722	Jorge Orta	.08	.06	.03
723	Randy Moffitt	.08	.06	.03
724	Johnny Grubb	.08	.06	.03
725	Dan Spillner	.08	.06	.03
726	Harvey Kuenn	.10	.08	.04
727	Chet Lemon	.10	.08	.04
728	Ron Reed	.08	.06	.03
729	Jerry Morales	.08	.06	.03
730	Jason Thompson	.08	.06	.03
731	Al Williams	.08	.06	.03
732	Dave Henderson	.15	.11	.06
733	Buck Martinez	.08	.06	.03
734	Steve Braun	.08	.06	.03
735	Tommy John	.25	.20	.10
736	Tommy John (Super Veteran)	.12	.09	.05
737	Mitchell Page	.08	.06	.03
738	Tim Foli	.08	.06	.03
739	Rick Ownbey	.08	.06	.03
740	Rusty Staub	.15	.11	.06
741	Rusty Staub (Super Veteran)	.10	.08	.04
742	Padres Batting/Pitching Leaders (Terry Kennedy, Tim Lollar)	.12	.09	.05
743	Mike Torrez	.10	.08	.04
744	Brad Mills	.08	.06	.03
745	Scott McGregor	.10	.08	.04
746	John Wathan	.10	.08	.04
747	Fred Breining	.08	.06	.03
748	Derrel Thomas	.08	.06	.03
749	Jon Matlack	.10	.08	.04
750	Ben Oglivie	.10	.08	.04
751	Brad Havens	.08	.06	.03
752	Luis Pujols	.08	.06	.03
753	Elias Sosa	.08	.06	.03
754	Bill Robinson	.08	.06	.03
755	John Candelaria	.12	.09	.05
756	Russ Nixon	.08	.06	.03
757	Rick Manning	.08	.06	.03
758	Aurelio Rodriguez	.10	.08	.04
759	Doug Bird	.08	.06	.03
760	Dale Murphy	.75	.60	.30
761	Gary Lucas	.08	.06	.03
762	Cliff Johnson	.08	.06	.03
763	Al Cowens	.08	.06	.03
764	Pete Falcone	.08	.06	.03
765	Bob Boone	.12	.09	.05
766	Barry Bonnell	.08	.06	.03
767	Duane Kuiper	.08	.06	.03
768	Chris Speier	.08	.06	.03
769	Checklist 661-792	.12	.09	.05
770	Dave Winfield	3.00	2.25	1.25
771	Twins Batting/Pitching Leaders (Bobby Castillo, Kent Hrbek)	.20	.15	.08
772	Jim Kern	.08	.06	.03
773	Larry Hisle	.10	.08	.04
774	Alan Ashby	.08	.06	.03
775	Burt Hooton	.10	.08	.04

		MT	NR MT	EX
776	Larry Parrish	.12	.09	.05
777	John Curtis	.08	.06	.03
778	Rich Hebner	.08	.06	.03
779	Rick Waits	.08	.06	.03
780	Gary Matthews	.12	.09	.05
781	Rick Rhoden	.12	.09	.05
782	Bobby Murcer	.12	.09	.05
783	Bobby Murcer (Super Veteran)	.10	.08	.04
784	Jeff Newman	.08	.06	.03
785	Dennis Leonard	.10	.08	.04
786	Ralph Houk	.10	.08	.04
787	Dick Tidrow	.08	.06	.03
788	Dane Iorg	.08	.06	.03
789	Bryan Clark	.08	.06	.03
790	Bob Grich	.12	.09	.05
791	Gary Lavelle	.08	.06	.03
792	Chris Chambliss	.10	.08	.04

1983 Topps All-Star Glossy Set Of 40

This set was a "consolation prize" in a scratch-off contest in regular packs of 1983 cards. The 2-1/2" by 3-1/2" cards have a large color photo surrounded by a yellow frame on the front. In very small type on a white border is printed the player's name. Backs carry the player's name, team, position and the card number along with a Topps identification. A major feature is that the surface of the front is glossy, which most collectors find very attractive. With many top stars, the set is a popular one, but the price has not moved too far above the issue price.

		MT	NR MT	EX
Complete Set:		13.00	9.75	5.25
Common Player:		.15	.11	.06
1	Carl Yastrzemski	1.00	.70	.40
2	Mookie Wilson	.15	.11	.06
3	Andre Thornton	.15	.11	.06
4	Keith Hernandez	.40	.30	.15
5	Robin Yount	.40	.30	.15
6	Terry Kennedy	.15	.11	.06
7	Dave Winfield	.60	.45	.25
8	Mike Schmidt	1.00	.70	.40
9	Buddy Bell	.20	.15	.08
10	Fernando Valenzuela	.50	.40	.20
11	Rich Gossage	.25	.20	.10
12	Bob Horner	.20	.15	.08
13	Toby Harrah	.15	.11	.06
14	Pete Rose	1.25	.90	.50
15	Cecil Cooper	.20	.15	.08
16	Dale Murphy	1.00	.70	.40
17	Carlton Fisk	.30	.25	.12
18	Ray Knight	.15	.11	.06
19	Jim Palmer	.40	.30	.15
20	Gary Carter	.50	.40	.20
21	Richard Zisk	.15	.11	.06
22	Dusty Baker	.15	.11	.06
23	Willie Wilson	.20	.15	.08
24	Bill Buckner	.15	.11	.06
25	Dave Stieb	.20	.15	.08
26	Bill Madlock	.20	.15	.08
27	Lance Parrish	.30	.25	.12
28	Nolan Ryan	1.00	.70	.40
29	Rod Carew	.60	.45	.25
30	Al Oliver	.20	.15	.08
31	George Brett	1.00	.70	.40
32	Jack Clark	.25	.20	.10
33	Rickey Henderson	.70	.50	.30
34	Dave Concepcion	.20	.15	.08
35	Kent Hrbek	.30	.25	.12
36	Steve Carlton	.50	.40	.20
37	Eddie Murray	.60	.45	.25
38	Ruppert Jones	.15	.11	.06
39	Reggie Jackson	.70	.50	.30
40	Bruce Sutter	.20	.15	.08

1983 Topps Traded

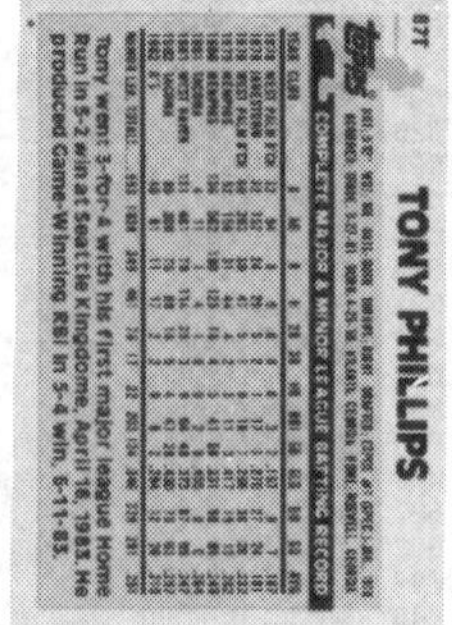

These 2-1/2" by 3-1/2" cards mark a continuation of the traded set introduced in 1981. The 132 cards retain the basic design of the year's regular issue, with their numbering being 1-132 with the "T" suffix. Cards in the set include traded players, new managers and promising rookies. Sold only through dealers, the set was in heavy demand as it contained the first cards of Darryl Strawberry, Ron Kittle, Julio Franco and Mel Hall. While some of those cards were very hot in 1983, it seems likely that some of the rookies may not live up to their initial promise.

		MT	NR MT	EX
Complete Set (132):		60.00	45.00	24.00
Common Player:		.10	.08	.04
1T	Neil Allen	.10	.08	.04
2T	Bill Almon	.10	.08	.04
3T	Joe Altobelli	.10	.08	.04
4T	Tony Armas	.10	.08	.04
5T	Doug Bair	.10	.08	.04
6T	Steve Baker	.10	.08	.04
7T	Floyd Bannister	.10	.08	.04
8T	Don Baylor	.30	.25	.12
9T	Tony Bernazard	.10	.08	.04
10T	Larry Biittner	.10	.08	.04
11T	Dann Bilardello	.10	.08	.04
12T	Doug Bird	.10	.08	.04
13T	Steve Boros	.10	.08	.04
14T	Greg Brock(FC)	.10	.08	.04
15T	Mike Brown	.10	.08	.04
16T	Tom Burgmeier	.10	.08	.04
17T	Randy Bush(FC)	.10	.08	.04
18T	Bert Campaneris	.20	.15	.08
19T	Ron Cey	.25	.20	.10
20T	Chris Codiroli(FC)	.10	.08	.04
21T	Dave Collins	.10	.08	.04
22T	Terry Crowley	.10	.08	.04
23T	Julio Cruz	.10	.08	.04
24T	Mike Davis	.10	.08	.04
25T	Frank DiPino	.10	.08	.04
26T	Bill Doran(FC)	1.00	.70	.40
27T	Jerry Dybzinski	.10	.08	.04
28T	Jamie Easterly	.10	.08	.04
29T	Juan Eichelberger	.10	.08	.04
30T	Jim Essian	.10	.08	.04
31T	Pete Falcone	.10	.08	.04
32T	Mike Ferraro	.10	.08	.04
33T	Terry Forster	.10	.08	.04
34T	Julio Franco(FC)	4.00	3.00	1.50
35T	Rich Gale	.10	.08	.04
36T	Kiko Garcia	.10	.08	.04
37T	Steve Garvey	1.50	1.25	.60
38T	Johnny Grubb	.10	.08	.04

		MT	NR MT	EX
39T	Mel Hall(FC)	.50	.40	.20
40T	Von Hayes	.50	.40	.20
41T	Danny Heep	.10	.08	.04
42T	Steve Henderson	.10	.08	.04
43T	Keith Hernandez	.50	.40	.20
44T	Leo Hernandez	.10	.08	.04
45T	Willie Hernandez	.10	.08	.04
46T	Al Holland	.10	.08	.04
47T	Frank Howard	.15	.11	.06
48T	Bobby Johnson	.10	.08	.04
49T	Cliff Johnson	.10	.08	.04
50T	Odell Jones	.10	.08	.04
51T	Mike Jorgensen	.10	.08	.04
52T	Bob Kearney	.10	.08	.04
53T	Steve Kemp	.10	.08	.04
54T	Matt Keough	.10	.08	.04
55T	Ron Kittle(FC)	.10	.08	.04
56T	Mickey Klutts	.10	.08	.04
57T	Alan Knicely	.10	.08	.04
58T	Mike Krukow	.10	.08	.04
59T	Rafael Landestoy	.10	.08	.04
60T	Carney Lansford	.10	.08	.04
61T	Joe Lefebvre	.10	.08	.04
62T	Bryan Little	.10	.08	.04
63T	Aurelio Lopez	.10	.08	.04
64T	Mike Madden	.10	.08	.04
65T	Rick Manning	.10	.08	.04
66T	Billy Martin	.20	.15	.08
67T	Lee Mazzilli	.10	.08	.04
68T	Andy McGaffigan	.10	.08	.04
69T	Craig McMurtry(FC)	.10	.08	.04
70T	John McNamara	.10	.08	.04
71T	Orlando Mercado	.10	.08	.04
72T	Larry Milbourne	.10	.08	.04
73T	Randy Moffitt	.10	.08	.04
74T	Sid Monge	.10	.08	.04
75T	Jose Morales	.10	.08	.04
76T	Omar Moreno	.10	.08	.04
77T	Joe Morgan	3.00	2.25	1.25
78T	Mike Morgan	.10	.08	.04
79T	Dale Murray	.10	.08	.04
80T	Jeff Newman	.10	.08	.04
81T	Pete O'Brien(FC)	.50	.40	.20
82T	Jorge Orta	.10	.08	.04
83T	Alejandro Pena(FC)	.50	.40	.20
84T	Pascual Perez	.20	.15	.08
85T	Tony Perez	1.50	1.25	.60
86T	Broderick Perkins	.10	.08	.04
87T	Tony Phillips(FC)	7.00	5.25	2.75
88T	Charlie Puleo	.10	.08	.04
89T	Pat Putnam	.10	.08	.04
90T	Jamie Quirk	.10	.08	.04
91T	Doug Rader	.10	.08	.04
92T	Chuck Rainey	.10	.08	.04
93T	Bobby Ramos	.10	.08	.04
94T	Gary Redus(FC)	.30	.25	.12
95T	Steve Renko	.10	.08	.04
96T	Leon Roberts	.10	.08	.04
97T	Aurelio Rodriguez	.10	.08	.04
98T	Dick Ruthven	.10	.08	.04
99T	Daryl Sconiers	.10	.08	.04
100T	Mike Scott	.25	.20	.10
101T	Tom Seaver	8.50	6.50	3.50
102T	John Shelby(FC)	.10	.08	.04
103T	Bob Shirley	.10	.08	.04
104T	Joe Simpson	.10	.08	.04
105T	Doug Sisk(FC)	.10	.08	.04
106T	Mike Smithson(FC)	.10	.08	.04
107T	Elias Sosa	.10	.08	.04
108T	Darryl Strawberry(FC)	35.00	26.00	14.00
109T	Tom Tellmann	.10	.08	.04
110T	Gene Tenace	.10	.08	.04
111T	Gorman Thomas	.10	.08	.04
112T	Dick Tidrow	.10	.08	.04
113T	Dave Tobik	.10	.08	.04
114T	Wayne Tolleson(FC)	.10	.08	.04
115T	Mike Torrez	.10	.08	.04
116T	Manny Trillo	.10	.08	.04
117T	Steve Trout	.10	.08	.04
118T	Lee Tunnell(FC)	.10	.08	.04
119T	Mike Vail	.10	.08	.04
120T	Ellis Valentine	.10	.08	.04
121T	Tom Veryzer	.10	.08	.04
122T	George Vukovich	.10	.08	.04
123T	Rick Waits	.10	.08	.04
124T	Greg Walker(FC)	.10	.08	.04
125T	Chris Welsh	.10	.08	.04
126T	Len Whitehouse	.10	.08	.04
127T	Eddie Whitson	.10	.08	.04
128T	Jim Wohlford	.10	.08	.04
129T	Matt Young(FC)	.10	.08	.04
130T	Joel Youngblood	.10	.08	.04
131T	Pat Zachry	.10	.08	.04
132T	Checklist 1-132	.10	.08	.04

1983 Topps Foldouts

Another Topps test issue, these 3-1/2" by 5-5/16" cards were printed in booklets like souvenier postcards. Each of the booklets have a theme of currently playing statistical leaders in a specific category such as home runs. The cards feature a color player photo on each side. A black strip at the bottom gives the player's name, position and team along with statistics in the particular category. A facsimile autograph crosses the photograph. Booklets carry nine cards, with eight having players on both sides and one doubling as the back cover, for a total of 17 cards per booklet. There are 85 cards in the set, although some players appear in more than one category. Naturally, most of the players pictured are stars. Even so, the set is a problem as it seems to be most valuable when complete and unseparated, so the cards are difficult to display.

		MT	NR MT	EX
Complete Set:		10.00	7.50	4.00
Common Folder:		1.25	.90	.50
1	Pitching Leaders (Vida Blue, Bert Blyleven, Steve Carlton, Fergie Jenkins, Tommy John, Jim Kaat, Jerry Koosman, Joe Niekro, Phil Niekro, Jim Palmer, Gaylord Perry, Jerry Reuss, Nolan Ryan, Tom Seaver, Paul Splittorff, Don Sutton, Mike Torrez)	1.75	1.25	.70
2	Home Run Leaders (Johnny Bench, Ron Cey, Darrell Evans, George Foster, Reggie Jackson, Dave Kingman, Greg Luzinski, John Mayberry, Rick Monday, Joe Morgan, Bobby Murcer, Graig Nettles, Tony Perez, Jim Rice, Mike Schmidt, Rusty Staub, Carl Yastrzemski)	2.50	2.00	1.00
3	Batting Leaders (George Brett, Rod Carew, Cecil Cooper, Steve Garvey, Ken Griffey, Pedro Guerrero, Keith Hernandez, Dane Iorg, Fred Lynn, Bill Madlock, Bake McBride, Al Oliver, Dave Parker, Jim Rice, Pete Rose, Lonnie Smith, Willie Wilson)	2.50	2.00	1.00
4	Relief Aces (Tom Burgmeier, Bill Campbell, Ed Farmer, Rollie Fingers, Terry Forster, Gene Garber, Rich Gossage, Jim Kern, Gary Lavelle, Tug McGraw, Greg Minton, Randy Moffitt, Dan Quisenberry, Ron Reed, Elias Sosa, Bruce Sutter, Kent Tekulve)	1.25	.90	.50
5	Stolen Base Leaders (Don Baylor, Larry Bowa, Al Bumbry, Rod Carew, Cesar Cedeno, Dave Concepcion, Jose Cruz, Julio Cruz, Rickey Henderson, Ron LeFlore, Davey Lopes, Garry Maddox, Omar Moreno, Joe Morgan, Amos Otis, Mickey Rivers, Willie Wilson)	1.25	.90	.50

A card number in parentheses () indicates the set is unnumbered.

1983 Topps Stickers

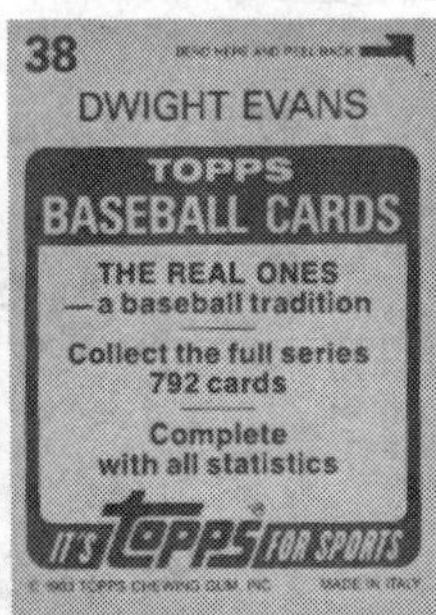

Topps increased the number of stickers in its set to 220 in 1983, but retained the same 1-15/16" by 2-9/16" size. The stickers are again numbered on both the front and back. Similar in style to previous sticker issues, the set includes 28 "foil" stickers, and various special stickers highlighting the 1982 season, playoffs and World Series. An album was also available.

	MT	NR MT	EX
Complete Set:	15.00	11.00	6.00
Common Player:	.03	.02	.01
Sticker Album:	.80	.60	.30

		MT	NR MT	EX
1	Hank Aaron	.40	.30	.15
2	Babe Ruth	.60	.45	.25
3	Willie Mays	.40	.30	.15
4	Frank Robinson	.30	.25	.12
5	Reggie Jackson	.20	.15	.08
6	Carl Yastrzemski	.25	.20	.10
7	Johnny Bench	.20	.15	.08
8	Tony Perez	.10	.08	.04
9	Lee May	.06	.05	.02
10	Mike Schmidt	.25	.20	.10
11	Dave Kingman	.08	.06	.03
12	Reggie Smith	.06	.05	.02
13	Graig Nettles	.06	.05	.02
14	Rusty Staub	.06	.05	.02
15	Willie Wilson	.06	.05	.02
16	LaMarr Hoyt	.03	.02	.01
17	Reggie Jackson, Gorman Thomas	.15	.11	.06
18	Floyd Bannister	.04	.03	.02
19	Hal McRae	.06	.05	.02
20	Rick Sutcliffe	.08	.06	.03
21	Rickey Henderson	.25	.20	.10
22	Dan Quisenberry	.06	.05	.02
23	Jim Palmer	.30	.25	.12
24	John Lowenstein	.03	.02	.01
25	Mike Flanagan	.04	.03	.02
26	Cal Ripken	.20	.15	.08
27	Rich Dauer	.03	.02	.01
28	Ken Singleton	.06	.05	.02
29	Eddie Murray	.20	.15	.08
30	Rick Dempsey	.04	.03	.02
31	Carl Yastrzemski	.40	.30	.15
32	Carney Lansford	.06	.05	.02
33	Jerry Remy	.03	.02	.01
34	Dennis Eckersley	.06	.05	.02
35	Dave Stapleton	.03	.02	.01
36	Mark Clear	.03	.02	.01
37	Jim Rice	.20	.15	.08
38	Dwight Evans	.08	.06	.03
39	Rod Carew	.20	.15	.08
40	Don Baylor	.08	.06	.03
41	Reggie Jackson	.40	.30	.15
42	Geoff Zahn	.03	.02	.01
43	Bobby Grich	.06	.05	.02
44	Fred Lynn	.10	.08	.04
45	Bob Boone	.04	.03	.02
46	Doug DeCinces	.06	.05	.02
47	Tom Paciorek	.03	.02	.01
48	Britt Burns	.03	.02	.01
49	Tony Bernazard	.03	.02	.01
50	Steve Kemp	.04	.03	.02
51	Greg Luzinski	.20	.15	.08
52	Harold Baines	.10	.08	.04
53	LaMarr Hoyt	.03	.02	.01
54	Carlton Fisk	.12	.09	.05
55	Andre Thornton	.15	.11	.06
56	Mike Hargrove	.04	.03	.02
57	Len Barker	.03	.02	.01
58	Toby Harrah	.04	.03	.02
59	Dan Spillner	.03	.02	.01
60	Rick Manning	.03	.02	.01
61	Rick Sutcliffe	.08	.06	.03
62	Ron Hassey	.03	.02	.01
63	Lance Parrish	.30	.25	.12
64	John Wockenfuss	.03	.02	.01
65	Lou Whitaker	.12	.09	.05
66	Alan Trammell	.15	.11	.06
67	Kirk Gibson	.15	.11	.06
68	Larry Herndon	.03	.02	.01
69	Jack Morris	.12	.09	.05
70	Dan Petry	.04	.03	.02
71	Frank White	.06	.05	.02
72	Amos Otis	.04	.03	.02
73	Willie Wilson	.25	.20	.10
74	Dan Quisenberry	.06	.05	.02
75	Hal McRae	.06	.05	.02
76	George Brett	.25	.20	.10
77	Larry Gura	.03	.02	.01
78	John Wathan	.04	.03	.02
79	Rollie Fingers	.10	.08	.04
80	Cecil Cooper	.08	.06	.03
81	Robin Yount	.30	.25	.12
82	Ben Oglivie	.06	.05	.02
83	Paul Molitor	.10	.08	.04
84	Gorman Thomas	.06	.05	.02
85	Ted Simmons	.06	.05	.02
86	Pete Vuckovich	.04	.03	.02
87	Gary Gaetti	.08	.06	.03
88	Kent Hrbek	.30	.25	.12
89	John Castino	.03	.02	.01
90	Tom Brunansky	.06	.05	.02
91	Bobby Mitchell	.03	.02	.01
92	Gary Ward	.04	.03	.02
93	Tim Laudner	.03	.02	.01
94	Ron Davis	.03	.02	.01
95	Willie Randolph	.06	.05	.02
96	Roy Smalley	.03	.02	.01
97	Jerry Mumphrey	.03	.02	.01
98	Ken Griffey	.06	.05	.02
99	Dave Winfield	.30	.25	.12
100	Rich Gossage	.10	.08	.04
101	Butch Wynegar	.04	.03	.02
102	Ron Guidry	.12	.09	.05
103	Rickey Henderson	.40	.30	.15
104	Mike Heath	.03	.02	.01
105	Dave Lopes	.06	.05	.02
106	Rick Langford	.03	.02	.01
107	Dwayne Murphy	.04	.03	.02
108	Tony Armas	.06	.05	.02
109	Matt Keough	.03	.02	.01
110	Dan Meyer	.03	.02	.01
111	Bruce Bochte	.03	.02	.01
112	Julio Cruz	.03	.02	.01
113	Floyd Bannister	.04	.03	.02
114	Gaylord Perry	.30	.25	.12
115	Al Cowens	.03	.02	.01
116	Richie Zisk	.04	.03	.02
117	Jim Essian	.03	.02	.01
118	Bill Caudill	.03	.02	.01
119	Buddy Bell	.20	.15	.08
120	Larry Parrish	.06	.05	.02
121	Danny Darwin	.03	.02	.01
122	Bucky Dent	.04	.03	.02
123	Johnny Grubb	.03	.02	.01
124	George Wright	.03	.02	.01
125	Charlie Hough	.06	.05	.02
126	Jim Sundberg	.04	.03	.02
127	Dave Stieb	.20	.15	.08
128	Willie Upshaw	.06	.05	.02
129	Alfredo Griffin	.04	.03	.02
130	Lloyd Moseby	.06	.05	.02
131	Ernie Whitt	.03	.02	.01
132	Jim Clancy	.04	.03	.02
133	Barry Bonnell	.03	.02	.01
134	Damaso Garcia	.04	.03	.02
135	Jim Kaat	.08	.06	.03
136	Jim Kaat	.06	.05	.02
137	Greg Minton	.03	.02	.01
138	Greg Minton	.03	.02	.01
139	Paul Molitor	.10	.08	.04
140	Paul Molitor	.08	.06	.03
141	Manny Trillo	.04	.03	.02
142	Manny Trillo	.04	.03	.02
143	Joel Youngblood	.03	.02	.01
144	Joel Youngblood	.03	.02	.01
145	Robin Yount	.15	.11	.06
146	Robin Yount	.12	.09	.05

		MT	NR MT	EX
147	Willie McGee	.08	.06	.03
148	Darrell Porter	.04	.03	.02
149	Darrell Porter	.04	.03	.02
150	Robin Yount	.15	.11	.06
151	Bruce Benedict	.03	.02	.01
152	Bruce Benedict	.03	.02	.01
153	George Hendrick	.04	.03	.02
154	Bruce Benedict	.03	.02	.01
155	Doug DeCinces	.06	.05	.02
156	Paul Molitor	.10	.08	.04
157	Charlie Moore	.03	.02	.01
158	Fred Lynn	.10	.08	.04
159	Rickey Henderson	.20	.15	.08
160	Dale Murphy	.25	.20	.10
161	Willie Wilson	.08	.06	.03
162	Jack Clark	.10	.08	.04
163	Reggie Jackson	.20	.15	.08
164	Andre Dawson	.15	.11	.06
165	Dan Quisenberry	.06	.05	.02
166	Bruce Sutter	.08	.06	.03
167	Robin Yount	.15	.11	.06
168	Ozzie Smith	.10	.08	.04
169	Frank White	.06	.05	.02
170	Phil Garner	.04	.03	.02
171	Doug DeCinces	.06	.05	.02
172	Mike Schmidt	.25	.20	.10
173	Cecil Cooper	.06	.05	.02
174	Al Oliver	.06	.05	.02
175	Jim Palmer	.15	.11	.06
176	Steve Carlton	.15	.11	.06
177	Carlton Fisk	.12	.09	.05
178	Gary Carter	.20	.15	.08
179	Joaquin Andujar	.04	.03	.02
180	Ozzie Smith	.10	.08	.04
181	Cecil Cooper	.06	.05	.02
182	Darrell Porter	.04	.03	.02
183	Darrell Porter	.04	.03	.02
184	Mike Caldwell	.03	.02	.01
185	Mike Caldwell	.03	.02	.01
186	Ozzie Smith	.10	.08	.04
187	Bruce Sutter	.08	.06	.03
188	Keith Hernandez	.12	.09	.05
189	Dane Iorg	.03	.02	.01
190	Dane Iorg	.03	.02	.01
191	Tony Armas	.04	.03	.02
192	Tony Armas	.04	.03	.02
193	Lance Parrish	.12	.09	.05
194	Lance Parrish	.12	.09	.05
195	John Wathan	.04	.03	.02
196	John Wathan	.04	.03	.02
197	Rickey Henderson	.12	.09	.05
198	Rickey Henderson	.12	.09	.05
199	Rickey Henderson	.12	.09	.05
200	Rickey Henderson	.12	.09	.05
201	Rickey Henderson	.12	.09	.05
202	Rickey Henderson	.12	.09	.05
203	Steve Carlton	.15	.11	.06
204	Steve Carlton	.12	.09	.05
205	Al Oliver	.06	.05	.02
206	Dale Murphy, Al Oliver	.20	.15	.08
207	Dave Kingman	.08	.06	.03
208	Steve Rogers	.04	.03	.02
209	Bruce Sutter	.08	.06	.03
210	Tim Raines	.20	.15	.08
211	Dale Murphy	.40	.30	.15
212	Chris Chambliss	.04	.03	.02
213	Gene Garber	.03	.02	.01
214	Bob Horner	.08	.06	.03
215	Glenn Hubbard	.03	.02	.01
216	Claudell Washington	.04	.03	.02
217	Bruce Benedict	.03	.02	.01
218	Phil Niekro	.12	.09	.05
219	Leon Durham	.20	.15	.08
220	Jay Johnstone	.04	.03	.02
221	Larry Bowa	.06	.05	.02
222	Keith Moreland	.06	.05	.02
223	Bill Buckner	.06	.05	.02
224	Fergie Jenkins	.08	.06	.03
225	Dick Tidrow	.03	.02	.01
226	Jody Davis	.06	.05	.02
227	Dave Concepcion	.06	.05	.02
228	Dan Driessen	.04	.03	.02
229	Johnny Bench	.20	.15	.08
230	Ron Oester	.03	.02	.01
231	Cesar Cedeno	.06	.05	.02
232	Alex Trevino	.03	.02	.01
233	Tom Seaver	.20	.15	.08
234	Mario Soto	.20	.15	.08
235	Nolan Ryan	.30	.25	.12
236	Art Howe	.03	.02	.01
237	Phil Garner	.04	.03	.02

		MT	NR MT	EX
238	Ray Knight	.06	.05	.02
239	Terry Puhl	.03	.02	.01
240	Joe Niekro	.06	.05	.02
241	Alan Ashby	.03	.02	.01
242	Jose Cruz	.06	.05	.02
243	Steve Garvey	.20	.15	.08
244	Ron Cey	.06	.05	.02
245	Dusty Baker	.04	.03	.02
246	Ken Landreaux	.03	.02	.01
247	Jerry Reuss	.06	.05	.02
248	Pedro Guerrero	.12	.09	.05
249	Bill Russell	.04	.03	.02
250	Fernando Valenzuela	.30	.25	.12
251	Al Oliver	.25	.20	.10
252	Andre Dawson	.15	.11	.06
253	Tim Raines	.20	.15	.08
254	Jeff Reardon	.08	.06	.03
255	Gary Carter	.20	.15	.08
256	Steve Rogers	.03	.02	.01
257	Tim Wallach	.08	.06	.03
258	Chris Speier	.03	.02	.01
259	Dave Kingman	.08	.06	.03
260	Bob Bailor	.03	.02	.01
261	Hubie Brooks	.06	.05	.02
262	Craig Swan	.03	.02	.01
263	George Foster	.08	.06	.03
264	John Stearns	.03	.02	.01
265	Neil Allen	.03	.02	.01
266	Mookie Wilson	.20	.15	.08
267	Steve Carlton	.30	.25	.12
268	Manny Trillo	.04	.03	.02
269	Gary Matthews	.06	.05	.02
270	Mike Schmidt	.25	.20	.10
271	Ivan DeJesus	.03	.02	.01
272	Pete Rose	.40	.30	.15
273	Bo Diaz	.04	.03	.02
274	Sid Monge	.03	.02	.01
275	Bill Madlock	.25	.20	.10
276	Jason Thompson	.03	.02	.01
277	Don Robinson	.03	.02	.01
278	Omar Moreno	.03	.02	.01
279	Dale Berra	.03	.02	.01
280	Dave Parker	.10	.08	.04
281	Tony Pena	.06	.05	.02
282	John Candelaria	.06	.05	.02
283	Lonnie Smith	.04	.03	.02
284	Bruce Sutter	.25	.20	.10
285	George Hendrick	.04	.03	.02
286	Tom Herr	.06	.05	.02
287	Ken Oberkfell	.03	.02	.01
288	Ozzie Smith	.10	.08	.04
289	Bob Forsch	.04	.03	.02
290	Keith Hernandez	.15	.11	.06
291	Garry Templeton	.06	.05	.02
292	Broderick Perkins	.03	.02	.01
293	Terry Kennedy	.20	.15	.08
294	Gene Richards	.03	.02	.01
295	Ruppert Jones	.03	.02	.01
296	Tim Lollar	.03	.02	.01
297	John Montefusco	.03	.02	.01
298	Sixto Lezcano	.03	.02	.01
299	Greg Minton	.03	.02	.01
300	Jack Clark	.25	.20	.10
301	Milt May	.03	.02	.01
302	Reggie Smith	.06	.05	.02
303	Joe Morgan	.10	.08	.04
304	John LeMaster	.03	.02	.01
305	Darrell Evans	.08	.06	.03
306	Al Holland	.03	.02	.01
307	Jesse Barfield	.08	.06	.03
308	Wade Boggs	.60	.45	.25
309	Tom Brunansky	.06	.05	.02
310	Storm Davis	.04	.03	.02
311	Von Hayes	.06	.05	.02
312	Dave Hostetler	.03	.02	.01
313	Kent Hrbek	.12	.09	.05
314	Tim Laudner	.03	.02	.01
315	Cal Ripken	.20	.15	.08
316	Andre Robertson	.03	.02	.01
317	Ed Vande Berg	.03	.02	.01
318	Glenn Wilson	.04	.03	.02
319	Chili Davis	.06	.05	.02
320	Bob Dernier	.03	.02	.01
321	Terry Francona	.03	.02	.01
322	Brian Giles	.03	.02	.01
323	David Green	.03	.02	.01
324	Atlee Hammaker	.03	.02	.01
325	Bill Laskey	.03	.02	.01
326	Willie McGee	.12	.09	.05
327	Johnny Ray	.06	.05	.02
328	Ryne Sandberg	.25	.20	.10

		MT	NR MT	EX
329	Steve Sax	.10	.08	.04
330	Eric Show	.04	.03	.02

1983 Topps Stickers Boxes

These eight cards were printed on the back panels of 1983 Topps sticker boxes, on card per box. The blank-backed cards measure the standard 2-1/2" by 3-1/2" and feature a full-color photo with the player's name at the top. The rest of the back panel advertises the sticker album, while the front of the box has an action photo of Reggie Jackson. The boxes are numbered on the front. Prices in the checklist that follows are for complete boxes.

		MT	NR MT	EX
Complete Set:		6.50	5.00	2.50
Common Player:		.75	.60	.30
1	Fernando Valenzuela	1.00	.70	.40
2	Gary Carter	1.25	.90	.50
3	Mike Schmidt	1.25	.90	.50
4	Reggie Jackson	1.25	.90	.50
5	Jim Palmer	1.00	.70	.40
6	Rollie Fingers	.75	.60	.30
7	Pete Rose	1.50	1.25	.60
8	Rickey Henderson	1.25	.90	.50

1984 Topps

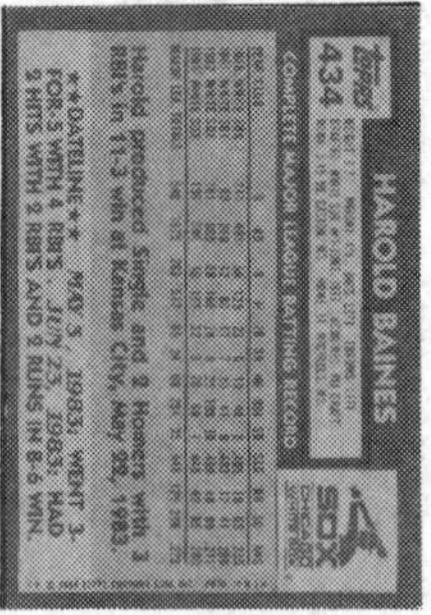

Another 792-card regular set from Topps. For the second straight year, the 2-1/2" by 3-1/2" cards featured a color action photo on the front along with a small portrait photo in the lower left. The team name runs in big letters down the left side, while the player's name and position runs under the large action photo. In the upper right-hand corner is the Topps logo. Backs have a team logo in the upper right corner, along with statistics, personal information and a few highlights. The backs have an unusual and hard-to-read red and purple coloring. Specialty cards include past season highlights, team leaders, major league statistical leaders, All-Stars, active career leaders and numbered checklists. Again, promising rookies were saved for the traded set. Late in 1984, Topps introduced a specially boxed "Tiffany" edition of the 1984 set, with the cards printed on white cardboard with a glossy finish. A total of 10,000 sets were produced. Prices for Tiffany edition super- stars can run from six to eight times the value of the "regular" edition, while common cards sell in the 40¢ range.

		MT	NR MT	EX
Complete Set (792):		75.00	56.00	30.00
Common Player:		.08	.06	.03
1	Steve Carlton (1983 Highlight)	.30	.25	.12
2	Rickey Henderson (1983 Highlight)	.50	.40	.20
3	Dan Quisenberry (1983 Highlight)	.10	.08	.04
4	Steve Carlton, Gaylord Perry, Nolan Ryan (1983 Highlight)	.30	.25	.12
5	Bob Forsch, Dave Righetti, Mike Warren (1983 Highlight)	.15	.11	.06
6	Johnny Bench, Gaylord Perry, Carl Yastrzemski (1983 Highlight)	.40	.30	.15
7	Gary Lucas	.08	.06	.03
8	*Don Mattingly*(FC)	12.00	9.00	4.75
9	Jim Gott	.10	.08	.04
10	Robin Yount	2.00	1.50	.80
11	Twins Batting & Pitching Leaders (Kent Hrbek, Ken Schrom)	.20	.15	.08
12	Billy Sample	.08	.06	.03
13	Scott Holman	.08	.06	.03
14	Tom Brookens	.08	.06	.03
15	Burt Hooton	.10	.08	.04
16	Omar Moreno	.08	.06	.03
17	John Denny	.08	.06	.03
18	Dale Berra	.08	.06	.03
19	*Ray Fontenot*(FC)	.10	.08	.04
20	Greg Luzinski	.12	.09	.05
21	Joe Altobelli	.08	.06	.03
22	Bryan Clark	.08	.06	.03
23	Keith Moreland	.10	.08	.04
24	John Martin	.08	.06	.03
25	Glenn Hubbard	.10	.08	.04
26	Bud Black	.10	.08	.04
27	Daryl Sconiers	.08	.06	.03
28	Frank Viola	.80	.60	.30
29	Danny Heep	.08	.06	.03
30	Wade Boggs	5.00	3.75	2.00
31	Andy McGaffigan	.08	.06	.03
32	Bobby Ramos	.08	.06	.03
33	Tom Burgmeier	.08	.06	.03
34	Eddie Milner	.08	.06	.03
35	Don Sutton	.30	.25	.12
36	Denny Walling	.08	.06	.03
37	Rangers Batting & Pitching Leaders (Buddy Bell, Rick Honeycutt)	.12	.09	.05
38	Luis DeLeon	.08	.06	.03
39	Garth Iorg	.08	.06	.03
40	Dusty Baker	.12	.09	.05
41	Tony Bernazard	.08	.06	.03
42	Johnny Grubb	.08	.06	.03
43	Ron Reed	.10	.08	.04
44	Jim Morrison	.08	.06	.03
45	Jerry Mumphrey	.08	.06	.03
46	Ray Smith	.08	.06	.03
47	Rudy Law	.08	.06	.03
48	Julio Franco(FC)	.60	.45	.25
49	John Stuper	.08	.06	.03
50	Chris Chambliss	.10	.08	.04
51	Jim Frey	.08	.06	.03
52	Paul Splittorff	.08	.06	.03
53	Juan Beniquez	.08	.06	.03
54	Jesse Orosco	.10	.08	.04
55	Dave Concepcion	.15	.11	.06
56	Gary Allenson	.08	.06	.03
57	Dan Schatzeder	.08	.06	.03
58	Max Venable	.08	.06	.03
59	Sammy Stewart	.08	.06	.03
60	Paul Molitor	1.75	1.25	.70
61	*Chris Codiroli*	.10	.08	.04
62	Dave Hostetler	.08	.06	.03
63	Ed Vande Berg	.08	.06	.03
64	Mike Scioscia	.08	.06	.03
65	Kirk Gibson	.40	.30	.15
66	Astros Batting & Pitching Leaders (Jose Cruz, Nolan Ryan)	.25	.20	.10
67	Gary Ward	.10	.08	.04
68	Luis Salazar	.08	.06	.03
69	Rod Scurry	.08	.06	.03
70	Gary Matthews	.12	.09	.05
71	Leo Hernandez	.08	.06	.03
72	Mike Squires	.08	.06	.03

		MT	NR MT	EX
73	Jody Davis	.10	.08	.04
74	Jerry Martin	.08	.06	.03
75	Bob Forsch	.10	.08	.04
76	Alfredo Griffin	.10	.08	.04
77	Brett Butler	.10	.08	.04
78	Mike Torrez	.10	.08	.04
79	Rob Wilfong	.08	.06	.03
80	Steve Rogers	.10	.08	.04
81	Billy Martin	.12	.09	.05
82	Doug Bird	.08	.06	.03
83	Richie Zisk	.10	.08	.04
84	Lenny Faedo	.08	.06	.03
85	Atlee Hammaker	.08	.06	.03
86	*John Shelby*(FC)	.10	.08	.04
87	Frank Pastore	.08	.06	.03
88	Rob Picciolo	.08	.06	.03
89	*Mike Smithson*(FC)	.15	.11	.06
90	Pedro Guerrero	.10	.08	.04
91	Dan Spillner	.08	.06	.03
92	Lloyd Moseby	.12	.09	.05
93	Bob Knepper	.10	.08	.04
94	Mario Ramirez	.08	.06	.03
95	Aurelio Lopez	.08	.06	.03
96	Royals Batting & Pitching Leaders (Larry Gura, Hal McRae)	.10	.08	.04
97	LaMarr Hoyt	.08	.06	.03
98	Steve Nicosia	.08	.06	.03
99	*Craig Lefferts*(FC)	.30	.25	.12
100	Reggie Jackson	1.50	1.25	.60
101	Porfirio Altamirano	.08	.06	.03
102	Ken Oberkfell	.08	.06	.03
103	Dwayne Murphy	.10	.08	.04
104	Ken Dayley	.08	.06	.03
105	Tony Armas	.12	.09	.05
106	Tim Stoddard	.08	.06	.03
107	Ned Yost	.08	.06	.03
108	Randy Moffitt	.08	.06	.03
109	Brad Wellman	.08	.06	.03
110	Ron Guidry	.10	.08	.04
111	Bill Virdon	.08	.06	.03
112	Tom Niedenfuer	.10	.08	.04
113	Kelly Paris	.08	.06	.03
114	Checklist 1-132	.08	.06	.03
115	Andre Thornton	.12	.09	.05
116	George Bjorkman	.08	.06	.03
117	Tom Veryzer	.08	.06	.03
118	Charlie Hough	.12	.09	.05
119	Johnny Wockenfuss	.08	.06	.03
120	Keith Hernandez	.15	.11	.06
121	*Pat Sheridan*(FC)	.10	.08	.04
122	Cecilio Guante(FC)	.10	.08	.04
123	Butch Wynegar	.08	.06	.03
124	Damaso Garcia	.08	.06	.03
125	Britt Burns	.08	.06	.03
126	Braves Batting & Pitching Leaders (Craig McMurtry, Dale Murphy)	.25	.20	.10
127	Mike Madden	.08	.06	.03
128	Rick Manning	.08	.06	.03
129	Bill Laskey	.08	.06	.03
130	Ozzie Smith	.70	.50	.30
131	Batting Leaders (Wade Boggs, Bill Madlock)	.50	.40	.20
132	Home Run Leaders (Jim Rice, Mike Schmidt)	.50	.40	.20
133	Runs Batted In Leaders (Cecil Cooper, Dale Murphy, Jim Rice)	.40	.30	.15
134	Stolen Base Leaders (Rickey Henderson, Tim Raines)	.30	.25	.12
135	Victory Leaders (John Denny, LaMarr Hoyt)	.10	.08	.04
136	Strikeout Leaders (Steve Carlton, Jack Morris)	.25	.20	.10
137	Earned Run Average Leaders (Atlee Hammaker, Rick Honeycutt)	.10	.08	.04
138	Leading Firemen (Al Holland, Dan Quisenberry)	.12	.09	.05
139	Bert Campaneris	.12	.09	.05
140	Storm Davis	.12	.09	.05
141	Pat Corrales	.08	.06	.03
142	Rich Gale	.08	.06	.03
143	Jose Morales	.08	.06	.03
144	Brian Harper	1.00	.70	.40
145	Gary Lavelle	.08	.06	.03
146	Ed Romero	.08	.06	.03
147	Dan Petry	.10	.08	.04
148	Joe Lefebvre	.08	.06	.03
149	Jon Matlack	.10	.08	.04
150	Dale Murphy	.70	.50	.30
151	Steve Trout	.08	.06	.03
152	Glenn Brummer	.08	.06	.03
153	Dick Tidrow	.08	.06	.03

		MT	NR MT	EX
154	Dave Henderson	.12	.09	.05
155	Frank White	.12	.09	.05
156	Athletics Batting & Pitching Leaders (Tim Conroy, Rickey Henderson)	.25	.20	.10
157	Gary Gaetti	.50	.40	.20
158	John Curtis	.08	.06	.03
159	Darryl Cias	.08	.06	.03
160	Mario Soto	.10	.08	.04
161	*Junior Ortiz*(FC)	.10	.08	.04
162	Bob Ojeda	.12	.09	.05
163	Lorenzo Gray	.08	.06	.03
164	Scott Sanderson	.08	.06	.03
165	Ken Singleton	.12	.09	.05
166	Jamie Nelson	.08	.06	.03
167	Marshall Edwards	.08	.06	.03
168	Juan Bonilla	.08	.06	.03
169	Larry Parrish	.12	.09	.05
170	Jerry Reuss	.12	.09	.05
171	Frank Robinson	.12	.09	.05
172	Frank DiPino	.08	.06	.03
173	*Marvell Wynne*(FC)	.08	.06	.03
174	Juan Berenguer	.08	.06	.03
175	Graig Nettles	.20	.15	.08
176	Lee Smith	.15	.11	.06
177	Jerry Hairston	.08	.06	.03
178	Bill Krueger	.08	.06	.03
179	Buck Martinez	.08	.06	.03
180	Manny Trillo	.10	.08	.04
181	Roy Thomas	.08	.06	.03
182	*Darryl Strawberry*	5.00	3.75	2.00
183	Al Williams	.08	.06	.03
184	Mike O'Berry	.08	.06	.03
185	Sixto Lezcano	.08	.06	.03
186	Cardinals Batting & Pitching Leaders (Lonnie Smith, John Stuper)	.10	.08	.04
187	Luis Aponte	.08	.06	.03
188	Bryan Little	.08	.06	.03
189	*Tim Conroy*(FC)	.12	.09	.05
190	Ben Oglivie	.10	.08	.04
191	Mike Boddicker	.12	.09	.05
192	*Nick Esasky*(FC)	.15	.11	.06
193	Darrell Brown	.08	.06	.03
194	Domingo Ramos	.08	.06	.03
195	Jack Morris	.30	.25	.12
196	Don Slaught(FC)	.12	.09	.05
197	Garry Hancock	.08	.06	.03
198	*Bill Doran*	.30	.25	.12
199	Willie Hernandez	.12	.09	.05
200	Andre Dawson	.60	.45	.25
201	Bruce Kison	.08	.06	.03
202	Bobby Cox	.08	.06	.03
203	Matt Keough	.08	.06	.03
204	*Bobby Meacham*(FC)	.15	.11	.06
205	Greg Minton	.08	.06	.03
206	*Andy Van Slyke*(FC)	3.00	2.25	1.25
207	Donnie Moore	.08	.06	.03
208	*Jose Oquendo*(FC)	.15	.11	.06
209	Manny Sarmiento	.08	.06	.03
210	Joe Morgan	.30	.25	.12
211	Rick Sweet	.08	.06	.03
212	Broderick Perkins	.08	.06	.03
213	Bruce Hurst	.15	.11	.06
214	Paul Householder	.08	.06	.03
215	Tippy Martinez	.08	.06	.03
216	White Sox Batting & Pitching Leaders (Richard Dotson, Carlton Fisk)	.15	.11	.06
217	Alan Ashby	.08	.06	.03
218	Rick Waits	.08	.06	.03
219	Joe Simpson	.08	.06	.03
220	Fernando Valenzuela	.20	.15	.08
221	Cliff Johnson	.08	.06	.03
222	Rick Honeycutt	.08	.06	.03
223	Wayne Krenchicki	.08	.06	.03
224	Sid Monge	.08	.06	.03
225	Lee Mazzilli	.10	.08	.04
226	Juan Eichelberger	.08	.06	.03
227	Steve Braun	.08	.06	.03
228	John Rabb	.08	.06	.03
229	Paul Owens	.08	.06	.03
230	Rickey Henderson	3.00	2.25	1.25
231	Gary Woods	.08	.06	.03
232	Tim Wallach	.15	.11	.06
233	Checklist 133-264	.08	.06	.03
234	Rafael Ramirez	.08	.06	.03
235	*Matt Young*	.15	.11	.06
236	Ellis Valentine	.08	.06	.03
237	John Castino	.08	.06	.03
238	Reid Nichols	.08	.06	.03
239	Jay Howell	.10	.08	.04
240	Eddie Murray	.80	.60	.30
241	Billy Almon	.08	.06	.03

		MT	NR MT	EX
242	Alex Trevino	.08	.06	.03
243	Pete Ladd	.08	.06	.03
244	Candy Maldonado(FC)	.15	.11	.06
245	Rick Sutcliffe	.15	.11	.06
246	Mets Batting & Pitching Leaders (Tom Seaver, Mookie Wilson)	.25	.20	.10
247	Onix Concepcion	.08	.06	.03
248	*Bill Dawley*(FC)	.10	.08	.04
249	Jay Johnstone	.10	.08	.04
250	Bill Madlock	.12	.09	.05
251	Tony Gwynn	3.00	2.25	1.25
252	Larry Christenson	.08	.06	.03
253	Jim Wohlford	.08	.06	.03
254	Shane Rawley	.12	.09	.05
255	Bruce Benedict	.08	.06	.03
256	Dave Geisel	.08	.06	.03
257	Julio Cruz	.08	.06	.03
258	Luis Sanchez	.08	.06	.03
259	Sparky Anderson	.12	.09	.05
260	Scott McGregor	.10	.08	.04
261	Bobby Brown	.08	.06	.03
262	*Tom Candiotti*(FC)	.25	.20	.10
263	Jack Fimple	.08	.06	.03
264	Doug Frobel	.08	.06	.03
265	*Donnie Hill*(FC)	.15	.11	.06
266	Steve Lubratich	.08	.06	.03
267	*Carmelo Martinez*(FC)	.25	.20	.10
268	Jack O'Connor	.08	.06	.03
269	Aurelio Rodriguez	.10	.08	.04
270	*Jeff Russell*(FC)	.20	.15	.08
271	Moose Haas	.08	.06	.03
272	Rick Dempsey	.10	.08	.04
273	Charlie Puleo	.08	.06	.03
274	Rick Monday	.10	.08	.04
275	Len Matuszek	.08	.06	.03
276	Angels Batting & Pitching Leaders (Rod Carew, Geoff Zahn)	.20	.15	.08
277	Eddie Whitson	.08	.06	.03
278	Jorge Bell	.50	.40	.20
279	Ivan DeJesus	.08	.06	.03
280	Floyd Bannister	.12	.09	.05
281	Larry Milbourne	.08	.06	.03
282	Jim Barr	.08	.06	.03
283	Larry Biittner	.08	.06	.03
284	Howard Bailey	.08	.06	.03
285	Darrell Porter	.10	.08	.04
286	Lary Sorensen	.08	.06	.03
287	Warren Cromartie	.08	.06	.03
288	Jim Beattie	.08	.06	.03
289	Randy S. Johnson	.08	.06	.03
290	Dave Dravecky	.10	.08	.04
291	Chuck Tanner	.08	.06	.03
292	Tony Scott	.08	.06	.03
293	Ed Lynch	.08	.06	.03
294	U.L. Washington	.08	.06	.03
295	Mike Flanagan	.12	.09	.05
296	Jeff Newman	.08	.06	.03
297	Bruce Berenyi	.08	.06	.03
298	Jim Gantner	.10	.08	.04
299	John Butcher	.08	.06	.03
300	Pete Rose	1.00	.70	.40
301	Frank LaCorte	.08	.06	.03
302	Barry Bonnell	.08	.06	.03
303	Marty Castillo	.08	.06	.03
304	Warren Brusstar	.08	.06	.03
305	Roy Smalley	.08	.06	.03
306	Dodgers Batting & Pitching Leaders (Pedro Guerrero, Bob Welch)	.15	.11	.06
307	Bobby Mitchell	.08	.06	.03
308	Ron Hassey	.08	.06	.03
309	*Tony Phillips*	1.00	.70	.40
310	Willie McGee	.20	.15	.08
311	Jerry Koosman	.12	.09	.05
312	Jorge Orta	.08	.06	.03
313	Mike Jorgensen	.08	.06	.03
314	Orlando Mercado	.08	.06	.03
315	Bob Grich	.12	.09	.05
316	Mark Bradley	.08	.06	.03
317	Greg Pryor	.08	.06	.03
318	Bill Gullickson	.08	.06	.03
319	Al Bumbry	.10	.08	.04
320	Bob Stanley	.08	.06	.03
321	Harvey Kuenn	.10	.08	.04
322	Ken Schrom	.08	.06	.03
323	Alan Knicely	.08	.06	.03
324	*Alejandro Pena*	.15	.11	.06
325	Darrell Evans	.15	.11	.06
326	Bob Kearney	.08	.06	.03
327	Ruppert Jones	.08	.06	.03
328	Vern Ruhle	.08	.06	.03
329	Pat Tabler(FC)	.12	.09	.05
330	John Candelaria	.12	.09	.05
331	Bucky Dent	.12	.09	.05
332	*Kevin Gross*(FC)	.15	.11	.06
333	Larry Herndon	.10	.08	.04
334	Chuck Rainey	.08	.06	.03
335	Don Baylor	.15	.11	.06
336	Mariners Batting & Pitching Leaders (Pat Putnam, Matt Young)	.10	.08	.04
337	Kevin Hagen	.08	.06	.03
338	Mike Warren	.08	.06	.03
339	Roy Lee Jackson	.08	.06	.03
340	Hal McRae	.12	.09	.05
341	Dave Tobik	.08	.06	.03
342	Tim Foli	.08	.06	.03
343	Mark Davis	.08	.06	.03
344	Rick Miller	.08	.06	.03
345	Kent Hrbek	.40	.30	.15
346	Kurt Bevacqua	.08	.06	.03
347	Allan Ramirez	.08	.06	.03
348	Toby Harrah	.10	.08	.04
349	Bob L. Gibson	.08	.06	.03
350	George Foster	.10	.08	.04
351	Russ Nixon	.08	.06	.03
352	Dave Stewart	.35	.25	.14
353	Jim Anderson	.08	.06	.03
354	Jeff Burroughs	.10	.08	.04
355	Jason Thompson	.08	.06	.03
356	Glenn Abbott	.08	.06	.03
357	Ron Cey	.12	.09	.05
358	Bob Dernier	.08	.06	.03
359	*Jim Acker*(FC)	.12	.09	.05
360	Willie Randolph	.12	.09	.05
361	Dave Smith	.10	.08	.04
362	David Green	.08	.06	.03
363	Tim Laudner	.08	.06	.03
364	Scott Fletcher(FC)	.15	.11	.06
365	Steve Bedrosian	.12	.09	.05
366	Padres Batting & Pitching Leaders (Dave Dravecky, Terry Kennedy)	.12	.09	.05
367	Jamie Easterly	.08	.06	.03
368	Hubie Brooks	.15	.11	.06
369	Steve McCatty	.08	.06	.03
370	Tim Raines	.50	.40	.20
371	Dave Gumpert	.08	.06	.03
372	Gary Roenicke	.08	.06	.03
373	Bill Scherrer	.08	.06	.03
374	Don Money	.08	.06	.03
375	Dennis Leonard	.10	.08	.04
376	*Dave Anderson*(FC)	.15	.11	.06
377	Danny Darwin	.08	.06	.03
378	Bob Brenly	.08	.06	.03
379	Checklist 265-396	.08	.06	.03
380	Steve Garvey	.50	.40	.20
381	Ralph Houk	.10	.08	.04
382	Chris Nyman	.08	.06	.03
383	Terry Puhl	.08	.06	.03
384	*Lee Tunnell*	.10	.08	.04
385	Tony Perez	.20	.15	.08
386	George Hendrick (All-Star)	.10	.08	.04
387	Johnny Ray (All-Star)	.12	.09	.05
388	Mike Schmidt (All-Star)	.50	.40	.20
389	Ozzie Smith (All-Star)	.15	.11	.06
390	Tim Raines (All-Star)	.25	.20	.10
391	Dale Murphy (All-Star)	.40	.30	.15
392	Andre Dawson (All-Star)	.20	.15	.08
393	Gary Carter (All-Star)	.30	.25	.12
394	Steve Rogers (All-Star)	.10	.08	.04
395	Steve Carlton (All-Star)	.25	.20	.10
396	Jesse Orosco (All-Star)	.10	.08	.04
397	Eddie Murray (All-Star)	.35	.25	.14
398	Lou Whitaker (All-Star)	.20	.15	.08
399	George Brett (All-Star)	.50	.40	.20
400	Cal Ripken, Jr. (All-Star)	1.00	.70	.40
401	Jim Rice (All-Star)	.30	.25	.12
402	Dave Winfield (All-Star)	.30	.25	.12
403	Lloyd Moseby (All-Star)	.12	.09	.05
404	Ted Simmons (All-Star)	.15	.11	.06
405	LaMarr Hoyt (All-Star)	.10	.08	.04
406	Ron Guidry (All-Star)	.20	.15	.08
407	Dan Quisenberry (All-Star)	.12	.09	.05
408	Lou Piniella	.15	.11	.06
409	*Juan Agosto*(FC)	.15	.11	.06
410	Claudell Washington	.10	.08	.04
411	Houston Jimenez	.08	.06	.03
412	Doug Rader	.08	.06	.03
413	*Spike Owen*(FC)	.20	.15	.08
414	Mitchell Page	.08	.06	.03
415	Tommy John	.25	.20	.10
416	Dane Iorg	.08	.06	.03
417	Mike Armstrong	.08	.06	.03
418	Ron Hodges	.08	.06	.03

		MT	NR MT	EX
419	John Henry Johnson	.08	.06	.03
420	Cecil Cooper	.15	.11	.06
421	Charlie Lea	.08	.06	.03
422	Jose Cruz	.12	.09	.05
423	Mike Morgan	.08	.06	.03
424	Dann Bilardello	.08	.06	.03
425	Steve Howe	.10	.08	.04
426	Orioles Batting & Pitching Leaders (Mike Boddicker, Cal Ripken, Jr.)	.25	.20	.10
427	Rick Leach	.08	.06	.03
428	Fred Breining	.08	.06	.03
429	*Randy Bush*	.15	.11	.06
430	Rusty Staub	.12	.09	.05
431	Chris Bando	.08	.06	.03
432	*Charlie Hudson*(FC)	.10	.08	.04
433	Rich Hebner	.08	.06	.03
434	Harold Baines	.25	.20	.10
435	Neil Allen	.08	.06	.03
436	Rick Peters	.08	.06	.03
437	Mike Proly	.08	.06	.03
438	Biff Pocoroba	.08	.06	.03
439	Bob Stoddard	.08	.06	.03
440	Steve Kemp	.10	.08	.04
441	Bob Lillis	.08	.06	.03
442	Byron McLaughlin	.08	.06	.03
443	Benny Ayala	.08	.06	.03
444	Steve Renko	.08	.06	.03
445	Jerry Remy	.08	.06	.03
446	Luis Pujols	.08	.06	.03
447	Tom Brunansky	.10	.08	.04
448	Ben Hayes	.08	.06	.03
449	Joe Pettini	.08	.06	.03
450	Gary Carter	.40	.30	.15
451	Bob Jones	.08	.06	.03
452	Chuck Porter	.08	.06	.03
453	Willie Upshaw	.10	.08	.04
454	Joe Beckwith	.08	.06	.03
455	Terry Kennedy	.10	.08	.04
456	Cubs Batting & Pitching Leaders (Fergie Jenkins, Keith Moreland)	.15	.11	.06
457	Dave Rozema	.08	.06	.03
458	Kiko Garcia	.08	.06	.03
459	Kevin Hickey	.08	.06	.03
460	Dave Winfield	2.00	1.50	.80
461	Jim Maler	.08	.06	.03
462	Lee Lacy	.08	.06	.03
463	Dave Engle	.08	.06	.03
464	Jeff Jones	.08	.06	.03
465	Mookie Wilson	.12	.09	.05
466	Gene Garber	.08	.06	.03
467	Mike Ramsey	.08	.06	.03
468	Geoff Zahn	.08	.06	.03
469	Tom O'Malley	.08	.06	.03
470	Nolan Ryan	7.00	5.25	2.75
471	Dick Howser	.08	.06	.03
472	Mike Brown	.08	.06	.03
473	Jim Dwyer	.08	.06	.03
474	Greg Bargar	.08	.06	.03
475	*Gary Redus*	.15	.11	.06
476	Tom Tellmann	.08	.06	.03
477	Rafael Landestoy	.08	.06	.03
478	Alan Bannister	.08	.06	.03
479	Frank Tanana	.12	.09	.05
480	Ron Kittle(FC)	.20	.15	.08
481	*Mark Thurmond*(FC)	.10	.08	.04
482	Enos Cabell	.08	.06	.03
483	Fergie Jenkins	.20	.15	.08
484	Ozzie Virgil	.08	.06	.03
485	Rick Rhoden	.12	.09	.05
486	Yankees Batting & Pitching Leaders (Don Baylor, Ron Guidry)	.15	.11	.06
487	Ricky Adams	.08	.06	.03
488	Jesse Barfield	.10	.08	.04
489	Dave Von Ohlen	.08	.06	.03
490	Cal Ripken, Jr.	7.00	5.25	2.75
491	Bobby Castillo	.08	.06	.03
492	Tucker Ashford	.08	.06	.03
493	Mike Norris	.08	.06	.03
494	Chili Davis	.12	.09	.05
495	Rollie Fingers	.25	.20	.10
496	Terry Francona	.08	.06	.03
497	Bud Anderson	.08	.06	.03
498	Rich Gedman	.10	.08	.04
499	Mike Witt	.15	.11	.06
500	George Brett	2.00	1.50	.80
501	Steve Henderson	.08	.06	.03
502	Joe Torre	.08	.06	.03
503	Elias Sosa	.08	.06	.03
504	Mickey Rivers	.10	.08	.04
505	Pete Vuckovich	.10	.08	.04
506	Ernie Whitt	.10	.08	.04

		MT	NR MT	EX
507	Mike LaCoss	.08	.06	.03
508	Mel Hall	.10	.08	.04
509	Brad Havens	.08	.06	.03
510	Alan Trammell	.40	.30	.15
511	Marty Bystrom	.08	.06	.03
512	Oscar Gamble	.10	.08	.04
513	Dave Beard	.08	.06	.03
514	Floyd Rayford	.08	.06	.03
515	Gorman Thomas	.10	.08	.04
516	Expos Batting & Pitching Leaders (Charlie Lea, Al Oliver)	.12	.09	.05
517	John Moses	.12	.09	.05
518	*Greg Walker*	.10	.08	.04
519	Ron Davis	.08	.06	.03
520	Bob Boone	.10	.08	.04
521	Pete Falcone	.08	.06	.03
522	Dave Bergman	.08	.06	.03
523	Glenn Hoffman	.08	.06	.03
524	Carlos Diaz	.08	.06	.03
525	Willie Wilson	.15	.11	.06
526	Ron Oester	.08	.06	.03
527	Checklist 397-528	.08	.06	.03
528	Mark Brouhard	.08	.06	.03
529	*Keith Atherton*(FC)	.20	.15	.08
530	Dan Ford	.08	.06	.03
531	Steve Boros	.08	.06	.03
532	Eric Show	.12	.09	.05
533	Ken Landreaux	.08	.06	.03
534	*Pete O'Brien*	.35	.25	.14
535	Bo Diaz	.10	.08	.04
536	Doug Bair	.08	.06	.03
537	Johnny Ray	.12	.09	.05
538	Kevin Bass	.15	.11	.06
539	George Frazier	.08	.06	.03
540	George Hendrick	.10	.08	.04
541	Dennis Lamp	.08	.06	.03
542	Duane Kuiper	.08	.06	.03
543	*Craig McMurtry*	.12	.09	.05
544	Cesar Geronimo	.08	.06	.03
545	Bill Buckner	.15	.11	.06
546	Indians Batting & Pitching Leaders (Mike Hargrove, Lary Sorensen)	.10	.08	.04
547	Mike Moore	.10	.08	.04
548	Ron Jackson	.08	.06	.03
549	*Walt Terrell*	.20	.15	.08
550	Jim Rice	.30	.25	.12
551	Scott Ullger	.08	.06	.03
552	Ray Burris	.08	.06	.03
553	Joe Nolan	.08	.06	.03
554	Ted Power(FC)	.12	.09	.05
555	Greg Brock	.15	.11	.06
556	Joey McLaughlin	.08	.06	.03
557	Wayne Tolleson	.10	.08	.04
558	Mike Davis	.10	.08	.04
559	Mike Scott	.20	.15	.08
560	Carlton Fisk	.70	.50	.30
561	Whitey Herzog	.10	.08	.04
562	Manny Castillo	.08	.06	.03
563	Glenn Wilson	.10	.08	.04
564	Al Holland	.08	.06	.03
565	Leon Durham	.10	.08	.04
566	Jim Bibby	.08	.06	.03
567	Mike Heath	.08	.06	.03
568	Pete Filson	.08	.06	.03
569	Bake McBride	.08	.06	.03
570	Dan Quisenberry	.12	.09	.05
571	Bruce Bochy	.08	.06	.03
572	Jerry Royster	.08	.06	.03
573	Dave Kingman	.15	.11	.06
574	Brian Downing	.12	.09	.05
575	Jim Clancy	.10	.08	.04
576	Giants Batting & Pitching Leaders (Atlee Hammaker, Jeff Leonard)	.10	.08	.04
577	Mark Clear	.08	.06	.03
578	Lenn Sakata	.08	.06	.03
579	Bob James	.08	.06	.03
580	Lonnie Smith	.10	.08	.04
581	*Jose DeLeon*(FC)	.15	.11	.06
582	Bob McClure	.08	.06	.03
583	Derrel Thomas	.08	.06	.03
584	Dave Schmidt	.08	.06	.03
585	Dan Driessen	.10	.08	.04
586	Joe Niekro	.15	.11	.06
587	Von Hayes	.15	.11	.06
588	Milt Wilcox	.08	.06	.03
589	Mike Easler	.10	.08	.04
590	Dave Stieb	.15	.11	.06
591	Tony LaRussa	.10	.08	.04
592	Andre Robertson	.08	.06	.03
593	Jeff Lahti	.08	.06	.03
594	Gene Richards	.08	.06	.03

No.	Card	MT	NR MT	EX
595	Jeff Reardon	.60	.45	.25
596	Ryne Sandberg	8.00	6.00	3.25
597	Rick Camp	.08	.06	.03
598	Rusty Kuntz	.08	.06	.03
599	*Doug Sisk*	.10	.08	.04
600	Rod Carew	.50	.40	.20
601	John Tudor	.12	.09	.05
602	John Wathan	.10	.08	.04
603	Renie Martin	.08	.06	.03
604	John Lowenstein	.08	.06	.03
605	Mike Caldwell	.08	.06	.03
606	Blue Jays Batting & Pitching Leaders (Lloyd Moseby, Dave Stieb)	.08	.06	.03
607	Tom Hume	.08	.06	.03
608	Bobby Johnson	.08	.06	.03
609	Dan Meyer	.08	.06	.03
610	Steve Sax	.10	.08	.04
611	Chet Lemon	.10	.08	.04
612	Harry Spilman	.08	.06	.03
613	Greg Gross	.08	.06	.03
614	Len Barker	.10	.08	.04
615	Garry Templeton	.12	.09	.05
616	Don Robinson	.10	.08	.04
617	Rick Cerone	.08	.06	.03
618	Dickie Noles	.08	.06	.03
619	Jerry Dybzinski	.08	.06	.03
620	Al Oliver	.20	.15	.08
621	Frank Howard	.10	.08	.04
622	Al Cowens	.08	.06	.03
623	Ron Washington	.08	.06	.03
624	Terry Harper	.08	.06	.03
625	Larry Gura	.10	.08	.04
626	Bob Clark	.08	.06	.03
627	Dave LaPoint	.10	.08	.04
628	Ed Jurak	.08	.06	.03
629	Rick Langford	.08	.06	.03
630	Ted Simmons	.15	.11	.06
631	Denny Martinez	.10	.08	.04
632	Tom Foley	.08	.06	.03
633	Mike Krukow	.10	.08	.04
634	Mike Marshall	.15	.11	.06
635	Dave Righetti	.10	.08	.04
636	Pat Putnam	.08	.06	.03
637	Phillies Batting & Pitching Leaders (John Denny, Gary Matthews)	.10	.08	.04
638	George Vukovich	.08	.06	.03
639	Rick Lysander	.08	.06	.03
640	Lance Parrish	.10	.08	.04
641	Mike Richardt	.08	.06	.03
642	Tom Underwood	.08	.06	.03
643	Mike Brown	.08	.06	.03
644	Tim Lollar	.08	.06	.03
645	Tony Pena	.12	.09	.05
646	Checklist 529-660	.08	.06	.03
647	Ron Roenicke	.08	.06	.03
648	Len Whitehouse	.08	.06	.03
649	Tom Herr	.12	.09	.05
650	Phil Niekro	.30	.25	.12
651	John McNamara	.08	.06	.03
652	Rudy May	.08	.06	.03
653	Dave Stapleton	.08	.06	.03
654	Bob Bailor	.08	.06	.03
655	Amos Otis	.10	.08	.04
656	Bryn Smith	.08	.06	.03
657	Thad Bosley	.08	.06	.03
658	Jerry Augustine	.08	.06	.03
659	Duane Walker	.08	.06	.03
660	Ray Knight	.12	.09	.05
661	Steve Yeager	.08	.06	.03
662	Tom Brennan	.08	.06	.03
663	Johnnie LeMaster	.08	.06	.03
664	Dave Stegman	.08	.06	.03
665	Buddy Bell	.08	.06	.03
666	Tigers Batting & Pitching Leaders (Jack Morris, Lou Whitaker)	.15	.11	.06
667	Vance Law	.10	.08	.04
668	Larry McWilliams	.08	.06	.03
669	Dave Lopes	.10	.08	.04
670	Rich Gossage	.10	.08	.04
671	Jamie Quirk	.08	.06	.03
672	Ricky Nelson	.08	.06	.03
673	Mike Walters	.08	.06	.03
674	Tim Flannery	.08	.06	.03
675	Pascual Perez	.10	.08	.04
676	Brian Giles	.08	.06	.03
677	Doyle Alexander	.12	.09	.05
678	Chris Speier	.08	.06	.03
679	Art Howe	.08	.06	.03
680	Fred Lynn	.25	.20	.10
681	Tom Lasorda	.12	.09	.05
682	Dan Morogiello	.08	.06	.03
683	*Marty Barrett*(FC)	.15	.11	.06
684	Bob Shirley	.08	.06	.03
685	Willie Aikens	.08	.06	.03
686	Joe Price	.08	.06	.03
687	Roy Howell	.08	.06	.03
688	George Wright	.08	.06	.03
689	Mike Fischlin	.08	.06	.03
690	Jack Clark	.10	.08	.04
691	*Steve Lake*(FC)	.10	.08	.04
692	Dickie Thon	.10	.08	.04
693	Alan Wiggins	.08	.06	.03
694	Mike Stanton	.08	.06	.03
695	Lou Whitaker	.40	.30	.15
696	Pirates Batting & Pitching Leaders (Bill Madlock, Rick Rhoden)	.15	.11	.06
697	Dale Murray	.08	.06	.03
698	Marc Hill	.08	.06	.03
699	Dave Rucker	.08	.06	.03
700	Mike Schmidt	2.50	2.00	1.00
701	NL Active Career Batting Leaders (Bill Madlock, Dave Parker, Pete Rose)	.35	.25	.14
702	NL Active Career Hit Leaders (Tony Perez, Pete Rose, Rusty Staub)	.35	.25	.14
703	NL Active Career Home Run Leaders (Dave Kingman, Tony Perez, Mike Schmidt)	.30	.25	.12
704	NL Active Career RBI Leaders (Al Oliver, Tony Perez, Rusty Staub)	.15	.11	.06
705	NL Active Career Stolen Bases Leaders (Larry Bowa, Cesar Cedeno, Joe Morgan)	.12	.09	.05
706	NL Active Career Victory Leaders (Steve Carlton, Fergie Jenkins, Tom Seaver)	.30	.25	.12
707	NL Active Career Strikeout Leaders (Steve Carlton, Nolan Ryan, Tom Seaver)	.35	.25	.14
708	NL Active Career ERA Leaders (Steve Carlton, Steve Rogers, Tom Seaver)	.25	.20	.10
709	NL Active Career Save Leaders (Gene Garber, Tug McGraw, Bruce Sutter)	.12	.09	.05
710	AL Active Career Batting Leaders (George Brett, Rod Carew, Cecil Cooper)	.30	.25	.12
711	AL Active Career Hit Leaders (Bert Campaneris, Rod Carew, Reggie Jackson)	.30	.25	.12
712	AL Active Career Home Run Leaders (Reggie Jackson, Greg Luzinski, Graig Nettles)	.20	.15	.08
713	AL Active Career RBI Leaders (Reggie Jackson, Graig Nettles, Ted Simmons)	.20	.15	.08
714	AL Active Career Stolen Bases Leaders (Bert Campaneris, Dave Lopes, Omar Moreno)	.10	.08	.04
715	AL Active Career Victory Leaders (Tommy John, Jim Palmer, Don Sutton)	.25	.20	.10
716	AL Active Strikeout Leaders (Bert Blyleven, Jerry Koosman, Don Sutton)	.15	.11	.06
717	AL Active Career ERA Leaders (Rollie Fingers, Ron Guidry, Jim Palmer)	.15	.11	.06
718	AL Active Career Save Leaders (Rollie Fingers, Rich Gossage, Dan Quisenberry)	.15	.11	.06
719	Andy Hassler	.08	.06	.03
720	Dwight Evans	.20	.15	.08
721	Del Crandall	.08	.06	.03
722	Bob Welch	.15	.11	.06
723	Rich Dauer	.08	.06	.03
724	Eric Rasmussen	.08	.06	.03
725	Cesar Cedeno	.12	.09	.05
726	Brewers Batting & Pitching Leaders (Moose Haas, Ted Simmons)	.12	.09	.05
727	Joel Youngblood	.08	.06	.03
728	Tug McGraw	.12	.09	.05
729	Gene Tenace	.10	.08	.04
730	Bruce Sutter	.20	.15	.08
731	Lynn Jones	.08	.06	.03
732	Terry Crowley	.08	.06	.03
733	Dave Collins	.10	.08	.04
734	Odell Jones	.08	.06	.03
735	Rick Burleson	.10	.08	.04
736	Dick Ruthven	.08	.06	.03
737	Jim Essian	.08	.06	.03
738	*Bill Schroeder*(FC)	.20	.15	.08
739	Bob Watson	.10	.08	.04
740	Tom Seaver	1.75	1.25	.70
741	Wayne Gross	.08	.06	.03
742	Dick Williams	.08	.06	.03
743	Don Hood	.08	.06	.03
744	Jamie Allen	.08	.06	.03
745	Dennis Eckersley	.15	.11	.06
746	Mickey Hatcher	.10	.08	.04

		MT	NR MT	EX
747	Pat Zachry	.08	.06	.03
748	Jeff Leonard	.12	.09	.05
749	Doug Flynn	.08	.06	.03
750	Jim Palmer	1.00	.70	.40
751	Charlie Moore	.08	.06	.03
752	Phil Garner	.10	.08	.04
753	Doug Gwosdz	.08	.06	.03
754	Kent Tekulve	.10	.08	.04
755	Garry Maddox	.10	.08	.04
756	Reds Batting & Pitching Leaders (Ron Oester, Mario Soto)	.10	.08	.04
757	Larry Bowa	.15	.11	.06
758	Bill Stein	.08	.06	.03
759	Richard Dotson	.12	.09	.05
760	Bob Horner	.15	.11	.06
761	John Montefusco	.08	.06	.03
762	Rance Mulliniks	.08	.06	.03
763	Craig Swan	.08	.06	.03
764	Mike Hargrove	.08	.06	.03
765	Ken Forsch	.08	.06	.03
766	Mike Vail	.08	.06	.03
767	Carney Lansford	.12	.09	.05
768	Champ Summers	.08	.06	.03
769	Bill Caudill	.08	.06	.03
770	Ken Griffey	.12	.09	.05
771	Billy Gardner	.08	.06	.03
772	Jim Slaton	.08	.06	.03
773	Todd Cruz	.08	.06	.03
774	Tom Gorman	.08	.06	.03
775	Dave Parker	.30	.25	.12
776	Craig Reynolds	.08	.06	.03
777	Tom Paciorek	.08	.06	.03
778	*Andy Hawkins*(FC)	.25	.20	.10
779	Jim Sundberg	.10	.08	.04
780	Steve Carlton	1.00	.70	.40
781	Checklist 661-792	.08	.06	.03
782	Steve Balboni	.10	.08	.04
783	Luis Leal	.08	.06	.03
784	Leon Roberts	.08	.06	.03
785	Joaquin Andujar	.10	.08	.04
786	Red Sox Batting & Pitching Leaders (Wade Boggs, Bob Ojeda)	.40	.30	.15
787	Bill Campbell	.08	.06	.03
788	Milt May	.08	.06	.03
789	Bert Blyleven	.20	.15	.08
790	Doug DeCinces	.12	.09	.05
791	Terry Forster	.10	.08	.04
792	Bill Russell	.10	.08	.04

1984 Topps All-Star Glossy Set Of 22

These 2-1/2" by 3-1/2" cards were a result of the success of Topps' efforts the previous year with glossy cards on a mail-in basis. A 22-card set, the cards are divided evenly between the two leagues. Each All-Star Game starter for both leagues, the managers and the honorary team captains have an All-Star Glossy card. The cards feature a large color photo on the front with an All-Star banner across the top and the league emblem in the lower left. The player's name and position appear below the photo. Backs have a name, team, position and card number along with the phrase "1983 All-Star Game Commemorative Set". The '84 Glossy All-Stars were distributed one card per pack in Topps rack packs that year.

		MT	NR MT	EX
Complete Set:		6.00	4.50	2.50
Common Player:		.20	.15	.08
1	Harvey Kuenn	.20	.15	.08
2	Rod Carew	.50	.40	.20
3	Manny Trillo	.20	.15	.08
4	George Brett	.80	.60	.30
5	Robin Yount	.40	.30	.15
6	Jim Rice	.50	.40	.20
7	Fred Lynn	.25	.20	.10
8	Dave Winfield	.50	.40	.20
9	Ted Simmons	.25	.20	.10
10	Dave Stieb	.25	.20	.10
11	Carl Yastrzemski	.80	.60	.30
12	Whitey Herzog	.20	.15	.08
13	Al Oliver	.25	.20	.10
14	Steve Sax	.30	.25	.12
15	Mike Schmidt	.80	.60	.30
16	Ozzie Smith	.30	.25	.12
17	Tim Raines	.50	.40	.20
18	Andre Dawson	.35	.25	.14
19	Dale Murphy	.80	.60	.30
20	Gary Carter	.50	.40	.20
21	Mario Soto	.20	.15	.08
22	Johnny Bench	.60	.45	.25

1984 Topps All-Star Glossy Set Of 40

For the second straight year in 1984, Topps produced a 40-card All-Star "Collector's Edition" set as a "consolation prize" for its sweepstakes game. By collecting game cards and sending them in with a bit of cash, the collector could receive one of eight different five-card series. As the previous year, the 2-1/2" by 3-1/2" cards feature a nearly full-frame color photo on its glossy finish front. Backs are printed in red and blue.

		MT	NR MT	EX
Complete Set:		16.00	12.00	6.50
Common Player:		.15	.11	.06
1	Pete Rose	1.25	.90	.50
2	Lance Parrish	.30	.25	.12
3	Steve Rogers	.15	.11	.06
4	Eddie Murray	.60	.45	.25
5	Johnny Ray	.20	.15	.08
6	Rickey Henderson	.70	.50	.30
7	Atlee Hammaker	.15	.11	.06
8	Wade Boggs	3.00	2.25	1.25
9	Gary Carter	.50	.40	.20
10	Jack Morris	.30	.25	.12
11	Darrell Evans	.20	.15	.08
12	George Brett	1.00	.70	.40
13	Bob Horner	.20	.15	.08
14	Ron Guidry	.30	.25	.12
15	Nolan Ryan	.50	.40	.20
16	Dave Winfield	.60	.45	.25
17	Ozzie Smith	.25	.20	.10
18	Ted Simmons	.20	.15	.08
19	Bill Madlock	.20	.15	.08
20	Tony Armas	.15	.11	.06

		MT	NR MT	EX
21	Al Oliver	.20	.15	.08
22	Jim Rice	.50	.40	.20
23	George Hendrick	.15	.11	.06
24	Dave Stieb	.20	.15	.08
25	Pedro Guerrero	.25	.20	.10
26	Rod Carew	.60	.45	.25
27	Steve Carlton	.50	.40	.20
28	Dave Righetti	.30	.25	.12
29	Darryl Strawberry	3.00	2.25	1.25
30	Lou Whitaker	.30	.25	.12
31	Dale Murphy	1.00	.70	.40
32	LaMarr Hoyt	.15	.11	.06
33	Jesse Orosco	.15	.11	.06
34	Cecil Cooper	.20	.15	.08
35	Andre Dawson	.35	.25	.14
36	Robin Yount	.40	.30	.15
37	Tim Raines	.50	.40	.20
38	Dan Quisenberry	.15	.11	.06
39	Mike Schmidt	1.00	.70	.40
40	Carlton Fisk	.30	.25	.12

1984 Topps Traded

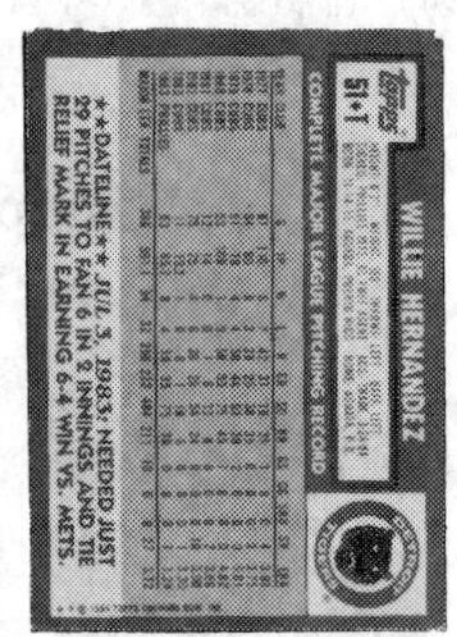

The popular Topps Traded set returned for its fourth year in 1984 with another 132-card set. The 2-1/2" by 3-1/2" cards have an identical design to the regular Topps cards except that the back cardboard is white and the card numbers carry a "T" suffix. As before, the set was sold only through hobby dealers. Also as before, players who changed teams, new managers and promising rookies are included in the set. The presence of several promising young rookies in especially high demand from investors and speculators had made this one of the most expensive Topps issues of recent years. A glossy-finish "Tiffany" version of the set was also issued, valued at four to five times the price of the normal Traded cards.

		MT	NR MT	EX
Complete Set (132):		60.00	45.00	24.00
Common Player:		.25	.20	.10
1T	Willie Aikens	.25	.20	.10
2T	Luis Aponte	.25	.20	.10
3T	Mike Armstrong	.25	.20	.10
4T	Bob Bailor	.25	.20	.10
5T	Dusty Baker	.50	.40	.20
6T	Steve Balboni	.25	.20	.10
7T	Alan Bannister	.25	.20	.10
8T	Dave Beard	.25	.20	.10
9T	Joe Beckwith	.25	.20	.10
10T	Bruce Berenyi	.25	.20	.10
11T	Dave Bergman	.25	.20	.10
12T	Tony Bernazard	.25	.20	.10
13T	Yogi Berra	.60	.45	.25
14T	Barry Bonnell	.25	.20	.10
15T	Phil Bradley(FC)	.25	.20	.10
16T	Fred Breining	.25	.20	.10
17T	Bill Buckner	.25	.20	.10
18T	Ray Burris	.25	.20	.10
19T	John Butcher	.25	.20	.10
20T	Brett Butler	.25	.20	.10
21T	Enos Cabell	.25	.20	.10
22T	Bill Campbell	.25	.20	.10
23T	Bill Caudill	.25	.20	.10
24T	Bob Clark	.25	.20	.10
25T	Bryan Clark	.25	.20	.10
26T	Jaime Cocanower	.25	.20	.10
27T	Ron Darling(FC)	1.00	.70	.40
28T	Alvin Davis(FC)	.25	.20	.10
29T	Ken Dayley	.25	.20	.10
30T	Jeff Dedmon(FC)	.25	.20	.10
31T	Bob Dernier	.25	.20	.10
32T	Carlos Diaz	.25	.20	.10
33T	Mike Easler	.25	.20	.10
34T	Dennis Eckersley	5.00	3.75	2.00
35T	Jim Essian	.25	.20	.10
36T	Darrell Evans	.25	.20	.10
37T	Mike Fitzgerald(FC)	.25	.20	.10
38T	Tim Foli	.25	.20	.10
39T	George Frazier	.25	.20	.10
40T	Rich Gale	.25	.20	.10
41T	Barbaro Garbey	.25	.20	.10
42T	Dwight Gooden(FC)	22.00	16.50	8.75
43T	Rich Gossage	.40	.30	.15
44T	Wayne Gross	.25	.20	.10
45T	Mark Gubicza(FC)	.90	.70	.35
46T	Jackie Gutierrez	.25	.20	.10
47T	Mel Hall	.30	.25	.12
48T	Toby Harrah	.25	.20	.10
49T	Ron Hassey	.25	.20	.10
50T	Rich Hebner	.25	.20	.10
51T	Willie Hernandez	.25	.20	.10
52T	Ricky Horton(FC)	.25	.20	.10
53T	Art Howe	.25	.20	.10
54T	Dane Iorg	.25	.20	.10
55T	Brook Jacoby(FC)	.25	.20	.10
56T	Mike Jeffcoat(FC)	.25	.20	.10
57T	Dave Johnson	.25	.20	.10
58T	Lynn Jones	.25	.20	.10
59T	Ruppert Jones	.25	.20	.10
60T	Mike Jorgensen	.25	.20	.10
61T	Bob Kearney	.25	.20	.10
62T	Jimmy Key(FC)	8.00	6.00	3.25
63T	Dave Kingman	.25	.20	.10
64T	Jerry Koosman	.25	.20	.10
65T	Wayne Krenchicki	.25	.20	.10
66T	Rusty Kuntz	.25	.20	.10
67T	Rene Lachemann	.25	.20	.10
68T	Frank LaCorte	.25	.20	.10
69T	Dennis Lamp	.25	.20	.10
70T	Mark Langston(FC)	12.00	9.00	4.75
71T	Rick Leach	.25	.20	.10
72T	Craig Lefferts	.25	.20	.10
73T	Gary Lucas	.25	.20	.10
74T	Jerry Martin	.25	.20	.10
75T	Carmelo Martinez	.25	.20	.10
76T	Mike Mason(FC)	.25	.20	.10
77T	Gary Matthews	.25	.20	.10
78T	Andy McGaffigan	.25	.20	.10
79T	Larry Milbourne	.25	.20	.10
80T	Sid Monge	.25	.20	.10
81T	Jackie Moore	.25	.20	.10
82T	Joe Morgan	3.00	2.25	1.25
83T	Graig Nettles	.25	.20	.10
84T	Phil Niekro	2.00	1.50	.80
85T	Ken Oberkfell	.25	.20	.10
86T	Mike O'Berry	.25	.20	.10
87T	Al Oliver	.30	.25	.12
88T	Jorge Orta	.25	.20	.10
89T	Amos Otis	.25	.20	.10
90T	Dave Parker	3.00	2.25	1.25
91T	Tony Perez	3.00	2.25	1.25
92T	Gerald Perry(FC)	1.50	1.25	.60
93T	Gary Pettis(FC)	.25	.20	.10
94T	Rob Picciolo	.25	.20	.10
95T	Vern Rapp	.25	.20	.10
96T	Floyd Rayford	.25	.20	.10
97T	Randy Ready(FC)	.25	.20	.10
98T	Ron Reed	.25	.20	.10
99T	Gene Richards	.25	.20	.10
100T	Jose Rijo(FC)	9.00	6.75	3.50
101T	Jeff Robinson(FC)	.25	.20	.10
102T	Ron Romanick(FC)	.25	.20	.10
103T	Pete Rose	8.00	6.00	3.25
104T	Bret Saberhagen(FC)	9.00	6.75	3.50
105T	Juan Samuel(FC)	.50	.40	.20
106T	Scott Sanderson	.25	.20	.10
107T	Dick Schofield(FC)	.25	.20	.10
108T	Tom Seaver	8.00	6.00	3.25
109T	Jim Slaton	.25	.20	.10
110T	Mike Smithson	.25	.20	.10
111T	Lary Sorensen	.25	.20	.10
112T	Tim Stoddard	.25	.20	.10
113T	Champ Summers	.25	.20	.10
114T	Jim Sundberg	.25	.20	.10
115T	Rick Sutcliffe	.50	.40	.20
116T	Craig Swan	.25	.20	.10

		MT	NR MT	EX
117T	Tim Teufel(FC)	.50	.40	.20
118T	Derrel Thomas	.25	.20	.10
119T	Gorman Thomas	.25	.20	.10
120T	Alex Trevino	.25	.20	.10
121T	Manny Trillo	.25	.20	.10
122T	John Tudor	.25	.20	.10
123T	Tom Underwood	.25	.20	.10
124T	Mike Vail	.25	.20	.10
125T	Tom Waddell	.25	.20	.10
126T	Gary Ward	.25	.20	.10
127T	Curt Wilkerson	.25	.20	.10
128T	Frank Williams(FC)	.25	.20	.10
129T	Glenn Wilson	.25	.20	.10
130T	Johnny Wockenfuss	.25	.20	.10
131T	Ned Yost	.25	.20	.10
132T	Checklist 1-132	.25	.20	.10

1984 Topps Gallery of Immortals

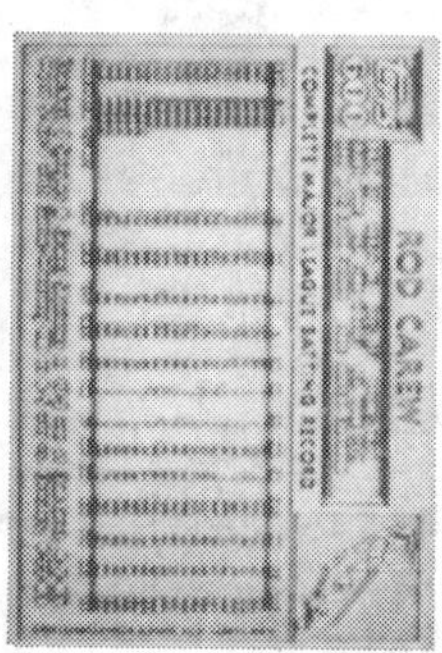

The Gallery of Immortals set of aluminum, bronze and silver replicas was the first miniature set of 12 from Topps and the start of an annual tradition (in 1985, the name was changed to Gallery of Champions). Each mini is an exact replica (one- quarter scale) of the featured player's official Topps baseball card card, both front and back, in minute detail. The bronze and silver sets include a dozen three-dimensional raised metal cards packaged in a velvet-lined case that bears the title of the set in gold-embossed letters. A certificate of authenticity is included with each set. A Tom Seaver pewter metal mini-card was given as a premium to dealers who purchsed bronze and silver sets (value $75). A Darryl Strawberry bronze was given as a premium to dealers who purchased cases of the 1984 Topps Traded sets (value $12). Additionally, a Steve Carlton bronze was issued as a premium in 1983 to dealers who purchased 1983 Topps Traded sets (value $50).

		MT	NR MT	EX
Complete Aluminum Set:		30.00	22.00	12.00
Complete Bronze Set:		175.00	131.00	70.00
Complete Silver Set:		600.00	450.00	240.00
(1a)	George Brett (aluminum)	1.50	1.25	.60
(1b)	George Brett (bronze)	15.00	11.00	6.00
(1c)	George Brett (silver)	80.00	60.00	32.00
(2a)	Rod Carew (aluminum)	1.50	1.25	.60
(2b)	Rod Carew (bronze)	12.50	9.50	5.00
(2c)	Rod Carew (silver)	50.00	37.00	20.00
(3a)	Steve Carlton (aluminum)	1.50	1.25	.60
(3b)	Steve Carlton (bronze)	12.50	9.50	5.00
(3c)	Steve Carlton (silver)	50.00	37.00	20.00
(4a)	Rollie Fingers (aluminum)	1.25	.90	.50
(4b)	Rollie Fingers (bronze)	10.00	7.50	4.00
(4c)	Rollie Fingers (silver)	20.00	15.00	8.00
(5a)	Steve Garvey (aluminum)	1.50	1.25	.60
(5b)	Steve Garvey (bronze)	12.50	9.50	5.00
(5c)	Steve Garvey (silver)	50.00	37.00	20.00
(6a)	Reggie Jackson (aluminum)	1.50	1.25	.60
(6b)	Reggie Jackson (bronze)	15.00	11.00	6.00
(6c)	Reggie Jackson (silver)	80.00	60.00	32.00
(7a)	Joe Morgan (aluminum)	1.25	.90	.50
(7b)	Joe Morgan (bronze)	10.00	7.50	4.00
(7c)	Joe Morgan (silver)	20.00	15.00	8.00
(8a)	Jim Palmer (aluminum)	1.25	.90	.50
(8b)	Jim Palmer (bronze)	10.00	7.50	4.00
(8c)	Jim Palmer (silver)	20.00	15.00	8.00
(9a)	Pete Rose (aluminum)	2.50	2.00	1.00
(9b)	Pete Rose (bronze)	25.00	18.50	10.00
(9c)	Pete Rose (silver)	110.00	82.00	44.00
(10a)	Nolan Ryan (aluminum)	1.50	1.25	.60
(10b)	Nolan Ryan (bronze)	12.50	9.50	5.00
(10c)	Nolan Ryan (silver)	80.00	60.00	33.00
(11a)	Mike Schmidt (aluminum)	1.50	1.25	.60
(11b)	Mike Schmidt (bronze)	15.00	11.00	6.00
(11c)	Mike Schmidt (silver)	80.00	60.00	32.00
(12a)	Tom Seaver (aluminum)	1.50	1.25	.60
(12b)	Tom Seaver (bronze)	12.50	9.50	5.00
(12c)	Tom Seaver (silver)	50.00	37.00	20.00

1984 Topps Rub Downs

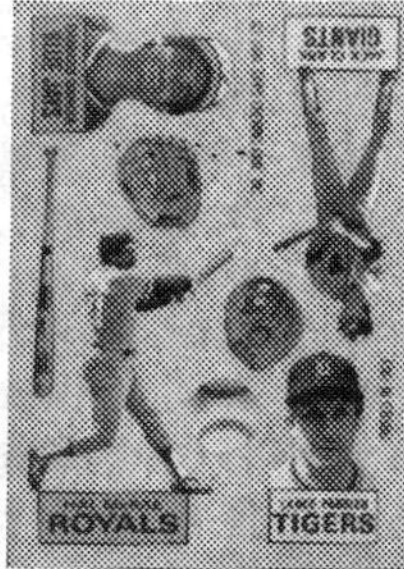

This set, produced by Topps in 1984, consists of 32 "Rub Down" sheets featuring 112 different players. Each sheet measures 2-3/8" by 3-15/16" and includes small, color baseball player figures along with bats, balls and gloves. The pictures can be transferred to another surface by rubbing the paper backing. The sheets, which were sold as a separate issue, are somewhat reminiscent of earlier tattoo sets issued by Topps. The sheets are not numbered.

		MT	NR MT	EX
Complete Set:		9.00	6.75	3.50
Common Player:		.10	.08	.04
(1)	Tony Armas, Harold Baines, Lonnie Smith	.10	.08	.04
(2)	Don Baylor, George Hendrick, Ron Kittle, Johnnie LeMaster	.10	.08	.04
(3)	Buddy Bell, Ray Knight, Lloyd Moseby	.10	.08	.04
(4)	Bruce Benedict, Atlee Hammaker, Frank White	.10	.08	.04
(5)	Wade Boggs, Rick Dempsey, Keith Hernandez	.60	.45	.25
(6)	George Brett, Andre Dawson, Paul Molitor, Alan Wiggins	.30	.25	.12
(7)	Tom Brunansky, Pedro Guerrero, Darryl Strawberry	.40	.30	.15
(8)	Bill Buckner, Rich Gossage, Dave Stieb, Rick Sutcliffe	.15	.11	.06
(9)	Rod Carew, Carlton Fisk, Johnny Ray, Matt Young	.25	.20	.10
(10)	Steve Carlton, Bob Horner, Dan Quisenberry	.25	.20	.10
(11)	Gary Carter, Phil Garner, Ron Guidry	.25	.20	.10
(12)	Ron Cey, Steve Kemp, Greg Luzinski, Kent Tekulve	.10	.08	.04
(13)	Chris Chambliss, Dwight Evans, Julio Franco	.15	.11	.06
(14)	Jack Clark, Damaso Garcia, Hal McRae, Lance Parrish	.20	.15	.08
(15)	Dave Concepcion, Cecil Cooper, Fred Lynn, Jesse Orosco	.15	.11	.06
(16)	Jose Cruz, Gary Matthews, Jack Morris, Jim Rice	.20	.15	.08
(17)	Ron Davis, Kent Hrbek, Tom Seaver	.25	.20	.10
(18)	John Denny, Carney Lansford, Mario Soto, Lou Whitaker	.10	.08	.04

		MT	NR MT	EX
(19)	Leon Durham, Dave Lopes, Steve Sax	.15	.11	.06
(20)	George Foster, Gary Gaetti, Bobby Grich, Gary Redus	.15	.11	.06
(21)	Steve Garvey, Bill Russell, Jerry REmy, George Wright	.20	.15	.08
(22)	Moose Haas, Bruce Sutter, Dickie Thon, Andre Thornton	.10	.08	.04
(23)	Toby Harrah, Pat Putnam, Tim Raines, Mike Schmidt	.30	.25	.12
(24)	Rickey Henderson, Dave Righetti, Pete Rose	.70	.50	.30
(25)	Steve Henderson, Bill Madlock, Alan Trammell	.20	.15	.08
(26)	LaMarr Hoyt, Larry Parrish, Nolan Ryan	.25	.20	.10
(27)	Reggie Jackson, Eric Show, Jason Thompson	.30	.25	.12
(28)	Tommy John, Terry Kennedy, Eddie Murray, Ozzie Smith	.25	.20	.10
(29)	Jeff Leonard, Dale Murphy, Ken Singleton, Dave Winfield	.30	.25	.12
(30)	Craig McMurtry, Cal Ripken, Steve Rogers, Willie Upshaw	.25	.20	.10
(31)	Ben Oglivie, Jim Palmer, Darrell Porter	.20	.15	.08
(32)	Tony Pena, Fernando Valenzuela, Robin Yount	.20	.15	.08

1984 Topps Stickers

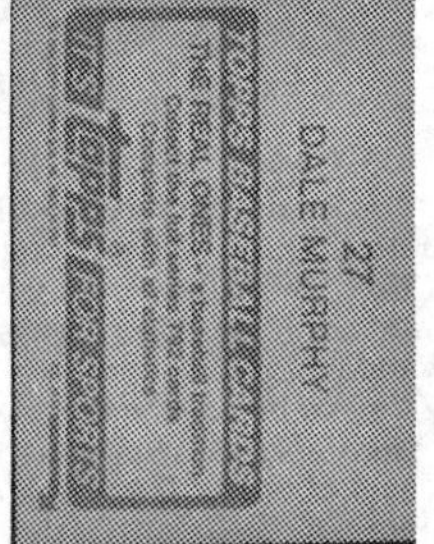

The largest sticker set issued by Topps, the 1984 set consists of 386 stickers, each measuring 1-15/16" by 2-9/16". The full color photos have stars in each of the corners and are numbered on both the front and the back. The back includes information about the sticker album and a promotion to order stickers through the mail.

	MT	NR MT	EX
Complete Set:	15.00	11.00	6.00
Common Player:	.03	.02	.01
Sticker Album:	.80	.60	.30

		MT	NR MT	EX
1	Steve Carlton	.15	.11	.06
2	Steve Carlton	.12	.09	.05
3	Rickey Henderson	.20	.15	.08
4	Rickey Henderson	.15	.11	.06
5	Fred Lynn	.12	.09	.05
6	Fred Lynn	.10	.08	.04
7	Greg Luzinski	.08	.06	.03
8	Greg Luzinski	.06	.05	.02
9	Dan Quisenberry	.08	.06	.03
10	Dan Quisenberry	.06	.05	.02
11	1983 Championship (LaMarr Hoyt)	.03	.02	.01
12	1983 Championship (Mike Flanagan)	.04	.03	.02
13	1983 Championship (Mike Boddicker)	.04	.03	.02
14	1983 Championship (Tito Landrum)	.03	.02	.01
15	1983 Championship (Steve Carlton)	.12	.09	.05
16	1983 Championship (Fernando Valenzuela)	.12	.09	.05
17	1983 Championship (Charlie Hudson)	.03	.02	.01
18	1983 Championship (Gary Matthews)	.04	.03	.02
19	1983 World Series (John Denny)	.03	.02	.01
20	1983 World Series (John Lowenstein)	.03	.02	.01
21	1983 World Series (Jim Palmer)	.10	.08	.04
22	1983 World Series (Benny Ayala)	.03	.02	.01
23	1983 World Series (Rick Dempsey)	.03	.02	.01
24	1983 World Series (Cal Ripken)	.15	.11	.06
25	1983 World Series (Sammy Stewart)	.03	.02	.01
26	1983 World Series (Eddie Murray)	.15	.11	.06
27	Dale Murphy	.25	.20	.10
28	Chris Chambliss	.04	.03	.02
29	Glenn Hubbard	.04	.03	.02
30	Bob Horner	.08	.06	.03
31	Phil Niekro	.12	.09	.05
32	Claudell Washington	.04	.03	.02
33	Rafael Ramirez	.03	.02	.01
34	Bruce Benedict	.04	.03	.02
35	Gene Garber	.03	.02	.01
36	Pascual Perez	.04	.03	.02
37	Jerry Royster	.03	.02	.01
38	Steve Bedrosian	.06	.05	.02
39	Keith Moreland	.06	.05	.02
40	Leon Durham	.06	.05	.02
41	Ron Cey	.06	.05	.02
42	Bill Buckner	.06	.05	.02
43	Jody Davis	.06	.05	.02
44	Lee Smith	.06	.05	.02
45	Ryne Sandberg	.10	.08	.04
46	Larry Bowa	.04	.03	.02
47	Chuck Rainey	.04	.03	.02
48	Fergie Jenkins	.06	.05	.02
49	Dick Ruthven	.03	.02	.01
50	Jay Johnstone	.04	.03	.02
51	Mario Soto	.06	.05	.02
52	Gary Redus	.04	.03	.02
53	Ron Oester	.04	.03	.02
54	Cesar Cedeno	.06	.05	.02
55	Dan Driessen	.04	.03	.02
56	Dave Concepcion	.06	.05	.02
57	Dann Bilardello	.03	.02	.01
58	Joe Price	.03	.02	.01
59	Tom Hume	.03	.02	.01
60	Eddie Milner	.03	.02	.01
61	Paul Householder	.04	.03	.02
62	Bill Scherrer	.04	.03	.02
63	Phil Garner	.04	.03	.02
64	Dickie Thon	.04	.03	.02
65	Jose Cruz	.06	.05	.02
66	Nolan Ryan	.15	.11	.06
67	Terry Puhl	.03	.02	.01
68	Ray Knight	.06	.05	.02
69	Joe Niekro	.06	.05	.02
70	Jerry Mumphrey	.10	.08	.04
71	Bill Dawley	.03	.02	.01
72	Alan Ashby	.04	.03	.02
73	Denny Walling	.04	.03	.02
74	Frank DiPino	.04	.03	.02
75	Pedro Guerrero	.12	.09	.05
76	Ken Landreaux	.03	.02	.01
77	Bill Russell	.04	.03	.02
78	Steve Sax	.10	.08	.04
79	Fernando Valenzuela	.15	.11	.06
80	Dusty Baker	.04	.03	.02
81	Jerry Reuss	.04	.03	.02
82	Alejandro Pena	.04	.03	.02
83	Rick Monday	.06	.05	.02
84	Rick Honeycutt	.03	.02	.01
85	Mike Marshall	.06	.05	.02
86	Steve Yeager	.04	.03	.02
87	Al Oliver	.06	.05	.02
88	Steve Rogers	.03	.02	.01
89	Jeff Reardon	.08	.06	.03
90	Gary Carter	.20	.15	.08
91	Tim Raines	.15	.11	.06
92	Andre Dawson	.12	.09	.05
93	Manny Trillo	.04	.03	.02
94	Tim Wallach	.06	.05	.02
95	Chris Speier	.03	.02	.01
96	Bill Gullickson	.04	.03	.02
97	Doug Flynn	.04	.03	.02
98	Charlie Lea	.03	.02	.01
99	Bill Madlock	.06	.05	.02
100	Wade Boggs	.25	.20	.10
101	Mike Schmidt	.15	.11	.06
102a	Jim Rice	.06	.05	.02
102b	Reggie Jackson	.06	.05	.02
103	Hubie Brooks	.06	.05	.02
104	Jesse Orosco	.04	.03	.02
105	George Foster	.08	.06	.03
106	Tom Seaver	.20	.15	.08
107	Keith Hernandez	.15	.11	.06

		MT	NR MT	EX
108	Mookie Wilson	.06	.05	.02
109	Bob Bailor	.03	.02	.01
110	Walt Terrell	.04	.03	.02
111	Brian Giles	.06	.05	.02
112	Jose Oquendo	.06	.05	.02
113	Mike Torrez	.03	.02	.01
114	Junior Ortiz	.03	.02	.01
115	Pete Rose	.40	.30	.15
116	Joe Morgan	.12	.09	.05
117	Mike Schmidt	.25	.20	.10
118	Gary Matthews	.06	.05	.02
119	Steve Carlton	.15	.11	.06
120	Bo Diaz	.04	.03	.02
121	Ivan DeJesus	.04	.03	.02
122	John Denny	.03	.02	.01
123	Garry Maddox	.03	.02	.01
124	Von Hayes	.08	.06	.03
125	Al Holland	.03	.02	.01
126	Tony Perez	.06	.05	.02
127	John Candelaria	.06	.05	.02
128	Jason Thompson	.03	.02	.01
129	Tony Pena	.06	.05	.02
130	Dave Parker	.12	.09	.05
131	Bill Madlock	.08	.06	.03
132	Kent Tekulve	.04	.03	.02
133	larry McWilliams	.03	.02	.01
134	Johnny Ray	.04	.03	.02
135	Marvell Wynne	.03	.02	.01
136	Dale Berra	.03	.02	.01
137	Mike Easler	.03	.02	.01
138	Lee Lacy	.03	.02	.01
139	George Hendrick	.04	.03	.02
140	Lonnie Smith	.04	.03	.02
141	Willie McGee	.08	.06	.03
142	Tom Herr	.06	.05	.02
143	Darrell Porter	.04	.03	.02
144	Ozzie Smith	.10	.08	.04
145	Bruce Sutter	.06	.05	.02
146	Dave LaPoint	.03	.02	.01
147	Neil Allen	.03	.02	.01
148	Ken Oberkfell	.04	.03	.02
149	David Green	.03	.02	.01
150	Andy Van Slyke	.04	.03	.02
151	Garry Templeton	.06	.05	.02
152	Juan Bonilla	.03	.02	.01
153	Alan Wiggins	.03	.02	.01
154	Terry Kennedy	.04	.03	.02
155	Dave Dravecky	.04	.03	.02
156	Steve Garvey	.15	.11	.06
157	Bobby Brown	.04	.03	.02
158	Ruppert Jones	.03	.02	.01
159	Luis Salazar	.03	.02	.01
160	Tony Gwynn	.12	.09	.05
161	Gary Lucas	.10	.08	.04
162	Eric Show	.04	.03	.02
163	Darrell Evans	.08	.06	.03
164	Gary Lavelle	.03	.02	.01
165	Atlee Hammaker	.03	.02	.01
166	Jeff Leonard	.06	.05	.02
167	Jack Clark	.10	.08	.04
168	Johnny LeMaster	.03	.02	.01
169	Duane Kuiper	.03	.02	.01
170	Tom O'Malley	.06	.05	.02
171	Chili Davis	.06	.05	.02
172	Bill Laskey	.03	.02	.01
173	Joel Youngblood	.06	.05	.02
174	Bob Brenly	.06	.05	.02
175	Atlee Hammaker	.15	.11	.06
176	Rick Honeycutt	.15	.11	.06
177	John Denny	.06	.05	.02
178	LaMarr Hoyt	.03	.02	.01
179	Tim Raines	.30	.25	.12
180	Dale Murphy	.40	.30	.15
181	Andre Dawson	.25	.20	.10
182	Steve Rogers	.15	.11	.06
183	Gary Carter	.30	.25	.12
184	Steve Carlton	.25	.20	.10
185	George Hendrick	.15	.11	.06
186	Johnny Ray	.15	.11	.06
187	Ozzie Smith	.20	.15	.08
188	Mike Schmidt	.40	.30	.15
189	Jim Rice	.30	.25	.12
190	Dave Winfield	.30	.25	.12
191	Lloyd Moseby	.15	.11	.06
192	LaMarr Hoyt	.15	.11	.06
193	Ted Simmons	.15	.11	.06
194	Ron Guidry	.20	.15	.08
195	Eddie Murray	.40	.30	.15
196	Lou Whitaker	.25	.20	.10
197	Cal Ripken	.40	.30	.15
198	George Brett	.40	.30	.15

		MT	NR MT	EX
199	Dale Murphy	.15	.11	.06
200a	Cecil Cooper	.03	.02	.01
200b	Jim Rice	.25	.20	.10
201	Tim Raines	.10	.08	.04
202	Rickey Henderson	.15	.11	.06
203	Eddie Murray	.20	.15	.08
204	Cal Ripken	.20	.15	.08
205	Gary Roenicke	.03	.02	.01
206	Ken Singleton	.06	.05	.02
207	Scott McGregor	.04	.03	.02
208	Tippy Martinez	.03	.02	.01
209	John Lowenstein	.04	.03	.02
210	Mike Flanagan	.04	.03	.02
211	Jim Palmer	.10	.08	.04
212	Dan Ford	.12	.09	.05
213	Rick Dempsey	.04	.03	.02
214	Rich Dauer	.03	.02	.01
215	Jerry Remy	.03	.02	.01
216	Wade Boggs	.50	.40	.20
217	Jim Rice	.20	.15	.08
218	Tony Armas	.06	.05	.02
219	Dwight Evans	.08	.06	.03
220	Bob Stanley	.04	.03	.02
221	Dave Stapleton	.06	.05	.02
222	Rich Gedman	.04	.03	.02
223	Glenn Hoffman	.06	.05	.02
224	Dennis Eckersley	.08	.06	.03
225	John Tudor	.06	.05	.02
226	Bruce Hurst	.04	.03	.02
227	Rod Carew	.20	.15	.08
228	Bobby Grich	.06	.05	.02
229	Doug DeCinces	.06	.05	.02
230	Fred Lynn	.10	.08	.04
231	Reggie Jackson	.20	.15	.08
232	Tommy John	.10	.08	.04
233	Luis Sanchez	.03	.02	.01
234	Bob Boone	.04	.03	.02
235	Bruce Kison	.04	.03	.02
236	Brian Downing	.04	.03	.02
237	Ken Forsch	.03	.02	.01
238	Rick Burleson	.04	.03	.02
239	Dennis Lamp	.03	.02	.01
240	LaMarr Hoyt	.03	.02	.01
241	Richard Dotson	.04	.03	.02
242	Harold Baines	.10	.08	.04
243	Carlton Fisk	.12	.09	.05
244	Greg Luzinski	.08	.06	.03
245	Rudy Law	.06	.05	.02
246	Tom Paciorek	.03	.02	.01
247	Floyd Bannister	.04	.03	.02
248	Julio Cruz	.04	.03	.02
249	Vance Law	.03	.02	.01
250	Scott Fletcher	.04	.03	.02
251	Toby Harrah	.04	.03	.02
252	Pat Tabler	.04	.03	.02
253	Gorman Thomas	.06	.05	.02
254	Rick Sutcliffe	.08	.06	.03
255	Andre Thornton	.06	.05	.02
256	Bake McBride	.03	.02	.01
257	Alan Bannister	.03	.02	.01
258	Jamie Easterly	.03	.02	.01
259	Lary Sorenson	.03	.02	.01
260	Mike Hargrove	.03	.02	.01
261	Bert Blyleven	.06	.05	.02
262	Ron Hassey	.04	.03	.02
263	Jack Morris	.12	.09	.05
264	Larry Herndon	.03	.02	.01
265	Lance Parrish	.12	.09	.05
266	Alan Trammell	.15	.11	.06
267	Lou Whitaker	.12	.09	.05
268	Aurelio Lopez	.03	.02	.01
269	Dan Petry	.04	.03	.02
270	Glenn Wilson	.04	.03	.02
271	Chet Lemon	.04	.03	.02
272	Kirk Gibson	.06	.05	.02
273	Enos Cabell	.04	.03	.02
274	Johnny Wockenfuss	.03	.02	.01
275	George Brett	.25	.20	.10
276	Willie Aikens	.03	.02	.01
277	Frank White	.04	.03	.02
278	Hal McRae	.06	.05	.02
279	Dan Quisenberry	.06	.05	.02
280	Willie Wilson	.08	.06	.03
281	Paul Splitorff	.03	.02	.01
282	U.L. Washington	.03	.02	.01
283	Bud Black	.06	.05	.02
284	John Wathan	.04	.03	.02
285	Larry Gura	.03	.02	.01
286	Pat Sheridan	.03	.02	.01
287a	Rusty Staub	.06	.05	.02
287b	Dave Righetti	.25	.20	.10

		MT	NR MT	EX
288a	Bob Forsch	.03	.02	.01
288b	Mike Warren	.06	.05	.02
289	Al Holland	.10	.08	.04
290	Dan Quisenberry	.15	.11	.06
291	Cecil Cooper	.06	.05	.02
292	Moose Haas	.03	.02	.01
293	Ted Simmons	.08	.06	.03
294	Paul Molitor	.10	.08	.04
295	Robin Yount	.15	.11	.06
296	Ben Oglivie	.04	.03	.02
297	Tom Tellmann	.50	.40	.20
298	Jim Gantner	.04	.03	.02
299	Rick Manning	.03	.02	.01
300	Don Sutton	.06	.05	.02
301	Charlie Moore	.04	.03	.02
302	Jim Slaton	.03	.02	.01
303	Gary Ward	.04	.03	.02
304	Tom Brunansky	.08	.06	.03
305	Kent Hrbek	.12	.09	.05
306	Gary Gaetti	.10	.08	.04
307	John Castino	.03	.02	.01
308	Ken Schrom	.03	.02	.01
309	Ron Davis	.03	.02	.01
310	Lenny Faedo	.03	.02	.01
311	Darrell Brown	.06	.05	.02
312	Frank Viola	.06	.05	.02
313	Dave Engle	.03	.02	.01
314	Randy Bush	.03	.02	.01
315	Dave Righetti	.12	.09	.05
316	Rich Gossage	.12	.09	.05
317	Ken Griffey	.06	.05	.02
318	Ron Guidry	.12	.09	.05
319	Dave Winfield	.15	.11	.06
320	Don Baylor	.08	.06	.03
321	Butch Wynegar	.03	.02	.01
322	Omar Moreno	.03	.02	.01
323	Andre Robertson	.03	.02	.01
324	Willie Randolph	.04	.03	.02
325	Don Mattingly	.50	.40	.20
326	Graig Nettles	.06	.05	.02
327	Rickey Henderson	.25	.20	.10
328	Carney Lansford	.08	.06	.03
329	Jeff Burroughs	.04	.03	.02
330	Chris Codiroli	.03	.02	.01
331	Dave Lopes	.06	.05	.02
332	Dwayne Murphy	.04	.03	.02
333	Wayne Gross	.03	.02	.01
334	Bill Almon	.03	.02	.01
335	Tom Underwood	.04	.03	.02
336	Dave Beard	.03	.02	.01
337	Mike Heath	.03	.02	.01
338	Mike Davis	.04	.03	.02
339	Pat Putnam	.03	.02	.01
340	Tony Bernazard	.03	.02	.01
341	Steve Henderson	.03	.02	.01
342	Richie Zisk	.04	.03	.02
343	Dave Henderson	.06	.05	.02
344	Al Cowens	.03	.02	.01
345	Bill Caudill	.03	.02	.01
346	Jim Beattie	.06	.05	.02
347	Ricky Nelson	.04	.03	.02
348	Roy Thomas	.06	.05	.02
349	Spike Owen	.04	.03	.02
350	Jamie Allen	.03	.02	.01
351	Buddy Bell	.06	.05	.02
352	Billy Sample	.03	.02	.01
353	George Wright	.03	.02	.01
354	Larry Parrish	.06	.05	.02
355	Jim Sundberg	.04	.03	.02
356	Charlie Hough	.06	.05	.02
357	Pete O'Brien	.06	.05	.02
358	Wayne Tolleson	.03	.02	.01
359	Danny Darwin	.03	.02	.01
360	Dave Stewart	.04	.03	.02
361	Mickey Rivers	.04	.03	.02
362	Bucky Dent	.04	.03	.02
363	Willie Upshaw	.06	.05	.02
364	Damaso Garcia	.04	.03	.02
365	Lloyd Moseby	.06	.05	.02
366	Cliff Johnson	.03	.02	.01
367	Jim Clancy	.04	.03	.02
368	Dave Stieb	.06	.05	.02
369	Alfredo Griffin	.04	.03	.02
370	Barry Bonnell	.04	.03	.02
371	Luis Leal	.03	.02	.01
372	Jesse Barfield	.06	.05	.02
373	Ernie Whitt	.03	.02	.01
374	Rance Mulliniks	.06	.05	.02
375	Mike Boddicker	.06	.05	.02
376	Greg Brock	.06	.05	.02
377	Bill Doran	.06	.05	.02
378	Nick Esasky	.06	.05	.02
379	Julio Franco	.08	.06	.03
380	Mel Hall	.06	.05	.02
381	Bob Kearney	.03	.02	.01
382	Ron Kittle	.06	.05	.02
383	Carmelo Martinez	.06	.05	.02
384	Craig McMurtry	.03	.02	.01
385	Darryl Strawberry	.30	.25	.12
386	Matt Young	.04	.03	.02

1984 Topps Stickers Boxes

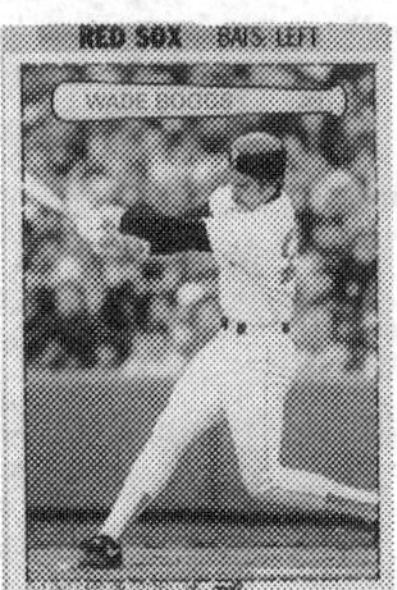

For the second straight year, Topps printed baseball cards on the back of its sticker boxes. The 1984 set, titled "The Super Bats" features 24 hitting leaders. The cards are blank-backed and measure 2-1/2" by 3-1/2". Two cards were printed on each of 12 different boxes. The player's name appears inside a bat above his photo. Prices listed are for complete boxes.

		MT	NR MT	EX
Complete Set:		8.50	6.50	3.50
Common Player:		.75	.60	.30
1	Al Oliver, Lou Whitaker	1.00	.70	.40
2	Ken Oberkfell, Ted Simmons	.75	.60	.30
3	Hal McRae, Alan Wiggins	.75	.60	.30
4	Lloyd Moseby, Tim Raines	1.00	.70	.40
5	Lonnie Smith, Willie Wilson	.75	.60	.30
6	Keith Hernandez, Robin Yount	.75	.60	.30
7	Wade Boggs, Johnny Ray	1.50	1.25	.60
8	Willie McGee, Ken Singleton	.75	.60	.30
9	Ray Knight, Alan Trammell	1.00	.70	.40
11	Rod Carew, George Hendrick	1.25	.90	.50
12	Bill Madlock, Eddie Murray	1.25	.90	.50
13	Jose Cruz, Cal Ripken, Jr.	1.25	.90	.50

1984 Topps Super

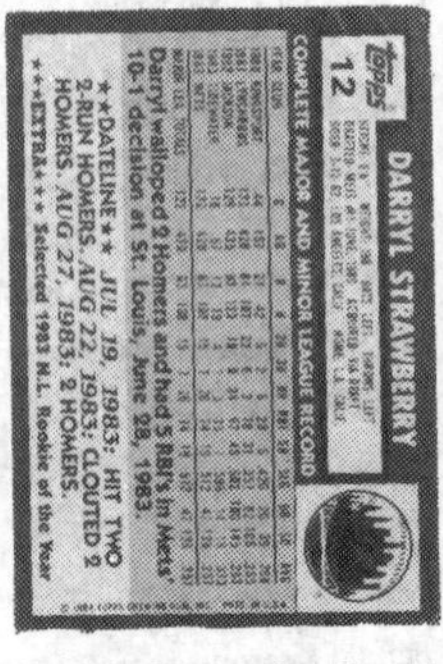

The next installment in Topps' continuing produc- tion of large-format cards, these 4-7/8" by 6-7/8" cards were sold in cellophane packs with a complete set being 30 cards. Other than their size and the change in card number on the back, there is nothing to distinguish the Supers from the regular 1984

Topps cards of the same players. One plus is that the players are all big name stars, and are likely to remain in demand.

		MT	NR MT	EX
Complete Set:		12.00	9.00	4.75
Common Player:		.25	.20	.10
1	Cal Ripken, Jr.	2.00	1.50	.80
2	Dale Murphy	.90	.70	.35
3	LaMarr Hoyt	.25	.20	.10
4	John Denny	.25	.20	.10
5	Jim Rice	.50	.40	.20
6	Mike Schmidt	.90	.70	.35
7	Wade Boggs	.75	.60	.30
8	Bill Madlock	.25	.20	.10
9	Dan Quisenberry	.25	.20	.10
10	Al Holland	.25	.20	.10
11	Ron Kittle	.25	.20	.10
12	Darryl Strawberry	.75	.60	.30
13	George Brett	.90	.70	.35
14	Bill Buckner	.25	.20	.10
15	Carlton Fisk	.30	.25	.12
16	Steve Carlton	.50	.40	.20
17	Ron Guidry	.35	.25	.14
18	Gary Carter	.50	.40	.20
19	Rickey Henderson	.90	.70	.35
20	Andre Dawson	.35	.25	.14
21	Reggie Jackson	.90	.70	.35
22	Steve Garvey	.50	.40	.20
23	Fred Lynn	.50	.40	.20
24	Pedro Guerrero	.25	.20	.10
25	Eddie Murray	.60	.45	.25
26	Keith Hernandez	.35	.25	.14
27	Dave Winfield	.50	.40	.20
28	Nolan Ryan	2.00	1.50	.80
29	Robin Yount	.90	.70	.35
30	Fernando Valenzuela	.40	.30	.15

1985 Topps

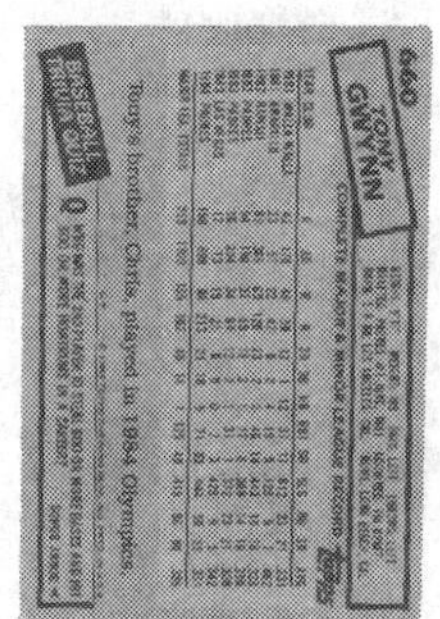

Holding the line at 792 cards, Topps did initiate some major design changes in its 2-1/2" by 3-1/2" cards in 1985. The use of two photos on the front was discontinued in favor of one large color photo. The Topps logo appears in the upper left-hand corner. At the bottom runs a diagonal rectangular box with the team name. It joins a team logo, and below that point runs the player's position and name. The backs feature statistics, biographical information and a trivia question. Some interesting specialty sets were introduced in 1985, including the revival of the father/son theme from 1976, a subset of the 1984 U.S. Olympic Baseball Team members and a set featuring #1 draft choices since the inception of the baseball draft in 1965. Again in 1985, a glossy-finish "Tiffany" edition of the regular set was produced, though the number was cut back to 5,000 sets. Values range from four times regular value for common cards to five-six times for high-demand stars and rookie cards.

	MT	NR MT	EX
Complete Set (792):	85.00	64.00	34.00
Common Player:	.06	.05	.02

		MT	NR MT	EX
1	Carlton Fisk (Record Breaker)	.25	.20	.10
2	Steve Garvey (Record Breaker)	.20	.15	.08
3	Dwight Gooden (Record Breaker)	.25	.20	.10
4	Cliff Johnson (Record Breaker)	.08	.06	.03
5	Joe Morgan (Record Breaker)	.15	.11	.06
6	Pete Rose (Record Breaker)	.60	.45	.25
7	Nolan Ryan (Record Breaker)	1.50	1.25	.60
8	Juan Samuel (Record Breaker)(FC)	.12	.09	.05
9	Bruce Sutter (Record Breaker)	.12	.09	.05
10	Don Sutton (Record Breaker)	.20	.15	.08
11	Ralph Houk	.08	.06	.03
12	Dave Lopes	.08	.06	.03
13	Tim Lollar	.06	.05	.02
14	Chris Bando	.06	.05	.02
15	Jerry Koosman	.10	.08	.04
16	Bobby Meacham	.06	.05	.02
17	Mike Scott	.15	.11	.06
18	Mickey Hatcher	.06	.05	.02
19	George Frazier	.06	.05	.02
20	Chet Lemon	.08	.06	.03
21	Lee Tunnell	.06	.05	.02
22	Duane Kuiper	.06	.05	.02
23	*Bret Saberhagen*	1.25	.90	.50
24	Jesse Barfield	.25	.20	.10
25	Steve Bedrosian	.12	.09	.05
26	Roy Smalley	.06	.05	.02
27	Bruce Berenyi	.06	.05	.02
28	Dann Bilardello	.06	.05	.02
29	Odell Jones	.06	.05	.02
30	Cal Ripken, Jr.	4.00	3.00	1.50
31	Terry Whitfield	.06	.05	.02
32	Chuck Porter	.06	.05	.02
33	Tito Landrum	.06	.05	.02
34	Ed Nunez(FC)	.08	.06	.03
35	Graig Nettles	.15	.11	.06
36	Fred Breining	.06	.05	.02
37	Reid Nichols	.06	.05	.02
38	Jackie Moore	.06	.05	.02
39	Johnny Wockenfuss	.06	.05	.02
40	Phil Niekro	.25	.20	.10
41	Mike Fischlin	.06	.05	.02
42	Luis Sanchez	.06	.05	.02
43	Andre David	.06	.05	.02
44	Dickie Thon	.08	.06	.03
45	Greg Minton	.06	.05	.02
46	Gary Woods	.06	.05	.02
47	Dave Rozema	.06	.05	.02
48	Tony Fernandez(FC)	.25	.20	.10
49	Butch Davis	.06	.05	.02
50	John Candelaria	.10	.08	.04
51	Bob Watson	.08	.06	.03
52	Jerry Dybzinski	.06	.05	.02
53	Tom Gorman	.06	.05	.02
54	Cesar Cedeno	.10	.08	.04
55	Frank Tanana	.10	.08	.04
56	Jim Dwyer	.06	.05	.02
57	Pat Zachry	.06	.05	.02
58	Orlando Mercado	.06	.05	.02
59	Rick Waits	.06	.05	.02
60	George Hendrick	.08	.06	.03
61	Curt Kaufman	.06	.05	.02
62	Mike Ramsey	.06	.05	.02
63	Steve McCatty	.06	.05	.02
64	*Mark Bailey*(FC)	.10	.08	.04
65	Bill Buckner	.12	.09	.05
66	Dick Williams	.06	.05	.02
67	*Rafael Santana*(FC)	.06	.05	.02
68	Von Hayes	.10	.08	.04
69	*Jim Winn*(FC)	.10	.08	.04
70	Don Baylor	.12	.09	.05
71	Tim Laudner	.06	.05	.02
72	Rick Sutcliffe	.12	.09	.05
73	Rusty Kuntz	.06	.05	.02
74	Mike Krukow	.08	.06	.03
75	Willie Upshaw	.08	.06	.03
76	Alan Bannister	.06	.05	.02
77	Joe Beckwith	.06	.05	.02
78	Scott Fletcher	.08	.06	.03
79	Rick Mahler	.06	.05	.02
80	Keith Hernandez	.12	.09	.05
81	Lenn Sakata	.06	.05	.02
82	Joe Price	.06	.05	.02
83	Charlie Moore	.06	.05	.02
84	Spike Owen	.08	.06	.03

		MT	NR MT	EX
85	Mike Marshall	.08	.06	.03
86	Don Aase	.06	.05	.02
87	David Green	.06	.05	.02
88	Bryn Smith	.06	.05	.02
89	Jackie Gutierrez	.06	.05	.02
90	Rich Gossage	.10	.08	.04
91	Jeff Burroughs	.08	.06	.03
92	Paul Owens	.06	.05	.02
93	*Don Schulze*(FC)	.06	.05	.02
94	Toby Harrah	.08	.06	.03
95	Jose Cruz	.10	.08	.04
96	Johnny Ray	.06	.05	.02
97	Pete Filson	.06	.05	.02
98	Steve Lake	.06	.05	.02
99	Milt Wilcox	.06	.05	.02
100	George Brett	1.75	1.25	.70
101	Jim Acker	.06	.05	.02
102	Tommy Dunbar	.06	.05	.02
103	Randy Lerch	.06	.05	.02
104	Mike Fitzgerald	.08	.06	.03
105	Ron Kittle	.06	.05	.02
106	Pascual Perez	.08	.06	.03
107	Tom Foley	.06	.05	.02
108	Darnell Coles(FC)	.06	.05	.02
109	Gary Roenicke	.06	.05	.02
110	Alejandro Pena	.08	.06	.03
111	Doug DeCinces	.10	.08	.04
112	Tom Tellmann	.06	.05	.02
113	Tom Herr	.10	.08	.04
114	Bob James	.06	.05	.02
115	Rickey Henderson	1.25	.90	.50
116	Dennis Boyd(FC)	.15	.11	.06
117	Greg Gross	.06	.05	.02
118	Eric Show	.08	.06	.03
119	Pat Corrales	.06	.05	.02
120	Steve Kemp	.08	.06	.03
121	Checklist 1-132	.06	.05	.02
122	Tom Brunansky	.12	.09	.05
123	Dave Smith	.08	.06	.03
124	Rich Hebner	.06	.05	.02
125	Kent Tekulve	.08	.06	.03
126	Ruppert Jones	.06	.05	.02
127	*Mark Gubicza*	.25	.20	.10
128	Ernie Whitt	.08	.06	.03
129	Gene Garber	.06	.05	.02
130	Al Oliver	.12	.09	.05
131	Father - Son (Buddy Bell, Gus Bell)	.12	.09	.05
132	Father - Son (Dale Berra, Yogi Berra)	.20	.15	.08
133	Father - Son (Bob Boone, Ray Boone)	.12	.09	.05
134	Father - Son (Terry Francona, Tito Francona)	.08	.06	.03
135	Father - Son (Bob Kennedy, Terry Kennedy)	.08	.06	.03
136	Father - Son (Bill Kunkel, Jeff Kunkel)(FC)	.08	.06	.03
137	Father - Son (Vance Law, Vern Law)	.10	.08	.04
138	Father - Son (Dick Schofield, Dick Schofield)	.08	.06	.03
139	Father - Son (Bob Skinner, Joel Skinner)	.08	.06	.03
140	Father - Son (Roy Smalley, Roy Smalley)	.08	.06	.03
141	Father - Son (Dave Stenhouse, Mike Stenhouse)	.08	.06	.03
142	Father - Son (Dizzy Trout, Steve Trout)	.08	.06	.03
143	Father - Son (Ossie Virgil, Ozzie Virgil)	.08	.06	.03
144	Ron Gardenhire	.06	.05	.02
145	*Alvin Davis*	.08	.06	.03
146	Gary Redus	.08	.06	.03
147	Bill Swaggerty	.06	.05	.02
148	Steve Yeager	.06	.05	.02
149	Dickie Noles	.06	.05	.02
150	Jim Rice	.15	.11	.06
151	Moose Haas	.06	.05	.02
152	Steve Braun	.06	.05	.02
153	Frank LaCorte	.06	.05	.02
154	Argenis Salazar(FC)	.06	.05	.02
155	Yogi Berra	.12	.09	.05
156	Craig Reynolds	.06	.05	.02
157	Tug McGraw	.10	.08	.04
158	Pat Tabler	.08	.06	.03
159	Carlos Diaz	.06	.05	.02
160	Lance Parrish	.25	.20	.10
161	Ken Schrom	.06	.05	.02
162	*Benny Distefano*(FC)	.10	.08	.04
163	Dennis Eckersley	.30	.25	.12

		MT	NR MT	EX
164	Jorge Orta	.06	.05	.02
165	Dusty Baker	.08	.06	.03
166	Keith Atherton	.06	.05	.02
167	Rufino Linares	.06	.05	.02
168	Garth Iorg	.06	.05	.02
169	Dan Spillner	.06	.05	.02
170	George Foster	.15	.11	.06
171	Bill Stein	.06	.05	.02
172	Jack Perconte	.06	.05	.02
173	Mike Young(FC)	.12	.09	.05
174	Rick Honeycutt	.06	.05	.02
175	Dave Parker	.25	.20	.10
176	Bill Schroeder	.06	.05	.02
177	Dave Von Ohlen	.06	.05	.02
178	Miguel Dilone	.06	.05	.02
179	Tommy John	.20	.15	.08
180	Dave Winfield	1.25	.90	.50
181	*Roger Clemens*(FC)	15.00	11.00	6.00
182	Tim Flannery	.06	.05	.02
183	Larry McWilliams	.06	.05	.02
184	Carmen Castillo(FC)	.10	.08	.04
185	Al Holland	.06	.05	.02
186	Bob Lillis	.06	.05	.02
187	Mike Walters	.06	.05	.02
188	Greg Pryor	.06	.05	.02
189	Warren Brusstar	.06	.05	.02
190	Rusty Staub	.12	.09	.05
191	Steve Nicosia	.08	.06	.03
192	Howard Johnson(FC)	.50	.40	.20
193	*Jimmy Key*	.75	.60	.30
194	Dave Stegman	.06	.05	.02
195	Glenn Hubbard	.06	.05	.02
196	Pete O'Brien	.12	.09	.05
197	Mike Warren	.06	.05	.02
198	Eddie Milner	.06	.05	.02
199	Denny Martinez	.08	.06	.03
200	Reggie Jackson	.80	.60	.30
201	Burt Hooton	.08	.06	.03
202	Gorman Thomas	.10	.08	.04
203	Bob McClure	.06	.05	.02
204	Art Howe	.06	.05	.02
205	Steve Rogers	.08	.06	.03
206	Phil Garner	.08	.06	.03
207	Mark Clear	.06	.05	.02
208	Champ Summers	.06	.05	.02
209	Bill Campbell	.06	.05	.02
210	Gary Matthews	.10	.08	.04
211	Clay Christiansen	.06	.05	.02
212	George Vukovich	.06	.05	.02
213	Billy Gardner	.06	.05	.02
214	John Tudor	.10	.08	.04
215	Bob Brenly	.06	.05	.02
216	Jerry Don Gleaton	.06	.05	.02
217	Leon Roberts	.06	.05	.02
218	Doyle Alexander	.10	.08	.04
219	Gerald Perry	.08	.06	.03
220	Fred Lynn	.20	.15	.08
221	Ron Reed	.06	.05	.02
222	Hubie Brooks	.10	.08	.04
223	Tom Hume	.06	.05	.02
224	Al Cowens	.06	.05	.02
225	Mike Boddicker	.10	.08	.04
226	Juan Beniquez	.06	.05	.02
227	Danny Darwin	.06	.05	.02
228	Dion James(FC)	.20	.15	.08
229	Dave LaPoint	.08	.06	.03
230	Gary Carter	.35	.25	.14
231	Dwayne Murphy	.08	.06	.03
232	Dave Beard	.06	.05	.02
233	Ed Jurak	.06	.05	.02
234	Jerry Narron	.06	.05	.02
235	Garry Maddox	.10	.08	.04
236	Mark Thurmond	.06	.05	.02
237	Julio Franco	.50	.40	.20
238	*Jose Rijo*	2.00	1.50	.80
239	Tim Teufel	.12	.09	.05
240	Dave Stieb	.12	.09	.05
241	Jim Frey	.06	.05	.02
242	Greg Harris	.06	.05	.02
243	Barbaro Garbey	.10	.08	.04
244	Mike Jones	.06	.05	.02
245	Chili Davis	.10	.08	.04
246	Mike Norris	.06	.05	.02
247	Wayne Tolleson	.06	.05	.02
248	Terry Forster	.08	.06	.03
249	Harold Baines	.15	.11	.06
250	Jesse Orosco	.08	.06	.03
251	Brad Gulden	.06	.05	.02
252	Dan Ford	.06	.05	.02
253	*Sid Bream*(FC)	.20	.15	.08
254	Pete Vuckovich	.08	.06	.03

		MT	NR MT	EX
255	Lonnie Smith	.08	.06	.03
256	Mike Stanton	.06	.05	.02
257	Brian Little (Bryan)	.06	.05	.02
258	Mike Brown	.06	.05	.02
259	Gary Allenson	.06	.05	.02
260	Dave Righetti	.10	.08	.04
261	Checklist 133-264	.06	.05	.02
262	*Greg Booker*(FC)	.12	.09	.05
263	Mel Hall	.08	.06	.03
264	Joe Sambito	.06	.05	.02
265	Juan Samuel(FC)	.12	.09	.05
266	Frank Viola	.10	.08	.04
267	*Henry Cotto*(FC)	.08	.06	.03
268	Chuck Tanner	.06	.05	.02
269	*Doug Baker*(FC)	.10	.08	.04
270	Dan Quisenberry	.10	.08	.04
271	Tim Foli (#1 Draft Pick)	.08	.06	.03
272	Jeff Burroughs (#1 Draft Pick)	.08	.06	.03
273	Bill Almon (#1 Draft Pick)	.08	.06	.03
274	Floyd Bannister (#1 Draft Pick)	.10	.08	.04
275	Harold Baines (#1 Draft Pick)	.15	.11	.06
276	Bob Horner (#1 Draft Pick)	.15	.11	.06
277	Al Chambers (#1 Draft Pick)	.08	.06	.03
278	Darryl Strawberry (#1 Draft Pick)	.30	.25	.12
279	Mike Moore (#1 Draft Pick)(FC)	.20	.15	.08
280	*Shawon Dunston* (#1 Draft Pick)	.40	.30	.15
281	*Tim Belcher* (#1 Draft Pick)	.60	.45	.25
282	*Shawn Abner* (#1 Draft Pick)(FC)	.10	.08	.04
283	Fran Mullins	.06	.05	.02
284	Marty Bystrom	.06	.05	.02
285	Dan Driessen	.08	.06	.03
286	Rudy Law	.06	.05	.02
287	Walt Terrell	.08	.06	.03
288	*Jeff Kunkel*(FC)	.10	.08	.04
289	Tom Underwood	.06	.05	.02
290	Cecil Cooper	.12	.09	.05
291	Bob Welch	.12	.09	.05
292	Brad Komminsk(FC)	.08	.06	.03
293	*Curt Young*(FC)	.08	.06	.03
294	*Tom Nieto*(FC)	.10	.08	.04
295	Joe Niekro	.10	.08	.04
296	Ricky Nelson	.06	.05	.02
297	Gary Lucas	.06	.05	.02
298	Marty Barrett	.08	.06	.03
299	Andy Hawkins	.08	.06	.03
300	Rod Carew	.50	.40	.20
301	John Montefusco	.06	.05	.02
302	Tim Corcoran	.06	.05	.02
303	*Mike Jeffcoat*	.08	.06	.03
304	Gary Gaetti	.12	.09	.05
305	Dale Berra	.06	.05	.02
306	Rick Reuschel	.10	.08	.04
307	Sparky Anderson	.08	.06	.03
308	John Wathan	.08	.06	.03
309	Mike Witt	.12	.09	.05
310	Manny Trillo	.08	.06	.03
311	Jim Gott	.06	.05	.02
312	Marc Hill	.06	.05	.02
313	Dave Schmidt	.06	.05	.02
314	Ron Oester	.06	.05	.02
315	Doug Sisk	.06	.05	.02
316	John Lowenstein	.06	.05	.02
317	*Jack Lazorko*(FC)	.06	.05	.02
318	Ted Simmons	.12	.09	.05
319	Jeff Jones	.06	.05	.02
320	Dale Murphy	.25	.20	.10
321	*Ricky Horton*	.08	.06	.03
322	Dave Stapleton	.06	.05	.02
323	Andy McGaffigan	.06	.05	.02
324	Bruce Bochy	.06	.05	.02
325	John Denny	.06	.05	.02
326	Kevin Bass	.10	.08	.04
327	Brook Jacoby	.08	.06	.03
328	Bob Shirley	.06	.05	.02
329	Ron Washington	.06	.05	.02
330	Leon Durham	.08	.06	.03
331	Bill Laskey	.06	.05	.02
332	Brian Harper	.06	.05	.02
333	Willie Hernandez	.08	.06	.03
334	Dick Howser	.06	.05	.02
335	Bruce Benedict	.06	.05	.02
336	Rance Mulliniks	.06	.05	.02
337	Billy Sample	.06	.05	.02
338	Britt Burns	.06	.05	.02
339	Danny Heep	.06	.05	.02
340	Robin Yount	1.00	.70	.40
341	Floyd Rayford	.06	.05	.02
342	Ted Power	.06	.05	.02
343	Bill Russell	.08	.06	.03
344	Dave Henderson	.10	.08	.04
345	Charlie Lea	.06	.05	.02
346	*Terry Pendleton*(FC)	2.50	2.00	1.00
347	Rick Langford	.06	.05	.02
348	Bob Boone	.08	.06	.03
349	Domingo Ramos	.06	.05	.02
350	Wade Boggs	1.75	1.25	.70
351	Juan Agosto	.06	.05	.02
352	Joe Morgan	.30	.25	.12
353	Julio Solano	.06	.05	.02
354	Andre Robertson	.06	.05	.02
355	Bert Blyleven	.12	.09	.05
356	Dave Meier	.06	.05	.02
357	Rich Bordi	.06	.05	.02
358	Tony Pena	.10	.08	.04
359	Pat Sheridan	.06	.05	.02
360	Steve Carlton	.60	.45	.25
361	Alfredo Griffin	.08	.06	.03
362	Craig McMurtry	.06	.05	.02
363	Ron Hodges	.06	.05	.02
364	Richard Dotson	.10	.08	.04
365	Danny Ozark	.06	.05	.02
366	Todd Cruz	.06	.05	.02
367	Keefe Cato	.06	.05	.02
368	Dave Bergman	.06	.05	.02
369	*R.J. Reynolds*(FC)	.10	.08	.04
370	Bruce Sutter	.12	.09	.05
371	Mickey Rivers	.08	.06	.03
372	Roy Howell	.06	.05	.02
373	Mike Moore	.06	.05	.02
374	Brian Downing	.10	.08	.04
375	Jeff Reardon	.12	.09	.05
376	Jeff Newman	.06	.05	.02
377	Checklist 265-396	.06	.05	.02
378	Alan Wiggins	.06	.05	.02
379	Charles Hudson	.08	.06	.03
380	Ken Griffey	.10	.08	.04
381	Roy Smith	.06	.05	.02
382	Denny Walling	.06	.05	.02
383	Rick Lysander	.06	.05	.02
384	Jody Davis	.10	.08	.04
385	Jose DeLeon	.08	.06	.03
386	*Dan Gladden*(FC)	.30	.25	.12
387	*Buddy Biancalana*(FC)	.12	.09	.05
388	Bert Roberge	.06	.05	.02
389	Rod Dedeaux (Team USA)	.06	.05	.02
390	Sid Akins (Team USA)(FC)	.10	.08	.04
391	Flavio Alfaro (Team USA)	.06	.05	.02
392	Don August (Team USA)(FC)	.08	.06	.03
393	*Scott Bankhead* (Team USA)	.25	.20	.10
394	Bob Caffrey (Team USA)(FC)	.08	.06	.03
395	Mike Dunne (Team USA)(FC)	.20	.15	.08
396	Gary Green (Team USA)(FC)	.08	.06	.03
397	John Hoover (Team USA)	.06	.05	.02
398	*Shane Mack* (Team USA)	2.00	1.50	.80
399	John Marzano (Team USA)(FC)	.10	.08	.04
400	Oddibe McDowell (Team USA)(FC)	.20	.15	.08
401	*Mark McGwire* (Team USA)	20.00	15.00	8.00
402	Pat Pacillo (Team USA)(FC)	.10	.08	.04
403	*Cory Snyder* (Team USA)	.75	.60	.30
404	*Billy Swift* (Team USA)	2.50	2.00	1.00
405	Tom Veryzer	.06	.05	.02
406	Len Whitehouse	.06	.05	.02
407	Bobby Ramos	.06	.05	.02
408	Sid Monge	.06	.05	.02
409	Brad Wellman	.06	.05	.02
410	Bob Horner	.08	.06	.03
411	Bobby Cox	.06	.05	.02
412	Bud Black	.06	.05	.02
413	Vance Law	.08	.06	.03
414	Gary Ward	.08	.06	.03
415	Ron Darling	.12	.09	.05
416	Wayne Gross	.06	.05	.02
417	*John Franco*(FC)	.30	.25	.12
418	Ken Landreaux	.06	.05	.02
419	Mike Caldwell	.06	.05	.02
420	Andre Dawson	.35	.25	.14
421	Dave Rucker	.06	.05	.02
422	Carney Lansford	.10	.08	.04
423	Barry Bonnell	.06	.05	.02
424	*Al Nipper*(FC)	.08	.06	.03
425	Mike Hargrove	.06	.05	.02
426	Verne Ruhle	.06	.05	.02
427	Mario Ramirez	.06	.05	.02
428	Larry Andersen	.06	.05	.02
429	Rick Cerone	.06	.05	.02
430	Ron Davis	.06	.05	.02
431	U.L. Washington	.06	.05	.02
432	Thad Bosley	.06	.05	.02
433	Jim Morrison	.06	.05	.02
434	Gene Richards	.06	.05	.02
435	Dan Petry	.08	.06	.03
436	Willie Aikens	.06	.05	.02

		MT	NR MT	EX
437	Al Jones	.06	.05	.02
438	Joe Torre	.08	.06	.03
439	Junior Ortiz	.06	.05	.02
440	Fernando Valenzuela	.08	.06	.03
441	Duane Walker	.06	.05	.02
442	Ken Forsch	.06	.05	.02
443	George Wright	.06	.05	.02
444	Tony Phillips	.15	.11	.06
445	Tippy Martinez	.06	.05	.02
446	Jim Sundberg	.08	.06	.03
447	Jeff Lahti	.06	.05	.02
448	Derrel Thomas	.06	.05	.02
449	*Phil Bradley*	.10	.08	.04
450	Steve Garvey	.25	.20	.10
451	Bruce Hurst	.12	.09	.05
452	John Castino	.06	.05	.02
453	Tom Waddell	.06	.05	.02
454	Glenn Wilson	.08	.06	.03
455	Bob Knepper	.08	.06	.03
456	Tim Foli	.06	.05	.02
457	Cecilio Guante	.06	.05	.02
458	Randy S. Johnson	.06	.05	.02
459	Charlie Leibrandt	.08	.06	.03
460	Ryne Sandberg	3.00	2.25	1.25
461	Marty Castillo	.06	.05	.02
462	Gary Lavelle	.06	.05	.02
463	Dave Collins	.08	.06	.03
464	*Mike Mason*(FC)	.06	.05	.02
465	Bob Grich	.10	.08	.04
466	Tony LaRussa	.08	.06	.03
467	Ed Lynch	.06	.05	.02
468	Wayne Krenchicki	.06	.05	.02
469	Sammy Stewart	.06	.05	.02
470	Steve Sax	.10	.08	.04
471	Pete Ladd	.06	.05	.02
472	Jim Essian	.06	.05	.02
473	Tim Wallach	.12	.09	.05
474	Kurt Kepshire	.06	.05	.02
475	Andre Thornton	.10	.08	.04
476	*Jeff Stone*(FC)	.12	.09	.05
477	Bob Ojeda	.10	.08	.04
478	Kurt Bevacqua	.06	.05	.02
479	Mike Madden	.06	.05	.02
480	Lou Whitaker	.25	.20	.10
481	Dale Murray	.06	.05	.02
482	Harry Spilman	.06	.05	.02
483	Mike Smithson	.06	.05	.02
484	Larry Bowa	.10	.08	.04
485	Matt Young	.06	.05	.02
486	Steve Balboni	.08	.06	.03
487	*Frank Williams*	.15	.11	.06
488	Joel Skinner(FC)	.08	.06	.03
489	Bryan Clark	.06	.05	.02
490	Jason Thompson	.06	.05	.02
491	Rick Camp	.06	.05	.02
492	Dave Johnson	.08	.06	.03
493	*Orel Hershiser*(FC)	1.25	.90	.50
494	Rich Dauer	.06	.05	.02
495	Mario Soto	.08	.06	.03
496	Donnie Scott	.06	.05	.02
497	Gary Pettis	.15	.11	.06
498	Ed Romero	.06	.05	.02
499	Danny Cox(FC)	.08	.06	.03
500	Mike Schmidt	1.50	1.25	.60
501	Dan Schatzeder	.06	.05	.02
502	Rick Miller	.06	.05	.02
503	Tim Conroy	.06	.05	.02
504	Jerry Willard	.06	.05	.02
505	Jim Beattie	.06	.05	.02
506	*Franklin Stubbs*(FC)	.10	.08	.04
507	Ray Fontenot	.06	.05	.02
508	John Shelby	.08	.06	.03
509	Milt May	.06	.05	.02
510	Kent Hrbek	.15	.11	.06
511	Lee Smith	.10	.08	.04
512	Tom Brookens	.06	.05	.02
513	Lynn Jones	.06	.05	.02
514	Jeff Cornell	.06	.05	.02
515	Dave Concepcion	.12	.09	.05
516	Roy Lee Jackson	.06	.05	.02
517	Jerry Martin	.06	.05	.02
518	Chris Chambliss	.08	.06	.03
519	Doug Rader	.06	.05	.02
520	LaMarr Hoyt	.06	.05	.02
521	Rick Dempsey	.08	.06	.03
522	Paul Molitor	.90	.70	.35
523	Candy Maldonado	.10	.08	.04
524	Rob Wilfong	.06	.05	.02
525	Darrell Porter	.08	.06	.03
526	Dave Palmer	.06	.05	.02
527	Checklist 397-528	.06	.05	.02
528	Bill Krueger	.06	.05	.02
529	Rich Gedman	.10	.08	.04
530	Dave Dravecky	.08	.06	.03
531	Joe Lefebvre	.06	.05	.02
532	Frank DiPino	.06	.05	.02
533	Tony Bernazard	.06	.05	.02
534	Brian Dayett(FC)	.06	.05	.02
535	Pat Putnam	.06	.05	.02
536	*Kirby Puckett*(FC)	21.00	15.50	8.50
537	Don Robinson	.08	.06	.03
538	Keith Moreland	.08	.06	.03
539	Aurelio Lopez	.06	.05	.02
540	Claudell Washington	.08	.06	.03
541	Mark Davis	.06	.05	.02
542	Don Slaught	.06	.05	.02
543	Mike Squires	.06	.05	.02
544	Bruce Kison	.06	.05	.02
545	Lloyd Moseby	.10	.08	.04
546	Brent Gaff	.06	.05	.02
547	Pete Rose	.60	.45	.25
548	Larry Parrish	.10	.08	.04
549	Mike Scioscia	.08	.06	.03
550	Scott McGregor	.08	.06	.03
551	Andy Van Slyke	.25	.20	.10
552	Chris Codiroli	.06	.05	.02
553	Bob Clark	.06	.05	.02
554	Doug Flynn	.06	.05	.02
555	Bob Stanley	.06	.05	.02
556	Sixto Lezcano	.06	.05	.02
557	Len Barker	.08	.06	.03
558	Carmelo Martinez	.08	.06	.03
559	Jay Howell	.08	.06	.03
560	Bill Madlock	.12	.09	.05
561	Darryl Motley	.06	.05	.02
562	Houston Jimenez	.06	.05	.02
563	Dick Ruthven	.06	.05	.02
564	Alan Ashby	.06	.05	.02
565	Kirk Gibson	.20	.15	.08
566	Ed Vande Berg	.06	.05	.02
567	Joel Youngblood	.06	.05	.02
568	Cliff Johnson	.06	.05	.02
569	Ken Oberkfell	.06	.05	.02
570	Darryl Strawberry	.60	.45	.25
571	Charlie Hough	.08	.06	.03
572	Tom Paciorek	.06	.05	.02
573	*Jay Tibbs*(FC)	.08	.06	.03
574	Joe Altobelli	.06	.05	.02
575	Pedro Guerrero	.10	.08	.04
576	Jaime Cocanower	.06	.05	.02
577	Chris Speier	.06	.05	.02
578	Terry Francona	.06	.05	.02
579	*Ron Romanick*	.10	.08	.04
580	Dwight Evans	.12	.09	.05
581	Mark Wagner	.06	.05	.02
582	Ken Phelps(FC)	.10	.08	.04
583	Bobby Brown	.06	.05	.02
584	Kevin Gross	.10	.08	.04
585	Butch Wynegar	.06	.05	.02
586	Bill Scherrer	.06	.05	.02
587	Doug Frobel	.06	.05	.02
588	Bobby Castillo	.06	.05	.02
589	Bob Dernier	.06	.05	.02
590	Ray Knight	.10	.08	.04
591	Larry Herndon	.08	.06	.03
592	*Jeff Robinson*	.10	.08	.04
593	Rick Leach	.06	.05	.02
594	Curt Wilkerson(FC)	.08	.06	.03
595	Larry Gura	.06	.05	.02
596	Jerry Hairston	.06	.05	.02
597	Brad Lesley	.06	.05	.02
598	Jose Oquendo	.06	.05	.02
599	Storm Davis	.10	.08	.04
600	Pete Rose	.60	.45	.25
601	Tom Lasorda	.10	.08	.04
602	*Jeff Dedmon*	.12	.09	.05
603	Rick Manning	.06	.05	.02
604	Daryl Sconiers	.06	.05	.02
605	Ozzie Smith	.75	.60	.30
606	Rich Gale	.06	.05	.02
607	Bill Almon	.06	.05	.02
608	Craig Lefferts	.08	.06	.03
609	Broderick Perkins	.06	.05	.02
610	Jack Morris	.15	.11	.06
611	Ozzie Virgil	.06	.05	.02
612	Mike Armstrong	.06	.05	.02
613	Terry Puhl	.06	.05	.02
614	Al Williams	.06	.05	.02
615	Marvell Wynne	.06	.05	.02
616	Scott Sanderson	.06	.05	.02
617	Willie Wilson	.12	.09	.05
618	Pete Falcone	.06	.05	.02

		MT	NR MT	EX
619	Jeff Leonard	.10	.08	.04
620	*Dwight Gooden*	3.00	2.25	1.25
621	Marvis Foley	.06	.05	.02
622	Luis Leal	.06	.05	.02
623	Greg Walker	.12	.09	.05
624	Benny Ayala	.06	.05	.02
625	*Mark Langston*	1.50	1.25	.60
626	German Rivera	.06	.05	.02
627	*Eric Davis*(FC)	2.50	2.00	1.00
628	Rene Lachemann	.06	.05	.02
629	Dick Schofield	.12	.09	.05
630	Tim Raines	.20	.15	.08
631	Bob Forsch	.08	.06	.03
632	Bruce Bochte	.06	.05	.02
633	Glenn Hoffman	.06	.05	.02
634	Bill Dawley	.06	.05	.02
635	Terry Kennedy	.08	.06	.03
636	Shane Rawley	.10	.08	.04
637	Brett Butler	.08	.06	.03
638	*Mike Pagliarulo*(FC)	.12	.09	.05
639	Ed Hodge	.06	.05	.02
640	Steve Henderson	.06	.05	.02
641	Rod Scurry	.06	.05	.02
642	Dave Owen	.06	.05	.02
643	Johnny Grubb	.06	.05	.02
644	Mark Huismann(FC)	.06	.05	.02
645	Damaso Garcia	.06	.05	.02
646	Scot Thompson	.06	.05	.02
647	Rafael Ramirez	.06	.05	.02
648	Bob Jones	.06	.05	.02
649	Sid Fernandez(FC)	.10	.08	.04
650	Greg Luzinski	.10	.08	.04
651	Jeff Russell	.08	.06	.03
652	Joe Nolan	.06	.05	.02
653	Mark Brouhard	.06	.05	.02
654	Dave Anderson	.06	.05	.02
655	Joaquin Andujar	.08	.06	.03
656	Chuck Cottier	.06	.05	.02
657	Jim Slaton	.06	.05	.02
658	Mike Stenhouse	.06	.05	.02
659	Checklist 529-660	.06	.05	.02
660	Tony Gwynn	2.00	1.50	.80
661	Steve Crawford	.06	.05	.02
662	Mike Heath	.06	.05	.02
663	Luis Aguayo	.06	.05	.02
664	*Steve Farr*(FC)	.30	.25	.12
665	Don Mattingly	3.00	2.25	1.25
666	Mike LaCoss	.06	.05	.02
667	Dave Engle	.06	.05	.02
668	Steve Trout	.06	.05	.02
669	Lee Lacy	.06	.05	.02
670	Tom Seaver	.40	.30	.15
671	Dane Iorg	.06	.05	.02
672	Juan Berenguer	.06	.05	.02
673	Buck Martinez	.06	.05	.02
674	Atlee Hammaker	.06	.05	.02
675	Tony Perez	.15	.11	.06
676	*Albert Hall*(FC)	.15	.11	.06
677	Wally Backman	.08	.06	.03
678	Joey McLaughlin	.06	.05	.02
679	Bob Kearney	.06	.05	.02
680	Jerry Reuss	.08	.06	.03
681	Ben Oglivie	.08	.06	.03
682	Doug Corbett	.06	.05	.02
683	Whitey Herzog	.08	.06	.03
684	Bill Doran	.12	.09	.05
685	Bill Caudill	.06	.05	.02
686	Mike Easler	.08	.06	.03
687	Bill Gullickson	.06	.05	.02
688	Len Matuszek	.06	.05	.02
689	Luis DeLeon	.06	.05	.02
690	Alan Trammell	.25	.20	.10
691	Dennis Rasmussen(FC)	.10	.08	.04
692	Randy Bush	.06	.05	.02
693	Tim Stoddard	.06	.05	.02
694	Joe Carter(FC)	5.00	3.75	2.00
695	Rick Rhoden	.10	.08	.04
696	John Rabb	.06	.05	.02
697	Onix Concepcion	.06	.05	.02
698	Jorge Bell	.20	.15	.08
699	Donnie Moore	.06	.05	.02
700	Eddie Murray	.50	.40	.20
701	Eddie Murray (All-Star)	.30	.25	.12
702	Damaso Garcia (All-Star)	.08	.06	.03
703	George Brett (All-Star)	.50	.40	.20
704	Cal Ripken, Jr. (All-Star)	1.00	.70	.40
705	Dave Winfield (All-Star)	.50	.40	.20
706	Rickey Henderson (All-Star)	.30	.25	.12
707	Tony Armas (All-Star)	.08	.06	.03
708	Lance Parrish (All-Star)	.15	.11	.06
709	Mike Boddicker (All-Star)	.08	.06	.03

		MT	NR MT	EX
710	Frank Viola (All-Star)	.12	.09	.05
711	Dan Quisenberry (All-Star)	.10	.08	.04
712	Keith Hernandez (All-Star)	.10	.08	.04
713	Ryne Sandberg (All-Star)	1.00	.70	.40
714	Mike Schmidt (All-Star)	.50	.40	.20
715	Ozzie Smith (All-Star)	.15	.11	.06
716	Dale Murphy (All-Star)	.30	.25	.12
717	Tony Gwynn (All-Star)	.50	.40	.20
718	Jeff Leonard (All-Star)	.06	.05	.02
719	Gary Carter (All-Star)	.20	.15	.08
720	Rick Sutcliffe (All-Star)	.12	.09	.05
721	Bob Knepper (All-Star)	.08	.06	.03
722	Bruce Sutter (All-Star)	.10	.08	.04
723	Dave Stewart	.12	.09	.05
724	Oscar Gamble	.08	.06	.03
725	Floyd Bannister	.10	.08	.04
726	Al Bumbry	.08	.06	.03
727	Frank Pastore	.06	.05	.02
728	Bob Bailor	.06	.05	.02
729	Don Sutton	.30	.25	.12
730	Dave Kingman	.15	.11	.06
731	Neil Allen	.06	.05	.02
732	John McNamara	.06	.05	.02
733	Tony Scott	.06	.05	.02
734	John Henry Johnson	.06	.05	.02
735	Garry Templeton	.08	.06	.03
736	Jerry Mumphrey	.06	.05	.02
737	Bo Diaz	.08	.06	.03
738	Omar Moreno	.06	.05	.02
739	Ernie Camacho	.06	.05	.02
740	Jack Clark	.08	.06	.03
741	John Butcher	.06	.05	.02
742	Ron Hassey	.06	.05	.02
743	Frank White	.10	.08	.04
744	Doug Bair	.06	.05	.02
745	Buddy Bell	.12	.09	.05
746	Jim Clancy	.08	.06	.03
747	Alex Trevino	.06	.05	.02
748	Lee Mazzilli	.08	.06	.03
749	Julio Cruz	.06	.05	.02
750	Rollie Fingers	.20	.15	.08
751	Kelvin Chapman	.06	.05	.02
752	Bob Owchinko	.06	.05	.02
753	Greg Brock	.08	.06	.03
754	Larry Milbourne	.06	.05	.02
755	Ken Singleton	.08	.06	.03
756	Rob Picciolo	.06	.05	.02
757	Willie McGee	.15	.11	.06
758	Ray Burris	.06	.05	.02
759	Jim Fanning	.06	.05	.02
760	Nolan Ryan	5.00	3.75	2.00
761	Jerry Remy	.06	.05	.02
762	Eddie Whitson	.06	.05	.02
763	Kiko Garcia	.06	.05	.02
764	Jamie Easterly	.06	.05	.02
765	Willie Randolph	.10	.08	.04
766	Paul Mirabella	.06	.05	.02
767	Darrell Brown	.06	.05	.02
768	Ron Cey	.10	.08	.04
769	Joe Cowley	.06	.05	.02
770	Carlton Fisk	.30	.25	.12
771	Geoff Zahn	.06	.05	.02
772	Johnnie LeMaster	.06	.05	.02
773	Hal McRae	.10	.08	.04
774	Dennis Lamp	.06	.05	.02
775	Mookie Wilson	.10	.08	.04
776	Jerry Royster	.06	.05	.02
777	Ned Yost	.06	.05	.02
778	Mike Davis	.08	.06	.03
779	Nick Esasky	.08	.06	.03
780	Mike Flanagan	.10	.08	.04
781	Jim Gantner	.08	.06	.03
782	Tom Niedenfuer	.08	.06	.03
783	Mike Jorgensen	.06	.05	.02
784	Checklist 661-792	.06	.05	.02
785	Tony Armas	.10	.08	.04
786	Enos Cabell	.06	.05	.02
787	Jim Wohlford	.06	.05	.02
788	Steve Comer	.06	.05	.02
789	Luis Salazar	.06	.05	.02
790	Ron Guidry	.10	.08	.04
791	Ivan DeJesus	.06	.05	.02
792	Darrell Evans	.12	.09	.05

Definitions for grading conditions are located in the Introduction of this price guide.

1985 Topps All-Star Glossy Set Of 22

This was the second straight year for this set of 22 cards featuring the starting players, the honorary captains and the managers in the All-Star Game. The set is virtually identical to that of the previous year in design with a color photo, All-Star banner, league emblem, and player's name and position on the front. What makes the cards special is their high gloss finish. The cards were available as inserts in Topps rack packs. With their combination of attractive appearance and big-name stars, these 2-1/2" by 3-1/2" cards will probably continue to enjoy a great deal of popularity.

		MT	NR MT	EX
Complete Set:		7.00	5.25	2.75
Common Player:		.20	.15	.08
1	Paul Owens	.20	.15	.08
2	Steve Garvey	.50	.40	.20
3	Ryne Sandberg	.40	.30	.15
4	Mike Schmidt	.60	.45	.25
5	Ozzie Smith	.30	.25	.12
6	Tony Gwynn	.60	.45	.25
7	Dale Murphy	.80	.60	.30
8	Darryl Strawberry	1.00	.70	.40
9	Gary Carter	.50	.40	.20
10	Charlie Lea	.20	.15	.08
11	Willie McCovey	.40	.30	.15
12	Joe Altobelli	.20	.15	.08
13	Rod Carew	.50	.40	.20
14	Lou Whitaker	.30	.25	.12
15	George Brett	.80	.60	.30
16	Cal Ripken	.60	.45	.25
17	Dave Winfield	.50	.40	.20
18	Chet Lemon	.20	.15	.08
19	Reggie Jackson	.60	.45	.25
20	Lance Parrish	.30	.25	.12
21	Dave Stieb	.25	.20	.10
22	Hank Greenberg	.20	.15	.08

1985 Topps All-Star Glossy Set Of 40

Similar to previous years' glossy sets, the 1985 All-Star "Collector's Edition" glossy set of 40 could be obtained through the mail in eight five-card subsets. To obtain the 2-1/2" by 3-1/2" cards, collectors had to accumulate sweepstakes insert cards from Topps packs, and pay 75¢ postage and handling. Under the circumstances, the complete set of 40 cards was not inexpensive. They are however, rather attractive and popular cards, and the set size enabled Topps to include some players who didn't make their 22-card set.

		MT	NR MT	EX
Complete Set:		18.00	13.50	7.25
Common Player:		.15	.11	.06
1	Dale Murphy	1.00	.70	.40
2	Jesse Orosco	.15	.11	.06
3	Bob Brenly	.15	.11	.06
4	Mike Boddicker	.15	.11	.06
5	Dave Kingman	.25	.20	.10
6	Jim Rice	.50	.40	.20
7	Frank Viola	.30	.25	.12
8	Alvin Davis	.35	.25	.14
9	Rick Sutcliffe	.20	.15	.08
10	Pete Rose	1.25	.90	.50
11	Leon Durham	.15	.11	.06
12	Joaquin Andujar	.15	.11	.06
13	Keith Hernandez	.40	.30	.15
14	Dave Winfield	.60	.45	.25
15	Reggie Jackson	.70	.50	.30
16	Alan Trammell	.35	.25	.14
17	Bert Blyleven	.20	.15	.08
18	Tony Armas	.15	.11	.06
19	Rich Gossage	.25	.20	.10
20	Jose Cruz	.15	.11	.06
21	Ryne Sandberg	.40	.30	.15
22	Bruce Sutter	.20	.15	.08
23	Mike Schmidt	1.00	.70	.40
24	Cal Ripken	.70	.50	.30
25	Dan Petry	.15	.11	.06
26	Jack Morris	.30	.25	.12
27	Don Mattingly	3.50	2.75	1.50
28	Eddie Murray	.60	.45	.25
29	Tony Gwynn	.60	.45	.25
30	Charlie Lea	.15	.11	.06
31	Juan Samuel	.30	.25	.12
32	Phil Niekro	.35	.25	.14
33	Alejandro Pena	.15	.11	.06
34	Harold Baines	.25	.20	.10
35	Dan Quisenberry	.15	.11	.06
36	Gary Carter	.50	.40	.20
37	Mario Soto	.15	.11	.06
38	Dwight Gooden	2.50	2.00	1.00
39	Tom Brunansky	.20	.15	.08
40	Dave Stieb	.20	.15	.08

1985 Topps Traded

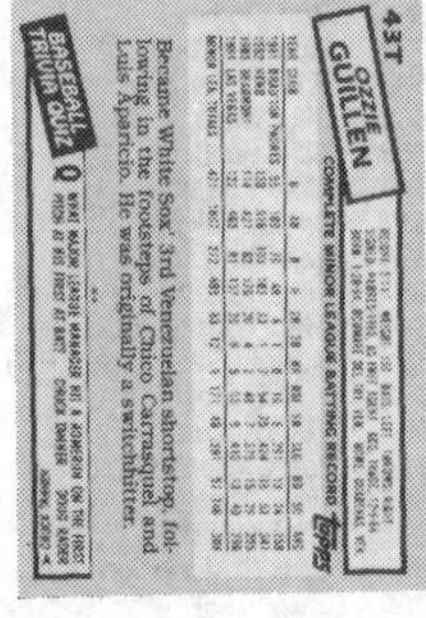

By 1985, the Topps Traded set had become a yearly feature, and Topps continued the tradition with another 132-card set. The 2-1/2" by 3-1/2" cards followed the pattern of being virtually identical in design to the regular cards issued by Topps. Sold only through established hobby dealers, the set features traded veterans and promising rookies. A glossy-finish "Tiffany" edition of the set is valued at four times normal Traded card value for commons, up to five or six times normal value for superstars and hot rookies.

		MT	NR MT	EX
Complete Set (132):		25.00	18.50	10.00
Common Player:		.10	.08	.04
1T	Don Aase	.10	.08	.04
2T	Bill Almon	.10	.08	.04
3T	Benny Ayala	.10	.08	.04
4T	Dusty Baker	.15	.11	.06
5T	George Bamberger	.10	.08	.04
6T	Dale Berra	.10	.08	.04
7T	Rich Bordi	.10	.08	.04
8T	Daryl Boston(FC)	.20	.15	.08
9T	Hubie Brooks	.25	.20	.10
10T	Chris Brown(FC)	.10	.08	.04
11T	Tom Browning(FC)	.60	.45	.25
12T	Al Bumbry	.10	.08	.04
13T	Ray Burris	.10	.08	.04
14T	Jeff Burroughs	.15	.11	.06
15T	Bill Campbell	.10	.08	.04
16T	Don Carman(FC)	.15	.11	.06
17T	Gary Carter	.60	.45	.25
18T	Bobby Castillo	.10	.08	.04
19T	Bill Caudill	.10	.08	.04
20T	Rick Cerone	.10	.08	.04
21T	Bryan Clark	.10	.08	.04
22T	Jack Clark	.12	.09	.05
23T	Pat Clements(FC)	.20	.15	.08
24T	Vince Coleman(FC)	.60	.45	.25
25T	Dave Collins	.15	.11	.06
26T	Danny Darwin	.15	.11	.06
27T	Jim Davenport	.10	.08	.04
28T	Jerry Davis	.10	.08	.04
29T	Brian Dayett	.10	.08	.04
30T	Ivan DeJesus	.10	.08	.04
31T	Ken Dixon	.10	.08	.04
32T	Mariano Duncan(FC)	.50	.40	.20
33T	John Felske	.10	.08	.04
34T	Mike Fitzgerald	.10	.08	.04
35T	Ray Fontenot	.10	.08	.04
36T	Greg Gagne(FC)	.35	.25	.14
37T	Oscar Gamble	.15	.11	.06
38T	Scott Garrelts(FC)	.15	.11	.06
39T	Bob L. Gibson	.10	.08	.04
40T	Jim Gott	.10	.08	.04
41T	David Green	.10	.08	.04
42T	Alfredo Griffin	.15	.11	.06
43T	Ozzie Guillen(FC)	1.50	1.25	.60
44T	Eddie Haas	.10	.08	.04
45T	Terry Harper	.10	.08	.04
46T	Toby Harrah	.15	.11	.06
47T	Greg Harris	.10	.08	.04
48T	Ron Hassey	.10	.08	.04
49T	Rickey Henderson	3.50	2.75	1.50
50T	Steve Henderson	.10	.08	.04
51T	George Hendrick	.15	.11	.06
52T	Joe Hesketh(FC)	.20	.15	.08
53T	Teddy Higuera(FC)	.25	.20	.10
54T	Donnie Hill	.10	.08	.04
55T	Al Holland	.10	.08	.04
56T	Burt Hooton	.15	.11	.06
57T	Jay Howell	.15	.11	.06
58T	Ken Howell(FC)	.15	.11	.06
59T	LaMarr Hoyt	.10	.08	.04
60T	Tim Hulett(FC)	.15	.11	.06
61T	Bob James	.10	.08	.04
62T	Steve Jeltz(FC)	.15	.11	.06
63T	Cliff Johnson	.10	.08	.04
64T	Howard Johnson	1.00	.70	.40
65T	Ruppert Jones	.10	.08	.04
66T	Steve Kemp	.15	.11	.06
67T	Bruce Kison	.10	.08	.04
68T	Alan Knicely	.10	.08	.04
69T	Mike LaCoss	.10	.08	.04
70T	Lee Lacy	.10	.08	.04
71T	Dave LaPoint	.10	.08	.04
72T	Gary Lavelle	.10	.08	.04
73T	Vance Law	.15	.11	.06
74T	Johnnie LeMaster	.10	.08	.04
75T	Sixto Lezcano	.10	.08	.04
76T	Tim Lollar	.10	.08	.04
77T	Fred Lynn	.30	.25	.12
78T	Billy Martin	.20	.15	.08
79T	Ron Mathis	.10	.08	.04
80T	Len Matuszek	.10	.08	.04
81T	Gene Mauch	.15	.11	.06
82T	Oddibe McDowell	.25	.20	.10
83T	Roger McDowell(FC)	.50	.40	.20
84T	John McNamara	.10	.08	.04
85T	Donnie Moore	.10	.08	.04
86T	Gene Nelson	.10	.08	.04
87T	Steve Nicosia	.10	.08	.04
88T	Al Oliver	.15	.11	.06
89T	Joe Orsulak(FC)	.20	.15	.08
90T	Rob Picciolo	.10	.08	.04
91T	Chris Pittaro	.10	.08	.04
92T	Jim Presley(FC)	.10	.08	.04
93T	Rick Reuschel	.10	.08	.04
94T	Bert Roberge	.10	.08	.04
95T	Bob Rodgers	.10	.08	.04
96T	Jerry Royster	.10	.08	.04
97T	Dave Rozema	.10	.08	.04
98T	Dave Rucker	.10	.08	.04
99T	Vern Ruhle	.10	.08	.04
100T	Paul Runge(FC)	.10	.08	.04
101T	Mark Salas(FC)	.10	.08	.04
102T	Luis Salazar	.10	.08	.04
103T	Joe Sambito	.10	.08	.04
104T	Rick Schu(FC)	.10	.08	.04
105T	Donnie Scott	.10	.08	.04
106T	Larry Sheets(FC)	.10	.08	.04
107T	Don Slaught	.10	.08	.04
108T	Roy Smalley	.10	.08	.04
109T	Lonnie Smith	.15	.11	.06
110T	Nate Snell	.10	.08	.04
111T	Chris Speier	.10	.08	.04
112T	Mike Stenhouse	.10	.08	.04
113T	Tim Stoddard	.10	.08	.04
114T	Jim Sundberg	.10	.08	.04
115T	Bruce Sutter	.25	.20	.10
116T	Don Sutton	.60	.45	.25
117T	Kent Tekulve	.15	.11	.06
118T	Tom Tellmann	.10	.08	.04
119T	Walt Terrell	.15	.11	.06
120T	Mickey Tettleton(FC)	8.00	6.00	3.25
121T	Derrel Thomas	.10	.08	.04
122T	Rich Thompson	.10	.08	.04
123T	Alex Trevino	.10	.08	.04
124T	John Tudor	.10	.08	.04
125T	Jose Uribe(FC)	.10	.08	.04
126T	Bobby Valentine	.10	.08	.04
127T	Dave Von Ohlen	.10	.08	.04
128T	U.L. Washington	.10	.08	.04
129T	Earl Weaver	.15	.11	.06
130T	Eddie Whitson	.10	.08	.04
131T	Herm Winningham(FC)	.10	.08	.04
132T	Checklist 1-132	.10	.08	.04

1985 Topps All-Time Record Holders

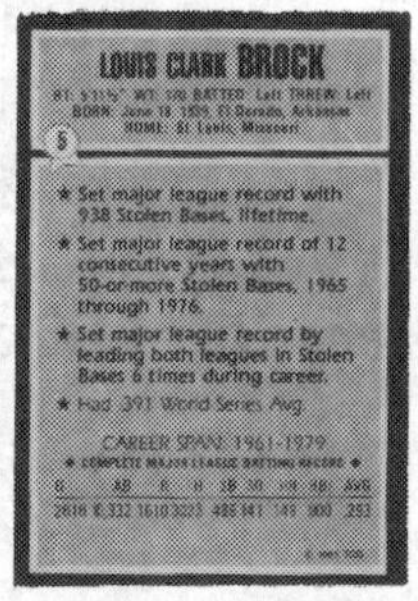

This 44-card boxed set was produced by Topps for the Woolworth's chain stores. Many hobbyists refer to this as the "Woolworth's" set, but that name does not appear anywhere on the cards. Featuring a combination of black and white and color photos of baseball record holders from all eras, the set is in the standard 2-1/2" by 3-1/2" format. Backs, printed in blue and orange, give career details and personal data. Because it combined old-timers with current players, the set did not achieve a great deal of collector popularity.

A card number in parentheses () indicates the set is unnumbered.

		MT	NR MT	EX
Complete Set:		5.00	3.75	2.00
Common Player:		.05	.04	.02
1	Hank Aaron	.25	.20	.10
2	Grover Alexander	.10	.08	.04
3	Ernie Banks	.12	.09	.05
4	Yogi Berra	.15	.11	.06
5	Lou Brock	.12	.09	.05
6	Steve Carlton	.12	.09	.05
7	Jack Chesbro	.07	.05	.03
8	Ty Cobb	.30	.25	.12
9	Sam Crawford	.07	.05	.03
10	Rollie Fingers	.07	.05	.03
11	Whitey Ford	.12	.09	.05
12	Johnny Frederick	.05	.04	.02
13	Frankie Frisch	.07	.05	.03
14	Lou Gehrig	.30	.25	.12
15	Jim Gentile	.05	.04	.02
16	Dwight Gooden	.60	.45	.25
17	Rickey Henderson	.15	.11	.06
18	Rogers Hornsby	.12	.09	.05
19	Frank Howard	.07	.05	.03
20	Cliff Johnson	.05	.04	.02
21	Walter Johnson	.15	.11	.06
22	Hub Leonard	.05	.04	.02
23	Mickey Mantle	1.00	.70	.40
24	Roger Maris	.12	.09	.05
25	Christy Mathewson	.12	.09	.05
26	Willie Mays	.20	.15	.08
27	Stan Musial	.20	.15	.08
28	Dan Quisenberry	.05	.04	.02
29	Frank Robinson	.12	.09	.05
30	Pete Rose	.40	.30	.15
31	Babe Ruth	.60	.45	.25
32	Nolan Ryan	.12	.09	.05
33	George Sisler	.10	.08	.04
34	Tris Speaker	.10	.08	.04
35	Ed Walsh	.07	.05	.03
36	Lloyd Waner	.07	.05	.03
37	Earl Webb	.05	.04	.02
38	Ted Williams	.30	.25	.12
39	Maury Wills	.07	.05	.03
40	Hack Wilson	.07	.05	.03
41	Owen Wilson	.05	.04	.02
42	Willie Wilson	.07	.05	.03
43	Rudy York	.05	.04	.02
44	Cy Young	.12	.09	.05

1985 Topps Gallery of Champions

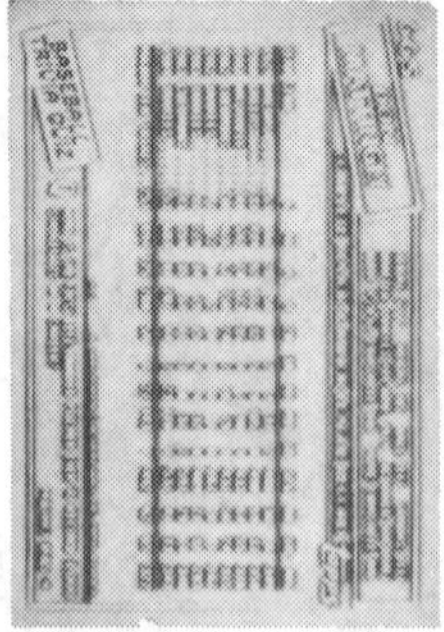

This second annual aluminum, bronze, and silver miniature issues honors 12 award winners from the previous season (MVP, Cy Young, Rookie of Year, Fireman, etc.). Each mini is an exact reproduction, at one-quarter scale of the player's official Topps baseball card, both front and back. The bronze and silver sets were issued in a specially-designed velvet-like case. Aluminum sets came cello-wrapped. A Dwight Gooden pewter replica was given as a premium to dealers who bought bronze and silver sets (value $75). A Pete Rose bronze was issued as a premium to dealers purchasing cases of 1985 Topps Traded sets (value $12).

		MT	NR MT	EX
Complete Aluminum Set:		30.00	22.00	12.00
Complete Bronze Set:		175.00	131.00	70.00
Complete Silver Set:		600.00	450.00	240.00
(1a)	Tony Armas (aluminum)	.70	.50	.30
(1b)	Tony Armas (bronze)	7.50	5.75	3.00
(1c)	Tony Armas (silver)	20.00	15.00	8.00
(2a)	Alvin Davis (aluminum)	1.00	.70	.40
(2b)	Alvin Davis (bronze)	10.00	7.50	4.00
(2c)	Alvin Davis (silver)	30.00	22.00	12.00
(3a)	Dwight Gooden (aluminum)	3.00	2.25	1.25
(3b)	Dwight Gooden (bronze)	25.00	18.50	10.00
(3c)	Dwight Gooden (silver)	125.00	94.00	50.00
(4a)	Tony Gwynn (aluminum)	1.25	.90	.50
(4b)	Tony Gwynn (bronze)	12.00	9.00	4.75
(4c)	Tony Gwynn (silver)	50.00	37.00	20.00
(5a)	Willie Hernandez (aluminum)	.70	.50	.30
(5b)	Willie Hernandez (bronze)	7.50	5.75	3.00
(5c)	Willie Hernandez (silver)	20.00	15.00	8.00
(6a)	Don Mattingly (aluminum)	8.00	6.00	3.25
(6b)	Don Mattingly (bronze)	50.00	37.00	20.00
(6c)	Don Mattingly (silver)	200.00	150.00	80.00
(7a)	Dale Murphy (aluminum)	1.50	1.25	.60
(7b)	Dale Murphy (bronze)	15.00	11.00	6.00
(7c)	Dale Murphy (silver)	80.00	60.00	32.00
(8a)	Dan Quisenberry (aluminum)	.70	.50	.30
(8b)	Dan Quisenberry (bronze)	7.50	5.75	3.00
(8c)	Dan Quisenberry (silver)	20.00	15.00	8.00
(9a)	Ryne Sandberg (aluminum)	1.25	.90	.50
(9b)	Ryne Sandberg (bronze)	12.50	9.50	5.00
(9c)	Ryne Sandberg (silver)	70.00	52.00	27.00
(10a)	Mike Schmidt (aluminum)	1.50	1.25	.60
(10b)	Mike Schmidt (bronze)	15.00	11.00	6.00
(10c)	Mike Schmidt (silver)	80.00	60.00	32.00
(11a)	Rick Sutcliffe (aluminum)	.70	.50	.30
(11b)	Rick Sutcliffe (bronze)	7.50	5.75	3.00
(11c)	Rick Sutcliffe (silver)	20.00	15.00	8.00
(12a)	Bruce Sutter (aluminum)	.70	.50	.30
(12b)	Bruce Sutter (bronze)	7.50	5.75	3.00
(12c)	Bruce Sutter (silver)	20.00	15.00	8.00

1985 Topps Rub Downs

Similar in size and design to the Rub Downs of the previous year, the 1985 set again consisted of 32 unnumbered sheets featuring 112 different players. The set was sold by Topps as a separate issue.

		MT	NR MT	EX
Complete Set:		6.00	4.50	2.50
Common Player:		.10	.08	.04
(1)	Tony Armas, Harold Baines, Lonnie Smith	.10	.08	.04
(2)	Don Baylor, George Hendrick, Ron Kittle, Johnnie LeMaster	.10	.08	.04
(3)	Buddy Bell, Tony Gwynn, Lloyd Moseby	.25	.20	.10
(4)	Bruce Benedict, Atlee Hammaker, Frank White	.10	.08	.04
(5)	Mike Boddicker, Rod Carew, Carlton Fisk, Johnny Ray	.25	.20	.10
(6)	Wade Boggs, Rick Dempsey, Keith Hernandez	.60	.45	.25
(7)	George Brett, Andre Dawson, Paul Molitor, Alan Wiggins	.30	.25	.12
(8)	Tom Brunansky, Pedro Guerrero, Darryl Strawberry	.40	.30	.15
(9)	Bill Buckner, Tim Raines, Ryne Sandberg, Mike Schmidt	.30	.25	.12

		MT	NR MT	EX
(10)	Steve Carlton, Bob Horner, Dan Quisenberry	.25	.20	.10
(11)	Gary Carter, Phil Garner, Ron Guidry	.25	.20	.10
(12)	Jack Clark, Damaso Garcia, Hal McRae, Lance Parrish	.20	.15	.08
(13)	Dave Concepcion, Cecil Cooper, Fred Lynn, Jesse Orosco	.15	.11	.06
(14)	Jose Cruz, Jack Morris, Jim Rice, Rick Sutcliffe	.20	.15	.08
(15)	Alvin Davis, Steve Kemp, Greg Luzinski, Kent Tekulve	.20	.15	.08
(16)	Ron Davis, Kent Hrbek, Juan Samuel	.20	.15	.08
(17)	John Denny, Carney Lansford, Mario Soto, Lou Whitaker	.15	.11	.06
(18)	Leon Durham, Willie Hernandez, Steve Sax	.15	.11	.06
(19)	Dwight Evans, Julio Franco, Dwight Gooden	.40	.30	.15
(20)	George Foster, Gary Gaetti, Bobby Grich, Gary Redus	.15	.11	.06
(21)	Steve Garvey, Jerry Remy, Bill Russell, George Wright	.20	.15	.08
(22)	Kirk Gibson, Rich Gossage, Don Mattingly, Dave Stieb	.90	.70	.35
(23)	Moose Haas, Bruce Sutter, Dickie Thon, Andre Thornton	.10	.08	.04
(24)	Rickey Henderson, Dave Righetti, Pete Rose	.70	.50	.30
(25)	Steve Henderson, Bill Madlock, Alan Trammell	.15	.11	.06
(26)	LaMarr Hoyt, Larry Parrish, Nolan Ryan	.25	.20	.10
(27)	Reggie Jackson, Eric Show, Jason Thompson	.30	.25	.12
(28)	Terry Kennedy, Eddie Murray, Tom Seaver, Ozzie Smith	.25	.20	.10
(29)	Mark Langston, Ben Oglivie, Darrell Porter	.15	.11	.06
(30)	Jeff Leonard, Gary Matthews, Dale Murphy, Dave Winfield	.30	.25	.12
(31)	Craig McMurtry, Cal Ripken, Steve Rogers, Willie Upshaw	.25	.20	.10
(32)	Tony Pena, Fernando Valenzuela, Robin Yount	.20	.15	.08

1985 Topps Stickers

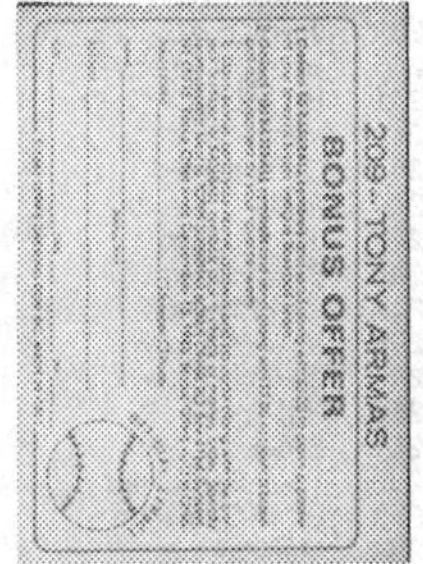

Topps went to a larger size for its stickers in 1985. Each of the 376 stickers measures 2-1/8" by 3" and is numbered on both the front and the back. The backs contain either an offer to obtain an autographed team ball or a poster. An album was also available.

	MT	NR MT	EX
Complete Set:	16.00	12.00	6.50
Common Player:	.03	.02	.01
Sticker Album:	.80	.60	.30

		MT	NR MT	EX
1	Steve Garvey	.25	.20	.10
2	Steve Garvey	.25	.20	.10
3	Dwight Gooden	.25	.20	.10
4	Dwight Gooden	.25	.20	.10
5	Joe Morgan	.10	.08	.04
6	Joe Morgan	.10	.08	.04
7	Don Sutton	.10	.08	.04
8	Don Sutton	.10	.08	.04
9	1984 A.L. Championships (Jack Morris)	.06	.05	.02
10	1984 A.L. Championships (Milt Wilcox)	.03	.02	.01
11	1984 A.L. Championships (Kirk Gibson)	.08	.06	.03
12	1984 N.L. Championships (Gary Matthews)	.04	.03	.02
13	1984 N.L. Championships (Steve Garvey)	.10	.08	.04
14	1984 N.L. Championships (Steve Garvey)	.15	.11	.06
15	1984 World Series (Jack Morris)	.06	.05	.02
16	1984 World Series (Kurt Bevacqua)	.03	.02	.01
17	1984 World Series (Milt Wilcox)	.03	.02	.01
18	1984 World Series (Alan Trammell)	.08	.06	.03
19	1984 World Series (Kirk Gibson)	.08	.06	.03
20	1984 World Series (Alan Trammell)	.12	.09	.05
21	1984 World Series (Chet Lemon)	.03	.02	.01
22	Dale Murphy	.25	.20	.10
23	Steve Bedrosian	.10	.08	.04
24	Bob Horner	.10	.08	.04
25	Claudell Washington	.06	.05	.02
26	Rick Mahler	.06	.05	.02
27	Rafael Ramirez	.04	.03	.02
28	Craig McMurtry	.04	.03	.02
29	Chris Chambliss	.04	.03	.02
30	Alex Trevino	.03	.02	.01
31	Bruce Benedict	.04	.03	.02
32	Ken Oberkfell	.03	.02	.01
33	Glenn Hubbard	.04	.03	.02
34	Ryne Sandberg	.15	.11	.06
35	Rick Sutcliffe	.08	.06	.03
36	Leon Durham	.06	.05	.02
37	Jody Davis	.06	.05	.02
38	Bob Dernier	.04	.03	.02
39	Keith Moreland	.06	.05	.02
40	Scott Sanderson	.04	.03	.02
41	Lee Smith	.06	.05	.02
42	Ron Cey	.06	.05	.02
43	Steve Trout	.06	.05	.02
44	Gary Matthews	.06	.05	.02
45	Larry Bowa	.04	.03	.02
46	Mario Soto	.06	.05	.02
47	Dave Parker	.12	.09	.05
48	Dave Concepcion	.06	.05	.02
49	Gary Redus	.06	.05	.02
50	Ted Power	.06	.05	.02
51	Nick Esasky	.04	.03	.02
52	Duane Walker	.06	.05	.02
53	Eddie Milner	.03	.02	.01
54	Ron Oester	.03	.02	.01
55	Cesar Cedeno	.04	.03	.02
56	Joe Price	.03	.02	.01
57	Pete Rose	.20	.15	.08
58	Nolan Ryan	.15	.11	.06
59	Jose Cruz	.06	.05	.02
60	Jerry Mumphrey	.04	.03	.02
61	Enos Cabell	.03	.02	.01
62	Bob Knepper	.04	.03	.02
63	Dickie Thon	.04	.03	.02
64	Phil Garner	.04	.03	.02
65	Craig Reynolds	.06	.05	.02
66	Frank DiPino	.03	.02	.01
67	Terry Puhl	.03	.02	.01
68	Bill Doran	.06	.05	.02
69	Joe Niekro	.04	.03	.02
70	Pedro Guerrero	.12	.09	.05
71	Fernando Valenzuela	.15	.11	.06
72	Mike Marshall	.08	.06	.03
73	Alejandro Pena	.04	.03	.02
74	Orel Hershiser	.10	.08	.04
75	Ken Landreaux	.06	.05	.02
76	Bill Russell	.06	.05	.02
77	Steve Sax	.06	.05	.02
78	Rick Honeycutt	.03	.02	.01
79	Mike Scioscia	.03	.02	.01
80	Tom Niedenfuer	.06	.05	.02
81	Candy Maldonado	.03	.02	.01
82	Tim Raines	.15	.11	.06
83	Gary Carter	.20	.15	.08
84	Charlie Lea	.03	.02	.01
85	Jeff Reardon	.08	.06	.03
86	Andre Dawson	.06	.05	.02
87	Tim Wallach	.04	.03	.02
88	Terry Francona	.04	.03	.02
89	Steve Rogers	.03	.02	.01
90	Bryn Smith	.03	.02	.01
91	Bill Gullickson	.04	.03	.02
92	Dan Driessen	.03	.02	.01
93	Doug Flynn	.03	.02	.01
94	Mike Schmidt	.20	.15	.08
95	Tony Armas	.30	.25	.12

		MT	NR MT	EX
96	Dale Murphy	.15	.11	.06
97	Rick Sutcliffe	.10	.08	.04
98	Keith Hernandez	.12	.09	.05
99	George Foster	.08	.06	.03
100	Darryl Strawberry	.30	.25	.12
101	Jesse Orosco	.04	.03	.02
102	Mookie Wilson	.04	.03	.02
103	Doug Sisk	.03	.02	.01
104	Hubie Brooks	.06	.05	.02
105	Ron Darling	.04	.03	.02
106	Wally Backman	.04	.03	.02
107	Dwight Gooden	.15	.11	.06
108	Mike Fitzgerald	.04	.03	.02
109	Walt Terrell	.03	.02	.01
110	Ozzie Virgil	.04	.03	.02
111	Mike Schmidt	.25	.20	.10
112	Steve Carlton	.15	.11	.06
113	Al Holland	.03	.02	.01
114	Juan Samuel	.06	.05	.02
115	Von Hayes	.04	.03	.02
116	Jeff Stone	.06	.05	.02
117	Jerry Koosman	.04	.03	.02
118	Al Oliver	.04	.03	.02
119	John Denny	.03	.02	.01
120	Charles Hudson	.03	.02	.01
121	Garry Maddox	.06	.05	.02
122	Bill Madlock	.06	.05	.02
123	John Candelaria	.06	.05	.02
124	Tony Pena	.06	.05	.02
125	Jason Thompson	.03	.02	.01
126	Lee Lacy	.04	.03	.02
127	Rick Rhoden	.06	.05	.02
128	Doug Frobel	.06	.05	.02
129	Kent Tekulve	.04	.03	.02
130	Johnny Ray	.04	.03	.02
131	Marvell Wynne	.08	.06	.03
132	Larry McWilliams	.03	.02	.01
133	Dale Berra	.03	.02	.01
134	George Hendrick	.06	.05	.02
135	Bruce Sutter	.08	.06	.03
136	Joaquin Andujar	.04	.03	.02
137	Ozzie Smith	.10	.08	.04
138	Andy Van Slyke	.04	.03	.02
139	Lonnie Smith	.06	.05	.02
140	Darrell Porter	.03	.02	.01
141	Willie McGee	.06	.05	.02
142	Tom Herr	.04	.03	.02
143	Dave LaPoint	.03	.02	.01
144	Neil Allen	.04	.03	.02
145	David Green	.03	.02	.01
146	Tony Gwynn	.20	.15	.08
147	Rich Gossage	.12	.09	.05
148	Terry Kennedy	.04	.03	.02
149	Steve Garvey	.15	.11	.06
150	Alan Wiggins	.03	.02	.01
151	Garry Templeton	.08	.06	.03
152	Ed Whitson	.04	.03	.02
153	Tim Lollar	.03	.02	.01
154	Dave Dravecky	.04	.03	.02
155	Graig Nettles	.04	.03	.02
156	Eric Show	.03	.02	.01
157	Carmelo Martinez	.03	.02	.01
158	Bob Brenly	.03	.02	.01
159	Gary Lavelle	.03	.02	.01
160	Jack Clark	.10	.08	.04
161	Jeff Leonard	.04	.03	.02
162	Chili Davis	.06	.05	.02
163	Mike Krukow	.03	.02	.01
164	Johnnie LeMaster	.03	.02	.01
165	Atlee Hammaker	.03	.02	.01
166	Dan Gladden	.06	.05	.02
167	Greg Minton	.03	.02	.01
168	Joel Youngblood	.03	.02	.01
169	Frank Williams	.04	.03	.02
170	Tony Gwynn	.20	.15	.08
171	Don Mattingly	.30	.25	.12
172	Bruce Sutter	.15	.11	.06
173	Dan Quisenberry	.10	.08	.04
174	Tony Gwynn	.40	.30	.15
175	Ryne Sandberg	.35	.25	.14
176	Steve Garvey	.30	.25	.12
177	Dale Murphy	.40	.30	.15
178	Mike Schmidt	.40	.30	.15
179	Darryl Strawberry	.50	.40	.20
180	Gary Carter	.30	.25	.12
181	Ozzie Smith	.20	.15	.08
182	Charlie Lea	.15	.11	.06
183	Lou Whitaker	.25	.20	.10
184	Rod Carew	.30	.25	.12
185	Cal Ripken	.40	.30	.15
186	Dave Winfield	.30	.25	.12
187	Reggie Jackson	.40	.30	.15
188	George Brett	.40	.30	.15
189	Lance Parrish	.25	.20	.10
190	Chet Lemon	.15	.11	.06
191	Dave Stieb	.15	.11	.06
192	Gary Carter	.20	.15	.08
193	Mike Schmidt	.30	.25	.12
194	Tony Armas	.15	.11	.06
195	Mike Witt	.10	.08	.04
196	Eddie Murray	.20	.15	.08
197	Cal Ripken	.20	.15	.08
198	Scott McGregor	.04	.03	.02
199	Rick Dempsey	.04	.03	.02
200	Tippy Martinez	.08	.06	.03
201	Ken Singleton	.04	.03	.02
202	Mike Boddicker	.06	.05	.02
203	Rich Dauer	.03	.02	.01
204	John Shelby	.04	.03	.02
205	Al Bumbry	.04	.03	.02
206	John Lowenstein	.04	.03	.02
207	Mike Flanagan	.04	.03	.02
209	Tony Armas	.04	.03	.02
210	Wade Boggs	.60	.45	.25
211	Bruce Hurst	.06	.05	.02
212	Dwight Evans	.06	.05	.02
213	Mike Easler	.04	.03	.02
214	Bill Buckner	.04	.03	.02
215	Bob Stanley	.04	.03	.02
216	Jackie Gutierrez	.03	.02	.01
217	Rich Gedman	.04	.03	.02
218	Jerry Remy	.03	.02	.01
219	Marty Barrett	.04	.03	.02
220	Reggie Jackson	.20	.15	.08
221	Geoff Zahn	.03	.02	.01
222	Doug DeCinces	.06	.05	.02
223	Rod Carew	.20	.15	.08
224	Brian Downing	.04	.03	.02
225	Fred Lynn	.06	.05	.02
226	Gary Pettis	.04	.03	.02
227	Mike Witt	.06	.05	.02
228	Bob Boone	.06	.05	.02
229	Tommy John	.06	.05	.02
230	Bobby Grich	.06	.05	.02
231	Ron Romanick	.04	.03	.02
232	Ron Kittle	.06	.05	.02
233	Richard Dotson	.06	.05	.02
234	Harold Baines	.08	.06	.03
235	Tom Seaver	.15	.11	.06
236	Greg Walker	.06	.05	.02
237	Roy Smalley	.04	.03	.02
238	Greg Luzinski	.06	.05	.02
239	Julio Cruz	.03	.02	.01
240	Scott Fletcher	.03	.02	.01
241	Rudy Law	.04	.03	.02
242	Vance Law	.03	.02	.01
243	Carlton Fisk	.20	.15	.08
244	Andre Thornton	.06	.05	.02
245	Julio Franco	.08	.06	.03
246	Brett Butler	.06	.05	.02
247	Bert Blyleven	.08	.06	.03
248	Mike Hargrove	.04	.03	.02
249	George Vukovich	.04	.03	.02
250	Pat Tabler	.04	.03	.02
251	Brook Jacoby	.06	.05	.02
252	Tony Bernazard	.03	.02	.01
253	Ernie Camacho	.03	.02	.01
254	Mel Hall	.06	.05	.02
255	Carmen Castillo	.04	.03	.02
256	Jack Morris	.12	.09	.05
257	Willie Hernandez	.06	.05	.02
258	Alan Trammell	.15	.11	.06
259	Lance Parrish	.12	.09	.05
260	Chet Lemon	.10	.08	.04
261	Lou Whitaker	.06	.05	.02
262	Howard Johnson	.06	.05	.02
263	Barbaro Garbey	.06	.05	.02
264	Dan Petry	.03	.02	.01
265	Aurelio Lopez	.03	.02	.01
266	Larry Herndon	.03	.02	.01
267	Kirk Gibson	.06	.05	.02
268	George Brett	.25	.20	.10
269	Dan Quisenberry	.06	.05	.02
270	Hal McRae	.06	.05	.02
271	Steve Balboni	.06	.05	.02
272	Pat Sheridan	.06	.05	.02
273	Jorge Orta	.04	.03	.02
274	Frank White	.04	.03	.02
275	Bud Black	.03	.02	.01
276	Darryl Motley	.03	.02	.01
277	Willie Wilson	.04	.03	.02
278	Larry Gura	.03	.02	.01

		MT	NR MT	EX
279	Don Slaught	.03	.02	.01
280	Dwight Gooden	.20	.15	.08
281	Mark Langston	.30	.25	.12
282	Tim Raines	.15	.11	.06
283	Rickey Henderson	.10	.08	.04
284	Robin Yount	.15	.11	.06
285	Rollie Fingers	.10	.08	.04
286	Jim Sundberg	.03	.02	.01
287	Cecil Cooper	.06	.05	.02
288	Jaime Cocanower	.04	.03	.02
289	Mike Caldwell	.03	.02	.01
290	Don Sutton	.06	.05	.02
291	Rick Manning	.04	.03	.02
292	Ben Oglivie	.04	.03	.02
293	Moose Haas	.15	.11	.06
294	Ted Simmons	.04	.03	.02
295	Jim Gantner	.03	.02	.01
296	Kent Hrbek	.12	.09	.05
297	Ron Davis	.03	.02	.01
298	Dave Engle	.03	.02	.01
299	Tom Brunansky	.06	.05	.02
300	Frank Viola	.06	.05	.02
301	Mike Smithson	.04	.03	.02
302	Gary Gaetti	.06	.05	.02
303	Tim Teufel	.04	.03	.02
304	Mickey Hatcher	.04	.03	.02
305	John Butcher	.03	.02	.01
306	Darrell Brown	.03	.02	.01
307	Kirby Puckett	.06	.05	.02
308	Dave Winfield	.15	.11	.06
309	Phil Niekro	.12	.09	.05
310	Don Mattingly	.70	.50	.30
311	Don Baylor	.08	.06	.03
312	Willie Randolph	.04	.03	.02
313	Ron Guidry	.06	.05	.02
314	Dave Righetti	.06	.05	.02
315	Bobby Meacham	.04	.03	.02
316	Butch Wynegar	.04	.03	.02
317	Mike Pagliarulo	.08	.06	.03
318	Joe Cowley	.03	.02	.01
319	John Montefusco	.03	.02	.01
320	Dave Kingman	.08	.06	.03
321	Rickey Henderson	.20	.15	.08
322	Bill Caudill	.03	.02	.01
323	Dwayne Murphy	.04	.03	.02
324	Steve McCatty	.04	.03	.02
325	Joe Morgan	.06	.05	.02
326	Mike Heath	.03	.02	.01
327	Chris Codiroli	.06	.05	.02
328	Ray Burris	.04	.03	.02
329	Tony Phillips	.03	.02	.01
330	Carney Lansford	.04	.03	.02
331	Bruce Bochte	.03	.02	.01
332	Alvin Davis	.15	.11	.06
333	Al Cowens	.03	.02	.01
334	Jim Beattie	.03	.02	.01
335	Bob Kearney	.03	.02	.01
336	Ed Vande Berg	.03	.02	.01
337	Mark Langston	.08	.06	.03
338	Dave Henderson	.04	.03	.02
339	Spike Owen	.03	.02	.01
340	Matt Young	.04	.03	.02
341	Jack Perconte	.04	.03	.02
342	Barry Bonnell	.03	.02	.01
343	Mike Stanton	.03	.02	.01
344	Pete O'Brien	.08	.06	.03
345	Charlie Hough	.06	.05	.02
346	Larry Parrish	.06	.05	.02
347	Buddy Bell	.08	.06	.03
348	Frank Tanana	.06	.05	.02
349	Curt Wilkerson	.03	.02	.01
350	Jeff Kunkel	.03	.02	.01
351	Billy Sample	.03	.02	.01
352	Danny Darwin	.03	.02	.01
353	Gary Ward	.03	.02	.01
354	Mike Mason	.03	.02	.01
355	Mickey Rivers	.04	.03	.02
356	Dave Stieb	.08	.06	.03
357	Damaso Garcia	.04	.03	.02
358	Willie Upshaw	.06	.05	.02
359	Lloyd Moseby	.08	.06	.03
360	George Bell	.08	.06	.03
361	Luis Leal	.04	.03	.02
362	Jesse Barfield	.06	.05	.02
363	Dave Collins	.03	.02	.01
364	Roy Lee Jackson	.04	.03	.02
365	Doyle Alexander	.04	.03	.02
366	Alfredo Griffin	.04	.03	.02
367	Cliff Johnson	.04	.03	.02
368	Alvin Davis	.15	.11	.06
369	Juan Samuel	.10	.08	.04
370	Brook Jacoby	.08	.06	.03
371	Dwight Gooden, Mark Langston	.30	.25	.12
372	Mike Fitzgerald	.04	.03	.02
373	Jackie Gutierrez	.03	.02	.01
374	Dan Gladden	.08	.06	.03
375	Carmelo Martinez	.06	.05	.02
376	Kirby Puckett	.20	.15	.08

1985 Topps Super

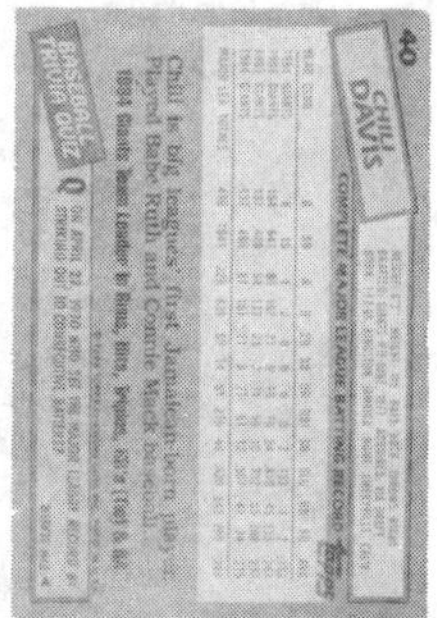

Still trying to sell collectors on the idea of jumbo-sized cards, Topps returned for a second year with its 4-7/8" by 6-7/8" "Super" set. In fact, the set size was doubled from the previous year, to 60 cards. The Supers are identical to the regular-issue 1985 cards of the same players, only the card numbers on back were changed. The cards were again sold three per pack for 50¢.

		MT	NR MT	EX
Complete Set:		17.50	13.00	7.00
Common Player:		.25	.20	.10
1	Ryne Sandberg	2.00	1.50	.80
2	Willie Hernandez	.25	.20	.10
3	Rick Sutcliffe	.25	.20	.10
4	Don Mattingly	.90	.70	.35
5	Tony Gwynn	.70	.50	.30
6	Alvin Davis	.25	.20	.10
7	Dwight Gooden	1.00	.70	.40
8	Dan Quisenberry	.25	.20	.10
9	Bruce Sutter	.25	.20	.10
10	Tony Armas	.25	.20	.10
11	Dale Murphy	.90	.70	.35
12	Mike Schmidt	.90	.70	.35
13	Gary Carter	.50	.40	.20
14	Rickey Henderson	.70	.50	.30
15	Tim Raines	.50	.40	.20
16	Mike Boddicker	.25	.20	.10
17	Alejandro Pena	.25	.20	.10
18	Eddie Murray	.60	.45	.25
19	Gary Matthews	.25	.20	.10
20	Mark Langston	.30	.25	.12
21	Mario Soto	.25	.20	.10
22	Dave Stieb	.25	.20	.10
23	Nolan Ryan	2.00	1.50	.80
24	Steve Carlton	.90	.70	.35
25	Alan Trammell	.50	.40	.20
26	Steve Garvey	.50	.40	.20
27	Kirk Gibson	.35	.25	.14
28	Juan Samuel	.35	.25	.14
29	Reggie Jackson	.90	.70	.35
30	Darryl Strawberry	.90	.70	.35
31	Tom Seaver	.90	.70	.35
32	Pete Rose	1.25	.90	.50
33	Dwight Evans	.30	.25	.12
34	Jose Cruz	.25	.20	.10
35	Bert Blyleven	.35	.25	.14
36	Keith Hernandez	.35	.25	.14
37	Robin Yount	.75	.60	.30
38	Joaquin Andujar	.25	.20	.10
39	Lloyd Moseby	.25	.20	.10
40	Chili Davis	.35	.25	.14
41	Kent Hrbek	.35	.25	.14
42	Dave Parker	.50	.40	.20
43	Jack Morris	.35	.25	.14
44	Pedro Guerrero	.30	.25	.12
45	Mike Witt	.25	.20	.10

		MT	NR MT	EX
46	George Brett	.90	.70	.35
47	Ozzie Smith	.75	.60	.30
48	Cal Ripken, Jr.	2.00	1.50	.80
49	Rich Gossage	.25	.20	.10
50	Jim Rice	.35	.25	.14
51	Harold Baines	.25	.20	.10
52	Fernando Valenzuela	.35	.25	.14
53	Buddy Bell	.25	.20	.10
54	Jesse Orosco	.25	.20	.10
55	Lance Parrish	.35	.25	.14
56	Jason Thompson	.25	.20	.10
57	Tom Brunansky	.25	.20	.10
58	Dave Righetti	.30	.25	.12
59	Dave Kingman	.25	.20	.10
60	Dave Winfield	.90	.70	.35

1985 Topps 3-D

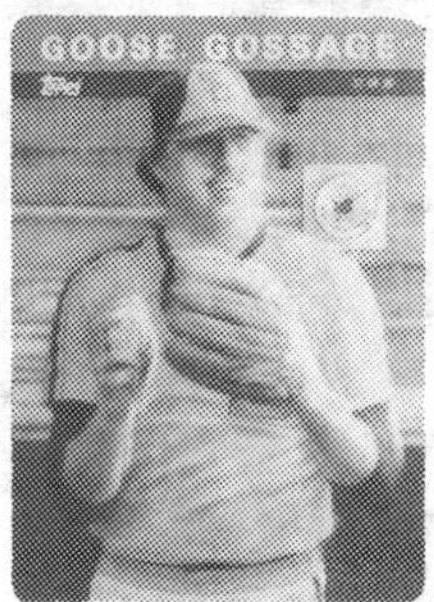

These 4-1/4" by 6" cards were something new. Printed on plastic, rather than paper, the player picture on the card is actually raised above the surface much like might be found on a relief map; a true 3-D baseball card. The plastic cards include the player's name, a Topps logo and card number across the top, and a team logo on the side. The backs are blank but have two peel-off adhesive strips so that the card may be attached to a flat surface. There are 30 cards in the set, the bulk of whom are stars.

		MT	NR MT	EX
Complete Set:		20.00	15.00	8.00
Common Player:		.25	.20	.10
1	Mike Schmidt	.90	.70	.35
2	Eddie Murray	.50	.40	.20
3	Dale Murphy	.90	.70	.35
4	George Brett	.90	.70	.35
5	Pete Rose	1.25	.90	.50
6	Jim Rice	.40	.30	.15
7	Ryne Sandberg	2.00	1.50	.80
8	Don Mattingly	.80	.60	.30
9	Darryl Strawberry	.60	.45	.25
10	Rickey Henderson	.80	.60	.30
11	Keith Hernandez	.35	.25	.14
12	Dave Kingman	.25	.20	.10
13	Tony Gwynn	.60	.45	.25
14	Reggie Jackson	.90	.70	.35
15	Gary Carter	.40	.30	.15
16	Cal Ripken, Jr.	2.00	1.50	.80
17	Tim Raines	.50	.40	.20
18	Dave Winfield	.90	.70	.35
19	Dwight Gooden	.75	.60	.30
20	Dave Stieb	.25	.20	.10
21	Fernando Valenzuela	.30	.25	.12
22	Mark Langston	.30	.25	.12
23	Bruce Sutter	.25	.20	.10
24	Dan Quisenberry	.25	.20	.10
25	Steve Carlton	.75	.60	.30
26	Mike Boddicker	.25	.20	.10
27	Goose Gossage	.30	.25	.12
28	Jack Morris	.30	.25	.12
29	Rick Sutcliffe	.25	.20	.10
30	Tom Seaver	.60	.45	.25

A card number in parentheses () indicates the set is unnumbered.

1986 Topps

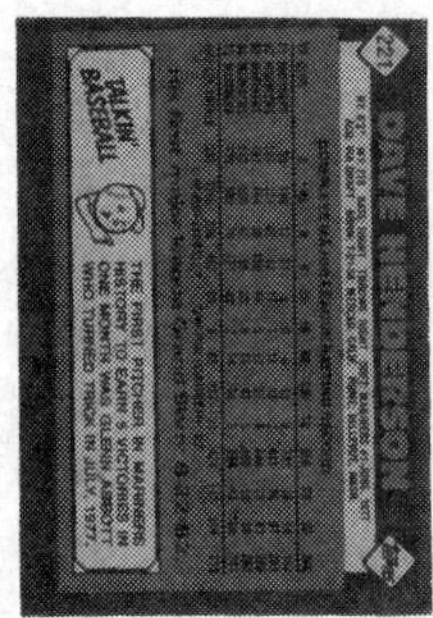

The 1986 Topps set consists of 792 cards. Fronts of the 2-1/2" by 3-1/2" cards feature color photos with the Topps logo in the upper right-hand corner while the player's position is in the lower left-hand corner. Above the picture is the team name, while below it is the player's name. The borders are a departure from previous practice, as the top 7/8" is black, while the remainder was white. There are no card numbers 51 and 171 in the set; the card that should have been #51, Bobby Wine, shares #57 with Bill Doran, while #171, Bob Rodgers, shares #141 with Chuck Cottier. Once again, a 5,000-set glossy-finish "Tiffany" edition was produced. Values are four to six times higher than the same card in the regular issue.

		MT	NR MT	EX
Complete Set (792):		35.00	26.00	14.00
Common Player:		.05	.04	.02
1	Pete Rose	.90	.70	.35
2	Pete Rose (Special 1963-66)	.30	.25	.12
3	Pete Rose (Special 1967-70)	.30	.25	.12
4	Pete Rose (Special 1971-1974)	.30	.25	.12
5	Pete Rose (Special 1975-78)	.30	.25	.12
6	Pete Rose (Special 1972-82)	.30	.25	.12
7	Pete Rose (Special 1983-85)	.30	.25	.12
8	Dwayne Murphy	.07	.05	.03
9	Roy Smith	.05	.04	.02
10	Tony Gwynn	1.00	.70	.40
11	Bob Ojeda	.07	.05	.03
12	*Jose Uribe*(FC)	.05	.04	.02
13	Bob Kearney	.05	.04	.02
14	Julio Cruz	.05	.04	.02
15	Eddie Whitson	.05	.04	.02
16	Rick Schu(FC)	.07	.05	.03
17	Mike Stenhouse	.05	.04	.02
18	Brent Gaff	.05	.04	.02
19	Rich Hebner	.05	.04	.02
20	Lou Whitaker	.12	.09	.05
21	George Bamberger	.05	.04	.02
22	Duane Walker	.05	.04	.02
23	*Manny Lee*(FC)	.15	.11	.06
24	Len Barker	.07	.05	.03
25	Willie Wilson	.12	.09	.05
26	Frank DiPino	.05	.04	.02
27	Ray Knight	.07	.05	.03
28	Eric Davis	.40	.30	.15
29	Tony Phillips	.05	.04	.02
30	Eddie Murray	.40	.30	.15
31	Jamie Easterly	.05	.04	.02
32	Steve Yeager	.05	.04	.02
33	Jeff Lahti	.05	.04	.02
34	Ken Phelps(FC)	.07	.05	.03
35	Jeff Reardon	.12	.09	.05
36	Tigers Leaders (Lance Parrish)	.12	.09	.05
37	Mark Thurmond	.05	.04	.02
38	Glenn Hoffman	.05	.04	.02
39	Dave Rucker	.05	.04	.02
40	Ken Griffey	.10	.08	.04
41	Brad Wellman	.05	.04	.02
42	Geoff Zahn	.05	.04	.02
43	Dave Engle	.05	.04	.02
44	*Lance McCullers*(FC)	.10	.08	.04
45	Damaso Garcia	.05	.04	.02
46	Billy Hatcher(FC)	.20	.15	.08
47	Juan Berenguer	.05	.04	.02

		MT	NR MT	EX
48	Bill Almon	.05	.04	.02
49	Rick Manning	.05	.04	.02
50	Dan Quisenberry	.07	.05	.03
51	Not Issued			
52	Chris Welsh	.05	.04	.02
53	*Len Dykstra*(FC)	3.00	2.25	1.25
54	John Franco	.12	.09	.05
55	Fred Lynn	.15	.11	.06
56	Tom Niedenfuer	.07	.05	.03
57a	Bobby Wine	.05	.04	.02
57b	Bill Doran	.10	.08	.04
58	Bill Krueger	.05	.04	.02
59	Andre Thornton	.07	.05	.03
60	Dwight Evans	.12	.09	.05
61	Karl Best	.05	.04	.02
62	Bob Boone	.07	.05	.03
63	Ron Roenicke	.05	.04	.02
64	Floyd Bannister	.10	.08	.04
65	Dan Driessen	.07	.05	.03
66	Cardinals Leaders (Bob Forsch)	.07	.05	.03
67	Carmelo Martinez	.07	.05	.03
68	Ed Lynch	.05	.04	.02
69	Luis Aguayo	.05	.04	.02
70	Dave Winfield	.60	.45	.25
71	Ken Schrom	.05	.04	.02
72	Shawon Dunston	.15	.11	.06
73	Randy O'Neal(FC)	.07	.05	.03
74	Rance Mulliniks	.05	.04	.02
75	Jose DeLeon	.07	.05	.03
76	Dion James	.07	.05	.03
77	Charlie Leibrandt	.07	.05	.03
78	Bruce Benedict	.05	.04	.02
79	Dave Schmidt	.07	.05	.03
80	Darryl Strawberry	.40	.30	.15
81	Gene Mauch	.07	.05	.03
82	Tippy Martinez	.05	.04	.02
83	Phil Garner	.07	.05	.03
84	Curt Young	.07	.05	.03
85	Tony Perez	.15	.11	.06
86	Tom Waddell	.05	.04	.02
87	Candy Maldonado	.10	.08	.04
88	Tom Nieto	.05	.04	.02
89	Randy St. Claire(FC)	.07	.05	.03
90	Garry Templeton	.07	.05	.03
91	Steve Crawford	.05	.04	.02
92	Al Cowens	.05	.04	.02
93	Scot Thompson	.05	.04	.02
94	Rick Bordi	.05	.04	.02
95	Ozzie Virgil	.05	.04	.02
96	Blue Jay Leaders (Jim Clancy)	.07	.05	.03
97	Gary Gaetti	.20	.15	.08
98	Dick Ruthven	.05	.04	.02
99	Buddy Biancalana	.05	.04	.02
100	Nolan Ryan	3.00	2.25	1.25
101	Dave Bergman	.05	.04	.02
102	*Joe Orsulak*	.15	.11	.06
103	Luis Salazar	.05	.04	.02
104	Sid Fernandez	.12	.09	.05
105	Gary Ward	.07	.05	.03
106	Ray Burris	.05	.04	.02
107	Rafael Ramirez	.05	.04	.02
108	Ted Power	.05	.04	.02
109	Len Matuszek	.05	.04	.02
110	Scott McGregor	.07	.05	.03
111	Roger Craig	.07	.05	.03
112	Bill Campbell	.05	.04	.02
113	U.L. Washington	.05	.04	.02
114	Mike Brown	.05	.04	.02
115	Jay Howell	.07	.05	.03
116	Brook Jacoby	.10	.08	.04
117	Bruce Kison	.05	.04	.02
118	Jerry Royster	.05	.04	.02
119	Barry Bonnell	.05	.04	.02
120	Steve Carlton	.40	.30	.15
121	Nelson Simmons	.05	.04	.02
122	Pete Filson	.05	.04	.02
123	Greg Walker	.10	.08	.04
124	Luis Sanchez	.05	.04	.02
125	Dave Lopes	.07	.05	.03
126	Mets Leaders (Mookie Wilson)	.07	.05	.03
127	*Jack Howell*(FC)	.05	.04	.02
128	John Wathan	.07	.05	.03
129	Jeff Dedmon(FC)	.05	.04	.02
130	Alan Trammell	.15	.11	.06
131	Checklist 1-132	.05	.04	.02
132	Razor Shines	.05	.04	.02
133	Andy McGaffigan	.05	.04	.02
134	Carney Lansford	.10	.08	.04
135	Joe Niekro	.10	.08	.04
136	Mike Hargrove	.05	.04	.02
137	Charlie Moore	.05	.04	.02
138	Mark Davis	.05	.04	.02
139	Daryl Boston	.10	.08	.04
140	John Candelaria	.10	.08	.04
141a	Bob Rodgers	.05	.04	.02
141b	Chuck Cottier	.05	.04	.02
142	Bob Jones	.05	.04	.02
143	Dave Van Gorder	.05	.04	.02
144	Doug Sisk	.05	.04	.02
145	Pedro Guerrero	.06	.05	.02
146	Jack Perconte	.05	.04	.02
147	Larry Sheets	.05	.04	.02
148	Mike Heath	.05	.04	.02
149	Brett Butler	.07	.05	.03
150	Joaquin Andujar	.07	.05	.03
151	Dave Stapleton	.05	.04	.02
152	Mike Morgan	.05	.04	.02
153	Ricky Adams	.05	.04	.02
154	Bert Roberge	.05	.04	.02
155	Bob Grich	.10	.08	.04
156	White Sox Leaders (Richard Dotson)	.07	.05	.03
157	Ron Hassey	.05	.04	.02
158	Derrel Thomas	.05	.04	.02
159	Orel Hershiser	.15	.11	.06
160	Chet Lemon	.07	.05	.03
161	Lee Tunnell	.05	.04	.02
162	Greg Gagne	.10	.08	.04
163	Pete Ladd	.05	.04	.02
164	Steve Balboni	.07	.05	.03
165	Mike Davis	.07	.05	.03
166	Dickie Thon	.07	.05	.03
167	Zane Smith(FC)	.15	.11	.06
168	Jeff Burroughs	.07	.05	.03
169	George Wright	.05	.04	.02
170	Gary Carter	.25	.20	.10
171	Not Issued			
172	Jerry Reed	.05	.04	.02
173	Wayne Gross	.05	.04	.02
174	Brian Snyder	.05	.04	.02
175	Steve Sax	.15	.11	.06
176	Jay Tibbs	.05	.04	.02
177	Joel Youngblood	.05	.04	.02
178	Ivan DeJesus	.05	.04	.02
179	*Stu Cliburn*(FC)	.10	.08	.04
180	Don Mattingly	.90	.70	.35
181	Al Nipper	.05	.04	.02
182	Bobby Brown	.05	.04	.02
183	Larry Andersen	.05	.04	.02
184	Tim Laudner	.05	.04	.02
185	Rollie Fingers	.30	.25	.12
186	Astros Leaders (Jose Cruz)	.07	.05	.03
187	Scott Fletcher	.07	.05	.03
188	Bob Dernier	.05	.04	.02
189	Mike Mason	.05	.04	.02
190	George Hendrick	.07	.05	.03
191	Wally Backman	.07	.05	.03
192	Milt Wilcox	.05	.04	.02
193	Daryl Sconiers	.05	.04	.02
194	Craig McMurtry	.05	.04	.02
195	Dave Concepcion	.12	.09	.05
196	Doyle Alexander	.10	.08	.04
197	Enos Cabell	.05	.04	.02
198	Ken Dixon	.05	.04	.02
199	Dick Howser	.05	.04	.02
200	Mike Schmidt	1.00	.70	.40
201	Vince Coleman (Record Breaker)(FC)	.12	.09	.05
202	Dwight Gooden (Record Breaker)	.20	.15	.08
203	Keith Hernandez (Record Breaker)	.08	.06	.03
204	Phil Niekro (Record Breaker)	.08	.06	.03
205	Tony Perez (Record Breaker)	.10	.08	.04
206	Pete Rose (Record Breaker)	.50	.40	.20
207	Fernando Valenzuela (Recored Breaker)	.08	.06	.03
208	Ramon Romero	.05	.04	.02
209	Randy Ready	.10	.08	.04
210	Calvin Schiraldi(FC)	.10	.08	.04
211	Ed Wojna	.05	.04	.02
212	Chris Speier	.05	.04	.02
213	Bob Shirley	.05	.04	.02
214	Randy Bush	.05	.04	.02
215	Frank White	.10	.08	.04
216	A's Leaders (Dwayne Murphy)	.07	.05	.03
217	Bill Scherrer	.05	.04	.02
218	Randy Hunt	.05	.04	.02
219	Dennis Lamp	.05	.04	.02
220	Bob Horner	.10	.08	.04
221	Dave Henderson	.10	.08	.04
222	Craig Gerber	.05	.04	.02
223	Atlee Hammaker	.05	.04	.02
224	Cesar Cedeno	.10	.08	.04
225	Ron Darling	.15	.11	.06

#	Player	MT	NR MT	EX
226	Lee Lacy	.05	.04	.02
227	Al Jones	.05	.04	.02
228	Tom Lawless	.05	.04	.02
229	Bill Gullickson	.05	.04	.02
230	Terry Kennedy	.07	.05	.03
231	Jim Frey	.05	.04	.02
232	Rick Rhoden	.10	.08	.04
233	Steve Lyons(FC)	.07	.05	.03
234	Doug Corbett	.05	.04	.02
235	Butch Wynegar	.05	.04	.02
236	Frank Eufemia	.05	.04	.02
237	Ted Simmons	.12	.09	.05
238	Larry Parrish	.10	.08	.04
239	Joel Skinner	.05	.04	.02
240	Tommy John	.20	.15	.08
241	Tony Fernandez	.20	.15	.08
242	Rich Thompson	.05	.04	.02
243	Johnny Grubb	.05	.04	.02
244	Craig Lefferts	.05	.04	.02
245	Jim Sundberg	.07	.05	.03
246	Phillies Leaders (Steve Carlton)	.15	.11	.06
247	Terry Harper	.05	.04	.02
248	Spike Owen	.05	.04	.02
249	Rob Deer(FC)	.10	.08	.04
250	Dwight Gooden	.50	.40	.20
251	Rich Dauer	.05	.04	.02
252	Bobby Castillo	.05	.04	.02
253	Dann Bilardello	.05	.04	.02
254	*Ozzie Guillen*	.30	.25	.12
255	Tony Armas	.07	.05	.03
256	Kurt Kepshire	.05	.04	.02
257	Doug DeCinces	.10	.08	.04
258	*Tim Burke*(FC)	.10	.08	.04
259	Dan Pasqua(FC)	.06	.05	.02
260	Tony Pena	.10	.08	.04
261	Bobby Valentine	.05	.04	.02
262	Mario Ramirez	.05	.04	.02
263	Checklist 133-264	.05	.04	.02
264	*Darren Daulton*(FC)	2.00	1.50	.80
265	Ron Davis	.05	.04	.02
266	Keith Moreland	.07	.05	.03
267	Paul Molitor	.60	.45	.25
268	Mike Scott	.15	.11	.06
269	Dane Iorg	.05	.04	.02
270	Jack Morris	.20	.15	.08
271	Dave Collins	.07	.05	.03
272	Tim Tolman	.05	.04	.02
273	Jerry Willard	.05	.04	.02
274	Ron Gardenhire	.05	.04	.02
275	Charlie Hough	.08	.06	.03
276	Yankees Leaders (Willie Randolph)	.07	.05	.03
277	Jaime Cocanower	.05	.04	.02
278	Sixto Lezcano	.05	.04	.02
279	Al Pardo	.05	.04	.02
280	Tim Raines	.12	.09	.05
281	Steve Mura	.05	.04	.02
282	Jerry Mumphrey	.05	.04	.02
283	Mike Fischlin	.05	.04	.02
284	Brian Dayett	.05	.04	.02
285	Buddy Bell	.10	.08	.04
286	Luis DeLeon	.05	.04	.02
287	*John Christensen*(FC)	.10	.08	.04
288	Don Aase	.05	.04	.02
289	Johnnie LeMaster	.05	.04	.02
290	Carlton Fisk	.30	.25	.12
291	Tom Lasorda	.07	.05	.03
292	Chuck Porter	.05	.04	.02
293	Chris Chambliss	.07	.05	.03
294	Danny Cox	.10	.08	.04
295	Kirk Gibson	.10	.08	.04
296	Geno Petralli(FC)	.07	.05	.03
297	Tim Lollar	.05	.04	.02
298	Craig Reynolds	.05	.04	.02
299	Bryn Smith	.05	.04	.02
300	George Brett	.50	.40	.20
301	Dennis Rasmussen	.12	.09	.05
302	Greg Gross	.05	.04	.02
303	Curt Wardle	.05	.04	.02
304	*Mike Gallego*(FC)	.12	.09	.05
305	Phil Bradley	.06	.05	.02
306	Padres Leaders (Terry Kennedy)	.07	.05	.03
307	Dave Sax	.05	.04	.02
308	Ray Fontenot	.05	.04	.02
309	John Shelby	.05	.04	.02
310	Greg Minton	.05	.04	.02
311	Dick Schofield	.05	.04	.02
312	Tom Filer	.05	.04	.02
313	Joe DeSa	.05	.04	.02
314	Frank Pastore	.05	.04	.02
315	Mookie Wilson	.10	.08	.04
316	Sammy Khalifa	.05	.04	.02

#	Player	MT	NR MT	EX
317	Ed Romero	.05	.04	.02
318	Terry Whitfield	.05	.04	.02
319	Rick Camp	.05	.04	.02
320	Jim Rice	.08	.06	.03
321	Earl Weaver	.07	.05	.03
322	Bob Forsch	.07	.05	.03
323	Jerry Davis	.05	.04	.02
324	Dan Schatzeder	.05	.04	.02
325	Juan Beniquez	.05	.04	.02
326	Kent Tekulve	.07	.05	.03
327	Mike Pagliarulo	.06	.05	.02
328	Pete O'Brien	.10	.08	.04
329	Kirby Puckett	4.00	3.00	1.50
330	Rick Sutcliffe	.12	.09	.05
331	Alan Ashby	.05	.04	.02
332	Darryl Motley	.05	.04	.02
333	Tom Henke(FC)	.20	.15	.08
334	Ken Oberkfell	.05	.04	.02
335	Don Sutton	.25	.20	.10
336	Indians Leaders (Andre Thornton)	.07	.05	.03
337	Darnell Coles	.07	.05	.03
338	Jorge Bell	.15	.11	.06
339	Bruce Berenyi	.05	.04	.02
340	Cal Ripken, Jr.	2.00	1.50	.80
341	Frank Williams	.05	.04	.02
342	Gary Redus	.05	.04	.02
343	Carlos Diaz	.05	.04	.02
344	Jim Wohlford	.05	.04	.02
345	Donnie Moore	.05	.04	.02
346	Bryan Little	.05	.04	.02
347	*Teddy Higuera*	.08	.06	.03
348	Cliff Johnson	.05	.04	.02
349	Mark Clear	.05	.04	.02
350	Jack Clark	.10	.08	.04
351	Chuck Tanner	.05	.04	.02
352	Harry Spilman	.05	.04	.02
353	Keith Atherton	.05	.04	.02
354	Tony Bernazard	.05	.04	.02
355	Lee Smith	.10	.08	.04
356	Mickey Hatcher	.05	.04	.02
357	Ed Vande Berg	.05	.04	.02
358	Rick Dempsey	.07	.05	.03
359	Mike LaCoss	.05	.04	.02
360	Lloyd Moseby	.10	.08	.04
361	Shane Rawley	.10	.08	.04
362	Tom Paciorek	.05	.04	.02
363	Terry Forster	.07	.05	.03
364	Reid Nichols	.05	.04	.02
365	Mike Flanagan	.10	.08	.04
366	Reds Leaders (Dave Concepcion)	.07	.05	.03
367	Aurelio Lopez	.05	.04	.02
368	Greg Brock	.07	.05	.03
369	Al Holland	.05	.04	.02
370	*Vince Coleman*	.25	.20	.10
371	Bill Stein	.05	.04	.02
372	Ben Oglivie	.07	.05	.03
373	*Urbano Lugo*(FC)	.07	.05	.03
374	Terry Francona	.05	.04	.02
375	Rich Gedman	.10	.08	.04
376	Bill Dawley	.05	.04	.02
377	Joe Carter	1.50	1.25	.60
378	Bruce Bochte	.05	.04	.02
379	Bobby Meacham	.05	.04	.02
380	LaMarr Hoyt	.05	.04	.02
381	Ray Miller	.05	.04	.02
382	*Ivan Calderon*(FC)	.50	.40	.20
383	*Chris Brown*	.15	.11	.06
384	Steve Trout	.05	.04	.02
385	Cecil Cooper	.10	.08	.04
386	*Cecil Fielder*(FC)	6.00	4.50	2.50
387	Steve Kemp	.07	.05	.03
388	Dickie Noles	.05	.04	.02
389	Glenn Davis(FC)	.12	.09	.05
390	Tom Seaver	.40	.30	.15
391	Julio Franco	.10	.08	.04
392	John Russell(FC)	.10	.08	.04
393	Chris Pittaro	.05	.04	.02
394	Checklist 265-396	.05	.04	.02
395	Scott Garrelts	.07	.05	.03
396	Red Sox Leaders (Dwight Evans)	.07	.05	.03
397	*Steve Buechele*(FC)	.20	.15	.08
398	*Earnie Riles*(FC)	.15	.11	.06
399	Bill Swift	.25	.20	.10
400	Rod Carew	.30	.25	.12
401	Turn Back The Clock (Fernando Valenzuela)	.15	.11	.06
402	Turn Back The Clock (Tom Seaver)	.15	.11	.06
403	Turn Back The Clock (Willie Mays)	.20	.15	.08
404	Turn Back The Clock (Frank Robinson)	.15	.11	.06
405	Turn Back The Clock (Roger Maris)	.20	.15	.08

		MT	NR MT	EX
406	Scott Sanderson	.05	.04	.02
407	Sal Butera	.05	.04	.02
408	Dave Smith	.07	.05	.03
409	*Paul Runge*	.07	.05	.03
410	Dave Kingman	.15	.11	.06
411	Sparky Anderson	.07	.05	.03
412	Jim Clancy	.07	.05	.03
413	Tim Flannery	.05	.04	.02
414	Tom Gorman	.05	.04	.02
415	Hal McRae	.10	.08	.04
416	Denny Martinez	.07	.05	.03
417	R.J. Reynolds	.07	.05	.03
418	Alan Knicely	.05	.04	.02
419	Frank Wills	.05	.04	.02
420	Von Hayes	.10	.08	.04
421	Dave Palmer	.05	.04	.02
422	Mike Jorgensen	.05	.04	.02
423	Dan Spillner	.05	.04	.02
424	Rick Miller	.05	.04	.02
425	Larry McWilliams	.05	.04	.02
426	Brewers Leaders (Charlie Moore)	.07	.05	.03
427	Joe Cowley	.05	.04	.02
428	Max Venable	.05	.04	.02
429	Greg Booker	.05	.04	.02
430	Kent Hrbek	.10	.08	.04
431	George Frazier	.05	.04	.02
432	Mark Bailey	.05	.04	.02
433	Chris Codiroli	.05	.04	.02
434	Curt Wilkerson	.05	.04	.02
435	Bill Caudill	.05	.04	.02
436	Doug Flynn	.05	.04	.02
437	Rick Mahler	.05	.04	.02
438	Clint Hurdle	.05	.04	.02
439	Rick Honeycutt	.05	.04	.02
440	Alvin Davis	.06	.05	.02
441	Whitey Herzog	.07	.05	.03
442	Ron Robinson(FC)	.12	.09	.05
443	Bill Buckner	.10	.08	.04
444	Alex Trevino	.05	.04	.02
445	Bert Blyleven	.12	.09	.05
446	Lenn Sakata	.05	.04	.02
447	Jerry Don Gleaton	.05	.04	.02
448	*Herm Winningham*	.15	.11	.06
449	Rod Scurry	.05	.04	.02
450	Graig Nettles	.15	.11	.06
451	Mark Brown	.05	.04	.02
452	Bob Clark	.05	.04	.02
453	Steve Jeltz	.07	.05	.03
454	Burt Hooton	.07	.05	.03
455	Willie Randolph	.10	.08	.04
456	Braves Leaders (Dale Murphy)	.25	.20	.10
457	*Mickey Tettleton*	1.00	.70	.40
458	Kevin Bass	.10	.08	.04
459	Luis Leal	.05	.04	.02
460	Leon Durham	.07	.05	.03
461	Walt Terrell	.07	.05	.03
462	Domingo Ramos	.05	.04	.02
463	Jim Gott	.05	.04	.02
464	Ruppert Jones	.05	.04	.02
465	Jesse Orosco	.07	.05	.03
466	Tom Foley	.05	.04	.02
467	Bob James	.05	.04	.02
468	Mike Scioscia	.07	.05	.03
469	Storm Davis	.10	.08	.04
470	Bill Madlock	.12	.09	.05
471	Bobby Cox	.05	.04	.02
472	Joe Hesketh	.07	.05	.03
473	Mark Brouhard	.05	.04	.02
474	John Tudor	.10	.08	.04
475	Juan Samuel	.12	.09	.05
476	Ron Mathis	.05	.04	.02
477	Mike Easler	.07	.05	.03
478	Andy Hawkins	.05	.04	.02
479	*Bob Melvin*(FC)	.05	.04	.02
480	*Oddibe McDowell*	.06	.05	.02
481	Scott Bradley(FC)	.10	.08	.04
482	Rick Lysander	.05	.04	.02
483	George Vukovich	.05	.04	.02
484	Donnie Hill	.05	.04	.02
485	Gary Matthews	.10	.08	.04
486	Angels Leaders (Bob Grich)	.07	.05	.03
487	Bret Saberhagen	.25	.20	.10
488	Lou Thornton	.05	.04	.02
489	Jim Winn	.05	.04	.02
490	Jeff Leonard	.07	.05	.03
491	Pascual Perez	.07	.05	.03
492	Kelvin Chapman	.05	.04	.02
493	Gene Nelson	.05	.04	.02
494	Gary Roenicke	.05	.04	.02
495	Mark Langston	.20	.15	.08
496	Jay Johnstone	.07	.05	.03
497	John Stuper	.05	.04	.02
498	Tito Landrum	.05	.04	.02
499	Bob L. Gibson	.05	.04	.02
500	Rickey Henderson	.60	.45	.25
501	Dave Johnson	.07	.05	.03
502	Glen Cook	.05	.04	.02
503	Mike Fitzgerald	.05	.04	.02
504	Denny Walling	.05	.04	.02
505	Jerry Koosman	.10	.08	.04
506	Bill Russell	.07	.05	.03
507	*Steve Ontiveros*(FC)	.12	.09	.05
508	Alan Wiggins	.05	.04	.02
509	Ernie Camacho	.05	.04	.02
510	Wade Boggs	.90	.70	.35
511	Ed Nunez	.05	.04	.02
512	Thad Bosley	.05	.04	.02
513	Ron Washington	.05	.04	.02
514	Mike Jones	.05	.04	.02
515	Darrell Evans	.12	.09	.05
516	Giants Leaders (Greg Minton)	.07	.05	.03
517	*Milt Thompson*(FC)	.06	.05	.02
518	Buck Martinez	.05	.04	.02
519	Danny Darwin	.05	.04	.02
520	Keith Hernandez	.12	.09	.05
521	Nate Snell	.05	.04	.02
522	Bob Bailor	.05	.04	.02
523	Joe Price	.05	.04	.02
524	Darrell Miller(FC)	.07	.05	.03
525	Marvell Wynne	.05	.04	.02
526	Charlie Lea	.05	.04	.02
527	Checklist 397-528	.05	.04	.02
528	Terry Pendleton	.20	.15	.08
529	Marc Sullivan	.05	.04	.02
530	Rich Gossage	.10	.08	.04
531	Tony LaRussa	.07	.05	.03
532	*Don Carman*	.08	.06	.03
533	Billy Sample	.05	.04	.02
534	Jeff Calhoun	.05	.04	.02
535	Toby Harrah	.07	.05	.03
536	Jose Rijo	.10	.08	.04
537	Mark Salas	.07	.05	.03
538	Dennis Eckersley	.20	.15	.08
539	Glenn Hubbard	.05	.04	.02
540	Dan Petry	.07	.05	.03
541	Jorge Orta	.05	.04	.02
542	Don Schulze	.05	.04	.02
543	Jerry Narron	.05	.04	.02
544	Eddie Milner	.05	.04	.02
545	Jimmy Key	.15	.11	.06
546	Mariners Leaders (Dave Henderson)	.07	.05	.03
547	*Roger McDowell*	.12	.09	.05
548	Mike Young	.05	.04	.02
549	Bob Welch	.12	.09	.05
550	Tom Herr	.10	.08	.04
551	Dave LaPoint	.07	.05	.03
552	Marc Hill	.05	.04	.02
553	Jim Morrison	.05	.04	.02
554	Paul Householder	.05	.04	.02
555	Hubie Brooks	.10	.08	.04
556	John Denny	.05	.04	.02
557	Gerald Perry	.12	.09	.05
558	Tim Stoddard	.05	.04	.02
559	Tommy Dunbar	.05	.04	.02
560	Dave Righetti	.08	.06	.03
561	Bob Lillis	.05	.04	.02
562	Joe Beckwith	.05	.04	.02
563	Alejandro Sanchez	.05	.04	.02
564	Warren Brusstar	.05	.04	.02
565	Tom Brunansky	.12	.09	.05
566	Alfredo Griffin	.07	.05	.03
567	Jeff Barkley	.05	.04	.02
568	Donnie Scott	.05	.04	.02
569	Jim Acker	.05	.04	.02
570	Rusty Staub	.10	.08	.04
571	Mike Jeffcoat	.05	.04	.02
572	Paul Zuvella	.05	.04	.02
573	Tom Hume	.05	.04	.02
574	Ron Kittle	.10	.08	.04
575	Mike Boddicker	.07	.05	.03
576	Expos Leaders (Andre Dawson)	.12	.09	.05
577	Jerry Reuss	.07	.05	.03
578	Lee Mazzilli	.07	.05	.03
579	Jim Slaton	.05	.04	.02
580	Willie McGee	.15	.11	.06
581	Bruce Hurst	.12	.09	.05
582	Jim Gantner	.07	.05	.03
583	Al Bumbry	.05	.04	.02
584	*Brian Fisher*(FC)	.06	.05	.02
585	Garry Maddox	.07	.05	.03
586	Greg Harris	.05	.04	.02

		MT	NR MT	EX
587	Rafael Santana	.05	.04	.02
588	Steve Lake	.05	.04	.02
589	Sid Bream	.10	.08	.04
590	Bob Knepper	.07	.05	.03
591	Jackie Moore	.05	.04	.02
592	Frank Tanana	.10	.08	.04
593	Jesse Barfield	.08	.06	.03
594	Chris Bando	.05	.04	.02
595	Dave Parker	.15	.11	.06
596	Onix Concepcion	.05	.04	.02
597	Sammy Stewart	.05	.04	.02
598	Jim Presley	.06	.05	.02
599	*Rick Aguilera*(FC)	.50	.40	.20
600	Dale Murphy	.15	.11	.06
601	Gary Lucas	.05	.04	.02
602	*Mariano Duncan*	.10	.08	.04
603	Bill Laskey	.05	.04	.02
604	Gary Pettis	.05	.04	.02
605	Dennis Boyd	.07	.05	.03
606	Royals Leaders (Hal McRae)	.07	.05	.03
607	Ken Dayley	.05	.04	.02
608	Bruce Bochy	.05	.04	.02
609	Barbaro Garbey	.05	.04	.02
610	Ron Guidry	.08	.06	.03
611	Gary Woods	.05	.04	.02
612	Richard Dotson	.05	.04	.02
613	Roy Smalley	.05	.04	.02
614	Rick Waits	.05	.04	.02
615	Johnny Ray	.05	.04	.02
616	Glenn Brummer	.05	.04	.02
617	Lonnie Smith	.07	.05	.03
618	Jim Pankovits	.05	.04	.02
619	Danny Heep	.05	.04	.02
620	Bruce Sutter	.12	.09	.05
621	John Felske	.05	.04	.02
622	Gary Lavelle	.05	.04	.02
623	Floyd Rayford	.05	.04	.02
624	Steve McCatty	.05	.04	.02
625	Bob Brenly	.05	.04	.02
626	Roy Thomas	.05	.04	.02
627	Ron Oester	.05	.04	.02
628	*Kirk McCaskill*(FC)	.15	.11	.06
629	*Mitch Webster*(FC)	.06	.05	.02
630	Fernando Valenzuela	.08	.06	.03
631	Steve Braun	.05	.04	.02
632	Dave Von Ohlen	.05	.04	.02
633	Jackie Gutierrez	.05	.04	.02
634	Roy Lee Jackson	.05	.04	.02
635	Jason Thompson	.05	.04	.02
636	Cubs Leaders (Lee Smith)	.07	.05	.03
637	Rudy Law	.05	.04	.02
638	John Butcher	.05	.04	.02
639	Bo Diaz	.07	.05	.03
640	Jose Cruz	.10	.08	.04
641	Wayne Tolleson	.05	.04	.02
642	Ray Searage	.05	.04	.02
643	Tom Brookens	.05	.04	.02
644	Mark Gubicza	.12	.09	.05
645	Dusty Baker	.07	.05	.03
646	Mike Moore	.05	.04	.02
647	Mel Hall	.07	.05	.03
648	Steve Bedrosian	.10	.08	.04
649	Ronn Reynolds	.05	.04	.02
650	Dave Stieb	.12	.09	.05
651	Billy Martin	.12	.09	.05
652	Tom Browning	.08	.06	.03
653	Jim Dwyer	.05	.04	.02
654	Ken Howell	.07	.05	.03
655	Manny Trillo	.07	.05	.03
656	Brian Harper	.05	.04	.02
657	Juan Agosto	.05	.04	.02
658	Rob Wilfong	.05	.04	.02
659	Checklist 529-660	.05	.04	.02
660	Steve Garvey	.15	.11	.06
661	Roger Clemens	3.50	2.75	1.50
662	Bill Schroeder	.05	.04	.02
663	Neil Allen	.05	.04	.02
664	Tim Corcoran	.05	.04	.02
665	Alejandro Pena	.07	.05	.03
666	Rangers Leaders (Charlie Hough)	.07	.05	.03
667	Tim Teufel	.05	.04	.02
668	Cecilio Guante	.05	.04	.02
669	Ron Cey	.10	.08	.04
670	Willie Hernandez	.07	.05	.03
671	Lynn Jones	.05	.04	.02
672	Rob Picciolo	.05	.04	.02
673	Ernie Whitt	.07	.05	.03
674	Pat Tabler	.07	.05	.03
675	Claudell Washington	.07	.05	.03
676	Matt Young	.05	.04	.02
677	Nick Esasky	.07	.05	.03

		MT	NR MT	EX
678	Dan Gladden	.07	.05	.03
679	Britt Burns	.05	.04	.02
680	George Foster	.15	.11	.06
681	Dick Williams	.05	.04	.02
682	Junior Ortiz	.05	.04	.02
683	Andy Van Slyke	.10	.08	.04
684	Bob McClure	.05	.04	.02
685	Tim Wallach	.12	.09	.05
686	Jeff Stone	.05	.04	.02
687	Mike Trujillo	.05	.04	.02
688	Larry Herndon	.07	.05	.03
689	Dave Stewart	.12	.09	.05
690	Ryne Sandberg	2.00	1.50	.80
691	Mike Madden	.05	.04	.02
692	Dale Berra	.05	.04	.02
693	Tom Tellmann	.05	.04	.02
694	Garth Iorg	.05	.04	.02
695	Mike Smithson	.05	.04	.02
696	Dodgers Leaders (Bill Russell)	.07	.05	.03
697	Bud Black	.05	.04	.02
698	Brad Komminsk	.05	.04	.02
699	Pat Corrales	.05	.04	.02
700	Reggie Jackson	.35	.25	.14
701	Keith Hernandez (All-Star)	.10	.08	.04
702	Tom Herr (All-Star)	.07	.05	.03
703	Tim Wallach (All-Star)	.07	.05	.03
704	Ozzie Smith (All-Star)	.15	.11	.06
705	Dale Murphy (All-Star)	.10	.08	.04
706	Pedro Guerrero (All-Star)	.12	.09	.05
707	Willie McGee (All-Star)	.12	.09	.05
708	Gary Carter (All-Star)	.20	.15	.08
709	Dwight Gooden (All-Star)	.12	.09	.05
710	John Tudor (All-Star)	.07	.05	.03
711	Jeff Reardon (All-Star)	.07	.05	.03
712	Don Mattingly (All-Star)	.20	.15	.08
713	Damaso Garcia (All-Star)	.05	.04	.02
714	George Brett (All-Star)	.35	.25	.14
715	Cal Ripken, Jr. (All-Star)	.80	.60	.30
716	Rickey Henderson (All-Star)	.25	.20	.10
717	Dave Winfield (All-Star)	.20	.15	.08
718	George Bell (All-Star)	.10	.08	.04
719	Carlton Fisk (All-Star)	.12	.09	.05
720	Bret Saberhagen (All-Star)	.15	.11	.06
721	Ron Guidry (All-Star)	.10	.08	.04
722	Dan Quisenberry (All-Star)	.07	.05	.03
723	Marty Bystrom	.05	.04	.02
724	Tim Hulett	.07	.05	.03
725	Mario Soto	.07	.05	.03
726	Orioles Leaders (Rick Dempsey)	.07	.05	.03
727	David Green	.05	.04	.02
728	Mike Marshall	.12	.09	.05
729	Jim Beattie	.05	.04	.02
730	Ozzie Smith	.40	.30	.15
731	Don Robinson	.07	.05	.03
732	*Floyd Youmans*(FC)	.12	.09	.05
733	Ron Romanick	.05	.04	.02
734	Marty Barrett	.10	.08	.04
735	Dave Dravecky	.07	.05	.03
736	Glenn Wilson	.07	.05	.03
737	Pete Vuckovich	.07	.05	.03
738	Andre Robertson	.05	.04	.02
739	Dave Rozema	.05	.04	.02
740	Lance Parrish	.08	.06	.03
741	Pete Rose	.40	.30	.15
742	Frank Viola	.15	.11	.06
743	Pat Sheridan	.05	.04	.02
744	Lary Sorensen	.05	.04	.02
745	Willie Upshaw	.07	.05	.03
746	Denny Gonzalez	.05	.04	.02
747	Rick Cerone	.05	.04	.02
748	Steve Henderson	.05	.04	.02
749	Ed Jurak	.05	.04	.02
750	Gorman Thomas	.10	.08	.04
751	Howard Johnson	.15	.11	.06
752	Mike Krukow	.07	.05	.03
753	Dan Ford	.05	.04	.02
754	*Pat Clements*	.12	.09	.05
755	Harold Baines	.15	.11	.06
756	Pirates Leaders (Rick Rhoden)	.07	.05	.03
757	Darrell Porter	.07	.05	.03
758	Dave Anderson	.05	.04	.02
759	Moose Haas	.05	.04	.02
760	Andre Dawson	.40	.30	.15
761	Don Slaught	.05	.04	.02
762	Eric Show	.07	.05	.03
763	Terry Puhl	.05	.04	.02
764	Kevin Gross	.07	.05	.03
765	Don Baylor	.12	.09	.05
766	Rick Langford	.05	.04	.02
767	Jody Davis	.10	.08	.04
768	Vern Ruhle	.05	.04	.02

		MT	NR MT	EX
769	*Harold Reynolds*(FC)	.30	.25	.12
770	Vida Blue	.10	.08	.04
771	John McNamara	.05	.04	.02
772	Brian Downing	.07	.05	.03
773	Greg Pryor	.05	.04	.02
774	Terry Leach	.05	.04	.02
775	Al Oliver	.10	.08	.04
776	Gene Garber	.05	.04	.02
777	Wayne Krenchicki	.05	.04	.02
778	Jerry Hairston	.05	.04	.02
779	Rick Reuschel	.10	.08	.04
780	Robin Yount	.60	.45	.25
781	Joe Nolan	.05	.04	.02
782	Ken Landreaux	.05	.04	.02
783	Ricky Horton	.07	.05	.03
784	Alan Bannister	.05	.04	.02
785	Bob Stanley	.05	.04	.02
786	Twins Leaders (Mickey Hatcher)	.07	.05	.03
787	Vance Law	.07	.05	.03
788	Marty Castillo	.05	.04	.02
789	Kurt Bevacqua	.05	.04	.02
790	Phil Niekro	.12	.09	.05
791	Checklist 661-792	.05	.04	.02
792	Charles Hudson	.06	.05	.02

1986 Topps All-Star Glossy Set Of 22

As in previous years, Topps continued to make the popular glossy-surfaced cards as an insert in rack packs. The All-Star Glossy set of 22 2-1/2" by 3-1/2" cards shows little design change from previous years. Cards feature a front color photo and All-Star banner at the top. The bottom has the player's name and position. The set includes the All-Star starting teams as well as the managers and honorary captains.

		MT	NR MT	EX
Complete Set:		6.00	4.50	2.50
Common Player:		.20	.15	.08
1	Sparky Anderson	.20	.15	.08
2	Eddie Murray	.50	.40	.20
3	Lou Whitaker	.30	.25	.12
4	George Brett	.80	.60	.30
5	Cal Ripken	.60	.45	.25
6	Jim Rice	.50	.40	.20
7	Rickey Henderson	.60	.45	.25
8	Dave Winfield	.50	.40	.20
9	Carlton Fisk	.30	.25	.12
10	Jack Morris	.30	.25	.12
11	A.L. All-Star Team	.20	.15	.08
12	Dick Williams	.20	.15	.08
13	Steve Garvey	.50	.40	.20
14	Tom Herr	.20	.15	.08
15	Graig Nettles	.20	.15	.08
16	Ozzie Smith	.30	.25	.12
17	Tony Gwynn	.60	.45	.25
18	Dale Murphy	.80	.60	.30
19	Darryl Strawberry	.80	.60	.30
20	Terry Kennedy	.20	.15	.08
21	LaMarr Hoyt	.20	.15	.08
22	N.L. All-Star Team	.20	.15	.08

1986 Topps All-Star Glossy Set Of 60

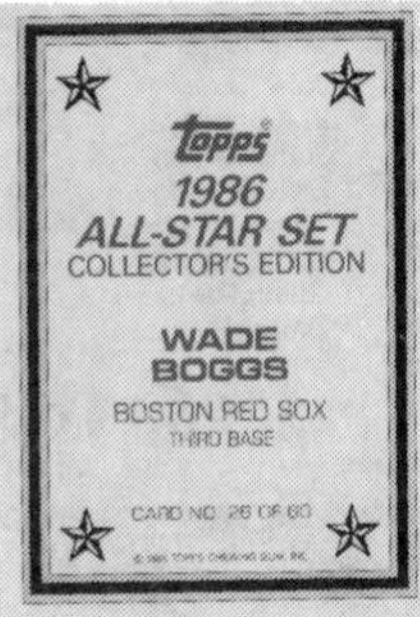

The Topps All-Star & Hot Prospects Glossy Set of 60 cards represents an expansion of a good idea. The 2-1/2" by 3-1/2" cards had a good following when they were limited to stars, but Topps realized that the addition of top young players would spice up the set even further, so in 1986 it was expanded from 40 to 60 cards. The cards themselves are basically all color glossy pictures with the player's name in very small print in the lower left-hand corner. To obtain the set, it was necessary to send $1 plus six special offer cards from wax packs to Topps for each series. At 60 cards, that meant the process had to be repeated six times as there were 10 cards in each series, making the set quite expensive from the outset.

		MT	NR MT	EX
Complete Set:		15.00	11.00	6.00
Common Player:		.15	.11	.06
1	Oddibe McDowell	.25	.20	.10
2	Reggie Jackson	.70	.50	.30
3	Fernando Valenzuela	.35	.25	.14
4	Jack Clark	.25	.20	.10
5	Rickey Henderson	.70	.50	.30
6	Steve Balboni	.15	.11	.06
7	Keith Hernandez	.40	.30	.15
8	Lance Parrish	.30	.25	.12
9	Willie McGee	.25	.20	.10
10	Chris Brown	.40	.30	.15
11	Darryl Strawberry	.90	.70	.35
12	Ron Guidry	.30	.25	.12
13	Dave Parker	.25	.20	.10
14	Cal Ripken	.70	.50	.30
15	Tim Raines	.50	.40	.20
16	Rod Carew	.60	.45	.25
17	Mike Schmidt	.90	.70	.35
18	George Brett	.90	.70	.35
19	Joe Hesketh	.15	.11	.06
20	Dan Pasqua	.20	.15	.08
21	Vince Coleman	1.00	.70	.40
22	Tom Seaver	.50	.40	.20
23	Gary Carter	.50	.40	.20
24	Orel Hershiser	.40	.30	.15
25	Pedro Guerrero	.30	.25	.12
26	Wade Boggs	1.25	.90	.50
27	Bret Saberhagen	.30	.25	.12
28	Carlton Fisk	.25	.20	.10
29	Kirk Gibson	.35	.25	.14
30	Brian Fisher	.20	.15	.08
31	Don Mattingly	3.00	2.25	1.25
32	Tom Herr	.15	.11	.06
33	Eddie Murray	.60	.45	.25
34	Ryne Sandberg	.40	.30	.15
35	Dan Quisenberry	.15	.11	.06
36	Jim Rice	.50	.40	.20
37	Dale Murphy	.90	.70	.35
38	Steve Garvey	.50	.40	.20
39	Roger McDowell	.25	.20	.10
40	Earnie Riles	.15	.11	.06
41	Dwight Gooden	1.25	.90	.50
42	Dave Winfield	.50	.40	.20
43	Dave Stieb	.20	.15	.08
44	Bob Horner	.20	.15	.08
45	Nolan Ryan	.50	.40	.20

		MT	NR MT	EX
46	Ozzie Smith	.25	.20	.10
47	Jorge Bell	.50	.40	.20
48	Gorman Thomas	.15	.11	.06
49	Tom Browning	.25	.20	.10
50	Larry Sheets	.20	.15	.08
51	Pete Rose	1.25	.90	.50
52	Brett Butler	.15	.11	.06
53	John Tudor	.20	.15	.08
54	Phil Bradley	.20	.15	.08
55	Jeff Reardon	.20	.15	.08
56	Rich Gossage	.25	.20	.10
57	Tony Gwynn	.60	.45	.25
58	Ozzie Guillen	.25	.20	.10
59	Glenn Davis	.35	.25	.14
60	Darrell Evans	.15	.11	.06

1986 Topps Traded

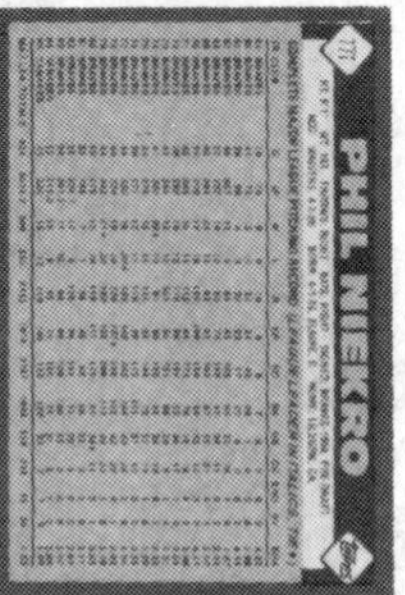

This 132-card set of 2-1/2" by 3-1/2" cards is one of the most popular sets of recent times. As always, the set features traded veterans, including such players as Phil Niekro and Tom Seaver. They are not, however, the reason for the excitement. The demand is there because of a better than usual crop of rookies who also appear in the sets. Among those are Jose Canseco, Wally Joyner, Pete Incaviglia, Todd Worrell and the first card of Bo Jackson. As in the previous two years, a glossy-finish "Tiffany" edition of 5,000 Traded sets was produced. The "Tiffany" cards are worth four to six times the value of the regular Traded cards.

		MT	NR MT	EX
Complete Set (132):		20.00	15.00	8.00
Common Player:		.08	.06	.03
1T	Andy Allanson(FC)	.10	.08	.04
2T	Neil Allen	.08	.06	.03
3T	Joaquin Andujar	.10	.08	.04
4T	Paul Assenmacher(FC)	.10	.08	.04
5T	Scott Bailes(FC)	.10	.08	.04
6T	Don Baylor	.15	.11	.06
7T	Steve Bedrosian	.15	.11	.06
8T	Juan Beniquez	.08	.06	.03
9T	Juan Berenguer	.08	.06	.03
10T	Mike Bielecki(FC)	.08	.06	.03
11T	Barry Bonds(FC)	8.00	6.00	3.25
12T	Bobby Bonilla(FC)	2.00	1.50	.80
13T	Juan Bonilla	.08	.06	.03
14T	Rich Bordi	.08	.06	.03
15T	Steve Boros	.08	.06	.03
16T	Rick Burleson	.08	.06	.03
17T	Bill Campbell	.08	.06	.03
18T	Tom Candiotti	.08	.06	.03
19T	John Cangelosi(FC)	.08	.06	.03
20T	Jose Canseco(FC)	3.50	2.75	1.50
21T	Carmen Castillo	.08	.06	.03
22T	Rick Cerone	.08	.06	.03
23T	John Cerutti(FC)	.08	.06	.03
24T	Will Clark(FC)	4.75	3.50	2.00
25T	Mark Clear	.08	.06	.03
26T	Darnell Coles	.12	.09	.05
27T	Dave Collins	.10	.08	.04
28T	Tim Conroy	.08	.06	.03
29T	Joe Cowley	.08	.06	.03
30T	Joel Davis(FC)	.12	.09	.05
31T	Rob Deer	.08	.06	.03
32T	John Denny	.08	.06	.03
33T	Mike Easler	.10	.08	.04
34T	Mark Eichhorn(FC)	.20	.15	.08
35T	Steve Farr	.08	.06	.03
36T	Scott Fletcher	.15	.11	.06
37T	Terry Forster	.10	.08	.04
38T	Terry Francona	.08	.06	.03
39T	Jim Fregosi	.08	.06	.03
40T	Andres Galarraga(FC)	1.75	1.25	.70
41T	Ken Griffey	.12	.09	.05
42T	Bill Gullickson	.08	.06	.03
43T	Jose Guzman(FC)	.35	.25	.14
44T	Moose Haas	.08	.06	.03
45T	Billy Hatcher	.20	.15	.08
46T	Mike Heath	.08	.06	.03
47T	Tom Hume	.08	.06	.03
48T	Pete Incaviglia(FC)	.75	.60	.30
49T	Dane Iorg	.08	.06	.03
50T	Bo Jackson(FC)	3.00	2.25	1.25
51T	Wally Joyner(FC)	1.00	.70	.40
52T	Charlie Kerfeld(FC)	.15	.11	.06
53T	Eric King(FC)	.20	.15	.08
54T	Bob Kipper(FC)	.12	.09	.05
55T	Wayne Krenchicki	.08	.06	.03
56T	John Kruk(FC)	2.00	1.50	.80
57T	Mike LaCoss	.08	.06	.03
58T	Pete Ladd	.08	.06	.03
59T	Mike Laga	.08	.06	.03
60T	Hal Lanier	.08	.06	.03
61T	Dave LaPoint	.12	.09	.05
62T	Rudy Law	.08	.06	.03
63T	Rick Leach	.08	.06	.03
64T	Tim Leary	.08	.06	.03
65T	Dennis Leonard	.10	.08	.04
66T	Jim Leyland	.08	.06	.03
67T	Steve Lyons	.12	.09	.05
68T	Mickey Mahler	.08	.06	.03
69T	Candy Maldonado	.15	.11	.06
70T	Roger Mason(FC)	.10	.08	.04
71T	Bob McClure	.08	.06	.03
72T	Andy McGaffigan	.08	.06	.03
73T	Gene Michael	.08	.06	.03
74T	Kevin Mitchell(FC)	.60	.45	.25
75T	Omar Moreno	.08	.06	.03
76T	Jerry Mumphrey	.08	.06	.03
77T	Phil Niekro	.20	.15	.08
78T	Randy Niemann	.08	.06	.03
79T	Juan Nieves(FC)	.06	.05	.02
80T	Otis Nixon(FC)	.25	.20	.10
81T	Bob Ojeda	.12	.09	.05
82T	Jose Oquendo	.08	.06	.03
83T	Tom Paciorek	.08	.06	.03
84T	Dave Palmer	.08	.06	.03
85T	Frank Pastore	.08	.06	.03
86T	Lou Piniella	.12	.09	.05
87T	Dan Plesac(FC)	.12	.09	.05
88T	Darrell Porter	.10	.08	.04
89T	Rey Quinones(FC)	.20	.15	.08
90T	Gary Redus	.10	.08	.04
91T	Bip Roberts	.40	.30	.15
92T	Billy Jo Robidoux(FC)	.15	.11	.06
93T	Jeff Robinson	.12	.09	.05
94T	Gary Roenicke	.08	.06	.03
95T	Ed Romero	.08	.06	.03
96T	Argenis Salazar	.08	.06	.03
97T	Joe Sambito	.08	.06	.03
98T	Billy Sample	.08	.06	.03
99T	Dave Schmidt	.08	.06	.03
100T	Ken Schrom	.08	.06	.03
101T	Tom Seaver	.60	.45	.25
102T	Ted Simmons	.20	.15	.08
103T	Sammy Stewart	.08	.06	.03
104T	Kurt Stillwell(FC)	.08	.06	.03
105T	Franklin Stubbs	.12	.09	.05
106T	Dale Sveum(FC)	.08	.06	.03
107T	Chuck Tanner	.08	.06	.03
108T	Danny Tartabull(FC)	1.00	.70	.40
109T	Tim Teufel	.08	.06	.03
110T	Bob Tewksbury(FC)	.60	.45	.25
111T	Andres Thomas(FC)	.12	.09	.05
112T	Milt Thompson	.12	.09	.05
113T	Robby Thompson(FC)	1.00	.70	.40
114T	Jay Tibbs	.08	.06	.03
115T	Wayne Tolleson	.08	.06	.03
116T	Alex Trevino	.08	.06	.03
117T	Manny Trillo	.10	.08	.04
118T	Ed Vande Berg	.08	.06	.03
119T	Ozzie Virgil	.08	.06	.03
120T	Bob Walk	.08	.06	.03
121T	Gene Walter(FC)	.12	.09	.05
122T	Claudell Washington	.12	.09	.05
123T	Bill Wegman(FC)	.20	.15	.08

		MT	NR MT	EX
124T	Dick Williams	.08	.06	.03
125T	Mitch Williams(FC)	.50	.40	.20
126T	Bobby Witt(FC)	.20	.15	.08
127T	Todd Worrell(FC)	.20	.15	.08
128T	George Wright	.08	.06	.03
129T	Ricky Wright	.08	.06	.03
130T	Steve Yeager	.08	.06	.03
131T	Paul Zuvella	.08	.06	.03
132T	Checklist	.08	.06	.03

1986 Topps Box Panels

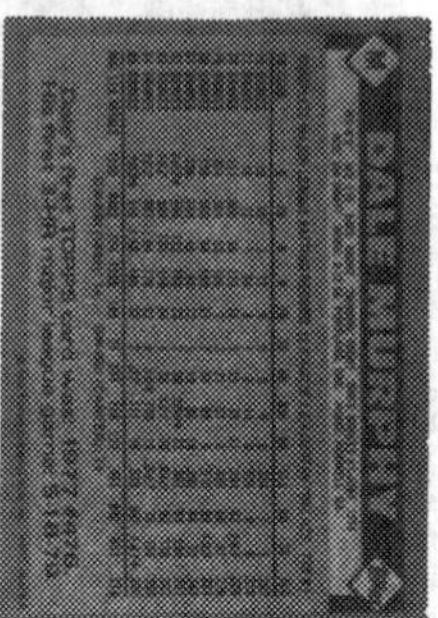

Following the lead of Donruss, which introduced the concept in 1985, Topps produced special cards on the bottom panels of wax boxes. Individual cards measure 2-1/2" by 3-1/2", the same as regular cards. Design of the cards is virtually identical with regular '86 Topps, though the top border is in red, rather than black. The cards are lettered "A" through "P", rather than numbered on the back.

		MT	NR MT	EX
Complete Panel Set:		10.00	7.50	4.00
Complete Singles Set:		5.00	3.75	2.00
Common Panel:		2.00	1.50	.80
Common Single Player:		.15	.11	.06
	Panel	3.50	2.75	1.50
A	Jorge Bell	.20	.15	.08
B	Wade Boggs	.60	.45	.25
C	George Brett	.35	.25	.14
D	Vince Coleman	.35	.25	.14
	Panel	2.00	1.50	.80
E	Carlton Fisk	.15	.11	.06
F	Dwight Gooden	.40	.30	.15
G	Pedro Guerrero	.15	.11	.06
H	Ron Guidry	.15	.11	.06
	Panel	3.50	2.75	1.50
I	Reggie Jackson	.30	.25	.12
J	Don Mattingly	.90	.70	.35
K	Oddibe McDowell	.15	.11	.06
L	Willie McGee	.15	.11	.06
	Panel	3.00	2.25	1.25
M	Dale Murphy	.35	.25	.14
N	Pete Rose	.50	.40	.20
O	Bret Saberhagen	.15	.11	.06
P	Fernando Valenzuela	.20	.15	.08

1986 Topps Gallery Of Champions

For the third consecutive year Topps issued 12 "metal mini-cards" as a dealer-ordering incentive. The metal replicas were minted 1/4-size (approxima- tely 1-1/4" by 1-3/4") of the regular cards and come in silver, aluminum and bronze. The bronze and silver sets were issued in leather-like velvet-lined display cases. A bronze 1952 Topps Mickey Mantle was given as a premium for dealers purchasing 1986 Traded sets, while a pewter Don Mattingly was issued as a premium to those ordering the aluminum, bronze and silver sets. The Mantle bronze is valued at $12 and

the Mattingly pewter at $100.

		MT	NR MT	EX
Complete Aluminum Set:		30.00	22.00	12.00
Complete Bronze Set:		175.00	131.00	70.00
Complete Silver Set:		650.00	487.00	260.00
(1a)	Wade Boggs (aluminum)	3.00	2.25	1.25
(1b)	Wade Boggs (bronze)	25.00	18.50	10.00
(1c)	Wade Boggs (silver)	125.00	94.00	50.00
(2a)	Vince Coleman (aluminum)	1.25	.90	.50
(2b)	Vince Coleman (bronze)	12.00	9.00	4.75
(2c)	Vince Coleman (silver)	50.00	37.00	20.00
(3a)	Darrell Evans (aluminum)	.70	.50	.30
(3b)	Darrell Evans (bronze)	7.50	5.75	3.00
(3c)	Darrell Evans (silver)	20.00	15.00	8.00
(4a)	Dwight Gooden (aluminum)	2.00	1.50	.80
(4b)	Dwight Gooden (bronze)	20.00	15.00	8.00
(4c)	Dwight Gooden (silver)	100.00	75.00	40.00
(5a)	Ozzie Guillen (aluminum)	.70	.50	.30
(5b)	Ozzie Guillen (bronze)	7.50	5.75	3.00
(5c)	Ozzie Guillen (silver)	20.00	15.00	8.00
(6a)	Don Mattingly (aluminum)	8.00	6.00	3.25
(6b)	Don Mattingly (bronze)	50.00	37.00	20.00
(6c)	Don Mattingly (silver)	200.00	150.00	80.00
(7a)	Willie McGee (aluminum)	1.00	.70	.40
(7b)	Willie McGee (bronze)	10.00	7.50	4.00
(7c)	Willie McGee (silver)	30.00	22.00	12.00
(8a)	Dale Murphy (aluminum)	1.50	1.25	.60
(8b)	Dale Murphy (bronze)	15.00	11.00	6.00
(8c)	Dale Murphy (silver)	80.00	60.00	32.00
(9a)	Dan Quisenberry (aluminum)	.70	.50	.30
(9b)	Dan Quisenberry (bronze)	7.50	5.75	3.00
(9c)	Dan Quisenberry (silver)	20.00	15.00	8.00
(10a)	Jeff Reardon (aluminum)	.70	.50	.30
(10b)	Jeff Reardon (bronze)	7.50	5.75	3.00
(10c)	Jeff Reardon (silver)	20.00	15.00	8.00
(11a)	Pete Rose (aluminum)	2.50	2.00	1.00
(11b)	Pete Rose (bronze)	25.00	18.50	10.00
(11c)	Pete Rose (silver)	110.00	82.00	44.00
(12a)	Bret Saberhagen (aluminum)	1.00	.70	.40
(12b)	Bret Saberhagen (bronze)	10.00	7.50	4.00
(12c)	Bret Saberhagen (silver)	30.00	22.00	12.00

1986 Topps Mini League Leaders

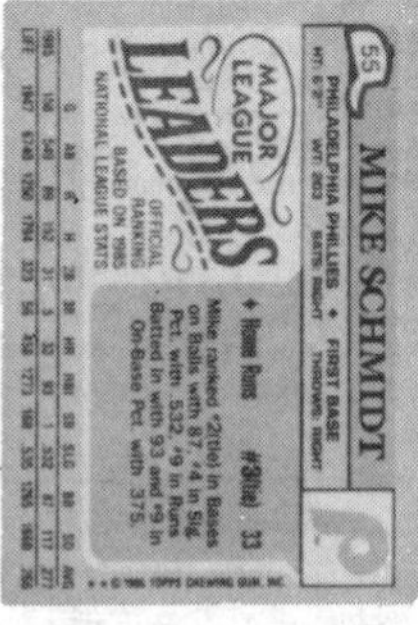

Topps had long experimented with bigger cards,

but in 1986, they also decided to try smaller ones. These 2-1/8" by 2-15/16" cards feature top players in a number of categories. Sold in plastic packs as a regular Topps issue, the 66-card set is attractive as well as innovative. The cards feature color photos and a minimum of added information on the fronts where only the player's name and Topps logo appear. Backs limited information as well, but do feature whatever information was required to justify the player's inclusion in a set of league leaders.

		MT	NR MT	EX
Complete Set:		8.00	6.00	3.25
Common Player:		.09	.07	.04
1	Eddie Murray	.40	.30	.15
2	Cal Ripken	.40	.30	.15
3	Wade Boggs	.80	.60	.30
4	Dennis Boyd	.09	.07	.04
5	Dwight Evans	.15	.11	.06
6	Bruce Hurst	.15	.11	.06
7	Gary Pettis	.09	.07	.04
8	Harold Baines	.15	.11	.06
9	Floyd Bannister	.09	.07	.04
10	Britt Burns	.09	.07	.04
11	Carlton Fisk	.20	.15	.08
12	Brett Butler	.15	.11	.06
13	Darrell Evans	.15	.11	.06
14	Jack Morris	.25	.20	.10
15	Lance Parrish	.25	.20	.10
16	Walt Terrell	.09	.07	.04
17	Steve Balboni	.09	.07	.04
18	George Brett	.50	.40	.20
19	Charlie Leibrandt	.09	.07	.04
20	Bret Saberhagen	.20	.15	.08
21	Lonnie Smith	.09	.07	.04
22	Willie Wilson	.15	.11	.06
23	Bert Blyleven	.15	.11	.06
24	Mike Smithson	.09	.07	.04
25	Frank Viola	.20	.15	.08
26	Ron Guidry	.20	.15	.08
27	Rickey Henderson	.40	.30	.15
28	Don Mattingly	1.25	.90	.50
29	Dave Winfield	.30	.25	.12
30	Mike Moore	.09	.07	.04
31	Gorman Thomas	.09	.07	.04
32	Toby Harrah	.09	.07	.04
33	Charlie Hough	.09	.07	.04
34	Doyle Alexander	.09	.07	.04
35	Jimmy Key	.15	.11	.06
36	Dave Stieb	.15	.11	.06
37	Dale Murphy	.50	.40	.20
38	Keith Moreland	.09	.07	.04
39	Ryne Sandberg	.30	.25	.12
40	Tom Browning	.15	.11	.06
41	Dave Parker	.20	.15	.08
42	Mario Soto	.09	.07	.04
43	Nolan Ryan	.30	.25	.12
44	Pedro Guerrero	.20	.15	.08
45	Orel Hershiser	.30	.25	.12
46	Mike Scioscia	.09	.07	.04
47	Fernando Valenzuela	.25	.20	.10
48	Bob Welch	.15	.11	.06
49	Tim Raines	.30	.25	.12
50	Gary Carter	.30	.25	.12
51	Sid Fernandez	.15	.11	.06
52	Dwight Gooden	.70	.50	.30
53	Keith Hernandez	.25	.20	.10
54	Juan Samuel	.20	.15	.08
55	Mike Schmidt	.50	.40	.20
56	Glenn Wilson	.09	.07	.04
57	Rick Reuschel	.15	.11	.06
58	Joaquin Andujar	.09	.07	.04
59	Jack Clark	.20	.15	.08
60	Vince Coleman	.60	.45	.25
61	Danny Cox	.09	.07	.04
62	Tom Herr	.09	.07	.04
63	Willie McGee	.15	.11	.06
64	John Tudor	.15	.11	.06
65	Tony Gwynn	.40	.30	.15
66	Checklist	.09	.07	.04

Definitions for grading conditions are located in the Introduction of this price guide.

1986 Topps Stickers

The 1986 Topps stickers are 2-1/8" by 3". The 200-piece set features 316 different subjects, with some stickers including two or three players. Numbers run only to 315, however. The set includes some specialty stickers such as League Championships and World Series themes. Stickers are numbered both front and back and included a chance to win a trip to spring training as well as an offer to buy a complete 1986 Topps regular set. An album for the stickers was available in stores.

		MT	NR MT	EX
Complete Set:		15.00	11.00	6.00
Common Player:		.03	.02	.01
Sticker Album:		.70	.50	.30
1	Pete Rose	.25	.20	.10
2	Pete Rose	.25	.20	.10
3	George Brett	.12	.09	.05
4	Rod Carew	.10	.08	.04
5	Vince Coleman	.12	.09	.05
6	Dwight Gooden	.15	.11	.06
7	Phil Niekro	.08	.06	.03
8	Tony Perez	.06	.05	.02
9	Nolan Ryan	.10	.08	.04
10	Tom Seaver	.10	.08	.04
11	N.L. Championship Series (Ozzie Smith)	.06	.05	.02
12	N.L. Championship Series (Bill Madlock)	.04	.03	.02
13	N.L. Championship Series (Cardinals Celebrate)	.03	.02	.01
14	A.L. Championship Series (Al Oliver)	.04	.03	.02
15	A.L. Championship Series (Jim Sundberg)	.03	.02	.01
16	A.L. Championship Series (George Brett)	.10	.08	.04
17	World Series (Bret Saberhagen)	.06	.05	.02
18	World Series (Dane Iorg)	.03	.02	.01
19	World Series (Tito Landrum)	.03	.02	.01
20	World Series (John Tudor)	.04	.03	.02
21	World Series (Buddy Biancalana)	.03	.02	.01
22	World Series (Darryl Motley, Darrell Porter)	.03	.02	.01
23	World Series (George Brett, Frank White)	.10	.08	.04
24	Nolan Ryan	.15	.11	.06
25	Bill Doran	.08	.06	.03
26	Jose Cruz	.04	.03	.02
27	Mike Scott	.08	.06	.03
28	Kevin Bass	.04	.03	.02
29	Glenn Davis	.10	.08	.04
30	Mark Bailey	.06	.05	.02
31	Dave Smith	.10	.08	.04
32	Phil Garner	.03	.02	.01
33	Dickie Thon	.06	.05	.02
34	Bob Horner	.12	.09	.05
35	Dale Murphy	.25	.20	.10
36	Glenn Hubbard	.04	.03	.02
37	Bruce Sutter	.08	.06	.03
38	Ken Oberkfell	.04	.03	.02
39	Claudell Washington	.04	.03	.02
40	Steve Bedrosian	.04	.03	.02
41	Terry Harper	.03	.02	.01
42	Rafael Ramirez	.06	.05	.02
43	Rick Mahler	.03	.02	.01

		MT	NR MT	EX
44	Joaquin Andujar	.06	.05	.02
45	Willie McGee	.10	.08	.04
46	Ozzie Smith	.06	.05	.02
47	Vince Coleman	.12	.09	.05
48	Danny Cox	.04	.03	.02
49	Tom Herr	.04	.03	.02
50	Jack Clark	.08	.06	.03
51	Andy Van Slyke	.04	.03	.02
52	John Tudor	.08	.06	.03
53	Terry Pendleton	.03	.02	.01
54	Keith Moreland	.06	.05	.02
55	Ryne Sandberg	.15	.11	.06
56	Lee Smith	.04	.03	.02
57	Steve Trout	.06	.05	.02
58	Jody Davis	.08	.06	.03
59	Gary Matthews	.04	.03	.02
60	Leon Durham	.04	.03	.02
61	Rick Sutcliffe	.06	.05	.02
62	Dennis Eckersley	.04	.03	.02
63	Bob Dernier	.03	.02	.01
64	Fernando Valenzuela	.15	.11	.06
65	Pedro Guerrero	.12	.09	.05
66	Jerry Reuss	.06	.05	.02
67	Greg Brock	.06	.05	.02
68	Mike Scioscia	.03	.02	.01
69	Ken Howell	.04	.03	.02
70	Bill Madlock	.04	.03	.02
71	Mike Marshall	.06	.05	.02
72	Steve Sax	.06	.05	.02
73	Orel Hershiser	.06	.05	.02
74	Andre Dawson	.12	.09	.05
75	Tim Raines	.12	.09	.05
76	Jeff Reardon	.06	.05	.02
77	Hubie Brooks	.04	.03	.02
78	Bill Gullickson	.04	.03	.02
79	Bryn Smith	.04	.03	.02
80	Terry Francona	.04	.03	.02
81	Vance Law	.03	.02	.01
82	Tim Wallach	.04	.03	.02
83	Herm Winningham	.04	.03	.02
84	Jeff Leonard	.06	.05	.02
85	Chris Brown	.20	.15	.08
86	Scott Garrelts	.03	.02	.01
87	Jose Uribe	.04	.03	.02
88	Manny Trillo	.04	.03	.02
89	Dan Driessen	.04	.03	.02
90	Dan Gladden	.06	.05	.02
91	Mark Davis	.04	.03	.02
92	Bob Brenly	.03	.02	.01
93	Mike Krukow	.04	.03	.02
94	Dwight Gooden	.35	.25	.14
95	Darryl Strawberry	.25	.20	.10
96	Gary Carter	.10	.08	.04
97	Wally Backman	.06	.05	.02
98	Ron Darling	.06	.05	.02
99	Keith Hernandez	.12	.09	.05
100	George Foster	.06	.05	.02
101	Howard Johnson	.06	.05	.02
102	Rafael Santana	.04	.03	.02
103	Roger McDowell	.06	.05	.02
104	Steve Garvey	.15	.11	.06
105	Tony Gwynn	.20	.15	.08
106	Graig Nettles	.06	.05	.02
107	Rich Gossage	.10	.08	.04
108	Andy Hawkins	.04	.03	.02
109	Carmelo Martinez	.04	.03	.02
110	Garry Templeton	.04	.03	.02
111	Terry Kennedy	.06	.05	.02
112	Tim Flannery	.08	.06	.03
113	LaMarr Hoyt	.03	.02	.01
114	Mike Schmidt	.25	.20	.10
115	Ozzie Virgil	.06	.05	.02
116	Steve Carlton	.10	.08	.04
117	Garry Maddox	.03	.02	.01
118	Glenn Wilson	.06	.05	.02
119	Kevin Gross	.03	.02	.01
120	Von Hayes	.04	.03	.02
121	Juan Samuel	.06	.05	.02
122	Rick Schu	.08	.06	.03
123	Shane Rawley	.06	.05	.02
124	Johnny Ray	.06	.05	.02
125	Tony Pena	.06	.05	.02
126	Rick Reuschel	.12	.09	.05
127	Sammy Khalifa	.06	.05	.02
128	Marvell Wynne	.04	.03	.02
129	Jason Thompson	.03	.02	.01
130	Rick Rhoden	.04	.03	.02
131	Bill Almon	.03	.02	.01
132	Joe Orsulak	.06	.05	.02
133	Jim Morrison	.06	.05	.02
134	Pete Rose	.40	.30	.15

		MT	NR MT	EX
135	Dave Parker	.12	.09	.05
136	Mario Soto	.03	.02	.01
137	Dave Concepcion	.10	.08	.04
138	Ron Oester	.03	.02	.01
139	Buddy Bell	.06	.05	.02
140	Ted Power	.03	.02	.01
141	Tom Browning	.06	.05	.02
142	John Franco	.08	.06	.03
143	Tony Perez	.06	.05	.02
144	Willie McGee	.08	.06	.03
145	Dale Murphy	.15	.11	.06
146	Tony Gwynn	.40	.30	.15
147	Tom Herr	.15	.11	.06
148	Steve Garvey	.30	.25	.12
149	Dale Murphy	.40	.30	.15
150	Darryl Strawberry	.40	.30	.15
151	Graig Nettles	.15	.11	.06
152	Terry Kennedy	.15	.11	.06
153	Ozzie Smith	.20	.15	.08
154	LaMarr Hoyt	.15	.11	.06
155	Rickey Henderson	.40	.30	.15
156	Lou Whitaker	.25	.20	.10
157	George Brett	.40	.30	.15
158	Eddie Murray	.40	.30	.15
159	Cal Ripken	.40	.30	.15
160	Dave Winfield	.30	.25	.12
161	Jim Rice	.30	.25	.12
162	Carlton Fisk	.25	.20	.10
163	Jack Morris	.25	.20	.10
164	Wade Boggs	.15	.11	.06
165	Darrell Evans	.06	.05	.02
166	Mike Davis	.06	.05	.02
167	Dave Kingman	.08	.06	.03
168	Alfredo Griffin	.04	.03	.02
169	Carney Lansford	.04	.03	.02
170	Bruce Bochte	.10	.08	.04
171	Dwayne Murphy	.08	.06	.03
172	Dave Collins	.04	.03	.02
173	Chris Codiroli	.10	.08	.04
174	Mike Heath	.03	.02	.01
175	Jay Howell	.12	.09	.05
176	Rod Carew	.20	.15	.08
177	Reggie Jackson	.20	.15	.08
178	Doug DeCinces	.10	.08	.04
179	Bob Boone	.12	.09	.05
180	Ron Romanick	.15	.11	.06
181	Bob Grich	.08	.06	.03
182	Donnie Moore	.06	.05	.02
183	Brian Downing	.10	.08	.04
184	Ruppert Jones	.10	.08	.04
185	Juan Beniquez	.04	.03	.02
186	Dave Stieb	.06	.05	.02
187	Jorge Bell	.20	.15	.08
188	Willie Upshaw	.08	.06	.03
189	Tom Henke	.04	.03	.02
190	Damaso Garcia	.10	.08	.04
191	Jimmy Key	.06	.05	.02
192	Jesse Barfield	.10	.08	.04
193	Dennis Lamp	.03	.02	.01
194	Tony Fernandez	.06	.05	.02
195	Lloyd Moseby	.04	.03	.02
196	Cecil Cooper	.08	.06	.03
197	Robin Yount	.15	.11	.06
198	Rollie Fingers	.08	.06	.03
199	Ted Simmons	.04	.03	.02
200	Ben Oglivie	.04	.03	.02
201	Moose Haas	.04	.03	.02
202	Jim Gantner	.03	.02	.01
203	Paul Molitor	.06	.05	.02
204	Charlie Moore	.03	.02	.01
205	Danny Darwin	.06	.05	.02
206	Brett Butler	.06	.05	.02
207	Brook Jacoby	.08	.06	.03
208	Andre Thornton	.12	.09	.05
209	Tom Waddell	.04	.03	.02
210	Tony Bernazard	.04	.03	.02
211	Julio Franco	.08	.06	.03
212	Pat Tabler	.04	.03	.02
213	Joe Carter	.08	.06	.03
214	George Vukovich	.03	.02	.01
215	Rich Thompson	.04	.03	.02
216	Gorman Thomas	.06	.05	.02
217	Phil Bradley	.10	.08	.04
218	Alvin Davis	.06	.05	.02
219	Jim Presley	.08	.06	.03
220	Matt Young	.04	.03	.02
221	Mike Moore	.04	.03	.02
222	Dave Henderson	.06	.05	.02
223	Ed Nunez	.04	.03	.02
224	Spike Owen	.03	.02	.01
225	Mark Langston	.06	.05	.02

		MT	NR MT	EX
226	Cal Ripken	.20	.15	.08
227	Eddie Murray	.20	.15	.08
228	Fred Lynn	.06	.05	.02
229	Lee Lacy	.03	.02	.01
230	Scott McGregor	.04	.03	.02
231	Storm Davis	.04	.03	.02
232	Rick Dempsey	.06	.05	.02
233	Mike Boddicker	.06	.05	.02
234	Mike Young	.06	.05	.02
235	Sammy Stewart	.06	.05	.02
236	Pete O'Brien	.08	.06	.03
237	Oddibe McDowell	.15	.11	.06
238	Toby Harrah	.04	.03	.02
239	Gary Ward	.04	.03	.02
240	Larry Parrish	.04	.03	.02
241	Charlie Hough	.04	.03	.02
242	Burt Hooton	.03	.02	.01
243	Don Slaught	.04	.03	.02
244	Curt Wilkerson	.04	.03	.02
245	Greg Harris	.03	.02	.01
246	Jim Rice	.15	.11	.06
247	Wade Boggs	.60	.45	.25
248	Rich Gedman	.04	.03	.02
249	Dennis Boyd	.04	.03	.02
250	Marty Barrett	.04	.03	.02
251	Dwight Evans	.06	.05	.02
252	Bill Buckner	.04	.03	.02
253	Bob Stanley	.03	.02	.01
254	Tony Armas	.04	.03	.02
255	Mike Easler	.10	.08	.04
256	George Brett	.25	.20	.10
257	Dan Quisenberry	.06	.05	.02
258	Willie Wilson	.06	.05	.02
259	Jim Sundberg	.06	.05	.02
260	Bret Saberhagen	.12	.09	.05
261	Bud Black	.06	.05	.02
262	Charlie Leibrandt	.06	.05	.02
263	Frank White	.04	.03	.02
264	Lonnie Smith	.06	.05	.02
265	Steve Balboni	.06	.05	.02
266	Kirk Gibson	.15	.11	.06
267	Alan Trammell	.15	.11	.06
268	Jack Morris	.10	.08	.04
269	Darrell Evans	.04	.03	.02
270	Dan Petry	.04	.03	.02
271	Larry Herndon	.04	.03	.02
272	Lou Whitaker	.06	.05	.02
273	Lance Parrish	.08	.06	.03
274	Chet Lemon	.03	.02	.01
275	Willie Hernandez	.10	.08	.04
276	Tom Brunansky	.08	.06	.03
277	Kent Hrbek	.12	.09	.05
278	Mark Salas	.03	.02	.01
279	Bert Blyleven	.06	.05	.02
280	Tim Teufel	.03	.02	.01
281	Ron Davis	.04	.03	.02
282	Mike Smithson	.06	.05	.02
283	Gary Gaetti	.08	.06	.03
284	Frank Viola	.06	.05	.02
285	Kirby Puckett	.12	.09	.05
286	Carlton Fisk	.12	.09	.05
287	Tom Seaver	.15	.11	.06
288	Harold Baines	.06	.05	.02
289	Ron Kittle	.04	.03	.02
290	Bob James	.03	.02	.01
291	Rudy Law	.04	.03	.02
292	Britt Burns	.03	.02	.01
293	Greg Walker	.06	.05	.02
294	Ozzie Guillen	.06	.05	.02
295	Tim Hulett	.03	.02	.01
296	Don Mattingly	.70	.50	.30
297	Rickey Henderson	.20	.15	.08
298	Dave Winfield	.10	.08	.04
299	Butch Wynegar	.03	.02	.01
300	Don Baylor	.06	.05	.02
301	Eddie Whitson	.03	.02	.01
302	Ron Guidry	.06	.05	.02
303	Dave Righetti	.08	.06	.03
304	Bobby Meacham	.06	.05	.02
305	Willie Randolph	.08	.06	.03
306	Vince Coleman	.15	.11	.06
307	Oddibe McDowell	.15	.11	.06
308	Larry Sheets	.06	.05	.02
309	Ozzie Guillen	.06	.05	.02
310	Earnie Riles	.04	.03	.02
311	Chris Brown	.10	.08	.04
312	Brian Fisher, Roger McDowell	.08	.06	.03
313	Tom Browning	.04	.03	.02
314	Glenn Davis	.10	.08	.04
315	Mark Salas	.03	.02	.01

1986 Topps Super

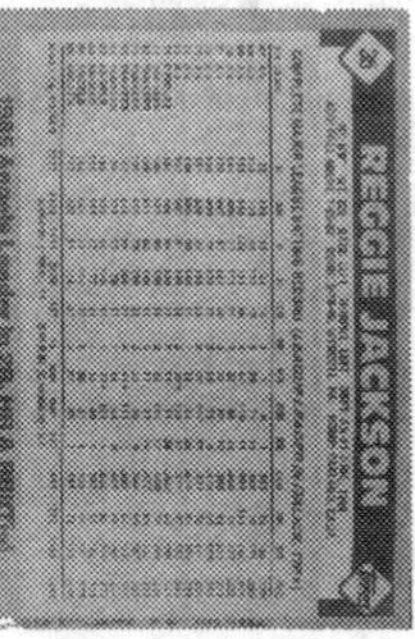

A third year of oversize, 4-7/8" by 6-7/8", versions of Topps' regular issue cards saw the set once again hit the 60-card mark. Besides being four times the size of a normal card, the Supers differ only in the number on the back of the card.

		MT	NR MT	EX
Complete Set:		16.00	12.00	6.50
Common Player:		.25	.20	.10
1	Don Mattingly	.75	.60	.30
2	Willie McGee	.35	.25	.14
3	Bret Saberhagen	.35	.25	.14
4	Dwight Gooden	.75	.60	.30
5	Dan Quisenberry	.25	.20	.10
6	Jeff Reardon	.25	.20	.10
7	Ozzie Guillen	.25	.20	.10
8	Vince Coleman	.35	.25	.14
9	Harold Baines	.25	.20	.10
10	Jorge Bell	.50	.40	.20
11	Bert Blyleven	.25	.20	.10
12	Wade Boggs	.75	.60	.30
13	Phil Bradley	.25	.20	.10
14	George Brett	.90	.70	.35
15	Hubie Brooks	.25	.20	.10
16	Tom Browning	.25	.20	.10
17	Bill Buckner	.25	.20	.10
18	Brett Butler	.25	.20	.10
19	Gary Carter	.50	.40	.20
20	Cecil Cooper	.25	.20	.10
21	Darrell Evans	.25	.20	.10
22	Dwight Evans	.25	.20	.10
23	Carlton Fisk	.30	.25	.12
24	Steve Garvey	.50	.40	.20
25	Kirk Gibson	.35	.25	.14
26	Rich Gossage	.25	.20	.10
27	Pedro Guerrero	.30	.25	.12
28	Ron Guidry	.30	.25	.12
29	Tony Gwynn	.60	.45	.25
30	Rickey Henderson	.70	.50	.30
31	Keith Hernandez	.30	.25	.12
32	Tom Herr	.25	.20	.10
33	Orel Hershiser	.50	.40	.20
34	Jay Howell	.25	.20	.10
35	Reggie Jackson	.90	.70	.35
36	Bob James	.25	.20	.10
37	Charlie Leibrandt	.25	.20	.10
38	Jack Morris	.35	.25	.14
39	Dale Murphy	.80	.60	.30
40	Eddie Murray	.60	.45	.25
41	Dave Parker	.75	.60	.30
42	Tim Raines	.50	.40	.20
43	Jim Rice	.35	.25	.14
44	Dave Righetti	.30	.25	.12
45	Cal Ripken, Jr.	2.00	1.50	.80
46	Pete Rose	1.00	.70	.40
47	Nolan Ryan	2.00	1.50	.80
48	Ryne Sandberg	2.00	1.50	.80
49	Mike Schmidt	.90	.70	.35
50	Tom Seaver	.80	.60	.30
51	Bryn Smith	.25	.20	.10
52	Lee Smith	.35	.25	.14
53	Ozzie Smith	.75	.60	.30
54	Dave Stieb	.25	.20	.10
55	Darryl Strawberry	.80	.60	.30
56	Gorman Thomas	.25	.20	.10
57	John Tudor	.25	.20	.10
58	Fernando Valenzuela	.30	.25	.12

		MT	NR MT	EX
59	Willie Wilson	.25	.20	.10
60	Dave Winfield	.75	.60	.30

1986 Topps Super Star

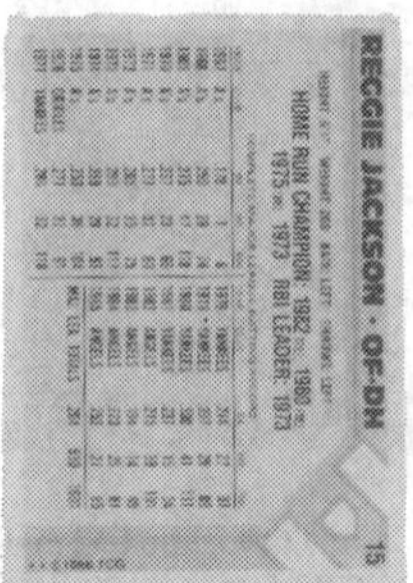

Labeled "Topps' Collector Series" in a red band at the top of the front, this set marked the second year of Topps' production of a special boxed set for the Woolworth chain of stores, though Woolworth's name does not appear anywhere on the card. The cards, which measure 2-1/2" by 3-1/2", feature a color photo with its lower right corner rolled up to reveal the words "Super Star" on a bright yellow border. The player's name appears in the lower left corner. The 66-card set features stars and retains a certain measure of popularity on that basis.

		MT	NR MT	EX
Complete Set:		5.00	3.75	2.00
Common Player:		.09	.07	.04
1	Tony Armas	.09	.07	.04
2	Don Baylor	.12	.09	.05
3	Wade Boggs	.80	.60	.30
4	George Brett	.40	.30	.15
5	Bill Buckner	.09	.07	.04
6	Rod Carew	.30	.25	.12
7	Gary Carter	.30	.25	.12
8	Cecil Cooper	.12	.09	.05
9	Darrell Evans	.12	.09	.05
10	Dwight Evans	.15	.11	.06
11	George Foster	.12	.09	.05
12	Bobby Grich	.09	.07	.04
13	Tony Gwynn	.35	.25	.14
14	Keith Hernandez	.25	.20	.10
15	Reggie Jackson	.30	.25	.12
16	Dave Kingman	.12	.09	.05
17	Carney Lansford	.09	.07	.04
18	Fred Lynn	.12	.09	.05
19	Bill Madlock	.12	.09	.05
20	Don Mattingly	1.50	1.25	.60
21	Willie McGee	.20	.15	.08
22	Hal McRae	.09	.07	.04
23	Dale Murphy	.40	.30	.15
24	Eddie Murray	.35	.25	.14
25	Ben Oglivie	.09	.07	.04
26	Al Oliver	.12	.09	.05
27	Dave Parker	.20	.15	.08
28	Jim Rice	.30	.25	.12
29	Pete Rose	.90	.70	.35
30	Mike Schmidt	.40	.30	.15
31	Gorman Thomas	.09	.07	.04
32	Willie Wilson	.12	.09	.05
33	Dave Winfield	.30	.25	.12

1986 Topps Tattoos

Topps returned to tattoos in 1986, marketing a set of 24 different tattoo sheets. Each sheet of tattoos measures 3-7/16" by 14" and includes both player and smaller action tattoos. As the action tattoos were uniform and not of any particular player, they add little value to the sheet.

The player tattoos measure 1-3/16" by 2-3/8". With 24 sheets, eight players per sheet, there are 192 players represented in the set. The sheets are numbered.

		MT	NR MT	EX
Complete Set:		5.00	3.75	2.00
Common Player:		.20	.15	.08
1	Julio Franco, Rich Gossage, Keith Hernandez, Charlie Leibrandt, Jack Perconte, Lee Smith, Dickie Thon, Dave Winfield	.25	.20	.10
2	Jesse Barfield, Shawon Dunston, Dennis Eckersley, Brian Fisher, Moose Haas, Mike Moore, Dale Murphy, Bret Saberhagen	.30	.25	.12
3	George Bell, Bob Brenly, Steve Carlton, Jose DeLeon, Bob Horner, Bob James, Dan Quisenberry, Andre Thornton	.25	.20	.10
4	Mike Davis, Leon Durham, Darrell Evans, Glenn Hubbard, Johnny Ray, Cal Ripken, Ted Simmons	.25	.20	.10
5	John Candelaria, Rick Dempsey, Steve Garvey, Ozzie Guillen, Gary Matthews, Jesse Orosco, Tony Pena	.25	.20	.10
6	Bruce Bochte, George Brett, Cecil Cooper, Sammy Khalifa, Ron Kittle, Scott McGregor, Pete Rose, Mookie Wilson	.45	.35	.20
7	John Franco, Carney Lansford, Don Mattingly, Graig Nettles, Rick Reuschel, Mike Schmidt, Larry Sheets, Don Sutton	.45	.35	.20
8	Cecilio Guante, Willie Hernandez, Mike Krukow, Fred Lynn, Phil Niekro, Ed Nunez, Ryne Sandberg, Pat Tabler	.25	.20	.10
9	Brett Butler, Chris Codiroli, Jim Gantner, Charlie Hough, Dave Parker, Rick Rhoden, Glenn Wilson, Robin Yount	.20	.15	.08
10	Tom Browning, Ron Darling, Von Hayes, Chet Lemon, Tom Seaver, Mike Smithson, Bruce Sutter, Alan Trammell	.25	.20	.10
11	Tony Armas, Jose Cruz, Jay Howell, Rick Mahler, Jack Morris, Rafael Ramirez, Dave Righetti, Mike Young	.20	.15	.08
12	Alvin Davis, Doug DeCinces, Andy Hawkins, Dennis Lamp, Keith Moreland, Jim Presley, Mario Soto, John Tudor	.20	.15	.08
13	Hubie Brooks, Jody Davis, Dwight Evans, Ron Hassey, Charles Hudson, Kirby Puckett, Jose Uribe	.20	.15	.08
14	Tony Bernazard, Phil Bradley, Bill Buckner, Brian Downing, Dan Driessen, Ron Guidry, LaMarr Hoyt, Garry Maddox	.20	.15	.08
15	Buddy Bell, Joe Carter, Tony Fernandez, Tito Landrum, Jeff Leonard, Hal McRae, Willie Randolph, Juan Samuel	.20	.15	.08
16	Dennis Boyd, Vince Coleman, Scott Garrelts, Alfredo Griffin, Donnie Moore, Tony Perez, Ozzie Smith, Frank White	.25	.20	.10
17	Rich Gedman, Kent Hrbek, Reggie Jackson, Mike Marshall, Terry Pendleton, Tim Raines, Mark Salas, Claudell Washington	.25	.20	.10
18	Chris Brown, Tom Brunansky, Glenn Davis, Ron Davis, Burt Hooton, Darryl Strawberry, Frank Viola, Tim Wallach	.30	.25	.12
19	Jack Clark, Bill Doran, Toby Harrah, Bill Madlock, Pete O'Brien, Larry Parrish, Mike Scioscia, Garry Templeton	.20	.15	.08
20	Gary Carter, Andre Dawson, Dwight Gooden, Orel Hershiser, Oddibe McDowell, Roger McDowell, Dwayne Murphy, Jim Rice	.40	.30	.15

		MT	NR MT	EX
21	Steve Balboni, Mike Easler, Charlie Lea, Lloyd Moseby, Steve Sax, Rick Sutcliffe, Gary Ward, Willie Wilson	.20	.15	.08
22	Wade Boggs, Dave Concepcion, Kirk Gibson, Tom Herr, Lance Parrish, Jeff Reardon, Bryn Smith, Gorman Thomas	.30	.25	.12
23	Carlton Fisk, Bob Grich, Pedro Guerrero, Willie McGee, Paul Molitor, Mike Scott, Dave Stieb, Lou Whitaker	.20	.15	.08
24	Bert Blyleven, Damaso Garcia, Phil Garner, Tony Gwynn, Rickey Henderson, Ben Oglivie, Nolan Ryan, Fernando Valenzuela	.30	.25	.12

1986 Topps 3-D

This set is a second effort in the production of over-size (4-1/2" by 6") plastic cards on which the player figure is embossed. Cards were sold one per pack for approximately 50¢. The 30 players in the set are among the game's top stars. The embossed color photo is bordered at bottom by a strip of contrasting color on which the player name appears. At the top, a row of white baseballs each contain a letter of the team nickname. Backs have no printing, and contain two self-adhesive strips with which the cards can be attached to a hard surface.

		MT	NR MT	EX
Complete Set:		15.00	11.00	6.00
Common Player:		.25	.20	.10
1	Bert Blyleven	.30	.25	.12
2	Gary Carter	.50	.40	.20
3	Wade Boggs	.75	.60	.30
4	Dwight Gooden	.75	.60	.30
5	George Brett	.90	.70	.35
6	Rich Gossage	.30	.25	.12
7	Darrell Evans	.25	.20	.10
8	Pedro Guerrero	.30	.25	.12
9	Ron Guidry	.30	.25	.12
10	Keith Hernandez	.30	.25	.12
11	Rickey Henderson	.70	.50	.30
12	Orel Hershiser	.50	.40	.20
13	Reggie Jackson	.90	.70	.35
14	Willie McGee	.30	.25	.12
15	Don Mattingly	.75	.60	.30
16	Dale Murphy	.60	.45	.25
17	Jack Morris	.30	.25	.12
18	Dave Parker	.60	.45	.25
19	Eddie Murray	.60	.45	.25
20	Jeff Reardon	.30	.25	.12
21	Dan Quisenberry	.25	.20	.10
22	Pete Rose	.90	.70	.35
23	Jim Rice	.35	.25	.14
24	Mike Schmidt	.90	.70	.35
25	Bret Saberhagen	.30	.25	.12
26	Darryl Strawberry	.80	.60	.30
27	Dave Stieb	.25	.20	.10
28	John Tudor	.25	.20	.10
29	Dave Winfield	.75	.60	.30
30	Fernando Valenzuela	.30	.25	.12

1987 Topps

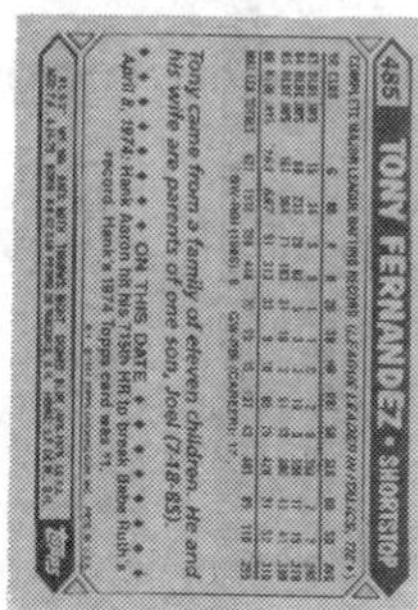

Many collectors feel that Topps' 1987 set of 792 card is a future classic. The 2-1/2" by 3-1/2" design is closely akin to the 1962 set in that the player photo is set against a woodgrain border. Instead of a rolling corner, as in 1962, the player photos in '87 feature a couple of clipped corners at top left and bottom right, where the team logo and player name appear. The player's position is not given on the front of the card. For the first time in several years, the trophy which designates members of Topps All-Star Rookie Team returned to the card design. As in the previous three years, Topps issued a glossy-finish "Tiffany" edition of their 792-card set. However, it was speculated that as many as 50,000 sets were produced as opposed to the 5,000 sets printed in 1985 and 1986. Because of the large print run, the values for the Tiffany cards are only 3-4 times higher than the same card in the regular issue.

		MT	NR MT	EX
Complete Set (792):		15.00	11.00	6.00
Common Player:		.05	.04	.02
1	Roger Clemens (Record Breaker)	.15	.11	.06
2	Jim Deshaies (Record Breaker)	.07	.05	.03
3	Dwight Evans (Record Breaker)	.07	.05	.03
4	Dave Lopes (Record Breaker)	.07	.05	.03
5	Dave Righetti (Record Breaker)	.07	.05	.03
6	Ruben Sierra (Record Breaker)	.25	.20	.10
7	Todd Worrell (Record Breaker)	.07	.05	.03
8	Terry Pendleton	.10	.08	.04
9	Jay Tibbs	.05	.04	.02
10	Cecil Cooper	.10	.08	.04
11	Indians Leaders (Jack Aker, Chris Bando, Phil Niekro)	.07	.05	.03
12	*Jeff Sellers*(FC)	.05	.04	.02
13	Nick Esasky	.07	.05	.03
14	Dave Stewart	.12	.09	.05
15	Claudell Washington	.07	.05	.03
16	Pat Clements	.05	.04	.02
17	Pete O'Brien	.10	.08	.04
18	Dick Howser	.05	.04	.02
19	Matt Young	.05	.04	.02
20	Gary Carter	.10	.08	.04
21	Mark Davis	.05	.04	.02
22	Doug DeCinces	.07	.05	.03
23	Lee Smith	.10	.08	.04
24	Tony Walker	.05	.04	.02
25	Bert Blyleven	.12	.09	.05
26	Greg Brock	.07	.05	.03
27	Joe Cowley	.05	.04	.02
28	Rick Dempsey	.07	.05	.03
29	Jimmy Key	.10	.08	.04
30	Tim Raines	.12	.09	.05
31	Braves Leaders (Glenn Hubbard, Rafael Ramirez)	.07	.05	.03
32	Tim Leary	.07	.05	.03
33	Andy Van Slyke	.12	.09	.05
34	Jose Rijo	.07	.05	.03
35	Sid Bream	.07	.05	.03
36	*Eric King*	.08	.06	.03
37	Marvell Wynne	.05	.04	.02
38	Dennis Leonard	.07	.05	.03
39	Marty Barrett	.07	.05	.03
40	Dave Righetti	.12	.09	.05
41	Bo Diaz	.07	.05	.03

#	Card	MT	NR MT	EX
42	Gary Redus	.05	.04	.02
43	Gene Michael	.05	.04	.02
44	Greg Harris	.05	.04	.02
45	Jim Presley	.10	.08	.04
46	Danny Gladden	.05	.04	.02
47	Dennis Powell	.07	.05	.03
48	Wally Backman	.07	.05	.03
49	Terry Harper	.05	.04	.02
50	Dave Smith	.07	.05	.03
51	Mel Hall	.07	.05	.03
52	Keith Atherton	.05	.04	.02
53	Ruppert Jones	.05	.04	.02
54	Bill Dawley	.05	.04	.02
55	Tim Wallach	.10	.08	.04
56	Brewers Leaders (Jamie Cocanower, Paul Molitor, Charlie Moore, Herm Starrette)	.07	.05	.03
57	*Scott Nielsen*(FC)	.10	.08	.04
58	Thad Bosley	.05	.04	.02
59	Ken Dayley	.05	.04	.02
60	Tony Pena	.07	.05	.03
61	*Bobby Thigpen*(FC)	.15	.11	.06
62	Bobby Meacham	.05	.04	.02
63	Fred Toliver(FC)	.07	.05	.03
64	Harry Spilman	.05	.04	.02
65	Tom Browning	.10	.08	.04
66	Marc Sullivan	.05	.04	.02
67	Bill Swift	.05	.04	.02
68	Tony LaRussa	.07	.05	.03
69	Lonnie Smith	.07	.05	.03
70	Charlie Hough	.07	.05	.03
71	*Mike Aldrete*(FC)	.15	.11	.06
72	Walt Terrell	.07	.05	.03
73	Dave Anderson	.05	.04	.02
74	Dan Pasqua	.10	.08	.04
75	Ron Darling	.12	.09	.05
76	Rafael Ramirez	.05	.04	.02
77	Bryan Oelkers	.05	.04	.02
78	Tom Foley	.05	.04	.02
79	Juan Nieves	.05	.04	.02
80	*Wally Joyner*	.40	.30	.15
81	Padres Leaders (Andy Hawkins, Terry Kennedy)	.07	.05	.03
82	*Rob Murphy*(FC)	.15	.11	.06
83	Mike Davis	.07	.05	.03
84	Steve Lake	.05	.04	.02
85	Kevin Bass	.07	.05	.03
86	Nate Snell	.05	.04	.02
87	Mark Salas	.05	.04	.02
88	Ed Wojna	.05	.04	.02
89	Ozzie Guillen	.08	.06	.03
90	Dave Stieb	.10	.08	.04
91	Harold Reynolds	.10	.08	.04
92a	Urbano Lugo (no trademark on front)	.30	.25	.12
92b	Urbano Lugo (trademark on front)	.07	.05	.03
93	Jim Leyland	.05	.04	.02
94	Calvin Schiraldi	.05	.04	.02
95	Oddibe McDowell	.07	.05	.03
96	Frank Williams	.05	.04	.02
97	Glenn Wilson	.07	.05	.03
98	Bill Scherrer	.05	.04	.02
99	Darryl Motley	.05	.04	.02
100	Steve Garvey	.12	.09	.05
101	*Carl Willis*(FC)	.10	.08	.04
102	Paul Zuvella	.05	.04	.02
103	Rick Aguilera	.06	.05	.02
104	Billy Sample	.05	.04	.02
105	Floyd Youmans	.07	.05	.03
106	Blue Jays Leaders (George Bell, Willie Upshaw)	.07	.05	.03
107	John Butcher	.05	.04	.02
108	Jim Gantner (photo reversed)	.07	.05	.03
109	R.J. Reynolds	.05	.04	.02
110	John Tudor	.10	.08	.04
111	Alfredo Griffin	.07	.05	.03
112	Alan Ashby	.05	.04	.02
113	Neil Allen	.05	.04	.02
114	Billy Beane	.05	.04	.02
115	Donnie Moore	.05	.04	.02
116	*Mike Stanley*	.10	.08	.04
117	Jim Beattie	.05	.04	.02
118	Bobby Valentine	.05	.04	.02
119	Ron Robinson	.05	.04	.02
120	Eddie Murray	.30	.25	.12
121	*Kevin Romine*(FC)	.12	.09	.05
122	Jim Clancy	.07	.05	.03
123	*John Kruk*	.60	.45	.25
124	Ray Fontenot	.05	.04	.02
125	Bob Brenly	.05	.04	.02
126	*Mike Loynd*(FC)	.15	.11	.06
127	Vance Law	.07	.05	.03
128	Checklist 1-132	.05	.04	.02
129	Rick Cerone	.05	.04	.02
130	Dwight Gooden	.15	.11	.06
131	Pirates Leaders (Sid Bream, Tony Pena)	.07	.05	.03
132	*Paul Assenmacher*	.15	.11	.06
133	Jose Oquendo	.05	.04	.02
134	*Rich Yett*(FC)	.12	.09	.05
135	Mike Easler	.07	.05	.03
136	Ron Romanick	.05	.04	.02
137	Jerry Willard	.05	.04	.02
138	Roy Lee Jackson	.05	.04	.02
139	*Devon White*(FC)	.60	.45	.25
140	Bret Saberhagen	.15	.11	.06
141	Herm Winningham	.05	.04	.02
142	Rick Sutcliffe	.10	.08	.04
143	Steve Boros	.05	.04	.02
144	Mike Scioscia	.07	.05	.03
145	Charlie Kerfeld	.07	.05	.03
146	*Tracy Jones*(FC)	.08	.06	.03
147	Randy Niemann	.05	.04	.02
148	Dave Collins	.07	.05	.03
149	Ray Searage	.05	.04	.02
150	Wade Boggs	.50	.40	.20
151	Mike LaCoss	.05	.04	.02
152	Toby Harrah	.07	.05	.03
153	*Duane Ward*(FC)	.40	.30	.15
154	Tom O'Malley	.05	.04	.02
155	Eddie Whitson	.05	.04	.02
156	Mariners Leaders (Bob Kearney, Phil Regan, Matt Young)	.07	.05	.03
157	Danny Darwin	.05	.04	.02
158	Tim Teufel	.05	.04	.02
159	Ed Olwine	.05	.04	.02
160	Julio Franco	.10	.08	.04
161	Steve Ontiveros	.05	.04	.02
162	*Mike LaValliere*	.12	.09	.05
163	Kevin Gross	.07	.05	.03
164	Sammy Khalifa	.05	.04	.02
165	Jeff Reardon	.10	.08	.04
166	Bob Boone	.07	.05	.03
167	*Jim Deshaies*	.12	.09	.05
168	Lou Piniella	.07	.05	.03
169	Ron Washington	.05	.04	.02
170	*Bo Jackson* (Future Stars)	1.00	.70	.40
171	*Chuck Cary*(FC)	.10	.08	.04
172	Ron Oester	.05	.04	.02
173	Alex Trevino	.05	.04	.02
174	Henry Cotto	.05	.04	.02
175	Bob Stanley	.05	.04	.02
176	Steve Buechele	.07	.05	.03
177	Keith Moreland	.07	.05	.03
178	Cecil Fielder	1.00	.70	.40
179	Bill Wegman	.10	.08	.04
180	Chris Brown	.07	.05	.03
181	Cardinals Leaders (Mike LaValliere, Ozzie Smith, Ray Soff)	.07	.05	.03
182	Lee Lacy	.05	.04	.02
183	Andy Hawkins	.05	.04	.02
184	*Bobby Bonilla*	.80	.60	.30
185	Roger McDowell	.10	.08	.04
186	Bruce Benedict	.05	.04	.02
187	Mark Huismann	.05	.04	.02
188	Tony Phillips	.05	.04	.02
189	Joe Hesketh	.05	.04	.02
190	Jim Sundberg	.07	.05	.03
191	Charles Hudson	.05	.04	.02
192	Cory Snyder(FC)	.10	.08	.04
193	Roger Craig	.07	.05	.03
194	Kirk McCaskill	.07	.05	.03
195	Mike Pagliarulo	.10	.08	.04
196	Randy O'Neal	.05	.04	.02
197	Mark Bailey	.05	.04	.02
198	Lee Mazzilli	.07	.05	.03
199	Mariano Duncan	.05	.04	.02
200	Pete Rose	.40	.30	.15
201	*John Cangelosi*	.12	.09	.05
202	Ricky Wright	.05	.04	.02
203	*Mike Kingery*(FC)	.15	.11	.06
204	Sammy Stewart	.05	.04	.02
205	Graig Nettles	.10	.08	.04
206	Twins Leaders (Tim Laudner, Frank Viola)	.07	.05	.03
207	George Frazier	.05	.04	.02
208	John Shelby	.05	.04	.02
209	Rick Schu	.05	.04	.02
210	Lloyd Moseby	.07	.05	.03
211	John Morris(FC)	.07	.05	.03
212	Mike Fitzgerald	.05	.04	.02
213	*Randy Myers*(FC)	.30	.25	.12

		MT	NR MT	EX
214	Omar Moreno	.05	.04	.02
215	Mark Langston	.12	.09	.05
216	*B.J. Surhoff* (Future Stars)	.15	.11	.06
217	Chris Codiroli	.05	.04	.02
218	Sparky Anderson	.07	.05	.03
219	Cecilio Guante	.05	.04	.02
220	Joe Carter	.25	.20	.10
221	Vern Ruhle	.05	.04	.02
222	Denny Walling	.05	.04	.02
223	Charlie Leibrandt	.07	.05	.03
224	Wayne Tolleson	.05	.04	.02
225	Mike Smithson	.05	.04	.02
226	Max Venable	.05	.04	.02
227	*Jamie Moyer*(FC)	.10	.08	.04
228	Curt Wilkerson	.05	.04	.02
229	*Mike Birkbeck*(FC)	.15	.11	.06
230	Don Baylor	.10	.08	.04
231	Giants Leaders (Bob Brenly, Mike Krukow)	.07	.05	.03
232	*Reggie Williams*	.10	.08	.04
233	*Russ Morman*(FC)	.10	.08	.04
234	Pat Sheridan	.05	.04	.02
235	Alvin Davis	.10	.08	.04
236	Tommy John	.15	.11	.06
237	Jim Morrison	.05	.04	.02
238	Bill Krueger	.05	.04	.02
239	Juan Espino	.05	.04	.02
240	Steve Balboni	.07	.05	.03
241	Danny Heep	.05	.04	.02
242	Rick Mahler	.05	.04	.02
243	Whitey Herzog	.07	.05	.03
244	Dickie Noles	.05	.04	.02
245	Willie Upshaw	.07	.05	.03
246	Jim Dwyer	.05	.04	.02
247	Jeff Reed(FC)	.07	.05	.03
248	Gene Walter	.07	.05	.03
249	Jim Pankovits	.05	.04	.02
250	Teddy Higuera	.15	.11	.06
251	Rob Wilfong	.05	.04	.02
252	Denny Martinez	.05	.04	.02
253	Eddie Milner	.05	.04	.02
254	*Bob Tewksbury*	.20	.15	.08
255	Juan Samuel	.10	.08	.04
256	Royals Leaders (George Brett, Frank White)	.10	.08	.04
257	Bob Forsch	.07	.05	.03
258	Steve Yeager	.05	.04	.02
259	*Mike Greenwell*(FC)	.50	.40	.20
260	Vida Blue	.07	.05	.03
261	*Ruben Sierra*(FC)	.90	.70	.35
262	Jim Winn	.05	.04	.02
263	Stan Javier(FC)	.07	.05	.03
264	Checklist 133-264	.05	.04	.02
265	Darrell Evans	.10	.08	.04
266	*Jeff Hamilton*(FC)	.08	.06	.03
267	Howard Johnson	.10	.08	.04
268	Pat Corrales	.05	.04	.02
269	Cliff Speck	.05	.04	.02
270	Jody Davis	.07	.05	.03
271	Mike Brown	.05	.04	.02
272	Andres Galarraga	.45	.35	.20
273	Gene Nelson	.05	.04	.02
274	*Jeff Hearron*(FC)	.05	.04	.02
275	LaMarr Hoyt	.05	.04	.02
276	Jackie Gutierrez	.05	.04	.02
277	Juan Agosto	.05	.04	.02
278	Gary Pettis	.05	.04	.02
279	*Dan Plesac*	.10	.08	.04
280	Jeffrey Leonard	.07	.05	.03
281	Bo Diaz, Bill Gullickson, Pete Rose (Reds TL)	.12	.09	.05
282	Jeff Calhoun	.05	.04	.02
283	*Doug Drabek*(FC)	.40	.30	.15
284	John Moses	.05	.04	.02
285	Dennis Boyd	.07	.05	.03
286	Mike Woodard(FC)	.07	.05	.03
287	Dave Von Ohlen	.05	.04	.02
288	Tito Landrum	.05	.04	.02
289	Bob Kipper	.07	.05	.03
290	Leon Durham	.07	.05	.03
291	*Mitch Williams*(FC)	.40	.30	.15
292	Franklin Stubbs	.07	.05	.03
293	Bob Rodgers	.05	.04	.02
294	Steve Jeltz	.05	.04	.02
295	Len Dykstra	.15	.11	.06
296	*Andres Thomas*	.15	.11	.06
297	Don Schulze	.05	.04	.02
298	Larry Herndon	.05	.04	.02
299	Joel Davis	.07	.05	.03
300	Reggie Jackson	.30	.25	.12
301	*Luis Aquino*(FC)	.10	.08	.04
302	Bill Schroeder	.05	.04	.02
303	Juan Berenguer	.05	.04	.02
304	Phil Garner	.05	.04	.02
305	John Franco	.10	.08	.04
306	Red Sox Leaders (Rich Gedman, John McNamara, Tom Seaver)	.07	.05	.03
307	*Lee Guetterman*(FC)	.15	.11	.06
308	Don Slaught	.05	.04	.02
309	Mike Young	.05	.04	.02
310	Frank Viola	.15	.11	.06
311	Turn Back The Clock (Rickey Henderson)	.12	.09	.05
312	Turn Back The Clock (Reggie Jackson)	.10	.08	.04
313	Turn Back The Clock (Roberto Clemente)	.10	.08	.04
314	Turn Back The Clock (Carl Yastrzemski)	.10	.08	.04
315	Turn Back The Clock (Maury Wills)	.07	.05	.03
316	Brian Fisher	.07	.05	.03
317	Clint Hurdle	.05	.04	.02
318	Jim Fregosi	.05	.04	.02
319	*Greg Swindell*(FC)	.30	.25	.12
320	*Barry Bonds*	3.00	2.25	1.25
321	Mike Laga	.05	.04	.02
322	Chris Bando	.05	.04	.02
323	*Al Newman*	.07	.05	.03
324	Dave Palmer	.05	.04	.02
325	Garry Templeton	.07	.05	.03
326	Mark Gubicza	.10	.08	.04
327	*Dale Sveum*	.08	.06	.03
328	Bob Welch	.10	.08	.04
329	Ron Roenicke	.05	.04	.02
330	Mike Scott	.12	.09	.05
331	Mets Leaders (Gary Carter, Keith Hernandez, Dave Johnson, Darryl Strawberry)	.10	.08	.04
332	Joe Price	.05	.04	.02
333	Ken Phelps	.07	.05	.03
334	*Ed Correa*	.05	.04	.02
335	Candy Maldonado	.07	.05	.03
336	*Allan Anderson*(FC)	.06	.05	.02
337	Darrell Miller	.05	.04	.02
338	Tim Conroy	.05	.04	.02
339	Donnie Hill	.05	.04	.02
340	Roger Clemens	.75	.60	.30
341	Mike Brown	.05	.04	.02
342	Bob James	.05	.04	.02
343	Hal Lanier	.05	.04	.02
344a	Joe Niekro (copyright outside yellow on back)	.30	.25	.12
344b	Joe Niekro (copyright inside yellow on back)	.07	.05	.03
345	Andre Dawson	.20	.15	.08
346	Shawon Dunston	.07	.05	.03
347	Mickey Brantley(FC)	.07	.05	.03
348	Carmelo Martinez	.07	.05	.03
349	Storm Davis	.10	.08	.04
350	Keith Hernandez	.10	.08	.04
351	Gene Garber	.05	.04	.02
352	Mike Felder(FC)	.07	.05	.03
353	Ernie Camacho	.05	.04	.02
354	Jamie Quirk	.05	.04	.02
355	Don Carman	.07	.05	.03
356	White Sox Leaders (Ed Brinkman, Julio Cruz)	.07	.05	.03
357	*Steve Fireovid*(FC)	.07	.05	.03
358	Sal Butera	.05	.04	.02
359	Doug Corbett	.05	.04	.02
360	Pedro Guerrero	.08	.06	.03
361	Mark Thurmond	.05	.04	.02
362	*Luis Quinones*(FC)	.12	.09	.05
363	Jose Guzman	.12	.09	.05
364	Randy Bush	.05	.04	.02
365	Rick Rhoden	.07	.05	.03
366	*Mark McGwire*	.90	.70	.35
367	Jeff Lahti	.05	.04	.02
368	John McNamara	.05	.04	.02
369	Brian Dayett	.05	.04	.02
370	Fred Lynn	.15	.11	.06
371	*Mark Eichhorn*	.15	.11	.06
372	Jerry Mumphrey	.05	.04	.02
373	Jeff Dedmon	.05	.04	.02
374	Glenn Hoffman	.05	.04	.02
375	Ron Guidry	.12	.09	.05
376	Scott Bradley	.05	.04	.02
377	John Henry Johnson	.05	.04	.02
378	Rafael Santana	.05	.04	.02
379	John Russell	.05	.04	.02
380	Rich Gossage	.15	.11	.06
381	Expos Leaders (Mike Fitzgerald, Bob Rodgers)	.07	.05	.03

		MT	NR MT	EX
382	Rudy Law	.05	.04	.02
383	Ron Davis	.05	.04	.02
384	Johnny Grubb	.05	.04	.02
385	Orel Hershiser	.12	.09	.05
386	Dickie Thon	.07	.05	.03
387	*T.R. Bryden*(FC)	.10	.08	.04
388	Geno Petralli	.05	.04	.02
389	Jeff Robinson	.07	.05	.03
390	Gary Matthews	.07	.05	.03
391	Jay Howell	.07	.05	.03
392	Checklist 265-396	.05	.04	.02
393	Pete Rose	.20	.15	.08
394	Mike Bielecki	.07	.05	.03
395	Damaso Garcia	.05	.04	.02
396	Tim Lollar	.05	.04	.02
397	Greg Walker	.07	.05	.03
398	Brad Havens	.05	.04	.02
399	Curt Ford(FC)	.07	.05	.03
400	George Brett	.35	.25	.14
401	Billy Jo Robidoux	.07	.05	.03
402	Mike Trujillo	.05	.04	.02
403	Jerry Royster	.05	.04	.02
404	Doug Sisk	.05	.04	.02
405	Brook Jacoby	.10	.08	.04
406	Yankees Leaders (Rickey Henderson, Don Mattingly)	.25	.20	.10
407	Jim Acker	.05	.04	.02
408	John Mizerock	.05	.04	.02
409	Milt Thompson	.07	.05	.03
410	Fernando Valenzuela	.08	.06	.03
411	Darnell Coles	.07	.05	.03
412	Eric Davis	.20	.15	.08
413	Moose Haas	.05	.04	.02
414	Joe Orsulak	.05	.04	.02
415	*Bobby Witt*	.12	.09	.05
416	Tom Nieto	.05	.04	.02
417	Pat Perry(FC)	.07	.05	.03
418	Dick Williams	.05	.04	.02
419	*Mark Portugal*(FC)	.12	.09	.05
420	*Will Clark*	1.75	1.25	.70
421	Jose DeLeon	.07	.05	.03
422	Jack Howell	.07	.05	.03
423	Jaime Cocanower	.05	.04	.02
424	Chris Speier	.05	.04	.02
425	Tom Seaver	.30	.25	.12
426	Floyd Rayford	.05	.04	.02
427	Ed Nunez	.05	.04	.02
428	Bruce Bochy	.05	.04	.02
429	*Tim Pyznarski* (Future Stars)(FC)	.10	.08	.04
430	Mike Schmidt	.40	.30	.15
431	Dodgers Leaders (Tom Niedenfuer, Ron Perranoski, Alex Trevino)	.07	.05	.03
432	Jim Slaton	.05	.04	.02
433	*Ed Hearn*(FC)	.10	.08	.04
434	Mike Fischlin	.05	.04	.02
435	Bruce Sutter	.12	.09	.05
436	*Andy Allanson*	.15	.11	.06
437	Ted Power	.05	.04	.02
438	*Kelly Downs*(FC)	.10	.08	.04
439	Karl Best	.05	.04	.02
440	Willie McGee	.10	.08	.04
441	*Dave Leiper*(FC)	.10	.08	.04
442	Mitch Webster	.07	.05	.03
443	John Felske	.05	.04	.02
444	Jeff Russell	.05	.04	.02
445	Dave Lopes	.07	.05	.03
446	*Chuck Finley*(FC)	.25	.20	.10
447	Bill Almon	.05	.04	.02
448	*Chris Bosio*(FC)	.20	.15	.08
449	*Pat Dodson* (Future Stars)(FC)	.10	.08	.04
450	Kirby Puckett	1.00	.70	.40
451	Joe Sambito	.05	.04	.02
452	Dave Henderson	.10	.08	.04
453	*Scott Terry*(FC)	.12	.09	.05
454	Luis Salazar	.05	.04	.02
455	Mike Boddicker	.07	.05	.03
456	A's Leaders (Carney Lansford, Tony LaRussa, Mickey Tettleton, Dave Von Ohlen)	.07	.05	.03
457	Len Matuszek	.05	.04	.02
458	Kelly Gruber(FC)	.15	.11	.06
459	Dennis Eckersley	.10	.08	.04
460	Darryl Strawberry	.15	.11	.06
461	Craig McMurtry	.05	.04	.02
462	Scott Fletcher	.07	.05	.03
463	Tom Candiotti	.05	.04	.02
464	Butch Wynegar	.05	.04	.02
465	Todd Worrell	.08	.06	.03
466	Kal Daniels(FC)	.10	.08	.04
467	Randy St. Claire	.05	.04	.02
468	George Bamberger	.05	.04	.02

		MT	NR MT	EX
469	*Mike Diaz*(FC)	.10	.08	.04
470	Dave Dravecky	.07	.05	.03
471	Ronn Reynolds	.05	.04	.02
472	Bill Doran	.07	.05	.03
473	Steve Farr	.05	.04	.02
474	Jerry Narron	.05	.04	.02
475	Scott Garrelts	.05	.04	.02
476	Danny Tartabull	.30	.25	.12
477	Ken Howell	.05	.04	.02
478	Tim Laudner	.05	.04	.02
479	*Bob Sebra*(FC)	.10	.08	.04
480	Jim Rice	.12	.09	.05
481	Phillies Leaders (Von Hayes, Juan Samuel, Glenn Wilson)	.07	.05	.03
482	Daryl Boston	.05	.04	.02
483	Dwight Lowry	.05	.04	.02
484	Jim Traber(FC)	.15	.11	.06
485	Tony Fernandez	.10	.08	.04
486	Otis Nixon	.10	.08	.04
487	Dave Gumpert	.05	.04	.02
488	Ray Knight	.07	.05	.03
489	Bill Gullickson	.05	.04	.02
490	Dale Murphy	.15	.11	.06
491	*Ron Karkovice*(FC)	.10	.08	.04
492	Mike Heath	.05	.04	.02
493	Tom Lasorda	.07	.05	.03
494	*Barry Jones*(FC)	.12	.09	.05
495	Gorman Thomas	.10	.08	.04
496	Bruce Bochte	.05	.04	.02
497	*Dale Mohorcic*(FC)	.15	.11	.06
498	Bob Kearney	.05	.04	.02
499	*Bruce Ruffin*(FC)	.08	.06	.03
500	Don Mattingly	.40	.30	.15
501	Craig Lefferts	.05	.04	.02
502	Dick Schofield	.05	.04	.02
503	Larry Andersen	.05	.04	.02
504	Mickey Hatcher	.05	.04	.02
505	Bryn Smith	.05	.04	.02
506	Orioles Leaders (Rich Bordi, Rick Dempsey, Earl Weaver)	.07	.05	.03
507	Dave Stapleton	.05	.04	.02
508	*Scott Bankhead*	.10	.08	.04
509	Enos Cabell	.05	.04	.02
510	Tom Henke	.07	.05	.03
511	Steve Lyons	.05	.04	.02
512	*Dave Magadan* (Future Stars)(FC)	.20	.15	.08
513	Carmen Castillo	.05	.04	.02
514	Orlando Mercado	.05	.04	.02
515	Willie Hernandez	.07	.05	.03
516	Ted Simmons	.10	.08	.04
517	Mario Soto	.07	.05	.03
518	Gene Mauch	.07	.05	.03
519	Curt Young	.07	.05	.03
520	Jack Clark	.15	.11	.06
521	Rick Reuschel	.10	.08	.04
522	Checklist 397-528	.05	.04	.02
523	Earnie Riles	.05	.04	.02
524	Bob Shirley	.05	.04	.02
525	Phil Bradley	.10	.08	.04
526	Roger Mason	.05	.04	.02
527	Jim Wohlford	.05	.04	.02
528	Ken Dixon	.05	.04	.02
529	*Alvaro Espinoza*(FC)	.07	.05	.03
530	Tony Gwynn	.30	.25	.12
531	Astros Leaders (Yogi Berra, Hal Lanier, Denis Menke, Gene Tenace)	.07	.05	.03
532	Jeff Stone	.05	.04	.02
533	Argenis Salazar	.05	.04	.02
534	Scott Sanderson	.05	.04	.02
535	Tony Armas	.07	.05	.03
536	*Terry Mulholland*(FC)	.35	.25	.14
537	Rance Mulliniks	.05	.04	.02
538	Tom Niedenfuer	.07	.05	.03
539	Reid Nichols	.05	.04	.02
540	Terry Kennedy	.07	.05	.03
541	*Rafael Belliard*(FC)	.10	.08	.04
542	Ricky Horton	.07	.05	.03
543	Dave Johnson	.07	.05	.03
544	Zane Smith	.07	.05	.03
545	Buddy Bell	.07	.05	.03
546	Mike Morgan	.05	.04	.02
547	Rob Deer	.10	.08	.04
548	*Bill Mooneyham*(FC)	.10	.08	.04
549	Bob Melvin	.05	.04	.02
550	*Pete Incaviglia*	.25	.20	.10
551	Frank Wills	.05	.04	.02
552	Larry Sheets	.07	.05	.03
553	*Mike Maddux*(FC)	.15	.11	.06
554	Buddy Biancalana	.05	.04	.02
555	Dennis Rasmussen	.10	.08	.04
556	Angels Leaders (Bob Boone, Marcel Lachemann, Mike Witt)	.07	.05	.03

		MT	NR MT	EX
557	*John Cerutti*	.15	.11	.06
558	Greg Gagne	.05	.04	.02
559	Lance McCullers	.07	.05	.03
560	Glenn Davis	.06	.05	.02
561	*Rey Quinones*	.15	.11	.06
562	*Bryan Clutterbuck*(FC)	.10	.08	.04
563	John Stefero	.05	.04	.02
564	Larry McWilliams	.05	.04	.02
565	Dusty Baker	.07	.05	.03
566	Tim Hulett	.05	.04	.02
567	*Greg Mathews*(FC)	.08	.06	.03
568	Earl Weaver	.07	.05	.03
569	Wade Rowdon(FC)	.07	.05	.03
570	Sid Fernandez	.10	.08	.04
571	Ozzie Virgil	.05	.04	.02
572	Pete Ladd	.05	.04	.02
573	Hal McRae	.07	.05	.03
574	Manny Lee	.05	.04	.02
575	Pat Tabler	.07	.05	.03
576	Frank Pastore	.05	.04	.02
577	Dann Bilardello	.05	.04	.02
578	Billy Hatcher	.07	.05	.03
579	Rick Burleson	.07	.05	.03
580	Mike Krukow	.07	.05	.03
581	Cubs Leaders (Ron Cey, Steve Trout)	.07	.05	.03
582	Bruce Berenyi	.05	.04	.02
583	Junior Ortiz	.05	.04	.02
584	Ron Kittle	.07	.05	.03
585	*Scott Bailes*	.15	.11	.06
586	Ben Oglivie	.07	.05	.03
587	Eric Plunk(FC)	.10	.08	.04
588	Wallace Johnson	.05	.04	.02
589	Steve Crawford	.05	.04	.02
590	Vince Coleman	.10	.08	.04
591	Spike Owen	.05	.04	.02
592	Chris Welsh	.05	.04	.02
593	Chuck Tanner	.05	.04	.02
594	Rick Anderson	.05	.04	.02
595	Keith Hernandez (All-Star)	.12	.09	.05
596	Steve Sax (All-Star)	.07	.05	.03
597	Mike Schmidt (All-Star)	.20	.15	.08
598	Ozzie Smith (All-Star)	.07	.05	.03
599	Tony Gwynn (All-Star)	.20	.15	.08
600	Dave Parker (All-Star)	.10	.08	.04
601	Darryl Strawberry (All-Star)	.10	.08	.04
602	Gary Carter (All-Star)	.15	.11	.06
603a	Dwight Gooden (All-Star, no trademark on front)	.80	.60	.30
603b	Dwight Gooden (All-Star, trademark on front)	.10	.08	.04
604	Fernando Valenzuela (All-Star)	.12	.09	.05
605	Todd Worrell (All-Star)	.10	.08	.04
606a	Don Mattingly (All-Star, no trademark on front)	1.25	.90	.50
606b	Don Mattingly (All-Star, trademark on front)	.25	.20	.10
607	Tony Bernazard (All-Star)	.05	.04	.02
608	Wade Boggs (All-Star)	.20	.15	.08
609	Cal Ripken, Jr. (All-Star)	.40	.30	.15
610	Jim Rice (All-Star)	.15	.11	.06
611	Kirby Puckett (All-Star)	.30	.25	.12
612	George Bell (All-Star)	.12	.09	.05
613	Lance Parrish (All-Star)	.10	.08	.04
614	Roger Clemens (All-Star)	.20	.15	.08
615	Teddy Higuera (All-Star)	.10	.08	.04
616	Dave Righetti (All-Star)	.10	.08	.04
617	Al Nipper	.05	.04	.02
618	Tom Kelly	.05	.04	.02
619	Jerry Reed	.05	.04	.02
620	Jose Canseco	.90	.70	.35
621	Danny Cox	.07	.05	.03
622	*Glenn Braggs*(FC)	.10	.08	.04
623	*Kurt Stillwell*(FC)	.12	.09	.05
624	Tim Burke	.05	.04	.02
625	Mookie Wilson	.07	.05	.03
626	Joel Skinner	.05	.04	.02
627	Ken Oberkfell	.05	.04	.02
628	Bob Walk	.05	.04	.02
629	Larry Parrish	.07	.05	.03
630	John Candelaria	.07	.05	.03
631	Tigers Leaders (Sparky Anderson, Mike Heath, Willie Hernandez)	.07	.05	.03
632	Rob Woodward(FC)	.07	.05	.03
633	Jose Uribe	.07	.05	.03
634	*Rafael Palmeiro*	1.75	1.25	.70
635	Ken Schrom	.05	.04	.02
636	Darren Daulton	.40	.30	.15
637	*Bip Roberts*	.10	.08	.04
638	Rich Bordi	.05	.04	.02
639	Gerald Perry	.10	.08	.04
640	Mark Clear	.05	.04	.02
641	Domingo Ramos	.05	.04	.02
642	Al Pulido	.05	.04	.02
643	Ron Shepherd	.05	.04	.02
644	John Denny	.05	.04	.02
645	Dwight Evans	.12	.09	.05
646	Mike Mason	.05	.04	.02
647	Tom Lawless	.05	.04	.02
648	*Barry Larkin*	.90	.70	.35
649	Mickey Tettleton	.20	.15	.08
650	Hubie Brooks	.07	.05	.03
651	Benny Distefano	.05	.04	.02
652	Terry Forster	.07	.05	.03
653	*Kevin Mitchell*	.35	.25	.14
654	Checklist 529-660	.05	.04	.02
655	Jesse Barfield	.15	.11	.06
656	Rangers Leaders (Bobby Valentine, Rickey Wright)	.07	.05	.03
657	Tom Waddell	.05	.04	.02
658	*Robby Thompson*	.30	.25	.12
659	Aurelio Lopez	.05	.04	.02
660	Bob Horner	.10	.08	.04
661	Lou Whitaker	.15	.11	.06
662	Frank DiPino	.05	.04	.02
663	Cliff Johnson	.05	.04	.02
664	Mike Marshall	.10	.08	.04
665	Rod Scurry	.05	.04	.02
666	Von Hayes	.07	.05	.03
667	Ron Hassey	.05	.04	.02
668	Juan Bonilla	.05	.04	.02
669	Bud Black	.05	.04	.02
670	Jose Cruz	.07	.05	.03
671a	Ray Soff (no "D-" before copyright line)	.20	.15	.08
671b	Ray Soff ("D-" before copyright line)	.05	.04	.02
672	Chili Davis	.07	.05	.03
673	Don Sutton	.12	.09	.05
674	Bill Campbell	.05	.04	.02
675	Ed Romero	.05	.04	.02
676	Charlie Moore	.05	.04	.02
677	Bob Grich	.07	.05	.03
678	Carney Lansford	.07	.05	.03
679	Kent Hrbek	.10	.08	.04
680	Ryne Sandberg	1.00	.70	.40
681	George Bell	.12	.09	.05
682	Jerry Reuss	.07	.05	.03
683	Gary Roenicke	.05	.04	.02
684	Kent Tekulve	.07	.05	.03
685	Jerry Hairston	.05	.04	.02
686	Doyle Alexander	.07	.05	.03
687	Alan Trammell	.12	.09	.05
688	Juan Beniquez	.05	.04	.02
689	Darrell Porter	.07	.05	.03
690	Dane Iorg	.05	.04	.02
691	Dave Parker	.10	.08	.04
692	Frank White	.07	.05	.03
693	Terry Puhl	.05	.04	.02
694	Phil Niekro	.10	.08	.04
695	Chico Walker	.05	.04	.02
696	Gary Lucas	.05	.04	.02
697	Ed Lynch	.05	.04	.02
698	Ernie Whitt	.07	.05	.03
699	Ken Landreaux	.05	.04	.02
700	Dave Bergman	.05	.04	.02
701	Willie Randolph	.07	.05	.03
702	Greg Gross	.05	.04	.02
703	Dave Schmidt	.05	.04	.02
704	Jesse Orosco	.07	.05	.03
705	Bruce Hurst	.10	.08	.04
706	Rick Manning	.05	.04	.02
707	Bob McClure	.05	.04	.02
708	Scott McGregor	.07	.05	.03
709	Dave Kingman	.10	.08	.04
710	Gary Gaetti	.15	.11	.06
711	Ken Griffey	.07	.05	.03
712	Don Robinson	.07	.05	.03
713	Tom Brookens	.05	.04	.02
714	Dan Quisenberry	.07	.05	.03
715	Bob Dernier	.05	.04	.02
716	Rick Leach	.05	.04	.02
717	Ed Vande Berg	.05	.04	.02
718	Steve Carlton	.15	.11	.06
719	Tom Hume	.05	.04	.02
720	Richard Dotson	.07	.05	.03
721	Tom Herr	.07	.05	.03
722	Bob Knepper	.07	.05	.03
723	Brett Butler	.07	.05	.03
724	Greg Minton	.05	.04	.02
725	George Hendrick	.07	.05	.03
726	Frank Tanana	.07	.05	.03

		MT	NR MT	EX
727	Mike Moore	.05	.04	.02
728	Tippy Martinez	.05	.04	.02
729	Tom Paciorek	.05	.04	.02
730	Eric Show	.07	.05	.03
731	Dave Concepcion	.10	.08	.04
732	Manny Trillo	.07	.05	.03
733	Bill Caudill	.05	.04	.02
734	Bill Madlock	.10	.08	.04
735	Rickey Henderson	.30	.25	.12
736	Steve Bedrosian	.10	.08	.04
737	Floyd Bannister	.07	.05	.03
738	Jorge Orta	.05	.04	.02
739	Chet Lemon	.07	.05	.03
740	Rich Gedman	.07	.05	.03
741	Paul Molitor	.25	.20	.10
742	Andy McGaffigan	.05	.04	.02
743	Dwayne Murphy	.07	.05	.03
744	Roy Smalley	.05	.04	.02
745	Glenn Hubbard	.05	.04	.02
746	Bob Ojeda	.07	.05	.03
747	Johnny Ray	.07	.05	.03
748	Mike Flanagan	.07	.05	.03
749	Ozzie Smith	.25	.20	.10
750	Steve Trout	.07	.05	.03
751	Garth Iorg	.05	.04	.02
752	Dan Petry	.07	.05	.03
753	Rick Honeycutt	.05	.04	.02
754	Dave LaPoint	.07	.05	.03
755	Luis Aguayo	.05	.04	.02
756	Carlton Fisk	.25	.20	.10
757	Nolan Ryan	1.25	.90	.50
758	Tony Bernazard	.05	.04	.02
759	Joel Youngblood	.05	.04	.02
760	Mike Witt	.07	.05	.03
761	Greg Pryor	.05	.04	.02
762	Gary Ward	.07	.05	.03
763	Tim Flannery	.05	.04	.02
764	Bill Buckner	.07	.05	.03
765	Kirk Gibson	.10	.08	.04
766	Don Aase	.05	.04	.02
767	Ron Cey	.07	.05	.03
768	Dennis Lamp	.05	.04	.02
769	Steve Sax	.15	.11	.06
770	Dave Winfield	.35	.25	.14
771	Shane Rawley	.07	.05	.03
772	Harold Baines	.12	.09	.05
773	Robin Yount	.35	.25	.14
774	Wayne Krenchicki	.05	.04	.02
775	Joaquin Andujar	.07	.05	.03
776	Tom Brunansky	.10	.08	.04
777	Chris Chambliss	.07	.05	.03
778	Jack Morris	.12	.09	.05
779	Craig Reynolds	.05	.04	.02
780	Andre Thornton	.07	.05	.03
781	Atlee Hammaker	.05	.04	.02
782	Brian Downing	.07	.05	.03
783	Willie Wilson	.10	.08	.04
784	Cal Ripken, Jr.	.90	.70	.35
785	Terry Francona	.05	.04	.02
786	Jimy Williams	.05	.04	.02
787	Alejandro Pena	.07	.05	.03
788	Tim Stoddard	.05	.04	.02
789	Dan Schatzeder	.05	.04	.02
790	Julio Cruz	.05	.04	.02
791	Lance Parrish	.15	.11	.06
792	Checklist 661-792	.05	.04	.02

1987 Topps All-Star Glossy Set Of 22

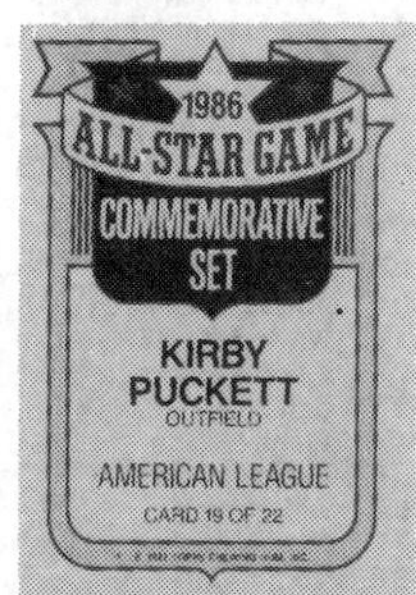

For the fourth consecutive year, Topps produced an All-Star Game commemorative set of 22 cards. The glossy cards, which measure 2-1/2" by 3-1/2", were included in rack packs. Using the same basic card design as in previous efforts with a few minor changes, the 1987 edition features American and National League logos on the card fronts. Card #'s 1- 12 feature representatives from the American League, while #'s 13-22 are National Leaguers.

		MT	NR MT	EX
Complete Set:		5.00	3.75	2.00
Common Player:		.15	.11	.06
1	Whitey Herzog	.15	.11	.06
2	Keith Hernandez	.40	.30	.15
3	Ryne Sandberg	.40	.30	.15
4	Mike Schmidt	.70	.50	.30
5	Ozzie Smith	.30	.25	.12
6	Tony Gwynn	.50	.40	.20
7	Dale Murphy	.50	.40	.20
8	Darryl Strawberry	.80	.60	.30
9	Gary Carter	.40	.30	.15
10	Dwight Gooden	.60	.45	.25
11	Fernando Valenzuela	.30	.25	.12
12	Dick Howser	.15	.11	.06
13	Wally Joyner	.70	.50	.30
14	Lou Whitaker	.30	.25	.12
15	Wade Boggs	.70	.50	.30
16	Cal Ripken	.50	.40	.20
17	Dave Winfield	.40	.30	.15
18	Rickey Henderson	.80	.60	.30
19	Kirby Puckett	.40	.30	.15
20	Lance Parrish	.30	.25	.12
21	Roger Clemens	.60	.45	.25
22	Teddy Higuera	.30	.25	.12

1987 Topps All-Star Glossy Set Of 60

Using the same design as the previous year, the 1987 Topps All-Star Glossy set includes 48 All-Star performers plus 12 potential superstars branded as "Hot Prospects". The card fronts are uncluttered, save the player's name found in very small print at the bottom. The set was available via a mail-in offer. Six subsets make up the 60-card set, with each subset being available for $1.00 plus six special offer cards that were found in wax packs.

		MT	NR MT	EX
Complete Set:		12.00	9.00	4.75
Common Player:		.15	.11	.06
1	Don Mattingly	2.50	2.00	1.00
2	Tony Gwynn	.60	.45	.25
3	Gary Gaetti	.25	.20	.10
4	Glenn Davis	.30	.25	.12
5	Roger Clemens	.70	.50	.30
6	Dale Murphy	.90	.70	.35
7	Lou Whitaker	.30	.25	.12
8	Roger McDowell	.15	.11	.06
9	Cory Snyder	.50	.40	.20
10	Todd Worrell	.20	.15	.08
11	Gary Carter	.50	.40	.20
12	Eddie Murray	.60	.45	.25

		MT	NR MT	EX
13	Bob Knepper	.15	.11	.06
14	Harold Baines	.20	.15	.08
15	Jeff Reardon	.20	.15	.08
16	Joe Carter	.25	.20	.10
17	Dave Parker	.25	.20	.10
18	Wade Boggs	1.25	.90	.50
19	Danny Tartabull	.35	.25	.14
20	Jim Deshaies	.20	.15	.08
21	Rickey Henderson	.70	.50	.30
22	Rob Deer	.15	.11	.06
23	Ozzie Smith	.25	.20	.10
24	Dave Righetti	.25	.20	.10
25	Kent Hrbek	.30	.25	.12
26	Keith Hernandez	.40	.30	.15
27	Don Baylor	.15	.11	.06
28	Mike Schmidt	.90	.70	.35
29	Pete Incaviglia	.50	.40	.20
30	Barry Bonds	.50	.40	.20
31	George Brett	.90	.70	.35
32	Darryl Strawberry	.90	.70	.35
33	Mike Witt	.15	.11	.06
34	Kevin Bass	.15	.11	.06
35	Jesse Barfield	.20	.15	.08
36	Bob Ojeda	.15	.11	.06
37	Cal Ripken	.70	.50	.30
38	Vince Coleman	.25	.20	.10
39	Wally Joyner	1.75	1.25	.70
40	Robby Thompson	.20	.15	.08
41	Pete Rose	1.25	.90	.50
42	Jim Rice	.50	.40	.20
43	Tony Bernazard	.15	.11	.06
44	Eric Davis	1.00	.70	.40
45	George Bell	.50	.40	.20
46	Hubie Brooks	.15	.11	.06
47	Jack Morris	.30	.25	.12
48	Tim Raines	.50	.40	.20
49	Mark Eichhorn	.20	.15	.08
50	Kevin Mitchell	.25	.20	.10
51	Dwight Gooden	.80	.60	.30
52	Doug DeCinces	.15	.11	.06
53	Fernando Valenzuela	.35	.25	.14
54	Reggie Jackson	.70	.50	.30
55	Johnny Ray	.15	.11	.06
56	Mike Pagliarulo	.20	.15	.08
57	Kirby Puckett	.50	.40	.20
58	Lance Parrish	.30	.25	.12
59	Jose Canseco	2.50	2.00	1.00
60	Greg Mathews	.25	.20	.10

1987 Topps Traded

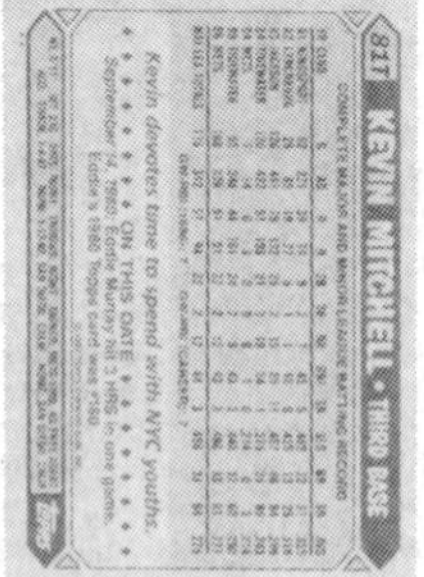

The Topps Traded set consists of 132 cards as have all Traded sets issued by Topps since 1981. The cards measure the standard 2 1/2" by 3 1/2" and are identical in design to the regular edition set. The purpose of the set is to update player trades and feature rookies not included in the regular issue. As they had done the previous three years, Topps produced a glossy-coated "Tiffany" edition of the Traded set. The Tiffany edition cards are valued at two to three times greater than the regular Traded cards.

	MT	NR MT	EX
Complete Set (132):	8.00	6.00	3.25
Common Player:	.06	.05	.02

		MT	NR MT	EX
1T	Bill Almon	.06	.05	.02
2T	Scott Bankhead	.08	.06	.03
3T	Eric Bell(FC)	.08	.06	.03
4T	Juan Beniquez	.06	.05	.02
5T	Juan Berenguer	.06	.05	.02
6T	Greg Booker	.06	.05	.02
7T	Thad Bosley	.06	.05	.02
8T	Larry Bowa	.10	.08	.04
9T	Greg Brock	.06	.05	.02
10T	Bob Brower(FC)	.06	.05	.02
11T	Jerry Browne(FC)	.10	.08	.04
12T	Ralph Bryant(FC)	.06	.05	.02
13T	DeWayne Buice(FC)	.06	.05	.02
14T	Ellis Burks(FC)	.80	.60	.30
15T	Ivan Calderon	.12	.09	.05
16T	Jeff Calhoun	.06	.05	.02
17T	Casey Candaele(FC)	.10	.08	.04
18T	John Cangelosi	.06	.05	.02
19T	Steve Carlton	.30	.25	.12
20T	Juan Castillo(FC)	.06	.05	.02
21T	Rick Cerone	.06	.05	.02
22T	Ron Cey	.10	.08	.04
23T	John Christensen	.06	.05	.02
24T	Dave Cone(FC)	.75	.60	.30
25T	Chuck Crim(FC)	.15	.11	.06
26T	Storm Davis	.06	.05	.02
27T	Andre Dawson	.40	.30	.15
28T	Rick Dempsey	.08	.06	.03
29T	Doug Drabek	.30	.25	.12
30T	Mike Dunne	.20	.15	.08
31T	Dennis Eckersley	.30	.25	.12
32T	Lee Elia	.06	.05	.02
33T	Brian Fisher	.10	.08	.04
34T	Terry Francona	.06	.05	.02
35T	Willie Fraser(FC)	.15	.11	.06
36T	Billy Gardner	.06	.05	.02
37T	Ken Gerhart(FC)	.15	.11	.06
38T	Danny Gladden	.06	.05	.02
39T	Jim Gott	.06	.05	.02
40T	Cecilio Guante	.06	.05	.02
41T	Albert Hall	.06	.05	.02
42T	Terry Harper	.06	.05	.02
43T	Mickey Hatcher	.06	.05	.02
44T	Brad Havens	.06	.05	.02
45T	Neal Heaton	.06	.05	.02
46T	Mike Henneman(FC)	.30	.25	.12
47T	Donnie Hill	.06	.05	.02
48T	Guy Hoffman	.06	.05	.02
49T	Brian Holton(FC)	.15	.11	.06
50T	Charles Hudson	.06	.05	.02
51T	Danny Jackson(FC)	.08	.06	.03
52T	Reggie Jackson	.50	.40	.20
53T	Chris James(FC)	.10	.08	.04
54T	Dion James	.10	.08	.04
55T	Stan Jefferson(FC)	.20	.15	.08
56T	Joe Johnson(FC)	.08	.06	.03
57T	Terry Kennedy	.08	.06	.03
58T	Mike Kingery	.08	.06	.03
59T	Ray Knight	.10	.08	.04
60T	Gene Larkin(FC)	.15	.11	.06
61T	Mike LaValliere	.10	.08	.04
62T	Jack Lazorko	.06	.05	.02
63T	Terry Leach	.06	.05	.02
64T	Tim Leary	.06	.05	.02
65T	Jim Lindeman(FC)	.15	.11	.06
66T	Steve Lombardozzi(FC)	.06	.05	.02
67T	Bill Long(FC)	.06	.05	.02
68T	Barry Lyons(FC)	.15	.11	.06
69T	Shane Mack	.40	.30	.15
70T	Greg Maddux(FC)	4.00	3.00	1.50
71T	Bill Madlock	.15	.11	.06
72T	Joe Magrane(FC)	.12	.09	.05
73T	Dave Martinez(FC)	.15	.11	.06
74T	Fred McGriff(FC)	3.00	2.25	1.25
75T	Mark McLemore(FC)	.10	.08	.04
76T	Kevin McReynolds(FC)	.10	.08	.04
77T	Dave Meads(FC)	.08	.06	.03
78T	Eddie Milner	.06	.05	.02
79T	Greg Minton	.06	.05	.02
80T	John Mitchell(FC)	.08	.06	.03
81T	Kevin Mitchell	.15	.11	.06
82T	Charlie Moore	.06	.05	.02
83T	Jeff Musselman(FC)	.12	.09	.05
84T	Gene Nelson	.06	.05	.02
85T	Graig Nettles	.12	.09	.05
86T	Al Newman	.06	.05	.02
87T	Reid Nichols	.06	.05	.02
88T	Tom Niedenfuer	.08	.06	.03
89T	Joe Niekro	.10	.08	.04
90T	Tom Nieto	.06	.05	.02
91T	Matt Nokes(FC)	.20	.15	.08

		MT	NR MT	EX
92T	Dickie Noles	.06	.05	.02
93T	Pat Pacillo	.15	.11	.06
94T	Lance Parrish	.10	.08	.04
95T	Tony Pena	.10	.08	.04
96T	Luis Polonia(FC)	.40	.30	.15
97T	Randy Ready	.06	.05	.02
98T	Jeff Reardon	.12	.09	.05
99T	Gary Redus	.08	.06	.03
100T	Jeff Reed	.06	.05	.02
101T	Rick Rhoden	.10	.08	.04
102T	Cal Ripken, Sr.	.06	.05	.02
103T	Wally Ritchie(FC)	.15	.11	.06
104T	Jeff Robinson(FC)	.10	.08	.04
105T	Gary Roenicke	.06	.05	.02
106T	Jerry Royster	.06	.05	.02
107T	Mark Salas	.06	.05	.02
108T	Luis Salazar	.06	.05	.02
109T	Benny Santiago(FC)	.35	.25	.14
110T	Dave Schmidt	.08	.06	.03
111T	Kevin Seitzer(FC)	.12	.09	.05
112T	John Shelby	.06	.05	.02
113T	Steve Shields(FC)	.08	.06	.03
114T	John Smiley(FC)	.25	.20	.10
115T	Chris Speier	.06	.05	.02
116T	Mike Stanley(FC)	.06	.05	.02
117T	Terry Steinbach(FC)	.20	.15	.08
118T	Les Straker(FC)	.08	.06	.03
119T	Jim Sundberg	.08	.06	.03
120T	Danny Tartabull	.25	.20	.10
121T	Tom Trebelhorn	.08	.06	.03
122T	Dave Valle(FC)	.12	.09	.05
123T	Ed Vande Berg	.06	.05	.02
124T	Andy Van Slyke	.20	.15	.08
125T	Gary Ward	.06	.05	.02
126T	Alan Wiggins	.06	.05	.02
127T	Bill Wilkinson(FC)	.15	.11	.06
128T	Frank Williams	.08	.06	.03
129T	Matt Williams(FC)	3.00	2.25	1.25
130T	Jim Winn	.06	.05	.02
131T	Matt Young	.06	.05	.02
132T	Checklist 1T-132T	.06	.05	.02

1987 Topps Box Panels

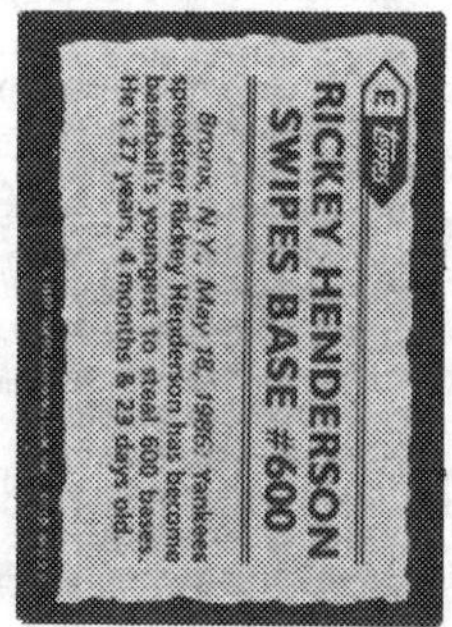

Offering baseball cards on retail boxes for a second straight year, Topps reduced the size of the cards to 2-1/8" by 3". Four different wax pack boxes were available, each featuring two cards that were placed on the sides of the boxes. The card fronts are identical in design to the regular issue cards. The backs are printed in blue and yellow and carry a commentary imitating a newspaper format. The cards are numbered A through H.

		MT	NR MT	EX
Complete Panel Set:		5.00	3.75	2.00
Complete Singles Set:		2.00	1.50	.80
Common Panel:		.75	.60	.30
Common Single Player:		.15	.11	.06
	Panel	1.25	.90	.50
A	Don Baylor	.15	.11	.06
B	Steve Carlton	.30	.25	.12
	Panel	.75	.60	.30
C	Ron Cey	.15	.11	.06
D	Cecil Cooper	.15	.11	.06
	Panel	1.75	1.25	.70
E	Rickey Henderson	.40	.30	.15
F	Jim Rice	.25	.20	.10
	Panel	1.25	.90	.50
G	Don Sutton	.20	.15	.08
H	Dave Winfield	.30	.25	.12

1987 Topps Baseball Highlights

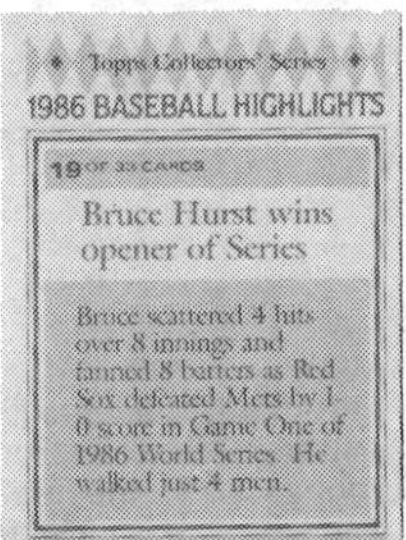

The "Baseball Highlights" boxed set of 33 cards was prepared by Topps for distribution at stores in the Woolworth's chain. Each card measures 2-1/2" by 3-1/2" in size and features a memorable baseball event that occurred during the 1986 season. The glossy set sold for $1.99 in Woolworth's stores.

		MT	NR MT	EX
Complete Set:		5.00	3.75	2.00
Common Player:		.09	.07	.04
1	Steve Carlton	.30	.25	.12
2	Cecil Cooper	.12	.09	.05
3	Rickey Henderson	.50	.40	.20
4	Reggie Jackson	.30	.25	.12
5	Jim Rice	.25	.20	.10
6	Don Sutton	.20	.15	.08
7	Roger Clemens	.50	.40	.20
8	Mike Schmidt	.35	.25	.14
9	Jesse Barfield	.15	.11	.06
10	Wade Boggs	.70	.50	.30
11	Tim Raines	.30	.25	.12
12	Jose Canseco	1.00	.70	.40
13	Todd Worrell	.15	.11	.06
14	Dave Righetti	.15	.11	.06
15	Don Mattingly	1.25	.90	.50
16	Tony Gwynn	.35	.25	.14
17	Marty Barrett	.09	.07	.04
18	Mike Scott	.12	.09	.05
19	World Series Game #1 (Bruce Hurst)	.12	.09	.05
20	World Series Game #1 (Calvin Schiraldi)	.09	.07	.04
21	World Series Game #2 (Dwight Evans)	.12	.09	.05
22	World Series Game #2 (Dave Henderson)	.09	.07	.04
23	World Series Game #3 (Len Dykstra)	.12	.09	.05
24	World Series Game #3 (Bob Ojeda)	.09	.07	.04
25	World Series Game #4 (Gary Carter)	.30	.25	.12
26	World Series Game #4 (Ron Darling)	.15	.11	.06
27	Jim Rice	.30	.25	.12
28	Bruce Hurst	.09	.07	.04
29	World Series Game #6 (Darryl Strawberry)	.35	.25	.14
30	World Series Game #6 (Ray Knight)	.09	.07	.04
31	World Series Game #6 (Keith Hernandez)	.25	.20	.10
32	World Series Games #7 (Mets Celebrate)	.12	.09	.05
33	Ray Knight	.09	.07	.04

1987 Topps Coins

For the first time since 1971, Topps issued a set of baseball "coins." Similar in design to the 1964 edition of Topps coins, the metal discs measure 1 1/2" in diameter. The aluminum coins were sold on a limited basis in retail outlets. Three coins and three sticks of gum were found in a pack. The coin fronts feature a full-color photo along with the player's name, team and position in a white band at the bottom of the coin. Gold-colored rims are found for American League players; National League players have silver-colored rims. Backs are silver in color and carry the coin number, player's name and personal and statistical information.

		MT	NR MT	EX
Complete Set:		10.00	7.50	4.00
Common Player:		.15	.11	.06
1	Harold Baines	.15	.11	.06
2	Jesse Barfield	.15	.11	.06
3	George Bell	.20	.15	.08
4	Wade Boggs	.70	.50	.30
5	George Brett	.30	.25	.12
6	Jose Canseco	1.00	.70	.40
7	Joe Carter	.15	.11	.06
8	Roger Clemens	.40	.30	.15
9	Alvin Davis	.15	.11	.06
10	Rob Deer	.15	.11	.06
11	Kirk Gibson	.20	.15	.08
12	Rickey Henderson	.25	.20	.10
13	Kent Hrbek	.20	.15	.08
14	Pete Incaviglia	.20	.15	.08
15	Reggie Jackson	.25	.20	.10
16	Wally Joyner	.60	.45	.25
17	Don Mattingly	1.25	.90	.50
18	Jack Morris	.20	.15	.08
19	Eddie Murray	.25	.20	.10
20	Kirby Puckett	.30	.25	.12
21	Jim Rice	.25	.20	.10
22	Dave Righetti	.20	.15	.08
23	Cal Ripken	.25	.20	.10
24	Cory Snyder	.25	.20	.10
25	Danny Tartabull	.20	.15	.08
26	Dave Winfield	.25	.20	.10
27	Hubie Brooks	.15	.11	.06
28	Gary Carter	.25	.20	.10
29	Vince Coleman	.20	.15	.08
30	Eric Davis	.70	.50	.30
31	Glenn Davis	.15	.11	.06
32	Steve Garvey	.25	.20	.10
33	Dwight Gooden	.40	.30	.15
34	Tony Gwynn	.30	.25	.12
35	Von Hayes	.15	.11	.06
36	Keith Hernandez	.20	.15	.08
37	Dale Murphy	.30	.25	.12
38	Dave Parker	.20	.15	.08
39	Tony Pena	.15	.11	.06
40	Nolan Ryan	.25	.20	.10
41	Ryne Sandberg	.20	.15	.08
42	Steve Sax	.15	.11	.06
43	Mike Schmidt	.30	.25	.12
44	Mike Scott	.15	.11	.06
45	Ozzie Smith	.15	.11	.06
46	Darryl Strawberry	.40	.30	.15
47	Fernando Valenzuela	.20	.15	.08
48	Todd Worrell	.15	.11	.06

1987 Topps Gallery Of Champions

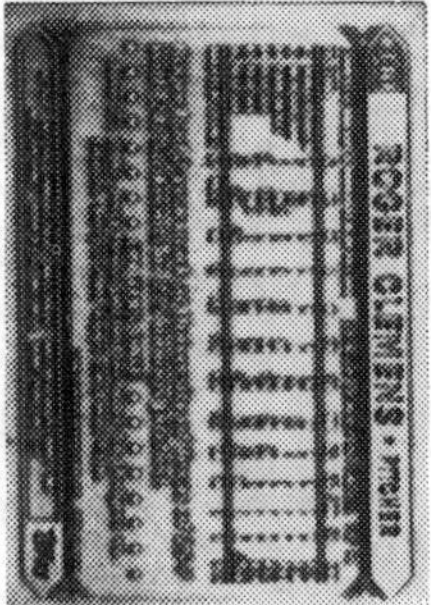

Designed as a tribute to the 1986 season's winners of baseball's most prestigious awards, the Gallery of Champions are metal "cards" that are one-quarter size replicas of the regular issue Topps cards. The bronze and silver sets were issued in leather-like velvet-lined display cases; the aluminum sets came cello-wrapped. Hobby dealers who purchased one bronze set or a 16-set case of aluminum "cards" received one free Jose Canseco pewter metal mini-card (value $60). The purchase of a silver set included five Canseco pewters. A 1953 Willie Mays bronze was given to dealers who brought cases of 1987 Topps Traded sets (value $10).

		MT	NR MT	EX
Complete Aluminum Set:		30.00	22.00	12.00
Complete Bronze Set:		175.00	131.00	70.00
Complete Silver Set:		700.00	525.00	280.00
(1a)	Jesse Barfield (aluminum)	.70	.50	.30
(1b)	Jesse Barfield (bronze)	7.50	5.75	3.00
(1c)	Jesse Barfield (silver)	20.00	15.00	8.00
(2a)	Wade Boggs (aluminum)	3.00	2.25	1.25
(2b)	Wade Boggs (bronze)	25.00	18.50	10.00
(2c)	Wade Boggs (silver)	125.00	94.00	50.00
(3a)	Jose Canseco (aluminum)	3.00	2.25	1.25
(3b)	Jose Canseco (bronze)	25.00	18.50	10.00
(3c)	Jose Canseco (silver)	125.00	94.00	50.00
(4a)	Joe Carter (aluminum)	.70	.50	.30
(4b)	Joe Carter (bronze)	7.50	5.75	3.00
(4c)	Joe Carter (silver)	20.00	15.00	8.00
(5a)	Roger Clemens (aluminum)	2.00	1.50	.80
(5b)	Roger Clemens (bronze)	20.00	15.00	8.00
(5c)	Roger Clemens (silver)	90.00	67.00	36.00
(6a)	Tony Gwynn (aluminum)	1.25	.90	.50
(6b)	Tony Gwynn (bronze)	12.00	9.00	4.75
(6c)	Tony Gwynn (silver)	50.00	37.00	20.00
(7a)	Don Mattingly (aluminum)	8.00	6.00	3.25
(7b)	Don Mattingly (bronze)	50.00	37.00	20.00
(7c)	Don Mattingly (silver)	200.00	150.00	80.00
(8a)	Tim Raines (aluminum)	1.00	.70	.40
(8b)	Tim Raines (bronze)	10.00	7.50	4.00
(8c)	Tim Raines (silver)	30.00	22.00	12.00
(9a)	Dave Righetti (aluminum)	1.00	.70	.40
(9b)	Dave Righetti (bronze)	10.00	7.50	4.00
(9c)	Dave Righetti (silver)	30.00	22.00	12.00
(10a)	Mike Schmidt (aluminum)	1.50	1.25	.60
(10b)	Mike Schmidt (bronze)	15.00	11.00	6.00
(10c)	Mike Schmidt (silver)	80.00	60.00	32.00
(11a)	Mike Scott (aluminum)	.70	.50	.30
(11b)	Mike Scott (bronze)	7.50	5.75	3.00
(11c)	Mike Scott (silver)	20.00	15.00	8.00
(12a)	Todd Worrell (aluminum)	.70	.50	.30
(12b)	Todd Worrell (bronze)	10.00	7.50	4.00
(12c)	Todd Worrell (silver)	20.00	15.00	8.00

1987 Topps Glossy Rookies

The 1987 Topps Glossy Rookies set of 22 cards was introduced with Topps' new 100-card "Jumbo Packs". Intended for sale in supermarkets, the jumbo packs contained one glossy card. Measuring the standard 2-1/2"

by 3-1/2" size, the special insert cards feature the top rookies from the previous season.

		MT	NR MT	EX
Complete Set:		12.00	9.00	4.75
Common Player:		.20	.15	.08
1	Andy Allanson	.20	.15	.08
2	John Cangelosi	.20	.15	.08
3	Jose Canseco	3.00	2.25	1.25
4	Will Clark	3.00	1.50	.90
5	Mark Eichhorn	.40	.30	.15
6	Pete Incaviglia	.70	.50	.30
7	Wally Joyner	1.00	.70	.40
8	Eric King	.30	.25	.12
9	Dave Magadan	.60	.45	.25
10	John Morris	.20	.15	.08
11	Juan Nieves	.40	.30	.15
12	Rafael Palmeiro	1.00	.70	.40
13	Billy Jo Robidoux	.20	.15	.08
14	Bruce Ruffin	.40	.30	.15
15	Ruben Sierra	1.25	.90	.50
16	Cory Snyder	.80	.60	.30
17	Kurt Stillwell	.60	.45	.25
18	Dale Sveum	.40	.30	.15
19	Danny Tartabull	.80	.60	.30
20	Andres Thomas	.40	.30	.15
21	Robby Thompson	.40	.30	.15
22	Todd Worrell	.40	.30	.15

1987 Topps Mini League Leaders

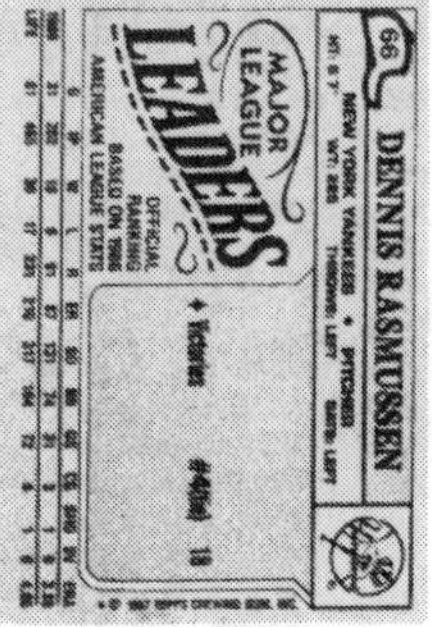

Returning for 1987, the Topps "Major League Leaders" set was increased in size from 66 to 76 cards. The 2-1/8" by 3" cards feature wood grain borders that encompass a white-bordered full-color photo. The card backs are printed in yellow, orange and brown and list the player's official ranking based on his 1986 American or National League statistics. The players featured are those who finished the top five in their leagues' various batting and pitching statistics. The cards were sold in plastic-wrapped packs, seven cards plus a game card per pack.

		MT	NR MT	EX
Complete Set:		8.00	6.00	3.25
Common Player:		.09	.07	.04
1	Bob Horner	.20	.15	.08
2	Dale Murphy	.50	.40	.20
3	Lee Smith	.09	.07	.04
4	Eric Davis	.60	.45	.25
5	John Franco	.15	.11	.06
6	Dave Parker	.20	.15	.08
7	Kevin Bass	.09	.07	.04
8	Glenn Davis	.20	.15	.08
9	Bill Doran	.15	.11	.06
10	Bob Knepper	.09	.07	.04
11	Mike Scott	.20	.15	.08
12	Dave Smith	.09	.07	.04
13	Mariano Duncan	.09	.07	.04
14	Orel Hershiser	.30	.25	.12
15	Steve Sax	.20	.15	.08
16	Fernando Valenzuela	.25	.20	.10
17	Tim Raines	.30	.25	.12
18	Jeff Reardon	.15	.11	.06
19	Floyd Youmans	.09	.07	.04
20	Gary Carter	.30	.25	.12
21	Ron Darling	.20	.15	.08
22	Sid Fernandez	.15	.11	.06
23	Dwight Gooden	.60	.45	.25
24	Keith Hernandez	.25	.20	.10
25	Bob Ojeda	.09	.07	.04
26	Darryl Strawberry	.50	.40	.20
27	Steve Bedrosian	.15	.11	.06
28	Von Hayes	.15	.11	.06
29	Juan Samuel	.20	.15	.08
30	Mike Schmidt	.50	.40	.20
31	Rick Rhoden	.09	.07	.04
32	Vince Coleman	.20	.15	.08
33	Danny Cox	.09	.07	.04
34	Todd Worrell	.15	.11	.06
35	Tony Gwynn	.40	.30	.15
36	Mike Krukow	.09	.07	.04
37	Candy Maldonado	.09	.07	.04
38	Don Aase	.09	.07	.04
39	Eddie Murray	.40	.30	.15
40	Cal Ripken	.40	.30	.15
41	Wade Boggs	.80	.60	.30
42	Roger Clemens	.60	.45	.25
43	Bruce Hurst	.15	.11	.06
44	Jim Rice	.30	.25	.12
45	Wally Joyner	.80	.60	.30
46	Donnie Moore	.09	.07	.04
47	Gary Pettis	.09	.07	.04
48	Mike Witt	.09	.07	.04
49	John Cangelosi	.09	.07	.04
50	Tom Candiotti	.09	.07	.04
51	Joe Carter	.20	.15	.08
52	Pat Tabler	.09	.07	.04
53	Kirk Gibson	.25	.20	.10
54	Willie Hernandez	.09	.07	.04
55	Jack Morris	.25	.20	.10
56	Alan Trammell	.30	.25	.12
57	George Brett	.50	.40	.20
58	Willie Wilson	.15	.11	.06
59	Rob Deer	.09	.07	.04
60	Teddy Higuera	.15	.11	.06
61	Bert Blyleven	.15	.11	.06
62	Gary Gaetti	.20	.15	.08
63	Kirby Puckett	.35	.25	.14
64	Rickey Henderson	.40	.30	.15
65	Don Mattingly	1.25	.90	.50
66	Dennis Rasmussen	.15	.11	.06
67	Dave Righetti	.20	.15	.08
68	Jose Canseco	1.00	.70	.40
69	Dave Kingman	.15	.11	.06
70	Phil Bradley	.15	.11	.06
71	Mark Langston	.15	.11	.06
72	Pete O'Brien	.09	.07	.04
73	Jesse Barfield	.15	.11	.06
74	George Bell	.25	.20	.10
75	Tony Fernandez	.15	.11	.06
76	Tom Henke	.09	.07	.04
77	Checklist	.09	.07	.04

1987 Topps Stickers

For the seventh consecutive year, Topps issued stickers to be housed in a specially designed yearbook. The stickers, which measure 2-1/8" by 3", offer a full-color front with a peel-off back printed in blue ink on white stock. The sticker fronts feature either one full-size

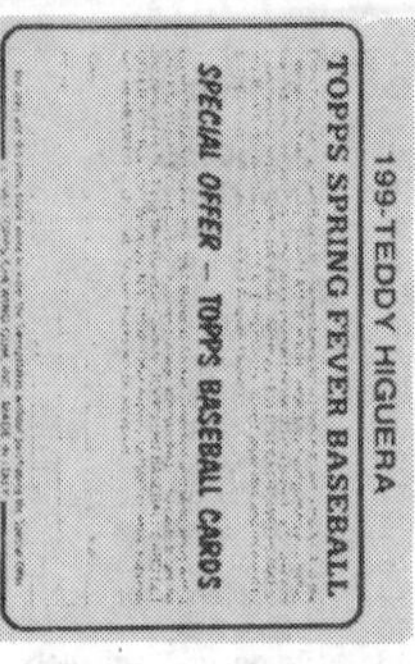

player picture or two half-size individual stickers. The sticker yearbook measures 9" by 10-3/4" and contains 36 glossy, magazine-style pages, all printed in full color. Mike Schmidt, 1986 National League MVP, is featured on the cover. The yearbook sold in retail outlets for 35¢, while stickers were sold five in a pack for 25¢. The number in parentheses in the following checklist is the sticker number the player shares the sticker with.

	MT	NR MT	EX
Complete Set:	18.00	13.50	7.25
Common Player:	.03	.02	.01
Sticker Album:	.70	.50	.30

		MT	NR MT	EX
1	1986 Highlights (Jim Deshaies) (172)	.04	.03	.02
2	1986 Highlights (Roger Clemens) (175)	.15	.11	.06
3	1986 Highlights (Roger Clemens) (176)	.15	.11	.06
4	1986 Highlights (Dwight Evans) (177)	.06	.05	.02
5	1986 Highlights (Dwight Gooden) (178)	.15	.11	.06
6	1986 Highlights (Dwight Gooden) (180)	.15	.11	.06
7	1986 Highlights (Dave Lopes) (181)	.03	.02	.01
8	1986 Highlights (Dave Righetti) (182)	.06	.05	.02
9	1986 Highlights (Dave Righetti) (183)	.10	.08	.04
10	1986 Highlights (Ruben Sierra) (185)	.15	.11	.06
11	1986 Highlights (Todd Worrell) (186)	.06	.05	.02
12	1986 Highlights (Todd Worrell) (187)	.06	.05	.02
13	N.L. Championship Series (Lenny Dykstra)	.06	.05	.02
14	N.L. Championship Series (Gary Carter)	.08	.06	.03
15	N.L. Championship Series (Mike Scott)	.06	.05	.02
16	A.L. Championship Series (Gary Pettis)	.03	.02	.01
17	A.L. Championship Series (Jim Rice)	.08	.06	.03
18	A.L. Championship Series (Bruce Hurst)	.04	.03	.02
19	1986 World Series (Bruce Hurst)	.04	.03	.02
20	1986 World Series (Wade Boggs)	.15	.11	.06
21	1986 World Series (Lenny Dykstra)	.06	.05	.02
22	1986 World Series (Gary Carter)	.08	.06	.03
23	1986 World Series (Dave Henderson)	.04	.03	.02
24	1986 World Series (Howard Johnson)	.04	.03	.02
25	1986 World Series (Mets Celebrate)	.08	.06	.03
26	Glenn Davis	.15	.11	.06
27	Nolan Ryan (188)	.10	.08	.04
28	Charlie Kerfeld (189)	.03	.02	.01
29	Jose Cruz (190)	.04	.03	.02
30	Phil Garner (191)	.06	.05	.02
31	Bill Doran (192)	.06	.05	.02
32	Bob Knepper (195)	.03	.02	.01
33	Denny Walling (196)	.10	.08	.04
34	Kevin Bass (197)	.04	.03	.02
35	Mike Scott	.10	.08	.04
36	Dale Murphy	.25	.20	.10
37	Paul Assenmacher (198)	.06	.05	.02
38	Ken Oberkfell (200)	.06	.05	.02
39	Andres Thomas (201)	.08	.06	.03
40	Gene Garber (202)	.03	.02	.01
41	Bob Horner	.08	.06	.03
42	Rafael Ramirez (203)	.03	.02	.01
43	Rick Mahler (204)	.03	.02	.01
44	Omar Moreno (205)	.03	.02	.01
45	Dave Palmer (206)	.03	.02	.01
46	Ozzie Smith	.12	.09	.05
47	Bob Forsch (207)	.03	.02	.01
48	Willie McGee (209)	.06	.05	.02
49	Tom Herr (210)	.06	.05	.02
50	Vince Coleman (211)	.08	.06	.03
51	Andy Van Slyke (212)	.06	.05	.02
52	Jack Clark (215)	.08	.06	.03
53	John Tudor (216)	.04	.03	.02
54	Terry Pendleton (217)	.03	.02	.01
55	Todd Worrell	.10	.08	.04
56	Lee Smith	.06	.05	.02
57	Leon Durham (218)	.03	.02	.01
58	Jerry Mumphrey (219)	.06	.05	.02
59	Shawon Dunston (220)	.06	.05	.02
60	Scott Sanderson (221)	.06	.05	.02
61	Ryne Sandberg	.15	.11	.06
62	Gary Matthews (222)	.04	.03	.02
63	Dennis Eckersley (225)	.06	.05	.02
64	Jody Davis (226)	.06	.05	.02
65	Keith Moreland (227)	.04	.03	.02
66	Mike Marshall (228)	.06	.05	.02
67	Bill Madlock (229)	.06	.05	.02
68	Greg Brock (230)	.04	.03	.02
69	Pedro Guerrero (231)	.08	.06	.03
70	Steve Sax	.12	.09	.05
71	Rick Honeycutt (232)	.03	.02	.01
72	Franklin Stubbs (235)	.03	.02	.01
73	Mike Scioscia (236)	.10	.08	.04
74	Mariano Duncan (237)	.03	.02	.01
75	Fernando Valenzuela	.15	.11	.06
76	Hubie Brooks	.06	.05	.02
77	Andre Dawson (238)	.08	.06	.03
78	Tim Burke (240)	.04	.03	.02
79	Floyd Youmans (241)	.03	.02	.01
80	Tim Wallach (242)	.04	.03	.02
81	Jeff Reardon (243)	.06	.05	.02
82	Mitch Webster (244)	.15	.11	.06
83	Bryn Smith (245)	.03	.02	.01
84	Andres Galarraga (246)	.12	.09	.05
85	Tim Raines	.15	.11	.06
86	Chris Brown	.08	.06	.03
87	Bob Brenly (247)	.03	.02	.01
88	Will Clark (249)	.25	.20	.10
89	Scott Garrelts (250)	.04	.03	.02
90	Jeffrey Leonard (251)	.06	.05	.02
91	Robby Thompson (252)	.06	.05	.02
92	Mike Krukow (255)	.03	.02	.01
93	Danny Gladden (256)	.03	.02	.01
94	Candy Maldonado (257)	.04	.03	.02
95	Chili Davis	.04	.03	.02
96	Dwight Gooden	.30	.25	.12
97	Sid Fernandez (258)	.04	.03	.02
98	Len Dykstra (259)	.06	.05	.02
99	Bob Ojeda (260)	.04	.03	.02
100	Wally Backman (261)	.04	.03	.02
101	Gary Carter	.15	.11	.06
102	Keith Hernandez (262)	.10	.08	.04
103	Darryl Strawberry (265)	.15	.11	.06
104	Roger McDowell (266)	.08	.06	.03
105	Ron Darling (267)	.08	.06	.03
106	Tony Gwynn	.20	.15	.08
107	Dave Dravecky (268)	.04	.03	.02
108	Terry Kennedy (269)	.08	.06	.03
109	Rich Gossage (270)	.10	.08	.04
110	Garry Templeton (271)	.04	.03	.02
111	Lance McCullers (272)	.04	.03	.02
112	Eric Show (275)	.04	.03	.02
113	John Kruk (276)	.12	.09	.05
114	Tim Flannery (277)	.06	.05	.02
115	Steve Garvey	.15	.11	.06
116	Mike Schmidt	.25	.20	.10
117	Glenn Wilson (278)	.06	.05	.02
118	Kent Tekulve (280)	.06	.05	.02
119	Gary Redus (281)	.08	.06	.03
120	Shane Rawley (282)	.03	.02	.01
121	Von Hayes	.06	.05	.02
122	Don Carman (283)	.04	.03	.02
123	Bruce Ruffin (285)	.04	.03	.02
124	Steve Bedrosian (286)	.06	.05	.02
125	Juan Samuel (287)	.06	.05	.02

		MT	NR MT	EX
126	Sid Bream (288)	.06	.05	.02
127	Cecilio Guante (289)	.03	.02	.01
128	Rick Reuschel (290)	.04	.03	.02
129	Tony Pena (291)	.04	.03	.02
130	Rick Rhoden	.06	.05	.02
131	Barry Bonds (292)	.10	.08	.04
132	Joe Orsulak (295)	.03	.02	.01
133	Jim Morrison (296)	.12	.09	.05
134	R.J. Reynolds (297)	.04	.03	.02
135	Johnny Ray	.06	.05	.02
136	Eric Davis	.30	.25	.12
137	Tom Browning (298)	.10	.08	.04
138	John Franco (300)	.06	.05	.02
139	Pete Rose (301)	.20	.15	.08
140	Bill Gullickson (302)	.04	.03	.02
141	Ron Oester (303)	.04	.03	.02
142	Bo Diaz (304)	.40	.30	.15
143	Buddy Bell (305)	.04	.03	.02
144	Eddie Milner (306)	.08	.06	.03
145	Dave Parker	.10	.08	.04
146	Kirby Puckett	.35	.25	.14
147	Rickey Henderson	.40	.30	.15
148	Wade Boggs	.60	.45	.25
149	Lance Parrish	.25	.20	.10
150	Wally Joyner	.70	.50	.30
151	Cal Ripken	.40	.30	.15
152	Dave Winfield	.30	.25	.12
153	Lou Whitaker	.25	.20	.10
154	Roger Clemens	.50	.40	.20
155	Tony Gwynn	.40	.30	.15
156	Ryne Sandberg	.25	.20	.10
157	Keith Hernandez	.25	.20	.10
158	Gary Carter	.30	.25	.12
159	Darryl Strawberry	.50	.40	.20
160	Mike Schmidt	.40	.30	.15
161	Dale Murphy	.40	.30	.15
162	Ozzie Smith	.20	.15	.08
163	Dwight Gooden	.50	.40	.20
164	Jose Canseco	.80	.60	.30
165	Curt Young (307)	.04	.03	.02
166	Alfredo Griffin (308)	.12	.09	.05
167	Dave Stewart (309)	.06	.05	.02
168	Mike Davis (310)	.06	.05	.02
169	Bruce Bochte (311)	.03	.02	.01
170	Dwayne Murphy (312)	.04	.03	.02
171	Carney Lansford (313)	.20	.15	.08
172	Joaquin Andujar (1)	.04	.03	.02
173	Dave Kingman	.08	.06	.03
174	Wally Joyner	.40	.30	.15
175	Gary Pettis (2)	.15	.11	.06
176	Dick Schofield (3)	.15	.11	.06
177	Donnie Moore (4)	.06	.05	.02
178	Brian Downing (5)	.15	.11	.06
179	Mike Witt	.06	.05	.02
180	Bob Boone (6)	.15	.11	.06
181	Kirk McCaskill (7)	.03	.02	.01
182	Doug DeCinces (8)	.06	.05	.02
183	Don Sutton (9)	.10	.08	.04
184	Jessie Barfield	.10	.08	.04
185	Tom Henke (10)	.15	.11	.06
186	Willie Upshaw (11)	.06	.05	.02
187	Mark Eichhorn (12)	.06	.05	.02
188	Damaso Garcia (27)	.10	.08	.04
189	Jim Clancy (28)	.03	.02	.01
190	Lloyd Moseby (29)	.04	.03	.02
191	Tony Fernandez (30)	.06	.05	.02
192	Jimmy Key (31)	.06	.05	.02
193	George Bell	.20	.15	.08
194	Rob Deer	.06	.05	.02
195	Mark Clear (32)	.03	.02	.01
196	Robin Yount (33)	.10	.08	.04
197	Jim Gantner (34)	.04	.03	.02
198	Cecil Cooper (37)	.06	.05	.02
199	Teddy Higuera	.08	.06	.03
200	Paul Molitor (38)	.08	.06	.03
201	Dan Plesac (39)	.08	.06	.03
202	Billy Jo Robidoux (40)	.03	.02	.01
203	Earnie Riles (42)	.03	.02	.01
204	Ken Schrom (43)	.03	.02	.01
205	Pat Tabler (44)	.03	.02	.01
206	Mel Hall (45)	.03	.02	.01
207	Tony Bernazard (47)	.03	.02	.01
208	Joe Carter	.10	.08	.04
209	Ernie Camacho (48)	.06	.05	.02
210	Julio Franco (49)	.06	.05	.02
211	Tom Candiotti (50)	.08	.06	.03
212	Brook Jacoby (51)	.06	.05	.02
213	Cory Snyder	.30	.25	.12
214	Jim Presley	.08	.06	.03
215	Mike Moore (52)	.08	.06	.03
216	Harold Reynolds (53)	.04	.03	.02

		MT	NR MT	EX
217	Scott Bradley (54)	.03	.02	.01
218	Matt Young (57)	.03	.02	.01
219	Mark Langston (58)	.06	.05	.02
220	Alvin Davis (59)	.06	.05	.02
221	Phil Bradley (60)	.06	.05	.02
222	Ken Phelps (62)	.04	.03	.02
223	Danny Tartabull	.20	.15	.08
224	Eddie Murray	.20	.15	.08
225	Rick Dempsey (63)	.06	.05	.02
226	Fred Lynn (64)	.06	.05	.02
227	Mike Boddicker (65)	.04	.03	.02
228	Don Aase (66)	.06	.05	.02
229	Larry Sheets (67)	.06	.05	.02
230	Storm Davis (68)	.04	.03	.02
231	Lee Lacy (69)	.08	.06	.03
232	Jim Traber (71)	.03	.02	.01
233	Cal Ripken	.20	.15	.08
234	Larry Parrish	.06	.05	.02
235	Gary Ward (72)	.03	.02	.01
236	Pete Incaviglia (73)	.10	.08	.04
237	Scott Fletcher (74)	.03	.02	.01
238	Greg Harris (77)	.08	.06	.03
239	Pete O'Brien	.06	.05	.02
240	Charlie Hough (78)	.04	.03	.02
241	Don Slaught (79)	.03	.02	.01
242	Steve Buechele (80)	.04	.03	.02
243	Oddibe McDowell (81)	.06	.05	.02
244	Roger Clemens (82)	.15	.11	.06
245	Bob Stanley (83)	.03	.02	.01
246	Tom Seaver (84)	.12	.09	.05
247	Rich Gedman (87)	.03	.02	.01
248	Jim Rice	.15	.11	.06
249	Dennis Boyd (88)	.25	.20	.10
250	Bill Buckner (89)	.04	.03	.02
251	Dwight Evans (90)	.06	.05	.02
252	Don Baylor (91)	.06	.05	.02
253	Wade Boggs	.40	.30	.15
254	George Brett	.25	.20	.10
255	Steve Farr (92)	.03	.02	.01
256	Jim Sundberg (93)	.03	.02	.01
257	Dan Quisenberry (94)	.04	.03	.02
258	Charlie Leibrandt (97)	.04	.03	.02
259	Argenis Salazar (98)	.06	.05	.02
260	Frank White (99)	.04	.03	.02
261	Willie Wilson (100)	.04	.03	.02
262	Lonnie Smith (102)	.10	.08	.04
263	Steve Balboni	.04	.03	.02
264	Darrell Evans	.06	.05	.02
265	Johnny Grubb (103)	.15	.11	.06
266	Jack Morris (104)	.08	.06	.03
267	Lou Whitaker (105)	.08	.06	.03
268	Chet Lemon (107)	.04	.03	.02
269	Lance Parrish (108)	.08	.06	.03
270	Alan Trammell (109)	.10	.08	.04
271	Darnell Coles (110)	.04	.03	.02
272	Willie Hernandez (111)	.04	.03	.02
273	Kirk Gibson	.15	.11	.06
274	Kirby Puckett	.20	.15	.08
275	Mike Smithson (112)	.04	.03	.02
276	Mickey Hatcher (113)	.12	.09	.05
277	Frank Viola (114)	.06	.05	.02
278	Bert Blyleven (117)	.06	.05	.02
279	Gary Gaetti	.10	.08	.04
280	Tom Brunansky (118)	.06	.05	.02
281	Kent Hrbek (119)	.08	.06	.03
282	Roy Smalley (120)	.03	.02	.01
283	Greg Gagne (122)	.04	.03	.02
284	Harold Baines	.10	.08	.04
285	Ron Hassey (123)	.04	.03	.02
286	Floyd Bannister (124)	.06	.05	.02
287	Ozzie Guillen (125)	.06	.05	.02
288	Carlton Fisk (126)	.06	.05	.02
289	Tim Hulett (127)	.03	.02	.01
290	Joe Cowley (128)	.04	.03	.02
291	Greg Walker (129)	.04	.03	.02
292	Neil Allen (131)	.10	.08	.04
293	John Cangelosi	.04	.03	.02
294	Don Mattingly	.90	.70	.35
295	Mike Easler (132)	.03	.02	.01
296	Rickey Henderson (133)	.12	.09	.05
297	Dan Pasqua (134)	.04	.03	.02
298	Dave Winfield (137)	.10	.08	.04
299	Dave Righetti	.12	.09	.05
300	Mike Pagliarulo (138)	.06	.05	.02
301	Ron Guidry (139)	.20	.15	.08
302	Willie Randolph (140)	.04	.03	.02
303	Dennis Rasmussen (141)	.04	.03	.02
304	Jose Canseco (142)	.40	.30	.15
305	Andres Thomas (143)	.04	.03	.02
306	Danny Tartabull (144)	.08	.06	.03
307	Robby Thompson (165)	.04	.03	.02

		MT	NR MT	EX
308	Pete Incaviglia, Cory Snyder (166)	.12	.09	.05
309	Dale Sveum (167)	.06	.05	.02
310	Todd Worrell (168)	.06	.05	.02
311	Andy Allanson (169)	.03	.02	.01
312	Bruce Ruffin (170)	.04	.03	.02
313	Wally Joyner (171)	.20	.15	.08

1988 Topps

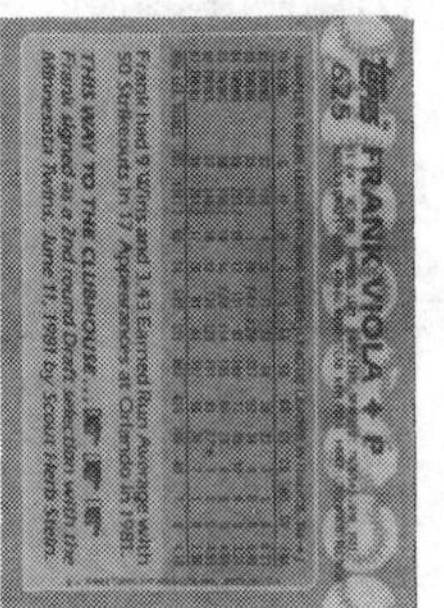

The 1988 Topps set features a clean, attractive design that should prove to be very popular with collectors for many years to come. The full-color player photo is surrounded by a thin yellow frame which is encompassed by a white border. The player's name appears in the lower right corner in a colored band which appears to wrap around the player photo. The player's team nickname is located in large letters at the top of the card. The Topps logo is placed in the lower left corner of the card. The card backs feature black print on orange and gray stock and includes the usual player personal and career statistics. Many of the cards contain a new feature entitled "This Way To The Clubhouse", which explains how the player joined his current team, be it by trade, free agency, etc. The 792-card set includes a number of special subsets including "Future Stars", "Turn Back The Clock", All-Star teams, All-Star rookie selections, and Record Breakers. All cards measure 2-1/2" by 3-1/2". For the fifth consecutive year, Topps issued a glossy "Tiffany" edition of its 792-card regular-issue set. The Tiffany cards have a value of 3-4 times greater than the same card in the regular issue. The Tiffany edition could be purchased by collectors directly from Topps for $99. The company placed ads for the Tiffany set in publications such as USA Today and The Sporting News.

		MT	NR MT	EX
Complete Set (792):		15.00	11.00	6.00
Common Player:		.04	.03	.02
1	Vince Coleman (Record Breakers)	.08	.06	.03
2	Don Mattingly (Record Breakers)	.15	.11	.06
3a	Mark McGwire (Record Breakers, white triangle by left foot)	.40	.30	.15
3b	Mark McGwire (Record Breakers, no white triangle)	.15	.11	.06
4a	Eddie Murray (Record Breakers, no mention of record on front)	.25	.20	.10
4b	Eddie Murray (Record Breakers, record mentioned on front)	.10	.08	.04
5	Joe Niekro, Phil Niekro (Record Breakers)	.10	.08	.04
6	Nolan Ryan (Record Breakers)	.40	.30	.15
7	Benito Santiago (Record Breakers)	.15	.11	.06
8	Kevin Elster (Future Stars)(FC)	.06	.05	.02
9	Andy Hawkins	.04	.03	.02
10	Ryne Sandberg	.50	.40	.20
11	Mike Young	.04	.03	.02
12	Bill Schroeder	.04	.03	.02
13	Andres Thomas	.06	.05	.02
14	Sparky Anderson	.06	.05	.02
15	Chili Davis	.06	.05	.02
16	Kirk McCaskill	.06	.05	.02
17	Ron Oester	.04	.03	.02
18a	*Al Leiter* (Future Stars, no "NY" on shirt, photo actually Steve George)(FC)	.40	.30	.15
18b	*Al Leiter* (Future Stars, "NY" on shirt, correct photo)(FC)	.10	.08	.04
19	*Mark Davidson*(FC)	.06	.05	.02
20	Kevin Gross	.06	.05	.02
21	Red Sox Leaders (Wade Boggs, Spike Owen)	.15	.11	.06
22	Greg Swindell	.15	.11	.06
23	Ken Landreaux	.04	.03	.02
24	Jim Deshaies	.06	.05	.02
25	Andres Galarraga	.15	.11	.06
26	Mitch Williams	.06	.05	.02
27	R.J. Reynolds	.04	.03	.02
28	*Jose Nunez*(FC)	.10	.08	.04
29	Argenis Salazar	.04	.03	.02
30	Sid Fernandez	.08	.06	.03
31	Bruce Bochy	.04	.03	.02
32	Mike Morgan	.04	.03	.02
33	Rob Deer	.06	.05	.02
34	Ricky Horton	.06	.05	.02
35	Harold Baines	.10	.08	.04
36	Jamie Moyer	.06	.05	.02
37	Ed Romero	.04	.03	.02
38	Jeff Calhoun	.04	.03	.02
39	Gerald Perry	.08	.06	.03
40	Orel Hershiser	.08	.06	.03
41	Bob Melvin	.04	.03	.02
42	*Bill Landrum*(FC)	.04	.03	.02
43	Dick Schofield	.04	.03	.02
44	Lou Piniella	.06	.05	.02
45	Kent Hrbek	.12	.09	.05
46	Darnell Coles	.06	.05	.02
47	Joaquin Andujar	.06	.05	.02
48	Alan Ashby	.04	.03	.02
49	Dave Clark(FC)	.10	.08	.04
50	Hubie Brooks	.08	.06	.03
51	Orioles Leaders (Eddie Murray, Cal Ripken, Jr.)	.25	.20	.10
52	Don Robinson	.06	.05	.02
53	Curt Wilkerson	.04	.03	.02
54	Jim Clancy	.06	.05	.02
55	Phil Bradley	.08	.06	.03
56	Ed Hearn	.04	.03	.02
57	*Tim Crews*(FC)	.15	.11	.06
58	Dave Magadan	.10	.08	.04
59	Danny Cox	.06	.05	.02
60	Rickey Henderson	.35	.25	.14
61	*Mark Knudson*(FC)	.10	.08	.04
62	Jeff Hamilton	.08	.06	.03
63	Jimmy Jones(FC)	.10	.08	.04
64	*Ken Caminiti*(FC)	.30	.25	.12
65	Leon Durham	.06	.05	.02
66	Shane Rawley	.06	.05	.02
67	Ken Oberkfell	.04	.03	.02
68	Dave Dravecky	.06	.05	.02
69	*Mike Hart*(FC)	.04	.03	.02
70	Roger Clemens	.50	.40	.20
71	Gary Pettis	.04	.03	.02
72	Dennis Eckersley	.10	.08	.04
73	Randy Bush	.04	.03	.02
74	Tom Lasorda	.06	.05	.02
75	Joe Carter	.15	.11	.06
76	Denny Martinez	.04	.03	.02
77	Tom O'Malley	.04	.03	.02
78	Dan Petry	.06	.05	.02
79	Ernie Whitt	.06	.05	.02
80	Mark Langston	.10	.08	.04
81	Reds Leaders (John Franco, Ron Robinson)	.06	.05	.02
82	*Darrel Akerfelds*(FC)	.04	.03	.02
83	Jose Oquendo	.04	.03	.02
84	Cecilio Guante	.04	.03	.02
85	Howard Johnson	.08	.06	.03
86	Ron Karkovice	.04	.03	.02
87	Mike Mason	.04	.03	.02
88	Earnie Riles	.04	.03	.02
89	*Gary Thurman*(FC)	.08	.06	.03
90	Dale Murphy	.10	.08	.04
91	*Joey Cora*(FC)	.12	.09	.05
92	Len Matuszek	.04	.03	.02
93	Bob Sebra	.04	.03	.02
94	*Chuck Jackson*(FC)	.04	.03	.02
95	Lance Parrish	.12	.09	.05
96	*Todd Benzinger*(FC)	.10	.08	.04
97	Scott Garrelts	.04	.03	.02
98	*Rene Gonzales*(FC)	.06	.05	.02
99	Chuck Finley	.06	.05	.02
100	Jack Clark	.06	.05	.02
101	Allan Anderson	.06	.05	.02
102	Barry Larkin	.12	.09	.05
103	Curt Young	.06	.05	.02

		MT	NR MT	EX
104	Dick Williams	.04	.03	.02
105	Jesse Orosco	.06	.05	.02
106	*Jim Walewander*(FC)	.04	.03	.02
107	Scott Bailes	.06	.05	.02
108	Steve Lyons	.04	.03	.02
109	Joel Skinner	.04	.03	.02
110	Teddy Higuera	.08	.06	.03
111	Expos Leaders (Hubie Brooks, Vance Law)	.06	.05	.02
112	*Les Lancaster*(FC)	.15	.11	.06
113	Kelly Gruber	.04	.03	.02
114	Jeff Russell	.04	.03	.02
115	Johnny Ray	.06	.05	.02
116	Jerry Don Gleaton	.04	.03	.02
117	*James Steels*(FC)	.04	.03	.02
118	Bob Welch	.08	.06	.03
119	*Robbie Wine*(FC)	.04	.03	.02
120	Kirby Puckett	.40	.30	.15
121	Checklist 1-132	.04	.03	.02
122	Tony Bernazard	.04	.03	.02
123	Tom Candiotti	.04	.03	.02
124	Ray Knight	.06	.05	.02
125	Bruce Hurst	.08	.06	.03
126	Steve Jeltz	.04	.03	.02
127	Jim Gott	.04	.03	.02
128	Johnny Grubb	.04	.03	.02
129	Greg Minton	.04	.03	.02
130	Buddy Bell	.08	.06	.03
131	Don Schulze	.04	.03	.02
132	Donnie Hill	.04	.03	.02
133	Greg Mathews	.06	.05	.02
134	Chuck Tanner	.04	.03	.02
135	Dennis Rasmussen	.08	.06	.03
136	Brian Dayett	.04	.03	.02
137	Chris Bosio	.06	.05	.02
138	Mitch Webster	.06	.05	.02
139	Jerry Browne	.06	.05	.02
140	Jesse Barfield	.10	.08	.04
141	Royals Leaders (George Brett, Bret Saberhagen)	.12	.09	.05
142	Andy Van Slyke	.10	.08	.04
143	Mickey Tettleton	.12	.09	.05
144	*Don Gordon*(FC)	.08	.06	.03
145	Bill Madlock	.08	.06	.03
146	*Donell Nixon*(FC)	.06	.05	.02
147	Bill Buckner	.08	.06	.03
148	Carmelo Martinez	.06	.05	.02
149	Ken Howell	.04	.03	.02
150	Eric Davis	.12	.09	.05
151	Bob Knepper	.06	.05	.02
152	*Jody Reed*(FC)	.15	.11	.06
153	John Habyan	.04	.03	.02
154	Jeff Stone	.04	.03	.02
155	Bruce Sutter	.10	.08	.04
156	Gary Matthews	.06	.05	.02
157	Atlee Hammaker	.04	.03	.02
158	Tim Hulett	.04	.03	.02
159	*Brad Arnsberg*(FC)	.12	.09	.05
160	Willie McGee	.10	.08	.04
161	Bryn Smith	.06	.05	.02
162	Mark McLemore	.06	.05	.02
163	Dale Mohorcic	.04	.03	.02
164	Dave Johnson	.06	.05	.02
165	Robin Yount	.20	.15	.08
166	*Rick Rodriguez*(FC)	.06	.05	.02
167	Rance Mulliniks	.04	.03	.02
168	Barry Jones	.04	.03	.02
169	*Ross Jones*(FC)	.04	.03	.02
170	Rich Gossage	.06	.05	.02
171	Cubs Leaders (Shawon Dunston, Manny Trillo)	.06	.05	.02
172	*Lloyd McClendon*(FC)	.10	.08	.04
173	Eric Plunk	.04	.03	.02
174	Phil Garner	.04	.03	.02
175	Kevin Bass	.06	.05	.02
176	Jeff Reed	.04	.03	.02
177	Frank Tanana	.06	.05	.02
178	Dwayne Henry(FC)	.06	.05	.02
179	Charlie Puleo	.04	.03	.02
180	Terry Kennedy	.06	.05	.02
181	Dave Cone(FC)	.10	.08	.04
182	Ken Phelps	.06	.05	.02
183	Tom Lawless	.04	.03	.02
184	Ivan Calderon	.08	.06	.03
185	Rick Rhoden	.06	.05	.02
186	Rafael Palmeiro	.20	.15	.08
187	Steve Kiefer(FC)	.06	.05	.02
188	John Russell	.04	.03	.02
189	*Wes Gardner*(FC)	.06	.05	.02
190	Candy Maldonado	.06	.05	.02
191	John Cerutti	.06	.05	.02

		MT	NR MT	EX
192	Devon White	.08	.06	.03
193	Brian Fisher	.06	.05	.02
194	Tom Kelly	.04	.03	.02
195	Dan Quisenberry	.06	.05	.02
196	Dave Engle	.04	.03	.02
197	Lance McCullers	.06	.05	.02
198	Franklin Stubbs	.06	.05	.02
199	*Dave Meads*	.06	.05	.02
200	Wade Boggs	.30	.25	.12
201	Rangers Leaders (Steve Buechele, Pete Incaviglia, Pete O'Brien, Bobby Valentine)	.06	.05	.02
202	Glenn Hoffman	.04	.03	.02
203	Fred Toliver	.04	.03	.02
204	Paul O'Neill(FC)	.12	.09	.05
205	*Nelson Liriano*(FC)	.08	.06	.03
206	Domingo Ramos	.04	.03	.02
207	*John Mitchell, John Mitchell*(FC)	.06	.05	.02
208	Steve Lake	.04	.03	.02
209	Richard Dotson	.06	.05	.02
210	Willie Randolph	.06	.05	.02
211	Frank DiPino	.04	.03	.02
212	Greg Brock	.06	.05	.02
213	Albert Hall	.04	.03	.02
214	Dave Schmidt	.04	.03	.02
215	Von Hayes	.06	.05	.02
216	Jerry Reuss	.06	.05	.02
217	Harry Spilman	.04	.03	.02
218	Dan Schatzeder	.04	.03	.02
219	Mike Stanley	.08	.06	.03
220	Tom Henke	.06	.05	.02
221	Rafael Belliard	.04	.03	.02
222	Steve Farr	.04	.03	.02
223	Stan Jefferson	.08	.06	.03
224	Tom Trebelhorn	.04	.03	.02
225	Mike Scioscia	.06	.05	.02
226	Dave Lopes	.06	.05	.02
227	Ed Correa	.04	.03	.02
228	Wallace Johnson	.04	.03	.02
229	Jeff Musselman	.08	.06	.03
230	Pat Tabler	.06	.05	.02
231	Pirates Leaders (Barry Bonds, Bobby Bonilla)	.10	.08	.04
232	Bob James	.04	.03	.02
233	Rafael Santana	.04	.03	.02
234	Ken Dayley	.04	.03	.02
235	Gary Ward	.06	.05	.02
236	Ted Power	.04	.03	.02
237	Mike Heath	.04	.03	.02
238	*Luis Polonia*	.30	.25	.12
239	Roy Smalley	.04	.03	.02
240	Lee Smith	.08	.06	.03
241	Damaso Garcia	.04	.03	.02
242	Tom Niedenfuer	.06	.05	.02
243	Mark Ryal(FC)	.04	.03	.02
244	Jeff Robinson	.04	.03	.02
245	Rich Gedman	.06	.05	.02
246	*Mike Campbell* (Future Stars)(FC)	.06	.05	.02
247	Thad Bosley	.04	.03	.02
248	Storm Davis	.08	.06	.03
249	Mike Marshall	.06	.05	.02
250	Nolan Ryan	.70	.50	.30
251	Tom Foley	.04	.03	.02
252	Bob Brower	.06	.05	.02
253	Checklist 133-264	.04	.03	.02
254	Lee Elia	.04	.03	.02
255	Mookie Wilson	.06	.05	.02
256	Ken Schrom	.04	.03	.02
257	Jerry Royster	.04	.03	.02
258	Ed Nunez	.04	.03	.02
259	Ron Kittle	.06	.05	.02
260	Vince Coleman	.08	.06	.03
261	Giants Leaders (Will Clark, Candy Maldonado, Kevin Mitchell, Robby Thompson, Jose Uribe)	.10	.08	.04
262	Drew Hall(FC)	.04	.03	.02
263	Glenn Braggs	.08	.06	.03
264	*Les Straker*	.04	.03	.02
265	Bo Diaz	.06	.05	.02
266	Paul Assenmacher	.04	.03	.02
267	*Billy Bean*(FC)	.04	.03	.02
268	Bruce Ruffin	.06	.05	.02
269	*Ellis Burks*	.40	.30	.15
270	Mike Witt	.06	.05	.02
271	Ken Gerhart	.06	.05	.02
272	Steve Ontiveros	.04	.03	.02
273	Garth Iorg	.04	.03	.02
274	Junior Ortiz	.04	.03	.02
275	Kevin Seitzer	.08	.06	.03
276	Luis Salazar	.04	.03	.02

		MT	NR MT	EX
277	Alejandro Pena	.06	.05	.02
278	Jose Cruz	.06	.05	.02
279	Randy St. Claire	.04	.03	.02
280	Pete Incaviglia	.08	.06	.03
281	Jerry Hairston	.04	.03	.02
282	Pat Perry	.04	.03	.02
283	Phil Lombardi(FC)	.06	.05	.02
284	Larry Bowa	.06	.05	.02
285	Jim Presley	.08	.06	.03
286	*Chuck Crim*	.12	.09	.05
287	Manny Trillo	.06	.05	.02
288	*Pat Pacillo*	.06	.05	.02
289	Dave Bergman	.04	.03	.02
290	Tony Fernandez	.10	.08	.04
291	Astros Leaders (Kevin Bass, Billy Hatcher)	.06	.05	.02
292	Carney Lansford	.08	.06	.03
293	*Doug Jones*(FC)	.25	.20	.10
294	*Al Pedrique*(FC)	.06	.05	.02
295	Bert Blyleven	.10	.08	.04
296	Floyd Rayford	.04	.03	.02
297	Zane Smith	.06	.05	.02
298	Milt Thompson	.04	.03	.02
299	Steve Crawford	.04	.03	.02
300	Don Mattingly	.30	.25	.12
301	Bud Black	.04	.03	.02
302	Jose Uribe	.04	.03	.02
303	Eric Show	.06	.05	.02
304	George Hendrick	.06	.05	.02
305	Steve Sax	.08	.06	.03
306	Billy Hatcher	.06	.05	.02
307	Mike Trujillo	.04	.03	.02
308	Lee Mazzilli	.06	.05	.02
309	*Bill Long*	.08	.06	.03
310	Tom Herr	.06	.05	.02
311	Scott Sanderson	.04	.03	.02
312	Joey Meyer (Future Stars)(FC)	.08	.06	.03
313	Bob McClure	.04	.03	.02
314	Jimy Williams	.04	.03	.02
315	Dave Parker	.12	.09	.05
316	Jose Rijo	.06	.05	.02
317	Tom Nieto	.04	.03	.02
318	Mel Hall	.06	.05	.02
319	Mike Loynd	.04	.03	.02
320	Alan Trammell	.10	.08	.04
321	White Sox Leaders (Harold Baines, Carlton Fisk)	.08	.06	.03
322	*Vicente Palacios*(FC)	.10	.08	.04
323	Rick Leach	.04	.03	.02
324	Danny Jackson	.10	.08	.04
325	Glenn Hubbard	.04	.03	.02
326	Al Nipper	.04	.03	.02
327	Larry Sheets	.06	.05	.02
328	*Greg Cadaret*(FC)	.06	.05	.02
329	Chris Speier	.04	.03	.02
330	Eddie Whitson	.04	.03	.02
331	Brian Downing	.06	.05	.02
332	Jerry Reed	.04	.03	.02
333	Wally Backman	.06	.05	.02
334	Dave LaPoint	.06	.05	.02
335	Claudell Washington	.06	.05	.02
336	Ed Lynch	.04	.03	.02
337	Jim Gantner	.04	.03	.02
338	Brian Holton	.08	.06	.03
339	Kurt Stillwell	.08	.06	.03
340	Jack Morris	.10	.08	.04
341	Carmen Castillo	.04	.03	.02
342	Larry Andersen	.04	.03	.02
343	Greg Gagne	.04	.03	.02
344	Tony LaRussa	.04	.03	.02
345	Scott Fletcher	.06	.05	.02
346	Vance Law	.06	.05	.02
347	Joe Johnson	.04	.03	.02
348	Jim Eisenreich	.04	.03	.02
349	Bob Walk	.04	.03	.02
350	Will Clark	.40	.30	.15
351	Cardinals Leaders (Tony Pena, Red Schoendienst)	.06	.05	.02
352	*Billy Ripken*(FC)	.06	.05	.02
353	Ed Olwine	.04	.03	.02
354	Marc Sullivan	.04	.03	.02
355	Roger McDowell	.08	.06	.03
356	Luis Aguayo	.04	.03	.02
357	Floyd Bannister	.06	.05	.02
358	Rey Quinones	.04	.03	.02
359	Tim Stoddard	.04	.03	.02
360	Tony Gwynn	.25	.20	.10
361	Greg Maddux	.70	.50	.30
362	Juan Castillo	.04	.03	.02
363	Willie Fraser	.06	.05	.02
364	Nick Esasky	.06	.05	.02

		MT	NR MT	EX
365	Floyd Youmans	.04	.03	.02
366	Chet Lemon	.06	.05	.02
367	Tim Leary	.06	.05	.02
368	*Gerald Young*(FC)	.08	.06	.03
369	Greg Harris	.04	.03	.02
370	Jose Canseco	.40	.30	.15
371	Joe Hesketh	.04	.03	.02
372	*Matt Williams*	1.50	1.25	.60
373	Checklist 265-396	.04	.03	.02
374	Doc Edwards	.04	.03	.02
375	Tom Brunansky	.08	.06	.03
376	*Bill Wilkinson*	.04	.03	.02
377	*Sam Horn*(FC)	.04	.03	.02
378	*Todd Frohwirth*(FC)	.08	.06	.03
379	Rafael Ramirez	.04	.03	.02
380	*Joe Magrane*	.10	.08	.04
381	Angels Leaders (Jack Howell, Wally Joyner)	.12	.09	.05
382	*Keith Miller*(FC)	.08	.06	.03
383	Eric Bell	.06	.05	.02
384	Neil Allen	.04	.03	.02
385	Carlton Fisk	.20	.15	.08
386	Don Mattingly (All-Star)	.15	.11	.06
387	Willie Randolph (All-Star)	.06	.05	.02
388	Wade Boggs (All-Star)	.12	.09	.05
389	Alan Trammell (All-Star)	.08	.06	.03
390	George Bell (All-Star)	.10	.08	.04
391	Kirby Puckett (All-Star)	.20	.15	.08
392	Dave Winfield (All-Star)	.15	.11	.06
393	Matt Nokes (All-Star)	.15	.11	.06
394	Roger Clemens (All-Star)	.15	.11	.06
395	Jimmy Key (All-Star)	.06	.05	.02
396	Tom Henke (All-Star)	.06	.05	.02
397	Jack Clark (All-Star)	.06	.05	.02
398	Juan Samuel (All-Star)	.06	.05	.02
399	Tim Wallach (All-Star)	.06	.05	.02
400	Ozzie Smith (All-Star)	.10	.08	.04
401	Andre Dawson (All-Star)	.10	.08	.04
402	Tony Gwynn (All-Star)	.15	.11	.06
403	Tim Raines (All-Star)	.12	.09	.05
404	Benny Santiago (All-Star)	.10	.08	.04
405	Dwight Gooden (All-Star)	.10	.08	.04
406	Shane Rawley (All-Star)	.06	.05	.02
407	Steve Bedrosian (All-Star)	.08	.06	.03
408	Dion James	.06	.05	.02
409	Joel McKeon(FC)	.04	.03	.02
410	Tony Pena	.06	.05	.02
411	Wayne Tolleson	.04	.03	.02
412	Randy Myers	.10	.08	.04
413	John Christensen	.04	.03	.02
414	John McNamara	.04	.03	.02
415	Don Carman	.06	.05	.02
416	Keith Moreland	.06	.05	.02
417	*Mark Ciardi*(FC)	.04	.03	.02
418	Joel Youngblood	.04	.03	.02
419	Scott McGregor	.06	.05	.02
420	Wally Joyner	.12	.09	.05
421	Ed Vande Berg	.04	.03	.02
422	Dave Concepcion	.06	.05	.02
423	*John Smiley*	.20	.15	.08
424	Dwayne Murphy	.06	.05	.02
425	Jeff Reardon	.08	.06	.03
426	Randy Ready	.04	.03	.02
427	*Paul Kilgus*(FC)	.08	.06	.03
428	John Shelby	.04	.03	.02
429	Tigers Leaders (Kirk Gibson, Alan Trammell)	.08	.06	.03
430	Glenn Davis	.06	.05	.02
431	Casey Candaele	.04	.03	.02
432	Mike Moore	.04	.03	.02
433	*Bill Pecota*(FC)	.08	.06	.03
434	Rick Aguilera	.04	.03	.02
435	Mike Pagliarulo	.08	.06	.03
436	Mike Bielecki	.04	.03	.02
437	*Fred Manrique*(FC)	.06	.05	.02
438	*Rob Ducey*(FC)	.06	.05	.02
439	Dave Martinez	.08	.06	.03
440	Steve Bedrosian	.10	.08	.04
441	Rick Manning	.04	.03	.02
442	*Tom Bolton*(FC)	.08	.06	.03
443	Ken Griffey	.06	.05	.02
444	Cal Ripken, Sr.	.04	.03	.02
445	Mike Krukow	.06	.05	.02
446	Doug DeCinces	.06	.05	.02
447	*Jeff Montgomery*(FC)	.50	.40	.20
448	Mike Davis	.06	.05	.02
449	*Jeff Robinson*	.06	.05	.02
450	Barry Bonds	.60	.45	.25
451	Keith Atherton	.04	.03	.02
452	Willie Wilson	.08	.06	.03
453	Dennis Powell	.04	.03	.02

		MT	NR MT	EX
454	Marvell Wynne	.04	.03	.02
455	*Shawn Hillegas*(FC)	.06	.05	.02
456	Dave Anderson	.04	.03	.02
457	Terry Leach	.04	.03	.02
458	Ron Hassey	.04	.03	.02
459	Yankees Leaders (Willie Randolph, Dave Winfield)	.08	.06	.03
460	Ozzie Smith	.12	.09	.05
461	Danny Darwin	.04	.03	.02
462	Don Slaught	.04	.03	.02
463	*Fred McGriff*	.20	.15	.08
464	Jay Tibbs	.04	.03	.02
465	Paul Molitor	.15	.11	.06
466	Jerry Mumphrey	.04	.03	.02
467	Don Aase	.04	.03	.02
468	Darren Daulton	.04	.03	.02
469	Jeff Dedmon	.04	.03	.02
470	Dwight Evans	.10	.08	.04
471	Donnie Moore	.04	.03	.02
472	Robby Thompson	.06	.05	.02
473	Joe Niekro	.06	.05	.02
474	Tom Brookens	.04	.03	.02
475	Pete Rose	.20	.15	.08
476	Dave Stewart	.08	.06	.03
477	Jamie Quirk	.04	.03	.02
478	Sid Bream	.06	.05	.02
479	Brett Butler	.06	.05	.02
480	Dwight Gooden	.10	.08	.04
481	Mariano Duncan	.04	.03	.02
482	Mark Davis	.04	.03	.02
483	*Rod Booker*(FC)	.04	.03	.02
484	Pat Clements	.04	.03	.02
485	Harold Reynolds	.06	.05	.02
486	*Pat Keedy*(FC)	.10	.08	.04
487	Jim Pankovits	.04	.03	.02
488	Andy McGaffigan	.04	.03	.02
489	Dodgers Leaders (Pedro Guerrero, Fernando Valenzuela)	.08	.06	.03
490	Larry Parrish	.06	.05	.02
491	B.J. Surhoff	.10	.08	.04
492	Doyle Alexander	.06	.05	.02
493	Mike Greenwell	.12	.09	.05
494	*Wally Ritchie*	.06	.05	.02
495	Eddie Murray	.25	.20	.10
496	Guy Hoffman	.04	.03	.02
497	Kevin Mitchell	.12	.09	.05
498	Bob Boone	.06	.05	.02
499	Eric King	.06	.05	.02
500	Andre Dawson	.15	.11	.06
501	Tim Birtsas(FC)	.06	.05	.02
502	Danny Gladden	.04	.03	.02
503	*Junior Noboa*(FC)	.04	.03	.02
504	Bob Rodgers	.04	.03	.02
505	Willie Upshaw	.06	.05	.02
506	John Cangelosi	.04	.03	.02
507	Mark Gubicza	.10	.08	.04
508	Tim Teufel	.04	.03	.02
509	Bill Dawley	.04	.03	.02
510	Dave Winfield	.20	.15	.08
511	Joel Davis	.04	.03	.02
512	Alex Trevino	.04	.03	.02
513	Tim Flannery	.04	.03	.02
514	Pat Sheridan	.04	.03	.02
515	Juan Nieves	.06	.05	.02
516	Jim Sundberg	.06	.05	.02
517	Ron Robinson	.04	.03	.02
518	Greg Gross	.04	.03	.02
519	Mariners Leaders (Phil Bradley, Harold Reynolds)	.06	.05	.02
520	Dave Smith	.06	.05	.02
521	Jim Dwyer	.04	.03	.02
522	*Bob Patterson*(FC)	.12	.09	.05
523	Gary Roenicke	.04	.03	.02
524	Gary Lucas	.04	.03	.02
525	Marty Barrett	.06	.05	.02
526	Juan Berenguer	.04	.03	.02
527	Steve Henderson	.04	.03	.02
528	Checklist 397-528,	.04	.03	.02
529	Tim Burke	.04	.03	.02
530	Gary Carter	.15	.11	.06
531	Rich Yett	.04	.03	.02
532	Mike Kingery	.04	.03	.02
533	*John Farrell*(FC)	.08	.06	.03
534	John Wathan	.06	.05	.02
535	Ron Guidry	.12	.09	.05
536	John Morris	.04	.03	.02
537	Steve Buechele	.04	.03	.02
538	Bill Wegman	.04	.03	.02
539	Mike LaValliere	.06	.05	.02
540	Bret Saberhagen	.10	.08	.04
541	Juan Beniquez	.04	.03	.02

		MT	NR MT	EX
542	*Paul Noce*(FC)	.04	.03	.02
543	Kent Tekulve	.06	.05	.02
544	Jim Traber	.06	.05	.02
545	Don Baylor	.08	.06	.03
546	John Candelaria	.06	.05	.02
547	*Felix Fermin*(FC)	.12	.09	.05
548	*Shane Mack*	.15	.11	.06
549	Braves Leaders (Ken Griffey, Dion James, Dale Murphy, Gerald Perry)	.08	.06	.03
550	Pedro Guerrero	.15	.11	.06
551	Terry Steinbach	.15	.11	.06
552	Mark Thurmond	.04	.03	.02
553	Tracy Jones	.06	.05	.02
554	Mike Smithson	.04	.03	.02
555	Brook Jacoby	.08	.06	.03
556	*Stan Clarke*(FC)	.04	.03	.02
557	Craig Reynolds	.04	.03	.02
558	Bob Ojeda	.06	.05	.02
559	*Ken Williams*(FC)	.08	.06	.03
560	Tim Wallach	.08	.06	.03
561	Rick Cerone	.04	.03	.02
562	Jim Lindeman	.04	.03	.02
563	Jose Guzman	.06	.05	.02
564	Frank Lucchesi	.04	.03	.02
565	Lloyd Moseby	.06	.05	.02
566	*Charlie O'Brien*(FC)	.04	.03	.02
567	Mike Diaz	.06	.05	.02
568	Chris Brown	.06	.05	.02
569	Charlie Leibrandt	.06	.05	.02
570	Jeffrey Leonard	.06	.05	.02
571	*Mark Williamson*(FC)	.06	.05	.02
572	Chris James	.06	.05	.02
573	Bob Stanley	.04	.03	.02
574	Graig Nettles	.08	.06	.03
575	Don Sutton	.12	.09	.05
576	*Tommy Hinzo*(FC)	.04	.03	.02
577	Tom Browning	.08	.06	.03
578	Gary Gaetti	.10	.08	.04
579	Mets Leaders (Gary Carter, Kevin McReynolds)	.08	.06	.03
580	Mark McGwire	.40	.30	.15
581	Tito Landrum	.04	.03	.02
582	*Mike Henneman*	.25	.20	.10
583	Dave Valle(FC)	.06	.05	.02
584	Steve Trout	.04	.03	.02
585	Ozzie Guillen	.06	.05	.02
586	Bob Forsch	.06	.05	.02
587	Terry Puhl	.04	.03	.02
588	*Jeff Parrett*(FC)	.06	.05	.02
589	Geno Petralli	.04	.03	.02
590	George Bell	.12	.09	.05
591	Doug Drabek	.06	.05	.02
592	Dale Sveum	.06	.05	.02
593	Bob Tewksbury	.04	.03	.02
594	Bobby Valentine	.04	.03	.02
595	Frank White	.06	.05	.02
596	John Kruk	.12	.09	.05
597	Gene Garber	.04	.03	.02
598	Lee Lacy	.04	.03	.02
599	Calvin Schiraldi	.04	.03	.02
600	Mike Schmidt	.40	.30	.15
601	Jack Lazorko	.04	.03	.02
602	Mike Aldrete	.06	.05	.02
603	Rob Murphy	.06	.05	.02
604	Chris Bando	.04	.03	.02
605	Kirk Gibson	.15	.11	.06
606	Moose Haas	.04	.03	.02
607	Mickey Hatcher	.04	.03	.02
608	Charlie Kerfeld	.04	.03	.02
609	Twins Leaders (Gary Gaetti, Kent Hrbek)	.08	.06	.03
610	Keith Hernandez	.06	.05	.02
611	Tommy John	.12	.09	.05
612	Curt Ford	.04	.03	.02
613	Bobby Thigpen	.08	.06	.03
614	Herm Winningham	.04	.03	.02
615	Jody Davis	.06	.05	.02
616	*Jay Aldrich*(FC)	.04	.03	.02
617	Oddibe McDowell	.06	.05	.02
618	Cecil Fielder	.35	.25	.14
619	*Mike Dunne*	.06	.05	.02
620	Cory Snyder	.08	.06	.03
621	Gene Nelson	.04	.03	.02
622	Kal Daniels	.06	.05	.02
623	Mike Flanagan	.06	.05	.02
624	Jim Leyland	.04	.03	.02
625	Frank Viola	.12	.09	.05
626	Glenn Wilson	.06	.05	.02
627	*Joe Boever*(FC)	.04	.03	.02
628	Dave Henderson	.08	.06	.03
629	Kelly Downs	.08	.06	.03

		MT	NR MT	EX
630	Darrell Evans	.08	.06	.03
631	Jack Howell	.06	.05	.02
632	*Steve Shields*	.04	.03	.02
633	*Barry Lyons*	.04	.03	.02
634	Jose DeLeon	.06	.05	.02
635	Terry Pendleton	.12	.09	.05
636	Charles Hudson	.04	.03	.02
637	*Jay Bell*(FC)	.50	.40	.20
638	Steve Balboni	.06	.05	.02
639	Brewers Leaders (Glenn Braggs, Tony Muser)	.06	.05	.02
640	Garry Templeton	.06	.05	.02
641	Rick Honeycutt	.04	.03	.02
642	Bob Dernier	.04	.03	.02
643	*Rocky Childress*(FC)	.04	.03	.02
644	Terry McGriff(FC)	.06	.05	.02
645	*Matt Nokes*	.10	.08	.04
646	Checklist 529-660	.04	.03	.02
647	Pascual Perez	.06	.05	.02
648	Al Newman	.04	.03	.02
649	*DeWayne Buice*	.04	.03	.02
650	Cal Ripken, Jr.	.40	.30	.15
651	*Mike Jackson*(FC)	.15	.11	.06
652	Bruce Benedict	.04	.03	.02
653	Jeff Sellers	.06	.05	.02
654	Roger Craig	.06	.05	.02
655	Len Dykstra	.12	.09	.05
656	Lee Guetterman	.04	.03	.02
657	Gary Redus	.04	.03	.02
658	Tim Conroy	.04	.03	.02
659	Bobby Meacham	.04	.03	.02
660	Rick Reuschel	.08	.06	.03
661	Turn Back The Clock (Nolan Ryan)	.25	.20	.10
662	Turn Back The Clock (Jim Rice)	.08	.06	.03
663	Turn Back The Clock (Ron Blomberg)	.04	.03	.02
664	Turn Back The Clock (Bob Gibson)	.08	.06	.03
665	Turn Back The Clock (Stan Musial)	.12	.09	.05
666	Mario Soto	.06	.05	.02
667	Luis Quinones	.04	.03	.02
668	Walt Terrell	.06	.05	.02
669	Phillies Leaders (Lance Parrish, Mike Ryan)	.06	.05	.02
670	Dan Plesac	.08	.06	.03
671	Tim Laudner	.04	.03	.02
672	*John Davis*(FC)	.04	.03	.02
673	Tony Phillips	.04	.03	.02
674	Mike Fitzgerald	.04	.03	.02
675	Jim Rice	.08	.06	.03
676	Ken Dixon	.04	.03	.02
677	Eddie Milner	.04	.03	.02
678	Jim Acker	.04	.03	.02
679	Darrell Miller	.04	.03	.02
680	Charlie Hough	.06	.05	.02
681	Bobby Bonilla	.15	.11	.06
682	Jimmy Key	.10	.08	.04
683	Julio Franco	.08	.06	.03
684	Hal Lanier	.04	.03	.02
685	Ron Darling	.04	.03	.02
686	Terry Francona	.04	.03	.02
687	Mickey Brantley	.04	.03	.02
688	Jim Winn	.04	.03	.02
689	*Tom Pagnozzi*(FC)	.10	.08	.04
690	Jay Howell	.06	.05	.02
691	Dan Pasqua	.08	.06	.03
692	Mike Birkbeck	.06	.05	.02
693	Benny Santiago	.12	.09	.05
694	*Eric Nolte*(FC)	.06	.05	.02
695	Shawon Dunston	.08	.06	.03
696	Duane Ward	.04	.03	.02
697	Steve Lombardozzi	.08	.06	.03
698	Brad Havens	.04	.03	.02
699	Padres Leaders (Tony Gwynn, Benny Santiago)	.12	.09	.05
700	George Brett	.12	.09	.05
701	Sammy Stewart	.04	.03	.02
702	Mike Gallego	.04	.03	.02
703	Bob Brenly	.04	.03	.02
704	Dennis Boyd	.06	.05	.02
705	Juan Samuel	.10	.08	.04
706	Rick Mahler	.04	.03	.02
707	Fred Lynn	.10	.08	.04
708	Gus Polidor(FC)	.06	.05	.02
709	George Frazier	.04	.03	.02
710	Darryl Strawberry	.15	.11	.06
711	Bill Gullickson	.04	.03	.02
712	John Moses	.04	.03	.02
713	Willie Hernandez	.06	.05	.02
714	Jim Fregosi	.04	.03	.02
715	Todd Worrell	.08	.06	.03
716	Lenn Sakata	.04	.03	.02

		MT	NR MT	EX
717	Jay Baller(FC)	.06	.05	.02
718	Mike Felder	.04	.03	.02
719	Denny Walling	.04	.03	.02
720	Tim Raines	.10	.08	.04
721	Pete O'Brien	.06	.05	.02
722	Manny Lee	.04	.03	.02
723	Bob Kipper	.04	.03	.02
724	Danny Tartabull	.10	.08	.04
725	Mike Boddicker	.06	.05	.02
726	Alfredo Griffin	.06	.05	.02
727	Greg Booker	.04	.03	.02
728	Andy Allanson	.06	.05	.02
729	Blue Jays Leaders (George Bell, Fred McGriff)	.10	.08	.04
730	John Franco	.08	.06	.03
731	Rick Schu	.04	.03	.02
732	Dave Palmer	.04	.03	.02
733	Spike Owen	.04	.03	.02
734	Craig Lefferts	.04	.03	.02
735	Kevin McReynolds	.10	.08	.04
736	Matt Young	.04	.03	.02
737	Butch Wynegar	.04	.03	.02
738	Scott Bankhead	.04	.03	.02
739	Daryl Boston	.04	.03	.02
740	Rick Sutcliffe	.08	.06	.03
741	Mike Easler	.06	.05	.02
742	Mark Clear	.04	.03	.02
743	Larry Herndon	.04	.03	.02
744	Whitey Herzog	.06	.05	.02
745	Bill Doran	.06	.05	.02
746	*Gene Larkin*	.10	.08	.04
747	Bobby Witt	.08	.06	.03
748	Reid Nichols	.04	.03	.02
749	Mark Eichhorn	.06	.05	.02
750	Bo Jackson	.40	.30	.15
751	Jim Morrison	.04	.03	.02
752	Mark Grant	.04	.03	.02
753	Danny Heep	.04	.03	.02
754	Mike LaCoss	.04	.03	.02
755	Ozzie Virgil	.04	.03	.02
756	Mike Maddux	.06	.05	.02
757	*John Marzano*	.06	.05	.02
758	*Eddie Williams*(FC)	.08	.06	.03
759	Athletics Leaders (Jose Canseco, Mark McGwire)	.20	.15	.08
760	Mike Scott	.10	.08	.04
761	Tony Armas	.06	.05	.02
762	Scott Bradley	.04	.03	.02
763	Doug Sisk	.04	.03	.02
764	Greg Walker	.06	.05	.02
765	Neal Heaton	.06	.05	.02
766	Henry Cotto	.04	.03	.02
767	*Jose Lind* (Future Stars)(FC)	.25	.20	.10
768	Dickie Noles	.04	.03	.02
769	Cecil Cooper	.08	.06	.03
770	Lou Whitaker	.10	.08	.04
771	Ruben Sierra	.15	.11	.06
772	Sal Butera	.04	.03	.02
773	Frank Williams	.04	.03	.02
774	Gene Mauch	.06	.05	.02
775	Dave Stieb	.08	.06	.03
776	Checklist 661-792	.04	.03	.02
777	Lonnie Smith	.06	.05	.02
778a	*Keith Comstock* (white team letters)(FC)	.60	.45	.25
778b	*Keith Comstock* (blue team letters)(FC)	.25	.20	.10
779	*Tom Glavine*(FC)	1.50	1.25	.60
780	Fernando Valenzuela	.15	.11	.06
781	*Keith Hughes*(FC)	.06	.05	.02
782	*Jeff Ballard*(FC)	.08	.06	.03
783	Ron Roenicke	.04	.03	.02
784	Joe Sambito	.04	.03	.02
785	Alvin Davis	.04	.03	.02
786	Joe Price	.04	.03	.02
787	Bill Almon	.04	.03	.02
788	Ray Searage	.04	.03	.02
789	Indians Leaders (Joe Carter, Cory Snyder)	.08	.06	.03
790	Dave Righetti	.06	.05	.02
791	Ted Simmons	.08	.06	.03
792	John Tudor	.08	.06	.03

A player's name in italic indicates a rookie card. An (FC) indicates a player's first card for that particular card company.

1988 Topps All-Star Glossy Set Of 22

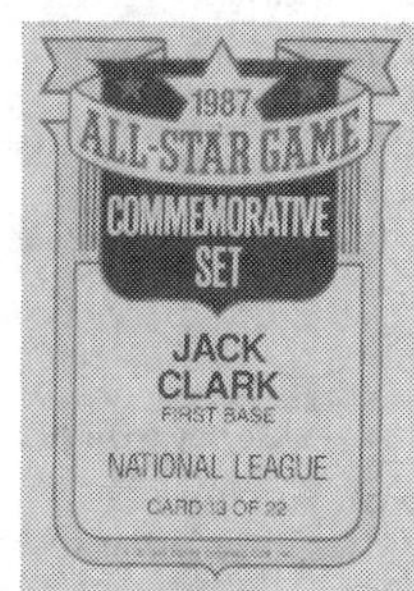

The fifth edition of Topps' special All-Star inserts (22 cards) was included in the company's 1988 rack packs. The 1987 American and National League All-Star lineup, plus honorary captains Jim Hunter and Billy Williams, are featured on the standard-size All-Star inserts. The glossy full-color card fronts contain player photos centered between a red and yellow "1987 All-Star" logo printed across the card top and the player name (also red and yellow) which is printed across the bottom margin. A National or American League logo appears in the lower left corner. Card backs are printed in red and blue on a white background, with the title and All-Star logo emblem printed above the player name and card number.

		MT	NR MT	EX
Complete Set:		4.00	3.00	1.50
Common Player:		.15	.11	.06
1	John McNamara	.15	.11	.06
2	Don Mattingly	1.00	.70	.40
3	Willie Randolph	.15	.11	.06
4	Wade Boggs	.80	.60	.30
5	Cal Ripken	.50	.40	.20
6	George Bell	.30	.25	.12
7	Rickey Henderson	.50	.40	.20
8	Dave Winfield	.40	.30	.15
9	Terry Kennedy	.15	.11	.06
10	Bret Saberhagen	.25	.20	.10
11	Jim Hunter	.25	.20	.10
12	Davey Johnson	.15	.11	.06
13	Jack Clark	.25	.20	.10
14	Ryne Sandberg	.40	.30	.15
15	Mike Schmidt	.60	.45	.25
16	Ozzie Smith	.25	.20	.10
17	Eric Davis	.60	.45	.25
18	Andre Dawson	.25	.20	.10
19	Darryl Strawberry	.60	.45	.25
20	Gary Carter	.40	.30	.15
21	Mike Scott	.15	.11	.06
22	Billy Williams	.25	.20	.10

1988 Topps All-Star Glossy Set Of 60

This standard-size collectors set includes 60 full-color glossy cards featuring All-Stars and Prospects in six separate 10-card sets. In 1986, Topps issued a similar set that included only All-Stars. Card fronts have a white border and a thin red line framing the player photo, with the player's name in the lower left corner. Card backs, in red and blue, include very basic player information (name, team and position), along with the card set logo and card number. Topps glossy collector sets were marketed via a special offer printed on a card packaged in all Topps wax packs. For six special offer cards and

$1.25, collectors received one of the six 10-card sets; 18 special offer cards and $7.50 earned the entire 60-card collection.

		MT	NR MT	EX
Complete Set:		14.00	10.50	5.50
Common Player:		.15	.11	.06
1	Andre Dawson	.30	.25	.12
2	Jesse Barfield	.20	.15	.08
3	Mike Schmidt	.70	.50	.30
4	Ruben Sierra	.40	.30	.15
5	Mike Scott	.20	.15	.08
6	Cal Ripken	.70	.50	.30
7	Gary Carter	.50	.40	.20
8	Kent Hrbek	.30	.25	.12
9	Kevin Seitzer	.70	.50	.30
10	Mike Henneman	.25	.20	.10
11	Don Mattingly	2.00	1.50	.80
12	Tim Raines	.40	.30	.15
13	Roger Clemens	.80	.60	.30
14	Ryne Sandberg	.40	.30	.15
15	Tony Fernandez	.20	.15	.08
16	Eric Davis	.80	.60	.30
17	Jack Morris	.30	.25	.12
18	Tim Wallach	.20	.15	.08
19	Mike Dunne	.25	.20	.10
20	Mike Greenwell	1.00	.70	.40
21	Dwight Evans	.20	.15	.08
22	Darryl Strawberry	.80	.60	.30
23	Cory Snyder	.30	.25	.12
24	Pedro Guerrero	.25	.20	.10
25	Rickey Henderson	.60	.45	.25
26	Dale Murphy	.70	.50	.30
27	Kirby Puckett	.50	.40	.20
28	Steve Bedrosian	.20	.15	.08
29	Devon White	.25	.20	.10
30	Benny Santiago	.25	.20	.10
31	George Bell	.40	.30	.15
32	Keith Hernandez	.40	.30	.15
33	Dave Stewart	.15	.11	.06
34	Dave Parker	.25	.20	.10
35	Tom Henke	.15	.11	.06
36	Willie McGee	.20	.15	.08
37	Alan Trammell	.30	.25	.12
38	Tony Gwynn	.60	.45	.25
39	Mark McGwire	.80	.60	.30
40	Joe Magrane	.25	.20	.10
41	Jack Clark	.25	.20	.10
42	Willie Randolph	.15	.11	.06
43	Juan Samuel	.25	.20	.10
44	Joe Carter	.25	.20	.10
45	Shane Rawley	.15	.11	.06
46	Dave Winfield	.50	.40	.20
47	Ozzie Smith	.25	.20	.10
48	Wally Joyner	.70	.50	.30
49	B.J. Surhoff	.20	.15	.08
50	Ellis Burks	.80	.60	.30
51	Wade Boggs	.80	.60	.30
52	Howard Johnson	.20	.15	.08
53	George Brett	.70	.50	.30
54	Dwight Gooden	.80	.60	.30
55	Jose Canseco	2.00	1.50	.80
56	Lee Smith	.15	.11	.06
57	Paul Molitor	.20	.15	.08
58	Andres Galarraga	.30	.25	.12
59	Matt Nokes	.40	.30	.15
60	Casey Candaele	.15	.11	.06

1988 Topps Traded

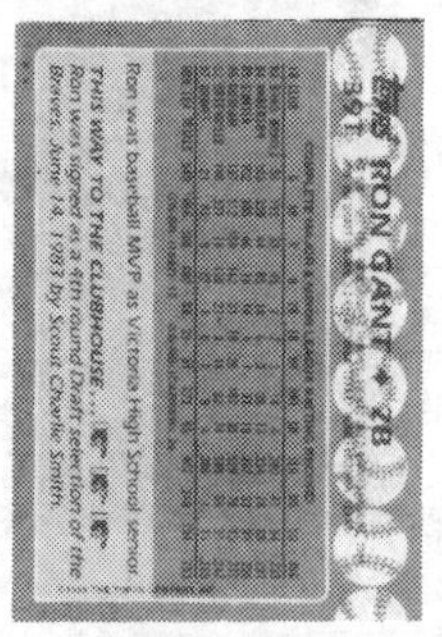

In addition to new players and traded veterans, 21 members of the U.S.A. Olympic Baseball team are showcased in this 132-card set, numbered 1T-132T. The standard-size (2-1/2" by 3-1/2") set follows the same design as the basic Topps issue - white borders, large full-color photos, team name (or U.S.A.) in large bold letters at the top of the card face, player name on a diagonal stripe across the lower right corner. Topps has issued its traded series each year since 1981 in boxed complete sets available through hobby dealers.

		MT	NR MT	EX
Complete Set (132):		30.00	22.00	12.00
Common Player:		.06	.05	.02
1T	Jim Abbott (USA)	6.00	4.50	2.50
2T	Juan Agosto	.06	.05	.02
3T	Luis Alicea(FC)	.15	.11	.06
4T	Roberto Alomar(FC)	10.00	7.50	4.00
5T	Brady Anderson(FC)	1.00	.70	.40
6T	Jack Armstrong	.25	.20	.10
7T	Don August	.15	.11	.06
8T	Floyd Bannister	.08	.06	.03
9T	Bret Barberie (USA)(FC)	.50	.40	.20
10T	Jose Bautista(FC)	.15	.11	.06
11T	Don Baylor	.10	.08	.04
12T	Tim Belcher	.20	.15	.08
13T	Buddy Bell	.10	.08	.04
14T	Andy Benes (USA)(FC)	4.50	3.50	1.75
15T	Damon Berryhill	.10	.08	.04
16T	Bud Black	.06	.05	.02
17T	Pat Borders	.40	.30	.15
18T	Phil Bradley	.10	.08	.04
19T	Jeff Branson (USA)(FC)	.06	.05	.02
20T	Tom Brunansky	.06	.05	.02
21T	Jay Buhner	1.50	1.25	.60
22T	Brett Butler	.10	.08	.04
23T	Jim Campanis (USA)(FC)	.20	.15	.08
24T	Sil Campusano(FC)	.10	.08	.04
25T	John Candelaria	.08	.06	.03
26T	Jose Cecena(FC)	.06	.05	.02
27T	Rick Cerone	.06	.05	.02
28T	Jack Clark	.08	.06	.03
29T	Kevin Coffman(FC)	.10	.08	.04
30T	Pat Combs (USA)	.10	.08	.04
31T	Henry Cotto	.06	.05	.02
32T	Chili Davis	.12	.09	.05
33T	Mike Davis	.08	.06	.03
34T	Jose DeLeon	.08	.06	.03
35T	Richard Dotson	.10	.08	.04
36T	Cecil Espy	.12	.09	.05
37T	Tom Filer	.06	.05	.02
38T	Mike Fiore (USA)(FC)	.10	.08	.04
39T	Ron Gant	2.00	1.50	.80
40T	Kirk Gibson	.10	.08	.04
41T	Rich Gossage	.15	.11	.06
42T	Mark Grace(FC)	2.50	2.00	1.00
43T	Alfredo Griffin	.08	.06	.03
44T	Ty Griffin (USA)(FC)	.10	.08	.04
45T	Bryan Harvey	1.50	1.25	.60
46T	Ron Hassey	.06	.05	.02
47T	Ray Hayward(FC)	.08	.06	.03
48T	Dave Henderson	.20	.15	.08
49T	Tom Herr	.10	.08	.04
50T	Bob Horner	.10	.08	.04
51T	Ricky Horton	.08	.06	.03
52T	Jay Howell	.08	.06	.03
53T	Glenn Hubbard	.06	.05	.02
54T	Jeff Innis(FC)	.10	.08	.04
55T	Danny Jackson	.15	.11	.06
56T	Darrin Jackson	.30	.25	.12
57T	Roberto Kelly	.75	.60	.30
58T	Ron Kittle	.10	.08	.04
59T	Ray Knight	.08	.06	.03
60T	Vance Law	.08	.06	.03
61T	Jeffrey Leonard	.08	.06	.03
62T	Mike Macfarlane	.25	.20	.10
63T	Scotti Madison(FC)	.15	.11	.06
64T	Kirt Manwaring(FC)	.20	.15	.08
65T	Mark Marquess (USA)	.06	.05	.02
66T	Tino Martinez (USA)	.75	.60	.30
67T	Billy Masse (USA)(FC)	.12	.09	.05
68T	Jack McDowell	3.00	2.25	1.25
69T	Jack McKeon	.06	.05	.02
70T	Larry McWilliams	.06	.05	.02
71T	Mickey Morandini (USA)	.50	.40	.20
72T	Keith Moreland	.08	.06	.03
73T	Mike Morgan	.06	.05	.02
74T	Charles Nagy (USA)	.75	.60	.30
75T	Al Nipper	.06	.05	.02
76T	Russ Nixon	.06	.05	.02
77T	Jesse Orosco	.08	.06	.03
78T	Joe Orsulak	.06	.05	.02
79T	Dave Palmer	.06	.05	.02
80T	Mark Parent(FC)	.20	.15	.08
81T	Dave Parker	.12	.09	.05
82T	Dan Pasqua	.10	.08	.04
83T	Melido Perez	.20	.15	.08
84T	Steve Peters(FC)	.15	.11	.06
85T	Dan Petry	.08	.06	.03
86T	Gary Pettis	.08	.06	.03
87T	Jeff Pico(FC)	.08	.06	.03
88T	Jim Poole (USA)	.10	.08	.04
89T	Ted Power	.06	.05	.02
90T	Rafael Ramirez	.06	.05	.02
91T	Dennis Rasmussen	.10	.08	.04
92T	Jose Rijo	.15	.11	.06
93T	Earnie Riles	.06	.05	.02
94T	Luis Rivera(FC)	.08	.06	.03
95T	Doug Robbins (USA)(FC)	.10	.08	.04
96T	Frank Robinson	.15	.11	.06
97T	Cookie Rojas	.06	.05	.02
98T	Chris Sabo(FC)	.75	.60	.30
99T	Mark Salas	.06	.05	.02
100T	Luis Salazar	.06	.05	.02
101T	Rafael Santana	.06	.05	.02
102T	Nelson Santovenia(FC)	.10	.08	.04
103T	Mackey Sasser(FC)	.10	.08	.04
104T	Calvin Schiraldi	.06	.05	.02
105T	Mike Schooler(FC)	.15	.11	.06
106T	Scott Servais (USA)(FC)	.10	.08	.04
107T	Dave Silvestri (USA)	.10	.08	.04
108T	Don Slaught	.06	.05	.02
109T	Joe Slusarski (USA)(FC)	.12	.09	.05
110T	Lee Smith	.12	.09	.05
111T	Pete Smith(FC)	.40	.30	.15
112T	Jim Snyder	.06	.05	.02
113T	Ed Sprague (USA)(FC)	.60	.45	.25
114T	Pete Stanicek(FC)	.15	.11	.06
115T	Kurt Stillwell	.10	.08	.04
116T	Todd Stottlemyre	.90	.70	.35
117T	Bill Swift	.20	.15	.08
118T	Pat Tabler	.08	.06	.03
119T	Scott Terry(FC)	.10	.08	.04
120T	Mickey Tettleton	.20	.15	.08
121T	Dickie Thon	.08	.06	.03
122T	Jeff Treadway	.10	.08	.04
123T	Willie Upshaw	.08	.06	.03
124T	Robin Ventura(FC)	6.00	4.50	2.50
125T	Ron Washington	.06	.05	.02
126T	Walt Weiss(FC)	.30	.25	.12
127T	Bob Welch	.10	.08	.04
128T	David Wells(FC)	.25	.20	.10
129T	Glenn Wilson	.08	.06	.03
130T	Ted Wood (USA)(FC)	.15	.11	.06
131T	Don Zimmer	.06	.05	.02
132T	Checklist 1T-132T	.06	.05	.02

1988 Topps Box Panels

After a one-year hiatus during which they appeared on the sides of Topps wax pack display boxes, Topps retail box cards returned to box bottoms in 1988. Topps first issued box-bottom cards in 1986,

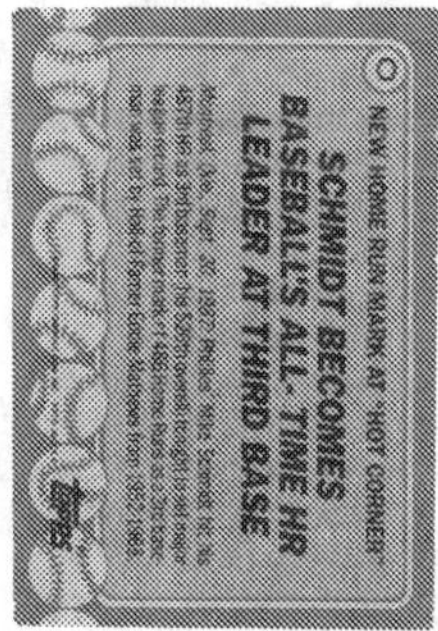

following the introduction of the concept by Donruss in 1985. Topps 1988 box-bottom series includes 16 standard-size baseball cards, four cards per each of four different display boxes. Card fronts follow the same design as the 1988 Topps basic issue; full-color player photos, framed in yellow, surrounded by a white border; diagonal player name lower right; team name in large letters at the top of the card front. Card backs are "numbered" A through P and are printed in black and orange.

		MT	NR MT	EX
Complete Panel Set:		7.00	5.25	2.75
Complete Singles Set:		3.00	2.25	1.25
Common Panel:		1.00	.70	.40
Common Single Player:		.08	.06	.03
	Panel	1.00	.70	.40
A	Don Baylor	.12	.09	.05
B	Steve Bedrosian	.12	.09	.05
C	Juan Beniquez	.08	.06	.03
D	Bob Boone	.08	.06	.03
	Panel	1.75	1.25	.70
E	Darrell Evans	.12	.09	.05
F	Tony Gwynn	.30	.25	.12
G	John Kruk	.15	.11	.06
H	Marvell Wynne	.08	.06	.03
	Panel	2.75	2.00	1.00
I	Joe Carter	.15	.11	.06
J	Eric Davis	.50	.40	.20
K	Howard Johnson	.12	.09	.05
L	Darryl Strawberry	.35	.25	.14
	Panel	2.50	2.00	1.00
M	Rickey Henderson	.50	.40	.20
N	Nolan Ryan	.35	.25	.14
O	Mike Schmidt	.08	.06	.03
P	Kent Tekulve	.08	.06	.03

1988 Topps American Baseball

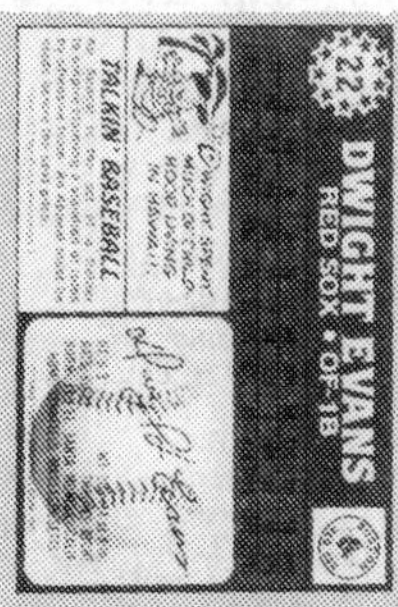

This 88-card set, unlike Topps' United Kingdom football cards, was made available for distribution by U.S. hobby dealers. The cards were packaged in checklist-backed boxes with an American flag on the top flap. The 2-1/4" by 3" cards feature full-color player photos printed on white stock with a red line framing the photo. The team name, printed in individual team colors, intersects the red frame at the top of the card. A bright yellow name banner appears below the photo. Card backs have bright blue borders and cartoon-style horizontal layouts. The card number appears within a circle of red stars upper left, beside the player's name and team logo. A red banner containing the player career stats runs the length of the card back. The lower half of the flip side features a caricature of the player and a one-line caption. Below the cartoon, a short "Talkin' Baseball" paragraph provides elementary baseball information, obviously designed to acquaint soccer-playing European collectors with American baseball rules and terminology. A glossy edition of the set was issued and is valued at 2-3 times greater than the regular issue.

		MT	NR MT	EX
Complete Set:		10.00	7.50	4.00
Common Player:		.08	.06	.03
1	Harold Baines	.15	.11	.06
2	Steve Bedrosian	.10	.08	.04
3	George Bell	.25	.20	.10
4	Wade Boggs	.70	.50	.30
5	Barry Bonds	.20	.15	.08
6	Bob Boone	.08	.06	.03
7	George Brett	.40	.30	.15
8	Hubie Brooks	.08	.06	.03
9	Ivan Calderon	.10	.08	.04
10	Jose Canseco	1.25	.90	.50
11	Gary Carter	.30	.25	.12
12	Joe Carter	.15	.11	.06
13	Jack Clark	.20	.15	.08
14	Will Clark	.50	.40	.20
15	Roger Clemens	.60	.45	.25
16	Vince Coleman	.20	.15	.08
17	Alvin Davis	.15	.11	.06
18	Eric Davis	.70	.50	.30
19	Glenn Davis	.20	.15	.08
20	Andre Dawson	.25	.20	.10
21	Mike Dunne	.15	.11	.06
22	Dwight Evans	.10	.08	.04
23	Tony Fernandez	.15	.11	.06
24	John Franco	.10	.08	.04
25	Gary Gaetti	.20	.15	.08
26	Kirk Gibson	.25	.20	.10
27	Dwight Gooden	.60	.45	.25
28	Pedro Guerrero	.20	.15	.08
29	Tony Gwynn	.35	.25	.14
30	Billy Hatcher	.08	.06	.03
31	Rickey Henderson	.35	.25	.14
32	Tom Henke	.08	.06	.03
33	Keith Hernandez	.25	.20	.10
34	Orel Hershiser	.30	.25	.12
35	Teddy Higuera	.10	.08	.04
36	Charlie Hough	.08	.06	.03
37	Kent Hrbek	.25	.20	.10
38	Brook Jacoby	.10	.08	.04
39	Dion James	.08	.06	.03
40	Wally Joyner	.50	.40	.20
41	John Kruk	.15	.11	.06
42	Mark Langston	.15	.11	.06
43	Jeffrey Leonard	.08	.06	.03
44	Candy Maldonaldo	.08	.06	.03
45	Don Mattingly	1.25	.90	.50
46	Willie McGee	.15	.11	.06
47	Mark McGwire	.80	.60	.30
48	Kevin Mitchell	.08	.06	.03
49	Paul Molitor	.15	.11	.06
50	Jack Morris	.15	.11	.06
51	Lloyd Moseby	.10	.08	.04
52	Dale Murphy	.40	.30	.15
53	Eddie Murray	.30	.25	.12
54	Matt Nokes	.40	.30	.15
55	Dave Parker	.20	.15	.08
56	Larry Parrish	.08	.06	.03
57	Kirby Puckett	.35	.25	.14
58	Tim Raines	.30	.25	.12
59	Willie Randolph	.08	.06	.03
60	Harold Reynolds	.08	.06	.03
61	Cal Ripken	.35	.25	.14
62	Nolan Ryan	.80	.60	.30
63	Bret Saberhagen	.20	.15	.08
64	Juan Samuel	.15	.11	.06
65	Ryne Sandberg	.25	.20	.10
66	Benny Santiago	.15	.11	.06
67	Mike Schmidt	.40	.30	.15

		MT	NR MT	EX
68	Mike Scott	.10	.08	.04
69	Kevin Seitzer	.40	.30	.15
70	Larry Sheets	.08	.06	.03
71	Ruben Sierra	.15	.11	.06
72	Ozzie Smith	.15	.11	.06
73	Zane Smith	.08	.06	.03
74	Cory Snyder	.15	.11	.06
75	Dave Stewart	.10	.08	.04
76	Darryl Strawberry	.50	.40	.20
77	Rick Sutcliffe	.15	.11	.06
78	Danny Tartabull	.20	.15	.08
79	Alan Trammell	.25	.20	.10
80	Fernando Valenzuela	.20	.15	.08
81	Andy Van Slyke	.15	.11	.06
82	Frank Viola	.15	.11	.06
83	Greg Walker	.10	.08	.04
84	Tim Wallach	.10	.08	.04
85	Dave Winfield	.30	.25	.12
86	Mike Witt	.08	.06	.03
87	Robin Yount	.25	.20	.10
88	Checklist	.08	.06	.03

1988 Topps Big Baseball

1988 Topps Big Baseball cards (2-5/8" by 3-3/4") were issued in three series, 88 cards per series (a total set of 264 cards). Each series features current star players, sold in 7-card packages. The glossy cards are similar in format, both front and back, to the 1956 Topps 340-card set. Each card features a posed head shot and a close-up action photo on the front, framed by a wide white border and a dark blue inner border. A white outlines highlights the player closeup. The player's name appears below his head shot, in reversed type on a splash of color that fades from yellow to orange to red to pink. On the card back, the player's name is printed in large red letters across the top, followed by his team name and position in black. Personal info is printed in a red rectangle beside a Topps baseball logo bearing the card number. A triple cartoon strip, in full-color, illustrates career highlights, performance, personal background, etc. A red, white and blue statistics box (pitching, batting, fielding) is printed across the bottom.

		MT	NR MT	EX
Complete Set:		20.00	15.00	8.00
Common Player:		.05	.04	.02
1	Paul Molitor	.12	.09	.05
2	Milt Thompson	.05	.04	.02
3	Billy Hatcher	.05	.04	.02
4	Mike Witt	.05	.04	.02
5	Vince Coleman	.12	.09	.05
6	Dwight Evans	.10	.08	.04
7	Tim Wallach	.10	.08	.04
8	Alan Trammell	.15	.11	.06
9	Will Clark	.80	.60	.30
10	Jeff Reardon	.08	.06	.03
11	Dwight Gooden	.50	.40	.20
12	Benny Santiago	.12	.09	.05
13	Jose Canseco	1.25	.90	.50
14	Dale Murphy	.30	.25	.12
15	George Bell	.20	.15	.08
16	Ryne Sandberg	.20	.15	.08
17	Brook Jacoby	.08	.06	.03
18	Fernando Valenzuela	.15	.11	.06
19	Scott Fletcher	.05	.04	.02
20	Eric Davis	.60	.45	.25
21	Willie Wilson	.10	.08	.04
22	B.J. Surhoff	.10	.08	.04
23	Steve Bedrosian	.08	.06	.03
24	Dave Winfield	.25	.20	.10
25	Bobby Bonilla	.15	.11	.06
26	Larry Sheets	.08	.06	.03
27	Ozzie Guillen	.08	.06	.03
28	Checklist 1-88	.05	.04	.02
29	Nolan Ryan	.80	.60	.30
30	Bob Boone	.05	.04	.02
31	Tom Herr	.08	.06	.03
32	Wade Boggs	.90	.70	.35
33	Neal Heaton	.05	.04	.02
34	Doyle Alexander	.05	.04	.02
35	Candy Maldonado	.08	.06	.03
36	Kirby Puckett	.25	.20	.10
37	Gary Carter	.20	.15	.08
38	Lance McCullers	.08	.06	.03
39a	Terry Steinbach (black Topps logo on front)	.12	.09	.05
39b	Terry Steinbach (white Topps logo on front)	.12	.09	.05
40	Gerald Perry	.10	.08	.04
41	Tom Henke	.05	.04	.02
42	Leon Durham	.05	.04	.02
43	Cory Snyder	.12	.09	.05
44	Dale Sveum	.05	.04	.02
45	Lance Parrish	.12	.09	.05
46	Steve Sax	.12	.09	.05
47	Charlie Hough	.05	.04	.02
48	Kal Daniels	.15	.11	.06
49	Bo Jackson	1.00	.70	.40
50	Ron Guidry	.10	.08	.04
51	Bill Doran	.08	.06	.03
52	Wally Joyner	.40	.30	.15
53	Terry Pendleton	.08	.06	.03
54	Marty Barrett	.08	.06	.03
55	Andres Galarraga	.15	.11	.06
56	Larry Herndon	.05	.04	.02
57	Kevin Mitchell	.08	.06	.03
58	Greg Gagne	.05	.04	.02
59	Keith Hernandez	.15	.11	.06
60	John Kruk	.10	.08	.04
61	Mike LaValliere	.08	.06	.03
62	Cal Ripken	.30	.25	.12
63	Ivan Calderon	.08	.06	.03
64	Alvin Davis	.10	.08	.04
65	Luis Polonia	.08	.06	.03
66	Robin Yount	.20	.15	.08
67	Juan Samuel	.12	.09	.05
68	Andres Thomas	.05	.04	.02
69	Jeff Musselman	.05	.04	.02
70	Jerry Mumphrey	.05	.04	.02
71	Joe Carter	.12	.09	.05
72	Mike Scioscia	.05	.04	.02
73	Pete Incaviglia	.10	.08	.04
74	Barry Larkin	.15	.11	.06
75	Frank White	.08	.06	.03
76	Willie Randolph	.08	.06	.03
77	Kevin Bass	.05	.04	.02
78	Brian Downing	.08	.06	.03
79	Willie McGee	.10	.08	.04
80	Ellis Burks	.40	.30	.15
81	Hubie Brooks	.08	.06	.03
82	Darrell Evans	.08	.06	.03
83	Robby Thompson	.05	.04	.02
84	Kent Hrbek	.15	.11	.06
85	Ron Darling	.12	.09	.05
86	Stan Jefferson	.05	.04	.02
87	Teddy Higuera	.10	.08	.04
88	Mike Schmidt	.30	.25	.12
89	Barry Bonds	.15	.11	.06
90	Jim Presley	.08	.06	.03
91	Orel Hershiser	.25	.20	.10
92	Jesse Barfield	.10	.08	.04
93	Tom Candiotti	.05	.04	.02
94	Bret Saberhagen	.12	.09	.05
95	Jose Uribe	.05	.04	.02
96	Tom Browning	.10	.08	.04
97	Johnny Ray	.08	.06	.03
98	Mike Morgan	.05	.04	.02
100	Jim Sundberg	.05	.04	.02
101	Roger McDowell	.08	.06	.03
102	Randy Ready	.05	.04	.02

		MT	NR MT	EX
103	Mike Gallego	.05	.04	.02
104	Steve Buechele	.05	.04	.02
105	Greg Walker	.08	.06	.03
106	Jose Lind	.12	.09	.05
107	Steve Trout	.05	.04	.02
108	Rick Rhoden	.08	.06	.03
109	Jim Pankovits	.05	.04	.02
110	Ken Griffey	.08	.06	.03
111	Danny Cox	.08	.06	.03
112	Franklin Stubbs	.05	.04	.02
113	Lloyd Moseby	.08	.06	.03
114	Mel Hall	.08	.06	.03
115	Kevin Seitzer	.25	.20	.10
116	Tim Raines	.25	.20	.10
117	Juan Castillo	.05	.04	.02
118	Roger Clemens	.50	.40	.20
119	Mike Aldrete	.08	.06	.03
120	Mario Soto	.05	.04	.02
121	Jack Howell	.05	.04	.02
122	Rick Schu	.05	.04	.02
123	Jeff Robinson	.10	.08	.04
124	Doug Drabek	.08	.06	.03
125	Henry Cotto	.05	.04	.02
126	Checklist 89-176	.05	.04	.02
127	Gary Gaetti	.12	.09	.05
128	Rick Sutcliffe	.10	.08	.04
129	Howard Johnson	.08	.06	.03
130	Chris Brown	.08	.06	.03
131	Dave Henderson	.08	.06	.03
132	Curt Wilkerson	.05	.04	.02
133	Mike Marshall	.10	.08	.04
134	Kelly Gruber	.05	.04	.02
135	Julio Franco	.10	.08	.04
136	Kurt Stillwell	.12	.09	.05
137	Donnie Hill	.05	.04	.02
138	Mike Pagliarulo	.10	.08	.04
139	Von Hayes	.08	.06	.03
140	Mike Scott	.10	.08	.04
141	Bob Kipper	.05	.04	.02
142	Harold Reynolds	.08	.06	.03
143	Bob Brenly	.05	.04	.02
144	Dave Concepcion	.08	.06	.03
145	Devon White	.12	.09	.05
146	Jeff Stone	.05	.04	.02
147	Chet Lemon	.05	.04	.02
148	Ozzie Virgil	.05	.04	.02
149	Todd Worrell	.10	.08	.04
150	Mitch Webster	.05	.04	.02
151	Rob Deer	.08	.06	.03
152	Rich Gedman	.08	.06	.03
153	Andre Dawson	.15	.11	.06
154	Mike Davis	.05	.04	.02
155	Nelson Liriano	.08	.06	.03
156	Greg Swindell	.10	.08	.04
157	George Brett	.30	.25	.12
158	Kevin McReynolds	.15	.11	.06
159	Brian Fisher	.08	.06	.03
160	Mike Kingery	.05	.04	.02
161	Tony Gwynn	.25	.20	.10
162	Don Baylor	.10	.08	.04
163	Jerry Browne	.05	.04	.02
164	Dan Pasqua	.08	.06	.03
165	Rickey Henderson	.25	.20	.10
166	Brett Butler	.08	.06	.03
167	Nick Esasky	.05	.04	.02
168	Kirk McCaskill	.05	.04	.02
169	Fred Lynn	.10	.08	.04
170	Jack Morris	.12	.09	.05
171	Pedro Guerrero	.12	.09	.05
172	Dave Stieb	.10	.08	.04
173	Pat Tabler	.08	.06	.03
174	Floyd Bannister	.05	.04	.02
175	Rafael Belliard	.05	.04	.02
176	Mark Langston	.10	.08	.04
177	Greg Mathews	.08	.06	.03
178	Claudell Washington	.05	.04	.02
179	Mark McGwire	1.00	.70	.40
180	Bert Blyleven	.10	.08	.04
181	Jim Rice	.20	.15	.08
182	Mookie Wilson	.08	.06	.03
183	Willie Fraser	.05	.04	.02
184	Andy Van Slyke	.10	.08	.04
185	Matt Nokes	.10	.08	.04
186	Eddie Whitson	.05	.04	.02
187	Tony Fernandez	.10	.08	.04
188	Rick Reuschel	.08	.06	.03
189	Ken Phelps	.05	.04	.02
190	Juan Nieves	.08	.06	.03
191	Kirk Gibson	.20	.15	.08
192	Glenn Davis	.15	.11	.06
193	Zane Smith	.05	.04	.02

		MT	NR MT	EX
194	Jose DeLeon	.08	.06	.03
195	Gary Ward	.05	.04	.02
196	Pascual Perez	.05	.04	.02
197	Carlton Fisk	.12	.09	.05
198	Oddibe McDowell	.08	.06	.03
199	Mark Gubicza	.10	.08	.04
200	Glenn Hubbard	.05	.04	.02
201	Frank Viola	.15	.11	.06
202	Jody Reed	.12	.09	.05
203	Len Dykstra	.08	.06	.03
204	Dick Schofield	.05	.04	.02
205	Sid Bream	.05	.04	.02
206	Guillermo Hernandez	.05	.04	.02
207	Keith Moreland	.05	.04	.02
208	Mark Eichhorn	.05	.04	.02
209	Rene Gonzales	.08	.06	.03
210	Dave Valle	.05	.04	.02
211	Tom Brunansky	.10	.08	.04
212	Charles Hudson	.05	.04	.02
213	John Farrell	.10	.08	.04
214	Jeff Treadway	.12	.09	.05
215	Eddie Murray	.25	.20	.10
216	Checklist 177-264	.05	.04	.02
217	Greg Brock	.08	.06	.03
218	John Shelby	.05	.04	.02
219	Craig Reynolds	.05	.04	.02
220	Dion James	.05	.04	.02
221	Carney Lansford	.08	.06	.03
222	Juan Berenguer	.05	.04	.02
223	Luis Rivera	.08	.06	.03
224	Harold Baines	.12	.09	.05
225	Shawon Dunston	.08	.06	.03
226	Luis Aguayo	.05	.04	.02
227	Pete O'Brien	.08	.06	.03
228	Ozzie Smith	.12	.09	.05
229	Don Mattingly	1.50	1.25	.60
230	Danny Tartabull	.15	.11	.06
231	Andy Allanson	.05	.04	.02
232	John Franco	.08	.06	.03
233	Mike Greenwell	.80	.60	.30
234	Bob Ojeda	.08	.06	.03
235	Chili Davis	.08	.06	.03
236	Mike Dunne	.12	.09	.05
237	Jim Morrison	.05	.04	.02
238	Carmelo Martinez	.05	.04	.02
239	Ernie Whitt	.05	.04	.02
240	Scott Garrelts	.05	.04	.02
241	Mike Moore	.05	.04	.02
242	Dave Parker	.10	.08	.04
243	Tim Laudner	.05	.04	.02
244	Bill Wegman	.05	.04	.02
245	Bob Horner	.08	.06	.03
246	Rafael Santana	.05	.04	.02
247	Alfredo Griffin	.05	.04	.02
248	Mark Bailey	.05	.04	.02
249	Ron Gant	.12	.09	.05
250	Bryn Smith	.05	.04	.02
251	Lance Johnson	.10	.08	.04
252	Sam Horn	.10	.08	.04
253	Darryl Strawberry	.40	.30	.15
254	Chuck Finley	.05	.04	.02
255	Darnell Coles	.08	.06	.03
256	Mike Henneman	.10	.08	.04
257	Andy Hawkins	.08	.06	.03
258	Jim Clancy	.08	.06	.03
259	Atlee Hammaker	.05	.04	.02
260	Glenn Wilson	.05	.04	.02
261	Larry McWilliams	.05	.04	.02
262	Jack Clark	.12	.09	.05
263	Walt Weiss	.80	.60	.30
264	Gene Larkin	.08	.06	.03

1988 Topps Coins

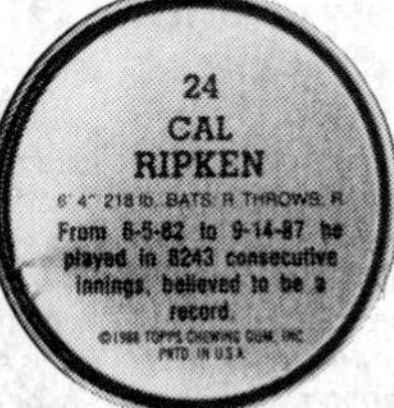

This edition of 60 lightweight metal coins is similar in design to Topps' 1964 set. The 1988 coins are 1 1/2" in diameter and feature full-color player closeups under crimped edges in silver, gold and pink. Curved under the photo is a red and white player name banner pinned by two gold stars. Coin backs list the coin number, player name, personal information and career summary in black letters on a silver background.

		MT	NR MT	EX
Complete Set:		8.00	6.00	3.25
Common Player:		.10	.08	.04
1	George Bell	.25	.20	.10
2	Roger Clemens	.40	.30	.15
3	Mark McGwire	.60	.45	.25
4	Wade Boggs	.70	.50	.30
5	Harold Baines	.15	.11	.06
6	Ivan Calderon	.10	.08	.04
7	Jose Canseco	.80	.60	.30
8	Joe Carter	.15	.11	.06
9	Jack Clark	.15	.11	.06
10	Alvin Davis	.15	.11	.06
11	Dwight Evans	.15	.11	.06
12	Tony Fernandez	.15	.11	.06
13	Gary Gaetti	.15	.11	.06
14	Mike Greenwell	.40	.30	.15
15	Charlie Hough	.10	.08	.04
16	Wally Joyner	.30	.25	.12
17	Jimmy Key	.10	.08	.04
18	Mark Langston	.15	.11	.06
19	Don Mattingly	1.00	.70	.40
20	Paul Molitor	.15	.11	.06
21	Jack Morris	.15	.11	.06
22	Eddie Murray	.20	.15	.08
23	Kirby Puckett	.25	.20	.10
24	Cal Ripken	.25	.20	.10
25	Bret Saberhagen	.15	.11	.06
26	Ruben Sierra	.15	.11	.06
27	Cory Snyder	.15	.11	.06
28	Terry Steinbach	.15	.11	.06
29	Danny Tartabull	.15	.11	.06
30	Alan Trammell	.15	.11	.06
31	Devon White	.15	.11	.06
32	Robin Yount	.15	.11	.06
33	Andre Dawson	.15	.11	.06
34	Steve Bedrosian	.15	.11	.06
35	Benny Santiago	.15	.11	.06
36	Tony Gwynn	.25	.20	.10
37	Bobby Bonilla	.15	.11	.06
38	Will Clark	.30	.25	.12
39	Eric Davis	.40	.30	.15
40	Mike Dunne	.15	.11	.06
41	John Franco	.10	.08	.04
42	Dwight Gooden	.40	.30	.15
43	Pedro Guerrero	.15	.11	.06
44	Dion James	.10	.08	.04
45	John Kruk	.15	.11	.06
46	Jeffrey Leonard	.10	.08	.04
47	Carmelo Martinez	.10	.08	.04
48	Dale Murphy	.30	.25	.12
49	Tim Raines	.20	.15	.08
50	Nolan Ryan	.20	.15	.08
51	Juan Samuel	.15	.11	.06
52	Ryne Sandberg	.20	.15	.08
53	Mike Schmidt	.30	.25	.12
54	Mike Scott	.15	.11	.06
55	Ozzie Smith	.15	.11	.06
56	Darryl Strawberry	.40	.30	.15
57	Rick Sutcliffe	.15	.11	.06
58	Fernando Valenzuela	.15	.11	.06
59	Tim Wallach	.15	.11	.06
60	Todd Worrell	.15	.11	.06

1988 Topps Gallery Of Champions

These bronze replicas are exact reproductions at one-quarter scale of Topps official 1988 cards, both front and back. The set includes 12 three-dimensional raised metal cards packaged in a velvet-lined case that bears the title of the set in gold embossed letters. A deluxe limited edition of the set (1,000) was produced in sterling silver and an economy version in aluminum.

Topps first issued the metal mini-cards in 1984 (the initial set was called Gallery of Immortals). Since 1985, the metal cards have honored award-winning players from the previous season. A Mark McGwire pewter replica was given as a premium to dealers ordering the aluminum, bronze and silver sets ($50 value). The special pewter card is distinguished from the regular issue by a diagonal name banner in the lower right corner (regular) replicas have a rectangular name banner printer parallel to the lower edge of the card). A 1955 Topps Duke Snider bronze (value $10) was available to dealers purchasing cases of the 1988 Topps Traded sets.

		MT	NR MT	EX
Complete Aluminum Set:		20.00	15.00	8.00
Complete Bronze Set:		125.00	94.00	50.00
Complete Silver Set:		500.00	375.00	200.00
(1a)	Steve Bedrosian (aluminum)	.70	.50	.30
(1b)	Steve Bedrosian (bronze)	7.50	5.75	3.00
(1c)	Steve Bedrosian (silver)	20.00	15.00	8.00
(2a)	George Bell (aluminum)	1.00	.70	.40
(2b)	George Bell (bronze)	10.00	7.50	4.00
(2c)	George Bell (silver)	20.00	15.00	8.00
(3a)	Wade Boggs (aluminum)	3.00	2.25	1.25
(3b)	Wade Boggs (bronze)	25.00	18.50	10.00
(3c)	Wade Boggs (silver)	125.00	94.00	50.00
(4a)	Jack Clark (aluminum)	1.00	.70	.40
(4b)	Jack Clark (bronze)	10.00	7.50	4.00
(4c)	Jack Clark (silver)	20.00	15.00	8.00
(5a)	Roger Clemens (aluminum)	2.00	1.50	.80
(5b)	Roger Clemens (bronze)	20.00	15.00	8.00
(5c)	Roger Clemens (silver)	90.00	67.00	36.00
(6a)	Andre Dawson (aluminum)	1.00	.70	.40
(6b)	Andre Dawson (bronze)	10.00	7.50	4.00
(6c)	Andre Dawson (silver)	20.00	15.00	8.00
(7a)	Tony Gwynn (aluminum)	1.25	.90	.50
(7b)	Tony Gwynn (bronze)	12.00	9.00	4.75
(7c)	Tony Gwynn (silver)	50.00	37.00	20.00
(8a)	Mark Langston (aluminum)	.70	.50	.30
(8b)	Mark Langston (bronze)	7.50	5.75	3.00
(8c)	Mark Langston (silver)	20.00	15.00	8.00
(9a)	Mark McGwire (aluminum)	3.00	2.25	1.25
(9b)	Mark McGwire (bronze)	25.00	18.50	10.00
(9c)	Mark McGwire (silver)	125.00	94.00	50.00
(10a)	Dave Righetti (aluminum)	1.00	.70	.40
(10b)	Dave Righetti (bronze)	10.00	7.50	4.00
(10c)	Dave Righetti (silver)	20.00	15.00	8.00
(11a)	Nolan Ryan (aluminum)	1.00	.70	.40
(11b)	Nolan Ryan (bronze)	10.00	7.50	4.00
(11c)	Nolan Ryan (silver)	20.00	15.00	8.00
(12a)	Benny Santiago (aluminum)	1.00	.70	.40
(12b)	Benny Santiago (bronze)	10.00	7.50	4.00
(12c)	Benny Santiago (silver)	20.00	15.00	8.00

1988 Topps Glossy Rookies

The Topps 1988 Rookies special insert cards follow the same basic design as the All-Star inserts. The set consists of 22 standard-size cards. Large, glossy color player photos are printed on a white background below

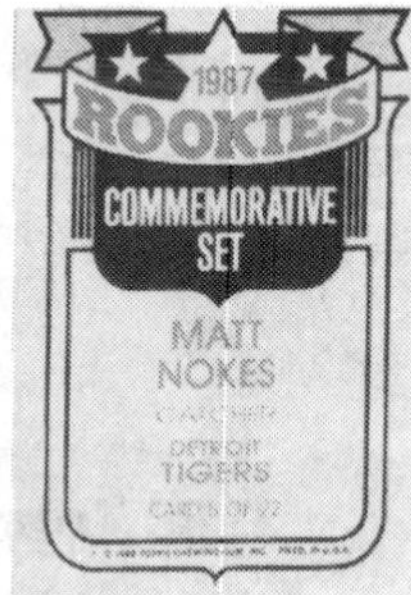

a red, yellow and blue "1987 Rookies" banner. A red and yellow player name appears beneath the photo. Red, white and blue card backs bear the title of the special insert set, the Rookies logo emblem, player name and card number.

		MT	NR MT	EX
Complete Set:		10.00	7.50	4.00
Common Player:		.20	.15	.08
1	Billy Ripken	.30	.25	.12
2	Ellis Burks	1.50	1.25	.60
3	Mike Greenwell	2.00	1.50	.80
4	DeWayne Buice	.20	.15	.08
5	Devon White	.40	.30	.15
6	Fred Manrique	.20	.15	.08
7	Mike Henneman	.40	.30	.15
8	Matt Nokes	.60	.45	.25
9	Kevin Seitzer	.80	.60	.30
10	B.J. Surhoff	.40	.30	.15
11	Casey Candaele	.20	.15	.08
12	Randy Myers	.60	.45	.25
13	Mark McGwire	1.50	1.25	.60
14	Luis Polonia	.25	.20	.10
15	Terry Steinbach	.40	.30	.15
16	Mike Dunne	.40	.30	.15
17	Al Pedrique	.20	.15	.08
18	Benny Santiago	.70	.50	.30
19	Kelly Downs	.40	.30	.15
20	Joe Magrane	.40	.30	.15
21	Jerry Browne	.20	.15	.08
22	Jeff Musselman	.25	.20	.10

1988 Topps Mini League Leaders

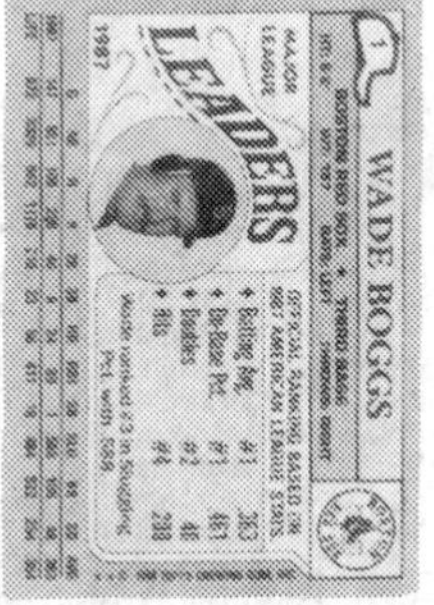

The third consecutive issue of Topps mini-cards (2-1/8" by 3") includes 77 cards spotlighting the top five ranked pitchers and batters. This set is unique in that it was the first time Topps included full-color player photos on both the front and back. Glossy action shots on the card fronts fade into a white border with a Topps logo in an upper corner. The player's name is printed in bold black letters beneath the photo. Horizontal reverses feature circular player photos on a blue and white background with the card number, player name, personal information, 1987 ranking and lifetime/1987 stats printed in red, black and yellow lettering.

		MT	NR MT	EX
Complete Set:		6.00	4.50	2.50
Common Player:		.09	.07	.04
1	Wade Boggs	.80	.60	.30
2	Roger Clemens	.60	.45	.25
3	Dwight Evans	.15	.11	.06
4	DeWayne Buice	.09	.07	.04
5	Brian Downing	.09	.07	.04
6	Wally Joyner	.60	.45	.25
7	Ivan Calderon	.15	.11	.06
8	Carlton Fisk	.20	.15	.08
9	Gary Redus	.09	.07	.04
10	Darrell Evans	.15	.11	.06
11	Jack Morris	.25	.20	.10
12	Alan Trammell	.30	.25	.12
13	Lou Whitaker	.20	.15	.08
14	Bret Saberhagen	.20	.15	.08
15	Kevin Seitzer	.50	.40	.20
16	Danny Tartabull	.25	.20	.10
17	Willie Wilson	.15	.11	.06
18	Teddy Higuera	.15	.11	.06
19	Paul Molitor	.20	.15	.08
20	Dan Plesac	.15	.11	.06
21	Robin Yount	.25	.20	.10
22	Kent Hrbek	.25	.20	.10
23	Kirby Puckett	.35	.25	.14
24	Jeff Reardon	.15	.11	.06
25	Frank Viola	.20	.15	.08
26	Rickey Henderson	.60	.45	.25
27	Don Mattingly	1.25	.90	.50
28	Willie Randolph	.15	.11	.06
29	Dave Righetti	.20	.15	.08
30	Jose Canseco	1.00	.70	.40
31	Mark McGwire	.90	.70	.35
32	Dave Stewart	.09	.07	.04
33	Phil Bradley	.15	.11	.06
34	Mark Langston	.15	.11	.06
35	Harold Reynolds	.09	.07	.04
36	Charlie Hough	.09	.07	.04
37	George Bell	.25	.20	.10
38	Tom Henke	.09	.07	.04
39	Jimmy Key	.15	.11	.06
40	Dion James	.09	.07	.04
41	Dale Murphy	.50	.40	.20
42	Zane Smith	.09	.07	.04
43	Andre Dawson	.25	.20	.10
44	Lee Smith	.09	.07	.04
45	Rick Sutcliffe	.15	.11	.06
46	Eric Davis	.60	.45	.25
47	John Franco	.15	.11	.06
48	Dave Parker	.20	.15	.08
49	Billy Hatcher	.09	.07	.04
50	Nolan Ryan	.60	.45	.25
51	Mike Scott	.20	.15	.08
52	Pedro Guerrero	.20	.15	.08
53	Orel Hershiser	.30	.25	.12
54	Fernando Valenzuela	.25	.20	.10
55	Bob Welch	.15	.11	.06
56	Andres Galarraga	.25	.20	.10
57	Tim Raines	.30	.25	.12
58	Tim Wallach	.15	.11	.06
59	Len Dykstra	.15	.11	.06
60	Dwight Gooden	.60	.45	.25
61	Howard Johnson	.15	.11	.06
62	Roger McDowell	.15	.11	.06
63	Darryl Strawberry	.50	.40	.20
64	Steve Bedrosian	.15	.11	.06
65	Shane Rawley	.09	.07	.04
66	Juan Samuel	.20	.15	.08
67	Mike Schmidt	.50	.40	.20
68	Mike Dunne	.15	.11	.06
69	Jack Clark	.25	.20	.10
70	Vince Coleman	.20	.15	.08
71	Willie McGee	.15	.11	.06
72	Ozzie Smith	.20	.15	.08
73	Todd Worrell	.15	.11	.06
74	Tony Gwynn	.40	.30	.15
75	John Kruk	.20	.15	.08
76	Rick Rueschel	.15	.11	.06
77	Checklist	.09	.07	.04

The values quoted are intended to reflect the market price.

1988 Topps Stickercards

Actually a part of the 1988 Topps Stickers issue, this set consists of 67 cards. The cards are the backs of the peel-off stickers and measure 2-1/8" by 3". To determine total value, combine the prices of the stickers (found in the 1988 Topps Stickers checklist) on the stickercard front with the value assigned to the stickercard in the following checklist.

		MT	NR MT	EX
Complete Set:		2.00	1.50	.80
Common Player:		.02	.02	.01
1	Jack Clark	.03	.02	.01
2	Andres Galarraga	.03	.02	.01
3	Keith Hernandez	.04	.03	.02
4	Tom Herr	.02	.02	.01
5	Juan Samuel	.03	.02	.01
6	Ryne Sandberg	.04	.03	.02
7	Terry Pendleton	.02	.02	.01
8	Mike Schmidt	.06	.05	.02
9	Tim Wallach	.02	.02	.01
10	Hubie Brooks	.02	.02	.01
11	Shawon Dunston	.02	.02	.01
12	Ozzie Smith	.03	.02	.01
13	Andre Dawson	.04	.03	.02
14	Eric Davis	.06	.05	.02
15	Pedro Guerrero	.03	.02	.01
16	Tony Gwynn	.05	.04	.02
17	Jeffrey Leonard	.02	.02	.01
18	Dale Murphy	.06	.05	.02
19	Dave Parker	.03	.02	.01
20	Tim Raines	.04	.03	.02
21	Darryl Strawberry	.06	.05	.02
22	Gary Carter	.04	.03	.02
23	Jody Davis	.02	.02	.01
24	Ozzie Virgil	.02	.02	.01
25	Dwight Gooden	.08	.06	.03
26	Mike Scott	.02	.02	.01
27	Rick Sutcliffe	.02	.02	.01
28	Sid Fernandez	.02	.02	.01
29	Neal Heaton	.02	.02	.01
30	Fernando Valenzuela	.03	.02	.01
31	Steve Bedrosian	.02	.02	.01
32	John Franco	.02	.02	.01
33	Lee Smith	.02	.02	.01
34	Wally Joyner	.06	.05	.02
35	Don Mattingly	.12	.09	.05
36	Mark McGwire	.08	.06	.03
37	Willie Randolph	.02	.02	.01
38	Lou Whitaker	.03	.02	.01
39	Frank White	.02	.02	.01
40	Wade Boggs	.10	.08	.04
41	George Brett	.06	.05	.02
42	Paul Molitor	.02	.02	.01
43	Tony Fernandez	.02	.02	.01
44	Cal Ripken	.06	.05	.02
45	Alan Trammell	.04	.03	.02
46	Jesse Barfield	.03	.02	.01
47	George Bell	.04	.03	.02
48	Jose Canseco	.10	.08	.04
49	Joe Carter	.03	.02	.01
50	Dwight Evans	.02	.02	.01
51	Rickey Henderson	.05	.04	.02
52	Kirby Puckett	.05	.04	.02
53	Cory Snyder	.03	.02	.01
54	Dave Winfield	.04	.03	.02
55	Terry Kennedy	.02	.02	.01
56	Matt Nokes	.03	.02	.01
57	B.J. Surhoff	.02	.02	.01
58	Roger Clemens	.08	.06	.03
59	Jack Morris	.03	.02	.01
60	Bret Saberhagen	.03	.02	.01
61	Ron Guidry	.03	.02	.01
62	Bruce Hurst	.02	.02	.01
63	Mark Langston	.02	.02	.01
64	Tom Henke	.02	.02	.01
65	Dan Plesac	.02	.02	.01
66	Dave Righetti	.03	.02	.01
67	Checklist	.02	.02	.01

1988 Topps Stickers

This set of 313 stickers (on 198 cards) offers a new addition for 1988 - 66 different players are pictured on the reverse of the sticker cards. The stickers come in two sizes (2-1/8" by 3" or 1-1/2" by 2-1/8"). Larger stickers fill an entire card, smaller ones are attached in pairs. A 36-page sticker yearbook produced by Topps has a designated space inside for each sticker,with one page per team and special pages of 1987 Highlights, World Series, All-Stars and Future Stars. No printing appears on the full-color action shot stickers except for a small black number in the lower left corner. Sticker card backs carry a Super Star header, player close-up and stats. Stickers were sold in packages of five (with gum) for 25 cents per pack. Unlike the 1987 Topps Stickers set, different pairings can be found, rather than the same two players/numbers always sharing the same sticker. To determine total value, combine the value of the stickercard (found in the 1988 Topps Stickercard checklist) with the values assigned the stickers in the following checklist.

		MT	NR MT	EX
Complete Set:		15.00	11.00	6.00
Common Player:		.02	.02	.01
Sticker Album:		.60	.45	.25
1	1987 Highlights (Mark McGwire)	.20	.15	.08
2	1987 Highlights (Benny Santiago)	.04	.03	.02
3	1987 Highlights (Don Mattingly)	.25	.20	.10
4	1987 Highlights (Vince Coleman)	.04	.03	.02
5	1987 Highlights (Bob Boone)	.02	.02	.01
6	1987 Highlights (Steve Bedrosian)	.02	.02	.01
7	1987 Highlights (Nolan Ryan)	.08	.06	.03
8	1987 Highlights (Darrell Evans)	.02	.02	.01
9	1987 Highlights (Mike Schmidt)	.10	.08	.04
10	1987 Highlights (Don Baylor)	.04	.03	.02
11	1987 Highlights (Eddie Murray)	.08	.06	.03
12	1987 Highlights (Juan Beniquez)	.02	.02	.01
13	1987 Championship Series (John Tudor)	.04	.03	.02
14	1987 Championship Series (Jeff Reardon)	.04	.03	.02
15	1987 Championship Series (Tom Brunansky)	.06	.05	.02
16	1987 Championship Series (Jeffrey Leonard)	.04	.03	.02
17	1987 Championship Series (Gary Gaetti)	.10	.08	.04
18	1987 Championship Series (Cardinals Celebrate)	.04	.03	.02
19	1987 World Series (Danny Gladden)	.04	.03	.02

		MT	NR MT	EX
20	1987 World Series (Bert Blyleven)	.08	.06	.03
21	1987 World Series (John Tudor)	.06	.05	.02
22	1987 World Series (Tom Lawless)	.04	.03	.02
23	1987 World Series (Curt Ford)	.04	.03	.02
24	1987 World Series (Kent Hrbek)	.12	.09	.05
25	1987 World Series (Frank Viola)	.10	.08	.04
26	Dave Smith	.02	.02	.01
27	Jim Deshaies	.02	.02	.01
28	Billy Hatcher	.02	.02	.01
29	Kevin Bass	.02	.02	.01
30	Mike Scott	.04	.03	.02
31	Danny Walling	.02	.02	.01
32	Alan Ashby	.02	.02	.01
33	Ken Caminiti	.02	.02	.01
34	Bill Doran	.02	.02	.01
35	Glenn Davis	.12	.09	.05
36	Ozzie Virgil	.02	.02	.01
37	Ken Oberkfell	.02	.02	.01
38	Ken Griffey	.02	.02	.01
39	Albert Hall	.02	.02	.01
40	Zane Smith	.02	.02	.01
41	Andres Thomas	.02	.02	.01
42	Dion James	.02	.02	.01
43	Jim Acker	.02	.02	.01
44	Tom Glavine	.04	.03	.02
45	Dale Murphy	.25	.20	.10
46	Jack Clark	.10	.08	.04
47	Vince Coleman	.04	.03	.02
48	Ricky Horton	.02	.02	.01
49	Terry Pendleton	.02	.02	.01
50	Tom Herr	.02	.02	.01
51	Joe Magrane	.04	.03	.02
52	Tony Pena	.02	.02	.01
53	Ozzie Smith	.04	.03	.02
54	Todd Worrell	.04	.03	.02
55	Willie McGee	.10	.08	.04
56	Andre Dawson	.15	.11	.06
57	Ryne Sandberg	.06	.05	.02
58	Keith Moreland	.02	.02	.01
59	Greg Maddux	.04	.03	.02
60	Jody Davis	.02	.02	.01
61	Rick Sutcliffe	.08	.06	.03
62	Jamie Moyer	.02	.02	.01
63	Leon Durham	.02	.02	.01
64	Lee Smith	.02	.02	.01
65	Shawon Dunston	.02	.02	.01
66	Franklin Stubbs	.02	.02	.01
67	Mike Scioscia	.02	.02	.01
68	Orel Hershiser	.06	.05	.02
69	Mike Marshall	.04	.03	.02
70	Fernando Valenzuela	.15	.11	.06
71	Mickey Hatcher	.02	.02	.01
72	Matt Young	.02	.02	.01
73	Bob Welch	.04	.03	.02
74	Steve Sax	.04	.03	.02
75	Pedro Guerrero	.12	.09	.05
76	Tim Raines	.15	.11	.06
77	Casey Candaele	.02	.02	.01
78	Mike Fitzgerald	.02	.02	.01
79	Andres Galarraga	.04	.03	.02
80	Neal Heaton	.02	.02	.01
81	Hubie Brooks	.02	.02	.01
82	Floyd Youmans	.02	.02	.01
83	Herm Winningham	.02	.02	.01
84	Denny Martinez	.02	.02	.01
85	Tim Wallach	.08	.06	.03
86	Jeffrey Leonard	.04	.03	.02
87	Will Clark	.10	.08	.04
88	Kevin Mitchell	.04	.03	.02
89	Mike Aldrete	.02	.02	.01
90	Scott Garrelts	.02	.02	.01
91	Jose Uribe	.02	.02	.01
92	Bob Brenly	.02	.02	.01
93	Robby Thompson	.02	.02	.01
94	Don Robinson	.02	.02	.01
95	Candy Maldonado	.04	.03	.02
96	Darryl Strawberry	.25	.20	.10
97	Keith Hernandez	.06	.05	.02
98	Ron Darling	.04	.03	.02
99	Howard Johnson	.04	.03	.02
100	Roger McDowell	.02	.02	.01
101	Dwight Gooden	.30	.25	.12
102	Kevin McReynolds	.04	.03	.02
103	Sid Fernandez	.02	.02	.01
104	Dave Magadan	.04	.03	.02
105	Gary Carter	.08	.06	.03
106	Carmelo Martinez	.02	.02	.01
107	Eddie Whitson	.02	.02	.01
108	Tim Flannery	.02	.02	.01
109	Stan Jefferson	.02	.02	.01
110	John Kruk	.10	.08	.04
111	Chris Brown	.04	.03	.02

		MT	NR MT	EX
112	Benny Santiago	.04	.03	.02
113	Garry Templeton	.02	.02	.01
114	Lance McCullers	.02	.02	.01
115	Tony Gwynn	.20	.15	.08
116	Steve Bedrosian	.06	.05	.02
117	Von Hayes	.02	.02	.01
118	Kevin Gross	.02	.02	.01
119	Bruce Ruffin	.02	.02	.01
120	Juan Samuel	.04	.03	.02
121	Shane Rawley	.02	.02	.01
122	Chris James	.04	.03	.02
123	Lance Parrish	.04	.03	.02
124	Glenn Wilson	.02	.02	.01
125	Mike Schmidt	.25	.20	.10
126	Andy Van Slyke	.08	.06	.03
127	Jose Lind	.04	.03	.02
128	Al Pedrique	.02	.02	.01
129	Bobby Bonilla	.04	.03	.02
130	Sed Bream	.02	.02	.01
131	Mike LaValliere	.02	.02	.01
132	Mike Dunne	.04	.03	.02
133	Jeff Robinson	.02	.02	.01
134	Doug Drabek	.02	.02	.01
135	Barry Bonds	.10	.08	.04
136	Dave Parker	.08	.06	.03
137	Nick Esasky	.02	.02	.01
138	Buddy Bell	.02	.02	.01
139	Kal Daniels	.04	.03	.02
140	Barry Larkin	.04	.03	.02
141	Eric Davis	.25	.20	.10
142	John Franco	.02	.02	.01
143	Bo Diaz	.02	.02	.01
144	Ron Oester	.02	.02	.01
145	Dennis Rasmussen	.02	.02	.01
146	Eric Davis	.40	.30	.15
147	Ryne Sandberg	.30	.25	.12
148	Andre Dawson	.20	.15	.08
149	Mike Schmidt	.40	.30	.15
150	Jack Clark	.20	.15	.08
151	Darryl Strawberry	.40	.30	.15
152	Gary Carter	.30	.25	.12
153	Ozzie Smith	.20	.15	.08
154	Mike Scott	.20	.15	.08
155	Rickey Henderson	.40	.30	.15
156	Don Mattingly	.90	.70	.35
157	Wade Boggs	.60	.45	.25
158	George Bell	.30	.25	.12
159	Dave Winfield	.30	.25	.12
160	Cal Ripken	.40	.30	.15
161	Terry Kennedy	.15	.11	.06
162	Willie Randolph	.15	.11	.06
163	Bret Saberhagen	.25	.20	.10
164	Mark McGwire	.35	.25	.14
165	Tony Phillips	.02	.02	.01
166	Jay Howell	.02	.02	.01
167	Carney Lansford	.02	.02	.01
168	Dave Stewart	.02	.02	.01
169	Alfredo Griffin	.02	.02	.01
170	Dennis Eckersley	.04	.03	.02
171	Mike Davis	.02	.02	.01
172	Luis Polonia	.02	.02	.01
173	Jose Canseco	.60	.45	.25
174	Mike Witt	.06	.05	.02
175	Jack Howell	.02	.02	.01
176	Greg Minton	.02	.02	.01
177	Dick Schofield	.02	.02	.01
178	Gary Pettis	.02	.02	.01
179	Wally Joyner	.25	.20	.10
180	DeWayne Buice	.02	.02	.01
181	Brian Downing	.02	.02	.01
182	Bob Boone	.02	.02	.01
183	Devon White	.04	.03	.02
184	Jim Clancy	.02	.02	.01
185	Willie Upshaw	.02	.02	.01
186	Tom Henke	.02	.02	.01
187	Ernie Whitt	.02	.02	.01
188	George Bell	.20	.15	.08
189	Lloyd Moseby	.02	.02	.01
190	Jimmy Key	.02	.02	.01
191	Dave Stieb	.02	.02	.01
192	Jesse Barfield	.04	.03	.02
193	Tony Fernandez	.10	.08	.04
194	Paul Molitor	.06	.05	.02
195	Jim Gantner	.02	.02	.01
196	Teddy Higuera	.04	.03	.02
197	Glenn Braggs	.02	.02	.01
198	Rob Deer	.02	.02	.01
199	Dale Sveum	.02	.02	.01
200	Bill Wegman	.02	.02	.01
201	Robin Yount	.06	.05	.02
202	B.J. Surhoff	.04	.03	.02

		MT	NR MT	EX
203	Dan Plesac	.06	.05	.02
204	Pat Tabler	.04	.03	.02
205	Mel Hall	.02	.02	.01
206	Scott Bailes	.02	.02	.01
207	Julio Franco	.04	.03	.02
208	Cory Snyder	.06	.05	.02
209	Chris Bando	.02	.02	.01
210	Greg Swindell	.04	.03	.02
211	Brook Jacoby	.02	.02	.01
212	Brett Butler	.02	.02	.01
213	Joe Carter	.10	.08	.04
214	Mark Langston	.08	.06	.03
215	Rey Quinones	.02	.02	.01
216	Ed Nunez	.02	.02	.01
217	Jim Presley	.02	.02	.01
218	Phil Bradley	.04	.03	.02
219	Alvin Davis	.10	.08	.04
220	Dave Valle	.02	.02	.01
221	Harold Reynolds	.02	.02	.01
222	Scott Bradley	.02	.02	.01
223	Gary Matthews	.02	.02	.01
224	Eric Bell	.02	.02	.01
225	Terry Kennedy	.02	.02	.01
226	Dave Schmidt	.02	.02	.01
227	Billy Ripken	.04	.03	.02
228	Cal Ripken	.20	.15	.08
229	Ray Knight	.02	.02	.01
230	Larry Sheets	.02	.02	.01
231	Mike Boddicker	.02	.02	.01
232	Tom Niedenfuer	.02	.02	.01
233	Eddie Murray	.20	.15	.08
234	Ruben Sierra	.12	.09	.05
235	Steve Buechele	.02	.02	.01
236	Charlie Hough	.02	.02	.01
237	Oddibe McDowell	.02	.02	.01
238	Mike Stanley	.02	.02	.01
239	Pete Incaviglia	.04	.03	.02
240	Pete O'Brien	.02	.02	.01
241	Scott Fletcher	.02	.02	.01
242	Dale Mohorcic	.02	.02	.01
243	Larry Parrish	.04	.03	.02
244	Wade Boggs	.35	.25	.14
245	Dwight Evans	.04	.03	.02
246	Sam Horn	.04	.03	.02
247	Jim Rice	.06	.05	.02
248	Marty Barrett	.02	.02	.01
249	Mike Greenwell	.15	.11	.06
250	Ellis Burks	.10	.08	.04
251	Roger Clemens	.12	.09	.05
252	Rich Gedman	.02	.02	.01
253	Bruce Hurst	.06	.05	.02
254	Bret Saberhagen	.15	.11	.06
255	Frank White	.02	.02	.01
256	Dan Quisenberry	.02	.02	.01
257	Danny Tartabull	.06	.05	.02
258	Bo Jackson	.08	.06	.03
259	George Brett	.25	.20	.10
260	Charlie Leibrandt	.02	.02	.01
261	Kevin Seitzer	.10	.08	.04
262	Mark Gubicza	.04	.03	.02
263	Willie Wilson	.04	.03	.02
264	Frank Tanana	.02	.02	.01
265	Darrell Evans	.02	.02	.01
266	Bill Madlock	.04	.03	.02
267	Kirk Gibson	.06	.05	.02
268	Jack Morris	.12	.09	.05
269	Matt Nokes	.06	.05	.02
270	Lou Whitaker	.04	.03	.02
271	Eric King	.02	.02	.01
272	Jim Morrison	.02	.02	.01
273	Alan Trammell	.20	.15	.08
274	Kent Hrbek	.12	.09	.05
275	Tom Brunansky	.04	.03	.02
276	Bert Blyleven	.04	.03	.02
277	Gary Gaetti	.04	.03	.02
278	Tim Laudner	.04	.03	.02
279	Gene Larkin	.02	.02	.01
280	Jeff Reardon	.02	.02	.01
281	Danny Gladden	.02	.02	.01
282	Frank Viola	.04	.03	.02
283	Kirby Puckett	.20	.15	.08
284	Ozzie Guillen	.06	.05	.02
285	Ivan Calderon	.02	.02	.01
286	Donnie Hill	.02	.02	.01
287	Ken Williams	.04	.03	.02
288	Jim Winn	.02	.02	.01
289	Bob James	.02	.02	.01
290	Carlton Fisk	.04	.03	.02
291	Richard Dotson	.02	.02	.01
292	Greg Walker	.02	.02	.01
293	Harold Baines	.10	.08	.04
294	Willie Randolph	.06	.05	.02
295	Mike Pagliarulo	.04	.03	.02
296	Ron Guidry	.04	.03	.02
297	Rickey Henderson	.10	.08	.04
298	Rick Rhoden	.02	.02	.01
299	Don Mattingly	.70	.50	.30
300	Dave Righetti	.04	.03	.02
301	Claudell Washington	.02	.02	.01
302	Dave Winfield	.08	.06	.03
303	Gary Ward	.02	.02	.01
304	Al Pedrique	.02	.02	.01
305	Casey Candaele	.02	.02	.01
306	Kevin Seitzer	.10	.08	.04
307	Mike Dunne	.04	.03	.02
308	Jeff Musselman	.02	.02	.01
309	Mark McGwire	.20	.15	.08
310	Ellis Burks	.10	.08	.04
311	Matt Nokes	.06	.05	.02
312	Mike Greenwell	.15	.11	.06
313	Devon White	.04	.03	.02

1989 Topps

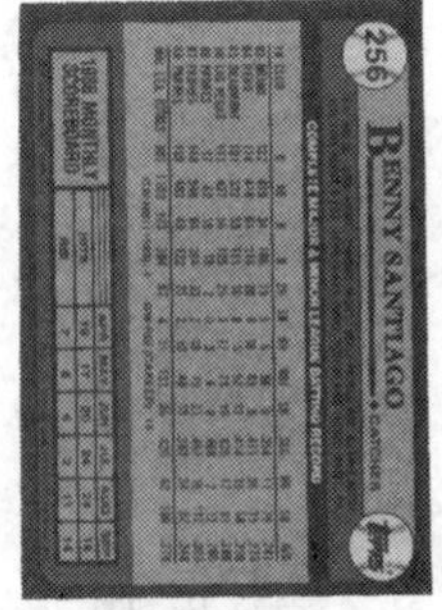

Ten top young players who led the June 1988 draft picks are featured on "#1 Draft Pick" cards in this full-color basic set of 792 standard-size baseball cards. An additional five cards salute 1989 Future Stars, 22 cards highlight All-Stars, seven contain Record Breakers, five are designated Turn Back The Clock, and six contain checklists. This set features the familiar white borders, but two inner photo corners (upper left and lower right) have been rounded off and the rectangular player name was replaced by a curved name banner in bright red or blue that leads to the team name in large script in the lower right corner. The card backs are printed in black on a red background and include personal information and complete minor and major league stats. Another new addition in this set is the special Monthly Scoreboard chart that lists monthly stats (April through September) in two of several categories (hits, run, home runs, stolen bases, RBIs, wins, strikeouts, games or saves).

	MT	NR MT	EX
Complete Set (792):	15.00	11.00	6.00
Common Player:	.03	.02	.01

		MT	NR MT	EX
1	George Bell (Record Breaker)	.08	.06	.03
2	Wade Boggs (Record Breaker)	.12	.09	.05
3	Gary Carter (Record Breaker)	.10	.08	.04
4	Andre Dawson (Record Breaker)	.08	.06	.03
5	Orel Hershiser (Record Breaker)	.10	.08	.04
6	Doug Jones (Record Breaker)	.06	.05	.02
7	Kevin McReynolds (Record Breaker)	.08	.06	.03
8	*Dave Eiland*(FC)	.03	.02	.01
9	Tim Teufel	.03	.02	.01
10	Andre Dawson	.15	.11	.06
11	Bruce Sutter	.08	.06	.03
12	Dale Sveum	.06	.05	.02
13	Doug Sisk	.03	.02	.01
14	Tom Kelly	.03	.02	.01
15	Robby Thompson	.06	.05	.02
16	Ron Robinson	.03	.02	.01
17	Brian Downing	.06	.05	.02

		MT	NR MT	EX
18	Rick Rhoden	.06	.05	.02
19	Greg Gagne	.03	.02	.01
20	Steve Bedrosian	.08	.06	.03
21	White Sox Leaders (Greg Walker)	.06	.05	.02
22	Tim Crews	.06	.05	.02
23	Mike Fitzgerald	.03	.02	.01
24	Larry Andersen	.03	.02	.01
25	Frank White	.06	.05	.02
26	Dale Mohorcic	.03	.02	.01
27	*Orestes Destrade*(FC)	.20	.15	.08
28	Mike Moore	.03	.02	.01
29	Kelly Gruber	.03	.02	.01
30	Doc Gooden	.08	.06	.03
31	Terry Francona	.03	.02	.01
32	Dennis Rasmussen	.08	.06	.03
33	B.J. Surhoff	.08	.06	.03
34	Ken Williams	.06	.05	.02
35	John Tudor	.08	.06	.03
36	Mitch Webster	.06	.05	.02
37	Bob Stanley	.03	.02	.01
38	Paul Runge	.03	.02	.01
39	Mike Maddux	.03	.02	.01
40	Steve Sax	.06	.05	.02
41	Terry Mulholland	.03	.02	.01
42	Jim Eppard(FC)	.08	.06	.03
43	Guillermo Hernandez	.06	.05	.02
44	Jim Snyder	.03	.02	.01
45	Kal Daniels	.03	.02	.01
46	Mark Portugal	.03	.02	.01
47	Carney Lansford	.06	.05	.02
48	Tim Burke	.03	.02	.01
49	*Craig Biggio*(FC)	.35	.25	.14
50	George Bell	.05	.04	.02
51	Angels Leaders (Mark McLemore)	.06	.05	.02
52	Bob Brenly	.03	.02	.01
53	Ruben Sierra	.15	.11	.06
54	Steve Trout	.03	.02	.01
55	Julio Franco	.08	.06	.03
56	Pat Tabler	.06	.05	.02
57	Alejandro Pena	.06	.05	.02
58	Lee Mazzilli	.06	.05	.02
59	Mark Davis	.03	.02	.01
60	Tom Brunansky	.06	.05	.02
61	Neil Allen	.03	.02	.01
62	Alfredo Griffin	.06	.05	.02
63	Mark Clear	.03	.02	.01
64	Alex Trevino	.03	.02	.01
65	Rick Reuschel	.08	.06	.03
66	Manny Trillo	.03	.02	.01
67	Dave Palmer	.03	.02	.01
68	Darrell Miller	.03	.02	.01
69	Jeff Ballard	.06	.05	.02
70	Mark McGwire	.25	.20	.10
71	Mike Boddicker	.06	.05	.02
72	John Moses	.03	.02	.01
73	Pascual Perez	.06	.05	.02
74	Nick Leyva	.03	.02	.01
75	Tom Henke	.06	.05	.02
76	*Terry Blocker*(FC)	.06	.05	.02
77	Doyle Alexander	.06	.05	.02
78	Jim Sundberg	.06	.05	.02
79	Scott Bankhead	.03	.02	.01
80	Cory Snyder	.15	.11	.06
81	Expos Leaders (Tim Raines)	.08	.06	.03
82	Dave Leiper	.03	.02	.01
83	Jeff Blauser(FC)	.15	.11	.06
84	*Bill Bene* (#1 Draft Pick)(FC)	.15	.11	.06
85	Kevin McReynolds	.12	.09	.05
86	Al Nipper	.03	.02	.01
87	Larry Owen	.03	.02	.01
88	*Darryl Hamilton*(FC)	.35	.25	.14
89	Dave LaPoint	.06	.05	.02
90	Vince Coleman	.12	.09	.05
91	Floyd Youmans	.03	.02	.01
92	Jeff Kunkel	.03	.02	.01
93	Ken Howell	.03	.02	.01
94	Chris Speier	.03	.02	.01
95	Gerald Young	.10	.08	.04
96	Rick Cerone	.03	.02	.01
97	Greg Mathews	.06	.05	.02
98	Larry Sheets	.06	.05	.02
99	*Sherman Corbett*(FC)	.12	.09	.05
100	Mike Schmidt	.35	.25	.14
101	Les Straker	.06	.05	.02
102	Mike Gallego	.03	.02	.01
103	Tim Birtsas	.03	.02	.01
104	Dallas Green	.03	.02	.01
105	Ron Darling	.10	.08	.04
106	Willie Upshaw	.06	.05	.02
107	Jose DeLeon	.06	.05	.02
108	Fred Manrique	.06	.05	.02
109	*Hipolito Pena*(FC)	.12	.09	.05

		MT	NR MT	EX
110	Paul Molitor	.20	.15	.08
111	Reds Leaders (Eric Davis)	.10	.08	.04
112	Jim Presley	.06	.05	.02
113	Lloyd Moseby	.06	.05	.02
114	Bob Kipper	.03	.02	.01
115	Jody Davis	.06	.05	.02
116	Jeff Montgomery	.06	.05	.02
117	Dave Anderson	.03	.02	.01
118	Checklist 1-132	.03	.02	.01
119	Terry Puhl	.03	.02	.01
120	Frank Viola	.12	.09	.05
121	Garry Templeton	.06	.05	.02
122	Lance Johnson(FC)	.10	.08	.04
123	Spike Owen	.03	.02	.01
124	Jim Traber	.06	.05	.02
125	Mike Krukow	.06	.05	.02
126	Sid Bream	.06	.05	.02
127	Walt Terrell	.06	.05	.02
128	Milt Thompson	.03	.02	.01
129	*Terry Clark*(FC)	.12	.09	.05
130	Gerald Perry	.08	.06	.03
131	Dave Otto(FC)	.08	.06	.03
132	Curt Ford	.03	.02	.01
133	Bill Long	.06	.05	.02
134	Don Zimmer	.03	.02	.01
135	Jose Rijo	.06	.05	.02
136	Joey Meyer	.08	.06	.03
137	Geno Petralli	.03	.02	.01
138	Wallace Johnson	.03	.02	.01
139	Mike Flanagan	.06	.05	.02
140	Shawon Dunston	.08	.06	.03
141	Indians Leaders (Brook Jacoby)	.06	.05	.02
142	Mike Diaz	.06	.05	.02
143	Mike Campbell	.08	.06	.03
144	Jay Bell	.06	.05	.02
145	Dave Stewart	.08	.06	.03
146	Gary Pettis	.03	.02	.01
147	DeWayne Buice	.03	.02	.01
148	Bill Pecota	.06	.05	.02
149	*Doug Dascenzo*(FC)	.08	.06	.03
150	Fernando Valenzuela	.06	.05	.02
151	Terry McGriff	.03	.02	.01
152	Mark Thurmond	.03	.02	.01
153	Jim Pankovits	.03	.02	.01
154	Don Carman	.06	.05	.02
155	Marty Barrett	.06	.05	.02
156	*Dave Gallagher*(FC)	.06	.05	.02
157	Tom Glavine	.50	.40	.20
158	Mike Aldrete	.06	.05	.02
159	Pat Clements	.03	.02	.01
160	Jeffrey Leonard	.06	.05	.02
161	*Gregg Olson* (#1 Draft Pick)	.40	.30	.15
162	John Davis	.03	.02	.01
163	Bob Forsch	.06	.05	.02
164	Hal Lanier	.03	.02	.01
165	Mike Dunne	.08	.06	.03
166	*Doug Jennings*(FC)	.12	.09	.05
167	Future Star (*Steve Searcy*)(FC)	.12	.09	.05
168	Willie Wilson	.08	.06	.03
169	Mike Jackson	.06	.05	.02
170	Tony Fernandez	.10	.08	.04
171	Braves Leaders (Andres Thomas)	.06	.05	.02
172	Frank Williams	.03	.02	.01
173	Mel Hall	.06	.05	.02
174	*Todd Burns*(FC)	.12	.09	.05
175	John Shelby	.03	.02	.01
176	Jeff Parrett	.08	.06	.03
177	*Monty Fariss* (#1 Draft Pick)	.12	.09	.05
178	Mark Grant	.03	.02	.01
179	Ozzie Virgil	.03	.02	.01
180	Mike Scott	.10	.08	.04
181	*Craig Worthington*(FC)	.12	.09	.05
182	Bob McClure	.03	.02	.01
183	Oddibe McDowell	.06	.05	.02
184	*John Costello*	.10	.08	.04
185	Claudell Washington	.06	.05	.02
186	Pat Perry	.03	.02	.01
187	Darren Daulton	.15	.11	.06
188	Dennis Lamp	.03	.02	.01
189	Kevin Mitchell	.10	.08	.04
190	Mike Witt	.06	.05	.02
191	*Sil Campusano*	.20	.15	.08
192	Paul Mirabella	.03	.02	.01
193	Sparky Anderson	.06	.05	.02
194	*Greg Harris*(FC)	.10	.08	.04
195	Ozzie Guillen	.06	.05	.02
196	Denny Walling	.03	.02	.01
197	Neal Heaton	.03	.02	.01
198	Danny Heep	.03	.02	.01
199	*Mike Schooler*	.10	.08	.04
200	George Brett	.30	.25	.12

		MT	NR MT	EX
201	Blue Jays Leaders (Kelly Gruber)	.06	.05	.02
202	*Brad Moore*(FC)	.12	.09	.05
203	Rob Ducey	.03	.02	.01
204	Brad Havens	.03	.02	.01
205	Dwight Evans	.10	.08	.04
206	Roberto Alomar	.75	.60	.30
207	Terry Leach	.03	.02	.01
208	Tom Pagnozzi	.06	.05	.02
209	*Jeff Bittiger*(FC)	.12	.09	.05
210	Dale Murphy	.10	.08	.04
211	Mike Pagliarulo	.08	.06	.03
212	Scott Sanderson	.03	.02	.01
213	Rene Gonzales	.06	.05	.02
214	Charlie O'Brien	.03	.02	.01
215	Kevin Gross	.06	.05	.02
216	Jack Howell	.06	.05	.02
217	Joe Price	.03	.02	.01
218	Mike LaValliere	.06	.05	.02
219	Jim Clancy	.06	.05	.02
220	Gary Gaetti	.12	.09	.05
221	Cecil Espy	.08	.06	.03
222	*Mark Lewis* (#1 Draft Pick)	.20	.15	.08
223	Jay Buhner	.15	.11	.06
224	Tony LaRussa	.06	.05	.02
225	*Ramon Martinez*(FC)	.20	.15	.08
226	Bill Doran	.06	.05	.02
227	John Farrell	.08	.06	.03
228	*Nelson Santovenia*	.15	.11	.06
229	Jimmy Key	.08	.06	.03
230	Ozzie Smith	.12	.09	.05
231	Padres Leaders (Roberto Alomar)	.10	.08	.04
232	Ricky Horton	.06	.05	.02
233	Gregg Jefferies (Future Star)(FC)	.30	.25	.12
234	Tom Browning	.08	.06	.03
235	John Kruk	.06	.05	.02
236	Charles Hudson	.03	.02	.01
237	Glenn Hubbard	.03	.02	.01
238	Eric King	.03	.02	.01
239	Tim Laudner	.03	.02	.01
240	Greg Maddux	.30	.25	.12
241	Brett Butler	.06	.05	.02
242	Ed Vande Berg	.03	.02	.01
243	Bob Boone	.06	.05	.02
244	Jim Acker	.03	.02	.01
245	Jim Rice	.10	.08	.04
246	Rey Quinones	.03	.02	.01
247	Shawn Hillegas	.06	.05	.02
248	Tony Phillips	.03	.02	.01
249	Tim Leary	.06	.05	.02
250	Cal Ripken, Jr.	.40	.30	.15
251	*John Dopson*(FC)	.10	.08	.04
252	Billy Hatcher	.06	.05	.02
253	*Jose Alvarez*(FC)	.08	.06	.03
254	Tom LaSorda	.06	.05	.02
255	Ron Guidry	.12	.09	.05
256	Benny Santiago	.12	.09	.05
257	Rick Aguilera	.03	.02	.01
258	Checklist 133-264	.03	.02	.01
259	Larry McWilliams	.03	.02	.01
260	Dave Winfield	.25	.20	.10
261	Cardinals Leaders (Tom Brunansky)	.06	.05	.02
262	*Jeff Pico*	.06	.05	.02
263	Mike Felder	.03	.02	.01
264	*Rob Dibble*(FC)	.40	.30	.15
265	Kent Hrbek	.15	.11	.06
266	Luis Aquino	.03	.02	.01
267	Jeff Robinson	.06	.05	.02
268	Keith Miller	.06	.05	.02
269	Tom Bolton	.06	.05	.02
270	Wally Joyner	.06	.05	.02
271	Jay Tibbs	.03	.02	.01
272	Ron Hassey	.03	.02	.01
273	Jose Lind	.08	.06	.03
274	Mark Eichhorn	.06	.05	.02
275	Danny Tartabull	.15	.11	.06
276	Paul Kilgus	.08	.06	.03
277	Mike Davis	.06	.05	.02
278	Andy McGaffigan	.03	.02	.01
279	Scott Bradley	.03	.02	.01
280	Bob Knepper	.06	.05	.02
281	Gary Redus	.03	.02	.01
282	*Cris Carpenter*(FC)	.15	.11	.06
283	Andy Allanson	.03	.02	.01
284	Jim Leyland	.03	.02	.01
285	John Candelaria	.06	.05	.02
286	Darrin Jackson	.08	.06	.03
287	Juan Nieves	.06	.05	.02
288	Pat Sheridan	.03	.02	.01
289	Ernie Whitt	.06	.05	.02
290	John Franco	.08	.06	.03

		MT	NR MT	EX
291	Mets Leaders (Darryl Strawberry)	.12	.09	.05
292	*Jim Corsi*(FC)	.08	.06	.03
293	Glenn Wilson	.06	.05	.02
294	Juan Berenguer	.03	.02	.01
295	Scott Fletcher	.06	.05	.02
296	Ron Gant	.40	.30	.15
297	*Oswald Peraza*(FC)	.08	.06	.03
298	Chris James	.08	.06	.03
299	*Steve Ellsworth*(FC)	.12	.09	.05
300	Darryl Strawberry	.20	.15	.08
301	Charlie Leibrandt	.06	.05	.02
302	Gary Ward	.06	.05	.02
303	Felix Fermin	.06	.05	.02
304	Joel Youngblood	.03	.02	.01
305	Dave Smith	.06	.05	.02
306	Tracy Woodson(FC)	.10	.08	.04
307	Lance McCullers	.06	.05	.02
308	Ron Karkovice	.03	.02	.01
309	Mario Diaz(FC)	.10	.08	.04
310	Rafael Palmeiro	.20	.15	.08
311	Chris Bosio	.03	.02	.01
312	Tom Lawless	.03	.02	.01
313	Denny Martinez	.06	.05	.02
314	Bobby Valentine	.03	.02	.01
315	Greg Swindell	.10	.08	.04
316	Walt Weiss	.20	.15	.08
317	*Jack Armstrong*	.12	.09	.05
318	Gene Larkin	.08	.06	.03
319	Greg Booker	.03	.02	.01
320	Lou Whitaker	.15	.11	.06
321	Red Sox Leaders (Jody Reed)	.06	.05	.02
322	John Smiley	.10	.08	.04
323	Gary Thurman	.10	.08	.04
324	*Bob Milacki*(FC)	.10	.08	.04
325	Jesse Barfield	.08	.06	.03
326	Dennis Boyd	.06	.05	.02
327	*Mark Lemke*(FC)	.12	.09	.05
328	Rick Honeycutt	.03	.02	.01
329	Bob Melvin	.03	.02	.01
330	Eric Davis	.12	.09	.05
331	Curt Wilkerson	.03	.02	.01
332	Tony Armas	.06	.05	.02
333	Bob Ojeda	.06	.05	.02
334	Steve Lyons	.03	.02	.01
335	Dave Righetti	.10	.08	.04
336	Steve Balboni	.06	.05	.02
337	Calvin Schiraldi	.03	.02	.01
338	Jim Adduci(FC)	.06	.05	.02
339	Scott Bailes	.03	.02	.01
340	Kirk Gibson	.15	.11	.06
341	Jim Deshaies	.03	.02	.01
342	Tom Brookens	.03	.02	.01
343	*Gary Sheffield* (Future Star)(FC)	1.25	.90	.50
344	Tom Trebelhorn	.03	.02	.01
345	Charlie Hough	.06	.05	.02
346	Rex Hudler(FC)	.06	.05	.02
347	John Cerutti	.06	.05	.02
348	Ed Hearn	.03	.02	.01
349	*Ron Jones*(FC)	.15	.11	.06
350	Andy Van Slyke	.12	.09	.05
351	Giants Leaders (Bob Melvin)	.06	.05	.02
352	Rick Schu	.03	.02	.01
353	Marvell Wynne	.03	.02	.01
354	Larry Parrish	.06	.05	.02
355	Mark Langston	.08	.06	.03
356	Kevin Elster	.08	.06	.03
357	Jerry Reuss	.06	.05	.02
358	*Ricky Jordan*(FC)	.06	.05	.02
359	Tommy John	.10	.08	.04
360	Ryne Sandberg	.30	.25	.12
361	Kelly Downs	.08	.06	.03
362	Jack Lazorko	.03	.02	.01
363	Rich Yett	.03	.02	.01
364	Rob Deer	.06	.05	.02
365	Mike Henneman	.08	.06	.03
366	Herm Winningham	.03	.02	.01
367	*Johnny Paredes*(FC)	.15	.11	.06
368	Brian Holton	.06	.05	.02
369	Ken Caminiti	.06	.05	.02
370	Dennis Eckersley	.10	.08	.04
371	Manny Lee	.03	.02	.01
372	Craig Lefferts	.03	.02	.01
373	Tracy Jones	.08	.06	.03
374	John Wathan	.06	.05	.02
375	Terry Pendleton	.08	.06	.03
376	Steve Lombardozzi	.03	.02	.01
377	Mike Smithson	.03	.02	.01
378	Checklist 265-396	.03	.02	.01
379	Tim Flannery	.03	.02	.01
380	Rickey Henderson	.30	.25	.12
381	Orioles Leaders (Larry Sheets)	.06	.05	.02

		MT	NR MT	EX
382	*John Smoltz*(FC)	.70	.50	.30
383	Howard Johnson	.08	.06	.03
384	Mark Salas	.03	.02	.01
385	Von Hayes	.08	.06	.03
386	Andres Galarraga (All-Star)	.08	.06	.03
387	Ryne Sandberg (All-Star)	.15	.11	.06
388	Bobby Bonilla (All-Star)	.08	.06	.03
389	Ozzie Smith (All-Star)	.12	.09	.05
390	Darryl Strawberry (All-Star)	.15	.11	.06
391	Andre Dawson (All-Star)	.10	.08	.04
392	Andy Van Slyke (All-Star)	.08	.06	.03
393	Gary Carter (All-Star)	.10	.08	.04
394	Orel Hershiser (All-Star)	.12	.09	.05
395	Danny Jackson (All-Star)	.08	.06	.03
396	Kirk Gibson (All-Star)	.08	.06	.03
397	Don Mattingly (All-Star)	.20	.15	.08
398	Julio Franco (All-Star)	.06	.05	.02
399	Wade Boggs (All-Star)	.15	.11	.06
400	Alan Trammell (All-Star)	.08	.06	.03
401	Jose Canseco (All-Star)	.15	.11	.06
402	Mike Greenwell (All-Star)	.15	.11	.06
403	Kirby Puckett (All-Star)	.20	.15	.08
404	Bob Boone (All-Star)	.06	.05	.02
405	Roger Clemens (All-Star)	.15	.11	.06
406	Frank Viola (All-Star)	.08	.06	.03
407	Dave Winfield (All-Star)	.12	.09	.05
408	Greg Walker	.06	.05	.02
409	Ken Dayley	.03	.02	.01
410	Jack Clark	.12	.09	.05
411	Mitch Williams	.06	.05	.02
412	Barry Lyons	.03	.02	.01
413	Mike Kingery	.03	.02	.01
414	Jim Fregosi	.03	.02	.01
415	Rich Gossage	.10	.08	.04
416	Fred Lynn	.10	.08	.04
417	Mike LaCoss	.03	.02	.01
418	Bob Dernier	.03	.02	.01
419	Tom Filer	.03	.02	.01
420	Joe Carter	.10	.08	.04
421	Kirk McCaskill	.06	.05	.02
422	Bo Diaz	.06	.05	.02
423	Brian Fisher	.06	.05	.02
424	Luis Polonia	.06	.05	.02
425	Jay Howell	.06	.05	.02
426	Danny Gladden	.03	.02	.01
427	Eric Show	.06	.05	.02
428	Craig Reynolds	.03	.02	.01
429	Twins Leaders (Greg Gagne)	.06	.05	.02
430	Mark Gubicza	.08	.06	.03
431	Luis Rivera	.06	.05	.02
432	*Chad Kreuter*(FC)	.15	.11	.06
433	Albert Hall	.03	.02	.01
434	*Ken Patterson*(FC)	.15	.11	.06
435	Len Dykstra	.10	.08	.04
436	Bobby Meacham	.03	.02	.01
437	*Andy Benes* (#1 Draft Pick)	.75	.60	.30
438	Greg Gross	.03	.02	.01
439	Frank DiPino	.03	.02	.01
440	Bobby Bonilla	.15	.11	.06
441	Jerry Reed	.03	.02	.01
442	Jose Oquendo	.03	.02	.01
443	*Rod Nichols*(FC)	.06	.05	.02
444	Moose Stubing	.03	.02	.01
445	Matt Nokes	.15	.11	.06
446	Rob Murphy	.03	.02	.01
447	Donell Nixon	.03	.02	.01
448	Eric Plunk	.03	.02	.01
449	Carmelo Martinez	.03	.02	.01
450	Roger Clemens	.40	.30	.15
451	Mark Davidson	.06	.05	.02
452	*Israel Sanchez*	.12	.09	.05
453	Tom Prince(FC)	.08	.06	.03
454	Paul Assenmacher	.03	.02	.01
455	Johnny Ray	.06	.05	.02
456	Tim Belcher	.08	.06	.03
457	Mackey Sasser	.06	.05	.02
458	*Donn Pall*(FC)	.12	.09	.05
459	Mariners Leaders (Dave Valle)	.06	.05	.02
460	Dave Stieb	.08	.06	.03
461	Buddy Bell	.06	.05	.02
462	Jose Guzman	.08	.06	.03
463	Steve Lake	.03	.02	.01
464	Bryn Smith	.03	.02	.01
465	Mark Grace	.20	.15	.08
466	Chuck Crim	.03	.02	.01
467	Jim Walewander	.03	.02	.01
468	Henry Cotto	.03	.02	.01
469	*Jose Bautista*	.06	.05	.02
470	Lance Parrish	.12	.09	.05
471	*Steve Curry*(FC)	.15	.11	.06
472	Brian Harper	.03	.02	.01

		MT	NR MT	EX
473	Don Robinson	.03	.02	.01
474	Bob Rodgers	.03	.02	.01
475	Dave Parker	.10	.08	.04
476	Jon Perlman(FC)	.06	.05	.02
477	Dick Schofield	.03	.02	.01
478	Doug Drabek	.06	.05	.02
479	*Mike Macfarlane*	.15	.11	.06
480	Keith Hernandez	.15	.11	.06
481	Chris Brown	.06	.05	.02
482	*Steve Peters*	.12	.09	.05
483	Mickey Hatcher	.03	.02	.01
484	Steve Shields	.03	.02	.01
485	Hubie Brooks	.08	.06	.03
486	Jack McDowell	.30	.25	.12
487	Scott Lusader(FC)	.08	.06	.03
488	Kevin Coffman	.06	.05	.02
489	Phillies Leaders (Mike Schmidt)	.12	.09	.05
490	*Chris Sabo*	.20	.15	.08
491	Mike Birkbeck	.03	.02	.01
492	Alan Ashby	.03	.02	.01
493	Todd Benzinger	.10	.08	.04
494	Shane Rawley	.06	.05	.02
495	Candy Maldonado	.06	.05	.02
496	Dwayne Henry	.03	.02	.01
497	Pete Stanicek	.12	.09	.05
498	Dave Valle	.03	.02	.01
499	*Don Heinkel*(FC)	.15	.11	.06
500	Jose Canseco	.20	.15	.08
501	Vance Law	.06	.05	.02
502	Duane Ward	.03	.02	.01
503	Al Newman	.03	.02	.01
504	Bob Walk	.03	.02	.01
505	Pete Rose	.20	.15	.08
506	Kirt Manwaring	.10	.08	.04
507	Steve Farr	.03	.02	.01
508	Wally Backman	.06	.05	.02
509	Bud Black	.03	.02	.01
510	Bob Horner	.08	.06	.03
511	Richard Dotson	.06	.05	.02
512	Donnie Hill	.03	.02	.01
513	Jesse Orosco	.06	.05	.02
514	Chet Lemon	.06	.05	.02
515	Barry Larkin	.10	.08	.04
516	Eddie Whitson	.03	.02	.01
517	Greg Brock	.06	.05	.02
518	Bruce Ruffin	.03	.02	.01
519	Yankees Leaders (Willie Randolph)	.03	.02	.01
520	Rick Sutcliffe	.08	.06	.03
521	Mickey Tettleton	.03	.02	.01
522	*Randy Kramer*(FC)	.06	.05	.02
523	Andres Thomas	.06	.05	.02
524	Checklist 397-528	.03	.02	.01
525	Chili Davis	.06	.05	.02
526	Wes Gardner	.06	.05	.02
527	Dave Henderson	.08	.06	.03
528	*Luis Medina*(FC)	.03	.02	.01
529	Tom Foley	.03	.02	.01
530	Nolan Ryan	.50	.40	.20
531	Dave Hengel(FC)	.08	.06	.03
532	Jerry Browne	.03	.02	.01
533	Andy Hawkins	.03	.02	.01
534	Doc Edwards	.03	.02	.01
535	Todd Worrell	.08	.06	.03
536	Joel Skinner	.03	.02	.01
537	Pete Smith	.08	.06	.03
538	Juan Castillo	.03	.02	.01
539	Barry Jones	.03	.02	.01
540	Bo Jackson	.30	.25	.12
541	Cecil Fielder	.30	.25	.12
542	Todd Frohwirth	.06	.05	.02
543	Damon Berryhill	.06	.05	.02
544	Jeff Sellers	.03	.02	.01
545	Mookie Wilson	.06	.05	.02
546	Mark Williamson	.06	.05	.02
547	Mark McLemore	.03	.02	.01
548	Bobby Witt	.08	.06	.03
549	Cubs Leaders (Jamie Moyer)	.03	.02	.01
550	Orel Hershiser	.08	.06	.03
551	Randy Ready	.03	.02	.01
552	Greg Cadaret	.06	.05	.02
553	Luis Salazar	.03	.02	.01
554	Nick Esasky	.06	.05	.02
555	Bert Blyleven	.10	.08	.04
556	Bruce Fields(FC)	.06	.05	.02
557	*Keith Miller*(FC)	.06	.05	.02
558	Dan Pasqua	.08	.06	.03
559	Juan Agosto	.03	.02	.01
560	Tim Raines	.08	.06	.03
561	Luis Aguayo	.03	.02	.01
562	Danny Cox	.06	.05	.02
563	Bill Schroeder	.03	.02	.01

		MT	NR MT	EX
564	Russ Nixon	.03	.02	.01
565	Jeff Russell	.03	.02	.01
566	Al Pedrique	.03	.02	.01
567	David Wells	.08	.06	.03
568	Mickey Brantley	.03	.02	.01
569	*German Jimenez*(FC)	.08	.06	.03
570	Tony Gwynn	.30	.25	.12
571	Billy Ripken	.06	.05	.02
572	Atlee Hammaker	.03	.02	.01
573	*Jim Abbott* (#1 Draft Pick)	1.00	.70	.40
574	Dave Clark	.06	.05	.02
575	Juan Samuel	.10	.08	.04
576	Greg Minton	.03	.02	.01
577	Randy Bush	.03	.02	.01
578	John Morris	.03	.02	.01
579	Astros Leaders (Glenn Davis)	.08	.06	.03
580	Harold Reynolds	.06	.05	.02
581	Gene Nelson	.03	.02	.01
582	Mike Marshall	.10	.08	.04
583	*Paul Gibson*(FC)	.06	.05	.02
584	Randy Velarde(FC)	.10	.08	.04
585	Harold Baines	.10	.08	.04
586	Joe Boever	.03	.02	.01
587	Mike Stanley	.03	.02	.01
588	*Luis Alicea*	.15	.11	.06
589	Dave Meads	.03	.02	.01
590	Andres Galarraga	.12	.09	.05
591	Jeff Musselman	.06	.05	.02
592	John Cangelosi	.03	.02	.01
593	Drew Hall	.10	.08	.04
594	Jimy Williams	.03	.02	.01
595	Teddy Higuera	.08	.06	.03
596	Kurt Stillwell	.06	.05	.02
597	*Terry Taylor*(FC)	.12	.09	.05
598	Ken Gerhart	.06	.05	.02
599	Tom Candiotti	.03	.02	.01
600	Wade Boggs	.25	.20	.10
601	Dave Dravecky	.06	.05	.02
602	Devon White	.10	.08	.04
603	Frank Tanana	.06	.05	.02
604	Paul O'Neill	.03	.02	.01
605a	Bob Welch (missing Complete Major League Pitching Record line)	3.00	2.25	1.25
605b	Bob Welch (contains Complete Major League Pitching Record line)	.08	.06	.03
606	Rick Dempsey	.06	.05	.02
607	*Willie Ansley* (#1 Draft Pick)	.15	.11	.06
608	Phil Bradley	.08	.06	.03
609	Tigers Leaders (Frank Tanana)	.06	.05	.02
610	Randy Myers	.08	.06	.03
611	Don Slaught	.03	.02	.01
612	Dan Quisenberry	.06	.05	.02
613	*Gary Varsho*(FC)	.15	.11	.06
614	Joe Hesketh	.03	.02	.01
615	Robin Yount	.25	.20	.10
616	*Steve Rosenberg*(FC)	.06	.05	.02
617	*Mark Parent*	.06	.05	.02
618	Rance Mulliniks	.03	.02	.01
619	Checklist 529-660	.03	.02	.01
620	Barry Bonds	.40	.30	.15
621	Rick Mahler	.03	.02	.01
622	Stan Javier	.03	.02	.01
623	Fred Toliver	.03	.02	.01
624	Jack McKeon	.03	.02	.01
625	Eddie Murray	.15	.11	.06
626	Jeff Reed	.03	.02	.01
627	Greg Harris	.03	.02	.01
628	Matt Williams	.10	.08	.04
629	Pete O'Brien	.06	.05	.02
630	Mike Greenwell	.08	.06	.03
631	Dave Bergman	.03	.02	.01
632	*Bryan Harvey*	.25	.20	.10
633	Daryl Boston	.03	.02	.01
634	Marvin Freeman(FC)	.08	.06	.03
635	Willie Randolph	.06	.05	.02
636	Bill Wilkinson	.06	.05	.02
637	Carmen Castillo	.03	.02	.01
638	Floyd Bannister	.06	.05	.02
639	Athletics Leaders (Walt Weiss)	.15	.11	.06
640	Willie McGee	.10	.08	.04
641	Curt Young	.06	.05	.02
642	Argenis Salazar	.03	.02	.01
643	*Louie Meadows*(FC)	.12	.09	.05
644	Lloyd McClendon	.03	.02	.01
645	Jack Morris	.12	.09	.05
646	Kevin Bass	.06	.05	.02
647	*Randy Johnson*(FC)	.75	.60	.30
648	*Sandy Alomar* (Future Star)(FC)	.40	.30	.15
649	Stewart Cliburn	.03	.02	.01
650	Kirby Puckett	.25	.20	.10
651	Tom Niedenfuer	.06	.05	.02

		MT	NR MT	EX
652	Rich Gedman	.06	.05	.02
653	*Tommy Barrett*(FC)	.06	.05	.02
654	Whitey Herzog	.06	.05	.02
655	Dave Magadan	.08	.06	.03
656	Ivan Calderon	.06	.05	.02
657	Joe Magrane	.08	.06	.03
658	R.J. Reynolds	.03	.02	.01
659	Al Leiter	.06	.05	.02
660	Will Clark	.50	.40	.20
661	Turn Back The Clock (Dwight Gooden)	.10	.08	.04
662	Turn Back The Clock (Lou Brock)	.08	.06	.03
663	Turn Back The Clock (Hank Aaron)	.15	.11	.06
664	Turn Back The Clock (Gil Hodges)	.06	.05	.02
665	Turn Back The Clock (Tony Oliva)	.06	.05	.02
666	Randy St. Claire	.03	.02	.01
667	Dwayne Murphy	.06	.05	.02
668	Mike Bielecki	.03	.02	.01
669	Dodgers Leaders (Orel Hershiser)	.12	.09	.05
670	Kevin Seitzer	.12	.09	.05
671	Jim Gantner	.03	.02	.01
672	Allan Anderson	.06	.05	.02
673	Don Baylor	.08	.06	.03
674	Otis Nixon	.03	.02	.01
675	Bruce Hurst	.08	.06	.03
676	Ernie Riles	.03	.02	.01
677	Dave Schmidt	.03	.02	.01
678	Dion James	.03	.02	.01
679	Willie Fraser	.03	.02	.01
680	Gary Carter	.15	.11	.06
681	Jeff Robinson	.10	.08	.04
682	Rick Leach	.03	.02	.01
683	*Jose Cecena*	.15	.11	.06
684	Dave Johnson	.06	.05	.02
685	Jeff Treadway	.10	.08	.04
686	Scott Terry	.08	.06	.03
687	Alvin Davis	.10	.08	.04
688	Zane Smith	.06	.05	.02
689	Stan Jefferson	.03	.02	.01
690	Doug Jones	.10	.08	.04
691	Roberto Kelly	.25	.20	.10
692	Steve Ontiveros	.03	.02	.01
693	*Pat Borders*	.30	.25	.12
694	Les Lancaster	.06	.05	.02
695	Carlton Fisk	.20	.15	.08
696	Don August	.08	.06	.03
697	Franklin Stubbs	.03	.02	.01
698	Keith Atherton	.03	.02	.01
699	Pirates Leaders (Al Pedrique)	.06	.05	.02
700	Don Mattingly	.25	.20	.10
701	Storm Davis	.08	.06	.03
702	Jamie Quirk	.03	.02	.01
703	Scott Garrelts	.03	.02	.01
704	*Carlos Quintana*(FC)	.15	.11	.06
705	Terry Kennedy	.06	.05	.02
706	Pete Incaviglia	.08	.06	.03
707	Steve Jeltz	.03	.02	.01
708	Chuck Finley	.03	.02	.01
709	Tom Herr	.06	.05	.02
710	Dave Cone	.15	.11	.06
711	*Candy Sierra*(FC)	.03	.02	.01
712	Bill Swift	.03	.02	.01
713	*Ty Griffin* (#1 Draft Pick)	.10	.08	.04
714	Joe M. Morgan	.03	.02	.01
715	Tony Pena	.06	.05	.02
716	Wayne Tolleson	.03	.02	.01
717	Jamie Moyer	.03	.02	.01
718	Glenn Braggs	.06	.05	.02
719	Danny Darwin	.03	.02	.01
720	Tim Wallach	.08	.06	.03
721	*Ron Tingley*(FC)	.03	.02	.01
722	Todd Stottlemyre	.15	.11	.06
723	Rafael Belliard	.03	.02	.01
724	Jerry Don Gleaton	.03	.02	.01
725	Terry Steinbach	.08	.06	.03
726	Dickie Thon	.03	.02	.01
727	Joe Orsulak	.03	.02	.01
728	Charlie Puleo	.03	.02	.01
729	Rangers Leaders (Steve Buechele)	.06	.05	.02
730	Danny Jackson	.12	.09	.05
731	Mike Young	.03	.02	.01
732	Steve Buechele	.03	.02	.01
733	*Randy Bockus*(FC)	.06	.05	.02
734	Jody Reed	.10	.08	.04
735	Roger McDowell	.08	.06	.03
736	Jeff Hamilton	.06	.05	.02
737	*Norm Charlton*(FC)	.30	.25	.12
738	Darnell Coles	.06	.05	.02
739	Brook Jacoby	.08	.06	.03
740	Dan Plesac	.08	.06	.03
741	Ken Phelps	.06	.05	.02

		MT	NR MT	EX
742	*Mike Harkey* (Future Star)(FC)	.15	.11	.06
743	Mike Heath	.03	.02	.01
744	Roger Craig	.06	.05	.02
745	Fred McGriff	.15	.11	.06
746	*German Gonzalez*(FC)	.06	.05	.02
747	Wil Tejada(FC)	.06	.05	.02
748	Jimmy Jones	.03	.02	.01
749	Rafael Ramirez	.03	.02	.01
750	Bret Saberhagen	.12	.09	.05
751	Ken Oberkfell	.03	.02	.01
752	Jim Gott	.03	.02	.01
753	Jose Uribe	.03	.02	.01
754	Bob Brower	.03	.02	.01
755	Mike Scioscia	.06	.05	.02
756	*Scott Medvin*(FC)	.06	.05	.02
757	*Brady Anderson*	.60	.45	.25
758	Gene Walter	.03	.02	.01
759	Brewers Leaders (Rob Deer)	.06	.05	.02
760	Lee Smith	.08	.06	.03
761	*Dante Bichette*(FC)	.40	.30	.15
762	Bobby Thigpen	.08	.06	.03
763	Dave Martinez	.06	.05	.02
764	*Robin Ventura* (#1 Draft Pick)	1.00	.70	.40
765	Glenn Davis	.06	.05	.02
766	Cecilio Guante	.03	.02	.01
767	*Mike Capel*(FC)	.03	.02	.01
768	Bill Wegman	.03	.02	.01
769	Junior Ortiz	.03	.02	.01
770	Alan Trammell	.08	.06	.03
771	Ron Kittle	.06	.05	.02
772	Ron Oester	.03	.02	.01
773	Keith Moreland	.06	.05	.02
774	Frank Robinson	.08	.06	.03
775	Jeff Reardon	.08	.06	.03
776	Nelson Liriano	.06	.05	.02
777	Ted Power	.03	.02	.01
778	Bruce Benedict	.03	.02	.01
779	Craig McMurtry	.03	.02	.01
780	Pedro Guerrero	.06	.05	.02
781	*Greg Briley*(FC)	.08	.06	.03
782	Checklist 661-792	.03	.02	.01
783	*Trevor Wilson*(FC)	.15	.11	.06
784	*Steve Avery* (#1 Draft Pick)(FC)	1.25	.90	.50
785	Ellis Burks	.10	.08	.04
786	Melido Perez	.08	.06	.03
787	*Dave West*(FC)	.15	.11	.06
788	Mike Morgan	.03	.02	.01
789	Royals Leaders (Bo Jackson)	.12	.09	.05
790	Sid Fernandez	.08	.06	.03
791	Jim Lindeman	.03	.02	.01
792	Rafael Santana	.03	.02	.01

1989 Topps All-Star Glossy Set Of 22

The glossy All-Stars were included in the Topps 1989 rack packs. Format was very similar to the sets produced since 1984. Besides the starting lineups of the 1988 All-Star Game, the set included the managers and honorary team captains, Bobby Doerr and Willie Stargell.

		MT	NR MT	EX
Complete set (22):		2.00	1.50	.75
Common player:		.05	.04	.02
1	Tom Kelly	.05	.04	.02
2	Mark McGwire	.15	.11	.06
3	Paul Molitor	.15	.11	.06
4	Wade Boggs	.15	.11	.06
5	Cal Ripken	.25	.20	.10
6	Jose Canseco	.20	.15	.08
7	Rickey Henderson	.15	.11	.06
8	Dave Winfield	.15	.11	.06
9	Terry Steinbach	.05	.04	.02
10	Frank Viola	.05	.04	.02
11	Bobby Doerr	.05	.04	.02
12	Whitey Herzog	.05	.04	.02
13	Will Clark	.15	.11	.06
14	Ryne Sandberg	.25	.20	.10
15	Bobby Bonilla	.10	.08	.04
16	Ozzie Smith	.10	.08	.04
17	Vince Coleman	.05	.04	.02
18	Andre Dawson	.10	.08	.04
19	Darryl Strawberry	.15	.11	.06
20	Gary Carter	.05	.04	.02
21	Dwight Gooden	.10	.08	.04
22	Willie Stargell	.10	.08	.04

1989 Topps Glossy Rookies Set Of 22

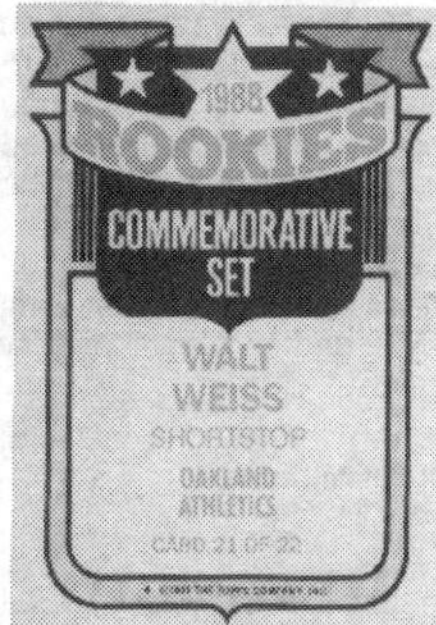

Bearing the same design and style of the past two years, Topps featured the top first-year players from the 1988 season in this glossy set. The full-color player photos appears beneath the "1988 Rookies" banner. The player's name is displayed beneath the photo. The flip side features the "1988 Rookies Commemorative Set" logo followed by the player's name, position, team, and card number.

		MT	NR MT	EX
Complete Set:		3.50	2.75	1.50
Common Player:		.15	.11	.06
1	Roberto Alomar	.25	.20	.10
2	Brady Anderson	.20	.15	.08
3	Tim Belcher	.20	.15	.08
4	Damon Berryhill	.15	.11	.06
5	Jay Buhner	.20	.15	.11
6	Kevin Elster	.15	.11	.06
7	Cecil Espy	.15	.11	.06
8	Dave Gallagher	.15	.11	.06
9	Ron Gant	.15	.11	.06
10	Paul Gibson	.15	.11	.06
11	Mark Grace	.60	.45	.25
12	Darrin Jackson	.15	.11	.06
13	Gregg Jefferies	.70	.50	.30
14	Ricky Jordan	.50	.40	.20
15	Al Leiter	.15	.11	.06
16	Melido Perez	.15	.11	.06
17	Chris Sabo	.35	.25	.14
18	Nelson Santovenia	.20	.15	.08
19	Mackey Sasser	.15	.11	.06
20	Gary Sheffield	.50	.40	.20
21	Walt Weiss	.15	.11	.06
22	David Wells	.15	.11	.06

Definitions for grading conditions are located in the Introduction of this price guide.

1989 Topps All-Star Glossy Set Of 60

For the seventh straight year Topps issued this "send-away" glossy set. Divided into six 10-card sets, it was available only by sending in special offer cards from the 1989 Topps wax packs. The 2-1/2" by 3-1/2" cards feature full-color photos bordered in white with a thin yellow frame. The player's name appears in small print in the lower right corner. Red-and-blue-printed flip sides provide basic information including player's name, team, and position. Any of the six 10-card sets were available for $1.25 and six special offer cards. The set was also made available in its complete 60-card set form for $7.50 and 18 special offer cards.

		MT	NR MT	EX
Complete Set:		10.00	7.50	4.00
Common Player:		.15	.11	.06
1	Kirby Puckett	.50	.40	.20
2	Eric Davis	.70	.50	.30
3	Joe Carter	.20	.15	.08
4	Andy Van Slyke	.20	.15	.08
5	Wade Boggs	.70	.50	.30
6	Dave Cone	.25	.20	.10
7	Kent Hrbek	.15	.11	.06
8	Darryl Strawberry	.70	.50	.30
9	Jay Buhner	.15	.11	.06
10	Ron Gant	.30	.25	.12
11	Will Clark	1.00	.70	.40
12	Jose Canseco	1.25	.90	.50
13	Juan Samuel	.15	.11	.06
14	George Brett	.25	.20	.10
15	Benny Santiago	.20	.15	.08
16	Dennis Eckersley	.15	.11	.06
17	Gary Carter	.15	.11	.06
18	Frank Viola	.20	.15	.08
19	Roberto Alomar	.30	.25	.12
20	Paul Gibson	.15	.11	.06
21	Dave Winfield	.20	.15	.08
22	Howard Johnson	.35	.25	.14
23	Roger Clemens	.40	.30	.15
24	Bobby Bonilla	.25	.20	.10
25	Alan Trammell	.20	.15	.08
26	Kevin McReynolds	.20	.15	.08
27	George Bell	.20	.15	.08
28	Bruce Hurst	.15	.11	.06
29	Mark Grace	.70	.50	.30
30	Tim Belcher	.20	.15	.08
31	Mike Greenwell	.70	.50	.30
32	Glenn Davis	.15	.11	.06
33	Gary Gaetti	.15	.11	.06
34	Ryne Sandberg	.70	.50	.30
35	Rickey Henderson	.70	.50	.30
36	Dwight Evans	.15	.11	.06
37	Doc Gooden	.50	.40	.20
38	Robin Yount	.25	.20	.10
39	Damon Berryhill	.15	.11	.06
40	Chris Sabo	.20	.15	.11
41	Mark McGwire	.70	.50	.30
42	Ozzie Smith	.25	.20	.10
43	Paul Molitor	.20	.15	.08
44	Andres Galarraga	.30	.25	.12
45	Dave Stewart	.15	.11	.06
46	Tom Browning	.15	.11	.06
47	Cal Ripken	.50	.40	.20
48	Orel Hershiser	.40	.30	.15
49	Dave Gallagher	.15	.11	.06
50	Walt Weiss	.20	.15	.08
51	Don Mattingly	1.50	1.25	.60
52	Tony Fernandez	.20	.15	.08
53	Rock Raines	.20	.15	.08
54	Jeff Reardon	.15	.11	.06
55	Kirk Gibson	.20	.15	.08
56	Jack Clark	.20	.15	.08
57	Danny Jackson	.15	.11	.06
58	Tony Gwynn	.60	.45	.25
59	Cecil Espy	.15	.11	.06
60	Jody Reed	.15	.11	.06

1989 Topps Traded

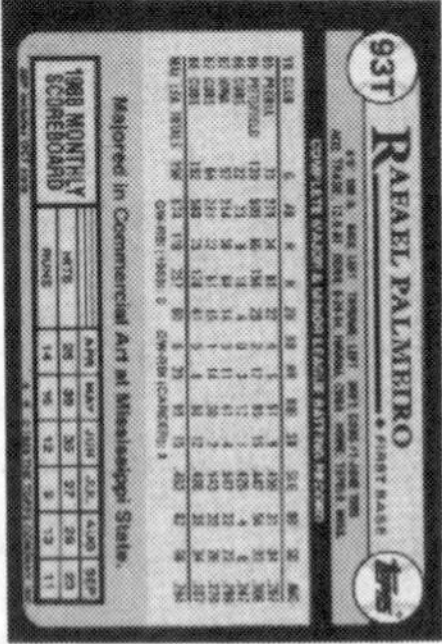

For the ninth straight year, Topps issued its annual 132-card "Traded" set at the end of the 1989 baseball season. The set, which was packaged in a special box and sold by hobby dealers, includes traded players and rookies who were not in the regular 1989 Topps set.

		MT	NR MT	EX
Complete Set (132):		6.00	4.50	2.50
Common Player:		.05	.04	.02
1T	Don Aase	.05	.04	.02
2T	Jim Abbott	1.00	.70	.40
3T	Kent Anderson(FC)	.05	.04	.02
4T	Keith Atherton	.05	.04	.02
5T	Wally Backman	.05	.04	.02
6T	Steve Balboni	.05	.04	.02
7T	Jesse Barfield	.05	.04	.02
8T	Steve Bedrosian	.05	.04	.02
9T	Todd Benzinger	.05	.04	.02
10T	Geronimo Berroa(FC)	.05	.04	.02
11T	Bert Blyleven	.05	.04	.02
12T	Bob Boone	.05	.04	.02
13T	Phil Bradley	.05	.04	.02
14T	Jeff Brantley(FC)	.05	.04	.02
15T	Kevin Brown(FC)	.05	.04	.02
16T	Jerry Browne	.05	.04	.02
17T	Chuck Cary	.05	.04	.02
18T	Carmen Castillo	.05	.04	.02
19T	Jim Clancy	.05	.04	.02
20T	Jack Clark	.05	.04	.02
21T	Bryan Clutterbuck	.05	.04	.02
22T	Jody Davis	.05	.04	.02
23T	Mike Devereaux(FC)	.30	.25	.12
24T	Frank DiPino	.05	.04	.02
25T	Benny Distefano	.05	.04	.02
26T	John Dopson	.05	.04	.02
27T	Len Dykstra	.15	.11	.06
28T	Jim Eisenreich	.05	.04	.02
29T	Nick Esasky	.05	.04	.02
30T	Alvaro Espinoza	.05	.04	.02
31T	Darrell Evans	.05	.04	.02
32T	Junior Felix(FC)	.30	.25	.12
33T	Felix Fermin	.05	.04	.02
34T	Julio Franco	.05	.04	.02
35T	Terry Francona	.05	.04	.02
36T	Cito Gaston	.05	.04	.02
37T	Bob Geren (photo actually Mike Fennell)(FC)	.05	.04	.02
38T	Tom Gordon(FC)	.05	.04	.02
39T	Tommy Gregg(FC)	.05	.04	.02
40T	Ken Griffey	.15	.11	.06
41T	Ken Griffey, Jr.(FC)	4.00	3.00	1.50

		MT	NR MT	EX
42T	Kevin Gross	.05	.04	.02
43T	Lee Guetterman	.05	.04	.02
44T	Mel Hall	.05	.04	.02
45T	Erik Hanson(FC)	.40	.30	.15
46T	Gene Harris(FC)	.05	.04	.02
47T	Andy Hawkins	.05	.04	.02
48T	Rickey Henderson	.05	.04	.02
49T	Tom Herr	.05	.04	.02
50T	Ken Hill(FC)	.05	.04	.02
51T	Brian Holman(FC)	.05	.04	.02
52T	Brian Holton	.05	.04	.02
53T	Art Howe	.05	.04	.02
54T	Ken Howell	.05	.04	.02
55T	Bruce Hurst	.05	.04	.02
56T	Chris James	.05	.04	.02
57T	Randy Johnson	.60	.45	.25
58T	Jimmy Jones	.05	.04	.02
59T	Terry Kennedy	.05	.04	.02
60T	Paul Kilgus	.05	.04	.02
61T	Eric King	.05	.04	.02
62T	Ron Kittle	.05	.04	.02
63T	John Kruk	.30	.25	.12
64T	Randy Kutcher(FC)	.05	.04	.02
65T	Steve Lake	.05	.04	.02
66T	Mark Langston	.25	.20	.10
67T	Dave LaPoint	.05	.04	.02
68T	Rick Leach	.05	.04	.02
69T	Terry Leach	.05	.04	.02
70T	Jim Levebvre	.05	.04	.02
71T	Al Leiter	.05	.04	.02
72T	Jeffrey Leonard	.05	.04	.02
73T	Derek Lilliquist(FC)	.05	.04	.02
74T	Rick Mahler	.05	.04	.02
75T	Tom McCarthy(FC)	.05	.04	.02
76T	Lloyd McClendon	.05	.04	.02
77T	Lance McCullers	.05	.04	.02
78T	Oddibe McDowell	.05	.04	.02
79T	Roger McDowell	.05	.04	.02
80T	Larry McWilliams	.05	.04	.02
81T	Randy Milligan	.10	.08	.04
82T	Mike Moore	.15	.11	.06
83T	Keith Moreland	.05	.04	.02
84T	Mike Morgan	.05	.04	.02
85T	Jamie Moyer	.05	.04	.02
86T	Rob Murphy	.05	.04	.02
87T	Eddie Murray	.30	.25	.12
88T	Pete O'Brien	.05	.04	.02
89T	Gregg Olson	.40	.30	.15
90T	Steve Ontiveros	.05	.04	.02
91T	Jesse Orosco	.05	.04	.02
92T	Spike Owen	.05	.04	.02
93T	Rafael Palmeiro	.50	.40	.20
94T	Clay Parker(FC)	.05	.04	.02
95T	Jeff Parrett	.05	.04	.02
96T	Lance Parrish	.05	.04	.02
97T	Dennis Powell	.05	.04	.02
98T	Rey Quinones	.05	.04	.02
99T	Doug Rader	.05	.04	.02
100T	Willie Randolph	.10	.08	.04
101T	Shane Rawley	.05	.04	.02
102T	Randy Ready	.05	.04	.02
103T	Bip Roberts	.05	.04	.02
104T	Kenny Rogers(FC)	.25	.20	.10
105T	Ed Romero	.05	.04	.02
106T	Nolan Ryan	1.50	1.25	.60
107T	Luis Salazar	.05	.04	.02
108T	Juan Samuel	.05	.04	.02
109T	Alex Sanchez(FC)	.05	.04	.02
110T	Deion Sanders(FC)	2.00	1.50	.80
111T	Steve Sax	.10	.08	.04
112T	Rick Schu	.05	.04	.02
113T	Dwight Smith(FC)	.15	.11	.06
114T	Lonnie Smith	.05	.04	.02
115T	Billy Spiers(FC)	.15	.11	.06
116T	Kent Tekulve	.05	.04	.02
117T	Walt Terrell	.05	.04	.02
118T	Milt Thompson	.05	.04	.02
119T	Dickie Thon	.05	.04	.02
120T	Jeff Torborg	.05	.04	.02
121T	Jeff Treadway	.05	.04	.02
122T	Omar Vizquel(FC)	.30	.25	.12
123T	Jerome Walton(FC)	.10	.08	.04
124T	Gary Ward	.05	.04	.02
125T	Claudell Washington	.05	.04	.02
126T	Curt Wilkerson	.05	.04	.02
127T	Eddie Williams	.05	.04	.02
128T	Frank Williams	.05	.04	.02
129T	Ken Williams	.05	.04	.02
130T	Mitch Williams	.20	.15	.08
131T	Steve Wilson(FC)	.10	.08	.04
132T	Checklist	.05	.04	.02

1989 Topps Box Panels

Continuing its practice of printing baseball cards on the bottom panels of its wax pack boxes, Topps in 1989 issued a special 16-card set, printing four cards on each of four different box-bottom panels. The cards are identical in design to the regular 1989 Topps cards. They are designated by letter (from A through P) rather than by number.

		MT	NR MT	EX
Complete Panel Set:		5.00	3.75	2.00
Complete Singles Set:		2.00	1.50	.80
Common Panel:		.50	.40	.20
Common Single Player:		.08	.06	.03
	Panel	.50	.40	.20
A	George Brett	.25	.20	.10
B	Bill Buckner	.08	.06	.03
C	Darrell Evans	.08	.06	.03
D	Rich Gossage	.08	.06	.03
	Panel	1.00	.70	.40
E	Greg Gross	.08	.06	.03
F	Rickey Henderson	.30	.25	.12
G	Keith Hernandez	.15	.11	.06
H	Tom Lasorda	.08	.06	.03
	Panel	2.50	2.00	1.00
I	Jim Rice	.15	.11	.06
J	Cal Ripken	.35	.25	.14
K	Nolan Ryan	.50	.40	.20
L	Mike Schmidt	.25	.20	.10
	Panel	1.00	.70	.40
M	Bruce Sutter	.15	.11	.06
N	Don Sutton	.10	.08	.04
O	Kent Tekulve	.08	.06	.03
P	Dave Winfield	.25	.20	.10

1989 Topps Batting Leaders

The active career batting leaders are showcased in this 22-card set. The standard-size cards are printed on super glossy stock with full-color photos. A unique left-handed or right-handed batter creates one of the vertical borders. The Topps logo appears in the upper left portion of the photo, while a "Top Active Career Batting

Leaders" cup is displayed in the lower left. The player's name appears above the photo. This set is specially numbered in accordance to career batting average. Wade Boggs is featured on card number one as the top active career batting leader. The flip sides present batting statistics. One batting leader card was included in each K-mart blister pack, which also includes 100 cards from the 1989 regular Topps set.

		MT	NR MT	EX
Complete Set:		25.00	18.00	9.00
Common Player:		.40	.30	.15
1	Wade Boggs	2.00	1.50	.80
2	Tony Gwynn	2.00	1.50	.80
3	Don Mattingly	2.00	1.50	.80
4	Kirby Puckett	2.50	2.00	1.00
5	George Brett	2.00	1.50	.80
6	Pedro Guerrero	.40	.30	.15
7	Rock Raines	.50	.40	.20
8	Keith Hernandez	.40	.30	.15
9	Jim Rice	.50	.40	.20
10	Paul Molitor	1.50	1.25	.60
11	Eddie Murray	1.00	.70	.40
12	Willie McGee	.40	.30	.15
13	Dave Parker	.40	.30	.15
14	Julio Franco	.40	.30	.15
15	Rickey Henderson	1.50	1.25	.60
16	Kent Hrbek	.40	.30	.15
17	Willie Wilson	.40	.30	.15
18	Johnny Ray	.40	.30	.15
19	Pat Tabler	.40	.30	.15
20	Carney Lansford	.40	.30	.15
21	Robin Yount	2.50	2.00	1.00
22	Alan Trammell	1.00	.70	.40

1989 Topps Big Baseball

Known by collectors as Topps "Big Baseball," the cards in this 330-card set measure 2-5/8" by 3-3/4" and are patterned after the 1956 Topps cards. The glossy card fronts are horizontally-designed and include two photos of each player, a posed head shot alongside an action photo. The backs include 1988 and career stats, but are dominated by a color cartoon featuring the player. The set was issued in three series of 110 cards each.

		MT	NR MT	EX
Complete Set:		20.00	15.00	8.00
Common Player:		.05	.04	.02
1	Orel Hershiser	.15	.11	.06
2	Harold Reynolds	.08	.06	.03
3	Jody Davis	.05	.04	.02
4	Greg Walker	.05	.04	.02
5	Barry Bonds	.08	.06	.03
6	Bret Saberhagen	.12	.09	.05
7	Johnny Ray	.05	.04	.02
8	Mike Fiore	.20	.15	.08
9	Juan Castillo	.05	.04	.02
10	Todd Burns	.05	.04	.02
11	Carmelo Martinez	.05	.04	.02
12	Geno Petralli	.05	.04	.02
13	Mel Hall	.05	.04	.02
14	Tom Browning	.08	.06	.03
15	Fred McGriff	.15	.11	.06
16	Kevin Elster	.05	.04	.02
17	Tim Leary	.05	.04	.02
18	Jim Rice	.05	.04	.02
19	Bret Barberie	.15	.11	.06
20	Jay Buhner	.05	.04	.02
21	Atlee Hammaker	.05	.04	.02
22	Lou Whitaker	.05	.04	.02
23	Paul Runge	.05	.04	.02
24	Carlton Fisk	.08	.06	.03
25	Jose Lind	.05	.04	.02
26	Mark Gubicza	.08	.06	.03
27	Billy Ripken	.05	.04	.02
28	Mike Pagliarulo	.05	.04	.02
29	Jim Deshaies	.05	.04	.02
30	Mark McLemore	.05	.04	.02
31	Scott Terry	.05	.04	.02
32	Franklin Stubbs	.05	.04	.02
33	Don August	.05	.04	.02
34	Mark McGwire	1.00	.70	.40
35	Eric Show	.05	.04	.02
36	Cecil Espy	.05	.04	.02
37	Ron Tingley	.05	.04	.02
38	Mickey Brantley	.05	.04	.02
39	Paul O'Neill	.05	.04	.02
40	Ed Sprague	.35	.25	.14
41	Len Dykstra	.05	.04	.02
42	Roger Clemens	.25	.20	.10
43	Ron Gant	.05	.04	.02
44	Dan Pasqua	.05	.04	.02
45	Jeff Robinson	.05	.04	.02
46	George Brett	.15	.11	.06
47	Bryn Smith	.05	.04	.02
48	Mike Marshall	.05	.04	.02
49	Doug Robbins	.15	.11	.06
50	Don Mattingly	1.50	1.25	.60
51	Mike Scott	.08	.06	.03
52	Steve Jeltz	.05	.04	.02
53	Dick Schofield	.05	.04	.02
54	Tom Brunansky	.08	.06	.03
55	Gary Sheffield	1.00	.70	.40
56	Dave Valle	.05	.04	.02
57	Carney Lansford	.08	.06	.03
58	Tony Gwynn	.15	.11	.06
59	Checklist	.05	.04	.02
60	Damon Berryhill	.05	.04	.02
61	Jack Morris	.05	.04	.02
62	Brett Butler	.05	.04	.02
63	Mickey Hatcher	.05	.04	.02
64	Bruce Sutter	.05	.04	.02
65	Robin Ventura	.80	.60	.30
66	Junior Oritiz	.05	.04	.02
67	Pat Tabler	.05	.04	.02
68	Greg Swindell	.08	.06	.03
69	Jeff Branson	.20	.15	.08
70	Manny Lee	.05	.04	.02
71	Dave Magadan	.05	.04	.02
72	Rich Gedman	.05	.04	.02
73	Rock Raines	.08	.06	.03
74	Mike Maddux	.05	.04	.02
75	Jim Presley	.05	.04	.02
76	Chuck Finley	.05	.04	.02
77	Jose Oquendo	.05	.04	.02
78	Rob Deer	.05	.04	.02
79	Jay Howell	.05	.04	.02
80	Terry Steinbach	.08	.06	.03
81	Eddie Whitson	.05	.04	.02
82	Ruben Sierra	.20	.15	.08
83	Bruce Benedict	.05	.04	.02
84	Fred Manrique	.05	.04	.02
85	John Smiley	.05	.04	.02
86	Mike Macfarlane	.05	.04	.02
87	Rene Gonzales	.05	.04	.02
88	Charles Hudson	.05	.04	.02
90	Les Straker	.05	.04	.02
91	Carmen Castillo	.05	.04	.02
92	Tracy Woodson	.05	.04	.02
93	Tino Martinez	.70	.50	.30
94	Herm Winningham	.05	.04	.02
95	Kelly Gruber	.05	.04	.02
96	Terry Leach	.05	.04	.02
97	Jody Reed	.05	.04	.02
98	Nelson Santovenia	.05	.04	.02
99	Tony Armas	.05	.04	.02
100	Greg Brock	.05	.04	.02
101	Dave Stewart	.05	.04	.02
102	Roberto Alomar	.08	.06	.03
103	Jim Sundberg	.05	.04	.02
104	Albert Hall	.05	.04	.02
105	Steve Lyons	.05	.04	.02
106	Sid Bream	.05	.04	.02

		MT	NR MT	EX
107	Danny Tartabull	.08	.06	.03
108	Rick Dempsey	.05	.04	.02
109	Rich Renteria	.05	.04	.02
110	Ozzie Smith	.08	.06	.03
111	Steve Sax	.08	.06	.03
112	Kelly Downs	.05	.04	.02
113	Larry Sheets	.05	.04	.02
114	Andy Benes	.50	.40	.20
115	Pete O'Brien	.05	.04	.02
116	Kevin McReynolds	.08	.06	.03
117	Juan Berenguer	.05	.04	.02
118	Billy Hatcher	.05	.04	.02
119	Rick Cerone	.05	.04	.02
120	Andre Dawson	.08	.06	.03
121	Storm Davis	.05	.04	.02
122	Devon White	.05	.04	.02
123	Alan Trammell	.08	.06	.03
124	Vince Coleman	.08	.06	.03
125	Al Leiter	.05	.04	.02
126	Dale Sveum	.05	.04	.02
127	Pete Incaviglia	.05	.04	.02
128	Dave Stieb	.08	.06	.03
129	Kevin Mitchell	.30	.25	.12
130	Dave Schmidt	.05	.04	.02
131	Gary Redus	.05	.04	.02
132	Ron Robinson	.05	.04	.02
133	Darnell Coles	.05	.04	.02
134	Benny Santiago	.08	.06	.03
135	John Farrell	.05	.04	.02
136	Willie Wilson	.05	.04	.02
137	Steve Bedrosian	.05	.04	.02
138	Don Slaught	.05	.04	.02
139	Darryl Strawberry	.25	.20	.10
140	Frank Viola	.10	.08	.04
141	Dave Silvestri	.20	.15	.08
142	Carlos Quintana	.05	.04	.02
143	Vance Law	.05	.04	.02
144	Dave Parker	.05	.04	.02
145	Tim Belcher	.05	.04	.02
146	Will Clark	.90	.70	.35
147	Mark Williamson	.05	.04	.02
148	Ozzie Guillen	.05	.04	.02
149	Kirk McCaskill	.05	.04	.02
150	Pat Sheridan	.05	.04	.02
151	Terry Pendleton	.05	.04	.02
152	Roberto Kelly	.05	.04	.02
153	Joey Meyer	.05	.04	.02
154	Mark Grant	.05	.04	.02
155	Joe Carter	.08	.06	.03
156	Steve Buechele	.05	.04	.02
157	Tony Fernandez	.08	.06	.03
158	Jeff Reed	.05	.04	.02
159	Bobby Bonilla	.08	.06	.03
160	Henry Cotto	.05	.04	.02
161	Kurt Stillwell	.05	.04	.02
162	Mickey Morandini	.25	.20	.10
163	Robby Thompson	.05	.04	.02
164	Rick Schu	.05	.04	.02
165	Stan Jefferson	.05	.04	.02
166	Ron Darling	.05	.04	.02
167	Kirby Puckett	.25	.20	.10
168	Bill Doran	.05	.04	.02
169	Dennis Lamp	.05	.04	.02
170	Ty Griffin	.60	.45	.25
171	Ron Hassey	.05	.04	.02
172	Dale Murphy	.08	.06	.03
173	Andres Galarraga	.08	.06	.03
174	Tim Flannery	.05	.04	.02
175	Cory Snyder	.05	.04	.02
176	Checklist	.05	.04	.02
177	Tommy Barrett	.05	.04	.02
178	Dan Petry	.05	.04	.02
179	Billy Masse	.20	.15	.08
180	Terry Kennedy	.05	.04	.02
181	Joe Orsulak	.05	.04	.02
182	Doyle Alexander	.05	.04	.02
183	Willie McGee	.05	.04	.02
184	Jim Gantner	.05	.04	.02
185	Keith Hernandez	.05	.04	.02
186	Greg Gagne	.05	.04	.02
187	Kevin Bass	.05	.04	.02
188	Mark Eichhorn	.05	.04	.02
189	Mark Grace	.25	.20	.10
190	Jose Canseco	1.00	.70	.40
191	Bobby Witt	.05	.04	.02
192	Rafael Santana	.05	.04	.02
193	Dwight Evans	.05	.04	.02
194	Greg Booker	.05	.04	.02
195	Brook Jacoby	.05	.04	.02
196	Rafael Belliard	.05	.04	.02
197	Candy Maldonado	.05	.04	.02

		MT	NR MT	EX
198	Mickey Tettleton	.08	.06	.03
199	Barry Larkin	.08	.06	.03
200	Frank White	.05	.04	.02
201	Wally Joyner	.15	.11	.06
202	Chet Lemon	.05	.04	.02
203	Joe Magrane	.05	.04	.02
204	Glenn Braggs	.05	.04	.02
205	Scott Fletcher	.05	.04	.02
206	Gary Ward	.05	.04	.02
207	Nelson Liriano	.05	.04	.02
208	Howard Johnson	.15	.11	.06
209	Kent Hrbek	.08	.06	.03
210	Ken Caminiti	.05	.04	.02
211	Mike Greenwell	.50	.40	.20
212	Ryne Sandberg	.25	.20	.10
213	Joe Slusarski	.25	.20	.10
214	Donnell Nixon	.05	.04	.02
215	Tim Wallach	.05	.04	.02
216	John Kruk	.05	.04	.02
217	Charles Nagy	.25	.20	.10
218	Alvin Davis	.08	.06	.03
219	Oswald Peraza	.05	.04	.02
220	Mike Schmidt	.30	.25	.12
221	Spike Owen	.05	.04	.02
222	Mike Smithson	.05	.04	.02
223	Dion James	.05	.04	.02
224	Ernie Whitt	.05	.04	.02
225	Mike Davis	.05	.04	.02
226	Gene Larkin	.05	.04	.02
227	Pat Combs	.50	.40	.20
228	Jack Howell	.05	.04	.02
229	Ron Oester	.05	.04	.02
230	Paul Gibson	.05	.04	.02
231	Mookie Wilson	.05	.04	.02
232	Glenn Hubbard	.05	.04	.02
233	Shawon Dunston	.05	.04	.02
234	Otis Nixon	.05	.04	.02
235	Melido Perez	.05	.04	.02
236	Jerry Browne	.05	.04	.02
237	Rick Rhoden	.05	.04	.02
238	Bo Jackson	.50	.40	.20
239	Randy Velarde	.05	.04	.02
240	Jack Clark	.05	.04	.02
241	Wade Boggs	.80	.60	.30
242	Lonnie Smith	.05	.04	.02
243	Mike Flanagan	.05	.04	.02
244	Willie Randolph	.05	.04	.02
245	Oddibe McDowell	.05	.04	.02
246	Ricky Jordan	.35	.25	.14
247	Greg Briley	.20	.15	.08
248	Rex Hudler	.05	.04	.02
249	Robin Yount	.20	.15	.08
250	Lance Parrish	.05	.04	.02
251	Chris Sabo	.20	.15	.08
252	Mike Henneman	.05	.04	.02
253	Gregg Jefferies	1.00	.70	.40
254	Curt Young	.05	.04	.02
255	Andy Van Slyke	.08	.06	.03
256	Rod Booker	.05	.04	.02
257	Rafael Palmeiro	.05	.04	.02
258	Jose Uribe	.05	.04	.02
259	Ellis Burks	.20	.15	.08
260	John Smoltz	.10	.08	.04
261	Tom Foley	.05	.04	.02
262	Lloyd Moseby	.05	.04	.02
263	Jim Poole	.15	.11	.06
264	Gary Gaetti	.08	.06	.03
265	Bob Dernier	.05	.04	.02
266	Harold Baines	.08	.06	.03
267	Tom Candiotti	.05	.04	.02
268	Rafael Ramirez	.05	.04	.02
269	Bob Boone	.05	.04	.02
270	Buddy Bell	.05	.04	.02
271	Rickey Henderson	.15	.11	.06
272	Willie Fraser	.05	.04	.02
273	Eric Davis	.25	.20	.10
274	Jeff Robinson	.05	.04	.02
275	Damaso Garcia	.05	.04	.02
276	Sid Fernandez	.05	.04	.02
277	Stan Javier	.05	.04	.02
278	Marty Barrett	.05	.04	.02
279	Gerald Perry	.05	.04	.02
280	Rob Ducey	.05	.04	.02
281	Mike Scioscia	.05	.04	.02
282	Randy Bush	.05	.04	.02
283	Tom Herr	.05	.04	.02
284	Glenn Wilson	.05	.04	.02
285	Pedro Guerrero	.10	.08	.04
286	Cal Ripken	.10	.08	.04
287	Randy Johnson	.15	.11	.06
288	Julio Franco	.08	.06	.03

		MT	NR MT	EX
289	Ivan Calderon	.05	.04	.02
290	Rich Yett	.05	.04	.02
291	Scott Servais	.20	.15	.08
292	Bill Pecota	.05	.04	.02
293	Ken Phelps	.05	.04	.02
294	Chili Davis	.05	.04	.02
295	Manny Trillo	.05	.04	.02
296	Mike Boddicker	.05	.04	.02
297	Geronimo Berroa	.05	.04	.02
298	Todd Stottlemyre	.05	.04	.02
299	Kirk Gibson	.05	.04	.02
300	Wally Backman	.05	.04	.02
301	Hubie Brooks	.05	.04	.02
302	Von Hayes	.05	.04	.02
303	Matt Nokes	.05	.04	.02
304	Doc Gooden	.20	.15	.08
305	Walt Weiss	.10	.08	.04
306	Mike LaValliere	.05	.04	.02
307	Cris Carpenter	.10	.08	.04
308	Ted Wood	.20	.15	.08
309	Jeff Russell	.05	.04	.02
310	Dave Gallagher	.05	.04	.02
311	Andy Allanson	.05	.04	.02
312	Craig Reynolds	.05	.04	.02
313	Kevin Seitzer	.08	.06	.03
314	Dave Winfield	.10	.08	.04
315	Andy McGaffigan	.05	.04	.02
316	Nick Esasky	.05	.04	.02
317	Jeff Blauser	.05	.04	.02
318	George Bell	.10	.08	.04
319	Eddie Murray	.10	.08	.04
320	Mark Davidson	.05	.04	.02
321	Juan Samuel	.05	.04	.02
322	Jim Abbott	.50	.40	.20
323	Kal Daniels	.05	.04	.02
324	Mike Brumley	.05	.04	.02
325	Gary Carter	.05	.04	.02
326	Dave Henderson	.05	.04	.02
327	Checklist	.05	.04	.02
328	Garry Templeton	.05	.04	.02
329	Pat Perry	.05	.04	.02
330	Paul Molitor	.08	.06	.03

1989 Topps Double Headers All-Stars

This scarce test issue was produced in two versions, an All-Stars set and a set of exclusively Mets and Yankees players. The "cards" are two-sided miniature (1-5/8" x 2-1/4") reproductions of the player's 1989 Topps card and his Topps rookie card, encased in a clear plastic s-tand.

		MT	NR MT	EX
Complete set (24):		65.00	49.00	26.00
Common player:		2.00	1.50	.80
(1)	Alan Ashby	2.00	1.50	.80
2	Wade Boggs	6.00	4.50	2.50
(3)	Bobby Bonilla	3.00	2.25	1.25
(4)	Jose Canseco	4.00	3.00	1.50
(5)	Will Clark	5.00	3.75	2.00
(6)	Roger Clemens	3.00	2.25	1.25
(7)	Andre Dawson	2.50	2.00	1.00
(9)	Carlton Fisk	2.50	2.00	1.00
(10)	John Franco	2.00	1.50	.80
(11)	Julio Franco	2.00	1.50	.80
(12)	Kirk Gibson	2.50	2.00	1.00
13	Mike Greenwell	2.50	2.00	1.00
(14)	Orel Hershiser	2.50	2.00	1.00
(15)	Danny Jackson	2.00	1.50	.80
(16)	Don Mattingly	6.00	4.50	2.25
(17)	Mark McGwire	4.00	3.00	1.50
(18)	Kirby Puckett	6.00	4.50	2.50
(19)	Ryne Sandberg	8.00	6.00	3.25
(20)	Ozzie Smith	3.00	2.25	1.25
(21)	Darryl Strawberry	2.50	2.00	1.00
(22)	Alan Trammell	3.00	2.25	1.25
(23)	Andy Van Slyke	2.50	2.00	1.00
(24)	Frank Viola	2.00	1.50	.80

1989 Topps Major League Debut

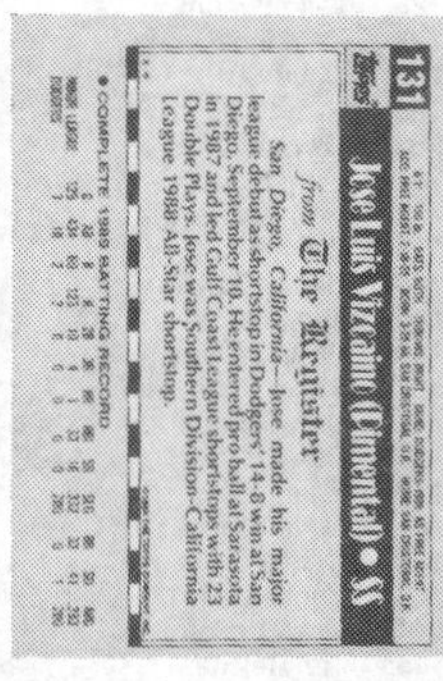

This 150-card set highlights the debut date of 1989 Major League rookies. Two checklist cards are also included in this boxed set. The checklist cards list the players in order of debut date, but the cards are numbered alphabetically. The card fronts resemble the 1990 Topps cards in style. A debut banner appears in an upper corner of the card. The flip sides are horizontal and are printed in black on yellow stock. An overview of the player's first game is provided on the card back. The set is packaged in an attractive red, blue, green and yellow collectors box. The set was available through select hobby dealers.

		MT	NR MT	EX
Complete Set:		18.00	13.50	7.25
Common Player:		.08	.06	.03
1	Jim Abbott	.30	.25	.12
2	Beau Allred	.15	.11	.06
3	Wilson Alvarez	.25	.20	.10
4	Kent Anderson	.08	.06	.03
5	Eric Anthony	.40	.30	.15
6	Kevin Appier	.25	.20	.10
7	Larry Arndt	.08	.06	.03
8	John Barfield	.08	.06	.03
9	Billy Bates	.08	.06	.03
10	Kevin Batiste	.10	.08	.04
11	Blaine Beatty	.20	.15	.08
12	Stan Belinda	.15	.11	.06
13	Juan Bell	.15	.11	.06
14	Joey Belle	.20	.15	.08
15	Andy Benes	.30	.25	.12
16	Mike Benjamin	.20	.15	.08
17	Geronimo Berroa	.08	.06	.03
18	Mike Blowers	.10	.08	.04
19	Brian Brady	.08	.06	.03
20	Francisco Cabrera	.25	.20	.10
21	George Canale	.08	.06	.03
22	Jose Cano	.08	.06	.03
23	Steve Carter	.10	.08	.04
24	Pat Combs	.30	.25	.12
25	Scott Coolbaugh	.15	.11	.06
26	Steve Cummings	.10	.08	.04
27	Pete Dalena	.08	.06	.03
28	Jeff Datz	.08	.06	.03
29	Bobby Davidson	.08	.06	.03
30	Drew Denson	.08	.06	.03
31	Gary DiSarcina	.20	.15	.08
32	Brian DuBois	.15	.11	.06
33	Mike Dyer	.10	.08	.04

		MT	NR MT	EX
34	Wayne Edwards	.10	.08	.04
35	Junior Felix	.30	.25	.12
36	Mike Fetters	.15	.11	.06
37	Steve Finley	.15	.11	.06
38	Darren Fletcher	.15	.11	.06
39	LaVel Freeman	.08	.06	.03
40	Steve Frey	.10	.08	.04
41	Mark Gardner	.20	.15	.08
42	Joe Girardi	.20	.15	.08
43	Juan Gonzalez	2.00	1.50	.80
44	Goose Gozzo	.15	.11	.06
45	Tommy Greene	.15	.11	.06
46	Ken Griffey,Jr.	3.50	2.75	1.50
47	Jason Grimsley	.20	.15	.08
48	Marquis Grissom	.40	.30	.15
49	Mark Guthrie	.10	.08	.04
50	Chip Hale	.08	.06	.03
51	John Hardy	.08	.06	.03
52	Gene Harris	.10	.08	.04
53	Mike Hartley	.10	.08	.04
54	Scott Hemond	.10	.08	.04
55	Xavier Hernandez	.10	.08	.04
56	Eric Hetzel	.15	.11	.06
57	Greg Hibbard	.25	.20	.10
58	Mark Higgins	.08	.06	.03
59	Glenallen Hill	.20	.15	.08
60	Chris Hoiles	.30	.25	.12
61	Shawn Holman	.10	.08	.04
62	Dann Howitt	.10	.08	.04
63	Mike Huff	.10	.08	.04
64	Terry Jorgenson	.10	.08	.04
65	Dave Justice	2.00	1.50	.80
66	Jeff King	.20	.15	.08
67	Matt Kinzer	.08	.06	.03
68	Joe Kraemer	.08	.06	.03
69	Marcus Lawton	.08	.06	.03
70	Derek Lilliquist	.15	.11	.06
71	Scott Little	.08	.06	.03
72	Greg Litton	.15	.11	.06
73	Rick Lueken	.10	.08	.04
74	Julio Machado	.15	.11	.06
75	Tom Magrann	.08	.06	.03
76	Kelly Mann	.20	.15	.08
77	Randy McCament	.08	.06	.03
78	Ben McDonald	.50	.40	.20
79	Chuck McElroy	.20	.15	.08
80	Jeff McKnight	.10	.08	.04
81	Kent Mercker	.25	.20	.10
82	Matt Merullo	.08	.06	.03
83	Hensley Meulens	.15	.11	.06
84	Kevin Mmahat	.08	.06	.03
85	Mike Munoz	.08	.06	.03
86	Dan Murphy	.08	.06	.03
87	Jaime Navarro	.20	.15	.08
88	Randy Nosek	.10	.08	.04
89	John Olerud	.50	.40	.20
90	Steve Olin	.10	.08	.04
91	Joe Oliver	.20	.15	.08
92	Francisco Oliveras	.10	.08	.04
93	Greg Olson	.15	.11	.06
94	John Orton	.10	.08	.04
95	Dean Palmer	.20	.15	.08
96	Ramon Pena	.08	.06	.03
97	Jeff Peterek	.08	.06	.03
98	Marty Pevey	.08	.06	.03
99	Rusty Richards	.08	.06	.03
100	Jeff Richardson	.08	.06	.03
101	Rob Richie	.08	.06	.03
102	Kevin Ritz	.10	.08	.04
103	Rosario Rodriguez	.25	.20	.10
104	Mike Roesler	.10	.08	.04
105	Kenny Rogers	.15	.11	.06
106	Bobby Rose	.20	.15	.08
107	Alex Sanchez	.15	.11	.06
108	Deion Sanders	.25	.20	.10
109	Jeff Schaefer	.08	.06	.03
110	Jeff Schulz	.10	.08	.04
111	Mike Schwabe	.10	.08	.04
112	Dick Scott	.08	.06	.03
113	Scott Scudder	.25	.20	.10
114	Rudy Seanez	.15	.11	.06
115	Joe Skalski	.08	.06	.03
116	Dwight Smith	.20	.15	.08
117	Greg Smith	.15	.11	.06
118	Mike Smith	.10	.08	.04
119	Paul Sorrento	.15	.11	.06
120	Sammy Sosa	.50	.40	.20
121	Billy Spiers	.15	.11	.06
122	Mike Stanton	.20	.15	.08
123	Phil Stephenson	.08	.06	.03
124	Doug Strange	.08	.06	.03
125	Russ Swan	.10	.08	.04
126	Kevin Tapani	.35	.25	.14
127	Stu Tate	.08	.06	.03
128	Greg Vaughn	.40	.30	.15
129	Robin Ventura	.25	.20	.10
130	Randy Veres	.08	.06	.03
131	Jose Vizcaino	.15	.11	.06
132	Omar Vizquel	.10	.08	.04
133	Larry Walker	.40	.30	.15
134	Jerome Walton	.50	.40	.20
135	Gary Wayne	.10	.08	.04
136	Lenny Webster	.10	.08	.04
137	Mickey Weston	.10	.08	.04
138	Jeff Wetherby	.08	.06	.03
139	John Wetteland	.25	.20	.10
140	Ed Whited	.08	.06	.03
141	Wally Whitehurst	.10	.08	.04
142	Kevin Wickander	.15	.11	.06
143	Dean Wilkins	.10	.08	.04
144	Dana Williams	.10	.08	.04
145	Paul Wilmet	.08	.06	.03
146	Craig Wilson	.15	.11	.06
147	Matt Winters	.08	.06	.03
148	Eric Yelding	.25	.20	.10
149	Clint Zavaras	.15	.11	.06
150	Todd Zeile	.50	.40	.20
---	Checklist (1 of 2)	.08	.06	.03
---	Checklist (2 of 2)	.08	.06	.03

1989 Topps Mini League Leaders

This 77-card set from Topps features baseball's statistical leaders from the 1988 season, and is referred to as a "mini" set because of the cards' small (2-1/8" by 3") size. The glossy cards feature action photos that have a soft focus on all edges. The player's team and name appear along the bottom of the card. The back features a head- shot of the player along with his 1988 season ranking and stats.

		MT	NR MT	EX
Complete Set:		6.00	4.50	2.50
Common Player:		.09	.07	.04
1	Dale Murphy	.35	.25	.14
2	Gerald Perry	.09	.07	.04
3	Andre Dawson	.20	.15	.08
4	Greg Maddux	.20	.15	.08
5	Rafael Palmeiro	.15	.11	.06
6	Tom Browning	.12	.09	.05
7	Kal Daniels	.15	.11	.06
8	Eric Davis	.60	.45	.25
9	John Franco	.09	.07	.04
10	Danny Jackson	.09	.07	.04
11	Barry Larkin	.15	.11	.06
12	Jose Rijo	.12	.09	.05
13	Chris Sabo	.20	.15	.08
14	Mike Scott	.09	.07	.04
15	Nolan Ryan	.50	.40	.20
16	Gerald Young	.09	.07	.04
17	Kirk Gibson	.12	.09	.05
18	Orel Hershiser	.25	.20	.10
19	Steve Sax	.12	.09	.05
20	John Tudor	.09	.07	.04

		MT	NR MT	EX
21	Hubie Brooks	.09	.07	.04
22	Andres Galarraga	.15	.11	.06
23	Otis Nixon	.09	.07	.04
24	Dave Cone	.15	.11	.06
25	Sid Fernandez	.12	.09	.05
26	Doc Gooden	.30	.25	.12
27	Kevin McReynolds	.20	.15	.08
28	Darryl Strawberry	.35	.25	.14
29	Juan Samuel	.09	.07	.04
30	Bobby Bonilla	.12	.09	.05
31	Sid Bream	.09	.07	.04
32	Andy Van Slyke	.12	.09	.05
33	Vince Coleman	.12	.09	.05
34	Jose DeLeon	.09	.07	.04
35	Joe Magrane	.12	.09	.05
36	Ozzie Smith	.12	.09	.05
37	Todd Worrell	.09	.07	.04
38	Tony Gwynn	.30	.25	.12
39	Brett Butler	.12	.09	.05
40	Will Clark	.80	.60	.30
41	Jim Gott	.09	.07	.04
42	Rick Reuschel	.12	.09	.05
43	Checklist	.09	.07	.04
44	Eddie Murray	.20	.15	.08
45	Wade Boggs	.80	.60	.30
46	Roger Clemens	.30	.25	.12
47	Dwight Evans	.12	.09	.05
48	Mike Greenwell	.70	.50	.30
49	Bruce Hurst	.12	.09	.05
50	Johnny Ray	.09	.07	.04
51	Doug Jones	.09	.07	.04
52	Greg Swindell	.15	.11	.06
53	Gary Pettis	.09	.07	.04
54	George Brett	.15	.11	.06
55	Mark Gubicza	.15	.11	.06
56	Willie Wilson	.09	.07	.04
57	Teddy Higuera	.12	.09	.05
58	Paul Molitor	.15	.11	.06
59	Robin Yount	.25	.20	.10
60	Allan Anderson	.09	.07	.04
61	Gary Gaetti	.12	.09	.04
62	Kirby Puckett	.40	.30	.15
63	Jeff Reardon	.09	.07	.04
64	Frank Viola	.12	.09	.05
65	Jack Clark	.12	.09	.05
66	Rickey Henderson	.25	.20	.10
67	Dave Winfield	.15	.11	.06
68	Jose Canseco	.80	.60	.30
69	Dennis Eckersley	.12	.09	.05
70	Mark McGwire	.80	.60	.30
71	Dave Stewart	.12	.09	.05
72	Alvin Davis	.12	.09	.05
73	Mark Langston	.12	.09	.05
74	Harold Reynolds	.12	.09	.05
75	George Bell	.15	.11	.06
76	Tony Fernandez	.15	.11	.06
77	Fred McGriff	.25	.20	.10

1989 Topps American Baseball

Photos not available at press time

For the second consecutive year Topps released an 88-card set of baseball cards available in both the United States and the United Kingdom. The mini-sized cards (2-1/4" by 3") feature full-color photos on the card fronts. The cards are printed on white stock with a low gloss finish. The player action photo is outlined in red, white, and blue and framed in white. The card backs are printed horizontally and include a characterization cartoon along with biographical information and statistics. The cards are sold in packs of five cards with a stick of bubble gum.

		MT	NR MT	EX
Complete Set:		8.00	6.00	3.25
Common Player:		.08	.06	.03
1	Brady Anderson	.08	.06	.03
2	Harold Baines	.15	.11	.06
3	George Bell	.15	.11	.06
4	Wade Boggs	1.00	.70	.40
5	Barry Bonds	.20	.15	.08
6	Bobby Bonilla	.20	.15	.08
7	George Brett	.15	.11	.06
8	Hubie Brooks	.08	.06	.03
9	Tom Brunansky	.08	.06	.03
10	Jay Buhner	.08	.06	.03
11	Brett Butler	.08	.06	.03
12	Jose Canseco	1.25	.90	.50
13	Joe Carter	.15	.11	.06
14	Jack Clark	.08	.06	.03
15	Will Clark	.80	.60	.30
16	Roger Clemens	.30	.25	.12
17	Dave Cone	.08	.06	.03
18	Alvin Davis	.08	.06	.03
19	Eric Davis	.30	.25	.12
20	Glenn Davis	.08	.06	.03
21	Andre Dawson	.12	.09	.05
22	Bill Doran	.08	.06	.03
23	Dennis Eckersley	.08	.06	.03
24	Dwight Evans	.08	.06	.03
25	Tony Fernandez	.08	.06	.03
26	Carlton Fisk	.08	.06	.03
27	John Franco	.08	.06	.03
28	Andres Galarraga	.15	.11	.06
29	Ron Gant	.08	.06	.03
30	Kirk Gibson	.08	.06	.03
31	Doc Gooden	.25	.20	.10
32	Mike Greenwell	.50	.40	.20
33	Mark Gubicza	.08	.06	.03
34	Pedro Gurrero	.12	.09	.05
35	Ozzie Guillen	.08	.06	.03
36	Tony Gwynn	.15	.11	.06
37	Rickey Henderson	.15	.11	.06
38	Orel Hershiser	.15	.11	.06
39	Teddy Higuera	.08	.06	.03
40	Charlie Hough	.08	.06	.03
41	Kent Hrbek	.12	.09	.05
42	Bruce Hurst	.08	.06	.03
43	Bo Jackson	.50	.40	.20
44	Gregg Jefferies	.60	.45	.25
45	Ricky Jordan	.25	.20	.10
46	Wally Joyner	.15	.11	.06
47	Mark Langston	.12	.09	.05
48	Mike Marshall	.08	.06	.03
49	Don Mattingly	2.00	1.50	.80
50	Fred McGriff	.35	.25	.14
51	Mark McGwire	1.00	.70	.40
52	Kevin McReynolds	.15	.11	.06
53	Paul Molitor	.08	.06	.03
54	Jack Morris	.08	.06	.03
55	Dale Murphy	.15	.11	.06
56	Eddie Murray	.10	.08	.04
57	Pete O'Brien	.08	.06	.03
58	Rafael Palmeiro	.08	.06	.03
59	Gerald Perry	.08	.06	.03
60	Kirby Puckett	.30	.25	.12
61	Rock Raines	.15	.11	.06
62	Johnny Ray	.08	.06	.03
63	Rick Reuschel	.08	.06	.03
64	Cal Ripken	.15	.11	.06
65	Chris Sabo	.15	.11	.06
66	Juan Samuel	.08	.06	.03
67	Ryane Sandberg	.15	.11	.06
68	Benny Santiago	.15	.11	.06
69	Steve Sax	.08	.06	.03
70	Mike Schmidt	.20	.15	.11
71	Ruben Sierra	.20	.15	.11
72	Ozzie Smith	.15	.11	.06
73	Cory Snyder	.08	.06	.03
74	Dave Stewart	.08	.06	.03
75	Darryl Strawberry	.25	.20	.10
76	Greg Swindell	.15	.11	.06
77	Alan Trammell	.15	.11	.06
78	Fernando Valenzuela	.08	.06	.03
79	Andy Van Slyke	.20	.15	.08
80	Frank Viola	.20	.15	.08
81	Claudell Washington	.08	.06	.03

		MT	NR MT	EX
82	Walt Weiss	.08	.06	.03
83	Lou Whitaker	.08	.06	.03
84	Dave Winfield	.20	.15	.08
85	Mike Witt	.08	.06	.03
86	Gerald Young	.08	.06	.03
87	Robin Yount	.20	.15	.08
88	Checklist	.08	.06	.03

1990 Topps

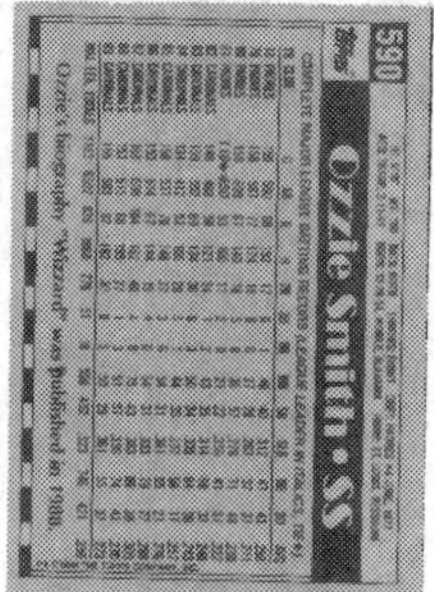

The 1990 Topps set again included 792 cards, and sported a newly-designed front that featured six different color schemes. The set led off with a special four-card salute to Nolan Ryan, and featured various other specials, including All-Stars, Number 1 Draft Picks, Record Breakers, manager cards, rookies, and "Turn Back the Clock" cards. The set also includes a special card commemorating A. Bartlett Giamatti, the late Baseball Commissioner. The backs are printed in black on a chartreuse background with the card number in the upper left corner. The set features 725 different individual player cards, the most ever, including 138 players making their first appearance in a regular Topps set.

	MT	NR MT	EX
Complete Set (792):	15.00	11.00	6.00
Common Player:	.03	.02	.01

		MT	NR MT	EX
1	Nolan Ryan	.35	.25	.14
2	Nolan Ryan (Mets)	.20	.15	.08
3	Nolan Ryan (Angels)	.20	.15	.08
4	Nolan Ryan (Astros)	.20	.15	.08
5	Nolan Ryan (Rangers)	.20	.15	.08
6	Vince Coleman (Record Breaker)	.10	.08	.04
7	Rickey Henderson (Record Breaker)	.20	.15	.08
8	Cal Ripken, Jr. (Record Breaker)	.15	.11	.06
9	Eric Plunk	.03	.02	.01
10	Barry Larkin	.15	.11	.06
11	Paul Gibson	.04	.03	.02
12	Joe Girardi(FC)	.15	.11	.06
13	Mark Williamson	.03	.02	.01
14	*Mike Fetters*(FC)	.20	.15	.08
15	Teddy Higuera	.06	.05	.02
16	*Kent Anderson*	.10	.08	.04
17	Kelly Downs	.05	.04	.02
18	Carlos Quintana	.09	.07	.04
19	Al Newman	.03	.02	.01
20	Mark Gubicza	.12	.09	.05
21	Jeff Torborg	.03	.02	.01
22	Bruce Ruffin	.03	.02	.01
23	Randy Velarde	.07	.05	.03
24	Joe Hesketh	.03	.02	.01
25	Willie Randolph	.08	.06	.03
26	Don Slaught	.03	.02	.01
27	Rick Leach	.03	.02	.01
28	Duane Ward	.04	.03	.02
29	John Cangelosi	.03	.02	.01
30	David Cone	.10	.08	.04
31	Henry Cotto	.03	.02	.01
32	John Farrell	.05	.04	.02
33	Greg Walker	.05	.04	.02
34	*Tony Fossas*(FC)	.07	.05	.03
35	Benito Santiago	.12	.09	.05
36	John Costello	.04	.03	.02
37	Domingo Ramos	.03	.02	.01

		MT	NR MT	EX
38	Wes Gardner	.04	.03	.02
39	Curt Ford	.04	.03	.02
40	Jay Howell	.06	.05	.02
41	Matt Williams	.15	.11	.06
42	Jeff Robinson	.05	.04	.02
43	Dante Bichette	.07	.05	.03
44	*Roger Salkeld* (#1 Draft Pick)	.25	.20	.10
45	Dave Parker	.09	.07	.04
46	Rob Dibble	.07	.05	.03
47	Brian Harper	.04	.03	.02
48	Zane Smith	.03	.02	.01
49	Tom Lawless	.03	.02	.01
50	Glenn Davis	.08	.06	.03
51	Doug Rader	.03	.02	.01
52	*Jack Daugherty*(FC)	.20	.15	.08
53	Mike LaCoss	.04	.03	.02
54	Joel Skinner	.04	.03	.02
55	Darrell Evans	.05	.04	.02
56	Franklin Stubbs	.04	.03	.02
57	*Greg Vaughn*(FC)	.60	.45	.25
58	Keith Miller	.10	.08	.04
59	Ted Power	.03	.02	.01
60	George Brett	.15	.11	.06
61	*Deion Sanders*	.30	.25	.12
62	Ramon Martinez	.30	.25	.12
63	Mike Pagliarulo	.04	.03	.02
64	Danny Darwin	.03	.02	.01
65	Devon White	.07	.05	.03
66	*Greg Litton*(FC)	.15	.11	.06
67	Scott Sanderson	.04	.03	.02
68	Dave Henderson	.06	.05	.02
69	Todd Frohwirth	.03	.02	.01
70	Mike Greenwell	.30	.25	.12
71	Allan Anderson	.05	.04	.02
72	*Jeff Huson*(FC)	.25	.20	.10
73	Bob Milacki	.05	.04	.02
74	*Jeff Jackson* (#1 Drast Pick)(FC)	.20	.15	.08
75	Doug Jones	.05	.04	.02
76	Dave Valle	.03	.02	.01
77	Dave Bergman	.03	.02	.01
78	Mike Flanagan	.04	.03	.02
79	Ron Kittle	.05	.04	.02
80	Jeff Russell	.05	.04	.02
81	Bob Rodgers	.03	.02	.01
82	Scott Terry	.04	.03	.02
83	Hensley Meulens	.30	.25	.12
84	Ray Searage	.03	.02	.01
85	Juan Samuel	.05	.04	.02
86	Paul Kilgus	.03	.02	.01
87	*Rick Luecken*(FC)	.15	.11	.06
88	Glenn Braggs	.05	.04	.02
89	*Clint Zavaras*(FC)	.15	.11	.06
90	Jack Clark	.06	.05	.02
91	*Steve Frey*(FC)	.20	.15	.08
92	Mike Stanley	.03	.02	.01
93	Shawn Hillegas	.03	.02	.01
94	Herm Winningham	.03	.02	.01
95	Todd Worrell	.05	.04	.02
96	Jody Reed	.04	.03	.02
97	Curt Schilling(FC)	.25	.20	.10
98	Jose Gonzalez(FC)	.10	.08	.04
99	*Rich Monteleone*(FC)	.15	.11	.06
100	Will Clark	.50	.40	.20
101	Shane Rawley	.04	.03	.02
102	Stan Javier	.04	.03	.02
103	Marvin Freeman	.09	.07	.04
104	Bob Knepper	.03	.02	.01
105	Randy Myers	.05	.04	.02
106	Charlie O'Brien	.03	.02	.01
107	Fred Lynn	.05	.04	.02
108	Rod Nichols	.04	.03	.02
109	Roberto Kelly	.08	.06	.03
110	Tommy Helms	.03	.02	.01
111	Ed Whited	.20	.15	.08
112	Glenn Wilson	.03	.02	.01
113	Manny Lee	.03	.02	.01
114	Mike Bielecki	.05	.04	.02
115	Tony Pena	.06	.05	.02
116	Floyd Bannister	.04	.03	.02
117	Mike Sharperson(FC)	.09	.07	.04
118	Erik Hanson	.10	.08	.04
119	Billy Hatcher	.04	.03	.02
120	John Franco	.05	.04	.02
121	Robin Ventura	.60	.45	.25
122	Shawn Abner	.03	.02	.01
123	Rich Gedman	.04	.03	.02
124	Dave Dravecky	.04	.03	.02
125	Kent Hrbek	.07	.05	.03
126	Randy Kramer	.03	.02	.01
127	Mike Devereaux	.06	.05	.02
128	Checklist 1-132	.03	.02	.01

		MT	NR MT	EX
129	Ron Jones	.10	.08	.04
130	Bert Blyleven	.05	.04	.02
131	Matt Nokes	.06	.05	.02
132	Lance Blankenship(FC)	.10	.08	.04
133	Ricky Horton	.03	.02	.01
134	*Earl Cunningham* (#1 Draft Pick)	.15	.11	.06
135	Dave Magadan	.05	.04	.02
136	Kevin Brown	.06	.05	.02
137	*Marty Pevey*(FC)	.15	.11	.06
138	Al Leiter	.04	.03	.02
139	Greg Brock	.04	.03	.02
140	Andre Dawson	.12	.09	.05
141	John Hart	.05	.04	.02
142	*Jeff Wetherby*(FC)	.15	.11	.06
143	Rafael Belliard	.03	.02	.01
144	Bud Black	.03	.02	.01
145	Terry Steinbach	.07	.05	.03
146	*Rob Richie*(FC)	.15	.11	.06
147	Chuck Finley	.04	.03	.02
148	Edgar Martinez(FC)	.09	.07	.04
149	Steve Farr	.04	.03	.02
150	Kirk Gibson	.09	.07	.04
151	Rick Mahler	.03	.02	.01
152	Lonnie Smith	.05	.04	.02
153	Randy Milligan	.05	.04	.02
154	Mike Maddux	.05	.04	.02
155	Ellis Burks	.25	.20	.10
156	Ken Patterson	.04	.03	.02
157	Craig Biggio	.15	.11	.06
158	Craig Lefferts	.04	.03	.02
159	Mike Felder	.03	.02	.01
160	Dave Righetti	.06	.05	.02
161	Harold Reynolds	.06	.05	.02
162	*Todd Zeile*(FC)	.60	.45	.25
163	Phil Bradley	.05	.04	.02
164	*Jeff Juden* (#1 Draft Pick)(FC)	.30	.25	.12
165	Walt Weiss	.08	.06	.03
166	Bobby Witt	.04	.03	.02
167	*Kevin Appier*(FC)	.35	.25	.14
168	Jose Lind	.04	.03	.02
169	Richard Dotson	.03	.02	.01
170	George Bell	.12	.09	.05
171	Russ Nixon	.03	.02	.01
172	Tom Lampkin(FC)	.10	.08	.04
173	Tim Belcher	.12	.09	.05
174	Jeff Kunkel	.03	.02	.01
175	Mike Moore	.07	.05	.02
176	Luis Quinones	.03	.02	.01
177	Mike Henneman	.05	.04	.02
178	Chris James	.06	.05	.02
179	Brian Holton	.04	.03	.02
180	Rock Raines	.10	.08	.04
181	Juan Agosto	.03	.02	.01
182	Mookie Wilson	.05	.04	.02
183	Steve Lake	.03	.02	.01
184	Danny Cox	.04	.03	.02
185	Ruben Sierra	.20	.15	.08
186	Dave LaPoint	.03	.02	.01
187	*Rick Wrona*(FC)	.12	.09	.05
188	Mike Smithson	.03	.02	.01
189	Dick Schofield	.04	.03	.02
190	Rick Reuschel	.06	.05	.02
191	Pat Borders	.08	.06	.03
192	Don August	.04	.03	.02
193	Andy Benes	.25	.20	.10
194	Glenallen Hill(FC)	.25	.20	.10
195	Tim Burke	.05	.04	.02
196	Gerald Young	.04	.03	.02
197	Doug Drabek	.07	.05	.03
198	Mike Marshall	.06	.05	.02
199	*Sergio Valdez*(FC)	.20	.15	.08
200	Don Mattingly	.40	.30	.15
201	Cito Gaston	.03	.02	.01
202	Mike Macfarlane	.03	.02	.01
203	*Mike Roesler*(FC)	.15	.11	.06
204	Bob Dernier	.03	.02	.01
205	Mark Davis	.09	.07	.04
206	Nick Esasky	.07	.05	.02
207	Bob Ojeda	.04	.03	.02
208	Brook Jacoby	.04	.03	.02
209	Greg Mathews	.04	.03	.02
210	Ryne Sandberg	.30	.25	.12
211	John Cerutti	.04	.03	.02
212	Joe Orsulak	.03	.02	.01
213	Scott Bankhead	.05	.04	.02
214	Terry Francona	.03	.02	.01
215	Kirk McCaskill	.04	.03	.02
216	Ricky Jordan	.20	.15	.08
217	Don Robinson	.04	.03	.02
218	Wally Backman	.04	.03	.02
219	Donn Pall	.03	.02	.01
220	Barry Bonds	.10	.08	.04
221	*Gary Mielke*(FC)	.15	.11	.06
222	Kurt Stillwell	.05	.04	.02
223	Tommy Gregg	.06	.05	.02
224	*Delino DeShields*(FC)	.60	.45	.25
225	Jim Deshaies	.05	.04	.02
226	Mickey Hatcher	.03	.02	.01
227	*Kevin Tapani*(FC)	.30	.25	.12
228	Dave Martinez	.03	.02	.01
229	David Wells	.03	.02	.01
230	Keith Hernandez	.07	.05	.03
231	Jack McKeon	.03	.02	.01
232	Darnell Coles	.04	.03	.02
233	Ken Hill	.10	.08	.06
234	Mariano Duncan	.05	.04	.02
235	Jeff Reardon	.04	.03	.02
236	Hal Morris(FC)	.50	.40	.20
237	*Kevin Ritz*(FC)	.15	.11	.06
238	Felix Jose(FC)	.10	.08	.04
239	Eric Show	.04	.03	.02
240	Mark Grace	.40	.30	.15
241	Mike Krukow	.04	.03	.02
242	Fred Manrique	.03	.02	.01
243	Barry Jones	.03	.02	.01
244	Bill Schroeder	.03	.02	.01
245	Roger Clemens	.25	.20	.10
246	Jim Eisenreich	.03	.02	.01
247	Jerry Reed	.03	.02	.01
248	Dave Anderson	.03	.02	.01
249	*Mike Smith*(FC)	.12	.09	.05
250	Jose Canseco	.70	.50	.30
251	Jeff Blauser	.05	.04	.02
252	Otis Nixon	.03	.02	.01
253	Mark Portugal	.03	.02	.01
254	Francisco Cabrera	.25	.20	.10
255	Bobby Thigpen	.07	.05	.03
256	Marvell Wynne	.03	.02	.01
257	Jose DeLeon	.07	.05	.03
258	Barry Lyons	.03	.02	.01
259	Lance McCullers	.05	.04	.02
260	Eric Davis	.30	.25	.12
261	Whitey Herzog	.03	.02	.01
262	Checklist 133-264	.03	.02	.01
263	*Mel Stottlemyre, Jr.*(FC)	.12	.09	.05
264	Bryan Clutterbuck	.03	.02	.01
265	Pete O'Brien	.06	.05	.02
266	German Gonzalez	.04	.03	.02
267	Mark Davidson	.03	.02	.01
268	Rob Murphy	.03	.02	.01
269	Dickie Thon	.03	.02	.01
270	Dave Stewart	.08	.06	.03
271	Chet Lemon	.05	.04	.02
272	Bryan Harvey	.04	.03	.02
273	Bobby Bonilla	.15	.11	.06
274	*Goose Gozzo*(FC)	.15	.11	.06
275	Mickey Tettleton	.07	.05	.03
276	Gary Thurman	.03	.02	.01
277	Lenny Harris(FC)	.12	.09	.05
278	Pascual Perez	.04	.03	.02
279	Steve Buechele	.04	.03	.02
280	Lou Whitaker	.07	.05	.03
281	Kevin Bass	.05	.04	.02
282	Derek Lilliquist	.10	.08	.04
283	*Albert Belle*(FC)	.70	.50	.30
284	*Mark Gardner*(FC)	.30	.25	.12
285	Willie McGee	.06	.05	.02
286	Lee Guetterman	.03	.02	.01
287	Vance Law	.03	.02	.01
288	Greg Briley	.15	.11	.06
289	Norm Charlton	.10	.08	.04
290	Robin Yount	.20	.15	.08
291	Dave Johnson	.03	.02	.01
292	Jim Gott	.04	.03	.02
293	Mike Gallego	.04	.03	.02
294	Craig McMurtry	.03	.02	.01
295	Fred McGriff	.25	.20	.10
296	Jeff Ballard	.07	.05	.03
297	Tom Herr	.06	.05	.02
298	Danny Gladden	.05	.04	.02
299	Adam Peterson(FC)	.09	.07	.04
300	Bo Jackson	.60	.45	.25
301	Don Aase	.03	.02	.01
302	*Marcus Lawton*(FC)	.08	.06	.03
303	Rick Cerone	.03	.02	.01
304	Marty Clary(FC)	.08	.06	.03
305	Eddie Murray	.15	.11	.06
306	Tom Niedenfuer	.03	.02	.01
307	Bip Roberts	.08	.06	.03
308	Jose Guzman	.05	.04	.02
309	*Eric Yelding*(FC)	.20	.15	.08
310	Steve Bedrosian	.05	.04	.02

		MT	NR MT	EX
311	Dwight Smith	.25	.20	.10
312	Dan Quisenberry	.05	.04	.02
313	Gus Polidor	.03	.02	.01
314	*Donald Harris* (#1 Draft Pick)	.20	.15	.08
315	Bruce Hurst	.06	.05	.02
316	Carney Lansford	.06	.05	.02
317	*Mark Guthrie*(FC)	.20	.15	.08
318	Wallace Johnson	.03	.02	.01
319	Dion James	.04	.03	.02
320	Dave Steib	.07	.05	.03
321	Joe M. Morgan	.03	.02	.01
322	Junior Ortiz	.03	.02	.01
323	Willie Wilson	.04	.03	.02
324	Pete Harnisch(FC)	.10	.08	.04
325	Robby Thompson	.06	.05	.02
326	*Tom McCarthy*	.10	.08	.04
327	Ken Williams	.03	.02	.01
328	Curt Young	.03	.02	.01
329	Oddibe McDowell	.06	.05	.02
330	Ron Darling	.09	.07	.04
331	*Juan Gonzalez*(FC)	2.00	1.50	.80
332	Paul O'Neill	.07	.05	.03
333	Bill Wegman	.03	.02	.01
334	Johnny Ray	.05	.04	.02
335	Andy Hawkins	.05	.04	.02
336	Ken Griffey, Jr.	1.00	.70	.40
337	Lloyd McClendon	.06	.05	.02
338	Dennis Lamp	.03	.02	.01
339	Dave Clark	.04	.03	.02
340	Fernando Valenzuela	.06	.05	.02
341	Tom Foley	.03	.02	.01
342	Alex Trevino	.03	.02	.01
343	Frank Tanana	.04	.03	.02
344	*George Canale*(FC)	.15	.11	.06
345	Harold Baines	.09	.07	.04
346	Jim Presley	.04	.03	.02
347	*Junior Felix*	.20	.15	.08
348	*Gary Wayne*(FC)	.12	.09	.05
349	*Steve Finley*(FC)	.30	.25	.12
350	Bret Saberhagen	.10	.08	.04
351	Roger Craig	.03	.02	.01
352	Bryn Smith	.05	.04	.02
353	Sandy Alomar	.25	.20	.10
354	*Stan Belinda*(FC)	.20	.15	.08
355	Marty Barrett	.05	.04	.02
356	Randy Ready	.03	.02	.01
357	Dave West	.20	.15	.08
358	Andres Thomas	.04	.03	.02
359	Jimmy Jones	.03	.02	.01
360	Paul Molitor	.09	.07	.04
361	*Randy McCament*(FC)	.15	.11	.06
362	Damon Berryhill	.06	.05	.02
363	Dan Petry	.03	.02	.01
364	Rolando Roomes(FC)	.15	.11	.06
365	Ozzie Guillen	.05	.04	.02
366	Mike Heath	.03	.02	.01
367	Mike Morgan	.03	.02	.01
368	Bill Doran	.06	.05	.02
369	Todd Burns	.04	.03	.02
370	Tim Wallach	.07	.05	.03
371	Jimmy Key	.08	.06	.03
372	Terry Kennedy	.03	.02	.01
373	Alvin Davis	.08	.06	.03
374	*Steve Cummings*(FC)	.15	.11	.06
375	Dwight Evans	.08	.06	.03
376	Checklist 265-396	.03	.02	.01
377	*Mickey Weston*(FC)	.15	.11	.06
378	Luis Salazar	.03	.02	.01
379	Steve Rosenberg	.03	.02	.01
380	Dave Winfield	.15	.11	.06
381	Frank Robinson	.03	.02	.01
382	Jeff Musselman	.03	.02	.01
383	John Morris	.04	.03	.02
384	*Pat Combs*	.20	.15	.08
385	Fred McGriff (All-Star)	.20	.15	.08
386	Julio Franco (All-Star)	.10	.08	.04
387	Wade Boggs (All-Star)	.20	.15	.08
388	Cal Ripken, Jr. (All-Star)	.15	.11	.06
389	Robin Yount (All-Star)	.20	.15	.08
390	Ruben Sierra (All-Star)	.20	.15	.08
391	Kirby Puckett (All-Star)	.20	.15	.08
392	Carlton Fisk (All-Star)	.08	.06	.03
393	Bret Saberhagen (All-Star)	.10	.08	.04
394	Jeff Ballard (All-Star)	.08	.06	.03
395	Jeff Russell (All-Star)	.08	.06	.03
396	A. Bartlett Giamatti	.30	.25	.12
397	Will Clark (All-Star)	.25	.20	.10
398	Ryne Sandberg (All-Star)	.15	.11	.06
399	Howard Johnson (All-Star)	.15	.11	.06
400	Ozzie Smith (All-Star)	.10	.08	.04
401	Kevin Mitchell (All-Star)	.10	.08	.04

		MT	NR MT	EX
402	Eric Davis (All-Star)	.10	.08	.04
403	Tony Gwynn (All-Star)	.15	.11	.06
404	Craig Biggio (All-Star)	.15	.11	.06
405	Mike Scott (All-Star)	.08	.06	.03
406	Joe Magrane (All-Star)	.08	.06	.03
407	Mark Davis (All-Star)	.08	.06	.03
408	Trevor Wilson	.06	.05	.02
409	Tom Brunansky	.09	.07	.04
410	Joe Boever	.06	.05	.02
411	Ken Phelps	.03	.02	.01
412	Jamie Moyer	.04	.03	.02
413	*Brian DuBois*(FC)	.15	.11	.06
414a	*Frank Thomas* (#1 Draft Pick, no name on front)	40.00	30.00	15.00
414b	*Frank Thomas* (#1 Draft Pick, name on front)	4.00	3.00	1.50
415	Shawon Dunston	.06	.05	.02
416	*Dave Johnson*(FC)	.12	.09	.05
417	Jim Gantner	.06	.05	.02
418	Tom Browning	.08	.06	.03
419	*Beau Allred*	.20	.15	.08
420	Carlton Fisk	.08	.06	.03
421	Greg Minton	.03	.02	.01
422	Pat Sheridan	.03	.02	.01
423	Fred Toliver	.03	.02	.01
424	Jerry Reuss	.05	.04	.02
425	Bill Landrum	.05	.04	.02
426	Jeff Hamilton	.05	.04	.02
427	Carmem Castillo	.03	.02	.01
428	*Steve Davis*(FC)	.12	.09	.05
429	Tom Kelly	.03	.02	.01
430	Pete Incaviglia	.06	.05	.02
431	Randy Johnson	.10	.08	.04
432	Damaso Garcia	.03	.02	.01
433	*Steve Olin*(FC)	.12	.08	.04
434	Mark Carreon(FC)	.09	.07	.04
435	Kevin Seitzer	.09	.07	.04
436	Mel Hall	.05	.04	.02
437	Les Lancaster	.05	.04	.02
438	Greg Myers(FC)	.10	.08	.04
439	Jeff Parrett	.06	.05	.02
440	Alan Trammell	.09	.07	.04
441	Bob Kipper	.03	.02	.01
442	Jerry Browne	.07	.05	.02
443	Cris Carpenter	.09	.07	.04
444	*Kyle Abbott* (FDP)	.20	.15	.08
445	Danny Jackson	.05	.04	.02
446	Dan Pasqua	.05	.04	.02
447	Atlee Hammaker	.03	.02	.01
448	Greg Gagne	.04	.03	.02
449	Dennis Rasmussen	.04	.03	.02
450	Rickey Henderson	.25	.20	.10
451	Mark Lemke(FC)	.10	.08	.04
452	Luis de los Santos(FC)	.10	.08	.04
453	Jody Davis	.03	.02	.01
454	Jeff King(FC)	.15	.11	.06
455	Jeffrey Leonard	.06	.05	.02
456	Chris Gwynn(FC)	.09	.07	.03
457	Gregg Jefferies	.30	.25	.12
458	Bob McClure	.03	.02	.01
459	Jim Lefebvre	.03	.02	.01
460	Mike Scott	.09	.07	.03
461	*Carlos Martinez*(FC)	.15	.11	.06
462	Denny Walling	.03	.02	.01
463	Drew Hall	.03	.02	.01
464	*Jerome Walton*	.25	.20	.10
465	Kevin Gross	.06	.05	.02
466	Rance Mulliniks	.03	.02	.01
467	Juan Nieves	.04	.03	.02
468	Billy Ripken	.04	.03	.02
469	John Kruk	.07	.05	.02
470	Frank Viola	.09	.07	.04
471	Mike Brumley	.03	.02	.01
472	Jose Uribe	.04	.03	.02
473	Joe Price	.03	.02	.01
474	Rich Thompson	.04	.03	.02
475	Bob Welch	.06	.05	.02
476	Brad Komminsk	.03	.02	.02
477	Willie Fraser	.03	.02	.02
478	Mike LaValliere	.04	.03	.02
479	Frank White	.06	.05	.02
480	Sid Fernandez	.09	.07	.04
481	Garry Templeton	.05	.04	.02
482	*Steve Carter*(FC)	.15	.11	.06
483	Alejandro Pena	.04	.03	.02
484	Mike Fitzgerald	.03	.02	.01
485	John Candelaria	.05	.04	.02
486	Jeff Treadway	.05	.04	.02
487	Steve Searcy	.05	.04	.02
488	Ken Oberkfell	.03	.02	.01
489	Nick Leyva	.03	.02	.01

		MT	NR MT	EX
490	Dan Plesac	.07	.05	.03
491	*Dave Cochrane*(FC)	.15	.11	.06
492	Ron Oester	.04	.03	.02
493	*Jason Grimsley*(FC)	.25	.20	.10
494	Terry Puhl	.03	.02	.01
495	Lee Smith	.06	.05	.02
496	Cecil Espy	.06	.05	.02
497	Dave Schmidt	.03	.02	.01
498	Rick Schu	.03	.02	.01
499	Bill Long	.04	.03	.02
500	Kevin Mitchell	.35	.25	.14
501	Matt Young	.03	.02	.01
502	Mitch Webster	.04	.03	.02
503	Randy St. Claire	.03	.02	.01
504	Tom O'Malley	.03	.02	.01
505	Kelly Gruber	.08	.06	.03
506	Tom Glavine	.20	.15	.08
507	Gary Redus	.04	.03	.02
508	Terry Leach	.03	.02	.01
509	Tom Pagnozzi	.03	.02	.01
510	Doc Gooden	.25	.20	.10
511	Clay Parker	.07	.05	.03
512	Gary Pettis	.03	.02	.01
513	Mark Eichhorn	.03	.02	.01
514	Andy Allanson	.03	.02	.01
515	Len Dykstra	.06	.05	.02
516	Tim Leary	.05	.04	.02
517	Roberto Alomar	.15	.11	.06
518	Bill Krueger	.03	.02	.01
519	Bucky Dent	.03	.02	.01
520	Mitch Williams	.09	.07	.03
521	Craig Worthington	.15	.11	.06
522	Mike Dunne	.04	.03	.02
523	Jay Bell	.03	.02	.01
524	Daryl Boston	.03	.02	.01
525	Wally Joyner	.20	.15	.08
526	Checklist 397-528	.03	.02	.01
527	Ron Hassey	.03	.02	.01
528	*Kevin Wickander*(FC)	.20	.15	.08
529	Greg Harris	.03	.02	.01
530	Mark Langston	.10	.08	.04
531	Ken Caminiti	.06	.05	.02
532	Cecilio Guante	.03	.02	.01
533	Tim Jones(FC)	.07	.05	.03
534	Louie Meadows	.07	.05	.03
535	John Smoltz	.15	.11	.06
536	*Bob Geren*	.15	.11	.06
537	Mark Grant	.03	.02	.01
538	*Billy Spiers*	.20	.15	.08
539	Neal Heaton	.03	.02	.01
540	Danny Tartabull	.09	.07	.03
541	Pat Perry	.03	.02	.01
542	Darren Daulton	.03	.02	.01
543	Nelson Liriano	.03	.02	.01
544	Dennis Boyd	.05	.04	.02
545	Kevin McReynolds	.09	.07	.04
546	Kevin Hickey	.05	.04	.02
547	Jack Howell	.05	.04	.02
548	Pat Clements	.03	.02	.01
549	Don Zimmer	.03	.02	.01
550	Julio Franco	.09	.07	.04
551	Tim Crews	.03	.02	.01
552	*Mike Smith*(FC)	.12	.09	.05
553	*Scott Scudder*(FC)	.20	.15	.11
554	Jay Buhner	.08	.06	.03
555	Jack Morris	.07	.05	.03
556	Gene Larkin	.03	.02	.01
557	*Jeff Innis*	.15	.11	.08
558	Rafael Ramirez	.04	.03	.02
559	Andy McGaffigan	.04	.03	.02
560	Steve Sax	.08	.06	.03
561	Ken Dayley	.03	.02	.01
562	Chad Kreuter	.10	.08	.04
563	Alex Sanchez	.10	.08	.04
564	*Tyler Houston* (#1 Draft Pick)	.20	.15	.08
565	Scott Fletcher	.05	.04	.02
566	Mark Knudson	.06	.05	.02
567	Ron Gant	.10	.08	.04
568	John Smiley	.07	.05	.03
569	Ivan Calderon	.05	.04	.02
570	Cal Ripken, Jr.	.35	.25	.14
571	Brett Butler	.06	.05	.02
572	Greg Harris	.09	.07	.04
573	Danny Heep	.03	.02	.01
574	Bill Swift	.04	.03	.02
575	Lance Parrish	.07	.05	.03
576	*Mike Dyer*(FC)	.20	.15	.08
577	Charlie Hayes(FC)	.10	.08	.04
578	Joe Magrane	.09	.07	.04
579	Art Howe	.03	.02	.01
580	Joe Carter	.15	.11	.06
581	Ken Griffey	.05	.04	.02
582	Rick Honeycutt	.03	.02	.01
583	Bruce Benedict	.03	.02	.01
584	*Phil Stephenson*(FC)	.09	.07	.04
585	Kal Daniels	.10	.08	.04
586	Ed Nunez	.03	.02	.01
587	Lance Johnson	.08	.06	.03
588	Rick Rhoden	.03	.02	.01
589	Mike Aldrete	.03	.02	.01
590	Ozzie Smith	.10	.08	.04
591	Todd Stottlemyre	.08	.06	.03
592	R.J. Reynolds	.03	.02	.01
593	Scott Bradley	.03	.02	.01
594	*Luis Sojo*(FC)	.20	.15	.08
595	Greg Swindell	.10	.08	.04
596	Jose DeJesus(FC)	.10	.08	.04
597	Chris Bosio	.07	.05	.03
598	Brady Anderson	.05	.04	.02
599	Frank Williams	.03	.02	.01
600	Darryl Strawberry	.30	.15	.08
601	Luis Rivera	.04	.03	.02
602	Scott Garrelts	.07	.05	.03
603	Tony Armas	.03	.02	.01
604	Ron Robinson	.03	.02	.01
605	Mike Scioscia	.07	.05	.03
606	Storm Davis	.07	.05	.03
607	Steve Jeltz	.03	.02	.01
608	*Eric Anthony*(FC)	.30	.25	.12
609	Sparky Anderson	.03	.02	.01
610	Pedro Guerrero	.12	.09	.05
611	Walt Terrell	.05	.04	.02
612	Dave Gallagher	.07	.05	.02
613	Jeff Pico	.04	.03	.02
614	Nelson Santovenia	.09	.07	.04
615	Rob Deer	.07	.05	.03
616	Brian Holman	.10	.08	.04
617	Geronimo Berroa	.08	.06	.03
618	Eddie Whitson	.05	.04	.02
619	Rob Ducey	.08	.06	.03
620	*Tony Castillo*(FC)	.20	.15	.08
621	Melido Perez	.07	.05	.03
622	Sid Bream	.05	.04	.02
623	Jim Corsi	.05	.04	.02
624	Darrin Jackson	.04	.03	.02
625	Roger McDowell	.07	.05	.03
626	Bob Melvin	.03	.02	.01
627	Jose Rijo	.07	.05	.03
628	Candy Maldonado	.04	.03	.02
629	Eric Hetzel(FC)	.10	.08	.04
630	Gary Gaetti	.10	.08	.04
631	*John Wetteland*(FC)	.25	.20	.10
632	Scott Lusader	.06	.05	.02
633	Dennis Cook(FC)	.25	.20	.10
634	Luis Polonia	.06	.05	.02
635	Brian Downing	.06	.05	.02
636	Jesse Orosco	.03	.02	.01
637	Craig Reynolds	.03	.02	.01
638	Jeff Montgomery	.07	.05	.03
639	Tony LaRussa	.03	.02	.01
640	Rick Sutcliffe	.06	.05	.02
641	*Doug Strange*(FC)	.15	.11	.06
642	Jack Armstrong	.04	.03	.02
643	Alfredo Griffin	.04	.03	.02
644	Paul Assenmacher	.04	.03	.02
645	Jose Oquendo	.06	.05	.02
646	Checklist 529-660	.03	.02	.01
647	Rex Hudler	.03	.02	.01
648	Jim Clancy	.03	.02	.01
649	*Dan Murphy*(FC)	.15	.11	.06
650	Mike Witt	.06	.05	.02
651	Rafael Santana	.06	.05	.02
652	Mike Boddicker	.06	.05	.02
653	John Moses	.03	.02	.01
654	*Paul Coleman* (#1 Draft Pick)	.20	.15	.08
655	Gregg Olson	.30	.25	.12
656	Mackey Sasser	.05	.04	.02
657	Terry Mulholland	.06	.05	.02
658	Donell Nixon	.03	.02	.01
659	Greg Cadaret	.03	.02	.01
660	Vince Coleman	.10	.08	.04
661	Turn Back The Clock - 1985 (Dick Howser)	.07	.05	.03
662	Turn Back The Clock - 1980 (Mike Schmidt)	.07	.05	.03
663	Turn Back The Clock - 1975 (Fred Lynn)	.07	.05	.03
664	Turn Back The Clock - 1970 (Johnny Bench)	.07	.05	.03
665	Turn Back The Clock - 1965 (Sandy Koufax)	.07	.05	.03
666	Brian Fisher	.05	.04	.02

		MT	NR MT	EX
667	Curt Wilkerson	.03	.02	.01
668	*Joe Oliver*(FC)	.30	.25	.12
669	Tom Lasorda	.03	.02	.01
670	Dennis Eckersley	.09	.07	.04
671	Bob Boone	.09	.07	.04
672	Roy Smith	.03	.02	.01
673	Joey Meyer	.03	.02	.01
674	Spike Owen	.05	.04	.02
675	Jim Abbott	.35	.25	.12
676	Randy Kutcher(FC)	.07	.05	.03
677	Jay Tibbs	.03	.02	.01
678	Kirt Manwaring	.10	.08	.04
679	Gary Ward	.04	.03	.02
680	Howard Johnson	.15	.11	.06
681	Mike Schooler	.07	.05	.03
682	Dann Bilardello	.03	.02	.01
683	*Kenny Rogers*	.10	.08	.04
684	*Julio Machado*(FC)	.20	.15	.08
685	Tony Fernandez	.09	.07	.04
686	Carmelo Martinez	.06	.05	.02
687	Tim Birtsas	.03	.02	.01
688	Milt Thompson	.06	.05	.02
689	Rich Yett	.03	.02	.01
690	Mark McGwire	.30	.25	.12
691	Chuck Cary	.03	.02	.01
692	Sammy Sosa	.50	.40	.20
693	Calvin Schiraldi	.03	.02	.01
694	*Mike Stanton*(FC)	.30	.25	.12
695	Tom Henke	.06	.05	.02
696	B.J. Surhoff	.07	.05	.03
697	Mike Davis	.03	.02	.01
698	*Omar Vizquel*	.10	.08	.04
699	Jim Leyland	.03	.02	.01
700	Kirby Puckett	.25	.20	.10
701	*Bernie Williams*(FC)	.30	.25	.12
702	Tony Phillips	.04	.03	.02
703	*Jeff Brantley*	.12	.09	.05
704	*Chip Hale*(FC)	.15	.11	.06
705	Claudell Washington	.07	.05	.03
706	Geno Petralli	.03	.02	.01
707	Luis Aquino	.03	.02	.01
708	Larry Sheets	.03	.02	.01
709	Juan Berneguer	.03	.02	.01
710	Von Hayes	.09	.07	.04
711	Rick Aguilera	.05	.04	.02
712	Todd Benzinger	.09	.07	.04
713	*Tim Drummond*(FC)	.15	.11	.06
714	*Marquis Grissom*(FC)	.50	.40	.20
715	Greg Maddux	.15	.11	.06
716	Steve Balboni	.03	.02	.01
717	Ron Kakovice	.03	.02	.01
718	Gary Sheffield	.30	.25	.12
719	*Wally Whitehurst*(FC)	.15	.11	.06
720	Andres Galarraga	.25	.20	.10
721	Lee Mazzilli	.03	.02	.01
722	Felix Fermin	.03	.02	.01
723	Jeff Robinson	.05	.04	.02
724	Juan Bell(FC)	.10	.08	.04
725	Terry Pendleton	.07	.05	.03
726	Gene Nelson	.03	.02	.01
727	Pat Tabler	.05	.04	.02
728	Jim Acker	.03	.02	.01
729	Bobby Valentine	.03	.02	.01
730	Tony Gwynn	.20	.15	.08
731	Don Carman	.05	.04	.02
732	Ernie Riles	.03	.02	.01
733	John Dopson	.09	.07	.04
734	Kevin Elster	.06	.05	.02
735	Charlie Hough	.06	.05	.02
736	Rick Dempsey	.03	.02	.01
737	Chris Sabo	.15	.11	.06
738	*Gene Harris*	.10	.08	.04
739	Dale Sveum	.04	.03	.02
740	Jesse Barfield	.08	.06	.03
741	Steve Wilson	.10	.08	.04
742	Ernie Whitt	.05	.04	.02
743	Tom Candiotti	.05	.04	.02
744	*Kelly Mann*(FC)	.20	.15	.08
745	Hubie Brooks	.06	.05	.02
746	Dave Smith	.06	.05	.02
747	Randy Bush	.03	.02	.01
748	Doyle Alexander	.06	.05	.02
749	Mark Parent	.04	.03	.02
750	Dale Murphy	.10	.08	.04
751	Steve Lyons	.04	.03	.02
752	Tom Gordon	.15	.11	.06
753	Chris Speier	.03	.02	.01
754	Bob Walk	.05	.04	.02
755	Rafael Palmeiro	.08	.06	.03
756	Ken Howell	.03	.02	.01
757	*Larry Walker*(FC)	.40	.30	.15

		MT	NR MT	EX
758	Mark Thurmond	.03	.02	.01
759	Tom Trebelhorn	.03	.02	.01
760	Wade Boggs	.25	.20	.10
761	Mike Jackson	.05	.04	.02
762	Doug Dascenzo	.07	.05	.03
763	Denny Martinez	.07	.05	.03
764	Tim Teufel	.05	.04	.02
765	Chili Davis	.07	.05	.03
766	Brian Meyer(FC)	.10	.08	.04
767	Tracy Jones	.06	.05	.02
768	Chuck Crim	.04	.03	.02
769	*Greg Hibbard*(FC)	.30	.25	.12
770	Cory Snyder	.09	.07	.04
771	Pete Smith	.06	.05	.02
772	Jeff Reed	.03	.02	.01
773	Dave Leiper	.03	.02	.01
774	*Ben McDonald*(FC)	.30	.25	.12
775	Andy Van Slyke	.09	.07	.04
776	Charlie Leibrandt	.04	.03	.02
777	Tim Laudner	.03	.02	.01
778	Mike Jeffcoat	.03	.02	.01
779	Lloyd Moseby	.06	.05	.02
780	Orel Hershiser	.15	.11	.06
781	Mario Diaz	.03	.02	.01
782	Jose Alvarez	.03	.02	.01
783	Checklist 661-792	.03	.02	.01
784	Scott Bailes	.03	.02	.01
785	Jim Rice	.07	.05	.03
786	Eric King	.04	.03	.02
787	Rene Gonzales	.03	.02	.01
788	Frank DiPino	.03	.02	.01
789	John Wathan	.03	.02	.01
790	Gary Carter	.07	.05	.03
791	Alvaro Espinoza	.15	.11	.06
792	Gerald Perry	.06	.05	.02

1990 Topps All-Star Glossy Set Of 22

One glossy All-Star card was included in each 1990 Topps rack pack. The cards measure 2-1/2" by 3-1/2" and feature a similar style to past glossy All-Star cards. Special cards of All-Star team captains Carl Yastrzemski and Don Drysdale are included in the set.

		MT	NR MT	EX
Complete Set:		3.50	2.75	1.50
Common Player:		.12	.09	.05
1	Tom Lasorda	.12	.09	.05
2	Will Clark	.35	.25	.14
3	Ryne Sandberg	.30	.25	.12
4	Howard Johnson	.15	.11	.06
5	Ozzie Smith	.15	.11	.06
6	Kevin Mitchell	.25	.20	.10
7	Eric Davis	.25	.20	.10
8	Tony Gwynn	.20	.15	.08
9	Benny Santiago	.15	.11	.06
10	Rick Rueschel	.12	.09	.05
11	Don Drysdale	.12	.09	.05
12	Tony LaRussa	.12	.09	.05
13	Mark McGwire	.30	.25	.12
14	Julio Franco	.15	.11	.06
15	Wade Boggs	.25	.20	.10
16	Cal Ripken	.20	.15	.08
17	Bo Jackson	.60	.45	.25
18	Kirby Puckett	.25	.20	.10

		MT	NR MT	EX
19	Ruben Sierra	.25	.20	.10
20	Terry Steinbach	.12	.09	.05
21	Dave Stewart	.15	.11	.06
22	Carl Yastrzemski	.15	.11	.06

1990 Topps All-Star Glossy Set Of 60

Sharp color photographs and a clutter-free design are features of the cards in this 60-card send away set. Topps initiated the redemption series in 1983 and increased the size of the set to 60 in 1986. Six special offer cards, which were included in Topps baseball wax packs, are necessary to obtain each of the six 10-card sets in the series.

		MT	NR MT	EX
Complete Set:		9.00	6.75	3.50
Common Player:		.10	.08	.04
1	Ryne Sandberg	.70	.50	.30
2	Nolan Ryan	.70	.50	.30
3	Glenn Davis	.15	.11	.06
4	Dave Stewart	.15	.11	.06
5	Barry Larkin	.15	.11	.06
6	Carney Lansford	.15	.11	.06
7	Darryl Strawberry	.60	.45	.25
8	Steve Sax	.15	.11	.06
9	Carlos Martinez	.10	.08	.04
10	Gary Sheffield	.40	.30	.15
11	Don Mattingly	.80	.60	.30
12	Mark Grace	.40	.30	.15
13	Bret Saberhagen	.20	.15	.08
14	Mike Scott	.10	.08	.04
15	Robin Yount	.20	.15	.08
16	Ozzie Smith	.15	.11	.06
17	Jeff Ballard	.10	.08	.04
18	Rick Reuschel	.10	.08	.04
19	Greg Briley	.10	.08	.04
20	Ken Griffey,Jr.	1.75	1.25	.70
21	Kevin Mitchell	.30	.25	.12
22	Wade Boggs	.60	.45	.25
23	Doc Gooden	.50	.40	.20
24	George Bell	.15	.11	.06
25	Eric Davis	.40	.30	.15
26	Ruben Sierra	.25	.20	.10
27	Roberto Alomar	.20	.15	.08
28	Gary Gaetti	.15	.11	.06
29	Gregg Olson	.20	.15	.08
30	Tom Gordon	.20	.15	.08
31	Jose Canseco	.80	.60	.30
32	Pedro Guerrero	.15	.11	.06
33	Joe Carter	.15	.11	.06
34	Mike Scioscia	.10	.08	.04
35	Julio Franco	.15	.11	.06
36	Joe Magrane	.10	.08	.04
37	Rickey Henderson	.40	.30	.15
38	Rock Raines	.15	.11	.06
39	Jerome Walton	.35	.25	.14
40	Bob Geren	.10	.08	.04
41	Andre Dawson	.20	.15	.08
42	Mark McGwire	.60	.45	.25
43	Howard Johnson	.20	.15	.08
44	Bo Jackson	.80	.60	.30
45	Shawon Dunston	.20	.15	.08
46	Carlton Fisk	.20	.15	.08
47	Mitch Williams	.15	.11	.06
48	Kirby Puckett	.35	.25	.14
49	Craig Worthington	.10	.08	.04
50	Jim Abbott	.20	.15	.08
51	Cal Ripken	.25	.20	.10
52	Will Clark	.70	.50	.30
53	Dennis Eckersley	.20	.15	.08
54	Craig Biggio	.15	.11	.06
55	Fred McGriff	.20	.15	.08
56	Tony Gwynn	.20	.15	.08
57	Mickey Tettleton	.10	.08	.04
58	Mark Davis	.10	.08	.04
59	Omar Vizquel	.10	.08	.04
60	Gregg Jefferies	.30	.25	.12

1990 Topps Traded

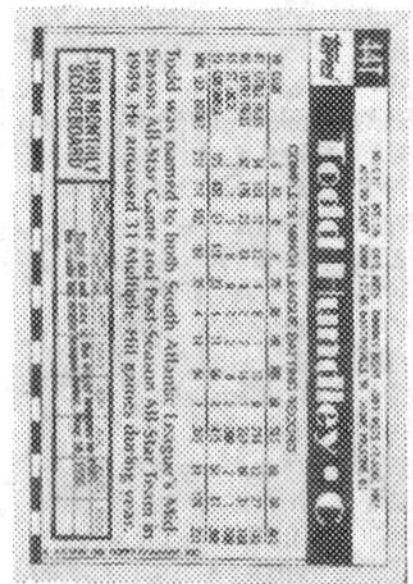

For the first time, Topps "Traded" series cards were made available nationwide in retail wax packs. The 132-card set was also sold in complete boxed form as it has been in recent years. The wax pack traded cards feature gray backs, while the boxed set cards feature white backs. The cards are numbered 1T-132T and showcase rookies, players who changed teams and new managers.

		MT	NR MT	EX
Complete Set (132):		8.00	6.00	3.25
Common Player:		.05	.04	.02
1T	Darrel Akerfelds	.05	.04	.02
2T	Sandy Alomar,Jr.	.20	.15	.08
3T	Brad Arnsberg	.05	.04	.02
4T	Steve Avery	.80	.60	.30
5T	Wally Backman	.05	.04	.02
6T	Carlos Baerga(FC)	1.25	.90	.50
7T	Kevin Bass	.06	.05	.02
8T	Willie Blair(FC)	.10	.08	.04
9T	Mike Blowers(FC)	.20	.15	.08
10T	Shawn Boskie(FC)	.20	.15	.08
11T	Daryl Boston	.05	.04	.02
12T	Dennis Boyd	.06	.05	.02
13T	Glenn Braggs	.06	.05	.02
14T	Hubie Brooks	.08	.06	.03
15T	Tom Brunansky	.08	.06	.03
16T	John Burkett(FC)	.40	.30	.15
17T	Casey Candaele	.05	.04	.02
18T	John Candelaria	.06	.05	.02
19T	Gary Carter	.10	.08	.04
20T	Joe Carter	.10	.08	.04
21T	Rick Cerone	.05	.04	.02
22T	Scott Coolbaugh(FC)	.15	.11	.06
23T	Bobby Cox	.05	.04	.02
24T	Mark Davis	.06	.05	.02
25T	Storm Davis	.06	.05	.02
26T	Edgar Diaz(FC)	.10	.08	.04
27T	Wayne Edwards(FC)	.20	.15	.08
28T	Mark Eichhorn	.05	.04	.02
29T	Scott Erickson(FC)	.40	.30	.15
30T	Nick Esasky	.06	.05	.02
31T	Cecil Fielder	.50	.40	.20
32T	John Franco	.08	.06	.03
33T	Travis Fryman(FC)	1.50	1.25	.60
34T	Bill Gullickson	.05	.04	.02
35T	Darryl Hamilton	.15	.11	.06
36T	Mike Harkey	.20	.15	.08
37T	Bud Harrelson	.05	.04	.02
38T	Billy Hatcher	.06	.05	.02
39T	Keith Hernandez	.08	.06	.03
40T	Joe Hesketh	.05	.04	.02

		MT	NR MT	EX
41T	Dave Hollins(FC)	.25	.20	.10
42T	Sam Horn	.08	.06	.03
43T	Steve Howard(FC)	.20	.15	.08
44T	Todd Hundley(FC)	.25	.20	.10
45T	Jeff Huson	.10	.08	.04
46T	Chris James	.05	.04	.02
47T	Stan Javier	.05	.04	.02
48T	Dave Justice(FC)	1.25	.90	.50
49T	Jeff Kaiser(FC)	.12	.09	.05
50T	Dana Kiecker(FC)	.20	.15	.08
51T	Joe Klink(FC)	.10	.08	.04
52T	Brent Knackert(FC)	.12	.09	.05
53T	Brad Komminsk	.05	.04	.02
54T	Mark Langston	.10	.08	.04
55T	Tim Layana(FC)	.25	.20	.10
56T	Rick Leach	.05	.04	.02
57T	Terry Leach	.05	.04	.02
58T	Tim Leary	.05	.04	.02
59T	Craig Lefferts	.05	.04	.02
60T	Charlie Leibrandt	.05	.04	.02
61T	Jim Leyritz(FC)	.20	.15	.08
62T	Fred Lynn	.06	.05	.02
63T	Kevin Maas(FC)	.60	.45	.25
64T	Shane Mack	.08	.06	.03
65T	Candy Maldonado	.06	.05	.02
66T	Fred Manrique	.05	.04	.02
67T	Mike Marshall	.05	.04	.02
68T	Carmelo Martinez	.05	.04	.02
69T	John Marzano	.06	.05	.02
70T	Ben McDonald	.60	.45	.25
71T	Jack McDowell	.08	.06	.03
72T	John McNamara	.05	.04	.02
73T	Orlando Mercado	.05	.04	.02
74T	Stump Merrill	.05	.04	.02
75T	Alan Mills(FC)	.20	.15	.08
76T	Hal Morris	.40	.30	.15
77T	Lloyd Moseby	.06	.05	.02
78T	Randy Myers	.08	.06	.03
79T	Tim Naehring(FC)	.35	.25	.14
80T	Junior Noboa	.06	.05	.02
81T	Matt Nokes	.06	.05	.02
82T	Pete O'Brien	.05	.04	.02
83T	John Olerud(FC)	1.25	.90	.50
84T	Greg Olson(FC)	.15	.11	.06
85T	Junior Ortiz	.05	.04	.02
86T	Dave Parker	.15	.11	.06
87T	Rick Parker(FC)	.15	.11	.06
88T	Bob Patterson	.05	.04	.02
89T	Alejandro Pena	.05	.04	.02
90T	Tony Pena	.08	.06	.03
91T	Pascual Perez	.05	.04	.02
92T	Gerald Perry	.05	.04	.02
93T	Dan Petry	.05	.04	.02
94T	Gary Pettis	.06	.05	.02
95T	Tony Phillips	.05	.04	.02
96T	Lou Pinella	.05	.04	.02
97T	Luis Polonia	.05	.04	.02
98T	Jim Presley	.06	.05	.02
99T	Scott Radinsky(FC)	.25	.20	.10
100T	Willie Randolph	.08	.06	.03
101T	Jeff Reardon	.08	.06	.03
102T	Greg Riddoch	.05	.04	.02
103T	Jeff Robinson	.05	.04	.02
104T	Ron Robinson	.05	.04	.02
105T	Kevin Romine	.05	.04	.02
106T	Scott Ruskin(FC)	.20	.15	.08
107T	John Russell	.05	.04	.02
108T	Bill Sampen(FC)	.20	.15	.08
109T	Juan Samuel	.08	.06	.03
110T	Scott Sanderson	.06	.05	.02
111T	Jack Savage(FC)	.10	.08	.04
112T	Dave Schmidt	.05	.04	.02
113T	Red Schoendienst	.05	.04	.02
114T	Terry Shumpert(FC)	.20	.15	.08
115T	Matt Sinatro	.05	.04	.02
116T	Don Slaught	.05	.04	.02
117T	Bryn Smith	.05	.04	.02
118T	Lee Smith	.08	.06	.03
119T	Paul Sorrento(FC)	.30	.25	.12
120T	Franklin Stubbs	.05	.04	.02
121T	Russ Swan(FC)	.20	.15	.08
122T	Bob Tewksbury	.05	.04	.02
123T	Wayne Tolleson	.05	.04	.02
124T	John Tudor	.06	.05	.02
125T	Randy Veres(FC)	.10	.08	.04
126T	Hector Villanueva(FC)	.20	.15	.08
127T	Mitch Webster	.05	.04	.02
128T	Ernie Whitt	.06	.05	.02
129T	Frank Wills	.06	.05	.02
130T	Dave Winfield	.15	.11	.06
131T	Matt Young	.05	.04	.02
132T	Checklist	.05	.04	.02

1990 Topps Box Panels

This special 16-card set features four cards on four different box-bottom panels. The cards are identical in design to the regular 1990 Topps cards. The cards are designated by letter.

		MT	NR MT	EX
Complete Panel Set:		3.00	2.25	1.25
Complete Singles Set:		1.50	1.25	.60
Common Panel:		.40	.30	.15
Common Single Player:		.06	.05	.02
	Panel	.60	.45	.25
A	Wade Boggs	.25	.20	.10
B	George Brett	.20	.15	.08
C	Andre Dawson	.15	.11	.06
D	Darrell Evans	.06	.05	.02
	Panel	.60	.45	.25
E	Doc Gooden	.25	.20	.10
F	Rickey Henderson	.25	.20	.10
G	Tom Lasorda	.06	.05	.02
H	Fred Lynn	.06	.05	.02
	Panel	.40	.30	.15
I	Mark McGwire	.25	.20	.10
J	Dave Parker	.10	.08	.04
K	Jeff Reardon	.06	.05	.02
L	Rick Reuschel	.06	.05	.02
	Panel	.60	.45	.25
M	Jim Rice	.06	.05	.02
N	Cal Ripken	.10	.08	.04
O	Nolan Ryan	.25	.20	.10
P	Ryne Sandberg	.25	.20	.10

1990 Topps Big Baseball

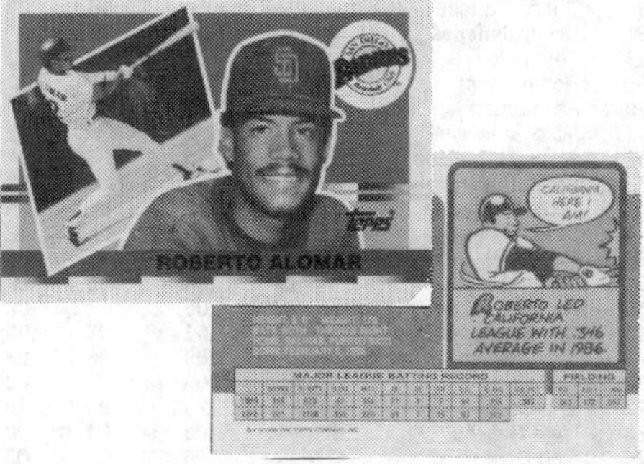

For the third consecutive year, Topps issued a 330-card set of the oversized cards (2-5/8" by 3-3/4"). The cards were issued in three 110-card series. The cards are reminiscent of Topps cards from the mid-1950s in that they feature players in portrait and action shots. The 1990 set has action photos in freeze frames. As in previous years, the cards are printed on white card stock with a glossy finish on the front. The card backs include

1989 and career hitting, fielding and pitching stats and a player cartoon.

	MT	NR MT	EX
Complete Set:	18.00	13.50	7.25
Common Player:	.05	.04	.02

#	Player	MT	NR MT	EX
1	Dwight Evans	.08	.06	.03
2	Kirby Puckett	.25	.20	.10
3	Kevin Gross	.06	.05	.02
4	Ron Hassey	.05	.04	.02
5	Lloyd McClendon	.05	.04	.02
6	Bo Jackson	.50	.40	.20
7	Lonnie Smith	.06	.05	.02
8	Alvaro Espinoza	.06	.05	.02
9	Roberto Alomar	.15	.11	.06
10	Glenn Braggs	.06	.05	.02
11	David Cone	.10	.08	.04
12	Claudell Washington	.05	.04	.02
13	Pedro Guerrero	.10	.08	.04
14	Todd Benzinger	.06	.05	.02
15	Jeff Russell	.06	.05	.02
16	Terry Kennedy	.05	.04	.02
17	Kelly Gruber	.15	.11	.06
18	Alfredo Griffin	.05	.04	.02
19	Mark Grace	.20	.15	.08
20	Dave Winfield	.12	.09	.05
21	Bret Saberhagen	.15	.11	.06
22	Roger Clemens	.30	.25	.12
23	Bob Walk	.05	.04	.02
24	Dave Magadan	.15	.11	.06
25	Spike Owen	.06	.05	.02
26	Jody Davis	.05	.04	.02
27	Kent Hrbek	.12	.09	.05
28	Mark McGwire	.50	.40	.20
29	Eddie Murray	.15	.11	.06
30	Paul O'Neill	.06	.05	.02
31	Jose DeLeon	.06	.05	.02
32	Steve Lyons	.05	.04	.02
33	Dan Plesac	.06	.05	.02
34	Jack Howell	.05	.04	.02
35	Greg Briley	.06	.05	.02
36	Andy Hawkins	.06	.05	.02
37	Cecil Espy	.05	.04	.02
38	Rick Sutcliffe	.08	.06	.03
39	Jack Clark	.12	.09	.05
40	Dale Murphy	.12	.09	.05
41	Mike Henneman	.06	.05	.02
42	Rick Honeycutt	.05	.04	.02
43	Willie Randolph	.06	.05	.02
44	Marty Barrett	.06	.05	.02
45	Willie Wilson	.06	.05	.02
46	Wallace Johnson	.05	.04	.02
47	Greg Brock	.06	.05	.02
48	Tom Browning	.06	.05	.02
49	Gerald Young	.05	.04	.02
50	Dennis Eckersley	.15	.11	.06
51	Scott Garrelts	.06	.05	.02
52	Gary Redus	.05	.04	.02
53	Al Newman	.05	.04	.02
54	Darryl Boston	.05	.04	.02
55	Ron Oester	.05	.04	.02
56	Danny Tartabull	.08	.06	.03
57	Gregg Jefferies	.30	.25	.12
58	Tom Foley	.05	.04	.02
59	Robin Yount	.20	.15	.08
60	Pat Borders	.06	.05	.02
61	Mike Greenwell	.30	.25	.12
62	Shawon Dunston	.10	.08	.04
63	Steve Buechele	.05	.04	.02
64	Dave Stewart	.12	.09	.05
65	Jose Oquendo	.05	.04	.02
66	Ron Gant	.20	.15	.08
67	Mike Scioscia	.06	.05	.02
68	Randy Velarde	.05	.04	.02
69	Charlie Hayes	.06	.05	.02
70	Tim Wallach	.08	.06	.03
71	Eric Show	.06	.05	.02
72	Eric Davis	.25	.20	.10
73	Mike Gallego	.05	.04	.02
74	Rob Deer	.06	.05	.02
75	Ryne Sandberg	.40	.30	.15
76	Kevin Seitzer	.08	.06	.03
77	Wade Boggs	.50	.40	.20
78	Greg Gagne	.06	.05	.02
79	John Smiley	.06	.05	.02
80	Ivan Calderon	.08	.06	.03
81	Pete Incaviglia	.06	.05	.02
82	Orel Hershiser	.12	.09	.05
83	Carney Lansford	.08	.06	.03
84	Mike Fitzgerald	.05	.04	.02
85	Don Mattingly	.60	.45	.25
86	Chet Lemon	.06	.05	.02
87	Rolando Roomes	.05	.04	.02
88	Bill Spiers	.06	.05	.02
89	Pat Tabler	.06	.05	.02
90	Danny Heep	.05	.04	.02
91	Andre Dawson	.15	.11	.06
92	Randy Bush	.05	.04	.02
93	Tony Gwynn	.15	.11	.06
94	Tom Brunansky	.08	.06	.03
95	Johnny Ray	.06	.05	.02
96	Matt Williams	.15	.11	.06
97	Barry Lyons	.05	.04	.02
98	Jeff Hamilton	.05	.04	.02
99	Tom Glavine	.06	.05	.02
100	Ken Griffey,Sr.	.06	.05	.02
101	Tom Henke	.06	.05	.02
102	Dave Righetti	.08	.06	.03
103	Paul Molitor	.12	.09	.05
104	Mike LaValliere	.06	.05	.02
105	Frank White	.06	.05	.02
106	Bob Welch	.08	.06	.03
107	Ellis Burks	.25	.20	.10
108	Andres Galarraga	.08	.06	.03
109	Mitch Williams	.08	.06	.03
110	Checklist	.05	.04	.02
111	Craig Biggio	.08	.06	.03
112	Dave Steib	.08	.06	.03
113	Ron Darling	.06	.05	.02
114	Bert Blyleven	.10	.08	.04
115	Dickie Thon	.05	.04	.02
116	Carlos Martinez	.06	.05	.02
117	Jeff King	.06	.05	.02
118	Terry Steinbach	.06	.05	.02
119	Frank Tanana	.06	.05	.02
120	Mark Lemke	.06	.05	.02
121	Chris Sabo	.10	.08	.04
122	Glenn Davis	.15	.11	.06
123	Mel Hall	.06	.05	.02
124	Jim Gantner	.06	.05	.02
125	Benito Santiago	.10	.08	.04
126	Milt Thompson	.06	.05	.02
127	Rafael Palmeiro	.12	.09	.05
128	Barry Bonds	.20	.15	.08
129	Mike Bielecki	.06	.05	.02
130	Lou Whitaker	.10	.08	.04
131	Bob Ojeda	.05	.04	.02
132	Dion James	.05	.04	.02
133	Denny Martinez	.06	.05	.02
134	Fred McGriff	.20	.15	.08
135	Terry Pendleton	.06	.05	.02
136	Pat Combs	.10	.08	.04
137	Kevin Mitchell	.30	.25	.12
138	Marquis Grissom	.50	.40	.20
139	Chris Bosio	.06	.05	.02
140	Omar Vizquel	.05	.04	.02
141	Steve Sax	.10	.08	.04
142	Nelson Liriano	.05	.04	.02
143	Kevin Elster	.06	.05	.02
144	Dan Pasqua	.06	.05	.02
145	Dave Smith	.06	.05	.02
146	Craig Worthington	.06	.05	.02
147	Dan Gladden	.06	.05	.02
148	Oddibe McDowell	.05	.04	.02
149	Bip Roberts	.06	.05	.02
150	Randy Ready	.05	.04	.02
151	Dwight Smith	.10	.08	.04
152	Ed Whitson	.06	.05	.02
153	George Bell	.12	.09	.05
154	Tim Raines	.15	.11	.06
155	Sid Fernandez	.08	.06	.03
156	Henry Cotto	.05	.04	.02
157	Harold Baines	.12	.09	.05
158	Willie McGee	.10	.08	.04
159	Bill Doran	.06	.05	.02
160	Steve Balboni	.05	.04	.02
161	Pete Smith	.06	.05	.02
162	Frank Viola	.12	.09	.05
163	Gary Sheffield	.25	.20	.10
164	Bill Landrum	.06	.05	.02
165	Tony Fernandez	.08	.06	.03
166	Mike Heath	.05	.04	.02
167	Jody Reed	.08	.06	.03
168	Wally Joyner	.08	.06	.03
169	Robby Thompson	.06	.05	.02
170	Ken Caminiti	.06	.05	.02
171	Nolan Ryan	.40	.30	.15
172	Ricky Jordan	.08	.06	.03
173	Lance Blankenship	.05	.04	.02
174	Dwight Gooden	.30	.25	.12
175	Ruben Sierra	.20	.15	.08

#	Player	MT	NR MT	EX
176	Carlton Fisk	.15	.11	.06
177	Garry Templeton	.06	.05	.02
178	Mike Devereaux	.06	.05	.02
179	Mookie Wilson	.06	.05	.02
180	Jeff Blauser	.06	.05	.02
181	Scott Bradley	.05	.04	.02
182	Luis Salazar	.05	.04	.02
183	Rafael Ramirez	.06	.05	.02
184	Vince Coleman	.08	.06	.03
185	Doug Drabek	.10	.08	.04
186	Darryl Strawberry	.30	.25	.12
187	Tim Burke	.06	.05	.02
188	Jesse Barfield	.08	.06	.03
189	Barry Larkin	.15	.11	.06
190	Alan Trammell	.10	.08	.04
191	Steve Lake	.05	.04	.02
192	Derek Lilliquist	.06	.05	.02
193	Don Robinson	.06	.05	.02
194	Kevin McReynolds	.08	.06	.03
195	Melido Perez	.06	.05	.02
196	Jose Lind	.06	.05	.02
197	Eric Anthony	.50	.40	.20
198	B.J. Surhoff	.06	.05	.02
199	John Olerud	.50	.40	.20
200	Mike Moore	.06	.05	.02
201	Mark Gubicza	.08	.06	.03
202	Phil Bradley	.06	.05	.02
203	Ozzie Smith	.12	.09	.05
204	Greg Maddux	.08	.06	.03
205	Julio Franco	.12	.09	.05
206	Tom Herr	.06	.05	.02
207	Scott Fletcher	.05	.04	.02
208	Bobby Bonilla	.15	.11	.06
209	Bob Geren	.06	.05	.02
210	Junior Felix	.20	.15	.08
211	Dick Schofield	.05	.04	.02
212	Jim Deshaies	.06	.05	.02
213	Jose Uribe	.06	.05	.02
214	John Kruk	.06	.05	.02
215	Ozzie Guillen	.08	.06	.03
216	Howard Johnson	.10	.08	.04
217	Andy Van Slyke	.08	.06	.03
218	Tim Laudner	.05	.04	.02
219	Manny Lee	.06	.05	.02
220	Checklist	.05	.04	.02
221	Cory Snyder	.08	.06	.03
222	Billy Hatcher	.06	.05	.02
223	Bud Black	.05	.04	.02
224	Will Clark	.40	.30	.15
225	Kevin Tapani	.20	.15	.08
226	Mike Pagliarulo	.06	.05	.02
227	Dave Parker	.12	.09	.05
228	Ben McDonald	.50	.40	.20
229	Carlos Baerga	.50	.40	.20
230	Roger McDowell	.06	.05	.02
231	Delino DeShields	.50	.40	.20
232	Mark Langston	.10	.08	.04
233	Wally Backman	.06	.05	.02
234	Jim Eisenreich	.06	.05	.02
235	Mike Schooler	.06	.05	.02
236	Kevin Bass	.06	.05	.02
237	John Farrell	.05	.04	.02
238	Kal Daniels	.10	.08	.04
239	Tony Phillips	.06	.05	.02
240	Todd Stottlemyre	.06	.05	.02
241	Greg Olson	.15	.11	.06
242	Charlie Hough	.06	.05	.02
243	Mariano Duncan	.06	.05	.02
244	Billy Ripken	.05	.04	.02
245	Joe Carter	.12	.09	.05
246	Tim Belcher	.08	.06	.03
247	Roberto Kelly	.08	.06	.03
248	Candy Maldonado	.08	.06	.03
249	Mike Scott	.08	.06	.03
250	Ken Griffey,Jr.	1.25	.90	.50
251	Nick Esasky	.06	.05	.02
252	Tom Gordon	.15	.11	.06
253	John Tudor	.06	.05	.02
254	Gary Gaetti	.10	.08	.04
255	Neal Heaton	.06	.05	.02
256	Jerry Browne	.06	.05	.02
257	Joe Rijo	.06	.05	.02
258	Mike Boddicker	.06	.05	.02
259	Brett Butler	.06	.05	.02
260	Andy Benes	.10	.08	.04
261	Kevin Brown	.08	.06	.03
262	Hubie Brooks	.08	.06	.03
263	Randy Milligan	.06	.05	.02
264	John Franco	.10	.08	.04
265	Sandy Alomar	.30	.25	.12
266	Dave Valle	.06	.05	.02

#	Player	MT	NR MT	EX
267	Jerome Walton	.25	.20	.10
268	Bob Boone	.08	.06	.03
269	Ken Howell	.06	.05	.02
270	Jose Canseco	.50	.40	.20
271	Joe Magrane	.08	.06	.03
272	Brian DuBois	.08	.06	.03
273	Carlos Quintana	.08	.06	.03
274	Lance Johnson	.06	.05	.02
275	Steve Bedrosian	.06	.05	.02
276	Brook Jacoby	.08	.06	.03
277	Fred Lynn	.06	.05	.02
278	Jeff Ballard	.06	.05	.02
279	Otis Nixon	.05	.04	.02
280	Chili Davis	.06	.05	.02
281	Joe Oliver	.12	.09	.05
282	Brian Holman	.08	.06	.03
283	Juan Samuel	.08	.06	.03
284	Rick Aguilera	.06	.05	.02
285	Jeff Reardon	.08	.06	.03
286	Sammy Sosa	.30	.25	.12
287	Carmelo Martinez	.06	.05	.02
288	Greg Swindell	.08	.06	.03
289	Erik Hanson	.15	.11	.06
290	Tony Pena	.08	.06	.03
291	Pascual Perez	.06	.05	.02
292	Rickey Henderson	.35	.25	.14
293	Kurt Stillwell	.06	.05	.02
294	Todd Zeile	.50	.40	.20
295	Bobby Thigpen	.10	.08	.04
296	Larry Walker	.30	.25	.12
297	Rob Murphy	.05	.04	.02
298	Mitch Webster	.05	.04	.02
299	Devon White	.06	.05	.02
300	Len Dykstra	.10	.08	.04
301	Keith Hernandez	.06	.05	.02
302	Gene Larkin	.06	.05	.02
303	Jeffrey Leonard	.06	.05	.02
304	Jim Presley	.06	.05	.02
305	Lloyd Moseby	.08	.06	.03
306	John Smoltz	.08	.06	.03
307	Sam Horn	.06	.05	.02
308	Greg Litton	.06	.05	.02
309	Dave Henderson	.08	.06	.03
310	Mark McLemore	.05	.04	.02
311	Gary Pettis	.06	.05	.02
312	Mark Davis	.05	.04	.02
313	Cecil Fielder	.50	.40	.20
314	Jack Armstrong	.08	.06	.03
315	Alvin Davis	.08	.06	.03
316	Doug Jones	.08	.06	.03
317	Eric Yelding	.08	.06	.03
318	Joe Orsulak	.06	.05	.02
319	Chuck Finley	.08	.06	.03
320	Glenn Wilson	.06	.05	.02
321	Harold Reynolds	.08	.06	.03
322	Teddy Higuera	.08	.06	.03
323	Lance Parrish	.08	.06	.03
324	Bruce Hurst	.06	.05	.02
325	Dave West	.06	.05	.02
326	Kirk Gibson	.10	.08	.04
327	Cal Ripken	.15	.11	.06
328	Rick Reuschel	.06	.05	.02
329	Jim Abbott	.15	.11	.06
330	Checklist	.05	.04	.02

1990 Topps Major League Debut

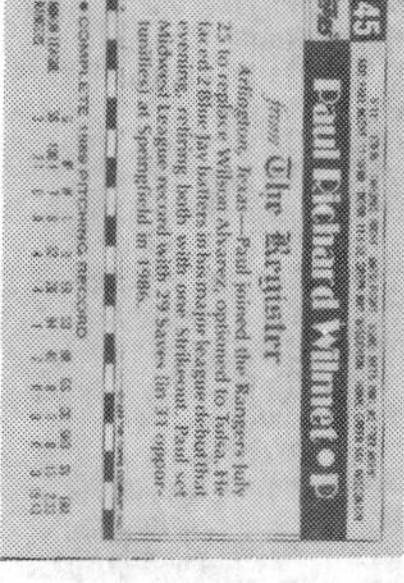

This 171-card set features the players who made their

Major League debut in 1990. The cards are styled like the 1991 Topps cards and are numbered in alphabetical order. The card backs are printed horizontally and feature information about the player's debut and statistics.

		MT	NR MT	EX
Complete Set:		15.00	11.00	6.00
Common Player:		.05	.04	.02
1	Paul Abbott	.06	.05	.02
2	Steve Adkins	.05	.04	.02
3	Scott Aldred	.08	.06	.03
4	Gerald Alexander	.06	.05	.02
5	Moises Alou	.25	.20	.10
6	Steve Avery	.80	.60	.30
7	Oscar Azocar	.05	.04	.02
8	Carlos Baerga	.30	.25	.12
9	Kevin Baez	.05	.04	.02
10	Jeff Baldwin	.05	.04	.02
11	Brian Barnes	.12	.09	.05
12	Kevin Bearse	.06	.05	.02
13	Kevin Belcher	.10	.08	.04
14	Mike Bell	.10	.08	.04
15	Sean Berry	.08	.06	.03
16	Joe Bitker	.08	.06	.03
17	Willie Blair	.06	.05	.02
18	Brian Bohanon	.06	.05	.02
19	Mike Bordick	.20	.15	.08
20	Shawn Boskie	.10	.08	.04
21	Rod Brewer	.06	.05	.02
22	Kevin Brown	.05	.04	.02
23	Dave Burba	.06	.05	.02
24	Jim Campbell	.05	.04	.02
25	Ozzie Canseco	.10	.08	.04
26	Chuck Carr	.08	.06	.03
27	Larry Casian	.06	.05	.02
28	Andujar Cedeno	.30	.25	.12
29	Wes Chamberlain	.30	.25	.12
30	Scott Chiamparino	.08	.06	.03
31	Steve Chitren	.08	.06	.03
32	Pete Coachman	.05	.04	.02
33	Alex Cole	.15	.11	.06
34	Jeff Conine	.15	.11	.06
35	Scott Cooper	.15	.11	.06
36	Milt Cuyler	.20	.15	.08
37	Steve Decker	.15	.11	.06
38	Rich DeLucia	.08	.06	.03
39	Delino DeShields	.35	.25	.14
40	Mark Dewey	.05	.04	.02
41	Carlos Diaz	.05	.04	.02
42	Lance Dickson	.10	.08	.04
43	Narciso Elvira	.06	.05	.02
44	Luis Encarnacion	.05	.04	.02
45	Scott Erickson	.40	.30	.15
46	Paul Faries	.06	.05	.02
47	Howard Farmer	.06	.05	.02
48	Alex Fernandez	.30	.25	.12
49	Travis Fryman	.80	.60	.30
50	Rich Garces	.06	.05	.02
51	Carlos Garcia	.05	.04	.02
52	Mike Gardiner	.08	.06	.03
53	Bernard Gilkey	.25	.20	.10
54	Tom Gilles	.05	.04	.02
55	Jerry Goff	.06	.05	.02
56	Leo Gomez	.30	.25	.12
57	Luis Gonzalez	.30	.25	.12
58	Joe Grahe	.15	.11	.06
59	Craig Grebeck	.10	.08	.04
60	Kip Gross	.08	.06	.03
61	Eric Gunderson	.06	.05	.02
62	Chris Hammond	.10	.08	.04
63	Dave Hansen	.10	.08	.04
64	Reggie Harris	.06	.05	.02
65	Bill Haselman	.05	.04	.02
66	Randy Hennis	.05	.04	.02
67	Carlos Hernandez	.10	.08	.04
68	Howard Hilton	.05	.04	.02
69	Dave Hollins	.25	.20	.10
70	Darren Holmes	.06	.05	.02
71	John Hoover	.05	.04	.02
72	Steve Howard	.06	.05	.02
73	Thomas Howard	.10	.08	.04
74	Todd Hundley	.20	.15	.08
75	Daryl Irvine	.10	.08	.04
76	Chris Jelic	.06	.05	.02
77	Dana Kiecker	.06	.05	.02
78	Brent Knackert	.05	.04	.02
79	Jimmy Kremers	.05	.04	.02
80	Jerry Kutzler	.05	.04	.02
81	Ray Lankford	.70	.50	.30
82	Tim Layana	.06	.05	.02

		MT	NR MT	EX
83	Terry Lee	.06	.05	.02
84	Mark Leiter	.08	.06	.03
85	Scott Leius	.15	.11	.06
86	Mark Leonard	.10	.08	.04
87	Darren Lewis	.20	.15	.08
88	Scott Lewis	.08	.06	.03
89	Jim Leyritz	.08	.06	.03
90	Dave Liddell	.05	.04	.02
91	Luis Lopez	.05	.04	.02
92	Kevin Maas	.35	.25	.14
93	Bob MacDonald	.06	.05	.02
94	Carlos Maldonado	.05	.04	.02
95	Chuck Malone	.05	.04	.02
96	Ramon Manon	.05	.04	.02
97	Jeff Manto	.08	.06	.03
98	Paul Marak	.06	.05	.02
99	Tino Martinez	.25	.20	.10
100	Derrick May	.25	.20	.10
101	Brent Mayne	.12	.09	.05
102	Paul McClellan	.08	.06	.03
103	Rodney McCray	.08	.06	.03
104	Tim McIntosh	.08	.06	.03
105	Brian McRae	.30	.25	.12
106	Jose Melendez	.06	.05	.02
107	Orlando Merced	.30	.25	.12
108	Alan Mills	.06	.05	.02
109	Gino Minutelli	.15	.11	.06
110	Mickey Morandini	.20	.15	.08
111	Pedro Munoz	.40	.30	.15
112	Chris Nabholz	.15	.11	.06
113	Tim Naehring	.10	.08	.04
114	Charles Nagy	.30	.25	.12
115	Jim Neidlinger	.08	.06	.03
116	Rafael Novoa	.08	.06	.03
117	Jose Offerman	.20	.15	.08
118	Omar Olivares	.10	.08	.04
119	Javier Ortiz	.08	.06	.03
120	Al Osuna	.08	.06	.03
121	Rick Parker	.06	.05	.02
122	Dave Pavlas	.05	.04	.02
123	Geronimo Pena	.20	.15	.08
124	Mike Perez	.08	.06	.03
125	Phil Plantier	.70	.50	.30
126	Jim Poole	.06	.05	.02
127	Tom Quinlan	.05	.04	.02
128	Scott Radinsky	.10	.08	.04
129	Darren Reed	.12	.09	.05
130	Karl Rhodes	.10	.08	.04
131	Jeff Richardson	.05	.04	.02
132	Rich Rodriguez	.06	.05	.02
133	Dave Rohde	.05	.04	.02
134	Mel Rojas	.08	.06	.03
135	Vic Rosario	.06	.05	.02
136	Rich Rowland	.06	.05	.02
137	Scott Ruskin	.08	.06	.03
138	Bill Sampen	.08	.06	.03
139	Andres Santana	.08	.06	.03
140	David Segui	.08	.06	.03
141	Jeff Shaw	.05	.04	.02
142	Tim Sherrill	.05	.04	.02
143	Terry Shumpert	.08	.06	.03
144	Mike Simms	.08	.06	.03
145	Daryl Smith	.05	.04	.02
146	Luis Sojo	.15	.11	.06
147	Steve Springer	.05	.04	.02
148	Ray Stephens	.05	.04	.02
149	Lee Stevens	.15	.11	.06
150	Mel Stottlemyre, Jr.	.05	.04	.02
151	Glenn Sutko	.05	.04	.02
152	Anthony Telford	.08	.06	.03
153	Frank Thomas	1.50	1.25	.60
154	Randy Tomlin	.20	.15	.08
155	Brian Traxler	.05	.04	.02
156	Efrain Valdez	.06	.05	.02
157	Rafael Valdez	.06	.05	.02
158	Julio Valera	.15	.11	.06
159	Jim Vatcher	.08	.06	.03
160	Hector Villanueva	.12	.09	.05
161	Hector Wagner	.05	.04	.02
162	Dave Walsh	.05	.04	.02
163	Steve Wapnick	.08	.06	.03
164	Colby Ward	.06	.05	.02
165	Turner Ward	.15	.11	.06
166	Terry Wells	.05	.04	.02
167	Mark Whiten	.20	.15	.08
168	Mike York	.05	.04	.02
169	Cliff Young	.08	.06	.03
170	Checklist	.05	.04	.02
171	Checklist	.05	.04	.02

1990 Topps TV All-Stars

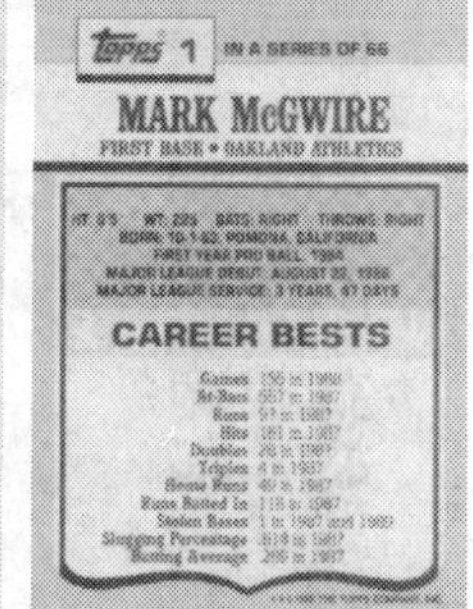

This 66-card boxed set was sold only through a television offer in limited markets. Consequently, production numbers are relatively low and single cards are seldom offered in the hobby market. Most of the game's top stars are included in the issue. Fronts feature a high-gloss surface. On the red-bordered backs there are several lines of biographical data plus each player's "Career Bests" in various statistical categories, set against a pastel background shield.

		MT	NR MT	EX
Complete set:		50.00	37.00	20.00
Common player:		1.00	.70	.40
1	Mark McGwire	3.00	2.25	1.25
2	Julio Franco	1.00	.70	.40
3	Ozzie Guillen	1.00	.70	.40
4	Carney Lansford	1.00	.70	.40
5	Bo Jackson	4.00	3.00	1.50
6	Kirby Puckett	5.00	3.75	2.00
7	Ruben Sierra	3.00	2.25	1.25
8	Carlton Fisk	2.50	2.00	1.00
9	Nolan Ryan	6.00	4.50	2.50
10	Rickey Henderson	4.00	3.00	1.50
11	Jose Canseco	2.50	2.00	1.00
12	Mark Davis	1.00	.70	.40
13	Dennis Eckersley	1.50	1.25	.60
14	Chuck Finley	1.00	.70	.40
15	Bret Saberhagen	1.00	.70	.40
16	Dave Stewart	1.00	.70	.40
17	Don Mattingly	3.00	2.25	1.25
18	Steve Sax	1.00	.70	.40
19	Cal Ripken, Jr.	5.00	3.75	2.00
20	Wade Boggs	3.00	2.25	1.25
21	George Bell	1.00	.70	.40
22	Mike Greenwell	1.00	.70	.40
23	Robin Yount	4.00	3.00	1.50
24	Mickey Tettleton	1.00	.70	.40
25	Roger Clemens	2.00	1.50	.80
26	Fred McGriff	2.50	2.00	1.00
27	Jeff Ballard	1.00	.70	.40
28	Dwight Evans	1.00	.70	.40
29	Paul Molitor	3.00	2.25	1.25
30	Gregg Olson	1.00	.70	.40
31	Dan Plesac	1.00	.70	.40
32	Greg Swindell	1.00	.70	.40
33	Cito Gaston, Tony LaRussa	1.00	.70	.40
34	Will Clark	3.50	2.75	1.50
35	Roberto Alomar	3.00	2.25	1.25
36	Barry Larkin	1.00	.70	.40
37	Ken Caminiti	1.00	.70	.40
38	Eric Davis	1.25	.90	.50
39	Tony Gwynn	1.50	1.25	.60
40	Kevin Mitchell	1.00	.70	.40
41	Craig Biggio	1.00	.70	.40
42	Mike Scott	1.00	.70	.40
43	Joe Carter	2.00	1.50	.80
44	Jack Clark	1.00	.70	.40
45	Glenn Davis	1.00	.70	.40
46	Orel Hershiser	1.50	1.25	.60
47	Jay Howell	1.00	.70	.40
48	Bruce Hurst	1.00	.70	.40
49	Dave Smith	1.00	.70	.40
50	Pedro Guerrero	1.00	.70	.40
51	Ryne Sandberg	5.00	3.75	2.00
52	Ozzie Smith	4.00	3.00	1.50
53	Howard Johnson	1.50	1.25	.60
54	Von Hayes	1.00	.70	.40
55	Tim Raines	1.75	1.25	.70
56	Darryl Strawberry	2.50	2.00	1.00
57	Mike LaValliere	1.00	.70	.40
58	Dwight Gooden	2.00	1.50	.80
59	Bobby Bonilla	2.00	1.50	.80
60	Tim Burke	1.00	.70	.40
61	Sid Fernandez	1.00	.70	.40
62	Andres Galarraga	1.75	1.25	.70
63	Mark Grace	2.00	1.50	.80
64	Joe Magrane	1.00	.70	.40
65	Mitch Williams	1.00	.70	.40
66	Roger Craig, Don Zimmer	1.00	.70	.40

1990 Topps TV Cardinals Team Set

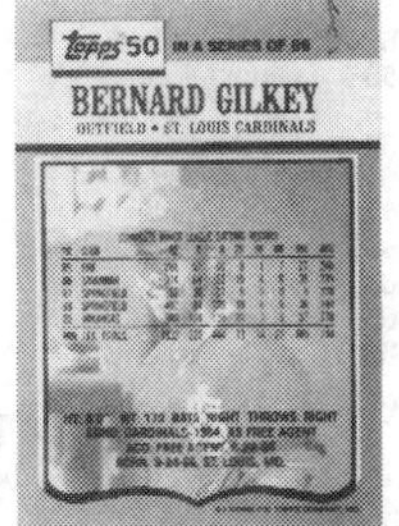

Available only as a boxed set via a limited television offer, this team set includes cards of all players on the opening day roster plus the manager, selected coaches and many of the organization's top prospects. In many cases this is the first card of a player in major league uniform, and in some cases represents the only card which will ever be issued of the player as a major leaguer. Cards feature a high-gloss front surface. Backs have a red border and feature a "ghost image" of the photo on the front as a background to the statistical and biographical data. Because of the relatively limited production and the fact it was sold as a boxed set only, single cards are seldom available.

		MT	NR MT	EX
Complete set:		60.00	45.00	24.00
Common player:		1.00	.70	.40
1	Whitey Herzog	2.00	1.50	.80
2	Steve Braun	1.00	.70	.40
3	Rich Hacker	1.00	.70	.40
4	Dave Ricketts	1.00	.70	.40
5	Jim Riggleman	1.00	.70	.40
6	Mike Roarke	1.00	.70	.40
7	Cris Carpenter	1.00	.70	.40
8	John Costello	1.00	.70	.40
9	Danny Cox	1.00	.70	.40
10	Ken Dayley	1.00	.70	.40
11	Jose DeLeon	1.00	.70	.40
12	Frank DiPino	1.00	.70	.40
13	Ken Hill	1.00	.70	.40
14	Howard Hilton	1.00	.70	.40
15	Ricky Horton	1.00	.70	.40
16	Joe Magrane	1.00	.70	.40
17	Greg Mathews	1.00	.70	.40
18	Bryn Smith	1.00	.70	.40
19	Scott Terry	1.00	.70	.40
20	Bob Tewksbury	2.50	2.00	1.00
21	John Tudor	1.00	.70	.40
22	Todd Worrell	1.50	1.25	.60
23	Tom Pagnozzi	1.00	.70	.40
24	Todd Zeile	2.00	1.50	.80
25	Pedro Guerrero	1.50	1.25	.60
26	Tim Jones	1.00	.70	.40
27	Jose Oquendo	1.50	1.25	.60
28	Terry Pendleton	3.00	2.25	1.25
29	Ozzie Smith	5.00	3.75	2.00
30	Denny Walling	1.00	.70	.40
31	Tom Brunansky	1.00	.70	.40
32	Vince Colemen	2.00	1.50	.80
33	Dave Collins	1.00	.70	.40
34	Willie McGee	2.50	2.00	1.00
35	John Morris	1.00	.70	.40
36	Milt Thompson	1.00	.70	.40
37	Gibson Alba	1.00	.70	.40

		MT	NR MT	EX
38	Scott Arnold	1.00	.70	.40
39	Rod Brewer	1.00	.70	.40
40	Greg Carmona	1.00	.70	.40
41	Mark Clark	1.50	1.25	.60
42	Stan Clarke	1.00	.70	.40
43	Paul Coleman	1.00	.70	.40
44	Todd Crosby	1.00	.70	.40
45	Brad DuVall	1.00	.70	.40
46	John Ericks	1.00	.70	.40
47	Bien Figueroa	1.00	.70	.40
48	Terry Francona	1.00	.70	.40
49	Ed Fulton	1.00	.70	.40
50	Bernard Gilkey	3.00	2.25	1.25
51	Ernie Camacho	1.00	.70	.40
52	Mike Hinkle	1.00	.70	.40
53	Ray Lankford	3.00	2.25	1.25
54	Julian Martinez	1.00	.70	.40
55	Jesus Mendez	1.00	.70	.40
56	Mike Milchin	1.00	.70	.40
57	Mauricio Nunez	1.00	.70	.40
58	Omar Olivares	2.00	1.50	.80
59	Geronimo Pena	2.00	1.50	.80
60	Mike Perez	2.00	1.50	.80
61	Gaylen Pitts	1.00	.70	.40
62	Mark Riggins	1.00	.70	.40
63	Tim Sherrill	1.00	.70	.40
64	Roy Silver	1.00	.70	.40
65	Ray Stephens	1.00	.70	.40
66	Craig Wilson	1.00	.70	.40

1990 Topps TV Cubs Team Set

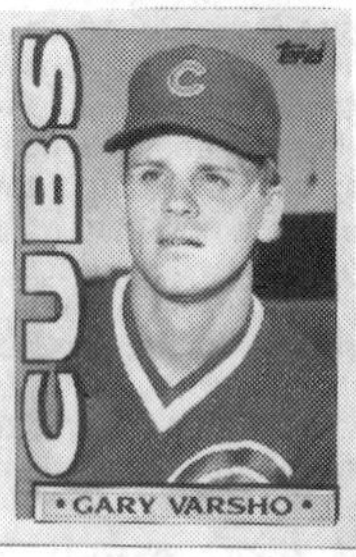

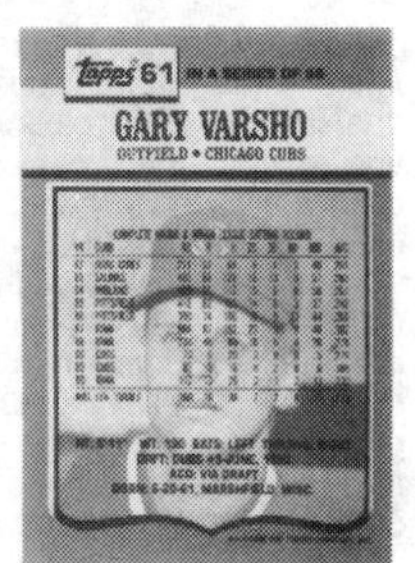

Sold only in boxed set form via a limited television offer, this 66-card issue includes all players on the team's 1990 opening day roster as well as the manager, selected coaches and some of the organization's top minor league prospects. For the latter group, this sets offers the first - and in many cases the only - card of the player in a major league uniform. The cards have a high-gloss front surface. Card backs feature a "ghost image" of the color photo used on the front as a background to the stats and biographical information. A red border completes the back design. Because the set was sold only in boxed form, and production was relatively low, single cards are seldom seen in the market.

	MT	NR MT	EX
Complete set:	60.00	45.00	24.00
Common player:	1.00	.70	.40

		MT	NR MT	EX
1	Don Zimmer	1.50	1.25	.60
2	Joe Altobelli	1.00	.70	.40
3	Chuck Cottier	1.00	.70	.40
4	Jose Martinez	1.00	.70	.40
5	Dick Pole	1.00	.70	.40
6	Phil Roof	1.00	.70	.40
7	Paul Assenmacher	1.00	.70	.40
8	Mike Bielecki	1.00	.70	.40
9	Mike Harkey	1.50	1.25	.60
10	Joe Kraemer	1.00	.70	.40
11	Les Lancaster	1.00	.70	.40
12	Greg Maddux	3.00	2.25	1.25
13	Jose Nunez	1.00	.70	.40
14	Jeff Pico	1.00	.70	.40
15	Rick Sutcliffe	1.50	1.25	.60
16	Dean Wilkins	1.00	.70	.40
17	Mitch Williams	2.00	1.50	.80
18	Steve Wilson	1.00	.70	.40
19	Damon Berryhill	1.00	.70	.40
20	Joe Girardi	1.50	1.25	.60
21	Rick Wrona	1.00	.70	.40
22	Shawon Dunston	2.00	1.50	.80
23	Mark Grace	3.00	2.25	1.25
24	Domingo Ramos	1.00	.70	.40
25	Luis Salazar	1.00	.70	.40
26	Ryne Sandberg	7.50	5.75	3.00
27	Greg Smith	1.00	.70	.40
28	Curtis Wilkerson	1.00	.70	.40
29	Dave Clark	1.00	.70	.40
30	Doug Dascenzo	1.00	.70	.40
31	Andre Dawson	4.00	3.00	1.50
32	Lloyd McClendon	1.00	.70	.40
33	Dwight Smith	1.50	1.25	.60
34	Jerome Walton	1.50	1.25	.60
35	Marvell Wynne	1.00	.70	.40
36	Alex Arias	2.00	1.50	.80
37	Bob Bafia	1.00	.70	.40
38	Brad Bierley	1.00	.70	.40
39	Shawn Boskie	2.50	2.00	1.00
40	Danny Clay	1.00	.70	.40
41	Rusty Crockett	1.00	.70	.40
42	Earl Cunningham	1.50	1.25	.60
43	Len Damian	1.00	.70	.40
44	Darrin Duffy	1.00	.70	.40
45	Ty Griffin	1.00	.70	.40
46	Brian Guinn	1.00	.70	.40
47	Phil Hannon	1.00	.70	.40
48	Phil Harrison	1.00	.70	.40
49	Jeff Hearron	1.00	.70	.40
50	Greg Kallevig	1.00	.70	.40
51	Cedric Landrum	1.00	.70	.40
52	Bill Long	1.00	.70	.40
53	Derrick May	3.00	2.25	1.25
54	Ray Mullino	1.00	.70	.40
55	Erik Pappas	1.50	1.25	.60
56	Steve Parker	1.00	.70	.40
57	Dave Pavlas	1.00	.70	.40
58	Laddie Renfroe	1.00	.70	.40
59	Jeff Small	1.00	.70	.40
60	Doug Strange	1.00	.70	.40
61	Gary Varsho	1.00	.70	.40
62	Hector Villanueva	1.50	1.25	.60
63	Rick Wilkins	3.00	2.25	1.25
64	Dana Williams	1.00	.70	.40
65	Bill Wrona	1.00	.70	.40
66	Fernando Zarranz	1.00	.70	.40

1990 Topps TV Mets Team Set

This late-season issue, sold only as a boxed set via a television offer in limited areas, features all of the players on the 1990 opening day roster, plus the manager, selected coaches and many of the organization's top minor league prospects. For many of the prospects, this is the first, if not the only, card on which they appear in major league uniform. A highlight of the back design is a "ghost image" full-color reproduction of the front photo, used as a background to the statistical and biographical information. A red border dominates the remainder of the back design. Because it was sold only as a boxed set, and production was relatively limited, single cards are seldom available.

	MT	NR MT	EX
Complete Set:	60.00	45.00	24.00
Common player:	1.00	.70	.40

1	Dave Johnson	1.00	.70	.40
2	Mike Cubbage	1.00	.70	.40
3	Doc Edwards	1.00	.70	.40
4	Bud Harrelson	1.00	.70	.40
5	Greg Pavlick	1.00	.70	.40
6	Mel Stottlemyre, Sr.	1.50	1.25	.60
7	Blaine Beatty	1.00	.70	.40
8	David Cone	2.00	1.50	.80
9	Ron Darling	2.00	1.50	.80
10	Sid Fernandez	2.00	1.50	.80
11	John Franco	2.00	1.50	.80
12	Dwight Gooden	4.00	3.00	1.50
13	Jeff Innis	1.00	.70	.40
14	Julio Machado	1.00	.70	.40
15	Jeff Musselman	1.00	.70	.40
16	Bob Ojeda	1.50	1.25	.60
17	Alejandro Pena	1.00	.70	.40
18	Frank Viola	2.50	2.00	1.00
19	Wally Whitehurst	1.00	.70	.40
20	Barry Lyons	1.00	.70	.40
21	Orlando Mercado	2.50	2.00	1.00
22	Mackey Sasser	1.00	.70	.40
23	Kevin Elster	1.00	.70	.40
24	Gregg Jefferies	3.00	2.25	1.25
25	Howard Johnson	2.50	2.00	1.00
26	Dave Magadan	2.00	1.50	.80
27	Mike Marshall	1.00	.70	.40
28	Tom O'Malley	1.00	.70	.40
29	Tim Teufel	1.00	.70	.40
30	Mark Carreon	1.50	1.25	.60
31	Kevin McReynolds	1.50	1.25	.60
32	Keith Miller	1.00	.70	.40
33	Darryl Strawberry	4.00	3.00	1.50
34	Lou Thornton	1.00	.70	.40
35	Shawn Barton	1.00	.70	.40
36	Tim Bogar	1.00	.70	.40
37	Terry Bross	1.00	.70	.40
38	Kevin Brown	1.00	.70	.40
39	Mike DeButch	1.00	.70	.40
40	Alex Diaz	1.00	.70	.40
41	Chris Donnels	1.00	.70	.40
42	Jeff Gardner	1.00	.70	.40
43	Denny Gonzalez	1.00	.70	.40
44	Kenny Graves	1.00	.70	.40
45	Manny Hernandez	1.00	.70	.40
46	Keith Hughes	1.00	.70	.40
47	Todd Hundley	2.00	1.50	.80
48	Chris Jelic	1.00	.70	.40
49	Dave Liddell	1.00	.70	.40
50	Terry McDaniel	1.00	.70	.40
51	Cesar Mejia	1.00	.70	.40
52	Scott Nielsen	1.00	.70	.40
53	Dale Plummer	1.00	.70	.40
54	Darren Reed	1.00	.70	.40
55	Gil Roca	1.00	.70	.40
56	Jaime Roseboro	1.00	.70	.40
57	Roger Samuels	1.00	.70	.40
58	Zoilo Sanchez	1.00	.70	.40
59	Pete Schourek	1.50	1.25	.60
60	Craig Shipley	1.00	.70	.40
61	Ray Soff	1.00	.70	.40
62	Steve Swisher	1.00	.70	.40
63	Kelvin Torve	1.00	.70	.40
64	Dave Trautwein	1.00	.70	.40
65	Julio Valera	1.00	.70	.40
66	Alan Zinter	1.00	.70	.40

1990 Topps TV Red Sox Team Set

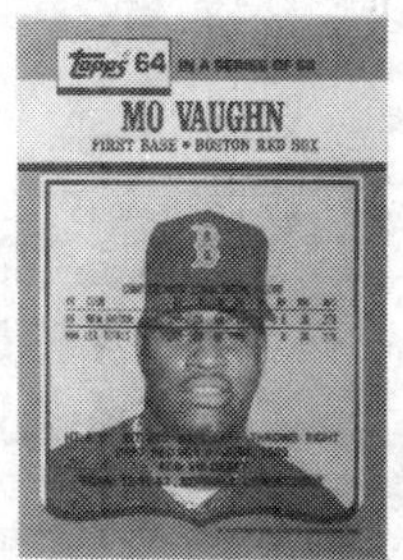

This 66-card set was available only via a television offer in certain limited areas. Production was relatively low and single cards are hard to find. Player selection includes all those on the team's opening day roster in 1990, plus the manager, selected coaches and the team's top minor league prospects. In many cases this represents the first, or even the only, appearance of these prospects on major league baseball cards. Fronts have a high-gloss surface. Card backs, bordered in red, feature a "ghost image" reproduction of the front photo as a background to the statistics and biographical data.

		MT	NR MT	EX
Complete set:		60.00	45.00	24.00
Common player:		1.00	.70	.40
1	Joe Morgan	1.00	.70	.40
2	Dick Berardino	1.00	.70	.40
3	Al Bumbry	1.00	.70	.40
4	Bill Fischer	1.00	.70	.40
5	Richie Hebner	1.00	.70	.40
6	Rac Slider	1.00	.70	.40
7	Mike Boddicker	1.00	.70	.40
8	Roger Clemens	5.00	3.75	2.00
9	John Dopson	1.00	.70	.40
10	Wes Gardner	1.00	.70	.40
11	Greg Harris	1.00	.70	.40
12	Dana Kiecker	1.00	.70	.40
13	Dennis Lamp	1.00	.70	.40
14	Rob Murphy	1.00	.70	.40
15	Jeff Reardon	1.50	1.25	.60
16	Mike Rochford	1.00	.70	.40
17	Lee Smith	3.00	2.25	1.25
18	Rich Gedman	1.00	.70	.40
19	John Marzano	1.00	.70	.40
20	Tony Pena	1.50	1.25	.60
21	Marty Barrett	1.00	.70	.40
22	Wade Boggs	5.00	3.75	2.00
23	Bill Buckner	1.00	.70	.40
24	Danny Heep	1.00	.70	.40
25	Jody Reed	1.50	1.25	.60
26	Luis Rivera	1.00	.70	.40
27	Billy Jo Robidoux	1.00	.70	.40
28	Ellis Burks	1.50	1.25	.60
29	Dwight Evans	1.50	1.25	.60
30	Mike Greenwell	2.00	1.50	.80
31	Randy Kutcher	1.00	.70	.40
32	Carlos Quintana	1.00	.70	.40
33	Kevin Romine	1.00	.70	.40
34	Ed Nottle	1.00	.70	.40
35	Mark Meleski	1.00	.70	.40
36	Steve Bast	1.00	.70	.40
37	Greg Blosser	1.00	.70	.40
38	Tom Bolton	1.00	.70	.40
39	Scott Cooper	2.00	1.50	.80
40	Zach Crouch	1.00	.70	.40
41	Steve Curry	1.00	.70	.40
42	Mike Dalton	1.00	.70	.40
43	John Flaherty	1.00	.70	.40
44	Angel Gonzalez	1.00	.70	.40
45	Eric Hetzel	1.00	.70	.40
46	Daryl Irvine	1.00	.70	.40
47	Joe Johnson	1.00	.70	.40
48	Rick Lancellotti	1.00	.70	.40
49	John Leister	1.00	.70	.40
50	Derek Livernois	1.00	.70	.40
51	Josias Manzanillo	1.00	.70	.40
52	Kevin Morton	1.00	.70	.40
53	Julius McDougal	1.00	.70	.40
54	Tim Naehring	1.50	1.25	.60
55	Jim Pankovits	1.00	.70	.40
56	Mickey Pina	1.00	.70	.40
57	Phil Plantier	3.00	2.25	1.25
58	Jerry Reed	1.00	.70	.40
59	Larry Shikles	1.00	.70	.40
60	Tito Stewart	1.00	.70	.40
61	Jeff Stone	1.00	.70	.40
62	John Trautwein	1.00	.70	.40
63	Gary Tremblay	1.00	.70	.40
64	Mo Vaughn	4.00	3.00	1.50
65	Scott Wade	1.00	.70	.40
66	Eric Wedge	1.00	.70	.40

A player's name in italic indicates a rookie card. An (FC) indicates a player's first card for that particular card company.

1990 Topps TV Yankees Team Set

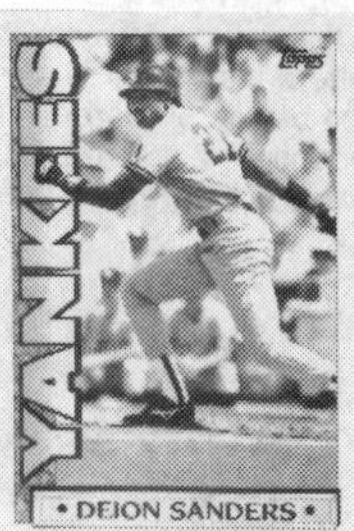

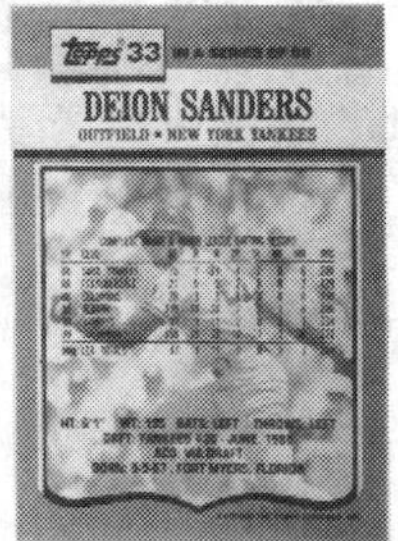

The first - and in many cases the only - baseball card appearance of top minor league prospects occurs in this special 66-card boxed set which was sold only via a special television offer in limited markets. The set also includes all players on the team's opening day roster, plus the manager and selected coaches. Card fronts have a high-gloss surface. On back, framed by a red border, the design features a "ghost image" of the color front photo, used as a background to the statistical and biographical information. Because the cards were sold only as a complete set, single cards are seldom available.

		MT	NR MT	EX
Complete set:		60.00	45.00	24.00
Common player:		1.00	.70	.40
1	Bucky Dent	1.50	1.25	.60
2	Mark Connor	1.00	.70	.40
3	Billy Connors	1.00	.70	.40
4	Mike Ferraro	1.00	.70	.40
5	Joe Sparks	1.00	.70	.40
6	Champ Summers	1.00	.70	.40
7	Greg Cadaret	1.00	.70	.40
8	Chuck Cary	1.00	.70	.40
9	Lee Guetterman	1.00	.70	.40
10	Andy Hawkins	1.00	.70	.40
11	Dave LaPoint	1.00	.70	.40
12	Tim Leary	1.00	.70	.40
13	Lance McCullers	1.00	.70	.40
14	Alan Mills	1.00	.70	.40
15	Clay Parker	1.00	.70	.40
16	Pascual Perez	1.00	.70	.40
17	Eric Plunk	1.00	.70	.40
18	Dave Righetti	1.50	1.25	.60
19	Jeff Robinson	1.00	.70	.40
20	Rick Cerone	1.00	.70	.40
21	Bob Geren	1.00	.70	.40
22	Steve Balboni	1.00	.70	.40
23	Mike Blowers	1.00	.70	.40
24	Alvaro Espinoza	1.00	.70	.40
25	Don Mattingly	5.00	3.75	2.00
26	Steve Sax	1.50	1.25	.60
27	Wayne Tolleson	1.00	.70	.40
28	Randy Velarde	1.00	.70	.40
29	Jesse Barfield	1.50	1.25	.60
30	Mel Hall	1.00	.70	.40
31	Roberto Kelly	2.00	1.50	.80
32	Luis Polonia	2.00	1.50	.80
33	Deion Sanders	4.00	3.00	1.50
34	Dave Winfield	5.00	3.75	2.00
35	Steve Adkins	1.00	.70	.40
36	Oscar Azocar	1.00	.70	.40
37	Bob Brower	1.00	.70	.40
38	Britt Burns	1.00	.70	.40
39	Bob Davidson	1.00	.70	.40
40	Brian Dorsett	1.00	.70	.40
41	Dave Eiland	1.00	.70	.40
42	John Fishel	1.00	.70	.40
43	Andy Fox	1.00	.70	.40
44	John Habyan	1.00	.70	.40
45	Cullen Hartzog	1.00	.70	.40
46	Sterling Hitchcock	2.00	1.50	.80
47	Brian Johnson	1.00	.70	.40
48	Jimmy Jones	1.00	.70	.40
49	Scott Kamieniecki	1.00	.70	.40
50	Mark Leiter	1.00	.70	.40
51	Jim Leyritz	2.00	1.50	.80
52	Jason Maas	1.00	.70	.40
53	Kevin Maas	1.50	1.25	.60
54	Hensley Meulens	1.50	1.25	.60
55	Kevin Mmahat	1.50	1.25	.60
56	Rich Monteleone	1.00	.70	.40
57	Vince Phillips	1.00	.70	.40
58	Carlos Rodriguez	1.00	.70	.40
59	Dave Sax	1.00	.70	.40
60	Willie Smith	1.00	.70	.40
61	Van Snider	1.00	.70	.40
62	Andy Stankiewicz	1.50	1.25	.60
63	Wade Taylor	1.00	.70	.40
64	Ricky Torres	1.00	.70	.40
65	Jim Walewander	1.00	.70	.40
66	Bernie Williams	2.00	1.50	.80

1990 Topps Heads Up!

Following up a much rarer test issue of the previous year, the Heads Up! Baseball Stars of 1990 was a 24-piece set which received rather wider distribution, but proved unpopular with collectors. On heavy cardboard, die-cut to approximately 5" x 6", these novelties featured only a head-and-cap photo of the player. Backs have the player's name and team, along with an adhesive strip and plastic suction cup which could be used to "hang" the player.

		MT	NR MT	EX
Complete set (24):		7.50	5.50	3.00
Common player:		.25	.20	.10
1	Tony Gwynn	.35	.25	.14
2	Will Clark	.50	.40	.20
3	Dwight Gooden	.25	.20	.10
4	Dennis Eckersley	.25	.20	.10
5	Ken Griffey, Jr.	2.00	1.50	.80
6	Craig Biggio	.25	.20	.10
7	Bret Saberhagen	.25	.20	.10
8	Bo Jackson	.40	.30	.15
9	Ryne Sandberg	1.00	.70	.40
10	Gregg Olson	.25	.20	.10
11	John Franco	.25	.20	.10
12	Rafael Palmeiro	.35	.25	.14
13	Gary Sheffield	.25	.20	.10
14	Mark McGwire	.35	.25	.14
15	Kevin Mitchell	.25	.20	.10
16	Jim Abbott	.35	.25	.14
17	Harold Reynolds	.25	.20	.10
18	Jose Canseco	.35	.25	.14
19	Don Mattingly	.60	.45	.25
20	Kirby Puckett	.35	.25	.14
21	Tom Gordon	.25	.20	.10
22	Craig Worthington	.25	.20	.10
23	Dwight Smith	.25	.20	.10
24	Jerome Walton	.25	.20	.10

1990 Topps Senior League

Topps was among several companies to produce a Senior League set in 1990. The set includes 132 cards and was sold as a boxed set. The card fronts have the Senior Baseball and Topps logo on top and the player's

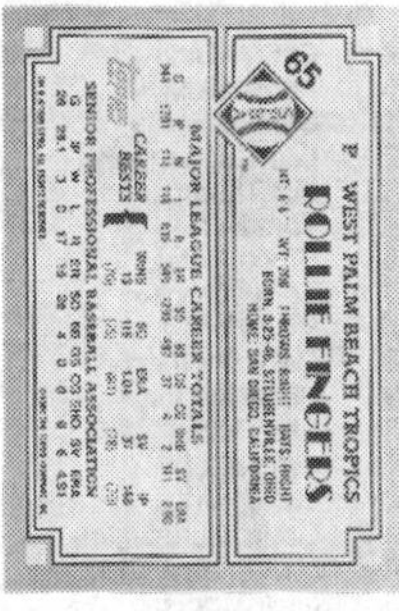

name and team logo on the bottom, with a woodgrain-like border surrounding the front photo. The backs of the card include traditional biographical information, plus career major league statistics, career ML bests and stats from any Senior League experience.

		MT	NR MT	EX
Complete Set:		9.00	6.75	3.50
Common Player:		.10	.08	.04
1	George Foster	.15	.11	.06
2	Dwight Lowry	.10	.08	.04
3	Bob Jones	.10	.08	.04
4	Clete Boyer	.10	.08	.04
5	Rafael Landestoy	.10	.08	.04
6	Bob Shirley	.10	.08	.04
7	Ivan Murrell	.10	.08	.04
8	Jerry White	.10	.08	.04
9	Steve Henderson	.10	.08	.04
10	Marty Castillo	.10	.08	.04
11	Bruce Kison	.10	.08	.04
12	George Hendrick	.10	.08	.04
13	Bernie Carbo	.10	.08	.04
14	Jerry Martin	.10	.08	.04
15	Al Hrabosky	.10	.08	.04
16	Luis Gomez	.10	.08	.04
17	Dick Drago	.10	.08	.04
18	Bobby Ramos	.10	.08	.04
19	Joe Pittman	.10	.08	.04
20	Ike Blessitt	.10	.08	.04
21	Bill Travers	.10	.08	.04
22	Dick Williams	.15	.11	.06
23	Randy Lerch	.10	.08	.04
24	Tom Spencer	.10	.08	.04
25	Graig Nettles	.15	.11	.06
26	Jim Gideon	.10	.08	.04
27	Al Bumbry	.10	.08	.04
28	Tom Murphy	.10	.08	.04
29	Rodney Scott	.10	.08	.04
30	Alan Bannister	.10	.08	.04
31	John D'Acquisto	.10	.08	.04
32	Bert Campaneris	.15	.11	.06
33	Bill Lee	.10	.08	.04
34	Jerry Grote	.10	.08	.04
35	Ken Reitz	.10	.08	.04
36	Al Oliver	.15	.11	.06
37	Tim Stoddard	.10	.08	.04
38	Lenny Randle	.10	.08	.04
39	Rick Manning	.10	.08	.04
40	Bobby Bonds	.15	.11	.06
41	Rick Wise	.10	.08	.04
42	Sal Butera	.10	.08	.04
43	Ed Figueroa	.10	.08	.04
44	Ron Washington	.10	.08	.04
45	Elias Sosa	.10	.08	.04
46	Dan Driessen	.10	.08	.04
47	Wayne Nordhagen	.10	.08	.04
48	Vida Blue	.15	.11	.06
49	Butch Hobson	.10	.08	.04
50	Randy Bass	.10	.08	.04
51	Paul Mirabella	.10	.08	.04
52	Steve Kemp	.10	.08	.04
53	Kim Allen	.10	.08	.04
54	Stan Cliburn	.10	.08	.04
55	Derrel Thomas	.10	.08	.04
56	Pete Falcone	.10	.08	.04
57	Willie Aikens	.10	.08	.04
58	Toby Harrah	.10	.08	.04
59	Bob Tolan	.10	.08	.04
60	Rick Waits	.10	.08	.04
61	Jim Morrison	.10	.08	.04
62	Stan Bahnsen	.10	.08	.04
63	Gene Richards	.10	.08	.04
64	Dave Cash	.10	.08	.04
65	Rollie Fingers	.50	.40	.20
66	Butch Benton	.10	.08	.04
67	Tim Ireland	.10	.08	.04
68	Rick Lysander	.10	.08	.04
69	Cesar Cedeno	.10	.08	.04
70	Jim Willoughby	.10	.08	.04
71	Bill Madlock	.15	.11	.06
72	Lee Lacy	.10	.08	.04
73	Milt Wilcox	.10	.08	.04
74	Ron Pruitt	.10	.08	.04
75	Wayne Krenchicki	.10	.08	.04
76	Earl Weaver	.25	.20	.10
77	Pedro Borbon	.10	.08	.04
78	Jose Cruz	.15	.11	.06
79	Steve Ontiveros	.10	.08	.04
80	Mike Easler	.10	.08	.04
81	Amos Otis	.10	.08	.04
82	Mickey Mahler	.10	.08	.04
83	Orlando Gonzalez	.10	.08	.04
84	Doug Simunic	.10	.08	.04
85	Felix Millan	.10	.08	.04
86	Garth Iorg	.10	.08	.04
87	Pete Broberg	.10	.08	.04
88	Roy Howell	.10	.08	.04
89	Dave LaRoche	.10	.08	.04
90	Jerry Manuel	.10	.08	.04
91	Tony Scott	.10	.08	.04
92	Larvell Blanks	.10	.08	.04
93	Joaquin Andujar	.10	.08	.04
94	Tito Landrum	.10	.08	.04
95	Joe Sambito	.10	.08	.04
96	Pat Dobson	.10	.08	.04
97	Dan Meyer	.10	.08	.04
98	Clint Hurdle	.10	.08	.04
99	Pete LaCock	.10	.08	.04
100	Bob Galasso	.10	.08	.04
101	Dave Kingman	.15	.11	.06
102	Jon Matlack	.10	.08	.04
103	Larry Harlow	.10	.08	.04
104	Rick Peterson	.10	.08	.04
105	Joe Hicks	.10	.08	.04
106	Bill Campbell	.10	.08	.04
107	Tom Paciorek	.10	.08	.04
108	Ray Burris	.10	.08	.04
109	Ken Landreaux	.10	.08	.04
110	Steve McCatty	.10	.08	.04
111	Ron LeFlore	.10	.08	.04
112	Joe Decker	.10	.08	.04
113	Leon Roberts	.10	.08	.04
114	Doug Corbett	.10	.08	.04
115	Mickey Rivers	.10	.08	.04
116	Dock Ellis	.10	.08	.04
117	Ron Jackson	.10	.08	.04
118	Bob Molinaro	.10	.08	.04
119	Fergie Jenkins	.50	.40	.20
120	U.L. Washington	.10	.08	.04
121	Roy Thomas	.10	.08	.04
122	Hal McRae	.20	.15	.08
123	Juan Eichelberger	.10	.08	.04
124	Gary Rajsich	.10	.08	.04
125	Dennis Leonard	.10	.08	.04
126	Walt Williams	.10	.08	.04
127	Rennie Stennett	.10	.08	.04
128	Jim Bibby	.10	.08	.04
129	Dyar Miller	.10	.08	.04
130	Luis Pujols	.10	.08	.04
131	Juan Beniquez	.10	.08	.04
132	Checklist	.10	.08	.04

1991 Topps

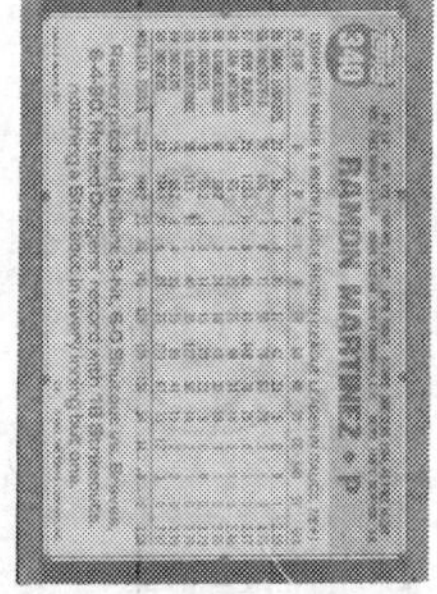

Topps celebrated its 40th anniversary in 1991 with

the biggest promotional campaign in baseball card history. More than 300,000 vintage Topps cards (or certificates which can be redeemed for valuable older cards) produced from 1952 to present were randomly inserted in packs. Also a grand prize winner will receive one complete set from each year, and others will receive a single set from 1952-present. The 1991 Topps card fronts feature the "Topps 40 Years of Baseball" logo in the upper left corner. Card borders frame the player photos. All players of the same team have cards with the same frame/border colors. Both action and posed shots appear in full-color on the card fronts. The flip sides are printed horizontally and feature complete statistics. Record Breakers and other special cards were once again included in the set. The cards measure 2-1/2" by 3-1/2". Several cards feature horizontal fronts. 6,313 forms of this set were released with gold "Operation Desert Shield" stamps on the fronts of the cards. The cards were released to U.S. troops serving in the Persian Gulf. Due to scarcity, these cards are quite valuable. Complete "Desert Shield" sets list for $2,500.

		MT	NR MT	EX
Complete Set (792):		18.00	13.50	7.25
Common Player:		.03	.02	.01
1	Nolan Ryan	.30	.25	.12
2	Record Breaker (George Brett)	.10	.08	.04
3	Record Breaker (Carlton Fisk)	.08	.06	.03
4	Record Breaker (Kevin Maas)	.10	.08	.04
5	Record Breaker (Cal Ripken, Jr.)	.10	.08	.04
6	Record Breaker (Nolan Ryan)	.20	.15	.08
7	RB (Ryne Sandberg)	.10	.08	.04
8	Record Breaker (Bobby Thigpen)	.08	.06	.03
9	Darrin Fletcher(FC)	.10	.08	.04
10	Gregg Olson	.08	.06	.03
11	Roberto Kelly	.08	.06	.03
12	Paul Assenmacher	.04	.03	.02
13	Mariano Duncan	.06	.05	.02
14	Dennis Lamp	.03	.02	.01
15	Von Hayes	.08	.06	.03
16	Mike Heath	.04	.03	.02
17	Jeff Brantley	.06	.05	.02
18	Nelson Liriano	.03	.02	.01
19	Jeff Robinson	.04	.03	.02
20	Pedro Guerrero	.08	.06	.03
21	Joe M. Morgan	.03	.02	.01
22	Storm Davis	.06	.05	.02
23	Jim Gantner	.04	.03	.02
24	Dave Martinez	.05	.04	.02
25	Tim Belcher	.08	.06	.03
26	Luis Sojo	.06	.05	.02
27	Bobby Witt	.08	.06	.03
28	Alvaro Espinoza	.05	.04	.02
29	Bob Walk	.03	.02	.01
30	Gregg Jefferies	.15	.11	.06
31	*Colby Ward*(FC)	.15	.11	.06
32	*Mike Simms*(FC)	.20	.15	.08
33	Barry Jones	.05	.04	.02
34	Atlee Hammaker	.03	.02	.01
35	Greg Maddux	.08	.06	.03
36	Donnie Hill	.03	.02	.01
37	Tom Bolton	.05	.04	.02
38	Scott Bradley	.03	.02	.01
39	*Jim Neidlinger*(FC)	.15	.11	.06
40	Kevin Mitchell	.20	.15	.08
41	Ken Dayley	.04	.03	.02
42	*Chris Hoiles*(FC)	.20	.15	.08
43	Roger McDowell	.06	.05	.02
44	Mike Felder	.04	.03	.02
45	Chris Sabo	.10	.08	.04
46	Tim Drummond	.06	.05	.02
47	Brook Jacoby	.06	.05	.02
48	Dennis Boyd	.05	.04	.02
49a	Pat Borders (40 stolen bases in 1986)	.20	.15	.08
49b	Pat Borders (0 stolen bases in 1986)	.15	.11	.06
50	Bob Welch	.08	.06	.03
51	Art Howe	.03	.02	.01
52	*Francisco Oliveras*(FC)	.10	.08	.04
53	Mike Sahrperson	.06	.05	.02
54	Gary Mielke	.05	.04	.02
55	Jeffrey Leonard	.05	.04	.02
56	Jeff Parrett	.04	.03	.02
57	Jack Howell	.04	.03	.02
58	Mel Stottlemyre	.08	.06	.03
59	Eric Yelding	.06	.05	.02
60	Frank Viola	.12	.09	.05
61	Stan Javier	.04	.03	.02
62	Lee Guetterman	.03	.02	.01
63	Milt Thompson	.04	.03	.02
64	Tom Herr	.05	.04	.02
65	Bruce Hurst	.06	.05	.02
66	Terry Kennedy	.03	.02	.01
67	Rick Honeycutt	.03	.02	.01
68	Gary Sheffield	.15	.11	.06
69	Steve Wilson	.06	.05	.02
70	Ellis Burks	.15	.11	.06
71	Jim Acker	.03	.02	.01
72	Junior Ortiz	.03	.02	.01
73	Craig Worthington	.06	.05	.02
74	*Shane Andrews*	.20	.15	.08
75	Jack Morris	.08	.06	.03
76	Jerry Browne	.05	.04	.02
77	Drew Hall	.03	.02	.01
78	Geno Petralli	.03	.02	.01
79	Frank Thomas	1.00	.70	.40
80	Fernando Valenzuela	.25	.20	.10
81	Cito Gaston	.03	.02	.01
82	Tom Glavine	.05	.04	.02
83	Daryl Boston	.03	.02	.01
84	Bob McClure	.03	.02	.01
85	Jesse Barfield	.08	.06	.03
86	Les Lancaster	.04	.03	.02
87	Tracy Jones	.03	.02	.01
88	Bob Tewksbury	.04	.03	.02
89	Darren Daulton	.06	.05	.02
90	Danny Tartabull	.08	.06	.03
91	*Greg Colbrunn*(FC)	.10	.08	.04
92	Danny Jackson	.06	.05	.02
93	Ivan Calderon	.08	.06	.03
94	John Dopson	.05	.04	.02
95	Paul Molitor	.10	.08	.04
96	Trevor Wilson	.04	.03	.02
97	Brady Anderson	.04	.03	.02
98	Sergio Valdez	.05	.04	.02
99	Chris Gwynn	.05	.04	.02
100a	Don Mattingly (10 hits in 1990)	.60	.45	.25
100b	Don Mattingly (101 hits in 1990)	.10	.08	.04
101	Rob Ducey	.04	.03	.02
102	Gene Larkin	.06	.05	.02
103	*Tim Costo*	.15	.11	.06
104	Don Robinson	.04	.03	.02
105	Kevin McReynolds	.05	.04	.02
106	Ed Nunez	.03	.02	.01
107	Luis Polonia	.04	.03	.02
108	Matt Young	.04	.03	.02
109	Greg Riddoch	.03	.02	.01
110	Tom Henke	.06	.05	.02
111	Andres Thomas	.03	.02	.01
112	Frank DiPino	.03	.02	.01
113	*Carl Everett*	.20	.15	.08
114	*Lance Dickson*(FC)	.10	.08	.04
115	Hubie Brooks	.08	.06	.03
116	Mark Davis	.05	.04	.02
117	Dion James	.03	.02	.01
118	*Tom Edens*(FC)	.10	.08	.04
119	Carl Nichols(FC)	.05	.04	.02
120	Joe Carter	.08	.06	.03
121	Eric King	.05	.04	.02
122	Paul O'Neill	.06	.05	.02
123	Greg Harris	.05	.04	.02
124	Randy Bush	.04	.03	.02
125	Steve Bedrosian	.06	.05	.02
126	*Bernard Gilkey*(FC)	.20	.15	.08
127	Joe Price	.03	.02	.01
128	*Travis Fryman*	.60	.45	.25
129	Mark Eichhorn	.03	.02	.01
130	Ozzie Smith	.08	.06	.03
131	Checklist 1	.03	.02	.01
132	Jamie Quirk	.03	.02	.01
133	Greg Briley	.08	.06	.03
134	Kevin Elster	.04	.03	.02
135	Jerome Walton	.08	.06	.03
136	Dave Schmidt	.03	.02	.01
137	Randy Ready	.03	.02	.01
138	Jamie Moyer	.04	.03	.02
139	Jeff Treadway	.05	.04	.02
140	Fred McGriff	.10	.08	.04
141	Nick Leyva	.03	.02	.01
142	Curtis Wilkerson	.04	.03	.02
143	John Smiley	.04	.03	.02
144	Dave Henderson	.06	.05	.02
145	Lou Whitaker	.08	.06	.03
146	Dan Plesac	.06	.05	.02
147	*Carlos Baerga*	.20	.15	.08
148	Rey Palacios	.04	.03	.02

		MT	NR MT	EX
149	*Al Osuna*(FC)	.15	.11	.06
150	Cal Ripken, Jr.	.12	.09	.05
151	Tom Browning	.06	.05	.02
152	Mickey Hatcher	.04	.03	.02
153	Bryan Harvey	.06	.05	.02
154	Jay Buhner	.06	.05	.02
155	Dwight Evans	.08	.06	.03
156	Carlos Martinez	.06	.05	.02
157	John Smoltz	.08	.06	.03
158	Jose Uribe	.04	.03	.02
159	Joe Boever	.03	.02	.01
160	Vince Coleman	.08	.06	.03
161	Tim Leary	.04	.03	.02
162	*Ozzie Canseco*(FC)	.15	.11	.06
163	Dave Johnson	.04	.03	.02
164	Edgar Diaz	.05	.04	.02
165	Sandy Alomar	.15	.11	.06
166	Harold Baines	.08	.06	.03
167	*Randy Tomlin*(FC)	.08	.06	.03
168	John Olerud	.40	.30	.15
169	Luis Aquino	.04	.03	.02
170	Carlton Fisk	.10	.08	.04
171	Tony LaRussa	.04	.03	.02
172	Pete Incaviglia	.06	.05	.02
173	Jason Grimsley	.06	.05	.02
174	Ken Caminiti	.05	.04	.02
175	Jack Armstrong	.08	.06	.03
176	John Orton(FC)	.06	.05	.02
177	*Reggie Harris*(FC)	.15	.11	.06
178	Dave Valle	.04	.03	.02
179	Pete Harnisch	.06	.05	.02
180	Tony Gwynn	.12	.09	.05
181	Duane Ward	.04	.03	.02
182	Junior Noboa	.04	.03	.02
183	Clay Parker	.04	.03	.02
184	Gary Green	.10	.08	.04
185	Joe Magrane	.06	.05	.02
186	Rod Booker	.03	.02	.01
187	Greg Cadaret	.03	.02	.01
188	Damon Berryhill	.06	.05	.02
189	*Daryl Irvine*(FC)	.15	.11	.06
190	Matt Williams	.15	.11	.06
191	*Willie Blair*	.10	.08	.04
192	Rob Deer	.06	.05	.02
193	Felix Fermin	.03	.02	.01
194	Xavier Hernandez(FC)	.08	.06	.03
195	Wally Joyner	.10	.08	.04
196	*Jim Vatcher*(FC)	.12	.09	.05
197	*Chris Nabholz*(FC)	.20	.15	.08
198	R.J. Reynolds	.04	.03	.02
199	Mike Hartley(FC)	.15	.11	.06
200	Darryl Strawberry	.15	.11	.06
201	Tom Kelly	.03	.02	.01
202	*Jim Leyritz*	.12	.09	.05
203	Gene Harris	.05	.04	.02
204	Herm Winningham	.04	.03	.02
205	*Mike Perez*(FC)	.15	.11	.06
206	Carlos Quintana	.08	.06	.03
207	Gary Wayne	.05	.04	.02
208	Willie Wilson	.06	.05	.02
209	Ken Howell	.05	.04	.02
210	Lance Parrish	.08	.06	.03
211	*Brian Barnes*(FC)	.15	.11	.06
212	Steve Finley	.06	.05	.02
213	Frank Wills	.06	.05	.02
214	Joe Girardi	.06	.05	.02
215	Dave Smith	.06	.05	.02
216	Greg Gagne	.04	.03	.02
217	Chris Bosio	.05	.04	.02
218	*Rick Parker*	.03	.02	.01
219	Jack McDowell	.06	.05	.02
220	Tim Wallach	.08	.06	.03
221	Don Slaught	.04	.03	.02
222	*Brian McRae*(FC)	.25	.20	.10
223	Allan Anderson	.04	.03	.02
224	Juan Gonzalez	.60	.45	.25
225	Randy Johnson	.06	.05	.02
226	Alfredo Griffin	.04	.03	.02
227	Steve Avery	.15	.11	.06
228	Rex Hudler	.04	.03	.02
229	Rance Mulliniks	.03	.02	.01
230	Sid Fernandez	.08	.06	.03
231	Doug Rader	.03	.02	.01
232	Jose DeJesus	.08	.06	.03
233	Al Leiter	.03	.02	.01
234	*Scott Erickson*	.12	.09	.05
235	Dave Parker	.10	.08	.04
236	Frank Tanana	.06	.05	.02
237	Rick Cerone	.03	.02	.01
238	Mike Dunne	.03	.02	.01
239	*Darren Lewis*(FC)	.25	.20	.10
240	Mike Scott	.08	.06	.03
241	Dave Clark	.04	.03	.02
242	Mike LaCoss	.03	.02	.01
243	Lance Johnson	.06	.05	.02
244	Mike Jeffcoat	.03	.02	.01
245	Kal Daniels	.08	.06	.03
246	Kevin Wickander	.05	.04	.02
247	Jody Reed	.08	.06	.03
248	Tom Gordon	.08	.06	.03
249	Bob Melvin	.03	.02	.01
250	Dennis Eckersley	.10	.08	.04
251	Mark Lemke	.05	.04	.02
252	*Mel Rojas*(FC)	.10	.08	.04
253	Garry Templeton	.04	.03	.02
254	*Shawn Boskie*	.15	.11	.06
255	Brian Downing	.05	.04	.02
256	Greg Hibbard	.08	.06	.03
257	Tom O'Malley	.03	.02	.01
258	Chris Hammond(FC)	.15	.11	.06
259	Hensley Meulens	.08	.06	.03
260	Harold Reynolds	.06	.05	.02
261	Bud Harrelson	.03	.02	.01
262	Tim Jones	.04	.03	.02
263	Checklist 2	.03	.02	.01
264	*Dave Hollins*	.25	.20	.10
265	Mark Gubicza	.06	.05	.02
266	Carmen Castillo	.03	.02	.01
267	Mark Knudson	.03	.02	.01
268	Tom Brookens	.04	.03	.02
269	Joe Hesketh	.03	.02	.01
270	Mark McGwire	.20	.15	.08
271	*Omar Olivares*(FC)	.15	.11	.06
272	Jeff King	.06	.05	.02
273	Johnny Ray	.05	.04	.02
274	Ken Williams	.03	.02	.01
275	Alan Trammell	.10	.08	.04
276	Bill Swift	.05	.04	.02
277	Scott Coolbaugh	.06	.05	.02
278	*Alex Fernandez*(FC)	.60	.45	.25
279a	Jose Gonzalez (photo of Billy Bean, left handed batter)	.20	.15	.08
279b	Jose Gonzalez (correct photo, right handed batter)	.12	.09	.05
280	Bret Saberhagen	.08	.06	.03
281	Larry Sheets	.04	.03	.02
282	Don Carman	.04	.03	.02
283	Marquis Grissom	.10	.08	.04
284	Bill Spiers	.06	.05	.02
285	Jim Abbott	.10	.08	.04
286	Ken Oberkfell	.04	.03	.02
287	Mark Grant	.03	.02	.01
288	Derrick May(FC)	.25	.20	.10
289	Tim Birtsas	.03	.02	.01
290	Steve Sax	.08	.06	.03
291	John Wathan	.03	.02	.01
292	Bud Black	.04	.03	.02
293	Jay Bell	.06	.05	.02
294	Mike Moore	.06	.05	.02
295	Rafael Palmeiro	.08	.06	.03
296	Mark Williamson	.04	.03	.02
297	Manny Lee	.04	.03	.02
298	Omar Vizquel	.04	.03	.02
299	*Scott Radinsky*	.15	.11	.06
300	Kirby Puckett	.20	.15	.08
301	Steve Farr	.04	.03	.02
302	Tim Teufel	.03	.02	.01
303	Mike Boddicker	.06	.05	.02
304	Kevin Reimer(FC)	.10	.08	.04
305	Mike Scioscia	.06	.05	.02
306	Lonnie Smith	.06	.05	.02
307	Andy Benes	.08	.06	.03
308	Tom Pagnozzi	.04	.03	.02
309	Norm Charlton	.08	.06	.03
310	Gary Carter	.08	.06	.03
311	Jeff Pico	.03	.02	.01
312	Charlie Hayes	.06	.05	.02
313	Ron Robinson	.06	.05	.02
314	Gary Pettis	.04	.03	.02
315	Roberto Alomar	.20	.15	.08
316	Gene Nelson	.03	.02	.01
317	Mike Fitzgerald	.03	.02	.01
318	Rick Aguilera	.06	.05	.02
319	Jeff McKnight(FC)	.06	.05	.02
320	Tony Fernandez	.08	.06	.03
321	Bob Rodgers	.03	.02	.01
322	*Terry Shumpert*	.15	.11	.06
323	Cory Snyder	.08	.06	.03
324	Ron Kittle	.08	.06	.03
325	Brett Butler	.06	.05	.02
326	Ken Patterson	.04	.03	.02
327	Ron Hassey	.03	.02	.01

		MT	NR MT	EX
328	Walt Terrell	.04	.03	.02
329	Dave Justice	.35	.25	.14
330	Doc Gooden	.20	.15	.08
331	Eric Anthony	.10	.08	.04
332	Kenny Rogers	.06	.05	.02
333	*Chipper Jones*	1.00	.70	.40
334	Todd Benzinger	.05	.04	.02
335	Mitch Williams	.08	.06	.03
336	Matt Nokes	.06	.05	.02
337	Keith Comstock	.03	.02	.01
338	Luis Rivera	.04	.03	.02
339	Larry Walker	.15	.11	.06
340	Ramon Martinez	.08	.06	.03
341	John Moses	.03	.02	.01
342	*Mickey Morandini*	.10	.08	.04
343	Jose Oquendo	.04	.03	.02
344	Jeff Russell	.06	.05	.02
345	Jose DeJesus	.06	.05	.02
346	Jesse Orosco	.04	.03	.02
347	Greg Vaughn	.10	.08	.04
348	Todd Stottlemyre	.06	.05	.02
349	Dave Gallagher	.04	.03	.02
350	Glenn Davis	.12	.09	.05
351	Joe Torre	.03	.02	.01
352	Frank White	.06	.05	.02
353	Tony Castillo	.05	.04	.02
354	Sid Bream	.05	.04	.02
355	Chili Davis	.06	.05	.02
356	Mike Marshall	.06	.05	.02
357	Jack Savage	.10	.08	.04
358	Mark Parent	.03	.02	.01
359	Chuck Cary	.04	.03	.02
360	Rock Raines	.15	.11	.06
361	Scott Garrelts	.05	.04	.02
362	*Hector Villanueva*	.15	.11	.06
363	Rick Mahler	.04	.03	.02
364	Dan Pasqua	.06	.05	.02
365	Mike Schooler	.06	.05	.02
366	Checklist 3	.03	.02	.01
367	*Dave Walsh*(FC)	.10	.08	.04
368	Felix Jose	.06	.05	.02
369	Steve Searcy	.06	.05	.02
370	Kelly Gruber	.10	.08	.04
371	Jeff Montgomery	.06	.05	.02
372	Spike Owen	.05	.04	.02
373	Darrin Jackson	.04	.03	.02
374	*Larry Casian*	.15	.11	.06
375	Tony Pena	.06	.05	.02
376	Mike Harkey	.08	.06	.03
377	Rene Gonzales	.03	.02	.01
378	*Wilson Alvarez*(FC)	.20	.15	.08
379	Randy Velarde	.04	.03	.02
380	Willie McGee	.08	.06	.03
381	Jose Lind	.05	.04	.02
382	Mackey Sasser	.05	.04	.02
383	Pete Smith	.06	.05	.02
384	Gerald Perry	.05	.04	.02
385	Mickey Tettleton	.05	.04	.02
386	Cecil Fielder (AS)	.10	.08	.04
387	Julio Franco (AS)	.08	.06	.03
388	Kelly Gruber (AS)	.08	.06	.03
389	Alan Trammell (AS)	.06	.05	.02
390	Jose Canseco (AS)	.10	.08	.04
391	Rickey Henderson (AS)	.10	.08	.04
392	Ken Griffey,Jr. (AS)	.30	.25	.12
393	Carlton Fisk (AS)	.08	.06	.03
394	Bob Welch (AS)	.06	.05	.02
395	Chuck Finley (AS)	.06	.05	.02
396	Bobby Thigpen (AS)	.08	.06	.03
397	Eddie Murray (AS)	.08	.06	.03
398	Ryne Sandberg (AS)	.10	.08	.04
399	Matt Williams (AS)	.08	.06	.03
400	Barry Larkin (AS)	.08	.06	.03
401	Barry Bonds (AS)	.15	.11	.06
402	Darryl Strawberry (AS)	.10	.08	.04
403	Bobby Bonilla (AS)	.10	.08	.04
404	Mike Scoscia (AS)	.06	.05	.02
405	Doug Drabek (AS)	.08	.06	.03
406	Frank Viola (AS)	.08	.06	.03
407	John Franco (AS)	.06	.05	.02
408	Ernie Riles	.04	.03	.02
409	Mike Stanley	.03	.02	.01
410	Dave Righetti	.08	.06	.03
411	Lance Blankenship	.04	.03	.02
412	Dave Bergman	.03	.02	.01
413	Terry Mulholland	.06	.05	.02
414	Sammy Sosa	.15	.11	.06
415	Rick Sutcliffe	.08	.06	.03
416	Randy Milligan	.06	.05	.02
417	Bill Krueger	.03	.02	.01
418	Nick Esasky	.06	.05	.02

		MT	NR MT	EX
419	Jeff Reed	.03	.02	.01
420	Bobby Thigpen	.08	.06	.03
421	Alex Cole(FC)	.20	.15	.08
422	Rick Rueschel	.06	.05	.02
423	Rafael Ramirez	.04	.03	.02
424	Calvin Schiraldi	.03	.02	.01
425	Andy Van Slyke	.08	.06	.03
426	*Joe Grahe*(FC)	.15	.11	.06
427	Rick Dempsey	.03	.02	.01
428	*John Barfield*(FC)	.10	.08	.04
429	Stump Merrill	.03	.02	.01
430	Gary Gaetti	.08	.06	.03
431	Paul Gibson	.03	.02	.01
432	Delino DeShields	.15	.11	.06
433	Pat Tabler	.04	.03	.02
434	Julio Machado(FC)	.10	.08	.04
435	Kevin Maas	.08	.06	.03
436	Scott Bankhead	.05	.04	.02
437	Doug Dascenzo	.04	.03	.02
438	Vicente Palacios	.05	.04	.02
439	Dickie Thon	.03	.02	.01
440	George Bell	.08	.06	.03
441	Zane Smith	.04	.03	.02
442	Charlie O'Brien	.04	.03	.02
443	Jeff Innis	.05	.04	.02
444	Glenn Braggs	.05	.04	.02
445	Greg Swindell	.06	.05	.02
446	*Craig Grebeck*(FC)	.08	.06	.03
447	John Burkett	.12	.09	.05
448	Craig Lefferts	.05	.04	.02
449	Juan Berenguer	.03	.02	.01
450	Wade Boggs	.12	.09	.05
451	Neal Heaton	.05	.04	.02
452	Bill Schroeder	.03	.02	.01
453	Lenny Harris	.05	.04	.02
454	Kevin Appier	.08	.06	.03
455	Walt Weiss	.06	.05	.02
456	Charlie Leibrandt	.05	.04	.02
457	*Todd Hundley*	.10	.08	.04
458	Brian Holman	.06	.05	.02
459	Tom Trebelhorn	.03	.02	.01
460	Dave Steib	.08	.06	.03
461	Robin Ventura	.15	.11	.06
462	Steve Frey	.06	.05	.02
463	Dwight Smith	.06	.05	.02
464	Steve Buechele	.04	.03	.02
465	Ken Griffey	.05	.04	.02
466	Charles Nagy(FC)	.10	.08	.04
467	Dennis Cook	.06	.05	.02
468	Tim Hulett	.04	.03	.02
469	Chet Lemon	.05	.04	.02
470	Howard Johnson	.10	.08	.04
471	*Mike Lieberthal*	.20	.15	.08
472	Kirt Manwaring	.05	.04	.02
473	Curt Young	.04	.03	.02
474	*Phil Plantier*(FC)	.50	.40	.20
475	Teddy Higuera	.08	.06	.03
476	Glenn Wilson	.05	.04	.02
477	Mike Fetters	.06	.05	.02
478	Kurt Stillwell	.05	.04	.02
479	Bob Patterson	.03	.02	.01
480	Dave Magadan	.10	.08	.04
481	Eddie Whitson	.05	.04	.02
482	Tino Martinez	.10	.08	.04
483	Mike Aldrete	.04	.03	.02
484	Dave LaPoint	.04	.03	.02
485	Terry Pendleton	.06	.05	.02
486	Tommy Greene(FC)	.10	.08	.04
487	Rafael Belliard	.03	.02	.01
488	Jeff Manto(FC)	.15	.11	.06
489	Bobby Valentine	.03	.02	.01
490	Kirk Gibson	.08	.06	.03
491	*Kurt Miller*	.30	.25	.12
492	Ernie Whitt	.05	.04	.02
493	Jose Rijo	.08	.06	.03
494	Chris James	.06	.05	.02
495	Charlie Hough	.04	.03	.02
496	Marty Barrett	.05	.04	.02
497	Ben McDonald	.12	.09	.05
498	Mark Salas	.03	.02	.01
499	Melido Perez	.06	.05	.02
500	Will Clark	.15	.11	.06
501	Mike Bielecki	.05	.04	.02
502	Carney Lansford	.06	.05	.02
503	Roy Smith	.04	.03	.02
504	*Julio Valera*(FC)	.10	.08	.04
505	Chuck Finley	.08	.06	.03
506	Darnell Coles	.04	.03	.02
507	Steve Jeltz	.03	.02	.01
508	*Mike York*(FC)	.15	.11	.06
509	Glenallen Hill	.06	.05	.02

		MT	NR MT	EX
510	John Franco	.08	.06	.03
511	Steve Balboni	.03	.02	.01
512	Jose Mesa(FC)	.05	.04	.02
513	Jerald Clark	.05	.04	.02
514	Mike Stanton	.08	.06	.03
515	Alvin Davis	.08	.06	.03
516	*Karl Rhodes*(FC)	.10	.08	.04
517	Joe Oliver	.06	.05	.02
518	Cris Carpenter	.05	.04	.02
519	Sparky Anderson	.04	.03	.02
520	Mark Grace	.10	.08	.04
521	Joe Orsulak	.05	.04	.02
522	Stan Belinda	.06	.05	.02
523	*Rodney McCray*(FC)	.08	.06	.03
524	Darrel Akerfelds	.04	.03	.02
525	Willie Randolph	.06	.05	.02
526	Moises Alou(FC)	.30	.25	.12
527	Checklist 4	.03	.02	.01
528	Denny Martinez	.06	.05	.02
529	*Mark Newfield*	.40	.30	.15
530	Roger Clemens	.20	.15	.08
531	*Dave Rhode*(FC)	.15	.11	.06
532	Kirk McCaskill	.06	.05	.02
533	Oddibe McDowell	.05	.04	.02
534	Mike Jackson	.04	.03	.02
535	Ruben Sierra	.15	.11	.06
536	Mike Witt	.04	.03	.02
537	Mike LaValliere	.05	.04	.02
538	Bip Roberts	.05	.04	.02
539	Scott Terry	.03	.02	.01
540	George Brett	.12	.09	.05
541	Domingo Ramos	.03	.02	.01
542	Rob Murphy	.03	.02	.01
543	Junior Felix	.08	.06	.03
544	Alejandro Pena	.03	.02	.01
545	Dale Murphy	.10	.08	.04
546	Jeff Ballard	.05	.04	.02
547	Mike Pagliarulo	.04	.03	.02
548	Jaime Navarro	.10	.08	.04
549	John McNamara	.03	.02	.01
550	Eric Davis	.15	.11	.06
551	Bob Kipper	.03	.02	.01
552	Jeff Hamilton	.04	.03	.02
553	*Joe Klink*	.10	.08	.04
554	Brian Harper	.06	.05	.02
555	*Turner Ward*(FC)	.10	.08	.04
556	Gary Ward	.04	.03	.02
557	Wally Whitehurst	.06	.05	.02
558	Otis Nixon	.03	.02	.01
559	Adam Peterson	.06	.05	.02
560	Greg Smith(FC)	.15	.11	.06
561	Tim McIntosh(FC)	.15	.11	.06
562	Jeff Kunkel	.03	.02	.01
563	*Brent Knackert*	.10	.08	.04
564	Dante Bichette	.08	.06	.03
565	Craig Biggio	.08	.06	.03
566	*Craig Wilson*(FC)	.15	.11	.06
567	Dwayne Henry	.03	.02	.01
568	Ron Karkovice	.04	.03	.02
569	Curt Schilling	.05	.04	.02
570	Barry Bonds	.30	.25	.12
571	Pat Combs	.08	.06	.03
572	Dave Anderson	.03	.02	.01
573	*Rich Rodriguez*(FC)	.15	.11	.06
574	John Marzano	.04	.03	.02
575	Robin Yount	.15	.11	.06
576	Jeff Kaiser(FC)	.10	.08	.04
577	Bill Doran	.06	.05	.02
578	Dave West	.06	.05	.02
579	Roger Craig	.03	.02	.01
580	Dave Stewart	.12	.09	.05
581	Luis Quinones	.03	.02	.01
582	Marty Clary	.03	.02	.01
583	Tony Phillips	.04	.03	.02
584	Kevin Brown	.06	.05	.02
585	Pete O'Brien	.04	.03	.02
586	Fred Lynn	.05	.04	.02
587	Jose Offerman(FC)	.10	.08	.04
588	*Mark Whiten*(FC)	.30	.25	.12
589	*Scott Ruskin*	.10	.08	.04
590	Eddie Murray	.12	.09	.05
591	Ken Hill	.05	.04	.02
592	B.J. Surhoff	.06	.05	.02
593	*Mike Walker*(FC)	.15	.11	.06
594	*Rich Garces*(FC)	.15	.11	.06
595	Bill Landrum	.05	.04	.02
596	*Ronnie Walden* (FDP)(FC)	.10	.08	.04
597	Jerry Don Gleaton	.03	.02	.01
598	Sam Horn	.05	.04	.02
599	Greg Myers	.04	.03	.02
600	Bo Jackson	.20	.15	.08

		MT	NR MT	EX
601	Bob Ojeda	.04	.03	.02
602	Casey Candaele	.04	.03	.02
603a	*Wes Chamberlain* (photo of Louie Meadows, no bat)(FC)	.50	.40	.20
603b	*Wes Chamberlain* (correct photo, holding bat)(FC)	.15	.11	.06
604	Billy Hatcher	.05	.04	.02
605	Jeff Reardon	.08	.06	.03
606	Jim Gott	.04	.03	.02
607	Edgar Martinez	.06	.05	.02
608	Todd Burns	.03	.02	.01
609	Jeff Torborg	.03	.02	.01
610	Andres Galarraga	.08	.06	.03
611	Dave Eiland	.04	.03	.02
612	Steve Lyons	.04	.03	.02
613	Eric Show	.04	.03	.02
614	Luis Salazar	.04	.03	.02
615	Bert Blyleven	.08	.06	.03
616	Todd Zeile	.15	.11	.06
617	Bill Wegman	.04	.03	.02
618	Sil Campusano	.04	.03	.02
619	David Wells	.04	.03	.02
620	Ozzie Guillen	.08	.06	.03
621	Ted Power	.03	.02	.01
622	Jack Daugherty	.05	.04	.02
623	Jeff Blauser	.04	.03	.02
624	Tom Candiotti	.04	.03	.02
625	Terry Steinbach	.06	.05	.02
626	Gerald Young	.03	.02	.01
627	*Tim Layana*	.15	.11	.06
628	Greg Litton	.05	.04	.02
629	Wes Gardner	.04	.03	.02
630	Dave Winfield	.10	.08	.04
631	Mike Morgan	.04	.03	.02
632	Lloyd Moseby	.06	.05	.02
633	Kevin Tapani	.10	.08	.04
634	Henry Cotto	.03	.02	.01
635	Andy Hawkins	.04	.03	.02
636	*Geronimo Pena*(FC)	.10	.08	.04
637	Bruce Ruffin	.04	.03	.02
638	Mike Macfarlane	.04	.03	.02
639	Frank Robinson	.05	.04	.02
640	Andre Dawson	.10	.08	.04
641	Mike Henneman	.06	.05	.02
642	Hal Morris	.15	.11	.06
643	Jim Presley	.06	.05	.02
644	Chuck Crim	.04	.03	.02
645	Juan Samuel	.06	.05	.02
646	*Andujar Cedeno*(FC)	.20	.15	.08
647	Mark Portugal	.04	.03	.02
648	Lee Stevens(FC)	.15	.11	.06
649	*Bill Sampen*	.15	.11	.06
650	Jack Clark	.08	.06	.03
651	*Alan Mills*	.12	.09	.05
652	Kevin Romine	.03	.02	.01
653	*Anthony Telford*(FC)	.20	.15	.08
654	Paul Sorrento(FC)	.15	.11	.06
655	Erik Hanson	.08	.06	.03
656	Checklist 5	.03	.02	.01
657	Mike Kingery	.03	.02	.01
658	*Scott Aldred*(FC)	.12	.09	.05
659	*Oscar Azocar*(FC)	.15	.11	.06
660	Lee Smith	.06	.05	.02
661	Steve Lake	.03	.02	.01
662	Rob Dibble	.08	.06	.03
663	Greg Brock	.05	.04	.02
664	John Farrell	.04	.03	.02
665	Jim Leyland	.03	.02	.01
666	Danny Darwin	.06	.05	.02
667	Kent Anderson	.04	.03	.02
668	Bill Long	.04	.03	.02
669	Lou Pinella	.04	.03	.02
670	Rickey Henderson	.12	.09	.05
671	Andy McGaffigan	.03	.02	.01
672	Shane Mack	.06	.05	.02
673	*Greg Olson*	.20	.15	.08
674	Kevin Gross	.06	.05	.02
675	Tom Brunansky	.08	.06	.03
676	*Scott Chiamparino*(FC)	.20	.15	.08
677	Billy Ripken	.04	.03	.02
678	Mark Davidson	.03	.02	.01
679	Bill Bathe(FC)	.04	.03	.02
680	David Cone	.06	.05	.02
681	*Jeff Schaefer*(FC)	.10	.08	.04
682	*Ray Lankford*(FC)	.40	.30	.15
683	Derek Lilliquist	.05	.04	.02
684	Milt Cuyler(FC)	.10	.08	.04
685	Doug Drabek	.08	.06	.03
686	Mike Gallego	.03	.02	.01
687	John Cerutti	.03	.02	.01
688	*Rosario Rodriguez*(FC)	.10	.08	.04

		MT	NR MT	EX
689	John Kruk	.06	.05	.02
690	Orel Hershiser	.10	.08	.04
691	Mike Blowers	.10	.08	.04
692	*Efrain Valdez*(FC)	.15	.11	.06
693	Francisco Cabrera	.08	.06	.03
694	Randy Veres	.03	.02	.01
695	Kevin Seitzer	.08	.06	.03
696	Steve Olin	.05	.04	.02
697	Shawn Abner	.04	.03	.02
698	Mark Guthrie	.05	.04	.02
699	Jim Lefebvre	.03	.02	.01
700	Jose Canseco	.15	.11	.06
701	Pascual Perez	.05	.04	.02
702	*Tim Naehring*	.20	.15	.08
703	Juan Agosto	.03	.02	.01
704	Devon White	.06	.05	.02
705	Robby Thompson	.05	.04	.02
706	Brad Arnsberg	.04	.03	.02
707	Jim Eisenreich	.04	.03	.02
708	John Mitchell(FC)	.12	.09	.05
709	Matt Sinatro	.03	.02	.01
710	Kent Hrbek	.08	.06	.03
711	Jose DeLeon	.05	.04	.02
712	Ricky Jordan	.06	.05	.02
713	Scott Scudder	.08	.06	.03
714	Marvell Wynne	.04	.03	.02
715	Tim Burke	.06	.05	.02
716	Bob Geren	.06	.05	.02
717	Phil Bradley	.06	.05	.02
718	Steve Crawford	.03	.02	.01
719	Keith Miller	.06	.05	.02
720	Cecil Fielder	.15	.11	.06
721	*Mark Lee*(FC)	.10	.08	.04
722	Wally Backman	.04	.03	.02
723	Candy Maldonado	.08	.06	.03
724	*David Segui*(FC)	.10	.08	.04
725	Ron Gant	.15	.11	.06
726	Phil Stephenson	.04	.03	.02
727	Mookie Wilson	.06	.05	.02
728	Scott Sanderson	.04	.03	.02
729	Don Zimmer	.04	.03	.02
730	Barry Larkin	.12	.09	.05
731	*Jeff Gray*(FC)	.15	.11	.06
732	Franklin Stubbs	.05	.04	.02
733	Kelly Downs	.04	.03	.02
734	John Russell	.03	.02	.01
735	Ron Darling	.06	.05	.02
736	Dick Schofield	.04	.03	.02
737	Tim Crews	.03	.02	.01
738	Mel Hall	.04	.03	.02
739	*Russ Swan*	.10	.08	.04
740	Ryne Sandberg	.20	.15	.08
741	Jimmy Key	.06	.05	.02
742	Tommy Gregg	.04	.03	.02
743	Bryn Smith	.04	.03	.02
744	Nelson Santovenia	.05	.04	.02
745	Doug Jones	.08	.06	.03
746	John Shelby	.03	.02	.01
747	Tony Fossas	.03	.02	.01
748	Al Newman	.03	.02	.01
749	Greg Harris	.04	.03	.02
750	Bobby Bonilla	.12	.09	.05
751	*Wayne Edwards*	.10	.08	.04
752	Kevin Bass	.05	.04	.02
753	*Paul Marak*(FC)	.15	.11	.06
754	Bill Pecota	.04	.03	.02
755	Mark Langston	.10	.08	.04
756	Jeff Huson	.05	.04	.02
757	Mark Gardner	.06	.05	.02
758	Mike Devereaux	.06	.05	.02
759	Bobby Cox	.03	.02	.01
760	Benny Santiago	.08	.06	.03
761	Larry Andersen	.04	.03	.02
762	Mitch Webster	.04	.03	.02
763	*Dana Kiecker*	.10	.08	.04
764	Mark Carreon	.05	.04	.02
765	Shawon Dunston	.08	.06	.03
766	Jeff Robinson	.05	.04	.02
767	#1 Draft Pick *(Dan Wilson)*(FC)	.30	.25	.12
768	Donn Pall	.04	.03	.02
769	*Tim Sherrill*(FC)	.10	.08	.04
770	Jay Howell	.06	.05	.02
771	Gary Redus	.03	.02	.01
772	Kent Mercker(FC)	.10	.08	.04
773	Tom Foley	.03	.02	.01
774	Dennis Rasmussen	.04	.03	.02
775	Julio Franco	.08	.06	.03
776	Brent Mayne(FC)	.15	.11	.06
777	John Candelaria	.05	.04	.02
778	Dan Gladden	.05	.04	.02
779	Carmelo Martinez	.04	.03	.02
780	Randy Myers	.08	.06	.03
781	Darryl Hamilton	.05	.04	.02
782	Jim Deshaies	.05	.04	.02
783	Joel Skinner	.03	.02	.01
784	Willie Fraser	.04	.03	.02
785	Scott Fletcher	.04	.03	.02
786	Eric Plunk	.03	.02	.01
787	Checklist 6	.03	.02	.01
788	Bob Milacki	.06	.05	.02
789	Tom Lasorda	.04	.03	.02
790	Ken Griffey,Jr.	.60	.45	.25
791	Mike Benjamin(FC)	.15	.11	.06
792	Mike Greenwell	.15	.11	.06

1991 Topps Wax Box Cards

Styled like the standard 1991 Topps cards, this 16-card set honors milestones of the featured players. The cards were found on the bottom of wax pack boxes. The cards are designated in alphabetical order by (A-P) and are not numbered.

		MT	NR MT	EX
	Complete Set:	2.50	2.00	1.00
	Common Player:	.08	.06	.03
(1)	Bert Blyleven	.08	.06	.03
(2)	George Brett	.20	.15	.08
(3)	Brett Butler	.10	.08	.04
(4)	Andre Dawson	.15	.11	.06
(5)	Dwight Evans	.10	.08	.04
(6)	Carlton Fisk	.20	.15	.08
(7)	Alfredo Griffin	.08	.06	.03
(8)	Rickey Henderson	.30	.25	.12
(9)	Willie McGee	.15	.11	.06
(10)	Dale Murphy	.20	.15	.08
(11)	Eddie Murray	.20	.15	.08
(12)	Dave Parker	.15	.11	.06
(13)	Jeff Reardon	.15	.11	.06
(14)	Nolan Ryan	.40	.30	.15
(15)	Juan Samuel	.08	.06	.03
(16)	Robin Yount	.20	.15	.08

1991 Topps Traded

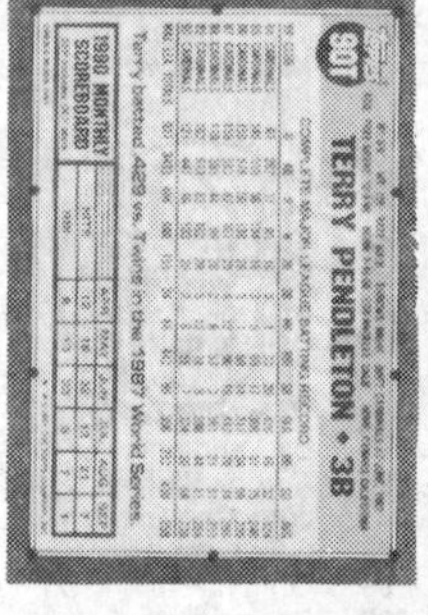

"Team USA" is featured in the 1991 Topps Traded set.

The cards feature the same style as the regular 1991 issue, including the 40th anniversary logo. The set includes 132 cards and showcases rookies and traded players along with "Team USA." The cards are numbered with a "T" designation in alphabetical order.

		MT	NR MT	EX
Complete Set (132):		15.00	11.00	6.00
Common Player:		.05	.04	.02
1	Juan Agosto	.05	.04	.02
2	Roberto Alomar	.25	.20	.10
3	Wally Backman	.05	.04	.02
4	Jeff Bagwell(FC)	2.00	1.50	.80
5	Skeeter Barnes(FC)	.15	.11	.06
6	Steve Bedrosian	.06	.05	.02
7	Derek Bell(FC)	.35	.25	.14
8	George Bell	.10	.08	.04
9	Rafael Belliard	.05	.04	.02
10	Dante Bichette	.06	.05	.02
11	Bud Black	.05	.04	.02
12	Mike Boddicker	.06	.05	.02
13	Sid Bream	.06	.05	.02
14	Hubie Brooks	.06	.05	.02
15	Brett Butler	.08	.06	.03
16	Ivan Calderon	.08	.06	.03
17	John Candelaria	.05	.04	.02
18	Tom Candiotti	.06	.05	.02
19	Gary Carter	.08	.06	.03
20	Joe Carter	.12	.09	.05
21	Rick Cerone	.05	.04	.02
22	Jack Clark	.08	.06	.03
23	Vince Coleman	.15	.11	.06
24	Scott Coolbaugh	.10	.08	.04
25	Danny Cox	.05	.04	.02
26	Danny Darwin	.05	.04	.02
27	Chili Davis	.08	.06	.03
28	Glenn Davis	.08	.06	.03
29	Steve Decker(FC)	.25	.20	.10
30	Rob Deer	.06	.05	.02
31	Rich DeLucia(FC)	.15	.11	.06
32	*John Dettmer* (USA)	.20	.15	.08
33	Brian Downing	.05	.04	.02
34	*Darren Dreifort* (USA)	1.00	.70	.40
35	Kirk Dressendorfer	.40	.30	.15
36	Jim Essian	.05	.04	.02
37	Dwight Evans	.08	.06	.03
38	Steve Farr	.06	.05	.02
39	Jeff Fassero	.20	.15	.08
40	Junior Felix	.08	.06	.03
41	Tony Fernandez	.08	.06	.03
42	Steve Finley	.08	.06	.03
43	Jim Fregosi	.05	.04	.02
44	Gary Gaetti	.06	.05	.02
45	*Jason Giambi* (USA)	.30	.25	.12
46	Kirk Gibson	.08	.06	.03
47	Leo Gomez(FC)	.30	.25	.12
48	Luis Gonzalez	.30	.25	.12
49	*Jeff Granger* (USA)	.80	.60	.30
50	*Todd Greene* (USA)	.20	.15	.08
51	*Jeffrey Hammonds* (USA)	2.00	1.50	.80
52	Mike Hargrove	.05	.04	.02
53	Pete Harnisch	.08	.06	.03
54	*Rick Helling* (USA)	.20	.15	.08
55	Glenallen Hill	.08	.06	.03
56	Charlie Hough	.06	.05	.02
57	Pete Incaviglia	.08	.06	.03
58	Bo Jackson	.50	.40	.20
59	Danny Jackson	.06	.05	.02
60	Reggie Jefferson(FC)	.30	.25	.12
61	*Charles Johnson* (USA)	1.25	.90	.50
62	Jeff Johnson(FC)	.20	.15	.08
63	*Todd Johnson* (USA)	.20	.15	.08
64	Barry Jones	.05	.04	.02
65	Chris Jones	.20	.15	.08
66	Scott Kamieniecki	.20	.15	.08
67	*Pat Kelly*	.25	.15	.08
68	Darryl Kile(FC)	.20	.15	.08
69	Chuck Knoblauch(FC)	.40	.30	.15
70	Bill Krueger	.05	.04	.02
71	Scott Leius(FC)	.15	.11	.06
72	*Donnie Leshnock* (USA)	.20	.15	.08
73	Mark Lewis	.30	.25	.12
74	Candy Maldonado	.06	.05	.02
75	*Jason McDonald* (USA)	.25	.20	.10
76	Willie McGee	.08	.06	.03
77	Fred McGriff	.10	.08	.04
78	*Billy McMillon* (USA)	.20	.15	.08
79	Hal McRae	.06	.05	.02
80	*Dan Melendez* (USA)	.30	.25	.12
81	Orlando Merced(FC)	.40	.30	.15
82	Jack Morris	.08	.06	.03
83	*Phil Nevin* (USA)	2.00	1.50	.80
84	Otis Nixon	.06	.05	.02
85	Johnny Oates	.05	.04	.02
86	Bob Ojeda	.05	.04	.02
87	Mike Pagliarulo	.05	.04	.02
88	Dean Palmer(FC)	.35	.25	.14
89	Dave Parker	.08	.06	.03
90	Terry Pendleton	.08	.06	.03
91	*Tony Phillips* (USA)	.20	.15	.08
92	Doug Piatt(FC)	.20	.15	.08
93	Ron Polk (U.S.A.)	.06	.05	.02
94	Rock Raines	.12	.09	.05
95	Willie Randolph	.06	.05	.02
96	Dave Righetti	.06	.05	.02
97	Ernie Riles	.05	.04	.02
98	*Chris Roberts* (USA)	.30	.25	.12
99	Jeff Robinson (Angels)	.05	.04	.02
100	Jeff Robinson (Orioles)	.05	.04	.02
101	*Ivan Rodriguez*	1.00	.70	.40
102	*Steve Rodriguez* (USA)	.20	.15	.08
103	Tom Runnells	.05	.04	.02
104	Scott Sanderson	.06	.05	.02
105	Bob Scanlan(FC)	.15	.11	.06
106	Pete Schourek(FC)	.15	.11	.06
107	Gary Scott(FC)	.35	.25	.14
108	*Paul Shuey* (USA)	.40	.30	.15
109	*Doug Simons*	.20	.15	.08
110	Dave Smith	.06	.05	.02
111	Cory Snyder	.05	.04	.02
112	Luis Sojo	.06	.05	.02
113	*Kennie Steenstra* (USA)	.20	.15	.08
114	Darryl Strawberry	.30	.25	.12
115	Franklin Stubbs	.05	.04	.02
116	*Todd Taylor* (USA)	.20	.15	.08
117	Wade Taylor(FC)	.20	.15	.08
118	Garry Templeton	.06	.05	.02
119	Mickey Tettleton	.06	.05	.02
120	Tim Teufel	.05	.04	.02
121	Mike Timlin	.20	.15	.08
122	*David Tuttle* (USA)	.20	.15	.08
123	Mo Vaughn(FC)	.50	.40	.20
124	Jeff Ware (USA)(FC)	.20	.15	.08
125	Devon White	.08	.06	.03
126	Mark Whiten	.20	.15	.08
127	Mitch Williams	.08	.06	.03
128	*Craig Wilson* (USA)	.20	.15	.08
129	Willie Wilson	.06	.05	.02
130	*Chris Wimmer* (USA)	.30	.25	.12
131	*Ivan Zweig* (USA)	.20	.15	.08
132	Checklist	.05	.04	.02

1991 Topps Babe Ruth

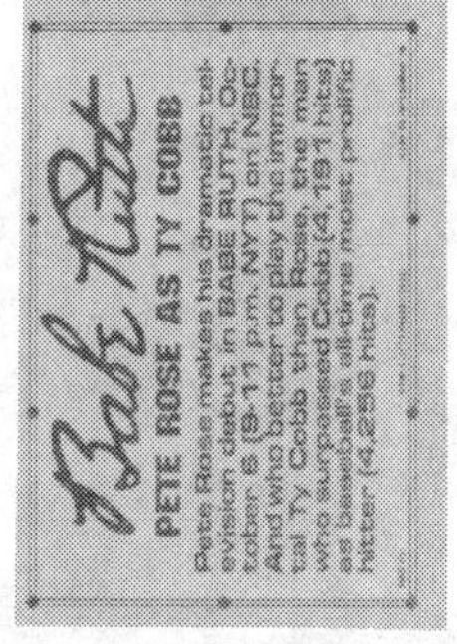

This 11-card set by Topps was released in honor of the NBC movie about Babe Ruth. The cards were released on a limited basis. The card fronts feature full-color photos from the movie, while the flip sides are printed horizontally and describe the front photo. The cards are numbered on the back.

		MT	NR MT	EX
Complete Set:		30.00	22.00	12.00
Common Player:		2.00	1.50	.80
1	Sunday October 6th NBC	2.00	1.50	.80
2	Stephen Lang as Babe Ruth	2.00	1.50	.80
3	Bruce Weitz as Miller Huggins	2.00	1.50	.80
4	Lisa Zane as Claire Ruth	2.00	1.50	.80
5	Donald Moffat as Jacob Ruppert	2.00	1.50	.80

		MT	NR MT	EX
6	Neil McDonough as Lou Gehrig	2.00	1.50	.80
7	Pete Rose as Ty Cobb	10.00	7.50	4.00
8	Rod Carew Baseball Consultant	6.00	4.50	2.50
9	Ruth and Manager Huggins	2.00	1.50	.80
10	Ruth In Action	2.00	1.50	.80
11	Babe Calls His Shot	2.00	1.50	.80

1991 Topps Major League Debut

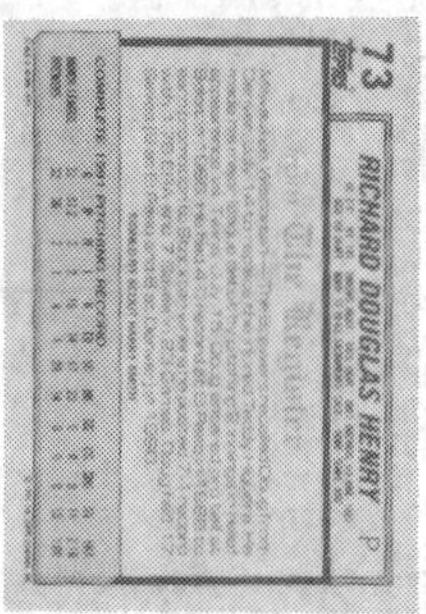

This 194-card set highlights the debut date of 1991 Major League rookies. Two checklist cards are also included in this boxed set. The card fronts resemble the 1992 Topps cards. A debut banner appears in the lower right hand corner of the card front. The set is packaged in an attractive collector box and the cards are numbered alphabetically. This set was available through select hobby dealers.

		MT	NR MT	EX
Complete Set:		15.00	11.00	6.00
Common Player:		.08	.06	.03
1	Kyle Abbott	.20	.15	.08
2	Dana Allison	.15	.11	.06
3	Rich Amaral	.08	.06	.03
4	Ruben Amaro	.10	.08	.04
5	Andy Ashby	.15	.11	.06
6	Jim Austin	.08	.06	.03
7	Jeff Bagwell	1.50	1.25	.60
8	Jeff Banister	.10	.08	.04
9	Willie Banks	.25	.20	.10
10	Bret Barberie	.20	.15	.08
11	Kim Batiste	.10	.08	.04
12	Chris Beasley	.10	.08	.04
13	Rodd Beck	.08	.06	.03
14	Derek Bell	.50	.40	.20
15	Esteban Beltre	.08	.06	.03
16	Freddie Benavides	.10	.08	.04
17	Rickey Bones	.10	.08	.04
18	Denis Boucher	.15	.11	.06
19	Ryan Bowen	.20	.15	.08
20	Cliff Brantley	.10	.08	.04
21	John Briscoe	.10	.08	.04
22	Scott Brosius	.10	.08	.04
23	Terry Bross	.08	.06	.03
24	Jarvis Brown	.10	.08	.04
25	Scott Bullett	.10	.08	.04
26	Kevin Campbell	.08	.06	.03
27	Amalio Carreno	.08	.06	.03
28	Matias Carrillo	.10	.08	.04
29	Jeff Carter	.08	.06	.03
30	Vinny Castilla	.10	.08	.04
31	Braulio Castillo	.10	.08	.04
32	Frank Castillo	.25	.20	.10
33	Darrin Chapin	.10	.08	.04
34	Mike Christopher	.08	.06	.03
35	Mark Clark	.15	.11	.06
36	Royce Clayton	.25	.20	.10
37	Stu Cole	.10	.08	.04
38	Gary Cooper	.08	.06	.03
39	Archie Corbin	.10	.08	.04
40	Rheal Cormier	.20	.15	.08
41	Chris Cron	.08	.06	.03
42	Mike Dalton	.08	.06	.03
43	Mark Davis	.08	.06	.03
44	Francisco de la Rosa	.08	.06	.03
45	Chris Donnels	.35	.25	.14
46	Brian Drahman	.25	.20	.10
47	Tom Drees	.15	.11	.06
48	Kirk Dressendorfer	.40	.30	.15
49	Bruce Egloff	.30	.25	.12
50	Cal Eldred	.30	.25	.12
51	Jose Escobar	.30	.25	.12
52	Tony Eusebio	.08	.06	.03
53	Hector Fajardo	.10	.08	.04
54	Monty Farriss	.10	.08	.04
55	Jeff Fassero	.15	.11	.06
56	Dave Fleming	.10	.08	.04
57	Kevin Flora	.10	.08	.04
58	Steve Foster	.10	.08	.04
59	Dan Gakeler	.08	.06	.03
60	Ramon Garcia	.15	.11	.06
61	Chris Gardner	.10	.08	.04
62	Jeff Gardner	.15	.11	.06
63	Chris George	.15	.11	.06
64	Ray Giannelli	.08	.06	.03
65	Tom Goodwin	.20	.15	.08
66	Mark Grater	.08	.06	.03
67	Johnny Guzman	.15	.11	.06
68	Juan Guzman	.60	.45	.25
69	Dave Haas	.08	.06	.03
70	Chris Haney	.25	.20	.10
71	Shawn Hare	.08	.06	.03
72	Donald Harris	.20	.15	.08
73	Doug Henry	.20	.15	.08
74	Pat Hentgen	.10	.08	.04
75	Gil Heredia	.20	.15	.08
76	Jeremy Hernandez	.20	.15	.08
77	Jose Hernandez	.08	.06	.03
78	Roberto Hernandez	.10	.08	.04
79	Bryan Hickerson	.15	.11	.06
80	Milt Hill	.08	.06	.03
81	Vince Horsman	.08	.06	.03
82	Wayne Housie	.08	.06	.03
83	Chris Howard	.15	.11	.06
84	David Howard	.20	.15	.08
85	Mike Humphreys	.15	.11	.06
86	Brian Hunter	.70	.50	.30
87	Jim Hunter	.08	.06	.03
88	Mike Ignasiak	.08	.06	.03
89	Reggie Jefferson	.35	.25	.14
90	Jeff Johnson	.20	.15	.08
91	Joel Johnson	.10	.08	.04
92	Calvin Jones	.15	.11	.06
93	Chris Jones	.25	.20	.10
94	Stacy Jones	.08	.06	.03
95	Jeff Juden	.25	.20	.10
96	Scott Kamieniecki	.20	.15	.08
97	Eric Karros	.60	.45	.25
98	Pat Kelly	.50	.40	.20
99	John Kiely	.08	.06	.03
100	Darryl Kile	.20	.15	.08
101	Wayne Kirby	.08	.06	.03
102	Garland Kiser	.10	.08	.04
103	Chuck Knoblauch	.60	.45	.25
104	Randy Knorr	.08	.06	.03
105	Tom Kramer	.08	.06	.03
106	Ced Landrum	.20	.15	.08
107	Patrick Lennon	.20	.15	.08
108	Jim Lewis	.08	.06	.03
109	Mark Lewis	.35	.25	.14
110	Doug Lindsey	.08	.06	.03
111	Scott Livingstone	.30	.25	.12
112	Kenny Lofton	.40	.30	.15
113	Ever Magallanes	.10	.08	.04
114	Mike Magnante	.10	.08	.04
115	Barry Manuel	.10	.08	.04
116	Josias Manzanillo	.10	.08	.04
117	Chito Martinez	.60	.45	.25
118	Terry Mathews	.08	.06	.03
119	Rob Mauer	.10	.08	.04
120	Tim Mauser	.08	.06	.03
121	Terry McDaniel	.20	.15	.08
122	Rusty Meacham	.15	.11	.06
123	Luis Mercedes	.25	.20	.10
124	Paul Miller	.15	.11	.06
125	Keith Mitchell	.25	.20	.10
126	Bobby Moore	.08	.06	.03
127	Kevin Morton	.30	.25	.12
128	Andy Mota	.25	.20	.10
129	Jose Mota	.15	.11	.06
130	Mike Mussina	.25	.20	.10
131	Jeff Mutis	.08	.06	.03
132	Denny Neagle	.40	.30	.15
133	Warren Newson	.15	.11	.06
134	Jim Olander	.08	.06	.03
135	Erik Pappas	.15	.11	.06
136	Jorge Pedre	.10	.08	.04
137	Yorkis Perez	.15	.11	.06

		MT	NR MT	EX
138	Mark Petkovsek	.15	.11	.06
139	Doug Piatt	.15	.11	.06
140	Jeff Plympton	.15	.11	.06
141	Harvey Pulliam	.15	.11	.06
142	John Ramos	.15	.11	.06
143	Mike Remlinger	.10	.08	.04
144	Laddie Renfroe	.10	.08	.04
145	Armando Reynoso	.10	.08	.04
146	Arthur Rhodes	.20	.15	.08
147	Pat Rice	.15	.11	.06
148	Nikco Riesgo	.10	.08	.04
149	Carlos Rodriguez	.10	.08	.04
150	Ivan Rodriguez	1.50	1.25	.60
151	Wayne Rosenthal	.10	.08	.04
152	Rico Rossy	.08	.06	.03
153	Stan Royer	.15	.11	.06
154	Rey Sanchez	.08	.06	.03
155	Reggie Sanders	.40	.30	.15
156	Mo Sanford	.35	.25	.14
157	Bob Scanlan	.15	.11	.06
158	Pete Schourek	.15	.11	.06
159	Gary Scott	.25	.20	.10
160	Tim Scott	.08	.06	.03
161	Tony Scruggs	.10	.08	.04
162	Scott Servais	.10	.08	.04
163	Doug Simons	.15	.11	.06
164	Heathcliff Slocumb	.10	.08	.04
165	Joe Slusarski	.10	.08	.04
166	Tim Spehr	.15	.11	.06
167	Ed Sprague	.10	.08	.04
168	Jeff Tackett	.08	.06	.03
169	Eddie Taubensee	.15	.11	.06
170	Wade Taylor	.15	.11	.06
171	Jim Thome	.60	.45	.25
172	Mike Timlin	.25	.20	.10
173	Jose Tolentino	.10	.08	.04
174	John Vander Wal	.08	.06	.03
175	Todd Van Poppel	.80	.60	.30
176	Mo Vaughn	.50	.40	.20
177	Dave Wainhouse	.15	.11	.06
178	Don Wakamatsu	.10	.08	.04
179	Bruce Walton	.08	.06	.03
180	Kevin Ward	.08	.06	.03
181	Dave Weathers	.08	.06	.03
182	Eric Wedge	.08	.06	.03
183	John Wehner	.25	.20	.10
184	Rick Wilkins	.30	.25	.12
185	Bernie Williams	.35	.25	.14
186	Brian Williams	.15	.11	.06
187	Ron Witmeyer	.08	.06	.03
188	Mark Wohlers	.25	.20	.10
189	Ted Wood	.20	.15	.08
190	Anthony Young	.50	.40	.20
191	Eddie Zosky	.20	.15	.08
192	Bob Zupcic	.15	.11	.06
193	Checklist	.08	.06	.03
194	Checklist	.08	.06	.03

1991 Topps Stadium Club

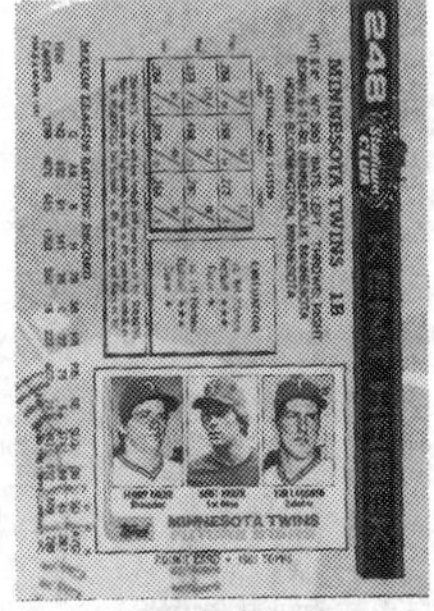

One of the most popular sets of 1991, this 600-card issue was released in two 300-card series. The cards were available in foil packs only. No factory sets were available. The cards feature borderless high gloss photos on the front and a player evaluation and card photo on the back. Stadium Club cards were considered scarce in many areas, thus driving up the price per pack. A special Stadium Club membership package was made available for $29.95 with 10 proof of purchase seals from wrappers.

		MT	NR MT	EX
Complete Set (600):		150.00	125.00	60.00
Common Player:		.20	.15	.08
1	Dave Stewart	1.00	.70	.40
2	Wally Joyner	.30	.25	.12
3	Shawon Dunston	.25	.20	.10
4	Darren Daulton	.20	.15	.08
5	Will Clark	2.00	1.50	.80
6	Sammy Sosa	2.50	2.00	1.00
7	Dan Plesac	.20	.15	.08
8	Marquis Grissom	2.00	1.50	.80
9	Erik Hanson	.30	.25	.12
10	Geno Petralli	.20	.15	.08
11	Jose Rijo	.25	.20	.10
12	Carlos Quintana	.20	.15	.08
13	Junior Ortiz	.20	.15	.08
14	Bob Walk	.20	.15	.08
15	Mike Macfarlane	.20	.15	.08
16	Eric Yelding	.20	.15	.08
17	Bryn Smith	.20	.15	.08
18	Bip Roberts	.20	.15	.08
19	Mike Scioscia	.20	.15	.08
20	Mark Williamson	.20	.15	.08
21	Don Mattingly	1.50	1.25	.60
22	John Franco	.20	.15	.08
23	Chet Lemon	.20	.15	.08
24	Tom Henke	.20	.15	.08
25	Jerry Browne	.20	.15	.08
26	Dave Justice	7.00	5.25	2.75
27	Mark Langston	.30	.25	.12
28	Damon Berryhill	.20	.15	.08
29	Kevin Bass	.20	.15	.08
30	Scott Fletcher	.20	.15	.08
31	Moises Alou	1.50	1.25	.60
32	Dave Valle	.20	.15	.08
33	Jody Reed	.20	.15	.08
34	Dave West	.20	.15	.08
35	Kevin McReynolds	.25	.20	.10
36	Pat Combs	.20	.15	.08
37	Eric Davis	.50	.40	.20
38	Bret Saberhagen	.30	.25	.12
39	Stan Javier	.20	.15	.08
40	Chuck Cary	.20	.15	.08
41	Tony Phillips	.20	.15	.08
42	Lee Smith	.25	.20	.10
43	Tim Teufel	.20	.15	.08
44	Lance Dickson	.30	.25	.12
45	Greg Litton	.20	.15	.08
46	Teddy Higuera	.25	.20	.10
47	Edgar Martinez	.30	.25	.12
48	Steve Avery	5.00	3.75	2.00
49	Walt Weiss	.20	.15	.08
50	David Segui	.30	.25	.12
51	Andy Benes	1.00	.70	.40
52	Karl Rhodes	.30	.25	.12
53	Neal Heaton	.20	.15	.08
54	Danny Gladden	.20	.15	.08
55	Luis Rivera	.20	.15	.08
56	Kevin Brown	.20	.15	.08
57	Frank Thomas	22.00	16.50	8.75
58	Terry Mulholland	.25	.20	.10
59	Dick Schofield	.20	.15	.08
60	Ron Darling	.20	.15	.08
61	Sandy Alomar, Jr.	.35	.25	.14
62	Dave Stieb	.20	.15	.08
63	Alan Trammell	.40	.30	.15
64	Matt Nokes	.20	.15	.08
65	Lenny Harris	.20	.15	.08
66	Milt Thompson	.20	.15	.08
67	Storm Davis	.20	.15	.08
68	Joe Oliver	.20	.15	.08
69	Andres Galarraga	.60	.45	.25
70	Ozzie Guillen	.25	.20	.10
71	Ken Howell	.20	.15	.08
72	Garry Templeton	.20	.15	.08
73	Derrick May	2.00	1.50	.80
74	Xavier Hernandez	.20	.15	.08
75	Dave Parker	.25	.20	.10
76	Rick Aguilera	.20	.15	.08
77	Robby Thompson	.20	.15	.08

		MT	NR MT	EX
78	Pete Incaviglia	.20	.15	.08
79	Bob Welch	.25	.20	.10
80	Randy Milligan	.25	.20	.10
81	Chuck Finley	.35	.25	.14
82	Alvin Davis	.20	.15	.08
83	Tim Naehring	.35	.25	.14
84	Jay Bell	.25	.20	.10
85	Joe Magrane	.25	.20	.10
86	Howard Johnson	.40	.30	.15
87	Jack McDowell	1.25	.90	.50
88	Kevin Seitzer	.20	.15	.08
89	Bruce Ruffin	.20	.15	.08
90	Fernando Valenzuela	.30	.25	.12
91	Terry Kennedy	.20	.15	.08
92	Barry Larkin	.80	.60	.30
93	Larry Walker	3.00	2.25	1.25
94	Luis Salazar	.20	.15	.08
95	Gary Sheffield	3.50	2.75	1.50
96	Bobby Witt	.20	.15	.08
97	Lonnie Smith	.20	.15	.08
98	Bryan Harvey	.25	.20	.10
99	Mookie Wilson	.25	.20	.10
100	Doc Gooden	.50	.40	.20
101	Lou Whitaker	.25	.20	.10
102	Ron Karkovice	.20	.15	.08
103	Jesse Barfield	.25	.20	.10
104	Jose DeJesus	.25	.20	.10
105	Benito Santiago	.25	.20	.10
106	Brian Holman	.20	.15	.08
107	Rafael Ramirez	.20	.15	.08
108	Ellis Burks	.50	.40	.20
109	Mike Bielecki	.20	.15	.08
110	Kirby Puckett	3.00	2.25	1.25
111	Terry Shumpert	.25	.20	.10
112	Chuck Crim	.20	.15	.08
113	Todd Benzinger	.20	.15	.08
114	Brian Barnes	.40	.30	.15
115	Carlos Baerga	5.00	3.75	2.00
116	Kal Daniels	.25	.20	.10
117	Dave Johnson	.20	.15	.08
118	Andy Van Slyke	.35	.25	.14
119	John Burkett	1.00	.70	.40
120	Rickey Henderson	1.50	1.25	.60
121	Tim Jones	.20	.15	.08
122	Daryl Irvine	.30	.25	.12
123	Ruben Sierra	1.50	1.25	.60
124	Jim Abbott	.80	.60	.30
125	Daryl Boston	.20	.15	.08
126	Greg Maddux	1.25	.90	.50
127	Von Hayes	.20	.15	.08
128	Mike Fitzgerald	.20	.15	.08
129	Wayne Edwards	.20	.15	.08
130	Greg Briley	.20	.15	.08
131	Rob Dibble	.30	.25	.12
132	Gene Larkin	.20	.15	.08
133	David Wells	.20	.15	.08
134	Steve Balboni	.20	.15	.08
135	Greg Vaughn	1.25	.90	.50
136	Mark Davis	.20	.15	.08
137	Dave Rohde	.20	.15	.08
138	Eric Show	.20	.15	.08
139	Bobby Bonilla	1.00	.70	.40
140	Dana Kiecker	.25	.20	.10
141	Gary Pettis	.20	.15	.08
142	Dennis Boyd	.20	.15	.08
143	Mike Benjamin	.20	.15	.08
144	Luis Polonia	.20	.15	.08
145	Doug Jones	.20	.15	.08
146	Al Newman	.20	.15	.08
147	Alex Fernandez	3.00	2.25	1.25
148	Bill Doran	.20	.15	.08
149	Kevin Elster	.20	.15	.08
150	Len Dykstra	.30	.25	.12
151	Mike Gallego	.20	.15	.08
152	Tim Belcher	.20	.15	.08
153	Jay Buhner	.20	.15	.08
154	Ozzie Smith	.70	.50	.30
155	Jose Canseco	1.50	1.25	.60
156	Gregg Olson	.30	.25	.12
157	Charlie O'Brien	.20	.15	.08
158	Frank Tanana	.20	.15	.08
159	George Brett	1.00	.70	.40
160	Jeff Huson	.20	.15	.08
161	Kevin Tapani	.35	.25	.14
162	Jerome Walton	.25	.20	.10
163	Charlie Hayes	.20	.15	.08
164	Chris Bosio	.20	.15	.08
165	Chris Sabo	.40	.30	.15
166	Lance Parrish	.20	.15	.08
167	Don Robinson	.20	.15	.08
168	Manuel Lee	.20	.15	.08

		MT	NR MT	EX
169	Dennis Rasmussen	.20	.15	.08
170	Wade Boggs	1.50	1.25	.60
171	Bob Geren	.20	.15	.08
172	Mackey Sasser	.20	.15	.08
173	Julio Franco	.50	.40	.20
174	Otis Nixon	.20	.15	.08
175	Bert Blyleven	.20	.15	.08
176	Craig Biggio	.40	.30	.15
177	Eddie Murray	.60	.45	.25
178	Randy Tomlin	.80	.60	.30
179	Tino Martinez	.80	.60	.30
180	Carlton Fisk	.80	.60	.30
181	Dwight Smith	.20	.15	.08
182	Scott Garrelts	.20	.15	.08
183	Jim Gantner	.20	.15	.08
184	Dickie Thon	.20	.15	.08
185	John Farrell	.20	.15	.08
186	Cecil Fielder	3.00	2.25	1.25
187	Glenn Braggs	.20	.15	.08
188	Allan Anderson	.20	.15	.08
189	Kurt Stillwell	.20	.15	.08
190	Jose Oquendo	.20	.15	.08
191	Joe Orsulak	.20	.15	.08
192	Ricky Jordan	.20	.15	.08
193	Kelly Downs	.20	.15	.08
194	Delino DeShields	1.25	.90	.50
195	Omar Vizquel	.20	.15	.08
196	Mark Carreon	.20	.15	.08
197	Mike Harkey	.20	.15	.08
198	Jack Howell	.20	.15	.08
199	Lance Johnson	.20	.15	.08
200	Nolan Ryan	15.00	11.00	6.00
201	John Marzano	.20	.15	.08
202	Doug Drabek	.30	.25	.12
203	Mark Lemke	.30	.25	.12
204	Steve Sax	.30	.25	.12
205	Greg Harris	.20	.15	.08
206	B.J. Surhoff	.20	.15	.08
207	Todd Burns	.20	.15	.08
208	Jose Gonzalez	.20	.15	.08
209	Mike Scott	.20	.15	.08
210	Dave Magadan	.30	.25	.12
211	Dante Bichette	.20	.15	.08
212	Trevor Wilson	.20	.15	.08
213	Hector Villanueva	.20	.15	.08
214	Dan Pasqua	.20	.15	.08
215	Greg Colbrunn	.30	.25	.12
216	Mike Jeffcoat	.20	.15	.08
217	Harold Reynolds	.25	.20	.10
218	Paul O'Neill	.25	.20	.10
219	Mark Guthrie	.25	.20	.10
220	Barry Bonds	5.00	3.75	2.00
221	Jimmy Key	.25	.20	.10
222	Billy Ripken	.20	.15	.08
223	Tom Pagnozzi	.20	.15	.08
224	Bo Jackson	2.00	1.50	.80
225	Sid Fernandez	.20	.15	.08
226	Mike Marshall	.20	.15	.08
227	John Kruk	.25	.20	.10
228	Mike Fetters	.20	.15	.08
229	Eric Anthony	.20	.15	.08
230	Ryne Sandberg	3.00	2.25	1.25
231	Carney Lansford	.20	.15	.08
232	Melido Perez	.20	.15	.08
233	Jose Lind	.20	.15	.08
234	Darryl Hamilton	.20	.15	.08
235	Tom Browning	.20	.15	.08
236	Spike Owen	.20	.15	.08
237	Juan Gonzalez	25.00	18.50	10.00
238	Felix Fermin	.20	.15	.08
239	Keith Miller	.20	.15	.08
240	Mark Gubicza	.20	.15	.08
241	Kent Anderson	.20	.15	.08
242	Alvaro Espinoza	.20	.15	.08
243	Dale Murphy	.50	.40	.20
244	Orel Hershiser	.30	.25	.12
245	Paul Molitor	1.25	.90	.50
246	Eddie Whitson	.20	.15	.08
247	Joe Girardi	.20	.15	.08
248	Kent Hrbek	.25	.20	.10
249	Bill Sampen	.20	.15	.08
250	Kevin Mitchell	.50	.40	.20
251	Mariano Duncan	.20	.15	.08
252	Scott Bradley	.20	.15	.08
253	Mike Greenwell	.30	.25	.12
254	Tom Gordon	.25	.20	.10
255	Todd Zeile	.80	.60	.30
256	Bobby Thigpen	.25	.20	.10
257	Gregg Jefferies	1.25	.90	.50
258	Kenny Rogers	.20	.15	.08
259	Shane Mack	.30	.25	.12

		MT	NR MT	EX
260	Zane Smith	.20	.15	.08
261	Mitch Williams	.25	.20	.10
262	Jim DeShaies	.20	.15	.08
263	Dave Winfield	1.00	.70	.40
264	Ben McDonald	1.00	.70	.40
265	Randy Ready	.20	.15	.08
266	Pat Borders	.20	.15	.08
267	Jose Uribe	.20	.15	.08
268	Derek Lilliquist	.20	.15	.08
269	Greg Brock	.20	.15	.08
270	Ken Griffey, Jr.	18.00	13.50	7.25
271	Jeff Gray	.25	.20	.10
272	Danny Tartabull	.40	.30	.15
273	Dennis Martinez	.20	.15	.08
274	Robin Ventura	3.00	2.25	1.25
275	Randy Myers	.20	.15	.08
276	Jack Daugherty	.20	.15	.08
277	Greg Gagne	.20	.15	.08
278	Jay Howell	.20	.15	.08
279	Mike LaValliere	.20	.15	.08
280	Rex Hudler	.20	.15	.08
281	Mike Simms	.50	.40	.20
282	Kevin Maas	.40	.30	.15
283	Jeff Ballard	.20	.15	.08
284	Dave Henderson	.30	.25	.12
285	Pete O'Brien	.20	.15	.08
286	Brook Jacoby	.20	.15	.08
287	Mike Henneman	.20	.15	.08
288	Greg Olson	.20	.15	.08
289	Greg Myers	.20	.15	.08
290	Mark Grace	1.50	1.25	.60
291	Shawn Abner	.20	.15	.08
292	Frank Viola	.30	.25	.12
293	Lee Stevens	.30	.25	.12
294	Jason Grimsley	.20	.15	.08
295	Matt Williams	1.50	1.25	.60
296	Ron Robinson	.20	.15	.08
297	Tom Brunansky	.20	.15	.08
298	Checklist	.20	.15	.08
299	Checklist	.20	.15	.08
300	Checklist	.20	.15	.08
301	Darryl Strawberry	.60	.45	.25
302	Bud Black	.20	.15	.08
303	Harold Baines	.30	.25	.12
304	Roberto Alomar	5.00	3.75	2.00
305	Norm Charlton	.20	.15	.08
306	Gary Thurman	.20	.15	.08
307	Mike Felder	.20	.15	.08
308	Tony Gwynn	2.00	1.50	.80
309	Roger Clemens	2.00	1.50	.80
310	Andre Dawson	.50	.40	.20
311	Scott Radinsky	.20	.15	.08
312	Bob Melvin	.20	.15	.08
313	Kirk McCaskill	.20	.15	.08
314	Pedro Guerrero	.35	.25	.14
315	Walt Terrell	.20	.15	.08
316	Sam Horn	.20	.15	.08
317	Wes Chamberlain	1.00	.70	.40
318	Pedro Munoz	.50	.40	.20
319	Roberto Kelly	.35	.25	.14
320	Mark Portugal	.20	.15	.08
321	Tim McIntosh	.20	.15	.08
322	Jesse Orosco	.20	.15	.08
323	Gary Green	.20	.15	.08
324	Greg Harris	.20	.15	.08
325	Hubie Brooks	.20	.15	.08
326	Chris Nabholz	.20	.15	.08
327	Terry Pendleton	.35	.25	.14
328	Eric King	.20	.15	.08
329	Chili Davis	.20	.15	.08
330	Anthony Telford	.20	.15	.08
331	Kelly Gruber	.35	.25	.14
332	Dennis Eckersley	.35	.25	.14
333	Mel Hall	.20	.15	.08
334	Bob Kipper	.20	.15	.08
335	Willie McGee	.30	.25	.12
336	Steve Olin	.20	.15	.08
337	Steve Buechele	.20	.15	.08
338	Scott Leius	.35	.25	.14
339	Hal Morris	.40	.30	.15
340	Jose Offerman	.40	.30	.15
341	Kent Mercker	.30	.25	.12
342	Ken Griffey	.20	.15	.08
343	Pete Harnisch	.20	.15	.08
344	Kirk Gibson	.30	.25	.12
345	Dave Smith	.20	.15	.08
346	Dave Martinez	.20	.15	.08
347	Atlee Hammaker	.20	.15	.08
348	Brian Downing	.20	.15	.08
349	Todd Hundley	.35	.25	.14
350	Candy Maldonado	.20	.15	.08

		MT	NR MT	EX
351	Dwight Evans	.30	.25	.12
352	Steve Searcy	.20	.15	.08
353	Gary Gaetti	.25	.20	.10
354	Jeff Reardon	.25	.20	.10
355	Travis Fryman	9.00	6.75	3.50
356	Dave Righetti	.20	.15	.08
357	Fred McGriff	1.50	1.25	.60
358	Don Slaught	.20	.15	.08
359	Gene Nelson	.20	.15	.08
360	Billy Spiers	.20	.15	.08
361	Lee Guetterman	.20	.15	.08
362	Darren Lewis	1.00	.70	.40
363	Duane Ward	.20	.15	.08
364	Lloyd Moseby	.20	.15	.08
365	John Smoltz	1.50	1.25	.60
366	Felix Jose	.80	.60	.30
367	David Cone	.30	.25	.12
368	Wally Backman	.20	.15	.08
369	Jeff Montgomery	.20	.15	.08
370	Rich Garces	.35	.25	.14
371	Billy Hatcher	.20	.15	.08
372	Bill Swift	.20	.15	.08
373	Jim Eisenreich	.20	.15	.08
374	Rob Ducey	.20	.15	.08
375	Tim Crews	.20	.15	.08
376	Steve Finley	.20	.15	.08
377	Jeff Blauser	.20	.15	.08
378	Willie Wilson	.20	.15	.08
379	Gerald Perry	.20	.15	.08
380	Jose Mesa	.20	.15	.08
381	Pat Kelly	2.00	1.50	.80
382	Matt Merullo	.20	.15	.08
383	Ivan Calderon	.30	.25	.12
384	Scott Chiamparino	.20	.15	.08
385	Lloyd McClendon	.20	.15	.08
386	Dave Bergman	.20	.15	.08
387	Ed Sprague	.40	.30	.15
388	Jeff Bagwell	10.00	7.50	4.00
389	Brett Butler	.25	.20	.10
390	Larry Andersen	.20	.15	.08
391	Glenn Davis	.30	.25	.12
392	Alex Cole (photo of Otis Nixon)	.30	.25	.12
393	Mike Heath	.20	.15	.08
394	Danny Darwin	.20	.15	.08
395	Steve Lake	.20	.15	.08
396	Tim Layana	.20	.15	.08
397	Terry Leach	.20	.15	.08
398	Bill Wegman	.20	.15	.08
399	Mark McGwire	.50	.40	.20
400	Mike Boddicker	.20	.15	.08
401	Steve Howe	.20	.15	.08
402	Bernard Gilkey	.40	.30	.15
403	Thomas Howard	.20	.15	.08
404	Rafael Belliard	.20	.15	.08
405	Tom Candiotti	.20	.15	.08
406	Rene Gonzalez	.25	.20	.10
407	Chuck McElroy	.25	.20	.10
408	Paul Sorrento	.25	.20	.10
409	Randy Johnson	1.25	.90	.50
410	Brady Anderson	.20	.15	.08
411	Dennis Cook	.20	.15	.08
412	Mickey Tettleton	.25	.20	.10
413	Mike Stanton	.20	.15	.08
414	Ken Oberkfell	.20	.15	.08
415	Rick Honeycutt	.20	.15	.08
416	Nelson Santovenia	.20	.15	.08
417	Bob Tewksbury	.20	.15	.08
418	Brent Mayne	.20	.15	.08
419	Steve Farr	.20	.15	.08
420	Phil Stephenson	.20	.15	.08
421	Jeff Russell	.20	.15	.08
422	Chris James	.20	.15	.08
423	Tim Leary	.20	.15	.08
424	Gary Carter	.30	.25	.12
425	Glenallen Hill	.30	.25	.12
426	Matt Young	.20	.15	.08
427	Sid Bream	.20	.15	.08
428	Greg Swindell	.30	.25	.12
429	Scott Aldred	.30	.25	.12
430	Cal Ripken, Jr.	2.50	2.00	1.00
431	Bill Landrum	.20	.15	.08
432	Ernie Riles	.20	.15	.08
433	Danny Jackson	.20	.15	.08
434	Casey Candaele	.20	.15	.08
435	Ken Hill	.20	.15	.08
436	Jaime Navarro	.20	.15	.08
437	Lance Blankenship	.20	.15	.08
438	Randy Velarde	.20	.15	.08
439	Frank DiPino	.20	.15	.08
440	Carl Nichols	.20	.15	.08
441	Jeff Robinson	.20	.15	.08

		MT	NR MT	EX
442	Deion Sanders	.35	.25	.14
443	Vincente Palacios	.20	.15	.08
444	Devon White	.30	.25	.12
445	John Cerutti	.20	.15	.08
446	Tracy Jones	.20	.15	.08
447	Jack Morris	.30	.25	.12
448	Mitch Webster	.20	.15	.08
449	Bob Ojeda	.20	.15	.08
450	Oscar Azocar	.20	.15	.08
451	Luis Aquino	.20	.15	.08
452	Mark Whiten	1.00	.70	.40
453	Stan Belinda	.20	.15	.08
454	Ron Gant	2.00	1.50	.80
455	Jose DeLeon	.20	.15	.08
456	Mark Salas	.20	.15	.08
457	Junior Felix	.20	.15	.08
458	Wally Whitehurst	.20	.15	.08
459	Phil Plantier	4.00	3.00	1.50
460	Juan Berenguer	.20	.15	.08
461	Franklin Stubbs	.20	.15	.08
462	Joe Boever	.20	.15	.08
463	Tim Wallach	.30	.25	.12
464	Mike Moore	.20	.15	.08
465	Albert Belle	5.00	3.75	2.00
466	Mike Witt	.20	.15	.08
467	Craig Worthington	.20	.15	.08
468	Jerald Clark	.20	.15	.08
469	Scott Terry	.20	.15	.08
470	Milt Cuyler	.60	.45	.25
471	John Smiley	.25	.20	.10
472	Charles Nagy	.25	.20	.10
473	Alan Mills	.20	.15	.08
474	John Russell	.20	.15	.08
475	Bruce Hurst	.20	.15	.08
476	Andujar Cedeno	2.00	1.50	.80
477	Dave Eiland	.20	.15	.08
478	Brian McRae	2.00	1.50	.80
479	Mike LaCoss	.20	.15	.08
480	Chris Gwynn	.20	.15	.08
481	Jamie Moyer	.20	.15	.08
482	John Olerud	5.00	3.75	2.00
483	Efrain Valdez	.20	.15	.08
484	Sil Campusano	.20	.15	.08
485	Pascual Perez	.20	.15	.08
486	Gary Redus	.20	.15	.08
487	Andy Hawkins	.20	.15	.08
488	Cory Snyder	.20	.15	.08
489	Chris Hoiles	.25	.20	.10
490	Ron Hassey	.20	.15	.08
491	Gary Wayne	.20	.15	.08
492	Mark Lewis	.80	.60	.30
493	Scott Coolbaugh	.20	.15	.08
494	Gerald Young	.20	.15	.08
495	Juan Samuel	.20	.15	.08
496	Willie Fraser	.20	.15	.08
497	Jeff Treadway	.20	.15	.08
498	Vince Coleman	.30	.25	.12
499	Cris Carpenter	.20	.15	.08
500	Jack Clark	.30	.25	.12
501	Kevin Appier	2.00	1.50	.80
502	Rafael Palmeiro	1.00	.70	.40
503	Hensley Meulens	.30	.25	.12
504	George Bell	.30	.25	.12
505	Tony Pena	.30	.25	.12
506	Roger McDowell	.20	.15	.08
507	Luis Sojo	.20	.15	.08
508	Mike Schooler	.20	.15	.08
509	Robin Yount	1.00	.70	.40
510	Jack Armstrong	.20	.15	.08
511	Rick Cerone	.20	.15	.08
512	Curt Wilkerson	.20	.15	.08
513	Joe Carter	1.00	.70	.40
514	Tim Burke	.20	.15	.08
515	Tony Fernandez	.25	.20	.10
516	Ramon Martinez	.50	.40	.20
517	Tim Hulett	.20	.15	.08
518	Terry Steinbach	.20	.15	.08
519	Pete Smith	.20	.15	.08
520	Ken Caminiti	.20	.15	.08
521	Shawn Boskie	.20	.15	.08
522	Mike Pagliarulo	.20	.15	.08
523	Tim Raines	.35	.25	.14
524	Alfredo Griffin	.20	.15	.08
525	Henry Cotto	.20	.15	.08
526	Mike Stanley	.20	.15	.08
527	Charlie Leibrandt	.20	.15	.08
528	Jeff King	.20	.15	.08
529	Eric Plunk	.20	.15	.08
530	Tom Lampkin	.20	.15	.08
531	Steve Bedrosian	.20	.15	.08
532	Tom Herr	.20	.15	.08
533	Craig Lefferts	.20	.15	.08
534	Jeff Reed	.20	.15	.08
535	Mickey Morandini	.35	.25	.14
536	Greg Cadaret	.20	.15	.08
537	Ray Lankford	2.00	1.50	.80
538	John Candelaria	.20	.15	.08
539	Rob Deer	.20	.15	.08
540	Brad Arnsberg	.20	.15	.08
541	Mike Sharperson	.20	.15	.08
542	Jeff Robinson	.20	.15	.08
543	Mo Vaughn	3.00	2.25	1.25
544	Jeff Parrett	.20	.15	.08
545	Willie Randolph	.20	.15	.08
546	Herm Winningham	.20	.15	.08
547	Jeff Innis	.20	.15	.08
548	Chuck Knoblauch	2.00	1.50	.80
549	Tommy Greene	.25	.20	.10
550	Jeff Hamilton	.20	.15	.08
551	Barry Jones	.20	.15	.08
552	Ken Dayley	.20	.15	.08
553	Rick Dempsey	.20	.15	.08
554	Greg Smith	.20	.15	.08
555	Mike Devereaux	.20	.15	.08
556	Keith Comstock	.20	.15	.08
557	Paul Faries	.20	.15	.08
558	Tom Glavine	5.00	3.75	2.00
559	Craig Grebeck	.20	.15	.08
560	Scott Erickson	1.00	.70	.40
561	Joel Skinner	.20	.15	.08
562	Mike Morgan	.20	.15	.08
563	Dave Gallagher	.20	.15	.08
564	Todd Stottlemyre	.25	.20	.10
565	Rich Rodriguez	.25	.20	.10
566	Craig Wilson	.25	.20	.10
567	Jeff Brantley	.25	.20	.10
568	Scott Kamieniecki	.30	.25	.12
569	Steve Decker	.80	.60	.30
570	Juan Agosto	.20	.15	.08
571	Tommy Gregg	.20	.15	.08
572	Kevin Wickander	.20	.15	.08
573	Jamie Quirk	.20	.15	.08
574	Jerry Don Gleaton	.20	.15	.08
575	Chris Hammond	.20	.15	.08
576	Luis Gonzalez	1.00	.70	.40
577	Russ Swan	.20	.15	.08
578	Jeff Conine	3.00	2.25	1.25
579	Charlie Hough	.20	.15	.08
580	Jeff Kunkel	.20	.15	.08
581	Darrel Akerfelds	.20	.15	.08
582	Jeff Manto	.25	.20	.10
583	Alejandro Pena	.20	.15	.08
584	Mark Davidson	.20	.15	.08
585	Bob MacDonald	.25	.20	.10
586	Paul Assenmacher	.20	.15	.08
587	Dan Wilson	.60	.45	.25
588	Tom Bolton	.20	.15	.08
589	Brian Harper	.20	.15	.08
590	John Habyan	.20	.15	.08
591	John Orton	.20	.15	.08
592	Mark Gardner	.20	.15	.08
593	Turner Ward	.40	.30	.15
594	Bob Patterson	.20	.15	.08
595	Edwin Nunez	.20	.15	.08
596	Gary Scott	.40	.30	.15
597	Scott Bankhead	.20	.15	.08
598	Checklist	.20	.15	.08
599	Checklist	.20	.15	.08
600	Checklist	.20	.15	.08

1991 "1953" Topps Archive

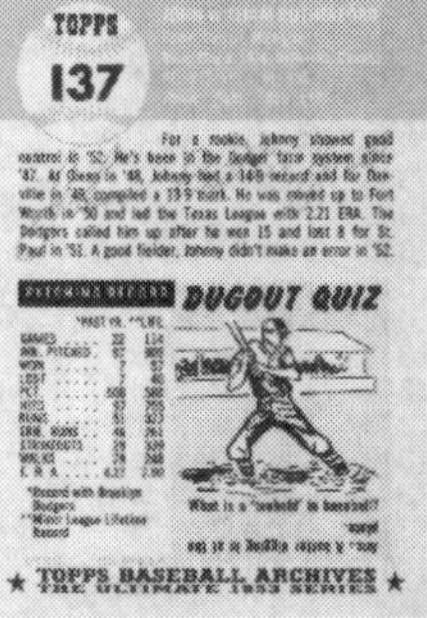

		MT	NR MT	EX
Complete Set:		60.00	45.00	25.00
Common Player:(1-337)		.20	.15	.08
1	Jackie Robinson	4.00	3.00	1.50
2	Luke Easter	.20	.15	.08
3	George Crowe	.20	.15	.08
4	Ben Wade	.20	.15	.08
5	Joe Dobson	.20	.15	.08
6	Sam Jones	.20	.15	.08
7	Bob Borkowski	.20	.15	.08
8	Clem Koshorek	.20	.15	.08
9	Joe Collins	.20	.15	.08
10	Smoky Burgess	.20	.15	.08
11	Sal Yvars	.20	.15	.08
12	Howie Judson	.20	.15	.08
13	Conrado Marrero	.20	.15	.08
14	Clem Labine	.20	.15	.08
15	Bobo Newsom	.20	.15	.08
16	Peanuts Lowrey	.20	.15	.08
17	Billy Hitchcock	.20	.15	.08
18	Ted Lepcio	.20	.15	.08
19	Mel Parnell	.20	.15	.08
20	Hank Thompson	.20	.15	.08
21	Billy Johnson	.20	.15	.08
22	Howie Fox	.20	.15	.08
23	Toby Atwell	.20	.15	.08
24	Ferris Fain	.20	.15	.08
25	Ray Boone	.20	.15	.08
26	Dale Mitchell	.25	.20	.10
27	Roy Campanella	2.50	2.00	1.00
28	Eddie Pellagrini	.20	.15	.08
29	Hal Jeffcoat	.20	.15	.08
30	Willard Nixon	.20	.15	.08
31	Ewell Blackwell	.20	.15	.08
32	Clyde Vollmer	.20	.15	.08
33	Bob Kennedy	.20	.15	.08
34	George Shuba	.20	.15	.08
35	Irv Noren	.20	.15	.08
37	Eddie Mathews	1.00	.70	.40
38	Jim Hearn	.20	.15	.08
39	Eddie Miksis	.20	.15	.08
40	John Lipon	.20	.15	.08
41	Enos Slaughter	.50	.40	.20
42	Gus Zernial	.20	.15	.08
43	Gil McDougald	.25	.20	.10
44	Ellis Kinder	.20	.15	.08
45	Grady Hatton	.20	.15	.08
46	Johnny Klippstein	.20	.15	.08
47	Bubba Church	.20	.15	.08
48	Bob Del Greco	.20	.15	.08
49	Faye Throneberry	.20	.15	.08
50	Chuck Dressen	.20	.15	.08
51	Frank Campos	.20	.15	.08
52	Ted Gray	.20	.15	.08
53	Sherman Lollar	.20	.15	.08
54	Bob Feller	1.00	.70	.40
55	Maurice McDermott	.20	.15	.08
56	Gerald Staley	.20	.15	.08
57	Carl Scheib	.20	.15	.08
58	George Metkovich	.20	.15	.08
59	Karl Drews	.20	.15	.08
60	Cloyd Boyer	.20	.15	.08
61	Early Wynn	.50	.40	.20
62	Monte Irvin	.50	.40	.20
63	Gus Niarhos	.20	.15	.08
64	Dave Philley	.20	.15	.08
65	Earl Harrist	.20	.15	.08
66	Orestes Minoso	.35	.25	.14
67	Roy Sievers	.20	.15	.08
68	Del Rice	.20	.15	.08
69	Dick Brodowski	.20	.15	.08
70	Ed Yuhas	.20	.15	.08
71	Tony Bartirome	.20	.15	.08
72	Fred Hutchinson	.20	.15	.08
73	Eddie Robinson	.20	.15	.08
74	Joe Rossi	.20	.15	.08
75	Mike Garcia	.20	.15	.08
76	Pee Wee Reese	2.00	1.50	.80
77	John Mize	.75	.60	.30
78	Al Schoendienst	.50	.40	.20
79	Johnny Wyrostek	.20	.15	.08
80	Jim Hegan	.20	.15	.08
81	Joe Black	.20	.15	.08
82	Mickey Mantle	15.00	11.00	6.00
83	Howie Pollet	.20	.15	.08
84	Bob Hooper	.20	.15	.08
85	Bobby Morgan	.20	.15	.08
86	Billy Martin	.35	.25	.14
87	Ed Lopat	.25	.20	.10
88	Willie Jones	.20	.15	.08
89	Chuck Stobbs	.20	.15	.08
90	Hank Edwards	.20	.15	.08
91	Ebba St. Claire	.20	.15	.08
92	Paul Minner	.20	.15	.08
93	Hal Rice	.20	.15	.08
94	William Kennedy	.20	.15	.08
95	Willard Marshall	.20	.15	.08
96	Virgil Trucks	.20	.15	.08
97	Don Kolloway	.20	.15	.08
98	Cal Abrams	.20	.15	.08
99	Dave Madison	.20	.15	.08
100	Bill Miller	.20	.15	.08
101	Ted Wilks	.20	.15	.08
102	Connie Ryan	.20	.15	.08
103	Joe Astroth	.20	.15	.08
104	Yogi Berra	2.50	2.00	1.00
105	Joe Nuxhall	.20	.15	.08
106	John Antonelli	.20	.15	.08
107	Danny O'Connell	.20	.15	.08
108	Bob Porterfield	.20	.15	.08
109	Alvin Dark	.20	.15	.08
110	Herman Wehmeier	.20	.15	.08
111	Hank Sauer	.20	.15	.08
112	Ned Garver	.20	.15	.08
113	Jerry Priddy	.20	.15	.08
114	Phil Rizzuto	2.00	1.50	.80
115	George Spencer	.20	.15	.08
116	Frank Smith	.20	.15	.08
117	Sid Gordon	.20	.15	.08
118	Gus Bell	.20	.15	.08
119	John Sain	.35	.25	.14
120	Davey Williams	.20	.15	.08
121	Walt Dropo	.20	.15	.08
122	Elmer Valo	.20	.15	.08
123	Tommy Byrne	.20	.15	.08
124	Sibby Sisti	.20	.15	.08
125	Dick Williams	.25	.20	.10
126	Bill Connelly	.20	.15	.08
127	Clint Courtney	.20	.15	.08
128	Wilmer Mizell	.20	.15	.08
129	Keith Thomas	.20	.15	.08
130	Turk Lown	.20	.15	.08
131	Harry Byrd	.20	.15	.08
132	Tom Morgan	.20	.15	.08
133	Gil Coan	.20	.15	.08
134	Rube Walker	.20	.15	.08
135	Al Rosen	.25	.20	.10
136	Ken Heintzelman	.20	.15	.08
137	John Rutherford	.20	.15	.08
138	George Kell	.50	.40	.20
139	Sammy White	.20	.15	.08
140	Tommy Glaviano	.20	.15	.08
141	Allie Reynolds	.35	.25	.14
142	Vic Wertz	.20	.15	.08
143	Billy Pierce	.25	.20	.10
144	Bob Schultz	.20	.15	.08
145	Harry Dorish	.20	.15	.08
146	Granville Hamner	.20	.15	.08
147	Warren Spahn	1.00	.70	.40
148	Mickey Grasso	.20	.15	.08
149	Dom DiMaggio	.25	.20	.10
150	Harry Simpson	.20	.15	.08
151	Hoyt Wilhelm	.75	.60	.30
152	Bob Adams	.20	.15	.08
153	Andy Seminick	.20	.15	.08
154	Dick Groat	.25	.20	.10
155	Dutch Leonard	.20	.15	.08
156	Jim Rivera	.20	.15	.08
157	Bob Addis	.20	.15	.08
158	John Logan	.20	.15	.08
159	Wayne Terwilliger	.20	.15	.08
160	Bob Young	.20	.15	.08
161	Vern Bickford	.20	.15	.08
162	Ted Kluszewski	.35	.25	.14
163	Fred Hatfield	.20	.15	.08
164	Frank Shea	.20	.15	.08
165	Billy Hoeft	.20	.15	.08
166	Bill Hunter	.20	.15	.08
167	Art Schult	.20	.15	.08
168	Willard Schmidt	.20	.15	.08
169	Dizzy Trout	.20	.15	.08
170	Bill Werle	.20	.15	.08
171	Bill Glynn	.20	.15	.08
172	Rip Repulski	.20	.15	.08
173	Preston Ward	.20	.15	.08
175	Ron Kline	.20	.15	.08
176	Don Hoak	.20	.15	.08
177	Jim Dyck	.20	.15	.08
178	Jim Waugh	.20	.15	.08
179	Gene Hermanski	.20	.15	.08
180	Virgil Stallcup	.20	.15	.08
181	Al Zarilla	.20	.15	.08

		MT	NR MT	EX
182	Bob Hofman	.20	.15	.08
183	Stu Miller	.20	.15	.08
184	Hal Brown	.20	.15	.08
185	Jim Pendleton	.20	.15	.08
186	Charlie Bishop	.20	.15	.08
187	Jim Fridley	.20	.15	.08
188	Andy Carey	.20	.15	.08
189	Ray Jablonski	.20	.15	.08
190	Dixie Walker	.20	.15	.08
191	Ralph Kiner	.50	.40	.20
192	Wally Westlake	.20	.15	.08
193	Mike Clark	.20	.15	.08
194	Eddie Kazak	.20	.15	.08
195	Ed McGhee	.20	.15	.08
196	Bob Keegan	.20	.15	.08
197	Del Crandall	.20	.15	.08
198	Forrest Main	.20	.15	.08
199	Marion Fricano	.20	.15	.08
200	Gordon Goldsberry	.20	.15	.08
201	Paul La Palme	.20	.15	.08
202	Carl Sawatski	.20	.15	.08
203	Cliff Fannin	.20	.15	.08
204	Dick Bokelmann	.20	.15	.08
205	Vern Benson	.20	.15	.08
206	Ed Bailey	.20	.15	.08
207	Whitey Ford	2.00	1.50	.80
208	Jim Wilson	.20	.15	.08
209	Jim Greengrass	.20	.15	.08
210	Bob Cerv	.20	.15	.08
211	J.W. Porter	.20	.15	.08
212	Jack Dittmer	.20	.15	.08
213	Ray Scarborough	.20	.15	.08
214	Bill Bruton	.20	.15	.08
215	Gene Conley	.20	.15	.08
216	Jim Hughes	.20	.15	.08
217	Murray Wall	.20	.15	.08
218	Les Fusselman	.20	.15	.08
219	Pete Runnels	.20	.15	.08
220	Satchell Paige	4.00	3.00	1.50
221	Bob Milliken	.20	.15	.08
222	Vic Janowicz	.20	.15	.08
223	John O'Brien	.20	.15	.08
224	Lou Sleater	.20	.15	.08
225	Bobby Shantz	.25	.20	.10
226	Ed Erautt	.20	.15	.08
227	Morris Martin	.20	.15	.08
228	Hal Newhouser	.20	.15	.08
229	Rocky Krshnich	.20	.15	.08
230	Johnny Lindell	.20	.15	.08
231	Solly Hemus	.20	.15	.08
232	Dick Kokos	.20	.15	.08
233	Al Aber	.20	.15	.08
234	Ray Murray	.20	.15	.08
235	John Hetki	.20	.15	.08
236	Harry Perkowski	.20	.15	.08
237	Clarence Podbielan	.20	.15	.08
238	Cal Hogue	.20	.15	.08
239	Jim Delsing	.20	.15	.08
240	Freddie Marsh	.20	.15	.08
241	Al Sima	.20	.15	.08
242	Charlie Silvera	.20	.15	.08
243	Carlos Bernier	.20	.15	.08
244	Willie Mays	.25	.20	.10
245	Bill Norman	.20	.15	.08
246	Roy Face	.20	.15	.08
247	Mike Sandlock	.20	.15	.08
248	Gene Stephens	.20	.15	.08
249	Ed O'Brien	.20	.15	.08
250	Bob Wilson	.20	.15	.08
251	Sid Hudson	.20	.15	.08
252	Henry Foiles	.20	.15	.08
254	Preacher Roe	.20	.15	.08
255	Dixie Howell	.20	.15	.08
256	Les Peden	.20	.15	.08
257	Bob Boyd	.20	.15	.08
258	Jim Gilliam	.35	.25	.14
259	Roy McMillan	.20	.15	.08
260	Sam Calderone	.20	.15	.08
262	Bob Oldis	.20	.15	.08
263	John Podres	.35	.25	.14
264	Gene Woodling	.35	.25	.14
265	Jackie Jensen	.35	.25	.14
266	Bob Cain	.20	.15	.08
269	Duane Pillette	.20	.15	.08
270	Vern Stephens	.20	.15	.08
272	Bill Antonello	.20	.15	.08
273	Harvey Haddix	.20	.15	.08
274	John Riddle	.20	.15	.08
276	Ken Raffensberger	.20	.15	.08
277	Don Lund	.20	.15	.08
278	Willie Miranda	.20	.15	.08

		MT	NR MT	EX
279	Joe Coleman	.20	.15	.08
280	Milt Bolling	.20	.15	.08
281	Jimmie Dykes	.20	.15	.08
282	Ralph Houk	.35	.25	.14
283	Frank J. Thomas	.20	.15	.08
284	Bob Lemon	.50	.40	.20
285	Joe Adcock	.20	.15	.08
286	Jimmy Piersall	.25	.20	.10
287	Mickey Vernon	.20	.15	.08
288	Robin Roberts	.50	.40	.20
289	Rogers Hornsby	.75	.60	.30
290	Hank Bauer	.20	.15	.08
291	Hoot Evers	.20	.15	.08
292	Whitey Lockman	.20	.15	.08
293	Ralph Branca	.25	.20	.10
294	Wally Post	.20	.15	.08
295	Phil Cavarretta	.20	.15	.08
296	Gil Hodges	.35	.25	.14
297	Roy Smalley	.20	.15	.08
298	Bob Friend	.20	.15	.08
299	Dusty Rhodes	.25	.20	.10
300	Eddie Stanky	.20	.15	.08
301	Harvey Kuenn	.25	.20	.10
302	Marty Marion	.20	.15	.08
303	Sal Maglie	.20	.15	.08
304	Lou Boudreau	.50	.40	.20
305	Carl Furillo	.35	.25	.14
306	Bobo Holloman	.20	.15	.08
307	Steve O'Neill	.20	.15	.08
308	Carl Erskine	.25	.20	.10
309	Leo Durocher	.25	.20	.10
310	Lew Burdette	.20	.15	.08
311	Richie Ashburn	.35	.25	.14
312	Hoyt Wilhelm	.60	.45	.25
313	Bucky Harris	.50	.40	.20
314	Joe Garagiola	.75	.60	.30
315	Johnny Pesky	.20	.15	.08
316	Fred Haney	.20	.15	.08
317	Hank Aaron	7.50	5.75	3.00
318	Curt Simmons	.20	.15	.08
319	Ted Williams	6.00	4.50	2.50
320	Don Newcombe	.35	.25	.14
321	Charlie Grimm	.20	.15	.08
322	Paul Richards	.20	.15	.08
323	Wes Westrum	.20	.15	.08
324	Vern Law	.20	.15	.08
325	Casey Stengel	1.00	.70	.40
326	Hall of Fame Inductees (Dizzy Dean, Al Simmons)	1.00	.70	.40
327	Duke Snider	1.50	1.25	.60
328	Bill Rigney	.20	.15	.08
329	Al Lopez	.50	.40	.20
330	Bobby Thomson	.35	.25	.14
331	Nellie Fox	.35	.25	.14
332	Eleanor Engle	.20	.15	.08
333	Larry Doby	.25	.20	.10
334	Billy Goodman	.20	.15	.08
335	Checklist 1-140	.20	.15	.08
336	Checklist 141-280	.20	.15	.08
337	Checklist 281-337	.20	.15	.08

1992 Topps

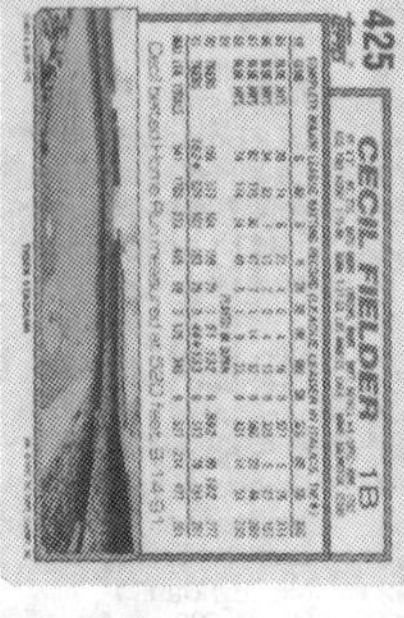

This 792-card set features white stock much like the 1991 issue. The card fronts feature full-color action and posed photos with a gray inner frame and the player name and position on the bottom. The backs feature biographical information, statistics and stadium photos on player cards where space is available. All-Star cards and

#1 Draft Pick cards are once again included. Topps brought back four-player rookie cards in 1992. Nine Top Prospect cards of this nature can be found within the set. Several cards can once again be found with horizontal fronts. "Match the Stats" game cards were inserted into packs of 1992 Topps cards. Special bonus cards were given away to winners of this insert game. Record Breaker cards are also featured in this set.

		MT	NR MT	EX
Complete Set (792):		20.00	15.00	8.00
Common Player:		.03	.02	.01
1	Nolan Ryan	.50	.40	.20
2	Record Breaker (Rickey Henderson)	.10	.08	.04
3	Record Breaker (Jeff Reardon)	.05	.04	.02
4	Record Breaker (Nolan Ryan)	.10	.08	.04
5	Record Breaker (Dave Winfield)	.06	.05	.02
6	*Brien Taylor* (FDP)	1.50	1.25	.60
7	*Jim Olander*(FC)	.10	.08	.04
8	*Bryan Hickerson*(FC)	.10	.08	.04
9	John Farrell	.03	.02	.01
10	Wade Boggs	.15	.11	.06
11	Jack McDowell	.08	.06	.03
12	Luis Gonzalez	.08	.06	.03
13	Mike Scioscia	.04	.03	.02
14	Wes Chamberlain	.08	.06	.03
15	Denny Martinez	.04	.03	.02
16	Jeff Montgomery	.04	.03	.02
17	Randy Milligan	.06	.05	.02
18	Greg Cadaret	.03	.02	.01
19	Jamie Quirk	.03	.02	.01
20	Bip Roberts	.05	.04	.02
21	Buck Rogers	.03	.02	.01
22	Bill Wegman	.04	.03	.02
23	Chuck Knoblauch	.10	.08	.04
24	Randy Myers	.05	.04	.02
25	Ron Gant	.15	.11	.06
26	Mike Bielecki	.03	.02	.01
27	Juan Gonzalez	.75	.60	.30
28	Mike Schooler	.04	.03	.02
29	Mickey Tettleton	.05	.04	.02
30	John Kruk	.06	.05	.02
31	Bryn Smith	.03	.02	.01
32	Chris Nabholz	.06	.05	.02
33	Carlos Baerga	.20	.15	.08
34	Jeff Juden	.15	.11	.06
35	Dave Righetti	.06	.05	.02
36	*Scott Ruffcorn* (FDP)	.30	.25	.12
37	Luis Polonia	.04	.03	.02
38	Tom Candiotti	.04	.03	.02
39	Greg Olson	.04	.03	.02
40	Cal Ripken, Jr.	.20	.15	.08
41	Craig Lefferts	.04	.03	.02
42	Mike Macfarlane	.04	.03	.02
43	Jose Lind	.04	.03	.02
44	Rick Aguilera	.05	.04	.02
45	Gary Carter	.08	.06	.03
46	Steve Farr	.04	.03	.02
47	Rex Hudler	.04	.03	.02
48	Scott Scudder	.05	.04	.02
49	Damon Berryhill	.04	.03	.02
50	Ken Griffey, Jr.	.75	.60	.30
51	Tom Runnells	.03	.02	.01
52	Juan Bell	.05	.04	.02
53	Tommy Gregg	.03	.02	.01
54	David Wells	.04	.03	.02
55	Rafael Palmeiro	.10	.08	.04
56	Charlie O'Brien	.03	.02	.01
57	Donn Pall	.03	.02	.01
58	Top Prospects-Catchers *(Brad Ausmus, Jim Campanis, Dave Nilsson, Doug Robbins)*	.20	.15	.08
59	Mo Vaughn	.25	.20	.10
60	Tony Fernandez	.05	.04	.02
61	Paul O'Neill	.06	.05	.02
62	Gene Nelson	.03	.02	.01
63	Randy Ready	.03	.02	.01
64	Bob Kipper	.03	.02	.01
65	Willie McGee	.08	.06	.03
66	FDP *(Scott Stahoviak)*	.30	.25	.12
67	Luis Salazar	.03	.02	.01
68	Marvin Freeman	.03	.02	.01
69	*Kenny Lofton*	.40	.30	.15
70	Gary Gaetti	.06	.05	.02
71	Erik Hanson	.08	.06	.03
72	Eddie Zosky(FC)	.10	.08	.04
73	Brian Barnes	.10	.08	.04
74	Scott Leius	.10	.08	.04
75	Bret Saberhagen	.08	.06	.03
76	Mike Gallego	.03	.02	.01
77	Jack Armstrong	.05	.04	.02
78	*Ivan Rodriguez*	.30	.25	.12
79	Jesse Orosco	.03	.02	.01
80	David Justice	.30	.25	.12
81	*Ced Landrum*(FC)	.15	.11	.06
82	*Doug Simons*	.10	.08	.04
83	Tommy Greene	.06	.05	.02
84	Leo Gomez	.15	.11	.06
85	Jose DeLeon	.04	.03	.02
86	Steve Finley	.06	.05	.02
87	*Bob MacDonald*(FC)	.15	.11	.06
88	Darrin Jackson	.04	.03	.02
89	Neal Heaton	.03	.02	.01
90	Robin Yount	.12	.09	.05
91	Jeff Reed	.03	.02	.01
92	Lenny Harris	.04	.03	.02
93	Reggie Jefferson	.15	.11	.06
94	Sammy Sosa	.08	.06	.03
95	Scott Bailes	.03	.02	.01
96	FDP *(Tom McKinnon)*	.15	.11	.06
97	Luis Rivera	.03	.02	.01
98	Mike Harkey	.06	.05	.02
99	Jeff Treadway	.04	.03	.02
100	Jose Canseco	.10	.08	.04
101	Omar Vizquel	.03	.02	.01
102	*Scott Kamieniecki*	.12	.09	.05
103	Ricky Jordan	.06	.05	.02
104	Jeff Ballard	.04	.03	.02
105	Felix Jose	.10	.08	.04
106	Mike Boddicker	.05	.04	.02
107	Dan Pasqua	.04	.03	.02
108	*Mike Timlin*	.12	.09	.05
109	Roger Craig	.04	.03	.02
110	Ryne Sandberg	.20	.15	.08
111	Mark Carreon	.03	.02	.01
112	Oscar Azocar	.04	.03	.02
113	Mike Greenwell	.10	.08	.04
114	Mark Portugal	.03	.02	.01
115	Terry Pendleton	.08	.06	.03
116	Willie Randolph	.05	.04	.02
117	Scott Terry	.03	.02	.01
118	Chili Davis	.08	.06	.03
119	Mark Gardner	.05	.04	.02
120	Alan Trammell	.10	.08	.04
121	Derek Bell	.15	.11	.06
122	Gary Varsho	.03	.02	.01
123	Bob Ojeda	.04	.03	.02
124	*Shawn Livsey* (FDP)	.15	.11	.06
125	Chris Hoiles	.08	.06	.03
126	Top Prospects-1st Baseman (Rico Brogna, *John Jaha, Ryan Klesko,* Dave Staton)(FC)	1.00	.70	.40
127	Carlos Quintana	.06	.05	.02
128	Kurt Stillwell	.04	.03	.02
129	Melido Perez	.04	.03	.02
130	Alvin Davis	.06	.05	.02
131	Checklist 1	.03	.02	.01
132	Eric Show	.03	.02	.01
133	Rance Mulliniks	.03	.02	.01
134	Darryl Kile	.08	.06	.03
135	Von Hayes	.05	.04	.02
136	Bill Doran	.05	.04	.02
137	Jeff Robinson	.03	.02	.01
138	Monty Fariss	.08	.06	.03
139	Jeff Innis	.05	.04	.02
140	Mark Grace	.12	.09	.05
141	Jim Leyland	.03	.02	.01
142	Todd Van Poppel(FC)	.30	.25	.12
143	Paul Gibson	.03	.02	.01
144	Bill Swift	.04	.03	.02
145	Danny Tartabull	.08	.06	.03
146	Al Newman	.03	.02	.01
147	Cris Carpenter	.04	.03	.02
148	*Anthony Young*(FC)	.25	.20	.10
149	*Brian Bohanon*(FC)	.15	.11	.06
150	Roger Clemens	.15	.11	.06
151	Jeff Hamilton	.03	.02	.01
152	Charlie Leibrandt	.04	.03	.02
153	Ron Karkovice	.04	.03	.02
154	Hensley Meulens	.08	.06	.03
155	Scott Bankhead	.04	.03	.02
156	*Manny Ramirez* (FDP)	1.00	.70	.40
157	Keith Miller	.03	.02	.01
158	Todd Frohwirth	.03	.02	.01
159	Darrin Fletcher	.05	.04	.02
160	Bobby Bonilla	.12	.09	.05
161	Casey Candaele	.03	.02	.01
162	Paul Faries(FC)	.10	.08	.04
163	Dana Kiecker	.03	.02	.01
164	Shane Mack	.08	.06	.03

		MT	NR MT	EX
165	Mark Langston	.10	.08	.04
166	Geronimo Pena	.06	.05	.02
167	Andy Allanson	.03	.02	.01
168	Dwight Smith	.04	.03	.02
169	Chuck Crim	.03	.02	.01
170	Alex Cole	.05	.04	.02
171	Bill Plummer	.03	.02	.01
172	Juan Berenguer	.03	.02	.01
173	Brian Downing	.04	.03	.02
174	Steve Frey	.03	.02	.01
175	Orel Hershiser	.08	.06	.03
176	*Ramon Garcia*(FC)	.15	.11	.06
177	Danny Gladden	.04	.03	.02
178	Jim Acker	.03	.02	.01
179	*Cesar Bernhardt, Bobby DeJardin, Armando Moreno, Andy Stankiewicz* (Moreno)	.25	.20	.10
180	Kevin Mitchell	.10	.08	.04
181	Hector Villanueva	.06	.05	.02
182	Jeff Reardon	.06	.05	.02
183	Brent Mayne	.06	.05	.02
184	Jimmy Jones	.03	.02	.01
185	Benny Santiago	.08	.06	.03
186	*Cliff Floyd* (FDP)	1.75	1.25	.70
187	Ernie Riles	.03	.02	.01
188	Jose Guzman	.05	.04	.02
189	Junior Felix	.06	.05	.02
190	Glenn Davis	.08	.06	.03
191	Charlie Hough	.04	.03	.02
192	*Dave Fleming*(FC)	.20	.15	.08
193	Omar Oliveras(FC)	.08	.06	.03
194	Eric Karros(FC)	.30	.25	.12
195	David Cone	.08	.06	.03
196	*Frank Castillo*(FC)	.12	.09	.05
197	Glenn Braggs	.04	.03	.02
198	Scott Aldred	.06	.05	.02
199	Jeff Blauser	.04	.03	.02
200	Len Dykstra	.08	.06	.03
201	Buck Showalter	.03	.02	.01
202	Rick Honeycutt	.03	.02	.01
203	Greg Myers	.03	.02	.01
204	Trevor Wilson	.05	.04	.02
205	Jay Howell	.04	.03	.02
206	Luis Sojo	.05	.04	.02
207	Jack Clark	.08	.06	.03
208	Julio Machado	.03	.02	.01
209	Lloyd McClendon	.03	.02	.01
210	Ozzie Guillen	.06	.05	.02
211	*Jeremy Hernandez*(FC)	.15	.11	.06
212	Randy Velarde	.03	.02	.01
213	Les Lancaster	.03	.02	.01
214	*Andy Mota*(FC)	.15	.11	.06
215	Rich Gossage	.05	.04	.02
216	*Brent Gates* (FDP)	.40	.30	.15
217	Brian Harper	.05	.04	.02
218	Mike Flanagan	.03	.02	.01
219	Jerry Browne	.04	.03	.02
220	Jose Rijo	.08	.06	.03
221	Skeeter Barnes	.04	.03	.02
222	Jaime Navarro	.04	.03	.02
223	Mel Hall	.04	.03	.02
224	*Brett Barberie*	.20	.15	.08
225	Roberto Alomar	.15	.11	.06
226	Pete Smith	.03	.02	.01
227	Daryl Boston	.03	.02	.01
228	Eddie Whitson	.04	.03	.02
229	Shawn Boskie	.04	.03	.02
230	Dick Schofield	.03	.02	.01
231	*Brian Drahman*(FC)	.10	.08	.04
232	John Smiley	.05	.04	.02
233	Mitch Webster	.04	.03	.02
234	Terry Steinbach	.05	.04	.02
235	Jack Morris	.08	.06	.03
236	Bill Pecota	.04	.03	.02
237	*Jose Hernandez*(FC)	.10	.08	.04
238	Greg Litton	.03	.02	.01
239	Brian Holman	.05	.04	.02
240	Andres Galarraga	.06	.05	.02
241	Gerald Young	.03	.02	.01
242	Mike Mussina(FC)	.50	.40	.20
243	Alvaro Espinoza	.03	.02	.01
244	Darren Daulton	.04	.03	.02
245	John Smoltz	.08	.06	.03
246	*Jason Pruitt* (FDP)	.15	.11	.06
247	Chuck Finley	.08	.06	.03
248	Jim Gantner	.04	.03	.02
249	Tony Fossas	.03	.02	.01
250	Ken Griffey	.05	.04	.02
251	Kevin Elster	.04	.03	.02
252	Dennis Rasmussen	.03	.02	.01
253	Terry Kennedy	.03	.02	.01
254	*Ryan Bowen*(FC)	.15	.11	.06
255	Robin Ventura	.15	.11	.06
256	Mike Aldrete	.03	.02	.01
257	Jeff Russell	.04	.03	.02
258	Jim Lindeman	.03	.02	.01
259	Ron Darling	.05	.04	.02
260	Devon White	.06	.05	.02
261	Tom Lasorda	.04	.03	.02
262	Terry Lee(FC)	.10	.08	.04
263	Bob Patterson	.03	.02	.01
264	Checklist 2	.03	.02	.01
265	Teddy Higuera	.05	.04	.02
266	Roberto Kelly	.08	.06	.03
267	Steve Bedrosian	.04	.03	.02
268	Brady Anderson	.03	.02	.01
269	*Ruben Amaro*(FC)	.15	.11	.06
270	Tony Gwynn	.12	.09	.05
271	Tracy Jones	.03	.02	.01
272	Jerry Don Gleaton	.03	.02	.01
273	Craig Grebeck	.04	.03	.02
274	*Bob Scanlan*	.10	.08	.04
275	Todd Zeile	.10	.08	.04
276	*Shawn Green* (FDP)	.25	.20	.10
277	Scott Chiamparino	.04	.03	.02
278	Darryl Hamilton	.04	.03	.02
279	Jim Clancy	.03	.02	.01
280	Carlos Martinez	.04	.03	.02
281	Kevin Appier	.05	.04	.02
282	*John Wehner*(FC)	.15	.11	.06
283	Reggie Sanders	.20	.15	.08
284	Gene Larkin	.04	.03	.02
285	Bob Welch	.06	.05	.02
286	Gilberto Reyes(FC)	.05	.04	.02
287	*Pete Schourek*	.15	.11	.06
288	Andujar Cedeno	.15	.11	.06
289	Mike Morgan	.04	.03	.02
290	Bo Jackson	.20	.15	.08
291	Phil Garner	.03	.02	.01
292	Ray Lankford	.15	.11	.06
293	Mike Henneman	.05	.04	.02
294	Dave Valle	.03	.02	.01
295	Alonzo Powell(FC)	.08	.06	.03
296	Tom Brunansky	.05	.04	.02
297	Kevin Brown	.05	.04	.02
298	Kelly Gruber	.08	.06	.03
299	Charles Nagy	.06	.05	.02
300	Don Mattingly	.15	.11	.06
301	Kirk McCaskill	.04	.03	.02
302	Joey Cora	.04	.03	.02
303	Dan Plesac	.04	.03	.02
304	Joe Oliver	.04	.03	.02
305	Tom Glavine	.08	.06	.03
306	*Al Shirley* (FDP)	.15	.11	.06
307	Bruce Ruffin	.03	.02	.01
308	*Craig Shipley*(FC)	.08	.06	.03
309	Dave Martinez	.04	.03	.02
310	Jose Mesa	.03	.02	.01
311	Henry Cotto	.03	.02	.01
312	Mike LaValliere	.04	.03	.02
313	Kevin Tapani	.08	.06	.03
314	Jeff Huson	.04	.03	.02
315	Juan Samuel	.06	.05	.02
316	Curt Schilling	.06	.05	.02
317	Mike Bordick(FC)	.06	.05	.02
318	Steve Howe	.04	.03	.02
319	Tony Phillips	.04	.03	.02
320	George Bell	.10	.08	.04
321	Lou Pinella	.03	.02	.01
322	Tim Burke	.04	.03	.02
323	Milt Thompson	.04	.03	.02
324	Danny Darwin	.04	.03	.02
325	Joe Orsulak	.03	.02	.01
326	Eric King	.04	.03	.02
327	Jay Buhner	.05	.04	.02
328	*Joel Johnson*(FC)	.15	.11	.06
329	Franklin Stubbs	.03	.02	.01
330	Will Clark	.20	.15	.08
331	Steve Lake	.03	.02	.01
332	*Chris Jones*	.10	.08	.04
333	Pat Tabler	.03	.02	.01
334	Kevin Gross	.03	.02	.01
335	Dave Henderson	.08	.06	.03
336	*Greg Anthony* (FDP)	.15	.11	.06
337	Alejandro Pena	.04	.03	.02
338	Shawn Abner	.03	.02	.01
339	Tom Browning	.06	.05	.02
340	Otis Nixon	.04	.03	.02
341	Bob Geren	.03	.02	.01
342	*Tim Spehr*(FC)	.10	.08	.04
343	*Jon Vander Wal*(FC)	.20	.15	.08
344	Jack Daugherty	.03	.02	.01

		MT	NR MT	EX
345	Zane Smith	.04	.03	.02
346	*Rheal Cormier*(FC)	.15	.11	.06
347	Kent Hrbek	.06	.05	.02
348	*Rick Wilkins*(FC)	.15	.11	.06
349	Steve Lyons	.03	.02	.01
350	Gregg Olson	.08	.06	.03
351	Greg Riddoch	.03	.02	.01
352	Ed Nunez	.03	.02	.01
353	*Braulio Castillo*(FC)	.08	.06	.03
354	Dave Bergman	.03	.02	.01
355	*Warren Newson*(FC)	.15	.11	.06
356	Luis Quinones	.03	.02	.01
357	Mike Witt	.04	.03	.02
358	*Ted Wood*	.15	.11	.06
359	Mike Moore	.04	.03	.02
360	Lance Parrish	.06	.05	.02
361	Barry Jones	.03	.02	.01
362	*Javier Ortiz*(FC)	.10	.08	.04
363	John Candelaria	.04	.03	.02
364	Glenallen Hill	.06	.05	.02
365	Duane Ward	.04	.03	.02
366	Checklist 3	.03	.02	.01
367	Rafael Belliard	.03	.02	.01
368	Bill Krueger	.03	.02	.01
369	*Steve Whitaker* (FDP)	.20	.15	.08
370	Shawon Dunston	.06	.05	.02
371	Dante Bichette	.04	.03	.02
372	*Kip Gross*(FC)	.10	.08	.04
373	Don Robinson	.03	.02	.01
374	Bernie Williams	.03	.02	.01
375	Bert Blyleven	.05	.04	.02
376	*Chris Donnels*(FC)	.15	.11	.06
377	*Bob Zupcic*(FC)	.30	.25	.12
378	Joel Skinner	.03	.02	.01
379	Steve Chitren	.06	.05	.02
380	Barry Bonds	.40	.30	.15
381	Sparky Anderson	.03	.02	.01
382	Sid Fernandez	.05	.04	.02
383	Dave Hollins	.06	.05	.02
384	Mark Lee	.03	.02	.01
385	Tim Wallach	.05	.04	.02
386	Will Clark (AS)	.10	.08	.04
387	Ryne Sandberg (AS)	.10	.08	.04
388	Howard Johnson (AS)	.05	.04	.02
389	Barry Larkin (AS)	.05	.04	.02
390	Barry Bonds (AS)	.10	.08	.04
391	Ron Gant (AS)	.08	.06	.03
392	Bobby Bonilla (AS)	.08	.06	.03
393	Craig Biggio (AS)	.05	.04	.02
394	Denny Martinez (AS)	.04	.03	.02
395	Tom Glavine (AS)	.05	.04	.02
396	Ozzie Smith (AS)	.08	.06	.03
397	Cecil Fielder (AS)	.10	.08	.04
398	Julio Franco (AS)	.08	.06	.03
399	Wade Boggs (AS)	.10	.08	.04
400	Cal Ripken, Jr. (AS)	.15	.11	.06
401	Jose Canseco (AS)	.10	.08	.04
402	Joe Carter (AS)	.08	.06	.03
403	Ruben Sierra (AS)	.10	.08	.04
404	Matt Nokes (AS)	.04	.03	.02
405	Roger Clemens (AS)	.12	.09	.05
406	Jim Abbott (AS)	.08	.06	.03
407	Bryan Harvey (AS)	.05	.04	.02
408	Bob Milacki	.03	.02	.01
409	Geno Petralli	.03	.02	.01
410	Dave Stewart	.08	.06	.03
411	Mike Jackson	.03	.02	.01
412	Luis Aquino	.03	.02	.01
413	Tim Teufel	.03	.02	.01
414	*Jeff Ware* (FDP)	.15	.11	.06
415	Jim Deshaies	.04	.03	.02
416	Ellis Burks	.10	.08	.04
417	Allan Anderson	.03	.02	.01
418	Alfredo Griffin	.03	.02	.01
419	Wally Whitehurst	.05	.04	.02
420	Sandy Alomar	.08	.06	.03
421	Juan Agosto	.03	.02	.01
422	Sam Horn	.03	.02	.01
423	*Jeff Fassero*	.10	.08	.04
424	*Paul McClellan*(FC)	.10	.08	.04
425	Cecil Fielder	.15	.11	.06
426	Rock Raines	.10	.08	.04
427	*Eddie Taubensee*(FC)	.20	.15	.08
428	Dennis Boyd	.05	.04	.02
429	Tony LaRussa	.03	.02	.01
430	Steve Sax	.06	.05	.02
431	Tom Gordon	.08	.06	.03
432	Billy Hatcher	.04	.03	.02
433	Cal Eldred(FC)	.25	.20	.10
434	Wally Backman	.03	.02	.01
435	Mark Eichhorn	.03	.02	.01

		MT	NR MT	EX
436	Mookie Wilson	.03	.02	.01
437	*Scott Servais*	.10	.08	.04
438	Mike Maddux	.03	.02	.01
439	*Chico Walker*(FC)	.10	.08	.04
440	Doug Drabek	.08	.06	.03
441	Rob Deer	.04	.03	.02
442	Dave West	.04	.03	.02
443	Spike Owen	.03	.02	.01
444	*Tyrone Hill* (FDP)	.25	.20	.10
445	Matt Williams	.12	.09	.05
446	Mark Lewis	.12	.09	.05
447	David Segui	.08	.06	.03
448	Tom Pagnozzi	.04	.03	.02
449	*Jeff Johnson*	.12	.09	.05
450	Mark McGwire	.12	.09	.05
451	Tom Henke	.05	.04	.02
452	Wilson Alvarez	.08	.06	.03
453	Gary Redus	.03	.02	.01
454	Darren Holmes	.03	.02	.01
455	Pete O'Brien	.03	.02	.01
456	Pat Combs	.04	.03	.02
457	Hubie Brooks	.04	.03	.02
458	Frank Tanana	.03	.02	.01
459	Tom Kelly	.03	.02	.01
460	Andre Dawson	.12	.09	.05
461	Doug Jones	.04	.03	.02
462	Rich Rodriguez	.04	.03	.02
463	*Mike Simms*	.10	.08	.04
464	Mike Jeffcoat	.03	.02	.01
465	Barry Larkin	.12	.09	.05
466	Stan Belinda	.04	.03	.02
467	Lonnie Smith	.04	.03	.02
468	Greg Harris	.03	.02	.01
469	Jim Eisenreich	.03	.02	.01
470	Pedro Guerrero	.08	.06	.03
471	Jose DeJesus	.04	.03	.02
472	*Rich Rowland*(FC)	.15	.11	.06
473	Top Prospects-3rd Baseman *(Frank Bolick, Craig Paquette, Tom Redington, Paul Russo)*(FC)	.35	.25	.14
474	*Mike Rossiter* (FDP)	.25	.20	.10
475	Robby Thompson	.04	.03	.02
476	Randy Bush	.03	.02	.01
477	Greg Hibbard	.04	.03	.02
478	Dale Sveum	.03	.02	.01
479	*Chito Martinez*(FC)	.10	.08	.04
480	Scott Sanderson	.04	.03	.02
481	Tino Martinez	.10	.08	.04
482	Jimmy Key	.05	.04	.02
483	Terry Shumpert	.03	.02	.01
484	Mike Hartley	.03	.02	.01
485	Chris Sabo	.08	.06	.03
486	Bob Walk	.03	.02	.01
487	John Cerutti	.03	.02	.01
488	Scott Cooper(FC)	.10	.08	.04
489	Bobby Cox	.03	.02	.01
490	Julio Franco	.10	.08	.04
491	Jeff Brantley	.04	.03	.02
492	Mike Devereaux	.04	.03	.02
493	Jose Offerman	.10	.08	.04
494	Gary Thurman	.03	.02	.01
495	Carney Lansford	.06	.05	.02
496	Joe Grahe	.04	.03	.02
497	*Andy Ashby*(FC)	.08	.06	.03
498	Gerald Perry	.03	.02	.01
499	Dave Otto	.03	.02	.01
500	Vince Coleman	.08	.06	.03
501	*Rob Mallicoat*(FC)	.06	.05	.02
502	Greg Briley	.03	.02	.01
503	Pascual Perez	.03	.02	.01
504	*Aaron Sele* (FDP)	1.50	1.25	.60
505	Bobby Thigpen	.08	.06	.03
506	Todd Benzinger	.04	.03	.02
507	Candy Maldonado	.04	.03	.02
508	Bill Gullickson	.05	.04	.02
509	Doug Dascenzo	.03	.02	.01
510	Frank Viola	.08	.06	.03
511	Kenny Rogers	.04	.03	.02
512	Mike Heath	.03	.02	.01
513	Kevin Bass	.04	.03	.02
514	*Kim Batiste*(FC)	.10	.08	.04
515	Delino DeShields	.08	.06	.03
516	*Ed Sprague*	.10	.08	.04
517	Jim Gott	.03	.02	.01
518	*Jose Melendez*(FC)	.10	.08	.04
519	Hal McRae	.03	.02	.01
520	*Jeff Bagwell*	.30	.25	.12
521	Joe Hesketh	.03	.02	.01
522	Milt Cuyler	.12	.09	.05
523	Shawn Hillegas	.03	.02	.01
524	Don Slaught	.03	.02	.01

		MT	NR MT	EX
525	Randy Johnson	.06	.05	.02
526	*Doug Piatt*	.10	.08	.04
527	Checklist 4	.03	.02	.01
528	*Steve Foster*(FC)	.15	.11	.06
529	Joe Girardi	.04	.03	.02
530	Jim Abbott	.10	.08	.04
531	Larry Walker	.08	.06	.03
532	Mike Huff	.04	.03	.02
533	Mackey Sasser	.03	.02	.01
534	*Benji Gil* (FDP)	.35	.25	.14
535	Dave Stieb	.06	.05	.02
536	Willie Wilson	.04	.03	.02
537	*Mark Leiter*(FC)	.10	.08	.04
538	Jose Uribe	.03	.02	.01
539	Thomas Howard	.03	.02	.01
540	Ben McDonald	.12	.09	.05
541	*Jose Tolentino*(FC)	.15	.11	.06
542	*Keith Mitchell*(FC)	.10	.08	.04
543	Jerome Walton	.08	.06	.03
544	*Cliff Brantley*(FC)	.15	.11	.06
545	Andy Van Slyke	.08	.06	.03
546	Paul Sorrento	.04	.03	.02
547	Herm Winningham	.03	.02	.01
548	Mark Guthrie	.04	.03	.02
549	Joe Torre	.03	.02	.01
550	Darryl Strawberry	.12	.09	.05
551	Top Prospects-Shortstops *(Manny Alexander, Alex Arias,* Wil Cordero, *Chipper Jones)*	.60	.45	.25
552	Dave Gallagher	.04	.03	.02
553	Edgar Martinez	.06	.05	.02
554	Donald Harris	.15	.11	.06
555	Frank Thomas	1.00	.70	.40
556	Storm Davis	.04	.03	.02
557	Dickie Thon	.03	.02	.01
558	Scott Garrelts	.03	.02	.01
559	Steve Olin	.03	.02	.01
560	Rickey Henderson	.15	.11	.06
561	Jose Vizcaino	.04	.03	.02
562	*Wade Taylor*	.10	.08	.04
563	Pat Borders	.04	.03	.02
564	*Jimmy Gonzalez* (FDP)	.20	.15	.08
565	Lee Smith	.05	.04	.02
566	Bill Sampen	.05	.04	.02
567	Dean Palmer	.12	.09	.05
568	Bryan Harvey	.05	.04	.02
569	Tony Pena	.05	.04	.02
570	Lou Whitaker	.06	.05	.02
571	Randy Tomlin	.06	.05	.02
572	Greg Vaughn	.12	.09	.05
573	Kelly Downs	.03	.02	.01
574	Steve Avery	.20	.15	.08
575	Kirby Puckett	.15	.11	.06
576	*Heathcliff Slocumb*(FC)	.10	.08	.04
577	Kevin Seitzer	.04	.03	.02
578	Lee Guetterman	.03	.02	.01
579	Johnny Oates	.03	.02	.01
580	Greg Maddux	.05	.04	.02
581	Stan Javier	.03	.02	.01
582	Vicente Palacios	.03	.02	.01
583	Mel Rojas	.03	.02	.01
584	*Wayne Rosenthal*(FC)	.10	.08	.04
585	Lenny Webster(FC)	.10	.08	.04
586	Rod Nichols	.03	.02	.01
587	Mickey Morandini	.08	.06	.03
588	Russ Swan	.03	.02	.01
589	Mariano Duncan	.04	.03	.02
590	Howard Johnson	.10	.08	.04
591	Top Prospects-Outfielders *(Jacob Brumfield, Jeremy Burnitz, Alan Cockrell,* D.J. Dozier)(FC)	.60	.45	.25
592	*Denny Neagle*(FC)	.15	.11	.06
593	Steve Decker	.10	.08	.04
594	*Brian Barber* (FDP)	.15	.11	.06
595	Bruce Hurst	.04	.03	.02
596	Kent Mercker	.04	.03	.02
597	*Mike Magnante*	.10	.08	.04
598	Jody Reed	.04	.03	.02
599	Steve Searcy	.03	.02	.01
600	Paul Molitor	.10	.08	.04
601	Dave Smith	.05	.04	.02
602	Mike Fetters	.04	.03	.02
603	*Luis Mercedes*(FC)	.10	.08	.04
604	Chris Gwynn	.03	.02	.01
605	Scott Erickson	.10	.08	.04
606	Brook Jacoby	.04	.03	.02
607	Todd Stottlemyre	.05	.04	.02
608	Scott Bradley	.03	.02	.01
609	Mike Hargrove	.03	.02	.01
610	Eric Davis	.12	.09	.05
611	*Brian Hunter*(FC)	.10	.08	.04

		MT	NR MT	EX
612	Pat Kelly	.10	.08	.04
613	Pedro Munoz(FC)	.15	.11	.06
614	Al Osuna	.04	.03	.02
615	Matt Merullo	.03	.02	.01
616	Larry Andersen	.03	.02	.01
617	Junior Ortiz	.03	.02	.01
618	*Cesar Hernandez,* Steve Hosey, Dan Peltier, *Jeff McNeely* (Hosey)	.60	.45	.25
619	Danny Jackson	.04	.03	.02
620	George Brett	.12	.09	.05
621	*Dan Gakeler*(FC)	.10	.08	.04
622	Steve Buechele	.04	.03	.02
623	Bob Tewksbury	.03	.02	.01
624	*Shawn Estes* (FDP)	.15	.11	.06
625	Kevin McReynolds	.08	.06	.03
626	*Chris Haney*(FC)	.08	.06	.03
627	Mike Sharperson	.03	.02	.01
628	Mark Williamson	.03	.02	.01
629	Wally Joyner	.10	.08	.04
630	Carlton Fisk	.12	.09	.05
631	*Armando Reynoso*(FC)	.10	.08	.04
632	Felix Fermin	.03	.02	.01
633	Mitch Williams	.05	.04	.02
634	Manuel Lee	.04	.03	.02
635	Harold Baines	.08	.06	.03
636	Greg Harris	.05	.04	.02
637	Orlando Merced	.12	.09	.05
638	Chris Bosio	.04	.03	.02
639	*Wayne Housie*(FC)	.10	.08	.04
640	Xavier Hernandez	.04	.03	.02
641	*David Howard*(FC)	.10	.08	.04
642	Tim Crews	.03	.02	.01
643	Rick Cerone	.03	.02	.01
644	Terry Leach	.03	.02	.01
645	Deion Sanders	.12	.09	.05
646	Craig Wilson	.04	.03	.02
647	Marquis Grissom	.12	.09	.05
648	Scott Fletcher	.03	.02	.01
649	Norm Charlton	.04	.03	.02
650	Jesse Barfield	.06	.05	.02
651	*Joe Slusarski*	.10	.08	.04
652	Bobby Rose	.04	.03	.02
653	Dennis Lamp	.03	.02	.01
654	*Allen Watson* (FDP)	.50	.40	.20
655	Brett Butler	.06	.05	.02
656	Top Prospects-Outfielders *(Rudy Pemberton,* Henry Rodriguez, *Lee Tinsley, Gerald Williams)*(FC)	.50	.40	.20
657	Dave Johnson	.03	.02	.01
658	Checklist 5	.03	.02	.01
659	Brian McRae	.10	.08	.04
660	Fred McGriff	.10	.08	.04
661	Bill Landrum	.03	.02	.01
662	*Juan Guzman*(FC)	.50	.40	.20
663	Greg Gagne	.03	.02	.01
664	Ken Hill	.04	.03	.02
665	*Dave Haas*(FC)	.10	.08	.04
666	Tom Foley	.03	.02	.01
667	*Roberto Hernandez*(FC)	.10	.08	.04
668	Dwayne Henry	.03	.02	.01
669	Jim Fregosi	.03	.02	.01
670	Harold Reynolds	.05	.04	.02
671	Mark Whiten	.10	.08	.04
672	Eric Plunk	.03	.02	.01
673	Todd Hundley	.10	.08	.04
674	*Mo Sanford*(FC)	.10	.08	.04
675	Bobby Witt	.04	.03	.02
676	Top Prospects-Pitchers *(Pat Mahomes, Sam Militello,* Roger Salkeld, *Turk Wendell)*(FC)	.30	.25	.12
677	John Marzano	.03	.02	.01
678	Joe Klink	.03	.02	.01
679	Pete Incaviglia	.04	.03	.02
680	Dale Murphy	.08	.06	.03
681	Rene Gonzales	.03	.02	.01
682	Andy Benes	.08	.06	.03
683	Jim Poole(FC)	.08	.06	.03
684	*Trever Miller* (FDP)	.15	.11	.06
685	*Scott Livingstone*(FC)	.12	.09	.05
686	Rich DeLucia	.04	.03	.02
687	*Harvey Pulliam*(FC)	.10	.08	.04
688	Tim Belcher	.04	.03	.02
689	Mark Lemke	.05	.04	.02
690	John Franco	.06	.05	.02
691	Walt Weiss	.06	.05	.02
692	Scott Ruskin	.04	.03	.02
693	Jeff King	.04	.03	.02
694	Mike Gardiner(FC)	.06	.05	.02
695	Gary Sheffield	.12	.09	.05
696	Joe Boever	.03	.02	.01
697	Mike Felder	.03	.02	.01

		MT	NR MT	EX
698	John Habyan	.03	.02	.01
699	Cito Gaston	.03	.02	.01
700	Ruben Sierra	.15	.11	.06
701	Scott Radinsky	.03	.02	.01
702	Lee Stevens	.06	.05	.02
703	*Mark Wohlers*(FC)	.10	.08	.04
704	Curt Young	.03	.02	.01
705	Dwight Evans	.06	.05	.02
706	Rob Murphy	.03	.02	.01
707	Gregg Jefferies	.10	.08	.04
708	Tom Bolton	.03	.02	.01
709	Chris James	.03	.02	.01
710	Kevin Maas	.12	.09	.05
711	*Ricky Bones*(FC)	.10	.08	.04
712	Curt Wilkerson	.03	.02	.01
713	Roger McDowell	.04	.03	.02
714	*Calvin Reese* (FDP)	.20	.15	.08
715	Craig Biggio	.08	.06	.03
716	*Kirk Dressendorfer*	.10	.08	.04
717	Ken Dayley	.03	.02	.01
718	B.J. Surhoff	.05	.04	.02
719	Terry Mulholland	.05	.04	.02
720	Kirk Gibson	.06	.05	.02
721	Mike Pagliarulo	.04	.03	.02
722	Walt Terrell	.03	.02	.01
723	Jose Oquendo	.03	.02	.01
724	Kevin Morton(FC)	.08	.06	.03
725	Doc Gooden	.12	.09	.05
726	Kirt Manwaring	.04	.03	.02
727	Chuck McElroy	.03	.02	.01
728	Dave Burba(FC)	.06	.05	.02
729	Art Howe	.03	.02	.01
730	Ramon Martinez	.10	.08	.04
731	Donnie Hill	.03	.02	.01
732	Nelson Santovenia	.03	.02	.01
733	Bob Melvin	.03	.02	.01
734	*Scott Hatteberg* (FDP)	.15	.11	.06
735	Greg Swindell	.05	.04	.02
736	Lance Johnson	.03	.02	.01
737	Kevin Reimer	.05	.04	.02
738	Dennis Eckersley	.08	.06	.03
739	Rob Ducey	.03	.02	.01
740	Ken Caminiti	.04	.03	.02
741	Mark Gubicza	.04	.03	.02
742	Billy Spiers	.04	.03	.02
743	Darren Lewis	.08	.06	.03
744	Chris Hammond	.05	.04	.02
745	Dave Magadan	.05	.04	.02
746	Bernard Gilkey	.10	.08	.04
747	Willie Banks(FC)	.10	.08	.04
748	Matt Nokes	.04	.03	.02
749	Jerald Clark	.04	.03	.02
750	Travis Fryman	.15	.11	.06
751	Steve Wilson	.03	.02	.01
752	Billy Ripken	.03	.02	.01
753	Paul Assenmacher	.03	.02	.01
754	Charlie Hayes	.04	.03	.02
755	Alex Fernandez	.15	.11	.06
756	Gary Pettis	.03	.02	.01
757	Rob Dibble	.08	.06	.03
758	Tim Naehring	.08	.06	.03
759	Jeff Torborg	.03	.02	.01
760	Ozzie Smith	.10	.08	.04
761	Mike Fitzgerald	.03	.02	.01
762	John Burkett	.04	.03	.02
763	Kyle Abbott	.06	.05	.02
764	*Tyler Green* (FDP)	.30	.25	.12
765	Pete Harnisch	.06	.05	.02
766	Mark Davis	.03	.02	.01
767	Kal Daniels	.06	.05	.02
768	*Jim Thome*(FC)	.20	.15	.08
769	Jack Howell	.03	.02	.01
770	Sid Bream	.05	.04	.02
771	*Arthur Rhodes*(FC)	.20	.15	.08
772	Garry Templeton	.04	.03	.02
773	Hal Morris	.12	.09	.05
774	Bud Black	.04	.03	.02
775	Ivan Calderon	.06	.05	.02
776	*Doug Henry*(FC)	.15	.11	.06
777	John Olerud	.12	.09	.05
778	Tim Leary	.04	.03	.02
779	Jay Bell	.05	.04	.02
780	Eddie Murray	.10	.08	.04
781	Paul Abbott(FC)	.08	.06	.03
782	Phil Plantier	.20	.15	.08
783	Joe Magrane	.05	.04	.02
784	Ken Patterson	.03	.02	.01
785	Albert Belle	.15	.11	.06
786	Royce Clayton(FC)	.25	.20	.10
787	Checklist 6	.03	.02	.01
788	Mike Stanton	.04	.03	.02
789	Bobby Valentine	.03	.02	.01
790	Joe Carter	.10	.08	.04
791	Danny Cox	.03	.02	.01
792	Dave Winfield	.12	.09	.05

1992 Topps Gold

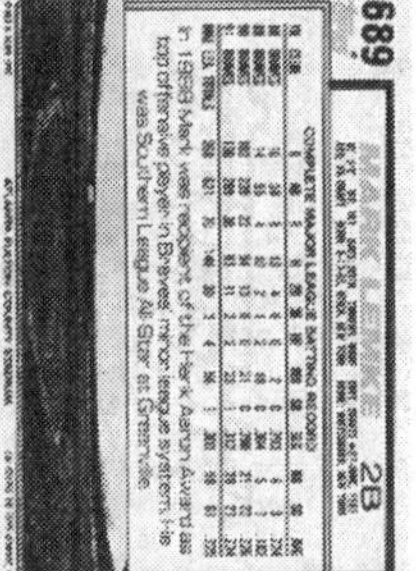

Two versions of each card in the regular Topps set were produced as premium cards with gold-foil enhancements. Topps Gold cards feature the same format as the regular card except the color bars beneath the photo with the player's name and team have been replaced with gold-foil elements. On back, the light blue Topps logo printed under the stats has been replaced with a gold "ToppsGold" logo. Topps Gold cards were random inserts in wax packs. Ten Gold cards were included in each Topps factory set, and complete factory sets of Gold cards were sold.

	MT	NR MT	EX
Complete Set (792):	375.00	225.00	125.00
Brien Taylor (autographed card)	50.00	40.00	20.00
Common Player:	.50	.40	.20
Stars: 5X-10X regular Topps			

1992 Topps Traded

Photos not available at press time

Members of the United States baseball team are featured in this 132-card boxed set released by Topps. The cards are styled after the regular 1992 Topps cards and are numbered alphabetically. Several United States baseball players featured in this set were also featuured in the 1991 Topps Traded set.

	MT	NR MT	EX
Complete Set (132):	15.00	11.00	6.00
Common Player:	.05	.04	.02

		MT	NR MT	EX
1	*Willie Adams* (USA)	.20	.15	.08
2	Jeff Alkire (USA)	1.00	.70	.40
3	Felipe Alou	.05	.04	.02
4	Moises Alou	.30	.25	.12
5	Ruben Amaro(FC)	.10	.08	.04
6	Jack Armstrong	.05	.04	.02

		MT	NR MT	EX
7	Scott Bankhead	.05	.04	.02
8	Tim Belcher	.08	.06	.03
9	George Bell	.08	.06	.03
10	Freddie Benavides(FC)	.12	.09	.05
11	Todd Benzinger	.05	.04	.02
12	Joe Boever	.05	.04	.02
13	Ricky Bones	.10	.08	.04
15	Hubie Brooks	.05	.04	.02
16	Jerry Browne	.05	.04	.02
17	Jim Bullinger	.10	.08	.04
18	Dave Burba	.05	.04	.02
19	Kevin Campbell(FC)	.12	.09	.05
20	Tom Candiotti	.05	.04	.02
21	Mark Carreon	.05	.04	.02
23	Archi Cianfrocco	.30	.25	.12
24	Phil Clark	.10	.08	.04
25	Chad Curtis	1.00	.70	.40
26	Eric Davis	.08	.06	.03
27	Tim Davis (USA)	.20	.15	.08
28	Gary DiSarcina	.05	.04	.02
29	Darren Dreifort (USA)	1.00	.70	.40
30	Mariano Duncan	.05	.04	.02
31	Mike Fitzgerald	.05	.04	.02
32	John Flaherty(FC)	.12	.09	.05
33	Darrin Fletcher	.05	.04	.02
34	Scott Fletcher	.05	.04	.02
35	Ron Fraser (USA)	.08	.06	.03
36	Andres Galarraga	.06	.05	.02
37	Dave Gallagher	.05	.04	.02
38	Mike Gallego	.05	.04	.02
39	Nomar Garciaparra (USA)	.20	.15	.08
40	Jason Giambi (USA)	.75	.60	.30
41	Danny Gladden	.05	.04	.02
42	Rene Gonzales	.05	.04	.02
43	Jeff Granger (USA)	.40	.30	.15
44	Rick Greene (USA)	.20	.15	.08
45	Jeffrey Hammonds (USA)	2.50	2.00	1.00
46	Charlie Hayes	.05	.04	.02
47	Von Hayes	.05	.04	.02
48	Rick Helling (USA)	.75	.60	.30
49	Butch Henry(FC)	.12	.09	.05
50	Carlos Hernandez(FC)	.12	.09	.05
51	Ken Hill	.08	.06	.03
52	Butch Hobson	.05	.04	.02
53	Vince Horsman(FC)	.10	.08	.04
54	Pete Incaviglia	.06	.05	.02
55	Gregg Jefferies	.08	.06	.03
56	Charles Johnson (USA)	.75	.60	.30
57	Doug Jones	.05	.04	.02
58	Brian Jordan	.30	.25	.12
59	Wally Joyner	.08	.06	.03
60	*Daron Kirkreit* (USA)	.20	.15	.08
61	Bill Krueger	.06	.05	.02
62	Gene Lamont	.06	.05	.02
63	Jim Lefebvre	.06	.05	.02
64	*Danny Leon*	.20	.15	.08
65	Pat Listach	.50	.40	.20
66	Kenny Lofton	1.00	.70	.40
67	Dave Martinez	.05	.04	.02
68	Derrick May	.10	.08	.04
69	Kirk McCaskill	.06	.05	.02
70	*Chad McConnell* (USA)	.75	.60	.30
71	Kevin McReynolds	.06	.05	.02
72	Rusty Meacham(FC)	.10	.08	.04
73	Keith Miller	.06	.05	.02
74	Kevin Mitchell	.08	.06	.03
75	*Jason Moler* (USA)	.60	.45	.25
76	Mike Morgan	.06	.05	.02
77	Jack Morris	.08	.06	.03
78	*Calvin Murray* (USA)	1.00	.70	.40
79	Eddie Murray	.08	.06	.03
80	Randy Myers	.06	.05	.02
81	Denny Neagle(FC)	.10	.08	.04
82	Phil Nevin (USA)	1.25	.90	.50
83	Dave Nilsson	.20	.15	.08
84	Junior Ortiz	.05	.04	.02
85	Donovan Osborne	.20	.15	.08
86	Bill Pecota	.05	.04	.02
87	Melido Perez	.05	.04	.02
88	Mike Perez(FC)	.10	.08	.04
89	Hipolito Pena(FC)	.10	.08	.04
90	Willie Randolph	.06	.05	.02
91	Darren Reed(FC)	.12	.09	.05
92	Bip Roberts	.08	.06	.03
93	Chris Roberts (USA)	.60	.45	.25
94	Steve Rodriguez (USA)	.12	.09	.05
95	Bruce Ruffin	.05	.04	.02
96	Scott Ruskin	.05	.04	.02
97	Bret Saberhagen	.08	.06	.03
98	Rey Sanchez(FC)	.12	.09	.05
99	Steve Sax	.08	.06	.03
100	Curt Schilling	.06	.05	.02
101	Dick Schofield	.05	.04	.02
102	Gary Scott	.10	.08	.04
103	Kevin Seitzer	.06	.05	.02
104	Frank Seminara(FC)	.12	.09	.05
105	Gary Sheffield	.30	.25	.12
106	John Smiley	.06	.05	.02
107	Cory Snyder	.06	.05	.02
108	Paul Sorrento	.06	.05	.02
109	Sammy Sosa	.20	.15	.08
110	Matt Stairs	.12	.09	.05
111	Andy Stankiewicz	.20	.15	.08
112	Kurt Stillwell	.06	.05	.02
113	Rick Sutcliffe	.06	.05	.02
114	Bill Swift	.06	.05	.02
115	Jeff Tackett(FC)	.12	.09	.05
116	Danny Tartabull	.08	.06	.03
117	Eddie Taubensee(FC)	.12	.09	.05
118	Dickie Thon	.05	.04	.02
119	*Michael Tucker* (USA)	1.75	1.25	.70
120	Scooter Tucker(FC)	.12	.09	.05
121	*Marc Valdes* (USA)	.20	.15	.08
122	Julio Valera(FC)	.10	.08	.04
123	*Jason Vilaitek* (USA)	.20	.15	.08
124	*Ron Villone* (USA)	.20	.15	.08
125	Frank Viola	.08	.06	.03
126	*B.J. Wallace* (USA)	1.00	.70	.40
127	Dan Walters(FC)	.12	.09	.05
128	Craig Wilson (USA)	.12	.09	.05
129	Chris Wimmer (USA)	.12	.09	.05
130	Dave Winfield	.15	.11	.06
131	Herm Winningham	.05	.04	.02
132	Checklist	.05	.04	.02

1992 Topps Kids

In a market which had increasingly become the province of adult collectors, Topps in 1992 offered an issue unashamedly aimed at the youngster. Called "Topps Kids," the 132-card set featured bright colors, garish graphics and the game's top stars. Sold at 35 cents per pack (with bubble gum), the issue was even priced for the young collector. Unfortunately, the concept was a flop and was not repeated in subsequent years. Card fronts featured player photos, sometimes only the player's head on a cartoon body, against a background of wild designs or cartoon ballplayers in action. Player names at bottom were rendered in superhero comic-book style. Backs featured a few 1991 and career stats, and/or a cartoon or two about the player or baseball trivia.

		MT	NR MT	EX
Complete Set (132):		8.00	6.00	3.25
Common Player:		.05	.04	.02
1	Ryne Sandberg	.25	.20	.10
2	Andre Dawson	.10	.08	.04
3	George Bell	.05	.04	.02
4	Mark Grace	.10	.08	.04
5	Shawon Dunston	.05	.04	.02
6	Tim Wallach	.05	.04	.02
7	Ivan Calderon	.05	.04	.02
8	Marquis Grissom	.05	.04	.02
9	Delino DeShields	.05	.04	.02
10	Denny Martinez	.05	.04	.02
11	Dwight Gooden	.10	.08	.04
12	Howard Johnson	.10	.08	.04
13	John Franco	.05	.04	.02
14	Gregg Jefferies	.15	.11	.06

		MT	NR MT	EX
15	Kevin McReynolds	.05	.04	.02
16	David Cone	.05	.04	.02
17	Len Dykstra	.10	.08	.04
18	John Kruk	.10	.08	.04
19	Von Hayes	.05	.04	.02
20	Mitch Williams	.05	.04	.02
21	Barry Bonds	.20	.15	.08
22	Bobby Bonilla	.10	.08	.04
23	Andy Van Slyke	.10	.08	.04
24	Doug Drabek	.05	.04	.02
25	Ozzie Smith	.20	.15	.08
26	Pedro Guerrero	.05	.04	.02
27	Todd Zelle	.05	.04	.02
28	Lee Smith	.05	.04	.02
29	Felix Jose	.05	.04	.02
30	Jose DeLeon	.05	.04	.02
31	David Justice	.15	.11	.06
32	Ron Gant	.10	.08	.04
33	Terry Pendleton	.05	.04	.02
34	Tom Glavine	.05	.04	.02
35	Otis Nixon	.05	.04	.02
36	Steve Avery	.10	.08	.04
37	Barry Larkin	.10	.08	.04
38	Eric Davis	.15	.11	.06
39	Chris Sabo	.10	.08	.04
40	Rob Dibble	.05	.04	.02
41	Paul O'Neill	.10	.08	.04
42	Jose Rijo	.10	.08	.04
43	Craig Biggio	.05	.04	.02
44	Jeff Bagwell	.10	.08	.04
45	Ken Caminiti	.05	.04	.02
46	Steve Finley	.05	.04	.02
47	Darryl Strawberry	.15	.11	.06
48	Ramon Martinez	.05	.04	.02
49	Brett Butler	.05	.04	.02
50	Eddie Murray	.15	.11	.06
51	Kal Daniels	.05	.04	.02
52	Orel Hershiser	.10	.08	.04
53	Tony Gwynn	.15	.11	.06
54	Benny Santiago	.05	.04	.02
55	Fred McGriff	.10	.08	.04
56	Bip Roberts	.05	.04	.02
57	Tony Fernandez	.05	.04	.02
58	Will Clark	.20	.15	.08
59	Kevin Mitchell	.05	.04	.02
60	Matt Williams	.10	.08	.04
61	Willie McGee	.05	.04	.02
62	Dave Righetti	.05	.04	.02
63	Cal Ripken, Jr.	.25	.20	.10
64	Ben McDonald	.05	.04	.02
65	Glenn Davis	.05	.04	.02
66	Gregg Olson	.05	.04	.02
67	Roger Clemens	.15	.11	.06
68	Wade Boggs	.20	.15	.08
69	Mike Greenwell	.10	.08	.04
70	Ellis Burks	.05	.04	.02
71	Sandy Alomar	.05	.04	.02
72	Greg Swindell	.05	.04	.02
73	Albert Belle	.10	.08	.04
74	Mark Whiten	.05	.04	.02
75	Alan Trammell	.15	.11	.06
76	Cecil Fielder	.20	.15	.08
77	Lou Whitaker	.10	.08	.04
78	Travis Fryman	.10	.08	.04
79	Tony Phillips	.05	.04	.02
80	Robin Yount	.20	.15	.08
81	Paul Molitor	.15	.11	.06
82	B.J. Surhoff	.05	.04	.02
83	Greg Vaughn	.05	.04	.02
84	Don Mattingly	.20	.15	.08
85	Steve Sax	.05	.04	.02
86	Kevin Maas	.05	.04	.02
87	Mel Hall	.05	.04	.02
88	Roberto Kelly	.10	.08	.04
89	Joe Carter	.10	.08	.04
90	Roberto Alomar	.15	.11	.06
91	Dave Stieb	.05	.04	.02
92	Kelly Gruber	.05	.04	.02
93	Tom Henke	.05	.04	.02
94	Chuck Finley	.05	.04	.02
95	Wally Joyner	.10	.08	.04
96	Dave Winfield	.20	.15	.08
97	Jim Abbott	.15	.11	.06
98	Mark Langston	.05	.04	.02
99	Frank Thomas	.35	.25	.14
100	Ozzie Guillen	.05	.04	.02
101	Bobby Thigpen	.05	.04	.02
102	Robin Ventura	.10	.08	.04
103	Bo Jackson	.20	.15	.08
104	Tim Raines	.10	.08	.04
105	George Brett	.20	.15	.08

		MT	NR MT	EX
106	Danny Tartabull	.10	.08	.04
107	Bret Saberhagen	.05	.04	.02
108	Brian McRae	.05	.04	.02
109	Kirby Puckett	.20	.15	.08
110	Scott Erickson	.05	.04	.02
111	Kent Hrbek	.10	.08	.04
112	Chuck Knoblauch	.05	.04	.02
113	Chili Davis	.10	.08	.04
114	Rick Aguilera	.05	.04	.02
115	Jose Canseco	.20	.15	.08
116	Dave Henderson	.05	.04	.02
117	Dave Stewart	.10	.08	.04
118	Rickey Henderson	.15	.11	.06
119	Dennis Eckersley	.10	.08	.04
120	Harold Baines	.05	.04	.02
121	Mark McGwire	.20	.15	.08
122	Ken Griffey, Jr.	.35	.25	.14
123	Harold Reynolds	.05	.04	.02
124	Erik Hanson	.05	.04	.02
125	Edgar Martinez	.10	.08	.04
126	Randy Johnson	.10	.08	.04
127	Nolan Ryan	.35	.25	.14
128	Ruben Sierra	.15	.11	.06
129	Julio Franco	.05	.04	.02
130	Rafael Palmeiro	.10	.08	.04
131	Juan Gonzalez	.20	.15	.08
132	Checklist	.05	.04	.02

1992 Topps Triple Header Photo Balls

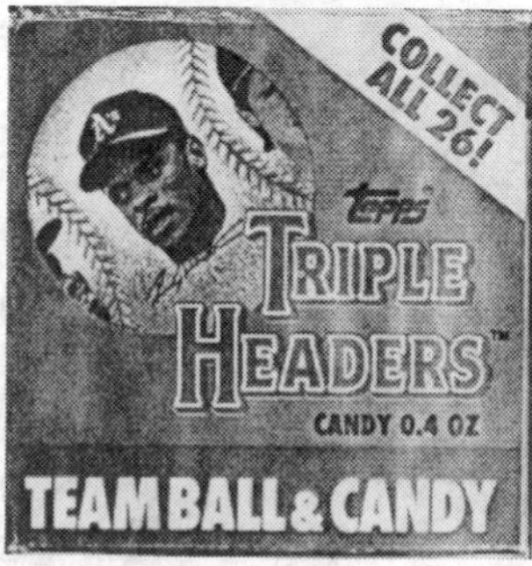

Picture a slightly oversize ping pong ball painted like a baseball with the heads and facsimile autographs of three different players on it and you've got the idea behind the Triple Headers test issue. Very limited in distribution, the team balls were sold in a small box with a package of candy.

	MT	NR MT	EX
Complete set (26):	75.00	56.00	30.00
Common ball:	3.00	2.25	1.25
(1) California Angels (Chuck Finley/ Dave Winfield/ Wally Joyner)	3.00	2.25	1.25
(2) Houston Astros (Jeff Bagwell/ Craig Biggio/ Ken Caminiti)	3.00	2.25	1.25
(3) Oakland Athletics (Jose Canseco/ Dave Henderson/ Rickey Henderson)	4.00	3.00	1.50
(4) Toronto Blue Jays (Roberto Alomar/ Kelly Gruber/ Joe Carter)	3.50	2.75	1.50
(5) Atlanta Braves (Ron Gant/ Tom Glavine/ Dave Justice)	3.50	2.75	1.50
(6) Milwaukee Brewers (Paul Molitor/ Robin Yount/ Greg Vaughn)	3.50	2.75	1.50
(7) St. Louis Cardinals (Pedro Guerrero/ Ozzie Smith/ Todd Zeile)	3.00	2.25	1.25
(8) Chicago Cubs (Ryne Sandberg/ George Bell/ Mark Grace)	5.00	3.75	2.00
(9) Los Angeles Dodgers (Ramon Martinez/ Eddie Murray/ Darryl Strawberry)	3.00	2.25	1.25
(10) Montreal Expos (Delino DeShields/ Dennis Martinez/ Ivan Calderon)	3.00	2.25	1.25
(11) San Francisco Giants (Will Clark/ Kevin Mitchell/ Matt Williams)	3.50	2.75	1.50
(12) Cleveland Indians (Sandy Alomar, Jr./ Alex Cole/ Mark Lewis)	3.00	2.25	1.25
(13) Seattle Mariners (Ken Griffey, Jr./ Harold Reynolds/ Ken Griffey Sr.)	5.00	3.75	2.00

	MT	NR MT	EX
(14) New York Mets (Vince Coleman/ Dwight Gooden/ Howard Johnson)	3.00	2.25	1.25
(15) Baltimore Orioles (Ben McDonald/ Cal Ripken, Jr./ Gregg Olson)	5.00	3.75	2.00
(16) San Diego Padres (Fred McGriff/ Tony Gwynn/ Benito Santiago)	3.00	2.25	1.25
(17) Philadelphia Phillies (Len Dykstra/ John Kruk/ Dale Murphy)	3.00	2.25	1.25
(18) Pittsburgh Pirates (Barry Bonds/ Bobby Bonilla/ Andy Van Slyke)	3.50	2.75	1.50
(19) Cincinnati Reds (Eric Davis/ Barry Larkin Chris Sabo)	3.00	2.25	1.25
(20) Boston Red Sox (Wade Boggs/ Mike Greenwell/ Roger Clemens)	3.50	2.75	1.50
(21) Kansas City Royals (George Brett/ Danny Tartabull/ Bret Saberhagen)	3.50	2.75	1.50
(22) Texas Rangers (Julio Franco/ Nolan Ryan Juan Gonzalez)	5.00	3.75	2.00
(23) Minnesota Twins (Scott Erickson/ Kirby Puckett/ Kent Hrbek)	3.50	2.75	1.50
(24) Detroit Tigers (Cecil Fielder/ Tony Phillips Alan Trammell)	3.00	2.25	1.25
(25) Chicago White Sox (Carlton Fisk/ Robin Ventura/ Frank Thomas)	5.00	3.75	2.00
(26) New York Yankees (Don Mattingly/ Steve Sax/ Willie Randolph)	3.50	2.75	1.50

1992 Topps Stadium Club Dome

This 200-card special Stadium Club set from Topps was uniquely packaged in a plastic replica of the Toronto Sky-Dome, the home of the 1991 All-Star Game. Featured in the set are members of Team USA, All-Stars, draft picks, top prospects and highlight cards from the World Series between the Twins and Braves. The cards are styled much like the regular Stadium Club cards.

		MT	NR MT	EX
Complete Set (200):		40.00	30.00	15.00
Common Player:		.20	.15	.08
1	Terry Adams	.30	.25	.12
2	Tommy Adams	.40	.30	.15
3	Rick Aguilera	.20	.15	.08
4	Ron Allen	.25	.20	.10
5	Roberto Alomar (AS)	.60	.45	.25
6	Sandy Alomar	.25	.20	.10
7	Greg Anthony	.40	.30	.15
8	James Austin	.25	.20	.10
9	Steve Avery	.40	.30	.15
10	Harold Baines	.20	.15	.08
11	Brian Barber	.80	.60	.30
12	Jon Barnes	.25	.20	.10
13	George Bell	.20	.15	.08
14	Doug Bennett	.25	.20	.10
15	Sean Bergman	.25	.20	.10
16	Bill Bliss	.25	.20	.10
17	Craig Biggio	.20	.15	.08
18	Wade Boggs (AS)	.20	.15	.08
19	Bobby Bonilla (AS)	.15	.11	.06
20	Russell Brock	.30	.25	.12
21	Tarrik Brock	.30	.25	.12
22	Tom Browning	.20	.15	.08
23	Brett Butler	.20	.15	.08
24	Ivan Calderon	.20	.15	.08
25	Joe Carter	.20	.15	.08
26	Joe Caruso	.25	.20	.10
27	Dan Cholowsky	.40	.30	.15
28	Will Clark (AS)	.30	.25	.12
29	Roger Clemens (AS)	.40	.30	.15
30	Shawn Curran	.25	.20	.10
31	Chris Curtis	.20	.15	.08
32	Chili Davis	.20	.15	.08
33	Andre Dawson	.20	.15	.08
34	Joe DeBerry	.25	.20	.10
35	John Dettmer	.40	.30	.15
36	Rob Dibble	.20	.15	.08
37	John Donati	.30	.25	.12
38	Dave Doorneweerd	.25	.20	.10
39	Darren Dreifort	1.50	1.25	.60
40	Mike Durant	.30	.25	.12
41	Chris Durkin	.30	.25	.12
42	Dennis Eckersley	.30	.25	.12
43	Brian Edmondson	.30	.25	.12
44	Vaughn Eshelman	.25	.20	.10
45	Shawn Estes	.35	.25	.14
46	Jorge Fabregas	.40	.30	.15
47	Jon Farrell	.35	.25	.14
48	Cecil Fielder (AS)	.25	.20	.10
49	Carlton Fisk	.20	.15	.08
50	Tim Flannelly	.25	.20	.10
51	Cliff Floyd	10.00	7.50	4.00
52	Julio Franco	.20	.15	.08
53	Greg Gagne	.20	.15	.08
54	Chris Gambs	.30	.25	.12
55	Ron Gant (NLCS)	.40	.30	.15
56	Brent Gates	1.50	1.25	.60
57	Dwayne Gerald	.30	.25	.12
58	Jason Giambi	.70	.50	.30
59	Benji Gil	1.00	.70	.40
60	Mark Gipner	.30	.25	.12
61	Danny Gladden	.20	.15	.08
62	Tom Glavine	.25	.20	.10
63	Jimmy Gonzalez	.25	.20	.10
64	Jeff Granger	1.50	1.25	.60
65	Dan Grapenthien	.25	.20	.10
66	Dennis Gray	.25	.20	.10
67	Shawn Green	.75	.60	.30
68	Tyler Green	.60	.45	.25
69	Todd Greene	.50	.40	.20
70	Ken Griffey, Jr. (AS)	2.00	1.50	.80
71	Kelly Gruber	.20	.15	.08
72	Ozzie Guillen	.20	.15	.08
73	Tony Gwynn (AS)	.30	.25	.12
74	Shane Halter	.25	.20	.10
75	Jeffrey Hammonds	6.00	4.50	2.50
76	Larry Hanlon	.25	.20	.10
77	Pete Harnisch	.20	.15	.08
78	Mike Harrison	.25	.20	.10
79	Bryan Harvey	.20	.15	.08
80	Scott Hatteberg	.60	.45	.25
81	Rick Helling	.30	.25	.12
82	Dave Henderson	.20	.15	.08
83	Rickey Henderson (AS)	.35	.25	.14
84	Tyrone Hill	1.00	.70	.40
85	Todd Hollandsworth	.60	.45	.25
86	Brian Holliday	.25	.20	.10
87	Terry Horn	.25	.20	.10
88	Jeff Hostetler	.30	.25	.12
89	Kent Hrbek	.20	.15	.08
90	Mark Hubbard	.25	.20	.10
91	Charles Johnson	2.00	1.50	.80
92	Howard Johnson	.20	.15	.08
93	Todd Johnson	.40	.30	.15
94	Bobby Jones	1.00	.70	.40
95	Dan Jones	.25	.20	.10
96	Felix Jose	.20	.15	.08
97	Dave Justice (WS)	.70	.50	.30
98	Jimmy Key	.20	.15	.08
99	Marc Kroom	.25	.20	.10
100	John Kruk	.20	.15	.08
101	Mark Langston	.20	.15	.08
102	Barry Larkin	.20	.15	.08
103	Mike LaValliere	.20	.15	.08
104	Scott Leius	.20	.15	.08
105	Mark Lemke	.20	.15	.08
106	Donnie Leshnock	.40	.30	.15
107	Jimmy Lewis	.25	.20	.10
108	Shawn Livesy	.40	.30	.15
109	Ryan Long	.40	.30	.15
110	Trevor Mallory	.25	.20	.10
111	Denny Martinez	.20	.15	.08
112	Justin Mashore	.25	.20	.10
113	Jason McDonald	.25	.20	.10
114	Jack McDowell	.25	.20	.10
115	Tom McKinnon	.35	.25	.14
116	Billy McKinnon	.25	.20	.10
117	Buck McNabb	.25	.20	.10

		MT	NR MT	EX
118	Jim Mecir	.25	.20	.10
119	Dan Melendez	.25	.20	.10
120	Shawn Miller	.25	.20	.10
121	Trever Miller	.25	.20	.10
122	Paul Molitor	.40	.30	.15
123	Vincent Moore	.25	.20	.10
124	Mike Morgan	.20	.15	.08
125	Jack Morris	.20	.15	.08
126	Jack Morris	.20	.15	.08
127	Sean Mulligan	.25	.20	.10
128	Eddie Murray	.25	.20	.10
129	Mike Neill	.60	.45	.25
130	Phil Nevin	4.00	3.00	1.50
131	Mark O'Brien	.25	.20	.10
132	Alex Ochoa	.25	.20	.10
133	Chad Ogea	.25	.20	.10
134	Greg Olson	.20	.15	.08
135	Paul O'Neill	.20	.15	.08
136	Jared Osentowski	.30	.25	.12
137	Mike Pagliarulo	.20	.15	.08
138	Rafael Palmeiro	.20	.15	.08
139	Rodney Pedraza	.25	.20	.10
140	Tony Phillips	.25	.20	.10
141	Scott Pisciotta	.30	.25	.12
142	Chris Pritchett	.30	.25	.12
143	Jason Pruitt	.25	.20	.10
144	Kirby Puckett (WS)	.60	.45	.25
145	Kirby Puckett (AS)	.60	.45	.25
146	Manny Ramirez	3.50	2.75	1.50
147	Eddie Ramos	.30	.25	.12
148	Mark Ratekin	.30	.25	.12
149	Jeff Reardon	.20	.15	.08
150	Sean Rees	.25	.20	.10
151	Calvin Reese	.80	.60	.30
152	Desmond Relaford	.25	.20	.10
153	Eric Richardson	.25	.20	.10
154	Cal Ripken, Jr. (AS)	.75	.60	.30
155	Chris Roberts	1.00	.70	.40
156	Mike Robertson	.35	.25	.14
157	Steve Rodriguez	.35	.25	.14
158	Mike Rossiter	.30	.25	.12
159	Scott Ruffcorn	1.50	1.25	.60
160	Chris Sabo	.20	.15	.08
161	Juan Samuel	.20	.15	.08
162	Ryne Sandberg (AS)	.75	.60	.30
163	Scott Sanderson	.20	.15	.08
164	Benito Santiago	.20	.15	.08
165	Gene Schall	.30	.25	.12
166	Chad Schoenvogel	.30	.25	.12
167	Chris Seelbach	.30	.25	.12
168	Aaron Sele	5.00	3.75	2.00
169	Basil Shabazz	.50	.40	.20
170	Al Shirley	1.00	.70	.40
171	Paul Shuey	.60	.45	.25
172	Ruben Sierra	.25	.20	.10
173	John Smiley	.30	.25	.12
174	Lee Smith	.30	.25	.12
175	Ozzie Smith	.30	.25	.12
176	Tim Smith	.25	.20	.10
177	Zane Smith	.20	.15	.08
178	John Smoltz	.20	.15	.08
179	Scott Stahoviak	.40	.30	.15
180	Kennie Steenstra	.60	.45	.25
181	Kevin Stocker	.20	.15	.08
182	Chris Stynes	.20	.15	.08
183	Danny Tartabull	.20	.15	.08
184	Brien Taylor	5.00	3.75	2.00
185	Todd Taylor	.30	.25	.12
186	Larry Thomas	.30	.25	.12
187	Ozzie Timmons	.30	.25	.12
188	David Tuttle	.30	.25	.12
189	Andy Van Slyke	.20	.15	.08
190	Frank Viola	.20	.15	.08
191	Michael Walkden	.30	.25	.12
192	Jeff Ware	.25	.20	.10
193	Allen Watson	3.50	2.75	1.50
194	Steve Whitaker	.40	.30	.15
195	Jerry Willard	.20	.15	.08
196	Craig Wilson	.25	.20	.10
197	Chris Wimmer	.25	.20	.10
198	Steve Wojciechowski	.30	.25	.12
199	Joel Wolfe	.25	.20	.10
200	Ivan Zweig	.50	.40	.20

Definitions for grading conditions are located in the Introduction of this price guide.

1992 Topps Stadium Club

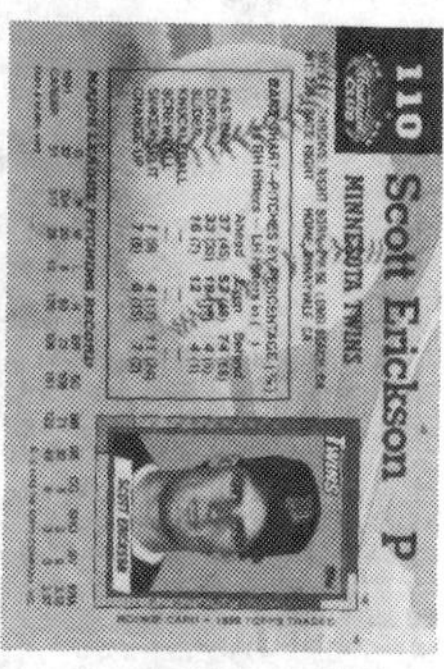

This 900-card set was released in three 300-card series. Like the 1991 issue, the cards feature borderless high gloss photos on the front. The flip sides feature the player's first Topps card and a player evaluation. Topps released updated cards in the third series for traded player and free agents. Several players appear on two cards. Special Members Choice cards are included in the set. Series III featured special inserts of the last three number one picks overall, Phil Nevin, Brien Taylor and Chipper Jones.

		MT	NR MT	EX
Complete Set (900):		70.00	50.00	30.00
Common Player:		.12	.09	.05
1	Cal Ripken, Jr.	1.00	.70	.40
2	Eric Yelding	.12	.09	.05
3	Geno Petralli	.12	.09	.05
4	Wally Backman	.12	.09	.05
5	Milt Cuyler	.12	.09	.05
6	Kevin Bass	.12	.09	.05
7	Dante Bichette	.12	.09	.05
8	Ray Lankford	.50	.40	.20
9	Mel Hall	.15	.11	.06
10	Joe Carter	.30	.25	.12
11	Juan Samuel	.12	.09	.05
12	Jeff Motngomery	.15	.11	.06
13	Glenn Braggs	.15	.11	.06
14	Henry Cotto	.12	.09	.05
15	Deion Sanders	.30	.25	.12
16	Dick Schofield	.12	.09	.05
17	David Cone	.20	.15	.08
18	Chili Davis	.20	.15	.08
19	Tom Foley	.12	.09	.05
20	Ozzie Guillen	.15	.11	.06
21	Luis Salazar	.12	.09	.05
22	Terry Steinbach	.15	.11	.06
23	Chris James	.12	.09	.05
24	Jeff King	.12	.09	.05
25	Carlos Quintana	.12	.09	.05
26	Mike Maddux	.12	.09	.05
27	Tommy Greene	.15	.11	.06
28	Jeff Russell	.15	.11	.06
29	Steve Finley	.20	.15	.08
30	Mike Flanagan	.12	.09	.05
31	Darren Lewis	.12	.09	.05
32	Mark Lee	.12	.09	.05
33	Willie Fraser	.12	.09	.05
34	Mike Henneman	.15	.11	.06
35	Kevin Maas	.30	.25	.12
36	Dave Hansen	.25	.20	.10
37	Erik Hanson	.12	.09	.05
38	Bill Doran	.12	.09	.05
39	Mike Boddicker	.12	.09	.05
40	Vince Coleman	.15	.11	.06
41	Devon White	.15	.11	.06
42	Mark Gardner	.12	.09	.05
43	Scott Lewis	.10	.08	.04
44	Juan Berenguer	.12	.09	.05

Regional interest may affect the value of a card.

		MT	NR MT	EX
45	Carney Lansford	.12	.09	.05
46	Curt Wilkerson	.12	.09	.05
47	Shane Mack	.15	.11	.06
48	Bip Roberts	.15	.11	.06
49	Greg Harris	.12	.09	.05
50	Ryne Sandberg	1.00	.70	.40
51	Mark Whiten	.30	.25	.12
52	Jack McDowell	.20	.15	.08
53	Jimmy Jones	.12	.09	.05
54	Steve Lake	.12	.09	.05
55	Bud Black	.12	.09	.05
56	Dave Valle	.12	.09	.05
57	Kevin Reimer	.12	.09	.05
58	Rich Gedman	.12	.09	.05
59	Travis Fryman	1.50	1.25	.60
60	Steve Avery	.75	.60	.30
61	Francisco DeLaRosa	.25	.20	.10
62	Scott Hemond	.12	.09	.05
63	Hal Morris	.12	.09	.05
64	Hensley Meulens	.12	.09	.05
65	Frank Castillo	.25	.20	.10
66	Gene Larkin	.12	.09	.05
67	Jose DeLeon	.12	.09	.05
68	Al Osuna	.12	.09	.05
69	Dave Cochrane	.12	.09	.05
70	Robin Ventura	1.00	.70	.40
71	John Cerutti	.12	.09	.05
72	Kevin Gross	.12	.09	.05
73	Ivan Calderon	.15	.11	.06
74	Mike Macfarlane	.12	.09	.05
75	Stan Belinda	.12	.09	.05
76	Shawn Hillegas	.12	.09	.05
77	Pat Borders	.12	.09	.05
78	Jim Vatcher	.12	.09	.05
79	Bobby Rose	.12	.09	.05
80	Roger Clemens	.80	.60	.30
81	Craig Worthington	.12	.09	.05
82	Jeff Treadway	.12	.09	.05
83	Jamie Quirk	.12	.09	.05
84	Randy Bush	.12	.09	.05
85	Anthony Young	.10	.08	.04
86	Trevor Wilson	.12	.09	.05
87	Jaime Navarro	.15	.11	.06
88	Les Lancaster	.12	.09	.05
89	Pat Kelly	.15	.11	.06
90	Alvin Davis	.12	.09	.05
91	Larry Andersen	.12	.09	.05
92	Rob Deer	.12	.09	.05
93	Mike Sharperson	.12	.09	.05
94	Lance Parrish	.12	.09	.05
95	Cecil Espy	.12	.09	.05
96	Tim Spehr	.15	.11	.06
97	Dave Stieb	.15	.11	.06
98	Terry Mulholland	.15	.11	.06
99	Dennis Boyd	.12	.09	.05
100	Barry Larkin	.30	.25	.12
101	Ryan Bowen	.12	.09	.05
102	Felix Fermin	.12	.09	.05
103	Luis Alicea	.12	.09	.05
104	Tim Hulett	.12	.09	.05
105	Rafael Belliard	.12	.09	.05
106	Mike Gallego	.12	.09	.05
107	Dave Righetti	.12	.09	.05
108	Jeff Schaefer	.12	.09	.05
109	Ricky Bones	.10	.08	.04
110	Scott Erickson	.10	.08	.04
111	Matt Nokes	.12	.09	.05
112	Bob Scanlan	.12	.09	.05
113	Tom Candiotti	.15	.11	.06
114	Sean Berry	.15	.11	.06
115	Kevin Morton	.30	.25	.12
116	Scott Fletcher	.12	.09	.05
117	B.J. Surhoff	.12	.09	.05
118	Dave Magadan	.12	.09	.05
119	Bill Gullickson	.12	.09	.05
120	Marquis Grissom	.25	.20	.10
121	Lenny Harris	.12	.09	.05
122	Wally Joyner	.20	.15	.08
123	Kevin Brown	.15	.11	.06
124	Braulio Castillo	.20	.15	.08
125	Eric King	.12	.09	.05
126	Mark Portugal	.12	.09	.05
127	Calvin Jones	.10	.08	.04
128	Mike Heath	.12	.09	.05
129	Todd Van Poppel	.50	.40	.20
130	Benny Santiago	.15	.11	.06
131	Gary Thurman	.12	.09	.05
132	Joe Girardi	.12	.09	.05
133	Dave Eiland	.12	.09	.05
134	Orlando Merced	.50	.40	.20
135	Joe Orsulak	.12	.09	.05

		MT	NR MT	EX
136	John Burkett	.12	.09	.05
137	Ken Dayley	.12	.09	.05
138	Ken Hill	.15	.11	.06
139	Walt Terrell	.12	.09	.05
140	Mike Scioscia	.12	.09	.05
141	Junior Felix	.12	.09	.05
142	Ken Caminiti	.12	.09	.05
143	Carlos Baerga	1.00	.70	.40
144	Tony Fossas	.12	.09	.05
145	Craig Grebeck	.12	.09	.05
146	Scott Bradley	.12	.09	.05
147	Kent Mercker	.12	.09	.05
148	Derrick May	.20	.15	.08
149	Jerald Clark	.15	.11	.06
150	George Brett	.40	.30	.15
151	Luis Quinones	.15	.11	.06
152	Mike Pagliarulo	.15	.11	.06
153	Jose Guzman	.15	.11	.06
154	Charlie O'Brien	.15	.11	.06
155	Darren Holmes	.15	.11	.06
156	Joe Boever	.15	.11	.06
157	Rich Monteleone	.15	.11	.06
158	Reggie Harris	.15	.11	.06
159	Roberto Alomar	1.00	.70	.40
160	Robby Thompson	.15	.11	.06
161	Chris Hoiles	.25	.20	.10
162	Tom Pagnozzi	.12	.09	.05
163	Omar Vizquel	.12	.09	.05
164	John Candelaria	.12	.09	.05
165	Terry Shumpert	.12	.09	.05
166	Andy Mota	.25	.20	.10
167	Scott Bailes	.12	.09	.05
168	Jeff Blauser	.12	.09	.05
169	Steve Olin	.12	.09	.05
170	Doug Drabek	.20	.15	.08
171	Dave Bergman	.12	.09	.05
172	Eddie Whitson	.12	.09	.05
173	Gilberto Reyes	.12	.09	.05
174	Mark Grace	.25	.20	.10
175	Paul O'Neill	.15	.11	.06
176	Greg Cadaret	.12	.09	.05
177	Mark Williamson	.12	.09	.05
178	Casey Candaele	.12	.09	.05
179	Candy Maldonado	.12	.09	.05
180	Lee Smith	.15	.11	.06
181	Harold Reynolds	.12	.09	.05
182	Dave Justice	1.25	.90	.50
183	Lenny Webster	.12	.09	.05
184	Donn Pall	.12	.09	.05
185	Gerald Alexander	.12	.09	.05
186	Jack Clark	.12	.09	.05
187	Stan Javier	.12	.09	.05
188	Ricky Jordan	.15	.11	.06
189	Franklin Stubbs	.12	.09	.05
190	Dennis Eckersley	.25	.20	.10
191	Danny Tartabull	.20	.15	.08
192	Pete O'Brien	.12	.09	.05
193	Mark Lewis	.10	.08	.04
194	Mike Felder	.12	.09	.05
195	Mickey Tettleton	.15	.11	.06
196	Dwight Smith	.12	.09	.05
197	Shawn Abner	.12	.09	.05
198	Jim Leyritz	.12	.09	.05
199	Mike Devereaux	.20	.15	.08
200	Craig Biggio	.15	.11	.06
201	Kevin Elster	.12	.09	.05
202	Rance Mulliniks	.12	.09	.05
203	Tony Fernandez	.15	.11	.06
204	Allan Anderson	.12	.09	.05
205	Herm Winningham	.12	.09	.05
206	Tim Jones	.12	.09	.05
207	Ramon Martinez	.10	.08	.04
208	Teddy Higuera	.12	.09	.05
209	John Kruk	.15	.11	.06
210	Jim Abbott	.30	.25	.12
211	Dean Palmer	1.00	.70	.40
212	Mark Davis	.12	.09	.05
213	Jay Buhner	.12	.09	.05
214	Jesse Barfield	.12	.09	.05
215	Kevin Mitchell	.15	.11	.06
216	Mike LaValliere	.15	.11	.06
217	Mark Wohlers	.10	.08	.04
218	Dave Henderson	.15	.11	.06
219	Dave Smith	.12	.09	.05
220	Albert Belle	.90	.70	.35
221	Spike Owen	.12	.09	.05
222	Jeff Gray	.12	.09	.05
223	Paul Gibson	.12	.09	.05
224	Bobby Thigpen	.15	.11	.06
225	Mike Mussina	2.00	1.50	.80
226	Darrin Jackson	.12	.09	.05

		MT	NR MT	EX
227	Luis Gonzalez	.10	.08	.04
228	Greg Briley	.12	.09	.05
229	Brent Mayne	.12	.09	.05
230	Paul Molitor	.30	.25	.12
231	Al Leiter	.12	.09	.05
232	Andy Van Slyke	.15	.11	.06
233	Ron Tingley	.12	.09	.05
234	Bernard Gilkey	.15	.11	.06
235	Kent Hrbek	.15	.11	.06
236	Eric Karros	1.50	1.25	.60
237	Randy Velarde	.12	.09	.05
238	Andy Allanson	.12	.09	.05
239	Willie McGee	.15	.11	.06
240	Juan Gonzalez	4.50	3.50	1.75
241	Karl Rhodes	.12	.09	.05
242	Luis Mercedes	.20	.15	.08
243	Billy Swift	.15	.11	.06
244	Tommy Gregg	.12	.09	.05
245	David Howard	.12	.09	.05
246	Dave Hollins	.50	.40	.20
247	Kip Gross	.10	.08	.04
248	Walt Weiss	.12	.09	.05
249	Mackey Sasser	.12	.09	.05
250	Cecil Fielder	.50	.40	.20
251	Jerry Browne	.12	.09	.05
252	Doug Dascenzo	.12	.09	.05
253	Darryl Hamilton	.12	.09	.05
254	Dann Bilardello	.12	.09	.05
255	Luis Rivera	.12	.09	.05
256	Larry Walker	.30	.25	.12
257	Ron Karkovice	.12	.09	.05
258	Bob Tewksbury	.15	.11	.06
259	Jimmy Key	.15	.11	.06
260	Bernie Williams	.20	.15	.08
261	Gary Wayne	.12	.09	.05
262	Mike Simms	.12	.09	.05
263	John Orton	.12	.09	.05
264	Marvin Freeman	.12	.09	.05
265	Mike Jeffcoat	.12	.09	.05
266	Roger Mason	.12	.09	.05
267	Edgar Martinez	.20	.15	.08
268	Henry Rodriguez	.20	.15	.08
269	Sam Horn	.12	.09	.05
270	Brian McRae	.30	.25	.12
271	Kirt Manwaring	.12	.09	.05
272	Mike Bordick	.15	.11	.06
273	Chris Sabo	.15	.11	.06
274	Jim Olander	.12	.09	.05
275	Greg Harris	.12	.09	.05
276	Dan Gakeler	.12	.09	.05
277	Bill Sampen	.12	.09	.05
278	Joel Skinner	.12	.09	.05
279	Curt Schilling	.12	.09	.05
280	Dale Murphy	.25	.20	.10
281	Lee Stevens	.12	.09	.05
282	Lonnie Smith	.12	.09	.05
283	Manuel Lee	.12	.09	.05
284	Shawn Boskie	.12	.09	.05
285	Kevin Seitzer	.12	.09	.05
286	Stan Royer	.15	.11	.06
287	John Dopson	.12	.09	.05
288	Scott Bullett	.35	.25	.14
289	Ken Patterson	.12	.09	.05
290	Todd Hundley	.15	.11	.06
291	Tim Leary	.12	.09	.05
292	Brett Butler	.12	.09	.05
293	Gregg Olson	.15	.11	.06
294	Jeff Brantley	.12	.09	.05
295	Brian Holman	.12	.09	.05
296	Brian Harper	.15	.11	.06
297	Brian Bohanon	.15	.11	.06
298	Checklist 1-100	.15	.11	.06
299	Checklist 101-200	.15	.11	.06
300	Checklist 201-300	.15	.11	.06
301	Frank Thomas	6.00	4.50	2.50
302	Lloyd McClendon	.15	.11	.06
303	Brady Anderson	.20	.15	.08
304	Julio Valera	.15	.11	.06
305	Mike Aldrete	.15	.11	.06
306	Joe Oliver	.15	.11	.06
307	Todd Stottlemyre	.15	.11	.06
308	Rey Sanchez	.15	.11	.06
309	Gary Sheffield	.60	.45	.25
310	Andujar Cedeno	.30	.25	.12
311	Kenny Rogers	.12	.09	.05
312	Bruce Hurst	.15	.11	.06
313	Mike Schooler	.12	.09	.05
314	Mike Benjamin	.12	.09	.05
315	Chuck Finley	.15	.11	.06
316	Mark Lemke	.12	.09	.05
317	Scott Livingstone	.15	.11	.06

		MT	NR MT	EX
318	Chris Nabholz	.12	.09	.05
319	Mike Humphreys	.15	.11	.06
320	Pedro Guerrero	.15	.11	.06
321	Willie Banks	.15	.11	.06
322	Tom Goodwin	.15	.11	.06
323	Hector Wagner	.10	.08	.04
324	Wally Ritchie	.12	.09	.05
325	Mo Vaughn	1.50	1.25	.60
326	Joe Klink	.12	.09	.05
327	Cal Eldred	.60	.45	.25
328	Daryl Boston	.12	.09	.05
329	Mike Huff	.12	.09	.05
330	Jeff Bagwell	1.50	1.25	.60
331	Bob Milacki	.12	.09	.05
332	Tom Prince	.12	.09	.05
333	Pat Tabler	.12	.09	.05
334	Ced Landrum	.12	.09	.05
335	Reggie Jefferson	.30	.25	.12
336	Mo Sanford	.35	.25	.14
337	Kevin Ritz	.12	.09	.05
338	Gerald Perry	.12	.09	.05
339	Jeff Hamilton	.12	.09	.05
340	Tim Wallach	.15	.11	.06
341	Jeff Huson	.15	.11	.06
342	Jose Melendez	.15	.11	.06
343	Willie Wilson	.15	.11	.06
344	Mike Stanton	.12	.09	.05
345	Joel Johnston	.15	.11	.06
346	Lee Guetterman	.12	.09	.05
347	Francisco Olivares	.12	.09	.05
348	Dave Burba	.12	.09	.05
349	Tim Crews	.12	.09	.05
350	Scott Leius	.15	.11	.06
351	Danny Cox	.12	.09	.05
352	Wayne Housie	.35	.25	.14
353	Chris Donnels	.10	.08	.04
354	Chris George	.10	.08	.04
355	Gerald Young	.12	.09	.05
356	Roberto Hernandez	.15	.11	.06
357	Neal Heaton	.12	.09	.05
358	Todd Frohwirth	.12	.09	.05
359	Jose Vizcaino	.12	.09	.05
360	Jim Thome	.75	.60	.30
361	Craig Wilson	.12	.09	.05
362	Dave Haas	.10	.08	.04
363	Billy Hatcher	.12	.09	.05
364	John Barfield	.12	.09	.05
365	Luis Aquino	.12	.09	.05
366	Charlie Leibrandt	.12	.09	.05
367	Howard Farmer	.12	.09	.05
368	Bryn Smith	.12	.09	.05
369	Mickey Morandini	.15	.11	.06
370	Jose Canseco	.50	.40	.20
371	Jose Uribe	.12	.09	.05
372	Bob MacDonald	.12	.09	.05
373	Luis Sojo	.12	.09	.05
374	Craig Shipley	.12	.09	.05
375	Scott Bankhead	.12	.09	.05
376	Greg Gagne	.12	.09	.05
377	Scott Cooper	.50	.40	.20
378	Jose Offerman	.12	.09	.05
379	Billy Spiers	.12	.09	.05
380	John Smiley	.15	.11	.06
381	Jeff Carter	.12	.09	.05
382	Heathcliff Slocumb	.12	.09	.05
383	Jeff Tackett	.10	.08	.04
384	John Kiely	.15	.11	.06
385	John Vander Wal	.25	.20	.10
386	Omar Olivares	.12	.09	.05
387	Ruben Sierra	.40	.30	.15
388	Tom Gordon	.12	.09	.05
389	Charles Nagy	.12	.09	.05
390	Dave Stewart	.15	.11	.06
391	Pete Harnisch	.15	.11	.06
392	Tim Burke	.12	.09	.05
393	Roberto Kelly	.12	.09	.05
394	Freddie Benavides	.12	.09	.05
395	Tom Glavine	.60	.45	.25
396	Wes Chamberlain	.20	.15	.08
397	Eric Gunderson	.12	.09	.05
398	Dave West	.12	.09	.05
399	Ellis Burks	.20	.15	.08
400	Ken Griffey, Jr.	4.50	3.50	1.75
401	Thomas Howard	.12	.09	.05
402	Juan Guzman	1.75	1.25	.70
403	Mitch Webster	.12	.09	.05
404	Matt Merullo	.12	.09	.05
405	Steve Buechele	.12	.09	.05
406	Danny Jackson	.12	.09	.05
407	Felix Jose	.12	.09	.05
408	Doug Piatt	.10	.08	.04

		MT	NR MT	EX
409	Jim Eisenreich	.12	.09	.05
410	Bryan Harvey	.15	.11	.06
411	Jim Austin	.15	.11	.06
412	Jim Poole	.12	.09	.05
413	Glenallen Hill	.15	.11	.06
414	Gene Nelson	.12	.09	.05
415	Ivan Rodriguez	1.00	.70	.40
416	Frank Tanana	.12	.09	.05
417	Steve Decker	.12	.09	.05
418	Jason Grimsley	.12	.09	.05
419	Tim Layana	.12	.09	.05
420	Don Mattingly	.60	.45	.25
421	Jerome Walton	.12	.09	.05
422	Rob Ducey	.12	.09	.05
423	Andy Benes	.25	.20	.10
424	John Marzano	.12	.09	.05
425	Gene Harris	.12	.09	.05
426	Rock Raines	.20	.15	.08
427	Bret Barberie	.10	.08	.04
428	Harvey Pulliam	.30	.25	.12
429	Cris Carpenter	.12	.09	.05
430	Howard Johnson	.10	.08	.04
431	Orel Hershiser	.12	.09	.05
432	Brian Hunter	.12	.09	.05
433	Kevin Tapani	.15	.11	.06
434	Rick Reed	.15	.11	.06
435	Ron Witmeyer	.15	.11	.06
436	Gary Gaetti	.15	.11	.06
437	Alex Cole	.15	.11	.06
438	Chito Martinez	.12	.09	.05
439	Greg Litton	.15	.11	.06
440	Julio Franco	.15	.11	.06
441	Mike Munoz	.15	.11	.06
442	Erik Pappas	.15	.11	.06
443	Pat Combs	.15	.11	.06
444	Lance Johnson	.15	.11	.06
445	Ed Sprague	.15	.11	.06
446	Mike Greenwell	.15	.11	.06
447	Milt Thompson	.15	.11	.06
448	Mike Magnante	.25	.20	.10
449	Chris Haney	.20	.15	.08
450	Robin Yount	.50	.40	.20
451	Rafael Ramirez	.15	.11	.06
452	Gino Minutelli	.15	.11	.06
453	Tom Lampkin	.15	.11	.06
454	Tony Perezchica	.15	.11	.06
455	Doc Gooden	.15	.11	.06
456	Mark Guthrie	.15	.11	.06
457	Jay Howell	.15	.11	.06
458	Gary DiSarcina	.15	.11	.06
459	John Smoltz	.25	.20	.10
460	Will Clark	.60	.45	.25
461	Dave Otto	.15	.11	.06
462	Rob Maurer	.20	.15	.08
463	Dwight Evans	.15	.11	.06
464	Tom Brunansky	.12	.09	.05
465	Shawn Hare	.30	.25	.12
466	Geronimo Pena	.20	.15	.08
467	Alex Fernandez	.50	.40	.20
468	Greg Myers	.12	.09	.05
469	Jeff Fassero	.12	.09	.05
470	Len Dykstra	.25	.20	.10
471	Jeff Johnson	.15	.11	.06
472	Russ Swan	.12	.09	.05
473	Archie Corbin	.30	.25	.12
474	Chuck McElroy	.12	.09	.05
475	Mark McGwire	.50	.40	.20
476	Wally Whitehurst	.12	.09	.05
477	Tim McIntosh	.12	.09	.05
478	Sid Bream	.12	.09	.05
479	Jeff Juden	.40	.30	.15
480	Carlton Fisk	.25	.20	.10
481	Jeff Plympton	.30	.25	.12
482	Carlos Martinez	.12	.09	.05
483	Jim Gott	.12	.09	.05
484	Bob McClure	.12	.09	.05
485	Tim Teufel	.12	.09	.05
486	Vicente Palacios	.12	.09	.05
487	Jeff Reed	.12	.09	.05
488	Tony Phillips	.15	.11	.06
489	Mel Rojas	.12	.09	.05
490	Ben McDonald	.30	.25	.12
491	Andres Santana	.15	.11	.06
492	Chris Beasley	.20	.15	.08
493	Mike Timlin	.15	.11	.06
494	Brian Downing	.12	.09	.05
495	Kirk Gibson	.12	.09	.05
496	Scott Sanderson	.12	.09	.05
497	Nick Esasky	.12	.09	.05
498	Johnny Guzman	.30	.25	.12
499	Mitch Williams	.15	.11	.06

		MT	NR MT	EX
500	Kirby Puckett	1.25	.90	.50
501	Mike Harkey	.12	.09	.05
502	Jim Gantner	.12	.09	.05
503	Bruce Egloff	.15	.11	.06
504	Josias Manzanillo	.20	.15	.08
505	Delino DeShields	.20	.15	.08
506	Rheal Cormier	.30	.25	.12
507	Jay Bell	.15	.11	.06
508	Rich Rowland	.25	.20	.10
509	Scott Servais	.15	.11	.06
510	Terry Pendleton	.20	.15	.08
511	Rich DeLucia	.12	.09	.05
512	Warren Newson	.12	.09	.05
513	Paul Faries	.12	.09	.05
514	Kal Daniels	.12	.09	.05
515	Jarvis Brown	.20	.15	.08
516	Rafael Palmeiro	.20	.15	.08
517	Kelly Downs	.12	.09	.05
518	Steve Chitren	.12	.09	.05
519	Moises Alou	.20	.15	.08
520	Wade Boggs	.30	.25	.12
521	Pete Schourek	.12	.09	.05
522	Scott Terry	.12	.09	.05
523	Kevin Appier	.20	.15	.08
524	Gary Redus	.12	.09	.05
525	George Bell	.15	.11	.06
526	Jeff Kaiser	.20	.15	.08
527	Alvaro Espinoza	.12	.09	.05
528	Luis Polonia	.12	.09	.05
529	Darren Daulton	.25	.20	.10
530	Norm Charlton	.20	.15	.08
531	John Olerud	2.00	1.50	.80
532	Dan Plesac	.12	.09	.05
533	Billy Ripken	.12	.09	.05
534	Rod Nichols	.12	.09	.05
535	Joey Cora	.12	.09	.05
536	Harold Baines	.10	.08	.04
537	Bob Ojeda	.12	.09	.05
538	Mark Leonard	.12	.09	.05
539	Danny Darwin	.12	.09	.05
540	Shawon Dunston	.15	.11	.06
541	Pedro Munoz	.12	.09	.05
542	Mark Gubicza	.15	.11	.06
543	Kevin Baez	.20	.15	.08
544	Todd Zeile	.15	.11	.06
545	Don Slaught	.12	.09	.05
546	Tony Eusebio	.20	.15	.08
547	Alonzo Powell	.12	.09	.05
548	Gary Pettis	.12	.09	.05
549	Brian Barnes	.15	.11	.06
550	Lou Whitaker	.15	.11	.06
551	Keith Mitchell	.12	.09	.05
552	Oscar Azocar	.12	.09	.05
553	Stu Cole	.15	.11	.06
554	Steve Wapnick	.10	.08	.04
555	Derek Bell	.50	.40	.20
556	Luis Lopez	.20	.15	.08
557	Anthony Telford	.15	.11	.06
558	Tim Mauser	.20	.15	.08
559	Glenn Sutko	.10	.08	.04
560	Darryl Strawberry	.20	.15	.08
561	Tom Bolton	.12	.09	.05
562	Cliff Young	.12	.09	.05
563	Bruce Walton	.12	.09	.05
564	Chico Walker	.12	.09	.05
565	John Franco	.15	.11	.06
566	Paul McClellan	.15	.11	.06
567	Paul Abbott	.15	.11	.06
568	Gary Varsho	.12	.09	.05
569	Carlos Maldonado	.20	.15	.08
570	Kelly Gruber	.10	.08	.04
571	Jose Oquendo	.12	.09	.05
572	Steve Frey	.12	.09	.05
573	Tino Martinez	.20	.15	.08
574	Bill Haselman	.12	.09	.05
575	Eric Anthony	.15	.11	.06
576	John Habyan	.12	.09	.05
577	Jeffrey McNeely	.30	.25	.12
578	Chris Bosio	.15	.11	.06
579	Joe Grahe	.15	.11	.06
580	Fred McGriff	.60	.45	.25
581	Rick Honeycutt	.12	.09	.05
582	Matt Williams	.25	.20	.10
583	Cliff Brantley	.20	.15	.08
584	Rob Dibble	.20	.15	.08
585	Skeeter Barnes	.12	.09	.05
586	Greg Hibbard	.12	.09	.05
587	Randy Milligan	.12	.09	.05
588	Checklist 301-400	.12	.09	.05
589	Checklist 401-500	.12	.09	.05
590	Checklist 501-600	.12	.09	.05

		MT	NR MT	EX
591	Frank Thomas (MC)	3.00	2.25	1.25
592	David Justice (MC)	.75	.60	.30
593	Roger Clemens (MC)	.50	.40	.20
594	Steve Avery (MC)	.50	.40	.20
595	Cal Ripken, Jr. (MC)	.75	.60	.30
596	Barry Larkin (MC)	.20	.15	.08
597	Jose Canseco (MC UER 370)	.30	.25	.12
598	Will Clark (MC)	.50	.40	.20
599	Cecil Fielder (MC)	.40	.30	.15
600	Ryne Sandberg (MC)	.75	.60	.30
601	Chuck Knoblauch (MC)	.25	.20	.10
602	Dwight Gooden (MC)	.50	.40	.20
603	Ken Griffey, Jr. (MC)	2.00	1.50	.80
604	Barry Bonds (MC)	1.00	.70	.40
605	Nolan Ryan (MC)	1.50	1.25	.60
606	Jeff Bagwell (MC)	.80	.60	.30
607	Robin Yount (MC)	.40	.30	.15
608	Bobby Bonilla (MC)	.20	.15	.08
609	George Brett (MC)	.60	.45	.25
610	Howard Johnson	.25	.20	.10
611	Esteban Beltre	.12	.09	.05
612	Mike Christopher	.20	.15	.08
613	Troy Afenir	.12	.09	.05
614	Mariano Duncan	.12	.09	.05
615	Doug Henry	.15	.11	.06
616	Doug Jones	.15	.11	.06
617	Alvin Davis	.12	.09	.05
618	Craig Lefferts	.12	.09	.05
619	Kevin McReynolds	.20	.15	.08
620	Barry Bonds	1.50	1.25	.60
621	Turner Ward	.20	.15	.08
622	Joe Magrane	.15	.11	.06
623	Mark Parent	.12	.09	.05
624	Tom Browning	.15	.11	.06
625	John Smiley	.15	.11	.06
626	Steve Wilson	.12	.09	.05
627	Mike Gallego	.12	.09	.05
628	Sammy Sosa	.15	.11	.06
629	Rico Rossy	.15	.11	.06
630	Royce Clayton	.60	.45	.25
631	Clay Parker	.12	.09	.05
632	Pete Smith	.12	.09	.05
633	Jeff McKnight	.12	.09	.05
634	Jack Daugherty	.12	.09	.05
635	Steve Sax	.20	.15	.08
636	Joe Hesketh	.12	.09	.05
637	Vince Horsman	.20	.15	.08
638	Joe Boever	.12	.09	.05
640	Jack Morris	.12	.09	.05
641	Arthur Rhodes	.20	.15	.08
642	Bob Melvin	.12	.09	.05
643	Rick Wilkins	.20	.15	.08
644	Scott Scudder	.12	.09	.05
645	Bip Roberts	.20	.15	.08
646	Julio Valera	.20	.15	.08
647	Kevin Campbell	.20	.15	.08
648	Steve Searcy	.12	.09	.05
649	Scott Kamieniecki	.12	.09	.05
650	Kurt Stillwell	.12	.09	.05
651	Bob Welch	.15	.11	.06
652	Andres Galarraga	.15	.11	.06
653	Mike Jackson	.12	.09	.05
654	Bo Jackson	.60	.45	.25
655	Sid Fernandez	.15	.11	.06
656	Mike Bielecki	.12	.09	.05
657	Jeff Reardon	.15	.11	.06
658	Wayne Rosenthal	.12	.09	.05
659	Eric Bullock	.12	.09	.05
660	Eric Davis	.25	.20	.10
661	Randy Tomlin	.20	.15	.08
662	Tom Edens	.12	.09	.05
663	Rob Murphy	.12	.09	.05
664	Leo Gomez	.12	.09	.05
665	Greg Maddux	.25	.20	.10
666	Greg Vaughn	.15	.11	.06
667	Wade Taylor	.12	.09	.05
668	Brad Arnsberg	.12	.09	.05
669	Mike Moore	.15	.11	.06
670	Mark Langston	.15	.11	.06
671	Barry Jones	.12	.09	.05
672	Bill Landrum	.12	.09	.05
673	Greg Swindell	.20	.15	.08
674	Wayne Edwards	.12	.09	.05
675	Greg Olson	.12	.09	.05
676	Bill Pulsipher	.20	.15	.08
677	Bobby Witt	.15	.11	.06
678	Mark Carreon	.12	.09	.05
679	Patrick Lennon	.30	.25	.12
680	Ozzie Smith	.40	.30	.15
681	John Briscoe	.20	.15	.08
682	Matt Young	.12	.09	.05
683	Jeff Conine	.20	.15	.08
684	Phil Stephenson	.12	.09	.05
685	Ron Darling	.15	.11	.06
686	Bryan Hickerson	.15	.11	.06
687	Dale Sveum	.12	.09	.05
688	Kirk McCaskill	.12	.09	.05
689	Rich Amaral	.15	.11	.06
690	Danny Tartabull	.15	.11	.06
691	Donald Harris	.15	.11	.06
692	Doug Davis	.20	.15	.08
693	John Farrell	.12	.09	.05
694	Paul Gibson	.12	.09	.05
695	Kenny Lofton	1.25	.90	.50
696	Mike Fetters	.12	.09	.05
697	Rosario Rodriguez	.12	.09	.05
698	Chris Jones	.15	.11	.06
699	Jeff Manto	.12	.09	.05
700	Rick Sutcliffe	.15	.11	.06
701	Scott Bankhead	.12	.09	.05
702	Donnie Hill	.12	.09	.05
703	Todd Worrell	.15	.11	.06
704	Rene Gonzales	.12	.09	.05
705	Rick Cerone	.12	.09	.05
706	Tony Pena	.12	.09	.05
707	Paul Sorrento	.12	.09	.05
708	Gary Scott	.15	.11	.06
709	Junior Noboa	.12	.09	.05
710	Wally Joyner	.20	.15	.08
711	Charlie Hayes	.15	.11	.06
712	Rich Rodriguez	.12	.09	.05
713	Rudy Seanez	.12	.09	.05
714	Jim Bullinger	.20	.15	.08
715	Jeff Robinson	.12	.09	.05
716	Jeff Branson	.25	.20	.10
717	Andy Ashby	.12	.09	.05
718	Dave Burba	.12	.09	.05
719	Rich Gossage	.20	.15	.08
720	Randy Johnson	.20	.15	.08
721	David Wells	.12	.09	.05
722	Paul Kilgus	.12	.09	.05
723	Dave Martinez	.12	.09	.05
724	Denny Neagle	.15	.11	.06
725	Andy Stankiewicz	.12	.09	.05
726	Rick Aguilera	.15	.11	.06
727	Junior Noboa	.12	.09	.05
728	Storm Davis	.12	.09	.05
729	Don Robinson	.12	.09	.05
730	Ron Gant	.40	.30	.15
731	Paul Assenmacher	.12	.09	.05
732	Mark Gardiner	.12	.09	.05
733	Milt Hill	.12	.09	.05
734	Jeremy Hernandez	.15	.11	.06
735	Ken Hill	.20	.15	.08
736	Xavier Hernandez	.12	.09	.05
737	Gregg Jefferies	.25	.20	.10
738	Dick Schofield	.12	.09	.05
739	Ron Robinson	.12	.09	.05
740	Sandy Alomar	.20	.15	.08
741	Mike Stanley	.12	.09	.05
742	Butch Henry	.12	.09	.05
743	Floyd Bannister	.12	.09	.05
744	Brian Drahman	.15	.11	.06
745	Dave Winfield	.60	.45	.25
746	Bob Walk	.12	.09	.05
747	Chris James	.12	.09	.05
748	Don Prybylinski	.20	.15	.08
749	Dennis Rasmussen	.12	.09	.05
750	Rickey Henderson	.50	.40	.20
751	Chris Hammond	.15	.11	.06
752	Bob Kipper	.12	.09	.05
753	Dave Rohde	.12	.09	.05
754	Hubie Brooks	.12	.09	.05
755	Bret Saberhagen	.20	.15	.08
756	Jeff Robinson	.12	.09	.05
757	Pat Listach	.90	.70	.35
758	Bill Wegman	.15	.11	.06
759	John Wetteland	.15	.11	.06
760	Phil Plantier	.60	.45	.25
761	Wilson Alvarez	.12	.09	.05
762	Scott Aldred	.12	.09	.05
763	Armando Reynoso	.30	.25	.12
764	Todd Benzinger	.12	.09	.05
765	Kevin Mitchell	.20	.15	.08
766	Gary Sheffield	.75	.60	.30
767	Allan Anderson	.12	.09	.05
768	Rusty Meacham	.15	.11	.06
769	Rick Parker	.12	.09	.05
770	Nolan Ryan	3.00	2.25	1.25
771	Jeff Ballard	.12	.09	.05
772	Cory Snyder	.12	.09	.05
773	Denis Boucher	.15	.11	.06

		MT	NR MT	EX
774	Jose Gonzales	.12	.09	.05
775	Juan Guerrero	.12	.09	.05
776	Ed Nunez	.12	.09	.05
777	Scott Ruskin	.12	.09	.05
778	Terry Leach	.12	.09	.05
779	Carl Willis	.12	.09	.05
780	Bobby Bonilla	.20	.15	.08
781	Duane Ward	.15	.11	.06
782	Joe Slusarski	.15	.11	.06
783	David Segui	.15	.11	.06
784	Kirk Gibson	.12	.09	.05
785	Frank Viola	.20	.15	.08
786	Keith Miller	.12	.09	.05
787	Mike Morgan	.12	.09	.05
788	Kim Batiste	.15	.11	.06
789	Sergio Valdez	.15	.11	.06
790	Eddie Taubensee	.15	.11	.06
791	Jack Armstrong	.12	.09	.05
792	Scott Fletcher	.12	.09	.05
793	Steve Farr	.12	.09	.05
794	Dan Pasqua	.12	.09	.05
795	Eddie Murray	.20	.15	.08
796	John Morris	.12	.09	.05
797	Francisco Cabrera	.12	.09	.05
798	Mike Perez	.20	.15	.08
799	Ted Wood	.20	.15	.08
800	Jose Rijo	.20	.15	.08
801	Danny Gladden	.12	.09	.05
802	Arci Cianfrocco	.25	.20	.10
803	Monty Fariss	.15	.11	.06
804	Roger McDowell	.12	.09	.05
805	Randy Myers	.15	.11	.06
806	Kirk Dressendorfer	.15	.11	.06
807	Zane Smith	.12	.09	.05
808	Glenn Davis	.15	.11	.06
809	Tory Lovullo	.12	.09	.05
810	Andre Dawson	.40	.30	.15
811	Bill Pecota	.12	.09	.05
812	Ted Power	.12	.09	.05
813	Willie Blair	.12	.09	.05
814	Dave Fleming	.90	.70	.35
815	Chris Gwynn	.12	.09	.05
816	Jody Reed	.12	.09	.05
817	Mark Dewey	.12	.09	.05
818	Kyle Abbott	.12	.09	.05
819	Tom Henke	.12	.09	.05
820	Kevin Seitzer	.12	.09	.05
821	Al Newman	.12	.09	.05
822	Tim Sherrill	.20	.15	.08
823	Chuck Crim	.12	.09	.05
824	Darren Reed	.15	.11	.06
825	Tony Gwynn	.50	.40	.20
826	Steve Foster	.20	.15	.08
827	Steve Howe	.12	.09	.05
828	Brook Jacoby	.12	.09	.05
829	Rodney McCray	.12	.09	.05
830	Chuck Knoblauch	.50	.40	.20
831	John Wehner	.15	.11	.06
832	Scott Garrelts	.12	.09	.05
833	Alejandro Pena	.12	.09	.05
834	Jeff Parrett	.12	.09	.05
835	Juan Bell	.12	.09	.05
836	Lance Dickson	.12	.09	.05
837	Darryl Kile	.15	.11	.06
838	Efrain Valdez	.15	.11	.06
839	Bob Zupcic	.60	.45	.25
840	George Bell	.15	.11	.06
841	Dave Gallagher	.12	.09	.05
842	Tim Belcher	.15	.11	.06
843	Jeff Shaw	.12	.09	.05
844	Mike Fitgerald	.12	.09	.05
845	Gary Carter	.20	.15	.08
846	John Russell	.12	.09	.05
847	Eric Hillman	.30	.25	.12
848	Mike Witt	.12	.09	.05
849	Curt Wilkerson	.12	.09	.05
850	Alan Trammell	.15	.11	.06
851	Rex Hudler	.12	.09	.05
852	Michael Walkden	.30	.25	.12
853	Kevin Ward	.15	.11	.06
854	Tim Naehring	.15	.11	.06
855	Bill Swift	.15	.11	.06
856	Damon Berryhill	.12	.09	.05
857	Mark Eichhorn	.12	.09	.05
858	Hector Villanueva	.12	.09	.05
859	Jose Lind	.12	.09	.05
860	Denny Martinez	.15	.11	.06
861	Bill Krueger	.12	.09	.05
862	Mike Kingery	.12	.09	.05
863	Jeff Innis	.12	.09	.05
864	Derek Lilliquist	.12	.09	.05
865	Reggie Sanders	1.00	.70	.40
866	Ramon Garcia	.20	.15	.08
867	Bruce Ruffin	.12	.09	.05
868	Dickie Thon	.12	.09	.05
869	Melido Perez	.15	.11	.06
870	Ruben Amaro	.15	.11	.06
871	Alan Mills	.12	.09	.05
872	Matt Sinatro	.12	.09	.05
873	Eddie Zosky	.20	.15	.08
874	Pete Incaviglia	.12	.09	.05
875	Tom Candiotti	.12	.09	.05
876	Bob Patterson	.12	.09	.05
877	Neal Heaton	.12	.09	.05
878	Terrel Hansen	.35	.25	.14
879	Dave Eiland	.12	.09	.05
880	Von Hayes	.12	.09	.05
881	Tim Scott	.20	.15	.08
882	Otis Nixon	.15	.11	.06
883	Herm Winningham	.12	.09	.05
884	Dion James	.12	.09	.05
885	Dave Wainhouse	.15	.11	.06
886	Frank DiPino	.12	.09	.05
887	Dennis Cook	.12	.09	.05
888	Jose Mesa	.12	.09	.05
889	Mark Leiter	.12	.09	.05
890	Willie Randolph	.15	.11	.06
891	Craig Colbert	.15	.11	.06
892	Dwayne Henry	.12	.09	.05
893	Jim Lindeman	.12	.09	.05
894	Charlie Hough	.12	.09	.05
895	Gil Heredia	.12	.09	.05
896	Scott Chiamparino	.12	.09	.05
897	Lance Blankenship	.12	.09	.05
898	Checklist 601-700	.12	.09	.05
899	Checklist 701-800	.12	.09	.05
900	Checklist 801-900	.12	.09	.05

1992 Stadium Club First Draft Picks

Issued as inserts with Stadium Club Series III, this three-card set features the No. 1 draft picks of 1990-92. Fronts have a full-bleed photo with S.C. logo and player name in the lower-right corner. At bottom-left in a red strip is a gold-foil stamping, "#1 Draft Pick of the '90's. An orange circle at upper-right has the year the player was the No. 1 choice. The basic red-and-black back has a color photo, afew biographical and draft details and a gold facsimile autograph among other gold-foil highlights.

		MT	NR MT	EX
Complete Set (3):		20.00	15.00	8.00
Common Player:		8.00	6.00	3.25
1	Chipper Jones	10.00	7.50	4.00
2	Brien Taylor	8.00	6.00	3.25
3	Phil Nevin	8.00	6.00	3.25

1993 Topps

Topps used a two series format in 1993. Series I featured cards 1-396. The card fronts feature full-color photos enclosed by a white border. The player's name

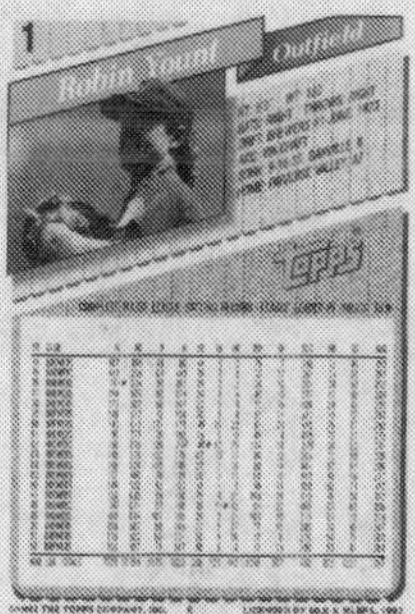

and team appear at the bottom. The backs feature an additional player photo and biographical information at the top. The bottom box includes statistics and player information. Like in recent years, several cards are printed horizontally. The cards are numbered in red on the back. The number appears in a yellow flag in the upper left corner of the card.

		MT	NR MT	EX
Complete Set (825):		30.00	22.00	12.00
Common Player:		.03	.02	.01
1	Robin Yount	.10	.08	.04
2	Barry Bonds	.20	.15	.08
3	Ryne Sandberg	.15	.11	.06
4	Roger Clemens	.15	.11	.06
5	Tony Gwynn	.12	.09	.05
6	*Jeff Tackett*	.12	.09	.05
7	Pete Incaviglia	.05	.04	.02
8	Mark Wohlers	.05	.04	.02
9	Kent Hrbek	.06	.05	.02
10	Will Clark	.15	.11	.06
11	Eric Karros	.15	.11	.06
12	Lee Smith	.06	.05	.02
13	Esteban Beltre	.05	.04	.02
14	Greg Briley	.03	.02	.01
15	Marquis Grissom	.08	.06	.03
16	Dan Plesac	.04	.03	.02
17	Dave Hollins	.08	.06	.03
18	Terry Steinbach	.06	.05	.02
19	Ed Nunez	.03	.02	.01
20	*Tim Salmon*	1.50	1.25	.60
21	Luis Salazar	.04	.03	.02
22	Jim Eisenreich	.03	.02	.01
23	Todd Stottlemyre	.05	.04	.02
24	Tim Naehring	.05	.04	.02
25	John Franco	.06	.05	.02
26	Skeeter Barnes	.06	.05	.02
27	*Carlos Garcia*	.25	.20	.10
28	Joe Orsulak	.04	.03	.02
29	Dwayne Henry	.03	.02	.01
30	Fred McGriff	.10	.08	.04
31	Derek Lilliquist	.03	.02	.01
32	Don Mattingly	.12	.09	.05
33	B.J. Wallace	.30	.25	.12
34	Juan Gonzalez	.50	.40	.20
35	John Smoltz	.08	.06	.03
36	Scott Servais	.08	.06	.03
37	Lenny Webster	.08	.06	.03
38	Chris James	.04	.03	.02
39	Roger McDowell	.04	.03	.02
40	Ozzie Smith	.10	.08	.04
41	Alex Fernandez	.08	.06	.03
42	Spike Owen	.03	.02	.01
43	Ruben Amaro	.05	.04	.02
44	Kevin Seitzer	.05	.04	.02
45	Dave Fleming	.10	.08	.04
46	*Eric Fox*	.12	.09	.05
47	Bob Scanlan	.03	.02	.01
48	Bert Blyleven	.06	.05	.02
49	Brian McRae	.06	.05	.02
50	Roberto Alomar	.12	.09	.05
51	Mo Vaughn	.05	.04	.02
52	Bobby Bonilla	.10	.08	.04
53	Frank Tanana	.04	.03	.02
54	Mike LaValliere	.04	.03	.02
55	Mark McLemore	.03	.02	.01
56	*Chad Mottola*	1.00	.70	.40
57	Norm Charlton	.06	.05	.02
58	Jose Melendez	.08	.06	.03
59	Carlos Martinez	.03	.02	.01
60	Roberto Kelly	.08	.06	.03
61	Gene Larkin	.03	.02	.01
62	Rafael Belliard	.03	.02	.01
63	Al Osuna	.03	.02	.01
64	Scott Chiamparino	.03	.02	.01
65	Brett Butler	.06	.05	.02
66	John Burkett	.04	.03	.02
67	Felix Jose	.08	.06	.03
68	Omar Vizquel	.03	.02	.01
69	*John Vander Wal*	.12	.09	.05
70	Roberto Hernandez	.08	.06	.03
71	Ricky Bones	.05	.04	.02
72	*Jeff Grotewold*	.12	.09	.05
73	Mike Moore	.05	.04	.02
74	Steve Buechele	.05	.04	.02
75	Juan Guzman	.10	.08	.04
76	Kevin Appier	.08	.06	.03
77	Junior Felix	.05	.04	.02
78	Greg Harris	.04	.03	.02
79	Dick Schofield	.04	.03	.02
80	Cecil Fielder	.10	.08	.04
81	Lloyd McClendon	.04	.03	.02
82	David Segui	.05	.04	.02
83	Reggie Sanders	.15	.11	.06
84	Kurt Stillwell	.04	.03	.02
85	Sandy Alomar	.08	.06	.03
86	John Habyan	.03	.02	.01
87	Kevin Reimer	.05	.04	.02
88	Mike Stanton	.05	.04	.02
89	Eric Anthony	.06	.05	.02
90	Scott Erickson	.08	.06	.03
91	Craig Colbert	.06	.05	.02
92	Tom Pagnozzi	.06	.05	.02
93	*Pedro Astacio*(FC)	.15	.11	.06
94	Lance Johnson	.04	.03	.02
95	Larry Walker	.10	.08	.04
96	Russ Swan	.03	.02	.01
97	Scott Fletcher	.03	.02	.01
98	*Derek Jeter*(FC)	.30	.25	.12
99	*Mike Williams*(FC)	.15	.11	.06
100	Mark McGwire	.10	.08	.04
101	*Jim Bullinger*	.12	.09	.05
102	Brian Hunter	.08	.06	.03
103	Jody Reed	.04	.03	.02
104	*Mike Butcher*(FC)	.15	.11	.06
105	Gregg Jefferies	.08	.06	.03
106	Howard Johnson	.08	.06	.03
107	*John Kiely*	.12	.09	.05
108	Jose Lind	.04	.03	.02
109	Sam Horn	.03	.02	.01
110	Barry Larkin	.08	.06	.03
111	Bruce Hurst	.05	.04	.02
112	Brian Barnes	.04	.03	.02
113	Thomas Howard	.04	.03	.02
114	Mel Hall	.06	.05	.02
115	Robby Thompson	.04	.03	.02
116	Mark Lemke	.04	.03	.02
117	Eddie Taubensee	.08	.06	.03
118	David Justice	.10	.08	.04
119	Pedro Munoz	.10	.08	.04
120	Ramon Martinez	.08	.06	.03
121	Todd Worrell	.05	.04	.02
122	Joey Cora	.03	.02	.01
123	Moises Alou	.08	.06	.03
124	Franklin Stubbs	.03	.02	.01
125	Pete O'Brien	.03	.02	.01
126	*Bob Aryault*(FC)	.12	.09	.05
127	Carney Lansford	.05	.04	.02
128	Kal Daniels	.05	.04	.02
129	Joe Grahe	.05	.04	.02
130	Jeff Montgomery	.05	.04	.02
131	Dave Winfield	.15	.11	.06
132	*Preston Wilson*(FC)	.40	.30	.15
133	Steve Wilson	.04	.03	.02
134	Lee Guetterman	.03	.02	.01
135	Mickey Tettleton	.08	.06	.03
136	Jeff King	.04	.03	.02
137	Alan Mills	.03	.02	.01
138	Joe Oliver	.04	.03	.02
139	Gary Gaetti	.04	.03	.02
140	Gary Sheffield	.10	.08	.04
141	Dennis Cook	.03	.02	.01
142	Charlie Hayes	.04	.03	.02
143	Jeff Huson	.04	.03	.02
144	Kent Mercker	.04	.03	.02
145	*Eric Young*(FC)	.15	.11	.06
146	Scott Leius	.04	.03	.02
147	Bryan Hickerson	.04	.03	.02
148	Steve Finley	.06	.05	.02
149	Rheal Cormier	.08	.06	.03
150	Frank Thomas	.75	.60	.30
151	*Archi Cianfrocco*	.15	.11	.06
152	Rich DeLucia	.04	.03	.02

		MT	NR MT	EX
153	Greg Vaughn	.06	.05	.02
154	Wes Chamberlain	.05	.04	.02
155	Dennis Eckersley	.08	.06	.03
156	Sammy Sosa	.04	.03	.02
157	Gary DiSarcina	.06	.05	.02
158	*Kevin Koslofski*(FC)	.12	.09	.05
159	*Doug Linton*(FC)	.12	.09	.05
160	Lou Whitaker	.06	.05	.02
161	Chad McDonnell	.12	.09	.05
162	Joe Hesketh	.03	.02	.01
163	*Tim Wakefield*	.10	.08	.04
164	Leo Gomez	.05	.04	.02
165	Jose Rijo	.06	.05	.02
166	*Tim Scott*(FC)	.12	.09	.05
167	Steve Olin	.05	.04	.02
168	Kevin Maas	.05	.04	.02
169	Kenny Rogers	.04	.03	.02
170	David Justice	.20	.15	.08
171	Doug Jones	.04	.03	.02
172	*Jeff Reboulet*(FC)	.12	.09	.05
173	Andres Galarraga	.05	.04	.02
174	Randy Velarde	.03	.02	.01
175	Kirk McCaskill	.04	.03	.02
176	Darren Lewis	.04	.03	.02
177	Lenny Harris	.04	.03	.02
178	Jeff Fassero	.04	.03	.02
179	Ken Griffey, Jr.	.50	.40	.20
180	Darren Daulton	.08	.06	.03
181	John Jaha	.12	.09	.05
182	Ron Darling	.05	.04	.02
183	Greg Maddux	.08	.06	.03
184	*Damion Easley*(FC)	.15	.11	.06
185	Jack Morris	.08	.06	.03
186	Mike Magnante	.05	.04	.02
187	John Dopson	.05	.04	.02
188	Sid Fernandez	.08	.06	.03
189	Tony Phillips	.08	.06	.03
190	Doug Drabek	.08	.06	.03
191	*Sean Lowe*(FC)	.15	.11	.06
192	Bob Milacki	.03	.02	.01
193	*Steve Foster*(FC)	.15	.11	.06
194	Jerald Clark	.05	.04	.02
195	Pete Harnisch	.06	.05	.02
196	Pat Kelly	.06	.05	.02
197	*Jeff Frye*(FC)	.12	.09	.05
198	Alejandro Pena	.04	.03	.02
199	Junior Ortiz	.03	.02	.01
200	Kirby Puckett	.15	.11	.06
201	Jose Uribe	.03	.02	.01
202	Mike Scioscia	.04	.03	.02
203	Bernard Gilkey	.06	.05	.02
204	Dan Pasqua	.04	.03	.02
205	Gary Carter	.08	.06	.03
206	Henry Cotto	.03	.02	.01
207	Paul Molitor	.08	.06	.03
208	Mike Hartley	.04	.03	.02
209	Jeff Parrett	.03	.02	.01
210	Mark Langston	.08	.06	.03
211	Doug Dascenzo	.03	.02	.01
212	Rick Reed	.03	.02	.01
213	Candy Maldonado	.05	.04	.02
214	Danny Darwin	.03	.02	.01
215	*Pat Howell*(FC)	.12	.09	.05
216	Mark Leiter	.03	.02	.01
217	Kevin Mitchell	.08	.06	.03
218	Ben McDonald	.08	.06	.03
219	Bip Roberts	.08	.06	.03
220	Benny Santiago	.08	.06	.03
221	Carlos Baerga	.10	.08	.04
222	Bernie Williams	.10	.08	.04
223	*Roger Pavlik*(FC)	.12	.09	.05
224	Sid Bream	.04	.03	.02
225	Matt Williams	.08	.06	.03
226	Willie Banks	.08	.06	.03
227	Jeff Bagwell	.12	.09	.05
228	Tom Goodwin	.08	.06	.03
229	Mike Perez	.08	.06	.03
230	Carlton Fisk	.08	.06	.03
231	John Wetteland	.08	.06	.03
232	Tino Martinez	.08	.06	.03
233	*Rick Greene*(FC)	.12	.09	.05
234	Tim McIntosh	.04	.03	.02
235	Mitch Williams	.06	.05	.02
236	*Kevin Campbell*	.10	.08	.04
237	Jose Vizcaino	.03	.02	.01
238	Chris Donnels	.05	.04	.02
239	Mike Boddicker	.04	.03	.02
240	John Olerud	.20	.15	.08
241	Mike Gardiner	.04	.03	.02
242	Charlie O'Brien	.03	.02	.01
243	Rob Deer	.04	.03	.02

		MT	NR MT	EX
244	Denny Neagle	.08	.06	.03
245	Chris Sabo	.08	.06	.03
246	Gregg Olson	.08	.06	.03
247	Frank Seminara	.08	.06	.03
248	Scott Scudder	.03	.02	.01
249	Tim Burke	.03	.02	.01
250	Chuck Knoblauch	.10	.08	.04
251	Mike Bielecki	.04	.03	.02
252	Xavier Hernandez	.03	.02	.01
253	Jose Guzman	.04	.03	.02
254	Cory Snyder	.04	.03	.02
255	Orel Hershiser	.08	.06	.03
256	Wil Cordero	.12	.09	.05
257	Luis Alicea	.04	.03	.02
258	Mike Schooler	.04	.03	.02
259	Craig Grebeck	.03	.02	.01
260	Duane Ward	.04	.03	.02
261	Bill Wegman	.04	.03	.02
262	Mickey Morandini	.08	.06	.03
263	*Vince Horsman*	.12	.09	.05
264	Paul Sorrento	.06	.05	.02
265	Andre Dawson	.10	.08	.04
266	Rene Gonzales	.03	.02	.01
267	Keith Miller	.04	.03	.02
268	Derek Bell	.10	.08	.04
269	*Todd Steverson*(FC)	.20	.15	.08
270	Frank Viola	.08	.06	.03
271	Wally Whitehurst	.04	.03	.02
272	*Kurt Knudsen*	.12	.09	.05
273	*Dan Walters*	.12	.09	.05
274	Rick Sutcliffe	.06	.05	.02
275	Andy Van Slyke	.08	.06	.03
276	Paul O'Neill	.06	.05	.02
277	Mark Whiten	.10	.08	.04
278	Chris Nabholz	.06	.05	.02
279	Todd Burns	.03	.02	.01
280	Tom Glavine	.10	.08	.04
281	*Butch Henry*(FC)	.12	.09	.05
282	Shane Mack	.08	.06	.03
283	Mike Jackson	.03	.02	.01
284	Henry Rodriguez	.06	.05	.02
285	Bob Tewksbury	.06	.05	.02
286	Ron Karkovice	.04	.03	.02
287	Mike Gallego	.04	.03	.02
288	Dave Cochrane	.03	.02	.01
289	Jesse Orosco	.03	.02	.01
290	Dave Stewart	.08	.06	.03
291	Tommy Greene	.08	.06	.03
292	Rey Sanchez	.08	.06	.03
293	Rob Ducey	.03	.02	.01
294	Brent Mayne	.04	.03	.02
295	Dave Stieb	.05	.04	.02
296	Luis Rivera	.03	.02	.01
297	Jeff Innis	.04	.03	.02
298	Scott Livingstone	.08	.06	.03
299	Bob Patterson	.03	.02	.01
300	Cal Ripken, Jr.	.20	.15	.08
301	Cesar Hernandez	.10	.08	.04
302	Randy Myers	.06	.05	.02
303	Brook Jacoby	.04	.03	.02
304	Melido Perez	.04	.03	.02
305	Rafael Palmeiro	.08	.06	.03
306	Damon Berryhill	.03	.02	.01
307	*Dan Serafini*(FC)	.20	.15	.08
308	Darryl Kile	.06	.05	.02
309	*J.T. Bruett*	.15	.11	.06
310	Dave Righetti	.05	.04	.02
311	Jay Howell	.05	.04	.02
312	Geronimo Pena	.05	.04	.02
313	Greg Hibbard	.05	.04	.02
314	Mark Gardner	.05	.04	.02
315	Edgar Martinez	.08	.06	.03
316	Dave Nilsson	.10	.08	.04
317	Kyle Abbott	.08	.06	.03
318	Willie Wilson	.06	.05	.02
319	Paul Assenmacher	.04	.03	.02
320	*Tim Fortugno*	.12	.09	.05
321	Rusty Meacham	.08	.06	.03
322	Pat Borders	.05	.04	.02
323	Mike Greenwell	.06	.05	.02
324	Willie Randolph	.06	.05	.02
325	Bill Gullickson	.05	.04	.02
326	Gary Varsho	.03	.02	.01
327	Tim Hulett	.03	.02	.01
328	Scott Ruskin	.03	.02	.01
329	Mike Maddux	.03	.02	.01
330	Danny Tartabull	.08	.06	.03
331	Kenny Lofton	.25	.20	.10
332	Geno Petralli	.03	.02	.01
333	Otis Nixon	.05	.04	.02
334	*Jason Kendall*(FC)	.30	.25	.12

		MT	NR MT	EX
335	Mark Portugal	.03	.02	.01
336	Mike Pagliarulo	.04	.03	.02
337	Kirt Manwaring	.04	.03	.02
338	Bob Ojeda	.04	.03	.02
339	*Mark Clark*(FC)	.12	.09	.05
340	John Kruk	.08	.06	.03
341	Mel Rojas	.04	.03	.02
342	Erik Hanson	.06	.05	.02
343	Doug Henry	.06	.05	.02
344	Jack McDowell	.08	.06	.03
345	Harold Baines	.08	.06	.03
346	Chuck McElroy	.03	.02	.01
347	Luis Sojo	.03	.02	.01
348	Andy Stankiewicz	.10	.08	.04
349	*Hipolito Pichardo*	.10	.08	.04
350	Joe Carter	.08	.06	.03
351	Ellis Burks	.06	.05	.02
352	Pete Schourek	.06	.05	.02
353	*Buddy Groom*(FC)	.20	.15	.08
354	Jay Bell	.06	.05	.02
355	Brady Anderson	.08	.06	.03
356	Freddie Benavides	.06	.05	.02
357	Phil Stephenson	.03	.02	.01
358	Kevin Wickander	.03	.02	.01
359	Mike Stanley	.03	.02	.01
360	Ivan Rodriguez	.12	.09	.05
361	Scott Bankhead	.04	.03	.02
362	Luis Gonzalez	.08	.06	.03
363	John Smiley	.06	.05	.02
364	Trevor Wilson	.04	.03	.02
365	Tom Candiotti	.04	.03	.02
366	Craig Wilson	.04	.03	.02
367	Steve Sax	.06	.05	.02
368	Delino Deshields	.06	.05	.02
369	Jaime Navarro	.06	.05	.02
370	Dave Valle	.03	.02	.01
371	Mariano Duncan	.04	.03	.02
372	Rod Nichols	.03	.02	.01
373	Mike Morgan	.05	.04	.02
374	Julio Valera	.08	.06	.03
375	Wally Joyner	.08	.06	.03
376	Tom Henke	.08	.06	.03
377	Herm Winningham	.03	.02	.01
378	Orlando Merced	.06	.05	.02
379	Mike Munoz	.08	.06	.03
380	Todd Hundley	.08	.06	.03
381	Mike Flanagan	.03	.02	.01
382	Tim Belcher	.06	.05	.02
383	Jerry Browne	.03	.02	.01
384	Mike Benjamin	.03	.02	.01
385	Jim Leyritz	.03	.02	.01
386	Ray Lankford	.12	.09	.05
387	Devon White	.06	.05	.02
388	Jeremy Hernandez	.08	.06	.03
389	Brian Harper	.06	.05	.02
390	Wade Boggs	.12	.09	.05
391	Derrick May	.10	.08	.04
392	Travis Fryman	.15	.11	.06
393	Ron Gant	.10	.08	.04
394	Checklist 1-132	.03	.02	.01
395	Checklist 133-264	.03	.02	.01
396	Checklist 265-396	.03	.02	.01
397	George Brett	.10	.08	.04
398	Bobby Witt	.03	.02	.01
399	Daryl Boston	.03	.02	.01
400	Bo Jackson	.15	.11	.06
401	Fred McGriff, Frank Thomas, Fred McGriff (AS)	.03	.02	.01
402	Ryne Sandberg, Carlos Baerga (AS)	.25	.20	.10
403	G. Sheffield, E. Martinez (AS)	.03	.02	.01
404	B. Larkin, T. Fryman (AS)	.03	.02	.01
405	Andy Van Slyke, Ken Griffey, Jr. (AS)	.25	.20	.10
406	L. Walker, K. Puckett (AS)	.03	.02	.01
407	B. Bonds, J. Carter (AS)	.15	.11	.06
408	D. Daulton, B. Harper (AS)	.03	.02	.01
409	G. Maddux, R. Clemens (AS)	.03	.02	.01
410	T. Glavine, D. Fleming (AS)	.03	.02	.01
411	L. Smith, D. Eckersley (AS)	.03	.02	.01
412	Jamie McAndrew	.03	.02	.01
413	Pete Smith	.03	.02	.01
414	Juan Guerrero	.03	.02	.01
415	Todd Frohwirth	.03	.02	.01
416	Randy Tomlin	.03	.02	.01
417	B.J. Surhoff	.03	.02	.01
418	Jim Gott	.03	.02	.01
419	Mark Thompson	.03	.02	.01
420	Kevin Tapani	.03	.02	.01
421	Curt Schilling	.03	.02	.01
422	*J.T. Snow*(FC)	.75	.60	.30

		MT	NR MT	EX
423	Top Prospects	.60	.45	.25
424	John Valentin	.03	.02	.01
425	Joe Girardi	.03	.02	.01
426	*Nigel Wilson*(FC)	.80	.60	.30
427	Bob MacDonald	.03	.02	.01
428	Todd Zeile	.03	.02	.01
429	Milt Cuyler	.03	.02	.01
430	Eddie Murray	.03	.02	.01
431	Rich Amaral	.03	.02	.01
432	Pete Young	.03	.02	.01
433	Rookies	.30	.25	.12
434	Jack Armstrong	.03	.02	.01
435	Willie McGee	.03	.02	.01
436	Greg Harris	.03	.02	.01
437	Chris Hammond	.03	.02	.01
438	*Ritchie Moody*(FC)	.15	.11	.06
439	Bryan Harvey	.03	.02	.01
440	Ruben Sierra	.15	.11	.06
441	D.Lemon T.Pridy	.40	.30	.15
442	Kevin McReynolds	.03	.02	.01
443	Terry Leach	.03	.02	.01
444	*David Nied*(FC)	.60	.45	.25
445	Dale Murphy	.03	.02	.01
446	Luis Mercedes	.03	.02	.01
447	*Keith Shepherd*	.15	.11	.06
448	Ken Caminiti	.03	.02	.01
449	James Austin	.03	.02	.01
450	Darryl Strawberry	.10	.08	.04
451	Gates/ Shave	.25	.20	.10
452	Bob Wickman	.20	.15	.08
453	Victor Cole	.03	.02	.01
454	*John Johnstone*(FC)	.20	.15	.08
455	Chili Davis	.03	.02	.01
456	Scott Taylor	.03	.02	.01
457	Tracy Woodson	.03	.02	.01
458	David Wells	.03	.02	.01
459	*Derek Wallace*(FC)	.20	.15	.08
460	Randy Johnson	.03	.02	.01
461	Steve Reed	.03	.02	.01
462	Felix Fermin	.03	.02	.01
463	Scott Aldred	.03	.02	.01
464	Greg Colbrunn	.03	.02	.01
465	Tony Fernandez	.03	.02	.01
466	Mike Felder	.03	.02	.01
467	Lee Stevens	.03	.02	.01
468	Matt Whiteside	.03	.02	.01
469	Dave Hansen	.03	.02	.01
470	Rob Dibble	.03	.02	.01
471	Dave Gallagher	.03	.02	.01
472	Chris Gwynn	.03	.02	.01
473	Dave Henderson	.03	.02	.01
474	Ozzie Guillen	.03	.02	.01
475	Jeff Reardon	.03	.02	.01
476	Voisard/ Scalzitti	.25	.20	.10
477	Jimmy Jones	.03	.02	.01
478	Greg Cadaret	.03	.02	.01
479	Todd Pratt	.03	.02	.01
480	Pat Listach	.10	.08	.04
481	*Ryan Luzinski*	.30	.25	.12
482	Darren Reed	.03	.02	.01
483	*Brian Griffiths*	.15	.11	.06
484	John Wehner	.03	.02	.01
485	Glenn Davis	.03	.02	.01
486	*Eric Wedge*	.25	.20	.10
487	Jesse Hollins	.03	.02	.01
488	Manuel Lee	.03	.02	.01
489	*Scott Fredrickson*	.15	.11	.06
490	Omar Olivares	.03	.02	.01
491	Shawn Hare	.03	.02	.01
492	Tom Lampkin	.03	.02	.01
493	Jeff Nelson	.03	.02	.01
494	K.Young/ Perez	.35	.25	.14
495	Ken Hill	.03	.02	.01
496	Reggie Jefferson	.03	.02	.01
497	M.Petersen/ W.Brown	.35	.25	.14
498	Bud Black	.03	.02	.01
499	Chuck Crim	.03	.02	.01
500	Jose Canseco	.10	.08	.04
501	Johnny Oates	.03	.02	.01
502	Butch Hobson	.03	.02	.01
503	Buck Rodgers	.03	.02	.01
504	Gene Lamont	.03	.02	.01
505	Mike Hargrove	.03	.02	.01
506	Sparky Anderson	.03	.02	.01
507	Hal McRae	.03	.02	.01
508	Phil Garner	.03	.02	.01
509	Tom Kelly	.03	.02	.01
510	Buck Showalter	.03	.02	.01
511	Tony LaRussa	.03	.02	.01
512	Lou Piniella	.03	.02	.01
513	Toby Harrah	.03	.02	.01

		MT	NR MT	EX
514	Cito Gaston	.03	.02	.01
515	Greg Swindell	.03	.02	.01
516	Alex Arias	.03	.02	.01
517	Bill Pecota	.03	.02	.01
518	*Benji Grigsby*	.20	.15	.08
519	David Howard	.03	.02	.01
520	Charlie Hough	.03	.02	.01
521	Kevin Flora	.03	.02	.01
522	Shane Reynolds	.03	.02	.01
523	*Doug Bochtler*	.15	.11	.06
524	Chris Hoiles	.03	.02	.01
525	Scott Sanderson	.03	.02	.01
526	Mike Sharperson	.03	.02	.01
527	Mike Fetters	.03	.02	.01
528	Paul Quantrill	.03	.02	.01
529	C.Jones/ Gil	.30	.25	.12
530	Sterling Hitchcock	.03	.02	.01
531	Joe Millette	.03	.02	.01
532	Tom Brunansky	.03	.02	.01
533	Frank Castillo	.03	.02	.01
534	Randy Knorr	.03	.02	.01
535	Jose Oquendo	.03	.02	.01
536	Dave Haas	.03	.02	.01
537	J.Hutchins/ R.Turner	.20	.15	.08
538	Jimmy Baron	.03	.02	.01
539	Kerry Woodson	.03	.02	.01
540	Ivan Calderon	.03	.02	.01
541	Denis Boucher	.03	.02	.01
542	Royce Clayton	.03	.02	.01
543	Reggie Williams	.03	.02	.01
544	Steve Decker	.03	.02	.01
545	Dean Palmer	.03	.02	.01
546	Hal Morris	.03	.02	.01
547	*Ryan Thompson*(FC)	.20	.15	.08
548	Lance Blankenship	.03	.02	.01
549	Hensley Meulens	.03	.02	.01
550	Scott Radinsky	.03	.02	.01
551	*Eric Young*(FC)	.20	.15	.08
552	Jeff Blauser	.03	.02	.01
553	Andujar Cedeno	.03	.02	.01
554	Arthur Rhodes	.03	.02	.01
555	Terry Mulholland	.03	.02	.01
556	Darryl Hamilton	.03	.02	.01
557	Pedro Martinez	.03	.02	.01
558	R.Whitman/ M.Skeels	.25	.20	.10
559	*Jamie Arnold*(FC)	.20	.15	.08
560	Zane Smith	.03	.02	.01
561	Matt Nokes	.03	.02	.01
562	Bob Zupcic	.03	.02	.01
563	Shawn Boskie	.03	.02	.01
564	Mike Timlin	.03	.02	.01
565	Jerald Clark	.03	.02	.01
566	Rod Brewer	.03	.02	.01
567	Mark Carreon	.03	.02	.01
568	Andy Benes	.03	.02	.01
569	Shawn Barton	.03	.02	.01
570	Tim Wallach	.03	.02	.01
571	Dave Mlicki	.03	.02	.01
572	Trevor Hoffman	.03	.02	.01
573	John Patterson	.03	.02	.01
574	De Shawn Warren	.03	.02	.01
575	Monty Fariss	.03	.02	.01
576	C.Floyd/ Buford	.60	.45	.25
577	Tim Costo	.03	.02	.01
578	Dave Magadan, Sean Berry	.03	.02	.01
579	N.Garret/ J.Bates, Charlie Hayes	.30	.25	.12
580	Walt Weiss	.03	.02	.01
581	Chris Haney	.03	.02	.01
582	Shawn Abner	.03	.02	.01
583	Marvin Freeman	.03	.02	.01
584	Casey Candaele	.03	.02	.01
585	Ricky Jordan	.03	.02	.01
586	Jeff Tabaka	.03	.02	.01
587	Manny Alexander	.03	.02	.01
588	Mike Trombley	.03	.02	.01
589	Carlos Hernandez	.03	.02	.01
590	Cal Eldred	.03	.02	.01
591	Alex Cole	.03	.02	.01
592	Phil Plantier	.03	.02	.01
593	Brett Merriman	.03	.02	.01
594	Jerry Nielsen	.03	.02	.01
595	Shawon Dunston	.03	.02	.01
596	Jimmy Key	.03	.02	.01
597	Gerald Perry	.03	.02	.01
598	Rico Brogna	.03	.02	.01
599	C. Nunez	.30	.25	.12
600	Bret Saberhagen	.03	.02	.01
601	Craig Shipley	.03	.02	.01
602	Henry Mercedes	.03	.02	.01
603	Jim Thome	.03	.02	.01
604	Rod Beck	.03	.02	.01

		MT	NR MT	EX
605	Chuck Finley	.03	.02	.01
606	J. Owens	.03	.02	.01
607	Dan Smith	.03	.02	.01
608	Bill Doran	.03	.02	.01
609	Lance Parrish	.03	.02	.01
610	Denny Martinez	.03	.02	.01
611	Tom Gordon	.03	.02	.01
612	Byron Mathews	.03	.02	.01
613	Joel Adamson	.03	.02	.01
614	Brian Williams	.03	.02	.01
615	Steve Avery	.03	.02	.01
616	Matt Mieske (TP)	.30	.25	.12
617	Craig Lefferts	.03	.02	.01
618	Tony Pena	.03	.02	.01
619	Billy Spiers	.03	.02	.01
620	Todd Benzinger	.03	.02	.01
621	M.Kotarski/ G.Boyd	.30	.25	.12
622	Ben Rivera	.03	.02	.01
623	*Al Martin*(FC)	.25	.20	.10
624	Sam Militello	.03	.02	.01
625	Rick Aguilera	.03	.02	.01
626	Danny Gladden	.03	.02	.01
627	Andres Berumen	.03	.02	.01
628	Kelly Gruber	.03	.02	.01
629	Cris Carpenter	.03	.02	.01
630	Mark Grace	.03	.02	.01
631	Jeff Brantley	.03	.02	.01
632	Chris Widger	.03	.02	.01
633	Three Russians	.25	.20	.10
634	Mo Sanford	.03	.02	.01
635	Albert Belle	.03	.02	.01
636	Tim Teufel	.03	.02	.01
637	Greg Myers	.03	.02	.01
638	Brian Bohanon	.03	.02	.01
639	Mike Bordick	.03	.02	.01
640	Doc Gooden	.03	.02	.01
641	P.Leahy/ G.Baugh	.20	.15	.08
642	Milt Hill	.03	.02	.01
643	Luis Aquino	.03	.02	.01
644	Dante Bichette	.03	.02	.01
645	Bobby Thigpen	.03	.02	.01
646	Rich Scheid	.03	.02	.01
647	Brian Sackinsky	.03	.02	.01
648	Ryan Hawblitzel	.03	.02	.01
649	Tom Marsh	.03	.02	.01
650	Terry Pendleton	.03	.02	.01
651	*Rafael Bourmigal*(FC)	.25	.20	.10
652	Dave West	.03	.02	.01
653	Steve Hosey	.03	.02	.01
654	Gerald Williams	.03	.02	.01
655	Scott Cooper	.03	.02	.01
656	Gary Scott	.03	.02	.01
657	Mike Harkey	.03	.02	.01
658	Top Prospects	.30	.25	.12
659	Ed Sprague	.03	.02	.01
660	Alan Trammell	.03	.02	.01
661	G.Alston/ M.Case	.25	.20	.10
662	Donovan Osborne	.03	.02	.01
663	Jeff Gardner	.03	.02	.01
664	Calvin Jones	.03	.02	.01
665	Darrin Fletcher	.03	.02	.01
666	Glenallen Hill	.03	.02	.01
667	Jim Rosenbohm	.03	.02	.01
668	Scott Lewis	.03	.02	.01
669	Kip Yaughn	.03	.02	.01
670	Julio Franco	.03	.02	.01
671	Dave Martinez	.03	.02	.01
672	Kevin Bass	.03	.02	.01
673	Todd Van Poppel	.03	.02	.01
674	Mark Gubicza	.03	.02	.01
675	Tim Raines	.03	.02	.01
676	Rudy Seanez	.03	.02	.01
677	Charlie Leibrandt	.03	.02	.01
678	Randy Milligan	.03	.02	.01
679	Kim Batiste	.03	.02	.01
680	Craig Biggio	.03	.02	.01
681	Darren Holmes	.03	.02	.01
682	John Candelaria	.03	.02	.01
683	Stafford/ Christian	.25	.20	.10
684	Pat Mahomes	.03	.02	.01
685	Bob Walk	.03	.02	.01
686	Russ Springer	.03	.02	.01
687	Tony Sheffield	.03	.02	.01
688	Dwight Smith	.03	.02	.01
689	Eddie Zosky	.03	.02	.01
690	Bien Figuerroa	.03	.02	.01
691	Jim Tatum	.03	.02	.01
692	Chad Kreuter	.03	.02	.01
693	Rich Rodriguez	.03	.02	.01
694	Shane Turner	.03	.02	.01
695	Kent Bottenfield	.03	.02	.01

		MT	NR MT	EX
696	Jose Mesa	.03	.02	.01
697	*Darrell Whitmore*	.20	.15	.08
698	Ted Wood	.03	.02	.01
699	Chad Curtis	.03	.02	.01
700	Nolan Ryan	.40	.30	.15
701	Mike Piazza (Delgado)	2.00	1.50	.80
702	*Tim Pugh*(FC)	.25	.20	.10
703	Jeff Kent	.03	.02	.01
704	J.Goodrich/ D.Figueroa	.20	.15	.08
705	Bob Welch	.03	.02	.01
706	Sherard Clinkscales	.03	.02	.01
707	Donn Pall	.03	.02	.01
708	Greg Olson	.03	.02	.01
709	Jeff Juden	.03	.02	.01
710	Mike Mussina	.25	.20	.10
711	Scott Chiamparino	.03	.02	.01
712	Stan Javier	.03	.02	.01
713	John Doherty	.03	.02	.01
714	Kevin Gross	.03	.02	.01
715	Greg Gagne	.03	.02	.01
716	Steve Cooke	.03	.02	.01
717	Steve Farr	.03	.02	.01
718	Jay Buchner	.03	.02	.01
719	Butch Henry	.03	.02	.01
720	David Cone	.03	.02	.01
721	Rick Wilkins	.03	.02	.01
722	Chuck Carr	.03	.02	.01
723	*Kenny Felder*(FC)	.30	.25	.12
724	Guillermo Velasquez	.03	.02	.01
725	Billy Hatcher	.03	.02	.01
726	Veneziale/ Kendrena	.20	.15	.08
727	Jonathan Hurst	.03	.02	.01
728	Steve Frey	.03	.02	.01
729	Mark Leonard	.03	.02	.01
730	Charles Nagy	.03	.02	.01
731	Donald Harris	.03	.02	.01
732	Travis Buckley	.03	.02	.01
733	Tom Browning	.03	.02	.01
734	Anthony Young	.03	.02	.01
735	Steve Shifflett	.03	.02	.01
736	Jeff Russell	.03	.02	.01
737	Wilson Alvarez	.03	.02	.01
738	Lance Painter	.03	.02	.01
739	Dave Weathers	.03	.02	.01
740	Len Dykstra	.03	.02	.01
741	Mike Devereaux	.03	.02	.01
742	Arocha/ Embree	.60	.45	.25
743	Dave Landaker	.03	.02	.01
744	Chris George	.03	.02	.01
745	Eric Davis	.03	.02	.01
746	Rookies	.25	.20	.10
747	Carl Willis	.03	.02	.01
748	Stan Belinda	.03	.02	.01
749	Scott Kamieniecki	.03	.02	.01
750	Rickey Henderson	.15	.11	.06
751	Eric Hillman	.03	.02	.01
752	Pat Hertgen	.03	.02	.01
753	Jim Corsi	.03	.02	.01
754	Brian Jordan	.15	.11	.06
755	Bill Swift	.03	.02	.01
756	Mike Henneman	.03	.02	.01
757	Harold Reynolds	.03	.02	.01
760	Luis Polonia	.03	.02	.01
761	Darrin Jackson	.03	.02	.01
762	Mark Lewis	.03	.02	.01
763	Rob Maurer	.03	.02	.01
764	Willie Greene	.03	.02	.01
765	Vince Coleman	.03	.02	.01
766	Todd Revenig	.03	.02	.01
767	Rich Ireland	.03	.02	.01
768	Mike MacFarlane	.03	.02	.01
769	Francisco Cabrera	.03	.02	.01
770	Robin Ventura	.03	.02	.01
771	Kevin Ritz	.03	.02	.01
772	Chito Martinez	.03	.02	.01
773	Cliff Brantley	.03	.02	.01
774	Curtis Leskanic	.03	.02	.01
775	Chris Bosio	.03	.02	.01
776	Jose Offerman	.03	.02	.01
777	Mark Guthrie	.03	.02	.01
778	Don Slaught	.03	.02	.01
779	Rich Monteleone	.03	.02	.01
780	Jim Abbott	.03	.02	.01
781	Jack Clark	.03	.02	.01
782	R.Mendoza/ D.Roman	.20	.15	.08
783	Heathcliff Slocumb	.03	.02	.01
784	Jeff Branson	.03	.02	.01
785	Kevin Brown	.03	.02	.01
786	Ryan/Tay/ Ganda	.25	.20	.10
787	Mike Matthews	.03	.02	.01
788	Mackey Sasser	.03	.02	.01

		MT	NR MT	EX
789	Jeff Conine	.03	.02	.01
790	George Bell	.03	.02	.01
791	Pat Rapp	.03	.02	.01
792	Joe Boever	.03	.02	.01
793	Jim Poole	.03	.02	.01
794	Andy Ashby	.03	.02	.01
795	Deion Sanders	.03	.02	.01
796	Scott Brosius	.03	.02	.01
797	Brad Pennington	.03	.02	.01
798	Greg Blosser	.03	.02	.01
799	Jim Edmonds	.03	.02	.01
800	Shawn Jeter	.03	.02	.01
801	Jesse Levis	.03	.02	.01
802	Phil Clark	.03	.02	.01
803	Ed Pierce	.03	.02	.01
804	Jose Valentin	.03	.02	.01
805	Terry Jorgensen	.03	.02	.01
806	Mark Hutton	.03	.02	.01
807	*Troy Neel*(FC)	.20	.15	.08
808	*Bret Boone*(FC)	.20	.15	.08
809	Chris Colon	.03	.02	.01
810	*Domingo Martinez*	.25	.20	.10
811	*Javy Lopez*(FC)	.30	.25	.12
812	Matt Walbeck	.03	.02	.01
813	Dan Wilson	.03	.02	.01
814	Scooter Tucker	.03	.02	.01
815	*Billy Ashley*(FC)	.30	.25	.12
816	*Tim Laker*(FC)	.20	.15	.08
817	*Bobby Jones*(FC)	.30	.25	.12
818	Brad Brink	.03	.02	.01
819	William Pennyfeather	.03	.02	.01
820	Stan Royer	.03	.02	.01
821	Doug Brocail	.03	.02	.01
822	Kevin Rogers	.03	.02	.01
823	Checklist 4 of 6	.03	.02	.01
824	Checklist 5 of 6	.03	.02	.01
825	Checklist 6 of 6	.03	.02	.01

1993 Topps Gold

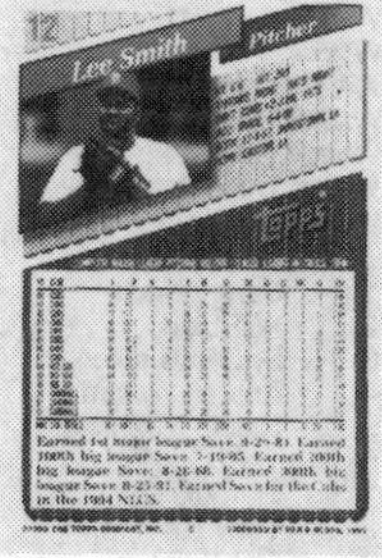

Expanding on the concept begun in 1992, Topps issued a "Gold" version of each of its regular 1993 cards as a premium insert. One Gold card was found in each wax packs; three per rack pack and five per jumbo. Ten Gold cards were included in each Topps factory set. Identical in format to the 1993 Topps regular-issue cards, the gold version replaces the black or white Topps logo in the card's upper corner with a Topps Gold logo in gold foil. The color bars and angled strips below the player photo which contain the player's name and team on a regular card are replaced with a gold-foil version on the inserts. Backs are identical to the regular cards.

	MT	NR MT	EX
Complete Set (825):	140.00	100.00	55.00
Common Gold card:	.15	.11	.06
Gold stars: 3X-5X regular Topps			

A player's name in italic indicates a rookie card. An (FC) indicates a player's first card for that particular card company.

1993 Topps Black Gold

Randomly inserted in regular 1993 Topps packs, as well as 10 per factory set, Black Gold cards are found in both single-player versions and "Winner" cards. The single-player cards feature an action photo set against a black background and highlighted at top and bottom with gold foil. Backs have another player photo at left, again on a black background. A career summary is printed in a blue box at right. A "Topps Black Gold" logo appears at top left, and the player's name is printed in gold foil in an art deco device at top right. The Winner cards picture tiny versions of the Black Gold player cards for which they could be redeemed by mail.

		MT	NR MT	EX
Complete Set (44):		30.00	22.00	12.00
Common Player:		.25	.20	.10
Winner A (1-11)		4.50	3.50	1.75
Winner B (12-22):		4.50	3.50	1.75
Winner C (23-33):		10.00	7.50	4.00
Winner D (34-44):		10.00	7.50	4.00
Winner AB (1-22):		10.00	7.50	4.00
Winner CD (23-44):		18.00	13.50	7.25
Winner ABCD (1-44):		25.00	18.50	10.00
1	Barry Bonds	2.50	2.00	1.00
2	Will Clark	1.00	.70	.40
3	Darren Daulton	.60	.45	.25
4	Andre Dawson	.50	.40	.20
5	Delino DeShields	.50	.40	.20
6	Tom Glavine	1.00	.70	.40
7	Marquis Grissom	1.00	.70	.40
8	Tony Gwynn	1.00	.70	.40
9	Eric Karros	1.00	.70	.40
10	Ray Lankford	.25	.20	.10
11	Barry Larkin	.40	.30	.15
12	Greg Maddux	.75	.60	.30
13	Fred McGriff	1.00	.70	.40
14	Joe Oliver	.25	.20	.10
15	Terry Pendleton	.25	.20	.10
16	Bip Roberts	.25	.20	.10
17	Ryne Sandberg	2.00	1.50	.80
18	Gary Sheffield	.75	.60	.30
19	Lee Smith	.25	.20	.10
20	Ozzie Smith	.75	.60	.30
21	Andy Van Slyke	.25	.20	.10
22	Larry Walker	.50	.40	.20
23	Roberto Alomar	2.00	1.50	.80
24	Brady Anderson	.25	.20	.10
25	Carlos Baerga	2.00	1.50	.80
26	Joe Carter	1.50	1.25	.60
27	Roger Clemens	1.25	.90	.50
28	Mike Devereaux	.25	.20	.10
29	Dennis Eckersley	.25	.20	.10
30	Cecil Fielder	1.00	.70	.40
31	Travis Fryman	2.00	1.50	.80
32	Juan Gonzalez	4.00	3.00	1.50
33	Ken Griffey Jr.	4.00	3.00	1.50
34	Brian Harper	.25	.20	.10
35	Pat Listach	.60	.45	.25
36	Kenny Lofton	1.50	1.25	.60
37	Edgar Martinez	.25	.20	.10
38	Jack McDowell	1.00	.70	.40
39	Mark McGwire	1.00	.70	.40
40	Kirby Puckett	2.00	1.50	.80
41	Mickey Tettleton	.25	.20	.10
42	Frank Thomas	5.00	3.75	2.00
43	Robin Ventura	1.00	.70	.40
44	Dave Winfield	1.00	.70	.40

1993 Topps Traded

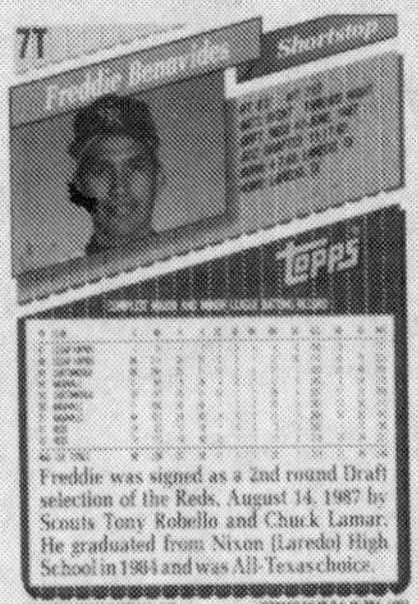

The 1993 Topps Traded baseball set features many players in their new uniforms. National League sluggers Fred McGriff and Gary Sheffield each appear in Atlanta and Florida uniforms, respectively. The set features 35 expansion players from the Colorado Rockies and Florida Marlins, as well as 22 Team USA members exclusive to Topps. The 132-card set is packed in a color deluxe printed box.

		MT	NR MT	EX
Complete Set (132):		14.00	10.50	5.50
Common Player:		.05	.04	.02
1	Barry Bonds	.50	.40	.20
2	Rich Renteria	.05	.04	.02
3	Aaron Sele	.60	.45	.25
4	*Carlton Loewer* (USA)	.30	.25	.12
5	Erik Pappas	.05	.04	.02
6	*Greg McMichael*	.15	.11	.06
7	Freddie Benavides	.05	.04	.02
8	Kirk Gibson	.05	.04	.02
9	Tony Fernandez	.05	.04	.02
10	*Jay Gainer* (USA)	.25	.20	.10
11	Orestes Destrade	.05	.04	.02
12	*A.J. Hinch* (USA)	.30	.25	.12
13	Bobby Munoz	.05	.04	.02
14	Tom Henke	.05	.04	.02
15	Rob Butler	.10	.08	.04
16	Gary Wayne	.05	.04	.02
17	David McCarty	.25	.20	.10
18	Walt Weiss	.05	.04	.02
19	*Todd Helton* (USA)	.50	.40	.20
20	Mark Whiten	.05	.04	.02
21	Ricky Gutierrez	.10	.08	.04
22	*Dustin Hermanson* (USA)	.25	.20	.10
23	*Sherman Obando*	.10	.08	.04
24	Mike Piazza	2.50	2.00	1.00
25	Jeff Russell	.05	.04	.02
26	Jason Bere	1.00	.70	.40
27	*Jack Voight*	.10	.08	.04
28	Chris Bosio	.05	.04	.02
29	Phil Hiatt	.15	.11	.06
30	*Matt Beaumont* (USA)	.25	.20	.10
31	Andres Galarraga	.10	.08	.04
32	Greg Swindell	.05	.04	.02
33	Vinny Castilla	.05	.04	.02
34	*Pat Clougherty* (USA)	.25	.20	.10
35	Greg Briley	.05	.04	.02
36	Dallas Green, Davey Johnson	.05	.04	.02
37	Tyler Green	.10	.08	.04
38	Craig Paquette	.10	.08	.04
39	Danny Sheaffer	.05	.04	.02
40	Jim Converse	.05	.04	.02
41	Terry Harvey	.05	.04	.02
42	Phil Plantier	.10	.08	.04
43	*Doug Saunders*	.10	.08	.04
44	Benny Santiago	.05	.04	.02
45	*Dante Powell* (USA)	.50	.40	.20
46	Jeff Parrett	.05	.04	.02
47	Wade Boggs	.10	.08	.04
48	Paul Molitor	.20	.15	.08
49	Turk Wendell	.05	.04	.02

		MT	NR MT	EX
50	David Wells	.05	.04	.02
51	Gary Sheffield	.10	.08	.04
52	Kevin Young	.15	.11	.06
53	Nelson Liriano	.05	.04	.02
54	Greg Maddux	.15	.11	.06
55	Derek Bell	.05	.04	.02
56	*Matt Turner*	.20	.15	.08
57	*Charlie Nelson* (USA)	.25	.20	.10
58	Mike Hampton	.05	.04	.02
59	*Troy O'Leary*	.15	.11	.06
60	Benji Gil	.15	.11	.06
61	*Mitch Lyden*	.15	.11	.06
62	J.T. Snow	.40	.30	.15
63	Damon Buford	.05	.04	.02
64	Gene Harris	.05	.04	.02
65	Randy Myers	.05	.04	.02
66	Felix Jose	.05	.04	.02
67	*Todd Dunn* (USA)	.25	.20	.10
68	Jimmy Key	.05	.04	.02
69	Pedro Castellano	.10	.08	.04
70	*Mark Merila* (USA)	.25	.20	.10
71	Rich Rodriguez	.05	.04	.02
72	Matt Mieske	.05	.04	.02
73	Pete Incaviglia	.05	.04	.02
74	Carl Everett	.10	.08	.04
75	Jim Abbott	.10	.08	.04
76	Luis Aquino	.05	.04	.02
77	*Rene Arocha*	.25	.20	.10
78	*Jon Shave*	.10	.08	.04
79	*Todd Walker* (USA)	1.25	.90	.50
80	Jack Armstrong	.05	.04	.02
81	Jeff Richardson	.05	.04	.02
82	Blas Minor	.05	.04	.02
83	Dave Winfield	.15	.11	.06
84	Paul O'Neill	.05	.04	.02
85	*Steve Reich* (USA)	.25	.20	.10
86	Chris Hammond	.05	.04	.02
87	*Hilly Hathaway*	.25	.20	.10
88	Fred McGriff	.20	.15	.08
89	*Dave Telgheder*	.10	.08	.04
90	*Richie Lewis*	.15	.11	.06
91	Brent Gates	.20	.15	.08
92	Andre Dawson	.05	.04	.02
93	*Andy Barkett* (USA)	.25	.20	.10
94	Doug Drabek	.05	.04	.02
95	Joe Klink	.05	.04	.02
96	Willie Blair	.05	.04	.02
97	*Danny Graves* (USA)	.25	.20	.10
98	Pat Meares	.10	.08	.04
99	Mike Lansing	.25	.20	.10
100	*Marcos Armas*	.25	.20	.10
101	*Darren Grass* (USA)	.25	.20	.10
102	Chris Jones	.05	.04	.02
103	*Ken Ryan*	.15	.11	.06
104	Ellis Burks	.05	.04	.02
105	Bobby Kelly	.05	.04	.02
106	Dave Magadan	.05	.04	.02
107	*Paul Wilson* (USA)	.40	.30	.15
108	Rob Natal	.05	.04	.02
109	Paul Wagner	.05	.04	.02
110	Jeromy Burnitz	.15	.11	.06
111	Monty Fariss	.05	.04	.02
112	Kevin Mitchell	.05	.04	.02
113	*Scott Pose*	.15	.11	.06
114	Dave Stewart	.05	.04	.02
115	*Russ Johnson* (USA)	.40	.30	.15
116	Armando Reynoso	.05	.04	.02
117	Geronimo Berroa	.05	.04	.02
118	*Woody Williams*	.15	.11	.06
119	*Tim Bogar*	.15	.11	.06
120	*Bob Scafa* (USA)	.30	.25	.12
121	Henry Cotto	.05	.04	.02
122	Gregg Jefferies	.10	.08	.04
123	Norm Charlton	.05	.04	.02
124	*Bret Wagner* (USA)	.25	.20	.10
125	David Cone	.05	.04	.02
126	Daryl Boston	.05	.04	.02
127	Tim Wallach	.05	.04	.02
128	*Mike Martin* (USA)	.25	.20	.10
129	*John Cummings*	.15	.11	.06
130	Ryan Bowen	.05	.04	.02
131	*John Powell* (USA)	.50	.40	.20
132	Checklist 1	.05	.04	.02

Definitions for grading conditions are located in the Introduction of this price guide.

1993 Topps Stadium Club

Topps' premium set for 1993 was issued in three series, two 300-card series and a final series of 150. Boxes contained 24 packs this year, compared to 36 in the past. Packs had 14 cards and an insert card. Each box had a 5" by 7" Master Photo card.

	MT	NR MT	EX
Complete Set (750):	65.00	45.00	25.00
Common Player:	.10	.08	.04

		MT	NR MT	EX
1	Pat Borders	.10	.08	.04
2	Greg Maddux	.30	.25	.12
3	Daryl Boston	.10	.08	.04
4	Bob Ayrault	.10	.08	.04
5	Tony Phillips	.10	.08	.04
6	Damion Easley	.30	.25	.12
7	Kip Gross	.10	.08	.04
8	Jim Thome	.10	.08	.04
9	Tim Belcher	.10	.08	.04
10	Gary Wayne	.10	.08	.04
11	Sam Militello	.50	.40	.20
12	Mike Magnante	.10	.08	.04
13	Tim Wakefield	.20	.15	.08
14	Tim Hulett	.10	.08	.04
15	Rheal Cormier	.10	.08	.04
16	Juan Guerrero	.30	.25	.12
17	Rich Gossage	.10	.08	.04
18	Tim Laker	.10	.08	.04
19	Darrin Jackson	.10	.08	.04
20	Jack Clark	.10	.08	.04
21	Roberto Hernandez	.10	.08	.04
22	Dean Palmer	.30	.25	.12
23	Harold Reynolds	.10	.08	.04
24	Dan Plesac	.10	.08	.04
25	Brent Mayne	.10	.08	.04
26	Pat Hentgen	.25	.20	.10
27	Luis Sojo	.10	.08	.04
28	Ron Gant	.25	.20	.10
29	Paul Gibson	.10	.08	.04
30	Bip Roberts	.10	.08	.04
31	Mickey Tettleton	.25	.20	.10
32	Randy Velarde	.10	.08	.04
33	Brian McRae	.10	.08	.04
34	Wes Chamberlain	.10	.08	.04
35	Wayne Kirby	.10	.08	.04
36	Rey Sanchez	.10	.08	.04
37	Jesse Orosco	.10	.08	.04
38	Mike Stanton	.10	.08	.04
39	Royce Clayton	.30	.25	.12
40	Cal Ripken, Jr.	.75	.60	.30
41	John Dopson	.10	.08	.04
42	Gene Larkin	.10	.08	.04
43	Tim Raines	.10	.08	.04
44	Randy Myers	.10	.08	.04
45	Clay Parker	.10	.08	.04
46	Mike Scioscia	.10	.08	.04
47	Pete Incaviglia	.10	.08	.04
48	Todd Van Poppel	.40	.30	.15
49	Ray Lankford	.25	.20	.10
50	Eddie Murray	.25	.20	.10
51	Barry Bonds	1.00	.70	.40
52	Gary Thurman	.10	.08	.04

		MT	NR MT	EX
53	Bob Wickman	.50	.40	.20
54	Joey Cora	.10	.08	.04
55	Kenny Rogers	.10	.08	.04
56	Mike Devereaux	.10	.08	.04
57	Kevin Seitzer	.10	.08	.04
58	Rafael Belliard	.10	.08	.04
59	David Wells	.10	.08	.04
60	Mark Clark	.10	.08	.04
61	Carlos Baerga	.50	.40	.20
62	Scott Brosius	.10	.08	.04
63	Jeff Grotewold	.25	.20	.10
64	Rick Wrona	.10	.08	.04
65	Kurt Knudsen	.10	.08	.04
66	Lloyd McClendon	.10	.08	.04
67	Omar Vizquel	.10	.08	.04
68	Jose Vizcaino	.10	.08	.04
69	Rob Ducey	.10	.08	.04
70	Casey Candaele	.10	.08	.04
71	Ramon Martinez	.25	.20	.10
72	Todd Hundley	.10	.08	.04
73	John Marzano	.10	.08	.04
74	Derek Parks	.10	.08	.04
75	Jack McDowell	.25	.20	.10
76	Tim Scott	.25	.20	.10
77	Mike Mussina	.60	.45	.25
78	Delino DeShields	.30	.25	.12
79	Chris Bosio	.10	.08	.04
80	Mike Bordick	.10	.08	.04
81	Rod Beck	.10	.08	.04
82	Ted Power	.10	.08	.04
83	John Kruk	.10	.08	.04
84	Steve Shifflett	.30	.25	.12
85	Danny Tartabull	.10	.08	.04
86	Mike Greenwell	.10	.08	.04
87	Jose Melendez	.10	.08	.04
88	Craig Wilson	.30	.25	.12
89	Melvin Nieves	.30	.25	.12
90	Ed Sprague	.10	.08	.04
91	Willie McGee	.10	.08	.04
92	Joe Orsulak	.10	.08	.04
93	Jeff King	.10	.08	.04
94	Dan Pasqua	.10	.08	.04
95	Brian Harper	.10	.08	.04
96	Joe Oliver	.10	.08	.04
97	Shane Turner	.30	.25	.12
98	Lenny Harris	.10	.08	.04
99	Jeff Parrett	.10	.08	.04
100	Luis Polonia	.10	.08	.04
101	Kent Bottenfield	.30	.25	.12
102	Albert Belle	.50	.40	.20
103	Mike Maddux	.10	.08	.04
104	Randy Tomlin	.10	.08	.04
105	Andy Stankiewicz	.10	.08	.04
106	Rico Rossy	.10	.08	.04
107	Joe Hesketh	.10	.08	.04
108	Dennis Powell	.10	.08	.04
109	Derrick May	.10	.08	.04
110	Pete Harnisch	.10	.08	.04
111	Kent Mercker	.10	.08	.04
112	Scott Fletcher	.10	.08	.04
113	Rex Hudler	.10	.08	.04
114	Chico Walker	.10	.08	.04
115	Rafael Palmeiro	.25	.20	.10
116	Mark Leiter	.10	.08	.04
117	Pedro Munoz	.25	.20	.10
118	Jim Bullinger	.10	.08	.04
119	Ivan Calderon	.10	.08	.04
120	Mike Timlin	.10	.08	.04
121	Rene Gonzales	.10	.08	.04
122	Greg Vaughn	.25	.20	.10
123	Mike Flanagan	.10	.08	.04
124	Mike Hartley	.10	.08	.04
125	Jeff Montgomery	.10	.08	.04
126	Mike Gallego	.10	.08	.04
127	Don Slaught	.10	.08	.04
128	Charlie O'Brien	.10	.08	.04
129	Jose Offerman	.25	.20	.10
130	Mark Wohlers	.10	.08	.04
131	Eric Fox	.25	.20	.10
132	Doug Strange	.10	.08	.04
133	Jeff Frye	.10	.08	.04
134	Wade Boggs	.30	.25	.12
135	Lou Whitaker	.10	.08	.04
136	Craig Grebeck	.10	.08	.04
137	Rich Rodriguez	.10	.08	.04
138	Jay Bell	.10	.08	.04
139	Felix Fermin	.10	.08	.04
140	Denny Martinez	.10	.08	.04
141	Eric Anthony	.10	.08	.04
142	Roberto Alomar	.70	.50	.30
143	Darren Lewis	.10	.08	.04

		MT	NR MT	EX
144	Mike Blowers	.10	.08	.04
145	Scott Bankhead	.10	.08	.04
146	Jeff Reboulet	.10	.08	.04
147	Frank Viola	.10	.08	.04
148	Bill Pecota	.10	.08	.04
149	Carlos Hernandez	.10	.08	.04
150	Bobby Witt	.10	.08	.04
151	Sid Bream	.10	.08	.04
152	Todd Zeile	.25	.20	.10
153	Dennis Cook	.10	.08	.04
154	Brian Bohanon	.10	.08	.04
155	Pat Kelly	.10	.08	.04
156	Milt Cuyler	.10	.08	.04
157	Juan Bell	.10	.08	.04
158	Randy Milligan	.10	.08	.04
159	Mark Gardner	.10	.08	.04
160	Pat Tabler	.10	.08	.04
161	Jeff Reardon	.10	.08	.04
162	Ken Patterson	.10	.08	.04
163	Bobby Bonilla	.15	.11	.06
164	Tony Pena	.10	.08	.04
165	Greg Swindell	.25	.20	.10
166	Kirk McCaskill	.10	.08	.04
167	Doug Drabek	.25	.20	.10
168	Franklin Stubbs	.10	.08	.04
169	Ron Tingley	.10	.08	.04
170	Willie Banks	.10	.08	.04
171	Sergio Valdez	.25	.20	.10
172	Mark Lemke	.10	.08	.04
173	Robin Yount	.40	.30	.15
174	Storm Davis	.10	.08	.04
175	Dan Walters	.10	.08	.04
176	Steve Farr	.10	.08	.04
177	Curt Wilkerson	.10	.08	.04
178	Luis Alicea	.10	.08	.04
179	Russ Swan	.10	.08	.04
180	Mitch Williams	.10	.08	.04
181	Wilson Alvarez	.10	.08	.04
182	Carl Willis	.10	.08	.04
183	Craig Biggio	.10	.08	.04
184	Sean Berry	.25	.20	.10
185	Trevor Wilson	.10	.08	.04
186	Jeff Tackett	.10	.08	.04
187	Ellis Burks	.25	.20	.10
188	Jeff Branson	.25	.20	.10
189	Matt Nokes	.10	.08	.04
190	John Smiley	.10	.08	.04
191	Danny Gladden	.10	.08	.04
192	Mike Boddicker	.10	.08	.04
193	Roger Pavlik	.10	.08	.04
194	Paul Sorrento	.10	.08	.04
195	Vince Coleman	.10	.08	.04
196	Gary DiSarcina	.10	.08	.04
197	Rafael Bournigal	.30	.25	.12
198	Mike Schooler	.10	.08	.04
199	Scott Ruskin	.10	.08	.04
200	Frank Thomas	4.00	3.00	1.50
201	Kyle Abbott	.10	.08	.04
202	Mike Perez	.10	.08	.04
203	Andre Dawson	.30	.25	.12
204	Bill Swift	.10	.08	.04
205	Alejandro Pena	.10	.08	.04
206	Dave Winfield	.30	.25	.12
207	Andujar Cedeno	.30	.25	.12
208	Terry Steinbach	.10	.08	.04
209	Chris Hammond	.10	.08	.04
210	Todd Burns	.10	.08	.04
211	Hipolito Pichardo	.10	.08	.04
212	John Kiely	.30	.25	.12
213	Tim Teufel	.10	.08	.04
214	Lee Guetterman	.10	.08	.04
215	Geronimo Pena	.10	.08	.04
216	Brett Butler	.10	.08	.04
217	Bryan Hickerson	.10	.08	.04
218	Rick Trlicek	.30	.25	.12
219	Lee Stevens	.10	.08	.04
220	Roger Clemens	.50	.40	.20
221	Carlton Fisk	.30	.25	.12
222	Chili Davis	.10	.08	.04
223	Walt Terrell	.10	.08	.04
224	Jim Eisenreich	.10	.08	.04
225	Ricky Bones	.10	.08	.04
226	Henry Rodriguez	.10	.08	.04
227	Ken Hill	.25	.20	.10
228	Rick Wilkins	.10	.08	.04
229	Ricky Jordan	.10	.08	.04
230	Bernard Gilkey	.10	.08	.04
231	Tim Fortugno	.10	.08	.04
232	Geno Petralli	.10	.08	.04
233	Jose Rijo	.10	.08	.04
234	Jim Leyritz	.10	.08	.04

		MT	NR MT	EX
235	Kevin Campbell	.10	.08	.04
236	Al Osuna	.10	.08	.04
237	Pete Smith	.10	.08	.04
238	Pete Schourek	.10	.08	.04
239	Moises Alou	.25	.20	.10
240	Donn Pall	.10	.08	.04
241	Denny Neagle	.10	.08	.04
242	Dan Peltier	.10	.08	.04
243	Scott Scudder	.10	.08	.04
244	Juan Guzman	.50	.40	.20
245	Dave Burba	.10	.08	.04
246	Rick Sutcliffe	.10	.08	.04
247	Tony Fossas	.10	.08	.04
248	Mike Munoz	.10	.08	.04
249	Tim Salmon	3.00	2.25	1.25
250	Rob Murphy	.10	.08	.04
251	Roger McDowell	.10	.08	.04
252	Lance Parrish	.10	.08	.04
253	Cliff Brantley	.10	.08	.04
254	Scott Leius	.10	.08	.04
255	Carlos Martinez	.10	.08	.04
256	Vince Horsman	.10	.08	.04
257	Oscar Azocar	.10	.08	.04
258	Craig Shipley	.10	.08	.04
259	Ben McDonald	.30	.25	.12
260	Jeff Brantley	.10	.08	.04
261	Damon Berryhill	.10	.08	.04
262	Joe Grahe	.10	.08	.04
263	Dave Hansen	.10	.08	.04
264	Rich Amaral	.30	.25	.12
265	Tim Pugh	.35	.25	.14
266	Dion James	.10	.08	.04
267	Frank Tanana	.10	.08	.04
268	Stan Belinda	.10	.08	.04
269	Jeff Kent	.10	.08	.04
270	Bruce Ruffin	.10	.08	.04
271	Xavier Hernandez	.10	.08	.04
272	Darrin Fletcher	.10	.08	.04
273	Tino Martinez	.10	.08	.04
274	Benny Santiago	.25	.20	.10
275	Scott Radinsky	.10	.08	.04
276	Mariano Duncan	.10	.08	.04
277	Kenny Lofton	.80	.60	.30
278	Dwight Smith	.10	.08	.04
279	Joe Carter	.40	.30	.15
280	Tim Jones	.10	.08	.04
281	Jeff Huson	.10	.08	.04
282	Phil Plantier	.40	.30	.15
283	Kirby Puckett	.75	.60	.30
284	Johnny Guzman	.10	.08	.04
285	Mike Morgan	.10	.08	.04
286	Chris Sabo	.10	.08	.04
287	Matt Williams	.10	.08	.04
288	Checklist 1-100	.10	.08	.04
289	Checklist 101-200	.10	.08	.04
290	Checklist 201-300	.10	.08	.04
291	Dennis Eckersley	.50	.40	.20
292	Eric Karros	.40	.30	.15
293	Pat Listach	.25	.20	.10
294	Andy Van Slyke	.25	.20	.10
295	Robin Ventura	.60	.45	.25
296	Tom Glavine	.60	.45	.25
297	Juan Gonzalez	1.00	.70	.40
298	Travis Fryman	.60	.45	.25
299	Larry Walker	.40	.30	.15
300	Gary Sheffield	.40	.30	.15
301	Chuck Finley	.10	.08	.04
302	Luis Gonzalez	.10	.08	.04
303	Darryl Hamilton	.10	.08	.04
304	Bien Figueroa	.10	.08	.04
305	Ron Darling	.10	.08	.04
306	Jonathan Hurst	.10	.08	.04
307	Mike Sharperson	.10	.08	.04
308	Mike Christopher	.10	.08	.04
309	Marvin Freeman	.10	.08	.04
310	Jay Buhner	.15	.11	.06
311	Butch Henry	.10	.08	.04
312	Greg Harris	.10	.08	.04
313	Darren Daulton	.15	.11	.06
314	Chuck Knoblauch	.15	.11	.06
315	Greg Harris	.10	.08	.04
316	John Franco	.10	.08	.04
317	John Wehner	.10	.08	.04
318	Donald Harris	.10	.08	.04
319	Benny Santiago	.10	.08	.04
320	Larry Walker	.25	.20	.10
321	Randy Knorr	.10	.08	.04
322	Ramon Martinez	.10	.08	.04
323	Mike Stanley	.10	.08	.04
324	Bill Wegman	.10	.08	.04
325	Tom Candiotti	.10	.08	.04

		MT	NR MT	EX
326	Glenn Davis	.10	.08	.04
327	Chuck Crim	.10	.08	.04
328	Scott Livingstone	.10	.08	.04
329	Eddie Taubensee	.10	.08	.04
330	George Bell	.10	.08	.04
331	Edgar Martinez	.10	.08	.04
332	Paul Assenmacher	.10	.08	.04
333	Steve Hosey	.40	.30	.15
334	Mo Vaughn	.50	.40	.20
335	Bret Saberhagen	.10	.08	.04
336	Mike Trombley	.10	.08	.04
337	Mark Lewis	.10	.08	.04
338	Terry Pendleton	.10	.08	.04
339	Dave Hollins	.25	.20	.10
340	Jeff Conine	.10	.08	.04
341	Bob Tewksbury	.10	.08	.04
342	Billy Ashley	.80	.60	.30
343	Zane Smith	.10	.08	.04
344	John Wetteland	.10	.08	.04
345	Chris Hoiles	.15	.11	.06
346	Frank Castillo	.10	.08	.04
347	Bruce Hurst	.10	.08	.04
348	Kevin McReynolds	.10	.08	.04
349	Dave Henderson	.10	.08	.04
350	Ryan Bowen	.10	.08	.04
351	Sid Fernandez	.10	.08	.04
352	Mark Whiten	.15	.11	.06
353	Nolan Ryan	2.00	1.50	.80
354	Rick Aguilera	.10	.08	.04
355	Mark Langston	.10	.08	.04
356	Jack Morris	.10	.08	.04
357	Rob Deer	.10	.08	.04
358	Dave Fleming	.20	.15	.08
359	Lance Johnson	.10	.08	.04
360	Joe Millette	.10	.08	.04
361	Wil Cordero	.25	.20	.10
362	Chito Martinez	.10	.08	.04
363	Scott Servais	.10	.08	.04
364	Bernie Williams	.10	.08	.04
365	Pedro Martinez	.25	.20	.10
366	Ryne Sandberg	.75	.60	.30
367	Brad Ausmus	.10	.08	.04
368	Scott Cooper	.10	.08	.04
369	Rob Dibble	.10	.08	.04
370	Walt Weiss	.10	.08	.04
371	Mark Davis	.10	.08	.04
372	Orlando Merced	.10	.08	.04
373	Mike Jackson	.10	.08	.04
374	Kevin Appier	.10	.08	.04
375	Esteban Beltre	.10	.08	.04
376	Joe Slusarski	.10	.08	.04
377	William Suero	.10	.08	.04
378	Pete O'Brien	.10	.08	.04
379	Alan Embree	.20	.15	.08
380	Lenny Webster	.10	.08	.04
381	Eric Davis	.10	.08	.04
382	Duane Ward	.10	.08	.04
383	John Habyan	.10	.08	.04
384	Jeff Bagwell	.50	.40	.20
385	Ruben Amaro	.10	.08	.04
386	Julio Valera	.10	.08	.04
387	Robin Ventura	.50	.40	.20
388	Archi Cianfrocco	.10	.08	.04
389	Skeeter Barnes	.10	.08	.04
390	Tim Costo	.15	.11	.06
391	Luis Mercedes	.10	.08	.04
392	Jeremy Hernandez	.10	.08	.04
393	Shawon Dunston	.10	.08	.04
394	Andy Van Slyke	.10	.08	.04
395	Kevin Maas	.10	.08	.04
396	Kevin Brown	.10	.08	.04
397	J.T. Bruett	.10	.08	.04
398	Darryl Strawberry	.10	.08	.04
399	Tom Pagnozzi	.10	.08	.04
400	Sandy Alomar	.10	.08	.04
401	Keith Miller	.10	.08	.04
402	Rich DeLucia	.10	.08	.04
403	Shawn Abner	.10	.08	.04
404	Howard Johnson	.10	.08	.04
405	Mike Benjamin	.10	.08	.04
406	*Roberto Mejia*	.60	.45	.25
407	Mike Butcher	.10	.08	.04
408	Deion Sanders	.30	.25	.12
409	Todd Stottlemyre	.10	.08	.04
410	Scott Kamieniecki	.10	.08	.04
411	Doug Jones	.10	.08	.04
412	John Burkett	.10	.08	.04
413	Lance Blankenship	.10	.08	.04
414	Jeff Parrett	.10	.08	.04
415	Barry Larkin	.15	.11	.06
416	Alan Trammell	.10	.08	.04

		MT	NR MT	EX
417	Mark Kiefer	.10	.08	.04
418	Gregg Olson	.10	.08	.04
419	Mark Grace	.25	.20	.10
420	Shane Mack	.10	.08	.04
421	Bob Walk	.10	.08	.04
422	Curt Schilling	.10	.08	.04
423	Erik Hanson	.10	.08	.04
424	George Brett	.20	.15	.08
425	Reggie Jefferson	.10	.08	.04
426	Mark Portugal	.10	.08	.04
427	Ron Karkovice	.10	.08	.04
428	Matt Young	.10	.08	.04
429	Troy Neel	.50	.40	.20
430	Hector Fajardo	.10	.08	.04
431	Dave Righetti	.10	.08	.04
432	Pat Listach	.20	.15	.08
433	Jeff Innis	.10	.08	.04
434	Bob McDonald	.10	.08	.04
435	Brian Jordan	.10	.08	.04
436	Jeff Blauser	.10	.08	.04
437	*Mike Myers*	.25	.20	.10
438	Frank Seminara	.10	.08	.04
439	Rusty Meacham	.10	.08	.04
440	Greg Briley	.10	.08	.04
441	Derek Lilliquist	.10	.08	.04
442	John Vander Wal	.10	.08	.04
443	Scott Erickson	.10	.08	.04
444	Bob Scanlan	.10	.08	.04
445	Todd Frohwirth	.10	.08	.04
446	Tom Goodwin	.10	.08	.04
447	William Pennyfeather	.10	.08	.04
448	Travis Fryman	.75	.60	.30
449	Mickey Morandini	.10	.08	.04
450	Greg Olson	.10	.08	.04
451	Trevor Hoffman	.10	.08	.04
452	Dave Magadan	.10	.08	.04
453	Shawn Jeter	.20	.15	.08
454	Andres Galarraga	.15	.11	.06
455	Ted Wood	.10	.08	.04
456	Freddie Benavides	.10	.08	.04
457	Junior Felix	.10	.08	.04
458	Alex Cole	.10	.08	.04
459	John Orton	.10	.08	.04
460	Eddie Zosky	.10	.08	.04
461	Dennis Eckersley	.10	.08	.04
462	Lee Smith	.10	.08	.04
463	John Smoltz	.15	.11	.06
464	Ken Caminiti	.10	.08	.04
465	Melido Perez	.10	.08	.04
466	Tom Marsh	.10	.08	.04
467	Jeff Nelson	.10	.08	.04
468	Jesse Levis	.10	.08	.04
469	Chris Nabholz	.10	.08	.04
470	Mike Mcfarlane	.10	.08	.04
471	Reggie Sanders	.25	.20	.10
472	Chuck McElroy	.10	.08	.04
473	Kevin Gross	.10	.08	.04
474	*Matt Whiteside*	.20	.15	.08
475	Cal Eldred	.25	.20	.10
476	Dave Gallagher	.10	.08	.04
477	Len Dykstra	.15	.11	.06
478	Mark McGwire	.25	.20	.10
479	David Segui	.10	.08	.04
480	Mike Henneman	.10	.08	.04
481	Bret Barberie	.10	.08	.04
482	Steve Sax	.10	.08	.04
483	Dave Valle	.10	.08	.04
484	Danny Darwin	.10	.08	.04
485	Devon White	.15	.11	.06
486	Eric Plunk	.10	.08	.04
487	Jim Gott	.10	.08	.04
488	Scooter Tucker	.10	.08	.04
489	Omar Oliveres	.10	.08	.04
490	Greg Myers	.10	.08	.04
491	Brian Hunter	.10	.08	.04
492	Kevin Tapani	.10	.08	.04
493	Rich Monteleone	.10	.08	.04
494	Steve Buechele	.10	.08	.04
495	Bo Jackson	.25	.20	.10
496	Mike LaValliere	.10	.08	.04
497	Mark Leonard	.10	.08	.04
498	Daryl Boston	.10	.08	.04
499	Jose Canseco	.20	.15	.08
500	Brian Barnes	.10	.08	.04
501	Randy Johnson	.15	.11	.06
502	Tim McIntosh	.10	.08	.04
503	Cecil Fielder	.40	.30	.15
504	Derek Bell	.20	.15	.08
505	Kevin Koslofski	.10	.08	.04
506	Darren Holmes	.10	.08	.04
507	Brady Anderson	.10	.08	.04
508	John Valentin	.40	.30	.15
509	Jerry Browne	.10	.08	.04
510	Fred McGriff	.60	.45	.25
511	Pedro Astacio	.50	.40	.20
512	Gary Gaetti	.10	.08	.04
513	*John Burke*	.30	.25	.12
514	Doc Gooden	.10	.08	.04
515	Thomas Howard	.10	.08	.04
516	*Darrell Whitmore*	1.00	.70	.40
517	Ozzie Guillen	.10	.08	.04
518	Darryl Kile	.10	.08	.04
519	Rich Rowland	.10	.08	.04
520	Carlos Delgado	2.00	1.50	.80
521	Doug Henry	.10	.08	.04
522	Greg Colbrunn	.10	.08	.04
523	Tom Gordon	.10	.08	.04
524	Ivan Rodriquez	.40	.30	.15
525	Kent Hrbek	.10	.08	.04
526	Eric Young	.40	.30	.15
527	Rod Brewer	.10	.08	.04
528	Eric Karros	.35	.25	.14
529	Marquis Grissom	.30	.25	.12
530	Rico Brogna	.10	.08	.04
531	Sammy Sosa	.20	.15	.08
532	Bret Boone	.20	.15	.08
533	Luis Rivera	.10	.08	.04
534	Hal Morris	.10	.08	.04
535	Monty Fariss	.10	.08	.04
536	Leo Gomez	.10	.08	.04
537	Wally Joyner	.10	.08	.04
538	Tony Gwynn	.25	.20	.10
539	Mike Williams	.10	.08	.04
540	Juan Gonzalez	3.00	2.25	1.25
541	Ryan Klesko	1.00	.70	.40
542	Ryan Thompson	.40	.30	.15
543	Chad Curtis	.30	.25	.12
544	Orel Hershiser	.10	.08	.04
545	Carlos Garcia	.15	.11	.06
546	Bob Welch	.10	.08	.04
547	Vinny Castilla	.10	.08	.04
548	Ozzie Smith	.25	.20	.10
549	Luis Salazar	.10	.08	.04
550	Mark Guthrie	.10	.08	.04
551	Charles Nagy	.10	.08	.04
552	Alex Fernandez	.25	.20	.10
553	Mel Rojas	.10	.08	.04
554	Orestes Destrade	.10	.08	.04
555	Mark Gubicza	.10	.08	.04
556	Steve Finley	.10	.08	.04
557	Don Mattingly	.40	.30	.15
558	Rickey Henderson	.25	.20	.10
559	Tommy Greene	.10	.08	.04
560	Arthur Rhodes	.10	.08	.04
561	Alfredo Griffin	.10	.08	.04
562	Will Clark	.30	.25	.12
563	Bob Zupcic	.10	.08	.04
564	Chuck Carr	.10	.08	.04
565	Henry Cotto	.10	.08	.04
566	Billy Spiers	.10	.08	.04
567	Jack Armstrong	.10	.08	.04
568	Kurt Stillwell	.10	.08	.04
569	David McCarty	1.25	.90	.50
570	Joe Vitiello	.40	.30	.15
571	Gerald Williams	.10	.08	.04
572	Dale Murphy	.10	.08	.04
573	Scott Aldred	.10	.08	.04
574	Bill Gullickson	.10	.08	.04
575	Bobby Thigpen	.10	.08	.04
576	Glenallen Hill	.10	.08	.04
577	Dwayne Henry	.10	.08	.04
578	Calvin Jones	.10	.08	.04
579	Al Martin	.50	.40	.20
580	Ruben Sierra	.25	.20	.10
581	Andy Benes	.10	.08	.04
582	Anthony Young	.10	.08	.04
583	Shawn Boskie	.10	.08	.04
584	*Scott Pose*	.40	.30	.15
585	Mike Piazza	5.00	3.75	2.00
586	Donovan Osborne	.15	.11	.06
587	James Austin	.10	.08	.04
588	Checklist 301-400	.10	.08	.04
589	Checklist 401-500	.10	.08	.04
590	Checklist 501-600	.10	.08	.04
591	MC (Ken Griffey Jr.)	1.75	1.25	.70
592	MC (Ivan Rodriguez)	.25	.20	.10
593	MC (Carlos Baerga)	.60	.45	.25
594	MC (Fred McGriff)	.40	.30	.15
595	MC (Mark McGwire)	.10	.08	.04
596	MC (Roberto Alomar)	.60	.45	.25
597	MC (Kirby Puckett)	.50	.40	.20
598	MC (Marquis Grissom)	.20	.15	.08

		MT	NR MT	EX
599	MC (John Smoltz)	.10	.08	.04
600	MC (Ryne Sandberg)	.50	.40	.20
601	Wade Boggs	.25	.20	.10
602	Jeff Reardon	.10	.08	.04
603	Billy Ripken	.10	.08	.04
604	Bryan Harvey	.10	.08	.04
605	Carlos Quintana	.10	.08	.04
606	Greg Hibbard	.10	.08	.04
607	Ellis Burks	.10	.08	.04
608	Greg Swindell	.10	.08	.04
609	Dave Winfield	.40	.30	.15
610	Charlie Hough	.10	.08	.04
611	Chili Davis	.10	.08	.04
612	Jody Reed	.10	.08	.04
613	Mark Williamson	.10	.08	.04
614	Phil Plantier	.20	.15	.08
615	Jim Abbott	.15	.11	.06
616	Dante Bichette	.10	.08	.04
617	Mark Eichhorn	.10	.08	.04
618	Gary Sheffield	.25	.20	.10
619	*Richie Lewis*	.20	.15	.08
620	Joe Girardi	.10	.08	.04
621	Jaime Navarro	.10	.08	.04
622	Willie Wilson	.10	.08	.04
623	Scott Fletcher	.10	.08	.04
624	Bud Black	.10	.08	.04
625	Tom Brunansky	.10	.08	.04
626	Steve Avery	.50	.40	.20
627	Paul Molitor	.30	.25	.12
628	Gregg Jefferies	.10	.08	.04
629	Dave Stewart	.10	.08	.04
630	Javy Lopez	1.00	.70	.40
631	Greg Gagne	.10	.08	.04
632	Bobby Kelly	.10	.08	.04
633	Mike Fetters	.10	.08	.04
634	Ozzie Canseco	.10	.08	.04
635	Jeff Russell	.10	.08	.04
636	Pete Incaviglia	.10	.08	.04
637	Tom Henke	.10	.08	.04
638	Chipper Jones	1.50	1.25	.60
639	Jimmy Key	.10	.08	.04
640	Dave Martinez	.10	.08	.04
641	Dave Stieb	.10	.08	.04
642	Milt Thompson	.10	.08	.04
643	Alan Mills	.10	.08	.04
644	Tony Fernandez	.10	.08	.04
645	Randy Bush	.10	.08	.04
646	Joe Magrane	.10	.08	.04
647	Ivan Calderon	.10	.08	.04
648	Jose Guzman	.10	.08	.04
649	John Olerud	1.00	.70	.40
650	Tom Glavine	.30	.25	.12
651	Julio Franco	.10	.08	.04
652	Armando Reynoso	.10	.08	.04
653	Felix Jose	.10	.08	.04
654	Ben Rivera	.10	.08	.04
655	Andre Dawson	.15	.11	.06
656	Mike Harkey	.10	.08	.04
657	Kevin Seitzer	.10	.08	.04
658	Lonnie Smith	.10	.08	.04
659	Norm Charlton	.10	.08	.04
660	Dave Justice	.75	.60	.30
661	Fernando Valezuela	.10	.08	.04
662	Dan Wilson	.15	.11	.06
663	Mark Gardner	.10	.08	.04
664	Doug Dascenzo	.10	.08	.04
665	Greg Maddux	.25	.20	.10
666	Harold Baines	.10	.08	.04
667	Randy Myers	.10	.08	.04
668	Harold Reynolds	.10	.08	.04
669	Candy Maldonado	.10	.08	.04
670	Al Leiter	.10	.08	.04
671	Jerald Clark	.10	.08	.04
672	Doug Drabek	.10	.08	.04
673	Kirk Gibson	.10	.08	.04
674	Steve Reed	.10	.08	.04
675	Mike Felder	.10	.08	.04
676	Ricky Gutierrez	.15	.11	.06
677	Spike Owen	.10	.08	.04
678	Otis Nixon	.10	.08	.04
679	Scott Sanderson	.10	.08	.04
680	Mark Carreon	.10	.08	.04
681	Troy Percival	.15	.11	.06
682	Kevin Stocker	2.00	1.50	.80
683	*Jim Converse*	.20	.15	.08
684	Barry Bonds	1.00	.70	.40
685	Greg Gohr	.10	.08	.04
686	Tim Wallach	.10	.08	.04
687	Matt Mieske	.15	.11	.06
688	Robby Thompson	.10	.08	.04
689	Brien Taylor	1.00	.70	.40

		MT	NR MT	EX
690	Kirt Manwaring	.10	.08	.04
691	*Mike Lansing*	.40	.30	.15
692	Steve Decker	.10	.08	.04
693	Mike Moore	.10	.08	.04
694	Kevin Mitchell	.10	.08	.04
695	Phil Hiatt	.40	.30	.15
696	*Tony Tarasco*	.60	.45	.25
697	Benji Gil	.50	.40	.20
698	Jeff Juden	.10	.08	.04
699	Kevin Reimer	.10	.08	.04
700	Andy Ashby	.10	.08	.04
701	John Jaha	.25	.20	.10
702	*Tim Bogar*	.25	.20	.10
703	David Cone	.10	.08	.04
704	Willie Greene	.35	.25	.14
705	*David Hulse*	.25	.20	.10
706	Cris Carpenter	.10	.08	.04
707	Ken Griffey, Jr	3.00	2.25	1.25
708	Steve Bedrosian	.10	.08	.04
709	Dave Nilsson	.10	.08	.04
710	Paul Wagner	.10	.08	.04
711	B.J. Surhoff			
712	*Rene Arocha*	.40	.30	.15
713	Manny Lee	.10	.08	.04
714	Brian Williams	.10	.08	.04
715	*Sherman Obando*	.25	.20	.10
716	Terry Mulholland	.10	.08	.04
717	Paul O'Neill	.10	.08	.04
718	David Nied	.60	.45	.25
719	J.T. Snow	1.25	.90	.50
720	Nigel Wilson	.60	.45	.25
721	Mike Bielecki	.10	.08	.04
722	Kevin Young	.35	.25	.14
723	Charlie Leibrandt	.10	.08	.04
724	Frank Bolick	.10	.08	.04
725	*Jon Shave*	.15	.11	.06
726	Steve Cooke	.25	.20	.10
727	*Domingo Martinez*	.25	.20	.10
728	Todd Worrell	.10	.08	.04
729	Jose Lind	.10	.08	.04
730	*Jim Tatum*	.25	.20	.10
731	Mike Hampton	.10	.08	.04
732	Mike Draper	.10	.08	.04
733	Henry Mercedes	.15	.11	.06
734	*John Johnstone*	.25	.20	.10
735	Mitch Webster	.10	.08	.04
736	Russ Springer	.10	.08	.04
737	Rob Natal	.10	.08	.04
738	Steve Howe	.10	.08	.04
739	*Darrell Sherman*	.25	.20	.10
740	Pat Mahomes	.10	.08	.04
741	Alex Arias	.10	.08	.04
742	Damon Buford	.10	.08	.04
743	Charlie Hayes	.10	.08	.04
744	Guillermo Velasquez	.25	.20	.10
745	Checklist 601-750	.10	.08	.04
746	Frank Thomas (MC)	2.00	1.50	.80
747	Barry Bonds (MC)	.50	.40	.20
748	Roger Clemens (MC)	.25	.20	.10
749	Joe Carter (MC)	.20	.15	.08
750	Greg Maddux (MC)	.10	.08	.04

1993 Stadium Club First Day Production

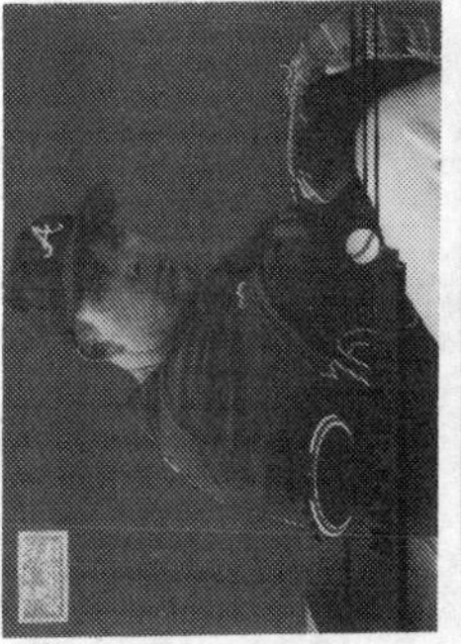

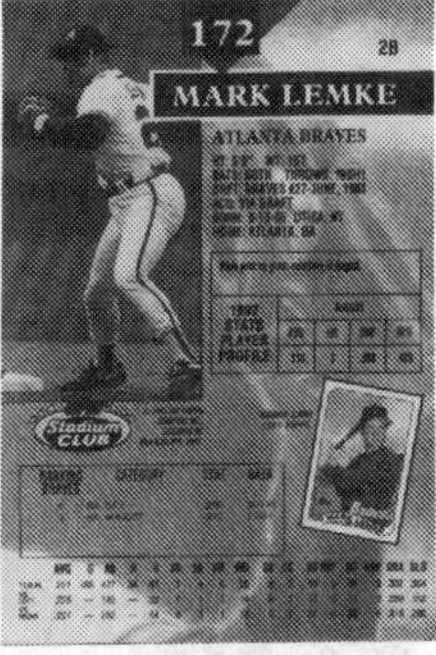

Inserted at the rate of about one per wax box, with an estimated production of about 2,000 apiece, Stadium Club First Day Production cards are regular-issue S.C.

cards to which an embossed silver holographic logo has been added in one of the upper corners. Because values for FDP-logo cards are 25 to 50 times greater than regular Stadium Club cards, collectors should be aware of fake FDP star cards made by cutting the logo off a common card and gluing it to a star player's card.

	MT	NR MT	EX
Complete Set (750):	6000.00	4500.00	2500.00
Common FDP card:	5.00	3.75	2.00
Stars: 25X to 50X S.C. price			

1993 Topps Stadium Club Special

Though the packaging and the cards themselves identify this 200-card set as a 1992 issue, it was not released until 1993 and is thought of by the hobby at large as a 1993 set. The set is sold in a plastic replica of Jack Murphy Stadium in San Diego, venue for the 1992 All-Star Game. Fifty-six of the cards feature players from that contest and are so identified by a line of gold-foil on the card front and an All-Star logo on back. Twenty-five members of the 1992 Team U.S.A. Olympic baseball squad are also included in the set, with appropriate logos and notations front and pack. There are 19 cards depicting action and stars of the 1992 League Championships and World Series. The other 100 cards in the set are 1992 draft picks. All cards have the same basic format as the regular-issue 1992 Topps Stadium Club cards, full-bleed photos on front and back, UV coating on both sides and gold-foil highlights on front. Besides the 200 standard-size cards, the Special Edition set included a dozen "Master Photos," 5" x 7" white-bordered premium cards.

		MT	NR MT	EX
Complete Set (200):		35.00	26.00	14.00
Common Player:		.10	.08	.04
1	Dave Winfield	.15	.11	.06
2	Juan Guzman	.10	.08	.04
3	Tony Gwynn	.20	.15	.08
4	Chris Roberts	.50	.40	.20
5	Benny Santiago	.10	.08	.04
6	Sherard Clinkscales	.20	.15	.08
7	Jonathan Nunnally	.20	.15	.08
8	Chuck Knoblauch	.10	.08	.04
9	Bob Wolcott	.20	.15	.08
10	Steve Rodriguez	.12	.09	.05
11	*Mark Williams*	.12	.09	.05
12	Danny Clyburn	.70	.50	.30
13	Darren Dreifort	1.00	.70	.40
14	Andy Van Slyke	.15	.11	.06
15	Wade Boggs	.25	.20	.10
16	Scott Patton	.10	.08	.04
17	Gary Sheffield	.15	.11	.06
18	Ron Villone	.30	.25	.12
19	Roberto Alomar	.35	.25	.14
20	Marc Valdes	.50	.40	.20
21	Daron Kirkreit	.40	.30	.15
22	Jeff Granger	.25	.20	.10
23	Levon Largusa	.25	.20	.10
24	Jimmy Key	.10	.08	.04
25	Kevin Pearson	.10	.08	.04
26	Michael Moore	.60	.45	.25
27	Preston Wilson	1.00	.70	.40
28	Kirby Puckett	.50	.40	.20
29	Tim Crabtree	.30	.25	.12
30	Bip Roberts	.10	.08	.04
31	Kelly Gruber	.10	.08	.04
32	Tony Fernandez	.10	.08	.04
33	Jason Angel	.30	.25	.12
34	Calvin Murray	.75	.60	.30
35	Chad McConnell	.50	.40	.20
36	Jason Moler	.30	.25	.12
37	Mark Lemke	.10	.08	.04
38	Tom Knauss	.10	.08	.04
39	Larry Mitchell	.30	.25	.12
40	Doug Mirabelli	.10	.08	.04
41	Everett Stull II	.30	.25	.12
42	Chris Wimmer	.10	.08	.04
43	Dan Serafini	.30	.25	.12
44	Ryne Sandberg	.30	.25	.12
45	Steve Lyons	.10	.08	.04
46	Ryan Freeburg	.30	.25	.12
47	Ruben Sierra	.10	.08	.04
48	David Mysel	.10	.08	.04
49	Joe Hamilton	.10	.08	.04
50	Steve Rodriguez	.10	.08	.04
51	Tim Wakefield	.20	.15	.08
52	Scott Gentile	.25	.20	.10
53	Doug Jones	.10	.08	.04
54	Willie Brown	.10	.08	.04
55	Chad Mottola	2.50	2.00	1.00
56	Ken Griffey, Jr	1.25	.90	.50
57	Jon Lieber	.10	.08	.04
58	Denny Martinez	.10	.08	.04
59	Joe Petcka	.10	.08	.04
60	Benji Simonton	.10	.08	.04
61	Brett Backlund	.80	.60	.30
62	Damon Berryhill	.10	.08	.04
63	Juan Guzman	.30	.25	.12
64	Doug Hecker	.30	.25	.12
65	Jamie Arnold	.30	.25	.12
66	Bob Tewksbury	.10	.08	.04
67	Tim Leger	.10	.08	.04
68	Todd Etler	.10	.08	.04
69	Lloyd McClendon	.10	.08	.04
70	Kurt Ehmann	.10	.08	.04
71	Rick Magdaleno	.10	.08	.04
72	Tom Pagnozzi	.10	.08	.04
73	Jeffrey Hammonds	2.00	1.50	.80
74	Joe Carter	.25	.20	.10
75	Chris Holt	.10	.08	.04
76	Charles Johnson	1.00	.70	.40
77	Bob Walk	.10	.08	.04
78	Fred McGriff	.25	.20	.10
79	Tom Evans	.10	.08	.04
80	Scott Klingenbeck	.10	.08	.04
81	Chad McConnell	.40	.30	.15
82	Chris Eddy	.10	.08	.04
83	Phil Nevin	2.00	1.50	.80
84	John Kruk	.10	.08	.04
85	Tony Sheffield	.10	.08	.04
86	John Smoltz	.10	.08	.04
87	Trevor Humphry	.10	.08	.04
88	Charles Nagy	.10	.08	.04
89	Sean Runyan	.10	.08	.04
90	Mike Gulan	.25	.20	.10
91	Darren Daulton	.10	.08	.04
92	Otis Nixon	.10	.08	.04
93	Nomar Garciaparra	.30	.25	.12
94	Larry Walker	.30	.25	.12
95	Hut Smith	.10	.08	.04
96	Rick Helling	.30	.25	.12
97	Roger Clemens	.60	.45	.25
98	Ron Gant	.10	.08	.04
99	Kenny Felder	.60	.45	.25
100	Steve Murphy	.10	.08	.04
101	Mike Smith	.10	.08	.04
102	Terry Pendleton	.10	.08	.04
103	Tim Davis	.10	.08	.04
104	Jeff Patzke	.10	.08	.04
105	Craig Wilson	.10	.08	.04
106	Tom Glavine	.10	.08	.04
107	Mark Langston	.10	.08	.04
108	Mark Thompson	.10	.08	.04
109	Eric Owens	.10	.08	.04
110	Keith Johnson	.10	.08	.04
111	Robin Ventura	.30	.25	.12

		MT	NR MT	EX
112	Ed Sprague	.10	.08	.04
113	Jeff Schmidt	.10	.08	.04
114	Don Wengert	.10	.08	.04
115	Craig Biggio	.10	.08	.04
116	Kenny Carlyle	.10	.08	.04
117	Derek Jeter	1.75	1.25	.70
118	Manuel Lee	.10	.08	.04
119	Jeff Haas	.10	.08	.04
120	Roger Bailey	.10	.08	.04
121	Sean Lowe	.40	.30	.15
122	Rick Aguilera	.10	.08	.04
123	Sandy Alomar	.10	.08	.04
124	Derek Wallace	.40	.30	.15
125	B.J. Wallace	.70	.50	.30
126	Greg Maddux	.10	.08	.04
127	Tim Moore	.10	.08	.04
128	Lee Smith	.10	.08	.04
129	Todd Steverson	.70	.50	.30
130	Chris Widger	.10	.08	.04
131	Paul Molitor	.25	.20	.10
132	Chris Smith	.10	.08	.04
133	Chris Gomez	.10	.08	.04
134	Jimmy Baron	.10	.08	.04
135	John Smoltz	.10	.08	.04
136	Pat Borders	.10	.08	.04
137	Donnie Leshnock	.10	.08	.04
138	Gus Gandarillos	.10	.08	.04
139	Will Clark	.40	.30	.15
140	Ryan Luzinski	.60	.45	.25
141	Cal Ripken, Jr.	.60	.45	.25
142	B.J. Wallace	2.00	1.50	.80
143	Trey Beamon	.80	.60	.30
144	Norm Charlton	.10	.08	.04
145	Mike Mussina	.80	.60	.30
146	Billy Owens	.50	.40	.20
147	Ozzie Smith	.15	.11	.06
148	Jason Kendall	.50	.40	.20
149	Mike Matthews	.50	.40	.20
150	David Spykstra	.10	.08	.04
151	Benji Grigsby	.50	.40	.20
152	Sean Smith	.10	.08	.04
153	Mark McGwire	.20	.15	.08
154	David Cone	.10	.08	.04
155	Shon Walker	.80	.60	.30
156	Jason McDowell	.10	.08	.04
157	Jack McDowell	.10	.08	.04
158	Paxton Briley	.10	.08	.04
159	Edgar Martinez	.10	.08	.04
160	Brian Sackinsky	.10	.08	.04
161	Barry Bonds	.50	.40	.20
162	Roberto Kelly	.10	.08	.04
163	Jeff Alkire	1.00	.70	.40
164	Mike Sharperson	.10	.08	.04
165	Jamie Taylor	.30	.25	.12
166	John Saffer	.30	.25	.12
167	Jerry Browne	.10	.08	.04
168	Travis Fryman	.40	.30	.15
169	Brady Anderson	.10	.08	.04
170	Chris Roberts	.10	.08	.04
171	Lloyd Peever	.10	.08	.04
172	Francisco Cabrera	.10	.08	.04
173	Ramiro Martinez	.10	.08	.04
174	Jeff Alkire	.10	.08	.04
175	Ivan Rodriguez	.15	.11	.06
176	Kevin Brown	.10	.08	.04
177	Chad Roper	.10	.08	.04
178	Rod Henderson	.10	.08	.04
179	Dennis Eckersley	.10	.08	.04
180	Shannon Stewart	.30	.25	.12
181	DeShawn Warren	.10	.08	.04
182	Lonnie Smith	.10	.08	.04
183	Willie Adams	.10	.08	.04
184	Jeff Montgomery	.10	.08	.04
185	Damon Hollins	.10	.08	.04
186	Byron Matthews	.10	.08	.04
187	Harold Baines	.10	.08	.04
188	Rick Greene	.30	.25	.12
189	Carlos Baerga	.30	.25	.12
190	Brandon Cromer	.10	.08	.04
191	Roberto Alomar	.40	.30	.15
192	Rich Ireland	.10	.08	.04
193	Steve Montgomery	.10	.08	.04
194	Brant Brown	.10	.08	.04
195	Ritchie Moody	.10	.08	.04
196	Michael Tucker	1.75	1.25	.70
197	Jason Varitek	1.25	.90	.50
198	David Manning	.10	.08	.04
199	Marquis Riley	.10	.08	.04
200	Jason Giambi	.30	.25	.12

1993 Topps Stadium Club Team Sets

This special edition of Stadium Club cards consists of 16 separate team sets of 30 cards each. Each blister-packed team set was priced around $6 and they sold exclusively at Wal-Mart. Fronts of the Uv-coated cards have a player photo that is borderless at the top, bottom and left. At right is a green stripe, at top of which is a partial baseball design and some othher striping in gold foil. Backs are basically green, with a light blue box at lower-right containing personal information and stats, along with the S.C. logo. A player photo is at upper-left, with his name superimposed on a bat. Cards are checklisted here within team set.

		MT	NR MT	EX
Complete set (480):		95.00	71.00	38.00
Common player:		.10	.08	.04
	ATLANTA BRAVES			
1	Tom Glavine	.50	.40	.20
2	Bill Pecota	.10	.08	.04
3	David Justice	.50	.40	.20
4	Mark Lemke	.10	.08	.04
5	Jeff Blauser	.10	.08	.04
6	Ron Gant	.50	.40	.20
7	Greg Olson	.10	.08	.04
8	Francisco Cabrera	.10	.08	.04
9	Chipper Jones	.50	.40	.20
10	Steve Avery	.50	.40	.20
11	Kent Mercker	.10	.08	.04
12	John Smoltz	.35	.25	.14
13	Pete Smith	.10	.08	.04
14	Damon Berryhill	.10	.08	.04
15	Sid Bream	.10	.08	.04
16	Otis Nixon	.10	.08	.04
17	Mike Stanton	.10	.08	.04
18	Greg Maddux	.50	.40	.20
19	Jay Howell	.10	.08	.04
20	Rafael Belliard	.10	.08	.04
21	Terry Pendleton	.10	.08	.04
22	Deion Sanders	.50	.40	.20
23	Brian Hunter	.10	.08	.04
24	Marvin Freeman	.10	.08	.04
25	.10 (Mark Wohlers)			
26	Ryan Klesko	.50	.40	.20
27	Javy Lopez	.25	.20	.10
28	Melvin Nieves	.25	.20	.10
29	Tony Tarasco	.25	.20	.10
30	Ramon Caraballo	.25	.20	.10
	CHICAGO CUBS			
1	Ryne Sandberg	1.00	.70	.40
2	Greg Hibbard	.10	.08	.04
4	Candy Maldonado	.10	.08	.04
5	Willie Wilson	.25	.20	.10
6	Dan Plesac	.10	.08	.04
7	Steve Buechele	.10	.08	.04
8	Mark Grace	.25	.20	.10
9	Shawon Dunston	.20	.15	.08
10	Steve Lake	.10	.08	.04
11	Dwight Smith	.10	.08	.04
12	Derrick May	.25	.20	.10
13	Paul Assenmacher	.10	.08	.04
14	Mike Harkey	.10	.08	.04
15	Lance Dickson	.10	.08	.04
16	Randy Myers	.25	.20	.10

		MT	NR MT	EX
17	Mike Morgan	.10	.08	.04
18	Chuck McElroy	.10	.08	.04
19	Jose Guzman	.10	.08	.04
20	Jose Vizcaino	.10	.08	.04
21	Frank Castillo	.10	.08	.04
22	Bob Scanlon	.10	.08	.04
23	Rick Wilkins	.25	.20	.10
24	Rey Sanchez	.10	.08	.04
25	Phil Dauphin	.15	.11	.06
26	Jim Bullinger	.10	.08	.04
27	Jessie Hollins	.15	.11	.06
28	Matt Walbeck	.25	.20	.10
29	Fernando Ramsey	.15	.11	.06
30	Jose Bautista	.15	.11	.06
	CALIFORNIA ANGELS			
1	J.T. Snow	.25	.20	.10
2	Chuck Crim	.10	.08	.04
3	Chili Davis	.25	.20	.10
4	Mark Langston	.25	.20	.10
5	Ron Tingley	.10	.08	.04
6	Eduardo Perez	.15	.11	.06
7	Scott Sanderson	.10	.08	.04
8	Jorge Fabregas	.15	.11	.06
9	Troy Percival	.15	.11	.06
10	Rod Carreia	.10	.08	.04
11	Greg Myers	.10	.08	.04
12	Steve Frey	.10	.08	.04
13	Tim Salmon	1.00	.70	.40
14	Scott Lewis	.10	.08	.04
15	Rene Gonzales	.10	.08	.04
16	Chuck Finley	.25	.20	.10
17	John Orton	.10	.08	.04
18	Joe Grahe	.10	.08	.04
19	Luis Polonia	.25	.20	.10
20	John Farrell	.10	.08	.04
21	Damion Easley	.20	.15	.08
22	Gene Nelson	.10	.08	.04
23	Chad Curtis	.50	.40	.20
24	Russ Springer	.10	.08	.04
25	De Shawn Warren	.15	.11	.06
26	Darryl Scott	.10	.08	.04
27	Gary DiSarcina	.10	.08	.04
28	Jerry Nielson	.15	.11	.06
29	Torey Lovullo	.10	.08	.04
30	Julio Valera	.10	.08	.04
	CHICAGO WHITE SOX			
1	Frank Thomas	1.50	1.25	.60
2	Bo Jackson	.50	.40	.20
3	Rod Bolton	.10	.08	.04
4	Dave Stieb	.20	.15	.08
5	Tim Raines	.25	.20	.10
6	Joey Cora	.10	.08	.04
7	Warren Newson	.10	.08	.04
8	Roberto Hernandez	.20	.15	.08
9	Brandon Wilson	.10	.08	.04
10	Wilson Alvarez	.20	.15	.08
11	Dan Pasqua	.10	.08	.04
12	Ozzie Guillen	.20	.15	.08
13	Robin Ventura	.35	.25	.14
14	Craig Grebeck	.10	.08	.04
15	Lance Johnson	.25	.20	.10
16	Carlton Fisk	.50	.40	.20
17	Ron Karkovice	.10	.08	.04
18	Jack McDowell	.50	.40	.20
19	Scott Radinsky	.20	.15	.08
20	Bobby Thigpen	.10	.08	.04
21	Donn Pall	.10	.08	.04
22	George Bell	.20	.15	.08
23	Alex Fernandez	.25	.20	.10
24	Mike Hiff	.10	.08	.04
25	Jason Bere	.50	.40	.20
26	Johnny Ruffin	.15	.11	.06
27	Ellis Burks	.20	.15	.08
28	Kirk McCaskill	.20	.15	.08
29	Terry Leach	.10	.08	.04
30	Shawn Gilbert	.15	.11	.06
	COLORADO ROCKIES			
1	David Nied	.50	.40	.20
2	Quinton McCracken	.15	.11	.06
3	Charlie Hayes	.20	.15	.08
4	Bryn Smith	.10	.08	.04
5	Dante Bichette	.25	.20	.10
6	Alex Cole	.20	.15	.08
7	Scott Aldred	.15	.11	.06
8	Roberto Mejia	.10	.08	.04
9	Jeff Parrett	.10	.08	.04
10	Joe Girardi	.20	.15	.08
11	Andres Galarraga	.50	.40	.20
12	Daryl Boston	.20	.15	.08
13	Jerald Clark	.10	.08	.04
14	Gerald Young	.10	.08	.04
15	Bruce Ruffin	.10	.08	.04
16	Rudy Seanez	.15	.11	.06
17	Darren Holmes	.15	.11	.06
18	Andy Ashby	.10	.08	.04
19	Chris Jones	.10	.08	.04
20	Mark Thompson	.10	.08	.04
21	Freddie Benavides	.10	.08	.04
22	Eric Wedge	.15	.11	.06
23	Vinny Castilla	.10	.08	.04
24	Butch Henry	.10	.08	.04
25	Jim Tatum	.10	.08	.04
26	Steve Reed	.10	.08	.04
27	Eric Young	.15	.11	.06
28	Danny Sheaffer	.10	.08	.04
29	Roger Bailey	.15	.11	.06
30	Brad Ausmus	.10	.08	.04
	FLORIDA MARLINS			
1	Nigel Wilson	.50	.40	.20
2	Bryan Harvey	.50	.40	.20
3	Bob McClure	.10	.08	.04
4	Alex Arias	.10	.08	.04
5	Walt Weiss	.20	.15	.08
6	Charlie Hough	.20	.15	.08
7	Scott Chiamparino	.20	.15	.08
8	Junior Felix	.10	.08	.04
9	Jack Armstrong	.10	.08	.04
10	Dave Magadan	.25	.20	.10
11	Cris Carpenter	.10	.08	.04
12	Benny Santiago	.35	.25	.14
13	Jeff Conine	.35	.25	.14
14	Jerry Don Gleaton	.10	.08	.04
15	Steve Decker	.10	.08	.04
16	Ryan Bowen	.20	.15	.08
17	Ramon Martinez	.15	.11	.06
18	Bret Barberie	.20	.15	.08
19	Monty Fariss	.20	.15	.08
20	Trevor Hoffman	.20	.15	.08
21	Scott Pose	.10	.08	.04
22	Mike Myers	.10	.08	.04
23	Geronimo Berroa	.10	.08	.04
24	Darrell Whitmore	.10	.08	.04
25	Chuck Carr	.20	.15	.08
26	Dave Weathers	.10	.08	.04
27	Matt Turner	.10	.08	.04
28	Jose Martinez	.10	.08	.04
29	Orestes Destrade	.25	.20	.10
30	Carl Everett	.10	.08	.04
	HOUSTON ASTROS			
1	Doug Drebek	.20	.15	.08
2	Eddie Taubensee	.10	.08	.04
3	James Mouton	.15	.11	.06
4	Ken Caminiti	.20	.15	.08
5	Chris James	.10	.08	.04
6	Jeff Juden	.25	.20	.10
7	Eric Anthony	.25	.20	.10
8	Jeff Bagwell	.50	.40	.20
9	Greg Swindall	.25	.20	.10
10	Steve Finley	.25	.20	.10
11	Al Osunea	.10	.08	.04
12	Gary Mota	.10	.08	.04
13	Scott Servais	.10	.08	.04
14	Craig Biggio	.50	.40	.20
15	Doug James	.10	.08	.04
16	Rob Mallicoat	.10	.08	.04
17	Darryl Kile	.50	.40	.20
18	Kevin Bass	.10	.08	.04
19	Pete Harnisch	.20	.15	.08
20	Andujar Cedeno	.20	.15	.08
21	Brian Hunter	.10	.08	.04
22	Brian Williams	.10	.08	.04
23	Chris Donnels	.10	.08	.04
24	Xavier Hernandez	.15	.11	.06
25	Todd Jones	.10	.08	.04
26	Luis Gonzalez	.10	.08	.04
27	Rick Parker	.15	.11	.06
28	Casey Candaele	.10	.08	.04
29	Tony Eusebio	.15	.11	.06
30	Mark Portugal	.10	.08	.04
	KANSAS CITY ROYALS			
1	George Brett	1.00	.70	.40
2	Mike MacFarlane	.25	.20	.10
3	Tom Gordon	.10	.08	.04
4	Waily Joyner	.50	.40	.20
5	Kevin Appier	.25	.20	.10
6	Phil Hiatt	.25	.20	.10
7	Keith Miller	.10	.08	.04
8	Hipolito Pichardo	.10	.08	.04
9	Chris Gwynn	.10	.08	.04
10	Jose Lind	.25	.20	.10
11	Mark Gubicza	.25	.20	.10
12	Dennis Rasmussen	.25	.20	.10
13	Mike Magnante	.15	.11	.06

		MT	NR MT	EX
14	Joe Vitiello	.15	.11	.06
15	Kevin McReynolds	.15	.11	.06
16	Greg Gagne	.15	.11	.06
17	David Cone	.20	.15	.08
18	Brent Mayne	.20	.15	.08
19	Jeff Montgomery	.25	.20	.10
20	Joe Randa	.10	.08	.04
21	Felix Jose	.25	.20	.10
22	Bill Sampen	.10	.08	.04
23	Curt Wilkerson	.10	.08	.04
24	Mark Gardner	.10	.08	.04
25	Brian McRae	.25	.20	.10
26	Hubie Brooks	.15	.11	.06
27	Chris Eddy	.15	.11	.06
28	Harvey Pulliam	.15	.11	.06
29	Rusty Meacham	.10	.08	.04
30	Danny Miceli	.15	.11	.06
	LOS ANGELES DODGERS			
1	Darryl Strawberry	.50	.40	.20
2	Pedro Martinez	.25	.20	.10
3	Jody Reed	.10	.08	.04
4	Carlos Hernandez	.50	.40	.20
5	Kevin Gross	.10	.08	.04
6	Mike Piazza	1.00	.70	.40
7	Jim Gott	.10	.08	.04
8	Eric Karros	.50	.40	.20
9	Mike Sharperson	.10	.08	.04
10	Ramon Martinez	.25	.20	.10
11	Tim Wallach	.25	.20	.10
12	Pedro Astacio	.15	.11	.06
13	Lenny Harris	.10	.08	.04
14	Brett Butler	.15	.11	.06
15	Raul Mondesi	.15	.11	.06
16	Todd Worrell	.10	.08	.04
17	Jose Offerman	.15	.11	.06
18	Mitch Webster	.10	.08	.04
19	Tom Candiotti	.10	.08	.04
20	Eric Davis	.35	.25	.14
21	Michael Moore	.10	.08	.04
22	Billy Ashley	.15	.11	.06
23	Orel Hershiser	.25	.20	.10
24	Roger Cedeno	.15	.11	.06
25	Roger McDowell	.15	.11	.06
26	Mike James	.15	.11	.06
27	Steve Wilson	.10	.08	.04
28	Todd Hollandsworth	.15	.11	.06
29	Cory Snyder	.10	.08	.04
30	Todd Williams	.15	.11	.06
	NEW YORK YANKEES			
1	Don Mattingly	.75	.60	.30
2	Jim Abbott	.50	.40	.20
3	Matt Nokes	.25	.20	.10
4	Danny Tartabull	.25	.20	.10
5	Wade Boggs	.75	.60	.30
6	Melido Perez	.10	.08	.04
7	Steve Farr	.10	.08	.04
8	Kevin Maas	.10	.08	.04
9	Randy Velarde	.10	.08	.04
10	Mike Humphreys	.10	.08	.04
11	Mike Gallego	.10	.08	.04
12	Mike Stanley	.10	.08	.04
13	Jimmy Key	.10	.08	.04
14	Paul O'Neill	.25	.20	.10
15	Spike Owen	.10	.08	.04
16	Pat Kelly	.25	.20	.10
17	Sterling Hitchcock	.25	.20	.10
18	Mike Witt	.10	.08	.04
19	Scott Kamieniecki	.10	.08	.04
20	John Habyan	.10	.08	.04
21	Bernie Williams	.10	.08	.04
22	Brien Taylor	.22	.15	.09
23	Rich Monteleone	.10	.08	.04
24	Mark Hutton	.10	.08	.04
25	Robert Eenhoorn	.15	.11	.06
26	Gerald Williams	.10	.08	.04
27	Sam Militello	.25	.20	.10
28	Bob Wickman	.25	.20	.10
29	Andy Stankiewicz	.20	.15	.08
30	Domingo Jean	.20	.15	.08
	OAKLAND A'S			
1	Dennis Eckersley	.50	.40	.20
2	Lance Blankenship	.10	.08	.04
3	Mike Mohler	.10	.08	.04
4	Jerry Browne	.10	.08	.04
5	Kevin Seitzer	.10	.08	.04
6	Storm Davis	.10	.08	.04
7	Mark McGwire	.60	.45	.25
8	Rickey Henderson	.75	.60	.30
9	Terry Steinbach	.10	.08	.04
10	Ruben Sierra	.40	.30	.15
11	Dave Henderson	.10	.08	.04
12	Bob Welch	.20	.15	.08
13	Rick Honeycutt	.10	.08	.04
14	Ron Darling	.10	.08	.04
16	Joe Boever	.10	.08	.04
17	Izzy Molina	.15	.11	.06
18	Mike Bordick	.10	.08	.04
19	Brent Gates	.10	.08	.04
20	Shawn Hillegas	.10	.08	.04
21	Scott Hammond	.10	.08	.04
22	Todd Van Poppel	.25	.20	.10
23	Johnny Guzman	.15	.11	.06
24	Scott Lydy	.10	.08	.04
25	Scott Baker	.10	.08	.04
26	Todd Revenig	.10	.08	.04
27	Scott Brosius	.10	.08	.04
28	Troy Neel	.15	.11	.06
29	Dale Sveum	.10	.08	.04
30	Mike Neill	.15	.11	.06
	PHILADELPHIA PHILLIES			
1	Darren Daulton	.25	.20	.10
2	Larry Anderson	.10	.08	.04
3	Kyle Abbott			
4	Chad McConnell	.15	.11	.06
5	Danny Jackson	.10	.08	.04
6	Kevin Stocker	.20	.15	.08
7	Jim Eisenreich	.10	.08	.04
8	Mickey Morandini	.10	.08	.04
9	Bob Ayrault	.10	.08	.04
10	Doug Lindsey	.15	.11	.06
11	Dave Hollins	.25	.20	.10
12	Dave West	.10	.08	.04
13	Wes Chamberlain	.10	.08	.04
14	Curt Schilling	.10	.08	.04
15	Len Dykstra	.50	.40	.20
16	Trevor Humphry	.15	.11	.06
17	Terry Mulholland	.25	.20	.10
18	Gene Schall	.15	.11	.06
19	Mike Lieberthal	.15	.11	.06
20	Ben Rivera	.10	.08	.04
21	Mariano Duncan	.20	.15	.08
22	Pete Incaviglia	.25	.20	.10
23	Ron Blazier	.15	.11	.06
24	Jeff Jackson	.15	.11	.06
25	Jose DeLeon	.10	.08	.04
26	Ron Lockett	.10	.08	.04
27	Tommy Greene	.25	.20	.10
28	Milt Thompson	.10	.08	.04
29	Mitch Williams	.50	.40	.20
30	John Kruk	.50	.40	.20
	ST. LOUIS CARDINALS			
1	Ozzie Smith	.75	.60	.30
2	Rene Arocha	.25	.20	.10
3	Bernard Gilkey	.25	.20	.10
4	Jose Oquendo	.10	.08	.04
5	Mike Perez	.10	.08	.04
6	Tom Pagnozzi	.10	.08	.04
7	Rod Brewer	.10	.08	.04
8	Joe Magrane	.10	.08	.04
9	Todd Zeile	.25	.20	.10
10	Bob Tewksbury	.15	.11	.06
11	Darrel Deak	.15	.11	.06
12	Gregg Jefferies	.50	.40	.20
13	Lee Smith	.25	.20	.10
14	Ozzie Canseco	.10	.08	.04
15	Tom Urbani	.15	.11	.06
16	Donovan Osborne	.10	.08	.04
17	Ray Lankford	.25	.20	.10
18	Rheal Cormier	.25	.20	.10
19	Allen Watson	.25	.20	.10
20	Geronimo Pena	.10	.08	.04
21	Rob Murphy	.10	.08	.04
22	Tracy Woodson	.10	.08	.04
23	Basil Shabazz	.15	.11	.06
24	Omar Olivares	.10	.08	.04
25	Brian Jordan	.15	.11	.06
26	Les Lancaster	.10	.08	.04
27	Sean Lowe	.15	.11	.06
28	Hector Villanueva	.10	.08	.04
29	Brian Barber	.15	.11	.06
30	Aaron Holbert	.15	.11	.06
	SAN FRANCISCO GIANTS			
1	Barry Bonds	.75	.60	.30
2	Dave Righetti	.25	.20	.10
3	Matt Williams	.40	.30	.15
4	Royce Clayton	.10	.08	.04
5	Salomon Torres	.15	.11	.06
6	Kirt Manwaring	.10	.08	.04
7	J.R. Phillips	.15	.11	.06
8	Kevin Rogers	.15	.11	.06
9	Will Clark	.75	.60	.30
10	John Burkett	.25	.20	.10

		MT	NR MT	EX
11	Willie McGee	.25	.20	.10
12	Rod Beck	.10	.08	.04
13	Jeff Reed	.10	.08	.04
14	Jeff Brantley	.10	.08	.04
15	Steve Hosey	.10	.08	.04
16	Chris Hancock	.15	.11	.06
17	Adell Davenport	.15	.11	.06
18	Mike Jackson	.10	.08	.04
19	Dave Martinez	.10	.08	.04
20	Bill Swift	.25	.20	.10
21	Steve Scarsone	.10	.08	.04
22	Trevor Wilson	.15	.11	.06
23	Mark Carreon	.10	.08	.04
24	Bud Black	.15	.11	.06
25	Darren Lewis	.25	.20	.10
26	Dan Carlson	.15	.11	.06
27	Craig Colbert	.15	.11	.06
28	Greg Brummet	.15	.11	.06
29	Bryan Hickerson	.10	.08	.04
30	Robby Thompson	.25	.20	.10
	SEATTLE MARINERS			
1	Ken Griffey Jr.	1.50	1.25	.60
2	Desi Realford	.15	.11	.06
3	Dave Weinhouse	.15	.11	.06
4	Rich Amaral	.10	.08	.04
5	Brian Deak	.10	.08	.04
6	Bret Boone	.25	.20	.10
7	Bill Haselman	.10	.08	.04
8	Dave Fleming	.10	.08	.04
9	Fernando Vina	.15	.11	.06
10	Greg Litton	.10	.08	.04
11	Mackey Sasser	.10	.08	.04
12	Lee Tinsley	.10	.08	.04
13	Norm Charlton	.25	.20	.10
14	Russ Swan	.10	.08	.04
15	Brian Holman	.10	.08	.04
16	Randy Johnson	.35	.25	.14
17	Erik Hanson	.10	.08	.04
18	Tino Martinez	.25	.20	.10
19	Marc Newfield	.25	.20	.10
20	Dave Valle	.10	.08	.04
21	John Cummings	.15	.11	.06
22	Mike Hampton	.15	.11	.06
23	Jay Buhner	.25	.20	.10
24	Edgar Martinez	.35	.25	.14
25	Omar Vizquel	.25	.20	.10
26	Pete O'Brien	.10	.08	.04
27	Brian Turang	.15	.11	.06
28	Chris Bosio	.15	.11	.06
29	Mike Felder	.10	.08	.04
30	Shawn Estes	.10	.08	.04
	TEXAS RANGERS			
1	Nolan Ryan	1.50	1.25	.60
2	Ritchie Moody	.15	.11	.06
3	Matt Whiteside	.10	.08	.04
4	David Hulse	.15	.11	.06
5	Roger Pavlik	.10	.08	.04
6	Dan Smith	.10	.08	.04
7	Donald Harris	.15	.11	.06
8	Butch Davis	.10	.08	.04
9	Benji Gil	.10	.08	.04
10	Ivan Rodriguez	.35	.25	.14
11	Dean Palmer	.25	.20	.10
12	Jeff Huson	.10	.08	.04
13	Rob Mauer	.10	.08	.04
14	Gary Redus	.10	.08	.04
15	Doug Dascenzo	.10	.08	.04
16	Charlie Liebrandt	.10	.08	.04
17	Tom Henke	.10	.08	.04
18	Manuel Lee	.10	.08	.04
19	Kenny Rogers	.10	.08	.04
20	Kevin Brown	.10	.08	.04
21	Juan Gonzalez	.75	.60	.30
22	Geno Petralli	.10	.08	.04
23	John Russell	.10	.08	.04
24	Robb Nen	.10	.08	.04
25	Julio Franco	.10	.08	.04
26	Rafael Palmeiro	.40	.30	.15
27	Todd Burns	.10	.08	.04
28	Jose Canseco	.40	.30	.15
29	Billy Ripken	.15	.11	.06
30	Dan Peltier	.10	.08	.04

A player's name in italic indicates a rookie card. An (FC) indicates a player's first card for that particular card company.

1993 Topps Finest

This 199-card set uses a process of multi-color metallization; this chromium technology adds depth and dimension to the card. The set has a 33-card subset of All-Stars; these cards (Refractors) were also recreated with refracting foil using the metallization enhancement process. There is one refracting foil card in every nine packs. Packs have five cards. Each 18-count box contains a 5" by 7" version of one of the 199 players in the regular set. Each jumbo card was produced using the metallization process, and one of every six will be enhanced with special refracting foil.

		MT	NR MT	EX
Complete Set (199):		500.00	375.00	200.00
Common Player:		1.75	1.25	.70
1	David Justice	13.00	9.75	5.25
2	Lou Whitaker	1.75	1.25	.70
3	Bryan Harvey	1.75	1.25	.70
4	Carlos Garcia	3.00	2.25	1.25
5	Sid Fernandez	1.75	1.25	.70
6	Brett Butler	1.75	1.25	.70
7	Scott Cooper	1.75	1.25	.70
8	B.J. Surhoff	1.75	1.25	.70
9	Steve Finley	1.75	1.25	.70
10	Curt Schilling	3.00	2.25	1.25
11	Jeff Bagwell	9.00	6.75	3.50
12	Alex Cole	1.75	1.25	.70
13	John Olerud	14.00	10.50	5.50
14	John Smiley	1.75	1.25	.70
15	Bip Roberts	1.75	1.25	.70
16	Albert Belle	11.00	8.25	4.50
17	Duane Ward	1.75	1.25	.70
18	Alan Trammell	1.75	1.25	.70
19	Andy Benes	2.50	2.00	1.00
20	Reggie Sanders	3.00	2.25	1.25
21	Todd Zeile	2.50	2.00	1.00
22	Rick Aguilera	1.75	1.25	.70
23	Dave Hollins	4.50	3.50	1.75
24	Jose Rijo	1.75	1.25	.70
25	Matt Williams	4.00	3.00	1.50
26	Sandy Alomar	1.75	1.25	.70
27	Alex Fernandez	3.50	2.75	1.50
28	Ozzie Smith	4.00	3.00	1.50
29	Ramon Martinez	1.75	1.25	.70
30	Bernie Williams	1.75	1.25	.70
31	Gary Sheffield	7.00	5.25	2.75
32	Eric Karros	4.50	3.50	1.75
33	Frank Viola	1.75	1.25	.70
34	Kevin Young	3.50	2.75	1.50
35	Ken Hill	1.75	1.25	.70
36	Tony Fernandez	1.75	1.25	.70
37	Tim Wakefield	1.75	1.25	.70
38	John Kruk	4.50	3.50	1.75
39	Chris Sabo	1.75	1.25	.70
40	Marquis Grissom	4.50	3.50	1.75
41	Glenn Davis	1.75	1.25	.70
42	Jeff Montgomery	1.75	1.25	.70
43	Kenny Lofton	7.00	5.25	2.75
44	John Burkett	1.75	1.25	.70
45	Darryl Hamilton	1.75	1.25	.70
46	Jim Abbott	3.00	2.25	1.25
47	Ivan Rodriguez	5.00	3.75	2.00
48	Eric Young	2.50	2.00	1.00
49	Mitch Williams	1.75	1.25	.70
50	Harold Reynolds	1.75	1.25	.70
51	Brian Harper	1.75	1.25	.70
52	Rafael Palmeiro	3.00	2.25	1.25
53	Bret Saberhagen	1.75	1.25	.70

		MT	NR MT	EX
54	Jeff Conine	1.75	1.25	.70
55	Ivan Calderon	1.75	1.25	.70
56	Juan Guzman	7.00	5.25	2.75
57	Carlos Baerga	13.00	9.75	5.25
58	Charles Nagy	1.75	1.25	.70
59	Wally Joyner	1.75	1.25	.70
60	Charles Hayes	1.75	1.25	.70
61	Shane Mack	1.75	1.25	.70
62	Pete Harnisch	1.75	1.25	.70
63	George Brett	12.00	9.00	4.75
64	Lance Johnson	1.75	1.25	.70
65	Ben McDonald	1.75	1.25	.70
66	Bobby Bonilla	2.00	1.50	.80
67	Terry Steinbach	1.75	1.25	.70
68	Ron Gant	3.50	2.75	1.50
69	Doug Jones	1.75	1.25	.70
70	Paul Molitor	7.50	5.75	3.00
71	Brady Anderson	1.75	1.25	.70
72	Chuck Finley	1.75	1.25	.70
73	Mark Grace	4.00	3.00	1.50
74	Mike Devereaux	1.75	1.25	.70
75	Tony Phillips	1.75	1.25	.70
76	Chuck Knoblauch	2.50	2.00	1.00
77	Tony Gwynn	6.00	4.50	2.50
78	Kevin Appier	1.75	1.25	.70
79	Sammy Sosa	4.00	3.00	1.50
80	Mickey Tettleton	1.75	1.25	.70
81	Felix Jose	1.75	1.25	.70
82	Mark Langston	1.75	1.25	.70
83	Gregg Jefferies	3.00	2.25	1.25
84	Andre Dawson (AS)	4.00	3.00	1.50
85	Greg Maddux (AS)	6.00	4.50	2.50
86	Rickey Henderson (AS)	6.00	4.50	2.50
87	Tom Glavine (AS)	7.00	5.25	2.75
88	Roberto Alomar (AS)	14.00	10.50	5.50
89	Darryl Strawberry (AS)	1.50	1.25	.60
90	Wade Boggs (AS)	5.00	3.75	2.00
91	Bo Jackson (AS)	5.00	3.75	2.00
92	Mark McGwire (AS)	4.00	3.00	1.50
93	Robin Ventura (AS)	7.00	5.25	2.75
94	Joe Carter (AS)	10.00	7.50	4.00
95	Lee Smith (AS)	1.75	1.25	.70
96	Cal Ripken, Jr. (AS)	11.00	8.25	4.50
97	Larry Walker (AS)	3.00	2.25	1.25
98	Don Mattingly (AS)	10.00	7.50	4.00
99	Jose Canseco (AS)	3.00	2.25	1.25
100	Dennis Eckersley (AS)	2.00	1.50	.80
101	Terry Pendleton (AS)	4.50	3.50	1.75
102	Frank Thomas (AS)	55.00	41.00	22.00
103	Barry Bonds (AS)	20.00	15.00	8.00
104	Roger Clemens	10.00	7.50	4.00
105	Ryne Sandberg (AS)	15.00	11.00	6.00
106	Fred McGriff (AS)	10.00	7.50	4.00
107	Nolan Ryan (AS)	40.00	30.00	16.00
108	Will Clark (AS)	9.00	6.75	3.50
109	Pat Listach (AS)	2.00	1.50	.80
110	Ken Griffey, Jr. (AS)	36.00	27.00	14.50
111	Cecil Fielder (AS)	7.50	5.75	3.00
112	Kirby Puckett (AS)	15.00	11.00	6.00
113	Doc Gooden (AS)	2.00	1.50	.80
114	Barry Larkin (AS)	3.00	2.25	1.25
115	David Cone (AS)	1.75	1.25	.70
116	Juan Gonzalez (AS)	36.00	27.00	14.50
117	Kent Hrbek	1.75	1.25	.70
118	Tim Wallach	1.75	1.25	.70
119	Craig Biggio	1.75	1.25	.70
120	Bobby Kelly	1.75	1.25	.70
121	Greg Olson	1.75	1.25	.70
122	Eddie Murray	3.00	2.25	1.25
123	Wil Cordero	3.00	2.25	1.25
124	Jay Buhner	1.75	1.25	.70
125	Carlton Fisk	2.50	2.00	1.00
126	Eric Davis	2.50	2.00	1.00
127	Doug Drabek	1.75	1.25	.70
128	Ozzie Guillen	1.75	1.25	.70
129	John Wetteland	1.75	1.25	.70
130	Andres Galarraga	4.00	3.00	1.50
131	Ken Caminiti	1.75	1.25	.70
132	Tom Candiotti	1.75	1.25	.70
133	Pat Borders	1.75	1.25	.70
134	Kevin Brown	1.75	1.25	.70
135	Travis Fryman	15.00	11.00	6.00
136	Kevin Mitchell	1.75	1.25	.70
137	Greg Swindell	1.75	1.25	.70
138	Benny Santiago	1.75	1.25	.70
139	Reggie Jefferson	1.75	1.25	.70
140	Chris Bosio	1.75	1.25	.70
141	Deion Sanders	6.00	4.50	2.50
142	Scott Erickson	1.75	1.25	.70
143	Howard Johnson	1.75	1.25	.70
144	Orestes Destrade	1.75	1.25	.70
145	Jose Guzman	1.75	1.25	.70
146	Chad Curtis	5.00	3.75	2.00
147	Cal Eldred	3.50	2.75	1.50
148	Willie Greene	1.75	1.25	.70
149	Tommy Greene	2.50	2.00	1.00
150	Erik Hanson	1.75	1.25	.70
151	Bob Welch	1.75	1.25	.70
152	John Jaha	3.00	2.25	1.25
153	Harold Baines	1.75	1.25	.70
154	Randy Johnson	4.00	3.00	1.50
155	Al Martin	3.00	2.25	1.25
156	J.T. Snow	10.00	7.50	4.00
157	Mike Mussina	10.00	7.50	4.00
158	Ruben Sierra	3.00	2.25	1.25
159	Dean Palmer	4.00	3.00	1.50
160	Steve Avery	12.00	9.00	4.75
161	Julio Franco	1.75	1.25	.70
162	Dave Winfield	9.00	6.75	3.50
163	Tim Salmon	32.00	24.00	13.00
164	Tom Henke	1.75	1.25	.70
165	Mo Vaughn	5.00	3.75	2.00
166	John Smoltz	3.00	2.25	1.25
167	Danny Tartabull	1.75	1.25	.70
168	Delino DeShields	3.00	2.25	1.25
169	Charlie Hough	1.75	1.25	.70
170	Paul O'Neill	1.75	1.25	.70
171	Darren Daulton	3.50	2.75	1.50
172	Jack McDowell	5.00	3.75	2.00
173	Junior Felix	1.75	1.25	.70
174	Jimmy Key	1.75	1.25	.70
175	George Bell	1.75	1.25	.70
176	Mike Stanton	1.75	1.25	.70
177	Len Dykstra	5.00	3.75	2.00
178	Norm Charlton	1.75	1.25	.70
179	Eric Anthony	1.75	1.25	.70
180	Bob Dibble	1.75	1.25	.70
181	Otis Nixon	1.75	1.25	.70
182	Randy Myers	1.75	1.25	.70
183	Tim Raines	1.75	1.25	.70
184	Orel Hershiser	1.75	1.25	.70
185	Andy Van Slyke	2.00	1.50	.80
186	*Mike Lansing*	3.00	2.25	1.25
187	Ray Lankford	1.75	1.25	.70
188	Mike Morgan	1.75	1.25	.70
189	Moises Alou	2.50	2.00	1.00
190	Edgar Martinez	1.75	1.25	.70
191	John Franco	1.75	1.25	.70
192	Robin Yount	8.00	6.00	3.25
193	Bob Tewksbury	1.75	1.25	.70
194	Jay Bell	1.75	1.25	.70
195	Luis Gonzalez	2.00	1.50	.80
196	Dave Fleming	2.00	1.50	.80
197	Mike Greenwell	1.75	1.25	.70
198	David Nied	6.00	4.50	2.50
199	Mike Piazza	60.00	45.00	24.00

1993 Topps Finest Refractors

This insert set features each of the cards from the regular Topps Finest set recreated with refracting foil using the metallization enhancement process. One refracting foil card was inserted in every nine packs, on average.

	MT	NR MT	EX
Complete Set (199):	9000.00	6500.00	3500.00
Common Player:	20.00	15.00	8.00

	MT	NR MT	EX
Stars: 8X to 12X Finest price			

1993 Topps Finest Jumbo All-Stars

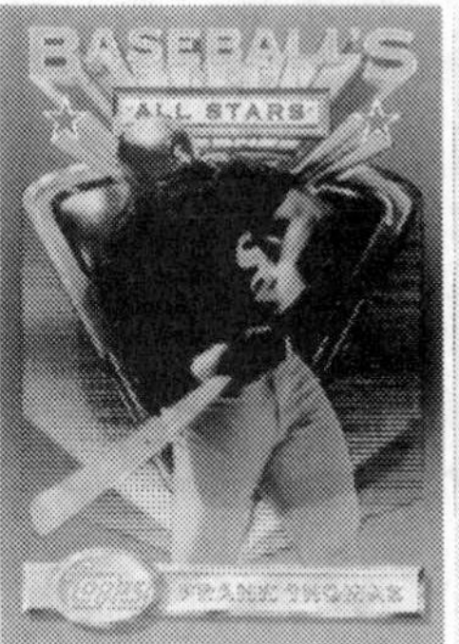

These 5" by 7" cards were produced using the metallization process. Each 18-count box contains one of the cards, while one of every six cards is enhanced with special refracting foil.

		MT	NR MT	EX
Complete Set (33):		875.00	656.00	350.00
Common Player (84-116):		15.00	11.00	6.00
84	Andre Dawson	15.00	11.00	6.00
85	Greg Maddux	30.00	22.00	12.00
86	Rickey Henderson	25.00	18.50	10.00
87	Tom Glavine	30.00	22.00	12.00
88	Roberto Alomar	50.00	37.00	20.00
89	Darryl Strawberry	15.00	11.00	6.00
90	Wade Boggs	25.00	18.50	10.00
91	Bo Jackson	25.00	18.50	10.00
92	Mark McGwire	20.00	15.00	8.00
93	Robin Ventura	25.00	18.50	10.00
94	Joe Carter	35.00	26.00	14.00
95	Lee Smith	15.00	11.00	6.00
96	Cal Ripken, Jr.	45.00	34.00	18.00
97	Larry Walker	15.00	11.00	6.00
98	Don Mattingly	30.00	22.00	12.00
99	Jose Canseco	20.00	15.00	8.00
100	Dennis Eckersley	15.00	11.00	6.00
101	Terry Pendleton	15.00	11.00	6.00
102	Frank Thomas	80.00	60.00	45.00
103	Barry Bonds	60.00	45.00	30.00
104	Roger Clemens	35.00	25.00	15.00
105	Ryne Sandberg	45.00	30.00	20.00
106	Fred McGriff	35.00	20.00	12.00
107	Nolan Ryan	85.00	60.00	45.00
108	Will Clark	25.00	15.00	10.00
109	Pat Listach	15.00	11.00	6.00
110	Ken Griffey, Jr.	70.00	50.00	25.00
111	Cecil Fielder	25.00	15.00	10.00
112	Kirby Puckett	40.00	30.00	20.00
113	Dwight Gooden	15.00	11.00	6.00
114	Barry Larkin	15.00	11.00	6.00
115	David Cone	15.00	11.00	6.00
116	Juan Gonzalez	70.00	50.00	30.00

1993 Topps Full Shot Super

Just as rivals Upper Deck and Donruss did, Topps issued a set of 21 oversized cards (3-1/2" by 5") that was available in retail outlets in packages that contained one of the large cards and two packs of regular issue Topps cards from the same year. The Topps Full Shot cards feature many of the top players in the game, and unlike the Upper Deck oversized cards, the Topps cards were not enlarged versions of existing cards but rather photos and a design that appeared only in this format.

		MT	NR MT	EX
Complete Set:		90.00	67.00	36.00
Common Player:		3.00	2.25	1.25
1	Frank Thomas	12.00	9.00	4.75
2	Ken Griffey, Jr.	12.00	9.00	4.75
3	Barry Bonds	8.00	6.00	3.25
4	Juan Gonzalez	9.00	6.75	3.50
5	Roberto Alomar	6.00	4.50	2.50
6	Mike Piazza	6.00	4.50	2.50
7	Tony Gwynn	4.00	3.00	1.50
8	Jeff Bagwell	4.00	3.00	1.50
9	Tim Salmon	6.00	4.50	2.50
10	John Olerud	4.00	3.00	1.50
11	Cal Ripken, Jr.	9.00	6.75	3.50
12	David McCarty	4.00	3.00	1.50
13	Darren Daulton	3.00	2.25	1.25
14	Carlos Baerga	5.00	3.75	2.00
15	Roger Clemens	4.00	3.00	1.50
16	John Kruk	3.00	2.25	1.25
17	Barry Larkin	3.00	2.25	1.25
18	Gary Sheffield	4.00	3.00	1.50
19	Tom Glavine	3.00	2.25	1.25
20	Andres Galarraga	4.00	3.00	1.50
21	Fred McGriff	4.00	3.00	1.50

1994 Topps Preview

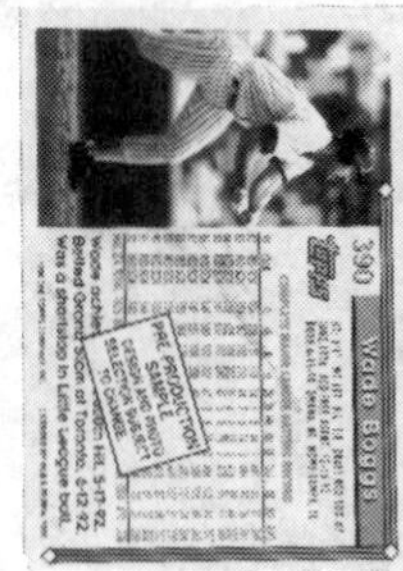

Two different versions of this nine-card set exist. A cello-wrapped version, designated (a) in the checklist, was given away to dealers and the hobby press. A second version, designated (b), was included in 1993 Topps factory sets. It is currently unknown which version, if either, will become more valuable due to demand and perceived scarcity. Both versions are similar to the regular-issue '94 Topps cards, except for the sample notation on back.

		MT	NR MT	EX
Complete set (a)(9):		7.50	5.75	3.00
Complete set (b) (9):		7.50	5.75	3.00
Common player (a):		.25	.20	.10
Common player (b):		.25	.20	.10
2a	Barry Bonds (vertical format)	1.75	1.25	.70
2b	Barry Bonds (horizontal)	1.75	1.25	.70
6a	Jeff Tackett (full bat label visible)	.25	.20	.10
6b	Jeff Tackett (partial bat label)	.25	.20	.10
34a	Juan Gonzalez (green triangle behind "Juan")	1.50	1.25	.60
34b	Juan Gonzalez (brown triangle)	1.50	1.25	.60
225a	Matt Williams (green triangle behind "Matt")	.50	.40	.20

		MT	NR MT	EX
225b	Matt Williams (blue triangle)	.50	.40	.20
294a	Carlos Quintana (team/position yellow)	.25	.20	.10
294b	Carlos Quintana (team/position black)	.25	.20	.10
331a	Ken Lofton (team/position white)	.25	.20	.10
331b	Ken Lofton (team/position black)	.25	.20	.10
390a	Wade Boggs (team/position yellow)	.75	.60	.30
390b	Wade Boggs (team/position black)	.75	.60	.30
397a	George Brett (vertical format)	1.00	.70	.40
397b	George Brett (horizontal)	1.00	.70	.40
700a	Nolan Ryan (vertical format)	2.00	1.50	.80
700b	Nolan Ryan (horizontal)	2.00	1.50	.80

1994 Topps

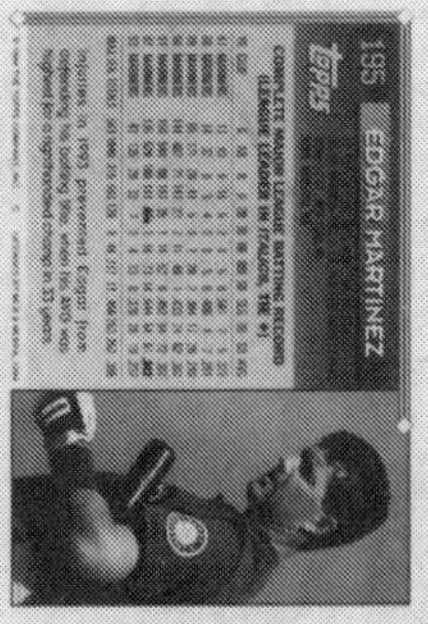

Once again released in two series, Topps basic baseball card for 1994 offers a standard mix of regular player cards, Future Stars, multi-player rookie cards and double-header All-Star cards. On the basic cards, the action player photo on front is framed in a home-plate shaped design. The player's name appears in script beneath the photo and a team color-coded strip at bottom carries the team and position designations. On back there is a player photo at the left or right end. A red box at top has biographical details while a marbled panel carries the stats and a career highlight. Cards are UV coated on each side. Inserts include a gold-enhanced card in every pack, plus random Black Gold cards.

		MT	NR MT	EX
Complete Set (396):		14.00	10.50	5.50
Common Player:		.04	.03	.02
1	Mike Piazza	1.50	1.25	.60
2	Bernie Williams	.04	.03	.02
3	Kevin Rogers	.04	.03	.02
4	Paul Carey	.04	.03	.02
5	Ozzie Guillen	.04	.03	.02
6	Derrick May	.04	.03	.02
7	Jose Mesa	.04	.03	.02
8	Todd Hundley	.04	.03	.02
9	Chris Haney	.04	.03	.02
10	John Olerud	.15	.11	.06
11	Andujar Cedeno	.04	.03	.02
12	John Smiley	.04	.03	.02
13	Phil Plantier	.04	.03	.02
14	Willie Banks	.04	.03	.02
15	Jay Bell	.04	.03	.02
16	Doug Henry	.04	.03	.02
17	Lance Blankenship	.04	.03	.02
18	Greg Harris	.04	.03	.02
19	Scott Livingstone	.04	.03	.02
20	Bryan Harvey	.04	.03	.02
21	Wil Cordero	.04	.03	.02
22	Roger Pavlik	.04	.03	.02
23	Mark Lemke	.04	.03	.02
24	Jeff Nelson	.04	.03	.02
25	Todd Zeile	.04	.03	.02
26	Billy Hatcher	.04	.03	.02
27	Joe Magrane	.04	.03	.02
28	Tony Longmire	.04	.03	.02
29	Omar Daal	.04	.03	.02

		MT	NR MT	EX
30	Kirt Manwaring	.04	.03	.02
31	Melido Perez	.04	.03	.02
32	Tim Hulett	.04	.03	.02
33	Jeff Schwarz	.04	.03	.02
34	Nolan Ryan	.40	.30	.15
35	Jose Guzman	.04	.03	.02
36	Felix Fermin	.04	.03	.02
37	Jeff Innis	.04	.03	.02
38	Brent Mayne	.04	.03	.02
39	Huck Flener	.04	.03	.02
40	Jeff Bagwell	.15	.11	.06
41	Kevin Wickander	.04	.03	.02
42	Ricky Gutierrez	.04	.03	.02
43	Pat Mahomes	.04	.03	.02
44	Jeff King	.04	.03	.02
45	Cal Eldred	.10	.08	.04
46	Craig Paquette	.04	.03	.02
47	Richie Lewis	.04	.03	.02
48	Tony Phillips	.04	.03	.02
49	Armando Reynoso	.04	.03	.02
50	Moises Alou	.08	.06	.03
51	Manuel Lee	.04	.03	.02
52	Otis Nixon	.04	.03	.02
53	*Billy Ashley*	.40	.30	.15
54	Mark Whiten	.04	.03	.02
55	Jeff Russell	.04	.03	.02
56	Chad Curtis	.04	.03	.02
57	*Kevin Stocker*	.50	.40	.20
58	Mike Jackson	.04	.03	.02
59	Matt Nokes	.04	.03	.02
60	Chris Bosio	.04	.03	.02
61	Damon Buford	.04	.03	.02
62	Tim Belcher	.04	.03	.02
63	Glenallen Hill	.04	.03	.02
64	Bill Wertz	.04	.03	.02
65	Eddie Murray	.04	.03	.02
66	Tom Gordon	.04	.03	.02
67	*Alex Gonzalez*	.50	.40	.20
68	Eddie Taubensee	.04	.03	.02
69	Jacob Brumfield	.04	.03	.02
70	Andy Benes	.04	.03	.02
71	Rich Becker	.04	.03	.02
72	Steve Cooke	.04	.03	.02
73	Billy Spiers	.04	.03	.02
74	Scott Brosius	.04	.03	.02
75	Alan Trammell	.04	.03	.02
76	Luis Aquino	.04	.03	.02
77	Jerald Clark	.04	.03	.02
78	Mel Rojas	.04	.03	.02
79	Billy Masse, Stanton Cameron, Tim Clark, Craig McClure	.04	.03	.02
80	Jose Canseco	.10	.08	.04
81	Greg McMichael	.10	.08	.04
82	Brian Turang	.04	.03	.02
83	Tom Urban	.04	.03	.02
84	Garret Anderson	.04	.03	.02
85	Tony Pena	.04	.03	.02
86	Ricky Jordan	.04	.03	.02
87	Jim Gott	.04	.03	.02
88	Pat Kelly	.04	.03	.02
89	Bud Black	.04	.03	.02
90	Robin Ventura	.10	.08	.04
91	Rick Sutcliffe	.04	.03	.02
92	Jose Bautista	.04	.03	.02
93	Bob Ojeda	.04	.03	.02
94	Phil Hiatt	.20	.15	.08
95	Tim Pugh	.04	.03	.02
96	Randy Knorr	.04	.03	.02
97	Todd Jones	.04	.03	.02
98	Ryan Thompson	.04	.03	.02
99	Tim Mauser	.04	.03	.02
100	Kirby Puckett	.20	.15	.08
101	Mark Dewey	.04	.03	.02
102	B.J. Surhoff	.04	.03	.02
103	Sterling Hitchcock	.04	.03	.02
104	Alex Arias	.04	.03	.02
105	David Wells	.04	.03	.02
106	Daryl Boston	.04	.03	.02
107	Mike Stanton	.04	.03	.02
108	Gary Redus	.04	.03	.02
109	Delino DeShields	.04	.03	.02
110	Lee Smith	.04	.03	.02
111	Greg Litton	.04	.03	.02
112	Frank Rodriguez	.10	.08	.04
113	Russ Springer	.04	.03	.02
114	Mitch Williams	.04	.03	.02
115	Eric Karros	.10	.08	.04
116	Jeff Brantley	.04	.03	.02
117	Jack Voight	.04	.03	.02
118	*Jason Bere*	.75	.60	.30
119	Kevin Roberson	.25	.20	.10
120	Jimmy Key	.04	.03	.02

		MT	NR MT	EX
121	Reggie Jefferson	.04	.03	.02
122	Jeremy Burnitz	.10	.08	.04
123	Billy Brewer	.04	.03	.02
124	Willie Canate	.04	.03	.02
125	Greg Swindell	.04	.03	.02
126	Hal Morris	.04	.03	.02
127	Brad Ausmus	.04	.03	.02
128	George Tsamis	.04	.03	.02
129	Denny Neagle	.04	.03	.02
130	Pat Listach	.10	.08	.04
131	Steve Karsay	.04	.03	.02
132	Bret Barberie	.04	.03	.02
133	Mark Leiter	.04	.03	.02
134	Greg Colbrunn	.04	.03	.02
135	David Nied	.10	.08	.04
136	Dean Palmer	.04	.03	.02
137	Steve Avery	.10	.08	.04
138	Bill Haselman	.04	.03	.02
139	Tripp Cromer	.04	.03	.02
140	Frank Viola	.04	.03	.02
141	Rene Gonzales	.04	.03	.02
142	Curt Schilling	.04	.03	.02
143	Tim Wallach	.04	.03	.02
144	Bobby Munoz	.04	.03	.02
145	Brady Anderson	.04	.03	.02
146	Rod Beck	.04	.03	.02
147	Mike LaValliere	.04	.03	.02
148	Greg Hibbard	.04	.03	.02
149	Kenny Lofton	.10	.08	.04
150	Doc Gooden	.04	.03	.02
151	Greg Gagne	.04	.03	.02
152	Ray McDavid	.04	.03	.02
153	Chris Donnels	.04	.03	.02
154	Dan Wilson	.04	.03	.02
155	Todd Stottlemyre	.04	.03	.02
156	David McCarty	.08	.06	.03
157	Paul Wagner	.04	.03	.02
158	Orlando Miller, Brandon Wilson, Derek Jeter, Mike Neal	.04	.03	.02
159	Mike Fetters	.04	.03	.02
160	Scott Lydy	.04	.03	.02
161	Darrell Whitmore	.15	.11	.06
162	Bob MacDonald	.04	.03	.02
163	Vinny Castilla	.04	.03	.02
164	Denis Boucher	.04	.03	.02
165	Ivan Rodriguez	.10	.08	.04
166	Ron Gant	.08	.06	.03
167	Tim Davis	.04	.03	.02
168	Steve Dixon	.04	.03	.02
169	Scott Fletcher	.04	.03	.02
170	Terry Mulholland	.04	.03	.02
171	Greg Myers	.04	.03	.02
172	Brett Butler	.04	.03	.02
173	Bob Wickman	.04	.03	.02
174	Dave Martinez	.04	.03	.02
175	Fernando Valenzuela	.04	.03	.02
176	Craig Grebeck	.04	.03	.02
177	Shawn Boskie	.04	.03	.02
178	Albie Lopez	.04	.03	.02
179	Butch Huskey	.04	.03	.02
180	George Brett	.15	.11	.06
181	Juan Guzman	.10	.08	.04
182	Eric Anthony	.04	.03	.02
183	Bob Dibble	.04	.03	.02
184	Craig Shipley	.04	.03	.02
185	Kevin Tapani	.04	.03	.02
186	Marcus Moore	.04	.03	.02
187	Graeme Lloyd	.10	.08	.04
188	Mike Bordick	.10	.08	.04
189	Chris Hammond	.04	.03	.02
190	Cecil Fielder	.10	.08	.04
191	Curtis Leskanic	.04	.03	.02
192	Lou Frazier	.04	.03	.02
193	Steve Dreyer	.04	.03	.02
194	Javy Lopez	.30	.25	.12
195	Edgar Martinez	.04	.03	.02
196	Allen Watson	.20	.15	.08
197	John Flaherty	.04	.03	.02
198	Kurt Stillwell	.04	.03	.02
199	Danny Jackson	.04	.03	.02
200	Cal Ripken	.25	.20	.10
201	Mike Bell	.04	.03	.02
202	*Alan Benes*	.15	.11	.06
203	Matt Farner	.04	.03	.02
204	*Jeff Granger*	.15	.11	.06
205	Brooks Kieschnick	.04	.03	.02
206	Jeremy Lee	.04	.03	.02
207	Charles Peterson, Andy Rice	.04	.03	.02
209	*Billy Wagner*	.10	.08	.04
210	Kelly Wunsch	.04	.03	.02
211	Tom Candiotti	.04	.03	.02
212	Domingo Jean	.10	.08	.04
213	John Burkett	.04	.03	.02
214	George Bell	.04	.03	.02
215	Dan Plesac	.04	.03	.02
216	Manny Ramirez	.15	.11	.06
217	Mike Maddux	.04	.03	.02
218	Kevin McReynolds	.04	.03	.02
219	Pat Borders	.04	.03	.02
220	Doug Drabek	.04	.03	.02
221	Larry Luebbers	.04	.03	.02
222	Trevor Hoffman	.04	.03	.02
223	Pat Meares	.04	.03	.02
224	Danny Miceli	.04	.03	.02
225	Greg Vaughn	.04	.03	.02
226	Scott Hemond	.04	.03	.02
227	Pat Rapp	.04	.03	.02
228	Kirk Gibson	.04	.03	.02
229	Lance Painter	.04	.03	.02
230	Larry Walker	.08	.06	.03
231	*Benji Gil*	.25	.20	.10
232	Mark Wohlers	.04	.03	.02
233	Rich Amaral	.06	.05	.02
234	Erik Pappas	.04	.03	.02
235	Scott Cooper	.04	.03	.02
236	Mike Butcher	.04	.03	.02
237	*Curtis Pride,* Shawn Green, Mark Sweeney, Eddie Davis	.04	.03	.02
238	Kim Batiste	.04	.03	.02
239	Paul Assenmacher	.04	.03	.02
240	Will Clark	.15	.11	.06
241	Jose Offerman	.04	.03	.02
242	Todd Frohwirth	.04	.03	.02
243	Tim Raines	.04	.03	.02
244	Rick Wilkins	.04	.03	.02
245	Bret Saberhagen	.04	.03	.02
246	Thomas Howard	.04	.03	.02
247	Stan Belinda	.04	.03	.02
248	Rickey Henderson	.10	.08	.04
249	Brian Williams	.04	.03	.02
250	Barry Larkin	.04	.03	.02
251	Jose Valentin	.04	.03	.02
252	Lenny Webster	.04	.03	.02
253	Blas Minor	.10	.08	.04
254	Tim Teufel	.04	.03	.02
255	Bobby Witt	.04	.03	.02
256	Walt Weiss	.04	.03	.02
257	Chad Kreuter	.04	.03	.02
258	Roberto Mejia	.10	.08	.04
259	Cliff Floyd	.50	.40	.20
260	Julio Franco	.04	.03	.02
261	Rafael Belliard	.04	.03	.02
262	Marc Newfield	.10	.08	.04
263	Gerald Perry	.04	.03	.02
264	Ken Ryan	.04	.03	.02
265	Chili Davis	.04	.03	.02
266	Dave West	.04	.03	.02
267	Royce Clayton	.04	.03	.02
268	Pedro Martinez	.10	.08	.04
269	Mark Hutton	.04	.03	.02
270	Frank Thomas	1.00	.70	.40
271	Brad Pennington	.04	.03	.02
272	Mike Harkey	.04	.03	.02
273	Sandy Alomar	.04	.03	.02
274	Dave Gallagher	.04	.03	.02
275	Wally Joyner	.04	.03	.02
276	Ricky Trlicek	.04	.03	.02
277	Al Osuna	.04	.03	.02
278	Calvin Reese	.04	.03	.02
279	Kevin Higgins	.04	.03	.02
280	Rick Aguilera	.04	.03	.02
281	Orlando Merced	.04	.03	.02
282	Mike Mohler	.04	.03	.02
283	John Jaha	.04	.03	.02
284	Robb Nen	.04	.03	.02
285	Travis Fryman	.10	.08	.04
286	Mark Thompson	.04	.03	.02
287	Mike Lansing	.10	.08	.04
288	Craig Lefferts	.04	.03	.02
289	Damon Berryhill	.04	.03	.02
290	Randy Johnson	.08	.06	.03
291	Jeff Reed	.04	.03	.02
292	Danny Darwin	.04	.03	.02
293	J.T. Snow	.40	.30	.15
294	Tyler Green	.04	.03	.02
295	Chris Hoiles	.04	.03	.02
296	Roger McDowell	.04	.03	.02
297	Spike Owen	.04	.03	.02
298	Salomon Torres	.10	.08	.04
299	Wilson Alvarez	.04	.03	.02
300	Ryne Sandberg	.20	.15	.08
301	Derek Lilliquist	.04	.03	.02

		MT	NR MT	EX
302	Howard Johnson	.04	.03	.02
303	Greg Cadaret	.04	.03	.02
304	Pat Hentgen	.04	.03	.02
305	Craig Biggio	.04	.03	.02
306	Scott Service	.04	.03	.02
307	Melvin Nieves	.04	.03	.02
308	Mike Trombley	.04	.03	.02
309	Carlos Garcia	.04	.03	.02
310	Robin Yount	.15	.11	.06
311	Marcos Armas	.04	.03	.02
312	Rich Rodriguez	.04	.03	.02
313	Justin Thompson	.04	.03	.02
314	Danny Sheaffer	.04	.03	.02
315	Ken Hill	.04	.03	.02
316	Chad Ogea, Duff Brumley, Terrell Wade, Chris Michalak	.04	.03	.02
317	Cris Carpenter	.04	.03	.02
318	Jeff Blauser	.04	.03	.02
319	Ted Power	.04	.03	.02
320	Ozzie Smith	.10	.08	.04
321	John Dopson	.04	.03	.02
322	Chris Turner	.04	.03	.02
323	Pete Incaviglia	.04	.03	.02
324	Alan Mills	.04	.03	.02
325	Jody Reed	.04	.03	.02
326	Rich Monteleone	.04	.03	.02
327	Mark Carreon	.04	.03	.02
328	Donn Pall	.04	.03	.02
329	Matt Walbeck	.04	.03	.02
330	Charles Nagy	.04	.03	.02
331	Jeff McKnight	.04	.03	.02
332	Jose Lind	.04	.03	.02
333	Mike Timlin	.04	.03	.02
334	Doug Jones	.04	.03	.02
335	Kevin Mitchell	.04	.03	.02
336	Luis Lopez	.04	.03	.02
337	Shane Mack	.04	.03	.02
338	Randy Tomlin	.04	.03	.02
339	Matt Mieske	.08	.06	.03
340	Mark McGwire	.10	.08	.04
341	Nigel Wilson	.10	.08	.04
342	Danny Gladden	.04	.03	.02
343	Mo Sanford	.04	.03	.02
344	Sean Berry	.04	.03	.02
345	Kevin Brown	.04	.03	.02
346	Greg Olson	.04	.03	.02
347	Dave Magadan	.04	.03	.02
348	Rene Arocha	.10	.08	.04
349	Carlos Quintana	.04	.03	.02
350	Jim Abbott	.04	.03	.02
351	Gary DiSarcina	.04	.03	.02
352	Ben Rivera	.04	.03	.02
353	Carlos Hernandez	.04	.03	.02
354	Darren Lewis	.04	.03	.02
355	Harold Reynolds	.04	.03	.02
356	Scott Ruffcorn	.04	.03	.02
357	Mark Gubicza	.04	.03	.02
358	Paul Sorrento	.04	.03	.02
359	Anthony Young	.04	.03	.02
360	Mark Grace	.08	.06	.03
361	Rob Butler	.04	.03	.02
362	Kevin Bass	.04	.03	.02
363	Eric Helfand	.04	.03	.02
364	Derek Bell	.04	.03	.02
365	Scott Erickson	.04	.03	.02
366	Al Martin	.10	.08	.04
367	Ricky Bones	.04	.03	.02
368	Jeff Branson	.04	.03	.02
369	Luis Ortiz, David Bell, Jason Giambi, George Arias	.04	.03	.02
370	Benny Santiago	.04	.03	.02
371	John Doherty	.04	.03	.02
372	Joe Girardi	.04	.03	.02
373	Tim Scott	.04	.03	.02
374	Marvin Freeman	.04	.03	.02
375	Deion Sanders	.10	.08	.04
376	Roger Salkeld	.04	.03	.02
377	Bernard Gilkey	.04	.03	.02
378	Tony Fossas	.04	.03	.02
379	Mark McLemore	.04	.03	.02
380	Darren Daulton	.04	.03	.02
381	Chuck Finley	.04	.03	.02
382	Mitch Webster	.04	.03	.02
383	Gerald Williams	.04	.03	.02
384	Frank Thomas, Fred McGriff	.15	.11	.06
385	Roberto Alomar, Robby Thompson	.04	.03	.02
386	Wade Boggs, Matt Williams	.04	.03	.02
387	Cal Ripken, Jeff Blauser	.04	.03	.02
388	Ken Griffey Jr., Len Dykstra	.10	.08	.04
389	Juan Gonzalez, David Justice	.20	.15	.08
390	Albert Belle, Barry Bonds	.35	.25	.14
391	Mike Stanley, Mike Piazza	1.50	1.25	.60
392	Jack McDowell, Greg Maddux	.10	.08	.04
393	Jimmy Key, Tom Glavine	.10	.08	.04
394	Jeff Montgomery, Randy Myers	.04	.03	.02
395	Checklist 1	.04	.03	.02
396	Checklist 2	.04	.03	.02

1987 Toys "R" Us

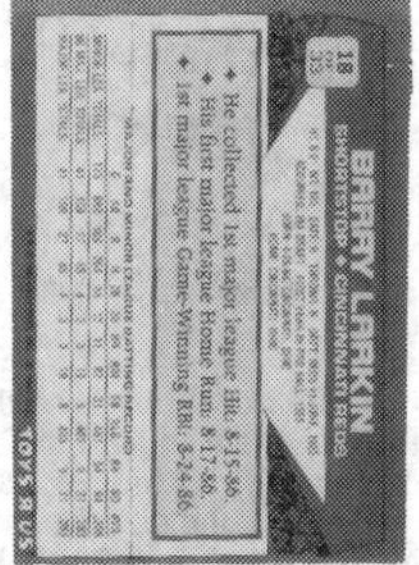

Marked as a collectors' edition set and titled "Baseball Rookies," the 1987 Toys "R" Us issue was produced by Topps for the toy store chain. The set is comprised of 33 glossy-coated cards, each measuring 2-1/2" by 3-1/2". The card fronts are very colorful, employing nine different colors including deep black borders. The backs, printed in blue and orange, contain career highlights and composite minor and major league statistics. The set was distributed in a specially designed box and sold for $1.99 in retail outlets.

		MT	NR MT	EX
Complete Set:		6.00	4.50	2.50
Common Player:		.10	.08	.04
1	Andy Allanson	.10	.08	.04
2	Paul Assenmacher	.12	.09	.05
3	Scott Bailes	.10	.08	.04
4	Barry Bonds	.60	.45	.25
5	Jose Canseco	.90	.70	.35
6	John Cerutti	.10	.08	.04
7	Will Clark	.90	.70	.35
8	Kal Daniels	.15	.11	.06
9	Jim Deshaies	.10	.08	.04
10	Mark Eichhorn	.10	.08	.04
11	Ed Hearn	.10	.08	.04
12	Pete Incaviglia	.12	.09	.05
13	Bo Jackson	.60	.45	.25
14	Wally Joyner	.60	.45	.25
15	Charlie Kerfeld	.10	.08	.04
16	Eric King	.10	.08	.04
17	John Kruk	.40	.30	.15
18	Barry Larkin	.50	.40	.20
19	Mike LaValliere	.10	.08	.04
20	Greg Mathews	.10	.08	.04
21	Kevin Mitchell	.20	.15	.08
22	Dan Plesac	.10	.08	.04
23	Bruce Ruffin	.10	.08	.04
24	Ruben Sierra	.50	.40	.20
25	Cory Snyder	.10	.08	.04
26	Kurt Stillwell	.10	.08	.04
27	Dale Sveum	.10	.08	.04
28	Danny Tartabull	.30	.25	.12
29	Andres Thomas	.10	.08	.04
30	Robby Thompson	.25	.20	.10
31	Jim Traber	.10	.08	.04
32	Mitch Williams	.15	.11	.06
33	Todd Worrell	.15	.11	.06

A player's name in italic indicates a rookie card. An (FC) indicates a player's first card for that particular card company.

1988 Toys "R" Us Rookies

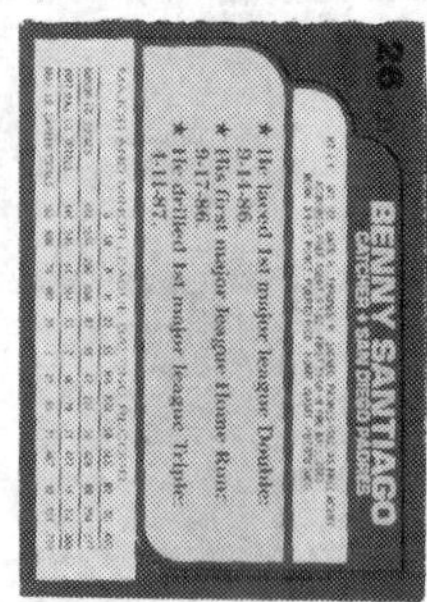

This 33-card boxed edition was produced by Topps for exclusive distribution at Toys "R" Us stores. The glossy standard-size cards spotlight rookies in both closeups and action photos on a bright blue background inlaid with yellow. The Toys "R" Us logo frames the top left corner, above a curving white banner that reads "Topps 1988 Collectors' Edition Rookies". A black Topps logo hugs the upper right-hand edge of the photo. The player name, red-lettered on a tube of yellow, frames the bottom. Card backs are horizontal, blue and pink on a bright pink background and include the player name, personal information and career highlights and stats.

		MT	NR MT	EX
Complete Set:		5.00	3.75	2.00
Common Player:		.10	.08	.04
1	Todd Benzinger	.20	.15	.08
2	Bob Brower	.10	.08	.04
3	Jerry Browne	.10	.08	.04
4	DeWayne Buice	.10	.08	.04
5	Ellis Burks	.30	.25	.12
6	Ken Caminiti	.20	.15	.08
7	Casey Candaele	.10	.08	.04
8	Dave Cone	.35	.25	.14
9	Kelly Downs	.15	.11	.06
10	Mike Dunne	.10	.08	.04
11	Ken Gerhart	.10	.08	.04
12	Mike Greenwell	.35	.25	.14
13	Mike Henneman	.12	.09	.05
14	Sam Horn	.10	.08	.04
15	Joe Magrane	.10	.08	.04
16	Fred Manrique	.10	.08	.04
17	John Marzano	.10	.08	.04
18	Fred McGriff	.25	.20	.10
19	Mark McGwire	.50	.40	.20
20	Jeff Musselman	.10	.08	.04
21	Randy Myers	.20	.15	.08
22	Matt Nokes	.25	.20	.10
23	Al Pedrique	.10	.08	.04
24	Luis Polonia	.15	.11	.06
25	Billy Ripken	.10	.08	.04
26	Benny Santiago	.30	.25	.12
27	Kevin Seitzer	.10	.08	.04
28	John Smiley	.12	.09	.05
29	Mike Stanley	.10	.08	.04
30	Terry Steinbach	.20	.15	.08
31	B.J. Surhoff	.20	.15	.08
32	Bobby Thigpen	.15	.11	.06
33	Devon White	.25	.20	.10

1989 Toys "R" Us Rookies

This glossy set of 33 top rookies was produced by Topps for the Toys "R" Us chain and was sold in a special box. Each player's name and position appear below the full-color photo, while the Toys "R" Us logo and "Topps 1989 Collector's Edition" appear along the top. Major

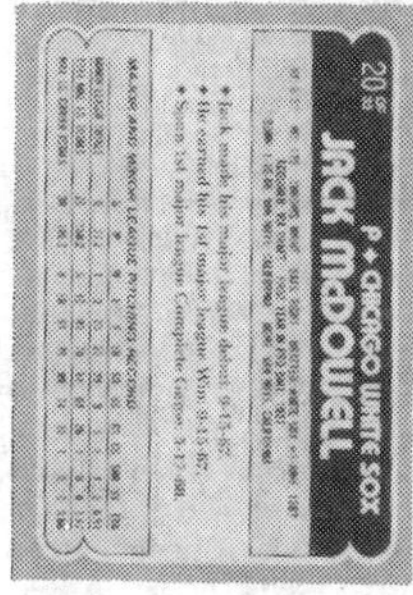

and minor league stats are on the back. The set is numbered alphabetically.

		MT	NR MT	EX
Complete Set:		4.00	3.00	1.50
Common Player:		.10	.08	.04
1	Roberto Alomar	.50	.40	.20
2	Brady Anderson	.15	.11	.06
3	Tim Belcher	.15	.11	.06
4	Damon Berryhill	.10	.08	.04
5	Jay Buhner	.12	.09	.05
6	Sherman Corbett	.10	.08	.04
7	Kevin Elster	.10	.08	.04
8	Cecil Espy	.10	.08	.04
9	Dave Gallagher	.12	.09	.05
10	Ron Gant	.35	.25	.14
11	Paul Gibson	.10	.08	.04
12	Mark Grace	.60	.45	.25
13	Bryan Harvey	.20	.15	.08
14	Darrin Jackson	.10	.08	.04
15	Gregg Jefferies	.60	.45	.25
16	Ron Jones	.10	.08	.04
17	Ricky Jordan	.10	.08	.04
18	Roberto Kelly	.30	.25	.12
19	Al Leiter	.10	.08	.04
20	Jack McDowell	.35	.25	.14
21	Melido Perez	.10	.08	.04
22	Jeff Pico	.10	.08	.04
23	Jody Reed	.10	.08	.04
24	Chris Sabo	.25	.20	.10
25	Nelson Santovenia	.10	.08	.04
26	Mackey Sasser	.10	.08	.04
27	Mike Schooler	.12	.09	.05
28	Gary Sheffield	.60	.45	.25
29	Pete Smith	.15	.11	.06
30	Pete Stanicek	.10	.08	.04
31	Jeff Treadway	.10	.08	.04
32	Walt Weiss	.25	.20	.10
33	Dave West	.15	.11	.06

1990 Toys "R" Us Rookies

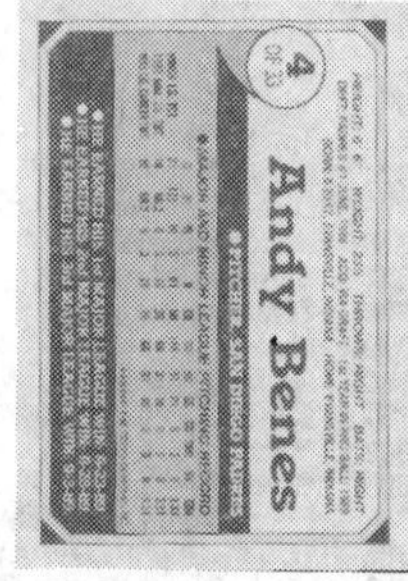

This 33-card set marks the fourth straigh year that Topps has produced a set to be sold exclusively at Toys "R"

Us stores. The card fronts contain full- color photos of 1989 rookies. The flip sides are horizontal and provide both minor and major league totals. The complete set is packaged in a special box which features a checklist uon the back.

		MT	NR MT	EX
Complete Set:		5.00	3.75	2.00
Common Player:		.10	.08	.04
1	Jim Abbott	.50	.40	.20
2	Eric Anthony	.40	.30	.15
3	Joey Belle	.50	.40	.20
4	Andy Benes	.20	.15	.08
5	Greg Briley	.15	.11	.06
6	Kevin Brown	.10	.08	.04
7	Mark Carreon	.10	.08	.04
8	Mike Devereaux	.15	.11	.06
9	Junior Felix	.25	.20	.10
10	Mark Gardner	.15	.11	.06
11	Bob Geren	.10	.08	.04
12	Tom Gordon	.10	.08	.04
13	Ken Griffey, Jr.	2.00	1.50	.80
14	Pete Harnisch	.10	.08	.04
15	Ken Hill	.10	.08	.04
16	Gregg Jefferies	.30	.25	.12
17	Derek Lilliquist	.10	.08	.04
18	Carlos Martinez	.10	.08	.04
19	Ramon Martinez	.30	.25	.12
20	Bob Milacki	.10	.08	.04
21	Gregg Olson	.15	.11	.06
22	Kenny Rogers	.10	.08	.04
23	Alex Sanchez	.10	.08	.04
24	Gary Sheffield	.30	.25	.12
25	Dwight Smith	.10	.08	.04
26	Billy Spiers	.10	.08	.04
27	Greg Vaughn	.30	.25	.12
28	Robin Ventura	.40	.30	.15
29	Jerome Walton	.10	.08	.04
30	Dave West	.10	.08	.04
31	John Wetteland	.15	.11	.06
32	Craig Worthington	.10	.08	.04
33	Todd Zeile	.20	.15	.08

1991 Toys "R" Us Rookies

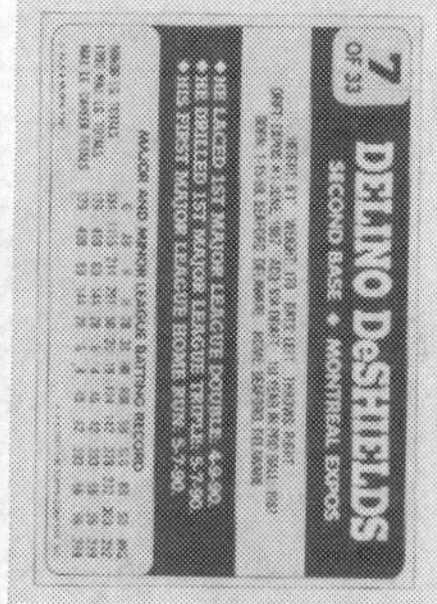

Produced by Topps, this 33-card set features baseball's top young players. The cards are styled much like past Toys "R" Us issues featuring glossy photos. The backs are printed horizontally and include player information and statistics. This set is the fifth of its kind produced by Topps for Toys "R" Us.

		MT	NR MT	EX
Complete Set:		5.00	3.75	2.00
Common Player:		.10	.08	.04
1	Sandy Alomar, Jr.	.15	.11	.06
2	Kevin Appier	.15	.11	.06
3	Steve Avery	.40	.30	.15
4	Carlos Baerga	.40	.30	.15
5	Alex Cole	.15	.11	.06
6	Pat Combs	.10	.08	.04
7	Delino DeShields	.30	.25	.12
8	Travis Fryman	.40	.30	.15
9	Marquis Grissom	.30	.25	.12
10	Mike Harkey	.10	.08	.04
11	Glenallen Hill	.10	.08	.04
12	Jeff Huson	.10	.08	.04
13	Felix Jose	.20	.15	.08
14	Dave Justice	.50	.40	.20
15	Dana Kiecker	.10	.08	.04
16	Kevin Maas	.15	.11	.06
17	Ben McDonald	.20	.15	.08
18	Brian McRae	.30	.25	.12
19	Kent Mercker	.10	.08	.04
20	Hal Morris	.20	.15	.08
21	Chris Nabholz	.10	.08	.04
22	Tim Naehring	.10	.08	.04
23	Jose Offerman	.15	.11	.06
24	John Olerud	.35	.25	.14
25	Scott Radinsky	.10	.08	.04
26	Bill Sampen	.10	.08	.04
27	Frank Thomas	2.00	1.50	.80
28	Randy Tomlin	.15	.11	.06
29	Greg Vaughn	.20	.15	.08
30	Robin Ventura	.40	.30	.15
31	Larry Walker	.30	.25	.12
32	Wally Whitehurst	.10	.08	.04
33	Todd Zeile	.20	.15	.08

1993 Toys "R" Us Topps Stadium Club

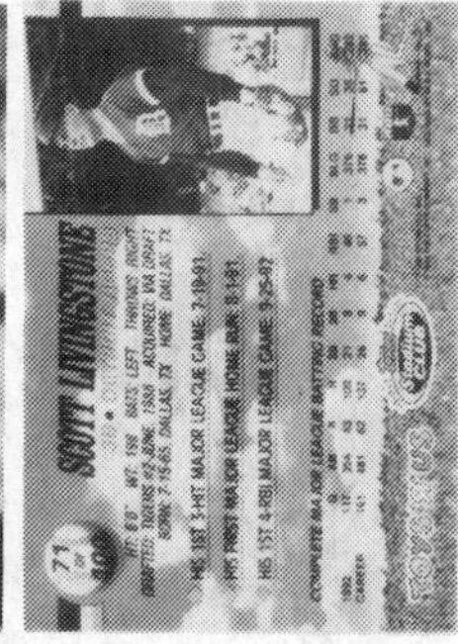

Featuring subsets labeled "Young Stars," "Future Stars" and "Rookie Stars," this 100-card set was sold in a plastic replica of a Toys "R" Us store, packaged with a dozen "Master Photos." Similar to regular 1993 Topps Stadium Club cards, the Toys "R" Us version features full-bleed photos on front, highlighed with goil-foil and a color Toys "R" Us logo in one of the upper corners. Backs have a background of a cloud-filled blue sky and green grass. A small player photo is at upper-right. Back information offers a few personal details, 1992 and career stats and a few career highlights. At bottom are the logos of all involved parties. The cards are UV-coated front and back. Each card is designated on the front as "Rookie Star," "Young Star" or "Future Star" in gold foil.

		MT	NR MT	EX
Complete Set:		9.00	6.75	3.50
Common Player:		.10	.08	.04
1	Ken Griffey, Jr.	1.50	1.25	.60
2	Chad Curtis	.15	.11	.06
3	Mike Bordick	.10	.08	.04
4	Ryan Klesko	.30	.25	.12
5	Pat Listach	.10	.08	.04
6	Jim Bullinger	.10	.08	.04
7	Tim Laker	.10	.08	.04
8	Mike Devereaux	.10	.08	.04
9	Kevin Young	.20	.15	.08
10	John Valentin	.10	.08	.04
11	Pat Mahomes	.15	.11	.06
12	Todd Hundley	.10	.08	.04
13	Roberto Alomar	.30	.25	.12
14	David Justice	.25	.20	.10
15	Mike Perez	.10	.08	.04
16	Royce Clayton	.10	.08	.04
17	Ryan Thompson	.10	.08	.04
18	Dave Hollins	.15	.11	.06
19	Brien Taylor	.40	.30	.15
20	Melvin Nieves	.20	.15	.08
21	Rheal Cormier	.20	.15	.08

		MT	NR MT	EX
22	Mike Piazza	.75	.60	.30
23	Larry Walker	.15	.11	.06
24	Tim Wakefield	.10	.08	.04
25	Tim Costo	.10	.08	.04
26	Pedro Munoz	.10	.08	.04
27	Reggie Sanders	.15	.11	.06
28	Arthur Rhodes	.15	.11	.06
29	Scott Cooper	.10	.08	.04
30	Marquis Grissom	.20	.15	.08
31	Dave Nilsson	.10	.08	.04
32	John Patterson	.10	.08	.04
33	Ivan Rodriguez	.20	.15	.08
34	Andy Stankiewicz	.12	.09	.05
35	Bret Boone	.12	.09	.05
36	Gerald Williams	.12	.09	.05
37	Mike Mussina	.20	.15	.08
38	Henry Rodriguez	.15	.11	.06
39	Chuck Knoblauch	.15	.11	.06
40	Bob Wickman	.10	.08	.04
41	Donovan Osborne	.10	.08	.04
42	Mike Timlin	.10	.08	.04
43	Damion Easley	.15	.11	.06
44	Pedro Astacio	.10	.08	.04
45	David Segui	.10	.08	.04
46	Willie Greene	.15	.11	.06
47	Mike Trombley	.10	.08	.04
48	Bernie Williams	.12	.09	.05
49	Eric Anthony	.15	.11	.06
50	Tim Naehring	.10	.08	.04
51	Carlos Baerga	.25	.20	.10
52	Brady Anderson	.12	.09	.05
53	Mo Vaughn	.15	.11	.06
54	Willie Banks	.12	.09	.05
55	Mark Wohlers	.10	.08	.04
56	Jeff Bagwell	.15	.11	.06
57	Frank Seminara	.10	.08	.04
58	Robin Ventura	.20	.15	.08
59	Alan Embree	.10	.08	.04
60	Rey Sanchez	.10	.08	.04
61	Delino DeShields	.15	.11	.06
62	Todd Van Poppel	.20	.15	.08
63	Eric Karros	.25	.20	.10
64	Gary Sheffield	.20	.15	.08
65	Dan Wilson	.12	.09	.05
66	Frank Thomas	1.50	1.25	.60
67	Tim Salmon	.90	.70	.35
68	Dan Smith	.15	.11	.06
69	Kenny Lofton	.15	.11	.06
70	Carlos Garcia	.15	.11	.06
71	Scott Livingstone	.15	.11	.06
72	Sam Militello	.10	.08	.04
73	Juan Guzman	.12	.09	.05
74	Greg Colbrunn	.10	.08	.04
75	David Hulse	.10	.08	.04
76	Rusty Meacham	.10	.08	.04
77	Dave Fleming	.10	.08	.04
78	Rene Arocha	.15	.11	.06
79	Derrick May	.15	.11	.06
80	Cal Eldred	.10	.08	.04
81	Bernard Gilkey	.15	.11	.06
82	Deion Sanders	.20	.15	.08
83	Reggie Jefferson	.10	.08	.04
84	Jeff Kent	.10	.08	.04
85	Juan Gonzalez	.60	.45	.25
86	Bill Ashley	.10	.08	.04
87	Travis Fryman	.20	.15	.08
88	Roberto Hernandez	.12	.09	.05
89	Hipolito Pichardo	.10	.08	.04
90	Wil Cordero	.20	.15	.08
91	John Jaha	.10	.08	.04
92	Javy Lopez	.20	.15	.08
93	Derek Bell	.15	.11	.06
94	Jeff Juden	.10	.08	.04
95	Steve Avery	.20	.15	.08
96	Moises Alou	.15	.11	.06
97	Brian Jordan	.15	.11	.06
98	Brian Williams	.10	.08	.04
99	Bob Zupcic	.10	.08	.04
100	Ray Lankford	.15	.11	.06

1993 Toys "R" Us Master Photos

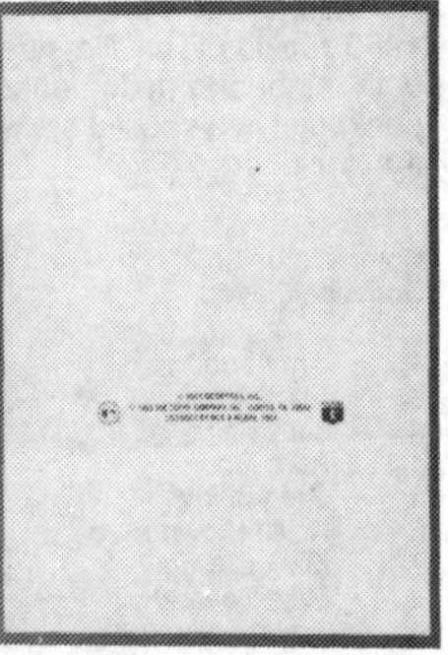

Each boxed set of Toys "R" Us Stadium Club cards comes with a set of 12 Master Photos. Similar to the regular 1993 S.C. Master Photos, they feature at center a larger 2-3/4" x 3-3/4"), uncropped version of the photo used on the Toys "R" Us card. A gold holographic box on the photo delineates the dimensions of the regular card, while another separates the photo from the 5" x 7" white background. Topps, Toys "R" Us, and Master Photo logos appear at the top of the card. Blank white backs have a few logos and copyrights printed in black.

		MT	NR MT	EX
Complete Set:		4.50	3.50	1.75
Common Player:		.50	.40	.20
(1)	Willie Greene	.50	.40	.20
(2)	Frank Thomas	1.50	1.25	.60
(3)	Chuck Knoblauch	.50	.40	.20
(4)	Marquis Grissom	.50	.40	.20
(5)	Scott Livingstone	.50	.40	.20
(6)	Ken Griffey, Jr.	1.50	1.25	.60
(7)	Carlos Baerga	.60	.45	.25
(8)	Ivan Rodriguez	.50	.40	.20
(9)	Moises Alou	.50	.40	.20
(10)	Sam Militello	.50	.40	.20
(11)	Eric Anthony	.50	.40	.20
(12)	Gary Sheffield	.60	.45	.25

1989 Upper Deck Promos

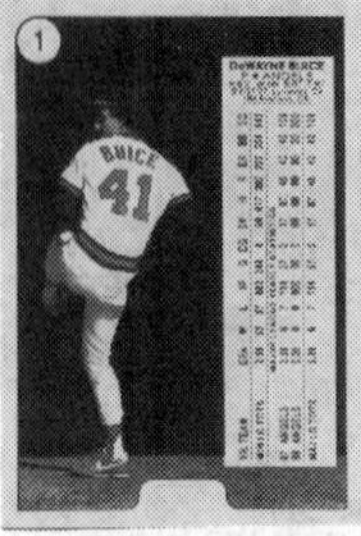

In 1988 Upper Deck produced a two-card test set to be distributed as samples for the 1989 set; 18,000 of each card were produced. The cards were distributed to dealers at the 1988 National Sports Collectors Convention. Two other variations of the promo cards exist. Both variations involve differences in how the hologram was produced. 2,000-5,000 of one of the hologram variations exist, while less than 1,000 of the third variation exist. These sets are valued at $300 and $500 respectively. Joyner and Buice were selected for the promo cards because of a reported investment interest in Upper Deck. Joyner and Buice were later required to sell their interest in the card company due to their active-player status.

		MT	NR MT	EX
Complete Set:		150.00	110.00	60.00
Common Player:		50.00	37.00	20.00
1	DeWayne Buice	50.00	37.00	20.00
700	Wally Joyner	75.00	55.00	30.00

Definitions for grading conditions are located in the Introduction of this price guide.

1989 Upper Deck

This premiere "Collector's Choice' issue from Upper Deck contains 700 cards (2-1/2" by 3-1/2") with full-color photos on both sides. The first 26 cards feature Star Rookies. The set also includes 26 special portrait cards with team checklist backs and seven numberical checklist cards (one for each 100 numbers). Team checklist cards feature individual player portraits by artist Vernon Wells. Major 1988 award winners (Cy Young, Rookie of Year, MVP) are honored on 10 cards in the set, in addition to their individual player cards. There are also special cards for the Most Valuable Players in both League Championship series and the World Series. The card fronts feature head-and-shoulder poses framed by a white border. A vertical brown and green artist's rendition of the runner's lane that leads from home plate to first base is found along the right margin. The backs carry full-color action poses that fill the card back, except for a compact (yet complete) stats chart. A high-number series, cards 701-800, featuring rookies and traded players, was released in mid- season in foil packs mixed within the complete set, in boxed complete sets and in high number set boxes.

		MT	NR MT	EX
Complete Set (700):		125.00	94.00	50.00
Common Player 1-700:		.08	.06	.03
Complete Set (800):		150.00	112.00	60.00
Common Player:701-800		.10	.08	.04
1	*Ken Griffey, Jr.*	52.00	39.00	21.00
2	*Luis Medina*	.12	.09	.05
3	*Tony Chance*	.15	.11	.06
4	*Dave Otto*	.08	.06	.03
5	*Sandy Alomar, Jr.*	.50	.40	.20
6	*Rolando Roomes*	.20	.15	.08
7	*David West*	.25	.20	.10
8	*Cris Carpenter*	.30	.25	.12
9	Gregg Jefferies	1.50	1.25	.60
10	*Doug Dascenzo*	.25	.20	.10
11	*Ron Jones*	.20	.15	.08
12	*Luis de los Santos*	.25	.20	.10
13a	*Gary Sheffield* (ERR)	10.00	7.50	4.00
13b	*Gary Sheffield* (COR)	10.00	7.50	4.00
14	*Mike Harkey*	.30	.25	.12
15	*Lance Blankenship*	.25	.20	.10
16	*William Brennan*	.15	.11	.06
17	*John Smoltz*	4.00	3.00	1.50
18	*Ramon Martinez*	1.25	.90	.50
19	*Mark Lemke*	.35	.25	.14
20	*Juan Bell*	.25	.20	.10
21	*Rey Palacios*	.15	.11	.06
22	*Felix Jose*	.75	.60	.30
23	*Van Snider*	.25	.20	.10
24	*Dante Bichette*	1.50	1.25	.60
25	*Randy Johnson*	2.00	1.50	.80
26	*Carlos Quintana*	.25	.20	.10
27	Star Rookie Checklist 1-26	.08	.06	.03
28	*Mike Schooler*	.10	.08	.04
29	Randy St. Claire	.08	.06	.03
30	*Jerald Clark*	.35	.25	.14
31	Kevin Gross	.08	.06	.03
32	*Dan Firova*	.20	.15	.08
33	Jeff Calhoun	.08	.06	.03
34	Tommy Hinzo	.08	.06	.03
35	*Ricky Jordan*	.30	.25	.12
36	Larry Parrish	.08	.06	.03
37	Bret Saberhagen	.15	.11	.06
38	Mike Smithson	.08	.06	.03
39	Dave Dravecky	.08	.06	.03
40	Ed Romero	.08	.06	.03
41	Jeff Musselman	.08	.06	.03
42	Ed Hearn	.08	.06	.03
43	Rance Mulliniks	.08	.06	.03
44	Jim Eisenreich	.08	.06	.03
45	*Sil Campusano*	.20	.15	.08
46	Mike Krukow	.08	.06	.03
47	*Paul Gibson*	.20	.15	.08
48	Mike LaCoss	.08	.06	.03
49	Larry Herndon	.08	.06	.03
50	Scott Garrelts	.08	.06	.03
51	Dwayne Henry	.08	.06	.03
52	Jim Acker	.08	.06	.03
53	Steve Sax	.15	.11	.06
54	Pete O'Brien	.08	.06	.03
55	Paul Runge	.08	.06	.03
56	Rick Rhoden	.08	.06	.03
57	*John Dopson*	.08	.06	.03
58	Casey Candaele	.08	.06	.03
59	Dave Righetti	.12	.09	.05
60	Joe Hesketh	.08	.06	.03
61	Frank DiPino	.08	.06	.03
62	Tim Laudner	.08	.06	.03
63	Jamie Moyer	.08	.06	.03
64	Fred Toliver	.08	.06	.03
65	Mitch Webster	.08	.06	.03
66	John Tudor	.10	.08	.04
67	John Cangelosi	.08	.06	.03
68	Mike Devereaux	.40	.30	.15
69	Brian Fisher	.08	.06	.03
70	Mike Marshall	.12	.09	.05
71	Zane Smith	.08	.06	.03
72a	Brian Holton (ball not visible on card front, photo actually Shawn Hillegas)	1.50	1.25	.60
72b	Brian Holton (ball visible, correct photo)	.15	.11	.06
73	Jose Guzman	.10	.08	.04
74	Rick Mahler	.08	.06	.03
75	John Shelby	.08	.06	.03
76	Jim Deshaies	.08	.06	.03
77	Bobby Meacham	.08	.06	.03
78	Bryn Smith	.08	.06	.03
79	Joaquin Andujar	.08	.06	.03
80	Richard Dotson	.08	.06	.03
81	Charlie Lea	.08	.06	.03
82	Calvin Schiraldi	.08	.06	.03
83	Les Straker	.08	.06	.03
84	Les Lancaster	.08	.06	.03
85	Allan Anderson	.08	.06	.03
86	Junior Ortiz	.08	.06	.03
87	Jesse Orosco	.08	.06	.03
88	Felix Fermin	.08	.06	.03
89	Dave Anderson	.08	.06	.03
90	Rafael Belliard	.08	.06	.03
91	Franklin Stubbs	.08	.06	.03
92	Cecil Espy	.08	.06	.03
93	Albert Hall	.08	.06	.03
94	Tim Leary	.08	.06	.03
95	Mitch Williams	.08	.06	.03
96	Tracy Jones	.10	.08	.04
97	Danny Darwin	.08	.06	.03
98	Gary Ward	.08	.06	.03
99	Neal Heaton	.08	.06	.03
100	Jim Pankovits	.08	.06	.03
101	Bill Doran	.08	.06	.03
102	Tim Wallach	.10	.08	.04
103	Joe Magrane	.10	.08	.04
104	Ozzie Virgil	.08	.06	.03
105	Alvin Davis	.12	.09	.05
106	Tom Brookens	.08	.06	.03
107	Shawon Dunston	.10	.08	.04
108	Tracy Woodson	.10	.08	.04
109	Nelson Liriano	.08	.06	.03
110	Devon White	.12	.09	.05
111	Steve Balboni	.08	.06	.03

		MT	NR MT	EX
112	Buddy Bell	.08	.06	.03
113	*German Jimenez*	.08	.06	.03
114	Ken Dayley	.08	.06	.03
115	Andres Galarraga	.50	.40	.20
116	Mike Scioscia	.08	.06	.03
117	Gary Pettis	.08	.06	.03
118	Ernie Whitt	.08	.06	.03
119	Bob Boone	.08	.06	.03
120	Ryne Sandberg	1.50	1.25	.60
121	Bruce Benedict	.08	.06	.03
122	Hubie Brooks	.10	.08	.04
123	Mike Moore	.08	.06	.03
124	Wallace Johnson	.08	.06	.03
125	Bob Horner	.10	.08	.04
126	Chili Davis	.08	.06	.03
127	Manny Trillo	.08	.06	.03
128	Chet Lemon	.08	.06	.03
129	John Cerutti	.08	.06	.03
130	Orel Hershiser	.10	.08	.04
131	Terry Pendleton	.30	.25	.12
132	Jeff Blauser	.30	.25	.12
133	Mike Fitzgerald	.08	.06	.03
134	Henry Cotto	.08	.06	.03
135	Gerald Young	.12	.09	.05
136	Luis Salazar	.08	.06	.03
137	Alejandro Pena	.08	.06	.03
138	Jack Howell	.08	.06	.03
139	Tony Fernandez	.12	.09	.05
140	Mark Grace	1.25	.90	.50
141	Ken Caminiti	.08	.06	.03
142	Mike Jackson	.08	.06	.03
143	Larry McWilliams	.08	.06	.03
144	Andres Thomas	.08	.06	.03
145	Nolan Ryan	4.00	3.00	1.50
146	Mike Davis	.08	.06	.03
147	DeWayne Buice	.08	.06	.03
148	Jody Davis	.08	.06	.03
149	Jesse Barfield	.10	.08	.04
150	Matt Nokes	.15	.11	.06
151	Jerry Reuss	.08	.06	.03
152	Rick Cerone	.08	.06	.03
153	Storm Davis	.10	.08	.04
154	Marvell Wynne	.08	.06	.03
155	Will Clark	1.50	1.25	.60
156	Luis Aguayo	.08	.06	.03
157	Willie Upshaw	.08	.06	.03
158	Randy Bush	.08	.06	.03
159	Ron Darling	.12	.09	.05
160	Kal Daniels	.15	.11	.06
161	Spike Owen	.08	.06	.03
162	Luis Polonia	.08	.06	.03
163	Kevin Mitchell	.20	.15	.08
164	*Dave Gallagher*	.25	.20	.10
165	Benito Santiago	.15	.11	.06
166	Greg Gagne	.08	.06	.03
167	Ken Phelps	.08	.06	.03
168	Sid Fernandez	.10	.08	.04
169	Bo Diaz	.08	.06	.03
170	Cory Snyder	.15	.11	.06
171	Eric Show	.08	.06	.03
172	Rob Thompson	.08	.06	.03
173	Marty Barrett	.08	.06	.03
174	Dave Henderson	.10	.08	.04
175	Ozzie Guillen	.08	.06	.03
176	Barry Lyons	.08	.06	.03
177	*Kelvin Torve*(FC)	.20	.15	.08
178	Don Slaught	.08	.06	.03
179	Steve Lombardozzi	.08	.06	.03
180	*Chris Sabo*	.60	.45	.25
181	Jose Uribe	.08	.06	.03
182	Shane Mack	.08	.06	.03
183	Ron Karkovice	.08	.06	.03
184	Todd Benzinger	.12	.09	.05
185	Dave Stewart	.10	.08	.04
186	Julio Franco	.10	.08	.04
187	Ron Robinson	.08	.06	.03
188	Wally Backman	.08	.06	.03
189	Randy Velarde	.08	.06	.03
190	Joe Carter	.75	.60	.30
191	Bob Welch	.10	.08	.04
192	Kelly Paris	.08	.06	.03
193	Chris Brown	.08	.06	.03
194	Rick Reuschel	.10	.08	.04
195	Roger Clemens	1.00	.70	.40
196	Dave Concepcion	.10	.08	.04
197	Al Newman	.08	.06	.03
198	Brook Jacoby	.10	.08	.04
199	Mookie Wilson	.08	.06	.03
200	Don Mattingly	1.00	.70	.40
201	Dick Schofield	.08	.06	.03
202	Mark Gubicza	.10	.08	.04

		MT	NR MT	EX
203	Gary Gaetti	.15	.11	.06
204	Dan Pasqua	.10	.08	.04
205	Andre Dawson	.40	.30	.15
206	Chris Speier	.08	.06	.03
207	Kent Tekulve	.08	.06	.03
208	Rod Scurry	.08	.06	.03
209	Scott Bailes	.08	.06	.03
210	Rickey Henderson	.75	.60	.30
211	Harold Baines	.12	.09	.05
212	Tony Armas	.08	.06	.03
213	Kent Hrbek	.10	.08	.04
214	Darrin Jackson	.08	.06	.03
215	George Brett	.75	.60	.30
216	Rafael Santana	.08	.06	.03
217	Andy Allanson	.08	.06	.03
218	Brett Butler	.08	.06	.03
219	Steve Jeltz	.08	.06	.03
220	Jay Buhner	.50	.40	.20
221	Bo Jackson	.70	.50	.30
222	Angel Salazar	.08	.06	.03
223	Kirk McCaskill	.08	.06	.03
224	Steve Lyons	.08	.06	.03
225	Bert Blyleven	.10	.08	.04
226	Scott Bradley	.08	.06	.03
227	Bob Melvin	.08	.06	.03
228	Ron Kittle	.08	.06	.03
229	Phil Bradley	.10	.08	.04
230	Tommy John	.12	.09	.05
231	Greg Walker	.08	.06	.03
232	Juan Berenguer	.08	.06	.03
233	Pat Tabler	.08	.06	.03
234	*Terry Clark*	.20	.15	.08
235	Rafael Palmeiro	1.50	1.25	.60
236	Paul Zuvella	.08	.06	.03
237	Willie Randolph	.08	.06	.03
238	Bruce Fields	.08	.06	.03
239	Mike Aldrete	.08	.06	.03
240	Lance Parrish	.15	.11	.06
241	Greg Maddux	1.25	.90	.50
242	John Moses	.08	.06	.03
243	Melido Perez	.10	.08	.04
244	Willie Wilson	.10	.08	.04
245	Mark McLemore	.08	.06	.03
246	Von Hayes	.10	.08	.04
247	Matt Williams	1.50	1.25	.60
248	John Candelaria	.08	.06	.03
249	Harold Reynolds	.08	.06	.03
250	Greg Swindell	.12	.09	.05
251	Juan Agosto	.08	.06	.03
252	Mike Felder	.08	.06	.03
253	Vince Coleman	.15	.11	.06
254	Larry Sheets	.08	.06	.03
255	George Bell	.25	.20	.10
256	Terry Steinbach	.10	.08	.04
257	*Jack Armstrong*	.20	.15	.08
258	Dickie Thon	.08	.06	.03
259	Ray Knight	.08	.06	.03
260	Darryl Strawberry	.30	.25	.12
261	Doug Sisk	.08	.06	.03
262	Alex Trevino	.08	.06	.03
263	Jeff Leonard	.08	.06	.03
264	Tom Henke	.08	.06	.03
265	Ozzie Smith	.40	.30	.15
266	Dave Bergman	.08	.06	.03
267	Tony Phillips	.08	.06	.03
268	Mark Davis	.08	.06	.03
269	Kevin Elster	.10	.08	.04
270	Barry Larkin	.40	.30	.15
271	Manny Lee	.08	.06	.03
272	Tom Brunansky	.12	.09	.05
273	*Craig Biggio*	1.50	1.25	.60
274	Jim Gantner	.08	.06	.03
275	Eddie Murray	.40	.30	.15
276	Jeff Reed	.08	.06	.03
277	Tim Teufel	.08	.06	.03
278	Rick Honeycutt	.08	.06	.03
279	Guillermo Hernandez	.08	.06	.03
280	John Kruk	.30	.25	.12
281	*Luis Alicea*	.20	.15	.08
282	Jim Clancy	.08	.06	.03
283	Billy Ripken	.08	.06	.03
284	Craig Reynolds	.08	.06	.03
285	Robin Yount	.75	.60	.30
286	Jimmy Jones	.08	.06	.03
287	Ron Oester	.08	.06	.03
288	Terry Leach	.08	.06	.03
289	Dennis Eckersley	.30	.25	.12
290	Alan Trammell	.10	.08	.04
291	Jimmy Key	.30	.25	.12
292	Chris Bosio	.08	.06	.03
293	Jose DeLeon	.08	.06	.03

		MT	NR MT	EX
294	Jim Traber	.08	.06	.03
295	Mike Scott	.12	.09	.05
296	Roger McDowell	.10	.08	.04
297	Garry Templeton	.08	.06	.03
298	Doyle Alexander	.08	.06	.03
299	Nick Esasky	.08	.06	.03
300	Mark McGwire	.70	.50	.30
301	*Darryl Hamilton*	.60	.45	.25
302	Dave Smith	.08	.06	.03
303	Rick Sutcliffe	.10	.08	.04
304	Dave Stapleton	.08	.06	.03
305	Alan Ashby	.08	.06	.03
306	Pedro Guerrero	.15	.11	.06
307	Ron Guidry	.12	.09	.05
308	Steve Farr	.08	.06	.03
309	Curt Ford	.08	.06	.03
310	Claudell Washington	.08	.06	.03
311	Tom Prince	.08	.06	.03
312	*Chad Kreuter*	.40	.30	.15
313	Ken Oberkfell	.08	.06	.03
314	Jerry Browne	.08	.06	.03
315	R.J. Reynolds	.08	.06	.03
316	Scott Bankhead	.08	.06	.03
317	Milt Thompson	.08	.06	.03
318	Mario Diaz	.10	.08	.04
319	Bruce Ruffin	.08	.06	.03
320	Dave Valle	.08	.06	.03
321a	*Gary Varsho* (batting righty on card back, photo actually Mike Bielecki)	2.00	1.50	.80
321b	*Gary Varsho* (batting lefty on card back, correct photo)	.30	.25	.12
322	Paul Mirabella	.08	.06	.03
323	Chuck Jackson	.08	.06	.03
324	Drew Hall	.10	.08	.04
325	Don August	.10	.08	.04
326	*Israel Sanchez*	.15	.11	.06
327	Denny Walling	.08	.06	.03
328	Joel Skinner	.08	.06	.03
329	Danny Tartabull	.30	.25	.12
330	Tony Pena	.08	.06	.03
331	Jim Sundberg	.08	.06	.03
332	Jeff Robinson	.12	.09	.05
333	Odibbe McDowell	.08	.06	.03
334	Jose Lind	.10	.08	.04
335	Paul Kilgus	.10	.08	.04
336	Juan Samuel	.12	.09	.05
337	Mike Campbell	.10	.08	.04
338	Mike Maddux	.08	.06	.03
339	Darnell Coles	.08	.06	.03
340	Bob Dernier	.08	.06	.03
341	Rafael Ramirez	.08	.06	.03
342	Scott Sanderson	.08	.06	.03
343	B.J. Surhoff	.10	.08	.04
344	Billy Hatcher	.08	.06	.03
345	Pat Perry	.08	.06	.03
346	Jack Clark	.15	.11	.06
347	Gary Thurman	.12	.09	.05
348	*Timmy Jones*	.20	.15	.08
349	Dave Winfield	.60	.45	.25
350	Frank White	.08	.06	.03
351	Dave Collins	.08	.06	.03
352	Jack Morris	.25	.20	.10
353	Eric Plunk	.08	.06	.03
354	Leon Durham	.08	.06	.03
355	Ivan DeJesus	.08	.06	.03
356	*Brian Holman*	.20	.15	.08
357a	Dale Murphy (reversed negative)	40.00	30.00	16.00
357b	Dale Murphy (corrected)	.35	.25	.14
358	Mark Portugal	.08	.06	.03
359	Andy McGaffigan	.08	.06	.03
360	Tom Glavine	2.50	2.00	1.00
361	Keith Moreland	.08	.06	.03
362	Todd Stottlemyre	.25	.20	.10
363	Dave Leiper	.08	.06	.03
364	Cecil Fielder	1.00	.70	.40
365	Carmelo Martinez	.08	.06	.03
366	Dwight Evans	.10	.08	.04
367	Kevin McReynolds	.15	.11	.06
368	Rich Gedman	.08	.06	.03
369	Len Dykstra	.25	.20	.10
370	Jody Reed	.12	.09	.05
371	Jose Canseco	.75	.60	.30
372	Rob Murphy	.08	.06	.03
373	Mike Henneman	.10	.08	.04
374	Walt Weiss	.10	.08	.04
375	*Rob Dibble*	.40	.30	.15
376	Kirby Puckett	1.50	1.25	.60
377	Denny Martinez	.08	.06	.03
378	Ron Gant	1.75	1.25	.70
379	Brian Harper	.08	.06	.03

		MT	NR MT	EX
380	*Nelson Santovenia*	.08	.06	.03
381	Lloyd Moseby	.08	.06	.03
382	Lance McCullers	.08	.06	.03
383	Dave Stieb	.10	.08	.04
384	Tony Gwynn	.80	.60	.30
385	Mike Flanagan	.08	.06	.03
386	Bob Ojeda	.08	.06	.03
387	Bruce Hurst	.10	.08	.04
388	Dave Magadan	.10	.08	.04
389	Wade Boggs	.60	.45	.25
390	Gary Carter	.10	.08	.04
391	Frank Tanana	.08	.06	.03
392	Curt Young	.08	.06	.03
393	Jeff Treadway	.10	.08	.04
394	Darrell Evans	.10	.08	.04
395	Glenn Hubbard	.08	.06	.03
396	Chuck Cary	.08	.06	.03
397	Frank Viola	.15	.11	.06
398	Jeff Parrett	.10	.08	.04
399	*Terry Blocker*	.15	.11	.06
400	Dan Gladden	.08	.06	.03
401	*Louie Meadows*	.15	.11	.06
402	Tim Raines	.25	.20	.10
403	Joey Meyer	.10	.08	.04
404	Larry Andersen	.08	.06	.03
405	Rex Hudler	.08	.06	.03
406	Mike Schmidt	2.00	1.50	.80
407	John Franco	.10	.08	.04
408	*Brady Anderson*	.90	.70	.35
409	Don Carman	.08	.06	.03
410	Eric Davis	.25	.20	.10
411	Bob Stanley	.08	.06	.03
412	Pete Smith	.10	.08	.04
413	Jim Rice	.10	.08	.04
414	Bruce Sutter	.10	.08	.04
415	Oil Can Boyd	.08	.06	.03
416	Ruben Sierra	.60	.45	.25
417	Mike LaValliere	.08	.06	.03
418	Steve Buechele	.08	.06	.03
419	Gary Redus	.08	.06	.03
420	Scott Fletcher	.08	.06	.03
421	Dale Sveum	.08	.06	.03
422	Bob Knepper	.08	.06	.03
423	Luis Rivera	.08	.06	.03
424	Ted Higuera	.10	.08	.04
425	Kevin Bass	.08	.06	.03
426	Ken Gerhart	.08	.06	.03
427	Shane Rawley	.08	.06	.03
428	Paul O'Neill	.08	.06	.03
429	Joe Orsulak	.08	.06	.03
430	Jackie Gutierrez	.08	.06	.03
431	Gerald Perry	.10	.08	.04
432	Mike Greenwell	.10	.08	.04
433	Jerry Royster	.08	.06	.03
434	Ellis Burks	.10	.08	.04
435	Ed Olwine	.08	.06	.03
436	Dave Rucker	.08	.06	.03
437	Charlie Hough	.08	.06	.03
438	Bob Walk	.08	.06	.03
439	Bob Brower	.08	.06	.03
440	Barry Bonds	2.00	1.50	.80
441	Tom Foley	.08	.06	.03
442	Rob Deer	.08	.06	.03
443	Glenn Davis	.08	.06	.03
444	Dave Martinez	.08	.06	.03
445	Bill Wegman	.08	.06	.03
446	Lloyd McClendon	.08	.06	.03
447	Dave Schmidt	.08	.06	.03
448	Darren Daulton	.40	.30	.15
449	Frank Williams	.08	.06	.03
450	Don Aase	.08	.06	.03
451	Lou Whitaker	.15	.11	.06
452	Goose Gossage	.12	.09	.05
453	Ed Whitson	.08	.06	.03
454	Jim Walewander	.08	.06	.03
455	Damon Berryhill	.12	.09	.05
456	Tim Burke	.08	.06	.03
457	Barry Jones	.08	.06	.03
458	Joel Youngblood	.08	.06	.03
459	Floyd Youmans	.08	.06	.03
460	Mark Salas	.08	.06	.03
461	Jeff Russell	.08	.06	.03
462	Darrell Miller	.08	.06	.03
463	Jeff Kunkel	.08	.06	.03
464	*Sherman Corbett*	.20	.15	.08
465	Curtis Wilkerson	.08	.06	.03
466	Bud Black	.08	.06	.03
467	Cal Ripken, Jr.	1.75	1.25	.70
468	John Farrell	.10	.08	.04
469	Terry Kennedy	.08	.06	.03
470	Tom Candiotti	.08	.06	.03

		MT	NR MT	EX
471	Roberto Alomar	5.00	3.75	2.00
472	Jeff Robinson	.12	.09	.05
473	Vance Law	.08	.06	.03
474	Randy Ready	.08	.06	.03
475	Walt Terrell	.08	.06	.03
476	Kelly Downs	.10	.08	.04
477	*Johnny Paredes*	.15	.11	.06
478	Shawn Hillegas	.08	.06	.03
479	Bob Brenly	.08	.06	.03
480	Otis Nixon	.08	.06	.03
481	Johnny Ray	.08	.06	.03
482	Geno Petralli	.08	.06	.03
483	Stu Cliburn	.08	.06	.03
484	Pete Incaviglia	.10	.08	.04
485	Brian Downing	.08	.06	.03
486	Jeff Stone	.08	.06	.03
487	Carmen Castillo	.08	.06	.03
488	Tom Niedenfuer	.08	.06	.03
489	Jay Bell	.30	.25	.12
490	Rick Schu	.08	.06	.03
491	*Jeff Pico*	.15	.11	.06
492	*Mark Parent*	.20	.15	.08
493	Eric King	.08	.06	.03
494	Al Nipper	.08	.06	.03
495	Andy Hawkins	.08	.06	.03
496	Daryl Boston	.08	.06	.03
497	Ernie Riles	.08	.06	.03
498	Pascual Perez	.08	.06	.03
499	Bill Long	.08	.06	.03
500	Kirt Manwaring	.10	.08	.04
501	Chuck Crim	.08	.06	.03
502	Candy Maldonado	.08	.06	.03
503	Dennis Lamp	.08	.06	.03
504	Glenn Braggs	.08	.06	.03
505	Joe Price	.08	.06	.03
506	Ken Williams	.08	.06	.03
507	Bill Pecota	.08	.06	.03
508	Rey Quinones	.08	.06	.03
509	*Jeff Bittiger*	.15	.11	.06
510	Kevin Seitzer	.08	.06	.03
511	Steve Bedrosian	.10	.08	.04
512	Todd Worrell	.10	.08	.04
513	Chris James	.10	.08	.04
514	Jose Oquendo	.08	.06	.03
515	David Palmer	.08	.06	.03
516	John Smiley	.12	.09	.05
517	Dave Clark	.08	.06	.03
518	Mike Dunne	.10	.08	.04
519	Ron Washington	.08	.06	.03
520	Bob Kipper	.08	.06	.03
521	Lee Smith	.10	.08	.04
522	Juan Castillo	.08	.06	.03
523	Don Robinson	.08	.06	.03
524	Kevin Romine	.08	.06	.03
525	Paul Molitor	.50	.40	.20
526	Mark Langston	.15	.11	.06
527	Donnie Hill	.08	.06	.03
528	Larry Owen	.08	.06	.03
529	Jerry Reed	.08	.06	.03
530	Jack McDowell	1.50	1.25	.60
531	Greg Mathews	.08	.06	.03
532	John Russell	.08	.06	.03
533	Don Quisenberry	.08	.06	.03
534	Greg Gross	.08	.06	.03
535	Danny Cox	.08	.06	.03
536	Terry Francona	.08	.06	.03
537	Andy Van Slyke	.15	.11	.06
538	Mel Hall	.08	.06	.03
539	Jim Gott	.08	.06	.03
540	Doug Jones	.10	.08	.04
541	Criag Lefferts	.08	.06	.03
542	Mike Boddicker	.08	.06	.03
543	Greg Brock	.08	.06	.03
544	Atlee Hammaker	.08	.06	.03
545	Tom Bolton	.08	.06	.03
546	*Mike Macfarlane*	.40	.30	.15
547	*Rich Renteria*	.15	.11	.06
548	John Davis	.08	.06	.03
549	Floyd Bannister	.08	.06	.03
550	Mickey Brantley	.08	.06	.03
551	Duane Ward	.08	.06	.03
552	Dan Petry	.08	.06	.03
553	Mickey Tettleton	.15	.11	.06
554	Rick Leach	.08	.06	.03
555	Mike Witt	.08	.06	.03
556	Sid Bream	.08	.06	.03
557	Bobby Witt	.10	.08	.04
558	Tommy Herr	.08	.06	.03
559	Randy Milligan	.08	.06	.03
560	*Jose Cecena*	.20	.15	.08
561	Mackey Sasser	.08	.06	.03
562	Carney Lansford	.08	.06	.03
563	Rick Aguilera	.08	.06	.03
564	Ron Hassey	.08	.06	.03
565	Dwight Gooden	.25	.20	.10
566	Paul Assenmacher	.08	.06	.03
567	Neil Allen	.08	.06	.03
568	Jim Morrison	.08	.06	.03
569	Mike Pagliarulo	.10	.08	.04
570	Ted Simmons	.10	.08	.04
571	Mark Thurmond	.08	.06	.03
572	Fred McGriff	1.25	.90	.50
573	Wally Joyner	.10	.08	.04
574	*Jose Bautista*	.20	.15	.08
575	Kelly Gruber	.08	.06	.03
576	Cecilio Guante	.08	.06	.03
577	Mark Davidson	.08	.06	.03
578	Bobby Bonilla	.25	.20	.10
579	Mike Stanley	.08	.06	.03
580	Gene Larkin	.10	.08	.04
581	Stan Javier	.08	.06	.03
582	Howard Johnson	.10	.08	.04
583a	Mike Gallego (photo on card back reversed)	1.00	.70	.40
583b	Mike Gallego (correct photo)	.15	.11	.06
584	David Cone	.35	.25	.14
585	*Doug Jennings*	.10	.08	.04
586	Charlie Hudson	.08	.06	.03
587	Dion James	.08	.06	.03
588	Al Leiter	.15	.11	.06
589	Charlie Puleo	.08	.06	.03
590	Roberto Kelly	.25	.20	.10
591	Thad Bosley	.08	.06	.03
592	Pete Stanicek	.10	.08	.04
593	*Pat Borders*	.40	.30	.15
594	*Bryan Harvey*	.90	.70	.35
595	Jeff Ballard	.10	.08	.04
596	Jeff Reardon	.10	.08	.04
597	Doug Drabek	.08	.06	.03
598	Edwin Correa	.08	.06	.03
599	Keith Atherton	.08	.06	.03
600	Dave LaPoint	.08	.06	.03
601	Don Baylor	.10	.08	.04
602	Tom Pagnozzi	.08	.06	.03
603	Tim Flannery	.08	.06	.03
604	Gene Walter	.08	.06	.03
605	Dave Parker	.12	.09	.05
606	Mike Diaz	.08	.06	.03
607	Chris Gwynn	.10	.08	.04
608	Odell Jones	.08	.06	.03
609	Carlton Fisk	.60	.45	.25
610	Jay Howell	.08	.06	.03
611	Tim Crews	.08	.06	.03
612	Keith Hernandez	.08	.06	.03
613	Willie Fraser	.08	.06	.03
614	Jim Eppard	.08	.06	.03
615	Jeff Hamilton	.08	.06	.03
616	Kurt Stillwell	.08	.06	.03
617	Tom Browning	.10	.08	.04
618	Jeff Montgomery	.40	.30	.15
619	Jose Rijo	.15	.11	.06
620	Jamie Quirk	.08	.06	.03
621	Willie McGee	.12	.09	.05
622	Mark Grant	.08	.06	.03
623	Bill Swift	.08	.06	.03
624	Orlando Mercado	.08	.06	.03
625	*John Costello*	.15	.11	.06
626	Jose Gonzalez	.08	.06	.03
627a	Bill Schroeder (putting on shin guards on card back, photo actually Ronn Reynolds)	1.25	.90	.50
627b	Bill Schroeder (arms crossed on card back, correct photo)	.15	.11	.06
628a	Fred Manrique (throwing on card back, photo actually Ozzie Guillen)	1.25	.90	.50
628b	Fred Manrique (batting on card back, correct photo)	.15	.11	.06
629	Ricky Horton	.08	.06	.03
630	Dan Plesac	.10	.08	.04
631	Alfredo Griffin	.08	.06	.03
632	Chuck Finley	.08	.06	.03
633	Kirk Gibson	.20	.15	.08
634	Randy Myers	.10	.08	.04
635	Greg Minton	.08	.06	.03
636	Herm Winningham	.08	.06	.03
637	Charlie Leibrandt	.08	.06	.03
638	Tim Birtsas	.08	.06	.03
639	Bill Buckner	.10	.08	.04
640	Danny Jackson	.15	.11	.06
641	Greg Booker	.08	.06	.03
642	Jim Presley	.08	.06	.03
643	Gene Nelson	.08	.06	.03

		MT	NR MT	EX
644	Rod Booker	.08	.06	.03
645	Dennis Rasmussen	.10	.08	.04
646	Juan Nieves	.08	.06	.03
647	Bobby Thigpen	.10	.08	.04
648	Tim Belcher	.10	.08	.04
649	Mike Young	.08	.06	.03
650	Ivan Calderon	.08	.06	.03
651	*Oswaldo Peraza*	.20	.15	.08
652a	Pat Sheridan (no position on front)	30.00	22.00	12.00
652b	Pat Sheridan (position on front)	.08	.06	.03
653	Mike Morgan	.08	.06	.03
654	Mike Heath	.08	.06	.03
655	Jay Tibbs	.08	.06	.03
656	Fernando Valenzuela	.08	.06	.03
657	Lee Mazzilli	.08	.06	.03
658	Frank Viola	.08	.06	.03
659	Jose Canseco	.40	.30	.15
660	Walt Weiss	.08	.06	.03
661	Orel Hershiser	.08	.06	.03
662	Kirk Gibson	.08	.06	.03
663	Chris Sabo	.15	.11	.06
664	Dennis Eckersley	.08	.06	.03
665	Orel Hershiser	.08	.06	.03
666	Kirk Gibson	.08	.06	.03
667	Orel Hershiser	.08	.06	.03
668	Wally Joyner (TC)	.08	.06	.03
669	Nolan Ryan (TC)	.60	.45	.25
670	Jose Canseco (TC)	.20	.15	.08
671	Fred McGriff (TC)	.15	.11	.06
672	Dale Murphy (TC)	.08	.06	.03
673	Paul Molitor (TC)	.15	.11	.06
674	Ozzie Smith (TC)	.08	.06	.03
675	Ryne Sandberg (TC)	.30	.25	.12
676	Kirk Gibson (TC)	.08	.06	.03
677	Andres Galarraga (TC)	.08	.06	.03
678	Will Clark (TC)	.30	.25	.12
679	Cory Snyder (TC)	.08	.06	.03
680	Alvin Davis (TC)	.08	.06	.03
681	Darryl Strawberry (TC)	.08	.06	.03
682	Cal Ripken, Jr. (TC)	.40	.30	.15
683	Tony Gwynn (TC)	.25	.20	.10
684	Mike Schmidt (TC)	.40	.30	.15
685	Andy Van Slyke (TC)	.08	.06	.03
686	Ruben Sierra (TC)	.08	.06	.03
687	Wade Boggs (TC)	.20	.15	.08
688	Eric Davis (TC)	.08	.06	.03
689	George Brett (TC)	.25	.20	.10
690	Alan Trammell (TC)	.08	.06	.03
691	Frank Viola (TC)	.08	.06	.03
692	Harold Baines (TC)	.08	.06	.03
693	Don Mattingly (TC)	.20	.15	.08
694	Checklist 1-100	.08	.06	.03
695	Checklist 101-200	.08	.06	.03
696	Checklist 201-300	.08	.06	.03
697	Checklist 301-400	.08	.06	.03
698	Checklist 401-500	.08	.06	.03
699	Checklist 501-600	.08	.06	.03
700	Checklist 601-700	.08	.06	.03
701	Checklist 701-800	.20	.15	.08
702	Jessie Barfield	.10	.08	.04
703	Walt Terrell	.10	.08	.04
704	Dickie Thon	.10	.08	.04
705	Al Leiter	.10	.08	.04
706	Dave LaPoint	.10	.08	.04
707	Charlie Hayes(FC)	1.50	1.25	.60
708	Andy Hawkins	.10	.08	.04
709	Mickey Hatcher	.10	.08	.04
710	Lance McCullers	.10	.08	.04
711	Ron Kittle	.10	.08	.04
712	Bert Blyleven	.10	.08	.04
713	Rick Dempsey	.10	.08	.04
714	Ken Williams	.10	.08	.04
715	Steve Rosenberg(FC)	.15	.11	.06
716	Joe Skalski(FC)	.20	.15	.08
717	Spike Owen	.10	.08	.04
718	Todd Burns	.10	.08	.04
719	Kevin Gross	.10	.08	.04
720	Tommy Herr	.10	.08	.04
721	Rob Ducey	.10	.08	.04
722	Gary Green(FC)	.15	.11	.06
723	Gregg Olson(FC)	1.00	.70	.40
724	Greg Harris(FC)	.15	.11	.06
725	Craig Worthington(FC)	.10	.08	.04
726	Tom Howard(FC)	.25	.20	.10
727	Dale Mohorcic	.10	.08	.04
728	Rich Yett	.10	.08	.04
729	Mel Hall	.10	.08	.04
730	Floyd Youmans	.10	.08	.04
731	Lonnie Smith	.15	.11	.06
732	Wally Backman	.10	.08	.04

		MT	NR MT	EX
733	Trevor Wilson	.10	.08	.04
734	Jose Alvarez	.10	.08	.04
735	Bob Milacki(FC)	.15	.11	.06
736	Tom Gordon(FC)	.30	.25	.12
737	Wally Whitehurst(FC)	.25	.20	.10
738	Mike Aldrete	.10	.08	.04
739	Keith Miller	.10	.08	.04
740	Randy Milligan	.10	.08	.04
741	Jeff Parrett	.10	.08	.04
742	Steve Finley(FC)	.35	.25	.14
743	Junior Felix(FC)	.25	.20	.10
744	Pete Harnisch(FC)	.50	.40	.20
745	Bill Spiers(FC)	.15	.11	.06
746	Hensley Meulens(FC)	.20	.15	.08
747	Juan Bell	.20	.15	.08
748	Steve Sax	.15	.11	.06
749	Phil Bradley	.10	.08	.04
750	Rey Quinones	.10	.08	.04
751	Tommy Gregg(FC)	.15	.11	.06
752	Kevin Brown(FC)	.40	.30	.15
753	Derek Lilliquist(FC)	.15	.11	.06
754	Todd Zeile(FC)	1.00	.70	.40
755	Jim Abbott(FC)	4.00	3.00	1.50
756	Ozzie Canseco(FC)	.10	.08	.04
757	Nick Esasky	.10	.08	.04
758	Mike Moore	.15	.11	.06
759	Rob Murphy	.10	.08	.04
760	Rick Mahler	.10	.08	.04
761	Fred Lynn	.10	.08	.04
762	Kevin Blankenship(FC)	.10	.08	.04
763	Eddie Murray	.50	.40	.20
764	Steve Searcy(FC)	.10	.08	.04
765	Jerome Walton(FC)	.10	.08	.04
766	Erik Hanson(FC)	.80	.60	.30
767	Bob Boone	.15	.11	.06
768	Edgar Martinez(FC)	.50	.40	.20
769	Jose DeJesus(FC)	.10	.08	.04
770	Greg Briley(FC)	.10	.08	.04
771	Steve Peters(FC)	.10	.08	.04
772	Rafael Palmeiro	1.25	.90	.50
773	Jack Clark	.15	.11	.06
774	Nolan Ryan	4.00	3.00	1.50
775	Lance Parrish	.10	.08	.04
776	Joe Girardi(FC)	.25	.20	.10
777	Willie Randolph	.10	.08	.04
778	Mitch Williams	.30	.25	.12
779	Dennis Cook(FC)	.15	.11	.06
780	Dwight Smith(FC)	.25	.20	.10
781	Lenny Harris(FC)	.40	.30	.15
782	Torey Lovullo(FC)	.15	.11	.06
783	Norm Charlton(FC)	.50	.40	.20
784	Chris Brown	.10	.08	.04
785	Todd Benzinger	.10	.08	.04
786	Shane Rawley	.10	.08	.04
787	Omar Vizquel(FC)	.40	.30	.15
788	LaVel Freeman(FC)	.25	.20	.10
789	Jeffrey Leonard	.10	.08	.04
790	Eddie Williams(FC)	.10	.08	.04
791	Jamie Moyer	.10	.08	.04
792	Bruce Hurst	.10	.08	.04
793	Julio Franco	.30	.25	.12
794	Claudell Washington	.10	.08	.04
795	Jody Davis	.10	.08	.04
796	Odibbe McDowell	.10	.08	.04
797	Paul Kilgus	.10	.08	.04
798	Tracy Jones	.10	.08	.04
799	Steve Wilson(FC)	.20	.15	.08
800	Pete O'Brien,			

1990 Upper Deck

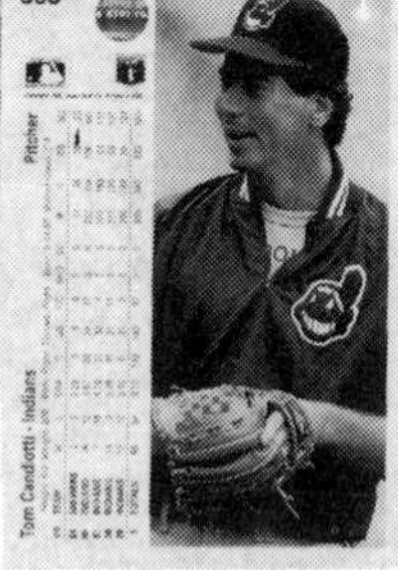

Following the success of its first issue, Upper Deck

released another 800-card set in 1990. The cards contain full-color photos on both sides and are 2-1/2" by 3-1/2" in size. The artwork of Vernon Wells is featured on the front of all team checklist cards. The 1990 set also introduces two new Wells illustrations - a tribute to Mike Schmidt upon his retirement and one commemorating Nolan Ryan's 5,000 career strikeouts. The cards are similar in design to the 1989 issue. The Wade Boggs card depicts the Red Sox star in four stages of his batting swing via a quad-action photograph, much like the Jim Abbott card of 1989. The high- number series (701-800) was released as a boxed set, in factory sets and in foil packs at mid-season.

	MT	NR MT	EX
Complete Set (800): 1-700	40.00	30.00	15.00
Common Player: 1-700	.06	.05	.02
Complete Set: 1-800	50.00	37.00	20.00
Common Player: 701-800	.10	.08	.04

		MT	NR MT	EX
1	Star Rookie Checklist	.06	.05	.02
2	*Randy Nosek*(FC)	.06	.05	.02
3	*Tom Dress*(FC)	.08	.06	.03
4	Curt Young	.06	.05	.02
5	Angels Checklist	.06	.05	.02
6	Luis Salazar	.06	.05	.02
7	Phillies Checklist	.06	.05	.02
8	Jose Bautista	.08	.06	.03
9	*Marquis Grissom*(FC)	2.00	1.50	.80
10	Dodgers Checklist	.06	.05	.02
11	Rick Aguilera	.08	.06	.03
12	Padres Checklist	.06	.05	.02
13	*Deion Sanders*(FC)	2.00	1.50	.80
14	Marvell Wynne	.06	.05	.02
15	David West	.15	.11	.06
16	Pirates Checklist	.06	.05	.02
17	*Sammy Sosa*(FC)	1.50	1.25	.60
18	Yankees Checklist	.06	.05	.02
19	Jack Howell	.06	.05	.02
20	Mike Schmidt (SPEC)	.50	.40	.20
21	Robin Ventura	1.50	1.25	.60
22	Brian Meyer(FC)	.20	.15	.08
23	*Blaine Beatty*(FC)	.08	.06	.03
24	Ken Griffey Jr. (TC)	.40	.30	.15
25	*Greg Vaughn*	1.00	.70	.40
26	*Xavier Hernandez*	.15	.11	.06
27	*Jason Grimsley*	.25	.20	.10
28	*Eric Anthony*	.70	.50	.30
29	Expos Checklist	.06	.05	.02
30	David Wells	.06	.05	.02
31	Hal Morris	.30	.25	.12
32	Bo Jackson (TC)	.25	.20	.10
33	*Kelly Mann*(FC)	.06	.05	.02
34	Nolan Ryan (SPEC)	1.25	.90	.50
35	*Scott Service*(FC)	.08	.06	.03
36	Athletics Checklist	.06	.05	.02
37	*Tino Martinez*	.40	.30	.15
38	Chili Davis	.09	.07	.04
39	Scott Sanderson	.06	.05	.02
40	Giants Checklist	.06	.05	.02
41	Tigers Checklist	.06	.05	.02
42	*Scott Coolbaugh*(FC)	.08	.06	.03
43	*Jose Cano*(FC)	.10	.08	.04
44	*Jose Vizcaino*	.30	.25	.12
45	*Bob Hamelin*	.20	.15	.08
46	*Jose Offerman*	.25	.20	.10
47	Kevin Blankenship	.10	.08	.04
48	Kirby Puckett (TC)	.20	.15	.08
49	*Tommy Greene*	1.00	.70	.40
50	Will Clark (SPEC)	.40	.30	.15
51	Rob Nelson(FC)	.09	.07	.04
52	*Chris Hammond*	.30	.25	.12
53	Indians Checklist	.06	.05	.02
54a	*Ben McDonald* (Orioles Logo)	15.00	11.00	6.00
54b	*Ben McDonald* (COR)	1.00	.70	.40
55	Andy Benes(FC)	.70	.50	.30
56	*John Olerud*(FC)	4.00	3.00	1.50
57	Red Sox Checklist	.06	.05	.02
58	Tony Armas	.06	.05	.02
59	*George Canale*(FC)	.06	.05	.02
60a	Orioles Checklist (Jamie Weston)	4.00	3.00	1.50
60b	Orioles Checklist (Mickey Weston)	.08	.06	.03
61	*Mike Stanton*(FC)	.20	.15	.08
62	Mets Checklist	.06	.05	.02
63	*Kent Mercker*(FC)	.20	.15	.08
64	*Francisco Cabrera*(FC)	.30	.25	.12
65	Steve Avery(FC)	3.00	2.25	1.25
66	Jose Canseco	.40	.30	.15
67	*Matt Merullo*(FC)	.08	.06	.03
68	Cardinals Checklist	.06	.05	.02
69	Ron Karkovice	.06	.05	.02
70	*Kevin Maas*(FC)	.20	.15	.08
71	Dennis Cook	.10	.08	.04
72	*Juan Gonzalez*(FC)	10.00	7.50	4.00
73	Cubs Checklist	.06	.05	.02
74	*Dean Palmer*(FC)	3.00	2.25	1.25
75	Bo Jackson (SPEC)	.60	.45	.25
76	*Rob Richie*(FC)	.20	.15	.08
77	*Bobby Rose*(FC)	.08	.06	.03
78	*Brian DuBois*(FC)	.08	.06	.03
79	White Sox Checklist	.06	.05	.02
80	Gene Nelson	.06	.05	.02
81	Bob McClure	.06	.05	.02
82	Rangers Checklist	.06	.05	.02
83	Greg Minton	.06	.05	.02
84	Braves Checklist	.06	.05	.02
85	Willie Fraser	.06	.05	.02
86	Neal Heaton	.06	.05	.02
87	*Kevin Tapani*(FC)	.25	.20	.10
88	Astros Checklist	.06	.05	.02
89a	Jim Gott (Incorrect Photo)	5.00	3.75	2.00
89b	Jim Gott (Photo of Gott)	.10	.08	.04
90	Lance Johnson(FC)	.09	.07	.04
91	Brewers Checklist	.06	.05	.02
92	Jeff Parrett	.08	.06	.03
93	*Julio Machado*(FC)	.06	.05	.02
94	Ron Jones	.10	.08	.04
95	Blue Jays Checklist	.06	.05	.02
96	Jerry Reuss	.06	.05	.02
97	Brian Fisher	.06	.05	.02
98	*Kevin Ritz*(FC)	.12	.09	.05
99	Reds Checklist	.06	.05	.02
100	Checklist 1-100	.06	.05	.02
101	Gerald Perry	.06	.05	.02
102	*Kevin Appier*(FC)	1.00	.70	.40
103	Julio Franco	.10	.08	.04
104	Craig Biggio	.20	.15	.08
105	Bo Jackson	.40	.30	.15
106	*Junior Felix*	.10	.08	.04
107	Mike Harkey(FC)	.08	.06	.03
108	Fred McGriff	.35	.25	.14
109	Rick Sutcliffe	.08	.06	.03
110	Pete O'Brien	.08	.06	.03
111	Kelly Gruber	.10	.08	.04
112	Pat Borders	.10	.08	.04
113	Dwight Evans	.10	.08	.04
114	Dwight Gooden	.10	.08	.04
115	*Kevin Batiste*(FC)	.15	.11	.06
116	Eric Davis	.12	.09	.05
117	Kevin Mitchell	.12	.09	.05
118	Ron Oester	.06	.05	.02
119	Brett Butler	.09	.07	.04
120	Danny Jackson	.06	.05	.02
121	Tommy Gregg	.06	.05	.02
122	Ken Caminiti	.08	.06	.03
123	Kevin Brown	.10	.08	.04
124	George Brett	.25	.20	.10
125	Mike Scott	.10	.08	.04
126	Cory Snyder	.10	.08	.04
127	George Bell	.15	.11	.06
128	Mark Grace	.30	.25	.12
129	Devon White	.10	.08	.04
130	Tony Fernandez	.15	.11	.06
131	Dan Aase	.06	.05	.02
132	Rance Mulliniks	.06	.05	.02
133	Marty Barrett	.08	.06	.03
134	Nelson Liriano	.07	.05	.03
135	Mark Carreon(FC)	.15	.11	.06
136	Candy Maldonado	.06	.05	.02
137	Tim Birtsas	.06	.05	.02
138	Tom Brookens	.06	.05	.02
139	John Franco	.08	.06	.03
140	Mike LaCoss	.06	.05	.02
141	Jeff Treadway	.07	.05	.03
142	Pat Tabler	.07	.05	.03
143	Darrell Evans	.06	.05	.02
144	Rafael Ramirez	.06	.05	.02
145	Oddibe McDowell	.09	.07	.04
146	Brian Downing	.09	.07	.04
147	Curtis Wilkerson	.06	.05	.02
148	Ernie Whitt	.07	.05	.03
149	Bill Schroeder	.06	.05	.02
150	Domingo Ramos	.06	.05	.02
151	Rick Honeycutt	.06	.05	.02
152	Don Slaught	.06	.05	.02
153	Mitch Webster	.06	.05	.02
154	Tony Phillips	.07	.05	.03
155	Paul Kilgus	.06	.05	.02
156	Ken Griffey, Jr.	4.00	3.00	1.50

		MT	NR MT	EX
157	Gary Sheffield	1.00	.70	.40
158	Wally Backman	.06	.05	.02
159	B.J. Surhoff	.08	.06	.03
160	Louie Meadows	.08	.06	.03
161	Paul O'Neill	.09	.07	.04
162	*Jeff McKnight*(FC)	.06	.05	.02
163	Alvaro Espinoza(FC)	.06	.05	.02
164	*Scott Scudder*(FC)	.08	.06	.03
165	Jeff Reed	.06	.05	.02
166	Gregg Jefferies	.40	.30	.15
167	Barry Larkin	.15	.11	.06
168	Gary Carter	.10	.08	.04
169	Robby Thompson	.09	.07	.04
170	Rolando Roomes	.15	.11	.06
171	Mark McGwire	.35	.25	.14
172	Steve Sax	.10	.08	.04
173	Mark Williamson	.06	.05	.02
174	Mitch Williams	.15	.11	.06
175	Brian Holton	.06	.05	.02
176	Rob Deer	.08	.06	.03
177	Tim Raines	.12	.09	.05
178	Mike Felder	.06	.05	.02
179	Harold Reynolds	.10	.08	.04
180	Terry Francona	.06	.05	.02
181	Chris Sabo	.15	.11	.06
182	Darryl Strawberry	.15	.11	.06
183	Willie Randolph	.10	.08	.04
184	Billy Ripken	.06	.05	.02
185	Mackey Sasser	.08	.06	.03
186	Todd Benzinger	.08	.06	.03
187	Kevin Elster	.07	.05	.03
188	Jose Uribe	.06	.05	.02
189	Tom Browning	.10	.08	.04
190	Keith Miller	.09	.07	.04
191	Don Mattingly	.35	.25	.14
192	Dave Parker	.12	.09	.05
193	Roberto Kelly	.15	.11	.06
194	Phil Bradley	.09	.07	.04
195	Ron Hassey	.07	.05	.03
196	Gerald Young	.06	.05	.02
197	Hubie Brooks	.08	.06	.03
198	Bill Doran	.09	.07	.04
199	Al Newman	.06	.05	.02
200	Checklist 101-200	.06	.05	.02
201	Terry Puhl	.06	.05	.02
202	Frank DiPino	.06	.05	.02
203	Jim Clancy	.06	.05	.02
204	Bob Ojeda	.07	.05	.03
205	Alex Trevino	.06	.05	.02
206	Dave Henderson	.10	.08	.04
207	Henry Cotto	.06	.05	.02
208	Rafael Belliard	.06	.05	.02
209	Stan Javier	.07	.05	.03
210	Jerry Reed	.06	.05	.02
211	Doug Dascenzo	.08	.06	.03
212	Andres Thomas	.07	.05	.03
213	Greg Maddux	.30	.25	.12
214	Mike Schooler	.09	.07	.04
215	Lonnie Smith	.09	.07	.04
216	Jose Rijo	.10	.08	.04
217	Greg Gagne	.08	.06	.03
218	Jim Gantner	.08	.06	.03
219	Allan Anderson	.09	.07	.04
220	Rick Mahler	.06	.05	.02
221	Jim Deshaies	.09	.07	.04
222	Keith Hernandez	.10	.08	.04
223	Vince Coleman	.12	.09	.05
224	David Cone	.20	.15	.08
225	Ozzie Smith	.20	.15	.08
226	Matt Nokes	.10	.08	.04
227	Barry Bonds	.80	.60	.30
228	Felix Jose	.20	.15	.08
229	Dennis Powell	.06	.05	.02
230	Mike Gallego	.06	.05	.02
231	Shawon Dunston	.09	.07	.04
232	Ron Gant	.40	.30	.15
233	*Omar Vizquel*	.10	.08	.04
234	Derek Lilliquist	.10	.08	.04
235	Erik Hanson	.10	.08	.04
236	Kirby Puckett	.75	.60	.30
237	*Bill Spiers*	.08	.06	.03
238	Dan Gladden	.07	.05	.03
239	Bryan Clutterbuck(FC)	.07	.05	.03
240	John Moses	.06	.05	.02
241	Ron Darling	.12	.09	.05
242	Joe Magrane	.12	.09	.05
243	Dave Magadan	.09	.07	.04
244	Pedro Guerrero	.06	.05	.02
245	Glenn Davis	.10	.08	.04
246	Terry Steinbach	.12	.09	.05
247	Fred Lynn	.09	.07	.04

		MT	NR MT	EX
248	Gary Redus	.06	.05	.02
249	Kenny Williams	.06	.05	.02
250	Sid Bream	.06	.05	.02
251	Bob Welch	.08	.06	.03
252	Bill Buckner	.07	.05	.03
253	Carney Lansford	.09	.07	.04
254	Paul Molitor	.25	.20	.10
255	Jose DeJesus	.15	.11	.06
256	Orel Hershiser	.10	.08	.04
257	Tom Brunansky	.10	.08	.04
258	Mike Davis	.06	.05	.02
259	Jeff Ballard	.12	.09	.05
260	Scott Terry	.09	.07	.04
261	Sid Fernandez	.10	.08	.04
262	Mike Marshall	.08	.06	.03
263	Howard Johnson	.08	.06	.03
264	Kirk Gibson	.09	.07	.04
265	Kevin McReynolds	.06	.05	.02
266	Cal Ripken, Jr.	.60	.45	.25
267	Ozzie Guillen	.07	.05	.03
268	Jim Traber	.06	.05	.02
269	Bobby Thigpen	.09	.07	.04
270	Joe Orsulak	.06	.05	.02
271	Bob Boone	.09	.07	.04
272	Dave Stewart	.09	.07	.04
273	Tim Wallach	.09	.07	.04
274	Luis Aquino	.06	.05	.02
275	Mike Moore	.10	.08	.04
276	Tony Pena	.08	.06	.03
277	Eddie Murray	.15	.11	.06
278	Milt Thompson	.07	.05	.03
279	Alejandro Pena	.06	.05	.02
280	Ken Dayley	.06	.05	.02
281	Carmen Castillo	.06	.05	.02
282	Tom Henke	.08	.06	.03
283	Mickey Hatcher	.06	.05	.02
284	Roy Smith(FC)	.06	.05	.02
285	Manny Lee	.06	.05	.02
286	Dan Pasqua	.07	.05	.03
287	Larry Sheets	.06	.05	.02
288	Garry Templeton	.07	.05	.03
289	Eddie Williams	.07	.05	.03
290	Brady Anderson	.15	.11	.06
291	Spike Owen	.07	.05	.03
292	Storm Davis	.09	.07	.04
293	Chris Bosio	.09	.07	.04
294	Jim Eisenreich	.07	.05	.03
295	Don August	.07	.05	.03
296	Jeff Hamilton	.07	.05	.03
297	Mickey Tettleton	.10	.08	.04
298	Mike Scioscia	.09	.07	.04
299	Kevin Hickey(FC)	.06	.05	.02
300	Checklist 201-300	.06	.05	.02
301	Shawn Abner	.06	.05	.02
302	Kevin Bass	.08	.06	.03
303	Bip Roberts(FC)	.08	.06	.03
304	Joe Girardi	.10	.08	.04
305	Danny Darwin	.06	.05	.02
306	Mike Heath	.06	.05	.02
307	Mike Macfarlane	.06	.05	.02
308	Ed Whitson	.08	.06	.03
309	Tracy Jones	.07	.05	.03
310	Scott Fletcher	.07	.05	.03
311	Darnell Coles	.07	.05	.03
312	Mike Brumley	.06	.05	.02
313	Bill Swift	.06	.05	.02
314	Charlie Hough	.07	.05	.03
315	Jim Presley	.08	.06	.03
316	Luis Polonia	.07	.05	.03
317	Mike Morgan	.06	.05	.02
318	Lee Guetterman	.06	.05	.02
319	Jose Oquendo	.08	.06	.03
320	Wayne Tollenson	.06	.05	.02
321	Jody Reed	.07	.05	.03
322	Damon Berryhill	.09	.07	.04
323	Roger Clemens	.50	.40	.20
324	Ryne Sandberg	.60	.45	.25
325	Benito Santiago	.10	.08	.04
326	Bret Saberhagen	.08	.06	.03
327	Lou Whitaker	.10	.08	.04
328	Dave Gallagher	.10	.08	.04
329	Mike Pagliarulo	.07	.05	.03
330	Doyle Alexander	.07	.05	.03
331	Jeffrey Leonard	.09	.07	.04
332	Torey Lovullo	.20	.15	.08
333	Pete Incaviglia	.09	.07	.04
334	Rickey Henderson	.30	.25	.12
335	Rafael Palmeiro	.20	.15	.08
336	Ken Hill	.40	.30	.15
337	Dave Winfield	.25	.20	.10
338	Alfredo Griffin	.07	.05	.03

		MT	NR MT	EX
339	Andy Hawkins	.07	.05	.03
340	Ted Power	.06	.05	.02
341	Steve Wilson	.10	.08	.04
342	Jack Clark	.10	.08	.04
343	Ellis Burks	.08	.06	.03
344	Tony Gwynn	.25	.20	.10
345	*Jerome Walton*	.06	.05	.02
346	Roberto Alomar	1.00	.70	.40
347	*Carlos Martinez*(FC)	.08	.06	.03
348	Chet Lemon	.07	.05	.03
349	Willie Wilson	.07	.05	.03
350	Greg Walker	.07	.05	.03
351	Tom Bolton	.06	.05	.02
352	German Gonzalez(FC)	.08	.06	.03
353	Harold Baines	.10	.08	.04
354	Mike Greenwell	.10	.08	.04
355	Ruben Sierra	.20	.15	.08
356	Anres Galarraga	.12	.09	.05
357	Andre Dawson	.15	.11	.06
358	*Jeff Brantley*(FC)	.10	.08	.04
359	Mike Bielecki	.08	.06	.03
360	Ken Oberkfell	.06	.05	.02
361	Kurt Stillwell	.07	.05	.03
362	Brian Holman	.09	.07	.04
363	Kevin Seitzer	.12	.09	.05
364	Alvin Davis	.06	.05	.02
365	Tom Gordon	.06	.05	.02
366	Bobby Bonilla	.12	.09	.05
367	Carlton Fisk	.10	.08	.04
368	*Steve Carter*(FC)	.08	.06	.03
369	Joel Skinner	.06	.05	.02
370	John Cangelosi	.06	.05	.02
371	Cecil Espy	.08	.06	.03
372	*Gary Wayne*(FC)	.08	.06	.03
373	Jim Rice	.08	.06	.03
374	*Mike Dyer*(FC)	.08	.06	.03
375	Joe Carter	.35	.25	.14
376	Dwight Smith	.06	.05	.02
377	*John Wetteland*(FC)	.35	.25	.14
378	Ernie Riles	.06	.05	.02
379	Otis Nixon	.06	.05	.02
380	Vance Law	.06	.05	.02
381	Dave Bergman	.06	.05	.02
382	Frank White	.07	.05	.03
383	Scott Bradley	.06	.05	.02
384	Israel Sanchez	.06	.05	.02
385	Gary Pettis	.06	.05	.02
386	Donn Pall(FC)	.06	.05	.02
387	John Smiley	.10	.08	.04
388	Tom Candiotti	.07	.05	.03
389	Junior Ortiz	.06	.05	.02
390	Steve Lyons	.06	.05	.02
391	Brian Harper	.06	.05	.02
392	Fred Manrique	.06	.05	.02
393	Lee Smith	.08	.06	.03
394	Jeff Kunkel	.06	.05	.02
395	Claudell Washington	.08	.06	.03
396	John Tudor	.07	.05	.03
397	Terry Kennedy	.07	.05	.03
398	Lloyd McClendon	.09	.07	.04
399	Craig Lefferts	.06	.05	.02
400	Checklist 301-400	.06	.05	.02
401	Keith Moreland	.06	.05	.02
402	Rich Gedman	.07	.05	.03
403	Jeff Robinson	.07	.05	.03
404	Randy Ready	.06	.05	.02
405	Rick Cerone	.06	.05	.02
406	Jeff Blauser	.07	.05	.03
407	Larry Andersen	.06	.05	.02
408	Joe Boever	.08	.06	.03
409	Felix Fermin	.06	.05	.02
410	Glenn Wilson	.06	.05	.02
411	Rex Hudler	.06	.05	.02
412	Mark Grant	.06	.05	.02
413	Dennis Martinez	.08	.06	.03
414	Darrin Jackson	.06	.05	.02
415	Mike Aldrete	.06	.05	.02
416	Roger McDowell	.09	.07	.04
417	Jeff Reardon	.10	.08	.04
418	Darren Daulton	.20	.15	.08
419	Tim Laudner	.08	.06	.03
420	Don Carman	.07	.05	.03
421	Lloyd Moseby	.09	.07	.04
422	Doug Drabek	.10	.08	.04
423	Lenny Harris	.09	.07	.04
424	Jose Lind	.07	.05	.03
425	*Dave Johnson*(FC)	.08	.06	.03
426	Jerry Browne	.09	.07	.04
427	*Eric Yelding*(FC)	.12	.09	.05
428	Brad Komminsk(FC)	.06	.05	.02
429	Jody Davis	.06	.05	.02

		MT	NR MT	EX
430	Mariano Duncan(FC)	.09	.07	.04
431	Mark Davis	.12	.09	.05
432	Nelson Santovenia	.10	.08	.04
433	Bruce Hurst	.10	.08	.04
434	*Jeff Huson*(FC)	.10	.08	.04
435	Chris James	.09	.07	.04
436	*Mark Guthrie*(FC)	.08	.06	.03
437	Charlie Hayes(FC)	.10	.08	.04
438	Shane Rawley	.08	.06	.03
439	Dickie Thon	.06	.05	.02
440	Juan Berenguer	.06	.05	.02
441	Kevin Romine	.06	.05	.02
442	Bill Landrum	.09	.07	.04
443	Todd Frohwirth	.07	.05	.03
444	Craig Worthington	.10	.08	.04
445	Fernando Valenzuela	.09	.07	.04
446	*Albert Belle*(FC)	3.00	2.25	1.25
447	*Ed Whited*(FC)	.08	.06	.03
448	Dave Smith	.09	.07	.04
449	Dave Clark	.07	.05	.03
450	Juan Agosto	.06	.05	.02
451	Dave Valle	.06	.05	.02
452	Kent Hrbek	.15	.11	.06
453	Von Hayes	.10	.08	.04
454	Gary Gaetti	.06	.05	.02
455	Greg Briley	.06	.05	.02
456	Glenn Braggs	.08	.06	.03
457	Kirt Manwaring	.10	.08	.04
458	Mel Hall	.07	.05	.03
459	Brook Jacoby	.08	.06	.03
460	Pat Sheridan	.06	.05	.02
461	Rob Murphy	.06	.05	.02
462	Jimmy Key	.10	.08	.04
463	Nick Esasky	.10	.08	.04
464	Rob Ducey	.09	.07	.04
465	Carlos Quintana	.09	.07	.04
466	*Larry Walker*(FC)	2.00	1.50	.80
467	Todd Worrell	.10	.08	.04
468	Kevin Gross	.09	.07	.04
469	Terry Pendleton	.09	.07	.04
470	Dave Martinez	.07	.05	.03
471	Gene Larkin	.06	.05	.02
472	Len Dykstra	.15	.11	.06
473	Barry Lyons	.06	.05	.02
474	Terry Mulholland(FC)	.10	.08	.04
475	*Chip Hale*(FC)	.08	.06	.03
476	Jesse Barfield	.08	.06	.03
477	Dan Plesac	.09	.07	.04
478a	Scott Garrelts (Photo actually Bill Bathe)	3.00	2.25	1.25
478b	Scott Garrelts (Correct photo)	.10	.08	.04
479	Dave Righetti	.10	.08	.04
480	Gus Polidor(FC)	.06	.05	.02
481	Mookie Wilson	.09	.07	.04
482	Luis Rivera	.06	.05	.02
483	Mike Flanagan	.07	.05	.03
484	Dennis "Oil Can" Boyd	.07	.05	.03
485	John Cerutti	.07	.05	.03
486	John Costello	.07	.05	.03
487	Pascual Perez	.07	.05	.03
488	Tommy Herr	.09	.07	.04
489	Tom Foley	.06	.05	.02
490	Curt Ford	.06	.05	.02
491	Steve Lake	.06	.05	.02
492	Tim Teufel	.06	.05	.02
493	Randy Bush	.06	.05	.02
494	Mike Jackson	.06	.05	.02
495	Steve Jeltz	.06	.05	.02
496	Paul Gibson	.08	.06	.03
497	Steve Balboni	.06	.05	.02
498	Bud Black	.06	.05	.02
499	Dale Sveum	.06	.05	.02
500	Checklist 401-500	.06	.05	.02
501	Timmy Jones	.06	.05	.02
502	Mark Portugal	.06	.05	.02
503	Ivan Calderon	.07	.05	.03
504	Rick Rhoden	.06	.05	.02
505	Willie McGee	.09	.07	.04
506	Kirk McCaskill	.08	.06	.03
507	Dave LaPoint	.07	.05	.03
508	Jay Howell	.10	.08	.04
509	Johnny Ray	.08	.06	.03
510	Dave Anderson	.06	.05	.02
511	Chuck Crim	.06	.05	.02
512	Joe Hesketh	.06	.05	.02
513	Dennis Eckersley	.10	.08	.04
514	Greg Brock	.08	.06	.03
515	Tim Burke	.08	.06	.03
516	Frank Tanana	.07	.05	.03
517	Jay Bell	.07	.05	.03
518	Guillermo Hernandez	.07	.05	.03

		MT	NR MT	EX
519	Randy Kramer(FC)	.08	.06	.03
520	Charles Hudson	.06	.05	.02
521	Jim Corsi(FC)	.08	.06	.03
522	Steve Rosenberg	.08	.06	.03
523	Cris Carpenter	.10	.08	.04
524	*Matt Winters*(FC)	.12	.09	.05
525	Melido Perez	.08	.06	.03
526	Chris Gwynn	.08	.06	.03
527	Bert Blyleven	.09	.07	.04
528	Chuck Cary	.07	.05	.03
529	Daryl Boston	.06	.05	.02
530	Dale Mohorcic	.06	.05	.02
531	Geronimo Berroa(FC)	.09	.07	.04
532	Edgar Martinez	.09	.07	.04
533	Dale Murphy	.10	.08	.04
534	Jay Buhner	.15	.11	.06
535	John Smoltz	.15	.11	.06
536	Andy Van Slyke	.15	.11	.06
537	Mike Henneman	.09	.07	.04
538	Miguel Garcia(FC)	.07	.05	.03
539	Frank Williams	.06	.05	.02
540	R.J. Reynolds	.06	.05	.02
541	Shawn Hillegas	.06	.05	.02
542	Walt Weiss	.10	.08	.04
543	*Greg Hibbard*(FC)	.15	.11	.06
544	Nolan Ryan	1.25	.90	.50
545	*Todd Zeile*	.40	.30	.15
546	Hensley Meulens	.08	.06	.03
547	Tim Belcher	.10	.08	.04
548	Mike Witt	.08	.06	.03
549	Greg Cadaret	.06	.05	.02
550	Franklin Stubbs	.06	.05	.02
551	*Tony Castillo*(FC)	.12	.09	.05
552	Jeff Robinson	.08	.06	.03
553	*Steve Olin*(FC)	.12	.09	.05
554	Alan Trammell	.10	.08	.04
555	Wade Boggs	.25	.20	.10
556	Will Clark	.40	.30	.15
557	Jeff King(FC)	.10	.08	.04
558	Mike Fitzgerald	.06	.05	.02
559	Ken Howell	.06	.05	.02
560	Bob Kipper	.06	.05	.02
561	Scott Bankhead	.09	.07	.04
562a	*Jeff Innis* (Photo actually David West)(FC)	3.00	2.25	1.25
562b	*Jeff Innis* (Corrected)(FC)	.08	.06	.03
563	Randy Johnson	.15	.11	.06
564	*Wally Whithurst*	.10	.08	.04
565	*Gene Harris*(FC)	.10	.08	.04
566	Norm Charlton	.09	.07	.04
567	Robin Yount	.40	.30	.15
568	*Joe Oliver*(FC)	.15	.11	.06
569	Mark Parent	.07	.05	.03
570	John Farrell	.07	.05	.03
571	Tom Glavine	.40	.30	.15
572	Rod Nichols(FC)	.06	.05	.02
573	Jack Morris	.09	.07	.04
574	Greg Swindell	.12	.09	.05
575	Steve Searcy(FC)	.09	.07	.04
576	Ricky Jordan	.08	.06	.03
577	Matt Williams	.35	.25	.14
578	Mike LaValliere	.07	.05	.03
579	Bryn Smith	.08	.06	.03
580	Bruce Ruffin	.06	.05	.02
581	Randy Myers	.08	.06	.03
582	*Rick Wrona*(FC)	.08	.06	.03
583	Juan Samuel	.09	.07	.04
584	Les Lancaster	.07	.05	.03
585	Jeff Musselman	.07	.05	.03
586	Rob Dibble	.09	.07	.04
587	Eric Show	.07	.05	.03
588	Jesse Orosco	.06	.05	.02
589	Herm Winningham	.06	.05	.02
590	Andy Allanson	.06	.05	.02
591	Dion James	.06	.05	.02
592	Carmelo Martinez	.08	.06	.03
593	Luis Quinones(FC)	.08	.06	.03
594	Dennis Rasmussen	.08	.06	.03
595	Rich Yett	.06	.05	.02
596	Bob Walk	.08	.06	.03
597	Andy McGaffigan	.07	.05	.03
598	Billy Hatcher	.07	.05	.03
599	Bob Knepper	.06	.05	.02
600	Checklist 501-600	.06	.05	.02
601	Joey Cora(FC)	.10	.08	.04
602	*Steve Finley*	.20	.15	.08
603	Kal Daniels	.10	.08	.04
604	Gregg Olson	.12	.09	.05
605	Dave Steib	.09	.07	.04
606	*Kenny Rogers*(FC)	.08	.06	.03
607	Zane Smith	.06	.05	.02

		MT	NR MT	EX
608	*Bob Geren*(FC)	.08	.06	.03
609	Chad Kreuter	.10	.08	.04
610	Mike Smithson	.06	.05	.02
611	*Jeff Wetherby*(FC)	.08	.06	.03
612	*Gary Mielke*(FC)	.08	.06	.03
613	Pete Smith	.08	.06	.03
614	*Jack Daugherty*(FC)	.08	.06	.03
615	Lance McCullers	.08	.06	.03
616	Don Robinson	.06	.05	.02
617	Jose Guzman	.06	.05	.02
618	Steve Bedrosian	.08	.06	.03
619	Jamie Moyer	.06	.05	.02
620	Atlee Hammaker	.06	.05	.02
621	*Rick Luecken*(FC)	.08	.06	.03
622	Greg W. Harris	.09	.07	.04
623	Pete Harnisch	.10	.08	.04
624	Jerald Clark	.10	.08	.04
625	Jack McDowell	.30	.25	.12
626	Frank Viola	.12	.09	.05
627	Ted Higuera	.09	.07	.04
628	*Marty Pevey*(FC)	.06	.05	.02
629	Bill Wegman	.06	.05	.02
630	Eric Plunk	.06	.05	.02
631	Drew Hall	.06	.05	.02
632	Doug Jones	.08	.06	.03
633	Geno Petralli	.06	.05	.02
634	Jose Alvarez	.06	.05	.02
635	Bob Milacki(FC)	.10	.08	.04
636	Bobby Witt	.07	.05	.03
637	Trevor Wilson	.08	.06	.03
638	Jeff Russell	.08	.06	.03
639	Mike Krukow	.07	.05	.03
640	Rick Leach	.06	.05	.02
641	Dave Schmidt	.06	.05	.02
642	Terry Leach	.06	.05	.02
643	Calvin Schiraldi	.06	.05	.02
644	Bob Melvin	.06	.05	.02
645	Jim Abbott	.25	.20	.10
646	*Jaime Navarro*(FC)	.30	.25	.12
647	Mark Langston	.10	.08	.04
648	Juan Nieves	.08	.06	.03
649	Damaso Garcia	.06	.05	.02
650	Charlie O'Brien	.06	.05	.02
651	Eric King	.06	.05	.02
652	Mike Boddicker	.08	.06	.03
653	Duan Ward	.07	.05	.03
654	Bob Stanley	.06	.05	.02
655	Sandy Alomar, Jr.	.10	.08	.04
656	Danny Tartabull	.15	.11	.06
657	Randy McCament	.06	.05	.02
658	Charlie Leibrandt	.07	.05	.03
659	Dan Quisenberry	.07	.05	.03
660	Paul Assenmacher	.06	.05	.02
661	Walt Terrell	.07	.05	.03
662	Tim Leary	.07	.05	.03
663	Randy Milligan	.08	.06	.03
664	Bo Diaz	.06	.05	.02
665	Mark Lemke	.07	.05	.03
666	Jose Gonzalez	.08	.06	.03
667	Chuck Finley	.07	.05	.03
668	John Kruk	.08	.06	.03
669	Dick Schofield	.07	.05	.03
670	Tim Crews	.06	.05	.02
671	John Dopson	.09	.07	.04
672	*John Orton*(FC)	.15	.11	.06
673	Eric Hetzel(FC)	.10	.08	.04
674	Lance Parrish	.08	.06	.03
675	Ramon Martinez	.12	.09	.05
676	Mark Gubicza	.10	.08	.04
677	Greg Litton	.20	.15	.08
678	Greg Mathews	.07	.05	.03
679	Dave Dravecky	.07	.05	.03
680	Steve Farr	.07	.05	.03
681	Mike Devereaux	.09	.07	.04
682	Ken Griffey, Sr.	.08	.06	.03
683a	*Mickey Weston* (Jamie)(FC)	4.00	3.00	1.50
683b	*Mickey Weston* (corrected)(FC)	.10	.08	.04
684	Jack Armstrong	.07	.05	.03
685	Steve Buechele	.07	.05	.03
686	Bryan Harvey	.07	.05	.03
687	Lance Blankenship	.09	.07	.04
688	Dante Bichette	.09	.07	.04
689	Todd Burns	.09	.07	.04
690	Dan Petry	.06	.05	.02
691	*Kent Anderson*(FC)	.08	.06	.03
692	Todd Stottlemyre	.08	.06	.03
693	Wally Joyner	.05	.04	.02
694	Mike Rochford(FC)	.10	.08	.04
695	Floyd Bannister	.07	.05	.03
696	Rick Reuschel	.09	.07	.04
697	Jose DeLeon	.09	.07	.04

		MT	NR MT	EX
698	Jeff Montgomery	.08	.06	.03
699	Jeff Montgomery	.08	.06	.03
700a	Checklist 601-700 (Jamie Weston)	.05	.04	.02
700b	Checklist 601-700 (Mickey Weston)	.10	.08	.04
701	Jim Gott	.10	.08	.04
702	"Rookie Threats" (Delino DeShields, Larry Walker, Marquis Grissom,)	1.00	.70	.40
703	Alejandro Pena	.10	.08	.04
704	Willie Randolph	.12	.09	.05
705	Tim Leary	.10	.08	.04
706	Chuck McElroy(FC)	.12	.09	.05
707	Gerald Perry	.10	.08	.04
708	Tom Brunansky	.12	.09	.05
709	John Franco	.15	.11	.06
710	Mark Davis	.10	.08	.04
711	Dave Justice(FC)	3.25	2.50	1.25
712	Storm Davis	.10	.08	.04
713	Scott Ruskin(FC)	.10	.08	.04
714	Glenn Braggs	.10	.08	.04
715	Kevin Bearse(FC)	.10	.08	.04
716	Jose Nunez(FC)	.15	.11	.06
717	Tim Layana(FC)	.08	.06	.03
718	Greg Myers(FC)	.12	.09	.05
719	Pete O'Brien	.10	.08	.04
720	John Candelaria	.10	.08	.04
721	Craig Grebeck(FC)	.25	.20	.10
722	Shawn Boskie(FC)	.12	.09	.05
723	Jim Leyritz(FC)	.20	.15	.08
724	Bill Sampen(FC)	.10	.08	.04
725	Scott Radinsky(FC)	.20	.15	.08
726	Todd Hundley(FC)	.15	.11	.06
727	Scott Hemond(FC)	.20	.15	.08
728	Lenny Webster(FC)	.10	.08	.04
729	Jeff Reardon	.12	.09	.05
730	Mitch Webster	.10	.08	.04
731	Brian Bohanon(FC)	.10	.08	.04
732	Rick Parker(FC)	.08	.06	.03
733	Terry Shumpert(FC)	.08	.06	.03
734a	Nolan Ryan (300-win stripe on front)	2.00	1.50	.80
734b	Nolan Ryan (no stripe)	8.00	6.00	3.25
735	John Burkett(FC)	.40	.30	.15
736	Derrick May(FC)	1.00	.70	.40
737	Carlos Baerga(FC)	3.50	2.75	1.50
738	Greg Smith(FC)	.15	.11	.06
739	Joe Kraemer(FC)	.15	.11	.06
740	Scott Sanderson	.10	.08	.04
741	Hector Villanueva(FC)	.10	.08	.04
742	Mike Fetters(FC)	.12	.09	.05
743	Mark Gardner(FC)	.30	.25	.12
744	Matt Nokes	.10	.08	.04
745	Dave Winfield	.25	.20	.10
746	Delino DeShields(FC)	1.00	.70	.40
747	Dann Howitt(FC)	.08	.06	.03
748	Tony Pena	.12	.09	.05
749	Oil Can Boyd	.12	.09	.05
750	Mike Benjamin(FC)	.10	.08	.04
751	Alex Cole(FC)	.80	.60	.30
752	Eric Gunderson(FC)	.20	.15	.08
753	Howard Farmer(FC)	.12	.09	.05
754	Joe Carter	.30	.25	.12
755	Ray Lankford(FC)	.75	.60	.30
756	Sandy Alomar,Jr.	.10	.08	.04
757	Alex Sanchez(FC)	.15	.11	.06
758	Nick Esasky	.10	.08	.04
759	Stan Belinda(FC)	.20	.15	.08
760	Jim Presley	.10	.08	.04
761	Gary DiSarcina(FC)	.20	.15	.08
762	Wayne Edwards(FC)	.20	.15	.08
763	Pat Combs(FC)	.20	.15	.08
764	Mickey Pina(FC)	.20	.15	.08
765	Wilson Alvarez(FC)	.60	.45	.25
766	Dave Parker	.15	.11	.06
767	Mike Blowers(FC)	.20	.15	.08
768	Tony Phillips	.10	.08	.04
769	Pascual Perez	.10	.08	.04
770	Gary Pettis	.10	.08	.04
771	Fred Lynn	.10	.08	.04
772	Mel Rojas(FC)	.20	.15	.08
773	David Segui(FC)	.30	.25	.12
774	Gary Carter	.15	.11	.06
775	Rafael Valdez(FC)	.15	.11	.06
776	Glenallen Hill(FC)	.15	.11	.06
777	Keith Hernandez	.12	.09	.05
778	Billy Hatcher	.12	.09	.05
779	Marty Clary(FC)	.10	.08	.04
780	Candy Maldonado	.12	.09	.05
781	Mike Marshall	.10	.08	.04
782	Billy Jo Robidoux(FC)	.10	.08	.04
783	Mark Langston	.12	.09	.05
784	Paul Sorrento(FC)	.80	.60	.30
785	Dave Hollins(FC)	2.00	1.50	.80
786	Cecil Fielder	.50	.40	.20
787	Matt Young	.10	.08	.04
788	Jeff Huson	.15	.11	.06
789	Lloyd Moseby	.12	.09	.05
790	Ron Kittle	.12	.09	.05
791	Hubie Brooks	.12	.09	.05
792	Craig Lefferts	.10	.08	.04
793	Kevin Bass	.10	.08	.04
794	Bryn Smith	.10	.08	.04
795	Juan Samuel	.12	.09	.05
796	Sam Horn(FC)	.15	.11	.06
797	Randy Myers	.12	.09	.05
798	Chris James	.10	.08	.04
799	Bill Gullickson	.10	.08	.04
800	Checklist 701-800	.10	.08	.04

1990 Upper Deck Reggie Jackson Heroes

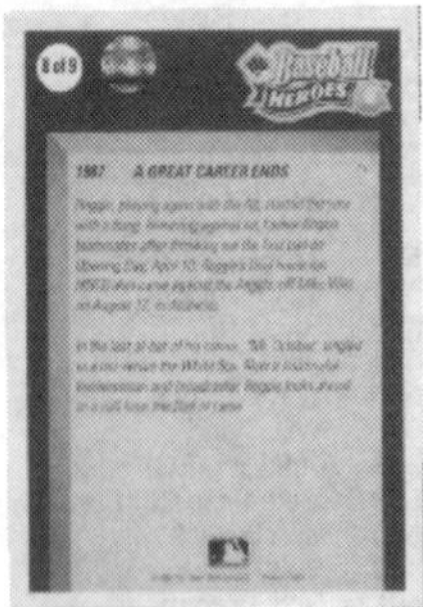

This Baseball Heroes set is devoted to Reggie Jackson. The cards, numbered 1-9, are the first in a continuing series of cards which have been issued in subsequent years. An unnumbered cover card that says "Baseball Heroes" was also issued. The Jackson cards were randomly inserted in high number foil packs only. Jackson also autographed 2,500 numbered cards, which were randomly included in high number packs.

	MT	NR MT	EX
Complete Set (10):	27.50	21.00	11.00
Common Reggie:	3.00	2.25	1.25
Autographed Card:	450.00	337.00	180.00

		MT	NR MT	EX
----	Header card	5.00	3.75	2.00
1	1969 Emerging Superstar (Reggie Jackson)	3.00	2.25	1.25
2	1973 An MVP Year (Reggie Jackson)	3.00	2.25	1.25
3	1977 "Mr. October" (Reggie Jackson)	3.00	2.25	1.25
4	1978 Jackson vs. Welch (Reggie Jackson)	3.00	2.25	1.25
5	1982 Under the Halo (Reggie Jackson)	3.00	2.25	1.25
6	1984 500! (Reggie Jackson)	3.00	2.25	1.25
7	1986 Moving Up the List (Reggie Jackson)	3.00	2.25	1.25
8	1987 A Great Career Ends (Reggie Jackson)	3.00	2.25	1.25
9	Heroes Checklist 1-9 (Reggie Jackson)	3.00	2.25	1.25

1991 Upper Deck

More than 110 rookies are included among the first 700 cards in the 1991 Upper Deck set. A 100-card high-number series was once again released in late summer. The 1991 Upper Deck cards feature high quality white stock and color photos on both the front and backs of the cards. A nine-card "Baseball Heroes" bonus set honor-

ing Nolan Ryan, is among the many insert specials in the 1991 Upper Deck set. Others include a card of Chicago Bulls superstar Michael Jordan. Along with the Ryan bonus cards, 2,500 limited-edition cards personally autographed and numbered by Ryan were randomly inserted. Upper Deck cards are packaged in tamper-proof foil packs. Each pack contains 15 cards and a 3-D team logo hologram sticker. The 1991 hologram stickers are full size.

	MT	NR MT	EX
Complete Set (800):	28.00	20.00	12.00
Common Player: 1-700	.05	.04	.02
Common Player: 701-800	.10	.08	.04

		MT	NR MT	EX
1	Star Rookie Checklist	.05	.04	.02
2	*Phil Plantier*(FC)	.70	.50	.30
3	*D.J. Dozier*(FC)	.10	.08	.04
4	Dave Hansen(FC)	.25	.20	.10
5	Maurice Vaughn(FC)	1.00	.70	.40
6	*Leo Gomez*(FC)	.25	.20	.10
7	*Scott Aldred*(FC)	.15	.11	.06
8	*Scott Chiamparino*(FC)	.30	.25	.12
9	*Lance Dickson*	.12	.09	.05
10	*Sean Berry*	.20	.15	.08
11	Bernie Williams(FC)	.40	.30	.15
12	*Brian Barnes*	.15	.11	.06
13	*Narciso Elvira*	.20	.15	.08
14	*Mike Gardiner*	.15	.11	.06
15	*Greg Colbrunn*	.30	.25	.12
16	*Bernard Gilkey*(FC)	.50	.40	.20
17	Mark Lewis(FC)	.15	.11	.06
18	*Mickey Morandini*	.15	.11	.06
19	Charles Nagy	.12	.09	.05
20	*Geronimo Pena*(FC)	.25	.20	.10
21	*Henry Rodriguez*	.30	.25	.12
22	Scott Cooper(FC)	.50	.40	.20
23	*Andujar Cedeno*(FC)	.40	.30	.15
24	*Eric Karros*	1.00	.70	.40
25	*Steve Decker*	.15	.11	.06
26	*Kevin Belcher*	.20	.15	.08
27	*Jeff Conine*	.50	.40	.20
28	Oakland Athletics Checklist	.10	.08	.04
29	Chicago White Sox Checklist	.08	.06	.03
30	Texas Rangers Checklist	.08	.06	.03
31	California Angels Checklist	.08	.06	.03
32	Seattle Mariners Checklist	.10	.08	.04
33	Kansas City Royals Checklist	.10	.08	.04
34	Minnesota Twins Checklist	.08	.06	.03
35	Scott Leius(FC)	.10	.08	.04
36	Neal Heaton	.06	.05	.02
37	*Terry Lee*(FC)	.20	.15	.08
38	Gary Redus	.05	.04	.02
39	Barry Jones	.06	.05	.02
40	Chuck Knoblauch(FC)	.80	.60	.30
41	Larry Andersen	.05	.04	.02
43	Darryl Hamilton	.06	.05	.02
44	Toronto Blue Jays Checklist	.08	.06	.03
45	Detroit Tigers Checklist	.10	.08	.04
46	Cleveland Indians Checklist	.08	.06	.03
47	Baltimore Orioles Checklist	.08	.06	.03
48	Milwaukee Brewers Checklist	.08	.06	.03
49	New York Yankees Checklist	.08	.06	.03
50	Top Prospect Checklist	.05	.04	.02
51	*Kyle Abbott*	.12	.09	.05
52	Jeff Juden(FC)	.25	.20	.10
53	*Todd Van Poppel*	.75	.60	.30
54	*Steve Karsay*	.60	.45	.25
55	*Chipper Jones*	1.50	1.25	.60
56	*Chris Johnson*(FC)	.25	.20	.10
57	*John Ericks*(FC)	.25	.20	.10

		MT	NR MT	EX
58	*Gary Scott*	.15	.11	.06
59	Kiki Jones(FC)	.12	.09	.05
60	*Wil Cordero*	.75	.60	.30
61	*Royce Clayton*(FC)	.90	.70	.35
62	*Tim Costo*	.30	.25	.12
63	Roger Salkeld(FC)	.40	.30	.15
64	*Brook Fordyce*	.25	.20	.10
65	*Mike Mussina*	2.50	2.00	1.00
66	*Dave Staton*	.25	.20	.10
67	*Mike Lieberthal*	.30	.25	.12
68	*Kurt Miller*	.30	.25	.12
69	*Dan Peltier*	.25	.20	.10
70	Greg Blosser(FC)	.25	.20	.10
71	*Reggie Sanders*	1.00	.70	.40
72	Brent Mayne(FC)	.15	.11	.06
73	*Rico Brogna*(FC)	.15	.11	.06
74	*Willie Banks*(FC)	.40	.30	.15
75	*Len Brutcher*	.10	.08	.04
76	*Pat Kelly*	.30	.25	.12
77	Cincinnati Reds Checklist	.08	.06	.03
78	Los Angeles Dodgers Checklist	.08	.06	.03
79	San Francisco Giants Checklist	.08	.06	.03
80	San Diego Padres Checklist	.08	.06	.03
81	Houston Astros Checklist	.08	.06	.03
82	Atlanta Braves Checklist	.10	.08	.04
83	"Fielder's Feat"	.20	.15	.08
84	*Orlando Merced*(FC)	.60	.45	.25
85	Domingo Ramos	.05	.04	.02
86	Tom Bolton	.05	.04	.02
87	*Andres Santana*(FC)	.12	.09	.05
88	John Dopson	.05	.04	.02
89	Kenny Williams	.05	.04	.02
90	Marty Barrett	.06	.05	.02
91	Tom Pagnozzi	.06	.05	.02
92	Carmelo Martinez	.06	.05	.02
93	"Save Master"	.10	.08	.04
94	Pittsburgh Pirates Checklist	.10	.08	.04
95	New York Mets Checklist	.10	.08	.04
96	Montreal Expos Checklist	.08	.06	.03
97	Philadelphia Phillies Checklist	.08	.06	.03
98	St. Louis Cardinals Checklist	.08	.06	.03
99	Chicago Cubs Checklist	.10	.08	.04
100	Checklist 1-100	.05	.04	.02
101	Kevin Elster	.06	.05	.02
102	Tom Brookens	.05	.04	.02
103	Mackey Sasser	.08	.06	.03
104	Felix Fermin	.05	.04	.02
105	Kevin McReynolds	.12	.09	.05
106	Dave Steib	.12	.09	.05
107	Jeffrey Leonard	.06	.05	.02
108	Dave Henderson	.08	.06	.03
109	Sid Bream	.06	.05	.02
110	Henry Cotto	.05	.04	.02
111	Shawon Dunston	.12	.09	.05
112	Mariano Duncan	.08	.06	.03
113	Joe Girardi	.08	.06	.03
114	Billy Hatcher	.08	.06	.03
115	Greg Maddux	.12	.09	.05
116	Jerry Browne	.08	.06	.03
117	Juan Samuel	.08	.06	.03
118	Steve Olin	.06	.05	.02
119	Alfredo Griffin	.06	.05	.02
120	Mitch Webster	.06	.05	.02
121	Joel Skinner	.05	.04	.02
122	Frank Viola	.15	.11	.06
123	Cory Snyder	.10	.08	.04
124	Howard Johnson	.12	.09	.05
125	*Carlos Baerga*	.60	.45	.25
126	Tony Fernandez	.12	.09	.05
127	Dave Stewart	.15	.11	.06
128	Jay Buhner	.08	.06	.03
129	Mike LaValliere	.06	.05	.02
130	Scott Bradley	.05	.04	.02
131	Tony Phillips	.06	.05	.02
132	Ryne Sandberg	.40	.30	.15
133	Paul O'Neill	.08	.06	.03
134	Mark Grace	.15	.11	.06
135	Chris Sabo	.12	.09	.05
136	Ramon Martinez	.10	.08	.04
137	Brook Jacoby	.08	.06	.03
138	Candy Maldonado	.08	.06	.03
139	Mike Scioscia	.08	.06	.03
140	Chris James	.08	.06	.03
141	Craig Worthington	.08	.06	.03
142	Manny Lee	.06	.05	.02
143	Tim Raines	.15	.11	.06
144	Sandy Alomar,Jr.	.15	.11	.06
145	John Olerud	.75	.60	.30
146	*Ozzie Canseco*	.15	.11	.06
147	Pat Borders	.06	.05	.02
148	Harold Reynolds	.10	.08	.04

		MT	NR MT	EX
149	Tom Henke	.08	.06	.03
150	R.J. Reynolds	.05	.04	.02
151	Mike Gallego	.05	.04	.02
152	Bobby Bonilla	.20	.15	.08
153	Terry Steinbach	.06	.05	.02
154	Barry Bonds	.30	.25	.12
155	Jose Canseco	.25	.20	.10
156	Gregg Jefferies	.15	.11	.06
157	Matt Williams	.20	.15	.08
158	Craig Biggio	.08	.06	.03
159	Daryl Boston	.05	.04	.02
160	Ricky Jordan	.08	.06	.03
161	Stan Belinda	.20	.15	.08
162	Ozzie Smith	.10	.08	.04
163	Tom Brunansky	.08	.06	.03
164	Todd Zeile	.30	.25	.12
165	Mike Greenwell	.15	.11	.06
166	Kal Daniels	.10	.08	.04
167	Kent Hrbek	.12	.09	.05
168	Franklin Stubbs	.06	.05	.02
169	Dick Schofield	.05	.04	.02
170	Junior Ortiz	.05	.04	.02
171	*Hector Villanueva*	.20	.15	.08
172	Dennis Eckersley	.15	.11	.06
173	Mitch Williams	.08	.06	.03
174	Mark McGwire	.35	.25	.14
175	Fernando Valenzuela	.10	.08	.04
176	Gary Carter	.10	.08	.04
177	Dave Magadan	.10	.08	.04
178	Robby Thompson	.08	.06	.03
179	Bob Ojeda	.05	.04	.02
180	Ken Caminiti	.06	.05	.02
181	Don Slaught	.05	.04	.02
182	Luis Rivera	.05	.04	.02
183	Jay Bell	.06	.05	.02
184	Jody Reed	.08	.06	.03
185	Wally Backman	.06	.05	.02
186	Dave Martinez	.06	.05	.02
187	Luis Polonia	.05	.04	.02
188	Shane Mack	.06	.05	.02
189	Spike Owen	.06	.05	.02
190	Scott Bailes	.05	.04	.02
191	John Russell	.05	.04	.02
192	Walt Weiss	.08	.06	.03
193	Jose Oquendo	.06	.05	.02
194	Carney Lansford	.08	.06	.03
195	Jeff Huson	.08	.06	.03
196	Keith Miller	.06	.05	.02
197	Eric Yelding	.10	.08	.04
198	Ron Darling	.06	.05	.02
199	John Kruk	.06	.05	.02
200	Checklist 101-200	.05	.04	.02
201	John Shelby	.05	.04	.02
202	Bob Geren	.06	.05	.02
203	Lance McCullers	.05	.04	.02
204	Alvaro Espinoza	.06	.05	.02
205	Mark Salas	.05	.04	.02
206	Mike Pagliarulo	.06	.05	.02
207	Jose Uribe	.06	.05	.02
208	Jim Deshaies	.06	.05	.02
209	Ron Karkovice	.05	.04	.02
210	Rafael Ramirez	.06	.05	.02
211	Donnie Hill	.05	.04	.02
212	Brian Harper	.08	.06	.03
213	Jack Howell	.05	.04	.02
214	Wes Gardner	.05	.04	.02
215	Tim Burke	.08	.06	.03
216	Doug Jones	.08	.06	.03
217	Hubie Brooks	.10	.08	.04
218	Tom Candiotti	.06	.05	.02
219	Gerald Perry	.06	.05	.02
220	Jose DeLeon	.06	.05	.02
221	Wally Whitehurst	.08	.06	.03
222	*Alan Mills*(FC)	.15	.11	.06
223	Alan Trammell	.12	.09	.05
224	Dwight Gooden	.25	.20	.10
225	*Travis Fryman*(FC)	2.00	1.50	.80
226	Joe Carter	.15	.11	.06
227	Julio Franco	.10	.08	.04
228	Craig Lefferts	.06	.05	.02
229	Gary Pettis	.06	.05	.02
230	Dennis Rasmussen	.06	.05	.02
231	Brian Downing	.06	.05	.02
232	Carlos Quintana	.10	.08	.04
233	Gary Gaetti	.12	.09	.05
234	Mark Langston	.15	.11	.06
235	Tim Wallach	.10	.08	.04
236	Greg Swindell	.10	.08	.04
237	Eddie Murray	.15	.11	.06
238	Jeff Manto(FC)	.20	.15	.08
239	Lenny Harris	.08	.06	.03

		MT	NR MT	EX
240	Jesse Orosco	.05	.04	.02
241	Scott Lusader	.05	.04	.02
242	Sid Fernandez	.08	.06	.03
243	*Jim Leyritz*	.08	.06	.03
244	Cecil Fielder	.20	.15	.08
245	Darryl Strawberry	.15	.11	.06
246	Frank Thomas(FC)	4.00	3.00	1.50
247	Kevin Mitchell	.20	.15	.08
248	Lance Johnson	.06	.05	.02
249	Rick Rueschel	.08	.06	.03
250	Mark Portugal	.05	.04	.02
251	Derek Lilliquist	.06	.05	.02
252	Brian Holman	.08	.06	.03
253	Rafael Valdez	.08	.06	.03
254	B.J. Surhoff	.06	.05	.02
255	Tony Gwynn	.15	.11	.06
256	Andy Van Slyke	.12	.09	.05
257	Todd Stottlemyre	.08	.06	.03
258	Jose Lind	.06	.05	.02
259	Greg Myers	.06	.05	.02
260	Jeff Ballard	.06	.05	.02
261	Bobby Thigpen	.10	.08	.04
262	*Jimmy Kremers*(FC)	.15	.11	.06
263	Robin Ventura	.30	.25	.12
264	John Smoltz	.10	.08	.04
265	Sammy Sosa	.20	.15	.08
266	Gary Sheffield	.15	.11	.06
267	Lenny Dykstra	.10	.08	.04
268	Bill Spiers	.06	.05	.02
269	Charlie Hayes	.08	.06	.03
270	Brett Butler	.08	.06	.03
271	Bip Roberts	.08	.06	.03
272	Rob Deer	.06	.05	.02
273	Fred Lynn	.08	.06	.03
274	Dave Parker	.15	.11	.06
275	Andy Benes	.10	.08	.04
276	Glenallen Hill	.08	.06	.03
277	*Steve Howard*(FC)	.12	.09	.05
278	Doug Drabek	.10	.08	.04
279	Joe Oliver	.08	.06	.03
280	Todd Benzinger	.06	.05	.02
281	Eric King	.06	.05	.02
282	Jim Presley	.06	.05	.02
283	Ken Patterson(FC)	.06	.05	.02
284	Jack Daugherty	.08	.06	.03
285	Ivan Calderon	.10	.08	.04
286	*Edgar Diaz*(FC)	.10	.08	.04
287	Kevin Bass	.08	.06	.03
288	Don Carman	.06	.05	.02
289	Greg Brock	.06	.05	.02
290	John Franco	.10	.08	.04
291	Joey Cora	.06	.05	.02
292	Bill Wegman	.06	.05	.02
293	Eric Show	.06	.05	.02
294	Scott Bankhead	.08	.06	.03
295	Garry Templeton	.06	.05	.02
296	Mickey Tettleton	.06	.05	.02
297	Luis Sojo(FC)	.15	.11	.06
298	Jose Rijo	.08	.06	.03
299	Dave Johnson	.06	.05	.02
300	Checklist 201-300	.05	.04	.02
301	Mark Grant	.05	.04	.02
302	Pete Harnisch	.08	.06	.03
303	Greg Olson(FC)	.10	.08	.04
304	*Anthony Telford*(FC)	.15	.11	.06
305	Lonnie Smith	.06	.05	.02
306	*Chris Hoiles*(FC)	.30	.25	.12
307	Bryn Smith	.06	.05	.02
308	Mike Devereaux	.06	.05	.02
309	Milt Thompson	.06	.05	.02
310	Bob Melvin	.05	.04	.02
311	Luis Salazar	.05	.04	.02
312	Ed Whitson	.06	.05	.02
313	Charlie Hough	.06	.05	.02
314	Dave Clark	.05	.04	.02
315	*Eric Gunderson*	.15	.11	.06
316	Dan Petry	.05	.04	.02
317	Dante Bichette	.08	.06	.03
318	Mike Heath	.05	.04	.02
319	Damon Berryhill	.06	.05	.02
320	Walt Terrell	.05	.04	.02
321	Scott Fletcher	.05	.04	.02
322	Dan Plesac	.08	.06	.03
323	Jack McDowell	.12	.09	.05
324	Paul Molitor	.15	.11	.06
325	Ozzie Guillen	.10	.08	.04
326	Gregg Olson	.10	.08	.04
327	Pedro Guerrero	.10	.08	.04
328	Bob Milacki	.06	.05	.02
329	John Tudor	.08	.06	.03
330	Steve Finley	.08	.06	.03

		MT	NR MT	EX
331	Jack Clark	.10	.08	.04
332	Jerome Walton	.15	.11	.06
333	Andy Hawkins	.06	.05	.02
334	Derrick May	.30	.25	.12
335	Roberto Alomar	.40	.30	.15
336	Jack Morris	.08	.06	.03
337	Dave Winfield	.15	.11	.06
338	Steve Searcy	.08	.06	.03
339	Chili Davis	.08	.06	.03
340	Larry Sheets	.06	.05	.02
341	Ted Higuera	.08	.06	.03
342	*David Segui*	.15	.11	.06
343	Greg Cadaret	.05	.04	.02
344	Robin Yount	.15	.11	.06
345	Nolan Ryan	.60	.45	.25
346	*Ray Lankford*	.40	.30	.15
347	Cal Ripken, Jr.	.40	.30	.15
348	Lee Smith	.08	.06	.03
349	Brady Anderson	.05	.04	.02
350	Frank DiPino	.05	.04	.02
351	Hal Morris	.10	.08	.04
352	Deion Sanders	.25	.20	.10
353	Barry Larkin	.10	.08	.04
354	Don Mattingly	.25	.20	.10
355	Eric Davis	.20	.15	.08
356	Jose Offerman	.12	.09	.05
357	*Mel Rojas*	.12	.09	.05
358	Rudy Seanez(FC)	.10	.08	.04
359	Oil Can Boyd	.06	.05	.02
360	Nelson Liriano	.05	.04	.02
361	Ron Gant	.20	.15	.08
362	*Howard Farmer*	.15	.11	.06
363	David Justice	.60	.45	.25
364	Delino DeShields	.30	.25	.12
365	Steve Avery	.25	.20	.10
366	David Cone	.12	.09	.05
367	lou Whitaker	.10	.08	.04
368	Von Hayes	.10	.08	.04
369	Frank Tanana	.06	.05	.02
370	Tim Teufel	.05	.04	.02
371	Randy Myers	.10	.08	.04
372	Roberto Kelly	.10	.08	.04
373	Jack Armstrong	.08	.06	.03
374	Kelly Gruber	.10	.08	.04
375	Kevin Maas	.10	.08	.04
376	Randy Johnson	.10	.08	.04
377	David West	.06	.05	.02
378	*Brent Knackert*(FC)	.12	.09	.05
379	Rick Honeycutt	.05	.04	.02
380	Kevin Gross	.08	.06	.03
381	Tom Foley	.05	.04	.02
382	Jeff Blauser	.06	.05	.02
383	*Scott Ruskin*	.15	.11	.06
384	Andres Thomas	.05	.04	.02
385	Dennis Martinez	.08	.06	.03
386	Mike Henneman	.08	.06	.03
387	Felix Jose	.15	.11	.06
388	Alejandro Pena	.05	.04	.02
389	Chet Lemon	.06	.05	.02
390	*Craig Wilson*(FC)	.20	.15	.08
391	Chuck Crim	.05	.04	.02
392	Mel Hall	.06	.05	.02
393	Mark Knudson	.05	.04	.02
394	Norm Charlton	.08	.06	.03
395	Mike Felder	.05	.04	.02
396	*Tim Layana*	.15	.11	.06
397	Steve Frey(FC)	.06	.05	.02
398	Bill Doran	.08	.06	.03
399	Dion James	.05	.04	.02
400	Checklist 301-400	.05	.04	.02
401	Ron Hassey	.05	.04	.02
402	Don Robinson	.06	.05	.02
403	Gene Nelson	.05	.04	.02
404	Terry Kennedy	.05	.04	.02
405	Todd Burns	.05	.04	.02
406	Roger McDowell	.08	.06	.03
407	Bob Kipper	.05	.04	.02
408	Darren Daulton	.08	.06	.03
409	Chuck Cary	.06	.05	.02
410	Bruce Ruffin	.06	.05	.02
411	Juan Berenguer	.05	.04	.02
412	Gary Ward	.05	.04	.02
413	Al Newman	.05	.04	.02
414	Danny Jackson	.08	.06	.03
415	Greg Gagne	.06	.05	.02
416	Tom Herr	.06	.05	.02
417	Jeff Parrett	.06	.05	.02
418	Jeff Reardon	.08	.06	.03
419	Mark Lemke	.06	.05	.02
420	Charlie O'Brien	.05	.04	.02
421	Willie Randolph	.08	.06	.03

		MT	NR MT	EX
422	Steve Bedrosian	.08	.06	.03
423	Mike Moore	.08	.06	.03
424	Jeff Brantley	.08	.06	.03
425	Bob Welch	.10	.08	.04
426	Terry Mulholland	.08	.06	.03
427	*Willie Blair*(FC)	.15	.11	.06
428	Darrin Fletcher(FC)	.10	.08	.04
429	Mike Witt	.06	.05	.02
430	Joe Boever	.05	.04	.02
431	Tom Gordon	.12	.09	.05
432	*Pedro Munoz*(FC)	.20	.15	.08
433	Kevin Seitzer	.10	.08	.04
434	Kevin Tapani	.15	.11	.06
435	Bret Saberhagen	.12	.09	.05
436	Ellis Burks	.20	.15	.08
437	Chuck Finley	.10	.08	.04
438	Mike Boddicker	.08	.06	.03
439	Francisco Cabrera	.08	.06	.03
440	*Todd Hundley*	.15	.11	.06
441	Kelly Downs	.06	.05	.02
442	*Dann Howitt*(FC)	.15	.11	.06
443	Scott Garrelts	.08	.06	.03
444	Rickey Henderson	.20	.15	.08
445	Will Clark	.30	.25	.12
446	Ben McDonald	.15	.11	.06
447	Dale Murphy	.12	.09	.05
448	Dave Righetti	.10	.08	.04
449	Dickie Thon	.05	.04	.02
450	Ted Power	.05	.04	.02
451	Scott Coolbaugh	.08	.06	.03
452	Dwight Smith	.08	.06	.03
453	Pete Incaviglia	.08	.06	.03
454	Andre Dawson	.15	.11	.06
455	Ruben Sierra	.20	.15	.08
456	Andres Galarraga	.10	.08	.04
457	Alvin Davis	.10	.08	.04
458	Tony Castillo	.06	.05	.02
459	Pete O'Brien	.06	.05	.02
460	Charlie Leibrandt	.06	.05	.02
461	Vince Coleman	.10	.08	.04
462	Steve Sax	.10	.08	.04
463	*Omar Oliveras*(FC)	.15	.11	.06
464	*Oscar Azocar*(FC)	.20	.15	.08
465	Joe Magrane	.08	.06	.03
466	*Karl Rhodes*(FC)	.30	.25	.12
467	Benito Santiago	.10	.08	.04
468	*Joe Klink*(FC)	.10	.08	.04
469	Sil Campusano	.05	.04	.02
470	Mark Parent	.05	.04	.02
471	*Shawn Boskie*	.20	.15	.08
472	Kevin Brown	.10	.08	.04
473	Rick Sutcliffe	.08	.06	.03
474	Rafael Palmeiro	.12	.09	.05
475	Mike Harkey	.10	.08	.04
476	Jaime Navarro	.15	.11	.06
477	Marquis Grissom	.20	.15	.08
478	Marty Clary	.05	.04	.02
479	Greg Briley	.10	.08	.04
480	Tom Glavine	.25	.20	.10
481	Lee Guetterman	.05	.04	.02
482	Rex Hudler	.06	.05	.02
483	Dave LaPoint	.06	.05	.02
484	Terry Pendleton	.08	.06	.03
485	Jesse Barfield	.08	.06	.03
486	Jose DeJesus	.08	.06	.03
487	*Paul Abbott*(FC)	.12	.09	.05
488	Ken Howell	.06	.05	.02
489	Greg W. Harris	.06	.05	.02
490	Roy Smith	.05	.04	.02
491	Paul Assenmacher	.05	.04	.02
492	Geno Petralli	.05	.04	.02
493	Steve Wilson	.08	.06	.03
494	Kevin Reimer(FC)	.08	.06	.03
495	Bill Long	.05	.04	.02
496	Mike Jackson	.06	.05	.02
497	Oddibe McDowell	.06	.05	.02
498	Bill Swift	.06	.05	.02
499	Jeff Treadway	.06	.05	.02
500	Checklist 401-500	.05	.04	.02
501	Gene Larkin	.06	.05	.02
502	Bob Boone	.08	.06	.03
503	Allan Anderson	.06	.05	.02
504	Luis Aquino	.06	.05	.02
505	Mark Guthrie	.06	.05	.02
506	Joe Orsulak	.06	.05	.02
507	*Dana Kiecker*(FC)	.15	.11	.06
508	Dave Gallagher	.05	.04	.02
509	Greg W. Harris	.06	.05	.02
510	Mark Williamson	.05	.04	.02
511	Casey Candaele	.05	.04	.02
512	Mookie Wilson	.06	.05	.02

		MT	NR MT	EX
513	Dave Smith	.08	.06	.03
514	*Chuck Carr*(FC)	.20	.15	.08
515	Glenn Wilson	.06	.05	.02
516	Mike Fitzgerald	.05	.04	.02
517	Devon White	.08	.06	.03
518	*Dave Hollins*	.25	.20	.10
519	Mark Eichhorn	.05	.04	.02
520	Otis Nixon	.05	.04	.02
521	*Terry Shumpert*	.20	.15	.08
522	*Scott Erickson*(FC)	.15	.11	.06
523	Danny Tartabull	.10	.08	.04
524	Orel Hershiser	.15	.11	.06
525	George Brett	.15	.11	.06
526	Greg Vaughn	.20	.15	.08
527	*Tim Naehring*(FC)	.10	.08	.04
528	Curt Schilling(FC)	.06	.05	.02
529	Chris Bosio	.06	.05	.02
530	Sam Horn	.08	.06	.03
531	Mike Scott	.10	.08	.04
532	George Bell	.15	.11	.06
533	Eric Anthony	.15	.11	.06
534	*Julio Valera*(FC)	.15	.11	.06
535	Glenn Davis	.15	.11	.06
536	Larry Walker	.25	.20	.10
537	Pat Combs	.15	.11	.06
538	*Chris Nabholz*(FC)	.20	.15	.08
539	Kirk McCaskill	.08	.06	.03
540	Randy Ready	.05	.04	.02
541	Mark Gubicza	.10	.08	.04
542	Rick Aguilera	.08	.06	.03
543	*Brian McRae*(FC)	.35	.25	.14
544	Kirby Puckett	.30	.25	.12
545	Bo Jackson	.25	.20	.10
546	Wade Boggs	.20	.15	.08
547	Tim McIntosh(FC)	.20	.15	.08
548	Randy Milligan	.08	.06	.03
549	Dwight Evans	.08	.06	.03
550	Billy Ripken	.05	.04	.02
551	Erik Hanson	.15	.11	.06
552	Lance Parrish	.10	.08	.04
553	Tino Martinez	.10	.08	.04
554	Jim Abbott	.15	.11	.06
555	Ken Griffey,Jr.	1.00	.70	.40
556	Milt Cuyler(FC)	.10	.08	.04
557	*Mark Leonard*(FC)	.10	.08	.04
558	Jay Howell	.08	.06	.03
559	Lloyd Moseby	.08	.06	.03
560	Chris Gwynn	.06	.05	.02
561	*Mark Whiten*(FC)	.40	.30	.15
562	Harold Baines	.10	.08	.04
563	Junior Felix	.15	.11	.06
564	*Darren Lewis*(FC)	.20	.15	.08
565	Fred McGriff	.25	.20	.10
566	Kevin Appier	.15	.11	.06
567	*Luis Gonzalez*(FC)	.40	.30	.15
568	Frank White	.08	.06	.03
569	Juan Agosto	.05	.04	.02
570	Mike Macfarlane	.06	.05	.02
571	Bert Blyleven	.10	.08	.04
572	Ken Griffey,Sr.	.10	.08	.04
573	Lee Stevens(FC)	.20	.15	.08
574	Edgar Martinez	.08	.06	.03
575	Wally Joyner	.10	.08	.04
576	Tim Belcher	.08	.06	.03
577	John Burkett	.10	.08	.04
578	Mike Morgan	.06	.05	.02
579	Paul Gibson	.05	.04	.02
580	Jose Vizcaino	.10	.08	.04
581	Duane Ward	.06	.05	.02
582	Scott Sanderson	.06	.05	.02
583	David Wells	.06	.05	.02
584	Willie McGee	.10	.08	.04
585	John Cerutti	.05	.04	.02
586	Danny Darwin	.08	.06	.03
587	Kurt Stillwell	.08	.06	.03
588	Rich Gedman	.05	.04	.02
589	Mark Davis	.08	.06	.03
590	Bill Gullickson	.06	.05	.02
591	Matt Young	.06	.05	.02
592	Bryan Harvey	.08	.06	.03
593	Omar Vizquel	.06	.05	.02
594	*Scott Lewis*(FC)	.15	.11	.06
595	Dave Valle	.06	.05	.02
596	Tim Crews	.05	.04	.02
597	Mike Bielecki	.06	.05	.02
598	Mike Sharperson	.06	.05	.02
599	Dave Bergman	.05	.04	.02
600	Checklist 501-600	.05	.04	.02
601	Steve Lyons	.06	.05	.02
602	Bruce Hurst	.08	.06	.03
603	Donn Pall	.05	.04	.02

		MT	NR MT	EX
604	*Jim Vatcher*(FC)	.15	.11	.06
605	Dan Pasqua	.06	.05	.02
606	Kenny Rogers	.08	.06	.03
607	*Jeff Schulz*(FC)	.15	.11	.06
608	Brad Arnsberg(FC)	.10	.08	.04
609	Willie Wilson	.08	.06	.03
610	Jamie Moyer	.06	.05	.02
611	Ron Oester	.05	.04	.02
612	Dennis Cook	.08	.06	.03
613	Rick Mahler	.05	.04	.02
614	Bill Landrum	.06	.05	.02
615	Scott Scudder	.15	.11	.06
616	*Tom Edens*(FC)	.08	.06	.03
617	"1917 Revisited"	.12	.09	.05
618	Jim Gantner	.06	.05	.02
619	Darrel Akerfelds(FC)	.06	.05	.02
620	Ron Robinson	.06	.05	.02
621	*Scott Radinsky*	.20	.15	.08
622	Pete Smith	.06	.05	.02
623	Melido Perez	.08	.06	.03
624	Jerald Clark	.06	.05	.02
625	Carlos Martinez	.08	.06	.03
626	*Wes Chamberlain*(FC)	.30	.25	.12
627	Bobby Witt	.08	.06	.03
628	Ken Dayley	.06	.05	.02
629	*John Barfield*(FC)	.10	.08	.04
630	Bob Tewksbury	.06	.05	.02
631	Glenn Braggs	.06	.05	.02
632	*Jim Neidlinger*(FC)	.20	.15	.08
633	Tom Browning	.08	.06	.03
634	Kirk Gibson	.12	.09	.05
635	Rob Dibble	.12	.09	.05
636	"Stolen Base Leaders"	.30	.25	.12
637	Jeff Montgomery	.08	.06	.03
638	Mike Schooler	.08	.06	.03
639	Storm Davis	.06	.05	.02
640	*Rich Rodriguez*(FC)	.15	.11	.06
641	Phil Bradley	.08	.06	.03
642	Kent Mercker	.15	.11	.06
643	Carlton Fisk	.12	.09	.05
644	*Mike Bell*(FC)	.10	.08	.04
645	*Alex Fernandez*(FC)	.50	.40	.20
646	Juan Gonzalez	1.00	.70	.40
647	Ken Hill	.06	.05	.02
648	Jeff Russell	.08	.06	.03
649	*Chuck Malone*(FC)	.15	.11	.06
650	Steve Buechele	.06	.05	.02
651	Mike Benjamin	.15	.11	.06
652	Tony Pena	.08	.06	.03
653	Trevor Wilson	.08	.06	.03
654	Alex Cole	.30	.25	.12
655	Roger Clemens	.25	.20	.10
656	"The Bashing Years"	.15	.11	.06
657	*Joe Grahe*(FC)	.20	.15	.08
658	Jim Eisenreich	.06	.05	.02
659	Dan Gladden	.06	.05	.02
660	Steve Farr	.06	.05	.02
661	*Bill Sampen*	.20	.15	.08
662	*Dave Rohde*(FC)	.15	.11	.06
663	Mark Gardner	.20	.15	.08
664	*Mike Simms*(FC)	.10	.08	.04
665	Moises Alou(FC)	.50	.40	.20
666	Mickey Hatcher	.06	.05	.02
667	Jimmy Key	.08	.06	.03
668	John Wetteland	.10	.08	.04
669	John Smiley	.06	.05	.02
670	Jim Acker	.05	.04	.02
671	Pascual Perez	.06	.05	.02
672	*Reggie Harris*(FC)	.30	.25	.12
673	Matt Nokes	.08	.06	.03
674	*Rafael Novoa*(FC)	.15	.11	.06
675	Hensley Meulens	.10	.08	.04
676	Jeff M. Robinson	.06	.05	.02
677	"Ground Breaking"	.25	.20	.10
678	Johnny Ray	.06	.05	.02
679	Greg Hibbard	.10	.08	.04
680	Paul Sorrento	.20	.15	.08
681	Mike Marshall	.06	.05	.02
682	Jim Clancy	.05	.04	.02
683	Rob Murphy	.05	.04	.02
684	Dave Schmidt	.05	.04	.02
685	*Jeff Gray*(FC)	.15	.11	.06
686	Mike Hartley(FC)	.20	.15	.08
687	Jeff King	.08	.06	.03
688	Stan Javier	.06	.05	.02
689	Bob Walk	.06	.05	.02
690	Jim Gott	.06	.05	.02
691	Mike LaCoss	.05	.04	.02
692	John Farrell	.06	.05	.02
693	Tim Leary	.06	.05	.02
694	*Mike Walker*(FC)	.20	.15	.08

		MT	NR MT	EX
695	Eric Plunk	.05	.04	.02
696	Mike Fetters(FC)	.15	.11	.06
697	Wayne Edwards	.10	.08	.04
698	Tim Drummond(FC)	.15	.11	.06
699	Willie Fraser	.05	.04	.02
700	Checklist 601-700	.05	.04	.02
701	Mike Heath	.10	.08	.04
702	"Rookie Threats"	.60	.45	.25
703	Jose Mesa	.10	.08	.04
704	Dave Smith	.10	.08	.04
705	Danny Darwin	.10	.08	.04
706	Rafael Belliard	.10	.08	.04
707	Rob Murphy	.10	.08	.04
708	Terry Pendleton	.15	.11	.06
709	Mike Pagliarulo	.10	.08	.04
710	Sid Bream	.12	.09	.05
711	Junior Felix	.12	.09	.05
712	Dante Bichette	.10	.08	.04
713	Kevin Gross	.10	.08	.04
714	Luis Sojo	.12	.09	.05
715	Bob Ojeda	.10	.08	.04
716	Julio Machado	.12	.09	.05
717	Steve Farr	.10	.08	.04
718	Franklin Stubbs	.10	.08	.04
719	Mike Boddicker	.12	.09	.05
720	Willie Randolph	.12	.09	.05
721	Willie McGee	.15	.11	.06
722	Chili Davis	.15	.11	.06
723	Danny Jackson	.12	.09	.05
724	Cory Snyder	.10	.08	.04
725	"MVP Lineup"	.15	.11	.06
726	Rob Deer	.10	.08	.04
727	Rich DeLucia(FC)	.15	.11	.06
728	Mike Perez(FC)	.15	.11	.06
729	Mickey Tettleton	.12	.09	.05
730	Mike Blowers	.10	.08	.04
731	Gary Gaetti	.12	.09	.05
732	Brett Butler	.12	.09	.05
733	Dave Parker	.15	.11	.06
734	Eddie Zosky(FC)	.10	.08	.04
735	Jack Clark	.12	.09	.05
736	Jack Morris	.12	.09	.05
737	Kirk Gibson	.12	.09	.05
738	Steve Bedrosian	.10	.08	.04
739	Candy Maldonado	.10	.08	.04
740	Matt Young	.10	.08	.04
741	Rich Garces(FC)	.12	.09	.05
742	George Bell	.15	.11	.06
743	Deion Sanders	.25	.20	.10
744	Bo Jackson	.50	.40	.20
745	Luis Mercedes(FC)	.40	.30	.15
746	Reggie Jefferson(FC)	.30	.25	.12
747	Pete Incaviglia	.10	.08	.04
748	Chris Hammond(FC)	.20	.15	.08
749	Mike Stanton	.12	.09	.05
750	Scott Sanderson	.10	.08	.04
751	Paul Faries(FC)	.20	.15	.08
752	Al Osuna(FC)	.15	.11	.06
753	Steve Chitren(FC)	.10	.08	.04
754	Tony Fernandez	.15	.11	.06
755	Jeff Bagwell(FC)	2.00	1.50	.80
756	Kirk Dressendorfer(FC)	.10	.08	.04
757	Glenn Davis	.15	.11	.06
758	Gary Carter	.12	.09	.05
759	Zane Smith	.10	.08	.04
760	Vance Law	.10	.08	.04
761	Denis Boucher(FC)	.20	.15	.08
762	Turner Ward(FC)	.10	.08	.04
763	Roberto Alomar	.50	.40	.20
764	Albert Belle	.40	.30	.15
765	Joe Carter	.15	.11	.06
766	Pete Schourek(FC)	.15	.11	.06
767	Heathcliff Slocumb(FC)	.15	.11	.06
768	Vince Coleman	.15	.11	.06
769	Mitch Williams	.12	.09	.05
770	Brian Downing	.10	.08	.04
771	Dana Allison(FC)	.15	.11	.06
772	Pete Harnisch	.12	.09	.05
773	Tim Raines	.15	.11	.06
774	Darryl Kile(FC)	.35	.25	.14
775	Fred McGriff	.25	.20	.10
776	Dwight Evans	.12	.09	.05
777	Joe Slusarski(FC)	.12	.09	.05
778	Dave Righetti	.12	.09	.05
779	Jeff Hamilton	.10	.08	.04
780	Ernest Riles	.10	.08	.04
781	Ken Dayley	.10	.08	.04
782	Eric King	.10	.08	.04
783	Devon White	.12	.09	.05
784	Beau Allred	.10	.08	.04
785	Mike Timlin(FC)	.12	.09	.05
786	Ivan Calderon	.15	.11	.06
787	Hubie Brooks	.12	.09	.05
788	Juan Agosto	.10	.08	.04
789	Barry Jones	.10	.08	.04
790	Wally Backman	.10	.08	.04
791	Jim Presley	.10	.08	.04
792	Charlie Hough	.10	.08	.04
793	Larry Andersen	.10	.08	.04
794	Steve Finley	.12	.09	.05
795	Shawn Abner	.10	.08	.04
796	Jeff M. Robinson	.10	.08	.04
797	Joe Bitker(FC)	.10	.08	.04
798	Eric Show	.10	.08	.04
799	Bud Black	.10	.08	.04
800	Checklist 701-800	.10	.08	.04
---	Michael Jordan (SP1)	9.00	6.75	3.50
---	A Day to Remember (Rickey Henderson/ Nolan Ryan) (SP2)	4.00	3.00	1.50
---	Hank Aaron hologram (HH1)	5.00	3.75	2.00

1991 Upper Deck Final Edition

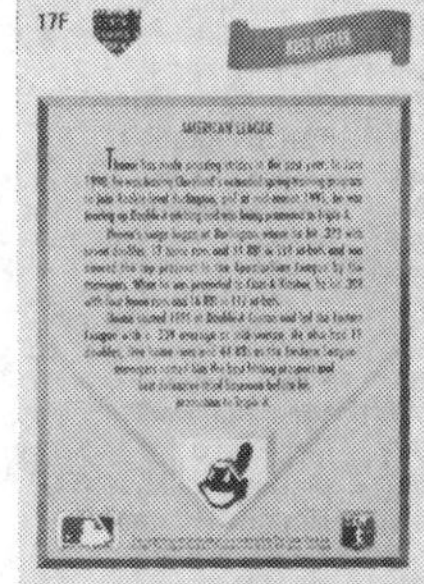

Upper Deck surprised the hobby with the release of this 100-card boxed set. The cards are numbered with an "F" designation. A special "Minor League Diamond Skills" subset (cards #1-21) features several top prospects. An All-Star subset (cards #79-99) is also included in this set. The cards are styled like the regular 1991 Upper Deck issue. Special team hologram cards are also included with the set.

	MT	NR MT	EX
Complete Set (100):	7.50	5.50	3.00
Common Player:	.05	.03	.01

		MT	NR MT	EX
1	Ryan Klesko/ Reggie Sanders (Minor League Diamond Skills Checklist)	.50	.40	.20
2	Pedro Martinez(FC)	.60	.45	.25
3	Lance Dickson	.10	.08	.04
4	Royce Clayton	.40	.30	.15
5	Scott Bryant(FC)	.35	.25	.14
6	Dan Wilson(FC)	.30	.25	.12
7	Dmitri Young(FC)	1.00	.70	.40
8	Ryan Klesko(FC)	1.50	1.25	.60
9	Tom Goodwin(FC)	.15	.11	.06
10	Rondell White(FC)	1.25	.90	.50
11	Reggie Sanders	.50	.40	.20
12	Todd Van Poppel	.50	.40	.20
13	Arthur Rhodes(FC)	.30	.25	.12
14	Eddie Zosky	.20	.15	.08
15	Gerald Williams(FC)	.40	.30	.15
16	Robert Eenhoorn(FC)	.12	.09	.05
17	Jim Thome(FC)	.60	.45	.25
18	Marc Newfield(FC)	1.00	.70	.40
19	Kerwin Moore(FC)	.25	.20	.10
20	Jeff McNeely(FC)	.30	.25	.12
21	Frankie Rodriguez(FC)	1.00	.70	.40
22	Andy Mota(FC)	.30	.25	.12
23	Chris Haney(FC)	.20	.15	.08
24	Kenny Lofton(FC)	1.50	1.25	.60
25	Dave Nilsson(FC)	.20	.15	.08
26	Derek Bell(FC)	.70	.50	.30
27	Frank Castillo(FC)	.50	.40	.20
28	Candy Maldonado	.20	.15	.08
29	Chuck McElroy	.20	.15	.08
30	Chito Martinez(FC)	.15	.11	.06
31	Steve Howe	.20	.15	.08
32	Freddie Benavides(FC)	.30	.25	.12

		MT	NR MT	EX
33	Scott Kamieniecki(FC)	.25	.20	.10
34	Denny Neagle(FC)	.15	.11	.06
35	Mike Humphreys(FC)	.20	.15	.08
36	Mike Remlinger(FC)	.25	.20	.10
37	Scott Coolbaugh	.20	.15	.08
38	Darren Lewis	.15	.11	.06
39	Thomas Howard(FC)	.20	.15	.08
40	John Candelaria	.20	.15	.08
41	Todd Benzinger	.20	.15	.08
42	Wilson Alvarez	.30	.25	.12
43	Patrick Lennon(FC)	.15	.11	.06
44	Rusty Meacham(FC)	.35	.25	.14
45	Ryan Bowen(FC)	.40	.30	.15
46	Rick Wilkins(FC)	.60	.45	.25
47	Ed Sprague(FC)	.30	.25	.12
48	Bob Scanlan(FC)	.20	.15	.08
49	Tom Candiotti	.20	.15	.08
50	Dennis Martinez (Perfecto)	.20	.15	.08
51	Oil Can Boyd	.20	.15	.08
52	Glenallen Hill	.30	.25	.12
53	Scott Livingstone(FC)	.30	.25	.12
54	Brian Hunter(FC)	.20	.15	.08
55	Ivan Rodriguez(FC)	1.00	.70	.40
56	Keith Mitchell(FC)	.15	.11	.06
57	Roger McDowell	.20	.15	.08
58	Otis Nixon	.20	.15	.08
59	Juan Bell	.20	.15	.08
60	Bill Krueger	.20	.15	.08
61	Chris Donnels(FC)	.12	.09	.05
62	Tommy Greene	.25	.20	.10
63	Doug Simons(FC)	.25	.20	.10
64	Andy Ashby(FC)	.20	.15	.08
65	Anthony Young(FC)	.15	.11	.06
66	Kevin Morton(FC)	.15	.11	.06
67	Bret Barberie(FC)	.15	.11	.06
68	Scott Servais(FC)	.25	.20	.10
69	Ron Darling	.20	.15	.08
70	Vicente Palacios	.20	.15	.08
71	Tim Burke	.20	.15	.08
72	Gerald Alexander(FC)	.20	.15	.08
73	Reggie Jefferson	.20	.15	.08
74	Dean Palmer	.60	.45	.25
75	Mark Whiten	.30	.25	.12
76	Randy Tomlin(FC)	.20	.15	.08
77	Mark Wohlers(FC)	.25	.20	.10
78	Brook Jacoby	.20	.15	.08
79	Ken Griffey, Jr./ Ryne Sandberg (All-Star Checklist)	.40	.30	.15
80	Jack Morris (AS)	.30	.25	.12
81	Sandy Alomar, Jr. (AS)	.25	.20	.10
82	Cecil Fielder (AS)	.30	.25	.12
83	Roberto Alomar (AS)	.30	.25	.12
84	Wade Boggs (AS)	.10	.08	.04
85	Cal Ripken, Jr. (AS)	.50	.40	.20
86	Rickey Henderson (AS)	.20	.15	.08
87	Ken Griffey, Jr. (AS)	.60	.45	.25
88	Dave Henderson (AS)	.25	.20	.10
89	Danny Tartabull (AS)	.25	.20	.10
90	Tom Glavine (AS)	.20	.15	.08
91	Benito Santiago (AS)	.25	.20	.10
92	Will Clark (AS)	.20	.15	.08
93	Ryne Sandberg (AS)	.30	.25	.12
94	Chris Sabo (AS)	.25	.20	.10
95	Ozzie Smith (AS)	.10	.08	.04
96	Ivan Calderon (AS)	.25	.20	.10
97	Tony Gwynn (AS)	.15	.11	.06
98	Andre Dawson (AS)	.10	.08	.04
99	Bobby Bonilla (AS)	.30	.25	.12
100	Checklist	.20	.15	.08

1991 Upper Deck Hank Aaron Heroes

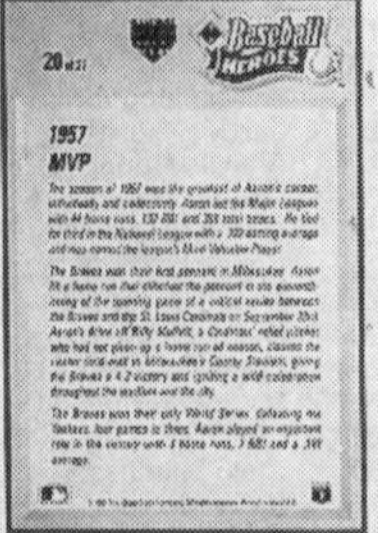

This set devoted to Hank Aaron is numbered 19-27 and includes an unnumbered cover card that says "Baseball Heroes." The cards are found in foil and jumbo packs of Upper Deck high number packs.

		MT	NR MT	EX
Complete Set (10):		7.00	5.25	2.75
Common Aaron:		.50	.40	.20
Autographed card:		400.00	300.00	160.00
1	Aaron Header:	4.00	3.00	1.50
19	1954 Rookie Year	.50	.40	.20
20	1957 MVP	.50	.40	.20
21	1966 Move to Atlanta	.50	.40	.20
22	1970 3,000'	.50	.40	.20
23	1974 715'	.50	.40	.20
24	1975 Return to Milwaukee	.50	.40	.20
25	1976 755'	.50	.40	.20
26	1982 Hall of Fame	.50	.40	.20
27	Checklist - Heroes 19-27	.50	.40	.20

1991 Upper Deck Nolan Ryan Heroes

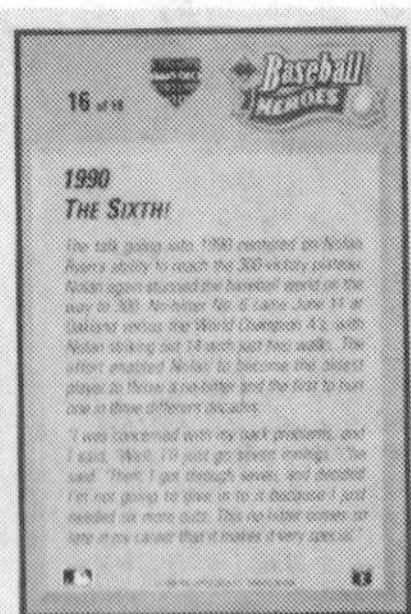

This set devoted to Nolan Ryan is numbered 10-18 and includes an unnumbered cover card that says "Baseball Heroes." The cards are found in foil, jumbo and boxes of low number Upper Deck packs.

	MT	NR MT	EX
Complete Set (10):	7.00	5.25	2.75
Common Ryan (1-9):	.50	.40	.20
Ryan Header NNO:	4.00	3.00	1.50
Autograph:	600.00	450.00	240.00

1991 Upper Deck Hall of Fame Heroes

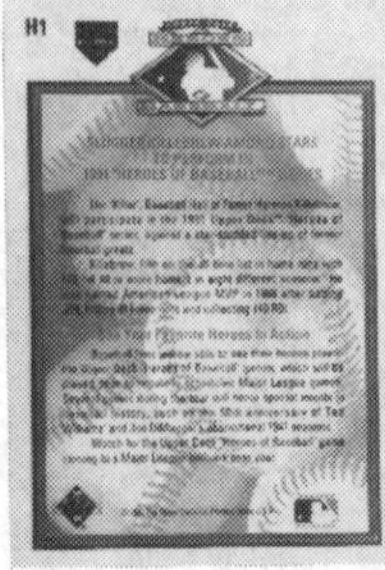

This four-card set features three members of Baseball's Hall of Fame: Harmon Killebrew, Gaylord Perry and Ferguson Jenkins. Each has a card for himself, plus there's a card which features all three players. The cards were found in specially-marked low number foil packs. The cards are numbered H1-H4. Upper Deck also produced 3,000 autographed and numbered cards for each player.

		MT	NR MT	EX
Complete Set (4):		45.00	30.00	15.00
Common HOF Hero (1-4):		15.00	10.00	5.00
Autograph:		120.00	80.00	40.00
1	Harmon Killebrew	15.00	10.00	5.00
2	Gaylord Perry	15.00	10.00	5.00
3	Ferguson Jenkins	15.00	10.00	5.00
4	Header Card:	15.00	10.00	5.00

1991 Upper Deck Silver Sluggers

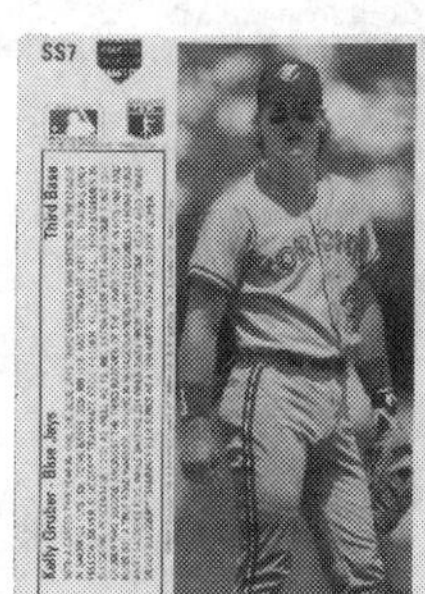

Each year the "Silver Slugger" award is presented to the player at each position with the highest batting average in the American and National Leagues. Upper Deck produced special cards in honor of the players who received this award for the 1990 season. The cards were randomly inserted in jumbo packs of Upper Deck cards. The cards feature a "SS" designation along with the card number. The cards are designed like the regular issue Upper Deck cards from 1991, but feature a Silver Slugger bat along the left border of the card.

		MT	NR MT	EX
Complete Set (18):		20.00	14.00	8.00
Common Player:		.50	.30	.15
1	Julio Franco	.50	.40	.20
2	Alan Trammell	.50	.40	.20
3	Rickey Henderson	1.50	1.25	.60
4	Jose Canseco	1.00	.70	.40
5	Barry Bonds	4.00	3.00	1.50
6	Eddie Murray	1.00	.70	.40
7	Kelly Gruber	.50	.40	.20
8	Ryne Sandberg	3.50	2.75	1.50
9	Darryl Strawberry	.75	.60	.30
10	Ellis Burks	.50	.40	.20
11	Lance Parrish	.50	.40	.20
12	Cecil Fielder	2.50	2.00	1.00
13	Matt Williams	.75	.60	.30
14	Dave Parker	.50	.40	.20
15	Bobby Bonilla	.75	.60	.30
16	Don Robinson	.50	.40	.20
17	Benito Santiago	.50	.40	.20
18	Barry Larkin	.75	.60	.30

1992 Upper Deck

Upper Deck introduced a new look in 1992. The baseline style was no longer used. The 1992 cards feature full-color action photos on white stock, with the player's name and the Upper Deck logo along the top border. The team name is inserted in the bottom right corner of the photo. Once again a 100-card high number series was released in late summer. Ted Williams autographed 2,500 Baseball Heroes cards which were randomly inserted into Upper Deck packs. Several subsets are also featured in the 1992 issue including Star Rookies and Top Prospects.

		MT	NR MT	EX
Complete Set (800):		40.00	30.00	15.00
Common Player:		.05	.04	.02
1	Star Rookie Checklist (Ryan Klesko/ Jim Thome)	.06	.05	.02
2	Royce Clayton (Star Rookie)	.20	.15	.08
3	*Brian Jordan* (Star Rookie)	.30	.25	.12
4	*Dave Fleming* (Star Rookie)	.20	.15	.08
5	*Jim Thome* (Star Rookie)	.25	.20	.10
6	Jeff Juden (Star Rookie)	.10	.08	.04
7	*Roberto Hernandez* (Star Rookie)	.10	.08	.04
8	Kyle Abbott (Star Rookie)(FC)	.10	.08	.04
9	*Chris George* (Star Rookie)	.20	.15	.08
10	*Rob Maurer* (Star Rookie)	.10	.08	.04
11	*Donald Harris* (Star Rookie)	.12	.09	.05
12	*Ted Wood* (Star Rookie)	.10	.08	.04
13	*Patrick Lennon* (Star Rookie)	.20	.15	.08
14	Willie Banks (Star Rookie)	.15	.11	.06
15	Roger Salkeld (Star Rookie)	.20	.15	.08
16	Wil Cordero (Star Rookie)	.25	.20	.10
17	*Arthur Rhodes* (Star Rookie)	.15	.11	.06
18	*Pedro Martinez* (Star Rookie)	.15	.11	.06
19	*Andy Ashby* (Star Rookie)	.10	.08	.04
20	Tom Goodwin (Star Rookie)	.15	.11	.06
21	*Braulio Castillo* (Star Rookie)	.10	.08	.04
22	Todd Van Poppel (Star Rookie)	.20	.15	.08
23	*Brian Williams* (Star Rookie)	.10	.08	.04
24	*Ryan Klesko* (Star Rookie)	.70	.50	.30
25	*Kenny Lofton* (Star Rookie)	.30	.25	.12
26	Derek Bell (Star Rookie)	.20	.15	.08
27	Reggie Sanders (Star Rookie)	.15	.11	.06
28	"Winfield's 400th" (Dave Winfield)	.10	.08	.04
29	Atlanta Braves Checklist (David Justice)	.05	.04	.02
30	Cincinnati Reds Checklist (Rob Dibble)	.05	.04	.02
31	Houston Astros Checklist (Craig Biggio)	.05	.04	.02
32	Los Angeles Dodgers Checklist (Eddie Murray)	.05	.04	.02
33	San Diego Padres Checklist (Fred McGriff)	.05	.04	.02
34	San Francisco Giants Checklist (Willie McGee)	.05	.04	.02
35	Chicago Cubs Checklist (Shawon Dunston)	.05	.04	.02
36	Montreal Expos Checklist (Delino DeShields)	.05	.04	.02
37	New York Mets Checklist (Howard Johnson)	.05	.04	.02
38	Philadelphia Phillies Checklist (John Kruk)	.05	.04	.02
39	Pittsburgh Pirates Checklist (Doug Drabeck)	.05	.04	.02
40	St. Louis Cardinals Checklist (Todd Zeile)	.05	.04	.02
41	"Playoff Perfection" (Steve Avery)	.10	.08	.04
42	*Jeremy Hernandez*	.20	.15	.08
43	*Doug Henry*	.20	.15	.08
44	*Chris Donnels*	.25	.20	.10
45	*Mo Sanford*(FC)	.20	.15	.08
46	*Scott Kamieniecki*	.15	.11	.06
47	Mark Lemke	.06	.05	.02
48	Steve Farr	.05	.04	.02
49	Francisco Oliveras	.05	.04	.02
50	*Ced Landrum*(FC)	.10	.08	.04
51	Top Prospect Checklist (Marc Newfield/ Rondell White)	.06	.05	.02
52	*Eduardo Perez* (Top Prospect)	.90	.70	.35
53	*Tom Nevers* (Top Prospect)	.20	.15	.08
54	*David Zancanaro* (Top Prospect)	.20	.15	.08
55	*Shawn Green* (Top Prospect)	.20	.15	.08
56	*Mark Wohlers* (Top Prospect)	.20	.15	.08
57	*Dave Nilsson* (Top Prospect)	.10	.08	.04
58	*Dmitri Young* (Top Prospect)	.25	.20	.10
59	*Ryan Hawblitzel* (Top Prospect)	.15	.11	.06
60	*Raul Mondesi* (Top Prospect)	.30	.25	.12
61	Rondell White (Top Prospect)	.75	.60	.30

		MT	NR MT	EX
62	Steve Hosey (Top Prospect)	.20	.15	.08
63	*Manny Ramirez* (Top Prospect)	1.00	.70	.40
64	Marc Newfield (Top Prospect)	.50	.40	.20
65	Jeromy Burnitz (Top Prospect)(FC)	.40	.30	.15
66	*Mark Smith* (Top Prospect)	.10	.08	.04
67	*Joey Hamilton* (Top Prospect)	.20	.15	.08
68	*Tyler Green* (Top Prospect)	.15	.11	.06
69	*John Farrell* (Top Prospect)	.15	.11	.06
70	*Kurt Miller* (Top Prospect)	.20	.15	.08
71	*Jeff Plympton* (Top Prosepct)	.10	.08	.04
72	Dan Wilson (Top Prospect)(FC)	.35	.25	.14
73	*Joe Vitiello* (Top Prospect)	.40	.30	.15
74	Rico Brogna (Top Prospect)(FC)	.10	.08	.04
75	*David McCarty* (Top Prospect)	1.50	1.25	.60
76	*Bob Wickman* (Top Prospect)	.40	.30	.15
77	*Carlos Rodriguez* (Top Prospect)	.15	.11	.06
78	"Stay in School" (Jim Abbott)	.10	.08	.04
79	Bloodlines (Ramon & Pedro Martinez)	.10	.08	.04
80	Bloodlines (Kevin & Keith Mitchell)	.10	.08	.04
81	Bloodlines (Sandy Jr. & Roberto Alomar)	.10	.08	.04
82	Bloodlines (Cal Jr. & Billy Ripken)	.15	.11	.06
83	Bloodlines (Tony & Chris Gwynn)	.10	.08	.04
84	Bloodlines (Dwight Gooden & Gary Sheffield)	.10	.08	.04
85	Bloodlines (Ken Sr., Ken Jr. & Craig Griffey)	.80	.60	.30
86	California Angels Checklist (Jim Abbott)	.05	.04	.02
87	Chicago White Sox Checklist (Frank Thomas)	.20	.15	.08
88	Kansas City Royals Checklist (Danny Tartabull)	.05	.04	.02
89	Minnesota Twins Checklist (Scott Erickson)	.05	.04	.02
90	Oakland Athletics Checklist (Rickey Henderson)	.05	.04	.02
91	Seattle Mariners Checklist (Edgar Martinez)	.05	.04	.02
92	Texas Rangers Checklist (Nolan Ryan)	.20	.15	.08
93	Baltimore Orioles Checklist (Ben McDonald)	.05	.04	.02
94	Boston Red Sox Checklist (Ellis Burks)	.05	.04	.02
95	Cleveland Indians Checklist (Greg Swindell)	.05	.04	.02
96	Detroit Tigers Checklist (Cecil Fielder)	.10	.08	.04
97	Milwaukee Brewers Checklist (Greg Vaughn)	.05	.04	.02
98	New York Yankees Checklist (Kevin Maas)	.05	.04	.02
99	Toronto Blue Jays Checklist (Dave Steib)	.05	.04	.02
100	Checklist 1-100	.05	.04	.02
101	Joe Oliver	.05	.04	.02
102	Hector Villanueva	.06	.05	.02
103	Ed Whitson	.05	.04	.02
104	Danny Jackson	.05	.04	.02
105	Chris Hammond	.06	.05	.02
106	Ricky Jordan	.06	.05	.02
107	Kevin Bass	.05	.04	.02
108	Darrin Fletcher	.05	.04	.02
109	Junior Ortiz	.05	.04	.02
110	Tom Bolton	.05	.04	.02
111	Jeff King	.06	.05	.02
112	Dave Magadan	.08	.06	.03
113	Mike LaValliere	.06	.05	.02
114	Hubie Brooks	.06	.05	.02
115	Jay Bell	.06	.05	.02
116	David Wells	.05	.04	.02
117	Jim Leyritz	.05	.04	.02
118	Manuel Lee	.05	.04	.02
119	Alvaro Espinoza	.05	.04	.02
120	B.J. Surhoff	.06	.05	.02
121	Hal Morris	.20	.15	.08
122	Shawon Dunston	.08	.06	.03
123	Chris Sabo	.10	.08	.04
124	Andre Dawson	.15	.11	.06
125	Eric Davis	.15	.11	.06
126	Chili Davis	.08	.06	.03
127	Dale Murphy	.10	.08	.04
128	Kirk McCaskill	.06	.05	.02
129	Terry Mulholland	.06	.05	.02
130	Rick Aguilera	.08	.06	.03
131	Vince Coleman	.10	.08	.04
132	Andy Van Slyke	.12	.09	.05
133	Gregg Jefferies	.15	.11	.06

		MT	NR MT	EX
134	Barry Bonds	.20	.15	.08
135	Dwight Gooden	.15	.11	.06
136	Dave Stieb	.08	.06	.03
137	Albert Belle	.25	.20	.10
138	Teddy Higuera	.08	.06	.03
139	Jesse Barfield	.08	.06	.03
140	Pat Borders	.06	.05	.02
141	Bip Roberts	.06	.05	.02
142	Rob Dibble	.10	.08	.04
143	Mark Grace	.15	.11	.06
144	Barry Larkin	.15	.11	.06
145	Ryne Sandberg	.25	.20	.10
146	Scott Erickson	.10	.08	.04
147	Luis Polonia	.06	.05	.02
148	John Burkett	.06	.05	.02
149	Luis Sojo	.06	.05	.02
150	Dickie Thon	.05	.04	.02
151	Walt Weiss	.06	.05	.02
152	Mike Scioscia	.06	.05	.02
153	Mark McGwire	.12	.09	.05
154	Matt Williams	.15	.11	.06
155	Rickey Henderson	.25	.20	.10
156	Sandy Alomar, Jr.	.10	.08	.04
157	Brian McRae	.25	.20	.10
158	Harold Baines	.08	.06	.03
159	Kevin Appier	.06	.05	.02
160	Felix Fermin	.05	.04	.02
161	Leo Gomez	.15	.11	.06
162	Craig Biggio	.10	.08	.04
163	Ben McDonald	.20	.15	.08
164	Randy Johnson	.08	.06	.03
165	Cal Ripken, Jr.	.30	.25	.12
166	Frank Thomas	1.00	.70	.40
167	Delino DeShields	.08	.06	.03
168	Greg Gagne	.05	.04	.02
169	Ron Karkovice	.05	.04	.02
170	Charlie Leibrandt	.05	.04	.02
171	Dave Righetti	.08	.06	.03
172	Dave Henderson	.10	.08	.04
173	Steve Decker	.15	.11	.06
174	Darryl Strawberry	.10	.08	.04
175	Will Clark	.25	.20	.10
176	Ruben Sierra	.15	.11	.06
177	Ozzie Smith	.15	.11	.06
178	Charles Nagy	.08	.06	.03
179	Gary Pettis	.05	.04	.02
180	Kirk Gibson	.08	.06	.03
181	Randy Milligan	.06	.05	.02
182	Dave Valle	.05	.04	.02
183	Chris Hoiles	.10	.08	.04
184	Tony Phillips	.05	.04	.02
185	Brady Anderson	.05	.04	.02
186	Scott Fletcher	.05	.04	.02
187	Gene Larkin	.05	.04	.02
188	Lance Johnson	.05	.04	.02
189	Greg Olson	.05	.04	.02
190	Melido Perez	.05	.04	.02
191	Lenny Harris	.05	.04	.02
192	Terry Kennedy	.05	.04	.02
193	Mike Gallego	.05	.04	.02
194	Willie McGee	.08	.06	.03
195	Juan Samuel	.06	.05	.02
196	Jeff Huson	.05	.04	.02
197	Alex Cole	.06	.05	.02
198	Ron Robinson	.06	.05	.02
199	Joel Skinner	.06	.05	.02
200	Checklist 101-200	.06	.05	.02
201	Kevin Reimer	.06	.05	.02
202	Stan Belinda	.05	.04	.02
203	Pat Tabler	.05	.04	.02
204	Jose Guzman	.05	.04	.02
205	Jose Lind	.05	.04	.02
206	Spike Owen	.05	.04	.02
207	Joe Orsulak	.05	.04	.02
208	Charlie Hayes	.05	.04	.02
209	Mike Devereaux	.06	.05	.02
210	Mike Fitzgerald	.05	.04	.02
211	Willie Randolph	.05	.04	.02
212	Rod Nichols	.05	.04	.02
213	Mike Boddicker	.05	.04	.02
214	Bill Spiers	.05	.04	.02
215	Steve Olin	.05	.04	.02
216	*David Howard*(FC)	.10	.08	.04
217	Gary Varsho	.05	.04	.02
218	Mike Harkey	.06	.05	.02
219	Luis Aquino	.05	.04	.02
220	Chuck McElroy	.05	.04	.02
221	Doug Drabek	.08	.06	.03
222	Dave Winfield	.15	.11	.06
223	Rafael Palmeiro	.12	.09	.05
224	Joe Carter	.12	.09	.05

		MT	NR MT	EX
225	Bobby Bonilla	.12	.09	.05
226	Ivan Calderon	.10	.08	.04
227	Gregg Olson	.10	.08	.04
228	Tim Wallach	.08	.06	.03
229	Terry Pendleton	.10	.08	.04
230	Gilberto Reyes(FC)	.08	.06	.03
231	Carlos Baerga	.10	.08	.04
232	Greg Vaughn	.10	.08	.04
233	Bret Saberhagen	.10	.08	.04
234	Gary Sheffield	.10	.08	.04
235	Mark Lewis	.10	.08	.04
236	George Bell	.10	.08	.04
237	Danny Tartabull	.10	.08	.04
238	Willie Wilson	.06	.05	.02
239	Doug Dascenzo	.05	.04	.02
240	Bill Pecota	.05	.04	.02
241	Julio Franco	.08	.06	.03
242	Ed Sprague	.10	.08	.04
243	Juan Gonzalez	.80	.60	.30
244	Chuck Finley	.10	.08	.04
245	*Ivan Rodriguez*	.50	.40	.20
246	Lenny Dykstra	.10	.08	.04
247	Deion Sanders	.15	.11	.06
248	Dwight Evans	.08	.06	.03
249	Larry Walker	.10	.08	.04
250	Billy Ripken	.05	.04	.02
251	Mickey Tettleton	.06	.05	.02
252	Tony Pena	.06	.05	.02
253	Benito Santiago	.08	.06	.03
254	Kirby Puckett	.20	.15	.08
255	Cecil Fielder	.20	.15	.08
256	Howard Johnson	.06	.05	.02
257	Andujar Cedeno	.06	.05	.02
258	Jose Rijo	.08	.06	.03
259	Al Osuna	.05	.04	.02
260	Todd Hundley	.06	.05	.02
261	Orel Hershiser	.08	.06	.03
262	Ray Lankford	.08	.06	.03
263	Robin Ventura	.15	.11	.06
264	Felix Jose	.10	.08	.04
265	Eddie Murray	.15	.11	.06
266	Kevin Mitchell	.08	.06	.03
267	Gary Carter	.10	.08	.04
268	Mike Benjamin	.05	.04	.02
269	Dick Schofield	.05	.04	.02
270	Jose Uribe	.05	.04	.02
271	Pete Incaviglia	.06	.05	.02
272	Tony Fernandez	.08	.06	.03
273	Alan Trammell	.10	.08	.04
274	Tony Gwynn	.15	.11	.06
275	Mike Greenwell	.10	.08	.04
276	*Jeff Bagwell*	.70	.50	.30
277	Frank Viola	.10	.08	.04
278	Randy Myers	.06	.05	.02
279	Ken Caminiti	.06	.05	.02
280	Bill Doran	.06	.05	.02
281	Dan Pasqua	.05	.04	.02
282	Alfredo Griffin	.05	.04	.02
283	Jose Oquendo	.05	.04	.02
284	Kal Daniels	.08	.06	.03
285	Bobby Thigpen	.08	.06	.03
286	Robby Thompson	.05	.04	.02
287	Mark Eichhorn	.05	.04	.02
288	Mike Felder	.05	.04	.02
289	Dave Gallagher	.05	.04	.02
290	Dave Anderson	.05	.04	.02
291	Mel Hall	.06	.05	.02
292	Jerald Clark	.06	.05	.02
293	Al Newman	.05	.04	.02
294	Rob Deer	.05	.04	.02
295	Matt Nokes	.06	.05	.02
296	Jack Armstrong	.06	.05	.02
297	Jim Deshaies	.05	.04	.02
298	Jeff Innis	.05	.04	.02
299	Jeff Reed	.05	.04	.02
300	Checklist 201-300	.05	.04	.02
301	Lonnie Smith	.05	.04	.02
302	Jimmy Key	.06	.05	.02
303	Junior Felix	.08	.06	.03
304	Mike Heath	.05	.04	.02
305	Mark Langston	.10	.08	.04
306	Greg W. Harris	.06	.05	.02
307	Brett Butler	.08	.06	.03
308	Luis Rivera	.05	.04	.02
309	Bruce Ruffin	.05	.04	.02
310	Paul Faries	.08	.06	.03
311	Terry Leach	.05	.04	.02
312	*Scott Brosius*(FC)	.15	.11	.06
313	Scott Leius	.08	.06	.03
314	Harold Reynolds	.08	.06	.03
315	Jack Morris	.10	.08	.04

		MT	NR MT	EX
316	David Segui	.10	.08	.04
317	Bill Gullickson	.06	.05	.02
318	Todd Frohwirth	.05	.04	.02
319	*Mark Leiter*(FC)	.10	.08	.04
320	Jeff M. Robinson	.05	.04	.02
321	Gary Gaetti	.08	.06	.03
322	John Smotlz	.10	.08	.04
323	Andy Benes	.10	.08	.04
324	Kelly Gruber	.08	.06	.03
325	Jim Abbott	.10	.08	.04
326	John Kruk	.06	.05	.02
327	Kevin Seitzer	.06	.05	.02
328	Darrin Jackson	.05	.04	.02
329	Kurt Stillwell	.05	.04	.02
330	Mike Maddux	.05	.04	.02
331	Dennis Eckersley	.10	.08	.04
332	Dan Gladden	.05	.04	.02
333	Jose Canseco	.10	.08	.04
334	Kent Hrbek	.06	.05	.02
335	Ken Griffey, Sr.	.06	.05	.02
336	Greg Swindell	.08	.06	.03
337	Trevor Wilson	.06	.05	.02
338	Sam Horn	.05	.04	.02
339	Mike Henneman	.06	.05	.02
340	Jerry Browne	.05	.04	.02
341	Glenn Braggs	.05	.04	.02
342	Tom Glavine	.10	.08	.04
343	Wally Joyner	.10	.08	.04
344	Fred McGriff	.10	.08	.04
345	Ron Gant	.15	.11	.06
346	Ramon Martinez	.15	.11	.06
347	Wes Chamberlain	.20	.15	.08
348	Terry Shumpert	.05	.04	.02
349	Tim Teufel	.05	.04	.02
350	Wally Backman	.05	.04	.02
351	Joe Girardi	.05	.04	.02
352	Devon White	.08	.06	.03
353	Greg Maddux	.08	.06	.03
354	*Ryan Bowen*	.15	.11	.06
355	Roberto Alomar	.25	.20	.10
356	Don Mattingly	.25	.20	.10
357	Pedro Guerrero	.10	.08	.04
358	Steve Sax	.10	.08	.04
359	Joey Cora	.05	.04	.02
360	Jim Gantner	.05	.04	.02
361	Brian Barnes	.10	.08	.04
362	Kevin McReynolds	.10	.08	.04
363	*Bret Barberie*(FC)	.15	.11	.06
364	David Cone	.08	.06	.03
365	Dennis Martinez	.08	.06	.03
366	*Brian Hunter*	.12	.09	.05
367	Edgar Martinez	.08	.06	.03
368	Steve Finley	.08	.06	.03
369	Greg Briley	.05	.04	.02
370	Jeff Blauser	.05	.04	.02
371	Todd Stottlemyre	.06	.05	.02
372	Luis Gonzalez	.08	.06	.03
373	*Rick Wilkins*	.25	.20	.10
374	*Darryl Kile*	.15	.11	.06
375	John Olerud	.25	.20	.10
376	Lee Smith	.08	.06	.03
377	Kevin Maas	.08	.06	.03
378	Dante Bichette	.06	.05	.02
379	Tom Pagnozzi	.06	.05	.02
380	Mike Flanagan	.05	.04	.02
381	Charlie O'Brien	.05	.04	.02
382	Dave Martinez	.05	.04	.02
383	Keith Miller	.05	.04	.02
384	Scott Ruskin	.05	.04	.02
385	Kevin Elster	.05	.04	.02
386	Alvin Davis	.08	.06	.03
387	Casey Candaele	.05	.04	.02
388	Pete O'Brien	.05	.04	.02
389	Jeff Treadway	.05	.04	.02
390	Scott Bradley	.05	.04	.02
391	Mookie Wilson	.05	.04	.02
392	Jimmy Jones	.05	.04	.02
393	Candy Maldonado	.05	.04	.02
394	Eric Yelding	.05	.04	.02
395	Tom Henke	.06	.05	.02
396	Franklin Stubbs	.05	.04	.02
397	Milt Thompson	.05	.04	.02
398	Mark Carreon	.05	.04	.02
399	Randy Velarde	.05	.04	.02
400	Checklist 301-400	.05	.04	.02
401	Omar Vizquel	.05	.04	.02
402	Joe Boever	.05	.04	.02
403	Bill Krueger	.05	.04	.02
404	Jody Reed	.06	.05	.02
405	Mike Schooler	.06	.05	.02
406	Jason Grimsley	.06	.05	.02

		MT	NR MT	EX
407	Greg Myers	.05	.04	.02
408	Randy Ready	.05	.04	.02
409	*Mike Timlin*	.08	.06	.03
410	Mitch Williams	.08	.06	.03
411	Garry Templeton	.06	.05	.02
412	Greg Cadaret	.05	.04	.02
413	Donnie Hill	.05	.04	.02
414	Wally Whitehurst	.05	.04	.02
415	Scott Sanderson	.06	.05	.02
416	Thomas Howard	.06	.05	.02
417	Neal Heaton	.05	.04	.02
418	Charlie Hough	.06	.05	.02
419	Jack Howell	.05	.04	.02
420	Greg Hibbard	.06	.05	.02
421	Carlos Quintana	.06	.05	.02
422	*Kim Batiste*(FC)	.10	.08	.04
423	Paul Molitor	.15	.11	.06
424	Ken Griffey, Jr.	.80	.60	.30
425	Phil Plantier	.18	.14	.07
426	*Denny Neagle*(FC)	.08	.06	.03
427	Von Hayes	.06	.05	.02
428	Shane Mack	.08	.06	.03
429	Darren Daulton	.06	.05	.02
430	Dwayne Henry	.05	.04	.02
431	Lance Parrish	.06	.05	.02
432	*Mike Humphreys*(FC)	.10	.08	.04
433	Tim Burke	.05	.04	.02
434	Bryan Harvey	.06	.05	.02
435	Pat Kelly	.10	.08	.04
436	Ozzie Guillen	.08	.06	.03
437	Bruce Hurst	.06	.05	.02
438	Sammy Sosa	.08	.06	.03
439	Dennis Rasmussen	.05	.04	.02
440	Ken Patterson	.05	.04	.02
441	Jay Buhner	.08	.06	.03
442	Pat Combs	.06	.05	.02
443	Wade Boggs	.15	.11	.06
444	George Brett	.15	.11	.06
445	Mo Vaughn	.35	.25	.14
446	Chuck Knoblauch	.35	.25	.14
447	Tom Candiotti	.06	.05	.02
448	Mark Portugal	.05	.04	.02
449	Mickey Morandini	.10	.08	.04
450	Duane Ward	.05	.04	.02
451	Otis Nixon	.05	.04	.02
452	Bob Welch	.08	.06	.03
453	*Rusty Meacham*(FC)	.10	.08	.04
454	*Keith Mitchell*	.10	.08	.04
455	Marquis Grissom	.10	.08	.04
456	Robin Yount	.20	.15	.08
457	*Harvey Pulliam*(FC)	.08	.06	.03
458	Jose DeLeon	.05	.04	.02
459	Mark Gubicza	.06	.05	.02
460	Darryl Hamilton	.06	.05	.02
461	Tom Browning	.08	.06	.03
462	Monty Fariss	.10	.08	.04
463	Jerome Walton	.10	.08	.04
464	Paul O'Neill	.08	.06	.03
465	Dean Palmer	.20	.15	.08
466	Travis Fryman	.20	.15	.08
467	John Smiley	.06	.05	.02
468	Lloyd Moseby	.05	.04	.02
469	*John Wehner*(FC)	.08	.06	.03
470	Skeeter Barnes(FC)	.06	.05	.02
471	Steve Chitren	.06	.05	.02
472	Kent Mercker	.06	.05	.02
473	Terry Steinbach	.06	.05	.02
474	Andres Galarraga	.08	.06	.03
475	Steve Avery	.20	.15	.08
476	Tom Gordon	.10	.08	.04
477	Cal Eldred	.15	.11	.06
478	Omar Olivares(FC)	.08	.06	.03
479	Julio Machado	.05	.04	.02
480	Bob Milacki	.05	.04	.02
481	Les Lancaster	.05	.04	.02
482	John Candelaria	.05	.04	.02
483	Brian Downing	.05	.04	.02
484	Roger McDowell	.05	.04	.02
485	Scott Scudder	.05	.04	.02
486	Zane Smith	.06	.05	.02
487	John Cerutti	.05	.04	.02
488	Steve Buechele	.06	.05	.02
489	Paul Gibson	.05	.04	.02
490	Curtis Wilkerson	.05	.04	.02
491	Marvin Freeman	.05	.04	.02
492	Tom Foley	.05	.04	.02
493	Juan Berenguer	.05	.04	.02
494	Ernest Riles	.05	.04	.02
495	Sid Bream	.06	.05	.02
496	Chuck Crim	.05	.04	.02
497	Mike Macfarlane	.05	.04	.02
498	Dale Sveum	.05	.04	.02
499	Storm Davis	.05	.04	.02
500	Checklist 401-500	.05	.04	.02
501	Jeff Reardon	.08	.06	.03
502	Shawn Abner	.05	.04	.02
503	Tony Fossas	.05	.04	.02
504	Cory Snyder	.05	.04	.02
505	Matt Young	.05	.04	.02
506	Allan Anderson	.05	.04	.02
507	Mark Lee	.05	.04	.02
508	Gene Nelson	.05	.04	.02
509	Mike Pagliarulo	.05	.04	.02
510	Rafael Belliard	.05	.04	.02
511	Jay Howell	.06	.05	.02
512	Bob Tewksbury	.05	.04	.02
513	Mike Morgan	.05	.04	.02
514	John Franco	.06	.05	.02
515	Kevin Gross	.05	.04	.02
516	Lou Whitaker	.08	.06	.03
517	Orlando Merced	.10	.08	.04
518	Todd Benzinger	.05	.04	.02
519	Gary Redus	.05	.04	.02
520	Walt Terrell	.05	.04	.02
521	Jack Clark	.08	.06	.03
522	Dave Parker	.10	.08	.04
523	Tim Naehring	.10	.08	.04
524	Mark Whiten	.15	.11	.06
525	Ellis Burks	.10	.08	.04
526	*Frank Castillo*	.10	.08	.04
527	Brian Harper	.06	.05	.02
528	Brook Jacoby	.06	.05	.02
529	Rick Sutcliffe	.06	.05	.02
530	Joe Klink	.05	.04	.02
531	Terry Bross	.05	.04	.02
532	Jose Offerman	.10	.08	.04
533	Todd Zeile	.12	.09	.05
534	Eric Karros	.30	.25	.12
535	*Anthony Young*	.08	.06	.03
536	Milt Cuyler	.10	.08	.04
537	Randy Tomlin	.08	.06	.03
538	*Scott Livingstone*	.08	.06	.03
539	Jim Eisenreich	.05	.04	.02
540	Don Slaught	.05	.04	.02
541	Scott Cooper(FC)	.08	.06	.03
542	Joe Grahe	.06	.05	.02
543	Tom Brunansky	.06	.05	.02
544	Eddie Zosky	.10	.08	.04
545	Roger Clemens	.20	.15	.08
546	David Justice	.30	.25	.12
547	Dave Stewart	.10	.08	.04
548	David West	.05	.04	.02
549	Dave Smith	.06	.05	.02
550	Dan Plesac	.06	.05	.02
551	Alex Fernandez	.20	.15	.08
552	Bernard Gilkey	.10	.08	.04
553	Jack McDowell	.10	.08	.04
554	Tino Martinez	.10	.08	.04
555	Bo Jackson	.30	.25	.12
556	Bernie Williams	.10	.08	.04
557	Mark Gardner	.06	.05	.02
558	Glenallen Hill	.08	.06	.03
559	Oil Can Boyd	.05	.04	.02
560	Chris James	.05	.04	.02
561	*Scott Servais*	.10	.08	.04
562	*Rey Sanchez*(FC)	.20	.15	.08
563	*Paul McClellan*(FC)	.08	.06	.03
564	*Andy Mota*	.08	.06	.03
565	Darren Lewis	.08	.06	.03
566	*Jose Melendez*(FC)	.08	.06	.03
567	Tommy Greene	.08	.06	.03
568	Rich Rodriguez	.06	.05	.02
569	*Heathcliff Slocumb*	.10	.08	.04
570	Joe Hesketh	.05	.04	.02
571	Carlton Fisk	.08	.06	.03
572	Erik Hanson	.10	.08	.04
573	Wilson Alvarez	.10	.08	.04
574	*Rheal Cormier*(FC)	.20	.15	.08
575	Tim Raines	.10	.08	.04
576	Bobby Witt	.06	.05	.02
577	Roberto Kelly	.10	.08	.04
578	Kevin Brown	.06	.05	.02
579	Chris Nabholz	.06	.05	.02
580	Jesse Orosco	.05	.04	.02
581	Jeff Brantley	.06	.05	.02
582	Rafael Ramirez	.05	.04	.02
583	Kelly Downs	.05	.04	.02
584	Mike Simms	.10	.08	.04
585	*Mike Remlinger*	.10	.08	.04
586	Dave Hollins	.08	.06	.03
587	Larry Andersen	.05	.04	.02
588	Mike Gardiner	.08	.06	.03

		MT	NR MT	EX
589	Craig Lefferts	.05	.04	.02
590	Paul Assenmacher	.05	.04	.02
591	Bryn Smith	.05	.04	.02
592	Donn Pall	.05	.04	.02
593	Mike Jackson	.05	.04	.02
594	Scott Radinsky	.05	.04	.02
595	Brian Holman	.06	.05	.02
596	Geronimo Pena	.08	.06	.03
597	Mike Jeffcoat	.05	.04	.02
598	Carlos Martinez	.05	.04	.02
599	Geno Petralli	.05	.04	.02
600	Checklist 501-600	.05	.04	.02
601	Jerry Don Gleaton	.05	.04	.02
602	Adam Peterson	.05	.04	.02
603	Craig Grebeck	.05	.04	.02
604	Mark Guthrie	.05	.04	.02
605	Frank Tanana	.05	.04	.02
606	Hensley Meulens	.08	.06	.03
607	Mark Davis	.05	.04	.02
608	Eric Plunk	.05	.04	.02
609	Mark Williamson	.05	.04	.02
610	Lee Guetterman	.05	.04	.02
611	Bobby Rose	.05	.04	.02
612	Bill Wegman	.06	.05	.02
613	Mike Hartley	.05	.04	.02
614	*Chris Beasley*(FC)	.10	.08	.04
615	Chris Bosio	.05	.04	.02
616	Henry Cotto	.05	.04	.02
617	*Chico Walker*(FC)	.10	.08	.04
618	Russ Swan	.05	.04	.02
619	Bob Walk	.05	.04	.02
620	Billy Swift	.05	.04	.02
621	*Warren Newson*	.15	.11	.06
622	Steve Bedrosian	.05	.04	.02
623	*Ricky Bones*(FC)	.08	.06	.03
624	Kevin Tapani	.10	.08	.04
625	*Juan Guzman*(FC)	.40	.30	.15
626	*Jeff Johnson*(FC)	.08	.06	.03
627	Jeff Montgomery	.06	.05	.02
628	Ken Hill	.06	.05	.02
629	Gary Thurman	.05	.04	.02
630	Steve Howe	.06	.05	.02
631	Jose DeJesus	.06	.05	.02
632	Bert Blyleven	.06	.05	.02
633	Jaime Navarro	.06	.05	.02
634	Lee Stevens	.08	.06	.03
635	Pete Harnisch	.08	.06	.03
636	Bill Landrum	.05	.04	.02
637	Rich DeLucia	.06	.05	.02
638	Luis Salazar	.05	.04	.02
639	Rob Murphy	.05	.04	.02
640	A.L. Diamond Skills Checklist (Rickey Henderson/ Jose Canseco)	.05	.04	.02
641	Roger Clemens (Diamond Skills)	.10	.08	.04
642	Jim Abbott (Diamond Skills)	.08	.06	.03
643	Travis Fryman (Diamond Skills)	.25	.20	.10
644	Jesse Barfield (Diamond Skills)	.10	.08	.04
645	Cal Ripken, Jr. (Diamond Skills)	.25	.20	.10
646	Wade Boggs (Diamond Skills)	.10	.08	.04
647	Cecil Fielder (Diamond Skills)	.10	.08	.04
648	Rickey Henderson (Diamond Skills)	.10	.08	.04
649	Jose Canseco (Diamond Skills)	.10	.08	.04
650	Ken Griffey, Jr. (Diamond Skills)	.50	.40	.20
651	Kenny Rogers	.05	.04	.02
652	*Luis Mercedes*(FC)	.10	.08	.04
653	Mike Stanton	.06	.05	.02
654	Glenn Davis	.10	.08	.04
655	Nolan Ryan	.40	.30	.15
656	Reggie Jefferson	.10	.08	.04
657	*Javier Ortiz*(FC)	.08	.06	.03
658	Greg A. Harris	.05	.04	.02
659	Mariano Duncan	.06	.05	.02
660	Jeff Shaw	.05	.04	.02
661	Mike Moore	.06	.05	.02
662	*Chris Haney*	.08	.06	.03
663	*Joe Slusarski*	.08	.06	.03
664	*Wayne Housie*(FC)	.20	.15	.08
665	Carlos Garcia(FC)	.08	.06	.03
666	Bob Ojeda	.05	.04	.02
667	*Bryan Hickerson*(FC)	.20	.15	.08
668	Tim Belcher	.06	.05	.02
669	Ron Darling	.06	.05	.02
670	Rex Hudler	.05	.04	.02
671	Sid Fernandez	.08	.06	.03
672	*Chito Martinez*	.08	.06	.03
673	*Pete Schourek*	.06	.05	.02
674	*Armando Renoso*(FC)	.15	.11	.06
675	Mike Mussina	.50	.40	.20
676	Kevin Morton(FC)	.08	.06	.03
677	Norm Charlton	.06	.05	.02
678	Danny Darwin	.05	.04	.02

		MT	NR MT	EX
679	Eric King	.05	.04	.02
680	Ted Power	.05	.04	.02
681	Barry Jones	.05	.04	.02
682	Carney Lansford	.08	.06	.03
683	Mel Rojas	.06	.05	.02
684	Rick Honeycutt	.05	.04	.02
685	*Jeff Fassero*(FC)	.10	.08	.04
686	Cris Carpenter	.06	.05	.02
687	Tim Crews	.05	.04	.02
688	Scott Terry	.05	.04	.02
689	Chris Gwynn	.05	.04	.02
690	Gerald Perry	.05	.04	.02
691	John Barfield	.05	.04	.02
692	Bob Melvin	.05	.04	.02
693	Juan Agosto	.05	.04	.02
694	Alejandro Pena	.06	.05	.02
695	Jeff Russell	.06	.05	.02
696	Carmelo Martinez	.05	.04	.02
697	Bud Black	.05	.04	.02
698	Dave Otto	.05	.04	.02
699	Billy Hatcher	.05	.04	.02
700	Checklist 601-700	.05	.04	.02
701	Clemente Nunez(FC)	.20	.15	.08
702	"Rookie Threats" (Donovan Osborne/ Brian Jordan/ Mark Clark)	.12	.09	.05
703	Mike Morgan	.06	.05	.02
704	Keith Miller	.06	.05	.02
705	Kurt Stillwell	.06	.05	.02
706	Damon Berryhill	.06	.05	.02
707	Von Hayes	.06	.05	.02
708	Rick Sutcliffe	.10	.08	.04
709	Hubie Brooks	.06	.05	.02
710	Ryan Turner(FC)	.30	.25	.12
711	N.L. Diamond Skills Checklist (Barry Bonds/ Andy Van Slyke)	.06	.05	.02
712	Jose Rijo (Diamond Skills)	.06	.05	.02
713	Tom Glavine (Diamond Skills)	.10	.08	.04
714	Shawon Dunston (Diamond Skills)	.08	.06	.03
715	Andy Van Slyke (Diamond Skills)	.08	.06	.03
716	Ozzie Smith (Diamond Skills)	.15	.11	.06
717	Tony Gwynn (Diamond Skills)	.20	.15	.08
718	Will Clark (Diamond Skills)	.20	.15	.08
719	Marquis Grissom (Diamond Skills)	.08	.06	.03
720	Howard Johnson (Diamond Skills)	.08	.06	.03
721	Barry Bonds (Diamond Skills)	.20	.15	.08
722	Kirk McCaskill	.06	.05	.02
723	Sammy Sosa	.06	.05	.02
724	George Bell	.08	.06	.03
725	Gregg Jefferies	.08	.06	.03
726	Gary DiSarcina	.06	.05	.02
727	Mike Bordick	.12	.09	.05
728	"400 Home Run Club" (Eddie Murray)	.12	.09	.05
729	Rene Gonzales	.06	.05	.02
730	Mike Bielecki	.06	.05	.02
731	Calvin Jones(FC)	.12	.09	.05
732	Jack Morris	.05	.04	.02
733	Frank Viola	.05	.04	.02
734	Dave Winfield	.15	.11	.06
735	Kevin Mitchell	.12	.09	.05
736	Billy Swift	.08	.06	.03
737	Dan Gladden	.06	.05	.02
738	Mike Jackson	.06	.05	.02
739	Mark Carreon	.06	.05	.02
740	Kirt Manwaring	.06	.05	.02
741	Randy Myers	.06	.05	.02
742	Kevin McReynolds	.08	.06	.03
743	Steve Sax	.08	.06	.03
744	Wally Joyner	.08	.06	.03
745	Gary Sheffield	.30	.25	.12
746	Danny Tartabull	.06	.05	.02
747	Julio Valera	.10	.08	.04
748	Denny Neagle	.10	.08	.04
749	Lance Blankenship	.06	.05	.02
750	Mike Gallego	.06	.05	.02
751	Bret Saberhagen	.05	.04	.02
752	Ruben Amaro(FC)	.15	.11	.06
753	Eddie Murray	.15	.11	.06
754	Kyle Abbott	.15	.11	.06
755	Bobby Bonilla	.15	.11	.06
756	Eric Davis	.15	.11	.06
757	Eddie Taubensee(FC)	.20	.15	.08
758	Andres Galarraga	.08	.06	.03
759	Pete Incaviglia	.08	.06	.03
760	Tom Candiotti	.08	.06	.03
761	Tim Belcher	.08	.06	.03
762	Ricky Bones	.15	.11	.06
763	Bip Roberts	.08	.06	.03
764	Pedro Munoz	.20	.15	.08
765	Greg Swindell	.08	.06	.03
766	Kenny Lofton	.25	.20	.10

		MT	NR MT	EX
767	Gary Carter	.08	.06	.03
768	Charlie Hayes	.06	.05	.02
769	Dickie Thon	.06	.05	.02
770	Diamond Debuts Checklist (Donovan Osborne)	.06	.05	.02
771	Bret Boone (Diamond Debuts)(FC)	.50	.40	.20
772	Archi Cianfrocco (Diamond Debuts)(FC)	.25	.20	.10
773	Mark Clark (Diamond Debuts)(FC)	.25	.20	.10
774	Chad Curtis (Diamond Debuts)(FC)	.70	.50	.30
775	Pat Listach (Diamond Debuts)(FC)	.40	.30	.15
776	Pat Mahomes (Diamond Debuts)(FC)	.15	.11	.06
777	Donovan Osborne (Diamond Debuts)(FC)	.15	.11	.06
778	John Patterson (Diamond Debuts)(FC)	.15	.11	.06
779	Andy Stankiewicz (Diamond Debuts)(FC)	.10	.08	.04
780	Turk Wendell (Diamond Debuts)(FC)	.10	.08	.04
781	Bill Krueger	.06	.05	.02
782	"Grand Theft" (Rickey Henderson)	.15	.11	.06
783	Kevin Seitzer	.06	.05	.02
784	Dave Martinez	.06	.05	.02
785	John Smiley	.08	.06	.03
786	Matt Stairs(FC)	.08	.06	.03
787	Scott Scudder	.06	.05	.02
788	John Wetteland	.10	.08	.04
789	Jack Armstrong	.06	.05	.02
790	Ken Hill	.08	.06	.03
791	Dick Schofield	.06	.05	.02
792	Mariano Duncan	.06	.05	.02
793	Bill Pecota	.06	.05	.02
794	Mike Kelly(FC)	.75	.60	.30
795	Willie Randolph	.06	.05	.02
796	Butch Henry(FC)	.20	.15	.08
797	Carlos Hernandez(FC)	.10	.08	.04
798	Doug Jones	.06	.05	.02
799	Melido Perez	.06	.05	.02
800	Checklist	.06	.05	.02
——	"Prime Time's Two" (Deion Sanders) (SP3)	4.00	3.00	1.50
——	"Mr. Baseball" (Tom Selleck/ Frank Thomas) (SP4)	5.00	3.75	2.00
——	Ted Williams hologram (HH2)	3.00	2.25	1.25

1992 Upper Deck College POY Holograms

This three-card hologram set features the College Player of the Year winners from 1989-91. Cards were randomly inserted in high number foil packs and have a CP prefix for numbering.

		MT	NR MT	EX
	Complete Set (3):	2.00	1.50	.80
	Common Player:	.40	.30	.15
1	David McCarty	1.00	.70	.40
2	Mike Kelly	.75	.60	.30
3	Ben McDonald	.40	.30	.15

A card number in parentheses () indicates the set is unnumbered.

1992 Upper Deck Ted Williams Heroes

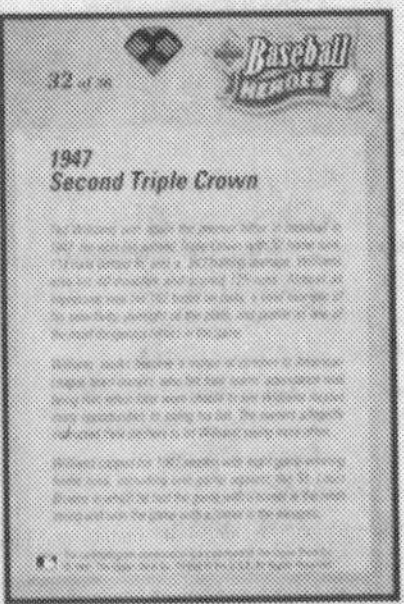

This Baseball Heroes set devoted to Ted Williams continues where previous efforts left off by numbering it from 28-36. An unnumbered cover card is also included that says "Baseball Heroes." Cards were found in low number foil and jumbo packs. Williams also autographed 2,500 cards, which were numbered and randomly inserted in low number packs.

		MT	NR MT	EX
	Complete Set (10):	7.50	5.75	3.00
	Common Williams:	.50	.40	.20
	Autographed Card:	450.00	337.00	180.00
——	Williams Header	4.00	3.00	1.50
28	1939 Rookie Year	.50	.40	.20
29	1941 .406!	.50	.40	.20
30	1942 Triple Crown Year	.50	.40	.20
31	1946 & 1949 MVP	.50	.40	.20
32	1947 Second Triple Crown	.50	.40	.20
33	1950s Player of the Decade	.50	.40	.30
34	1960 500 Home Run Club	.50	.40	.20
35	1966 Hall of Fame	.50	.40	.20
36	Checklist - Heroes 28-36	.50	.40	.20

1992 Upper Deck Bench/Morgan Heroes

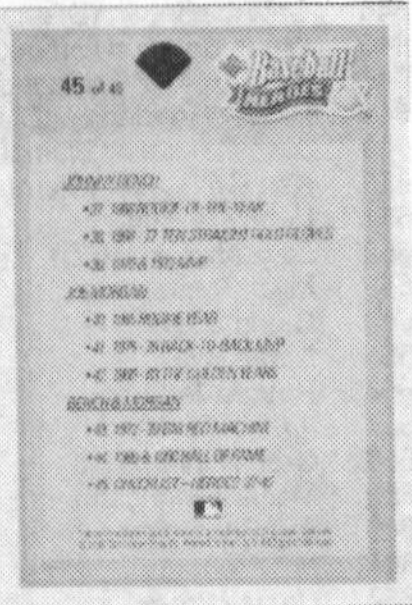

This set is devoted to two of the vital cogs in Cincinnati's Big Red Machine: Hall of Famers Johnny Bench and Joe Morgan. Cards, numbered 37-45, were included in high number packs. An unnumbered cover card was also produced, as were 2,500 cards numbered and signed by both players. They were also randomly inserted in high number packs.

	MT	NR MT	EX
Complete Set (10):	14.00	10.50	5.50
Common Card:	1.00	.70	.40
Header Card:	7.50	5.50	3.00
Autograph:	300.00	225.00	125.00

1992 Upper Deck Hall of Fame Heroes

Photos not available at press time

This set features three top players from the 1970s: Vida Blue, Lou Brock and Rollie Fingers. The cards continue from last year's set by using numbers H5-H8. The three players are each on one card; the fourth card features all three. They were found in low foil packs and specially-marked jumbo packs. Both types of packs could also contain autographed cards; each player signed 3,000 cards.

		MT	NR MT	EX
Complete Set (4):		35.00	26.00	14.00
Common Player:		8.00	6.00	3.25
Vida Blue Autograph:		75.00	56.00	30.00
Lou Brock Autograph:		100.00	75.00	40.00
Rollie Fingers Autograph:		90.00	67.00	36.00
5	Vida Blue	8.00	6.00	3.25
6	Lou Brock	10.00	7.50	4.00
7	Rollie Fingers	9.00	6.75	3.50
8	Vida Blue/Lou Brock/ Rollie Fingers	10.00	7.50	4.00

1992 Upper Deck Home Run Heroes

This 26-card set features a top home run hitter from each major league team. The cards, numbered HR1-HR26, were found in low number jumbo packs, one per pack.

		MT	NR MT	EX
Complete Set (26):		22.00	16.50	8.75
Common Player:		.50	.40	.20
1	Jose Canseco	.60	.45	.25
2	Cecil Fielder	1.00	.70	.40
3	Howard Johnson	.50	.40	.20
4	Cal Ripken, Jr.	2.00	1.50	.80
5	Matt Williams	.75	.60	.30
6	Joe Carter	1.25	.90	.50
7	Ron Gant	.75	.60	.30
8	Frank Thomas	5.00	3.75	2.00
9	Andre Dawson	.60	.45	.25
10	Fred McGriff	1.50	1.25	.60
11	Danny Tartabull	.50	.40	.20
12	Chili Davis	.50	.40	.20
13	Albert Belle	2.00	1.50	.80
14	Jack Clark	.50	.40	.20
15	Paul O'Neill	.50	.40	.20
16	Darryl Strawberry	.60	.45	.25
17	Dave Winfield	1.00	.70	.40
18	Jay Buhner	.50	.40	.20
19	Juan Gonzalez	4.00	3.00	1.50
20	Greg Vaughn	.60	.45	.25
21	Barry Bonds	2.50	2.00	1.00
22	Matt Nokes	.50	.40	.20
23	John Kruk	.60	.45	.25
24	Ivan Calderon	.50	.40	.20
25	Jeff Bagwell	2.00	1.50	.80
26	Todd Zeile	.50	.40	.20

1992 Upper Deck Scouting Report

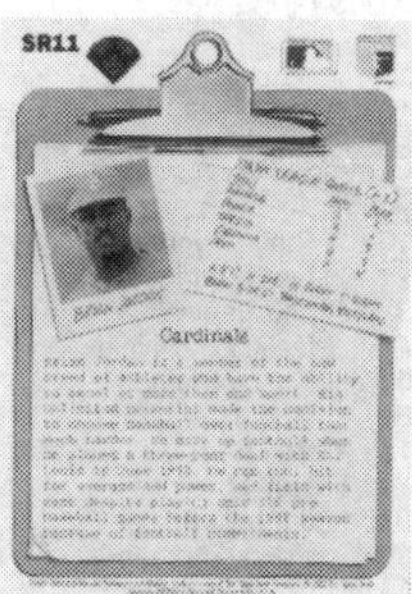

These cards were randomly inserted in Upper Deck high number jumbo packs. The set is numbered SR1-SR25 and features 25 top prospects, including 1992 Rookies of the Year Pat Listach and Eric Karros. "Scouting Report" is written down the side on the front in silver lettering. The back features a clipboard which shows a photo, a player profile and a major league scouting report.

		MT	NR MT	EX
Complete Set (25):		20.00	15.00	8.00
Common Player:		.40	.30	.15
1	Andy Ashby	.40	.30	.15
2	Willie Banks	.50	.40	.20
3	Kim Batiste	.40	.30	.15
4	Derek Bell	1.50	1.25	.60
5	Archi Cianfrocco	.50	.40	.20
6	Royce Clayton	2.00	1.50	.80
7	Gary DiSarcina	.40	.30	.15
8	Dave Fleming	2.00	1.50	.80
9	Butch Henry	.50	.40	.20
10	Todd Hundley	.40	.30	.15
11	Brian Jordan	2.00	1.50	.80
12	Eric Karros	2.00	1.50	.80
13	Pat Listach	.90	.70	.35
14	Scott Livingstone	.40	.30	.15
15	Kenny Lofton	4.00	3.00	1.50
16	Pat Mahomes	.60	.45	.25
17	Denny Neagle	.40	.30	.15
18	Dave Nilsson	.50	.40	.20
19	Donovan Osborne	1.25	.90	.50
20	Reggie Sanders	2.00	1.50	.80
21	Andy Stankiewicz	.50	.40	.20
22	Jim Thome	3.50	2.75	1.50
23	Julio Valera	.40	.30	.15
24	Mark Wohlers	.50	.40	.20
25	Anthony Young	.40	.30	.15

1992 Upper Deck FanFest

This 54-card boxed set was made available through special offers at the 1992 National Sports Collectors Convention and at the 1992 All-Star FanFest in San

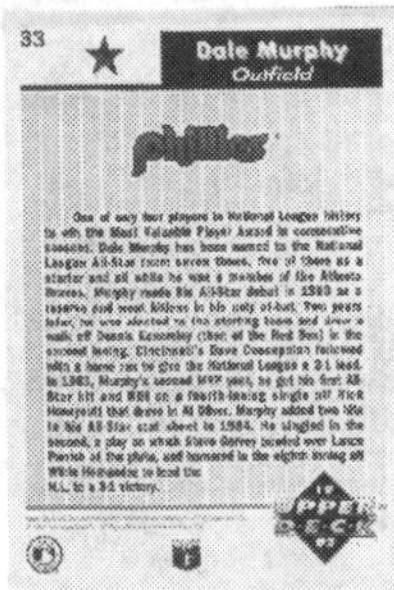

Diego. Card fronts feature a glossy UV finish, silver-foil stamping and the All-Star FanFest logo. The card backs include a player profile. Both "Future Heroes" and past and present "All-Star Heroes" are featured. The complete set was packaged in an attractive blue box with white pinstripes.

		MT	NR MT	EX
Complete Set:		16.00	12.00	6.50
Common Player:		.10	.08	.04
1	Steve Avery	.30	.25	.12
2	Ivan Rodriguez	.60	.45	.25
3	Jeff Bagwell	.30	.25	.12
4	Delino DeShields	.15	.11	.06
5	Royce Clayton	.25	.20	.10
6	Robin Ventura	.30	.25	.12
7	Phil Plantier	.25	.20	.10
8	Ray Lankford	.20	.15	.08
9	Juan Gonzalez	.60	.45	.25
10	Frank Thomas	1.25	.90	.50
11	Roberto Alomar	.80	.60	.30
12	Sandy Alomar, Jr.	.10	.08	.04
13	Wade Boggs	.30	.25	.12
14	Barry Bonds	.25	.20	.10
15	Bobby Bonilla	.25	.20	.10
16	George Brett	.30	.25	.12
17	Jose Canseco	.60	.45	.25
18	Will Clark	.60	.45	.25
19	Roger Clemens	.30	.25	.12
20	Eric Davis	.10	.08	.04
21	Rob Dibble	.10	.08	.04
22	Cecil Fielder	.25	.20	.10
23	Dwight Gooden	.20	.15	.08
24	Ken Griffey, Jr.	1.00	.70	.40
25	Tony Gwynn	.60	.45	.25
26	Bryan Harvey	.10	.08	.04
27	Rickey Henderson	.30	.25	.12
28	Howard Johnson	.10	.08	.04
29	Wally Joyner	.10	.08	.04
30	Barry Larkin	.20	.15	.08
31	Don Mattingly	.25	.20	.10
32	Mark McGwire	.35	.25	.14
33	Dale Murphy	.10	.08	.04
34	Rafael Palmeiro	.10	.08	.04
35	Kirby Puckett	.50	.40	.20
36	Cal Ripken, Jr.	1.00	.70	.40
37	Nolan Ryan	.80	.60	.30
38	Chris Sabo	.10	.08	.04
39	Ryne Sandberg	.60	.45	.25
40	Benito Santiago	.10	.08	.04
41	Ruben Sierra	.25	.20	.10
42	Ozzie Smith	.30	.25	.12
43	Darryl Strawberry	.25	.20	.10
44	Robin Yount	.30	.25	.12
45	Rollie Fingers	.30	.25	.12
46	Reggie Jackson	.60	.45	.25
47	Billy Williams	.10	.08	.04
48	Lou Brock	.30	.25	.12
49	Gaylord Perry	.25	.20	.10
50	Ted Williams	.70	.50	.30
51	Brooks Robinson	.50	.40	.20
52	Bob Gibson	.25	.20	.10
53	Bobby Bonds	.10	.08	.04
54	Robin Roberts	.10	.08	.04

Regional interest may affect the value of a card.

1992 Upper Deck Ted Williams' Best

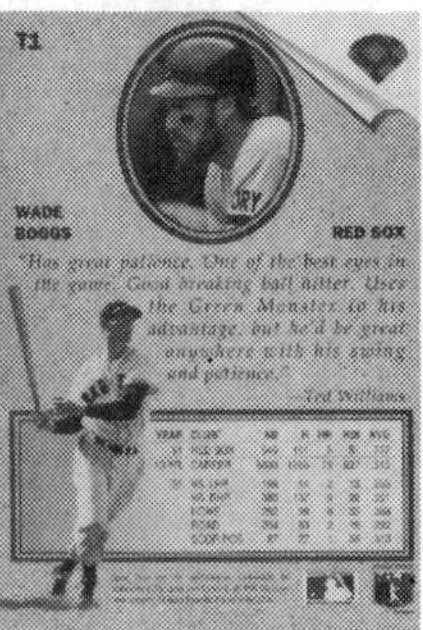

Twenty of the best hitters in baseball according to legend Ted Williams are featured in this special insert set from Upper Deck. The cards are styled much like the 1992 FanFest cards and showcase each chosen player. Each card is numbered with a "T" designation.

		MT	NR MT	EX
Complete Set (20):		30.00	22.00	12.00
Common Player:		.75	.60	.30
1	Wade Boggs	1.00	.70	.40
2	Barry Bonds	3.00	2.25	1.25
3	Jose Canseco	.90	.70	.35
4	Will Clark	1.25	.90	.50
5	Cecil Fielder	1.25	.90	.50
6	Tony Gwynn	1.00	.70	.40
7	Rickey Henderson	1.00	.70	.40
8	Fred McGriff	2.00	1.50	.80
9	Kirby Puckett	2.50	2.00	1.00
10	Ruben Sierra	1.00	.70	.40
11	Roberto Alomar	3.00	2.25	1.25
12	Jeff Bagwell	2.00	1.50	.80
13	Albert Belle	2.50	2.00	1.00
14	Juan Gonzalez	7.50	5.75	3.00
15	Ken Griffey, Jr.	7.50	5.75	3.00
16	Chris Hoiles	.75	.60	.30
17	David Justice	3.00	2.25	1.25
18	Phil Plantier	1.50	1.25	.60
19	Frank Thomas	10.00	7.50	4.00
20	Robin Ventura	1.50	1.25	.60

1993 Upper Deck

Upper Deck introduced its 1993 set in a two-series format to adjust to expansion. Cards 1-420 make up the first series. Special subsets in series one include rookies, teammates and community heroes. The card fronts feature full-color player photos surrounded by a white border. "Upper Deck" appears at the top of the photo and the player's name, team and position appear at the bottom. The backs feature vertical photos, which is a change from the past, and more complete statistics than what Upper Deck has had in the past. The hologram appears in the lower left corner on the card back.

		MT	NR MT	EX
Complete Set (840):		50.00	37.00	20.00
Common Player:		.05	.04	.02
1	Star Rookie Checklist (Tim Salmon)	.05	.04	.02
2	*Mike Piazza* (Star Rookie)(FC)	4.00	3.00	1.50
3	Rene Arocha (Star Rookie)(FC)	.50	.40	.20
4	Willie Greene (Star Rookie)(FC)	.15	.11	.06
5	*Manny Alexander* (Star Rookie)(FC)	.25	.20	.10
6	Dan Wilson (Star Rookie)	.12	.09	.05
7	*Dan Smith* (Star Rookie)(FC)	.20	.15	.08
8	*Kevin Rogers* (Star Rookie)(FC)	.20	.15	.08
9	*Nigel Wilson* (Star Rookie)(FC)	1.50	1.25	.60
10	*Joe Vitko* (Star Rookie)(FC)	.15	.11	.06
11	Tim Costo (Star Rookie)	.15	.11	.06
12	*Alan Embree* (Star Rookie)(FC)	.30	.25	.12
13	*Jim Tatum* (Star Rookie)(FC)	.25	.20	.10
14	*Cris Colon* (Star Rookie)(FC)	.15	.11	.06
15	Steve Hosey (Star Rookie)(FC)	.12	.09	.05
16	*Sterling Hitchcock* (Star Rookie)(FC)	.50	.40	.20
17	*Dave Mlicki* (Star Rookie)(FC)	.15	.11	.06
18	*Jessie Hollins* (Star Rookie)(FC)	.15	.11	.06
19	*Bobby Jones* (Star Rookie)(FC)	.30	.25	.12
20	*Kurt Miller* (Star Rookie)(FC)	.15	.11	.06
21	*Melvin Nieves* (Star Rookie)(FC)	.40	.30	.15
22	*Billy Ashley* (Star Rookie)(FC)	.20	.15	.08
23	*J.T. Snow* (Star Rookie)(FC)	1.50	1.25	.60
24	Chipper Jones (Star Rookie)	.75	.60	.30
25	*Tim Salmon* (Star Rookie)(FC)	3.00	2.25	1.25
26	*Tim Pugh* (Star Rookie)(FC)	.15	.11	.06
27	*Dave Nied* (Star Rookie)(FC)	1.00	.70	.40
28	*Mike Trombley* (Star Rookie)(FC)	.20	.15	.08
29	*Javy Lopez* (Star Rookie)(FC)	.75	.60	.30
30	Community Heroes Checklist (Jim Abbott)	.05	.04	.02
31	Jim Abbott (Community Heroes)	.10	.08	.04
32	Dale Murphy (Community Heroes)	.10	.08	.04
33	Tony Pena (Community Heroes)	.10	.08	.04
34	Kirby Puckett (Community Heroes)	.20	.15	.08
35	Harold Reynolds (Community Heroes)	.10	.08	.04
36	Cal Ripken, Jr. (Community Heroes)	.20	.15	.08
37	Nolan Ryan (Community Heroes)	.20	.15	.08
38	Ryne Sandberg (Community Heroes)	.20	.15	.08
39	Dave Stewart (Community Heroes)	.10	.08	.04
40	Dave Winfield (Community Heroes)	.15	.11	.06
41	Teammates Checklist (Joe Carter/ Mark McGwire)	.05	.04	.02
42	Blockbuster Trade (Joe Carter/ Roberto Alomar)	.12	.09	.05
43	Brew Crew (Paul Molitor/ Pat Listach/ Robin Yount)	.12	.09	.05
44	Iron and Steal (Cal Ripken, Jr./ Brady Anderson)	.12	.09	.05
45	Youthful Tribe (Albert Belle/ Sandy Alomar, Jr./ Jim Thome/ Carlos Baerga/ Kenny Lofton)	.12	.09	.05
46	Motown Mashers (Cecil Fielder/ Mickey Tettleton)	.12	.09	.05
47	Yankee Pride (Roberto Kelly/ Don Mattingly)	.12	.09	.05
48	Boston Cy Sox (Frank Viola/ Roger Clemens)	.12	.09	.05
49	Bash Brothers (Ruben Sierra/ Mark McGwire)	.12	.09	.05
50	Twin Titles (Kent Hrbek/ Kirby Puckett)	.12	.09	.05
51	Southside Sluggers (Robin Ventura/ Frank Thomas)	.50	.40	.20
52	Latin Stars (Juan Gonzalez/ Jose Canseco/ Ivan Rodriguez/ Rafael Palmeiro)	.40	.30	.15
53	Lethal Lefties (Mark Langston/ Jim Abbott/ Chuck Finley)	.12	.09	.05
54	Royal Family (Wally Joyner/ George Brett Gregg Jefferies)	.12	.09	.05
55	Pacific Sox Exchange (Kevin Mitchell/ Jay Buhner/ Ken Griffey, Jr.)	.12	.09	.05
56	George Brett	.15	.11	.06
57	Scott Cooper	.08	.06	.03
58	Mike Maddux	.05	.04	.02
59	*Rusty Meacham*(FC)	.12	.09	.05
60	Wilfredo Cordero	.15	.11	.06
61	Tim Teufel	.05	.04	.02
62	Jeff Montgomery	.06	.05	.02

		MT	NR MT	EX
63	Scott Livingstone	.08	.06	.03
64	Doug Dascenzo	.05	.04	.02
65	Bret Boone	.40	.30	.15
66	*Tim Wakefield*(FC)	.20	.15	.08
67	Curt Schilling	.08	.06	.03
68	Frank Tanana	.05	.04	.02
69	Lenny Dykstra	.08	.06	.03
70	Derek Lilliquist	.05	.04	.02
71	Anthony Young	.08	.06	.03
72	*Hipolito Pichardo*(FC)	.12	.09	.05
73	Rob Beck	.06	.05	.02
74	Kent Hrbek	.08	.06	.03
75	Tom Glavine	.12	.09	.05
76	Kevin Brown	.08	.06	.03
77	Chuck Finley	.08	.06	.03
78	Bob Walk	.05	.04	.02
79	Rheal Cormier	.10	.08	.04
80	Rick Sutcliffe	.08	.06	.03
81	Harold Baines	.08	.06	.03
82	Lee Smith	.08	.06	.03
83	Geno Petralli	.05	.04	.02
84	Jose Oquendo	.05	.04	.02
85	Mark Gubicza	.06	.05	.02
86	Mickey Tettleton	.08	.06	.03
87	Bobby Witt	.06	.05	.02
88	Mark Lewis	.06	.05	.02
89	Kevin Appier	.08	.06	.03
90	Mike Stanton	.05	.04	.02
91	Rafael Belliard	.05	.04	.02
92	Kenny Rogers	.05	.04	.02
93	Randy Velarde	.05	.04	.02
94	Luis Sojo	.05	.04	.02
95	Mark Leiter	.05	.04	.02
96	Jody Reed	.06	.05	.02
97	Pete Harnisch	.06	.05	.02
98	Tom Candiotti	.06	.05	.02
99	Mark Portugal	.05	.04	.02
100	Dave Valle	.05	.04	.02
101	Shawon Dunston	.08	.06	.03
102	B.J. Surhoff	.08	.06	.03
103	Jay Bell	.08	.06	.03
104	Sid Bream	.05	.04	.02
105	Checklist 1-105 (Frank Thomas)	.05	.04	.02
106	Mike Morgan	.05	.04	.02
107	Bill Doran	.05	.04	.02
108	Lance Blankenship	.05	.04	.02
109	Mark Lemke	.05	.04	.02
110	Brian Harper	.06	.05	.02
111	Brady Anderson	.08	.06	.03
112	Bip Roberts	.08	.06	.03
113	Mitch Williams	.08	.06	.03
114	Craig Biggio	.08	.06	.03
115	Eddie Murray	.08	.06	.03
116	Matt Nokes	.06	.05	.02
117	Lance Parrish	.06	.05	.02
118	Bill Swift	.06	.05	.02
119	Jeff Innis	.05	.04	.02
120	Mike LaValliere	.05	.04	.02
121	Hal Morris	.08	.06	.03
122	Walt Weiss	.06	.05	.02
123	Ivan Rodriguez	.15	.11	.06
124	Andy Van Slyke	.08	.06	.03
125	Roberto Alomar	.15	.11	.06
126	Robby Thompson	.06	.05	.02
127	Sammy Sosa	.06	.05	.02
128	Mark Langston	.06	.05	.02
129	Jerry Browne	.05	.04	.02
130	Chuck McElroy	.05	.04	.02
131	Frank Viola	.08	.06	.03
132	Leo Gomez	.08	.06	.03
133	Ramon Martinez	.10	.08	.04
134	Don Mattingly	.12	.09	.05
135	Roger Clemens	.15	.11	.06
136	Rickey Henderson	.15	.11	.06
137	Darren Daulton	.12	.09	.05
138	Ken Hill	.08	.06	.03
139	Ozzie Guillen	.08	.06	.03
140	Jerald Clark	.08	.06	.03
141	Dave Fleming	.15	.11	.06
142	Delino DeShields	.12	.09	.05
143	Matt Williams	.15	.11	.06
144	Larry Walker	.20	.15	.08
145	Ruben Sierra	.12	.09	.05
146	Ozzie Smith	.12	.09	.05
147	Chris Sabo	.08	.06	.03
148	*Carlos Hernandez*(FC)	.12	.09	.05
149	Pat Borders	.08	.06	.03
150	Orlando Merced	.08	.06	.03
151	Royce Clayton	.08	.06	.03
152	Kurt Stillwell	.06	.05	.02
153	Dave Hollins	.10	.08	.04

		MT	NR MT	EX
154	Mike Greenwell	.08	.06	.03
155	Nolan Ryan	.50	.40	.20
156	Felix Jose	.08	.06	.03
157	Junior Felix	.06	.05	.02
158	Derek Bell	.10	.08	.04
159	Steve Buechele	.06	.05	.02
160	John Burkett	.06	.05	.02
161	*Pat Howell*(FC)	.15	.11	.06
162	Milt Cuyler	.06	.05	.02
163	Terry Pendleton	.10	.08	.04
164	Jack Morris	.10	.08	.04
165	Tony Gwynn	.15	.11	.06
166	Deion Sanders	.15	.11	.06
167	Mike Devereaux	.08	.06	.03
168	Ron Darling	.08	.06	.03
169	Orel Hershiser	.08	.06	.03
170	Mike Jackson	.05	.04	.02
171	Doug Jones	.06	.05	.02
172	*Dan Walters*(FC)	.12	.09	.05
173	Darren Lewis	.08	.06	.03
174	Carlos Baerga	.12	.09	.05
175	Ryne Sandberg	.15	.11	.06
176	Gregg Jefferies	.12	.09	.05
177	John Jaha(FC)	.20	.15	.08
178	Luis Polonia	.05	.04	.02
179	Kirt Manwaring	.05	.04	.02
180	Mike Magnante	.08	.06	.03
181	Billy Ripken	.05	.04	.02
182	Mike Moore	.06	.05	.02
183	Eric Anthony	.06	.05	.02
184	Lenny Harris	.05	.04	.02
185	Tony Pena	.06	.05	.02
186	Mike Felder	.05	.04	.02
187	Greg Olson	.05	.04	.02
188	Rene Gonzales	.05	.04	.02
189	Mike Bordick	.08	.06	.03
190	Mel Rojas	.05	.04	.02
191	Todd Frohwirth	.05	.04	.02
192	Darryl Hamilton	.08	.06	.03
193	Mike Fetters	.05	.04	.02
194	Omar Olivares	.05	.04	.02
195	Tony Phillips	.08	.06	.03
196	Paul Sorrento	.08	.06	.03
197	Trevor Wilson	.06	.05	.02
198	Kevin Gross	.05	.04	.02
199	Ron Karkovice	.05	.04	.02
200	Brook Jacoby	.05	.04	.02
201	Mariano Duncan	.05	.04	.02
202	Dennis Cook	.05	.04	.02
203	Daryl Boston	.05	.04	.02
204	Mike Perez	.08	.06	.03
205	Manuel Lee	.05	.04	.02
206	Steve Olin	.05	.04	.02
207	Charlie Hough	.05	.04	.02
208	Scott Scudder	.05	.04	.02
209	Charlie O'Brien	.05	.04	.02
210	Checklist 106-210 (Barry Bonds)	.05	.04	.02
211	Jose Vizcaino	.05	.04	.02
212	Scott Leius	.05	.04	.02
213	Kevin Mitchell	.08	.06	.03
214	Brian Barnes	.08	.06	.03
215	Pat Kelly	.08	.06	.03
216	Chris Hammond	.08	.06	.03
217	Rob Deer	.06	.05	.02
218	Cory Snyder	.06	.05	.02
219	Gary Carter	.10	.08	.04
220	Danny Darwin	.05	.04	.02
221	Tom Gordon	.05	.04	.02
222	Gary Sheffield	.10	.08	.04
223	Joe Carter	.10	.08	.04
224	Jay Buhner	.06	.05	.02
225	Jose Offerman	.06	.05	.02
226	Jose Rijo	.06	.05	.02
227	Mark Whiten	.08	.06	.03
228	Randy Milligan	.05	.04	.02
229	Bud Black	.05	.04	.02
230	Gary DiSarcina	.05	.04	.02
231	Steve Finley	.08	.06	.03
232	Dennis Martinez	.08	.06	.03
233	Mike Mussina	.40	.30	.15
234	Joe Oliver	.06	.05	.02
235	*Chad Curtis*	.40	.30	.15
236	Shane Mack	.08	.06	.03
237	Jaime Navarro	.08	.06	.03
238	Brian McRae	.08	.06	.03
239	Chili Davis	.06	.05	.02
240	Jeff King	.06	.05	.02
241	Dean Palmer	.06	.05	.02
242	Danny Tartabull	.10	.08	.04
243	Charles Nagy	.15	.11	.06
244	Ray Lankford	.15	.11	.06
245	Barry Larkin	.15	.11	.06
246	Steve Avery	.15	.11	.06
247	John Kruk	.08	.06	.03
248	Derrick May	.08	.06	.03
249	Stan Javier	.05	.04	.02
250	Roger McDowell	.05	.04	.02
251	Dan Gladden	.05	.04	.02
252	Wally Joyner	.08	.06	.03
253	Pat Listach	.15	.11	.06
254	Chuck Knoblauch	.10	.08	.04
255	Sandy Alomar Jr.	.10	.08	.04
256	Jeff Bagwell	.15	.11	.06
257	Andy Stankiewicz	.15	.11	.06
258	Darrin Jackson	.06	.05	.02
259	Brett Butler	.08	.06	.03
260	Joe Orsulak	.06	.05	.02
261	Andy Benes	.10	.08	.04
262	Kenny Lofton	.35	.25	.14
263	Robin Ventura	.15	.11	.06
264	Ron Gant	.15	.11	.06
266	Juan Guzman	.15	.11	.06
267	Wes Chamberlain	.08	.06	.03
268	John Smiley	.06	.05	.02
269	Franklin Stubbs	.05	.04	.02
270	Tom Browning	.06	.05	.02
271	Dennis Eckersley	.12	.09	.05
272	Carlton Fisk	.12	.09	.05
273	Lou Whitaker	.08	.06	.03
274	Phil Plantier	.15	.11	.06
275	Bobby Bonilla	.10	.08	.04
276	Ben McDonald	.10	.08	.04
277	Bob Zupcic	.10	.08	.04
278	Terry Steinbach	.06	.05	.02
279	Terry Mulholland	.06	.05	.02
280	Lance Johnson	.06	.05	.02
281	Willie McGee	.06	.05	.02
282	Bret Saberhagen	.08	.06	.03
283	Randy Myers	.08	.06	.03
284	Randy Tomlin	.08	.06	.03
285	Mickey Morandini	.08	.06	.03
286	Brian Williams	.08	.06	.03
287	Tino Martinez	.08	.06	.03
288	Jose Melendez	.08	.06	.03
289	Jeff Huson	.05	.04	.02
290	Joe Grahe	.05	.04	.02
291	Mel Hall	.06	.05	.02
292	Otis Nixon	.06	.05	.02
293	Todd Hundley	.08	.06	.03
294	Casey Candaele	.05	.04	.02
295	Kevin Seitzer	.06	.05	.02
296	Eddie Taubensee	.10	.08	.04
297	Moises Alou	.10	.08	.04
298	Scott Radinsky	.05	.04	.02
299	Thomas Howard	.05	.04	.02
300	Kyle Abbott	.08	.06	.03
301	Omar Vizquel	.05	.04	.02
302	Keith Miller	.05	.04	.02
303	Rick Aguilera	.08	.06	.03
304	Bruce Hurst	.08	.06	.03
305	Ken Caminiti	.06	.05	.02
306	Mike Pagiarulo	.05	.04	.02
307	Frank Seminara(FC)	.12	.09	.05
308	Andre Dawson	.15	.11	.06
309	Jose Lind	.06	.05	.02
310	Joe Boever	.05	.04	.02
311	Jeff Parrett	.05	.04	.02
312	Alan Mills	.05	.04	.02
313	Kevin Tapani	.08	.06	.03
314	Daryl Kile	.08	.06	.03
315	Checklist 211-315 (Will Clark)	.05	.04	.02
316	Mike Sharperson	.05	.04	.02
317	John Orton	.05	.04	.02
318	Bob Tewksbury	.08	.06	.03
319	Xavier Hernandez	.05	.04	.02
320	Paul Assenmacher	.05	.04	.02
321	John Franco	.08	.06	.03
322	Mike Timlin	.06	.05	.02
323	Jose Guzman	.06	.05	.02
324	Pedro Martinez	.15	.11	.06
325	Bill Spiers	.06	.05	.02
326	Melido Perez	.06	.05	.02
327	Mike Macfarlane	.06	.05	.02
328	Ricky Bones	.06	.05	.02
329	Scott Bankhead	.06	.05	.02
330	Rich Rodriguez	.05	.04	.02
331	Geronimo Pena	.06	.05	.02
332	Bernie Williams	.10	.08	.04
333	Paul Molitor	.10	.08	.04
334	Roger Mason	.05	.04	.02
335	David Cone	.10	.08	.04
336	Randy Johnson	.06	.05	.02

		MT	NR MT	EX
337	Pat Mahomes	.15	.11	.06
338	Erik Hanson	.08	.06	.03
339	Duane Ward	.06	.05	.02
340	*Al Martin*(FC)	.15	.11	.06
341	Pedro Munoz	.10	.08	.04
342	Greg Colbrunn	.06	.05	.02
343	Julio Valera	.06	.05	.02
344	John Olerud	.10	.08	.04
345	George Bell	.10	.08	.04
346	Devon White	.08	.06	.03
347	Donovan Osborne	.15	.11	.06
348	Mark Gardner	.06	.05	.02
349	Zane Smith	.06	.05	.02
350	Wilson Alvarez	.06	.05	.02
351	*Kevin Koslofski*(FC)	.15	.11	.06
352	Roberto Hernandez	.10	.08	.04
353	Glenn Davis	.08	.06	.03
354	Reggie Sanders	.15	.11	.06
355	Ken Griffey Jr.	.60	.45	.25
356	Marquis Grissom	.12	.09	.05
357	Jack McDowell	.12	.09	.05
358	Jimmy Key	.06	.05	.02
359	Stan Belinda	.05	.04	.02
360	Gerald Williams	.10	.08	.04
361	Sid Fernandez	.08	.06	.03
362	Alex Fernandez	.08	.06	.03
363	John Smoltz	.10	.08	.04
364	Travis Fryman	.15	.11	.06
365	Jose Canseco	.25	.20	.10
366	David Justice	.15	.11	.06
367	*Pedro Astacio*(FC)	.25	.20	.10
368	Tim Belcher	.08	.06	.03
369	Steve Sax	.08	.06	.03
370	Gary Gaetti	.06	.05	.02
371	*Jeff Frye*(FC)	.12	.09	.05
372	Bob Wickman	.20	.15	.08
373	*Ryan Thompson*(FC)	.40	.30	.15
374	David Hulse	.15	.11	.06
375	Cal Eldred	.20	.15	.08
376	Ryan Klesko	.20	.15	.08
377	*Damion Easley*(FC)	.20	.15	.08
378	*John Kiely*(FC)	.20	.15	.08
379	*Jim Bullinger*(FC)	.12	.09	.05
380	Brian Bohanon	.08	.06	.03
381	Rod Brewer	.08	.06	.03
382	*Fernando Ramsey*(FC)	.15	.11	.06
383	Sam Militello	.15	.11	.06
384	Arthur Rhodes	.15	.11	.06
385	Eric Karros	.30	.25	.12
386	Rico Brogna	.12	.09	.05
387	*John Valentin*(FC)	.12	.09	.05
388	*Kerry Woodson*(FC)	.12	.09	.05
389	*Ben Rivera*(FC)	.12	.09	.05
390	*Matt Whiteside*(FC)	.15	.11	.06
391	Henry Rodriguez	.08	.06	.03
392	John Wetteland	.08	.06	.03
393	Kent Mercker	.06	.05	.02
394	Bernard Gilkey	.08	.06	.03
395	Doug Henry	.08	.06	.03
396	Mo Vaughn	.12	.09	.05
397	Scott Erickson	.08	.06	.03
398	Bill Gullickson	.08	.06	.03
399	Mark Guthrie	.05	.04	.02
400	Dave Martinez	.05	.04	.02
401	*Jeff Kent*	.15	.11	.06
402	Chris Hoiles	.15	.11	.06
403	Mike Henneman	.08	.06	.03
404	Chris Nabholz	.08	.06	.03
405	Tom Pagnozzi	.08	.06	.03
406	Kelly Gruber	.08	.06	.03
407	Bob Welch	.08	.06	.03
408	Frank Castillo	.08	.06	.03
409	John Dopson	.05	.04	.02
410	Steve Farr	.06	.05	.02
411	Henry Cotto	.05	.04	.02
412	Bob Patterson	.05	.04	.02
413	Todd Stottlemyre	.06	.05	.02
414	Greg A. Harris	.05	.04	.02
415	Denny Neagle	.08	.06	.03
416	Bill Wegman	.06	.05	.02
417	Willie Wilson	.06	.05	.02
418	Terry Leach	.05	.04	.02
419	Willie Randolph	.06	.05	.02
420	Checklist 316-420 (Mark McGwire)	.05	.04	.02
421	Checklist 422-449 Top Prospects (Calvin Murray)	.25	.20	.10
422	Pete Janicki (Top Prospect)	.15	.11	.06
423	Todd Jones (Top Prospect)	.06	.05	.02
424	Mike Neill (Top Prospect)	.15	.11	.06
425	Carlos Delgado (Top Prospect)	1.25	.90	.50
426	Jose Oliva (Top Prospect)	.20	.15	.08

		MT	NR MT	EX
427	Tyrone Hill (Top Prospect)	.15	.11	.06
428	Dmitri Young (Top Prospect)	.50	.40	.20
429	Derek Wallace (Top Prospect)	.30	.25	.12
430	Michael Moore (Top Prospect)	.50	.40	.20
431	Cliff Floyd (Top Prospect)	2.50	2.00	1.00
432	Calvin Murray (Top Prospect)	.30	.25	.12
433	Manny Ramiez (Top Prospect)	.80	.60	.30
434	Marc Newfield (Top Prospect)	.20	.15	.08
435	Charles Johnson (Top Prospect)	.50	.40	.20
436	Butch Huskey (Top Prospect)	.50	.40	.20
437	Brad Pennington (Top Prospect)	.08	.06	.03
438	Ray McDavid (Top Prospect)	.30	.25	.12
439	Chad McConnell (Top Prospect)	.25	.20	.10
440	Midre Cummings (Top Prospect)	.40	.30	.15
441	Benji Gil (Top Prospect)	.30	.25	.12
442	Frank Rodriguez (Top Prospect)	.30	.25	.12
443	Chad Mottola (Top Prospect)	1.50	1.25	.60
444	John Burke (Top Prospect)	.25	.20	.10
445	Michael Tucker (Top Prospect)	.60	.45	.25
446	Rick Greene (Top Prospect)	.15	.11	.06
447	Rich Becker (Top Prospect)	.20	.15	.08
448	Mike Robertson (Top Prospect)	.08	.06	.03
449	Derek Jeter (Top Prospect)	.60	.45	.25
450	Checklist 451-470 Inside the Numbers (David McCarty/ Ivan Rodriguez)	.25	.20	.10
451	Jim Abbott (Inside the Numbers)	.10	.08	.04
452	Jeff Bagwell (Inside the Numbers)	.12	.09	.05
453	Jason Bere (Inside the Numbers)	.75	.60	.30
454	Delino DeShields (Inside the Numbers)	.08	.06	.03
455	Travis Fryman (Inside the Numbers)	.15	.11	.06
456	Alex Gonzalez (Inside the Numbers)	.40	.30	.15
457	Phil Hiatt (Inside the Numbers)	.15	.11	.06
458	Dave Hollins (Inside the Numbers)	.10	.08	.04
459	Chipper Jones (Inside the Numbers)	.50	.40	.20
460	David Justice (Inside the Numbers)	.25	.20	.10
461	Ray Lankford (Inside the Numbers)	.08	.06	.03
462	David McCarty (Inside the Numbers)	.20	.15	.08
463	Mike Mussina (Inside the Numbers)	.15	.11	.06
464	Jose Offerman (Inside the Numbers)	.08	.06	.03
465	Dean Palmer (Inside the Numbers)	.12	.09	.05
466	Geronimo Pena (Inside the Numbers)	.06	.05	.02
467	Eduardo Perez (Inside the Numbers)	.30	.25	.12
468	Ivan Rodriguez (Inside the Numbers)	.12	.09	.05
470	Bernie Williams (Inside the Numbers)	.08	.06	.03
471	Checklist 472-485 Team Stars (Barry Bonds/ Matt Williams/ Will Clark)	.20	.15	.08
472	Strike Force (Greg Maddux/ Steve Avery John Smoltz/ Tom Glavine)	.20	.15	.08
473	Red October (Jose Rijo/ Rob Dibble/ Roberto Kelly/ Reggie Sanders/ Barry Larkin)	.08	.06	.03
474	Four Corners (Gary Sheffield/ Phil Plantier/ Tony Gwynn/ Fred McGriff tier/)	.20	.15	.08
475	Shooting Stars (Doug Drabek/ Craig Biggio/ Jeff Bagwell)	.06	.05	.02
476	Giant Sticks (Will Clark/ Barry Bonds/ Matt Williams)	.20	.15	.08
477	Boyhood Friends (Eric Davis/ Darryl Strawberry)	.06	.05	.02
478	Rock Solid (Dante Bichette/ Dave Nied/ Andres Galarraga)	.25	.20	.10
479	Inaugural Catch (Dave Magadan/ Orestes Destrade/ Bret Barbarie/ Jeff Conine)	.20	.15	.08
480	Steel City Champions (Tim Wakefield/ Andy Van Slyke/ Jay Bell)	.06	.05	.02
481	"Les Grandes Etoiles" (Marquis Grissom/ Delino DeShields/ Dennis Martinez/ Larry Walker)	.15	.11	.06
482	Runnin' Redbirds (Geronimo Pena/ Ray Lankford/ Ozzie Smith/ Bernard Gilkey)	.06	.05	.02
483	Ivy Leaguers (Randy Myers/ Ryne Sandberg/ Mark Grace)	.20	.15	.08
484	Big Apple Power Switch (Eddie Murray/ Howard Johnson/ Bobby Bonilla)	.08	.06	.03
485	Hammers & Nails (John Kruk/ Dave Hollins/ Darren Daulton/ Lenny Dykstra)	.25	.20	.10
486	Barry Bonds (Award Winners)	.30	.25	.12

#	Player	MT	NR MT	EX
487	Dennis Eckersley (Award Winners)	.06	.05	.02
488	Greg Maddux (Award Winners)	.10	.08	.04
489	Dennis Eckersley (Award Winners)	.06	.05	.02
490	Eric Karros (Award Winners)	.10	.08	.04
491	Pat Listach (Award Winners)	.10	.08	.04
492	Gary Sheffield (Award Winners)	.10	.08	.04
493	Mark MCGwire (Award Winners)	.08	.06	.03
494	Gary Sheffield (Award Winners)	.10	.08	.04
495	Edgar Martinez (Award Winners)	.06	.05	.02
496	Fred McGriff (Award Winners)	.15	.11	.06
497	Juan Gonzalez (Award Winners)	.50	.40	.20
498	Darren Daulton (Award Winners)	.08	.06	.03
499	Cecil Fielder (Award Winners)	.10	.08	.04
500	Checklist 501-510 Diamond Debuts (Brent Gates)	.20	.15	.08
501	Tavo Alvarez (Diamond Debuts)	.08	.06	.03
502	Rod Bolton (Diamond Debuts)	.06	.05	.02
503	*John Cummings* (Diamond Debuts)	.15	.11	.06
504	Brent Gates (Diamond Debuts)	.30	.25	.12
505	Tyler Green (Diamond Debuts)	.10	.08	.04
506	*Jose Martinez* (Diamond Debuts)	.15	.11	.06
507	Troy Percival (Diamond Debuts)	.08	.06	.03
508	Kevin Stocker (Diamond Debuts)	.90	.70	.35
509	Matt Walbeck (Diamond Debuts)	.25	.20	.10
510	Rondell White (Diamond Debuts)	.75	.60	.30
511	Billy Ripken	.06	.05	.02
512	Mike Moore	.06	.05	.02
513	Jose Lind	.06	.05	.02
514	Chito Martinez	.06	.05	.02
515	Jose Guzman	.06	.05	.02
516	Kim Batiste	.06	.05	.02
517	Jeff Tackett	.06	.05	.02
518	Charlie Hough	.06	.05	.02
519	Marvin Freeman	.06	.05	.02
520	Carlos Martinez	.06	.05	.02
521	Eric Young	.30	.25	.12
522	Pete Incaviglia	.06	.05	.02
523	Scott Fletcher	.06	.05	.02
524	Orestes Destrade	.08	.06	.03
525	Checklist 421-525 (Ken Griffey, Jr.)	.06	.05	.02
526	Ellis Burks	.06	.05	.02
527	Juan Samuel	.06	.05	.02
528	Dave Magadan	.06	.05	.02
529	Jeff Parrett	.06	.05	.02
530	Bill Krueger	.06	.05	.02
531	Frank Bolick	.06	.05	.02
532	Alan Trammell	.09	.07	.04
533	Walt Weiss	.06	.05	.02
534	David Cone	.06	.05	.02
535	Greg Maddux	.15	.11	.06
536	Kevin Young	.40	.30	.15
537	Dave Hansen	.08	.06	.03
538	Alex Cole	.06	.05	.02
539	Greg Hibbard	.06	.05	.02
540	Gene Larkin	.06	.05	.02
541	Jeff Reardon	.06	.05	.02
542	Felix Jose	.06	.05	.02
543	Jimmy Key	.06	.05	.02
544	Reggie Jefferson	.06	.05	.02
545	Gregg Jefferies	.08	.06	.03
546	Dave Stewart	.08	.06	.03
547	Tim Wallach	.06	.05	.02
548	Spike Owen	.06	.05	.02
549	Tommy Greene	.06	.05	.02
550	Fernando Valenzuela	.06	.05	.02
551	Rich Amaral	.06	.05	.02
552	Bret Barberie	.06	.05	.02
553	Edgar Martinez	.06	.05	.02
554	Jim Abbott	.12	.09	.05
555	Frank Thomas	1.25	.90	.50
556	Wade Boggs	.10	.08	.04
557	Tom Henke	.06	.05	.02
558	Milt Thompson	.06	.05	.02
559	Lloyd McClendon	.06	.05	.02
560	Vinny Castilla	.06	.05	.02
561	Ricky Jordan	.06	.05	.02
562	Andujar Cedeno	.06	.05	.02
563	Greg Vaughn	.08	.06	.03
564	Cecil Fielder	.15	.11	.06
565	Kirby Puckett	.25	.20	.10
566	Mark McGwire	.12	.09	.05
567	Barry Bonds	.50	.40	.20
568	Jody Reed	.06	.05	.02
569	Todd Zeile	.06	.05	.02
570	Mark Carreon	.06	.05	.02
571	Joe Girardi	.06	.05	.02
572	Luis Gonzalez	.06	.05	.02
573	Mark Grace	.10	.08	.04
574	Rafael Palmeiro	.10	.08	.04
575	Darryl Strawberry	.08	.06	.03

#	Player	MT	NR MT	EX
576	Will Clark	.20	.15	.08
577	Fred McGriff	.25	.20	.10
578	Kevin Reimer	.06	.05	.02
579	Dave Righetti	.06	.05	.02
580	Juan Bell	.06	.05	.02
581	Jeff Brantley	.06	.05	.02
582	Brian Hunter	.06	.05	.02
583	Tim Naehring	.06	.05	.02
584	Glenallen Hill	.06	.05	.02
585	Cal Ripken, Jr.	.30	.25	.12
586	Albert Belle	.45	.35	.20
587	Robin Yount	.20	.15	.08
588	Chris Bosio	.06	.05	.02
589	Pete Smith	.06	.05	.02
590	Chuck Carr	.08	.06	.03
591	Jeff Blauser	.06	.05	.02
592	Kevin McReynolds	.06	.05	.02
593	Andres Galarraga	.08	.06	.03
594	Kevin Maas	.06	.05	.02
595	Eric Davis	.08	.06	.03
596	Brian Jordan	.10	.08	.04
597	Tim Raines	.06	.05	.02
598	Rick Wilkins	.06	.05	.02
599	Steve Cooke	.20	.15	.08
600	Mike Gallego	.06	.05	.02
601	Mike Munoz	.06	.05	.02
602	Luis Rivera	.06	.05	.02
603	Junior Ortiz	.06	.05	.02
604	Brent Mayne	.06	.05	.02
605	Luis Alicea	.08	.06	.03
606	Damon Berryhill	.06	.05	.02
607	Dave Henderson	.06	.05	.02
608	Kirk McCaskill	.06	.05	.02
609	Jeff Fassero	.08	.06	.03
610	Mike Harkey	.06	.05	.02
611	Francisco Cabrera	.06	.05	.02
612	Rey Sanchez	.06	.05	.02
613	Scott Servais	.06	.05	.02
614	Darrin Fletcher	.06	.05	.02
615	Felix Fermin	.06	.05	.02
616	Kevin Seitzer	.06	.05	.02
617	Bob Scanlan	.06	.05	.02
618	Billy Hatcher	.06	.05	.02
619	John Vander Wal	.06	.05	.02
620	Joe Hesketh	.06	.05	.02
621	Hector Villanueva	.06	.05	.02
622	Randy Milligan	.06	.05	.02
623	*Tony Tarasco*	.75	.60	.30
624	Russ Swan	.06	.05	.02
625	Willie Wilson	.06	.05	.02
626	Frank Tanana	.06	.05	.02
627	Pete O'Brien	.06	.05	.02
628	Lenny Webster	.06	.05	.02
629	Mark Clark	.08	.06	.03
630	Checklist 526-630 (Roger Clemens)	.06	.05	.02
631	Alex Arias	.10	.08	.04
632	Chris Gwynn	.06	.05	.02
633	Tom Bolton	.06	.05	.02
634	Greg Briley	.06	.05	.02
635	Kent Bottenfield	.06	.05	.02
636	Kelly Downs	.06	.05	.02
637	Manuel Lee	.06	.05	.02
638	Al Leiter	.06	.05	.02
639	Jeff Gardner	.06	.05	.02
640	Mike Gardiner	.06	.05	.02
641	Mark Gardner	.06	.05	.02
642	Jeff Branson	.06	.05	.02
643	Paul Wagner	.06	.05	.02
644	Sean Berry	.10	.08	.04
645	Phil Hiatt	.30	.25	.12
646	Kevin Mitchell	.06	.05	.02
647	Charlie Hayes	.08	.06	.03
648	Jim Deshaies	.06	.05	.02
649	Dan Pasqua	.06	.05	.02
650	Mike Maddux	.06	.05	.02
651	*Domingo Martinez*	.30	.25	.12
652	*Greg McMichael*	.30	.25	.12
653	*Eric Wedge*	.20	.15	.08
654	Mark Whiten	.08	.06	.03
655	Bobby Kelly	.08	.06	.03
656	Julio Franco	.07	.05	.03
657	Gene Harris	.06	.05	.02
658	Pete Schourek	.06	.05	.02
659	Mike Bielecki	.06	.05	.02
660	Ricky Gutierrez	.10	.08	.04
661	Chris Hammond	.08	.06	.03
662	Tim Scott	.08	.06	.03
663	Norm Charlton	.06	.05	.02
664	Doug Drabek	.07	.05	.03
665	Dwight Gooden	.08	.06	.03

		MT	NR MT	EX
666	Jim Gott	.06	.05	.02
667	Randy Myers	.06	.05	.02
668	Darren Holmes	.06	.05	.02
669	Tim Spehr	.06	.05	.02
670	Bruce Ruffin	.06	.05	.02
671	Bobby Thigpen	.06	.05	.02
672	Tony Fernandez	.06	.05	.02
673	Darrin Jackson	.08	.06	.03
674	Gregg Olson	.06	.05	.02
675	Rob Dibble	.06	.05	.02
676	Howard Johnson	.08	.06	.03
677	*Mike Lansing*	.30	.25	.12
678	Charlie Leibrandt	.06	.05	.02
679	Kevin Bass	.06	.05	.02
680	Hubie Brooks	.06	.05	.02
681	Scott Brosius	.08	.06	.03
682	Randy Knorr	.06	.05	.02
683	Dante Bichette	.06	.05	.02
684	Bryan Harvey	.08	.06	.03
685	Greg Gohr	.06	.05	.02
686	Willie Banks	.06	.05	.02
687	Robb Nen	.06	.05	.02
688	Mike Scioscia	.06	.05	.02
689	John Farrell	.06	.05	.02
690	John Candelaria	.06	.05	.02
691	Damon Buford	.10	.08	.04
692	Todd Worrell	.06	.05	.02
693	Pat Hentgen	.50	.40	.20
694	John Smiley	.06	.05	.02
695	Greg Swindell	.06	.05	.02
696	Derek Bell	.12	.09	.05
697	Terry Jorgensen	.06	.05	.02
698	Jimmy Jones	.06	.05	.02
699	David Wells	.06	.05	.02
700	Dave Martinez	.06	.05	.02
701	Steve Bedrosian	.06	.05	.02
702	Jeff Russell	.06	.05	.02
703	Joe Magrane	.06	.05	.02
704	Matt Mieske	.06	.05	.02
705	Paul Molitor	.10	.08	.04
706	Dale Murphy	.06	.05	.02
707	Steve Howe	.06	.05	.02
708	Greg Gagne	.06	.05	.02
709	Dave Eiland	.06	.05	.02
710	David West	.06	.05	.02
711	Luis Aquino	.06	.05	.02
712	Joe Orsulak	.06	.05	.02
713	Eric Plunk	.06	.05	.02
714	Mike Felder	.06	.05	.02
715	Joe Klink	.06	.05	.02
716	Lonnie Smith	.06	.05	.02
717	Monty Fariss	.06	.05	.02
718	Craig Lefferts	.06	.05	.02
719	John Habyan	.06	.05	.02
720	Willie Blair	.06	.05	.02
721	Darnell Coles	.06	.05	.02
722	Mark Williamson	.06	.05	.02
723	Bryn Smith	.06	.05	.02
724	Greg W. Harris	.06	.05	.02
725	*Graeme Lloyd*	.20	.15	.08
726	Cris Carpenter	.06	.05	.02
727	Chico Walker	.06	.05	.02
728	Tracy Woodson	.06	.05	.02
729	Jose Uribe	.06	.05	.02
730	Stan Javier	.06	.05	.02
731	Jay Howell	.06	.05	.02
732	Freddie Benavides	.06	.05	.02
733	Jeff Reboulet	.06	.05	.02
734	Scott Sanderson	.06	.05	.02
735	Checklist 631-735 (Ryne Sandberg)	.06	.05	.02
736	Archi Cianfrocco	.06	.05	.02
737	Daryl Boston	.06	.05	.02
738	Craig Grebeck	.06	.05	.02
739	Doug Dascenzo	.06	.05	.02
740	Gerald Young	.08	.06	.03
741	Candy Maldonado	.06	.05	.02
742	Joey Cora	.06	.05	.02
743	Don Slaught	.06	.05	.02
744	Steve Decker	.06	.05	.02
745	Blas Minor	.06	.05	.02
746	Storm Davis	.06	.05	.02
747	Carlos Quintna	.06	.05	.02
748	Vince Coleman	.06	.05	.02
749	Todd Burns	.06	.05	.02
750	Steve Frey	.06	.05	.02
751	Ivan Calderon	.06	.05	.02
752	*Steve Reed*	.15	.11	.06
753	Danny Jackson	.06	.05	.02
754	Jeff Conine	.08	.06	.03
755	Juan Gonzalez	1.00	.70	.40

		MT	NR MT	EX
756	Mike Kelly	.25	.20	.10
757	John Doherty	.20	.15	.08
758	Jack Armstrong	.06	.05	.02
759	John Wehner	.06	.05	.02
760	Scott Bankhead	.06	.05	.02
761	Jim Tatum	.15	.11	.06
762	Scott Pose	.15	.11	.06
763	Andy Ashby	.06	.05	.02
764	Ed Sprague	.06	.05	.02
765	Harold Baines	.06	.05	.02
766	Kirk Gibson	.06	.05	.02
767	Troy Neel	.30	.25	.12
768	Dick Schofield	.06	.05	.02
769	Dickie Thon	.06	.05	.02
770	Butch Henry	.06	.05	.02
771	Junior Felix	.06	.05	.02
772	*Ken Ryan*	.20	.15	.08
773	Trevor Hoffman	.06	.05	.02
774	Phil Plantier	.15	.11	.06
775	Bo Jackson	.20	.15	.08
776	Benito Santiago	.06	.05	.02
777	Andre Dawson	.06	.05	.02
778	Bryan Hickerson	.06	.05	.02
779	Dennis Moeller	.06	.05	.02
780	Ryan Bowen	.08	.06	.03
781	Eric Fox	.06	.05	.02
782	Joe Kmak	.06	.05	.02
783	Mike Hampton	.06	.05	.02
784	*Darrell Sherman*	.30	.25	.12
785	J.T. Snow	.75	.60	.30
786	Dave Winfield	.15	.11	.06
787	Jim Austin	.08	.06	.03
788	Craig Shipley	.06	.05	.02
789	Greg Myers	.06	.05	.02
790	Todd Benzinger	.06	.05	.02
791	Cory Snyder	.06	.05	.02
792	David Segui	.06	.05	.02
793	Armando Reynoso	.06	.05	.02
794	Chili Davis	.06	.05	.02
795	Dave Nilsson	.06	.05	.02
796	Paul O'Neill	.06	.05	.02
797	Jerald Clark	.06	.05	.02
798	Jose Mesa	.06	.05	.02
799	Brian Holman	.06	.05	.02
800	Jim Eisenreich	.06	.05	.02
801	Mark McLemore	.06	.05	.02
802	Luis Sojo	.06	.05	.02
803	Harold Reynolds	.06	.05	.02
804	Dan Plesac	.06	.05	.02
805	Dave Stieb	.06	.05	.02
806	Tom Brunansky	.06	.05	.02
807	Kelly Gruber	.06	.05	.02
808	Bob Ojeda	.06	.05	.02
809	Dave Burba	.06	.05	.02
810	Joe Boever	.06	.05	.02
811	Jeremy Hernandez	.08	.06	.03
812	Angels Checklist (Tim Salmon)	.60	.45	.25
813	Astros Checklist (Jeff Bagwell)	.15	.11	.06
814	Athletics Checklist (Mark McGwire)	.08	.06	.03
815	Blue Jays Checklist (Roberto Alomar)	.25	.20	.10
816	Braves Checklist (Steve Avery)	.15	.11	.06
817	Brewers Checklist (Pat Listach)	.08	.06	.03
818	Cardinals Checklist (Gregg Jefferies)	.06	.05	.02
819	Cubs Checklist (Sammy Sosa)	.06	.05	.02
820	Dodgers Checklist (Darryl Strawberry)	.08	.06	.03
821	Expos Checklist (Dennis Martinez)	.06	.05	.02
822	Ginats Checklist (Robby Thompson)	.08	.06	.03
823	Indians Checklist (Albert Belle)	.25	.20	.10
824	Mariners Checklist (Randy Johnson)	.08	.06	.03
825	Marlins Checklist (Nigel Wilson)	.30	.25	.12
826	Mets Checklist (Bobby Bonilla)	.06	.05	.02
827	Orioles Checklist (Glenn Davis)	.08	.06	.03
828	Padres Checklist (Gary Sheffield)	.10	.08	.04
829	Phillies Checklist (Darren Daulton)	.08	.06	.03
830	Pirates Checklist (Jay Bell)	.06	.05	.02
831	Rangers Checklist (Juan Gonzalez)	.60	.45	.25
832	Red Sox Checklist (Andre Dawson)	.06	.05	.02
833	Reds Checklist (Hal Morris)	.08	.06	.03
834	Rockies Checklist (David Nied)	.20	.15	.08
835	Royals Checklist (Felix Jose)	.06	.05	.02
836	Tigers Checklist (Travis Fryman)	.20	.15	.08
837	Twins Checklist (Shane Mack)	.06	.05	.02
838	White Sox Checklist (Robin Ventura)	.10	.08	.04
839	Yankees Checklist (Danny Tartabull)	.06	.05	.02

		MT	NR MT	EX
840	Checklist 736-840 (Roberto Alomar)	.06	.05	.02
----	3,000 Hits (Robin Yount/ George Brett) (SP5)	4.00	3.00	1.50

1993 Upper Deck Clutch Performers

Reggie Jackson has selected the players who perform the best under pressure for this 20-card insert set. Cards were available only in Series II retail packs and use the prefix R for numbering. Fronts have a black bottom panel with "Clutch Performers" printed in dark gray. Jackson's facsimile autograph is overprinted in gold foil. On back, under a second player photo, is Jackson's picture and his assessment of the player. There are a few lines of stats to support the player's selection to this exclusive company.

		MT	NR MT	EX
Complete Set (20):		35.00	26.00	14.00
Common Player:		1.00	.70	.40
1	Roberto Alomar	3.50	2.75	1.50
2	Wade Boggs	1.25	.90	.50
3	Barry Bonds	5.00	3.75	2.00
4	Jose Canseco	1.25	.90	.50
5	Joe Carter	3.00	2.25	1.25
6	Will Clark	2.00	1.50	.80
7	Roger Clemens	3.00	2.25	1.25
8	Dennis Eckersley	1.00	.70	.40
9	Cecil Fielder	1.75	1.25	.70
10	Juan Gonzalez	7.50	5.75	3.00
11	Ken Griffey Jr.	7.50	5.75	3.00
12	Rickey Henderson	1.25	.90	.50
13	Barry Larkin	1.00	.70	.40
14	Don Mattingly	3.00	2.25	1.25
15	Fred McGriff	3.00	2.25	1.25
16	Terry Pendleton	1.00	.70	.40
17	Kirby Puckett	3.50	2.75	1.50
18	Ryne Sandberg	3.50	2.75	1.50
19	John Smoltz	1.00	.70	.40
20	Frank Thomas	10.00	7.50	4.00

1993 Upper Deck 5th Anniversary

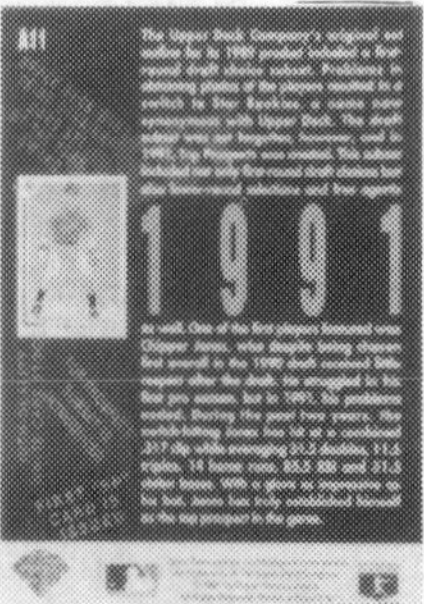

This 15-card insert set features 15 of Upper Deck's most popular cards from its first five years. Foil stamping and a fifth anniversary logo appear on the cards, which are reproductions of the originals. The prefix A appears before each card number. The cards were available in Series II hobby packs only.

		MT	NR MT	EX
Complete Set (15):		24.00	18.00	9.50
Common Player:		1.00	.70	.40
1	Ken Griffey Jr.	8.00	6.00	3.25
2	Gary Sheffield	1.50	1.25	.60
3	Roberto Alomar	3.00	2.25	1.25
4	Jim Abbott	1.00	.70	.40
5	Nolan Ryan	5.00	3.75	2.00
6	Juan Gonzalez	5.00	3.75	2.00
7	David Justice	2.00	1.50	.80
8	Carlos Baerga	2.00	1.50	.80
9	Reggie Jackson	2.00	1.50	.80
10	Eric Karros	1.50	1.25	.60
11	Chipper Jones	2.00	1.50	.80
12	Ivan Rodriguez	1.50	1.25	.60
13	Pat Listach	1.00	.70	.40
14	Frank Thomas	7.50	5.75	3.00
15	Tim Salmon	3.00	2.25	1.25

1993 Upper Deck Future Heroes

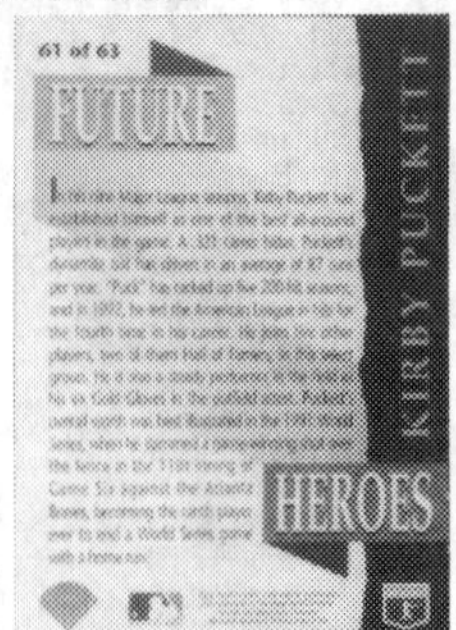

This insert set includes eight player cards, a checklist and an unnumbered header card. The cards are numbered 55-63 as a continuation of previous Heroes sets, but this one features more than one player; previous sets featured only one player. Card fronts have a Future Heroes logo and a facsimile autograph. The player's name is revealed using a peeled-back paper effect. Cards were randomly inserted in Series II foil packs.

		MT	NR MT	EX
Complete Set (10):		15.00	11.00	6.00
Common Player:		1.00	.70	.40
Header card:		4.00	3.00	1.50
55	Roberto Alomar	2.00	1.50	.80
56	Barry Bonds	2.50	2.00	1.00
57	Roger Clemens	1.50	1.25	.60
58	Juan Gonzalez	4.00	3.00	1.50
59	Ken Griffey Jr.	5.00	3.75	2.00
60	Mark McGwire	1.00	.70	.40
61	Kirby Puckett	2.00	1.50	.80
62	Frank Thomas	6.00	4.50	2.50
63	Checklist	1.00	.70	.40

1993 Upper Deck Home Run Heroes

This 28-card insert set features the top home run hitters from each team for 1992. Cards, inserted in Series I jumbo packs, are numbered with an HR prefix. The card fronts say Home Run Heroes along the side; a bat with the player's name and an Upper Deck trademark appears along the bottom.

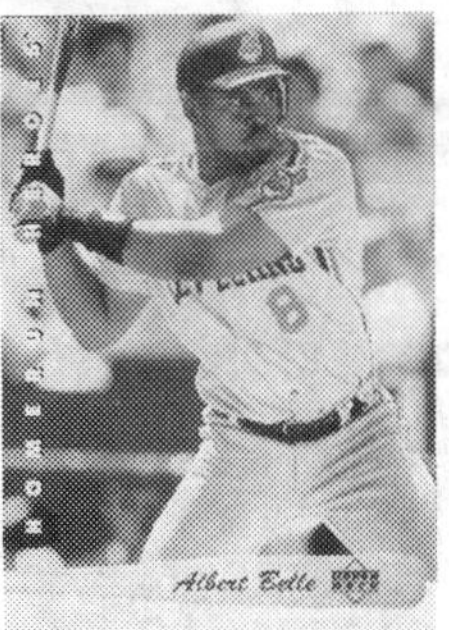

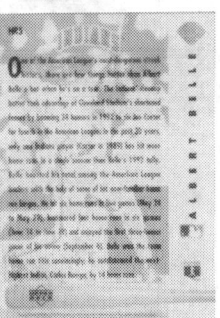

		MT	NR MT	EX
Complete Set (28):		22.00	16.50	8.75
Common Player:		.50	.40	.20
1	Juan Gonzalez	4.50	3.50	1.75
2	Mark McGwire	1.00	.70	.40
3	Cecil Fielder	1.50	1.25	.60
4	Fred McGriff	2.00	1.50	.80
5	Albert Belle	2.00	1.50	.80
6	Barry Bonds	3.00	2.25	1.25
7	Joe Carter	2.00	1.50	.80
8	Darren Daulton	1.00	.70	.40
9	Ken Griffey Jr.	6.00	4.50	2.50
10	Dave Hollins	1.00	.70	.40
11	Ryne Sandberg	2.50	2.00	1.00
12	George Bell	.50	.40	.20
13	Danny Tartabull	.50	.40	.20
14	Mike Devereaux	.50	.40	.20
15	Greg Vaughn	.50	.40	.20
16	Larry Walker	.90	.70	.35
17	David Justice	2.50	2.00	1.00
18	Terry Pendleton	.50	.40	.20
19	Eric Karros	1.50	1.25	.60
20	Ray Lankford	.50	.40	.20
21	Matt Williams	1.00	.70	.40
22	Eric Anthony	.50	.40	.20
23	Bobby Bonilla	.50	.40	.20
24	Kirby Puckett	2.50	2.00	1.00
25	Mike Macfarlane	.50	.40	.20
26	Tom Brunansky	.50	.40	.20

1993 Upper Deck Iooss Collection

Sports photographer Walter Iooss Jr. has captured 26 current players in this insert set featuring their candid portraits. Cards have full-bleed photos and gold foil stamping. Backs have biographical sketches and are numbered using a WI prefix. They are available in Series I retail packs.

		MT	NR MT	EX
Complete Set (27):		36.00	27.00	14.50
Common Player:		.75	.60	.30
Header card:		4.00	3.00	1.50
1	Tim Salmon	6.00	4.50	2.50
2	Jeff Bagwell	2.00	1.50	.80
3	Mark McGwire	1.00	.70	.40
4	Roberto Alomar	3.50	2.75	1.50
5	Steve Avery	2.50	2.00	1.00
6	Paul Molitor	2.00	1.50	.80
7	Ozzie Smith	2.00	1.50	.80
8	Mark Grace	1.00	.70	.40
9	Eric Karros	1.50	1.25	.60
10	Delino DeShields	.75	.60	.30
11	Will Clark	2.00	1.50	.80
12	Albert Belle	3.00	2.25	1.25
13	Ken Griffey Jr.	8.00	6.00	3.25
14	Howard Johnson	.75	.60	.30
15	Cal Ripken, Jr.	3.00	2.25	1.25
16	Fred McGriff	2.00	1.50	.80
17	Darren Daulton	1.50	1.25	.60
18	Andy Van Slyke	.75	.60	.30
19	Nolan Ryan	8.00	6.00	3.25
20	Wade Boggs	1.50	1.25	.60
21	Barry Larkin	.75	.60	.30
22	George Brett	3.00	2.25	1.25
23	Cecil Fielder	1.50	1.25	.60
24	Kirby Puckett	3.50	2.75	1.50
25	Frank Thomas	9.00	6.75	3.50
26	Don Mattingly	3.00	2.25	1.25

1993 Upper Deck Willie Mays Heroes

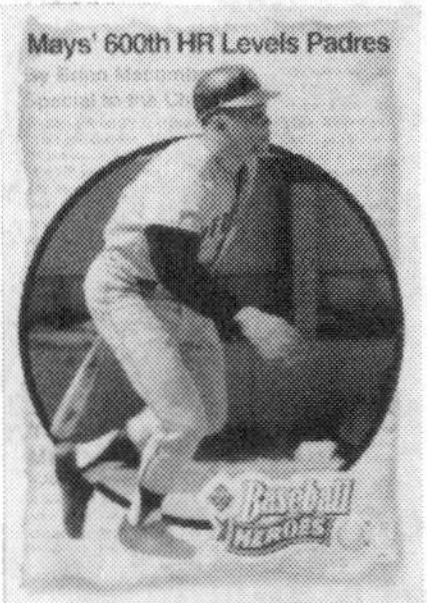

This 10-card insert set includes eight individually-titled cards, an illustrated checklist and one header card. The set is a continuation of Upper Deck's previous Heroes efforts, honoring greats such as Hank Aaron, Nolan Ryan and Reggie Jackson, and is numbered 46-54. Cards were randomly inserted into Series I foil packs.

		MT	NR MT	EX
Complete Set (10):		5.00	3.75	2.00
Common Mays:		.50	.40	.20
---	Header card	3.00	2.25	1.25
46	1951 Rookie-of-the-Year	.50	.40	.20
47	1954 The Catch	.50	.40	.20
48	1956-57 30-30 Club	.50	.40	.20
49	1961 Four-Homer Game	.50	.40	.20
50	1965 Most Valuable Player	.50	.40	.20
51	1969 600-Home Run Club	.50	.40	.20
52	1972 New York Homecoming	.50	.40	.20
53	1979 Hall of Fame	.50	.40	.20
54	Checklist - Heroes 46-54	.50	.40	.20

1993 Upper Deck On Deck

These UV-coated cards feature 25 of the game's top players. Each card has a full-bleed photo on the front and questions and answers on the back. Available only in Series II jumbo packs, the cards have a D prefix for numbering.

		MT	NR MT	EX
Complete Set (25):		24.00	18.00	9.50
Common Player:		.50	.40	.20
1	Jim Abbott	.75	.60	.30
2	Roberto Alomar	2.00	1.50	.80

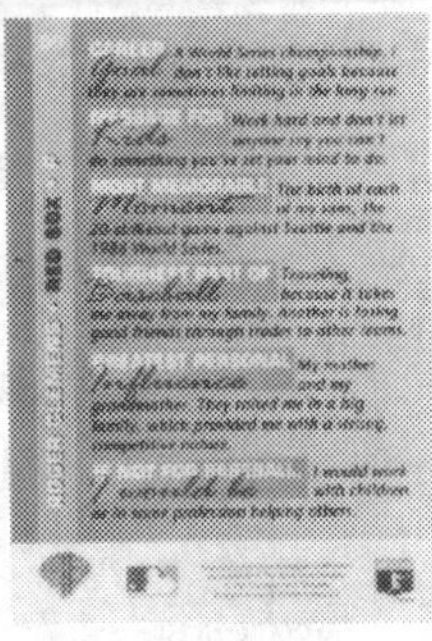

3	Carlos Baerga	1.75	1.25	.70
4	Albert Belle	1.75	1.25	.70
5	Wade Boggs	.75	.60	.30
6	George Brett	1.75	1.25	.70
7	Jose Canseco	.75	.60	.30
8	Will Clark	1.00	.70	.40
9	Roger Clemens	1.50	1.25	.60
10	Dennis Eckersley	.50	.40	.20
11	Cecil Fielder	1.00	.70	.40
12	Juan Gonzalez	4.00	3.00	1.50
13	Ken Griffey Jr.	4.50	3.50	1.75
14	Tony Gwynn	.75	.60	.30
15	Bo Jackson	.75	.60	.30
16	Chipper Jones	2.00	1.50	.80
17	Eric Karros	.75	.60	.30
18	Mark McGwire	.75	.60	.30
19	Kirby Puckett	2.00	1.50	.80
20	Nolan Ryan	4.50	3.50	1.75
21	Tim Salmon	4.00	3.00	1.50
22	Ryne Sandberg	2.00	1.50	.80
23	Darryl Strawberry	.50	.40	.20
24	Frank Thomas	6.00	4.50	2.50
25	Andy Van Slyke	.50	.40	.20

1993 Upper Deck Then And Now

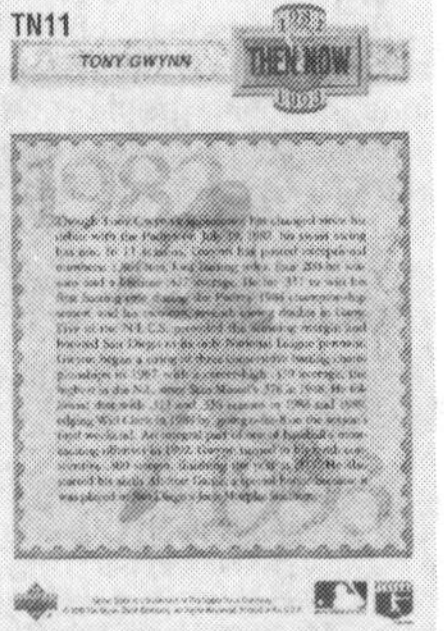

This 18-card lithogram set features both Hall of Famers and current players. The cards feature a combination of four-color player photos and a holographic background. They were random inserts in both Series I and Series II packs. Numbering includes the prefix TN.

		MT	NR MT	EX
Complete Set (18):		70.00	52.00	28.00
Common Player:		2.00	1.50	.80
1	Wade Boggs	2.00	1.50	.80
2	George Brett	4.00	3.00	1.50
3	Rickey Henderson	2.00	1.50	.80
4	Cal Ripken, Jr.	5.00	3.75	2.00
5	Nolan Ryan	11.00	8.25	4.50
6	Ryne Sandberg	5.00	3.75	2.00
7	Ozzie Smith	2.00	1.50	.80
8	Darryl Strawberry	2.00	1.50	.80
9	Dave Winfield	3.00	2.25	1.25
10	Dennis Eckersley	2.00	1.50	.80
11	Tony Gwynn	2.00	1.50	.80
12	Howard Johnson	2.00	1.50	.80
13	Don Mattingly	3.00	2.25	1.25
14	Eddie Murray	2.00	1.50	.80
15	Robin Yount	3.00	2.25	1.25
16	Reggie Jackson	5.00	3.75	2.00
17	Mickey Mantle	18.00	13.50	7.25
18	Willie Mays	10.00	7.50	4.00

1993 Upper Deck "Highlights"

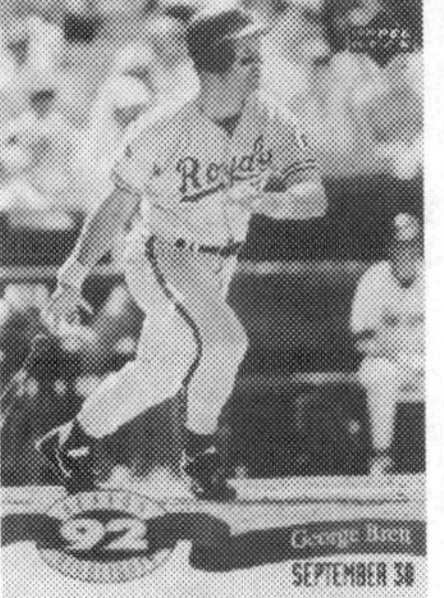

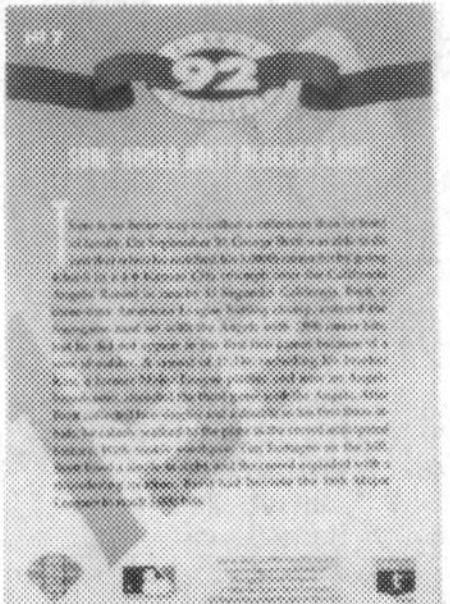

These 20 insert cards commemorate highlights from the 1992 season. Cards, which were randomly inserted in 1993 Upper Deck Series II packs, have a '92 Season Highlights logo on the bottom, with the player's name inside a banner trailing from the logo. The date of the significant event is under the player's name. Card backs have the logo at the top and are numbered with an HI prefix. A headline desscribes what highlight occurred, while the text describes the event. 1992 is faded across the background.

		MT	NR MT	EX
Complete Set (20):		55.00	41.00	22.00
Common Player:		1.00	.70	.40
1	Roberto Alomar	6.00	4.50	2.50
2	Steve Avery	3.00	2.25	1.25
3	Harold Baines	1.00	.70	.40
4	Damon Berryhill	1.00	.70	.40
5	Barry Bonds	9.00	6.75	3.50
6	Bret Boone	1.50	1.25	.60
7	George Brett	4.00	3.00	1.50
8	Francisco Cabrera	1.00	.70	.40
9	Ken Griffey Jr.	12.00	9.00	4.75
10	Rickey Henderson	3.00	2.25	1.25
11	Kenny Lofton	3.50	2.75	1.50
12	Mickey Morandini	1.00	.70	.40
13	Eddie Murray	2.00	1.50	.80
14	David Nied	4.00	3.00	1.50
15	Jeff Reardon	1.00	.70	.40
16	Bip Roberts	1.00	.70	.40
17	Nolan Ryan	12.00	9.00	4.75
18	Ed Sprague	1.00	.70	.40
19	Dave Winfield	3.00	2.25	1.25
20	Robin Yount	3.50	2.75	1.50

1993 Upper Deck All-Time Heroes

This 1993 Upper Deck set pays homage to one of the classiest, turn-of-the-century card sets, the T202 Hassan Triple Folders. The All-Time Heroes cards are 2-1/4" by 5-1/4" and feature two side panels and a larger middle panel, which features an action shot of the player. A portrait of the player and the Baseball Assistance Team (BAT) logo flank the action photo. Card backs have a biography and career summary. A Classic Combinations subset of 35 cards features artwork or photographs of two or more great players together, plus individual photos on the side panels. Production was limited to 5,140 numbered cases; cards were packaged in 12-card foil packs. Ten T202 reprints were also produced and were randomly inserted in the foil packs.

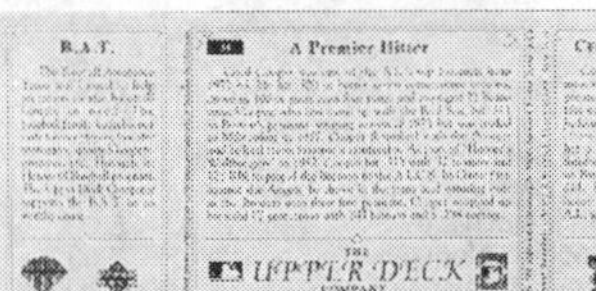

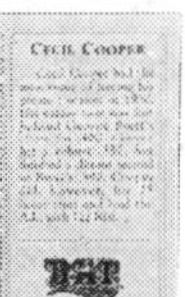

		MT	NR MT	EX
Complete Set:		45.00	34.00	18.00
Common Player:		.10	.08	.04
1	Hank Aaron	2.00	1.50	.80
2	Tommie Agee	.10	.08	.04
3	Bob Allison	.10	.08	.04
4	Matty Alou	.10	.08	.04
5	Sal Bando	.10	.08	.04
6	Hank Bauer	.10	.08	.04
7	Don Baylor	.10	.08	.04
8	Glenn Beckert	.10	.08	.04
9	Yogi Berra	.50	.40	.20
10	Buddy Biancalana	.10	.08	.04
11	Jack Billingham	.10	.08	.04
12	Joe Black	.15	.11	.06
13	Paul Blair	.10	.08	.04
14	Steve Blass	.10	.08	.04
15	Ray Boone	.10	.08	.04
16	Lou Boudreau	.25	.20	.10
17	Ken Brett	.10	.08	.04
18	Nellie Briles	.10	.08	.04
19	Bobby Brown	.15	.11	.06
20	Bill Buckner	.10	.08	.04
21	Don Buford	.10	.08	.04
22	Al Bumbry	.10	.08	.04
23	Lew Burdette	.10	.08	.04
24	Jeff Burroughs	.10	.08	.04
25	Johnny Callison	.10	.08	.04
26	Bert Campaneris	.10	.08	.04
27	Rico Carty	.10	.08	.04
28	Dave Cash	.10	.08	.04
29	Cesar Cedeno	.10	.08	.04
30	Frank Chance	.25	.20	.10
31	Joe Charboneau	.10	.08	.04
32	Ty Cobb	2.00	1.50	.80
33	Jerry Coleman	.10	.08	.04
34	Cecil Cooper	.10	.08	.04
35	Frankie Crossetti	.10	.08	.04
36	Alvin Dark	.10	.08	.04
37	Tommy Davis	.10	.08	.04
38	Dizzy Dean	.35	.25	.14
39	Doug DeCinces	.10	.08	.04
40	Bucky Dent	.10	.08	.04
41	Larry Dierker	.10	.08	.04
42	Larry Doby	.10	.08	.04
43	Moe Drabowsky	.10	.08	.04
44	Dave Dravecky	.10	.08	.04
45	Del Ennis	.10	.08	.04
46	Carl Erskine	.10	.08	.04
47	Johnny Evers	.25	.20	.10
48	Elroy Face	.10	.08	.04
49	Rick Ferrell	.25	.20	.10
50	Mark Fidrych	.10	.08	.04
51	Curt Flood	.10	.08	.04
52	Whitey Ford	.50	.40	.20
53	George Foster	.10	.08	.04
54	Jimmie Foxx	.25	.20	.10
55	Jim Fregosi	.10	.08	.04
56	Phil Garner	.10	.08	.04
57	Ralph Garr	.10	.08	.04
58	Lou Gehrig	2.00	1.50	.80
59	Bobby Grich	.10	.08	.04
60	Jerry Grote	.10	.08	.04
61	Harvey Haddix	.10	.08	.04
62	Toby Harrah	.10	.08	.04
63	Bud Harrelson	.10	.08	.04
64	Jim Hegan	.10	.08	.04
65	Gil Hodges	.25	.20	.10
66	Ken Holtzman	.10	.08	.04
67	Bob Horner	.10	.08	.04
68	Rogers Hornsby	.25	.20	.10
69	Carl Hubbell	.25	.20	.10
70	Ron Hunt	.10	.08	.04
71	Monte Irvin	.25	.20	.10
72	Reggie Jackson	.50	.40	.20
73	Larry Jansen	.10	.08	.04
74	Ferguson Jenkins	.25	.20	.10
75	Tommy John	.15	.11	.06
76	Cliff Johnson	.10	.08	.04
77	Davey Johnson	.10	.08	.04
78	Walter Johnson	.50	.40	.20
79	George Kell	.25	.20	.10
80	Don Kessinger	.10	.08	.04
81	Vern Law	.10	.08	.04
82	Dennis Leonard	.10	.08	.04
83	Johnny Logan	.10	.08	.04
84	Mickey Lolich	.10	.08	.04
85	Jim Lonborg	.10	.08	.04
86	Bill Madlock	.10	.08	.04
87	Mickey Mantle	3.00	2.25	1.25
88	Billy Martin	.25	.20	.10
89	Christy Mathewson	.50	.40	.20
90	Lee May	.10	.08	.04
91	Willie Mays	2.00	1.50	.80
92	Bill Mazeroski	.15	.11	.06
93	Gil McDougald	.10	.08	.04
94	Sam McDowell	.10	.08	.04
95	Minnie Minoso	.10	.08	.04
96	Johnny Mize	.25	.20	.10
97	Rick Monday	.10	.08	.04
98	Wally Moon	.10	.08	.04
99	Manny Mota	.10	.08	.04
100	Bobby Murcer	.10	.08	.04
101	Ron Necciai	.10	.08	.04
102	Al Oliver	.10	.08	.04
103	Mel Ott	.25	.20	.10
104	Mel Parnell	.10	.08	.04
105	Jimmy Piersall	.10	.08	.04
106	Johnny Podres	.10	.08	.04
107	Bobby Richardson	.15	.11	.06
108	Robin Roberts	.25	.20	.10
109	Al Rosen	.10	.08	.04
110	Babe Ruth	4.00	3.00	1.50
111	Joe Sambito	.10	.08	.04
112	Manny Sanguillen	.10	.08	.04
113	Ron Santo	.10	.08	.04
114	Bill Skowron	.15	.11	.06
115	Enos Slaughter	.25	.20	.10
116	Warren Spahn	.25	.20	.10
117	Tris Speaker	.25	.20	.10
118	Frank Thomas	.10	.08	.04
119	Bobby Thomson	.10	.08	.04
120	Andre Thornton	.10	.08	.04
121	Marv Throneberry	.10	.08	.04
122	Luis Tiant	.10	.08	.04
123	Joe Tinker	.25	.20	.10
124	Honus Wagner	.50	.40	.20
125	Bill White	.10	.08	.04
126	Ted Williams	1.00	.70	.40
127	Earl Wilson	.10	.08	.04
128	Joe Wood	.10	.08	.04
129	Cy Young	.50	.40	.20
130	Richie Zisk	.10	.08	.04
131	Babe Ruth, Lou Gehrig	2.00	1.50	.80
132	Ted Williams, Rogers Hornsby	.50	.40	.20
133	Lou Gehrig, Babe Ruth	2.00	1.50	.80
134	Babe Ruth, Mickey Mantle	3.00	2.25	1.25
135	Mickey Mantle, Reggie Jackson	1.50	1.25	.60
136	Mel Ott, Carl Hubbell	.25	.20	.10
137	Mickey Mantle, Willie Mays	2.00	1.50	.80
138	Cy Young, Walter Johnson	.50	.40	.20
139	Honus Wagner, Rogers Hornsby	.50	.40	.20
140	Mickey Mantle, Whitey Ford	1.50	1.25	.60
141	Mickey Mantle, Billy Martin	1.50	1.25	.60
142	Cy Young, Walter Johnson	.50	.40	.20
143	Christy Mathewson, Walter Johnson	.50	.40	.20
144	Warren Spahn, Christy Mathewson	.50	.40	.20
145	Honus Wagner, Ty Cobb	1.00	.70	.40
146	Babe Ruth, Ty Cobb	2.00	1.50	.80
147	Joe Tinker, Johnny Evers	.50	.40	.20
148	Johnny Evers, Frank Chance	.50	.40	.20
149	Hank Aaron, Babe Ruth	2.00	1.50	.80
150	Willie Mays, Hank Aaron	1.00	.70	.40
151	Babe Ruth, Willie Mays	1.50	1.25	.60
152	Babe Ruth, Whitey Ford	1.50	1.25	.60
153	Larry Doby, Minnie Minoso	.10	.08	.04
154	Joe Black, Monte Irvin	.10	.08	.04
155	Joe Wood, Christy Mathewson	.25	.20	.10
156	Christy Mathewson, Cy Young	.50	.40	.20
157	Cy Young, Joe Wood	.25	.20	.10
158	Cy Young, Whitey Ford	.25	.20	.10
159	Cy Young, Ferguson Jenkins	.25	.20	.10

		MT	NR MT	EX
160	Ty Cobb, Rogers Hornsby	1.00	.70	.40
161	Tris Speaker, Ted Williams	.50	.40	.20
162	Rogers Hornsby, Ted Williams	.50	.40	.20
163	Willie Mays, Monte Irvin	.50	.40	.20
164	Willie Mays, Bobby Thomson	.50	.40	.20
165	Reggie Jackson, Mickey Mantle	1.50	1.25	.60

1993 Upper Deck All-Time Heroes T202 Reprints

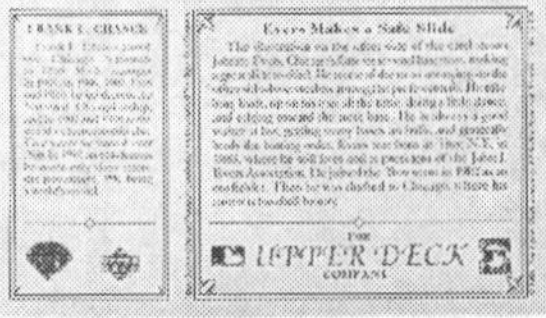

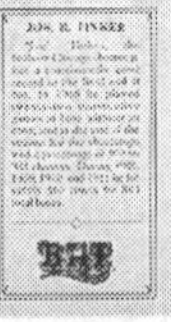

A series of 10 reprints of the classic 1912 Hassan "Triplefolders" baseball cards on which the All-Time Heroes set was patterned was included as random inserts in the Upper Deck old-timers set. The reprints measure 5-1/4" x 2-1/4" (same as the originals). The Hassan cigarette ads on the backs of the originals have been replaced on the reprints by an Upper Deck hologram and the logos of the card company, B.A.T., Major League Baseball and the Cooperstown Collection. The Hassan cards are known as T202, their designation in the "American Card Catalog." The reprints are unnumbered and are checklisted here alphabetically in order of the player appearing on the left end of each card.

		MT	NR MT	EX
Complete set (10):		10.00	7.50	4.00
Common player:		.50	.40	.20
(1)	Art Devlin/ Christy Mathewson	1.00	.70	.40
(2)	Hugh Jennings/ Ty Cobb	2.00	1.50	.80
(3)	John Kling/ Cy Young	1.00	.70	.40
(4)	Jack Knight/ Walter Johnson	.75	.60	.30
(5)	John McGraw/ Hugh Jennings	.50	.40	.20
(6)	George Moriarty/ Ty Cobb	2.00	1.50	.80
(7)	Charley O'Leary/ Ty Cobb	2.00	1.50	.80
(8)	Charley O'Leary/ Ty Cobb	2.00	1.50	.80
(9)	Joe Tinker/ Frank Chance	1.00	.70	.40
(10)	Joe Wood/ Tris Speaker	.50	.40	.20

1993 Upper Deck Iooss Collection Super

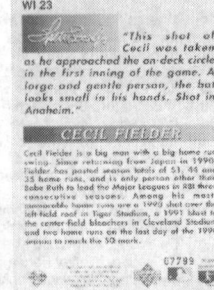

The Upper Deck Co. issued a series of 27 individually numbered oversized cards identical to the Iooss Collection insert cards in the regular Upper Deck set in 1993. The cards are 3-1/2" by 5" and each card is numbered to a limit of 10,000. The cards were available in retail outlets such as WalMart, packaged in blister packs with two foil packs of 1993 Upper Deck cards for a retail price of around $4.97.

		MT	NR MT	EX
Complete Set:		85.00	64.00	34.00
Common Player:		3.00	2.25	1.25
1	Tim Salmon	6.00	4.50	2.50
2	Jeff Bagwell	4.00	3.00	1.50
3	Mark McGwire	5.00	3.75	2.00
4	Roberto Alomar	5.00	3.75	2.00
5	Steve Avery	4.00	3.00	1.50
6	Paul Molitor	4.00	3.00	1.50
7	Ozzie Smith	4.00	3.00	1.50
8	Mark Grace	3.00	2.25	1.25
9	Eric Karros	4.00	3.00	1.50
10	Delino DeShields	3.00	2.25	1.25
11	Will Clark	4.00	3.00	1.50
12	Albert Belle	3.00	2.25	1.25
13	Ken Griffey, Jr.	7.50	5.75	3.00
14	Howard Johnson	3.00	2.25	1.25
15	Cal Ripken, Jr.	6.00	4.50	2.50
16	Fred McGriff	3.50	2.75	1.50
17	Darren Daulton	3.00	2.25	1.25
18	Andy Van Slyke	3.00	2.25	1.25
19	Nolan Ryan	7.50	5.75	3.00
20	Wade Boggs	4.00	3.00	1.50
21	Barry Larkin	3.50	2.75	1.50
22	George Brett	5.00	3.75	2.00
23	Cecil Fielder	4.00	3.00	1.50
24	Kirby Puckett	4.00	3.00	1.50
25	Frank Thomas	7.50	5.75	3.00
26	Don Mattingly	4.00	3.00	1.50
27	Iooss Header	3.00	2.25	1.25

1993 Upper Deck 5th Anniversary Super

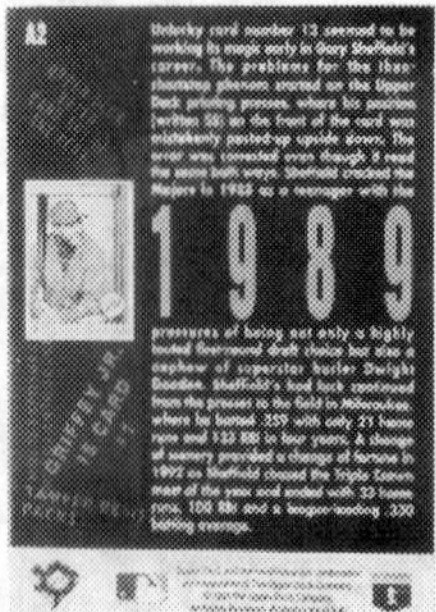

This set of oversized (3-1/2" by 5") cards is simply an enlarged version of the Upper Deck 5th Anniversary subset that was inserted with the company's 1993 cards. There are 15 cards in the set, which are reprinted versions of some of the most popular cards in the last five years from Upper Deck. Each of the cards carries a number on the back out of a limit of 10,000 total. The cards were sold individually in blister packs at retail outlets along with two packs of 1993 Upper Deck.

		MT	NR MT	EX
Complete Set:		52.50	39.00	21.00
Common Player:		3.00	2.25	1.25
1	Ken Griffey, Jr.	9.00	6.75	3.50
2	Gary Sheffield	3.00	2.25	1.25
3	Roberto Alomar	4.00	3.00	1.50
4	Jim Abbott	4.00	3.00	1.50
5	Nolan Ryan	7.50	5.75	3.00
6	Juan Gonzalez	5.00	3.75	2.00
7	David Justice	4.00	3.00	1.50
8	Carlos Baerga	3.50	2.75	1.50
9	Reggie Jackson	4.00	3.00	1.50
10	Eric Karros	3.50	2.75	1.50
11	Chipper Jones	3.00	2.25	1.25

		MT	NR MT	EX
12	Ivan Rodriguez	3.00	2.25	1.25
13	Pat Listach	3.00	2.25	1.25
14	Frank Thomas	7.50	5.75	3.00
15	Tim Salmon	6.00	4.50	2.50

1993 Upper Deck Reggie Jackson Heroes Super

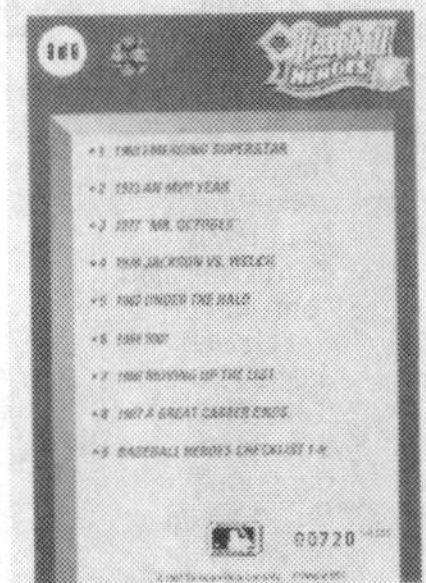

Upper Deck issued a large version of its 1990 Heroes Reggie Jackson cards that was available in retail outlets. Just as in the case of the regular issue Jackson insert cards, there are 10 cards (nine numbered and one un-numbered header card). The cards are 3-1/2" by 5" and identical to the smaller Heroes cards in every other respect. Each of the individual cards carries a sequential number out of a limit of 10,000. The cards were sold one to a package that also included two packs of 1993 Upper Deck cards for about $4.97.

		MT	NR MT	EX
Complete set:		35.00	26.00	14.00
Common card:		5.00	3.75	2.00
1	1969 Emerging Superstar (Reggie Jackson)	5.00	3.75	2.00
2	1973 An MVP Year (Reggie Jackson)	5.00	3.75	2.00
3	1977 "Mr. October" (Reggie Jackson)	5.00	3.75	2.00
4	1978 Jackson vs. Welch (Reggie Jackson)	5.00	3.75	2.00
5	1982 Under the Halo (Reggie Jackson)	5.00	3.75	2.00
6	1984 500! (Reggie Jackson)	5.00	3.75	2.00
7	1986 Moving Up the List (Reggie Jackson)	5.00	3.75	2.00
8	1987 A Great Career Ends (Reggie Jackson)	5.00	3.75	2.00
9	Heroes Checklist (Reggie Jackson)	5.00	3.75	2.00
—	Header card	5.00	3.75	2.00

1993 Upper Deck Triple Crown

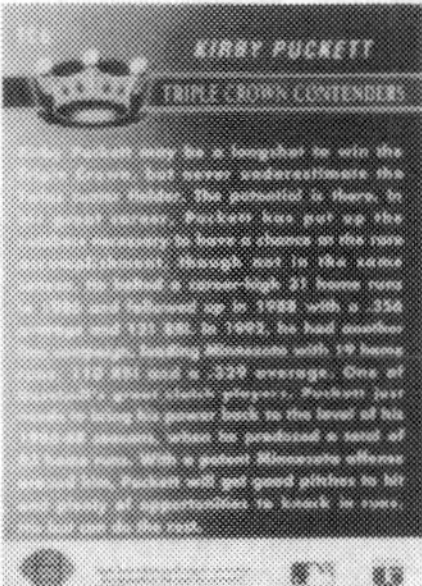

These insert cards were available in 1993 Upper Deck Series I foil packs sold by hobby dealers. The set features 10 players who are candidates to win baseball's Triple Crown. Card fronts have a crown and the player's name at the bottom. Backs put that material at the top and explain why the player might lead the league in home runs, batting average and runs batted in.

		MT	NR MT	EX
Complete Set (10):		36.00	27.00	14.50
Common Player:		1.75	1.25	.70
1	Barry Bonds	5.00	3.75	2.00
2	Jose Canseco	2.00	1.50	.80
3	Will Clark	2.50	2.00	1.00
4	Ken Griffey Jr.	9.00	6.75	3.50
5	Fred McGriff	3.00	2.25	1.25
6	Kirby Puckett	4.50	3.50	1.75
7	Cal Ripken, Jr.	4.50	3.50	1.75
8	Gary Sheffield	2.50	2.00	1.00
9	Frank Thomas	10.00	7.50	4.00
10	Larry Walker	1.75	1.25	.70

1993 Upper Deck Diamond Gallery

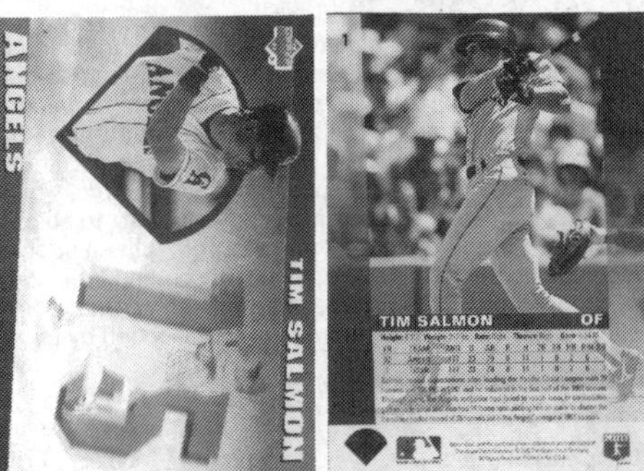

Utilizing something the company calls lithogram technology, Upper Deck produced a 36-card set in 1993 that combined four-colr photography and a holographic image. It featured one star from each of the 28 teams, along with a subset spot- lighting top rookies from 1993 and cards saluting Nolan Ryan, Rickey Henderson and Ozzie Smith. The set came in a specially- designed box, with a numbered checklist card. The set was limited to a total of 123,600.

		MT	NR MT	EX
Complete Set:		35.00	26.00	14.00
Common Player:		.50	.40	.20
1	Tim Salmon	3.00	2.25	1.25
2	Jeff Bagwell	.75	.60	.30
3	Mark McGwire	1.50	1.25	.60
4	Roberto Alomar	2.00	1.50	.80
5	Terry Pendleton	.50	.40	.20
6	Robin Yount	3.00	2.25	1.25
7	Ray Lankford	.75	.60	.30
8	Ryne Sandberg	4.00	3.00	1.50
9	Darryl Strawberry	1.00	.70	.40
10	Marquis Grissom	.50	.40	.20
11	Barry Bonds	3.00	2.25	1.25
12	Carlos Baerga	1.00	.70	.40
13	Ken Griffey, Jr.	5.00	3.75	2.00
14	Benito Santiago	.75	.60	.30
15	Dwight Gooden	.75	.60	.30
16	Cal Ripken, Jr.	4.00	3.00	1.50
17	Tony Gwynn	1.00	.70	.40
18	Dave Hollins	.50	.40	.20
19	Andy Van Slyke	.75	.60	.30
20	Juan Gonzalez	3.50	2.75	1.50
21	Roger Clemens	1.50	1.25	.60
22	Barry Larkin	1.00	.70	.40
23	Dave Nied	1.50	1.25	.60
24	George Brett	4.00	3.00	1.50
25	Travis Fryman	.75	.60	.30
26	Kirby Puckett	3.00	2.25	1.25
27	Frank Thomas	5.00	3.75	2.00
28	Don Mattingly	3.00	2.25	1.25

		MT	NR MT	EX
29	Rickey Henderson	3.00	2.25	1.25
30	Nolan Ryan	5.00	3.75	2.00
31	Ozzie Smith	3.00	2.25	1.25
32	Wilfredo Cordero	1.50	1.25	.60
33	Phil Hyatt	1.50	1.25	.60
34	Mike Piazza	3.50	2.75	1.50
35	J.T. Snow	1.50	1.25	.60
36	Kevin Young	1.50	1.25	.60

1993 Upper Deck SP

This is Upper Deck's first ever super premium baseball card set. There are 290 cards in the single-series set; 252 are individual player cards, while the remainder includes a Premier Prospects subset featuring top prospects (20 cards), 18 All-Stars and a Platinum Power insert set of 20 top home run hitters. Cards, which were available in 12-card foil packs, feature full-bleed color photos and UV coating on the front, plus a special logo using lenticular printing. Foil is also used intricately in the design. Backs have a larger color photo and statistics. Cards are numbered and color-coded by team.

		MT	NR MT	EX
Complete Set (290):		48.00	36.00	19.00
Common Player:		.10	.08	.04
1	Roberto Alomar	.75	.60	.30
2	Wade Boggs	.25	.20	.10
3	Joe Carter	.35	.25	.14
4	Ken Griffey Jr.	3.00	2.25	1.25
5	Mark Langston	.10	.08	.04
6	John Olerud	1.00	.70	.40
7	Kirby Puckett	.90	.70	.35
8	Cal Ripken, Jr.	1.00	.70	.40
9	Ivan Rodriguez	.40	.30	.15
10	Barry Bonds	1.50	1.25	.60
11	Darren Daulton	.20	.15	.08
12	Marquis Grissom	.20	.15	.08
13	David Justice	.80	.60	.30
14	John Kruk	.10	.08	.04
15	Barry Larkin	.15	.11	.06
16	Terry Mulholland	.10	.08	.04
17	Ryne Sandberg	.80	.60	.30
18	Gary Sheffield	.40	.30	.15
19	Chad Curtis	.60	.45	.25
20	Chili Davis	.10	.08	.04
21	Gary DiSarcina	.10	.08	.04
22	Damion Easley	.10	.08	.04
23	Chuck Finley	.10	.08	.04
24	Luis Polonia	.10	.08	.04
25	Tim Salmon	4.00	3.00	1.50
26	*J.T. Snow*	1.50	1.25	.60
27	Russ Springer	.10	.08	.04
28	Jeff Bagwell	.60	.45	.25
29	Craig Biggio	.10	.08	.04
30	Ken Caminiti	.10	.08	.04
31	Andujar Cedeno	.15	.11	.06
32	Doug Drabek	.10	.08	.04
33	Steve Finley	.10	.08	.04
34	Luis Gonzalez	.20	.15	.08
35	Pete Harnisch	.10	.08	.04
36	Darryl Kile	.10	.08	.04
37	Mike Bordick	.10	.08	.04
38	Dennis Eckersley	.10	.08	.04
39	Brent Gates	.50	.40	.20
40	Rickey Henderson	.30	.25	.12
41	Mark McGwire	.30	.25	.12
42	Craig Paquette	.10	.08	.04
43	Ruben Sierra	.25	.20	.10
44	Terry Steinbach	.10	.08	.04
45	Todd Van Poppel	.25	.20	.10
46	Pat Borders	.10	.08	.04
47	Tony Fernandez	.10	.08	.04
48	Juan Guzman	.60	.45	.25
49	Pat Hentgen	.70	.50	.30
50	Paul Molitor	.40	.30	.15
51	Jack Morris	.10	.08	.04
52	Ed Sprague	.10	.08	.04
53	Duane Ward	.10	.08	.04
54	Devon White	.10	.08	.04
55	Steve Avery	.40	.30	.15
56	Jeff Blauser	.10	.08	.04
57	Ron Gant	.25	.20	.10
58	Tom Glavine	.35	.25	.14
59	Greg Maddux	.30	.25	.12
60	Fred McGriff	.50	.40	.20
61	Terry Pendleton	.10	.08	.04
62	Deion Sanders	.25	.20	.10
63	John Smoltz	.15	.11	.06
64	Cal Eldred	.25	.20	.10
65	Darryl Hamilton	.10	.08	.04
66	John Jaha	.20	.15	.08
67	Pat Listach	.20	.15	.08
68	Jaime Navarro	.10	.08	.04
69	Kevin Reimer	.10	.08	.04
70	B.J. Surhoff	.10	.08	.04
71	Greg Vaughn	.10	.08	.04
72	Robin Yount	.50	.40	.20
73	*Rene Arocha*	.50	.40	.20
74	Bernard Gilkey	.10	.08	.04
75	Gregg Jefferies	.20	.15	.08
76	Ray Lankford	.15	.11	.06
77	Tom Pagnozzi	.10	.08	.04
78	Lee Smith	.10	.08	.04
79	Ozzie Smith	.25	.20	.10
80	Bob Tewksbury	.10	.08	.04
81	Mark Whiten	.15	.11	.06
82	Steve Buechele	.10	.08	.04
83	Mark Grace	.15	.11	.06
84	Jose Guzman	.10	.08	.04
85	Derrick May	.10	.08	.04
86	Mike Morgan	.10	.08	.04
87	Randy Myers	.10	.08	.04
88	Kevin Roberson	.40	.30	.15
89	Sammy Sosa	.15	.11	.06
90	Rick Wilkins	.10	.08	.04
91	Brett Butler	.10	.08	.04
92	Eric Davis	.10	.08	.04
93	Orel Hershiser	.10	.08	.04
94	Eric Karros	.35	.25	.14
95	Ramon Martinez	.10	.08	.04
96	Raul Mondesi	.30	.25	.12
97	Jose Offerman	.10	.08	.04
98	Mike Piazza	6.00	4.50	2.50
99	Darryl Strawberry	.15	.11	.06
100	Moises Alou	.20	.15	.08
101	Wilfredo Cordero	.20	.15	.08
102	Delino DeShields	.15	.11	.06
103	Darrin Fletcher	.10	.08	.04
104	Ken Hill	.10	.08	.04
105	*Mike Lansing*	.60	.45	.25
106	Dennis Martinez	.10	.08	.04
107	Larry Walker	.25	.20	.10
108	John Wetteland	.10	.08	.04
109	Rod Beck	.10	.08	.04
110	John Burkett	.10	.08	.04
111	Will Clark	.40	.30	.15
112	Royce Clayton	.20	.15	.08
113	Darren Lewis	.10	.08	.04
114	Willie McGee	.10	.08	.04
115	Bill Swift	.10	.08	.04
116	Robby Thompson	.10	.08	.04
117	Matt Williams	.20	.15	.08
118	Sandy Alomar Jr.	.10	.08	.04
119	Carlos Baerga	.80	.60	.30
120	Albert Belle	.60	.45	.25
121	Reggie Jefferson	.10	.08	.04
122	Kenny Lofton	.50	.40	.20
123	Wayne Kirby	.10	.08	.04
124	Carlos Martinez	.10	.08	.04
125	Charles Nagy	.10	.08	.04
126	Paul Sorrento	.10	.08	.04
127	Rich Amaral	.10	.08	.04
128	Jay Buhner	.10	.08	.04
129	Norm Charlton	.10	.08	.04
130	Dave Fleming	.25	.20	.10
131	Erik Hanson	.10	.08	.04
132	Randy Johnson	.15	.11	.06
133	Edgar Martinez	.10	.08	.04

		MT	NR MT	EX
134	Tino Martinez	.10	.08	.04
135	Omar Vizquel	.10	.08	.04
136	Bret Barberie	.10	.08	.04
137	Chuck Carr	.10	.08	.04
138	Jeff Conine	.10	.08	.04
139	Orestes Destrade	.10	.08	.04
140	Chris Hammond	.10	.08	.04
141	Bryan Harvey	.10	.08	.04
142	Benito Santiago	.10	.08	.04
143	Walt Weiss	.10	.08	.04
144	*Darrell Whitmore*	.50	.40	.20
145	*Tim Bolger*	.25	.20	.10
146	Bobby Bonilla	.10	.08	.04
147	Jerome Burnitz	.30	.25	.12
148	Vince Coleman	.10	.08	.04
149	Dwight Gooden	.10	.08	.04
150	Todd Hundley	.10	.08	.04
151	Howard Johnson	.10	.08	.04
152	Eddie Murray	.10	.08	.04
153	Bret Saberhagen	.10	.08	.04
154	Brady Anderson	.10	.08	.04
155	Mike Devereaux	.10	.08	.04
156	Jeffrey Hammonds	2.50	2.00	1.00
157	Chris Hoiles	.10	.08	.04
158	Ben McDonald	.10	.08	.04
159	Mark McLemore	.10	.08	.04
160	Mike Mussina	.90	.70	.35
161	Gregg Olson	.10	.08	.04
162	David Segui	.10	.08	.04
163	Derek Bell	.10	.08	.04
164	Andy Benes	.10	.08	.04
165	Archi Cianfrocco	.10	.08	.04
166	Ricky Gutierrez	.10	.08	.04
167	Tony Gwynn	.30	.25	.12
168	Gene Harris	.10	.08	.04
169	Trevor Hoffman	.10	.08	.04
170	*Ray McDavid*	.75	.60	.30
171	Phil Plantier	.20	.15	.08
172	Mariano Duncan	.10	.08	.04
173	Lenny Dykstra	.15	.11	.06
174	Tommy Greene	.10	.08	.04
175	Dave Hollins	.25	.20	.10
176	Pete Incaviglia	.10	.08	.04
177	Mickey Morandini	.10	.08	.04
178	Curt Schilling	.10	.08	.04
179	Kevin Stocker	1.75	1.25	.70
180	Mitch Williams	.10	.08	.04
181	Stan Belinda	.10	.08	.04
182	Jay Bell	.10	.08	.04
183	Steve Cooke	.10	.08	.04
184	Carlos Garcia	.60	.45	.25
185	Jeff King	.10	.08	.04
186	Orlando Merced	.10	.08	.04
187	Don Slaught	.10	.08	.04
188	Andy Van Slyke	.15	.11	.06
189	Kevin Young	.40	.30	.15
190	Kevin Brown	.10	.08	.04
191	Jose Canseco	.20	.15	.08
192	Julio Franco	.10	.08	.04
193	Benji Gil	.50	.40	.20
194	Juan Gonzalez	3.00	2.25	1.25
195	Tom Henke	.10	.08	.04
196	Rafael Palmeiro	.25	.20	.10
197	Dean Palmer	.30	.25	.12
198	Nolan Ryan	2.50	2.00	1.00
199	Roger Clemens	.60	.45	.25
200	Scott Cooper	.10	.08	.04
201	Andre Dawson	.15	.11	.06
202	Mike Greenwell	.10	.08	.04
203	Carlos Quintana	.10	.08	.04
204	Jeff Russell	.10	.08	.04
205	Aaron Sele	1.75	1.25	.70
206	Mo Vaughn	.50	.40	.20
207	Frank Viola	.10	.08	.04
208	Rob Dibble	.10	.08	.04
209	Roberto Kelly	.10	.08	.04
210	Kevin Mitchell	.10	.08	.04
211	Hal Morris	.10	.08	.04
212	Joe Oliver	.10	.08	.04
213	Jose Rijo	.10	.08	.04
214	Bip Roberts	.10	.08	.04
215	Chris Sabo	.10	.08	.04
216	Reggie Sanders	.20	.15	.08
217	Dante Bichette	.10	.08	.04
218	Jerald Clark	.10	.08	.04
219	Alex Cole	.10	.08	.04
220	Andres Galarraga	.15	.11	.06
221	Joe Girardi	.10	.08	.04
222	Charlie Hayes	.10	.08	.04
223	*Robert Mejia*	.60	.45	.25
224	Armando Reynoso	.10	.08	.04

		MT	NR MT	EX
225	Eric Young	.30	.25	.12
226	Kevin Appier	.10	.08	.04
227	George Brett	.50	.40	.20
228	David Cone	.10	.08	.04
229	Phil Hiatt	.40	.30	.15
230	Felix Jose	.10	.08	.04
231	Wally Joyner	.10	.08	.04
232	Mike Macfarlane	.10	.08	.04
233	Brian McRae	.10	.08	.04
234	Jeff Montgomery	.10	.08	.04
235	Rob Deer	.10	.08	.04
236	Cecil Fielder	.40	.30	.15
237	Travis Fryman	.80	.60	.30
238	Mike Henneman	.10	.08	.04
239	Tony Phillips	.10	.08	.04
240	Mickey Tettleton	.10	.08	.04
241	Alan Trammell	.10	.08	.04
242	David Wells	.10	.08	.04
243	Lou Whitaker	.10	.08	.04
244	Rick Aguilera	.10	.08	.04
245	Scott Erickson	.10	.08	.04
246	Brian Harper	.10	.08	.04
247	Kent Hrbek	.10	.08	.04
248	Chuck Knoblauch	.20	.15	.08
249	Shane Mack	.10	.08	.04
250	David McCarty	1.00	.70	.40
251	Pedro Munoz	.10	.08	.04
252	Dave Winfield	.35	.25	.14
253	Alex Fernandez	.15	.11	.06
254	Ozzie Guillen	.10	.08	.04
255	Bo Jackson	.25	.20	.10
256	Lance Johnson	.10	.08	.04
257	Ron Karkovice	.10	.08	.04
258	Jack McDowell	.30	.25	.12
259	Tim Raines	.10	.08	.04
260	Frank Thomas	4.00	3.00	1.50
261	Robin Ventura	.40	.30	.15
262	Jim Abbott	.10	.08	.04
263	Steve Farr	.10	.08	.04
264	Jimmy Key	.10	.08	.04
265	Don Mattingly	.30	.25	.12
266	Paul O'Neill	.10	.08	.04
267	Mike Stanley	.10	.08	.04
268	Danny Tartabull	.10	.08	.04
269	Bob Wickman	.25	.20	.10
270	Bernie Williams	.10	.08	.04
271	Jason Bere	1.50	1.25	.60
272	*Roger Cedeno*	.50	.40	.20
273	*Johnny Damon*	1.00	.70	.40
274	*Russ Davis*	.60	.45	.25
275	Carlos Delgado	2.50	2.00	1.00
276	Carl Everett	.20	.15	.08
277	Cliff Floyd	4.00	3.00	1.50
278	Alex Gonzalez	.80	.60	.30
279	*Derek Jeter*	1.00	.70	.40
280	Chipper Jones	1.50	1.25	.60
281	Javy Lopez	1.25	.90	.50
282	*Chad Mottola*	2.00	1.50	.80
283	Marc Newfield	.50	.40	.20
284	Eduardo Perez	1.00	.70	.40
285	Manny Ramirez	2.00	1.50	.80
286	*Todd Steverson*	.75	.60	.30
287	Michael Tucker	1.00	.70	.40
288	Allen Watson	1.00	.70	.40
289	Rondell White	2.00	1.50	.80
290	Dmitri Young	.60	.45	.25

1993 Upper Deck SP Platinum Power

This 20-card insert set features 20 of the game's top home run hitters. The top of each insert card features a special die cut treatment. Backs are numbered with a PP prefix.

		MT	NR MT	EX
Complete Set (20):		160.00	120.00	64.00
Common Player:		4.00	3.00	1.50
1	Albert Belle	10.00	7.50	4.00
2	Barry Bonds	14.00	10.50	5.50
3	Joe Carter	8.00	6.00	3.25
4	Will Clark	7.00	5.25	2.75
5	Darren Daulton	4.00	3.00	1.50
6	Cecil Fielder	7.50	5.75	3.00
7	Ron Gant	4.50	3.50	1.75
8	Juan Gonzalez	16.00	12.00	6.50
9	Ken Griffey Jr.	18.00	13.50	7.25
10	Dave Hollins	4.00	3.00	1.50
11	David Justice	11.00	8.25	4.50
12	Fred McGriff	8.00	6.00	3.25
13	Mark McGwire	4.00	3.00	1.50
14	Dean Palmer	4.50	3.50	1.75
15	Mike Piazza	30.00	22.00	12.00
16	Tim Salmon	20.00	15.00	8.00
17	Ryne Sandberg	10.00	7.50	4.00
18	Gary Sheffield	7.00	5.25	2.75
19	Frank Thomas	22.00	16.50	8.75
20	Matt Williams	4.50	3.50	1.75

1993 Upper Deck Fun Packs

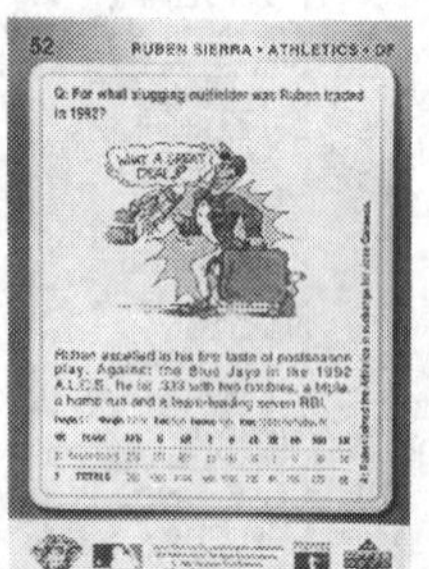

Aimed at the younger audience, this Upper Deck product features 150 "regular" player cards and 75 specialty cards in a varietty of subsets, plus two different types of insert cards. The basic player cards feature a photo (generally an action shot) set onto a background of purple, green and red, highlighted by yellow and orange stripes. On back is a white panel set against a red, yellow and orange blended stripes. In the panel are a cartoon, a trivia question and answer about the player, and some brief biographical details, stats and career summary. The basic player cards are arranged within the set in alphabetical order by team. The teams are also arranged alphabetically, according to their popular nickname. Leading off each team's roster in the set is a "Glow Stars" sticker. These feature a color player photo against a parti-colored background. The area around the photo is die-cut to allow the player's picture to be separated from the background and stuck to a wall, where the white and green outlines glow in the dark. Cards #1-9 are designated as "Stars of Tomorrow". Both front and back have a background of a star-studded purple sky. On front, the player's name appears in white in a stadium setting at bottom. The player is pictured in an action pose above the stadium, outlined as a constellation. On back is a portrait photo, a prediction of future greatness and a few stats and biographical details. Cards 10-21 are "Hot Shots" - heat-sensitive cards. When touched the black textured ink which surrounds the player photo turns clear, revealing a colored pattern beneath. Backs, which are not heat-sensitive, have a short career write-up. Cards 22-27 are "Kid Stars" and feature a childhood photo and a clue to the player's identity against a background of blue, pink and purple question marks. Pink and orange backs have a color photo of the player. Cards 28-37 are checklisted as "Upper Deck Heroes", though that designation does not appear on the cards. The subset is done in comic-book art style, and feature a blackboard motiff on front and back, on which player photos are superimposed and annotated with basketball playing tips. Cards 216-220 are designated "Foldouts" and are double-size (2-1/2"x7"). Fronts have a purple background photo of the player, with a full-color action photo superimposed. The player's name and position are in blue on a vertical yellow band at right. Backs have previous year and career stats and a player profile. Inside the Foldout is a full-color version of the front background photo, showing the playing leadping or diving to make a play. Yellow strips at left and right have the player's name. The five checklist cards which conclude the set have player photos on front.

		MT	NR MT	EX
Complete Set (225):		30.00	22.00	12.00
Common Player:		.10	.08	.04
1	Wil Cordero (Stars of Tomorrow)	.50	.40	.20
2	Brent Gates (Stars of Tomorrow)	.20	.15	.08
3	Benji Gil (Stars of Tomorrow)	.20	.15	.08
4	Phil Hiatt (Stars of Tomorrow)	.20	.15	.08
5	David McCarty (Stars of Tomorrow)	.25	.20	.10
6	Mike Piazza (Stars of Tomorrow)	2.00	1.50	.80
7	Tim Salmon (Stars of Tomorrow)	1.50	1.25	.60
8	J.T. Snow (Stars of Tomorrow)	.40	.30	.15
9	Kevin Young (Stars of Tomorrow)	.50	.40	.20
10	Roberto Alomar (Hot Shots)	.50	.40	.20
11	Barry Bonds (Hot Shots)	.60	.45	.25
12	Jose Canseco (Hot Shots)	.20	.15	.08
13	Will Clark (Hot Shots)	.50	.40	.20
14	Roger Clemens (Hot Shots)	.35	.25	.14
15	Juan Gonzalez (Hot Shots)	.50	.40	.20
16	Ken Griffey, Jr. (Hot Shots)	.80	.60	.30
17	Mark McGwire (Hot Shots)	.35	.25	.14
18	Nolan Ryan (Hot Shots)	.80	.60	.30
19	Ryne Sandberg (Hot Shots)	.60	.45	.25
20	Gary Sheffield (Hot Shots)	.25	.20	.10
21	Frank Thomas (Hot Shots)	.80	.60	.30
22	Roberto Alomar (Kid Stars)	.10	.08	.04
23	Roger Clemens (Kid Stars)	.10	.08	.04
24	Ken Griffey, Jr. (Kid Stars)	.25	.20	.10
25	Gary Sheffield (Kid Stars)	.10	.08	.04
26	Nolan Ryan (Kid Stars)	.25	.20	.10
27	Frank Thomas (Kid Stars)	.25	.20	.10
28	Reggie Jackson (Heroes)	.15	.11	.06
29	Roger Clemens (Heroes)	.10	.08	.04
30	Ken Griffey, Jr. (Heroes)	.25	.20	.10
31	Bo Jackson (Heroes)	.15	.11	.06
32	Cal Ripken, Jr. (Heroes)	.15	.11	.06
33	Nolan Ryan (Heroes)	.25	.20	.10
34	Deion Sanders (Heroes)	.15	.11	.06
35	Ozzie Smith (Heroes)	.10	.08	.04
36	Frank Thomas (Heroes)	.10	.08	.04
37	Tim Salmon (Glow Stars)	.25	.20	.10
38	Chili Davis	.10	.08	.04
39	Chuck Finley	.10	.08	.04
40	Mark Langston	.10	.08	.04
41	Luis Polonia	.10	.08	.04
42	Jeff Bagwell (Glow Stars)	.20	.15	.08
43	Jeff Bagwell	.15	.11	.06
44	Craig Biggio	.10	.08	.04
45	Ken Caminiti	.10	.08	.04
46	Doug Drabek	.10	.08	.04
47	Steve Finley	.12	.09	.05
48	Mark McGwire (Glow Stars)	.25	.20	.10
49	Dennis Eckersley	.12	.09	.05
50	Rickey Henderson	.20	.15	.08
51	Mark McGwire	.20	.15	.08
52	Ruben Sierra	.15	.11	.06
53	Terry Steinbach	.10	.08	.04
54	Roberto Alomar (Glow Stars)	.25	.20	.10
55	Roberto Alomar	.25	.20	.10
56	Joe Carter	.15	.11	.06
57	Juan Guzman	.10	.08	.04
58	Paul Molitor	.25	.20	.10
59	Jack Morris	.12	.09	.05
60	John Olerud	.20	.15	.08
61	Tom Glavine (Glow Stars)	.15	.11	.06
62	Steve Avery	.15	.11	.06
63	Tom Glavine	.12	.09	.05
64	David Justice	.20	.15	.08
65	Greg Maddux	.15	.11	.06
66	Terry Pendleton	.10	.08	.04

		MT	NR MT	EX
67	Deion Sanders	.20	.15	.08
68	John Smoltz	.12	.09	.05
69	Robin Yount (Glow Stars)	.25	.20	.10
70	Cal Eldred	.12	.09	.05
71	Pat Listach	.10	.08	.04
72	Greg Vaughn	.10	.08	.04
73	Robin Yount	.35	.25	.14
74	Ozzie Smith (Glow Stars)	.20	.15	.08
75	Gregg Jefferies	.20	.15	.08
76	Ray Lankford	.15	.11	.06
77	Lee Smith	.12	.09	.05
78	Ozzie Smith	.20	.15	.08
79	Bob Tewksbury	.10	.08	.04
80	Ryne Sandberg (Glow Stars)	.25	.20	.10
81	Mark Grace	.15	.11	.06
82	Mike Morgan	.10	.08	.04
83	Randy Myers	.10	.08	.04
84	Ryne Sandberg	.75	.60	.30
85	Sammy Sosa	.15	.11	.06
86	Eric Karros (Glow Stars)	.20	.15	.08
87	Brett Butler	.10	.08	.04
88	Orel Hershiser	.15	.11	.06
89	Eric Karros	.20	.15	.08
90	Ramon Martinez	.10	.08	.04
91	Jose Offerman	.10	.08	.04
92	Darryl Strawberry	.20	.15	.08
93	Marquis Grissom (Glow Stars)	.15	.11	.06
94	Delino DeShields	.20	.15	.08
95	Marquis Grissom	.15	.11	.06
96	Ken Hill	.10	.08	.04
97	Dennis Martinez	.12	.09	.05
98	Larry Walker	.15	.11	.06
99	Barry Bonds (Glow Stars)	.25	.20	.10
100	Barry Bonds	.35	.25	.14
101	Will Clark	.35	.25	.14
102	Bill Swift	.10	.08	.04
103	Robby Thompson	.10	.08	.04
104	Matt Williams	.15	.11	.06
105	Carlos Baerga (Glow Stars)	.20	.15	.08
106	Sandy Alomar, Jr.	.10	.08	.04
107	Carlos Baerga	.25	.20	.10
108	Albert Belle	.20	.15	.08
109	Kenny Lofton	.15	.11	.06
110	Charles Nagy	.10	.08	.04
111	Ken Griffey, Jr. (Glow Stars)	.50	.40	.20
112	Jay Buhner	.15	.11	.06
113	Dave Fleming	.10	.08	.04
114	Ken Griffey, Jr.	1.00	.70	.40
115	Randy Johnson	.15	.11	.06
116	Edgar Martinez	.15	.11	.06
117	Benito Santiago (Glow Stars)	.20	.15	.08
118	Bret Barberie	.10	.08	.04
119	Jeff Conine	.15	.11	.06
120	Brian Harvey	.12	.09	.05
121	Benito Santiago	.20	.15	.08
122	Walt Weiss	.10	.08	.04
123	Dwight Gooden (Glow Stars)	.20	.15	.08
124	Bobby Bonilla	.15	.11	.06
125	Tony Fernandez	.12	.09	.05
126	Dwight Gooden	.20	.15	.08
127	Howard Johnson	.15	.11	.06
128	Eddie Murray	.15	.11	.06
129	Bret Saberhagen	.12	.09	.05
130	Cal Ripken, Jr. (Glow Stars)	.25	.20	.10
131	Brady Anderson	.12	.09	.05
132	Mike Devereaux	.10	.08	.04
133	Ben McDonald	.10	.08	.04
134	Mike Mussina	.15	.11	.06
135	Cal Ripken, Jr.	.75	.60	.30
136	Fred McGriff (Glow Stars)	.20	.15	.08
137	Andy Benes	.12	.09	.05
138	Tony Gwynn	.20	.15	.08
139	Fred McGriff	.20	.15	.08
140	Phil Plantier	.10	.08	.04
141	Gary Sheffield	.20	.15	.08
142	Darren Daulton (Glow Stars)	.15	.11	.06
143	Darren Daulton	.12	.09	.05
144	Len Dykstra	.15	.11	.06
145	Dave Hollins	.12	.09	.05
146	John Kruk	.15	.11	.06
147	Mitch Williams	.10	.08	.04
148	Andy Van Slyke (Glow Stars)	.15	.11	.06
149	Jay Bell	.15	.11	.06
150	Zane Smith	.10	.08	.04
151	Andy Van Slyke	.15	.11	.06
152	Tim Wakefield	.10	.08	.04
153	Juan Gonzalez (Glow Stars)	.25	.20	.10
154	Kevin Brown	.10	.08	.04
155	Jose Canseco	.20	.15	.08
156	Juan Gonzalez	.35	.25	.14
157	Rafael Palmeiro	.20	.15	.08
158	Dean Palmer	.15	.11	.06
159	Ivan Rodriguez	.15	.11	.06
160	Nolan Ryan	1.00	.70	.40
161	Roger Clemens (Glow Stars)	.20	.15	.08
162	Roger Clemens	.20	.15	.08
163	Andre Dawson	.20	.15	.08
164	Mike Greenwell	.15	.11	.06
165	Tony Pena	.10	.08	.04
166	Frank Viola	.10	.08	.04
167	Barry Larkin (Glow Stars)	.15	.11	.06
168	Rob Dibble	.10	.08	.04
169	Roberto Kelly	.15	.11	.06
170	Barry Larkin	.15	.11	.06
171	Kevin Mitchell	.12	.09	.05
172	Bip Roberts	.10	.08	.04
173	Andres Galarrage (Glow Stars)	.20	.15	.08
174	Dante Bichette	.12	.09	.05
175	Jerald Clark	.10	.08	.04
176	Andres Galarraga	.20	.15	.08
177	Charlie Hayes	.12	.09	.05
178	David Nied	.12	.09	.05
179	David Cone (Glow Stars)	.15	.11	.06
180	Kevin Appler	.10	.08	.04
181	George Brett	.60	.45	.25
182	David Cone	.10	.08	.04
183	Felix Jose	.10	.08	.04
184	Wally Joyner	.15	.11	.06
185	Cecil Fielder (Glow Stars)	.20	.15	.08
186	Cecil Fielder	.20	.15	.08
187	Travis Fryman	.15	.11	.06
188	Tony Phillips	.10	.08	.04
189	Mickey Telleton	.12	.09	.05
190	Lou Whitaker	.15	.11	.06
191	Kirby Puckett (Glow Stars)	.25	.20	.10
192	Scott Erickson	.12	.09	.05
193	Chuck Knoblauch	.12	.09	.05
194	Shane Mack	.12	.09	.05
195	Kirby Puckett	.25	.20	.10
196	Dave Winfield	.35	.25	.14
197	Frank Thomas (Glow Stars)	.50	.40	.20
198	George Bell	.10	.08	.04
199	Bo Jackson	.20	.15	.08
200	Jack McDowell	.15	.11	.06
201	Tim Raines	.15	.11	.06
202	Frank Thomas	1.00	.70	.40
203	Robin Ventura	.20	.15	.08
204	Jim Abbott (Glow Stars)	.25	.20	.10
205	Jim Abbott	.20	.15	.08
206	Wade Boggs	.25	.20	.10
207	Jimmy Key	.10	.08	.04
208	Don Mattingly	.25	.20	.10
209	Danny Tartabull	.15	.11	.06
210	Brett Butler (All-Star Advice)	.10	.08	.04
211	Tony Gwynn (All-Star Advice)	.10	.08	.04
212	Rickey Henderson (All-Star Advice)	.10	.08	.04
213	Ramon Martinez (All-Star Advice)	.10	.08	.04
214	Nolan Ryan (All-Star Advice)	.35	.25	.14
215	Ozzie Smith (All-Star Advice)	.10	.08	.04
216	Marquis Grissom (Fold-Out)	.20	.15	.08
217	Dean Palmer (Fold-Out)	.20	.15	.08
218	Cal Ripken, Jr. (Fold-Out)	.50	.40	.20
219	Deion Sanders (Fold-Out)	.35	.25	.14
220	Darryl Strawberry (Fold-Out)	.25	.20	.10
221	David McCarty (Checklist)	.10	.08	.04
222	Barry Bonds (Checklist)	.10	.08	.04
223	Juan Gonzalez (Checklist)	.10	.08	.04
224	Ken Griffey, Jr. (Checklist)	.10	.08	.04
225	Frank Thomas (Checklist)	.10	.08	.04

1993 Fun Packs All-Star Scratch-Offs

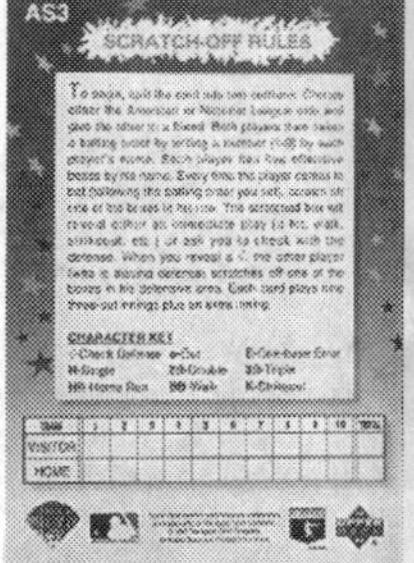

Randomly inserted into Fun Packs was a series of nine

"All-Star Scratch-Off" game cards. Fronts and backs have a star-studded blue background. Inside the folded, double-size (2-1/2" x 7") cards are American and National League line-ups which can be used to play a baseball game, the rules of which are explained on the card backs. On front are photos of two of the players in the line-up, matched by position from each league. The inserts are numbered with an "AS" prefix.

		MT	NR MT	EX
Complete set (9):		21.00	15.50	8.50
Common card:		1.00	.70	.40
1	Fred McGriff vs. Frank Thomas	5.00	3.75	2.00
2	Darren Daulton vs. Ivan Rodriguez	1.00	.70	.40
3	Mark McGwire vs. Will Clark	2.50	2.00	1.00
4	Ryne Sandberg vs. Roberto Alomar	3.00	2.25	1.25
5	Robin Ventura vs. Terry Pendleton	1.00	.70	.40
6	Cal Ripken, Jr. vs. Ozzie Smith	4.00	3.00	1.50
7	Barry Bonds vs. Juan Gonzalez	4.00	3.00	1.50
8	Marquis Grissom vs. Ken Griffey, Jr.	5.00	3.75	2.00
9	Tony Gwynn vs. Kirby Puckett	2.00	1.50	.80

1993 Fun Packs Mascot Madness

Upper Deck's high-tech lithogram process of combining color photos and holograms was used to create the five-card "Mascot Madness" inserts which were randomly found in Fun Packs. The mascot's name appears in pink and purple boxes vertically at left. Against a fading orange background are a color photo and a hologram of the mascot. Backs have a description of the mascot and explain his role with the team.

		MT	NR MT	EX
Complete set (5):		5.00	3.75	2.00
Common card:		1.00	.70	.40
1	Phillie Phanatic	1.00	.70	.40
2	Pirate Parrot	1.00	.70	.40
3	Fredbird	1.00	.70	.40
4	BJ Birdy	1.00	.70	.40
5	Youppi	1.00	.70	.40

1994 Upper Deck Collector's Choice

This 1994 Upper Deck set, released in two series, is more widely available than the regular 1994 UD-brand set. The cards, which feature the traditional UV coating and holograms, have large photos with a narrow, pinstripe-border. Backs have stats and a color photo. Series I has 320 cards and subsets titled Rookie Class, Draft Picks and Top Performers. Each of the regular set's 320 cards is also printed with either a gold (1 in 36 packs) or silver-foil replica signature card. Silver

cards appear in every pack, unless a gold Signature card is included. "You Crash the Card" instant win game cards were also included at least one per box. The contest allows one winner to appear with Ken Griffey, Jr. on his

		MT	NR MT	EX
Complete Set (320):		17.00	12.50	6.75
Common Player:		.05	.04	.02
1	*Rich Becker*	.15	.11	.06
2	Greg Blosser	.15	.11	.06
3	Midre Cummings	.30	.25	.12
4	Carlos Delgado	.90	.70	.35
5	*Steve Dreyer*	.15	.11	.06
6	*Carl Everett*	.15	.11	.06
7	Cliff Floyd	1.00	.70	.40
8	Alex Gonzalez	1.00	.70	.40
9	Shawn Green	.20	.15	.08
10	*Butch Huskey*	.10	.08	.04
11	*Mark Hutton*	.15	.11	.06
12	*Miguel Jimenez*	.15	.11	.06
13	Steve Karsay	.15	.11	.06
14	Marc Newfield	.15	.11	.06
15	Luis Ortiz	.10	.08	.04
16	Manny Ramirez	.60	.45	.25
17	Johnny Ruffin	.15	.11	.06
18	*Scott Stahoviak*	.15	.11	.06
19	Salomon Torres	.10	.08	.04
20	*Gabe White*	.10	.08	.04
21	*Brian Anderson*	.15	.11	.06
22	*Wayne Gomes*	.15	.11	.06
23	*Jeff Granger*	.20	.15	.08
24	*Steve Soderstrom*	.20	.15	.08
25	*Trot Nixon*	.25	.20	.10
26	*Kirk Presley*	.15	.11	.06
27	*Matt Brunson*	.15	.11	.06
28	*Brooks Kieschnick*	.15	.11	.06
29	*Billy Wagner*	.15	.11	.06
30	*Matt Drews*	.15	.11	.06
31	Kurt Abbott	.05	.04	.02
32	Luis Alicea	.05	.04	.02
33	Roberto Alomar	.20	.15	.08
34	Sandy Alomar Jr.	.05	.04	.02
35	Moises Alou	.05	.04	.02
36	Wilson Alvarez	.05	.04	.02
37	Rich Amaral	.05	.04	.02
38	Eric Anthony	.05	.04	.02
39	Luis Aquino	.05	.04	.02
40	Jack Armstrong	.05	.04	.02
41	Rene Arocha	.10	.08	.04
42	Rich Aude	.05	.04	.02
43	Brad Ausmus	.05	.04	.02
44	Steve Avery	.15	.11	.06
45	Bob Ayrault	.05	.04	.02
46	Willie Banks	.05	.04	.02
47	Bret Barberie	.05	.04	.02
48	Kim Batiste	.05	.04	.02
49	Rod Beck	.05	.04	.02
50	*Jason Bere*	1.00	.70	.40
51	Sean Berry	.05	.04	.02
52	Dante Bichette	.05	.04	.02
53	Jeff Blauser	.05	.04	.02
54	Mike Blowers	.05	.04	.02
55	Tim Bogar	.05	.04	.02
56	Tom Bolton	.05	.04	.02
57	Ricky Bones	.05	.04	.02
58	Bobby Bonilla	.05	.04	.02
59	Bret Boone	.05	.04	.02
60	Pat Borders	.05	.04	.02
61	Mike Bordick	.05	.04	.02
62	Daryl Boston	.05	.04	.02

		MT	NR MT	EX
63	Ryan Bowen	.05	.04	.02
64	Jeff Branson	.05	.04	.02
65	George Brett	.15	.11	.06
66	Steve Buechele	.05	.04	.02
67	Dave Burba	.05	.04	.02
68	John Burkett	.05	.04	.02
69	Jeromy Burnitz	.10	.08	.04
70	Brett Butler	.05	.04	.02
71	Rob Butler	.05	.04	.02
72	Ken Caminiti	.05	.04	.02
73	Cris Carpenter	.05	.04	.02
74	Vinny Castilla	.05	.04	.02
75	Andujar Cedeno	.05	.04	.02
76	Wes Chamberlain	.05	.04	.02
77	Archi Cianfrocco	.05	.04	.02
78	Dave Clark	.05	.04	.02
79	Jerald Clark	.05	.04	.02
80	Royce Clayton	.10	.08	.04
81	David Cone	.05	.04	.02
82	Jeff Conine	.05	.04	.02
83	Steve Cooke	.05	.04	.02
84	Scott Cooper	.05	.04	.02
85	Joey Cora	.05	.04	.02
86	Tim Costa	.05	.04	.02
87	Chad Curtis	.10	.08	.04
88	Ron Darling	.05	.04	.02
89	Danny Darwin	.05	.04	.02
90	Rob Deer	.05	.04	.02
91	Jim Deshaies	.05	.04	.02
92	Delino DeShields	.05	.04	.02
93	Rob Dibble	.05	.04	.02
94	Gary DiSarcina	.05	.04	.02
95	Doug Drabek	.05	.04	.02
96	Scott Erickson	.05	.04	.02
97	Rikkert Faneyte	.05	.04	.02
98	Jeff Fassero	.15	.11	.06
99	Alex Fernandez	.10	.08	.04
100	Cecil Fielder	.15	.11	.06
101	Dave Fleming	.05	.04	.02
102	Darrin Fletcher	.05	.04	.02
103	Scott Fletcher	.05	.04	.02
104	Mike Gallego	.05	.04	.02
105	Carlos Garcia	.05	.04	.02
106	Jeff Gardner	.05	.04	.02
107	Brent Gates	.15	.11	.06
108	Benji Gil	.20	.15	.08
109	Bernard Gilkey	.05	.04	.02
110	Chris Gomez	.05	.04	.02
111	Luis Gonzalez	.05	.04	.02
112	Tom Gordon	.05	.04	.02
113	Jim Gott	.05	.04	.02
114	Mark Grace	.05	.04	.02
115	Tommy Greene	.05	.04	.02
116	Willie Greene	.05	.04	.02
117	Ken Griffey Jr.	.75	.60	.30
118	Bill Gullickson	.05	.04	.02
119	Ricky Gutierrez	.05	.04	.02
120	Juan Guzman	.05	.04	.02
121	Chris Gwynn	.05	.04	.02
122	Tony Gwynn	.20	.15	.08
123	Jeffrey Hammonds	.25	.20	.10
124	Erik Hanson	.05	.04	.02
125	Gene Harris	.05	.04	.02
126	Greg Harris	.05	.04	.02
127	Bryan Harvey	.05	.04	.02
128	Billy Hatcher	.05	.04	.02
129	Hilly Hathaway	.05	.04	.02
130	Charlie Hayes	.05	.04	.02
131	Rickey Henderson	.15	.11	.06
132	Mike Henneman	.05	.04	.02
133	Pat Hentgen	.05	.04	.02
134	Roberto Hernandez	.05	.04	.02
135	Orel Hershiser	.05	.04	.02
136	Phil Hiatt	.15	.11	.06
137	Glenallen Hill	.05	.04	.02
138	Ken Hill	.05	.04	.02
139	Eric Hillman	.05	.04	.02
140	Chris Hoiles	.05	.04	.02
141	Dave Hollins	.05	.04	.02
142	David Hulse	.15	.11	.06
143	Todd Hundley	.05	.04	.02
144	Pete Incaviglia	.05	.04	.02
145	Danny Jackson	.05	.04	.02
146	John Jaha	.05	.04	.02
147	Domingo Jean	.05	.04	.02
148	Gregg Jefferies	.05	.04	.02
149	Reggie Jefferson	.05	.04	.02
150	Lance Johnson	.05	.04	.02
151	Bobby Jones	.05	.04	.02
152	Chipper Jones	.25	.20	.10
153	Todd Jones	.05	.04	.02

		MT	NR MT	EX
154	Brian Jordan	.05	.04	.02
155	Wally Joyner	.05	.04	.02
156	David Justice	.25	.20	.10
157	Ron Karkovice	.05	.04	.02
158	Eric Karros	.15	.11	.06
159	Jeff Kent	.05	.04	.02
160	Jimmy Key	.05	.04	.02
161	Mark Kiefer	.05	.04	.02
162	Darryl Kile	.05	.04	.02
163	Jeff King	.05	.04	.02
164	Wayne Kirby	.05	.04	.02
165	Ryan Klesko	.20	.15	.08
166	Chuck Knoblauch	.05	.04	.02
167	Chad Kreuter	.05	.04	.02
168	John Kruk	.10	.08	.04
169	Mark Langston	.05	.04	.02
170	Mike Lansing	.10	.08	.04
171	Barry Larkin	.05	.04	.02
172	Manuel Lee	.05	.04	.02
173	Phil Leftwich	.05	.04	.02
174	Darren Lewis	.05	.04	.02
175	Derek Lilliquist	.05	.04	.02
176	Jose Lind	.05	.04	.02
177	Albie Lopez	.05	.04	.02
178	Javier Lopez	.35	.25	.14
179	Torey Lovullo	.05	.04	.02
180	Scott Lydy	.05	.04	.02
181	Mike Macfarlane	.05	.04	.02
182	Shane Mack	.05	.04	.02
183	Shane Maddux	.05	.04	.02
184	Dave Magadan	.05	.04	.02
185	Joe Magrane	.05	.04	.02
186	Kirt Manwaring	.05	.04	.02
187	Al Martin	.10	.08	.04
188	Pedro A. Martinez	.05	.04	.02
189	Pedro J. Martinez	.10	.08	.04
190	Ramon Martinez	.05	.04	.02
191	Tino Martinez	.05	.04	.02
192	Don Mattingly	.15	.11	.06
193	Derrick May	.05	.04	.02
194	David McCarty	.10	.08	.04
195	Ben McDonald	.05	.04	.02
196	Roger McDowell	.05	.04	.02
197	Fred McGriff	.20	.15	.08
198	Mark McLemore	.05	.04	.02
199	Greg McMichael	.10	.08	.04
200	Jeff McNeely	.10	.08	.04
201	Brian McRae	.05	.04	.02
202	Pat Meares	.05	.04	.02
203	Roberto Mejia	.05	.04	.02
204	Orlando Merced	.05	.04	.02
205	Jose Mesa	.05	.04	.02
206	Blas Minor	.05	.04	.02
207	Angel Miranda	.05	.04	.02
208	Paul Molitor	.20	.15	.08
209	Raul Mondesi	.15	.11	.06
210	Jeff Montgomery	.05	.04	.02
211	Mickey Morandini	.05	.04	.02
212	Mike Morgan	.05	.04	.02
213	Jamie Moyer	.05	.04	.02
214	Bobby Munoz	.05	.04	.02
215	Troy Neel	.20	.15	.08
216	Dave Nilsson	.05	.04	.02
217	John O'Donoghue	.05	.04	.02
218	Paul O'Neill	.05	.04	.02
219	Jose Offerman	.05	.04	.02
220	Joe Oliver	.05	.04	.02
221	Greg Olson	.05	.04	.02
222	Donovan Osborne	.05	.04	.02
223	Jayhawk Owens	.05	.04	.02
224	Mike Pagliarulo	.05	.04	.02
225	Craig Paquette	.05	.04	.02
226	Roger Pavlik	.05	.04	.02
227	Brad Pennington	.05	.04	.02
228	Eduardo Perez	.05	.04	.02
229	Mike Perez	.05	.04	.02
230	Tony Phillips	.05	.04	.02
231	Hipolito Pichardo	.05	.04	.02
232	Phil Plantier	.05	.04	.02
233	*Curtis Pride*	.25	.20	.10
234	Tim Pugh	.05	.04	.02
235	Scott Radinsky	.05	.04	.02
236	Pat Rapp	.05	.04	.02
237	Kevin Reimer	.05	.04	.02
238	Armando Reynoso	.05	.04	.02
239	Jose Rijo	.05	.04	.02
240	Cal Ripken Jr.	.25	.20	.10
241	Kevin Roberson	.25	.20	.10
242	Kenny Rogers	.05	.04	.02
243	Kevin Rogers	.05	.04	.02
244	Mel Rojas	.05	.04	.02

Last minute additions

Checklists for the card sets in this section were received from manufacturers just prior to publication. The possibility that changes may occur before cards are printed should be recognized.

Because cards were not actually in the market when this catalog went to press, it is impossible to quote values.

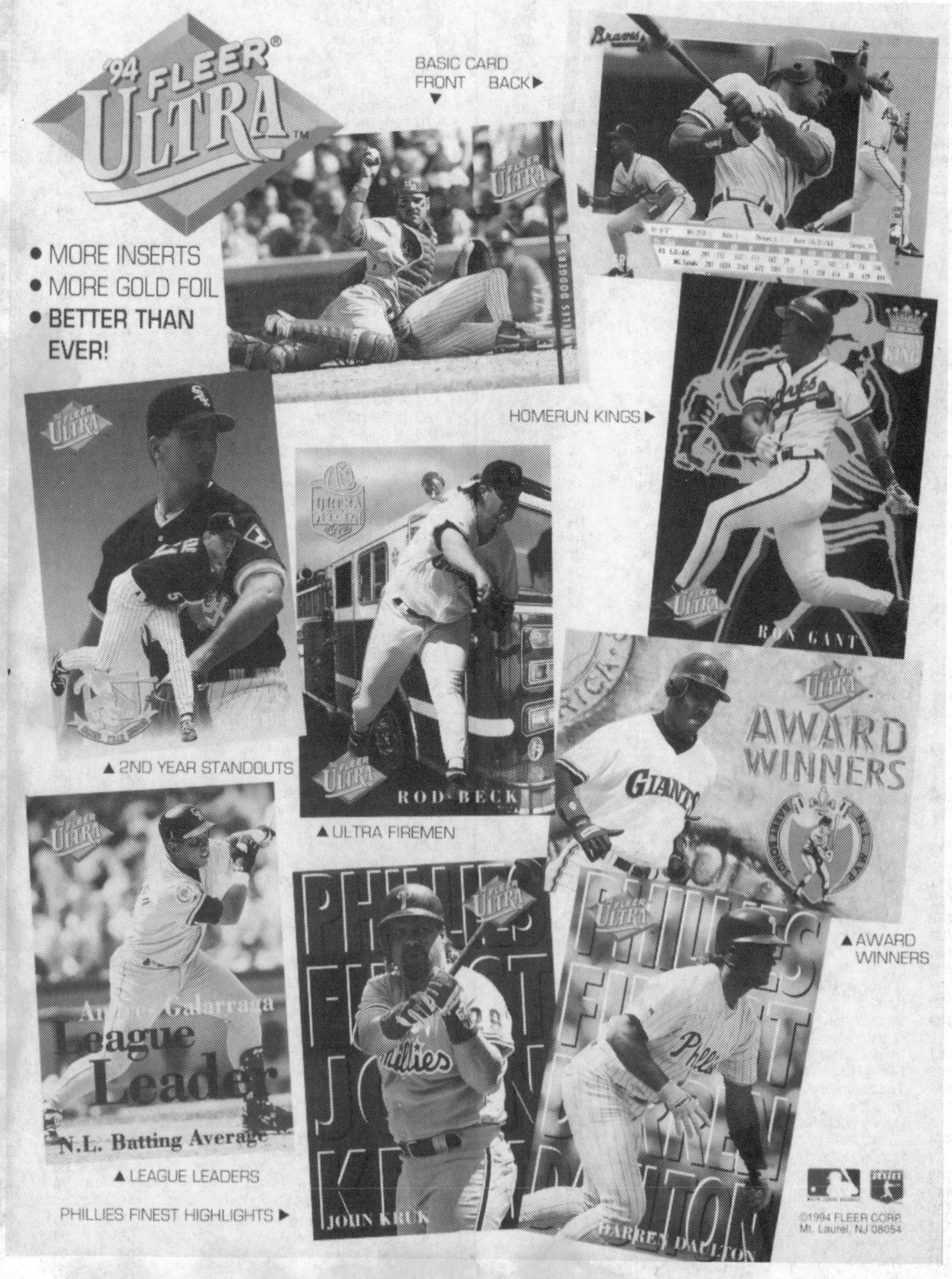

1994 Fleer Ultra

1 Jeffrey Hammonds
2 Chris Hoiles
3 Ben McDonald
4 Mark McLemore
5 Alan Mills
6 Jamie Moyer
7 Brad Pennington
8 Jim Poole
9 Cal Ripken Jr.
10 Jack Voigt
11 Roger Clemens
12 Danny Darwin
13 Andre Dawson
14 Scott Fletcher
15 Greg Harris
16 Billy Hatcher
17 Jeff Russell
18 Aaron Sele
19 Mo Vaughn
20 Mike Butcher
21 Rod Correia
22 Steve Frey
23 Phil Leftwich
24 Torey Lovullo
25 Ken Patterson
26 Eduardo Perez
27 Tim Salmon
28 J.T. Snow
29 Chris Turner
30 Wilson Alvarez
31 Jason Bere
32 Joey Cora
33 Alex Fernandez
34 Roberto Hernandez
35 Lance Johnson
36 Ron Karkovice
37 Kirk McCaskill
38 Jeff Schwarz
39 Frank Thomas
40 Sandy Alomar Jr.
41 Albert Belle
42 Felix Fermin
43 Wayne Kirby
44 Tom Kramer
45 Kenny Lofton
46 Jose Mesa
47 Eric Plunk
48 Paul Sorrento
49 Jim Thome
50 Bill Wertz
51 John Doherty
52 Cecil Fielder
53 Travis Fryman
54 Chris Gomez
55 Mike Henneman
56 Chad Kreuter
57 Bob MacDonald
58 Mike Moore
59 Tony Phillips
60 Lou Whitaker
61 Kevin Appier
62 Greg Gagne
63 Chris Gwynn
64 Bob Hamelin
65 Chris Haney
66 Phil Hiatt
67 Felix Jose
68 Jose Lind
69 Mike Macfarlane
70 Jeff Montgomery
71 Hipolito Pichardo
72 Juan Bell
73 Cal Eldred
74 Darryl Hamilton
75 Doug Henry
76 Mike Ignasiak
77 John Jaha
78 Graeme Lloyd
79 Angel Miranda
80 Dave Nilsson
81 Troy O'Leary
82 Kevin Reimer
83 Willie Banks
84 Larry Casian
85 Scott Erickson
86 Eddie Guardado
87 Kent Hrbek
88 Terry Jorgensen
89 Chuck Knoblauch
90 Pat Meares
91 Mike Trombley
92 Dave Winfield
93 Wade Boggs
94 Scott Kamieniecki
95 Pat Kelly
96 Jimmy Key
97 Jim Leyritz
98 Bobby Munoz
99 Paul O'Neill
100 Melido Perez
101 Mike Stanley
102 Danny Tartabull
103 Bernie Williams
104 Kurt Abbott
105 Mike Bordick
106 Ron Darling
107 Brent Gates
108 Miguel Jimenez
109 Steve Karsay
110 Scott Lydy
111 Mark McGwire
112 Troy Neel
113 Craig Paquette
114 Bob Welch
115 Bobby Witt
116 Rich Amaral
117 Mike Blowers
118 Jay Buhner
119 Dave Fleming
120 Ken Griffey Jr.
121 Tino Martinez
122 Marc Newfield
123 Ted Power
124 Mackey Sasser
125 Omar Vizquel
126 Kevin Brown
127 Juan Gonzalez
128 Tom Henke
129 David Hulse
130 Dean Palmer
131 Roger Pavlik
132 Ivan Rodriguez
133 Kenny Rogers
134 Doug Strange
135 Pat Borders
136 Joe Carter
137 Darnell Coles
138 Pat Hentgen
139 Al Leiter
140 Paul Molitor
141 John Olerud
142 Ed Sprague
143 Dave Stewart
144 Mike Timlin
145 Duane Ward
146 Devon White
147 Steve Avery
148 Steve Bedrosian
149 Damon Berryhill
150 Jeff Blauser
151 Tom Glavine
152 Chipper Jones
153 Mark Lemke
154 Fred McGriff
155 Greg McMichael
156 Deion Sanders
157 John Smoltz
158 Mark Wohlers
159 Jose Bautista
160 Steve Buechele
161 Mike Harkey
162 Greg Hibbard
163 Chuck McElroy
164 Mike Morgan
165 Kevin Roberson
166 Ryne Sandberg
167 Jose Vizcaino
168 Rick Wilkins
169 Willie Wilson
170 Willie Greene
171 Roberto Kelly
172 Larry Luebbers
173 Kevin Mitchell
174 Joe Oliver
175 John Roper
176 Johnny Ruffin
177 Reggie Sanders
178 John Smiley
179 Jerry Spradlin
180 Freddie Benavides
181 Dante Bichette
182 Willie Blair
183 Kent Bottenfield
184 Jerald Clark
185 Joe Girardi
186 Roberto Mejia
187 Steve Reed
188 Armando Reynoso
189 Bruce Ruffin
190 Eric Young
191 Luis Aquino
192 Bret Barberie
193 Ryan Bowen
194 Chuck Carr
195 Orestes Destrade
196 Richie Lewis
197 Dave Magadan
198 Bob Natal
199 Gary Sheffield
200 Matt Turner
201 Darrell Whitmore
202 Eric Anthony
203 Jeff Bagwell
204 Andujar Cedeno
205 Luis Gonzalez
206 Xavier Hernandez
207 Doug Jones
208 Darryl Kile
209 Scott Servais
210 Greg Swindell
211 Brian Williams
212 Pedro Astacio
213 Brett Butler
214 Omar Daal
215 Jim Gott
216 Raul Mondesi
217 Jose Offerman
218 Mike Piazza
219 Cory Snyder
220 Tim Wallach
221 Todd Worrell
222 Moises Alou
223 Sean Berry
224 Wil Cordero
225 Jeff Fassero
226 Darrin Fletcher
227 Cliff Floyd
228 Marquis Grissom
229 Ken Hill
230 Mike Lansing
231 Kirk Rueter
232 John Wetteland
233 Rondell White
234 Tim Bogar
235 Jeromy Burnitz
236 Dwight Gooden
237 Todd Hundley
238 Jeff Kent
239 Josias Manzanillo
240 Joe Orsulak
241 Ryan Thompson
242 Kim Batiste
243 Darren Daulton
244 Tommy Greene
245 Dave Hollins
246 Pete Incaviglia
247 Danny Jackson
248 Ricky Jordan
249 John Kruk
250 Mickey Morandini
251 Terry Mulholland
252 Ben Rivera
253 Kevin Stocker
254 Jay Bell
255 Steve Cooke
256 Jeff King
257 Al Martin
258 Danny Micelli
259 Blas Minor
260 Don Slaught
261 Paul Wagner
262 Tim Wakefield
263 Kevin Young
264 Rene Arocha
265 Richard Batchelor
266 Gregg Jefferies
267 Brian Jordan
268 Jose Oquendo
269 Donovan Osborne
270 Erik Pappas
271 Mike Perez
272 Bob Tewksbury

273 Mark Whiten
274 Todd Zeile
275 Andy Ashby
276 Brad Ausmus
277 Phil Clark
278 Jeff Gardner
279 Ricky Gutierrez
280 Tony Gwynn
281 Tim Mauser
282 Scott Sanders
283 Frank Seminara
284 Wally Whitehurst
285 Rod Beck
286 Barry Bonds
287 Dave Burba
288 Mark Carreon
289 Royce Clayton
290 Mike Jackson
291 Darren Lewis
292 Kirt Manwaring
293 Dave Martinez
294 Billy Swift
295 Salomon Torres
296 Matt Williams
297 Checklist
298 Checklist
299 Checklist
300 Checklist

1994 Fleer Ultra Award Winners

1 Ivan Rodriguez
2 Don Mattingly
3 Roberto Alomar
4 Robin Ventura
5 Omar Vizquel
6 Ken Griffey Jr.
7 Kenny Lofton
8 Devon White
9 Mark Langston
10 Kirt Manwaring
11 Mark Grace
12 Robby Thompson
13 Matt Williams
14 Jay Bell
15 Barry Bonds
16 Marquis Grissom
17 Larry Walker
18 Greg Maddux
19 Frank Thomas
20 Barry Bonds
21 Paul Molitor
22 Jack McDowell
23 Greg Maddux
24 Tim Salmon
25 Mike Piazza

1994 Fleer Ultra Home Run Kings

1 Juan Gonzalez
2 Ken Griffey Jr.
3 Frank Thomas
4 Albert Belle
5 Rafael Palmeiro
6 Joe Carter
7 Barry Bonds
8 David Justice
9 Matt Williams
10 Fred McGriff
11 Ron Gant
12 Mike Piazza

1994 Fleer Ultra RBI Kings

1 Albert Belle
2 Frank Thomas
3 Joe Carter
4 Juan Gonzalez
5 Cecil Fielder
6 Carlos Baerga
7 Barry Bonds
8 David Justice
9 Ron Gant
10 Mike Piazza
11 Matt Williams
12 Darren Daulton

1994 Fleer Ultra League Leaders

1 John Olerud
2 Rafael Palmeiro
3 Kenny Lofton
4 Jack McDowell
5 Randy Johnson
6 Andres Galarraga
7 Lenny Dykstra
8 Chuck Carr
9 Tom Glavine
10 Jose Rijo

1994 Fleer Ultra Second Year Standouts

1 Jason Bere
2 Brent Gates
3 Jeffrey Hammonds
4 Tim Salmon
5 Aaron Sele
6 Chuck Carr
7 Jeff Conine
8 Greg McMichael
9 Mike Piazza
10 Kevin Stocker

1994 Fleer Ultra Phillies Finest

1 Darren Daulton, John Kruk
2 Darren Daulton, John Kruk
3 Darren Daulton, John Kruk
4 Darren Daulton, John Kruk
5 Darren Daulton, John Kruk
6 Darren Daulton, John Kruk
7 Darren Daulton, John Kruk
8 Darren Daulton, John Kruk
9 Darren Daulton, John Kruk
10 Darren Daulton, John Kruk